Langenscheidt's German-English English-German Dictionary

Second Edition

Includes new German spelling

Edited by the
Langenscheidt editorial staff

POCKET BOOKS

New York   London   Toronto   Sydney

Pocket Books
A Division of Simon & Schuster, Inc.
1230 Avenue of the Americas
New York, NY 10020

Copyright 1952 © 1969, 1970, 1993, 2007 by Langenscheidt KG, Berlin and Munich, Germany
Originally published in Germany by Langenscheidt KG, Berlin and Munich

All rights reserved, including the right to reproduce this book or portions thereof in any form whatsoever. For information, address Pocket Books Subsidiary Rights Department, 1230 Avenue of the Americas, New York, NY 10020.

This Pocket Books paperback edition June 2009

POCKET and colophon are registered trademarks of Simon & Schuster, Inc.

For information about special discounts for bulk purchases, please contact Simon & Schuster Special Sales at 1-866-506-1949 or business@simonandschuster.com.

The Simon & Schuster Speakers Bureau can bring authors to your live event. For more information or to book an event, contact the Simon & Schuster Speakers Bureau at 1-866-248-3049 or visit our website at www.simonspeakers.com.

Manufactured in the United States of America

20 19 18 17 16 15 14 13 12

ISBN: 978-1-4391-4166-3

Preface

This new dictionary of English and German is a tool with more than 55,000 references for those who work with these languages at beginner's or intermediate level.

Languages are in a constant process of change. Therefore many words which have entered German and English in the last few years have been included in the vocabulary, e.g. *abgasfrei*, *Blog*, *chatten*, *DVD-Player*, *Handynummer*, *Kanzlerin*, *Lausch-angriff*, *SMS*, *Vogelgrippe*; *blog*, *cell* (*phone*), *chat*, *coach class*, *digital camera*, *Internet access*, *low-calorie*, *snowboarding*, *text message*.

The easy-to-read, clearly laid out typography with all the head-words in blue makes for good readability and allows the user to find words and expressions and their translations more quickly. The **new German spelling** has been used and detailed notes for the user have been included.

The A–Z part of this dictionary contains many important German and English proper names and abbreviations. Another feature is the special quick-reference sections listing the States of Germany and Austria and the Cantons of Switzerland, German weights and measures, examples of German declension and conjugation and alphabetical lists of German and English irregular verbs.

Designed for the widest possible variety of uses, this dictionary will be of great value to students, teachers and tourists, and will find a place in home and office libraries alike.

Contents

How to use this dictionary

This dictionary endeavors to do everything it can to help you find the words and translations you are looking for as quickly and as easily as possible.

To enable you to get the most out of your dictionary, you will be shown exactly where and how to find the information that will help you choose the right translation in every situation – whether at school or at home, in your profession, when writing letters, or in everyday conversation.

1. German and English headwords

1.1 When you are looking for a particular word it is important to know that the dictionary entries are arranged in strict **alphabetical order:**

Aal – ab
beugen – biegen
hay – haze

In the German-English section the letters **ä**, **ö** and **ü** are treated on the same basis as **a**, **o** and **u**. **ß** is treated as **ss**.

1.2 Besides the headwords and their derivatives and compounds, the past tense and past participle of irregular German verbs are also given as individual entries in alphabetical order in the German-English section, e.g. **ging, gegangen.**

1.3 Many German and English proper names and abbreviations are included in the vocabulary.

1.4 How then do you go about finding a particular word? Take a look at the words in bold print at the top of each page. These are the so-called **catchwords** and they serve as a guide to tracing your word as quickly as possible. The catchword on the top left gives you the first headword on the left-hand page, while the one on the top right gives you the last word on the right-hand page, e.g.

Griechenland – gut

1.5 What about entries comprising hyphenated expressions or two or more words, such as **DVD-Player, left-handed** or **mass media?** Expressions of this kind are treated in the same way as single words and thus appear in strict alphabetical order. Should you be unable to find a compound in the dictionary, just break it down into its components and look these up separately. In this way the meaning of many compound expressions can be derived indirectly.

When using the dictionary you will notice many 'word families', or groups of words stemming from a common root, which have been collated within one article in order to save space:

> **Einkaufs... – ~bummel – ~preis – ~wagen – ~zentrum**
> **amend – amendment – amends**

2. Spelling

2.1 Where American and British spelling of a word differs, the American spelling is given first as in

> **center,** *Br* **centre**
> **center** (*Br* **centre**) **forward**
> **dialog,** *Br* **dialogue**
> **analy|ze,** *Br* **-se** etc.

or in the English-German section as a separate headword, e.g. **theater, defense** etc.

A 'u' or an 'l' in parentheses in a word also indicates variant spellings:

> **colo(u)red** means: American **colored,** British **coloured**
> **travel(l)er** means: American **traveler,** British **traveller**

2.2 Word division in a German word is possible after each syllable, e.g.

> **ein-hül-len, Zu-cker, ba-cken, tes-ten**

In the English-German section the centered dots within a headword indicate syllabification breaks.

3. The different typefaces and their functions

3.1 Bold type is used for the German and English headwords and for Arabic numerals separating different parts of speech (nouns, transitive and intransitive verbs, adjectives and adverbs etc.) and different grammatical forms of a word:

> **bieten 1.** *v/t* ... **2.** *v/i* ...
> **hängen 1.** *v/i* (*irr, ge-, h*) hang (***an*** *dat* on...); **2.** *v/t* (*ge-, h*) hang (***an*** *acc* on)
> **feed 1.** Futter *n* ; ... **2.** *v/t* füttern

3.2 *Italics* are used for

a) grammatical and other abbreviations: *v/t, v/i, adj, adv, appr, fig* etc.
b) gender labels (masculine, feminine and neuter): *m, f, n*
c) grammatical references in brackets in the German-English section
d) any additional information preceding or following a translation (including dative or accusative objects):

> **knacken** *v/t and v/i* ... *twig*: snap; *fire, radio*: crackle
> **Etikett** *n* ... label (*a. fig*)
> **Gedanke** *m* (*-n; -n*) ...
> **geben** (*irr, ge-, h*) ...
> **befolgen** ... follow, take (*advice*); observe (*rule etc*)
> **file** ... *Briefe etc* ablegen
> **labored** schwerfällig (*style etc*); mühsam (*breathing etc*)

3.3 *Boldface italics* are used for phraseology etc., notes on German grammar and prepositions taken by the headword:

> **Lage** *f* ... ***in der ~ sein zu*** *inf* be able to *inf*
> **BLZ** ... *abbr of **Bankleitzahl***
> **abheben** (*irr, **heben**, sep, -ge-, h*)
> **abfahren** ... (*irr, **fahren**, sep, -ge-, **sein***) leave, depart (*both: **nach*** for)
> **line** ... ***hold the ~*** TEL bleiben Sie am Apparat
> **agree** ... sich einigen (***on*** über *acc*)

3.4 Normal type is used for translations of the headwords.

4. Pronunciation

When you have found the headword you are looking for in the German-English section, you will notice that very often this word is followed by certain symbols enclosed in square brackets. This is the phonetic transcription of the word, which tells you how it is pronounced. And one phonetic alphabet has come to be used internationally, namely that of the International Phonetic Association. This phonetic system is known by the abbreviation **IPA**. The symbols used in this dictionary are listed in the following tables on page 9 and 10.

4.1 The length of vowels is indicated by [ː] following the vowel symbol.

4.1.1 Stress is indicated by ['] or [ˌ] preceding the stressed syllable. ['] stands for strong stress, [ˌ] for weak stress:

> **Kabel** ['kaːbəl] – **Kabine** [ka'biːnə]
> **'nachsehen – Be'sitz – be'sprechen**
> **Jus'tizminisˌterium – Mi'nisterpräsiˌdent**

4.1.2 The glottal stop [ʔ] is the forced stop between one word or syllable and a following one beginning with a vowel, as in

> **Analphabet** [anʔalfa'beːt]
> **beeindrucken** [bəʔ'ʔaindrʊkən]

4.2 No transcription of compounds is given if the parts appear as separate entries. Each individual part should be looked up, as with

> **'Blumenbeet** (= **Blume** and **Beet**)

4.3 Guide to pronunciation for the German-English section

A. Vowels

[a] as in French *carte*: **Mann** [man]

[aː] as in *father*: **Wagen** ['vaːgən]

[e] as in *bed*: **Tenor** [te'noːɐ]

[eː] resembles the first sound in English [eɪ]: **Weg** [veːk]

[ə] unstressed e as in *ago*: **Bitte** ['bɪtə]

[ɛ] as in *fair*: **männlich** ['mɛnlɪç], **Geld** [gɛlt]

[ɛː] same sound but long: **zählen** ['tsɛːlən]

[ɪ] as in *it*: **Wind** [vɪnt]

[i] short, otherwise like [iː]: **Kapital** [kapi'taːl]

[iː] long, as in *meet*: **Vieh** [fiː]

[ɔ] as in *long*: **Ort** [ɔrt]

[o] as in *molest*: **Moral** [mo'raːl]

[oː] resembles the English sound in *go* [gəʊ] but without the [ʊ]: **Boot** [boːt]

[øː] as in French *feu*. The sound may be acquired by saying [e] through closely rounded lips: **schön** [ʃøːn]

[ø] same sound but short: **ökumenisch** [øku'meːnɪʃ]

[œ] as in French *neuf*. The sound resembles the English vowel in *her*. Lips, however, must be well rounded as for [ɒ]: **öffnen** ['œfnən]

[ʊ] as in *book*: **Mutter** ['mʊtɐ]

[u] short, otherwise like [uː]: **Musik** [mu'ziːk]

[uː] long, as in *boot*: **Uhr** [uːɐ]

[ʏ] short, opener than [yː]: **Hütte** ['hʏtə]

[y] almost like the French u as in *sur*. It may be acquired by saying [ɪ] through fairly closely rounded lips: **Büro** [by'roː]

[yː] same sound but long: **führen** ['fyːrən]

B. Diphthongs

[aɪ] as in *like*: **Mai** [maɪ]

[aʊ] as in *mouse*: **Maus** [maʊs]

[ɔy] as in *boy*: **Beute** ['bɔytə], **Läufer** ['lɔyfɐ]

C. Consonants

[b] as in *better*: **besser** ['bɛsɐ]

[d] as in *dance*: **du** [duː]

[f] as in *find*: **finden** ['fɪndən], **Vater** ['faːtɐ], **Philosoph** [filo'zoːf]

[g] as in *gold*: **Gold** [gɔlt]

[ʒ] as in *measure*: **Genie** [ʒe'niː]

[h] as in *house* but not aspirated: **Haus** [haʊs]

[ç] an approximation to this sound may be acquired by assuming the mouth-configuration for [ɪ] and emitting a strong current of breath: **Licht** [lɪçt], **Mönch** [mœnç], **lustig** ['lʊstɪç]

[x] as in Scottish *loch*, Whereas [ç] is pronounced at the front of the mouth, [x] is pronounced in the throat: **Loch** [lɔx]

[j] as in *year*: **ja** [jaː]

[k] as in *kick*: **keck** [kɛk], **Tag** [taːk], **Chronik** ['kroːnɪk], **Café** [ka'feː]

[l] as in *lump*. Pronounced like English initial "clear l": **lassen** ['lasən]

[m] as in *mouse*: **Maus** [maʊs]

[n] as in *not*: **nein** [naɪn]

[ŋ] as in *sing*, *drink*: **singen** ['zɪŋən], **trinken** ['trɪŋkən]

[p] as in *pass*: **Pass** [pas], **Trieb** [triːp], **obgleich** [ɔp'glaɪç]

[r] as in *rot*. There are two pronunciations: the frontal or lingual r: **rot** [roːt] and the uvular r [ʀ] (unknown in the

English language): **Mauer** ['maur]

[s] as in *miss*. Unvoiced when final, doubled, or next a voiceless consonant: **Glas** [gla:s], **Masse** ['masə], **Mast** [mast], **nass** [nas]

[z] as in *zero*. S voiced when initial in a word or syllable: **Sohn** [zo:n], **Rose** ['ro:zə]

[ʃ] as in *ship*: **Schiff** [ʃif], **Charme**

[ʃarm], **Spiel** [ʃpi:l], **Stein** [ʃtain]

[t] as in *tea*: **Tee** [te:], **Thron** [tro:n], **Stadt** [ʃtat], **Bad** [ba:t], **Findling** ['fintliŋ], **Wind** [vint]

[v] as in *vast*: **Vase** ['va:ze], **Winter** ['vintɐ]

[ã, ɛ̃, õ] are nasalized vowels. Examples: **Ensemble** [ã'sã:bəl], **Terrain** [tɛ'rɛ̃:], **Bonbon** [bõ'bõ:]

4.3.1 Phonetic changes in plurals

singular		plural		example
-g	[-k]	-ge	[-gə]	Flug – Flüge
-d	[-t]	-de	[-də]	Grund – Gründe, Abend – Abende
-b	[-p]	-be	[-bə]	Stab – Stäbe
-s	[-s]	-se	[-zə]	Los – Lose
-ch	[-x]	-che	[-çə]	Bach – Bäche
-iv	[-i:f]	-ive	[-i:və]	Stativ – Stative

4.3.2 The German alphabet

a [a:], b [be:], c [tse:], d [de:], e [e:], f [ɛf], g [ge:], h [ha:], i [i:], j [jɔt], k [ka:], l [ɛl], m [ɛm], n [ɛn], o [o:], p [pe:], q [ku:], r [ɛr], s [ɛs], t [te:], u [u:], v [fau], w [ve:], x [iks], y ['ʏpsilɔn], z [tsɛt]

4.3.3 List of suffixes

The German suffixes are not transcribed unless they are parts of headwords.

-bar	[-ba:ɐ]	-isch	[-iʃ]
-chen	[-çən]	-ist	[-ist]
-d	[-t]	-keit	[-kait]
-de	[-də]	-lich	[-liç]
-ei	[-ai]	-ling	[-liŋ]
-en	[-ən]	-losigkeit	[-lo:ziçkait]
-end	[-ənt]	-nis	[-nis]
-er	[-ɐ]	-sal	[-za:l]
-haft	[-haft]	-sam	[-za:m]
-heit	[-hait]	-schaft	[-ʃaft]
-icht	[-içt]	-sieren	[-zi:rən]
-ie	[-i:]	-ste	[-stə]
-ieren	[-i:rən]	-tät	[-tɛ:t]
-ig	[-iç]	-tum	[-tu:m]
-ik	[-ik]	-ung	[-ʊŋ]
-in	[-in]	-ungs-	[-ʊŋs-]
		-wärts	[-vɛrts]

5. The tilde (~)

5.1 A symbol you will repeatedly come across in the dictionary articles is the so-called tilde (~), which serves as a replacement mark. For reasons of space, related words are often combined in groups with the help of the tilde. In these cases, the tilde represents either the complete headword or that part of the word up to a vertical line (|):

> **Ski ... ~fahrer(in)** (= *Skifahrer, Skifahrerin*)
> **Ess|löffel ... ~stäbchen** (= *Essstäbchen*)
> **jet ... ~ engine** (= *jet engine*)
> **natural| resources ... ~ science** (= *natural science*)

5.2 In the case of the phrases in boldface italics, the tilde represents the headword immediately preceding, which itself may also have been formed with the help of a tilde:

> **kommen ...** *zu spät* **~** (= *kommen*)
> **ange|bracht ... ~gossen ...** *wie* **~** (= *angegossen*) *sitzen*
> **foreign ... ~** (= *foreign*) *affairs*
> **break ...** *take a* **~** (= *break*)

6. Abbreviations of grammatical terms and subject areas are designed to help the user choose the appropriate headword or translation of a word.

Words which are predominantly used in British English are marked by the abbreviation *Br*:

> **Bürgersteig** *m* sidewalk, *Br* pavement
> **girl guide** *Br* Pfadfinderin *f*

List of abbreviations

a.	*also*, auch	GASTR	*gastronomy*, Kochkunst
abbr	*abbreviation*, Abkürzung	*gen*	*genitive (case)*, Genitiv
acc	*accusative (case)*, Akkusativ	GEOGR	*geography*, Geografie
adj	*adjective*, Adjektiv	GEOL	*geology*, Geologie
adv	*adverb*, Adverb	*ger*	*gerund*, Gerundium
AGR	*agriculture*, Landwirtschaft	GR	*grammar*, Grammatik
Am	*American English*, amerikanisches Englisch		
		h	*haben*, have
ANAT	*anatomy*, Anatomie	*hist*	*historically*, historisch
appr	*approximately*, etwa	HIST	*history*, Geschichte
ARCH	*architecture*, Architektur	HUMOR	*humorous*, humorvoll
art	*article*, Artikel		
ASTR	*astrology*, Astrologie; *astronomy*, Astronomie	*impers*	*impersonal*, unpersönlich
		indef	*indefinite*, unbestimmt
attr	*attributively* , attributiv	*inf*	*infinitive (mood)*, Infinitiv
AVIAT	*aviation*, Luftfahrt	*int*	*interjection*, Interjektion
		interr	*interrogative*, fragend
BIOL	*biology*, Biologie	*irr*	*irregular*, unregelmäßig
BOT	*botany*, Botanik	IT	*information technology*, Informationstechnologie
Br	*British English*, britisches Englisch		
		j-m	*jemandem*, to someone
CHEM	*chemistry*, Chemie	*j-n*	*jemanden*, someone
cj	*conjunction*, Konjunktion	*j-s*	*jemandes*, someone's
coll	*collectively*, als Sammelwort	JUR	*jurisprudence*, Recht
comp	*comparative*, Komparativ		
contp	*contemptuously*, verächtlich	LING	*linguistics*, Sprachwissenschaft
cpds	*compounds*, Zusammensetzungen	*lit*	*literary*, nur in der Schriftsprache vorkommend
dat	*dative (case)*, Dativ	*m*	*masculine*, männlich
		MAR	*maritime term*, Schifffahrt
ECON	*economy*, Wirtschaft	MATH	*mathematics*, Mathematik
e-e	*a(n)*, eine	*m-e*	*my*, meine
e.g.	*for example*, zum Beispiel	MED	*medicine*, Medizin
ELECTR	*electrical engineering*, Elektrotechnik	METEOR	*meteorology*, Meteorologie
		MIL	*military term*, militärisch
e-m	*einem*, to a(n)	MOT	*motoring*, Kraftfahrwesen
e-n	*einen*, a(n)	*m-r*	*meiner*, of my, to my
e-r	*einer*, of a(n), to a(n)	*mst*	*mostly* , *usually*, meistens
e-s	*eines*, of a(n)	MUS	*music*, Musik
esp.	*especially*, besonders		
et., *et.*	etwas, *something*	*n*	*neuter*, sächlich
etc	*et cetera*, *and so on*, usw., und so weiter	*neg!*	*negative, usually considered offensive*, kann als beleidigend empfunden werden
F	*colloquial*, umgangssprachlich	*nom*	*nominative (case)*, Nominativ
f	*feminine*, weiblich	*num*	*numeral*, Zahlwort
fig	*figuratively*, übertragen		

OPT	*optics*, Optik	*s-m*	*seinem*, to his, to one's
o.s., *o.s.*	*oneself*, sich	*s-n*	*seinen*, his, one's
		s.o., *s.o.*	*someone*, jemand(en)
PAINT	*painting*, Malerei	SPORT	*sports*, Sport
PARL	*parliamentary term*, parlamentarischer Ausdruck	*s-r*	*seiner*, of his, of one's, to his, to one's
pass	*passive voice*, Passiv	*s-s*	*seines*, of his, of one's
PED	*pedagogy*, Schulwesen	s.th., *s.th.*	*something*, etwas
pers	*personal*, persönlich	*su*	*substantive*, Substantiv
PHARM	*pharmacy*, Pharmazie	*subj*	*subjunctive* (*mood*), Konjunktiv
PHIL	*philosophy*, Philosophie		
PHOT	*photography*, Fotografie	*sup*	*superlative*, Superlativ
PHYS	*physics*, Physik		
pl	*plural*, Plural	TECH	*technology*, Technik
POET	*poetry*, Dichtung	TEL	*telephony*, Telefon; *telecommunications*, Telekommunikation
POL	*politics*, Politik		
poss	*possessive*, besitzanzeigend		
POST	*post and telecommunications*, Postwesen	THEA	*theater*, Theater
		TV	*television*, Fernsehen
pp	*past participle*, Partizip Perfekt		
pred	*predicative*, prädikativ	u., *u.*	*und*, and
pres	*present*, Präsens	UNIV	*university*, Hochschulwesen
pres p	*present participle*, Partizip Präsens		
		V	*vulgar*, vulgär, unanständig
pret	*preterit(e)*, Präteritum	*v/aux*	*auxiliary verb*, Hilfsverb
PRINT	*printing*, Druckwesen	*vb*	*verb*, Verb
pron	*pronoun*, Pronomen	VET	*veterinary medicine*, Veterinärmedizin, Tiermedizin
prp	*preposition*, Präposition		
PSYCH	*psychology*, Psychologie	*v/i*	*intransitive verb*, intransitives Verb
RAIL	*railroad*, *railway*, Eisenbahn	*v/refl*	*reflexive verb*, reflexives Verb
refl	*reflexive*, reflexiv	*v/t*	*transitive verb*, transitives Verb
REL	*religion*, Religion		
RHET	*rhetoric*, Rhetorik	ZO	*zoology*, Zoologie
s-e	*seine*, his, one's	→	*see*, *refer to*, siehe
sep	*separable*, abtrennbar		
sg	*singular*, Singular	®	*registered trademark*, eingetragene Marke
sl	*slang*, Slang		

7. Translations and phraseology

After the boldface headword in the German-English section, the phonetic transcription of this word, its part of speech label, and its grammar, we finally come to the most important part of the entry: **the translation(s)**.

7.1 It is quite rare for a headword to be given just one translation. Usually a word will have several related translations, which are separated by a **comma**.

7.2 Different senses of a word are indicated by

a) **semicolons:**

> **Fest** ... celebration; party; REL festival
> **balance** ... Waage *f*; Gleichgewicht *n*

b) italics for **definitions:**

> **Läufer** ... runner (*a . carpet*); *chess*: bishop
> **call** ... Berufung *f* (**to** in *ein Amt*; auf *einen Lehrstuhl*)
> **cake** ... Tafel *f Schokolade*, Stück *n Seife*

c) **abbreviations** of subject areas:

> **Bug** *m* ... MAR bow; AVIAT nose
> **Gespräch** *n* talk (*a.* POL); ... TEL call
> **daisy** BOT Gänseblümchen *n*
> **duck** ... ZO Ente *f*

7.2.1 Where a word has fundamentally different meanings, it very often appears as two or more separate entries distinguished by **exponents** or raised figures:

> **betreten**[1] *v/t* ... step on; enter
> **betreten**[2] *adj* embarrassed
> **Bauer**[1] *m* ... farmer
> **Bauer**[2] *n, m* ... (bird)cage
> **chap**[1] ... Riss *m*
> **chap**[2] ... *Br* F Bursche *m*

This does not apply to senses which have directly evolved from the primary meaning of the word.

7.3 When a headword can be several different parts of speech, these are distinguished by boldface **Arabic numerals** (see also the section on p.7, paragraph 3.1 concerning the different typefaces):

geräuschlos	1. *adj* noiseless (*adjective*)
	2. without a sound (*adverb*)
work	1. Arbeit *f* (*noun*)
	2. *v/i* arbeiten (*verb*)
green	1. grün (*adjective*)
	2. Grün *n* (*noun*)

7.3.1 In the German-English section boldface Arabic numerals are also used to distinguish between transitive, intransitive
and reflexive verbs (if this affects their translation) and to show
that where there is a change of meaning a verb may be differently
conjugated:

> **fahren** (*irr*, *ge-*) **1.** *v/i* (*sein*) go; *bus etc*: run; ... **2.** *v/t* (*h*) drive (*car etc*) ...

If grammatical indications come before the subdivision they
refer to all translations that follow:

> **bauen** (*ge-*, *h*) **1.** *v/t* build ...; **2.** *fig v/i*: ~ *auf* ...

7.3.2 Boldface Arabic numerals are also used to indicate the
different meanings of nouns which can occur in more than one
gender and to show that where there is a change of meaning a
noun may be differently inflected:

> **Halfter 1.** *m*, *n* (*-s*; *-*) halter; **2.** *n* (*-s*; *-*), *f* (*-*; *-n*) holster

7.4 Illustrative phrases in boldface italics are generally given
within the respective categories of the dictionary article:

> **baden 1.** *v/i* ... ~ *gehen* go swimming; **2.** *v/t* ...
> **good 1.** ... *real* ~ F echt gut (= *adjective*); **2.** ... *for* ~ für immer (= *noun*)

8. Grammatical references

Knowing what to do with the grammatical information available in the dictionary will enable the user to get the most out
of this dictionary.

8.1 verbs (see the list of irregular German verbs on page 654).

Verbs have been treated in the following ways:

a) **bändigen** *v/t* (*ge-*, *h*)

The past participle of this word is formed by means of the
prefix *ge-* and the auxiliary verb *haben*: **er hat gebändigt.**

b) **abfassen** *v/t* (*sep*, *-ge-*, *h*)

In conjugation the prefix *ab* must be separated from the primary verb *fassen*: *sie fasst ab*; *sie hat abgefasst*.

c) **finden** *v/t* (*irr*, *ge-*, *h*)

irr following a verb means that it is an irregular verb. The principal parts of this particular word can be found as an individual headword in the main part of the German-English section and in the list of irregular German verbs on page 654: *sie fand*; *sie hat gefunden*.

d) **abfallen** *v/i* (*irr*, **fallen**, *sep*, *-ge-*, *sein*)

A reference such as *irr*, **fallen** indicates that the compound word **abfallen** is conjugated in exactly the same way as the primary verb **fallen** as given in the list of irregular German verbs on page 654: *er fiel ab*; *er ist abgefallen*.

e) **senden** *v/t* ([*irr*,] *ge-*, *h*)

The square brackets indicate that **senden** can be treated as a regular or an irregular verb: *sie sandte* or *sie sendete*; *sie hat gesandt* or *sie hat gesendet*.

8.2 nouns

The inflectional forms (*genitive singular*; *nominative plural*) follow immediately after the indication of gender. No forms are given for compounds if the parts appear as separate headwords.

The horizontal stroke replaces the part of the word which remains unchanged in the inflection:

Affäre *f* (-; *-n*)
Keks *m*, *n* (*-es*; *-e*)
Bau *m* (*-[e]s*; *Bauten*)
Blatt *n* (*-[e]s*; *Blätter* ['blɛtɐ])

The inflectional forms of German nouns ending in **-in** are given in the following ways:

Ärztin *f* (-; *-nen*)
Chemiker(in) (*-s*; *-/-*; *-nen*) = **Chemiker** *m* (*-s*; -) and **Chemikerin** *f* (-; *-nen*)

8.3 Prepositions

If, for instance, a headword (verb, adjective or noun) is governed by certain prepositions, these are given in boldface italics and in brackets together with their English or German translations and placed next to the appropriate translation. If the German or English preposition is the same for all or several translations, it is given only once before or after the first translation and then also applies to the translations which follow it:

> **abrücken** ... 1. *v/t* (*h*) move away (*von* from)
> **befestigen** *v/t* (*no* -ge-, *h*) fasten (*an dat* to), fix (to), attach (to)
> **dissent** ... 2. anderer Meinung sein (*from* als)
> **dissimilar** (*to*) unähnlich (*dat*); verschieden (von)

With German prepositions which can take the dative or the accusative, the case is given in brackets:

> **fürchten** ... *sich* ~ ... be afraid (*vor dat* of)
> **bauen** ... ~ *auf* (*acc*) rely *or* count on

We hope that this somewhat lengthy introduction has shown you that this dictionary contains a great deal more than simple one-to-one translations, and that you are now well-equipped to make the most of all it has to offer.

GERMAN – ENGLISH

A

à [a] *prp* **5 Karten ~ 20 Euro** 5 tickets at 20 euros each *or* a piece

Aal [a:l] *m* (-[e]s; -e) zo eel

aalen ['a:lən] *v/refl* (*ge-*, *h*) **sich in der Sonne ~** bask in the sun

'aal'glatt *fig adj* (as) slippery as an eel

Aas [a:s] *m* (-[e]s; -e) *no pl* carrion; F *contp pl* **Äser** beast, *sl* bastard

'Aasgeier *m* zo vulture (*a. fig*)

ab [ap] *prp and adv:* **München ~ 13.55** departure from Munich (at) 1.55; **~ 7 Uhr** from 7 o'clock (on); **~ morgen (1. März)** starting tomorrow (March 1st); **von jetzt ~** from now on; **~ und zu** now and then; **ein Film ~ 18** an X (-rated) film; **ein Knopf ist ~** a button has come off

'abarbeiten *v/t* (*sep*, *-ge-*, *h*) work out *or* off (*debts*); **sich ~** wear o.s. out

Abart ['ap²art] *f* (-; *en*) variety

abartig ['ap²artıç] *adj* abnormal

Abb. *abbr of* **Abbildung** fig., illustration

'Abbau *m* (-[e]s; *no pl*) mining; TECH dismantling; *fig* overcoming (*of prejudices etc*); reduction (*of expenditure, staff etc*); **'abbauen** *v/t* (*sep*, *-ge-*, *h*) mine; TECH dismantle; *fig* overcome (*prejudices etc*); reduce (*expenditure, staff etc*); **sich ~** BIOL break down

'abbeißen *v/t* (*irr*, *beißen*, *sep*, *-ge-*, *h*) bite off

'abbeizen *v/t* (*sep*, *-ge-*, *h*) remove *old paint etc* with corrosives

'abbekommen *v/t* (*irr*, *kommen*, *sep*, *no -ge-*, *h*) get off; **s-n Teil** *or* **et. ~** get one's share; **et. ~** *fig* get hurt, get damaged

'abberufen *v/t* (*irr*, *rufen*, *sep*, *no -ge-*, *h*), **'Abberufung** *f* recall

'abbestellen *v/t* (*sep*, *no -ge-*, *h*) cancel one's subscription (*or* order) for

'Abbestellung *f* cancellation

'abbiegen *v/i* (*irr*, *biegen*, *sep*, *-ge-*, *sein*) turn (off); **nach rechts (links) ~** turn right (left)

'abbilden *v/t* (*sep*, *-ge-*, *h*) show, depict

'Abbildung *f* (-; *-en*) picture, illustration

'Abbitte *f* apology; **j-m ~ leisten wegen** apologize to s.o. for

'abblasen F *v/t* (*irr*, *blasen*, *sep*, *-ge-*, *h*) call off, cancel

'abblättern *v/i* (*sep*, *-ge-*, *sein*) *paint etc:* flake off

'abblenden 1. *v/t* (*sep*, *-ge-*, *h*) dim **2.** *v/i* MOT dim (*Br* dip) the headlights

'Abblendlicht *n* MOT dimmed (*Br* dipped) headlights *pl*, low beam

'abbrechen *v/t* (*irr*, *brechen*, *sep*, *-ge-*) **1.** *v/t* (*h*) break off (*a. fig*); pull down, demolish (*building etc*); strike (*camp*, *tent*) **2.** *v/i* (*sein*) break off; (*h*) *fig* stop; **'abbremsen** *v/t* (*sep*, *-ge-*, *h*) slow down; **'abbrennen** *v/t* (*irr*, *brennen*, *sep*, *-ge-*) **1.** *v/i* (*sein*) burn down **2.** *v/t* (*h*) burn down (*building etc*); let *or* set off (*fireworks*); **'abbringen** *v/t* (*irr*, *bringen*, *sep*, *-ge-*, *h*) **j-n von e-r Sache ~** talk s.o. out of (doing) s.th.; **j-n vom Thema ~** get s.o. off a subject

'Abbruch *m* (-[e]s; *no pl*) breaking off; demolition; **'abbruchreif** *adj* derelict, due for demolition

'abbuchen *v/t* (*sep*, *-ge-*, *h*) debit (**von** to); **'Abbuchung** *f* debit

'abbürsten *v/t* (*sep*, *-ge-*, *h*) brush off (*dust etc*); brush (*coat etc*)

Abc [a:be:'tse:] *n* (-; *no pl*) ABC, alphabet; **ABC-Waffen** *pl* MIL nuclear, biological and chemical weapons

'abdanken *v/i* (*sep*, *-ge-*, *h*) resign; *king etc:* abdicate; **'Abdankung** *f* (-; *-en*) resignation; abdication

'abdecken *v/t* (*sep*, *-ge-*, *h*) uncover; untile (*roof*); unroof (*house*); clear (*the table*); ECON cover (up)

'abdichten *v/t* (*sep*, *-ge-*, *h*) TECH seal

'abdrängen *v/t* (*sep*, *-ge-*, *h*) push aside

'abdrehen 1. *v/t* (*sep*, *-ge-*, *h*) turn *or* switch off (*light, water etc*) **2.** *v/i* (*a. sein*) *ship, plane:* change one's course

'Abdruck *m* print, mark

'abdrucken *v/t* (*sep*, *-ge-*, *h*) print

'abdrücken (*sep*, *-ge-*, *h*) **1.** *v/t* fire (*gun*) **2.** *v/i* pull the trigger

Abend ['a:bənt] *m* (-s; -e) evening; **am ~** in the evening, at night; **heute ~** tonight; **morgen (gestern) ~** tomorrow (last) night; → **bunt, essen**; **~brot** *n* (-[e]s; *no pl*), **~essen** *n* supper, dinner, *Br a.* high tea; **~kasse** *f* THEA *etc* box office; **~kleid** n evening dress or gown; **~kurs** m evening classes pl

'**Abendland** n (-[e]s; no pl) West, Occident; '**abendländisch** ['a:bəntlɛndɪʃ] adj Western, Occidental

'**Abendmahl** n (-[e]s; no pl) the (Holy) Communion, the Lord's Supper; **das ~ empfangen** receive Communion

abends ['a:bənts] adv in the evening, at night; **dienstags ~** (on) Tuesday evenings

'**Abendschule** f evening classes pl, night school

Abenteuer ['a:bəntɔʏɐ] n (-s; -) adventure (a. in cpds ...ferien, ...spielplatz)

'**abenteuerlich** adj adventurous; fig risky; fantastic

Abenteurer ['a:bəntɔʏrɐ] m (-s; -) adventurer; '**Abenteurerin** ['a:bəntɔʏrə-rɪn] f (-; -nen) adventuress

aber ['a:bɐ] cj and adv but; **oder ~** or else; **~, ~!** now then!; **~ nein!** not at all!

'**Aberglaube** m superstition

abergläubisch ['a:bɐglɔʏbɪʃ] adj superstitious

'**aberkennen** v/t (irr, **kennen**, sep, no -ge-, h) **j-m et. ~** deprive s.o. of sth. (a. JUR); '**Aberkennung** f (-; -en) deprivation (a. JUR)

abermalig ['a:bɐma:lɪç] adj repeated

abermals ['a:bɐma:ls] adv once more or again

'**aber'tausend** adj: **tausende und ~e** thousands upon thousands

'**abfahren** (irr, **fahren**, sep, -ge-) 1. v/i (sein) leave, depart (both: **nach** for); F (**voll**) **~ auf** (acc) really go for 2. v/t (h) carry or cart away

'**Abfahrt** f departure (**nach** for), start (for); skiing: descent

'**Abfahrts|lauf** m downhill skiing (or race); **~zeit** f (time of) departure

'**Abfall** m waste, refuse, garbage, trash, Br a. rubbish; **~beseitigung** f waste disposal; **~eimer** m → **Mülleimer**

'**abfallen** v/i (irr, **fallen**, sep, -ge-, sein) fall (off); terrain: slope (down); fig fall away (**von** from); esp POL secede (from); **vom Glauben~** renounce one's faith; **~ gegen** compare badly with

'**abfällig** 1. adj derogatory 2. adv: **~ von j-m sprechen** run s.o. down

'**Abfallpro,dukt** n waste product

'**abfälschen** v/t (sep, -ge-, h) SPORT deflect; '**abfangen** v/t (irr, **fangen**, sep, -ge-, h) catch, intercept; MOT, AVIAT right; '**abfärben** v/i (sep, -ge-, h) color etc: run, material: a. bleed; fig **~ auf** (acc) rub off on; '**abfassen** v/t (sep, -ge-, h) compose, word, write

'**abfertigen** v/t (sep, -ge-, h) dispatch; customs: clear; serve (customers); check in (passengers etc); **j-n kurz ~** be short with s.o.; '**Abfertigung** f dispatch; clearance; check-in

'**abfeuern** v/t (sep, -ge-, h) fire (off); launch (rocket)

'**abfinden** v/t (irr, **finden**, sep, -ge-, h) ECON pay off (creditor); buy out (partner); compensate; **sich mit e-r Sache~** put up with s.th.; '**Abfindung** f (-; -en) ECON satisfaction; compensation

'**abflachen** v/t and v/refl (sep, -ge-, h) flatten; '**abflauen** v/i (sep, -ge-, h) wind etc: drop (a. fig); '**abfliegen** v/i (irr, **fliegen**, sep, -ge-, sein) AVIAT leave, depart; '**abfließen** v/i (irr, **fließen**, sep, -ge-, sein) flow off, drain (off or away)

'**Abflug** m AVIAT departure

'**Abfluss** m (-es; Abflüsse) no pl flowing off; TECH drain

'**Abflussrohr** n wastepipe, drain(pipe)

'**abfragen** v/t (sep, -ge-, h) quiz or question s.o. (**über** acc about), test s.o. orally

Abfuhr ['apfu:ɐ] f (-; -en) removal; **j-m e-e ~ erteilen** rebuff (F SPORT lick) s.o.

'**abführen** (sep, -ge-, h) 1. v/t lead or take away; ECON pay (over) (**an** acc to); 2. v/i MED-move one's bowels; act as a laxative; '**abführend** adj, '**Abführmittel** n MED laxative

'**abfüllen** v/t (sep, -ge-, h) bottle; can

'**Abgabe** f (-; -n) no pl handing in; SPORT pass; ECON rate; duty

'**abgabenfrei** adj tax-free

'**abgabenpflichtig** adj dutiable

'**Abgang** m (-[e]s; Abgänge) no pl departure; Am graduation, Br school-leaving; THEA exit (a. fig); SPORT dismount; '**Abgänger** ['apgɛŋɐ] m (-s; -) Am graduate, Br school-leaver

'**Abgas** n waste gas; pl emission(s pl); MOT exhaust fumes pl

'**abgasfrei** adj emission-free

'**Abgasuntersuchung** f MOT Am emissions test, Br exhaust emission test

'**abgearbeitet** adj worn out

'abgeben v/t (irr, **geben**, sep, -ge-, h) leave (**bei** with); hand in; deposit (one's baggage etc), hand over (ticket etc) (**an** acc to); cast (vote); pass (ball); give off, emit (heat etc); make (offer, statement etc); **j-m et. ~ von** share s.th. with s.o.; **sich ~ mit** concern o.s. with s.th., associate with s.o.

'abge|brannt adj burnt down; F fig broke; **~brüht** fig adj hard-boiled; **~droschen** adj hackneyed; **~fahren** adj tires: worn out; **~griffen** adj worn; **~hackt** fig adj disjointed; **~hangen** adj: **gut~es Fleisch** well-hung meat; **~härtet** adj hardened (**gegen** to)

'abgehen v/i (irr, **gehen**, sep, -ge-, sein) train etc: leave; mail, goods: get off; THEA go off (stage); button etc: come off; path etc: branch off; **von der Schule~** leave school; **~ von** drop (plan etc); **von s-r Meinung ~** change one's mind or opinion; **ihm geht … ab** he lacks …; **gut ~** end well, pass off well

'abge|hetzt, ~kämpft adj exhausted, worn out; **~kartet** ['apgəkartət] F adj: **~e Sache** put-up job; **~legen** adj remote, distant; **~macht** adj fixed; **~!** it's a deal!; **~magert** adj emaciated; **~neigt** adj: **e-r Sache ~ sein** be averse to s.th.; **ich wäre nicht ~, et. zu tun** I wouldn't mind doing s.th.; **~nutzt** adj worn out

Abgeordnete ['apgəˈɔrdnətə] m, f (-n; -n) Am representative, congress|man (-woman), Br Member of Parliament (abbr MP); **'Abgeordnetenhaus** n Am House of Representatives, Br House of Commons

'abgepackt adj prepack(ag)ed

'abgeschieden adj secluded

'Abgeschiedenheit f (-; no pl) seclusion

'abge|schlossen adj completed; **~e Wohnung** self-contained apartment (Br flat); **~sehen** adj: **~ von** aside (Br a. apart) from; **ganz ~ von** not to mention, let alone; **~spannt** adj exhausted, weary; **~standen** adj stale; **~storben** adj dead (tree etc); numb (leg etc); **~stumpft** adj insensitive, indifferent (**gegen** to); **~tragen, ~wetzt** adj worn out; threadbare, shabby

abgewöhnen v/t (sep, -ge-, h) **j-m et. ~** make s.o. give up s.th.; **sich** (dat) **das**

Rauchen ~ stop or give up smoking

'Abgott m idol (a. fig); **abgöttisch** ['apɡœtɪʃ] adv: **j-n ~ lieben** idolize s.o.

'abgrasen v/t (sep, -ge-, h) graze; fig scour

'abgrenzen v/t (sep, -ge-, h) mark off; delimit (**gegen** from)

'Abgrund m abyss, chasm, gulf (all a. fig); **am Rande des ~s** fig on the brink of disaster; **'abgrund'tief** adj abysmal

'abgucken F v/t (sep, -ge-, h) **j-m et. ~** learn s.th. from (watching) s.o.; → **abschreiben**

'Abguss m cast

'abhaben F v/t (irr, **haben**, sep, -ge-, h) **willst du et. ~?** do you want some (of it)? **'abhacken** v/t (sep, -ge-, h) chop or cut off; **'abhaken** v/t (sep, -ge-, h) check (Br tick) off; F forget; **'abhalten** v/t (irr, **halten**, sep, -ge-, h) hold (meeting etc); **j-n von der Arbeit ~** keep s.o. from his work; **j-n davon ~, et. zu tun** keep s.o. from doing s.th.

'abhandeln v/t (sep, -ge-, h) treat (subject etc); **j-m et. ~** make a deal with s.o. for s.th.; **'Abhandlung** f treatise (**über** acc on)

'Abhang m slope

'abhängen¹ v/t (sep, -ge-, h) take down (picture etc); RAIL etc uncouple; F shake s.o. off

'abhängen² v/i (irr, **hängen**, sep, -ge-, h) **~ von** depend on; **das hängt davon ab** that depends

abhängig ['aphɛŋɪç] adj: **~ von** dependent on; a. addicted to drugs etc

'Abhängigkeit f (-; -en) dependence (**von** on); addiction (to)

'abhärten v/t (sep, -ge-, h) **sich ~** harden o.s. (**gegen** to)

'abhauen (irr, **hauen**, sep, -ge-) **1.** v/t (h) cut or chop off **2.** F v/i (sein) make off (**mit** with), run away (with); **hau ab!** beat it!, scram!

'abheben (irr, **heben**, sep, -ge-, h) **1.** v/t lift or take off; pick up (receiver); (with)draw (money); cut (cards); **sich ~** stand out (**von** among, from), fig a. contrast with **2.** v/i cut the cards; answer the phone; plane: take (esp rocket: lift) off

'abheften v/t (sep, -ge-, h) file

'abheilen v/i (sep, -ge-, sein) heal (up)

'abhetzen v/refl (sep, -ge-, h) wear o.s.

out

'Abhilfe f remedy; **~ schaffen** take remedial measures

'Abholdienst m pickup service

'abholen v/t (sep, -ge-, h) pick up, collect; **j-n von der Bahn ~** meet s.o. at the station; **'abholzen** v/t (sep, -ge-, h) fell, cut down (trees); deforest (area); '**abhorchen** v/t (sep, -ge-, h) MED auscultate, sound; **'abhören** v/t (sep, -ge-, h) listen in on, tap (telephone conversation), F bug; → **abfragen**

'Abhörgerät n bugging device, F bug

Abitur [abi'tuːɐ] n (-s; -e) school-leaving examination (qualifying for university entrance)

'abjagen v/t (sep, -ge-, h) **j-m et. ~** recover s.th. from s.o.; '**abkanzeln** F v/t (sep, -ge-, h) tell s.o. off; **'abkaufen** v/t (sep, -ge-, h) **j-m et. ~** buy s.th. from s.o.

Abkehr ['apkeːɐ] f (-; no pl) break (**von** with); **'abkehren** v/refl (sep, -ge-, h) **sich ~ von** turn away from

'abklingen v/i (irr, klingen, sep, -ge-, sein) fade away; pain etc: ease off

'abklopfen v/t (sep, -ge-, h) MED sound

'abknallen F v/t (sep, -ge-, h) pick off

'abknicken v/t (sep, -ge-, h) snap or break off; bend

'abkochen v/t (sep, -ge-, h) boil

'abkomman,dieren v/t (sep, no -ge-, h) MIL detach (**zu** for)

'abkommen v/i (irr, kommen, sep, -ge-, sein) **~ von** get off; drop (plan etc); **vom Thema ~** stray from the point; → **Weg**

Abkommen n (-s; -) agreement, treaty; **ein ~ schließen** make an agreement

Abkömmling ['apkœmlɪŋ] m (-s; -e) descendant

'abkoppeln v/t (sep, -ge-, h) uncouple (**von** from); undock (spacecraft)

'abkratzen (sep, -ge-) **1.** v/t (h) scrape off **2.** F v/i (sein) kick the bucket

'abkühlen v/t and v/refl (sep, -ge-, h) cool down (a. fig)

'Abkühlung f cooling

'abkürzen v/t (sep, -ge-, h) shorten; abbreviate; **den Weg ~** take a short cut

Abkürzung f abbreviation; short cut

'abladen v/t (irr, laden, sep, -ge-, h) unload; dump (waste etc)

Ablage f (-; -n) no pl filing; filing tray; Swiss → **Zweigstelle**

'ablagern (sep, -ge-, h) **1.** v/t season

(wood); let wine age; GEOL etc deposit; **sich ~** settle, be deposited **2.** v/i (a. sein) season; age; **'Ablagerung** f (-; -en) CHEM, GEOL deposit, sediment

'ablassen (irr, lassen, sep, -ge-, h) **1.** v/t drain off (liquid); let off (steam); drain (pond etc) **2.** v/i: **von et. (j-m) ~** stop doing s.th. (leave s.o. alone)

'Ablauf m (-[e]s; Abläufe) course; process; order of events; no pl expiration, Br expiry; → **Abfluss**

'ablaufen (irr, laufen, sep, -ge-) **1.** v/i (sein) water etc: run off; performance etc: go, proceed; come to an end; period, passport etc: expire; time, record, tape: run out; clock: run down; **gut ~** turn out well **2.** v/t (h) wear down

'ablecken v/t (sep, -ge-, h) lick (off)

'ablegen (sep, -ge-, h) **1.** v/t take off (clothes); file (letters etc); give up (habit etc); take (examination, oath); **abgelegte Kleider** cast-offs pl **2.** v/i take off one's (hat and) coat; MAR put out, sail

'Ableger m (-s; -) BOT layer; offshoot (a. fig)

'ablehnen v/t (sep, -ge-, h) refuse; turn down (application etc); PARL reject; object to; condemn; **~d** adj negative

'Ablehnung f (-; -en) refusal; rejection; objection (gen to)

'ableiten v/t (sep, -ge-, h) divert; LING, MATH derive (**aus** dat, **von** from) (a. fig)

'Ableitung f diversion; LING, MATH derivation (a. fig)

'ablenken v/t (sep, -ge-, h) divert (**von** from); soccer: turn away (ball); deflect (rays etc); **j-n von der Arbeit ~** distract s.o. from his work; **er lässt sich leicht ~** he is easily diverted

'Ablenkung f diversion

'ablesen v/t (irr, lesen, sep, -ge-, h) read

'abliefern v/t (sep, -ge-, h) deliver (**bei** to, at); hand over (to)

'ablösbar adj detachable; **'ablösen** v/t (sep, -ge-, h) detach; take off; take s.o.'s place, take over from s.o.; esp MIL relieve; replace; **sich ~** take turns (driving etc); **'Ablösesumme** f SPORT transfer fee; **'Ablösung** f relief

'abmachen v/t (sep, -ge-, h) remove, take off; settle, arrange

'Abmachung f (-; -en) arrangement, agreement, deal

'abmagern *v/i* (*sep*, *-ge-*, *sein*) get thin

'Abmagerung *f* (*-*; *-en*) emaciation

'Abmagerungskur *f* slimming diet

'abmähen *v/t* (*sep*, *-ge-*, *h*) mow

'abmalen *v/t* (*sep*, *-ge-*, *h*) copy

'Abmarsch *m* (*-[e]s*; *no pl*) start; MIL marching off; **'abmar,schieren** *v/i* (*sep*, *no -ge-*, *sein*) start; MIL march off

'abmelden *v/t* (*sep*, *-ge-*, *h*) cancel the registration of (*car etc*); cancel s.o.'s membership (*in a club etc*); give notice of s.o.'s withdrawal (*from school*); **sich** ~ give notice of change of address; report off duty; **'Abmeldung** *f* notice of withdrawal; notice of change of address

'abmessen *v/t* (*irr*, **messen**, *sep*, *-ge-*, *h*) measure; **'Abmessung** *f* measurement; *pl* dimensions

'abmon,tieren *v/t* (*sep*, *no -ge-*, *h*) take off; take down; TECH dismantle

'abmühen *v/refl* (*sep*, *-ge-*, *h*) work very hard; try hard (*to do s.th.*); struggle (**mit** with)

'abnagen *v/t* (*sep*, *-ge-*, *h*) gnaw (at)

Abnahme ['apnaːmə] *f* (*-*; *-n*) reduction, decrease; loss (*a. of weight*); ECON purchase; TECH acceptance

'abnehmbar *adj* removable

'abnehmen (*irr*, **nehmen**, *sep*, *-ge-*, *h*) **1.** *v/t* take off (*a.* MED), remove; pick up (*receiver*); TECH accept; ECON buy; **j-m et.** ~ take s.th. (away) from s.o. **2.** *v/i* decrease, diminish; lose weight; answer the phone; *moon*: wane

'Abnehmer *m* (*-s*; *-*) buyer; customer

'Abneigung *f* (**gegen**) dislike (of, for); aversion (to)

abnorm [ap'nɔrm] *adj* abnormal; exceptional, unusual; **Abnormität** [apnɔrmi'tɛːt] *f* (*-*; *-en*) abnormality

'abnutzen, **'abnützen** *v/t and v/refl* (*sep*, *-ge-*, *h*) wear out

'Abnutzung, **'Abnützung** *f* (*-*; *no pl*) wear (and tear) (*a.* fig)

Abonnement [abɔnə'maː:] *n* (*-s*; *-s*) subscription (**auf** *acc* to); **Abonnent** [abɔ'nɛnt] *m* (*-en*; *-en*) subscriber; THEA season-ticket holder; **abonnieren** [abɔ'niːrən] *v/t* (*no -ge-*, *h*) subscribe to

Abordnung *f* (*-*; *-en*) delegation

Abort [a'bɔrt] *m* (*-[e]s*; *-e*) lavatory, toilet

'abpassen *v/t* (*sep*, *-ge-*, *h*) watch or wait for (*s.o.*, *s.th.*); waylay *s.o.* (*a.* fig)

'abpfeifen *v/t and v/i* (*irr*, **pfeifen**, *sep*, *-ge-*, *h*) SPORT blow the final whistle; stop the game

'abplagen *v/refl* (*sep*, *-ge-*, *h*) struggle (**mit** with)

'abprallen *v/i* (*sep*, *-ge-*, *sein*) rebound, bounce (off); *bullet*: ricochet

'abputzen *v/t* (*sep*, *-ge-*, *h*) wipe off; clean

'abraten *v/i* (*irr*, **raten**, *sep*, *-ge-*, *h*) **j-m** ~ **von** advise or warn s.o. against

'abräumen *v/t* (*sep*, *-ge-*, *h*) clear away; clear (*the table*)

'abrea,gieren *v/t* (*sep*, *no -ge-*, *h*) work off (*one's anger etc*) (**an** *dat* on); **sich** ~ F let off steam

'abrechnen (*sep*, *-ge-*, *h*) **1.** *v/t* deduct, subtract; claim (*expenses*) **2.** *v/i*: **mit j-m** ~ settle accounts (*fig a.* get even) with s.o.; **'Abrechnung** *f* settlement; F *fig* showdown

'abreiben *v/t* (*irr*, **reiben**, *sep*, *-ge-*, *h*) rub off; rub down (*body*); polish

'Abreise *f* departure (**nach** for)

'abreisen *v/i* (*sep*, *-ge-*, *sein*) depart, leave, start, set out (*all*: **nach** for)

'Abreisetag *m* day of departure

'abreißen (*irr*, **reißen**, *sep*, *-ge-*) **1.** *v/t* (*h*) tear or pull off; pull down (*building*) **2.** *v/i* (*sein*) break; *button etc*: come off

'Abreiß,kalender *m* tear-off calendar

'abrichten *v/t* (*sep*, *-ge-*, *h*) train (*animal*), *a.* break *a horse* in

'abriegeln *v/t* (*sep*, *-ge-*, *h*) block off, cordon off

'Abriss *m* (*-es*; *-e*) (*no pl*) demolition; outline, summary

'abrollen *v/i* (*sep*, *-ge-*, *sein*) and *v/t* (*h*) unroll (*a.* fig)

'abrücken (*sep*, *-ge-*) **1.** *v/t* (*h*) move away (**von** from); **2.** *v/i* (*sein*) draw away (**von** from); MIL march off

'Abruf *m*: **auf** ~ ECON on call

'abrufen *v/t* (*irr*, **rufen**, *sep*, *-ge-*, *h*) call away; IT recall, fetch, retrieve

'abrunden *v/t* (*sep*, *-ge-*, *h*) round (off)

'abrupfen *v/t* (*sep*, *-ge-*, *h*) pluck (off)

abrupt [ap'rʊpt] *adj* abrupt

'abrüsten *v/i* (*sep*, *-ge-*, *h*) MIL disarm

'Abrüstung *f* (*-*; *no pl*) MIL disarmament

'abrutschen *v/i* (*sep*, *-ge-*, *sein*) slide down; slip (off) (**von** from)

ABS [aːbeːˈɛs] → **Antiblockiersystem**

Absage [ˈapzaːgə] f (-; -n) refusal; cancellation; **'absagen** (sep, -ge-, h) **1.** v/t call off, cancel (event etc) **2.** v/i call off; **j-m ~ a.** cancel one's appointment with s.o.; decline (the invitation)

'absägen v/t (sep, -ge-, h) saw off; F fig oust, sack s.o.

'absahnen F v/i (sep, -ge-, h) cash in

'Absatz m paragraph; ECON sales pl; shoe: heel; stairs: landing

'abschaben v/t (sep, -ge-, h) scrape off

'abschaffen v/t (sep, -ge-, h) do away with, abolish; repeal (law); put an end to (abuses etc); **'Abschaffung** f (-; no pl) abolition; repeal

'abschalten (sep, -ge-, h) **1.** v/t switch or turn off **2.** F v/i relax, switch off

'abschätzen v/t (sep, -ge-, h) estimate; assess; size up; **abschätzig** [ˈapʃɛtsɪç] adj contemptuous; derogatory

Abschaum m (-s; no pl) scum (a. fig)

'Abscheu m (-s; no pl) disgust (**vor, gegen** at, for); **e-n ~ haben vor** abhor, detest; **~ erregend** → **abscheuerregend**; **'abscheuerregend** adj revolting, repulsive

ab'scheulich adj abominable, despicable (a. person), a. atrocious (crime)

'abschicken v/t (sep, -ge-, h) → **absenden**

'abschieben fig v/t (irr, schieben, sep, -ge-, h) push away; get rid of; deport; **et. auf j-n ~** shove s.th. off on (to) s.o.

Abschied [ˈapʃiːt] m (-[e]s; -e) parting, farewell; **~ nehmen (von)** say goodbye (to), take leave (of); **s-n ~ nehmen** resign, retire

'Abschiedsfeier f farewell party

'Abschiedskuss m goodbye kiss

'abschießen v/t (irr, schießen, sep, -ge-, h) shoot off (AVIAT down); launch (rocket); shoot, kill (deer); F pick s.o. off; fig oust; get rid of s.o.

'abschirmen v/t (sep, -ge-, h) shield (**gegen** from); fig protect (**gegen** against, from); **'Abschirmung** f (-; -en) shield, screen; fig protection

'abschlachten v/t (sep, -ge-, h) slaughter (a. fig)

'Abschlag m SPORT kickout; ECON down payment; **'abschlagen** v/t (irr, schlagen, sep, -ge-, h) knock off; cut off (head); cut down (tree); refuse (request

etc), turn s.th. down

'abschleifen v/t (irr, schleifen, sep, -ge-, h) grind off; sand(paper), smooth

'Abschleppdienst m MOT emergency road (Br breakdown) service

'abschleppen v/t (sep, -ge-, h) MOT (give s.o. a) tow; police: tow away

'Abschlepp|seil n towrope; **~wagen** m Am tow truck, Br breakdown lorry

'abschließen (irr, schließen, sep, -ge-, h) **1.** v/t lock (up); close, finish; complete; take out (insurance); conclude (research etc); **e-n Handel ~** strike a bargain; **sich ~** shut o.s. off; → **Wette 2.** v/i close, finish; **~d 1.** adj concluding; final **2.** adv: **~ sagte er** he concluded by saying

'Abschluss m conclusion, close; **~prüfung** f final examination, finals pl, esp Am a. graduation; **s-e ~ machen** graduate (**an** dat from); **~zeugnis** n Am diploma, Br school-leaving certificate

'abschmecken v/t (sep, -ge-, h) season

'abschmieren v/t (sep, -ge-, h) TECH lubricate, grease

'abschminken v/t (sep, -ge-, h) **sich ~** remove one's make-up

'abschnallen v/t (sep, -ge-, h) undo; take off (skis); **sich ~** MOT, AVIAT unfasten one's seat belt

'abschneiden (irr, schneiden, sep, -ge-, h) **1.** v/t cut (off) (a. fig); **j-m das Wort ~** cut s.o. short **2.** v/i: **gut ~** come off well

'Abschnitt m passage, section (of book etc); paragraph; MATH, BIOL segment; period (of time), stage (of journey), phase (of development); coupon, slip, stub (of check etc)

'abschnittweise adv section by section

'abschrauben v/t (sep, -ge-, h) unscrew

'abschrecken v/t (sep, -ge-, h) deter (**von** from); GASTR douse eggs etc with cold water; **~d** adj deterrent; **~es Beispiel** n warning example

'Abschreckung f (-; -en) deterrence

'abschreiben v/t (irr, schreiben, sep, -ge-, h) copy; PED crib; ECON write off (a. F fig); **'Abschrift** f copy, duplicate

'abschürfen v/t (sep, -ge-, h) graze

'Abschürfung f (-; -en) abrasion

Abschuss m launch(ing) (of rocket); AVIAT shooting down, downing; kill;

~basis f MIL launching base

abschüssig ['apʃʏsɪç] adj sloping; steep

'Abschussliste F f: *auf der~ stehen* be on the hit list

'Abschussrampe f MIL launching pad

'abschütteln v/t (sep, -ge-, h) shake off

'abschwächen v/t (sep, -ge-, h) lessen, diminish

'abschweifen fig v/i (sep, -ge-, sein) digress (*von* from)

'Abschweifung f (-; -en) digression

absehbar ['apzeːbaːɐ] adj foreseeable; *in ~er (auf~e) Zeit* in the (for the) foreseeable future

'absehen v/t (irr, *sehen*, sep, -ge-, h) foresee; *es ist kein Ende abzusehen* there is no end in sight; *es abgesehen haben auf* (acc) be after; *~ von* refrain from

'abseilen v/refl (sep, -ge-, h) descend by a rope, Br a. abseil; F make a getaway

abseits ['apzaɪts] adv and prp away or remote from

'Abseitsfalle f soccer: offside trap

abseitsstehen v/i (irr, *stehen*, sep, -ge-, h) soccer: be left out

'absenden v/t ([irr, *senden*,] sep, -ge-, h) send (off), dispatch; mail, esp Br post (*letter etc*)

'Absender m (-s; -) sender

absetzbar ['apzɛtsbaːɐ] adj: *steuerlich ~* deductible from tax

'absetzen (sep, -ge-, h) **1.** v/t take off (*hat, glasses etc*); set or put down (*bag etc*); drop (*passenger*); dismiss (*employee*); THEA, film: take off; deduct (*from tax*); depose (*king etc*); ECON sell; *sich ~* CHEM, GEOL settle; be deposited **2.** v/i: *ohne abzusetzen* without stopping

'Absetzung f (-; -en) dismissal; deposition; THEA, film: withdrawal

'Absicht f (-; -en) intention; *mit ~* on purpose; **'absichtlich 1.** adj intentional **2.** adv on purpose

'absitzen (irr, *sitzen*, sep, -ge-) **1.** v/i (sein) dismount (*von* from); **2.** v/t (h) serve (*sentence*); F sit out (*play etc*)

absolut [apzoˈluːt] adj absolute

Absolvent [apzɔlˈvɛnt] m (-en; -en), **Absol'ventin** f (-; -nen) graduate; **absolvieren** [apzɔlˈviːrən] v/t (no -ge-, h) attend (*school*); complete (*studies*);

graduate from (*college etc*)

'absondern v/t (sep, -ge-, h) separate; MED, BIOL secrete; *sich ~* cut o.s. off (*von* from); **'Absonderung** f (-; -en) separation; MED, BIOL secretion

absorbieren [apzɔrˈbiːrən] v/t (no -ge-, h) absorb (a. fig)

'abspeichern v/t (sep, -ge-, h) IT store, save

abspenstig ['apʃpɛnstɪç] adj: *j-m die Freundin ~ machen* steal s.o.'s girlfriend

absperren v/t (sep, -ge-, h) lock; turn off (*water, gas etc*); block off (*road*); cordon off; **'Absperrung** f (-; -en) barrier; cordon

'abspielen v/t (sep, -ge-, h) play (*record etc*); SPORT pass (*the ball*); *sich ~* happen, take place

'Absprache f agreement

'absprechen v/t (irr, *sprechen*, sep, -ge-, h) agree upon; arrange; *j-m die Fähigkeit etc ~* dispute s.o.'s ability etc

'abspringen v/i (irr, *springen*, sep, -ge-, sein) jump off; AVIAT jump, bail out; fig back out (*von* of)

'Absprung m jump; SPORT take-off; fig *den ~ schaffen* make it

'abspülen v/t (sep, -ge-, h) rinse; wash up

abstammen v/i (sep, no past participle) be descended (*von* from); CHEM, LING derive; **'Abstammung** f (-; no pl) descent; derivation; **'Abstammungslehre** f theory of the origin of species

'Abstand m distance (a. fig); interval; *~ halten* keep one's distance; fig *mit~* by far

abstatten ['apʃtatən] v/t (sep, -ge-, h) *j-m e-n Besuch ~* pay a visit to s.o.

'abstauben v/t (sep, -ge-, h) dust; F fig sponge; swipe

'Abstauber F m (-s;-), **'Abstaubertor** n SPORT opportunist goal

'abstechen (irr, *stechen*, sep, -ge-, h) **1.** v/t stick (*pig etc*) **2.** v/i contrast (*von* with); **'Abstecher** m (-s; -) side-trip, excursion (a. fig)

'abstecken v/t (sep, -ge-, h) mark out

'abstehen v/i (irr, *stehen*, sep, -ge-, h) stick out, protrude; → *abgestanden*

'absteigen v/i (irr, *steigen*, sep, -ge-, sein) get off (a horse etc); climb down;

stay (*in dat* at); SPORT *Am* be moved down to a lower division, *Br* be relegated; '**Absteiger** *m* (-*s*; -) SPORT *Br* relegated club

'**abstellen** *v/t* (*sep*, -*ge*-, *h*) put down; leave (*s.th. with s.o.*); turn off (*gas etc*); park (*car*); *fig* put an end to *s.th.*

'**Abstellgleis** *n* RAIL siding; *j-n aufs ~ schieben* F push s.o. aside

'**Abstellraum** *m* storeroom

'**abstempeln** *v/t* (*sep*, -*ge*-, *h*) stamp

'**absterben** *v/i* (*irr*, *sterben*, *sep*, -*ge*-, *sein*) die off; *limb*: go numb

Abstieg ['apʃtiːk] *m* (-[*e*]*s*; -*e*) descent; *fig* decline; SPORT *Br* relegation

'**abstimmen** *v/i* (*sep*, -*ge*-, *h*) vote (*über acc* on)

'**Abstimmung** *f* vote; *radio*: tuning

Abstinenzler [apstiˈnɛntslɐ] *m* (-*s*; -) teetotal(l)er

'**Abstoß** *m* SPORT goal-kick

'**abstoßen** *v/t* (*irr*, *stoßen*, *sep*, -*ge*-, *h*) repel; MED reject; push off (*boat*); F get rid of *s.th.*; *~d fig adj* repulsive

abstrakt [apˈstrakt] *adj* abstract

'**abstreiten** *v/t* (*irr*, *streiten*, *sep*, -*ge*-, *h*) deny

'**Abstrich** *m* MED smear; *pl* ECON cuts; *fig* reservations

'**abstufen** *v/t* (*sep*, -*ge*-, *h*) graduate; gradate (*colors*)

'**abstumpfen** (*sep*, -*ge*-) **1.** *v/t* (*h*) blunt, dull (*a. fig*) **2.** *fig v/i* (*sein*) become unfeeling

'**Absturz** *m*, '**abstürzen** *v/i* (*sep*, -*ge*-, *sein*) fall; AVIAT, IT crash

'**absuchen** *v/t* (*sep*, -*ge*-, *h*) search (*nach* for)

absurd [apˈzʊrt] *adj* absurd, preposterous

Abszess [apsˈtsɛs] *m* (-*es*; -*e*) MED abscess

Abt [apt] *m* (-[*e*]*s*; *Äbte* ['ɛptə]) REL abbot

'**abtasten** *v/t* (*sep*, -*ge*-, *h*) feel (for); MED palpate; frisk; TECH, IT scan

'**abtauen** *v/t* (*sep*, -*ge*-, *h*) defrost

Abtei [apˈtai] *f* (-; -*en*) REL abbey

Abteil [apˈtail] *n* (-[*e*]*s*; -*e*) RAIL compartment

'**abteilen** *v/t* (*sep*, -*ge*-, *h*) divide; ARCH partition off

Ab'teilung *f* (-; -*en*) department (*a.* ECON); ward (*of hospital*); MIL detachment; **Ab'teilungsleiter** *m* head of (a) department; *Am* floorwalker, *Br* shopwalker

Äbtissin [ɛpˈtɪsɪn] *f* (-; -*nen*) REL abbess

'**abtöten** *v/t* (*sep*, -*ge*-, *h*) kill (*bacteria etc*); *fig* deaden (*feelings etc*)

'**abtragen** *v/t* (*irr*, *tragen*, *sep*, -*ge*-, *h*) wear out (*clothes*); clear away (*dishes etc*); pay off (*debt*)

'**Abtrans,port** *m* transportation

'**abtreiben** (*irr*, *treiben*, *sep*, -*ge*-) **1.** *v/i* MED (*h*) have an abortion; MAR, AVIAT (*sein*) be blown off course **2.** *v/t* (*h*) MED abort; '**Abtreibung** *f* (-; -*en*) abortion; *e-e ~ vornehmen* perform an abortion

'**abtrennen** *v/t* (*sep*, -*ge*-, *h*) detach; separate; MED sever

'**abtreten** (*irr*, *treten*, *sep*, -*ge*-) **1.** *v/t* (*h*) wear down (*heels*); wipe (*one's feet*); *fig* give up (*an acc* to); **2.** *v/i* (*sein*) resign; THEA; exit; '**Abtreter** *m* (-*s*; -) doormat

'**abtrocknen** (*sep*, -*ge*-, *h*) **1.** *v/t* dry; *sich ~* dry o.s. off **2.** *v/i* dry the dishes, *Br a.* dry up

abtrünnig ['aptrʏnɪç] *adj* unfaithful, disloyal; '**Abtrünnige** ['aptrʏnɪgə] *m*, *f* (-*n*; -*n*) renegade, turncoat

abtun *v/t* (*irr*, *tun*, *sep*, -*ge*-, *h*) dismiss (*als* as), brush *s.o.*, *s.th.* aside

abwägen ['apvɛːgən] *v/t* (*irr*, *wägen*, *sep*, -*ge*-, *h*) weigh (*gegen* against)

'**abwählen** *v/t* (*sep*, -*ge*-, *h*) vote out

'**abwälzen** *v/t* (*sep*, -*ge*-, *h*) *et. auf j-n ~* shove s.th. off on (to) s.o.

'**abwandeln** *v/t* (*sep*, -*ge*-, *h*) vary, modify

'**abwandern** *v/i* (*sep*, -*ge*-, *sein*) migrate (*von* from; *nach* to); '**Abwanderung** *f* migration

'**Abwandlung** *f* modification, variation

'**Abwärme** *f* TECH waste heat

Abwart ['apvart] *m* (-*s*; -*e*) *Swiss →* **Hausmeister**

'**abwarten** (*sep*, -*ge*-, *h*) **1.** *v/t* wait for, await **2.** *v/i* wait; *warten wir ab!* let's wait and see!; *wart nur ab!* just wait!

abwärts ['apvɛrts] *adv* down, downward(s)

Abwasch ['apvaʃ] *m* (-[*e*]*s*; *no pl*) *den ~ machen* do the washing-up

'**abwaschbar** *adj* washable

'**abwaschen** (*irr*, *waschen*, *sep*, -*ge*-, *h*) **1.** *v/t* wash off **2.** *v/i* do the dishes, *Br a.*

wash up
'Abwaschwasser n dishwater
'Abwasser n TECH waste water, sewage; **~aufbereitung** f TECH sewage treatment
'abwechseln v/i (sep, -ge-, h) alternate; **sich mit j-m ~** take turns (**bei et.** at [doing] s.th.); **~d** adv by turns
'Abwechslung f (-; -en) change; **zur ~** for a change; **'abwechslungsreich** adj varied; colo(u)rful
'Abweg m: **auf ~e geraten** go astray
abwegig ['apveːɡɪç] adj absurd, unrealistic
'Abwehr f (-; no pl) defen|se, Br -ce (a. SPORT); warding off (of blow etc); save (of ball)
'abwehren v/t (sep, -ge-, h) ward off (blow etc); beat off; SPORT block
'Abwehr|fehler m SPORT defensive error; **~kräfte** pl MED resistance; **~spieler** m SPORT defender; **~stoffe** pl MED antibodies
'abweichen v/i (irr, weichen, sep, -ge-, sein) deviate (**von** from); digress
'Abweichung f (-; -en) deviation
'abweisen v/t (irr, weisen, sep, -ge-, h) turn away; rebuff; decline, turn down (request, offer etc); **~d** adj unfriendly
'abwenden v/t ([irr, wenden,] sep, -ge-, h) turn away (a. **sich ~**) (**von** from); avert (tragedy etc)
'abwerfen v/t (irr, werfen, sep, -ge-, h) throw off; AVIAT drop; BOT shed (leaves); ECON yield (profit)
'abwerten v/t (sep, -ge-, h) ECON devalue; **~d** fig adj disparaging
'Abwertung f ECON devaluation
'abwesend adj absent
'Abwesenheit f (-; no pl) absence
abwickeln v/t (sep, -ge-, h) unwind; ECON handle; transact (business)
'abwiegen v/t (irr, wiegen, sep, -ge-, h) weigh (out)
'abwimmeln F v/t (sep, -ge-, h) **j-n ~** get rid of s.o., give s.o. the elbow
'abwischen v/t (sep, -ge-, h) wipe (off)
'Abwurf m dropping; soccer: throw-out
'abwürgen F v/t (sep, -ge-, h) MOT stall; fig stifle; **'abzahlen** v/t (sep, -ge-, h) make monthly etc payments for; pay off; **'abzählen** v/t (sep, -ge-, h) count
'Abzahlung f: **et. auf ~ kaufen** Am buy s.th. on the instalment plan (Br on hire

purchase)
'abzapfen v/t (sep, -ge-, h) tap, draw off
'Abzeichen n badge; medal
'abzeichnen v/t (sep, -ge-, h) copy, draw; sign, initial; **sich ~** (begin to) show; stand out (**gegen** against)
'Abziehbild n Am decal, Br transfer
'abziehen (irr, ziehen, sep, -ge-) 1. v/t (h) take off, remove; MATH subtract; strip (bed); take out (key); **das Fell ~** skin 2. v/i (sein) go away; MIL withdraw; smoke: escape; storm, clouds: move off
'Abzug m ECON deduction; discount; MIL withdrawal; PRINT copy; PHOT print; gun: trigger; TECH vent, outlet; cooker hood
abzüglich ['aptsyːklɪç] prp less, minus
'abzweigen (sep, -ge-) 1. v/t (h) divert (resources etc) (**für** to); 2. v/i (sein) path etc: branch off
'Abzweigung f (-; -en) junction
ach [ax] int oh!; **~ je!** oh dear!; **~ so!** I see; **~ was!** surprised: really?, annoyed: of course not!, nonsense!
Achse ['aksə] f (-; -n) TECH axle; MATH etc axis; F **auf ~ sein** be on the move
Achsel ['aksəl] f (-; -n) ANAT shoulder; **die ~n zucken** shrug one's shoulders
'Achselhöhle f ANAT armpit
'Achsenbruch m MOT broken axle
acht [axt] adj eight; **heute in ~ Tagen** a week from today, esp Br today week; (**heute**) **vor ~ Tagen** a week ago (today)
Acht f: **~ geben → achtgeben; außer ~ lassen** disregard; **sich in ~ nehmen** be careful, look or watch out (**vor** dat for)
achte ['axtə] adj eighth
'achteckig adj octagonal
Achtel ['axtəl] n (-s; -) eighth (part)
achten (ge-, h) 1. v/t respect 2. v/i: **~ auf** (acc) pay attention to; keep an eye on; watch; be careful with; **darauf ~, dass** see to it that
ächten ['ɛçtən] v/t (ge-, h) ban; esp HIST outlaw
Achter ['axtɐ] m (-s; -) rowing: eight
'Achterbahn f roller coaster
'achtfach adj and adv eightfold
achtgeben v/i (irr, geben, sep, -ge-, h) be careful; pay attention (**auf** acc to); take care (**auf** acc of); **gib acht!** look or watch out!, be careful!
'achtlos adj careless, heedless
'Achtung f (-; no pl) respect (**vor** dat

for); **~!** look out!; MIL attention!; **~! ~!** attention please!; **~! Fertig! Los!** On your marks! Get set! Go!; **~ Stufe!** Am caution: step!, Br mind the step!

'achtzehn adj eighteen

'achtzehnte adj eighteenth

achtzig ['axtsıç] adj eighty; **die ~er Jahre** the eighties; **~ste** adj eightieth

ächzen ['ɛçtsən] v/i (ge-, h) groan (*vor* dat with)

Acker ['akɐ] m (-s; Äcker ['ɛkɐ]) field; **~bau** m (-[e]s; no pl) agriculture; farming; **~ und Viehzucht** crop and stock farming; **~land** n (-[e]s; no pl) farmland

'ackern F v/i (ge-, h) slog (away)

Adapter [a'daptɐ] m (-s; -) TECH adapter

addieren [a'di:rən] v/t (no -ge-, h) add (up); **Addition** [adi'tsio:n] f (-; -en) addition, adding up

Adel ['a:dəl] m (-s; no pl) aristocracy

'adeln v/t (ge-, h) ennoble (a. fig); Br knight

Ader ['a:dɐ] f (-; -n) ANAT blood vessel, vein

Adjektiv ['atjɛktiːf] n (-s; -e) LING adjective

Adler ['a:dlɐ] m (-s; -) ZO eagle

adlig ['a:dlıç] adj noble; **Adlige** ['a:dlıgə] m, f (-n; -n) noble|man (-woman)

Admiral [atmi'ra:l] m (-s; -e) MAR admiral

adoptieren [adɔp'tiːrən] v/t (no -ge-, h) adopt; **Adoptivkind** [adɔp'tiːfkɪnt] n adopted child

Adressbuch [a'drɛsbuːx] n directory

Adresse [a'drɛsə] f (-; -n) address

adressieren [adrɛ'siːrən] v/t (no -ge-, h) address (*an* acc to)

Advent [at'vɛnt] m (-[e]s; no pl) REL Advent; Advent Sunday

Ad'ventszeit f Christmas season

Adverb [at'vɛrp] n (-s; Adverbien [at-'vɛrbiən]) LING adverb

Aerobic [ɛ'ro:bık] n (-s; no pl) aerobics

Affäre [a'fɛːrə] f (-; -n) affair

Affe ['afə] m (-n; -n) ZO monkey; ape

Affekt [a'fɛkt] m (-[e]s; -e) **im ~** in the heat of passion (a. JUR)

affektiert [afɛk'tiːɐt] adj affected

Afrika ['a:frika] Africa; **Afrikaner** [afri-'ka:nɐ] m (-s; -), **Afrikanerin** [afri-'ka:nərın] f (-; -nen), **afri'kanisch** adj African

After ['aftɐ] m (-s; -) ANAT anus

AG abbr of **Aktiengesellschaft** Am (stock) corporation, Br PLC, public limited company

Agent [a'gɛnt] m (-en; -en), **A'gentin** f (-; -nen) agent; POL (secret) agent

Agentur [agɛn'tuːɐ] f (-; -en) agency

Aggression [agrɛ'sio:n] f (-; -en) aggression; **aggressiv** [agrɛ'siːf] adj aggressive; **Aggressivität** [agrɛsivi'tɛːt] f (-; no pl) aggressiveness

Agitator [agi'ta:to:ɐ] m (-s; -en [agita-'to:rən]) agitator

ah [a:] int ah!

äh [ɛː] int er; *disgusted:* ugh!

aha [a'ha] int I see!, oh!

A'ha-Erlebnis n aha-experience

Ahn [a:n] m (-[e]s; -en; -en) ancestor, pl **~en** forefathers

ähneln ['ɛːnəln] v/i (ge-, h) resemble, look like

ahnen ['a:nən] v/t (ge-, h) suspect; foresee, know

ähnlich ['ɛːnlıç] adj similar (*dat* to); **j-m ~ sehen** look like s.o.

'Ähnlichkeit f (-; -en) likeness, resemblance, similarity (*mit* to)

'Ahnung f (-; -en) presentiment, a. foreboding; notion, idea; **ich habe keine ~** I have no idea; **'ahnungslos** adj unsuspecting, innocent

Ahorn ['a:hɔrn] m (-s, -e) BOT maple

Ähre ['ɛːrə] f (-; -n) BOT ear; spike

Aids [eıdz] n (-; no pl) MED AIDS

'Aids|-Kranke m, f MED AIDS victim or sufferer; **~test** m MED AIDS test

Airbag ['ɛəbæg] m (-s; -s) MOT airbag

Akademie [akade'mi:] f (-; -n) academy, college; **Akademiker(in)** [aka-'de:mikɐ, aka'de:mikɐrın] m(f) (-s; -/-; -nen) university graduate; **akademisch** [aka'de:mıʃ] adj academic

akklimatisieren [aklimati'zi:rən] v/refl (no -ge-, h) acclimatize (*an* acc to)

Akkord [a'kɔrt] m (-[e]s; -e) MUS chord; **im ~** ECON by the piece or job; **~arbeit** f ECON piecework; **~arbeiter(in)** ECON pieceworker

Akkordeon [a'kɔrdeɔn] n (-s; -s) MUS accordion

Ak'kordlohn m ECON piece wages

Akku ['aku] F m (-s; -s), **Akkumulator** [akumu'la:to:ɐ] m (-s; -en [akumula-'to:rən]) TECH (storage) battery, Br a.

accumulator

Akkusativ ['akuzatiːf] *m* (*-s*; *-e*) LING accusative (case)

Akne ['aknə] *f* (*-*; *-n*) MED acne

Akrobat [akro'baːt] *m* (*-en*; *-en*), **Akro·'batin** *f* (*-*; *-nen*) acrobat; **akro'batisch** *adj* acrobatic

Akt [akt] *m* (*-[e]s*; *-e*) act(ion); THEA act; PAINT, PHOT nude

Akte ['aktə] *f* (*-*; *-n*) file; *pl.* files, records; **zu den ~n legen** file

'Akten|deckel *m* folder; **~koffer** *m* attaché case; **~ordner** *m* file; **~tasche** *f* briefcase; **~zeichen** *n* reference (number)

Aktie ['aktsiə] *f* (*-*; *-n*) ECON share, *esp Am* stock; **'Aktiengesellschaft** *f Am* corporation, *Br* joint-stock company

Aktion [ak'tsioːn] *f* (*-*; *-en*) campaign, drive; MIL *ect* operation; **in ~** in action

Aktionär [aktsio'nɛːɐ̯] *m* (*-s*; *-e*), **Aktio·'närin** *f* (*-*; *-nen*) ECON shareholder, *esp Am* stockholder

aktiv [ak'tiːf] *adj* active

Aktiv ['aktiːf] *n* (*-s*; *no pl*) LING active voice; **aktivieren** *v/t* (*no -ge-*, *h*) activate; **Aktivist** [akti'vist] *m* (*-en*; *-en*) *esp* POL activist

Ak'tivurlaub *m* activity vacation

aktualisieren [aktuali'ziːrən] *v/t* (*no -ge-*, *h*) update

aktuell [aktü'ɛl] *adj* topical; current; up-to-date; TV, *radio*: **e-e ~e Sendung** a current affairs *or* news feature

Akupunktur [akupuŋnk'tuːɐ̯] *f* (*-*; *-en*) MED acupuncture

Akustik [a'kustɪk] *f* (*-*; *no pl*) acoustics

a'kustisch *adj* acoustic

akut [a'kuːt] *adj* urgent (*problem etc*); *a.* MED acute

Akzent [ak'tsɛnt] *m* (*-[e]s*; *-e*) accent; stress (*a. fig*)

akzeptabel [aktsɛp'taːbəl] *adj* acceptable; reasonable (*price etc*)

akzeptieren [aktsɛp'tiːrən] *v/t* (*no -ge-*, *h*) accept

Alarm [a'larm] *m* (*-[e]s*; *-e*) alarm; **~ schlagen** sound the alarm; **~anlage** *f* alarm system; **~bereitschaft** *f*: **in ~** on standby, on the alert

alarmieren [alar'miːrən] *v/t* (*no -ge-*, *h*) call; alert; **~d** *adj* alarming

albern ['albɐn] *adj* silly, foolish

Album ['albʊm] *n* (*-s*; *Alben* ['albən]) album (*a. record*)

Algebra ['algəbra] *f* (*-*; *no pl*) MATH algebra

Algen ['algən] *pl* BOT algae; **~pest** *f* plague *of* algae, algal bloom

Alibi ['aːlibi] *n* (*-s*; *-s*) JUR alibi

Alimente [ali'mɛntə] *pl* JUR alimony

Alkohol ['alkohoːl] *m* (*-s*; *no pl*) alcohol; **'alkoholfrei** *adj* nonalcoholic, soft; **Alkoholiker(in)** [alko'hoːlikɐ, alko'hoːlikərin] *m*(*f*) (*-s*; *-/-*; *-nen*) alcoholic; **alko'holisch** *adj* alcoholic; **Alkoholismus** [alkoho'lɪsmʊs] *m* (*-*; *no pl*) alcoholism; **alkoholsüchtig** *adj* addicted to alcohol; **Alkoholtest** *m* alcohol test, *Br* breathalyser® test

All *n* (*-s*; *no pl*) universe; (outer) space

alle¹ ['alə] *indef pron and adj* all; **~s (Beliebige)** anything; **~** (**Leute**) everybody; anybody; **~ beide** both of them; **wir ~** all of us; **~s in ~m** all in all; **auf ~ Fälle** in any case; **~ drei Tage** every three days; → **Art, Gute, vor**;

alle² ['alə] F *adj*: **~ sein** be all gone; **mein Geld ist ~** I'm out of money

Allee [a'leː] *f* (*-*; *-n*) avenue

allein [a'lain] *adj and adv* alone; lonely; by o.s.; **ganz ~** all alone; **er hat es ganz ~ gemacht** he did it all by himself; **~ stehend** → **alleinstehend**

Al'lein|erziehende *m*, *f* (*-n*; *-n*) single parent; **~gang** *m*: **im ~** single-handedly, solo

alleinig [a'lainıç] *adj* sole

Al'leinsein *n* (*-s*; *no pl*) loneliness

alleinstehend *adj* single

Allerbeste ['alə'bɛstə]: **der (die, das) ~** the best of all, the very best

allerdings ['alɐ'dıŋs] *adv* however, though; **~!** certainly!, *esp Am* F sure!

'aller'erste *adj* very first

Allergie [alɛr'giː] *f* (*-*; *-n*) MED allergy (**gegen** to); **allergisch** [a'lɛrgıʃ] *adj* allergic (**gegen** to)

'aller'hand F *adj* a good deal (of); **das ist ja ~!** that's a bit much!

'Aller'heiligen *n* REL All Saints' Day

allerlei ['alə'lai] *adj* all kinds *or* sorts of

'aller'letzte *adj* last of all, very last; **~'liebst 1.** *adj* (most) lovely **2.** *adv*: **am ~en mögen** like best of all; **~'meiste** *adj* (by far the) most; **~'nächste** *adj* very next; **in ~r Zeit** in the very near future; **~'neu(e)ste** *adj* very latest

'Aller'seelen *n* REL All Souls' Day

allerseits [ˈalɐˈzaits] *adv* F: *Tag~!* hi, everybody!

'aller'wenigst *adv*: *am ~en* least of all

alles everything

allesamt [ˈaləˈzamt] *adv* all together

'allge'mein 1. *adj* general; common; universal **2.** *adv*: *im Allgemeinen* in general, generally; *~ verständlich* intelligible (to all), popular

Allge'mein|arzt *m*, **Allge'meinärztin** *f* Br GP, Am family practitioner; *~bildung* *f* general education

'Allge'meinheit *f* (-; *no pl*) (general) public

allgemeinver'ständlich *adj* → *allgemein*

All'heilmittel *n* cure-all (*a. fig*)

Allianz [aˈljants] *f* (-; *-en*) alliance

Alligator [aliˈgaːtoːɐ] *m* (*-s*; *-en*) alligator

Alliierte [aliˈiːɐtə]: *die ~n pl* POL the Allies

'all|'jährlich *adv* every year; *~ stattfindend* annual; *~'mächtig* *adj* omnipotent; Almighty (*God*)

allmählich [alˈmɛːlɪç] **1.** *adj* gradual **2.** *adv* gradually

'Allradantrieb *m* MOT four-wheel drive

allseitig [ˈalzaitɪç] *adv*: *~ interessiert sein* have all-round interests

'Alltag *m* everyday life

'all|'täglich *adj* everyday; *fig a.* ordinary; *~'wissend* *adj* omniscient

'allzu *adv* (all) too; *~ viel* too much

Alm [alm] *f* (-; *-en*) alpine pasture, alp

Almosen [ˈalmoːzən] *n* (*-s*; -) alms

'Alpdruck *m* (*-[e]s*; *no pl*) nightmare (*a. fig*)

Alphabet [alfaˈbeːt] *n* (*-[e]s*; *-e*) alphabet; **alpha'betisch** *adj* alphabetical

alpin [alˈpiːn] *adj* alpine

'Alptraum *m* nightmare (*a. fig*)

als [als] *cj time*: when; while; *after comp*: than; *~ ich ankam* when I arrived; *~ Kind* (*Geschenk*) as a child (present); *älter ~* older than; *~ ob* as if, as though; *nichts ~* nothing but

also [ˈalzo] *cj* so, therefore; F well, you know; *~ gut!* very well (then)!, all right (then)!; *~ doch* so … after all; *du willst ~ gehen* etc*?* so you want to go *etc?*

alt [alt] *adj* old; HIST ancient; classical (*language*); *ein 12 Jahre ~er Junge* a

twelve-year-old boy

Alt *m* (*-s*; *no pl*) MUS alto

Altar [alˈtaːɐ] *m* (*-s*; *Altäre* [alˈtɛːrə]) REL altar

'Alte *m*, *f* (*-n*; *-n*) *der ~* the old man (*a. fig*); the boss; *die ~* the old woman (*a. fig*); *die ~n pl* the old

Altenheim *n* → *Altersheim*

'Altenpfleger(in) geriatric nurse

Alter [ˈaltɐ] *n* (*-s*; *no pl*) age; old age; *im ~ von …* at the age of …; *er ist in deinem ~* he's your age

älter [ˈɛltɐ] *adj* older; *mein ~er Bruder* my elder brother; *ein ~er Herr* an elderly gentleman

'altern *v/i* (*ge-*, *sein*) grow old, age

alternativ [altɐnaˈtiːf] *adj* alternative; POL ecological, green; *a.* counter-culture (*movement etc*)

Alternative¹ [altɐnaˈtiːvə] *f* (-; *-n*) alternative; option, choice

Alterna'tive² *m*, *f* (*-n*; *-n*) ecologist, member of the counterculture movement

'Alters|grenze *f* age limit; retirement age; *~heim* *n* old people's home; *~rente* *f* old-age pension; *~schwäche* *f* (-; *no pl*) infirmity; *an ~ sterben* die of old age; *~versorgung* *f* old age pension (scheme)

'Altertum *n* (*-s*; *no pl*) antiquity

'Altglascon,tainer *m Am* glass recycling bin, *Br* bottle bank

'altklug *adj* precocious

'Altlasten *pl* residual pollution

'Altme,tall *n* scrap (metal)

'altmodisch *adj* old-fashioned

'Altöl *n* waste oil

'Altpa,pier *n* waste paper

'altsprachlich *adj*: *~es Gymnasium appr* classical secondary school

'Altstadt *f* old town; *~sa,nierung* *f* town-cent|er (*Br* -re) rehabilitation

'Altwarenhändler *m* second-hand dealer

Alt'weibersommer *m* Indian summer; gossamer

Aluminium [aluˈmiːnjʊm] *n* (*-s*; *no pl*) alumin(i)um

am [am] *prp* at the (*window etc*); *time*: in the (*morning etc*); at the (*weekend etc*); on (*Sunday etc*); *~ 1. Mai* on May 1st; *~ Tage* during the day; *~ Himmel* in the sky; *~ meisten* most; *~ Leben* alive

Amateur [ama'tøːɐ] *m* (*-s*; *-e*) amateur; **~funker** *m* radio amateur, F radio ham

Amboss ['ambɔs] *m* (*-es*; *-e*) anvil

ambulant [ambu'lant] *adv*: **~ behandelt werden** MED get outpatient treatment

Ambulanz [ambu'lants] *f* (*-*; *-en*) MED outpatients' department; MOT ambulance

Ameise ['aːmaizə] *f* (*-*; *-n*) ZO ant

'Ameisenhaufen *m* ZO anthill

Amerika [a'meːrika] America

Amerikaner [ameri'kaːnɐ] *m* (*-s*; *-*), **Ameri'kanerin** [ameri'kaːnərin] *f* (*-*; *-nen*), **ameri'kanisch** *adj* American

Amnestie [amnɛs'tiː] *f* (*-*; *-n*), **amnes'tieren** *v/t* (*no -ge-*, *h*) JUR amnesty

Amok ['aːmɔk] *m*: **~ laufen** run amok

Ampel ['ampəl] *f* (*-*; *-n*) traffic light(s)

Amphibie [am'fiːbjə] *f* (*-*; *-n*) ZO amphibian

Ampulle [am'pulə] *f* (*-*; *-n*) ampoule

Amputation [amputa'tsjoːn] *f* (*-*; *-en*) MED amputation; **amputieren** [ampu-'tiːrən] *v/t* (*no -ge-*, *h*) MED amputate

Amsel ['amzəl] *f* (*-*; *-n*) ZO blackbird

Amt [amt] *n* (*-[e]s*; *Ämter* ['ɛmtɐ]) office, department, *esp Am* bureau; position; duty, function; TEL exchange

'amtlich *adj* official

'Amts|arzt *m* medical examiner (*Br* officer); **~einführung** *f* inauguration; **~geheimnis** *n* official secret; **~geschäfte** *pl* official duties; **~zeichen** *n* TEL dial (*Br* dialling) tone; **~zeit** *f* term (of office)

Amulett [amu'lɛt] *n* (*-[e]s*; *-e*) amulet, (lucky) charm

amüsant [amy'zant] *adj* amusing, entertaining

amüsieren [amy'ziːrən] *v/t* (*no -ge-*, *h*) amuse; **sich ~** enjoy o.s., have a good time; **sich ~ über** (*acc*) laugh at

an [an] **1.** *prp*: **~ der Themse** (*Küste*, *Wand*) on the Thames (coast, wall); **~ s-m Schreibtisch** at his desk; **~ der Hand** by the hand; **~ der Arbeit** at work; **~ den Hausaufgaben sitzen** sit over one's homework; *et.* **schicken ~** (*acc*) send s.th. to; **sich lehnen ~** (*acc*) lean against; **~ die Tür etc klopfen** knock at the door *etc*; **~ e-m Sonntagmorgen** on a Sunday morning; **~ dem Tag, ...** on the day ...; **~ Weihnachten** *etc* at Christmas *etc*; **• Mangel, Stelle,**

sterben 2. *adv* on (*a. light etc*); **von jetzt** (*da*, *heute*) **~** from now (that time, today) on; **München ~ 16.45** arrival Munich 4.45 p.m.

Anabolikum [ana'boːlikum] *n* (*-s*; *-ka*) PHARM anabolic steroid

analog [ana'loːk] *adj* analogous

Ana'log... *in cpds* analog(ue) (*computer etc*)

Analphabet [anʔalfa'beːt] *m* (*-en*; *-en*), **Analpha'betin** *f* (*-*; *-nen*) illiterate (person)

Analyse [ana'lyːzə] *f* (*-*; *-n*) analysis

analysieren [analy'ziːrən] *v/t* (*no -ge-*, *h*) analy|ze, *Br* -se

Ananas ['ananas] *f* (*-*; *-*, *-se*) BOT pineapple

Anarchie [anar'çiː] *f* (*-*; *-n*) anarchy

Anatomie [anato'miː] *f* (*-*; *-n*) anatomy

anatomisch [ana'toːmɪʃ] *adj* anatomical

'anbahnen *v/t* (*sep*, *-ge-*, *h*) pave the way for; **sich ~** be developing; be impending

'Anbau *m* (*-[e]s*; *-ten*) AGR (*no pl*) cultivation; ARCH annex, extension

'anbauen *v/t* (*sep*, *-ge-*, *h*) AGR cultivate, grow; ARCH add (**an** *acc* to), build on

'anbehalten *v/t* (*irr*, **halten**, *sep*, *no -ge-*, *h*) keep on

an'bei *adv* ECON enclosed

'anbeißen (*irr*, **beißen**, *sep*, *-ge-*, *h*) **1.** *v/t* take a bite of **2.** *v/i fish*: bite; *fig* take the bait; **'anbellen** *v/t* (*sep*, *-ge-*, *h*) bark at; **'anbeten** *v/t* (*sep*, *-ge-*, *h*) adore, worship (*a. fig*)

'Anbetracht *m*: **in ~** (**dessen**, **dass**) considering (that)

'anbetteln *v/t* (*sep*, *-ge-*, *h*) **j-n um et.** ~ beg s.o. for s.th.; **anbiedern** ['anbiːdɐn] *v/refl* (*sep*, *-ge-*, *h*) curry favo(u)r (**bei** with); **'anbieten** *v/t* (*irr*, **bieten**, *sep*, *-ge-*, *h*) offer; **'anbinden** *v/t* (*irr*, **binden**, *sep*, *-ge-*, *h*) tie up; **~ an** (*acc or dat*) tie to

'Anblick *m* sight; **'anblicken** *v/t* (*sep*, *-ge-*, *h*) look at; glance at

'anbohren *v/t* (*sep*, *-ge-*, *h*) tap

'anbrechen (*irr*, **brechen**, *sep*, *-ge-*) **1.** *v/t* (*h*) break into (*supplies*); open **2.** *v/i* (*sein*) begin; *day*: break; *night*: fall

'anbrennen *v/i* (*irr*, **brennen**, *sep*, *-ge-*, *sein*) burn (*a.* **~ lassen**)

'anbringen *v/t* (*irr*, **bringen**, *sep*, *-ge-*, *h*) fix (*an dat* to)

'**Anbruch** *m* (-[e]*s*; *no pl*) beginning; *bei ~ der Nacht* at nightfall

'**anbrüllen** *v/t* (*sep*, -ge-, *h*) roar at

Andacht ['andaxt] *f* (-; -en) REL (*no pl*) devotion; service; prayers

andächtig ['andɛçtɪç] *adj* REL devout

'**andauern** *v/i* (*sep*, -ge-, *h*) continue, go on, last; **~d** *adj and adv* → *dauernd*

'**Andenken** *n* (-*s*; -) keepsake; souvenir (*both*: **an** *acc* of); *zum ~ an* (*acc*) in memory of

andere ['andərə] *adj and indef pron* other; different; *mit ~n Worten* in other words; *am ~n Morgen* the next morning; *et.* (*nichts*) *~s* s.th.; *nichts ~s als* nothing but; *die ~n* the others; *alle ~n* everybody else

andererseits ['andərə'zaɪts] *adv* on the other hand

ändern ['ɛndɐn] *v/t* (*ge*-, *h*) change; alter (*clothes*) *ich kann es nicht ~* I can't help it; *sich ~* change

'**andern'falls** *adv* otherwise

anders ['andɐs] *adv* different(ly); *jemand ~* somebody else; *~ werden* change; *~ sein* (*als*) be different (from); *es geht nicht ~* there is no other way; *~herum* **1.** *adv* the other way round **2.** F *adj* queer; *~wo(hin)* *adv* elsewhere

anderthalb ['andɐt'halp] *adj* one and a half

'**Änderung** *f* (-; -en) change; alteration

'**andeuten** *v/t* (*sep*, -ge-, *h*) hint (at), suggest; indicate; *j-m ~, dass* give s.o. a hint that

'**Andeutung** *f* (-; -en) hint, suggestion

'**Andrang** *m* (-[e]*s*; *no pl*) crush; ECON rush (*nach* for), run (*zu, nach* on)

'**andrehen** *v/t* (*sep*, -ge-, *h*) turn on; F *j-m et. ~* fob s.th. off on s.o.

'**androhen** *v/t* (*sep*, -ge-, *h*) *j-m et. ~* threaten s.o. with s.th.

'**aneignen** *v/refl* (*sep*, -ge-, *h*) acquire; *esp* JUR appropriate

anei'nander *adv* tie etc together; *~ denken* think of each other; *~geraten* *v/t* (*irr*, *geraten*, *sep*, *sein*) clash (*mit* with)

Anekdote [anɛk'do:tə] *f* (-; -n) anecdote

'**anekeln** *v/t* (*sep*, -ge-, *h*) disgust, sicken; *es ekelt mich an* it makes me sick

'**anerkannt** *adj* acknowledged, recognized

'**anerkennen** *v/t* (*irr*, *kennen*, *sep*, *no* -ge-, *h*) acknowledge, recognize; appreciate; *~d* *adj* appreciative

'**Anerkennung** *f* (-; -en) acknowledg(e)ment, recognition; appreciation

'**anfahren** (*irr*, *fahren*, *sep*, -ge-) **1.** *v/i* (*sein*) start **2.** *v/t* (*h*) deliver; MOT *etc* hit, *car etc*: a. run into; *fig j-n ~* jump on s.o.; '**Anfahrt** *f* journey, ride

'**Anfall** *m* MED fit, attack

'**anfallen** *v/t* (*irr*, *fallen*, *sep*, -ge-, *h*) attack, assault; *dog*: go for

'**anfällig** *adj* delicate; *~ für* susceptible to

'**Anfang** *m* beginning, start; *am ~* at the beginning; *~ Mai* early in May; *~ nächsten Jahres* early next year; *~ der neunziger Jahre* in the early nineties; *er ist ~ 20* he is in his early twenties; *von ~ an* from the beginning *or* start; '**anfangen** *v/t and v/i* (*irr*, *fangen*, *sep*, -ge-, *h*) begin, start; do; '**Anfänger** *m* (-*s*; -), '**Anfängerin** *f* (-; -*nen*) beginner

'**anfangs** *adv* at first

'**Anfangs|buchstabe** *m* initial (letter); *großer ~* capital (letter); *~stadium* *n*: *im ~* at an early stage

'**anfassen** *v/t* (*sep*, -ge-, *h*) touch; take (hold of); *sich ~* take each other by the hands; F *zum Anfassen* everyman's

'**anfechtbar** *adj* contestable; '**anfechten** *v/t* (*irr*, *fechten*, *sep*, -ge-, *h*) contest; '**Anfechtung** *f* (-; -en) contesting

'**anfertigen** *v/t* (*sep*, -ge-, *h*) make, manufacture

'**anfeuchten** *v/t* (*sep*, -ge-, *h*) moisten

'**anfeuern** *fig v/t* (*sep*, -ge-, *h*) cheer

'**anflehen** *v/t* (*sep*, -ge-, *h*) implore

'**anfliegen** *v/t* (*irr*, *fliegen*, *sep*, -ge-, *h*) AVIAT approach; fly (regularly) to

'**Anflug** *m* AVIAT approach; *fig* touch

'**anfordern** *v/t* (*sep*, -ge-, *h*) demand; request; '**Anforderung** *f* (-; -en) demand; request; *pl* requirements, qualifications

'**Anfrage** *f* (-; -*n*) inquiry

'**anfragen** *v/i* (*sep*, -ge-, *h*) inquire (*bei j-m nach et.* of s.o. about s.th.)

'**anfreunden** *v/refl* (*sep*, -ge-, *h*) make friends (*mit* with)

'**anfühlen** *v/refl* (*sep*, -ge-, *h*) feel; *es*

fühlt sich weich an it feels soft
'**anführen** *v/t (sep, -ge-, h)* lead; state; F fool; '**Anführer(in)** leader
'**Anführungszeichen** *pl* quotation marks, inverted commas
'**Angabe** *f (-; -n)* statement; indication; F big talk; *tennis:* service; *pl* information, data; TECH specifications
'**angeben** *(irr, geben, sep, -ge-, h)* **1.** *v/t* give, state; *customs:* declare; indicate; quote *(price)* **2.** *v/i* F fig brag, show off; *tennis:* serve; '**Angeber** F *m (-s; -)* braggart, show-off; **Angeberei** [angeːbəˈraɪ] F *f (-; no pl)* bragging, showing off
angeblich [ˈangeːplɪç] *adj* alleged; *~ ist er …* he is said to be …
'**angeboren** *adj* innate, inborn; MED congenital
'**Angebot** *n (-[e]s, -e)* offer *(a.* ECON*); ~ und Nachfrage* supply and demand
'**ange|bracht** *adj* appropriate; *~bunden adj: kurz ~* curt; *~gossen* F *adj: wie ~ sitzen* fit like a glove; *~heitert adj* tipsy, Br *a.* (slightly) merry
'**angehen** *(irr, gehen, sep, -ge-, sein)* **1.** F *v/i* light etc: go on **2.** *v/t* concern; *das geht dich nichts an* that is none of your business; *~d adj* future; *~er Arzt* doctor-to-be
'**angehören** *v/i (sep, no -ge-, h)* belong to; '**Angehörige** *m, f (-n; -n)* relative; member; *die nächsten ~n* the next of kin
'**Angeklagte** *m, f (-n; -n)* JUR defendant
Angel [ˈaŋəl] *f (-; -n)* fishing tackle; TECH hinge
'**Angelegenheit** *f (-; -en)* matter, affair
angelehnt *adj door etc:* ajar
'**angelernt** *adj* semi-skilled *(worker)*
'**Angelhaken** *m* fishhook
'**angeln** *(ge-, h)* **1.** *v/i (nach* for) fish, angle *(both a. fig)* **2.** *v/t* catch, hook
'**Angelrute** *f* fishing rod
Angelsachse [ˈaŋəlzaksə] *m (-n; -n)*, **angelsächsisch** [ˈaŋəlzɛksɪʃ] *adj* Anglo-Saxon
'**Angelschein** *m* fishing permit
'**Angelschnur** *f* fishing line
angemessen *adj* proper, suitable; just *(punishment)*; reasonable *(price)*
'**angenehm** *adj* pleasant, agreeable; *~!* pleased to meet you
'**ange|nommen** *cj* (let's) suppose, supposing; *~regt adj* animated; lively;

~schrieben adj: bei j-m gut (schlecht) ~ sein be in s.o.'s good (bad) books; *~sehen adj* respected
'**angesichts** *prp (gen)* in view of
'**Angestellte** *m, f (-n; -n)* employee *(bei* with), *pl* the staff
'**ange|tan** *adj: ganz ~ sein von* be taken with; *~trunken adj* (slightly) drunk; *in ~em Zustand* under the influence of alcohol; *~wandt adj* applied; *~wiesen adj: ~ auf (acc)* dependent (up)on
'**angewöhnen** *v/t (sep, no -ge-, h) sich (j-m) ~, et. zu tun* get (s.o.) used to doing s.th.; *sich das Rauchen ~* take to smoking; '**Angewohnheit** *f* habit
Angina [aŋˈgiːna] *f (-; -nen)* MED tonsillitis
'**angleichen** *v/t (irr, gleichen, sep, -ge-, h)* adjust *(an acc* to)
Angler [ˈaŋlɐ] *m (-s; -)* angler
Anglist [aŋˈglɪst] *m (-en; -en)*, **An-**'**glistin** *f (-; -nen)* student of *(or* graduate in) English
'**angreifen** *v/t (irr, greifen, sep, -ge-, h)* attack *(a.* SPORT *and fig);* affect *(health etc);* touch *(supplies)*
'**Angreifer** *m (-s; -)* attacker, SPORT *a.* offensive player; *esp* POL aggressor
'**angrenzend** *adj* adjacent *(an acc* to)
'**Angriff** *m* attack *(a.* SPORT *and fig);* MIL assault, charge; *in ~ nehmen* set about
'**angriffslustig** *adj* aggressive
Angst [aŋst] *f (-; Ängste* [ˈɛŋstə]*)* fear *(vor dat* of)*; ~ haben (vor dat* be afraid *or* scared (of)*; j-m ~ einjagen* frighten *or* scare s.o.; *(hab) keine Angst!* don't be afraid!; *~hase* F *m* chicken
ängstigen [ˈɛŋstɪgən] *v/t (ge-, h)* frighten, scare; *sich ~* be afraid *(vor dat* of); be worried *(um* about)
ängstlich [ˈɛŋstlɪç] *adj* timid, fearful; anxious
'**anhaben** F *v/t (irr, haben, sep, -ge-, h)* have on *(a.* light etc)*, a.* wear, be wearing *(dress etc)*
'**anhalten** *(irr, halten, sep, -ge-, h)* **1.** *v/t* stop; *den Atem ~* hold one's breath **2.** *v/i* stop; continue; *~d adj* continual
'**Anhalter** *m (-s; -)* hitchhiker; F *per ~ fahren* hitchhike
'**Anhaltspunkt** *m* clue
an'hand *prp (gen)* by means of
'**Anhang** *m* appendix; *(no pl)* relations;
'**anhängen** *v/t (sep, -ge-, h)* add; hang

up; RAIL, MOT couple (**an** acc to);
'**Anhänger** m (-s; -) follower, supporter
(a. SPORT); pendant; label, tag; MOT
trailer; '**anhänglich** adj affectionate;
contp clinging

'**anhäufen** v/t and v/refl (sep, -ge-, h)
heap up, accumulate

'**Anhäufung** f (-; -en) accumulation

'**anheben** v/t (irr, **heben**, sep, -ge-, h) lift,
raise (a. price); MOT jack up

'**anheften** v/t (sep, -ge-, h) attach, tack
(both: **an** acc to)

Anhieb m: **auf ~** on the first try

'**anhimmeln** F v/t (sep, -ge-, h) idolize,
worship

'**Anhöhe** f rise, hill, elevation

anhören v/t (sep, -ge-, h) listen to; **mit ~**
overhear; **es hört sich ... an** it sounds
...; '**Anhörung** f (-; -en) hearing

animieren [ani'miːrən] v/t (no -ge-, h)
encourage; stimulate

'**ankämpfen** v/i (sep, -ge-, h) **~ gegen**
fight s.th.

'**Ankauf** m purchase

Anker ['aŋkɐ] m (-s; -) MAR anchor; **vor ~
gehen** drop anchor

'**ankern** v/i (ge-, h) MAR anchor

'**anketten** v/t (sep, -ge-, h) chain up

'**Anklage** f (-; no pl) JUR accusation,
charge (a. fig); '**anklagen** v/t (sep,
-ge-, h) JUR accuse (**wegen** of), charge
(with) (both a. fig.)

'**anklammern** v/t (sep, -ge-, h) clip s.th.
on; **sich ~** (**an** acc) cling (to)

Anklang m: **~ finden** meet with approval

'**ankleben** v/t (sep, -ge-, h) stick on (**an**
dat or acc to)

'**anklicken** v/t (sep, -ge-, h) IT click

'**anklopfen** v/i (sep, -ge-, h) knock (**an**
dat or acc at)

'**anknipsen** v/t (sep, -ge-, h) switch on

'**anknüpfen** v/t (sep, -ge-, h) tie (**an** acc
to); fig begin; **Beziehungen ~** (**zu**) establish contacts (with)

'**ankommen** v/i (irr, **kommen**, sep, -ge-,
sein) arrive; **nicht gegen j-n ~** be no
match for s.o.; **es kommt** (**ganz**) **darauf an** it (all) depends; **es kommt darauf an, dass** what matters is; **darauf
kommt es nicht an** that doesn't matter; **es darauf ~ lassen** take a chance;
gut ~ (**bei**) fig go down well (with)

'**ankündigen** v/t (sep, -ge-, h) announce;

advertise; '**Ankündigung** f announcement; advertisement

Ankunft ['ankʊnft] f (-; no pl) arrival

'**anlächeln**, '**anlachen** v/t (sep, -ge-, h)
smile at

'**Anlage** f arrangement; facility; plant;
TECH system; (stereo etc) set; ECON investment; enclosure; fig gift; pl park,
gardens; **sanitäre ~n** sanitary facilities

Anlass ['anlas] m (-es; **Anlässe** ['an-
lɛsə]) occasion; cause

'**anlassen** v/t (irr, **lassen**, sep, -ge-, h)
MOT start; F keep on, leave on (a. light
etc); '**Anlasser** m (-s; -) MOT starter

anlässlich ['anlɛslɪç] prp (gen) on the
occasion of

'**Anlauf** m SPORT run-up; fig start

'**anlaufen** (irr, **laufen**, sep, -ge-) **1.** v/i
(sein) run up; fig start; metal: tarnish;
glasses etc: steam up **2.** v/t (h) MAR call
or touch at

'**anlegen** (sep, -ge-, h) **1.** v/t put on (dress
etc); lay out (garden etc); build (road
etc); invest (money); found (town etc);
MED apply (dressing etc); lay in (supplies); **sich mit j-m ~** pick a quarrel with
s.o. **2.** v/i MAR land; moor; **es ~ auf** (acc)
aim at; '**Anleger** m (-s; -) ECON inves-
tor; MAR landing stage

'**anlehnen** v/t (sep, -ge-, h) lean (**an** acc
against); leave door etc ajar; **sich ~ an**
(acc) lean against, fig lean on s.o.

Anleihe ['anlaiə] f (-; -n) ECON loan

'**Anleitung** f (-; -en) guidance, instruction; written instructions

'**Anliegen** n (-s; -) request; message (of a
film etc)

Anlieger ['anliːgɐ] m (-s; -) resident

'**anlocken** v/t (sep, -ge-, h) attract, lure

'**anmachen** v/t (sep, -ge-, h) light (fire
etc); turn on (light etc); dress (salad);
F chat s.o. up; turn s.o. on

'**anmalen** v/t (sep, -ge-, h) paint

'**Anmarsch** m: **im ~** on the way

anmaßen v/t (sep, -ge-, h) **sich ~** assume; claim (right); **sich ~, et. zu tun**
presume to do s.th.; **~d** adj arrogant

'**anmelden** v/t (sep, -ge-, h) announce
(visitor); register (birth etc); customs:
declare; **sich ~** enrol(l) (for classes
etc); register (at a hotel); **sich ~ bei**
make an appointment with (doctor etc)

'**Anmeldung** f announcement; registration, enrol(l)ment

'**anmerken** v/t (sep, -ge-, h) **j-m et. ~** notice s.th. in s.o.; **sich et. (nichts) ~ lassen** (not) let it show; '**Anmerkung** f (-; -en) note; annotation, footnote

Anmut ['anmuːt] f (-; no pl) grace

'**anmutig** adj graceful

'**annähen** v/t (sep, -ge-, h) sew on (**an** acc to)

'**annähernd** adv approximately

'**Annäherung** f (-; -en) approach (**an** acc to); '**Annäherungsversuche** pl advances, F pass

Annahme ['annaːmə] f (-; -n) (no pl) acceptance (a. fig); assumption

'**annehmbar** adj acceptable; reasonable (price etc); '**annehmen** v/t (irr, **nehmen**, sep, -ge-, h) accept; suppose; adopt (child, name); take (ball); take on (color, look etc); **sich e-r Sache** or **j-s ~** take care of s.th. or s.o.; '**Annehmlichkeiten** pl comforts, amenities

Annonce [a'noːsə] f (-; -n) advertisement

annullieren [anʊ'liːrən] v/t (no -ge-, h) annul; ECON cancel

anöden ['anˈøːdən] F v/t (sep, -ge-, h) bore s.o. to death

anonym [ano'nyːm] adj anonymous

Anonymität [anonymi'tɛːt] f (-; no pl) anonymity

Anorak ['anorak] m (-s; -s) anorak

'**anordnen** v/t (sep, -ge-, h) arrange; give order(s), order; '**Anordnung** f (-; -en) arrangement; direction, order

'**anorganisch** adj CHEM inorganic

'**anpacken** F fig (sep, -ge-, h) **1.** v/t tackle **2.** v/i: **mit ~** lend a hand

'**anpassen** v/t (sep, -ge-, h) adapt, adjust (both a. **sich ~**) (dat, **an** acc to)

'**Anpassung** f (-; -en) adaptation, adjustment

'**anpassungsfähig** adj adaptable

'**Anpassungsfähigkeit** f adaptability

'**Anpfiff** m SPORT starting whistle; F fig dressing-down

'**anpflanzen** v/t (sep, -ge-, h) cultivate, plant; '**Anpflanzung** f cultivation

'**anpöbeln** v/t (sep, -ge-, h) accost; shout abuse at; **anprangern** ['anpraŋɐn] v/t (sep, -ge-, h) denounce; '**anpreisen** v/t (irr, **preisen**, sep, -ge-, h) push; plug; '**anpro‚bieren** v/t (no -ge-, h) try on; '**anpumpen** F v/t (sep, -ge-, h) touch

s.o. (**um** for); '**anraten** v/t (irr, **raten**, sep, -ge-, h) advise; '**anrechnen** v/t (sep, -ge-, h) charge; allow

'**Anrecht** n: **ein ~ haben auf** (acc) be entitled to

'**Anrede** f address; '**anreden** v/t (sep, -ge-, h) address (**mit Namen** by name)

'**anregen** v/t (sep, -ge-, h) stimulate; suggest; **~d** adj stimulating

'**Anregung** f stimulation; suggestion

'**Anregungsmittel** n PHARM stimulant

'**Anreise** f (Anfahrt) journey; (Ankunft) arrival

'**anreisen** v/i (sep, -ge-, sein) arrive

'**Anreisetag** m day of arrival

'**Anreiz** m incentive

'**anrichten** v/t (sep, -ge-, h) GASTR prepare, dress; cause, do (damage etc)

anrüchig ['anrʏçiç] adj disreputable

'**Anruf** m call (a. TEL); **~beantworter** m TEL answering machine

'**anrufen** v/t (irr, **rufen**, sep, -ge-, h) TEL call or ring up, phone

'**anrühren** v/t (sep, -ge-, h) touch; mix

'**Ansage** f announcement; '**ansagen** v/t (sep, -ge-, h) announce; **Ansager** ['anzaːgɐ] m (-s; -), **Ansagerin** ['anzaːgərɪn] f (-; -nen) announcer

'**ansammeln** v/t and v/refl (sep, -ge-, h) accumulate; '**Ansammlung** f collection, accumulation; crowd

'**Ansatz** m start (**zu** of); attempt (**zu** at); approach; TECH attachment; MATH set--up; pl first signs

'**anschaffen** v/t (sep, -ge-, h) get; **sich et. ~** buy or get (o.s.) s.th.

'**Anschaffung** f (-; -en) purchase, buy

'**anschauen** v/t (sep, -ge-, h) → **ansehen**; '**anschaulich** adj graphic (account etc); '**Anschauung** f (-; -en) (**von**) view (of), opinion (about, of)

'**Anschauungsmateri‚al** n PED visual aids

'**Anschein** m (-[e]s; no pl) appearance; **allem ~ nach** to all appearances; **den ~ erwecken, als (ob)** give the impression of ...; '**anscheinend** adv apparently

'**anschieben** v/t (irr, **shieben**, sep, -ge-, h) give a push (a. MOT)

'**Anschlag** m attack; poster; bill, notice; typewriter: stroke; MUS, swimming: touch; **e-n ~ auf j-n verüben** make an attempt on s.o.'s life; **~brett** n bulletin (esp Br notice) board

'anschlagen (*irr, schlagen, sep, -ge-, h*) **1.** *v/t* post; MUS strike; chip (*cup etc*) **2.** *v/i* dog: bark; take (effect) (*a.* MED); swimming: touch the wall

'anschließen *v/t* (*irr, schließen, sep, -ge-, h*) ELECTR, TECH connect; **sich ~** follow; agree with; **sich j-m** *or* **e-r Sache ~** join s.o. or s.th.; **~d 1.** *adj* following **2.** *adv* then, afterwards

'Anschluss *m* connection; **im ~ an** (*acc*) following; **~ finden** (**bei**) make contact *or* friends (with); **~ bekommen** TEL get through

'anschmiegen *v/refl* (*sep, -ge-, h*) snuggle up (**an** *acc* to)

'anschmiegsam *adj* affectionate

'anschnallen *v/t* (*sep, -ge-, h*) strap on, put on (*a.* ski); **sich ~** AVIAT, MOT fasten one's seat belt; **'anschnauzen** F *v/t* (*sep, -ge-, h*) tell *s.o.* off, *Am a.* bawl *s.o.* out; **'anschneiden** *v/t* (*irr, schneiden, sep, -ge-, h*) cut; *fig* bring up; **'anschrauben** *v/t* (*sep, -ge-, h*) screw on (**an** *acc* to); **'anschreiben** *v/t* (*irr, schreiben, sep, -ge-, h*) write on the (black)board; **j-n ~** write to s.o.; (**et.**) **~ lassen** buy (s.th.) on credit; → **angeschrieben**; **'anschreien** *v/t* (*irr, schreien, sep, -ge-, h*) shout at

'Anschrift *f* address

'Anschuldigung *f* (*-; -en*) accusation

'anschwellen *v/i* (*irr, schwellen, sep, -ge-, sein*) swell (*a. fig*); **'anschwemmen** *v/t* (*sep, -ge-, h*) wash ashore

'ansehen *v/t* (*irr, sehen, sep, -ge-, h*) look at, have *or* take a look at; watch; see (*all a.* **sich** [*dat*] **~**); **~ als** look upon as; **et. mit ~** watch *or* witness s.th.; **man sieht ihm an, dass ...** one can see that ...; **'Ansehen** *n* (*-s; no pl*) reputation

ansehnlich ['anzeːnlɪç] *adj* considerable

'anseilen *v/t and v/refl* (*sep, -ge-, h*) rope

'ansetzen (*sep, -ge-, h*) **1.** *v/t* put (**an** *acc* to); put on, add; fix, set (*date etc*); **Fett** *etc* **~** put on weight *etc* **2.** *v/i:* **~ zu** prepare for (*landing etc*)

'Ansicht *f* (*-; -en*) view, *a.* opinion, *a.* sight; **der ~ sein, dass ...** be of the opinion that ...; **meiner ~ nach** in my opinion; **zur ~** ECON on approval

'Ansichts|karte *f* picture postcard; **~sache** *f* matter of opinion

'anspannen *v/t* (*sep, -ge-, h*) strain

'Anspannung *f* (*-; -en*) strain, exertion

'anspielen *v/i* (*sep, -ge-, h*) soccer: kick off; **~ auf** (*acc*) allude to, hint at

'Anspielung *f* (*-; -en*) allusion, hint

'anspitzen *v/t* (*sep, -ge-, h*) sharpen

'Ansporn *m* (*-[e]s; no pl*) incentive

'anspornen *v/t* (*sep, -ge-, h*) encourage, spur *s.o.* on

'Ansprache *f* address, speech; **e-e ~ halten** deliver an address

'ansprechen *v/t* (*irr, sprechen, sep, -ge-, h*) address, speak to; *fig* appeal to; **~d** *adj* attractive

'Ansprechpartner *m* s.o. to talk to, contact

'anspringen (*irr, springen, sep, -ge-*) **1.** *v/i* (*sein*) engine: start **2.** *v/t* (*h*) jump (up)on

'anspritzen *v/t* (*sep, -ge-, h*) spatter

'Anspruch *m* claim (**auf** *acc* to) (*a.* JUR); **~ haben auf** (*acc*) be entitled to; **~ erheben auf** (*acc*) claim; **Zeit in ~ nehmen** take up time

'anspruchslos *adj* modest; light, undemanding (*reading etc*); *contp* trivial

'anspruchsvoll *adj* demanding; sophisticated, refined (*tastes etc*)

Anstalt ['anʃtalt] *f* (*-; -en*) establishment, institution; mental hospital; **~en machen zu** get ready for

'Anstand *m* (*-[e]s; no pl*) decency; manners; **'anständig** *adj* decent (*a. fig*)

'anstandslos *adv* unhesitatingly; without difficulty

'anstarren *v/t* (*sep, -ge-, h*) stare at

an'statt *prp* (*gen*) *and cj* instead of

'anstechen *v/t* (*irr, stechen, sep, -ge-, h*) tap (*barrel*)

'anstecken *v/t* (*sep, -ge-, h*) stick on; put on (*ring*); light; set fire to; MED infect; **sich bei j-m ~** MED catch s.th. from s.o.; **~d** *adj* MED infectious, contagious, catching (*all a. fig*)

'Anstecknadel *f* pin, button

'Ansteckung *f* (*-; no pl*) MED infection, contagion

'anstehen *v/i* (*irr, stehen, sep, -ge-, h*) (**nach** for) stand in line, *Br* queue up

'ansteigen *v/i* (*irr, steigen, sep, -ge-, sein*) rise

'anstellen *v/t* (*sep, -ge-, h*) engage, employ; TV *etc*: turn on; MOT start; F be up to (*s.th. illegal etc*); make (*inquiries etc*);

sich ~ line up (*nach* for), *Br* queue up (for); F (make a) fuss

'**Anstellung** *f* job, position; *e-e* ~ *finden* find employment

Anstieg ['anʃtiːk] *m* (-[e]s; *no pl*) rise, increase

'**anstiften** *v/t* (*sep*, -ge-, *h*) incite

'**Anstifter** *m* instigator

'**Anstiftung** *f* incitement

'**anstimmen** *v/t* (*sep*, -ge-, *h*) MUS strike up

'**Anstoß** *m soccer*: kickoff; *fig* initiative, impulse; offen|se, *Br* -ce; ~ *erregen* give offense (*bei* to); ~ *nehmen an* take offense at; *den* ~ *zu et. geben* start s.th., initiate s.th.; '**anstoßen** (*irr*, *stoßen*, *sep*, -ge-) 1. *v/t* (*h*) nudge s.o. 2. *v/i* (*sein*) knock, bump; (*h*) clink glasses; ~ *auf* (*acc*) drink to s.o. or s.th.

anstößig ['anʃtøːsɪç] *adj* offensive

'**anstrahlen** *v/t* (*sep*, -ge-, *h*) illuminate; beam at s.o.

'**anstreichen** *v/t* (*irr*, *streichen*, *sep*, -ge-, *h*) paint; PED mark (*mistakes etc*)

'**Anstreicher** *m* (house)painter

'**anstrengen** *v/refl* (*sep*, -ge-, *h*) try (hard), make an effort; ~**d** *adj* strenuous, hard

'**Anstrengung** *f* (-; -en) exertion, strain; effort

Ansturm *fig m* (-[e]s; *no pl*) rush (*auf acc* for)

'**Anteil** *m* share (*a. ECON*), portion; ~ *nehmen an* (*dat*) take an interest in; sympathize with; ~**nahme** ['annaːmə] *f* (-; *no pl*) sympathy; interest

Antenne [an'tɛnə] *f* (-; -n) antenna, *Br* aerial

Anti..., **anti...** *in cpds* anti...

Anti|alko'holiker *m* teetotal(l)er; ~'**babypille** F *f* birth control pill, F the pill; ~'**biotikum** *n* MED antibiotic; ~**blo-** '**ckiersys,tem** *n* MOT anti-lock braking system

antik [an'tiːk] *adj* antique, HIST *a.* ancient; **An'tike** *f* (-; *no pl*) ancient world

'**Antikörper** *m* MED antibody

Antilope [anti'loːpə] *f* (-; -n) zo antelope

Antipathie [antipa'tiː] *f* (-; -n) antipathy

Antiquariat [antikva'rjaːt] *n* (-[e]s; -e) second-hand bookshop

antiquarisch [anti'kvaːrɪʃ] *adj and adv* second-hand

Antiquitäten [antikvi'tɛːtən] *pl* antiques; ~**laden** *m* antique shop

Antisemit [antize'miːt] *m* (-en; -en) anti-Semite; **antise'mitisch** *adj* anti-Semitic; **Antisemitismus** [antizemi-'tɪsmʊs] *m* (-; *no pl*) anti-Semitism

Antrag ['antraːk] *m* (-[e]s; *Anträge* ['antrɛːgə]) application; PARL motion; proposal; ~ *stellen auf* (*acc*) make an application for; PARL move for; ~**steller(in)** ['antraːkʃtɛlə, 'antraːk-ʃtɛlərɪn] *m* (-s; -/-; -nen) applicant; PARL mover

'**antreiben** (*irr*, *treiben*, *sep*, -ge-) 1. *v/t* (*h*) TECH drive; urge s.o. (on) 2. *v/i* (*sein*) float ashore

'**antreten** (*irr*, *treten*, *sep*, -ge-) 1. *v/t* (*h*) enter upon (*office etc*); take up (*position*); set out on (*journey*) 2. *v/i* (*sein*) take one's place; MIL line up

'**Antrieb** *m* TECH drive (*a. fig*), propulsion; *fig* motive, impulse; *aus eigenem* ~ of one's own accord

'**antun** *v/t* (*irr*, *tun*, *sep*, -ge-, *h*) *j-m et.* ~ do s.th. to s.o.; *sich et.* ~ lay hands on o.s.

Antwort ['antvɔrt] *f* (-; -en) answer (*auf acc* to), reply (to)

'**antworten** *v/i* (ge-, *h*) answer (*j-m* s.o., *auf et.* s.th.), reply (to s.o. or s.th.)

'**anvertrauen** *v/t* (*sep*, *no* -ge-, *h*) *j-m et.* ~ (en)trust s.o. with s.th.; confide s.th. to s.o.

'**anwachsen** *v/i* (*irr*, *wachsen*, *sep*, -ge-, *sein*) BOT take root; *fig* increase

Anwalt ['anvalt] *m* (-[e]s; *Anwälte* ['an-vɛltə]) → *Rechtsanwalt*

'**Anwärter** *m* candidate (*auf acc* for)

'**anweisen** *v/t* (*irr*, *weisen*, *sep*, -ge-, *h*) instruct; direct, order

'**Anweisung** *f* instruction; order

'**anwenden** *v/t* ([irr, *wenden*,] *sep*, -ge-, *h*) use; apply (*auf acc* to)

'**Anwendung** *f* use; application

'**anwerben** *v/t* (*irr*, *werben*, *sep*, -ge-, *h*) recruit (*a. fig*)

'**Anwesen** *n* (-s; -) estate; property

'**anwesend** *adj* present

'**Anwesenheit** *f* (-; *no pl*) presence; PED attendance; *die* ~ *feststellen* call the roll; '**Anwesenheitsliste** *f* attendance record (*Br* list)

anwidern ['anviːdɐn] *v/t* (*sep*, -ge-, *h*) make s.o. sick

'**Anzahl** *f* (-; *no pl*) number, quantity

'**anzahlen** *v/t* (*sep*, *-ge-*, *h*) pay on account; '**Anzahlung** *f* down payment

'**anzapfen** *v/t* (*sep*, *-ge-*, *h*) tap

'**Anzeichen** *n* symptom (*a.* MED), sign

Anzeige ['antsaigə] *f* (-; *-n*) advertisement; announcement; JUR information; IT display; TECH reading

'**anzeigen** *v/t* (*sep*, *-ge-*, *h*) announce; report to the police; TECH indicate, show

'**anziehen** *v/t* (*irr*, *ziehen*, *sep*, *-ge-*, *h*) put on (*dress etc*); dress *s.o.*; *fig* attract, draw; tighten (*screw*); pull (*lever etc*); *sich ~* get dressed; dress; **~d** *adj* attractive

'**Anziehung** *f* (-; *no pl*), '**Anziehungskraft** *f* (-; *no pl*) PHYS attraction, *fig a.* appeal

'**Anzug** *m* suit

anzüglich ['antsy:klɪç] *adj* suggestive (*joke*); personal, offensive (*remark etc*)

'**anzünden** *v/t* (*sep*, *-ge-*, *h*) light; set on fire

apart [a'part] *adj* striking

Apartment [a'partmənt] *n* (-*s*; -*s*) studio (apartment *or Br* flat)

apathisch [a'pa:tɪʃ] *adj* apathetic

Apfel ['apfəl] *m* (-*s*; *Äpfel* ['ɛpfəl]) BOT apple; **~mus** *n* GASTR apple sauce

Apfelsine [apfəl'zi:nə] *f* (-; *-n*) BOT orange

'**Apfelwein** *m* cider

Apostel [a'pɔstəl] *m* (-*s*; -) REL apostle

Apostroph [apo'stro:f] *m* (-*s*; -*e*) apostrophe

Apotheke [apo'te:kə] *f* (-; *-n*) pharmacy, drugstore, *Br* chemist's

Apotheker [apo'te:kɐ] *m* (-*s*; -), **Apo-'thekerin** *f* (-; *-nen*) pharmacist, druggist, *Br* chemist

App. *abbr of Apparat* TEL ext., extension

Apparat [apa'ra:t] *m* (-[*e*]*s*; -*e*) apparatus; device; (tele)phone; radio; TV set; camera; POL *etc* machine(ry); *am ~!* TEL speaking!; *am ~ bleiben* TEL hold the line

Appell [a'pɛl] *m* (-*s*; -*e*) appeal (*an acc* to); MIL roll call

appellieren [apɛ'li:rən] *v/i* (*no -ge-*, *h*) (make an) appeal (*an acc* to)

Appetit [ape'ti:t] *m* (-[*e*]*s*; *no pl*) appetite (*auf acc* for); *~ auf et. haben* feel like s.th.; *guten ~!* enjoy your meal!

appe'titanregend *adj* appetizing

Appe'tithappen *m* GASTR appetizer

appe'titlich *adj* appetizing, savo(u)ry, *fig a.* inviting

applaudieren [aplau'di:rən] *v/i* (*no -ge-*, *h*) applaud; **Applaus** [a'plaus] *m* (-*es*; *no pl*) applause

Aprikose [apri'ko:zə] *f* (-; *-n*) BOT apricot

April [a'prɪl] *m* (-[*s*]; *no pl*) April; *~! ~!* April fool!

Aqua|jogging ['akvadʒɔgɪŋ] *n* (-*s*; *no pl*) SPORT aqua jogging; **~planing** [kva'pla:nɪŋ] *n* (-[*s*]; *no pl*) MOT hydroplaning, *Br* aquaplaning

Aquarell [akva'rɛl] *n* (-*s*; -*e*) watercolo(u)r

Aquarium [a'kva:rjʊm] *n* (-*s*; *-ien*) aquarium

Äquator [ɛ'kva:to:ɐ] *m* (-*s*; *no pl*) equator

Ära ['ɛ:ra] *f* (-; *no pl*) era

Araber ['arabɐ] *m* (-*s*; -), **Araberin** ['arabərɪn] *f* (-; *-nen*) Arab

arabisch [a'ra:bɪʃ] *adj* Arabian; Arabic

Arbeit ['arbait] *f* (-; *-en*) work, ECON, POL *a.* labo(u)r; employment, job; PED test; scientific *etc* paper; workmanship; *bei der ~* at work; *zur ~ gehen or fahren* go to work; *gute ~ leisten* make a good job of it; *sich an die ~ machen* set to work; '**arbeiten** *v/i* (*ge-*, *h*) work (*an dat* at, on)

'**Arbeiter** *m* (-*s*; -), '**Arbeiterin** *f* (-; *-nen*) worker

'**Arbeitgeber** *m* (-*s*; -) employer

'**Arbeitnehmer** *m* (-*s*; -) employee

'**Arbeits|agentur** *f Am* (un)employment agency, *Br* employment agency; **~amt** *n Am* employment office, *Br* job centre; **~blatt** *n* PED worksheet; **~erlaubnis** *f* green card, *Br* work permit

'**arbeitsfähig** *adj* fit for work

'**Arbeits|gang** *m* TECH operation; **~gemeinschaft** *f* work *or* study group; **~gericht** *n* JUR labor court, *Br* industrial tribunal; **~hose** *f* overalls; **~kleidung** *f* working clothes; **~kräfte** *pl* workers, labo(u)r

'**arbeitslos** *adj* unemployed, out of work; '**Arbeitslose** *m*, *f* (-*n*; -*n*) *die ~n pl* the unemployed

'**Arbeitslosengeld** *n* unemployment compensation (*Br* benefit); *~ beziehen* F be on the dole

'**Arbeitslosigkeit** *f* (-; *no pl*) unemploy-

ment
'**Arbeits|markt** *m* labo(u)r market; **∼mi-**
,nister *m Am* Secretary of Labor; *Br*
Minister of Labour; **∼niederlegung** *f*
strike, walkout; **∼pause** *f* break, intermission; **∼platz** *m* workplace; job
'**arbeitsscheu** *adj* work-shy
'**Arbeits|speicher** *m* IT main memory;
∼suche *f*: *er ist auf ∼* he is looking
for a job; **∼süchtige** *m, f* workaholic;
∼tag *m* workday
'**arbeitsunfähig** *adj* unfit for work; *per-*
manently disabled
'**Arbeits|weise** *f* method (of working);
∼zeit *f*, (*gleitende* flexible) working
hours; **∼zeitverkürzung** *f* fewer working hours; **∼zimmer** *n* study
Archäologe [arçεo'lo:gə] *m* (*-n; -n*)
arch(a)eologist; **Archäologie**
[arçεolo'gi:] *f* (*-; no pl*) arch(a)eology;
Archäo'login *f* (*-; -nen*) arch(a)e-
ologist
Arche ['arçə] *f* (*-; -n*) ark; *die ∼ Noah*
Noah's ark
Architekt [arçi'tεkt] *m* (*-en; -en*), **Archi-**
'**tektin** *f* (*-; -nen*) architect; **architekto-**
nisch [arçitεk'to:nɪʃ] *adj* architectural; **Architektur** [arçitεk'tu:r] *f* (*-; -en*)
architecture
Archiv [ar'çi:f] *n* (*-s; -e*) archives; record
office
Arena [a're:na] *f* (*-; -nen*) ring
Ärger ['εrgɐ] *m* (*-s; no pl*) anger (*über*
acc at); trouble; F *j-m ∼ machen* cause
s.o. trouble; '**ärgerlich** *adj* angry
(*über, auf acc* at s.th.; with *s.o.*); annoying; '**ärgern** *v/t* (*ge-, h*) annoy; *sich ∼* be
annoyed (*über acc* at, about s.th., with
s.o.); '**Ärgernis** *n* (*-ses; -se*) nuisance
arglos ['arklo:s] *adj* innocent
Argwohn ['arkvo:n] *m* (*-[e]s; no pl*) suspicion (*gegen* of)
argwöhnisch ['arkvø:nɪʃ] *adj* suspicious
Arie ['a:rjə] *f* (*-; -n*) MUS aria
Aristokratie [arɪstokra'ti:] *f* (*-; -n*) aristocracy
arm [arm] *adj* poor; *die Armen* the poor
Arm *m* (*-[e]s; -e*) ANAT arm; GEOGR
branch; F *j-n auf den ∼ nehmen* pull
s.o.'s leg
Armaturen [arma'tu:rən] *pl* TECH in-
struments; (plumbing) fixtures; **∼brett**
n MOT dashboard

'**Armband** *n* bracelet
'**Armbanduhr** *f* wrist-watch
Armee [ar'me:] *f* (*-; -n*) MIL armed forces; army
Ärmel ['εrməl] *m* (*-s; -*) sleeve
ärmlich ['εrmlıç] *adj* poor (*a. fig*); shabby
'**Armreif(en)** *m* bangle
'**armselig** *adj* wretched, miserable
Armut ['armu:t] *f* (*-; no pl*) poverty; *∼ an*
(*dat*) lack of
Aroma [a'ro:ma] *n* (*-s; -men*) flavo(u)r;
aroma
Arrest [a'rεst] *m* (*-[e]s; -e*) PED deten-
tion; *∼ bekommen* be kept in
arrogant [aro'gant] *adj* arrogant, conceited
Arsch [arʃ] V *m* (*-es; Ärsche* ['εrʃə]) ass,
Br arse; **∼loch** V *n* asshole, *Br* arsehole
Art [art] *f* (*-; -en*) way, manner; kind,
sort; BIOL species; *auf diese ∼* (in) this
way; *e-e ∼ ...* a sort of ...; *Geräte aller ∼*
all kinds *or* sorts of tools
'**Artenschutz** *m* protection of endangered species
Arterie [ar'te:rjə] *f* (*-; -n*) ANAT artery
Ar'terienverkalkung *f* MED arterioscle-
rosis
Arthritis [ar'tri:tɪs] *f* (*-; -tiden*) MED arthritis
artig ['artıç] *adj* good, well-behaved; *sei*
∼! be good!, be a good boy (*or* girl)!
Artikel [ar'ti:kəl] *m* (*-s; -*) article
Artillerie ['artıləri:] *f* (*-; no pl*) MIL artil-
lery
Artist [ar'tɪst] *m* (*-en; -en*), **Ar'tistin** *f* (*-;*
-nen) acrobat, (circus) performer
Arznei [a:ɐts'nai] *f* (*-; -en*), **∼mittel** *n*
medicine, drug
Arzt [a:ɐtst] *m* (*-es; Ärzte* ['ε:ɐtstə])
doctor, physician; **Ärztin** ['ε:ɐtstɪn] *f*
(*-; -nen*) (lady) doctor *or* physician
'**ärztlich** *adj* medical; *sich ∼ behandeln*
lassen undergo treatment
As [as] *n* (*-; -*) MUS A flat
Asbest [as'bεst] *m* (*-[e]s; -e*) asbestos
Asche ['aʃə] *f* (*-; -n*) ash(es)
'**Aschen|bahn** *f* SPORT cinder-track, MOT
dirt track; **∼becher** *m* ashtray
Ascher'mittwoch *m* Ash Wednesday
äsen ['ε:zən] *v/i* (*ge-, h*) HUNT feed,
browse
Asiat [a'zja:t] *m* (*-en; -en*), **Asi'atin** *f* (*-;*
-nen) Asian; **asi'atisch** *adj* Asian, Asi-

atic; **Asien** ['aːzjən] n (-s; no pl) Asia

Asket [as'keːt] m (-en; -en), **as'ketisch** adj ascetic

'**asozial** adj antisocial

Asphalt [as'falt] m (-s; -e) asphalt

asphaltieren [asfal'tiːrən] v/t (no -ge-, h) (cover with) asphalt

Ass [as] n (-es; -e) ace (a. tennis and fig)

aß [aːs] pret of **essen**

Assistent [asis'tɛnt] m (-en; -en), **Assis'tentin** f (-; -nen) assistant

Assis'tenzarzt m Am intern, Br houseman

Ast [ast] m (-es; Äste ['ɛstə]) BOT branch

Astronaut [astro'naut] m (-en; -en), **Astro'nautin** f (-; -nen) astronaut

Astronom [astro'noːm] m (-en; -en) astronomer; **Astronomie** [astrono'miː] f (-; no pl) astronomy

ASU [aːzu] abbr of **Abgas-Sonder-Untersuchung** MOT Am emissions test, Br exhaust emission test

Asyl [a'zyːl] n (-s; -e) asylum; **Asylant** [azy'lant] m (-en; -en), **Asy'lantin** f (-; -nen) asylum seeker, (political) refugee

A'syl|bewerber(in) asylum seeker; **~recht** n right of (political) asylum

Atelier [ate'ljeː] n (-s; -s) studio

Atem ['aːtəm] m (-s; no pl) breath; **außer** out of breath; **(tief) ~ holen** take a (deep) breath; '**atemberaubend** adj breathtaking; '**Atemgerät** n MED respirator; '**atemlos** adj breathless; '**Atempause** f F breather; '**Atemzug** m breath

Äther ['ɛːtɐ] m (-s; no pl) CHEM ether; radio etc: air

Athlet [at'leːt] m (-en; -en), **Ath'letin** f (-; -nen) SPORT athlete

ath'letisch adj athletic

Atlas ['atlas] m (-ses; -se, Atlanten) atlas

atmen ['aːtmən] v/i and v/t (ge-, h) breathe

Atmosphäre [atmo'sfɛːrə] f (-; -n) atmosphere

'**Atmung** f (-; no pl) breathing, respiration

Atoll [a'tɔl] n (-s; -e) atoll

Atom [a'toːm] n (-s; -e) atom

A'tom... in cpds -energie, -forschung, -kraft, -krieg, -müll, -rakete, -reaktor, -waffen etc nuclear ...

atomar [ato'maːɐ] adj atomic, nuclear

A'tombombe f MIL atom(ic) bomb

A'tomkern m PHYS (atomic) nucleus

a'tomwaffenfrei adj nuclear-free

Attentat ['atəntaːt] n (-[e]s; -e) assassination attempt, attempt on s.o.'s life; **Opfer e-s ~s werden** be assassinated

'**Attentäter** m (-s; -) assassin

Attest [a'tɛst] n (-[e]s; -e) (doctor's) certificate

Attraktion [atrak'tsjoːn] f (-; -en) attraction; **attraktiv** [atrak'tiːf] adj attractive

Attrappe [a'trapə] f (-; -n) dummy

Attribut [atri'buːt] n (-[e]s; -e) LING attribute (a. fig)

ätzend ['ɛtsənt] adj corrosive, caustic (a. fig), F gross; **das ist echt ~** it's the pits

au [au] int ouch!; **~ fein!** oh, good!

Aubergine [obɛr'ʒiːnə] f (-; -n) BOT eggplant, Br aubergine

auch [aux] cj also, too, as well; **ich ~** so am (or do) I, F me too; **~ nicht** not ... either; **wenn ~** even if; **wo ~ (immer)** wherever; **ist es ~ wahr?** is it really true?

Audienz [au'djɛnts] f (-; -en) audience (**bei** with)

auf [auf] prp (dat and acc) and adv on; in; at; open; up; **~ Seite 20** on page 20; **~ der Straße** on (Br in) the street; on the road; **~ der Welt** in the world; **~ See** at sea; **~ dem Lande** in the country; **~ dem Bahnhof** etc at the station etc; **~ Urlaub** on vacation; **die Uhr stellen ~** (acc) set the watch to; **~ deutsch** in German; **~ deinen Wunsch** at your request; **~ die Sekunde genau** to the second; **~ und ab** up and down

'**auf|arbeiten** v/t (sep, -ge-, h) catch up on (backlog); refurbish; **~atmen** v/i (sep, -ge-, h) heave a sigh of relief

'**Aufbau** m (-[e]s; no pl) building (up); structure; '**aufbauen** v/t (sep, -ge-, h) build (up) (a. fig); set up; construct

'**auf|bauschen** v/t (sep, -ge-, h) exaggerate; **~bekommen** v/t (irr, **kommen**, sep, no -ge-, h) get door etc open; be given (a task etc); **~bereiten** v/t (sep, no -ge-, h) process, clean, treat; **~bessern** v/t (sep, -ge-, h) raise (salary etc); **~bewahren** v/t (sep, no -ge-, h) keep; **~bieten** v/t (irr, **bieten**, sep, -ge-, h) muster; **~blasen** v/t (irr, **blasen**, sep,

-ge-, h) blow up; **~bleiben** *v/i* (*irr, bleiben, sep, -ge-, sein*) stay up; *door etc*: remain open; **~blenden** *v/i* (*sep, -ge-, h*) MOT turn the headlights up; **~blicken** *v/i* (*sep, -ge-, h*) look up (**zu** at) (*a. fig*); **~blitzen** *v/i* (*sep, -ge-, h, sein*) flash (*a. fig*)

'aufbrausen *v/i* (*sep, -ge-, sein*) fly into a temper; **~d** *adj* irascible

'aufbrechen (*irr, brechen, sep, -ge-*) **1.** *v/t* (*h*) break *or* force open **2.** *v/i* (*sein*) burst open; *fig* leave (**nach** for)

'aufbringen *v/t* (*irr, bringen, sep, -ge-, h*) raise (*money*); muster (*courage etc*); start (*fashion etc*); → *aufgebracht*

'Aufbruch *m* (*-[e]s; no pl*) departure, start

'auf|brühen *v/t* (*sep, -ge-, h*) make; **~bürden** *v/t* (*sep, -ge-, h*) *j-m et.* **~** burden s.o. with s.th.; **~decken** *v/t* (*sep, -ge-, h*) uncover; **~drängen** *v/t* (*sep, -ge-, h*) *j-m et.* **~** force s.th. on s.o.; *sich j-m* **~** impose on s.o.; *sich* **~** *fig* suggest itself; **~drehen** F (*sep, -ge-, h*) **1.** *v/t* turn on **2.** *v/i* MOT step on the gas

'aufdringlich *adj* obtrusive

'Aufdruck *m* imprint; *on stamps*: overprint, surcharge

aufei'nander *adv* on top of each other; one after another; **~folgend** *adj* successive

Aufenthalt ['aufɛnthalt] *m* (*-[e]s; -e*) stay; RAIL stop

'Aufenthalts|genehmigung *f* residence permit; **~raum** *m* lounge, recreation room

'auferstehen *v/i* (*irr, stehen, sep, no -ge-, sein*) rise (from the dead)

'Auferstehung *f* (*-; -en*) REL resurrection

'aufessen *v/t* (*irr, essen, sep, -ge-, h*) eat up

'auffahren *v/i* (*irr, fahren, sep, -ge-, sein*) crash (**auf** *acc* into); *fig* start up;

'Auffahrt *f* approach; driveway, *Br* drive; **'Auffahrunfall** *m* MOT rear-end collision; pileup

'auffallen *v/i* (*irr, fallen, sep, -ge-, sein*) attract attention; *j-m* **~** strike s.o.

'auffallend, 'auffällig *adj* striking; conspicuous; flashy (*clothes*)

'auffangen *v/t* (*irr, fangen, sep, -ge-, h*) catch (*a. fig*)

'auffassen *v/t* (*sep, -ge-, h*) understand

(**als** as)

'Auffassung *f* view; interpretation

'auffinden *v/t* (*irr, finden, sep, -ge-, h*) find, discover

'auffordern *v/t* (*sep, -ge-, h*) *j-n* **~**, *et. zu tun* ask (*or* tell) s.o. to do s.th.

'Aufforderung *f* request; demand

'auffrischen *v/t* (*sep, -ge-, h*) freshen up; brush up

'aufführen *v/t* (*sep, -ge-, h*) THEA *etc* perform, present; state; *sich* **~** behave

'Aufführung *f* THEA *etc* performance; *film*: showing

'Aufgabe *f* task, job; duty; PED task, assignment; MATH problem; *fig* surrender; *es sich zur* **~** *machen* make it one's business

'Aufgang *m* staircase; AST rising

'aufgeben (*irr, geben, sep, -ge-, h*) **1.** *v/t* give up; mail, send, *Br* post; check (*baggage*); PED set, give, assign (*homework etc*); ECON place (*order etc*) **2.** *v/i* give up *or* in

'aufge|bracht *adj* furious; **~dreht** F *adj* excited; **~dunsen** ['aufɡədʊnzən] *adj* puffed(-up)

'aufgehen *v/i* (*irr, gehen, sep, -ge-, sein*) open; *sun, dough etc*: rise; MATH come out even; *in Flammen* **~** go up in flames

'aufge|hoben *fig adj*: *gut* **~** *sein bei* be in good hands with; **~legt** *adj*: *zu et.* **~** *sein* feel like (doing) s.th.; *gut* (*schlecht*) **~** in a good (bad) mood; **~regt** *adj* excited; nervous; **~schlossen** *fig adj* open-minded; **~** *für* open to; **~weckt** *fig adj* bright

'aufgreifen *v/t* (*irr, greifen, sep, -ge-, h*) pick up

auf'grund (*gen*) because of

'auf|haben F *v/t* (*irr, haben, sep, -ge-, h*) have on, wear; PED have *homework etc* to do; **~halten** *v/t* (*irr, halten, sep, -ge-, h*) stop, hold up (*a. traffic, thief etc*); keep open; *sich* **~** (*bei j-m*) stay (with s.o.); **~hängen** *v/t* (*sep, -ge-, h*) hang (up); *j-n* **~** hang s.o.; **~heben** *v/t* (*irr, heben, sep, -ge-, h*) pick up; keep; abolish (*law etc*); break up (*meeting etc*); *sich gegenseitig* **~** neutralize each other; → *aufgehoben*

'Aufheben *n* (*-s; no pl*) *viel* **~** *s machen* make a fuss (*von* about)

'auf|heitern *v/t* (*sep, -ge-, h*) cheer up;

sich ~ *weather:* clear up; **~helfen** *v/i* (*irr, helfen, sep,* -ge-, *h*) help *s.o.* up; **~hellen** *v/t and v/refl* (*sep,* -ge-, *h*) brighten; **~hetzen** *v/t* (*sep,* -ge-, *h*) *j-n* ~ *gegen* set s.o. against; **~holen** (*sep,* -ge-, *h*) **1.** *v/t* make up for **2.** *v/i* catch up (*gegen* with); **~horchen** *v/i* (*sep,* -ge-, *h*) prick (up) one's ears; ~ *lassen* make *s.o.* sit up; **~hören** *v/i* (*sep,* -ge-, *h*) stop, end, finish, quit; *mit et.* ~ stop (doing) s.th.; *hör(t) auf!* stop it!; **~kaufen** *v/t* (*sep,* -ge-, *h*) buy up

'**aufklären** *v/t* (*sep,* -ge-, *h*) clear up, *a.* solve (*crime*); *j-n* ~ *über* (*acc*) inform s.o. about; *j-n* (*sexuell*) ~ F tell s.o. the facts of life; '**Aufklärung** *f* (-; *no pl*) clearing up, solution; information; sex education; PHILOS Enlightenment; MIL reconnaissance

'**aufkleben** *v/t* (*sep,* -ge-, *h*) paste *or* stick on; '**Aufkleber** *m* (-*s*; -) sticker

'**aufknöpfen** *v/t* (*sep,* -ge-, *h*) unbutton

'**aufkommen** *v/i* (*irr, kommen, sep,* -ge-, *sein*) come up; come into fashion *or* use; *rumo(u)r etc*: arise; ~ *für* pay (for)

'**Aufladegerät** *n* charger

'**aufladen** *v/t* (*irr, laden, sep,* -ge-, *h*) load; ELECTR charge; (*prepaid card etc*) top up

'**Auflage** *f* edition; circulation

'**auf**|**lassen** F *v/t* (*irr, lassen, sep,* -ge-, *h*) leave *door etc* open; keep *one's hat etc* on; **~lauern** *v/i* (*sep,* -ge-, *h*) *j-m* ~ waylay s.o.

'**Auflauf** *m* crowd; GASTR soufflé, pudding

'**auf**|**laufen** *v/i* (*irr, laufen, sep,* -ge-, *sein*) MAR run aground; **~leben** *v/i* (*sep,* -ge-, *sein*) *a.* (*wieder*) ~ *lassen* revive; **~legen** (*sep,* -ge-, *h*) **1.** *v/t* put on, lay on **2.** *v/i* TEL hang up

'**auflehnen** *v/t and v/refl* (*sep,* -ge-, *h*) lean (*auf acc* on); *sich* ~ rebel, revolt (*gegen* against); '**Auflehnung** *f* (-; -en) rebellion, revolt

'**auf**|**lesen** *v/t* (*irr, lesen, sep,* -ge-, *h*) pick up (*a. fig*); **~leuchten** *v/i* (*sep,* -ge-, *h*) flash (up); **~listen** *v/t* (*sep,* -ge-, *h*) list (a. IT); **~lockern** *v/t* (*sep,* -ge-, *h*) loosen up; *fig* liven up

'**auflösen** *v/t* (*sep,* -ge-, *h*) dissolve; solve (*a.* MATH); disintegrate; '**Auflösung** *f* (dis)solution; disintegration

'**aufmachen** F *v/t* (*sep,* -ge-, *h*) open;

sich ~ set out; '**Aufmachung** *f* (-; -en) get-up

'**aufmerksam** *adj* attentive (*auf acc* to); thoughtful; *j-n* ~ *machen auf* (*acc*) call s.o.'s attention to

'**Aufmerksamkeit** *f* (-; -en) (*no pl*) attention; (*gift*) small present

'**aufmuntern** *v/t* (*sep,* -ge-, *h*) encourage; cheer up

Aufnahme ['aufnaːmə] *f* (-; -*n*) taking up; reception (*a.* MED *etc*); admission; photo(graph); recording; *film:* shooting

'**aufnahmefähig** *adj* receptive (*für* of)

'**Aufnahme**|**gebühr** *f* admission fee; **~prüfung** *f* entrance exam(ination)

'**aufnehmen** *v/t* (*irr, nehmen, sep,* -ge-, *h*) take up (*a. post etc*); pick up; put *s.o.* up; hold; take *s.th.* in; receive; PED *etc* admit; PHOT take a picture of; record; take (*the ball*); *es* ~ *mit* be a match for

'**aufpassen** *v/i* (*sep,* -ge-, *h*) pay attention; take care; ~ *auf* (*acc*) take care of, look after; keep an eye on; *pass auf!* look out!

'**Aufprall** *m* (-[*e*]*s; no pl*) impact

'**aufprallen** *v/i* (*sep,* -ge-, *sein*) ~ *auf* (*dat or acc*) hit

'**aufpumpen** *v/t* (*sep,* -ge-, *h*) pump up

'**aufputschen** *v/t* (*sep,* -ge-, *h*) pep up

'**Aufputschmittel** *n* PHARM stimulant, pep pill

'**auf**|**raffen** *v/refl* (*sep,* -ge-, *h*) *sich* ~ *zu* bring o.s. to *do s.th.*; **~räumen** *v/t* (*sep,* -ge-, *h*) tidy up; clear

'**aufrecht** *adj and adv* upright (*a. fig*); **~erhalten** *v/t* (*irr, halten, sep, no* -ge-, *h*) maintain, keep up

'**aufregen** *v/t* (*sep,* -ge-, *h*) excite, upset; *sich* ~ get excited *or* upset (*über acc* about); **~d** *adj* exciting

'**Aufregung** *f* excitement; fuss

'**aufreiben** *fig v/t* (*irr, reiben, sep,* -ge-, *h*) wear down; **~d** *adj* stressful

'**aufreißen** *v/t* (*irr, reißen, sep,* -ge-, *h*) tear open; fling *door etc* open; open *one's eyes* wide; F pick *s.o.* up

'**aufreizend** *adj* provocative

'**aufrichten** *v/t* (*sep,* -ge-, *h*) put up, raise; *sich* ~ straighten up; sit up

'**aufrichtig** *adj* sincere; frank

'**Aufrichtigkeit** *f* (-; *no pl*) sincerity; frankness

'**Aufriss** *m* (-*es*; -*e*) ARCH elevation

'**aufrollen** v/t and v/refl (sep, -ge-, h) roll up

'**Aufruf** m call; appeal (**zu** for)

'**aufrufen** v/t (irr, **rufen**, sep, -ge-, h) call on

Aufruhr ['aufruːɐ] m (-s; no pl) revolt; riot; turmoil; '**Aufrührer** m (-s; -) rebel; rioter; **aufrührerisch** ['aufryːrərɪʃ] adj rebellious

'**aufrunden** v/t (sep, -ge-, h) round off

'**aufrüsten** v/t and v/i (sep, -ge-, h) (re)arm; '**Aufrüstung** f (re)armament

'**auf|rütteln** fig v/t (sep, -ge-, h) shake up, rouse; ~**sagen** v/t (sep, -ge-, h) say; a. recite (poem)

aufsässig ['aufzɛsɪç] adj rebellious

'**Aufsatz** m PED essay, Am a. theme; (newspaper etc) article; TECH top

'**auf|saugen** v/t (sep, -ge-, h) absorb (a. fig); ~**scheuern** v/t (sep, -ge-, h) chafe; ~**schichten** v/t (sep, -ge-, h) pile up; ~**schieben** fig v/t (irr, **schieben**, sep, -ge-, h) put off, postpone; delay

'**Aufschlag** m impact; ECON extra charge; lapel; cuff, Br turnup; tennis: service; '**aufschlagen** (irr, **schlagen**, sep, -ge-, h) **1.** v/t open (book, eyes etc); pitch (tent); cut (one's knee etc); **Seite 3** ~ open at page 3 **2.** v/i tennis: serve; **auf dem Boden** ~ hit the ground

'**auf|schließen** v/t (irr, **schließen**, sep, -ge-, h) unlock, open; ~**schlitzen** v/t (sep, -ge-, h) slit or rip open

'**Aufschluss** m information (**über** acc on)

'**auf|schnappen** F fig v/t (sep, -ge-, h) pick up; ~**schneiden** (irr, **schneiden**, sep, -ge-, h) **1.** v/t cut open; GASTR cut up **2.** F fig v/i brag, boast, talk big

'**Aufschnitt** m (-[e]s; no pl) GASTR cold cuts, Br (slices of) cold meat

'**auf|schnüren** v/t (sep, -ge-, h) untie; unlace; ~**schrauben** v/t (sep, -ge-, h) unscrew; ~**schrecken** (sep, -ge-) **1.** v/t (h) startle **2.** v/i (sein) start (up)

'**Aufschrei** m yell; scream, outcry (a. fig)

'**auf|schreiben** v/t (irr, **schreiben**, sep, -ge-, h) write down; ~**schreien** v/i (irr, **schreien**, sep, -ge-, h) cry out, scream

'**Aufschrift** f inscription

'**Aufschub** m postponement; delay; adjournment; respite

'**Aufschwung** m SPORT swing-up; esp ECON recovery, upswing; boom

'**Aufsehen** n (-s; no pl) ~ **erregen** attract attention; cause a sensation; ~ **erregend** → **aufsehenerregend**; '**aufsehenerregend** adj sensational

'**Aufseher** m (-s; -), '**Aufseherin** f (-; -nen) guard

'**aufsetzen** (sep, -ge-, h) **1.** v/t put on; draw up (letter etc); **sich** ~ sit up **2.** v/i AVIAT touch down

'**Aufsetzer** m (-s; -) SPORT awkward bouncing ball

'**Aufsicht** f (-; no pl) supervision, control; ~ **führen** PED etc be on (break) duty; proctor, Br invigilate

'**Aufsichts|behörde** f supervisory board; ~**rat** m ECON board of directors; supervisory board

'**auf|sitzen** v/i (irr, **sitzen**, sep, -ge-, sein) mount; ~**spannen** v/t (sep, -ge-, h) stretch; put up (umbrella); spread; ~**sparen** v/t (sep, -ge-, h) save; ~**sperren** v/t (sep, -ge-, h) unlock; F open wide; ~**spielen** v/refl (sep, -ge-, h) show off; **sich** ~ **als** play; ~**spießen** v/t (sep, -ge-, h) spear, skewer; animal: gore; ~**springen** v/i (irr, **springen**, sep, -ge-, sein) jump up; door etc: fly open; lips etc: chap; ~**spüren** v/t (sep, -ge-, h) track down; ~**stacheln** v/t (sep, -ge-, h) goad (s.o. into doing s.th.); ~**stampfen** v/i (sep, -ge-, h) stamp (one's foot)

'**Aufstand** m revolt, rebellion

'**Aufständische** m, f (-n; -n) rebel

'**auf|stapeln** v/t (sep, -ge-, h) pile up; ~**stechen** v/t (irr, **stechen**, sep, -ge-, h) puncture, prick open; MED lance; ~**stecken** v/t (sep, -ge-, h) put up (hair); F fig give up; ~**stehen** v/i (irr, **stehen**, sep, -ge-, sein) get up, rise; ~**steigen** v/i (irr, **steigen**, sep, -ge-, sein) rise (a. fig); get on (horse, bicycle); be promoted; SPORT Am a. be moved up to a higher division

'**aufstellen** v/t (sep, -ge-, h) set up, put up; post (guard); set (trap, record etc); nominate s.o.; draw up (table, list etc)

'**Aufstellung** f putting up; nomination; list; SPORT line-up

Aufstieg ['aufʃtiːk] m (-[e]s; -e) ascent, fig a. rise

'**auf|stöbern** fig v/t (sep, -ge-, h) ferret out; ~**stoßen** (irr, **stoßen**, sep, -ge-,

aufstützen 46

h) **1.** *v/t* push open **2.** *v/i* belch; **~stützen** *v/refl* (*sep*, *-ge-*, *h*) lean (**auf** *acc or dat* on); **~suchen** *v/t* (*sep*, *-ge-*, *h*) visit; see

'**Auftakt** *m* MUS upbeat; *fig* prelude

'**auf|tanken** *v/t* (*sep*, *-ge-*, *h*) fill up; MOT, AVIAT refuel; **~tauchen** *v/i* (*sep*, *-ge-*, *sein*) appear; MAR surface; **~tauen** *v/t* (*sep*, *-ge-*, *h*) thaw; GASTR defrost; **~teilen** *v/t* (*sep*, *-ge-*, *h*) divide (up)

Auftrag ['auftra:k] *m* (-[*e*]*s*; *Aufträge* ['auftrɛ:gə]) instructions, order (*a.* ECON); MIL mission; *im ~ von* on behalf of; **auftragen** *v/t* (*irr*, *tragen*, *sep*, *-ge-*, *h*) serve (up) (*food*); apply (*paint*); *j-m et. ~* ask (*or* tell) s.o. to do s.th; F *dick~* exaggerate; '**Auftraggeber** *m* (-*s*; -) principal; customer

'**auf|treffen** *v/i* (*irr*, *treffen*, *sep*, *-ge-*, *sein*) strike, hit; **~treiben** F *v/t* (*irr*, *treiben*, *sep*, *-ge-*, *h*) get hold of; raise (*money*); **~trennen** *v/t* (*sep*, *-ge-*, *h*) undo (*seam*), cut open; **~treten** *v/i* (*irr*, *treten*, *sep*, *-ge-*, *sein*) THEA *etc* appear (*als* as); behave, act; occur

'**Auftreten** *n* (-*s*; *no pl*) appearance; behavio(u)r; occurrence

'**Auftrieb** *m* (-[*e*]*s*; *no pl*) PHYS buoyancy (*a. fig*); AVIAT lift; *fig* impetus

'**Auftritt** *m* THEA entrance

'**auf|tun** *v/refl* (*irr*, *tun*, *sep*, *-ge-*, *h*) open (*a. fig*); *abyss*: yawn; **~türmen** *v/t* (*sep*, *-ge-*, *h*) pile *or* heap up; *sich ~* pile up; **~wachen** *v/i* (*sep*, *-ge-*, *sein*) wake up; **~wachsen** *v/i* (*irr*, *wachsen*, *sep*, *-ge-*, *sein*) grow up

Aufwand ['aufvant] *m* (-[*e*]*s*; *no pl*) expenditure (**an** *dat* of), *a.* expense; pomp

aufwändig ['aufvɛndɪç] *adj* costly; extravagant (*lifestyle*)

'**aufwärmen** *v/t* (*sep*, *-ge-*, *h*) warm up; F *fig contp* bring up

aufwärts ['aufvɛrts] *adv* upward(s); **~gehen** *v/i* (*irr*, *gehen*, *sep*, *-ge-*, *sein*) *fig* improve

'**auf|wecken** *v/t* (*sep*, *-ge-*, *h*) wake (up); **~weichen** *v/t* (*sep*, *-ge-*, *h*) soften; soak; **~weisen** *v/t* (*irr*, *weisen*, *sep*, *-ge-*, *h*) show, have; **~wenden** *v/t* ([*irr*, *wenden*,] *sep*, *-ge-*, *h*) spend (*für* on); *Mühe ~* take pains

aufwendig → *aufwändig*

'**aufwerfen** *v/t* (*irr*, *werfen*, *sep*, *-ge-*, *h*) raise (*question etc*)

'**aufwerten** *v/t* (*sep*, *-ge-*, *h*) ECON revalue; *fig* increase the value of

'**Aufwertung** *f* revaluation

'**aufwickeln** *v/t and v/refl* (*sep*, *-ge-*, *h*) wind up, roll up; put *hair* in curlers

aufwiegeln ['aufvi:gəln] *v/t* (*sep*, *-ge-*, *h*) stir up, incite, instigate

'**aufwiegen** *v/t* (*irr*, *wiegen*, *sep*, *-ge-*, *h*) make up for

Aufwiegler ['aufvi:glɐ] *m* (-*s*; -) agitator; instigator

'**Aufwind** *m* upwind; *im ~ fig* on the upswing

'**auf|wirbeln** *v/t* (*sep*, *-ge-*, *h*) whirl up; *fig* (*viel*) *Staub ~* make (quite) a stir; **~wischen** *v/t* (*sep*, *-ge-*, *h*) wipe up; **~wühlen** *fig v/t* (*sep*, *-ge-*, *h*) stir, move

'**aufzählen** *v/t* (*sep*, *-ge-*, *h*) name (one by one), list; '**Aufzählung** *f* enumeration, list

'**aufzeichnen** *v/t* (*sep*, *-ge-*, *h*) TV, *radio etc*: record; tape; draw; '**Aufzeichnung** *f* recording; *pl* notes

'**aufzeigen** *v/t* (*sep*, *-ge-*, *h*) show; demonstrate; point out (*mistake etc*)

'**aufziehen** (*irr*, *ziehen*, *sep*, *-ge-*) **1.** *v/t* (*h*) draw *or* pull up; (pull) open; bring up (*child*); wind (up) (*clock*); mount (*photo etc*); **~** tease s.o. **2.** *v/i* (*sein*) come up; '**Aufzug** *m* elevator, *Br* lift; THEA act; F *contp* get-up

'**aufzwingen** *v/t* (*irr*, *zwingen*, *sep*, *-ge-*, *h*) *j-n et. ~* force s.th. upon s.o.

Augapfel ['auk'apfəl] *m* ANAT eyeball

Auge ['augə] *n* (-*s*; -*n*) ANAT eye; *ein blaues ~* a black eye; *mit bloßem ~* with the naked eye; *mit verbundenen ~n* blindfold; *in meinen ~n* in my view; *mit anderen ~n* in a different light; *aus den ~n verlieren* lose sight of; *ein ~ zudrücken* turn a blind eye; *unter vier ~n* in private; F *ins ~ gehen* go wrong

'**Augenarzt** *m* eye specialist

'**Augenblick** *m* moment, instant

'**augenblicklich 1.** *adj* present; immediate; momentary **2.** *adv* at present, at the moment; immediately

'**Augen|braue** *f* eyebrow; **~licht** *n* (-[*e*]*s*; *no pl*) eyesight; **~lid** *n* eyelid; **~maß** *n*: *ein gutes ~* a sure eye; *nach dem ~* by the eye; **~merk** *n*: *sein ~ richten auf* (*acc*) turn one's attention to, *fig a.* have in view; **~schein** *m* (-*s*; *no pl*) appearance; **in ~ nehmen** examine, inspect; **~zeuge** *m* eyewitness

August [au'gʊst] *m* (-; *no pl*) August

Auktion [auk'tsjoːn] *f* (-; *-en*) auction

Auktionator [auktsjo'naːtoːɐ] *m* (-*s*; *-en* [auktsjona'toːrən]) auctioneer

Aula ['aula] *f* (-; *-s*, *Aulen*) auditorium, *Br* (assembly) hall

aus [aus] *prp* (*dat*) *and adv mst* out of, from; of (*silk etc*); out of (*spite etc*); *light etc*: out, off; *play etc*: over, finished; SPORT out; **~ dem Fenster** *etc* out of the window *etc*; **~ München** from Munich; **~ Holz** (made) of wood; **~ Mitleid** out of pity; **~ Spaß** for fun; **~ Versehen** by mistake; **~ diesem Grunde** for this reason; **von hier~** from here; F **von mir ~!** I don't care!; **~ der Mode** out of fashion; F **~ sein** be over; be out; **~ sein auf** (*acc*) be out for; be after (*s.o.'s money etc*); **die Schule** (**das Spiel**) **ist~** school (the game) is over; **einl~** TECH on / off

Aus *n*: **im ~** *ball*: out of play

aus|arbeiten *v/t* (*sep*, *-ge-*, *h*) work out; prepare; **~arten** *v/i* (*sep*, *-ge-*, *sein*) get out of hand; **~atmen** *v/t and v/i* (*sep*, *-ge-*, *h*) breathe out; **~baden** F *v/t* (*sep*, *-ge-*, *h*) **et. ~ müssen** take the rap for s.th.

Ausbau *m* (-[*e*]*s*; *no pl*) extension; completion; removal; **ausbauen** *v/t* (*sep*, *-ge-*, *h*) extend; complete; remove; improve; **ausbaufähig** *adj*: **et. ist~** there is potential for growth *or* development

ausbessern *v/t* (*sep*, *-ge-*, *h*) mend, repair, F *a*. fix; **Ausbesserung** *f* (-; *-en*) repair(ing)

Ausbeute *f* (-; *no pl*) gain, profit; yield; **ausbeuten** *v/t* (*sep*, *-ge-*, *h*) exploit (*a. contp*); **Ausbeutung** *f* (-; *no pl*) exploitation

ausbilden *v/t* (*sep*, *-ge-*, *h*) train, instruct; **j-n ~ zu** train s.o. to be

Ausbilder *m* (-*s*; -) instructor

Ausbildung *f* (-; *-en*) training, instruction

ausbleiben *v/i* (*irr*, **bleiben**, *sep*, *-ge-*, *sein*) stay out; fail to come; **es konnte nicht ~** it was inevitable

Ausblick *m* view (**auf** *acc* of); *fig* outlook (**for**)

ausbrechen *v/i* (*irr*, **brechen**, *sep*, *-ge-*, *sein*) break out (*a. fig*); **in Tränen ~** burst into tears; **Ausbrecher** *m* (-*s*; -) escaped prisoner

ausbreiten *v/t* (*sep*, *-ge-*, *h*) spread (out); **sich ~** spread; **Ausbreitung** *f* (-; *no pl*) spreading

ausbrennen *v/i* (*irr*, **brennen**, *sep*, *-ge-*, *sein*) burn out

Ausbruch *m* escape, breakout; outbreak (*of fire etc*); eruption (*of volcano*); (out)burst (*of resentment etc*)

ausbrüten *v/t* (*sep*, *-ge-*, *h*) hatch (*a. fig*)

Ausdauer *f* perseverance, stamina, *esp* SPORT *a*. staying power; **ausdauernd** *adj* persevering; SPORT tireless

ausdehnen *v/t and v/refl* (*sep*, *-ge-*, *h*) stretch; *fig* expand, extend

Ausdehnung *f* expansion; extension

ausdenken *v/t* (*irr*, **denken**, *sep*, *-ge-*, *h*) think *s.th*. up; invent (*a. fig*)

Ausdruck *m* expression, term; IT printout; **ausdrucken** *v/t* (*sep*, *-ge-*, *h*) IT print out

ausdrücken *v/t* (*sep*, *-ge-*, *h*) stub out (*cigarette etc*); *fig* express

ausdrücklich ['ausdrʏklɪç] *adj* express, explicit

ausdrucks|los *adj* expressionless, blank; **~voll** *adj* expressive

Ausdrucksweise *f* language, style

Ausdünstung *f* (-; *-en*) exhalation; perspiration; odo(u)r

auseinander [aus?ai'nandɐ] *adv* apart; separate(d); **~bringen** *v/t* (*irr*, **bringen**, *sep*, *-ge-*, *h*) separate, **~gehen** *v/i* (*irr*, **gehen**, *sep*, *-ge-*, *sein*) part; *meeting etc*: break up; *opinions etc*: differ; *married couple*: separate; **~halten** *v/t* (*irr*, **halten**, *sep*, *-ge-*, *h*) tell apart; **~nehmen** *v/t* (*irr*, **nehmen**, *sep*, *-ge-*, *h*) take apart (*a. fig*); **~setzen** *v/t* (*irr*, **setzen**, *sep*, *-ge-*, *h*) explain; **sich ~ setzen mit** *v/refl* deal with; argue with *s.o*.

Ausei'nandersetzung *f* (-; *-en*) argument

auserlesen *adj* choice, exquisite

ausfahren (*irr*, **fahren**, *sep*, *-ge-*) **1.** *v/i* (*sein*) go for a drive *or* ride **2.** *v/t* (*h*) take *s.o*. out; AVIAT extend (*landing gear*); **Ausfahrt** *f* drive, ride; MOT exit

Ausfall *m* TECH, MOT, SPORT failure; loss

ausfallen *v/i* (*irr*, **fallen**, *sep*, *-ge-*, *sein*) fall out; not take place, be cancelled; TECH, MOT break down, fail; **gut** *etc* **~** turn out well *etc*; **~ lassen** cancel;

die Schule fällt aus there is no school
'**ausfallend**, '**ausfällig** *adj* insulting
'**ausfertigen** *v/t* (*sep*, -ge-, *h*) draw up
(*contract etc*); make out (*check etc*)
'**Ausfertigung** *f* drawing up; copy; *in
doppelter ~* in duplicate
'**ausfindig** *adj*: *~ machen* find
ausflippen ['ausflɪpən] F *v/i* (*sep*, -ge-,
sein) freak out
Ausflüchte ['ausflʏçtə] *pl* excuses
'**Ausflug** *m* trip, excursion, outing
Ausflügler ['ausflyːklɐ] *m* (-*s*; -) day
tripper
'**Ausfluss** *m* TECH outlet; MED discharge
'**aus|fragen** *v/t* (*sep*, -ge-, *h*) question
(*über acc* about); sound out; **~fransen**
v/i (*sep*, -ge-, *sein*) fray; **~fressen** F *v/t*
(*irr*, *fressen*, *sep*, -ge-, *h*) *et. ~* be up to
no good
Ausfuhr ['ausfuːɐ] *f* (-; -*en*) ECON export
(-ation); '**ausführbar** *adj* practicable;
'**ausführen** *v/t* (*sep*, -ge-, *h*) take *s.o.*
out; carry out (*task etc*); ECON export;
explain
ausführlich ['ausfyːɐlɪç] **1.** *adj*
detailed; comprehensive **2.** *adv* in detail; '**Ausführlichkeit** *f*: *in aller ~* in
great detail
'**Ausführung** *f* execution, performance;
type, model, design
'**ausfüllen** *v/t* (*sep*, -ge-, *h*) fill out (*Br* in)
(*form*)
'**Ausgabe** *f* distribution; edition; expense; issue; IT output
'**Ausgang** *m* exit, way out; end; result,
outcome; TECH, ELECTR output, outlet
'**Ausgangs|punkt** *m* starting point;
~sperre *f* POL curfew
'**ausgeben** *v/t* (*irr*, *geben*, *sep*, -ge-, *h*)
give out; spend; F *j-m e-n ~* buy *s.o.*
a drink; *sich ~ als* pass o.s. off as
'**ausge|beult** *adj* baggy; **~bildet** *adj*
trained, skilled; **~bucht** *adj* booked
up; **~dehnt** *adj* extensive; **~dient** *adj*:
~ haben *fig* have had its day; **~fallen**
adj odd, unusual; **~glichen** *adj* (well-)
balanced
'**ausgehen** *v/i* (*irr*, *gehen*, *sep*, -ge-, *sein*)
go out; end; *hair:* fall out; *money, supplies:* run out; *leer ~* get nothing; *~ von*
start from *or* at; come from; *davon ~*,
dass assume that; *ihm ging das Geld
aus* he ran out of money
'**ausge|kocht** *fig adj* cunning; out-and-

-out (*villain etc*); **~lassen** *fig adj* cheerful; hilarious; *~ sein* be in high spirits;
~macht *adj* agreed(-on); downright
(*nonsense*); **~prägt** *adj* marked, pronounced; **~rechnet** *adv*: *~ er* he of all
people; *~ heute* today of all days;
~schlossen *adj* out of the question;
~storben *adj* extinct; **~sucht** *adj* select, choice; **~wachsen** *adj* fullgrown;
~wogen *adj* (well-)balanced; **~zeich-
net** *adj* excellent
ausgiebig ['ausgiːbɪç] *adj* extensive,
thorough; substantial (*meal*)
'**ausgießen** *v/t* (*irr*, *gießen*, *sep*, -ge-, *h*)
pour out
'**Ausgleich** *m* (-[*e*]*s*; *no pl*) compensation; SPORT even score, *Br* equalization;
tennis: deuce; '**ausgleichen** *v/t and v/i*
(*irr*, *gleichen*, *sep*, -ge-, *h*) compensate;
equalize (*Br a.* SPORT); ECON balance;
SPORT make the score even
'**Ausgleichs|sport** *m* remedial exercis-
es; **~tor** *n*, **~treffer** *m* SPORT tying point,
Br equalizer
'**ausgraben** *v/t* (*irr*, *graben*, *sep*, -ge-, *h*)
dig out *or* up (*a. fig*)
'**Ausgrabungen** *pl* excavations
'**ausgrenzen** *v/t* (*sep*, -ge-, *h*) isolate
'**Ausguss** *m* (kitchen) sink
'**aushalten** (*irr*, *halten*, *sep*, -ge-, *h*) **1.** *v/t*
bear, stand; keep (*mistress etc*); *nicht
auszuhalten sein* be unbearable **2.**
v/i hold out
aushändigen ['aushɛndɪgən] *v/t* (*sep*,
-ge-, *h*) hand over
'**Aushang** *m* notice; bulletin
'**aushängen** *v/t* (*sep*, -ge-, *h*) hang out,
put up; unhinge (*door*)
'**aus|heben** *v/t* (*irr*, *heben*, *sep*, -ge-, *h*)
dig (*trench*); raid (*place etc*); **~helfen** *v/i*
(*irr*, *helfen*, *sep*, -ge-, *h*) help out
'**Aushilfe** *f* (temporary) help
'**Aushilfs...** *in cpds -kellner etc*: temporary
'**aus|holen** *v/i* (*sep*, -ge-, *h*) *zum Schlag
~* swing (to strike); *fig weit ~* go far
back; **~horchen** *v/t* (*sep*, -ge-, *h*) sound
(*über acc* on); **~hungern** *v/t* (*sep*, -ge-,
h) starve out; **~kennen** *v/refl* (*irr*, *kennen*, *sep*, -ge-, *h*) *sich ~* (*in dat*) know
one's way (about); *fig* know a lot
(about); **~klingen** *v/i* (*irr*, *klingen*,
sep, -ge-, *sein*) draw to a close; **~klop-
fen** *v/t* (*sep*, -ge-, *h*) knock out; **~kom-**

men *v/i* (*irr*, **kommen**, *sep*, *-ge-*, *sein*) get by; **~ mit** manage with *s.th.*; get along with *s.o.*

Auskunft ['auskʊnft] *f* (-; *Auskünfte* ['auskʏnftə]) information; (*no pl*) information desk; TEL inquiries

'**aus|lachen** *v/t* (*sep*, *-ge-*, *h*) laugh at (**wegen** for); **~laden** *v/t* (*irr*, **laden**, *sep*, *-ge-*, *h*) unload

'**Auslage** *f* window display; *pl* expenses

'**Ausland** *n* (-[*e*]*s*; *no pl*) **das ~** foreign countries; **ins ~**, **im ~** abroad

Ausländer ['auslɛndɐ] *m* (-*s*; -) foreigner; **~feindlichkeit** *f* hostility to foreigners, xenophobia

Ausländerin ['auslɛndərɪn] *f* (-; *-nen*) foreigner

ausländisch ['auslɛndɪʃ] *adj* foreign

'**Auslands|gespräch** *n* international call; **~korrespondent(in)** foreign correspondent

'**auslassen** *v/t* (*irr*, **lassen**, *sep*, *-ge-*, *h*) leave out; melt (*butter etc*); let out (*seam*); **s-n Zorn an j-m ~** take it out on *s.o.*; **sich ~ über** (*acc*) express o.s. on

'**Auslassung** *f* (-; *-en*) omission

'**Auslassungszeichen** *n* LING apostrophe

'**Auslauf** *m* room to move about; *dog*: exercise; '**auslaufen** *v/i* (*irr*, **laufen**, *sep*, *-ge-*, *sein*) MAR leave port; *pot etc*: leak; *liquid etc*: run out; '**Ausläufer** *m* METEOR ridge, trough; *pl* GEOGR foothills; '**Auslaufmo,dell** *n* ECON close-out (*Br* phase-out) model

'**auslegen** *v/t* (*sep*, *-ge-*, *h*) lay out; carpet; line (*with paper etc*); display (*goods*); interpret (*text etc*); advance (*money*)

'**Auslegung** *f* (-; *-en*) interpretation

'**aus|leihen** *v/t* (*irr*, **leihen**, *sep*, *-ge-*, *h*) lend (out), loan; **sich** (*dat*) **et. ~** borrow *s.th.*; **~lernen** *v/i* (*sep*, *-ge-*, *h*) complete one's training; **man lernt nie aus** we live and learn

'**Auslese** *f* choice, selection; *fig* pick

'**auslesen** *v/t* (*irr*, **lesen**, *sep*, *-ge-*, *h*) pick out, select; finish (*book etc*)

'**ausliefern** *v/t* (*sep*, *-ge-*, *h*) hand *or* turn over, deliver (up); POL extradite; '**Auslieferung** *f* delivery; extradition

'**aus|liegen** *v/i* (*irr*, **liegen**, *sep*, *-ge-*, *h*) be laid out; **~löschen** *v/t* (*sep*, *-ge-*, *h*) put out; *fig* wipe out; **~losen** *v/t* (*sep*, *-ge-*, *h*) draw (lots) for

'**auslösen** *v/t* (*sep*, *-ge-*, *h*) TECH release; ransom, redeem; cause, start, trigger *s.th.* off; '**Auslöser** *m* (PHOT shutter) release; trigger

'**ausmachen** *v/t* (*sep*, *-ge-*, *h*) put out (*fire*); turn off (*light etc*); arrange (*date etc*); agree on (*price etc*); make up; amount to; settle (*dispute*); sight, spot; **macht es Ihnen et. aus** (, **wenn…**)? do you mind (if …)?; **es macht mir nichts aus** I don't mind; **das macht** (*gar*) **nichts aus** that doesn't matter (at all)

'**ausmalen** *v/t* (*sep*, *-ge-*, *h*) paint; **sich et. ~** imagine s.th.

'**Ausmaß** *n* extent; *pl* proportions

aus|merzen ['ausmɛrtsən] *v/t* (*sep*, *-ge-*, *h*) eliminate; **~messen** *v/t* (*irr*, **messen**, *sep*, *-ge-*, *h*) measure

Ausnahme ['ausnaːmə] *f* (-; *-n*) exception; **~zustand** *m* POL state of emergency

'**ausnahmslos** *adv* without exception

'**ausnahmsweise** *adv* by way of exception; just this once

'**ausnehmen** *v/t* (*irr*, **nehmen**, *sep*, *-ge-*, *h*) clean (*chicken etc*); except; F *contp* fleece *s.o.*; **~d** *adv* exceptionally

'**aus|nutzen** *v/t* (*sep*, *-ge-*, *h*) use; take advantage of (*a. contp*); exploit; **~packen** (*sep*, *-ge-*, *h*) **1.** *v/t* unpack **2.** F *v/i* talk; **~pfeifen** *v/t* (*irr*, **pfeifen**, *sep*, *-ge-*, *h*) boo, hiss; **~plaudern** *v/t* (*sep*, *-ge-*, *h*) blab out; **~plündern** *v/t* (*sep*, *-ge-*, *h*) plunder, rob; **~pro,bieren** *v/t* (*sep*, *no -ge-*, *h*) try (out), test

'**Auspuff** *m* MOT exhaust; **~gase** *pl* MOT exhaust fumes; **~rohr** *n* MOT exhaust pipe; **~topf** *m* MOT muffler, *Br* silencer

'**aus|quar,tieren** *v/t* (*sep*, *no -ge-*, *h*) move out; **~ra,dieren** *v/t* (*sep*, *no -ge-*, *h*) erase; *fig* wipe out; **~ran,gieren** *v/t* (*sep*, *no -ge-*, *h*) discard; **~rauben** *v/t* (*sep*, *-ge-*, *h*) rob; **~räumen** *v/t* (*sep*, *-ge-*, *h*) empty; clear out (*room etc*); *fig* clear up (*doubt etc*); **~rechnen** *v/t* (*sep*, *-ge-*, *h*) work out

'**Ausrede** *f* excuse

'**ausreden** (*sep*, *-ge-*, *h*) **1.** *v/i* finish speaking; **j-n ~ lassen** hear s.o. out **2.** *v/t*: **j-m et. ~** talk s.o. out of s.th.

'**ausreichen** *v/t* (*sep*, *-ge-*, *h*) be enough; **~d** *adj* sufficient, enough; *grade*: (barely) passing, only average, weak, D

'**Ausreise** f departure; '**ausreisen** v/i (sep, -ge-, sein) leave (a or one's country); '**Ausreisevisum** n exit visa

'**ausreißen** (irr, **reißen**, sep, -ge-) **1.** v/t (h) pull or tear out **2.** F v/i (sein) run away; '**Ausreißer** m (-s; -) runaway

'**aus|renken** v/t (sep, -ge-, h) MED dislocate; **~richten** v/t (sep, -ge-, h) tell s.o. s.th.; deliver (message); accomplish; arrange (party etc); **richte ihr e-n Gruß von mir aus!** give her my regards!; **kann et. ~?** can I take a message

'**ausrotten** v/t (sep, -ge-, h) exterminate '**Ausrottung** f (-; -en) extermination

'**ausrücken** v/i (sep, -ge-, sein) F run away; MIL march out

'**Ausruf** m cry, shout; '**ausrufen** v/t (irr, **rufen**, sep, -ge-, h) cry, shout, exclaim; call out (name); POL proclaim; '**Ausrufung** f (-; -en) POL proclamation; '**Ausrufungszeichen** n LING exclamation mark

'**ausruhen** v/i, v/t and v/refl (sep, -ge-, h) rest

'**ausrüsten** v/t (sep, -ge-, h) equip; '**Ausrüstung** f equipment

'**ausrutschen** v/i (sep, -ge-, sein) slip '**Aussage** f statement; JUR evidence

'**aussagen** v/t (sep, -ge-, h) state, declare; JUR testify

'**ausschalten** v/t (sep, -ge-, h) switch off; fig eliminate

'**Ausschau** f: **~ halten nach** → '**ausschauen** v/i (sep, -ge-, h) **~ nach** look out for, watch out for

'**ausscheiden** (irr, **scheiden**, sep, -ge-) **1.** v/i (sein) be ruled out; SPORT etc drop out (aus dat of); retire (aus dat from office etc); **~ aus** (dat) leave (a firm etc) **2.** v/t (h) eliminate; MED etc secrete, exude; '**Ausscheidung** f elimination (a. SPORT); MED secretion

'**Ausscheidungs...** in cpds ...spiel etc: SPORT qualifying ...

'**aus|schlachten** fig v/t (sep, -ge-, h) salvage, Br a. cannibalize; contp exploit; **~schlafen** (irr, **schlafen**, sep, -ge-, h) **1.** v/i sleep in **2.** v/t sleep off

'**Ausschlag** m MED rash; TECH deflection; **den ~ geben** decide it

'**ausschlagen** (irr, **schlagen**, sep, -ge-, h) **1.** v/t knock out (tooth etc); fig refuse, decline (offer etc) **2.** v/i horse: kick; BOT bud; TECH deflect

'**ausschlaggebend** adj decisive

'**ausschließen** v/t (irr, **schließen**, sep, -ge-, h) lock out; fig exclude; expel; SPORT disqualify

'**ausschließlich** adj exclusive

'**Ausschluss** m exclusion; expulsion; SPORT disqualification; **unter ~ der Öffentlichkeit** in closed session

'**aus|schmücken** v/t (sep, -ge-, h) decorate; fig embellish; **~schneiden** v/t (irr, **schneiden**, sep, -ge-, h) cut out

'**Ausschnitt** m clothing: neck; (press) clipping (Br cutting); fig part; extract; **mit tiefem ~** low-necked

'**ausschreiben** v/t (irr, **schreiben**, sep, -ge-, h) write out (a. check etc); advertise (post etc); '**Ausschreibung** f advertisement

'**Ausschreitungen** pl violence, riots

'**Ausschuss** m committee, board; TECH (no pl) refuse, waste, rejects

'**aus|schütteln** v/t (sep, -ge-, h) shake out; **~schütten** v/t (sep, -ge-, h) pour out (a. fig); spill; ECON pay; **sich vor Lachen ~** split one's sides

'**ausschweifend** adj dissolute

'**Ausschweifung** f (-; -en) debauchery, excess

'**aussehen** v/i (irr, **sehen**, sep, -ge-, h) look; **krank (traurig) ~** look ill (sad); **~ wie ...** look like ...; **wie sieht er aus?** what does he look like? '**Aussehen** n (-s; no pl) look(s), appearance

außen ['ausən] adv outside; **nach ~ (hin)** outward(s); fig outwardly

'**Außenbordmotor** m outboard motor

aussenden v/t ([irr, **senden**,] sep, -ge-, h) send out

'**Außen|dienst** m field service; **~handel** m foreign trade; **~mi,nister** m Am Secretary of State, Br Foreign Secretary; **~minis,terium** n Am State Department, Br Foreign Office; **~poli,tik** f foreign affairs; foreign policy

'**außenpo,litisch** adj foreign-policy

'**Außenseite** f outside

Außenseiter ['ausənzaitɐ] m (-s; -) outsider

'**Außen|spiegel** m MOT outside rearview mirror; **~stände** pl ECON receivables; **~stelle** f branch; **~stürmer** m SPORT winger; **~welt** f outside world

außer ['ausɐ] **1.** prp (dat) out of; aside

from, *Br* beside(s); except; ~ *sich sein*
be beside o.s. (*vor Freude* with joy); *alle* ~ *e–m* all but one; → *Betrieb, Gefahr*
2. *cj:* ~ *dass* except that; ~ *wenn* unless

'**außerdem** *cj* besides, moreover

äußere ['ɔysərə] *adj* exterior, outer, outward; '**Äußere** *n* (*-n; no pl*) exterior,
outside; (outward) appearance

'**außergewöhnlich** *adj* unusual

'**außerhalb** *prp* (*gen*) *and adv* outside;
out of; beyond

'**außerirdisch** *adj* extraterrestrial

'**äußerlich** *adj* external, outward

'**Äußerlichkeit** *f* (*-; -en*) formality; minor detail

äußern ['ɔysən] *v/t* (*ge-, h*) utter, express; *sich* ~ say s.th.; *sich* ~ *zu or über*
(*acc*) express o.s. on

'**außer'ordentlich** *adj* extraordinary

'**außerplanmäßig** *adj* unscheduled

äußerst ['ɔysəst] **1.** *adj* outermost; *fig*
extreme; *im ~en Fall* at (the) worst;
at (the) most **2.** *adv* extremely

außer'stande *adj:* ~ *sein* be unable

'**Äußerung** *f* (*-; -en*) utterance, remark

'**aussetzen** (*sep, -ge-, h*) **1.** *v/t* abandon;
expose (*dat* to); *et. auszusetzen ha-
ben an* (*dat*) find fault with **2.** *v/i* stop,
break off; MOT, TECH fail

'**Aussicht** *f* view (*auf acc* of); *fig* prospect (of), chance (*auf Erfolg* of success); '**aussichtslos** *adj* hopeless, desperate; '**Aussichtspunkt** *m* vantage
point; '**aussichtsreich** *adj* promising;
'**Aussichtsturm** *m* lookout tower

'**Aussiedler** *m* resettler, evacuee

'**aussitzen** *v/t* (*irr, sitzen, sep, -ge-, h*) sit
s.th. out

aussöhnen ['auszøːnən] *v/refl* (*sep,
-ge-, h*) *sich* ~ (*mit*) become reconciled
(with), F make it up (with)

'**Aussöhnung** *f* (*-; -en*) reconciliation

'**aus|sor,tieren** *v/t* (*sep, no -ge-, h*) sort
out; ~**spannen** (*sep, -ge-, h*) **1.** *v/t* un-
harness **2.** *fig v/i* (take a) rest, relax

'**aussperren** *v/t* (*sep, -ge-, h*) lock out (*a.
ECON*); '**Aussperrung** *f* (*-; -en*) ECON
lock-out

'**aus|spielen** (*sep, -ge-, h*) **1.** *v/t* play; *j-n
gegen j-n* ~ play s.o. off against s.o. **2.**
v/i card game: lead; *er hat ausgespielt*
fig he is done for; ~**spio,nieren** *v/t* (*sep,
no -ge-, h*) spy out

'**Aussprache** *f* pronunciation; discus-

sion; *private* heart-to-heart (talk)

'**aussprechen** *v/t* (*irr, sprechen, sep,
-ge-, h*) pronounce; express; *sich* ~
für (*gegen*) speak for (against); *sich
mit j-m gründlich* ~ have a heart-to-
-heart talk with s.o.

'**Ausspruch** *m* saying; remark

'**aus|spucken** *v/i and v/t* (*sep, -ge-, h*)
spit out; ~**spülen** *v/t* (*sep, -ge-, h*) rinse

'**Ausstand** *m* strike, F walkout

'**ausstatten** *v/t* (*sep, -ge-, h*) fit out,
equip, furnish; '**Ausstattung** *f* (*-; -en*)
equipment, furnishings; design

'**aus|stechen** *v/t* (*irr, stechen, sep, -ge-,
h*) GASTR cut out (*a. fig*); put out (*eyes*);
~**stehen** (*irr, stehen, sep, -ge-, h*) **1.** *v/t*
stand, endure; F *ich kann ihn* (*es*)
nicht ~ I can't stand him (it) **2.** *v/i:*
(*noch*) ~ be outstanding *or* overdue

'**aussteigen** *v/i* (*irr, steigen, sep, -ge-,
sien*) get out (*aus dat* of); (*a.* ~ *aus
dat*) get off *a* bus, train; F *fig* drop
out; '**Aussteiger** *m* (*-s; -*) drop-out

'**ausstellen** *v/t* (*sep, -ge-, h*) exhibit, display, show; make out (*check etc*); issue
(*passport*); '**Aussteller** *m* (*-s; -*) exhib-
itor; issuer; drawer (*of check*)

'**Ausstellung** *f* exhibition, show

'**aussterben** *v/i* (*irr, sterben, sep, -ge-,
sein*) die out, become extinct (*both a.
fig*)

'**Aussteuer** *f* trousseau; dowry

'**aussteuern** *v/t* (*sep, -ge-, h*) ELECTR
modulate; '**Aussteuerung** *f* ELECTR
modulation; level control

Ausstieg ['ausʃtiːk] *m* (*-[e]s; -e*) exit; *fig*
withdrawal (*aus dat* from)

'**ausstopfen** *v/t* (*sep, -ge-, h*) stuff; pad

'**Ausstoß** *m* TECH, PHYS discharge, ejection; ECON output

'**ausstoßen** *v/t* (*irr, stoßen, sep, -ge-, h*)
TECH, PHYS give off, eject, emit; ECON
turn out; give (*cry, sigh*); expel

'**aus|strahlen** *v/t* (*sep, -ge-, h*) radiate
(*happiness etc*); TV, *radio:* broadcast,
transmit; '**Ausstrahlung** *f* radiation;
broadcast; *fig* magnetism, charisma

'**aus|strecken** *v/t* (*sep, -ge-, h*) stretch
(out); ~**streichen** *v/t* (*irr, streichen,
sep, -ge-, h*) strike out; ~**strömen** *v/i*
(*sep, -ge-, sein*) escape (*aus dat* from);
~**suchen** *v/t* (*sep, -ge-, h*) choose, pick

'**Austausch** *m* (*-[e]s; no pl*) exchange

'**austauschbar** *adj* exchangeable

'**austauschen** v/t (sep, -ge-, h) exchange (**gegen** for)

'**Austauschschüler(in)** exchange student

'**austeilen** v/t (sep, -ge-, h) distribute, hand out; deal (out) (cards, blows)

Auster ['austɐ] f (-; -n) zo oyster

'**austragen** v/t (irr, **tragen**, sep, -ge-, h) deliver (mail); settle (dispute etc); hold (contest etc); **das Kind ~** have the baby

'**Austragungsort** m SPORT venue

Australien [aus'traːljən] Australia

Australier [aus'traːljɐ] m (-s; -), **Australierin** [aus'traːljərɪn] f (-; -nen), **aust'ralisch** adj Australian

'**aus|treiben** v/t (irr, **treiben**, sep, -ge-, h) exorcise; F **j-m et. ~** cure s.o. of s.th.; **~treten** (irr, **treten**, sep, -ge-) **1.** v/t (h) tread or stamp out (fire); wear out (shoes) **2.** v/i (sein) escape (**aus** dat from); F go to the bathroom (Br toilet); **~ aus** (dat) leave (a club etc); resign from; **~trinken** v/t (irr, **trinken**, sep, -ge-, h) drink up; empty

'**Austritt** m leaving; resignation; escape

'**austrocknen** v/t (sep, -ge-, h) and v/i (sein) dry up

'**ausüben** v/t (sep, -ge-, h) practi|ce, Br -se; hold (office); exercise (power etc); exert (pressure etc); '**Ausübung** f (-; no pl) practice; exercise

'**Ausverkauf** m ECON (clearance) sale

'**ausverkauft** adj ECON, THEA sold out; **vor ~em Haus spielen** play to a full house

'**Auswahl** f choice, selection (both a. ECON); SPORT representative team

'**auswählen** v/t (sep, -ge-, h) choose, select

'**Auswanderer** m emigrant

'**auswandern** v/i (sep, -ge-, sein) emigrate; '**Auswanderung** f emigration

auswärtig ['ausvɛrtɪç] adj out-of-town; POL foreign

'**auswärts** adv out of town

'**Auswärts|sieg** m SPORT away victory; **~spiel** n SPORT away game

'**auswechseln** v/t (sep, -ge-, h) exchange (**gegen** for); change (tire); replace; **A gegen B ~** SPORT substitute B for A; **wie ausgewechselt** (like) a different person; '**Auswechselspieler** m SPORT substitute

'**Ausweg** m way out; '**auswegios** adj

hopeless; '**Ausweglosigkeit** f (-; no pl) hopelessness

'**ausweichen** v/i (irr, **weichen**, sep, -ge-, sein) make way (dat for); fig avoid s.o.; evade (question); **~d** adj evasive

'**ausweinen** v/refl (sep, -ge-, h) have a good cry

Ausweis ['ausvais] m (-es; -e) identification (card); card

'**ausweisen** v/t (irr, **weisen**, sep, -ge-, h) expel; **sich ~** identify o.s.

'**Ausweispa,piere** pl documents

'**Ausweisung** f (-; -en) expulsion

'**ausweiten** fig v/t (sep, -ge-, h) expand

'**auswendig** adv by heart; **et. ~ können** know s.th. by heart; **~ lernen** memorize; learn by heart

'**auswerfen** v/t (irr, **werfen**, sep, -ge-, h) throw out; cast (anchor); TECH eject

'**auswerten** v/t (sep, -ge-, h) evaluate, analyze, interpret; utilize, exploit; '**Auswertung** f evaluation; utilization

'**auswickeln** v/t (sep, -ge-, h) unwrap

'**auswirken** v/refl (sep, -ge-, h) **sich ~ auf** (acc) affect; **sich positiv ~** have a favo(u)rable effect; '**Auswirkung** f effect

'**auswischen** v/t (sep, -ge-, h) wipe out

'**auswringen** v/t (irr, **wringen**, sep, -ge-, h) wring out

Auswuchs m (-es; Auswüchse ['ausvyːksə]) excrescence; fig pl excesses

'**aus|wuchten** v/t (sep, -ge-, h) TECH balance; **~zahlen** v/t (sep, -ge-, h) pay (out); pay s.o. off; **sich ~ pay; ~zählen** v/t (sep, -ge-, h) count; boxing: count out

'**Auszahlung** f payment; paying off

'**auszeichnen** v/t (sep, -ge-, h) price, mark (out) (goods); **sich ~** distinguish o.s.; **j-n mit et. ~** award s.th. to s.o.; '**Auszeichnung** f marking; fig distinction, hono(u)r; award; decoration

'**ausziehen** (irr, **ziehen**, sep, -ge-) **1.** v/t (h) take off (coat etc); pull out (table etc); **sich ~** undress **2.** v/i (sein) move out

'**Auszubildende** m, f (-n; -n) apprentice, trainee

'**Auszug** m move, removal; extract, excerpt; statement (of account)

authentisch [au'tɛntɪʃ] adj authentic, genuine

Autismus [au'tɪsmʊs] m PSYCH autism

autistisch [au'tɪstɪʃ] adj PSYCH autistic

Auto ['auto] n (-s; -s) car, auto(mobile); (*mit dem*) ~ **fahren** drive, go by car

'**Autobahn** f Am expressway, Br motorway; ~**dreieck** n interchange; ~**gebühr** f toll; ~**kreuz** n interchange

Autobiogra'phie f autobiography

'**Auto|bombe** f car bomb; ~**bus** m → *Bus*; ~**fähre** f car ferry; ~**fahrer(in)** motorist, driver; ~**fahrt** f drive; ~**friedhof** F m car dump, auto junkyard

Autogramm [auto'gram] n autograph; ~**jäger** m autograph hunter

'**Auto|karte** f road map; ~**kino** n drive-in theater (Br cinema)

Automat [auto'maːt] m (-en; -en) vending (Br a. slot) machine; TECH robot; → *Spielautomat*; **Automatik** [auto-'maːtɪk] f (-; no pl) automatic (system or control); MOT automatic transmission; automatic; **Automation**

[automa'tsjoːn] f (-; no pl) automation; **auto'matisch** adj automatic

'**Autome,chaniker** m car mechanic

autonom [auto'noːm] adj autonomous

'**Autonummer** f license (Br licence) number

Autor ['autoːɐ] m (-s; -en [au'toːrən]) author

'**Autorepara,turwerkstatt** f garage, car repair shop

Autorin [au'toːrɪn] f (-; -nen) author(ess)

autorisieren [autori'ziːrən] v/t (no -ge-, h) authorize; **autoritär** [autori'tɛːɐ] adj authoritarian; **Autorität** [autori'tɛːt] f (-; -en) authority

'**Auto|tele,fon** n car phone; ~**vermietung** f car rental (Br hire) service; ~**waschanlage** f car wash

Axt [akst] f (-; Äxte ['ɛkstə]) ax(e)

B

Baby ['beːbi] n (-s; -s) baby; ~**bett** n crib, Br cot; ~**fläschchen** n baby's bottle; ~**nahrung** f baby food; ~**sitter(in)** babysitter; ~**sitz** m child seat; ~**wickelraum** m baby-changing room

Bach [bax] m (-[e]s; Bäche ['bɛçə]) brook, stream, Am a. creek

'**Backblech** n baking sheet

'**Backbord** n (-s; no pl) MAR port

Backe ['bakə] f (-; -n) ANAT cheek

backen v/t and v/i ([irr, **backen**,] -ge-, h) bake

'**Backenzahn** m ANAT molar (tooth)

Bäcker ['bɛkɐ] m (-s; -) baker; **beim** ~ at the baker's; **Bäckerei** [bɛkə'rai] f (-; -en) bakery, baker's (shop)

'**Back|form** f baking tin; ~**hendl** ['bak-hɛndl] *Austrian* n (-s; -n) fried chicken; ~**obst** n dried fruit; ~**ofen** m oven; ~**pflaume** f prune; ~**pulver** n baking powder; ~**stein** m brick

backte ['baktə] pret of **backen**

'**Backwaren** pl breads and pastries

Bad [baːt] n (-[e]; Bäder ['bɛːdɐ]) bath; swim; bathroom; → *Badeort*; **ein** ~ **nehmen** → *baden* 1

'**Bade|anstalt** f swimming pool, public baths; ~**anzug** m swimsuit; ~**hose** f

bathing trunks; ~**kappe** f bathing cap; ~**mantel** m bathrobe; ~**meister** m pool or bath attendant

baden ['baːdən] (ge-, h) **1.** v/i bathe, take or have a bath; swim; ~ **gehen** go swimming **2.** v/t bathe (a. MED); Br a. bath

'**Bade|ort** m seaside (or health) resort; ~**sachen** Pl swimming things; ~**schaum** m bubble bath, bath foam; ~**tuch** n bath towel; ~**wanne** f bathtub; ~**zeug** n swimming gear; ~**zimmer** n bathroom

Badminton ['bɛtmɪntn] n (-; no pl) badminton

baff [baf] adj: F ~ **sein** be flabbergasted

Bagatelle [baga'tɛlə] f (-; -n) trifle

Baga'tellschaden m superficial damage

Bagger ['bagɐ] m (-s; -) TECH excavator; dredge(r); ~**baggern** v/i (ge-, h) TECH excavate; dredge

Bahn [baːn] f (-; -en) railroad, Br railway; train; way, path, course; SPORT track; **mit der** ~ by rail; ~ **frei!** make way!; cpds → a. **Eisenbahn**

'**bahnbrechend** adj epoch-making

BahnCard® [baːn'kaːt] f (-; -s) rail card (*allowing 50% or 25% reduction on* *tickets*)

'**Bahndamm** *m* railroad (*Br* railway) embankment

'**bahnen** *v/t* (*ge-, h*) **den Weg ~** clear the way (*dat* for *s.o.* or *s.th.*); **sich e-n Weg ~** force *or* work one's way

'**Bahn|hof** *m* (railroad, *Br* railway) station; **~linie** *f* railroad (*Br* railway) line; **~steig** ['baːnʃtaik] *m* (-[e]s; -e) platform; **~übergang** *m* grade (*Br* level) crossing

Bahre ['baːrə] *f* (-; -n) stretcher; bier

Baisse ['bɛːsə] *f* (-; -n) ECON fall, slump

Bakterien [bak'teːrjən] *pl* MED bacteria, germs

balancieren [balaˈsiːrən] *v/t and v/i* (*no -ge-, h*) balance

bald [balt] *adv* soon; F almost, nearly; **so ~ wie möglich** as soon as possible

baldig ['baldɪç] *adj* speedy; **~e Antwort** ECON early reply; **auf(ein)es Wiedersehen!** see you again soon!

balgen ['balgən] *v/refl* (*ge-, h*) scuffle (*um* for)

Balken ['balkən] *m* (-s; -) beam

Balkon [balˈkɔŋ] *m* (-s; -s, -e [balˈkoːnə]) balcony; **~tür** *f* French window

Ball [bal] *m* (-[e]s; **Bälle** ['bɛlə]) ball; dance; **am ~ sein** SPORT have the ball; **am ~ bleiben** *fig* stick to it

Ballade [baˈlaːdə] *f* (-; -n) ballad

Ballast ['balast] *m* (-[e]s; *no pl*) ballast, *fig a.* burden; **~stoffe** *pl* MED roughage, bulk

ballen ['balən] *v/t* (*ge-, h*) clench (*Fist*)

'**Ballen** *m* (-s; -) bale; ANAT ball

Ballett [baˈlɛt] *n* (-[e]s; -e) ballet

Ballon [baˈlɔŋ] *m* (-s; -s) balloon

'**Ballungs|raum** *m*, **~zentrum** *n* congested area, conurbation

Balsam ['balzaːm] *m* (-s; *no pl*) balm

Bambus ['bambʊs] *m* (-ses, -; -se) BOT bamboo; **~rohr** *n* BOT bamboo (cane)

banal [baˈnaːl] *adj* banal, trite

Banane [baˈnaːnə] *f* (-; -n) BOT banana

Banause [baˈnauzə] *m* (-n; -n) philistine

band [bant] *pret of* **binden**

Band[1] *n* (-[e]s; **Bänder** ['bɛndɐ]) ribbon; tape; (*hat*) band; ANAT ligament; *fig* tie, link; **auf ~ aufnehmen** tape; **am laufenden ~** *fig* continuously

Band[2] *m* (-[e]s; **Bände** ['bɛndə]) volume

Bandage [banˈdaːʒə] *f* (-; -n) bandage

bandagieren [bandaˈʒiːrən] *v/t* (*no* -ge-, *h*) bandage (up)

'**Bandbreite** *f* ELECTR bandwidth; *fig* range

Bande ['bandə] *f* (-; -n) gang; *billiards*: cushions; *ice hockey*: boards; *bowling*: gutter

'**Bänderriss** *m* MED torn ligament

bändigen ['bɛndɪgən] *v/t* (*ge-, h*) tame (*a. fig*); restrain, control (*children etc*)

Bandit [banˈdiːt] *m* (-en; -en) bandit, outlaw

'**Band|maß** *n* tape measure; **~scheibe** *f* ANAT (intervertebral) disk (*Br* disc); **~scheibenschaden** *m*, **~scheibenvorfall** *m* MED slipped disk; **~wurm** *m* ZO tapeworm

bange ['baŋə] *adj* afraid; anxious

'**Bange** *f*: **j-m ~ machen** frighten *or* scare *s.o.*; **keine ~!** (have) no fear!

'**bangen** *v/i* (*ge-, h*) be anxious *or* worried (*um* about)

Bank[1] [baŋk] *f* (-; **Bänke** ['bɛŋkə]) bench; F **durch die ~** without exception; **auf die lange ~ schieben** put off

Bank[2] *f* (-; -en) bank; **auf der ~** in the bank

'**Bankangestellte** *m, f* bank clerk *or* employee

'**Bankauto,mat** *m* → **Geldautomat**

Bankett [baŋˈkɛt] *n* (-[e]s; -e) banquet

'**Bankgeschäfte** *pl* banking transactions

Bankier [baŋˈkjeː] *m* (-s; -s) banker

'**Bank|konto** *n* bank(ing) account; **~leitzahl** *f* A.B.A. number, *Br* bank (sorting) code; **~note** *f* bill, *Br* (bank) note; **~raub** *m* bank robbery

bankrott [baŋˈkrɔt] *adj* ECON bankrupt

Bank'rott *m* (-[e]s; -e) ECON bankruptcy; **~ machen** go bankrupt

'**Bankverbindung** *f* account(s), account details

Bann [ban] *m* (-[e]s; *no pl*) ban; spell

'**bannen** *v/t* (*ge-, h*) ward off; (*wie*) **gebannt** spellbound

Banner ['banɐ] *n* (-s; -) banner (*a. fig*)

bar [baːɐ] *adj* (in) cash; **gegen ~** for cash

Bar *f* (-; -s) bar; nightclub

Bär [bɛːɐ] *m* (-en; -en) ZO bear

Baracke [baˈrakə] *f* (-; -n) hut; *contp* shack

Barbar [barˈbaːɐ] *m* (-en; -en) barbarian; **barbarisch** [barˈbaːrɪʃ] *adj* barbarous, *a.* atrocious (*crime etc*)

'**Bardame** *f* barmaid

'**barfuß** *adj and adv* barefoot

barg [bark] *pret of* **bergen**

'**Bargeld** *n* cash

'**bargeldlos** *adj* noncash

'**Barhocker** *m* bar stool

Bariton ['baːritɔn] *m* (-s; -e ['baːritoːnə]) MUS baritone

Barkasse [bar'kasə] *f* (-; -n) MAR launch

barm'herzig *adj* merciful; charitable

Barm'herzigkeit *f* (-; *no pl*) mercy; charity

'**Barmixer** *m* barman

Barometer [baro'meːtɐ] *n* (-s; -) barometer

Baron [ba'roːn] *m* (-s; -e) baron

Ba'ronin *f* (-; -nen) baroness

Barren ['barən] *m* (-s; -) bar, ingot, *a.* gold, silver bullion; SPORT parallel bars

Barriere [ba'rjeːrə] *f* (-; -n) barrier

Barrikade [bari'kaːdə] *f* (-; -n) barricade

barsch [barʃ] *adj* rough, gruff, brusque

Barsch *m* (-[e]s; -e) ZO perch

'**Barscheck** *m* (negotiable) check, *Br* open cheque

barst [barst] *pret of* **bersten**

Bart [baːɐt] *m* (-[e]s; *Bärte* ['bɛːɐtə]) beard; TECH bit; *sich e-n ~ wachsen lassen* grow a beard

bärtig ['bɛːɐtɪç] *adj* bearded

'**Barzahlung** *f* cash payment

Basar [ba'zaːɐ] *m* (-s; -e) bazaar

Base ['baːzə] *f* (-; -n) cousin; CHEM base

basieren [ba'ziːrən] *v/i* (*no -ge-, h*) *~ auf* (*dat*) be based on

Basis ['baːzɪs] *f* (-; *Basen*) basis; MIL, ARCH base

Baskenmütze ['baskənmʏtsə] *f* beret

Bass [bas] *m* (-es; *Bässe* ['bɛsə]) MUS bass

Bassin [ba'sɛ̃ː] *n* (-s; -s) basin; (swimming) pool

Bassist [ba'sɪst] *m* (-en; -en) MUS bass singer *or* player

Bast [bast] *m* (-[e]s; -e) bast; HUNT velvet

Bastard ['bastart] *m* (-s; -e) BIOL hybrid; mongrel; V bastard

basteln ['bastəln] (*ge-, h*) **1.** *v/i* make *or* repair things o.s. **2.** *v/t* build, make

Bastler ['bastlɐ] *m* (-s; -) home handyman, do-it-yourselfer

bat [baːt] *pret of* **bitten**

Batik ['baːtɪk] *m* (-s; -en), *f* (-; -en) batik

Batist [ba'tɪst] *m* (-[e]s; -e) cambric

Batterie [batə'riː] *f* (-; -n) ELECTR, MIL battery

Bau [bau] *m* (-[e]s; *Bauten*) (*no pl*) building, construction; build, frame; building; ZO (*pl Baue*) hole, den; *im ~* under construction; **~arbeiten** *pl* construction work; road works; **~arbeiter** *m* construction worker; **~art** *f* style (of construction); type, model

Bauch [baux] *m* (-[e]s; *Bäuche* ['bɔʏçə]) belly (*a. fig*); ANAT abdomen; F tummy

'**bauchig** *adj* bulgy

'**Bauch|landung** *f* AVIAT belly landing; **~redner** *m* ventriloquist; **~schmerzen** *pl* stomachache; **~tanz** *m* belly dancing

bauen ['bauən] (*ge-, h*) **1.** *v/t* build, construct, *a.* make (*furniture etc*) **2.** *fig v/i: ~ auf* (*acc*) rely *or* count on

Bauer¹ ['bauɐ] *m* (-n; -n) farmer; *chess*: pawn

'**Bauer²** *n*, *m* (-s; -) (bird)cage

Bäuerin ['bɔʏərɪn] *f* (-; -nen) farmer's wife; farmer

bäuerlich ['bɔʏɐlɪç] *adj* rural; rustic

'**Bauern|fänger** *contp m* trickster, conman; **~haus** *n* farmhouse; **~hof** *m* farm; **~möbel** *pl* rustic furniture

'**baufällig** *adj* dilapidated

'**Bau|firma** *f* builders and contractors; **~genehmigung** *f* building permit; **~gerüst** *n* scaffold(ing); **~herr** *m* owner; **~holz** *n* lumber, *Br a.* timber; **~inge,nieur** *m* civil engineer; **~jahr** *n* year of construction; *~ 1995* 1995 model; **~kasten** *m* box of building blocks (*Br* bricks); TECH construction set; kit; **~leiter** *m* building supervisor

'**baulich** *adj* structural

Baum [baum] *m* (-[e]s; *Bäume* ['bɔʏmə]) BOT tree

'**Baumarkt** *m* do-it-yourself superstore

baumeln ['bauməln] *v/i* (*ge-, h*) dangle, swing; *mit den Beinen ~* dangle one's legs

'**Baum|schule** *f* nursery; **~stamm** *m* trunk; log; **~wolle** *f* cotton

'**Bau|plan** *m* architectural drawing; blueprints; **~platz** *m* building site

Bausch [bauʃ] *m* (-[e]s; -e) wad, ball; *in ~ und Bogen* lock, stock and barrel

'**Bausparkasse** *f* building and loan association, *Br* building society

'**Bau|stein** *m* brick; (building) block; *fig*

element; **∼stelle** f building site; MOT construction zone, Br roadworks; **∼stil** m (architectural) style; **∼stoff** m building material; **∼techniker** m engineer; **∼teil** n component (part), unit, module; **∼unternehmer** m building contractor; **∼vorschriften** pl building regulations; **∼werk** n building; **∼zaun** m hoarding; **∼zeichner** m draftsman, Br draughtsman

Bayer ['baiɐ] m (-n; -n), **Bayerin** ['baiə-rɪn] f (-; -nen), **bay(e)risch** ['bai(ə)rɪʃ] adj Bavarian; **Bayern** ['baiɐn] Bavaria.

Bazillus [ba'tsɪlʊs] m (-; -len) MED bacillus, germ

beabsichtigen [bə'ʔapzɪçtɪɡən] v/t (no -ge-, h) intend, plan; **es war beabsichtigt** it was intentional

be'achten v/t (no -ge-, h) pay attention to; observe, follow (rule etc); **∼ Sie, dass ...** note that ...; **nicht ∼** take no notice of; disregard; **be'achtlich** adj remarkable; considerable

Be'achtung f (-; no pl) attention; consideration; observance

Beamte [bə'ʔamtə] m (-n; -n), **Be'amtin** f (-; -nen) official; (police etc) officer; civil servant

be'ängstigend adj alarming

beanspruchen [bə'ʔanʃpruxən] v/t (no -ge-, h) claim; take up (time etc); TECH stress; **Be'anspruchung** f (-; -en) claim; TECH stress, strain (a. fig)

beanstanden [bə'ʔanʃtandən] v/t (no -ge-, h) complain about; object to

beantragen [bə'ʔantraːɡən] v/t (no -ge-, h) apply for; JUR, PARL move (for); propose

be'antworten v/t (no -ge-, h) answer, reply to

be'arbeiten v/t (no -ge-, h) work; AGR till; hew (stone); process; be in charge of (a case etc); treat (subject); revise; THEA adapt (nach from); esp MUS arrange; F **j-n ∼** work on s.o.

Be'arbeitung f (-; -en) working; revision; THEA adaptation; esp MUS arrangement; TECH processing, treatment

be'atmen v/t (no -ge-, h) MED give artificial respiration to s.o.

beaufsichtigen [bə'ʔaufzɪçtɪɡən] v/t (no -ge-, h) supervise; look after; **Be-'aufsichtigung** f (-; -en) supervision;

looking after

be'auftragen v/t (no -ge-, h) commission; instruct; **∼ mit** put s.o. in charge of; **Beauftragte** [bə'ʔauftraːktə] m, f (-n; -n) agent; representative; commissioner

be'bauen v/t (no -ge-, h) build on; AGR cultivate

beben ['beːbən] v/i (ge-, h) shake, tremble; shiver (all: **vor** with); earth: quake

bebildern [bə'bɪldən] v/t (no -ge-, h) illustrate

Becher ['bɛçɐ] m (-s; -) cup, mug

Becken ['bɛkən] n (-s; -) basin, bowl; pool; ANAT pelvis; MUS cymbal(s)

bedacht [bə'daxt] adj: **darauf ∼ sein zu** inf be anxious to inf

bedächtig [bə'dɛçtɪç] adj deliberate; measured

bedang [bə'daŋ] pret of **bedingen**

be'danken v/refl (no -ge-, h) **sich bei j-m für et. ∼** thank s.o. for s.th.

Bedarf [bə'darf] m (-[e]s; no pl) need (an dat of), want (of); ECON demand (for); **bei ∼** if necessary

Be'darfshaltestelle f request stop

bedauerlich [bə'dauɐlɪç] adj regrettable; **be'dauerlicher'weise** adv unfortunately

be'dauern v/t (no -ge-, h) feel or be sorry for s.o., pity s.o.; regret s.th.; **Be-'dauern** n (-s; no pl) regret (über acc at); **be'dauernswert** adj pitiable, deplorable

be'decken v/t (no -ge-, h) cover

be'deckt adj METEOR overcast

be'denken v/t (irr, denken, no -ge-, h) consider, think s.th. over; **Be'denken** pl doubts; scruples; objections

be'denkenlos adv unhesitatingly; without scruples

be'denklich adj doubtful; serious, critical; alarming

Be'denkzeit f: **e-e Stunde ∼** one hour to think it over

be'deuten v/t (no -ge-, h) mean; **∼d** adj important; considerable; distinguished

Be'deutung f (-; -en) meaning; importance; **be'deutungslos** adj insignificant; meaningless; **be'deutungsvoll** adj significant; meaningful

be'dienen (no -ge-, h) **1.** v/t serve, wait on s.o.; TECH operate, work; **sich ∼** help o.s.; ~ *Sie sich!* help yourself! **2.** *v/i* serve; wait (at table); *card games*: follow suit; **Be'dienung** *f* (-; -en) (*no pl*) service; waiter, waitress; shop assistant, clerk; TECH operation, control; **Be-'dienungsanleitung** *f* operating instructions

bedingen [bə'dıŋən] *v/t* ([*irr*,] *no -ge-, h*) require; cause; imply, involve; **be-'dingt** *adj*: ~ *durch* caused by, due to

Be'dingung *f* (-; -en) condition; *pl* ECON terms; requirements; conditions; *unter einer* ~ on one condition

be'dingungslos *adj* unconditional

be'drängen *v/t* (*no -ge-, h*) press (hard)

be'drohen *v/t* (*no -ge-, h*) threaten, menace; **be'drohlich** *adj* threatening; **Be'drohung** *f* threat, menace (*gen* to)

be'drücken *v/t* (*no -ge-, h*) depress, sadden

bedungen [bə'dʊŋən] *pp of* **bedingen**

Bedürfnis [bə'dʏrfnɪs] *n* (-ses; -se) need, necessity (*für, nach* for); ~**anstalt** *f* comfort station, *Br* public convenience (*or* toilets)

be'dürftig *adj* needy, poor

be'eilen *v/refl* (*no -ge-, h*) hurry (up)

beeindrucken [bə'ʔaindrʊkən] *v/t* (*no -ge-, h*) impress

beeinflussen [bə'ʔainflʊsən] *v/t* (*no -ge-, h*) influence; affect

beeinträchtigen [bə'ʔaintrɛçtıgən] *v/t* (*no -ge-, h*) affect, impair

be'end(ig)en *v/t* (*no -ge-, h*) (bring to an) end, finish, conclude, close

beengen [bə'ɛŋən] *v/t* (*no -ge-, h*) make *s.o.* (feel) uncomfortable; **be'engt** *adj*: ~ *wohnen* live in cramped quarters

be'erben *v/t* (*no -ge-, h*) *j-n* ~ be s.o.'s heir

beerdigen [bə'ʔeːrdıgən] *v/t* (*no -ge-, h*) bury; **Be'erdigung** *f* (-; -en) burial, funeral

Beere ['beːrə] *f* (-; -n) BOT berry; grape

Beet [beːt] *n* (-[e]s; -e) bed, patch

befähigen [bə'fɛːıgən] *v/t* (*no -ge-, h*) enable; qualify (*für, zu* for); **be'fähigt** *adj* (cap)able; *zu et.* ~ fit *or* qualified for s.th.; **Be'fähigung** *f* (-; *no pl*) qualification(s), (cap)ability

befahl [bə'faːl] *pret of* **befehlen**

be'fahrbar *adj* passable, practicable; MAR navigable

be'fahren *v/t* (*irr*, **fahren**, *no -ge-, h*) drive *or* travel on; MAR navigate

be'fallen *v/t* (*irr*, **fallen**, *no -ge-, h*) attack, seize (*a. fig*)

be'fangen *adj* self-conscious; prejudiced, JUR *a.* bias(s)ed

Be'fangenheit *f* (-; *no pl*) self-consciousness; JUR bias, prejudice

be'fassen *v/refl* (*no -ge-, h*) *sich ~ mit* engage *or* occupy o.s. with; work on *s.th.*; deal with *s.o., s.th.*

Befehl [bə'feːl] *m* (-[e]s; -e) order; command (*über acc* of); **be'fehlen** *v/t* (*irr*, *no -ge-, h*) order; command

Be'fehlshaber *m* (-s; -) MIL commander

be'festigen *v/t* (*no -ge-, h*) fasten (*an dat* to), fix (to), attach (to); MIL fortify; **Be'festigung** *f* (-; -en) fixing, fastening; MIL fortification

be'feuchten *v/t* (*no -ge-, h*) moisten, damp

be'finden *v/refl* (*irr*, **finden**, *no -ge-, h*) be (situated); **Be'finden** *n* (-s; *no pl*) (state of) health

be'flecken *v/t* (*no -ge-, h*) stain; *fig a.* sully

befohlen [bə'foːlən] *pp of* **befehlen**

be'folgen *v/t* (*no -ge-, h*) follow, take (*advice*); observe (*rule etc*); REL keep; **Be'folgung** *f* (-; *no pl*) following; observance

be'fördern *v/t* (*no -ge-, h*) carry, transport; haul, ship; promote (*zu* to)

Be'förderung *f* (-; -en) (*no pl*) transport (-ation); shipment; promotion

be'fragen *v/t* (*no -ge-, h*) question, interview

be'freien *v/t* (*no -ge-, h*) free, liberate; rescue; exempt (*von* from); **Be'freiung** *f* (-; *no pl*) liberation; exemption

Befremden [bə'frɛmdən] *n* (-s; *no pl*) irritation, displeasure; **be'fremdet** *adj* irritated, displeased

befreunden [bə'frɔyndən] *v/refl* (*no -ge-, h*) *sich ~ mit* make friends with; *fig* warm to; **be'freundet** *adj* friendly; ~ *sein* be friends

befriedigen [bə'friːdıgən] *v/t* (*no -ge-, h*) satisfy; *sich selbst* ~ masturbate; ~**d** *adj* satisfactory; *grade*: fair

befriedigt [bə'friːdıçt] *adj* satisfied, pleased

Be'friedigung *f* (-; *no pl*) satisfaction

be'fristet *adj* limited (*auf acc* to), tem-

befruchten 58

porary

be'fruchten v/t (no -ge-, h) BIOL fertilize, inseminate; **Be'fruchtung** f (-; -en) BIOL fertilization, insemination

Befugnis [bə'fu:knɪs] f (-; -se) authority; esp JUR competence; **befugt** [bə-'fu:kt] adj authorized; competent

be'fühlen v/t (no -ge-, h) feel, touch

Be'fund m finding(s) (a. MED, JUR)

be'fürchten v/t (no -ge-, h) fear, be afraid of; suspect; **Be'fürchtung** f (-; -en) fear, suspicion

befürworten [bə'fy:ɐvɔrtən] v/t (no -ge-, h) advocate, speak or plead for; **Be'fürworter** m (-s; -) advocate

begabt [bə'ga:pt] adj gifted, talented **Be'gabung** f (-; -en) gift, talent(s)

begann [bə'gan] pret of **beginnen**

be'geben v/refl (irr, **geben**, no -ge-, h) **sich in Gefahr** ~ expose o.s. to danger **Be'gebenheit** f (-; -en) incident, event

begegnen [bə'ge:gnən] v/i (no -ge-, sein) meet (a. fig **mit** with); **sich** ~ meet **Be'gegnung** f (-; -en) meeting, encounter (a. SPORT)

be'gehen v/t (irr, **gehen**, no -ge-, h) walk (on); celebrate (birthday etc); commit (crime); make (mistake); **ein Unrecht** ~ do wrong

begehren [bə'ge:rən] v/t (no -ge-, h) desire; **be'gehrenswert** adj desirable

be'gehrlich adj desirous, covetous

begehrt [bə'ge:ɐt] adj (very) popular, (much) in demand

begeistern [bə'gaistɐn] v/t (no -ge-, h) fill with enthusiasm; carry away (audience); **sich** ~ **für** be enthusiastic about

be'geistert adj enthusiastic

Be'geisterung f (-; no pl) enthusiasm

Begierde [bə'gi:ɐdə] f (-; -n) desire (**nach** for), appetite (for)

be'gierig adj greedy; eager (**nach, auf** acc for; **zu** inf to inf)

be'gießen v/t (irr, **gießen**, no -ge-, h) water; GASTR baste; F fig celebrate s.th. (with a drink)

Beginn [bə'gɪn] m (-[e]s; no pl) beginning, start; **zu** ~ at the beginning

be'ginnen v/t and v/i (irr, no -ge-, h) begin, start

beglaubigen [bə'glaubɪgən] v/t (no -ge-, h) attest, certify; **Be'glaubigung** f (-; -en) attestation, certification

be'gleichen v/t (irr, **gleichen**, no -ge-, h)

pay, settle

be'gleiten v/t (no -ge-, h) accompany (a. MUS **auf** dat on); **j-n nach Hause** ~ see s.o. home; **Be'gleiter(in)** (-s; -/-; -nen) companion; MUS accompanist

Be'gleit|erscheinung f concomitant; MED side effect; ~**schreiben** n covering letter

Be'gleitung f (-; -en) company; esp MIL escort; MUS accompaniment

be'glückwünschen v/t (no -ge-, h) congratulate (**zu** on)

begnadigen [bə'gna:dɪgən] v/t (no -ge-, h), **Be'gnadigung** f (-; -en) JUR pardon; amnesty

begnügen [bə'gny:gən] v/refl (no -ge-, h) **sich** ~ **mit** be satisfied with; make do with

begonnen [bə'gɔnən] pp of **beginnen**

be'graben v/t (irr, **graben**, no -ge-, h) bury (a. fig); **Begräbnis** [bə'grɛ:pnɪs] n (-ses; -se) burial; funeral

begradigen [bə'gra:dɪgən] v/t (no -ge-, h) straighten

be'greifen v/t (irr, **greifen**, no -ge-, h) comprehend, understand

be'greiflich adj understandable

be'grenzen v/t (no -ge-, h) limit, restrict (**auf** acc to); **be'grenzt** adj limited

Be'griff m (-[e]s; -e) idea, notion; term (a. MATH); **im** ~ **sein zu** inf be about to inf; **be'griffsstutzig** contp adj F slow on the uptake

be'gründen v/t (no -ge-, h) give reasons for; **be'gründet** adj well-founded, justified; **Be'gründung** f (-; -en) reasons, arguments

be'grünen v/t (no -ge-, h) landscape

be'grüßen v/t (no -ge-, h) greet, welcome (a. fig); **Be'grüßung** f (-; -en) greeting, welcome

begünstigen [bə'gʏnstɪgən] v/t (no -ge-, h) favo(u)r

be'gutachten v/t (no -ge-, h) give an (expert's) opinion on; examine; ~ **lassen** obtain expert opinion on

begütert [bə'gy:tɐt] adj wealthy

be'haart adj hairy

behäbig [bə'hɛ:bɪç] adj slow; portly

be'haftet adj: **mit Fehlern** ~ flawed

behagen [bə'ha:gən] v/i (no -ge-, h) **j-m** ~ please or suit s.o.; **Be'hagen** n (-s; no pl) pleasure, enjoyment; **behaglich** [bə'ha:klɪç] adj comfortable; cozy, snug

be'halten v/t (irr, **halten**, no -ge-, h) keep (fig **für sich** to o.s.); remember

Behälter [bə'hɛltə] m (-s; -) container, receptacle

be'handeln v/t (no -ge-, h) handle; treat (a. MED); **sich** (**ärztlich**) ~ **lassen** undergo (medical) treatment

Be'handlung f (-; -en) handling; a. MED treatment

beharren [bə'harən] v/i (no -ge-, h) insist (**auf** dat on)

be'harrlich adj persistent

behaupten [bə'hauptən] v/t (no -ge-, h) claim; pretend; **Be'hauptung** f (-; -en) statement, claim

be'heben v/t (irr, **heben**, no -ge-, h) repair (damage etc)

be'heizen v/t (no -ge-, h) heat

be'helfen v/refl (irr, **helfen**, no -ge-, h) **sich ~ mit** make do with; **sich ~ ohne** do without

Be'helfs... in cpds mst temporary

beherbergen [bə'hɛrbɛrgən] v/t (no -ge-, h) accommodate

be'herrschen v/t (no -ge-, h) rule (over), govern; ECON dominate, control; have (a good) command of (language); **sich ~** control o.s.; **Be'herrschung** f (-; no pl) command, control

beherzigen [bə'hɛrtsɪgən] v/t (no -ge-, h) take to heart, mind

be'hilflich adj: **j-m ~ sein** help s.o. (**bei** with, in)

be'hindern v/t (no -ge-, h) hinder; obstruct (a. SPORT); **be'hindert** adj MED handicapped; disabled

Be'hinderung f (-; -en) obstruction; MED handicap

Behörde [bə'høːɐdə] f (-; -n) authority, mst the authorities; board

be'hüten v/t (no -ge-, h) guard (**vor** dat from)

behutsam [bə'huːtzaːm] adj careful; gentle

bei [bai] prp (dat) near; at; with; by; time: during; at; ~ **München** near Munich; **wohnen ~** stay (or live) with; ~ **mir** (**ihr**) at my (her) place; ~ **uns** (**zu Hause**) at home; **arbeiten ~** work for; **e-e Stelle ~** a job with; ~ **der Marine** in the navy; ~ **Familie Müller** at the Müllers'; ~ **Müller** c/o Müller; **ich habe kein Geld ~ mir** I have no money with

or on me; ~ **e-r Tasse Tee** over a cup of tea; **wir haben Englisch ~ Herrn X** we have Mr X for English; ~ **Licht** by light; ~ **Tag** during the day; ~ **Nacht** (**Sonnenaufgang**) at night (sunrise); ~ **s-r Geburt** at his birth; ~ **Regen** (**Gefahr**) in case of rain (danger); ~ **100 Grad** at a hundred degrees; → **Arbeit, beim, weit**

'beibehalten v/t (irr, **halten**, sep, no -ge-, h) keep up, retain

'beibringen v/t (irr, **bringen**, sep, no -ge-, h) teach; tell; inflict (dat on)

Beichte ['baiçtə] f (-; -n) REL confession

'beichten v/t and v/i (ge-, h) REL confess (a. fig)

'Beichtstuhl m REL confessional

beide ['baidə] adj and pron both; **m-e~n Brüder** my two brothers; **wir ~** the two of us; both of us; **keiner von ~n** neither of them; **30 ~** tennis: 30 all

beei'nander adv together

'Beifahrer m front(-seat) passenger

'Beifall m (-[e]s; no pl) applause; fig approval

'Beifallssturm m (standing) ovation

'beifügen v/t (sep, -ge-, h) enclose (dat with)

beige [beːʃ] adj beige

'beigeben (irr, **geben**, sep, -ge-, h) **1.** v/t add **2.** F v/i: **klein ~** knuckle under

'Bei|geschmack m smack (**von** of) (a. fig); **~hilfe** f aid, allowance; JUR aiding and abetting

Beil [bail] n (-[e]s; -e) hatchet; ax(e)

'Beilage f supplement; GASTR side dish; vegetables

'beiläufig adj casual

'beilegen v/t (sep, -ge-, h) add (dat to); enclose (with); settle (dispute)

'Beilegung f (-; -en) settlement

'Beileid n (-[e]s; no pl) condolence; **herzliches ~** my deepest sympathy

'beiliegen v/i (irr, **liegen**, sep, -ge-, h) be enclosed (dat with)

beim [baim] prp: ~ **Bäcker** at the baker's; ~ **Sprechen** etc while speaking etc; ~ **Spielen** at play; → a. **bei**

'beimessen v/t (irr, **messen**, sep, -ge-, h) attach importance etc (dat to)

Bein [bain] n (-[e]s; -e) ANAT leg; bone

beinah(e) ['baina:(ə)] adv almost, nearly

'Beinbruch m MED fracture of the leg

'beipflichten v/i (sep, -ge-, h) agree (dat

with)
be'irren v/t (no -ge-, h) confuse
beisammen [bai'zamən] adv together
Bei'sammensein n: **geselliges ~** get-
-together
'Beischlaf m JUR sexual intercourse
bei'seite adv aside; **~schaffen** v/t (sep,
-ge-, h) remove; liquidate s.o.
'beisetzen v/t (sep, -ge-, h) bury
'Beisetzung f (-; -en) funeral
'Beispiel n (-[e]s; -e) example; **zum ~** for
example, for instance; **sich an j-m ein
~ nehmen** follow s.o.'s example
'beispiel|haft adj exemplary; **~los** adj
unprecedented, unparalleled
'beispielsweise adv such as
beißen ['baisən] v/t and v/i (irr, -ge-, h)
bite (a. fig); **sich ~ colors**: clash; **~d** adj
biting, pungent (both a. fig)
'Beistand m (-[e]s; no pl) assistance
'bei|stehen v/i (irr, **stehen**, sep, -ge-, h)
j-m ~ assist or help s.o.; **~steuern** v/t
(sep, -ge-, h) contribute (**zu** to)
Beitrag ['baitra:k] m (-[e]s; Beiträge
['baitrɛ:gə]) contribution; dues, Br
subscription; **'beitragen** v/t (irr, **tragen**, sep, -ge-, h) contribute (**zu** to)
'beitreten v/i (irr, **treten**, sep, -ge-, sein)
join; **'Beitritt** m (-[e]s; -e) joining
'Beiwagen m MOT sidecar
bei'zeiten adv early, in good time
beizen ['baitsən] v/t (ge-, h) stain
(wood); pickle (meat)
bejahen [bə'ja:ən] v/t (no -ge-, h) answer in the affirmative, affirm; **~d**
adj affirmative
be'kämpfen v/t (no -ge-, h) fight
(against)
bekannt [bə'kant] adj (well-)known; familiar; **et. ~ geben** announce s.th.; **j-n
mit j-m ~ machen** introduce s.o. to s.o.;
Be'kannte m, f (-n; -n) acquaintance,
mst friend
be'kanntgeben v/t (irr, **geben**, sep, -ge-,
h) →**bekannt**
be'kanntlich adv as you know
be'kanntmachen v/t (sep, -ge-, h) →**bekannt**; **Be'kanntmachung** f (-; -en) announcement
Be'kanntschaft f (-; -en) acquaintance
be'kehren v/t (no -ge-, h) convert
be'kennen v/t (irr, **kennen**, no -ge-, h)
confess (a. REL); admit; **sich schuldig
~** JUR plead guilty; **sich ~ zu** profess

s.th.; claim responsibility for; **Be-
'kennerbrief** m letter claiming responsibility
Be'kenntnis n (-ses; -se) confession, REL
a. denomination
be'klagen v/t (no -ge-, h) deplore; **sich ~**
complain (**über** acc about)
be'klagenswert adj deplorable
be'kleben v/t (no -ge-, h) stick (or paste)
on s.th.; **mit Etiketten ~** label s.th.
be'kleckern F v/t (no -ge-, h) stain; **sich
~ mit** spill s.th. over o.s.
Be'kleidung f (-; -en) clothing, clothes
be'kommen (irr, **kommen**, no -ge-) **1.**
v/t (h) get, receive; feel; be hav-
ing (baby) **2.** v/i (sein) **j-m (gut) ~** agree
with s.o.; **bekömmlich** [bə'kœmlıç] adj
wholesome
be'kräftigen v/t (no -ge-, h) confirm
be'kreuzigen v/refl (no -ge-, h) cross o.s.
bekümmert [bə'kymɐt] adj worried
be'laden v/t (irr, **laden**, no -ge-, h) load,
fig a. burden
Belag [bə'la:k] m (-[e]s; Beläge [bə-
'lɛ:gə]) covering; TECH coat(ing); MOT
lining; (road) surface; MED fur; plaque;
GASTR topping; spread; (sandwich) filling
be'lagern v/t (no -ge-, h) MIL besiege (a.
fig); **Be'lagerung** f (-; -en) MIL siege
be'langlos adj irrelevant
be'lassen v/t (irr, **lassen**, no -ge-, h)
leave; **es dabei ~** leave it at that
be'lastbar adj resistant to strain or
stress; TECH loadable; **be'lasten** v/t
(no -ge-, h) load; fig burden; JUR in-
criminate; pollute; damage; **j-s Konto
~ mit** charge s.th. to s.o.'s account
belästigen [bə'lɛstıgən] v/t (no -ge-, h)
molest; annoy; disturb, bother; **Be-
'lästigung** f (-; -en) molestation; annoyance; disturbance
Be'lastung f (-; -en) load (a. TECH); fig
burden; strain; stress; JUR incrimina-
tion; pollution, contamination
Be'lastungszeuge m JUR witness for
the prosecution
be'laufen v/refl (irr, **laufen**, no -ge-, h)
sich ~ auf (acc) amount to
be'lauschen v/t (no -ge-, h) eavesdrop
on
be'leben fig v/t (no -ge-, h) stimulate; **~d**
adj stimulating
belebt [bə'le:pt] adj busy, crowded

Beleg [bə'leːk] *m* (-[*e*]*s*; -*e*) proof; receipt; document; **be'legen** *v/t* (*no -ge-, h*) cover; reserve (*seat*); prove; enrol(l) for, take (*classes*); GASTR put s.th. on; **den ersten** *etc* **Platz ~** SPORT take first *etc* place

Be'legschaft *f* (-; -*en*) staff

be'legt *adj* taken, occupied; *hotel etc*: full; TEL busy, *Br* engaged; MED coated; **~es Brot** sandwich

be'lehren *v/t* (*no -ge-, h*) teach, instruct, inform; **sich ~ lassen** take advice

beleidigen [bə'laidɪɡən] *v/t* (*no -ge-, h*) offend (*a. fig*), insult; **~d** *adj* offensive, insulting

Be'leidigung *f* (-; -*en*) offense, *Br* offence, insult

be'lesen *adj* well-read

be'leuchten *v/t* (*no -ge-, h*) light (up), illuminate (*a. fig*); *fig* throw light on

Be'leuchtung *f* (-; -*en*) light(ing); illumination

Belgien ['bɛlɡjən] Belgium; **Belgier** ['bɛlɡjɐ] *m* (-*s*; -), **Belgierin** ['bɛlɡjərɪn] *f* (-; -*nen*), **'belgisch** *adj* Belgian

be'lichten *v/t* (*no -ge-, h*) PHOT expose

Be'lichtungsmesser *m* PHOT exposure meter

Be'lieben *n*: **nach ~** at will

beliebig [bə'liːbɪç] *adj* any; optional; **jeder ~e** anyone

beliebt [bə'liːpt] *adj* popular (**bei** with)

Be'liebtheit *f* (-; *no pl*) popularity

be'liefern *v/t* (*no -ge-, h*) supply, furnish (**mit** with); **Be'lieferung** *f* supply

bellen ['bɛlən] *v/i* (*ge-, h*) bark (*a. fig*)

be'lohnen *v/t* (*no -ge-, h*) reward

Be'lohnung *f* (-; -*en*) reward; **zur ~** as a reward

be'lügen *v/t* (*irr*, **lügen**, *no -ge-, h*) **j-n ~** lie to s.o.

belustigen [bə'lʊstɪɡən] *v/t* (*no -ge-, h*) amuse; **belustigt** [bə'lʊstɪçt] *adj* amused; **Be'lustigung** *f* (-; -*en*) amusement

bemächtigen [bə'mɛçtɪɡən] *v/refl* (*no -ge-, h*) get hold of, seize

be'malen *v/t* (*no -ge-, h*) paint

bemängeln [bə'mɛŋəln] *v/t* (*no -ge-, h*) find fault with

bemannt [bə'mant] *adj* manned

be'merkbar *adj* noticeable; **sich ~ machen** draw attention to o.s.; begin to show; **be'merken** *v/t* (*no -ge-, h*) notice;

remark; **be'merkenswert** *adj* remarkable; **Be'merkung** *f* (-; -*en*) remark (**über** *acc* about)

be'mitleiden *v/t* (*no -ge-, h*) pity, feel sorry for; **be'mitleidenswert** *adj* pitiable

be'mühen *v/refl* (*no -ge-, h*) try (hard); **sich ~ um** try to get *s.th.*; try to help *s.o.*; **bitte ~ Sie sich nicht!** please don't bother; **Be'mühung** *f* (-; -*en*) effort; **danke für Ihre ~en!** thank you for your trouble

be'muttern *v/t* (*no -ge-, h*) mother *s.o.*

be'nachbart *adj* neighbo(u)ring

benachrichtigen [bə'naːxrɪçtɪɡən] *v/t* (*no -ge-, h*) inform, notify

Be'nachrichtigung *f* (-; -*en*) information, notification

benachteiligen [bə'naːxtailɪɡən] *v/t* (*no -ge-, h*) place *s.o.* at a disadvantage; discriminate against *s.o.*; **benachteiligt** [bə'naːxtailɪçt] *adj* disadvantaged; **die Benachteiligten** the underprivileged; **Be'nachteiligung** *f* (-; -*en*) disadvantage; discrimination

be'nehmen *v/refl* (*irr*, **nehmen**, *no -ge-, h*) behave (o.s.); **Be'nehmen** *n* (-*s*; *no pl*) behavio(u)r; manners

be'neiden *v/t* (*no -ge-, h*) **j-n um et. ~** envy s.o. s.th.

be'neidenswert *adj* enviable

BENELUX ['beːneluks] *abbr of* **Belgien, Niederlande, Luxemburg** Belgium, the Netherlands and Luxembourg

be'nennen *v/t* (*irr*, **nennen**, *no -ge-, h*) name

Bengel ['bɛŋəl] *m* (-*s*; -) (little) rascal, urchin

benommen [bə'nɔmən] *adj* dazed, F dopey

be'noten *v/t* (*no -ge-, h*) grade, *Br* mark

be'nötigen *v/t* (*no -ge-, h*) need, want, require

be'nutzen *v/t* (*no -ge-, h*) use

Be'nutzer *m* (-*s*; -) user

be'nutzerfreundlich *adj* user-friendly

Be'nutzeroberfläche *f* IT user interface

Be'nutzung *f* use

Benzin [bɛn'tsiːn] *n* (-*s*; -*e*) gasoline, F gas, *Br* petrol

beobachten [bə'ʔoːbaxtən] *v/t* (*no -ge-, h*) watch; observe

Be'obachter *m* (-*s*; -) observer

Be'obachtung f (-; -en) observation

be'pflanzen v/t (no -ge-, h) plant (*mit* with)

bequem [bə'kveːm] adj comfortable; easy; lazy; **be'quemen** v/refl (no -ge-, h) **sich ~ zu** inf bring o.s. to inf

Be'quemlichkeit f (-; -en) comfort; **alle ~en** all conveniences; (no pl) laziness

be'raten v/t (irr, **raten**, no -ge-, h) advise s.o.; debate, discuss s.th.; **sich ~** confer (*mit j-m* with s.o.; *über et.* on s.th.); **Be'rater** m (-s; -) adviser, consultant; **Be'ratung** f (-; -en) advice (a. MED); debate; consultation, conference; **Be'ratungsstelle** f counsel(l)ing center (*Br* centre)

be'rauben v/t (no -ge-, h) rob

be'rauschend adj intoxicating; F fig **nicht gerade ~!** not so hot!; **bo 'rauscht** fig adj: **~ von** drunk with

be'rechnen v/t (no -ge-, h) calculate; ECON charge (**zu** at); **~d** adj calculating

Be'rechnung f calculation (a. fig)

berechtigen [bə'rɛçtɪgən] v/t: **j-n ~ zu** entitle (*or* authorize) s.o. to; **berechtigt** [bə'rɛçtɪçt] adj entitled (**zu** to); authorized (to); legitimate; **Be'rechtigung** f (-; no pl) right (**zu** to); authority

Beredsamkeit [bə'reːtzaːmkait] f (-; no pl) eloquence

beredt [bə'reːt] adj eloquent (a. fig)

Be'reich m (-[e]s; -e) area; range; field

bereichern [bə'raiçɐn] v/t (no -ge-, h) enrich; **sich ~** get rich (**an** dat on); **Be'reicherung** [bə'raiçərʊŋ] f (-; no pl) enrichment

Be'reifung f (-; -en) (set of) tires (*Br* tyres)

be'reinigen v/t (no -ge-, h) settle

be'reisen v/t (no -ge-, h) tour; cover

bereit [bə'rait] adj ready, prepared; willing; **be'reiten** v/t (no -ge-, h) prepare; cause; **be'reithalten** v/t (irr, **halten**, sep, -ge-, h) have s.th. ready; **sich ~** stand by; **be'reits** adv already; **Be'reitschaft** f (-; no pl) readiness; **in ~** on standby; **Be'reitschaftsdienst** m: **~ haben** doctor etc: be on call; **be'reitstellen** v/t (sep, -ge-, h) provide; **be'reitwillig** adj ready, willing

be'reuen v/t (no -ge-, h) repent (of); regret

Berg [bɛrk] m (-[e]s; -e) mountain; **~e von** F loads of; **die Haare standen ihm zu ~e** his hair stood on end

berg'ab adv downhill (a. fig)

'Bergarbeiter m miner

berg'auf adv uphill

'Berg|bahn f mountain railroad (*Br* railway); **~bau** m (-[e]s; no pl) mining

bergen ['bɛrgən] v/t (irr, ge- h) rescue, save s.o.; salvage s.th.; recover (body)

'Bergführer m mountain guide

bergig ['bɛrgɪç] adj mountainous

'Berg|kette f mountain range; **~mann** m (-[e]s; -leute) miner; **~rutsch** m landslide; **~schuhe** pl mountain(eering) boots; **~spitze** f (mountain) peak; **~steigen** n mountaineering, (mountain) climbing; **~steiger** m (-s; -) mountaineer, (mountain) climber

'Bergung f (-; -en) recovery; rescue

'Bergungsarbeiten pl rescue work; salvage operations

'Bergwacht f alpine rescue service

'Bergwerk n mine

Bericht [bə'rɪçt] m (-[e]s; -e) report (*über* acc on), account (of)

be'richten v/t and v/i (no -ge-, h) report (*über* acc on); **j-m et. ~** inform s.o. of s.th.; tell s.o. about s.th.

Be'richt|erstatter m (-s; -) reporter; correspondent; **~erstattung** f (-; -en) report(ing)

berichtigen [bə'rɪçtɪgən] v/t (no -ge-, h) correct; **Be'richtigung** f (-; -en) correction

be'rieseln v/t (no -ge-, h) sprinkle

Bernstein ['bɛrnʃtain] m (-s; no pl) amber

bersten ['bɛrstən] v/i (irr, -ge-, sein) burst (fig **vor** dat with)

berüchtigt [bə'rʏçtɪçt] adj notorious (**wegen** for)

berücksichtigen [bə'rʏkzɪçtɪgən] v/t (no -ge-, h) take into consideration; **nicht ~** disregard

Be'rücksichtigung f: **unter ~** (gen) in consideration of

Be'ruf m (-[e]s; -e) job, occupation; trade; profession; **be'rufen** v/t (irr, **rufen**, no -ge-, h) appoint (**zu** [as] to s.th.); **sich ~ auf** (acc) refer to

be'ruflich adj professional; **~ unterwegs** away on business

Be'rufs... in cpds ...sportler etc: professional ...; **~ausbildung** f vocational (or professional) training; **~berater** m careers advisor; **~beratung** f careers guidance; **~bezeichnung** f job designation or title; **~kleidung** f work clothes; **~krankheit** f occupational disease; **~schule** f vocational school

be'rufstätig adj: **~ sein** (go to) work, have a job; **Be'rufstätige** m, f (-n; -n) working person, pl working people

Be'rufsverkehr m rush-hour traffic

Be'rufung f (-; -en) appointment (zu to); JUR appeal (bei to); **unter ~ auf** (acc) with reference to; on the grounds of

be'ruhen v/i (no -ge-, h) **~ auf** (dat) be based on; **et. auf sich ~ lassen** let s.th. rest

beruhigen [bə'ruːɪɡən] v/t (no -ge-, h) quiet(en), calm, soothe; reassure s.o.; **sich ~** calm down; **~d** adj reassuring; MED sedative

Be'ruhigung f (-; -en) calming (down); soothing; relief; **Be'ruhigungsmittel** n MED sedative; tranquil(l)izer

berühmt [bə'ryːmt] adj famous (**wegen** for); **Be'rühmtheit** f (-; -en) (no pl) fame; celebrity, star

be'rühren v/t (no -ge-, h) touch (a. fig); concern; **Be'rührung** f (-; -en) touch; **in ~ kommen** come into contact

Be'rührungs|angst f fear of contact; **~punkt** m point of contact

besänftigen [bə'zɛnftɪɡən] v/t (no -ge-, h) appease, calm, soothe

Be'satzung f (-; -en) AVIAT, MAR crew; MIL occupying forces

Be'satzungs|macht f MIL occupying power; **~truppen** pl MIL occupying forces

be'saufen F v/refl (irr, **saufen**, no -ge-, h) get drunk, get bombed

be'schädigen v/t (no -ge-, h) damage

Be'schädigung f (-; -en) damage

be'schaffen v/t (no -ge-, h) provide, get; raise (money); **Be'schaffenheit** f (-; no pl) state, condition

beschäftigen [bə'ʃɛftɪɡən] v/t (no -ge-, h) employ; keep s.o. busy; **sich ~** occupy o.s.; **beschäftigt** [bə'ʃɛftɪçt] adj busy, occupied; **Be'schäftigte** m, f (-n; -n) employed person, pl employed people; **Be'schäftigung** f (-; -en) employment; occupation

be'schämen v/t (no -ge-, h) shame s.o., make s.o. feel ashamed; **~d** adj shameful; humiliating

be'schämt adj ashamed (**über** acc of)

be'schatten fig v/t (no -ge-, h) shadow, F tail

Bescheid [bə'ʃait] m (-[e]s; -e) answer; JUR decision; information (**über** acc on, about); **sagen Sie mir ~** let me know; (**gut**) **~ wissen über** (acc) know all about

be'scheiden adj modest (a. fig); humble; **Be'scheidenheit** f (-; no pl) modesty

bescheinigen [bə'ʃainɪɡən] v/t (no -ge-, h) certify

Be'scheinigung f (-; -en) (no pl) certification; certificate

be'scheißen V v/t (irr, **scheißen**, no -ge-, h) cheat; **j-n ~ um** do s.o. out of

be'schenken v/t (no -ge-, h) **j-n** (**reich**) **~** give s.o. (shower s.o. with) presents

Be'scherung f (-; -en) distribution of (Christmas) presents; F fig mess

be'schichten v/t (no -ge-, h) TECH coat

Be'schichtung f (-; -en) TECH coat

be'schießen v/t (irr, **schießen**, no -ge-, h) MIL fire or shoot at; bombard (a. PHYS), shell

be'schimpfen v/t (no -ge-, h) abuse, insult; swear at; **Be'schimpfung** f (-; -en) abuse, insult

be'schissen V adj lousy, rotten

Be'schlag m TECH metal fitting(s); **in ~ nehmen** fig monopolize s.o.; bag; occupy; **be'schlagen** (irr, **schlagen**, no -ge-) **1.** v/t (h) cover; TECH fit, mount; shoe (horse) **2.** v/i (sein) window etc: steam up **3.** adj steamed-up; fig well-versed (**auf**, **in** dat in)

Be'schlagnahme [bə'ʃlaːknaːmə] f (-; -n) confiscation; **be'schlagnahmen** v/t (no -ge-, h) confiscate

beschleunigen [bə'ʃlɔynɪɡən] v/t and v/i (no -ge-, h) accelerate, speed up; **Be'schleunigung** f (-; -en) acceleration

be'schließen v/t (irr, **schließen**, no -ge-, h) decide (on); pass (law); conclude; **Be'schluss** m decision

be'schmieren v/t (no -ge-, h) smear, soil; scrawl all over; cover wall etc with graffiti; spread (toast etc)

be'schmutzen v/t (no -ge-, h) soil (a.

fig), dirty

be'schneiden *v/t* (*irr,* **schneiden,** *no* *-ge-, h*) clip, cut (*a. fig*); prune; MED circumcise

be'schönigen [bəˈʃøːnɪɡən] *v/t* (*no* *-ge-, h*) gloss over

beschränken [bəˈʃrɛŋkən] *v/t* (*no -ge-, h*) confine, limit, restrict; **sich ~ auf** (*acc*) confine o.s. to; **be'schränkt** *adj* limited; *contp* dense; narrow-minded

Be'schränkung *f* (-; *-en*) limitation, restriction

be'schreiben *v/t* (*irr,* **schreiben,** *no* *-ge-, h*) describe; write on

Be'schreibung *f* (-; *-en*) description

be'schriften *v/t* (*no -ge-, h*) inscribe; mark (*goods*); **Be'schriftung** *f* (-; *-en*) inscription

beschuldigen [bəˈʃʊldɪɡən] *v/t* (*no* *-ge-, h*) blame; **j-n e-r Sache ~** accuse s.o. of s.th. (*a.* JUR); **Be'schuldigung** *f* (-; *-en*) accusation

be'schummeln F *v/t* (*no -ge-, h*) cheat

Be'schuss *m*: **unter ~** MIL under fire

be'schützen *v/t* (*no -ge-, h*) protect, shelter, guard (**vor** *dat* from)

Be'schützer *m* (-*s*; -) protector

Beschwerde [bəˈʃveːrdə] *f* (-; *-n*) complaint (**über** *acc* about; **bei** to); *pl* MED complaints, trouble

beschweren [bəˈʃveːrən] *v/t* (*no -ge-, h*) weight *s.th.*; **sich ~** complain (**über** *acc* about; **bei** to)

be'schwerlich *adj* hard, arduous

beschwichtigen [bəˈʃvɪçtɪɡən] *v/t* (*no* *-ge-, h*) appease (*a.* POL), calm

be'schwindeln *v/t* (*no -ge-, h*) tell a fib *or* lie; cheat

beschwingt [bəˈʃvɪŋt] *adj* buoyant; MUS lively, swinging

beschwipst [bəˈʃvɪpst] F *adj* tipsy

be'schwören *v/t* (*irr,* **schwören,** *no* *-ge-, h*) swear to; implore; conjure up

beseitigen [bəˈzaitɪɡən] *v/t* (*no -ge-, h*) remove (*a. s.o.*), *a.* dispose of (*waste etc*); eliminate; POL liquidate

Be'seitigung *f* (-; *no pl*) removal; disposal; elimination

Besen ['beːzən] *m* (-*s*; -) broom

'Besenstiel *m* broomstick

besessen [bəˈzɛsən] *adj* obsessed (**von** by, with); **wie ~** like mad

be'setzen *v/t* (*no -ge-, h*) occupy (*a.* MIL); fill (*post etc*); THEA cast; trim;

squat in; **be'setzt** *adj* occupied; *seat*: taken; *bus etc*: full up; TEL busy, *Br* engaged; **Be'setztzeichen** *n* TEL busy signal, *Br* engaged tone; **Be'setzung** *f* (-; *-en*) THEA cast; MIL occupation

besichtigen [bəˈzɪçtɪɡən] *v/t* (*no -ge-, h*) visit, see the sights of; inspect

Be'sichtigung *f* (-; *-en*) sightseeing; visit (*gen* to); inspection (of)

be'siedeln *v/t* (*no -ge-, h*) settle; colonize; populate; **be'siedelt** *adj*: **dicht** (**dünn**) **~** densely (sparsely) populated; **Be'siedlung** *f* (-; *-en*) settlement; colonization; population

be'siegeln *v/t* (*no -ge-, h*) seal

be'siegen *v/t* (*no -ge-, h*) defeat, beat; conquer (*a. fig*)

besinnen *v/refl* (*irr,* **sinnen,** *no -ge-, h*) remember; think (**auf** *acc* about); **sich anders ~** change one's mind

be'sinnlich *adj* contemplative

Be'sinnung *f* (-; *no pl*) MED consciousness; (**wieder**) **zur ~ kommen** MED come round; *fig* come to one's senses

be'sinnungslos *adj* MED unconscious

Be'sitz *m* (-*es*; *no pl*) possession; property; **~ ergreifen von** take possession of; **be'sitzanzeigend** *adj* LING possessive; **be'sitzen** *v/t* (*irr,* **sitzen,** *no -ge-, h*) possess, own; **Be'sitzer** *m* (-*s*; -) possessor, owner; **den ~ wechseln** change hands

besoffen [bəˈzɔfən] F *adj* drunk, plastered, stoned

besohlen [bəˈzoːlən] *v/t* (*no -ge-, h*) **~ lassen** have (re)soled

Be'soldung *f* (-; *-en*) pay; salary

besondere [bəˈzɔndərə] *adj* special, particular; peculiar

Be'sonderheit *f* (-; *-en*) peculiarity

be'sonders *adv* especially, particularly; chiefly, mainly

be'sonnen *adj* prudent, level-headed

be'sorgen *v/t* (*no -ge-, h*) get, buy; → **erledigen; Be'sorgnis** [bəˈzɔrknɪs] *f* (-; *-se*) concern, alarm, anxiety (**über** *acc* about; at); **~ erregend → besorgniserregend;** **be'sorgniserregend** *adj* alarming; **besorgt** [bəˈzɔrkt] *adj* worried, anxious; **Be'sorgung** *f* (-; *-en*) **~en machen** go shopping

be'spielen *v/t* (*no -ge-, h*) make a recording on

be'spitzeln *v/t* (*no -ge-, h*) spy on *s.o.*

be'sprechen v/t (irr, **sprechen**, no -ge-, h) discuss, talk s.th. over; review (book etc); **Be'sprechung** f (-; -en) discussion, talk(s); meeting, conference; review

be'spritzen v/t (no -ge-, h) spatter

besser ['bɛsɐ] adj and adv better; **es ist ~, wir fragen ihn** we had better ask him; **immer ~** better and better; **es geht ihm ~** he is better; **oder ~ gesagt** or rather; **es ~ wissen** know better; **es ~ machen als** do better than; **~ ist ~** just to be on the safe side

'bessern v/refl (ge-, h) improve, get better; **'Besserung** f (-; no pl) improvement; **auf dem Wege der ~** on the way to recovery; **gute ~!** get better soon

Besserwisser ['bɛsɐvɪsɐ] m (-s; -) F smart aleck

Be'stand m (no pl) (continued) existence; stock; **~ haben** last, be lasting

be'ständig adj constant, steady (a. character); settled; **...beständig** in cpds ...-resistant, ...-proof

Be'standsaufnahme f ECON stocktaking (a. fig); **~ machen** take stock (a. fig)

Be'standteil m part, component

be'stärken v/t (no -ge-, h) confirm, strengthen, encourage (**in** dat in)

bestätigen [bə'ʃtɛtɪgən] v/t (no -ge-, h) confirm; certify; acknowledge (receipt); **sich ~** prove (to be) true; come true; **sich bestätigt fühlen** feel affirmed; **Be'stätigung** f (-; -en) confirmation; certificate; acknowledg(e)ment; letter of confirmation

bestatten [bə'ʃtatən] v/t (no -ge-, h) bury; **Be'stattungsinsti,tut** n funeral home, Br undertakers

be'stäuben v/t (no -ge-, h) dust; BOT pollinate

beste ['bɛstə] adj and adv best; **am ~n** best; **welches gefällt dir am ~n?** which one do you like best?; **am ~n nehmen Sie den Bus** it would be best to take a bus; **Beste** m, f (-n; -n), n (-n; no pl) the best; **das ~ geben** do one's best; **das ~ machen aus** make the best of; (**nur**) **zu deinem ~n** for your own good

be'stechen v/t (irr, **stechen**, no -ge-, h) bribe; fascinate (**durch** by)

be'stechlich adj corrupt

Be'stechung f (-; -en) bribery, corruption; **Be'stechungsgeld** n bribe

Besteck [bə'ʃtɛk] n (-[e]s; -e) (set of) knife, fork and spoon; cutlery

be'stehen (irr, **stehen**, no -ge-, h) **1.** v/t pass (examination etc) **2.** v/i be, exist; **~ auf** (dat) insist on; **~ aus** (**in**) (dat) consist of (in); **~ bleiben** last, survive

Be'stehen n (-s; no pl) existence

be'stehlen v/t (irr, **stehlen**, no -ge-, h) **j-n ~** steal s.o.'s money etc

be'steigen v/t (irr, **steigen**, no -ge-, h) climb; get on a bus etc; ascend (the throne)

be'stellen v/t (no -ge-, h) order; book (room etc); reserve (seat etc); call (taxi); give, send (message etc); AGR cultivate; **kann ich et. ~?** can I take a message?; **~ Sie ihm bitte, ...** please tell him ...

Be'stellschein m ECON order form

Be'stellung f (-; -en) booking; reservation; ECON order; **auf ~** to order

'bestenfalls adv at best

'bestens adv very well

bestialisch [bɛs'tjaːlɪʃ] adj fig bestial

Bestie ['bɛstjə] f (-; -n) beast, fig a. brute

be'stimmen v/t (no -ge-, h) determine, decide; define; choose, pick; **zu ~ haben** be in charge, F be the boss; **bestimmt für** meant for; **be'stimmt 1.** adj determined, firm; LING definite (article); **~e Dinge** certain things **2.** adv certainly; **ganz ~** definitely; **er ist ~ ...** he must be ...; **Be'stimmung** f (-; -en) regulation; destiny

Be'stimmungsort m destination

'Bestleistung f SPORT (personal) record

be'strafen v/t (no -ge-, h) punish

Be'strafung f (-; -en) punishment

be'strahlen v/t (no -ge-, h) irradiate (a. MED); **Be'strahlung** f (-; -en) irradiation; MED ray treatment, radiotherapy

be'streichen v/t (irr, **streichen**, no -ge-, h) spread; **be'streiten** (irr, **streiten**, no -ge-, h) challenge; deny; pay for, finance; **be'streuen** v/t (no -ge-, h) sprinkle (**mit** with); **be'stürmen** v/t (no -ge-, h) urge; bombard

be'stürzt adj dismayed (**über** acc at); **Be'stürzung** f (-; no pl) consternation, dismay

Besuch [bə'zuːx] m (-[e]s; -e) visit (gen, **bei**, **in** dat to); call (**bei** on; **in** dat at); attendance (gen at); **~ haben** have company or guests; **be'suchen** v/t (*no -ge-*, *h*) visit; call on, (go to) see; look *s.o.* up; attend (*meeting etc*); go to (*pub etc*); **Be'sucher(in)** (*-s*; *-/-*; *-nen*) visitor, guest; **Be'suchszeit** *f* visiting hours; **be'sucht** *adj*: **gut** (**schlecht**) ~ well (poorly) attended; much (little) frequented

betagt [bə'taːkt] *adj* aged

be'tasten *v/t* (*no -ge-*, *h*) touch, feel

be'tätigen *v/t* (*no -ge-*, *h*) TECH operate; apply (*brake*); **sich** ~ be active

Be'tätigung *f* (*-*; *-en*) activity

betäuben [bə'tɔybən] *v/t* (*no -ge-*, *h*) stun (*a. fig*), daze; MED an(a)esthetize

Be'täubung *f* (*-*; *-en*) MED an(a)esthetization; an(a)esthesia; *fig* daze, stupor

Be'täubungsmittel *n* MED an(a)esthetic; narcotic

Bete ['beːtə] *f* (*-*; *-n*) **rote** ~ BOT beet, *Br* beetroot

beteiligen [bə'tailɡən] *v/t* (*no -ge-*, *h*) **j-n** ~ give s.o. a share (**an** *dat* in); **sich** ~ take part (**an** *dat*, **bei** in), participate (in) (*a.* JUR); **beteiligt** [bə'tailɪçt] *adj* concerned; ~ **sein an** (*dat*) be involved in; ECON have a share in; **Be'teiligung** *f* (*-*; *-en*) participation (*a.* JUR, ECON); involvement; share (*a.* ECON)

beten ['beːtən] *v/i* (*ge-*, *h*) pray (**um** for), say one's prayers; say grace

beteuern [bə'tɔyɐn] *v/t* (*no -ge-*, *h*) protest (*one's innocence etc*)

Beton [be'tɔŋ] *m* (*-s*; *-s*, *-e* [be'toːnə]) concrete

betonen [bə'toːnən] *v/t* (*no -ge-*, *h*) stress, *fig a.* emphasize

betonieren [beto'niːrən] *v/t* (*no -ge-*, *h*) (cover with) concrete

Be'tonung *f* (*-*; *-en*) stress; *fig* emphasis

betören [bə'tøːrən] *v/t* (*no -ge-*, *h*) infatuate, bewitch

Betr. *abbr of* **betrifft** re

Betracht [bə'traxt] *m*: **in** ~ **ziehen** take into consideration; **nicht in** ~ **kommen** be out of the question

be'trachten *v/t* (*no -ge-*, *h*) look at, *fig a.* view; ~ **als** look upon *or* regard as, consider; **Be'trachter** *m* (*-s*; *-*) viewer

beträchtlich [bə'trɛçtlɪç] *adj* considerable

Be'trachtung *f* (*-*; *-en*) view; **bei näherer** ~ on closer inspection

Betrag [bə'traːk] *m* (*-[e]s*; *Beträge* [bə-

'trɛːɡə]) amount, sum; **be'tragen** (*irr*, **tragen**, *no -ge-*, *h*) **1.** *v/t* amount to **2.** *v/refl* behave (o.s.); **Be'tragen** *n* (*-s*; *no pl*) behavio(u)r, conduct

be'trauen *v/t* (*no -ge-*, *h*) entrust (**mit** ·with)

be'treffen *v/t* (*irr*, **treffen**, *no -ge-*, *h*) concern; refer to; **was ... betrifft** as for ..., as to ...; **betrifft** (*abbr* **Betr.**) re; ~**d** *adj* concerning; **die** ~**en Personen** *etc* the people *etc* concerned

be'treiben *v/t* (*irr*, **treiben**, *no -ge-*, *h*) operate, run; go in for (*sport etc*)

be'treten[1] *v/t* (*irr*, **treten**, *no -ge-*, *h*) step on; enter; **Betreten (des Rasens) verboten!** keep out! (keep off the grass!)

be'treten[2] *adj* embarrassed

betreuen [bə'trɔyən] *v/t* (*no -ge-*, *h*) look after, take care of; **Be'treuung** *f* (*-*; *no pl*) care (*gen* of, for)

Betrieb [bə'triːp] *m* (*-[e]s*; *-e*) business, firm, company; (*no pl*) operation, running; (*no pl*) rush; **in** ~ **sein** (**setzen**) be in (put into) operation; **außer** ~ out of order; **im Geschäft war viel** ~ the shop was very busy

Be'triebs|anleitung *f* operating instructions; ~**berater** *m* business consultant; ~**ferien** *pl* company (*Br a.* works) holiday; ~**fest** *n* annual company fête; ~**kapi‚tal** *n* working capital; ~**klima** *n* working atmosphere; ~**kosten** *pl* operating costs; ~**leitung** *f* management; ~**rat** *m* works council

be'triebssicher *adj* safe to operate

Be'triebs|störung *f* TECH breakdown; ~**sys‚tem** *n* IT operating system; ~**unfall** *m* industrial accident; ~**wirtschaft** *f* business administration

be'trinken *v/refl* (*irr*, **trinken**, *no -ge-*, *h*) get drunk

betroffen [bə'trɔfən] *adj* affected, concerned; dismayed, shocked; **Be'troffenheit** *f* (*-*; *no pl*) dismay, shock

betrübt [bə'tryːpt] *adj* sad, grieved (**über** *acc* at)

Betrug [bə'truːk] *m* (*-[e]s*; *no pl*) cheat; JUR fraud; deceit; **be'trügen** *v/t* (*irr*, **trügen**, *no -ge-*, *h*) deceive; cheat (**beim Kartenspiel** at cards); swindle, trick (**um et.** out of s.th.); be unfaithful to; **Be'trüger(in)** (*-s*; *-/-*; *-nen*) swindler, trickster

betrunken [bə'trʊŋkən] *adj* drunken; ~

sein be drunk

Be'trunkene *m*, *f* (*-n*; *-n*) drunk

Bett [bɛt] *n* (*-[e]s*; *-en*) bed; *am ~* at the bedside; *ins ~ gehen* (*bringen*) go (put) to bed; *~bezug* *m* comforter case, *Br* duvet cover; *~decke* *f* blanket; quilt

betteln ['bɛtəln] *v/i* (*ge-*, *h*) beg (*um* for)

'Bettgestell *n* bedstead

bettlägerig ['bɛtlɛːɡərɪç] *adj* bedridden

'Bettlaken *n* sheet

Bettler ['bɛtlɐ] *m* (*-s*; *-*) beggar

Bett|nässer ['bɛtnɛsɐ] *m* (*-s*; *-*) MED bed wetter; *~ruhe* *f* bed rest; *j-m ~ verordnen* tell s.o. to stay in bed; *~vorleger* *m* bedside rug; *~wäsche* *f* bed linen; *~zeug* *n* bedding, bedclothes

beugen ['bɔyɡən] *v/t* (*ge-*, *h*) bend; LING inflect; *sich ~* (*vor* *dat* to) bend, bow

Beule ['bɔylə] *f* (*-*; *-n*) MED bump; MOT dent

beunruhigen [bə'ʔʊnruːɪɡən] *v/t* (*no -ge-*, *h*) alarm, worry

beurlauben [bə'ʔuːɐlaubən] *v/t* give s.o. leave *or* time off; suspend; *sich ~ lassen* ask for leave; **beurlaubt** [bə'ʔuːɐlaupt] *adj* on leave

be'urteilen *v/t* (*no -ge-*, *h*) judge (*nach* by); rate; **Be'urteilung** *f* (*-*; *-en*) judg(e)ment; evaluation

Beute ['bɔytə] *f* (*-*; *no pl*) booty, loot; ZO prey (*a. fig*); HUNT bag; *fig a.* victim

Beutel ['bɔytəl] *m* (*-s*; *-*) bag; pouch

bevölkern [bə'fœlkɐn] *v/t* (*no -ge-*, *h*) populate; **be'völkert** *adj* → *besiedelt*; **Be'völkerung** *f* (*-*; *-en*) population

bevollmächtigen [bə'fɔlmɛçtɪɡən] *v/t* (*no -ge-*, *h*) authorize

be'vor *cj* before

bevor|munden [bə'foːɐmʊndən] *v/t* (*no -ge-*, *h*) patronize; *~stehen* *v/i* (*irr*, *stehen*, *sep*, *-ge-*, *h*) be approaching; lie ahead; be imminent; *j-m ~* be in store for s.o., await s.o.

bevorzugen [bə'foːɐtsuːɡən] *v/t* (*no -ge-*, *h*) prefer; favo(u)r; **Be'vorzugung** *f* (*-*; *-en*) preferential treatment

be'wachen *v/t* (*no -ge-*, *h*) guard, watch over; **Be'wacher** *m* (*-s*; *-*) guard; SPORT marker; **Be'wachung** *f* (*-*; *-en*) (*no pl*) guarding; SPORT marking; guard

bewaffnen [bə'vafnən] *v/t* (*no -ge-*, *h*) arm (*a. fig*); **Be'waffnung** *f* (*-*; *-en*) armament; arms

be'wahren *v/t* (*no -ge-*, *h*) keep; *~ vor* (*dat*) keep *or* save from

be'währen *v/refl* (*no -ge-*, *h*) prove successful; *sich ~ als* prove to be

bewährt [bə'vɛːɐt] *adj* (well-)tried, reliable; experienced; **Be'währung** *f* (*-*; *-en*) JUR probation

Be'währungs|frist *f* JUR (period of) probation; *~helfer* *m* JUR probation officer; *~probe* *f* (acid) test

bewaldet [bə'valdət] *adj* wooded, woody

bewältigen [bə'vɛltɪɡən] *v/t* (*no -ge-*, *h*) manage, cope with; cover (*distance*)

be'wandert *adj* (well-)versed (*in* *dat* in)

be'wässern *v/t* (*no -ge-*, *h*) irrigate; **Be-'wässerung** *f* (*-*; *-en*) irrigation

bewegen [bə'veːɡən] *v/t and v/refl* (*no -ge-*, *h*) move (*a. fig*); *nicht ~!* don't move!; (*irr*) *j-n zu et. ~* get s.o. to do s.th.

Be'weggrund *m* motive

beweglich [bə'veːklɪç] *adj* movable; agile; flexible; TECH moving (*parts*); **Be'weglichkeit** *f* (*-*; *no pl*) mobility; agility; **be'wegt** *adj* rough (*sea*); choked (*voice*); eventful (*life*); *fig* moved, touched; **Be'wegung** *f* (*-*; *-en*) movement (*a.* POL); motion (*a.* PHYS); exercise; *fig* emotion; *in ~ setzen* set in motion; **Be-'wegungsfreiheit** *f* (*-*; *no pl*) freedom of movement (*fig a.* of action); **be-'wegungslos** *adj* motionless

Beweis [bə'vais] *m* (*-es*; *-e*) proof (*für* of); *~(e)* evidence (*esp* JUR)

be'weisen *v/t* (*irr*, *weisen*, *no -ge-*, *h*) prove; show

Be'weismittel *n* JUR (piece of) evidence

Be'weisstück *n* (piece of) evidence, JUR exhibit

be'wenden *v/i*: *es dabei ~ lassen* leave it at that

be'werben *v/refl* (*irr*, *werben*, *no -ge-*, *h*) *sich ~ um* apply for; **Be'werber(in)** (*-s*; *-/-*; *-nen*) applicant; **Be'werbung** *f* (*-*; *-en*) application; **Be-'werbungsschreiben** *n* (letter of) application

be'werten *v/t* (*no -ge-*, *h*) assess; judge; **Be'wertung** *f* (*-*; *-en*) assessment

bewilligen [bə'vɪlɪɡən] *v/t* (*no -ge-*, *h*) grant, allow; **be'wirken** *v/t* (*no -ge-*, *h*) cause; **bewirten** [bə'vɪrtən] *v/t (no -ge-, h)* entertain

be'wirtschaften *v/t (no -ge-, h)* run; AGR farm; **be'wirtschaftet** *adj* open (to the public)

Be'wirtung *f (-; -en)* catering; service; hospitality

bewog [bə'voːk] *pret of* **bewegen**

bewogen [bə'voːgən] *pp of* **bewegen**

be'wohnen *v/t (no -ge-, h)* live in; inhabit; **Be'wohner(in)** *(-s; -/-; -nen)* inhabitant; occupant; **be'wohnt** *adj* inhabited; occupied

bewölken [bə'vœlkən] *v/refl (no -ge-, h)* METEOR cloud over (*a. fig*); **be'wölkt** *adj* METEOR cloudy, overcast

Be'wölkung *f (-; no pl)* METEOR clouds

Bewunderer [bə'vʊndərɐ] *m (-s; -)* admirer; **bewundern** *v/t (no -ge-, h)* admire (**wegen** for); **be'wundernswert** *adj* admirable; **Be'wunderung** *f (-; no pl)* admiration

bewusst [bə'vʊst] *adj* conscious; intentional; **sich e-r Sache ~ sein** be conscious *or* aware of s.th., realize s.th.; **j-m et. ~ machen** make s.o. realize s.th.

be'wusstlos *adj* MED unconscious

be'wusstmachen *v/t* → **bewusst**

Be'wusstsein *n (-s; no pl)* MED consciousness; **bei ~** conscious

be'zahlen *v/t (no -ge-, h)* pay; pay for (*a. fig*); **be'zahlt** *adj*: **~er Urlaub** paid leave; **es macht sich ~** it pays; **Be'zahlung** *f (-; no pl)* payment; pay

be'zaubern *v/t (no -ge-, h)* charm; **~d** *adj* charming, F sweet, darling

be'zeichnen *v/t (no -ge-, h)* **~ als** call, describe as; **~d** *adj* characteristic, typical (**für** of)

Be'zeichnung *f (-; -en)* name, term

be'zeugen *v/t (no -ge-, h)* JUR testify to

be'ziehen *v/t (irr, ziehen, no -ge-, h)* cover; put clean sheets on (*bed*); move into; receive; subscribe to (*paper etc*); **~ auf** (*acc*) relate to; **sich ~** cloud over; **sich ~ auf** (*acc*) refer to; **Be'ziehung** *f (-; -en)* relation (**zu** to s.th.; with s.o.); connection (**zu** with); relationship; respect; **~en haben** have connections

be'ziehungsweise *cj* respectively; or; or rather

Bezirk [bə'tsɪrk] *m (-[e]s; -e)* precinct, Br *a.* district

Bezug [bə'tsuːk] *m (-[e]s; Bezüge* [bə-'tsyːgə]) cover(ing); case, slip; (*no pl*) ECON purchase; subscription (*gen* to); *pl* earnings; **~ nehmen auf** (*acc*) refer to; **in ~ auf** (*acc*) → **bezüglich**

bezüglich [bə'tsyːklɪç] *prp (gen)* regarding, concerning

Be'zugs|per,son *f* PSYCH person to relate to, role model; **~punkt** *m* reference point; **~quelle** *f* source (of supply)

be'zwecken *v/t (no -ge-, h)* aim at, intend; **be'zweifeln** *v/t (no -ge-, h)* doubt, question; **be'zwingen** *v/t (irr, zwingen, no -ge-, h)* conquer, defeat

Bibel ['biːbəl] *f (-; -n)* Bible

Biber ['biːbɐ] *m (-s; -)* ZO beaver

Bibliothek [biblio'teːk] *f (-; -en)* library

Bibliothekar [bibliote'kaːɐ] *m (-s; -e)*, **Bibliothe'karin** *f (-; -nen)* librarian

biblisch ['biːblɪʃ] *adj* biblical

bieder ['biːdɐ] *adj* honest; square

biegen ['biːgən] *v/t (irr, ge-, h) and v/i (sein)* bend (*a. sich ~*), road: *a.* turn; **um die Ecke ~** turn (round) the corner

biegsam ['biːkzaːm] *adj* flexible

'Biegung *f (-; -en)* curve

Biene ['biːnə] *f (-; -n)* ZO bee

'Bienen|königin *f* ZO queen (bee); **~korb** *m*, **~stock** *m* (bee)hive; **~wachs** *n* beeswax

Bier [biːɐ] *n (-[e]s; -e)* beer; **~ vom Faß** draft (*Br* draught) beer; **~deckel** *m* coaster, beer mat; **~krug** *m* beer mug, stein

Biest [biːst] F *fig n (-[e]s; -er)* beast; (*kleines*) **~** brat, little devil, stinker

bieten ['biːtən] *v/t (irr, ge-, h)* **1.** *v/t* offer; **sich ~** present itself **2.** *v/i* auction: (make a) bid

Bigamie [biga'miː] *f (-; -n)* bigamy

Bikini [bi'kiːni] *m (-s; -s)* bikini

Bilanz [bi'lants] *f (-; -en)* ECON balance; *fig* result; **~ ziehen aus** (*dat*) *fig* take stock of

Bild [bɪlt] *n (-[e]s; -er* ['bɪldɐ]) picture; image; **sich ein ~ machen von** get an idea of; **~ausfall** *m* TV blackout; **~bericht** *m* photo(graphic) essay (*Br* report)

bilden ['bɪldən] *v/t (ge-, h)* form (*a. sich ~*); shape; *fig* educate (*sich* o.s.), be, constitute

'Bilderbuch *n* picture book

'Bildfläche *f*: F **auf der ~ erscheinen** (**von der ~ verschwinden**) appear on (disappear from) the scene

'Bildhauer *m* (*-s*; *-*), **'Bildhauerin** *f* (*-*; *-nen*) sculptor

'bildlich *adj* graphic; figurative

'Bildnis *n* (*-ses*; *-se*) portrait

'Bildplatte *f* videodisk (*Br* -disc)

'Bildröhre *f* picture tube

'Bildschirm *m* TV screen, IT *a.* display, monitor; **~schoner** *m* (*-s*; *-*) screen saver; **~text** *m* videotext, *Br* viewdata

'bild'schön *adj* most beautiful

'Bildung *f* (*-*; *-en*) (*no pl*) education; formation

'Bildungs... *in cpds* **...chancen,** **...reform,** **...urlaub** *etc*: educational ...; **~lücke** *f* gap in one's knowledge

'Bildunterschrift *f* caption

Billard ['bɪljart] *n* (*-s*; *-e*) billiards, pool; **~kugel** *f* billiard ball; **~stock** *m* cue

Billett [bɪl'jɛt] *n* (*-[e]s*; *-e*) *Swiss* ticket

billig ['bɪlɪç] *adj* cheap (*a. contp*), inexpensive

billigen ['bɪlɪgən] *v/t* (*ge-*, *h*) approve of; **'Billigung** *f* (*-*; *no pl*) approval

Billion [bɪ'ljoːn] *f* (*-*; *-en*) trillion

bimmeln ['bɪməln] F *v/i* (*ge-*, *h*) jingle; TEL ring

binär [bi'nɛːɐ] *adj* MATH, PHYS *etc* binary

Binde ['bɪndə] *f* (*-*; *-n*) bandage; sling; → **Damenbinde**; **~gewebe** *n* ANAT connective tissue; **~glied** *n* (connecting) link

'Bindehaut *f* ANAT conjunctiva; **~entzündung** *f* MED conjunctivitis

binden (*irr*, *ge-*, *h*) **1.** *v/t* bind (*a. book*), tie (*an acc* to); make (*wreath etc*); knot (*tie*); **sich ~** bind or commit o.s. **2.** *v/i* bind

'Bindestrich *m* LING hyphen

'Bindewort *n* LING conjunction

Bindfaden ['bɪntfaːdən] *m* string

'Bindung *f* (*-*; *-en*) tie, link, bond; *skiing*: binding

Binnen|hafen ['bɪnənhaːfən] *m* inland port; **~handel** *m* domestic trade; **~markt** *m*: **Europäischer ~** European single market; **~schifffahrt** *f* inland navigation; **~verkehr** *m* inland traffic *or* transport

Binse ['bɪnzə] *f* (*-*; *-n*) BOT rush

'Binsenweisheit *f* (*-*; *-en*) truism

Bio..., **bio...** [bio-] *in cpds* **...chemie,**

...dynamisch, **...sphäre** *etc*: bio...

Biografie, **Biographie** [biogra'fiː] *f* (*-*; *-n*) biography

bio'grafisch, **bio'graphisch** *adj* biographic(al)

Bioladen ['biːolaːdən] *m* health food shop *or* store

Biologe [bio'loːgə] *m* (*-n*; *-n*) biologist

Biologie [biolo'giː] *f* (*-*; *no pl*) biology

Bio'login *f* (*-*; *-nen*) biologist

biologisch [bio'loːgɪʃ] *adj* biological; AGR organic; **~ abbaubar** biodegradable

'Biorhythmus *m* biorhythms

Biotechnik *f* (*-*; *no pl*) biotechnology

Biotop [bio'toːp] *n* (*-s*; *-e*) biotope

Birke ['bɪrkə] *f* (*-*; *-n*) BOT birch (tree)

Birne ['bɪrnə] *f* (*-*; *-n*) BOT pear; ELECTR (light) bulb

bis [bɪs] *prp* (*acc*) *and adv* and *cj* time: till, until, (up) to; *space*: (up) to, as far as; **von ... ~ ...** from ... to ...; **~ auf** (*acc*) except; **~ zu** up to; **~ später!** see you later!; **~ jetzt** up to now, so far; **~ Montag** by Monday; **zwei ~ drei** two or three; **wie weit ist es ~ ...?** how far is it to ...?

Bischof ['bɪʃɔf] *m* (*-s*; *Bischöfe* ['bɪʃœfə]) REL bishop

bisexuell [bizɛ'ksuɛl] *adj* bisexual

bis'her *adv* up to now, so far; **wie ~** as before

bisherig [bɪs'heːrɪç] *adj* previous

Biskuit [bɪs'kviːt] *n* (*-[e]s*; *-e*) sponge cake (mix)

biss [bɪs] *pret of* **beißen**

Biss *m* (*-es*; *-e*) bite (*a. fig*)

bisschen ['bɪsçən] *adj and adv*: **ein ~** a little, a (little) bit (of); **nicht ein ~** not in the least

Bissen ['bɪsən] *m* (*-s*; *-*) bite; **keinen ~** not a thing

bissig ['bɪsɪç] *adj fig* cutting; **ein ~er Hund** a dog that bites; **Vorsicht, ~er Hund!** beware of the dog!

Bistum ['bɪstuːm] *n* (*-s*; *Bistümer* ['bɪstyːmɐ]) REL bishopric, diocese

bis'weilen *adv* at times, now and then

Bit [bɪt] *n* (*-[s]*; *-[s]*) IT bit

bitte ['bɪtə] *adv* please; **~ nicht!** please don't!; **~** (**schön**)**!** that's all right, not at all, you're welcome; here you are; (**wie**) **~?** pardon?; **~ sehr?** can I help you?; **'Bitte** *f* (*-*; *-n*) request (**um** for);

bitten

ich habe e-e ~ (an dich) I have a favo(u)r to ask of you; **'bitten** v/t (irr, ge-, h) **j-n um et. ~** ask s.o. for s.th.; **darf ich ~?** may I have (the pleasure of) this dance?; → **Erlaubnis**

bitter ['bɪtɐ] adj bitter (a. fig), a. biting (cold); **~'kalt** adj bitterly cold

blähen ['blɛːən] v/refl (ge-, h) swell

'Blähungen pl MED flatulence, Br a. wind

blamabel [bla'maːbəl] adj embarrassing; **Blamage** [bla'maːʒə] f (-; -n) disgrace, shame; **blamieren** [bla'miːrən] v/t (no -ge-, h) **j-n ~** make s.o. look like a fool; **sich ~** make a fool of o.s.

blank [blaŋk] adj shining, shiny, bright; polished; F broke

Blanko... ['blaŋko] in cpds ECON blank

Bläschen ['blɛːsçən] n (-s; -) MED vesicle, small blister

Blase ['blaːzə] f (-; -n) bubble; ANAT bladder; MED blister

'Blasebalg m (pair of) bellows

'blasen v/t (irr, ge-, h) blow (a. MUS)

'Blas|instru,ment n MUS wind instrument; **~ka,pelle** f brass band; **~rohr** n blowpipe

blass [blas] adj pale (vor with); **~ werden** turn pale; **Blässe** ['blɛsə] f (-; no pl) paleness, pallor

Blatt [blat] n (-[e]s; Blätter ['blɛtɐ]) BOT leaf; piece, sheet (a. MUS); (news)paper; card games: hand; **blättern** ['blɛtɐn] v/i (ge-, h) **~ in** (dat) leaf through

'Blätterteig m puff pastry

blau [blau] adj blue; F loaded, stoned; **~es Auge** black eye; **~er Fleck** bruise; **Fahrt ins Blaue** mystery tour

blauäugig ['blauɔygɪç] adj blue-eyed; fig starry-eyed

'Blaubeere f BOT blueberry, Br bilberry

'blaugrau adj bluish-gray (Br -grey)

'Blauhelme pl MIL UN soldiers

bläulich ['blɔylɪç] adj bluish

'Blaulicht n (-[e]s; -er) flashing light(s)

'blaumachen F v/i (sep, -ge-, h) stay away from work or school

'Blausäure f CHEM prussic acid

Blech [blɛç] n (-[e]s; -e) sheet metal; in cpds ...dach, ...löffel etc: tin ...; ...instrument: MUS brass ...

'Blech|büchse, ~dose f can, Br a. tin

'blechen F v/t and v/i (ge-, h) shell out

'Blechschaden m MOT bodywork damage

Blei [blai] n (-[e]s; -e) lead; **aus ~** leaden

Bleibe ['blaibə] f (-; -n) place to stay

'bleiben v/i (irr, ge-, sein) stay, remain; **~ bei** stick to; F **et. ~ lassen** not do s.th.; **lass das ~!** stop that!; **das wirst du schön ~ lassen!** you'll do nothing of the sort!; → **Apparat, ruhig**; **~d** adj lasting, permanent

'bleibenlassen v/i → **bleiben**

bleich [blaiç] adj pale (vor with)

'bleichen v/t ([irr,] ge-, h) bleach

bleiern ['blaiɐn] adj lead(en fig)

'bleifrei adj MOT unleaded

'Bleistift m pencil; **~spitzer** m pencil sharpener

Blende ['blɛndə] f (-; -n) blind; PHOT aperture; (bei) **~ 8** (at) f-8

'blenden v/t (ge-, h) blind, dazzle (both a. fig); **~d** adj dazzling (a. fig); brilliant; **~ aussehen** look great

'blendfrei adj OPT antiglare

blich [blɪç] pret of **bleichen**

Blick [blɪk] m (-[e]s; -e) look (auf acc at); view (of); **flüchtiger ~** glance; **auf den ersten ~** at first sight; **'blicken** v/i (ge-, h) look, glance (both: auf acc, nach at)

'Blickfang m eye-catcher

'Blickfeld n field of vision

blieb [bliːp] pret of **bleiben**

blies [bliːs] pret of **blasen**

blind [blɪnt] adj blind (a. fig **gegen, für** to; **vor** dat with); dull (mirror etc); **~er Alarm** false alarm; **~er Passagier** stowaway; **auf e-m Auge ~** blind in one eye; **ein Blinder** a blind man; **e-e Blinde** a blind woman; **die Blinden** the blind

'Blinddarm m ANAT appendix; **~entzündung** f MED appendicitis; **~operati,on** f MED appendectomy

Blinden|hund ['blɪndənhʊnt] m seeing eye (Br guide) dog; **~schrift** f braille

Blindgänger ['blɪntgɛŋɐ] m (-s; -) MIL dud

'Blindheit f (-; no pl) blindness

blindlings ['blɪntlɪŋs] adv blindly

'Blindschleiche f ZO blindworm

blinken ['blɪŋkən] v/i (ge-, h) sparkle, shine; twinkle; flash (a signal); MOT indicate; **Blinker** ['blɪŋkɐ] m (-s; -) MOT turn signal, Br indicator

blinzeln ['blɪntsəln] v/i (ge-, h) blink (one's eyes)

Blitz [blɪts] *m* (*-es*; *-e*) (flash of) lightning; PHOT flash; **~ableiter** *m* (*-s*; *-*) lightning conductor

'blitzen *v/i* (*ge-*, *h*) flash; *es blitzt* it's lightening

'Blitz|gerät *n* PHOT (electronic) flash; **~lampe** *f* PHOT flashbulb; flash cube; **~licht** *n* (*-[e]s*; *-er*) PHOT flash(light); **~schlag** *m* lightning stroke

'blitz'schnell *adj and adv* like a flash; *attr* split-second

Block [blɔk] *m* (*-[e]s*; *Blöcke* ['blœkə]) block; POL, ECON bloc; (*writing*) pad

Blockade [blɔ'ka:də] *f* (*-*; *-n*) MAR, MIL blockade

'Blockflöte *f* recorder

'Blockhaus *n* log cabin

blockieren [blɔ'ki:rən] *v/t and v/i* (*no -ge-*, *h*) block; MOT lock

'Blockschrift *f* block letters

blöde ['blø:də] F *adj* silly, stupid

'blödeln *v/i* (*ge-*, *h*) fool *or* clown around

Blödheit ['blø:thait] *f* (*-*; *no pl*) stupidity

'Blödsinn F *m* (*-[e]s*; *no pl*) rubbish, nonsense

'blödsinnig F *adj* stupid, idiotic

Blog [blɔk] *m*, *n* (*-s*; *-s*) blog

blöken ['blø:kən] *v/i* (*ge-*, *h*) ZO bleat

blond [blɔnt] *adj* blond, fair

Blondine [blɔn'di:nə] *f* (*-*; *-n*) blonde

bloß [blo:s] **1.** *adj* bare; naked (*eye*); mere; **~ legen** *v/t* (*sep*, *-ge-*, *h*) lay bare, expose **2.** *adv* only, just, merely

Blöße ['blø:sə] *f* (*-*; *-n*) nakedness; *sich e-e ~ geben* lay o.s. open to attack *or* criticism

'bloß|legen *v/t* → *bloß*; **~stellen** *v/t* (*sep*, *-ge-*, *h*) expose, compromise, unmask; *sich ~* compromise o.s.

blühen ['bly:ən] *v/i* (*ge-*, *h*) (be in) bloom; (be in) blossom; *fig* flourish

Blume ['blu:mə] *f* (*-*; *-n*) flower; GASTR bouquet; head, froth

'Blumen|beet *n* flowerbed; **~händler** *m* florist; **~kohl** *m* BOT cauliflower; **~laden** *m* flower shop, florist's; **~strauß** *m* bunch of flowers; bouquet; **~topf** *m* flowerpot; **~vase** *f* vase

Bluse ['blu:zə] *f* (*-*; *-n*) blouse

Blut [blu:t] *n* (*-[e]s*; *no pl*) blood

'blutarm *adj* MED an(a)emic (*a. fig*)

'Blut|armut *f* MED an(a)emia; **~bad** *n* massacre; **~bahn** *f* ANAT bloodstream; **~bank** *f* (*-*; *-en*) MED blood bank

'blutbefleckt *adj* bloodstained

'Blut|bild *n* MED blood count; **~blase** *f* MED blood blister; **~druck** *m* MED blood pressure

Blüte ['bly:tə] *f* (*-*; *-n*) flower; bloom (*a. fig*); blossom; *fig* height, heyday; *in (voller) ~* in (full) bloom

Blutegel *m* ZO leech

'bluten *v/i* (*ge-*, *h*) bleed (*aus dat* from)

'Blüten|blatt *n* petal; **~staub** *m* pollen

Bluter ['blu:tə] *m* (*-s*; *-*) MED h(a)emophiliac

'Blut|erguss *m* bruise; MED h(a)ematoma; **~gefäß** *n* ANAT blood vessel; **~gerinnsel** *n* MED blood clot; **~gruppe** *f* MED blood group; **~hund** *m* ZO bloodhound

'blutig *adj* bloody; **~er Anfänger** rank beginner, F greenhorn

'Blut|körperchen *n* MED blood corpuscle; **~kreislauf** *m* MED (blood) circulation; **~lache** *f* pool of blood

'blutleer *adj* bloodless

'Blutprobe *f* MED blood test

blutrünstig ['blu:trynstɪç] *adj* bloodthirsty, gory

'Blutschande *f* JUR incest

'Blutspender *m* blood donor

'Blutsverwandte *m*, *f* blood relation

'Blutübertragung *f* MED blood transfusion

'Blutung *f* (*-*; *-en*) MED bleeding, h(a)emorrhage

'blutunterlaufen *adj* bloodshot

'Blut|vergießen *n* (*-s*; *no pl*) bloodshed; **~vergiftung** *f* MED blood poisoning; **~wurst** *f* black sausage (*Br* pudding)

BLZ [be:ɛl'tsɛt] *abbr of Bankleitzahl* A.B.A. number, *Br* bank (sorting) code

Bö [bø:] *f* (*-*; *-en*) gust, squall

Bob [bɔp] *m* (*-s*; *-s*) bob(sled); **~bahn** *f* bob run; **~fahrer** *m* bobber

Bock [bɔk] *m* (*-[e]s*; *Böcke* ['bœkə]) ZO buck; he-goat, billy-goat; ram; SPORT buck; *e-n ~ schießen* (make a) blunder; F *keinen* (*or null*) *~ auf et. haben* have zero interest in s.th.

'bocken *v/i* (*ge-*, *h*) buck; sulk

'bockig *adj* obstinate; sulky

'Bockspringen *n* leapfrog

Boden ['bo:dən] *m* (*-s*; *Böden* ['bø:dən]) ground; AGR soil; bottom; floor; attic

'**Boden|perso,nal** *n* AVIAT ground crew; **~schätze** *pl* mineral resources; **~stati,on** *f* AVIAT ground control; **~turnen** *n* floor exercises

Body ['bɔdi] *m* (-*s*; -*s*) bodysuit

bog [bo:k] *pret of* **biegen**

Bogen ['bo:gən] *m* (-*s*; *Bögen* ['bø:gən]) bend, curve; MATH arc; ARCH arch; *skiing:* turn; bow; sheet; **~schießen** *n* archery; **~schütze** *m* archer

Bohle ['bo:lə] *f* (-; -*n*) plank

Bohne ['bo:nə] *f* (-; -*n*) BOT bean; *grüne ~n* green (*Br a.* French) beans

'**Bohnenstange** *f* beanpole (*a.* F)

bohnern ['bo:nɐn] *v/t* (*ge-*, *h*) polish, wax; '**Bohnerwachs** *n* floor polish

bohren ['bo:rən] *v/t* (*ge-*, *h*) bore, drill (*a. dentist*); **~d** *fig adj* piercing (*look*); insistent (*questions etc*)

Bohrer ['bo:rɐ] *m* (-*s*; -*) TECH drill

'**Bohr|insel** *f* oil rig; **~loch** *n* borehole, well(head); **~ma,schine** *f* (electric) drill; **~turm** *m* derrick

'**Bohrung** *f* (-; -*en*) drilling; bore

Boje ['bo:jə] *f* (-; -*n*) MAR buoy

Bolzen ['bɔltsən] *m* (-*s*; -) TECH bolt

bombardieren [bɔmbar'di:rən] *v/t* (*no -ge-*, *h*) bomb; *fig* bombard

Bombe ['bɔmbə] *f* (-; -*n*) bomb; *fig* bombshell

'**Bomben|angriff** *m* air raid; **~anschlag** *m* bomb attack; **~erfolg** F *m* roaring success; THEA *etc* smash hit; **~geschäft** F *n* super deal

'**Bombenleger** *m* (-*s*; -) bomber

'**bombensicher** *adj* bombproof

Bomber ['bɔmbɐ] F *m* (-*s*; -) MIL bomber (*a.* SPORT)

Bon [bɔŋ] *m* (-*s*; -*s*) coupon, voucher

Bonbon [bɔŋ'bɔŋ] *m*, *n* (-*s*; -*s*) candy, *Br* sweet

Boot [bo:t] *n* (-[*e*]*s*; -*e*) boat

'**Bootsmann** *m* (-[*e*]*s*; -*leute*) boatswain

Bord¹ [bɔrt] *n* (-[*e*]*s*; -*e*) shelf

Bord² *m*: *an ~* AVIAT, MAR on board; *über ~* MAR overboard; *von ~ gehen* MAR disembark

Bordell [bɔr'dɛl] *n* (-*s*; -*e*) brothel, F whorehouse

'**Bordkarte** *f* AVIAT boarding pass

'**Bordstein** *m* curb, *Br* kerb

borgen ['bɔrgən] *v/t* (*ge-*, *h*) borrow; *sich et. von j-m ~* borrow s.th. from s.o.; *j-m et. ~* lend s.th. to s.o.

Borke ['bɔrkə] *f* (-; -*n*) BOT bark

borniert [bɔr'ni:ɐt] *adj* narrow-minded

Börse ['bœrzə] *f* (-; -*n*) ECON stock exchange

'**Börsen|bericht** *m* market report; **~kurs** *m* quotation; **~makler** *m* stockbroker; **~speku,lant** *m* stock-jobber

Borste ['bɔrstə] *f* (-; -*n*) bristle

'**borstig** *adj* bristly

Borte ['bɔrtə] *f* (-; -*n*) border; braid, lace

bösartig ['bø:sartıç] *adj* vicious; MED malignant

Böschung ['bœʃʊŋ] *f* (-; -*en*) slope, bank; RAIL embankment

böse ['bø:zə] *adj* bad, evil, wicked; angry (*über acc* about; *auf j-n* with s.o.), mad (*auf acc* at); *er meint es nicht ~* he means no harm

'**Böse** *n* (-*n*; *no pl*) (the) evil

'**Bösewicht** *m* (-[*e*]*s*; -*er*) villain

boshaft ['bo:shaft] *adj* malicious

Bosheit ['bo:shait] *f* (-; *no pl*) malice

'**böswillig** *adj* malicious, JUR *a.* wil(l)ful

bot [bo:t] *pret of* **bieten**

Botanik [bo'ta:nık] *f* (-; *no pl*) botany

Bo'taniker *m* (-*s*; -) botanist

bo'tanisch *adj* botanical

Bote ['bo:tə] *m* (-*n*; -*n*) messenger

'**Botengang** *m* errand; *Botengänge machen* run errands

Botschaft ['bo:tʃaft] *f* (-; -*en*) message; POL embassy

'**Botschafter** *m* (-*s*; -) POL ambassador (*in dat* to); '**Botschafterin** *f* (-; -*nen*) POL ambassadress (*in dat* to)

Bottich ['bɔtıç] *m* (-*s*; -*e*) tub, vat

Bouillon [bul'jɔŋ] *f* (-; -*s*) consommé, bouillon, broth

Boulevard|blatt [bulə'va:ɐblat] *n*, **~zeitung** *f* tabloid

Bowle ['bo:lə] *f* (-; -*n*) (cold) punch; bowl

boxen ['bɔksən] (*ge-*, *h*) **1.** *v/i* box **2.** *v/t* punch; '**Boxen** *n* (-*s*; *no pl*) boxing; **Boxer** ['bɔksɐ] *m* (-*s*; -) boxer

'**Box|handschuh** *m* boxing glove; **~kampf** *m* boxing match, fight; **~sport** *m* boxing

Boykott [bɔy'kɔt] *m* (-[*e*]*s*; -*e*), **boykottieren** [bɔyko'ti:rən] *v/t* (*no -ge-*, *h*) boycott

brach [bra:x] *pret of* **brechen**

brachliegend *adj* AGR fallow

brachte ['braxtə] *pret of* **bringen**

Branche ['brã:ʃə] *f* (-; *-n*) ECON line (of business); '**Branchenverzeichnis** *n* TEL yellow pages

Brand [brant] *m* (-[e]*s*; *Brände* ['brɛndə]) fire; **in ~ geraten** catch fire; **in ~ stecken** set fire to; **~blase** *f* MED blister

branden ['brandən] *v/i* (*ge-, sein*) surge (**gegen** against)

'**Brand|fleck** *m* burn; **~mal** *n* brand

'**brandmarken** *fig v/t* (*ge-, h*) brand, stigmatize

'**Brand|mauer** *f* fire wall; **~stätte** *f*, **~stelle** *f* scene of fire; **~stifter** *m* arsonist; **~stiftung** *f* arson

'**Brandung** *f* (-; *no pl*) surf, surge, breakers

'**Brandwunde** *f* MED burn; scald

brannte ['brantə] *pret of* **brennen**

'**Branntwein** *m* brandy, spirits

braten ['bra:tən] *v/t* (*irr, ge-, h*) roast; grill, broil; fry; **am Spieß ~** roast on a spit, barbecue

'**Braten** *m* (-*s*; -) roast (meat); joint; **~fett** *n* dripping; **~soße** *f* gravy

'**Brat|fisch** *m* fried fish; **~huhn** *n* roast chicken; **~kar,toffeln** *pl* fried potatoes; **~ofen** *m* oven; **~pfanne** *f* frying pan

Bratsche ['bra:tʃə] *f* (-; *-n*) MUS viola

'**Bratwurst** *f* grilled sausage

Brauch [braux] *m* (-[e]*s*; *Bräuche* ['brɔʏçə]) custom; habit, practice

'**brauchbar** *adj* useful

'**brauchen** *v/t* (*ge-, h*) need; require; take (*time*); use; **wie lange wird er ~?** how long will it take him?; **du brauchst es nur zu sagen** just say the word; **ihr braucht es nicht zu tun** you don't have to do it; **er hätte nicht zu kommen ~** he need not have come

brauen ['brauən] *v/t* (*ge-, h*) brew

Brauerei [brauə'rai] *f* (-; *-en*) brewery

braun [braun] *adj* brown; (sun)tanned; **~ werden** (get a) tan

Bräune ['brɔʏnə] *f* (-; *no pl*) (sun)tan

'**bräunen** (*ge-, h*) 1. *v/t* brown, tan 2. *v/i* (get a) tan

'**Braunkohle** *f* brown coal, lignite

'**bräunlich** *adj* brownish

Brause ['brauzə] *f* (-; *-n*) shower; → **Limonade**; '**brausen** *v/i* (*ge-, h*) roar; (*sein*) rush; (*h*) → **duschen**

Braut [braut] *f* (-; *Bräute* ['brɔʏtə]) bride; fiancée; **Bräutigam** ['brɔʏtɪgam] *m* (-*s*; *-e*) (bride)groom; fiancé

'**Braut|jungfer** *f* bridesmaid; **~kleid** *n* wedding-dress; **~paar** *n* bride and (bride)groom; engaged couple

brav [bra:f] *adj* good; honest; **sei(d) ~!** be good!

BRD [be:ʔɛr'de:] *abbr of* **Bundesrepublik Deutschland** FRG, Federal Republic of Germany

brechen ['brɛçən] (*irr, ge-*) 1. *v/t* (*h*) break (*a. fig*); MED vomit; **sich ~** OPT be refracted; **sich den Arm ~** break one's arm 2. *v/i* (*h*) MED vomit, F throw up, *Br a.* be sick; **mit j-m ~** break with s.o.; **~d voll** crammed, packed; (*sein*) break, get broken, fracture

'**Brechreiz** *m* MED nausea

'**Brechstange** *f* crowbar

'**Brechung** *f* (-; *-en*) OPT refraction

Brei [brai] *m* (-[e]*s*; *-e*) pulp, mash; pap; porridge; pudding

'**breiig** *adj* pulpy, mushy

breit [brait] *adj* wide; broad (*a. fig*)

'**breitbeinig** *adj* with legs (wide) apart

Breite ['braitə] *f* (-; *-n*) width, breadth; ASTR, GEOGR latitude

'**breiten** *v/t* (*ge-, h*) spread

'**Breiten|grad** *m* degree of latitude; **~kreis** *m* parallel (of latitude)

breitmachen *v/refl* (*sep, -ge-, h*): **sich ~** F spread o.s., take up room

'**Breitwand** *f film*: wide screen

Bremsbelag ['brɛmsbəla:k] *m* brake lining

Bremse ['brɛmzə] *f* (-; *-n*) TECH brake; ZO gadfly; '**bremsen** (*ge-, h*) 1. *v/i* MOT brake, put on the brake(s); slow down 2. *v/t* MOT brake; *fig* curb

'**Brems|licht** *n* (-[e]*s*; *-er*) MOT stop light; **~pe,dal** *n* MOT brake pedal; **~spur** *f* MOT skid marks; **~weg** *m* MOT stopping distance

'**brennbar** *adj* combustible; (in)flammable; **brennen** ['brɛnən] (*irr, ge-, h*) 1. *v/t* burn; distil(l) (*whisky etc*); bake (*bricks*) 2. *v/i* burn; be on fire; *wound, eyes*: smart, burn; F *darauf ~ zu inf* be dying to *inf*; **es brennt!** fire!; **Brenner** ['brɛnɐ] *m* (-*s*; -) burner

'**Brenn|holz** *n* firewood; **~materi,al** *n* fuel; **~nessel** *f* BOT (stinging) nettle; **~punkt** *m* focus, focal point; **~spiritus** *m* methylated spirit; **~stab** *m* TECH fuel rod; **~stoff** *m* fuel

brenzlig ['brɛntslɪç] *adj* burnt; *fig* hot

Bresche ['brɛʃə] *f* (-; -*n*) breach (*a. fig*), gap

Brett [brɛt] *n* (-[*e*]*s*; -*er*) board

'Bretterzaun *m* wooden fence

'Brettspiel *n* board game

Brezel ['breːtsəl] *f* (-; -*n*) pretzel

Brief [briːf] *m* (-[*e*]*s*; -*e*) letter; **~beschwerer** *m* (-*s*; -) paperweight; **~bogen** *m* sheet of (note)paper; **~freund(in)** pen pal (*Br* friend); **~kasten** *m* mailbox, *Br* letterbox

'brieflich *adj and adv* by letter

'Brief|marke *f* (postage) stamp; **~markensammlung** *f* stamp collection; **~öffner** *m* letter opener, *Br* paper knife; **~pa,pier** *n* stationery; **~tasche** *f* wallet; **~taube** *f* zo carrier pigeon; **~träger(in)** (-*s*; -/-; -*nen*) mailman (mailwoman), *Br* postman (postwoman); **~umschlag** *m* envelope; **~wahl** *f* postal vote; **~wechsel** *m* correspondence

briet [briːt] *pret of* **braten**

Brikett [bri'kɛt] *n* (-*s*; -*s*) briquet(te)

brillant [brɪl'jant] *adj* brilliant

Bril'lant *m* (-*en*; -*en*) (cut) diamond

Bril'lantring *m* diamond ring

Brille ['brɪlə] *f* (-; -*n*) (pair of) glasses, spectacles; goggles; toilet seat

'Brillen|etui *n* eyeglass (*Br* spectacle) case; **~träger(in)** (-*s*; -/-; -*nen*) ~ **sein** wear glasses

bringen ['brɪŋən] *v/t* (*irr*, *ge-*, *h*) bring; take; cause; make (*sacrifice*); yield (*profit*); *j-n nach Hause ~* see (*or* take) s.o. home; *in Ordnung ~* put in order; *das bringt mich auf e-e Idee* that gives me an idea; *j-n dazu ~, et. zu tun* get s.o. to do s.th.; *et. mit sich ~* involve s.th.; *j-n um et. ~* deprive s.o. of s.th.; *j-n zum Lachen ~* make s.o. laugh; *j-n wieder zu sich ~* bring s.o. round; *es zu et. (nichts) ~* go far (get nowhere); F *es ~* make it; *das bringt nichts* it's no use

Brise ['briːzə] *f* (-; -*n*) breeze

Brite ['brɪtə] *m* (-*n*; -*n*), **'Britin** *f* (-; -*nen*) Briton; *die Briten pl* the British

'britisch *adj* British

bröckeln ['brœkəln] *v/i* (*ge-*, *h*, *sein*) crumble

Brocken ['brɔkən] *m* (-*s*; -) piece; lump; rock; GASTR chunk; morsel; *ein paar ~*

Englisch a few scraps of English; F *ein harter ~* a hard nut to crack

Brombeere ['brɔmbeːrə] *f* BOT blackberry

Bronchitis [brɔn'çiːtɪs] *f* (-; -*tiden* [brɔnçi'tiːdən]) MED bronchitis

Bronze ['broːsə] *f* (-; -*n*) bronze; **~zeit** *f* (-; *no pl*) HIST Bronze Age

Brosche ['brɔʃə] *f* (-; -*n*) brooch, pin

broschiert [brɔ'ʃiːrt] *adj* paperback

Broschüre [brɔ'ʃyːrə] *f* (-; -*n*) pamphlet; brochure

Brot [broːt] *n* (-[*e*]*s*; -*e*) bread; sandwich; *ein (Laib) ~* a loaf (of bread); *e-e Scheibe ~* a slice of bread; *sein ~ verdienen* earn one's living

Brötchen ['brøːtçən] *n* (-*s*; -) roll

'Brot|rinde *f* crust; **~(schneide)ma,schine** *f* bread cutter

Bruch [brux] *m* (-[*e*]*s*; *Brüche* ['bryçə]) break; MED fracture; hernia; MATH fraction; GEOL fault; *fig* breach (*of promise etc*); JUR violation; *zu ~ gehen* be wrecked; **~bude** F *f* dump, hovel

brüchig ['bryçɪç] *adj* brittle

'Bruch|landung *f* AVIAT crash landing; **~rechnung** *f* MATH fractional arithmetic, F fractions

'bruchsicher *adj* breakproof

'Bruch|strich *m* MATH fraction bar; **~stück** *n* fragment; **~teil** *m* fraction; *im ~ e-r Sekunde* in a split second; **~zahl** *f* MATH fraction(al) number

Brücke ['brykə] *f* (-; -*n*) bridge (*a.* SPORT); rug; **'Brückenpfeiler** *m* pier

Bruder ['bruːdə] *m* (-*s*; *Brüder* ['bryːdə]) brother (*a.* REL); **~krieg** *m* civil war

brüderlich ['bryːdəlɪç] **1.** *adj* brotherly **2.** *adv*: ~ *teilen* share and share alike

'Brüderlichkeit *f* (-; *no pl*) brotherhood

'Brüderschaft *f*: ~ *trinken* agree to use the familiar 'du' form of address

Brühe ['bryːə] *f* (-; -*n*) broth; stock; F dishwater; slops; F filthy water, bilge

'Brühwürfel *m* beef cube

brüllen ['brylən] *v/i* (*ge-*, *h*) roar (*vor Lachen* with laughter); zo bellow; F bawl; **~des Gelächter** roars of laughter

brummen ['brumən] *v/i* (*ge-*, *h*) growl; zo hum, buzz (*a. engine etc*); *head*: be buzzing; **'brummig** *adj* grumpy

brünett [bry'nɛt] *adj* brunette, dark-haired

Brunnen ['brunən] *m* (-*s*; -) well, spring,

fountain

Brunstzeit ['brʊnsttsait] *f* zo rutting season

Brust [brʊst] *f* (-; *Brüste* ['brʏstə]) ANAT (*no pl*) chest; breast(s), bosom; **~bein** *n* ANAT breastbone; **~beutel** *m* neck pouch, *Br* money bag

brüsten ['brʏstən] *v/refl* (*ge-, h*) boast, brag (*mit* of)

'**Brust|kasten** *m*, **~korb** *m* ANAT chest, thorax; **~schwimmen** *n* breaststroke

'**Brüstung** *f* (-; *-en*) parapet

'**Brustwarze** *f* ANAT nipple

Brut [bru:t] *f* (-; *-en*) zo brooding; brood (*a.* F), hatch; fry

brutal [bru'ta:l] *adj* brutal; **Brutalität** [brutali'tɛːt] *f* (-; *-en*) brutality

'**Brutappa,rat** *m* zo incubator

brüten ['bry:tən] *v/i* (*ge-, h*) zo brood, sit (on eggs); **~ über** (*dat*) *fig* brood over

'**Brutkasten** *m* MED incubator

brutto ['brʊto] *adv* ECON gross

'**Brutto|einkommen** *n* ECON gross earnings; **~sozi,alpro,dukt** *n* ECON gross national product

Bube ['bu:bə] *m* (*-n; -n*) boy, lad; *card game*: knave, jack

Buch [bu:x] *n* (*-[e]s; Bücher* ['by:çɐ]) book; **~binder** *m* (*-s; -*) (book)binder; **~drucker** *m* printer; **~druckerei** *f* print shop, *Br* printing office

Buche ['bu:xə] *f* (-; *-n*) BOT beech

'**buchen** *v/t* (*ge-, h*) book; ECON enter

Bücherbord ['by:çɐbɔrt] *n* bookshelf

Bücherei [by:çə'rai] *f* (-; *-en*) library

'**Bücherre,gal** *n* bookshelf

'**Bücherschrank** *m* bookcase

'**Buch|fink** *m* zo chaffinch; **~halter(in)** bookkeeper; **~haltung** *f* (-; *no pl*) bookkeeping; **~händler(in)** booksell-er; **~handlung** *f* bookstore, *Br* book-shop; **~macher** *m* bookmaker

Büchse ['bʏksə] *f* (-; *-n*) can, *Br* tin; box; rifle

'**Büchsen|fleisch** *n* canned (*Br* tinned) meat; **~öffner** *m* can (*Br* tin) opener

Buchstabe ['bu:xʃta:bə] *m* (*-n; -n*) let-ter; *großer* (*kleiner*) **~** capital (small) letter; **buchstabieren** [bu:xʃta'bi:rən] *v/t* (*no -ge-, h*) spell; **buchstäblich** ['bu:xʃtɛːplɪç] *adv* literally

'**Buchstütze** *f* bookend

Bucht ['bʊxt] *f* (-; *-en*) bay; creek, inlet

'**Buchung** *f* (-; *-en*) booking; ECON entry

Buckel ['bʊkəl] *m* (*-s; -*) hump, hunch; **e-n ~ machen** hump *or* hunch one's back

bücken ['bʏkən] *v/refl* (*ge-, h*) bend (down), stoop

bucklig ['bʊklɪç] *adj* hunchbacked

Bucklige ['bʊkligə] *m*, *f* (*-n; -n*) hunch-back

Bückling ['bʏklɪŋ] *m* (*-s; -e*) smoked herring, *Br* kipper

Buddhismus [bʊ'dɪsmʊs] *m* (-; *no pl*) Buddhism; **Buddhist** ['bʊdɪst] *m* (*-en; -en*), **bud'dhistisch** *adj* Buddhist

Bude ['bu:də] *f* (*-n; -n*) stall, booth; hut; F pad, *Br* digs; *contp* shack, dump, hole

Budget [by'dʒeː] *n* (*-s; -s*) budget

Büfett [by'fɛt] *n* (*-[e]s; -s, -e*) counter, bar, buffet; sideboard, cupboard; **kal-tes ~** GASTR cold buffet (meal)

Büffel ['bʏfəl] *m* (*-s; -*) zo buffalo

'**büffeln** F *v/i* (*ge-, h*) grind, cram, swot

Bug [bu:k] *m* (*-[e]s; -e*) MAR bow; AVIAT nose; zo, GASTR shoulder

Bügel ['by:gəl] *m* (*-s; -*) hanger; bow; **~brett** *n* ironing board; **~eisen** *n* iron; **~falte** *f* crease

'**bügelfrei** *adj* no(n)-iron

'**bügeln** *v/t* (*ge-, h*) iron, press

buh [bu:] *int* boo!

buhen ['bu:ən] *v/i* (*ge-, h*) boo

Bühne ['by:nə] *f* (-; *-n*) stage, *fig a.* scene

'**Bühnen|bild** *n* (stage) set(ting); **~bildner(in)** (*-s; -/-; -nen*) stage design-er

'**Buhrufe** *pl* boos

Bullauge ['bʊlaugə] *n* MAR porthole

'**Bulldogge** *f* zo bulldog

Bulle ['bʊlə] *m* (*-n; -n*) zo bull (*a. fig*); F *contp* cop, *pl* the fuzz

Bummel ['bʊməl] F *m* (*-s; -*) stroll; **Bummelei** [bʊmə'lai] *f* (-; *no pl*) F *contp* dawdling; slackness; '**bummeln** F *v/i* (*ge-, sein*) stroll, saunter; (*ge-, h*) *contp* dawdle; ECON go slow; '**Bummelstreik** *m* ECON slowdown, *Br* go-slow (strike); **Bummler** ['bʊmlɐ] F *m* (*-s; -*) stroller; *contp* dawdler, slow-poke, *Br* slowcoach

bumsen ['bʊmzən] *v/i and v/t* (*ge-, h*) F → *krachen*; V screw

Bund[1] [bʊnt] *m* (*-[e]s; Bünde* ['bʏndə]) union, federation, alliance; associa-tion; (waist)band; *der ~* POL the Feder-al Government; F → *Bundeswehr*

Bund² *n* (-[e]s; -e) bundle; bunch
Bündel ['byndəl] *n* (-s; -) bundle
'**bündeln** *v/t* (*ge-*, *h*) bundle (up)
Bundes... ['bundəs-] *in cpds* Federal
...; German ...; **~bahn** *f* Federal Rail-
road(s); **~genosse** *m* ally; **~kanzler(in)**
Federal Chancellor; **~land** *n appr* (federal) state, Land; **~liga** *f* SPORT First Division; **~präsi,dent** *m* Federal President; **~rat** *m* Bundesrat, Upper House
of German Parliament; **~repu,blik** *f*
Federal Republic; **~staat** *m* federal
state; confederation; **~straße** *f* Federal
Highway; **~tag** *m* (-[e]s; *no pl*) Bundestag, Lower House of German Parliament; **~trainer** *m* coach of the (German) national team; **~verfassungsge-
richt** *n* Federal Constitutional Court,
Am appr Supreme Court; **~wehr** *f* (-;
no pl) MIL (German Federal) Armed
Forces
bündig ['byndıç] *adj* TECH flush; *kurz
und* **~** terse(ly); point-blank
Bündnis ['byntnıs] *n* (-ses; -se) alliance
Bunker ['bunkɐ] *m* (-s; -) air-raid shelter, bunker
bunt [bunt] *adj* colo(u)red; multi-
colo(u)red; colo(u)rful (*a. fig*); varied;
~er Abend evening of entertainment;
F *mir wird's zu* **~** that's all I can take
'**Buntstift** *m* colo(u)red pencil, crayon
Bürde ['byrdə] *f* (-; -*n*) burden (*für j-n* to
s.o.)
Burg [burk] *f* (-; -*en*) castle
Bürge ['byrgə] *m* (-*n*; -*n*) JUR guarantor
(*a. fig*); '**bürgen** *v/i* (*ge-*, *h*) *für j-n* **~** JUR
stand surety for s.o.; *für et.* **~** guarantee
s.th.
Bürger ['byrgɐ] *m* (-s; -), '**Bürgerin** *f* (-;
-*nen*) citizen; **~initia,tive** *f* (citizen's *or*
local) action group; **~krieg** *m* civil war
'**bürgerlich** *adj* civil; middle-class; *esp
contp* bourgeois; **~e Küche** home
cooking; '**Bürgerliche** *m*, *f* (-*n*; -*n*)
commoner

'**Bürger|meister** *m* mayor; **~rechte** *pl*
civil rights; **~steig** ['byrgɐʃtaik] *m*
(-[e]s; -e) sidewalk, *Br* pavement
'**Bürgschaft** *f* (-; -*en*) JUR surety; bail
Büro [by'ro:] *n* (-s; -s) office; **~ange-
stellte** *m*, *f* (-*n*; -*n*) clerk, office worker;
~klammer *f* (paper) clip
Bürokrat [byro'kra:t] *m* (-*en*; -*en*) bu-
reaucrat; **Bürokratie** [byrokra'ti:] *f*
(-; -*n*) bureaucracy; *contp* red tape
Bü'rostunden *pl* office hours
Bursche ['burʃə] *m* (-*n*; -*n*) fellow, guy
burschikos [burʃi'ko:s] *adj* (tom)boy-
ish, pert
Bürste ['byrstə] *f* (-; -*n*) brush
'**bürsten** *v/t* (*ge-*, *h*) brush
'**Bürstenschnitt** *m* crew cut
Bus [bus] *m* (-ses; -se) bus; coach
Busch [buʃ] *m* (-[e]s; *Büsche* ['byʃə])
BOT bush, shrub
Büschel ['byʃəl] *n* (-s; -) bunch; tuft
'**buschig** *adj* bushy
Busen ['bu:zən] *m* (-s; -) ANAT bosom,
breast(s)
'**Busfahrer** *m* bus driver
'**Bushaltestelle** *f* bus stop
Bussard ['busart] *m* (-s; -e) ZO buzzard
Buße ['bu:sə] *f* (-; -*n*) REL penance; re-
pentance; **~ tun** do penanc
büßen ['by:sən] *v/t* (*ge-*, *h*) pay *or* suffer
for *s.th.*; REL repent
'**Bußgeld** *n* fine, penalty
'**Bußtag** *m* REL day of repentance
Büste ['by:stə] *f* (-; -*n*) bust
'**Büstenhalter** *m* bra
Butter ['butɐ] *f* (-; *no pl*) butter; **~blume**
f BOT buttercup; **~brot** *n* (slice *or* piece
of) bread and butter; F *für ein* **~** for a
song; **~brotpa,pier** *n* greaseproof paper; **~dose** *f* butter dish; **~milch** *f* but-
termilk
b.w. *abbr of* **bitte wenden** PTO, please
turn over
bzw. *abbr of* **beziehungsweise** resp.,
respectively

C

C *abbr of* **Celsius** C, Celsius, centigrade

ca. *abbr of* **circa** approx., approximately

Café [ka'feː] *n* (-s; -s) café, coffee house

Cafeteria [kafetə'riːa] *f* (-; -s *or* -ien) cafeteria

campen ['kɛmpən] *v/i* (ge-, h) camp

Camper ['kɛmpɐ] *m* (-s; -) camper

Camping... ['kɛmpɪŋ-] *in cpds* ...**bett**, ...**tisch** *etc* camp ...; **~bus** *m* camper (van *Br*); **~platz** *m* campground, *Br* campsite

Cappuccino [kapu'tʃino] *m* (-[s]; -[s]) cappuccino

Casino [ka'ziːno] *n* → **Kasino**

Catcher ['kɛtʃɐ] *m* (-s; -) wrestler

C'D [tseː'deː] *f* (-; -s) CD, compact disk (*Br* disc); **C'D-Brenner** *m* CD burner, CD writer; **C'D-Player** *m* CD player; **CD-'ROM** CD-ROM; **CD-'ROM-Laufwerk** *n* CD-ROM drive; **C'D-Spieler** *m* CD player

Cellist [tʃɛ'lɪst] *m* (-en; -en), **Cel'listin** *f* (-; -nen) MUS cellist

Cello ['tʃɛlo] *n* (-s; -s, *Celli*) MUS cello

Celsius ['tsɛlzjʊs] *5 Grad ~* (*abbr 5° C*) five degrees centigrade *or* Celsius

Cembalo ['tʃɛmbalo] *n* (-s; -s, -li) MUS harpsichord

Champagner® [ʃam'panjɐ] *m* (-s; -) champagne

Champignon ['ʃampɪnjɔŋ] *m* (-s; -) BOT mushroom

Chance ['ʃãːsə] *f* (-; -n) chance; *die ~n stehen gleich (3 zu 1)* the odds are even (three to one); **'Chancengleichheit** *f* equal opportunities

Chaos ['kaːɔs] *n* (-; *no pl*) chaos

Chaot [ka'oːt] *m* (-en; -en) chaotic person; POL anarchist, *pl a.* lunatic fringe

cha'otisch *adj* chaotic

Charakter [ka'raktɐ] *m* (-s; -e [karak-'teːrə]) character, nature; **charakterisieren** [karakteri'ziːrən] *v/t* (*no -ge-*, h) characterize, describe (*als* as); **charakteristisch** [karakte'rɪstɪʃ] *adj* characteristic, typical (*für* of); **Cha-'rakterzug** *m* trait

charmant [ʃar'mant] *adj* charming

Charme [ʃarm] *m* (-s; *no pl*) charm

Charterflug ['tʃartɐfluːk] *m* (-[e]s; -flüge) charter flight

chartern ['tʃartɐn] *v/t* (ge-, h) charter

Chassis [ʃa'siː] *n* (-; -) TECH chassis

Chat [tʃɛt] *m* (-s; -s) IT chat

chatten ['tʃɛtən] *v/t* (ge-, h) IT chat

Chauffeur [ʃɔ'føːɐ] *m* (-s; -e) chauffeur, driver

Chauvi ['ʃoːvi] *m* (-s; -s) F male chauvinist (pig)

Chauvinismus [ʃovi'nɪsmʊs] *m* (-; *no pl*) chauvinism, POL *a.* jingoism

checken ['tʃɛkən] *v/t* (ge-, h) check; F (*understand*) get

Chef [ʃɛf] *m* (-s; -s) head, chief, F boss; **~arzt** *m* medical director, *Br* senior consultant; **~sekre,tärin** *f* executive secretary

Chemie [çe'miː] *f* (-; *no pl*) chemistry; **~faser** *f* synthetic fiber (*Br* fibre)

Chemikalien [çemi'kaːljən] *pl* chemicals; **Chemiker(in)** ['çeːmikɐ, 'çeːmikərɪn] *m(f)* (-s; -/-; -nen) (analytical) chemist; **chemisch** ['çeːmɪʃ] *adj* chemical; **~e Reinigung** dry cleaning

Chemothera'pie [çemotera'piː] *f* MED chemotherapy

Chiffre ['ʃɪfrə] *f* (-; -n) code, cipher; box (number); **chiffrieren** [ʃɪ'friːrən] *v/t* (*no -ge-*, h) (en)code

China ['çiːna] China; **Chinese** [çi-'neːzə] *m* (-n; -n), **Chi'nesin** *f* (-; nen), **chi'nesisch** *adj* Chinese

Chinin [çi'niːn] *n* (-s; *no pl*) PHARM quinine

Chip [tʃɪp] *m* (-s; -s) *a.* IT chip; GASTR *pl* chips, *Br* crisps

Chirurg [çi'rʊrk] *m* (-en; -en) surgeon

Chirurgie [çirʊr'giː] *f* (-; -n) surgery

Chirurgin [çi'rʊrgɪn] *f* (-; -nen) surgeon

chirurgisch [çi'rʊrgɪʃ] *adj* surgical

Chlor [kloːɐ] *n* (-s; *no pl*) CHEM chlorine

chloren ['kloːrən] *v/t* (ge-, h) chlorinate

Cholera ['koːlera] *f* (-; *no pl*) MED cholera; **cholerisch** [ko'leːrɪʃ] *adj* choleric

Cholesterin [çoleste'riːn] *n* (-s; *no pl*) MED cholesterol

Chor [koːɐ] *m* (-[e]s; *Chöre* ['køːrə]) MUS choir (*a.* ARCH); *im ~* in chorus

Choral [ko'raːl] *m* (-s; *Chöräle* [ko-

're:lə]) MUS, REL chorale, hymn

Christ [krɪst] *m* (*-en*; *-en*) REL Christian;
~**baum** *m* Christmas tree

'**Christenheit:** *die* ~ REL Christendom

'**Christentum** *n* (*-s*; *no pl*) REL Christianity

Christin ['krɪstɪn] *f* (*-*; *-nen*) REL Christian

'**Christkind** *n* Infant Jesus; Father Christmas, Santa Claus

'**christlich** *adj* REL Christian

Christus ['krɪstʊs] REL Christ; *vor* ~ B.C.; *nach* ~ A.D.

Chrom [kro:m] *n* (*-s*; *no pl*) chrome, CHEM *a.* chromium

Chromosom [kromo'zo:m] *n* (*-s*; *-en*) BIOL chromosome

Chronik ['kro:nɪk] *f* (*-*; *-en*) chronicle

chronisch ['kro:nɪʃ] *adj* MED chronic

chronologisch [krono'lo:gɪʃ] *adj* chronological

circa → **zirka**

City ['sɪtɪ] *f* (*-*; *-s*) downtown, (city) center, *Br* centre

Clique ['klɪkə] *f* (*-*; *-n*) F group, set; *contp* clique

Clou [klu:] F *m* (*-s*; *-s*) highlight, climax;

der ~ *daran* the whole point of it

Compact Disc, **Compact Disk** ['kəmpæktdɪsk] *f* (*-*; *-s*) compact disk (*Br* disc)

Computer [kɔm'pju:tɐ] *m* (*-s*; *-*) computer; ~**ausdruck** *m* computer printout

com'puter|gesteuert *adj* computer-controlled; ~**gestützt** *adj* computer-aided

Com'putergrafik *f* computer graphics

computerisieren [kɔmpjutəri'zi:rən] *v/t* (*no* -ge-, *h*) computerize

Com'puter|spiel *n* computer game; ~**virus** *m* computer virus

Conférencier [ko-fera-'sje:] *m* (*-s*; *-s*) master of ceremonies, F emcee, MC, *Br* compère

Cord *etc* → **Kord** *etc*

Couch [kautʃ] *f* (*-*; *-s*) couch

Coupé [ku'pe:] *n* (*-s*; *-s*) MOT coupé

Coupon → **Kupon**

Cousin [ku'zɛ-:] *m* (*-s*; *-s*), **Cousine** [ku'zi:nə] *f* (*-*; *-n*) cousin

Creme [kre:m] *f* (*-*; *-s*) cream (*a. fig*)

Curry ['kari] *m* (*-s*; *-s*) curry powder

Cursor ['kɜ:sə] *m* (*-s*; *-s*) IT cursor

D

da [da:] **1.** *adv* space: there; here; *time*: then, at that time; ~ *drüben* (*draußen, hinten*) over (out, back) there; *von* ~ *aus* from there; *das ...* ~ that ... (over there); ~ *kommt er* here he comes; ~ *bin ich* here I am; ~ *sein* be there; exist; *ist noch ...* ~? is any ... left?; *noch nie* ~ *gewesen* unprecedented; *er ist gleich wieder* ~ he'll be right back; *von* ~ *an* or *ab* from then on **2.** *cj* as, since, because

'**dabehalten** *v/t* (*irr*, *halten*, *sep*, *no* -ge-, *h*) keep; *j-n* ~ keep s.o. in

dabei [da'bai] *adv* there, present; near *or* close by; at the same time; included with it; ~ *sein* be there; take part; be in on it; *ich bin* ~! count me in!; *er ist gerade* ~ *zu gehen* he's just leaving; *es ist nichts* ~ there's nothing to it; there's no harm in it; *was ist schon* ~? (so) what of it?; *lassen wir es* ~!

let's leave it at that!; ~**bleiben** *v/i* (*irr*, *bleiben*, *sep*, *-ge-*, *sein*) stick to it; ~**haben** F *v/t* (*irr*, *haben*, *sep*, *-ge-*, *h*) have with (*or* on) one

'**dableiben** *v/i* (*irr*, *bleiben*, *sep*, *-ge-*, *sein*) stay

Dach [dax] *n* (*-[e]s*; *Dächer* ['dɛçɐ]) roof

'**Dach|boden** *m* attic; ~**decker** ['daxdekɐ] *m* (*-s*; *-*) roofer; ~**fenster** *n* dormer window; ~**gepäckträger** *m* MOT roof-rack

'**Dachgeschoss** *n*, '**Dachgeschoß** *Austrian n* attic; ~**wohnung** *f* loft apartment, *Br* attic flat

'**Dach|kammer** *f* garret; ~**luke** *f* skylight; ~**pappe** *f* roofing felt; ~**rinne** *f* gutter

Dachs [daks] *m* (*-es*; *-e*) ZO badger

'**Dachstuhl** *m* roof framework

dachte ['daxtə] *pret of* **denken**

'**Dachter,rasse** *f* roof terrace

'**Dachverband** *m* ECON *etc* umbrella organization

Dackel ['dakǝl] *m* (-*s*; -) ZO dachshund

'**dadurch** *adv and cj* this *or* that way; for this reason, so; ~, **dass** due to the fact that

dafür [da'fyːɐ] *adv* for it, for that; instead; in return, in exchange; ~ **sein** be in favo(u)r of it; **er kann nichts** ~ it is not his fault; ~ **sorgen, dass** see to it that

da'gegen *adv and cj* against it; however, on the other hand; ~ **sein** be against (*or* opposed to) it; **haben Sie et. ~, dass ich ...?** do you mind if I ...?; **wenn Sie nichts ~ haben** if you don't mind; **... ist nichts ~** ... can't compare

da'heim *adv* at home

'**daher** *adv and cj* from there; that's why

da'hin *adv* there, to that place; gone, past; **bis ~** till then; up to there

da'hinten *adv* back there

da'hinter *adv* behind it; **es steckt nichts ~** there is nothing to it; F ~ **kommen** find out (about it)

'**dalassen** F *v/t* (*irr*, *lassen*, *sep*, -*ge*-, *h*) leave behind

damalig ['daːmaːlɪç] *adj* then

damals ['daːmaːls] *adv* then, at that time

Dame ['daːmǝ] *f* (-; -*n*) lady; partner; *cards*, *chess*: queen; checkers, *Br* draughts

'**Damen...** *in cpds* ladies' ...; SPORT women's ...; **~binde** *f* sanitary napkin (*Br* towel)

'**damenhaft** *adj* ladylike

'**Damen|toi,lette** *f* ladies' room (*Br* toilet), *the ladies*; **~wahl** *f* ladies' choice

damit 1. ['daːmɪt] *adv* with it *or* that; by it, with it; **was will er ~ sagen?** what's he trying to say?; **wie steht es ~?** how about it?; ~ **einverstanden sein** have no objections **2.** [da'mɪt] *cj* so that; in order to *inf*; ~ **nicht** so as not to *inf*

Damm [dam] *m* (-[*e*]*s*; *Dämme* ['dɛmǝ]) dam; embankment

dämmerig ['dɛmǝrɪç] *adj* dim

'**Dämmerlicht** *n* (-[*e*]*s*; *no pl*) twilight

dämmern ['dɛmɐn] *v/i* (*ge*-, *h*) dawn (*a.* F *j-m* on s.o.); get dark *or* dusky

'**Dämmerung** *f* (-; -*en*) dusk; dawn

Dämon ['dɛːmɔn] *m* (-*s*; -*en* [dɛ-'moːnǝn]) demon; **dämonisch** [dɛ-'moːnɪʃ] *adj* demoniac(al)

Dampf [dampf] *m* (-[*e*]*s*; *Dämpfe* ['dɛmpfǝ]) steam; PHYS vapo(u)r

'**dampfen** *v/i* (*ge*-, *h and sein*) steam

dämpfen ['dɛmpfǝn] *v/t* (*ge*-, *h*) deaden; muffle (*voice*); soften (*light*, *sound*, *blow*); GASTR steam, stew; steam-iron; *fig* put a damper on; curb (*a.* ECON)

Dampfer ['dampfɐ] *m* (-*s*; -) steamer, steamship

'**Dampf|kochtopf** *m* pressure cooker; **~ma,schine** *f* steam engine; **~schiff** *n* steamer, steamship

da'nach *adv* after it *or* that; afterwards; for it; according to it; **ich fragte ihn ~** I asked him about it; F **mir ist nicht ~** I don't feel like it

Däne ['dɛːnǝ] *m* (-*n*; -*n*) Dane

da'neben *adv* next to it, beside it; besides, as well, at the same time; beside the mark; **~benehmen** F *v/refl* (*irr*, *nehmen*, *sep*, *no* -*ge*-, *h*) step out of line; **~gehen** F *v/i* (*irr*, *gehen*, *sep*, -*ge*-, *sien*) miss (the target); F misfire

'**Dänemark** Denmark

Dänin ['dɛːnɪn] *f* (-; -*nen*) Danish woman *or* girl; '**dänisch** *adj* Danish

dank [daŋk] *prp* (*gen*) thanks to

Dank *m* (-[*e*]*s*; *no pl*) thanks; **Gott sei ~!** thank God!; **vielen ~!** many thanks!

'**dankbar** *adj* grateful (*j-m* to s.o.); rewarding (*task etc*)

'**Dankbarkeit** *f* (-; *no pl*) gratitude

'**danken** *v/i* (*ge*-, *h*) thank (*j-m für et.* s.o. for s.th.); **danke** (**schön**) thank you (very much); (**nein**,) **danke** no, thank you; **nichts zu ~** not at all

dann [dan] *adv* then; ~ **und wann** (every) now and then

daran [da'ran] *adv* on it; **die, think etc** of it; *believe etc* in it; *suffer etc* from it; → **liegen**

darauf [da'rauf] *adv* on (top of) it; after (that); *listen, drink etc* to it; *proud etc* of it; *wait etc* for it; **am Tage ~** the day after; **zwei Jahre ~** two years later; ~ **kommt es an** that's what matters

darauf'hin *adv* after that; as a result

daraus [da'raus] *adv* from (*or* out of) it; **was ist ~ geworden?** what has become of it?; ~ **wird nichts!** F nothing doing!

Darbietung ['daːɐbiːtʊŋ] *f* (-; -*en*) presentation; performance

darin [da'rɪn] *adv* in it; ['daːrɪn] in that

darlegen ['daːɐleːgən] *v/t* (*sep*, *-ge-*, *h*) explain, set out

Darlehen ['daːɐleːən] *n* (*-s*; *-*) loan; *ein~ geben* grant a loan

Darm [darm] *m* (*-[e]s*; *Därme* ['dɛrmə]) ANAT bowel(s), intestine(s); GASTR skin; *~grippe* *f* MED intestinal flu

darstellen ['daːɐʃtɛlən] *v/t* (*sep*, *-ge-*, *h*) represent, show, depict; describe; THEA play, do; trace, graph; **'Darsteller(in)** (*-s*; *-/-*; *-nen*) THEA performer, actor (actress); **'Darstellung** *f* (*-*; *-en*) representation; description; account; portrayal

darüber [daˈryːbɐ] *adv* over *or* above it; across it; in the meantime; *write, talk etc* about it; *... und ~ ...* and more; *~ werden Jahre vergehen* that will take years

darum [daˈrʊm] *adv and cj* (a)round it; because of it, that's why; *~ bitten* ask for it; → *gehen*

darunter [daˈrʊntɐ] *adv* under *or* below it, underneath; among them; including; *... und ~ ...* and less; *was verstehst du ~?* what do you understand by it?

das [das] → *der*

'Dasein *n* (*-s*; *no pl*) life, existence

dass [das] *cj* that; so (that); *es sei denn, ~* unless; *nicht ~ ich wüsste* not that I know of

'dastehen *v/i* (*irr*, *stehen*, *sep*, *-ge-*, *h*) stand (there)

Datei [daˈtai] *f* (*-*; *-en*) IT file; *~verwaltung* *f* IT file management

Daten ['daːtən] *pl* data (*a*. IT), facts; particulars; *~bank* *f* (*-*; *-en*) database, data bank; *~schutz* *m* JUR data protection; *~speicher* *m* data memory *or* storage; *~träger* *m* data medium *or* carrier; *~übertragung* *f* data transfer; *~verarbeitung* *f* data processing

datieren [daˈtiːrən] *v/t and v/i* (*no -ge-*, *h*) date

Dativ ['daːtiːf] *m* (*-s*; *-e*) dative (case)

Dattel ['datəl] *f* (*-*; *-n*) date

Datum ['daːtʊm] *n* (*-s*; *Daten* ['daːtən]) date; *welches ~ haben wir heute?* what's the date today?

Dauer ['dauɐ] *f* (*-*; *no pl*) duration; continuance; *auf die ~* in the long run; *für die ~ von* for a period *or* term of; *von ~ sein* last; *~arbeitslosigkeit* *f* long-term unemployment; *~auftrag* *m* ECON standing order; *~geschwindigkeit* *f* MOT *etc* cruising speed

'dauerhaft *adj* lasting; durable

'Dauer|karte *f* season ticket; *~lauf* *m* SPORT jogging; *im ~* at a jog; *~lutscher* *m* lollipop

dauern *v/i* (*-ge-*, *h*) last, take; → *lange*

'Dauerwelle *f* permanent, *Br* perm

Daumen ['daumən] *m* (*-s*; *-*) ANAT thumb; F *j-m den ~ halten* keep one's fingers crossed (for s.o.); *am ~ lutschen* suck one's thumb

Daunen ['daunən] *pl* down

'Daunendecke *f* eiderdown

da'von *adv* (away) from it; by it; about it; away; of it *or* them; *et. ~ haben* get s.th. out of it; *das kommt ~!* there you are!, that will teach you!; *~kommen* *v/i* (*irr*, *kommen*, *sep*, *-ge-*, *sein*) escape, get away; *~laufen* *v/i* (*irr*, *laufen*, *sep*, *-ge-*, *sein*) run away

da'vor *adv* before it; in front of it; *be afraid*, *warn s.o. etc* of it

da'zu *adv* for it, for that purpose; in addition; *noch ~* into the bargain; *~ ist es da* that's what it's there for; *Salat ~?* a salad with it?; → *kommen*, *Lust*; *~gehören* *v/i* (*sep*, *no -ge-*, *h*) belong to it, be part of it; *~gehörig* *adj* belonging to it; *~kommen* *v/i* (*irr*, *kommen*, *sep*, *-ge-*, *sein*) join *s.o.*; be added

da'zwischen *adv* between (them); in between; among them; *~kommen* *v/i* (*irr*, *kommen*, *sep*, *-ge-*, *sein*) intervene, happen; *wenn nichts dazwischenkommt* if all goes well

DB [deːˈbeː] *abbr of* **Deutsche Bahn** German Rail

dealen ['diːlən] *v/i* (*-ge-*, *h*) F push drugs

Dealer ['diːlɐ] *m* (*-s*; *-*) drug dealer, F pusher

Debatte [deˈbatə] *f* (*-*; *-n*) debate

debattieren [debaˈtiːrən] *v/i* (*no -ge-*, *h*) debate (*über acc* on)

Debüt [deˈbyː] *n* (*-s*; *-s*) debut; *sein ~ geben* make your debut

dechiffrieren [deʃiˈfriːrən] *v/t* (*no -ge-*, *h*) decipher, decode

Deck [dɛk] *n* (*-[e]s*; *-s*) MAR deck

Decke ['dɛkə] *f* (*-*; *-n*) blanket; quilt; ARCH ceiling

Deckel ['dɛkəl] *m* (*-s*; *-*) lid, cover, top

'decken *v/t and v/i* (*-ge-*, *h*) cover (*a*. ZO), SPORT *a*. mark; *sich ~ (mit)* coincide (with); → *Tisch*

'Deckung *f* (-; *no pl*) cover; *boxing*: guard; *in ~ gehen* take cover

defekt [de'fɛkt] *adj* defective, faulty; TECH out of order; **De'fekt** *m* (-[e]s; -e) defect, fault

defensiv [defɛn'si:f] *adj*, **Defensive** [defɛn'zi:və] *f* (-; *no pl*) defensive

definieren [defi'ni:rən] *v/t* (*no -ge-, h*) define; **Definition** [defini'tsjo:n] *f* (-; -en) definition

Defizit ['de:fitsɪt] *n* (-s; -e) deficit; deficiency

Degen ['de:gən] *m* (-s; -) sword; *fencing*: épée

degradieren [degra'di:rən] *v/t* (*no -ge-, h*) degrade (*a. fig*)

dehnbar ['de:nba:ɐ] *adj* flexible, elastic (*a. fig*); **dehnen** ['de:nən] *v/t* (*ge-, h*) stretch (*a. fig*).

Deich [daiç] *m* (-[e]s; -e) dike

Deichsel ['daiksəl] *f* (-; -n) pole, shaft

dein [dain] *poss pron* your; **~er, ~e, ~(e)s** yours; **deinerseits** ['dainɐ'zaits] *adv* on your part; **deines'gleichen** ['dai-nəsglaiçən] *pron contp* the likes of you **deinetwegen** ['dainɐt've:gən] *adv* for your sake; because of you

Dekan [de'ka:n] *m* (-s; -e), **De'kanin** *f* (-; -nen) REL, UNIV dean

Deklination [deklina'tsjo:n] *f* (-; -en) LING declension; **deklinieren** [dekli-'ni:rən] *v/t* (*no -ge-, h*) decline

Dekolleté [dekɔl'te:] *n* (-s; -s) low neck-line

Dekorateur [dekora'tø:ɐ] *m* (-s; -e), **Dekora'teurin** *f* (-; -nen) decorator; window dresser; **Dekoration** [dekora-'tsjo:n] *f* (-; -en) decoration; (window) display; THEA scenery; **dekorativ** [dckora'ti:f] *adj* decorative; **dekorie-ren** [deko'ri:rən] *v/t* (*no -ge-, h*) deco-rate; dress

Delfin → *Delphin*

delikat [deli'ka:t] *adj* delicious, exquis-ite; *fig* delicate, ticklish

Delikatesse [delika'tɛsə] *f* (-; -n) delica-cy; **Delika'tessenladen** *m* delicates-sen, F deli

Delphin [dɛl'fi:n] *m* (-s; -e) zo dolphin

Dementi [de'mɛnti] *n* (-s; -s) (official) denial; **dementieren** [demɛn'ti:rən] *v/t* (*no -ge-, h*) deny (officially)

dementsprechend,   demgemäß

['de:mgəmɛ:s] *adv* accordingly

'demnach *adv* according to that

'demnächst *adv* shortly, before long

Demo ['de:mo] F *f f* (-; -s) demo

Demokrat [demo'kra:t] *m* (-en; -en) democrat; **Demokratie** [demokra'ti:] *f* (-; -n) democracy; **Demo'kratin** *f* (-; -nen) democrat; **demo'kratisch** *adj* democratic

demolieren [demo'li:rən] *v/t* (*no -ge-, h*) demolish, wreck

Demonstrant [demɔn'strant] *m* (-en; -en), **Demon'strantin** *f* (-; -nen) dem-onstrator; **Demonstration** [demɔnstra'tsjo:n] *f* (-; -en) demon-stration; **demonstrieren** [demɔn-'stri:rən] *v/t and v/i* (*no -ge-, h*) demon-strate

demontieren [demɔn'ti:rən] *v/t* (*no -ge-, h*) dismantle

demoralisieren [demorali'zi:rən] *v/t* (*no -ge-, h*) demoralize

Demoskopie [demosko'pi:] *f* (-; -n) public opinion research

Demut ['de:mu:t] *f* (-; *no pl*) humility, humbleness; **demütig** ['de:my:tɪç] *adj* humble; **demütigen** ['de:my:tɪ-gən] *v/t* (*ge-, h*) humiliate; **'Demütigung** *f* (-; -en) humiliation

denkbar ['dɛŋkba:ɐ] **1.** *adj* conceivable **2.** *adv*: **~ einfach** most simple

denken ['dɛŋkən] *v/t and v/i* (*irr, ge-, h*) think (**an** *acc*, **über** *acc* of, about); **da-ran ~** (**zu** *inf*) remember (to *inf*)

'Denkfa,brik *f* think tank

'Denkmal *n* monument; memorial

'denkwürdig *adj* memorable

denn [dɛn] *cj and adv* for, because; *es sei ~, dass* unless; *mehr ~ je* more than ever; **dennoch** ['dɛnnɔx] *cj* yet, still, nevertheless

Denunziant [denun'tsjant] *m* (-en; -en) informer; **denunzieren** [denun-'tsi:rən] *v/t* (*no -ge-, h*) inform on *or* against

Deodorant [deʔodo'rant] *n* (-s; -e, -s) deodorant

Deponie [depo'ni:] *f* (-; -n) dump, waste disposal site

deponieren [depo'ni:rən] *v/t* (*no -ge-, h*) deposit, leave

Depot [de'po:] *n* (-s; -s) depot (*a.* MIL); *Swiss*: deposit

Depression [deprɛ'sjo:n] *f* (-; -en) depression (a. ECON)

depressiv [deprɛ'siːf] adj depressive

deprimieren [depri'miːrən] v/t (no -ge-, h) depress; **~d** adj depressing

deprimiert [depri'miːɐt] adj depressed

der [deːɐ], **die** [diː], **das** [das] **1.** art the **2.** dem pron that, this; he, she, it; **die** pl these, those, they **3.** rel pron who, which, that; '**derartig 1.** adv so (much); like that **2.** adj such (as this)

derb [dɛrp] adj coarse; tough, sturdy

'**der'gleichen** dem pron: **nichts ~** nothing of the kind

derjenige ['deːɐje:nɪgə], **diejenige** ['diːje:nɪgə], **dasjenige** ['dasje:nɪgə] dem pron the one; **diejenigen** pl the ones, those

dermaßen ['deːɐ'maːsən] adv so (much), like that

Dermatologe [dɛrmato'loːgə] m (-n; -n), **Dermato'login** f (-; -nen) dermatologist **derselbe** [dɛr'zɛlbə], **dieselbe** [diː'zɛlbə], **dasselbe** [das'zɛlbə] dem pron the same

Deserteur [dezɛr'tøːɐ] m (-s; -e) MIL deserter; **desertieren** [dezɛr'tiːrən] v/i (no -ge-, sein) MIL desert

deshalb ['dɛs'halp] cj and adv therefore, for that reason, that is why, so

Desinfektionsmittel [dɛsʔɪnfɛk-'tsjoːnsmɪtəl] n MED disinfectant

desinfizieren [dɛsʔɪnfi'tsiːrən] v/t (no -ge-, h) MED disinfect

'**Desinteresse** n (-s; no pl) indifference

'**desinteres‚siert** adj uninterested, indifferent

destillieren [dɛstɪ'liːrən] v/t (no -ge-, h) distil(l)

desto ['dɛsto] cj and adv → **je**

'**des'wegen** cj and adv → **deshalb**

Detail [de'tai] n (-s; -s) detail

detailliert [deta'jiːɐt] adj detailed

Detektiv [detɛk'tiːf] m (-s; -e) detective

deuten ['dɔytən] (ge-, h) **1.** v/t interpret **2.** v/i: **~ auf** (acc) point at

'**deutlich** adj clear, distinct, plain

deutsch [dɔytʃ] adj German; **auf Deutsch** in German

'**Deutsche** m, f (-n; -n) German

'**Deutschland** Germany

Devise [de'viːzə] f (-; -n) motto

De'visen pl ECON foreign currency

Dezember [de'tsɛmbɐ] m (-[s]; -) December

dezent [de'tsɛnt] adj discreet, unobtrusive; conservative (clothes etc); soft (music etc)

Dezimal... [detsi'maːl-] MATH in cpds ...bruch, ...system etc: decimal ...; **~stelle** f MATH decimal (place)

DGB [deːgeː'beː] abbr of **Deutscher Gewerkschaftsbund** Federation of German Trade Unions

d. h. abbr of **das heißt** i. e., that is

Dia ['diːa] n (-s; -s) PHOT slide

Diagnose [dia'gnoːzə] f (-; -n) diagnosis

diagonal [diago'naːl] adj, **Diago'nale** f (-; -n) diagonal

Dialekt [dia'lɛkt] m (-[e]s; -e) dialect

Dialog [dia'loːk] m (-[e]s; -e) dialog, Br dialogue

Diamant [dia'mant] m (-en; -en) diamond

'**Diapro‚jektor** m slide projector

Diät [di'ɛːt] f (-; -en) diet; **e-e ~ machen (Diät leben)** be on (keep to) a diet

Di'äten pl PARL allowance

dich [dɪç] pers pron you; **~ (selbst)** yourself

dicht [dɪçt] **1.** adj dense, a. thick (fog); heavy (traffic); F closed, shut **2.** adv: **~ an** (dat) or **bei** close to

'**dichten** v/t and v/i (ge-, h) write (poetry); **Dichter(in)** ['dɪçtɐ, 'dɪçtərɪn] m(f) (-s; -/-; -nen) poet; writer; **dichterisch** ['dɪçtərɪʃ] adj poetic; **~e Freiheit** poetic licen|se, Br -ce

'**dichthalten** F v/i (irr, **halten**, sep, -ge-, h) keep mum

'**Dichtung**[1] f (-; -en) TECH seal(ing)

'**Dichtung**[2] f (-; -en) poetry

dick [dɪk] adj thick; fat; **es macht ~** it's fattening

'**Dicke** f (-; -n) thickness; fatness;

'**dickfellig** F adj thick-skinned

'**dickflüssig** adj thick; TECH viscous

Dickicht ['dɪkɪçt] n (-[e]s; -e) thicket

'**Dick|kopf** m stubborn or pig-headed person; **~milch** f soured milk

Dieb [diːp] m (-[e]s; -e [-'biːbə]), **Diebin** ['diːbɪn] f (-; -nen) thief

diebisch ['diːbɪʃ] adj thievish; fig malicious (glee etc)

Diebstahl ['diːpʃtaːl] m (-[e]s; -stähle ['diːpʃtɛːlə]) theft; JUR mst larceny

Diele ['diːlə] f (-; -n) board, plank; hallway, Br a. hall

dienen ['diːnən] v/i (ge-, h) serve (**j-m**

s.o.; *als* as); **Diener** ['di:nɐ] *m* (-*s*; -) servant; *fig* bow (*vor dat* to)

Dienst [di:nst] *m* (-[*e*]*s*; -*e*) service; work; ~ **haben** be on duty; *im* (*außer*) ~ on (off) duty; ~ *tuend* on duty; ~... *in cpds* ...wagen, ...wohnung *etc*: official ..., company ..., business ...

'**Dienstag** *m* (-[*e*]*s*; -*e*) Tuesday

'**Dienstalter** *n* seniority, length of service

'**dienstbereit** *adj* on duty

diensteifrig *adj* (*contp* over-)eager

'**Dienstgrad** *m* grade, rank (*a*. MIL)

'**Dienstleistung** *f* service

'**dienstlich** *adj* official

'**Dienstreise** *f* business trip

'**Dienststunden** *pl* office hours

'**Dienstweg** *m* official channels

dies [di:s], **dieser** ['di:zɐ], **diese** ['di:zə], **dieses** ['di:zəs] *dem pron* this; this one; *diese pl* these

diesig ['di:zɪç] *adj* hazy, misty

diesjährig ['di:sjɛːrɪç] *adj* this year's

'**diesmal** *adv* this time

diesseits ['di:szaits] *prp* (*gen*) on this side of; '**Diesseits** *n* (-; *no pl*) this life *or* world

Dietrich ['di:trɪç] *m* (-*s*; -*e*) TECH picklock, skeleton key

Differenz [dɪfə'rɛnts] *f* (-; -*en*) difference; disagreement

differenzieren [dɪfərɛn'tsiːrən] *v/i* (*no -ge-*, *h*) distinguish

Digital... [digi'ta:l] *in cpds* ...anzeige, ...uhr *etc*: digital ...

Diktat [dɪk'ta:t] *n* (-[*e*]*s*; -*e*) dictation; **Diktator** [dɪk'ta:to:ɐ] *m* (-*s*; -*en*) [dɪkta'to:rən] dictator; **diktatorisch** [dɪkta'to:rɪʃ] *adj* dictatorial; **Diktatur** [dɪkta'tu:ɐ] *f* (-; -*en*) dictatorship; **diktieren** [dɪk'ti:rən] *v/t and v/i* (*no -ge-*, *h*) dictate

Dik'tiergerät *n* Dictaphone®

Dilettant [dile'tant] *m* (-*en*; -*en*) amateur; **dilet'tantisch** *adj* amateurish

DIN® [di:n] *abbr of* **Deutsches Institut für Normung** German Institute for Standardization

Ding [dɪŋ] *n* (-[*e*]*s*; -*e*) thing; *vor allen ~en* above all; F *ein ~ drehen* pull a job

'**Dings(bums)** *m*, *f*, *n*, **Dingsda** *m*, *f*, *n* F thingamajig, whatchamacallit

Dinosaurier [dino'zaurjɐ] *m* (-*s*; -) ZO dinosaur

Dioxid ['di:ʔɔksy:t] *n* (-*s*; -*e*) CHEM dioxide

Dioxin [dio'ksi:n] *n* (-*s*; -*e*) CHEM dioxin

Diphtherie [dɪfte'ri:] *f* (-; -*n*) MED diphtheria

Diplom [di'plo:m] *n* (-*s*; -*e*) diploma, degree; ~... *in cpds* ...ingenieur *etc*: qualified ..., graduate ...

Diplomat [diplo'ma:t] *m* (-*en*; -*en*) diplomat; **Diplomatie** [diploma'ti:] *f* (-; *no pl*) diplomacy; **Diplo'matin** *f* (-; -*nen*) diplomat; **diplo'matisch** *adj* diplomatic (*a*. *fig*)

dir [di:ɐ] *pers pron* (to) you; ~ (*selbst*) yourself

direkt [di'rɛkt] **1.** *adj* direct; TV live **2.** *adv* direct; *fig* directly, right; TV live; ~ *gegenüber* (*von*) right across

Direktion [dirɛk'tsjo:n] *f* (-; -*en*) management

Direktor [di'rɛkto:ɐ] *m* (-*s*; -*en* [dirɛk'to:rən]) director, manager; PED principal, *Br* headmaster; **Direktorin** [dirɛk'to:rɪn] (-; -*nen*) director, manager; PED principal, *Br* headmistress

Di'rektübertragung *f* TV live transmission *or* broadcast

Dirigent [diri'gɛnt] *m* (-*en*; -*en*) conductor; **dirigieren** [diri'gi:rən] *v/t and v/i* (*no -ge-*, *h*) MUS conduct; *fig* direct

Dirne ['dɪrnə] *f* (-; -*n*) prostitute, whore

Discman® *m* (-*s*; -*men*) portable CD player, Discman®

Disharmo'nie [dɪsharmo'ni:] *f* MUS dissonance (*a*. *fig*); **dishar'monisch** *adj* MUS discordant

Diskette [dɪs'kɛtə] *f* (-; -*n*) diskette, floppy (disk); **Dis'kettenlaufwerk** *n* disk drive

Disko ['dɪsko] *f* (-; -*s*) disco

Diskont [dɪs'kɔnt] *m* (-*s*; -*e*) ECON discount

Diskothek [dɪsko'te:k] (-; -*en*) disco, discotheque

diskret [dɪs'kre:t] *adj* discreet; **Diskretion** [dɪskre'tsjo:n] *f* (-; *no pl*) discretion

diskriminieren [dɪskrimi'ni:rən] *v/t* (*no -ge-*, *h*) discriminate against

Diskri'minierung *f* (-; -*en*) discrimination (*von* against)

Diskussion [dɪsku'sjo:n] *f* (-; -*en*) discussion, debate

Diskussi'ons|leiter *m* (panel) chair-

man; **~runde** f, **~teilnehmer** pl panel
Diskuswerfen ['dɪskʊsvɛrfən] n (-s; no pl) SPORT discus throwing
diskutieren [dɪsku'tiːrən] v/t and v/i (no -ge-, h) discuss
Disqualifikati'on f SPORT disqualification (**wegen** for); **disqualifi'zieren** v/t (no -ge-, h) SPORT disqualify
Dissident [dɪsi'dɛnt] m (-en; -en), **Dissi'dentin** f (-; -nen) POL dissident
Distanz [dɪs'tants] f (-; -en) distance
distanzieren [dɪstan'tsiːrən] v/refl (no -ge-, h) distance o.s. (**von** from)
Distel ['dɪstəl] f (-; -n) BOT thistle
Distrikt [dɪs'trɪkt] m (-[e]s; -e) district
Disziplin [dɪstsi'pliːn] f (-; -en) (no pl) discipline; SPORT event; **diszipliniert** [dɪstsipli'niːrt] adj disciplined
divers [di'vɛrs] adj various; several
Dividende [divi'dɛndə] f (-; -n) ECON dividend
dividieren [divi'diːrən] v/t (no -ge-, h) MATH divide (**durch** by)
Division [divi'zjoːn] f (-; -en) MATH, MIL division
DJH [deːjɔt'haː] abbr of **Deutsches Jugendherbergswerk** German Youth Hostel Association
DM [deːˈɛm] abbr of **Deutsche Mark** hist (former monetary unit of Germany) German mark(s)
doch [dɔx] cj and adv but, however, yet; **kommst du nicht (mit)? - ~!** aren't you coming? - (oh) yes, I am!; **ich war es nicht - ~!** I didn't do it - yes, you did!; **er kam also ~?** so he did come after all?; **du kommst ~?** you're coming, aren't you?; **kommen Sie ~ herein!** do come in!; **wenn ~ ...!** if only ...!
Docht [dɔxt] m (-[e]s; -e) wick
Dock [dɔk] n (-s; -s) MAR dock
Dogge ['dɔgə] f (-; -n) ZO mastiff; Great Dane
Dogma ['dɔgma] n (-s; Dogmen ['dɔgmən]) dogma; **dogmatisch** [dɔg'maːtɪʃ] adj dogmatic
Dohle ['doːlə] f (-; -n) ZO (jack)daw
Doktor ['dɔktoːr] m (-s; -en [dɔk'toːrən]) doctor; UNIV doctor's degree; **~arbeit** f UNIV (doctoral or PhD) thesis
Dokument [doku'mɛnt] n (-[e]s; -e) document
Dokumentar... [dokumɛn'taːr-] in cpds ...spiel etc: documentary ...; **~film**

m documentary (film)
Dolch [dɔlç] m (-[e]s; -e) dagger
Dollar ['dɔlar] m (-[s]; -s) dollar
dolmetschen ['dɔlmɛtʃən] v/i (ge-, h) interpret; **'Dolmetscher(in)** (-s; -/-; -nen) interpreter
Dom [doːm] m (-[e]s; -e) cathedral
dominierend [domi'niːrənt] adj (pre-) dominant
Dompteur [dɔmp'tøːr] m (-s; -e), **Dompteuse** [dɔmp'tøːzə] f (-; -n) animal tamer or trainer
Donner ['dɔnɐ] m (-s; no pl) thunder
'donnern v/i (ge-, h) thunder (a. fig)
'Donnerstag m (-[e]s; -e) Thursday
'Donnerwetter F n (-s; -) dressing-down; **~!** wow!
doof [doːf] F adj stupid, dumb
Doppel ['dɔpəl] n (-s; -) duplicate; tennis etc: doubles; **~...** in cpds ...bett, ...zimmer etc: double ...
Doppeldecker ['dɔpəldɛkɐ] m (-s; -) AVIAT biplane; MOT double-decker (bus)
Doppelgänger ['dɔpəlgɛŋɐ] m (-s; -) double, look-alike
'Doppel|pass m soccer: wall pass; **~punkt** m LING colon; **~stecker** m ELECTR two-way adapter
doppelt adj double; **~ so viel (wie)** twice as much (as)
'Doppelverdiener pl two-income family
Dorf [dɔrf] n (-[e]s; Dörfer ['dœrfɐ]) village; **~bewohner** m villager
Dorn [dɔrn] m (-[e]s; -en) BOT thorn (a. fig); TECH tongue; spike
'dornig adj thorny (a. fig)
Dorsch [dɔrʃ] m (-[e]s; -e) ZO cod(fish)
dort [dɔrt] adv there
'dorther adv from there
'dorthin adv there
Dose ['doːzə] f (-; -n) can, Br a. tin
'Dosen... in cpds canned, Br a. tinned
dösen ['døːzən] F v/i (ge-, h) doze
'Dosenöffner m can (Br tin) opener
Dosis ['doːzɪs] f (-; Dosen) MED dose
Dotter ['dɔtɐ] m, n (-s; -) yolk
Double ['duːbəl] n (-s; -s) film: stunt man (or woman)
Dozent [do'tsɛnt] m (-en; -en), **Do'zentin** f (-; -nen) (university) lecturer, assistant professor

Dr. *abbr of* **Doktor** Dr., Doctor

Drache ['draxə] *m* (*-n*; *-n*) dragon

'**Drachen** *m* (*-s*; *-*) kite; SPORT hang glider; **e-n ~ steigen lassen** fly a kite; **~fliegen** *n* SPORT hang gliding

Draht [dra:t] *m* (*-[e]s*; **Drähte** ['drɛ:tə]) wire; F **auf ~ sein** be on the ball

drahtig ['dra:tɪç] *fig adj* wiry

'**drahtlos** *adj* wireless

'**Drahtseil** *n* TECH cable; *circus*: tightrope; **~bahn** *f* cable railway

'**Drahtzieher** *fig m* (*-s*; *-*) wirepuller

drall [dral] *adj* buxom, strapping

Drall *m* (*-[e]s*; *no pl*) twist, spin

Drama ['dra:ma] *n* (*-s*; **Dramen**) drama

Dramatiker [dra'ma:tikɐ] *m* (*-s*; *-*) dramatist, playwright

dra'matisch *adj* dramatic

dran [dran] F *adv* → **daran**; **du bist ~** it's your turn; *fig* you're in for it

drang [draŋ] *pret of* **dringen**

Drang *m* (*-[e]s*; *no pl*) urge, drive (**nach** for)

drängeln ['drɛŋəln] F *v/t and v/i* (*ge-*, *h*) push, shove

drängen ['drɛŋən] *v/t and v/i* (*ge-*, *h*) push, shove; **j-n zu et. ~** press *or* urge s.o. to do s.th.; **sich ~** press; force one's way; **~d** *adj* pressing

'**drankommen** F *v/i* (*irr*, **kommen**, *sep*, *-ge-*, *sein*) have one's turn; **als erster ~** be first

drastisch ['drastɪʃ] *adj* drastic

drauf [drauf] F *adv* → **darauf**; **~ und dran sein, et. zu tun** be just about to do s.th.; **Draufgänger** ['draufɡɛŋɐ] *m* (*-s*; *-*) daredevil

draus [draus] F *adv* → **daraus**

draußen ['drausən] *adv* outside; outdoors; **da ~** out there; **bleib(t) ~!** keep out!

drechseln ['drɛksəln] *v/t* (*ge-*, *h*) turn (on a lathe)

Drechsler ['drɛkslɐ] *m* (*-s*; *-*) turner

Dreck [drɛk] F *m* (*-[e]s*; *no pl*) dirt; filth (*a. fig*); mud; *fig* trash; **dreckig** ['drɛkɪç] F *adj* dirty; filthy (*both a. fig*)

Dreh|arbeiten ['dre:arbaitən] *pl film*: shooting; **~bank** *f* (*-*; *-bänke*) TECH lathe

'**drehbar** *adj* revolving, rotating

'**Drehbuch** *n film*: script

drehen ['dre:ən] *v/t* (*ge-*, *h*) turn; *film*: shoot; roll; **sich ~** turn, rotate; spin; **sich ~ um** *fig* be about; → **Ding**

Dreher ['dre:ɐ] *m* (*-s*; *-*) TECH turner

'**Dreh|kreuz** *n* turnstile; **~orgel** *f* barrel organ; **~ort** *m film*: location; **~strom** *m* ELECTR three-phase current; **~stuhl** *m* swivel chair; **~tür** *f* revolving door

'**Drehung** *f* (*-*; *-en*) turn; rotation

'**Drehzahl** *f* TECH (number of) revolutions; **~messer** *m* MOT rev(olution) counter

drei [drai] *adj* three

Drei *f* (*-*; *-en*) three; *grade*: fair, C

'**drei|beinig** *adj* three-legged; **~dimensio.nal** *adj* three-dimensional

'**Dreieck** *n* (*-[e]s*; *-e*) triangle

'**dreieckig** *adj* triangular

dreierlei ['draiɐlai] *adj* three kinds of

'**dreifach** *adj* threefold, triple

'**Drei|gang...** TECH *in cpds* three-speed ...; **~kampf** *m* SPORT triathlon; **~rad** *n* tricycle; **~satz** *m* (*-es*; *no pl*) MATH rule of three; **~sprung** *m* (*-[e]s*; *no pl*) SPORT triple jump

dreißig ['draisɪç] *adj* thirty

'**dreißigste** *adj* thirtieth

dreist [draist] *adj* brazen, impertinent

dreistufig ['draiʃtu:fɪç] *adj* three-stage

'**dreizehn(te)** *adj* thirteen(th)

Dresche ['drɛʃə] F *f* (*-*; *no pl*) thrashing

'**dreschen** *v/t and v/i* (*irr*, *ge-*, *h*) AGR thresh; thrash; '**Dreschma,schine** *f* AGR threshing machine

dressieren [drɛ'si:rən] *v/t* (*no -ge-*, *h*) train

Dressman ['drɛsmən] *m* (*-s*; *-men*) male model

Dressur [drɛ'su:ɐ] *f* (*-*; *-en*) training; act; **~reiten** *n* dressage

dribbeln ['drɪbəln] *v/i* (*ge-*, *h*), **Dribbling** *n* (*-s*; *-s*) SPORT dribble

drillen ['drɪlən] *v/t* (*ge-*, *h*) MIL drill (*a. fig*)

Drillinge ['drɪlɪŋə] *pl* triplets

drin [drɪn] F *adv* → **darin**; **das ist nicht ~!** no way!

dringen ['drɪŋən] *v/i* (*irr*, *ge-*, *h*) **~ auf** (*acc*) insist on; **~ aus** come from; **~ durch** force one's way through, penetrate, pierce; **~ in** (*acc*) penetrate into; **darauf~, dass** urge that; **~d** *adj* urgent, pressing; strong (*suspicion etc*)

drinnen ['drɪnən] F *adv* inside; indoors

dritte ['drɪtə] *adj* third; **wir sind zu dritt** there are three of us; **die Dritte Welt** the Third World; '**Drittel** *n* (*-s*; *-*) third;

'**drittens** *adv* thirdly; '**Dritte-Welt-Laden** *m* third world shop

Droge ['dro:gə] *f* (-; *-n*) drug

'**drogenabhängig** *adj* addicted to drugs; **~ sein** be a drug addict

'**Drogen|abhängige** *m, f* (-*n*; -*n*) drug addict; **~missbrauch** *m* drug abuse

'**drogensüchtig** → **drogenabhängig**

'**Drogentote** *m, f* drug victim

Drogerie [drogə'ri:] *f* (-; *-n*) drugstore, *Br* chemist's (shop)

Drogist [dro'gɪst] *m* (-*en*; -*en*), **Drogistin** *f* (-; *-nen*) chemist

drohen ['dro:ən] *v/i* (ge-, *h*) threaten, menace

dröhnen ['drø:nən] *v/i* (ge-, *h*) roar

'**Drohung** *f* (-; *-en*) threat (**gegen** to)

drollig ['drɔlɪç] *adj* funny, droll

Dromedar [dromə'da:ɐ] *n* (-*s*; -*e*) ZO dromedary

drosch [drɔʃ] *pret of* **dreschen**

Drossel ['drɔsəl] *f* (-; *-n*) ZO thrush

'**drosseln** *v/t* (ge-, *h*) TECH throttle

drüben ['dry:bən] *adv* over there (*a. fig*)

drüber ['dry:bɐ] F *adv* → **darüber, drunter**

Druck [druk] *m* (-[*e*]*s*; -*e*) pressure; printing; print

'**Druckbuchstabe** *m* block letter

Drückeberger ['drykəbergɐ] F *m* (-*s*; -) shirker

'**drucken** *v/t* (ge-, *h*) print; **et. ~ lassen** have s.th. printed *or* published

drücken ['drykən] (ge-, *h*) **1.** *v/t* press; push; *fig* force down; **j-m die Hand ~** shake hands with s.o. **2.** *v/i* pinch **3.** F *v/refl:* **sich vor et. ~** shirk (doing) s.th.; **~d** *adj* heavy, oppressive

Drucker ['drukɐ] *m* (-*s*; -) printer (*a.* IT)

Drücker ['drykɐ] *m* (-*s*; -) latch; trigger; F hawker

Druckerei [drukə'rai] *f* (-; *-en*) printers

'**Druck|fehler** *m* misprint; **~kammer** *f* pressurized cabin; **~knopf** *m* snap fastener, *Br* press stud; TECH (push) button; **~luft** *f* TECH compressed air; **~sache** *f* printed (*or* second-class) matter; **~schrift** *f* block letters; **~taste** *f* TECH push button

drunter ['druntɐ] F *adv* → **darunter; es ging ~ und drüber** it was absolutely chaotic

Drüse ['dry:zə] *f* (-; *-n*) ANAT gland

Dschungel ['dʒuŋəl] *m* (-*s*; -) jungle (*a.* *fig*)

Dschunke ['dʒuŋkə] *f* (-; *-n*) MAR junk

du [du:] *pers pron* you

Dübel ['dy:bəl] *m* (-*s*; -), '**dübeln** *v/t* (*ge-, h*) TECH dowel

ducken ['dukən] *v/refl* (ge-, *h*) duck; *fig* cringe (**vor** *dat* before); crouch

Duckmäuser ['dukmɔyzɐ] *m* (-*s*; -) coward; yes-man

Dudelsack ['du:dəlzak] *m* MUS bagpipes

Duell [du'ɛl] *n* (-*s*; -*e*) duel; **duellieren** [duɛ'li:rən] *v/refl* (*no -ge-, h*) fight a duel

Duett [du'ɛt] *n* (-[*e*]*s*; -*e*) MUS duet

Duft [duft] *m* (-[*e*]*s*; *Düfte* ['dyftə]) scent, fragrance, smell (**nach** of); '**duften** *v/i* (ge-, *h*) smell (**nach** of); '**duftend** *adj* fragrant; '**duftig** *adj* dainty

dulden ['duldən] *v/t* (ge-, *h*) tolerate, put up with; suffer

duldsam ['dultza:m] *adj* tolerant

dumm [dum] *adj* stupid, F dumb

'**Dummheit** *f* (-; *-en*) (*no pl*) stupidity, ignorance; stupid *or* foolish thing

'**Dummkopf** *m contp* fool, blockhead

dumpf [dumpf] *adj* dull; *fig* vague

Düne ['dy:nə] *f* (-; *-n*) (sand) dune

Dung [duŋ] *m* (-[*e*]*s*; *no pl*) dung, manure

düngen ['dyŋən] *v/t* (ge-, *h*) fertilize; manure; **Dünger** ['dyŋɐ] *m* (-*s*; -) fertilizer; manure

dunkel ['duŋkəl] *adj* dark (*a. fig*)

'**Dunkelheit** *f* (-; *no pl*) dark(ness)

'**Dunkel|kammer** *f* PHOT darkroom; **~ziffer** *f* number of unreported cases

dünn [dyn] *adj* thin; weak (*coffee etc*)

Dunst [dunst] *m* (-[*e*]*s*; *Dünste* ['dynstə]) haze, mist; CHEM vapo(u)r; **dünsten** ['dynstən] *v/t* (ge-, *h*) GASTR stew, braise; '**dunstig** *adj* hazy, misty

Duplikat [dupli'ka:t] *n* (-[*e*]*s*; -*e*) duplicate; copy

Dur [du:ɐ] *n* (-; *no pl*) MUS major (key)

durch [durç] *prp* (*acc*) *and adv* through; across; MATH divided by; GASTR (well) done; **~ j-n** (**et.**) by s.o. (s.th.); **~ und ~** through and through

'**durcharbeiten** (*sep, -ge-, h*) **1.** *v/t* study thoroughly; **sich ~ durch** work (one's way) through a *text etc* **2.** *v/i* work without a break

durch'aus *adv* absolutely, quite; ~ *nicht* by no means

'durchblättern *v/t* (*sep*, *-ge-*, *h*) leaf *or* thumb through

'Durchblick *fig m* grasp *of s.th.*

'durchblicken *v/i* (*sep*, *-ge-*, *h*) look through; ~ *lassen* give to understand; *ich blicke* (*da*) *nicht durch* I don't get it

durch'bohren *v/t* (*no -ge-*, *h*) pierce; perforate

'durchbraten *v/t* (*irr*, *braten*, *sep*, *-ge-*, *h*) roast thoroughly

'durchbrechen[1] (*irr*, *brechen*, *sep*, *-ge-*) 1. *v/t* (*h*) break (in two) 2. *v/i* (*sein*) break through *or* apart

durch'brechen[2] *v/t* (*irr*, *brechen*, *no -ge-*, *h*) break through

'durch|brennen *v/i* (*irr*, *brennen*, *sep*, *-ge-*, *sein*) ELECTR blow; *reactor*: melt down; F run away

'durchbringen *v/t* (*irr*, *bringen*, *sep*, *-ge-*, *h*) get (MED pull) *s.o.* through; go through *one's money*; support (*family*)

'Durchbruch *m* breakthrough (*a. fig*)

durch'dacht *adj* (well) thought-out

'durchdrehen (*sep*, *-ge-*, *h*) 1. *v/i wheels*: spin; F *fig* crack up, flip 2. *v/t* GASTR grind, *Br* mince

'durchdringend *adj* piercing

durchei'nander *adv* confused; (in) a mess; ~*bringen* *v/t* (*irr*, *bringen*, *sep*, *-ge-*, *h*) confuse, mix up; mess up; **Durchei'nander** *n* (*-s*; *no pl*) confusion, mess

durch'fahren[1] *v/t* (*irr*, *fahren*, *no -ge-*, *h*) go (*or* pass, drive) through

'durchfahren[2] *v/i* (*irr*, *fahren*, *sep*, *-ge-*, *sein*) go (*or* pass, drive) through

'Durchfahrt *f* passage; ~ *verboten* no thoroughfare

'Durchfall *m* MED diarrh(o)ea

'durch|fallen *v/i* (*irr*, *fallen*, *sep*, *-ge-*, *sein*) fall through; fail, F flunk (*test etc*); F be a flop; *j-n* ~ *lassen* fail (F flunk) *s.o.*; ~*fragen* *v/refl* (*sep*, *-ge-*, *h*) ask one's way (*nach*, *zu* to)

'durchführbar *adj* practicable, feasible

'durchführen *v/t* (*sep*, *-ge-*, *h*) carry out, do

'Durchgang *m* passage

'Durchgangs... *in cpds* *...verkehr etc*: through ...; *...lager etc*: transit ...

'durchgebraten *adj* well done

'durchgehen (*irr*, *gehen*, *sep*, *-ge-*, *sein*) 1. *v/i* go through (*a.* RAIL *and* PARL); *fig* run away (*mit* with); *horse*: bolt 2. *v/t* go *or* look through; ~ *lassen* tolerate; ~*d* *adj* continuous; ~*er Zug* through train; ~ *geöffnet* open all day

'durchgreifen *fig v/i* (*irr*, *greifen*, *sep*, *-ge-*, *h*) take drastic measures; ~*d* *adj* drastic; radical

'durchhalten (*irr*, *halten*, *sep*, *-ge-*, *h*) 1. *v/t* keep up 2. *v/i* hold out

'durchhängen *v/i* (*irr*, *hängen*, *sep*, *-ge-*, *h*) sag; F have a low

'durchkämpfen *v/t* (*sep*, *-ge-*, *h*) fight out; *sich* ~ fight one's way through

'durchkommen *v/i* (*irr*, *kommen*, *sep*, *-ge-*, *sein*) come through (*a.* MED); get through; get along; get away (*mit e-r Lüge etc* with a lie *etc*)

durch'kreuzen *v/t* (*no -ge-*, *h*) cross, thwart

'durchlassen *v/t* (*irr*, *lassen*, *sep*, *-ge-*, *h*) let pass, let through

'durchlässig *adj* permeable (*für* to)

'durchlaufen[1] (*irr*, *laufen*, *sep*, *-ge-*) 1. *v/i* (*sein*) run through 2. *v/t* (*h*) wear through

durch'laufen[2] *v/t* (*irr*, *laufen*, *no -ge-*, *h*) pass through

'Durchlauferhitzer *m* (*-s*; *-*) (instant) water heater, *Br a.* geyser

'durchlesen *v/t* (*irr*, *lesen*, *sep*, *-ge-*, *h*) read through

durch|'leuchten *v/t* (*no -ge-*, *h*) MED X-ray; *fig* screen; ~*löchern* [durç-'lœçɐn] *v/t* (*no -ge-*, *h*) perforate, make holes in

'durchmachen F *v/t* (*sep*, *-ge-*, *h*) go through; *viel* ~ suffer a lot; *die Nacht* ~ make a night of it

'Durchmesser *m* (*-s*; *-*) diameter

durch'nässen *v/t* (*no -ge-*, *h*) soak

'durchnehmen *v/t* (*irr*, *nehmen*, *sep*, *-ge-*, *h*) PED do, deal with

'durchpausen *v/t* (*sep*, *-ge-*, *h*) trace

durch'queren *v/t* (*no*, *-ge-*, *h*) cross

'Durchreiche *f* (*-*; *-n*) hatch

'Durchreise *f*: *ich bin nur auf der* ~ I'm only passing through; **'durchreisen** *v/i* (*sep*, *-ge-*, *sein*) travel through

'Durchreisevisum *n* transit visa

'durch|reißen (*irr*, *reißen*, *sep*, *-ge-*) 1. *v/t* (*h*) tear (in two) 2. *v/i* (*sein*) tear, break; **~ringen** v/refl (irr, **ringen**, sep, -ge-, h) **sich ~, et. zu tun** bring o.s. to do s.th.

'Durchsage f announcement

durch'schauen v/t (no -ge-, h) see through s.o. or s.th.

'durchscheinen v/i (irr, **scheinen**, sep, -ge-, h) shine through; **~d** adj transparent

'durchscheuern v/t (sep, -ge-, h) chafe; wear through

'durchschlafen v/i (irr, **schlafen**, sep, -ge-, h) sleep through

'Durchschlag m (carbon) copy

durch'schlagen[1] v/t (irr, **schlagen**, no -ge-, h) cut in two; bullet etc: go through, pierce

'durchschlagen[2] (irr, **schlagen**, sep, -ge-) **1.** v/refl (h): **sich ~ nach** make one's way to **2.** v/i (sein) come through (a. fig); **~d** adj sweeping; effective

'Durch|schlagpa,pier n carbon paper; **~schlagskraft** fig f force, impact

'durchschneiden v/t (irr, **schneiden**, sep, -ge-, h) cut (through)

'Durchschnitt m average; **im (über, unter dem) ~** on an (above, below) average; **im ~ betragen (verdienen** etc) average

'durchschnittlich 1. adj average; ordinary **2.** adv on an average

'Durchschnitts... in cpds average ...

'Durchschrift f (carbon) copy

'durch|sehen v/t (irr, **sehen**, sep, -ge-, h) look or go through; check; **~setzen** v/t (sep, -ge-, h) put (or push) s.th. through; **s-n Kopf ~** have one's way; **sich ~** get one's way; be successful; **sich ~ können** have authority (**bei** over)

durch'setzt adj: **~ mit** interspersed with

'durchsichtig adj transparent (a. fig); clear; see-through

'durchsickern v/i (sep, -ge-, sein) seep through; fig leak out

'durchstarten v/i (sep, -ge-, sein) AVIAT climb and reaccelerate

durch'stechen v/t (irr, **stechen**, no -ge-, h) pierce

'durch|stecken v/t (sep, -ge-, h) stick through; **~stehen** v/t (irr, **stehen**, sep, -ge-, h) go through

durch'stoßen v/t (irr, **stoßen**, no -ge-, h) break through

'durchstreichen v/t (irr, **streichen**, sep, -ge-, h) cross out

durch'suchen v/t (no -ge-, h) search, F frisk; **Durch'suchung** f (-; -en) search; **Durch'suchungsbefehl** m search warrant

durch|trieben [dʊrç'tri:bən] adj cunning, sly; **~wachsen** adj GASTR streaky

'Durchwahl f (-; no pl) TEL direct dial(l)ing; **'durchwählen** v/i (sep, -ge-, h) TEL dial direct

durchweg ['dʊrçvɛk] adv without exception

durch'weicht adj soaked, drenched

durch'wühlen v/t (no -ge-, h) rummage through

'durch|zählen v/t (sep, -ge-, h) count off (Br up); **~ziehen** (irr, **ziehen**, sep, -ge-) **1.** v/i (sein) pass through **2.** v/t (h) pull s.th. through; fig carry s.th. through (to the end)

durch'zucken v/t (no -ge-, h) flash through

'Durchzug m (-[e]s; no pl) draft, Br draught

dürfen ['dʏrfən] **1.** v/aux (irr, no -ge-, h) be allowed or permitted to inf; **darf ich gehen?** may I go?; **ja(, du darfst)** yes, you may; **du darfst nicht** you must not, you aren't allowed to; **dürfte ich ...?** could I ...?; **das dürfte genügen** that should be enough **2.** v/i (irr, ge-, h) **er darf (nicht)** he is (not) allowed to inf

durfte ['dʊrftə] pret of **dürfen**

dürftig ['dʏrftɪç] adj poor; scanty

dürr [dʏr] adj dry; barren, arid; skinny

Dürre ['dʏrə] f (-; -n) drought; (no pl) barrenness

Durst [dʊrst] m (-[e]s; no pl) thirst (**auf** acc for); **~ haben** be thirsty

'durstig adj thirsty

Dusche ['dʊʃə] f (-; -n) shower

'duschen v/refl and v/i (ge-, h) have or take a shower

Düse ['dy:zə] f (-; -n) TECH nozzle; jet

'düsen F v/i (ge-, sein) jet

'Düsen|antrieb m jet propulsion; **mit ~** jet-propelled; **~flugzeug** n jet (plane); **~jäger** m MIL jet fighter; **~triebwerk** n jet engine

düster ['dy:stɐ] adj dark, gloomy (both a. fig); dim (light); fig dismal

Dutzend ['dʊtsənt] n (-s; -e) dozen

'dutzendweise adv by the dozen

duzen ['duːtsən] *v/t* (*ge-*, *h*) use the familiar 'du' with s.o.; **sich ~** be on 'du' terms

DVD [deːfauˈdeː] *abbr of Digital Versatile Disk* DVD; **~-Player** *m* (*-s*; *-*) DVD player; **~-Rekorder** *m* (*-s*; *-*) DVD recorder

Dynamik [dyˈnaːmɪk] *f* (*-*; *no pl*) PHYS dynamics; *fig* dynamism

dyˈnamisch *adj* dynamic

Dynamit [dynaˈmiːt] *n* (*-s*; *no pl*) dynamite

Dynamo [dyˈanːmo] *m* (*-s*; *-s*) ELECTR dynamo, generator

D-Zug ['deːtsuːk] *m* express train

E

Ebbe ['ɛbə] *f* (*-*; *-n*) ebb, low tide

eben ['eːbən] **1.** *adj* even; flat; MATH plane; **zu ~er Erde** on the first (*Br* ground) floor **2.** *adv* just; **an ~ dem Tag** on that very day; **so ist es ~** that's the way it is; **gerade ~ so** or **noch** just barely

'Ebenbild *n* image

ebenbürtig ['eːbənbyrtɪç] *adj:* **j-m ~ sein** be a match for s.o., be s.o.'s equal

Ebene ['eːbənə] *f* (*-*; *-n*) GEOGR plain; MATH plane; *fig* level

'ebenerdig *adj and adv* at street level; on the first (*Br* ground) floor

'ebenfalls *adv* as well, too

'Ebenholz *n* ebony

'Ebenmaß *n* (*-es; no pl*) symmetry; harmony; regularity; **'ebenmäßig** *adj* symmetrical; harmonious; regular

'ebenso *adv and cj* just as; as well; **~ wie** in the same way as; **~ gern**, **~ gut** just as well; **~ sehr**, **~ viel** just as much; **~ wenig** just as little *or* few

Eber ['eːbɐ] *m* (*-s*; *-*) ZO boar

ebnen ['eːbnən] *v/t* (*ge-*, *h*) even, level; *fig* smooth

Echo ['ɛço] *n* (*-s*; *-s*) echo; *fig* response

echt [ɛçt] *adj* genuine (*a. fig*), real; true; pure; fast (*color*); authentic; F **~ gut** real good; **'Echtheit** *f* (*-*; *no pl*) genuineness; authenticity

Eckball ['ɛkbal] *m* SPORT corner (kick)

Ecke ['ɛkə] *f* (*-*; *-n*) corner; edge; SPORT **lange** (**kurze**) **~** far (near) corner; → **Eckball**; **eckig** ['ɛkɪç] *adj* square, angular; *fig* awkward

'Eckzahn *m* canine tooth

Economyclass [iˈkɔnəmiklaːs] *f* (*-; no pl*) coach (class)

edel ['eːdəl] *adj* noble; MIN precious

'Edelme,tall *n* precious metal

'Edelstahl *m* stainless steel

'Edelstein *m* precious stone; gem

EDV [eːdeːˈfau] *abbr of Elektronische Datenverarbeitung* electronic data processing

Efeu ['eːfɔy] *m* (*-s*; *no pl*) BOT ivy

Effekt [ɛˈfɛkt] *m* (*-[e]s*; *-e*) effect

effektiv [ɛfɛkˈtiːf] **1.** *adj* effective **2.** *adv* actually; **Effektivität** [ɛfɛktiviˈtɛːt] *f* (*-*; *no pl*) effectiveness

efˈfektvoll *adj* effective, striking

Effet [ɛˈfeː] *m* (*-s*; *-s*) SPORT spin

EG [eːˈgeː] *hist abbr of Europäische Gemeinschaft* EC, European Community

egal [eˈgaːl] F *adj:* **~ ob** (**warum, wer** *etc*) no matter if (why, who, *etc*); **das ist ~** it doesn't matter; **das ist mir ~** I don't care, it's all the same to me

Egge ['ɛgə] *f* (*-*; *-n*), **'eggen** *v/t* (*ge-*, *h*) AGR harrow

Egoismus [egoˈɪsmʊs] *m* (*-; no pl*) ego(t)ism; **Egoist(in)** [egoˈɪst(ɪn)] (*-en; -en/-; -nen*) ego(t)ist; **ego'istisch** *adj* selfish, ego(t)istic(al)

ehe ['eːə] *cj* before; **nicht ~** not until

Ehe ['eːə] *f* (*-; -n*) marriage (**mit** to); **~beratung** *f* marriage counseling (*Br* guidance)

'Ehe|bruch *m* adultery; **~frau** *f* wife; **~leute** *pl* married couple

'ehelich *adj* conjugal; JUR legitimate

ehemalig ['eːəmaːlɪç] *adj* former, ex-...

ehemals ['eːəmaːls] *adv* formerly

'Ehemann *m* husband

'Ehepaar *n* (married) couple

eher ['eːɐ] *adv* earlier, sooner; **je ~, desto lieber** the sooner the better; **nicht ~ als** not until *or* before

'Ehering *m* wedding ring

ehrbar ['eːrbaːɐ] *adj* respectable

Ehre ['eːrə] *f* (-; -*n*) hono(u)r; **zu ~n** (*von*) in hono(u)r of

'ehren *v/t* (*ge-, h*) hono(u)r; respect

'ehrenamtlich *adj* honorary

'Ehren|bürger *m* honorary citizen; **~doktor** *m* UNIV honorary doctor; **~gast** *m* guest of hono(u)r; **~kodex** *m* code of hono(u)r; **~mann** *m* man of hono(u)r; **~mitglied** *n* honorary member; **~platz** *m* place of hono(u)r; **~rechte** *pl* civil rights; **~rettung** *f* rehabilitation

'ehrenrührig *adj* defamatory

'Ehren|runde *f esp* SPORT lap of hono(u)r; **~sache** *f* point of hono(u)r; **~tor** *n*, **~treffer** *m* SPORT consolation goal

'ehrenwert *adj* hono(u)rable

'Ehrenwort *n* (-[*e*]*s*; -*e*) word of hono(u)r; F **~!** cross my heart!

ehrerbietig ['eːrʔɛɐbiːtɪç] *adj* respectful

Ehrfurcht ['eːrfʊrçt] *f* (-; *no pl*) respect (**vor** *dat* for); awe (of); **~ gebietend** awe-inspiring, awesome; **ehrfürchtig** ['eːrfʏrçtɪç] *adj* respectful

'Ehrgefühl *n* (-[*e*]*s*; *no pl*) sense of hono(u)r

'Ehrgeiz *m* ambition; **'ehrgeizig** *adj* ambitious

'ehrlich *adj* honest; frank; fair; **'Ehrlichkeit** *f* (-; *no pl*) honesty; fairness

'Ehrung *f* (-; -*en*) hono(u)r(ing)

'ehrwürdig *adj* venerable

Ei [ai] *n* (-[*e*]*s*; *Eier* ['aiɐ]) egg; V *pl* balls

Eiche ['aiçə] *f* (-; -*n*) oak(-tree)

Eichel ['aiçəl] *f* (-; -*n*) BOT acorn; *card games*: club(s); ANAT glans (penis)

eichen ['aiçən] *v/t* (*ge-, h*) ga(u)ge

Eichhörnchen ['aiçhœrnçən] *n* (-*s*; -) zo squirrel

Eid [ait] *m* (-[*e*]*s*; -*e*) oath; **e-n ~ ablegen** take an oath

Eidechse ['aidɛksə] *f* (-; -*n*) zo lizard

eidesstattlich ['aidəsʃtatlɪç] *adj*: **~e Erklärung** JUR statutory declaration

'Eidotter *m, n* (egg) yolk

'Eier|becher *m* eggcup; **~kuchen** *m* pancake; **~li,kör** *m* eggnog; **~schale** *f* eggshell; **~stock** *m* ANAT ovary; **~uhr** *f* egg timer

Eifer ['aifɐ] *m* (-*s*; *no pl*) zeal, eagerness; **glühender ~** ardo(u)r

'Eifersucht *f* (-; *no pl*) jealousy

'eifersüchtig *adj* jealous (**auf** *acc* of)

eifrig *adj* eager, zealous; ardent

'Eigelb *n* (-[*e*]*s*; -*e*) (egg) yolk

eigen ['aigən] *adj* own, of one's own; peculiar; particular, F fussy; **...eigen** *in cpds* staatseigen *etc*: ...-owned

'Eigenart *f* peculiarity

'eigenartig *adj* peculiar; strange

'Eigenbedarf *m* personal needs

'Eigengewicht *n* dead weight

eigenhändig ['aigənhɛndɪç] **1.** *adj* personal **2.** *adv* personally, with one's own hands

'Eigen|heim *n* home (of one's own); **~liebe** *f* self-love; **~lob** *n* self-praise

'eigenmächtig *adj* arbitrary

'Eigenname *m* proper noun

'Eigennutz *m* (-*es*; *no pl*) self-interest

eigennützig ['aigənnʏtsɪç] *adj* selfish

'eigens *adv* (e)specially, expressly

'Eigenschaft *f* (-; -*en*) quality; TECH, PHYS, CHEM property; **in s-r ~ als** in his capacity as; **'Eigenschaftswort** *n* (-[*e*]*s*; -*wörter*) LING adjective

'Eigensinn *m* (-[*e*]*s*; *no pl*) stubbornness; **'eigensinnig** *adj* stubborn, obstinate

eigentlich ['aigəntlɪç] **1.** *adj* actual, true, real; exact **2.** *adv* actually, really; originally

'Eigentor *n* SPORT own goal (*a. fig*)

'Eigentum *n* (-[*e*]*s*; *no pl*) property

Eigentümer ['aigəntyːmɐ] *m* (-*s*; -), **'Eigentümerin** *f* (-; -*nen*) owner, proprietor (proprietress)

eigentümlich ['aigəntyːmlɪç] *adj* peculiar; strange, odd; **'Eigentümlichkeit** *f* (-; -*en*) peculiarity

'Eigentumswohnung *f* condominium, F condo, *Br* owner-occupied flat

'eigenwillig *adj* wil(l)ful; individual, original (*style etc*)

eignen ['aignən] *v/refl* (*ge-, h*) **sich ~ für** be suited *or* fit for; **'Eignung** *f* (-; *no pl*) suitability; aptitude, qualification

'Eignungs|prüfung *f*, **~test** *m* aptitude test

Eil|bote ['ailboːtə] *m*: **durch ~n** by special delivery; **~brief** *m* special delivery (*Br* express) letter

Eile ['ailə] *f* (-; *no pl*) haste, hurry; **'eilen**

v/i (*ge-*, *sein*) hurry, hasten, rush; (*ge-*, *h*) be urgent; **eilig** *adj* hurried, hasty; urgent; *es ~ haben* be in a hurry

Eimer ['aimɐ] *m* (*-s*; *-*) bucket, pail

ein [ain] **1.** *adj* one **2.** *indef art* a, an **3.** *adv*: *"einlaus"* "on / off"; *~ und aus gehen* come and go; *nicht mehr ~ noch aus wissen* be at one's wits' end

einander [ai'nandɐ] *pron* each other, one another

'**einarbeiten** *v/t* (*sep*, *-ge-*, *h*) train, acquaint *s.o.* with his work, F break *s.o.* in; *sich ~* work o.s. in

'**einarmig** ['ainarmɪç] *adj* one-armed

einäschern ['ainʔɛʃɐn] *v/t* (*sep*, *-ge-*, *h*) cremate; **Einäscherung** ['ainʔɛʃ(ə)ruŋ] *f* (*-*; *-en*) cremation

'**einatmen** *v/t* (*sep*, *-ge-*, *h*) inhale, breathe

'**einäugig** ['ainɔygɪç] *adj* one-eyed

'**Einbahnstraße** *f* one-way street

einbalsamieren ['ainbalzami:rən] *v/t* (*no -ge-*, *h*) embalm

'**Einband** *m* (*-[e]s*; *-bände*) binding, cover

'**Einbau** *m* (*-[e]s*; *-bauten*) installation, fitting; *~... in cpds ...möbel etc*: built-in ...; '**einbauen** *v/t* (*sep*, *-ge-*, *h*) build in, instal(l), fit

'**einberufen** *v/t* (*irr*, *rufen*, *sep*, *no -ge-*, *h*) MIL draft, *Br* call up; call (*meeting etc*); '**Einberufung** *f* (*-*; *-en*) MIL draft, *Br* call-up

'**ein|beziehen** *v/t* (*irr*, *ziehen*, *sep*, *no -ge-*, *h*) include; *~biegen* *v/i* (*irr*, *biegen*, *sep*, *-ge-*, *sein*) turn (*in acc* into)

'**einbilden** *v/refl* (*sep*, *-ge-*, *h*) imagine; *sich et. ~ auf* (*acc*) be conceited about; '**Einbildung** *f* (*-*; *no pl*) imagination, fancy; conceit

'**einblenden** *v/t* (*sep*, *-ge-*, *h*) TV fade in

'**Einblick** *m* insight (*in acc* into)

'**einbrechen** *v/i* (*irr*, *brechen*, *sep*, *-ge-*, *sein*) collapse; *winter*: set in; *~ in* (*acc*) break into, burgle; fall through (the ice); '**Einbrecher** *m* (*-s*; *-*) burglar

'**einbringen** *v/t* (*irr*, *bringen*, *sep*, *-ge-*, *h*) bring in; yield (*profit etc*)

'**Einbruch** *m* burglary; *bei ~ der Nacht* at nightfall

einbürgern ['ainbʏrgɐn] *v/t* (*sep*, *-ge-*, *h*) naturalize; *sich ~ fig* come into use

'**Einbürgerung** *f* (*-*; *-en*) naturalization

'**Einbuße** *f* (*-*; *-n*) loss

'**einbüßen** *v/t* (*sep*, *-ge-*, *h*) lose

eindämmen ['aindɛmən] *v/t* (*sep*, *-ge-*, *h*) dam (up), *fig a.* get under control

'**eindecken** *fig v/t* (*sep*, *-ge-*, *h*) provide (*mit* with)

'**eindeutig** ['aindɔytɪç] *adj* clear

'**eindrehen** *v/t* (*sep*, *-ge-*, *h*) put *hair* in curlers

'**eindringen** *v/i* (*irr*, *dringen*, *sep*, *-ge-*, *sein*) *~ in* (*acc*) enter (*a. fig*); force one's way into; MIL invade; '**eindringlich** *adj* urgent; '**Eindringling** *m* (*-s*; *-e*) intruder; MIL invader

'**Eindruck** *m* impression; '**eindrücken** *v/t* (*sep*, *-ge-*, *h*) break *or* push in

'**eindrucksvoll** *adj* impressive

eineiig ['ainʔaiç] *adj* identical (*twins*)

'**einein'halb** *adj* one and a half

einengen ['ainʔɛŋən] *v/t* (*sep*, *-ge-*, *h*) confine, restrict

einer ['ainɐ], **eine** ['ainə], **ein(e)s** ['ain(ə)s] *indef pron* one

'**Einer** *m* (*-s*; *-*) MATH unit; *rowing*: single sculls

einerlei ['ainɐ'lai] *adj*: *ganz ~* all the same; *~ ob* no matter if; '**Einer'lei** *n*: *das tägliche ~* the daily grind *or* rut

'**einer'seits** *adv* on the one hand

'**einfach** *adj* simple; easy; plain; one--way (*Br* single) (*ticket*)

'**Einfachheit** *f* (*-*; *no pl*) simplicity

einfädeln ['ainfɛːdəln] *v/t* (*sep*, *-ge-*, *h*) thread; F start, set afoot; MOT merge

'**einfahren** (*irr*, *fahren*, *sep*, *-ge-*) **1.** *v/t* (*h*) MOT run in; bring in (*harvest*) **2.** *v/i* (*sein*) come in, RAIL *a.* pull in

'**Einfahrt** *f* entrance, way in

'**Einfall** *m* idea; MIL invasion

'**einfallen** *v/i* (*irr*, *fallen*, *sep*, *-ge-*, *sein*) fall in; collapse; MUS join in; *~ in* (*acc*) MIL invade; *ihm fiel ein, dass* it came to his mind that; *mir fällt nichts ein* I have no ideas; *es fällt mir nicht ein* I can't think of it; *dabei fällt mir ein* that reminds me; *was fällt dir ein?* what's the idea?

einfältig ['ainfɛltɪç] *adj* simple-minded; stupid

Einfa'milienhaus *n* detached house

'**einfarbig** *adj* solid-colored, *Br* self-coloured

'**ein|fassen** *v/t* (*sep*, *-ge-*, *h*) border; *~fetten* *v/t* (*sep*, *-ge-*, *h*) grease; *~finden* *v/refl* (*irr*, *finden*, *sep*, *-ge-*, *h*) appear, arrive; **~flechten** *fig v/t (irr, **flechten**, sep, -ge-, h)* work in; **~fliegen** *v/t (irr, **fliegen**, sep, -ge-, h)* fly in; **~fließen** *v/i (irr, **fließen**, sep, -ge-, sein) fig et. ~ lassen* slip s.th. in; **~flößen** *v/t (sep, -ge-, h)* pour *(j-m* into s.o.'s mouth); *fig* fill with *(awe etc)*

'**Einfluss** *fig m* influence

'**einflussreich** *adj* influential

einförmig ['ainfœrmɪç] *adj* uniform

'**einfrieren** *(irr, **frieren**, sep, -ge-)* **1.** *v/i (sein)* freeze (in) **2.** *v/t (h)* freeze *(a. fig)*

'**einfügen** *v/t (sep, -ge-, h)* put in; *fig* insert; *sich ~* fit in; adjust (o.s.) *(in acc* to); '**Einfügetaste** *f* IT insert key

einfühlsam ['ainfy:lza:m] *adj* sympathetic; '**Einfühlungsvermögen** *n (-s; no pl)* empathy

Einfuhr ['ainfu:ɐ] *f (-; -en)* ECON *(no pl)* importation; import

'**einführen** *v/t (sep, -ge-, h)* introduce; instal(l); ECON import

'**Einfuhrstopp** *m* ECON import ban

'**Einführung** *f (-; -en)* introduction

'**Einführungs...** *in cpds ...kurs, ...preis etc:* introductory ...

'**Eingabe** *f* petition; IT input; **~taste** *f* IT enter *or* return key

'**Eingang** *m* entrance; ECON arrival; receipt; '**eingängig** *adj* catchy *(tune etc)*

'**eingangs** *adv* at the beginning

'**eingeben** *v/t (irr, **geben**, sep, -ge-, h)* MED administer *(dat* to); IT feed, enter

'**eingebildet** *adj* imaginary; conceited *(auf acc* of)

'**Eingeborene** *m, f (-n; -n)* native

'**Eingebung** *f (-; -en)* inspiration; impulse

'**eingefallen** *adj* sunken, hollow

'**eingefleischt** *adj* confirmed

'**eingehen** *(irr, **gehen**, sep, -ge-, sein)* **1.** *v/i* ECON come in, arrive; BOT, ZO die; *fabric:* shrink; *~ auf (acc)* agree to; go into *(detail)*; listen to *s.o.* **2.** *v/t* enter into *(a contract etc)*; make *(a bet)*; take *(a risk etc)*; **~d** *adj* thorough; detailed

'**eingemacht** *adj* preserved

eingemeinden ['aingəmaindən] *v/t (sep, no -ge-, h)* incorporate *(in acc* into)

'**einge|nommen** *adj* partial *(für* to); prejudiced *(gegen* against); *von sich ~* full of o.s.; **~schlossen** *adj* locked in; trapped; ECON included; **~schnappt**

F *adj* in a huff; **~schrieben** *adj* registered; **~spielt** *adj:* *(gut) aufeinander ~ sein* work well together, be a good team; **~stellt** *adj:* *~ auf (acc)* prepared for; *~ gegen* opposed to

Eingeweide ['aingəvaidə] *pl* ANAT intestines, guts

'**Eingeweihte** *m, f (-n; -n)* insider

'**eingewöhnen** *v/refl (sep, no -ge-, h) sich ~ in (acc)* get used to, settle in

'**eingießen** *v/t (irr, **gießen**, sep, -ge-, h)* pour

eingleisig ['ainglaizɪç] *adj* single-track

'**eingliedern** *v/t (sep, -ge-, h)* integrate

'**Eingliederung** *f* integration

'**ein|graben** *v/t (irr, **graben**, sep, -ge-, h)* bury; **~gra,vieren** *v/t (sep, no -ge-, h)* engrave

'**eingreifen** *v/i (irr, **greifen**, sep, -ge-, h)* step in, interfere; '**Eingriff** *m* intervention, interference; MED operation

'**einhaken** *v/t (sep, -ge-, h)* hook in; *sich ~* link arms, take s.o.'s arm

'**Einhalt** *m:* *~ gebieten* put a stop *(dat* to); '**einhalten** *v/t (irr, **halten**, sep, -ge-, h)* keep

'**einhängen** *(sep, -ge-, h)* **1.** *v/t* hang in; TEL hang up *(receiver); sich ~ → einhaken* **2.** *v/i* TEL hang up

'**einheimisch** *adj* native, local; ECON home, domestic; '**Einheimische** *m, f (-n; -n)* local, native

'**Einheit** *f (-; -en)* unit; POL unity

'**einheitlich** *adj* uniform; homogeneous

'**Einheits...** *in cpds ...preis etc:* standard

einhellig ['ainhɛlɪç] *adj* unanimous

'**einholen** *v/t (sep, -ge-, h)* catch up with *(a. fig)*; make up for *lost time*; make *(inquiries) (über* acc about); seek *(advice) (bei* from); ask for *permission etc*; strike *(sail); ~ gehen* go shopping

'**Einhorn** *n* MYTH unicorn

'**einhüllen** *v/t (sep, -ge-, h)* wrap (up); *fig* shroud

einig ['ainɪç] *adj:* *sich ~ sein* agree; *sich nicht ~ sein* disagree, differ

einige ['ainɪgə] *indef pron* some, a few, several

einigen ['ainɪgən] *v/t (ge-, h) sich ~ über (acc)* agree on

einigermaßen ['ainɪgɐ'ma:sən] *adv* quite, fairly; not too bad

'**einiges** *indef pron* some, something; quite a lot

'**Einigkeit** f (-; *no pl*) unity; agreement

'**Einigung** f (-; -en) agreement, settlement; POL unification

'**einjagen** v/t (*sep, -ge-, h*) **j-m e-n Schrecken** ~ give s.o. a fright, frighten *or* scare s.o.

einjährig ['aɪnjɛːrɪç] *adj* one-year-old; ~**e Pflanze** annual

'**einkalku,lieren** v/t (*no -ge-, h*) take into account, allow for

'**Einkauf** m purchase; *Einkäufe machen* → *einkaufen* 2; '**einkaufen** (*sep, -ge-, h*) **1.** v/t buy, ECON *a.* purchase **2.** v/i go shopping

'**Einkaufs...** *in cpds* shopping ...; ~**bummel** m shopping spree; ~**preis** m ECON purchase price; ~**wagen** m grocery *or* shopping cart, *Br* (supermarket) trolley; ~**zentrum** n (shopping) mall, *Br* shopping centre

'**ein|kehren** v/i (*sep, -ge-, sein*) stop (*in dat* at); ~**klammern** v/t (*sep, -ge-, h*) put in brackets

'**Einklang** m (-[e]s; *no pl*) MUS unison; *fig* harmony

'**ein|kleiden** v/t (*sep, -ge-, h*) clothe (*a. fig*); ~**klemmen** v/t (*sep, -ge-, h*) squeeze, jam; *eingeklemmt sein* be stuck, be jammed; ~**kochen** (*sep, -ge-*) **1.** v/t (*h*) preserve **2.** v/i (*sein*) boil down

'**Einkommen** n (-s; -) income; ~**steuererklärung** f income-tax return

'**einkreisen** v/t (*sep, -ge-, h*) encircle, surround

Einkünfte ['aɪnkʏnftə] *pl* income

'**einladen** v/t (*irr, laden, sep, -ge-, h*) invite; load; ~**d** *adj* inviting

'**Einladung** f (-; -en) invitation

'**Einlage** f (-; -n) ECON investment; MED arch support; THEA, MUS interlude

Einlass ['aɪnlas] m (-es; *no pl*) admission, admittance; '**einlassen** v/t (*irr, lassen, sep, -ge-, h*) let in; run (*a bath*); *sich* ~ *auf* (*acc*) get involved in; let o.s. in for; agree to; *sich mit j-m* ~ get involved with s.o.

'**Einlauf** m SPORT finish; MED enema

'**einlaufen** (*irr, laufen, sep, -ge-*) **1.** v/i (*sein*) come in (*a. SPORT*); *water:* run in; MAR enter port; *fabric:* shrink **2.** v/t (*h*) break *new shoes* in; *sich* ~ warm up

'**einleben** v/refl (*sep, -ge-, h*) settle in

'**einlegen** v/t (*sep, -ge-, h*) put in; set (*hair*); GASTR pickle; MOT change into

'**Einlegesohle** f insole

'**einleiten** v/t (*sep, -ge-, h*) start; introduce; MED induce; TECH dump, discharge (*sewage*); ~**d** *adj* introductory

'**Einleitung** f introduction

'**ein|lenken** v/i (*sep, -ge-, h*) come round; ~**leuchten** v/i (*sep, -ge-, h*) be evident, be obvious; *das leuchtet mir* (*nicht*) *ein* that makes (doesn't make) sense to me; ~**liefern** v/t (*sep, -ge-, h*) take (*ins Gefängnis* to prison; *in die Klinik* to [the] hospital); ~**lösen** v/t (*sep, -ge-, h*) redeem; cash (*check*); ~**machen** v/t (*sep, -ge-, h*) preserve

'**einmal** *adv* once; some *or* one day, sometime; *auf* ~ suddenly; at the same time, at once; *noch* ~ once more *or* again; *noch* ~ *so* ... (*wie*) twice as ... (as); *es war* ~ once (upon a time) there was; *haben Sie schon* ~ ...? have you ever ...?; *schon* ~ *dort gewesen sein* have been there before; *nicht* ~ not even

'**Einmal...** *in cpds* disposable ...

Einmal'eins n (-; *no pl*) multiplication table

einmalig ['aɪnmaːlɪç] *adj* single; *fig* unique; F fabulous

'**Einmann...** *in cpds* one-man ...

'**Einmarsch** m entry; MIL invasion

'**einmar,schieren** v/i (*no -ge-, sein*) march in; ~ *in* (*acc*) MIL invade

'**einmischen** v/refl (*sep, -ge-, h*) meddle (*in acc* in, with), interfere (with)

'**Einmündung** f junction

einmütig ['aɪnmyːtɪç] *adj* unanimous

'**Einmütigkeit** f (-; *no pl*) unanimity

Einnahmen ['aɪnnaːmən] *pl* takings, receipts; '**einnehmen** v/t (*irr, nehmen, sep, -ge-, h*) take (*a. MIL*); earn, make; '**einnehmend** *adj* engaging

'**einnicken** v/i (*sep, -ge-, sein*) doze off

'**einnisten** v/refl (*sep, -ge-, h*) *sich bei j-m* ~ park o.s. on s.o.

'**Einöde** f (-; -n) desert, wilderness

'**ein|ordnen** v/t (*sep, -ge-, h*) put in its proper place; file; *sich* ~ MOT get in lane; ~**packen** v/t (*sep, -ge-, h*) pack (up); wrap up; ~**parken** v/t *and* v/i (*sep, -ge-, h*) park (between two cars); ~**pferchen** v/t (*sep, -ge-, h*) pen in; coop up; ~**pflanzen** v/t (*sep, -ge-, h*) plant; *fig* implant (*a.* MED); **~planen** *v/t* (*sep, -ge-, h*) allow for; **~prägen** *v/t* (*sep, -ge-, h*) impress; **sich et. ~** keep s.th. in mind; memorize s.th.; **~quartieren** F *v/t* (*no -ge-, h*) put *s.o.* up (**bei j-m** at s.o.'s place); **sich ~ bei** (*dat*) move in with; **~rahmen** *v/t* (*sep, -ge-, h*) frame; **~räumen** *v/t* (*sep, -ge-, h*) put away; furnish; *fig* grant, concede; **~reden** (*sep, -ge-, h*) 1. *v/t:* **j-m et. ~** talk s.o. into (believing) s.th. 2. *v/i:* **auf j-n ~** keep on at s.o.; **~reiben** *v/t* (*irr, reiben, sep, -ge-, h*) rub; **~reichen** *v/t* (*sep, -ge-, h*) hand *or* send in; **~reihen** *v/t* (*sep, -ge-, h*) place (among); **sich ~** take one's place

einreihig ['ainraiiç] *adj* single-breasted

'**Einreise** *f* entry (*a.* in *cpds*)

'**einreisen** *v/i* (*sep, -ge-, sein*) enter (**in ein Land** a country)

'**ein|reißen** (*irr, reißen, sep, -ge-*) 1. *v/t* (*h*) tear; pull down 2. *v/i* (*sein*) tear; *fig* spread; **~renken** *v/t* (*sep, -ge-, h*) MED set; *fig* straighten out

'**einrichten** *v/t* (*sep, -ge-, h*) furnish; establish; arrange; **sich ~** furnish one's home; **sich ~ auf** (*acc*) prepare for; '**Einrichtung** *f* (*-; -en*) furnishings; fittings; TECH installation(s), facilities; institution, facility

'**einrücken** (*sep, -ge-*) 1. *v/i* (*sein*) MIL join the forces; march in 2. *v/t* (*h*) PRINT indent

eins [ains] *pron and adj* one; one thing; **es ist alles ~** it's all the same (thing)

Eins *f* (*-; -en*) one; *grade:* excellent, A

einsam ['ainza:m] *adj* lonely, lonesome; solitary; '**Einsamkeit** *f* (*-; no pl*) loneliness; solitude

'**einsammeln** *v/t* (*sep, -ge-, h*) collect

'**Einsatz** *m* TECH inset, insert; stake(s) (*a. fig*); MUS entry; *fig* effort(s), zeal; use, employment; MIL action, mission; deployment; **im ~** in action; **unter ~ des Lebens** at the risk of one's life

'**einsatz|bereit** *adj* ready for action; **~freudig** *adj* dynamic, zealous

'**einschalten** *v/t* (*sep, -ge-, h*) ELECTR switch *or* turn on; call *s.o.* in; **sich ~** step in; '**Einschaltquote** *f* TV rating

'**ein|schärfen** *v/t* (*sep, -ge-, h*) urge (**j-m et.** s.o. to do s.th.); **~schätzen** *v/t* (*sep, -ge-, h*) estimate; judge, rate; **falsch ~** misjudge; **~schenken** *v/t* (*sep, -ge-, h*) pour (out); **~schicken** *v/t* (*sep, -ge-, h*)

send in; **~schieben** *v/t* (*irr, schieben, sep, -ge-, h*) slip in; insert

einschl. *abbr of* **einschließlich** incl., including

'**ein|schlafen** *v/i* (*irr, schlafen, sep, -ge-, sein*) fall asleep, go to sleep; **~schläfern** ['ainʃlɛ:fən] *v/t* (*sep, -ge-, h*) put to sleep

'**Einschlag** *m* strike, impact; *fig* touch

'**einschlagen** (*irr, schlagen, sep, -ge-, h*) 1. *v/t* knock in (*or* out); break (in), smash; wrap up; take (*road etc*); turn (*wheels*); → **Laufbahn** 2. *v/i* lightning *etc:* strike; *fig* be a success

einschlägig ['ainʃlɛ:giç] *adj* relevant

'**ein|schleusen** *fig v/t* (*sep, -ge-, h*) infiltrate (**in** *acc* into); **~schließen** *v/t* (*irr, schließen, sep, -ge-, h*) lock in *or* up; enclose; MIL surround, encircle; *fig* include; **~schließlich** *prp* (*gen*) including, ... included; **~schmeicheln** *v/refl* (*sep, -ge-, h*) **sich ~ bei** ingratiate o.s. with; **~schnappen** *v/i* (*sep, -ge-, sein*) snap shut; *fig* go into a huff; → **eingeschnappt**

'**einschneidend** *fig adj* drastic; far-reaching; '**Einschnitt** *m* cut; notch; *fig* break

'**einschränken** *v/t* (*sep, -ge-, h*) restrict, reduce (*both:* **auf** *acc* to); cut down on; **sich ~** economize; '**Einschränkung** *f* (*-; -en*) restriction, reduction, cut; **ohne ~** without reservation

'**Einschreibebrief** *m* registered letter

'**einschreiben** *v/t* (*irr, schreiben, sep, -ge-, h*) enter; book; enrol(l) (*a.* MIL); (**sich**) **~ lassen** (**für**) enrol(l) (o.s.) (for)

'**einschreiten** *fig v/i* (*irr, schreiten, sep, -ge-, sein*) step in, intervene; **~** (**gegen**) take (legal) measures (against)

'**einschüchtern** *v/t* (*sep, -ge-, h*) intimidate; bully; '**Einschüchterung** *f* (*-; -en*) intimidation

'**einschulen** *v/t* (*sep, -ge-, h*) **eingeschult werden** start school

'**Einschuss** *m* bullet hole

'**einschweißen** *v/t* (*sep, -ge-, h*) shrink-wrap

'**einsegnen** *v/t* (*sep, -ge-, h*) REL consecrate; confirm; '**Einsegnung** *f* (*-; -en*) REL consecration; confirmation

'**einsehen** *v/t* (*irr, sehen, sep, -ge-, h*) see, realize; **das sehe ich nicht ein!** I don't see why!; '**Einsehen** *n:* **ein ~ ha-**

ben show some understanding

'einseifen v/t (sep, -ge-, h) soap; lather; F fig **j-n ~** take s.o. for a ride

einseitig ['ainzaitiç] adj one-sided; MED, POL, JUR unilateral

'einsenden v/t ([irr, **senden**,] sep, -ge-, h) send in; **'Einsendeschluss** m closing date (for entries)

'einsetzen (sep, -ge-, h) **1.** v/t put in, insert; appoint; use, employ; TECH put into service; ECON invest, stake; bet; risk; **sich ~** try hard, make an effort; **sich ~ für** stand up for **2.** v/i set in, start

'Einsicht f (-; -en) insight; (no pl) understanding; **zur ~ kommen** listen to reason; **~ nehmen in** (acc) take a look at; **'einsichtig** adj understanding; reasonable

'Einsiedler m (-s; -) hermit

einsilbig ['ainzilbiç] adj monosyllabic; fig taciturn

'ein|spannen v/t (sep, -ge-, h) harness; TECH clamp, fix; F rope s.o. in; **~sparen** v/t (sep, -ge-, h) save, economize on; **~sperren** v/t (sep, -ge-, h) lock or shut up; **~spielen** v/t (sep, -ge-, h) bring in; **sich ~** warm up; fig get going; → **eingespielt**

'Einspielergebnisse pl film: box office returns

'einspringen v/i (irr, **springen**, sep, -ge-, sein) **für j-n ~** take s.o.'s place

'Einspritz... in cpds MOT fuel-injection

'Einspruch m objection (a. JUR), protest; POL veto; appeal

einspurig ['ainʃpuːrɪç] adj RAIL single-track; MOT single-lane

einst [ainst] adv once, at one time

'Einstand m start; tennis: deuce

'ein|stecken v/t (sep, -ge-, h) pocket (a. fig); ELECTR plug in; mail, post; fig take; **~stehen** v/i (irr, **stehen**, sep, -ge-, h) **für** stand up for; **~steigen** v/i (irr, **steigen**, sep, -ge-, sein) get in; get on (bus etc); **alles ~!** RAIL all aboard!; **~stellen** v/t (sep, -ge-, h) engage, employ, hire; give up; stop; SPORT equal; TECH adjust (**auf** acc to); radio: tune in (to); OPT, PHOT focus (on); **die Arbeit ~** (go on) strike, walk out; **das Feuer ~** MIL cease fire; **sich ~ auf** (acc) adjust to; be prepared for

'Einstellung f attitude (**zu** towards); employment; cessation; TECH adjust-

ment; OPT, PHOT focus(s)ing; film: take

'Einstellungsgespräch n interview

Einstieg ['ainʃtiːk] m (-[e]s; -e) entrance, entry (a. ECON)

'Einstiegsdroge f gateway drug

einstig ['ainstɪç] adj former, one-time

'einstimmen v/i (sep, -ge-, h) MUS join in

einstimmig ['ainʃtɪmɪç] adj unanimous

einstöckig ['ainʃtœkɪç] adj one-storied, Br one-storey(ed)

'ein|stu,dieren v/t (no -ge-, h) THEA rehearse; **~stufen** v/t (sep, -ge-, h) grade, rate

einstufig ['ainʃtuːfɪç] adj single-stage

'Einstufungsprüfung f placement test

'Einsturz m, **'einstürzen** v/i (sep, -ge-, sein) collapse

einst'weilen adv for the present

einstweilig ['ainstvailiç] adj temporary

'ein|tauschen v/t (sep, -ge-, h) exchange (**gegen** for); **~teilen** v/t (sep, -ge-, h) divide (**in** acc into); organize

einteilig ['aintailiç] adj one-piece

'Einteilung f (-; -en) division; organization; arrangement

eintönig ['aintøːnɪç] adj monotonous

'Eintönigkeit f (-; no pl) monotony

'Eintopf m GASTR stew

'Eintracht f (-; no pl) harmony, unity

'einträchtig adj harmonious, peaceful

Eintrag ['aintraːk] m (-[e]s; Einträge ['aintrɛːɡə]) entry (a. ECON), registration; **'eintragen** v/t (irr, **tragen**, sep, -ge-, h) enter (**in** acc in); register (**bei** with); enrol(l) (with); fig earn; **sich ~** register, hotel: a. check in

einträglich ['aintrɛːklɪç] adj profitable

'ein|treffen v/i (irr, **treffen**, sep, -ge-, sein) arrive; happen; come true; **~treiben** fig v/t (irr, **treiben**, sep, -ge-, h) collect; **~treten** (irr, **treten**, sep, -ge-) **1.** v/i (sein) enter; happen, take place; **~ für** stand up for, support; **~ in** (acc) join (club etc) **2.** v/t (h) kick in (door etc); **sich et. ~** run s.th. into one's foot

'Eintritt m entry; admission; **~ frei!** admission free!; **~ verboten!** keep out!

'Eintritts|geld n entrance or admission (fee); **~karte** f (admission) ticket

'einüben v/t (sep, -ge-, h) practise; rehearse

'einverstanden adj: **~ sein** agree (**mit** to); **~!** agreed!; **'Einverständnis** n (-ses; no pl) agreement

Einwand ['ainvant] *m* (-[e]s; *Einwände* ['ainvɛndə]) objection (*gegen* to)

'**Einwanderer** *m*, '**Einwanderin** *f* immigrant; '**einwandern** *v/i* (*sep, -ge-, sein*) immigrate; '**Einwanderung** *f* immigration

'**einwandfrei** *adj* perfect, faultless

einwärts ['ainverts] *adv* inward(s)

'**Einweg...** ...*rasierer,* ...*spritze etc*: disposable; **~flasche** *f* non-returnable bottle; **~packung** *f* throwaway pack

'**einweichen** *v/t* (*sep, -ge-, h*) soak

'**einweihen** *v/t* (*sep, -ge-, h*) dedicate, *Br* inaugurate; *j-n* **~** *in* (*acc*) F let s.o. in on; '**Einweihung** *f* (-; *-en*) dedication, *Br* inauguration

'**einweisen** *v/t* (*irr,* **weisen**, *sep, -ge-, h*) *j-n* **~** *in* (*acc*) send (*esp* JUR commit) s.o. to; instruct s.o. in, brief s.o. on

'**einwenden** *v/t* ([*irr,* **wenden**,] *sep, -ge-, h*) object (*gegen* to)

'**Einwendung** *f* (-; *-en*) objection

'**einwerfen** *v/t* (*irr,* **werfen**, *sep, -ge-, h*) throw in (*a. fig,* SPORT *a. v/i*); break (*window*); mail, *Br* post; insert (*coin*)

'**einwickeln** *v/t* (*sep, -ge-, h*) wrap (up); F take s.o. in

'**Einwickelpa,pier** *n* wrapping-paper

einwilligen ['ainvɪlɪgən] *v/i* (*sep, -ge-, h*) consent (*in acc* to), agree (to)

'**Einwilligung** *f* (-; *-en*) consent (*in acc* to), agreement

'**einwirken** *v/i* (*sep, -ge-, h*) **~** *auf* (*acc*) act (up)on; *fig* work on s.o.

'**Einwirkung** *f* effect, influence

Einwohner ['ainvo:nɐ] *m* (-s; -), '**Einwohnerin** *f* (-; *-nen*) inhabitant; '**Einwohnermeldeamt** *n* registration office

'**Einwurf** *m* slot; SPORT throw-in

'**Einzahl** *f* (-; *no pl*) LING singular

'**einzahlen** *v/t* (*sep, -ge-, h*) pay in

'**Einzahlung** *f* payment, deposit

einzäunen ['aintsɔynən] *v/t* (*sep, -ge-, h*) fence in

Einzel ['aintsəl] *n* (-s; -) *tennis*: singles

'**Einzel...** *in cpds* ...*bett,* ...*zimmer etc*: single ...; **~fall** *m* special case; **~gänger** ['aintsəlgɛŋɐ] *m* (-s; -) F loner; **~haft** *f* solitary confinement; **~handel** *m* retail trade; **~händler** *m* retailer; **~haus** *n* detached house

'**Einzelheit** *f* (-; *-en*) detail

'**einzeln** *adj* single; odd (*shoe etc*); *Ein-*

zelne *pl* several, some; *der Einzelne* the individual; **~ eintreten** enter one at a time; **~ angeben** specify; *im Einzelnen* in detail; *jeder Einzelne* each and every one

'**einziehen** (*irr,* **ziehen**, *sep, -ge-*) **1.** *v/t* (*h*) draw in; *esp* TECH retract; duck; strike (*sail etc*); MIL draft, *Br* call up; confiscate; withdraw (*license etc*); make (*inquiries*) **2.** *v/i* (*sein*) move in; march in; soak in

einzig ['aintsɪç] *adj* only; single; *kein Einziger* ... not a single ...; *das Einzige* the only thing; *der* (*die*) *Einzige* the only one; **~artig** *adj* unique, singular

'**Einzug** *m* moving in; entry

Eis [ais] *n* (-es; *no pl*) ice; GASTR ice cream; **~ am Stiel** ice lolly; **~bahn** *f* skating rink; **~bär** *m* ZO polar bear; **~becher** *m* sundae; **~bein** *n* GASTR (pickled) pork knuckles; **~berg** *m* iceberg; **~brecher** *m* (-s; -) MAR icebreaker; **~diele** *f* ice-cream parlo(u)r

Eisen ['aizən] *n* (-s; -) iron

'**Eisenbahn** *f* railroad, *Br* railway; train set; **Eisenbahner** ['aizənba:nɐ] *m* (-s; -) railroadman, *Br* railwayman

'**Eisenbahnwagen** *m* (railroad) car, *Br* coach, railway carriage

'**Eisen|erz** *n* iron ore; **~gießerei** *f* iron foundry; **~hütte** *f* TECH ironworks

'**Eisenwaren** *pl* hardware, ironware; **~handlung** *f* hardware store, *Br* ironmonger's

eisern ['aizɐn] *adj* iron (*a. fig*), of iron

'**eisgekühlt** *adj* iced

'**Eishockey** *n* hockey, *Br* ice hockey

eisig ['aizɪç] *adj* icy (*a. fig*)

'**eis'kalt** *adj* ice-cold

'**Eiskunst|lauf** *m* (-[e]s; *no pl*) figure skating; **~läufer(in)** figure skater

'**Eis|meer** *n* polar sea; **~re,vue** *f* ice show; **~schnelllauf** *m* speed skating; **~scholle** *f* ice floe; **~verkäufer** *m* iceman; **~würfel** *m* ice cube; **~zapfen** *m* icicle; **~zeit** *f* (-; *no pl*) GEOL ice age

eitel ['aitəl] *adj* vain; '**Eitelkeit** *f* (-; *no pl*) vanity

Eiter ['aitɐ] *m* (-s; *no pl*) MED pus

'**Eiterbeule** *f* MED abscess, boil

'**eitern** *v/i* (*ge-, h*) MED fester

eitrig ['aitrɪç] *adj* MED purulent, festering

'**Eiweiß** *n* (-es; *no pl*) white of egg; BIOL

protein

'eiweiß|arm *adj* low in protein, low-protein; ~reich *adj* rich in protein, high-protein

'Eizelle *f* BIOL egg cell, ovum

Ekel ['e:kəl] **1.** *m* (-*s*; *no pl*) disgust (*vor dat* at), loathing (for); ~ erregend → ekelhaft **2.** F *n* (-*s*; -) beast; ekelerregend *adj* → ekelhaft

'ekelhaft, 'ek(e)lig *adj* sickening, disgusting, repulsive

'ekeln *v/refl and v/impers* (*ge-*, *h*) ich ekle mich davor it makes me sick

Ekstase [ɛk'sta:zə] *f* (-; -*n*) ecstasy

Elan [e'la:n] *m* (-*s*; *no pl*) vigo(u)r

elastisch [e'lastɪʃ] *adj* elastic, flexible

Elch [ɛlç] *m* (-[*e*]*s*; -*e*) ZO elk; moose

Elefant [ele'fant] *m* (-*en*; -*en*) ZO elephant; Ele'fantenhochzeit F *f* ECON jumbo merger

elegant [ele'gant] *adj* elegant

Eleganz [ele'gants] *f* (-; *no pl*) elegance

Elektriker [e'lɛktrɪkɐ] *m* (-*s*; -) electrician; elektrisch [e'lɛktrɪʃ] *adj* electrical; electric; elektrisieren [elɛktri'zi:rən] *v/t* (*no -ge-*, *h*) electrify

Elektrizität [elɛktritsi'tɛːt] *f* (-; *no pl*) electricity; Elektrizi'tätswerk *n* (electric) power station

Elektrogerät [e'lɛktrogərɛːt] *n* electric appliance

Elektronik [elɛk'tro:nɪk] *f* electronics; electronic system; elektronisch [elɛk'tro:nɪʃ] *adj* electronic

E'lektrora,sierer *m* (-*s*; -) electric razor

Elektro|'technik *f* electrical engineering; ~'techniker *m* electrical engineer

Element [ele'mɛnt] *n* (-[*e*]*s*; -*e*) element

elementar [elemɛn'taːɐ] *adj* elementary

elend ['e:lɛnt] *adj* miserable

'Elend *n* (-*s*; *no pl*) misery

'Elendsviertel *n* slum

elf [ɛlf] *adj* eleven

Elf *f* (-; -*en*) eleven; *soccer*: team

Elfe ['ɛlfə] *f* (-; -*n*) elf, fairy

'Elfenbein *n* ivory

Elf'meter *m* (-*s*; -) *soccer*: penalty; ~punkt *m* penalty spot; ~schießen *n* penalty shoot-out

'elfte *adj* eleventh

Elite [e'li:tə] *f* (-; -*n*) elite

Ellbogen ['ɛlbo:gən] *m* ANAT elbow

Elster ['ɛlstɐ] *f* (-; -*n*) ZO magpie

elterlich ['ɛltɐlɪç] *adj* parental

Eltern ['ɛltɐn] *pl* parents

'Elternhaus *n* (one's parents') home

'elternlos *adj* orphan(ed)

'Eltern|teil *m* parent; ~vertretung *f* appr Parent-Teacher Association; ~zeit *f* parental leave

Email [e'mai] *n* (-*s*; -*s*), Emaille [e'maljə] *f* (-; -*n*) enamel

Emanzipation [emantsipa'tsjo:n] *f* (-; -*en*) emancipation; women's lib (-eration); emanzipieren [emantsi'pi:rən] *v/refl* (*no -ge-*, *h*) become emancipated

Embargo [ɛm'bargo] *n* (-*s*; -*s*) ECON embargo

Embolie [ɛmbo'li:] *f* (-; -*n*) MED embolism

Embryo ['ɛmbryo] *m* (-*s*; -*en* [ɛmbry'o:nən]) BIOL embryo

Emigrant [emi'grant] *m* (-*en*; -*en*), Emi'grantin *f* (-; -*nen*) emigrant, *esp* POL refugee; Emigration [emigra'tsjo:n] *f* (-; -*en*) emigration; in der ~ in exile; emigrieren [emi'gri:rən] *v/i* (*no -ge-*, *sein*) emigrate

Emission [emi'sjo:n] *f* (-; -*en*) PHYS emission; ECON issue

empfahl [ɛm'pfa:l] *pret of* empfehlen

Empfang [ɛm'pfaŋ] *m* (-[*e*]*s*; *Empfänge* [ɛm'pfɛŋə]) reception (a. radio, hotel), welcome; receipt (nach, bei on)

emp'fangen *v/t* (*irr*, fangen, *no -ge-*, *h*) receive; welcome; Emp'fänger(in) (-*s*; -/-; -*nen*) receiver (*m a. radio*); addressee

emp'fänglich *adj* susceptible (für to)

Empfängnis [ɛm'pfɛŋnɪs] *f* (-; *no pl*) MED conception; ~verhütung *f* MED contraception, birth control

Emp'fangs|bescheinigung *f* receipt; ~dame *f* receptionist

empfehlen [ɛm'pfe:lən] *v/t* (*irr*, *no -ge-*, *h*) recommend; emp'fehlenswert *adj* advisable; Emp'fehlung *f* (-; -*en*) recommendation

empfinden [ɛm'pfɪndən] *v/t* (*irr*, finden, *no -ge-*, *h*) feel (als ... to be ...); empfindlich [ɛm'pfɪntlɪç] *adj* sensitive (für, gegen to) (*a.* PHOT, CHEM); tender, delicate; touchy; irritable (*a.* MED); severe (*punishment etc*); ~e Stelle sore spot

Emp'findlichkeit *f* (-; -*en*) sensitivity;

PHOT speed; delicacy; touchiness

empfindsam [ɛm'pfɪntza:m] *adj* sensitive

Emp'findung *f* (-; -en) sensation; perception; feeling, emotion

empfohlen [ɛm'pfo:lən] *pp of* **empfehlen**

empor [ɛm'po:ɐ] *adv* up, upward(s)

empören [ɛm'pø:rən] *v/t* (*no -ge-, h*) outrage; shock; **sich ~ (über** *acc*) be outraged *or* shocked (at); **~d** *adj* shocking, outrageous

Emporkömmling [ɛm'po:ɐkœmlɪŋ] *contp m* (-s; -e) upstart

empört [ɛm'pø:ɐt] *adj* indignant (**über** *acc* at), shocked (at); **Em'pörung** *f* (-; *no pl*) indignation

Ende ['ɛndə] *n* (-s; *no pl*) end; *film:* ending; **am ~** at the end; in the end, finally; **zu ~** over; *time:* up; **zu ~ gehen** come to an end; **zu ~ lesen** finish reading; **er ist ~ zwanzig** he is in his late twenties; **~ Mai** at the end of May; **~ der achtziger Jahre** in the late eighties; *radio:* **~!** over!; **'enden** *v/i* (*ge-, h*) (come to an) end; stop, finish; F **~ als** end up as

'Endergebnis *n* final result

'endgültig *adj* final, definitive

Endlagerung ['ɛntla:gərʊŋ] *f* final disposal (*of radioactive waste*)

'endlich *adv* finally, at last

'endlos *adj* endless

'End|runde *f*, **~spiel** *n* SPORT final(s); **~spurt** *m* SPORT final spurt (*a. fig*); **~stati,on** *f* RAIL terminus, terminal; **~summe** *f* (sum) total

'Endung *f* (-; -en) LING ending

Energie [enɛr'gi:] *f* (-; -n) energy; TECH, ELECTR power; **~sparen** *n* energy saving, conservation of energy

ener'giebewusst *adj* energy-conscious

Ener'giekrise *f* energy crisis

ener'gielos *adj* lacking in energy

Ener'gie|quelle *f* source of energy; **~versorgung** *f* power supply

energisch [e'nɛrgɪʃ] *adj* energetic, vigorous

eng [ɛŋ] *adj* narrow; tight; cramped; *fig* close; **~ beieinander** close(ly) together

Engagement [ã:ga3ə'mã:] *n* (-s; -s) THEA *etc* engagement; POL commitment; **engagieren** [ã:ga'3i:rən] *v/t* (*no -ge-, h*) engage; **sich ~ für** be very involved in; **engagiert** [ã:ga'3i:ɐt] *adj*

involved, committed

Enge ['ɛŋə] *f* (-; *no pl*) narrowness; cramped conditions; **in die ~ treiben** drive into a corner

Engel ['ɛŋəl] *m* (-s; -) angel

'England England; **Engländer** ['ɛŋlendɐ] *m* (-s; -) Englishman; **die ~** *pl* the English; **Engländerin** ['ɛŋlɛndərɪn] *f* (-; -nen) Englishwoman

'englisch *adj* English; **auf Englisch** in English

'Englischunterricht *m* English lesson(s) *or* class(es); teaching of English

'Engpass *m* bottleneck (*a. fig*)

engstirnig ['ɛŋʃtɪrnɪç] *adj* narrow-minded

Enkel ['ɛŋkəl] *m* (-s; -) grandchild; grandson

'Enkelin *f* (-; -nen) granddaughter

enorm [e'nɔrm] *adj* enormous; F terrific

Ensemble [ã:'sã:bl] *n* (-s; -s) THEA company; cast

entarten [ɛnt'ʔa:ɐtən] *v/i* (*no -ge-, sein*), **ent'artet** *adj* degenerate; **Ent'artung** *f* (-; -en) degeneration

entbehren [ɛnt'be:rən] *v/t* (*no -ge-, h*) do without; spare; miss; **entbehrlich** [ɛnt'be:ɐlɪç] *adj* dispensable; superfluous; **Ent'behrung** *f* (-; -en) want, privation

ent'binden (*irr, binden, no -ge-, h*) **1.** *v/i* MED have the baby **2.** *v/t:* **j-n ~ von** *fig* relieve s.o. of; **entbunden werden von** MED give birth to

Ent'bindung *f* (-; -en) MED delivery

Ent'bindungsstati,on *f* MED maternity ward

entblößen [ɛnt'blø:sən] *v/t* (*no -ge-, h*) bare, uncover

ent'decken *v/t* (*no -ge-, h*) discover

Ent'decker *m* (-s; -), **Ent'deckerin** *f* (-; -nen) discoverer

Ent'deckung *f* (-; -en) discovery

Ente ['ɛntə] *f* (-; -n) ZO duck; F *fig* hoax

ent'ehren *v/t* (*no -ge-, h*) dishono(u)r

enteignen [ɛnt'ʔaignən] *v/t* (*no -ge-, h*) expropriate; dispossess *s.o.*

Ent'eignung *f* (-; -en) expropriation; dispossession

ent'erben *v/t* (*no -ge-, h*) disinherit

entern ['ɛntɐn] *v/t* (*ge-, h*) MAR board

ent|fachen [ɛnt'faxən] *v/t* (*no -ge-, h*) kindle, *fig a.* rouse; **~fallen** *v/i* (*irr, fallen, no -ge-, sein*) be cancelled; **~ auf**

(acc) fall to s.o. ('s share); *es ist mir ~* it has slipped my memory; **~falten** v/t *(no -ge-, h)* unfold; *fig* develop; **sich ~** unfold; *fig* develop *(zu* into)

entfernen [ɛnt'fɛrnən] v/t *(no -ge-, h)* remove *(a. fig)*; **sich ~** leave; **ent'fernt** *adj* distant *(a. fig)*; **weit** *(zehn Meilen)* **~** far (10 miles) away; **Ent'fernung** f *(-; -en)* distance; removal

Ent'fernungsmesser m *(-s; -)* PHOT range finder

ent'flammbar *adj* (in)flammable

entfremden [ɛnt'frɛmdən] v/t *(no -ge-, h)* estrange *(dat* from); **Ent'fremdung** f *(-; -en)* estrangement, alienation

ent'führen v/t *(no -ge-, h)* kidnap; AVIAT hijack; **Ent'führer** m *(-s; -)* kidnapper; AVIAT hijacker; **Ent'führung** f *(-; -en)* kidnapping; AVIAT hijacking

ent'gegen *prp (dat)* and *adv* contrary to; toward(s); **~gehen** v/i *(irr, gehen, sep, -ge-, sein)* go to meet

ent'gegengesetzt *adj* opposite

ent'gegenkommen v/i *(irr, kommen, sep, -ge-, sein)* come to meet; *fig* **j-m ~** meet s.o. halfway; **~d** *fig adj* obliging

ent'gegen|nehmen v/t *(irr, nehmen, sep, -ge-, h)* accept, receive; **~sehen** v/i *(irr, sehen, sep, -ge-, h)* await; look forward to s.th.; **~setzen** v/t *(sep, -ge-, h)* **j-m Widerstand ~** put up resistance to s.o.; **~treten** v/i *(irr, treten, sep, -ge-, sein)* walk towards; oppose; face

entgegnen [ɛnt'ge:gnən] v/i *(no -ge-, h)* reply, answer; retort

Ent'gegnung f *(-; -en)* reply; retort

ent'gehen v/i *(irr, gehen, no -ge-, sein)* escape; miss

entgeistert [ɛnt'gaistɐt] *adj* aghast

Entgelt [ɛnt'gɛlt] n *(-[e]s; -e)* remuneration; fee

ent|giften [ɛnt'gɪftən] v/t *(no -ge-, h)* decontaminate; **~gleisen** [ɛnt'glaizən] v/i *(no -ge-, sein)* RAIL be derailed; *fig* blunder; **~gleiten** *fig* v/i *(irr, gleiten, no -ge-, sein)* get out of control; **~gräten** [ɛnt'grɛːtən] v/t *(no -ge-, h)* bone, fil(l)et

ent'halten v/t *(irr, halten, no -ge-, h)* contain, hold; include; **sich ~** *(gen)* abstain *or* refrain from; **ent'haltsam** *adj* abstinent; moderate; **Ent'haltsamkeit** f *(-; no pl)* abstinence; moderation

Ent'haltung f *(-; -en)* abstention

ent'härten v/t *(no -ge-, h)* soften

enthaupten [ɛnt'hauptən] v/t *(no -ge-, h)* behead, decapitate

ent'hüllen v/t *(no -ge-, h)* uncover; unveil; *fig* reveal, disclose; **Ent'hüllung** f *(-; -en)* unveiling; *fig* revelation, disclosure

Enthusiasmus [ɛntu'zjasmʊs] m *(-; no pl)* enthusiasm; **Enthusiast(in)** [ɛntu-'zjast(-ɪn)] *(-en, -en/-; -nen)* enthusiast; *film*, SPORT F fan; **enthusi'astisch** *adj* enthusiastic

ent|'kleiden v/t and v/refl *(no -ge-, h)* undress, strip; **~'kommen** v/i *(irr, kommen, no -ge-, sein)* escape *(dat* from); **~'korken** v/t *(no -ge-, h)* uncork

entkräften [ɛnt'krɛftən] v/t *(no -ge-, h)* weaken *(a. fig)*; **Ent'kräftung** f *(-; -en)* weakening, exhaustion

ent'laden v/t *(irr, laden, no -ge-, h)* unload; *esp* ELECTR discharge; **sich ~** *esp* ELECTR discharge; *fig* explode

Ent'ladung f *(-; -en)* unloading; *esp* ELECTR discharge; *fig* explosion

ent'lang *prp (dat)* and *adv* along; *hier ~, bitte!* this way, please!; *die Straße etc ~* along the street *etc*

entlarven [ɛnt'larfən] v/t *(no -ge-, h)* unmask, expose

ent'lassen v/t *(irr, lassen, no -ge-, h)* dismiss, F fire, give *s.o.* the sack; MED discharge; JUR release

Ent'lassung f *(-; -en)* dismissal; MED discharge; JUR release

ent'lasten v/t *(no -ge-, h)* relieve *s.o.* of some of his work; JUR exonerate, clear *s.o.* of a charge; *den Verkehr ~* relieve the traffic congestion; **Ent'lastung** f *(-; -en)* relief; JUR exoneration

Ent'lastungszeuge m JUR witness for the defense *(Br* defence)

ent'laufen v/i *(irr, laufen, no -ge-, sein)* run away *(dat* from)

ent'legen *adj* remote, distant

ent|'locken v/t *(no -ge-, h)* draw, elicit *(dat* from); **~'lohnen** v/t *(no -ge-, h)* pay (off); **~'lüften** v/t *(no -ge-, h)* ventilate; **~machten** [ɛnt'maxtən] v/t *(no -ge-, h)* deprive *s.o.* of his power; **~militarisieren** [ɛntmilitari'ziːrən] v/t *(no -ge-, h)* demilitarize; **~mündigen** [ɛnt-'mʏndɪgən] v/t *(no -ge-, h)* JUR place under disability; **~mutigen** [ɛnt-'muːtɪgən] v/t *(no -ge-, h)* discourage;

~'nehmen *v/t* (*irr*, *nehmen*, *no -ge-*, *h*) take (*dat* from); **~ aus** (with-)draw from; *fig* gather *or* learn from; **~ 'puppen** *v/refl* (*no -ge-*, *h*) **sich ~ als** turn out to be; **~'rahmen** *v/t* (*no -ge-*, *h*) skim; **~'reißen** *v/t* (*irr*, *reißen*, *no -ge-*, *h*) snatch (away) (*dat* from); **~ 'rinnen** *v/i* (*irr*, *rinnen*, *no -ge-*, *sein*) escape (*dat* from); **~'rollen** *v/t* (*no -ge-*, *h*) unroll

ent'rüsten *v/t* (*no -ge-*, *h*) fill with indignation; **sich ~** become indignant (**über** *acc* at *s.th.*, with *s.o.*); **ent'rüstet** *adj* indignant (**über** *acc* at *s.th.*, with *s.o.*;) **Ent'rüstung** *f* (*-*; *-en*) indignation

Entsafter [ɛnt'zaftɐ] *m* (*-s*; *-*) juice extractor

ent'salzen *v/t* (*no -ge-*, *h*) desalinize

ent'schädigen *v/t* (*no -ge-*, *h*) compensate; **Ent'schädigung** *f* (*-*; *-en*) compensation

ent'schärfen *v/t* (*no -ge-*, *h*) defuse (*a. fig*)

ent'scheiden *v/t and v/i and v/refl* (*irr*, *scheiden*, *no -ge-*, *h*) decide (**für** on, in favo[u]r of; **gegen** against); settle; **er kann sich nicht ~** he can't make up his mind; **~d** *adj* decisive; crucial

Ent'scheidung *f* (*-*; *-en*) decision

entschieden [ɛnt'ʃiːdən] *adj* decided, determined, resolute; **~ dafür** strongly in favo(u)r of it; **Ent'schiedenheit** *f* (*-*; *no pl*) determination

ent'schließen *v/refl* (*irr*, *schließen*, *no -ge-*, *h*) decide, determine, make up one's mind; **Ent'schließung** *f* (*-*; *-en*) POL resolution

entschlossen [ɛnt'ʃlɔsən] *adj* determined, resolute; **Ent'schlossenheit** *f* (*-*; *no pl*) determination, resoluteness

Ent'schluss *m* decision, resolution

entschlüsseln [ɛnt'ʃlʏsəln] *v/t* (*no -ge-*, *h*) decipher, decode

entschuldigen [ɛnt'ʃʊldɪgən] *v/t* (*no -ge-*, *h*) excuse; **sich ~** apologize (**bei** to; **für** for); excuse o.s.; **~ Sie!** (I'm) sorry!; excuse me!; **Ent'schuldigung** *f* (*-*; *-en*) excuse; apology; **um ~ bitten** apologize; **~!** (I'm) sorry!; excuse me!

ent'setzen *v/t* (*no -ge-*, *h*) shock; horrify; **Ent'setzen** *n* (*-s*; *no pl*) horror, terror; **ent'setzlich** *adj* horrible, dreadful, terrible; atrocious; **ent'setzt** *adj* shocked; horrified

ent|'sichern *v/t* (*no -ge-*, *h*) release the safety catch of; **~'sinnen** *v/refl* (*irr*, *sinnen*, *no -ge-*, *h*) remember, recall

ent'sorgen *v/t* (*no -ge-*, *h*) dispose of

Ent'sorgung *f* (*-*; *-en*) (waste) disposal

ent'spannen *v/t and v/refl* (*no -ge-*, *h*) relax; **sich ~ a.** take it easy; *fig* ease (up); **ent'spannt** *adj* relaxed

Ent'spannung *f* (*-*; *-en*) relaxation; POL détente

ent'spiegelt *adj* OPT non-glare

ent'sprechen *v/i* (*irr*, *sprechen*, *no -ge-*, *h*) correspond to; answer to *a description*; meet (*requirements etc*); **~d** *adj* corresponding (*dat* to); appropriate

Ent'sprechung *f* (*-*; *-en*) equivalent

ent'springen *v/i* (*irr*, *springen*, *no -ge-*, *sein*) river: rise

entstehen *v/i* (*irr*, *stehen*, *no -ge-*, *sein*) come into being; arise; emerge, develop; **~ aus** originate from

Ent'stehung *f* (*-*; *-en*) origin

ent'stellen *v/t* (*no -ge-*, *h*) disfigure, deform; *fig* distort; **Ent'stellung** *f* (*-*; *-en*) disfigurement, deformation, distortion (*a. fig*)

entstört [ɛnt'ʃtøːɐt] *adj* ELECTR interference-free

ent'täuschen *v/t* (*no -ge-*, *h*) disappoint; **Ent'täuschung** *f* (*-*; *-en*) disappointment

entwaffnen [ɛnt'vafnən] *v/t* (*no -ge-*, *h*) disarm

Ent'warnung *f* all clear (signal)

ent'wässern *v/t* (*no -ge-*, *h*) drain; **Ent'wässerung** *f* (*-*; *-en*) drainage; CHEM dehydration

'entweder *cj*: **~ ... oder** either ... or

ent|'weichen *v/i* (*irr*, *weichen*, *no -ge-*, *sein*) escape (**aus** from); **~'weihen** *v/t* (*no -ge-*, *h*) desecrate; **~'wenden** *v/t* (*no -ge-*, *h*) pilfer, steal; **~'werfen** *v/t* (*irr*, *werfen*, *no -ge-*, *h*) design; draw up

ent'werten *v/t* (*no -ge-*, *h*) lower the value of (*a. fig*); cancel; **Ent'wertung** *f* (*-*; *-en*) devaluation; cancellation

ent'wickeln *v/t and v/refl* (*no -ge-*, *h*) develop (*a.* PHOT) (**zu** into); **Ent'wicklung** *f* (*-*; *-en*) development; BIOL *a.* evolution; adolescence, age of puberty

Ent'wicklungs|helfer *m*, **~helferin** *f* POL, ECON development aid volunteer; Peace Corps volunteer, *Br* VSO worker; **~hilfe** *f* development aid; **~land** *n* POL developing country

ent|wirren [ɛnt'vɪrən] *v/t (no -ge-, h)* disentangle (*a. fig*); **~'wischen** *v/i (no -ge-, sein)* get away

ent'würdigend *adj* degrading

Ent'wurf *m* outline, (rough) draft, plan; design; sketch

ent|'wurzeln *v/t (no -ge-, h)* uproot; **~ 'ziehen** *v/t (irr, ziehen, no -ge-, h)* take away (*dat* from); revoke (*license etc*); deprive of *rights etc*; CHEM extract; **sich j-m (e-r Sache) ~** evade s.o. (s.th.)

Ent'ziehungs|anstalt *f* substance (*Br* drug) abuse clinic; **~kur** *f* detoxi(fi)-cation (treatment), *a*. F drying out

entziffern [ɛnt'tsɪfɐn] *v/t (no -ge-, h)* decipher, make out

ent'zücken *v/t (no -ge-, h)* charm, delight; **Ent'zücken** *n (-s; no pl)* delight; **ent'zückend** *adj* delightful, charming, F sweet; **ent'zückt** *adj* delighted (*über acc, von* at, with)

Ent'zug *m* withdrawal; revocation

Ent'zugserscheinung *f* MED withdrawal symptom

entzündbar [ɛnt'tsʏntbaːɐ] *adj* (in)-flammable; **ent'zünden** *v/refl (no -ge-, h)* catch fire; MED become inflamed; **Ent'zündung** *f (-; -en)* MED inflammation

ent'zwei *adv* in two, to pieces

Enzyklopädie [ɛntsyklope'diː] *f (-; -n)* encyclop(a)edia

Epidemie [epide'miː] *f (-; -n)* MED epidemic (disease)

Epilog [epi'loːk] *m (-[e]s; -e* [epi'loːgə]) epilog, *Br* epilogue

episch ['eːpɪʃ] *adj* epic

Episode [epi'zoːdə] *f (-; -n)* episode

Epoche [e'pɔxə] *f (-; -n)* epoch, period, era

Epos ['eːpɔs] *n (-; Epen* ['eːpən]) epic (poem)

er [eːɐ] *pers pron* he; it

Er'achten *n*: *meines ~s* in my opinion

Erbanlage ['ɛrpʔanlaːgə] *f* BIOL genes, genetic code

erbarmen [ɛɐ'barmən] *v/refl (no -ge-, h)* **sich j-s ~** take pity on s.o.

erbärmlich [ɛɐ'bɛrmlɪç] *adj* pitiful, pitiable; miserable; mean

er'barmungslos *adj* pitiless, merciless

er'bauen *v/t (no -ge-, h)* build, con-

struct; **Er'bauer** *m (-s; -)* builder, constructor

er'baulich *adj* edifying; **Er'bauung** *fig f (-; -en)* edification, uplift

Erbe ['ɛrbə] **1.** *m (-n; -n)* heir **2.** *n (-s; no pl)* inheritance, heritage

erben ['ɛrbən] *v/t (ge-, h)* inherit

erbeuten [ɛɐ'bɔytən] *v/t (no -ge-, h)* MIL capture; *thief*: get away with

'Erbfaktor *m* BIOL gene

Erbin ['ɛrbɪn] *f (-; -nen)* heir, heiress

er'bitten *v/t (irr, bitten, no -ge-, h)* ask for, request

erbittert [ɛɐ'bɪtɐt] *adj* fierce, furious

'Erbkrankheit *f* MED hereditary disease

erblich ['ɛrplɪç] *adj* hereditary

er'blicken *v/t (no -ge-, h)* see, catch sight of

erblinden [ɛɐ'blɪndən] *v/i (no -ge-, sein)* go blind

er'brechen *v/t and v/refl (irr, brechen, no -ge-, h)* MED vomit

Erbschaft ['ɛrpʃaft] *f (-; -en)* inheritance, heritage

Erbse ['ɛrpsə] *f (-; -n)* BOT pea; *(grüne)* **~n** green peas

'Erbstück *n* heirloom

Erd|apfel ['eːɐtapfəl] *Austrian m* potato; **~ball** *m (-[e]s; no pl)* globe; **~beben** *n (-s; -)* earthquake; **~beere** *f* BOT strawberry; **~boden** *m* earth, ground

Erde ['eːɐdə] *f (-; -n) (no pl)* earth; ground, soil; → **eben**; **'erden** *v/t (ge-, h)* ELECTR earth, ground

erdenklich [ɛɐ'dɛŋklɪç] *adj* imaginable

Erd|gas ['eːɐtgaːs] *n* natural gas; **~geschoss** *n*, **~geschoß** *Austrian n* first (*Br* ground) floor

er'dichten *v/t (no -ge-, h)* invent, make up; **er'dichtet** *adj* invented, made-up

erdig ['eːɐdɪç] *adj* earthy

'Erd|klumpen *m* clod, lump of earth; **~kruste** *f* earth's crust; **~kugel** *f* globe; **~kunde** *f (-; no pl)* geography; **~leitung** *f* ELECTR ground (*Br* earth) connection; underground pipe(line); **~nuss** *f* BOT peanut; **~öl** *n* (mineral) oil, petroleum; **~reich** *n* ground, earth

erdreisten [ɛɐ'draɪstən] *v/refl (no -ge-, h)* F have the nerve

er'drosseln *v/t (no -ge-, h)* throttle

er'drücken *v/t (no -ge-, h)* crush (to death); **~d** *fig adj* overwhelming

'Erd|rutsch *m (-[e]s; -e)* landslide (*a.*

POL); **~teil** *m* GEOGR continent

er'dulden *v/t* (*no -ge-, h*) suffer, endure

'Erdumlaufbahn *f* earth orbit

'Erdung *f* (-; *-en*) ELECTR grounding, *Br* earthing

'Erdwärme *f* GEOL geothermal energy

er'eifern *v/refl* (*no -ge-, h*) get excited

ereignen [ɛɐ'ʔaignən] *v/refl* (*no -ge-, h*) happen, occur; **Ereignis** [ɛɐ'ʔaignɪs] *n* (*-ses; -se*) event, occurrence

er'eignisreich *adj* eventful

Erektion [erɛk'tsjoːn] *f* (-; *-en*) erection

Eremit [ere'miːt] *m* (*-en; -en*) hermit, anchorite

er'fahren¹ *v/t* (*irr, fahren, no -ge-, h*) hear; learn; experience

er'fahren² *adj* experienced

Er'fahrung *f* (-; *-en*) (work) experience

Er'fahrungsaustausch *m* exchange of experience; **er'fahrungsgemäß** *adv* as experience shows

er'fassen *v/t* (*no -ge-, h*) grasp; record, register; cover, include; IT collect

er'finden *v/t* (*irr, finden, no -ge-, h*) invent; **Er'finder(in)** (*-s; -/-; -nen*) inventor; **erfinderisch** [ɛɐ'fɪndərɪʃ] *adj* inventive; **Er'findung** *f* (-; *-en*) invention; **Er'findungskraft** *f* (-; *no pl*) inventiveness

Erfolg [ɛɐ'fɔlk] *m* (*-[e]s; -e*) success; result; **viel ~!** good luck!; **~ versprechend** promising; **er'folgen** *v/i* (*no -ge-, sein*) happen, take place; **er'folglos** *adj* unsuccessful; futile; **Er'folglosigkeit** *f* (-; *no pl*) lack of success; **er'folgreich** *adj* successful; **Er'folgserlebnis** *n* sense of achievement

erforderlich [ɛɐ'fɔrdəlɪç] *adj* necessary, required; **er'fordern** *v/t* (*no -ge-, h*) require, demand; **Erfordernis** [ɛɐ'fɔrdɐnɪs] *n* (*-ses; -se*) requirement, demand

er'forschen *v/t* (*no -ge-, h*) explore; investigate, study; **Er'forscher** *m* explorer; **Er'forschung** *f* exploration

er'freuen *v/t* (*no -ge-, h*) please

erfreulich [ɛɐ'frɔylɪç] *adj* pleasing, pleasant; gratifying

er'freut *adj* pleased (*über acc* at, about); **sehr ~!** pleased to meet you

er'frieren *v/i* (*irr, frieren, no -ge-, sein*) freeze to death; **Er'frierung** *f* (-; *-en*) MED frostbite

er'frischen *v/t and v/refl* (*no -ge-, h*) re-

fresh (o.s.); **~d** *adj* refreshing

Er'frischung *f* (-; *-en*) refreshment

erfroren [ɛɐ'froːrən] *adj* frostbitten; BOT killed by frost

er'füllen *fig v/t* (*no -ge-, h*) fulfil(l); keep (*promise etc*); serve (*purpose etc*); meet (*requirements etc*); **~ mit** fill with; **sich ~** be fulfilled, come true; **Er'füllung** *f* (-; *-en*) fulfil(l)ment; **in ~ gehen** come true

ergänzen [ɛɐ'gɛntsən] *v/t* (*no -ge-, h*) complement (**einander** each other); supplement, add; **~d** *adj* complementary, supplementary

Er'gänzung *f* (-; *-en*) completion; supplement, addition

ergattern [ɛɐ'gatɐn] F *v/t* (*no -ge-, h*) (manage to) get hold of

er'geben (*irr, geben, no -ge-, h*) **1.** *v/t* amount *or* come to **2.** *v/refl* surrender; *fig* arise; **sich ~ aus** result from; **sich ~ in** (*acc*) resign o.s. to

Er'gebenheit *f* (-; *no pl*) devotion

Ergebnis [ɛɐ'geːpnɪs] *n* (*-ses; -se*) result, SPORT *a.* score; outcome

er'gebnislos *adj* without result

er'gehen *v/i* (*irr, gehen, no -ge-, sein*) *order etc*: be issued (**an** *acc* to); **wie ist es dir ergangen?** how did things go with you?; **et. über sich ~ lassen** (patiently) endure s.th.

ergiebig [ɛɐ'giːbɪç] *adj* productive, rich; **Er'giebigkeit** *f* (-; *no pl*) (high) yield; productiveness

er'gießen *v/refl* (*irr, gießen, no -ge-, h*) **sich ~ über** (*acc*) pour down on

er'grauen *v/i* (*no -ge-, sein*) turn gray (*Br* grey)

er'greifen *v/t* (*irr, greifen, no -ge-, h*) seize, grasp, take hold of; take (*measures etc*); take up; *fig* move, touch

ergriffen [ɛɐ'grɪfən] *fig adj* moved

Er'griffenheit *f* (-; *no pl*) emotion

er'gründen *v/t* (*no -ge-, h*) find out, fathom

er'haben *adj* raised, elevated; *fig* sublime; **~ sein über** (*acc*) be above

er'halten¹ *v/t* (*irr, halten, no -ge-, h*) get, receive; keep, preserve; protect; support, maintain (*family etc*)

er'halten² *adj*: **gut ~** in good condition

erhältlich [ɛɐ'hɛltlɪç] *adj* obtainable, available

Er'haltung *f* (-; *no pl*) preservation; upkeep

er'hängen v/t (no -ge-, h) hang (**sich** o.s.)

er'heben v/t (irr, **heben**, no -ge-, h) raise (a. voice), lift; **sich ~** rise up (**gegen** against)

erheblich [ɛɐ'heːplɪç] adj considerable

Er'hebung f (-; -en) survey; revolt

erheitern [ɛɐ'haitən] v/t (no -ge-, h) cheer up, amuse; **erhellen** [ɛɐ'hɛlən] v/t (no -ge-, h) light up; fig throw light upon; **erhitzen** [ɛɐ'hɪtsən] v/t (no -ge-, h) heat; **sich ~** get hot; **er'hoffen** v/t (no -ge-, h) hope for

erhöhen [ɛɐ'høːən] v/t (no -ge-, h) raise; increase; **Er'höhung** f (-; -en) increase

er'holen v/refl (no -ge-, h) recover; relax, rest; **erholsam** [ɛɐ'hoːlzaːm] adj restful, relaxing; **Er'holung** f (-; no pl) recovery; relaxation

Er'holungsheim n rest home

erinnern [ɛɐ'ʔɪnɐn] v/t (no -ge-, h) j-n ~ **an** (acc) remind s.o. of; **sich ~ an** (acc) remember, recall; **Erinnerung** [ɛɐ-'ɪnərʊŋ] f (-; -en) memory (**an** acc of); remembrance, souvenir; keepsake; **zur ~ an** (acc) in memory of

erkalten [ɛɐ'kaltən] v/i (no -ge-, sein) cool down (a. fig)

erkälten [ɛɐ'kɛltən] v/refl (no -ge-, h) **sich ~** catch (a) cold; (**stark**) **erkältet sein** have a (bad) cold; **Er'kältung** f (-; -en) cold

erkennbar [ɛɐ'kɛnbaːɐ] adj recognizable; **er'kennen** v/t (irr, **kennen**, no -ge-, h) recognize (**an** dat by), know (by); see, realize; **er'kenntlich** adj: **sich** (j-m) **~ zeigen** show (s.o.) one's gratitude; **Er'kenntnis** f (-; -se) realization; discovery; pl findings

Er'kennungs|dienst m (police) records department; **~melo,die** f signature tune; **~zeichen** n badge; AVIAT markings

Erker ['ɛrkɐ] m (-s; -) ARCH bay; **~fenster** n ARCH bay window

er'klären v/t (no -ge-, h) explain (j-m to s.o.); declare; j-n (offiziell) **für ... ~** pronounce s.o. ...; **~d** adj explanatory

erklärlich [ɛɐ'klɛːɐlɪç] adj explainable; **er'klärt** adj declared; **Er'klärung** f (-; -en) explanation; declaration; definition; **e-e ~ abgeben** make a statement

er'klingen v/i (irr, **klingen**, no -ge-, sein) (re)sound, ring (out)

erkranken [ɛɐ'kraŋkən] v/i (no -ge-, sein) fall ill, get sick; **~ an** (dat) get; **Er-'krankung** f (-; -en) illness, sickness

erkunden [ɛɐ'kʊndən] v/t (no -ge-, h) explore

erkundigen [ɛɐ'kʊndɪgən] v/refl (no -ge-, h) inquire (**nach** about s.th.; after s.o.); make inquiries (about); **sich** (**bei j-m**) **nach dem Weg ~** ask (s.o.) the way; **Er'kundigung** f (-; -en) inquiry

Er'kundung f (-; -en) exploration; MIL reconnaissance

Erlagschein [ɛɐ'laːkʃain] Austrian m money-order form

er'lahmen v/i (no -ge-, sein) flag

Erlass [ɛɐ'las] m (-es; -e) decree; JUR remission; **er'lassen** v/t (irr, **lassen**, no -ge-, h) issue; enact (bill etc); **j-m et. ~** release s.o. from s.th.

erlauben [ɛɐ'laubən] v/t (no -ge-, h) allow, permit; **sich et. ~** permit o.s. (or dare) to do s.th.; treat o.s. to s.th.

Erlaubnis [ɛɐ'laupnɪs] f (-; no pl) permission; authority; **um ~ bitten** ask s.o.'s permission; **~schein** m permit

erläutern [ɛɐ'lɔytɐn] v/t (no -ge-, h) explain, illustrate; **Er'läuterung** f (-; -en) explanation; annotation

Erle ['ɛrlə] f (-; -n) BOT alder

er'leben v/t (no -ge-, h) experience; go through; see; have; **das werden wir nicht mehr ~** we won't live to see that

Erlebnis [ɛɐ'leːpnɪs] n (-ses; -se) experience; adventure

er'lebnisreich adj eventful

erledigen [ɛɐ'leːdɪgən] v/t (no -ge-, h) take care of, do, handle; settle; F finish s.o. (a. SPORT); do s.o. in; **erledigt** [ɛɐ-'leːdɪçt] adj finished, settled; F worn out; F **der ist ~!** he is done for

Er'ledigung f (-; -en) (no pl) settlement; pl things to do, shopping

er'legen v/t (no -ge-, h) HUNT shoot

erleichtern [ɛɐ'laiçtɐn] v/t (no -ge-, h) ease, relieve; **er'leichtert** adj relieved; **Erleichterung** [ɛɐ'laiçtərʊŋ] f (-; no pl) relief (**über** acc at)

er'leiden v/t (irr, **leiden**, no -ge-, h) suffer

er'lesen adj choice, select

er'leuchten v/t (no -ge-, h) illuminate

er'liegen v/i (irr, **liegen**, no -ge-, sein) succumb to

Er'liegen *n*: **zum ~ kommen** (**bringen**) come (bring) to a standstill

erlogen [ɛɐˈloːgən] *adj* false; **~ sein** be a lie

Erlös [ɛɐˈløːs] *m* (*-es*; *-e*) proceeds; profit(s)

erlosch [ɛɐˈlɔʃ] *pret of* **erlöschen**

erloschen [ɛɐˈlɔʃən] **1.** *pp of* **erlöschen 2.** *adj* extinct (*volcano*)

er'löschen *v/i* (*irr, no -ge-, sein*) go out; *fig* die; JUR lapse, expire

er'lösen *v/t* (*no -ge-, h*) deliver, free (*both: von* from); **Erlöser** [ɛɐˈløːzɐ] *m* (*-s; no pl*) REL Savio(u)r; **Er'lösung** *f* (*-; no pl*) REL salvation; relief

ermächtigen [ɛɐˈmɛçtɪgən] *v/t* (*no -ge-, h*) authorize; **Er'mächtigung** *f* (*-; -en*) authorization; authority

er'mahnen *v/t* (*no -ge-, h*) admonish; reprove, warn (*a.* SPORT)

Er'mahnung *f* (*-; -en*) admonition; warning; *esp* SPORT (first) caution

Er'mangelung *f*: **in ~** (*gen*) for want of

ermäßigt [ɛɐˈmɛːsɪçt] *adj* reduced, cut; **Er'mäßigung** *f* (*-; -en*) reduction, cut

er'messen *v/t* (*irr, messen, no -ge-, h*) assess; judge; **Er'messen** *n* (*-s; no pl*) discretion; **nach eigenem ~** at one's own discretion

er'mitteln (*no -ge-, h*) **1.** *v/t* find out; determine **2.** *v/i esp* JUR investigate; **Er'mittlung** *f* (*-; -en*) finding; JUR investigation

er'möglichen *v/t* (*no -ge-, h*) make possible

er'morden *v/t* (*no -ge-, h*) murder; *esp* POL assassinate; **Er'mordung** *f* (*-; -en*) murder; *esp* POL assassination

ermüden [ɛɐˈmyːdən] (*no -ge-*) **1.** *v/t* (*h*) tire, fatigue **2.** *v/i* (*sein*) tire, get tired, fatigue (*a.* TECH); **Er'müdung** *f* (*-; no pl*) fatigue, tiredness

er'muntern [ɛɐˈmʊntɐn] *v/t* (*no -ge-, h*) encourage; stimulate; **Er'munterung** *f* (*-; -en*) encouragement; incentive

ermutigen [ɛɐˈmuːtɪgən] *v/t* (*no -ge-, h*) encourage; **~d** *adj* encouraging **Er'mutigung** *f* (*-; -en*) encouragement

er'nähren *v/t* (*no -ge-, h*) feed; support (*family etc*); **sich ~ von** live on; **Er'nährer** *m* (*-s; -*) breadwinner, supporter; **Er'nährung** *f* (*-; no pl*) nutrition, food, diet

er'nennen *v/t* (*irr, nennen, no -ge-, h*)

j-n ~ zu appoint s.o. (to be)

Er'nennung *f* (*-; -en*) appointment

erneuern [ɛɐˈnɔʏɐn] *v/t* (*no -ge-, h*) renew; **Er'neuerung** *f* (*-; -en*) renewal

er'neut 1. *adj* renewed **2.** *adv* once more

erniedrigen [ɛɐˈniːdrɪgən] *v/t* (*no -ge-, h*) humiliate; **sich ~** degrade o.s. **Er'niedrigung** *f* (*-; -en*) humiliation

ernst [ɛrnst] *adj* serious, earnest; **~ nehmen** take s.o. *or* s.th. seriously

Ernst *m* (*-es; no pl*) seriousness, earnest; **im ~**(?) seriously(?); **ist das dein ~?** are you serious?

'ernsthaft, 'ernstlich *adj* serious

Ernte [ˈɛrntə] *f* (*-; -n*) harvest; crop(s) **'Erntedankfest** *n* Thanksgiving (Day), *Br* harvest festival

'ernten *v/t* (*ge-, h*) harvest, reap (*a. fig*)

er'nüchtern *v/t* (*no -ge-, h*) sober, *fig a.* disillusion; **Er'nüchterung** *f* (*-; -en*) sobering up; *fig* disillusionment

Eroberer [ɛɐˈʔoːbərɐ] *m* (*-s; -*) conqueror; **erobern** [ɛɐˈʔoːbɐn] *v/t* (*no -ge-, h*) conquer; **Er'oberung** *f* (*-; -en*) conquest (*a. fig*)

er'öffnen *v/t* (*no -ge-, h*) open; inaugurate; disclose *s.th.* (*j-m* to s.o.)

Er'öffnung *f* (*-; -en*) opening; inauguration; disclosure

erörtern [ɛɐˈʔœrtɐn] *v/t* (*no -ge-, h*) discuss; **Er'örterung** *f* (*-; -en*) discussion

Erotik [eˈroːtɪk] *f* (*-; no pl*) eroticism

erotisch [eˈroːtɪʃ] *adj* erotic

er'pressen *v/t* (*no -ge-, h*) blackmail; extort; **Er'presser(in)** (*-s; -/-; -nen*) blackmailer; **Er'pressung** *f* (*-; -en*) blackmail(ing); extortion

er'proben *v/t* (*no -ge-, h*) try, test

er'raten *v/t* (*irr, raten, no -ge-, h*) guess

er'rechnen *v/t* (*no -ge-, h*) calculate, work *s.th.* out

erregbar [ɛɐˈreːkbaːɐ] *adj* excitable; irritable

er'regen *v/t* (*no -ge-, h*) excite, *sexually: a.* arouse; *fig* rouse; cause; **sich ~** get excited; **~d** *adj* exciting, thrilling

Er'reger *m* (*-s; -*) MED germ, virus

Er'regung *f* (*-; -en*) excitement

erreichbar [ɛɐˈraɪçbaːɐ] *adj* within reach (*a. fig*); available; **leicht ~** within easy reach; **nicht ~** out of reach; not available; **er'reichen** *v/t* (*no -ge-, h*) reach; catch (*train etc*); **es ~, dass ...** succeed in doing *s.th.*; **et. ~** get some-

where; **telefonisch zu ~ sein** have a
(*Br* be on the) phone

er'**richten** *v/t* (*no -ge-, h*) put up, erect;
fig found, *esp* ECON set up

Er'**richtung** *f* (-; *-en*) erection; *fig* establishment

er'**ringen** *v/t* (*irr, ringen, no -ge-, h*) win,
gain; achieve

er'**röten** *v/i* (*no -ge-, sein*) blush

Errungenschaft [ɛɛ'ruŋənʃaft] *f* (-;
-en) achievement; *m-e neueste ~* my
latest acquisition

Ersatz [ɛɛ'zats] *m* (*-es; no pl*) replacement; substitute; surrogate; compensation; damages; *als ~ für* in exchange
for; *~dienst m → Zivildienst*; *~mann
m* (*-[e]s; -leute*) substitute (*a.* SPORT);
~mine f refill; *~reifen m* MOT spare tire
(*Br* tyre); *~spieler m* SPORT substitute;
~teil n TECH spare part

er'**schaffen** *v/t* (*irr, schaffen, no -ge-, h*)
create

er'**schallen** *v/i* ([*irr, schallen,*] *no -ge-,
sein*) (re)sound, ring (out)

er'**scheinen** *v/i* (*irr, scheinen, no -ge-,
sein*) appear, F turn up; be published;
Er'scheinen *n* (*-s; no pl*) appearance;
publication; **Er'scheinung** *f* (-; *-en*) appearance; apparition; phenomenon

er'**schießen** *v/t* (*irr, schießen, no -ge-,
h*) shoot (dead); **erschlaffen** [ɛɛ-
'ʃlafən] *v/i* (*no -ge-, sein*) go limp; *fig*
weaken; er'**schlagen** *v/t* (*irr, schlagen, no -ge-, h*) kill; er'**schließen** *v/t*
(*irr, schließen, no -ge-, h*) open up; develop

erschollen [ɛɛ'ʃɔlən] *pp of* **erschallen**

er'**schöpfen** *v/t* (*no -ge-, h*) exhaust; er
'**schöpft** *adj* exhausted

Er'**schöpfung** *f* (-; *no pl*) exhaustion

erschrak [ɛɛ'ʃraːk] *pret of* **erschrecken**
2

er'**schrecken** 1. *v/t* (*no -ge-, h*) frighten,
scare 2. *v/i* (*irr, no -ge-, sein*) be frightened (*über acc* at); *~d adj* alarming;
terrible

erschrocken [ɛɛ'ʃrɔkən] *pp of* **erschrecken** 2

erschüttern [ɛɛ'ʃʏtɐn] *v/t* (*no -ge-, h*)
shake; *fig a.* shock; *fig* move

Er'**schütterung** *f* (-; *-en*) shock (*a. fig*);
TECH vibration

erschweren [ɛɛ'ʃveːrən] *v/t* (*no -ge-, h*)
make more difficult; aggravate

er'**schwindeln** *v/t* (*no -ge-, h*) obtain
s.th. by fraud; (*sich*) *et. von j-m ~* swindle s.o. out of s.th.

er'**schwingen** *v/t* (*irr, schwingen, no
-ge-, h*) afford; er'**schwinglich** *adj*
within one's means, affordable; reasonable (*price*)

er'**sehen** *v/t* (*irr, sehen, no -ge-, h*) see,
learn, gather (*all: aus* from)

ersetzbar [ɛɛ'zɛtsbaːɐ] *adj* replaceable; reparable; er'**setzen** *v/t* (*no -ge-,
h*) replace (*durch* by); compensate
for; *j-m et. ~* reimburse s.o. for s.th.

er'**sichtlich** *adj* evident, obvious

er'**sparen** *v/t* (*no -ge-, h*) save; *j-m et. ~*
spare s.o. s.th.

Ersparnisse [ɛɛ'ʃpaːɐnɪsə] *pl* savings

erst [eːɐst] *adv* first; at first; *~ jetzt
(gestern)* only now (yesterday); *~
nächste Woche* not before *or* until
next week; *es ist ~ neun Uhr* it's only
nine o'clock; *eben ~* just (now); *~ recht*
all the more; *~ recht nicht* even less; →
einmal

er'**starren** *v/i* (*no -ge-, sein*) stiffen; *fig*
freeze; er'**starrt** *adj* stiff; numb

erstatten [ɛɛ'ʃtatən] *v/t* (*no -ge-, h*) refund, reimburse (*j-m et.* s.o. for s.th.);
Bericht ~ (give a) report (*über acc*
on); *Anzeige ~* report to the police

'**Erstaufführung** *f* THEA first night *or*
performance, premiere, *film: a.* first
run

er'**staunen** *v/t* (*no -ge-, h*) surprise, astonish; **Er'staunen** *n* (*-s; no pl*) surprise, astonishment; *in ~ (ver)setzen*
astonish; er'**staunlich** *adj* surprising,
astonishing; er'**staunt** *adj* astonished

'**Erstausgabe** *f* first edition

'**erst**'**beste** *adj* first; any old

'**erste** *adj* first; *auf den ~n Blick* at first
sight; *fürs Erste* for the time being; *als
Erste(r)* first; *zum ~n Mal(e)* for the
first time; *am Ersten* on the first

er'**stechen** *v/t* (*irr, stechen, no -ge-, h*)
stab

'**erstens** *adv* first(ly), in the first place

'**Erstere**: *der (die, das) ~* the former

er'**sticken** *v/t* (*no -ge-, h*) *and v/i* (*sein*)
choke, suffocate; **Er'stickung** *f* (-; *no
pl*) suffocation

erst|**klassig** ['eːɐstklasɪç] *adj* first-
-class, F *a.* super; *~malig* ['eːɐstmaːlɪç]
adj first; *~mals* ['eːɐstmaːls] *adv* for

the first time
er'streben v/t (no -ge-, h) strive after
er'strebenswert adj desirable
er'strecken v/refl (no -ge-, h) extend, stretch (**bis, auf** acc to; **über** acc over); **sich ~ über** (acc) a. cover
'Erstschlag m MIL first strike
er'suchen v/t (no -ge-, h) request
er'tappen v/t (no -ge-, h) catch; → **Tat**
er'tönen v/i (no -ge-, sein) (re)sound
Ertrag [ɛɐ̯'traːk] m (-[e]s; Erträge [ɛɐ̯-'trɛːɡə]) AGR yield, produce, TECH a. output; ECON proceeds, returns
er'tragen v/t (irr, tragen, no -ge-, h) bear, endure; stand
erträglich [ɛɐ̯'trɛːklɪç] adj bearable, tolerable
er'tränken v/t (no -ge-, h) drown
er'trinken v/i (irr, trinken, no -ge-, sein) drown
erübrigen [ɛɐ̯'ʔyːbrɪɡən] v/t (no -ge-, h) spare; **sich ~** be unnecessary
Erw. abbr of **Erwachsene(r)** adult(s)
er'wachen v/i (no -ge-, sein) wake (up); esp fig awake, awaken
er'wachsen[1] v/i (irr, wachsen, no -ge-, sein) arise (**aus** from)
er'wachsen[2] adj grown-up, adult
Er'wachsene m, f (-n; -n) adult; **nur für ~!** adults only!; **Er'wachsenenbildung** f adult education
erwägen [ɛɐ̯'vɛːɡən] v/t (irr, wägen, no -ge-, h) consider, think s.th. over; **Er-'wägung** f (-; -en) consideration; **in ~ ziehen** take into consideration
erwähnen [ɛɐ̯'vɛːnən] v/t (no -ge-, h) mention; **Er'wähnung** f (-; -en) mention(ing)
er'wärmen v/t and v/refl (no -ge-, h) warm (up); fig **sich ~ für** warm to
Er'wärmung f (-; -en) warming up; **~ der Erdatmosphäre** global warming
er'warten v/t (no -ge-, h) expect; wait for, await; **Er'wartung** f (-; -en) expectation, anticipation
er'wartungsvoll adj and adv full of expectation, expectant(ly)
er'wecken fig v/t (no -ge-, h) awaken; arouse; → **Anschein**
er'weisen v/t (irr, weisen, no -ge-, h) do (service etc); show (respect etc); **sich ~ als** prove to be
erweitern [ɛɐ̯'vaitɐn] v/t and v/refl (no -ge-, h) extend, enlarge; esp ECON ex-

pand; **Er'weiterung** f (-; -en) extension, enlargement, expansion
Erwerb [ɛɐ̯'vɛrp] m (-[e]s; -e) acquisition; purchase; income; **er'werben** v/t (irr, werben, no -ge-, h) acquire (a. fig); purchase
er'werbs|los adj unemployed; **~tätig** adj (gainfully) employed, working; **~unfähig** adj unable to work
Er'werbung f (-; -en) acquisition; purchase
erwidern [ɛɐ̯'viːdɐn] v/t (no -ge-, h) reply, answer; return (visit etc)
Er'widerung f (-; -en) reply, answer; return
er'wischen v/t (no -ge-, h) catch, get; **ihn hat's erwischt** he's had it
er'wünscht adj desired; desirable; welcome
er'würgen v/t (no -ge-, h) strangle
Erz [eːɐ̯ts] n (-es; -e) ore
er'zählen v/t (no -ge-, h) tell; narrate; **man hat mir erzählt** I was told
Er'zähler m (-s; -), **Er'zählerin** f (-; -nen) narrator
Er'zählung f (-; -en) (short) story, tale
'Erzbischof m REL archbishop
'Erzbistum n REL archbishopric
'Erzengel m REL archangel
er'zeugen v/t (no -ge-, h) ECON produce (a. fig); TECH make, manufacture; ELECTR generate; fig cause, create; **Er-'zeuger** m (-s; -) ECON producer; **Er-'zeugnis** n (-ses; -se) ECON product (a. fig); **Er'zeugung** f (-; -en) ECON production
er'ziehen v/t (irr, ziehen, no -ge-, h) bring up, raise; educate; **j-n zu et. ~** teach s.o. to be or to do s.th.
Erzieher [ɛɐ̯'tsiːɐ] m (-s; -), **Erzieherin** [ɛɐ̯'tsiːərɪn] f (-; -nen) educator; teacher; (qualified) kindergarten teacher; **er'zieherisch** adj educational, pedagogic(al); **Er'ziehung** f (-; no pl) upbringing; education
Er'ziehungs|anstalt f reform (Br approved) school; **~berechtigte** m, f (-n; -n) parent or guardian; **~wesen** n (-s; no pl) educational system
er'zielen v/t (no -ge-, h) achieve; SPORT score
erzogen [ɛɐ̯'tsoːɡən] adj: **gut ~ sein** be well-bred; **schlecht ~ sein** be ill-bred
er'zwingen v/t (irr, zwingen, no -ge-, h)

(en)force

es [ɛs] *pers pron* it; he; she; ~ *gibt* there is, there are; *ich bin* ~ it's me; *ich hoffe* ~ I hope so; *ich kann* ~ I can (do it)

Esche ['ɛʃə] *f* (-; *-n*) BOT ash (tree)

Esel ['eːzəl] *m* (*-s*; -) ZO donkey, ass (*a.* F)

'Eselsbrücke *f* mnemonic

'Eselsohr *fig n* dog-ear

Eskorte [ɛs'kɔrtə] *f* (-; *-n*) MIL escort, MAR *a.* convoy

essbar ['ɛsbaːɐ] *adj* eatable; edible

essen ['ɛsən] *v/t and v/i* (*irr, ge-, h*) eat; *zu Mittag* ~ (have) lunch; *zu Abend* ~ have supper (*or* dinner); ~ *gehen* eat *or* dine out; *'Essen n* (*-s*; -) food; meal; dish; dinner

'Essens|marke *f* meal ticket; ~*zeit f* lunchtime; dinner *or* supper time

Essig ['ɛsɪç] *m* (*-s*; *-e*) vinegar

'Essiggurke *f* pickled gherkin, pickle

Ess|löffel *m* tablespoon; ~*stäbchen pl* chopsticks; ~*tisch m* dining table; ~*zimmer n* dining room

Estrich ['ɛstrɪç] *m* (*-s*; *-e*) ARCH flooring, subfloor; *Swiss:* loft, attic, garret

etablieren [eta'bliːrən] *v/refl* (*no -ge-, h*) establish o.s.

Etage [e'taːʒə] *f* (-; *-n*) floor, stor(e)y; *auf der ersten* ~ on the second (*Br* first) floor; **E'tagenbett** *n* bunk bed

Etappe [e'tapə] *f* (-; *-n*) stage, SPORT *a.* leg

Etat [e'taː] *m* (*-s*; *-s*) budget

Ethik ['eːtɪk] *f* (-; *no pl*) ethics

ethisch ['eːtɪʃ] *adj* ethical

ethnisch ['ɛtnɪʃ] *adj* ethnic

Etikett [eti'kɛt] *n* (*-[e]s*; *-e[n]*) label (*a. fig*); (price) tag; **Eti'kette** *f* (-; *-n*) etiquette; **etikettieren** [etikɛ'tiːrən] *v/t* (*no -ge-, h*) label

etliche ['ɛtlɪçə] *indef pron* several, quite a few

Etui [ɛt'viː] *n* (*-s*; *-s*) case

etwa ['ɛtva] *adv* about, around; perhaps, by any chance; *nicht* ~*, dass* not that; **etwaig** ['ɛtvaɪç] *adj* any

etwas ['ɛtvas] **1.** *indef pron* something; anything **2.** *adj* some; any **3.** *adv* a little, somewhat

EU [eː'uː] *abbr of* **Europäische Union** EU, European Union

euch [ɔʏç] *pers pron* you; ~ (*selbst*) yourselves; **euer** ['ɔʏɐ] *poss pron* your; *der* (*die, das*) *Eu(e)re* yours

Eule ['ɔʏlə] *f* (-; *-n*) ZO owl; ~*n nach A-then tragen* carry coals to Newcastle

euresgleichen ['ɔʏrəs'glaɪçən] *pron* people like you, F *contp* the likes of you

Euro... ['ɔʏro] *in cpds ...cheque etc:* Euro...

Europa [ɔʏ'roːpa] Europe; ~*... in cpds* European; **Europäer** [ɔʏro'pɛːɐ] *m* (*-s*; -), **Europäerin** [ɔʏro'pɛːərɪn] *f* (-; *-nen*), **euro'päisch** *adj* European; *Europäische Gemeinschaft* European Community

Euter ['ɔʏtɐ] *n* (*-s*; -) udder

ev. *abbr of* **evangelisch** Prot., Protestant

evakuieren [evaku'iːrən] *v/t* (*no -ge-, h*) evacuate

evangelisch [evaŋ'geːlɪʃ] *adj* REL Protestant; ~*-lutherisch* Lutheran

Evangelium [evaŋ'geːljʊm] *n* (*-s*; *-lien*) Gospel

eventuell [evɛntu'ɛl] **1.** *adj* possible **2.** *adv* possibly, perhaps

evtl. *abbr of* **eventuell** poss., possibly

ewig ['eːvɪç] *adj* eternal; F constant, endless; *auf* ~ for ever; **'Ewigkeit** *f* (-; *no pl*) eternity; F *eine* ~ (for) ages

exakt [ɛ'ksakt] *adj* exact, precise

Ex'aktheit *f* (-; *no pl*) exactness, precision

Examen [ɛ'ksaːmən] *n* (*-s*; *Examina* [ɛ-'ksaːmina]) exam, examination

Exekutive [ɛkseku'tiːvə] *f* (-; *-n*) POL executive (power)

Exemplar [ɛksɛm'plaːɐ] *n* (*-s*; *-e*) specimen; copy

exerzieren [ɛksɛr'tsiːrən] *v/i* (*no -ge-, h*) MIL drill

Exil [ɛ'ksiːl] *n* (*-s*; *-e*) exile

Existenz [ɛksɪs'tɛnts] *f* (-; *-en*) existence; living, livelihood; ~*kampf m* struggle for survival; ~*minimum n* subsistence level

existieren [ɛksɪs'tiːrən] *v/i* (*no -ge-, h*) exist; live (*von* on)

exklusiv [ɛksklu'ziːf] *adj* exclusive, select

exotisch [ɛ'ksoːtɪʃ] *adj* exotic

Expansion [ɛkspan'zjoːn] *f* (-; *-en*) expansion

Expedition [ɛkspedi'tsjoːn] *f* (-; *-en*) expedition

Experiment [ɛksperi'mɛnt] *n* (*-[e]s*; *-e*), **experimentieren** [ɛksperimɛn'tiːrən]

v/i (*no -ge-, h*) experiment
Experte [ɛks'pɛrtə] *m* (*-n; -n*), **Ex-**
'**pertin** *f* (*-; -nen*) expert (**für** on)
explodieren [ɛksplo'diːrən] *v/i* (*no -ge-,
sein*) explode (*a. fig*), burst; **Explosion**
[ɛksplo'zjoːn] *f* (*-; -en*) explosion (*a.
fig*); **explosiv** [ɛksplo'ziːf] *adj* explosive
Export [ɛks'pɔrt] *m* (*-[e]s; -e*) (*no pl*)
export(ation); exports
exportieren [ɛkspɔr'tiːrən] *v/t* (*no -ge-,
h*) export
Express [ɛks'prɛs] *m* (*-es; no pl*) RAIL
express; **per ~** by special delivery, *Br*
express

extra ['ɛkstra] *adv* extra; separately; F
on purpose; **~ für dich** especially for
you
Extra *n* (*-s; -s*), **~blatt** *n* extra
Extrakt [ɛks'trakt] *m* (*-[e]s; -e*) extract
extravagant [ɛkstrava'gant] *adj* flam-
boyant
extrem [ɛks'treːm] *adj*, **Ex'trem** *n* (*-s;
-e*) extreme; **Extremist(in)** [ɛkstre-
'mɪst(ɪn)] (*-en; -en/-; -nen*), **extre-**
'**mistisch** *adj* extremist, ultra
Exzellenz [ɛkstsɛ'lɛnts] *f* (*-; -en*) Excel-
lency
exzentrisch [ɛks'tsɛntrɪʃ] *adj* eccentric
Exzess [ɛks'tsɛs] *m* (*-ses; -se*) excess

F

Fa. *abbr of* **Firma** firm; Messrs.
Fabel ['faːbəl] *f* (*-; -n*) fable (*a. fig*)
'**fabelhaft** *adj* fantastic, wonderful
Fabrik [fa'briːk] *f* (*-; -en*) factory, works,
shop; **Fabrikant** [fabri'kant] *m* (*-en;
-en*) factory owner; manufacturer
Fa'brikarbeiter *m* factory worker
Fabrikat [fabri'kaːt] *n* (*-[e]s; -e*) make,
brand; product
Fabrikation [fabrika'tsjoːn] *f* (*-; -en*)
manufacturing, production
Fabrikati'onsfehler *m* flaw
Fa'brik|besitzer *m* factory owner; **~wa-**
re *f* manufactured product(s)
Fach [fax] *n* (*-[e]s; Fächer* ['fɛçɐ] compartment; pigeonhole; shelf; PED, UNIV
subject; *fig* **Fachgebiet**; **~arbeiter** *m*
skilled worker; **~arzt** *m*, **~ärztin** *f* specialist (**für** in); **~ausbildung** *f* professional training; **~ausdruck** *m* technical
term; **~buch** *n* (cap)ability; specialist book
Fächer ['fɛçɐ] *m* (*-s; -*) fan
'**Fach|frau** *f* expert; **~gebiet** *n* line, field;
trade, business; **~geschäft** *n* dealer
(specializing in ...); **~hochschule** *f*
appr (technial) college, *esp Br* poly-
technic; **~kenntnisse** *pl* specialized
knowledge
'**fachkundig** *adj* competent, expert
'**fachlich** *adj* professional, specialized
'**Fach|litera,tur** *f* specialized literature;
~mann *m* (*-[e]s; -leute*) expert
fachmännisch ['faxmɛnɪʃ] *adj* expert

'**Fachschule** *f* technical school *or* college
fachsimpeln ['faxzɪmpəln] *v/i* (*ge-, h*)
talk shop
'**Fach|werk** *n* framework; **~werkhaus** *n*
half-timbered house; **~zeitschrift** *f*
(professional *or* specialist) journal
Fackel ['fakəl] *f* (*-; -n*) torch; **~zug** *m*
torchlight procession
fade ['faːdə] *adj* GASTR tasteless, flat;
stale; *fig* dull, boring
Faden ['faːdən] *m* (*-s; Fäden* ['fɛːdən])
thread (*a. fig*); **~fadenscheinig** *adj*
threadbare; *fig* flimsy (*excuse etc*)
fähig ['fɛːɪç] *adj* capable (**zu** of [*doing*]
s.th.), able (to *do s.th.*); '**Fähigkeit** *f* (*-;
-en*) (cap)ability; talent, gift
fahl [faːl] *adj* pale; ashen (*face*)
fahnden ['faːndən] *v/i* (*ge-, h*) search
(**nach** for); '**Fahndung** *f* (*-; -en*) search;
'**Fahndungsliste** *f* wanted list
Fahne ['faːnə] *f* (*-; -n*) flag; *mst fig* banner; F **e-e ~ haben** reek of alcohol
'**Fahnen|flucht** *f* (*-; no pl*) MIL deser-
tion; **~stange** *f* flagpole, flagstaff
Fahrbahn ['faːɐ̯baːn] *f* road(way), pavement; MOT lane
'**fahrbar** *adj* mobile
Fähre ['fɛːrə] *f* (*-; -n*) ferry(boat)
fahren ['faːrən] (*irr, ge-*) **1.** *v/i* (*sein*) go;
bus etc: run; leave; MOT drive; ride; **mit
dem Auto** (**Zug, Bus** *etc*) **~** go by car
(train, bus *etc*); **über e-e Brücke** *etc*

~ cross a bridge *etc*; *mit der Hand über et.* ~ run one's hand over s.th.; *was ist denn in dich gefahren?* what's got into you? **2.** *v/t* (*h*) drive (*car etc*); ride (*bicycle etc*); carry

Fahrer ['faːrɐ] *m* (*-s*; -) driver; **~flucht** *f* hit-and-run offense (*Br* offence)

'**Fahrerin** *f* (-; -*nen*) driver

Fahr|gast ['faːɐɡast] *m* passenger; **~geld** *n* fare; **~gelegenheit** *f* means of transport(ation); **~gemeinschaft** *f* car pool; **~gestell** *n* MOT chassis; AVIAT → *Fahrwerk*; **~karte** *f* ticket

'**Fahrkarten|auto,mat** *m* ticket machine; **~entwerter** *m* (*-s*; -) ticket-cancel(l)ing machine; **~schalter** *m* ticket window

'**fahrlässig** *adj* careless, reckless (*a.* JUR); **grob ~** grossly negligent

'**Fahrlehrer** *m* driving instructor

'**Fahrplan** *m* timetable, schedule

'**fahrplanmäßig 1.** *adj* scheduled **2.** *adv* according to schedule; on time

'**Fahr|preis** *m* fare; **~prüfung** *f* driving test; **~rad** *n* bicycle, F bike; **~schein** *m* ticket; **~schule** *f* driving school; **~schüler** *m* MOT student driver, *Br* learner (driver); PED non-local student; **~stuhl** *m* elevator, *Br* lift; **~stunde** *f* driving lesson

Fahrt [faːɐt] *f* (-; -*en*) ride, MOT *a.* drive, trip, journey, MAR voyage, cruise; speed (*a.* MOT); *in voller ~* at full speed

Fährte ['fɛːɐtə] *f* (-; -*n*) track (*a. fig*)

'**Fahrtenschreiber** *m* MOT tachograph

'**Fahrwasser** *n* MAR fairway

'**Fahrwerk** *n* AVIAT landing gear

'**Fahrzeug** *n* (-[*e*]*s*; -*e*) vehicle

Fairness ['fɛːɐnɪs] *f* (-; *no pl*) fair play

Faktor ['faktoːɐ] *m* (-*s*; -*en* [fak'toːrən]) factor

Fakultät [fakʊl'tɛːt] *f* (-; -*en*) UNIV faculty, department

Falke ['falkə] *m* (-*n*; -*n*) ZO hawk, falcon

Fall [fal] *m* (-[*e*]*s*; *Fälle* ['fɛlə]) fall; LING, JUR, MED case; *auf jeden ~* in any case; *auf keinen ~* on no account; *für den ~, dass ...* in case ...; *gesetzt den ~, dass* suppose (that); *zu ~ bringen* fig defeat

Falle ['falə] *f* (-; -*n*) trap (*a. fig*)

fallen ['falən] *v/i* (*irr, ge-, sein*) fall (*a. rain etc*), drop; ~ *lassen* drop (*a. fig*); MIL be killed (in action); *ein Tor fiel* SPORT a goal was scored

fällen ['fɛlən] *v/t* (*ge-, h*) fell, cut down (*tree*); JUR pass (*sentence*); make (*a decision etc*)

'**fallenlassen** ['faləlasən] *v/i* (*irr, fallen, no ge-, h*) *fig* drop

fällig ['fɛlɪç] *adj* due; payable

'**Fall|obst** *n* windfall; **~rückzieher** *m* soccer: overhead kick

falls [fals] *cj* if, in case; ~ *nicht* unless

'**Fallschirm** *m* parachute; **~jäger** *m* MIL paratrooper; **~springen** *n* MIL parachuting; SPORT skydiving; **~springer** *m* MIL parachutist; SPORT skydiver

'**Falltür** *f* trapdoor

falsch [falʃ] *adj and adv* wrong; false (*a. fig*); forged; ~ *gehen* watch: be wrong; *et.* ~ *aussprechen (schreiben, verstehen etc)* mispronounce (misspell, misunderstand *etc*) s.th.; ~ *verbunden!* TEL sorry, wrong number

fälschen ['fɛlʃən] *v/t* (*ge-, h*) forge, fake; counterfeit; '**Fälscher** *m* (-*s*; -) forger

'**Falsch|geld** *n* counterfeit *or* false money; **~spieler** *m* cheat

'**Fälschung** *f* (-; -*en*) forgery; counterfeit; '**fälschungssicher** *adj* forgery-proof

Falt... ['falt-] *in cpds* ...*bett*, ...*boot etc*: folding ...; **Falte** ['faltə] *f* (-; -*n*) fold; wrinkle; pleat; crease; '**falten** *v/t* (*ge-, h*) fold; '**Faltenrock** *m* pleated skirt

Falter ['faltɐ] *m* (-*s*; -) ZO butterfly

faltig ['faltɪç] *adj* wrinkled

familiär [fami'ljɛːɐ] *adj* personal; informal; **~e Probleme** family problems

Familie [fa'miːljə] *f* (-; -*n*) family (*a.* ZO, BOT)

Fa'milien|angelegenheit *f* family affair; **~anschluss** *m*: ~ *haben* live as one of the family; **~name** *m* family (*or* last) name, surname; **~packung** *f* family size (package); **~planung** *f* family planning; **~stand** *m* marital status; **~vater** *m* family man

Fanatiker [fa'naːtikɐ] *m* (-*s*; -), **Fa'natikerin** *f* (-; -*nen*), **fa'natisch** *adj* fanatic; **Fanatismus** [fana'tɪsmʊs] *m* (-; *no pl*) fanaticism

fand [fant] *pret of* **finden**

Fang [faŋ] *m* (-[*e*]*s*; *Fänge* ['fɛŋə]) catch (*a. fig*); '**fangen** *v/t* (*irr, ge-, h*) catch (*a. fig*); *sich wieder* ~ get a grip on o.s. again; *Fangen spielen* play tag (*Br* catch); '**Fangzahn** *m* zo fang

Fantasie [fanta'zi:] *f* (-; -*n*) imagination; fantasy; **fanta'sielos** *adj* unimaginative; **fanta'sieren** *v/i* (*no* -ge-, *h*) daydream; MED be delirious; F talk nonsense; **fanta'sievoll** *adj* imaginative; **Fantast** [fan'tast] *m* (-*en*; -*en*) dreamer; **fan'tastisch** *adj* fantastic, F *a*. great, terrific

Farbband ['farpbant] *n* (typewriter) ribbon

Farbe ['farbə] *f* (-; -*n*) colo(u)r; paint; complexion; tan; *card games:* suit

'**farbecht** *adj* colo(u)r-fast

färben ['fɛrbən] *v/t* (ge-, *h*) dye; *esp fig* colo(u)r; **sich rot ~** turn red; → **abfärben**

'**farben|blind** *adj* colo(u)r-blind; **~froh**, **~prächtig** *adj* colo(u)rful

Farb|fernsehen *n* colo(u)r television; **~fernseher** *m* colo(u)r TV set; **~film** *m* colo(u)r film; **~foto** *n* colo(u)r photo

farbig ['farbɪç] *adj* colo(u)red; stained (*glass*); *fig* colo(u)rful; **Farbige** ['farbɪgə] *m*, *f* (-*n*; -*n*) → **Schwarze**

'**Farbkasten** *m* paintbox

'**farblos** *adj* colo(u)rless (*a. fig*)

'**Farbstift** *m* colo(u)red pencil, crayon

'**Farbstoff** *m* dye; GASTR colo(u)ring

'**Farbton** *m* shade, tint

'**Färbung** *f* (-; -*en*) colo(u)ring; hue

Farnkraut ['farnkraut] *n* BOT fern

Fasan [fa'za:n] *m* (-[*e*]*s*; -*e*[*n*]) zo pheasant

Faschismus [fa'ʃɪsmʊs] *m* (-; *no pl*) POL fascism; **Faschist** [fa'ʃɪst] *m* (-*en*; -*en*), **fa'schistisch** *adj* POL fascist

faseln ['fa:zəln] *v/i* (ge-, *h*) drivel

Faser ['fa:zɐ] *f* (-; -*n*) fiber, *Br* fibre; grain; **faserig** ['fa:zərɪç] *adj* fibrous; '**fasern** *v/i* (ge-, *h*) fray

Fass [fas] *n* (-*es*; *Fässer* ['fɛsɐ]) cask, barrel; **vom ~** on tap

Fassade [fa'sa:də] *f* (-; -*n*) ARCH facade, front (*a. fig*)

'**Fassbier** *n* draft (*Br* draught) beer

fassen ['fasən] (ge-, *h*) **1.** *v/t* take hold of, grasp; seize; catch (*criminal*); hold, take; set (*jewels*); *fig* grasp, understand; pluck up (*courage*); make (*a decision*); **sich ~** compose o.s.; **sich kurz ~** be brief; **es ist nicht zu ~** that's incredible **2.** *v/i:* **~ nach** reach for

'**Fassung** *f* (-; -*en*) setting; frame (*of*

glasses); ELECTR socket; draft(ing); wording, version; (*no pl*) composure; **die ~ verlieren** lose one's composure; **j-n aus der ~ bringen** put s.o. out

'**fassungslos** *adj* stunned; speechless

'**Fassungsvermögen** *n* capacity

fast [fast] *adv* almost, nearly; **~ nie** (**nichts**) hardly ever (anything)

fasten ['fastən] *v/i* (ge-, *h*) fast

'**Fastenzeit** *f* REL Lent

'**Fastnacht** *f* → **Karneval**

fatal [fa'ta:l] *adj* unfortunate; awkward; disastrous

fauchen ['fauxən] *v/i* (ge-, *h*) zo hiss

faul [faul] *adj* rotten, bad, GASTR *a*. spoiled; *fig* lazy; F fishy; **~e Ausrede** lame excuse; '**faulen** *v/i* (ge-, *h*, *sein*) rot, go bad; decay

faulenzen ['faulɛntsən] *v/i* (ge-, *h*) laze, loaf (about); '**Faulenzer**(**in**) ['faulɛntsɐ, 'faulɛntsərɪn] (-*s*; -/-; -*nen*) lazybones; *contp* loafer

'**Faulheit** *f* (-; *no pl*) laziness

faulig ['faulɪç] *adj* rotten

Fäulnis ['fɔylnɪs] *f* (-; *no pl*) rottenness, decay (*a. fig*)

'**Faulpelz** F *m* → **Faulenzer**

'**Faultier** *n* zo sloth

Faust [faust] *f* (-; *Fäuste* ['fɔystə]) fist; **auf eigene ~** on one's own initiative; **~handschuh** *m* mitten; **~regel** *f* (**als ~** as a) rule of thumb; **~schlag** *m* punch

Favorit [favo'ri:t] *m* (-*en*; -*en*), **Favo'ritin** *f* (-; -*nen*) favo(u)rite

Fax [faks] *n* (-; -[*e*]) fax; fax machine

faxen ['faksən] *v/i and v/t* (ge-, *h*) fax, send a fax (to)

'**Faxgerät** *n* fax machine

FCKW [ɛftse:ka:'ve:] *abbr of* **Fluorchlorkohlenwasserstoff** chlorofluorocarbon, CFC

Feber ['fe:bɐ] *Austrian m* (-*s*; -), **Februar** ['fe:brua:ɐ] *m* (-*s*; -*e*) February

fechten ['fɛçtən] *v/i* (*irr*, ge-, *h*) SPORT fence; *fig* fight; '**Fechten** *n* (-*s*; *no pl*) SPORT fencing; **Fechter**(**in**) ['fɛçtɐ, 'fɛçtərɪn] *m(f)* (-*s*; -/-; -*nen*) SPORT fencer

Feder ['fe:dɐ] *f* (-; -*n*) feather; plume; nib; TECH spring; **~ball** *m* SPORT badminton; shuttlecock; **~bett** *n* comforter, *Br* duvet; **~gewicht** *n* SPORT featherweight; **~halter** *m* penholder

'**feder|leicht** *adj* (as) light as a feather

Federmäppchen ['feːdɛmɛpçən] *n* (*-s*; *-*) pencil case

'**federn** (*ge-*, *h*) **1.** *v/i* be springy **2.** *v/t* TECH spring; **~d** *adj* springy, elastic

'**Federstrich** *m* stroke of the pen

Federung ['feːdərʊŋ] *f* (*-*; *-en*) springs; MOT suspension; *e-e gute ~ haben* be well sprung

'**Federzeichnung** *f* pen-and-ink drawing

Fee [feː] *f* (*-*; *-n*) fairy

fegen ['feːgən] *v/t* (*ge-*, *h*) *and fig v/i* (*sein*) sweep

fehl [feːl] *adj*: *~ am Platze* out of place

'**Fehlbetrag** *m* deficit

'**fehlen** *v/i* (*ge-*, *h*) be missing; be absent; *ihm fehlt* (*es an*) … he is lacking …; *du fehlst uns* we miss you; *was dir fehlt, ist* … what you need is …; *was fehlt Ihnen?* what's wrong with you?

Fehler ['feːlɐ] *m* (*-s*; *-*) mistake; fault, TECH *a.* defect, flaw; IT error

'**fehlerfrei** *adj* faultless, flawless

'**fehlerhaft** *adj* faulty; full of mistakes; TECH defective

'**Fehlermeldung** *f* IT error message

'**Fehl|ernährung** *f* malnutrition; **~geburt** *f* MED miscarriage; **~griff** *m* mistake; wrong choice

'**Fehlschlag** *m* failure; '**fehlschlagen** *v/i* (*irr, schlagen, sep, -ge-, sein*) fail

'**Fehl|start** *m* false start; **~tritt** *m* slip; *fig* lapse; **~zündung** *f* MOT backfire (*a. ~ haben*)

Feier ['faɪɐ] *f* (*-*; *-n*) celebration; party

'**Feierabend** *m* end of a day's work; closing time; evening (at home); *~ machen* finish (work), F knock off; *nach~* after work

'**feierlich** *adj* solemn; festive

'**Feierlichkeit** *f* (*-*; *-en*) (*no pl*) solemnity; ceremony

'**feiern** *v/t and v/i* (*ge-*, *h*) celebrate; have a party

'**Feiertag** *m* holiday; *gesetzlicher ~* public (*or* legal, *Br a.* bank) holiday

feig [faɪk], **feige** ['faɪgə] *adj* cowardly; *~ sein* be a coward

Feige ['faɪgə] *f* (*-*; *-n*) BOT fig

'**Feigheit** *f* (*-*; *no pl*) cowardice

'**Feigling** *m* (*-s*; *-e*) coward

Feile ['faɪlə] *f* (*-*; *-n*), '**feilen** *v/t and v/i* (*ge-*, *h*) file

feilschen ['faɪlʃən] *v/i* (*ge-*, *h*) haggle

(*um* about, over)

fein [faɪn] *adj* fine; choice, excellent; keen (*ear*); delicate; distinguished, F posh; *~! good!*, okay!

Feind [faɪnt] *m* (*-[e]s*; *-e* ['faɪndə]) enemy (*a. fig*); **~bild** *n* enemy image

Feindin ['faɪndɪn] *f* (*-*; *-nen*) enemy

'**feindlich** *adj* hostile; MIL enemy

'**Feindschaft** *f* (*-*; *no pl*) hostility

'**feindselig** *adj* hostile (*gegen* to)

'**Feindseligkeit** *f* (*-*; *no pl*) hostility

feinfühlig ['faɪnfyːlɪç] *adj* sensitive

'**Feingefühl** *n* (*-[e]s*; *no pl*) sensitiveness

'**Feinheit** *f* (*-*; *-en*) (*no pl*) fineness; keenness; delicacy; *pl* niceties

'**Fein|kostgeschäft** *n* delicatessen; **~me,chaniker** *m* precision mechanic

'**Feinschmecker** *m* (*-s*; *-*) gourmet

feist [faɪst] *adj* fat, stout

Feld [fɛlt] *n* (*-[e]s*; *-er* ['fɛldə]) field (*a. fig*); *chess:* square; **~arbeit** *f* AGR work in the fields; fieldwork; **~bett** *n* cot, *Br* camp bed; **~flasche** *f* water bottle, canteen; **~lerche** *f* ZO skylark; **~marschall** *m* MIL field marshal

Feldstecher ['fɛltʃtɛçɐ] *m* (*-s*; *-*) field glasses

Feldwebel ['fɛltveːbəl] *m* (*-s*; *-*) MIL sergeant

'**Feldzug** *m* MIL campaign (*a. fig*)

Felge ['fɛlgə] *f* (*-*; *-n*) rim; SPORT circle

Fell [fɛl] *n* (*-[e]s*; *-e*) ZO coat; skin, fur

Fels [fɛls] *m* (*-en*; *-en*) rock

'**Felsbrocken** *m* boulder

Felsen ['fɛlzən] *m* (*-s*; *-*) rock

felsig ['fɛlzɪç] *adj* rocky

'**Felsspalte** *f* crevice

'**Felsvorsprung** *m* ledge

feminin [femiˈniːn] *adj* feminine (*a.* LING); *contp* effeminate; **Feminismus** [femiˈnɪsmʊs] *m* (*-*; *no pl*) feminism; **Feministin** [femiˈnɪstɪn] *f* (*-*; *-nen*), **femi'nistisch** *adj* feminist

Fenchel ['fɛnçəl] *m* (*-s*; *no pl*) BOT fennel

Fenster ['fɛnstɐ] *n* (*-s*; *-*) window; **~bank** *f* (*-*; *-bänke*), **~brett** *n* windowsill; **~flügel** *m* casement; **~laden** *m* shutter; **~rahmen** *m* window frame; **~scheibe** *f* (window)pane

Ferien ['feːrjən] *pl* vacation, *esp Br* holiday(s *pl*); *~ haben* be on vacation; **~haus** *n* vacation home, cottage; **~la-**

ger *n* summer camp; **~wohnung** *f* vacation rental, *Br* holiday apartment

Ferkel ['fɛrkəl] *n* (-s; -) ZO piglet; F pig

fern [fɛrn] *adj and adv* far(away), far-off, distant; **von ~** from a distance

'Fernamt *n* telephone exchange

'Fernbedienung *f* remote control

'fernbleiben *v/i* (*irr*, *bleiben*, *sep*, *-ge-*, *sein*) stay away (*dat* from)

Ferne ['fɛrnə] *f* (-; *no pl*) distance; **aus der ~** from a distance

ferner ['fɛrnɐ] *adv* further(more); in addition, also

'Fern|fahrer *m* long-haul truck driver, F trucker, *Br* long-distance lorry driver; **~gespräch** *n* TEL long-distance call

'ferngesteuert *adj* remote-controlled; MIL guided (*missile etc*)

'Fernglas *n* binoculars

'fernhalten *v/t* (*irr*, *halten*, *sep*, *-ge-*, *h*) keep away (**von** from)

Fern|heizung *f* district heating; **~kurs** *m* correspondence course; **~laster** F *m* (-s; -) MOT longhaul truck, *Br* long--distance lorry; **~lenkung** *f* remote control; **~licht** *n* MOT full (*or* high) beam

'fernliegen *v/i* (*irr*, *liegen*, *sep*, *-ge-*, *h*): **es liegt mir fern zu** far be it from me to

'Fernmelde|satel,lit *m* communications satellite; **~technik** *f*, **~wesen** *n* (-s; *no pl*) telecommunications

'Fern|rohr *n* telescope; **~schreiben** *n*, **~schreiber** *m* telex

'fernsehen *v/i* (*irr*, *sehen*, *sep*, *-ge-*, *h*) watch television; **'Fernsehen** *n* (-s; *no pl*) television (**im** on); **'Fernseher** F *m* (-s; -) TV (set); TV viewer

'Fernseh|schirm *m* (TV) screen; **~sendung** *f* TV program(me)

'Fernsteuerung *f* remote control

'Fernverkehr *m* long-distance traffic

Ferse ['fɛrzə] *f* (-; *-n*) ANAT heel (*a. fig*)

fertig ['fɛrtɪç] *adj* ready; finished; **~ bringen** manage; *iro* be capable of; **~ machen** finish (*a.* F *s.o.*); get *s.th.* ready; F give *s.o.* hell, do *s.o.* in; **sich ~ machen** get ready (**mit et.**) **~ sein** have finished (s.th.); **mit et. ~ werden** cope with *a problem etc*; F **völlig ~** dead beat

'fertigbringen *v/t* (*irr*, *bringen*, *sep*, *-ge-*, *h*) → **fertig**

'Fertig|gericht *n* ready(-to-serve) meal; **~haus** *n* prefabricated house, F prefab

'Fertigkeit *f* (-; *-en*) skill

'fertigmachen *v/t* (*irr*, *bringen*, *sep*, *-ge-*, *h*) → **fertig**

'Fertigstellung *f* (-; *no pl*) completion

'fertigwerden *v/t* (*irr*, *bringen*, *sep*, *-ge-*, *sein*) → **fertig**

fesch [fɛʃ] *Austrian adj* smart, chic

Fessel ['fɛsəl] *f* (-; *-n*) shackle (*a. fig*); ANAT ankle; **'fesseln** *v/t* (*ge-*, *h*) bind, tie (up); *fig* fascinate

fest [fɛst] *adj* firm (*a. fig*); solid; fast; *fig* fixed (*date etc*); sound (*sleep*); steady (*girlfriend etc*); **~ schlafen** be fast asleep

Fest *n* (-[e]s; *-e*) celebration; party; REL festival, feast; → **froh**

'festbinden *v/t* (*irr*, *binden*, *sep*, *-ge-*, *h*) fasten, tie (**an** *dat* to)

'Festessen *n* banquet, feast

'festfahren *v/refl* (*irr*, *fahren*, *sep*, *-ge-*, *h*) get stuck

'Festhalle *f* (festival) hall

'festhalten (*irr*, *halten*, *sep*, *-ge-*, *h*) **1.** *v/i*: **~ an** (*dat*) stick to **2.** *v/t* hold on to; hold *s.o. or s.th.* tight; **sich ~ an** (*dat*) hold on to

festigen ['fɛstɪgən] *v/t* (*ge-*, *h*) strengthen; **sich ~** grow firm *or* strong

Festigkeit ['fɛstɪçkaɪt] *f* (-; *no pl*) firmness; strength

'Festland *n* mainland; *the* Continent

'festlegen *v/t* (*sep*, *-ge-*, *h*) fix, set; **sich ~ auf** (*acc*) commit o.s. to *s.th.*

'festlich *adj* festive

'festmachen *v/t* (*sep*, *-ge-*, *h*) fasten, fix (**an** *dat* to); MAR moor; ECON fix

Festnahme ['fɛstnaːmə] *f* (-; *-n*), **'festnehmen** *v/t* (*irr*, *nehmen*, *sep*, *-ge-*, *h*) arrest

'Festplatte *f* IT hard disk

'fest|schrauben *v/t* (*sep*, *-ge-*, *h*) screw (on) tight; **~setzen** *v/t* (*sep*, *-ge-*, *h*) fix; **~sitzen** *v/i* (*irr*, *sitzen*, *sep*, *-ge-*, *h*) be stuck; be (left) stranded

'Festspiele *pl* festival

'feststehen *v/i* (*irr*, *stehen*, *sep*, *-ge-*, *h*) be certain; *date etc*: be fixed; **~d** *adj* established (*fact etc*); set (*phrase etc*)

'feststellen *v/t* (*sep*, *-ge-*, *h*) find (out); establish; see, notice; state; TECH lock, arrest; **'Feststellung** *f* (-; *-en*) finding(s); realization; statement

'Festtag *m* holiday; REL religious holiday; F red-letter day

'Festung *f* (-; *-en*) fortress

'Festzug *m* procession

fett [fɛt] *adj* fat (*a. fig*); PRINT bold; **~ ge- druckt** boldface, in bold type (*or* print); **Fett** *n* (-[e]s; -e) fat; dripping; shorten- ing; TECH grease; **'fettarm** *adj* low-fat, *pred* low in fat; **'Fettfleck** *m* grease spot; **fettig** ['fɛtɪç] *adj* greasy

'Fettnäpfchen *n*: **ins ~ treten** put one's foot in it

Fetzen ['fɛtsən] *m* (-s; -) shred; rag; scrap (*of paper etc*)

feucht [fɔʏçt] *adj* moist, damp; humid

Feuchtigkeit ['fɔʏçtɪçkait] *f* (-; *no pl*) moisture; dampness; humidity

feudal [fɔʏ'daːl] *adj* POL feudal; F posh, *Br* swish

Feuer ['fɔʏɐ] *n* (-s; -) fire (*a. fig*); **j-m ~ geben** give s.o. a light; **~ fangen** catch fire; *fig* fall for *s.o.*; **~,larm** *m* fire alarm; **~bestattung** *f* cremation

'feuerfest *adj* fireproof, fire-resistant

'Feuergefahr *f* danger of fire

'feuergefährlich *adj* inflammable

'Feuer|leiter *f* fire escape; **~löscher** ['fɔʏɐlœʃɐ] *m* (-s; -) fire extinguisher; **~melder** ['fɔʏɐmɛldɐ] *m* (-s; -) fire alarm

feuern ['fɔʏɐn] *v/i and v/t* (ge-, h) fire (*a. F s.o.*)

'feuer'rot *adj* blazing red; crimson

'Feuer|schiff *n* lightship; **~stein** *m* flint; **~wache** *f* fire station; **~waffe** *f* firearm, gun; **~wehr** *f* (-; -en) fire brigade (*or* de- partment); fire truck (*Br* fire engine); **~wehrmann** *m* (-[e]s, -männer, -leute) fireman, fire fighter; **~werk** *n* fire- works; **~werkskörper** *m* firework, fire- cracker; **~zeug** *n* (cigarette) lighter

feurig ['fɔʏrɪç] *adj* fiery, ardent

Fiasko ['fjasko] *n* (-s; -s) fiasco, (com- plete) failure

Fibel ['fiːbəl] *f* (-; -n) primer, first reader

Fiber ['fiːbɐ] *f* fiber, *Br* fibre; **~glas** *n* fi- berglass, *Br* fibreglass

Fichte ['fɪçtə] *f* (-; -n) BOT spruce, F *mst* pine *or* fir (tree)

ficken ['fɪkən] V *v/i and v/t* (ge-, h) fuck

Fieber ['fiːbɐ] *n* (-s; *no pl*) MED temper- ature, fever (*a. fig*); **~ haben** (**messen**) have a (take *s.o.'s*) temperature; **~ sen- kend** MED antipyretic

'fieberhaft *adj* MED feverish (*a. fig*)

'fiebern *v/i* (ge-, h) MED have *or* run a temperature; **~ nach** *fig* crave for

'Fieberthermo,meter *n* fever (*Br* clini- cal) thermometer

fiel [fiːl] *pret of* **fallen**

fies [fiːs] F *adj* mean, nasty

Figur [fi'guːɐ] *f* (-; -en) figure

Filet [fi'leː] *n* (-s; -s) GASTR fil(l)et

Filiale [fi'ljaːlə] *f* (-; -n) branch

Film [fɪlm] *m* (-[e]s; -e) film; movie, *esp Br* (motion) picture; *the* movies, *Br the* cinema; **~aufnahme** *f* filming, shoot- ing; take, shot

filmen ['fɪlmən] (ge-, h) **1.** *v/t* film, shoot **2.** *v/i* make a film

'Film|gesellschaft *f* motion-picture (*Br* film) company; **~kamera** *f* mo- tion-picture (*Br* film) camera; **~kas- ,sette** *f* film magazine, cartridge; **~pro- ,jektor** *m* film (*or* movie) projector; **~regis,seur** *m* film director; **~schauspieler(in)** film (*or* screen, movie) actor (actress); **~studio** *n* film studio(s); **~the,ater** *n* → **Kino**; **~verleih** *m* film distributors; **~vorführer** *m* (-s; -) projectionist

Filter ['fɪltɐ] *m*, *esp* TECH *n* (-s; -) filter

'Filterkaffee *m* filter coffee

'filtern *v/t* (ge-, h) filter

'Filterziga,rette *f* filter(-tipped) ciga- rette, filter tip

Filz [fɪlts] *m* (-es; -e) felt; F POL corrup- tion, sleaze; **'filzen** F *v/t* (ge-, h) frisk

'Filz|schreiber ['fɪltsʃraibɐ] *m* (-s; -), **~stift** *m* felt(-tipped) pen

Finale [fi'naːlə] *n* (-s; -) finale; SPORT fi- nal(s)

Finanz|amt [fi'nants'amt] *n* tax office; Internal (*Br* Inland) Revenue; **~beam- te** *m* tax officer

Finanzen [fi'nantsən] *pl* finances

finanziell [finan'tsjɛl] *adj* financial

finanzieren [finan'tsiːrən] *v/t* (*no* -ge-, h) finance

Fi'nanz|mi,nister *m* minister of fi- nance; Secretary of the Treasury, *Br* Chancellor of the Exchequer; **~minis- ,terium** *n* ministry of finance; Treasury Department, *Br* Treasury; **~wesen** *n* (-s; *no pl*) finance

Findelkind ['fɪndəlkɪnt] *n* JUR found- ling

finden *v/t* (*irr, ge-, h*) find; think, believe; **ich finde ihn nett** I think he's nice; **wie ~ Sie ...?** how do you like ...?; **~ Sie (nicht)?** do (don't) you think so?;

das wird sich ~ we'll see
Finder ['fɪndɐ] *m* (-s; -) finder
'**Finderlohn** *m* finder's reward
findig ['fɪndɪç] *adj* clever
fing [fɪŋ] *pret of* **fangen**
Finger ['fɪŋɐ] *m* (-s; -) ANAT finger; ~**abdruck** *m* fingerprint; ~**fertigkeit** *f* (-; *no pl*) manual skill; ~**hut** *m* thimble; BOT foxglove; ~**nagel** *m* ANAT fingernail; ~**spitze** *f* fingertip; ~**spitzengefühl** *n* (-[e]s; *no pl*) sure instinct; tact
fingiert [fɪn'giːɐt] *adj* faked; fictitious
Fink [fɪŋk] *m* (-en; -en) ZO finch
Finne ['fɪnə] *m* (-n; -n), **Finnin** ['fɪnɪn] *f* (-; -nen) Finn; '**finnisch** *adj* Finnish
Finnland ['fɪnlant] Finland
finster ['fɪnstɐ] *adj* dark, gloomy; *fig* grim; shady
'**Finsternis** *f* (-; -se) darkness, gloom
Finte ['fɪntə] *f* (-; -n) trick; SPORT feint
Firma ['fɪrma] (-; -men) firm, company
firmen ['fɪrmən] *v/t* (ge-, h) REL confirm
'**Firmung** *f* (-; -en) REL confirmation
First [fɪrst] *m* (-[e]s; -e) ARCH ridge
Fisch [fɪʃ] *m* (-[e]s; -e) ZO fish; *pl* ASTR Pisces; *er ist (ein)* ~ he's (a) Pisces
'**Fischdampfer** *m* trawler
fischen ['fɪʃən] *v/t and v/i* (ge-, h) fish
Fischer ['fɪʃɐ] *m* (-s; -) fisherman; ~... *in cpds* ...boot, ...dorf *etc*: fishing ...
Fischerei [fɪʃə'raɪ] *f* (-; *no pl*) fishing
'**Fisch|fang** *m* (-[e]s; *no pl*) fishing; ~**gräte** *f* fishbone; ~**grätenmuster** *n* herring-bone (pattern); ~**gründe** *pl* fishing grounds; ~**händler** *m* fish dealer, *esp Br* fishmonger; ~**kutter** *m* smack; ~**laich** *m* spawn; ~**stäbchen** *n* GASTR fish stick (*Br* finger); ~**zucht** *f* fish farming; ~**zug** *m* catch, haul (*both a. fig*)
Fisole [fi'zoːlə] *Austrian f* (-; -n) BOT string bean
Fistel ['fɪstəl] *f* (-; -n) MED fistula
'**Fistelstimme** *f* falsetto
fit [fɪt] *adj* fit; *sich* ~ *halten* keep fit
'**Fitness** *f* (-; *no pl*) fitness; ~**center** *n* health club, fitness center, gym
fix [fɪks] *adj* ECON fixed; F quick; F smart, bright; F ~ *und fertig sein* be dead beat; be a nervous wreck; ~**e Idee** PSYCH obsession
fixen ['fɪksən] F *v/i* (ge-, h) shoot, fix; be a junkie; **Fixer** ['fɪksɐ] F *m* (-s; -) junkie, mainliner

fixieren [fɪ'ksiːrən] *v/t* (*no -ge-*, h) fix (*a.* PHOT); stare at *s.o.*
'**Fixstern** *m* ASTR fixed star
FKK [ɛfka:'ka:] *abbr of* **Freikörperkultur** nudism
FK'K-Strand *m* nudist beach
flach [flax] *adj* flat; level, even, plane; *fig* shallow
Fläche ['flɛçə] *f* (-; -n) surface (*a.* MATH); area (*a.* MATH); expanse, space
'**flächendeckend** *adj* exhaustive
'**Flächen|inhalt** *m* MATH (surface) area; ~**maß** *n* square *or* surface measure
'**Flachland** *n* (-[e]s; *no pl*) lowland, plain
Flachs [flaks] *m* (-es; *no pl*) BOT flax
flackern ['flakɐn] *v/i* (ge-, h) flicker
Fladenbrot ['fla:dənbro:t] *n* round flat bread (*or* loaf)
Flagge ['flagə] *f* (-; -n) flag
'**flaggen** *v/i* (ge-, h) fly a flag *or* flags
Flak [flak] *f* (-; -) MIL anti-aircraft gun
Flamme ['flamə] *f* (-; -n) flame (*a. fig*)
Flanell [fla'nɛl] *m* (-s; -e) flannel
Flanke ['flaŋkə] *f* (-; -n) flank, side; *soccer*: cross; SPORT flank vault
flankieren [flaŋ'ki:rən] *v/t* (*no -ge-*, h) flank
Flasche ['flaʃə] *f* (-; -n) bottle; baby's bottle; F *contp* dead loss
'**Flaschen|bier** *n* bottled beer; ~**hals** *m* neck of a bottle; ~**öffner** *m* bottle opener; ~**pfand** *n* (bottle) deposit; ~**zug** *m* TECH block and tackle, pulley
flatterhaft ['flatɐhaft] *adj* fickle, flighty
flattern ['flatɐn] *v/i* (ge-, sein) flutter; TECH (h) wobble
flau [flau] *adj* queasy; *fig* flat; ECON slack
Flaum [flaum] *m* (-[e]s; *no pl*) down, fluff, fuzz
Flausch [flauʃ] *m* (-es; -e) fleece
flauschig ['flauʃɪç] *adj* fleecy, fluffy
Flausen ['flauzən] F *pl* (funny) ideas
Flaute ['flautə] *f* (-; -n) MAR calm; ECON slack period
Flechte ['flɛçtə] *f* (-; -n) plait, braid; BOT, MED lichen; '**flechten** *v/t* (*irr*, ge-, h) plait, braid (*hair*); weave (*basket*)
Fleck [flɛk] *m* (-[e]s; -e) stain, mark; speck; dot; blot(ch); *fig* place, spot; patch; *blauer* ~ bruise; *vom* ~ *weg* on the spot; *nicht vom* ~ *kommen* not get anywhere; '**Flecken** *m* → **Fleck**

'**Fleckenentferner** *m* stain remover

'**fleckenlos** *adj* spotless (*a. fig*)

fleckig ['flɛkɪç] *adj* spotted; stained

Fledermaus ['fleːdɐmaus] *f* zo bat

Flegel ['fleːgəl] *m* (*-s*; *-*) lout, boor

'**flegelhaft** *adj* loutish

'**Flegeljahre** *pl* awkward age

'**flegeln** F *contp v/refl* (*ge-*, *h*) lounge

flehen ['fleːən] *v/i* (*ge-*, *h*) beg; pray (**um** for); **flehentlich** ['fleːəntlɪç] *adj* imploring, entreating

Fleisch [flaɪʃ] *n* (*-[e]s*; *no pl*) flesh (*a. fig*); GASTR meat; **~ fressend→ fleischfressend**; **~brühe** *f* (meat) broth, consommé

Fleischer ['flaɪʃɐ] *m* (*-s*; *-*) butcher

Fleischerei [flaɪʃə'raɪ] *f* (*-*; *-en*) butcher's (shop)

'**fleischfressend** *adj* BOT, ZO carnivorous

Fleischhauer ['flaɪʃhauɐ] *Austrian m* (*-s*; *-*) butcher

fleischig ['flaɪʃɪç] *adj* fleshy

'**Fleisch|klößchen** *n* (*-s*; *-*) meatball; **~kon,serven** *pl* canned (*Br* tinned) meat

'**fleischlos** *adj* meatless

'**Fleischwolf** *m* meat grinder, *Br* mincer

Fleiß [flaɪs] *m* (*-es*; *no pl*) diligence, hard work; **fleißig** ['flaɪsɪç] *adj* diligent, hard-working; **~ sein** work hard

fletschen ['flɛtʃən] *v/t* (*ge-*, *h*) bare

flexibel [flɛ'ksiːbəl] *adj* flexible

Flexibilität [flɛksibili'tɛːt] *f* (*-*; *no pl*) flexibility

flicken ['flɪkən] *v/t* (*ge-*, *h*) mend, repair, *a. fig* patch (up); '**Flicken** *m* (*-s*; *-*) patch; '**Flickwerk** *n* patchwork (*a. fig*); '**Flickzeug** *n* TECH repair kit

Flieder ['fliːdɐ] *m* (*-s*; *-*) BOT lilac

Fliege ['fliːgə] *f* (*-*; *-n*) zo fly; bow tie

'**fliegen** *v/i* (*irr, ge-*, *sein*) and *v/t* (*h*) fly (*a.* **~ lassen**); F fall; F be fired; F get the sack; be kicked out *of school*; F **~ auf** (*acc*) really go for; F *in die Luft* **~** blow up

'**Fliegen** *n* (*-s*; *no pl*) flying; aviation

'**Fliegen|fänger** *m* flypaper; **~fenster** *n* flyscreen; **~gewicht** *n* SPORT flyweight; **~gitter** *n* wire mesh (screen); **~klatsche** *f* flyswatter; **~pilz** *m* BOT fly agaric

Flieger ['fliːgɐ] *m* (*-s*; *-*) MIL airman; F plane; *cycling*: sprinter; **~a,larm** *m* air-raid warning

fliehen ['fliːən] *v/i* (*irr, ge-*, *sein*) flee, run away (*both*: **vor** *dat* from)

'**Fliehkraft** *f* PHYS centrifugal force

Fliese ['fliːzə] *f* (*-*; *-n*), '**fliesen** *v/t* (*ge-*, *h*) tile; '**Fliesenleger** *m* (*-s*; *-*) tiler

Fließband ['fliːsbant] *n* (*-[e]s*; *-bänder*) TECH assembly line; conveyor belt

fließen ['fliːsən] *v/i* (*irr, ge-*, *sein*) flow (*a. fig*); run; **~d 1.** *adj* flowing; running; LING fluent **2.** *adv*: **er spricht ~ Englisch** he speaks English fluently *or* fluent English

'**Fließheck** *n* MOT fastback

flimmern ['flɪmɐn] *v/i* (*ge-*, *h*) shimmer; *film*: flicker

flink [flɪŋk] *adj* quick, nimble

Flinte ['flɪntə] *f* (*-*; *-n*) shotgun; F gun

Flipper ['flɪpɐ] F *m* (*-s*; *-*) pinball machine; '**flippern** *v/i* (*ge-*, *h*) play pinball

Flirt [flœrt] *m* (*-s*; *-s*) flirtation

flirten ['flœrtən] *v/i* (*ge-*, *h*) flirt

Flittchen ['flɪtçən] F *n* (*-s*; *-*) floozie

Flitter ['flɪtɐ] *m* (*-s*; *-*) tinsel (*a. fig*), spangles; **~wochen** *pl* honeymoon

flitzen ['flɪtsən] F *v/i* (*ge-*, *sein*) flit, whizz, shoot

flocht [flɔxt] *pret of* **flechten**

Flocke ['flɔkə] *f* (*-*; *-n*) flake

flockig ['flɔkɪç] *adj* fluffy, flaky

flog [floːk] *pret of* **fliegen**

floh [floː] *pret of* **fliehen**

Floh *m* (*-[e]s*; *Flöhe* ['fløːə]) zo flea

'**Flohmarkt** *m* flea market

Florett [flo'rɛt] *n* (*-[e]s*; *-e*) foil

florieren [flo'riːrən] *v/i* (*no -ge-*, *h*) flourish, prosper

Floskel ['flɔskəl] *f* (*-*; *-n*) empty *or* cliché(d) phrase

floss [flɔs] *pret of* **fließen**

Floß [floːs] *n* (*-es*; *Flöße* ['fløːsə]) raft, float

Flosse ['flɔsə] *f* (*-*; *-n*) zo fin, *a.* SPORT flipper

Flöte ['fløːtə] *f* (*-*; *-n*) MUS flute; recorder

flott [flɔt] *adj* brisk (*pace*); F smart, chic; MAR afloat

Flotte ['flɔtə] *f* (*-*; *-n*) MAR fleet; navy

'**Flottenstützpunkt** *m* MIL naval base

Fluch [fluːx] *m* (*-[e]s*; *Flüche* ['flyːçə]) curse; swear word; **fluchen** ['fluːxən] *v/i* (*ge-*, *h*) swear, curse

Flucht [fluxt] *f* (*-*; *-en*) flight (**vor** *dat* from); escape, getaway (**aus** *dat* from)

'**fluchtartig** *adv* hastily

Fluchtauto

'**Fluchtauto** n getaway car

flüchten ['flʏçtən] v/i (ge-, sein) flee (**nach, zu** to), run away; escape, get away; **flüchtig** ['flʏçtɪç] adj quick; superficial; careless; fugitive, criminal etc: on the run, at large; **~er Blick** glance; **~er Eindruck** glimpse

'**Flüchtigkeitsfehler** m slip

Flüchtling ['flʏçtlɪŋ] m fugitive; POL refugee

'**Flüchtlingslager** n refugee camp

Flug [fluːk] m (-[e]s; Flüge ['flyːgə]) flight; **im ~(e)** rapidly, quickly; **~abwehrra,kete** f MIL anti-aircraft missile; **~bahn** f trajectory; **~ball** m tennis: volley; **~begleiter(in)** flight attendant; **~blatt** n handbill, leaflet; **~dienst** m air service

Flügel ['flyːgəl] m (-s; -) zo wing (a. SPORT); TECH blade; windmill: sail; MUS grand piano; **~mutter** f TECH wing nut; **~schraube** f TECH thumb screw; **~stürmer** m SPORT wing forward; **~tür** f folding door

'**Fluggast** m (air) passenger

flügge ['flʏgə] adj full-fledged

'**Flug|gesellschaft** f airline; **~hafen** m airport; **~linie** f air route; → **Fluggesellschaft**; **~lotse** m air traffic controller; **~nummer** f flight number; **~plan** m flight schedule; **~platz** m airfield, airport; **~schein** m (flight) ticket; **~schreiber** m (-s; -) flight recorder, black box; **~sicherung** f air traffic control; **~ticket** n (flight) ticket; **~verbindung** f flight connection; **~verkehr** m air traffic; **~zeit** f flying time

'**Flugzeug** n (-[e]s; -e) (air)plane, aircraft, Br a. aeroplane; **mit dem ~** by air or plane; **~absturz** m air or plane crash; **~entführung** f hijacking, skyjacking; **~halle** f hangar; **~träger** m MAR MIL aircraft carrier

Flunder ['flʊndɐ] f (-; -n) zo flounder

flunkern ['flʊŋkɐn] v/i (ge-, h) fib; brag

Fluor ['fluːoːɐ] n (-s; no pl) CHEM fluorine; fluoride

'**Fluorchlorkohlenwasserstoff** m CHEM chlorofluorocarbon, CFC

Flur [fluːɐ] m (-[e]s; -e) hall; corridor

Fluss [flʊs] m (-es; Flüsse ['flʏsə]) river; stream; **im ~** fig in (a state of) flux

fluss'abwärts adv downstream

fluss'aufwärts adv upstream

'**Flussbett** n river bed

flüssig ['flʏsɪç] adj liquid; melted; fig fluent; ECON available; '**Flüssigkeit** f (-; -en) liquid; (no pl) liquidity; fig fluency; '**Flüssigkris,tallanzeige** f liquid crystal display, LCD; '**Flüssigseife** f liquid soap

'**Fluss|lauf** m course of a river; **~pferd** n zo hippopotamus, F hippo; **~ufer** n riverbank, riverside

flüstern ['flʏstɐn] v/i and v/t (ge-, h) whisper

Flut [fluːt] f (-; -en) flood (a. fig); high tide; **es ist ~** the tide is in; **~licht** n floodlights; **~welle** f tidal wave

focht [fɔxt] pret of **fechten**

Fohlen ['foːlən] n (-s; -) zo foal; colt; filly

Föhn[1] [føːn] m (-[e]s; -e) hairdrier

Föhn[2] m (-[e]s; -e) METEOR foehn, föhn

föhnen ['føːnən] v/t (ge-, h) blow-dry

Folge ['fɔlgə] f (-; -n) result, consequence; effect; succession; order; series; TV etc: sequel, episode; aftermath; MED aftereffect

folgen ['fɔlgən] v/i (ge-, sein) follow; obey; **hieraus folgt, dass** from this it follows that; **wie folgt** as follows; **~d** adj following, subsequent

folgendermaßen ['fɔlgəndɐ'maːsən] adv as follows

'**folgenschwer** adj momentous

'**folgerichtig** adj logical; consistent

folgern ['fɔlgɐn] v/t (ge-, h) conclude (**aus** dat from); **Folgerung** ['fɔlgərʊŋ] f (-; -en) conclusion

folglich ['fɔlklɪç] cj consequently, thus, therefore

folgsam ['fɔlkzaːm] adj obedient

Folie ['foːljə] f (-; -n) foil; transparency

Folter ['fɔltɐ] f (-; -n) torture; **auf die ~ spannen** tantalize; '**foltern** v/t (ge-, h) torture, fig a. torment

Fön® m → **Föhn**[1]

Fonds [fõ:] m (-; -) ECON fund

fönen v/t → **föhnen**

Fontäne [fɔn'tɛːnə] f (-; -n) jet, spout; gush

Förder|band ['fœrdɐbant] n TECH conveyor belt; **~korb** m mining: cage

fordern ['fɔrdɐn] v/t (ge-, h) demand, esp JUR a. claim; ECON ask, charge

fördern ['fœrdɐn] v/t (ge-, h) promote; support (a. UNIV), sponsor; PED tutor, provide remedial classes for; TECH mine

Forderung ['fɔrdərʊŋ] *f* (-; -en) demand; claim (*a.* JUR); ECON charge

Förderung ['fœrdərʊŋ] *f* (-; -en) promotion, advancement; support, sponsorship; UNIV *etc*: grant; PED tutoring, remedial classes; TECH mining

Forelle [fo'rɛlə] *f* (-; -n) ZO trout

Form [fɔrm] *f* (-; -en) form, shape, SPORT *a.* condition; TECH mo(u)ld; *gut in ~* in great form; **formal** [fɔr'maːl] *adj* formal; **Formalität** [fɔrmali'tɛːt] *f* (-; -en) formality

Format [fɔr'maːt] *n* (-[e]s; -e) size; format; *fig* caliber, *Br* calibre

formatieren [fɔrma'tiːrən] *v/t* (*no -ge-*, *h*) IT format; **Forma'tierung** *f* (-; -en) IT formatting

Formel ['fɔrməl] *f* (-; -n) formula

formell [fɔr'mɛl] *adj* formal

formen ['fɔrmən] *v/t* (*ge-*, *h*) shape, form; *fig* mo(u)ld

'**Formfehler** *m* irregularity

formieren [fɔr'miːrən] *v/t and v/refl* (*no -ge-*, *h*) form (up)

förmlich ['fœrmlɪç] **1.** *adj* formal; *fig* regular **2.** *adv* formally; *fig* literally

'**formlos** *adj* shapeless; *fig* informal

'**formschön** *adj* well-designed

Formular [fɔrmu'laːɐ] *n* (-s; -e) form, blank

formulieren [fɔrmu'liːrən] *v/t* (*no -ge-*, *h*) word, phrase; formulate; express

Formu'lierung *f* (-; -en) wording, phrasing; formulation; expression, phrase

forsch [fɔrʃ] *adj* dashing

forschen ['fɔrʃən] *v/i* (*ge-*, *h*) research, do research; *~ nach* search for

Forscher ['fɔrʃɐ] *m* (-s; -), '**Forscherin** *f* (-; -nen) explorer; (research) scientist; **Forschung** ['fɔrʃʊŋ] *f* (-; -en) research (work)

Forst [fɔrst] *m* (-[e]s; -e[n]) forest

Förster ['fœrstɐ] *m* (-s; -) forester; forest ranger

'**Forstwirtschaft** *f* (-; *no pl*) forestry

fort [fɔrt] *adv* off, away; gone; missing

Fort [foːɐ] *n* (-s; -s) MIL fort

'**fortbestehen** *v/i* (*irr, stehen, sep, no -ge-*, *h*) continue

'**fortbewegen** *v/refl* (*sep, no -ge-*, *h*) move; '**Fortbewegung** *f* moving; (loco)motion

'**Fortbildung** *f* (-, *no pl*) further education *or* training

'**fort|fahren** *v/i* (*irr, fahren, sep, -ge-*) (*sein*) leave, go away, MOT *a.* drive off; (*h*) continue, go *or* keep on (*et. zu tun* doing s.th.); *~führen* *v/t* (*sep, -ge-*, *h*) continue, carry on; *~gehen* *v/i* (*irr, gehen, sep, -ge-, sein*) go away, leave

'**fortgeschritten** *adj* advanced

'**fortlaufend** *adj* consecutive, successive

'**fortpflanzen** *v/refl* (*sep, -ge-, h*) BIOL reproduce; *fig* spread; '**Fortpflanzung** *f* BIOL reproduction

'**fortschreiten** *v/i* (*irr, schreiten, sep, -ge-, sein*) advance, proceed, progress; *~d adj* progressive

'**Fortschritt** *m* progress

'**fortschrittlich** *adj* progressive

'**fortsetzen** *v/t* (*sep, -ge-, h*) continue, go on with; '**Fortsetzung** *f* (-; -en) continuation; *film etc*: sequel; *~ folgt* to be continued; '**Fortsetzungsro,man** *m* serialized novel

'**fortwährend** *adj* continual, constant

fossil [fɔ'siːl] *adj*, **Fos'sil** *n* (-s; -ien) GEOL fossil (*a. fig* F)

Foto ['foːto] *n* (-s; -s) photo(graph); *ein ~ machen (von)* take a photo (of)

'**Fotoalbum** *n* photo album

'**Fotoappa,rat** *m* camera

Fotograf [foto'graːf] *m* (-en; -en) photographer; **Fotografie** [fotogra'fiː] *f* (-; -n) (*no pl*) photography; photograph, picture; **fotografieren** [fotogra-'fiːrən] *v/t and v/i* (*no -ge-*, *h*) take a photo(graph) *or* picture (of); *sich ~ lassen* have one's picture taken; **Foto-'grafin** *f* (-; -nen) photographer

'**Fotohandy** *n* camera phone

Fotoko'pie *f* photocopy; **fotoko'pieren** *v/t* (*no -ge-*, *h*) (photo)copy

'**Fotomo,dell** *n* model

'**Fotozelle** *f* photoelectric cell

Fotze ['fɔtsə] V *f* (-; -n) cunt

Foul [faul] *n* (-s; -s) SPORT foul; **foulen** ['faulən] *v/t and v/i* (*ge-*, *h*) SPORT foul

Foyer [foa'jeː] *n* (-s; -s) foyer, lobby, lounge

Fr. *abbr of* **Frau** Mrs, Ms

Fracht [fraxt] *f* (-; -en) freight, load, MAR, AVIAT *a.* cargo; ECON freight, *Br* carriage; ECON freight, *Br* consignment note; *~brief* *m* RAIL bill of lading (*a. MAR*), *Br* consignment note

Frachter ['fraxtɐ] *m* (*-s*; -) MAR freighter

Frack [frak] *m* (-[*e*]*s*; *Fräcke* ['frɛkə]) tails, tailcoat

Frage ['fra:gə] *f* (*-*; *-n*) question; *e-e ~ stellen* ask a question; → *infrage*

'**Fragebogen** *m* question(n)aire

'**fragen** *v/t and v/i* (*ge-*, *h*) ask (*nach* for; *wegen* about); *nach dem Weg* (*der Zeit*) ~ ask the way (time); *sich ~* wonder

'**Frage|wort** *n* LING interrogative; *~zeichen* *n* LING question mark

fraglich ['fra:klɪç] *adj* doubtful, uncertain; ... in question

fraglos ['fra:klo:s] *adv* undoubtedly, unquestionably

Fragment [fra'gmɛnt] *n* (-[*e*]*s*; *-e*) fragment

fragwürdig ['fra:kvʏrdɪç] *adj* dubious, F shady

Fraktion [frak'tsjo:n] *f* (*-*; *-en*) (parliamentary) group *or* party

Frakti'onsführer *m* PARL floor leader, *Br* chief whip

Franc [fra:] *m* (*-*; *-s*), **Franken** ['fraŋkən] *m* (*-*; -) franc

frankieren [fraŋ'ki:rən] *v/t* (*no -ge-*, *h*) stamp; frank

Frankreich ['fraŋkraiç] France

Franse ['franzə] *f* (*-*; *-n*) fringe

fransig ['franzɪç] *adj* frayed

Franzose [fran'tso:zə] *m* (*-n*; *-n*) Frenchman; *die ~n pl* the French

Französin [fran'tsø:zɪn] *f* (*-*; *-nen*) Frenchwoman

französisch [fran'tsø:zɪʃ] *adj* French

fraß [fra:s] *pret of* **fressen**

Fraß F *contp m* (*-es*; *no pl*) muck

Fratze ['fratsə] *f* (*-*; *-n*) grimace

Frau [frau] *f* (*-*; *-en*) woman; wife; ~ *X* Mrs (*or* Ms) X

Frauchen ['frauçən] *n* mistress (*of dog*)

'**Frauen|arzt** *m*, *~ärztin* *f* gyn(a)ecologist; *~bewegung* *f*: *die* ~ POL women's lib(eration)

'**frauenfeindlich** *adj* sexist

'**Frauen|haus** *n* women's shelter (*Br* refuge); *~klinik* *f* gyn(a)ecological hospital; *~rechtlerin* ['frauənrɛçtlərɪn] *f* (*-*; *-nen*) feminist

Fräulein ['frɔʏlain] *n* (*-s*; -) Miss

'**fraulich** *adj* womanly, feminine

frech [frɛç] *adj* sassy, *Br* cheeky

'**Frechheit** *f* (*-*; *no pl*) F *Br* cheek

Freeclimbing ['fri:klaimɪŋ] *n* (*-s*; *no pl*) free climbing

frei [frai] *adj* free (*von* from, of); independent; freelance; vacant; candid, frank; SPORT unmarked; *ein ~er Tag* a day off; *morgen haben wir* ~ there is no school tomorrow; *im Freien* outdoors; → *Fuß*; *sich ~ machen* undress; *sich ~ machen von* free o.s. from; → *a*. *freibekommen, freigeben, freihaben*; *~ halten* keep clear (*exit*), → *freihalten*

'**Freibad** *n* open-air swimming-pool

'**freibekommen** *v/t* (*irr*, *kommen*, *sep*, *no -ge-*, *h*) get *a day etc* off

'**freiberuflich** *adj* freelance, self-employed

'**Freiexem,plar** *n* free copy

'**Freigabe** *f* (*-*; *no pl*) release

'**freigeben** (*irr*, *geben*, *sep*, *-ge-*, *h*) **1.** *v/t* release; *e-n Tag etc ~* give a day *etc* off **2.** *v/i*: *j-m ~* give s.o. time off

freigebig ['fraige:bɪç] *adj* generous

'**Freigepäck** *n* AVIAT baggage allowance

'**freihaben** F *v/i* (*irr*, *haben*, *sep*, *-ge-*, *h*) have a day off (*Br a*. a holiday)

'**Freihafen** *m* free port

'**freihalten** *v/t* (*irr*, *halten*, *sep*, *-ge-*, *h*) keep, save (*seat etc*); treat (*s.o.*)

'**Frei|handel** *m* free trade; *~handelszone* *f* free trade area

freihändig ['fraihɛndɪç] *adv* with no hands

'**Freiheit** *f* (*-*; *-en*) freedom, liberty; *sich ~en herausnehmen gegen* take liberties with

'**Freiheitsstrafe** *f* JUR prison sentence

'**Freikarte** *f* free ticket

'**freikaufen** *v/t* (*sep*, *-ge-*, *h*) ransom

'**Freikörperkul,tur** *f* (*-*; *no pl*) nudism

'**freilassen** *v/t* (*irr*, *lassen*, *sep*, *-ge-*, *h*) release, set free; '**Freilassung** *f* (*-*; *-en*) release

'**Freilauf** *m* freewheel (*a*. *im ~ fahren*)

'**freilich** *adv* indeed, of course

'**Freilicht...** *in cpds* open-air ...

'**freimachen** *v/t* (*sep*, *-ge-*, *h*) *post*: stamp; *sich ~* undress; *sich ~ von* o.s. from; → *frei*; → *Oberkörper*

'**Freimaurer** *m* freemason

freimütig ['fraimy:tɪç] *adj* candid, frank

'**freischaffend** *adj* freelance

'**freischwimmen** *v/refl* (*irr*, *schwimmen*, *sep*, *-ge-*, *h*) pass a 15-minute swimming test

'**Freisprechanlage** f hands-free kit

'**freisprechen** v/t (irr, **sprechen**, sep, -ge-, h) esp REL absolve (**von** from); JUR acquit (of); '**Freispruch** m JUR acquittal

'**Freistaat** m POL free state

'**frei|stehen** v/i (irr, **stehen**, sep, -ge-, h) be unoccupied; SPORT be unmarked; **es steht dir frei zu** inf you are free to inf; **~stellen** v/t (sep, -ge-, h) j-n ~ exempt s.o. (**von** from) (a. MIL); **j-m et. ~** leave s.th. (up) to s.o.

'**Frei|stil** m freestyle; **~stoß** m soccer: free kick; **~stunde** f PED free period; **~tag** m Friday; **~tod** m suicide; **~treppe** f outdoor stairs; **~wild** fig n fair game

'**freiwillig** adj voluntary; **sich ~ melden** volunteer (**zu** for); **Freiwillige** ['frai-viliɡə] m, f (-n; -n) volunteer

'**Freizeit** f free or leisure time; **~gestaltung** f leisure-time activities; **~kleidung** f leisurewear; **~park** m amusement park; **~zentrum** n leisure center (Br centre)

'**freizügig** adj permissive; film etc: explicit

fremd [frɛmt] adj strange; foreign; unknown; **ich bin auch ~ hier** I'm a stranger here myself; '**fremdartig** adj strange, exotic; **Fremde** ['frɛmdə] m, f (-n; -n) stranger; foreigner

'**Fremden|führer** m, **~führerin** f (-; -nen) (tourist) guide; **~hass** m xenophobia; **~legi,on** f Foreign Legion; **~verkehr** m tourism; **~verkehrsbü,ro** n tourist office; **~zimmer** n guest room; **~ (zu vermieten)** rooms to let

'**fremdgehen** F v/i (irr, **gehen**, sep, -ge-, sein) be unfaithful (to one's wife or husband), play around

'**Fremd|körper** m MED foreign body; fig alien element; **~sprache** f foreign language; **~sprachensekre,tärin** f bilingual secretary

'**fremd|sprachig, ~sprachlich** adj foreign-language

'**Fremdwort** n (-[e]s; -wörter) foreign word

Frequenz [fre'kvɛnts] f (-; -en) PHYS frequency

Fresse ['frɛsə] V f (-; -n) big (fat) mouth

'**fressen** v/t (irr, ge-, h) ZO eat, feed on; F gobble (up); fig devour

Freude ['frɔydə] f (-; -n) joy, delight; pleasure; **~ haben an** (dat) take pleasure in

'**Freuden|geschrei** n shouts of joy, cheers; **~haus** F n brothel; **~tränen** pl tears of joy

'**freudestrahlend** adj radiant (with joy)

freudig ['frɔydɪç] adj joyful, cheerful; happy (event etc)

freudlos ['frɔytloːs] adj joyless, cheerless

freuen ['frɔyən] v/t (ge-, h) **es freut mich, dass** I'm glad or pleased (that); **sich ~ über** (acc) be pleased or glad about; **sich ~ auf** (acc) look forward to

Freund [frɔynt] m (-[e]s; -e ['frɔyndə]) friend; boyfriend; **Freundin** ['frɔyn-dɪn] f (-; -nen) friend; girlfriend

'**freundlich** adj friendly, kind, nice; fig cheerful (room etc); '**Freundlichkeit** f (-; no pl) friendliness, kindness

'**Freundschaft** f (-; -en) friendship; **~ schließen** make friends

'**freundschaftlich** adj friendly

'**Freundschaftsspiel** n SPORT friendly (game)

Frevel ['freːfəl] m (-s; -) outrage (**an** dat, **gegen** on)

Frieden ['friːdən] m (-s; no pl) peace; **im ~** in peacetime; **lass mich in ~!** leave me alone!

'**Friedens|bewegung** f peace movement; **~forschung** f peace studies; **~verhandlungen** pl peace negotiations or talks; **~vertrag** m peace treaty

friedfertig ['friːtfɛrtɪç] adj peaceable

'**Friedhof** m cemetery, graveyard

'**friedlich** adj peaceful

'**friedliebend** adj peace-loving

frieren ['friːrən] v/i (irr, ge , h) freeze; **ich friere** I am or feel cold; I'm freezing

Fries [friːs] m (-es; -e) ARCH frieze

Frikadelle [frika'dɛlə] f (-; -n) meatball

frisch [frɪʃ] adj fresh; clean (shirt etc); **~ gestrichen!** wet (or fresh) paint!

Frische ['frɪʃə] f (-; no pl) freshness

'**Frischhalte|beutel** m polythene bag; **~folie** f plastic wrap, Br. cling film

Friseur [fri'zøːɐ] m (-s; -e) hairdresser; barber; **~sa,lon** m hairdresser's (shop), barber's shop

Friseuse [fri'zøːzə] f (-; -n) hairdresser

frisieren [fri'ziːrən] v/t (no -ge-, h) do s.o.'s hair; F MOT soup up

Frisör *etc* → **Friseur** *etc*

Frist [frɪst] *f* (-; -en) (fixed) period of time; deadline; extension (*a.* ECON)

fristen ['frɪstən] *v/t* (ge-, h) **sein Dasein** ~ scrape a living

'**fristlos** *adj* without notice

Frisur [fri'zuːɐ] *f* (-; -en) hairstyle, hairdo

Fritten ['frɪtən] F *pl* fries, *Br* chips; **frittieren** [fri'tiːrən] *v/t* (*no* -ge-, h) deep fry

frivol [fri'voːl] *adj* frivolous; suggestive

froh [froː] *adj* glad (**über** *acc* about); cheerful; happy; **~es Fest!** happy holiday!; Merry Christmas!

fröhlich ['frøːlɪç] *adj* cheerful, happy; merry; '**Fröhlichkeit** *f* (-; *no pl*) cheerfulness, merriment

fromm [frɔm] *adj* pious, devout; meek; steady (*horse*); **~er Wunsch** pious hope

Frömmigkeit ['frœmɪçkait] *f* (-; *no pl*) religiousness, piety

Fronleichnam [froːn'laiçnaːm] *m* (-[e]s; *no pl*) REL Corpus Christi

Front [frɔnt] *f* (-; -en) front (*a.* fig), ARCH *a.* face, MIL *a.* line; **in ~ liegen** SPORT be ahead

frontal [frɔn'taːl] *adj* MOT head-on

Fron'talzusammenstoß *m* MOT head-on collision

'**Frontantrieb** *m* MOT front-wheel drive

fror [froːɐ] *pret of* **frieren**

Frosch [frɔʃ] *m* (-[e]s; *Frösche* ['frœʃə]) ZO frog; **~mann** *m* frogman; **~perspek- ,tive** *f* worm's-eye view

Frost [frɔst] *m* (-[e]s; *Fröste* ['frœstə]) frost; **~beule** *f* chilblain

frösteln ['frœstəln] *v/i* (ge-, h) feel chilly, shiver (*a.* fig)

'**frostig** *adj* frosty, fig *a.* chilly

'**Frostschutzmittel** *n* MOT antifreeze

Frottee [frɔ'teː] *n, m* (-[s]; -s) terry (-cloth); **frottieren** [frɔ'tiːrən] *v/t* (*no* -ge-, h) rub down

Frucht [fruxt] *f* (-; *Früchte* ['fryçtə]) BOT fruit (*a.* fig); '**fruchtbar** *adj* BIOL fertile, *esp* fig *a.* fruitful; '**Fruchtbarkeit** *f* (-; *no pl*) fertility; *fig* fruitfulness

'**fruchtlos** *adj* fruitless, futile

'**Fruchtsaft** *m* fruit juice

früh [fryː] *adj and adv* early; **zu ~ kom- men** be early; **~ genug** soon enough; **heute** (**morgen**) **~** this (tomorrow) morning; '**Frühaufsteher** *m* (-s; -) early riser (F bird); **Frühe** ['fryːə] *f: in aller* **~** (very) early in the morning

früher ['fryːɐ] **1.** *adj* former; previous **2.** *adv* in former times, at one time; **~ oder später** sooner or later; **ich habe ~** (**ein- mal**) … I used to …

'**frühestens** *adv* at the earliest

'**Früh|geburt** *f* MED premature birth; premature baby; **~jahr** *n* spring; **~jahrsputz** *m* spring cleaning

früh'morgens *adv* early in the morning

'**frühreif** *adj* precocious

'**Frühstück** *n* breakfast (**zum** for)

'**frühstücken** *v/i* (ge-, h) (have) breakfast

Frust [frʊst] F *m* (-[e]s; *no pl*) frustration

Frustration [frʊstra'tsjoːn] *f* (-; -en) frustration; **frustrieren** [frʊs'triːrən] *v/t* (*no* -ge-, h) frustrate

frz. *abbr of* **französisch** Fr., French

Fuchs [fʊks] *m* (-es; *Füchse* ['fʏksə]) ZO fox (*a.* fig); sorrel; **~jagd** *f* foxhunt(ing); **~schwanz** *m* TECH handsaw

'**fuchs'teufels'wild** F *adj* hopping mad

fuchteln ['fʊxtəln] *v/i* (ge-, h) **~ mit** wave s.th. around

Fuge ['fuːgə] *f* (-; -n) TECH joint; MUS fugue

fügen ['fyːgən] *v/t/refl* (ge-, h) submit (**in** *acc*, *dat* to s.th.)

fühlbar ['fyːlbaːɐ] *fig adj* noticeable; considerable; **fühlen** ['fyːlən] *v/t and v/i and v/refl* (ge-, h) feel, fig *a.* sense; **sich wohl ~** → **wohlfühlen**

Fühler ['fyːlɐ] *m* (-s; -) ZO feeler (*a.* fig)

fuhr [fuːɐ] *pret of* **fahren**

führen ['fyːrən] (ge-, h) **1.** *v/t* lead; guide; take; run, manage; ECON sell, deal in; keep (*account, books etc*); have (*a talk etc*); bear (*name etc*); MIL command; **j-n ~ durch** show s.o. round; **sich ~** conduct o.s. **2.** *v/i* lead (**zu** to, *a.* fig), SPORT *a.* be leading, be ahead; **~d** *adj* leading

Führer ['fyːrɐ] *m* (-s; -) leader (*a.* POL); guide; head, chief; guide(book)

'**Führerschein** *m* MOT driver's license, *Br* driving licence

'**Führung** *f* (-; -en) (*no pl*) leadership, control; ECON management; (guided) tour; **gute ~** good conduct; **in ~ gehen** (**sein**) SPORT take (be in) the lead;

'**Führungszeugnis** n certificate of (good) conduct

Fuhrunternehmen ['fuːɐʔʊntɐneːmən] n trucking company, Br haulage contractors

'**Fuhrwerk** n horse-drawn vehicle

Fülle ['fʏlə] f (-; no pl) crush; fig wealth, abundance; GASTR body

'**füllen** v/t and v/refl (ge-, h) fill (a. MED), stuff (a. GASTR)

Füller ['fʏlɐ] m (-s; -), '**Füllfederhalter** m fountain pen

füllig ['fʏlɪç] adj stout, portly

'**Füllung** f (-; -en) filling (a. MED), stuffing (a. GASTR)

fummeln ['fʊməln] F v/i (ge-, h) fiddle, tinker (both: **an** dat with); F grope

Fund [fʊnt] m (-[e]s; -e ['fʊndə]) discovery; find

Fundament [fʊndaˈmɛnt] n (-[e]s; -e) ARCH foundation(s), fig a. basis

Fundamentalist [fʊndamɛntaˈlɪst] m (-en; -en) fundamentalist

'**Fundbü,ro** n lost and found (office), Br lost-property office

'**Fundgrube** fig f treasure trove

Fundi ['fʊndi] F m (-s; -s) POL radical Green

fundiert [fʊnˈdiːɐt] adj well-founded (argument etc); sound (knowledge)

fünf [fʏnf] adj five; grade: F, N, Br fail, poor, E; '**Fünfeck** n (-[e]s; -e) pentagon; '**fünffach** adj fivefold

'**Fünfkampf** m SPORT pentathlon

'**Fünflinge** pl quintuplets

'**fünfte** adj fifth; '**Fünftel** n (-s; -) fifth

'**fünftens** adv fifth(ly), in the fifth place

'**fünfzehn(te)** adj fifteen(th)

fünfzig ['fʏnftsɪç] adj fifty

'**fünfzigste** adj fiftieth

fungieren [fʊŋˈgiːrən] v/i (no -ge-, h) **als** act as, function as

Funk [fʊŋk] m (-s; no pl) radio; **über** or **durch** ~ by radio

'**Funkama,teur** m radio ham

Funke ['fʊŋkə] m (-n; -n) spark; fig a. glimmer; **funkeln** ['fʊŋkəln] v/i (ge-, h) sparkle, glitter; twinkle

'**funken** v/t (ge-, h) radio, transmit

Funker ['fʊŋkɐ] m (-s; -) radio operator

'**Funk|gerät** n radio set; ~**haus** n broadcasting center (Br centre); ~**sig,nal** n radio signal; ~**spruch** m radio message; ~**stati,on** f radio station; ~**streife**

f (radio) patrol car; ~**tele,fon** n cellular phone

Funktion [fʊŋkˈtsjoːn] f (-; -en) function; **Funktionär** [fʊŋktsjoˈnɛːɐ] m (-s; -e) functionary, official (a. SPORT); **funktionieren** [fʊŋktsjoˈniːrən] v/i (no -ge-, h) work

'**Funkturm** m radio tower

'**Funkverkehr** m radio communication

für [fyːɐ] prp (acc) for; in favo(u)r of; on behalf of; ~ **immer** forever; **Tag** ~ **Tag** day by day; **Wort** ~ **Wort** word by word; **jeder** ~ **sich** everyone by himself; **was** ~ **...?** what (kind or sort of) ...?; **das Für und Wider** the pros and cons

Furche ['fʊrçə] f (-; -n) furrow; rut

Furcht [fʊrçt] f (-; no pl) fear, dread (both: **vor** dat of); **aus** ~(**dass**) for fear (that); ~ **erregend** → **furchterregend**

'**furchtbar** adj terrible, awful

fürchten ['fʏrçtən] v/t and v/i (ge-, h) fear, be afraid of; dread; ~ **um** fear for; **sich** ~ be scared; be afraid (**vor** dat of); **ich fürchte, ...** I'm afraid ...

fürchterlich ['fʏrçtɐlɪç] → **furchtbar**

'**furcht|erregend** adj frightening; ~**los** adj fearless; ~**sam** adj timid

füreiˈnander adv for each other

Furnier [fʊrˈniːɐ] n (-[e]s; -e), **furnieren** [fʊrˈniːrən] v/t (no -ge-, h) veneer

'**Fürsorge** f (-; no pl) care; **öffentliche** ~ (public) welfare (work); ~**empfänger** m social security beneficiary

fürsorglich ['fyːɐzɔrklɪç] adj considerate

'**Für|sprache** f intercession (**für** for; **bei** with); ~**sprech** m (-[e]s; -e) Swiss: lawyer; ~**sprecher(in)** advocate (a. fig)

Fürst [fʏrst] m (-en; -en) prince

'**Fürstentum** n (-s; -tümer ['fʏrstəntyːmɐ]) principality

'**Fürstin** f (-; -nen) princess

'**fürstlich** adj princely (a. fig)

Furt [fʊrt] f (-; -en) ford

Furunkel [fuˈrʊŋkəl] m (-s; -) MED boil, furuncle

'**Fürwort** n (-[e]s; -wörter) LING pronoun

Furz [fʊrts] m (-es; -e), '**furzen** v/i (ge-, h) fart

Fusion [fuˈzjoːn] f (-; -en) ECON merger, amalgamation

fusionieren [fuzjoˈniːrən] v/i (no -ge-, h) ECON merge, amalgamate

Fuß [fuːs] m (-es; Füße) ['fyːsə] ANAT

foot; stand; stem; **zu**~ on foot; **zu**~ **ge-hen** walk; **gut zu**~ **sein** be a good walk-er; ~ **fassen** become established; **auf freiem** ~ at large

'**Fußball** m (no pl) soccer, Br football; soccer ball, Br football

Fußballer ['fuːsbalɐ] m (-s; -) footballer

'**Fußball|feld** n football field; ~**rowdy** m (football) hooligan; ~**spiel** n soccer or football match; ~**spieler(in)** football player, footballer; ~**toto** n football pools

'**Fußboden** m floor; flooring; ~**heizung** f underfloor heating

'**Fußbremse** f MOT footbrake

Fussel ['fʊsəl] f (-; -n), m (-s; -[n]) piece of lint (Br fluff); pl lint, Br fluff; '**fusselig** ['fʊsəlɪç] adj linty, Br cov-ered in fluff; '**fusseln** v/i (ge-, h) shed a lot of lint (Br fluff), F mo(u)lt

Fußgänger ['fuːsɡɛŋɐ] m (-s; -), '**Fußgängerin** f (-; -nen) pedestrian; '**Fußgängerzone** f (pedestrian or

shopping) mall, Br pedestrian precinct

'**Fußgeher** Austrian m → **Fußgänger**

'**Fuß|gelenk** n ANAT ankle; ~**matte** f doormat; ~**note** f footnote; ~**pflege** f pedicure; MED podiatry, Br. chiropody; ~**pfleger(in)** podiatrist, Br chiropodist; ~**pilz** m MED athlete's foot; ~**sohle** f ANAT sole (of the foot); ~**spur** f foot-print; track; ~**stapfen** pl: **in j-s** ~ **treten** follow in s.o.'s footsteps; ~**tritt** m kick; ~**weg** m foothpath; **e-e Stunde** ~ an hour's walk

Futter[1] ['fʊtɐ] n (-s; no pl) AGR feed, fod-der, food

'**Futter**[2] n (-s; -) lining

Futteral [fʊtəˈraːl] n (-s; -e) case; cover

füttern[1] ['fʏtɐn] v/t (ge-, h) AGR feed

'**füttern**[2] v/t (ge-, h) line

'**Futternapf** m (feeding) bowl

Fütterung ['fʏtərʊŋ] f (-; -en) feeding (time)

Futur [fuˈtuːɐ] n (-s; -e) future (a. LING)

G

gab [ɡaːp] pret of **geben**

Gabe ['ɡaːbə] f (-; -n) gift, present; MED dose; fig talent, gift; **milde** ~ alms

Gabel ['ɡaːbəl] f (-; -n) fork; TEL cradle

'**gabeln** v/refl (ge-, h) fork, branch

Gabelstapler ['ɡaːbəlʃtaːplɐ] m (-s; -) TECH fork-lift (truck)

Gabelung ['ɡaːbəlʊŋ] f (-; -en) fork(ing)

gackern ['ɡakɐn] v/i (ge-, h) cluck, cack-le (a. fig)

gaffen ['ɡafən] v/i (ge-, h) gawk, gawp, F rubberneck; **Gaffer** ['ɡafɐ] m (-s; -) F rubberneck(er), Br nosy parker

Gage ['ɡaːʒə] f (-; -n) fee

gähnen ['ɡɛːnən] v/i (ge-, h) yawn

Gala ['ɡaːla] f (-; -s) gala

galant [ɡaˈlant] adj gallant, courteous

Galeere [ɡaˈleːrə] f (-; -n) MAR galley

Galerie [ɡaləˈriː] f (-; -n) gallery

Galgen ['ɡalɡən] m (-s; -) gallows; ~**frist** f reprieve; ~**hu**~**mor** m gallows hu-mo(u)r; ~**vogel** F m crook

Galle ['ɡalə] f (-; -n) ANAT gall; bile

'**Gallen|blase** f ANAT gall bladder; ~**stein** m MED gallstone

Gallert ['ɡalɐt] n (-[es]; -e), **Gallerte** [ɡaˈlɛrtə] f (-; -n) jelly

Galopp [ɡaˈlɔp] m (-s; -s, -e) gallop

galoppieren [ɡalɔˈpiːrən] v/i (nu -ge-, sein) gallop

galt [ɡalt] pret of **gelten**

gammeln ['ɡaməln] F v/i (ge-, h) loaf (about), bum around; **Gammler(in)** ['ɡamlɐ, 'ɡamlərɪn] m(f) F (-s; -/-; -nen) loafer, bum

Gämse ['ɡɛmzə] f (-; -n) ZO chamois

gang [ɡaŋ] adj: ~ **und gäbe** nothing un-usual, (quite) usual

Gang [ɡaŋ] m (-[e]s; Gänge ['ɡɛŋə]) walk, gait, way s.o. walks; ARCH pas-sage, a. AVIAT etc aisle; corridor; MOT gear; GASTR course; **et. in** ~ **bringen** get s.th. going, start s.th.; **in** ~ **kommen** get started; **im** ~**(e) sein** be (going) on, be in progress; **in vollem** ~**(e)** in full swing

gängeln ['ɡɛŋəln] v/t (ge-, h) lead s.o. by the nose

gängig ['ɡɛŋɪç] adj current; ECON sal(e)-able

'**Gangschaltung** f MOT gears
Ganove [ga'noːvə] F m (-n; -n) crook
Gans [gans] f (-; Gänse ['gɛnzə]) ZO goose
Gänse|blümchen ['gɛnzəblyːmçən] n BOT daisy; **~braten** m roast goose; **~haut** f (-; no pl) gooseflesh; **dabei kriege ich e-e ~** F it gives me the creeps; **~marsch** m (-[e]s; no pl) single or Indian file
Gänserich ['gɛnzərɪç] m (-s; -e) ZO gander
ganz [gants] 1. adj whole, entire, total; F undamaged; full (hour etc); **den ~en Tag** all day; **die ~e Zeit** all the time; **auf der ~en Welt** all over the world; **sein ~es Geld** all his money 2. adv completely, totally; very; quite, rather, fairly; **~ allein** all by oneself; **~ aus Holz** etc all wood etc; **~ und gar** completely, totally; **~ und gar nicht** not at all, by no means; **~ wie du willst** just as you like; **nicht ~** not quite; → **voll**
Ganze ['gantsə] n (-n; no pl) whole; **das ~** the whole thing; **im ~n** in all, altogether; **im großen und ~n** on the whole; **aufs ~ gehen** go all out
gänzlich ['gɛntslɪç] adv completely, entirely
'**Ganztags|beschäftigung** f full-time job; **~schule** f all-day school(ing)
gar [gaːɐ] 1. adj GASTR done 2. adv: **~ nicht** not at all; **~ nichts** nothing at all; **~ zu ...** (a bit) too ...
Garage [ga'raːʒə] f (-; -n) garage
Garantie [garan'tiː] f (-; -n) guarantee, esp ECON warranty; **garantieren** [garan'tiːrən] v/t and v/i (no -ge-, h) guarantee (**für et.** s.th.)
Garbe ['garbə] f (-; -n) AGR sheaf
Garde ['gardə] f (-; -n) guard; MIL (the) Guards
Garderobe [gardə'roːbə] f (-; -n) (no pl) wardrobe, clothes; checkroom, Br cloakroom; THEA dressing room
Garde'roben|frau f checkroom (Br cloakroom) attendant; **~marke** f coat check (Br cloakroom) ticket; **~ständer** m coat stand or rack
Gardine [gar'diːnə] f (-; -n) curtain
Gar'dinenstange f curtain rod
gären ['gɛːrən] v/i ([irr,] ge-, h, sein) ferment, work
Garn [garn] n (-[e]s; -e) yarn; thread;

cotton
Garnele [gar'neːlə] f (-; -n) ZO shrimp; prawn
garnieren [gar'niːrən] v/t (no -ge-, h) garnish (a. fig)
Garnison [garni'zoːn] f (-; -en) MIL garrison, post
Garnitur [garni'tuːɐ] f (-, -en) set; suite
Garten ['gartən] m (-s; Gärten ['gɛrtən]) garden; **~arbeit** f gardening; **~bau** m (-[e]s; no pl) horticulture; **~erde** f (garden) mo(u)ld; **~fest** n garden party; **~geräte** pl gardening tools; **~haus** n summerhouse; **~lo,kal** n beer garden; outdoor restaurant; **~schere** f pruning shears; **~stadt** f garden city; **~zwerg** m (garden) gnome
Gärtner ['gɛrtnɐ] m (-s; -) gardener
Gärtnerei [gɛrtnə'rai] f (-; -en) truck farm, Br market garden
'**Gärtnerin** f (-; -nen) gardener
Gärung ['gɛːrʊŋ] f (-; -en) fermentation
Gas [gaːs] n (-es; -e ['gaːzə]) gas; **~ geben** MOT accelerate, F step on the gas
gasförmig ['gaːsfœrmɪç] adj gaseous
'**Gas|hahn** m gas valve (or cock, Br tap); **~heizung** f gas heating; **~herd** m gas cooker or stove; **~kammer** f gas chamber; **~la,terne** f gas (street) lamp; **~leitung** f gas main; **~maske** f gas mask; **~ofen** m gas stove; **~pe,dal** n MOT gas pedal, Br accelerator (pedal)
Gasse ['gasə] f (-; -n) lane, alley
Gast [gast] m (-[e]s; Gäste ['gɛstə]) guest; visitor; customer
'**Gastarbeiter** m, '**Gastarbeiterin** f foreign worker
Gästebuch ['gɛstəbuːx] n visitors' book
'**Gästezimmer** n guest (or spare) room
'**gastfreundlich** adj hospitable
'**Gastfreundschaft** f hospitality
Gastgeber ['gastgeːbɐ] m (-s; -) host
Gastgeberin ['gastgeːbərɪn] f (-; -nen) hostess
'**Gast|haus** n, **~hof** m restaurant, inn
gastieren [gas'tiːrən] v/i (no -ge-, h) give performances; THEA guest, give a guest performance
'**gastlich** adj hospitable
'**Gast|mannschaft** f SPORT visiting team; **~spiel** n THEA guest performance; **~stätte** f restaurant; **~stube** f taproom; restaurant; **~wirt** m landlord;

~wirtschaft f restaurant, inn

'Gaswerk n TECH gasworks

'Gaszähler m TECH gas meter

Gatte ['gatə] m (-n; -n) husband

Gatter ['gatɐ] n (-s; -) fence; gate

Gattin ['gatɪn] f (-; -nen) wife

Gattung ['gatʊŋ] f (-; -en) type, class, sort; BIOL genus; species

GAU [gau] (ABBR of *größter anzunehmender Unfall*) m (-[s]; no pl) worst case scenario, Br maximum credible accident, MCA

Gaul [gaul] m (-[e]s; *Gäule* ['gɔylə]) nag

Gaumen ['gaumən] m (-s; -) ANAT palate

Gauner ['gaunɐ] m (-s; -), **'Gaunerin** f (-; -nen) F crook

Gaze ['ga:zə] f (-; -n) gauze

Gazelle [ga'tsɛlə] f (-; -n) ZO gazelle

geb. abbr of *geboren* b., born

Gebäck [gə'bɛk] n (-[e]s; -e) pastry; cookies, Br biscuits

ge'backen pp of *backen*

Gebälk [gə'bɛlk] n (-[e]s; -e) timberwork, beams

gebar [gə'ba:ɐ] pret of *gebären*

Gebärde [gə'bɛːɐdə] f (-; -n) gesture

ge'bärden v/refl (no -ge-, h) behave, act (*wie* like)

gebären [gə'bɛːrən] v/t (irr, no -ge-, h) give birth to; **Gebärmutter** [gə-'bɛːrmʊtɐ] f ANAT uterus, womb

Gebäude [gə'bɔydə] n (-s; -) building, structure

Ge'beine pl bones, mortal remains

geben ['ge:bən] v/t (irr, ge-, h) give (*j-m et.* s.o. s.th.); hand, pass; deal (*cards*); make; *sich ~* pass; get better; *von sich ~* utter, let out; *j-m die Schuld ~* blame s.o.; *es gibt* there is, there are; *was gibt es?* what's up?; what's for *lunch etc?*; TV *etc* what's on?; *das gibt's nicht* that can't be true; that's out

Gebet [gə'be:t] n (-[e]s; -e) prayer

ge'beten pp of *bitten*

Gebiet [gə'bi:t] n (-[e]s; -e) region, area; *esp* POL territory; *fig* field

ge'bieterisch adj imperious

ge'bietsweise adv regionally; **~ Regen** local showers

Gebilde [gə'bɪldə] n (-s; -) thing, object

gebildet [gə'bɪldət] adj educated

Gebirge [gə'bɪrgə] n (-s; -) mountains

gebirgig [gə'bɪrgɪç] adj mountainous

Ge'birgs|bewohner m mountain-dweller; **~zug** m mountain range

Ge'biss n (-es; -e) (set of) teeth; (set of) false teeth, denture(s)

ge'bissen pp of *beißen*

Gebläse [gə'blɛːzə] n (-s; -) TECH blower, (MOT air) fan

ge'blasen pp of *blasen*

geblichen [gə'blɪçən] pp of *bleichen*

geblieben [gə'bli:bən] pp of *bleiben*

geblümt [gə'bly:mt] adj floral

gebogen [gə'bo:gən] 1. pp of *biegen* 2. adj bent, curved

geboren [gə'bo:rən] 1. pp of *gebären* 2. adj born; **~e Smith** née Smith; **ich bin am ... ~** I was born on the ...

geborgen [gə'bɔrgən] 1. pp of *bergen* 2. adj safe, secure; **Ge'borgenheit** f (-; no pl) safety, security

geborsten [gə'bɔrstən] pp of *bersten*

Gebot [gə'bo:t] n (-[e]s; -e) REL commandment; *fig* rule; necessity; *auction etc*: bid

geboten [gə'bo:tən] pp of *bieten*

gebracht [gə'braxt] pp of *bringen*

gebrannt [gə'brant] pp of *brennen*

ge'braten pp of *braten*

Ge'brauch m (-[e]s; no pl) use; application; **ge'brauchen** v/t (no -ge-, h) use; employ; *gut (nicht) zu ~ sein* be useful (useless); *ich könnte ... ~* I could do with ...; **gebräuchlich** [gə'brɔyçlɪç] adj in use; common, usual; current

Ge'brauchsanweisung f directions *or* instructions for use

ge'brauchsfertig adj ready for use; instant (*coffee etc*)

Ge'brauchsgrafiker m commercial artist

ge'braucht adj used, ECON *a.* second-hand

Ge'brauchtwagen m MOT used *or* second-hand car; **~händler** m used car dealer

Ge'brechen n (-s; -) defect, handicap

gebrechlich [gə'brɛçlɪç] adj frail; infirm; **Ge'brechlichkeit** f (-; no pl) frailty; infirmity

gebrochen [gə'brɔxən] pp of *brechen*

Ge'brüder pl brothers

Gebrüll [gə'bryl] n (-[e]s; no pl) roar (-ing)

Gebühr [gə'by:ɐ] f (-; -en) charge (*a.* TEL), fee; postage; due; **gebührend** [gə'by:rənt] adj due; proper

ge'bühren\frei *adj* free of charge; TEL toll-free, *Br* nonchargeable; **~pflichtig** *adj* chargeable; **~e Straße** toll road; **~e Verwarnung** fine

gebunden [gə'bʊndən] **1.** *pp of* **binden 2.** *adj* bound, *fig a.* tied

Geburt [gə'bu:ɐt] *f* (-; -en) birth

Ge'burten\kon,trolle *f*, **~regelung** *f* birth control

ge'burten\schwach *adj* low-birthrate; **~stark** *adj*: **~e Jahrgänge** baby boom

Ge'burtenziffer *f* birthrate

gebürtig [gə'bʏrtɪç] *adj* by birth

Ge'burts\anzeige *f* birth announcement; **~datum** *n* date of birth; **~fehler** *m* congenital defect; **~helfer(in)** obstetrician; **~jahr** *n* year of birth; **~land** *n* native country; **~ort** *m* birthplace; **~tag** *m* birthday; **~tagsfeier** *f* birthday party; **~tagskind** *n* birthday boy (*or* girl); **~urkunde** *f* birth certificate

Gebüsch [gə'bʏʃ] *n* (-[e]s; -e) bushes, shrubbery

gedacht [gə'daxt] *pp of* **denken**

Gedächtnis [gə'dɛçtnɪs] *n* (-ses; -se) memory; **aus dem ~** from memory; **zum ~ an** (*acc*) in memory (*or* commemoration) of; **im ~ behalten** keep in mind, remember; **~lücke** *f* memory lapse; **~schwund** *m* MED amnesia; blackout; **~stütze** *f* memory aid

Gedanke [gə'daŋkə] *m* (-n; -n) thought; idea; **was für ein ~!** what an idea!; **in ~n** absorbed in thought; absent-minded; **sich ~n machen über** (*acc*) think about; be worried *or* concerned about; **j-s ~n lesen** read s.o.'s mind

Ge'danken\austausch *m* exchange of ideas; **~gang** *m* train of thought

ge'dankenlos *adj* thoughtless

Ge'danken\strich *m* dash; **~übertragung** *f* telepathy

Gedeck [gə'dɛk] *n* (-[e]s; -e) cover; **ein ~ auflegen** set a place

gedeihen [gə'daiən] *v/i* (*irr, no -ge-, sein*) thrive, prosper; grow; flourish

ge'denken *v/i* (*irr, denken, no -ge-, h*) (*gen*) think of; commemorate; mention

Gedenk\feier [gə'dɛŋkfaiɐ] *f* commemoration; **~mi,nute** *f*: **e-e ~** a moment's (*Br* minute's) silence; **~stätte** *f*, **~stein** *m* memorial; **~tafel** *f* plaque

Gedicht [gə'dɪçt] *n* (-[e]s; -e) poem

gediegen [gə'di:gən] *adj* solid; tasteful

gedieh [gə'di:] *pret of* **gedeihen**

gediehen [gə'di:ən] *pp of* **gedeihen**

Gedränge [gə'drɛŋə] *n* (-s; -) crowd, F crush; **ge'drängt** *fig adj* concise

gedroschen [gə'drɔʃən] *pp of* **dreschen**

ge'drückt *fig adj* depressed

gedrungen [gə'drʊŋən] **1.** *pp of* **dringen 2.** *adj* squat, stocky; thickset

Geduld [gə'dʊlt] *f* (-; *no pl*) patience; **ge'dulden** *v/refl* (*no -ge-, h*) wait (patiently); **geduldig** [gə'dʊldɪç] *adj* patient; **Ge'duldspiel** *n* puzzle (*a. fig*)

gedurft [gə'dʊrft] *pp of* **dürfen**

geehrt [gə'ʔe:ɐt] *adj* hono(u)red; **Sehr ~er Herr N.** Dear Mr N.

geeignet [gə'ʔaignət] *adj* suitable; suited, qualified; right

Gefahr [gə'fa:ɐ] *f* (-; -en) danger; threat; risk; **auf eigene ~** at one's own risk; **außer ~** out of danger, safe

gefährden [gə'fɛ:ɐdən] *v/t* (*no -ge-, h*) endanger; risk, jeopardize

ge'fahren *pp of* **fahren**

gefährlich [gə'fɛ:ɐlɪç] *adj* dangerous; risky

ge'fahrlos *adj* without risk, safe

Gefährte [gə'fɛ:ɐtə] *m* (-n; -n), **Ge'fährtin** *f* (-; -nen) companion

Gefälle [gə'fɛlə] *n* (-s; -) fall, slope, descent; gradient (*a. PHYS*)

ge'fallen 1. *pp of* **fallen 2.** *v/i* (*irr, fallen, no -ge-, h*) please; **es gefällt mir (nicht)** I (don't) like it; **wie gefällt dir ...?** how do you like ...?; **sich et. ~ lassen** put up with s.th.

Ge'fallen¹ *m* (-s; -) favo(u)r; **j-n um e-n ~ bitten** ask a favo(u)r of s.o.

Ge'fallen² *n*: **~ finden an** (*dat*) enjoy, like

ge'fällig *adj* pleasant, agreeable; obliging, kind; **j-m ~ sein** do s.o. a favo(u)r

Ge'fälligkeit *f* (-; -en) (*no pl*) kindness; favo(u)r

ge'fangen 1. *pp of* **fangen 2.** *adj* captive; imprisoned; **~ halten** keep s.o. prisoner; **~ nehmen** take s.o. prisoner; *fig* captivate; **Ge'fangene** *m*, *f* (-n; -n) prisoner; convict; **Ge'fangennahme** *f* (-; *no pl*) capture; **Ge'fangenschaft** *f* (-; *no pl*) captivity, imprisonment; **in ~ sein** be a prisoner of war

Gefängnis [gə'fɛŋnɪs] *n* (-ses; -se) prison, jail, *Br a.* gaol; **ins ~ kommen** go to jail *or* prison; **~di,rektor** *m* governor, warden; **~strafe** *f* (sentence *or* term of) imprisonment; **~wärter** *m* prison guard

Gefäß [gə'fɛːs] *n* (-es; -e) vessel (*a.* ANAT), container

gefasst [gə'fast] *adj* composed; **~ auf** (*acc*) prepared for

Gefecht [gə'fɛçt] *n* (-[e]s; -e) MIL combat, action

gefedert [gə'feːdɐt] *adj*: **gut~ sein** MOT have good suspension

gefeit [gə'fait] *adj*: **~ gegen** immune to

Gefieder [gə'fiːdɐ] *n* (-s; -) ZO plumage, feathers

geflochten [gə'flɔxtən] *pp of* **flechten**

geflogen [gə'floːgən] *pp of* **fliegen**

geflohen [gə'floːən] *pp of* **fliehen**

geflossen [gə'flɔsən] *pp of* **fließen**

Ge'flügel *n* (-s; *no pl*) poultry

ge'flügelt *adj*: **~es Wort** saying

gefochten [gə'fɔxtən] *pp of* **fechten**

Ge'folge *n* (-s; -) entourage, retinue, train; **Gefolgschaft** [gə'fɔlkʃaft] *f* (-; -en) followers

gefragt [gə'fraːkt] *adj* in demand, popular

gefräßig [gə'frɛːsɪç] *adj* greedy, voracious

Gefreite [gə'fraitə] *m* (-n; -n) MIL private first class, *Br* lance corporal

ge'fressen *pp of* **fressen**

ge'frieren *v/i* (*irr,* **frieren**, *no* -ge-, *sein*) freeze

Gefrierfach [gə'friːɐfax] *n* freezer, freezing compartment

ge'friergetrocknet *adj* freeze-dried

Ge'frier|punkt *m* freezing point; **~truhe** *f* freezer, deep-freeze

gefroren [gə'froːrən] *pp of* **frieren**

Ge'frorene *Austrian n* (-n; *no pl*) ice cream

Gefüge [gə'fyːgə] *n* (-s; -) structure, texture

gefügig [gə'fyːgɪç] *adj* pliant

Ge'fügigkeit *f* (-; *no pl*) pliancy

Gefühl [gə'fyːl] *n* (-[e]s; -e) feeling; sense; sensation; emotion; **ge'fühllos** *adj* insensible, numb; unfeeling, heartless; **ge'fühlsbetont** *adj* (highly) emotional; **ge'fühlvoll** *adj* (full of) feeling; tender; sentimental

gefunden [gə'fundən] *pp of* **finden**

gegangen [gə'gaŋən] *pp of* **gehen**

gegeben [gə'geːbən] *pp of* **geben**

gegen ['geːgən] *prp* (*acc*) against, JUR, SPORT *a.* versus; about, around; (in return) for; MED *etc* for; compared with

'Gegen... *in cpds* ...aktion, ...angriff, ...argument, ...frage *etc*: counter-...; **~besuch** *m* return visit

Gegend ['geːgənt] *f* (-; -en) region, area; countryside; neighbo(u)rhood

gegenei'nander *adv* against one another *or* each other

'Gegen|fahrbahn *f* MOT opposite *or* oncoming lane; **~gewicht** *n* counterweight; **ein ~ bilden zu et.** counterbalance s.th.; **~kandi,dat** *m* rival candidate; **~leistung** *f* quid pro quo; **als ~** in return; **~licht** *n* (-[e]s; *no pl*) PHOT back light; **im** *or* **bei ~** against the light; **~maßnahme** *f* countermeasure; **~mittel** *n* MED antidote (*a. fig*); **~par,tei** *f* other side; POL opposition; SPORT opposite side; **~richtung** *f* opposite direction

'Gegensatz *m* contrast; opposite; **im ~ zu** in contrast to *or* with; **gegensätzlich** ['geːgənzɛtslɪç] *adj* contrary, opposite

'Gegenseite *f* opposite side

gegenseitig ['geːgənzaitɪç] *adj* mutual

'Gegenseitigkeit *f*: **auf ~ beruhen** be mutual

'Gegen|spieler *m*, **~spielerin** *f* SPORT opponent (*a. fig*); **~sprechanlage** *f* intercom (system)

'Gegenstand *m* object (*a. fig*); *fig* subject; **gegenständlich** ['geːgənʃtɛntlɪç] *adj art*: representational; **'gegenstandslos** *adj* invalid; irrelevant; *art*: abstract, nonrepresentational

'Gegen|stimme *f* PARL vote against, no; **nur drei ~n** only three noes; **~stück** *n* counterpart

'Gegenteil *n* opposite; **im ~** on the contrary; **'gegenteilig** *adj* contrary, opposite

gegen'über *adv and prp* (*dat*) opposite; *fig* to, toward(s); compared with

Gegen'über *n* (-s; -) person opposite; neighbo(u)r across the street

gegen'überstehen *v/i* (*irr,* **stehen**, *sep,* -ge-, *h*) face, be faced with

Gegen'überstellung *f* confrontation

'Gegenverkehr *m* oncoming traffic

Gegenwart ['ge:gənvart] *f* (-; *no pl*) present (time); presence; LING present (tense)

gegenwärtig ['ge:gənvɛrtɪç] **1.** *adj* present, current **2.** *adv* at present

Gegen|wehr ['ge:gənve:ɐ] *f* (-; *no pl*) resistance; ~wert *m* equivalent (value); ~wind *m* head wind

'**gegenzeichnen** *v/t* (*sep*, *-ge-*, *h*) countersign

'**Gegenzug** *m* countermove; RAIL train coming from the opposite direction

gegessen [gə'gesən] *pp of* **essen**

geglichen [gə'glɪçən] *pp of* **gleichen**

geglitten [gə'glɪtən] *pp of* **gleiten**

geglommen [gə'glɔmən] *pp of* **glimmen**

Gegner ['ge:gnɐ] *m* (*-s*; *-*), '**Gegnerin** *f* (-; *-nen*) opponent (*a.* SPORT), adversary; MIL enemy

'**gegnerisch** *adj* opposing; MIL (of the) enemy, hostile

'**Gegnerschaft** *f* (-; *-en*) opposition

gegolten [gə'gɔltən] *pp of* **gelten**

gegoren [gə'go:rən] *pp of* **gären**

gegossen [gə'gɔsən] *pp of* **gießen**

ge'graben *pp of* **graben**

gegriffen [gə'grɪfən] *pp of* **greifen**

gehabt [gə'ha:pt] *pp of* **haben**

Gehackte [gə'haktə] *n* → **Hackfleisch**

Gehalt [gə'halt] **1.** *m* (*-[e]s*; *-e*) content **2.** *n* (*-[e]s*; *Gehälter* [gə'hɛltɐ]) salary

ge'halten *pp of* **halten**

Ge'halts|empfänger *m* salaried employee; ~erhöhung *f* raise, *Br* increase *or* rise in salary

ge'haltvoll *adj* substantial; nutritious

gehangen [gə'haŋən] *pp of* **hängen** 1

gehässig [gə'hɛsɪç] *adj* malicious, spiteful; **Ge'hässigkeit** *f* (-; *no pl*) malice, spite(fulness)

ge'hauen *pp of* **hauen**

Gehäuse [gə'hɔyzə] *n* (*-s*; *-*) case, box; TECH casing; ZO shell; BOT core

Gehege [gə'he:gə] *n* (*-s*; *-*) enclosure

geheim [gə'haim] *adj* secret; *et.* ~ **halten** keep s.th. (a) secret

Ge'heim|a,gent *m* secret agent; ~dienst *m* secret service

Geheimnis [gə'haimnɪs] *n* (*-ses*; *-se*) secret; mystery

ge'heimnisvoll *adj* mysterious

Ge'heim|nummer *f* TEL unlisted (*Br* ex--directory) number; ~poli,zei *f* secret

police; ~schrift *f* code, cipher

ge'heißen *pp of* **heißen**

gehemmt [gə'hɛmt] *adj* inhibited, self--conscious

gehen ['ge:ən] *v/i* (*irr*, *ge-*, *sein*) go; walk; leave; TECH work (*a. fig*); ECON sell; *fig* last; *einkaufen* (*schwimmen*) ~ go shopping (swimming); ~ *wir!* let's go!; *wie geht es dir* (*Ihnen*)? how are you?; *es geht mir gut* (*schlecht*) I'm fine (not feeling well); ~ *in* (*acc*) go into; ~ *nach* *road etc*: lead to; *window etc*: face; *fig* go *or* judge by; *das geht nicht* that's impossible; *das geht schon* that's o.k.; *es geht nichts über* (*acc*) ... there is nothing like ...; *worum geht es?* what is it about?; *darum geht es* (*nicht*) that's (not) the point; *sich* ~ *lassen* let o.s. go

'**gehenlassen** *v/refl* (*irr*, *lassen*, *sep*, *no* *-ge-*, *h*) → **gehen**

geheuer [gə'hɔyɐ] *adj*: *nicht* (*ganz*) ~ eerie, creepy, F fishy

Geheul [gə'hɔyl] *n* (*-[e]s*; *no pl*) howling

Ge'hirn *n* (*-[e]s*; *-e*) ANAT brain(s); ~er-schütterung *f* MED concussion (of the brain); ~schlag *m* MED (cerebral) apoplexy; ~wäsche *f* brainwashing

gehoben [gə'ho:bən] **1.** *pp of* **heben** **2.** *adj* elevated; high(er); ~e *Stimmung* high spirits

Gehöft [gə'hœft] *n* (*-[e]s*; *-e*) farm (-stead)

geholfen [gə'hɔlfən] *pp of* **helfen**

Gehölz [gə'hœlts] *n* (*-es*; *-e*) wood, coppice, copse

Gehör [gə'hø:ɐ] *n* (*-[e]s*; *-e*) (sense of) hearing; ear; *nach dem* ~ by ear; *sich* ~ *verschaffen* make o.s. heard

ge'horchen *v/i* (*no -ge-*, *h*) obey; *nicht* ~ disobey

ge'hören *v/i* (*no -ge-*, *h*) belong (*dat or* *zu* to); *gehört dir das?* is this yours?; *es gehört sich* (*nicht*) it is proper *or* right (not done); *das gehört nicht hierher* that's not to the point

ge'hörig **1.** *adj* due, proper; necessary; decent; *zu et.* ~ belonging to s.th. **2.** *adv* properly, thoroughly

ge'hörlos *adj* deaf; *die Gehörlosen* the deaf

gehorsam [gə'ho:rza:m] *adj* obedient

Ge'horsam *m* (*-s*; *no pl*) obedience

'**Gehsteig** *m*, '**Gehweg** *m* sidewalk, *Br*

pavement

Geier ['gaiɐ] *m* (-s; -) zo vulture, buzzard

Geige ['gaigə] *f* (-; -n) MUS violin, F fiddle; *(auf der)* ~ *spielen* play (on) the violin

'**Geigen|bogen** *m* MUS (violin) bow; ~**kasten** *m* MUS violin case

'**Geiger** ['gaigɐ] *m* (-s; -), **Geigerin** ['gaigərɪn] *f* (-; -nen) MUS violinist

'**Geigerzähler** *m* PHYS Geiger counter

geil [gail] *adj* V hot, horny; *contp* lecherous, lewd; BOT rank; F awesome, *Br* brill, ace

Geisel ['gaizəl] *f* (-; -n) hostage; ~**nehmer** ['gaizəlne:mɐ] *m* (-s; -) kidnap(p)er

Geißel ['gaisəl] *fig f* (-; -n) scourge

Geist [gaist] *m* (-[e]s; -er) (*no pl*) spirit; soul; mind; intellect; wit; ghost; *der Heilige* ~ REL the Holy Ghost *or* Spirit

Geister|bahn ['gaistɐba:n] *f* tunnel of horror, *Br* ghost train; ~**fahrer** F *m* MOT wrong-way driver

'**geisterhaft** *adj* ghostly

'**geistesabwesend** *adj* absent-minded

'**Geistes|arbeiter** *m* brainworker; ~**blitz** *m* brainstorm, *Br* brainwave

'**Geistesgegenwart** *f* presence of mind; '**geistesgegenwärtig** *adj* alert; quick--witted

'**geistesgestört** *adj* mentally disturbed, deranged

'**geisteskrank** *adj* mentally ill

'**Geisteskrankheit** *f* mental illness

'**geistesschwach** *adj* feeble-minded

'**Geisteswissenschaften** *pl* the arts, *the* humanities

'**Geisteszustand** *m* mental state

geistig ['gaistɪç] *adj* mental; intellectual; spiritual; ~ *behindert* mentally handicapped

'**geistlich** *adj* religious; spiritual; ecclesiastical; clerical; '**Geistliche** *m* (-n; -n) clergyman; priest; minister; *die* ~*n* the clergy

'**geistlos** *adj* trivial, inane, silly

'**geistreich**, '**geistvoll** *adj* witty, clever

Geiz [gaits] *m* (-es; *no pl*) stinginess

'**Geizhals** *m* miser, niggard

geizig ['gaitsɪç] *adj* stingy, miserly

Ge'jammer F *n* (-s; *no pl*) wailing, complaining

gekannt [gə'kant] *pp of* **kennen**

Gekläff [gə'klɛf] F *n* (-[e]s; *no pl*) yapping

Geklapper [gə'klapɐ] F *n* (-s; *no pl*) clatter(ing)

Geklimper F *n* (-s; *no pl*) tinkling

geklungen [gə'kluŋən] *pp of* **klingen**

gekniffen [gə'knɪfən] *pp of* **kneifen**

ge'kommen *pp of* **kommen**

gekonnt [gə'kɔnt] 1. *pp of* **können** 2. *adj* masterly

gekränkt [gə'krɛŋkt] *adj* hurt, offended

Gekritzel [gə'krɪtsəl] *contp n* (-s; *no pl*) scrawl, scribble

gekrochen [gə'krɔxən] *pp of* **kriechen**

gekünstelt [gə'kʏnstəlt] *adj* affected; artificial

Gelächter [gə'lɛçtɐ] *n* (-s; *no pl*) laughter

ge'laden *pp of* **laden**

Ge'lage *n* (-s; -) feast; carouse

Gelände [gə'lɛndə] *n* (-s; -) area, country, ground; site; *auf dem* ~ on the premises; ~... *in cpds* ...*lauf,* ...*ritt,* ...*wagen etc:* cross-country ...

Geländer [gə'lɛndɐ] *n* (-s; -) banisters; handrail, rail(ing); parapet

ge'lang *pret of* **gelingen**

ge'langen *v/i* (*no -ge-, sein*) ~ *an* (*acc*) *or nach* reach, arrive at, get *or* come to; ~ *in* (*acc*) get *or* come into; *fig zu et.* ~ gain *or* win *or* achieve s.th.

ge'lassen 1. *pp of* **lassen** 2. *adj* calm, composed, cool

Gelatine [ʒela'ti:nə] *f* (-; *no pl*) gelatin(e)

ge'laufen *pp of* **laufen**

ge'läufig *adj* common, current; familiar

gelaunt [gə'launt] *adj: schlecht* (*gut*) ~ *sein* be in a bad (good) mood

gelb [gɛlp] *adj* yellow

'**gelblich** *adj* yellowish

'**Gelbsucht** *f* (-; *no pl*) MED jaundice

Geld [gɛlt] *n* (-[e]s; -er ['gɛldɐ]) money; *zu* ~ *machen* turn into cash

'**Geld|angelegenheiten** *pl* money *or* financial matters *or* affairs; ~**anlage** *f* investment; ~**ausgabe** *f* expense; ~**auto-mat** *m* automatic teller machine, ATM, autoteller, *Br* cash dispenser; ~**beutel** *m*, ~**börse** *f* purse; ~**buße** *f* fine, penalty; ~**geber(in)** ['gɛltge:bɐ, gɛltge:bərɪn] (-s; -/-; -nen) financial backer; investor '**geldgierig** adj greedy for money

'**Geld|knappheit** f, **~mangel** m lack of money; ECON (financial) stringency; **~mittel** pl funds, means, resources; **~schein** m bill, Br (bank)note; **~schrank** m safe; **~sendung** f remittance; **~strafe** f fine; **~stück** n coin; **~verlegenheit** f financial embarrassment; **~verschwendung** f waste of money; **~waschanlage** f money laundering scheme; **bei ~** on occasion of money; **~wechselautomat** m, **~wechsler** ['gɛltvɛkslɐ] m (-s; -) change machine

Gelee [ʒe'le:] n, m (-s; -s) jelly; gel

ge'**legen 1.** pp of **liegen 2.** adj situated, located; fig convenient, opportune; **Ge'legenheit** f (-; -en) occasion; opportunity, chance; **bei ~** on occasion

Ge'legenheits|arbeit f casual or odd job; **~arbeiter** m casual labo(u)rer, odd-job man; **~kauf** m bargain

gelegentlich [gə'le:gəntlɪç] adv occasionally

gelehrig [gə'le:rɪç] adj docile

Gelehrsamkeit [gə'le:ɐza:mkaɪt] f (-; no pl) learning; **gelehrt** [gə'le:ɐt] adj learned; **Ge'lehrte** m, f (-n; -n) scholar, learned man or woman

Geleise [gə'laɪzə] n → **Gleis**

Geleit [gə'laɪt] n (-[e]s; -e) escort

ge'**leiten** v/t (no -ge-, h) accompany, conduct, escort

Ge'leitzug m MAR, MIL convoy

Gelenk [gə'lɛŋk] n (-[e]s; -e) ANAT, TECH joint; **ge'lenkig** adj flexible (a. TECH); lithe, supple

gelernt [gə'lɛrnt] adj skilled, trained

ge'**lesen** pp of **lesen**

geliebt [gə'li:pt] adj (be)loved, dear

Ge'liebte 1. m (-n; -n) lover **2.** f (-n; -n) mistress

geliehen [gə'li:ən] pp of **leihen**

gelingen [gə'lɪŋən] v/i (irr, no -ge-, sein) succeed, manage; turn out well; **es gelang mir, et. zu tun** I succeeded in doing (I managed to do) s.th.; **Ge'lingen** n (-s; no pl) success; **gutes ~!** good luck!

gelitten [gə'lɪtən] pp of **leiden**

gelogen [gə'lo:gən] pp of **lügen**

gelten ['gɛltən] v/i and v/t (irr, ge-, h) be worth; fig count for; be valid; SPORT count; ECON be effective; **~ für** apply

to; **~ als** be regarded or looked upon as, be considered or supposed to be; **~ lassen** accept (**als** as); **~d** adj accepted; **~ machen** assert; **s-n Einfluss** (**bei j-m**) **~ machen** bring one's influence to bear (on s.o.)

'**Geltung** f (-; no pl) prestige; weight; **zur ~ kommen** show to advantage

'**Geltungsbedürfnis** n (-ses; no pl) need for recognition

Gelübde [gə'lʏpdə] n (-s; -) vow

gelungen [gə'lʊŋən] **1.** pp of **gelingen 2.** adj successful, a success

gemächlich [gə'mɛːçlɪç] adj leisurely

ge'**mahlen** pp of **mahlen**

Gemälde [gə'mɛːldə] n (-s; -) painting, picture; **~gale,rie** f art (or picture) gallery

gemäß [gə'mɛːs] prp (dat) according to

gemäßigt [gə'mɛːsɪçt] adj moderate; temperate (climate etc)

gemein [gə'maɪn] adj mean; dirty, filthy (joke etc); BOT, ZO common

Gemeinde [gə'maɪndə] f (-; -n) POL municipality; local government; REL parish; congregation; **~rat** m (member of the) city (Br local) council; **~rätin** [gə-'maɪndərɛ:tɪn] f (-; -nen) member of the city (Br local) council; **~steuern** pl local taxes, Br (local) rates

ge'**meingefährlich** adj: **~er Mensch** public enemy

Ge'meinheit f (-; -en) (no pl) meanness; mean thing (to do or say), F dirty trick

gemeinnützig [gə'maɪnnʏtsɪç] adj non--profit, Br non-profitmaking

Ge'meinplatz m commonplace

ge'meinsam 1. adj common, joint; mutual **2.** adv together

Ge'meinschaft f (-; -en) community

Ge'meinschafts|arbeit f teamwork; **~kunde** f (-; no pl) PED social studies; **~produkti,on** f coproduction; **~raum** m recreation room, lounge

Ge'meinsinn m (-[e]s; no pl) public spirit; (sense of) solidarity

ge'**meinverständlich** adj popular

Ge'meinwohl n public welfare

ge'**messen 1.** pp of **messen 2.** adj measured; formal; grave

Gemetzel [gə'mɛtsəl] n (-s; -) slaughter, massacre

gemieden [gə'mi:dən] pp of **meiden**

Gemisch [gə'mɪʃ] *n* (-[e]s; -e) mixture (*a.* CHEM)

gemocht [gə'mɔxt] *pp of* **mögen**

gemolken [gə'mɔlkən] *pp of* **melken**

Gemse → **Gämse**

Gemurmel [gə'murməl] *n* (-s; *no pl*) murmur, mutter

Gemüse [gə'my:zə] *n* (-s; -) vegetable(s); greens; **~händler** *m* greengrocer('s)

gemusst [gə'must] *pp of* **müssen**

Gemüt [gə'my:t] *n* (-[e]s; -er) mind, soul; heart; nature, mentality

ge'mütlich *adj* comfortable, snug, cozy, *Br* cosy; peaceful, pleasant, relaxed; **mach es dir ~** make yourself at home; **Ge'mütlichkeit** *f* (-; *no pl*) snugness, coziness, *Br* cosiness; cozy (*Br* cosy) *or* relaxed atmosphere

Ge'mütsbewegung *f* emotion

ge'mütskrank *adj* emotionally disturbed

Ge'mütszustand *m* state of mind

Gen [ge:n] *n* (-s; -e) BIOL gene

genannt [gə'nant] *pp of* **nennen**

genas [gə'na:s] *pret of* **genesen** 1

genau [gə'nau] **1.** *adj* exact, precise, accurate; careful, close; strict; **Genaueres** further details **2.** *adv:* **~ um 10 Uhr** at 10 o'clock sharp; **~ der ...** that very ...; **~ zuhören** listen closely; **es ~ nehmen (mit et.)** be particular (about s.th.); **Ge'nauigkeit** *f* (-; *no pl*) accuracy, precision, exactness

ge'nauso *adv* → **ebenso**

genehmigen [gə'ne:mɪgən] *v/t* (*no -ge-, h*) permit, allow; approve

Ge'nehmigung *f* (-; *-en*) permission; approval; permit; licen|se, *Br* -ce

geneigt [gə'naikt] *adj* inclined (**zu** to)

General [gena'ra:l] *m* (-s; *Generäle* [gena'rɛ:lə]) MIL general; **~di,rektor** *m* ECON president, *Br* chairman; **~konsul** *m* consul general; **~konsu,lat** *n* consulate general; **~probe** *f* THEA dress rehearsal; **~sekre,tär** *m* secretary-general; **~stab** *m* MIL general staff; **~streik** *m* general strike; **~versammlung** *f* general meeting; **~vertreter** *m* ECON sole agent

Generation [genəra'tsjo:n] *f* (-; *-en*) generation; **Generati'onenkon,flikt** *m* generation gap

Generator [gena'ra:tɐ] *m* (-s; *-en* [genəra'to:rən]) ELECTR generator

generell [genə'rɛl] *adj* general, universal

genesen [gə'ne:zən] **1.** *v/i* (*irr, no -ge-, sein*) recover (**von** from), get well **2.** *pp of* **genesen** 1

Ge'nesung *f* (-; *no pl*) recovery

Genetik [ge'ne:tɪk] *f* (-; *no pl*) BIOL genetics; **ge'netisch** *adj* BIOL genetic; **~er Fingerabdruck** genetic fingerprint

genial [ge'nja:l] *adj* brilliant, of genius

Genialität [genjali'tɛ:t] *f* (-; *no pl*) genius

Genick [gə'nɪk] *n* (-[e]s; -e) ANAT (back *or* nape of the) neck

Genie [ʒe'ni:] *n* (-s; -s) genius

genieren [ʒe'ni:rən] *v/refl* (*no -ge-, h*) be embarrassed

genießen [gə'ni:sən] *v/t* (*irr, no -ge-, h*) enjoy

Genießer [gə'ni:sɐ] *m* (-s; -) gourmet

Genitiv ['ge:niti:f] *m* (-s; -e) LING genitive *or* possessive (case)

genommen [gə'nɔmən] *pp of* **nehmen**

genormt [gə'nɔrmt] *adj* standardized

genoss [gə'nɔs] *pret of* **genießen**

Genosse [gə'nɔsə] *m* (-n; -n) POL comrade; F pal, buddy, *Br* mate

genossen [gə'nɔsən] *pp of* **genießen**

Ge'nossenschaft *f* (-; *-en*) cooperative

Ge'nossin *f* (-; *-nen*) POL comrade

'Gentechnik *f*, **'Gentechnolo,gie** *f* genetic engineering

genug [gə'nu:k] *adj* enough, sufficient

Genüge [gə'ny:gə] *f*: **zur ~** (well) enough, sufficiently

ge'nügen *v/i* (*no -ge-, h*) be enough, be sufficient; **das genügt** that will do; **~d** *adj* enough, sufficient; plenty of

genügsam [gə'ny:kza:m] *adj* easily satisfied; frugal; modest; **Ge'nügsamkeit** *f* (-; *no pl*) modesty; frugality

Ge'nugtuung *f* (-; *no pl*) satisfaction

Genus ['ge:nus] *n* (-; *Genera* ['ge:nera]) LING gender

Genuss [gə'nus] *m* (-es; *Genüsse* [gə-'nysə]) pleasure; (*no pl*) consumption; **ein ~** a real treat; *food:* **a.** delicious; **~mittel** *n* excise item, *Br* (semi-)luxury

Geografie, Geographie [geogra'fi:] *f* (-; *no pl*) geography; **geografisch, geographisch** [geo'gra:fɪʃ] *adj* geographic(al)

Geologe [geoˈloːgə] m (-n; -n) geologist; **Geologie** [geoloˈgiː] f (-; no pl) geology; **Geoˈlogin** f (-; -nen) geologist; **geologisch** [geoˈloːgɪʃ] adj geologic(al)

Geometrie [geomeˈtriː] f (-; no pl) geometry; **geometrisch** [geoˈmeːtrɪʃ] adj geometric(al)

Gepäck [gəˈpɛk] n (-[e]s; no pl) baggage, luggage; **~ablage** f baggage (or luggage) rack; **~aufbewahrung** f baggage room, Br left-luggage office; **~kon,trolle** f baggage check, Br luggage inspection; **~schalter** m baggage (or luggage) counter; **~schein** m baggage check, Br luggage ticket; **~träger** m porter; bicycle: carrier

gepanzert [gəˈpantsɐt] adj MOT armo(u)red

Gepard [ˈgeːpart] m (-s; -e) zo cheetah

gepfiffen [gəˈpfɪfən] pp of pfeifen

gepflegt [gəˈpfleːkt] adj well-groomed, neat; fig cultivated

Gepflogenheit [gəˈpfloːgənhait] f (-; -en) habit, custom

Geplapper [gəˈplapɐ] F n (-s; no pl) babbling, chatter(ing)

Geplauder [gəˈplaudɐ] n (-s; no pl) chat (-ting)

Gepolter [gəˈpɔltɐ] n (-s; no pl) rumble

gepriesen [gəˈpriːzən] pp of preisen

Gequassel [gəˈkvasəl] F n (-s; no pl), **Gequatsche** [gəˈkvatʃə] F n (-s; no pl) blather, blather

gequollen [gəˈkvɔlən] pp of quellen

gerade [gəˈraːdə] 1. adj straight (a. fig); even (number); direct; upright, erect (posture) 2. adv just; nicht ~ not exactly; das ist es ja ~! that's just it!; ~ deshalb that's just why; ~ rechtzeitig just in time; warum ~ ich? why me of all people?; da wir ~ von ... sprechen speaking of ...; **Ge'rade** f (-n; -n) MATH (straight) line; SPORT straight; linke (rechte) ~ boxing: straight left (right)

gerade|'aus adv straight on or ahead; **~he'raus** adj straightforward, frank

ge'radestehen v/i (irr, stehen, sep, -ge-, h) stand straight; ~ für answer for

ge'radewegs adv straight, directly

ge'radezu adv simply

gerannt [gəˈrant] pp of rennen

Gerät [gəˈrɛːt] n (-[e]s; -e) device; F gadget; appliance; (kitchen) utensil;

radio, TV set; coll, a. SPORT etc equipment; SPORT apparatus; TECH tool; instrument

ge'raten 1. pp of raten **2.** v/i (irr, raten, no -ge-, sein) turn out (gut well); ~ an (acc) come across; ~ in (acc) get into; in Brand ~ catch fire

Ge'räteturnen n apparatus gymnastics

Ge'ratewohl n: aufs ~ at random

geräumig [gəˈrɔymɪç] adj spacious, roomy

Geräusch [gəˈrɔyʃ] n (-[e]s; -e) sound, noise; **ge'räuschlos 1.** adj noiseless (a. TECH); **2.** adv without a sound; **ge'räuschvoll** adj noisy

gerben [ˈgɛrbən] v/t (ge-, h) tan

Gerberei [gɛrbəˈrai] f (-; -en) tannery

ge'recht adj just, fair; (j-m, e-r Sache) ~ werden do justice to; meet (demands etc); **Ge'rechtigkeit** f (-; no pl) justice

Ge'rede F n (-s; no pl) talk; gossip

gereizt [gəˈraitst] adj irritated

Ge'reiztheit f (-; no pl) irritability

Gericht¹ [gəˈrɪçt] n (-[e]s; -e) GASTR dish

Ge'richt² n (-[e]s; -e) JUR court; vor ~ stehen (stellen) stand (bring to) trial; vor ~ gehen go to court

ge'richtlich adj JUR judicial, legal

Ge'richtsbarkeit f (-; no pl) JUR jurisdiction

Ge'richts|gebäude n JUR law court(s), courthouse; **~hof** m JUR law court; **~medi,zin** f JUR forensic medicine; **~saal** m JUR courtroom; **~verfahren** n JUR lawsuit; **~verhandlung** f JUR hearing; trial; **~vollzieher** [gəˈrɪçtsfɔltsiːɐ] m (-s; -) JUR marshal, Br bailiff

gerieben [gəˈriːbən] pp of reiben

gering [gəˈrɪŋ] adj little, small; slight, minor; low; ~ schätzen think little of

ge'ringfügig adj slight, minor; petty

ge'ring|schätzen v/t (sep, -ge-, h) → **ge'ring;~schätzig** [gəˈrɪŋʃɛtsɪç] adj contemptuous

ge'ringst adj least; nicht im Geringsten not in the least

ge'rinnen v/i (irr, rinnen, no -ge-, sein) coagulate; curdle; clot

Ge'rippe n (-s; -) skeleton (a. fig); TECH framework

gerissen [gəˈrɪsən] **1.** pp of reißen **2.** F adj cunning, smart

geritten [gəˈrɪtən] pp of reiten

germanisch [gɛr'ma:nɪʃ] *adj* Germanic; **Germanist(in)** [gɛrma'nɪst(ɪn)] (*-en; -en/-; -nen*) student of (*or* graduate in) German

gern [gɛrn] *adv* willingly, gladly; **et. (sehr) ~ tun** like (love) to do s.th. *or* doing s.th.; **ich möchte ~** I'd like (to); **~ geschehen!** not at all, (you're) welcome

gernhaben *v/t* (*irr, haben, sep, -ge-, h*) like, be fond of

gerochen [gə'rɔxən] *pp of* **riechen**

Geröll [gə'rœl] *n* (*-[e]s; -e*) scree; boulders

geronnen [gə'rɔnən] *pp of* **rinnen**

Gerste ['gɛrstə] *f* (*-; -n*) BOT barley

'**Gerstenkorn** *n* MED sty(e)

Gerte ['gɛrtə] *f* (*-; -n*) switch, rod, twig

Geruch [gə'rʊx] *m* (*-[e]s; Gerüche* [gə-'ryçə]) smell; odo(u)r; scent

ge'ruchlos *adj* odo(u)rless

Ge'ruchssinn *m* (sense of) smell

Gerücht [gə'rʏçt] *n* (*-[e]s; -e*) rumo(u)r

ge'rufen *pp of* **rufen**

gerührt [gə'ry:ɐt] *adj* touched, moved

Gerümpel [gə'rʏmpəl] *n* (*-s; no pl*) lumber, junk

Gerundium [ge'rʊndiʊm] *n* (*-s; -ien*) LING gerund

gerungen [gə'rʊŋən] *pp of* **ringen**

Gerüst [gə'rʏst] *n* (*-[e]s; -e*) frame (-work); scaffold(ing); stage

ge'salzen *pp of* **salzen**

gesamt [gə'zamt] *adj* whole, entire, total, all

Ge'samt... *in cpds* ...*ergebnis etc: mst* total ...; **~ausgabe** *f* complete edition; **~schule** *f* comprehensive school

gesandt [gə'zant] *pp of* **senden**

Gesandte [gə'zantə] *m, f* (*-n; -n*) POL envoy; **Ge'sandtschaft** *f* (*-; -en*) legation, mission

Gesang [gə'zaŋ] *m* (*-[e]s; Gesänge* [gə-'zɛŋə]) singing; song; voice; **~buch** *n* REL hymn book; **~(s)lehrer(in)** singing teacher; **~verein** *m* choral society, glee club

Gesäß [gə'zɛːs] *n* (*-es; -e*) ANAT buttocks, bottom

ge'schaffen *pp of* **schaffen¹**

Geschäft [gə'ʃɛft] *n* (*-[e]s; -e*) business; store, *Br* shop; bargain

ge'schäftig *adj* busy, active

Ge'schäftigkeit *f* (*-; no pl*) activity

ge'schäftlich 1. *adj* business ...; commercial **2.** *adv* on business

Ge'schäfts|brief *m* business letter; **~frau** *f* businesswoman; **~freund** *m* business friend; **~führer(in)** managing director; (*of shop*) manager; **~inhaber(in)** proprietor; **~leitung** *f* executive board; **~mann** *m* businessman

ge'schäftsmäßig *adj* businesslike

Ge'schäfts|ordnung *f* PARL standing orders; rules (of procedure); **~partner(in)** (business) partner; **~räume** *pl* (business) premises; **~reise** *f* business trip; **~schluss** *m* closing time; **nach ~** a. after business hours; **~stelle** *f* office; **~straße** *f* shopping street

'**ge'schäftüchtig** *adj* efficient, smart

Ge'schäfts|verbindung *f* business connection; **~viertel** *n* commercial district; downtown; **~zeit** *f* office *or* business hours; **~zweig** *m* branch *or* line (of business)

geschah [gə'ʃa:] *pret of* **geschehen** 1

geschehen [gə'ʃe:ən] **1.** *v/i* (*irr, no -ge-, sein*) happen, occur, take place; be done; **es geschieht ihm recht** it serves him right **2.** *pp of* **geschehen** 1

gescheit [gə'ʃait] *adj* clever, bright, F brainy

Geschenk [gə'ʃɛŋk] *n* (*-[e]s; -e*) present, gift; **~gutschein** *m* gift voucher; **~packung** *f* gift box; **~papier** *n* gift wrap

Geschichte [gə'ʃɪçtə] *f* (*-; -n*) story; (*no pl*) history; F business, thing

ge'schichtlich *adj* historical

Ge'schichts|schreiber *m* (*-s; -*), **~wissenschaftler** *m* historian

Geschick [gə'ʃɪk] *n* (*-[e]s; -e*) fate, destiny; → **Ge'schicklichkeit** *f* (*-; no pl*) skill; dexterity; **~schickt** *adj* skil(l)ful, skilled; dext(e)rous; clever

geschieden [gə'ʃi:dən] **1.** *pp of* **scheiden 2.** *adj* divorced, *marriage:* dissolved

geschienen [gə'ʃi:nən] *pp of* **scheinen**

Geschirr [gə'ʃɪr] *n* (*-[e]s; -e*) dishes, china; (*no pl*) kitchen utensils, pots and pans, crockery; harness; **~ spülen** wash *or* do the dishes

Ge'schirrspüler *m* (*-s; -*) dishwasher

geschissen [gə'ʃɪsən] *pp of* **scheißen**

ge'schlafen *pp of* **schlafen**

ge'schlagen *pp of* **schlagen**

Geschlecht [gə'ʃlɛçt] *n* (-[e]s; -er) (*no pl*) sex; kind, species; family, line(age); generation; LING gender

Ge'schlechts|krankheit *f* MED sexually transmitted disease, venereal disease; **~teile** *pl* genitals; **~trieb** *m* sexual instinct *or* urge; **~verkehr** *m* (sexual) intercourse; **~wort** *n* LING article

geschlichen [gə'ʃliçən] *pp of schleichen*

geschliffen [gə'ʃlifən] **1.** *pp of schleifen²* **2.** *adj* cut; *fig* polished

geschlossen [gə'ʃlɔsən] **1.** *pp of schließen* **2.** *adj* closed

geschlungen [gə'ʃluŋən] *pp of schlingen*

Geschmack [gə'ʃmak] *m* (-[e]s; *Ge-schmäcke* [gə'ʃmɛkə]) taste (*a. fig*); flavo(u)r; **~ finden an** (*dat*) develop a taste for; **ge'schmacklos** *adj a. fig* tasteless; **Ge'schmacklosigkeit** *f* (-; *no pl*) tastelessness; **Ge'schmack(s)-sache** *f* matter of taste; **ge-'schmackvoll** *adj* tasteful, in good taste

geschmeidig [gə'ʃmaidiç] *adj* supple, pliant

geschmissen [gə'ʃmisən] *pp of schmeißen*

geschmolzen [gə'ʃmɔltsən] *pp of schmelzen*

geschnitten [gə'ʃnitən] *pp of schneiden*

geschoben [gə'ʃoːbən] *pp of schieben*

Geschöpf [gə'ʃœpf] *n* (-[e]s; -e) creature

geschoren [gə'ʃoːrən] *pp of scheren*

Geschoss [gə'ʃɔs] *n* (-es; -e), **Geschoß** [gə'ʃoːs] *Austrian n* (-es; -e) projectile, missile; stor(e)y, floor

ge'schossen *pp of schießen*

Ge'schrei *f n* (-s; *no pl*) shouting, yelling; screams; crying; *fig* fuss

geschrieben [gə'ʃriːbən] *pp of schreiben*

geschrie(e)n [gə'ʃriː(ə)n] *pp of schreien*

geschritten [gə'ʃritən] *pp of schreiten*

geschunden [gə'ʃundən] *pp of schinden*

Geschütz [gə'ʃyts] *n* (-es; -e) MIL gun, cannon

Geschwader [gə'ʃvaːdɐ] *n* (-s; -) MIL MAR squadron; AVIAT group, *Br* wing

Geschwätz [gə'ʃvɛts] F *n* (-es; *no pl*) chatter, babble; gossip; *fig* nonsense

ge'schwätzig *adj* talkative; gossipy

geschweige [gə'ʃvaigə] *cj*: **~ (denn)** let alone

geschwiegen [gə'ʃviːgən] *pp of schweigen*

geschwind [gə'ʃvint] *adj* quick, swift

Geschwindigkeit [gə'ʃvindiçkait] *f* (-; -en) speed; fastness, quickness; PHYS velocity; **mit e-r ~ von ...** at a speed *or* rate of ...

Ge'schwindigkeits|begrenzung *f* speed limit; **~überschreitung** *f* MOT speeding

Geschwister [gə'ʃvistɐ] *pl* brother(s) and sister(s); JUR siblings

geschwollen [gə'ʃvɔlən] **1.** *pp of schwellen* 1 **2.** *adj* MED swollen; *fig* bombastic, pretentious, pompous

geschwommen [gə'ʃvɔmən] *pp of schwimmen*

geschworen [gə'ʃvoːrən] *pp of schwören*; **Ge'schworene** *m, f* (-n; -n) member of a jury; **die ~n** the jury

Geschwulst [gə'ʃvulst] *f* (-; *Ge-schwülste* [gə'ʃvylstə]) MED growth, tumo(u)r

geschwunden [gə'ʃvundən] *pp of schwinden*

geschwungen [gə'ʃvuŋən] *pp of schwingen*

Geschwür [gə'ʃvyːɐ] *n* (-s; -e) MED abscess, ulcer

ge'sehen *pp of sehen*

Geselchte [gə'zɛlçtə] *Austrian n* (-n; *no pl*) GASTR smoked meat

Geselle [gə'zɛlə] *m* (-n; -n) journeyman

ge'sellen *v/refl* (*no -ge-, h*) **sich zu j-m ~** join s.o.

ge'sellig *adj* sociable; ZO *etc* social; **~es Beisammensein** get-together

Ge'sellin *f* (-; -nen) trained woman *hairdresser etc*, journeywoman

Gesellschaft [gə'zɛlʃaft] *f* (-; -en) society; company; party; ECON company, corporation; **j-m ~ leisten** keep s.o. company

ge'sellschaftlich *adj* social

Ge'sellschafts... *in cpds* **...kritik,** **...ordnung** *etc*: social ...; **~spiel** *n* parlo(u)r game; **~tanz** *m* ballroom dance

gesessen [gə'zɛsən] *pp of sitzen*

Gesetz [gə'zɛts] *n* (-es; -e) JUR law; act;

~buch *n* JUR code (of law); **~entwurf** *m* PARL bill

ge'setzgebend *adj* JUR legislative

Ge'setzgeber *m* (*-s*; *-*) JUR legislator

Ge'setzgebung *f* (*-*; *-en*) JUR legislation

ge'setzlich 1. *adj* legal; lawful **2.** *adv:* ~ **geschützt** JUR patented, registered

ge'setzlos *adj* lawless

ge'setzmäßig *adj* legal, lawful

gesetzt [gə'zɛtst] **1.** *adj* staid, dignified; mature (*age*) **2.** *cj:* ~ **den Fall**(, **dass**) ... supposing (that)

ge'setzwidrig *adj* illegal, unlawful

Gesicht [gə'zɪçt] *n* (*-[e]s*; *-er*) face; **zu~ bekommen** catch sight of

Ge'sichts|ausdruck *m* look, expression; **~creme** *f* face cream; **~farbe** *f* complexion; **~punkt** *m* point of view, aspect, angle; **~wasser** *n* toner; **~zug** *m* feature

Gesindel [gə'zɪndəl] *n* (*-s*; *no pl*) trash, *the* riff-raff

gesinnt [gə'zɪnt] *adj* minded; **j-m feindlich** ~ **sein** be ill-disposed towards s.o.

Ge'sinnung *f* (*-*; *-en*) mind; attitude; POL conviction(s)

ge'sinnungslos *adj* unprincipled

ge'sinnungstreu *adj* loyal

Ge'sinnungswechsel *m* about-face, *Br* about-turn

gesittet [gə'zɪtət] *adj* civilized, well--mannered

gesoffen [gə'zɔfən] *pp of* **saufen**

gesogen [gə'zoːgən] *pp of* **saugen**

gesotten [gə'zɔtən] *pp of* **sieden**

gespalten [gə'ʃpaltən] *pp of* **spalten**

Gespann [gə'ʃpan] *n* (*-[e]s*; *-e*) team (*a. fig*)

gespannt [gə'ʃpant] *adj* tense (*a. fig*); ~ **sein auf** (*acc*) be anxious to see; **ich bin** ~, **ob** (**wie**) I wonder if (how)

Gespenst [gə'ʃpɛnst] *n* (*-[e]s*; *-er*) ghost, apparition, *esp fig* specter, *Br* spectre

ge'spenstisch *adj* ghostly, F spooky

gespie(e)n [gə'ʃpiː(ə)n] *pp of* **speien**

Gespinst [gə'ʃpɪnst] *n* (*-[e]s*; *-e*) web, tissue (*both a. fig*)

gesponnen [gə'ʃpɔnən] *pp of* **spinnen**

Gespött [gə'ʃpœt] *n* (*-[e]s*; *no pl*) mockery, ridicule; **j-n zum~ machen** make a laughingstock of s.o.

Gespräch [gə'ʃprɛːç] *n* (*-[e]s*; *-e*) talk (*a. POL*), conversation; TEL call

ge'sprächig *adj* talkative

gesprochen [gə'ʃprɔxən] *pp of* **sprechen**

gesprossen [gə'ʃprɔsən] *pp of* **sprießen**

gesprungen [gə'ʃprʊŋən] *pp of* **springen**

Gespür [gə'ʃpyːɐ] *n* (*-s*; *no pl*) flair, nose

Gestalt [gə'ʃtalt] *f* (*-*; *-en*) shape, form; figure; **ge'stalten** *v/t* (*no -ge-, h*) arrange; design; **Ge'staltung** *f* (*-*; *-en*) arrangement; design; decoration

gestanden [gə'ʃtandən] *pp of* **stehen**

ge'ständig *adj:* ~ **sein** confess; have confessed

Geständnis [gə'ʃtɛntnɪs] *n* (*-ses*; *-se*) confession (*a. fig*)

Gestank [gə'ʃtaŋk] *m* (*-[e]s*; *no pl*) stench, stink

gestatten [gə'ʃtatən] *v/t* (*no -ge-, h*) allow, permit

Geste ['gɛstə] *f* (*-*; *-n*) gesture (*a. fig*)

ge'stehen *v/t and v/i* (*irr*, **stehen**, *no -ge-, h*) confess

Ge'stein *n* (*-[e]s*; *-e*) rock, stone

Gestell [gə'ʃtɛl] *n* (*-[e]s*; *-e*) stand, base, pedestal; shelves; frame

gestern ['gɛstən] *adv* yesterday; ~ **Abend** last night

gestiegen [gə'ʃtiːgən] *pp of* **steigen**

gestochen [gə'ʃtɔxən] *pp of* **stechen**

gestohlen [gə'ʃtoːlən] *pp of* **stehlen**

gestorben [gə'ʃtɔrbən] *pp of* **sterben**

ge'stoßen *pp of* **stoßen**

gestreift [gə'ʃtraift] *adj* striped

gestrichen [gə'ʃtrɪçən] *pp of* **streichen**

gestrig ['gɛstrɪç] *adj* yesterday's, of yesterday

gestritten [gə'ʃtrɪtən] *pp of* **streiten**

Gestrüpp [gə'ʃtrʏp] *n* (*-[e]s*; *-e*) brushwood, undergrowth; *fig* jungle, maze

gestunken [gə'ʃtʊŋkən] *pp of* **stinken**

Gestüt [gə'ʃtyːt] *n* (*-[e]s*; *-e*) stud

Gesuch [gə'zuːx] *n* (*-[e]s*; *-e*) application, request

gesund [gə'zʊnt] *adj* healthy; healthful, *fig a.* sound; **~er Menschenverstand** common sense; (**wieder**) ~ **werden** get well (again), recover; **Ge'sundheit** *f* (*-*; *no pl*) health; **auf j-s** ~ **trinken** drink to s.o.'s health; **~!** bless you!; **ge'sundheitlich 1.** *adj:* **~er Zustand** state of health; **aus ~en Grün-**

den for health reasons **2.** *adv*: **~ geht es ihm gut** he is in good health

Ge'sundheitsamt *n* Public Health Department (*Br* Office)

Ge'sundheitsschädlich *adj* bad for one's health

Ge'sundheits|zeugnis *n* health certificate; **~zustand** *m* state of health

gesungen [gə'zʊŋən] *pp of* **singen**

gesunken [gə'zʊŋkən] *pp of* **sinken**

getan [gə'ta:n] *pp of* **tun**

Getöse [gə'tø:zə] *n* (*-s; no pl*) din, (deafening) noise

ge'tragen *pp of* **tragen**

Getränk [gə'trɛŋk] *n* (*-[e]s; -e*) drink, beverage; **Ge'tränkeauto,mat** *m* drinks machine

Getreide [gə'traidə] *n* (*-s; -*) cereals, grain, *Br a.* corn; **~ernte** *f* grain harvest (*or* crop)

ge'treten *pp of* **treten**

Getriebe [gə'tri:bə] *n* (*-s; -*) MOT transmission

ge'trieben [gə'tri:bən] *pp of* **treiben**

getroffen [gə'trɔfən] *pp of* **treffen**

getrogen [gə'tro:gən] *pp of* **trügen**

getrost [gə'tro:st] *adv* safely

getrunken [gə'trʊŋkən] *pp of* **trinken**

Getue [gə'tu:ə] F *n* (*-s; no pl*) fuss

Getümmel [gə'tʏməl] *n* (*-s; -*) turmoil

Gewächs [gə'vɛks] *n* (*-es; -e*) plant; MED growth

ge'wachsen 1. *pp of* **wachsen¹ 2.** *fig adj*: **j-m ~ sein** be a match for s.o.; **e-r Sache ~ sein** be equal to s.th., be able to cope with s.th.

Ge'wächshaus *n* greenhouse, hothouse

gewagt [gə'va:kt] *adj* daring; *fig* risqué

gewählt [gə'vɛ:lt] *adj* refined

Gewähr [gə'vɛ:ɐ] *f*: **~ übernehmen (für)** guarantee; **ge'währen** *v/t* (*no -ge-, h*) grant, allow; **ge'währleisten** *v/t* (*no -ge-, h*) guarantee

Gewahrsam [gə'va:ɐza:m] *m*: **et. (j-n) in ~ nehmen** take s.th. in safekeeping (s.o. into custody)

Gewalt [gə'valt] *f* (*-; -en*) (*no pl*) force, violence; power; **mit ~** by force; **höhere ~** act of God; **häusliche ~** domestic violence; **in s-e ~ bringen** seize by force; **die ~ verlieren über** (*acc*) lose control over; **~herrschaft** *f* tyranny

ge'waltig *adj* powerful, mighty; enormous

ge'waltlos *adj* nonviolent; **Ge-'waltlosigkeit** *f* (*-; no pl*) nonviolence

ge'waltsam 1. *adj* violent **2.** *adv* by force; **~ öffnen** force open

ge'walttätig *adj* violent

Ge'walttätigkeit *f* (*-; -en*) (*no pl*) violence; act of violence

Ge'waltverbrechen *n* crime of violence

Gewand [gə'vant] *n* (*-[e]s; Gewänder* [gə'vɛndɐ]) robe, gown; REL vestment

gewandt [gə'vant] **1.** *pp of* **wenden** (*v/refl*) **2.** *adj* nimble; skil(l)ful; clever

Ge'wandtheit *f* (*-; no pl*) nimbleness; skill; ease

gewann [gə'van] *pret of* **gewinnen**

ge'waschen *pp of* **waschen**

Gewässer [gə'vɛsɐ] *n* (*-s; -*) body of water; *pl* waters

Gewebe [gə've:bə] *n* (*-s; -*) fabric; BIOL tissue

Gewehr [gə've:ɐ] *n* (*-[e]s; -e*) gun; rifle; shotgun; **~kolben** *m* (rifle) butt; **~lauf** *m* (rifle *or* gun) barrel

Geweih [gə'vai] *n* (*-[e]s; -e*) ZO antlers, horns

Gewerbe [gə'vɛrbə] *n* (*-s; -*) trade, business; **~schein** *m* trade licen|se, *Br* -ce

gewerblich [gə'vɛrplɪç] *adj* commercial, industrial; **gewerbsmäßig** [gə'vɛrpsmɛ:sɪç] *adj* professional

Gewerkschaft [gə'vɛrkʃaft] *f* (*-; -en*) labor union, *Br* (trade) union

Ge'werkschaft(l)er *m* (*-s; -*), **Ge-'werkschaft(l)erin** *f* (*-; -nen*) labor (*Br* trade) unionist; **ge'werkschaftlich** *adj*, **Ge'werkschafts...** *in cpds* labor (*Br* trade) union ...

ge'wesen *pp of* **sein¹**

gewichen [gə'vɪçən] *pp of* **weichen**

Gewicht [gə'vɪçt] *n* (*-[e]s; -e*) weight; importance; **~ legen auf** (*acc*) stress

gewiesen [gə'vi:zən] *pp of* **weisen**

gewillt [gə'vɪlt] *adj* willing, ready

Gewimmel [gə'vɪməl] *n* (*-s; no pl*) throng

Gewinde [gə'vɪndə] *n* (*-s; -*) TECH thread; **ein ~ bohren in** (*acc*) tap

Gewinn [gə'vɪn] *m* (*-[e]s; -e*) ECON profit (*a. fig*); gain(s); prize; winnings; **~ bringend → gewinnbringend**

ge'winnbringend *adj* profitable

ge'winnen *v/t and v/i* (*irr, no -ge-, h*)

win; gain; **~d** *fig adj* winning, engaging
Gewinner [gǝ'vɪnɐ] *m* (*-s*; *-*), **Ge-**
'winnerin *f* (*-*; *-nen*) winner
Ge'winnzahl *f* winning number
Gewirr [gǝ'vɪr] *n* (*-[e]s*; *no pl*) tangle;
maze
gewiss [gǝ'vɪs] **1.** *adj* certain **2.** *adv* certainly
Ge'wissen *n* (*-s*; *-*) conscience
ge'wissenhaft *adj* conscientious
ge'wissenlos *adj* unscrupulous
Ge'wissens|bisse *pl* pricks *or* pangs of
conscience; **~frage** *f* question of conscience; **~gründe** *pl*: **aus ~n** for reasons of conscience
Ge'wissheit *f* (*-*; *no pl*) certainty; **mit ~**
know etc for certain *or* sure
Gewitter [gǝ'vɪtɐ] *n* (*-s*; *-*) thunder-
storm; **~regen** *m* thundershower;
~wolke *f* thundercloud
gewoben [gǝ'voːbǝn] *pp of* **weben**
gewogen [gǝ'voːgǝn] *pp of* **wiegen¹**
and **wägen**
gewöhnen [gǝ'vøːnǝn] *v/t and v/refl*
(*no -ge-*, *h*) **sich** (*j-n*) **an** (*acc*) get
(s.o.) used to; **Gewohnheit** [gǝ-
'voːnhaɪt] *f* (*-*; *-en*) habit (**et. zu tun**
of doing s.th.); **ge'wohnheitsmäßig**
adj habitual
gewöhnlich [gǝ'vøːnlɪç] *adj* common,
ordinary, usual; vulgar, F common
gewohnt [gǝ'voːnt] *adj* usual; **et.** (**zu**
tun) **~ sein** be used *or* accustomed to
(doing) s.th.
Gewölbe [gǝ'vœlbǝ] *n* (*-s*; *-*) vault
gewölbt [gǝ'vœlpt] *adj* arched
gewonnen [gǝ'vɔnǝn] *pp of* **gewinnen**
geworben [gǝ'vɔrbǝn] *pp of* **werben**
geworden [gǝ'vɔrdǝn] *pp of* **werden**
geworfen [gǝ'vɔrfǝn] *pp of* **werfen**
gewrungen [gǝ'vrʊŋǝn] *pp of* **wringen**
Gewühl [gǝ'vyːl] *n* (*-[e]s*; *no pl*) crowd,
crush
gewunden [gǝ'vʊndǝn] **1.** *pp of* **winden**
2. *adj* winding
Gewürz [gǝ'vʏrts] *n* (*-es*; *-e*) spice;
~gurke *f* pickle(d gherkin)
gewusst [gǝ'vʊst] *pp of* **wissen**
gezackt [gǝ'tsakt] *adj* jagged, serrated
Ge'zeiten *pl* tide(s)
Gezeter [gǝ'tseːtɐ] *contp n* (*-s*; *no pl*)
(shrill) clamo(u)r; nagging
geziert [gǝ'tsiːɐt] *adj* affected
gezogen [gǝ'tsoːgǝn] *pp of* **ziehen**

Gezwitscher [gǝ'tsvɪtʃɐ] *n* (*-s*; *no pl*)
chirp(ing), twitter(ing)
gezwungen [gǝ'tsvʊŋǝn] **1.** *pp of* **zwin-**
gen 2. *adj* forced, unnatural
Gicht [gɪçt] *f* (*-*; *no pl*) MED gout
Giebel ['giːbǝl] *m* (*-s*; *-*) gable
Gier [giːɐ] *f* (*-*; *no pl*) greed(iness) (**nach**
for); **gierig** ['giːrɪç] *adj* greedy (**nach**,
auf *acc* for, after)
gießen ['giːsǝn] *v/t and v/i* (*irr*, *ge-*, *h*)
pour; TECH cast; water
Gieße'rei *f* (*-*; *-en*) TECH foundry
'Gießkanne *f* watering pot (*Br* can)
Gift [gɪft] *n* (*-[e]s*; *-e*) poison, ZO *a*. ven-
om (*a. fig*); **'giftig** *adj* poisonous; venomous (*a. fig*); poisoned; TECH toxic
'Gift|müll *m* toxic waste; **~mülldepo,nie**
f toxic waste dump; **~schlange** *f* ZO
poisonous *or* venomous snake; **~stoff**
m poisonous *or* toxic substance; pollutant; **~zahn** *m* ZO poison fang
Gigant [gi'gant] *m* (*-en*; *-en*) giant
gi'gantisch *adj* gigantic
ging [gɪŋ] *pret of* **gehen**
Gipfel ['gɪpfǝl] *m* (*-s*; *-*) top, peak, summit, *fig a*. height; **~konfe,renz** *f* POL
summit (meeting *or* conference)
'gipfeln *v/i* (*ge-*, *h*) culminate (**in** *dat* in)
Gips [gɪps] *m* (*-es*; *-e*) plaster (of Paris);
in ~ MED in (a) plaster (cast); **~abdruck**
m, **~abguss** *m* plaster cast
'gipsen *v/t* (*ge-*, *h*) plaster (*a*. F MED)
'Gipsverband *m* MED plaster cast
Giraffe [gi'rafǝ] *f* (*-*; *-n*) ZO giraffe
Girlande [gɪr'landǝ] *f* (*-*; *-n*) garland,
festoon
Girokonto ['ʒiːrokɔnto] *n* checking (*or*
current) account; postal check (*Br* gi-
ro) account
Gischt [gɪʃt] *m* (*-[e]s*; *-e*), *f* (*-*; *-en*) (sea)
spray, spindrift
Gitarre [gi'tarǝ] *f* (*-*; *-n*) MUS guitar
Gitarrist [gita'rɪst] *m* (*-en*; *-en*) guitarist
Gitter ['gɪtɐ] *n* (*-s*; *-*) lattice; grating; F
hinter ~n (**sitzen**) (be) behind bars
'Gitterbett *n* crib, *Br* cot
'Gitterfenster *n* lattice (window)
Glanz [glants] *m* (*-es*; *no pl*) shine, gloss
(*a*. TECH), luster, *Br* lustre, brilliance (*a.*
fig), *fig* splendo(u)r, glamo(u)r
glänzen ['glɛntsǝn] *v/i* (*ge-*, *h*) shine,
gleam; glitter, glisten; **~d** *adj* shining,
shiny, bright; PHOT glossy; *fig* brilliant,
excellent

'**Glanz|leistung** f brilliant achievement; **~zeit** f heyday

Glas [glaːs] n (-es; Gläser ['glɛːzɐ]) glass

Glaser ['glaːzɐ] m (-s; -) glazier

gläsern ['glɛːzɐn] adj (of) glass

'**Glas|faser** f, **~fiber** f glass fiber (Br fibre); **~hütte** f TECH glassworks

glasieren [glaˈziːrən] v/t (no -ge-, h) glaze; GASTR ice, frost

glasig ['glaːzɪç] adj glassy

'**glasklar** adj crystal-clear (a. fig)

'**Glasscheibe** f (glass) pane

Glasur [glaˈzuːɐ] f (-; -en) glaze; GASTR icing

glatt [glat] adj smooth (a. fig); slippery; fig clear; **Glätte** ['glɛtə] f (-; no pl) smoothness (a. fig); slipperiness

'**Glatteis** n (glare, Br black) ice; **es herrscht~** the roads are icy; F **j-n aufs ~ führen** mislead s.o.

glätten ['glɛtən] v/t (ge-, h) smooth; Swiss: → **bügeln**

'**glattgehen** v/i (irr, sep, -ge-, sein) F work (out well), go (off) well

Glatze ['glatsə] f (-; -n) bald head; **e-e ~ haben** be bald

Glaube ['glaubə] m (-ns; no pl) belief, esp REL faith (both: **an** acc in)

'**glauben** v/t and v/i (ge-, h) believe; think, guess; **~ an** (acc) believe in (a. REL)

'**Glaubens|bekenntnis** n REL creed, profession or confession of faith; **~lehre** f, **~satz** m dogma, doctrine

glaubhaft ['glauphaft] adj credible, plausible

gläubig ['glɔybɪç] adj religious; devout; **die Gläubigen** the faithful

Gläubiger ['glɔybɪgɐ] m (-s; -), '**Gläubigerin** f (-; -nen) ECON creditor

'**glaubwürdig** adj credible; reliable

gleich [glaiç] **1.** adj same; equal (right etc); **auf die ~e Art** (in) the same way; **zur ~en Zeit** at the same time; **das ist mir ~** it's all the same to me; **ganz ~, wann** etc no matter when etc; **das Gleiche** the same; **(ist) ~ ...** MATH equals ..., is ...; **~ bleibend → gleichbleibend**; **~ gesinnt** like-minded; **~ lautend → gleichlautend 2.** adv equally, alike; at once, right away; in a moment or minute; **~ groß (alt)** of the same size (age); **~ nach (neben)** right after (next to); **~ gegenüber** just opposite or across the street; **es ist ~ 5 Uhr** it's almost 5 o'clock; **~ aussehen (gekleidet sein)** look (be dressed) alike; **bis ~!** see you soon or later!; **gleichaltrig** ['glaiçʔaltrɪç] adj (of) the same age

gleichberechtigt adj equal, having equal rights; '**Gleichberechtigung** f (-; no pl) equal rights

'**gleichbleibend** adj constant, steady

'**gleichen** v/i (irr, ge-, h) (dat) be or look like

'**gleichfalls** adv also, likewise; **danke, ~!** (thanks,) the same to you

gleichförmig ['glaiçfœrmɪç] adj uniform

'**Gleichgewicht** n (-[e]s; no pl) balance (a. fig)

'**gleichgültig** adj indifferent (**gegen** to); careless; **das (er) ist mir ~** I don't care (for him); '**Gleichgültigkeit** f (-; no pl) indifference

'**Gleichheit** f (-; no pl) equality

'**gleichkommen** v/i (irr, kommen, sep, -ge-, sein) **e-r Sache ~** amount to s.th.; **j-m ~** equal s.o. (**an** dat in)

'**gleichlautend** adj identical

'**gleichmäßig** adj regular; constant; even

gleichnamig ['glaiçnaːmɪç] adj of the same name

'**Gleichnis** n (-ses; -se) parable

gleichsam adv as it were, so to speak

gleichseitig ['glaiçzaitɪç] adj MATH equilateral

'**gleich|setzen**, **~stellen** v/t (sep, -ge-, h) equate (**dat** to, with); put s.o. on an equal footing (with)

'**Gleichstrom** m ELECTR direct current

'**Gleichung** f (-; -en) MATH equation

'**gleichwertig** adj equally good; **j-m ~ sein** be a match for s.o. (a. SPORT)

'**gleichzeitig** adj simultaneous; **beide ~** both at the same time

Gleis [glais] n (-es; -e) RAIL rail(s), track(s), line; platform, gate

gleiten ['glaitən] v/i (irr, ge-, sein) glide, slide; **~d** adj: **~e Arbeitszeit** flexible working hours, flextime, Br a. flexitime

'**Gleitflug** m glide

'**Gleitschirm|fliegen** n paragliding; **~flieger** m paraglider

Gletscher ['glɛtʃɐ] m (-s; -) glacier; **~spalte** f crevasse

glich [glɪç] *pret of* **gleichen**

Glied [gliːt] *n* (*-es; Glieder* ['gliːdɐ]) ANAT limb; penis; TECH link

gliedern ['gliːdɐn] *v/t* (*ge-, h*) structure; divide (*in acc* into)

Gliederung ['gliːdərʊŋ] *f* (*-; -en*) structure, arrangement; outline

'Gliedmaßen *pl* ANAT limbs, extremities

glimmen ['glɪmən] *v/i* ([*irr,*] *ge-, h*) glow; smo(u)lder

'Glimmstängel F *m* (*-s; -*) cigarette, *Br sl* fag

glimpflich ['glɪmpflɪç] **1.** *adj* lenient, mild **2.** *adv:* ~ **davonkommen** get off lightly

glitschig ['glɪtʃɪç] *adj* slippery

glitt [glɪt] *pret of* **gleiten**

glitzern ['glɪtsɐn] *v/i* (*ge-, h*) glitter, sparkle, glint

global [gloˈbaːl] *adj* global

Globus ['gloːbʊs] *m* (*-[ses]; -se*) globe

Glocke ['glɔkə] *f* (*-; -n*) bell

'Glocken|blume *f* bluebell; ~**spiel** *n* chimes; ~**turm** *m* bell tower, belfry

glomm [glɔm] *pret of* **glimmen**

glorreich ['gloː ʀaɪç] *adj* glorious

Glotze ['glɔtsə] F *f* (*-; -n*) TV the tube, *Br* goggle box; **glotzen** F *v/i* (*ge-, h*) goggle, gape, stare

Glück [glʏk] *n* (*-[e]s; no pl*) (good) luck, fortune; happiness; ~ **haben** be lucky; **zum** ~ fortunately; **viel** ~! good luck!

Glucke ['glʊkə] *f* (*-; -n*) ZO sitting hen; *fig* hen

gluckern ['glʊkɐn] *v/i* (*ge-, h*) gurgle

'glücklich *adj* happy; ~**er Zufall** lucky chance

'glücklicher'weise *adv* fortunately

'Glücks|bringer *m* (*-s; -*) lucky charm; ~**fall** *m* lucky chance; ~**pfennig** *m* lucky penny; ~**pilz** *m* lucky fellow; ~**spiel** *n* game of chance; *coll* gambling; ~**spieler** *m* gambler; ~**tag** *m* lucky day

'glückstrahlend *adj* radiant

'Glückwunsch *m* congratulations; **herzlichen** ~! congratulations!; happy birthday!

Glühbirne ['glyːbɪrnə] *f* ELECTR light bulb

glühen ['glyːən] *v/i* (*ge-, h*) glow (*a. fig*)

glühend ['glyːənt] *adj* glowing; red-hot (*iron*); *fig* burning; ~ **heiß** blazing hot

'Glühwein *m* mulled wine

Glut [gluːt] *f* (*-; -en*) (glowing) fire; embers; live coals; *fig* ardo(u)r

'Gluthitze *f* blazing heat

GmbH [geːˀɛmbeːˈhaː] *abbr of* **Gesellschaft mit beschränkter Haftung** private limited liability company

Gnade ['gnaːdə] *f* (*-; -n*) mercy, *esp* REL *a.* grace; favo(u)r

'Gnaden|frist *f* reprieve; ~**gesuch** *n* JUR petition for mercy

'gnadenlos *adj* merciless

gnädig ['gnɛːdɪç] *adj* gracious; *esp* REL merciful

Gold [gɔlt] *n* (*-[e]s; no pl*) gold; ~**barren** *m* gold bar *or* ingot; *coll* bullion

golden ['gɔldən] *adj* gold; *fig* golden

'Goldfisch *m* ZO goldfish

'goldgelb *adj* golden (yellow)

'Gold|gräber ['gɔltgrɛːbɐ] *m* (*-s; -*) gold digger; ~**grube** *fig f* goldmine, bonanza

goldig ['gɔldɪç] F *adj* sweet, lovely, cute

'Gold|mine *f* goldmine; ~**münze** *f* gold coin; ~**schmied** *m* goldsmith; ~**stück** *n* gold coin

Golf¹ [gɔlf] *m* (*-[e]s; -e*) GEOGR gulf

Golf² *n* (*-s; no pl*) SPORT golf; ~**platz** *m* golf course; ~**schläger** *m* golf club; ~**spieler** *m* golfer

Gondel ['gɔndəl] *f* (*-; -n*) gondola; cabin

Gong [gɔŋ] *m* (*-s; -s*) gong

gönnen ['gœnən] *v/t* (*ge-, h*) **j-m et.** ~ not (be)grudge s.o. s.th.; **j-m et. nicht** ~ (be)grudge s.o. s.th.; **sich et.** ~ allow o.s. s.th., treat o.s. to s.th.

gönnerhaft ['gœnɐhaft] *adj* patronizing

gor [goːɐ] *pret of* **gären**

Gorilla [goˈrɪla] *m* (*-s; -s*) ZO gorilla

goss [gɔs] *pret of* **gießen**

Gosse ['gɔsə] *f* (*-; -n*) gutter (*a. fig*)

Gotik ['goːtɪk] *f* (*-; no pl*) ARCH Gothic style *or* period; **'gotisch** *adj* Gothic

Gott [gɔt] *m* (*-[e]s; Götter* ['gœtɐ]) REL God, Lord; MYTH god; ~ **sei Dank**(!) thank God(!); **um** ~**es Willen!** for heaven's sake!; **gottergeben** *adj* resigned (to the will of God)

'Gottesdienst *m* REL (divine) service

gottesfürchtig ['gɔtəsfʏrçtɪç] *adj* godfearing

Gotteslästerer ['gɔtəslɛstərɐ] *m* (*-s; -*) blasphemer; **'Gotteslästerung** *f* (*-; -en*) blasphemy

'Gottheit *f* (*-; -en*) deity, divinity

Göttin ['gœtɪn] *f* (*-; -nen*) goddess

'**göttlich** ['gœtlɪç] *adj* divine
gott'lob *int* thank God *or* goodness!
'**gottlos** *adj* godless, wicked
'**gottverlassen** F *adj* godforsaken
'**Gottvertrauen** *n* trust in God
Götze ['gœtsə] *m* (-*n*; -*n*), '**Götzenbild** *n* idol
Gouverneur [guvɛr'nøːɐ] *m* (-*s*; -*e*) governor
Grab [graːp] *n* (-[*e*]*s*; *Gräber* ['grɛːbɐ]) grave; tomb
graben ['graːbən] *v/t and v/i* (*irr*, *ge*-, *h*) dig, ZO *a*. burrow; '**Graben** *m* (-*s*; *Gräben* ['grɛːbən]) ditch; MIL trench
'**Grab|mal** *n* monument; tomb; ~**rede** *f* funeral address; ~**schrift** *f* epitaph; ~**stätte** *f* burial place; grave, tomb; ~**stein** *m* tombstone, gravestone
Grad [graːt] *m* (-[*e*]*s*; -*e*) degree; MIL *etc* rank, grade; *15* ~ *Kälte* 15 degrees below zero; ~**einteilung** *f* graduation
graduell [gra'duɛl] *adj* in degree
Graf [graːf] *m* (-*en*; -*en*) count, *Br* earl
Graffiti [gra'fiːti] *pl* graffiti
Grafik ['graːfɪk] *f* (-; -*en*) (*no pl*) graphic arts; print; MATH, TECH graph, diagram; (*no pl*) art(work), illustrations; (*no pl*) IT graphics
'**Grafiker** *m* (-*s*; -), '**Grafikerin** *f* (-; -*nen*) graphic artist
Gräfin ['grɛːfɪn] *f* (-; -*nen*) countess
grafisch ['graːfɪʃ] *adj* graphic
Grafologie *f* → *Graphologie*
'**Grafschaft** *f* (-; -*en*) county
Gramm [gram] *n* (-*s*; -*e*) gram
Grammatik [gra'matɪk] *f* (-; -*en*) grammar; **gram'matisch** *adj* grammatical
Granat [gra'naːt] *m* (-[*e*]*s*; -*e*) MIN garnet
Gra'nate *f* (-; -*n*) MIL shell
Gra'nat|splitter *m* MIL shell splinter; ~**werfer** *m* MIL mortar
grandios [gran'djoːs] *adj* magnificent, grand
Granit [gra'niːt] *m* (-*s*; -*e*) granite
Graphik *f etc* → *Grafik etc*
Graphologie [grafolo'giː] *f* (-; *no pl*) graphology
Gras [graːs] *n* (-*es*; *Gräser* ['grɛːzɐ]) grass; **grasen** ['graːzən] *v/i* (*ge*-, *h*) graze; '**Grashalm** *m* blade of grass
grassieren [gra'siːrən] *v/i* (*no -ge-*, *h*) rage, be rife
grässlich ['grɛslɪç] *adj* hideous, atrocious

Gräte ['grɛːtə] *f* (-; -*n*) (fish)bone
Gratifikation [gratifika'tsjoːn] *f* (-; -*en*) gratuity, bonus
gratis ['graːtɪs] *adv* free (of charge)
Grätsche ['grɛːtʃə] *f* (-; -*n*), '**grätschen** *v/i* (*ge*-, *h*) straddle; *soccer*: stride tackle
Gratulant [gratu'lant] *m* (-*en*; -*en*), **Gratu'lantin** *f* (-; -*nen*) congratulator; **Gratulation** [gratula'tsjoːn] *f* (-; -*en*) congratulation; **gratulieren** [gratu'liːrən] *v/i* (*no -ge-*, *h*) congratulate (*j-m zu et.* s.o. on s.th.); *j-m zum Geburtstag* ~ wish s.o. many happy returns (of the day)
grau [grau] *adj* gray, *Br* grey
'**Graubrot** *n* rye bread
Gräuel ['grɔyəl] *m* (-*s*; -) horror
'**Gräueltat** *f* atrocity
'**grauen** *v/i* (*ge*-, *h*) *mir graut es vor* (*dat*) I dread (the thought of)
'**Grauen** *n* (-*s*; -) horror
'**grauenhaft**, '**grauenvoll** *adj* horrible, horrifying
Graupel ['graupəl] *f* (-; -*n*) sleet, soft hail
grausam ['grauzaːm] *adj* cruel
'**Grausamkeit** *f* (-; -*en*) cruelty
grausig ['grauzɪç] *adj* → **grauenhaft**
'**Grauzone** *f fig* gray (*Br* grey) area
gravieren [gra'viːrən] *v/t* (*no -ge-*, *h*) engrave; ~**d** *adj* serious
Gravur [gra'vuːɐ] *f* (-; -*en*) engraving
Grazie ['graːtsjə] *f* (-; *no pl*) grace
graziös [gra'tsjøːs] *adj* graceful
greifen ['graifən] (*irr*, *ge*-, *h*) **1.** *v/t* seize, grasp, grab, take *or* catch hold of **2.** *v/i fig* take effect; ~ *nach* reach for; grasp at
Greis [grais] *m* (-*es*; -*e*) (very) old man; **greisenhaft** ['graizənhaft] *adj* senile (*a.* MED); **Greisin** ['graizɪn] *f* (-; -*nen*) (very) old woman
grell [grɛl] *adj* glaring; shrill
Grenze ['grɛntsə] *f* (-; -*n*) border; boundary; *fig* limit; '**grenzen** *v/i* (*ge*-, *h*) ~ *an* (*acc*) border on
'**grenzenlos** *adj* boundless
'**Grenz|fall** *m* borderline case; ~**land** *n* borderland, frontier; ~**linie** *f* borderline, POL demarcation line; ~**stein** *m* boundary stone; ~**übergang** *m* frontier crossing (point), checkpoint
Greuel *m* → **Gräuel**
Grieche ['griːçə] *m* (-*n*; -*n*) Greek;

ˈ**Griechenland** Greece; ˈ**Griechin** f (-;
-nen), ˈ**griechisch** adj Greek

Grieß [griːs] m (-es; -e) semolina

griff [grɪf] pret of **greifen**

Griff m (-[e]s; -e) grip, grasp; handle

ˈ**griffbereit** adj at hand, handy

Grill [grɪl] m (-s; -s) grill

Grille [ˈgrɪlə] f (-; -n) zo cricket

ˈ**grillen** v/t (ge-, h) grill, barbecue

Grimasse [griˈmasə] f (-; -n) grimace;
~**n schneiden** pull faces

grimmig [ˈgrɪmɪç] adj grim

grinsen [ˈgrɪnzən] v/i (ge-, h) grin (**über**
acc at); **höhnisch** or **spöttisch** ~ (**über**
acc) sneer (at); ˈ**Grinsen** n (-s; no pl)
grin; **höhnisches** or **spöttisches** ~
sneer

Grippe [ˈgrɪpə] f (-; -n) MED influenza, F
flu

Grips [grɪps] F m (-es; no pl) brains

grob [groːp] **1.** adj coarse (a. fig); fig
gross; crude; rude; rough **2.** adv: ~ **ge-
schätzt** at a rough estimate

ˈ**Grobheit** f (-; no pl) coarseness; roughness; rudeness

grölen [ˈɡrøːlən] F v/t and v/i (ge-, h)
bawl

Groll [grɔl] m (-[e]s; no pl) grudge, ill
will; ˈ**grollen** v/i (ge-, h) **j-m** ~ bear
s.o. a grudge

Groschen [ˈgrɔʃən] m (-s; -) hist (former monetary unit of Austria) groschen; F ten-pfennig piece, ten pfen-
nigs

groß [groːs] adj big; large (a. family);
tall; grown-up; F big (brother etc); fig
great (a. fun, trouble, pain etc); capital
(letter); ~**es Geld** bills, Br notes; ~**e Ferien** summer vacation, Br summer hol-
iday(s); **Groß und Klein** young and old;
im Großen und Ganzen on the whole;
F ~ **in et. sein** be great at (doing) s.th.;
wie ~ **ist es?** what size is it?; **wie** ~ **bist
du?** how tall are you?

ˈ**großartig** adj great, F a. terrific

ˈ**Großaufnahme** f film: close-up

Größe [ˈgrøːsə] f (-; -n) size; height; esp
MATH quantity; fig greatness; celebrity

ˈ**Großeltern** pl grandparents

ˈ**großen'teils** adv to a large or great extent, largely

ˈ**Größenwahn** m megalomania (a. fig)

ˈ**Groß|fa͵milie** f extended family; ~**han-
del** m ECON wholesale (trade); ~**händ-**
ler m ECON wholesale dealer, wholesal-
er; ~**handlung** f ECON wholesale business; ~**indus͵trie** f big industry; big
business; ~**industri͵elle** m big industrialist, F tycoon; ~**macht** f POL great power; ~**markt** m ECON hypermarket;
wholesale market; ~**maul** F n braggart;
~**mutter** f grandmother; ~**raum** m con-
urbation, metropolitan area; **der** ~
München Greater Munich, the Greater Munich area; ~**raumflugzeug** n
wide-bodied jet

ˈ**großschreiben** v/t (irr, **schreiben**, sep,
-ge-, h) capitalize; ˈ**Großschreibung** f
(use of) capitalization

großsprecherisch [ˈgroːsʃprɛçərɪʃ]
adj boastful

großspurig [ˈgroːsʃpuːrɪç] adj arrogant

ˈ**Großstadt** f big city; ˈ**großstädtisch**
adj of or in a big city; urban

ˈ**größten'teils** adv mostly, mainly

ˈ**großtun** v/i (irr, **tun**, sep, -ge-, h) show
off; **sich mit et.** ~ brag about s.th.

ˈ**Großvater** m grandfather

ˈ**Großverdiener** m (-s; -) big earner

ˈ**Großwild** n big game

ˈ**großziehen** v/t (irr, **ziehen**, sep, -ge-, h)
raise, rear; bring up

ˈ**großzügig** adj generous, liberal; ... on
a large scale; spacious

ˈ**Großzügigkeit** f (-; no pl) generosity,
liberality; spaciousness

grotesk [groˈtɛsk] adj grotesque

Grotte [ˈgrɔtə] f (-; -n) grotto

grub [gruːp] pret of **graben**

Grübchen [ˈgryːpçən] n (-s; -) dimple

Grube [ˈgruːbə] f (-; -n) pit; mine

Grübelei [gryːbəˈlaɪ] f (-; -en) ponder-
ing, musing

grübeln [ˈgryːbəln] v/i (ge-, h) ponder,
muse (**über** acc on, over)

Gruft [grʊft] f (-; **Grüfte** [ˈgrʏftə]) tomb,
vault

grün [gryːn] adj green; **Grün** n (-s; -)
green; **im** ~**en** in the country

ˈ**Grünanlage** f park

Grund [grʊnt] m (-[e]s; **Gründe** [ˈgrʏn-
də]) reason; cause; ground, AGR a. soil;
bottom; ~ **und Boden** property, land;
aus diesem ~**(e)** for this reason; **von**
~ **auf** entirely; **im** ~**e (genommen)** actually, basically; → **aufgrund**; → **zugrunde**

ˈ**Grund...** in cpds ...**bedeutung**, ...**be-**

dingung, …regel, …prinzip, …wort-schatz etc: *mst* basic …; **~begriffe** *pl* basics, fundamentals; **~besitz** *m* property, land; **~besitzer** *m* landowner

gründen ['gryndən] *v/t* (*ge-, h*) found (*a. family*), set up, establish; **sich ~ auf** (*dat*) be based *or* founded on

Gründer ['gryndɐ] *m* (*-s; -*), **'Gründerin** *f* (*-; -nen*) founder

'grund'falsch *adj* absolutely wrong

'Grund|fläche *f* MATH base; ARCH area; **~gedanke** *m* basic idea; **~geschwindigkeit** *f* AVIAT ground speed; **~gesetz** *n* POL Basic (Constitutional) Law (for the Federal Republic of Germany); **~lage** *f* foundation, *fig a.* basis; *pl* (basic) elements

'grundlegend *adj* fundamental, basic

gründlich ['gryntlɪç] *adj* thorough

'Grundlinie *f* tennis etc: base line

'grundlos *adj* groundless, unfounded

'Grundmauer *f* foundation

Grün'donnerstag *m* REL Maundy *or* Holy Thursday

'Grund|rechnungsart *f* MATH basic arithmetical operation; **~riss** *m* ARCH ground plan; **~satz** *m* principle

grundsätzlich ['gruntsetslɪç] **1.** *adj* fundamental **2.** *adv*: **ich bin ~ dagegen** I am against it on principle

'Grund|schule *f* elementary (*or* grade) school, *Br* primary (*or* junior) school; **~stein** *m* ARCH foundation stone; *fig* foundations; **~stück** *n* plot (of land), lot; (building) site; premises; **~stücksmakler** *m* realtor, *Br* real estate agent

'Gründung *f* (*-; -en*) foundation, establishment, setting up

'grundver'schieden *adj* totally different

'Grund|wasser *n* ground water; **~zahl** *f* cardinal number; **~zug** *m* main feature, characteristic

Grüne ['gry:nə] *m, f* (*-n; -n*) POL Green

'Grünfläche *f* green space

'grünlich *adj* greenish

'Grünspan *m* (*-[e]s; no pl*) verdigris

grunzen ['gruntsən] *v/i and v/t* (*ge-, h*) grunt

Gruppe ['grupə] *f* (*-; -n*) group

'Gruppenreise *f* group tour

gruppieren [gru'pi:rən] *v/t* (*no -ge-, h*) group, arrange in groups; **sich ~** form groups

Grusel… ['gru:zəl-] *in cpds …film etc*: horror …; **'gruselig** *adj* eerie, creepy; spine-chilling; **'gruseln** *v/t and v/refl* (*ge-, h*) **es gruselt mich** F it gives me the creeps

Gruß [gru:s] *m* (*-es; Grüße* ['gry:sə]) greeting(s); MIL salute; **viele Grüße an** (*acc*) … give my regards (*or* love) to …; **mit freundlichen Grüßen** yours sincerely; **herzliche Grüße** best wishes; love

grüßen ['gry:sən] *v/t* (*ge-, h*) greet, F say hello to; MIL salute; **~ Sie ihn von mir** give my regards (*or* love) to him

gucken ['gukən] *v/i* (*ge-, h*) look

'Guckloch *n* peephole

Güggeli ['gygəli] *n* (*-s; -*) *Swiss* chicken

gültig ['gyltɪç] *adj* valid; current

'Gültigkeit *f* (*-; no pl*) validity; **s-e ~ verlieren** expire

Gummi ['gumi] *m, n* (*-s; -[s]*) rubber; **~band** *n* (*-[e]s; -bänder*) rubber (*esp Br a.* elastic) band; **~bärchen** *pl* gummy bears; **~baum** *m* BOT rubber tree; rubber plant

gummieren [gu'mi:rən] *v/t* (*no -ge-, h*) gum

'Gummi|knüppel *m* truncheon; **~stiefel** *m* rubber boot, *esp Br* wellington (boot); **~zug** *m* elastic

Gunst [gunst] *f* (*-; no pl*) favo(u)r, goodwill; → **zugunsten**

günstig ['gynstɪç] *adj* favo(u)rable (**für** to); convenient; **im ~sten Fall** at best; **~e Gelegenheit** chance

Gurgel ['gurgəl] *f* (*-; -n*) throat; **j-m an die ~ springen** fly at s.o.'s throat; **'gurgeln** *v/i* (*ge-, h*) MED gargle

Gurke ['gurkə] *f* (*-; -n*) BOT cucumber

gurren ['gurən] *v/i* (*ge-, h*) ZO coo

Gurt [gurt] *m* (*-[e]s; -e*) belt (*a.* MOT *and* AVIAT); strap

Gürtel ['gyrtəl] *m* (*-s; -*) belt; **~reifen** *m* MOT radial (tire, *Br* tyre)

GUS [gus, ge:?u:'?ɛs] *abbr of* **Gemeinschaft Unabhängiger Staaten** CIS, Commonwealth of Independent States

Guss [gus] *m* (*-es; Güsse* ['gysə]) downpour; TECH casting; GASTR icing; *fig* **aus e-m ~** of a piece; **'Gusseisen** *n* cast iron; **'gusseisern** *adj* cast-iron

gut [gu:t] **1.** *adj* good; fine; **ganz ~** not bad; **also ~!** all right (then)!; **schon ~!** never mind!; (**wieder**) **~ werden**

come right (again), be all right; **~e Rei-se!** have a nice trip!; **sei bitte so ~ und ...** would you be so good as to or good enough to ...; **in et. ~ sein** be good at (doing) s.th. **2.** adv well; look, taste etc good; **du hast es ~** you are lucky; **es ist ~ möglich** it may well be; **es gefällt mir ~** I (do) like it; **~ gebaut** well-built; **~ gelaunt** in a good mood; **~ gemacht!** well done!; **mach's ~!** take care (of yourself)!; **~ gehen** go (off) well, work out well or all right; **wenn alles ~ geht** if nothing goes wrong; **mir geht es ~** I'm (doing) well; **Gut** n (-[e]s; **Güter** ['gy:tɐ]) estate; pl goods

'**Gutachten** n (-s; -) (expert) opinion; certificate; **Gutachter** ['gu:tʔaxtɐ] m (-s; -) expert

'**gutartig** adj good-natured; MED benign

Gutdünken ['gu:tdʏŋkən] n: **nach ~** at one's discretion

Gute ['gu:tə] n (-n; no pl) good; **~s tun** do good; **alles ~!** all the best!, good luck!

Güte ['gy:tə] f (-; no pl) goodness, kindness; ECON quality; F **meine ~!** good gracious!

Güter|bahnhof ['gy:tɐba:nho:f] m freight depot, Br goods station; **~gemeinschaft** f JUR community of property; **~trennung** f JUR separation of property; **~verkehr** m freight (Br goods) traffic; **~wagen** m freight car, Br goods wag(g)on; **~zug** m freight (Br goods) train

'**gutgläubig** adj credulous

'**Guthaben** n (-s; -) ECON credit (balance)

'**gutheißen** v/t (irr, **heißen**, sep, -ge-, h) approve (of)

'**gutherzig** adj kind(-hearted)

gütig ['gy:tɪç] adj good, kind(ly)

gütlich ['gy:tlɪç] adv: **sich ~ einigen** come to an amicable settlement

'**gutmachen** v/t (sep, -ge-, h) make up for, repay

gutmütig ['gu:tmy:tɪç] adj good-natured

'**Gutmütigkeit** f (-; no pl) good nature

'**Gutsbesitzer** m, '**Gutsbesitzerin** f (-; -nen) estate owner

'**Gutschein** m coupon, esp Br voucher

'**gutschreiben** v/t (irr, **schreiben**, sep, -ge-, h) **j-m et. ~** credit s.th. to s.o.'s account; '**Gutschrift** f credit

'**Gutshaus** n manor (house)

'**Gutshof** m estate, manor

'**gutstehen** v/refl (irr, **stehen**, sep, -ge-, h): **sich ~** be well off; F **sich gut mit j-m stehen → stehen**

'**Gutsverwalter** m steward, manager

'**gutwillig** adj willing

Gymnasium [gʏm'na:zjʊm] n (-s; -ien) high school, Br appr grammar school

Gymnastik [gʏm'nastɪk] f (-; no pl) exercises, gymnastics; **gym'nastisch** adj: **~e Übungen** physical exercises

Gynäkologe [gynɛko'lo:gə] m (-n; -n), **Gynäko'login** f (-; -nen) MED gyn(a)ecologist

H

Haar [ha:ɐ] n (-[e]s; -e ['ha:rə]) hair; **sich die ~e kämmen (schneiden lassen)** comb one's hair (have one's hair cut); **sich aufs ~ gleichen** look absolutely identical; **um ein ~** by a hair's breadth

'**Haarausfall** m loss of hair

'**Haarbürste** f hairbrush

haaren ['ha:rən] v/i and v/refl (ge-, h) ZO lose its hair; fur: shed hairs

'**Haaresbreite** f: **um ~** by a hair's breadth

'**haarfein** adj (as) fine as a hair

'**Haarfestiger** m (-s; -) setting lotion

'**Haargefäß** n ANAT capillary (vessel)

'**haargenau** F adv precisely; **(stimmt) ~!** dead right!

haarig ['ha:rɪç] adj hairy

'**haarklein** F adv to the last detail

'**Haar|klemme** f bobby pin, Br hair clip; **~nadel** f hairpin; **~nadelkurve** f hairpin bend; **~netz** n hair-net

'**haarscharf** F adv by a hair's breadth

'**Haar|schnitt** m haircut; **~spalterei** f (-; no pl) hair-splitting; **~spange** f barrette, Br (hair) slide; **~spray** m, n hair-

spray
'**haarsträubend** adj hair-raising
'**Haar|teil** n hairpiece; **~trockner** m hair
dryer; **~wäsche** f, **~waschmittel** n
shampoo; **~wasser** n hair tonic;
~wuchs m: **starken ~ haben** have a
lot of hair; **~wuchsmittel** n hair restor-
er
haben ['ha:bən] v/t (irr, ge-, h) have
(got); **Hunger ~** be hungry; **Durst ~**
be thirsty; **Ferien** (**Urlaub**) **~** be on vacation (Br holiday); **er hat Geburtstag**
it's his birthday; **welche Farbe hat ...?**
what colo(u)r is ...?; **zu ~ sein** be available; F **sich ~** make a fuss; F **was hast
du?** what's the matter with you?; F **da ~
wir's!** there we are!; → **Datum**
'**Haben** n (-s; no pl) ECON credit
Habgier ['ha:pgi:ɐ] f greed(iness)
'**habgierig** adj greedy
Habicht ['ha:bɪçt] m (-s; -e) ZO hawk
'**Habseligkeiten** pl belongings
Hacke ['hakə] f (-; -n) AGR hoe; (pick-)
axe; ANAT heel; '**hacken** v/t (ge-, h)
chop; AGR hoe; ZO peck
'**Hackentrick** m soccer: backheeler
Hacker ['hakɐ] m (-s; -) IT hacker
'**Hack|fleisch** n ground (Br minced)
meat; **~ordnung** f ZO pecking order
Hafen ['ha:fən] m (-s; **Häfen** ['hɛ:fən])
harbo(u)r, port; **~arbeiter** m docker,
longshoreman; **~stadt** f (sea)port
Hafer ['ha:fɐ] m (-s; -) BOT oats; **~brei** m
oatmeal, Br porridge; **~flocken** pl
(rolled) oats; **~schleim** m gruel
Haft [haft] f (-; no pl) JUR confinement,
imprisonment; **in ~** under arrest
'**haftbar** adj responsible, JUR liable
'**Haftbefehl** m JUR warrant of arrest
'**haften** v/i (ge-, h) stick, adhere (**an** dat
to); **~ für** JUR answer for, be liable for
Häftling ['hɛftlɪŋ] m (-s; -e) prisoner,
convict
'**Haftpflicht** f JUR liability; **~versiche-
rung** f liability insurance; MOT third
party insurance
'**Haftung** f (-; -en) responsibility, JUR liability; **mit beschränkter ~** limited
Hagel ['ha:gəl] m (-s; no pl) hail, fig a.
shower, volley; '**Hagelkorn** n hail-
stone; '**hageln** v/i (ge-, h) hail (a. fig);
'**Hagelschauer** m hail shower
hager ['ha:gɐ] adj lean, gaunt, haggard
Hahn [ha:n] m (-[e]s; **Hähne** ['hɛ:nə]) ZO

cock, rooster; TECH (water) tap, faucet
Hähnchen ['hɛ:nçən] n (-s; -) ZO chick-
en
'**Hahnenkamm** m ZO cockscomb
Hai [hai] m (-[e]s; -e), **~fisch** m ZO shark
häkeln ['hɛ:kəln] v/t and v/i (ge-, h) cro-
chet
Haken ['ha:kən] m (-s; -) hook (a. boxing), peg; check, Br tick; F snag, catch
'**Hakenkreuz** n swastika
halb [halp] adj and adv half; **e-e ~e
Stunde** half an hour; **ein ~es Pfund**
half a pound; **zum ~en Preis** at half-
-price; **auf ~em Wege** (**entgegenkommen**) (meet) halfway; **~ so viel** half as
much; F (**mit j-m**) **halbe-halbe machen** go halves or fifty-fifty (with
s.o.); **~ gar** GASTR underdone
'**Halbbruder** m half-brother
'**Halbdunkel** n semi-darkness
Halbe ['halbə] f (-n; -n) pint (of beer)
'**halbfett** adj GASTR medium-fat; PRINT
semi-bold
'**Halbfi,nale** n SPORT semifinal
'**Halbgott** m demigod
'**halbherzig** adj half-hearted
halbieren [hal'bi:rən] v/t (no -ge-, h)
halve; MATH bisect
'**Halbinsel** f peninsula
'**Halbjahr** n six months; **halbjährig**
['halpjɛ:rɪç] adj six-month;
'**halbjährlich 1.** adj half-yearly **2.** adv
half-yearly, twice a year
'**Halbkreis** m semicircle
'**Halbkugel** f hemisphere
'**halblaut 1.** adj low, subdued **2.** adv in an
undertone
'**Halbleiter** m ELECTR semiconductor
'**halbmast** adv (at) half-mast
'**Halb|mond** m half-moon, crescent;
~pensi,on f (-; no pl) esp Br half board;
~schlaf m doze; **~schuh** m (low) shoe;
~schwester f half-sister
'**halbtags** adv: **~ arbeiten** work part-
-time; '**Halbtagsarbeit** f (-; no pl)
part-time job; '**Halbtagskraft** f part-
-time worker, F part-timer
halbwegs ['halpve:ks] adv reasonably
Halbwüchsige ['halpvy:ksɪgə] m, f (-n;
-n) adolescent
'**Halbzeit** f SPORT half (time); **~stand** m
SPORT half-time score
Halde ['haldə] f (-; -n) slope; dump
half [half] pret of **helfen**

Hälfte ['hɛlftə] f (-; -n) half; **die ~ von** half of

Halfter ['halftɐ] **1.** m, n (-s; -) halter **2.** n (-s; -), f (-; -n) holster

Halle ['halə] f (-; -n) hall; lounge; **in der~** SPORT etc indoors

'**hallen** v/i (ge-, h) resound, reverberate

'**Hallenbad** n indoor swimming pool

'**Hallensport** m indoor sports

Halm [halm] m (-[e]s; -e) BOT blade; ha(u)lm, stalk; straw

Hals [hals] m (-es; Hälse ['hɛlzə]) ANAT neck; throat; **~ über Kopf** helter-skelter; F **sich vom ~ schaffen** get rid of; F **es hängt mir zum ~(e) (he)raus** I'm fed up with it; fig **bis zum ~** up to one's neck; **~band** n (-[e]s; -bänder) necklace; collar; **~entzündung** f MED sore throat; **~kette** f necklace; **~schmerzen** pl: **~ haben** have a sore throat

halsstarrig ['halsʃtarɪç] adj stubborn, obstinate

'**Halstuch** n neckerchief; scarf

Halt m (-[e]s; -e, -s) (no pl) hold; support (a. fig); fig stability; stop

halt [halt] int stop!, MIL halt!

'**haltbar** adj durable; GASTR not perishable; fig tenable; **~ bis ...** best before ...

'**Haltbarkeitsdatum** n best-by (or best--before) date

halten ['haltən] (irr, ge-, h) **1.** v/t hold; keep (animal, promise etc); make (speech); give (lecture); take (Br a. in) a paper etc; SPORT save; **~ für** regard as; (mis)take for; **viel (wenig) ~ von** think highly (little) of; **sich ~** last; GASTR keep; **sich gut ~** fig do well; **sich ~ an** (acc) keep to **2.** v/i hold, last; stop, halt; ice: bear; rope etc: hold; **~ zu** stand by, F stick to; **Halter(in)** ['haltɐ, 'haltərɪn] m(f) (-s; -/-; -nen) owner; TECH holder

'**Haltestelle** f stop, RAIL a. station

'**Halteverbot** n MOT no stopping (area)

'**haltlos** adj unsteady; fig baseless

'**haltmachen** v/i (sep, -ge-, h) stop; fig **vor nichts ~** stop at nothing

'**Haltung** f (-; -en) posture; fig attitude (**zu** towards)

hämisch ['hɛːmɪʃ] adj malicious, sneering

Hammel ['haməl] m (-s; -) ZO wether

'**Hammelfleisch** n GASTR mutton

Hammer ['hamɐ] m (-s; Hämmer ['hɛmɐ]) hammer (a. SPORT); **hämmern** ['hɛmɐn] v/t and v/i (ge-, h) hammer

Hämorrhoiden, Hämorriden [hɛmɔro-'iːdən] pl MED h(a)emorrhoids, F Br piles

Hampelmann ['hampəlman] m jumping jack

Hamster ['hamstɐ] m (-s; -) ZO hamster

'**hamstern** v/t and v/i (ge-, h) hoard

Hand [hant] f (-; Hände ['hɛndə]) hand; **von ~, mit der ~** by hand; **an ~ von** (or gen) by means of; **zur ~** at hand; **aus erster (zweiter) ~** first-hand (second--hand); **an die ~ nehmen** take by the hand; **sich die ~ geben** shake hands; **aus der ~ legen** lay aside; **~ breit →** **handbreit**; **~ voll → handvoll**; **Hände hoch (weg)!** hands up (off)!; **~arbeit** f (no pl) manual labo(u)r; needlework; **es ist ~** it is handmade; **~ball** m SPORT (European) handball; **~betrieb** m TECH manual operation; **~breit** f (-; -) hand's breadth; **~bremse** f MOT handbrake; **~buch** n manual, handbook

Händedruck ['hɛndədrʊk] m (-[e]s; -drücke) handshake

Handel ['handəl] m (-s; no pl) commerce, business; trade; market; transaction, deal, bargain; **~ treiben** ECON trade (**mit** with s.o.); '**handeln** v/i (ge-, h) act, take action; bargain (**um** for), haggle (over); **mit j-m ~** ECON trade with s.o.; **~ mit** deal in; **~ von** deal with, be about; **es handelt sich um** it concerns, it is about; it is a matter of

'**Handels|abkommen** n trade agreement; **~bank** f (-; -banken) commercial bank; **~bi,lanz** f balance of trade

'**handelseinig** adj: **~ werden** come to terms

'**Handels|gesellschaft** f (trading) company; **~kammer** f chamber of commerce; **~schiff** n merchant ship; **~schule** f commercial school; **~vertreter** m (traveling) salesman, Br sales representative; **~ware** f commodity, merchandise

'**Hand|feger** ['hantfeːgɐ] m (-s; -) handbrush; **~fertigkeit** f manual skill

'**handfest** adj solid

'**Handfläche** f ANAT palm

'**handgearbeitet** adj handmade

'**Hand|gelenk** *n* ANAT wrist; **~gepäck** *n* hand baggage (*Br* luggage); **~gra,nate** *f* MIL hand grenade

handgreiflich ['hantgraiflɪç] *adj:* **~ werden** turn violent, get tough

'**handhaben** *v/t* (*ge-*, *h*) handle, manage; TECH operate

Händler ['hɛndlɐ] *m* (*-s*; *-*), '**Händlerin** *f* (*-*; *-nen*) dealer, trader

'**handlich** *adj* handy, manageable

Handlung ['handlʊŋ] *f* (*-*; *-en*) act, action; *film etc*: story, plot

'**Handlungs|reisende** *m* sales representative, travel(l)ing salesman; **~weise** *f* conduct, behavio(u)r

'**Hand|rücken** *m* ANAT back of the hand; **~schellen** *pl* handcuffs; *j-m* **~ anlegen** handcuff s.o.; **~schlag** *m* handshake; **~schrift** *f* hand(writing)

'**handschriftlich** *adj* handwritten

'**Hand|schuh** *m* glove; **~spiel** *n* soccer: hand ball; **~stand** *m* handstand; **~tasche** *f* handbag, purse; **~tuch** *n* towel; **~voll** *f* handful; **~wagen** *m* handcart; **~werk** *n* craft, trade

Handwerker ['hantvɛrkɐ] *m* (*-s*; *-*) craftsman; workman

'**Handwerkszeug** *n* (kit of) tools

'**Handwurzel** *f* ANAT wrist

Handy ['hɛndi] *n* (*-s*; *-s*) *Br* mobile (phone), *Am* cell (phone); **~nummer** *f Br* mobile number, *Am* cell phone number

Hanf [hanf] *m* (*-es*; *no pl*) BOT hemp; cannabis

Hang [haŋ] *m* (*-[e]s*; *Hänge* ['hɛŋə]) slope; (*no pl*) *fig* inclination (*zu* for), tendency (towards)

Hänge|brücke ['hɛŋəbrʏkə] *f* suspension bridge; **~lampe** *f* hanging lamp; **~matte** *f* hammock

hängen ['hɛŋən] **1.** *v/i* (*irr*, *ge-*, *h*) hang (*an dat* on *the wall etc*; from *the ceiling etc*); **~ bleiben** get stuck (*a. fig*); **~ bleiben an** (*dat*) get caught on; **~ an** (*dat*) be fond of; be devoted to; *alles, woran ich hänge* everything that is dear to me **2.** *v/t* (*ge-*, *h*) hang (*an acc* on); **~bleiben** *v/i* (*irr*, *bleiben*, *sep*, *-ge-*, *sein*) fig get stuck; → **hängen**

hänseln ['hɛnzəln] *v/t* (*ge-*, *h*) tease (*wegen* about)

Hanswurst [hans'vʊrst] *m* (*-[e]s*; *-e*) fool, clown

Hantel ['hantəl] *f* (*-*; *-n*) dumbbell

hantieren [han'tiːrən] *v/i* (*no -ge-*, *h*) **~ mit** handle; **~ an** (*dat*) fiddle about with

Happen ['hapən] *m* (*-s*; *-*) morsel, bite; snack

Hardware ['hɑːdwɛə] *f* (*-*; *-s*) IT hardware

Harfe ['harfə] *f* (*-*; *-n*) MUS harp

Harfenist [harfə'nɪst] *m* (*-en*; *-en*), **Harfe'nistin** *f* (*-*; *-nen*) MUS harpist

Harke ['harkə] *f* (*-*; *-n*), '**harken** *v/t* (*ge-*, *h*) rake

harmlos ['harmloːs] *adj* harmless

Harmonie [harmo'niː] *f* (*-*; *-n*) harmony (*a.* MUS); **harmo'nieren** *v/i* (*no -ge-*, *h*) harmonize (*mit* with); **harmonisch** [har'moːnɪʃ] *adj* harmonious

Harn [harn] *m* (*-[e]s*; *-e*) MED urine

'**Harnblase** *f* ANAT (urinary) bladder

'**Harnröhre** *f* ANAT urethra

Harpune [har'puːnə] *f* (*-*; *-n*) harpoon

harpunieren [harpu'niːrən] *v/t* (*no -ge-*, *h*) harpoon

hart [hart] **1.** *adj* hard, F *a.* tough; SPORT rough; severe; **~ gekocht** hard-boiled **2.** *adv* hard

Härte ['hɛrtə] *f* (*-*; *-n*) hardness; toughness; roughness; severity; *esp* JUR hardship; **~fall** *m* case of hardship

'**härten** *v/t* (*ge-*, *h*) harden

'**Hartfaserplatte** *f* hardboard

'**Hartgeld** *n* coin(s)

hartgesotten ['hartgəzɔtən] *adj* hard-boiled

'**hartherzig** *adj* hard-hearted

hartnäckig ['hartnɛkɪç] *adj* stubborn, obstinate; persistent

Harz [haːɐts] *n* (*-es*; *-e*) resin; rosin

'**harzig** *adj* resinous

Hasch [haʃ] F *n* (*-s*; *no pl*) hash

'**haschen** F *v/i* (*ge-*, *h*) smoke hash

Haschisch ['haʃɪʃ] *n* (*-[s]*; *no pl*) hashish

Hase ['haːzə] *m* (*-n*; *-n*) ZO hare

Haselmaus ['haːzəlmaus] *f* ZO dormouse

'**Haselnuss** *f* BOT hazelnut

'**Hasenscharte** *f* MED harelip

Hass [has] *m* (*-es*; *no pl*) hatred, hate (*auf acc*, *gegen* of, for)

hassen ['hasən] *v/t* (*ge-*, *h*) hate

hässlich ['hɛslɪç] *adj* ugly, *fig a.* nasty

Hast [hast] *f* (*-*; *no pl*) hurry, haste; rush

hasten ['hastən] *v/i* (*ge-*, *sein*) hurry,

hastig

hasten, rush

'**hastig** *adj* hasty, hurried

hätscheln ['hɛːt ʃəln] *v/t* (*ge*-, *h*) fondle;
contp pamper

hatte ['hatə] *pret of* **haben**

Haube ['haubə] *f* (-; -*n*) bonnet (*a. Br*
MOT); cap; ZO crest; MOT hood

Hauch [haux] *m* (-[*e*]*s*; -*e*) breath; whiff;
fig touch, trace; **hauchen** ['hauxən] *v/t*
(*ge*-, *h*) breathe

hauen F *v/t* ([*irr*,] *ge*-, *h*) hit, beat, thrash;
TECH hew; *sich* ~ (have a) fight

Haufen ['haufən] *m* (-*s*; -) heap, pile
(*both a.* F); F crowd; **häufen** ['hɔyfən]
v/t (*ge*-, *h*) heap (up), pile (up); *sich* ~
fig become more frequent, be on the
increase; **häufig** ['hɔyfiç] **1.** *adj* frequent **2.** *adv* frequently, often

Haupt [haupt] *n* (-[*e*]*s*; *Häupter* ['hɔyp-
tɐ]) head, *fig a.* leader; ~**bahnhof** *m*
main *or* central station; ~**beschäftigung** *f* chief occupation; ~**bestandteil**
m chief ingredient; ~**darsteller(in)**
leading actor (actress), lead

Häuptelsalat ['hɔyptəlzalaːt] *Austrian*
m BOT lettuce

'**Haupt|fach** *n* UNIV major, *Br* main sub-
ject; ~**film** *m* feature (film); ~**gericht** *n*
GASTR main course; ~**gewinn** *m* first
prize; ~**grund** *m* main reason; ~**leitung**
f TECH main

Häuptling ['hɔyptlɪŋ] *m* (-*s*; -*e*) chief

'**Haupt|mann** *m* (-[*e*]*s*; -*leute*) MIL cap-
tain; ~**me,nü** *n* IT main menu; ~**merkmal** *n* chief characteristic; ~**per,son** F
f center (*Br* centre) of attention;
~**quar,tier** *n* headquarters; ~**rolle** *f*
THEA *etc* lead(ing part)

'**Hauptsache** *f* main thing *or* point

'**hauptsächlich** *adj* main, chief, principal

'**Haupt|satz** *m* LING main clause; ~**sen-
dezeit** *f* TV prime time, *Br* peak time (*or*
viewing hours); ~**speicher** *m* IT main
memory; ~**stadt** *f* capital; ~**straße** *f*
main street; main road; ~**verkehrs-
straße** *f* arterial road; ~**verkehrszeit**
f rush *or* peak hour(s); ~**versammlung**
f general meeting; ~**wohnsitz** *m* main
place of residence; ~**wort** *n* (-[*e*]*s*; -*wörter*) LING noun

Haus [haus] *n* (-*es*; *Häuser* ['hɔyzɐ])
house; building; *zu* ~*e* at home, in;
nach ~*e* **kommen** (*bringen*) come *or*

get (take) home; ~**angestellte** *m*, *f* domestic (servant); ~**apo,theke** *f* medicine cabinet; ~**arbeit** *f* housework;
~**arzt** *m*, ~**ärztin** *f* family doctor; ~**auf-
gaben** *pl* PED homework, assignment;
s-e ~ *machen a. fig* do one's homework; ~**bar** *f* cocktail cabinet; ~**beset-
zer** *m* (-*s*; -) squatter; ~**besetzung** *f*
squatting; ~**besitzer** *m* house owner;
~**einweihung** *f* house-warming (party)

hausen ['hauzən] *v/i* (*ge*-, *h*) live; *fig*
play havoc

'**Hausflur** *m* (entrance) hall, hallway

'**Hausfrau** *f* housewife

'**Hausfriedensbruch** *m* JUR trespass

'**hausgemacht** *adj* homemade

'**Haushalt** *m* (-[*e*]*s*; -*e*) household; PARL
budget; (*j-m*) *den* ~ *führen* keep house
(for s.o.); **Haushälterin** ['haushɛltərin]
f (-; -*nen*) housekeeper

'**Haushalts|geld** *n* housekeeping mon-
ey; ~**plan** *m* PARL budget; ~**waren** *pl*
household articles

'**Haus|herr** *m* head of the household;
host; ~**herrin** *f* lady of the house; hostess

'**haushoch** *adj* huge; crushing (*defeat*
etc)

hausieren [hau'ziːrən] *v/i* (*no -ge*-, *h*)
peddle, hawk (*mit et.* s.th.) (*a. fig*);
Hau'sierer *m* (-*s*; -) pedlar, hawker

häuslich ['hɔyslɪç] *adj* domestic; home-
loving

'**Haus|mädchen** *n* (house)maid;
~**mann** *m* house husband; ~**manns-
kost** *f* plain fare; ~**meister** *m* caretaker,
janitor; ~**mittel** *n* household remedy;
~**ordnung** *f* house rules; ~**rat** *m*
(-[*e*]*s*; *no pl*) household effects;
~**schlüssel** *m* front-door key; ~**schuh**
m slipper

Hausse ['hoːs(ə)] *f* (-; -*n*) ECON rise,
boom

'**Haus|suchung** *f* (-; -*en*) house search;
~**tier** *n* domestic animal; ~**tür** *f* front
door; ~**verwaltung** *f* property management; ~**wirt** *m* landlord; ~**wirtin** *f* landlady; ~**wirtschaft** *f* (-; *no pl*) house-
keeping; ~**wirtschaftslehre** *f* domestic
science, home economics; ~**wirt-
schaftsschule** *f* domestic science (*or*
home economics) school

Haut [haut] *f* (-; *Häute* ['hɔytə]) skin;
complexion; *bis auf die* ~ *durchnässt*

soaked to the skin; **~abschürfung** *f* MED abrasion; **~arzt** *m*, **~ärztin** *f* dermatologist; **~ausschlag** *m* MED rash

'**hauteng** *adj* skin-tight

'**Haut|farbe** *f* colo(u)r of the skin; complexion; **~krankheit** *f* skin disease; **~pflege** *f* skin care; **~schere** *f* cuticle scissors

Hbf. *abbr of* **Hauptbahnhof** cent. sta., central station

H-Bombe ['ha:bɔmbə] *f* MIL H-bomb

Hebamme ['he:pʔamə] *f* (-; *-n*) midwife

Hebebühne ['he:bəby:nə] *f* MOT car hoist

Hebel ['he:bəl] *m* (-*s*; -) TECH lever

heben ['he:bən] *v/t* (*irr, ge-, h*) lift, raise (*a. fig*); heave; hoist; *fig a.* improve; *sich ~* rise, go up

Hecht [hɛçt] *m* (-[*e*]*s*; -*e*) ZO pike

'**hechten** *v/i* (*ge-, sein*) dive (*nach* for); SPORT do a long-fly

Heck [hɛk] *n* (-[*e*]*s*; -*e*) MAR stern; AVIAT tail; MOT rear

Hecke ['hɛkə] *f* (-; *-n*) BOT hedge

'**Heckenrose** *f* BOT dogrose

'**Heckenschütze** *m* MIL sniper

'**Heckscheibe** *f* MOT rear window

Heer [he:ɐ] *n* (-[*e*]*s*; -*e*) MIL army, *fig a.* host

Hefe ['he:fə] *f* (-; *-n*) yeast

Heft [hɛft] *n* (-[*e*]*s*; -*e*) notebook; exercise book; booklet; issue, number

heften ['hɛftən] *v/t* (*ge-, h*) fix, fasten, attach (**an** *acc* to); pin (to); tack, baste; stitch

Hefter ['hɛftɐ] *m* (-*s*; -) stapler; file

heftig ['hɛftɪç] *adj* violent, fierce; heavy

'**Heftklammer** *f* staple

'**Heftpflaster** *n* bandage, Band Aid®, *Br* (adhesive *or* sticking) plaster

Hehl [he:l] *n:* **kein ~ aus et. machen** make no secret of s.th.

Hehler ['he:lɐ] *m* (-*s*; -) JUR receiver of stolen goods, *sl* fence

Hehlerei [he:lə'rai] *f* (-; *-en*) JUR receiving stolen goods

Heide[1] ['haidə] *m* (-*n*; *-n*) REL heathen

'**Heide**[2] *f* (-; *-n*) heath(land)

'**Heidekraut** *n* (-[*e*]*s*; *no pl*) BOT heather, heath

'**Heiden|angst** F *f: e-e ~ haben* be scared stiff; **~geld** F *n: ein ~* a fortune; **~lärm** F *m: ein ~* a hell of a noise; **~spaß** F *m: e-n ~ haben* have a ball

'**Heidentum** *n* (-*s*; *no pl*) REL heathenism; **Heidin** ['haidɪn] *f* (-; *-nen*), '**heidnisch** ['haidnɪʃ] *adj* REL heathen

heikel ['haikəl] *adj* delicate, tricky; tender; F fussy

heil [hail] *adj* safe, unhurt; undamaged, whole, intact; **Heil** *n* (-*s*; *no pl*) REL grace

Heiland ['hailant] *m* (-[*e*]*s*; *no pl*) REL Savio(u)r, Redeemer

'**Heilbad** *n* health resort, spa

'**heilbar** *adj* curable

heilen ['hailən] **1.** *v/t* (*ge-, h*) cure **2.** *v/i* (*ge-, sein*) heal (up)

'**Heilgym,nastik** *f* physiotherapy

heilig ['hailɪç] *adj* REL holy; sacred (*a. fig*)

Heilig'abend *m* Christmas Eve

Heilige ['hailɪgə] *m*, *f* (-*n*; *-n*) REL saint

heiligen ['hailɪgən] *v/t* (*ge-, h*) REL sanctify (*a. fig*), hallow

'**heiligsprechen** *v/t* (*irr, sprechen, sep, -ge-, h*) canonize

'**Heiligtum** *n* (-*s*; *-tümer* ['hailɪçty:mɐ]) REL sanctuary, shrine

'**Heilkraft** *f* healing *or* curative power; '**heilkräftig** *adj* curative

'**Heilkraut** *n* BOT medicinal herb

'**heillos** *fig adj* utter, hopeless

'**Heil|mittel** *n* remedy, cure (*both a. fig*); **~praktiker(in)** ['hailpraktikɐ, 'hailpraktikərɪn] · (-*s*; -/-; *-nen*) non-medical practitioner; **~quelle** *f* (medicinal) mineral spring

'**heilsam** *fig adj* salutary

'**Heilsar,mee** *f* Salvation Army

'**Heilung** *f* (-; *-en*) cure; healing

heim [haim] *adv* home

Heim *n* (-[*e*]*s*; -*e*) (*no pl*) home; hostel; **Heim...** *in cpds* ...*mannschaft*, ...*sieg*, ...*spiel etc*: home

Heimat ['haima:t] *f* (-; *no pl*) home; home country; home town; *in der* (*meiner*) *~* at home; '**heimatlos** *adj* homeless; '**Heimatstadt** *f* home town; '**Heimatvertriebene** *m*, *f* expellee

heimisch ['haimɪʃ] *adj* home, domestic; BOT, ZO *etc* native; *fig* homelike, hom(e)y; *sich ~ fühlen* feel at home

Heimkehr ['haimke:ɐ] *f* (-; *no pl*) return (home); '**heimkehren** *v/i* (*sep, -ge-, sein*) return home, come back

'**heimlich** *adj* secret; '**Heimlichkeit** *f* (-;

-*en*) (*no pl*) secrecy; *pl* secrets

'**Heimreise** *f* journey home

'**heimsuchen** *v/t* (*sep*, *-ge-*, *h*) strike

'**heimtückisch** *adj* insidious (*a.* MED); treacherous

heimwärts ['haimvɛrts] *adv* homeward(s)

'**Heimweg** *m* way home

'**Heimweh** *n* (*-s*; *no pl*) homesickness; ~ **haben** be homesick

Heimwerker ['haimvɛrkɐ] *m* (*-s*; -) do--it-yourselfer

Heirat ['haira:t] *f* (-; *-en*) marriage

heiraten ['haira:tən] *v/t and v/i* (*ge-*, *h*) marry, get married (to)

'**Heirats|antrag** *m* proposal (of marriage); *j-m e-n* ~ *machen* propose to s.o.; ~**schwindler** *m* marriage impostor; ~**vermittler(in)** (*-s*; *-/-*; *-nen*) marriage broker; ~**vermittlung** *f* marriage bureau

heiser ['haizɐ] *adj* hoarse, husky

'**Heiserkeit** *f* (-; *no pl*) hoarseness, huskiness

heiß [hais] *adj* hot, *fig a.* passionate, ardent; *mir ist* ~ I am *or* feel hot

heißen ['haisən] *v/i* (*irr*, *ge-*, *h*) be called; mean; *wie* ~ *Sie?* what's your name?; *wie heißt das?* what do you call this?; *was heißt ... auf Englisch?* what is ... in English?; *es heißt im Text* it says in the text; *das heißt* that is (*abbr d. h.* i. e.)

heiter ['haitɐ] *adj* cheerful; humorous (*film etc*); METEOR fair; *fig aus* ~*em Himmel* out of the blue; '**Heiterkeit** *f* (-; *no pl*) cheerfulness; amusement

heizbar ['haitsba:rɐ] *adj* heated; **heizen** ['haitsən] *v/t and v/i* (*ge-*, *h*) heat; *mit Kohlen* ~ burn coal; **Heizer** ['haitsɐ] *m* (*-s*; -) MAR, RAIL stoker

'**Heiz|kessel** *m* boiler; ~**kissen** *n* electric cushion; ~**körper** *m* radiator; ~**kraftwerk** *n* thermal power-station; ~**materi,al** *n* fuel; ~**öl** *n* fuel oil

'**Heizung** *f* (-; *-en*) heating

Held [hɛlt] *m* (*-en*; *-en* ['hɛldən]) hero

heldenhaft ['hɛldənhaft] *adj* heroic

'**Heldentat** *f* heroic deed

'**Heldentum** *n* (*-s*; *no pl*) heroism

Heldin ['hɛldɪn] *f* (-; *-nen*) heroine

helfen ['hɛlfən] *v/i* (*irr*, *ge-*, *h*) help, aid; assist; *j-m bei et.* ~ help s.o. with *or* in (doing) s.th.; ~ *gegen* MED *etc* be good

for; *er weiß sich zu* ~ he can manage; *es hilft nichts* it's no use

Helfer ['hɛlfɐ] *m* (*-s*; -), '**Helferin** *f* (-; *-nen*) helper, assistant

'**Helfershelfer** *contp m* accomplice

hell [hɛl] *adj* bright (*light*, *flame etc*); light (*color etc*); light-colo(u)red (*dress etc*); clear (*voice etc*); pale (*beer*); *fig* bright, clever; *es wird schon* ~ it's getting light already; ~**blau** *adj* light blue; ~**blond** *adj* very fair; ~**hörig** *adj* quick of hearing; ARCH poorly soundproofed; ~ *werden* prick up one's ears

'**Hellseher** *m* (*-s*; -), '**Hellseherin** *f* (-; *-nen*) clairvoyant

Helm [hɛlm] *m* (*-[e]s*; *-e*) helmet

Hemd [hɛmt] *n* (*-[e]s*; *-en* ['hɛmdən]) shirt; vest; ~**bluse** *f* shirt; ~**blusenkleid** *n* shirtwaist, *Br* shirt-waister

Hemisphäre [hemi'sfɛ:rə] *f* (-; *-n*) hemisphere

hemmen ['hɛmən] *v/t* (*ge-*, *h*) check, stop; hamper; '**Hemmung** *f* (-; *-en*) PSYCH inhibition; scruple

'**hemmungslos** *adj* unrestrained; unscrupulous

Hengst [hɛŋst] *m* (*-[e]s*; *-e*) zo stallion

Henkel ['hɛŋkəl] *m* (*-s*; -) handle

Henker ['hɛŋkɐ] *m* (*-s*; -) hangman, executioner

Henne ['hɛnə] *f* (-; *-n*) zo hen

her [he:ɐ] *adv* here; *das ist lange* ~ that was a long time ago

herab [hɛ'rap] *adv* down; ~**lassen** *fig v/refl* (*irr*, *lassen*, *sep*, *-ge-*, *h*) condescend; ~**lassend** *adj* condescending; ~**sehen** *fig v/i* (*irr*, *sehen*, *sep*, *-ge-*, *h*) ~ *auf* (*acc*) look down upon; ~**setzen** *v/t* (*sep*, *-ge-*, *h*) reduce; *fig* disparage

heran [hɛ'ran] *adv* close, near; ~ *an* (*acc*) up *or* near to; ~**gehen** *v/i* (*irr*, *gehen*, *sep*, *-ge-*, *sein*) ~ *an* (*acc*) walk up to; *fig* set about *a task etc*; ~**kommen** *v/i* (*irr*, *kommen*, *sep*, *-ge-*, *sein*) come near (*a. fig*); ~**wachsen** *v/i* (*irr*, *wachsen*, *sep*, *-ge-*, *sein*) grow (up) (*zu* into)

He'ranwachsende *m, f* (*-n*; *-n*) adolescent

he'ranwinken *v/t* (*sep*, *-ge-*, *h*) hail (*taxi etc*)

herauf [hɛ'rauf] *adv* up (here); upstairs; ~**beschwören** *v/t* (*irr*, *schwören*, *sep*, *no -ge-*, *h*) call up; bring on, provoke

heraus [hɛ'raus] *adv* out; *fig aus* (*dat*)

... ~ out of ...; ***zum Fenster*** ~ out of the window; ~ ***mit der Sprache!*** speak out!, out with it!; **~bekommen** *v/t* (*irr*, **kommen**, *sep, no -ge-, h*) get out; get back (*change*); *fig* find out; **~bringen** *v/t* (*irr*, **bringen**, *sep, -ge-, h*) bring out; PRINT publish; THEA stage; *fig* find out; **~finden** (*irr*, **finden**, *sep, -ge-, h*) **1.** *v/t* find; *fig* find out, discover **2.** *v/i* find one's way out

He'rausforderer *m* (*-s; -*) challenger; **he'rausfordern** *v/t* (*sep, -ge-, h*) challenge; provoke, F ask for it; **He-'rausforderung** *f* challenge; provocation

he'rausgeben *v/t* (*irr*, **geben**, *sep, -ge-, h*) give back; give up; PRINT publish; issue; give change (**auf** *acc* for); **He-'rausgeber(in)** [hɛ'rausge:bɐ, hɛ-'rausge:bərɪn] *m(f)* (*-s; -/-; -nen*) publisher

he'raus|kommen *v/i* (*irr*, **kommen**, *sep, -ge-, kommen*) come out; *book:* be published; *stamps:* be issued; ~ **aus** get out of; F **groß** ~ be a great success; **~nehmen** *v/t* (*irr*, **nehmen**, *sep, -ge-, h*) take out; SPORT take *s.o.* off the team; *fig* **sich et.** ~ take liberties, go too far; **~putzen** *v/t and v/refl* (*sep, -ge-, h*) spruce (o.s.) up; **~reden** *v/refl* (*sep, -ge-, h*) make excuses; talk one's way out; **~stellen** *v/t* (*sep, -ge-, h*) put out; *fig* emphasize; **sich** ~ **als** turn out *or* prove to be; **~strecken** *v/t* (*sep, -ge-, h*) stick out; **~suchen** *v/t* (*sep, -ge-, h*) pick out; **j-m et.** ~ find *s.o. s.th.*

herb [hɛrp] *adj* tart; dry (*wine etc*); *fig* harsh; bitter

her'bei *adv* up, over, here; **~eilen** *v/i* (*sep, -ge-, sein*) come running up; **~führen** *fig v/t* (*sep, -ge-, h*) cause, bring about

Herberge ['hɛrbɛrgə] *f* (*-; -n*) inn; lodging; hostel

Herbst [hɛrpst] *m* (*-[e]s; -e*) fall, autumn

Herd [he:ɐt] *m* (*-[e]s; -e* ['he:ɐdə]) cooker, stove; *fig* center, *Br* centre; MED focus, seat

Herde ['he:ɐdə] *f* (*-; -n*) ZO herd (*a. fig contp*); flock (*of sheep, geese etc*)

herein [hɛ'rain] *adv* in (here); **~!** come in!; **~brechen** *v/i* (*irr*, **brechen**, *sep, -ge-, sein*) night: fall; ~ **über** (*acc*) befall

s.o.; **~fallen** F *v/i* (*irr*, **fallen**, *sep, -ge-, sein*) be taken in (**auf** *acc* by); **~legen** F *v/t* (*sep, -ge-, h*) take *s.o.* in

'herfallen *v/i* (*irr*, **fallen**, *sep, -ge-, sein*) ~ **über** (*acc*) attack (*a. fig*)

'Hergang *m:* **j-m den** ~ **schildern** tell *s.o.* what happened

'hergeben *v/t* (*irr*, **geben**, *sep, -ge-, h*) give up, part with; **sich** ~ **zu** lend o.s. to

Hering ['he:rɪŋ] *m* (*-s; -e*) ZO herring

'herkommen *v/i* (*irr*, **kommen**, *sep, -ge-, sein*) come (here); ~ **von** come from, *fig a.* be caused by

herkömmlich ['he:ɐkœmlɪç] *adj* conventional (*a.* MIL)

Herkunft ['he:ɐkʊnft] *f* (*-; no pl*) origin; birth, descent

heroisch [he'ro:ɪʃ] *adj* heroic

Herr [hɛr] *m* (*-n; -en*) gentleman; master; REL *the* Lord; ~ **Brown** Mr Brown; ~ **der Lage** master of the situation

'Herren|bekleidung *f* menswear; **~doppel** *n tennis:* men's doubles; **~einzel** *n tennis:* men's singles

'herrenlos *adj* abandoned; stray (*dog*)

'Herrentoi,lette *f* men's restroom (*Br* toilet *or* lavatory)

'herrichten *v/t* (*sep, -ge-, h*) get ready, F fix

herrisch ['hɛrɪʃ] *adj* imperious

herrlich ['hɛrlɪç] *adj* marvel(l)ous, wonderful, F fantastic; **'Herrlichkeit** *f* (*-; -en*) glory

'Herrschaft *f* (*-; no pl*) rule, power, control (*a. fig*) (**über** *acc* over); **die** ~ **verlieren über** (*acc*) lose control of

herrschen ['hɛrʃən] *v/i* (*ge-, h*) rule; **es herrschte ...** there was ...; **Herrscher(in)** ['hɛrʃɐ, 'hɛrʃərɪn] *m(f)* (*-s; -/-; -nen*) ruler; sovereign, monarch; **'herrschsüchtig** *adj* domineering, F bossy

'herrühren *v/i* (*sep, -ge-, h*) ~ **von** come from, be due to

'herstellen *v/t* (*sep, -ge-, h*) make, produce; *fig* establish; **Herstellung** *f* (*-; no pl*) production; *fig* establishment; **'Herstellungskosten** *pl* production cost(s)

herüber [hɛ'ry:bɐ] *adv* over (here), across

herum [hɛ'rʊm] *adv* (a)round; F **anders** ~ the other way round; **~führen** *v/t* (*sep, -ge-, h*) **j-n** (**in der Stadt** *etc*) ~ show *s.o.*

(a)round (the town *etc*); **~kommen** F *v/i* (*irr*, **kommen**, *sep*, *-ge-*, *sein*) (*weit or viel*) **~** get around; **um et. ~** *fig* get (a)round s.th.; **~kriegen** F *v/t* (*sep*, *-ge-*, *h*) **j-n zu et. ~** get s.o. round to (do-ing) s.th.; **~lungern** F *v/i* (*sep*, *-ge-*, *h*) loaf *or* hang around; **~reichen** *v/t* (*sep*, *-ge-*, *h*) pass *or* hand round; **~sprechen** *v/refl* (*irr*, **sprechen**, *sep*, *-ge-*, *h*) get around; **~treiben** F *v/refl* (*irr*, **treiben**, *sep*, *-ge-*, *h*) gad *or* knock about

He'rumtreiber F *m* (*-s*; *-*), **He-'rumtreiberin** F *f* (*-*; *-nen*) tramp, loafer

herunter [hɛ'rʊntɐ] *adv* down; down-stairs; **~gekommen** *adj* run-down; seedy, shabby; **~hauen** F *v/t* (*sep*, *-ge-*, *h*) **j-m e-e ~** smack *or* slap s.o. ('s face); **~machen** F *v/t* (*sep*, *-ge-*, *h*) run *s.o. or s.th.* down; **~spielen** F *v/t* (*sep*, *-ge-*, *h*) play *s.th.* down

hervor [hɛɐ'foːɐ] *adv* out of *or* from, forth; **~bringen** *v/t* (*irr*, **bringen**, *sep*, *-ge-*, *h*) bring out, produce (*a. fig*); yield; utter; **~gehen** *v/i* (*irr*, **gehen**, *sep*, *-ge-*, *sein*) **~ aus** (*dat*) follow from; **als Sieger ~** come off victorious; **~heben** *v/t* (*irr*, **heben**, *sep*, *-ge-*, *h*) stress, emphasize; **~ragend** *adj* outstanding, excellent, superior; prominent, emi-nent; **~rufen** *v/t* (*irr*, **rufen**, *sep*, *-ge-*, *h*) cause, bring about; create; **~ste-chend** *adj* striking; **~tretend** *adj* prom-inent; protruding, bulging; **~tun** *v/refl* (*irr*, **tun**, *sep*, *-ge-*, *h*) distinguish o.s. (**als** as)

Herz [hɛrts] *n* (*-ens*; *-en*) ANAT heart (*a. fig*); *cards*: heart(s); **j-m das ~ brechen** break s.o.'s heart; **sich ein ~ fassen** take heart; **mit ganzem ~en** whole-heartedly; **schweren ~ens** with a heavy heart; **sich et. zu ~en nehmen** take s.th. to heart; **es nicht übers ~ bringen zu** *inf* not have the heart to *inf*; **et. auf dem ~en haben** have s.th. on one's mind; **ins ~ schließen** take to one's heart; **~anfall** *m* heart attack

'Herzens|lust *f*: **nach ~** to one's heart's content; **~wunsch** *m* heart's desire, dearest wish

'Herzfehler *m* cardiac defect

'herzhaft *adj* hearty; savo(u)ry

'herzig *adj* sweet, lovely, cute

'Herz|in,farkt *m* MED cardiac infarct

(-ion), F *mst* heart attack, coronary; **~klopfen** *n* (*-s*; *no pl*) palpitation; **er hatte ~** (*vor dat*) his heart was throb-bing (with)

'herzkrank *adj* suffering from (a) heart disease

'herzlich 1. *adj* cordial, hearty; warm, friendly **2.** *adv*: **~ gern** with pleasure

'herzlos *adj* heartless

Herzog ['hɛrtsoːk] *m* (*-s*; *Herzöge* ['hɛrtsøːgə]) duke; **Herzogin** ['hɛrt-soːgɪn] *f* (*-*; *-nen*) duchess

'Herz|schlag *m* heartbeat; MED heart failure; **~schrittmacher** *m* MED (cardi-ac) pacemaker; **~transplantati,on** *f* MED heart transplant

'herzzerreißend *adj* heart-rending

heterosexuell [heterozɛksʊ'ɛl] *adj* het-erosexual

Hetze ['hɛtsə] *f* (*-*; *no pl*) hurry, rush; POL *etc* agitation, campaign(ing) (**gegen** against); **'hetzen 1.** *v/t* (*ge-*, *h*) rush; ZO hunt, chase; **e-n Hund auf j-n ~** set a dog on s.o. **2.** *v/i* (*ge-*, *sein*) hurry, rush; (*ge-*, *h*) POL *etc* agitate (**gegen** against); **'hetzerisch** *adj* inflam-matory; **'Hetzjagd** *f* hunt(ing), chase (*a. fig*); *fig* rush; **'Hetzkam,pagne** *f* POL smear campaign

Heu [hɔy] *n* (*-[e]s*; *no pl*) hay

'Heuboden *m* hayloft

Heuchelei [hɔyçə'lai] *f* (*-*; *-en*) hypocri-sy; cant; **heucheln** ['hɔyçəln] *v/i and v/t* (*ge-*, *h*) feign, simulate; **Heuch-ler(in)** ['hɔyçlɐ (-lərɪn)] (*-s*; *-/-*; *-nen*) hypocrite; **heuchlerisch** ['hɔyçlərɪʃ] *adj* hypocritical

heuer ['hɔyɐ] *Austrian adv* this year

Heuer ['hɔyɐ] *f* (*-*; *-n*) MAR pay; **'heuern** *v/t* (*ge-*, *h*) hire, MAR *a.* sign on

heulen ['hɔylən] *v/i* (*ge-*, *h*) howl; F *contp* bawl; MOT roar; *siren*: whine

'Heuschnupfen *m* MED hay fever

'Heuschrecke *f* (*-*; *-n*) ZO grasshopper; locust

heute ['hɔytə] *adv* today; **~ Abend** this evening, tonight; **~ früh**, **~ Morgen** this morning; **~ in acht Tagen** a week from now; **~ vor acht Tagen** a week ago to-day; **heutig** ['hɔytɪç] *adj* today's; of to-day, present(-day); **'heutzutage** *adv* nowadays, these days

Hexe ['hɛksə] *f* (*-*; *-n*) witch (*a. fig*); **alte ~** (old) hag; **'hexen** *v/i* (*ge-*, *h*) practice

hing

witchcraft; F work miracles

'**Hexen|kessel** *m* inferno; **~schuss** *m* (*-es*; *no pl*) MED lumbago

hieb [hi:p] *pret of* **hauen**

Hieb [hi:p] *m* (*-[e]s*; *-e* ['hi:bə]) blow, stroke; punch; lash, cut; *pl* beating; thrashing

hielt [hi:lt] *pret of* **halten**

hier [hi:ɐ] *adv* here, in this place; present; **~ entlang!** this way!

hieran ['hi:'ran] *adv* from *or* in this; **hierauf** ['hi:'rauf] *adv* on it *or* this; after this, then; **hieraus** ['hi:'raus] *adv* from *or* out of this; '**hier'bei** *adv* here, in this case; on this occasion; '**hier'durch** *adv* by this, hereby, this way; '**hier'für** *adv* for this; '**hier'her** *adv* (over) here, this way; **bis~** so far; **hierin** ['hi:'rɪn] *adv* in this; '**hier'mit** *adv* with this; '**hier'nach** *adv* after this; according to this; **hierüber** ['hi:'ry:bɐ] *adv* about this (subject); **hierunter** ['hi:'rʊntɐ] *adv* under this; among these; *understand etc* by this *or* that; '**hier'von** *adv* of *or* from this; '**hier'zu** *adv* for this; to this

hiesig ['hi:zɪç] *adj* local; **ein Hiesiger** one of the locals

hieß [hi:s] *pret of* **heißen**

Hilfe ['hɪlfə] *f* (*-*; *-n*) help; aid (*a.* ECON), assistance (*a.* MED), relief (*für* to); **Erste ~** first aid; **um ~ rufen** cry for help; **~!** help!; → **mithilfe**; **~me,nü** *n* IT help menu; **~ruf** *m* call (*or* cry) for help; **~stellung** *f* support (*a. fig*)

'**hilf|los** *adj* helpless; **~reich** *adj* helpful

'**Hilfsakti,on** *f* relief action

'**Hilfsarbeiter** *m*, '**Hilfsarbeiterin** *f* unskilled worker

'**hilfsbedürftig** *adj* needy

'**hilfsbereit** *adj* helpful, ready to help; '**Hilfsbereitschaft** *f* (*-*; *no pl*) readiness to help, helpfulness

'**Hilfs|mittel** *n* aid, TECH *a.* device; **~organisati,on** *f* relief organization; **~verb** *n* LING auxiliary (verb)

Himbeere ['hɪmbe:rə] *f* BOT raspberry

Himmel ['hɪməl] *m* (*-s*; *-*) sky; REL heaven (*a. fig*); **um ~s willen** for Heaven's sake; → **heiter**

'**Himmelfahrt** REL Ascension (Day)

'**Himmels|körper** *m* AST celestial body; **~richtung** *f* direction; cardinal point

himmlisch ['hɪmlɪʃ] *adj* heavenly, *fig a.* marvel(l)ous

hin [hɪn] **1.** *adv* there; **bis ~ zu** as far as; **noch lange ~** still a long way off; **auf s-e Bitte (s-n Rat) ~** at his request (advice); **~ und her** to and fro, back and forth; **~ und wieder** now and then; **~ und zurück** there and back; RAIL round trip, round-trip ticket, *esp Br* return (ticket) **2.** F *pred adj* ruined; done for; gone

hi'nab *adv* → **hinunter**

'**hinarbeiten** *v/i* (*sep*, *-ge-*, *h*) **~ auf** (*acc*) work towards

hi'nauf *adv* up (there); upstairs; **die Straße** *etc* **~** up the street *etc*; **~gehen** *v/i* (*irr*, **gehen**, *sep*, *-ge-*, *sein*) go up, *fig a.* rise

hi'naus *adv* out; **aus ... ~** out of ...; **in** (*acc*) **... ~** out into ...; **~ (mit dir)!** (get) out!, out you go!; **~gehen** *v/i* (*irr*, **gehen**, *sep*, *-ge-*, *sein*) go out(side); **~ über** (*acc*) go beyond; **~ auf** (*acc*) window *etc*: look out onto; **~laufen** *v/i* (*irr*, **laufen**, *sep*, *-ge-*, *sein*) run out(side); **~ auf** (*acc*) come *or* amount to; **~schieben** *v/t* (*irr*, **schieben**, *sep*, *-ge-*, *h*) put off, postpone; **~stellen** *v/t* (*sep*, *-ge-*, *h*) SPORT send *s.o.* off (the field); **~werfen** *v/t* (*irr*, **werfen**, *sep*, *-ge-*, *h*) throw out (**aus** of), *fig a.* kick out; (give *s.o.* the) sack, fire; **~wollen** *v/i* (*sep*, *-ge-*, *h*) **~ auf** (*acc*) aim (*or* drive *or* get) at; **hoch ~** aim high

'**Hinblick** *m*: **im ~ auf** (*acc*) in view of, with regard to

'**hinbringen** *v/t* (*irr*, **bringen**, *sep*, *-ge-*, *h*) take there

hinderlich ['hɪndɐlɪç] *adj* hindering, impeding; **j-m ~ sein** be in *s.o.'s* way

hindern ['hɪndɐn] *v/t* (*ge-*, *h*) hinder, hamper; **~ an** (*dat*) prevent from

Hindernis ['hɪndɐnɪs] *n* (*-ses*; *-se*) obstacle (*a. fig*); **~rennen** *n* steeplechase

Hindu ['hɪndu] *m* (*-[s]*; *-[s]*) Hindu

Hinduismus [hɪndu'ɪsmʊs] *m* (*-*; *no pl*) hinduism

hin'durch *adv* through; **das ganze Jahr** *etc* **~** throughout the year *etc*

hi'nein *adv* in; **~ mit dir!** in you go!; **~gehen** *v/i* (*irr*, **gehen**, *sep*, *-ge-*, *sein*) go in; **~ in** (*acc*) go into

'**hinfallen** *v/i* (*irr*, **fallen**, *sep*, *-ge-*, *sein*) fall (down)

'**hinfällig** *adj* frail, infirm; invalid

hing [hɪŋ] *pret of* **hängen** 1

'Hingabe f (-; no pl) devotion (**an** acc to); **'hingeben** v/t (irr, **geben**, sep, -ge-, h) give (up); **sich ~** (dat) give o.s. to; devote o.s. to

'hinhalten v/t (irr, **halten**, sep, -ge-, h) hold out; **j-n ~** put s.o. off

hinken ['hɪŋkən] v/i (ge-, h) (walk with a) limp; (ge-, sein) limp

'hin|kommen v/i (irr, **kommen**, sep, -ge-, sein) get there; **~kriegen** F v/t (sep, -ge-, h) manage

'hinlänglich adj sufficient

'hin|legen v/t (sep, -ge-, h) lay or put down; **sich ~** lie down; **~nehmen** v/t (irr, **nehmen**, sep, -ge-, h) put up with

'hinreißen v/t (irr, **reißen**, sep, -ge-, h) carry away; **~d** adj entrancing; breathtaking

'hinrichten v/t (sep, -ge-, h) execute; **'Hinrichtung** f (-; -en) execution

'hinsetzen v/t (sep, -ge-, h) set or put down; **sich ~** sit down

'Hinsicht f (-; no pl) respect; **in gewisser ~** in a way; **'hinsichtlich** prp (gen) with respect or regard to

'Hinspiel n SPORT first leg

'hinstellen v/t (sep, -ge-, h) put (down); **~ als** make s.o. or s.th. appear to be

hinten ['hɪntən] adv at the back; MOT in the back; **von ~** from behind

hinter ['hɪntɐ] prp (dat) behind

'Hinter... in cpds ...achse, ...eingang, ...rad etc: rear ...; **~bein** n hind leg

Hinterbliebenen [hɪntɐ'bliːbənən] pl the bereaved; esp JUR surviving dependents

hintere'nander adv one after the other; **dreimal ~** three times in a row

'Hintergedanke m ulterior motive

hinter'gehen v/t (irr, **gehen**, no -ge-, h) deceive

'Hintergrund m background (a. fig)

'Hinterhalt m ambush; **hinterhältig** ['hɪntɐhɛltɪç] adj insidious, underhand(ed)

'Hinterhaus n rear building

hinter'her adv behind, after; afterwards

'Hinterhof m backyard

'Hinterkopf m back of the head

hinter'lassen v/t (irr, **lassen**, no -ge-, h) leave (behind); **Hinter'lassenschaft** f (-; -en) property (left), estate

hinter'legen v/t (no -ge-, h) deposit (**bei** with)

'Hinterlist f deceit(fulness); (underhanded) trick; **'hinterlistig** adj deceitful; underhand(ed)

'Hintermann m person (car etc) behind (one); fig mst pl person behind the scenes, brain(s), mastermind

'Hintern F m (-s; -) bottom, backside, behind, Br bum

hinterrücks ['hɪntɐryks] adv from behind

'Hinter|seite f back; **~teil** F n → **Hintern**; **~treppe** f back stairs; **~tür** f back door

hinter'ziehen v/t (irr, **ziehen**, no -ge-, h) evade (taxes)

'Hinterzimmer n back room

hi'nüber adv over, across; **~ sein** F be ruined; GASTR be spoilt

hi'nunter adv down; downstairs; **die Straße ~** down the road

Hinweg ['hɪnveːk] m way there

hinweg [hɪn'vɛk] adv: **über** (acc) ... **~** over ...; **~kommen** v/i (irr, **kommen** sep, -ge-, sein) **~ über** (acc) get over; **~sehen** v/i (irr, **sehen**, sep, -ge-, h) **~ über** (acc) ignore; **~setzen** v/refl (sep, -ge-, h) **sich ~ über** (acc) ignore, disregard

Hinweis ['hɪnvais] m (-es; -e) reference (**auf** acc to); hint, tip (as to, regarding); indication (of), clue (as to); **'hinweisen** (irr, **weisen**, sep, -ge-, h) **1.** v/t: **j-n ~ auf** (acc) draw or call s.o.'s attention to **2.** v/i: **~ auf** (acc) point at or to, indicate; fig point out, indicate; hint at

'Hinweis|schild n, **~tafel** f sign, notice

'hin|werfen v/t (irr, **werfen**, sep, -ge-, h) throw down; **~ziehen** v/refl (irr, **ziehen**, sep, -ge-, h) extend (**bis zu** to), stretch (to); drag on

hin'zu|fügen v/t (sep, -ge-, h) add (**zu** to) (a. fig); **~kommen** v/i (irr, **kommen**, sep, -ge-, sein) be added; **hinzu kommt, dass** add to this ..., and what is more, ...; **~ziehen** v/t (irr, **ziehen**, sep, -ge-, h) call in, consult

Hirn [hɪrn] n (-[e]s; -e) ANAT brain; fig brain(s), mind; **~gespinst** n fantasy

Hirsch [hɪrʃ] m (-[e]s; -e) ZO stag; **~geweih** n ZO antlers; **~kuh** f ZO hind

Hirse ['hɪrzə] f (-; -n) BOT millet

Hirte ['hɪrtə] m (-n; -n) herdsman; shepherd (a. fig)

hissen ['hɪsən] v/t (ge-, h) hoist

Historiker [hɪs'toːrikɐ] *m* (*-s*; *-*), **His-**
'torikerin *f* (*-*; *-nen*) historian; **his-**
'torisch *adj* historical; historic (*event*
etc)

Hitliste ['hɪtlɪstə] *f* top 40 *etc*, charts

Hitze ['hɪtsə] *f* (*-*; *no pl*) heat

'Hitzewelle *f* heat wave

'hitzig *adj* hot-tempered, peppery; heated (*debate etc*)

'Hitzkopf *m* hothead

'Hitzschlag *m* MED heatstroke

HIV|-negativ [haː?iːfauˈneːgatiːf] *adj*
MED HIV negative; **~-positiv** *adj* MED
HIV positive; **~-Positive** *m*, *f* (*-n*; *-n*)
MED HIV carrier

H-Milch ['haːmɪlç] *f Br* long-life milk

hob [hoːp] *pret of* **heben**

Hobby ['hɔbi] *n* (*-s*; *-s*) hobby

'Hobby... *in cpds* amateur ...

Hobel ['hoːbəl] *m* (*-s*; *-*) TECH plane

'Hobelbank *f* (*-*; *-bänke*) TECH carpenter's bench

'hobeln *v/t* (*ge-*, *h*) TECH plane

hoch [hoːx] *adj and adv* high; tall; *fig*
heavy (*fine etc*); distinguished (*guest*);
great, old (*age*); deep (*snow*); **10 ~ 4**
MATH 10 to the power of 4; **3000 Meter**
~ *fly etc* at an altitude of 3,000 meters;
in hohem Maße highly, greatly; **~** *ver-*
schuldet heavily in debt; F *das ist mir*
zu ~ that's above me

Hoch *n* (*-s*; *-s*) METEOR high (*a. fig*)

'Hochachtung *f* (deep) respect (*vor dat*
for); **'hochachtungsvoll** *adv* Yours
sincerely

'Hoch|bau *m* (*-[e]s*; *no pl*) **Hoch- und**
Tiefbau structural and civil engineering; **~betrieb** F *m* (*-[e]s*; *no pl*) rush

'hochdeutsch *adj* High *or* standard
German

'Hoch|druck *m* high pressure (*a. fig*);
~ebene *f* plateau, tableland; **~form** *f*:
in ~ in top form *or* shape; **~fre,quenz**
f ELECTR high frequency; **~gebirge** *n*
high mountains; **~genuss** *m* real treat

'hochgezüchtet *adj* ZO, TECH highbred,
TECH *a.* sophisticated; MOT tuned up, F
souped up

hochhackig ['hoːxhakɪç] *adj* high-
-heeled

'Hoch|haus *n* high rise, tower block;
~konjunk,tur *f* ECON boom; **~land** *n*
highlands; **~leistungs...** *in cpds*
...*sport etc*: high-performance ...

'Hochmut *m* arrogance; **hochmütig**
['hoːxmyːtɪç] *adj* arrogant

'Hochofen *m* TECH blast furnace

'hochpro,zentig *adj* high-proof

'Hoch|rechnung *f* projection; POL com-
puter prediction; **~sai,son** *f* peak (*or*
height of the) season; **~schulab-**
schluss *m* degree; **~schulausbildung**
f higher education; **~schule** *f* university; college; academy; **~seefischerei** *f*
deep-sea fishing; **~sommer** *m* mid-
summer; **~spannung** *f* ELECTR high
tension (*a. fig*) *or* voltage; **~sprung**
m SPORT high jump

höchst [høːçst] **1.** *adj* highest, *fig a.* supreme; extreme **2.** *adv* highly, most, extremely; **'Höchst...** *in cpds mst* maximum ..., top ...

Hochstapler ['hoːxʃtaːplɐ] *m* (*-s*; *-*),
'Hochstaplerin *f* (*-*; *-nen*) impostor,
swindler

'höchstens *adv* at (the) most, at best

'Höchst|form *f* SPORT top form *or* shape;
~geschwindigkeit *f* top speed (*mit* at);
speed limit; **~leistung** *f* SPORT record
(performance); TECH maximum out-
put; **~maß** *n* maximum (*an an* of)

'höchstwahr'scheinlich *adv* most
likely *or* probably

'Hochtechnolo,gie *f* high technology,
hi tech

'hochtrabend *adj* pompous

'Hochverrat *m* high treason

'Hochwasser *n* high tide; flood

hochwertig ['hoːxveːɐtɪç] *adj* high-
-grade, high-quality

Hochzeit ['hɔxtsait] *f* (*-*; *-en*) wedding

'Hochzeits... *in cpds* ...*geschenk*,
...*kleid*, ...*tag etc*: wedding ...; **~reise**
f honeymoon

Hocke ['hɔkə] *f* (*-*; *-n*) crouch, squat

'hocken *v/i* (*ge-*, *h*) squat, crouch; F sit

Hocker ['hɔkɐ] *m* (*-s*; *-*) stool

Höcker ['hœkɐ] *m* (*-s*; *-*) ZO hump

Hockey ['hɔki] *n* (*-s*; *no pl*) SPORT field
hockey, *Br* hockey

Hoden ['hoːdən] *m* (*-s*; *-*) ANAT testicle

Hof [hoːf] *m* (*-[e]s*; *Höfe* ['høːfə]) yard;
AGR farm; court(yard); court; **~dame** *f*
lady-in-waiting

hoffen ['hɔfən] *v/i and v/t* (*ge-*, *h*) hope
(*auf acc* for); trust (in); *das Beste ~*
hope for the best; *ich hoffe es* I hope
so; *ich hoffe nicht, ich will es nicht ~* I

hope not; '**hoffentlich** *adv* I hope, let's hope, hopefully; '**Hoffnung** *f* (-; *-en*) hope (*auf acc* of); *sich ~en machen* have hopes; *die ~ aufgeben* lose hope

'**hoffnungslos** *adj* hopeless

'**hoffnungsvoll** *adj* hopeful; promising

höflich ['høːflɪç] *adj* polite, courteous (*zu* to); '**Höflichkeit** *f* (-; *no pl*) politeness, courtesy

Höhe ['høːə] *f* (-; *-n*) height; AVIAT, MATH, ASTR, GEOGR altitude; peak (*a. fig*); *fig* amount; level; extent (*of damage etc*); MUS pitch; *auf gleicher ~ mit* on a level with; *in die ~* up; F *ich bin nicht ganz auf der ~* I'm not feeling up to the mark

Hoheit ['hoːhait] *f* (-; *no pl*) POL sovereignty; Highness

'**Hoheits|gebiet** *n* territory; *~gewässer pl* territorial waters; *~zeichen* *n* national emblem

'**Höhen|luft** *f* mountain air; *~messer* *m* altimeter; *~ruder* *n* AVIAT elevator; *~sonne®* *f* MED ultraviolet lamp, sunlamp; *~zug* *m* mountain chain

'**Höhepunkt** *m* climax, culmination, height, peak; highlight

hohl [hoːl] *adj* hollow (*a. fig*)

Höhle ['høːlə] *f* (-; *-n*) cave, cavern; ZO hole, burrow; den, lair

'**Hohl|maß** *n* measure of capacity; *~raum* *m* hollow, cavity; *~spiegel* *m* concave mirror

Hohn [hoːn] *m* (-[*e*]*s*; *no pl*) derision, scorn; '**Hohngelächter** *n* jeers, jeering laughter; **höhnisch** ['høːnɪʃ] *adj* derisive, scornful; *~es Lächeln* sneer

holen ['hoːlən] *v/t* (*ge-*, *h*) (go and) get, fetch, go for; draw (*breath*); call (*s.o., the police etc*); *~ lassen* send for; *sich ~* catch, get (*a cold etc*); seek (*advice*)

Holland ['hɔlant] Holland, *the* Netherlands; **Holländer** ['hɔlɛndɐ] *m* (-*s*; -) Dutchman; **Hol'länderin** ['hɔlɛndərɪn] *f* (-; *-nen*) Dutchwoman; '**holländisch** *adj* Dutch

Hölle ['hœlə] *f* (-; *no pl*) hell

'**Höllenlärm** F *m* a hell of a noise

Holler ['hɔlɐ] *Austrian m* (-*s*; -) BOT elder

höllisch ['hœlɪʃ] *adj* infernal, F hellish

holperig ['hɔlpərɪç] *adj* bumpy (*a. fig*), rough, uneven; *fig* clumsy (*style etc*)

holpern ['hɔlpɐn] *v/i* (*ge-*, *sein*) jolt, bump; *fig* be bumpy

Holunder [hoˈlʊndɐ] *m* (-*s*; -) BOT elder

Holz [hɔlts] *n* (-*es*; *Hölzer* ['hœltsɐ]) wood; lumber, Br *a.* timber; *aus ~* (made) of wood, wooden; *~ hacken* chop wood; *~blasinstru‚ment* *n* MUS woodwind (instrument)

hölzern ['hœltsɐn] *adj* wooden, *fig a.* clumsy

'**Holz|fäller** ['hɔltsfɛlɐ] *m* (-*s*; -) woodcutter, lumberjack; *~hammer* *m* mallet; *fig* sledgehammer

holzig ['hɔltsɪç] *adj* woody; stringy

'**Holz|kohle** *f* charcoal; *~schnitt* *m* woodcut; *~schnitzer* *m* wood carver; *~schuh* *m* clog; *~weg* *fig m*: *auf dem ~ sein* be barking up the wrong tree; *~wolle* *f* wood shavings, excelsior; *~wurm* *m* ZO woodworm

homöopathisch [homøoˈpaːtɪʃ] *adj* hom(o)eopathic

homosexuell [homozɛˈksuɛl] *adj* homosexual

Honig ['hoːnɪç] *m* (-*s*; *-e*) honey

'**Honigwabe** *f* honeycomb

Honorar [honoˈraːr] *n* (-*s*; *-e*) fee

honorieren [honoˈriːrən] *v/t* (*no -ge-*, *h*) pay (a fee to); *fig* appreciate, reward

Hopfen ['hɔpfən] *m* (-*s*; -) BOT hop; *brewing*: hops

hoppla ['hɔpla] *int* (wh)oops!

hopsen ['hɔpsən] F *v/i* (*ge-*, *sein*) hop, jump

Hörappa‚rat ['høːrɛʔaparaːt] *m* hearing aid

hörbar ['høːrbaːr] *adj* audible

horchen ['hɔrçən] *v/i* (*ge-*, *h*) listen (*auf acc* to); eavesdrop; **Horcher** ['hɔrçɐ] *m* (-*s*; -) eavesdropper

Horde ['hɔrdə] *f* (-; *-n*) horde (*a.* ZO), *contp a.* mob, gang

hören ['høːrən] *v/i and v/t* (*ge-*, *h*) hear; listen to; obey, listen; *~ auf* (*acc*) listen to; *von j-m ~* hear from (*or* of, about) s.o.; *er hört schwer* his hearing is bad; *hör(t) mal!* listen!; look (here)!; *nun or also hör(t) mal!* wait a minute!, now look *or* listen here!; **Hörer** ['høːrɐ] *m* (-*s*; -) listener; TEL receiver; '**Hörerin** ['høːrərɪn] *f* (-; *-nen*) listener

'**Hör|fehler** ['høːrɛfeːlɐ] *m* MED hearing defect; *~gerät* *n* hearing aid

hörig ['høːrɪç] *adj*: *j-m ~ sein* be s.o.'s slave

Horizont [horiˈtsɔnt] *m* (-[*e*]*s*; *-e*) horizon (a. fig); **s-n ~ erweitern** broaden one's mind; **das geht über meinen ~** that's beyond me; **horizontal** [horitsɔn'taːl] adj horizontal

Hormon [hɔr'moːn] n (-s; -e) hormone

Horn [hɔrn] n (-[e]s; Hörner ['hœrnə]) horn; **~haut** f horny skin, callus(es); ANAT cornea

Hornisse [hɔr'nisə] f (-; -n) ZO hornet

Horoskop [horo'skoːp] n (-s; -e) horoscope

Hör|rohr ['høːˌɾoːɐ] n MED stethoscope; **~saal** m lecture hall, auditorium; **~spiel** n radio play; **~weite** f: **in (au-ßer) ~** within (out of) earshot

Höschen ['høːsçən] n (-s; -) panties

Hose ['hoːzə] f (-; -n) (**e-e ~** a pair of) pants, Br trousers; slacks; shorts

'Hosen|anzug m pants (Br trouser) suit; **~schlitz** m fly; **~tasche** f trouser pocket; **~träger** pl (a pair of) suspenders or Br braces

Hospital [hɔspi'taːl] n (-s; -täler [hɔspi-'tɛːlɐ]) hospital

Hostie ['hɔstjə] f (-; -n) REL host

Hotel [ho'tɛl] n (-s; -s) hotel; **~di,rektor** m hotel manager; **~fach** n (-[e]s; no pl) hotel business; **~zimmer** n hotel room

HP abbr of **Halbpension** half-board

Hr(n). abbr of **Herrn** Mr

Hubraum ['huːpraum] m MOT cubic capacity

hübsch [hypʃ] adj pretty, nice (-looking), cute; fig nice, lovely

Hubschrauber ['huːpʃraubɐ] m (-s; -) helicopter; **~landeplatz** m heliport

Huf [huːf] m (-[e]s; -e) ZO hoof

'Hufeisen n horseshoe

Hüfte ['hyftə] f (-; -n) ANAT hip

'Hüftgelenk n ANAT hip joint

'Hüftgürtel m girdle

Hügel ['hyːgəl] m (-s; -) hill; **'hügelig** adj hilly; **'Hügelland** n downs

Huhn [huːn] n (-[e]s; Hühner ['hyːnɐ]) ZO chicken; hen; **Hühnchen** ['hyːnçən] n (-s; -) chicken; F **mit j-m ein ~ zu rup-fen haben** have a bone to pick with s.o.

'Hühner|auge n MED corn; **~brühe** f chicken broth; **~ei** n hen's egg; **~farm** f poultry or chicken farm; **~hof** m poultry or chicken yard; **~leiter** f chicken ladder; **~stall** m henhouse

huldigen ['huldɪgən] v/i (ge-, h) pay homage to; fig indulge in

Hülle ['hylə] f (-; -n) cover(ing), wrap (-ping); jacket, Br sleeve; sheath; **in ~ und Fülle** in abundance; **'hüllen** v/t (ge-, h) **~ in** (acc) wrap (up) in, cover in

Hülse ['hylzə] f (-; -n) BOT pod; husk; TECH case; **'Hülsenfrüchte** pl pulse

human [hu'maːn] adj humane

humanitär [humani'tɛːɐ] adj humanitarian; **Humanität** [humani'tɛːt] f (-; no pl) humanity

Hummel ['huməl] f (-; -n) ZO bumblebee

Hummer ['humɐ] m (-s; -) ZO lobster

Humor [hu'moːɐ] m (-s; no pl) humo(u)r; (**keinen**) **~ haben** have a (no) sense of humo(u)r; **Humorist** [humo'rɪst] m (-en; -en) humorist; **humo'ristisch, hu'morvoll** adj humorous

humpeln ['humpəln] v/i (ge-, h) hobble; (ge-, sein) limp

Hund [hunt] m (-[e]s; -e) ZO dog

Hunde|hütte ['hundəhytə] f doghouse, Br kennel; **~kuchen** m dog biscuit; **~leine** f lead, leash

'hunde'müde adj dog-tired

hundert ['hundɐt] adj a or one hundred; **zu hunderten** by the hundreds

'hundertfach adj hundredfold

Hundert'jahrfeier f centenary, centennial; **hundertjährig** ['hundɐtjɛːrɪç] adj a hundred years old; a hundred years of

'hundertste adj hundredth

Hündin ['hyndɪn] f (-; -nen) ZO bitch

hündisch ['hyndɪʃ] adj doglike, slavish

Hüne ['hyːnə] m (-n; -n) giant

'Hünengrab n dolmen

Hunger ['huŋɐ] m (-s; no pl) hunger; **~ bekommen** get hungry; **~ haben** be hungry; **vor ~ sterben** die of starvation, starve to death

'Hungerlohn m starvation wages

'hungern v/i (ge-, h) go hungry, starve

'Hungersnot f famine

'Hungerstreik m hunger strike

'Hungertod m (death from) starvation

hungrig ['huŋrɪç] adj hungry (**nach, auf** acc for)

Hupe ['huːpə] f (-; -n) MOT horn

'hupen v/i (ge-, h) MOT sound one's horn, hoot, honk

hüpfen ['hypfən] v/i (ge, sein) hop, skip; ball etc: bounce

Hürde ['hyrdə] f (-; -n) hurdle, fig a. obstacle; zo fold, pen

'Hürdenlauf *m* SPORT hurdles

'Hürdenläufer *m*, **'Hürdenläuferin** *f*
SPORT hurdler

Hure ['huːrə] *f* (-; *-n*) whore, prostitute

huschen ['huʃən] *v/i* (*ge-, sein*) flit, dart

hüsteln ['hyːstəln] *v/i* (*ge-, h*) cough
slightly; *iro* hem; **husten** ['huːstən]
v/i (*ge-, h*), **'Husten** *m* (*-s; no pl*) cough

'Husten|bon,bon *m*, *n* cough drop;
~saft *m* PHARM cough syrup

Hut¹ [huːt] *m* (-[*e*]*s; Hüte* ['hyːtə]) hat;
den ~ aufsetzen (*abnehmen*) put on
(take off) one's hat

Hut² *f: auf der ~ sein* be on one's guard
(*vor dat* against)

hüten ['hyːtən] *v/t* (*ge-, h*) guard, protect, watch over; zo herd, mind; look
after; *das Bett ~* be confined to (one's)
bed; *sich ~ vor* (*dat*) beware of; *sich ~,
et. zu tun* be careful not to do s.th.

'Hutkrempe *f* (hat) brim

hutschen ['huːtʃən] *Austrian v/t and v/i*
→ *schaukeln*

Hütte ['hyːtə] *f* (-; *-n*) hut; *contp* shack;

cottage, cabin; mountain hut; TECH
ironworks

Hyäne ['hyːnə] *f* (-; *-n*) zo hy(a)ena

Hyazinthe [hya'tsɪntə] *f* (-; *-n*) BOT hya-
cinth

Hydrant [hy'drant] *m* (*-en; -en*) hydrant

hydraulisch [hy'draulɪʃ] *adj* hydraulic

Hydrokultur ['hyːdrokʊltuːɐ] *f* hydro-
ponics

Hygiene [hy'gjeːnə] *f* (-; *no pl*) hygiene

hygienisch [hy'gjeːnɪʃ] *adj* hygienic

Hypnose [hyp'noːzə] *f* (-; *-n*) hypnosis;
Hypnotiseur [hypnoti'zøːɐ] *m* (*-s; -e*)
hypnotist; **hypnotisieren** [hypnoti-
'ziːrən] *v/t* (*no -ge-, h*) hypnotize

Hypotenuse [hypote'nuːzə] *f* (-; *-n*)
MATH hypotenuse

Hypothek [hypo'teːk] *f* (-; *-en*) ECON
mortgage; *e-e ~ aufnehmen* take out
a mortgage

Hypothese [hypo'teːzə] *f* (-; *-n*) hypoth-
esis, supposition; **hypothetisch** [hypo-
'teːtɪʃ] *adj* hypothetical

Hysterie [hyste'riː] *f* (-; *-n*) hysteria

hysterisch [hys'teːrɪʃ] *adj* hysterical

I

i. A. *abbr of im Auftrag* p. p., per proc-
uration

ICE® [iːtseː'ʔeː] *abbr of Intercityex-
presszug* intercity express (train)

ich [ɪç] *pers pron* I; *~ selbst* (I) myself; *~
bin's* it's me

ideal [ide'aːl] *adj*, **Ide'al** *n* (*-s; -e*) ideal;
Idealismus [idea'lɪsmʊs] *m* (-; *no pl*)
idealism; **Idea'list(in)** (*-en; -en/-;
-nen*) idealist

Idee [i'deː] *f* (-; *-n*) idea

identifizieren [identifi'tsiːrən] *v/t* (*no
-ge-, h*) identify; *sich ~ mit* identify
with; **identisch** [i'dɛntɪʃ] *adj* identical

Identitätskarte [idɛntiˈtɛːtskartə] *Austrian f* identity card

Ideologe [ideo'loːgə] *m* (*-n; -n*) ideolo-
gist; **Ideologie** [ideolo'giː] *f* (-; *-n*) ide-
ology; **ideo'logisch** *adj* ideological

idiomatisch [idio'maːtɪʃ] *adj* LING idio-
matic; *~er Ausdruck* idiom

Idiot [i'djoːt] *m* (*-en; -en*) idiot

Idi'otenhügel F *m* skiing: nursery slope

idi'otisch *adj* idiotic

Idol [i'doːl] *n* (*-s; -e*) idol

Idyll [i'dyl] *n* (*-s; -e*), **I'dylle** *f* (-; *-n*)
idyl(l); **i'dyllisch** *adj* idyllic

Igel ['iːgəl] *m* (*-s; -*) zo hedgehog

Iglu ['iːglu] *m* (*-s; -s*) igloo

ignorieren [ɪgno'riːrən] *v/t* (*no -ge-, h*)
ignore, disregard

i. H. *abbr of im Hause* on the premises

ihr [iːɐ] *poss pron* her; *pl* their; *Ihr* your;
ihrerseits ['iːrɐzaits] *adv* on her (*pl*
their) part; **ihresgleichen** ['iːrəsglai-
çən] *indef pron* her (*pl* their) equals,
people like herself (*pl* themselves); **ih-
retwegen** ['iːrətveːgən] *adv* for her (*pl*
their) sake

Ikone [i'koːnə] *f* (-; *-n*) icon

illegal ['ɪlegaːl] *adj* JUR illegal

illegitim [ɪlegi'tiːm] *adj* JUR illegitimate

Illusion [ɪlu'zjoːn] *f* (-; *-en*) illusion

illusorisch [ɪlu'zoːrɪʃ] *adj* illusory

Illustration [ɪlustra'tsjoːn] *f* (-; *-en*) illustration; **illustrieren** [ɪlus'triːrən]

v/t (*no* -ge-, *h*) illustrate; **Illustrierte** [ɪlʊs'triːɐtə] *f* (-*n*; -*n*) magazine

im [ɪm] *prep in the*; ~ **Bett** in bed; ~ **Kino** *etc* at the cinema *etc*; ~ **Erdgeschoss** on the first (*Br* ground) floor; ~ **Mai** in May; ~ **Jahre 1997** in (the year) 1997; ~ **Stehen** (while) standing up; → **in**

imaginär [imagi'nɛːɐ] *adj* imaginary

Imbiss ['ɪmbɪs] *m* (-*es*; -*e*) snack

'Imbissstube *f* snack bar

imitieren [imi'tiːrən] *v/t* (*no* -ge-, *h*) imitate

Imker ['ɪmkɐ] *m* (-*s*; -) beekeeper

immatrikulieren [ɪmatriku'liːrən] *v/t and v/refl* (*no* -ge-, *h*) UNIV enrol(l), register

immer ['ɪmɐ] *adv* always, all the time; ~ **mehr** more and more; ~ **wieder** again and again; **für** ~ for ever, for good

'Immergrün *n* BOT evergreen

'immer'hin *adv* after all

'immer'zu *adv* all the time, constantly

Immigrant [ɪmi'grant] *m* (-*en*; -*en*), **Immi'grantin** *f* (-; -*nen*) immigrant

Immissionen [ɪmi'sjoːnən] *pl* (harmful effects of) noise, pollutants *etc*

Immobilien [ɪmo'biːliən] *pl* real estate; ~**makler** *m* realtor, real estate agent

immun [ɪ'muːn] *adj* immune (**gegen** to, against, from); ~ **machen** → **immunisieren** [ɪmuni'ziːrən] *v/t* (*no* -ge-, *h*) immunize; **Immunität** [ɪmuni'tɛːt] *f* (-; *no pl*) immunity; **Im'munschwäche** *f* (-; -*n*) MED immunodeficiency; **Im'munsystem** *n* (-*s*; -*e*) MED immune system

Imperativ ['ɪmperatiːf] *m* (-*s*; -*e*) LING imperative (mood)

Imperfekt ['ɪmpɛrfɛkt] *n* (-*s*; -*e*) LING past (tense)

Imperialismus [ɪmperja'lɪsmʊs] *m* (-; *no pl*) imperialism; **Imperialist** [ɪmperja'lɪst] *m* (-*en*; -*en*), **imperia'listisch** *adj* imperialist

impfen ['ɪmpfən] *v/t* (ge-, *h*) MED vaccinate

'Impf|pass *m* MED vaccination card; ~**schein** *m* MED vaccination certificate; ~**stoff** *m* MED vaccine, serum

'Impfung *f* (-; -*en*) MED vaccination

imponieren [ɪmpo'niːrən] *v/i* (*no* -ge-, *h*) **j-m** ~ impress s.o.

Import [ɪm'pɔrt] *m* (-[*e*]*s*; -*e*) ECON import(ation); **Importeur** [ɪmpɔr'tøːɐ] *m* (-*s*; -*e*) ECON importer; **importieren** [ɪmpɔr'tiːrən] *v/t* (*no* -ge-, *h*) ECON import

imposant [impo'zant] *adj* impressive, imposing

imprägnieren [ɪmprɛ'gniːrən] *v/t* (*no* -ge-, *h*), **imprägniert** [ɪmprɛ'gniːɐt] *adj* waterproof

improvisieren [ɪmprovi'ziːrən] *v/t and v/i* (*no* -ge-, *h*) improvise

Impuls [ɪm'pʊls] *m* (-*es*; -*e*) impulse; stimulus

impulsiv [ɪmpʊl'ziːf] *adj* impulsive

imstande [ɪm'ʃtandə] *adj*: ~ **sein zu** *inf* be capable of *ger*

in [ɪn] *prp* (*dat and acc*) **1.** in, at; within, inside; into, in; **überall** ~ all over; ~ **der Stadt** in town; ~ **der Schule** at school; ~ **die Schule** to school; ~**s Kino** to the cinema; ~**s Bett** to bed; **warst du schon mal** ~ **...?** have you ever been to ...?; → **im 2.** in, at, during; ~ **dieser** (**der nächsten**) **Woche** this (next) week; ~ **diesem Alter** (**Augenblick**) at this age (moment); ~ **der Nacht** at night; **heute** ~ **acht Tagen** a week from now; **heute** ~ **e-m Jahr** this time next year; → **im 3.** in, at; **gut sein** ~ (*dat*) be good at; ~ **Eile** in a hurry; ~ **Behandlung** (**Reparatur**) under treatment (repair); ~**s Deutsche** into German; → **im 4.** F ~ **sein** be in

'Inbegriff *m* epitome

'inbegriffen *adj* ECON included

in'dem *cj* while, as; by doing *s.th.*

Inder ['ɪndɐ] *m* (-*s*; -), **Inderin** ['ɪndərɪn] *f* (-; -*nen*) Indian

Indian ['ɪndjaːn] *Austrian m* (-*s*; -*e*) ZO turkey (cock)

Indianer [ɪn'djaːnɐ] *m* (-*s*; -), **Indianerin** [ɪn'djaːnərɪn] *f* (-; -*nen*) Native American, (American) Indian

Indien ['ɪndjən] India

Indikativ ['ɪndikatiːf] *m* (-*s*; -*e*) LING indicative (mood)

indirekt ['ɪndirɛkt] *adj* indirect, LING *a*. reported

indisch ['ɪndɪʃ] *adj* Indian

indiskret ['ɪndɪskreːt] *adj* indiscreet

Indiskretion [ɪndɪskre'tsjoːn] *f* (-; -*en*) indiscretion

indiskutabel [ɪndɪsku'taːbəl] *adj* out of the question

individuell [ɪndivi'duɛl] *adj*, **Individu-um** [ɪndi'vi:duɒm] *n* (-s; -en) individual

indiz [ɪn'di:ts] *n* (-es; -ien) indication, sign; *pl* JUR circumstantial evidence

industrialisieren [ɪndʊstriali'zi:rən] *v/t* (*no* -ge-, *h*) industrialize; **Industriali'sierung** *f* (-; *no pl*) industrialization

Industrie [ɪndʊs'tri:] *f* (-; -n) industry

Indus'triegebiet *n* industrial area

industriell [ɪndʊstri'ɛl] *adj* industrial

Industri'elle *m* (-n; -n) industrialist

inei'nander *adv* into one another; **~ verliebt** in love with each other; **~ greifen** *v/t* (*irr*, **greifen**, *sep*, -ge-, *h*) TECH interlock (*a. fig*)

Infanterie [ɪnfantəri:] *f* (-; -n) MIL infantry; **Infanterist** ['ɪnfantərɪst] *m* (-en; -en) MIL infantryman

Infektion [ɪnfɛk'tsjo:n] *f* (-; -en) MED infection; **Infekti'onskrankheit** *f* infectious disease

Infinitiv ['ɪnfiniti:f] *m* (-s; -e) LING infinitive (mood)

infizieren [ɪnfi'tsi:rən] *v/t* (*no* -ge-, *h*) MED infect

Inflation [ɪnfla'tsjo:n] *f* (-; -en) inflation

in'folge *prp* (*gen*) owing to, due to

infolge'dessen *adv* consequently

Informatik [ɪnfɔr'ma:tɪk] *f* (-; *no pl*) computer science; **Infor'matiker(in)** [ɪnfɔr'ma:tikɐ, ɪnfɔr'ma:tikərɪn] *m(f)* (-s; -/-; -nen) computer scientist

Information [ɪnfɔrma'tsjo:n] *f* (-; -en) information; **die neuesten ~en** the latest information

informieren [ɪnfɔr'mi:rən] *v/t* (*no* -ge-, *h*) inform; **falsch ~** misinform

in'frage: ~ stellen question; put in jeopardy; **~ kommen** be possible (*person*: eligible); **nicht ~ kommen** be out of the question

infrarot ['ɪnfraro:t] *adj* PHYS infrared

'Infrastruk,tur *f* infrastructure

Ing. *abbr of* **Ingenieur** eng., engineer

Ingenieur [ɪnʒe'njø:ɐ] *m* (-s; -e), **Inge-'nieurin** [ɪnʒe'njø:rɪn] *f* (-; -nen) engineer

Ingwer ['ɪŋvɐ] *m* (-s; *no pl*) ginger

Inhaber ['ɪnha:bɐ] *m* (-s; -), **'Inhaberin** *f* (-; -nen) owner, proprietor (proprietress); holder

Inhalt ['ɪnhalt] *m* (-[e]s; -e) contents;

volume, capacity; *fig* meaning

'Inhalts|angabe *f* summary; **~verzeich-nis** *n* table of contents

Initiative [initsja'ti:və] *f* (-; -n) initiative; **die ~ ergreifen** take the initiative

inklusive [ɪnklu'zi:və] *prp* ECON including

inkonsequent ['ɪnkɔnzekvɛnt] *adj* inconsistent

In-'Kraft-Treten *n* (-s; *no pl*) coming into force, taking effect

'Inland *n* (-[e]s; *no pl*) home (country); **~flug** *m* domestic (*or* internal) flight

inländisch ['ɪnlɛndɪʃ] *adj* domestic, home, inland

Inlett ['ɪnlɛt] *n* (-[e]s; -e) ticking

in'mitten *prp* (*gen*) in the middle of

innen ['ɪnən] *adv* inside; **nach ~** inwards

'Innen|archi,tekt *m*, **~archi,tektin** *f* interior designer; **~architek,tur** *f* interior design; **~mi,nister(in)** minister of the interior; Secretary of the Interior, *Br* Home Secretary; **~minis,terium** *n* ministry of the interior; Department of the Interior, *Br* Home Office; **~poli-,tik** *f* domestic politics

'innenpo,litisch *adj* domestic, internal

'Innenseite *f*: **auf der ~** (on the) inside

'Innenstadt *f* downtown, (city *or* town) center *or Br* centre

inner ['ɪnɐ] *adj* inside; *fig* inner; MED, POL internal; **Innere** ['ɪnərə] *n* (-n; *no pl*) interior, inside

Innereien [ɪnə'raiən] *pl* GASTR offal

'innerhalb *prp* (*gen*) within

'innerlich *adj* internal (*a.* MED)

innert ['ɪnɐt] *Swiss prp* (*gen or dat*) with in

innig ['ɪnɪç] *adj* tender, affectionate

Innung ['ɪnʊŋ] *f* (-; -en) guild

'inoffiziell *adj* unofficial

ins [ɪns] → **in**

Insasse ['ɪnzasə] *m* (-n; -n) inmate; MOT passenger; **'Insassenversicherung** *f* MOT passenger insurance; **'Insassin** *f* (-; -nen) inmate; MOT passenger

insbe'sondere *adv* (e)specially

'Inschrift *f* inscription, legend

Insekt [ɪn'zɛkt] *n* (-s; -en) ZO insect, bug

In'sektenstich *m* insect bite

Insel ['ɪnzəl] *f* (-; -n) island

'Inselbewohner *m* islander

Inserat [ɪnze'ra:t] *n* (-[e]s; -e) advertisement, F ad; **inserieren** [ɪnze'ri:rən] *v/t* *and* v/i (*no -ge-, h*) advertise

insge'heim *adv* secretly

insge'samt *adv* altogether, in all

inso'fern 1. *adv* as far as that goes **2.** *cj:* ~ **als** in so far as

Inspektion [ɪnspɛk'tsjoːn] *f* (-; *-en*) inspection; MOT service

Inspektor [ɪn'spɛktoːɐ] *m* (*-s*; *-en* [ɪnspɛk'toːrən]), **Inspek'torin** *f* (-; *-nen*) inspector

inspizieren [ɪnspi'tsiːrən] v/t (*no -ge-, h*) inspect

Installateur [ɪnstala'tøːɐ] *m* (*-s*; *-e*) plumber; (gas *or* electrical) fitter

installieren [ɪnsta'liːrən] v/t (*no -ge-, h*) put in, fit, instal(l)

instand [ɪn'ʃtant] *adv:* ~ **halten** keep in good condition *or* repair; TECH maintain; ~ **setzen** repair

In'standhaltung *f* (-; *no pl*) maintenance

'inständig *adv:* **j-n** ~ **bitten** implore s.o.

In'standsetzung *f* (-; *-en*) repair

Instanz [ɪn'stants] *f* (-; *-en*) authority; JUR instance

Instinkt [ɪn'stɪŋkt] *m* (*-[e]s*; *-e*) instinct

instinktiv [ɪnstɪŋk'tiːf] *adv* instinctively

Institut [ɪnsti'tuːt] *n* (*-[e]s*; *-e*) institute

Institution [ɪnstitu'tsjoːn] *f* (-; *-en*) institution

Instrument [ɪnstru'mɛnt] *n* (*-[e]s*; *-e*) instrument

inszenieren [ɪnstse'niːrən] v/t (*no -ge-, h*) (put on) stage; *film:* direct; *fig* stage

Insze'nierung *f* (-; *-en*) production

intellektuell [ɪntɛlɛk'tuɛl] *adj*, **Intellektu'elle** *m, f* (*-n; -n*) intellectual, F highbrow

intelligent [ɪnteli'gɛnt] *adj* intelligent

Intelligenz [ɪnteli'gɛnts] *f* (-; *-en*) intelligence; **~quoti,ent** *m* I.Q.

Intendant [ɪntɛn'dant] *m* (*-en; -en*), **Inten'dantin** *f* (-; *-nen*) THEA *etc* director

intensiv [ɪntɛn'ziːf] *adj* intensive; intense; **Inten'sivkurs** *m* crash course

interessant [ɪntərɛ'sant] *adj* interesting; **Interesse** [ɪntə'rɛsə] *n* (*-s; -n*) interest (*an dat, für* in)

Inte'ressengebiet *n* field of interest

Interessent [ɪntərɛ'sɛnt] *m* (*-en; -en*), **Interes'sentin** *f* (-; *-nen*) interested person; ECON prospect, *Br* prospective buyer

interessieren [ɪntərɛ'siːrən] v/t (*no -ge-, h*) interest (*für* in); **sich** ~ **für** take an interest in; be interested in

intern [ɪn'tɛrn] *adj* internal

Internat [ɪntɛr'naːt] *n* (*-[e]s; -e*) boarding school

internatio'nal [ɪntɛrnatsjo'naːl] *adj* international

Internet ['ɪntɛnɛt] *n* (*-[s]; no pl*) Internet

Internist [ɪntɛr'nɪst] *m* (*-en; -en*), **Inter'nistin** *f* (-; *-nen*) MED internist

Interpretation [ɪntɛrpreta'tsjoːn] *f* (-; *-en*) interpretation; analysis

interpretieren [ɪntɛrpre'tiːrən] v/t (*no -ge-, h*) interpret, ana,lyze, *Br* -lyse

Interpunktion [ɪntɛrpʊŋk'tsjoːn] *f* (-; *no pl*) punctuation

Intervall [ɪntɛr'val] *n* (*-[e]s; -e*) interval

intervenieren [ɪntɛrve'niːrən] v/i (*no -ge-, h*) intervene

Interview ['ɪntɛrvjuː] *n* (*-s; -s*), **interviewen** [ɪntɛr'vjuːən] v/t (*no -ge-, h*) interview

intim [ɪn'tiːm] *adj* intimate (*mit* with) (*a. sexually*); **Intimität** [ɪntimi'tɛːt] *f* (-; *no pl*) intimacy; **In'timsphäre** *f* privacy

intolerant ['ɪntolerant] *adj* intolerant (*gegen* of); **Intoleranz** ['ɪntolerants] *f* (-; *no pl*) intolerance

intransitiv ['ɪntranzitiːf] *adj* LING intransitive

Intrige [ɪn'triːgə] *f* (-; *-n*) intrigue, scheme, plot; **intrigieren** [ɪntri'giːrən] v/i (*no -ge-, h*) (plot and) scheme

Invalide [ɪnva'liːdə] *m* (*-n; -n*) invalid; **Inva'lidenrente** *f* disability pension

Invalidität [ɪnvalidi'tɛːt] *f* (-; *no pl*) disablement, disability

Inventar [ɪnvɛn'taːɐ] *n* (*-s; -e*) inventory, stock

Inventur [ɪnvɛn'tuːɐ] *f* (-; *-en*) ECON stocktaking; ~ **machen** take stock

investieren [ɪnvɛs'tiːrən] v/t (*no -ge-, h*) ECON invest (*a. fig*); **Investition** [ɪnvɛsti'tsjoːn] *f* (-; *-en*) ECON investment

inwiefern [ɪnvi'fɛrn] *cj and adv* in what respect *or* way

inwieweit *cj and adv* to what extent

'Inzucht *f* inbreeding

in'zwischen *adv* meanwhile, in the meantime; by now

irdisch ['ɪrdɪʃ] *adj* earthly, worldly

Ire ['i:rə] m (-n; -n) Irishman; pl the Irish

irgend ['ɪrgənt] adv in cpds: some...; any...; **wenn ~ möglich** if at all possible; **wenn du ~ kannst** if you possibly can; F ~ **so ein ...** some ...; **~'ein(e)** indef pron some(one); any(one); **~'ein(e)s** indef pron some; any; **~etwas** something; anything; **~jemand** someone, somebody; anyone, anybody; **~'wann** adv sometime (or other); (at) any time; **~'wie** adv somehow (or other); **~'wo** adv somewhere; anywhere

Irin ['i:rɪn] f (-; -nen) Irishwoman; **irisch** ['i:rɪʃ] adj Irish; **Irland** ['ɪrlant] Ireland

Ironie [iro'ni:] f (-; no pl) irony

ironisch [i'ro:nɪʃ] adj ironic(al)

irre ['ɪrə] adj mad, crazy, insane; confused; F super, terrific

'Irre m, f (-n; -n) madman (madwoman), lunatic; **wie ein ~r** like mad or a madman

'irreführen v/t (sep, -ge-, h) mislead, lead astray; **~d** adj misleading

'irre|gehen v/i (irr, gehen, sep, -ge-, sein) go astray, fig a. be wrong; **~machen** v/t (sep, -ge-, h) confuse

irren ['ɪrən] **1.** v/refl (ge-, h) be wrong, be mistaken; **sich ~** be wrong; **sich in et. ~** get s.th. wrong **2.** v/i (ge-, sein) wander, stray, err

irritieren [ɪri'ti:rən] v/t (no -ge-, h) irritate; F confuse

'Irrlicht n (-[e]s; -er) will-o'-the-wisp

'Irrsinn m (-[e]s; no pl) madness

'irrsinnig adj insane, mad; F terrific

Irrtum ['ɪrtu:m] m (-s; Irrtümer ['ɪrty:mə]) error, mistake; **im ~ sein** be mistaken; **'irrtümlich** adv by mistake

Ischias ['ɪʃjas] m, n, f (-; no pl) MED sciatica

Islam [ɪs'la:m] m (-[s]; no pl) Islam

Island ['i:slant] Iceland

Isländer ['i:slɛndə] m (-s; -), **'Isländerin** ['i:slɛndərɪn] f (-; -nen) Icelander

'isländisch adj Icelandic

Isolierband [izo'li:ɐbant] n (-[e]s; -bänder) insulating tape; **isolieren** [izo'li:rən] v/t (no -ge-, h) isolate; ELECTR, TECH insulate; **Iso'lierstati,on** f MED isolation ward; **Iso'lierung** f (-; -en) isolation; ELECTR, TECH insulation

Israel ['ɪsrae:l] Israel

Israeli [ɪsra'e:li] m (-[s]; -[s]), f (-; -[s]), **israelisch** [ɪsra'e:lɪʃ] adj Israeli

Italien [i'ta:ljən] Italy; **Italiener** [ita-'lje:nɐ] m (-s; -), **Itali'enerin** [ita-'lje:nərɪn] f (-; -nen), **itali'enisch** adj Italian

J

ja [ja:] adv yes, F a. yeah; PARL yea, aye; **wenn ~** if so; **da ist er ~!** well, there he is!; **ich sagte es Ihnen ~** I told you so; **ich bin ~ (schließlich) ...** after all, I am ...; **tut es 'ja nicht!** don't you dare do it!; **sei 'ja vorsichtig!** do be careful!; **vergessen Sie es 'ja nicht!** be sure not to forget it!; **~, weißt du nicht?** why, don't you know?; **du kommst doch, ~?** you're coming, aren't you?

Jacht [jaxt] f (-; -en) MAR yacht

Jacke ['jakə] f (-; -n) jacket; coat

Jackett [ʒa'kɛt] n (-s; -s) jacket, coat

Jagd [ja:kt] f (-; -en) hunt(ing) (a. fig); shoot(ing); fig chase; → **Jagdrevier**; **auf (die) ~ gehen** go hunting or shooting; **~ machen auf** (acc) hunt (for); a. chase s.o.; **~aufseher** m gamekeeper; **~flugzeug** n MIL fighter (plane); **~hund**

m ZO hound; **~hütte** f (hunting) lodge; **~re,vier** n hunting ground; **~schein** m hunting or shooting licen|se, Br -ce

jagen ['ja:gən] v/t and v/i (ge-, h) hunt; shoot; fig race, dash; hunt, chase; **j-n aus dem Haus** etc ~ drive or chase s.o. out of the house etc

Jäger ['jɛ:gɐ] m (-s; -) hunter, huntsman

Jaguar ['ja:gua:ɐ] m (-s; -e) ZO jaguar

jäh [jɛ:] adj sudden; steep

Jahr [ja:ɐ] n (-[e]s; -e ['ja:rə]) year; **ein drei viertel ~** nine months; **einmal im ~** once a year; **im ~e 1995** in (the year) 1995; **ein 10 ~e altes Auto** a ten--year-old car; **mit 18 ~en, im Alter von 18 ~en** at (the age of) eighteen; **heute vor e-m ~** a year ago today; **die 80er-Jahre** the eighties

jahr'aus *adv*: ~, **jahrein** year in, year out; year after year

'Jahrbuch *n* yearbook, annual

jahrelang ['ja:rəlaŋ] **1.** *adj* longstanding, (many) years of **2.** *adv* for (many) years

Jahres... ['ja:rəs-] *in cpds* ...bericht, ...bilanz, ...einkommen *etc*: annual ...; ~anfang *m* beginning of the year; ~ende *n* end of the year; ~tag *m* anniversary; ~wechsel *m* turn of the year; ~zahl *f* date, year; ~zeit *f* season, time of (the) year

'Jahrgang *m* age group; PED year, class (**1995** of '95); GASTR vintage

Jahr'hundert *n* (-s; -e) century; ~wende *f* turn of the century

jährlich ['jɛ:rlɪç] **1.** *adj* annual, yearly **2.** *adv* every year, yearly, once a year

'Jahrmarkt *m* fair

Jahr'tausend *n* (-s; -e) millennium

Jahr'zehnt *n* (-[e]s; -e) decade

'Jähzorn *m* violent (fit of) temper

'jähzornig *adj* hot-tempered

Jalousie [ʒalu'zi:] *f* (-; -n) (venetian) blind

Jammer ['jamɐ] *m* (-s; *no pl*) misery; *es ist ein* ~ it is a pity; **jämmerlich** ['jɛmɐlɪç] *adj* miserable, wretched; pitiful, sorry; ~ *versagen* fail miserably; **'jammern** *v/i* (ge-, h) moan, lament (*über acc* over, about); complain (of, about); **jammer'schade** *adj*: *es ist* ~, *dass* it's a crying shame that

Janker ['jaŋkɐ] *Austrian m* (-s; -) jacket

Jänner ['jɛnɐ] *Austrian m* (-s; -), **Januar** ['janua:ɐ] *m* (-[s]; -e) January

Japan ['ja:pan] Japan; **Japaner** [ja-'pa:nɐ] *m* (-s; -), **Ja'panerin** [ja-'pa:nərɪn] *f* (-; -nen), **ja'panisch** *adj* Japanese

Jargon [ʒar'goː:] *m* (-s; -s) jargon; slang

'Jastimme *f* PARL aye, yea

jäten ['jɛ:tən] *v/t* (ge-, h) weed

Jauche ['jauxə] *f* (-; -n) liquid manure

jauchzen ['jauxtsən] *v/i* (ge-, h) shout for *or* with joy; exult, rejoice

Jause ['jauzə] *Austrian f* (-; -n) snack

ja'wohl *adv* (that's) right, (yes,) indeed

je [je:] *adv* and *cj* ever; each; per; *der beste Film, den ich* ~ *gesehen habe* the best film I have ever seen; ~ *zwei* (*Pfund*) two (pounds) each; *drei Euro* ~ *Kilo* three euros per kilo; ~ *nach Grö-*

ße (**Geschmack**) according to size (taste); ~ *nachdem*(, *wie*) it depends (on how); ~ ..., *desto* ... the ... the ...

Jeans [dʒiːnz] *pl*, *a. f* (-; -) (*e-e* ~ a pair of) jeans; ~jacke *f* denim jacket

jede ['je:də], **jeder** ['je:dɐ], **jedes** ['je:dəs] *indef pron* every; each; either; *jeder weiß* (*das*) everybody knows; *du kannst jeden fragen* (you can) ask anyone; *jeder von uns* (*euch*) each of us (you); *jeder, der* whoever; *jeden zweiten Tag* every other day; *jeden Augenblick* any moment now; *jedes Mal* every time; *jedes Mal wenn* whenever

'jeden'falls *adv* in any case, anyhow

'jedermann *indef pron* everyone, everybody

'jeder'zeit *adv* any time, always

je'doch *cj* however

je'her *adv*: *von* ~ always

jemals ['je:ma:ls] *adv* ever

jemand ['je:mant] *indef pron* someone, somebody; anyone, anybody

jene ['je:nə], **jener** ['je:nɐ], **jenes** ['je:nəs] *dem pron* that (one); *pl* those; *dies und jenes* this and that

jenseitig ['je:nzaitɪç] *adj* opposite

jenseits ['je:nzaits] *adv and prp* (*gen*) on the other side (of), beyond (*a. fig*)

'Jenseits *n* (-; *no pl*) next world, hereafter

jetzig ['jɛtsɪç] *adj* present; existing

jetzt [jɛtst] *adv* now, at present; *bis* ~ up to now, so far; *erst* ~ only now; ~ *gleich* right away *or* away; *von* ~ *an* from now on

jeweilig ['je:'vailɪç] *adj* respective

jeweils ['je:'vails] *adv* each; at a time

Jh. *abbr of Jahrhundert* cent., century

Jochbein ['jɔxbain] *n* ANAT cheekbone

Jockel ['dʒɔke] *m* (-s; -s) jockey

Jod [joːt] *n* (-[e]s; *no pl*) CHEM iodine

jodeln ['joːdəln] *v/i* (ge-, h) yodel

Joga → Yoga

joggen ['dʒɔgən] *v/i* (ge-, h) jog

Jogger ['dʒɔgɐ] *m* (-s; -) jogger

Jogging ['dʒɔgɪŋ] *n* (-s; *no pl*) jogging; ~anzug *m* tracksuit; ~hose *f* tracksuit trousers

Joghurt, Jogurt ['joːgʊrt] *m*, *n* (-[s]; -[s]) yog(h)urt, yoghourt

Johannisbeere [jo'hanɪsbeːrə] *f*: *rote* ~ redcurrant; *schwarze* ~ blackcurrant

johlen ['jo:lən] v/i (ge-, h) howl, yell
Jolle ['jɔlə] f (-; -n) MAR dinghy
Jongleur [ʒɔ-'glø:ɐ] m (-s; -e) juggler
jonglieren [ʒɔ-'gli:rən] v/t and v/i (no -ge-, h) juggle
Joule [dʒu:l] n (-[s]; -) PHYS joule
Journalismus [ʒʊrna'lɪsmʊs] m (-; no pl) journalism; **Journalist(in)** [ʒʊrna-'lɪst(ɪn)] (-en; -en/-; -nen) journalist
jr. → **jun.**
Jubel ['ju:bəl] m (-s; no pl) cheering, cheers; rejoicing; '**jubeln** v/i (ge-, h) cheer, shout for joy; rejoice
Jubiläum [jubi'lɛ:ʊm] n (-s; -läen) anniversary; **50-jähriges ~** fiftieth anniversary, (golden) jubilee
jucken ['jʊkən] v/t and v/i (ge-, h) itch; **es juckt mich am ...** my ... itches
Jude ['ju:də] m (-n; -n) Jewish person; **er ist ~** he is Jewish; **Jüdin** ['jy:dɪn] f (-; -nen) Jewish woman or girl; **sie ist ~** she is Jewish; **jüdisch** ['jy:dɪʃ] adj Jewish
Judo ['ju:do] n (-[s]; no pl) SPORT judo
Jugend ['ju:gənt] f (-; no pl) youth; **die ~** young people; **~amt** n youth welfare office; **~arbeitslosigkeit** f youth unemployment
'**jugendfrei** adj: **~er Film** G(-rated) (Br U(-rated)) film; **nicht ~** X-rated
'**Jugend|fürsorge** f youth welfare; **~gericht** n JUR juvenile court; **~herberge** f youth hostel; **~klub** m youth club; **~kriminali,tät** f juvenile delinquency
'**jugendlich** adj youthful, young
'**Jugendliche** m, f (-n; -n) young person, m a. youth, JUR a. juvenile
'**Jugend|stil** m (-s; no pl) Art Nouveau; **~strafanstalt** f detention center (Br centre), reformatory; **~verbot** n for adults only; → **jugendfrei**, **~zentrum** n youth center (Br centre)
Juli ['ju:li] m (-[s]; -s) July
Jumbojet ['jʊmbojet] m jumbo (jet)
jun. abbr of **junior** Jun., jun., Jnr., Jr., junior
jung [jʊŋ] adj young

Junge[1] ['jʊŋə] m (-n; -n) boy; lad; cards: jack, knave
'**Junge**[2] n (-n; -n) ZO young; puppy; kitten; cub; **~ bekommen** or **werfen** have young
'**jungenhaft** adj boyish
'**Jungenstreich** m boyish prank
jünger ['jyŋɐ] adj younger
'**Jünger** m (-s; -) REL disciple (a. fig)
'**Jungfern|fahrt** f MAR maiden voyage; **~flug** m AVIAT maiden flight
'**Jung|frau** f virgin; ASTR Virgo; **er ist ~** he's (a) Virgo; **~geselle** m bachelor, single (man); **~gesellin** f bachelor girl, single (woman); esp JUR spinster
jüngste ['jyŋstə] adj youngest; fig latest; **in ~r Zeit** lately, recently; **das Jüngste Gericht** the Last Judg(e)ment; **der Jüngste Tag** Doomsday
Juni ['ju:ni] m (-[s]; -s) June
junior ['ju:njo:ɐ] adj, '**Junior** m (-s; -en [ju'njo:rən]), **Juni'orin** f (-; -nen) junior (a. SPORT)
Jupe [ʒy:p] Swiss m (-s; -s) skirt
Jura ['ju:ra]: **~ studieren** study (the) law
juridisch [ju'ri:dɪʃ] Austrian → **juristisch**; **Jurist(in)** [ju'rɪst(ɪn)] (-en; -en/-; -nen) lawyer; law student; **ju'ristisch** adj legal
Jurorenkomitee [ju'ro:rənkomite:] Austrian n → **Jury**
Jury [ʒy'ri:] f (-; -s) jury
justieren [jʊs'ti:rən] v/t (no -ge-, h) TECH adjust, set
Justiz [jʊs'ti:ts] f (-; no pl) (administration of) justice, (the) law; **~beamte** m judicial officer; **~irrtum** m error of justice; **~mi,nister** m minister of justice; Attorney General, Br Lord Chancellor; **~minis,terium** n ministry of justice; Department of Justice
Jute ['ju:tə] f (-; no pl) jute
Juwel [ju've:l] m, n (-s; -en) jewel, gem (both a. fig); pl jewel(le)ry
Juwelier [juve'li:ɐ] m (-s; -e) jewel(l)er

K

Kabarett [kaba'rɛt] n (-s; -s) (political) revue

Kabel ['ka:bəl] n (-s; -) cable

'Kabelfernsehen n cable TV

Kabeljau ['ka:bəljau] m (-s; -e, -s) ZO cod(fish)

Kabine [ka'bi:nə] f (-; -n) cabin; cubicle; SPORT dressing room; TECH car; TEL etc booth; **Ka'binenbahn** f cable railway

Kabinett [kabi'nɛt] n (-s; -e) POL cabinet

Kabis ['ka:bɪs] Swiss m (-; no pl) green cabbage

Kabriolett [kabrio'lɛt] n (-s; -s) MOT convertible

Kachel ['kaxəl] f (-; -n), **'kacheln** v/t (ge-, h) tile; **'Kachelofen** m tiled stove

Kadaver [ka'da:vɐ] m (-s; -) carcass

Kadett [ka'dɛt] m (-en; -en) MIL cadet

Käfer ['kɛ:fɐ] m (-s; -) ZO beetle, bug

Kaffee ['kafe] m (-s; -s) coffee; **~ kochen** make coffee; **~ mit Milch** white coffee; **~auto,mat** m coffee machine; **~bohne** f coffee bean; **~haus** [ka-'fe:haus] Austrian n café, coffee house; **~kanne** f coffee pot; **~ma,schine** f cofffeemaker; **~mühle** f coffee grinder

Käfig ['kɛ:fɪç] m (-s; -e) cage (a. fig)

kahl [ka:l] adj bald; fig bare (rock, wall etc); barren, bleak (landscape)

Kahn [ka:n] m (-[e]s; Kähne ['kɛ:nə]) boat; barge

Kai [kai] m (-s; -s) quay, wharf

Kaiser ['kaizɐ] m (-s; -) emperor

Kaiserin ['kaizərɪn] f (-; -nen) empress

'Kaiserreich n empire

Kajüte [ka'jy:tə] f (-; -n) MAR cabin

Kakao [ka'kau] m (-s; -s) cocoa; (hot) chocolate; chocolate milk

Kaktee [kak'te:] f (-; -n), **Kaktus** ['kak-tʊs] m (-; Kakteen) BOT cactus

Kalb [kalp] n (-[e]s; Kälber ['kɛlbɐ]) ZO calf; **kalben** ['kalbən] v/i (ge-, h) calve

'Kalbfleisch n veal

'Kalbs|braten m roast veal; **~schnitzel** n veal cutlet; escalope (of veal)

Kaldaunen [kal'daunən] pl GASTR tripe

Kalender [ka'lɛndɐ] m (-s; -) calendar; **~jahr** n calendar year

Kali ['ka:li] n (-s; no pl) CHEM potash

Kaliber [ka'li:bɐ] n (-s; -) caliber, Br cal-ibre (a. fig)

Kalk [kalk] m (-[e]s; -e) lime; GEOL limestone, chalk; MED calcium; **'kalken** v/t (ge-, h) whitewash; AGR lime; **'kalkig** adj limy; **'Kalkstein** m limestone

Kalorie [kalo'ri:] f (-; -n) calorie

kalo'rien|arm adj, **~redu,ziert** adj low--calorie, low in calories; **~reich** adj high-calorie, high or rich in calories

kalt [kalt] adj cold; **mir ist ~** I'm cold; **es (mir) wird ~** it's (I'm) getting cold; **~ bleiben** fig keep (one's) cool; **das lässt mich kalt** that leaves me cold

kaltblütig ['kaltbly:tɪç] **1.** adj cold--blooded (a. fig) **2.** adv in cold blood

Kälte ['kɛltə] f (-; no pl) cold; fig coldness; **vor ~ zittern** shiver with cold; **fünf Grad ~** five degrees below zero; **~einbruch** m cold snap; **~grad** m degree below zero; **~peri,ode** f cold spell

'kaltmachen F v/t (sep, -ge-, h) bump off

kam [ka:m] pret of **kommen**

Kamee [ka'me:ə] f (-; -n) cameo

Kamel [ka'me:l] n (-s; -e) ZO camel

Ka'melhaar n (-[e]s; no pl) camelhair

Kamera ['kamərа] f (-; -s) camera

Kamerad [kamə'ra:t] m (-en; -en [kamə'ra:dən]) companion, F mate, pal, buddy; **Kameradin** [kamə'ra:dɪn] f (-; -nen) companion

Kame'radschaft f (-; no pl) comradeship

'Kameramann m cameraman

'Kamerare,korder m (-s; -) camcorder

Kamille [ka'mɪlə] f (-; -n) BOT camomile

Kamin [ka'mi:n] m (-s; -e) fireplace; chimney (a. MOUNT); **am ~** by the fire (-side); **~kehrer** [ka'mi:nke:rɐ] m (-s; -) chimney sweep; **~sims** m, n mantelpiece

Kamm [kam] m (-[e]s; Kämme ['kɛmə]) comb, ZO a. crest (a. fig)

kämmen ['kɛmən] v/t (ge-, h) comb; **sich (die Haare) ~** comb one's hair

Kammer ['kamɐ] f (-; -n) (small) room; storeroom, closet; garret; POL, ECON chamber; JUR division

'Kammermu,sik f chamber music

'Kammgarn n worsted (yarn)

Kampagne [kam'panjə] f (-; -n) campaign

Kampf [kampf] *m* (-[e]s; *Kämpfe* ['kɛmpfə]) fight (*a. fig*), struggle (*a. fig*), *esp* MIL combat, battle (*a. fig*); SPORT contest, match; *boxing:* fight, bout; *fig* conflict; **'kampfbereit** *adj* ready for battle (MIL combat); **kämpfen** ['kɛmpfən] *v/i* (*ge-, h*) fight (*gegen* against; *mit* with; *um* for) (*a. fig*); struggle (*a. fig*); *fig* contend, wrestle

Kampfer ['kampfɐ] *m* (-s; *no pl*) CHEM camphor

Kämpfer ['kɛmpfɐ] *m* (-s; -), **'Kämpferin** *f* (-; -nen) fighter (*a. fig*); **kämpferisch** ['kɛmpfərɪʃ] *adj* fighting, aggressive

'Kampfflugzeug *n* MIL combat aircraft; **~kraft** *f* (-; *no pl*) fighting strength; **~richter** *m* SPORT judge; **~sportarten** *pl* martial arts

Kanada ['kanada] Canada; **Kanadier** [ka'na:djɐ] *m* (-s; -), **Ka'nadierin** [ka-'na:djərɪn] *f* (-; -nen), **ka'nadisch** *adj* Canadian

Kanal [ka'na:l] *m* (-s; *Kanäle* [ka'nɛ:lə]) canal; channel (*a.* TV, TECH, EDP); sewer, drain; *der ~* the (English) Channel

Kanalisation [kanaliza'tsjo:n] *f* (-; -en) sewerage (system); canalization

kanalisieren [kanali'zi:rən] *v/t* (*no -ge-, h*) sewer; canalize; *fig* channel

Ka'naltunnel *m* Channel Tunnel, F Chunnel

Kanarienvogel [ka'na:rjənfo:gəl] *m* canary

Kandidat [kandi'da:t] *m* (-en; -en), **Kandi'datin** *f* (-; -nen) candidate; **Kandidatur** [kandida'tu:ɐ] *f* (-; -en) candidacy, *Br a.* candidature; **kandidieren** [kandi'di:rən] *v/i* (*no -ge-, h*) stand *or* run for election; *~ für ...* run for the office of ...

Känguru, Känguruh ['kɛŋguru] *n* (-s; -s) ZO kangaroo

Kaninchen [ka'ni:nçən] *n* (-s; -) ZO rabbit

Kanister [ka'nɪstɐ] *m* (-s; -) (fuel) can

Kanne ['kanə] *f* (-; -n) pot; can

Kannibale [kani'ba:lə] *m* (-n; -n) cannibal

kannte ['kantə] *pret of* **kennen**

Kanon ['ka:nɔn] *m* (-s; -s) MUS canon

Kanone [ka'no:nə] *f* (-; -n) MIL gun; cannon; F ace, *esp* SPORT *a.* crack

Kante ['kantə] *f* (-; -n) edge; **'kanten** *v/t* (*ge-, h*) set on edge; tilt; edge (*skis*)

'Kanten *m* (-s; -) crust

kantig ['kantɪç] *adj* angular, square(d)

Kantine [kan'ti:nə] *f* (-; -n) canteen

Kanton [kan'to:n] *m* (-s; -e) POL canton

Kanu ['ka:nu] *n* (-s; -s) canoe

Kanüle [ka'ny:lə] *f* (-; -n) MED cannula, (drain) tube

Kanzel ['kantsəl] *f* (-; -n) REL pulpit; AVIAT cockpit

Kanzlei [kants'lai] *f* (-; -en) office

Kanzler ['kantslɐ] *m* (-s; -) chancellor

Kanzlerin ['kantslərɪn] *f* (-; -nen) chancellor

Kap [kap] *n* (-s; -s) cape, headland

Kapazität [kapatsi'tɛ:t] *f* (-; -en) capacity; *fig* authority

Kapelle [ka'pɛlə] *f* (-; -n) REL chapel; MUS band

Ka'pellmeister *m* MUS conductor

kapern ['ka:pɐn] *v/t* (*ge-, h*) MAR capture, seize

kapieren [ka'pi:rən] F *v/t* (*no -ge-, h*) get; *kapiert?* got it?

Kapital [kapi'ta:l] *n* (-s; -e, -ien) ECON capital, funds; **~anlage** *f* investment

Kapitalismus [kapita'lɪsmʊs] *m* (-; *no pl*) capitalism; **Kapita'list** *m* (-en; -en), **kapita'listisch** *adj* capitalist

Kapi'talverbrechen *n* capital crime, JUR felony

Kapitän [kapi'tɛ:n] *m* (-s; -e) captain (*a.* SPORT)

Kapitel [ka'pɪtəl] *n* (-s; -) chapter (*a. fig*); F *fig* story

Kapitulation [kapitula'tsjo:n] *f* (-; -en) capitulation, surrender (*a. fig*)

kapitulieren [kapitu'li:rən] *v/i* (*no -ge-, h*) capitulate, surrender (*a. fig*)

Kaplan [ka'pla:n] *m* (-s; *Kapläne* [ka-'plɛ:nə]) REL curate

Kappe ['kapə] *f* (-; -n) cap, TECH *a.* top, hood; **'kappen** *v/t* (*ge-, h*) cut (*rope*); lop, top (*tree*)

Kapsel ['kapsəl] *f* (-; -n) capsule

kaputt [ka'pʊt] F *adj* broken (*a. fig*); TECH out of order; *fig* dead beat; ruined; *~ machen* F *v/t* (*sep, -ge-, h*) break, wreck (*a. fig*), ruin; *fig → ~machen*; **~gehen** F *v/i* (*irr, gehen, sep, -ge-, sein*) break; MOT *etc* break down; *fig* break up; **~machen** *v/t* (*sep, -ge-, h*) F *fig* wreck, ruin

Kapuze [ka'puːtsə] *f* (-; -*n*) hood; cowl

Karabiner [kara'biːnɐ] *m* (-*s*; -) carbine; **~haken** *m* karabiner, snaplink

Karaffe [ka'rafə] *f* (-; -*n*) decanter

Karambolage [karambo'laːʒə] *f* (-; -*n*) collision, crash

Karat [ka'raːt] *n* (-[*e*]*s*; -*e*) carat

Karate [ka'raːtə] *n* (-[*s*]; *no pl*) SPORT karate

Karawane [kara'vaːnə] *f* (-; -*n*) caravan

Kardinal [kardi'naːl] *m* (-*s*; *Kardinäle* [kardi'nɛːlə]) REL cardinal

Karfiol [kar'fjoːl] *Austrian m* (-*s*; *no pl*) BOT cauliflower

Kar'freitag [kaːɐ'fraitaːk] *m* REL Good Friday

karg [kark], **kärglich** ['kɛrklɪç] *adj* meag|er, *Br* -re, scanty; frugal; poor

kariert [ka'riːɐt] *adj* checked, checkered, *Br* chequered; squared

Karies ['kaːrjɛs] *f* (-; *no pl*) MED (dental) caries

Karikatur [karika'tuːɐ] *f* (-; -*en*) *mst* cartoon, *esp fig* caricature; **Karikaturist** [karikatu'rɪst] *m* (-*en*; -*en*) cartoonist

karikieren [kari'kiːrən] *v/t* (*no* -*ge*-, *h*) caricature

Karneval ['karnəval] *m* (-*s*; -*e*, -*s*) carnival

Karo ['kaːro] *n* (-*s*; -*s*) square, check; *cards*: diamonds

Karosserie [karɔsə'riː] *f* (-; -*n*) MOT body

Karotte [ka'rɔtə] *f* (-; -*n*) BOT carrot

Karpfen ['karpfən] *m* (-*s*; -) ZO carp

Karre ['karə] *f* (-; -*n*), **'Karren** *m* (-*s*; -) cart; wheelbarrow; F MOT jalopy

Karriere [ka'rjeːrə] *f* (-; -*n*) career; **~ machen** work one's way up, get to the top

Karte ['kartə] *f* (-; -*n*) card; ticket; GEOGR map; chart; GASTR menu; **gute (schlechte) ~n** a good (bad) hand

Kartei [kar'tai] *f* (-; -*en*) card index; **~karte** *f* index *or* file card

'Karten|haus *n* house of cards (*a. fig*); MAR chartroom; **~spiel** *n* card game; deck (*Br* pack) of cards; **~tele,fon** *n* cardphone; **~vorverkauf** *m* advance booking; box office

Kartoffel [kar'tɔfəl] *f* (-; -*n*) BOT potato; **~brei** *m* mashed potatoes; **~chips** *pl* (potato) chips, *Br* crisps; **~kloß** *m*, **~knödel** *m* potato dumpling; **~puffer** *m* potato fritter; **~schalen** *pl* potato peelings; **~schäler** *m* potato peeler

Karton [kar'tɔŋ] *m* (-*s*; -*s*) cardboard; pasteboard; cardboard box

Karussell [karu'sɛl] *n* (-*s*; -*s*) roundabout, car(r)ousel, merry-go-round

Karwoche ['kaːɐvɔxə] *f* REL Holy Week

Kaschmir ['kaʃmiːɐ] *m* (-*s*; -*e*) cashmere

Käse ['kɛːzə] *m* (-*s*; -) cheese

Kaserne [ka'zɛrnə] *f* (-; -*n*) barracks

Ka'sernenhof *m* barrack square

käsig ['kɛːzɪç] *adj* cheesy; pasty

Kasino [ka'ziːno] *n* (-*s*; -*s*) casino; MIL (officers') mess

Kasperle ['kaspɐlə] *n*, *m* (-*s*; -) Punch; **~the,ater** *n* Punch and Judy show

Kassa ['kasa] *Austrian f* (-; *Kassen*), **Kasse** ['kasə] *f* (-; -*n*) till; cash register; checkout (counter); cash desk; cashier's counter; THEA *etc* box office; F **gut (knapp) bei Kasse sein** be flush (be a bit hard up)

'Kassen|beleg *m*, **~bon** *m* sales slip, *Br* receipt; **~erfolg** *m* THEA *etc* box-office success; **~pati,ent** *m* MED health plan (*Am* medicaid, *Br* NHS) patient; **~schlager** F *m* blockbuster; **~wart** ['kasənvart] *m* (-[*e*]*s*; -*e*) treasurer

Kassette [ka'sɛtə] *f* (-; -*n*) box, case; MUS, TV, PHOT *etc* cassette; casket

Kas'setten... *in cpds* **...rekorder** *etc*: cassette...

kassieren [ka'siːrən] *v/t and v/i* (*no* -*ge*-, *h*) collect, take (the money)

Kassierer [ka'siːɐ] *m* (-*s*; -), **Kas'siererin** *f* (-; -*nen*) cashier; teller; collector

Kastanie [kas'taːnjə] *f* (-; -*n*) BOT chestnut

Kasten ['kastən] *m* (-*s*; *Kästen* ['kɛstən]) box (*a.* F TV, SPORT *etc*); case; chest

kastrieren [kas'triːrən] *v/t* (*no* -*ge*-, *h*) MED, VET castrate

Kasus ['kaːzus] *m* (-; -) LING case

Katalog [kata'loːk] *m* (-[*e*]*s*; -*e*) catalog(ue *Br*)

Katalysator [kataly'zaːtoːɐ] *m* (-*s*; -*en* [katalyza'toːrən]) CHEM catalyst; MOT catalytic converter

Katapult [kata'pult] *m*, *n* (-[*e*]*s*; -*e*), **katapultieren** [katapul'tiːrən] *v/t* (*no* -*ge*-, *h*) catapult

katastrophal [katastro'faːl] *adj* disastrous (*a. fig*); **Katastrophe** [katas-

'tro:fə] f (-; -n) catastrophe, disaster (a. fig)

Kata'strophen|gebiet n disaster area; **~schutz** m disaster control

Katechismus [katɛ'çɪsmʊs] m (-; -men) REL catechism

Kategorie [katego'ri:] f (-; -n) category

Kater ['ka:tɐ] m (-s; -) ZO male cat, tomcat; F hangover

kath. abbr of **katholisch** Cath., Catholic

Kathedrale [kate'dra:lə] f (-; -n) cathedral

Katholik [kato'li:k] m (-en; -en), **Katho-** '**likin** f (-; -nen), **katholisch** [ka'to:lɪʃ] adj (Roman) Catholic

Kätzchen ['kɛtsçən] n (-s; -) ZO kitten, pussy (a. BOT)

Katze ['katsə] f (-; -n) ZO cat; kitten

Kauderwelsch ['kaudɐvɛlʃ] n (-[s]; no pl) gibberish

kauen ['kauən] v/t and v/i (ge-, h) chew

kauern ['kauɐn] v/i and v/refl (ge-, h) crouch, squat

Kauf [kauf] m (-[e]s; Käufe ['kɔyfə]) purchase (a. ECON), F buy; purchasing, buying; **ein guter ~** a bargain, F a good buy; **zum ~ anbieten** offer for sale

'**kaufen** v/t (ge-, h) buy (a. fig), purchase

Käufer ['kɔyfɐ] m (-s; -), '**Käuferin** f (-; -nen) buyer; customer

'**Kauffrau** f (-; -en) businesswoman

'**Kauf|haus** n department store; **~kraft** f (-; no pl) ECON purchasing power

käuflich ['kɔyflɪç] adj for sale; fig venal

'**Kaufmann** m (-[e]s; -leute) businessman; dealer, trader, merchant; storekeeper, Br mst shopkeeper; grocer

kaufmännisch ['kaufmɛnɪʃ] adj commercial, business; **~er Angestellter** clerk

'**Kaufvertrag** m contract of sale

'**Kaugummi** m (-s; -s) chewing gum

kaum [kaum] adv hardly; **~ zu glauben** hard to believe

Kaution [kau'tsjo:n] f (-; -en) security; JUR bail

Kautschuk ['kautʃʊk] m (-s; -e) (india) rubber

Kavalier [kava'li:ɐ] m (-s; -e) gentleman

Kaviar ['ka:vjar] m (-s; -e) caviar(e)

keck [kɛk] adj cheeky, saucy, pert

Kegel ['ke:gəl] m (-s; -) skittle, pin; MATH, TECH cone; **~bahn** f bowling (esp Br skittle) alley

'**kegelförmig** ['ke:gəlfœrmɪç] adj conical

'**Kegelkugel** f bowling (esp Br skittle) ball

'**kegeln** v/i (ge-, h) bowl, go bowling, esp Br play (at) skittles or ninepins

Kehle ['ke:lə] f (-; -n) ANAT throat

'**Kehlkopf** m ANAT larynx

Kehre ['ke:rə] f (-; -n) (sharp) bend

'**kehren** v/t (ge-, h) sweep; **j-m den Rücken ~** turn one's back on s.o.

Kehricht ['ke:rɪçt] m (-s; no pl) sweepings; **~schaufel** f dustpan

kehrtmachen ['ke:ɐtmaxən] v/i (sep, -ge-, h) turn back

keifen ['kaifən] v/i (ge-, h) nag, bitch

Keil [kail] m (-[e]s; -e) wedge; gusset

Keiler ['kailɐ] m (-s; -) ZO wild boar

'**Keilriemen** m MOT fan belt

Keim [kaim] m (-[e]s; -e) BIOL, MED germ; BOT bud, sprout; fig seed(s)

'**keimen** v/i (ge-, h) BOT germinate, sprout; fig form, grow; stir

'**keimfrei** adj MED sterile

'**keimtötend** adj MED germicidal

'**Keimzelle** f BIOL germ cell

kein [kain] indef pron **1.** adj: **~(e)** no, not any; **~ anderer** no one else; **~(e) ... mehr** not any more ...; **~ Geld (~e Zeit)** mehr no money (time) left; **~ Kind mehr** no longer a child **2.** su: **~er, ~e, ~(e)s** none, no one, nobody; **~er von beiden** neither (of the two); **~er von uns** none of us; '**keines'falls** adv by no means, under no circumstances; '**keineswegs** [kainəs've:ks] adv by no means, not in the least; '**keinmal** adv not once, not a single time

Keks [ke:ks] m, n (-es, -e) cookie, Br biscuit

Kelch [kɛlç] m (-[e]s; -e) cup (a. BOT); REL chalice

Kelle ['kɛlə] f (-; -n) GASTR ladle, scoop; TECH trowel; signaling disk

Keller ['kɛlɐ] m (-s; -) cellar; → **~geschoss** n, **~geschoß** Austrian n basement; **~wohnung** f basement (apartment, esp Br flat)

Kellner ['kɛlnɐ] m (-s; -) waiter

Kellnerin ['kɛlnərɪn] f (-; -nen) waitress

keltern ['kɛltɐn] v/t (ge-, h) press

kennen ['kɛnən] v/t (irr, ge-, h) know, be acquainted with; **~ lernen** → **kennenlernen**

'**kennenlernen** v/t (sep, -ge-, h) get to know, become acquainted with; meet s.o.; **als ich ihn kennenlernte** when I first met him

Kenner ['kɛnɐ] m (-s; -), '**Kennerin** f (-; -nen) expert; **kenntlich** ['kɛntlɪç] adj recognizable (**an** dat by); **Kenntnis** f (-; -se) knowledge; **gute ~se in** (dat) a good knowledge of

'**Kennwort** n password

'**Kennzeichen** n mark, sign; (distinguishing) feature, characteristic; MOT license (Br registration) number

'**kennzeichnen** v/t (ge-, h) mark; fig characterize

kentern ['kɛntɐn] v/i (ge-, sein) MAR capsize

Keramik [ke'ra:mɪk] f (-; -en) ceramics

Kerbe ['kɛrbə] f (-; -n) notch

Kerker ['kɛrkɐ] m (-s; -) dungeon

Kerl [kɛrl] F m (-s; -e) fellow, guy; **armer ~** poor devil; **ein anständiger ~** a decent sort

Kern [kɛrn] m (-[e]s; -e) BOT pip, seed, stone, kernel; TECH core (a. fig); PHYS nucleus; **~...** in cpds ...energie, ...forschung, ...physik, ...reaktor, ...technik etc: nuclear ...; **~fach** n PED basic subject; **~fa,milie** f nuclear family; **~gehäuse** n BOT core

'**kernge'sund** adj F (as) sound as a bell

kernig ['kɛrnɪç] adj full of seeds (Br pips); fig robust; pithy

'**Kernkraft** f PHYS nuclear power; **~gegner** m anti-nuclear activist; **~werk** n nuclear power station or plant

'**kernlos** adj BOT seedless

'**Kernspaltung** f PHYS nuclear fission

'**Kernwaffen** pl MIL nuclear weapons; '**kernwaffenfrei** adj: **~e Zone** MIL nuclear-free zone; '**Kernwaffenversuch** m MIL nuclear test

'**Kernzeit** f ECON core time

Kerze ['kɛrtsə] f (-; -n) candle; SPORT shoulder stand

kess [kɛs] F adj cheeky, saucy, pert

Kessel ['kɛsəl] m (-s; -) kettle; TECH boiler; tank

Kette ['kɛtə] f (-; -n) chain (a. fig); necklace; **e-e ~ bilden** form a line

'**Ketten|...** in cpds ...antrieb, ...laden, ...rauchen, ...raucher, ...reaktion etc: chain ...

'**ketten** v/t (ge-, h) chain (**an** acc to)

'**Kettenfahrzeug** n tracked vehicle

Ketzer ['kɛtsɐ] m (-s; -) heretic

Ketzerei [kɛtsə'rai] f (-; -en) heresy

keuchen ['kɔʏçən] v/i (ge-, h) pant, gasp

'**Keuchhusten** m MED whooping cough

Keule ['kɔʏlə] f (-; -n) club; GASTR leg

keusch [kɔʏʃ] adj chaste

'**Keuschheit** f (-; no pl) chastity

Kfz [ka:ʔɛf'tsɛt] abbr of **Kraftfahrzeug** motor vehicle; **Kf'z-Brief** m, **Kf'z--Schein** m vehicle registration document; **Kf'z-Steuer** f road or automobile tax; **Kf'z-Werkstatt** f garage

KG [ka:'ge:] abbr of **Kommanditgesellschaft** ECON limited partnership

kichern ['kɪçɐn] v/i (ge-, h) giggle

Kiebitz ['ki:bɪts] m (-es; -e) ZO peewit, lapwing; F kibitzer

Kiefer[1] ['ki:fɐ] m (-s; -) ANAT jaw(bone)

'**Kiefer**[2] f (-; -n) BOT pine(tree)

Kiel [ki:l] m (-[e]s; -e) MAR keel; **~flosse** f AVIAT tail fin; **~raum** m MAR bilge; **~wasser** n (-s; -) MAR wake (a. fig)

Kieme ['ki:mə] f (-n; -n) ZO gill

Kies [ki:s] m (-es; -e) gravel (a. **mit ~ bestreuen**); F dough

Kiesel ['ki:zəl] m (-s; -) pebble

Kilo ['ki:lo] n (-s; -) → **Kilogramm**

Kilo|'gramm [kilo'gram] n kilogram(me); **~hertz** [kilo'hɛrts] n (-; -) kilohertz; **~'meter** m kilometer, Br kilometre; **~'watt** n ELECTR kilowatt

Kind [kɪnt] n (-[e]s; -er ['kɪndɐ]) child; **ein ~ erwarten** be expecting a baby

'**Kinder|arzt** m, **~ärztin** f p(a)ediatrician; **~garten** m kindergarten, nursery school; **~gärtnerin** ['kɪndɐgɛrtnərɪn] f (-; -nen) nursery-school or kindergarten teacher; **~geld** n child benefit; **~hort** m ['kɪndɐhɔrt] m (-[e]s; -e), **~krippe** f day nursery; **~lähmung** f MED polio(-myelitis)

'**kinderlieb** adj fond of children

'**kinderlos** adj childless

'**Kinder|mädchen** n nurse(maid), nanny; **~spiel** fig n: **ein ~ sein** be child's play; **~stube** fig f manners, upbringing; **~wagen** m baby carriage, buggy, Br pram; **~zimmer** n children's room

Kindes|alter ['kɪndəs'altɐ] n childhood; infancy; **~entführung** f kidnap-(p)ing; **~misshandlung** f child abuse

'**Kindheit** f (-; no pl) (**von ~ an** from) childhood

kindisch ['kɪndɪʃ] *adj* childish
'kindlich *adj* childlike
Kinn [kɪn] *n* (-[e]s; -e) ANAT chin; **~backe** *f*, **~backen** *m* (-s; -) ANAT jaw(-bone); **~haken** *m* boxing: hook (to the chin), uppercut
Kino ['ki:no] *n* (-s; -s) (*no pl*) motion pictures, *esp Br* cinema, F *the* movies; movie theater, *esp Br* cinema
'Kinobesucher *m*, **'Kinogänger** ['ki:nogɛŋɐ] *m* (-s; -) moviegoer, *Br* cinemagoer
Kippe ['kɪpə] *f* (-; -n) F butt, *esp Br* stub; SPORT upstart
'kippen 1. *v/i* (ge-, *sein*) tip *or* topple (over) 2. *v/t* (ge-, *h*) tilt, tip over *or* up
Kirche ['kɪrçə] *f* (-; -n) church; **in die ~ gehen** go to church
'Kirchen|buch *n* parish register; **~diener** *m* sexton; **~gemeinde** *f* parish; **~jahr** *n* Church *or* ecclesiastical year; **~lied** *n* hymn; **~mu,sik** *f* sacred *or* church music; **~schiff** *n* ARCH nave; **~steuer** *f* church tax; **~stuhl** *m* pew; **~tag** *m* church congress
'Kirchgang *m* churchgoing; **Kirchgänger** ['kɪrçgɛŋɐ] *m* (-s; -) churchgoer
'kirchlich *adj* church, ecclesiastical
'Kirchturm *m* steeple; spire; church tower
Kirsche ['kɪrʃə] *f* (-; -n) BOT cherry
Kissen ['kɪsən] *n* (-s; -) pillow; cushion; **~bezug** *m*, **~hülle** *f* pillowcase, pillowslip
Kiste ['kɪstə] *f* (-; -n) box, chest; crate
Kitsch [kɪtʃ] *m* (-[e]s; *no pl*) kitsch; trash; F slush
'kitschig *adj* kitschy; trashy; slushy
Kitt [kɪt] *m* (-[e]s; -e) cement; putty
Kittel ['kɪtəl] *m* (-s; -) smock; overall; MED (white) coat
'kitten *v/t* (ge-, *h*) cement; putty
Kitzel ['kɪtsəl] *m* (-s; -) tickle, *fig a.* thrill, kick; **'kitzeln** *v/i and v/t* (ge-, *h*) tickle; **Kitzler** ['kɪtslɐ] *m* (-s; -) ANAT clitoris; **kitzlig** ['kɪtslɪç] *adj* ticklish (*a. fig*)
kläffen ['klɛfən] *v/i* (ge-, *h*) yap, yelp
klaffend ['klafənt] *adj* gaping; yawning
Klage ['kla:gə] *f* (-; -n) complaint; lament; JUR action, (law)suit
'klagen *v/i* (ge-, *h*) complain (**über** *acc* of, about; **bei** to); lament; JUR go to court; **gegen j-n ~** JUR sue s.o.

Kläger ['klɛ:gɐ] *m* (-s; -), **'Klägerin** *f* (-; -nen) JUR plaintiff
kläglich ['klɛ:klɪç] → **jämmerlich**
Klamauk [kla'mauk] *m* (-s; *no pl*) racket; THEA *etc* slapstick
klamm [klam] *adj* numb; clammy
Klammer ['klamɐ] *f* (-; -n) TECH cramp, clamp; clip; clothespin, *Br* (clothes) peg; MED brace; MATH, PRINT bracket(s); **'klammern** *v/t* (ge-, *h*) fasten *or* clip together; **sich ~ an** (*acc*) cling to
klang [klaŋ] *pret of* **klingen**
Klang *m* (-[e]s; Klänge ['klɛŋə]) sound; tone; clink; ringing
'klangvoll *adj* sonorous; *fig* illustrious
Klappe ['klapə] *f* (-; -n) flap; hinged lid; MOT tailgate, *Br* tailboard; TECH, BOT, ANAT valve; F trap; **'klappen** (ge-, *h*) 1. *v/t*: **nach oben ~** lift up, raise; put *or* fold up; **nach unten ~** lower, put down; **es lässt sich** (**nach hinten**) ~ it folds (backward) 2. *v/i* clap, clack; F work, work out (well)
Klapper ['klapɐ] *f* (-; -n) rattle
'klappern *v/i* (ge-, *h*) clatter, rattle (**mit et.** s.th.)
'Klapperschlange *f* ZO rattlesnake
Klapp|fahrrad ['klapfaːraːt] *n* folding bicycle; **~fenster** *n* top-hung window; **~messer** *n* jack knife, clasp knife
klapprig ['klaprɪç] *adj* MOT rattly, ramshackle; F shaky
'Klappsitz *m* folding *or* tip-up seat
'Klappstuhl *m* folding chair
'Klapptisch *m* folding table
Klaps [klaps] *m* (-es; -e) slap, pat; smack
klar [klaːr] *adj* clear (*a. fig*); **ist dir ~, dass ...?** do you realize that ...?; **das ist mir** (**nicht ganz**) ~ I (don't quite) understand; (**na**) ~! of course!; **alles ~?** everything okay?
Kläranlage ['klɛːrʔanlaːgə] *f* sewage works
klären ['klɛːrən] *v/t* (ge-, *h*) TECH purify, treat; *fig* clear up; settle; SPORT clear
'Klarheit *f* (-; *no pl*) clearness, *fig a.* clarity
Klarinette [klari'nɛtə] *f* (-; -n) MUS clarinet
'Klarsicht... *in cpds* transparent
Klasse ['klasə] *f* (-; -n) class (*a.* POL), PED *a.* grade, *Br* form; classroom; F **klasse sein** be super, be fantastic
'Klassen|arbeit *f* (classroom) test;

~buch n classbook, Br (class) register; **~kame,rad** m classmate; **~lehrer(in)** homeroom teacher, Br form teacher, a. form master (mistress); **~sprecher** m class representative; **~zimmer** n classroom

klassifizieren [klasifi'tsi:rən] v/t (no -ge-, h) classify; **Klassifi'zierung** f (-; -en) classification

Klassiker ['klasɪkɐ] m (-s; -) classic

klassisch ['klasɪʃ] adj classic(al)

Klatsch [klatʃ] F m (-es; no pl) gossip

'Klatschbase f gossip

'klatschen v/i and v/t (ge-, h) clap, applaud; F slap, bang; splash; F gossip; **in die Hände ~** clap one's hands

'klatschhaft adj gossipy

'Klatschmaul F n (old) gossip

'klatsch'nass F adj soaking wet

klauben ['klaubən] Austrian v/t (ge-, h) pick; gather

Klaue ['klauə] f (-; -n) zo claw; pl fig clutches

klauen ['klauən] F v/t (ge-, h) pinch

Klausel ['klauzəl] f (-; -n) JUR clause; condition

Klausur [klau'zu:ɐ] f (-; -en) test (paper), exam(ination)

Klavier [kla'vi:ɐ] n (-s; -e) MUS piano; **~ spielen** play the piano; **~kon,zert** n MUS piano concerto; piano recital

Klebeband ['kle:bəbant] n (-[e]s; -bänder) adhesive tape; **kleben** ['kle:bən] (ge-, h) **1.** v/t glue, paste; stick **2.** v/i stick, cling (**an** dat to) (a. fig); **klebrig** ['kle:brɪç] adj sticky

Kleb|stoff ['kle:pʃtɔf] m adhesive; glue; **~streifen** m adhesive tape

kleckern ['klɛkɐn] F (ge-, h) **1.** v/i make a mess **2.** v/t spill

Klecks [klɛks] F m (-es; -e) (ink)blot; blob; **klecksen** ['klɛksən] F v/i (ge-, h) blot, make blots

Klee [kle:] m (-s; no pl) BOT clover

'Kleeblatt n cloverleaf

Kleid [klait] n (-[e]s; -er ['klaidɐ]) dress; pl clothes; **kleiden** ['klaidən] v/t (ge-, h) dress, clothe; **j-n gut ~** suit s.o.; **sich gut** etc **~** dress well etc

Kleider|bügel ['klaidɐby:gəl] m (coat) hanger; **~bürste** f clothes brush; **~haken** m coat hook; **~schrank** m wardrobe; **~ständer** m coat stand; **~stoff** m dress material

'kleidsam adj becoming

'Kleidung f (-; no pl) clothes, clothing

'Kleidungsstück n article of clothing

Kleie ['klaiə] f (-; -n) AGR bran

klein [klain] adj small, esp F little (a. finger, brother); short; **von ~ auf** from an early age; **ein ~ wenig** a little bit; **Groß und Klein** young and old; **die Kleinen** the little ones; **~ schneiden** cut up (into small pieces)

'Klein|anzeige f want ad, Br small ad; **~bildkamera** f 35 mm camera; **~fa,milie** f nuclear family; **~geld** n (small) change; **~holz** n matchwood

Kleinigkeit ['klainɪçkait] f (-; -en) little thing, trifle; little something; **e-e ~ sein** be nothing, be child's play

'Kleinkind n baby, infant

'Kleinkram F m odds and ends

'kleinlaut adj subdued

'kleinlich adj small-minded, petty; mean; pedantic, fussy

'kleinschneiden v/t (irr, **schneiden**, sep, -ge-, h) → **klein**

'Kleinstadt f small town; **'kleinstädtisch** adj small-town, provincial

'Kleintrans,porter m MOT pick-up

'Kleinwagen m MOT small or compact car, F runabout

Kleister ['klaistɐ] m (-s; -) paste

Klemme ['klɛmə] f (-; -n) TECH clamp; (hair) clip; F **in der ~ sitzen** be in a fix or tight spot; **'klemmen** v/i and v/t (ge-, h) jam; stick; be stuck, be jammed; **sich ~** jam one's finger or hand

Klempner ['klɛmpnɐ] m (-s; -) plumber

Klepper ['klɛpɐ] m (-s; -) zo nag

Klerus ['kle:rʊs] m (-; no pl) REL clergy

Klette ['klɛtə] f (-; -n) BOT bur(r); fig leech

klettern ['klɛtɐn] v/i (ge-, sein) climb; **auf e-n Baum ~** climb (up) a tree

'Kletterpflanze f BOT climber

Klient [kli'ɛnt] m (-en; -en), **Kli'entin** f (-; -nen) client

Klima ['kli:ma] n (-s; -s) climate, fig a. atmosphere

'Klimaanlage f air-conditioning

klimatisch [kli'ma:tɪʃ] adj climatic

klimpern ['klɪmpɐn] v/i (ge-, h) jingle, chink (**mit et.** s.th.); F MUS strum (away) (**auf** dat on)

Klinge ['klɪŋə] *f* (-; -*n*) blade

Klingel ['klɪŋəl] *f* (-; -*n*) bell

'**Klingelknopf** *m* bell (push)

'**klingeln** *v/i* (*ge*-, *h*) ring (the bell); *es klingelt* the (door)bell is ringing

'**klingen** *v/i* (*irr, ge*-, *h*) sound; *bell, metal etc*: ring; *glasses etc*: clink

Klinik ['kliːnɪk] *f* (-; -*en*) hospital; clinic

klinisch ['kliːnɪʃ] *adj* clinical

Klinke ['klɪŋkə] *f* (-; -*n*) (door) handle

Klippe ['klɪpə] *f* (-; -*n*) cliff, rock(s); *fig* obstacle

klirren ['klɪrən] *v/i* (*ge*-, *h*) *window*: rattle; *glasses etc*: clink; *broken glass*: tinkle; *swords*: clash; *keys, coins*: jingle

Klischee [kli'ʃeː] *n* (-s; -s) cliché

klobig ['kloːbɪç] *adj* bulky, clumsy

klopfen ['klɔpfən] (*ge*-, *h*) **1.** *v/i heart etc*: beat, throb; knock (*an acc* at, on); tap; pat; *es klopft* there's a knock at the door **2.** *v/t* beat; knock; drive (*nail etc*)

Klosett [klo'zɛt] *n* (-s; -s) lavatory, toilet

Kloß [kloːs] *m* (-es; *Klöße* ['kløːsə]) clod, lump (*a. fig*); GASTR dumpling

Kloster ['kloːstɐ] *n* (-s; *Klöster* ['kløːstɐ]) REL monastery; convent

Klotz [klɔts] *m* (-es; *Klötze* ['klœtsə]) block; log

Klub [klʊp] *m* (-s; -s) club

'**Klubsessel** *m* lounge chair

Kluft [klʊft] *f* (-; *Klüfte* ['klʏftə]) gap (*a. fig*); abyss

klug [kluːk] *adj* intelligent, clever, F bright, smart; wise; *daraus* (*aus ihm*) *werde ich nicht ~* I don't know what to make of it (him)

'**Klugheit** *f* (-; *no pl*) intelligence, cleverness, F brains; good sense; knowledge

Klumpen ['klʊmpən] *m* (-s; -) lump; clod; nugget; '**Klumpfuß** *m* MED club foot; '**klumpig** *adj* lumpy; cloddish

knabbern ['knabɐn] *v/t and v/i* (*ge*-, *h*) nibble, gnaw

Knabe ['knaːbə] *m* (-n; -n) boy

'**knabenhaft** *adj* boyish

Knäckebrot ['knɛkəbroːt] *n* crispbread

knacken ['knakən] *v/t and v/i* (*ge*-, *h*) crack; *twig*: snap; *fire, radio*: crackle

Knacks F *m* (-es; -e) crack; *fig* defect

Knall [knal] *m* (-[e]s; -e) bang; crack, report; pop; F *e-n ~ haben* be nuts

'**Knallbon,bon** *m, n* cracker

'**knallen** *v/i and v/t* (*ge*-, *h*) bang; slam; crack; pop; F crash (*gegen* into); F *j-m e-e ~* slap s.o.('s face)

'**knallig** F *adj* flashy, loud

'**Knallkörper** *m* firecracker

knapp [knap] *adj* scarce; scanty, meager, *Br* meagre (*food, pay etc*); bare (*a. majority etc*); limited (*time etc*); narrow (*escape etc*); tight (*dress etc*); brief; *~ an Geld* (*Zeit etc*) short of money (*time etc*); *mit ~er Not* only just, barely

Knappe ['knapə] *m* (-n; -n) miner

'**knapphalten** *v/t* (*irr, halten, sep, -ge-, h*): *j-n ~* keep s.o. short

'**Knappheit** *f* (-; *no pl*) shortage

Knarre ['knarə] *f* (-; -*n*) rattle; F gun

'**knarren** *v/i* (*ge*-, *h*) creak

Knast [knast] F *m* (-[e]s; *Knäste* ['knɛstə]) *sl* clink

knattern ['knatɐn] *v/i* (*ge*-, *h*) crackle; MOT roar

Knäuel ['knɔʏəl] *m, n* (-s; -) ball; tangle

Knauf [knauf] *m* (-[e]s; *Knäufe* ['knɔʏfə]) knob; pommel

knaus(e)rig ['knauz(ə)rɪç] F *adj* stingy

knautschen ['knautʃən] *v/t and v/i* (*ge*-, *h*) crumple

'**Knautschzone** *f* MOT crumple zone

Knebel ['kneːbəl] *m* (-s; -), '**knebeln** *v/t* (*ge*-, *h*) gag (*a. fig*)

kneifen ['knaifən] *v/t and v/i* (*irr, ge*-, *h*) pinch (*j-m in den Arm* s.o.'s arm); F chicken out; '**Kneifzange** *f* pincers

Kneipe ['knaipə] F *f* (-; -*n*) saloon, bar, *esp Br* pub

kneten ['kneːtən] *v/t* (*ge*-, *h*) knead; mo(u)ld; '**Knetmasse** *f* Plasticine®, Play-Doh®

Knick [knɪk] *m* (-[e]s; -e, -s) fold, crease; bend; '**knicken** *v/t* (*ge*-, *h*) fold, crease; bend; break; *nicht ~!* do not bend!

Knicks [knɪks] *m* (-es; -e) curts(e)y; *e-n ~ machen* → '**knicksen** *v/i* (*ge*-, *h*) curts(e)y (*vor dat* to)

Knie [kniː] *n* (-s; - ['kniːə, kniː]) ANAT knee; *~beuge* *f* SPORT knee bend; *~kehle* *f* ANAT hollow of the knee

knien [kniːn] *v/i* (*ge*-, *h*) kneel, be on one's knees (*vor dat* before)

'**Kniescheibe** *f* ANAT kneecap

'**Kniestrumpf** *m* knee(-length) sock

kniff [knɪf] *pret of* **kneifen**

Kniff *m* (-[e]s; -e) crease, fold; pinch; trick, knack

kniff(e)lig ['knɪf(ə)lɪç] *adj* tricky

knipsen ['knɪpsən] *v/t and v/i* (ge-, h) F PHOT take a picture (of); punch, clip

Knirps [knɪrps] *m* (-es; -e) little guy

knirschen ['knɪrʃən] *v/i* (ge-, h) crunch; **mit den Zähnen** ~ grind *or* gnash one's teeth

knistern ['knɪstɐn] *v/i* (ge-, h) crackle, rustle

knittern ['knɪtɐn] *v/t and v/i* (ge-, h) crumple, crease, wrinkle

Knoblauch ['kno:plaux] *m* (-[e]s; *no pl*) BOT garlic

Knöchel ['knœçəl] *m* (-s; -) ANAT ankle; knuckle

Knochen ['knɔxən] *m* (-s; -) ANAT bone

'Knochenbruch *m* MED fracture

knochig ['knɔxɪç] *adj* bony

Knödel ['knø:dəl] *m* (-s; -) dumpling

Knolle ['knɔlə] *f* (-; -n) BOT tuber; bulb

Knopf [knɔpf] *m* (-es; *Knöpfe* ['knœp-fə]), **knöpfen** ['knœpfən] *v/t* (ge-, h) button

'Knopfloch *n* buttonhole

Knorpel ['knɔrpəl] *m* (-s; -) GASTR gristle; ANAT cartilage

knorrig ['knɔrɪç] *adj* gnarled, knotted

Knospe ['knɔspə] *f* (-; -n), **'knospen** *v/i* (ge-, h) BOT bud

knoten [kno:tən] *v/t* (ge-, h) knot, make a knot in; **'Knoten** *m* (-s; -) knot (*a. fig*); **'Knotenpunkt** *m* center, *Br* centre; RAIL junction

knüllen ['knʏlən] *v/t and v/i* (ge-, h) crumple

Knüller ['knʏlɐ] F *m* (-s; -) smash (hit); scoop

knüpfen ['knʏpfən] *v/t* (ge-, h) tie; weave

Knüppel ['knʏpəl] *m* (-s; -) stick, cudgel; truncheon; **~schaltung** *f* floor shift

knurren ['knʊrən] *v/i* (ge-, h) growl, snarl; *fig* grumble (**über** *acc* at); *stomach*: rumble

knusp(e)rig ['knʊsp(ə)rɪç] *adj* crisp, crunchy

knutschen ['knu:tʃən] F *v/i* (ge-, h) pet, neck, smooch

k.o. [ka:'ʔo:] *adj* knocked out; *fig* beat ✓

Koalition [koali'tsjo:n] *f* (-; -en) *esp* POL coalition; **Große** ~ grand coalition

Kobold ['ko:bɔlt] *m* (-[e]s; -e) (hob)goblin, imp (*a. fig*)

Koch [kɔx] *m* (-[e]s; *Köche* ['kœçə]) cook; chef; **~buch** *n* cookbook, *Br* cookery book

'kochen (ge-, h) **1.** *v/t* cook; boil (*eggs etc*); make (*coffee etc*) **2.** *v/i* cook, do the cooking; boil (*a. fig*); **gut** ~ be a good cook; F **vor Wut** ~ boil with rage; **~d heiß** boiling hot

Kocher ['kɔxɐ] *m* (-s; -) ELECTR cooker

Köchin ['kœçɪn] *f* (-; -nen) cook; chef

'Koch|löffel *m* (wooden) spoon; **~ni-sche** *f* kitchenette; **~platte** *f* hotplate; **~salz** *n* common salt; **~topf** *m* saucepan, pot

Köder ['kø:dɐ] *m* (-s; -) bait, decoy (*both a. fig*), lure; **'ködern** *v/t* (ge-, h) bait, decoy (*both a. fig*)

Kodex ['ko:dɛks] *m* (-es; -, -e) code

kodieren [ko'di:rən] *v/t* (*no* -ge-, h) (en)code; **Ko'dierung** *f* (-; -en) (en)coding

Koffein [kɔfe'i:n] *n* (-s; *no pl*) caffeine

Koffer ['kɔfɐ] *m* (-s; -) (suit)case; trunk; **~radio** *n* portable (radio); **~raum** *m* MOT trunk, *Br* booth

Kognak® ['kɔnjak] *m* (-s; -s) cognac® brandy from the Cognac region in France

Kohl [ko:l] *m* (-[e]s; -e) BOT cabbage

Kohle ['ko:lə] *f* (-; -n) coal; ELECTR carbon; F dough

'Kohlehy,drat *n* carbohydrate

'Kohlen... *in cpds* ...*dioxid etc*: CHEM carbon ...; **~bergwerk** *n* coalmine, colliery; **~ofen** *m* coal-burning stove

'Kohlensäure *f* CHEM carbonic acid; GASTR F fizz; **'kohlensäurehaltig** *adj* carbonated, F fizzy

'Kohlen|stoff *m* CHEM carbon; **~was-serstoff** *m* CHEM hydrocarbon

'Kohle|pa,pier *n* carbon paper; **~zeich-nung** *f* charcoal drawing

Kohlrabi [ko:l'ra:bi] *m* (-s; -s) BOT kohlrabi

Koje ['ko:jə] *f* (-; -n) MAR berth, bunk

Kokain [koka'i:n] *n* (-s; *no pl*) cocaine

kokettieren [kokɛ'ti:rən] *v/i* (*no* -ge-, h) flirt; *fig* ~ **mit** toy with

Kokosnuss ['ko:kɔsnʊs] *f* BOT coconut

Koks [ko:ks] *m* (-es; *no pl*) coke; F dough; *sl* coke, snow

Kolben ['kɔlbən] *m* (-s; -) butt; TECH piston; **~stange** *f* TECH piston rod

Kolibri ['ko:libri] *m* (-s; -s) ZO humming bird

Kolleg [kɔ'le:k] *n* (-s; -s) UNIV course (of lectures)

Kollege

Kollege [kɔ'le:gə] *m* (-*n*; -*n*), **Kol'legin** *f* (-; -*nen*) colleague

Kollegium [kɔ'le:gjʊm] *n* (-*s*; -*ien*) UNIV faculty, *Br* teaching staff

Kollekte [kɔ'lɛktə] *f* (-; -*n*) REL collection

Kollektion [kɔlɛk'tsjoːn] *f* (-; -*en*) ECON collection; range

kollektiv [kɔlɛk'tiːf] *adj*, **Kollek'tiv** *n* (-*s*; -*e*) collective (*a. in cpds*)

Koller ['kɔlɐ] F *m* (-*s*; -) fit; rage

kollidieren [kɔli'diːrən] *v/i* (*no -ge-, sein*) collide; **Kollision** [kɔli'zjoːn] *f* (-; -*en*) collision, *fig a.* clash, conflict

Kölnischwasser ['kœlnɪʃvasɐ] *n* (-*s*; -) (eau de) cologne

Kolonie [kolo'niː] *f* (-; -*n*) colony

kolonisieren [koloni'ziːrən] *v/t* (*no -ge-, h*) colonize; **Koloni'sierung** *f* (-; -*en*) colonization

Kolonne [ko'lɔnə] *f* (-; -*n*) column; MIL convoy; gang, crew

Koloss [ko'lɔs] *m* (-*es*; -*e*) colossus, *fig a.* giant (of a man)

kolossal [kolɔ'saːl] *adj* gigantic

Kombi ['kɔmbi] *m* (-[*s*]; -*s*) MOT station wagon, *Br* estate (car)

Kombination [kɔmbina'tsjoːn] *f* (-; -*en*) combination; set; coveralls, *Br* overalls; flying suit; *soccer:* combined move

kombinieren [kɔmbi'niːrən] (*no -ge-, h*) **1.** *v/t* combine **2.** *v/i* reason

Kombüse [kɔm'byːzə] *f* (-; -*n*) MAR galley

Komet [ko'meːt] *m* (-*en*; -*en*) ASTR comet

Komfort [kɔm'foːɐ] *m* (-*s*; *no pl*) (modern) conveniences; luxury

komfortabel [kɔmfɔr'taːbəl] *adj* comfortable; well-appointed; luxurious

Komik ['koːmɪk] *f* (-; *no pl*) humo(u)r; comic effect; **Komiker** ['koːmikɐ] *m* (-*s*; -) comedian; **komisch** ['koːmɪʃ] *adj* comic(al), funny; strange, odd

Komitee [komi'teː] *n* (-*s*; -*s*) committee

Komma ['kɔma] *n* (-*s*; -*s*, -*ta*) comma; **sechs ~ vier** six point four

Kommandant [kɔman'dant] *m* (-*en*; -*en*), **Kommandeur** [kɔman'døːɐ] *m* (-*s*; -*e*) MIL commander, commanding officer; **kommandieren** [kɔman-'diːrən] *v/i and v/t* (*no -ge-, h*) command, be in command of; **Kommando** [kɔ'mando] *n* (-*s*; -*s*) command; order;

MIL commando; **Kom'mandobrücke** *f* MAR (navigating) bridge

kommen ['kɔmən] *v/i* (*irr, ge-, sein*) come; arrive; get; reach; **zu spät ~** be late; **weit ~** get far; **zur Schule ~** start school; **ins Gefängnis ~** go to jail; **~ lassen** send for *s.o.*, call *s.o.*; order *s.th.*; **~ auf** (*acc*) think of, hit upon; remember; **hinter et. ~** find s.th. out; **um et. ~** lose s.th.; miss s.th.; **zu et. ~** come by s.th.; **wieder zu sich ~** come round *or* to; **wohin kommt ...?** where does ... go?; **daher kommt es, dass** that's why; **woher kommt es, dass ...?** why is it that ...?, F how come ...?

Kommentar [kɔmɛn'taːɐ] *m* (-*s*; -*e*) commentary; **kein ~!** no comment

Kommentator [kɔmɛn'taːtoːɐ] *m* (-*s*; -*en* [kɔmɛnta'toːrən]), **Kommentatorin** [kɔmɛnta'toːrɪn] *f* (-; -*nen*) commentator

kommentieren [kɔmɛn'tiːrən] *v/t* (*no -ge-, h*) comment (on)

kommerzialisieren [kɔmɛrtsjali-'ziːrən] *v/t* (*no -ge-, h*) commercialize

Kommissar [kɔmɪ'saːɐ] *m* (-*s*; -*e*) commissioner; superintendent

Kommission [kɔmɪ'sjoːn] *f* (-; -*en*) commission; committee

Kommode [kɔ'moːdə] *f* (-; -*n*) bureau, *Br* chest (of drawers)

Kommunal... [kɔmu'naːl-] *in cpds* ...*politik etc:* local ...; **Kommune** [kɔ'muːnə] *f* (-; -*n*) commune

Kommunikation [kɔmunika'tsjoːn] *f* (-; *no pl*) communication

Kommunion [kɔmu'njoːn] *f* (-; -*en*) REL (Holy) Communion

Kommunismus [kɔmu'nɪsmʊs] *m* (-; *no pl*) POL communism; **Kommunist** [kɔmu'nɪst] *m* (-*en*; -*en*), **Kommunistin** *f* (-; -*nen*), **kommu'nistisch** *adj* POL communist

Komödie [ko'møːdjə] *f* (-; -*n*) comedy; **~ spielen** put on an act, play-act

kompakt [kɔm'pakt] *adj* compact

Kom'paktanlage *f* stereo system, music center (*Br* centre)

Kompanie [kɔmpa'niː] *f* (-; -*n*) MIL company

Kompass ['kɔmpas] *m* (-*es*; -*e*) compass

kompatibel [kɔmpa'tiːbəl] *adj* compatible (*a.* IT)

komplett [kɔm'plɛt] *adj* complete

Komplex [kɔm'plɛks] *m* (*-es*; *-e*) complex (*a.* PSYCH)

Kompliment [kɔmpli'mɛnt] *n* (-[*e*]*s*; *-e*) compliment; *j-m ein~ machen* pay s.o. a compliment

Komplize [kɔm'pliːtsə] *m* (*-n*; *-n*) accomplice

komplizieren [kɔmpli'tsiːrən] *v/t* (*no -ge-, h*) complicate; **kompliziert** [kɔmpli'tsiːɐt] *adj* complicated, complex

Kom'plizin *f* (-; *-nen*) accomplice

Komplott [kɔm'plɔt] *n* (-[*e*]*s*; *-e*) plot, conspiracy

komponieren [kɔmpo'niːrən] *v/t and v/i* (*no -ge-, h*) MUS compose; write; **Komponist** [kɔmpo'nɪst] *m* (*-en*; *-en*) MUS composer; **Komposition** [kɔmpozi'tsjoːn] *f* (-; *-en*) MUS composition

Kompott [kɔm'pɔt] *n* (-[*e*]*s*; *-e*) GASTR compot(e), stewed fruit

Kompresse [kɔm'prɛsə] *f* (-; *-n*) MED compress

komprimieren [kɔmpri'miːrən] *v/t* (*no -ge-, h*) compress

Kompromiss [kɔmpro'mɪs] *m* (*-es*; *-e*) compromise; **kompro'misslos** *adj* uncompromising

kompromittieren [kɔmprɔmɪ'tiːrən] *v/t* (*no -ge-, h*) compromise (*sich* o.s.); **~d** *adj* compromising

Kondensator [kɔndɛn'zaːtoːɐ] *m* (*-s*; *-en* [kɔndɛnza'toːrən]) ELECTR capacitor; TECH condenser; **kondensieren** [kɔndɛn'ziːrən] *v/t* (*no -ge-, h*) condense

Kondensmilch [kɔn'dɛnsmɪlç] *f* condensed milk

Kondition [kɔndi'tsjoːn] *f* (-; *-en*) condition; (*no pl*) SPORT condition, shape, form; *gute~* (great) stamina

konditional [kɔnditsjo'naːl] *adj* LING conditional

Konditi'onstraining *n* fitness training

Konditor [kɔn'diːtoːɐ] *m* (*-s*; *-en* [kɔndi'toːrən]) confectioner; pastrycook

Konditorei [kɔndito'rai] *f* (-; *-en*) cake shop; café, tearoom; *~waren pl* confectionery

Kondom [kɔn'doːm] *n, m* (*-s*; *-e*) condom

Kondukteur [kɔndʊk'tøːɐ] *Swiss m* (*-s*; *-e*) → *Schaffner*

Konfekt [kɔn'fɛkt] *n* (-[*e*]*s*; *-e*) sweets, chocolates

Konfektion [kɔnfɛk'tsjoːn] *f* (-; *no pl*) ready-made clothing; **Konfekti'ons...** *in cpds* ready-made ..., off-the-peg ...

Konferenz [kɔnfe'rɛnts] *f* (-; *-en*) conference

Konfession [kɔnfɛ'sjoːn] *f* (-; *-en*) religion, denomination; **konfessionell** [kɔnfɛsjo'nɛl] *adj* confessional, denominational; **Konfessi'onsschule** *f* denominational school

Konfirmand [kɔnfɪr'mant] *m* (*-en*; *-en*), **Konfir'mandin** *f* (-; *-nen*) REL confirmand; **Konfirmation** [kɔnfɪrma'tsjoːn] *f* (-; *-en*) REL confirmation; **konfirmieren** [kɔnfɪr'miːrən] *v/t* (*no -ge-, h*) confirm

konfiszieren [kɔnfɪs'tsiːrən] *v/t* (*no -ge-, h*) JUR confiscate

Konfitüre [kɔnfi'tyːrə] *f* (-; *-n*) jam

Konflikt [kɔn'flɪkt] *m* (-[*e*]*s*; *-e*) conflict

konfrontieren [kɔnfrɔn'tiːrən] *v/t* (*no -ge-, h*) confront

konfus [kɔn'fuːs] *adj* confused, mixed-up

Kongress [kɔn'grɛs] *m* (*-es*; *-e*) convention, *Br* congress

König ['køːnɪç] *m* (*-s*; *-e*) king

Königin ['køːnɪgɪn] *f* (-; *-nen*) queen

königlich ['køːnɪklɪç] *adj* royal

Königreich ['køːnɪkraiç] *n* kingdom

Konjugation [kɔnjuga'tsjoːn] *f* (-; *-en*) LING conjugation; **konjugieren** [kɔnju'giːrən] *v/t* (*no -ge-, h*) LING conjugate

Konjunktiv ['kɔnjʊŋktiːf] *m* (*-s*; *-e*) LING subjunctive (mood)

Konjunktur [kɔnjʊŋk'tuːɐ] *f* (-; *-en*) economic situation

konkret [kɔn'kreːt] *adj* concrete

Konkurrent [kɔnkʊ'rɛnt] *m* (*-en*; *-en*), **Konkur'rentin** *f* (-; *-nen*) competitor, rival; **Konkurrenz** [kɔnkʊ'rɛnts] *f* (-; *no pl*) competition; *die~* one's competitors; *außer~* not competing; → *konkurrenzlos*

konkur'renzfähig *adj* competitive

Konkur'renzkampf *m* competition

konkur'renzlos *adj* without competition, unrival(l)ed

konkurrieren [kɔnkʊ'riːrən] *v/i* (*no -ge-, h*) compete

Konkurs [kɔn'kʊrs] *m* (*-es*; *-e*) ECON, JUR bankruptcy; *in~ gehen* go bankrupt;

~masse *f* JUR bankrupt's estate

können ['kœnən] *v/t and v/i* (*irr*, ge-, *h*), *v/aux* (*irr, no -ge-, h*) can, be able to; may, be allowed to; *kann ich gehen etc?* can *or* may I go *etc?*; *du kannst nicht* you cannot *or* can't; *ich kann nicht mehr* I can't go on; I can't manage *or* eat any mòre; *es kann sein* it may be; *ich kann nichts dafür* it's not my fault; *e-e Sprache ~* know *or* speak a language

'Können *n* (*-s; no pl*) ability, skill

Könner ['kœnɐ] *m* (*-s; -*), **'Könnerin** *f* (*-; -nen*) master, expert; *esp* SPORT ace, crack

konnte ['kɔntə] *pret of* **können**

konsequent [kɔnze'kvɛnt] *adj* consistent; **Konsequenz** [kɔnze'kvɛnts] *f* (*-; -en*) (*no pl*) consistency; consequence

konservativ [kɔnzɛrva'tiːf] *adj* conservative

Konserven [kɔn'zɛrvən] *pl* canned (*Br a.* tinned) foods; **~büchse** *f*, **~dose** *f* can, *Br a.* tin; **~fa,brik** *f* cannery

konservieren [kɔnzɛr'viːrən] *v/t* (*no -ge-, h*) preserve; **Konser-'vierungsmittel** *n* preservative

Konsonant [kɔnzo'nant] *m* (*-en; -en*) LING consonant

konstruieren [kɔnstru'iːrən] *v/t* (*no -ge-, h*) construct; design

Konstrukteur [kɔnstrʊk'tøːɐ] *m* (*-s; -e*) TECH designer; **Konstruktion** [kɔnstrʊk'tsjoːn] *f* (*-; -en*) construction

Konsul ['kɔnzʊl] *m* (*-s; -n*) consul

Konsulat [kɔnzu'laːt] *n* (*-[e]s; -e*) consulate

konsultieren [kɔnzʊl'tiːrən] *v/t* (*no -ge-, h*) consult

Konsum[1] [kɔn'zuːm] *m* (*-s; no pl*) consumption

Konsum[2] ['kɔnzuːm] *m* (*-s; -s*) cooperative (society *or* store), F co-op

Konsument [kɔnzu'mɛnt] *m* (*-en; -en*), **Konsu'mentin** *f* (*-; -nen*) consumer; **Kon'sumgesellschaft** *f* consumer society; **konsumieren** [kɔnzu'miːrən] *v/t* (*no -ge-, h*) consume

Kontakt [kɔn'takt] *m* (*-[e]s; -e*) contact (*a.* ELECTR); **~ aufnehmen** get in touch; **~ haben** *or* **in ~ stehen mit** be in contact *or* touch with; **den ~ verlieren** lose

touch; **kon'taktfreudig** *adj* sociable

Kon'taktlinsen *pl* OPT contact lenses

Konter ['kɔntɐ] *m* (*-s; -*), **'kontern** *v/i* (*ge-, h*) counter (*a. fig*)

Kontinent [kɔnti'nɛnt] *m* (*-[e]s; -e*) continent

Konto ['kɔnto] *n* (*-s; Konten*) account

'Kontoauszug *m* (bank) statement

Kontrast [kɔn'trast] *m* (*-[e]s; -e*) contrast (*a.* PHOT, TV *etc*)

Kontrolle [kɔn'trɔlə] *f* (*-; -n*) control; supervision; check(up)

Kontrolleur [kɔntrɔ'løːɐ] *m* (*-s; -e*), **Kontrol'leurin** *f* (*-; -nen*) inspector, RAIL *a.* conductor

kontrollieren [kɔntrɔ'liːrən] *v/t* (*no -ge-, h*) check; check up on *s.o.*; control

Kon'trollpunkt *m* checkpoint

Kontroverse [kɔntro'vɛrzə] *f* (*-; -n*) controversy

konventionell [kɔnvɛntsjo'nɛl] *adj* conventional

Konversation [kɔnvɛrza'tsjoːn] *f* (*-; -en*) conversation; **Konversati-'onslexikon** *n* encyclop(a)edia

Konzentration [kɔntsɛntra'tsjoːn] *f* (*-; -en*) concentration

Konzentrati'onslager *n* concentration camp

konzentrieren [kɔntsɛn'triːrən] *v/t and v/refl* (*no -ge-, h*) concentrate; *sich auf et.* **~** concentrate on s.th.

Konzept [kɔn'tsɛpt] *n* (*-[e]s; -e*) (rough) draft; conception; *j-n aus dem ~ bringen* put s.o. out

Konzern [kɔn'tsɛrn] *m* (*-[e]s; -e*) ECON combine, group

Konzert [kɔn'tsɛrt] *n* (*-[e]s; -e*) MUS concert; concerto; **~halle** *f*, **~saal** *m* concert hall, auditorium

Konzession [kɔntse'sjoːn] *f* (*-; -en*) concession; license, *Br* licence

Kopf [kɔpf] *m* (*-[e]s; Köpfe* ['kœpfə]) head (*a. fig*); top; *fig a.* brains, mind; **~ hoch!** chin up!; *j-m ~ über den ~ wachsen* outgrow s.o.; *fig* be too much for s.o.; *sich den ~ zerbrechen* (*über acc*) rack one's brains (over); *sich et. aus dem ~ schlagen* put s.th. out of one's mind; **~ an ~** neck and neck; **~ball** *m* SPORT header; headed goal; **~bede-ckung** *f* headgear; *ohne ~* bareheaded

köpfen ['kœpfən] *v/t* (*ge-, h*) behead, decapitate; SPORT head (*ins Tor* home)

'**Kopf|ende** *n* head; **~hörer** *pl* headphones; **~jäger** *m* headhunter; **~kissen** *n* pillow

'**kopflos** *adj* headless; *fig* panicky

'**Kopf|rechnen** *n* mental arithmetic; **~sa,lat** *m* BOT lettuce; **~schmerzen** *pl* headache; **~sprung** *m* SPORT header; **~stand** *m* SPORT headstand; **~tuch** *n* scarf, (head)kerchief

kopf'über *adv* headfirst (*a. fig*)

'**Kopfweh** *n* → **Kopfschmerzen**

'**Kopfzerbrechen** *n*: *j-m ~ machen* give s.o. a headache

Kopie [ko'pi:] *f* (-; -n), **ko'pieren** *v/t* (*no -ge-*, *h*) copy; **Kopiergerät** [ko-'pi:ɐgəre:t] *n* copier

Koppel[1] ['kɔpəl] *f* (-; -n) paddock

'**Koppel**[2] *n* (-s; -) MIL belt

'**koppeln** *v/t* (*ge-*, *h*) couple; dock

Koralle [ko'ralə] *f* (-; -n) ZO coral

Korb [kɔrp] *m* (-[e]s; *Körbe* ['kœrbə]) basket

Kord [kɔrt] *m* (-[e]s; -e) corduroy

Kordel ['kɔrdəl] *f* (-; -n) cord

'**Kordhose** *f* corduroys

Korinthe [ko'rıntə] *f* (-; -n) currant

Kork [kɔrk] *m* (-[e]s; -e) BOT cork

'**Korkeiche** *f* BOT cork oak

Korken ['kɔrkən] *m* (-s; -) cork; **~zieher** ['kɔrkəntsi:ɐ] *m* (-s; -) corkscrew

Korn[1] [kɔrn] *n* (-[e]s; *Körner* ['kœrnɐ]) BOT grain; seed; (*no pl*) grain, *Br a.* corn; (*pl -e*) TECH front sight

Korn[2] F *m* (-[e]s; -e) (grain) schnapps

körnig ['kœrnıç] *adj* grainy

Körper ['kœrpɐ] *m* (-s; -) body (*a.* PHYS, CHEM), MATH *a.* solid, **~bau** *m* (-[e]s; *no pl*) build, physique

'**körperbehindert** *adj* (physically) disabled *or* handicapped

'**Körper|geruch** *m* body odo(u)r, BO; **~größe** *f* height; **~kraft** *f* physical strength

'**körperlich** *adj* physical

'**Körperpflege** *f* personal hygiene

'**Körperschaft** *f* (-; -en) corporation, (corporate) body

'**Körper|teil** *m* part of the body; **~verletzung** *f* JUR bodily injury

korrekt [kɔ'rɛkt] *adj* correct

Korrektur [kɔrɛk'tu:ɐ] *f* (-; -en) correction; PED *etc* grading, *Br* marking

Korrespondent [kɔrɛspɔn'dɛnt] *m* (-en; -en), **Korrespon'dentin** *f* (-;

-nen) correspondent; **Korrespondenz** [kɔrɛspɔn'dɛnts] *f* (-; -en) correspondence; **korrespondieren** [kɔrɛspɔn-'di:rən] *v/i* (*no -ge-*, *h*) correspond (*mit* with)

Korridor ['kɔridoːɐ] *m* (-s; -e) corridor; hall

korrigieren [kɔri'gi:rən] *v/t* (*no -ge-*, *h*) correct; PED *etc* grade, *Br* mark

korrupt [kɔ'rʊpt] *adj* corrupt(ed)

Korruption [kɔrʊp'tsjoːn] *f* (-; -en) corruption

Korsett [kɔr'zɛt] *n* (-s; -s) corset (*a. fig*)

Kosename ['koːzənaːmə] *m* pet name

Kosmetik [kɔs'meːtɪk] *f* (-; *no pl*) beauty culture; cosmetics, toiletries

Kosmetikerin [kɔs'meːtikərın] *f* (-; -nen) beautician, cosmetician

Kost [kɔst] *f* (-; *no pl*) food, diet; board

'**kostbar** *adj* precious, valuable; costly

'**Kostbarkeit** *f* (-; -en) precious object, treasure (*a. fig*)

kosten[1] ['kɔstən] *v/t* (*ge-*, *h*) cost, be; *fig* take (*time etc*); *was or wie viel kostet …?* how much it …?

'**kosten**[2] *v/t* (*ge-*, *h*) taste, try

'**Kosten** *pl* cost(s); price; expenses; charges; *auf j-s ~* at s.o.'s expense

'**kostenlos 1.** *adj* free **2.** *adv* free of charge

köstlich ['kœstlıç] *adj* delicious; *fig* priceless; *sich~ amüsieren* have great fun, F have a ball

'**Kostprobe** *f* taste, sample (*a. fig*)

'**kostspielig** *adj* expensive, costly

Kostüm [kɔs'tyːm] *n* (-s; -e) costume, dress; suit; **~fest** *n* fancy-dress ball

Kot [koːt] *m* (-[e]s; *no pl*) excrement, zo *a.* droppings

Kotelett [kotə'lɛt] *n* (-s; -s) chop, cutlet

Koteletten [kotə'lɛtən] *pl* sideburns

'**Kotflügel** *m* MOT fender, *Br* wing

kotzen ['kɔtsən] V *v/i* (*ge-*, *h*) puke

Krabbe ['krabə] *f* (-; -n) ZO shrimp; prawn

krabbeln ['krabəln] *v/i* (*ge-*, *sein*) crawl

Krach [krax] *m* (-[e]s; *Kräche* ['krɛçə]) crash, bang; (*no pl*) noise; F quarrel, fight

'**krachen** *v/i* (*ge-*, *h*) crack, bang, crash

Kracher ['kraxɐ] *m* (-s; -) (fire)cracker

krächzen ['krɛçtsən] *v/t and v/i* (*ge-*, *h*) croak

Kraft [kraft] *f* (-; *Kräfte* ['krɛftə])

strength, force (*a.* POL), power (*a.*
ELECTR, TECH, POL); *in ~ sein (setzen,
treten)* JUR *etc* be in (put into, come into) force; *~brühe f* GASTR consommé,
clear soup; *~fahrer(in)* driver, motor-
ist; *~fahrzeug n* motor vehicle

kräftig ['krɛftɪç] *adj* strong (*a.* fig), powerful; substantial (*food*); good

'**kraftlos** *adj* weak, feeble

'**Kraft|probe** *f* test of strength; *~stoff m*
MOT fuel; *~verschwendung f* waste of
energy; *~werk n* power station

Kragen ['kraːgən] *m* (*-s;* -) collar

Krähe ['krɛːə] *f* (*-;* -*n*) ZO crow

krähen ['krɛːən] *v/i* (ge-, *h*) crow

Krake ['kraːkə] *m* (*-n;* -*n*) ZO octopus

Kralle ['kralə] *f* (*-;* -*n*) ZO claw (*a.* fig)

'**krallen** *v/refl* (ge-, *h*) cling (*an acc* on),
clutch (at)

Kram [kraːm] F *m* (*-[e]s; no pl*) stuff,
(one's) things

Krampf [krampf] *m* (*-[e]s; Krämpfe*
['krɛmpfə]) MED cramp; spasm, convulsion; *~ader f* MED varicose vein

'**krampfhaft** *fig adj* forced (*smile etc*);
desperate (*attempt etc*)

Kran [kraːn] *m* (*-[e]s; Kräne* ['krɛːnə])
TECH crane

Kranich ['kraːnɪç] *m* (*-s;* -*e*) ZO crane

krank [kraŋk] *adj* ill, sick; *~ werden* get
sick, *Br* fall ill; '**Kranke** *m, f*(*-n;* -*n*) sick
person, patient; *die ~n* the sick

kränken ['krɛŋkən] *v/t* (ge-, *h*) hurt
(*s.o.'s* feelings), offend

'**Kranken|bett** *n* sickbed; *~geld n* sick-
ness benefit; *~gym,nastik f* physiotherapy; *~haus n* hospital; *~kasse f*
health insurance scheme; *in e-r ~ sein*
be a member of a health insurance
scheme *or* plan; *~pflege f* nursing;
~pfleger m male nurse; *~schein m*
health insurance certificate; *~schwe-
ter f* nurse; *~versicherung f* health insurance; *~wagen m* ambulance; *~zim-
mer n* sickroom

'**krankhaft** *adj* morbid (*a.* fig)

'**Krankheit** *f*(*-;* -*en*) illness, sickness, disease

'**Krankheitserreger** *m* germ

kränklich ['krɛŋklɪç] *adj* sickly, ailing

Kränkung ['krɛŋkʊŋ] *f*(*-;* -*en*) insult, offense, *Br* offence

Kranz [krants] *m* (*-es; Kränze*
['krɛntsə]) wreath; *fig* ring, circle

krass [kras] *adj* crass, gross; blunt

Krater ['kraːtɐ] *m* (*-s;* -) crater

kratzen ['kratsən] *v/t and v/refl* (ge-, *h*)
scratch (o.s.); scrape (*von* off)

Kratzer ['kratsɐ] *m* (*-s;* -) scratch (*a.*
MED)

kraulen ['kraulən] **1.** *v/t* (ge-, *h*) stroke;
run one's fingers through **2.** *v/i* (ge-,
sein) SPORT do the crawl

kraus [kraus] *adj* curly (*hair*); wrinkled

Krause ['krauzə] *f* (*-;* -*n*) ruff; friz(z)

kräuseln ['krɔyzəln] *v/t and v/refl* (ge-,
h) curl, friz(z); *water:* ripple

Kraut [kraut] *n* (*-[e]s; Kräuter* ['krɔytɐ])
BOT herb; tops, leaves; cabbage

Krawall [kra'val] *m* (*-s;* -*e*) riot; F row,
racket

Krawatte [kra'vatə] *f* (*-;* -*n*) tie

kreativ [krea'tiːf] *adj* creative

Kreativität [kreativi'tɛːt] *f*(*-; no pl*) cre-
ativity

Kreatur [krea'tuːɐ] *f* (*-;* -*en*) creature

Krebs [kreːps] *m* ZO crayfish; MED cancer; AST Cancer; *sie ist (ein)* ~ she's (a)
Cancer; *~ erregend* → krebserregend

Krebs... MED cancerous; **krebserregend** *adj* MED carcinogenic; *~ge-
schwulst f* MED carcinoma; *~kranke
m, f* cancer patient

Kredit [kre'diːt] *m* (*-[e]s;* -*e*) ECON credit; loan; *~karte f* credit card, *pl coll* F
plastic money

Kreide ['kraidə] *f* (*-;* -*n*) chalk; crayon

Kreis [krais] *m* (*-es;* -*e*) circle (*a.* fig); POL
district, county; *~bahn f* AST orbit

kreischen ['kraiʃən] *v/i* (ge-, *h*) screech;
squeal

Kreisel ['kraizəl] *m* (*-s;* -) (spinning)
top; PHYS gyro(scope); '**kreiseln** *v/i*
(ge-, *h, sein*) spin around

kreisen ['kraizən] *v/i* (ge-, *h, sein*) (move
in a) circle, revolve, rotate; circulate

kreisförmig ['kraisfœrmɪç] *adj* circular

'**Kreislauf** *m* MED, ECON circulation; BIOL
cycle (*a.* fig), TECH, ELECTR *a.* circuit;
~störungen pl MED circulatory trouble

'**Kreis|säge** *f* circular saw; *~verkehr m*
traffic circle, *Br* roundabout

Krempe ['krɛmpə] *f* (*-;* -*n*) brim

Kren [kreːn] *Austrian m* (*-[e]s; no pl*)
GASTR horseradish

Krepp [krɛp] *m* (*-s;* -*s*) crepe

Kreuz [krɔyts] *n* (*-es;* -*e*) cross (*a.* fig);
ANAT (small of the) back; *cards:* club(s);

MUS sharp; *über~* crosswise; F *j-n aufs ~ legen* take s.o. in; **kreuzen** ['krɔytsən] **1.** *v/t and v/i/refl (ge-, h)* cross; clash **2.** *v/i (ge-, sein)* MAR cruise
Kreuzer ['krɔytsɐ] *m (-s; -)* MAR cruiser
'**Kreuzfahrer** *m* HIST crusader
'**Kreuzfahrt** *f* MAR cruise
kreuzigen ['krɔytsɪgən] *v/t (ge-, h)* crucify; '**Kreuzigung** *f (-; -en)* crucifixion
'**Kreuzotter** *f* ZO adder
'**Kreuzschmerzen** *pl* backache
'**Kreuzung** *f (-; -en)* RAIL, MOT crossing, junction; intersection, crossroads; BIOL cross(breed)ing; cross(breed); *fig* cross
'**Kreuzverhör** *n* JUR cross-examination; *ins ~ nehmen* cross-examine
'**kreuzweise** *adv* crosswise, crossways
'**Kreuz|worträtsel** *n* crossword (puzzle); *~zug* HIST *m* crusade
kriechen ['kri:çən] *v/i (irr, ge-, sein)* creep, crawl; *fig vor j-m ~* toady to s.o.
Kriecher ['kri:çɐ] *contp m (-s; -)* toady
'**Kriechspur** *f* MOT slow lane
Krieg [kri:k] *m (-[e]s; -e* ['kri:gə]*)* war; *~ führen gègen* be at war with
kriegen ['kri:gən] F *v/t (ge-, h)* get; catch
Krieger ['kri:gɐ] *m (-s; -)* warrior
'**Kriegerdenkmal** *n* war memorial
kriegerisch ['kri:gərɪʃ] *adj* warlike, martial
'**Kriegführung** *f (-; no pl)* warfare
'**Kriegs|beil** *fig n: das ~ begraben* bury the hatchet; *~dienstverweigerer* *m (-s; -)* conscientious objector; *~erklärung f* declaration of war; *~gefangene m* prisoner of war, P.O.W.; *~gefangenschaft f* captivity; *~recht n* JUR martial law; *~schauplatz m* theater (*Br* theatre) of war; *~schiff n* warship; *~teilnehmer m* (war) veteran, *Br* ex-serviceman; *~verbrechen n* war crime; *~verbrecher m* war criminal
Krimi ['kri:mi] F *m (-s; -s)* (crime) thriller, detective novel
Kriminal|beamte [krimi'na:lbə ʔamtə] *m* detective, plain-clothesman; *~polizei f* criminal investigation department; *~roman m →* **Krimi**
kriminell [krimi'nɛl] adj, **Krimi'nelle** *m, f (-n; -n)* criminal
Krippe ['krɪpə] *f (-; -n)* crib, manger (*a.* REL); REL crèche, *Br* crib
Krise ['kri:zə] *f (-; -n)* crisis
'**Krisenherd** *m esp* POL trouble spot

Kristall[1] [krɪs'tal] *m (-s; -e)* crystal
Kris'tall[2] *n (s; no pl)*, *~glas n* crystal
kristallisieren [krɪstali'zi:rən] *v/i and v/i/refl (no -ge-, h)* crystallize
Kriterium [kri'te:rjʊm] *n (-s; -ien)* criterion (*für* of)
Kritik [kri'ti:k] *f (-; -en)* criticism; THEA, MUS *etc* review, critique; *gute ~en* a good press; *~ üben an (dat)* criticize;
Kritiker(in) ['kri:tikɐ, 'kri:tikərɪn] *m(f) (-s; -/-; -nen)* critic; **kri'tiklos** *adj* uncritical; **kritisch** ['kri:tɪʃ] *adj* critical (*a. fig*) (*gegenüber* of); **kritisieren** [kriti'zi:rən] *v/t (no -ge-, h)* criticize
kritzeln ['krɪtsəln] *v/t and v/i (ge-, h)* scrawl, scribble
kroch [krɔx] *pret of* **kriechen**
Krokodil [kroko'di:l] *n (-s; -e)* ZO crocodile
Krone ['kro:nə] *f (-; -n)* crown; coronet
krönen ['krø:nən] *v/t (ge-, h)* crown; *j-n zum König ~* crown s.o. king
'**Kronleuchter** *m* chandelier
'**Kronprinz** *m* crown prince
'**Kronprin,zessin** *f* crown princess
'**Krönung** *f (-; -en)* coronation; *fig* crowning event, climax, high point
Kropf [krɔpf] *m (-[e]s; Kröpfe* ['krœpfə]*)* MED goiter, *Br* goitre; ZO crop
Kröte ['krø:tə] *f (-; -n)* ZO toad
Krücke ['krʏkə] *f (-; -n)* crutch
Krug [kru:k] *m (-[e]s; Krüge* ['kry:gə]*)* jug, pitcher; mug, stein; tankard
Krümel ['kry:məl] *m (-s; -)* crumb
krümelig ['kry:məlɪç] *adj* crumbly
'**krümeln** *v/t and v/i (ge-, h)* crumble
krumm [krʊm] *adj* crooked (*a. fig*), bent
krummbeinig ['krʊmbainɪç] *adj* bow-legged
krümmen ['krʏmən] *v/t (ge-, h)* bend (*a.* TECH), crook; *sich ~* bend; writhe (with pain); '**Krümmung** *f (-; -en)* bend, curve; GEOGR, MATH, MED curvature
Krüppel ['krʏpəl] *m (-s; -)* cripple
Kruste ['krʊstə] *f (-; -n)* crust
Kto. *abbr of* **Konto** a/c, account
Kübel ['ky:bəl] *m (-s; -)* bucket, pail; tub
Kubik|meter [ku'bi:kme:tɐ] *m, n* cubic meter (*Br* metre); *~wurzel f* MATH cube root
Küche ['kʏçə] *f (-; -n)* kitchen; GASTR cooking, cuisine; *kalte (warme) ~* cold (hot) meals

Kuchen ['ku:xən] *m* (*-s*; *-*) cake; tart, pie

'**Küchen|geräte** *pl* kitchen utensils (*or* appliances); **~geschirr** *n* kitchen crockery, kitchenware; **~herd** *m* cooker; **~schrank** *m* (kitchen) cupboard

Kuckuck ['kʊkʊk] *m* (*-s*; *-s*) zo cuckoo

Kufe ['ku:fə] *f* (*-*; *-n*) runner; aviat skid

Kugel ['ku:gəl] *f* (*-*; *-n*) ball; bullet; math, geogr sphere; sport shot

kugelförmig ['ku:gəlfœrmɪç] *adj* ball-shaped, *esp* astr, math spheric(al)

'**Kugelgelenk** *n* tech, anat ball (and socket) joint

'**Kugellager** *n* tech ball bearing

'**kugeln** *v/i* (*ge-*, *sein*) *and* *v/t* (*h*) roll

Kugelschreiber ['ku:gəlʃraibɐ] *m* (*-s*; *-*) ballpoint (pen)

'**kugelsicher** *adj* bulletproof

'**Kugelstoßen** *n* (*-s*; *no pl*) sport shot put(ting); **Kugelstoßer** ['ku:gəlʃtoːsɐ] *m* (*-s*; *-*), **Kugelstoßerin** ['ku:gəlʃtoːsərɪn] *f* (*-*; *-nen*) sport shot-putter

Kuh [ku:] *f* (*-*; **Kühe** ['ky:ə]) zo cow

kühl [ky:l] *adj* cool (*a. fig*); '**Kühle** *f* (*-*; *no pl*) cool(ness); '**kühlen** *v/t* (*ge-*, *h*) cool; chill; refrigerate; refresh

Kühler ['ky:lɐ] *m* (*-s*; *-*) mot radiator

'**Kühlerhaube** *f* mot hood, *Br* bonnet

'**Kühlmittel** *n* coolant

'**Kühlraum** *m* cold-storage room

'**Kühlschrank** *m* fridge, refrigerator

'**Kühltruhe** *f* deep-freeze, freezer

'**Kühlwasser** *n* mot cooling water

kühn [ky:n] *adj* bold

'**Kühnheit** *f* (*-*; *no pl*) boldness

'**Kuhstall** *m* cowshed

Küken ['ky:kən] *n* (*-s*; *-*) zo chick (*a. fig*)

Kukuruz ['kukurʊts] *Austrian m* → **Mais**

Kuli ['ku:li] F *m* (*-s*; *-s*) ballpoint

Kulissen [ku'lɪsən] *pl* thea wings; scenery; **hinter den ~** backstage, *esp fig* behind the scenes

Kult [kʊlt] *m* (*-[e]s*; *-e*) cult; rite, ritual (act)

kultivieren [kʊlti'vi:rən] *v/t* (*no -ge-*, *h*) cultivate

Kultur [kʊl'tu:ɐ] *f* (*-*; *-en*) culture (*a. biol*), civilization; agr cultivation

Kul'turbeutel *m* toilet bag

kulturell [kʊltu'rɛl] *adj* cultural

Kul'tur|geschichte *f* history of civilization; **~zentrum** *n* cultural center (*Br* centre)

Kultusmi,nister ['kʊltʊsministɐ] *m* minister of education and cultural affairs

Kummer ['kʊmɐ] *m* (*-s*; *no pl*) grief, sorrow; trouble, worry; **~ haben mit** have trouble *or* problems with

kümmerlich ['kymɐlɪç] *adj* miserable; poor, scanty; **kümmern** ['kymɐn] *v/refl and v/t* (*ge-*, *h*) **sich ~ um** look after, take care of, mind; care *or* worry about, be interested in

Kumpel ['kʊmpəl] *m* (*-s*; *-*) miner; F mate, buddy, pal

Kunde ['kʊndə] *m* (*-n*; *-n*) customer, client; '**Kundendienst** *m* after-sales service; (customer) service; service department; tech servicing

Kundgebung ['kʊntge:bʊŋ] *f* (*-*; *-en*) meeting, rally, demonstration

kündigen ['kyndɪgən] *v/i and v/t* (*ge-*, *h*) cancel; **j-m ~** give s.o. his / her / one's notice; dismiss s.o., F sack *or* fire s.o.

'**Kündigung** *f* (*-*; *-en*) cancellation; (period of) notice

Kundin ['kʊndɪn] *f* (*-*; *-nen*) customer, client

Kundschaft ['kʊntʃaft] *f* (*-*; *-en*) customers, clients

Kunst [kʊnst] *f* (*-*; **Künste** ['kynstə]) art; skill; **~...** *in cpds* **...herz**, **...leder**, **...licht** *etc*: artificial; **~akade,mie** *f* academy of arts; **~ausstellung** *f* art exhibition; **~dünger** *m* agr artificial fertilizer; **~erziehung** *f* ped art (education); **~faser** *f* man-made *or* synthetic fiber (*Br* fibre); **~fehler** *m* professional blunder; **~fliegen** *n* stunt flying, aerobatics; **~geschichte** *f* history of art; **~gewerbe** *n*, **~handwerk** *n* arts and crafts

Künstler ['kynstlɐ] *m* (*-s*; *-*), **Künstlerin** ['kynstlərɪn] *f* (*-*; *-nen*) artist, mus, thea *a.* performer

künstlerisch ['kynstlərɪʃ] *adj* artistic

künstlich ['kynstlɪç] *adj* artificial; false; synthetic; man-made

'**Kunst|schwimmen** *n* water ballet; **~seide** *f* rayon; **~springen** *n* springboard diving; **~stoff** *m* plastic; **~stück** *n* trick, stunt, *esp fig* feat; gymnastics; **~turnen** *n* gymnastics; **~turner** *m* gymnast

'**kunstvoll** *adj* artistic; elaborate

'**Kunstwerk** *n* work of art

Kupfer ['kʊpfɐ] *n* (*-s*; *no pl*) copper (*aus*

of); **~stich** *m* copperplate (engraving)
Kupon [ku'põː] *m* (-*s*; -*s*) coupon
Kuppe ['kʊpə] *f* (-; -*n*) (rounded) hilltop; ANAT head
Kuppel ['kʊpəl] *f* (-; -*n*) ARCH dome; cupola
Kuppelei [kʊpə'lai] *f* (-; -*en*) JUR procuring
'**kuppeln** *v/i* (*ge*-, *h*) MOT put the clutch in *or* out; **Kupplung** ['kʊplʊŋ] *f* (-; -*en*) MOT clutch
Kur [kuːɐ] *f* (-; -*en*) course of treatment; cure
Kür [kyːɐ] *f* (-; -*en*) SPORT free skating; free exercises
Kurbel ['kʊrbəl] *f* (-; -*n*) crank, handle; '**kurbeln** *v/t* (*ge*-, *h*) crank; wind (up *etc*); '**Kurbelwelle** *f* TECH crankshaft
Kürbis ['kʏrbɪs] *m* (-*ses*; -*se*) BOT pumpkin, gourd, squash
'**Kurgast** *m* visitor
kurieren [ku'riːrən] *v/t* (*no* -*ge*-, *h*) cure (***von*** of)
kurios [ku'rjoːs] *adj* curious, odd, strange
'**Kürlauf** *m* SPORT free skating
'**Kurort** *m* health resort, spa
Kurpfuscher ['kuːɐpfʊʃɐ] *m* (-*s*; -) quack (doctor)
Kurs [kʊrs] *m* (-*es*; -*e*) AVIAT, MAR course (*a. fig*); PED *etc* class(es); ECON (exchange) rate; (stock) price
Kürschner ['kʏrʃnɐ] *m* (-*s*; -) furrier
kursieren [kʊr'ziːrən] *v/i* (*no* -*ge*-, *h*) circulate (*a. fig*)
Kurve ['kʊrvə] *f* (-; -*n*) curve (*a.* MATH *and fig*); bend, turn; '**kurvenreich** *adj* winding, full of bends; F curvaceous
kurz [kʊrts] *adj* short; brief; ***~e Hose*** shorts; (***bis***) ***vor ~em*** (until) recently; (***erst***) ***seit ~em*** (only) for a short time; ***~ vorher*** (***darauf***) shortly before (after[wards]); ***~ vor uns*** just ahead of us; ***~ nacheinander*** in quick succession; ***~ fortgehen*** *etc* go away for a short time *or* a moment; ***~ gesagt*** in short; ***zu ~ kommen*** go short; ***~ angebunden*** curt
'**Kurzarbeit** *f* ECON short time
'**kurzarbeiten** *v/i* (*sep*, *ge*-, *h*) ECON work short time
kurzatmig ['kʊrtsʔaːtmɪç] *adj* short of breath
Kürze ['kʏrtsə] *f* (-; *no pl*) shortness; brevity; ***in ~*** soon, shortly, before long
'**kürzen** *v/t* (*ge*-, *h*) shorten (***um*** by); abridge; cut, reduce (*a.* MATH)
kurzerhand ['kʊrtsɐ'hant] *adv* without hesitation, on the spot
'**kurzfassen** *v/refl* (*sep*, -*ge*-, *h*): ***sich ~*** be brief, put it briefly
'**kurzfristig 1.** *adj* short-term **2.** *adv* at short notice
'**Kurzgeschichte** *f* short story
kurzlebig ['kʊrtsleːbɪç] *adj* short-lived
kürzlich ['kʏrtslɪç] *adv* recently, not long ago
'**Kurz|nachrichten** *pl* news summary; **~schluss** *m* ELECTR short circuit, F short; **~schrift** *f* shorthand
'**kurzsichtig** *adj* nearsighted, *Br* shortsighted
'**Kurzstrecke** *f* short distance
'**Kürzung** *f* (-; -*en*) cut, reduction (*a.* MATH)
'**Kurzwaren** *pl* notions, *Br* haberdashery
kurzweilig ['kʊrtsvailɪç] *adj* entertaining
'**Kurzwelle** *f* PHYS, *radio*: short wave
kuschelig ['kʊʃəlɪç] F *adj* cozy, *Br* cosy, snug; **kuscheln** ['kʊʃəln] *v/refl* (*ge*-, *h*) snuggle, cuddle (***an*** *acc* up to; ***in*** *acc* in)
Kusine *f* → ***Cousine***
Kuss [kʊs] *m* (-*es*; *Küsse* ['kʏsə]) kiss
'**kussecht** *adj* kiss-proof
küssen ['kʏsən] *v/t* (*ge*-, *h*) kiss
Küste ['kʏstə] *f* (-; -*n*) coast, shore; ***an der ~*** on the coast; ***an die ~*** ashore
'**Küsten|gewässer** *pl* coastal waters; **~schifffahrt** *f* coastal shipping; **~schutz** *m*, **~wache** *f* coast guard
Küster ['kʏstɐ] *m* (-*s*; -) REL verger, sexton
Kutsche ['kʊtʃə] *f* (-; -*n*) carriage, coach; **Kutscher** ['kʊtʃɐ] *m* (-*s*; -) coachman
Kutte ['kʊtə] *f* (-; -*n*) (monk's) habit
Kutteln ['kʊtəln] *pl* GASTR tripe
Kutter ['kʊtɐ] *m* (-*s*; -) MAR cutter
Kuvert [ku'veːɐ] *n* (-*s*; -*s*) envelope
Kybernetik [kybɛr'neːtɪk] *f* (-; *no pl*) cybernetics

L

labil [la'biːl] *adj* unstable

Labor [la'boːɐ] *n* (-s; -e) laboratory, F lab; **Laborant(in)** [labo'rant(ɪn)] (-en; -en/-; -nen) laboratory assistant

Labyrinth [laby'rɪnt] *n* (-[e]s; -e) labyrinth, maze (*both a. fig*)

Lache [laxa] *f* (-; -n) pool, puddle

lächeln ['lɛçəln] *v/i* (ge-, h), **'Lächeln** *n* (-s; *no pl*) smile

lachen ['laxən] *v/i* (ge-, h) laugh (*über acc* at); **Lachen** *n* (-s; *no pl*) laugh (-ter); **j-n zum ~ bringen** make s.o. laugh; **lächerlich** ['lɛçɐlɪç] *adj* ridiculous; **~ machen** ridicule, make fun of; **sich ~ machen** make a fool of o.s.

Lachs [laks] *m* (-es; -e) zo salmon

Lack [lak] *m* (-[e]s; -e) varnish; lacquer; MOT paint(work)

lackieren [la'kiːrən] *v/t* (*no* -ge-, h) varnish; lacquer; paint (*a.* MOT)

'Lackschuhe *pl* patent-leather shoes

Ladefläche ['laːdəflɛçə] *f* loading space

'Ladegerät *n* ELECTR battery charger

'Ladehemmung *f* MIL jam

laden ['laːdən] *v/t* (*irr*, ge-, h) load; ELECTR charge; IT boot (up); *fig et.* **auf sich ~** burden o.s. with s.th.

'Laden *m* (-s; *Läden* ['lɛːdən]) store, *Br* shop; shutter; **~dieb** *m* shoplifter; **~diebstahl** *m* shoplifting; **~inhaber** *m* storekeeper, *Br* shopkeeper; **~kasse** *f* till; **~schluss** *m* closing time; **nach ~** after hours; **~tisch** *m* counter

'Laderampe *f* loading platform *or* ramp

'Laderaum *m* loading space; MAR hold

'Ladung *f* (-; -en) load, freight; AVIAT, MAR cargo; ELECTR, MIL charge; **e-e ~ ... a load of ...**

lag [laːk] *pret of* **liegen**

Lage ['laːgə] *f* (-; -n) situation, position (*both a. fig*); location; layer; round (*of beer etc*); **in schöner** (*ruhiger*) **~** beautifully (peacefully) situated; **in der ~ sein zu** *inf* be able to *inf*, be in a position to *inf*

Lager ['laːgɐ] *n* (-s; -) bed; camp (*a. fig*); ECON stock, store; GEOL deposit; TECH bearing; **et. auf ~ haben** have s.th. in store (*a. fig for s.o.*); **~feuer** *n* campfire; **~haus** *n* warehouse

'lagern (*ge-, h*) 1. *v/i* camp; ECON be stored 2. *v/t* store, keep; MED lay, rest; **kühl ~** keep in a cool place

'Lagerraum *m* storeroom

Lagerung ['laːgərʊŋ] *f* (-; *no pl*) storage

Lagune [la'guːnə] *f* (-; -n) lagoon

lahm [laːm] *adj* lame; **lahmen** ['laːmən] *v/i* (ge-, h) be lame (*auf dat* in)

lähmen ['lɛːmən] *v/t* (ge-, h) paralyze, *Br* paralyse; bring *traffic etc* to a standstill

'lahmlegen *v/t* (sep, -ge-, h) → **lähmen**

'Lähmung *f* (-; -en) MED paralysis

Laib [laip] *m* (-[e]s; -e ['laibə]) loaf

Laich [laiç] *m* (-[e]s; -e), **laichen** ['laiçən] *v/i* (ge-, h) spawn

Laie ['laiə] *m* (-n; -n) layman; amateur

'laienhaft *adj* amateurish

'Laienspiel *n* amateur play

Laken ['laːkən] *n* (-s; -) sheet; bath towel

Lakritze [la'krɪtsə] *f* (-; -n) liquorice

lallen ['lalən] *v/i and v/t* (ge-, h) speak drunkenly; *baby:* babble

Lamm [lam] *n* (-[e]s; *Lämmer* ['lɛmɐ]) zo lamb; **~fell** *n* lambskin

Lampe ['lampə] *f* (-; -n) lamp, light; bulb

'Lampenfieber *n* stage fright

'Lampenschirm *m* lampshade

Lampion [lam'pjoː-] *m* (-s; -s) Chinese lantern

Land [lant] *n* (-[e]s; *Länder* ['lɛndɐ]) land; country; AGR ground, soil; ECON land, property; **an ~ gehen** MAR go ashore; **auf dem ~e** in the country; **aufs ~ fahren** go into the country; **außer ~es gehen** go abroad; **~arbeiter** *m* farmhand; **~bevölkerung** *f* country *or* rural population

Landebahn ['landəbaːn] *f* AVIAT runway

land'einwärts *adv* up-country, inland

landen ['landən] *v/i* (ge-, sein) land; *fig v/i* **in** (*dat*) end up in

'Landenge *f* neck of land, isthmus

'Landeplatz *m* AVIAT landing field

Länderspiel ['lɛndɐʃpiːl] *n* SPORT international match

'Landes|grenze *f* national border; **~innere** *n* interior; **~re,gierung** *f* Land (*Austrian* Provincial) government;

~sprache f national language

'**landesüblich** adj customary

'**Landesverrat** m treason

'**Land|flucht** f rural exodus; **~friedens-bruch** m JUR breach of the public peace; **~gericht** n JUR appr regional superior court; **~haus** n country house, cottage; **~karte** f map; **~kreis** m district

'**landläufig** adj customary, current, common

ländlich ['lɛntlɪç] adj rural; rustic

'**Land|rat** m, **~rätin** ['lantrɛːtɪn] f (-; -nen) appr District Administrator

'**Landschaft** f (-; -en) countryside; scenery; esp PAINT landscape

'**landschaftlich** adj scenic

'**Landsmann** m (-[e]s; -leute) (fellow) countryman; **Landsmännin** ['lantsmɛnɪn] f (-; -nen) fellow countrywoman

'**Land|straße** f country (or ordinary) road; **~streicher(in)** tramp; **~streitkräfte** pl MIL land forces; **~tag** m Land parliament

'**Landung** f (-; -en) landing, AVIAT a. touchdown

'**Landungssteg** m MAR gangway

'**Land|vermesser** ['lantfɛɐmɛsɐ] m (-s; -) land surveyor; **~vermessung** f (-; -en) land surveying; **~weg** m: **auf dem ~e** by land; **~wirt(in)** farmer

'**Landwirtschaft** f (-; no pl) agriculture, farming; '**landwirtschaftlich** adj agricultural

'**Landzunge** f GEOGR promontory, spit

lang [laŋ] adj and adv long; F tall; **drei Jahre (einige Zeit) ~** for three years (some time); **den ganzen Tag ~** all day long; **seit ~em** for a long time; **vor ~er Zeit** (a) long (time) ago; **über kurz oder ~** sooner or later; **~ ersehnt** long-hoped-for; **~ erwartet** long-awaited; **gleich ~** the same length

langatmig ['laŋʔaːtmɪç] adj long-winded

lange ['laŋə] adv (for a) long (time); **es ist schon ~ her(, seit)** it has been a long time (since); **(noch) nicht ~ her** not long ago; **noch ~ hin** still a long way off; **es dauert nicht ~** it won't take long; **ich bleibe nicht ~ fort** I won't be long; **wie ~ noch?** how much longer?

Länge ['lɛŋə] f (-; -n) length; GEOGR longitude; **der ~ nach** (at) full length;

(sich) in die ~ ziehen stretch (a. fig)

langen ['laŋən] F v/i (ge-, h) reach (**nach** for); be enough; **mir langt es** I've had enough, fig a. I'm sick of it

'**Längen|grad** m GEOGR degree of longitude; **~maß** n linear measure

'**Langeweile** f (-; no pl) boredom; **~ haben** be bored; **aus ~** to pass the time

'**langfristig** adj long-term

'**langjährig** ['laŋjɛːrɪç] adj long-standing; **~e Erfahrung** many years of experience

'**Langlauf** m (-[e]s; no pl) SPORT cross-country (skiing)

langlebig ['laŋleːbɪç] adj long-lived

länglich ['lɛŋlɪç] adj longish, oblong

längs [lɛŋs] **1.** prp (gen) along(side) **2.** adv lengthwise

'**langsam** adj slow; **~er werden** or **fahren** slow down

'**Langschläfer** ['laŋʃlɛːfɐ] m (-s; -), **~schläferin** ['laŋʃlɛːfərɪn] f (-; -nen) late riser

längst [lɛŋst] adv long ago or before; **~ vorbei** long time past; **ich weiß es ~** I have known it for a long time; **längstens** ['lɛŋstəns] adv at (the) most

'**Langstrecken...** in cpds long-distance ...; AVIAT, MIL long-range ...

'**langweilen** v/t (ge-, h) bore; **sich ~** be bored; **langweilig** ['laŋvailɪç] adj boring, dull

'**Langwelle** f PHYS, radio: long wave

langwierig ['laŋviːrɪç] adj lengthy, protracted (a. MED)

Lanze ['lantsə] f (-; -n) lance, spear

Lappalie [laˈpaːljə] f (-; -n) trifle

Lappen ['lapən] m (-s; -) (piece of) cloth; rag (a. fig)

läppisch ['lɛpɪʃ] adj silly; ridiculous

Lärche ['lɛrçə] f (-; -n) BOT larch

Lärm [lɛrm] m (-s; no pl) noise

lärmen ['lɛrmən] v/i (ge-, h) be noisy; **~d** adj noisy

Larve ['larfə] f (-; -n) mask; ZO larva

las [laːs] pret of **lesen**

lasch [laʃ] F adj slack, lax

Lasche ['laʃə] f (-; -n) flap; tongue

Laser ['leːzɐ] m (-s; -) PHYS laser; **~drucker** m IT laser printer; **~strahl** m PHYS laser beam; **~technik** f laser technology

lassen ['lasən] v/t (irr, ge-, h) and v/aux

(*irr, no -ge-, h*) let, leave; *j-n et. tun* ~ let s.o. do s.th.; allow s.o. to do s.th.; make s.o. do s.th.; *j-n* (*et.*) *zu Hause* ~ leave s.o. (s.th.) at home; *j-n allein* (*in Ruhe*) ~ leave s.o. alone; *sich die Haare schneiden* ~ have *or* get one's hair cut; *sein Leben* ~ (*für*) lose (give) one's life (for); *rufen* ~ send for, call in; *es lässt sich machen* it can be done; *lass alles so, wie* (*wo*) *es ist* leave everything as (where) it is; *er kann das Rauchen etc nicht* ~ he can't stop smoking *etc*; *lass das!* stop it! → *grüßen, kommen*

lässig ['lɛsɪç] *adj* casual; careless

Last [last] *f* (-; *-en*) load, burden, weight (*all a. fig*); *j-m zur* ~ *fallen* be a burden to s.o.; *j-m et. zur* ~ *legen* charge s.o. with s.th.; **lasten** ['lastən] *v/i* (*ge-, h*) ~ *auf* (*dat*) *a. fig* weigh *or* rest (up)on

'**Lastenaufzug** *m* freight elevator, *Br* goods lift

Laster[1] ['lastɐ] *m* (*-s; -*) → *Lastwagen*

Laster[2] *n* (*-s; -*) vice

lästern ['lɛstɐn] *v/i* (*ge-, h*) ~ *über* (*acc*) run down

lästig ['lɛstɪç] *adj* troublesome, annoying; (*j-m*) ~ *sein* be a nuisance (to s.o.)

'**Last|kahn** *m* barge; ~**tier** *n* pack animal; ~**wagen** *m* MOT truck, *Br a.* lorry; ~**wagenfahrer** *m* MOT truck (*Br a.* lorry) driver, trucker

Latein [la'tain] *n* (*-s; no pl*) Latin

La'teina,merika Latin America; **La'teinameri,kaner(in)**, **la'teinameri,kanisch** *adj* Latin American

la'teinisch *adj* Latin

Laterne [la'tɛrnə] *f* (-; *-n*) lantern; streetlight

La'ternenpfahl *m* lamppost

Latte ['latə] *f* (-; *-n*) lath; pale; SPORT bar

'**Lattenzaun** *m* paling, picket fence

Lätzchen ['lɛtsçən] *n* (*-s; -*) bib

Laub [laup] *n* (*-[e]s; no pl*) foliage, leaves; '**Laubbaum** *m* deciduous tree

Laube ['laubə] *f* (-; *-n*) arbo(u)r

'**Laubfrosch** *m* ZO tree frog

'**Läubsäge** *f* fretsaw

Lauch [laux] *m* (*-[e]s; -e*) BOT leek

Lauer ['lauɐ] *f*: *auf der* ~ *liegen or sein* lie in wait; '**lauern** *v/i* (*ge-, h*) lurk; ~ *auf* (*acc*) lie in wait for

Lauf [lauf] *m* (*-[e]s; Läufe* ['lɔyfə]) run; course; *gun:* barrel; *im* ~(*e*) *der Zeit* in the course of time; ~**bahn** *f* career; ~**diszi,plin** *f* SPORT track event

laufen ['laufən] *v/i and v/t* (*irr, ge-, sein*) run (*a.* TECH, MOT, ECON); walk; *fig* work, run; *j-n* ~ *lassen* let s.o. go; let s.o. off; ~**d 1.** *fig adj* present, current (*a.* ECON); continual; *auf dem Laufenden sein* be up to date **2.** *adv* continuously; regularly; always

'**laufenlassen** *v/t* (*irr, lassen, sep, no -ge-, h*) → *laufen*

Läufer ['lɔyfɐ] *m* (*-s; -*) runner (*a. carpet*); *chess:* bishop; '**Läuferin** *f* (-; *-nen*) runner

'**Lauf|gitter** *n* playpen; ~**masche** *f* run, *Br* ladder; ~**schuhe** *pl* walking shoes; SPORT trainers; ~**steg** *m* footbridge; TECH, *fashion:* catwalk; MAR gangway

Lauge ['laugə] *f* (-; *-n*) suds; CHEM lye

Laune ['launə] *f* (-; *-n*) mood, temper; *gute* (*schlechte*) ~ *haben* be in a good (bad) mood *or* temper; **launenhaft**, '**launisch** *adj* moody; bad-tempered

Laus [laus] *f* (-; *Läuse* ['lɔyzə]) ZO louse

Lauschangriff ['lauʃʔaŋgrɪf] *m* bugging operation; **lauschen** ['lauʃən] *v/i* (*ge-, h*) listen (*dat* to); eavesdrop

lauschig ['lauʃɪç] *adj* snug, cozy, *Br* cosy

laut[1] [laut] **1.** *adj* loud; noisy **2.** *adv* loud(ly); ~ *vorlesen* read (out) aloud; (*sprich*) ~*er, bitte!* speak up, please!

laut[2] *prp* (*gen or dat*) according to

Laut *m* (*-[e]s; -e*) sound, noise

lauten ['lautən] *v/i* (*ge-, h*) read; be

läuten ['lɔytən] *v/i and v/t* (*ge-, h*) ring; *es läutet* (*an der Tür*) the (door)bell is ringing

lauter ['lautɐ] *adv* sheer (*nonsense etc*); nothing but; (*so*) many

'**lautlos** *adj* silent, soundless; hushed

'**Lautschrift** *f* phonetic transcription

'**Lautsprecher** *m* TECH (loud)speaker

'**Lautstärke** *f* loudness, ELECTR *a.* (sound) volume; *mit voller* ~ (at) full blast; ~**regler** *m* volume control

lauwarm ['lauvarm] *adj* lukewarm (*a. fig*)

Lava ['laːva] *f* (-; *Laven*) GEOL lava

Lavabo [la'vaːbo] *Swiss n* → *Waschbecken*

Lavendel [la'vɛndəl] *m* (*-s; -*) BOT lavender

Lawine [la'viːnə] *f* (-; *-n*) avalanche

Lehnsessel

Lazarett [latsa'rɛt] *n* (-[e]s; -e) (military) hospital

leben ['le:bən] (ge-, h) **1.** *v/i* live; be alive; **von et. ~** live on s.th. **2.** *v/t* live; '**Leben** *n* (-s; -) life; **am ~ bleiben** stay alive; survive; **am ~ sein** be alive; **sich das ~ nehmen** take one's (own) life, commit suicide; **ums ~ kommen** lose one's life, be killed; **um sein ~ laufen** (**kämpfen**) run (fight) for one's life; **das tägliche ~** everyday life; **mein ~ lang** all my life; '**lebend** *adj* living; **lebendig** [le'bɛndɪç] *adj* living, alive; *fig* lively

'**Lebens|abend** *m* old age, the last years of one's life; **~bedingungen** *pl* living conditions; **~dauer** *f* life-span; TECH (service) life; **~erfahrung** *f* experience of life; **~erwartung** *f* life expectancy

'**lebensfähig** *adj* MED viable (*a. fig*)

'**Lebensgefahr** *f* mortal danger; **in** (**unter**) **~** in danger (at the risk) of one's life; '**lebensgefährlich** *adj* dangerous (to life), perilous

'**lebensgroß** *adj* life-size(d)

'**Lebensgröße** *f*: **e-e Statue in ~** a life-size(d) statue

'**Lebenshaltungskosten** *pl* cost of living

'**lebenslänglich 1.** *adj* lifelong; **~e Freiheitsstrafe** JUR life sentence **2.** *adv* for life

'**Lebenslauf** *m* personal record, curriculum vitae

'**lebenslustig** *adj* fond of life

'**Lebensmittel** *pl* food(stuffs); groceries; **~geschäft** *n* grocery, supermarket

'**lebensmüde** *adj* tired of life

'**Lebens|notwendigkeit** *f* vital necessity; **~retter(in)** lifesaver, rescuer; **~standard** *m* standard of living; **~unterhalt** *m* livelihood; **s-n ~ verdienen** earn one's living (**als** as; **mit** out of, by); **~versicherung** *f* life insurance; **~weise** *f* way of life

'**lebenswichtig** *adj* vital, essential

'**Lebenszeichen** *n* sign of life

'**Lebenszeit** *f* lifetime; **auf ~** for life

Leber ['le:bɐ] *f* (-; -n) ANAT liver; **~fleck** *m* mole; **~tran** *m* cod-liver oil

'**Lebewesen** *n* living being, creature

lebhaft ['le:phaft] *adj* lively; heavy (*traffic etc*)

'**Lebkuchen** *m* gingerbread

'**leblos** *adj* lifeless (*a. fig*)

'**Lebzeiten** *pl*: **zu s-n ~** in his lifetime

lechzen ['lɛçtsən] *v/i* (ge-, h) **~ nach** thirst for

leck [lɛk] *adj* leaking, leaky

Leck *n* (-[e]s; -s) leak

lecken[1] ['lɛkən] *v/t and v/i* (ge-, h) *a.* **~ an** (*dat*) lick

'**lecken**[2] *v/i* (ge-, h) leak

lecker ['lɛkɐ] *adj* delicious, tasty, F yummy; '**Leckerbissen** *m* delicacy, treat (*a. fig*)

Leder ['le:dɐ] *n* (-s; -) leather; '**ledern** *adj* leather(n); '**Lederwaren** *pl* leather goods

ledig ['le:dɪç] *adj* single, unmarried

lediglich ['le:dɪklɪç] *adv* only, merely

Lee [le:] *f* (-; *no pl*) MAR lee; **nach ~** leeward

leer [le:ɐ] **1.** *adj* empty (*a. fig*); vacant (*house etc*); blank (*page etc*); ELECTR dead, *Br* flat; **~ stehend** unoccupied, vacant **2.** *adv*: **~ laufen** TECH idle; **Leere** ['le:rə] *f* (-; *no pl*) emptiness (*a. fig*); '**leeren** *v/t and v/refl* (ge-, h) empty; '**Leergut** *n* empties; '**Leerlauf** *m* TECH idling; neutral (gear); *fig* running on the spot; '**Leertaste** *f* space bar; '**Leerung** *f* (-; -en) post collection

legal [le'ga:l] *adj* legal, lawful

legalisieren [legali'zi:rən] *v/t* (*no -ge-, h*) legalize; **Legali'sierung** *f* (-; -en) legalization

Legasthenie [legaste'ni:] *f* (-; -n) PSYCH dyslexia, F word blindness

Legastheniker [legas'te:nikɐ] *m* (-s; -), **Legas'thenikerin** *f* (-; -nen) PSYCH dyslexic

legen ['le:gən] *v/t and v/i* (ge-, h) lay (*a. eggs*); place, put; set (*hair*); **sich ~** lie down; *fig* calm down; *pain*: wear off

Legende [le'gɛndə] *f* (-; -n) legend

leger [le'ʒe:ɐ] *adj* casual, informal

Legislative [legɪsla'ti:və] *f* (-; -n) legislative power

legitim [legi'ti:m] *adj* legitimate

Lehm [le:m] *m* (-[e]s; -e) loam; clay

lehmig ['le:mɪç] *adj* loamy, F muddy

Lehne ['le:nə] *f* (-; -n) back(rest); arm (-rest); '**lehnen** *v/t and v/i* lean (*a. sich ~*) rest (**an** *acc*, **gegen** against; **auf** *acc* on); **sich aus dem Fenster ~** lean out of the window; '**Lehnsessel** *m*, '**Lehnstuhl** *m* armchair, easy chair

Lehrbuch ['leːɐ̯buːx] n textbook

Lehre ['leːrə] f (-; -n) science; theory; REL, POL teachings, doctrine; moral; ECON apprenticeship; **in der ~ sein** be apprenticed (**bei** to); **das wird ihm e-e ~ sein** that will teach him a lesson

'**lehren** v/t (ge-, h) teach, instruct; show

Lehrer ['leːrɐ] m (-s; -) teacher, instructor, Br a. master; **~ausbildung** f teacher training

Lehrerin ['leːrərɪn] f (-; -nen) (lady) teacher, Br a. mistress

'**Lehrer|kol,legium** n (teaching) staff; **~zimmer** n staff or teachers' room

'**Lehr|gang** m course (of instruction or study); training course; **~jahr** n year (of apprenticeship)

Lehrling ['leːɐ̯lɪŋ] m (-s; -e) apprentice, trainee

'**Lehr|meister** m, **~meisterin** f master; fig teacher; **~mittel** pl teaching aids; **~plan** m curriculum, syllabus; **~probe** f demonstration lesson

'**lehrreich** adj informative, instructive

'**Lehr|stelle** f apprenticeship; vacancy for an apprentice; **~stuhl** m professorship; **~tochter** Swiss f apprentice; **~vertrag** m indenture(s); **~zeit** f apprenticeship

Leib [laip] m (-[e]s; Leiber ['laibɐ]) body; belly, ANAT abdomen; stomach; **bei lebendigem ~e** alive; **mit ~ und Seele** (with) heart and soul

'**Leibgericht** n GASTR favo(u)rite dish

leibhaftig [laip'haftɪç] adj: **der ~e Teufel** the devil incarnate; **~es Ebenbild** living image; **ich sehe ihn noch ~ vor mir** I can see him (before me) now

'**leiblich** adj physical

'**Leib|rente** f life annuity; **~wache** f, **~wächter** m bodyguard; **~wäsche** f underwear

Leiche ['laiçə] f (-; -n) (dead) body, corpse

'**leichen'blass** adj deadly pale

'**Leichen|halle** f mortuary; **~schauhaus** n morgue; **~verbrennung** f cremation; **~wagen** m hearse

leicht [laiçt] adj light (a. fig); easy, simple; slight, minor; TECH light(weight); **~ möglich** quite possible; **~ gekränkt** easily offended; **es fällt mir (nicht) ~ (zu inf)** I find it easy (difficult) (to inf); **das ist ~ gesagt** it's not as easy

as that; **es geht ~ kaputt** it breaks easily; **~ verständlich** easy to understand

'**Leicht|ath,let** m SPORT (track-and-field) athlete; **~ath,letik** f SPORT track and field (events), athletics; **~ath,letin** f SPORT (track-and-field) athlete; **~gewicht** n SPORT lightweight

'**leichtgläubig** adj credulous

Leichtigkeit ['laiçtıçkait] f: **mit ~** easily, with ease

leichtlebig ['laiçtleːbɪç] adj happy-go-lucky

'**Leichtme,tall** n light metal

'**leichtnehmen** v/t (irr, nehmen, sep, -ge-, h): **et. ~** not worry about s.th.; make light of s.th.; **nimm's leicht!** never mind!, don't worry about it!

'**Leichtsinn** m (-[e]s; no pl) carelessness; recklessness; '**leichtsinnig** adj careless; reckless

'**leichtverständlich** adj → **leicht**

Leid [lait] n (-[e]s; no pl) sorrow, grief; pain; **es tut mir ~** I'm sorry (**um** for; **wegen** about; **dass ich zu spät komme** for being late)

leiden ['laidən] v/t and v/i (irr, ge-, h) suffer (**an** dat, **unter** dat from); **j-n gut ~ können** like s.o.; **ich kann ... nicht ~** I don't like ...; I can't stand ...; '**Leiden** n (-s; -) suffering(s); MED disease

'**Leidenschaft** f (-; -en) passion

'**leidenschaftlich** adj passionate; vehement

'**Leidensgenosse** m,
'**Leidensgenossin** f fellow sufferer

leider ['laidɐ] adv unfortunately; **~ ja (nein)** I'm afraid so (not)

'**leidlich** adj passable, F so-so

'**Leidtragende** m, f (-n; -n) mourner; **er ist der ~ dabei** he is the one who suffers for it

'**Leidwesen** n: **zu m-m ~** to my regret

Leierkasten ['laiɐkastən] m barrel organ; **~mann** m organ grinder

leiern ['laiɐn] v/i and v/t (ge-, h) crank (up); fig drone

Leihbücherei ['laibyːçərai] f public library

leihen ['laiən] v/t (irr, ge-, h) lend; rent (Br hire) out; borrow (**von** from); rent, hire

'**Leih|gebühr** f rental, lending fee; **~haus** n pawnshop, pawnbroker's (shop); **~mutter** F *f* surrogate mother; **~wagen** *m* MOT rented (*Br* hire) car

'leihweise *adv* on loan

Leim [laim] *m* (-[e]s; -e), **leimen** ['laimən] *v/t* (ge-, h) glue

Leine ['lainə] *f* (-; -n) line; lead, leash

Leinen ['lainən] *n* (-s; -) linen; canvas; *in ~ gebunden* clothbound

'Leinenschuh *m* canvas shoe

'Lein|samen *m* BOT linseed; **~tuch** *n* (linen) sheet; **~wand** *f* linen; PAINT canvas; screen

leise ['laizə] *adj* quiet, *a.* low, soft (*voice, a. music etc*); *fig* slight, faint; **~r stellen** turn (the volume) down

Leiste ['laistə] *f* (-; -n) ledge; ANAT groin

'leisten *v/t* (ge-, h) do, work; achieve, accomplish; render (*service etc*); take (*oath*); *gute Arbeit ~* do a good job; *sich et. ~* treat o.s. to s.th.; *ich kann es mir (nicht) ~* I can('t) afford it

'Leistung *f* (-; -en) performance; achievement, PED *a.* (piece of) work, result, TECH *a.* output; service; benefit

'Leistungsdruck *m* (-[e]s; *no pl*) pressure, stress

'leistungsfähig *adj* efficient; (physically) fit; **'Leistungsfähigkeit** *f* (-; *no pl*) efficiency (*a.* TECH, ECON); fitness

'Leistungs|kon,trolle *f* (achievement or proficiency) test; **~kurs** *m* PED *appr* special subject; **~sport** *m* competitive sport(s)

Leitar,tikel ['lait?arti:kəl] *m* editorial, *esp Br* leader, leading article

leiten ['laitən] *v/t* (ge-, h) lead, guide (*a. fig*), conduct (*a.* PHYS, MUS); run (*a.* PED), be in charge of, manage; TV *etc* direct; host; **~d** *adj* leading; PHYS conductive; **~e Stellung** key position; **~er Angestellter** executive

Leiter[1] ['laitɐ] *f* (-; -n) ladder

'Leiter[2] *m* (-s; -) leader; conductor (*a.* PHYS, MUS); ECON *etc* head, manager; chairman; → *Schulleiter*

Leiterin ['laitərin] *f* (-; -nen) leader; head; chairwoman

'Leit|faden *m* manual, guide; **~planke** *f* MOT guardrail, *Br* crash barrier; **~spruch** *m* motto

'Leitung *f* (-; -en) ECON management; head office; administration; chairmanship; organization; THEA *etc* direction; TECH main, pipe(s); ELECTR, TEL line;

die ~ haben be in charge; *unter der ~ von* MUS conducted by

'Leitungsrohr *n* pipe

'Leitungswasser *n* tap water

Lektion [lɛk'tsjo:n] *f* (-; -en) lesson

Lektüre [lɛk'ty:rə] *f* (-; -n) reading (matter); PED reader

Lende ['lɛndə] *f* (-; -n) ANAT loin; GASTR sirloin

lenken ['lɛŋkən] *v/t* (ge-, h) steer, drive; *fig* guide *s.o.*; direct (*traffic etc*)

Lenker ['lɛŋkɐ] *m* (-s; -) handlebar

'Lenkrad *n* MOT steering wheel

'Lenkung *f* (-; -en) MOT steering (system)

Leopard [leo'part] *m* (-en; -en) ZO leopard

Lerche ['lɛrçə] *f* (-; -n) ZO lark

lernen ['lɛrnən] *v/t and v/i* (ge-, h) learn; study; *er lernt leicht* he is a quick learner; *lesen ~* learn (how) to read

'Lernmittelfreiheit *f* free books *etc*

lesbar ['le:sba:ɐ] *adj* readable

Lesbierin ['lɛsbjərin] *f* (-; -nen), **lesbisch** ['lɛsbiʃ] *adj* lesbian

Lesebuch ['le:zəbu:x] *n* reader

Leselampe *f* reading lamp

lesen ['le:zən] *v/i and v/t* (*irr*, ge-, h) read; AGR harvest

'lesenswert *adj* worth reading

Leser ['le:zɐ] *m* (-s; -) reader

Leseratte F *f* bookworm

'Leserbrief *m* letter to the editor

'Leserin *f* (-; -nen) reader

'leserlich *adj* legible

'Lesestoff *m* reading matter

'Lesezeichen *n* bookmark

'Lesung *f* (-; -en) reading (*a.* PARL)

Letzt [lɛtst] *f*: *zu guter ~* in the end

letzte ['lɛtstə] *adj* last; latest; *zum ~n Mal(e)* for the last time; *in ~r Zeit* recently; *als Letzter ankommen etc* arrive *etc* last; *Letzter sein* be last (*a.* SPORT); *das ist das Letzte!* that's the limit!; **'letztens** *adv* finally; *erst ~* just recently; **letztere** ['lɛtstərə] *adj* latter; *der* (*die, das*) *Letztere* the latter

Leuchtanzeige ['lɔʏçt?antsaigə] *f* luminous *or* LED display light; **leuchten** ['lɔʏçtən] *v/i* (ge-, h) shine; glow; **'Leuchten** *n* (-s; *no pl*) shining; glow; **'leuchtend** *adj* shining (*a. fig*); bright; **Leuchter** ['lɔʏçtɐ] *m* (-s; -) candlestick

'Leucht|farbe *f* luminous paint; **~re,klame** *f* neon sign(s); **~(stoff)röhre** *f*

ELECTR fluorescent lamp; **~turm** *m* lighthouse; **~ziffer** *f* luminous figure

leugnen ['lɔygnən] *v/t and v/i* (ge-, h) deny (*et. getan zu haben* having done s.th.)

Leute ['lɔytə] *pl* people, F folks

Leutnant ['lɔytnant] *m* (-s; -s) MIL second lieutenant

Lexikon ['lɛksikɔn] *n* (-s; -ka, -ken) encyclop(a)edia; dictionary

Libelle [li'bɛlə] *f* (-; -n) ZO dragonfly

liberal [libe'raːl] *adj* liberal

Libero ['liːbero] *m* (-s; -s) *soccer:* sweeper

licht ['lɪçt] *adj* bright; *fig* lucid

Licht *n* (-[e]s; -er ['lɪçtɐ]) light; (*no pl*) brightness; **~ machen** switch *or* turn on the light(s)

'**Licht|bild** *n* photo(graph); slide; **~bildervortrag** *m* slide lecture; **~blick** *m* ray of hope; bright moment

'**lichtempfindlich** *adj* sensitive to light; PHOT sensitive; '**Lichtempfindlichkeit** *f* (light) sensitivity; PHOT speed

lichten ['lɪçtən] *v/t* (ge-, h) clear; **den Anker ~** MAR weigh anchor; **sich ~** get thin(ner); *fig* be thinning (out)

'**Licht|geschwindigkeit** *f* speed of light; **~hupe** *f* MOT (headlight) flash(er); **die ~ betätigen** flash one's lights; **~jahr** *n* light year; **~ma,schine** *f* MOT generator; **~orgel** *f* colo(u)r organ; **~pause** *f* blueprint; **~schacht** *m* well; **~schalter** *m* (light) switch

'**lichtscheu** *fig adj* shady

'**Licht|schutzfaktor** *m* sun protection factor, SPF; **~strahl** *m* ray *or* beam of light (*a. fig*)

'**Lichtung** *f* (-; -en) clearing

Lid [liːt] *n* (-[e]s; Lider ['liːdɐ]) ANAT (eye)lid; **~schatten** *m* eye shadow

lieb [liːp] *adj* dear; sweet; nice, kind; good; **~ gewinnen** get fond of; **~ haben** love, be fond of; **Liebe** ['liːbə] *f* (-; *no pl*) love (**zu** of, for); **aus ~ zu** out of love for; **~ auf den ersten Blick** love at first sight; '**lieben** *v/t* (ge-, h) love, *a.* be in love with *s.o.*; make love to

'**liebenswert** *adj* lovable, charming, sweet

'**liebenswürdig** *adj* kind; '**Liebenswürdigkeit** *f* (-; *no pl*) kindness

lieber ['liːbɐ] *adv* rather, sooner; **~ ha-ben** prefer, like better; **ich möchte ~** (**nicht**) ... I'd rather (not) ...; **du solltest ~** (**nicht**) ... you had better (not) ...

'**Liebes|brief** *m* love letter; **~erklärung** *f*: *j-m e-e ~ machen* declare one's love to s.o.; **~kummer** *m*: **~ haben** be lovesick; **~paar** *n* lovers

'**liebevoll** *adj* loving, affectionate

'**liebgewinnen** *v/t* (*irr*, **gewinnen**, *sep*, *h*) → **lieb**

'**liebhaben** *v/t* (*irr*, **haben**, *sep*, *-ge-*, *h*) → **lieb**; **Liebhaber** ['liːphaːbɐ] *m* (-s; -) lover (*a. fig*); **~... in cpds ...preis, ...stück etc:** collector's ...; **Liebhaberei** [liːphaːbə'raɪ] *f* (-; -en) hobby

Liebkosung [liːp'koːzʊŋ] *f* (-; -en) caress

'**lieblich** *adj* lovely, charming, sweet (*a. wine*)

'**Liebling** *m* (-s; -e) darling; favo(u)rite

'**Lieblings...** in cpds mst favo(u)rite

'**lieblos** *adj* unloving, cold; unkind (*words etc*); *fig* careless

Lied [liːt] *n* (-[e]s; -er ['liːdɐ]) song; tune

liederlich ['liːdɐlɪç] *adj* slovenly, sloppy

Liedermacher ['liːdɐmaxɐ] *m* (-s; -) singer-songwriter

lief [liːf] *pret of* **laufen**

Lieferant [lifə'rant] *m* (-en; -en) ECON supplier; **lieferbar** ['liːfɐbaːɐ] *adj* ECON available; '**Lieferfrist** *f* ECON term of delivery; **liefern** ['liːfɐn] *v/t* (ge-, h) ECON deliver; *j-m et.* **~** supply s.o. with s.th.; **Lieferung** ['liːfərʊŋ] *f* (-; -en) ECON delivery; supply

'**Lieferwagen** *m* MOT (delivery) van

Liege ['liːgə] *f* (-; -n) couch

liegen ['liːgən] *v/i* (*irr*, ge-, h) lie, *a.* be (situated); (*krank*) **im Bett ~** be (ill) in bed; *nach Osten* (*der Straße*) **~** face east (the street); *daran liegt es*(, *dass*) that's (the reason) why; *es* (*er*) *liegt mir nicht* F it (he) is not my cup of tea; *mir liegt viel* (*wenig*) *daran* it means a lot (doesn't mean much) to me; **~ bleiben** stay in bed; be left behind; **~ lassen** leave (behind); F *j-n* *links ~ lassen* ignore s.o., give s.o. the cold shoulder

'**liegenbleiben** *v/i* (*irr*, **bleiben**, *sep*, *-ge-*, *sein*) → **liegen**; **~lassen** *v/i* (*irr*, **lassen**, *sep*, *no -ge-*, *h*) → **liegen**

'**Liege|sitz** *m* reclining seat; **~stuhl** *m* deckchair; **~stütz** *m* (-es; -e) SPORT push-up, *Br* press-up; **~wagen** *m* RAIL couchette

lieh [liː] *pret of* **leihen**

ließ [liːs] *pret of* **lassen**

Lift [lɪft] *m* (-[e]s; -e, -s) elevator, *Br* lift; ski lift

Liga ['liːga] *f* (-; Ligen) league, SPORT *a.* division

Likör [li'køːɐ] *m* (-s; -e) liqueur

lila ['liːla] *adj* purple, violet

Lilie ['liːljə] *f* (-; -n) BOT lily

Liliputaner [lilipu'taːnɐ] *m* (-s; -) dwarf, midget

Limonade [limo'naːdə] *f* (-; -n) pop; lemon soda, *Br* lemonade

Limousine [limu'ziːnə] *f* (-; -n) MOT sedan, *Br* saloon car; limousine

Linde ['lɪndə] *f* (-; -n) BOT lime (tree), linden

lindern ['lɪndɐn] *v/t* (ge-, h) relieve, ease, alleviate; **Linderung** ['lɪndərʊŋ] *f* (-; *no pl*) relief, alleviation

Lineal [line'aːl] *n* (-s; -e) ruler

Linie ['liːnjə] *f* (-; -n) line; **auf s-e ~ achten** watch one's weight

'Linien|flug *m* AVIAT scheduled flight; **~richter** *m* SPORT linesman

'linientreu *adj* POL: **~ sein** follow the party line

linieren [li'niːrən], **liniieren** [lini'iːrən] *v/t* (*no* -ge-, h) rule, line

linke ['lɪŋkə] *adj* left (*a.* POL); **auf der ~n Seite** on the left(-hand side); **'Linke** *m, f* (-n; -n) POL leftist, left-winger

linkisch ['lɪŋkɪʃ] *adj* awkward, clumsy

links [lɪŋks] *adv* on the left (*a.* POL); on the wrong side; **nach ~** (to the) left; **~ von** to the left of

Links... *in cpds* ...*verkehr etc*: left-hand

Links'außen *m* (-; -) SPORT outside left, left wing

Linkshänder ['lɪŋkshɛndɐ] *m* (-s; -), **'Linkshänderin** *f* (-; -nen) left-hander

'Linksradi,kale *m, f* (-n; -n) POL left-wing extremist

Linse ['lɪnzə] *f* (-; -n) BOT lentil; OPT lens

Lippe ['lɪpə] *f* (-; -n) ANAT lip

'Lippenstift *m* lipstick

liquidieren [likvi'diːrən] *v/t* (*no* -ge-, h) ECON liquidate (*a.* POL)

lispeln ['lɪspəln] *v/i* (ge-, h) (have a) lisp

List [lɪst] *f* (-; -en) trick; (*no pl*) cunning

Liste ['lɪstə] *f* (-; -n) list; roll

listig ['lɪstɪç] *adj* cunning, tricky, sly

Liter ['liːtɐ] *n, m* (-s; -) liter, *Br* litre

literarisch [lɪtə'raːrɪʃ] *adj* literary

Literatur [lɪtəra'tuːɐ] *f* (-; -en) literature; **~... in cpds** ...*kritik etc*: mst literary

Litfaßsäule ['lɪtfaszɔylə] *f* advertising pillar

litt [lɪt] *pret of* **leiden**

Lizenz [li'tsɛnts] *f* (-; -en) license, *Br* licence

Lkw, LKW ['ɛlkaveː] *m* (-[s]; -) *abbr of* **Lastkraftwagen** truck, *Br a.* lorry

Lob [loːp] *n* (-[e]s; *no pl*) praise; **loben** ['loːbən] *v/t* (ge-, h) praise; **'lobenswert** *adj* praiseworthy, laudable

Loch [lɔx] *n* (-[e]s; Löcher ['lœçɐ]) hole (*a. fig*); puncture; **lochen** ['lɔxən] *v/t* (ge-, h) punch (*a.* TECH); **Locher** ['lɔxɐ] *m* (-s; -) punch

Locke ['lɔkə] *f* (-; -n) curl; lock

locken¹ ['lɔkən] *v/t and v/refl* (ge-, h) curl

locken² *v/t* (ge-, h) lure, entice, *fig a.* attract, tempt

'Locken|kopf *m* curly head; **~wickler** ['lɔkənvɪklɐ] *m* (-s; -) curler, roller

locker ['lɔkɐ] *adj* loose; slack; *fig* relaxed; **'lockern** *v/t* (ge-, h) loosen, slacken; relax (*a. fig*); **sich ~** loosen, (be)come loose; SPORT limber up; *fig* relax

lockig ['lɔkɪç] *adj* curly, curled

'Lockvogel *m* decoy (*a. fig*)

lodern ['loːdɐn] *v/i* (ge-, h) blaze, flare

Löffel ['lœfəl] *m* (-s; -) spoon; ladle

'löffeln *v/t* (ge-, h) spoon up

log [loːk] *pret of* **lügen**

Logbuch ['lɔkbuːx] *n* MAR log

Loge ['loːʒə] *f* (-; -n) THEA box; lodge

Logik ['loːgɪk] *f* (-; *no pl*) logic

logisch ['loːgɪʃ] *adj* logical

'logischer'weise *adv* obviously

Lohn [loːn] *m* (-[e]s; Löhne ['løːnə]) ECON wages, pay(ment); *fig* reward; **~empfänger** *m* wageworker, *Br* wage earner

lohnen ['loːnən] *v/refl* (ge-, h) be worth (-while), pay; **es (die Mühe) lohnt sich** it's worth it (the trouble); **das Buch (der Film) lohnt sich** the book (film) is worth reading (seeing); **~d** *adj* paying; *fig* rewarding

'Lohn|erhöhung *f* raise, *Br* increase in

wages, rise; **~steuer** f income tax;
~stopp m wage freeze

Loipe ['lɔʏpə] f (-; -n) (cross-country)
course

Lok [lɔk] f (-; -s) → **Lokomotive**

Lokal [lo'ka:l] n (-s; -e) restaurant; bar,
saloon, esp Br pub

Lo'kal... in cpds mst local

Lokführer m RAIL engineer, Br train
driver

Lokomotive [lokomo'ti:və] f (-; -n) RAIL
engine

Lorbeer ['lɔrbe:ɐ] m (-s; -en) BOT laurel;
GASTR bay leaf

Lore ['lo:rə] f (-; -n) TECH tipcart

los [lo:s] adj and adv off; dog etc: loose;
~ sein be rid of; **was ist ~?** what's the
matter?, F what's up?; what's going on
(here)?; **hier ist nicht viel ~** there's
nothing much going on here; F **da ist
was ~!** that's where the action is!; F **also ~!** okay, let's go!

Los [lo:s] n (-es; -e ['lo:zə]) lot, fig a.
fate; (lottery) ticket, number

losbinden ['lo:s...] v/t (irr, **binden**, sep, -ge-, h)
untie

Löschblatt ['lœʃblat] n blotting paper

löschen ['lœʃən] v/t (ge-, h) extinguish,
put out; quench (thirst); blot (ink);
wipe off the blackboard; erase, IT a. de-
lete; slake (lime); MAR unload

Löschpa,pier n blotting paper

lose ['lo:zə] adj loose

Lösegeld ['lø:zəgelt] n ransom

losen ['lo:zən] v/i (ge-, h) draw lots (**um**
for)

lösen ['lø:zən] v/t (ge-, h) undo (knot
etc); loosen, relax; TECH release; take
off; solve (problem etc); settle (conflict
etc); buy, get (ticket etc); dissolve (a.
CHEM); **sich ~** come loose or undone;
fig free o.s. (**von** from)

losfahren ['lo:s...] v/i (irr, **fahren**, sep, -ge-,
sein) leave; drive off; **~gehen** v/i (irr,
gehen, sep, -ge-, sein) leave; start, begin; shot etc: go off; **auf j-n ~** go for s.o.;
ich gehe jetzt los I'm off now; **~ketten**
v/t (sep, -ge-, h) unchain; **~kommen** v/i
(irr, **kommen**, sep, -ge-, sein) get away
(**von** from); **~lassen** v/t (irr, **lassen**,
sep, -ge-, h) let go; **den Hund ~ auf**
(acc) set the dog on; **~legen** F v/i
(sep, -ge-, h) get cracking

löslich ['lø:slɪç] adj CHEM soluble

los|machen v/t (sep, -ge-, h) → **lösen**;
~reißen v/t (irr, **reißen**, sep, -ge-, h) tear
off; **sich ~** break away; esp fig tear o.s.
away (**both**: **von** from); **~sagen** v/refl
(sep, -ge-, h) **sich ~ von** break with;
~schlagen v/i (irr, **schlagen**, sep,
-ge-, h) strike (**auf j-n** out at s.o.);
~schnallen v/t (sep, -ge-, h) unbuckle;
sich ~ MOT, AVIAT unfasten one's seat
belt; **~stürzen** v/i (sep, -ge-, sein) **~
auf** (acc) rush at

Losung ['lo:zʊŋ] f (-; -en) MIL password;
fig slogan

Lösung ['lø:zʊŋ] f (-; -en) solution (a.
fig); settlement

Lösungsmittel n solvent

loswerden v/t (irr, **werden**, sep, -ge-,
sein) get rid of; spend (money); lose

losziehen v/i (irr, **ziehen**, sep, -ge-,
sein) set out, take off, march away

Lot [lo:t] n (-[e]s; -e) plumbline

löten ['lø:tən] v/t (ge-, h) TECH solder

Lotion [lo'tsjo:n] f (-; -en) lotion

Lotse ['lo:tsə] m (-n; -n), **lotsen** v/t (ge-,
h) MAR pilot

Lotterie [lɔtə'ri:] f (-; -n) lottery; **~ge-
winn** m prize; **~los** n lottery ticket

Lotto ['lɔto] n (-s; -s) lotto, bingo; Br national lottery; in Germany: Lotto; (**im**)
~ spielen do Lotto; **~schein** m Lotto
coupon; **~ziehung** f Lotto draw

Löwe ['lø:və] m (-n; -n) ZO lion; AST Leo;
er ist (ein) ~ he's (a) Leo

Löwenzahn m BOT dandelion

Löwin ['lø:vɪn] f (-; -nen) ZO lioness

loyal [loa'ja:l] adj loyal, faithful

Luchs [lʊks] m (-es; -e) ZO lynx

Lücke ['lʏkə] f (-; -n) gap (a. fig);
Lückenbüßer m stopgap;
lückenhaft adj full of gaps; fig incomplete; **lückenlos** adj without a gap; fig
complete; **Lückentest** m PSYCH completion or fill-in test

lud [lu:t] pret of **laden**

Luft [lʊft] f (-; no pl) air; **an der frischen
~** (out) in the fresh air; (**frische**) **~
schöpfen** get a breath of fresh air;
die ~ anhalten catch (esp fig a. hold)
one's breath; **tief ~ holen** take a deep
breath; **in die ~ sprengen** (F **fliegen**)
blow up

Luft|angriff m air raid; **~ballon** m bal-
loon; **~bild** n aerial photograph or
view; **~blase** f air bubble; **~brücke** f

airlift
'**luftdicht** adj airtight
'**Luft|druck** m (-[e]s; no pl) PHYS, TECH
air pressure
lüften ['lʏftən] v/t and v/i (ge-, h) air,
ventilate; fig reveal
'**Luft|fahrt** f (-; no pl) aviation, aeronautics; **~feuchtigkeit** f (atmospheric) humidity; **~gewehr** n airgun
'**luftig** adj airy; breezy; light (dress etc)
'**Luft|kissen** n air cushion; **~kissen-fahrzeug** n hovercraft; **~krankheit** f
air-sickness; **~krieg** m air warfare;
~kurort m (climatic) health resort
'**luftleer** adj: **~er Raum** vacuum
'**Luft|linie** f: **50 km ~** 50 km as the crow
flies; **~post** f air mail; **~pumpe** f air
pump; bicycle pump; **~röhre** f ANAT
windpipe, trachea; **~schlange** f
streamer; **~schloss** n castle in the
air; **~sprünge** pl: **~ machen vor Freu-de** jump for joy
'**Lüftung** f (-; -en) airing; TECH ventilation
'**Luft|veränderung** f change of air;
~verkehr m air traffic; **~verschmut-zung** f air pollution; **~waffe** f MIL air
force; **~weg** m: **auf dem ~** by air;
~zug m draft, Br draught
Lüge ['lyːgə] f (-; -n) lie; '**lügen** v/i (irr,
ge-, h) lie, tell a lie or lies; **das ist ge-logen** that's a lie; **Lügner(in)** ['lyːgnɐ,
'lyːgnərɪn] m(f) (-s; -/-; -nen) liar; **lüg-nerisch** ['lyːgnərɪʃ] adj false
Luke ['luːkə] f (-; -n) hatch; skylight
Lümmel ['lʏməl] F m (-s; -) rascal
lumpen ['lʊmpən] F v/t: **sich nicht ~ las-sen** be generous
'**Lumpen** m (-s; -) rag; **in ~** in rags
lumpig ['lʊmpɪç] F adj: **für ~e zwei Euro**
for a paltry two euros
Lunge ['lʊŋə] f (-; -n) ANAT lungs; **(auf) ~**

rauchen inhale
'**Lungen|entzündung** f MED pneumonia; **~flügel** m ANAT lung; **~zug** m:
e-n ~ machen inhale
Lupe ['luːpə] f (-; -n) magnifying glass;
unter die ~ nehmen scrutinize (closely)
Lust [lʊst] f (-; Lüste ['lʏstə]) (no pl)
desire, interest; pleasure, delight;
lust; **~ haben auf et. (et. zu tun)** feel
like (doing) s.th.; **hättest du ~ auszu-gehen?** would you like to go out?,
how about going out?; **ich habe
keine ~** I don't feel like it, I'm not
in the mood for it; **die ~ an et. verlie-ren (j-m die ~ an et. nehmen)** (make
s.o.) lose all interest in s.th.
lüstern ['lʏstɐn] adj greedy (**nach** for)
lustig ['lʊstɪç] adj funny; cheerful; **er ist
sehr ~** he is full of fun; **es war sehr ~** it
was great fun; **sich ~ machen über**
(acc) make fun of
'**lustlos** adj listless, indifferent
'**Lustmord** m sex murder
'**Lustspiel** n THEA comedy
lutschen ['lʊtʃən] v/i and v/t (ge-, h)
suck
Luv [luːf] f (-; no pl) MAR windward,
weather side
luxuriös [lʊksuˈrjøːs] adj luxurious
Luxus ['lʊksʊs] m (-; no pl) luxury; **~ar-,tikel** m luxury (article); **~ausführung** f
deluxe version; **~ho,tel** n five-star (or
luxury) hotel
Lymphdrüse ['lʏmfdryːzə] f ANAT
lymph gland
lynchen ['lʏnçən] v/t (ge-, h) lynch
Lyrik ['lyːrɪk] f (-; no pl) poetry
Lyriker ['lyːrɪkɐ] m (-s; -), '**Lyrikerin** f (-;
-nen) (lyric) poet
lyrisch ['lyːrɪʃ] adj lyrical (a. fig)

M

machbar ['maxbaːɐ] adj feasible
machen ['maxən] v/t (ge-, h) do; make;
GASTR make, prepare; fix (a. fig); be,
come to, amount to; take, pass (test
etc); make, go on (a trip etc); **Hausauf-gaben ~** do one's homework; **da**

(-**gegen**) **kann man nichts ~** it can't
be helped; **mach, was du willst!** do
as you please!; (**nun**) **mach mal** or
schon! hurry up!, come on or along
now!; **mach's gut!** take care (of yourself)!, good luck!; (**das**) **macht nichts**

it doesn't matter; *mach dir nichts d-(a)raus!* never mind!, don't worry!; *das macht mir nichts aus* I don't mind or care; *was or wie viel macht das?* how much is it?; *sich et. (nichts) ~ aus* (not) care about; (not) care for

'**Machenschaften** *pl* machinations; *unsaubere* ~ sleaze (*esp* POL)

Macher ['maxɐ] *m* (*-s*; *-*) man of action, doer

Macho ['matʃo] *m* (*-s*; *-s*) macho

Macht [maxt] *f* (*-*; *Mächte* ['mɛçtə]) power (*über acc* of); *an der* ~ in power; *mit aller* ~ with all one's might

Machthaber ['maxthaːbɐ] *m* (*-s*; *-*) POL ruler

mächtig ['mɛçtɪç] *adj* powerful, mighty (*a.* F); enormous, huge

'**Machtkampf** *m* struggle for power

'**machtlos** *adj* powerless

'**Macht|missbrauch** *m* abuse of power; ~**poli,tik** *f* power politics; ~**übernahme** *f* takeover; ~**wechsel** *m* transition of power

Mädchen ['mɛːtçən] *n* (*-s*; *-*) girl; maid

'**mädchenhaft** *adj* girlish

'**Mädchen|name** *m* girl's name; maiden name; ~**schule** *f* girls' school

Made ['maːdə] *f* (*-*; *-n*) ZO maggot; worm

Mädel ['mɛːdəl] *n* (*-s*; *-s*) girl

'**madig** *adj* maggoty, worm-eaten; F'**madigmachen** *v/t* (*sep*, *-ge-*, *h*): F *j-m et.* ~ spoil s.th. for s.o.

Magazin [maga'tsiːn] *n* (*-s*; *-e*) magazine (*a.* MIL, PHOT, TV); store(room), warehouse

Magd [maːkt] *f* (*-*; *Mägde* ['mɛːktə]) (female) farmhand

Magen ['maːgən] *m* (*-s*; *Mägen* ['mɛːgən]) ANAT stomach; ~**beschwerden** *pl* MED stomach trouble; ~**geschwür** *n* MED (stomach) ulcer; ~**schmerzen** *pl* stomachache

mager ['maːgɐ] *adj* lean, thin, skinny; GASTR low-fat (*cheese*), lean (*meat*), skim (*milk*); *fig* meager, *Br* meagre

Magie [ma'giː] *f* (*-*; *no pl*) magic

magisch ['maːgɪʃ] *adj* magic(al)

Magister [ma'gɪstɐ] *m* (*-s*; *-*) UNIV Master of Arts *or* Science; *Austrian* → *Apotheker*

Magistrat [magɪs'traːt] *m* (*-[e]s*; *-e*) municipal council

Magnet [ma'gneːt] *m* (*-[e]s*, *-en*; *-e[n]*)

magnet (*a. fig*); ~**...** *in cpds* ...**band**, ...**feld**, ...**nadel** *etc*: magnetic ...

mag'netisch *adj* magnetic (*a. fig*)

magnetisieren [magneti'ziːrən] *v/t* (*no -ge-*, *h*) magnetize

Mahagoni [maha'goːni] *n* (*-s*; *no pl*) mahogany

Mähdrescher ['mɛːdrɛʃɐ] *m* (*-s*; *-*) AGR combine (harvester); **mähen** ['mɛːən] *v/t* (*ge-*, *h*) mow; cut; AGR reap

mahlen ['maːlən] *v/t* (*irr*, *ge-*, *h*) grind; mill

'**Mahlzeit** *f* (*-*; *-en*) meal; feed(ing)

Mähne ['mɛːnə] *f* (*-*; *-n*) ZO mane (*a.* F)

mahnen ['maːnən] *v/t* (*ge-*, *h*) remind; ECON send *s.o.* a reminder

'**Mahngebühr** *f* reminder fee

'**Mahnmal** *n* memorial

'**Mahnung** *f* (*-*; *-en*) reminder

Mai [mai] *m* (*-[e]s*; *-e*) May; *der Erste* ~ May Day; ~**baum** *m* maypole; ~**glöckchen** *n* BOT lily of the valley; ~**käfer** *m* ZO cockchafer

Mais [mais] *m* (*-es*; *-e*) BOT corn, *Br* maize

Majestät [majes'tɛːt] *f*: *Seine* (*Ihre*, *Eure*) ~ His (Her, Your) Majesty

majes'tätisch *adj* majestic

Majonäse *f* → *Mayonnaise*

Major [ma'joːɐ] *m* (*-s*; *-e*) MIL major

makaber [ma'kaːbɐ] *adj* macabre

Makel ['maːkəl] *m* (*-s*; *-*) blemish (*a. fig*)

mäkelig ['mɛːkəlıç] F *adj* picky, *esp Br* choos(e)y

'**makellos** *adj* immaculate (*a. fig*)

mäkeln ['mɛːkəln] F *v/i* (*ge-*, *h*) carp, pick, nag (*an dat* at)

Makler ['maːklɐ] *m* (*-s*; *-*) ECON real estate agent; broker; ~**gebühr** *f* fee, commission

'**Maklerin** *f* (*-*; *-nen*) ECON → *Makler*

mal [maːl] *adv* MATH times, multiplied by; by; F → *einmal*; *12* ~ *5 ist* (*gleich*) *60* 12 times *or* multiplied by 5 is *or* equals 60; *ein 7* ~ *4 Meter großes Zimmer* a room 7 meters by 4

Mal[1] *n* (*-[e]s*; *-e*) time; *zum ersten* (*letzten*) ~(*e*) for the first (last) time; *mit e-m* ~(*e*) all of a sudden; *ein für alle* ~(*e*) once and for all

Mal[2] *n* mark

malen ['maːlən] *v/t* (*ge-*, *h*) paint

Maler ['maːlɐ] *m* (*-s*; *-*) painter

Malerei [maːlə'rai] *f* (*-*; *-en*) painting

Malerin ['maːlərɪn] f (-; -nen) (woman) painter

'malerisch fig adj picturesque

'Malkasten m paintbox

'malnehmen → *multiplizieren*

Malz [malts] n (-es; no pl) malt

'Malzbier n malt beer

Mama ['mama] F f (-; -s) mom(my), Br mum(my)

Mammut ['mamʊt] n (-s; -e, -s) ZO mammoth

man [man] indef pron you, one; they, people; *wie schreibt ~ das?* how do you spell it?; *~ sagt, dass* they or people say (that); *~ hat mir gesagt* I was told

Manager ['mɛnɪdʒɐ] m (-s; -), **'Managerin** f (-; -nen) ECON executive; SPORT manager

manch [manç], **~er** ['mançɐ], **~e** ['mançə], **~es** ['mançəs] indef pron (mst pl) some; quite a few, many

'manchmal adv sometimes, occasionally

Mandant [man'dant] m (-en; -en), **Man'dantin** f (-; -nen) JUR client

Mandarine [manda'riːnə] f (-; -n) BOT tangerine

Mandat [man'daːt] n (-[e]s; -e) POL mandate; seat; **Mandatar** [manda'taːɐ] Austrian m → *Abgeordnete*

Mandel ['mandəl] f (-; -n) BOT almond; ANAT tonsil; **~entzündung** f MED tonsillitis

Manege [ma'neːʒə] f (-; -n) (circus) ring

Mangel¹ ['maŋəl] m (-s; Mängel ['mɛŋəl]) (no pl) lack (*an dat* of), shortage; TECH defect, fault; shortcoming; *aus ~ an (dat)* for lack of

'Mangel² f (-; -n) mangle

'mangelhaft adj poor (*quality etc*); defective (*goods etc*); PED poor, unsatisfactory, failing

'mangeln v/t (ge-, h) mangle

'mangels prp (gen) for lack or want of

'Mangelware f: *~ sein* be scarce

Manie [ma'niː] f (-; -n) mania (a. fig)

Manieren [ma'niːrən] pl manners

manierlich [ma'niːrlɪç] adv: *sich ~ betragen* behave (decently)

Manifest [mani'fɛst] n (-[e]s; -e) manifesto

manipulieren [manipu'liːrən] v/t (no -ge-, h) manipulate

Mann [man] m (-[e]s; Männer ['mɛnɐ]) man; husband

Männchen ['mɛnçən] n (-s; -) ZO male

'Manndeckung f SPORT man-to-man marking

Mannequin ['manəkɛ̃ː] n (-s; -s) model

mannigfach ['manɪçfax], **'mannigfaltig** adj many and various

männlich ['mɛnlɪç] adj BIOL male; masculine (a. LING)

'Mannschaft f (-; -en) SPORT team; MAR, AVIAT crew

Manöver [ma'nøːvɐ] n (-s; -), **manövrieren** [manø'vriːrən] v/i (no -ge-, h) maneuver, Br manoeuvre

Mansarde [man'zardə] f (-; -n) room or apartment in the attic

Manschette [man'ʃɛtə] f (-; -n) cuff; TECH gasket

Man'schettenknopf m cuff-link

Mantel ['mantəl] m (-s; Mäntel ['mɛntəl]) coat; tire: casing, bicycle: tire (Br tyre) cover; TECH jacket, shell

Manuskript [manu'skrɪpt] n (-[e]s; -e) manuscript; copy

Mappe ['mapə] f (-; -n) briefcase; school bag, satchel; folder

Märchen ['mɛːɐçən] n (-s; -) fairytale (a. fig); **~land** n (-[e]s; no pl) fairyland

Marder ['mardɐ] m (-s; -) ZO marten

Margarine [marga'riːnə] f (-; no pl) margarine

Margerite [margə'riːtə] f (-; -n) BOT marguerite

Marienkäfer [ma'riːənkɛːfɐ] m ZO ladybug, Br ladybird

Marihuana [mari'huaːna] n (-s; no pl) marijuana, sl grass; **~ziga,rette** f sl joint

Marille [ma'rɪlə] Austrian f (-; -n) BOT apricot

Marine [ma'riːnə] f (-; -n) MIL navy

ma'rineblau adj navy blue

Marionette [marjo'nɛtə] f (-; -n) puppet (a. fig); **Mario'nettenthe,ater** n puppet show

Mark¹ n (-[e]s; no pl) marrow; BOT pulp

Mark² [mark] f (-; -) hist (former monetary unit of Germany) mark

Marke ['markə] f (-; -n) ECON brand; TECH make; trademark; stamp; badge, tag; mark; **markieren** [mar'kiːrən] v/t (no -ge-, h) mark (a. SPORT); F fig act; **Mar'kierung** f (-; -en) mark

Markise [mar'kiːzə] f (-; -n) awning, sun

blind

Markt [markt] *m* (-[e]s; *Märkte* ['mɛrktə]) ECON market; **auf den ~ bringen** put on the market; **~platz** *m* market place; **~wirtschaft** *f* market economy

Marmelade [marmə'laːdə] *f* (-; -*n*) jam

Marmor ['marmoːɐ] *m* (-*s*; -*e*) marble

Marsch[1] [marʃ] *m* (-[e]s; *Märsche* ['mɛrʃə]) march (*a.* MUS)

Marsch[2] *f* (-; -*en*) GEOGR marsh, fen

Marschall ['marʃal] *m* (-*s*; *Marschälle* ['marʃɛlə]) MIL marshal

'**Marschbefehl** *m* MIL marching orders

marschieren [mar'ʃiːrən] *v/i* (*no -ge-, sein*) march

Marsmensch ['marsmɛnʃ] *m* Martian

Marter ['martɐ] *f* (-; -*n*) torture

'**martern** *v/t* (*ge-, h*) torture

'**Marterpfahl** *m* stake

Martinshorn ['martiːnshɔrn] *n* (police *etc*) siren

Märtyrer ['mɛrtyrɐ] *m* (-*s*; -), '**Märtyrerin** ['mɛrtyrərɪn] *f* (-; -*nen*) martyr (*a. fig*)

Marxismus [mar'ksɪsmus] *m* (-; *no pl*) POL Marxism; **Marxist** [mar'ksɪst] *m* (-*en*; -*en*), **mar'xistisch** *adj* POL Marxist

März [mɛrts] *m* (-[*es*]; -*e*) March

Marzipan [martsi'paːn] *n* (-*s*; -*e*) marzipan

Masche ['maʃə] *f* (-; -*n*) stitch; mesh; F trick

'**Maschendraht** *m* wire netting

Maschine [ma'ʃiːnə] *f* (-; -*n*) machine; MOT engine; AVIAT plane; motorcycle

Ma'schinen|bau *m* (-[e]s; *no pl*) mechanical engineering; **~gewehr** *n* MIL machinegun

ma'schinenlesbar *adj* machine-readable

Ma'schinen|öl *n* engine oil; **~pis,tole** *f* MIL submachine gun, machine pistol; **~schaden** *m* engine trouble *or* failure; **~schlosser** *m* (engine) fitter

Masern ['maːzɐn] *pl* MED measles

Maserung ['maːzərʊŋ] *f* (-; -*en*) grain

Maske ['maskə] *f* (-; -*n*) mask (*a.* IT)

'**Maskenball** *m* fancy-dress ball

Maskenbildner ['maskənbɪldnɐ] *m* (-*s*; -), '**Maskenbildnerin** *f* (-; -*nen*) THEA *etc* make-up artist

maskieren [mas'kiːrən] *v/t* (*no -ge-, h*) mask; **sich ~** put on a mask

maskulin [masku'liːn] *adj* masculine (*a.* LING)

maß [maːs] *pret of* **messen**

Maß[1] *n* (-*es*; -*e*) measure (**für** of); dimensions, measurements, size; *fig* extent, degree; **~e und Gewichte** weights and measures; **nach ~** (**gemacht**) made to measure; **in gewissem** (**hohem**) **~e** to a certain (high) degree; **in zunehmendem ~e** increasingly; **~ halten → maßhalten**

Maß[2] *f* (-; -[*e*]) liter (*Br* litre) of beer

Massage [ma'saːʒə] *f* (-; -*n*) massage

Massaker [ma'saːkɐ] *n* (-*s*; -) massacre

Masse ['masə] *f* (-; -*n*) mass; substance; bulk; F **e-e~** *Geld etc* loads *or* heaps of; **die** (**breite**) **~**, POL **die ~n** *pl* the masses

'**Maßeinheit** *f* unit of measure(ment)

'**Massen...** *in cpds* ...*medien*, ...*mörder etc*: mass ...; **~andrang** *m* crush

'**massenhaft** F *adv* masses *or* loads of

'**Massen|karambo,lage** *f* MOT pileup; **~produkti,on** *f* ECON mass production

Masseur [ma'søːɐ] *m* (-*s*; -*e*) masseur

Masseurin [ma'søːrɪn] *f* (-; -*nen*), **Masseuse** [ma'søːzə] *f* (-; -*n*) masseuse

'**maßgebend, maßgeblich** ['maːsgeːplɪç] *adj* authoritative

'**maßhalten** *v/i* (*irr*, **halten**, *sep, -ge-, h*) be moderate (**in** *dat* in)

massieren [ma'siːrən] *v/t* (*no -ge-, h*) massage

massig ['masɪç] *adj* massive, bulky

mäßig ['mɛːsɪç] *adj* moderate; poor

mäßigen ['mɛːsɪgən] *v/t and v/refl* (*ge-, h*) moderate; '**Mäßigung** *f* (-; *no pl*) moderation; restraint

massiv [ma'siːf] *adj* solid

Mas'siv *n* (-*s*; -*e*) GEOL massif

'**Maßkrug** *m* beer mug, stein

'**maßlos** *adj* immoderate; gross (*exaggeration*)

Maßnahme ['maːsnaːmə] *f* (-; -*n*) measure, step

'**Maßregel** *f* rule; '**maßregeln** *v/t* (*ge-, h*) reprimand; discipline

'**Maßstab** *m* scale; *fig* standard; **im ~ 1:10** on the scale of 1:10

maßstabgetreu *adj* true to scale

'**maßvoll** *adj* moderate

Mast[1] [mast] *m* (-[e]s; -*en*) MAR, TECH mast

Mast[2] *f* (-; -*en*) AGR fattening

'**Mastdarm** *m* ANAT rectum

                                                  mehr

mästen ['mɛstən] v/t (ge-, h) AGR fatten;
F stuff s.o.

masturbieren [mastʊr'biːrən] v/i (no
-ge-, h) masturbate

Match [mɛtʃ] n (-[e]s; -s, -e) game, Br.
match; **~ball** m tennis: match point

Material [mate'rjaːl] n (-s; -ien) material
(a. fig); TECH materials

Materialismus [materja'lɪsmʊs] m (-;
no pl) PHILOS materialism; **Materialist**
[materja'lɪst] m (-en; -en) materialist;
materia'listisch adj materialistic

Materie [ma'teːrjə] f (-; -n) matter (a.
fig); fig subject (matter); **materiell**
[mate'rjɛl] adj material

Mathematik [matema'tiːk] f (-; no pl)
mathematics; **Mathematiker** [mate-
'maːtikɐ] m (-s; -) mathematician;
mathe'matisch adj mathematical

Matinee [mati'neː] f (-; -n) THEA etc
morning performance

Matratze [ma'tratsə] f (-; -n) mattress

Matrize [ma'triːtsə] f (-; -n) stencil

Matrose [ma'troːzə] m (-n; -n) MAR sail-
or, seaman

Matsch [matʃ] F m (-[e]s; no pl) mud,
slush; **'matschig** adj muddy, slushy

matt [mat] adj weak; exhausted, worn
out; dull, pale (color); PHOT mat(t);
frosted (glass); chess: checkmate

Matte ['matə] f (-; -n) mat

Mattigkeit ['matɪçkait] f (-; no pl) exhaustion, weakness

'Mattscheibe f screen; PHOT focus(s)ing
screen; F (boob) tube, Br telly, box

Matura [ma'tuːra] Austrian, Swiss f →
Abitur

Mauer ['mauɐ] f (-; -n) wall; **~blümchen**
fig n wallflower

'mauern v/i (ge-, h) lay bricks

Mauerwerk n (-[e]s; no pl) masonry,
brickwork

Maul [maul] n (-[e]s; Mäuler ['mɔylɐ])
zo mouth; sl **halt's ~!** shut up!

maulen ['maulən] F v/i (ge-, h) grumble,
sulk, pout

'Maul|korb m muzzle (a. fig); **~tier** n
mule; **~wurf** m zo mole; **~wurfshau-
fen** m, **~wurfshügel** m molehill

Maurer ['maurɐ] m (-s; -) bricklayer;
~kelle f trowel; **~meister** m master
bricklayer

Maus [maus] f (-; Mäuse ['mɔyzə]) zo
mouse (a. IT)

'Mausefalle ['mauzəfalə] f mousetrap

Mauser ['mauzɐ] f (-; no pl) zo mo(u)lt
(-ing); **in der ~ sein** be mo(u)lting

Maut [maut] Austrian f (-; -en) toll;
~straße f turnpike, toll road

maximal [maksi'maːl] **1.** adj maximum
2. adv at (the) most; **Maximum** ['mak-
simʊm] n (-s; -ma) maximum

Mayonnaise [majɔ'nɛːzə] f (-; -n) GASTR
mayonnaise

Mäzen [mɛ'tseːn] m (-s; -e) patron;
SPORT sponsor

Mechanik [me'çaːnɪk] f (-; -en) (no pl)
PHYS mechanics; TECH mechanism; **Mechaniker** [me'çaːnikɐ] m (-s; -) mechanic; **mechanisch** [me'çaːnɪʃ] adj
TECH mechanical; **mechanisieren**
[meçani'ziːrən] v/t (no -ge-, h) mecha-
nize; **Mechani'sierung** f (-; -en) mech-
anization; **Mechanismus** [meça-
'nɪsmʊs] m (-; -men) TECH mechanism;
works

meckern ['mɛkɐn] v/i (ge-, h) zo bleat; F
grumble, bitch (**über** acc at, about)

Medaille [me'daljə] f (-; -n) medal

Me'daillengewinner m medal(l)ist

Medaillon [medal'joː] n (-s; -s) locket

Medien ['meːdjən] pl mass media;
teaching aids; audio-visual aids

Medikament [medika'mɛnt] n (-[e]s; -e)
drug; medicine

meditieren [medi'tiːrən] v/i (no -ge-, h)
meditate (**über** acc on)

Medizin [medi'tsiːn] f (-; -en) (no pl)
(science of) medicine; medicine,
remedy (**gegen** for)

Mediziner [medi'tsiːnɐ] m (-s; -), **Medi-
'zinerin** f (-; -nen) (medical) doctor;
UNIV medical student

medizinisch [medi'tsiːnɪʃ] adj medical

Meer [meːɐ] n (-[e]s; -e [ˈmeːrə]) sea (a.
fig), ocean; **~enge** f GEOGR straits

Meeres|boden ['meːrəsboːdən] m
seabed; **~früchte** pl GASTR seafood;
~spiegel m sea level

'Meerjungfrau f MYTH mermaid

'Meerrettich m (-s; -e) horseradish

Meerschweinchen ['meːɐʃvainçən] n
(-s; -) zo guinea pig

Megabyte [mega'bait] n IT megabyte

Mehl [meːl] n (-[e]s; -e) flour; meal

mehlig ['meːlɪç] adj mealy

'Mehlspeise Austrian f sweet (dish)

mehr [meːɐ] indef pron and adv more;

immer ~ more and more; *nicht* ~ no longer, not any longer (*or* more); *noch* ~ even more; *es ist kein ... ~ da* there isn't any ... left

mehrdeutig ['meːɐdɔytɪç] *adj* ambiguous

mehrere ['meːrərə] *adj and indef pron* several

'**Mehrheit** *f* (-; -en) majority

'**Mehrkosten** *pl* extra costs

'**mehrmals** *adv* several times

'**Mehr|wegflasche** *f* returnable (*or* deposit) bottle; **~wertsteuer** *f* ECON value-added tax (*abbr* VAT); **~zahl** *f* (-; *no pl*) majority; LING plural (form)

'**Mehrzweck...** *in cpds ...fahrzeug etc*: multi-purpose ...

meiden ['maidən] *v/t* (*irr, ge-, h*) avoid

Meile ['mailə] *f* (-; -n) mile

'**meilenweit** *adv* (for) miles

mein [main] *poss pron and adj* my; *das ist ~er* (~e, ~[e]s) that's mine

'**Meineid** *m* JUR perjury

meinen ['mainən] *v/t* (*ge-, h*) think, believe; mean; say; ~ *Sie wirklich?* do you (really) think so?; *wie* ~ *Sie das?* what do you mean by that?; *sie* ~ *es gut* they mean well; *ich habe es nicht so gemeint* I didn't mean it; *wie* ~ *Sie?* (I beg your) pardon?

'**meinetwegen** ['mainətveːɡən] *adv* for my sake; because of me; F I don't mind *or* care!

'**Meinung** *f* (-; -en) opinion (*über acc, von* about, of); *meiner* ~ *nach* in my opinion; *der* ~ *sein, dass* be of the opinion that, feel *or* believe that; *s-e* ~ *äußern* express one's opinion; *s-e* ~ *ändern* change one's mind; *ich bin Ihrer* (*anderer*) ~ I (don't) agree with you; *j-m die* ~ *sagen* give s.o. a piece of one's mind

'**Meinungs|austausch** *m* exchange of views (*über acc* on); **~forscher** *m* pollster; **~freiheit** *f* (-; *no pl*) freedom of speech *or* opinion; **~umfrage** *f* opinion poll; **~verschiedenheit** *f* disagreement (*über acc* about)

Meise ['maizə] *f* (-; -n) ZO titmouse

Meißel ['maisəl] *m* (-s; -) chisel

'**meißeln** *v/t and v/i* (*ge-, h*) chisel, carve

meist [maist] **1.** *adj* most; *das ~e* (*davon*) most of it; *die ~en* (*von ihnen*) most of them; *die ~en Leute* most peo-

ple; *die ~e Zeit* most of the time **2.** *adv* → **meistens**; *am ~en* (the) most; most (of all); **meistens** ['maistəns] *adv* usually; most of the time

Meister ['maistɐ] *m* (-s; -) master (*a. fig*); SPORT champion, F champ

'**meisterhaft 1.** *adj* masterly **2.** *adv* in a masterly manner *or* way

'**Meisterin** *f* (-; -nen) master (*a. fig*); SPORT champion

meistern ['maistɐn] *v/t* (*ge-, h*) master

'**Meisterschaft** *f* (-; -en) (*no pl*) mastery; SPORT championship, cup; title

'**Meister|stück** *n*, **~werk** *n* masterpiece

Melancholie [melaŋkoˈliː] *f* (-; *no pl*) melancholy; **melancholisch** [melaŋˈkoːlɪʃ] *adj* melancholy; ~ *sein* feel depressed, F have the blues

Melange [meˈlãːˌʒə] *Austrian f* (-; -n) coffee with milk

melden ['mɛldən] (*ge-, h*) **1.** *v/t* report *s.th. or s.o.* (*bei* to); *radio etc*: announce, report; *j-m et.* ~ notify s.o. of s.th. **2.** *v/refl*: *sich* ~ report (*bei* to, *für, zu* for); register (*bei* with); PED *etc*: put up one's hand; TEL answer the phone; SPORT enter (*für, zu* for); volunteer (*für, zu* for)

'**Meldung** *f* (-; -en) report, news, announcement; information; notice; notification; registration (*bei* with); SPORT entry (*für, zu* for)

melken ['mɛlkən] *v/t* ([*irr,*] *ge-, h*) milk

Melodie [meloˈdiː] *f* (-; -n) MUS melody, tune; **melodisch** [meˈloːdɪʃ] *adj* MUS melodious, melodic

Melone [meˈloːnə] *f* (-; -n) BOT melon; F derby, *Br* bowler (hat)

Memoiren [memoˈaːrən] *pl* memoirs

Menge ['mɛŋə] *f* (-; -n) amount, quantity; MATH set; F *e-e* ~ *Geld* plenty (*or* lots) of money; → **Menschenmenge**

'**Mengenlehre** *f* (-; *no pl*) MATH set theory; PED new math(ematics)

Mensa ['mɛnza] *f* (-; -s, *Mensen*) cafeteria, *Br* refectory, canteen

Mensch [mɛnʃ] *m* (-en; -en) human being; man; person, individual; *pl* people; mankind; *j-m* ~, nobody!; *~!* wow!

Menschen|affe *m* ZO ape; **~fresser** *m* cannibal; **~freund** *m* philanthropist; **~handel** *m* slave trade; **~kenntnis** *f*: ~ *haben* know human nature; **~leben** *n* human life

'**menschenleer** *adj* deserted
'**Menschen|menge** *f* crowd; **~rechte** *pl* human rights; **~seele** *f*: **keine ~** not a (living) soul
'**menschenunwürdig** *adj* degrading; *housing etc*: unfit for human beings
'**Menschen|verstand** *m*: **gesunder ~** common sense; **~würde** *f* human dignity
Menschheit: **die ~** mankind, the human race
'**menschlich** *adj* human; humane
'**Menschlichkeit** *f* (-; *no pl*) humanity
Menstruation [menstrua'tsjo:n] *f* (-; *-en*) MED menstruation
Mentalität [mɛntali'tɛːt] *f* (-; *-en*) mentality
Menü [me'ny:] *n* (-s; *-s*) set meal (*or* lunch); IT menu
Meridian [meri'dja:n] *m* (-s; *-e*) GEOGR, ASTR meridian
merkbar ['mɛrkbaːɐ] *adj* marked, distinct; noticeable; '**Merkblatt** *n* leaflet; **merken** ['mɛrkən] *v/t* (*ge-, h*) notice; feel; find (out), discover; **sich etc. ~** remember s.th., keep *or* bear s.th. in mind; '**merklich** *adj* → **merkbar**; '**Merkmal** *n* sign; feature, trait
'**merkwürdig** *adj* strange, odd, curious
'**merkwürdiger'weise** *adv* strangely enough
messbar ['mɛsbaːɐ] *adj* measurable
'**Messbecher** *m* measuring cup
Messe ['mɛsə] *f* (-; *-n*) ECON fair; REL mass; MIL, MAR mess
messen ['mɛsən] *v/t* (*irr, ge-, h*) measure; take (*temperature etc*); **sich nicht mit j-m ~ können** be no match for s.o.; **gemessen an** (*dat*) compared with
Messer ['mɛsɐ] *n* (-s; -) knife; **bis aufs ~** to the knife; **auf des ~s Schneide stehen** be on a razor edge, be touch and go (**ob** whether)
Messerstecherei [mɛsɐʃteçə'rai] *f* (-; *-en*) knife fight
'**Messerstich** *m* stab (with a knife)
Messing ['mɛsɪŋ] *n* (-s; *-e*) brass
'**Messinstru,ment** *n* measuring instrument
'**Messung** *f* (-; *-en*) measuring; reading
Metall [me'tal] *n* (-s; *-e*) metal
metallen [me'talən] , **me'tallisch** *adj* metallic
Me'tallwaren *pl* hardware

Metamorphose [metamɔr'foːzə] *f* (-; *-n*) metamorphosis
Metastase [meta'sta:zə] *f* (-; *-n*) MED metastasis
Meteor [mete'oːɐ] *m* (-s; *-e*) ASTR meteor
Meteorit [meteo'riːt] *m* (-en; *-e[n]*) ASTR meteorite
Meteorologe [meteoro'loːgə] *m* (-n; *-n*) meteorologist; **Meteorologie** [meteorolo'giː] *f* (-; *no pl*) meteorology; **Meteoro'login** *f* (-; *-nen*) meteorologist
Meter ['meːtɐ] *n, m* (-s; -) meter, *Br* metre; **~maß** *n* tape measure
Methode [me'toːdə] *f* (-; *-n*) method, TECH *a.* technique; **methodisch** [me'toːdɪʃ] *adj* methodical
metrisch ['meːtrɪʃ] *adj* metric; **~es Maßsystem** metric system
Metropole [metro'poːlə] *f* (-; *-n*) metropolis
Metzger ['mɛtsgɐ] *m* (-s; -) butcher
Metzgerei [mɛtsgə'rai] *f* (-; *-en*) butcher's (shop)
Meute ['mɔytə] *f* (-; *-n*) pack (of hounds); *fig* mob, pack
Meuterei [mɔytə'rai] *f* (-; *-en*) mutiny; **Meuterer** ['mɔytərɐ] *m* (-s; -) mutineer; **meutern** ['mɔytɐn] *v/i* (*ge-, h*) mutiny (**gegen** against)
MEZ *abbr of* **Mitteleuropäische Zeit** CET, Central European Time
miau [mi'au] *int* zo meow, *Br* miaow
miauen [mi'auən] *v/i* (*no -ge-, h*) zo meow, *Br* miaow
mich [mɪç] *pers pron* me; **~ (selbst)** myself
mied [miːt] *pret of* **meiden**
Mieder ['miːdɐ] *n* (-s; -) corset(s); bodice; **~höschen** *n* pantie girdle; **~waren** *pl* foundation garments
Miene ['miːnə] *f* (-; *-n*) expression, look, air; **gute ~ zum bösen Spiel machen** grin and bear it
mies [miːs] F *adj* rotten, lousy
Miete ['miːtə] *f* (-; *-n*) rent; hire charge; **zur ~ wohnen** be a tenant; lodge (**bei** with); '**mieten** *v/t* (*ge-, h*) rent; (take on) lease; AVIAT, MAR charter; **ein Auto etc ~** rent (*Br* hire) a car *etc*; **Mieter(in)** ['miːtɐ, 'miːtərɪn] *m(f)* (-s; -/-; *-nen*) tenant, lodger
'**Mietshaus** *n* apartment building *or* house, *Br* block of flats, tenement

'**Mietvertrag** *m* lease (contract)

'**Mietwohnung** *f* apartment, *Br* (rented) flat

Migräne [mi'grɛːnə] *f* (-; -n) MED migraine

Mikro ['miːkro] F *n* (-*s*; -*s*) mike

Mikro... ['miːkro-] *in cpds* ...chip, ...computer, ...elektronik, ...film, ...prozessor *etc*: micro...

Mikrofon [mikro'foːn] *n* (-*s*; -*e*) microphone

Mikroskop [mikro'skoːp] *n* (-*s*; -*e*) microscope; **mikro'skopisch** *adj* microscopic(al)

Mikrowelle ['miːkrovɛlə] F *f*, '**Mikrowellenherd** *m* microwave oven

Milbe ['mɪlbə] *f* (-; -*n*) ZO mite

Milch [mɪlç] *f* (-; *no pl*) milk; **~geschäft** *n* dairy, creamery; **~glas** *n* frosted glass

milchig ['mɪlçɪç] *adj* milky

'**Milch|kaffee** *m* white coffee; **~kännchen** *n* (milk) jug; **~kanne** *f* milk can; **~mann** F *m* milkman; **~mixgetränk** *n* milk shake; **~pro,dukte** *pl* dairy products; **~pulver** *n* powdered milk; **~reis** *m* rice pudding; **~straße** *f* ASTR Milky Way, Galaxy; **~tüte** *f* milk carton; **~wirtschaft** *f* dairy farming; **~zahn** *m* milk tooth

mild [mɪlt] *adj* mild, soft; gentle

milde ['mɪldə] *adv* mildly; **~ ausgedrückt** to put it mildly

'**Milde** *f* (-; *no pl*) mildness, gentleness; leniency, mercy

mildern ['mɪldɐn] *v/t* (*ge*-, *h*) lessen, soften; **~d** *adj*: **~e Umstände** JUR mitigating circumstances

'**mildtätig** *adj* charitable

Milieu [mi'ljøː] *n* (-*s*; -*s*) environment; social background

Militär [mili'tɛːɐ] *n* (-*s*; *no pl*) the military, armed forces; army; **~dienst** *m* (-[*e*]*s*; *no pl*) military service; **~dikta,tur** *f* military dictatorship; **~gericht** *n* court martial

militärisch [mili'tɛːrɪʃ] *adj* military

Militarismus [milita'rɪsmʊs] *m* (-; *no pl*) militarism; **Militarist** [milita'rɪst] *m* (-*en*; -*en*) militarist; **milita'ristisch** *adj* militaristic

'**Mili'tärre'gierung** *f* military government

Milliarde [mɪ'ljardə] *f* (-; -*n*) billion, *Br old use a.* a thousand million(s)

Millimeter ['mɪlimeːtɐ] *n*, *m* (-*s*; -) millimet|er, *Br* -re; **~pa,pier** *n* graph paper

Million [mɪ'lioːn] *f* (-; -*en*) million

Millionär [mɪljo'nɛːɐ] *m* (-*s*; -*e*), **Millio'närin** *f* (-; -*nen*) millionaire

Milz [mɪlts] *f* (-; *no pl*) ANAT spleen

Mimik ['miːmɪk] *f* (-; *no pl*) facial expression

minder ['mɪndɐ] **1.** *adj* → **geringer, weniger 2.** *adv* less; **nicht ~** no less

'**Minderheit** *f* (-; -*en*) minority

minderjährig ['mɪndɐjɛːrɪç] *adj*: **~ sein** be under age, be a minor; **Minderjährige** ['mɪndɐjɛːrɪgə] *m*, *f* (-*n*; -*n*) minor

'**Minderjährigkeit** *f* (-; *no pl*) minority

'**minderwertig** *adj* inferior, of inferior quality; '**Minderwertigkeit** *f* (-; *no pl*) inferiority; ECON inferior quality

'**Minderwertigkeitskom,plex** *m* PSYCH inferiority complex

mindest ['mɪndəst] *adj* least; **das Mindeste** the (very) least; **nicht im Mindesten** not in the least, not at all

'**Mindest...** *in cpds* ...alter, ...einkommen, ...lohn *etc*: minimum ...

mindestens ['mɪndəstəns] *adv* at least

'**Mindest|haltbarkeitsdatum** *n* pull date, *Br* best-before (*or* best-by, sell-by) date; **~maß** *n* minimum; **auf ein ~ herabsetzen** reduce to a minimum

Mine ['miːnə] *f* (-; -*n*) mine (*a.* MAR, MIL); lead; cartridge; refill

Mineral [mine'raːl] *n* (-*s*; -*e*, -*ien*) mineral; **Mineralogie** [mineralo'giː] *f* (-; *no pl*) mineralogy

Mine'ralöl *n* mineral oil

Mine'ralwasser *n* mineral water

Miniatur [minja'tuːɐ] *f* (-; -*en*) miniature

Minigolf ['mɪnigɔlf] *n* miniature (*Br* crazy) golf

minimal [mini'maːl] *adj*, *adv* minimal; minimum; at least; **Minimum** ['miːnimʊm] *n* (-*s*; -*ma*) minimum

Minirock ['mɪnirɔk] *m* miniskirt

Minister [mi'nɪstɐ] *m* (-*s*; -), **Mi'nisterin** *f* (-; -*nen*) minister, secretary, *Br a.* secretary of state

Ministerium [minɪs'teːriʊm] *n* (-*s*; -*ien*) ministry, department, *Br a.* office

Mi'nisterpräsi,dent *m*, **Mi'nisterpräsi,dentin** *f* prime minister

minus ['miːnʊs] *adv* MATH minus; **bei 10 Grad ~** at 10 degrees below zero

Minute [mi'nuːtə] *f* (-; -*n*) minute

Mi'nutenzeiger *m* minute hand

Mio *abbr of* **Million(en)** m, million

mir [miːɐ] *pers pron* (to) me

Mischbatte,rie ['mɪʃbatəriː] *f* mixing faucet, *Br* mixer tap

'Mischbrot *n* wheat and rye bread

mischen ['mɪʃən] *v/t* (*ge-, h*) mix; blend (*tea etc*); shuffle (*cards*); **sich ~** mingle *or* mix (**unter** with)

'Mischling *m* (*-s; -e*) *esp contp* half-caste; BOT, ZO hybrid; mongrel

'Mischmasch F *m* (*-[e]s; -e*) hotch-potch, jumble

'Misch|ma,schine *f* TECH mixer; **~pult** *n* radio, TV: mixer, mixing console

'Mischung *f* (*-; -en*) mixture; blend; assortment

'Mischwald *m* mixed forest

miserabel [mizə'raːbəl] F *adj* lousy, rotten

miss'achten [mɪsʔ'axtən] *v/t* (*no -ge-, h*) disregard, ignore; despise

Miss'achtung *f* disregard; contempt; neglect (*all: gen of*)

'Missbildung *f* (*-; -en*) deformity, malformation

miss'billigen *v/t* (*no -ge-, h*) disapprove of

'Missbrauch *m* abuse (*a.* JUR); misuse; **miss'brauchen** *v/t* (*no -ge-, h*) abuse; misuse

miss'deuten *v/t* (*no -ge-, h*) misinterpret

'Misserfolg *m* failure; F flop

'Missernte *f* bad harvest, crop failure

miss'fallen *v/i* (*irr,* **fallen,** *no -ge-, h*) *j-m* **~** displease s.o.; **'Missfallen** *n* (*-s; no pl*) displeasure, dislike

'missgebildet *adj* deformed, malformed; **'Missgeburt** *f* deformed child *or* animal; freak

'Missgeschick *n* (*-[e]s; -e*) mishap

miss'glücken *v/i* (*no -ge-, sein*) fail

miss'gönnen *v/t* (*no -ge-, h*) *j-m et.* **~** envy s.o. s.th.

'Missgriff *m* mistake

miss'handeln *v/t* (*no -ge-, h*) ill-treat, maltreat (*a. fig*); batter

Miss'handlung *f* ill-treatment, maltreatment, *esp* JUR assault and battery

Mission [mɪ'sjoːn] *f* (*-; -en*) mission (*a.* POL *and fig*); **Missionar(in)** [mɪsjo-'naːɐ, mɪsjo'naːrɪn] *m(f)* (*-s; -e/-; -nen*) missionary

'Missklang *m* dissonance, discord (*both a. fig*)

'Misskre,dit *m* discredit

misslang [mɪs'laŋ] *pret of* **misslingen;** **misslingen** [mɪs'lɪŋən] *v/i* (*irr, no -ge-, sein*) fail; **misslungen** [mɪs'luŋən] *pp of* **misslingen;** **das ist mir ~** I've bungled it

'missmutig *adj* bad-tempered, grumpy, glum

miss'raten 1. *v/i* (*irr,* **raten,** *no -ge-, sein*) fail; turn out badly **2.** *adj* wayward

miss'trauen *v/i* (*no -ge-, h*) distrust; **'Misstrauen** *n* (*-s; no pl*) distrust, suspicion (*both:* **gegenüber** of *)

'Misstrauens|antrag *m* PARL motion of no confidence; **~votum** *n* PARL vote of no confidence

misstrauisch ['mɪstrauɪʃ] *adj* distrustful, suspicious

'Missverhältnis *n* disproportion

'Missverständnis *n* (*-ses; -se*) misunderstanding; **'missverstehen** *v/t* (*irr,* **stehen,** *no -ge-, h*) misunderstand

'Misswahl *f* beauty contest *or* competition

Mist [mɪst] *m* (*-[e]s; no p*) AGR dung, manure; F trash, rubbish

'Mistbeet *n* AGR hotbed

Mistel ['mɪstəl] *f* (*-; -n*) BOT mistletoe

'Mistgabel *f* AGR dung fork

'Misthaufen *m* AGR manure heap

mit [mɪt] *prp* (*dat*) *and adv* with; **~ Gewalt** by force; **~ Absicht** on purpose; **~ dem Auto** (*der Bahn etc*) by car (train *etc*); **~ 20 Jahren** at (the age of) 20; **~ 100 Stundenkilometern** at 100 kilometers per hour; **~ einem Mal(e)** all of a sudden; (all) at the same time; **~ lauter Stimme** in a loud voice; **~ anderen Worten** in other words; **ein Mann ~ dem Namen ...** a man by the name of ...; *j-n* **~ Namen kennen** know s.o. by name; **~ der Grund dafür, dass** one of the reasons why; **~ der Beste** one of the best

'Mitarbeit *f* cooperation; assistance; PED activity, class participation

'Mitarbeiter *m*, **'Mitarbeiterin** *f* colleague; employee; assistant; **freie(r)** **Mitarbeiter(in)** freelance

'mit|bekommen F *v/t* (*irr,* **kommen,** *sep, no -ge-, h*) get; catch; **~benutzen** *v/t* (*sep, no -ge-, h*) share

'**Mit|bestimmungsrecht** *n* (right of) codetermination, worker participation; **~bewerber(in)** (rival) competitor; fellow applicant; **~bewohner(in)** roommate, *Br* flatmate

'**mitbringen** *v/t* (*irr*, *bringen*, *sep*, *-ge-*, *h*) bring *s.th. or s.o.* with one; **j-m et. ~** bring s.o. s.th.; **Mitbringsel** ['mɪtbrɪŋzəl] *F n* (*-s*; *-*) little present; souvenir

'**Mitbürger** *m*, '**Mitbürgerin** *f* fellow citizen

mitei'nander *adv* with each other, with one another; together, jointly

'**miterleben** *v/t* (*sep*, *no -ge-*, *h*) live to see

'**Mitesser** *m* MED blackhead

'**mitfahren** *v/i* (*irr*, *fahren*, *sep*, *-ge-*, *sein*) **mit j-m ~** drive or go with s.o.; **j-n ~ lassen** give s.o. a lift

'**Mitfahr|gelegenheit** *f* lift; **~zen,trale** *f* car pool(ing) service

'**mitfühlend** *adj* sympathetic

'**mitgeben** *v/t* (*irr*, *geben*, *sep*, *-ge-*, *h*) **j-m et. ~** give s.o. s.th. (to take along)

'**Mitgefühl** *n* (*-[e]s*; *no pl*) sympathy

'**mitgehen** *v/i* (*irr*, *gehen*, *sep*, *-ge-*, *sein*) **mit j-m ~** go or come along with s.o.; **F et. ~ lassen** walk off with s.th.

'**Mitgift** *f* (*-*; *-en*) dowry

'**Mitglied** *n* member (**bei** of)

'**Mitgliedsbeitrag** *m* subscription

'**Mitgliedschaft** *f* (*-*; *-en*) membership

'**mithaben** *v/t* (*irr*, *haben*, *sep*, *-ge-*, *h*) **ich habe kein Geld mit** I haven't got any money with me or on me

'**Mithilfe** *f* (*-*; *no pl*) assistance, help, cooperation (**bei** in; **von** of)

mit'hilfe *prp*: **~ von** (or gen) with the help of, *fig a.* by means of

'**mithören** *v/t* (*sep*, *-ge-*, *h*) listen in to; overhear

'**Mitinhaber** *m*, '**Mitinhaberin** *f* joint owner

'**mitkommen** *v/i* (*irr*, *kommen*, *sep*, *-ge-*, *sein*) come along (**mit** with); *fig* keep pace (**mit** with), follow; PED get on, keep up (with the class)

'**Mitlaut** *m* LING consonant

'**Mitleid** *n* (*-[e]s*; *no pl*) pity (**mit** for); **aus ~** out of pity; **~ haben mit** feel sorry for

mitleidig ['mɪtlaidɪç] *adj* compassionate, sympathetic

'**mitleidslos** *adj* pitiless

'**mitmachen** (*sep*, *-ge-*, *h*) **1.** *v/i* join in **2.** *v/t* take part in; follow (*a fashion etc*); F go through

'**Mitmenschen**: **die ~** one's fellow human beings; people

'**mitnehmen** *v/t* (*irr*, *nehmen*, *sep*, *-ge-*, *h*) take *s.th. or s.o.* with one; **j-n (im Auto) ~** give s.o. a lift

'**mitreden** *v/t* (*sep*, *-ge-*, *h*) **et. mitzureden haben** (**bei**) have a say (in)

'**mitreißen** *v/t* (*irr*, *reißen*, *sep*, *-ge-*, *h*) drag along; *fig* carry away (*mst passive*); **~d** *fig adj* electrifying (*speech etc*)

'**mitschneiden** *v/t* (*irr*, *schneiden*, *sep*, *-ge-*, *h*) radio, TV record, tape(-record)

'**mitschreiben** (*irr*, *schreiben*, *sep*, *-ge-*, *h*) **1.** *v/t* take down; take, do (*a test*) **2.** *v/i* take notes

'**Mitschuld** *f* (*-*; *no pl*) partial responsibility; '**mitschuldig** *adj*: **~ sein** be partly to blame (**an** *dat* for)

'**Mitschüler** *m*, '**Mitschülerin** *f* classmate; schoolmate, fellow student

'**mitspielen** *v/i* (*sep*, *-ge-*, *h*) SPORT, MUS play; join in (*a game etc*); **in e-m Film** *etc* **~** be or appear in a film *etc*

'**Mitspieler** *m*, '**Mitspielerin** *f* partner, SPORT *a.* team-mate

Mittag ['mɪtaːk] *m* (*-s*; *-e*) noon, midday; **heute ~** at noon today; **zu ~ essen** (have) lunch; **~essen** *n* lunch; **was gibt es zum ~?** what's for lunch?

'**mittags** *adv* at noon; **12 Uhr ~** 12 o'clock noon

'**Mittags|pause** *f* lunch break; **~ruhe** *f* midday rest; **~schlaf** *m* after-dinner nap; **~zeit** *f* lunchtime

Mitte ['mɪtə] *f* (*-*; *no pl*) middle; center, *Br* centre (*a.* POL); **~ Juli** in the middle of July; **~ dreißig** in one's mid thirties

'**mitteilen** *v/t* (*sep*, *-ge-*, *h*) **j-m et. ~** inform s.o. of s.th.; '**mitteilsam** *adj* communicative; '**Mitteilung** *f* (*-*; *-en*) report, information, message

Mittel ['mɪtəl] *n* (*-s*; *-*) means, way; measure; PHARM remedy (**gegen** for) (*a. fig*); average; MATH mean; PHYS medium; *pl* means, money

'**Mittelalter** *n* (*-s*; *no pl*) Middle Ages

'**mittelalterlich** *adj* medi(a)eval

'**Mittel|ding** *n* cross (**zwischen** between); **~feld** *n* SPORT midfield; **~feldspieler(in)** midfield player, midfielder; **~finger** *m* ANAT middle finger '**mittelfristig** *adj* medium-term

'**Mittelgewicht** *n* (-[e]s; *no pl*) SPORT middleweight (class)

'**mittelgroß** *adj* of medium height; medium-sized

'**Mittel|klasse** *f* middle class (*a.* MOT); **~linie** *f* SPORT halfway line

'**mittellos** *adj* without means

'**mittelmäßig** *adj* average

'**Mittelpunkt** *m* center, *Br* centre (*a. fig*)

'**mittels** *prp* (*gen*) by (means of), through

'**Mittelschule** *f* → **Realschule**

'**Mittel|strecke** *f* SPORT middle distance; **~streckenra‚kete** *f* MIL medium-range missile; **~streifen** *m* MOT median strip, *Br* central reservation; **~stufe** *f* PED junior highschool, *Br* middle school; **~stürmer(in)** SPORT center (*Br* centre) forward; **~weg** *m* middle course; **~welle** *f* radio: medium wave (*abbr* AM); **~wort** *n* (-[e]s; *-wörter*) LING participle

mitten ['mɪtən] *adv:* **~ in** (**auf, unter** *dat*) in the midst *or* middle of

mitten'drin F *adv* right in the middle

mitten'durch F *adv* right through (the middle); right in two

Mitternacht ['mɪtɛnaxt] *f* midnight

mittlere ['mɪtlərə] *adj* middle, central; average, medium

mittlerweile ['mɪtlɐ'vaɪlə] *adv* meanwhile, (in the) meantime

Mittwoch ['mɪtvɔx] *m* (-[s]; *-e*) Wednesday

mit'unter *adv* now and then

'**Mitverantwortung** *f* share of the responsibility

'**mitwirken** *v/i* (*sep, -ge-, h*) take part (**bei** in); '**Mitwirkende** *m, f* (-*n; -n*) THEA, MUS performer; *pl* THEA the cast; '**Mitwirkung** *f* (-; *no pl*) participation

'**Mixbecher** *m* shaker

mixen ['mɪksən] *v/t* (*ge-, h*) mix

Mixer ['mɪksɐ] *m* (-*s; -*) mixer; '**Mixgetränk** *n* mixed drink, cocktail, shake

Möbel ['mø:bəl] *pl* furniture; **~spediti‚on** *f* removal firm; **~stück** *n* piece of furniture; **~wagen** *m* moving (*Br* furniture) van

mobil [mo'bi:l] *adj* mobile; **~ machen** MIL mobilize

Mobiliar [mobi'ljaːɐ] *n* (-*s; no pl*) furniture

Mo'biltele‚fon *n* mobile phone

möblieren [mø'bliːrən] *v/t* (*no -ge-, h*) furnish

mochte ['mɔxtə] *pret of* **mögen**

Mode ['moːdə] *f* (-; *-n*) fashion; **in ~** in fashion; **~ sein** be in fashion, F be in; **die neueste ~** the latest fashion; **mit der ~ gehen** follow the fashion; **in** (**aus der**) **~ kommen** come into (go out of) fashion

Modell [mo'dɛl] *n* (-*s; -e*) model; **j-m ~ stehen** *or* **sitzen** pose *or* sit for s.o.; **~bau** *m* model construction; **~baukasten** *m* model construction kit; **~eisenbahn** *f* model railway

modellieren [modɛ'liːrən] *v/t* (*no -ge-, h*) model

Modem ['moːdɛm] *m, n* (-*s; -s*) IT modem

'**Modenschau** *f* fashion show

Moderator [mode'raːtoːɐ] *m* (-*s; -en* [modera'toːrən]), **Modera'torin** *f* (-; *-nen*) TV *etc* presenter, host, anchorman (anchorwoman)

moderieren [mode'riːrən] *v/t* (*no -ge-, h*) TV *etc* present, host

moderig ['moːdərɪç] *adj* musty, mo(u)ldy

modern[1] ['moːdɐn] *v/i* (*ge-, h, sein*) mo(u)ld, rot, decay

modern[2] [mo'dɛrn] *adj* modern; fashionable

modernisieren [modɛrni'ziːrən] *v/t* (*no -ge-, h*) modernize, bring up to date

'**Mode|schmuck** *n* costume jewel(le)ry; **~schöpfer(in)** fashion designer; **~waren** *pl* fashionwear; **~wort** *n* (-[e]s; *-wörter*) vogue word, F in word; **~zeichner(in)** fashion designer; **~zeitschrift** *f* fashion magazine

modisch ['moːdɪʃ] *adj* fashionable, stylish

Modul[1] [mo'duːl] *n* (-*s; -e*) IT module

Modul[2] ['moːdʊl] *m* (-*s;-n*) MATH, TECH module

Mofa ['moːfa] *n* (-*s; -s*) (small) moped, motorized bicycle

mogeln ['moːgəln] F *v/i* (*ge-, h*) cheat; crib

mögen ['møːgən] *v/t* (*irr, ge-, h*) *and v/aux* (*irr, no -ge-, h*) like; **er mag sie** (**nicht**) he likes (doesn't like) her; **lieber ~** like better, prefer; **nicht ~** dislike; **was möchten Sie?** what would you

like?; **ich möchte, dass du es weißt**
I'd like you to know (it); **ich möchte
lieber bleiben** I'd rather stay; **es
mag sein (, dass)** it may be (that)
möglich ['møːklɪç] **1.** *adj* possible; **alle
~en** all sorts of; **sein Möglichstes
tun** do what one can; do one's utmost;
nicht ~! you don't say (so)!; **so bald
(schnell, oft) wie ~** as soon (quickly,
often) as possible **2.** *adv:* **~st bald** *etc*
as soon *etc* as possible;
'möglicher'weise *adv* possibly;
'Möglichkeit *f* (-; -en) possibility; opportunity; chance; **nach ~** if possible
Mohammedaner [mohame'daːnɐ] *m*
(-s; -), **mohamme'danisch** *adj* Muslim
Mohn [moːn] *m* (-[e]s; -e) BOT poppy
Möhre ['møːrə] *f* (-; -n), **Mohrrübe**
['moːryːbə] *f* BOT carrot
Molch [mɔlç] *m* (-[e]s; -e) ZO salaman-
der
Mole ['moːlə] *f* (-; -n) MAR mole, jetty
Molekül [mole'kyːl] *n* (-s; -e) CHEM mol-
ecule
molk [mɔlk] *pret of* **melken**
Molkerei [mɔlkə'rai] *f* (-; -en) dairy
Moll [mɔl] *n* (-; *no pl*) MUS minor (key);
a-Moll A minor
mollig ['mɔlɪç] F *adj* snug, cozy, *Br* cosy;
plump, chubby
Moment [mo'mɛnt] *m* (-[e]s; -e) moment; **(e-n) ~ bitte!** just a moment
please!; **im ~** at the moment
Monarch [mo'narç] *m* (-en; -en) monarch; **Monarchie** [monar'çiː] *f* (-; -n)
monarchy; **Monarchin** [mo'narçɪn] *f*
(-; -nen) monarch; **Monarchist**
[monar'çɪst] *m* (-en; -en) monarchist
Monat ['moːnat] *m* (-[e]s; -e) month;
zweimal im *or* **pro ~** twice a month
'monatelang *adv* for months
'monatlich *adj and adv* monthly
'Monats|binde *f* sanitary napkin (*Br*
towel); **~karte** *f* commuter ticket, *Br*
(monthly) season ticket
Mönch [mœnç] *m* (-[e]s; -e) monk; friar
Mond [moːnt] *m* (-[e]s; -e ['moːndə])
moon; **~finsternis** *f* lunar eclipse
'mondhell *adj* moonlit
'Mond|landefähre *f* lunar module;
~landung *f* moon landing; **~oberflä-
che** *f* moon surface, lunar soil;
~schein *m* (-[e]s; *no pl*) moonlight;
~sichel *f* crescent; **~umkreisung** *f,*

~umlaufbahn *f* lunar orbit
Monitor ['moːnitoːɐ] *m* (-s; -en [moni-
'toːrən]) TV *etc* monitor
Monolog [mono'loːk] *m* (-[e]s; -e) mon-
olog(ue *Br*)
Monopol [mono'poːl] *n* (-s; -e) ECON
monopoly
monoton [mono'toːn] *adj* monotonous
Monotonie [monoto'niː] *f* (-; -n) monotony
Monoxid ['moːnɔksiːt] *n* CHEM monox-
ide
Monster ['mɔnstɐ] *n* (-s; -) monster
Montag ['moːntaːk] *m* (-[e]s; -e) Monday
Montage [mɔn'taːʒə] *f* (-; -n) TECH assembly; installation; **auf ~ sein** be
away on a field job; **~band** *n* (-[e]s;
-bänder) TECH assembly line; **~halle** *f*
TECH assembly shop
Monteur [mɔn'tøːɐ] *m* (-s; -e) TECH fitter; *esp* MOT, AVIAT mechanic
montieren [mɔn'tiːrən] *v/t* (*no -ge-, h*)
TECH assemble; fit, attach; install(l)
Moor [moːɐ] *n* (-[e]s; -e) bog, moor
(-land); **moorig** ['moːrɪç] *adj* boggy
Moos [moːs] *n* (-es; -e) BOT moss
moosig ['moːzɪç] *adj* mossy
Moped ['moːpɛt] *n* (-s; -s) moped
Mops [mɔps] *m* (-es; **Möpse** ['mœpsə])
ZO pug(dog)
Moral [mo'raːl] *f* (-; *no pl*) morals, moral
standards; MIL *etc* morale; **mo'ralisch**
adj moral; **moralisieren** [morali-
'ziːrən] *v/i* (*no -ge-, h*) moralize
Morast [mo'rast] *m* (-[e]s; -e) morass;
mire, mud
Mord [mɔrt] *m* (-[e]s; -e ['mɔrdə]) murder (**an** *dat* of); **e-n ~ begehen** commit
murder; **~anschlag** *m esp* POL assassination attempt
Mörder ['mœrdɐ] *m* (-s; -), **'Mörderin** *f*
(-; -nen) murderer; (hired) killer; *esp*
POL assassin
'Mord|kommissi,on *f* homicide divi-
sion, *Br* murder squad; **~pro,zess** *m*
JUR murder trial
'Mords|angst F *f*: **e-e ~ haben** be scared
stiff; **~glück** F *n* stupendous luck; **~kerl**
F *m* devil of a fellow; **~wut** F *f*: **e-e ~
haben** be in a hell of a rage
'Mord|verdacht *m* suspicion of murder;
~versuch *m* attempted murder
morgen ['mɔrgən] *adv* tomorrow; **~**

Abend (*früh*) tomorrow night (morning); **~** *Mittag* at noon tomorrow; **~** *in e-r Woche* a week from tomorrow; **~** *um diese Zeit* this time tomorrow; ... *von* **~** tomorrow's ..., ... of tomorrow

'**Morgen** *m* (-*s*; -) morning; AGR acre; *heute* **~** this morning; *am* (*frühen*) **~** (early) in the morning; *am nächsten* **~** the next morning; **~essen** *Swiss n* breakfast; **~grauen** *n* dawn; *im* or *bei* **~** at dawn; **~land** *n* (-[*e*]*s*; *no pl*) Orient; **~mantel** *m*, **~rock** *m* dressing gown

'**morgens** *adv* in the morning; *von* **~** *bis abends* from morning till night

morgig ['mɔrgɪç] *adj* tomorrow's ...

Morphium ['mɔrfjʊm] *n* (-*s*; *no pl*) PHARM morphine

morsch [mɔrʃ] *adj* rotten; **~** *werden* rot

Morsealpha,bet ['mɔrzəalfabeːt] *n* Morse code

Mörser ['mœrzɐ] *m* (-*s*; -) mortar (*a.* MIL)

'**Morsezeichen** *n* Morse signal

Mörtel ['mœrtəl] *m* (-*s*; -) mortar

Mosaik [moza'iːk] *n* (-*s*; -*en*) mosaic

Mosa'ikstein *m* piece

Moschee [mɔ'ʃeː] *f* (-; -*n*) mosque

Moskito [mɔs'kiːto] *m* (-*s*; -*s*) ZO mosquito

Moslem ['mɔslɛm] *m* (-*s*; -*s*), **moslemisch** [mɔs'leːmɪʃ] *adj*, **Moslime** [mɔs'liːmə] *f* (-; -*n*) Muslim

Most [mɔst] *m* (-[*e*]*s*; -*e*) grape juice; cider

Motiv [mo'tiːf] *n* (-*s*; -*e*) motive; PAINT, MUS motif; **Motivation** [motiva'tsjoːn] *f* (-; -*en*) motivation; **motivieren** [moti'viːrən] *v/t* (*no -ge-, h*) motivate

Motor ['moːtoːɐ, mo'toːɐ] *m* (-*s*; -*en* [mo'toːrən]) motor, engine; **~boot** *n* motor boat; **~haube** *f* hood, *Br* bonnet

motorisieren [motori'ziːrən] *v/t* (*no -ge-, h*) motorize

'**Motor|leistung** *f* (engine) performance; **~rad** *n* motorcycle, F motorbike; **~** *fahren* ride a motorcycle; **~radfahrer(in)** motorcyclist, biker; **~roller** *m* (motor) scooter; **~säge** *f* power saw; **~schaden** *m* engine trouble (*or* failure)

Motte ['mɔtə] *f* (-; -*n*) ZO moth

'**Mottenkugel** *f* mothball

'**mottenzerfressen** *adj* moth-eaten

Motto ['mɔto] *n* (-*s*; -*s*) motto

Möwe ['møːvə] *f* (-; -*n*) ZO (sea)gull

Mücke ['mʏkə] *f* (-; -*n*) ZO gnat, midge, mosquito; *aus e-r* **~** *e-n Elefanten machen* make a mountain out of a molehill; '**Mückenstich** *m* gnat bite

müde ['myːdə] *adj* tired; weary; sleepy; **~** *sein* (*werden*) be (get) tired (*fig e-r Sache* of s.th.)

'**Müdigkeit** *f* (-; *no pl*) tiredness

Muff [mʊf] *m* (-[*e*]*s*; -*e*) muff

Muffe ['mʊfə] *f* (-; -*n*) TECH sleeve, socket

Muffel ['mʊfəl] F *m* (-*s*; -) sourpuss

muff(e)lig ['mʊf(ə)lɪç], **muffig** ['mʊfɪç] F *adj* musty; *contp* sulky, sullen

Mühe ['myːə] *f* (-; -*n*) trouble; effort; difficulty (*mit* with s.th.); (*nicht*) *der* **~** *wert* (not) worth the trouble; *j-m* **~** *machen* give s.o. trouble; *sich* **~** *geben* try hard; *sich die* **~** *sparen* save o.s. the trouble; *mit* **~** *und Not* (just) barely

'**mühelos** *adv* without difficulty

mühen ['myːən] *v/refl* (*ge-, h*) struggle, work hard

'**mühevoll** *adj* laborious

Mühle ['myːlə] *f* (-; -*n*) mill; morris

Mühsal ['myːzaːl] *f* (-; -*e*) toil

mühsam ['myːzaːm], '**mühselig 1.** *adj* laborious **2.** *adv* with difficulty

Mulatte [mu'latə] *m* (-*n*; -*n*), **Mu'lattin** *f* (-; -*nen*) mulatto

Mulde ['mʊldə] *f* (-; -*n*) hollow

Mull [mʊl] *m* (-[*e*]*s*; -*e*) muslin; *esp* MED gauze

Müll [mʏl] *m* (-*s*; *no pl*) garbage, trash, *Br* refuse, rubbish; **~abfuhr** *f* garbage (*Br* refuse) collection; **~beseitigung** *f* waste disposal; **~beutel** *m* garbage bag, *Br* dustbin liner

'**Mullbinde** *f* MED gauze bandage

'**Müll|con,tainer** *m* garbage (*Br* rubbish) skip; **~depo,nie** *f* dump; **~eimer** *m* garbage can, *Br* dustbin; **~fahrer** *m* garbage man, *Br* dustman; **~halde** *f* dump; **~haufen** *m* garbage (*Br* rubbish) heap; **~kippe** *f* dump; **~schlucker** *m* garbage (*Br* refuse) chute; **~tonne** *f* garbage can, *Br* dustbin; **~verbrennungsanlage** *f* (waste) incineration plant; **~wagen** *m* garbage truck, *Br* dustcart

Multiplikation [mʊltiplika'tsjoːn] *f* (-; -*en*) MATH multiplication; **multiplizieren** [mʊltipli'tsiːrən] *v/t* (*no -ge-, h*)

MATH multiply (*mit* by)

Mumie ['muːmjə] *f* (-; *-n*) mummy

Mumps [mʊmps] *m*, *f* (-; *no pl*) MED mumps

Mund [mʊnt] *m* (-[e]s; *Münder* ['mʏn-də]) mouth; F **den ~ vollnehmen** talk big; **halt den ~!** shut up!; **~art** *f* dialect

münden ['mʏndən] *v/i* (*ge-*, *h*, *sein*) **~ in** (*acc*) river etc: flow into; road etc: lead into

'**Mundgeruch** *m* bad breath

'**Mundhar,monika** *f* MUS mouth organ, harmonica

mündig ['mʏndɪç] *adj* emancipated; **~ (werden)** JUR (come) of age

mündlich ['mʏntlɪç] *adj* oral; verbal

'**Mundstück** *n* mouthpiece; tip

'**Mündung** *f* (-; *-en*) river: mouth; gun: muzzle

'**Mund|wasser** *n* mouthwash; **~werk** F *n*: **ein loses ~** a loose tongue; **~winkel** *m* corner of the mouth

'**Mund-zu-'Mund-Beatmung** *f* (-; *-en*) MED mouth-to-mouth resuscitation, F kiss of life

Munition [muni'tsjoːn] *f* (-; *-en*) ammunition

munkeln ['mʊŋkəln] F *v/t* (*ge-*, *h*) **man munkelt, dass** rumo(u)r has it that

Münster ['mʏnstɐ] *n* (-s; -) cathedral, minster

munter ['mʊntɐ] *adj* awake; lively; merry

Münze ['mʏntsə] *f* (-; *-n*) coin; medal

'**Münz|einwurf** *m* (coin) slot; **~fernsprecher** *m* pay phone; **~tank(auto,mat)** *m* coin-operated (gas, Br petrol) pump; **~wechsler** *m* (-s; -) change machine

mürbe ['mʏrbə] *adj* tender; brittle; GASTR crisp; '**Mürbeteig** *m* short pastry; shortcake

Murmel ['mʊrməl] *f* (-; *-n*) marble

'**murmeln** *v/t and v/i* (*ge-*, *h*) murmur

'**Murmeltier** *n* ZO marmot

murren ['mʊrən] *v/i* (*ge-*, *h*) complain (**über** *acc* about)

mürrisch ['mʏrɪʃ] *adj* sullen; grumpy

Mus [muːs] *n* (-es; *-e*) mush; stewed fruit

Muschel ['mʊʃəl] *f* (-; *-n*) ZO mussel; shell

Museum [mu'zeːʊm] *n* (-s; *Museen*) museum

Musik [mu'ziːk] *f* (-; *no pl*) music

musikalisch [muzi'kaːlɪʃ] *adj* musical

Mu'sik|anlage *f* hi-fi *or* stereo set; **~auto,mat** *m*, **~box** *f* juke box

Musiker ['muːzikɐ] *m* (-s; -), '**Musikerin** *f* (-; *-nen*) musician

Mu'sik|instru,ment *n* musical instrument; **~ka,pelle** *f* band; **~kas,sette** *f* music cassette; **~lehrer(in)** music teacher; **~stunde** *f* music lesson

musisch ['muːzɪʃ] *adv*: **~ interessiert (begabt)** fond of (gifted for) fine arts and music

musizieren [muzi'tsiːrən] *v/i* (*no -ge-*, *h*) make music

Muskat [mʊs'kaːt] *m* (-[e]s; *-e*), **~nuss** *f* BOT nutmeg

Muskel ['mʊskəl] *m* (-s; *-n*) ANAT muscle; **~kater** F *m* aching muscles; **~zerrung** *f* MED pulled muscle

muskulös [mʊsku'løːs] *adj* muscular, brawny

Müsli ['myːsli] *n* (-s; -) GASTR granola, Br muesli

Muss *n* (-; *no pl*) necessity; **es ist ein ~** it is a must

Muße ['muːsə] *f* (-; *no pl*) leisure; spare time

müssen ['mʏsən] *v/i* (*irr*, *ge-*, *h*) and *v/aux* (*irr*, *no -ge-*, *h*) must, have (got) to; **du musst den Film sehen!** you must see the film!; **ich muss jetzt (m-e) Hausaufgaben machen** I have (got) to do my homework now; **sie muss krank sein** she must be ill; **du musst es nicht tun** you need not do it; **das müsstest du (doch) wissen** you ought to know (that); **sie müsste zu Hause sein** she should (ought to) be (at) home; **das müsste schön sein!** that would be nice!; **du hättest ihm helfen ~** you ought to have helped him

müßig ['myːsɪç] *adj* idle; useless

musste ['mʊstə] *pret of* **müssen**

Muster ['mʊstɐ] *n* (-s; -) pattern; sample; model

'**muster|gültig**, **~haft** *adj* exemplary; **sich ~ benehmen** behave perfectly

'**Musterhaus** *n* showhouse

'**mustern** *v/t* (*ge-*, *h*) eye *s.o.*; size *s.o.* up; MIL **gemustert werden** F have one's medical; **Musterung** ['mʊstərʊŋ] *f* (-; *-en*) MIL medical (examination for military service)

Mut [muːt] *m* (-[e]s; *no pl*) courage; **j-m**

~ **machen** encourage s.o.; **den ~ verlieren** lose courage; → **zumute**

mutig ['mu:tıç] *adj* courageous, brave

'**mutlos** *adj* discouraged

'**mutmaßen** *v/t* (*ge-, h*) speculate

'**mutmaßlich** *adj* probable; presumed

'**Mutprobe** *f* test of courage

Mutter ['mʊtɐ] *f* (-; *Mütter* ['mʏtɐ]) mother; TECH nut; ~**boden** *m*, ~**erde** *f* AGR topsoil

mütterlich ['mʏtɐlıç] *adj* motherly

'**mütterlicherseits** *adv*: **Onkel** *etc* ~ maternal uncle *etc*

'**Mutterliebe** *f* motherly love

'**mutterlos** *adj* motherless

'**Mutter|mal** *n* birthmark, mole; ~**milch** *f* mother's milk; ~**schaftsurlaub** *m* maternity leave; ~**schutz** *m* JUR legal protection of expectant and nursing mothers; ~**söhnchen** *contp n* sissy; ~**sprache** *f* mother tongue; ~**sprachler** ['mʊtɐʃpraːxlɐ] *m* (-*s*; -) native speaker; ~**tag** *m* Mother's Day

Mutti ['mʊti] F *f* (-; -*s*) mom(my), *esp Br* mum(my)

'**mutwillig** *adj* wanton

Mütze ['mʏtsə] *f* (-; -*n*) cap

MwSt *abbr of* **Mehrwertsteuer** VAT, value-added tax

mysteriös [mʏste'rjøːs] *adj* mysterious

mystisch ['mʏstıʃ] *adj* mystic(al)

mythisch ['myːtıʃ] *adj* mythical

Mythologie [mytolo'giː] *f* (-; -*n*) mythology

Mythos ['myːtɔs] *m* (-; *Mythen*) myth

N

N *abbr of* **Nord(en)** N, north

na [na] *int* well; ~ **und?** so what?; ~ **gut!** all right then; ~ **ja** (oh) well; ~(, ~)**!** come on!, come now!; ~ **so (et)was!** what do you know!, *Br* I say!; ~, **dann nicht!** oh, forget it!; ~ **also!** there you are!; ~, **warte!** just you wait!

Nabe ['naːbə] *f* (-; -*n*) TECH hub

Nabel ['naːbəl] *m* (-*s*; -) ANAT navel

'**Nabelschnur** *f* ANAT umbilical chord

nach [naːx] *prp* (*dat*) *and adv* to, toward(s), for; after; *time*: after, past; according to, by; ~ **Hause** home; *abfahren* ~ leave for; ~ **rechts** (*Süden*) to the right (south); ~ **oben** up(stairs); ~ **unten** down(stairs); ~ **vorn** (*hinten*) to the front (back); *der Reihe* ~ one after the other; *s-e Uhr* ~ *dem Radio stellen* set one's watch by the radio; ~ **m-r Uhr** by my watch; *suchen* (*fragen*) ~ look (ask) for; ~ **Gewicht** (*Zeit*) by weight (the hour); *riechen* (*schmecken*) ~ smell (taste) of; ~ **und** ~ gradually; ~ **wie vor** as before, still

nachahmen ['naːxaːmən] *v/t* (*sep, -ge-, h*) imitate, copy; take off

'**Nachahmung** *f* (-; -*en*) imitation

Nachbar ['naxbaːɐ] *m* (-*n*; -*n*), '**Nachbarin** *f* (-; -*nen*) neighbo(u)r; '**Nachbarschaft** *f* (-; *no pl*) neighbo(u)rhood, vicinity

'**Nachbau** *m* (-[*e*]*s*; -*ten*) TECH reproduction; '**nachbauen** *v/t* (*sep, -ge-, h*) copy, reproduce

'**Nachbildung** *f* (-; -*en*) copy, imitation; replica; dummy

'**nachblicken** *v/i* (*sep, -ge-, h*) look after

nach'dem *cj* after, when; *je* ~ *wie* depending on how

'**nachdenken** *v/i* (*irr, denken, sep, -ge-, h*) think; ~ **über** (*acc*) think about, think *s.th.* over

'**nachdenklich** *adj* thoughtful; *es macht e-n* ~ it makes you think

'**Nachdruck**[1] *m* (-[*e*]*s*; *no pl*) emphasis, stress

'**Nachdruck**[2] (-[*e*]*s*; -*e*) reprint

'**nachdrucken** *v/t* (*sep, -ge-, h*) reprint

nachdrücklich ['naːxdrʏklıç] *adj* emphatic; forceful; ~ **raten** (*empfehlen*) advise (recommend) strongly

'**nacheifern** *v/i* (*sep, -ge-, h*) *j-m* ~ emulate s.o.

nachei'nander *adv* one after the other, in (*or* by) turns

'**nacherzählen** *v/t* (*sep, no -ge-, h*) retell; '**Nacherzählung** *f* (-; -*en*) PED reproduction

'**Nachfolge** *f* (-; *no pl*) succession; *j-s* ~ *antreten* succeed s.o.; '**nachfolgen** *v/i*

(*sep, -ge-, sein*) (*dat*) succeed *s.o.*;
'Nachfolger(in) ['na:xfɔlgɐ,
'na:xfɔlgərɪn] (*-s; -/-; -nen*) successor
'nachforschen *v/i* (*sep, -ge-, h*) investigate; **'Nachforschung** *f* (*-; -en*) investigation, inquiry
'Nachfrage *f* (*-; -n*) inquiry; ECON demand; **'nachfragen** *v/i* (*sep, -ge-, h*) inquire, ask
'nach|fühlen *v/t* (*sep, -ge-, h*) *j-m et.* ~ understand how s.o. feels; **~füllen** *v/t* (*sep, -ge-, h*) refill; **~geben** *v/i* (*irr, geben, sep, -ge-, h*) give (way); *fig* give in
'Nachgebühr *f* (*-; -en*) *post* surcharge
'nachgehen *v/i* (*irr, gehen, sep, -ge-, sein*) follow (*a. fig*); *watch*: be slow; *e-r Sache* ~ investigate s.th.; *s-r Arbeit* ~ go about one's work
'Nachgeschmack *m* (*-[e]s; no pl*) aftertaste (*a. fig*)
nachgiebig ['na:xgi:bɪç] *adj* yielding, soft (*both a. fig*); **'Nachgiebigkeit** *f* (*-; no pl*) yieldingness, softness (*both a. fig*)
nachhaltig ['na:xhaltɪç] *adj* lasting, enduring
nach'hause → *Haus*
nach'her *adv* afterwards; *bis* ~! see you later!, so long!
'Nachhilfe *f* help, assistance; PED → **~stunden** *pl,* **~unterricht** *m* PED private lesson(s), coaching
'nachholen *v/t* (*sep, -ge-, h*) make up for, catch up on
'Nachkomme *m* (*-n; -n*) descendant, *pl esp* JUR issue; **'nachkommen** *v/i* (*irr, kommen, sep, -ge-, sein*) follow, come later; (*dat*) comply with
'Nachkriegs... *in cpds* postwar ...
Nachlass ['na:xlas] *m* (*-es; -lässe* ['na:xlɛsə]) ECON reduction, discount; JUR estate
'nachlassen *v/i* (*irr, lassen, sep, -ge-, h*) decrease, diminish, go down; *effect etc*: wear off; *student etc*: slacken one's effort; *interest etc*: flag; *health etc*: fail, deteriorate
'nachlässig *adj* careless, negligent
'nach|laufen *v/i* (*irr, laufen, sep, -ge-, sein*) run after; **~lesen** *v/t* (*irr, lesen, sep, -ge-, h*) look up; **~machen** *v/t* (*sep, -ge-, h*) imitate, copy; counterfeit, forge
'Nachmittag *m* afternoon; *heute* ~ this

afternoon
'nachmittags *adv* in the afternoon
Nachnahme ['na:xna:mə] *f* (*-; -n*) ECON cash on delivery; *per* ~ *schicken* send C.O.D.
'Nach|name *m* surname, last (*or* family) name; **~porto** *n* surcharge
'nachprüfen *v/t* (*sep, -ge-, h*) check (up), make sure (of)
'nachrechnen *v/t* (*sep, -ge-, h*) check
'Nachrede *f*: *üble* ~ malicious gossip; JUR defamation (of character), slander
Nachricht ['na:xrɪçt] *f* (*-; -en*) news; message; report; information, notice; *pl* news (report), newscast; *e-e gute* (*schlechte*) ~ good (bad) news; *Sie hören* ~*en* here is the news
'Nachrichten|dienst *m* news service; MIL intelligence service; **~satel,lit** *m* communications satellite; **~sprecher(in)** newscaster, *esp Br* newsreader; **~technik** *f* telecommunications
'Nachruf *m* obituary
'nach|rüsten *v/i* (*sep, -ge-, h*) POL, MIL close the armament gap; **~sagen** *v/t* (*sep, -ge-, h*) *j-m Schlechtes* ~ speak badly of s.o.; *man sagt ihm nach, dass er ...* he is said to *inf*
'Nachsai,son *f* off-peak season; *in der* ~ out of season
'nachschlagen (*irr, schlagen, sep, -ge-, h*) **1.** *v/t* look up **2.** *v/i*: ~ *in* (*dat*) consult; **'Nachschlagewerk** *n* reference book
'Nach|schlüssel *m* duplicate (*or* skeleton) key; **~schrift** *f* postscript; dictation; **~schub** *m esp* MIL supplies
'nach|sehen (*irr, sehen, sep, - ge-, h*) **1.** *v/i* follow with one's eyes; (have a) look; ~ *ob* (go and) see whether **2.** *v/t* look *or* go over *or* through; correct, mark; *check* (*a.* TECH); **~senden** *v/t* ([*irr, senden,*] *sep, -ge-, h*) send on, forward; *bitte* ~! *post* please forward!
'Nachsilbe *f* LING suffix
'nachsitzen *v/i* (*irr, sitzen, sep, -ge-, h*) stay in (after school), be kept in; ~ *lassen* keep in, detain
'Nachspann *m* (*-[e]s; -e*) *film*: credits *pl*
'Nachspiel *n* sequel, consequences
'nachspielen *v/i* (*sep, -ge-, h*) SPORT *5 Minuten* ~ *lassen* allow 5 minutes for injury time; **'Nachspielzeit** *f esp soccer*: injury time
'nach|spio,nieren *v/i* (*no -ge-, h*) spy

(up)on; **~sprechen** *v/t* (*irr*, **sprechen**, *sep*, *-ge-*, *h*) *j-m et.* **~** say *or* repeat s.th. after s.o.

nächst'beste [nɛːçst'bɛstə] *adj* first, F any old; next-best, second-best

nächste ['nɛːçstə] *adj* next; nearest (*a. relative*); **in den ~n Tagen (Jahren)** in the next few days (years); **in ~r Zeit** in the near future; *was kommt als Nächstes?* what comes next?; *der Nächste, bitte!* next please!

'**nachstehen** *v/i* (*irr*, **stehen**, *sep*, *-ge-*, *h*) *j-m in nichts ~* be in no way inferior to s.o.

'**nachstellen** (*sep*, *-ge-*, *h*) **1.** *v/t* put back (*watch*); TECH (re)adjust **2.** *v/i*: *j-m ~* be after s.o.; '**Nachstellung** *f* (*-*; *-en*) persecution

'**Nächstenliebe** *f* charity

Nacht [naxt] *f* (*-*; *Nächte* ['nɛçtə]) night; *Tag und ~* night and day; *die ganze ~* all night (long); *heute Nacht* tonight; last night

'**Nachtdienst** *m* night duty; **~ haben** PHARM be open all night

'**Nachteil** *m* disadvantage, drawback; *im ~ sein* be at a disadvantage (*gegenüber* compared with); **nachteilig** ['naːxtaɪlɪç] *adj* disadvantageous

'**Nacht|essen** *Swiss n* → **Abendbrot**; **~falter** *m* ZO moth; **~hemd** *n* nightgown, nightdress, F nightie; nightshirt

Nachtigall ['naxtigal] *f* (*-*; *-en*) ZO nightingale

'**Nachtisch** *m* (*-[e]s*; *no pl*) dessert; sweet

nächtlich ['nɛçtlɪç] *adj* nightly; at *or* by night

'**Nachtlo,kal** *n* nightclub

Nachtrag ['naːxtraːk] *m* (*-[e]s*; *-träge* ['naːxtrɛːgə]) supplement; '**nachtragen** *fig v/t* (*irr*, **tragen**, *sep*, *-ge-*, *h*) *j-m et.* **~** bear s.o. a grudge; '**nachtragend** *adj* unforgiving; **nachträglich** ['naːxtrɛːklɪç] *adj* additional; later; belated

nachts *adv* at night, in the night(time)

'**Nachtschicht** *f* night shift; **~ haben** be on night shift

'**nachtschlafend** *adj*: *zu ~er Zeit* in the middle of the night

'**Nachttisch** *m* bedside table

'**Nachttopf** *m* chamber pot

'**Nachtwächter** *m* night watchman

'**nachwachsen** *v/i* (*irr*, **wachsen**, *sep*, *-ge-*, *sein*) grow again

'**Nachwahl** *f* PARL special election, *Br* by-election

Nachweis ['naːxvaɪs] *m* (*-es*; *-e*) proof, evidence; '**nachweisbar** *adj* demonstrable; *esp* CHEM *etc* detectable

'**nachweisen** *v/t* (*irr*, **weisen**, *sep*, *-ge-*, *h*) prove; *esp* CHEM *etc* detect

'**nachweislich** *adv* as can be proved

'**Nach|welt** *f* (*-*; *no pl*) posterity; **~wirkung** *f* aftereffect(s), *pl a.* aftermath; **~wort** *n* (*-[e]s*; *-worte*) epilog(ue)

'**Nachwuchs** *m* (*-es*; *no pl*) young talent, F new blood; **~...** *in cpds* ...*autor*, ...*schauspieler etc*: talented *or* promising young ..., up-and-coming ...

'**nach|zahlen** *v/t* (*sep*, *-ge-*, *h*) pay extra; **~zählen** *v/t* (*sep*, *-ge-*, *h*) count over (again), check

'**Nachzahlung** *f* additional *or* extra payment

Nachzügler ['naːxtsyːklɐ] *m* (*-s*; *-*) straggler, latecomer

Nacken ['nakən] *m* (*-s*; *-*) ANAT (back *or* nape of the) neck; **~stütze** *f* headrest

nackt [nakt] *adj* naked; *esp* PAINT, PHOT nude; bare (*a. fig*); *fig* plain; *völlig ~* stark naked; *sich ~ ausziehen* strip; *~ baden* swim in the nude; *j-n ~ malen* paint s.o. in the nude

Nadel ['naːdəl] *f* (*-*; *-n*) needle; pin; brooch; **~baum** *m* BOT conifer(ous tree); **~öhr** *n* eye of a needle; **~stich** *m* pinprick (*a. fig*)

Nagel ['naːgəl] *m* (*-s*; *Nägel* ['nɛːgəl]) nail; *an den Nägeln kauen* bite one's nails; **~lack** *m* nail varnish *or* polish

'**nageln** *v/t* (*ge-*, *h*) nail (*an acc*, *auf acc* to)

'**nagel'neu** F *adj* brand-new

'**Nagelpflege** *f* manicure

nagen ['naːgən] (*ge-*, *h*) **1.** *v/i* gnaw (*an dat* at); *an e-m Knochen ~* pick a bone **2.** *v/t* gnaw; '**Nagetier** *n* ZO rodent

'**Nahaufnahme** *f* PHOT *etc* close-up

nahe [naːə] *adj* near, close (*bei* to); nearby; **~ kommen** (*dat*) come close to; *fig* → *nahekommen*; → *nahelegen*; → *naheliegen*; → *naheliegend*; **Nähe** ['nɛːə] *f* (*-*; *no pl*) nearness; neighbo(u)rhood, vicinity; *in der ~ des Bahnhofs* near the station; *ganz in der ~* quite near, close by; *in deiner*

~ near you

nahegehen v/i (irr, **gehen**, sep, -ge-, sein): **j-m ~** affect s.o. deeply

'**nahekommen** v/i (irr, **kommen**, sep, -ge-, sein) fig come close to

'**nahelegen** v/t (sep, -ge-, h) suggest

'**naheliegen** v/i (irr, **liegen**, sep, -ge-, h) seem likely; '**naheliegend** adj likely, obvious

nahen ['na:ən] v/i (ge-, sein) approach

nähen ['nɛ:ən] v/t and v/i (ge-, h) sew; make

Nähere ['nɛ:ərə] n (-n; no pl) details, particulars

nähern ['nɛ:ən] v/refl (ge-, h) approach, get near(er) or close(r) (dat to)

'**nahezu** adv nearly, almost

'**Nähgarn** n (sewing) cotton

'**Nahkampf** m MIL close combat

nahm [na:m] pret of **nehmen**

'**Nähma,schine** f sewing machine

'**Nähnadel** f (sewing) needle

nähren ['nɛ:rən] v/t (ge-, h) feed; fig nurture

nahrhaft ['na:ɐhaft] adj nutritious, nourishing

Nährstoff ['nɛ:ɐʃtɔf] m nutrient

Nahrung ['na:rʊŋ] f (-; no pl) food, nourishment; AGR feed; diet

'**Nahrungsmittel** pl food(stuffs)

Nährwert ['nɛ:ɐveːɐt] m nutritional value

Naht [na:t] f (-; **Nähte** ['nɛ:tə]) seam; MED suture

'**Nahverkehr** m local traffic; '**Nahverkehrszug** m local or commuter train

'**Nähzeug** n sewing kit

naiv [na'i:f] adj naive; **Naivität** [naivi-'tɛ:t] f (-; no pl) naivety

Name ['na:mə] m (-ns; -n) name; **im ~n von** on behalf of; **nur dem ~n nach** in name only; '**namenlos** adj nameless, fig a. unspeakable; '**namens** adv by (the) name of, named, called

'**Namens|tag** m name day; **~vetter** m namesake; **~zug** m signature

namentlich ['na:məntlɪç] adj and adv by name

nämlich ['nɛ:mlɪç] adv that is (to say), namely; you see or know

nannte ['nantə] pret of **nennen**

Napf [napf] m (-[e]s; **Näpfe** ['nɛpfə]) ~wl, basin

Narbe ['narbə] f (-; -n) scar

narbig ['narbɪç] adj scarred

Narkose [nar'ko:zə] f (-; -n) MED an(a)esthesia; **in ~** under an an(a)esthetic

Narr [nar] m (-en; -en) fool; **j-n zum ~en halten** fool s.o.; '**narrensicher** adj foolproof; **närrisch** ['nɛrɪʃ] adj foolish; **~ vor** (dat) mad with

Narzisse [nar'tsɪsə] f (-; -n) BOT daffodil

nasal [na'za:l] adj nasal

naschen ['naʃən] v/i and v/t (ge-, h) nibble (**an** dat at); **gern ~** have a sweet tooth; **Naschereien** [naʃə'raiən] pl dainties, goodies, sweets; '**naschhaft** adj sweet-toothed

Nase ['na:zə] f (-; -n) ANAT nose (a. fig); **sich die ~ putzen** blow one's nose; **in der ~ bohren** pick one's nose; F **die ~ voll haben (von)** be fed up (with)

'**Nasen|bluten** n MED nosebleed; **~loch** n nostril; **~spitze** f tip of the nose

Nashorn n ZO rhinoceros, F rhino

nass [nas] adj wet; **triefend ~** soaking (wet); **Nässe** ['nɛsə] f (-; no pl) wet (-ness); '**nässen** (ge-, h) **1.** v/t wet **2.** v/i MED weep

'**nasskalt** adj damp and cold, raw

Nation [na'tsjoːn] f (-; -en) nation

national [natsjo'na:l] adj national; **Natio'nalhymne** f national anthem

Nationalismus [natsjona'lɪsmʊs] m (-; no pl) nationalism; **Nationalität** [natsjonali'tɛ:t] f (-; -en) nationality

Natio'nal|mannschaft f SPORT national team; **~park** m national park

Natio'nalsozia,lismus m HIST National Socialism, contp Nazism; **Natio'nalsozia,list** m, **natio'nalsozia,listisch** adj HIST National Socialist, contp Nazi

Natter ['natɐ] f (-; -n) ZO adder, viper (a. fig)

Natur [na'tu:ɐ] f (-; -en) nature; **von ~ (aus)** by nature

Naturalismus [natura'lɪsmʊs] m (-; no pl) naturalism

Na'tur|ereignis n, **~erscheinung** f natural phenomenon; **~forscher** m naturalist; **~geschichte** f natural history; **~gesetz** n law of nature

na'turgetreu adj true to life; lifelike

Na'turkata,strophe f (natural) catastrophe or disaster, act of God

natürlich [na'ty:ɐlɪç] **1.** adj natural **2.**

adv naturally, of course

Na'tur|schätze *pl* natural resources; **~schutz** *m* nature conservation; **unter ~** protected; **~schützer** [na'tu:ɐʃytsɐ] *m* (-*s*; -) conservationist; **~schutzgebiet** *n* nature reserve; national park; **~wissenschaft** *f* (natural) science

n. Chr. *abbr of* **nach Christus** AD, Anno Domini

Nebel ['ne:bəl] *m* (-*s*; -) fog; mist; haze; smoke; **~horn** *n* foghorn; **~leuchte** *f* MOT fog light

neben ['ne:bən] *prp* (*dat and acc*) beside, next to; besides, apart from; compared with; **~ anderem** among other things; **setz dich ~ mich** sit by me or by my side

neben'an *adv* next door

neben'bei *adv* in addition, at the same time; **~ (gesagt)** by the way

'Nebenberuf *m* second job, sideline; **'nebenberuflich** *adv* as a sideline

Nebenbuhler ['ne:bənbu:lɐ] *m* (-*s*; -), **'Nebenbuhlerin** *f* (-; -*nen*) rival

'nebenei'nander *adv* side by side; next (door) to each other; **~ bestehen** coexist

'Neben|einkünfte *pl*, **~einnahmen** *pl* extra money; **~fach** *n* PED *etc* minor (subject); *Br* subsidiary subject; **~fluss** *m* tributary; **~gebäude** *n* next-door or adjoining building; annex(e); **~haus** *n* house next door; **~kosten** *pl* extras; **~mann** *m*: **dein ~** the person next to you; **~pro,dukt** *n* by-product; **~rolle** *f* THEA supporting role, minor part (*a. fig*); cameo (role); **~sache** *f* minor matter; **das ist ~** that's of little or no importance

'nebensächlich *adj* unimportant

'Neben|satz *m* LING subordinate clause; **~stelle** *f* TEL extension; **~straße** *f* side street; minor road; **~strecke** *f* RAIL branch line; **~tisch** *m* next table; **~verdienst** *m* extra earnings; **~wirkung** *f* side effect; **~zimmer** *n* adjoining room

neblig ['ne:blɪç] *adj* foggy; misty; hazy

necken ['nɛkən] *v/t* (*ge-*, *h*) tease

Neckerei [nɛkə'rai] *f* (-; -*en*) teasing .

'neckisch *adj* playful, teasing

Neffe ['nɛfə] *m* (-*n*; -*n*) nephew

negativ ['ne:gati:f] *adj* negative

'Negativ *n* (-*s*; -*e*) PHOT negative

nehmen ['ne:mən] *v/t* (*irr, ge-, h*) take (*a.*

sich ~); **j-m et. ~** take s.th. (away) from s.o. (*a. fig*); **sich e-n Tag frei ~** take a day off; **j-n an die Hand ~** take s.o. by the hand

Neid [nait] *m* (-*es*; *no pl*) envy; **reiner ~** sheer envy; **neidisch** ['naidɪʃ] *adj* envious (**auf** *acc* of)

Neige ['naigə] *f*: **zur ~ gehen** draw to its close; run out

'neigen (*ge-*, *h*) **1.** *v/t and refl* bend, incline **2.** *v/i*: **zu et. ~** tend to (do) s.th.

'Neigung *f* (-; -*en*) inclination (*a. fig*), slope, incline; *fig* tendency

nein [nain] *adv* no

Nektar ['nɛkta:ɐ] *m* (-*s*; -*e*) BOT nectar

Nelke ['nɛlkə] *f* (-; -*n*) BOT carnation; GASTR clove

nennen ['nɛnən] *v/t* (*irr, ge-, h*) name, call; mention; **sich ~** call o.s., be called; **man nennt ihn ...** he is called ...; **das nenne ich ...!** that's what I call ...!

'nennenswert *adj* worth mentioning

Nenner ['nɛnɐ] *m* (-*s*; -) MATH denominator

'Nennwert *m* ECON nominal or face value; **zum ~** at par

Neo..., neo... [neo-] *in cpds* ...**faschist** *etc*: neo-...

Neon ['ne:ɔn] *n* (-*s*; *no pl*) CHEM neon

'Neonröhre *f* neon tube

Nepp [nɛp] F *m* (-*s*; *no pl*) rip-off

neppen ['nɛpən] F *v/t* (*ge-*, *h*) fleece, rip *s.o.* off

Nerv [nɛrf] *m* (-*s*; -*en*) ANAT nerve; **j-m auf die ~en fallen** or **gehen** get on s.o.'s nerves; **die ~en behalten** (**verlieren**) keep (lose) one's head

nerven ['nɛrfən] F *v/t and v/i* (*ge-*, *h*) be a pain in the neck (**j-n** to s.o.)

'Nervenarzt *m*, **'Nervenärztin** *f* neurologist

'nervenaufreibend *adj* nerve-racking

'Nerven|belastung *f* nervous strain; **~kitzel** *m* thrill, F kick(s)

'nervenkrank *adj* mentally ill

'Nerven|säge F *f* pain in the neck; **~system** *n* nervous system; **~zusammenbruch** *m* nervous breakdown

nervös [nɛr'vø:s] *adj* nervous

Nervosität [nɛrvozi'tɛ:t] *f* (-; *no pl*) nervousness

Nerz [nɛrts] *m* (-*es*; -*e*) ZO mink

Nessel ['nɛsəl] *f* (-; -*n*) BOT nettle

Nest [nɛst] *n* (-[*e*]*s*; -*er* ['nɛstɐ]) ZO nest;

F *contp* one-horse town

nett [nɛt] *adj* nice; kind; *so ~ sein und et.* (*or et. zu*) *tun* be so kind as to do s.th.

netto ['nɛto] *adv* ECON net

Netz [nɛts] *n* (*-es*; *-e*) net; RAIL, TEL, IT network; ELECTR mains; **~haut** *f* ANAT retina; **~karte** *f* RAIL area season ticket

neu [nɔy] *adj* new; fresh; *fig* modern; *neuere Sprachen* modern languages; *neueste Nachrichten* (*Mode*) latest news (fashion); *von neuem* anew, afresh; *seit neu(st)em* since (very) recently; *viel Neues* a lot of new things; *was gibt es Neues?* what's the news?, what's new?; **'neuartig** *adj* novel

'Neubau *m* (*-[e]s*; *-ten*) new building; **~gebiet** *n* new housing estate

neuerdings ['nɔyɐ'dɪŋs] *adv* lately, recently

Neuerer ['nɔyərɐ] *m* (*-s*; *-*) innovator; **'Neuerung** *f* (*-*; *-en*) innovation

'Neugestaltung *f* reorganization, reformation

'Neugier *f*, **Neugierde** ['nɔygiːɐdə] *f* (*-*; *no pl*) curiosity; **'neugierig** *adj* curious (*auf acc* about); F *contp* nos(e)y; *ich bin ~, ob* I wonder if; **Neugierige** ['nɔygiːrɪgə] *contp pl* rubbernecks

'Neuheit *f* (*-*; *-en*) novelty

Neuigkeit ['nɔyıçkaıt] *f* (*-*; *-en*) (piece of) news

'Neujahr *n* New Year('s Day); *Prost ~!* Happy New Year!

'neulich *adv* the other day

Neuling ['nɔylıŋ] *m* (*-s*; *-e*) newcomer, F greenhorn

'neumodisch *contp adj* newfangled

'Neumond *m* new moon

neun [nɔyn] *adj* nine; **'neunte** *adj* ninth; **'Neuntel** *n* (*-s*; *-*) ninth (part); **'neuntens** *adv* ninthly; **'neunzehn** *adj* nineteen; **'neunzehnte** *adj* nineteenth; **'neunzig** *adj* ninety; **'neunzigste** *adj* ninetieth

Neurose [nɔy'roːzə] *f* (*-*; *-n*) MED neurosis; **neurotisch** [nɔy'roːtıʃ] *adj* MED neurotic

'neusprachlich *adj* modern-language

'neutral [nɔy'traːl] *adj* neutral

Neutralität [nɔytraliˈtɛːt] *f* (*-*; *no pl*) neutrality

Neutronen... [nɔy'troːnən-] PHYS *in cpds* ...*bombe etc*: neutron ...

Neutrum ['nɔytrʊm] *n* (*-s*; *-tra*) LING neuter

'Neuverfilmung *f* remake

'neuwertig *adj* as good as new

'Neuzeit *f* (*-*; *no pl*) modern times

nicht [nıçt] *adv* not; *überhaupt ~* not at all; **~ (ein)mal, gar ~** not even; **~ mehr** not any more *or* longer; *sie ist nett* (*wohnt hier*), **~** (*wahr*)? she's nice (lives here), isn't (doesn't) she?; **~ so ... wie** not as ... as; *noch ~* not yet; **~ besser** (*als*) no (*or* not any) better (than); *ich* (*auch*) **~** I don't *or* I'm not (either); (*bitte*) **~!** (please) don't!

'Nicht... *in cpds* ...*mitglied, ...schwimmer etc*: *mst* non-...; **~beachtung** *f* disregard; non-observance

Nichte ['nıçtə] *f* (*-*; *-n*) niece

nichtig ['nıçtıç] *adj* trivial; JUR void, invalid

'Nichtraucher *m*, **'Nichtraucherin** *f* non-smoker

nichts *indef pron* nothing, not anything; **~** (*anderes*) *als* nothing but; *gar ~* nothing at all; F *das ist ~* that's no good; **~ sagend** meaningless; **Nichts** *n* (*-s*; *no pl*) nothing(ness); *aus dem ~ appear etc* from nowhere; *build etc* from nothing

nichtsdesto'weniger *adv* nevertheless

nichtsnutzig ['nıçtsnʊtsıç] *adj* good--for-nothing, worthless

'nichtssagend *adj* meaningless

Nichtstuer ['nıçtstuːɐ] *m* (*-s*; *-*) do--nothing, F bum

nicken ['nıkən] *v/i* (*ge-*, *h*) nod (one's head)

nie [niː] *adv* never, at no time; *fast ~* hardly ever; *~ und nimmer* never ever

nieder ['niːdɐ] **1.** *adj* low **2.** *adv* down

'Niedergang *m* (*-[e]s*; *no pl*) decline

'niedergeschlagen *adj* depressed, (feeling) down

'Niederlage *f* defeat, F beating

'niederlassen *v/refl* (*irr, lassen, sep, -ge-, h*) settle (down); ECON set up (*als* as); **'Niederlassung** *f* (*-*; *-en*) ECON establishment; branch

'nieder|legen *v/t* (*sep, -ge-, h*) lay down (*a. office etc*); *die Arbeit ~* (go on) strike, down tools, F walk out; *sich ~* lie down; go to bed; **~metzeln** *v/t* (*sep, -ge-, h*) massacre

'Niederschlag *m* METEOR rain(fall);

PHYS fallout; CHEM precipitate; *boxing*: knock-down; **'niederschlagen** *v/t* (*irr*, **schlagen**, *sep*, *-ge-*, *h*) knock down; cast down (*eyes*); *fig* put down (*revolt etc*); JUR quash; **sich ~** CHEM precipitate

'niederschmettern *fig v/t* (*sep*, *-ge-*, *h*) shatter, crush

'niederträchtig *adj* base, mean

Niederung ['ni:dəruŋ] *f* (*-*; *-en*) lowland(s)

niedlich ['ni:tlıç] *adj* pretty, sweet, cute

niedrig ['ni:drıç] *adj* low (*a. fig*); *fig* light (*sentence etc*); **~ fliegen** fly low

niemals ['ni:ma:ls] → *nie*

niemand ['ni:mant] *indef pron* nobody, no one, not anybody; **~ von ihnen** none of them; **'Niemandsland** *n* (*-[e]s*; *no pl*) no-man's-land

Niere ['ni:rə] *f* (*-*; *-n*) ANAT kidney

nieseln ['ni:zəln] *v/i* (*ge-*, *h*) drizzle

'Nieselregen *m* drizzle

niesen ['ni:zən] *v/i* (*ge-*, *h*) sneeze

Niete[1] ['ni:tə] *f* (*-*; *-n*) TECH rivet

'Niete[2] *f* (*-*; *-n*) blank; F failure

Nikolaustag ['nıkolausta:k] *m* St. Nicholas' Day

Nikotin [niko'ti:n] *n* (*-s*; *no pl*) CHEM nicotine

Nilpferd ['ni:lpfe:ɐrt] *n* ZO hippopotamus, F hippo

Nippel ['nıpəl] *m* (*-s*; *-*) TECH nipple

nippen ['nıpən] *v/i* (*ge-*, *h*) sip (**an** *dat* at)

nirgends ['nırgənts] *adv* nowhere

Nische ['ni:ʃə] *f* (*-*; *-n*) niche, recess

nisten ['nıstən] *v/i* (*ge-*, *h*) ZO nest

'Nistplatz *m* ZO nesting place

Niveau [ni'vo:] *n* (*-s*; *-s*) level, *fig a.* standard

Nixe ['nıksə] *f* (*-*; *-n*) water nymph, mermaid

noch [nɔx] *adv* still; **~ nicht** not yet; **~ nie** never before; *er hat nur* **~ 5 Euro** (*Minuten*) he has only 5 euros (minutes) left; (*sonst*) **~ et. ?** anything else?; *ich möchte* **~ et.** (**Tee**) I'd like some more (tea); **~ ein**(**e**, **-n**)..., *bitte* another ..., please; **~ einmal** once more *or* again; **~ zwei Stunden** another two hours, two hours to go; **~ besser** (*schlimmer*) even better (worse); **~ gestern** only yesterday; *und wenn es* **~ so ... ist** however (*or* no matter how) ... it may be

nochmalig ['nɔxma:lıç] *adj* new, re-newed

'nochmals *adv* once more *or* again

Nockerl ['nɔkɐl] *Austrian n* (*-s*; *-n*) GASTR small dumpling

Nomade [no'ma:də] *m* (*-n*; *-n*), **No'madin** *f* (*-*; *-nen*) nomad

Nominativ ['no:minati:f] *m* (*-s*; *-e*) LING nominative (case)

nominieren [nomi'ni:rən] *v/t* (*no -ge-*, *h*) nominate

Nonne ['nɔnə] *f* (*-*; *-n*) REL nun

'Nonnenkloster *n* REL convent

Norden ['nɔrdən] *m* (*-s*; *no pl*) north; *nach* **~** north(wards); **nordisch** ['nɔrdıʃ] *adj* northern; SPORT **~e Kombination** Nordic Combined

nördlich ['nœrtlıç] **1.** *adj* north(ern); northerly **2.** *adv:* **~ von** north of

Nordlicht ['nɔrtlıçt] *n* (*-[e]s*; *-er*) ASTR northern lights

Nord'osten *m* northeast; **nord'östlich** *adj* northeast(ern); northeasterly

'Nordpol *m* North Pole

Nord'westen *m* northwest

nord'westlich *adj* northwest(ern); northwesterly

'Nordwind *m* north wind

nörgeln ['nœrgəln] *v/i* (*ge-*, *h*) nag (**an** *dat* at)

Nörgler ['nœrglɐ] *m* (*-s*; *-*), **'Nörglerin** *f* (*-*; *-nen*) nagger

Norm [nɔrm] *f* (*-*; *-en*) standard, norm

normal [nɔr'ma:l] *adj* normal; F *nicht ganz* **~** not quite right in the head

Nor'mal... *esp* TECH *in cpds* ...*maß*, ...*zeit etc*: standard ...; **~ben,zin** *n* regular (gas, *Br* petrol)

normalerweise [nɔr'ma:lɐ'vaizə] *adv* normally, usually

normalisieren [nɔrmali'zi:rən] *v/refl* (*no -ge-*, *h*) return to normal

normen ['nɔrmən] *v/t* (*ge-*, *h*) standardize

Norwegen ['nɔrve:gən] Norway

Norweger ['nɔrve:gɐ] *m* (*-s*; *-*), **'Norwegerin** ['nɔrve:gərın] *f* (*-*; *-nen*), **'norwegisch** *adj* Norwegian

Not [no:t] *f* (*-*; *Nöte* ['nø:tə]) need; want; poverty; hardship, misery; difficulty; emergency; distress; **~ leidend** needy; *in* **~** *sein* be in trouble; *zur* **~** if need be, if necessary

Notar [no'ta:ɐ] *m* (*-s*; *-e*), **No'tarin** *f* (*-*; *-nen*) JUR notary (public)

'**Not|aufnahme** f MED emergency room, Br casualty; **~ausgang** m emergency exit; **~behelf** m (-[e]s; -e) makeshift, expedient; **~bremse** f emergency brake; **~dienst** m emergency duty

'**notdürftig** adj scanty; temporary

Note ['noːtə] f (-; -n) note (a. MUS and POL); ECON bill, esp Br (bank)note; PED grade, Br mark; pl MUS (sheet) music; **~n lesen** read music

Notebook ['noʊtbʊk] n (-s; -s) IT notebook

'**Notendurchschnitt** m PED etc average

'**Notenständer** m music stand

'**Notfall** m emergency

'**notfalls** adv if necessary

'**notgedrungen** adv: **et. ~ tun** be forced to do s.th.

notieren [noˈtiːrən] v/t (no -ge-, h) make a note of, note (down); ECON quote

nötig ['nøːtɪç] adj necessary; **~ haben** need; **~ brauchen** need badly; **das Nötigste** the (bare) necessities or essentials; **nötigen** ['nøːtɪgən] v/t (ge-, h) force, compel; press, urge; '**Nötigung** f (-; -en) coercion; JUR intimidation

Notiz [noˈtiːts] f (-; -en) note; **keine ~ nehmen von** take no notice of, ignore; **sich ~en machen** take notes; **~block** m memo pad, Br notepad; **~buch** n notebook

'**Notlage** f awkward (or difficult) situation; difficulties; emergency

'**notlanden** v/i (-ge-, sein) AVIAT make an emergency landing; '**Notlandung** f AVIAT emergency landing

'**Notlösung** f expedient

'**Notlüge** f white lie

notorisch [noˈtoːrɪʃ] adj notorious

'**Not|ruf** m TEL emergency call; **~rufsäule** f TEL emergency phone; **~sig,nal** n emergency or distress signal; **~stand** m state of (national) emergency; **~standsgebiet** n disaster area; ECON depressed area; **~standsgesetze** pl POL emergency laws; **~verband** m MED emergency dressing

'**Notwehr** f (-; no pl) JUR self-defense, Br self-defence

'**notwendig** adj necessary

'**Notwendigkeit** f (-; -en) necessity

'**Notzucht** f (-; no pl) JUR rape

Novelle [noˈvɛlə] f (-; -n) novella; PARL amendment

November [noˈvɛmbɐ] m (-[s]; -) November

Nr. abbr of **Nummer** No., no., number

Nu [nuː] m: **im ~** in no time

Nuance ['nyaˑːsə] f shade

nüchtern ['nyçtɐn] adj sober (a. fig); matter-of-fact; **auf ~en Magen** on an empty stomach; **~ werden (machen)** sober up

'**Nüchternheit** f (-; no pl) sobriety

Nudel ['nuːdəl] f (-; -n) noodle

nuklear [nukleˈaːɐ] adj nuclear

null [nʊl] adj zero, Br nought; TEL 0; SPORT nil, nothing; tennis: love; **~ Grad** zero degrees; **~ Fehler** no mistakes; **gleich Null sein** be nil

'**Null|di,ät** f low-calorie (or F starvation) diet; **~punkt** m zero (point or fig level); **~ta,rif** m free fare(s); **zum ~** free (of charge)

Numerus clausus ['nuːmerʊs 'klaʊzʊs] m (-; no pl) UNIV restricted admission(s)

Nummer ['nʊmɐ] f (-; -n) number; issue; size; **nummerieren** [nʊməˈriːrən] v/t (no -ge-, h) number

'**Nummernschild** n MOT license plate, Br numberplate

nun [nuːn] adv now; well

nur [nuːɐ] adv only, just; merely; nothing but; **er tut ~ so** he's just pretending; **~ so (zum Spaß)** just for fun; **warte ~!** just you wait!; **mach ~!, ~ zu!** go ahead!; → **Erwachsene**

Nuss [nʊs] f (-; Nüsse ['nʏsə]) BOT nut; **~baum** m walnut (tree); **~knacker** m nutcracker; **~schale** f nutshell

Nüstern ['nyːstɐn] pl ZO nostrils

Nutte ['nʊtə] F f (-; -n) hooker, sl tart

Nutzanwendung ['nʊtsʔanvɛndʊŋ] f practical application; '**nutzbar** adj usable; **~ machen** utilize; exploit; harness; '**nutzbringend** adj profitable, useful

nütze ['nʏtsə] adj useful; **zu nichts ~ sein** be (of) no use; be good for nothing

Nutzen ['nʊtsən] m (-s; -) use; profit, gain; advantage; **~ ziehen aus** (dat) benefit or profit from or by; **zum ~ von** (or gen) for the benefit of

'**nutzen, 'nützen** (ge-, h) **1.** v/i: **j-m ~** be of use to s.o.; **es nützt nichts (es zu tun)** it's no use (doing it) **2.** v/t use, make use of; take advantage of

nützlich ['nʏtslɪç] *adj* useful, helpful; advantageous; **sich ~ machen** make o.s. useful

'**nutzlos** *adj* useless, (of) no use

'**Nutzung** *f* (-; -en) use, utilization

Nylon® ['nailɔn] *n* (-s; *no pl*) nylon®; **~strümpfe** *pl* nylon® stockings

Nymphe ['nʏmfə] *f* (-; -n) nymph

O

O *abbr of* **Osten** E, east

o *int* oh!; **o weh!** oh dear!

o. Ä. *abbr of* **oder Ähnliche(s)** or the like

Oase [o'a:zə] *f* (-; -n) oasis (*a. fig*)

ob [ɔp] *cj* whether, if; **als ~** as if, as though; **und ~!** and how!, you bet!

Obacht ['o:baxt] *f*: **~ geben auf** (*acc*) pay attention to; (**gib**) **~!** watch out!

Obdach ['ɔpdax] *n* (-[e]s; *no pl*) shelter

'**obdachlos** *adj* homeless, without shelter; '**Obdachlose** *m, f* (-n; -n) homeless person; '**Obdachlosen,syl** *n* shelter for the homeless

Obduktion [ɔpdʊk'tsjoːn] *f* (-; -en) MED autopsy

obduzieren [ɔpdu'tsiːrən] *v/t* (*no -ge-, h*) MED perform an autopsy on

oben ['o:bən] *adv* above; up; on (the) top; at the top (*a. fig*); on the surface; upstairs; **da ~** up there; **von ~ bis unten** from top to bottom (*or* toe); **links ~** (at the) top left; **siehe ~** see above; F **~ ohne** topless; **von ~ herab** *fig* patronizing(ly), condescending(ly); **~ erwähnt** *or* **genannt** above-mentioned; **~'an** *adv* at the top; **~'auf** *adv* on the top; on the surface; F feeling great; **~'drein** *adv* besides, into the bargain, at that; **~'hin** *adv* superficially

Ober ['o:bɐ] *m* (-s; -) waiter

'**Ober|arm** *m* ANAT upper arm; **~arzt** *m*, **~ärztin** *f* assistant medical director; **~befehl** *m* MIL supreme command; **~begriff** *n* generic term; **~bürgermeister** *m* mayor, *Br* Lord Mayor

obere ['o:bərə] *adj* upper, top, *fig a.* superior

'**Oberfläche** *f* surface (*a. fig*) (**an** *dat* on); '**oberflächlich** *adj* superficial

'**oberhalb** *prp* (*gen*) above

'**Ober|hand** *f*: **die ~ gewinnen** (**über** *acc*) get the upper hand (of); **~haupt** *n* head, chief; **~haus** *n* (-es; *no pl*) *Br*

PARL House of Lords; **~hemd** *n* shirt; **~herrschaft** *f* (-; *no pl*) supremacy

Oberin ['o:bərɪn] *f* (-; -nen) REL Mother Superior

'**oberirdisch** *adj* above ground; ELECTR overhead

'**Ober|kellner** *m* head waiter; **~kiefer** *m* ANAT upper jaw; **~körper** *m* upper part of the body; **den ~ frei machen** strip to the waist; **~leder** *n* uppers; **~leitung** *f* chief management; ELECTR overhead contact line; **~lippe** *f* ANAT upper lip

Obers ['o:bɐs] *Austrian n* (-; *no pl*) GASTR cream

'**Oberschenkel** *m* ANAT thigh

'**Oberschule** *f appr* highschool, *Br* grammar school

Oberst ['o:bɐst] *m* (-en; -en) MIL colonel

oberste ['o:bɐstə] *adj* up(per)most, top (-most); highest; *fig* chief, first

'**Ober|stufe** *f appr* senior highschool, *Br appr* senior classes; **~teil** *n* top

ob'gleich *cj* (al)though

Obhut ['ɔphuːt] *f* (-; *no pl*) care, charge; **in s-e ~ nehmen** take care *or* charge of

obig ['o:bɪç] *adj* above(-mentioned)

Objekt [ɔp'jɛkt] *n* (-[e]s; -e) object (*a.* LING); ECON property

objektiv [ɔpjɛk'tiːf] *adj* objective; impartial, unbias(s)ed

Objek'tiv *n* (-s; -e) PHOT (object) lens

Objektivität [ɔpjɛktivi'tɛːt] *f* (-; *no pl*) objectivity; impartiality

Oblate [o'bla:tə] *f* (-; -n) wafer; REL host

obligatorisch [obliga'to:rɪʃ] *adj* compulsory

Oboe [o'bo:ə] *f* (-; -n) MUS oboe

Oboist [obo'ɪst] *m* (-en; -en) MUS oboist

Observatorium [ɔpzɛrva'to:rjʊm] *n* (-s; -ien) ASTR observatory

Obst [o:pst] *n* (-[e]s; *no pl*) fruit; **~garten** *m* orchard; **~kon,serven** *pl* canned fruit; **~laden** *m* fruit store, *esp Br* fruiterer's (shop); **~torte** *f*

fruit pie (*Br* flan)

obszön [ɔps'tsøːn] *adj* obscene, filthy

ob'wohl *cj* (al)though

Occasion [ɔka'zjoːn] *Swiss f* (-; *-en*) bargain, good buy

Ochse ['ɔksə] *m* (*-n*; *-n*) zo ox, bullock; F blockhead

od. *abbr of* **oder** or

öde ['øːdə] *adj* deserted, desolate; waste; *fig* dull, dreary, tedious

oder ['oːdɐ] *cj* or; ~ **aber** or else, otherwise; ~ **vielmehr** or rather; ~ **so** or so; **er kommt doch, ~?** he's coming, isn't he?; **du kennst ihn ja nicht, ~ doch?** you don't know him, or do you?

Ofen ['oːfən] *m* (*-s*; *Öfen* ['øːfən]) stove; oven; TECH furnace; **~heizung** *f* stove heating; **~rohr** *n* stovepipe

offen ['ɔfən] **1.** *adj* open (*a. fig*); vacant (*post*); *fig* frank **2.** *adv*: ~ **gesagt** frankly (speaking); ~ **s-e Meinung sagen** speak one's mind (freely); ~ **stehen** be open; ECON be outstanding

'offenbar *adj* obvious, evident; apparent; **offenbaren** [ɔfən'baːrən] *v/t* (*ge-*, *h*) reveal, disclose, show; **Offen-'barung** *f* (-; *-en*) revelation

'Offenheit *f* (-; *no pl*) openness, frankness

'offenherzig *adj* open-hearted, frank, candid; *fig* revealing (*dress*)

'offensichtlich *adj* → *offenbar*

offensiv [ɔfɛn'ziːf] *adj*, **Offensive** [ɔfɛn'ziːvə] *f* (-; *-n*) offensive

'offenstehen *v/i* (*irr, stehen, sep, -ge-, h*): *j-m* ~ *fig* be open to s.o.

öffentlich ['œfəntlɪç] *adj* public; **~e Verkehrsmittel** *pl* public transport; **~e Schulen** *pl* public (*Br* state) schools; ~ **auftreten** appear in public

'Öffentlichkeit *f* (-; *no pl*) the public; **in aller** ~ in public, openly; **an die** ~ **bringen** make public

offiziell [ɔfi'tsjɛl] *adj* official

Offizier [ɔfi'tsiːɐ] *m* (*-s*; *-e*) MIL (commissioned) officer

öffnen ['œfnən] *v/t and v/refl* (*ge-*, *h*) open; **Öffner** ['œfnɐ] *m* (*-s*; -) opener; 'Öffnung *f* (-; *-en*) opening

'Öffnungszeiten *pl* business *or* office hours

oft [ɔft] *adv* often, frequently

oh [oː] *int* o(h)!

ohne ['oːnə] *prp* (*acc*) *and cj* without; ~

mich! count me out!; ~ **ein Wort** (**zu sagen**) without (saying) a word

ohne|'gleichen *adv* unequal(l)ed, unparalleled; **~'hin** *adv* anyhow, anyway

Ohnmacht ['oːnmaxt] *f* (-; *-en*) MED unconsciousness; *fig* helplessness; **in** ~ **fallen** faint, pass out; **'ohnmächtig** *adj* MED unconscious; *fig* helpless; ~ **werden** faint, pass out

Ohr [oːɐ] *n* (*-[e]s*; *-en* ['oːrən]) ANAT ear; F *j-n* **übers** ~ **hauen** cheat s.o.; **bis über die** ~**en verliebt** (**verschuldet**) head over heels in love (over your head in debt)

Öhr [øːɐ] *n* (*-[e]s*; *-e* ['øːrə]) eye

Ohrenarzt ['oːrən'ʔaːɐtst] *m* ear specialist

'ohrenbetäubend *adj* deafening

'Ohren|schmerzen *pl* earache; **~schützer** *pl* earmuffs; **~zeuge** *m* earwitness

'Ohrfeige *f* slap in the face (*a. fig*); **ohrfeigen** ['oːɐfaigən] *v/t* (*ge-*, *h*) *j-n* ~ slap s.o.'s face

'Ohr|läppchen ['oːɐlɛpçən] *n* (*-s*; -) ANAT earlobe; **~ring** *m* earring

oje [o'jeː] *int* oh dear!, dear me!

Ökologe [øko'loːgə] *m* (*-n*; *-n*) ecologist; **Ökologie** [økolo'giː] *f* (-; *no pl*) ecology; **ökologisch** [øko'loːgɪʃ] *adj* ecological

Ökonomie [økono'miː] *f* (-; *no pl*) economy; ECON economics; **ökonomisch** [øko'noːmɪʃ] *adj* economical; ECON economic

Ökosys,tem ['øːkozysteːm] *n* ecosystem

Oktave [ɔk'taːvə] *f* (-; *-n*) MUS octave

Oktober [ɔk'toːbɐ] *m* (*-[s]*; -) October

ökumenisch [øku'meːnɪʃ] *adj* REL ecumenical

Öl [øːl] *n* (*-[e]s*; *Öle*) oil; petroleum; **nach** ~ **bohren** drill for oil; **auf** ~ **stoßen** strike oil; **'Ölbaum** *m* BOT olive (tree)

Oldtimer ['ouldtaimə] *m* (*-s*; -) MOT veteran car

ölen ['øːlən] *v/t* (*ge-*, *h*) oil, TECH *a.* lubricate

'Öl|farbe *f* oil (paint); **~feld** *n* oilfield; **~förderland** *n* oil-producing country; **~förderung** *f* oil production; **~gemälde** *n* oil painting; **~heizung** *f* oil heating

ölig ['øːlɪç] *adj* oily, greasy (*both a. fig*)

oliv [o'li:f] *adj* olive

Olive [o'li:və] *f* (-; *-n*) BOT olive

'Öl‖leitung *f* (oil) pipeline; **∼messtab** *m* MOT dipstick; **∼pest** *f* oil pollution; **∼quelle** *f* oil well; **∼sar,dine** *f* canned (*Br a*. tinned) sardine; **∼stand** *m* oil level; **∼tanker** *m* MAR oil tanker; **∼teppich** *m* oil slick

'Ölung *f* (-; *no pl*) oiling, TECH *a*. lubrication; *Letzte* **∼** REL extreme unction

'Öl‖wanne *f* MOT oil pan, *Br* sump; **∼wechsel** *m* MOT oil change

Olympia... [o'lʏmpja-] *in cpds ...mannschaft, ...medaille etc*: Olympic ...

Olympiade [olʏm'pja:də] *f* (-; *-n*) SPORT Olympic Games, Olympics

'Ölzeug *n* oilskins

Oma ['o:ma] F *f* (-; *-s*) grandma

Omi ['o:mi] F *f* (-; *-s*) granny

Omnibus ['ɔmnibʊs] *m* → *Bus*

onanieren [ona'ni:rən] *v/i* (*no -ge-*, *h*) masturbate

Onkel ['ɔŋkəl] *m* (-s; -) uncle

Online... ['ɔnlain-] IT online ...

Opa ['o:pa] F *m* (-s; *-s*) grandpa

Oper ['o:pɐ] *f* (-; *-n*) MUS opera; opera (house)

Operation [opəra'tsjo:n] *f* (-; *-en*) MED operation; *e-e* **∼** *vornehmen* perform an operation; **Operati'onssaal** *m* MED operating room (*Br* theatre)

Operette [opə'rɛtə] *f* (-; *-n*) MUS operetta

operieren [opə'ri:rən] (*no -ge-*, *h*) **1.** *v/t* MED *j-n* **∼** operate on s.o. (*wegen* for); *operiert werden* be operated on, have an operation; *sich* **∼** *lassen* undergo an operation **2.** *v/i* MED, MIL operate; proceed

'Opernsänger(in) opera singer

Opfer ['ɔpfɐ] *n* (-s; -) sacrifice; offering; victim; *ein* **∼** *bringen* make a sacrifice; (*dat*) *zum* **∼** *fallen* fall victim to

'opfern *v/t and v/i* (*ge-*, *h*) sacrifice

Opium ['o:pjʊm] *n* (-s; *no pl*) opium

Opposition [ɔpozi'tsjo:n] *f* (-; *-en*) opposition (*a*. PARL)

Optik ['ɔptik] *f* (-; *no pl*) optics; PHOT optical system

Optiker ['ɔptikɐ] *m* (-s; -), **'Optikerin** *f* (-; *-nen*) optician

optimal [ɔpti'ma:l] *adj* optimum, best

Optimismus [ɔpti'mɪsmʊs] *m* (-; *no pl*) optimism; **Optimist(in)** [ɔpti'mɪst(ɪn)] (*-en*; *-en*/-; *-nen*) optimist; opti-

'mistisch *adj* optimistic

Option [ɔp'tsjo:n] *f* (-; *-en*) option

optisch ['ɔptiʃ] *adj* optical

Orange [o'ra..ːʒə] *f* (-; *-n*) BOT orange

Orchester [ɔr'kɛstɐ] *n* (-s; -) MUS orchestra

Orchidee [ɔrçi'de:] *f* (-; *-n*) bot orchid

Orden ['ɔrdən] *m* (-s; -) medal, decoration; *esp* REL order

'Ordensschwester *f* REL sister, nun

ordentlich ['ɔrdəntliç] **1.** *adj* tidy, neat, orderly; proper; thorough; decent (*a*. F); respectable; full (*member etc*); JUR ordinary; reasonable (*performance etc*); F good, sound **2.** *adv*: *s-e Sache* **∼** *machen* do a good job; *sich* **∼** *benehmen* (*anziehen*) behave (dress) properly *or* decently

ordinär [ɔrdi'nɛːɐ] *adj* vulgar; common

ordnen ['ɔrdnən] *v/t* (*ge-*, *h*) put in order; arrange, sort (out); file; settle

Ordner ['ɔrdnɐ] *m* (-s; -) file; folder; attendant, guard

'Ordnung *f* (-; *no pl*) order; orderliness, tidiness; arrangement; system, set-up; class; *in* **∼** all right; TECH *etc in* (good) order; *in* **∼** *bringen* put right (*a*. *fig*); tidy up; repair, fix (*a*. *fig*); (*in*) **∼** *halten* keep (in) order; *et. ist nicht in* **∼** (*mit*) there is s.th. wrong (with)

'ordnungsgemäß 1. *adj* correct, regular **2.** *adv* duly, properly

'Ordnungs‖strafe *f* JUR fine, penalty; **∼zahl** *f* MATH ordinal number

Organ [ɔr'ga:n] *n* (-s; *-e*) organ; **∼empfänger** *m* MED organ recipient; **∼handel** *m* sale of (transplant) organs

Organisation [ɔrganiza'tsjo:n] *f* (-; *-en*) organization; **Organisator** [ɔrgani'za:to:ɐ] *m* (-s; *-en* [ɔrganiza'to:rən]) organizer; **Organisa'torin** *f* (-; *-nen*) organizer; **organisatorisch** [ɔrganiza'to:rɪʃ] *adj* organizational

organisch [ɔr'ga:nɪʃ] *adj* organic

organisieren [ɔrgani'zi:rən] *v/t* organize; F get (hold of); *sich* **∼** organize; ECON unionize; **organisiert** [ɔrgani'zi:ɐt] *adj* organized; ECON unionized

Organismus [ɔrga'nɪsmʊs] *m* (-; *-men*) BIOL organism

Organist [ɔrga'nɪst] *m* (*-en*; *-en*), **Orga'nistin** *f* (-; *-nen*) MUS organist

Or'ganspender *m* MED (organ) donor

Orgasmus [ɔr'gasmʊs] *m* (-; *-men*) or-

gasm
Orgel ['ɔrgəl] *f* (-; -n) MUS organ
'Orgelpfeife *f* MUS organ pipe
Orgie ['ɔrgjə] *f* (-; -n) orgy
Orientale [orjɛn'taːlə] *m* (-n; -n), **Orien-'talin** *f* (-; -nen), **orien'talisch** *adj* oriental
orientieren [orjɛn'tiːrən] *v/t* (*no -ge-, h*) inform (*über acc* about), brief (on); *sich ~* orient(ate) o.s. (*a. fig*) (*nach* by); inform o.s.; **Orien'tierung** *f* (-; *no pl*) orientation, *fig a.* information; *die ~ verlieren* lose one's bearings
Orien'tierungssinn *m* (-[e]s; *no pl*) sense of direction
original [origi'naːl] *adj* original; real, genuine; TV live; **Origi'nal** *n* (-s; -e) original; *fig* real (*or* quite a) character
Origi'nal... *in cpds* ...*aufnahme*, ...*ausgabe etc*: original ...; *~übertragung f* live broadcast *or* program(me)
originell [origi'nɛl] *adj* original; ingenious; witty
Orkan [ɔr'kaːn] *m* (-[e]s; -e) hurricane
or'kanartig *adj* violent; *fig* thunderous
Ort [ɔrt] *m* (-[e]s; -e) place; village, (small) town; spot, point; scene; *vor ~ mining*: at the (pit) face; *fig* in the field, on the spot
orten ['ɔrtən] *v/t* (*ge-, h*) locate, spot
orthodox [ɔrto'dɔks] *adj* orthodox
Orthographie [ɔrtogra'fiː] *f* (-; -n) orthography
Orthopäde [ɔrto'pɛːdə] *m* (-n; -n), **Ortho'pädin** *f* (-; -nen) MED orthop(a)edic specialist
örtlich ['œrtlɪç] *adj* local
'Ortsbestimmung *f* AVIAT, MAR location; LING adverb of place

'Ortschaft *f* → *Ort*
'Ortsgespräch *n* TEL local call
'Ortskenntnis *f*: *~ besitzen* know a place
'Ortsnetz *n* TEL local exchange
'Ortszeit *f* local time
Öse ['øːzə] *f* (-; -n) eye; eyelet
Ostblock ['ɔstblɔk] *m* (-[e]s; *no pl*) HIST POL East(ern) Bloc
Osten ['ɔstən] *m* (-s; *no pl*) east; POL *the* East; *nach ~* east(wards)
Oster|ei ['oːstɐʔai] *n* Easter egg; *~hase m* Easter bunny *or* rabbit
Ostern ['oːstɐn] *n* (-; -) Easter (*zu, an* at); *frohe ~!* Happy Easter!
Österreicher ['øːstəraiçɐ] *m* (-s; -), **'Österreicherin** ['øːstəraiçərɪn] *f* (-; -nen), **'österreichisch** *adj* Austrian
östlich ['œstlɪç] **1.** *adj* east(ern); easterly **2.** *adv*: *~ von* (to the) east of
ostwärts ['ɔstvɛrts] *adv* east(wards)
'Ostwind *m* east wind
Otter ['ɔtɐ] ZO **1.** *m* (-s; -) otter **2.** *f* (-; -n) adder, viper
outen ['autən] *v/t* (*ge-, h*) out
Ouvertüre [uvɐr'tyːrə] *f* (-; -n) MUS overture
oval [o'vaːl] *adj*, **O'val** *n* (-s; -e) oval
Oxid [ɔ'ksiːt] *n* (-[e]s; -e [ɔ'ksiːdə]) CHEM oxide; **oxidieren** [ɔksi'diːrən] *v/t* (*no -ge-, h*) *and v/i* (*h, sein*) CHEM oxidize; **Oxyd** *n* → *Oxid*
Ozean ['oːtsean] *m* (-s; -e) ocean, sea
Ozon [o'tsoːn] *n* (-s; *no pl*) CHEM ozone
o'zonfreundlich *adj* ozone-friendly
O'zon|loch *n* ozone hole; *~schicht f* ozone layer; *~schild m* ozone shield; *~werte pl* ozone levels

P

paar [paːɐ] *indef pron*: *ein ~* a few, some, F a couple of; *ein ~ Mal* a few times
Paar *n* (-[e]s; -e) pair; couple; *ein ~ (neue) Schuhe* a (new) pair of shoes
paaren ['paːrən] *v/t and v/refl* (*ge-, h*) ZO mate; *fig* combine
'Paarlauf *m* SPORT pair skating
'Paarung *f* (-; -en) ZO mating, copulation; SPORT matching

'paarweise *adv* in pairs, in twos
Pacht [paxt] *f* (-; -en) lease; rent
'pachten *v/t* (*ge-, h*) (take on) lease
Pächter ['pɛçtɐ] *m* (-s; -), **'Pächterin** *f* (-; -nen) leaseholder; AGR tenant
'Pacht|vertrag *m* lease; *~zins m* rent
Pack¹ [pak] *m* → *Packen*
Pack² *contp n* (-[e]s; *no pl*) rabble
Päckchen ['pɛkçən] *n* (-s; -) pack, *Br*

packet; small parcel; **packen** ['pakən] v/t and v/i (ge-, h) pack; make up (parcel etc); grab, seize (**an** dat by); fig grip; '**Packen** m (-s; -) pack, pile (a. fig); **Packer** ['pakɐ] m (-s; -) packer; removal man; '**Packpa,pier** n packing or brown paper; '**Packung** f (-; -en) package, box; pack, Br packet

Pädagoge [pɛda'goːgə] m (-n; -n), **Päda'gogin** f (-; -nen) teacher; education(al)ist

päda'gogisch adj pedagogic, educational; **~e Hochschule** college of education

Paddel ['padəl] n (-s; -) paddle
'**Paddelboot** n canoe
'**paddeln** v/i (ge-, h, sein) paddle, canoe

Page ['paːʒə] m (-n; -n) page(boy)

Paket [pa'keːt] n (-[e]s; -e) package; parcel; **~karte** f parcel post slip, Br parcel mailing form; **~post** f parcel post; **~schalter** m parcel counter; **~zustellung** f parcel delivery

Pakt [pakt] m (-[e]s; -e) POL pact

Palast [pa'last] m (-[e]s; Paläste [pa-'lɛstə]) palace

Palme ['palmə] f (-; -n) BOT palm (tree)
Palm'sonntag m REL Palm Sunday

Pampelmuse ['pampəlmuːzə] f (-; -n) BOT grapefruit

paniert [pa'niːɐt] adj GASTR breaded

Panik ['paːnɪk] f (-; -en) panic; **in ~ geraten** (**versetzen**) panic; **in ~** panic-stricken, F panicky; **panisch** ['paːnɪʃ] adj: **~e Angst** mortal terror

Panne ['panə] f (-; -n) breakdown, MOT a. engine trouble; fig mishap

'**Pannenhilfe** f MOT breakdown service

Panter, Panther ['pantɐ] m (-s; -) ZO panther

Pantoffel [pan'tɔfəl] m (-s; -n) slipper; **~held** F m henpecked husband

Pantomime [panto'miːmə] THEA **1.** f (-; -n) mime, dumb show **2.** m (-n; -n) mime (artist); **panto'mimisch** adv: **~ darstellen** mime

Panzer ['pantsɐ] m (-s; -) armo(u)r (a. fig); MIL tank; ZO shell; **~glas** n bullet-proof glass

'**panzern** v/t (ge-, h) armo(u)r; → **gepanzert**

'**Panzerschrank** m safe

Panzerung ['pantsəruŋ] f (-; -en) armo(u)r plating

Papa [pa'paː] F m (-s; -s) dad(dy), pa

Papagei [papa'gai] m (-en; -en) ZO parrot

Papeterie [papɛtə'riː] Swiss f (-; -n) stationer('s shop)

Papier [pa'piːɐ] n (-s; -e) paper; pl papers, documents; identification (paper)

Pa'pier... in cpds ...geld, ...handtuch, ...serviette, ...tüte etc: mst paper ...; **~geschäft** n stationer('s store, Br shop); **~korb** m wastepaper basket; **~krieg** F m red tape; **~schnitzel** pl scraps of paper; **~waren** pl stationery

Pappe ['papə] f (-; -n) cardboard, pasteboard

Pappel ['papəl] f (-; -n) BOT poplar

'**Papp|kar,ton** m cardboard box, carton; **~teller** m paper plate

Paprika ['paprika] m (-s; -[s]) BOT sweet pepper; (no pl) GASTR paprika

Papst [paːpst] m (-[e]s; Päpste ['pɛːpstə]) pope; '**päpstlich** adj papal

Parade [pa'raːdə] f (-; -n) parade; soccer etc: save; boxing, fencing: parry

Paradeiser [para'daizɐ] Austrian m (-s; -) BOT tomato

Paradies [para'diːs] n (-es; -e) paradise

paradiesisch [para'diːzɪʃ] fig adj heavenly, delightful

paradox [para'dɔks] adj paradoxical

Paragraph [para'graːf] m (-en; -en) JUR article, section; paragraph

parallel [para'leːl] adj, **Paral'lele** f (-; -n) parallel

Parasit [para'ziːt] m (-en; -en) parasite

Parfüm [par'fyːm] n (-s; -s) perfume, Br a. scent; **Parfümerie** [parfymə'riː] f (-; -n) perfumery; **parfümieren** [parfy-'miːrən] v/t (no -ge-, h) perfume, scent; **sich ~** put on perfume

parieren [pa'riːrən] v/t and v/i (no -ge-, h) SPORT parry, fig a. counter (**mit** with); pull up (horse); obey

Park [park] m (-s; -s) park

parken ['parkən] v/t and v/i (ge-, h) MOT park; **Parken verboten!** no parking!

Parkett [par'kɛt] n (-[e]s; -e, -s) parquet (floor); THEA orchestra, Br stalls; dance floor

'**Park|gebühr** f parking fee; **~(hoch)haus** n parking garage, Br multi-storey car park

parkieren [par'kiːrən] Swiss v/t and v/i

Parkkralle

→ *parken*

'**Park|kralle** *f* wheel clamp; **~lücke** *f* parking space; **~platz** *m* parking lot, *Br* car park; → *Parklücke*; **e-n ~ su-chen (finden)** look for (find) somewhere to park the car; **~scheibe** *f* parking disk (*Br* disc); **~sünder** *m* parking offender; **~uhr** *f* MOT parking meter; **~wächter** *m* park keeper; MOT parking lot (*Br* car park) attendant

Parlament [parla'mɛnt] *n* (-[e]s; -e) parliament; **parlamentarisch** [parlamɛn-'taːrɪʃ] *adj* parliamentary

Parodie [paro'diː] *f* (-; -n), **paro'dieren** *v/t* (*no -ge-, h*) parody

Parole [pa'roːlə] *f* (-n; -n) MIL password; *fig* watchword, POL *a.* slogan

Partei [par'tai] *f* (-; -en) party (*a.* POL); **j-s ~ ergreifen** take sides with s.o., side with s.o.; **par'teiisch** *adj* partial (*für* to); prejudiced (*gegen* against)

par'teilos *adj* POL independent

Par'tei|mitglied *n* POL party member; **~pro,gramm** *n* POL platform; **~tag** *m* POL convention; **~zugehörigkeit** *f* POL party membership

Parterre [par'tɛrə] *n* (-s; -s) first (*Br* ground) floor

Partie [par'tiː] *f* (-; -n) game, SPORT *a.* match; part, passage (*a.* MUS); **e-e gute** *etc* **~ sein** be a good *etc* match

Partisan [parti'zaːn] *m* (-s; -en; -en), **Parti'sanin** *f* (-; -nen) MIL partisan, guerilla

Partitur [parti'tuːr] *f* (-; -en) MUS score

Partizip [parti'tsiːp] *n* (-s; -ien) LING participle

Partner ['partnɛ] *m* (-s; -), '**Partnerin** *f* (-; -nen) partner

'**Partnerschaft** *f* (-; -en) partnership

'**Partnerstadt** *f* twin town

paschen ['paʃən] *Austrian v/t and v/i* (*ge-, h*) smuggle; **Pascher** ['paʃɐ] *Austrian m* (-s; -) smuggler

Pass [pas] *m* (-es; *Pässe* ['pɛsə]) passport; SPORT, GEOGR pass; **langer ~** SPORT long ball

Passage [pa'saːʒə] *f* (-; -n) passage

Passagier [pasa'ʒiːɐ] *m* (-s; -e) passenger; **~flugzeug** *n* passenger plane; airliner

Passa'gierin *f* (-; -nen) passenger

Passah ['pasa] *n* (-s; *no pl*), '**Passahfest** *n* REL Passover

Passant [pa'sant] *m* (-en; -en), **Pas-'santin** *f* (-; -nen) passerby

'**Passbild** *n* passport photo(graph)

passen ['pasən] *v/i* (*ge-, h*) fit (*j-m* s.o.; *auf or für or zu et.* s.th.); suit (*j-m* s.o.), be convenient; *cards*, SPORT pass; **~ zu** go with, match; **sie ~ gut zueinander** they are well suited to each other; **passt es Ihnen morgen?** would to-morrow suit you *or* be all right (with you)?; **das (es) passt mir gar nicht** I don't like that (him) at all; **das passt (nicht) zu ihm** that's just like him (not like him, not his style); **~d** *adj* fitting; matching; suitable, right

passierbar [pa'siːrbaːr] *adj* passable

passieren [pa'siːrən] (*no -ge-*) **1.** *v/i* (*sein*) happen **2.** *v/t* (*h*) pass (through)

Pas'sierschein *m* pass, permit

Passion [pa'sjoːn] *f* (-; -en) passion; REL Passion

passiv ['pasiːf] *adj* passive

'**Passiv** *n* (-s; *no pl*) LING passive (voice)

Paste ['pastə] *f* (-; -n) paste

Pastell [pas'tɛl] *n* (-[e]s; -e) PAINT pastel

Pastete [pas'teːtə] *f* (-; -n) GASTR pie

Pate ['paːtə] *m* (-n; -n) godfather; '**Patenkind** *n* godchild

'**Patenschaft** *f* (-; -en) sponsorship

Patent [pa'tɛnt] *n* (-[e]s; -e) patent; MIL commission; **~amt** *n* patent office; **~anwalt** *m* JUR patent agent

patentieren [patɛn'tiːrən] *v/t* (*no -ge-, h*) patent; **(sich) et. ~ lassen** take out a patent for s.th.

Pa'tentinhaber *m* patentee

pathetisch [pa'teːtɪʃ] *adj* pompous

Patient [pa'tsjɛnt] *m* (-en; -en), **Pa-'tientin** *f* (-; -nen) MED patient

Patin ['paːtɪn] *f* (-; -nen) godmother

Patriot [patri'oːt] *m* (-en; -en) patriot

patri'otisch *adj* patriotic

Patrone [pa'troːnə] *f* (-; -n) cartridge

Patrouille [pa'trʊljə] *f* (-; -n) MIL patrol; **patrouillieren** [patrʊl'jiːrən] *v/i* (*no -ge-, h*) MIL patrol

Patsche ['patʃə] F *f*: **in der ~ sitzen** be in a fix *or* jam

'**patschen** F *v/i* (*ge-, h*) (s)plash

'**patsch'nass** *adj* soaking wet

patzen ['patsən] F *v/i* (*ge-, h*), **Patzer** ['patsɐ] F *m* (-s; -) blunder

Pauke ['paukə] *f* (-; -n) MUS bass drum; kettledrum

'**pauken** F *v/i and v/t* (*ge-, h*) cram
Pauschale [pau'ʃaːlə] *f* (*-; -n*) lump sum
Pau'schal|gebühr *f* flat rate; **~reise** *f* package tour; **~urteil** *n* sweeping judg(e)ment
Pause[1] ['pauzə] *f* (*-; -n*) recess, *Br* break, *esp* THEA, SPORT intermission, *Br* interval; pause; rest (*a.* MUS)
'**Pause**[2] *f* (*-; -n*) TECH tracing
'**pausen** *v/t* (*ge-, h*) TECH trace
'**pausenlos** *adj* uninterrupted, nonstop
'**Pausenzeichen** *n radio*: interval signal; PED bell
pausieren [pau'ziːrən] *v/i* (*no -ge-, h*) pause, rest
Pavian ['paːvjaːn] *m* (*-s; -e*) ZO baboon
Pavillon ['pavıljɔŋ] *m* (*-s; -s*) pavilion
Pazifist [patsi'fıst] *m* (*-en; -en*), **Pazi'fistin** *f* (*-; -nen*), **pazi'fistisch** *adj* pacifist
PC [peː'tseː] *m* (*-[s]; -[s]*) *abbr of personal computer* PC
Pech [pɛç] *n* (*-s; no pl*) pitch; F bad luck; **~strähne** F *f* run of bad luck; **~vogel** F *m* unlucky fellow
pedantisch [pe'dantıʃ] *adj* pedantic, fussy
Pegel ['peːgəl] *m* (*-s; -*) level (*a. fig*)
peilen ['paılən] *v/t* (*ge-, h*) sound
peinigen ['paınıgən] *v/t* (*ge-, h*) torment
Peiniger ['paınıgɐ] *m* (*-s; -*) tormentor
peinlich ['paınlıç] *adj* embarrassing; **~ genau** meticulous (*bei, in dat* in); *es war mir ~* I was *or* felt embarrassed
Peitsche ['paıtʃə] *f* (*-; -n*), '**peitschen** *v/t* (*ge-, h*) whip
'**Peitschenhieb** *m* lash
Pelle ['pɛlə] *f* (*-; -n*) skin; peel; '**pellen** *v/t* (*ge-, h*) peel; '**Pellkar,toffeln** *pl* potatoes (boiled) in their jackets
Pelz [pɛlts] *m* (*-es; -e*) fur; skin
'**pelzgefüttert** *adj* fur-lined
'**Pelzgeschäft** *n* fur(rier's) store (*Br* shop)
pelzig ['pɛltsıç] *adj* furry; MED furred
'**Pelzmantel** *m* fur coat
'**Pelztiere** *pl* furred animals, furs
Pendel ['pɛndəl] *n* (*-s; -*) pendulum
'**pendeln** *v/i* (*ge-, h*) swing; RAIL *etc* shuttle; commute
'**Pendeltür** *f* swing door
'**Pendelverkehr** *m* RAIL *etc* shuttle service; commuter traffic; **Pendler(in)** ['pɛndlɐ, 'pɛndlərın] *m(f)* (*-s; -/-;*

-nen) RAIL *etc* commuter
Penis ['peːnıs] *m* (*-s; -se*) ANAT penis
Penner ['pɛnɐ] F *m* (*-s; -*) tramp, bum
Pension [pa'sjoːn] *f* (*-; -en*) (old age) pension; boarding-house, private hotel; *in ~ sein* be retired; **Pensionär(in)** [pa,sjo'nɛːɐ, pa,sjo'nɛːrın] *m(f)* (*-s; -e/-; -nen*) (old age) pensioner; boarder; **Pensionat** [pa,sjo'naːt] *n* (*-[e]s; -e*) boarding school
pensionieren [pa,sjo'niːrən] *v/t* (*no -ge-, h*) pension (off); *sich ~ lassen* retire; **Pensio'nierung** *f* (*-; -en*) retirement
Pensionist [pa,sjo'nıst] *Austrian*, *Swiss m* (*-en; -en*) (old age) pensioner
Pensi'onsgast *m* boarder
Pensum ['pɛnzʊm] *n* (*-s; Pensen, Pensa*) (work) quota, stint
per [pɛr] *prp* (*acc*) per; by
perfekt [pɛr'fɛkt] *adj* perfect; **~ machen** settle
'**Perfekt** *n* (*-s; -e*) LING present perfect
Pergament [pɛrga'mɛnt] *n* (*-[e]s; -e*) parchment
Periode [pe'rjoːdə] *f* (*-; -n*) period, MED *a.* menstruation
periodisch [pe'rjoːdıʃ] *adj* periodic(al)
Peripherie [perife'riː] *f* (*-; -n*) periphery, outskirts; **~geräte** *pl* IT peripheral equipment
Perle ['pɛrlə] *f* (*-; -n*) pearl; bead
'**perlen** *v/i* (*ge-, h*) sparkle, bubble
'**Perlenkette** *f* pearl necklace
'**Perlmuschel** *f* ZO pearl oyster
Perlmutt ['pɛrlmʊt] *n* (*-s; no pl*) mother-of-pearl
Perron [pɛ'roː] *m* (*-s; -s*) *Swiss* platform
Perser ['pɛrzɐ] *m* (*-s; -*) Persian; Persian carpet; **Perserin** ['pɛrzərın] *f* (*-; -nen*) Persian (woman); **Persien** ['pɛrzjən] Persia; **persisch** ['pɛrzıʃ] *adj* Persian
Person [pɛr'zoːn] *f* (*-; -en*) person, THEA *etc a.* character; *ein Tisch für drei ~en* a table for three
Personal [pɛrzo'naːl] *n* (*-s; no pl*) staff, personnel; *zu wenig ~ haben* be understaffed; **~abbau** *m* staff reduction; **~abteilung** *f* personnel department; **~ausweis** *m* identity card; **~chef** *m* staff manager
Personalien [pɛrzo'naːljən] *pl* particulars, personal data

Personalpronomen 218

Perso'nalpro,nomen *n* LING personal pronoun

Per'sonen|(kraft)wagen (*abbr PKW*) *m* (*Br a.* motor)car, auto(mobile); **~zug** *m* passenger train; local *or* commuter train

personifizieren [pɛrzonifi'tsi:rən] *v/t* (*no -ge-, h*) personify

persönlich [pɛr'zøːnlıç] *adj* personal

Per'sönlichkeit *f* (-; -*en*) personality

Perücke [pe'rʏkə] *f* (-; -*n*) wig

pervers [pɛr'vɛrs] *adj* perverted; **~er Mensch** pervert

Pessimismus [pɛsi'mısmʊs] *m* (-; *no pl*) pessimism; **Pessimist(in)** [pɛsi-'mıst(ın)] (-*en*; -*en*/-; -*nen*) pessimist; **pessi'mistisch** *adj* pessimistic

Pest [pɛst] *f* (-; *no pl*) MED plague

Pestizid [pɛsti'tsi:t] *n* (-*s*; -*e*) pesticide

Petersilie [peːtɐ'zi:ljə] *f* (-; -*n*) BOT parsley

Petroleum [pe'tro:leum] *n* (-*s*; *no pl*) kerosene, *Br* paraffin; **~lampe** *f* kerosene (*Br* paraffin) lamp

petzen ['pɛtsən] F *v/i* (*ge-, h*) tell tales, *Br a.* sneak

Pfad [pfaːt] *m* (-[*e*]*s*; -*e* ['pfaːdə]) path, track; **~finder** *m* boy scout; **~finderin** ['pfaːtfındərın] *f* (-; -*nen*) girl scout, *Br* girl guide

Pfahl [pfaːl] *m* (-[*e*]*s*; *Pfähle* ['pfɛːlə]) stake; post; pole

Pfand [pfant] *n* (-[*e*]*s*; *Pfänder* ['pfɛn-də]) security; pawn, pledge; deposit; forfeit

'Pfandbrief *m* ECON mortgage bond

pfänden ['pfɛndən] *v/t* (*ge-, h*) seize

'Pfandhaus *n* → *Leihhaus*

Pfandleiher ['pfantlaiɐ] *m* (-*s*; -) pawnbroker

'Pfandschein *m* pawn ticket

'Pfändung *f* (-; -*en*) JUR seizure

Pfanne ['pfanə] *f* (-; -*n*) pan, skillet

'Pfannkuchen *m* pancake

Pfarrbezirk ['pfarbətsɪrk] *m* parish

Pfarrer ['pfarɐ] *m* (-*s*; -) vicar; pastor; (parish) priest

'Pfarr|gemeinde *f* parish; **~haus** *n* parsonage; rectory, vicarage; **~kirche** *f* parish church

Pfau [pfau] *m* (-[*e*]*s*; -*en*) ZO peacock

Pfeffer ['pfɛfɐ] *m* (-*s*; -) pepper; **~kuchen** *m* gingerbread; **~minze** ['pfɛf-ɐmıntsə] *f* (-; *no pl*) BOT peppermint

'pfeffern *v/t* (*ge-, h*) pepper

'Pfefferstreuer *m* (-*s*; -) pepper caster

pfeffrig ['pfɛfrıç] *adj* peppery

Pfeife ['pfaifə] *f* (-; -*n*) whistle; pipe (*a.* MUS); **'pfeifen** *v/i and v/t* (*irr, ge-, h*) whistle (*j-m* to s.o.); F **~ auf** (*acc*) not give a damn about

Pfeil [pfail] *m* (-[*e*]*s*; -*e*) arrow

Pfeiler ['pfailɐ] *m* (-*s*; -) pillar; pier

Pfennig ['pfɛnıç] *m* (-*s*; -*e*) hist (*former monetary unit of Germany*) pfennig; *fig* penny

Pferch [pfɛrç] *m* (-[*e*]*s*; -*e*) fold, pen

'pferchen *v/t* (*ge-, h*) cram (*in acc* into)

Pferd [pfeːrt] *n* (-[*e*]*s*; -*e*) ZO horse (*a.* SPORT); **zu ~e** on horseback

Pferde|geschirr ['pfeːɐdəgəʃır] *n* harness; **~koppel** *f* paddock; **~rennen** *n* horserace; **~stall** *m* stable; **~stärke** *f* TECH horsepower; **~wagen** *m* (horse-drawn) carriage

pfiff [pfıf] *pret of pfeifen*

Pfiff *m* (-[*e*]*s*; -*e*) whistle

pfiffig ['pfıfıç] *adj* smart

Pfingsten ['pfıŋstən] *n* (-; -) REL Pentecost, *Br* Whitsun (**zu, an** at)

Pfingst'montag *m* REL Whit Monday

'Pfingstrose *f* BOT peony

Pfingst'sonntag *m* REL Pentecost, *Br* Whit Sunday

Pfirsich ['pfırzıç] *m* (-*s*; -*e*) BOT peach

Pflanze ['pflantsə] *f* (-; -*n*) plant; **~n fressend** ZO herbivorous

'pflanzen *v/t* (*ge-, h*) plant

'Pflanzenfett *n* vegetable fat

'pflanzlich *adj* vegetable

'Pflanzung *f* (-; -*en*) plantation

'Pflaster ['pflastɐ] *n* (-*s*; -) pavement; MED Band-Aid®, *Br* plaster

'pflastern *v/t* (*ge-, h*) pave

'Pflasterstein *m* paving stone

Pflaume ['pflaumə] *f* (-; -*n*) BOT plum

Pflege ['pfleːgə] *f* (-; *no pl*) care; MED nursing; *fig* cultivation; TECH maintenance; *j-n* **in ~ nehmen** take s.o. into one's care; **~...** in *cpds* ...**eltern**, ...**kind**, ...**sohn** *etc*: foster ...; ...**heim**, ...**kosten**, ...**personal** *etc*: nursing ...

'pflegebedürftig *adj* needing care

'Pflegefall *m* constant-care patient

'pflegeleicht *adj* wash-and-wear, easy-care

'pflegen *v/t* (*ge-, h*) care for, look after, *esp* MED *a.* nurse; TECH maintain; *fig* cultivate; keep up (*custom etc*); **sie pflegte zu sagen** she used to *or* would say; **Pfleger** ['pfleːgɐ] *m* (-*s*; -) male nurse; **Pflegerin** ['pfleːgərɪn] *f* (-; -*nen*) nurse; '**Pflegestelle** *f* nursing place

Pflicht [pflɪçt] *f* (-; -*en*) duty (**gegen** to); SPORT compulsory events

'**pflichtbewusst** *adj* conscientious

'**Pflicht|bewusstsein** *n* sense of duty; **~erfüllung** *f* performance of one's duty; **~fach** *n* PED compulsory subject

'**pflicht|gemäß, ~getreu** *adj* dutiful; **~vergessen** *adv*: **~ handeln** neglect one's duty

'**Pflichtversicherung** *f* compulsory insurance

Pflock ['pflɔk] *m* (-[*e*]*s*; *Pflöcke* ['pflœkə]) peg, pin; plug

pflücken ['pflʏkən] *v/t* (ge-, h) pick, gather

Pflug [pfluːk] *m* (-[*e*]*s*; *Pflüge* ['pflyːgə]), **pflügen** ['pflyːgən] *v/t and v/i* (ge-, h) plow, *Br* plough

Pforte ['pfɔrtə] *f* (-; -*n*) gate, door, entrance; **Pförtner** ['pfœrtnɐ] *m* (-*s*; -) doorman, doorkeeper, porter

Pfosten ['pfɔstən] *m* (-*s*; -) post

Pfote ['pfoːtə] *f* (-; -*n*) ZO paw (*a*. F)

pfropfen ['pfrɔpfən] *v/t* (ge-, h) stopper; cork; plug; AGR graft; F cram, stuff

'**Pfropfen** *m* (-*s*; -) stopper; cork; plug; MED clot

pfui [pfui] *int* ugh!; *audience*: boo!

Pfund [pfʊnt] *n* (-[*e*]*s*; -*e* ['pfʊndə]) pound (*453,59 g*); pound (sterling); **10 ~** ten pounds

'**pfundweise** *adv* by the pound

pfuschen ['pfʊʃən] F *v/i* (ge-, h), **Pfuscherei** [pfʊʃə'rai] F *f* (-; -*en*) bungle, botch

Pfütze ['pfʏtsə] *f* (-; -*n*) puddle, pool

Phänomen [fɛnoˈmeːn] *n* (-*s*; -*e*) phenomenon; **phänomenal** [fɛnomeˈnaːl] *adj* phenomenal

Phantasie *etc* → **Fantasie** *etc*

pharmazeutisch [farmaˈtsɔytɪʃ] *adj* pharmaceutic(al)

Phase ['faːzə] *f* (-; -*n*) phase (*a*. ELECTR), stage

Philosoph [filoˈzoːf] *m* (-*en*; -*en*) philosopher; **Philosophie** [filozoˈfiː] *f* (-; -*n*) philosophy; **philosophieren** [filozoˈfiːrən] *v/i* (*no* -ge-, h) philoso-

phize (**über** *acc* on); **Philo'sophin** *f* (-; -*nen*) (woman) philosopher; **philosophisch** [filoˈzoːfɪʃ] *adj* philosophical

phlegmatisch [flɛˈgmatɪʃ] *adj* phlegmatic

Phonetik [foˈneːtɪk] *f* (-; *no pl*) phonetics; **phoˈnetisch** *adj* phonetic

Phosphor ['fɔsfoːɐ] *m* (-*s*; -*e*) CHEM phosphorus

Photo... → **Foto...**

Phrase ['fraːzə] *contp f* (-; -*n*) cliché (phrase)

Physik [fyˈziːk] *f* (-; *no pl*) physics

physikalisch [fyziˈkaːlɪʃ] *adj* physical

Physiker ['fyːzikɐ] *m* (-*s*; -), '**Physikerin** *f* (-; -*nen*) physicist

physisch ['fyːzɪʃ] *adj* physical

Pianist [pjaˈnɪst] *m* (-*en*; -*en*), **Piaˈnistin** *f* (-; -*nen*) MUS pianist

Piano ['pjaːno] *n* (-*s*; -*s*) MUS piano

Picke ['pɪkə] *f* (-; -*n*) TECH pick(axe)

Pickel[1] ['pɪkəl] *m* (-*s*; -) TECH pick(axe)

'**Pickel**[2] *m* (-*s*; -) MED pimple; **pickelig** ['pɪkəlɪç] *adj* MED pimpled, pimply

picken ['pɪkən] *v/i and v/t* (ge-, h) ZO peck, pick

Picknick ['pɪknɪk] *n* (-*s*; -*e*, -*s*) picnic

'**picknicken** *v/i* (ge-, h) (have a) picnic

piekfein ['piːkfain] F *adj* posh

piep(s)en ['piːp(s)ən] *v/i* (ge-, h) chirp, cheep; ELECTR bleep

Pietät [pjeˈtɛːt] *f* (-; *no pl*) reverence; piety; **pie'tätlos** *adj* irreverent; **pie'tätvoll** *adj* reverent

Pik [piːk] *n* (-[*s*]; -[*s*]) *cards*: spade(s)

pikant [piˈkant] *adj* piquant, spicy (*both a. fig*)

Pilger ['pɪlgɐ] *m* (-*s*; -) pilgrim; '**Pilgerfahrt** *f* pilgrimage; '**Pilgerin** *f* (-; -*nen*) pilgrim; '**pilgern** *v/i* (ge-, *sein*) (go on a) pilgrimage

Pille ['pɪlə] *f* (-; -*n*) pill; F **die ~ nehmen** be on the pill

Pilot [piˈloːt] *m* (-*en*; -*en*), **Piˈlotin** *f* (-; -*nen*) pilot

Pilz [pɪlts] *m* (-*es*; -*e*) BOT mushroom (*a. fig*); toadstool; MED fungus; **~e suchen (gehen)** go mushrooming

Pinguin ['pɪŋguiːn] *m* (-*s*; -*e*) ZO penguin

pinkeln ['pɪŋkəln] F *v/i* (ge-, h) (have a) pee, piddle

Pinsel ['pɪnzəl] *m* (-*s*; -) (paint)brush

'Pinselstrich m brushstroke
Pinzette [pɪn'tsɛtə] f (-; -n) tweezers
Pionier [pjo'niːɐ] m (-s; -e) pioneer, MIL a. engineer
Pirat [pi'raːt] m (-en; -en) pirate
Pisse [ˈpɪsə] V f (-; no pl), **'pissen** V v/i (ge-, h) piss
Piste [ˈpɪstə] f (-; -n) course; AVIAT runway
Pistole [pɪsˈtoːlə] f (-; -n) pistol, gun
Pkw, PKW [ˈpeːkaːveː] abbr of **Personenkraftwagen** (Br a. motor)car, automobile
Plache [ˈplaxə] Austrian f (-; -n) awning, tarpaulin
placieren etc → **platzieren** etc
plädieren [plɛˈdiːrən] v/i (no -ge-, h) JUR plead (**für** for); **Plädoyer** [plɛdoaˈjeː] n (-s; -s) JUR final speech, pleading
Plage [ˈplaːɡə] f (-; -n) trouble, misery; plague; nuisance, F pest; **'plagen** v/t (ge-, h) trouble; bother; pester; **sich** ~ toil, drudge
Plakat [plaˈkaːt] n (-[e]s; -e) poster, placard, bill
Plakette [plaˈkɛtə] f (-; -n) plaque, badge
Plan [plaːn] m (-[e]s; **Pläne** [ˈplɛːnə]) plan; intention
Plane [ˈplaːnə] f (-; -n) awning, tarpaulin
'planen v/t (ge-, h) plan, make plans for
Planet [plaˈneːt] m (-en; -en) ASTR planet
planieren [plaˈniːrən] v/t (no -ge-, h) TECH level, plane, grade
Planke [ˈplaŋkə] f (-; -n) plank, (thick) board
plänkeln [ˈplɛŋkəln] v/i (ge-, h) skirmish
'planlos adj without plan; aimless
'planmäßig 1. adj scheduled (arrival etc) **2.** adv according to plan
Plan(t)schbecken [ˈplanʃbɛkən] n paddling pool
plan(t)schen [ˈplanʃən] v/i (ge-, h) splash
Plantage [planˈtaːʒə] f (-; -n) plantation
Plappermaul [ˈplapɐmaul] F n chatterbox
plappern [ˈplapɐn] F v/i (ge-, h) chatter, prattle, babble, jabber
plärren [ˈplɛrən] F v/i and v/t (ge-, h) blubber; bawl; radio: blare
Plastik¹ [ˈplastɪk] f (-; -en) sculpture
'Plastik² n (-s; no pl) plastic; **~...** in cpds ...besteck etc: plastic ...

plastisch [ˈplastɪʃ] adj plastic; three-dimensional; fig graphic
Platin [ˈplaːtiːn] n (-s; no pl) platinum
plätschern [ˈplɛtʃɐn] v/i (ge-, h) ripple (a. fig), splash
platt [plat] adj flat, level, even; fig trite; F flabbergasted
Platte [ˈplatə] f (-; -n) sheet, plate; slab; board; panel; MUS record, disk, Br disc; IT disk; GASTR dish; F bald pate; **kalte ~** GASTR plate of cold cuts (Br meats)
plätten [ˈplɛtən] v/t (ge-, h) iron, press
'Platten|spieler m record player; **~teller** m turntable
'Plattform f platform
'Plattfuß m MED flat foot
'Plattheit fig f (-; -en) triviality; platitude
Plättli [ˈplɛtli] Swiss n (-s; -s) tile
Platz [plats] m (-es; **Plätze** [ˈplɛtsə]) place, spot; site; room, space; square; circus; seat; **es ist (nicht) genug ~** there's (there isn't) enough room; **~ machen für** make room for; make way for; **~ nehmen** take a seat, sit down; **ist dieser ~ noch frei?** is this seat taken?; **j-n vom ~ stellen** SPORT send s.o. off; **auf eigenem ~** SPORT at home; **auf die Plätze, fertig, los!** SPORT on your marks, get set, go!
'Platz|anweiser m (-s; -) usher; **~anweiserin** f (-; -nen) usherette
Plätzchen [ˈplɛtsçən] n (-s; -) (little) place, spot; GASTR cookie, Br biscuit
platzen [ˈplatsən] v/i (ge-, sein) burst (a. fig); crack, split; explode (a. fig **vor** dat with), blow up; F come to grief or nothing, fall through, blow up, sl go phut; break up
platzieren [plaˈtsiːrən] v/t (no -ge-, h) place; **sich ~** SPORT be placed
Plat'zierung f (-; -en) place, placing
'Platzkarte f reservation (ticket)
Plätzli [ˈplɛtsli] Swiss n (-s; -) cutlet
'Platz|pa,trone f blank (cartridge); **~regen** m cloudburst, downpour; **~reser,vierung** f seat reservation; **~verweis** m: **e-n ~ erhalten** SPORT be sent off; **~wart** m (-s; -e) SPORT groundskeeper, Br groundsman; **~wunde** f MED cut, laceration
Plauderei [plaudəˈrai] f (-; -en) chat
plaudern [ˈplaudɐn] v/i (ge-, h) (have a) chat

plauschen ['plauʃən] *Austrian v/i* (have a) chat

pleite ['plaitə] F *adj* broke

'**Pleite** F *f* (-; *-n*) bankruptcy; *fig* flop; **pleitegehen** go broke

Plombe ['plɔmbə] *f* (-; *-n*) TECH seal; MED filling; **plombieren** [plɔm'biːrən] *v/t* (*no -ge-, h*) TECH seal; MED fill

plötzlich ['plœtslɪç] **1.** *adj* sudden **2.** *adv* suddenly, all of a sudden

plump [plʊmp] *adj* clumsy; **plumps** *int* thud, plop; **plumpsen** ['plʊmpsən] *v/i* (*ge-, sein*) thud, plop, flop

Plunder ['plʊndɐ] F *m* (*-s; no pl*) trash, junk

Plünderer ['plʏndərɐ] *m* (*-s; -*) looter, plunderer; **plündern** ['plʏndɐn] *v/i and v/t* (*ge-, h*) plunder, loot

Plural ['pluːraːl] *m* (*-s; -e*) LING plural

plus [plʊs] *adv* plus

Plusquamperfekt ['plʊskvampɛrfɛkt] *n* (*-s; -e*) LING past perfect

Pneu [pnɔy] *Swiss m* (*-s; -s*) tire, *Br* tyre

Po [poː] F *m* (*-s; -s*) bottom, behind

Pöbel ['pøːbəl] *m* (*-s; no pl*) mob, rabble

pochen ['pɔxən] *v/i* (*ge-, h*) knock, rap (*both: **an** acc* at)

Pocke ['pɔkə] *f* (-; *-n*) MED pock

'**Pocken** *pl* MED smallpox; **~impfung** *f* MED smallpox vaccination

Podest [po'dɛst] *n, m* (*-[e]s; -e*) platform; *fig* pedestal

Podium ['poːdjʊm] *n* (*-s; -ien*) podium, platform; '**Podiumsdiskussi,on** *f* panel discussion

Poesie [poe'ziː] *f* (-; *-n*) poetry

Poet [po'eːt] *m* (*-en; -en*), **Po'etin** *f* (-; *-nen*) poet

poetisch [po'eːtɪʃ] *adj* poetic(al)

Pointe ['poɛ̃ːtə] *f* (-; *-n*) point, punch line

Pokal [po'kaːl] *m* (*-s; -e*) goblet; SPORT cup; **~endspiel** *n* SPORT cup final; **~sieger** *m* SPORT cup winner; **~spiel** *n* SPORT cup tie

pökeln ['pøːkəln] *v/t* (*ge-, h*) salt

Pol [poːl] *m* (*-s; -e*) GEOGR pole

polar [po'laːɐ] *adj* polar

Pole ['poːlə] *m* (*-n; -n*) Pole

Polemik [po'leːmɪk] *f* (-; *-en*) polemic(s); **po'lemisch** *adj* polemic(al)

polemisieren [polemi'ziːrən] *v/i* (*no -ge-, h*) polemize

'**Polen** Poland

Police [po'liːsə] *f* (-; *-n*) policy

Polier [po'liːɐ] *m* (*-s; -e*) TECH foreman

polieren [po'liːrən] *v/t* (*no -ge-, h*) polish

Polin ['poːlɪn] *f* (-; *-nen*) Pole, Polish woman

Politik [poli'tiːk] *f* (-; *no pl*) politics; policy (*a. fig*); **Politiker(in)** [po'liːtikɐ, po'liːtikərɪn] *m(f)* (*-s; -/-; -nen*) politician; **politisch** [po'liːtɪʃ] *adj* political; **politisieren** [politi'ziːrən] *v/i* (*no -ge-, h*) talk politics

Polizei [poli'tsai] *f* (-; *no pl*) police; **~auto** *n* police car; **~beamt|e** *m*, **-in** *f* police officer

poli'zeilich *adj* (of *or* by the) police

Poli'zei|prä,sidium *n* police headquarters; **~re,vier** *n* police station; precinct, *Br* district; **~schutz** *m*: *unter ~* under police guard; **~streife** *f* police patrol; **~stunde** *f* closing time; **~wache** *f* police station

Polizist [poli'tsɪst] *m* (*-en; -en*) policeman; **Poli'zistin** *f* (-; *-nen*) policewoman

polnisch ['pɔlnɪʃ] *adj* Polish

Polster ['pɔlstɐ] *n* (*-s; -*) upholstery; cushion; pad(ding); *fig* bolster; **~garni,tur** *f* three-piece suite; **~möbel** *pl* upholstered furniture

'**polstern** *v/t* (*ge-, h*) upholster; pad

'**Polster|sessel** *m* easy chair, armchair; **~stuhl** *m* upholstered chair

Polsterung ['pɔlstərʊŋ] *f* (-; *-en*) upholstery; padding

poltern ['pɔltɐn] *v/i* (*ge-, h*) rumble; *fig* bluster

Pommes frites [pɔm'frɪt] *pl* French fries, French fried potatoes, *Br* chips

Pomp [pɔmp] *m* (*-[e]s; no pl*) pomp

pompös [pɔm'pøːs] *adj* showy

Pony¹ ['pɔni] *n* (*-s; -s*) ZO pony

'**Pony²** *m* (*-s; -s*) fringe, bangs

Popgruppe ['pɔpɡrʊpə] *f* MUS pop group

'**Popmu,sik** *f* pop music

populär [popu'lɛːɐ] *adj* popular

Popularität [populari'tɛːt] *f* (-; *no pl*) popularity

Pore ['poːrə] *f* (-; *-n*) pore

Porno ['pɔrno] F *m* (*-s; -s*), **~film** *m* porn (film), blue movie; **~heft** *n* porn magazine

porös [po'røːs] *adj* porous

Portemonnaie [pɔrtmɔ'neː] *n* (*-s; -s*)

purse

Portier [pɔr'tjeː] *m* (-s; -s) doorman, porter

Portion [pɔr'tsjoːn] *f* (-; -en) portion, share; helping, serving

Portmonee *n* → **Portemonnaie**

Porto ['pɔrto] *n* (-s; -s, -ti) postage

Porträt [pɔr'trɛː] *n* (-s; -s) portrait

porträtieren [pɔrtrɛ'tiːrən] *v/t* (*no* -ge-, *h*) portray

Portugal ['pɔrtugal] Portugal

Portugiese [pɔrtu'giːzə] *m* (-n; -n), **Portu'giesin** *f* (-; -nen), **portu-'giesisch** *adj* Portuguese

Porzellan [pɔrtsɛ'laːn] *n* (-s; -e) china, porcelain

Posaune [po'zaunə] *f* (-; -n) MUS trombone; *fig* trumpet

Pose ['poːzə] *f* (-; -n) pose, attitude

Position [pozi'tsjoːn] *f* (-; -en) position (*a. fig*)

positiv ['poːzitiːf] *adj* positive

possessiv [pɔsɛ'siːf] *adj* LING possessive; **Posses'sivpro,nomen** *n* LING possessive pronoun

Post® [pɔst] *f* (-; *no pl*) mail, *esp Br* post; letters; *mit der Post®* by post *or* mail; **Postamt** *n* post office; **Postanweisung** *f* money order; **Postbote** *m* mailman, *Br* postman

Posten ['pɔstən] *m* (-s; -) post; job, position; MIL sentry; ECON item; lot, parcel

'Postfach *n* (PO) box

postieren [pɔs'tiːrən] *v/t* (*no* -ge-, *h*) post, station, place; *sich ~* station o.s.

'Postkarte *f* postcard

'Postkutsche *f* stagecoach

'postlagernd *adj* (in care of) general delivery, *Br* poste restante

'Post|leitzahl *f* zip code, *Br* post(al) code; **~sparbuch** *n* post-office savings book; **~stempel** *m* postmark

'postwendend *adv* by return mail, *Br* by return (of post)

'Post|wertzeichen *n* (postage) stamp; **~zustellung** *f* postal *or* mail delivery

Potenz [po'tɛnts] *f* (-; -en) (*no pl*) MED potency; MATH power

Pracht [praxt] *f* (-; *no pl*) splendo(u)r, magnificence

prächtig ['prɛçtɪç] *adj* splendid, magnificent, *fig a.* great, super

Prädikat [prɛdi'kaːt] *n* (-[e]s; -e) LING predicate

prägen ['prɛːgən] *v/t* (*ge-, h*) stamp, coin (*a. fig*)

prahlen ['praːlən] *v/i* (*ge-, h*) brag, boast (*both: mit* of), talk big, show off; **Prahler** ['praːlɐ] *m* (-s; -) boaster, braggart; **Prahlerei** [praːlə'rai] *f* (-; -en) boasting, bragging; *fig* **'prahlerisch** *adj* boastful; showy

Praktikant [prakti'kant] *m* (-en; -en), **Prakti'kantin** *f* (-; -nen) trainee; **Praktiken** ['praktikən] *pl* practices; **'Praktikum** *n* (-s; -ka) practical training; **'praktisch 1.** *adj* practical; useful, handy; **~er Arzt** general practitioner **2.** *adv* practically; virtually; **praktizieren** [prakti'tsiːrən] *v/t* (*no* -ge-, *h*) practice (*Br* practise) medicine *or* law

Prälat [prɛ'laːt] *m* (-en; -en) REL prelate

Praline [pra'liːnə] *f* (-; -n) chocolate

prall [pral] *adj* tight; well-rounded; bulging; blazing (*sun*)

prallen ['pralən] *v/i* (*ge-, sein*) **~ gegen** (*or auf acc*) crash *or* bump into

Prämie ['prɛːmjə] *f* (-; -n) premium; prize; bonus; **prämieren** [prɛ'miːrən], **prämiieren** [prɛmi'iːrən] *v/t* (*no* -ge-, *h*) award a prize to

Pranke ['praŋkə] *f* (-; -n) ZO paw (*a. F*)

Präparat [prɛpa'raːt] *n* (-[e]s; -e) preparation

präparieren [prɛpa'riːrən] *v/t* (*no* -ge-, *h*) prepare; MED, BOT, ZO dissect

Präposition [prɛpozi'tsjoːn] *f* (-; -en) LING preposition

Prärie [prɛ'riː] *f* (-; -n) prairie

Präsens ['prɛːzɛns] *n* (-; -sentia [prɛ-'zɛntsja]) LING present (tense)

präsentieren [prɛzɛn'tiːrən] *v/t* (*no* -ge-, *h*) present; offer

Präservativ [prɛzɛrva'tiːf] *n* (-s; -e) condom

Präsident [prɛzi'dɛnt] *m* (-en; -en), **Präsi'dentin** *f* (-; -nen) president; chairman (chairwoman); **präsidieren** [prɛzi'diːrən] *v/i* preside (*in dat* over)

Präsidium [prɛ'ziːdjʊm] *n* (-s; -ien) presidency

prasseln ['prasəln] *v/i* (*ge-, h*) rain etc: patter; *fire:* crackle

Präteritum [prɛ'teːrɪtʊm] *n* (-s; -ta) LING past (tense)

Praxis ['praksɪs] *f* (-; *Praxen*) (*no pl*) practice (*a.* MED, JUR); MED doctor's office, *Br* surgery

Präzedenzfall [prɛtse'dɛntsfal] *m* precedent

präzis [prɛ'tsiːs], **präzise** [prɛ'tsiːzə] *adj* precise; **Präzision** [prɛtsi'zjoːn] *f* (-; *no pl*) precision

predigen ['preːdɪɡən] *v/i and v/t* (*ge-, h*) preach

Prediger ['preːdɪɡɐ] *m* (-*s*; -), '**Predigerin** *f* (-; *-nen*) preacher

Predigt ['preːdɪçt] *f* (-; *-en*) sermon

Preis [prais] *m* (-*es*; *-e*) price (*a. fig*); prize; *film etc*: award; reward; **um jeden ~** at all costs

'**Preisausschreiben** *n* competition

Preiselbeere ['praizəlbeːrə] *f* BOT cranberry

preisen ['praizən] *v/t* (*irr, ge-, h*) praise

'**Preiserhöhung** *f* rise *or* increase in price(s)

'**preisgeben** *v/t* (*irr, geben, sep, -ge-, h*) abandon; reveal, give away

'**preisgekrönt** *adj* prize-winning; *film etc*: award-winning

'**Preis|gericht** *n* jury; **~lage** *f* price range; **~liste** *f* price list; **~nachlass** *m* discount; **~rätsel** *n* competition; **~richter(in)** judge; **~schild** *n* price tag; **~stopp** *m* price freeze; **~träger(in)** prizewinner

'**preiswert** *adj* cheap

prellen ['prɛlən] *v/t* (*ge-, h*) *fig* cheat (**um** out of); **sich et. ~** MED bruise s.th.; '**Prellung** *f* (-; *-en*) MED contusion, bruise

Premiere [prə'mjeːrə] *f* (-; *-n*) THEA *etc* first night, première

Premiermi,nister [prə'mjeːministɐ] *m*, **Pre'miermi,nisterin** [prə'mjeːministɐrin] *f* prime minister

Presse ['prɛsə] *f* (-; *-n*) (*no pl*) press; squeezer; **~...** *in cpds* ...*agentur*, ...*konferenz*, ...*fotograf etc*: press ...; **~freiheit** *f* freedom of the press; **~meldung** *f* news item

'**pressen** *v/t* (*ge-, h*) press; squeeze

'**Presse|tri,büne** *f* press box; **~vertreter** *m* reporter

'**Pressluft** *f* compressed air; **~...** *in cpds* ...*bohrer*, ...*hammer etc*: pneumatic ...

Prestige [prɛs'tiːʒə] *n* (-*s*; *no pl*) prestige; **~verlust** *m* loss of prestige *or* face

Preuße ['prɔʏsə] *m* (-*n*; -*n*), '**Preußin** *f* (-; *-nen*), '**preußisch** *adj* Prussian

prickeln ['prɪkəln] *v/i* (*ge-, h*) prickle; tingle

pries [priːs] *pret of* **preisen**

Priester ['priːstɐ] *m* (-*s*; -) priest; **Priesterin** ['priːstərɪn] *f* (-; *-nen*) priestess; '**priesterlich** *adj* priestly

prima ['priːma] F *adj* great, super

primär [pri'mɛːɐ] *adj* primary

Primar|arzt [pri'maːɐ'aːɐtst] *Austrian m* → **Oberarzt**; **~schule** *Swiss f* → **Grundschule**

Primel ['priːməl] *f* (-; *-n*) BOT primrose

primitiv [primi'tiːf] *adj* primitive

Prinz [prɪnts] *m* (-*en*; -*en*) prince

Prinzessin [prɪn'tsɛsɪn] *f* (-; *-nen*) princess

'**Prinzgemahl** *m* prince consort

Prinzip [prɪn'tsiːp] *n* (-*s*; -*ien*) principle (**aus** on; **im** in); **prinzipiell** [prɪntsi-'pjɛl] *adv* as a matter of principle

Prise ['priːzə] *f* (-; *-n*) **e-e ~ Salz** *etc* a pinch of salt *etc*

Prisma ['prɪsma] *n* (-*s*; -*men*) prism

Pritsche ['prɪtʃə] *f* (-; *-n*) plank bed; MOT platform

privat [pri'vaːt] *adj* private; personal

Pri'vat... *in cpds* ...*leben*, ...*schule*, ...*detektiv etc*: private ...; **~angelegenheit** *f* personal *or* private matter *or* affair; **das ist m-e ~** that's my own business

Privileg [privi'leːk] *n* (-[*e*]*s*; -*gien* [privi-'leːɡjən]) privilege

pro [proː] *prp* (*acc*) per; **2 Euro ~ Stück** two euros each

Pro *n*: **das ~ und Kontra** the pros and cons

Probe ['proːbə] *f* (-; *-n*) trial, test; sample; THEA rehearsal; MATH proof; **auf ~** on probation; **auf die ~ stellen** put to the test; **~alarm** *m* test alarm, fire drill; **~aufnahmen** *pl film*: screen test; **~fahrt** *f* test drive; **~flug** *m* test flight

'**proben** *v/i and v/t* (*ge-, h*) THEA *etc* rehearse

'**probeweise** *adv* on trial; on probation

'**Probezeit** *f* (time of) probation

probieren [pro'biːrən] *v/t* (*no -ge-, h*) try; taste

Problem [pro'bleːm] *n* (-*s*; -*e*) problem

problematisch [proble'maːtɪʃ] *adj* problematic(al)

Produkt [pro'dʊkt] *n* (-[*e*]*s*; -*e*) product (*a.* MATH); result

Produktion [produk'tsjoːn] *f* (-; *-en*)
production; output

produktiv [produk'tiːf] *adj* productive

Produktivität [produktivi'tɛːt] *f* (-; *no pl*) productivity

Produzent [produ'tsɛnt] *m* (*-en*; *-en*), **Produ'zentin** *f* (-; *-nen*) producer; **produzieren** [produ'tsiːrən] *v/t* (*no -ge-, h*) produce

professionell [professjo'nɛl] *adj* professional

Professor [pro'fɛsoːɐ] *m* (-s; *-en* [profɛ'soːrən]), **Profes'sorin** *f* (-; *-nen*) professor

Professur [profɛ'suːɐ] *f* (-; *-en*) professorship, chair (*für* of)

Profi ['proːfi] *m* (-s; *-s*) pro; **~...** *in cpds* ...*boxer*, ...*fußballer etc*: professional

Profil [pro'fiːl] *n* (-s; *-e*) profile; MOT tread; **profilieren** [profi'liːrən] *v/refl* (*no -ge-, h*) distinguish o.s.

Profit [pro'fiːt] *m* (-[e]s; *-e*) profit

profitieren [profi'tiːrən] *v/i* (*no -ge-, h*) profit (*von or bei et.* from *or* by s.th.)

Prognose [pro'gnoːzə] *f* (-; *-n*) prediction; METEOR forecast; MED prognosis

Programm [pro'gram] *n* (-s; *-e*) program(me *Br*); TV *a.* channel; IT program; **~fehler** *m* IT program error, bug

programmieren [progra'miːrən] *v/t* (*no -ge-, h*) program (*a.* IT)

Programmierer [progra'miːrɐ] *m* (-s; -), **Program'miererin** *f* (-; *-nen*) IT programmer

Projekt [pro'jɛkt] *n* (-[e]s; *-e*) project

Projektion [projɛk'tsjoːn] *f* (-; *-en*) projection; **Projektor** [pro'jɛktoːɐ] *m* (-s; *-en* [projɛk'toːrən]) projector

proklamieren [prokla'miːrən] *v/t* (*no -ge-, h*) proclaim

Prokurist [proku'rist] *m* (*-en*; *-en*), **Proku'ristin** *f* (-; *-nen*) authorized signatory

Proletarier [prole'taːrjɐ] *m* (-s; -), **proletarisch** [prole'taːrɪʃ] *adj* proletarian

Prolog [pro'loːk] *m* (-[e]s; *-e*) prologue

Promillegrenze [pro'mɪləgrɛntsə] *f* (blood) alcohol limit

prominent [promi'nɛnt] *adj* prominent

Prominenz [promi'nɛnts] *f* (-; *no pl*) notables; high society

Promotion [promo'tsjoːn] *f* (-; *-en*) UNIV doctorate; **promovieren** [promo-'viːrən] *v/i* (*no -ge-, h*) do one's doctorate

prompt [prompt] *adj* prompt; quick

Pronomen [pro'noːmən] *n* (-s; *-mina*) LING pronoun

Propeller [pro'pɛlɐ] *m* (-s; -) propeller

Prophet [pro'feːt] *m* (*-en*; *-en*) prophet; **pro'phetisch** *adj* prophetic

prophezeien [profe'tsaiən] *v/t* (*no -ge-, h*) prophesy, predict; **Prophe'zeiung** *f* (-; *-en*) prophecy, prediction

Proportion [propor'tsjoːn] *f* (-; *-en*) proportion

Proporz [pro'ports] *m* (*-es*; *-e*) POL proportional representation

Prosa ['proːza] *f* (-; *no pl*) prose

Prospekt [pro'spɛkt] *m* (-[e]s; *-e*) prospectus; brochure, pamphlet

prost [proːst] *int* cheers!

Prostituierte [prostitu'iːɐtə] *f* (-n; -n) prostitute

Protest [pro'tɛst] *m* (-[e]s; *-e*) protest; **aus ~** in (*or* as a) protest

Protestant [protɛs'tant] *m* (*-en*; *-en*), **Protes'tantin** *f* (-; *-nen*), **protes-'tantisch** *adj* REL Protestant

protestieren [protɛs'tiːrən] *v/i* (*no -ge-, h*) protest

Prothese [pro'teːzə] *f* (-; *-n*) MED artificial limb; denture

Protokoll [proto'kɔl] *n* (-s; *-e*) record, minutes; protocol; (*das*) **~ führen** take *or* keep the minutes; **zu ~ nehmen** JUR record; **~führer** *m* keeper of the minutes

protokollieren [protokɔ'liːrən] *v/t and v/i* (*no -ge-, h*) take the minutes (of); JUR record

protzen ['protsən] F *v/i* (*ge-, h*) show off (*mit et.* s.th.)

protzig ['protsɪç] *adj* showy, flashy

Proviant [pro'vjant] *m* (-s; *no pl*) provisions, food

Provinz [pro'vɪnts] *f* (-; *-en*) province; *fig* country; **provinziell** [provɪn'tsjɛl] *adj* provincial (*a. contp*)

Provision [provi'zjoːn] *f* (-; *-en*) ECON commission

provisorisch [provi'zoːrɪʃ] *adj* provisional, temporary

provozieren [provo'tsiːrən] *v/t* (*no -ge-, h*) provoke

Prozent [pro'tsɛnt] *n* (-[e]s; *-e*) per cent; F *pl* discount; **~satz** *m* percentage

prozentual [protsɛn'tuaːl] *adj* proportional; **~er Anteil** percentage

Prozess [pro'tsɛs] *m* (*-es*; *-e*) process (*a.* TECH, CHEM *etc*); JUR action; lawsuit, case; trial; **j-m den ~ machen** take s.o. to court; **e-n ~ gewinnen (verlieren)** win (lose) a case; **prozessieren** [protsɛ'siːrən] *v/i* (*no -ge-, h*) JUR go to court; **gegen j-n ~** bring an action against s.o., take s.o. to court

Prozession [protsɛ'sjoːn] *f* (*-; -en*) procession

Prozessor [pro'tsɛsoːɐ] *m* (*-s; -en* [protsɛ'soːrən] IT processor

prüde ['pryːdə] *adj* prudish; **~ sein** be a prude

prüfen ['pryːfən] *v/t* (*ge-, h*) PED *etc* examine, test (*a.* TECH); check; inspect (*a.* TECH); *fig* consider; **~d** *adj* searching

Prüfer ['pryːfɐ] *m* (*-s; -*), **'Prüferin** *f* (*-; -nen*) PED *etc* examiner; *esp* TECH tester

Prüfling ['pryːflɪŋ] *m* (*-s; -e*) candidate

'Prüfstein *m* touchstone (**für** of)

'Prüfung *f* (*-; -en*) examination, F exam; test; check(ing), inspection; **e-e ~ machen (bestehen, nicht bestehen)** take (pass, fail) an exam(ination)

'Prüfungsarbeit *f* examination *or* test paper

Prügel ['pryːgəl] F *pl* (*e-e Tracht*) **~ bekommen** get a (good) beating *or* hiding *or* thrashing; **Prüge'lei** F *f* (*-; -en*) fight; **'prügeln** F *v/t* (*ge-, h*) beat, flog; **sich ~** (have a) fight; **'Prügelstrafe** *f* corporal punishment

Prunk [prʊŋk] *m* (*-[e]s; no pl*) splendo(u)r, pomp; **'prunkvoll** *adj* splendid, magnificent

PS [peː'ʔɛs] *abbr of* **Pferdestärke** horsepower, HP

Psalm [psalm] *m* (*-s; -en*) REL psalm

Pseudonym [psɔydo'nyːm] *n* (*-s; -e*) pseudonym

pst [pst] *int* sh!, ssh!; psst!

Psyche ['psyːçə] *f* (*-; -n*) mind, psyche

Psychiater [psy'çjaːtɐ] *m* (*-s; -*), **Psy'chiaterin** *f* (*-; -nen*) psychiatrist; **psy'chiatrisch** [psy'çjaːtrɪʃ] *adj* psychiatric

psychisch ['psyːçɪʃ] *adj* mental, MED *a.* psychic

Psychoana'lyse ['psyçoanalyːzə] *f* psychoanalysis

Psychologe [psyço'loːgə] *m* (*-n; -n*) psychologist (*a. fig*); **Psychologie**

[psyçolo'giː] *f* (*-; no pl*) psychology; **Psycho'login** *f* (*-; -nen*) psychologist; **psycho'logisch** *adj* psychological

Psychose [psy'çoːzə] *f* (*-; -n*) MED psychosis

psychosomatisch [psyçozo'maːtɪʃ] *adj* MED psychosomatic

Pubertät [puber'tɛːt] *f* (*-; no pl*) puberty

Publikum ['puːblikʊm] *n* (*-s; no pl*) audience, TV *a.* viewers, *radio: a.* listeners; SPORT crowd, spectators; ECON customers; public

publizieren [publi'tsiːrən] *v/t* (*no -ge-, h*) publish

Pudding ['pʊdɪŋ] *m* (*-s; -e, -s*) pudding, *esp Br* blancmange

Pudel ['puːdəl] *m* (*-s; -*) ZO poodle

Puder ['puːdɐ] *m* (*-s; -*) powder

'Puderdose *f* powder compact

'pudern *v/t* (*ge-, h*) powder; **sich ~** powder one's face

'Puderzucker *m* confectioner's (*Br* icing) sugar

Puff¹ [pʊf] F *m* (*-s; -s*) brothel

Puff² *m* (*-[e]s; Püffe* ['pyfə]) hump; poke

Puffer ['pʊfɐ] *m* (*-s; -*) RAIL buffer (*a. fig*)

'Puffmais *m* popcorn

Pulli ['pʊli] F *m* (*-s; -s*) (light) sweater

Pullover [pʊ'loːvɐ] *m* (*-s; -*) sweater, pullover

Puls [pʊls] *m* (*-es; -e*) MED pulse; pulse rate; **~ader** *f* ANAT artery

pulsieren [pʊl'ziːrən] *v/i* (*no -ge-, h*) MED pulsate (*a. fig*)

Pult [pʊlt] *n* (*-[e]s; -e*) desk

Pulver ['pʊlvɐ] *n* (*-s; -*) powder; F cash, *sl* dough; **pulv(e)rig** ['pʊlv(ə)rɪç] *adj* powdery; **pulverisieren** [pʊlveri'ziːrən] *v/t* (*no -ge-, h*) pulverize

'Pulverkaffee *m* instant coffee

'Pulverschnee *m* powder snow

pumm(e)lig ['pʊm(ə)lɪç] F *adj* chubby, plump, tubby

Pumpe ['pʊmpə] *f* (*-; -n*) TECH pump

'pumpen *v/i and v/t* TECH pump; F lend; borrow

Punker ['paŋkɐ] F *m* (*-s; -*), **'Punkerin** *f* (*-; -nen*) punk

Punkt [pʊŋkt] *m* (*-[e]s; -e*) point (*a. fig*); dot; full stop, period; *fig* spot, place; **um ~ zehn (Uhr)** at ten (o'clock) sharp; **nach ~en gewinnen** *etc* SPORT win *etc* on points

punktieren [pʊŋk'tiːrən] *v/t (no -ge-, h)* dot; MED puncture

pünktlich ['pʏŋktlıç] *adj* punctual; **~ sein** be on time; '**Pünktlichkeit** *f (-; no pl)* punctuality

'**Punkt|sieger** *m* SPORT winner on points; **~spiel** *n* SPORT league game

Pupille [pu'pılə] *f (-; -n)* ANAT pupil

Puppe ['pʊpə] *f (-; -n)* doll, F *a.* chick; THEA puppet (*a. fig*); MOT dummy; ZO chrysalis, pupa

'**Puppen|spiel** *n* puppet show; **~stube** *f* doll's house; **~wagen** *m* doll carriage, *Br* doll's pram

pur [puːɐ] *adj* pure (*a. fig*); *whisky etc*: straight, *Br* neat

Purpur ['pʊrpur] *m (-s; no pl)* crimson

'**purpurrot** *adj* crimson

Purzelbaum ['pʊrtsəlbaum] *m* somersault; **e-n ~ schlagen** turn a somersault

purzeln ['pʊrtsəln] *v/i (ge-, sein)* tumble

Pute ['puːtə] *f (-; -n)* ZO turkey (hen)

Puter ['puːtɐ] *m (-s; -)* ZO turkey (cock)

Putsch [pʊtʃ] *m (-[e]s; -e)* putsch, coup (d'état); '**putschen** *v/i (ge-, h)* revolt, make a putsch

Putz [pʊts] *m (-es; no pl)* ARCH plaster (-ing); **unter ~** ELECTR concealed

putzen ['pʊtsən] *(ge-, h)* **1.** *v/t* clean; polish; wipe; **sich die Nase ~** blow one's nose; **sich die Zähne ~** brush one's teeth **2.** *v/i* do the cleaning; **~ (gehen)** work as a cleaner

'**Putzfrau** *f* cleaner, cleaning woman *or* lady

putzig ['pʊtsıç] *adj* funny, cute

'**Putzlappen** *m* cleaning rag

'**Putzmittel** *n* clean(s)er; polish

Puzzle ['pazəl] *n (-s; -s)* jigsaw (puzzle)

Pyjama [py'dʒaːma] *m (-s; -s)* pajamas, *Br* pyjamas

Pyramide [pyra'miːdə] *f (-; -n)* pyramid

Q

Quacksalber ['kvakzalbɐ] *m (-s; -)* quack (doctor)

Quadrat [kva'draːt] *n (-[e]s; -e)* square; **ins~ erheben** MATH square; **~... in** *cpds* ...**meile,** ...**meter,** ...**wurzel,** ...**zahl** *etc*: square ...; **qua'dratisch** *adj* square; MATH quadratic

quaken ['kvaːkən] *v/i (ge-, h)* duck: quack; *frog*: croak

quäken ['kvɛːkən] *v/i (ge-, h)* squeak

Qual [kvaːl] *f (-; -en)* pain, torment, agony; anguish

quälen ['kvɛːlən] *v/t (ge-, h)* torment (*a. fig*); torture; *fig* pester, plague

Qualifikation [kvalifika'tsjoːn] *f (-; -en)* qualification; **Qualifikati'ons...** *in cpds* ...**spiel** *etc*: qualifying ...

qualifizieren [kvalifi'tsiːrən] *v/t and v/refl (no -ge-, h)* qualify

Qualität [kvali'tɛːt] *f (-; -en)* quality

qualitativ [kvalita'tiːf] *adj and adv* in quality

Quali'täts... *in cpds* ...**arbeit,** ...**waren** *etc*: high-quality ...

Qualm [kvalm] *m (-[e]s; no pl)* (thick) smoke; **qualmen** ['kvalmən] *v/i (ge-,*

h) smoke; F be a heavy smoker

'**qualvoll** *adj* very painful; agonizing

Quantität [kvanti'tɛːt] *f (-; -en)* quantity; **quantitativ** [kvantita'tiːf] *adj and adv* in quantity

Quantum ['kvantʊm] *n (-s; Quanten)* amount, *fig a.* share

Quarantäne [karan'tɛːnə] *f (-; -n)* (**unter ~ stellen** put in) quarantine

Quark [kvark] *m (-s; no pl)* curd, cottage cheese

Quartal [kvar'taːl] *n (-s; -e)* quarter (of a year)

Quartett [kvar'tɛt] *n (-[e]s; -e)* MUS quartet(te)

Quartier [kvar'tiːɐ] *n (-s; -e)* accommodation; *Swiss:* quarter

Quarz [kvaːɐts] *m (-es; -e)* MIN quartz

Quatsch [kvatʃ] F *m (-[e]s; no pl)* nonsense, rubbish, *sl* rot, crap, bullshit; **~ machen** fool around; joke, F kid

quatschen ['kvatʃən] F *v/i (ge-, h)* talk rubbish; chat

Quecksilber ['kvɛkzılbɐ] *n (-s; no pl)* mercury, quicksilver

Quelle ['kvɛlə] *f (-; -n)* spring, source (*a.*

fig), well, *fig a.* origin; **'quellen** *v/i* (*irr*, *ge-*, *sein*) pour (**aus** from)

'Quellenangabe *f* reference

quengeln ['kvɛŋəln] F *v/i* (*ge-*, *h*) whine

quer [kveːɐ] *adv* across; crosswise; **kreuz und ~** all over the place; **kreuz und ~ durch Deutschland fahren** travel all over Germany; **Quere** ['kveːrə] *f*: F **j-m in die ~ kommen** get in s.o.'s way

Querfeld'einlauf *m* SPORT cross-country race

'Querlatte *f* SPORT crossbar

'Querschläger *m* MIL ricochet

'Querschnitt *m* cross-section (*a. fig*)

'querschnitt(s)gelähmt *adj* MED paraplegic

'Querstraße *f* intersecting road; **zweite ~ rechts** second turning on the right

Querulant [kveru'lant] *m* (*-en*; *-en*), **Queru'lantin** *f* (*-*; *-nen*) querulous person

quetschen ['kvɛtʃən] *v/t and v/refl* (*ge-*, *h*) squeeze; MED bruise (o.s.)

'Quetschung *f* (*-*; *-en*) MED bruise

quiek(s)en ['kviːk(s)ən] *v/i* (*ge-*, *h*) squeak, squeal

quietschen ['kviːtʃən] *v/i* (*ge-*, *h*) squeal; screech; squeak, creak

quitt [kvɪt] *adj*: **mit j-m ~ sein** be quits *or* even with s.o. (*a. fig*)

quittieren [kvɪ'tiːrən] *v/t* (*no -ge-*, *h*) ECON give a receipt for

'Quittung *f* (*-*; *-en*) receipt; *fig* answer

quoll [kvɔl] *pret of* **quellen**

Quote ['kvoːtə] *f* (*-*; *-n*) quota; share; rate

'Quotenregelung *f* quota system

Quotient [kvo'tsjɛnt] *m* (*-en*; *-en*) MATH quotient

R

Rabatt [ra'bat] *m* (*-[e]s*; *-e*) ECON discount, rebate

Rabe ['raːbə] *m* (*-n*; *-n*) ZO raven

rabiat [ra'bjaːt] *adj* rough, tough

Rache ['raxə] *f* (*-*; *no pl*) revenge; **aus ~ für** in revenge for

Rachen ['raxən] *m* (*-s*; *-*) ANAT throat

rächen ['rɛçən] *v/t* (*ge-*, *h*) avenge *s.th.*; revenge *s.o.*; **sich an j-m für et. ~** revenge o.s. *or* take revenge on s.o. for s.th.; **Rächer** ['rɛçɐ] *m* (*-s*; *-*) avenger

rachsüchtig ['raxzʏçtɪç] *adj* revengeful, vindictive

Rad [raːt] *n* (*-[e]s*; *Räder* ['rɛːdɐ]) wheel; bicycle, F bike; **~ fahren** cycle, ride a bicycle, F bike; **ein ~ schlagen** peacock: spread its tail; SPORT turn a (cart)wheel

Radar [ra'daːɐ] *m*, *n* (*-s*; *-e*) radar; **~falle** *f* MOT speed trap; **~kon,trolle** *f* MOT radar speed check; **~schirm** *m* radar screen; **~stati,on** *f* radar station

radeln ['raːdəln] F *v/i* (*ge-*, *sein*) bike

Rädelsführer ['rɛːdəlsfyːrɐ] *m* ringleader

Räderwerk ['rɛːdɐvɛrk] *n* TECH gearing

'Radfahrer *m* (*-s*; *-*), **'Radfahrerin** *f* (*-*; *-nen*) cyclist

radieren [ra'diːrən] *v/t* (*no -ge-*, *h*) erase, rub out; *art*: etch

Radiergummi [ra'diːɐgʊmi] *m* eraser, *Br a.* rubber

Ra'dierung *f* (*-*; *-en*) *art*: etching

Radieschen [ra'diːsçən] *n* (*-s*; *-*) BOT (red) radish

radikal [radi'kaːl] *adj*, **Radi'kale** *m*, *f* (*-n*; *-n*) radical; **Radikalismus** [radika-'lɪsmʊs] *m* (*-*; *no pl*) radicalism

Radio ['raːdjo] *n* (*-s*; *-s*) radio; **im ~** on the radio; **~ hören** listen to the radio

radioak'tiv [radjoak'tiːf] *adj* PHYS radioactive; **~er Niederschlag** fall-out

Radioaktivi'tät *f* (*-*; *no pl*) radioactivity

'Radiowecker *m* clock radio

Radius ['raːdjʊs] *m* (*-*; *Radien*) radius

'Rad|kappe *f* hubcap; **~rennbahn** *f* cycling track; **~rennen** *n* cycle race; **~sport** *m* cycling; **~sportler** *m* cyclist; **~weg** *m* cycle track *or* path, bikeway

raffen ['rafən] *v/t* (*ge-*, *h*) gather up; **an sich ~** grab

Raffinerie [rafinə'riː] *f* (*-*; *-n*) CHEM refinery

Raffinesse [rafi'nɛsə] *f* (*-*; *-n*) (*no pl*) shrewdness; refinement

raffiniert [rafi'niːɐt] *adj* refined (*a. fig*);

fig shrewd, clever

ragen ['ra:gən] *v/i* (*ge-*, *h*) tower (up), rise (high)

Rahe ['ra:ə] *f* (-; -*n*) MAR yard

Rahm [ra:m] *m* (-[*e*]*s*; *no pl*) cream

rahmen ['ra:mən] *v/t* (*ge-*, *h*) frame; PHOT mount; **'Rahmen** *m* (-*s*; -) frame; *fig* framework; setting; scope; *aus dem ~ fallen* be out of the ordinary

Rakete [ra'ke:tə] *f* (-; -*n*) rocket, MIL *a.* missile; *ferngelenkte ~* guided missile; *e-e ~ abfeuern* (*starten*) launch a rocket *or* missile

Ra'keten|antrieb *m* rocket propulsion; *mit ~* rocket-propelled; **~basis** *f* MIL rocket *or* missile base *or* site

rammen ['ramən] *v/t* (*ge-*, *h*) ram; MOT *etc* hit, collide with

Rampe ['rampə] *f* (-; -*n*) (loading) ramp

'Rampenlicht *n* (-[*e*]*s*; *no pl*) THEA footlights; *fig* limelight

Ramsch [ramʃ] F *m* (-*es*; *no pl*) junk

Rand [rant] *m* (-[*e*]*s*; *Ränder* ['rɛndɐ]) edge, border; brink (*a. fig*); rim; brim; margin; *am ~(e) des Ruins etc* on the brink of ruin *etc*

randalieren [randa'li:rən] *v/i* (*no -ge-*, *h*) kick up a racket; **Randalierer** [randa'li:rɐ] *m* (-*s*; -) rowdy, hooligan

'Rand|bemerkung *f* marginal note; *fig* comment; **~gruppe** *f* fringe group

'randlos *adj* rimless

'Randstreifen *m* MOT shoulder

rang [raŋ] *pret of* **ringen**

Rang *m* (-[*e*]*s*; *Ränge* ['rɛŋə]) position, rank (*a.* MIL); THEA balcony, *Br* circle; *pl* SPORT terraces

rangieren [raŋ'ʒi:rən] (*no -ge-*, *h*) **1.** *v/t* RAIL switch, *Br* shunt **2.** *fig v/i* rank (*vor j-m* before s.o.)

'Rangordnung *f* hierarchy

Ranke ['raŋkə] *f* (-; -*n*) BOT tendril

'ranken *v/refl* (*ge-*, *h*) BOT creep, climb

rann [ran] *pret of* **rinnen**

rannte ['rantə] *pret of* **rennen**

Ranzen ['rantsən] *m* (-*s*; -) knapsack; satchel

ranzig ['rantsɪç] *adj* rancid, rank

Rappe ['rapə] *m* (-*n*; -*n*) ZO black horse

rar [ra:r] *adj* rare, scarce

Rarität [rari'tɛ:t] *f* (-; -*en*) curiosity; (*no pl*) rarity

rasch [raʃ] *adj* quick, swift; prompt

rascheln ['raʃəln] *v/i* (*ge-*, *h*) rustle

rasen ['ra:zən] *v/i* (*ge-*, *sein*) F MOT race, tear, speed; (*ge-*, *h*) rage; *~ vor Begeisterung* roar with enthusiasm

'Rasen *m* (-*s*; -) lawn, grass

'rasend *adj* breakneck; raging; agonizing; splitting; thunderous

'Rasen|mäher *m* lawn mower; **~platz** *m* lawn; *tennis*: grass court

Raserei [ra:zə'rai] *f* (-; -*en*) (*no pl*) frenzied rage; frenzy, madness; F MOT reckless driving

Rasier|appa,rat [ra'zi:ɐapara:t] *m* (safety) razor; *esp elektrischer ~* shaver; **~creme** *f* shaving cream

rasieren [ra'zi:rən] *v/t and v/refl* (*no -ge-*, *h*) shave

Ra'sier|klinge *f* razor blade; **~messer** *n* (straight) razor; **~pinsel** *m* shaving brush; **~seife** *f* shaving soap; **~wasser** *n* aftershave (lotion)

Rasse ['rasə] *f* (-; -*n*) race; ZO breed

'Rassehund *m* ZO pedigree dog

Rassel ['rasəl] *f* (-; -*n*), **'rasseln** *v/i* (*ge-*, *h*) rattle

'Rassen... *in cpds* ...*diskriminierung*, ...*konflikt*, ...*probleme etc*: *mst* racial ...; **~trennung** *f* POL (racial) segregation; HIST apartheid; **~unruhen** *pl* race riots

rassig ['rasɪç] *adj* classy

rassisch ['rasɪʃ] *adj* racial

Rassismus [ra'sɪsmʊs] *m* (-; *no pl*) POL racism; **Ras'sist(in)** ᘙ(-*en*; -*en*/-; -*nen*), **ras'sistisch** *adj* POL racist

Rast [rast] *f* (-; -*en*) rest, stop; break; **rasten** ['rastən] *v/i* (*ge-*, *h*) rest, stop, take a break; **'rastlos** *adj* restless

'Rastplatz *m* resting place; MOT rest area, *Br* lay-by

'Raststätte *f* MOT service area

Rasur [ra'zu:r] *f* (-; -*en*) shave

Rat [ra:t] *m* (-[*e*]*s*; *Räte* ['rɛ:tə]) (*no pl*) (piece of) advice; council; *j-n um ~ fragen* ask s.o.'s advice; *j-s ~ befolgen* take s.o.'s advice

Rate ['ra:tə] *f* (-; -*n*) rate; ECON instal(l)-ment; *auf ~n* by instal(l)ments

raten ['ra:tən] *v/t and v/i* (*irr*, *ge-*, *h*) advise; guess; solve; *j-m zu et. ~* advise s.o. to do s.th.; *rate mal!* (have a) guess!

'Ratenzahlung *f* → *Abzahlung*

'Rateteam *n* TV *etc* panel

Ratgeber ['ra:tge:bɐ] *m* (-*s*; -),

'**Ratgeberin** f (-; -nen) adviser, counsel(l)or; m guide (**über** acc to)
'**Rathaus** n city (Br town) hall
ratifizieren [ratifi'tsiːrən] v/t (no -ge-, h) ratify
Ration [ra'tsjoːn] f (-; -en) ration
rational [ratsjo'naːl] adj rational
rationell [ratsjo'nɛl] adj efficient; economical
rationieren [ratsjo'niːrən] v/t (no -ge-, h) ration
'**ratlos** adj at a loss
'**ratsam** adj advisable, wise
'**Ratschlag** m piece of advice; **ein paar gute Ratschläge** some good advice
Rätsel ['rɛːtsəl] n (-s; -) puzzle; riddle (both a. fig); mystery
'**rätselhaft** adj puzzling; mysterious
Ratte ['ratə] f (-; -n) zo rat (a. contp)
rattern ['ratɐn] v/i (ge-, h, sein) rattle, clatter
rau [rau] adj rough, rugged (both a. fig); harsh; chapped; sore
Raub [raup] m (-[e]s; no pl) robbery; loot, booty; prey; **~bau** m (-[e]s; no pl) overexploitation (**an** dat of); **~ mit s-r Gesundheit treiben** ruin one's health
rauben ['raubən] v/t (ge-, h) rob, steal; kidnap; **j-m et. ~** rob s.o. of s.th. (a. fig)
Räuber ['rɔybɐ] m (-s; -) robber
'**Raub|fisch** m predatory fish; **~mord** m murder with robbery; **~mörder** m murderer and robber; **~tier** n beast of prey; **~überfall** m holdup, (armed) robbery; mugging; **~vogel** m bird of prey; **~zug** m raid
Rauch [raux] m (-[e]s; no pl) smoke; CHEM etc fume; **rauchen** ['rauxən] v/i and v/t (ge-, h) smoke; CHEM etc fume; **Rauchen verboten!** no smoking; **Pfeife ~** smoke a pipe; **Raucher(in)** ['rauxɐ, 'rauxərɪn] m(f) (-s; -/-; -nen) smoker (m a. RAIL)
Räucher... ['rɔyçɐ-] in cpds ...aal, ...speck etc: smoked ...
'**räuchern** v/t (ge-, h) smoke
'**Räucherstäbchen** n joss stick
'**Rauchfahne** f trail of smoke
rauchig ['rauxɪç] adj smoky
'**Rauch|waren** pl tobacco products; furs; **~zeichen** n smoke signal
Räude ['rɔydə] f (-; -n) VET mange
'**räudig** adj VET mangy

raufen ['raufən] (ge-, h) 1. v/t: **sich die Haare ~** tear one's hair 2. v/i fight, scuffle; **Rauferei** [raufə'rai] f (-; -en) fight, scuffle
Raum [raum] m (-[e]s; Räume ['rɔymə]) room; space; area; (outer) space; **~anzug** m spacesuit; **~deckung** f SPORT zone marking
räumen ['rɔymən] v/t (ge-, h) leave, move out of; check out of; clear (**von** of); evacuate (a. MIL); **s-e Sachen in ... (**acc**) ~** put one's things (away) in ...
'**Raum|fähre** f space shuttle; **~fahrer** F m spaceman; **~fahrt** f (-; no pl) space travel or flight; astronautics; **~fahrt...** in cpds ...technik, ...zentrum etc: space ...; **~flug** m space flight; **~inhalt** m volume; **~kapsel** f space capsule; **~la,bor** n space lab
räumlich ['rɔymlɪç] adj three-dimensional
'**Raum|schiff** n spacecraft; spaceship; **~sonde** f space probe; **~stati,on** f space station
'**Räumung** f (-; -en) clearance; evacuation (a. MIL); JUR eviction
'**Räumungsverkauf** m ECON clearance sale
raunen ['raunən] v/i (ge-, h) whisper, murmur
Raupe ['raupə] f (-; -n) ZO caterpillar; TECH a. track; '**Raupenschlepper** m MOT caterpillar® tractor
'**Raureif** m hoarfrost
raus [raus] F int get out (of here)!
Rausch [rauʃ] m (-es; Räusche ['rɔyʃə]) drunkenness, intoxication; F high; fig ecstasy; **e-n ~ haben** be drunk; **s-n ~ ausschlafen** sleep it off
rauschen ['rauʃən] v/i (ge-, h) water etc: rush; brook: murmur; storm: roar; (ge-, sein) sweep; **~d** adj thunderous (applause); **~es Fest** lavish celebration
'**Rauschgift** n drug(s), narcotic(s); **~dezer,nat** n narcotics or drugs squad; **~handel** m drug traffic(king); **~händler** m drug trafficker, F pusher
räuspern ['rɔyspɐn] v/refl (ge-, h) clear one's throat
Razzia ['ratsja] f (-; -ien) raid, roundup
Reagenzglas [rea'gɛntsglaːs] n CHEM test tube
reagieren [rea'giːrən] v/i (no -ge-, h) CHEM, MED react (**auf** acc to), fig a. re-

spond (to)); **Reaktion** [reak'tsjoːn] *f* (-; -en) CHEM, MED, PHYS, POL reaction (*auf acc* to), *fig a.* response (to)

Reaktor [re'aktoːɐ] *m* (-s; -en [reak-'toːrən]) PHYS (nuclear *or* atomic) reactor

real [re'aːl] *adj* real; concrete

realisieren [reali'ziːrən] *v/t* (*no -ge-, h*) realize

Realismus [rea'lɪsmʊs] *m* (-; *no pl*) realism; **rea'listisch** *adj* realistic

Realität [reali'tɛːt] *f* (-; *no pl*) reality

Re'alschule *f appr* (junior) highschool, *Br* secondary school

Rebe ['reːbə] *f* (-; -n) BOT vine

Rebell [re'bɛl] *m* (-en; -en) rebel

rebellieren [rebɛ'liːrən] *v/i* (*no -ge-, h*) rebel, revolt, rise (*all:* **gegen** against)

Re'bellin *f* (-; -nen) rebel

re'bellisch *adj* rebellious

Rebhuhn ['reːphuːn] *n* ZO partridge

'**Rebstock** *m* BOT vine

Rechen ['rɛçən] *m* (-s; -), '**rechen** *v/t* (*ge-, h*) rake

'**Rechen|aufgabe** *f* MATH (arithmetical) problem; **~fehler** *m* MATH arithmetical error, miscalculation; **~ma,schine** *f* calculator; computer

'**Rechenschaft** *f*: **~ ablegen über** (*acc*) account for; **zur ~ ziehen** call to account (**wegen** for)

'**Rechen|schieber** *m* MATH slide rule; **~werk** *n* IT arithmetic unit; **~zentrum** *n* computer center (*Br* centre)

rechnen ['rɛçnən] *v/i and v/t* (*ge-, h*) calculate, reckon; work out, do sums; count; **~ mit** *fig* expect; count on; **mit mir kannst du nicht ~!** count me out!

'**Rechnen** *n* (-s; *no pl*) arithmetic

Rechner ['rɛçnɐ] *m* (-s; -) calculator; computer

rechnerisch ['rɛçnərɪʃ] *adj* arithmetical

'**Rechnung** *f* (-; -en) MATH calculation; problem, sum; ECON invoice, bill, check; **die ~, bitte!** can I have the check, please?; **das geht auf m-e ~** that's on me

recht [rɛçt] **1.** *adj* right; correct; POL right-wing; **auf der ~en Seite** on the right(-hand side); **mir ist es ~** I don't mind **2.** *adv* right(ly), correctly; rather, quite; **ich weiß nicht ~** I don't really know; **es geschieht ihm ~** it serves

him right; **erst ~** all the more; **erst ~ nicht** even less; **du kommst gerade ~ (zu)** you're just in time (for); **j-m ~ geben** agree with s.o.; **~ haben** be right

Recht *n* (-[e]s; -e) right, claim (*both: auf acc* to); (*no pl*) JUR law; justice; **gleiches ~** equal rights; **~ haben → recht**; **j-m ~ geben → recht**; **im ~ sein** be in the right; **er hat es mit (vollem) ~ getan** he was (perfectly) right to do so; **ein ~ auf et. haben** be entitled to s.th.

'**Rechteck** *n* (-[e]s; -e) rectangle

'**rechteckig** *adj* rectangular

'**rechtfertigen** *v/t* (*ge-, h*) justify

'**Rechtfertigung** *f* (-; -en) justification

'**rechtlich** *adj* JUR legal

'**rechtlos** *adj* without rights; outcast

'**rechtmäßig** *adj* JUR lawful; legitimate; legal; '**Rechtmäßigkeit** *f* (-; *no pl*) JUR lawfulness, legitimacy

rechts [rɛçts] *adv* on the right(-hand side); **nach ~** to the right

Rechts... *in cpds* POL right-wing ...; **~anspruch** *m* legal claim (*auf acc* to); **~anwalt** *m*, **~anwältin** ['rɛçtsan-vɛltɪn] *f* (-; -nen) lawyer

Rechts'außen *m* (-; -) *soccer:* outside right

'**rechtschaffen** *adj* honest

'**Recht|schreibfehler** *m* spelling mistake; **~schreibung** *f* (-; *no pl*) spelling, orthography

'**rechtsextre,mistisch** *adj* POL extreme right

'**Rechtsfall** *m* JUR (law) case

Rechtshänder ['rɛçtshɛndɐ] *m* (-s; -), '**Rechtshänderin** *f* (-; -nen) right-handed person; **sie ist Rechtshänderin** she is right-handed

'**Rechtsprechung** *f* (-; *no pl*) jurisdiction

'**rechtsradi,kal** *adj* POL extreme right-wing

'**Rechtsschutz** *m* legal protection; legal costs insurance

'**rechtswidrig** *adj* JUR illegal, unlawful

'**rechtwink(e)lig** *adj* rectangular

'**rechtzeitig 1.** *adj* punctual **2.** *adv* in time (**zu** for)

Reck [rɛk] *n* (-[e]s; -e) horizontal bar

recken ['rɛkən] *v/t* (*ge-, h*) stretch; **sich ~** stretch o.s.

recyceln [ri'saikəln] *v/t* (*no -ge-, h*) recycle; **Recyclingpa,pier** [ri-

'saiklıŋpapi:ɐ] n recycled paper

Redakteur [redak'tøːɐ] m (-s; -e), **Redak'teurin** f (-; -nen) editor

Redaktion [redak'tsjoːn] f (-; -en) (no pl) editing; editorial staff, editors; editorial office or department

redaktionell [redaktsjoˈnɛl] adj editorial

Rede ['reːdə] f (-; -n) speech, address; talk (**von** of); **e-e ~ halten** make a speech; **direkte** (**indirekte**) **~** LING direct (reported or indirect) speech; **j-n zur ~ stellen** take s.o. to task; **nicht der ~ wert** not worth mentioning

'**redegewandt** adj eloquent

reden ['reːdən] v/i and v/t (ge-, h) talk, speak (both: **mit** to; **über** acc about, of); **ich möchte mit dir ~** I'd like to talk to you; **die Leute~** people talk; **j-n zum Reden bringen** make s.o. talk

'**Redensart** f saying, phrase

redlich ['reːtlıç] adj upright, honest; **sich ~(e) Mühe geben** do one's best

Redner ['reːdnɐ] m (-s; -), '**Rednerin** f (-; -nen) speaker

'**Rednerpult** n speaker's desk

redselig ['reːtzeːlıç] adj talkative

reduzieren [redu'tsiːrən] v/t (no -ge-, h) reduce (**auf** acc to)

Reeder ['reːdɐ] m (-s; -) shipowner

Reederei [reːdəˈrai] f (-; -en) shipping company

reell [reˈɛl] adj reasonable, fair (price); real (chance); solid (firm)

Referat [refeˈraːt] n (-[e]s; -e) paper; report; lecture; **ein ~ halten** read a paper

Referendar [referɛnˈdaːɐ] m (-s; -e), **Referen'darin** f (-; -nen) appr trainee teacher

Referent [refeˈrɛnt] m (-en; -en), **Refe'rentin** f (-; -nen) speaker; **Referenz** [refeˈrɛnts] f (-; -en) reference; **referieren** [refeˈriːrən] v/i (no -ge-, h) (give a) report or lecture (**über** acc on)

reflektieren [reflɛkˈtiːrən] v/t and v/i (no -ge-, h) reflect (fig **über** acc [up]on)

Reflex [reˈflɛks] m (-es; -e) reflex

reflexiv [reflɛˈksiːf] adj LING reflexive

Reform [reˈfɔrm] f (-; -en) reform

Reformator [refɔrˈmaːtoːɐ] m (-s; -en [reˈfɔrmɐ, reˈfɔrmərın] m(f) (-s; -/-; -nen) reformer

Re'formhaus n health food store (Br shop)

reformieren [refɔrˈmiːrən] v/t (no -ge-, h) reform

Refrain [rəˈfrɛ͂ː] m (-s; -s) refrain, chorus

Regal [reˈgaːl] n (-s; -e) shelf (unit), shelves·

rege ['reːgə] adj lively; busy; active

Regel ['reːgəl] f (-; -n) rule; MED period, menstruation; **in der ~** as a rule

'**regelmäßig** adj regular

'**regeln** ['reːgəln] v/t (ge-, h) regulate, TECH a. adjust; ECON settle

'**regelrecht** adj regular (a. F)

'**Regeltechnik** f control engineering

'**Regelung** f (-; -en) regulation; adjustment; ECON settlement; TECH control

'**regelwidrig** adj against the rule(s); SPORT unfair; **~es Spiel** foul play

regen ['reːgən] v/t and v/refl (ge-, h) move, stir

'**Regen** m (-s; -) rain; **starker ~** heavy rain(fall); **~bogen** m rainbow; **~bogenhaut** f ANAT iris; **~guss** m (heavy) shower, downpour; **~mantel** m raincoat; **~schauer** m shower; **~schirm** m umbrella; **~tag** m rainy day; **~tropfen** m raindrop; **~wald** m rain forest; **~wasser** n rainwater; **~wetter** n rainy weather; **~wurm** m ZO earthworm; **~zeit** f rainy season, the rains

Regie [reˈʒiː] f (-; no pl) THEA, film etc: direction; **unter der ~ von** directed by

Re'gieanweisung f stage direction

regieren [reˈgiːrən] (no -ge-, h) **1.** v/i reign **2.** v/t govern (a. LING), rule

Re'gierung f (-; -en) government, administration; reign

Re'gierungs|bezirk m administrative district; **~chef** m head of government; **~wechsel** m change of government

Regime [reˈʒiːm] n (-s; -) POL regime

Re'gimekritiker m POL dissident

Regiment [regiˈmɛnt] n (-[e]s; -er) (no pl) rule (a. fig); MIL regiment

Regisseur [reʒıˈsøːɐ] m (-s; -e), **Regis'seurin** f (-; -nen) THEA, film etc: director, THEA Br a. producer

Register [reˈgıstɐ] n (-s; -) register (a. MUS), record; index; **registrieren** [regısˈtriːrən] v/t (no -ge-, h) register, record; fig note; **Registrierkasse** [regısˈtriːɐkasə] f cash register

Reglement [regləˈmaː] n (-s; -s) regulation, order, rule

Regler ['reːɡlɐ] *m* (-*s*; -) TECH control

regnen ['reːɡnən] *v/i* (ge-, *h*) rain (*a. fig*); **es regnet in Strömen** it's pouring with rain; '**regnerisch** *adj* rainy

regulär [reguˈlɛːɐ] *adj* regular; normal

regulierbar [reguˈliːɐbaːɐ] *adj* adjustable; controllable

regulieren [reguˈliːrən] *v/t* (*no -ge-*, *h*) regulate, adjust; control

'**Regung** *f* (-; -en) movement, motion; emotion; impulse

'**regungslos** *adj* motionless

Reh [reː] *n* (-[*e*]*s*; -*e*) ZO deer, roe; doe; GASTR venison

rehabilitieren [rehabiliˈtiːrən] *v/t* (*no -ge-*, *h*) rehabilitate

'**Reh|bock** *m* ZO (roe)buck; **~keule** *f* GASTR leg of venison; **~kitz** *n* ZO fawn

Reibe ['raibə] *f* (-; -*n*), **Reibeisen** ['raipʔaizən] *n* (-*s*; -) grater, rasp

reiben ['raibən] *v/i and v/t* (*irr*, ge-, *h*) rub; grate, grind; **sich die Augen** (*Hände*) **~** rub one's eyes (hands)

'**Reibung** *f* (-; -en) TECH *etc* friction

'**reibungslos** *adj* TECH *etc* frictionless; *fig* smooth

reich [raiç] *adj* rich (**an** *dat* in), wealthy; abundant

Reich *n* (-[*e*]*s*; -*e*) empire, kingdom (*a.* REL, BOT, ZO); *fig* world

reichen ['raiçən] (ge-, *h*) **1.** *v/t* reach; hand, pass; give, hold out (*one's hand*); **2.** *v/i* last, do; **~ bis** reach *or* come up to; **das reicht** that will do; F **mir reicht's!** I've had enough

'**reichhaltig** *adj* rich

'**reichlich 1.** *adj* rich, plentiful; plenty of **2.** *adv* rather; generously

'**Reichtum** *m* (-*s*; *no pl*) wealth (**an** *dat* of) (*a. fig*)

'**Reichweite** *f* reach; AVIAT, MIL *etc* range; **in** (**außer**) (*j-s*) **~** within (out of) (s.o.'s) reach

reif [raif] *adj* ripe, *esp fig* mature

Reif *m* (-[*e*]*s*; *no pl*) white frost, hoar-frost

Reife ['raifə] *f* (-; *no pl*) ripeness, *esp fig* maturity; '**reifen** *v/i* (ge-, *sein*) ripen, mature (*both a. fig*)

Reifen ['raifən] *m* (-*s*; -) hoop; MOT *etc* tire, *Br* tyre; **~panne** *f* MOT flat tire (*Br* tyre), puncture, F flat

'**Reifeprüfung** *f* → **Abitur**

'**reiflich** *adj* careful

Reihe ['raiə] *f* (-; -*n*) line, row; number; series; **der ~ nach** in turn; **ich bin an der ~** it's my turn

'**Reihenfolge** *f* order

'**Reihenhaus** *n* row (*Br* terraced) house

'**reihenweise** *adv* in rows; F *fig* by the dozen

Reiher ['raiɐ] *m* (-*s*; -) ZO heron

Reim [raim] *m* (-[*e*]*s*; -*e*) rhyme

reimen ['raimən] *v/t and v/refl* (ge-, *h*) rhyme (**auf** *acc* with)

rein [rain] *adj* pure (*a. fig*); clean; *fig* clear (*conscience*); plain (*truth*); mere, sheer, nothing but

'**Reinfall** F *m* flop; let-down

'**Reingewinn** *m* ECON net profit

'**reinhauen** F *v/i* (*sep, -ge-*, *h*) tuck in

'**Reinheit** *f* (-; *no pl*) purity (*a. fig*); cleanness

reinigen ['rainɪɡən] *v/t* (ge-, *h*) clean; cleanse (*a.* MED); dry-clean; *fig* purify

'**Reinigung** *f* (-; -en) clean(s)ing; *fig* purification; (dry) cleaners; **chemische ~** dry cleaning; dry cleaner's

'**Reinigungsmittel** *n* cleaning agent, cleaner, detergent

'**reinlich** *adj* clean; cleanly

'**reinrassig** *adj* ZO purebred, pedigree; thoroughbred

'**Reinschrift** *f* fair copy

Reis [rais] *m* (-*es*; -*e*) BOT rice

Reise ['raizə] *f* (-; -*n*) trip; journey; tour; MAR voyage; **auf ~n sein** be travel(l)ing; **e-e ~ machen** take a trip; **gute ~!** have a nice trip!; **~andenken** *n* souvenir; **~bü,ro** *n* travel agency *or* bureau; **~führer** *m* guide(book); **~gesellschaft** *f* tourist party; tour operator; **~kosten** *pl* travel(l)ing expenses; **~krankheit** *f* travel sickness; **~leiter(in)** tour guide *or* manager, *Br* courier

'**reisen** *v/i* (ge-, *sein*) travel; **durch Frankreich ~** tour France; **ins Ausland ~** go abroad; '**Reisende** *m*, *f* (-*n*; -*n*) travel(l)er; tourist; passenger

'**Reise|pass** *m* passport; **~scheck** *m* travel(l)er's check (*Br* cheque); **~tasche** *f* travel(l)ing bag, holdall

Reisig ['raiziç] *n* (-*s*; *no pl*) brushwood

'**Reißbrett** ['raisbrɛt] *n* drawing board

reißen ['raisən] (*irr*, ge-) **1.** *v/t* (*h*) tear (**in Stücke** to pieces), rip; pull, drag; ZO kill; F crack (*jokes*); SPORT knock down;

an sich ~ seize, snatch, grab **2.** *v/i (sein)* break, burst; *sich um et. ~* scramble for (*or* to get) s.th.; **~d** *adj* torrential

Reißer ['raisɐ] F *m (-s; -)* thriller; hit

reißerisch ['raisərɪʃ] *adj* sensational, loud

'Reiß|verschluss *m* zipper; *den ~ an et. öffnen (schließen)* unzip (zip up) s.th.; **~zwecke** *f* thumbtack, *Br* drawing pin

reiten ['raitən] *(irr, ge-)* **1.** *v/i (sein)* ride, go on horseback **2.** *v/t (h)* ride

'Reiten *n (-s; no pl)* horseback riding

Reiter ['raitɐ] *m (-s; -)* rider, horseman

Reiterin ['raitərɪn] *f (-; -nen)* rider, horsewoman

'Reitpferd *n* saddle *or* riding horse

Reiz [raits] *m (-es; -e)* charm, attraction, appeal; thrill; MED, PSYCH stimulus; *(für j-n) den ~ verlieren* lose one's appeal (for s.o.); **'reizbar** *adj* irritable, excitable; **reizen** ['raitsən] *(ge-, h)* **1.** *v/t* irritate (*a.* MED), annoy; ZO bait; provoke; appeal to, attract; tempt; challenge **2.** *v/i cards:* bid; **'reizend** *adj* charming, delightful; lovely, sweet, cute; **'reizlos** *adj* unattractive

'Reizung *f (-; -en)* irritation (*a.* MED)

'reizvoll *adj* attractive; challenging

'Reizwort *n (-[e]s; -wörter)* emotive word

rekeln ['reːkəln] F *v/refl (ge-, h)* loll

Reklamation [reklamaˈtsjoːn] *f (-; -en)* complaint

Reklame [reˈklaːmə] *f (-; -n)* advertising, publicity; advertisement, F ad; *~ machen für* advertise, promote

reklamieren [reklaˈmiːrən] *v/i (no -ge-, h)* complain (*wegen* about), protest (against)

Rekord [reˈkɔrt] *m (-[e]s; -e)* record; *e-n ~ aufstellen* set *or* establish a record

Rekrut [reˈkruːt] *m (-en; -en)* MIL recruit

rekrutieren [rekruˈtiːrən] *v/t (no -ge-, h)* recruit

Rektor ['rɛktoːɐ] *m (-s; -en* [rɛkˈtoːrən]) principal, *Br* headmaster; UNIV president, *Br* rector; **Rektorin** [rɛkˈtoːrɪn] *f (-; -nen)* principal, *Br* headmistress; UNIV president, *Br* rector

relativ [relaˈtiːf] *adj* relative

Relief [reˈljɛf] *n (-s; -s)* relief

Religion [reliˈgjoːn] *f (-; -en)* religion

religiös [reliˈgjøːs] *adj* religious

Reling ['reːlɪŋ] *f (-; -s)* MAR rail

Reliquie [reˈliːkvjə] *f (-; -n)* relic

Rempelei [rɛmpəˈlai] F *f (-; -en)*, **rempeln** ['rɛmpəln] F *v/t (ge-, h)* jostle

Rennbahn ['rɛnbaːn] *f* racecourse, racetrack; cycling track

'Rennboot *n* racing boat; speedboat

rennen ['rɛnən] *v/i and v/t (irr, ge-, sein)* run; **Rennen** *n (-s; -)* race (*a. fig*); heat

'Renn|fahrer *m*, **~fahrerin** *f* racing driver; racing cyclist; **~läufer** *m* ski racer; **~pferd** *n* racehorse, racer; **~rad** *n* racing bicycle, racer; **~sport** *m* racing; **~stall** *m* racing stable; **~wagen** *m* race (*Br* racing) car, racer

renommiert [renoˈmiːɐt] *adj* renowned

renovieren [renoˈviːrən] *v/t (no -ge-, h)* renovate, F do up; redecorate

rentabel [rɛnˈtaːbəl] *adj* ECON profitable, paying

Rente ['rɛntə] *f (-; -n)* (old age) pension; *in ~ gehen* retire

'Renten|alter *n* retirement age; **~versicherung** *f* pension scheme

Rentier ['rɛntiːɐ] *n (-s; -e)* ZO reindeer

rentieren [rɛnˈtiːrən] *v/refl (no -ge-, h)* ECON pay; *fig* be worth it

Rentner ['rɛntnɐ] *m (-s; -)*, **'Rentnerin** ['rɛntnərɪn] *f (-; -nen)* (old age) pensioner

Reparatur [reparaˈtuːɐ] *f (-; -en)* repair; **~werkstatt** *f* repair shop; MOT garage

reparieren [repaˈriːrən] *v/t (no -ge-, h)* repair, mend, F fix

Reportage [repɔrˈtaːʒə] *f (-; -n)* report

Reporter [reˈpɔrtɐ] *m (-s; -)*, **Re-'porterin** *f (-; -nen)* reporter

Repräsentant [reprɛzɛnˈtant] *m (-en; -en)* representative; **Repräsentantenhaus** *n* PARL House of Representatives; **Repräsen'tantin** *f (-;-nen)* representative; **repräsentieren** [reprɛzɛnˈtiːrən] *v/t (no -ge-, h)* represent

Repressalie [reprɛˈsaːljə] *f (-; -n)* reprisal

Reproduktion [reprodukˈtsjoːn] *f (-; -en)* reproduction, print

reproduzieren [reproduˈtsiːrən] *v/t (no -ge-, h)* reproduce

Reptil [rɛpˈtiːl] *n (-s; -ien)* ZO reptile

Republik [repuˈbliːk] *f (-; -en)* republic

Republikaner [republiˈkaːnɐ] *m (-s; -)*, **Republi'kanerin** *f (-; -nen)*, **republi-'kanisch** *adj* POL republican

Reservat [rezɛrˈvaːt] *n (-[e]s; -e)* (p)reserve; reservation

Reserve [re'zɛrvə] *f* (-; -*n*) réserve (*a.* MIL); **~...** *in cpds* ...kanister, ...rad *etc*: spare ...

reservieren [rezɛr'viːrən] *v/t* (*no* -ge-, *h*) reserve (*a.* ~ *lassen*); *j-m e-n Platz* ~ keep *or* save a seat for s.o.; **reserviert** [rezɛr'viːrt] *adj* reserved (*a. fig*); aloof; **Reser'viertheit** *f* (-; *no pl*) aloofness

Residenz [rezi'dɛnts] *f* (-; -*en*) residence

Resignation [rezɪgna'tsjoːn] *f* (-; *no pl*) resignation; **resignieren** [rezɪ'gniːrən] *v/i* (*no* -ge-, *h*) give up; **resigniert** [rezɪ'gniːrt] *adj* resigned

Resoziali'sierung *f* (-; -*en*) rehabilitation

Respekt [re'spɛkt] *m* (-[*e*]*s*; *no pl*) respect (*vor dat* for); **respektieren** [respɛk'tiːrən] *v/t* (*no* -ge-, *h*) respect; **re'spektlos** *adj* irreverent, disrespectful; **re'spektvoll** *adj* respectful

Ressort [re'soːr] *n* (-*s*; -*s*) department, province

Rest [rɛst] *m* (-[*e*]*s*; -*e*) rest; *pl* remains, remnants; GASTR leftovers; F *das gab ihm den* ~ that finished him (off)

Restaurant [rɛsto'raː ̃] *n* (-*s*; -*s*) restaurant

restaurieren [rɛsto'riːrən] *v/t* (*no* -ge-, *h*) restore

'Restbetrag *m* remainder

'restlich *adj* remaining

'restlos *adv* completely

Resultat [rezʊl'taːt] *n* (-[*e*]*s*; -*e*) result (*a.* SPORT), outcome

Retorte [re'tɔrtə] *f* (-; -*n*) CHEM retort

Re'tortenbaby F *n* test-tube baby

retten ['rɛtən] *v/t* (ge-, *h*) save, rescue (*both*: *aus dat*, *vor dat* from)

Retter ['rɛtɐ] *m* (-*s*; -), **'Retterin** *f* (-; -*nen*) rescuer

Rettich ['rɛtɪç] *m* (-*s*; -*e*) BOT radish

'Rettung *f* (-; -*en*) rescue (*aus dat*, *vor dat* from); *das war s-e* ~ that saved him

'Rettungs|boot *n* lifeboat; **~mannschaft** *f* rescue party; **~ring** *m* life belt, life buoy; **~schwimmer** *m* lifeguard

Reue ['rɔyə] *f* (-; *no pl*) remorse, repentance (*both*: *über acc* for)

reumütig ['rɔymyːtɪç] *adj* repentant

Revanche [re'vaːʃ(ə)] *f* (-; -*n*) revenge

revanchieren [reva-'ʃiːrən] *v/refl* (*no* -ge-, *h*) have one's revenge (*bei*, *an dat* on); make it up (*bei j-m* to s.o.)

Revers [re'veːr] *n*, *m* (-; -) lapel

revidieren [revi'diːrən] *v/t* (*no* -ge-, *h*) revise; ECON audit

Revier [re'viːr] *n* (-*s*; -*e*) district; ZO territory (*a. fig*); → *Polizeirevier*

Revision [revi'zjoːn] *f* (-; -*en*) revision; ECON audit; JUR appeal

Revolte [re'vɔltə] *f* (-; -*n*), **revoltieren** [revɔl'tiːrən] *v/i* (*no* -ge-, *h*) revolt

Revolution [revolu'tsjoːn] *f* (-; -*en*) revolution; **revolutionär** [revolutsjo-'nɛːr] *adj*, **Revolutio'när(in)** (-*s*; -*e*/-; -*nen*) revolutionary

Revolver [re'vɔlvɐ] *m* (-*s*; -) revolver, F gun

Revue [re'vyː] *f* (-; -*n*) THEA (musical) show

Rezept [re'tsɛpt] *n* (-[*e*]*s*; -*e*) MED prescription; GASTR recipe (*a. fig*)

Rezession [retsɛ'sjoːn] *f* (-; -*en*) ECON recession

Rhabarber [ra'barbɐ] *m* (-*s*; *no pl*) BOT rhubarb

rhetorisch [re'toːrɪʃ] *adj* rhetorical

Rheuma ['rɔyma] *n* (-*s*; *no pl*) MED rheumatism

rhythmisch ['rʏtmɪʃ] *adj* rhythmic(al)

Rhythmus ['rʏtmʊs] *m* (-; -*men*) rhythm

Ribisel ['riːbiːzəl] *Austrian f* (-; -[*n*]) → *Johannisbeere*

richten ['rɪçtən] *v/t* (ge-, *h*) fix; get *s.th.* ready, prepare; do (*room, one's hair*); (*sich*) ~ *an* (*acc*) address (o.s.) to; put *a question* to; ~ *auf* (*acc*) direct *or* turn to; point *or* aim *camera, gun etc* at; ~ *gegen* direct against; *sich* ~ *nach* go by, act according to; follow (*fashion etc*); depend on; *ich richte mich ganz nach dir* I leave it to you

Richter(in) ['rɪçtɐ, 'rɪçtərɪn] *m(f)* (-*s*; -/-; -*nen*) judge

'richterlich *adj* judicial

'Richtgeschwindigkeit *f* MOT recommended speed

richtig ['rɪçtɪç] **1.** *adj* right; correct, proper; true; real **2.** *adv*: ~ *nett* (*böse*) really nice (angry); *et.* ~ *machen* do s.th. right; *m-e Uhr geht* ~ my watch is right

'Richtigkeit *f* (-; *no pl*) correctness

richtigstellen *v/t* (*sep*, -ge-, *h*) *fig* put *or* set right

'Richt|linien *pl* guidelines; **~preis** *m*

ECON recommended price
'**Richtung** *f* (-; -en) direction; POL leaning; PAINT *etc* style; '**richtungslos** *adj* aimless, disorient(at)ed
'**richtungweisend** *adj* pioneering
rieb [riːp] *pret of* **reiben**
riechen ['riːçən] *v/i and v/t* (irr, ge-, h) smell (**nach** of; **an** *dat* at)
rief [riːf] *pret of* **rufen**
Riegel ['riːɡəl] *m* (-s; -) bolt, bar
Riemen ['riːmən] *m* (-s; -) strap; TECH belt; MAR oar
Riese ['riːzə] *m* (-n; -n) giant (*a. fig*)
rieseln ['riːzəln] *v/i* (ge-, sein) trickle; *rain:* drizzle; *snow:* fall gently
Riesen... *in cpds mst* giant ..., gigantic ..., enormous ...; **~erfolg** *m* huge success, *film etc:* a. smash hit
'**riesengroß**, '**riesenhaft** → **riesig**
'**Riesenrad** *n* Ferris wheel
riesig ['riːzɪç] *adj* enormous, gigantic, giant
'**Riesin** *f* (-; -nen) giantess (*a. fig*)
riet [riːt] *pret of* **raten**
Riff [rɪf] *n* (-[e]s; -e) GEOGR reef
Rille ['rɪlə] *f* (-; -n) groove
Rind [rɪnt] *n* (-[e]s; -er ['rɪndɐ]) ZO cow, *pl* cattle; GASTR beef
Rinde ['rɪndə] *f* (-; -n) BOT bark; GASTR rind; crust
Rinder|braten ['rɪndɐbraːtən] *m* roast beef; **~herde** *f* herd of cattle
'**Rind|fleisch** *n* GASTR beef; **~(s)leder** *n* cowhide; **~vieh** *n* ZO cattle
Ring [rɪŋ] *m* (-[e]s; -e) ring (*a. fig*); MOT ring road; *subway etc:* circle (line)
'**Ringbuch** *n* loose-leaf *or* ring binder
ringeln ['rɪŋəln] *v/refl* (ge-, h) curl, coil (*a.* ZO)
'**Ringelnatter** *f* ZO grass snake
'**Ringelspiel** *Austrian n* → **Karussell**
ringen ['rɪŋən] (irr, ge-, h) **1.** *v/i* SPORT wrestle (**mit** with), *fig a.* struggle (against, with; **um** for); **nach Atem ~** gasp (for breath) **2.** *v/t* wring
'**Ringen** *n* (-s; *no pl*) SPORT wrestling
Ringer ['rɪŋɐ] *m* (-s; -) SPORT wrestler
ringförmig ['rɪŋfœrmɪç] *adj* circular
'**Ringkampf** *m* SPORT wrestling match
'**Ringrichter** *m* SPORT referee
rings *adv:* **~ um** around
'**ringshe'rum**, '**rings'um**, '**ringsum'her** *adv* all around; everywhere
Rinne ['rɪnə] *f* (-; -n) groove, channel; gutter; '**rinnen** *v/i* (irr, ge-, sein) run; flow, stream; **Rinnsal** ['rɪnzaːl] *n* (-s; -e) trickle
'**Rinnstein** *m* gutter
Rippe ['rɪpə] *f* (-; -n) ANAT rib
'**Rippenfell** *n* ANAT pleura; **~entzündung** *f* MED pleurisy
'**Rippenstoß** *m* nudge in the ribs
Risiko ['riːziko] *n* (-s; -s, -ken) risk; **ein** (**kein**) **~ eingehen** take a risk (no risks); **auf eigenes ~** at one's own risk
riskant [rɪsˈkant] *adj* risky
riskieren [rɪsˈkiːrən] *v/t* (no -ge-, h) risk
riss [rɪs] *pret of* **reißen**
Riss *m* (-es; -e) tear, rip, split (*a. fig*); crack; MED chap, laceration; **rissig** ['rɪsɪç] *adj* chapped; cracky, cracked
Rist [rɪst] *m* (-es; -e) ANAT instep
ritt [rɪt] *pret of* **reiten**
Ritt *m* (-[e]s; -e) ride (on horseback)
Ritter ['rɪtɐ] *m* (-s; -) knight; **j-n zum ~ schlagen** knight s.o.
'**ritterlich** *fig adj* chivalrous
Ritz [rɪts] *m* (-es; -e), **Ritze** ['rɪtsə] *f* (-; -n) crack, chink; gap
Rivale [riˈvaːlə] *m* (-n; -n), **Ri'valin** *f* (-; -nen) rival; **rivalisieren** [rivaliˈziːrən] *v/i* (no -ge-, h) compete; **Rivalität** [rivaliˈtɛːt] *f* (-; -en) rivalry
rk., r.-k. *abbr of* **römisch-katholisch** RC, Roman Catholic
Robbe ['rɔbə] *f* (-; -n) ZO seal
Robe ['roːbə] *f* (-; -n) robe, gown
Roboter ['roːbɔtɐ] *m* (-s; -) robot
robust [roˈbust] *adj* robust, strong, tough
roch [rɔx] *pret of* **riechen**
röcheln ['rœçəln] (ge-, h) **1.** *v/i* moan **2.** *v/t* gasp
Rock [rɔk] *m* (-[e]s; Röcke ['rœkə]) skirt
Rodelbahn ['roːdəlbaːn] *f* toboggan run
rodeln ['roːdəln] *v/i* (ge-, sein) sled(ge), coast; SPORT toboggan
'**Rodelschlitten** *m* sled(ge); toboggan
roden ['roːdən] *v/t* (ge-, h) clear; stub
Rogen ['roːɡən] *m* (-s; -) (hard) roe
Roggen ['rɔɡən] *m* (-s; -) BOT rye
roh [roː] *adj* raw; rough; *fig* brutal; **mit ~er Gewalt** with brute force
'**Rohbau** *m* (-[e]s; -ten) carcass
'**Rohkost** *f* raw vegetables and fruit
'**Rohling** *m* (-s; -e) TECH blank; *fig* brute
'**Rohmateri‚al** *n* raw material

'**Rohöl** n crude (oil)

Rohr [roːɐ] n (-[e]s; -e ['roːrə]) TECH pipe, tube; duct; BOT reed; cane

Röhre ['røːrə] f (-; -n) pipe, tube (a. TV), TV etc valve

'**Rohr|leitung** f duct, pipe(s); plumbing; pipeline; **~stock** m cane; **~zucker** m cane sugar

'**Rohstoff** m raw material

Rollbahn ['rɔlbaːn] f AVIAT runway

Rolle ['rɔlə] f (-; -n) roll (a. SPORT), TECH a. roller; coil; caster, castor; THEA part, role (both a. fig); **e-e ~ Garn** a spool of thread, Br a reel of cotton; **das spielt keine ~** that doesn't matter, that makes no difference; **Geld spielt k-e ~** money is no object

'**rollen** v/i (ge-, sein) and v/t (ge-, h) roll

Roller ['rɔlɐ] m (-s; -) (motor) scooter

'**Roll|film** m PHOT roll film; **~kragen** m turtleneck, esp Br polo neck; **~laden** m rolling shutter

Rollo ['rɔlo] n (-s; -s) shades, Br (roller) blind

'**Rollschuh** m roller skate; **~ laufen** roller-skate; **~bahn** f roller-skating rink; **~läufer** m roller skater

'**Rollstuhl** m wheelchair

'**Rolltreppe** f escalator

Roman [ro'maːn] m (-s; -e) novel

Romanik [ro'maːnɪk] f (-; no pl) ARCH Romanesque (style or period)

romanisch [ro'maːnɪʃ] adj LING Romance; ARCH Romanesque

Romanist [roma'nɪst] m (-en; -en), **Roma'nistin** f (-; -nen) student of Romance languages

Ro'manschriftsteller m, **Ro'manschriftstellerin** f novelist

Romantik [ro'mantɪk] f (-; no pl) romance; HIST Romanticism

romantisch [ro'mantɪʃ] adj romantic

Römer ['røːmɐ] m (-s; -), '**Römerin** f (-; -nen), **römisch** ['røːmɪʃ] adj Roman

Rommee ['rɔme] n (-s; -s) rummy

röntgen ['rœntgən] v/t (ge-, h) MED X-ray

'**Röntgen|appa,rat** m MED X-ray apparatus; **~aufnahme** f, **~bild** n MED X-ray; **~strahlen** pl PHYS X-rays; **~untersuchung** f MED X-ray

rosa ['roːza] adj pink; fig rose-colo(u)red; **Rose** ['roːzə] f (-; -n) BOT rose

'**Rosenkohl** m BOT Brussels sprouts

'**Rosenkranz** m REL rosary

rosig ['roːzɪç] adj rosy (a. fig)

Rosine [ro'ziːnə] f (-; -n) raisin

'**Rosshaar** n (-[e]s; no pl) horsehair

Rost [rɔst] m (-[e]s; -e) (no pl) CHEM rust; TECH grate; GASTR grid(iron), grill; **rosten** ['rɔstən] v/i (ge-, sein) rust

rösten ['rœstən] v/t (ge-, h) roast (a. F); toast; fry

'**Rostfleck** m rust stain; '**rostfrei** adj rustproof, stainless; '**rostig** adj rusty

rot [roːt] adj red (a. POL); **~ glühend** red-hot; **~ werden** blush; **in den ~en Zahlen** ECON in the red

Rot n (-s; -) red; **die Ampel steht auf ~** the lights are red; **bei ~** at red

'**rotblond** adj sandy(-haired)

Röte ['røːtə] f (-; no pl) redness, red (colo[u]r); fig blush

Röteln ['røːtəln] pl MED German measles

röten ['røːtən] v/refl (ge-, h) redden; flush

'**rothaarig** adj red-haired

'**Rothaarige** m, f (-n; -n) redhead

rotieren [ro'tiːrən] v/i (no -ge-, h) rotate

Rotkehlchen n (-s; -) zo robin

'**Rotkohl** m BOT red cabbage

rötlich ['røːtlɪç] adj reddish

'**Rot|stift** m red crayon or pencil; **~wein** m red wine; **~wild** n zo (red) deer

Rotznase ['rɔtsnaːzə] F f snotty nose

Route ['ruːtə] f (-; -n) route

Routine [ru'tiːnə] f (-; no pl) routine; experience; **~sache** f routine (matter)

routiniert [ruti'niːɐt] adj experienced

Rübe ['ryːbə] f (-; -n) BOT turnip; (sugar) beet

Rubin [ru'biːn] m (-s; -e) MIN ruby

Rübli ['ryːpli] Swiss n (-s; -) BOT carrot

Rubrik [ru'briːk] f (-; -en) heading; column

Ruck [rʊk] m (-[e]s; -e) jerk, jolt, start; fig POL swing

Rückantwortschein ['rʏkantvɔrtʃain] m reply coupon

'**ruckartig** adj jerky, abrupt

'**rückbezüglich** adj LING reflexive

'**Rückblende** f flashback (auf acc to)

'**Rückblick** m review (auf acc of); **im ~** in retrospect

rücken ['rʏkən] **1.** v/t (ge-, h) move, shift, push **2.** v/i (ge-, sein) move; move over; **näher ~** approach

'**Rücken** *m* (*-s; -*) ANAT back (*a. fig*); **~de-ckung** *fig f* backing, support; **~lehne** *f* back(rest); **~mark** *n* ANAT spinal cord; **~schmerzen** *pl* backache; **~schwimmen** *n* backstroke; **~wind** *m* following wind, tailwind; **~wirbel** *m* ANAT dorsal vertebra

'**Rück|erstattung** *f* (*-; -en*) refund; **~fahrkarte** *f* round-trip ticket, *Br a.* return (ticket); **~fahrt** *f* return trip; *auf der ~* on the way back; **~fall** *m* relapse

'**rückfällig** *adj*: **~ werden** relapse

'**Rückflug** *m* return flight

'**Rückgabe** *f* (*-; no pl*) return

'**Rückgang** *m* drop, fall; ECON recession

'**rückgängig** *adj*: **~ machen** cancel

'**Rück|gewinnung** *f* (*-; no pl*) recovery; **~grat** *n* ANAT spine, backbone (*both a. fig*); **~halt** *m* (*-[e]s; no pl*) support; **~hand** *f*, **~handschlag** *m* tennis: backhand; **~kauf** *m* ECON repurchase

'**Rückkehr** ['rʏkkeːɐ] *f* (*-; no pl*) return; *nach s-r ~ aus ...* on his return from ...

'**Rück|kopplung** *f* ELECTR feedback (*a. fig*); **~lage** *f* (*-; -n*) reserve(s); savings; **~lauf** *m* TECH rewind

'**rückläufig** *adj* falling, downward

'**Rücklicht** *n* (*-[e]s; -er*) MOT rear light, taillight

'**rücklings** ['rʏklɪŋs] *adv* backward(s); from behind

'**Rückporto** *n* return postage

'**Rückreise** *f* → *Rückfahrt*

'**Rucksack** ['rʊkzak] *m* rucksack, backpack; **~tou,rismus** *m* backpacking; **~tou,rist** *m* backpacker

'**Rück|schlag** *m* SPORT return; *fig* setback; **~schluss** *m* conclusion; **~schritt** *m fig* step back(ward); **~seite** *f* back; reverse; flip side; **~sendung** *f* return

'**Rücksicht** *f* (*-; -en*) consideration, regard; *aus (ohne) ~ auf (acc)* out of (without any) consideration *or* regard for; *~ nehmen auf (acc)* show consideration for; '**rücksichtslos** *adj* inconsiderate (*gegen* of), thoughtless (of); ruthless; reckless; '**rücksichtsvoll** *adj* considerate (*gegen* of), thoughtful

'**Rück|sitz** *m* MOT back seat; **~spiegel** *m* MOT rear-view mirror; **~spiel** *n* SPORT return match; **~stand** *m* CHEM residue; *mit der Arbeit (e-m Tor) im ~ sein* be behind with one's work (down by one goal)

'**rückständig** *adj* backward; underdeveloped; **~e Miete** arrears of rent

'**Rück|stau** *m* MOT tailback; **~stelltaste** *f* backspace key; **~tritt** *m* resignation; withdrawal; TECH → **~trittbremse** *f* coaster (*Br* back-pedal) brake

rückwärts ['rʏkverts] *adv* backward(s); *~ aus (dat) ... fahren* back out of ...; *~ in (acc) ... fahren* back into ...

'**Rückwärtsgang** *m* MOT reverse (gear)

'**Rückweg** *m* way back

'**ruckweise** *adv* jerkily, in jerks

'**rückwirkend** *adj* retroactive

'**Rück|wirkung** *f* reaction (*auf acc* upon); **~zahlung** *f* repayment; **~zieher** *m* (*-s; -*) soccer: overhead kick; F *e-n ~ machen* back (*or* chicken) out (*von* of); **~zug** *m* retreat

Rüde ['ryːdə] *m* (*-n; -n*) ZO male (dog ect)

Rudel ['ruːdəl] *n* (*-s; -*) ZO pack; herd

Ruder ['ruːdɐ] *n* (*-s; -*) AVIAT, MAR rudder; SPORT oar; *am ~* at the helm (*a. fig*); **~boot** *n* rowing boat, rowboat

Ruderer ['ruːdərɐ] *m* (*-s; -*) rower, oarsman; '**Ruderin** *f* (*-; -nen*) rower, oarswoman; '**rudern** *v/i* and *v/t* (*ge-, h*) row

'**Ruder|re,gatta** *f* (rowing) regatta, boat race; **~sport** *m* rowing

Ruf [ruːf] *m* (*-[e]s; -e*) call (*a. fig*); cry, shout; *fig* reputation; **rufen** *v/i* and *v/t* (*irr, ge-, h*) call (*a. doctor etc*); cry, shout; *~ nach* call for (*a. fig*); *~ lassen* send for; *um Hilfe ~* call *or* cry for help

'**Rufnummer** *f* telephone number

'**Rufweite** *f*: *in (außer) ~* within (out of) call(ing distance)

Rüge ['ryːgə] *f* (*-; -n*) reproof, reproach (*both: wegen* for); '**rügen** *v/t* (*ge-, h*) reprove, reproach

Ruhe ['ruːə] *f* (*-; no pl*) quiet, calm; silence; rest; peace; calm(ness); *zur ~ kommen* come to rest; *j-n in ~ lassen* leave s.o. in peace; *lass mich in ~!* leave me alone!; *et. in ~ tun* take one's time (doing s.th.); *die ~ behalten* F keep (one's) cool, play it cool; *sich zur ~ setzen* retire; *~, bitte!* (be) quiet, please!; '**ruhelos** *adj* restless

'**ruhen** *v/i* (*ge-, h*) rest (*auf dat* on)

'**Ruhe|pause** *f* break; **~stand** *m* (*-[e]s; no pl*) retirement; **~tag** *m* a day's rest; *Montag ~* closed on Mondays

ruhig ['ruːɪç] *adj* quiet; silent; calm;

cool; TECH smooth; **~ bleiben** F keep (one's) cool, play it cool

Ruhm [ru:m] *m* (-[e]*s*; *no pl*) fame, *esp* POL, MIL *etc* glory; **rühmen** ['ry:mən] *v/t* (*ge-*, *h*) praise (**wegen** for); **sich e-r Sache ~** boast of s.th.; **rühmlich** ['ry:mlıç] *adj* laudable, praiseworthy

'ruhmlos *adj* inglorious

'ruhmreich *adj* glorious

Ruhr [ru:ɐ] *f* (-; *no pl*) MED dysentery

Rühreier ['ry:ɐ²aiɐ] *pl* scrambled eggs

rühren ['ry:rən] *v/t* (*ge-*, *h*) stir; move (*a. fig*); *fig* touch, affect; **das rührt mich gar nicht** that leaves me cold; **rührt euch!** MIL (stand) at ease!; **~d** *fig adj* touching, moving; very kind

rührig ['ry:rıç] *adj* active, busy

rührselig ['ry:ɐze:lıç] *adj* sentimental

'Rührung *f* (-; *no pl*) emotion

Ruin [ru'i:n] *m* (-*s*; *no pl*) ruin

Ruine [ru'i:nə] *f* (-; *-n*) ruin

ruinieren [rui'ni:rən] *v/t* (*no -ge-*, *h*) ruin

rülpsen ['rylpsən] *v/i* (*ge-*, *h*), **Rülpser** ['rylpsɐ] *m* (-*s*; -) belch

Rumäne [ru'mɛ:nə] *m* (-*n*; -*n*) Romanian; **Rumänien** Romania; **Ru'mänin** *f* (-; *-nen*), **ru'mänisch** *adj* Romanian

Rummel ['ruməl] F *m* (-*s*; *no pl*) (hustle and) bustle; F ballyhoo; **~platz** F *m* amusement park, fairground

rumoren [ru'mo:rən] *v/i* (*no -ge-*, *h*) rumble

Rumpelkammer ['rumpəlkamɐ] F *f* lumber room

rumpeln ['rumpəln] F *v/i* (*ge-*, *h*, *sein*) rumble

Rumpf [rumpf] *m* (-*es*; *Rümpfe* ['rympfə]) ANAT trunk; MAR hull; AVIAT fuselage

rümpfen ['rympfən] *v/t* (*ge-*, *h*) **die Nase ~** turn up one's nose (**über** *acc* at), sneer (at)

rund [runt] **1.** *adj* round (*a. fig*) **2.** *adv* about; **~ um** (a)round; **'Rundblick** *m* panorama; **Runde** ['rundə] *f* (-; *-n*) round (*a. fig and* SPORT); *racing*: lap; **s-e ~ machen** in (*dat*) patrol; **die ~ machen** go the round(s)

'Rundfahrt *f* tour (**durch** round)

'Rundfunk *m* (-*s*; *no pl*) radio; broad-

casting corporation; **im ~** on the radio; **im ~ übertragen** *or* **senden** broadcast; **~hörer(in)** listener, *pl a.* (radio) audience; **~sender** *m* broadcasting *or* radio station

'Rundgang *m* tour (**durch** of)

'rundhe'raus *adv* frankly, plainly

'rundhe'rum *adv* all around

'rundlich *adj* plump, chubby

'Rund|reise *f* tour (**durch** of); **~schau** *f* review; **~schreiben** *n* circular (letter); **~spruch** *Swiss m* → **Rundfunk**

'Rundung *f* (-; *-en*) curve

rundweg [runt'vɛk] *adv* flatly, plainly

runter ['runtɐ] F *adv* → **herunter**

Runzel ['runtsəl] *f* (-; *-n*) wrinkle

runz(e)lig ['runts(ə)lıç] *adj* wrinkled

'runzeln *v/t* (*ge-*, *h*) **die Stirn ~** frown (**über** *acc* at)

Rüpel ['ry:pəl] *m* (-*s*; -) lout

rupfen ['rupfən] *v/t* (*ge-*, *h*) pluck

Rüsche ['ry:ʃə] *f* (-; *-n*) frill, ruffle

Ruß [ru:s] *m* (-*es*; *no pl*) soot

Russe ['rusə] *m* (-*n*; *-n*) Russian

Rüssel ['rysəl] *m* (-*s*; -) ZO trunk; snout

rußen ['ru:sən] *v/i* (*ge-*, *h*) smoke

rußig ['ru:sıç] *adj* sooty

Russin ['rusın] *f* (-; *-nen*), **russisch** ['rusıʃ] *adj* Russian

'Russland Russia

rüsten ['rystən] (*ge-*, *h*) **1.** *v/i* MIL arm **2.** *v/refl* get ready, prepare (**zu**, **für** for); arm o.s. (**gegen** for)

rüstig ['rystıç] *adj* vigorous, sprightly

rustikal [rusti'ka:l] *adj* rustic

'Rüstung *f* (-; *-en*) MIL armament; armo(u)r

'Rüstungs|indus,trie *f* armament industry; **~wettlauf** *m* arms race

'Rüstzeug *n* equipment

Rute ['ru:tə] *f* (-; *-n*) rod (*a. fig*), switch

Rutschbahn ['rutʃba:n] *f*, **Rutsche** ['rutʃə] *f* (-; *-n*) slide, chute; **'rutschen** *v/i* (*ge-*, *sein*) slide, slip; glide; MOT *etc* skid; **rutschig** ['rutʃıç] *adj* slippery

'rutschsicher *adj* MOT *etc* non-skid

rütteln ['rytəln] (*ge-*, *h*) **1.** *v/t* shake **2.** *v/i* jolt; **an der Tür ~** rattle at the door

S

S *abbr of* **Süd(en)** S, south

S. *abbr of* **Seite** p., page

s. *abbr of* **siehe** see

Saal [zaːl] *m* (-[e]*s*; **Säle** ['zɛːlə]) hall

Saat [zaːt] *f* (-; -*en*) (*no pl*) sowing; seed(s) (*a. fig*); crop(s)

Sabbat ['zabat] *m* (-*s*; -*e*) sabbath (day)

sabbern ['zabɐn] F *v/i* (*ge-, h*) slobber, slaver

Säbel ['zɛːbəl] *m* (-*s*; -) saber, *Br* sabre (*a.* SPORT), sword; **'säbeln** F *v/t* (*ge-, h*) cut, hack

Sabotage [zabo'taːʒə] *f* (-; -*n*) sabotage; **Saboteur** [zabo'tøːɐ] *m* (-*s*; -*e*) saboteur; **sabotieren** [zabo'tiːrən] *v/t* (*no -ge-, h*) sabotage

Sach|bearbeiter ['zaxbəʔarbaitɐ] *m*, **~bearbeiterin** ['zaxbəʔarbaitərɪn] *f* official in charge; **~beschädigung** *f* damage to property; **~buch** *n* specialized book, *pl coll* nonfiction

'sachdienlich *adj*: **~e Hinweise** relevant information

Sache ['zaxə] *f* (-; -*n*) thing; matter, business; issue, problem, question; cause; JUR matter, case; *pl* things, clothes; **zur ~ kommen** (**bei der ~ bleiben**) come (keep) to the point; **nicht zur ~ gehören** be irrelevant

'sachgerecht *adj* proper

'Sachkenntnis *f* expert knowledge

'sachkundig *adj* expert

'sachlich *adj* matter-of-fact, business-like; unbias(s)ed, objective; practical, technical; **~ richtig** factually correct

sächlich ['zɛçlɪç] *adj* LING neuter

'Sach re,gister *n* (subject) index

'Sachschaden *m* damage to property

sacht [zaxt] *adj* soft, gentle; slow

'Sach|verhalt *m* (-[e]*s*; -*e*) facts (of the case); **~verstand** *m* know-how; **~verständige** *m, f* (-*n*; -*n*) expert; JUR expert witness; **~wert** *m* (-[e]*s*; *no pl*) real value; **~zwänge** *pl* inherent necessities

Sack [zak] *m* (-[e]*s*; **Säcke** ['zɛkə]) sack, bag; V balls; **sacken** F *v/i* (*ge-, sein*) sink; **'Sackgasse** *f* blind alley (*a. fig*), dead end (*a. fig*), *fig* impasse

Sadismus [za'dɪsmʊs] *m* (-; *no pl*) sadism; **Sadist** [za'dɪst] *m* (-*en*; -*en*) sad-

ist; **sa'distisch** *adj* sadistic

säen ['zɛːən] *v/t and v/i* (*ge-, h*) sow (*a. fig*)

Safari [za'faːri] *f* (-; -*s*) safari; **~park** *m* wildlife reserve, safari park

Saft [zaft] *m* (-[e]*s*; **Säfte** ['zɛftə]) juice; BOT sap (*both a. fig*); **saftig** ['zaftɪç] *adj* juicy (*a. fig*); lush; F fancy (*prices etc*)

Sage ['zaːgə] *f* (-; -*n*) legend, myth

Säge ['zɛːgə] *f* (-; -*n*) saw

'Sägemehl *n* sawdust

sagen ['zaːgən] *v/i and v/t* (*ge-, h*) say; **j-m et. ~** tell s.o. s.th.; **die Wahrheit ~** tell the truth; **er lässt dir ~** he asked me to tell you; **~ wir ...** (let's) say ...; **man sagt, er sei reich** he is said to be rich; **er lässt sich nichts ~** he will not listen to reason; **das hat nichts zu ~** it doesn't matter; **et. (nichts) zu ~ haben** (**bei**) have a say (no say) (in); **das sagt mir nichts** it doesn't mean anything to me; **unter uns gesagt** between you and me

sägen ['zɛːgən] *v/t and v/i* (*ge-, h*) saw

'sagenhaft *adj* legendary; F fabulous, incredible, fantastic

'Sägespäne *pl* sawdust

'Sägewerk *n* sawmill

sah [zaː] *pret of* **sehen**

Sahne ['zaːnə] *f* (-; *no pl*) cream

Saison [zɛ'zɔ̃ː] *f* (-; -*s*) season; **in der ~** in season

sai'sonbedingt *adj* seasonal

Saite ['zaitə] *f* (-; -*n*) MUS string, chord (*a. fig*); **'Saiteninstru,ment** *n* MUS string(ed) instrument

Sakko ['zako] *m, n* (-*s*; -*s*) (sports) jacket, sport(s) coat

Sakristei [zakrɪs'tai] *f* (-; -*en*) REL vestry, sacristy

Salat [za'laːt] *m* (-[e]*s*; -*e*) BOT lettuce; GASTR salad; **~sauce** *f* salad dressing

Salbe ['zalbə] *f* (-; -*n*) ointment

'Salbung *f* (-; -*en*) unction

'salbungsvoll *adj* unctuous

Saldo ['zaldo] *m* (-*s*; -*s*, -*di*) ECON balance

Salon [za'lɔ̃ː] *m* (-*s*; -*s*) salon; MAR saloon; drawing room

salopp [za'lɔp] *adj* casual; *contp* sloppy

Salpeter [zal'pe:tɐ] *m* (-*s*; *no pl*) CHEM salt|peter (*Br* -petre), niter, *Br* nitre
Salto ['zalto] *m* (-*s*; -*s*, -*ti*) somersault
Salut [za'lu:t] *m* (-[*e*]*s*; -*e*) MIL salute; ~ **schießen** fire a salute
salutieren [zalu'ti:rən] *v/i* (*no -ge-, h*) MIL (give a) salute
Salve ['zalvə] *f* (-; -*n*) MIL volley (*a. fig*); salute
Salz [zalts] *n* (-*es*; -*e*) salt
'Salzbergwerk *n* salt mine
salzen ['zaltsən] *v/t* ([*irr*,] *ge-, h*) salt
salzfrei ['zaltsfrai] *adj* salt-free, no-salt *diet*
salzig ['zaltsɪç] *adj* salty
'Salz|kar,toffeln *pl* boiled potatoes; **~säure** *f* (-; *no pl*) CHEM hydrochloric acid; **~stange** *f* pretzel (*Br* salt) stick; **~streuer** *m* (-*s*; -) salt shaker, *Br* salt cellar; **~wasser** *n* salt water
Same ['za:mə] *m* (-*n*; -*n*), **'Samen** *m* (-*s* -) BOT seed (*a. fig*); BIOL sperm, semen
'Samen|bank *f* (-; -*en*) MED, VET sperm bank; **~erguss** *m* ejaculation; **~korn** *n* BOT seedcorn
Sammel... ['zaməl-] *in cpds* ...*begriff*, ...*bestellung*, ...*konto etc*: collective ...; **~büchse** *f* collecting box
'sammeln *v/t* (*ge-, h*) collect; gather; pick; accumulate; **sich ~** assemble; *fig* compose o.s.
Sammler ['zamlɐ] *m* (-*s*; -), **'Sammlerin** *f* (-; -*nen*) collector
'Sammlung *f* (-; -*en*) collection
Samstag ['zamsta:k] *m* (-[*e*]*s*; -*e*) Saturday
samt [zamt] *prp* (*dat*) together *or* along with
Samt *m* (-[*e*]*s*; -*e*) velvet
sämtlich ['zɛmtlɪç] *adj*: **~e** *pl* all the; the complete *works etc*
Sanatorium [zana'to:rjʊm] *n* (-*s*; -*ien*) sanatorium, sanitarium
Sand [zant] *m* (-[*e*]*s*; -*e*) sand
Sandale [zan'da:lə] *f* (-; -*n*) sandal
Sandalette [zanda'lɛtə] *f* (-; -*n*) high--heeled sandal
'Sand|bahn *f* SPORT dirt track; **~bank** *f* (-; -*bänke*) sandbank; **~boden** *m* sandy soil; **~burg** *f* sandcastle
sandig ['zandɪç] *adj* sandy
'Sand|mann *m*, **~männchen** *n* sandman; **~pa,pier** *n* sandpaper; **~sack** *m* sand bag; **~stein** *m* sandstone; **~strand**

m sandy beach
sandte ['zantə] *pret of* **senden**
'Sanduhr *f* hourglass
sanft [zanft] *adj* gentle, soft; mild; easy (*death*)
sanftmütig ['zanftmy:tɪç] *adj* gentle, mild
sang [zaŋ] *pret of* **singen**
Sänger ['zɛŋɐ] *m* (-*s*; -), **Sängerin** ['zɛŋərɪn] *f* (-; -*nen*) singer
sanieren [za'ni:rən] *v/t* (*no -ge-, h*) redevelop (*a*. ECON), rehabilitate (*a*. ARCH)
Sa'nierung *f* (-; -*en*) redevelopment, rehabilitation; **Sa'nierungsgebiet** *n* redevelopment area
sanität [zani'tɛ:ɐ] *adj* sanitary
Sanitäter [zani'tɛ:tɐ] *m* (-*s*; -) paramedic; MIL medic, *Br* medical orderly
sank [zaŋk] *pret of* **sinken**
Sankt [zaŋkt] Saint, ABBR St
Sardelle [zar'dɛlə] *f* (-; -*n*) ZO anchovy
Sardine [zar'di:nə] *f* (-; -*n*) ZO sardine
Sarg [zark] *m* (-[*e*]*s*; *Särge* ['zɛrgə]) casket, *esp Br* coffin
Sarkasmus [zar'kasmʊs] *m* (-; *no pl*) sarcasm; **sar'kastisch** *adj* sarcastic
saß [za:s] *pret of* **sitzen**
Satan ['za:tan] *m* (-*s*; -*e*) Satan; *fig* devil
Satellit [zatɛ'li:t] *m* (-*en*; -*en*) satellite (*a. fig*); **über ~** by *or* via satellite
Satel'liten... *in cpds* ...*bild*, ...*staat*, ...*stadt*, ...-*TV*: satellite ...
Satin [za'tɛ̃:] *m* (-*s*; -*s*) satin; sateen
Satire [za'ti:rə] *f* (-; -*n*) satire (**auf** *acc* upon); **Satiriker** [za'ti:rikɐ] *m* (-*s*; -) satirist; **sa'tirisch** *adj* satiric(al)
satt [zat] *adj* F full (up); **ich bin ~** I've had enough, F I'm full (up); **sich ~ essen** eat one's fill (**an** *dat* of)
Sattel ['zatəl] *m* (-*s*; *Sättel* ['zɛtəl]) saddle; **'satteln** *v/t* (*ge-, h*) saddle; **'Sattelschlepper** *m* MOT semi-trailer truck, *Br* articulated lorry
'satthaben *v/t* (*irr*, **haben**, *sep*, -*ge-, h*) F be tired *or* F sick of, be fed up with
sättigen ['zɛtɪgən] (*ge-, h*) **1.** *v/t* satisfy; feed; CHEM, PHYS saturate **2.** *v/i* be substantial, be filling; **'Sättigung** *f* (-; -*en*) satiety; CHEM, ECON saturation (*a. fig*)
Sattler ['zatlɐ] *m* (-*s*; -) saddler
Sattlerei [zatlə'rai] *f* (-; -*en*) saddlery
Satz [zats] *m* (-*es*; *Sätze* ['zɛtsə]) leap; LING sentence; *tennis etc*: set; ECON rate; MUS movement; **~aussage** *f* LING

predicate; **~bau** *m* (-[e]*s*; *no pl*) LING
syntax; construction; **~gegenstand** *m*
LING subject
Satzung ['zatsʊŋ] *f* (-; -*en*) statute
'Satzzeichen *n* LING punctuation mark
Sau [zau] *f* (-; *Säue* ['zɔʏə]) ZO sow;
HUNT wild sow; F swine, pig
sauber ['zaubɐ] *adj* clean (*a.* F *fig*);
pure; neat (*a. fig*), tidy; decent; *iro* fine,
nice; **~ halten** keep clean (*sich* o.s.); **~**
machen clean (up); **'Sauberkeit** *f* (-;
no pl) clean(li)ness; tidiness, neatness;
purity; decency; **'saubermachen** *v/t*
and v/i (*sep*, -*ge*-, *h*) → **sauber**; **säu-**
bern ['zɔʏbɐn] *v/t* (*ge*-, *h*) clean (up);
cleanse (*a.* MED)
sauer ['zauɐ] *adj* sour (*a. fig*), acid (*a.*
CHEM); GASTR pickled; F mad (*auf acc*
at), cross (with); **~ werden** turn sour;
F get mad; **saurer Regen** acid rain
säuerlich ['zɔʏɐlɪç] *adj* sharp; F wry
'Sauerstoff *m* (-[e]*s*; *no pl*) CHEM oxygen; **~gerät** *n* MED oxygen apparatus;
~zelt *n* MED oxygen tent
'Sauerteig *m* leaven
saufen ['zaufən] *v/t and v/i* (*irr*, *ge*-, *h*)
ZO drink; F booze; **Säufer(in)** ['zɔʏfɐ,
'zɔʏfərɪn] *m(f)* F (-*s*; -/-; -*nen*) drunk-
ard, F boozer
saugen ['zaugən] *v/i and v/t* ([*irr*,] *ge*-,
h) suck (*an et.* [at] s.th.)
säugen ['zɔʏgən] *v/t* (*ge*-, *h*)· suckle (*a.*
ZO), nurse, breastfeed
'Säugetier *n* mammal
saugfähig ['zaukfɛːɪç] *adj* absorbent
Säugling ['zɔʏklɪŋ] *m* (-*s*; -*e*) baby, infant
'Säuglings|heim *n* (baby) nursery;
~pflege *f* infant care; **~schwester** *f* baby nurse; **~stati,on** *f* neonatal care
unit; **~sterblichkeit** *f* infant mortality
Säule ['zɔʏlə] *f* (-; -*n*) column; pillar (*a.*
fig); **'Säulengang** *m* colonnade
Saum [zaum] *m* (-[e]*s*; *Säume* ['zɔʏmə])
hem(line); seam; **säumen** ['zɔʏmən]
v/t (*ge*-, *h*) hem; border, edge; line
Sauna ['zauna] *f* (-; -*s*, *Saunen*) sauna
Säure ['zɔʏrə] *f* (-; -*n*) CHEM acid
säurehaltig ['zɔʏrəhaltɪç] *adj* acid
sausen ['zauzən] *v/i* (*ge*-, *sein*) F rush,
dash; (*ge*-, *h*) *ears*: buzz; *wind*: howl
'Saustall *m* pigsty (*a.* F *contp*)
Saxophon [zakso'foːn] *n* (-*s*; -*e*) MUS
saxophone, F sax

S-Bahn ['ɛsbaːn] *f* rapid transit, *Br* sub-
urban train
Schabe ['ʃaːbə] *f* (-; -*n*) ZO cockroach
'schaben *v/t* (*ge*-, *h*) scrape (*von* from)
schäbig ['ʃɛːbɪç] *adj* shabby, *fig a.*
mean
Schablone [ʃa'bloːnə] *f* (-; -*n*) stencil;
fig stereotype
Schach [ʃax] *n* (-*s*; *no pl*) chess; **~!**
check!; **~ und matt!** checkmate!; *j-n*
in ~ halten keep s.o. in check; **~brett**
n chessboard; **~feld** *n* square; **~fi,gur**
f chessman, piece
schach'matt *adj*: *j-n* **~ setzen** checkmate s.o.
'Schachspiel *n* (game of) chess; chessboard and men
Schacht [ʃaxt] *m* (-[e]*s*; *Schächte*
['ʃɛçtə]) shaft, *mining*: *a.* pit
Schachtel ['ʃaxtəl] *f* (-; -*n*) box; carton;
e-e **~ Zigaretten** a pack (*esp Br* packet)
of cigarettes
'Schachzug *m* move (*a. fig*)
schade ['ʃaːdə] *pred adj*: *es ist* **~** it's a
pity; *wie* **~!** what a pity *or* shame!; *zu*
~ sein für be too good for
Schädel ['ʃɛːdəl] *m* (-*s*; -) ANAT skull;
~bruch *m* MED fracture of the skull
schaden ['ʃaːdən] *v/i* (*ge*-, *h*) damage,
do damage to, harm, hurt; *der Ge-*
sundheit **~** be bad for one's health;
das schadet nichts it doesn't matter;
es könnte ihm nicht **~** it wouldn't hurt
him
'Schaden *m* (-*s*; *Schäden* ['ʃɛːdən])
damage (*an dat* to); *esp* TECH trouble,
defect (*a.* MED); *fig* disadvantage; ECON
loss; *j-m* **~ zufügen** do s.o. harm; **~er-**
satz *m* damages; **~ leisten** pay damages; **~freude** *f*: **~ empfinden über** (*acc*)
gloat over
'schadenfroh *adv* gloatingly
schadhaft ['ʃaːthaft] *adj* damaged; defective, faulty; leaking (*pipes*)
schädigen ['ʃɛːdɪgən] *v/t* (*ge*-, *h*) damage, harm
schädlich ['ʃɛːtlɪç] *adj* harmful, injuri-
ous; bad (for your health)
Schädling ['ʃɛːtlɪŋ] *m* (-*s*; -*e*) BIOL pest
'Schädlings|bekämpfung *f* pest con-
trol; **~bekämpfungsmittel** *n* pesticide
Schadstoff ['ʃaːtʃtɔf] *m* harmful substance; pollutant
'schadstoffarm *adj* MOT low-emission

Schaf [ʃaːf] n (-[e]s; -e) zo sheep

'Schafbock m zo ram

Schäfer ['ʃɛːfɐ] m (-s; -) shepherd; **~hund** m sheepdog; **Deutscher ~** German shepherd, esp Br Alsatian

'Schaffell n sheepskin; zo fleece

schaffen[1] ['ʃafən] v/t (irr, ge-, h) create

'schaffen[2] (ge-, h) **1.** v/t cause, bring about; manage, get s.th. done; take; **es ~** make it, a. succeed **2.** v/i work; **j-m zu ~ machen** cause s.o. trouble; **sich zu ~ machen an** (dat) tamper with

Schaffner ['ʃafnɐ] m (-s; -), **'Schaffnerin** f (-; -nen) conductor; Br RAIL guard

Schafott [ʃaˈfɔt] n (-[e]s; -e) scaffold

Schaft [ʃaft] m (-[e]s; Schäfte ['ʃɛftə]) shaft; stock; shank; leg

'Schafwolle f sheep's wool

'Schafzucht f sheep breeding

schäkern ['ʃɛːkɐn] v/i (ge-, h) joke; flirt

schal [ʃaːl] adj stale, flat, fig a. empty

Schal m (-s; -s) scarf

Schale ['ʃaːlə] f (-; -n) bowl, dish; GASTR shell; peel, skin; **schälen** ['ʃɛːlən] v/t (ge-, h) peel, pare; **sich ~ skin**: peel (off)

Schall [ʃal] m (-[e]s; -e) sound; **~dämpfer** m silencer (a. Br MOT), MOT muffler

'schalldicht adj soundproof

schallen ['ʃalən] v/i ([irr,] ge-, h) sound; ring (out); **~des Gelächter** roars of laughter

'Schall|geschwindigkeit f speed of sound; **~mauer** f sound barrier; **~platte** f record, disk, Br disc; **~welle** f PHYS sound wave

schalten ['ʃaltən] v/i and v/t (ge-, h) switch, turn; MOT shift (esp Br change) gear; F get it; react; **Schalter** ['ʃaltɐ] m (-s; -) counter; RAIL ticket window; AVIAT desk; ELECTR switch

'Schalt|hebel m MOT gear lever; TECH, AVIAT control lever; ELECTR switch lever; **~jahr** n leap year; **~tafel** f ELECTR switchboard, control panel; **~uhr** f time switch

'Schaltung f (-; -en) MOT gearshift; ELECTR circuit

Scham [ʃaːm] f (-; no pl) shame; **vor ~** with shame; **schämen** ['ʃɛːmən] v/refl (ge-, h) be or feel ashamed (gen, **wegen** of); **du solltest dich (was) ~!** you ought to be ashamed of yourself!

'Scham|gefühl n (-[e]s; no pl) sense of shame; **~haare** pl pubic hair

'schamhaft adj bashful

'schamlos adj shameless; indecent

Schande ['ʃandə] f (-; no pl) shame, disgrace; **schänden** ['ʃɛndən] v/t (ge-, h) disgrace; desecrate; rape

Schandfleck ['ʃantflɛk] m eyesore

schändlich ['ʃɛntlɪç] adj disgraceful

'Schandtat f atrocity

Schanze ['ʃantsə] f (-; -n) SPORT ski jump

Schar [ʃaːɐ] f (-; -en ['ʃaːrən]) troop, band; F horde; crowd; zo flock

'scharen v/refl (ge-, h) **sich ~ um** gather round

scharf [ʃarf] adj sharp (a. fig), PHOT a. in focus; clear; savage, fierce (dog); live (ammunition), armed (bomb etc); GASTR hot; F hot, sexy; F **~ sein auf** (acc) be keen on; **~ (ein)stellen** PHOT focus; F **~e Sachen** hard liquor

Schärfe ['ʃɛrfə] f (-; -n) sharpness (a. PHOT); fig severity, fierceness

'schärfen v/t (ge-, h) sharpen

'Scharf|richter m executioner; **~schütze** m sharpshooter; sniper

'scharfsichtig adj sharp-sighted; fig clear-sighted

'Scharfsinn m (-[e]s; no pl) acumen

'scharfsinnig adj sharp-witted, shrewd

'scharfstellen v/t (sep, -ge-, h) → **scharf**

Scharlach ['ʃarlax] m (-s; no pl) scarlet; MED scarlet fever

'scharlachrot adj scarlet

Scharlatan ['ʃarlatan] m (-s; -e) charlatan, fraud

Scharnier [ʃarˈniːɐ] n (-s; -e) TECH hinge

Schärpe ['ʃɛrpə] f (-; -n) sash

scharren ['ʃarən] v/i (ge-, h) scrape, scratch

schartig ['ʃartɪç] adj jagged, notchy

Schaschlik ['ʃaʃlɪk] m, n (-s; -s) GASTR shish kebab

Schatten ['ʃatən] m (-s; -) shadow (a. fig); shade; **im ~** in the shade

'schattenhaft adj shadowy

Schattierung [ʃaˈtiːrʊŋ] f (-; -en) shade; fig colo(u)r

schattig ['ʃatɪç] adj shady

Schatz [ʃats] m (-es; Schätze ['ʃɛtsə]) treasure; fig darling; **~amt** n POL Treasury Department, Br Treasury

schätzen ['ʃɛtsən] v/t (ge-, h) estimate,

value (*both*: **auf** *acc* at); appreciate; think highly of; F reckon, guess

'**Schatz|kammer** *f* treasury (*a. fig*); **~kanzler** *m* Chancellor of the Exchequer; **~meister(in)** treasurer

'**Schätzung** *f* (-; *-en*) estimate; valuation

Schau [ʃau] *f* (-; *-en*) show, exhibition; **zur ~ stellen** exhibit, display

Schauder ['ʃaudɐ] *m* (-*s*; -) shudder

'**schauderhaft** *adj* horrible, dreadful

'**schaudern** *v/i* (*ge-*, *h*) shudder, shiver (*both*: **vor** *dat* with)

schauen ['ʃauən] *v/i* (*ge-*, *h*) look (**auf** *acc* at)

Schauer ['ʃauɐ] *m* (-*s*; -) METEOR shower; shudder, shiver; **~geschichte** *f* horror story (*a. fig*)

'**schauerlich** *adj* dreadful, horrible

Schaufel ['ʃaufəl] *f* (-; *-n*) shovel; dustpan; '**schaufeln** *v/t* (*ge-*, *h*) shovel; dig

'**Schaufenster** *n* shop window; **~ausla·ge** *f* window display; **~bummel** *m*: **e-n ~ machen** go window-shopping; **~dekorati·on** *f* window dressing

Schaukel ['ʃaukəl] *f* (-; *-n*) swing

'**schaukeln** ['ʃaukəln] **1.** *v/i* swing; *boat etc*: rock **2.** *v/t* rock

'**Schaukel|pferd** *n* rocking horse; **~stuhl** *m* rocking chair, rocker

Schaulustige ['ʃaulustɪɡə] *pl* (curious) onlookers, F rubbernecks

Schaum [ʃaum] *m* (-[*e*]*s*; *Schäume* ['ʃɔymə]) foam; GASTR froth, head; lather; spray; **schäumen** ['ʃɔymən] *v/i* (*ge-*, *h*) foam (*a. fig*), froth; lather; spray

'**Schaumgummi** *m* foam rubber

schaumig ['ʃaumɪç] *adj* foamy, frothy

'**Schaumlöscher** *m* foam extinguisher

'**Schauplatz** *m* scene

'**Schaupro·zess** *m* JUR show trial

schaurig ['ʃaurɪç] *adj* creepy; horrible

'**Schauspiel** *n* THEA play; *fig* spectacle

'**Schauspieler(in)** actor (actress)

'**Schauspielschule** *f* drama school

Schausteller ['ʃauʃtɛlɐ] *m* (-*s*; -) showman

Scheck [ʃɛk] *m* (-*s*; -*s*) ECON check, *Br* cheque; **~heft** *n* checkbook, *Br* chequebook

scheckig ['ʃɛkɪç] *adj* spotty

'**Scheckkarte** *f* check cashing (*Br* cheque) card

scheffeln ['ʃɛfəln] F *v/t* (*ge-*, *h*) rake in

Scheibe ['ʃaibə] *f* (-; *-n*) disk, *Br* disc; slice; pane; target

'**Scheiben|bremse** *f* MOT disk (*Br* disc) brake; **~wischer** *m* MOT windshield (*Br* windscreen) wiper

Scheide ['ʃaidə] *f* (-; *-n*) sheath; scabbard; ANAT vagina; '**scheiden** (*irr*, *ge-*) **1.** *v/t* (*h*) separate, part (*both*: **von** from); divorce; **sich ~ lassen** get a divorce, **von j-m**: divorce s.o. **2.** *v/i* (*sein*) part; **~ aus** (*dat*) retire from

'**Scheideweg** *m* crossroads

'**Scheidung** *f* (-; *-en*) divorce

'**Scheidungsklage** *f* JUR divorce suit

Schein¹ [ʃain] *m* (-[*e*]*s*; -*e*) certificate; blank, *Br* form; bill, *Br* note

Schein² *m* (-[*e*]*s*; *no pl*) light; *fig* appearance; **et. (nur) zum ~ tun** (only) pretend to do s.th.

'**scheinbar** *adj* seeming, apparent

scheinen ['ʃainən] *v/i* (*irr*, *ge-*, *h*) shine; *fig* seem, appear, look

'**scheinheilig** *adj* hypocritical

'**Scheinwerfer** *m* searchlight; MOT headlight; THEA spotlight

Scheiß... [ʃais-] V *in cpds* damn ..., fucking ..., *esp Br* bloody ...

Scheiße ['ʃaisə] V *f* (-; *no pl*), '**scheißen** V *v/i* (*irr*, *ge-*, -*e*) shit, crap

Scheit [ʃait] *n* (-[*e*]*s*; -*e*) piece of wood

Scheitel ['ʃaitəl] *m* (-*s*; -) parting

'**scheiteln** *v/t* (*ge-*, *h*) part

Scheiterhaufen ['ʃaitɐhaufən] *m* pyre; HIST stake

scheitern ['ʃaitɐn] *v/i* (*ge-*, *sein*) fail, go wrong

Schelle ['ʃɛlə] *f* (-; *-n*) (little) bell; TECH clamp, clip

Schellfisch ['ʃɛlfɪʃ] *m* ZO haddock

Schelm [ʃɛlm] *m* (-[*e*]*s*; -*e*) rascal

schelmisch ['ʃɛlmɪʃ] *adj* impish

Schema ['ʃeːma] *n* (-*s*; -*s*, -*ta*) pattern, system; **schematisch** [ʃeˈmaːtɪʃ] *adj* schematic; mechanical

Schemel ['ʃeːməl] *m* (-*s*; -) stool

schemenhaft ['ʃeːmənhaft] *adj* shadowy

Schenkel ['ʃɛŋkəl] *m* (-*s*; -) ANAT thigh; shank; MATH leg

schenken ['ʃɛŋkən] *v/t* (*ge-*, *h*) give (as a present) (**zu** for)

'**Schenkung** *f* (-; *-en*) JUR donation

Scherbe ['ʃɛrbə] *f* (-; *-n*), '**Scherben** *m* (-*s*; -) (broken) piece, fragment

Schere

Schere ['ʃeːrə] f (-; -n) scissors; zo claw

scheren¹ ['ʃeːrən] v/t (irr, ge-, h) zo shear; bot clip; cut

'**scheren²** v/refl (ge-, h) **sich ~ um** bother about

Scherereien [ʃeːrə'raiən] pl trouble, bother

Schermaus ['ʃeːɐmaus] Austrian f zo mole

Scherz [ʃɛrts] m (-es; -e) joke; **im (zum)** ~ for fun; **scherzen** ['ʃɛrtsən] v/i (ge-, h) joke (**über** acc at); '**scherzhaft** adj joking; ~ **gemeint** meant as a joke

scheu [ʃɔy] adj shy (a. zo); bashful; ~ **machen** frighten; **Scheu** f (-; no pl) shyness; awe; **scheuen** ['ʃɔyən] (ge-, h) **1.** v/i shy (**vor** dat at), take fright (at) **2.** v/t shun, avoid; fear; **sich ~, et. zu tun** be afraid of doing s.th.

scheuern ['ʃɔyɐn] v/t and v/i (ge-, h) scrub, scour; chafe

'**Scheuertuch** n floor cloth

'**Scheuklappen** pl blinders, Br blinkers (both a. fig)

'**scheumachen** v/t (sep, -ge-, h) → **scheu**

Scheune ['ʃɔynə] f (-; -n) barn

Scheusal ['ʃɔyzaːl] n (-s; -e) monster (a. fig); fig beast

scheußlich ['ʃɔyslɪç] adj horrible (a. F), atrocious

Schicht [ʃɪçt] f (-; -en) layer; coat; film; econ shift; class; **schichten** ['ʃɪçtən] v/t (ge-, h) arrange in layers, pile up

'**schichtweise** adv in layers

schick [ʃɪk] adj smart, chic, stylish

schicken ['ʃɪkən] v/t (ge-, h) send (**nach, zu** to); **das schickt sich nicht** that isn't done

Schickeria [ʃɪkəˈriːa] F f (-; no pl) smart set, beautiful people, trendies

Schickimicki [ʃɪkiˈmɪki] F contp m (-s; -s) trendy

Schicksal ['ʃɪkzaːl] n (-s; -e) fate, destiny; lot

Schiebe|dach ['ʃiːbədax] n mot sliding roof, sunroof; ~**fenster** n sliding window; sash window

schieben ['ʃiːbən] v/t (irr, ge-, h) push

Schieber ['ʃiːbɐ] m (-s; -) tech slide; bolt; F profiteer

'**Schiebetür** f sliding door

'**Schiebung** F f (-; -en) swindle, fix (a. sport)

schied [ʃiːt] pret of **scheiden**

'**Schiedsrichter** ['ʃiːtsrɪçtɐ] m, '**Schiedsrichterin** f soccer: referee; tennis: umpire; judge, esp pl a. jury

schief [ʃiːf] adj crooked, not straight; sloping, oblique (a. math); leaning; fig false

Schiefer ['ʃiːfɐ] m (-s; -) geol slate

'**Schiefertafel** f slate

'**schiefgehen** v/i (irr, **gehen**, sep, -ge-, sein) F go wrong

schielen ['ʃiːlən] v/i (ge-, h) squint, be cross-eyed

schien [ʃiːn] pret of **scheinen**

Schienbein ['ʃiːnbain] n anat shin (-bone)

Schiene ['ʃiːnə] f (-; -n) tech etc rail; med splint

'**schienen** v/t (ge-, h) med splint

Schießbude ['ʃiːsbuːdə] f shooting gallery

schießen ['ʃiːsən] v/i and v/t (irr, ge-, h) shoot, fire (both: **auf** acc at); sport score; **Schießerei** [ʃiːsəˈrai] f (-; -en) shooting; gunfight

'**Schieß|pulver** n gunpowder; ~**scharte** f mil loophole, embrasure; ~**scheibe** f target; ~**stand** m shooting range

Schiff [ʃɪf] n (-[e]s; -e) mar ship, boat; arch nave; **mit dem** ~ by boat

Schiffahrt → **Schifffahrt**

'**schiffbar** adj navigable

'**Schiffbau** m (-[e]s; no pl) shipbuilding

'**Schiffbruch** m shipwreck (a. fig); ~ **erleiden** be shipwrecked

Schiffer ['ʃɪfɐ] m (-s; -) sailor; skipper

'**Schifffahrt** f (-; no pl) shipping, navigation

'**Schiffs|junge** m ship's boy; ~**ladung** f shipload; cargo; ~**schraube** f (ship's) propeller; ~**werft** f shipyard

Schikane [ʃiˈkaːnə] f (-; -n) a. pl harassment; **aus reiner** ~ out of sheer spite; F **mit allen ~n** with all the trimmings

schikanieren [ʃikaˈniːrən] v/t (no -ge-, h) harass; bully

Schild¹ [ʃɪlt] n (-[e]s; -er ['ʃɪldɐ]) sign, plate

Schild² m (-[e]s; -e) shield

'**Schilddrüse** f anat thyroid (gland)

schildern ['ʃɪldɐn] v/t (ge-, h) describe; depict, portray

Schilderung ['ʃɪldərʊŋ] f (-; -en) description, portrayal; account

'Schildkröte f zo tortoise; turtle

Schilf [ʃɪlf] n (-[e]s; no pl) BOT reed(s)

schillern ['ʃɪlɐn] v/i (ge-, h) be iridescent; **~d** adj iridescent; fig dubious

Schimmel ['ʃɪməl] m zo white horse; BOT mo(u)ld; **schimm(e)lig** ['ʃɪm(ə)lɪç] adj mo(u)ldy, musty; **'schimmeln** v/i (ge-, h, sein) (be) mo(u)ldy

Schimmer ['ʃɪmɐ] m (-s; -) glimmer (a. fig), gleam, fig a. trace, touch

'schimmern v/i (ge-, h) shimmer, glimmer, gleam

Schimpanse [ʃɪm'panzə] m (-n; -n) zo chimpanzee

schimpfen ['ʃɪmpfən] v/i and v/t (ge-, h) scold (mit j-m s.o.); F tell s.o. off, bawl s.o. out; **~ über** (acc) complain about

'Schimpfwort n swearword

Schindel ['ʃɪndəl] f (-; -n) shingle

schinden ['ʃɪndən] v/t (irr, ge-, h) maltreat; slave-drive; **sich ~** drudge, slave away; **Schinder** ['ʃɪndɐ] m (-s; -) slave driver; **Schinderei** [ʃɪndə'raɪ] f (-; -en) slavery, drudgery

Schinken ['ʃɪŋkən] m (-s; -) ham

Schippe ['ʃɪpə] f (-; -n), **'schippen** v/t (ge-, h) shovel

Schirm [ʃɪrm] m (-[e]s; -e) umbrella; sunshade; TV, IT etc: screen; shade; peak, visor; **~herr(in)** patron, sponsor; **~herrschaft** f patronage, sponsorship; **unter der ~ von** under the auspices of; **~mütze** f peaked cap; **~ständer** m umbrella stand

schiss [ʃɪs] pret of scheißen

Schlacht [ʃlaxt] f (-; -en) battle (bei of)

'schlachten v/t (ge-, h) slaughter, kill, butcher

Schlachter ['ʃlaxtɐ] m (-s; -) butcher

'Schlacht|feld n MIL battlefield, battleground; **~haus** n, **~hof** m slaughterhouse; **~plan** m MIL plan of action (a. fig); **~schiff** n MIL battleship

Schlacke ['ʃlakə] f (-; -n) cinders; GEOL, METALL slag

Schlaf [ʃlaːf] m (-[e]s; no pl) sleep; **e-n leichten (festen) ~ haben** be a light (sound) sleeper; F fig **im ~** blindfold

'Schlafanzug m pajamas, Br pyjamas

Schläfe ['ʃlɛːfə] f (-; -n) ANAT temple

schlafen ['ʃlaːfən] v/i (irr, ge-, h) sleep (a. fig); **~ gehen, sich ~ legen** go to bed; **fest ~** be fast asleep; **j-n ~ legen** put s.o. to bed or to sleep

schlaff [ʃlaf] adj slack (a. fig); flabby; limp

'Schlaf|gelegenheit f sleeping accommodation; **~krankheit** f MED sleeping sickness; **~lied** n lullaby

'schlaflos adj sleepless

'Schlaflosigkeit f (-; no pl) sleeplessness, MED insomnia

'Schlafmittel n MED sleeping pill(s)

'Schlafmütze fig f sleepyhead; slowpoke, Br slowcoach

schläfrig ['ʃlɛːfrɪç] adj sleepy, drowsy

'Schlaf|saal m dormitory; **~sack** m sleeping bag; **~ta,blette** f sleeping pill

'schlaftrunken adj (very) drowsy

'Schlaf|wagen m RAIL sleeping car, sleeper; **~wandler(in)** [ʃlaːfvandlɐ, ʃlaːfvandlərɪn] (-s; -/-; -nen) sleepwalker, somnambulist; **~zimmer** n bedroom

Schlag [ʃlaːk] m (-[e]s; Schläge ['ʃlɛːgə]) blow (a. fig); slap; punch; pat, tap; a. tennis: stroke; ELECTR shock (a. fig); MED beat; pl beating; → **Schlaganfall**; **~ader** f ANAT artery; **~anfall** m MED (apoplectic) stroke

'schlagartig 1. adj sudden, abrupt **2.** adv all of a sudden, abruptly

'Schlagbaum m barrier

'Schlagbohrer m TECH percussion drill

schlagen ['ʃlaːgən] (irr, ge-, h) **1.** v/t hit, beat (a. GASTR and fig), strike, knock, fell, cut (down); **sich ~** fight (um over); **sich geschlagen geben** admit defeat **2.** v/i hit, beat (a. heart etc), strike (a. clock), knock; **an or gegen et. ~** hit s.th., bump or crash into s.th.

Schlager ['ʃlaːgɐ] m (-s; -) MUS hit (a. fig), (pop) song

Schläger ['ʃlɛːgɐ] m (-s; -) tennis etc: racket; table tennis, cricket, baseball: bat; golf: club; hockey: stick; contp thug; **Schlägerei** [ʃlɛːgə'raɪ] f (-; -en) fight, brawl

'schlagfertig adj quick-witted; **~e Antwort** (witty) repartee

'Schlag|instru,ment n MUS percussion instrument; **~kraft** f (-; no pl) striking power (a. MIL); **~loch** n pot-hole; **~obers** Austrian n, **~sahne** f whipped cream; **~seite** f MAR list; **~ haben** be listing; **~stock** m baton, truncheon; **~wort** n catchword, slogan; **~zeile** f headline

'Schlagzeug n MUS drums

Schlagzeuger ['ʃlaːktsɔʏgɐ] m (-s; -)

MUS drummer
schlaksig ['ʃlaːksɪç] *adj* lanky, gangling
Schlamm [ʃlam] *m* (-[e]s; -e) mud
schlammig ['ʃlamɪç] *adj* muddy
Schlampe ['ʃlampə] F *f* (-; -n) slut
schlampig ['ʃlampɪç] F *adj* sloppy
schlang [ʃlaŋ] *pret of* **schlingen**
Schlange ['ʃlaŋə] *f* (-; -n) ZO snake, serpent (*a. fig*); *fig* line, *esp Br* queue; ~ **stehen** line up, stand in line, *esp Br* queue (up) (**nach** for); **schlängeln** ['ʃlɛŋəln] *v/refl* (ge-, h) wind *or* weave (one's way), *person*: worm one's way
'**Schlangenlinie** *f* serpentine line; *in* ~*n* **fahren** weave
schlank [ʃlaŋk] *adj* slim, slender; *j-n* ~ **machen** make s.o. look slim; ~**e Unternehmensstruktur** ECON lean management; '**Schlankheitskur** *f*: **e-e** ~ **machen** be slimming; '**schlankmachen** *v/t* (*sep, -ge-, h*): *j-n* ~ → **schlank**
schlapp [ʃlap] F *adj* worn out; weak; **Schlappe** ['ʃlapə] F *f* (-; -n) setback, beating; '**schlappmachen** F *v/i* (*sep, -ge-, h*) flake out; '**Schlappschwanz** F *m* weakling, wimp
schlau [ʃlau] *adj* clever, smart, bright; sly, cunning, crafty
Schlauch [ʃlaux] *m* (-[e]s; *Schläuche* ['ʃlɔʏçə]) tube; hose; ~**boot** *n* (inflatable *or* rubber) dinghy
Schlaufe ['ʃlaufə] *f* (-; -n) loop
schlecht [ʃlɛçt] *adj* bad; poor; *mir ist* (**wird**) ~ I feel (I'm getting) sick to my stomach; ~ **aussehen** look ill; *sich* ~ *fühlen* feel bad; ~ *werden* GASTR go bad; *es geht ihm sehr* ~ he is in a bad way; ~ *gelaunt* in a bad temper *or* mood, bad-tempered; F *j-n* ~ *machen* run s.o. down, backbite s.o.
'**schlechtmachen** *v/t* (*sep, -ge-, h*): F *j-n* ~ *machen* run s.o. down, backbite s.o.
schleichen ['ʃlaiçən] *v/i* (irr, ge-, sein) creep (*a. fig*), sneak; '**Schleichweg** *m* secret path; '**Schleichwerbung** *f* plugging; *für et.* ~ *machen* plug s.th.
Schleier ['ʃlaiɐ] *m* (-s; -) veil (*a. fig*); haze; '**schleierhaft** *adj*: F *es ist mir* ~ it's a mystery to me
Schleife ['ʃlaifə] *f* (-; -n) bow; ribbon; AVIAT, IT, ELECTR, GEOGR loop
schleifen[1] ['ʃlaifən] *v/t and v/i* (ge-, h) drag (along); rub
'**schleifen**[2] *v/t* (irr, ge-, h) grind (*a.*

TECH), sharpen; sand(paper); cut; F drill *s.o.* hard
Schleifer ['ʃlaifɐ] *m* (-s; -), '**Schleifma,schine** *f* TECH grinder
'**Schleifpa,pier** *n* sandpaper
'**Schleifstein** *m* grindstone; whetstone
Schleim [ʃlaim] *m* (-[e]s; -e) slime; MED mucus; '**Schleimhaut** *f* ANAT mucous membrane; **schleimig** ['ʃlaimɪç] *adj* slimy (*a. fig*); MED mucous
schlemmen ['ʃlɛmən] *v/i* (ge-, h) feast
schlendern ['ʃlɛndɐn] *v/i* (ge-, sein) stroll, saunter, amble
schlenkern ['ʃlɛŋkɐn] *v/i and v/t* (ge-, h) dangle, swing (**mit den Armen** one's arms)
schleppen ['ʃlɛpən] *v/t* (ge-, h) drag (*a. fig*); MOT, MAR tow; *sich* ~ drag (on); ~**d** *adj* dragging; *fig* drawling
Schlepper ['ʃlɛpɐ] *m* (-s; -) MAR tug; MOT tractor
'**Schlepp**|**lift** *m* T-bar (lift), drag lift, ski tow; ~**tau** *n* tow-rope; *im* (*ins*) ~ in tow (*a. fig*)
Schleuder ['ʃlɔʏdɐ] *f* (-; -n) catapult, slingshot; TECH spin drier
'**schleudern** (ge-, h) **1.** *v/t* fling, hurl (*both a. fig*); spin-dry **2.** *v/i* MOT skid
'**Schleudersitz** *m* AVIAT ejection (*esp Br* ejector) seat
schleunigst ['ʃlɔʏnɪçst] *adv* immediately
Schleuse ['ʃlɔʏzə] *f* (-; -n) sluice; lock
schlich [ʃlɪç] *pret of* **schleichen**
schlicht [ʃlɪçt] *adj* plain, simple
schlichten ['ʃlɪçtən] *v/t* (ge-, h) settle
'**Schlichtung** *f* (-; -en) settlement
schlief [ʃliːf] *pret of* **schlafen**
schließen ['ʃliːsən] *v/t and v/i* (irr, ge-, h) shut, close (down); *fig* close, finish; ~ *aus* (*dat*) conclude from; *nach ... zu* ~ judging by ...
Schließfach ['ʃliːsfax] *n* safe-deposit box; RAIL *etc*: (left luggage) locker
schließlich ['ʃliːslɪç] *adv* finally; eventually, in the end; after all
schliff [ʃlɪf] *pret of* **schleifen**[2]
Schliff *m* (-[e]s; -e) cut; polish (*a. fig*)
schlimm [ʃlɪm] *adj* bad; awful; *das ist nicht or halb so* ~ it's not as bad as that; *das Schlimme daran* the bad thing about it
'**schlimmsten**'**falls** *adv* at (the) worst
Schlinge ['ʃlɪŋə] *f* (-; -n) loop; noose;

HUNT snare (*a. fig*); MED sling

Schlingel ['ʃlɪŋəl] *m* (*-s; -*) rascal

schlingen ['ʃlɪŋən] *v/t* (*irr, ge-, h*) wind, twist; tie; wrap (*um* [a]round); gobble; **sich um et. ~** wind (a)round s.th.

schlingern ['ʃlɪŋɐn] *v/i* (*ge-, h*) MAR roll

'**Schlingpflanze** *f* BOT creeper, climber

Schlips [ʃlɪps] *m* (*-es; -e*) necktie, *esp Br* tie

schlitteln ['ʃlɪtəln] *Swiss v/i* (*ge-, sein*) go sledging, go tobogganing

Schlitten ['ʃlɪtən] *m* (*-s; -*) sled, *Br* sledge; sleigh; SPORT toboggan; **~ fahren** go sledging, go tobogganing

Schlittschuh ['ʃlɪtʃuː] *m* ice-skate (*a. ~ laufen*); '**Läufer(in)** ice-skater

Schlitz [ʃlɪts] *m* (*-es; -e*) slit; slot

schlitzen ['ʃlɪtsən] (*v/t ge-, h*) slit, slash

schloss [ʃlɔs] *pret of* **schließen**

Schloss *n* (*-es; Schlösser* ['ʃlœsɐ]) TECH lock; ARCH castle, palace; **ins ~ fallen** *door:* slam shut; **hinter ~ und Riegel** locked up, under lock and key

Schlosser ['ʃlɔsɐ] *m* (*-s; -*) metal-worker; locksmith; **Schlosserei** [ʃlɔsə'raɪ] *f* (*-; -en*) metalwork shop

schlottern ['ʃlɔtɐn] *v/i* (*ge-, h*) shake, tremble (*both: vor dat* with); bag

Schlucht [ʃlʊxt] *f* (*-; -en*) canyon, gorge, ravine

schluchzen ['ʃlʊxtsən] *v/i* (*ge-, h*), **Schluchzer** ['ʃlʊxtsɐ] *m* (*-s; -*) sob

Schluck [ʃlʊk] *m* (*-[e]s; -e*) draught, swallow; sip; gulp; '**Schluckauf** *m* (*-s; no pl*) hiccups; (*e-n*) **~ haben** have (the) hiccups; **schlucken** ['ʃlʊkən] *v/t and v/i* (*ge-, h*) swallow (*a. fig*)

'**Schluckimpfung** *f* MED oral vaccination

schlug [ʃluːk] *pret of* **schlagen**

Schlummer ['ʃlʊmɐ] *m* (*-s; no pl*) slumber; '**schlummern** *v/i* (*ge-, h*) lie asleep; *fig* slumber

schlüpfen ['ʃlʏpfən] *v/i* (*ge-, sein*) slip, slide; ZO hatch (out); **Schlüpfer** ['ʃlʏpfɐ] *m* (*-s; -*) briefs, panties

schlüpfrig ['ʃlʏpfrɪç] *adj* slippery; *contp* risqué, off-colo(u)r

Schlupfwinkel ['ʃlʊpfvɪŋkəl] *m* hiding place

schlurfen ['ʃlʊrfən] *v/i* (*ge-, sein*) shuffle (along)

schlürfen ['ʃlʏrfən] *v/t and v/i* (*ge-, h*) slurp

Schluss [ʃlʊs] *m* (*-es; no pl*) end; conclusion; ending; **~ machen** finish; break up; **~ machen mit** stop s.th., put an end to s.th.; **zum ~** finally; (**ganz**) **bis zum ~** to the (very) end; **für heute!** that's all for today!

Schlüssel ['ʃlʏsəl] *m* (*-s; -*) key (**für, zu** to); **~bein** *n* ANAT collarbone; **~blume** *f* BOT cowslip, primrose; **~bund** *m, n* bunch of keys; **~kind** F *n* latchkey child; **~loch** *n* keyhole; **~wort** *n* keyword, IT *a.* password

'**Schlussfolgerung** *f* conclusion

schlüssig ['ʃlʏsɪç] *adj* conclusive; **sich ~ werden** make up one's mind (**über** *acc* about)

'**Schluss|licht** *n* MOT *etc:* tail-light; **~pfiff** *m* SPORT final whistle; **~phase** *f* final stage(s); **~verkauf** *m* ECON (end--of-season) sale

schmächtig ['ʃmɛçtɪç] *adj* slight, thin, frail

schmackhaft ['ʃmakhaft] *adj* tasty

schmal [ʃmaːl] *adj* narrow; thin, slender (*a. fig*); **schmälern** ['ʃmɛːlɐn] *v/t* (*ge-, h*) detract from

'**Schmalfilm** *m* cinefilm

'**Schmalspur** *f* RAIL narrow ga(u)ge

'**Schmalspur...** *fig in cpds* small-time ...

Schmalz [ʃmalts] *n* (*-es; -e*) grease; lard

schmalzig ['ʃmaltsɪç] F *adj* schmaltzy, mushy, *Br* soapy

schmarotzen [ʃma'rɔtsən] F *v/i* (*no -ge-, h*) sponge (**bei** on)

Schmarotzer [ʃma'rɔtsɐ] *m* (*-s; -*) BOT, ZO parasite, *fig a.* sponger

schmatzen ['ʃmatsən] *v/i* smack (one's lips), eat noisily

schmecken ['ʃmɛkən] *v/i and v/t* (*ge-, h*) taste (**nach** of); **gut** (**schlecht**) **~** taste good (bad); (**wie**) **schmeckt dir ...?** (how) do you like ...? (*a. fig*); **es schmeckt süß** (**nach nichts**) it has a sweet (no) taste

Schmeichelei [ʃmaiçə'laɪ] *f* (*-; -en*) flattery; '**schmeichelhaft** *adj* flattering; '**schmeicheln** *v/i* (*ge-, h*) flatter (**j-m** s.o.); **Schmeichler(in)** ['ʃmaiçlɐ, 'ʃmaiçlərɪn] *m(f)* (*-s; -/-; -nen*) flatterer; **schmeichlerisch** [ʃmaiçlərɪʃ] *adj* flattering

schmeißen ['ʃmaisən] F *v/t and v/i* (*irr, ge-, h*) throw, chuck; slam; **mit Geld um**

sich ~ throw one's money about

'**Schmeißfliege** *f* zo blowfly, bluebottle

schmelzen ['ʃmɛltsən] *v/i* (*irr, ge-, sein*) *and v/t* (*h*) melt; thaw; TECH smelt

'**Schmelz|ofen** *m* (s)melting furnace; ~**tiegel** *m* melting pot (*a. fig*)

Schmerz [ʃmɛrts] *m* (*-es; -en*) pain (*a. fig*), ache; *fig* grief, sorrow

schmerzen ['ʃmɛrtsən] *v/i and v/t* (*ge-, h*) hurt (*a. fig*), ache; *esp fig* pain

'**schmerzfrei** *adj* without pain

'**schmerzhaft** *adj* painful

'**schmerzlich** *adj* painful, sad

'**schmerzlos** *adj* painless

'**Schmerzmittel** *n* PHARM painkiller

'**schmerzstillend** *adj* painkilling

Schmetterling ['ʃmɛtɐlɪŋ] *m* (*-s; -e*) zo butterfly

schmettern ['ʃmɛtɐn] (*ge-, h*) **1.** *v/t* smash (*a. tennis*); F MUS belt out **2.** *v/i* (*sein*) crash, slam; MUS blare

Schmied [ʃmiːt] *m* (*-[e]s; -e*) (black)-smith; **Schmiede** ['ʃmiːdə] *f* (*-; -n*) forge, smithy; '**Schmiedeeisen** *n* wrought iron; '**schmieden** *v/t* (*ge-, h*) forge; *fig* make (*plans etc*)

schmiegen ['ʃmiːɡən] *v/refl* (*ge-, h*) *sich* ~ *an* (*acc*) snuggle up to; *dress etc*: cling to

Schmiere ['ʃmiːrə] *f* (*-; -n*) grease

'**schmieren** *v/t* (*ge-, h*) TECH grease, oil, lubricate; spread (*butter etc*); *contp* scribble, scrawl; **Schmiererei** [ʃmiːrə-'rai] *f* (*-; -en*) scrawl; graffiti

schmierig ['ʃmiːrɪç] *adj* greasy; dirty; filthy; *contp* slimy

Schmiermittel ['ʃmiːrmɪtəl] *n* TECH lubricant

Schminke ['ʃmɪŋkə] *f* (*-; -n*) make-up (*a.* THEA); '**schminken** *v/t* (*ge-, h*) make *s.o.* up; *sich* ~ make o.s. or one's face up

Schmirgelpa,pier ['ʃmɪrɡəlpapiːɐ] *n* emery paper

schmiss [ʃmɪs] *pret of* **schmeißen**

schmollen ['ʃmɔlən] *v/i* (*ge-, h*) sulk, be sulky, pout

schmolz [ʃmɔlts] *pret of* **schmelzen**

schmoren ['ʃmoːrən] *v/t and v/i* (*ge-, h*) GASTR braise, stew (*a. fig*)

Schmuck [ʃmʊk] *m* (*-[e]s; no pl*) jewel-(le)ry, jewels; decoration(s), orna-ment(s); **schmücken** ['ʃmʏkən] *v/t* (*ge-, h*) decorate; '**schmucklos** *adj* un-adorned; plain; '**Schmuckstück** *n* piece of jewel(le)ry; *fig* gem

Schmuggel ['ʃmʊɡəl] *m* (*-; no pl*), **Schmuggelei** [ʃmʊɡə'lai] *f* (*-; -en*) smuggling; '**schmuggeln** *v/t and v/i* (*ge-, h*) smuggle; '**Schmuggelware** *f* smuggled goods; **Schmuggler** ['ʃmʊɡ-lɐ] *m* (*-s; -*) smuggler

schmunzeln ['ʃmʊntsəln] *v/i* (*ge-, h*) smile to o.s.

schmusen ['ʃmuːzən] F *v/i* (*ge-, h*) (kiss and) cuddle, smooch

Schmutz [ʃmʊts] *m* (*-es; no pl*) dirt, filth, *fig a.* smut; ~**fleck** *m* smudge

schmutzig ['ʃmʊtsɪç] *adj* dirty, filthy (*both a. fig*); ~ *werden, sich* ~ *machen* get dirty

Schnabel ['ʃnaːbəl] *m* (*-s; Schnäbel* ['ʃnɛːbəl]) zo bill, beak

Schnalle ['ʃnalə] *f* (*-; -n*) buckle

'**schnallen** *v/t* (*ge-, h*) buckle; *et.* ~ *an* (*acc*) strap s.th. to

schnalzen ['ʃnaltsən] *v/i* (*ge-, h*) snap one's fingers; click one's tongue

schnappen ['ʃnapən] (*ge-, h*) **1.** *v/i* snap, snatch (*both: nach* at); F *nach Luft* ~ gasp for breath **2.** F *v/t* catch

'**Schnappschuss** *m* PHOT snapshot

Schnaps [ʃnaps] *m* (*-es; Schnäpse* ['ʃnɛpsə]) spirits, schnapps, F booze

schnarchen ['ʃnarçən] *v/i* (*ge-, h*) snore

schnarren ['ʃnarən] *v/i* (*ge-, h*) rattle; *voice*: rasp

schnattern ['ʃnatɐn] *v/i* (*ge-, h*) zo cack-le; chatter (*a.* F)

schnauben ['ʃnaubən] *v/i and v/t* (*ge-, h*) snort; *sich die Nase* ~ blow one's nose

schnaufen ['ʃnaufən] *v/i* (*ge-, h*) breathe hard, pant, puff

Schnauze ['ʃnautsə] *f* (*-; -n*) zo snout, mouth, muzzle; F AVIAT, MOT nose; TECH spout; V trap, kisser; V *die* ~ *halten* keep one's trap shut

Schnecke ['ʃnɛkə] *f* (*-; -n*) zo snail; slug

'**Schnecken|haus** *n* zo snail shell; ~**tempo** *n*: *im* ~ at a snail's pace

Schnee [ʃneː] *m* (*-s; no pl*) snow (*a. sl*); ~ *räumen* remove snow; ~**ball** *m* snow-ball; ~**ballschlacht** *f* snowball fight

'**schneebedeckt** *adj* snow-capped

'**Schnee|fall** *m* snowfall; ~**flocke** *f* snowflake; ~**gestöber** ['ʃneːɡəʃtøːbɐ] *n* (*-s; -*) snow flurry; ~**glöckchen** *n*

BOT snowdrop; **~grenze** *f* snow line; **~mann** *m* snowman; **~matsch** *m* slush; **~mo,bil** *n* snowmobile; **~pflug** *m* snowplow, *Br* snowplough; **~regen** *m* sleet; **~sturm** *m* snowstorm, blizzard; **~verwehung** *f* snowdrift

'**schnee'weiß** *adj* snow-white

Schneewittchen [ʃneːˈvɪtçən] *n* (-*s*; *no pl*) Snow White

Schneid [ʃnait] F *m* (-[*e*]*s*; *no pl*) grit, guts; **~brenner** *m* TECH cutting torch

Schneide [ˈʃnaidə] *f* (-; -*n*) edge

'**schneiden** *v/t and v/i* (*irr, ge-, h*) cut (*a. fig*), *film etc*: *a.* edit; GASTR carve

Schneider [ˈʃnaidɐ] *m* (-*s*; -) tailor; **Schneiderei** [ʃnaidəˈrai] *f* (-; -*en*) (*no pl*) tailoring, dressmaking; tailor's *or* dressmaker's shop; '**Schneiderin** *f* (-; -*nen*) dressmaker; seamstress; '**schneidern** *v/i and v/t* (*ge-, h*) do dressmaking; make, sew

'**Schneidezahn** *m* incisor

schneidig [ˈʃnaidɪç] *adj* dashing; smart

schneien [ˈʃnaiən] *v/i* (*ge-, h*) snow

schnell [ʃnɛl] *adj* fast, quick; prompt; rapid; **es geht ~** it won't take long; **(mach[**f**]) ~!** hurry up!

'**Schnell...** *in cpds* ...*dienst*, ...*paket*, ...*zug etc: mst* express ...

schnellen [ˈʃnɛlən] *v/t* (*ge-, h*) *and v/i* (*ge-, sein*) shoot, spring

'**Schnellhefter** *m* folder

Schnelligkeit [ˈʃnɛlɪçkait] *f* (-; *no pl*) speed; quickness, rapidity

'**Schnell|imbiss** *m* snack bar; **~straße** *f* expressway, thruway, *Br* motorway

schnetzeln [ˈʃnɛtsəln] *esp Swiss v/t* (*ge-, h*) GASTR chop up

schnippisch [ˈʃnɪpɪʃ] *adj* sassy, pert

schnipsen [ˈʃnɪpsən] *v/i* (*ge-, h*) snap one's fingers

schnitt [ʃnɪt] *pret of* **schneiden**

Schnitt *m* (-[*e*]*s*; -*e*) cut (*a. fig*); average

'**Schnittblumen** *pl* cut flowers

Schnitte [ˈʃnɪtə] *f* (-; -*n*) slice; open sandwich

schnittig [ˈʃnɪtɪç] *adj* stylish; MOT sleek

Schnitt|lauch *m* BOT chives; **~muster** *n* pattern; **~punkt** *m* (point of) intersection; **~stelle** *f* *film etc*: cut; IT interface; **~wunde** *f* MED cut

Schnitzel[1] [ˈʃnɪtsəl] *n* (-*s*; -) GASTR cutlet; **Wiener ~** schnitzel

'**Schnitzel**[2] *n, m* (-*s*; -) chip; scrap

schnitzen [ˈʃnɪtsən] *v/t* (*ge-, h*) carve, cut (in wood); **Schnitzer** [ˈʃnɪtsɐ] *m* (-*s*; -) (wood) carver; **Schnitzerei** [ʃnɪtsəˈrai] *f* (-; -*en*) (wood) carving

Schnorchel [ˈʃnɔrçəl] *m* (-*s*; -), '**schnorcheln** *v/i* (*ge-, h*) snorkel

Schnörkel [ˈʃnœrkəl] *m* (-*s*; -) flourish; ARCH scroll

schnorren [ˈʃnɔrən] F *v/t* (*ge-, h*) mooch, *Br* cadge

schnüffeln [ˈʃnʏfəln] *v/i* (*ge-, h*) sniff (**an** *dat* at); F snoop (about or around)

Schnuller [ˈʃnʊlɐ] *m* (-*s*; -) pacifier, *Br* dummy

Schnulze [ˈʃnʊltsə] F *f* (-; -*n*) tearjerker; schmal(t)zy song

'**Schnulzensänger**   F   *m*, '**Schnulzensängerin** *f* crooner

schnulzig [ˈʃnʊltsɪç] F *adj* schmal(t)zy

Schnupfen [ˈʃnʊpfən] *m* (-*s*; -) MED cold; **e-n ~ haben** (**bekommen**) have a (catch [a]) cold

'**Schnupftabak** *m* snuff

schnuppern [ˈʃnʊpɐn] *v/i* (*ge-, h*) sniff (**an** *et.* [at] s.th.)

Schnur [ʃnuːɐ] *f* (-; **Schnüre** [ˈʃnyːrə]) string, cord; ELECTR flex

Schnürchen [ˈʃnyːrçən] *n*: **wie am ~** like clockwork

schnüren [ˈʃnyːrən] *v/t* (*ge-, h*) lace (up); tie up

'**schnurgerade** *adv* dead straight

'**schnurlos** *adj*: **~es Telefon** cordless phone

Schnürlsamt [ˈʃnyːɐlzamt] *Austrian m* corduroy

Schnurrbart [ˈʃnʊrbaːɐt] *m* m(o)ustache

schnurren [ˈʃnʊrən] *v/i* (*ge-, h*) purr

Schnür|schuh [ˈʃnyːɐʃuː] *m* laced shoe; **~senkel** [ˈʃnyːɐzɛŋkəl] *m* (-*s*; -) shoestring, *Br* shoelace

schnurstracks [ˈʃnuːɐˈʃtraks] *adv* direct(ly), straight; straight away

schob [ʃoːp] *pret of* **schieben**

Schober [ˈʃoːbɐ] *m* (-*s*; -) haystack, hayrick; barn

Schock [ʃɔk] *m* (-[*e*]*s*; -*s*) MED shock; **unter ~ stehen** be in (a state of) shock

schocken [ˈʃɔkən] F *v/t* (*ge-, h*) shock

schockieren [ʃɔˈkiːrən] *v/t* (*no -ge-, h*) shock

Schokolade [ʃokoˈlaːdə] *f* (-; -*n*) chocolate; **e-e Tafel ~** a bar of chocolate

scholl [ʃɔl] *pret of* **schallen**

Scholle ['ʃɔlə] *f* (-; -n) clod; (ice)floe; zo flounder, *Br* plaice

schon [ʃoːn] *adv* already; ever; even; ~ *damals* even then; ~ *1968* as early as 1968; ~ *der Gedanke* the very idea; *ist sie* ~ *da* (*zurück*)? has she come (is she back) yet?; *habt ihr* ~ *gegessen?* have you eaten yet?; *bist du* ~ *einmal dort gewesen?* have you ever been there?; *ich wohne hier* ~ *seit zwei Jahren* I've been living here for two years now; *ich kenne ihn* ~, *aber* I do know him, but; *er macht das* ~ he'll do it all right; ~ *gut!* never mind!, all right!

schön [ʃøːn] **1.** *adj* beautiful, lovely; METEOR *a.* fine, fair; nice (*a.* F iro); (*na*,) ~ all right **2.** *adv*: ~ *warm* (*kühl*) nice and warm (cool); *ganz* ~ *teuer* (*schnell*) pretty expensive (fast); *j-n ganz* ~ *erschrecken* (*überraschen*) give s.o. quite a start (surprise)

schonen ['ʃoːnən] *v/t* (ge-, h) take care of, go easy on (*a.* TECH); spare; *sich* ~ take it easy; save o.s. *or* one's strength; **~d 1.** *adj* gentle; mild **2.** *adv*: ~ *umgehen mit* take (good) care of; handle with care; go easy on

'**Schönheit** *f* (-; -en) beauty

'**Schönheitspflege** *f* beauty care

'**Schonung** *f* (-; -en) (*no pl*) (good) care; rest; preservation; tree nursery

'**schonungslos** *adj* relentless, brutal

schöpfen ['ʃœpfən] *v/t* (ge-, h) scoop, ladle; draw (*water*); → *Luft*, *Verdacht*

Schöpfer ['ʃœpfɐ] *m* (-s; -), '**Schöpferin** *f* (-; -nen) creator

schöpferisch ['ʃœpfərɪʃ] *adj* creative

'**Schöpfung** *f* (-; -en) creation

schor [ʃoːɐ] *pret of* **scheren**

Schorf [ʃɔrf] *m* (-[e]s; -e) MED scab

Schornstein ['ʃɔrnʃtain] *m* chimney; MAR, RAIL funnel; **~feger** *m* chimney sweep

schoss [ʃɔs] *pret of* **schießen**

Schoß [ʃoːs] *m* (-es; *Schöße* ['ʃøːsə]) lap; womb

Schote ['ʃoːtə] *f* (-; -n) BOT pod, husk

Schotte ['ʃɔtə] *m* (-n; -n) Scot(sman); *pl* the Scots, the Scottish (people)

Schotter ['ʃɔtɐ] *m* (-s; -) gravel, road metal

Schottin ['ʃɔtɪn] *f* (-; -nen) Scotswoman

'**schottisch** *adj* Scots, Scottish; Scotch

'**Schottland** Scotland

schräg [ʃrɛːk] **1.** *adj* slanting, sloping, oblique; diagonal **2.** *adv*: ~ *gegenüber* diagonally opposite

Schramme ['ʃramə] *f* (-; -n), '**schrammen** *v/t and v/i* (ge-, h) scratch (*a.* MED)

Schrank [ʃraŋk] *m* (-[e]s; *Schränke* ['ʃrɛŋkə]) cupboard; closet; wardrobe

Schranke ['ʃraŋkə] *f* (-; -n) barrier (*a.* fig), RAIL *a.* gate; JUR bar; *pl* limits, bounds

'**schrankenlos** *fig adj* boundless

'**Schrankenwärter** *m* RAIL gatekeeper

'**Schrankwand** *f* wall units

Schraube ['ʃraubə] *f* (-; -n), '**schrauben** *v/t* (ge-, h) TECH screw

'**Schrauben|schlüssel** *m* TECH spanner, wrench; **~zieher** *m* TECH screwdriver

Schraubstock ['ʃraupʃtɔk] *m* vise, *Br* vice

Schreck [ʃrɛk] *m* (-[e]s; -e) fright, shock; *j-m e-n* ~ *einjagen* give s.o. a fright, scare s.o.

Schrecken ['ʃrɛkən] *m* (-s; -) terror, fright; horror(s); '**Schreckensnachricht** *f* dreadful news

'**schreckhaft** *adj* jumpy; skittish

'**schrecklich** *adj* awful, terrible; horrible, dreadful, atrocious

Schrei [ʃrai] *m* (-[e]s; -e) cry, shout, yell, scream (*all*: *um*, *nach* for)

schreiben ['ʃraibən] *v/t and v/i* (*irr*, ge-, h) write (*j-m* to s.o.; *über* acc about); type; spell; *falsch* ~ misspell; *wie schreibt man ...?* how do you spell ...?

'**Schreiben** *n* (-s; -) letter

'**Schreib|fehler** *m* spelling mistake; **~heft** *n* exercise book; **~kraft** *f* typist; **~ma,schine** *f* typewriter; **~materi,al** *n* writing materials, stationery; **~schutz** *m* IT write *or* file protection; **~tisch** *m* desk

'**Schreibung** *f* (-; -en) spelling

'**Schreibwaren** *pl* stationery; **~geschäft** *n* stationer's, stationery shop

'**Schreibzen,trale** *f* typing pool

schreien ['ʃraiən] *v/i and v/t* (*irr*, ge-, h) cry, shout, yell, scream (*all*: *um*, *nach* [out] for); ~ *vor Schmerz* (*Angst*) cry out with pain (in terror); *es war* *zum Schreien* it was a scream; **~d** *fig adj* loud (*colors*); flagrant (*abuse etc*), glaring (*injustices etc*)

Schreiner ['ʃrainɐ] *m* (*-s*; *-*) → *Tischler*

schreiten ['ʃraitən] *v/i* (*irr, ge-, sein*) stride

schrie [ʃriː] *pret of* **schreien**

schrieb [ʃriːp] *pret of* **schreiben**

Schrift [ʃrɪft] *f* (*-*; *-en*) (hand)writing, hand; PRINT type; character, letter; *pl* works, writings; *die Heilige* **~** REL the Scriptures; **~art** *f* script; PRINT typeface; **~deutsch** *n* standard German

'**schriftlich** *adj* written; **~** *übersetzen* translate in writing

Schriftsteller ['ʃrɪftʃtɛlɐ] *m* (*-s*; *-*), '**Schriftstellerin** *f* (*-*; *-nen*) author, writer

'**Schrift|verkehr** *m*, **~wechsel** *m* correspondence; **~zeichen** *n* character, letter

schrill [ʃrɪl] *adj* shrill (*a. fig*), piercing

schritt [ʃrɪt] *pret of* **schreiten**

Schritt *m* (*-[e]s*; *-e*) step (*a. fig*); pace; *fig* **~e unternehmen** take steps; **~** *fahren!* MOT dead slow; **~macher** *m* SPORT pacemaker (*a.* MED), pacesetter

'**schrittweise** *adv* step by step, gradually

schroff [ʃrɔf] *adj* steep; jagged; *fig* gruff

Schrot [ʃroːt] *m, n* (*-[e]s*; *-e*) (*no pl*) coarse meal; HUNT (small) shot; pellet; **~flinte** *f* shotgun

Schrott [ʃrɔt] *m* (*-[e]s*; *-e*) scrap (metal)

'**Schrotthaufen** *m* scrap heap

'**Schrottplatz** *m* scrapyard

schrubben ['ʃrʊbən] *v/t* (*ge-, h*) scrub, scour

schrumpfen ['ʃrʊmpfən] *v/i* (*ge-, sein*) shrink

Schub [ʃuːp] *m* (*-[e]s*; *Schübe* ['ʃyːbə]) → *Schubkraft*; **~fach** *n* drawer; **~karren** *m* wheelbarrow; **~kasten** *m* drawer; **~kraft** *f* PHYS, TECH thrust; **~lade** *f* drawer

Schubs [ʃʊps] F *m* (*-es*; *-e*), **schubsen** ['ʃʊpsən] F *v/t* (*ge-, h*) push

schüchtern ['ʃʏçtɐn] *adj* shy, bashful

'**Schüchternheit** *f* (*-*; *no pl*) shyness, bashfulness

schuf [ʃuːf] *pret of* **schaffen**[1]

Schuft [ʃʊft] *m* (*-[e]s*; *-e*) *contp* bastard

schuften ['ʃʊftən] F *v/i* (*ge-, h*) slave away, drudge

Schuh [ʃuː] *m* (*-[e]s*; *-e*) shoe; *j-m et. in die ~e schieben* put the blame for s.th. on s.o.; **~anzieher** *m* shoehorn; **~creme** *f* shoe polish; **~geschäft** *n* shoe store (*Br* shop); **~löffel** *m* shoehorn; **~macher** *m* shoemaker; **~putzer** ['ʃuːpʊtsɐ] *m* (*-s*; *-*) shoeshine boy

'**Schul|abbrecher** *m* (*-s*; *-*) dropout; **~abgänger** ['ʃuːlapgɛŋɐ] *m* (*-s*; *-*) school leaver; **~amt** *n* school board, *Br* education authority; **~arbeit** *f* schoolwork; *pl* homework; **~besuch** *m* (school) attendance; **~bildung** *f* education; **~buch** *n* textbook

Schuld [ʃʊlt] *f* (*-*; *-en* ['ʃʊldən]) (*no pl*) JUR guilt, *esp* REL sin; *mst pl* debt; *j-m die ~ (an et.) geben* blame s.o. (for s.th.); *es ist (nicht) deine ~* it is(n't) your fault; *~en haben (machen)* be in (run into) debt; → *zuschulden*

'**schuldbewusst** *adj*: **~e Miene** guilty look; **~en** ['ʃʊldən] *v/t* (*ge-, h*) *j-m et.* **~** owe s.o. s.th.; **schuldig** ['ʃʊldɪç] *adj esp* JUR guilty (*an dat* of); responsible *or* to blame (for); *j-m et.* **~** *sein* owe s.o. s.th.; **Schuldige** ['ʃʊldɪgə] *m, f* (*-n*; *-n*) culprit; JUR guilty person, offender

'**schuldlos** *adj* innocent

Schuldner ['ʃʊldnɐ] *m* (*-s*; *-*); '**Schuldnerin** *f* (*-*; *-nen*) debtor

'**Schuldschein** *m* ECON promissory note, IOU (= I owe you)

Schule ['ʃuːlə] *f* (*-*; *-n*) school (*a. fig*); *höhere ~ appr* (senior) high school, *Br* secondary school; *auf or in der ~* at school; *in die or zur ~ gehen (kommen)* go to (start) school

'**schulen** *v/t* (*ge-, h*) train, school

Schüler ['ʃyːlɐ] *m* (*-s*; *-*) student, schoolboy, *esp Br a.* pupil; **~austausch** *m* student exchange (program[me])

Schülerin ['ʃyːlərɪn] *f* (*-*; *-nen*) student, schoolgirl, *esp Br a.* pupil

'**Schülervertretung** *f appr* student government (*Br* council)

'**Schul|ferien** *pl* vacation, *Br* holidays; **~fernsehen** *n* educational TV; **~funk** *m* schools programmes; **~gebäude** *n* school (building); **~geld** *n* school fee(s), tuition; **~heft** *n* exercise book; **~hof** *m* school yard, playground; **~kame,rad** *m* schoolfellow; **~leiter** *m* principal, *Br* headmaster, head teacher; **~leiterin** f principal, *Br* headmistress; **~mappe** f schoolbag; satchel; **~ordnung** f school regulations

'**schulpflichtig** *adj*: **~es Kind** school--age child

'**Schul|schiff** n training ship; **~schluss** m end of school (*or* term); **nach ~** after school; **~schwänzer** ['ʃuːlʃvɛntsɐ] m (-*s*; -) truant; **~stunde** f lesson, class, period; **~tasche** f schoolbag

Schulter ['ʃultɐ] f (-; -n) ANAT shoulder

'**Schulterblatt** n ANAT shoulder-blade

'**schulterfrei** *adj* strapless

'**schultern** v/t (ge-, h) shoulder

'**Schultertasche** f shoulder bag

'**Schulwesen** n (-s; no pl) education(al system)

schummeln ['ʃumǝln] F v/i (ge-, h) cheat

Schund [ʃʊnt] m (-[e]s; no pl) trash, rubbish, junk

schund [ʃʊnt] pret of **schinden**

Schuppe ['ʃupǝ] f (-; -n) ZO scale; pl MED dandruff

'**Schuppen** m (-s; -) shed, esp F contp shack

schuppig ['ʃupɪç] adj ZO scaly

schüren ['ʃyːrǝn] v/t (ge-, h) stir up (a. fig)

schürfen ['ʃyrfǝn] v/i (ge-, h) prospect (**nach** for)

'**Schürfwunde** f MED graze, abrasion

Schurke ['ʃʊrkǝ] m (-n; -n) esp THEA etc villain

Schurwolle ['ʃuːɐvɔlǝ] f virgin wool

Schürze ['ʃyrtsǝ] f (-; -n) apron

Schuss [ʃʊs] m (-es; Schüsse ['ʃysǝ]) shot; GASTR dash; SPORT shot, soccer: a. strike; skiing: schuss (**a. ~ fahren**); sl shot, fix; F **gut in ~ sein** be in good shape

Schüssel ['ʃysǝl] f (-; -n) bowl, dish; basin

'**Schuss|waffe** f firearm; **~wunde** f MED gunshot *or* bullet wound

Schuster ['ʃuːstɐ] m (-s; -) shoemaker

Schutt [ʃʊt] m (-[e]s; no pl) rubble, debris

'**Schüttelfrost** m MED shivering fit, *the* shivers

schütteln ['ʃytǝln] v/t (ge-, h) shake

schütten ['ʃytǝn] v/t (ge-, h) pour; throw

Schutz [ʃʊts] m (-es; no pl) protection (**gegen, vor** dat against), defense, Br

defence (against, from); shelter (from); safeguard (against); cover; **~blech** n fender, Br mudguard; **~brille** f goggles

Schütze ['ʃytsǝ] m (-n; -n) MIL rifleman; hunter; SPORT scorer; ASTR Sagittarius; **er ist (ein) ~** he's (a) Sagittarius; **ein guter ~** a good shot

schützen ['ʃytsǝn] v/t (ge-, h) protect (**gegen, vor** dat against, from), defend (against, from), guard (against, from); shelter (from); safeguard

'**Schutzengel** m guardian angel

'**Schützengraben** m MIL trench

'**Schutzgeld** n protection money; **~erpressung** f protection racket

'**Schutz|haft** f JUR protective custody; **~heilige** m, f patron (saint); **~impfung** f MED protective inoculation; vaccination; **~kleidung** f protective clothing

Schützling ['ʃytslɪŋ] m (-s; -e) protégé(e)

'**schutzlos** *adj* unprotected; defenseless, Br defenceless

'**Schutz|maßnahme** f safety measure; **~pa,tron** m REL patron (saint); **~umschlag** m dust cover; **~zoll** m ECON protective duty (*or* tariff)

schwach [ʃvax] adj weak (a. fig); poor; faint; delicate, frail; **schwächer werden** grow weak; decline; fail; fade

Schwäche ['ʃvɛçǝ] f weakness (a. fig); MED infirmity; fig drawback, shortcoming; **e-e ~ haben für** be partial to; '**schwächen** v/t (ge-, h) weaken (a. fig); lessen; '**schwächlich** adj weakly, feeble; delicate, frail; '**Schwächling** m (-s; -e) weakling (a. fig), softy, sissy

'**schwachsinnig** adj feeble-minded; F stupid, idiotic

'**Schwachstrom** m ELECTR low-voltage current

Schwager ['ʃvaːgɐ] m (-s; Schwäger ['ʃvɛːgɐ]) brother-in-law; **Schwägerin** ['ʃvɛːgǝrɪn] f (-; -nen) sister-in-law

Schwalbe ['ʃvalbǝ] f (-; -n) ZO swallow; soccer: dive

Schwall [ʃval] m (-[e]s; -e) gush, esp fig a. torrent

schwamm [ʃvam] pret of **schwimmen**

Schwamm m (-[e]s; Schwämme ['ʃvɛmǝ]) sponge; BOT fungus; F dry rot

Schwammerl ['ʃvamɐl] Austrian m (-s; -[n]) → **Pilz**

schwammig ['ʃvamıç] *adj* spongy; puffy; *fig* woolly

Schwan [ʃva:n] *m* (-[e]s; *Schwäne* ['ʃvɛ:nə]) zo swan

schwand [ʃvant] *pret of* **schwinden**

schwang [ʃvaŋ] *pret of* **schwingen**

schwanger ['ʃvaŋɐ] *adj* pregnant

'Schwangerschaft *f* (-; -en) pregnancy; **'Schwangerschaftsabbruch** *m* abortion

schwanken ['ʃvaŋkən] *v/i* (ge-, h) sway, roll (*a.* MAR); stagger; *fig* ~ **zwischen ... und ...** waver between ... and ...; *prices*: range from ... to ...; **'Schwankung** *f* (-; -en) change, variation (*a.* ECON)

Schwanz [ʃvants] *m* (-es; *Schwänze* ['ʃvɛntsə]) zo tail (*a.* AVIAT, ASTR); V cock

schwänzen ['ʃvɛntsən] *v/i and v/t* (ge-, h) (**die Schule**) ~ play truant (F hooky)

Schwarm [ʃvarm] *m* (-[e]s; *Schwärme* ['ʃvɛrmə]) swarm; crowd, F bunch; zo shoal, school; F dream; idol

schwärmen ['ʃvɛrmən] *v/i* (ge-, sein) zo swarm; (ge-, h) ~ **für** be mad about; dream of; have a crush on *s.o.*; ~ **von** rave about

Schwarte ['ʃvartə] *f* (-; -n) rind; F *contp* (old) tome

schwarz [ʃvarts] *adj* black (*a. fig*); **Schwarzes Brett** bulletin board, *Br* notice board; ~ **auf weiß** in black and white

'Schwarzarbeit *f* (-; *no pl*) illicit work

'Schwarzbrot *n* rye bread

Schwarze ['ʃvartsə] *m, f* (-n; -n) black (man *or* woman); *pl* the Blacks

schwärzen ['ʃvɛrtsən] *v/t* (ge-, h) blacken

'Schwarz|fahrer *m* fare dodger; ~**händler** *m* black marketeer; ~**markt** *m* black market; ~**seher** *m* pessimist; (TV) license (*Br* licence) dodger

Schwarz'weiß... *in cpds* ...film, ...fernseher *etc*: black-and-white ...

schwatzen ['ʃvatsən], **schwätzen** ['ʃvɛtsən] *v/i* (ge-, h) chat(ter); PED talk

Schwätzer ['ʃvɛtsɐ] *contp m* (-s; -), **'Schwätzerin** *f* (-; -nen) loudmouth

schwatzhaft ['ʃvatshaft] *adj* chatty

Schwebe|bahn ['ʃve:bəba:n] *f* cableway, ropeway; ~**balken** *m* SPORT beam

schweben ['ʃve:bən] *v/i* (ge-, h) be suspended; zo, AVIAT hover (*a. fig*); glide;

esp JUR be pending; **in Gefahr** ~ be in danger

Schwede ['ʃve:də] *m* (-n; -n) Swede

Schweden ['ʃve:dən] Sweden

Schwedin ['ʃve:dın] *f* (-; -nen) Swede

'schwedisch *adj* Swedish

Schwefel ['ʃve:fəl] *m* (-s; *no pl*) CHEM sulfur, *Br* sulphur; ~**säure** *f* CHEM sulfuric (*Br* sulphuric) acid

Schweif [ʃvaif] *m* (-[e]s; -e) zo tail (*a.* ASTR); **schweifen** ['ʃvaifən] *v/i* (ge-, sein) wander (*a. fig*), roam

schweigen ['ʃvaigən] *v/i* (*irr*, ge-, h) be silent; **'Schweigen** *n* (-s; *no pl*) silence; **'schweigend** *adj* silent

schweigsam ['ʃvaikza:m] *adj* quiet, taciturn, reticent

Schwein [ʃvain] *n* (-[e]s; -e) zo pig, hog; F *contp* (filthy) pig; swine, bastard; F ~ **haben** be lucky; **'Schweinebraten** *m* roast pork; **'Schweinefleisch** *n* pork; **Schweinerei** [ʃvainə'rai] F *f* (-; -en) mess; *fig* dirty trick; dirty *or* crying shame; filth(y story *or* joke)

'Schweinestall *m* pigsty (*a. fig*)

'schweinisch F *adj* filthy, obscene

'Schweinsleder *n* pigskin

Schweiß [ʃvais] *m* (-es; *no pl*) sweat, perspiration

schweißen *v/t* (ge-, h) TECH weld

Schweißer *m* (-s; -) TECH welder

'schweißgebadet *adj* soaked in sweat

'Schweißgeruch *m* body odo(u)r, BO

Schweiz [ʃvaits] Switzerland

Schweizer ['ʃvaitsɐ] *m* (-s; -), *adj* Swiss

Schweizerin ['ʃvaitsərın] *f* (-; -nen) Swiss woman *or* girl

schweizerisch ['ʃvaitsərıʃ] *adj* Swiss

schwelen ['ʃve:lən] *v/i* (ge-, h) smo(u)lder (*a. fig*)

schwelgen ['ʃvɛlgən] *v/i* (ge-, h) ~ **in** (*dat*) revel in

Schwelle ['ʃvɛlə] *f* (-; -n) threshold (*a. fig*); RAIL tie, *Br* sleeper

'schwellen 1. *v/i* (*irr*, ge-, sein) swell **2.** *v/t* (ge-, h) swell

'Schwellung *f* (-; -en) MED swelling

Schwemme ['ʃvɛmə] *f* (-; -n) ECON glut, oversupply; **schwemmen** *v/t* (ge-, h) **an Land** ~ wash ashore

Schwengel ['ʃvɛŋəl] *m* (-s; -) clapper; handle

schwenken ['ʃvɛŋkən] *v/t* (ge-, h) and *v/i* (ge-, sein) swing, wave

schwer [ʃveːɐ] **1.** *adj* heavy; *fig* difficult, hard; GASTR strong, rich; MED *etc* serious, severe; heavy, violent (*storm etc*); **~e Zeiten** hard times; **es ~ haben** have a bad time; **100 Pfund ~ sein** weigh a hundred pounds **2.** *adv:* **~ arbeiten** work hard; → **schwerfallen**; → **hören;** **~ beschädigt** → **schwerbeschädigt**; **~ verdaulich** indigestible, heavy (*both a. fig*); **~ verständlich** difficult *or* hard to understand; **~ verwundet** seriously wounded

'schwerbeschädigt *adj* seriously disabled

Schwere [ʃveːrə] *f* (-; *no pl*) weight (*a. fig*); *fig* seriousness

'schwerfallen *v/i* (*irr, fallen, sep, -ge-, sein*): **j-m ~** be difficult for s.o.; **es fällt ihm schwer zu** ... he finds it difficult to ...

'schwerfällig *adj* awkward, clumsy

'Schwergewicht *n* (-[e]s; *no pl*) heavyweight; *fig* (main) emphasis

'schwerhörig *adj* hard of hearing

'Schwer|indus,trie *f* heavy industry; **~kraft** *f* (-; *no pl*) PHYS gravity; **~me,tall** *n* heavy metal

schwermütig ['ʃveːɐmyːtɪç] *adj* melancholy; **~ sein** have the blues

'Schwerpunkt *m* center (*Br* centre) of gravity; *fig* (main) emphasis

Schwert [ʃveːɐt] *n* (-[e]s; -er) sword

'Schwerverbrecher *m* dangerous criminal, JUR felon

'schwer|verdaulich *adj* → **schwer**; **~verständlich** *adj* → **schwer**; **~ver,wundet** *adj* → **schwer**

'schwerwiegend *fig adj* weighty, serious

Schwester ['ʃvɛstɐ] *f* (-; -n) sister, REL *a.* nun; MED nurse

schwieg [ʃviːk] *pret of* **schweigen**

Schwieger... ['ʃviːgɐ-] *in cpds* ...**eltern**, ...**mutter**, ...**sohn** *etc*: ...-in-law

Schwiele ['ʃviːlə] *f* (-; -n) MED callus

schwielig ['ʃviːlɪç] *adj* horny

schwierig ['ʃviːrɪç] *adj* difficult, hard

'Schwierigkeit *f* (-; -en) difficulty, trouble; **in ~en geraten** get *or* run into trouble; **~en haben, et. zu tun** have difficulty in doing s.th.

Schwimmbad ['ʃvɪmbaːt] *n* (indoor) swimming pool; **schwimmen** ['ʃvɪmən] *v/i* (*irr, ge-, sein*) swim; float; **~**

gehen go swimming

'Schwimm|flosse *f* swimfin, *Br* flipper; **~gürtel** *m* swimming belt; **~haut** *f* ZO web; **~lehrer** *m* swimming instructor; **~weste** *f* life jacket

Schwindel ['ʃvɪndəl] *m* (-s; *no pl*) MED giddiness, dizziness; F swindle, fraud; **~ erregend** dizzy; **'schwindeler,regend** *adj* dizzy

'schwindeln F *v/i* (*ge-, h*) fib, tell fibs

schwinden ['ʃvɪndən] *v/i* (*irr, ge-, sein*) dwindle, decline

Schwindler ['ʃvɪndlɐ] F *m* (-s; -), **'Schwindlerin** *f* (-; -nen) swindler, crook; liar

schwindlig ['ʃvɪndlɪç] *adj* MED dizzy, giddy; **mir ist ~** I feel dizzy

Schwinge ['ʃvɪŋə] *f* (-; -n) ZO wing

'schwingen *v/i and v/t* (*irr, ge-, h*) swing; wave; PHYS oscillate; vibrate

'Schwingung *f* (-; -en) PHYS oscillation; vibration

Schwips [ʃvɪps] F *m:* **e-n ~ haben** be tipsy

schwirren ['ʃvɪrən] *v/i* (*ge-, sein*) whirr, whizz, *esp* ZO buzz (*a. fig*); (*ge-, h*) **mir schwirrt der Kopf** my head is buzzing

schwitzen ['ʃvɪtsən] *v/i* (*ge-, h*) sweat, perspire

schwoll [ʃvɔl] *pret of* **schwellen** 1

schwor [ʃvoːɐ] *pret of* **schwören**

schwören ['ʃvøːrən] *v/t and v/i* (*irr, ge-, h*) swear; JUR take an *or* the oath; *fig* **~ auf** (*acc*) swear by

schwul [ʃvuːl] F *adj* gay; *contp* queer

schwül [ʃvyːl] *adj* sultry (*a. fig*), close

schwülstig ['ʃvyːlstɪç] *adj* bombastic, pompous

Schwung [ʃvʊŋ] *m* (-[e]s; *Schwünge* ['ʃvʏŋə]) swing; *fig* verve, pep; drive; **in ~ kommen** get going; **et. in ~ bringen** get s.th. going; **'schwungvoll** *adj* full of energy *or* verve; MUS swinging

Schwur [ʃvuːɐ] *m* (-[e]s; *Schwüre* ['ʃvyːrə]) oath; **~gericht** *n* JUR jury court

sechs [zɛks] *adj* six; *grade:* F, *Br a.* poor; **'Sechseck** *n* (-[e]s; -e) hexagon; **'sechseckig** *adj* hexagonal; **'sechsfach** *adj* sixfold; **'sechsmal** *adv* six times; **Sechs'tagerennen** *n* SPORT six-day race; **sechstägig** ['zɛkstɛːgɪç] *adj* lasting *or* of six days; **'sechste** *adj* sixth; **Sechstel** ['zɛkstəl] *n* (-*s*; -) sixth (part); **'sechstens** *adv* sixthly, in the sixth place; **sechzehn(te)** ['zɛçtseːn(tə)] *adj* sixteen(th); **sechzig** ['zɛçtsɪç] *adj* sixty; **'sechzigste** *adj* sixtieth

See¹ [zeː] *m* (-*s*; -*n*) lake

See² *f* (-; *no pl*) sea, ocean; **auf ~** at sea; **auf hoher ~** on the high seas; **an der ~** at the seaside; **zur ~ gehen (fahren)** go to sea (be a sailor); **in ~ stechen** put to sea; **~bad** *n* seaside resort; **~fahrt** *f* navigation; **~gang** *m* (-[*e*]*s*; *no pl*): **hoher ~** heavy sea; **~hafen** *m* seaport; **~hund** *m* zo seal; **~karte** *f* nautical chart

'seekrank *adj* seasick

'Seekrankheit *f* seasickness

Seele ['zeːlə] *f* (-; -*n*) soul (*a. fig*)

'seelenlos *adj* soulless

'Seelenruhe *f* peace of mind; **in aller ~** as cool as you please

seelisch ['zeːlɪʃ] *adj* mental

'Seelsorge *f* (-; *no pl*) pastoral care

Seelsorger ['zeːlzɔrgɐ] *m* (-*s*; -), **'Seelsorgerin** *f* (-; -*nen*) pastor

See|macht *f* sea power; **~mann** *m* (-[*e*]*s*; -*leute*) seaman, sailor; **~meile** *f* nautical mile; **~not** *f* (-; *no pl*) distress (at sea); **~notkreuzer** *m* MAR rescue cruiser; **~räuber** *m* pirate; **~reise** *f* voyage, cruise; **~rose** *f* BOT water lily; **~sack** *m* kit bag; **~schlacht** *f* MIL naval battle; **~streitkräfte** *pl* MIL naval forces, navy

'seetüchtig *adj* seaworthy

'See|warte *f* naval observatory; **~weg** *m* sea route; **auf dem ~** by sea; **~zeichen** *n* seamark; **~zunge** *f* zo sole

Segel ['zeːgəl] *n* (-*s*; -) sail; **~boot** *n* sailboat, *Br* sailing boat; **~fliegen** *n* gliding; **~flugzeug** *n* glider

'segeln *v/i* (*ge-*, *sein*) sail, SPORT *a.* yacht

'Segel|schiff *n* sailing ship; sailing vessel; **~sport** *m* sailing, yachting; **~tuch** *n* canvas, sailcloth

Segen ['zeːgən] *m* (-*s*; -) blessing (*a. fig*)

Segler ['zeːglɐ] *m* (-*s*; -) yachtsman

Seglerin ['zeːglərɪn] *f* (-; -*nen*) yachtswoman

segnen ['zeːgnən] *v/t* (*ge-*, *h*) bless

'Segnung *f* (-; -*nen*) blessing

Sehbeteiligung ['zeːbətailɪgʊŋ] *f* (TV) ratings

sehen ['zeːən] *v/i and v/t* (*irr, ge-, h*) see; watch; notice; **~ nach** look after; look for; **sich ~ lassen** show up; **das sieht man (kaum)** it (hardly) shows; **siehst du** (you) see; I told you; **siehe oben (unten, Seite ...)** see above (below, page ...); **'sehenlassen** *v/refl* (*irr, lassen, sep, no -ge-, h*) → **sehen**; **'sehenswert** *adj* worth seeing; **'Sehenswürdigkeit** *f* (-; -*en*) place *etc* worth seeing, sight, *pl* sights

'Sehkraft *f* (-; *no pl*) eyesight, vision

Sehne ['zeːnə] *f* (-; -*n*) ANAT sinew; string

sehnen ['zeːnən] *v/refl* (*ge-*, *h*) long (**nach** for), yearn (for); **sich danach ~ zu** *inf* be longing to *inf*

'Sehnerv *m* ANAT optic nerve

sehnig ['zeːnɪç] *adj* sinewy, GASTR *a.* stringy

sehnlichst ['zeːnlɪçst] *adj* dearest

'Sehnsucht *f*, **'sehnsüchtig** *adj* longing, yearning

sehr [zeːɐ] *adv before adj and adv*: very; *with verbs*: very much, greatly

'Sehtest *m* sight test

seicht [zaiçt] *adj* shallow (*a. fig*)

Seide ['zaidə] *f* (-; -*n*), **'seiden** *adj* silk

'Seidenpa,pier *n* tissue paper

'Seidenraupe *f* zo silkworm

seidig ['zaidɪç] *adj* silky

Seife ['zaifə] *f* (-; -*n*) soap

'Seifen|blase *f* soap bubble; **~lauge** *f* (soap)suds; **~oper** *f* TV soap opera; **~schale** *f* soap dish; **~schaum** *m* lather

seifig ['zaifɪç] *adj* soapy

Seil [zail] *n* (-[*e*]*s*; -*e*) rope

'Seilbahn *f* cable railway

'seilspringen *v/i* (*only inf*) skip

sein¹ [zain] *v/i* (*irr, ge-, sein*) be; exist; *et.* **~ lassen** stop *or* quit (doing) s.th.

sein² *poss pron* his, her, its; **~er, ~e, ~(e)s** his, hers

Sein *n* (-*s*; *no pl*) being; existence

seiner|seits ['zainɐzaits] *adv* for his part; **~zeit** *adv* then, in those days

seines'gleichen ['zainəsglaiçən] *pron* his equals

seinet'wegen ['zainətveːgən] → **meinetwegen**

'seinlassen *v/t* (*irr, sep, -ge-, h*): *et.* **~** → **sein**

seit [zait] *prp and cj* since; **~ 2002** since 2002; **~ drei Jahren** for three years (now); **~ langem (kurzem)** for a long (short) time; **~dem 1.** *adv* since then, since that time, ever since **2.** *cj* since

Seite ['zaitə] *f* (-; -*n*) side (*a. fig*); page; *auf der linken ~* on the left(-hand side); *fig auf der e-n* (*anderen*) *~* on the one (other) hand

'**Seiten|ansicht** *f* side view, profile; **~blick** *m* sidelong glance; **~hieb** *m* sideswipe; **~linie** *f esp soccer:* touchline

seitens ['zaitəns] *prp* (*gen*) on the part of, by

'**Seitensprung** F *m:* *e-n ~ machen* cheat (on one's wife *or* husband)

'**Seitenstechen** *n* (-*s; no pl*) MED a stitch (in the side)

'**seitlich** *adj* side ..., at the side(s)

seitwärts ['zaitvɛrts] *adv* sideways, to the side

Sekretär [zekre'tɛːɐ] *m* (-*s; -e*) secretary; bureau; **Sekretariat** [zekreta-'rjaːt] *n* (-[*e*]*s; -e*) (secretary's) office; **Sekretärin** [zekre'tɛːrɪn] *f* (-; -*nen*) secretary

Sekt [zɛkt] *m* (-[*e*]*s; -e*) sparkling wine

Sekte ['zɛktə] *f* (-; -*n*) sect

Sektion [zɛk'tsjoːn] *f* (-; -*en*) section; MED autopsy

Sektor ['zɛktoːɐ] *m* (-*s; -en* [zɛk-'toːrən]) sector; *fig* field

Sekunde [ze'kʊndə] *f* (-; -*n*) second; *auf die ~* to the second

Se'kundenzeiger *m* second(s) hand

selbe ['zɛlbə] *adj* same

selber ['zɛlbɐ] *pron →* **selbst** *1*

selbst [zɛlbst] **1.** *pron:* *ich* (*du etc*) *~* I (you *etc*) myself (yourself *etc*); *mach es ~* do it yourself; *et. ~ tun* do s.th. by oneself; *von ~* by itself; *~ gemacht* homemade **2.** *adv* even

'**Selbstachtung** *f* self-respect

'**selbständig** *etc →* **selbstständig** *etc*

'**Selbstbedienung** *f* self-service; **~sladen** *m* self-service store (*Br* shop)

'**Selbst|befriedigung** *f* masturbation; **~beherrschung** *f* self-control; **~bestimmung** *f* self-determination

'**selbstbewusst** *adj* self-confident, self--assured; '**Selbstbewusstsein** *n* self--confidence

'**Selbst|bildnis** *n* self-portrait; **~erhaltungstrieb** *m* survival instinct; **~erkenntnis** *f* (-; *no pl*) self-knowledge

'**selbstgerecht** *adj* self-righteous

'**Selbst|hilfe** *f* self-help; **~hilfegruppe** *f*

self-help group; **~kostenpreis** *m:* *zum ~* ECON at cost (price)

'**selbstkritisch** *adj* self-critical

'**Selbstlaut** *m* LING vowel

'**selbstlos** *adj* unselfish

'**Selbst|mord** *m,* **~mörder(in)** suicide

'**selbstmörderisch** *adj* suicidal

'**selbstsicher** *adj* self-confident, self--assured

'**selbstständig** *adj* independent, self--reliant; self-employed; '**Selbstständigkeit** *f* (-; *no pl*) independence

'**Selbststudium** *n* (-*s; no pl*) self-study

'**selbst|süchtig** *adj* selfish, ego(-t)istic(al); **~tätig** *adj* automatic

'**Selbsttäuschung** *f* self-deception

'**selbstverständlich 1.** *adj* natural; *das ist ~* that's a matter of course **2.** *adv* of course, naturally; *~! a.* by all means!; '**Selbstverständlichkeit** *f* (-; -*en*) matter of course

'**Selbst|verteidigung** *f* self-defense, *Br* self-defence; **~vertrauen** *n* self-confidence, self-reliance; **~verwaltung** *f* self-government, autonomy

'**selbstzufrieden** *adj* self-satisfied

selchen ['zɛlçən] *Austrian →* **räuchern**

selig ['zeːlɪç] *adj* REL blessed; late; *fig* overjoyed

Sellerie ['zɛləri] *m* (-*s; -[s]*), *f* (-; -) BOT celeriac; celery

selten ['zɛltən] **1.** *adj* rare; *~ sein* be rare, be scarce **2.** *adv* rarely, seldom

'**Seltenheit** *f* (-; *no pl*) rarity

seltsam ['zɛltzaːm] *adj* strange, odd

Semester [ze'mɛstɐ] *n* (-*s; -*) UNIV semester, *esp Br* term

Semikolon [zemi'koːlɔn] *n* (-*s; -s*) LING semicolon

Seminar [zemi'naːɐ] *n* (-*s; -e*) UNIV department; seminar; REL seminary; teacher training college

sen. *abbr of* **senior** sen., Sen., Sr, Snr, senior

Senat [ze'naːt] *m* (-[*e*]*s; -e*) senate

Senator [ze'naːtoːɐ] *m* (-*s; -en* [zena-'toːrən]), **Sena'torin** *f* (-; -*nen*) senator

Sendemast *m* ELECTR mast

senden ['zɛndən] *v/t* ([*irr,*] *ge-, h*) send (*mit der Post®* by mail, *Br* by post); ELECTR broadcast, transmit, *a.* televise

Sender ['zɛndɐ] *m* (-*s; -*) radio *or* television station; ELECTR transmitter

'**Sende|reihe** f TV or radio series; **~schluss** m close-down, F sign-off; **~zeichen** n call letters (Br sign); **~zeit** f air time

'**Sendung** f (-; -en) broadcast, program (-me), a. telecast; ECON consignment, shipment; **auf ~ sein** be on the air

Senf [zɛnf] m (-[e]s; -e) mustard (a. BOT)

senil [ze'ni:l] adj senile; **Senilität** [zenili'tɛ:t] f (-; no pl) senility

Senior ['ze:njoːɐ] **1.** m (-s; -en [ze-'njoːrən]) senior (a. SPORT); senior citizen **2.** adj senior

Seni'orenheim n old people's home

Seni'orin f (-; -nen) senior citizen

Senke ['zɛŋkə] f (-; -n) GEOGR depression, hollow; '**senken** v/t (ge-, h) lower (a. one's voice), a. bow (one's head); ECON a. reduce, cut; **sich ~** drop, go or come down

'**senkrecht** adj vertical

Sensation [zɛnza'tsjoːn] f (-; -en) sensation; **sensationell** [zɛnzatsjo'nɛl] adj, **Sensati'ons...** in cpds ...**blatt** etc: sensational (...)

Sense ['zɛnzə] f (-; -n) AGR scythe

sensibel [zɛn'zi:bəl] adj sensitive

sensibilisieren [zɛnzibili'zi:rən] v/t (no -ge-, h) sensitize (**für** to)

sentimental [zɛntimen'taːl] adj sentimental; **Sentimentalität** [zɛntimɛntali'tɛːt] f (-; -en) sentimentality

September [zɛp'tɛmbɐ] m (-[s]; -) September

Serenade [zere'naːdə] f (-; -n) MUS serenade

Serie ['zeːrjə] f (-; -n) series, TV etc a. serial; set; **in ~** produce etc in series

'**serienmäßig** adj series(-produced); standard

'**Serien|nummer** f serial number; **~wagen** m MOT standard-type car

seriös [ze'rjøːs] adj respectable; honest; serious

Serum ['zeːrum] n (-s; -ren, -ra) serum

Service[1] [zɛr'viːs] n (-[s]; -) set; service

Service[2] ['zøːɐvis] m, n (-; -s) service

servieren [zɛr'viːrən] v/t (no -ge-, h) serve; **Serviererin** [zɛr'viːrərin] f (-; -nen) waitress; **Serviertochter** [zɛr-'viːɐtɔxtɐ] Swiss f waitress

Serviette [zɛr'vjɛtə] f (-; -n) napkin, esp Br serviette

Servo|bremse ['zɛrvobrɛmzə] f MOT servo or power brake; **~lenkung** f MOT servo(-assisted) or power steering

Sessel ['zɛsəl] m (-s; -) armchair, easy chair; **~lift** m chair lift

sesshaft ['zɛshaft] adj: **~ werden** settle (down)

Set [zɛt] n, m (-s; -s) place mat

setzen ['zɛtsən] v/t and v/i (ge-, h) put, set (a. PRINT, AGR, MAR), AGR a. plant; place; seat s.o.; **~ über** (acc) jump over; cross (river); **~ auf** (acc) bet on, back; **sich ~** sit down; CHEM etc settle; **sich ~ auf** (acc) get on, mount; **sich ~ in** (acc) get into; **sich zu j-m ~** sit beside or with s.o.; **~ Sie sich bitte!** take or have a seat!

Setzer ['zɛtsɐ] m (-s; -) PRINT compositor, typesetter; **Setzerei** [zɛtsə'rai] f (-; -en) PRINT composing room

Seuche ['zɔʏçə] f (-; -en) epidemic (disease)

seufzen ['zɔʏftsən] v/i (ge-, h), **Seufzer** ['zɔʏftsɐ] m (-s; -) sigh

Sexismus [zɛ'ksɪsmus] m (-; no pl) sexism; **Sexist** [zɛ'ksɪst] m (-en; -en), **se-'xistisch** adj sexist

Sexual... [zɛ'ksuaːl-] in cpds ...**erziehung**, ...**leben**, ...**trieb** etc: sex(ual) ...; **~verbrechen** n sex crime

sexuell [zɛ'ksuɛl] adj sexual; **~e Belästigung** (sexual) harassment

sexy ['zɛksi] adj sexy

sezieren [ze'tsiːrən] v/t (no -ge-, h) MED dissect (a. fig); perform an autopsy on

Showgeschäft ['ʃougəʃɛft] n (-[e]s; no pl) show business

sich [zɪç] refl pron oneself; himself, herself, itself; pl themselves; yourself, pl yourselves; **~ ansehen** look at oneself; look at each other

Sichel ['zɪçəl] f (-; -n) AGR sickle; ASTR crescent

sicher ['zɪçɐ] **1.** adj safe (**vor** dat from), secure (from); esp TECH proof (**gegen** against); fig certain, sure; reliable; (**sich**) **~ sein** be sure (**e-r Sache** of s.th.; **dass** that); **2.** adv safely; **~!** of course, sure(ly); certainly; probably; **du hast** (**bist**) **~ ...** you must have (be) ...

'**Sicherheit** f (-; -en) (no pl) security (a. MIL, POL, ECON); safety (a. TECH); fig certainty; skill; (**sich**) **in ~ bringen** get to safety; ECON cover

'**Sicherheits...** esp TECH in cpds ...glas, ...nadel, ...schloss etc: safety ...; ~**gurt** m seat belt, safety belt; ~**maßnahme** f safety (POL security) measure

'**sicherlich** adv → **sicher** 2

'**sichern** v/t (ge-, h) protect, safeguard; secure (a. MIL, TECH); IT save; **sich** ~ secure o.s. (**gegen, vor** dat against, from); '**sicherstellen** v/t (sep, -ge-, h) secure; guarantee; **Sicherung** ['zɪçə-rʊŋ] f (-; -en) securing; safeguard(-ing); TECH safety device; ELECTR fuse

'**Sicherungs|kasten** m ELECTR fuse box; ~**ko,pie** f IT backup; **e-e** ~ **machen** (**von**) back up

Sicht [zɪçt] f (-; no pl) visibility; view; **in** ~ **kommen** come into sight or view; **auf lange** ~ in the long run; '**sichtbar** adj visible; **sichten** ['zɪçtən] v/t (ge-, h) sight; fig sort (through or out)

'**Sichtkarte** f season ticket

'**sichtlich** adv visibly

'**Sichtweite** f visibility; **in** (**außer**) ~ within (out of) sight

sickern ['zɪkɐn] v/i (ge-, sein) trickle, ooze, seep

sie [zi:] pers pron she; it; pl they; **Sie** you

Sieb [zi:p] n (-[e]s; -e) sieve; strainer

sieben[1] ['zi:bən] v/t (ge-, h) sieve, sift

'**sieben**[2] adj seven

Sieben'meter m SPORT penalty shot or throw

siebte ['zi:ptə] adj, '**Siebtel** n (-s; -) seventh; **siebzehn(te)** ['zi:ptse:ntə] adj seventeen(th); **siebzig** ['zi:ptsɪç] adj seventy; '**siebzigste** adj seventieth

siedeln ['zi:dəln] v/i (ge-, h) settle

sieden ['zi:dən] v/t and v/i ([irr,] ge-, h) boil, simmer

'**Siedepunkt** m boiling point (a. fig)

Siedler ['zi:dlɐ] m (-s; -) settler

Siedlung ['zi:dlʊŋ] f (-; -en) settlement; housing development

Sieg [zi:k] m (-[e]s; -e) victory, SPORT a. win

Siegel ['zi:gəl] n (-s; -) seal, signet

'**Siegellack** m sealing wax

'**siegeln** v/t (ge-, h) seal

siegen ['zi:gən] v/i (ge-, h) win

Sieger ['zi:gɐ] m (-s; -), **Siegerin** ['zi:gərɪn] f (-; -nen) winner

'**siegreich** adj winning; victorious

Signal [zɪ'gna:l] n (-s; -e), **signalisieren** [zɪgnali'zi:rən] v/t (no -ge-, h) signal

signieren [zɪ'gni:rən] v/t (no -ge-, h) sign

Silbe ['zɪlbə] f (-; -n) syllable

'**Silbentrennung** f LING syllabification

Silber ['zɪlbɐ] n (-s; no pl) silver; silver-ware; '**silbergrau** adj silver-gray (Br -grey); '**Silberhochzeit** f silver wedding; '**silbern** adj silver

Silhouette [zi'luɛtə] f (-; -n) silhouette; skyline

Silikon [zili'ko:n] n (-s; -e) CHEM silicone

Silizium [zi'li:tsjʊm] n (-s; no pl) CHEM silicon

Silvester [zɪl'vɛstɐ] n (-s; -) New Year's Eve

Sims [zɪms] m, n (-es; -e) ledge; windowsill

simulieren [zimu'li:rən] v/t and v/i TECH etc simulate; sham

simultan [zimʊl'ta:n] adj simultaneous

Sinfonie [zɪnfo'ni:] f (-; -n) MUS symphony

singen ['zɪŋən] v/t and v/i (irr, ge-, h) sing (**richtig** [**falsch**] in [out of] tune)

Singular ['zɪŋgulaɐ] m (-s; -e) LING singular

Singvogel ['zɪŋfo:gəl] m ZO songbird

sinken ['zɪŋkən] v/i (irr, ge-, sein) sink (a. fig), go down (a. ECON), ASTR a. set; prices etc: fall, drop

Sinn [zɪn] m (-[e]s; -e) sense (**für** of); mind; meaning; point, idea; **im** ~ **haben** have in mind; **es hat keinen** ~ (**zu warten** etc) it's no use or good (waiting etc); '**Sinnbild** n symbol

'**sinnentstellend** adj distorting

Sinnes|organ ['zɪnəsˀɔrga:n] n sense organ; ~**täuschung** f hallucination; ~**wandel** m change of mind

'**sinnlich** adj sensuous; sensory; sensual; '**Sinnlichkeit** f (-; no pl) sensuality

'**sinnlos** adj senseless; useless

'**sinnverwandt** adj synonymous

'**sinnvoll** adj meaningful; useful; wise, sensible

Sintflut ['zɪntflu:t] f the Flood

Sippe ['zɪpə] f (-; -n) (extended) family, clan

Sirene [zi're:nə] f (-; -n) siren

Sirup ['zi:rʊp] m (-s; -e) sirup, Br syrup; treacle, molasses

Sitte ['zɪtə] f (-; -n) custom, tradition; pl morals; manners

soff

'**Sittenlosigkeit** *f* (-; *no pl*) immorality
'**Sittenpoli**,**zei** *f* vice squad
'**sittenwidrig** *adj* immoral
'**Sittlichkeitsverbrechen** *n* sex crime
Situation [zitua'tsjoːn] *f* (-; -*en*) situation; position
Sitz [zɪts] *m* (-*es*; -*e*) seat; fit; ~**blo**,**ckade** *f* sit-down demonstration
sitzen ['zɪtsən] *v/i* (*irr*, *ge-*, *h*) sit (*an dat* at; *auf dat* on); be; fit; F do time; ~ **bleiben** keep one's seat; PED have to repeat a year; F ~ **bleiben auf** (*dat*) be left with; F *j-n* ~ **lassen** leave s.o. in the lurch, let s.o. down
'**sitzen|bleiben** *v/i* (*irr*, **bleiben**, *sep*, -*ge-*, *sein*) → **sitzen**; ~**lassen** *v/i* (*irr*, **lassen**, *sep*, *no -ge-*, *sein*) a. *fig* → **sitzen**
'**Sitzplatz** *m* seat
'**Sitzstreik** *m* sit-down strike
'**Sitzung** *f* (-; -*en*) session (*a.* PARL), meeting, conference
Skala ['skaːla] *f* (-; -*en*) scale, *fig a.* range
Skalp [skalp] *m* (-*s*; -*e*), **skalpieren** [skal'piːrən] *v/t* (*no -ge-*, *h*) scalp
Skandal [skan'daːl] *m* (-*s*; -*e*) scandal; *ein* ~ *sein* be scandalous; **skandalös** [skanda'løːs] *adj* scandalous, shocking
Skelett [ske'lɛt] *n* (-[*e*]*s*; -*e*) skeleton
Skepsis ['skɛpsɪs] *f* (-; *no pl*) skepticism, *Br* scepticism; **Skeptiker** ['skɛptikɐ] *m* (-*s*; -) skeptic, *Br* sceptic; **skeptisch** ['skɛptɪʃ] *adj* skeptical, *Br* sceptical
Ski [ʃiː] *m* (-*s*; -*er* ['ʃiːɐ]) ski; ~ *laufen* or *fahren* ski; ~**brille** *f* ski goggles; ~**fahren** *n* skiing; ~**fahrer(in)** skier; ~**fliegen** *n* ski flying; ~**gebiet** *n* skiing area; ~**kurs** *m* skiing course; ~**läufer(in)** skier; ~**lehrer(in)** ski instructor; ~**lift** *m* ski lift; ~**schuh** *m* ski boot; ~**sport** *m* skiing; ~**springen** *n* ski jumping; ~**stock** *m* ski pole
Skizze ['skɪtsə] *f* (-; -*n*), **skizzieren** [skɪ'tsiːrən] *v/t* (*no -ge-*, *h*) sketch
Sklave ['sklaːvə] *m* (-*n*; -*n*) slave (*a. fig*); **Sklaverei** [sklaːvə'raɪ] *f* (-; *no pl*) slavery; '**Sklavin** *f* (-; -*nen*) slave (*a. fig*); '**sklavisch** *adj* slavish (*a. fig*)
Skonto ['skɔnto] *m*, *n* (-*s*; -*s*) ECON (cash) discount
Skorpion [skɔr'pjoːn] *m* (-*s*; -*e*) ZO scorpion; ASTR Scorpio; *er ist* (*ein*) ~ he's (a) Scorpio

Skrupel ['skruːpəl] *m* (-*s*; -) scruple, qualm; '**skrupellos** *adj* unscrupulous
Skulptur [skʊlp'tuːɐ] *f* (-; -*en*) sculpture
Slalom ['slaːlɔm] *m* (-*s*; -*s*) slalom
Slawe ['slaːvə] *m* (-*n*; -*n*), '**Slawin** *f* (-; -*nen*) Slav; '**slawisch** *adj* Slav(ic)
Slip [slɪp] *m* (-*s*; -*s*) briefs, panties
'**Slipeinlage** *f* panty liner
Slipper ['slɪpɐ] *m* (-*s*; -) loafer, *esp Br* slip-on (shoe)
Slowake [slo'vaːkə] *m* (-*n*; -*n*) Slovak
Slowakei [slova'kaɪ] *f* Slovakia
Slo'wakin *f* (-; -*nen*), **slo'wakisch** *adj* Slovak
Smaragd [sma'rakt] *m* (-[*e*]*s*; -*e*) MIN, **sma'ragdgrün** *adj* emerald
Smiley ['smaili] *n* (-*s*; -*s*) smiley
Smog [smɔk] *m* (-[*s*]; -*s*) smog; **Smogalarm** *m* smog alert
Smoking ['smoːkɪŋ] *m* (-*s*; -*s*) tuxedo, *Br* dinner jacket
SMS [ɛsɛm'ɛs] *f* (-; -) text (message); *ich schicke dir eine* ~ I'll text you, I'll send you a text (message)
Snob [snɔp] *m* (-*s*; -*s*) snob; **Snobismus** [sno'bɪsmus] *m* (-; *no pl*) snobbery; **sno'bistisch** *adj* snobbish
Snowboard ['snoːboːɐt] *n* (-*s*; -*s*) snowboard; **Snowboardfahren** *n* snowboarding
so [zoː] **1.** *adv* so; like this *or* that, this *or* that way; thus; such; (*nicht*) ~ *groß wie* (not) as big as; ~ *ein*(*e*) such a; ~ *sehr* so (F that) much; *und* ~ *weiter* and so on; *oder* ~ *et.* or s.th. like that; *oder* ~ or so; ~, *fangen wir an!* well *or* all right, let's begin!; F ~ *weit sein* be ready; *es ist* ~ *weit* it's time; ~ *genannt* so-called; *doppelt* ~ *viel* twice as much; ~ *viel wie möglich* as much as possible **2.** *cj* so, therefore; ~ *dass* so that **3.** *int*: ~*!* all right!, o.k.!; that's it!; *ach* ~*!* I see
s.o. *abbr of* **siehe oben** see above
so'bald [zo'balt] *cj* as soon as
Socke ['zɔkə] *f* (-; -*n*) sock
Sockel ['zɔkəl] *m* (-*s*; -) base; pedestal
Sodbrennen ['zoːtbrɛnən] *n* (-*s*; *no pl*) MED heartburn
soeben [zo'eːbən] *adv* just (now)
Sofa ['zoːfa] *n* (-*s*; -*s*) sofa, settee, davenport
sofern [zo'fɛrn] *cj* if, provided that; ~ *nicht* unless
soff [zɔf] *pret of* **saufen**

sofort [zo'fɔrt] *adv* at once, immediately, right away

So'fortbildkamera *f* PHOT instant camera

Software ['zɔftwɛːɐ] *f* IT software; **~pa-,ket** *n* software package

sog [zoːk] *pret of* **saugen**

Sog *m* (-[e]s; -e) suction, MAR *a.* wake

sogar [zo'gaːɐ] *adv* even

sogenannt ['zoːɡənant] *adj* so-called

Sohle ['zoːlə] *f* (-; -n) sole; *mining:* floor

Sohn [zoːn] *m* (-[e]s; *Söhne* ['zøːnə]) son

Sojabohne ['zoːjaboːnə] *f* BOT soybean

so'lange [zo'laŋə] *cj* as long as

Solar... [zo'laːɐ-] *in cpds* ...energie *etc*: solar ...

solch [zɔlç] *dem pron* such, like this *or* that

Sold [zɔlt] *m* (-[e]s; -e) MIL pay

Soldat [zɔl'daːt] *m* (-en; -en), **Sol'datin** *f* (-; -nen) soldier

Söldner ['zœldnɐ] *m* (-s; -) MIL mercenary

Sole ['zoːlə] *f* (-; -n) brine, salt water

solidarisch [zoli'daːrɪʃ] *adj:* **sich ~ er-klären mit** declare one's solidarity with

solide [zo'liːdə] *adj* solid, *fig a.* sound; reasonable (*prices*); steady (*person*)

Solist [zo'lɪst] *m* (-en; -en), **So'listin** *f* (-; -nen) soloist

Soll [zɔl] *n* (-[s]; -[s]) ECON debit; target, quota; **~ und Haben** debit and credit

sollen ['zɔlən] *v/i* (ge-; h) *and v/aux* (*irr, no -ge-, h*) be to; be supposed to; (*was*) **soll ich ...?** (what) shall I ...?; **du soll-test** (**nicht**) ... you should(n't) ...; you ought(n't) to; **was soll das?** what's the idea?

Solo ['zoːlo] *n* (-s, -s, *Soli*) *esp* MUS solo; *SPORT* solo attempt *etc*

so'mit [zo'mɪt] *cj* thus, so, consequently

Sommer ['zɔmɐ] *m* (-s; -) summer (time); **im ~** in (the) summer; **~ferien** *pl* summer vacation (*Br* holidays); **~fri-sche** *f* summer resort

'sommerlich *adj* summery

'Sommersprosse *f* freckle

'sommersprossig *adj* freckled

'Sommerzeit *f* summertime; daylight saving (*Br* summer) time

Sonate [zo'naːtə] *f* (-; -n) MUS sonata

Sonde ['zɔndə] *f* (-; -n) probe (*a.* MED)

Sonder... ['zɔndɐ-] *in cpds* ...angebot,

...ausgabe, ...flug, ...preis, ...wunsch, ...zug *etc*: special ...

'sonderbar *adj* strange, F funny

'Sonderling *m* (-s; -e) eccentric

'Sondermüll *m* hazardous (*or* special toxic) waste; **~depo,nie** *f* special waste dump

sondern ['zɔndɐn] *cj* but; **nicht nur ...,** **~ auch ...** not only ... but also ...

'Sonderschule *f* special school (for the handicapped *etc*)

Sonnabend ['zɔnʔaːbənt] *m* Saturday

Sonne ['zɔnə] *f* (-; -n) sun

sonnen ['zɔnən] *v/refl* (*ge-, h*) sunbathe

'Sonnenaufgang *m* (*bei ~* at) sunrise

'Sonnen|bad *n:* **ein ~ nehmen** sunbathe; **~bank** *f* (-; *-bänke*) sunbed; **~blume** *f* BOT sunflower; **~brand** *m* sunburn; **~bräune** *f* suntan; **~brille** *f* sunglasses; **~creme** *f* suntan lotion, *Br* sun cream; **~ener,gie** *f* solar energy; **~finsternis** *f* solar eclipse

'sonnen|klar F *adj* (as) clear as daylight

'Sonnen|kol,lektor *m* solar panel; **~licht** *n* (-[e]s, *no pl*) sunlight; **~öl** *n* suntan oil; **~schein** *m* sunshine; **~schirm** *m* sunshade; **~schutz** *m* suntan lotion; **~seite** *f* sunny side (*a. fig*); **~stich** *m* sunstroke; **~strahl** *m* sunbeam; **~sys,tem** *n* solar system; **~uhr** *f* sundial; **~untergang** *m* sunset

sonnig ['zɔnɪç] *adj* sunny (*a. fig*)

Sonntag ['zɔntaːk] *m* Sunday; (*am*) **~** on Sunday; **'sonntags** *adv* on Sundays

'Sonntagsfahrer *contp m* MOT Sunday driver

sonst [zɔnst] *adv* else; otherwise, or (else); normally, usually; **~ noch et.** (*je-mand*)? anything (anyone) else?; **~ noch Fragen?** any other questions?; **~ nichts** nothing else; **alles wie ~** everything as usual; **nichts ist wie ~** nothing is as it used to be; **'sonstig** *adj* other

Sopran [zo'praːn] *m* (-s; -e) MUS, **Sopra-nistin** [zopra'nɪstɪn] *f* (-; -nen) MUS soprano

Sorge ['zɔrɡə] *f* (-; -n) worry; sorrow; trouble; care; **sich ~n machen** (*um*) worry *or* be worried (about); **keine ~!** don't worry!; **sorgen** ['zɔrɡən] (*ge-, h*) **1.** *v/i:* **~ für** care for, take care of; **da-für ~, dass** see (to it) that **2.** *v/refl:* **sich ~ um** worry *or* be worried about

'Sorgenkind *n* problem child

Sorgfalt ['zɔrkfalt] f (-; no pl) care
sorgfältig ['zɔrkfɛltɪç] adj careful
sorglos ['zɔrkloːs] adj carefree; careless
Sorte ['zɔrtə] f (-; -n) sort, kind, type; **sortieren** [zɔr'tiːrən] v/t (no -ge-, h) sort; arrange; **Sortiment** [zɔrti'mɛnt] n (-[e]s; -e) ECON assortment
Soße ['zoːsə] f (-; -n) sauce; gravy
sott [zɔt] pret of **sieden**
Souffleur [zu'fløːɐ] m (-s; -e), **Souffleuse** [zu'fløːzə] f (-; -n) THEA prompter; **soufflieren** [zu'fliːrən] v/i (no -ge-, h) THEA prompt (j-m s.o.)
souverän [zuvə'rɛːn] adj POL sovereign
Souveränität [zuvərɛni'tɛːt] f (-; no pl) POL sovereignty
so'viel [zo'fiːl] cj as far as; → **so**; **so-'weit** cj as far as; → **so**; **so'wie** cj as well as, and ... as well; as soon as; **sowie'so** adv anyway, anyhow, in any case
so'wohl [zo'voːl] cj: ~ *Lehrer als (auch) Schüler* both teachers and students
sozial [zo'tsjaːl] adj social
Sozi'al... in cpds ...arbeiter, ...demokrat, ...versicherung etc: social ...; **~hilfe** f welfare, Br social security; **~ beziehen** be on welfare (Br social security)
Sozialismus [zotsja'lɪsmus] m (-; no pl) socialism; **Sozialist(in)** [-en/-; -en / -nen), **sozia'listisch** adj socialist
Sozi'alkunde f PED social studies
Sozi'alstaat m welfare state
Soziologe [zotsjo'loːgə] m (-n; -n) sociologist; **Soziologie** [zotsjolo'giː] f (-; no pl) sociology; **Sozio'login** f (-; -nen) sociologist; **soziologisch** [zotsjo'loːgɪʃ] adj sociological
sozu'sagen adv so to speak
Spagat [ʃpa'gaːt] m: ~ *machen* do the splits
Spalier [ʃpa'liːɐ] n (-s; -e) BOT espalier; MIL etc lane
Spalt [ʃpalt] m (-[e]s; -e) crack, gap; **Spalte** ['ʃpaltə] f (-; -n) → **Spalt**; PRINT column; **'spalten** v/t ([irr,] ge-, h) split (a. fig); POL divide; **sich** ~ split (up); **'Spaltung** f (-; -en) split(ting); PHYS fission; fig split; POL division
Span [ʃpaːn] m (-[e]s; Späne ['ʃpɛːnə]) chip; pl TECH shavings
Spange ['ʃpaŋə] f (-; -n) clasp
Spaniel ['ʃpaːnjəl] m (-s; -s) ZO spaniel
Spanien ['ʃpaːnjən] Spain

Spanier ['ʃpaːnjɐ] m (-s; -), **Spanierin** ['ʃpaːnjərin] f (-; -nen) Spaniard
spanisch ['ʃpaːnɪʃ] adj Spanish
spann [ʃpan] pret of **spinnen**
Spann m (-[e]s; -e) ANAT instep
Spanne ['ʃpanə] f (-; -n) span
'spannen (ge-, h) **1.** v/t stretch, tighten; put up (line); cock (gun); draw, bend (bow) **2.** v/i be (too) tight; **~d** adj exciting, thrilling, gripping
'Spannung f (-; -en) tension (a. TECH, POL, PSYCH); ELECTR voltage; fig suspense, excitement
'Spannweite f span, fig a. range
Spar|buch ['ʃpaːɐbuːx] n savings book; **~büchse** f esp Br money box
sparen ['ʃpaːrən] v/i and v/t (ge-, h) save; economize; **~ für** or **auf** (acc) save up for; **Sparer(in)** ['ʃpaːrɐ, 'ʃpaːrərin] m(f) (-s; -/-; -nen) saver
Spargel ['ʃpargəl] m (-s; -) BOT asparagus
'Sparkasse f savings bank
'Sparkonto n savings account
spärlich ['ʃpɛːrlɪç] adj sparse, scant; scanty; poor (attendance)
sparsam ['ʃpaːrzaːm] adj economical (**mit** of); **~ leben** lead a frugal life; **~ umgehen mit** use sparingly; go easy on
'Sparsamkeit f (-; no pl) economy
'Sparschwein(chen) n piggy bank
Spaß [ʃpaːs] m (-es; Späße ['ʃpɛːsə]), Austrian a. **Spass** for; joke; **aus** (nur zum) ~ (just) for fun; **es macht viel (keinen)** ~ it's great (no) fun; **j-m den** ~ verderben spoil s.o.'s fun; **er macht nur** ~ he is only joking (F kidding); **keinen** ~ verstehen have no sense of humo(u)r
spaßen ['ʃpaːsən] v/i (ge-, h) joke
spaßig ['ʃpaːsɪç] adj funny
'Spaßvogel m joker
spät [ʃpɛːt] adj and adv late; **am ~en Nachmittag** late in the afternoon; **wie ~ ist es?** what time is it?; **von früh bis ~** from morning till night; **(fünf Minuten) zu ~ kommen** be (five minutes) late; **bis ~er!** see you (later)!; → **früher**
Spaten ['ʃpaːtən] m (-s; -) spade
'spätestens adv at the latest
Spatz [ʃpats] m (-en; -en) ZO sparrow
spazieren [ʃpa'tsiːrən]: ~ *fahren* go (take s.o.) for a drive; take s.o. out; ~ *gehen* go for a walk

Spazierfahrt [ʃpa'tsiːɐfaːɐt] *f* drive, ride

Spa'ziergang *m* walk; **e-n ~ machen** go for a walk; **Spa'ziergänger(in)** [ʃpa-'tsiːɐgɛŋɐ, ʃpa'tsiːɐgɛŋ(ə)rɪn] (*-s*; *-/-*; *-nen*) walker

Specht [ʃpɛçt] *m* (*-[e]s*; *-e*) ZO woodpecker

Speck [ʃpɛk] *m* (*-[e]s*; *-e*) bacon

speckig [ʃpɛkɪç] *fig adj* greasy

Spediteur [ʃpedi'tøːɐ] *m* (*-s*; *-e*) shipping agent; remover

Spedition [ʃpedi'tsjoːn] *f* (*-*; *-en*) shipping agency; moving (*Br* removal) firm

Speer [ʃpeːɐ] *m* (*-[e]s*; *-e*) spear; SPORT javelin

Speiche [ʃpaiçə] *f* (*-*; *-n*) spoke

Speichel [ʃpaiçəl] *m* (*-s*; *no pl*) saliva, spit

Speicher [ʃpaiçɐ] *m* (*-s*; *-*) storehouse; tank, reservoir; ARCH attic; IT memory, store; **~dichte** *f* IT bit density; **~kapazi-tät** *f* IT memory capacity

'speichern *v/t* (*ge-*, *h*) store (up)

Speicherung [ʃpaiçəruŋ] *f* (*-*; *-en*) storage

speien [ʃpaiən] *v/t* (*irr*, *ge-*, *h*) spit; spout; *volcano etc*: belch

Speise [ʃpaizə] *f* (*-*; *-n*) food; dish; **~eis** *n* ice cream; **~kammer** *f* larder, pantry; **~karte** *f* menu

'speisen (*ge-*, *h*) **1.** *v/i* dine **2.** *v/t* feed (*a.* ELECTR *etc*)

'Speise|röhre *f* ANAT gullet; **~saal** *m* dining hall; **~wagen** *m* RAIL diner, *esp Br* dining car

Spekulant [ʃpeku'lant] *m* (*-en*; *-en*) ECON speculator

Spekulation [ʃpekula'tsjoːn] *f* (*-*; *-en*) speculation, ECON *a.* venture

spekulieren [ʃpeku'liːrən] *v/i* (*no -ge-*, *h*) ECON speculate (**auf** *acc* on; **mit** in)

Spende [ʃpɛndə] *f* (*-*; *-n*) gift; contribution; donation; **'spenden** *v/t* (*ge-*, *h*) give (*a. fig*); donate (*a.* MED); **Spender** [ʃpɛndɐ] *m* (*-s*; *-*) giver; donor (*a.* MED), **Spenderin** *f* (*-*; *-nen*) donor (*a.* MED)

spendieren [ʃpɛn'diːrən] *v/t* (*no -ge-*, *h*) **j-m et. ~** treat s.o. to s.th.

Spengler [ʃpɛŋlɐ] *Austrian m* → **Klempner**

Sperling [ʃpɛrlɪŋ] *m* (*-s*; *-e*) ZO sparrow

Sperre [ʃpɛrə] *f* (*-*; *-n*) barrier, RAIL *a.*

gate; *fig* stop; TECH lock(ing device); barricade; SPORT suspension; PSYCH mental block; ECON embargo

'sperren *v/t* (*ge-*, *h*) close; ECON embargo; cut off; stop (*check*); SPORT suspend; obstruct; **~ in** (*acc*) lock (up) in

'Sperr|holz *n* plywood; **~müllabfuhr** *f* removal of bulky refuse

'Sperrung *f* (*-*; *-en*) closing

Spesen [ʃpeːzən] *pl* expenses

Spezi [ʃpeːtsi] F *m* (*-s*; *-[s]*) buddy, pal

Spezial|ausbildung [ʃpe-'tsjaːlʔausbɪlduŋ] *f* special training; **~gebiet** *n* special field, special(i)ty; **~geschäft** *n* specialized shop or store

spezialisieren [ʃpetsjali'ziːrən] *v/refl* (*no -ge-*, *h*) specialize (**auf** *acc* in); **Spezialist(in)** [ʃpetsja'lɪst(ɪn)] (*-en*; *-en/-*; *-nen*) specialist; **Spezialität** [ʃpetsjali'tɛːt] *f* (*-*; *-en*) special(i)ty; **speziell** [ʃpe'tsjɛl] *adj* specific, particular

spezifisch [ʃpe'tsiːfɪʃ] *adj* specific; **~es Gewicht** specific gravity

Sphäre [ʃfɛːrə] *f* (*-*; *-n*) sphere (*a. fig*)

spicken [ʃpɪkən] (*ge-*, *h*) **1.** *v/t* GASTR lard (*a. fig*) **2.** F *v/i* PED crib

spie [ʃpiː] *pret of* **speien**

Spiegel [ʃpiːgəl] *m* (*-s*; *-*) mirror (*a. fig*)

'Spiegelbild *n* reflection (*a. fig*)

'Spiegelei *n* GASTR fried egg

'spiegel|glatt *adj* glassy; icy

'spiegeln *v/i* and *v/t* (*ge-*, *h*) reflect (*a. fig*); shine; **sich ~** be reflected (*a. fig*)

'Spiegelung *f* (*-*; *-en*) reflection

Spiel [ʃpiːl] *n* (*-[e]s*; *-e*) game (*a. fig*); match; play (*a.* THEA *etc*); gambling; *fig* gamble; **auf dem ~ stehen** be at stake; **aufs ~ setzen** risk; **'Spiel|ca,sino** *n* casino; **spielen** [ʃpiː-lən] *v/i and v/t* (*ge-*, *h*) play (*a. fig*) (**um** for); THEA act; perform; gamble; do (*the pools etc*); *Klavier etc* **~** play the piano *etc*; **'spielend** *fig adv* easily; **Spieler** [ʃpiːlɐ] *m* (*-s*; *-*), **Spielerin** [ʃpiːlə-rɪn] *f* (*-*; *-nen*) player; gambler

'Spiel|feld *n* (playing) field, pitch; **~film** *m* feature film; **~halle** *f* amusement arcade, game room; **~kame,rad(in)** playmate; **~karte** *f* playing card; **~ka,sino** *n* casino; **~marke** *f* counter, chip; **~plan** *m* THEA *etc* program(me); **~platz** *m* playground; **~raum** *fig m* play, scope; **~regel** *f* rule (of the game); **~sachen**

pl toys; **⁓stand** *m* score; **⁓uhr** *f* music (*Br* musical) box; **⁓verderber(in)** (*-s*; *-/-*; *-nen*) spoilsport; **⁓waren** *pl* toys; **⁓zeit** *f* THEA, SPORT season; playing (*film*: running) time

'**Spielzeug** *n* toy(s); **⁓...** *in cpds* ...pistole *etc*: toy ...

Spieß [ʃpiːs] *m* (*-es*; *-e*) MIL spear; GASTR spit; skewer

spießen ['ʃpiːsən] *v/t* (*ge-*, *h*) skewer

Spießer ['ʃpiːsɐ] F *contp m* (*-s*; *-*), '**spießig** F *contp adj* philistine

Spinat [ʃpi'naːt] *m* (*-[e]s*; *-e*) BOT spinach

Spind [ʃpɪnt] *n*, *m* (*-[e]s*; *-e*) locker

Spindel ['ʃpɪndəl] *f* (*-*; *-n*) spindle

Spinne ['ʃpɪnə] *f* (*-*; *-n*) zo spider

'**spinnen** (*irr*, *ge-*, *h*) **1.** *v/t* spin (*a. fig*) **2.** F *contp v/i* be nuts; talk nonsense

Spinner ['ʃpɪnɐ] *m* (*-s*; *-*), '**Spinnerin** F (*-*; *-nen*) spinner; F *contp* nut, crackpot

'**Spinnrad** *n* spinning wheel

'**Spinnwebe** *f* (*-*; *-n*) cobweb

Spion [ʃpjoːn] *m* (*-s*; *-e*) spy

Spionage [ʃpjo'naːʒə] *f* (*-*; *no pl*) espionage; **spionieren** [ʃpjo'niːrən] *v/i* (*no -ge-*, *h*) spy; F snoop

Spi'onin *f* (*-*; *-nen*) spy

Spirale [ʃpi'raːlə] *f* (*-*; *-n*), **spiralförmig** [ʃpi'raːlfœrmɪç] *adj* spiral

Spirituosen [ʃpiri'tuoːzən] *pl* spirits

Spiritus ['ʃpiːritus] *m* spirit

Spital [ʃpi'taːl] *Austrian*, *Swiss n* (*-s*; *Spitäler* [ʃpi'tɛːlɐ]) hospital

spitz [ʃpɪts] *adj* pointed (*a. fig*); MATH acute; **⁓e Zunge** sharp tongue

'**Spitzbogen** *m* ARCH pointed arch

Spitze ['ʃpɪtsə] *f* (*-*; *-n*) point; tip; ARCH spire; BOT, GEOGR top; head (*a. fig*); lace; F MOT top speed; **spitze sein** F be super, be (the) tops; **an der ⁓** at the top (*a. fig*)

Spitzel ['ʃpɪtsəl] *m* (*-s*; *-*) informer, F stoolpigeon

spitzen ['ʃpɪtsən] *v/t* (*ge-*, *h*) point, sharpen; purse; zo prick up (*its ears*)

'**Spitzen...** *in cpds* top ...; hi-tech ...; **⁓technolo,gie** *f* high technology, hi tech

'**spitzfindig** *adj* quibbling

'**Spitzfindigkeit** *f* (*-*; *-en*) subtlety

'**Spitzhacke** *f* pickax(e), pick

'**Spitzname** *m* nickname

Splitter ['ʃplɪtɐ] *m* (*-s*; *-*), '**splittern** *v/i*

(*ge-*, *h*, *sein*) splinter

'**splitter'nackt** F *adj* stark naked

sponsern ['ʃpɔnzɐn] *v/t* (*ge-*, *h*) sponsor

Sponsor ['ʃpɔnzɐ] *m* (*-s*; *-en* [ʃpɔn'zoːrən]) sponsor

spontan [ʃpɔn'taːn] *adj* spontaneous

Sporen ['ʃpoːrən] *pl* spurs (*a.* ZO); BIOL spores

Sport [ʃpɔrt] *m* (*-[e]s*; *no pl*) sport(s); PED physical education; **⁓ treiben** do sports

'**Sport...** *in cpds* ...ereignis, ...geschäft, ...hemd, ...verein, ...zentrum *etc*: mst sports ...; **⁓kleidung** *f* sportswear

'**Sportler** ['ʃpɔrtlɐ] *m* (*-s*; *-*), **Sportlerin** ['ʃpɔrtlərɪn] *f* (*-*; *-nen*) athlete

'**sportlich** *adj* athletic; casual, sporty

'**Sport|nachrichten** *pl* sports news; **⁓platz** *m* sports grounds; **⁓tauchen** *n* scuba diving; **⁓wagen** *m* stroller, *Br* pushchair; MOT sports car

Spott [ʃpɔt] *m* (*-[e]s*; *no pl*) mockery; derision

'**spott'billig** F *adj* dirt cheap

spotten ['ʃpɔtən] *v/i* (*ge-*, *h*) mock (*über acc* at), scoff (at); make fun (of)

Spötter ['ʃpœtɐ] *m* (*-s*; *-*) mocker, scoffer; '**spöttisch** *adj* mocking, derisive

'**Spottpreis** *m*: **für e-n ⁓** dirt cheap

sprach [ʃpraːx] *pret of* **sprechen**

Sprache ['ʃpraːxə] *f* (*-*; *-n*) language (*a. fig*); speech; **zur ⁓ kommen** (**bringen**) come up (bring *s.th.* up)

'**Sprach|fehler** *m* speech defect; **⁓gebrauch** *m* usage; **⁓lehrer(in)** language teacher

'**sprachlich 1.** *adj* language ... **2.** *adv*: **⁓ richtig** grammatically correct

'**sprachlos** *adj* speechless

'**Sprach|rohr** *fig n* mouthpiece; **⁓unterricht** *m* language teaching; **⁓wissenschaft** *f* linguistics

sprang [ʃpraŋ] *pret of* **springen**

Spraydose ['ʃpreːdoːzə] *f* spray can, aerosol (can)

Sprechanlage ['ʃpreçanlaːgə] *f* intercom

sprechen ['ʃpreçən] *v/t and v/i* (*irr*, *ge-*, *h*) speak (*j-n, mit j-m* to s.o.); talk (to) (*both*: *über acc*, *von* about, of); **nicht zu ⁓ sein** be busy; **Sprecher(in)** ['ʃpreçɐ, 'ʃpreçərɪn] *m(f)* (*-s*; *-/-*; *-nen*) speaker; announcer; spokesman (spokeswoman); '**Sprechstunde** *f* office hours; MED office (*Br* consulting) hours, *Br* surgery; '**Sprechzimmer** *n* office, *Br a.* consulting room

spreizen ['ʃpraitsən] *v/t* (*ge-, h*) spread

sprengen ['ʃprɛŋən] *v/t* (*ge-, h*) blow up; blast; sprinkle; water; *fig* break up

'**Sprengkopf** *m* MIL warhead

'**Sprengstoff** *m* MIL explosive

'**Sprengung** *f* (-; *-en*) blasting; blowing up

sprenkeln ['ʃprɛŋkəln] *v/t* (*ge-, h*) speck(le), spot, dot

Spreu [ʃprɔy] *f* (-; *no pl*) chaff (*a. fig*)

Sprichwort ['ʃprɪçvɔrt] *n* proverb, saying

'**sprichwörtlich** *adj* proverbial (*a. fig*)

sprießen ['ʃpriːsən] *v/i* (*irr, ge-, sein*) BOT sprout

'**Springbrunnen** *m* fountain

springen ['ʃprɪŋən] *v/i* (*irr, ge-, sein*) jump, leap; *ball etc*: bounce; SPORT dive; *glass etc*: crack; break; burst; **in die Höhe** (**zur Seite**) ~ jump up (aside)

Springer ['ʃprɪŋɐ] *m* (-*s*; -) jumper; diver; *chess*: knight

'**Springflut** *f* spring tide

'**Springreiten** *n* show jumping

Spritze ['ʃprɪtsə] *f* (-; *-n*) MED injection, F shot; syringe; '**spritzen 1.** *v/i and v/t* (*ge-, h*) splash; spray (*a.* TECH, AGR); MED inject; give *s.o.* an injection of **2.** *v/i* (*ge-, sein*) spatter; gush (**aus** from); **Spritzer** ['ʃprɪtsɐ] *m* (-*s*; -) splash; dash

'**Spritzpis,tole** *f* TECH spray gun

'**Spritztour** F *f* MOT spin

spröde ['ʃprøːdə] *adj* brittle (*a. fig*); rough

spross [ʃprɔs] *pret of* **sprießen**

Sprosse ['ʃprɔsə] *f* (-; *-n*) rung

Spruch [ʃprʊx] *m* (-[*e*]*s*; *Sprüche* ['ʃprʏçə]) saying; decision; ~**band** *n* banner

Sprudel ['ʃpruːdəl] *m* (-*s*; -) mineral water; '**sprudeln** *v/i* (*ge-, sein*) bubble

Sprühdose ['ʃpryːdoːzə] *f* spray can, aerosol (can); **sprühen** ['ʃpryːən] *v/t and v/i* (*ge-, h*) spray; throw out (*sparks*)

'**Sprühregen** *m* drizzle

Sprung [ʃprʊŋ] *m* (-[*e*]*s*; *Sprünge* ['ʃprʏŋə]) jump, leap; SPORT dive; crack, fissure; ~**brett** *n* SPORT diving board; springboard; *fig* stepping stone; ~**schanze** *f* ski jump

Spucke ['ʃpʊkə] F *f* (-; *no pl*) spit

'**spucken** *v/i and v/t* (*ge-, h*) spit; F throw up

Spuk [ʃpuːk] *m* (-[*e*]*s*; *-e*) apparition, ghost; **spuken** ['ʃpuːkən] *v/i* (*ge-, h*) ~ **in** (*dat*) haunt; **hier spukt es** this place is haunted

Spule ['ʃpuːlə] *f* (-; *-n*) spool, reel; bobbin; ELECTR coil; '**spulen** *v/t* (*ge-, h*) spool, wind, reel

spülen ['ʃpyːlən] *v/t and v/i* (*ge-, h*) wash up, do the dishes; rinse; flush the toilet

'**Spülma,schine** *f* dishwasher

Spur [ʃpuːɐ] *f* (-; *-en*) track(s); trail; print; lane; trace (*a. fig*); *j-m auf der ~ sein* be on s.o.'s trail; **spüren** ['ʃpyːrən] *v/t* (*ge-, h*) feel, sense; notice

'**spurlos** *adv* without leaving a trace

'**Spurweite** *f* RAIL ga(u)ge; MOT track

St. *abbr of* **Sankt** St, Saint

Staat [ʃtaːt] *m* (-[*e*]*s*; *-en*) state; POL government; '**Staatenbund** *m* confederacy, confederation; '**staatenlos** *adj* stateless; '**staatlich 1.** *adj* state ...; public, national **2.** *adv*: ~ **geprüft** qualified, registered

'**Staats|angehörige** *m, f* national, citizen, subject; ~**angehörigkeit** *f* (-; *no pl*) nationality; ~**anwalt** *m* JUR district attorney, *Br* (public) prosecutor; ~**besuch** *m* official *or* state visit; ~**bürger(in)** citizen; ~**chef** *m* head of state; ~**dienst** *m* civil (*or* public) service

'**staatseigen** *adj* state-owned

'**Staatsfeind** *m* public enemy

'**Staats|haushalt** *m* budget; ~**kasse** *f* treasury; ~**mann** *m* statesman; ~**oberhaupt** *n* head of (the) state; ~**sekre,tär(in)** undersecretary of state; ~**streich** *m* coup d'état; ~**vertrag** *m* treaty; ~**wissenschaft** *f* political science

Stab [ʃtaːp] *m* (-[*e*]*s*; *Stäbe* ['ʃtɛːbə]) staff (*a. fig*); bar; SPORT, MUS baton; SPORT pole

Stäbchen ['ʃtɛːpçən] *pl* chopstick

'**Stabhochsprung** *m* SPORT pole vault

stabil [ʃtaˈbiːl] *adj* stable (*a.* ECON, POL); solid, strong; sound; **stabilisieren** [ʃtabiliˈziːrən] *v/t* (*no -ge-, h*) stabilize; **Stabilität** [ʃtabiliˈtɛːt] *f* (-; *no pl*) stability

stach [ʃtaːx] *pret of* **stechen**

Stachel ['ʃtaxəl] *m* (-*s*; *-n*) BOT, ZO spine; prick; ZO sting; ~**beere** *f* BOT gooseberry; ~**draht** *m* barbed wire

stachelig ['ʃtaxəlɪç] *adj* prickly

'**Stachelschwein** *n* zo porcupine

Stadel ['ʃtɑːdəl] *Austrian m* (-s; -[n]) barn

Stadion ['ʃtɑːdjɔn] *n* (-s; -ien) stadium

Stadium ['ʃtɑːdjʊm] *n* (-s; -ien) stage, phase

Stadt [ʃtat] *f* (-; *Städte* ['ʃtɛːtə]) town; city; *die ~ Berlin* the city of Berlin; *in die ~ fahren* go downtown, *esp Br* go (in)to town; ~**bahn** *f* urban railway

Städter ['ʃtɛːtɐ] *m* (-s; -), '**Städterin** *f* (-; -nen) city dweller, F townie, *often contp* city slicker

'**Stadt|gebiet** *n* urban area; ~**gespräch** *fig n* talk of the town

städtisch ['ʃɛːtɪʃ] *adj* urban; POL municipal

'**Stadt|plan** *m* city map; ~**rand** *m* outskirts; ~**rat** *m* town council; city councilman, *Br* town council(l)or; ~**rundfahrt** *f* sightseeing tour; ~**streicher(in)** city vagrant; ~**teil** *m*, ~**viertel** *n* quarter

Staffel ['ʃtafəl] *f* (-; -n) SPORT relay race *or* team; MIL, AVIAT squadron

Staffelei [ʃtafə'lai] *f* (-; -en) PAINT easel

'**staffeln** *v/t* (ge-, *h*) grade, scale

stahl [ʃtɑːl] *pret of* **stehlen**

Stahl *m* (-[e]s; *Stähle* ['ʃtɛːlə]) steel

'**Stahlwerk** *n* steelworks

stak [ʃtɑːk] *pret of* **stecken** 2

Stall [ʃtal] *m* (-[e]s; *Ställe* ['ʃtɛlə]) stable

'**Stallknecht** *m* stableman

Stamm [ʃtam] *m* (-[e]s; *Stämme* ['ʃtɛmə]) BOT stem (*a.* LING), trunk; tribe, stock; *fig* regulars; ~**...** *in cpds* ...*gast*, ...*kunde*, ...*spieler etc*: regular ...; ~**baum** *m* family tree; zo pedigree

stammeln ['ʃtaməln] *v/t* (ge-, *h*) stammer

stammen ['ʃtamən] *v/i* (ge-, *h*) ~ *aus* (**von**) come from; be from; ~ *von work of art etc*: be by

'**Stammformen** *pl* LING principal parts, *mst* tenses

stämmig ['ʃtɛmɪç] *adj* sturdy; stout

'**Stammkneipe** F *f Br* local

stampfen ['ʃtampfən] (ge-, *h*) **1.** *v/t* mash **2.** *v/i* stamp (*mit dem Fuß* one's foot)

stand [ʃtant] *pret of* **stehen**

Stand *m* (-[e]s; *Stände* ['ʃtɛndə]) (*no pl*) stand(ing), standing *or* upright position; footing, foothold; ASTR position;

TECH *etc*: height, level (*a. fig*); reading; SPORT score; *racing*: standings; *fig* state; social standing, status; stand, stall; class; profession; *auf den neuesten ~ bringen* bring up to date; *e-n schweren ~ haben* have a hard time (of it); → *außerstande*; → *imstande*; → *instand*; → *zustande*

Standard ['ʃtandart] *m* (-s; -s) standard

'**Standbild** *n* statue

Ständchen ['ʃtɛntçən] *n* (-s; -) MUS serenade

Ständer ['ʃtɛndɐ] *m* (-s; -) stand; rack

Standesamt ['ʃtandəsamt] *n* marriage license bureau, *Br* registry office; '**standesamtlich** *adj*: ~*e Trauung* civil marriage; '**Standesbeamt|e** *m*, -**in** *f* civil magistrate, *Br* registrar

'**Standfoto** *n* still

'**standhaft** *adj* steadfast, firm; ~ *bleiben* resist temptation

'**standhalten** *v/i* (*irr, halten, sep, -ge-, h*) withstand, resist

ständig ['ʃtɛndɪç] *adj* constant; permanent (*address*)

'**Stand|licht** *n* (-[e]s; *no pl*) MOT parking light; ~**ort** *m* position; location; MIL post, garrison; ~**pauke** F *f: j-m e-e ~ halten* give s.o. a talking-to; ~**platz** *m* stand; ~**punkt** *m* (point of) view, standpoint; ~**spur** *f* MOT (*Br* hard) shoulder; ~**uhr** *f* grandfather clock

Stange ['ʃtaŋə] *f* (-; -n) pole; staff; rod, bar; carton (*of cigarettes*)

Stängel ['ʃtɛŋəl] *m* (-s; -) BOT stalk, stem

stank [ʃtaŋk] *pret of* **stinken**

Stanniol [ʃta'njoːl] *n* (-s; -e) tin foil

Stanze ['ʃtantsə] *f* (-; -n), '**stanzen** *v/t* (ge-, *h*) TECH punch

Stapel ['ʃtɑːpəl] *m* (-s; -) pile, stack; heap; *vom ~ lassen* MAR launch (*a. fig*); *vom ~ laufen* MAR be launched

'**Stapellauf** *m* MAR launch

'**stapeln** *v/t* (ge-, *h*) pile (up), stack

stapfen ['ʃtapfən] *v/i* (ge-, *sein*) trudge

Star[1] [ʃtaːɐ] *m* (-[e]s; -e) zo starling; MED cataract

Star[2] *m* (-s; -s) THEA *etc*: star

starb [ʃtarp] *pret of* **sterben**

stark [ʃtark] **1.** *adj* strong (*a.* GASTR); powerful; *fig* heavy; F super, great **2.** *adv*: ~ *beeindruckt* greatly impressed; ~ *beschädigt* badly damaged; **Stärke** ['ʃtɛrkə] *f* (-; -n) (*no pl*) strength, power; intensity; degree; CHEM starch; **'stärken** v/t (ge-, h) strengthen (a. fig); starch; **sich ~** take some refreshment; **'Starkstrom** m ELECTR high--voltage (or heavy) current; **Stärkung** f (-; -en) strengthening; refreshment; **'Stärkungsmittel** n MED tonic

starr [ʃtar] adj stiff; rigid (a. TECH); frozen (face); **~er Blick** (fixed) stare; **~ vor Kälte (Entsetzen)** frozen (scared) stiff; **'starren** v/i (ge-, h) stare (**auf** acc at); **starrköpfig** ['ʃtarkœpfɪç] adj stubborn, obstinate; **'Starrsinn** m (-[e]s; no pl) stubbornness, obstinacy

Start [ʃtart] m (-[e]s; -s) start (a. fig); AVIAT take-off; rocket: lift-off

'Startbahn f AVIAT runway

'startbereit adj ready to start; AVIAT ready for take-off

starten ['ʃtartən] v/i (ge-, sein) and v/t (ge-, h) start (a. F); AVIAT take off; lift off; launch (a. fig)

Station [ʃta'tsjoːn] f (-; -en) station; MED ward; **stationär** [ʃtatsjoˈnɛːɐ] adj: **~er Patient** MED in-patient; **stationieren** [ʃtatsjoˈniːrən] v/t (no -ge-, h) MIL station; deploy; **Stationsvorsteher** m RAIL stationmaster

Statist [ʃta'tɪst] m (-en; -en) THEA extra

Statistik [ʃta'tɪstɪk] f (-; -en) statistics; **Sta'tistiker** [ʃta'tɪstɪkə] m (-s; -) statistician; **sta'tistisch** adj statistical

Stativ [ʃta'tiːf] n (-s; -e) PHOT tripod

statt [ʃtat] prp instead of.; **~ et. zu tun** instead of doing s.th.; **~'dessen** instead

Stätte ['ʃtɛtə] f (-; -n) place; scene

'stattfinden v/i (irr, finden, sep, -ge-, h) take place; happen

'stattlich adj imposing; handsome

Statue ['ʃtaːtuə] f (-; -n) statue

Statur [ʃta'tuːɐ] f (-; -en) build

Status ['ʃtaːtus] m (-; -) state; status; **~sym,bol** n status symbol; **~zeile** f IT status line

Stau [ʃtau] m (-[e]s; -s, -e) MOT traffic jam or congestion

Staub [ʃtaup] m (-[e]s; TECH -e, Stäube ['ʃtɔybə]) dust (a. **~ wischen**)

'Staubecken n reservoir

stauben ['ʃtaubən] v/i (ge-, h) give off or make dust; **staubig** ['ʃtaubɪç] adj dusty; **'staubsaugen** v/i and v/t (ge-, h) vacuum, F Br hoover;

'Staubsauger m vacuum cleaner, F Br hoover; **'Staubtuch** n duster

'Staudamm m dam

Staude ['ʃtaudə] f (-; -n) BOT herbacious plant

stauen ['ʃtauən] v/t (ge-, h) dam up; **sich ~** MOT etc be stacked up

staunen ['ʃtaunən] v/i (ge-, h) be astonished or surprised (**über** acc at)

'Staunen n (-s; no pl) astonishment, amazement

Staupe ['ʃtaupə] f (-; -n) VET distemper

'Stausee m reservoir

stechen ['ʃtɛçən] v/i and v/t (irr, ge-, h) prick; zo sting, bite; stab; pierce; **mit et. ~ in** (acc) stick s.th. in(to); **sich ~** prick o.s.; **~d** fig adj piercing (look); stabbing (pain)

'Stechuhr f time clock

Steckbrief ['ʃtɛkbriːf] m JUR „wanted" poster

'steckbrieflich adv: **er wird ~ gesucht** JUR a warrant is out against him

'Steckdose f ELECTR (wall) socket

stecken ['ʃtɛkən] (ge-, h) **1.** v/t stick; put; esp TECH insert (**in** acc into); pin (**an** acc to, on); AGR set, plant **2.** v/i ([irr]) be; stick, be stuck; **~ bleiben** get stuck; **'steckenbleiben** v/i (irr, bleiben, sep, -ge-, sein) fig get stuck

'Steckenpferd n hobby horse; fig hobby

Stecker ['ʃtɛkə] m (-s; -) ELECTR plug; **'Steck|kon,takt** m ELECTR plug (connection); **~nadel** f pin; **~platz** m IT slot

Steg [ʃteːk] m (-[e]s; -e) footbridge

Stegreif ['ʃteːkraif] m: **aus dem ~** extempore, ad-lib; **aus dem ~ sprechen** or **spielen** etc extemporize, ad-lib

stehen ['ʃteːən] v/i (irr, ge-, h) stand; be; stand up; **es steht ihr** it suits (or looks well on) her; **wie steht es** (or **das Spiel**)**?** what's the score?; **hier steht, dass** it says here that; **wo steht das?** where does it say so or that?; **wie steht es mit ...?** what about ...?; F **darauf stehe ich** it turns me on; **~ bleiben** stop; esp TECH come to a standstill (a. fig); **~ lassen** leave (untouched); leave behind; **alles~ und liegen lassen** drop everything; **sich e-n Bart ~ lassen** grow a beard

'stehen|bleiben v/i (irr, bleiben, sep, -ge-, sein) → **stehen**; **~lassen** v/t (irr, *lassen*, *sep*, *no -ge-*, *h*) → *stehen*

'Steh|kragen *m* stand-up collar; ~lampe *f* floor (*Br* standard) lamp; ~leiter *f* step ladder

stehlen ['ʃteːlən] *v/t and v/i* (*irr, ge-, h*) steal (*a. fig sich ~*)

'Stehplatz *m* standing ticket; *pl* standing room

steif [ʃtaif] *adj* stiff (*vor dat* with)

Steigbügel ['ʃtaikbyːgə] *m* stirrup

steigen ['ʃtaigən] *v/i* (*irr, ge-, sein*) go, step; climb (*a.* AVIAT); *fig* rise, go up; ~ *in* (*auf*) (*acc*) get on (*bus, bike etc*); ~ *aus* (*von*) get off (*bus, horse etc*); *aus dem Bett* ~ get out of bed

steigern ['ʃtaigən] *v/t* (*ge-, h*) raise, increase; heighten; improve; LING compare; *sich* ~ improve, get better

Steigerung ['ʃtaigərʊŋ] *f* (*-; -en*) rise, increase; heightening; improvement; LING comparison

'Steigung *f* (*-; -en*) gradient; slope

steil [ʃtail] *adj* steep (*a. fig*)

Stein [ʃtain] *m* (*-[e]s; -e*) stone (*a.* BOT, MED), rock; ~bock *m* ZO rock goat; ASTR Capricorn; *er ist* (*ein*) ~ he's (a) Capricorn; ~bruch *m* quarry

steinern ['ʃtainən] *adj* (of) stone; *fig* stony

'Steingut *n* (*-[e]s; -e*) earthenware

steinig ['ʃtainɪç] *adj* stony

steinigen ['ʃtainɪɡən] *v/t* (*ge-, h*) stone

'Steinkohle *f* (hard) coal

Steinmetz ['ʃtainmɛts] *m* (*-en; -en*) stonemason

'Steinzeit *f* (*-; no pl*) Stone Age

Stellage [ʃtɛˈlaːʒə] *Austrian f* (*-; -n*) stand, rack, shelf

Stelle ['ʃtɛlə] *f* (*-; -n*) place; spot; point; job; authority; MATH figure; *freie* ~ vacancy, opening; *auf der* (*zur*) ~ on the spot; *der erste* ~ *stehen* (*kommen*) be (come) first; *an j-s* ~ in s.o.'s place; *ich an deiner* ~ if I were you

'stellen *v/t* (*ge-, h*) put; set (*trap, clock, task etc*); turn (*up, down etc*); ask (*question*); provide; corner, hunt down (*criminal etc*); *sich* ~ give o.s. up, turn o.s. in; *sich gegen* (*hinter*) *j-n* ~ *fig* oppose (back) s.o.; *sich schlafend etc* ~ pretend to be asleep *etc*; *stell dich dorthin!* (go and) stand over there!

'Stellen|angebot *n* vacancy; *ich habe ein* ~ I was offered a job; ~anzeige *f*

job ad(vertisement), employment ad; ~gesuch *n* application for a job

'stellenweise *adv* partly, in places

'Stellung *f* (*-; -en*) position; post, job; ~ *nehmen zu* comment on, give one's opinion of; ~nahme ['ʃtɛlʊŋnaːmə] *f* (*-; -n*) comment, opinion (*both: zu* to)

'stellungslos *adj* unemployed, jobless

'stellvertretend *adj* acting, deputy, vice-...; 'Stellvertreter(in) (*-s; -/-; -nen*) representative; deputy

Stelze ['ʃtɛltsə] *f* (*-; -n*) stilt

'stelzen *v/i* (*ge-, sein*) stalk

stemmen ['ʃtɛmən] *v/t* (*ge-, h*) lift (*weight*); *sich* ~ *gegen* press o.s. against; *fig* resist *or* oppose s.th.

Stempel ['ʃtɛmpəl] *m* (*-s; -*) stamp; postmark; hallmark; BOT pistil

'Stempelkissen *n* ink pad

'stempeln (*ge-, h*) 1. *v/t* stamp; cancel; hallmark 2. F *v/i*: ~ *gehen* be on the dole

Stengel → *Stängel*

Stenografie [ʃtenograˈfiː] *f* (*-;-n*) shorthand; stenogra'fieren *v/t* (*no -ge-, h*) take down in shorthand

Stenogramm [ʃtenoˈgram] *n* (*-[e]s; -e*) shorthand notes; Stenotypistin [ʃtenotyˈpɪstɪn] *f* (*-; -nen*) shorthand typist

Steppdecke ['ʃtɛpdɛkə] *f* quilt; steppen ['ʃtɛpən] (*ge-, h*) 1. *v/t* quilt; stitch 2. *v/i* tap dance; 'Stepptanz *m* tap dancing

Sterbebett ['ʃtɛrbəbɛt] *n* deathbed

'Sterbeklinik *f* MED hospice

sterben ['ʃtɛrbən] *v/i* (*irr, ge-, sein*) die (*an dat* of) (*a. fig*); *im Sterben liegen* be dying

sterblich ['ʃtɛrplɪç] *adj* mortal

'Sterblichkeit *f* (*-; no pl*) mortality

Stereo ['ʃteːreo] *n* (*-s; -s*) stereo

steril [ʃteˈriːl] *adj* sterile; Sterilisation [ʃterilizaˈtsjoːn] *f* (*-; -en*) sterilization; sterilisieren [ʃteriliˈziːrən] *v/t* (*no -ge-, h*) sterilize

Stern [ʃtɛrn] *m* (*-[e]s; -e*) star (*a. fig*)

'Sternbild *n* ASTR constellation; sign of the zodiac

'Sternchen *n* (*-s; -*) PRINT asterisk

'Sternenbanner *n* Star-Spangled Banner, Stars and Stripes

'Sternenhimmel *m* starry sky

'sternklar *adj* starry

'Stern|kunde *f* (-; *no pl*) astronomy; ~schnuppe *f* (-; *-n*) shooting *or* falling star; ~warte *f* (-; *-n*) observatory

stetig ['ʃteːtɪç] *adj* continual, constant; steady; stets [ʃteːts] *adv* always

Steuer¹ ['ʃtɔʏɐ] *n* (*-s*; *-*) MOT (steering) wheel; MAR helm, rudder

'Steuer² *f* (-; *-n*) tax (*auf acc* on)

'Steuer|beamte *m* revenue officer; ~berater *m* tax adviser

'Steuerbord *n* MAR starboard

'Steuer|erklärung *f* tax return; ~ermäßigung *f* tax allowance

'steuerfrei *adj* tax-free

'Steuerhinterziehung *f* tax evasion

'Steuer|knüppel *m* AVIAT control column *or* stick; ~mann *m* MAR helmsman; *rowing:* cox, coxswain

'steuern *v/t and v/i* (*ge-*, *h*) steer, AVIAT, MAR *a.* navigate, pilot, MOT *a.* drive; TECH control (*a. fig*); *fig* direct

'steuerpflichtig *adj* taxable

'Steuerrad *n* MOT steering wheel

'Steuerruder *n* MAR helm, rudder

'Steuersenkung *f* tax reduction

Steuerung ['ʃtɔʏɐʊŋ] *f* (-; *-en*) steering (system); ELECTR, TECH control (*a. fig*)

'Steuerzahler *m*, 'Steuerzahlerin *f* taxpayer

Stich [ʃtɪç] *m* (*-[e]s*; *-e*) prick; ZO sting, bite; stab; stitch; *cards:* trick; engraving; *im ~ lassen* desert *or* abandon *s.o.*, *s.th.*, leave *s.o.* in the lurch, let *s.o.* down

Stichelei [ʃtɪçə'laɪ] F *f* (-; *-en*) dig, gibe

sticheln ['ʃɪçəln] F *v/i* (*ge-*, *h*) make digs, gibe (*gegen* at)

'Stichflamme *f* jet of flame

'stichhaltig *adj* valid, sound; watertight; *nicht ~ sein* F not hold water

'Stich|probe *f* spot check; ~tag *m* cutoff date; deadline; ~wahl *f* POL run-off; ~wort *n* (*-[e]s*; *-e*) THEA cue; (*-[e]s*; *-wörter*) headword; ~e *pl* notes; *das Wichtigste in ~en* an outline of the main points; ~wortverzeichnis *n* index; ~wunde *f* MED stab

sticken ['ʃtɪkən] *v/t and v/i* (*ge-*, *h*) embroider; Stickerei [ʃtɪkə'raɪ] *f* (-; *-en*) embroidery

stickig ['ʃtɪkɪç] *adj* stuffy

'Stickstoff *m* (*-[e]s*; *no pl*) CHEM nitrogen

Stief... [ʃtiːf-] *in cpds* ...*mutter etc*:

step...

Stiefel ['ʃtiːfəl] *m* (*-s*; *-*) boot

Stiefmütterchen ['ʃtiːfmʏtɐçən] *n* (*-s*; *-*) BOT pansy

stieg [ʃtiːk] *pret of* **steigen**

Stiege ['ʃtiːɡə] *Austrian f* (-; *-n*) → **Treppe**

Stiel [ʃtiːl] *m* (*-[e]s*; *-e*) handle; stick; stem; BOT stalk

Stier [ʃtiːɐ] *m* (*-[e]s*; *-e*) ZO bull; ASTR Taurus; *er ist ~* he's (a) Taurus

'Stierkampf *m* bullfight

stieß [ʃtiːs] *pret of* **stoßen**

Stift [ʃtɪft] *m* (*-[e]s*; *-e*) pen; pencil; crayon; TECH pin; peg

stiften ['ʃtɪftən] *v/t* (*ge-*, *h*) donate; *fig* cause; 'Stiftung *f* (-; *-en*) donation

Stil [ʃtiːl] *m* (*-[e]s*; *-e*) style (*a. fig*); *in großem ~* in (grand) style; *fig* on a large scale; stilistisch [ʃti'lɪstɪʃ] *adj* stylistic

still [ʃtɪl] *adj* quiet, silent; still; *sei(d) ~!* be quiet!; *halt ~!* keep still!; *sich ~ verhalten* keep quiet (*or* still)

Stille ['ʃtɪlə] *f* (-; *no pl*) silence, quiet (-ness); *in aller ~* quietly; secretly

Stilleben *n* → **Stillleben**

stillen ['ʃtɪlən] *v/t* (*ge-*, *h*) nurse, breastfeed; *fig* relieve (*pain*); satisfy (*curiosity etc*); quench (*one's thirst*)

'stillhalten *v/i* (*irr*, *halten*, *sep*, *-ge-*, *h*) keep still

'Stillleben *n* PAINT still life

'stilllegen *v/t* (*sep*, *-ge-*, *h*) close down

'stillos *adj* lacking style, tasteless

'stillschweigend *adj* tacit

'Stillstand *m* (*-[e]s*; *no pl*) standstill, stop, *fig a.* stagnation (*a.* ECON); deadlock; 'stillstehen *v/i* (*irr*, *stehen*, *sep*, *-ge-*, *h*) (have) stop(ped), (have) come to a standstill

'Stilmöbel *pl* period furniture

'stilvoll *adj* stylish; *~ sein* have style

'Stimmband *n* ANAT vocal cord

'stimmberechtigt *adj* entitled to vote

Stimme ['ʃtɪmə] *f* (-; *-n*) voice; POL vote; *sich der ~ enthalten* abstain

'stimmen (*ge-*, *h*) **1.** *v/i* be right, be true, be correct; POL vote (*für* for; *gegen* against); *es stimmt et. nicht* (*damit or mit ihm*) there's s.th. wrong (with it *or* him); **2.** *v/t* MUS tune; *j-n traurig etc ~* make *s.o.* sad *etc*

'Stimmenthaltung *f* abstention

'**Stimmrecht** *n* right to vote

'**Stimmung** *f* (-; *-en*) mood; atmosphere; feeling

'**stimmungsvoll** *adj* atmospheric

'**Stimmzettel** *m* ballot (paper)

stinken ['ʃtɪŋkən] *v/i* (*irr, ge-, h*) stink (*a. fig*) (**nach** of)

Stipendium [ʃti'pɛndjʊm] *n* (*-s; -ien*) UNIV scholarship, grant

stippen ['ʃtɪpən] *v/t* (*ge-, h*) dip

'**Stippvi,site** *F f* flying visit

Stirn [ʃtɪrn] *f* (-; *-en*) ANAT forehead; **die ~ runzeln** frown

stöbern ['ʃtøːbən] *F v/i* (*ge-, h*) rummage (about)

stochern ['ʃtɔxən] *v/i* (*ge-, h*) **im Feuer ~** poke the fire; **im Essen ~** pick at one's food; **in den Zähnen ~** pick one's teeth

Stock [ʃtɔk] *m* (*-[e]s; Stöcke* ['ʃtœkə]) stick; cane; ARCH stor(e)y, floor; **im ersten ~** on the second (*Br* first) floor

'**stock'dunkel** *F adj* pitch-dark

stocken ['ʃtɔkən] *v/i* (*ge-, h*) stop (short); falter; *traffic*: be jammed; **~d 1.** *adj* halting **2.** *adv*: **~ lesen** stumble through a text; **~ sprechen** speak haltingly

'**Stockfleck** *m* mo(u)ld stain

'**Stockung** *f* (-; *-en*) holdup, delay

'**Stockwerk** *n* stor(e)y, floor

Stoff [ʃtɔf] *m* (*-[e]s; -e*) material, stuff (*a. F*); fabric, textile; cloth; CHEM, PHYS *etc* substance; *fig* subject (matter)

'**stofflich** *adj* material

'**Stofftier** *n* soft toy animal

'**Stoffwechsel** *m* BIOL metabolism

stöhnen ['ʃtøːnən] *v/i* (*ge-, h*) groan, moan (*a. fig*)

Stollen ['ʃtɔlən] *m* (*-s; -*) tunnel, gallery

stolpern ['ʃtɔlpən] *v/i* (*ge-, sein*) stumble (**über** *acc* over), trip (over) (*both a. fig*)

stolz [ʃtɔlts] *adj* proud (**auf** *acc* of)

Stolz *m* (*-es; no pl*) pride (**auf** *acc* in)

stolzieren [ʃtɔl'tsiːrən] *v/i* (*no -ge-, sein*) strut, stalk

stopfen ['ʃtɔpfən] *v/t* (*ge-, h*) darn, mend; stuff, fill (*a. pipe*)

Stoppel ['ʃtɔpəl] *f* (-; *-n*) stubble

'**Stoppelbart** *F m* stubbly beard

'**stoppelig** *adj* stubbly, bristly

'**Stoppelzieher** *Austrian m* corkscrew

stoppen ['ʃtɔpən] *v/i and v/t* (*ge-, h*) stop (*a. fig*); *esp* SPORT time

'**Stopp|licht** *n* (*-[e]s; -er*) MOT stop light; **~schild** *n* stop sign; **~uhr** *f* stopwatch

Stöpsel ['ʃtœpsəl] *m* (*-s; -*) stopper; plug

Storch [ʃtɔrç] *m* (*-[e]s; Störche* ['ʃtœrçəl]) zo stork

stören ['ʃtøːrən] *v/t and v/i* (*ge-, h*) disturb; trouble; bother, annoy; be in the way; **lassen Sie sich nicht ~!** don't let me disturb you!; **darf ich Sie kurz ~?** may I trouble you for a minute?; **es (er) stört mich nicht** it (he) doesn't bother me, I don't mind (him); **stört es Sie(, wenn ich rauche)?** do you mind (my smoking *or* if I smoke)?

'**Störenfried** ['ʃtøːrənfriːt] *m* (*-[e]s; -e*) troublemaker; intruder

Störfall ['ʃtøːrfal] *m* TECH accident

störrisch ['ʃtœrɪʃ] *adj* stubborn, obstinate

'**Störung** *f* (-; *-en*) disturbance; trouble (*a.* TECH); TECH breakdown; TV, *radio*: interference

Stoß [ʃtoːs] *m* (*-es; Stöße* ['ʃtøːsə]) push, shove; thrust; kick; butt; blow, knock; shock; MOT jolt; bump, *esp* TECH, PHYS impact; pile, stack; '**Stoßdämpfer** *m* MOT shock absorber; **stoßen** ['ʃtoːsən] *v/t* (*irr, ge-, h*) *and v/i* (*sein*) push, shove; thrust; kick; butt; knock, strike; pound; **~ gegen** *or* **an** (*acc*) bump *or* run into *or* against; **sich den Kopf ~ (an** *dat*) knock one's head (against); **~ auf** (*acc*) strike (*oil etc*); *fig* come across; meet with; '**stoßgesichert** *adj* shockproof, shock-resistant; '**Stoßstange** *f* MOT bumper; '**Stoßzahn** *m* ZO tusk; '**Stoßzeit** *f* rush hour, peak hours

stottern ['ʃtɔtən] *v/i and v/t* (*ge-, h*) stutter

Str. *abbr of* **Straße** St, Street; Rd, Road

'**Strafanstalt** *f* prison, penitentiary; '**strafbar** *adj* punishable, penal; **sich ~ machen** commit an offense (*Br* offence); **Strafe** ['ʃtraːfə] *f* (-; *-n*) punishment; JUR, ECON, SPORT penalty (*a. fig*); fine; **30 Euro ~ zahlen müssen** be fined 30 euros; **zur ~** as a punishment; '**strafen** *v/t* (*ge-, h*) punish

straff [ʃtraf] *adj* tight; *fig* strict

'**straffrei** *adj*: **~ ausgehen** go unpunished

'**Straf|gefangene** *m*, *f* prisoner, convict; **~gesetz** *n* criminal law

sträflich [ˈʃtrɛːflɪç] **1.** *adj* inexcusable **2.** *adv*: **~ vernachlässigen** neglect badly

'**Straf|mi‚nute** *f* SPORT penalty minute; **~pro‚zess** *m* JUR criminal action, trial; **~raum** *m* SPORT penalty area (F box); **~stoß** *m* SPORT penalty kick; **~tat** *f* JUR criminal offense (*Br* offence); crime; **~zettel** *m* ticket

Strahl [ʃtraːl] *m* (-[e]s, -en) ray (*a. fig*); beam; flash; jet; **strahlen** [ˈʃtraːlən] *v/i* (*ge-*, *h*) radiate; shine (brightly); *fig* beam (*vor* with); '**Strahlen...** in *cpds* PHYS ...*schutz etc*: radiation ...

'**Strahlung** *f* (-; -en) PHYS radiation

Strähne [ˈʃtrɛːnə] *f* (-; -n) strand; streak

stramm [ʃtram] *adj* tight; **~stehen** MIL stand to attention

strampeln [ˈʃtrampəln] *v/i* (*ge-*, *h*) kick

Strand [ʃtrant] *m* (-[e]s; *Strände* [ˈʃtrɛn-də]) beach; **am ~** on the beach

stranden [ˈʃtrandən] *v/i* (*ge-*, *sein*) MAR strand; *fig* fail

'**Strand|gut** *n* flotsam and jetsam (*a. fig*); **~korb** *m* roofed wicker beach chair

Strang [ʃtraŋ] *m* (-[e]s; *Stränge* [ˈʃtrɛŋə]) rope; *esp* ANAT cord

Strapaze [ʃtraˈpaːtsə] *f* (-; -n) strain, exertion, hardship; **strapazieren** [ʃtrapa-ˈtsiːrən] *v/t* (*no -ge-*, *h*) wear *s.o.* or *s.th.* out, be hard on; **strapazierfähig** *adj* longwearing, *Br* hardwearing

strapaziös [ʃtrapaˈtsjøːs] *adj* strenuous

Straße [ˈʃtraːsə] *f* (-; -n) road; street; GEOGR strait; **auf der ~** on the road; on (*Br a.* in) the street

'**Straßen|arbeiten** *pl* roadworks; **~bahn** *f* streetcar, *Br* tram; **~ca‚fé** *n* sidewalk (*Br* pavement) café; **~karte** *f* road map; **~kehrer** [ˈʃtraːsənkeːrɐ] *m* (-s; -) street sweeper; **~kreuzung** *f* crossroads; intersection; **~lage** *f* MOT roadholding; **~rand** *m* roadside; **am ~** at *or* by the roadside; **~sperre** *f* road block

strategisch [ʃtraˈteːgɪʃ] *adj* strategic

sträuben [ˈʃtrɔybən] *v/t and v/refl* (*ge-*, *h*) ruffle (up); bristle (up); **sich ~ gegen** struggle against

Strauch [ʃtraux] *m* (-[e]s; *Sträucher* [ˈʃtrɔyçɐ]) BOT shrub, bush

straucheln [ˈʃtrauxəln] *v/i* (*ge-*, *sein*) stumble

Strauß[1] [ʃtraus] *m* (-es; -e) ZO ostrich

Strauß[2] *m* (-es; *Sträuße* [ˈʃtrɔysə]) bunch, bouquet

Strebe [ˈʃtreːbə] *f* (-; -n) prop, stay (*a.* AVIAT, MAR); '**streben** *v/i* (*ge-*, *h*) strive (*nach* for, after); **Streber** [ˈʃtreːbɐ] *m* (-s; -) pusher; PED *etc* grind, *Br* swot; **strebsam** [ˈʃtreːpzaːm] *adj* ambitious

Strecke [ˈʃtrɛkə] *f* (-; -n) distance (*a.* SPORT, MATH), way; route; RAIL line; SPORT course; stretch; **zur ~ bringen** kill; *esp fig* hunt down; '**strecken** *v/t* (*ge-*, *h*) stretch (out), extend

Streich [ʃtraiç] *m* (-[e]s; -e) trick, prank, practical joke; **j-m e-n ~ spielen** play a trick *or* joke on s.o.

streicheln [ˈʃtraiçəln] *v/t* (*ge-*, *h*) stroke, caress

streichen [ˈʃtraiçən] *v/t and v/i* (*irr, ge-*, *h*) paint; spread; cross out; cancel; MAR strike; MUS bow; **mit der Hand ~ über** (*acc*) run one's hand over; **~ durch** roam (*acc*); **Streicher(in)** [ˈʃtraiçɐ, ˈʃtraiçərɪn] *m(f)* (-s; -/-; -nen) MUS string player, *pl* the strings

'**Streich|holz** *n* match; **~instru‚ment** *n* MUS string instrument; **~or‚chester** *n* MUS string orchestra

'**Streichung** *f* (-; -en) cancellation; cut

Streife [ˈʃtraifə] *f* (-; -n) patrol; **auf ~ gehen** go on patrol; **auf ~ sein** in (*dat*) patrol

'**streifen** *v/t and v/i* (*ge-*, *h*) touch, brush (against); MOT scrape against; graze; slip (*von* off); *fig* touch on; **~ durch** roam (*acc*), wander through

'**Streifen** *m* (-s; -) stripe; strip

'**Streifenwagen** *m* squad (*Br* patrol) car

'**Streifschuss** *m* MED graze

'**Streifzug** *m* tour (*durch* of)

Streik [ʃtraik] *m* (-[e]s; -s) strike, walk-out

'**Streikbrecher** *m* strikebreaker, *Br* blackleg, *contp* scab

streiken [ˈʃtraikən] *v/i* (*ge-*, *h*) (go *or* be on) strike; F *fig* refuse (to work etc)

'**Streikende** *m*, *f* (-n; -n) striker

'**Streikposten** *m* picket

Streit [ʃtrait] *m* (-[e]s; -e) quarrel; argument; fight; POL *etc* dispute; **~ anfangen** pick a fight *or* quarrel; **~ suchen** be looking for trouble; **streiten** [ˈʃtrai-tən] *v/i and v/refl* (*irr, ge-*, *h*) quarrel, argue, fight (*all:* **wegen, über** *acc* about, over); **sich ~ um** fight for

'**Streitfrage** *f* (point at) issue

streitig ['ʃtraitiç] *adj:* **j-m et. ~ machen** dispute s.o.'s right to s.th.

'**Streitkräfte** *pl* MIL (armed) forces

'**streitsüchtig** *adj* quarrelsome

streng [ʃtrɛŋ] *adj* strict; severe; harsh; rigid; **~ genommen** strictly speaking

Strenge ['ʃtrɛŋə] *f* (-; *no pl*) strictness; severity; harshness; rigidity

'**strenggläubig** *adj* REL orthodox

Stress [ʃtrɛs] *m* (-es; *no pl*) stress; **im ~** under stress

Streu [ʃtrɔy] *f* (-; -en) AGR litter

'**streuen** *v/t and v/i* (ge-, h) scatter (*a.* PHYS); spread; sprinkle; grit

streunen ['ʃtrɔynən] *v/i* (ge-, sein), **~d** *adj* stray

strich [ʃtriç] *pret of* **streichen**

Strich *m* (-[e]s; -e) line; stroke; F red-light district; F **auf den ~ gehen** walk the streets; **~junge** F *m* male prostitute; **~kode** *m* bar code

'**strichweise** *adv* in parts; **~ Regen** scattered showers

Strick [ʃtrik] *m* (-[e]s; -e) cord; rope

stricken ['ʃtrikən] *v/t and v/i* (ge-, h) knit

'**Strick|jacke** *f* cardigan; **~leiter** *f* rope ladder; **~nadel** *f* knitting needle; **~waren** *pl* knitwear; **~zeug** *n* knitting (things)

Striemen ['ʃtriːmən] *m* (-s; -) welt, weal

stritt [ʃtrit] *pret of* **streiten**

strittig ['ʃtritiç] *adj* controversial; **~er Punkt** point at issue

Stroh [ʃtroː] *n* (-[e]s; *no pl*) straw; thatch; **~dach** *n* thatch(ed) roof; **~halm** *m* straw; **~hut** *m* straw hat; **~witwe** F *f* grass widow; **~witwer** F *m* grass widower

Strom [ʃtroːm] *m* (-[e]s; *Ströme* ['ʃtrøːmə]) (large) river; current (*a.* ELECTR); **ein ~ von** a stream of (*a. fig*); **es gießt in Strömen** it's pouring (with rain)

strom'ab(wärts) *adv* downstream

strom'auf(wärts) *adv* upstream

'**Stromausfall** *m* ELECTR power failure, blackout

strömen ['ʃtrøːmən] *v/i* (ge-, sein) stream (*a. fig*), flow, run; pour (*a. fig*)

'**Stromkreis** *m* ELECTR circuit

'**stromlinienförmig** *adj* streamlined

'**Stromschnelle** *f* (-; -n) GEOGR rapid

'**Stromstärke** *f* ELECTR amperage

'**Strömung** *f* (-; -en) current, *fig a.* trend

Strophe ['ʃtroːfə] *f* (-; -n) stanza, verse

strotzen ['ʃtrɔtsən] *v/i* (ge-, h) **~ von** be full of, abound with; **~ vor** (*dat*) be bursting with

Strudel ['ʃtruːdəl] *m* (-s; -) whirlpool (*a. fig*), eddy

Struktur [ʃtrʊk'tuːɐ] *f* (-; -en) structure, pattern

Strumpf [ʃtrʊmpf] *m* (-[e]s; *Strümpfe* ['ʃtrʏmpfə]) stocking

'**Strumpfhose** *f* pantyhose, Br tights

struppig ['ʃtrʊpiç] *adj* shaggy

Stück [ʃtyk] *n* (-[e]s; -e) piece; part; lump; AGR head (*a. pl*); THEA play; **2 Euro das ~** 2 euros each; **im** or **am ~** in one piece; **in ~e schlagen (reißen)** smash (tear) to pieces; '**stückweise** *adv* bit by bit (*a. fig*); ECON by the piece

Student [ʃtu'dɛnt] *m* (-en; -en), Stu-'**dentin** *f* (-; -nen) student; **Studie** ['ʃtuːdjə] *f* (-; -n) study (**über** *acc* of); '**Studienplatz** *m* university or college place; **studieren** [ʃtu'diːrən] *v/t and v/i* (*no* -ge-, h) study, be a student (of) (**an** *dat* at); **Studium** ['ʃtuːdjʊm] *n* (-s; -ien) studies

Stufe ['ʃtuːfə] *f* (-; -n) step; level; stage

'**Stufenbarren** *m* SPORT uneven parallel bars

Stuhl [ʃtuːl] *m* (-[e]s; *Stühle* ['ʃtyːlə]) chair; MED stool; **~gang** *m* (-[e]s; *no pl*) MED (bowel) movement; **~lehne** *f* back of a chair

stülpen ['ʃtʏlpən] *v/t* (ge-, h) put (**auf** *acc*, **über** *acc* over, on)

stumm [ʃtʊm] *adj* dumb, mute; *fig* silent

Stummel ['ʃtʊməl] *m* (-s; -) stub, stump, butt

'**Stummfilm** *m* silent film

Stümper ['ʃtʏmpɐ] F *m* (-s; -) bungler

stumpf [ʃtʊmpf] *adj* blunt, dull (*a. fig*)

Stumpf *m* (-[e]s; *Stümpfe* ['ʃtʏmpfə]) stump, stub

'**stumpfsinnig** *adj* dull; monotonous

Stunde ['ʃtʊndə] *f* (-; -n) hour; PED class, lesson; period

'**Stundenkilo,meter** *m* kilometer (*Br* kilometre) per hour

'**stundenlang 1.** *adj:* **nach ~em Warten** after hours of waiting **2.** *adv* for hours

(and hours)

'**Stunden|lohn** *m* hourly wage; **~plan** *m* schedule, *Br* timetable

'**stundenweise** *adv* by the hour

'**Stundenzeiger** *m* hour hand

stündlich ['ʃtʏntlɪç] **1.** *adj* hourly **2.** *adv* hourly, every hour

Stupsnase ['ʃtupsnaːzə] F *f* snub nose

stur [ʃtuːɐ̯] F *adj* pigheaded

Sturm [ʃtʊrm] *m* (-[e]s; *Stürme* ['ʃtʏrmə]) storm (*a. fig*); **stürmen** ['ʃtʏrmən] *v/t* (ge-, h) *and v/i* (ge-, *sein*) storm; SPORT attack; rush; **Stürmer(in)** ['ʃtʏrmɐ, 'ʃtʏrmərɪn] *m(f)* (-s; -/-; -nen) SPORT forward; *esp soccer*: striker; **stürmisch** ['ʃtʏrmɪʃ] *adj* stormy; *fig* wild, vehement

Sturz [ʃtʊrts] *m* (-es; *Stürze* ['ʃtʏrtsə]) fall (*a. fig*); POL etc: overthrow

stürzen ['ʃtʏrtsən] **1.** *v/i* (ge-, *sein*) fall; crash; rush, dash; **schwer~** have a bad fall **2.** *v/t* (ge-, h) throw; POL etc: overthrow; *j-n ins Unglück~* ruin s.o.; *sich stürzen aus* throw o.s. out of; *sich ~ auf* (*acc*) throw o.s. at

'**Sturzflug** *m* AVIAT nosedive

'**Sturzhelm** *m* crash helmet

Stute ['ʃtuːtə] *f* (-; -n) ZO mare

Stütze ['ʃtʏtsə] *f* (-; -n) support, prop; *fig a.* aid

stutzen ['ʃtʊtsən] (ge-, h) **1.** *v/t* trim, clip **2.** *v/i* stop short; (begin to) wonder

stützen ['ʃtʏtsən] *v/t* (ge-, h) support (*a. fig*); *sich ~ auf* (*acc*) lean on; *fig* be based on

'**Stütz|pfeiler** *m* ARCH supporting column; **~punkt** *m* MIL base (*a. fig*)

Styropor® [ʃtyro'poːɐ̯] *n* (-s; *no pl*) Styrofoam®, *Br* polystyrene®

s. u. *abbr of* *siehe unten* see below

Subjekt [zʊp'jɛkt] *n* (-[e]s; -e) LING subject; *contp* character

subjektiv [zʊpjɛk'tiːf] *adj* subjective

Substantiv ['zʊpstantiːf] *n* (-s; -e) LING noun

Substanz [zʊp'stants] *f* (-; -en) substance (*a. fig*)

subtrahieren [zʊptra'hiːrən] *v/t* (no -ge-, h) MATH subtract; **Subtraktion** [zʊptrak'tsjoːn] *f* (-; -en) MATH subtraction

subventionieren [zʊpvɛntsjo'niːrən] *v/t* (no -ge-, h) subsidize

Suche ['zuːxə] *f* (-; *no pl*) search (*nach*

for); *auf der ~ nach* in search of; '**suchen** *v/t and v/i* (ge-, h) look for; search for; *gesucht:* ... wanted: ...; *was hat er hier zu ~?* what's he doing here?; *er hat hier nichts zu ~* he has no business to be here; **Sucher** ['zuːxɐ] *m* (-s; -) PHOT viewfinder

Sucht [zʊxt] *f* (-; *Süchte* ['zʏçtə]) addiction (*nach* to); mania (for); **süchtig** ['zʏçtɪç] *adj:* ~ *sein* be addicted to *drugs etc*, be a *drug etc* addict; **Süchtige** ['zʏçtɪgə] *m*, *f* (-n; -n) addict

Süden ['zyːdən] *m* (-s; *no pl*) south; *nach ~* south(wards)

Südfrüchte ['zyːtfrʏçtə] *pl* tropical *or* southern fruits

'**südlich 1.** *adj* south(ern); southerly **2.** *adv:* ~ *von* (to the) south of

Süd'osten *m* southeast; **süd'östlich** *adj* southeast(ern); southeasterly

'**Südpol** *m* South Pole

'**südwärts** ['zyːdvɛrts] *adv* southward(s)

Süd'westen *m* southwest; **süd'westlich** *adj* southwest(ern); southwesterly

'**Südwind** *m* south wind

Sülze ['zʏltsə] *f* (-; -n) GASTR jellied meat

Summe ['zʊmə] *f* (-; -n) sum (*a. fig*); amount; (sum) total

summen ['zʊmən] *v/i and v/t* (ge-, h) buzz, hum

summieren [zʊ'miːrən] *v/refl* (no -ge-, h) add up (*auf acc* to)

Sumpf [zʊmpf] *m* (-es; *Sümpfe* ['zʏmpfə]) swamp, bog

'**sumpfig** *adj* swampy, marshy

Sünde ['zʏndə] *f* (-; -n) sin (*a. fig*)

'**Sündenbock** F *m* scapegoat

Sünder ['zʏndɐ] *m* (-s; -), '**Sünderin** *f* (-; -nen) sinner

sündig ['zʏndɪç] *adj* sinful; **sündigen** ['zʏndɪgən] *v/i* (ge-, h) (commit a) sin

Super... ['zuːpɐ-] *in cpds* ...*macht etc:* *mst* super...

'**Super** *n* (-s; *no pl*), **~ben,zin** *n* super *or* premium (gasoline), *Br* four-star (petrol)

Superlativ ['zuːpɐlatiːf] *m* (-s; -e) LING superlative (*a. fig*)

'**Supermarkt** *m* supermarket

Suppe ['zʊpə] *f* (-; -n) soup

'**Suppen...** *in cpds* ...*löffel,* ...*teller,* ...*küche etc:* soup ...

Surfbrett ['zøːɛfbrɛt] *n* sail board; surfboard; '**surfen** *v/i* (*ge-*, *h*) surf
surren ['zʊrən] *v/i* (*ge-*, *h*) whirr; buzz
süß [zyːs] *adj* sweet, sugary (*both a. fig*)
Süße ['zyːsə] *f* (*-*; *no pl*) sweetness
'**süßen** *v/t* (*ge-*, *h*) sweeten
Süßigkeiten ['zyːsɪçkaitən] *pl* sweets,
candy
'**süßlich** *adj* sweetish; *contp* mawkish,
sugary
'**süß**'**sauer** *adj* GASTR sweet-and-sour
'**Süßstoff** *m* sweetener
'**Süßwasser** *n* fresh water
Symbol [zym'boːl] *n* (*-s*; *-e*) symbol;
Symbolik [zym'boːlɪk] *f* (*-*; *no pl*) sym-
bolism; **sym**'**bolisch** *adj* symbolic(al)
Symmetrie [zyme'triː] *f* (*-*; *-n*) symmetry; **symmetrisch** [zy'meːtrɪʃ] *adj*
symmetric(al)
Sympathie [zympa'tiː] *f* (*-*; *-n*) liking
(*für* for); sympathy; **Sympathisant(in)**
[zympati'zant(ɪn)] (*-en*; *-en/-*; *-nen*)
sympathizer; **sympathisch** [zym-
'paːtɪʃ] *adj* nice, likable; *er ist mir ~*
I like him
Symphonie [zymfo'niː] *f* (*-*; *-n*) *etc* →
Sinfonie
Symptom [zymp'toːm] *n* (*-s*; *-e*) symptom
Synagoge [zyna'goːgə] *f* (*-*; *-n*) syna-
gogue
synchron [zyn'kroːn] *adj* TECH synchro-
nous; **synchronisieren** [zynkroni-
'ziːrən] *v/t* (*no -ge-*, *h*) synchronize;
film etc: dub
synonym [zyno'nyːm] *adj* synonymous
Syno'**nym** *n* (*-s*; *-e*) synonym
Synthese [zyn'teːzə] *f* (*-*; *-n*) synthesis
synthetisch [zyn'teːtɪʃ] *adj* synthetic
System [zys'teːm] *n* (*-s*; *-e*) system
systematisch [zyste'maːtɪʃ] *adj* sys-
tematic, methodical
Sys'**temfehler** *m* IT system error
Szene ['stseːnə] *f* (*-*; *-n*) scene (*a. fig*)
Szenerie [stsenə'riː] *f* (*-*; *-n*) scenery;
setting

T

Tabak ['taːbak] *m* (*-s*; *-e*) tobacco; **~ge-
schäft** *n* tobacconist's; **~waren** *pl* to-
bacco products
Tabelle [ta'bɛlə] *f* (*-*; *-n*) table (*a. MATH,
SPORT*)
Ta'bellen|kalkulati,on *f* IT spreadsheet;
~platz *m* SPORT position
Tablett [ta'blɛt] *n* (*-[e]s*; *-s*) tray
Tablette [ta'blɛtə] *f* (*-*; *-n*) tablet
tabu [ta'buː] *adj*, **Ta'bu** *n* (*-s*; *-s*) taboo
Tabulator [tabu'laːtoːɐ] *m* (*-s*; *-en*
[tabula'toːrən]) tabulator
Tachometer [taxo'meːtɐ] *m*, *n* (*-s*; *-*)
MOT speedometer
Tadel ['taːdəl] *m* (*-s*; *-*) blame; censure,
reproof, rebuke; '**tadellos** *adj* faultless; blameless; excellent; perfect
'**tadeln** *v/t* (*ge-*, *h*) criticize, blame; censure, reprove, rebuke (*all: wegen* for)
Tafel ['taːfəl] *f* PED *etc*: blackboard; (bulletin, *esp Br* notice) board; sign; tablet,
plaque; GASTR bar (*of chocolate*)
täfeln ['tɛːfəln] *v/t* (*ge-*, *h*) panel
'**Täfelung** *f* (*-*; *-en*) panel(l)ing
Taft [taft] *m* (*-[e]s*; *-e*) taffeta

Tag [taːk] *m* (*-[e]s*; *-e* ['taːgə]) day; daylight; *welchen ~ haben wir heute?*
what day is it today?; *heute* (*morgen*)
in 14 ~en two weeks from today (tomorrow); *e-s ~es* one day; *den ganzen ~* all day; *am ~e* during the day;
~ und Nacht night and day; *am helllichten ~* in broad daylight; *ein freier
~* a day off; *guten ~!* hello!, hi!; how
do you do?; (*j-m*) *guten ~ sagen* say
hello (to s.o.); F *sie hat ihre ~e* she
has her period; *unter ~e* underground;
→ **zutage**
Tage|bau ['taːgəbau] *m* (*-[e]s*; *-e*) open-
cast mining; **~buch** *n* diary; **~ führen**
keep a diary
'**tagelang** *adv* for days
'**tagen** *v/i* (*ge-*, *h*) meet, hold a meeting;
JUR be in session
'**Tages|anbruch** *m*: *bei ~* at daybreak, at
dawn; **~gespräch** *n* talk of the day;
~karte *f* day ticket; GASTR menu for
the day; **~licht** *n* (*-[e]s*; *no pl*) daylight;
~mutter *f* childminder; **~ordnung** *f*
agenda; **~stätte** *f* day care center (*Br*

centre); **~tour** f day trip; **~zeit** f time of day; **zu jeder ~** at any hour; **~zeitung** f daily (paper)

'**tageweise** adv by the day

täglich ['tɛːklɪç] adj and adv daily

'**Tagschicht** f ECON day shift

'**tagsüber** adv during the day

'**Tagung** f (-; -en) conference

Taille ['taljə] f (-; -n) waist; waistline

tailliert [ta'jiːɐt] adj waisted, tapered

Takelage [takə'laːʒə] f (-; -n) MAR rigging

Takt [takt] m (-[e]s; -e) (no pl) MUS time, measure, beat; MUS bar; MOT stroke; (no pl) tact; **den ~ halten** MUS keep time

Taktik ['taktɪk] f (-; -en) MIL tactics (a. fig); '**taktisch** adj tactical

'**taktlos** adj tactless

'**Taktstock** m MUS baton

'**Taktstrich** m MUS bar

'**taktvoll** adj tactful

Tal [taːl] n (-[e]s; Täler ['tɛːlɐ]) valley

Talar [ta'laːɐ] m (-s; -e) robe, gown

Talent [ta'lɛnt] n (-[e]s; -e) talent (a. person), gift; **talentiert** [talɛn'tiːɐt] adj talented, gifted

Talg [talk] m (-[e]s; -e) tallow; GASTR suet

Talisman ['taːlɪsman] m (-s; -e) talisman, charm

Talk|master ['tɔːkmaːstɐ] m (-s; -) TV talk (Br chat) show host; **~show** ['tɔːkʃoʊ] f (-; -s) TV talk (Br chat) show

'**Talsperre** ['taːlʃpɛrə] f dam, barrage

Tampon ['tampɔn] m (-s; -s) tampon

Tandler ['tandlɐ] Austrian m (-s; -) second-hand dealer

Tang [taŋ] m (-[e]s; -e) BOT seaweed

Tank [taŋk] m (-s; -s) tank; **tanken** ['taŋkən] v/t (ge-, h) get some gasoline (Br petrol), fill up; **Tanker** ['taŋkɐ] m (-s; -) MAR tanker; '**Tankstelle** f filling (or gas, Br petrol) station; '**Tankwart** m (-[e]s; -e) gas station (Br petrol pump) attendant

Tanne ['tanə] f (-; -n) BOT fir (tree)

'**Tannenbaum** m Christmas tree

'**Tannenzapfen** m BOT fir cone

Tante ['tantə] f (-; -n) aunt; **~ Lindy** Aunt Lindy; **~-Emma-Laden** F m mom-and-pop store, Br corner shop

Tantiemen [ta'tjeːmən] pl royalties

Tanz [tants] m (-es; Tänze ['tɛntsə]), **tanzen** ['tantsən] v/i (ge-, h, sein) and v/t (ge-, h) dance; **Tänzer** ['tɛntsɐ] m (-s; -), **Tänzerin** ['tɛntsərɪn] f (-; -nen) dancer

'**Tanz|fläche** f dance floor; **~kurs** m dancing lessons; **~mu,sik** f dance music; **~schule** f dancing school

Tapete [ta'peːtə] f (-; -n), **tapezieren** [tape'tsiːrən] v/t (no -ge-, h) wallpaper

tapfer ['tapfɐ] adj brave; courageous

'**Tapferkeit** f (-; no pl) bravery; courage

Tarif [ta'riːf] m (-[e]s; -e) rate(s), tariff; (wage) scale; **~lohn** m standard wage(s); **~verhandlungen** pl wage negotiations, collective bargaining

tarnen ['tarnən] v/t (ge-, h) camouflage; fig disguise

'**Tarnung** f (-; -en) camouflage

Tasche ['taʃə] f (-; -n) bag; pocket

'**Taschen|buch** n paperback; **~dieb** m pickpocket; **~geld** n allowance, Br pocket money; **~lampe** f flashlight, Br torch; **~messer** n penknife, pocket-knife; **~rechner** m pocket calculator; **~schirm** m telescopic umbrella; **~tuch** n handkerchief, F hankie; **~uhr** f pocket watch

Tasse ['tasə] f (-; -n) cup; **e-e ~ Tee** etc a cup of tea etc

Tastatur [tasta'tuːɐ] f (-; -en) keyboard, keys; **Taste** ['tastə] f (-; -n) key

tasten ['tastən] (ge-, h) **1.** v/i grope (**nach** for), feel (for); fumble (for) **2.** v/t touch, feel; **sich ~** feel or grope (a. fig) one's way

'**Tastentele,fon** n push-button phone

'**Tastsinn** m (-[e]s; no pl) sense of touch

tat [taːt] pret of **tun**

Tat f (-; -en) act, deed; action; JUR offense, Br offence; **j-n auf frischer ~ er-tappen** catch s.o. in the act

'**tatenlos** adj inactive, passive

Täter ['tɛːtɐ] m (-s; -), **Täterin** f (-; -nen) culprit; JUR offender

tätig ['tɛːtɪç] adj active; busy; **~ sein bei** be employed with; **~ werden** act, take action; '**Tätigkeit** f (-; -en) activity; work; occupation, job

'**Tatkraft** f (-; no pl) energy

'**tatkräftig** adj energetic, active

tätlich ['tɛːtlɪç] adj violent; **~ werden gegen** assault; '**Tätlichkeiten** pl (acts of) violence; JUR assault (and battery)

'**Tatort** m JUR scene of the crime

tätowieren [tɛto'viːrən] v/t (no -ge-, h), **Täto'wierung** f (-; -en) tattoo

'**Tatsache** *f* fact

'**tatsächlich 1.** *adj* actual, real **2.** *adv* actually, in fact; really

tätscheln ['tɛːtʃəln] *v/t* (ge-, h) pat, pet

Tatze ['tatsə] *f* (-; -n) zo paw (*a. fig*)

Tau¹ [tau] *n* (-[e]s; -e) rope

Tau² *m* (-[e]s; *no pl*) dew

taub [taup] *adj* deaf (*fig* **gegen** to); numb, benumbed

Taube ['taubə] *f* (-; -n) zo pigeon; *esp fig* dove; '**Taubenschlag** *m* pigeonhouse

'**Taubheit** *f* (-; *no pl*) deafness; numbness

'**taubstumm** *adj* deaf-and-dumb

'**Taubstumme** *m, f* (-n; -n) deaf mute

tauchen ['tauxən] **1.** *v/i* (ge-, h, sein) dive (**nach** for); SPORT skin-dive; *submarine*: *a.* submerge; stay underwater **2.** *v/t* (h) dip (**in** *acc* into); duck; **Taucher** ['tauxɐ] *m* (-s; -) (SPORT skin) diver; '**Tauchsport** *m* skin diving

tauen ['tauən] *v/i* (ge-, sein) *and v/t* (ge-, h) thaw, melt

Taufe ['taufə] *f* (-; -n) baptism, christening; '**taufen** *v/t* (ge-, h) baptize, christen; '**Taufpate** *m* godfather; '**Taufpatin** *f* godmother; '**Taufschein** *m* certificate of baptism

taugen ['taugən] *v/i* (ge-, h) be good *or* fit *or* of use *or* suited (*all:* **zu, für** for); **nichts**~ be no good; F **taugt es was?** is it any good?; **tauglich** ['tauklɪç] *adj esp* MIL fit (*for service*)

Taumel ['tauməl] *m* (-s; *no pl*) dizziness; rapture, ecstasy; '**taumelig** *adj* dizzy; '**taumeln** *v/i* (ge-, sein) stagger, reel

Tausch [tauʃ] *m* (-[e]s; -e) exchange, F swap; **tauschen** ['tauʃən] *v/t* (ge-, h) exchange, F swap (*both:* **gegen** for); switch; change; **ich möchte nicht mit ihm** ~ I wouldn't like to be in his shoes

täuschen ['tɔyʃən] *v/t* (ge-, h) deceive, fool; delude; cheat; *a.* SPORT feint; **sich** ~ deceive o.s.; be mistaken; **sich** ~ **lassen von** be taken in by; ~**de Ähnlichkeit** striking similarity; '**Täuschung** *f* (-; -en) deception; delusion; JUR deceit; *a.* PED cheating

tausend ['tauzənt] *adj* a thousand

'**tausendst** *adj* thousandth

'**Tausendstel** *n* (-s; -) thousandth (part)

'**Tautropfen** *m* dewdrop

'**Tauwetter** *n* thaw

'**Tauziehen** *n* (-s; *no pl*) SPORT tug-of-war (*a. fig*)

Taxi ['taksi] *n* (-s; -s) taxi(cab), cab

taxieren [ta'ksiːrən] *v/t* (no -ge-, h) rate, estimate (**auf** *acc* at)

'**Taxistand** *m* cabstand, *esp Br* taxi rank

Technik ['tɛçnɪk] *f* (-; -en) (*no pl*) technology, engineering; technique (*a.* SPORT *etc*), MUS execution

Techniker ['tɛçnɪkɐ] *m* (-s; -), '**Technikerin** *f* (-; -nen) engineer; technician (*a.* SPORT *etc*)

technisch ['tɛçnɪʃ] *adj* technical; technological; ~**e Hochschule** school *etc* of technology

Technologie [tɛçnolo'giː] *f* (-; -n) technology; **technologisch** [tɛçno'loːgɪʃ] *adj* technological

Tee [teː] *m* (-s; -s) tea; (**e-n**) ~ **trinken** have some tea; (**e-n**) ~ **machen** *or* **kochen** make some tea; ~**beutel** *m* teabag; ~**kanne** *f* teapot; ~**löffel** *m* teaspoon

Teer [teːɐ] *m* (-[e]s; -e), **teeren** ['teːrən] *v/t* (ge-, h) tar

'**Teesieb** *n* tea strainer

'**Teetasse** *f* teacup

Teich [taiç] *m* (-[e]s; -e) pool, pond

Teig [taik] *m* (-[e]s; -e) dough, paste

teigig ['taigɪç] *adj* doughy, pasty

'**Teigwaren** *pl* pasta

Teil [tail] *m, n* (-[e]s; -e) part; portion, share; component; **zum** ~ partly, in part; ~**...** *in cpds* ~**erfolg** *etc*: partial ...

'**teilbar** *adj* divisible

'**Teilchen** *n* (-s; -) particle

teilen ['tailən] *v/t* (ge-, h) divide; share

'**teilhaben** *v/i* (*irr*, **haben**, sep, -ge-, h) ~ **an** (*dat*) (have a) share in; '**Teilhaber(in)** ['tailhaːbɐ (-bərɪn)] (-s; -/-; -nen) ECON partner

'**Teilnahme** ['tailnaːmə] *f* (-; *no pl*) participation (**an** *dat* in); *fig* interest (in); sympathy (for)

'**teilnahmslos** *adj* indifferent; *esp* MED apathetic; '**Teilnahmslosigkeit** *f* (-; *no pl*) indifference; apathy

'**teilnehmen** *v/i* (*irr*, **nehmen**, sep, -ge-, h) ~ **an** (*dat*) take part *or* participate in; share (in); '**Teilnehmer(in)** ['tailneːmɐ (-mərɪn)] (-s; -/-; -nen) participant; UNIV student; SPORT competitor

teils *adv* partly

'**Teilstrecke** *f* stage, leg

'**Teilung** *f* (-; -en) division

'teilweise *adv* partly, in part

'Teilzahlung *f* → *Abzahlung, Rate*

Teint [tɛ̃:] *m* (*-s; -s*) complexion

Tel. *abbr of* **Telefon** tel., telephone

Telefon [tele'fo:n] *n* (*-s; -e*) telephone, phone; **am ~** on the (tele)phone; **~ haben** have a (*Br* be on the) (tele)phone; **ans ~ gehen** answer the (tele)phone; **~anruf** *m* (tele)phone call; **~anschluss** *m* telephone connection; **~appa,rat** *m* telephone, phone

Telefonat [telefo'na:t] *n* (*-[e]s; -e*) → *Telefongespräch*

Tele'fon|buch *n* telephone directory, phone book; **~gebühr** *f* telephone charge; **~gespräch** *n* (tele)phone call

telefonieren [telefo'ni:rən] *v/i* (*no -ge-, h*) (tele)phone; be on the phone; **mit j-m ~** talk to s.o. on the phone

telefonisch [tele'fo:nɪʃ] **1.** *adj* telephonic, telephone ... **2.** *adv* by (tele)phone, over the (tele)phone

Tele'fon|karte *f* phonecard; **~leitung** *f* telephone line; **~netz** *n* telephone network; **~nummer** *f* (tele)phone number; **~zelle** *f* (tele)phone booth, *esp Br* (tele)phone box, *Br* call box; **~zen,trale** *f* switchboard

Telegramm [tele'gram] *n* (*-s; -e*) telegram, wire, cable(gram)

Teleobjektiv ['te:leɔpjɛkti:f] *n* telephoto lens

Telephon *n* → *Telefon*

Teletext ['te:lətɛkst] *m* teletext

Teller ['tɛlɐ] *m* (*-s; -*) plate; **~wäscher** ['tɛlɐvɛʃɐ] *m* (*-s; -*) dishwasher

Tempel ['tɛmpəl] *m* (*-s; -*) temple

Temperament [tɛmpəra'mɛnt] *n* (*-[e]s; -e*) temper(ament); life; F pep

tempera'ment|los *adj* lifeless, dull; **~voll** *adj* full of life *or* F pep

Temperatur [tɛmpəra'tu:ɐ] *f* (*-; -en*) temperature; **j-s ~ messen** take s.o.'s temperature

Tempo ['tɛmpo] *n* (*-s; -s, -pi*) speed; MUS time; **mit ~** ... at a speed of ... an hour

Tendenz [tɛn'dɛnts] *f* (*-; -en*) tendency, trend; leaning; **tendenziös** [tɛndɛn-'tsjø:s] *adj* tendentious; **tendieren** [tɛn'di:rən] *v/i* (*no -ge-, h*) tend (**zu** towards; **dazu, et. zu tun** to do s.th.)

Tennis ['tɛnɪs] *n* (*-; no pl*) tennis; **~platz** *m* tennis court; **~schläger** *m* tennis racket; **~spieler(in)** tennis player

Tenor [te'no:ɐ] *m* (*-s; Tenöre* [te'nø:rə]) MUS tenor

Teppich ['tɛpɪç] *m* (*-s; -e*) carpet

'Teppichboden *m* fitted carpet, wall-to--wall carpeting

Termin [tɛr'mi:n] *m* (*-s; -e*) date; deadline; engagement; **e-n ~ vereinbaren (einhalten, absagen)** make (keep, cancel) an appointment

Terminal ['tø:rmɪnəl] *m, n* (*-s; -s*) AVIAT terminal; *n* (*-s; -s*) IT terminal

Terrasse [tɛ'rasə] *f* (*-; -n*) terrace

ter'rassenförmig [tɛ'rasənfœrmɪç] *adj* terraced, in terraces

Terrine [tɛ'ri:nə] *f* (*-; -n*) tureen

Territorium [tɛri'to:rjʊm] *n* (*-s; -ien*) territory

Terror ['tɛro:ɐ] *m* (*-s; no pl*) terror

terrorisieren [tɛrori'zi:rən] *v/t* (*no -ge-, h*) terrorize

Terrorismus [tɛro'rɪsmʊs] *m* (*-; no pl*) terrorism; **Terrorist(in)** [tɛro'rɪst(ɪn)] (*-en; -en/-; -nen*), **terro'ristisch** *adj* terrorist

Testament [tɛsta'mɛnt] *n* (*-[e]s; -e*) (last) will; JUR last will and testament

testamentarisch [tɛstamen'ta:rɪʃ] *adv* by will

Testa'mentsvollstrecker *m* executor

Testbild ['tɛstbɪlt] *n* TV test card

testen ['tɛstən] *v/t* (*no -ge-, h*) test

'Testpi,lot *m* test pilot

Tetanus ['te:tanʊs] *m* (*-; no pl*) MED tetanus

teuer ['tɔʏɐ] *adj* expensive; **wie~ ist es?** how much is it?

Teufel ['tɔʏfəl] *m* (*-s; -*) devil (*a. fig*); **wer (wo, was) zum ~ ...?** who (where, what) the hell ...? **'Teufelskerl** F *m* devil of a fellow; **'Teufelskreis** *m* vicious circle; **teuflisch** ['tɔʏflɪʃ] *adj* devilish, diabolic(al)

Text [tɛkst] *m* (*-[e]s; -e*) text; MUS words, lyrics

Texter ['tɛkstɐ] *m* (*-s; -*), **'Texterin** *f* (*-; -nen*) MUS songwriter

Textil... [tɛks'ti:l-] *in cpds* textile ...

Textilien [tɛks'ti:ljən] *pl* textiles

'Textverarbeitung *f* word processing

Theater [te'a:tɐ] *n* (*-s; -*) theater, *Br* theatre; F **~ machen (um)** make a fuss (about); **~besucher** *m* theatergoer, *Br* theatregoer; **~karte** *f* theater (*Br* theatre) ticket; **~kasse** *f* box office;

~stück n play

Thema ['te:ma] n (-s; Themen) subject, topic; MUS theme; **das ~ wechseln** change the subject

Theologe [teo'lo:gə] m (-n; -n) theologian; **Theologie** [teolo'gi:] f (-; -n) theology; **Theo'login** f (-; -nen) theologian; **theo'logisch** adj theological

Theoretiker [teo're:tikɐ] m (-s; -) theorist; **theo'retisch** adj theoretical

Theorie [teo'ri:] f (-; -n) theory

Therapeut [tera'pɔyt] m (-en; -en), **Thera'peutin** f (-; -nen) therapist; **Therapie** [tera'pi:] f (-; -n) therapy

Thermometer [tɛrmo'me:tɐ] n (-s; -) thermometer

Thermosflasche® ['tɛrmosflaʃə] f thermos®

These ['te:zə] f (-; -n) thesis

Thon [to:n] Swiss m (-s; -s) tuna (fish)

Thrombose [trɔm'bo:zə] f (-; -n) MED thrombosis

Thron [tro:n] m (-[e]s; -e) throne

'Thronfolger ['tro:nfɔlgɐ] m (-s; -), **'Thronfolgerin** ['tro:nfɔlgərɪn] f (-; -nen) successor to the throne

Thunfisch ['tu:nfɪʃ] m tuna (fish)

Tick [tɪk] F m (-[e]s; -s) quirk

ticken ['tɪkən] v/i (ge-, h) tick

Tiebreak, Tie-Break ['taɪbreɪk] m, n tennis: tiebreak(er)

tief [ti:f] adj deep (a. fig); low

Tief n (-s; -s) METEOR depression (a. PSYCH, ECON), low (a. fig)

Tiefe ['ti:fə] f (-; -n) depth (a. fig)

'Tief|ebene f lowland(s); **~flieger** m low-flying air plane; **~gang** m MAR draft, Br draught; fig depth; **~ga,rage** f parking or underground garage, Br underground car park

'tiefgekühlt adj deep-frozen

'Tiefkühl|fach n freezing compartment; **~kost** f frozen foods; **~schrank** m, **~truhe** f freezer, deep-freeze

Tier [ti:ɐ] n (-[e]s; -e) animal; F hohes ~ bigwig, big shot; **~arzt** m, **-ärztin** f veterinarian, Br veterinary surgeon, F vet; **~freund** m animal lover; **~garten** m → Zoo; **~heim** n animal shelter

tierisch ['ti:rɪʃ] adj animal; fig bestial, brutish

'Tierkreis m ASTR zodiac; **~zeichen** n sign of the zodiac

'Tiermedi,zin f veterinary medicine

Tierquäle'rei f cruelty to animals

'Tier|reich n animal kingdom; **~schutz** m protection of animals; **~schutzverein** m society for the prevention of cruelty to animals; **~versuch** m MED experiment with animals

Tiger ['ti:gɐ] m (-s; -) zo tiger

Tigerin ['ti:gərɪn] f (-; -nen) zo tigress

tilgen ['tɪlgən] v/t (ge-, h) ECON pay off

Tinte ['tɪntə] f (-; -n) ink

'Tintenfisch m zo squid

Tipp [tɪp] m (-s; -s) hint, tip; tip-off; j-m e-n ~ geben tip s.o. off

tippen ['tɪpən] v/i and v/t (ge-, h) tap; type; F guess; do lotto etc

Tisch [tɪʃ] m (-[e]s; -e) table; **am ~ sitzen** sit at the table; **bei ~** at table; **den ~ decken (abräumen)** lay (clear) the table; **~decke** f tablecloth; **~gebet** n REL grace: **das ~ sprechen** say grace

Tischler ['tɪʃlɐ] m (-s; -) joiner; cabinet-maker

'Tisch|platte f tabletop; **~tennis** n table tennis; **~tuch** n tablecloth

Titel ['ti:təl] m (-s; -) title; **~bild** n cover picture; **~blatt** n, **~seite** f title page; cover, front page

Toast [to:st] m (-[e]s; -s), **toasten** ['to:stən] v/t (ge-, h) toast

toben ['to:bən] v/i (ge-, h) rage (a. fig); romp; **tobsüchtig** ['to:pzʏçtɪç] adj raving mad; **'Tobsuchtsanfall** m tantrum

Tochter ['tɔxtɐ] f (-; Töchter ['tœçtɐ]) daughter; **~gesellschaft** f ECON subsidiary (company)

Tod [to:t] m (-[e]s; no pl) death (a. fig) (**durch** from); **tod...** in cpds **...ernst**, **...müde**, **...sicher**: dead ...:

Todes|ängste ['to:dəsɛŋstə] pl: ~ **ausstehen** be scared to death; **~anzeige** f obituary (notice); **~fall** m (case of) death; **~kampf** m agony; **~opfer** n casualty; **~strafe** f JUR capital punishment; death penalty; **~ursache** f cause of death; **~urteil** n JUR death sentence

'Todfeind m deadly enemy

'tod'krank adj mortally ill

tödlich ['tø:tlɪç] adj fatal; deadly; esp fig mortal

'Todsünde f mortal or deadly sin

Toilette [toa'lɛtə] f (-; -n) bathroom, Br toilet, lavatory; pl rest rooms, Br ladies' or men's rooms

Toi'letten... *in cpds* ...*papier*, ...*seife etc*: toilet ...; **~tisch** *m* dressing table

tolerant [tole'rant] *adj* tolerant (*gegen* of, towards); **Toleranz** [tole'rants] *f* (-; -en) tolerance (*a.* TECH); **tolerieren** [tole'ri:rən] *v/t* (*no -ge-, h*) tolerate

toll [tɔl] *adj* wild; F great, fantastic

'tollkühn *adj* daredevil

'Tollwut *f* VET rabies; **'tollwütig** ['tɔlvy:-tɪç] *adj* VET rabid

Tomate [to'ma:tə] *f* (-; -n) BOT tomato

Ton¹ [to:n] *m* (-[e]s; -e) clay

Ton² *m* (-[e]s; **Töne** ['tø:nə]) tone (*a.* MUS, PAINT), PAINT *a.* shade; sound (*a.* TV, *film*); note; stress; **kein ~** not a word; **~art** *f* MUS key; **~band** *n* (-[e]s; -bänder) (recording) tape; **~bandgerät** *n* tape recorder

tönen ['tø:nən] (*ge-, h*) **1.** *v/i* sound, ring **2.** *v/t* tinge, tint, shade

'Ton|fall *m* tone (of voice); accent; **~film** *m* sound film; **~kopf** *m* ELECTR (magnetic) head; **~lage** *f* MUS pitch; **~leiter** *f* MUS scale

Tonne ['tɔnə] *f* (-; -n) barrel; (metric) ton

Tontechniker *m* sound engineer

'Tönung *f* (-; -en) tint, tinge, shade

Topf [tɔpf] *m* (-[e]s; **Töpfe** ['tœpfə]) pot; saucepan

Topfen ['tɔpfən] *Austrian m* (-s; *no pl*) GASTR curd(s)

Töpfer ['tœpfɐ] *m* (-s; -) potter

Töpferei [tœpfə'rai] *f* (-; -en) pottery

'Töpferin *f* (-; -nen) potter

'Töpferscheibe *f* potter's wheel

'Töpferware *f* pottery, earthenware

Tor [to:ɐ] *n* (-[e]s; -e) gate; *soccer etc*: goal; **ein ~ schießen** score (a goal); **im ~ stehen** keep goal

Torf [tɔrf] *m* (-[e]s; -e) peat

'Torfmull *m* peat dust

'Torhüter ['to:ɐhy:tɐ] *m* → *Torwart*

torkeln ['tɔrkəln] F *v/i* (*ge-, h, sein*) reel, stagger

'Torlatte *f* SPORT crossbar

'Torlinie *f* SPORT goal line

torpedieren [tɔrpe'di:rən] *v/t* (*no -ge-, h*) MIL torpedo (*a. fig*)

'Tor|pfosten *m* SPORT goalpost; **~raum** *m* SPORT goalmouth; **~schuss** *m* SPORT shot at goal; **~schütze** *m* SPORT scorer

Torte ['tɔrtə] *f* (-; -n) pie, *esp Br* flan; cream cake, gateau

'Torwart ['to:ɐvart] *m* (-[e]s; -e) SPORT

goalkeeper, F goalie

tosen ['to:zən] *v/i* (*ge-, h*) roar; thunder; **~d** *adj* thunderous (*applause*)

tot [to:t] *adj* dead (*a. fig*); late; **~ geboren** MED stillborn; **~ umfallen** drop dead

total [to'ta:l] *adj* total, complete

totalitär [totali'tɛ:ɐ] *adj* POL totalitarian

'Tote *m, f* (-n; -n) dead man *or* woman; (dead) body, corpse; *mst pl* casualty; *pl the* dead; **töten** ['tø:tən] *v/t* (*ge-, h*) kill

'Totenbett *n* deathbed

'toten'blass *adj* deadly pale

'Toten|gräber ['to:təngrɛ:bɐ] *m* (-s; -) gravedigger; **~kopf** *m* skull; skull and crossbones; **~maske** *f* death mask; **~messe** *f* REL mass for the dead, requiem (*a. MUS*); **~schädel** *m* skull; **~schein** *m* death certificate

'toten'still *adj* deathly still

'totlachen F *v/refl* (*sep, -ge-, h*) kill o.s. laughing

Toto ['to:to] *m*, F *n* (-s; -s) football pools

'Totschlag *m* (-[e]s; *no pl*) JUR manslaughter; **'totschlagen** *v/t* (*irr, schlagen, sep, -ge-, h*) kill; *j-n ~* beat s.o. to death; *die Zeit ~* kill time

'totschweigen *v/t* (*irr, schweigen, sep, -ge-, h*) hush up

Toupet [tu'pe:] *n* (-s; -s) toupee

toupieren [tu'pi:rən] *v/t* (*no -ge-, h*) Br backcomb

Tour [tu:ɐ] *f* (-; -en) tour (*durch* of), trip; excursion; TECH turn, revolution; *auf ~en kommen* MOT pick up speed; F *krumme ~en* underhand methods

Touren... ['tu:rən-] *in cpds* ...*rad etc*: touring ...

Tourismus [tu'rɪsmʊs] *m* (-; *no pl*) tourism; **~geschäft** *n* tourist industry

Tourist [tu'rɪst] *m* (-en; -en), **Tou'ristin** *f* (-; -nen) tourist; **tou'ristisch** *adj* touristic

Tournee [tʊr'ne:] *f* (-; -s, -n) tour; *auf ~ gehen* go on tour

Trab [tra:p] *m* (-[e]s; *no pl*) trot

Trabant [tra'bant] *m* (-en; -en) ASTR satellite; **Tra'bantenstadt** *f* satellite town

traben ['tra:bən] *v/i* (*ge-, h, sein*) trot

Traber ['tra:bɐ] *m* (-s; -) ZO trotter

'Trabrennen *n* trotting race

Tracht [traxt] *f* (-; -en) costume; uniform; dress; F *e-e ~ Prügel* a thrashing

trächtig ['trɛçtɪç] *adj* ZO with young,

pregnant

Tradition [tradi'tsjo:n] *f* (-; *-en*) tradition; **traditionell** [traditsjo'nɛl] *adj* traditional

traf [tra:f] *pret of* **treffen**

Trafik [tra'fɪk] *Austrian f* (-; *-en*) → **Tabakgeschäft**; **Trafikant** [trafi'kant] *Austrian m* (*-en*; *-en*) tobacconist

Tragbahre ['tra:kba:rə] *f* stretcher

'**tragbar** *adj* portable; wearable; *fig* bearable; *person:* acceptable

Trage ['tra:gə] *f* (-; *-n*) stretcher

träge ['trɛ:gə] *adj* lazy, indolent; PHYS inert (*a. fig*)

tragen [tra:gən] (*irr, ge-, h*) **1.** *v/t* carry; wear; *fig* bear; **sich gut ~** wear well **2.** *v/i* BOT bear fruit; *fig* hold; **~d** *adj* ARCH supporting; THEA leading

Träger ['trɛ:gɐ] *m* (*-s*; *-*) carrier; porter; (shoulder) strap; TECH support; ARCH girder; *fig* bearer

'**trägerlos** *adj* strapless

'**Tragetasche** *f* carrier bag; carrycot

'**tragfähig** *adj* load-bearing; *fig* sound

'**Tragfläche** *f* AVIAT wing

Trägheit ['trɛ:khait] *f* (-; *no pl*) laziness, indolence; PHYS inertia (*a. fig*)

Tragik ['tra:gɪk] *f* (-; *no pl*) tragedy

tragisch ['tra:gɪʃ] *adj* tragic

Tragödie [tra'gø:djə] *f* (-; *-n*) tragedy

'**Tragriemen** *m* strap; sling

'**Tragweite** *f* range; *fig* significance

Trainer ['trɛ:nɐ] *m* (*-s*; *-*), '**Trainerin** *f* (-; *-nen*) SPORT trainer, coach; **trainieren** [trɛ'ni:rən] *v/i and v/t* (*no -ge-, h*) SPORT train, coach

'**Training** *n* (*-s*; *-s*) training

'**Trainingsanzug** *m* track suit

Traktor ['trakto:ɐ] *m* (*-s*; *-en* [trak-'to:rən]) MOT tractor

trällern ['trɛlɐn] *v/t and v/i* (*ge-, h*) warble, trill

Tram [tram] *Austrian f* (-; *-s*), *Swiss n* (*-s*; *-s*) streetcar, *Br* tram

trampeln ['trampəln] *v/i* (*ge-, h*) trample, stamp

'**Trampelpfad** *m* beaten track

trampen ['trɛmpən] *v/i* (*ge-, sein*) hitchhike; **Tramper(in)** ['trɛmpɐ, 'trɛmpərɪn] (*-s*; *-/-*; *-nen*) hitchhiker

Träne ['trɛ:nə] *f* (-; *-n*) tear; **in ~n ausbrechen** burst into tears; '**tränen** *v/i* (*ge-, h*) water; '**Tränengas** *n* tear gas

trank [traŋk] *pret of* **trinken**

Tränke ['trɛŋkə] *f* (-; *-n*) watering place

'**tränken** *v/t* (*ge-, h*) ZO water; soak, drench

Transfer [trans'fe:ɐ] *m* (*-s*; *-s*) transfer (*a.* SPORT)

Transformator [transfɔr'ma:to:ɐ] *m* (*-s*; *-en* [transfɔrma'to:rən]) ELECTR transformer

Transfusion [transfu'zjo:n] *f* (-; *-en*) MED transfusion

Transistor [tran'zɪsto:ɐ] *m* (*-s*; *-en* [tranzɪs'to:rən]) ELECTR transistor

Transit [tran'zi:t] *m* (*-s*; *-e*) transit

transitiv ['tranziti:f] *adj* LING transitive

transparent [transpa'rɛnt] *adj* transparent

Transpa'rent *n* (*-[e]s*; *-e*) banner

Transplantation [transplanta'tsjo:n] *f* (-; *-en*), **transplantieren** [transplan-'ti:rən] *v/t* (*no -ge-, h*) MED transplant

Transport [trans'pɔrt] *m* (*-[e]s*; *-e*) transport; shipment; **transportabel** [transpɔr'ta:bəl], **trans'portfähig** *adj* transportable; **transportieren** [transpɔr'ti:rən] *v/t* (*no -ge-, h*) transport, ship, carry, MOT *a.* haul

Trans'port|mittel *n* (means of) transport(ation); **~unternehmen** *n* hauler, *Br* haulier

Trapez [tra'pe:ts] *n* (*-es*; *-e*) MATH trapezoid, *Br* trapezium; SPORT trapeze

trappeln ['trapəln] *v/i* (*ge-, sein*) clatter; patter

trat [tra:t] *pret of* **treten**

Traube ['traubə] *f* (-; *-n*) BOT bunch of grapes; grape; *pl* grapes; *fig* cluster

Traubensaft *m* grape juice

'**Traubenzucker** *m* glucose

trauen ['trauən] (*ge-, h*) **1.** *v/t* marry **2.** *v/i* trust (*j-m* s.o.); **sich ~**, *et. zu tun* dare (to) do s.th.; **ich traute meinen Augen nicht** I couldn't believe my eyes

Trauer ['trauɐ] *f* (-; *no pl*) grief, sorrow; mourning; **in ~** in mourning; **~fall** *m* death; **~feier** *f* funeral service; **~marsch** *m* MUS funeral march

'**trauern** *v/i* (*ge-, h*) mourn (**um** for)

'**Trauerrede** *f* funeral oration

'**Trauerzug** *m* funeral procession

träufeln ['trɔyfəln] *v/t* (*ge-, h*) drip, trickle

Traum [traum] *m* (*-[e]s*; *Träume* ['trɔymə]) dream (*a. fig*); **~...** *in cpds* *...beruf, ...mann etc:* dream ..., ... of one's dreams; **träumen** ['trɔymən] *v/i and v/t* (*ge-, h*) dream (*a. fig*) (**von** about, of); **schlecht** ~ have bad dreams; **Träumer** ['trɔymɐ] *m* (*-s; -*) dreamer (*a. fig*); **Träumerei** [trɔymə-'rai] *fig f* (day)dream(s), reverie (*a. MUS*)

träumerisch ['trɔyməriʃ] *adj* dreamy

traurig ['trauriç] *adj* sad (**über** *acc*, **wegen** about)

'**Traurigkeit** *f* (*-; no pl*) sadness

Trauring ['trauriŋ] *m* wedding ring

'**Trauschein** *m* marriage certificate

'**Trauung** *f* (*-; -en*) marriage, wedding

'**Trauzeuge** *m*, '**Trauzeugin** *f* witness to a marriage

Trecker ['trɛkɐ] *m* (*-s; -*) MOT tractor

Treff [trɛf] F *m* (*-s; -s*) meeting place

treffen ['trɛfən] *v/t and v/i* (*irr, ge-, h*) hit (*a. fig*); hurt; meet *s.o.*; take (*measures etc*); **nicht** ~ miss; **sich** ~ (**mit** *j-m*) meet (*s.o.*); **gut** ~ PHOT *etc*: capture well; '**Treffen** *n* (*-s; -*) meeting; '**treffend 1.** *adj* apt (*remark etc*) **2.** *adv:* ~ **gesagt** well put; **Treffer** ['trɛfɐ] *m* (*-s; -*) hit (*a. fig*); SPORT goal; win; '**Treffpunkt** *m* meeting place

Treibeis ['traip'ʔais] *n* drift ice

treiben ['traibən] (*irr, ge-*) **1.** *v/t* (*h*) drive (*a. TECH and fig*); SPORT *etc:* do; push, press *s.o.*; BOT put forth; F do, be up to **2.** *v/i* (*sein*) drift (*a. fig*), float; BOT shoot (up); **sich** ~ **lassen** drift along (*a. fig*); **~de Kraft** driving force; '**Treiben** *n* (*-s; no pl*) doings, goingson; **geschäftiges** ~ bustle

'**treibenlassen** *v/refl* (*irr, lassen, sep, no -ge-, h*) → **treiben**

'**Treib|haus** *n* hothouse; **~hausef,fekt** *m* greenhouse effect; **~holz** *n* driftwood; **~riemen** *m* TECH driving belt; **~sand** *m* quicksand; **~stoff** *m* fuel

trennen ['trɛnən] *v/t* (*ge-, h*) separate; sever; part; divide (*a. LING, POL*); segregate; TEL disconnect; **sich** ~ separate (**von** from), part (*a. fig*); **sich** ~ **von** part with *s.th.*; leave *s.o.*; '**Trennung** *f* (*-; -en*) separation; division; segregation

'**Trennwand** *f* partition

Treppe ['trɛpə] *f* (*-; -n*) staircase, stairs

'**Treppen|absatz** *m* landing; **~geländer** *n* banisters; **~haus** *n* staircase; hall

Tresor [tre'zo:ɐ] *m* (*-s; -e*) safe; strongroom, vault

treten ['tre:tən] *v/i and v/t* (*irr, ge-, h*) kick; step (**aus** out of; **in** *acc* into; **auf** *acc* on[to]); pedal (away)

treu [trɔy] *adj* faithful (*a. fig*); loyal; devoted; **Treue** ['trɔyə] *f* (*-; no pl*) fidelity, faithfulness, loyalty

'**Treuhänder(in)** ['trɔyhɛndɐ, 'trɔyhɛndərin] *m(f)* (*-s; -/-; -nen*) JUR trustee

'**treulos** *adj* faithless, disloyal, unfaithful (*all:* **gegen** to)

Tribüne [tri'by:nə] *f* (*-; -n*) platform; stand

Trichter ['triçtɐ] *m* (*-s; -*) funnel; crater

Trick [trik] *m* (*-s; -s*) trick; **~aufnahme** *f* trick shot; **~betrüger(in)** confidence trickster

trieb [tri:p] *pret of* **treiben**

Trieb *m* (*-[e]s; -e* ['tri:bə]) BOT (young) shoot, sprout; *fig* impulse, drive; sex drive; **~feder** *f* mainspring (*a. fig*)

triefen ['tri:fən] *v/i* (*ge-, h*) drip, be dripping (**von** with)

triftig ['triftiç] *adj* weighty; good

Trikot [tri'ko:] *n* (*-s; -s*) SPORT shirt, jersey; leotard

Triller ['trilɐ] *m* (*-s; -*) MUS trill; '**trillern** *v/i and v/t* (*ge-, h*) trill; ZO warble

trimmen ['trimən] *v/i/refl* (*ge-, h*) keep fit

'**Trimmpfad** *m* fitness trail

trinkbar ['triŋkba:ɐ] *adj* drinkable

trinken ['triŋkən] *v/t and v/i* (*irr, ge-, h*) drink (**auf** *acc* to); have; **et. zu** ~ a drink; **Trinker(in)** ['triŋkɐ (-kərin)] (*-s; -/-; -nen*) drinker, alcoholic

'**Trink|geld** *n* tip; *j-m* (**zwei Euro**) ~ **geben** tip *s.o.* (two euros); **~spruch** *m* toast; **~wasser** *n* drinking water

Trio ['tri:o] *n* (*-s; -s*) MUS trio (*a. fig*)

trippeln ['tripəln] *v/i* (*ge-, sein*) mince

Tripper ['tripɐ] *m* (*-s; -*) MED gonorrh(o)ea

Tritt [trit] *m* (*-[e]s; -e*) kick; step

'**Trittbrett** *n* step; MOT running board

'**Trittleiter** *f* stepladder

Triumph [tri'umf] *m* (*-[e]s; -e*) triumph

triumphal [trium'fa:l] *adj* triumphant

triumphieren [trium'fi:rən] *v/i* (*no -ge-, h*) triumph (**über** *acc* over)

trocken ['trɔkən] *adj* dry (*a. fig*)

'**Trocken...** *in cpds* dried ...; drying ...

'**Trockenhaube** *f* hairdryer

'**Trockenheit** *f* (*-; no pl*) dryness; AGR drought

'**trockenlegen** v/t (sep, -ge-, h) drain; change (a baby)

trocknen ['trɔknən] v/t (ge-, h) and v/i (sein) dry

Trockner ['trɔknɐ] m (-s; -) dryer

Troddel ['trɔdəl] f (-; -n) tassel

Trödel ['trø:dəl] m (-s; no pl) junk

trödeln ['trø:dəln] v/i (ge-, h) dawdle

Trödler ['trø:dlɐ] m (-s; -) junk dealer; dawdler

trog [tro:k] pret of **trügen**

Trog m (-[e]s; Tröge ['trø:gə]) trough

Trommel ['trɔməl] f (-; -n) MUS drum (a. TECH); **~fell** n ANAT eardrum

'**trommeln** v/i and v/t (ge-, h) drum

Trommler ['trɔmlɐ] m (-s; -) drummer

Trompete [trɔm'pe:tə] f (-; -n) MUS trumpet; **trom'peten** v/i and v/t (no -ge-, h) trumpet (a. ZO); **Trompeter** [trɔm'pe:tɐ] m (-s; -) trumpeter

Tropen ['tro:pən]: **die ~** pl the tropics

'**Tropen...** in cpds tropical ...

Tropf [trɔpf] m (-[e]s; Tröpfe ['trœpfə]) MED drip

Tröpfchen ['trœpfçən] n (-s; -) droplet

tröpfeln ['trœpfəln] v/i and v/t (ge-, h) drip; **es tröpfelt** it's spitting

tropfen ['trɔpfən] v/i and v/t (ge-, h) drip, drop; '**Tropfen** m (-s; -) drop (a. fig); **ein ~ auf den heißen Stein** a drop in the bucket; '**tropfenweise** adv in drops, drop by drop

Trophäe [tro'fɛ:ə] f (-; -n) trophy (a. fig)

tropisch ['tro:pɪʃ] adj tropical

Trosse ['trɔsə] f (-; -n) cable

Trost [tro:st] m (-[e]s; no pl) comfort, consolation; **ein schwacher ~** cold comfort

trösten ['trø:stən] v/t (ge-, h) comfort, console; **sich ~** console o.s. (mit with)

tröstlich ['trø:stlɪç] adj comforting

'**trostlos** adj miserable; desolate

Trott [trɔt] m (-[e]s; -e) trot; F **der alte ~** the old routine

Trottel ['trɔtəl] F m (-s; -) dope

trottelig ['trɔtəlɪç] F adj dopey

trotten ['trɔtən] v/i (ge-, sein) trot

Trottinett ['trɔtinɛt] Swiss n (-s; -e) scooter

Trottoir [trɔ'toa:ɐ] Swiss n (-s; -e, -s) sidewalk, Br pavement

trotz [trɔts] prp (gen) in spite of, despite

Trotz m (-es; no pl) defiance; **j-m zum ~** to spite s.o.

'**trotzdem** adv in spite of it, nevertheless, F anyhow, anyway

trotzen ['trɔtsən] v/i (ge-, h) defy (dat s.o. or s.th.); sulk

trotzig ['trɔtsɪç] adj defiant; sulky

trüb [try:p], **trübe** ['try:bə] adj cloudy; muddy; dim; dull, fig a. gloomy

Trubel ['tru:bəl] m (-s; no pl) (hustle and) bustle

trüben ['try:bən] v/t (ge-, h) cloud; fig spoil, mar

Trübsal ['try:pza:l] f: **~ blasen** mope

'**trübselig** adj sad, gloomy; dreary

'**Trübsinn** m (-[e]s; no pl) melancholy, gloom, low spirits; '**trübsinnig** adj melancholy, gloomy

trug [tru:k] pret of **tragen**

trügen ['try:gən] (irr, ge-, h) **1.** v/t deceive **2.** v/i be deceptive

trügerisch ['try:gərɪʃ] adj deceptive

'**Trugschluss** m fallacy

Truhe ['tru:ə] f (-; -n) chest

Trümmer ['trymɐ] pl ruins; debris; pieces, bits

Trumpf [trʊmpf] m (-[e]s; Trümpfe ['trympfə]) trump (card) (a. fig); **~ sein** be trumps; fig **s-n ~ ausspielen** play one's trump card

Trunkenheit ['trʊŋkənhait] f (-; no pl) esp JUR: **~ am Steuer** drunk (Br drink) driving

'**Trunksucht** f (-; no pl) alcoholism

Trupp [trʊp] m (-s; -s) band, party; group; **Truppe** ['trʊpə] f (-; -n) MIL troop, pl troops, forces; THEA company, troupe

'**Truppen|gattung** f MIL branch (of service); **~übungsplatz** m training area

Truthahn ['tru:tha:n] m ZO turkey

Tscheche ['tʃɛçə] m (-n; -n) Czech; **Tschechien** ['tʃɛçjən] Czech Republic; '**Tschechin** f (-; -nen) Czech; '**tschechisch** adj Czech; **Tschechische Republik** Czech Republic

Tube ['tu:bə] f (-; -n) tube

Tuberkulose [tuberku'lo:zə] f (-; -n) MED tuberculosis

Tuch [tu:x] n (-[e]s) (pl -e) cloth; (pl Tücher ['ty:çɐ]) scarf

'**Tuchfühlung** f: **auf ~** in close contact

tüchtig ['tyçtɪç] adj (cap)able, competent; skil(l)ful; efficient; F fig good

'**Tüchtigkeit** f (-; no pl) (cap)ability, qualities; skill; efficiency

tückisch

tückisch ['tʏkɪʃ] *adj* malicious; MED insidious; treacherous

tüfteln ['tʏftəln] F *v/i* (*ge-*, *h*) puzzle (*an dat* over)

Tugend ['tu:gənt] *f* (-; *-en*) virtue (*a. fig*)

Tulpe ['tʊlpə] *f* (-; *-n*) BOT tulip

Tumor ['tu:mo:ɐ] *m* (-*s*; *-en* [tu'mo:rən]) MED tumo(u)r

Tümpel ['tʏmpəl] *m* (-*s*; -) pool

Tumult [tu'mʊlt] *m* (*-[e]s*; *-e*) tumult, uproar

tun [tu:n] *v/t and v/i* (*irr*, *ge-*, *h*) do; take (*a step etc*); F put; *zu ~ haben* have work to do; be busy; *ich weiß* (*nicht*), *was ich ~ soll or muss* I (don't) know what to do; *so ~*, *als ob* pretend to *inf*

Tünche ['tʏnçə] *f* (-; *-n*), **'tünchen** *v/t* (*ge-*, *h*) whitewash

Tunfisch *m* → **Thunfisch**

Tunke ['tʊŋkə] *f* (-; *-n*) sauce

Tunnel ['tʊnəl] *m* (-*s*; -) tunnel

Tüpfelchen ['tʏpfəlçən] *n*: *das ~ auf dem i* the icing on the cake

tupfen ['tʊpfən] *v/t* (*ge-*, *h*) dab

'Tupfen *m* (-*s*; -) dot, spot

Tupfer ['tʊpfɐ] *m* (-*s*; -) MED swab

Tür [ty:ɐ] *f* (-; *-en* [ty:rən]) door (*a. fig*); *die ~(en) knallen* slam the door(s); F *j-n vor die ~ setzen* throw s.o. out; *Tag der offenen ~* open house (*Br* day)

Turban ['tʊrba:n] *m* (-*s*; *-e*) turban

Turbine [tʊr'bi:nə] *f* (-; *-n*) TECH turbine

Turbolader ['tʊrbola:dɐ] *m* (-*s*; -) MOT turbo(charger)

Türke ['tʏrkə] *m* (-*n*; *-n*) Turk; **Türkei** [tʏr'kai] *f* Turkey; **Türkin** ['tʏrkɪn] *f* (-; *-nen*) Turk(ish woman); **'türkisch** *adj* Turkish

'Tür|klingel *f* doorbell; **~klinke** *f* door handle; **~knauf** *m* doorknob

Turm [tʊrm] *m* (*-[e]s*; *Türme* ['tʏrmə]) tower; steeple; *chess*: castle, rook

türmen ['tʏrmən] *v/t* (*ge-*, *h*) pile up (*a. sich ~*)

'Turmspitze *f* spire

'Turmspringen *n* SPORT platform diving

turnen ['tʊrnən] *v/i* (*ge-*, *h*) SPORT do gymnastics; **'Turnen** *n* (-*s*; *no pl*) SPORT gymnastics; PED physical education (*abbr* PE); **Turner** ['tʊrnɐ] *m* (-*s*; -), **Turnerin** ['tʊrnərɪn] *f* (-; *-nen*) SPORT gymnast

'Turnhalle *f* gymnasium, F gym

'Turnhemd *n* gym shirt

'Turnhose *f* gym shorts

Turnier [tʊr'ni:ɐ] *n* (-*s*; *-e*) tournament

Tur'niertanz *m* ballroom dancing

'Turn|lehrer(in) gym(nastics) *or* PE teacher; **~schuh** *m* sneaker, *Br* trainer; **~verein** *m* gymnastics club

'Tür|pfosten *m* doorpost; **~rahmen** *m* doorframe; **~schild** *n* doorplate; **~sprechanlage** *f* entryphone

Tusche ['tʊʃə] *f* (-; *-n*) Indian ink; watercolo(u)r

'Tuschkasten *m* paintbox

Tüte ['ty:tə] *f* (-; *-n*) (paper *or* plastic) bag; *e-e ~ ...* a bag of ...

TÜV [tʏf] *abbr of* **Technischer Überwachungs-Verein** *Br appr* MOT (test), compulsory car inspection; (*nicht*) *durch den ~ kommen* pass (fail) its *or* one's MOT

Typ [ty:p] *m* (-*s*; *-en*) type; model; F fellow, guy; **Type** ['ty:pə] *f* (-; *-n*) TECH type; F character

Typhus ['ty:fʊs] *m* (-; *no pl*) MED typhoid (fever)

typisch ['ty:pɪʃ] *adj* typical (*für* of)

Tyrann [ty'ran] *m* (*-en*; *-en*) tyrant

Tyrannei [tyra'nai] *f* (-; *-en*) tyranny

tyrannisch [ty'ranɪʃ] *adj* tyrannical

tyrannisieren [tyrani'zi:rən] *v/t* (*no -ge-*, *h*) tyrannize, bully

U

u. a. *abbr of* **unter anderem** among other things; **und andere** and others

U-Bahn ['u:ba:n] *f* underground, subway, *in London*: tube

übel ['y:bəl] *adj* bad; *mir ist ~* I feel sick; *et. ~ nehmen* be offended by s.th.; *~*

riechend foul-smelling, foul

'Übel *n* (-*s*; -) evil

'Übelkeit *f* (-; *-en*) nausea

'übelnehmen *v/t* (*irr*, *nehmen*, *sep*, *-ge-*, *h*) → **übel**

'Übeltäter *m*, **'Übeltäterin** *f esp iro* culprit

üben ['y:bən] *v/t and v/i* (*ge-*, *h*) practice, *Br* practise; **Klavier** *etc* ~ practice the piano *etc*

über ['y:bɐ] *prp* (*dat or acc*) over; above (*a. fig*); more than; across; *fig* about, of, *lecture etc a.* on; **sprechen** (**nachdenken** *etc*) ~ (*acc*) talk (think *etc*) about; ~ **Nacht bleiben** stay overnight; ~ **München nach Rom** to Rome via Munich

über'all *adv* everywhere; ~ **in** ... (*dat*) *a.* throughout ..., all over ...

über'anstrengen *v/t and v/refl* (*no -ge-*, *h*) overstrain (o.s.)

über'arbeiten *v/t* (*no -ge-*, *h*) revise; **sich** ~ overwork o.s.

'überaus *adv* most, extremely

'überbelichten *v/t* (*no -ge-*, *h*) PHOT overexpose

über'bieten *v/t* (*irr*, *bieten*, *no -ge-*, *h*) at *auction*: outbid (**um** by); *fig* beat, *a.* outdo *s.o.*

'Überblick *m* view; *fig* overview (**über** *acc* of); general idea, outline

über|'blicken *v/t* (*no -ge-*, *h*) overlook; *fig* be able to calculate

über'bringen *v/t* (*irr*, *bringen*, *no -ge-*, *h*) deliver; **Über'bringer(in)** (*-s*; *-/-*; *-nen*) ECON bearer

über|'brücken *v/t* (*no -ge-*, *h*) bridge (*a. fig*); **~dacht** [y:bɐ'daxt] *adj* roofed, covered; **~'dauern** *v/t* (*no -ge-*, *h*) outlast, survive; **~'denken** *v/t* (*irr*, *denken*, *no -ge-*, *h*) think *s.th.* over

'überdimensio,nal *adj* oversized

'Überdosis *f* MED overdose

'überdrüssig ['y:bɐdrysɪç] *adj*: ~ **sein** be weary or sick (*gen* of)

'über|durchschnittlich *adj* above--average; **~eifrig** *adj* overzealous

über'eilen *v/t* (*no -ge-*, *h*) rush; **nichts** ~! don't rush things!; **über'eilt** *adj* rash, hasty

überei'nander *adv* on top of each other; *talk etc* about one another; **~schlagen** *v/t* (*irr*, *schlagen*, *sep*, *-ge-*, *h*): **die Beine** ~ cross one's legs

über'einkommen *v/i* (*irr*, *kommen*, *sep*, *-ge-*, *sein*) agree; **Über'einkommen** *n* (*-s*; *-*), **Über'einkunft** *f* (*-*; *-künfte*) agreement

über'einstimmen *v/i* (*sep*, *-ge-*, *h*) tally, correspond (with); **mit j-m** ~ agree with

s.o. (**in** *dat* on); **Über'einstimmung** *f* (*-*; *-en*) agreement; correspondence; **in** ~ **mit** in accordance with

über'fahren *v/t* (*irr*, *fahren*, *no -ge-*, *h*) run *s.o.* over, knock *s.o.* down

'Überfahrt *f* MAR crossing

'Überfall *m* assault (*auf acc* on); hold-up (on, of); mugging (of); MIL raid (on); invasion (of); **über'fallen** *v/t* (*irr*, *fallen*, *no -ge-*, *h*) attack, assault; hold up; mug; MIL raid; invade

'überfällig *adj* overdue

über'fliegen *v/t* (*irr*, *fliegen*, *no -ge-*, *h*) fly over *or* across; *fig* glance over, skim (through)

'überfließen *v/i* (*irr*, *fließen*, *sep*, *-ge-*, *sein*) overflow

'Überfluss *m* (*-es*; *no pl*) abundance (**an** *dat* of); affluence; **im** ~ **haben** abound in; **'überflüssig** *adj* superfluous

über|'fluten *v/t* (*no -ge-*, *h*) flood (*a. fig*); **~'fordern** *v/t* (*no -ge-*, *h*) overtax

überfragt [y:bɐ'fra:kt] *adj*: F **da bin ich** ~ you've got me there

über'führen *v/t* (*no -ge-*, *h*) transport; JUR convict (**e-r Tat** of a crime)

Über'führung *f* (*-*; *-en*) transfer; JUR conviction; MOT overpass, *Br* flyover; footbridge

über'füllt *adj* overcrowded, packed

über'füttern *v/t* (*no -ge-*, *h*) overfeed

'Übergang *m* crossing; *fig* transition

über'geben *v/t* (*irr*, *geben*, *no -ge-*, *h*) hand over; MIL surrender; **sich** ~ vomit

über'gehen[1] *v/t* (*irr*, *gehen*, *no -ge-*, *h*) pass over, ignore

'übergehen[2] *v/i* (*irr*, *gehen*, *sep*, *-ge-*, *sein*) pass (**zu** on to); ~ **in** (*acc*) change *or* turn (in)to

'übergeschnappt F *adj* cracked

'Übergewicht *n* (~ **haben** be) overweight; *fig* predominance

'übergewichtig *adj* overweight

'überglücklich *adj* overjoyed

'übergreifen *v/i* (*irr*, *greifen*, *sep*, *-ge-*, *h*) ~ **auf** (*acc*) spread to

'Übergriff *m* infringement (**auf** *acc* of); (act of) violence

'Übergröße *f* outsize; **in** ~**n** outsized, oversize(d)

über'handnehmen *v/i* (*irr*, *nehmen*, *sep*, *-ge-*, *h*) become rampant

über'häufen *v/t* (*no -ge-*, *h*) swamp; shower

über'haupt *adv* ... at all; anyway; ~ **nicht** (*nichts*) not (nothing) at all

überheblich [y:bɐ'he:plɪç] *adj* arrogant

Über'heblichkeit *f* (-; *no pl*) arrogance

über'|hitzen *v/t* (*no -ge-, h*) overheat (*a. fig*); **~höht** [y:bɐ'hø:t] *adj* excessive; **~'holen** *v/t* (*no -ge-, h*) pass, overtake (*a.* SPORT); TECH overhaul, service; **~'holt** *adj* outdated, antiquated; **~'hören** *v/t* (*no -ge-, h*) miss, not catch *or* get; ignore

'überirdisch *adj* supernatural

über'kleben *v/t* (*no -ge-, h*) paste up, cover

'überkochen *v/i* (*sep, -ge-, sein*) boil over

über'|kommen *v/t* (*irr, kommen, no -ge-, h*) ... **überkam ihn** he was seized with *or* overcome by ...; **~'laden** *v/t* (*irr, laden, no -ge-, h*) overload (*a.* ELECTR); *fig* clutter; **~'lassen** *v/t* (*irr, lassen, no -ge-, h*) *j-m et.* ~ let s.o. have s.th., leave s.th. to s.o. (*a. fig*); *j-n sich selbst* ~ leave s.o. to himself; *j-n s-m Schicksal* ~ leave s.o. to his fate; **~'lasten** *v/t* (*no -ge-, h*) overload (*a.* ELECTR); *fig* overburden

'überlaufen¹ *v/i* (*irr, laufen, sep, -ge-, sein*) run *or* flow over; MIL desert

über'laufen² *v/t* (*irr, laufen, no -ge-, h*) *es überlief mich heiß und kalt* I went hot and cold

über'laufen³ *adj* overcrowded

'Überläufer *m* MIL deserter; POL defector

über'leben *v/t and v/i* (*no -ge-, h*) survive (*a. fig*); live through s.th.

Über'lebende *m, f* (*-n; -n*) survivor

'überlebensgroß *adj* larger than life

über'legen¹ *v/t and v/i* (*no -ge-, h*) think about s.th., think s.th. over; consider; *lassen Sie mich* ~ let me think; *ich habe es mir* (*anders*) *überlegt* I've made up (changed) my mind

über'legen² *adj* superior (*j-m* to s.o.)

Über'legenheit *f* (-; *no pl*) superiority

über'legt *adj* deliberate; prudent

Über'legung *f* (-; *-en*) consideration, reflection

'überleiten *v/i* (*sep, -ge-, h*) ~ *zu* lead up *or* over to

über'liefern *v/t* (*no -ge-, h*) hand down, pass on; **Über'lieferung** *f* (-; *-en*) tradition

über'listen *v/t* (*no -ge-, h*) outwit

'Übermacht *f* (-; *no pl*) superiority; *esp* MIL superior forces; *in der* ~ *sein* be superior in numbers; **'übermächtig** *adj* superior; *fig* overpowering

'Übermaß *n* (*-es; no pl*) excess (*an dat* of); **'übermäßig** *adj* excessive

'übermenschlich *adj* superhuman

über'mitteln *v/t* (*no -ge-, h*) convey

'übermorgen *adv* the day after tomorrow

über'müdet *adj* overtired

'übermütig [y:bɐmy:tɪç] *adj* high-spirited

'übernächst *adj the* next but one; **~e Woche** the week after next

übernachten [y:bɐ'naxtən] *v/i* (*no -ge-, h*) stay overnight (*bei j-m* at s.o.'s [house], with s.o.), spend the night (at, with)

Über'nachtung *f* (-; *-en*) night; ~ *und Frühstück* bed and breakfast

Übernahme ['y:bɐna:mə] *f* (-; *-n*) taking (over); adoption

'überna,türlich *adj* supernatural

über'nehmen *v/t* (*irr, nehmen, no -ge-, h*) take over; adopt; take (*responsibility etc*); undertake *to do*

über'prüfen *v/t* (*no -ge-, h*) check, examine; verify; *esp* POL screen

Über'prüfung *f* check, examination; verification; screening

über'|queren *v/t* (*no -ge-, h*) cross; **~'ragen** *v/t* (*no -ge-, h*) tower above (*a. fig*); **~'ragend** *adj* outstanding

überraschen [y:bɐ'raʃən] *v/t* (*no -ge-, h*) surprise; *j-n bei et.* ~ *a.* catch s.o. doing s.th.; **Über'raschung** *f* (-; *-en*) surprise

über'reden *v/t* (*no -ge-, h*) persuade (*et. zu tun* to do s.th.); *j-n zu et.* ~ talk s.o. into (doing) s.th.; **Über'redung** *f* (-; *no pl*) persuasion

'überregio,nal *adj* national

über'|reichen *v/t* (*no -ge-, h*) present, hand *s.th.* over (*dat* to); **~'reizen** *v/t* (*no -ge-, h*) overexcite; **~'reizt** *adj* overwrought, F on edge

'Überrest *m* remains; *pl* relics; GASTR leftovers

über'|rumpeln *v/t* (*no -ge-, h*) (take *s.o.* by) surprise; **~'runden** *v/t* (*no -ge-, h*) SPORT lap

übersät [y:bɐ'zɛ:t] *adj*: ~ *mit* strewn

with *garbage*; studded with *stars*

übersättigt [y:bɐˈzɛtɪçt] *adj* sated, surfeited

'**Überschall...** *in cpds* supersonic ...

über|'**schatten** *v/t (no -ge-, h)* overshadow (*a. fig*); **~'schätzen** *v/t (no -ge-, h)* overrate, overestimate

'**Überschlag** *m* AVIAT loop; SPORT somersault; ECON rough estimate

'**überschlagen¹** (*irr, schlagen, sep, -ge-*) **1.** *v/t (h)* cross (*one's legs*); **2.** *v/i (sein) fig ~ in (acc)* turn into

über'**schlagen²** (*no -ge-, h*) **1.** *v/t* skip; ECON make a rough estimate of **2.** *v/refl* turn (right) over; go head over heels; *voice*: break

'**überschnappen** F *v/i (no -ge-, sein)* crack up

über|'**schneiden** *v/refl (irr, schneiden, no -ge-, h)* overlap (*a. fig*); intersect; **~**'**schreiben** *v/t (irr, schreiben, no -ge-, h)* make *s.th.* over (*dat* to); **~**'**schreiten** *v/t (irr, schreiten, no -ge-, h)* cross; *fig* go beyond; pass; break (*the speed limit etc*)

'**Überschrift** *f* heading, title; headline; caption

'**Überschuss** *m*, '**überschüssig** [ˈy:bɐˌʃʏsɪç] *adj* surplus

über|'**schütten** *v/t (no -ge-, h)* **~** *mit* cover with; shower with; heap *s.th.* on

'**überschwänglich** [ˈy:bɐˌʃvɛŋlɪç] *adj* effusive

über'**schwemmen** *v/t (no -ge-, h),* **Über**'**schwemmung** *f (-; -en)* flood

'**überschwenglich** → *überschwänglich*

'**Übersee:** *in (nach)* **~** oversea

über'**sehen** *v/t (irr, sehen, no -ge-, h)* overlook; ignore

über'**setzen¹** *v/t (no -ge-, h)* translate (*in acc* into)

'**übersetzen²** (*sep, -ge-*) **1.** *v/i (h, sein)* cross (*über e-n Fluss* a river); **2.** *v/t (h)* take over

Über'**setzer** [y:bɐˈzɛtsɐ] *m (-s; -),* **Über**'**setzerin** *f (-; -nen)* translator

Über'**setzung** *f (-; -en)* translation (*aus dat* from; *in acc* into)

'**Übersicht** *f (-; -en)* overview (*über acc* of); outline, summary

'**übersichtlich** *adj* clear(ly arranged)

'**übersiedeln** *v/i (sep, -ge-, sein)* move (*nach* to); '**Übersied(e)lung** *f* move

über'**spannen** *v/t (no -ge-, h)* span

über'**spannt** *fig adj* eccentric; extravagant

über'**spielen** *v/t (no -ge-, h)* record; tape; *fig* cover up

über'**spitzt** *adj* exaggerated

über'**springen** *v/t (irr, springen, no -ge-, h)* jump (over), *esp* SPORT *a.* clear; *fig* skip

über'**stehen¹** *v/t (irr, stehen, no -ge-, h)* get over; survive (*a. fig*), live through

'**überstehen²** *v/i (irr, stehen, sep, -ge-, h)* jut out

über'**steigen** *fig v/t (irr, steigen, no -ge-, h)* exceed; **~**'**stimmen** *v/t (no -ge-, h)* outvote

'**über**|**streifen** *v/t (sep, -ge-, h)* slip *s.th.* on; **~strömen** *v/i (sep, -ge-, sein)* overflow (*vor dat* with)

'**Überstunden** *pl* overtime; **~** *machen* work overtime

über|'**stürzen** *v/t (no -ge-, h)* **et. ~** rush things; *sich* **~** *events:* follow in rapid succession; **~**'**stürzt** *adj* (over)hasty; rash; **~**'**teuert** *adj* overpriced; **~**'**tönen** *v/t (no -ge-, h)* drown (out)

über'**tragbar** *adj* transferable; MED contagious

über'**tragen¹** *adj* figurative

über'**tragen²** *v/t (irr, tragen, no -ge-, h)* broadcast, *a.* televise; translate; MED, TECH transmit; MED transfuse (*blood*); JUR, ECON transfer

Über'**tragung** *f (-; -en)* radio, TV broadcast; transmission; translation; MED transfusion; JUR, ECON transfer

über'**treffen** *v/t (irr, treffen, no -ge-, h)* outstrip, outdo, surpass, beat

über'**treiben** *v/i and v/t (irr, treiben, no -ge-, h)* exaggerate; overdo

Über'**treibung** *f (-; -en)* exaggeration

'**übertreten¹** *v/i (irr, treten, sep, -ge-, sein)* **~** *zu* go over to, REL convert to

über'**treten²** *v/t (irr, treten, no -ge-, h)* **1.** *v/t* break, violate **2.** *v/i* SPORT foul (a jump *or* throw); **Über**'**tretung** *f (-; -en)* violation, JUR *a.* offen|se, *Br* -ce

'**Übertritt** *m* change (*zu* to); REL, POL conversion (to)

übervölkert [y:bɐˈfœlkɐt] *adj* overpopulated

über'**wachen** *v/t (no -ge-, h)* supervise, oversee; control; observe

Über'**wachung** *f (-; -en)* supervision,

control; observance; surveillance

überwältigen [y:bɛ'vɛltɪgən] *v/t (no -ge-, h)* overwhelm, overpower, *fig a.* overcome; **~d** *adj* overwhelming, overpowering

über'weisen *v/t (irr, weisen, no -ge-, h)* ECON transfer (**an j-n** to s.o.'s account); remit; MED refer (**an** *acc* to)

Über'weisung *f (-; -en)* ECON transfer; remittance; MED referral

'überwerfen¹ *v/t (irr, werfen, sep, -ge-, h)* slip s.th. on

über'werfen² *v/refl (irr, werfen, no -ge-, h)* **sich ~ (mit j-m)** fall out with each other (with s.o.)

über'wiegen *v/i (irr, wiegen, no -ge-, h)* predominate; **~d** *adj* predominant; vast (*majority*)

über'|winden *v/t (irr, winden, no -ge-, h)* overcome (*a. fig*); defeat; **sich ~ zu** *inf* bring o.s. to *inf*; **~wintern** [y:bɛ-'vɪntɐn] *v/i (no -ge-, h)* spend the winter (*in dat* in); **~'wuchern** *v/t (no -ge-, h)* overgrow

'Überzahl *f (-; no pl)* majority; **in der ~ sein** outnumber *s.o.*

über'zeugen *v/t (no -ge-, h)* convince (**von** of), persuade; **sich ~, dass** make sure that; **sich selbst ~** (go and) see for o.s.; **überzeugt** [y:bɛ'tsɔykt] *adj* convinced; **~ sein** *a.* be *or* feel (quite) sure; **Über'zeugung** *f (-; -en)* conviction

'überziehen¹ *v/t (irr, ziehen, sep, -ge-, h)* put s.th. on

über'ziehen² *v/t (irr, ziehen, no, -ge-, h)* TECH cover; ECON overdraw

Über'ziehungskre,dit *m* ECON overdraft (facility)

'Überzug *m* cover; coat(ing)

üblich ['y:plɪç] *adj* usual, normal; **es ist ~** it's the custom; **wie ~** as usual

'U-Boot *n* submarine

übrig ['y:brɪç] *adj* remaining; **die Übrigen** *pl* the others, the rest; **~ sein** (**haben**) be (have) left; **~ bleiben** be left, remain; **es bleibt mir nichts anderes ~ (als zu** *inf*) there is nothing else I can do (but *inf*); **~ lassen** leave

übrigens ['y:brɪgəns] *adv* by the way

'übriglassen *v/i (irr, lassen, sep, -ge-, sein) (a. fig) → übrig*

Übung ['y:bʊŋ] *f (-; -en)* exercise; practice; **in (aus der) ~** in (out of) practice

Ufer ['u:fɐ] *n (-s; -)* shore; bank; **ans ~** ashore

Uhr [u:ɐ] *f (-; -en* ['u:rən]) clock; watch; **um vier ~** at four o'clock

'Uhr|armband *n* watchstrap; **~macher** *m (-s; -)* watchmaker; **~werk** *n* clockwork; **~zeiger** *m* hand; **~zeigersinn** *m*: **im ~** clockwise; **entgegen dem ~** counterclockwise, *Br* anticlockwise

Uhu ['u:hu] *m (-s; -s)* ZO eagle owl

UKW [u:ka:'ve:] *abbr of Ultrakurzwelle* VHF, very high frequency

Ulk [ʊlk] *m (-s; -e)* joke; hoax

ulkig ['ʊlkɪç] *adj* funny

Ulme ['ʊlmə] *f (-; -n)* BOT elm

Ultimatum [ʊlti'ma:tʊm] *n (-s; -ten)* ultimatum; **j-m ein ~ stellen** deliver an ultimatum to s.o.

um [ʊm] *prp (acc) and cj* (a)round; at; about, around; **~ Geld** for money; **e-e Stunde (10 cm)** by an hour (10 cm); **~ ... willen** for the sake of ...; **~ zu** *inf* (in order) to *inf*; **~ sein** F be over; **die Zeit ist ~** time's up; **→ umso**

umarmen [ʊm'ˀarmən] *v/t (no -ge-, h) (a. sich ~)* embrace, hug

Um'armung *f (-; -en)* embrace, hug

'Umbau *m (-[e]s; -e, -ten)* rebuilding, reconstruction; **'umbauen** *v/t (sep, -ge-, h)* rebuild, reconstruct

'um|binden *v/t (irr, binden, sep, -ge-, h)* put s.th. on; **~blättern** *v/i (sep, -ge-, h)* turn (over) the page; **~bringen** *v/t (irr, bringen, sep, -ge-, h)* kill; **sich ~** kill o.s.; **~buchen** *v/t (sep, -ge-, h)* change; ECON transfer (**auf** *acc* to); **~denken** *v/i (irr, denken, sep, -ge-, h)* change one's way of thinking; **~dispo,nieren** *v/i (sep, no -ge-, h)* change one's plans; **~drehen** *v/t (sep, -ge-, h)* turn (round); **sich ~** turn round

Um'drehung *f (-; -en)* turn; PHYS, TECH rotation, revolution

umei'nander *adv* care *etc* about *or* for each other

'umfahren¹ *v/t (irr, fahren, sep, -ge-, h)* run down

um'fahren² *v/t (irr, fahren, no -ge-, h)* drive (MAR sail) round

'umfallen *v/i (irr, fallen, sep, -ge-, sein)* fall down *or* over; collapse; **tot ~** drop dead

'Umfang *m* circumference; size; extent; **in großem ~** on a large scale

'umfangreich *adj* extensive; voluminous

um'fassen *fig v/t* (*no -ge-, h*) cover; include; **~d** *adj* comprehensive; complete

'**umformen** *v/t* (*sep*, *-ge-, h*) turn, change; ELECTR, LING, MATH *a.* transform, convert (*all:* **in** *acc* [in]to)

'**Umformer** *m* (*-s*; *-*) ELECTR converter

'**Umfrage** *f* opinion poll

'**Umgang** *m* (*-[e]s*; *no pl*) company; **~ haben mit** associate with; **beim ~ mit** when dealing with

'**umgänglich** ['ʊmgɛnlɪç] *adj* sociable

'**Umgangs|formen** *pl* manners; **~sprache** *f* colloquial speech; **die englische ~** colloquial English

um'geben *v/t* (*irr*, **geben**, *no -ge-, h*) surround (**mit** with); **Um'gebung** *f* (*-; -en*) surroundings; environment

'**umgehen¹** *v/i* (*irr*, **gehen**, *sep*, *-ge-, sein*) **~ mit** deal with, handle; **~ können mit** have a way with, be good with

um'gehen² *v/t* (*irr*, **gehen**, *no -ge-, h*) avoid; bypass

'**umgehend** *adv* immediately

Um'gehungsstraße *f* bypass; beltway, *Br* ring road

umgekehrt ['ʊmgəkeːɐt] **1.** *adj* reverse; opposite; (**genau**) **~** (just) the other way round **2.** *adv* the other way round; **und ~** and vice versa

'**umgraben** *v/t* (*irr*, **graben**, *sep*, *-ge-, h*) dig (up), break up

'**Umhang** *m* cape; '**umhängen** *v/t* (*sep*, *-ge-, h*) put around *or* over s.o.'s shoulders *etc*; rehang

'**umhauen** *v/t* (*irr*, **hauen**, *sep*, *-ge-, h*) fell, cut down; F knock *s.o.* out

um'her *adv* (a)round, about

um'herstreifen *v/i* (*sep*, *-ge-, sein*) roam *or* wander around

'**umkehren** (*sep*, *-ge-*) **1.** *v/i* (*sein*) turn back **2.** *v/t* (*h*) reverse

'**Umkehrung** *f* (*-; -en*) reversal (*a. fig*)

'**umkippen** (*sep*, *-ge-*) **1.** *v/t* (*h*) tip over, upset **2.** *v/i* (*sein*) fall down *or* over, overturn

um'klammern *v/t* (*no -ge-, h*), **Um-'klammerung** *f* (*-; -en*) clasp, clutch, clench

'**Umkleide|ka,bine** *f* changing cubicle; **~raum** *m esp* SPORT changing *or* locker room; THEA dressing room

'**umkommen** *v/i* (*irr*, **kommen**, *sep*, *-ge-,*

sein) be killed (**bei** in), die (in); F **~ vor** (*dat*) be dying with

'**Umkreis** *m:* **im ~ von** within a radius of; **um'kreisen** *v/t* (*no -ge-, h*) circle; ASTR revolve around; *satellite etc:* orbit

'**umkrempeln** *v/t* (*sep*, *-ge-, h*) roll up

'**Umlauf** *m* circulation; PHYS, TECH rotation; ECON circular; **im** (**in**) **~ sein** (**bringen**) be in (put into) circulation, circulate; **~bahn** *f* ASTR orbit

um|laufen *v/i* (*irr*, **laufen**, *sep*, *-ge-, sein*) circulate; **~legen** *v/t* (*sep*, *-ge-, h*) put on; move; share (*expenses etc*); TECH pull; F do *s.o.* in, bump *s.o.* off

'**umleiten** *v/t* (*sep*, *-ge-, h*) divert; '**Umleitung** *f* (*-; -en*) detour, *Br* diversion

'**umliegend** *adj* surrounding

'**umpacken** *v/t* (*sep*, *-ge-, h*) repack

'**umpflanzen** *v/t* (*sep*, *-ge-, h*) repot

umranden ['ʊm'randən] *v/t* (*no -ge-, h*), **Um'randung** *f* (*-; -en*) edge, border

'**umräumen** *v/t* (*sep*, *-ge-, h*) rearrange

'**umrechnen** *v/t* (*sep*, *-ge-, h*) convert (**in** *acc* into); '**Umrechnung** *f* (*-; -en*) conversion; '**Umrechnungskurs** *m* exchange rate

'**umreißen** *v/t* (*irr*, **reißen**, *sep*, *-ge-, h*) knock *s.o.* down

um'ringen *v/t* (*no -ge-, h*) surround

'**Umriss** *m* outline (*a. fig*), contour

'**um|rühren** *v/t* (*sep*, *-ge-, h*) stir; **~rüsten** *v/t* (*sep*, *-ge-, h*) TECH convert (*auf acc* to); **~satteln** F *v/i* (*sep*, *-ge-, h*) **~ von ... auf** (*acc*) ... switch from ... to ...

'**Umsatz** *m* ECON sales

'**umschalten** *v/t* and *v/i* (*sep*, *-ge-, h*) switch (over) (*auf acc* to) (*a. fig*)

'**Umschlag** *m* envelope; cover, wrapper; jacket; cuff, *Br* turn-up; MED compress; ECON handling; '**umschlagen** (*irr*, **schlagen**, *sep*, *-ge-*) **1.** *v/t* (*h*) cut down, fell; turn up; turn down; ECON handle **2.** *v/i* (*sein*) turn over; *fig* change (suddenly)

'**Umschlagplatz** *m* trading center (*Br* centre)

'**umschnallen** *v/t* (*sep*, *-ge-, h*) buckle on

'**umschreiben¹** *v/t* (*irr*, **schreiben**, *sep*, *-ge-, h*) rewrite

um'schreiben² *v/t* (*irr*, **schreiben**, *no -ge-, h*) paraphrase

Um'schreibung *f* (*-; -en*) paraphrase

'**Umschrift** *f* transcription

'**umschulen** v/t (sep, -ge-, h) retrain; transfer to another school

umschwärmt [ʊm'ʃvɛrmt] adj idolized

'**Umschwung** m (drastic) change, esp POL a. swing

um'segeln v/t (no -ge-, h) sail round; circumnavigate

'**um|sehen** v/refl (irr, sehen, sep, -ge-, h) look around (**in e-m Laden** a shop; **nach** for); look back (**nach** at); **sich ~ nach** be looking for; **~setzen** v/t (sep, -ge-, h) move (a. PED); ECON sell; **~ in** (acc) convert (in)to; **in die Tat ~** put into action; **sich ~** change places

'**umsiedeln** v/i (sep, -ge-, sein) and v/t (h) resettle; → **umziehen**

'**Umsied(e)lung** f (-; -en) resettlement

'**Umsiedler** m (-s; -) resettler

'**umso 1.** **je später** etc, **~ schlechter** etc the later etc the worse etc **2. ~ besser** so much the better

um'sonst adv free (of charge), for nothing; F for free; fig in vain

um'spannen v/t (no -ge-, h) span (a. fig)

'**umspringen** v/i (irr, springen, sep, -ge-, sein) shift, change (suddenly) (a. fig); **~ mit** treat (badly)

'**Umstand** m circumstance; fact; detail; **unter diesen (keinen) Umständen** under the (no) circumstances; **unter Umständen** possibly; **keine Umstände machen** not cause s.o. any trouble; not go to any trouble; no put o.s. out; **in anderen Umständen sein** be expecting

umständlich ['ʊmʃtɛntlɪç] adj awkward; complicated; long-winded; **das ist (mir) viel zu ~** that's far too much trouble (for me)

'**Umstands|kleid** n maternity dress; **~wort** n (-[e]s; -wörter) LING adverb

'**Umstehende: die ~n** pl the bystanders

'**umsteigen** v/i (irr, steigen, sep, -ge-, sein) change (**nach** for), RAIL a. change trains (for)

'**umstellen** v/t (sep, -ge-, h) change (**auf** acc to), make a change or changes in, esp TECH a. switch (over) (to), convert (to); adjust (to); rearrange (a. furniture), reorganize; reset (watch); **sich ~ auf** (acc) change or switch (over) to; adjust (o.s.) to, get used to

'**Umstellung** f (-; -en) change; switch; conversion; adjustment; rearrange-

ment, reorganization

'**umstimmen** v/t (sep, -ge-, h) **j-n ~** change s.o.'s mind

'**umstoßen** v/t (irr, stoßen, sep, -ge-, h) knock over, upset (a. fig)

umstritten [ʊm'ʃtrɪtən] adj controversial

'**Umsturz** m overthrow; '**umstürzen** v/i (sep, -ge-, sein) overturn, fall over

'**Umtausch** m, '**umtauschen** v/t (sep, -ge-, h) exchange (**gegen** for)

'**umwälzend** adj revolutionary

'**Umwälzung** f (-; -en) radical change

'**umwandeln** v/t (sep, -ge-, h) turn (**in** acc into), transform (into); esp CHEM, ELECTR, PHYS a. convert ([in]to)

'**Umwandlung** f (-; -en) transformation, conversion

'**Umweg** m roundabout route or way (a. fig), esp MOT a. detour; **ein ~ von 10 Minuten** ten minutes out of the way; fig **auf ~en** in a roundabout way

'**Umwelt** f (-; no pl) environment

'**Umwelt...** in cpds mst environmental ...; **~forschung** f ecology

'**umwelt|freundlich** adj environment friendly, non-polluting; **~schädlich** adj harmful, noxious, polluting

'**Umwelt|schutz** m conservation, environmental protection, pollution control; **~schützer** m environmentalist, conservationist; **~schutzpa,pier** n recycled paper; **~sünder** m (environmental) polluter; **~verschmutzer** m (-s; -) polluter; **~verschmutzung** f (environmental) pollution; **~zerstörung** f ecocide

'**umziehen** (irr, ziehen, sep -ge-) **1.** v/i (sein) move (**nach** to); **2.** v/refl (h) change (one's clothes)

umzingeln [ʊm'tsɪŋəln] v/t (no -ge-, h) surround, encircle

'**Umzug** m move (**nach** to), removal (to); parade

unabhängig ['ʊnaphɛŋɪç] adj independent (**von** of); **~ davon, ob (was)** regardless of whether (what); '**Unabhängigkeit** f (-; no pl) independence (**von** from)

'**unabsichtlich** adj unintentional; **et. ~ tun** do s.th. by mistake

unab'wendbar adj inevitable

'**unachtsam** adj careless, negligent

'**Unachtsamkeit** f (-; no pl) careless-

ness, negligence
unan'fechtbar *adj* incontestable
'un|angebracht *adj* inappropriate; ~ **sein** be out of place; ~**angemessen** *adj* unreasonable; inadequate; ~**angenehm** *adj* unpleasant; embarrassing
unan'nehmbar *adj* unacceptable
Unannehmlichkeiten ['ʊn?anneːmlɪkkaitən] *pl* trouble, difficulties
'unansehnlich *adj* unsightly
'unanständig *adj* indecent, obscene
unan'tastbar *adj* inviolable
'unappetitlich *adj* unappetizing
Unart ['ʊn?art] *f* (-; *-en*) bad habit
'unartig *adj* naughty, bad
'unaufdringlich *adj* unobtrusive
'unauffällig *adj* inconspicuous, unobtrusive
unauf'findbar *adj* not to be found, untraceable
'unaufgefordert *adv* without being asked, of one's own accord
unaufhörlich [ʊn?auf'høːɐlɪç] *adj* continuous
'unaufmerksam *adj* inattentive
'Unaufmerksamkeit *f* (-; *no pl*) inattention, inattentiveness
'unaufrichtig *adj* insincere
unaus|löschlich [ʊn?aus'lœʃlɪç] *adj* indelible; ~**stehlich** [ʊn?aus'ʃteːlɪç] *adj* unbearable
'unbarmherzig *adj* merciless
'un|beabsichtigt *adj* unintentional; ~**beachtet** *adj* unnoticed; ~**beaufsichtigt** *adj* unattended; ~**bebaut** *adj* undeveloped; ~**bedacht** ['ʊnbədaxt] *adj* thoughtless; ~**bedenklich** 1. *adj* safe 2. *adv* without hesitation; ~**bedeutend** *adj* insignificant; minor; ~**bedingt** 1. *adj* unconditional, absolute 2. *adv* by all means, absolutely; *need etc* badly; ~**befahrbar** *adj* impassable; ~**befangen** *adj* unprejudiced, unbias(s)ed; unembarrassed; ~**befriedigend** *adj* unsatisfactory; ~**befriedigt** *adj* dissatisfied; ~**begabt** *adj* untalented; ~**begreiflich** *adj* inconceivable, incomprehensible; ~**begrenzt** *adj* unlimited, boundless; ~**begründet** *adj* unfounded
'Unbehagen *n* (-s; *no pl*) uneasiness, discomfort; **'unbehaglich** *adj* uneasy, uncomfortable
unbehelligt [ʊnbə'hɛlɪçt] *adj* unmolested

'un|beherrscht *adj* uncontrolled, lacking self-control; ~**beholfen** ['ʊnbəhɔlfən] *adj* clumsy, awkward; ~**beirrt** *adj* unwavering; ~**bekannt** *adj* unknown
'Unbekannte *f* (-; *-n*) MATH unknown quantity
'un|bekümmert *adj* light-hearted, cheerful; ~**belehrbar** *adj*: *er ist* ~ he'll never learn; ~**beliebt** *adj* unpopular; *er ist überall* ~ nobody likes him; ~**bemannt** *adj* unmanned; ~**bemerkt** *adj* unnoticed; ~**benutzt** *adj* unused; ~**bequem** *adj* uncomfortable; inconvenient; ~**berechenbar** *adj* unpredictable; ~**berechtigt** *adj* unauthorized; unjustified; ~**beschädigt** *adj* undamaged; ~**bescheiden** *adj* immodest
un|be'schränkt *adj* unlimited; absolute (*power*); ~**beschreiblich** ['ʊnbə-'ʃraiplɪç] *adj* indescribable; ~**be'sehen** *adv* unseen; ~**besiegbar** ['ʊnbə'ziːkbaːɐ] *adj* invincible
'un|besonnen *adj* thoughtless, imprudent; rash; ~**be'spielbar** *adj* SPORT unplayable; ~**beständig** *adj* unstable; METEOR changeable, unsettled; ~**bestätigt** *adj* unconfirmed
unbe'stechlich *adj* incorruptible
'unbestimmt *adj* indefinite (*a.* LING); uncertain; vague
un|be'streitbar *adj* indisputable; ~**bestritten** [ʊnbə'ʃtrɪtən] *adj* undisputed
'un|beteiligt *adj* not involved; indifferent; ~**betont** *adj* unstressed
unbeugsam [ʊn'bɔykzaːm] *adj* inflexible
'un|bewacht *adj* unwatched, unguarded (*a.* fig); ~**bewaffnet** *adj* unarmed; ~**beweglich** *adj* immovable; motionless
unbe'wohnbar *adj* uninhabitable
'unbewohnt *adj* uninhabited; unoccupied, vacant
'unbewusst *adj* unconscious
unbe'zahlbar *fig adj* invaluable, priceless; **'unbezahlt** *adj* unpaid
'unblutig 1. *adj* bloodless 2. *adv* without bloodshed
'unbrauchbar *adj* useless
und [ʊnt] *cj* and; F *na* ~? so what?
'undankbar *adj* ungrateful (*gegen* to); thankless; **'Undankbarkeit** *f* (-; *no pl*) ingratitude, ungratefulness
undefi'nierbar *adj* undefinable
un'denkbar *adj* unthinkable

'undeutlich *adj* indistinct; inarticulate; *fig* vague

'undicht *adj* leaky

'unduldsam *adj* intolerant; **'Unduldsamkeit** *f* (-; *no pl*) intolerance

undurch|'dringlich *adj* impenetrable; ~**'führbar** *adj* impracticable

'undurch|lässig *adj* impervious, impermeable; ~**sichtig** *adj* opaque; *fig* mysterious

'uneben *adj* uneven; **'Unebenheit** *f* (-; *no pl*) unevenness; (-; *-en*) bump

'unecht *adj* false; artificial; imitation ...; F *contp* fake, phon(e)y

'unehelich *adj* illegitimate

'unehrenhaft *adj* dishono(u)rable

'unehrlich *adj* dishonest

'uneigennützig *adj* unselfish

'uneinig *adj*: (**sich**) ~ **sein** disagree (**über** *acc* on); **'Uneinigkeit** *f* (-; *no pl*) disagreement; dissension

unein'nehmbar *adj* impregnable

'un|empfänglich *adj* insusceptible (**für** to); ~**empfindlich** *adj* insensitive (**gegen** to)

un'endlich *adj* infinite; endless; never-ending; **Un'endlichkeit** *f* (-; *no pl*) infinity (*a. fig*)

unent|behrlich [ʊnʔɛnt'beːɐlɪç] *adj* indispensable; ~**geltlich** [ʊnʔɛnt'gɛltlɪç] *adj and adv* free (of charge)

'unentschieden *adj* undecided; ~ **enden** SPORT end in a draw *or* tie; **es steht** ~ the score is even; **'Unentschieden** *n* (-s; -) SPORT draw, tie

'unentschlossen *adj* irresolute

unent'schuldbar *adj* inexcusable

unentwegt [ʊnʔɛnt'veːkt] *adv* untiringly; continuously

'un|erfahren *adj* inexperienced; ~**erfreulich** *adj* unpleasant; ~**erfüllt** *adj* unfulfilled; ~**ergiebig** *adj* unproductive; ~**erheblich** *adj* irrelevant (**für** to); insignificant

unerhört ['ʊnʔɛːɐ'høːɐt] *adj* outrageous

'un|erkannt *adj* unrecognized; ~**erklärlich** *adj* inexplicable; ~**erlässlich** *adj* essential, indispensable; ~**erlaubt** *adj* unallowed; unauthorized; ~**erledigt** *adj* unsettled (*a.* ECON)

uner'messlich *adj* immeasurable

unermüdlich [ʊnʔɛɐ'myːtlɪç] *adj* indefatigable; untiring

uner'reichbar *adj* inaccessible; *esp fig* unattainable; **uner'reicht** *adj* unequal(l)ed

unersättlich [ʊnʔɛɐ'zɛtlɪç] *adj* insatiable

'unerschlossen *adj* undeveloped

uner|schöpflich [ʊnʔɛɐ'ʃœpflɪç] *adj* inexhaustible; ~**schütterlich** [ʊnʔɛɐ-'ʃʏtɐlɪç] *adj* imperturbable; ~**schwinglich** [ʊnʔɛɐ'ʃvɪŋlɪç] *adj* exorbitant; **für j-n** ~ **sein** be beyond s.o.'s means; ~**setzlich** [ʊnʔɛɐ'zɛtslɪç] *adj* irreplaceable; ~**träglich** [ʊnʔɛɐ-'trɛːklɪç] *adj* unbearable

'unerwartet *adj* unexpected

'unerwünscht *adj* unwanted

'unfähig *adj* incompetent; incapable (**zu tun** of doing), unable (to *inf*) **'Unfähigkeit** *f* (-; *no pl*) incompetence; incapacity, inability

'Unfall *m* accident; crash

'Unfallstelle *f* scene of the accident

un'fehlbar *adj* infallible (*a.* REL); unfailing

unförmig ['ʊnfœrmɪç] *adj* shapeless; misshapen; monstrous

'unfrankiert *adj* unstamped

'unfrei *adj* not free; *post* unpaid

'unfreiwillig *adj* involuntary; unconscious (*humor*)

'unfreundlich *adj* unfriendly (**zu** to), unkind (to); *fig* cheerless

'Unfrieden *m* (-s; *no pl*) discord; ~ **stiften** make mischief

'unfruchtbar *adj* infertile; **'Unfruchtbarkeit** *f* (-; *no pl*) infertility

Unfug ['ʊnfuːk] *m* (-[e]s; *no pl*) nonsense; ~ **treiben** be up to mischief, fool around

Ungar ['ʊŋɡar] *m* (-n; -n), **'Ungarin** *f* (-; -*nen*), **'ungarisch** *adj* Hungarian; **'Ungarn** Hungary

'ungastlich *adj* inhospitable

'un|geachtet *prp* (*gen*) regardless of; despite; ~**geahnt** *adj* unthought-of; ~**gebeten** *adj* uninvited, unasked; ~**gebildet** *adj* uneducated; ~**geboren** *adj* unborn; ~**gebräuchlich** *adj* uncommon, unusual; ~**gebührlich** ['ʊnɡə-byːɐlɪç] *adj* unseemly; ~**gebunden** *fig adj* free, independent; **frei und** ~ footloose and fancy-free; ~**gedeckt** *adj* ECON uncovered; SPORT unmarked

'**Ungeduld** f (-; *no pl*) impatience
'**ungeduldig** *adj* impatient
'**ungeeignet** *adj* unfit; unqualified; inappropriate
ungefähr ['ʊngəfɛːɐ] **1.** *adj* approximate; rough **2.** *adv* approximately, roughly, about, around, ... or so; *so* ~ something like that
'**ungefährlich** *adj* harmless; safe
'**ungeheuer** *adj* enormous (*a. fig*), huge, vast
'**Ungeheuer** n (-s; -) monster (*a. fig*)
unge'heuerlich *adj* monstrous
'**ungehindert** *adj and adv* unhindered
'**ungehobelt** *fig adj* uncouth, rough
'**ungehörig** *adj* improper, unseemly
'**ungehorsam** *adj* disobedient
Ungehorsam m (-s; *no pl*) disobedience
'**un|gekocht** *adj* uncooked; **~gekünstelt** *adj* unaffected; **~gekürzt** *adj* unabridged; **~gelegen** *adj* inconvenient; *j-m* ~ *kommen* be inconvenient for s.o.
ungelenk ['ʊngəlɛŋk] *adj* awkward, clumsy
'**ungelernt** *adj* unskilled
'**ungemütlich** *adj* uncomfortable; F ~ *werden* get nasty
'**ungenau** *adj* inaccurate; *fig* vague; '**Ungenauigkeit** f (-; -en) inaccuracy
ungeniert ['ʊnʒeniːɐt] *adj* uninhibited
'**un|genießbar** *adj* uneatable; undrinkable; F unbearable; **~genügend** *adj* insufficient; PED poor, unsatisfactory; *grade: a.* F; **~gepflegt** *adj* neglected; untidy, unkempt; **~gerade** *adj* uneven; odd; **~gerecht** *adj* unfair, unjust
'**Ungerechtigkeit** f (-; *no pl*) injustice, unfairness
'**ungern** *adv* unwillingly; *et.* ~ *tun* hate *or* not like to do s.th.
'**un|geschehen** *adj:* ~ *machen* undo; **~geschickt** *adj* awkward, clumsy; **~geschliffen** *adj* uncut (*diamond etc*); unpolished (*a. fig*); **~geschminkt** *adj* without make-up; *fig* unvarnished, plain (*truth*); **~gesetzlich** *adj* illegal, unlawful; **~gestört** *adj* undisturbed; **~gestraft** *adj:* ~ *davonkommen* get off unpunished (F scot-free); **~gesund** *adj* unhealthy (*a. fig*); **~geteilt** *adj* undivided (*a. fig*)
Ungetüm ['ʊngətyːm] n (-s; -e) monster, *fig a.* monstrosity

'**ungewiss** *adj* uncertain; *j-n im Ungewissen lassen* keep s.o. in the dark (*über acc* about); '**Ungewissheit** f (-; *no pl*) uncertainty
'**ungewöhnlich** *adj* unusual
'**ungewohnt** *adj* strange, unfamiliar;
Ungeziefer ['ʊngətsiːfɐ] n (-s; *no pl*) vermin
'**ungezogen** *adj* naughty, bad; spoilt
'**ungezwungen** *adj* relaxed, informal; easygoing
'**ungläubig** *adj* incredulous, unbelieving (*a.* REL)
unglaublich [ʊn'glauplɪç] *adj* incredible, unbelievable
'**unglaubwürdig** *adj* implausible; unreliable (*witness etc*)
'**ungleich** *adj* unequal, different; unlike; **~mäßig** *adj* uneven; irregular
'**Unglück** n (-[e]s; -e) (*no pl*) bad luck, misfortune; misery; accident; disaster; '**unglücklich** *adj* unhappy, miserable; unfortunate; '**unglücklicher'weise** *adv* unfortunately
'**ungültig** *adj* invalid; *für* ~ *erklären* JUR invalidate
'**Ungunst** f: *zu* ~*en* → *zuungunsten*; '**ungünstig** *adj* unfavo(u)rable; disadvantageous
'**ungut** *adj:* ~*es Gefühl* misgivings (*bei et.* about s.th.); *nichts für* ~*!* no offense (*Br* offence) meant!
'**unhaltbar** *adj* untenable; intolerable; SPORT unstoppable
'**unhandlich** *adj* unwieldy
'**unhar,monisch** *adj* MUS discordant
'**Unheil** n (-s; *no pl*) mischief; evil; disaster; '**unheilbar** *adj* MED incurable
'**unheilvoll** *adj* disastrous; sinister
'**unheimlich** *adj* creepy, spooky, eerie; F tremendous; F ~ *gut* terrific, fantastic
'**unhöflich** *adj* impolite; rude
'**Unhöflichkeit** f (-; *no pl*) impoliteness, rudeness
un'hörbar *adj* inaudible
'**unhygienisch** *adj* insanitary
Uniform [uni'fɔrm] f (-; -en) uniform
'**uninteressant** *adj* uninteresting
uninteressiert ['ʊnʔɪntərɛsiːɐt] *adj* uninterested (*an dat* in)
Union [u'njoːn] f (-; -en) union
Universität [univɛrzi'tɛːt] f (-; -en) university

Universum [uni'vɛrzʊm] *n* (*-s*; *no pl*) universe

Unke ['ʊŋkə] *f* (*-*; *-n*) zo toad

'unkenntlich *adj* unrecognizable

'Unkenntnis *f* (*-*; *no pl*) ignorance

'unklar *adj* unclear; uncertain; confused, muddled; *im Unklaren sein* (*lassen*) be (leave *s.o.*) in the dark

'unklug *adj* imprudent, unwise

'Unkosten *pl* expenses, costs

'Unkraut *n* (*-[e]s*; *no pl*) weed(s); *~ jäten* weed (the garden)

unkündbar ['ʊnkyntbaːɐ] *adj* permanent (*post*)

'unlängst *adv* lately, recently

'unleserlich *adj* illegible

'unlogisch *adj* illogical

un'lösbar *adj* insoluble

'unmännlich *adj* unmanly, effeminate

'unmäßig *adj* excessive

'Unmenge *f* vast quantity *or* number(s) (*von* of), F loads (of), tons (of)

'Unmensch *m* monster, brute

'unmenschlich *adj* inhuman, cruel

'Unmenschlichkeit *f* (*-*; *-en*) (*no pl*) inhumanity; cruelty

un'merklich *adj* imperceptible

'unmissverständlich *adj* unmistakable

'unmittelbar 1. *adj* immediate, direct **2.** *adv*: *~ nach* (*hinter*) right after (behind)

'unmöbliert *adj* unfurnished

'unmodern *adj* out of fashion *or* style

'unmöglich 1. *adj* impossible **2.** *adv*: *ich kann es ~ tun* I can't possibly do it

'unmoralisch *adj* immoral

'unmündig *adj* JUR under age

'unmusikalisch *adj* unmusical

'unnachahmlich *adj* inimitable

'unnachgiebig *adj* unyielding

'unnachsichtig *adj* strict, severe

unnahbar [ʊn'naːbaːɐ] *adj* standoffish, cold

'unnatürlich *adj* unnatural (*a. fig*); affected

'unnötig *adj* unnecessary, needless

unnütz ['ʊnnʏts] *adj* useless

'unordentlich *adj* untidy; *~ sein* room *etc*: be (in) a mess; **'Unordnung** *f* (*-*; *no pl*) disorder, mess

'unparteiisch *adj* impartial, unbias(s)ed; **'Unparteiische** *m*, *f* (*-n*; *-n*) SPORT referee

'unpassend *adj* unsuitable; improper; inappropriate

'unpassierbar *adj* impassable

unpässlich ['ʊnpɛslɪç] *adj* indisposed

'unpersönlich *adj* impersonal (*a.* LING)

'unpolitisch *adj* unpolitical

'unpraktisch *adj* impractical

'unpünktlich *adj* unpunctual

'unrecht *adj* wrong; *~ haben* be wrong; *j-m ~ tun* do s.o. wrong; **'Unrecht** *n* (*-[e]s*; *no pl*) injustice, wrong; *zu ~* wrong(ful)ly; *~ haben* → *unrecht*; *~ tun* → *unrecht*

'unrechtmäßig *adj* unlawful

'unregelmäßig *adj* irregular (*a.* LING)

'Unregelmäßigkeit *f* (*-*; *-en*) irregularity

'unreif *adj* unripe; *fig* immature

'Unreife *fig f* immaturity

'unrein *adj* unclean; impure (*a.* REL)

'Unreinheit *f* (*-*; *-en*) impurity

'unrichtig *adj* incorrect, wrong

'Unruhe *f* (*-*; *-n*) (*no pl*) restlessness, unrest (*a.* POL); anxiety, alarm; *pl* disturbances, riots

'unruhig *adj* restless; uneasy; worried, alarmed; MAR rough

uns [ʊns] *pers pron* (to) us; each other; *~ (selbst)* (to) ourselves; *ein Freund von ~* a friend of ours

'un|sachgemäß *adj* improper; *~sachlich* *adj* unobjective; *~sanft* *adj* rude, rough; *~sauber* *adj* unclean, *esp fig a.* impure; SPORT unfair; *fig* underhand; *~schädlich* *adj* harmless; *~scharf* *adj* PHOT blurred, out of focus

un'schätzbar *adj* inestimable, invaluable

'un|scheinbar *adj* inconspicuous; plain; *~schlüssig* *adj* irresolute; undecided; *~schön* *adj* unsightly; *fig* unpleasant

'Unschuld *f* (*-*; *no pl*) innocence; *fig* virginity

'unschuldig *adj* innocent (*an dat* of)

'unselbstständig *adj* dependent on others; **'Unselbstständigkeit** *f* lack of independence, dependence on others

unser ['ʊnzɐ] *poss pron* our; *~er, ~e, ~es* ours

'unsicher *adj* unsafe, insecure; self--conscious; uncertain; **'Unsicherheit** *f* (*-*; *-en*) (*no pl*) insecurity, unsafeness;

self-consciousness; uncertainty
'unsichtbar *adj* invisible
'Unsinn *m* (-[e]s; *no pl*) nonsense
'unsinnig *adj* nonsensical, stupid; absurd
'Unsitte *f* bad habit; abuse
'unsittlich *adj* immoral, indecent
'unsozial *adj* unsocial
'unsportlich *adj* unathletic; *fig* unfair
'unsterblich 1. *adj* immortal (*a. fig*) **2.** *adv*: ~ **verliebt** madly in love (*in acc* with); **'Unsterblichkeit** *f* immortality
'Unstimmigkeit *f* (-; -en) discrepancy; *pl* disagreements
'unsympathisch *adj* disagreeable; *er* (*es*) *ist mir* ~ I don't like him (it)
'untätig *adj* inactive; idle; **'Untätigkeit** *f* (-; *no pl*) inactivity
'untauglich *adj* unfit (*a. MIL*); incompetent
un'teilbar *adj* indivisible
unten ['ʊntən] *adv* (down) below, down (*a. nach ~*); downstairs; ~ *auf* (*dat*) at the bottom of *the page etc*; *siehe* ~ see below; *von oben bis* ~ from top to bottom
unter ['ʊntɐ] *prp* under; below (*a. fig*); among; *fig* less than; ~ *anderem* among other things; ~ *uns* (*gesagt*) between you and me; ~ *Wasser* underwater
'Unterarm *m* ANAT forearm
'unter|belichtet *adj* PHOT underexposed; **~besetzt** *adj* understaffed
'Unterbewusstsein *n* subconscious; *im* ~ subconsciously
unter|'bieten *v/t* (*irr, bieten, no -ge-, h*) underbid; undercut; beat (*record*); **~'binden** *fig v/t* (*irr, binden, no -ge-, h*) put a stop to; prevent
unter'brechen *v/t* (*irr, brechen, no -ge-, h*) interrupt; **Unter'brechung** *f* (-; *-en*) interruption
'unterbringen *v/i* (*irr, bringen, sep, -ge-, h*) accommodate, put *s.o.* up; find a place for, put (*in acc* into); **'Unterbringung** *f* (-; *-en*) accommodation
unter'dessen *adv* in the meantime, meanwhile
unter'drücken *v/t* (*no -ge-, h*) oppress; suppress; **Unter'drücker** *m* (*-s; -*) oppressor; **Unter'drückung** *f* (-; *-en*) oppression; suppression

untere ['ʊntərə] *adj* lower (*a. fig*)
'unterentwickelt *adj* underdeveloped
'unterernährt *adj* undernourished, underfed; **'Unterernährung** *f* (-; *no pl*) undernourishment, malnutrition
Unter'führung *f* (-; *-en*) underpass, *Br a.* subway
'Untergang *m* ASTR setting; MAR sinking; *fig* downfall; decline; fall; **'untergehen** *v/i* (*irr, gehen, sep, -ge-, sein*) go down (*a. fig*), ASTR *a.* set, MAR *a.* sink
'untergeordnet *adj* subordinate, inferior; secondary
'Untergewicht *n* (-[e]s; *no pl*), **'untergewichtig** *adj* underweight
unter'graben *fig v/t* (*irr, graben, no -ge-, h*) undermine
'Untergrund *m* subsoil; POL underground; *in den* ~ *gehen* go underground; **~bahn** *f* → **U-Bahn**
'unterhalb *prp* (*gen*) below, under
'Unterhalt *m* (-[e]s; *no pl*) support, maintenance (*a. JUR*); **unter'halten** *v/t* (*irr, halten, no -ge-, h*) entertain; support; *sich* ~ (*mit*) talk (to, with); *sich* (*gut*) ~ enjoy o.s., have a good time; **unter'haltsam** *adj* entertaining; **Unter'haltung** *f* (-; *-en*) talk, conversation; entertainment; **Unter'haltungsindus,trie** *f* show business
'Unter|händler *m* negotiator; **~haus** *n* (*-es; no pl*) *Br* PARL House of Commons; **~hemd** *n* undershirt, *Br* vest; **~holz** *n* (*-es; no pl*) undergrowth; **~hose** *f* shorts, *esp Br* underpants, panties, *Br* pants; *e-e lange ~, lange ~n* (a pair of) long johns
'unterirdisch *adj* underground
'Unterkiefer *m* ANAT lower jaw
'Unterkleid *n* slip
'unterkommen *v/i* (*irr, kommen, sep, -ge-, sein*) find accommodation; find work *or* a job (*bei* with)
Unterkunft ['ʊntɐkʊnft] *f* (-; *-künfte* ['ʊntɐkʏnftə]) accommodation, lodging(s); MIL quarters; ~ *und Verpflegung* board and lodging
'Unterlage *f* TECH base; *pl* documents; data
unter'lassen *v/t* (*irr, lassen, no -ge-, h*) omit, fail to do *s.th.*; stop *or* quit doing *s.th.*; **Unter'lassung** *f* (-; *-en*) omission (*a. JUR*)

'**unterlegen**¹ v/t (sep, -ge-, h) underlay
unter'legen² adj inferior (dat to)
Unter'legenheit f (-; no pl) inferiority
'**Unterleib** m ANAT abdomen, belly
unter'liegen v/i (irr, liegen, no -ge-, sein) be defeated (j-m by s.o.), lose (to s.o.); fig be subject to
'**Unterlippe** f ANAT lower lip
'**Untermieter** m, '**Untermieterin** f roomer, Br lodger
unter'nehmen v/t (irr, nehmen, no -ge-, h) make, take, go on a trip etc; **et. ~** do s.th. (**gegen** about s.th.), take action (against s.o.); **Unter'nehmen** n (-s; -) firm, business; venture; undertaking, enterprise; MIL operation; **Unter-'nehmensberater(in)** management consultant; **Unter'nehmer** m (-s; -) businessman, entrepreneur; employer; **Unter'nehmerin** f (-; -nen) businesswoman; **unter'nehmungslustig** adj active, dynamic; adventurous
'**Unteroffizier** m MIL non-commissioned officer
'**unterordnen** v/t and v/refl (sep, -ge-, h) subordinate (o.s.) (dat to)
Unter'redung f (-; -en) talk(s)
Unterricht ['ʊntərɪçt] m (-[e]s; no pl) instruction, teaching; PED school, classes, lessons; **unter'richten** v/i and v/t (no -ge-, h) teach; give lessons; inform (**über** acc of); '**Unterrichtsstunde** f lesson, PED a. class, period
'**Unterrock** m slip
unter'sagen v/t (no -ge-, h) prohibit
unter'schätzen v/t (no -ge-, h) underestimate; underrate
unter'scheiden v/t and v/i (irr, scheiden, no -ge-, h) distinguish (**zwischen** between; **von** from); tell apart; **sich ~** differ (**von** from; **in** dat in; **durch** by); **Unter'scheidung** f (-; -en) distinction; **Unterschied** ['ʊntərʃiːt] m (-[e]s; -e) difference; **im ~ zu** unlike, as opposed to; '**unterschiedlich** adj different; varying
unter'schlagen v/t (irr, schlagen, no -ge-, h) embezzle; **Unter'schlagung** f (-; -en) embezzlement
Unterschlupf ['ʊntərʃlʊpf] m (-[e]s; no pl) hiding place
unter'schreiben v/t and v/i (irr, schreiben, no -ge-, h) sign
'**Unterschrift** f signature; caption

'**Unterseeboot** n → **U-Boot**
Untersetzer ['ʊntərzɛtsə] m (-s; -) coaster; saucer
unter'setzt adj thickset, stocky
'**Unterstand** m shelter, MIL a. dugout
unter'stehen (irr, stehen, no -ge-, h) **1.** v/i (dat) be under (the control of) **2.** v/refl dare; **~ Sie sich (et. zu tun)!** don't you dare ([to] do s.th.)!
'**unterstellen**¹ v/t (sep, -ge-, h) put s.th. in; store; **sich ~** take shelter
unter'stellen² v/t (no -ge-, h) assume; **j-m ~, dass er ...** insinuate that s.o. ...; **Unter'stellung** f (-; -en) insinuation
unter'streichen v/t (irr, streichen, no -ge-, h) underline (a. fig)
unter'stützen v/t (no -ge-, h) support; back (up); **Unter'stützung** f (-; -en) support; aid; welfare (payments)
unter'suchen v/t (no -ge-, h) examine (a. MED), investigate (a. JUR); search; CHEM analyze; **Unter'suchung** f (-; -en) examination (a. MED), investigation (a. JUR), a. (medical) checkup; CHEM analysis
Unter'suchungs|gefangene m, f JUR prisoner on remand; **~gefängnis** n JUR remand prison; **~haft** f: **in ~ sein** JUR be on remand; **~richter** m JUR examining magistrate
Untertan ['ʊntərtaːn] m (-s; -en) subject
'**Untertasse** f saucer
'**untertauchen** (sep, -ge-) **1.** v/i (sein) dive, submerge; fig disappear; esp POL go underground **2.** v/t (h) duck
'**Unterteil** n, m lower part, bottom
unter'teilen v/t (no -ge-, h) subdivide; **Unter'teilung** f (-; -en) subdivision
'**Untertitel** m subtitle, film: a. caption
'**Unterton** m undertone
Unter'treibung f (-; -en) understatement
'**untervermieten** v/t (no -ge-, h) sublet
unter'wandern v/t (no -ge-, h) infiltrate
'**Unterwäsche** f underwear
'**Unterwasser...** in cpds underwater ...
unterwegs [ʊntər'veːks] adv on the or one's way (**nach** to)
unter'weisen v/t (irr, weisen, no -ge-, h) instruct; **Unter'weisung** f (-; -en) instruction
'**Unterwelt** f (-; no pl) underworld
unter'werfen v/t (irr, werfen, no -ge-, h) subject (dat to); subjugate; **sich ~** sub-

mit (to); **Unter'werfung** *f* (-; *-en*) subjection; submission (*unter acc* to)

unterwürfig [ʊntɐ'vʏrfɪç] *adj* servile

unter'zeichnen *v/t* (*no -ge-, h*) sign; **Unter'zeichnete** *m, f* (*-n; -n*) the undersigned; **Unter'zeichnung** *f* (-; *-en*) signing

'unterziehen¹ *v/t* (*irr, ziehen, sep, -ge-, h*) put *s.th.* on underneath

unter'ziehen² *v/t* (*irr, ziehen, no -ge-, h*) *sich e-r Behandlung, Prüfung etc* ~ undergo (*treatment etc*), take (*an examination etc*)

'Untiefe *f* shallow, shoal

un|'tragbar *adj* unbearable, intolerable; ~**'trennbar** *adj* inseparable

'untreu *adj* unfaithful (*dat* to)

un|'tröstlich *adj* inconsolable; ~**trüglich** [ʊn'try:klɪç] *adj* unmistakable

'Untugend *f* vice, bad habit

'unüber|legt *adj* thoughtless; ~**sichtlich** *adj* blind (*bend etc*)

unüber|'trefflich [ʊnʔy:bɐ'trɛflɪç] *adj* unsurpassable, matchless; ~**troffen** [ʊnʔy:bɐ'trɔfən] *adj* unequal(l)ed; ~**windlich** [ʊnʔy:bɐ'vɪntlɪç] *adj* insuperable, invincible

unum|gänglich [ʊnʔʊm'gɛŋlɪç] *adj* inevitable; ~**schränkt** [ʊnʔʊm'ʃrɛŋkt] *adj* unlimited; POL absolute; ~**stritten** [ʊnʔʊm'ʃtrɪtən] *adj* undisputed; ~**wunden** [ʊnʔʊm'vʊndən] *adv* straight out, frankly

ununterbrochen [ʊnʔʊntɐbrɔxən] *adj* uninterrupted; continuous

un|ver'änderlich *adj* unchanging; ~**ver'antwortlich** *adj* irresponsible; ~**ver'besserlich** *adj* incorrigible; ~**ver'bindlich** *adj* noncommittal, ECON not binding; ~**ver'daulich** *adj* indigestible (*a. fig*)

'unverdient *adj* undeserved

'unverdünnt *adj* undiluted; straight

unver'einbar *adj* incompatible

'unverfälscht *adj* unadulterated

'unverfänglich *adj* harmless

'unverfroren *adj* brazen, impertinent

'unvergänglich *adj* immortal, eternal

unver'gesslich *adj* unforgettable

'unver'gleichlich *adj* incomparable

'unverhältnismäßig *adv* disproportionately; ~ *hoch* excessive

'unverheiratet *adj* unmarried, single

unverhofft [ʊnfɐɐhɔft] *adj* unhoped-

for; unexpected

unverhohlen ['ʊnfɐɐho:lən] *adj* undisguised, open

'unverkäuflich *adj* not for sale; unsal(e)able

unver'kennbar *adj* unmistakable

'unverletzt *adj* unhurt

unvermeidlich [ʊnfɐɐ'maitlɪç] *adj* inevitable

'unvermindert *adj* undiminished

'unvermittelt *adj* abrupt, sudden

'Unvermögen *n* (*-s; no pl*) inability, incapacity

'unvermutet *adj* unexpected

'unvernünftig *adj* unreasonable; foolish

'unverschämt *adj* rude, impertinent; outrageous (*price etc*); **'Unverschämtheit** *f* (-; *-en*) impertinence; *die ~ haben zu inf* have the nerve to *inf*

'unverschuldet *adj* through no fault of one's own

unversehens ['ʊnfɐɐze:əns] *adv* unexpectedly, all of a sudden

'un|versehrt *adj* unhurt, undamaged; ~**versöhnlich** *adj* irreconcilable (*a. fig*), implacable; ~**versorgt** *adj* unprovided for; ~**verständlich** *adj* unintelligible; *es ist mir ~* I can't see how *or* why, F it beats me; ~**versucht** *adj*: *nichts ~ lassen* leave nothing undone

unver'wundbar *adj* invulnerable

unver|'wüstlich [ʊnfɐɐ'vy:stlɪç] *adj* indestructible; ~**zeihlich** [ʊnfɐɐ'tsailɪç] *adj* inexcusable; ~**züglich** [ʊnfɐɐ'tsy:klɪç] **1.** *adj* immediate, prompt **2.** *adv* immediately, without delay

'unvollendet *adj* unfinished

'unvollkommen *adj* imperfect

'unvollständig *adj* incomplete

'unvorbereitet *adj* unprepared

'unvoreingenommen *adj* unprejudiced, unbias(s)ed

'unvorhergesehen *adj* unforeseen

'unvorhersehbar *adj* unforeseeable

'unvorsichtig *adj* careless; **'Unvorsichtigkeit** *f* (-; *no pl*) carelessness

unvor'stellbar *adj* unthinkable

'unvorteilhaft *adj* unbecoming

'unwahr *adj* untrue; **'Unwahrheit** *f* untruth; **'unwahrscheinlich** *adj* improbable, unlikely; F fantastic

unwegsam ['ʊnveːkzaːm] *adj* difficult, rough (*terrain*)

unweigerlich [ʊn'vaigɐlɪç] *adv* inevitably

'**unweit** *prp* (*gen*) not far from

'**Unwetter** *n* (-s; -) disastrous (thunder)-storm

'**unwichtig** *adj* unimportant

unwider|legbar [ʊnviːdɐ'leːkbaɐ] *adj* irrefutable; **~ruflich** [ʊnviːdɐ'ruːflɪç] *adj* irrevocable; **~stehlich** [ʊnviːdɐ-'fteːlɪç] *adj* irresistible

'**Unwille(n)** *m* indignation (*über acc* at); '**unwillig** *adj* indignant (*über acc* at); unwilling, reluctant

'**unwillkürlich** *adj* involuntary

'**unwirklich** *adj* unreal

'**unwirksam** *adj* ineffective

unwirsch ['ʊnvɪrʃ] *adj* surly, gruff

unwirtlich ['ʊnvɪrtlɪç] *adj* inhospitable

'**unwirtschaftlich** *adj* uneconomic(al)

'**unwissend** *adj* ignorant

'**Unwissenheit** *f* (-; *no pl*) ignorance

'**unwohl** *adj* unwell; uneasy

'**unwürdig** *adj* unworthy (*gen* of)

unzählig [ʊn'tsɛːlɪç] *adj* innumerable, countless

unzer'brechlich *adj* unbreakable

unzer'reißbar *adj* untearable

unzer'störbar *adj* indestructible

unzer'trennlich *adj* inseparable

'**Unzucht** *f* (-; *no pl*) sexual offense (*Br* offence); '**unzüchtig** *adj* indecent; obscene

'**unzufrieden** *adj* discontent(ed) (*mit* with), dissatisfied (with); '**Unzufriedenheit** *f* discontent, dissatisfaction

'**unzugänglich** *adj* inaccessible

'**unzulänglich** *adj* inadequate

'**unzulässig** *adj* inadmissible

unzu'mutbar *adj* unacceptable; unreasonable

'**unzurechnungsfähig** *adj* JUR irresponsible; '**Unzurechnungsfähigkeit** *f* (-; *no pl*) JUR irresponsibility

'**unzureichend** *adj* insufficient

'**unzusammenhängend** *adj* incoherent

'**unzuverlässig** *adj* unreliable, untrustworthy; uncertain

üppig ['ʏpɪç] *adj* luxuriant, lush (*both a.*

fig); voluptuous, luscious; opulent; rich

uralt ['uːɐʔalt] *adj* ancient (*a. iro*)

Uran [u'raːn] *n* (-s; *no pl*) uranium

'**Uraufführung** *f* première, first performance (*film:* showing)

urbar ['uːɐbaːɐ] *adj* arable; **~ machen** cultivate; reclaim

'**Urbevölkerung** *f*, '**Ureinwohner** *pl* aboriginal inhabitants; *in Australia:* Aborigines

'**Urenkel** *m* great-grandson

'**Urenkelin** *f* great-granddaughter

'**Urgroß...** *in cpds* ...eltern, ...mutter, ...vater: great-grand...

Urheberrecht ['uːɐheːbɐrɛçt] *n* copyright (*an dat* on, for)

Urin [u'riːn] *m* (-s; -e) urine; **urinieren** [uri'niːrən] *v/i* (*no -ge-*, *h*) urinate

Urkunde ['uːɐkʊndə] *f* (-; -n) document; diploma; '**Urkundenfälschung** *f* forgery of documents

Urlaub ['uːɐlaup] *m* (-[e]s; -e) vacation, *Br* holiday(s); MIL leave; *in or im ~ sein* (*auf ~ gehen*) be (go) on vacation (*Br* holiday); *e-n Tag* (*ein paar Tage*) *~ nehmen* take a day (a few days) off; **Urlauber(in)** ['uːɐlaubɐ, 'uːɐlaubərɪn] *m(f)* (-s; -/-; -nen) vacationist, vacationer, *Br* holidaymaker

Urne ['ʊrnə] *f* (-; -n) urn; ballot box

'**Ursache** *f* (-; -n) cause; reason; *keine ~!* not at all, you're welcome

'**Ursprung** *m* origin

ursprünglich ['uːɐfprʏŋlɪç] *adj* original; natural, unspoilt

Urteil ['ʊrtail] *n* (-[e]s; -e) judg(e)ment; JUR sentence; *sich ein ~ bilden* form a judg(e)ment (*über acc* about)

'**urteilen** *v/i* (*ge-*, *h*) judge (*über j-n, et.* s.o., s.th.; *nach* by)

'**Urwald** *m* primeval forest; jungle

urwüchsig ['uːɐvyːksɪç] *adj* coarse, earthy

'**Urzeit** *f* prehistoric times

usw. *abbr of* **und so weiter** etc, and so on

Utensilien [utɛn'ziːljən] *pl* utensils

Utopie [uto'piː] *f* (-; -n) illusion

utopisch [u'toːpɪʃ] *adj* utopian; fantastic

V

Vagabund [vaga'bʊnt] *m* (*-en; -en*) vagabond, tramp, F bum

vage ['vaːgə] *adj* vague

Vakuum ['vaːkuʊm] *n* (*-s; -kua, -kuen*) vacuum

Vampir ['vampiːɐ] *m* (*-s; -e*) zo vampire (*a. fig*)

Vanille [va'nɪljə] *f* (*-; no pl*) vanilla

variabel [va'rjaːbəl] *adj* variable

Variante [va'rjantə] *f* (*-; -n*) variant

Variation [varja'tsioːn] *f* (*-; -en*) variation

Varietee, *a.* **Variété** [varje'teː] *n* (*-s; -s*) vaudeville, *Br* variety theatre, music hall

variieren [vari'iːrən] *v/i and v/t* (*no -ge-, h*) vary

Vase ['vaːzə] *f* (*-; -n*) vase

Vater ['faːtɐ] *m* (*-s; Väter* ['fɛːtɐ]) father

'Vaterland *n* native country

'Vaterlandsliebe *f* patriotism

väterlich ['fɛːtəlɪç] *adj* fatherly, paternal

'Vaterschaft *f* (*-; -en*) JUR paternity

'Vater'unser *n* (*-s; -*) REL Lord's Prayer

V-Ausschnitt ['fauʔausʃnɪt] *m* V-neck

v. Chr. *abbr of* **vor Christus** BC, before Christ

Vegetarier [vege'taːrjɐ] *m* (*-s; -*), **Vegetarierin** *f* (*-; -nen*), **vegetarisch** [vege'taːrɪʃ] *adj* vegetarian

Vegetation [vegeta'tsioːn] *f* (*-; -en*) vegetation; **vegetieren** [vege'tiːrən] *v/i* (*no -ge-, h*) vegetate

Veilchen ['failçən] *n* (*-s; -*) BOT violet

Velo ['veːlo] *Swiss n* (*-s; -s*) bicycle, F bike

Ventil [vɛn'tiːl] *n* (*-s; -e*) TECH valve; *fig* vent, outlet

Ventilation [vɛntila'tsioːn] *f* (*-; -en*) ventilation; **Ventilator** [vɛnti'laːtoːɐ] *m* (*-s; -en* [vɛntila'toːrən]) fan

verabreden [fɛɐ'ʔapreːdən] *v/t* (*no -ge-, h*) agree (up)on, arrange; appoint, fix; *sich ~* make a date (*or* an appointment) (*mit* with); **Ver'abredung** *f* (*-; -en*) appointment; date

ver'abreichen *v/t* (*no -ge-, h*) give; MED administer; **ver'abscheuen** *v/t* (*no -ge-, h*) loathe, detest

verabschieden [fɛɐ'ʔapʃiːdən] *v/t* (*no -ge-, h*) say goodbye to (*a. sich ~ von*); dismiss; JUR pass; **Ver'abschiedung** *f* (*-; -en*) dismissal; JUR passing

ver'achten *v/t* (*no -ge-, h*) despise; **verächtlich** [fɛɐ'ʔɛçtlɪç] *adj* contemptuous; **Ver'achtung** *f* (*-; no pl*) contempt

verallgemeinern [fɛɐ'ʔalgə'mainɐ] *v/t* (*no -ge-, h*) generalize

ver'altet *adj* antiquated, out of date

Veranda [ve'randa] *f* (*-; -den*) porch, *Br* veranda(h)

veränderlich [fɛɐ'ʔɛndəlɪç] *adj* changeable (*a.* METEOR), variable (*a.* MATH, LING); **ver'ändern** *v/t and v/refl* (*no -ge-, h*), **Ver'änderung** *f* change

verängstigt [fɛɐ'ʔɛŋstɪçt] *adj* frightened, scared

ver'anlagen *v/t* (*no -ge-, h*) ECON assess; **veranlagt** [fɛɐ'ʔanlaːkt] *adj* inclined (*zu, für* to); **künstlerisch (musikalisch) ~ sein** have a gift *or* bent for art (music); **Ver'anlagung** *f* (*-; -en*) (pre)disposition (*a.* MED); talent, gift; ECON assessment

ver'anlassen *v/t* (*no -ge-, h*) make arrangements (*or* arrange) for *s.th.*; *j-n zu et. ~* make s.o. do s.th.

Ver'anlassung *f* (*-; -en*) cause (*zu* for)

ver'|anschaulichen *v/t* (*no -ge-, h*) illustrate; **~'anschlagen** *v/t.* (*no -ge-, h*) estimate (*auf acc* at)

ver'anstalten *v/t* (*no -ge-, h*) arrange, organize; hold, give (*concert, party etc*); **Ver'anstaltung** *f* (*-; -en*) event, SPORT *a.* meet, *Br* meeting

ver'antworten *v/t* (*no -ge-, h*) take the responsibility for; **ver'antwortlich** *adj* responsible; *j-n ~ machen für* hold s.o. responsible for; **Ver'antwortung** *f* (*-; no pl*) responsibility; *auf eigene ~* at one's own risk; *j-n zur ~ ziehen* call s.o. to account; **Ver'antwortungsgefühl** *n* (*-[e]s; no pl*) sense of responsibility; **ver'antwortungslos** *adj* irresponsible

ver'|arbeiten *v/t* (*no -ge-, h*) process; *fig* digest; *et. ~ zu* manufacture (*or* make) s.th. into; **~'ärgern** *v/t* (*no -ge-, h*) make *s.o.* angry, annoy

ver'armt *adj* impoverished

ver'arschen *v/t (no -ge-, h)* **j-n ~** take the piss out of s.o.

Verb [vɛrp] *n (-s; -en* ['vɛrbən]) LING verb

Verband [fɛɐ'bant] *m (-es; Verbände* [fɛɐ'bɛndə]) MED dressing, bandage; ECON association; MIL formation, unit; **~(s)kasten** *m* MED first-aid kit *or* box; **~(s)zeug** *n* MED dressing material

ver'bannen *v/t (no -ge-, h)* banish (*a. fig*), exile; **Ver'bannung** *f (-; -en)* banishment, exile

verbarrika'dieren *v/t (no -ge-, h)* barricade; block

ver'bergen *v/t (irr, bergen, no -ge-, h)* hide (*a. sich ~*), conceal

ver'bessern *v/t (no -ge-, h)* improve; correct; **Ver'besserung** *f (-; -en)* improvement; correction

ver'beugen *v/refl (no -ge-, h)*, **Ver'beugung** *f (-; -en)* bow (*vor* to)

ver'|biegen *v/t (irr, biegen, no -ge-, h)* twist; **~'bieten** *v/t (irr, bieten, no -ge-, h)* forbid; prohibit; → **verboten**

ver'billigen *v/t (no -ge-, h)* reduce in price; **verbilligt** [fɛɐ'bɪlɪçt] *adj* reduced, at reduced prices

verbinden *v/t (irr, binden, no -ge-, h)* MED dress, bandage; bandage *s.o.* up; *a.* TECH connect, join, link (up); TEL put *s.o.* through (*mit* to); combine (*a.* CHEM *sich ~*); *fig* unite; associate; **j-m die Augen ~** blindfold s.o.; *damit sind beträchtliche Kosten verbunden* that involves considerable cost(s *pl*); *falsch verbunden!* wrong number!

verbindlich [fɛɐ'bɪntlɪç] *adj* obligatory, compulsory (*a.* PED); obliging

Ver'bindlichkeit *f (-; -en) (no pl)* obligingness; *pl* ECON liabilities

Ver'bindung *f (-; -en)* connection; combination; CHEM compound; UNIV fraternity, *Br* society; *sich in ~ setzen mit* get in touch with; *in ~ stehen* (*bleiben*) be (keep) in touch

verbissen [fɛɐ'bɪsən] *adj* dogged

ver'bittert *adj* bitter, embittered

verblassen [fɛɐ'blasən] *v/i (no -ge-, sein)* fade (*a. fig*)

Verbleib [fɛɐ'blaip] *m (-[e]s; no pl)* whereabouts; **ver'bleiben** *v/i (irr, blei-*

ben, no -ge-, sein) remain

verbleit [fɛɐ'blait] *adj* leaded

ver'blendet *fig adj* blind

Ver'blendung *fig f (-; -en)* blindness

verblichen [fɛɐ'blɪçən] *adj* faded

verblüffen [fɛɐ'blʏfən] *v/t (no -ge-, h)* amaze, F flabbergast

Ver'blüffung *f (-; -en)* amazement

ver'blühen *v/i (no -ge-, sein)* fade, wither (*both a. fig*)

ver'bluten *v/i (no -ge-, sein)* MED bleed to death

verborgen [fɛɐ'bɔrgən] *adj* hidden, concealed; *im Verborgenen* in secret

Verbot [fɛɐ'boːt] *n (-[e]s; -e)* prohibition, ban (on *s.th.*); **ver'boten** *adj*: *Rauchen ~* no smoking

Ver'brauch *m (-[e]s; no pl)* consumption (*an dat* of); **ver'brauchen** *v/t (no -ge-, h)* consume, use up

Verbraucher [fɛɐ'brauxə] *m (-s; -),* **'braucherin** *f (-; -nen)* consumer; **~schutz** *m* consumer protection

Ver'brechen *n (-s; -)* crime; *ein ~ begehen* commit a crime; **Ver'brecher(in)** *(-s; -/-; -nen),* **ver'brecherisch** *adj* criminal

ver'breiten *v/t and v/refl (no -ge-, h)* spread (*in dat, über* acc over, through); circulate

verbreitern [fɛɐ'braitən] *v/t and v/refl (no -ge-, h)* widen, broaden

Ver'breitung *f (-; no pl)* spread(ing); circulation

ver'brennen *v/i (irr, brennen, no -ge-, sein) and v/t (h)* burn (up); cremate

Ver'brennung *f (-; -en)* burning; cremation; TECH combustion; MED burn

ver'bringen *v/t (irr, bringen, no -ge-, h)* spend, pass

verbrüdern [fɛɐ'bryːdən] *v/refl (no -ge-, h)* fraternize; **Verbrüderung** [fɛɐ'bryːdərʊŋ] *f (-; -en)* fraternization

ver'brühen *v/t (no -ge-, h)* scald

ver'buchen *v/t (no -ge-, h)* book

verbünden [fɛɐ'byndən] *v/refl (no -ge-, h)* ally o.s. (*mit* to, with)

Ver'bündete *m, f (-n; -n)* ally (*a. fig*)

ver'bürgen *v/refl (no -ge-, h) sich ~ für* vouch for, guarantee

ver'büßen *v/t (no -ge-, h) e-e Strafe ~* serve a sentence, serve time

verchromt [fɛɐ'kroːmt] *adj* chromium--plated

Verdacht [fɛɐˈdaxt] *m* (-[e]s; -e) suspicion; **~ schöpfen** become suspicious

verdächtig [fɛɐˈdɛçtɪç] *adj* suspicious, suspect; **Verdächtige** [fɛɐˈdɛçtɪgə] *m*, *f* (-n; -n) suspect; **ver'dächtigen** *v/t* (*no -ge-*, *h*) suspect (**j-n e-r Tat** s.o. of [doing] s.th.); **Ver'dächtigung** *f* (-; -en) suspicion

verdammen [fɛɐˈdamən] *v/t* (*no-ge-*, *h*) condemn (**zu** to), damn (*a*. REL); **Ver'dammnis** *f* (-; *no pl*) REL damnation; **ver'dammt 1.** *adj* damned, F *a*. damn, darn(ed), *Br sl a*. bloody; F **~ (noch mal)!** damn (it)! **2.** *adv*: **~ gut** *etc* damn (*Br sl a*. bloody) good *etc*; **Ver'dammung** *f* (-; -en) condemnation; REL damnation

ver'dampfen *v/t* (*no-ge-*, *h*) and *v/i* (*sein*) evaporate

ver'danken *v/t* (*no-ge-*, *h*) **j-m (e-m Umstand) et. ~** owe s.th. to s.o. (s.th.)

verdarb [fɛɐˈdarp] *pret of* **verderben**

verdauen [fɛɐˈdauən] *v/t* (*no-ge-*, *h*) digest (*a. fig*)

ver'daulich *adj* digestible; **leicht (schwer) ~** easy (hard) to digest

Ver'dauung *f* (-; *no pl*) digestion

Ver'deck *n* (-[e]s; -e) top; **ver'decken** *v/t* (*no-ge-*, *h*) cover (up) (*a. fig*)

ver'denken *v/t* (*irr, denken, no-ge-, h*) **ich kann es ihm nicht ~(, dass er …)** I can't blame him (for *doing*)

verderben [fɛɐˈdɛrbən] (*irr, no-ge-*) **1.** *v/i* (*sein*) spoil (*a. fig*); GASTR go bad **2.** *v/t* (*h*) spoil (*a. fig*), ruin; **sich den Magen ~** upset one's stomach

Ver'derben *n* (-s; *no pl*) ruin

verderblich [fɛɐˈdɛrplɪç] *adj* perishable; **leicht ~e Lebensmittel** perishables

ver'dichten *v/t* (*no-ge-*, *h*) compress, condense

ver'dienen *v/t* (*no-ge-*, *h*) earn, make; *fig* deserve

Ver'dienst¹ *m* (-[e]s; -e) earnings; salary; wages; gain, profit

Ver'dienst² *n* (-[e]s; -e) merit; **es ist sein ~, dass** it is thanks to him that

ver'dient *adj* (well-)deserved

ver'doppeln *v/t* and *v/refl* (*no-ge-*, *h*) double

verdorben [fɛɐˈdɔrbən] **1.** *pp of* **verderben 2.** *adj* GASTR spoilt, bad (*both a. fig*); MED upset

ver'dorren [fɛɐˈdɔrən] *v/i* (*no-ge-*, *sein*) wither, dry up; **~'drängen** *v/t* (*no-ge-*, *h*) supplant, supersede; replace; PHYS displace; PSYCH repress, suppress; **~'drehen** *v/t* (*no-ge-*, *h*) twist, *fig a*. distort; **die Augen ~** roll one's eyes; **j-m den Kopf ~** turn s.o.'s head; **~'dreht** F *fig adj* mixed up; **~'dreifachen** *v/t* and *v/refl* (*no-ge-*, *h*) treble, triple

verdrießen [fɛɐˈdriːsən] *v/t* (*irr, no-ge-*, *h*) annoy; **verdrießlich** [fɛɐˈdriːslɪç] *adj* glum, morose, sullen; **verdross** [fɛɐˈdrɔs] *pret of* **verdrießen**; **verdrossen** [fɛɐˈdrɔsən] **1.** *pp of* **verdrießen 2.** *adj* grumpy, sullen; **Verdruss** [fɛɐˈdrʊs] *m* (-es; -e) annoyance

ver'dummen (*no-ge-*) **1.** *v/t* (*h*) make stupid, stultify **2.** *v/i* (*sein*) become stultified

ver'dunkeln *v/t* and *v/refl* (*no-ge-*, *h*) darken; black out; *fig* obscure

Ver'dunk(e)lung *f* (-; -en) darkening; blackout; JUR collusion

ver'dünnen *v/t* (*no-ge-*, *h*) dilute

ver'dunsten *v/i* (*no-ge-*, *sein*) evaporate

ver'dursten *v/i* (*no-ge-*, *sein*) die of thirst

verdutzt [fɛɐˈdʊtst] *adj* puzzled

ver'edeln *v/t* (*no-ge-*, *h*) BOT graft; TECH process, refine; **Ver'ed(e)lung** *f* (-; -en) BOT grafting; TECH processing, refinement

ver'ehren *v/t* (*no-ge-*, *h*) admire; adore, worship (*both a. fig*), *esp* REL *a*. revere, venerate; **Ver'ehrer(in)** (-s; -/-; -nen) admirer, *esp* film *etc*: *a*. fan; **Ver'ehrung** *f* (-; *no pl*) admiration; adoration, worship; *esp* REL reverence, veneration

vereidigen [fɛɐˈʔaidigən] *v/t* (*no-ge-*, *h*) swear *s.o.* in; JUR put *s.o.* under an oath

Verein [fɛɐˈʔain] *m* (-[e]s; -e) club (*a.* SPORT); society, association

vereinbar [fɛɐˈʔainbaːɐ] *adj* compatible (**mit** with); **vereinbaren** [fɛɐˈʔainbaːrən] *v/t* (*no-ge-*, *h*) agree (up)on, arrange; **Ver'einbarung** *f* (-; -en) agreement, arrangement

ver'einen → vereinigen

ver'einfachen *v/t* (*no-ge-*, *h*) simplify

Ver'einfachung *f* (-; -en) simplification

ver'einheitlichen *v/t* (*no-ge-*, *h*) standardize

ver'einigen v/t and v/refl (no -ge-, h) unite (**zu** into); combine, join

Ver'einigung f (-; -en) union; combination; alliance

ver'einsamen v/i (no -ge-, sein) become lonely or isolated

vereinzelt [fɛɛ'ʔaintsəlt] adj occasional, odd; **~ Regen** scattered showers

ver'|eiteln v/t (no -ge-, h) prevent; frustrate; **~'enden** v/i (no -ge-, sein) esp zo die, perish; **~'engen** v/t and v/refl (no -ge-, h) narrow

ver'erben v/t (no -ge-, h) **j-m et. ~** leave (BIOL transmit) s.th. to s.o.; **sich ~ (auf** acc) be passed on or down (to) (a. BIOL and fig); **Ver'erbung** f (-; no pl) BIOL heredity; **Ver'erbungslehre** f BIOL genetics

verewigen [fɛɛ'ʔeːvɪgən] v/t (no -ge-, h) immortalize

ver'fahren (irr, fahren, no -ge-) **1.** v/i (sein) proceed; **~ mit** deal with **2.** v/refl (h) MOT get lost

Ver'fahren n (-s; -) procedure, method, esp TECH a. technique, way; JUR (legal) proceedings (**gegen** against)

Ver'fall m (-[e]s; no pl) decay (a. fig); dilapidation; fig decline; ECON etc expiry; **ver'fallen** (irr, fallen, no -ge-, sein) **1.** v/i decay (a. fig), dilapidate; esp fig decline; ECON expire; MED waste away; become addicted to; (**wieder**) **~ in** (acc) fall (back) into; **~ auf** (acc) hit (up)on **2.** adj decayed; dilapidated; **Ver'fallsdatum** n expiry date; GASTR pull date, Br best-before (or best-by) date; PHARM sell-by date

ver'fälschen v/t (no -ge-, h) falsify; distort; GASTR adulterate

verfänglich [fɛɛ'fɛŋlɪç] adj delicate, tricky; embarrassing, compromising

ver'färben v/refl (no -ge-, h) discolo(u)r

ver'fassen v/t (no -ge-, h) write

Verfasser [fɛɛ'fasɐ] m (-s; -), **Ver'fasserin** f (-; -nen) author

Ver'fassung f (-; -en) state (of health or of mind), condition; POL constitution

ver'fassungs|mäßig adj POL constitutional; **~widrig** adj unconstitutional

ver'faulen v/i (no -ge-, sein) rot, decay

ver'fechten v/t (irr, fechten, no -ge-, h), **Ver'fechter(in)** (-s; -/-; -nen) advocate

ver'fehlen v/t (no -ge-, h) miss (**sich**

each other); **Ver'fehlung** f (-; -en) offense, Br offence

verfeinden [fɛɛ'faindən] v/refl (no -ge-, h) become enemies; **ver'feindet** adj hostile; **~ sein** be enemies

verfeinern [fɛɛ'fainɐn] v/t and v/refl (no -ge-, h) refine

ver'filmen v/t (no -ge-, h) film; **Ver'filmung** f (-; -en) filming; film version

ver'flechten v/t (irr, flechten, no -ge-, h) intertwine (a. **sich ~**)

ver'fluchen v/t (no -ge-, h) curse

ver'flucht → verdammt

ver'folgen v/t (no -ge-, h) pursue (a. fig); chase, hunt (both a. fig); POL, REL persecute; follow (track etc); fear etc: haunt s.o.; **j-n gerichtlich ~** prosecute s.o.; **Verfolger** [fɛɛ'fɔlgɐ] m (-s; -) pursuer; persecutor; **Ver'folgung** f (-; -en) pursuit (a. cycling); chase, hunt, persecution; **gerichtliche ~** prosecution

ver'frachten v/t (no -ge-, h) freight, ship; F bundle s.o., s.th. (**in** acc into)

verfremden [fɛɛ'frɛmdən] v/t (no -ge-, h) esp art: alienate

ver'früht adj premature

verfügbar [fɛɛ'fyːkbaːɐ] adj available; **ver'fügen** (no -ge-, h) **1.** v/t decree, order **2.** v/i: **~ über** (acc) have at one's disposal; **Ver'fügung** f (-; -en) decree, order; (no pl) disposal; **j-m zur ~ stehen** (**stellen**) be (place) at s.o. 's disposal

ver'führen v/t (no -ge-, h) seduce (**et. zu tun** into doing s.th.); **Ver'führer** m (-s; -) seducer; **Ver'führerin** f (-; -nen) seductress; **ver'führerisch** adj seductive; tempting; **Ver'führung** f (-; -en) seduction

vergangen [fɛɛ'gaŋən] adj gone, past; **im ~en Jahr** last year; **Ver'gangenheit** f (-; no pl) past; LING past tense

vergänglich [fɛɛ'gɛŋlɪç] adj transitory, transient

vergasen [fɛɛ'gaːzən] v/t (no -ge-, h) gas; CHEM gasify; **Vergaser** [fɛɛ'gaːzɐ] m (-s; -) MOT carburet(t)or

vergaß [fɛɛ'gaːs] pret of **vergessen**

ver'geben v/t (irr, geben, no -ge-, h) give away (a. fig); award (prize etc); forgive; **ver'gebens** adv in vain; **vergeblich** [fɛɛ'geːplɪç] **1.** adj futile **2.** adv in vain; **Ver'gebung** f (-; -en) forgiveness, pardon

ver'gehen (*irr*, *gehen*, *no -ge-, sein*) **1.** *v/i time etc*: go by, pass; *pain*, *effect etc*: wear off; **~ vor** (*dat*) be dying with; *wie die Zeit vergeht!* how time flies! **2.** *v/refl sich ~ an* (*dat*) violate; rape

Vergehen *n* (*-s*; *-*) JUR offen|se, *Br* -ce

ver'gelten *v/t* (*irr*, *gelten*, *no -ge-, h*) repay; reward; **Ver'geltung** *f* (*-; -en*) retaliation (*a.* MIL)

vergessen [fɛɐ̯'gɛsən] **1.** *v/t* (*irr*, *no -ge-, h*) forget; leave **2.** *pp of* **vergessen** 1; **Ver'gessenheit** *f: in ~ geraten* fall into oblivion; **vergesslich** [fɛɐ̯'gɛslɪç] *adj* forgetful

vergeuden [fɛɐ̯'gɔʏdən] *v/t* (*no -ge-, h*), **Ver'geudung** *f* (*-; -en*) waste

vergewaltigen [fɛɐ̯gə'valtɪgən] *v/t* (*no -ge-, h*) rape, violate (*a. fig*)

Verge'waltigung *f* (*-; -en*) rape, violation (*a. fig*)

vergewissern [fɛɐ̯gə'vɪsɐn] *v/refl* (*no -ge-, h*) make sure (*e-r Sache* of s.th.; *ob* whether; *dass* that)

ver'gießen *v/t* (*irr*, *gießen*, *no -ge-, h*) shed (*blood*, *tears*); spill

ver'giften *v/t* (*no -ge-, h*) poison (*a. fig*); contaminate; **Ver'giftung** *f* (*-; -en*) poisoning (*a. fig*); contamination

ver'gittert *adj* barred (*window etc*)

Ver'gleich *m* (*-[e]s*; *-e*) comparison; JUR compromise; **ver'gleichbar** *adj* comparable (*mit* to, with); **ver'gleichen** *v/t* (*irr*, *gleichen*, *no -ge-, h*) compare (*mit* with *or* to); *... ist nicht zu ~ mit ...* cannot be compared to; *...* cannot compare with; *verglichen mit* compared to *or* with; **ver'gleichsweise** *adv* comparatively, relatively

ver'glühen *v/i* (*no -ge-, sein*) burn out (*or* up)

vergnügen [fɛɐ̯'gny:gən] *v/refl* (*no -ge-, h*) enjoy o.s. (*mit et.* doing s.th.)

Ver'gnügen *n* (*-s*; *-*) pleasure, enjoyment, fun; *mit ~* with pleasure; *viel ~!* have fun!, have a good time!

vergnügt [fɛɐ̯'gny:kt] *adj* cheerful

Ver'gnügung *f* (*-; -en*) pleasure, amusement, entertainment

Ver'gnügungspark *m* amusement park

ver'gnügungssüchtig *adj* pleasure--seeking

Ver'gnügungsviertel *n* nightlife district

ver|'golden *v/t* (*no -ge-, h*) gild; **~göt-**

tern [fɛɐ̯'gœtɐn] *v/t* (*no -ge-, h*) idolize, adore; **~'graben** *v/t* (*irr*, *graben*, *no -ge-, h*) bury (*a. fig*)

ver'greifen *v/refl* (*irr*, *greifen*, *no -ge-, h*) *sich ~ an* (*dat*) lay hands on

vergriffen [fɛɐ̯'grɪfən] *adj* out of print

vergrößern [fɛɐ̯'grøːsɐn] *v/t* (*no -ge-, h*) enlarge (*a.* PHOT); increase; OPT magnify; *sich ~* increase, grow, expand; **Ver'größerung** *f* (*-; -en*) increase; PHOT enlargement; OPT magnification; **Ver'größerungsglas** *n* OPT magnifying glass

Vergünstigung [fɛɐ̯'gʏnstɪgʊŋ] *f* (*-; -en*) privilege

vergüten [fɛɐ̯'gyːtən] *v/t* (*no -ge-, h*) reimburse, pay (for); **Ver'gütung** *f* (*-; -en*) reimbursement

ver'haften *v/t* (*no -ge-, h*), **Ver'haftung** *f* (*-; -en*) arrest

ver'halten¹ *v/refl* (*irr*, *halten*, *no -ge-, h*) behave, conduct o.s., act; *sich ruhig ~* keep quiet

ver'halten² *adj* restrained; subdued

Ver'halten *n* (*-s*; *no pl*) behavio(u)r, conduct; **Ver'haltensforschung** *f* behavio(u)ral science; **ver'haltensgestört** *adj* disturbed, maladjusted

Verhältnis [fɛɐ̯'hɛltnɪs] *n* (*-ses*; *-se*) relationship, relations; attitude; proportion, relation, *esp* MATH ratio; F affair; *pl* circumstances, conditions; *über j-s ~se* beyond s.o.'s means; **ver'hältnismäßig** *adv* comparatively, relatively

Ver'hältniswort *n* (*-[e]s*; *-wörter*) LING preposition

ver'handeln *no* (*-ge-, h*) **1.** *v/i* negotiate **2.** *v/t* JUR hear; **Ver'handlung** *f* (*-; -en*) negotiation, talk; JUR hearing; trial; **Ver'handlungsbasis** *f* ECON asking price

ver'hängen *v/t* (*no -ge-, h*) cover (*mit* with); impose (*über acc* on)

Verhängnis [fɛɐ̯'hɛŋnɪs] *n* (*-ses*; *-se*) fate; disaster; **ver'hängnisvoll** *adj* fatal, disastrous

verharmlosen [fɛɐ̯'harmloːzən] *v/t* (*no -ge-, h*) play *s.th.* down

verhärmt [fɛɐ̯'hɛrmt] *adj* careworn

ver'hasst *adj* hated; hateful

ver'hätscheln *v/t* (*no -ge-, h*) coddle, pamper, spoil

verhauen 302

ver'hauen F *v/t* (*no -ge-, h*) spank
verheerend [fɛɐˈheːrənt] *adj* disastrous
ver'heilen *v/i* (*no -ge-, sein*) heal (up)
verheimlichen [fɛɐˈhaimlɪçən] *v/t* (*no -ge-, h*) hide, conceal
ver'heiraten *v/t* (*no -ge-, h*) marry (*s.o.* off) (*mit* to); **sich ~** get married
ver'heiratet *adj* married (*mit* to)
ver'heißungsvoll *adj* promising
ver'helfen *v/i* (*irr, helfen, no -ge-, h*) *j-m zu et.* **~** help s.o. to get s.th.
ver'herrlichen *v/t* (*no -ge-, h*) glorify, *contp a.* idolize; **Ver'herrlichung** *f* (-; *-en*) glorification
ver'hexen *v/t* (*no -ge-, h*) bewitch
ver'hindern *v/t* (*no -ge-, h*) prevent (*dass j. et. tut* s.o. from doing s.th.); **ver'hindert** *adj* unable to come; F *ein ~er ...* a would-be ...; **Ver'hinderung** *f* (-; *-en*) prevention
ver'höhnen *v/t* (*no -ge-, h*) deride, mock (at), jeer (at)
Verhör [fɛɐˈhøːɐ] *n* (-[*e*]*s*; *-e*) JUR interrogation; **ver'hören** (*no -ge-, h*) **1.** *v/t* interrogate, question **2.** *v/refl* get it wrong
ver'hüllen *v/t* (*no -ge-, h*) cover, veil
ver'hungern *v/i* (*no -ge-, sein*) die of hunger, starve (to death)
Ver'hungern *n* (-*s*; *no pl*) starvation
ver'hüten *v/t* (*no -ge-, h*) prevent
Ver'hütung *f* (-; *-en*) prevention
Ver'hütungsmittel *n* MED contraceptive
ver'irren *v/refl* (*no -ge-, h*) get lost, lose one's way, go astray (*a. fig*)
Ver'irrung *f* (-; *-en*) aberration
ver'jagen *v/t* (*no -ge-, h*) chase *or* drive away
verjähren [fɛɐˈjɛːrən] *v/i* (*no -ge-, sein*) JUR come under the statute of limitations; **ver'jährt** *adj* JUR statute-barred
verjüngen [fɛɐˈjʏŋən] *v/t* (*no -ge-, h*) make *s.o.* (look) younger, rejuvenate; **sich ~** ARCH, TECH taper (off)
ver'kabeln *v/t* (*no -ge-, h*) ELECTR cable
Ver'kauf *m* sale; **ver'kaufen** *v/t* (*no -ge-, h*) sell; **zu ~** for sale; **sich gut ~** sell well; **Ver'käufer** *m* (-*s*; -) (sales)clerk, salesman, *Br* shop assistant; ECON seller; **Ver'käuferin** *f* (-; *-nen*) (sales)clerk, saleslady, *Br* shop assistant; **ver'käuflich** *adj* for sale; **schwer ~** hard to sell
Verkehr [fɛɐˈkeːɐ] *m* (-*s*; *no pl*) traffic;

transportation, *Br* transport; *fig* contact, dealings; intercourse; circulation; **starker** (**schwacher**) **~** heavy (light) traffic; **ver'kehren** (*no -ge-, h*) **1.** *v/i* bus *etc*: run; **~ in** (*dat*) frequent; **~ mit** associate *or* mix with; have intercourse with **2.** *v/t* turn (*in acc* into); **ins Gegenteil ~** reverse
Ver'kehrs|ader *f* arterial road; **~ampel** *f* traffic light(s); **~behinderung** *f* hold--up, delay; JUR obstruction of traffic; **~de,likt** *n* traffic offense (*Br* offence); **~flugzeug** *n* airliner; **~funk** *m* traffic bulletin; **~insel** *f* traffic island; **~meldung** *f* traffic announcement, flash; **~mi,nister** *m* minister of transportation; **~minis,terium** *n* ministry of transportation; **~mittel** *n* means of transportation; **öffentliche ~** public transportation; **~opfer** *n* road casualty; **~poli,zei** *f* traffic police; **~rowdy** *m* F road hog
ver'kehrssicher *adj* MOT roadworthy
Ver'kehrs|sicherheit *f* MOT road safety; roadworthiness; **~stau** *m* traffic jam; **~sünder(in)** F traffic offender; **~teilnehmer(in)** road user; **~unfall** *m* traffic accident; (car) crash; **~unterricht** *m* traffic instruction; **~zeichen** *n* traffic sign
ver'kehrt *adj and adv* wrong; upside down; inside out
ver'kennen *v/t* (*irr, kennen, no -ge-, h*) mistake, misjudge; **~'klagen** *v/t* (*no -ge-, h*) JUR sue (*auf acc, wegen* for); **~'klappen** *v/t* (*no -ge-, h*) dump (into the sea); **~'kleben** *v/t* (*no -ge-, h*) glue (together)
ver'kleiden *v/t* (*no -ge-, h*) disguise (*als* as), dress *s.o.* up (as); TECH cover, (en)case; panel; **sich ~** disguise o.s., dress (o.s.) up; **Ver'kleidung** *f* (-; *-en*) disguise; TECH cover, encasement; panel-(l)ing; MOT fairing
verkleinern [fɛɐˈklainɐn] *v/t* (*no -ge-, h*) make smaller, reduce, diminish; **Ver'kleinerung** [fɛɐˈklainərʊŋ] *f* (-; *-en*) reduction
ver'klingen *v/i* (*irr, klingen, no -ge-, sein*) die away
ver'knallt F *adj*: **~ sein in** (*acc*) be madly in love with, have a crush on
ver'|knoten *v/t* (*no -ge-, h*) knot; **~'knüpfen** *v/t* (*no -ge-, h*) knot together;

fig connect, combine; ~**'kohlen** *v/i* (*no -ge-*, *sein*) char; ~**'kommen 1.** *v/i* (*irr*, **kommen**, *no -ge-*, *sein*) become run--down *or* dilapidated; go to seed; GASTR go bad **2.** *adj* run-down, dilapidated; neglected; depraved, rotten (to the core); ~**'korken** *v/t* (*no -ge-*, *h*) cork (up); ~**'körpern** *v/t* (*no -ge-*, *h*) personify; embody; *esp* THEA impersonate; ~**'kriechen** *v/refl* (*irr*, **kriechen**, *no -ge-*, *h*) hide; ~**'krümmt** *adj* crooked, curved (*a.* MED); ~**'krüppelt** *adj* crippled; ~**'kümmern** *v/i* (*no -ge-*, *sein*) BIOL become stunted; ~**'kümmert** *adj* BIOL stunted

verkünden [fɛɐ'kʏndən] *v/t* (*no -ge-*, *h*) announce; proclaim; JUR pronounce; REL preach; **Ver'kündung** *f* (*-*; *-en*) announcement; proclamation; JUR pronouncement; REL preaching

ver|**'kürzen** *v/t* (*no -ge-*, *h*) shorten; reduce; ~**'krümmt** *adj* crooked; ~**'laden** *v/t* (*irr*, **laden**, *no -ge-*, *h*) load (**auf** *acc* onto; **in** *acc* into)

Verlag [fɛɐ'la:k] *m* (*-[e]s*; *-e* [fɛɐ'la:gə]) publishing house *or* company, publisher(s)

ver'lagern *v/t and v/refl* (*no -ge-*, *h*) shift (**auf** *acc* to)

ver'langen *v/t* (*no -ge-*, *h*) ask for; demand; claim; charge; take, call for; **Ver'langen** *n* (*-s*; *-*) desire (**nach** for); longing (for), yearning (for); **auf** ~ by request; ECON on demand

verlängern [fɛɐ'lɛŋɐn] *v/t* (*no -ge-*, *h*) lengthen, make longer; prolong, extend (*a.* ECON); **Verlängerung** [fɛɐ-'lɛŋərʊŋ] *f* (*-*; *-en*) lengthening; prolongation, extension; SPORT overtime, *Br* extra time

ver'langsamen *v/t and v/refl* (*no -ge-*, *h*) slacken, slow down (*both a. fig*)

ver'lassen (*irr*, **lassen**, *no -ge-*, *h*) **1.** *v/t* leave; abandon, desert **2.** *v/refl*: **sich** ~ **auf** (*acc*) rely *or* depend on

verlässlich [fɛɐ'lɛslɪç] *adj* reliable, dependable

Ver'lauf *m* course; **ver'laufen** (*irr*, **laufen**, *no -ge-*) **1.** *v/i* (*sein*) run; go; end (up) **2.** *v/refl* (*h*) get lost, lose one's way

ver'leben *v/t* (*no -ge-*, *h*) spend; have

ver'legen[1] *v/t* (*no -ge-*, *h*) move; mislay; TECH lay; put off, postpone; publish

ver'legen[2] *adj* embarrassed

Ver'legenheit *f* (*-*; *-en*) (*no pl*) embar-

rassment; embarrassing situation

Verleger [fɛɐ'le:gɐ] *m* (*-s*; *-*), **Ver-'legerin** *f* (*-*; *-nen*) publisher

Verleih [fɛɐ'lai] *m* (*-[e]s*; *-e*) (*no pl*) hire, rental; *film*: distributor(s)

ver'leihen *v/t* (*irr*, **leihen**, *no -ge-*, *h*) lend, loan; MOT *etc* rent (*Br* hire) out; award (*prize etc*); grant (*privilege etc*); **Ver'leihung** *f* (*-*; *-en*) award(ing), presentation; grant(ing)

ver'leiten *v/t* (*no -ge-*, *h*) **j-n zu et.** ~ make s.o. do s.th., lead s.o. to do s.th.

ver'lernen *v/t* (*no -ge-*, *h*) forget

ver'lesen (*irr*, **lesen**, *no -ge-*, *h*) **1.** *v/t* read (*or* call) out **2.** *v/refl* make a slip (in reading); misread *s.th.*

verletzen [fɛɐ'lɛtsən] *v/t* (*no -ge-*, *h*) hurt, injure, *fig a.* offend; **sich** ~ hurt o.s., get hurt; ~**d** *adj* offensive

Ver'letzte *m, f* (*-n*; *-n*) injured person; *pl* the injured; **Ver'letzung** *f* (*-*; *-en*) injury, *esp pl a.* hurt; JUR violation

ver'leugnen *v/t* (*no -ge-*, *h*) deny; renounce

verleumden [fɛɐ'lɔymdən] *v/t* (*no -ge-*, *h*) defame; JUR slander, libel; ~**'leumderisch** *adj* JUR slanderous, libel-(l)ous; **Ver'leumdung** *f* (*-*; *-en*) JUR slander; libel

ver'lieben *v/refl* (*no -ge-*, *h*) fall in love (**in** *acc* with); **verliebt** [fɛɐ'li:pt] *adj* in love (**in** *acc* with); amorous (*look etc*); **Ver'liebte** *m, f* (*-n*; *-n*) lover

verlieren [fɛɐ'li:rən] *v/t and v/i* (*irr*, *no -ge-*, *h*) lose; **Ver'lierer(in)** (*-s*; *-/-*; *-nen*) loser

ver'loben *v/refl* (*no -ge-*, *h*) get engaged (**mit** to); **Verlobte** [fɛɐ'lo:ptə] **1.** *m* (*-n*; *-n*) fiancé **2.** *f* (*-n*; *-n*) fiancée; **Ver-'lobung** *f* (*-*; *-en*) engagement

ver'locken *v/t* (*no -ge-*, *h*) tempt; ~**d** *adj* tempting

Ver'lockung *f* (*-*; *-en*) temptation

verlogen [fɛɐ'lo:gən] *adj* untruthful, lying

verlor [fɛɐ'lo:ɐ] *pret of* **verlieren**

verloren [fɛɐ'lo:rən] **1.** *pp of* **verlieren** **2.** *adj* lost; wasted; ~ **gehen** be *or* get lost; **ver'lorengehen** *v/i* (*irr*, **gehen**, *sep*, *-ge-*, *sein*) → **verloren**

ver'losen *v/t* (*no -ge-*, *h*) raffle (off); **Ver'losung** *f* (*-*; *-en*) raffle

Verlust [fɛɐ'lʊst] *m* (*-[e]s*; *-e*) loss (*a. fig*); *pl esp* MIL casualties

ver'machen v/t (no -ge-, h) leave, will

Vermächtnis [fɛɐˈmɛçtnɪs] n (-ses; -se) legacy (a. fig)

ver'markten v/t (no -ge-, h) market, merchandize; **Ver'marktung** f (-; -en) marketing, merchandizing

ver'mehren v/t and v/refl increase (**um** by), multiply (by) (a. BIOL); BIOL reproduce, esp ZO a. breed; **Ver'mehrung** f (-; -en) increase; BIOL reproduction

vermeidbar [fɛɐˈmaitbaːɐ] adj avoidable; **ver'meiden** v/t (irr, **meiden**, no -ge-, h) avoid

vermeintlich [fɛɐˈmaintɪç] adj supposed, alleged

ver'mengen v/t (no -ge-, h) mix, mingle, blend

Vermerk [fɛɐˈmɛrk] m (-[e]s; -e) note

ver'merken v/t (no -ge-, h) make a note of

ver'messen[1] v/t (irr, **messen**, no -ge-, h) measure; survey

ver'messen[2] adj presumptuous

Ver'messung f (-; -en) measuring; survey(ing)

ver'mieten v/t (no -ge-, h) let, rent, lease (out); rent (Br hire) out (cars etc); **zu ~** for rent, Br to let, for hire

Ver'mieter m (-s; -) landlord

Ver'mieterin f (-; -nen) landlady

Ver'mietung f (-; -en) letting, renting

ver'mischen v/t and v/refl (no -ge-, h) mix, mingle, blend (**mit** with); **ver-'mischt** adj mixed; miscellaneous

vermissen [fɛɐˈmɪsən] v/t (no -ge-, h) miss; **ver'misst** adj missing; **die Ver-missten** pl the missing

ver'mitteln (no -ge-, h) **1.** v/t arrange; give, convey (impression etc); **j-m et. ~** get or find s.o. s.th. **2.** v/i mediate (**zwischen** between); **Ver'mittler** m (-s; -) mediator, go-between; ECON agent, broker; **Ver'mittlung** f (-; -en) mediation; arrangement; agency, office; (telephone) exchange; operator

ver'modern v/i (no -ge-, sein) rot, mo(u)lder

Ver'mögen n (-s; -) fortune, property, possessions; ECON assets

ver'mögend adj well-to-do, well-off

vermummen [fɛɐˈmʊmən] v/refl (no -ge-, h) mask o.s., disguise o.s.

vermuten [fɛɐˈmuːtən] v/t (no -ge-, h) suppose, expect, think, guess; **ver-**

'mutlich adv probably; **Ver'mutung** f (-; -en) supposition; speculation

vernachlässigen [fɛɐˈnaːxlɛsɪɡən] v/t (no -ge-, h), **Ver'nachlässigung** f (-; -en) neglect

ver'narben v/i (no -ge-, sein) scar over; fig heal

ver'narrt adj: **~ in** (acc) mad or crazy about

ver'nehmen v/t (irr, **nehmen**, no -ge-, h) JUR question, interrogate

ver'nehmlich adj clear, distinct

Ver'nehmung f (-; -en) JUR interrogation, examination

ver'neigen v/refl (no -ge-, h), **Ver-'neigung** f (-; -en) bow (**vor** dat to) (a. fig)

ver'neinen (no -ge-, h) **1.** v/t deny **2.** v/i say no, answer in the negative; **~d** adj negative

Ver'neinung f (-; -en) denial, negative (a. LING)

ver'nichten v/t (no -ge-, h) destroy; **~d** adj devastating (a. fig); crushing

Ver'nichtung f (-; -en) destruction; extermination

Vernunft [fɛɐˈnʊnft] f (-; no pl) reason; **~ annehmen** listen to reason; **j-n zur ~ bringen** bring s.o. to reason

vernünftig [fɛɐˈnʏnftɪç] adj sensible, reasonable (a. ECON); F decent

ver'öden v/i (no -ge-, sein) become deserted

ver'öffentlichen v/t (no -ge-, h) publish; **Ver'öffentlichung** f (-; -en) publication

ver'ordnen v/t (no -ge-, h) order, MED a. prescribe (**gegen** for); **Ver'ordnung** f (-; -en) order; MED prescription

ver'pachten v/t (no -ge-, h) lease

Ver'pächter m lessor

ver'packen v/t (no -ge-, h) pack (up); TECH package; wrap up

Ver'packung f (-; -en) pack(ag)ing; wrapping; **Ver'packungsmüll** m superfluous packaging

ver'|passen v/t (no -ge-, h) miss; **~-'patzen** F v/t (no -ge-, h) mess up, spoil; **~pesten** [fɛɐˈpɛstən] v/t (no -ge-, h) pollute, foul, contaminate; stink up (Br out); **~'petzen** F v/t (no -ge-, h) **j-n ~** tell on s.o. (**bei** to); **~'pfänden** v/t (no -ge-, h) pawn; fig pledge

ver'pflanzen v/t (no -ge-, h), **Ver-'pflanzung** f (-; -en) transplant (a. MED)

ver'pflegen v/t (no -ge-, h) feed

Ver'pflegung f (-; -en) food

ver'pflichten v/t (no -ge-, h) oblige; engage; *sich ~, et. zu tun* undertake (ECON agree) to do s.th.; **ver'pflichtet** adj: *~ sein* (*sich ~ fühlen*) *et. zu tun* be (feel) obliged to do s.th.; **Ver'pflichtung** f (-; -en) obligation; duty; ECON, JUR liability; engagement, commitment

ver'pfuschen F v/t (no -ge-, h) bungle, botch

ver'plappern v/refl (no -ge-, h) blab

verpönt [fɛɛ'pøːnt] adj taboo

ver'prügeln F v/t (no -ge-, h) beat s.o. up

Ver'putz m (-es; no pl), **ver'putzen** v/t (no -ge-, h) ARCH plaster

verquollen [fɛɛ'kvɔlən] adj face etc: puffy, swollen; wood: warped

Verrat [fɛɛ'raːt] m (-[e]s; no pl) betrayal (*an dat* of); treachery (to); JUR treason (to); **ver'raten** v/t (irr, *raten*, no -ge-, h) betray, give away (*both a. fig*); *sich ~* betray o.s., give o.s. away

Verräter [fɛɛ'rɛːtɐ] m (-s; -), **Ver'räterin** f (-; -nen) traitor

verräterisch [fɛɛ'rɛːtərɪʃ] adj treacherous; fig telltale

ver'rechnen (no -ge-, h) **1.** v/t offset (*mit* against); **2.** v/refl miscalculate, make a mistake (*a. fig*); *sich um zwei Euro ~* be two euros out

Ver'rechnungsscheck m ECON voucher check, Br crossed cheque

ver'regnet adj rainy

ver'reisen v/i (no -ge-, sein) go away (*geschäftlich* on business); **ver'reist** adj away (*geschäftlich* on business)

verrenken [fɛɛ'rɛŋkən] v/t (no -ge-, h) MED dislocate, luxate; *sich et. ~* MED dislocate s.th.; *sich den Hals ~* crane one's neck; **Ver'renkung** f (-; -en) MED dislocation, luxation

ver'richten v/t (no -ge-, h) do, perform, carry out

ver'riegeln v/t (no -ge-, h) bolt, bar

verringern [fɛɛ'rɪŋɐn] v/t (no -ge-, h) decrease, lessen (*both a. sich ~*), reduce, cut down; **Ver'ringerung** f (-; -en) reduction, decrease

ver'rosten v/t (no -ge-, sein) rust, get rusty (*a. fig*)

verrotten [fɛɛ'rɔtən] v/i (no -ge-, sein) rot; **ver'rottet** adj rotten

ver'rücken v/t (no -ge-, h) move, shift

ver'rückt adj mad, crazy (*both a. fig nach* about); *wie ~* like mad; *~ werden* go mad, go crazy; *j-n ~ machen* drive s.o. mad; **Ver'rückte** m, f (-n; -n) madman (madwoman), lunatic, maniac (*all a. F*); **Ver'rücktheit** f (-; -en) (no pl) madness, craziness; crazy thing

Ver'ruf m: *in ~ bringen* bring discredit (up)on; *in ~ kommen* get into discredit

ver'rufen adj disreputable, notorious

ver'rutschen v/i (no -ge-, sein) slip, get out of place

Vers [fɛrs] m (-es; -e ['fɛrzə]) verse; line

ver'sagen (no -ge-, h) **1.** v/i fail (*a.* MED, MOT etc *a.* break down; gun etc: misfire **2.** v/t deny, refuse; **Ver'sagen** n (-s; no pl) failure; **Ver'sager** m (-s; -) failure

ver'salzen v/t (no -ge-, h) oversalt

ver'sammeln v/t (no -ge-, h) gather, assemble; *sich ~ a.* meet; **Ver'sammlung** f (-; -en) assembly, meeting

Versand [fɛɛ'zant] m (-[e]s; no pl) dispatch, shipment; *~... in cpds ...haus, ...katalog etc:* mail-order ...

ver'säumen v/t (no -ge-, h) miss; *~ et. zu tun* fail to do s.th.; **Versäumnis** [fɛɛ'zɔymnɪs] n (-ses; -se) omission

ver'schaffen v/t (no -ge-, h) get, find; *sich ~ a.* obtain; *~schämt* adj bashful; *~schanzen* v/refl (no -ge-, h) entrench o.s. (*a. fig hinter* behind); *~schärfen* v/t (no -ge-, h) aggravate; tighten up; increase; *sich ~* get worse; *~schenken* v/t (no -ge-, h) give away (*a. fig*); *~'scherzen* v/t (no -ge-, h) forfeit; *~'scheuchen* v/t (no -ge-, h) chase away (*a. fig*); *~'schicken* v/t (no -ge-, h) send off, esp ECON *a.* dispatch

ver'schieben v/t (irr, *schieben*, no -ge-, h) move, shift (*a. sich ~*); postpone, put off; **Ver'schiebung** f (-; -en) shift(ing); postponement

verschieden [fɛɛ'ʃiːdən] adj different (*von* from); *~e ... pl* various ..., several...; *~artig* adj different; various

Ver'schiedenheit f (-; -en) difference

ver'schiedentlich adv repeatedly

ver'schiffen v/t (no -ge-, h) ship

Ver'schiffung f (-; -en) shipment

ver'schimmeln v/i (no -ge-, sein) get mo(u)ldy; **ver'schlafen** (irr, *schlafen*, no -ge-, h) **1.** v/i oversleep **2.** v/t sleep through **3.** adj sleepy (*a. fig*)

Ver'schlag *m* shed

ver'schlagen[1] *v/t* (*irr, schlagen, no -ge-, h*) **j-m den Atem ~** take s.o.'s breath away; **j-m die Sprache ~** leave s.o. speechless; **es hat ihn nach X ~** he ended up in X

ver'schlagen[2] *adj* sly, cunning

verschlechtern [fɛɐˈʃlɛçtɐn] *v/t and v/refl* (*no -ge-, h*) make (*refl* get) worse, worsen, deteriorate

Ver'schlechterung *f* (-; *-en*) deterioration; change for the worse

ver'schleiern *v/t* (*no -ge-, h*) veil (*a. fig*)

Verschleiß [fɛɐˈʃlais] *m* (*-es; no pl*) wear (and tear); **ver'schleißen** *v/t* (*irr, no -ge-, h*) wear out

ver|'schleppen *v/t* (*no -ge-, h*) carry off; POL displace; draw out, delay; MED neglect; **~'schleudern** *v/t* (*no -ge-, h*) waste; ECON sell dirt cheap; **~ 'schließen** *v/t* (*irr, schließen, no -ge-, h*) close (*a. fig one's eyes*); lock (up)

ver'schlingen *v/t* (*irr, schlingen, no -ge-, h*) devour (*a. fig*); gulp (down)

verschliss [fɛɐˈʃlis] *pret of* **verschleißen**; **verschlissen** [fɛɐˈʃlisən] *pp of* **verschleißen**

verschlossen [fɛɐˈʃlɔsən] *adj* closed; *fig* aloof, reserved; **Ver'schlossenheit** *f* (-; *no pl*) aloofness

ver'schlucken (*no -ge-, h*) **1.** *v/t* swallow (*fig up*); **2.** *v/refl* choke; **ich habe mich verschluckt** it went down the wrong way

Ver'schluss *m* fastener; clasp; catch; lock; cover, lid; cap, top; PHOT shutter; **unter ~** under lock and key

ver'schlüsseln *v/t* (*no -ge-, h*) (en)code, (en)cipher

verschmähen [fɛɐˈʃmɛːən] *v/t* (*no -ge-, h*) disdain, scorn

ver'schmelzen *v/i* (*irr, schmelzen, no -ge-, sein*) *and v/t* (*h*) merge, fuse (*both a.* ECON, POL *etc*), melt; **Ver-'schmelzung** *f* (-; *-en*) fusion (*a. fig*)

ver|'schmerzen *v/t* (*no -ge-, h*) get over s.th.; **~'schmieren** *v/t* (*no -ge-, h*) smear, smudge

verschmitzt [fɛɐˈʃmɪtst] *adj* mischievous

ver|'schmutzen (*no -ge-*) **1.** *v/t* (*h*) soil, dirty; pollute **2.** *v/i* (*sein*) get dirty; get polluted; **~'schnaufen** F *v/i and v/refl*

(*no -ge-, h*) stop for breath

ver'schneit *adj* snow-covered, snowy

Ver'schnitt *m* blend; waste

verschnupft [fɛɐˈʃnʊpft] *adj*: **~ sein** MED have a cold; F be in a huff

ver'schnüren *v/t* (*no -ge-, h*) tie up

verschollen [fɛɐˈʃɔlən] *adj* missing; JUR presumed dead

ver'schonen *v/t* (*no -ge-, h*) spare; **j-n mit et. ~** spare s.o. s.th.

verschönern [fɛɐˈʃøːnɐn] *v/t* (*no -ge-, h*) embellish; **Verschönerung** [fɛɐ-ˈʃøːnərʊŋ] *f* (-; *-en*) embellishment

verschossen [fɛɐˈʃɔsən] *adj* faded; F **~ sein in** (*acc*) have a crush on

verschränken [fɛɐˈʃrɛŋkən] *v/t* (*no -ge-, h*) fold; cross (*one's legs*)

ver'schreiben (*irr, schreiben, no -ge-, h*) **1.** *v/t* MED prescribe (**gegen** for); **2.** *v/refl* make a slip of the pen

ver'schreibungspflichtig *adj* PHARM available on prescription only

verschroben [fɛɐˈʃroːbən] *adj* eccentric, odd

ver'schrotten *v/t* (*no -ge-, h*) scrap

ver'schüchtert *adj* intimidated

ver'schulden *v/t* (*no -ge-, h*) be responsible for, cause, be the cause of; **sich ~** get into debt; **ver'schuldet** *adj* in debt

ver'schütten *v/t* (*no -ge-, h*) spill; bury s.o. (alive)

verschwägert [fɛɐˈʃvɛːgɐt] *adj* related by marriage

ver'schweigen *v/t* (*irr, schweigen, no -ge-, h*) keep s.th. a secret, hide

verschwenden [fɛɐˈʃvɛndən] *v/t* (*no -ge-, h*) waste; **Verschwender** [fɛɐ-ˈʃvɛndɐ] *m* (-s; -) spendthrift; **ver-schwenderisch** [fɛɐˈʃvɛndərɪʃ] *adj* wasteful, extravagant; lavish; **Ver-'schwendung** *f* (-; *-en*) waste

verschwiegen [fɛɐˈʃviːgən] *adj* discreet; hidden; secret; **Ver-'schwiegenheit** *f* (-; *no pl*) secrecy, discretion

ver'schwimmen *v/i* (*irr, schwimmen, no -ge-, sein*) become blurred

ver'schwinden *v/i* (*irr, schwinden, no -ge-, sein*) disappear, vanish; F **verschwinde!** beat it!; **Ver'schwinden** *n* (-s; *no pl*) disappearance

verschwommen [fɛɐˈʃvɔmən] *adj* blurred (*a.* PHOT), *fig a.* vague, hazy

ver'schwören *v/refl* (*irr, schwören, no*

-ge-, h) conspire, plot; **Verschwörer** [fɛɐˈʃvøːrɐ] m (-s; -) conspirator; **Ver-** **'schwörung** f (-; -en) conspiracy, plot

verschwunden [fɛɐˈʃvʊndən] adj missing

ver'sehen (irr, **sehen**, no -ge-, h) **1.** v/t hold (an office etc); ~ **mit** provide with **2.** v/refl make a mistake; **Ver'sehen** n (-s; -) mistake, error; **aus** ~ → **versehentlich** [fɛɐˈzeːəntlɪç] adv by mistake, unintentionally

Versehrte [fɛɐˈzeːɐtə] m, f (-n; -n) disabled person

ver|'sengen v/t (no -ge-, h) singe, scorch; ~**'senken** v/t (no -ge-, h) sink; **sich** ~ **in** (acc) become absorbed in

versessen [fɛɐˈzɛsən] adj: ~ **auf** (acc) keen on, mad or crazy about

ver'setzen v/t (no -ge-, h) move, shift; transfer; PED promote, Br move s.o. up; give (s.o. a kick etc); pawn; AGR transplant; F **j-n** ~ stand s.o. up; **j-n in die Lage** ~ **zu** inf put s.o. in a position to inf, enable s.o. to inf; **sich in j-s Lage** ~ put o.s. in s.o.'s place; **Ver-** **'setzung** f (-; -en) transfer; PED promotion

ver'seuchen v/t (no -ge-, h) contaminate; **Ver'seuchung** f (-; -en) contamination

ver'sichern v/t (no -ge-, h) ECON insure (**bei** with); assure (**j-m et.** s.o. s.th.), assert; **sich** ~ insure o.s.; make sure (**dass** that); **Ver'sicherte** m, f (-n; -n) the insured; **Ver'sicherung** f (-; -en) insurance; assurance, assertion

Ver'sicherungs|gesellschaft f insurance company; ~**po.lice** f, ~**schein** m insurance policy

ver|'sickern v/i (no -ge-, sein) trickle away; ~**'siegeln** v/t (no -ge-, h) seal; ~**'siegen** v/i (no -ge-, sein) dry up, run dry; ~**'silbern** v/t (no -ge-, h) silver- -plate; F turn s.th. into cash; ~**'sinken** v/i (irr, **sinken**, no -ge-, sein) sink; → **versunken**

Version [vɛrˈzjoːn] f (-; -en) version

'Versmaß n meter, Br metre

versöhnen [fɛɐˈzøːnən] v/t (no -ge-, h) reconcile; **sich** (**wieder**) ~ make it up (**mit** with); **ver'söhnlich** adj conciliatory; **Ver'söhnung** f (-; -en) reconciliation; esp POL appeasement

ver'sorgen v/t (no -ge-, h) provide (**mit** with), supply (with); support; take care of, look after; **Ver'sorgung** f (-; no pl) supply (**mit** with); support; care

ver'späten v/refl (no -ge-, h) be late; **ver'spätet** adj belated, late, RAIL etc a. delayed; **Ver'spätung** f (-; -en) being or coming late, RAIL etc delay; **20 Minu-** **ten** ~ **haben** be 20 minutes late

ver'speisen v/t (no -ge-, h) eat (up)

ver'sperren v/t (no -ge-, h) bar, block (up), obstruct (a. view); lock

ver'spielen v/t (no -ge-, h) lose; **ver-** **'spielt** adj playful

ver'spotten v/t (no -ge-, h) make fun of, ridicule

ver'sprechen (irr, **sprechen**, no -ge-, h) **1.** v/t promise (a. fig); **sich zu viel** ~ (**von**) expect too much (of) **2.** v/refl make a mistake or slip; **Ver'sprechen** n (-s; -) promise; **ein** ~ **geben** (**halten**, **brechen**) make (keep, break) a promise; **Ver'sprecher** F m (-s; -) slip (of the tongue)

ver'staatlichen v/t (no -ge-, h) ECON nationalize; **Ver'staatlichung** f (-; -en) ECON nationalization

Verstädterung [fɛɐˈʃtɛːtərʊŋ] f (-; -en) urbanization

Verstand [fɛɐˈʃtant] m (-[e]s; no pl) mind, intellect; reason, (common) sense; intelligence, brains; **nicht bei** ~ out of one's mind, not in one's right mind; **den** ~ **verlieren** go out of one's mind; **verstandesmäßig** [fɛɐˈʃtandəsmɛːsɪç] adj rational

ver'ständig adj reasonable, sensible

verständigen [fɛɐˈʃtɛndɪɡən] v/t (no -ge-, h) inform (**von** of), notify (of); call (doctor, police etc); **sich** ~ communicate; come to an agreement (**über** acc on); **Ver'ständigung** f (-; no pl) communication (a. TEL); agreement

verständlich [fɛɐˈʃtɛntlɪç] adj audible; intelligible; comprehensible; understandable; **schwer** (**leicht**) ~ difficult (easy) to understand; **j-m et.** ~ **machen** make s.th. clear to s.o.; **sich** ~ **machen** make o.s. understood

Verständnis [fɛɐˈʃtɛntnɪs] n (-ses; no pl) comprehension, understanding; sympathy; (**viel**) ~ **haben** be (very) understanding; ~ **haben für** understand; appreciate

ver'ständnislos adj uncomprehending; blank (*look etc*)

ver'ständnisvoll *adj* understanding, sympathetic; knowing (*look etc*)

ver'stärken *v/t* (*no -ge-, h*) reinforce (*a.* TECH, MIL); strengthen (*a.* TECH); *radio*, PHYS amplify; intensify; **Ver'stärker** *m* (*-s; -*) amplifier; **Ver'stärkung** *f* (*-; -en*) strengthening; reinforcement(s MIL); amplification; intensification

ver'stauben *v/i* (*no -ge-, sein*) get dusty

verstauchen [fɛɐˈʃtauxən] *v/t* (*no -ge-, h*), **Ver'stauchung** *f* (*-; -en*) MED sprain

ver'stauen *v/t* (*no -ge-, h*) stow away

Versteck [fɛɐˈʃtɛk] *n* (*-[e]s; -e*) hiding place, hideout, hideaway

ver'stecken *v/t and v/refl* (*no -ge-, h*) hide (*a. fig*); **Verstecken spielen** play (at) hide-and-seek

ver'stehen (*irr*, **stehen**, *no -ge-, h*) understand, F get; catch; see; realize; know; *es ~ zu inf* know how to *inf*; *zu ~ geben* give s.o. to understand, suggest; *ich verstehe!* I see!; *falsch ~* misunderstand; *was ~ Sie unter …?* what do you mean *or* understand by …?; *sich (gut) ~* get along (well) (*mit* with); *es versteht sich von selbst* it goes without saying

ver'steifen (*no -ge-, h*) **1.** *v/t* stiffen (*a. sich ~*); TECH strut, brace **2.** *v/refl: sich auf et. ~* insist on (doing) s.th.

ver'steigern *v/t* (*no -ge-, h*) auction off

Ver'steigerung *f* (*-; -en*) auction (sale)

ver'steinern *v/i* (*no -ge-, sein*) petrify (*a. fig*)

ver'stellbar *adj* adjustable

ver'stellen *v/t* (*no -ge-, h*) block; move; set *s.th.* wrong *or* the wrong way; TECH adjust, regulate; disguise (*one's voice etc*); *sich ~* pretend

Ver'stellung *f* (*-; no pl*) disguise, make--believe, (false) show

ver'steuern *v/t* (*no -ge-, h*) pay duty *or* tax on

verstiegen [fɛɐˈʃtiːɡən] *adj* high-flown

ver'stimmen *v/t* (*no -ge-, h*) MUS put out of tune; *fig* annoy; **ver'stimmt** *adj* annoyed; MUS out of tune; MED upset; **Ver'stimmung** *f* (*-; -en*) annoyance

ver'stockt [fɛɐˈʃtɔkt] *adj* stubborn, obstinate; **~stohlen** [fɛɐˈʃtoːlən] *adj* furtive, stealthy

ver'stopfen *v/t* (*no -ge-, h*) plug (up); block, jam; MED constipate; **ver'stopft**

adj MED constipated; **Ver'stopfung** *f* (*-; -en*) block(age); MED constipation

verstorben [fɛɐˈʃtɔrbən] *adj* late, deceased; **Ver'storbene** *m, f* (*-n; -n*) the deceased; *die ~n* the deceased

verstört [fɛɐˈʃtøːɐt] *adj* upset; distracted; wild (*look etc*)

Ver'stoß *m* offense, *Br* offence (*gegen* against), violation (of)

ver'stoßen (*irr*, **stoßen**, *no -ge-, h*) **1.** *v/t* expel (*aus* from); disown **2.** *v/i: ~ gegen* offend against, violate

ver'strahlt *adj* (radioactively) contaminated

ver'streichen (*irr*, **streichen**, *no -ge-*) **1.** *v/i* (*sein*) time: pass, go by; *date*: expire **2.** *v/t* (*h*) spread

ver'streuen *v/t* (*no -ge-, h*) scatter

verstümmeln [fɛɐˈʃtyməln] *v/t* (*no -ge-, h*) mutilate (*a. fig*); **Ver'stümmelung** *f* (*-; -en*) mutilation (*a. fig*)

ver'stummen *v/i* (*no -ge-, sein*) grow silent; stop; die down

Versuch [fɛɐˈzuːx] *m* (*-[e]s; -e*) attempt, try; trial, test; PHYS experiment; *mit et.* (*j-m*) *e-n ~ machen* give s.th. (s.o.) a try; **ver'suchen** *v/t* (*no -ge-, h*) try, attempt; taste; REL tempt; *es ~* have a try (at it)

Ver'suchs… *in cpds* …*bohrung etc*: test …, trial …; **~ka,ninchen** *n* guinea pig; **~stadium** *n* experimental stage; **~tier** *n* laboratory *or* test animal

ver'suchsweise *adv* by way of trial

Ver'suchung *f* (*-; -en*) temptation; *j-n in ~ führen* tempt s.o.

versunken [fɛɐˈzʊŋkən] *fig adj: ~ in* (*acc*) absorbed *or* lost in

ver'süßen *v/t* (*no -ge-, h*) sweeten

ver'tagen *v/t and v/refl* (*no -ge-, h*) adjourn; **Ver'tagung** *f* (*-; -en*) adjournment

ver'tauschen *v/t* (*no -ge-, h*) exchange (*mit* for)

verteidigen [fɛɐˈtaidɪɡən] *v/t* (*no -ge-, h*) defend (*sich* o.s.); **Verteidiger(in)** [fɛɐˈtaidɪɡɐ (-ɡərɪn)] (*-s; -/-; -nen*) defender, SPORT *a.* back; *fig* advocate; **Ver'teidigung** *f* (*-; -en*) defense, *Br* defence

Ver'teidigungs… *in cpds* …*politik etc*: *mst* defense …, *Br* defence …; **~mi,nister** *m* Secretary of Defense, *Br* Minister of Defence; **~minis,terium**

n Department of Defense, *Br* Ministry of Defence

ver'teilen *v/t* (*no -ge-, h*) distribute; hand out; **Ver'teiler** *m* (*-s;* -) distributor; **Ver'teilung** *f* (*-; -en*) distribution

ver'tiefen *v/t and v/refl* (*no -ge-, h*) deepen (*a. fig*); **sich ~ in** (*acc*) become absorbed in; **Ver'tiefung** *f* (*-; -en*) hollow, depression, dent; *fig* deepening

vertikal [vɛrti'ka:l] *adj*, **Verti'kale** *f* (*-; -n*) vertical

ver'tilgen *v/t* (*no -ge-, h*) exterminate; F consume; **Ver'tilgung** *f* (*-; no pl*) extermination

vertonen [fɛɛ'to:nən] *v/t* (*no -ge-, h*) set to music

Vertrag [fɛɛ'tra:k] *m* (*-[e]s; Verträge* [fɛɛ'trɛ:gə]) contract; POL treaty

ver'tragen *v/t* (*irr, tragen, no -ge-, h*) endure, bear, stand; **ich kann ... nicht ~** ... doesn't agree with me; I can't stand ...; **er kann viel ~** he can take a lot; he can hold his drink; F **ich (es) könnte ... ~** I (it) could do with ...; **sich (gut) ~** get along (well) (**mit** with); **sich wieder ~** make it up

ver'traglich *adv* by contract

verträglich [fɛɛ'trɛ:klıç] *adj* easy to get on with; GASTR (easily) digestible

ver'trauen *v/i* (*no -ge-, h*) trust (**auf** *acc* in); **Ver'trauen** *n* (*-s; no pl*) confidence, trust, faith; **im ~** (**gesagt**) between you and me; **wenig ~ erweckend aussehen** inspire little confidence

Ver'trauens|frage *f:* **die ~ stellen** PARL ask for a vote of confidence; **~sache** *f:* **das ist ~** that is a matter of confidence; **~stellung** *f* position of trust

ver'trauensvoll *adj* trustful, trusting

Ver'trauensvotum *n* PARL vote of confidence

ver'trauenswürdig *adj* trustworthy

ver'traulich *adj* confidential; familiar

ver'traut *adj* familiar; close

Ver'traute *m, f* (*-n; -n*) confidant(e *f*)

Ver'trautheit *f* (*-; no pl*) familiarity

ver'treiben *v/t* (*irr, treiben, no -ge-, h*) drive *or* chase away (*a. fig*); pass (*the time*); ECON sell; **~ aus** drive out of; **Ver'treibung** *f* (*-; -en*) expulsion (**aus** from)

ver'treten *v/t* (*irr, treten, no -ge-, h*) substitute for, replace, stand in for; POL, ECON represent, PARL *a.* sit for; JUR

act for *s.o.*; **j-s Sache ~** JUR plead s.o.'s cause; **die Ansicht ~, dass** argue that; **sich den Fuß ~** sprain one's ankle; F **sich die Beine ~** stretch one's legs

Ver'treter *m* (*-s;* -), **Ver'treterin** *f* (*-; -nen*) substitute, deputy; POL, ECON representative, ECON *a.* agent; MED locum

Ver'tretung *f* (*-; -en*) substitution, replacement; substitute, stand-in, *a.* supply teacher; ECON, POL representation

Vertrieb [fɛɛ'tri:p] *m* (*-[e]s; no pl*) ECON sale, distribution

Vertriebene [fɛɛ'tri:bənə] *m, f* (*-n; -n*) POL expellee, refugee

ver'trocknen *v/i* (*no -ge-, sein*) dry up; **~trödeln** F *v/t* (*no -ge-, h*) dawdle away, waste; **~trösten** *v/t* (*no -ge-, h*) put *s.o.* off; **~tuschen** F *v/t* (*no -ge-, h*) cover up; **~übeln** *v/t* (*no -ge-, h*) take amiss; **ich kann es ihr nicht ~** I can't blame her for it; **~üben** *v/t* (*no -ge-, h*) commit

verunglücken [fɛɛ'ʔʊnglʏkən] *v/i* (*no -ge-, sein*) have an accident; *fig* go wrong; **tödlich ~** die in an accident

ver'ursachen *v/t* (*no -ge-, h*) cause

ver'urteilen *v/t* (*no -ge-, h*) condemn (**zu** to) (*a. fig*), sentence (to), convict (**wegen** of); **Ver'urteilung** *f* (*-; -en*) condemnation (*a. fig*)

ver'vielfachen *v/t* (*no -ge-, h*) multiply

vervielfältigen [fɛɛ'fi:lfɛltıgən] *v/t* (*no -ge-, h*) copy, duplicate; **Ver'vielfältigung** *f* (*-; -en*) duplication; copy

ver'vollkommnen *v/t* (*no -ge-, h*) perfect; improve

vervollständigen [fɛɛ'fɔlʃtɛndıgən] *v/t* (*no -ge-, h*) complete

ver'|wachsen *adj* MED deformed, crippled; *fig* **~ mit** deeply rooted in, bound up with; **~'wackelt** F *adj* PHOT blurred

ver'wahren *v/t* (*no -ge-, h*) keep (in a safe place); **sich ~ gegen** protest against

verwahrlost [fɛɛ'va:ɛlo:st] *adj* uncared-for, neglected

ver'walten *v/t* (*no -ge-, h*) manage, *esp* POL *a.* administer; **Ver'walter** *m* (*-s;* -) manager; administrator; **Ver'waltung** *f* (*-; -en*) administration, management; **Ver'waltungs...** *in cpds* ...*gericht*, ...*kosten etc*: administrative ...

ver'wandeln v/t (no -ge-, h) change, turn (both a. **sich ~**), esp PHYS, CHEM a. transform, convert (all: **in** acc into); **Ver'wandlung** f (-; -en) change, transformation; conversion

verwandt [fɛɐ'vant] adj related (**mit** to); **Ver'wandte** m, f (-n; -n) relative; (**alle**) **m-e ~n** (all) my relatives or relations; **der nächste ~** the next of kin; **Ver'wandtschaft** f (-; -en) relationship; (no pl) relations

ver'warnen v/t (no -ge-, h) caution; SPORT book; **Ver'warnung** f (-; -en) Br caution; SPORT booking

ver'waschen adj washed-out

ver'wässern v/t (no -ge-, h) water down (a. fig)

ver'wechseln v/t (no -ge-, h) confuse (**mit** with), mix up (with), mistake (for); **Ver'wechs(e)lung** f (-; -en) mistake, F mix-up

ver'wegen adj daring, bold

Ver'wegenheit f (-; no pl) boldness, daring

ver'weichlicht adj soft

ver'weigern v/t (no -ge-, h) refuse; disobey; **Ver'weigerung** f (-; -en) denial, refusal

ver'weilen v/i (no -ge-, h) stay; fig rest

Verweis [fɛɐ'vais] m (-es; -e) reprimand, reproof; reference (**auf** acc to)

ver'weisen v/t (irr, weisen, no -ge-, h) refer (**auf** acc, **an** acc to); expel (gen from)

ver'welken v/i (no -ge-, sein) wither, fig a. fade

ver'wenden v/t (no -ge-, h) use; spend (time etc) (**auf** acc on); **Ver'wendung** f (-; -en) use; **keine ~ haben für** have no use for

ver'werfen v/t (irr, werfen, no -ge-, h) drop, give up; reject

ver'werten v/t (no -ge-, h) use, make use of

verwesen [fɛɐ'veːzən] v/i (no -ge-, sein), **Ver'wesung** f (-; no pl) decay

ver'wickeln fig v/t (no -ge-, h) involve; **sich ~ in** (acc) get caught in; **ver-'wickelt** fig adj complicated; **~ sein** (**werden**) **in** (acc) be (get) involved in; **Ver'wicklung** fig f (-; -en) involvement; complication

ver'wildern v/i (no -ge-, sein) grow (or run) wild; **ver'wildert** adj wild (a.

fig), overgrown

ver'winden v/t (irr, winden, no -ge-, h) get over s.th.

ver'wirklichen v/t (no -ge-, h) realize; **sich ~** come true; **sich selbst ~** fulfil(l) o.s.; **Ver'wirklichung** f (-; -en) realization

ver'wirren v/t (no -ge-, h) tangle (up); fig confuse; **ver'wirrt** fig adj confused; **Ver'wirrung** fig f (-; -en) confusion

ver'wischen v/t (no -ge-, h) blur (a. fig); cover (track etc)

verwittern [fɛɐ'vɪtən] v/i (no -ge-, sein) GEOL weather

ver'witwet adj widowed

verwöhnen [fɛɐ'vøːnən] v/t (no -ge-, h) spoil; **ver'wöhnt** adj spoilt

verworren [fɛɐ'vɔrən] adj confused, muddled; complicated

verwundbar [fɛɐ'vʊntbaːɐ] adj vulnerable (a. fig); **ver'wunden** v/t (no -ge-, h) wound

ver'wunderlich adj surprising

Verwunderung [fɛɐ'vʊndəruŋ] f (-; no pl) (**zu m-r** etc ~ to my etc) surprise

Ver'wundete m, f (-n; -n) wounded (person), casualty

Ver'wundung f (-; -en) wound, injury

ver'wünschen v/t (no -ge-, h), **Ver-'wünschung** f (-; -en) curse

ver'wüsten v/t (no -ge-, h) lay waste, devastate, ravage; **Ver'wüstung** f (-; -en) devastation, ravage

ver'zählen v/refl (no -ge-, h) count wrong; **~'zaubern** v/t (no -ge-, h) enchant, fig a. charm; **~ in** (acc) turn into; **~'zehren** v/t (no -ge-, h) consume (a. fig)

ver'zeichnen v/t (no -ge-, h) record, keep a record of, list; fig achieve; suffer; **Ver'zeichnis** n (-ses; -se) list, catalog(ue); record, register; index

verzeihen [fɛɐ'tsaiən] v/t and v/i (irr, no -ge-, h) forgive s.o.; pardon, excuse s.th.; **ver'zeihlich** adj pardonable; **Ver-'zeihung** f (-; no pl) pardon; (**j-n**) **um ~ bitten** apologize (to s.o.); **~!** (I'm) sorry!; excuse me!

ver'zerren v/t (no -ge-, h) distort (a. fig); **sich ~** become distorted

Ver'zerrung f (-; -en) distortion

Verzicht [fɛɐ'tsɪçt] m (-[e]s; -e) renunciation (**auf** acc of); mst giving up, doing without etc

ver'zichten v/i (no -ge-, h) **~ auf** (acc) do without; give up; renounce (a. JUR)

verzieh [fɛɐ'tsiː] pret of **verzeihen**

ver'ziehen (irr, **ziehen**, no -ge-) **1.** v/i (sein) move (**nach** to); **2.** v/t (h) spoil; **das Gesicht ~** make a face; **sich ~** wood: warp; storm etc: pass (over); F disappear **3.** pp of **verzeihen**

ver'zieren v/t (no -ge-, h) decorate

Ver'zierung f (-; -en) decoration, ornament

ver'zinsen v/t (no -ge-, h) pay interest on; **sich ~** yield interest

Ver'zinsung f (-; -en) interest

ver'zögern v/t (no -ge-, h) delay; **sich ~** be delayed; **Ver'zögerung** f (-; -en) delay

ver'zollen v/t (no -ge-, h) pay duty on; **et. (nichts) zu ~ haben** have s.th. (nothing) to declare

verzückt [fɛɐ'tsʏkt] adj ecstatic; **Ver'zückung** f (-; -en) ecstasy; **in ~ geraten** go into ecstasies or raptures (**wegen**, **über** acc over)

Verzug [fɛɐ'tsuːk] m (-[e]s; no pl) delay; ECON default

ver'zweifeln v/i (no -ge-, h) despair (**an** dat of); **ver'zweifelt** adj desperate, despairing

Ver'zweiflung f (-; no pl) despair; **j-n zur ~ bringen** drive s.o. to despair

verzweigen [fɛɐ'tsvaigən] v/refl (no -ge-, h) branch

verzwickt [fɛɐ'tsvɪkt] F adj tricky

Veteran [vete'raːn] m (-en; -en) MIL veteran (a. fig)

Veterinär [veteri'nɛːɐ] m (-s; -e), **Veteri'närin** f (-; -nen) veterinarian, Br veterinary surgeon, F vet

Veto ['veːto] n (-s; -s) veto; **(s)ein ~ einlegen gegen** veto

Vetter ['fɛtɐ] m (-s; -n) cousin

'Vetternwirtschaft f (-; no pl) nepotism

vgl. abbr of **vergleiche** cf., confer

VHS abbr of **Volkshochschule** adult education program(me); adult evening classes

Vibration [vibra'tsjoːn] f (-; -en) vibration; **vibrieren** [vi'briːrən] v/i (no -ge-, h) vibrate

Video ['viːdeo] n (-s; -s) video (a. in cpds …aufnahme, …clip, …kamera, …kassette, …recorder etc); **auf ~ aufnehmen** video(tape), tape; **~band** n videotape;

~text m teletext

Videothek [video'teːk] f (-; -en) video (-tape) library; video store (Br shop)

Vieh [fiː] n (-[e]s; no pl) cattle; **20 Stück ~** 20 head of cattle; **~bestand** m livestock; **~händler** m cattle dealer

'viehisch contp adj bestial, brutal

'Vieh|markt m cattle market; **~zucht** f cattle breeding, stockbreeding; **~züchter** m cattle breeder, stockbreeder

viel [fiːl] adj and adv a lot (of), plenty (of), F lots of; **~e** many; **nicht ~** not much; **nicht ~e** not many; **sehr ~** a great deal (of); **sehr ~e** very many, a lot (of); **das ~e Geld** all that money; **ziemlich ~** quite a lot (of); **ziemlich ~e** quite a few; **~ besser** much better; **~ teurer** much more expensive; **e-r zu ~** one too many; **~ zu ~** far too much; **~ zu wenig** not nearly enough; **~ lieber** much rather; **wie ~** how much (pl many); **~ beschäftigt** very busy; **~ sagend** meaningful; **~ versprechend** promising; **'vieldeutig** [-dɔytɪç] adj ambiguous; **vielerlei** ['fiːlɐ'lai] adj all kinds or sorts of; **'vielfach 1.** adj multiple **2.** adv in many cases, (very) often; **'Vielfalt** f (-; no pl) (great) variety (gen of); **'vielfarbig** adj multicolo(u)red

vielleicht [fi'laiçt] adv perhaps, maybe; **~ ist er …** he may or might be …

'vielmals adv: **(ich) danke (Ihnen) ~** thank you very much; **entschuldigen Sie ~** I'm very sorry, I do apologize

viel'mehr cj rather

'viel|sagend adj meaningful; **~seitig** ['fiːlzaitɪç] adj versatile

'Vielseitigkeit f (-; no pl) versatility

'vielversprechend adj promising

vier [fiːɐ] adj four; **zu viert sein** be four; **auf allen ~en** on all fours; **unter ~ Augen** in private, privately

'Vierbeiner [-bainɐ] m (-s; -) zo quadruped, four-legged animal

'vierbeinig adj four-legged

'Viereck n quadrangle, quadrilateral

'viereckig adj quadrangular, square

Vierer ['fiːrɐ] m (-s; -) rowing: four

'vierfach adj fourfold; **~e Ausfertigung** four copies

'vierfüßig ['fiːɐfyːsɪç] adj four-footed

'Vierfüßler ['fiːɐfyːslɐ] m (-s; -) zo quadruped

'vierhändig ['fiːɐhɛndɪç] adj MUS four-handed

'vierjährig ['fiːɐjɛːrɪç] *adj* four-year-old, of four

Vierlinge ['fiːɐlɪŋə] *pl* quadruplets, quads

'viermal *adv* four times

'Vierradantrieb *m* MOT four-wheel drive

'vierseitig ['fiːɐzaitɪç] *adj* MATH quadrilateral

'vierspurig ['fiːɐʃpuːrɪç] *adj* MOT four-lane

'vierstöckig ['fiːɐʃtœkɪç] *adj* four-storied, *Br* four-storey ...

'Viertaktmotor *m* four-stroke engine

vierte ['fiːɐtə] *adj* fourth

Viertel ['fɪrtəl] *n* (-*s*; -) fourth (part); quarter; (*ein*) ~ *vor* (*nach*) (a) quarter to (past); ~**fi,nale** *n* SPORT quarter finals

Vierteljahr *n* three months

'vierteljährlich 1. *adj* quarterly **2.** *adv* every three months, quarterly

vierteln ['fɪrtəln] *v/t* (*ge-*, *h*) quarter

'Viertel|note *f* MUS quarter note, *Br* crotchet; ~**pfund** *n* quarter of a pound

'Viertel'stunde *f* quarter of an hour

viertens ['fiːɐtəns] *adv* fourthly

vierzehn ['fɪrtseːn] *adj* fourteen; ~ *Tage* two weeks, *esp Br a.* a fortnight

'vierzehnte *adj* fourteenth

vierzig ['fɪrtsɪç] *adj* forty

'vierzigste *adj* fortieth

Villa ['vɪla] *f* (-; *Villen*) villa

violett [vio'lɛt] *adj* violet, purple

Violine [vio'liːnə] *f* (-; -*n*) MUS violin

Virtuelle Realität [vɪr'tuɛlə] *f* virtual reality, Cyberspace

virtuos [vɪr'tuoːs] *adj* virtuoso ..., masterly; **Virtuose** [vɪr'tuoːzə] *m* (-*n*; -*n*) virtuoso; **Virtuosität** [vɪrtuoziˈtɛːt] *f* (-; *no pl*) virtuosity

Virus ['viːrʊs] *n*, *m* (-; *Viren*) MED virus

Visier [vi'ziːɐ] *n* (-*s*; -*e*) sights; visor

Vision [vi'zjoːn] *f* (-; -*en*) vision

Visite [vi'ziːtə] *f* (-; -*n*) MED round

Vi'sitenkarte *f* (visiting) card

Visum ['viːzʊm] *n* (-*s*; *Visa*) visa

vital [vi'taːl] *adj* vigorous; **Vitalität** [vitaliˈtɛːt] *f* (-; *no pl*) vigo(u)r

Vitamin [vita'miːn] *n* (-*s*; -*e*) vitamin

Vitrine [vi'triːnə] *f* (-; -*n*) (glass) cabinet; showcase

Vize... ['fiːtsə-] *in cpds* vice(-)...

Vogel ['foːgəl] *m* (-*s*; *Vögel* ['føːgəl]) ZO bird

'Vogelbauer *n* birdcage

'vogelfrei *adj* outlawed

'Vogel|futter *n* birdseed; ~**grippe** *f* bird flu, avian flu; ~**käfig** *m* birdcage; ~**kunde** *f* ornithology

vögeln ['føːgəln] V *v/t and v/i* (*ge-*, *h*) screw

'Vogel|nest *n* bird's nest; ~**perspektive** *f* bird's-eye view; ~**scheuche** *f* scarecrow (*a. fig*); ~**schutzgebiet** *n* bird sanctuary; ~**warte** *f* ornithological station; ~**zug** *m* bird migration

Vokabel [vo'kaːbəl] *f* (-; -*n*) word; *pl* → **Vokabular** [vokabu'laːɐ] *n* (-*s*; -*e*) vocabulary

Vokal [vo'kaːl] *m* (-*s*; -*e*) LING vowel

Volant [vo'lãː] *Austrian m* → **Lenkrad**

Volk [fɔlk] *n* (-[*e*]*s*; *Völker* ['fœlkɐ]) people, nation; *the* people; ZO swarm; *ein Mann aus dem* ~*e* a man of the people

Völker|kunde ['fœlkɐkʊndə] *f* ethnology; ~**mord** *m* genocide; ~**recht** *n* (-[*e*]*s*; *no pl*) international law; ~**wanderung** *f* migration of peoples; F mass exodus

'Volks|abstimmung *f* POL referendum; ~**fest** *n* funfair; ~**hochschule** *f* adult evening classes; ~**lied** *n* folk song; ~**mund** *m*: *im* ~ in the vernacular; ~**mu,sik** *f* folk music; ~**repu,blik** *f* people's republic; ~**schule** HIST *f* → **Grundschule**; ~**sport** *m* popular sport; ~**sprache** *f* vernacular; ~**stamm** *m* tribe, race; ~**tanz** *m* folk dance; ~**tracht** *f* national costume

'volkstümlich ['fɔlkstyːmlɪç] *adj* popular, folk ...; traditional

'Volks|versammlung *f* public meeting; ~**wirt** *m* economist; ~**wirtschaft** *f* (national) economy; → ~**wirtschaftslehre** *f* economics; ~**zählung** *f* census

voll [fɔl] **1.** *adj* full (*a. fig*); full up (*a.* F); F plastered; thick, rich (*hair*); ~*er* full of, filled with, *a.* covered with *dirt etc* **2.** *adv* fully; completely, totally, wholly; *pay etc* in full, the full price; *hit etc* full, straight, right; ~ *entwickelt* fully developed; (*nicht*) *für* ~ *nehmen* (not) take seriously

'vollauf *adv* perfectly, quite

'vollauto,matisch *adj* fully automatic

'Vollbart *m* (full) beard

'Vollbeschäftigung *f* full employment

'Vollblut... *in cpds* full-blooded (*a. fig*)

'Vollblüter ['fɔlblyːtɐ] *m* (-*s*; -) ZO thoroughbred

voll'bringen *v/t* (*irr*, **bringen**, *no* -*ge*-, *h*) accomplish, achieve; perform

'Volldampf *m* full steam; F *mit* ~ (at) full blast

voll'enden *v/t* (*no* -*ge*-, *h*) finish, complete; **voll'endet** *adj* completed; *fig* perfect; **vollends** ['fɔlɛnts] *adv* completely; **Voll'endung** *f* (-; *no pl*) finishing, completion; *fig* perfection

voll'führen *v/t* (*no* -*ge*-, *h*) perform

'vollfüllen *v/t* (*sep*, -*ge*-, *h*) (**gießen**) fill (up)

'Vollgas *n* (-*es*; *no pl*) MOT full throttle; ~ **geben** F step on it

völlig ['fœlɪç] **1.** *adj* complete, absolute, total **2.** *adv* completely; ~ **unmöglich** absolutely impossible

'volljährig ['fɔljɛːrɪç] *adj* JUR ~ **sein** (**werden**) be (come) of age; **noch nicht** ~ under age; **'Volljährigkeit** *f* (-; *no pl*) JUR majority

voll'kommen *adj* perfect; → **völlig**

Voll'kommenheit *f* (-; *no pl*) perfection

'Vollkornbrot *n* wholemeal bread

'vollmachen *v/t* (*sep*, -*ge*-, *h*) fill (up); F soil, dirty; **um das Unglück voll zu machen** to crown it all

Voll|macht *f* (-; -*en*) full power(s), authority; JUR power of attorney; ~ **haben** be authorized; ~**milch** *f* full-cream milk; ~**mond** *m* full moon

'vollpacken *v/t* (*sep*, -*ge*-, *h*) load (**mit** with) (*a. fig*)

'Vollpensi,on *f* full board

'vollschlank *adj* plump

'vollständig *adj* complete; → **völlig**

'vollstopfen *v/t* (*sep*, -*ge*-, *h*) stuff, *fig a.* cram, pack (*all*: **mit** with)

voll'strecken *v/t* (*no* -*ge*-, *h*) JUR execute; **Voll'streckung** *f* (-; -*en*) JUR execution

'volltanken *v/t* (*sep*, -*ge*-, *h*): **bitte** ~*!* MOT fill her up, please!

'Voll|treffer *m* direct hit; bull's eye (*a. fig*); ~**versammlung** *f* plenary session

'vollwertig *adj* full

'Vollwertkost *f* wholefoods

vollzählig ['fɔltsɛːlɪç] *adj* complete

voll'ziehen *v/t* (*irr*, **ziehen**, *no* -*ge*-, *h*) execute; perform; **sich** ~ take place; **Voll'ziehung** *f* (-; *no pl*), **Voll'zug** *m* (-[*e*]*s*; *no pl*) execution

Volontär [volɔn'tɛːɐ] *m* (-*s*, -*e*), **Volon-**

'tärin *f* (-; -*nen*) unpaid trainee

Volt [vɔlt] *n* (-; -) ELECTR volt

Volumen [vo'luːmən] *n* (-*s*; -, -*mina*) volume; size

von [fɔn] *prp* from; *instead of gen*: of; *passive*: by; about *s.o. or s.th.*; **südlich** ~ south of; **weit** ~ far from; ~ **Hamburg** from Hamburg; ~ **nun an** from now on; **ein Freund** ~ **mir** a friend of mine; **die Freunde** ~ **Alice** Alice's friends; **ein Brief** (**Geschenk**) ~ **Tom** a letter (gift) from Tom; **ein Buch** (**Bild**) ~ **Orwell** (**Picasso**) a book (painting) by Orwell (Picasso); **der König** (**Bürgermeister** *etc*) ~ ... the King (Mayor *etc*) of ...; **ein Kind** ~ **10 Jahren** a child of ten; **müde** ~ **der Arbeit** tired from work; **es war nett** (**gemein**) ~ **dir** it was nice (mean) of you; **reden** (**hören**) ~ talk (hear) about *or* of; ~ **Beruf** (**Geburt**) by profession (birth); ~ **selbst** by itself; ~ **mir aus!** I don't mind *or* care

von'stattengehen *v/i* (*irr*, **gehen**, *sep*, -*ge*-, *sein*) go, come off

vor [foːɐ] *prp* (*dat and acc*) in front of; outside; before; ... ago; with, for; ~ **der Klasse** in front of the class; ~ **der Schule** in front of *or* outside the school; before school; ~ **kurzem** (**e-r Stunde**) a short time (an hour) ago; **5 Minuten** ~ **12** five (minutes) to twelve; ~ **j-m liegen** be *or* lie ahead of s.o. (*a. fig and* SPORT); ~ **sich hin** smile *etc* to o.s.; **sicher** ~ safe from; ~ **Kälte** with cold; ~ **Angst** for fear; ~ **allem** above all; ~ **sich gehen** go on, happen

'Vorabend *m* eve (*a. fig*)

'Vorahnung *f* presentiment, foreboding

voran [fo'ran] *adv* at the head (*dat* of), in front (of), before; **Kopf** ~ head first; ~**gehen** *v/i* (*irr*, **gehen**, *sep*, -*ge*-, *sein*) go in front *or* first; *esp fig* lead the way; ~**kommen** *v/i* (*irr*, **kommen**, *sep*, -*ge*-, *sein*) get on *or* along (*a. fig*), make headway

'Voranzeige *f* preannouncement; *film*: trailer

'vorarbeiten *v/i* (*sep*, -*ge*-, *h*) work in advance; *fig* pave the way

'Vorarbeiter *m* foreman

voraus [fo'raus] *adv* ahead (*dat* of); *im* **Voraus** in advance, beforehand

vo'rausgehen *v/i* (*irr*, **gehen**, *sep*, -*ge*-,

sein) precede; → *vorangehen*

vo'rausgesetzt *cj*: ~, *dass* provided that

Vo'raussage *f* (-; *-n*) prediction; METEOR forecast; vo'raussagen *v/t* (*sep*, *-ge-*, *h*) predict; forecast

vo'raus|schicken *v/t* (*sep*, *-ge-*, *h*) send on ahead; ~sehen *v/t* (*irr*, *sehen*, *sep*, *-ge-*, *h*) foresee, see *s.th.* coming

vo'raussetzen *v/t* (*sep*, *-ge-*, *h*) assume; take *s.th.* for granted

Vo'raussetzung *f* (-; *-en*) condition, prerequisite; assumption; *die* ~en er-*füllen* meet the requirements

Vo'raussicht *f* (-; *no pl*) foresight; *aller* ~ *nach* in all probability

vo'raussichtlich *adv* probably; *er kommt* ~ *morgen* he is expected to arrive tomorrow

Vo'rauszahlung *f* advance payment

'Vorbedeutung *f* omen

'Vorbedingung *f* prerequisite

Vorbehalt ['foːɐbəhalt] *m* (-[*e*]*s*; *-e*) reservation; 'vorbehalten 1. *v/t* (*irr*, *hal-ten*, *sep*, *no* *-ge-*, *h*) *sich* (*das Recht*) ~ *zu inf* reserve the right to *inf* 2. *adj* reserved; 'vorbehaltlos 1. *adj* unconditional 2. *adv* without reservation

vor'bei *adv* time: over, past; finished; gone; space: past, by; *jetzt ist alles* ~ it's all over now; ~*!* missed!; ~fahren *v/i* (*irr*, *fahren*, *sep*, *-ge-*, *sein*) go (*or* drive) past (*an dat s.o. or s.th.*), pass (*s.o. or s.th.*); ~gehen *v/i* (*irr*, *gehen*, *sep*, *-ge-*, *sein*) walk past; *a. fig* go by, pass; *shot etc*: miss; ~ *kommen v/i* (*irr*, *kommen*, *sep*, *-ge-*, *sein*) pass (*an dat s.th.*); get past (*an obstacle etc*); F drop in (*bei j-m* on *s.o.*); *fig* avoid; ~las-*sen v/t* (*irr*, *lassen*, *sep*, *-ge-*, *h*) let *s.o.* pass

'Vorbemerkung *f* preliminary remark

'vorbereiten *v/t and v/refl* (*sep*, *no -ge-*, *h*) prepare (*auf acc* for); 'Vorbereitung *f* (-; *-en*) preparation (*auf acc* for)

'vorbestellen *v/t* (*sep*, *no -ge-*, *h*) book (*or* order) in advance; reserve (*room*, *seat etc*); 'Vorbestellung *f* (-; *-en*) advance booking; reservation

'vorbestraft *adj*: ~ *sein* have a police record

'vorbeugen (*sep*, *-ge-*, *h*) 1. *v/i* prevent (*e-r Sache s.th.*); 2. *v/refl* bend forward; ~d *adj* preventive, MED *a.* pro-

phylactic

'Vorbeugung *f* (-; *-en*) prevention

'Vorbild *n* model, pattern; (*j-m*) *ein* ~ *sein* set an example (to *s.o.*); *sich j-n zum* ~ *nehmen* follow *s.o.*'s example

'vorbildlich *adj* exemplary

'Vorbildung *f* education(al background)

'vor|bringen *v/t* (*irr*, *bringen*, *sep*, *-ge-*, *h*) bring forward; say, state; ~da,tieren *v/t* (*no -ge-*, *h*) antedate; postdate

Vorder... ['fɔrdɐ-] *in cpds* ...achse, ...rad, ...sitz, ...tür, ...zahn *etc*: front ...

vordere ['fɔrdərə] *adj* front

'Vorder|grund *m* foreground (*a. fig*); ~mann *m*: *mein* ~ the man *or* boy in front of me; ~seite *f* front (side); head

'vor|dränge(l)n *v/refl* (*sep*, *-ge-*, *h*) cut into line, *Br* jump the queue; ~dringen *v/i* (*irr*, *dringen*, *sep*, *-ge-*, *sein*) advance; ~ (*bis*) *zu* work one's way through to (*a. fig*)

'Vordruck *m* (-[*e*]*s*; *-e*) form, blank

'voreilig *adj* hasty, rash, precipitate; ~*e Schlüsse ziehen* jump to conclusions

'voreingenommen *adj* prejudiced, bias(s)ed; 'Voreingenommenheit *f* (-; *no pl*) prejudice, bias

'vorenthalten *v/t* (*irr*, *halten*, *sep*, *no -ge-*, *h*) keep back, withhold (*both*: *j-m et. s.th.* from *s.o.*)

'Vorentscheidung *f* preliminary decision

'vorerst *adv* for the present, for the time being

Vorfahr ['foːɐfaːɐ] *m* (*-en*; *-en*) ancestor

'vorfahren *v/i* (*irr*, *fahren*, *sep*, *-ge-*, *sein*) drive up (*or* on); 'Vorfahrt *f* (-; *no pl*) right of way, priority

'Vorfall *m* incident, occurrence, event

'vor|fallen *v/i* (*irr*, *fallen*, *sep*, *-ge-*, *sein*) happen, occur; ~finden *v/t* (*irr*, *finden*, *sep*, *-ge-*, *h*) find

'Vorfreude *f* anticipation

'vorführen *v/t* (*sep*, *-ge-*, *h*) show, present; perform (*trick etc*); demonstrate; JUR bring (*j-m* before *s.o.*); 'Vorführer *m* demonstrator; 'Vorführung *f* presentation, show(ing); performance; demonstration; JUR production

'Vorführwagen *m* MOT demonstrator, *Br* demonstration car

'Vorgabe *f* handicap

'Vorgang *m* event, occurrence, happening; file, record(s); BIOL, TECH process; **e-n ~ schildern** give an account of what happened; **Vorgänger(in)** ['foːɐ-gɛŋɐ, 'foːɐgɛŋərɪn] *m(f)* (-s; -/-; -nen) predecessor

'**Vorgarten** *m* front yard (*Br* garden)
'**vorgeben** *v/t* (*irr, geben, sep, -ge-, h* SPORT give; *fig* use s.th. as a pretext
'**Vorgebirge** *n* foothills
'**vorgefasst** *adj* preconceived
'**vorgefertigt** *adj* prefabricated
'**Vorgefühl** *n* presentiment
'**vorgehen** *v/i* (*irr, gehen, sep, -ge-, sein*) go on; come first; act; JUR sue (**gegen j-n** s.o.); proceed; *watch*: be fast; '**Vorgehen** *n* (*-s; no pl*) procedure
'**vorgeschichtlich** *adj* prehistoric
'**Vor|geschmack** *m* foretaste (**auf** *acc* of); **~gesetzte** *m, f* (*-n; -n*) superior, F boss
'**vorgestern** *adv* the day before yesterday
'**vorgreifen** *v/i* (*irr, greifen, sep, -ge-, h*) anticipate *s.o. or s.th.*
'**vorhaben** *v/t* (*irr, haben, sep, -ge-, h*) plan, intend; **haben Sie heute Abend et. vor?** have you anything on tonight?; **was hat er jetzt wieder vor?** what is he up to now?; '**Vorhaben** *n* (*-s; -*) plan(s), intention; TECH, ECON *a.* project
'**Vorhalle** *f* (entrance) hall, lobby
'**vorhalten** (*irr, halten, sep, -ge-, h*) **1.** *v/t*: **j-m et. ~** hold s.th. in front of s.o.; *fig* blame s.o. for (doing) s.th. **2.** *v/i* last; '**Vorhaltungen** *pl* reproaches; **j-m ~ machen (für et.)** reproach s.o. (with s.th., for being ...)
'**Vorhand** *f* (*-; no pl*) *tennis*: forehand
vorhanden [foːɐ'handən] *adj* available; in existence; **~ sein** exist; **es ist nichts mehr ~** there's nothing left; **Vor'handensein** *n* (*-s; no pl*) existence
'**Vorhang** *m* curtain
'**Vorhängeschloss** *n* padlock
vor'her *adv* before, earlier; in advance, beforehand
vor'herbestimmen *v/t* (*sep, no -ge-, h*) predetermine
vorherig [foːɐ'heːrɪç] *adj* previous
'**Vorherrschaft** *f* (*-; no pl*) predominance; '**vorherrschen** *v/i* (*sep, -ge-, h*) predominate, prevail; '**vorherrschend** *adj* predominant, prevailing

vor'hersehbar *adj* foreseeable
vor'hersehen *v/t* (*irr, sehen, sep, -ge-, h*) foresee
vor'hin *adv* a (little) while ago
'**Vorhut** *f* (*-; -en*) MIL vanguard
vorig ['foːrɪç] *adj* last; former, previous
vorjährig ['foːɐjɛːrɪç] *adj* of last year, last year' ...
'**Vorkämpfer** *m*, '**Vorkämpferin** *f* champion, pioneer
Vorkehrungen ['foːɐkeːrʊŋən] *pl*: **~ treffen** take precautions
'**Vorkenntnisse** *pl* previous knowledge *or* experience (**in** *dat* of)
'**vorkommen** *v/i* (*irr, kommen, sep, -ge-, sein*) be found; happen; **es kommt mir ... vor** it seems ... to me
'**Vorkommen** *n* (*-s; -*) MIN deposit(s)
Vorkommnis ['foːɐkɔmnɪs] *n* (*-ses; -se*) occurrence, incident, event
'**Vorkriegs...** *in cpds* prewar ...
'**vorladen** *v/t* (*irr, laden, sep, -ge-, h*) JUR summon; '**Vorladung** *f* (*-; -en*) JUR summons
'**Vorlage** *f* model; pattern; copy; presentation; PARL bill; *soccer etc*: pass
'**vorlassen** *v/t* (*irr, lassen, sep, -ge-, h*) let *s.o.* go first; let *s.o.* pass; **vorgelassen werden** be admitted (**bei** to)
'**Vorlauf** *m* recorder: fast-forward; SPORT (preliminary) heat; '**Vorläufer** *m* forerunner, precursor; '**vorläufig 1.** *adj* provisional, temporary **2.** *adv* for the present, for the time being
'**vorlaut** *adj* pert, cheeky
'**Vorleben** *n* (*-s; no pl*) former life, past
'**vorlegen** *v/t* (*sep, -ge-, h*) present; produce; show
'**Vorleger** *m* (*-s; -*) rug; mat
'**vorlesen** *v/t* (*irr, lesen, sep, -ge-, h*) read out (aloud); **j-m et. ~** read s.th. to s.o.; '**Vorlesung** *f* (*-; -en*) lecture (**über** *acc* on; **vor** *dat* to); **e-e ~ halten** (give a) lecture
'**vorletzte** *adj* last but one; **~ Nacht** (**Woche**) the night (week) before last
'**Vorliebe** *f* (*-; -n*) preference, special liking
'**vorliebnehmen** *v/i* (*irr, nehmen, sep, -ge-, h*) **mit** make do with
'**vorliegen** *v/i* (*irr, liegen, sep, -ge-, h*) **es liegen (keine) ... vor** there are (no) ...; **was liegt gegen ihn vor?** what is he charged with?; **~d** *adj* present, in ques-

tion

'**vor|lügen** v/t (irr, **lügen**, sep, -ge-, h) **j-m et. ~** tell s.o. lies; **~machen** v/t (sep, -ge-, h) **j-m et. ~** show s.th. to s.o., show s.o. how to do s.th.; fig fool s.o.

'**Vormachtstellung** f supremacy

'**Vormarsch** m MIL advance (a. fig)

'**vormerken** v/t (sep, -ge-, h) **j-n ~** put s.o.'s name down

'**Vormittag** m morning; **heute ~** this morning

'**vormittags** adv in the morning; **sonntags ~** on Sunday mornings

'**Vormund** m (-[e]s; -e) JUR guardian; **~schaft** f (-; -en) JUR guardianship

vorn [fɔrn] adv in front; **nach ~** forward; **von ~** from the front; from the beginning; **j-n von ~(e) sehen** see s.o.'s face; **noch einmal von ~(e) (anfangen)** (start) all over again

'**Vorname** m first or Christian name, forename

vornehm ['foːɐneːm] adj distinguished; noble; fashionable, exclusive, F smart, posh; **die ~e Gesellschaft** (high) society; **~ tun** put on airs

'**vornehmen** v/t (irr, **nehmen**, sep, -ge-, h) carry out, do; make (changes etc); **sich et. ~** decide or resolve to do s.th.; make plans for s.th.; **sich fest vorgenommen haben zu** inf have the firm intention to inf, be determined to inf

'**vornherein** adv: **von ~** from the start or beginning

'**Vorort** m suburb

'**Vorposten** m outpost (a. MIL)

'**vorprogram,mieren** v/t (sep, no -ge-, sein) (pre)program(me); fig **das war vorprogrammiert** that was bound to happen

'**Vorrang** m (-[e]s; no pl) precedence (**vor** dat over), priority (over)

'**Vorrat** m (-[e]s; -räte) store, stock, supply (**all: an** dat of); GASTR provisions; ECON resources, reserves; **e-n ~ anlegen an** (dat) stockpile; **vorrätig** ['foːɐrɛːtɪç] adj available; ECON in stock

'**Vorrecht** n privilege

'**Vorredner** m previous speaker

'**Vorrichtung** f TECH device

'**vorrücken** (sep, -ge-) **1.** v/t (h) move forward **2.** v/i (sein) advance

'**Vorrunde** f SPORT preliminary round

'**vorsagen** v/i (sep, -ge-, h) **j-m ~** prompt s.o.

'**Vorsai,son** f off-peak season

'**Vorsatz** m resolution; intention; JUR intent; **vorsätzlich** ['foːɐzɛtslɪç] adj intentional; esp JUR wil(l)ful

'**Vorschau** f preview (**auf** acc of), film, TV a. trailer

'**Vorschein** m: **zum ~ bringen** produce; fig bring out; **zum ~ kommen** appear; fig come to light

'**vor|schieben** v/t (irr, **schieben**, sep, -ge-, h) push forward; slip (bolt); fig use as a pretext; **~schießen** F v/t (irr, **schießen**, sep, -ge-, h) advance (money)

'**Vorschlag** m suggestion, proposal (a. PARL etc); **den ~ machen** → '**vorschlagen** v/t (irr, **schlagen**, sep, -ge-, h) suggest, propose

'**Vorschlussrunde** f SPORT semifinal

'**vorschnell** adj hasty, rash

'**vorschreiben** fig v/t (irr, **schreiben**, sep, -ge-, h) prescribe; tell; **ich lasse mir nichts ~** I won't be dictated to; '**Vorschrift** f rule, regulation; instruction, direction; **Dienst nach ~ machen** work to rule

'**vorschrifts|mäßig** adj correct, proper; **~widrig** adj and adv contrary to regulations

'**Vorschub** m: **~ leisten** (dat) encourage; JUR aid and abet

'**Vorschul...** in cpds pre-school ...

'**Vorschule** f preschool

'**Vorschuss** m advance

'**vorschützen** v/t (sep, -ge-, h) use s.th. as a pretext

'**vorsehen** (irr, **sehen**, sep, -ge-, h) **1.** v/t plan; JUR provide; **~ für** intend (or designate) for **2.** v/refl be careful, take care, watch out (**vor** dat for)

'**Vorsehung** f (-; no pl) providence

'**vorsetzen** v/t (sep, -ge-, h) **j-m et. ~** put s.th. before s.o.; offer s.o. s.th.

'**Vorsicht** f (-; no pl) caution, care; **~!** look or watch out!, (be) careful!; **~, Stufe!** mind the step!; '**vorsichtig** adj careful, cautious; '**vorsichtshalber** ['foːɐzɪçtshalbɐ] adv to be on the safe side; '**Vorsichtsmaßnahme** f precaution, precautionary measure; **~n treffen** take precautions

'**Vorsilbe** f LING prefix

'**vorsingen** v/t and v/i (irr, **singen**, sep, -ge-, h) **j-m et. ~** sing s.th. to s.o.; (have an) audition

'**Vorsitz** m chair(manship), presidency; **den ~ haben** (**übernehmen**) be in (take) the chair, preside (**bei** over, at)

'**Vorsitzende** m, f (-n; -n) chairman (chairwoman), president

'**Vorsorge** f (-; no pl) precaution; **~ treffen** take precautions; **~untersuchung** f MED preventive checkup

'**vorsorglich 1.** adj precautionary **2.** adv as a precaution

'**Vorspann** m (-[e]s; -e) film etc: credits

'**Vorspeise** f hors d'œuvre, Br starter

'**Vorspiel** n MUS prelude (a. fig); foreplay; '**vorspielen** v/t (sep, -ge-, h) **j-m et. ~** play s.th. to s.o.

'**vorsprechen** (irr, **sprechen**, sep, -ge-, h) **1.** v/t pronounce (**j-m** for s.o.); **2.** v/i call (**bei** at); THEA (have an) audition

'**vorspringen** fig v/i (irr, **springen**, sep, -ge-, sein) project, protrude (both a. ARCH); '**Vorsprung** m ARCH projection; SPORT lead; **e-n ~ haben** be leading (**von** by); esp fig **e-n ~ von zwei Jahren haben** be two years ahead

'**Vorstadt** f suburb

'**Vorstand** m ECON board (of directors); managing committee (of a club etc)

'**vorstehen** v/i (irr, **stehen**, sep, -ge-, h) project, protrude

'**vorstellen** v/t (sep, -ge-, h) introduce (**sich** o.s.; **j-n j-m** s.o. to s.o.); put watch forward (**um** by); fig mean; **sich et.** (**j-n als …**) **~** imagine s.th. (s.o. as …); **so stelle ich mir … vor** that's my idea of …; **sich ~ bei** have an interview with a firm etc; '**Vorstellung** f (-; -en) introduction; interview; THEA performance, film etc: a. show; idea; expectation

'**Vorstellungs\kraft** f (-; no pl), **~vermögen** n (-s; no pl) imagination

Vorstopper ['fo:ɐʃtɔpɐ] m (-s; -) SPORT center (Br centre) back

'**Vorstoß** m MIL advance; fig attempt

'**Vorstrafe** f previous conviction

'**vorstrecken** v/t (sep, -ge-, h) advance (money)

'**Vorstufe** f preliminary stage

'**vortäuschen** v/t (sep, -ge-, h) feign, fake

'**Vorteil** m advantage (a. SPORT); benefit, profit; **die ~e und Nachteile** the pros

and cons; '**vorteilhaft** adj advantageous, profitable; '**Vorteilsregel** f SPORT advantage rule

Vortrag ['fo:ɐtra:k] m (-[e]s; Vorträge ['fo:ɐtrɛ:gə]) talk, esp UNIV lecture; MUS etc recital; **e-n ~ halten** give a talk or lecture (**vor** dat to; **über** acc on)

'**vortragen** v/t (irr, **tragen**, sep, -ge-, h) express, state; MUS etc perform, play; recite (poem etc)

'**vortreten** v/i (irr, **treten**, sep, -ge-, sein) step forward; fig protrude, stick out

'**Vortritt** m (-[e]s; no pl) precedence; **j-m den ~ lassen** let s.o. go first

vorüber [fo:'ry:bɐ] adv: **~ sein** be over; **~gehen** v/i (irr, **gehen**, sep, -ge-, sein) pass, go by; **~gehend** adj temporary

'**Vorübung** f preparatory exercise

'**Voruntersuchung** f JUR, MED preliminary examination

'**Vorurteil** n prejudice; '**vorurteilslos** adj unprejudiced, unbias(s)ed

'**Vorverkauf** m THEA advance booking

'**vorverlegen** v/t (sep, no -ge-, h) advance

'**Vorwahl** f TEL area (Br STD or dialling) code; POL primary, Br preliminary election

'**Vorwand** m pretext, excuse

vorwärts ['fo:ɐvɛrts] adv forward, on (-ward), ahead; **~!** come on!, let's go!; '**vorwärtskommen** v/i (irr, **kommen**, sep, -ge-, sein) make headway (a. fig)

vorweg [fo:ɐ'vɛk] adv beforehand

vor'wegnehmen v/t (irr, **nehmen**, sep, -ge-, h) anticipate

'**vor\weisen** v/t (irr, **weisen**, sep, -ge-, h) produce, show; **et. ~ können** boast s.th.; **~werfen** fig v/t (irr, **werfen**, sep, -ge-, h) **j-m et. ~** reproach s.o. with s.th.

'**vorwiegend** adv predominantly, chiefly, mainly, mostly

'**vorwitzig** adj cheeky, pert

'**Vorwort** n (-[e]s; -e) foreword; preface

'**Vorwurf** m reproach; **j-m Vorwürfe machen** (**wegen**) reproach s.o. (for); '**vorwurfsvoll** adj reproachful

'**Vorzeichen** n omen, sign (a. MATH)

'**vorzeigen** v/t (sep, -ge-, h) show; produce

'**vorzeitig** adj premature, early

'**vorziehen** v/t (irr, **ziehen**, sep, -ge-, h) draw; fig prefer

'Vorzimmer *n* anteroom; outer office; *Austrian* → *Hausflur*

'Vorzug *m* advantage; merit

vorzüglich [foːɐ'tsyːklɪç] *adj* excellent, exquisite

'vorzugsweise *adv* preferably

Votum ['voːtʊm] *n* (-s; -ta, -ten) vote

VP *abbr of* **Vollpension** full board; (full) board and lodging

vulgär [vʊl'gɛːɐ] *adj* vulgar

Vulkan [vʊl'kaːn] *m* (-s; -e) volcano; **~ausbruch** *m* volcanic eruption

vul'kanisch *adj* volcanic

W

W *abbr of* **West(en)** W, west; **Watt** W, watt(s)

Waage ['vaːgə] *f* (-; -n) scale(s *Br*); balance; ASTR Libra; **sich die ~ halten** balance each other; **er ist (e-e) ~** he's (a) Libra; **'waagerecht** *adj* horizontal

Waagschale ['vaːkʃaːlə] *f* scale

Wabe ['vaːbə] *f* (-; -n) honeycomb

wach [vax] *adj* awake; **~ rütteln** rouse; *fig* → **wachrütteln**; **~ werden** wake (up), *esp fig* → **wachwerden**

Wache ['vaxə] *f* (-; -n) guard (*a.* MIL); sentry; MAR, MED *etc* watch; police station; **~ haben** be on guard (MAR watch); **~ halten** keep watch; **'wachen** *v/i* (ge-, *h*) (keep) watch (**über** *acc* over)

'Wachhund *m* watchdog

'Wachmann *m* (-[e]s; -männer, -leute) watchman; *Austrian* → **Polizist**

Wacholder [va'xɔldɐ] *m* (-s; -) BOT juniper

'wach|rufen *v/t* (*irr*, *rufen*, *sep*, -ge-, *h*) call up, evoke; **~rütteln** *v/t* (*sep*, -ge-, *h*) *fig* rouse (*a. fig*)

Wachs [vaks] *n* (-es; -e) wax

wachsam ['vaxzaːm] *adj* watchful, on one's guard, vigilant; **'Wachsamkeit** *f* (-; *no pl*) watchfulness, vigilance

wachsen[1] ['vaksən] *v/i* (*irr*, ge-, *sein*) grow (*a.* **sich ~ lassen**), *fig a.* increase

'wachsen[2] *v/t* (ge-, *h*) wax

'Wachs|fi,gurenkabi,nett *n* waxworks; **~tuch** *n* oilcloth

'Wachstum *n* (-s; *no pl*) growth, *fig a.* increase

Wachtel ['vaxtəl] *f* (-; -n) ZO quail

Wächter ['vɛçtɐ] *m* (-s; -) guard

'Wachtmeister *m* (-s; *no pl*) patrolman, *Br* (police) constable

'Wach(t)turm *m* watchtower

'wachwerden *v/i* (*irr*, *werden*, *sep*, -ge-,

sein) *fig* awake; → **wach**

wackelig ['vakəlɪç] *adj* shaky (*a. fig*); loose (*tooth*); **'wackeln** *v/i* (ge-, *h*) shake; *table etc*: wobble; *tooth*: be loose; PHOT move; **~ mit** waggle

Wade ['vaːdə] *f* (-; -n) ANAT calf

Waffe ['vafə] *f* (-; -n) weapon (*a. fig*), *pl a.* arms

Waffel ['vafəl] *f* (-; -n) waffle; wafer

'Waffen|gewalt *f*: **mit ~** by force of arms; **~schein** *m* gun license (*Br* licence); **~stillstand** *m* armistice (*a. fig*); truce

wagen ['vaːgən] *v/t* (ge-, *h*) dare; risk; **sich ~** venture

'Wagen *m* (-s; -) MOT car; RAIL car, *Br* carriage

wägen ['vɛːgən] *lit v/t* (*irr*, ge-, *h*) weigh (*one's words etc*)

'Wagen|heber *m* TECH jack; **~ladung** *f* cartload

Waggon [va'goː] *m* (-s, -s) (railroad) car, *Br* (railway) carriage; freight car, *Br* goods waggon

Wagnis ['vaːknɪs] *n* (-ses; -se) venture, risk

Wa'gon *m* → **Waggon**

Wahl [vaːl] *f* (-; -en) choice; alternative; selection; POL election; voting, poll; vote; **die ~ haben (s-e ~ treffen)** have the (make one's) choice; **keine (andere) ~ haben** have no choice *or* alternative; **'wahlberechtigt** *adj* POL entitled to vote; **'Wahlbeteiligung** *f* POL poll, (voter) turnout; **hohe (niedrige) ~** heavy (light) poll; **'Wahlbezirk** *m* → **Wahlkreis**

wählen ['vɛːlən] *v/t and v/i* (ge-, *h*) choose, pick, select; POL vote (for); elect; TEL dial; **'Wähler** *m* (-s; -) voter

'Wahlergebnis *n* election result

wählerisch ['vɛːlərɪʃ] *adj* F picky (**in** *dat*

about), *esp Br* choos(e)y

'**Wählerschaft** *f* (-; *-en*) electorate, voters

'**Wahl|fach** *n* PED *etc* elective, optional subject; **~ka,bine** *f* voting (*esp Br* polling) booth; **~kampf** *m* election campaign; **~kreis** *m* electoral district, *Br* constituency; **~lo,kal** *n* polling place (*Br* station)

'**wahllos** *adj* indiscriminate

'**Wahl|pro,gramm** *n* election platform; **~recht** *n* (-[*e*]*s*; *no pl*) (right to) vote, suffrage, franchise; **~rede** *f* election speech

'**Wählscheibe** *f* TEL dial

'**Wahl|sieg** *m* election victory; **~sieger** *m* election winner; **~spruch** *m* motto; **~urne** *f* ballot box; **~versammlung** *f* election rally

'**Wahnsinn** *m* (-[*e*]*s*; *no pl*) madness (*a.* F), insanity

'**wahnsinnig** 1. *adj* mad (*a.* F), insane, F *a.* crazy; F awful, terrible 2. F *adv* terribly, awfully; madly (*in love*)

'**Wahnsinnige** *m*, *f* (-*n*; -*n*) madman (madwoman), lunatic, maniac (*all a.* F)

'**Wahnvorstellung** *f* delusion, hallucination

wahr [vaːɐ] *adj* true; real; genuine

wahren ['vaːrən] *v/t* (*ge-*, *h*) protect; **den Schein ~** keep up appearances

während ['vɛːrənt] 1. *prp* (*gen*) during 2. *cj* while; whereas

'**wahrhaft, wahr'haftig** *adv* really, truly

'**Wahrheit** *f* (-; *-en*) truth

'**wahrheits|gemäß, ~getreu** *adj* true, truthful; **~liebend** *adj* truthful

wahrnehmbar ['vaːɐneːmbaːɐ] *adj* noticeable, perceptible; '**wahrnehmen** *v/t* (*irr*, *nehmen*, *sep*, -*ge*-, *h*) perceive; notice; seize, take (*chance etc*); look after (*s.o.'s interests etc*); '**Wahrnehmung** *f* (-; *-en*) perception

'**wahrsagen** *v/i* (*sep*, -*ge*-, *h*) *j-m* **~** tell s.o. his fortune; **sich ~ lassen** have one's fortune told; '**Wahrsager(in)** ['vaːɐzaːɡɐ, 'vaːɐzaːɡərɪn] *m* (*f*) (-*s*; -/-; -*nen*) fortune-teller

wahr'scheinlich 1. *adj* probable, likely 2. *adv* probably, (very *or* most) likely; **~ gewinnt er** (**nicht**) he is (not) likely to win; **Wahr'scheinlichkeit** *f* (-; *-en*) probability, likelihood

Währung ['vɛːrʊŋ] *f* (-; *-en*) currency

'**Währungs...** *in cpds* ...*politik*, ...*reform etc*: monetary ...

'**Wahrzeichen** *n* landmark

Waise ['vaizə] *f* (-; *-n*) orphan

'**Waisenhaus** *n* orphanage

Wal [vaːl] *m* (-[*e*]*s*; -*e*) zo whale

Wald [valt] *m* (-[*e*]*s*; *Wälder* ['vɛldɐ]) wood(s), forest; **~brand** *m* forest fire

'**waldreich** *adj* wooded

'**Waldsterben** *n* dying of forests

'**Walfang** *m* whaling

'**Walfänger** *m* whaler

Walkman® *m* (-*s*; -*men*) personal stereo, Walkman®

Wall [val] *m* (-[*e*]*s*; *Wälle* ['vɛlə]) mound; MIL rampart

Wallach ['valax] *m* (-[*e*]*s*; -*e*) zo gelding

wallen ['valən] *v/i* (*ge-*, *sein*) flow

'**Wallfahrer** *m*, '**Wallfahrerin** *f* pilgrim

'**Wallfahrt** *f* pilgrimage

'**Walnuss** *f* BOT walnut

'**Walross** *n* zo walrus

Walze ['valtsə] *f* (-; -*n*) roller; cylinder; TECH, MUS barrel

'**walzen** *v/t* (*ge-*, *h*) roll (*a.* TECH)

wälzen ['vɛltsən] *v/t* (*ge-*, *h*) roll (*a. sich ~*); *fig* turn *s.th.* over in one's mind

Walzer ['valtsɐ] *m* (-*s*; -) MUS waltz (*a. ~ tanzen*)

wand [vant] *pret of* **winden**

Wand *f* (-; *Wände* ['vɛndə]) wall, *fig a.* barrier

Wandale [van'daːlə] *m* (-*n*; -*n*) vandal; **Wandalismus** [vanda'lɪsmʊs] *m* (-; *no pl*) vandalism

Wandel ['vandəl] *m* (-*s*; *no pl*), '**wandeln** *v/t* and *v/i/refl* (*ge-*, *h*) change

Wanderer ['vandərɐ] *m* (-*s*; -), '**Wanderin** *f* (-; -*nen*) hiker

wandern ['vandɐn] *v/i* (*ge-*, *sein*) hike; ramble (about); *eyes etc:* roam, wander

'**Wander|po,kal** *m* challenge cup; **~preis** *m* challenge trophy; **~schuhe** *pl* walking shoes; **~tag** *m* (school) outing *or* excursion

'**Wanderung** *f* (-; *-en*) walking tour, hike; zo *etc* migration

'**Wand|gemälde** *n* mural; **~ka,lender** *m* wall calendar; **~karte** *f* wallchart

Wandlung ['vandlʊŋ] *f* (-; *-en*) change

'**Wand|schrank** *m* closet, *Br* built-in cupboard; **~tafel** *f* blackboard

wandte ['vantə] *pret of* **wenden**

'**Wandteppich** *m* tapestry

Wange ['vaŋə] *f* (-; -*n*) ANAT cheek

Wankelmotor ['vaŋkəlmoːtoːɐ] *m* rotary piston *or* Wankel engine

wankelmütig ['vaŋkəlmyːtɪç] *adj* fickle

wanken ['vaŋkən] *v/i* (ge-, *sein*) stagger, reel; *fig* rock

wann [van] *interr adv* when, (at) what time; *seit ~?* (for) how long?, since when?

Wanne ['vanə] *f* (-; -*n*) tub (*a.* F); bath (-tub)

Wanze ['vantsə] *f* (-; -*n*) zo bug (*a.* F)

Wapitihirsch [va'piːtihɪrʃ] *m* zo elk

Wappen ['vapən] *n* (-*s*; -) (coat of) arms

'Wappenkunde *f* heraldry

wappnen ['vapnən] *fig v/refl* (ge-, *h*) arm o.s.

war [vaːɐ] *pret of sein¹*

warb [varp] *pret of werben*

Ware ['vaːrə] *f* (-; -*n*) *coll mst* goods; article; product

'Waren|haus *n* department store; **~la-ger** *n* stock; **~probe** *f* sample; **~zeichen** *n* trademark

warf [varf] *pret of werfen*

warm [varm] *adj* warm (*a. fig*); GASTR hot; *schön ~* nice and warm; *~ halten* keep warm; *~ machen* warm (up)

Wärme ['vɛrmə] *f* (-; *no pl*) warmth; PHYS heat; **~iso,lierung** *f* heat insulation

'wärmen *v/t* (ge-, *h*) warm

'Wärmflasche *f* hot-water bottle

'warmherzig *adj* warm-hearted

'warmmachen *v/t* (sep, -ge-, *h*) → *warm*

Warm'wasser|bereiter *m* (-*s*; -) water heater; **~versorgung** *f* hot-water supply

'Warn|blinkanlage *f* MOT warning flasher; **~dreieck** *n* MOT warning triangle

warnen ['varnən] *v/t* (ge-, *h*) warn (*vor dat* of, against); *j-n davor ~, et. zu tun* warn s.o. not to do s.th.

'Warn|schild *n* danger sign; **~sig,nal** *n* warning signal; **~streik** *m* token strike

'Warnung *f* (-; -*en*) warning

'Warteliste *f* waiting list

warten¹ ['vartən] *v/i* (ge-, *h*) wait (*auf acc* for); *j-n ~ lassen* keep s.o. waiting

'warten² *v/t* (ge-, *h*) TECH service, maintain

Wärter ['vɛrtɐ] *m* (-*s*; -), **'Wärterin** *f* (-; -*nen*) attendant; zo keeper

'Warte|saal *m*, **~zimmer** *n* waiting room

'Wartung *f* (-; -*en*) TECH maintenance

warum [va'rʊm] *interr adv* why

Warze ['vartsə] *f* (-; -*n*) MED wart

was [vas] **1.** *interr pron* what; *~ gibt's?* what is it?, F what's up?; what's for lunch *etc*?; **~ soll's?** so what?; *~ ma-chen Sie?* what are you doing?; *~* do you do?; *~ kostet …?* how much is …?; *~ für …?* what kind *or* sort of …?; *~ für e-e Farbe (Größe)?* what colo(u)r (size)?; *~ für ein Unsinn* what nonsense!; *~ für e-e gute Idee!* what a good idea! **2.** *rel pron* what; *~ (auch) immer* whatever; *alles, ~ ich habe (brauche)* all I have (need); *ich weiß nicht, ~ ich tun (sagen) soll* I don't know what to do (say); *…, ~ mich är-gerte…*, which made me angry **3.** F *indef pron →* **etwas**

waschbar ['vaʃbaːɐ] *adj* washable

'Waschbecken *n* washbowl, *Br* wash-basin

Wäsche ['vɛʃə] *f* (-; -*n*) washing; (*no pl*) laundry; linen; underwear; *in der ~* in the wash; *schmutzige ~ waschen* wash one's dirty linen in public

'waschecht *adj* washable; fast (*color*); *fig* trueborn, genuine

'Wäsche|klammer *f* clothespin, *Br* clothes peg; **~leine** *f* clothesline

waschen ['vaʃən] *v/t and v/refl* (irr, ge-, *h*) wash; *sich die Haare (Hände) ~* wash one's hair (hands)

Wäscherei [vɛʃə'rai] *f* (-; -*en*) laundry

'Wasch|lappen *m* washcloth, *Br* flannel, facecloth; **~ma,schine** *f* washing machine, F washer

'waschma,schinenfest *adj* machine--washable

Wasch|mittel *n*, **~pulver** *n* washing powder; **~raum** *m* lavatory, washroom; **~sa,lon** *m* laundromat, *Br* launderette; **~straße** *f* MOT car wash

Wasser ['vasɐ] *n* (-*s*; -) water; **~ball** *m* beach ball; SPORT water polo; **~bett** *n* water bed; **~dampf** *m* steam

'wasserdicht *adj* waterproof; *esp* MAR watertight (*a. fig*)

'Wasser|fall *m* waterfall; falls; **~farbe** *f* water colo(u)r; **~flugzeug** *n* seaplane; **~graben** *m* SPORT water jump; **~hahn** *m* tap, faucet

wässerig ['vɛsərɪç] *adj* watery; *j-m den Mund ~ machen* make s.o.'s mouth wa-

ter
'Wasser|kessel *m* kettle; **~klo‚sett** *n*
water closet, W.C.; **~kraft** *f* (-; *no pl*)
water power; **~kraftwerk** *n* hydroelec-
tric power station *or* plant; **~lauf** *m* wa-
tercourse; **~leitung** *f* waterpipe(s);
~mangel *m* (-*s*; *no pl*) water shortage;
~mann *m* (-[*e*]*s*; *no pl*) ASTR Aquarius;
er ist (ein) **~** he's (an) Aquarius
'wassern *v/i* (*ge-, h*) AVIAT touch down
on water; *spacecraft:* splash down
wässern ['vɛsɐn] *v/t* (*ge-, h*) water; AGR
irrigate; GASTR soak; PHOT rinse
'Wasserpflanze *f* BOT aquatic plant
'Wasserrohr *n* TECH water pipe
'Wasserscheide *f* GEOGR watershed
'wasserscheu *adj* afraid of water
'Wasser|ski 1. *m* water ski **2.** *n* (-*s*; *no pl*)
water skiing; **~ fahren** water-ski;
~spiegel *m* water level; **~sport** *m* water *or* aquatic sports, aquatics; **~spü-
lung** *f* TECH flushing cistern; **Toilette
mit~** (flush) toilet, W.C.; **~stand** *m* water level; **~stoff** *m* (-[*e*]*s*; *no pl*) CHEM
hydrogen; **~stoffbombe** *f* MIL hydrogen bomb, H-bomb; **~strahl** *m* jet of
water; **~straße** *f* waterway; **~tier** *n*
aquatic animal; **~verschmutzung** *f*
water pollution; **~versorgung** *f* water
supply; **~waage** *f* (*Br* spirit) level;
~weg *m* waterway; **auf dem~** by water;
~welle *f* water wave; **~werk(e)** *n(pl)*
waterworks; **~zeichen** *n* watermark
waten ['vaːtən] *v/i* (*ge-, sein*) wade
watscheln ['vaːtʃəln] *v/i* (*ge-, sein*)
waddle
Watt¹ [vat] *n* (-*s*; -) ELECTR watt
Watt² *n* (-[*e*]*s*; -*en*) GEOGR mud flats
Watte ['vatə] *f* (-; -*n*) cotton wool
wattiert [va'tiːɐt] *adj* padded; quilted
weben ['veːbən] *v/t and v/i* ([*irr,*] *ge-, h*)
weave; **Weber** ['veːbɐ] *m* (-*s*; -) weaver; **Weberei** [veːbə'raɪ] *f* (-; -*en*) weav-
ing mill; **'Weberin** *f* (-; -*nen*) weaver;
Webstuhl ['veːpʃtuːl] *m* loom
Wechsel ['vɛksəl] *m* (-*s*; -) change; exchange; ECON bill of exchange; allowance; **Wechselgeld** *n* (small) change
wechselhaft *adj* changeable
'Wechseljahre *pl* MED menopause
'Wechselkurs *m* ECON exchange rate
'wechseln *v/t and v/i* (*ge-, h*) change; exchange; vary; **~d** *adj* varying
'wechselseitig ['vɛksəlzaɪtɪç] *adj* mu-

tual, reciprocal
'Wechsel|strom *m* ELECTR alternating
current; **~stube** *f* ECON exchange office; **~wirkung** *f* interaction
wecken ['vɛkən] *v/t* (*ge-, h*) wake (up), F
call; *fig* awaken (*memories etc*); rouse
(*s.o.'s curiosity etc*)
Wecker ['vɛkɐ] *m* (-*s*; -) alarm (clock)
wedeln ['veːdəln] *v/i* (*ge-, h*) wave (**mit
et.** s.th.); *skiing:* wedel; **mit dem
Schwanz~** wag its tail
weder ['veːdɐ] *cj:* **~ ... noch ...** neither
... nor ...
Weg [veːk] *m* (- [*e*]*s*; -*e* ['veːgə]) way (*a.
fig*); road (*a. fig*); path; route; walk; **auf
friedlichem (legalem)~e** by peaceful
(legal) means; **j-m aus dem~ gehen**
get (*fig* keep) out of s.o.'s way; **j-n
aus dem~ räumen** put s.o. out of
the way; **vom~ abkommen** lose one's
way; → **halb**
weg [vɛk] *adv* away; gone; off; F in raptures (**von** over, about); **Finger~!**
(keep your) hands off!; **nichts wie~!**
let's get out of here!; F **~ sein** be out;
~bleiben F *v/i* (*irr, bleiben, sep, -ge-,
sein*) stay away; be left out; **~bringen**
F *v/t* (*irr, bringen, sep, -ge-, h*) take
away; **~ von** get *s.o.* away from
wegen ['veːgən] *prp* (*gen*) because of;
for the sake of; due *or* owing to; JUR for
wegfahren ['vɛkfaːrən] (*irr, fahren,
sep, -ge-*) **1.** *v/i* (*sein*) leave **2.** *v/t* (*h*) take
away, remove
'wegfallen *v/i* (*irr, fallen, sep, -ge-, sein*)
be dropped; stop, be stopped
Weggang ['vɛkgaŋ] *m* (-[*e*]*s*; *no pl*)
leaving; **'weggehen** *v/i* (*irr, gehen,
sep, -ge-, sein*) go away (*a. fig*), leave;
stain etc: come off; ECON sell
weg|jagen ['vɛkjaːgən] *v/t* (*sep, -ge-, h*)
drive *or* chase away; **~kommen** F *v/i*
(*irr, kommen, sep, -ge-, sein*) get away;
get lost; **gut~** come off well; **mach,
dass du wegkommst!** get out of here!,
sl get lost!; **~lassen** *v/t* (*irr, lassen, sep,
-ge-, h*) let *s.o.* go; leave *s.th.* out; **~lau-
fen** *v/i* (*irr, laufen, sep, -ge-, sein*) run
away ([**vor**] *j-m* from s.o.) (*a. fig*); **~le-
gen** *v/t* (*sep, -ge-, h*) put away; **~neh-
men** *v/t* (*irr, nehmen, sep, -ge-, h*) take
away (**von** from); take up (*room, time*);
steal (*a. s.o.'s girlfriend etc*); **j-m et.~**
take s.th. (away) from s.o.; **~räumen**

v/t (*sep*, *-ge-*, *h*) clear away, remove; **~schaffen** *v/t* (*sep*, *-ge-*, *h*) remove; **~schicken** *v/t* (*sep*, *-ge-*, *h*) send away *or* off; **~sehen** *v/i* (*irr*, *sehen*, *sep*, *-ge-*, *h*) look away; **~setzen** *v/t* (*sep*, *-ge-*, *h*) move

Wegweiser ['veːkvaizɐ] *m* (*-s*; -) signpost; *fig* guide

Wegwerf... ['vɛkvɛrf-] *in cpds* ...*geschirr*, ...*besteck*, ...*rasierer etc*: throwaway ..., disposable ...; ...*flasche etc*: non-returnable ...; **'wegwerfen** *v/t* (*irr*, *werfen*, *sep*, *-ge-*, *h*) throw away

weg|wischen ['vɛkvɪʃən] *v/t* (*sep*, *-ge-*, *h*) wipe off; **~ziehen** (*irr*, *ziehen*, *sep*, *-ge-*) **1.** *v/i* (*sein*) move away **2.** *v/t* (*h*) pull away

weh [veː] *adv*: **~ tun** → **wehtun**

wehen ['veːən] *v/i* (*ge-*, *h*) blow; wave

'Wehen *pl* labo(u)r

wehmütig ['veːmyːtɪç] *adj* melancholy; wistful

Wehr¹ [veːɐ] *n* (*-[e]s*; *-e* ['veːrə]) weir

Wehr² *f*: *sich zur ~ setzen* → *wehren*

'Wehrdienst *m* (*-[e]s*; *no pl*) military service; **~verweigerer** *m* (*-s*; -) conscientious objector

wehren ['veːrən] *v/refl* (*ge-*, *h*) defend o.s. (*gegen* against), fight (*a. fig gegen et.* s.th.); **'wehrlos** *adj* defenseless, *Br* defenceless; *fig* helpless

'Wehrpflicht *f* (-; *no pl*) compulsory military service; **'wehrpflichtig** *adj* liable to military service; **'Wehrpflichtige** *m* (*-n*; *-n*) draftee, *Br* conscript

'wehtun hurt (*j-m* s.o.; *fig* s.o.'s feelings); be aching; *sich* (*am Finger*) **~** hurt o.s. (hurt one's finger)

Weib [vaip] *n* (*-[e]s*; *-er* ['vaibɐ]) *contp* woman; bitch; **'Weibchen** *n* (*-s*; -) zo female; **weibisch** ['vaibɪʃ] *adj* effeminate, F sissy; **'weiblich** *adj* female; feminine (*a.* LING)

weich [vaiç] *adj* soft (*a. fig*), tender; GASTR done; soft-boiled (*egg*); **~ werden** soften; *fig* give in

Weiche ['vaiçə] *f* (-; *-n*) RAIL switch, points

weichen ['vaiçən] *v/i* (*irr*, *ge-*, *sein*) give way (*dat* to), yield (to); go (away)

'weichlich *adj* soft, effeminate, F sissy

'Weichling *m* (*-s*; *-e*) weakling, F softy, sissy

'weichmachen *v/t* (*sep*, *-ge-*, *h*): F *j-n* **~** soften s.o. up

'Weichspüler *m* (*-s*; -) fabric softener

'Weichtier *n* zo mollusk, *Br* mollusc

Weide¹ ['vaidə] *f* (-; *-n*) BOT willow

Weide² *f* (-; *-n*) AGR pasture; *auf die* (*der*) **~** to (at) pasture; **'Weideland** *n* pasture(land), range; **'weiden** *v/t and v/i* (*ge-*, *h*) graze, pasture; *fig* *sich* **~** *an* (*dat*) feast on; *contp* gloat over

weigern ['vaigɐn] *v/refl* (*ge-*, *h*) refuse

Weigerung ['vaigərʊŋ] *f* (-; *-en*) refusal

Weihe ['vaiə] *f* (-; *-n*) REL consecration; ordination; **'weihen** *v/t* (*ge-*, *h*) consecrate; *zum Priester* **~** ordain *s.o.* priest

Weiher ['vaiɐ] *m* (*-s*; -) pond

Weihnachten ['vainaxtən] *n* (-; -) Christmas, F Xmas

'Weihnachts|abend *m* Christmas Eve; **~baum** *m* Christmas tree; **~einkäufe** *pl* Christmas shopping; **~geschenk** *n* Christmas present; **~lied** *n* (Christmas) carol; **~mann** *m* Father Christmas, Santa Claus; **~markt** *m* Christmas fair; **~tag** *m* Christmas Day; *zweiter* **~** day after Christmas, *esp Br* Boxing Day; **~zeit** *f* Christmas season

'Weih|rauch *m* REL incense; **~wasser** *n* (*-s*; *no pl*) REL holy water

weil [vail] *cj* because; since, as

'Weilchen *n*: *ein* **~** a little while

Weile ['vailə] *f*: *e-e* **~** a while

Wein [vain] *m* (*-[e]s*; *-e*) wine; BOT vine; **~(an)bau** *m* (*-[e]s*; *no pl*) wine growing; **~beere** *f* grape; **~berg** *m* vineyard; **~brand** *m* brandy

weinen ['vainən] *v/i* (*ge-*, *h*) cry (*vor dat* with; *nach* for; *wegen* about, over); weep (*um* for, over; *über acc* at; *vor dat* for, with); **weinerlich** ['vainɐlɪç] *adj* tearful; whining

'Wein|fass *n* wine cask *or* barrel; **~flasche** *f* wine bottle; **~händler** *m* wine merchant; **~hauer** *Austrian m* → *Winzer*; **~karte** *f* wine list; **~keller** *m* wine cellar *or* vault, vaults; **~kellerei** *f* winery; **~kenner** *m* wine connoisseur; **~lese** *f* vintage; **~presse** *f* wine press; **~probe** *f* wine tasting; **~rebe** *f* BOT vine

'weinrot *adj* claret

'Weinstock *m* BOT vine

'Weintraube *f* → *Traube*

weise ['vaizə] *adj* wise

'Weise *f* (-; *-n*) way; MUS tune; *auf diese*

(*die gleiche*) ~ this (the same) way; *auf m-e* (*s-e*) ~ my (his) way

weisen ['vaizən] *v/t and v/i* (*irr, ge-, h*) show; *j-n von der Schule* ~ expel s.o. from school; ~ *auf* (*acc*) point to *or* at; *von sich* ~ reject; repudiate

Weisheit ['vaishait] *f* (-; *-en*) wisdom; *mit s-r* ~ *am Ende sein* be at one's wit's end

'**Weisheitszahn** *m* wisdom tooth

weismachen ['vaismaxən] F *v/t: j-m* ~, *dass* make s.o. believe that; *du kannst mir nichts* ~ you can't fool me

weiß [vais] *adj* white; ~ *werden or machen* whiten; '**Weißbrot** *n* white bread; '**Weiße** *m, f* (-*n*; *-n*) white, white man (woman), *pl the* whites

'**weißen** *v/t* (*ge-, h*) whitewash

'**Weißkohl** *m,* '**Weißkraut** *n* BOT (green, *Br* white) cabbage

'**weißlich** *adj* whitish

'**weißmachen** *v/t* (*sep, -ge-, h*) → *weiß*

'**Weißwein** *m* white wine

Weisung ['vaizuŋ] *f* (-; *-en*) instruction, directive

weit [vait] **1.** *adj* wide, *clothes: a.* big; long (*way, trip etc*) **2.** *adv* far, a long way (*a. time and fig*); ~ *weg* far away (*von* from); *von* ~ *em* from a distance; ~ *und breit* far and wide; *bei* ~ *em* by far; *bei* ~ *em nicht so ...* not nearly as ...; ~ *über* (*acc*) well over; ~ *besser* far *or* much better; *zu* ~ *gehen* go too far; *es* ~ *bringen* go far; *wir haben es* ~ *gebracht* we have come a long way; ~ *blickend* *fig* farsighted; ~ *reichend* far-reaching; ~ *verbreitet* widespread

'**weit'ab** *adv* far away (*von* from)

'**weit'aus** *adv* (by) far, much

Weite ['vaitə] *f* (-; *-n*) width; vastness, expanse; *esp* SPORT distance

'**weiten** *v/t and v/refl* (*ge-, h*) widen

weiter ['vaitɐ] *adv* on, further; (*mach*) ~*!* go on!; (*geh*) ~*!* move on!; *und so* ~ and so on *or* forth, et cetera; *nichts* ~ nothing else; ~*arbeiten* *v/i* (*sep, -ge-, h*) go on working; ~*bilden* *v/refl* (*sep, -ge-, h*) improve one's knowledge; continue one's education *or* training

'**Weiterbildung** *f* (-; *no pl*) further education *or* training

weitere ['vaitərə] *adj* further, additional; *alles Weitere* the rest; *bis auf* ~*s* until further notice; *ohne* ~*s* easily;

Weiteres more, (further) details

'**weiter**|**geben** *v/t* (*irr, geben, sep, -ge-, h*) pass (*dat, an acc* to) (*a. fig*); ~**gehen** *v/i* (*irr, gehen, sep, -ge-, sein*) move on; *fig* continue, go on

'**weiter'hin** *adv* further(more); *et.* ~ *tun* go on doing s.th., continue to do s.th.

'**weiter**|**kommen** *v/i* (*irr, kommen, sep, -ge-, sein*) get on (*fig* in life); ~**leben** *v/i* (*sep, -ge-, h*) live on, *fig a.* survive; ~**machen** *v/t and v/i* (*sep, -ge-, h*) go *or* carry on, continue

'**Weiterverkauf** *m* resale

'**weit**|**gehend 1.** *adj* considerable **2.** *adv* largely; ~**läufig** *adj* spacious; distant (*relative*); ~**sichtig** *adj* MED farsighted (*a. fig*), *Br* longsighted

'**Weitsprung** *m* broad (*Br* long) jump

'**Weitwinkelobjek,tiv** *n* PHOT wide-angle lens

Weizen ['vaitsən] *m* (-*s*; -) BOT wheat

welche ['vɛlçə], **welcher** ['vɛlçɐ], **welches** ['vɛlçəs] **1.** *interr pron* what, which; *welcher* which one?; *welcher von beiden?* which of the two? **2.** *rel pron* who, that; which, that **3.** F *welche indef pron* some, any

welk [vɛlk] *adj* faded, withered; flabby

welken ['vɛlkən] *v/i* (*ge-, sein*) fade, wither

Wellblech ['vɛlblɛç] *n* corrugated iron

Welle ['vɛlə] *f* (-; *-n*) wave (*a.* PHYS *and fig*); TECH shaft; '**wellen** *v/t and v/refl* (*ge-, h*) wave

'**Wellenlänge** *f* ELECTR wavelength

'**Wellensittich** ['vɛlənzitiç] *m* (-*s*; *-e*) ZO budgerigar, F budgie

wellig ['vɛlɪç] *adj* wavy

Welt [vɛlt] *f* (-; *-en*) world; *die ganze* ~ the whole world; *auf der ganzen* ~ all over *or* throughout the world; *das beste etc* ... *der* ~ the best *etc* ... in the world, the world's best *etc* ...; *zur* ~ *kommen* be born; *zur* ~ *bringen* give birth to

'**Weltall** *n* universe

'**weltberühmt** *adj* world-famous

Weltergewicht ['vɛltɐɡəvɪçt] *n* (-[*e*]*s*; *no pl*), '**Weltergewichtler** *m* (-*s*; -) SPORT welterweight

'**weltfremd** *adj* naive, unrealistic

'**Weltfriede(n)** *m* world peace

'**Weltgeschichte** *f* world history

'**weltklug** *adj* worldlywise

'**Weltkrieg** *m* world war; *der Zweite* ~ World War II

'**Weltkugel** *f* globe

'**weltlich** *adj* worldly

'**Welt|litera,tur** *f* world literature; **~macht** *f* POL world power; **~markt** *m* ECON world market; **~meer** *n* ocean; **~meister(in)** world champion; **~meisterschaft** *f* world championship; *esp soccer*: World Cup; **~raum** *m* (-[*e*]*s*; *no pl*) (outer) space; **~reich** *n* empire; **~reise** *f* world trip; **~re,kord** *m* world record; **~stadt** *f* metropolis; **~untergang** *m* end of the world

'**weltweit** *adj* worldwide

'**Weltwirtschaft** *f* world economy

'**Weltwirtschaftskrise** *f* worldwide economic crisis

'**Weltwunder** *n* wonder of the world

Wende ['vɛndə] *f* (-; -*n*) turn (*a. swimming*); change; **~kreis** *m* ASTR, GEOGR tropic; MOT turning circle

Wendeltreppe ['vɛndəltrɛpə] *f* spiral staircase

'**wenden** *v/t and v/i* (ge-, *h*) *and v/refl* ([*irr*,] *ge*-, *h*) turn (*nach* to; *gegen* against); MOT turn (round); GASTR turn over; *sich an j-n um Hilfe* ~ turn to s.o. for help; *bitte* ~ please turn over, pto

'**Wendepunkt** *m* turning point

wendig ['vɛndɪç] *adj* MOT, MAR maneuverable, *Br* manoeuvrable; *fig* nimble

'**Wendung** *f* (-; -*en*) turn, *fig a.* change; expression, phrase

wenig ['ve:nɪç] *indef pron and adv* little; **~(e)** *pl* few; *nur* **~e** only few; only a few; (*in*) **~er als** (in) less than; *am* **~sten** of all; *er spricht* ~ he doesn't talk much; (*nur*) *ein* (*klein*) ~ (just) a little (bit)

'**wenigstens** *adv* at least

wenn [vɛn] *cj* when; if; ~ **...** *nicht* if ... not, unless; ~ *auch* (al)though, even though; *wie or als* ~ as though, as if; ~ *ich nur ... wäre!* if only I were ...!; ~ *auch noch so ...* no matter how ...; *und* ~ *nun ...?* what if ...?

wer [ve:ɐ] **1.** *interr pron* who, which; ~ *von euch?* which of you? **2.** *rel pron* who; ~ *auch* (*immer*) who(so)ever **3.** F *indef pron* somebody, anybody

Werbe|abteilung ['vɛrbəaptailʊŋ] *f* publicity department; **~agen,tur** *f* advertising agency; **~feldzug** *m* advertis-

ing campaign; **~fernsehen** *n* commercial television; **~film** *m* promotion(al) film; **~funk** *m* radio commercials

werben ['vɛrbən] (*irr, ge-, h*) **1.** *v/i* advertise (*für et.* s.th.), promote (s.th.), give *s.th. or s.o.* publicity; *esp* POL make propaganda (*für* for), canvass (for); ~ *um* court (*a. fig*) **2.** *v/t* recruit; canvass, solicit

'**Werbesendung** *f*, '**Werbespot** ['vɛrbəspɔt] *m* (-*s*; -*s*) (TV) commercial

'**Werbung** *f* (-; *no pl*) advertising, (sales) promotion; *a.* POL *etc* publicity, propaganda; recruitment; ~ *machen für et.* advertise s.th.

Werdegang ['ve:ɐdəgaŋ] *m* career

werden ['ve:ɐdən] *v/i* (*irr, ge-, sein*) *and v/aux* become, get; turn, go; grow; turn out; *wir* ~ we will (*or* shall), we are going to; *geliebt* ~ be loved (*von* by); *was willst du* ~? what do you want to be?; *mir wird schlecht* I'm going to be sick; F *es wird schon wieder* (~) it'll be all right

werfen ['vɛrfən] *v/i and v/t* (*irr, ge-, h*) throw (*a.* ZO) ([*mit*] *et. nach* s.th. at); drop (*bombs*); cast (*shadow*)

Werft [vɛrft] *f* (-; -*en*) MAR shipyard, dockyard

Werk [vɛrk] *n* (-[*e*]*s*; -*e*) work, deed; TECH mechanism; ECON works, factory; *ans* ~ *gehen* set *or* go to work; **~bank** *f* (-; -*bänke*) TECH workbench; **~meister** *m* TECH foreman

'**Werkstatt** *f* (-; -*stätten*) workshop; MOT garage

'**Werktag** *m* workday

'**werktags** *adv* on workdays

'**werktätig** *adj* working

'**Werkzeug** *n* tool (*a. fig*); *coll* tools; instrument; **~macher** *m* toolmaker

wert [ve:ɐt] *adj* worth; *die Mühe* (*e-n Versuch*) ~ worth the trouble (a try); *fig nichts* ~ no good; Wert *m* (-[*e*]*s*; -*e*) value, *esp fig a.* worth; use; *pl* data, figures; ... *im* ~(*e*) *von 20 Dollar* 20 dollars' worth of ...; *großen* ~ *legen auf* (*acc*) set great store by

werten ['ve:ɐtən] *v/t* (ge-, *h*) value; *a.* SPORT rate, judge

'**Wertgegenstand** *m* article of value

'**wertlos** *adj* worthless

'**Wertpa,piere** *pl* securities

'**Wertsachen** *pl* valuables

'Wertung f (-; -en) valuation; a. SPORT rating, judging; score, points

'wertvoll adj valuable

Wesen ['ve:zən] n (-s; -) being, creature; fig essence; nature, character

'wesentlich adj essential; considerable; **im Wesentlichen** on the whole

weshalb [vɛs'halp] interr adv → **warum**

Wespe ['vɛspə] f (-; -n) ZO wasp

Weste ['vɛstə] f (-; -n) vest, Br waistcoat

Westen ['vɛstən] m (-s; no pl) west; POL West

Western ['vɛstɐn] m (-s; -) western

'westlich 1. adj western; westerly; POL West(ern) **2.** adv: **~ von** (to the) west of

'Westwind m west(erly) wind

Wettbewerb ['vɛtbəvɛrp] m (-[e]s; -e) competition (a. ECON), contest

Wettbü,ro n betting office

Wette ['vɛtə] f (-; -n) bet; **e-e ~ abschließen** make a bet; **um die ~ laufen** etc race (**mit j-m** s.o.)

'wetteifern v/i (ge-, h) compete (**mit** with; **um** for)

'wetten v/i and v/t (ge-, h) bet; **mit j-m um 10 Dollar ~** bet s.o. ten dollars; **~ auf** (acc) bet on, back

Wetter ['vɛtɐ] n (-s; -) weather

'Wetterbericht m weather report

'Wetterfahne f weather vane

'wetterfest adj weatherproof

'Wetter|karte f weather chart; **~lage** f weather situation; **~leuchten** n sheet lightning; **~vorhersage** f weather forecast; **~warte** f weather station

'Wett|kampf m competition, contest; **~kämpfer(in)** contestant, competitor; **~lauf** m race (a. fig **mit** against); **~läufer(in)** runner

'wettmachen v/t (sep, -ge-, h) make up for

'Wettrennen n race

'Wettrüsten n (-s; no pl) arms race

'Wettstreit m contest, competition

wetzen ['vɛtsən] v/t (ge-, h) whet, sharpen

wich [vɪç] pret of **weichen**

wichtig ['vɪçtɪç] adj important

'Wichtigkeit f (-; no pl) importance

'wickeln v/t (ge-, h) change (baby); **~ in** (acc) wrap in; **~ um** wrap (a)round

Widder ['vɪdɐ] m (-s; -) ZO ram; ASTR Aries; **er ist (ein) ~** he's (an) Aries

wider ['vi:dɐ] prp (acc) **~ Willen** against

one's will; **~ Erwarten** contrary to expectations

'Widerhaken m barb

'widerhallen v/i (sep, -ge-, h) resound (**von** with)

wider'legen v/t (no -ge-, h) refute, disprove

'widerlich adj sickening, disgusting

'widerrechtlich adj illegal, unlawful

'Widerruf m JUR revocation; withdrawal; **wider'rufen** v/t (irr, **rufen**, no -ge-, h) revoke; withdraw

Widersacher ['vi:dɐzaxɐ] m (-s; -) adversary, rival

'Widerschein m reflection

wider'setzen v/refl (no -ge-, h) (dat) oppose, resist

'widersinnig adj absurd

widerspenstig ['vi:dɐʃpɛnstɪç] adj unruly, stubborn

'widerspiegeln v/t (sep, -ge-, h) reflect (a. fig); **sich ~ in** (dat) be reflected in

wider'sprechen v/i (irr, **sprechen**, no -ge-, h) (dat) contradict

'Widerspruch m contradiction

widersprüchlich ['vi:dɐʃprYçlɪç] adj contradictory

'widerspruchslos adv without contradiction

'Widerstand m resistance (a. ELECTR), opposition; **~ leisten** offer resistance (dat to); **'widerstandsfähig** adj resistant (a. TECH); **wider'stehen** v/i (irr, **stehen**, no -ge-, h) (dat) resist

wider'streben v/i (no -ge-, h) **es widerstrebt mir, dies zu tun** I hate doing or to do that; **~d** adv reluctantly

widerwärtig ['vi:dɐvɛrtɪç] adj disgusting

'Widerwille m aversion (**gegen** to), dislike (of, for); disgust (at)

'widerwillig adj reluctant, unwilling

widmen ['vɪtmən] v/t (ge-, h) dedicate; **'Widmung** f (-; -en) dedication

wie [vi:] **1.** interr adv how; **~ geht es Gordon?** how is Gordon?; **~ ist er?** what's he like?; **~ ist das Wetter?** what's the weather like?; **~ heißen Sie?** what's your name?; **~ nennt man ...?** what do you call ...?; **~ wäre (ist, steht) es mit ...?** what or how about ...?; **~ viele ...?** how many ...? **2.** cj like; as; **~ neu (verrückt)** like new (mad); **doppelt so ... ~** twice as ... as; **~ (zum Beispiel)**

such as, like; **~ üblich** as usual; **~ er sagte** as he said; **ich zeige (sage) dir, ~ (...)** I'll show (tell) you how (...)

wieder ['viːdɐ] *adv* again; *in cpds often* re...; **immer ~** again and again; **~ aufbauen** reconstruct; **~ aufnehmen** resume; **~ beleben** MED resuscitate, revive (*a. fig*); **~ erkennen** recognize (**an** *dat* by); **~ finden** find (what one has lost); *fig* regain; **~ gutmachen** make up for; **~ herstellen** restore; **~ sehen** see or meet again; **~ verwendbar** reusable; **~ verwerten** TECH recycle

Wieder|'aufbau *m* (-[e]*s*; *no pl*) reconstruction, rebuilding; **~'aufbereitung** *f* TECH recycling; reprocessing (*a.* NUCL); **~'aufbereitungsanlage** *f* TECH reprocessing plant; **~'aufleben** *n* (-*s*; *no pl*) revival; **~'aufnahme** *f* (-; *no pl*) resumption

'wiederbekommen *v/t* (*irr, kommen, sep, no -ge-, h*) get back

'Wieder|belebung *f* (-; -*en*) MED resuscitation; **~belebungsversuch** *m* MED attempt at resuscitation

'wiederbringen *v/t* (*irr, bringen, sep, -ge-, h*) bring back; return

Wieder'einführung *f* reintroduction

'Wiederentdeckung *f* rediscovery

'Wiedergabe *f* TECH reproduction, playback; **'wiedergeben** *v/t* (*irr, geben, sep, -ge-, h*) give back, return; *fig* describe; TECH play back, reproduce

Wieder'gutmachung *f* (-; -*en*) reparation

'wiederholen[1] *v/t* (*sep, -ge-, h*) (go and) get *s.o.* or *s.th.* back

wieder'holen[2] *v/t* (*no -ge-, h*) repeat; PED revise, review; THEA replay; **sich ~** repeat o.s. (*a. fig*); **wieder'holt** *adv* repeatedly, several times

Wieder'holung *f* (-; -*en*) repetition; PED review; TV *etc* rerun; SPORT replay

Wiederkehr ['viːdɐkeːɐ] *f* (-; *no pl*) return; recurrence; **'wiederkehren** *v/i* (*sep, -ge-, sein*) return; recur

'wiederkommen *v/i* (*irr, kommen, sep, -ge-, sein*) come back, return

'Wiedersehen *n* (-*s*; -) seeing *s.o.* again; reunion; **auf ~!** goodbye!

wiederum ['viːdərʊm] *adv* again; on the other hand

'Wieder|vereinigung *f* reunion, *esp* POL *a.* reunification; **~verkauf** *m* resale;

~verwendung *f* reuse; **~verwertung** *f* (-; -*en*) TECH recycling; **~wahl** *f* POL re-election

Wiege ['viːgə] *f* (-; -*n*) cradle

wiegen[1] ['viːgən] *v/t and v/i* (*irr, ge-, h*) weigh

'wiegen[2] *v/t* (*ge-, h*) rock (**in den Schlaf** to sleep)

'Wiegenlied *n* lullaby

wiehern ['viːɐn] *v/i* (*ge-, h*) ZO neigh

wies [viːs] *pret of* **weisen**

Wiese ['viːzə] *f* (-; -*n*) meadow

Wiesel ['viːzəl] *n* (-*s*; -) ZO weasel

wieso [viˈzoː] *interr adv* → **warum**

wievielt [viˈfiːlt] *adj*: **zum ~en Male?** how many times?

wild [vɪlt] *adj* wild (*a. fig*) (F **auf** *acc* about); violent

Wild *n* (-[e]*s*; *no pl*) HUNT game; GASTR *mst* venison; **~bach** *m* torrent

Wilde ['vɪldə] *m, f* (-*n*; -*n*) savage; F **wie ein ~r** like mad

Wilderer ['vɪldərɐ] *m* (-*s*; -) poacher

wildern ['vɪldɐn] *v/i* (*ge-, h*) poach

'Wildhüter *m* gamekeeper

'Wildkatze *f* ZO wild cat

'Wildleder *n* suede

'Wildnis *f* (-; -*se*) wilderness

'Wild|park *m*, **~reser,vat** *n* game park *or* reserve; **~schwein** *n* ZO wild boar

Wille ['vɪlə] *m* (-*ns*; -*n*) will; intention; **s-n ~n durchsetzen** have *or* get one's own way; **j-m s-n ~n lassen** let s.o. have his (own) way

'willenlos *adj* weak(-willed)

'Willenskraft *f* (-; *no pl*) willpower; **durch ~ erzwingen** will

'willensstark *adj* strong-willed

willig ['vɪlɪç] *adj* willing

will'kommen *adj* welcome (*a.* **~ heißen**) (**in** *dat* to)

willkürlich ['vɪlkyːɐlɪç] *adj* arbitrary; random

wimmeln ['vɪməln] *v/i* (*ge-, h*) **~ von** be teeming with

wimmern ['vɪmɐn] *v/i* (*ge-, h*) whimper

Wimpel ['vɪmpəl] *m* (-*s*; -) pennant

Wimper ['vɪmpɐ] *f* (-; -*n*) eyelash; **ohne mit der ~ zu zucken** without turning a hair; **'Wimperntusche** *f* mascara

Wind [vɪnt] *m* (-[e]*s*; -*e* ['vɪndə]) wind

Winde ['vɪndə] *f* (-; -*n*) winch, windlass, hoist

Windel ['vɪndəl] *f* (-; -*n*) diaper, *Br* nappy

winden ['vɪndən] v/t (irr, ge-, h) wind, TECH a. hoist; **sich ~** wind (one's way); writhe (with pain etc)

'**Windhund** m ZO greyhound

windig ['vɪndɪç] adj windy

'**Wind|mühle** f windmill; **~pocken** pl MED chickenpox; **~richtung** f direction of the wind; **~schutzscheibe** f MOT windshield, Br windscreen; **~stärke** f wind force

'**windstill** adj, '**Windstille** f calm

'**Windstoß** m gust

'**Windsurfen** n windsurfing

Windung f (-; -en) bend, turn (a. TECH)

Wink [vɪŋk] m (-[e]s; -e) sign; fig hint

Winkel ['vɪŋkəl] m (-s; -) corner; MATH angle; '**winkelig** adj angular; crooked

winken ['vɪŋkən] v/i (ge-, h) wave (one's hand etc), signal; beckon

winseln ['vɪnzəln] v/i (ge-, h) whimper, whine

Winter ['vɪntɐ] m (-s; -) winter

'**winterlich** adj wintry

'**Winter|reifen** m MOT snow tire (Br tyre); **~schlaf** m ZO hibernation; **~spiele** pl: **Olympische~** SPORT Winter Olympics; **~sport** m winter sports

Winzer ['vɪntsɐ] m (-s; -) winegrower

winzig ['vɪntsɪç] adj tiny, diminutive

Wipfel ['vɪpfəl] m (-s; -) (tree)top

Wippe ['vɪpə] f (-; -n), '**wippen** v/i (ge-, h) seesaw

wir [viːɐ] pers pron we; **~ drei** the three of us; F **~ sind's!** it's us!

Wirbel ['vɪrbəl] m (-s; -) whirl (a. fig); ANAT vertebra

'**wirbeln** v/i (ge-, sein) whirl

'**Wirbel|säule** f ANAT spinal column, spine; **~sturm** m cyclone, tornado; **~tier** n vertebrate; **~wind** m whirlwind

wirken ['vɪrkən] (ge-, h) **1.** v/i work; be effective (**gegen** against); look; **anregend** etc **~** have a stimulating etc effect (**auf** acc [up]on); **~ als** act as **2.** v/t weave; fig work (miracles etc)

wirklich ['vɪrklɪç] adj real, actual; true, genuine; '**Wirklichkeit** f (-; -en) reality; **in ~** in reality, actually

wirksam ['vɪrkzaːm] adj effective

'**Wirkung** f (-; -en) effect

'**wirkungslos** adj ineffective

'**wirkungsvoll** adj effective

wirr [vɪr] adj confused, mixed up; hair:

tousled; **Wirren** ['vɪrən] pl disorder, confusion; **Wirrwarr** ['vɪrvar] m (-s; no pl) confusion, mess, welter

Wirt [vɪrt] m (-[e]s; -e) landlord; '**Wirtin** f (-; -nen) landlady; '**Wirtschaft** f (-; -en) ECON, POL economy; business; → **Gastwirtschaft**; '**wirtschaften** v/i (ge-, h) keep house; manage one's money or affairs or business; economize; **gut** (**schlecht**) **~** be a good (bad) manager; '**Wirtschafterin** f (-; -nen) housekeeper; '**wirtschaftlich** adj economic; economical; '**Wirtschafts...** ECON in cpds ...gemeinschaft, ...gipfel, ...krise, ...system, ...wunder etc: economic ...

'**Wirtshaus** n → **Gastwirtschaft**

wischen ['vɪʃən] v/t (ge-, h) wipe; **Staub ~** dust

wispern ['vɪspɐn] v/t and v/i (ge-, h) whisper

wissbegierig ['vɪsbəgiːrɪç] adj curious

wissen ['vɪsən] v/t and v/i (irr, ge-, h) know; **ich möchte ~** I'd like to know, I wonder; **soviel ich weiß** as far as I know; **weißt du** you know; **weißt du noch?** (do you) remember?; **woher weißt du das?** how do you know?; **man kann nie ~** you never know; **ich will davon** (**von ihm**) **nichts ~** I don't want anything to do with it (him)

'**Wissen** n (-s; no pl) knowledge; know-how; **m-s ~s** as far as I know

'**Wissenschaft** f (-; -en) science

'**Wissenschaftler** m (-s; -), '**Wissenschaftlerin** f (-; -nen) scientist

'**wissenschaftlich** adj scientific

'**wissenswert** adj worth knowing; **Wissenswertes** useful facts; **alles Wissenswerte** (**über** acc) all you need to know (about)

wittern ['vɪtɐn] v/t (ge-, h) scent, smell (both a. fig)

Witwe ['vɪtvə] f (-; -n) widow

Witwer ['vɪtvɐ] m (-s; -) widower

Witz [vɪts] m (-es; -e) joke; **~e reißen** crack jokes

witzig ['vɪtsɪç] adj funny, witty

wo [voː] adv where; **~ ... doch** when, although

wob [voːp] pret of **weben**

wobei [vo'bai] adv: **~ bist du?** what are you at?; **~ mir einfällt** which reminds me

Woche ['vɔxə] f (-; -n) week

'**Wochen...** in cpds ...*lohn*, ...*markt*, ...*zeitung etc*: weekly ...; **~ende** n weekend; **am ~** on (Br at) the weekend

'**wochenlang 1.** adj: **~es Warten** (many) weeks of waiting **2.** adv for weeks

'**Wochenschau** f film: newsreel

'**Wochentag** m weekday

wöchentlich ['vœçəntliç] **1.** adj weekly **2.** adv weekly, every week; **einmal ~** once a week

wodurch [vo'durç] adv how; through which

wofür [vo'fy:ɐ] adv for which; **~?** what (...) for?

wog [vo:k] pret of **wiegen**[1] and **wägen**

Woge ['vo:gə] f (-; -n) wave, esp fig a. surge; breaker; '**wogen** v/i (ge-, h) surge, heave (both a. fig)

woher [vo'he:ɐ] adv where ... from; **~ weißt du (das)?** how do you know?

wohin [vo'hɪn] adv where (... to)

wohl [vo:l] adv and cj well; probably, I suppose; **sich ~ fühlen → wohlfühlen**; **~ oder übel** willy-nilly, whether you etc like it or not; **~ kaum** hardly

Wohl n (-[e]s; no pl) well-being; **auf j-s ~ trinken** drink to s.o.('s health); **zum ~!** to your health!; F cheers!

'**wohlbehalten** adv safely

'**Wohlfahrtsstaat** m welfare state

'**wohlfühlen** v/refl (sep, -ge-, h): **sich ~** feel well, be well; feel good; feel at home (**bei** with); **ich fühle mich nicht wohl** I don't feel well

'**wohl|gemerkt** adv mind you; **~genährt** adj well-fed; **~gesinnt** adj: **j-m ~ sein** be well-disposed towards s.o.; **~habend** adj well-off, well-to-do

wohlig ['vo:liç] adj snug, cozy, Br cosy

'**Wohl|stand** m (-[e]s; no pl) prosperity, affluence; **~standsgesellschaft** f affluent society

'**Wohltat** f (-; no pl) pleasure; relief; blessing; '**Wohltäter(in)** benefactor (benefactress); '**wohltätig** adj charitable; **für ~e Zwecke** for charity

'**Wohltätigkeits...** in cpds ...*ball*, ...*konzert etc*: charity ...

'**wohltun** v/i (irr, tun, sep, -ge-, h): **j-m ~** do s.o. good

'**wohlverdient** adj well-deserved

'**wohlwollend** adj benevolent

wohnen ['vo:nən] v/i (ge-, h) live (**in** dat in; **bei j-m** with s.o.); stay (**in** dat at; **bei** with)

'**Wohngebiet** n residential area

'**Wohngemeinschaft** f: (**mit j-m**) **in e-r ~ leben** share an apartment (Br a flat) or a house (with s.o.)

wohnlich ['vo:nliç] adj comfortable, snug, cozy, Br cosy

'**Wohnmo,bil** n (-s; -e) camper, motor home (Br caravan)

'**Wohn|siedlung** f housing development (Br estate); **~sitz** m residence; **ohne festen ~** of no fixed abode

'**Wohnung** f (-; -en) apartment, Br flat; **m-e** etc **~** my etc place

'**Wohnungs|amt** n housing office; **~bau** m (-[e]s; no pl) house building; **~not** f housing shortage

'**Wohnwagen** m trailer, Br caravan; mobile home

'**Wohnzimmer** n sitting or living room

wölben ['vœlbən] v/refl (ge-, h), '**Wölbung** f (-; -en) vault, arch

Wolf [volf] m (-[e]s; Wölfe ['vœlfə]) zo wolf

Wolke ['volkə] f (-; -n) cloud

'**Wolkenbruch** m cloudburst

'**Wolkenkratzer** m (-s; -) skyscraper

'**wolkenlos** adj cloudless

wolkig ['volkiç] adj cloudy, clouded

'**Woll...** in cpds ...*schal*, ...*socken etc*: wool(l)en ...; **~decke** f blanket

Wolle ['volə] f (-; -n) wool

wollen ['volən] v/t and v/i (ge-, h) and v/aux (no -ge-, h) want (to); **lieber ~** prefer; **~ wir (gehen** etc**)?** shall we (go etc)?; **~ Sie bitte ...** will or would you please ...; **wie (was, wann) du willst** as (whatever, whenever) you like; **sie will, dass ich komme** she wants me to come; **ich wollte, ich wäre (hätte) ...** I wish I were (had) ...

womit [vo'mɪt] adv with which; **~?** what ... with?

Wonne ['vonə] f (-; -n) joy, delight

woran [vo'ran] adv: **~ denkst du?** what are you thinking of?; **~ liegt es, dass ...?** how is it that ...?; **~ sieht man, welche (ob) ...?** how can you tell which (if) ...?

worauf [vo'rauf] adv after which; on which; **~?** what ... on?; **~ wartest du?** what are you waiting for?

woraus [vo'raus] adv from which; **~ ist es?** what's it made of?

worin [voˈrɪn] *adv* in which; **~?** where?

Wort [vɔrt] *n* (-[e]s; -e, **Wörter** [ˈvœrtɐ]) word; **mit anderen ~en** in other words; **sein ~ geben (halten, brechen)** give (keep, break) one's word; **j-n beim ~ nehmen** take s.o. at his word; **ein gutes ~ einlegen für** put in a good word for; **j-m ins ~ fallen** cut s.o. short

'Wortart *f* LING part of speech

Wörter|buch [ˈvœrtɐbuːx] *n* dictionary; **~verzeichnis** *n* vocabulary, list of words

'Wortführer *m* spokesman; **'Wortführerin** *f* spokeswoman

'wortkarg *adj* taciturn

wörtlich [ˈvœrtlɪç] *adj* literal; **~e Rede** LING direct speech

'Wort|schatz *m* vocabulary; **~spiel** *n* pun; **~stellung** *f* LING word order

worüber [voˈryːbɐ] *adv* about which; **~ lachen Sie?** what are you laughing at *or* about?

worum [voˈrʊm] *adv* about which; **~ handelt es sich?** what is it about?

worunter [voˈrʊntɐ] *adv* among which; **~?** what ... under?

wovon [voˈfɔn] *adv* about which; **~ redest du?** what are you talking about?

wovor [voˈfoːɐ] *adv* of which; **~ hast du Angst?** what are you afraid of?

wozu [voˈtsuː] *adv:* **~ er mir rät** what he advised me to do; **~?** what (...) for?; why?

Wrack [vrak] *n* (-[e]s; -s) MAR wreck (*a. fig*)

wrang [vraŋ] *pret of* **wringen**

wringen [ˈvrɪŋən] *v/t* (*irr, ge-, h*) wring

Wucher [ˈvuːxɐ] *m* (-s; *no pl*) usury

Wucherer [ˈvuːxərɐ] *m* (-s; -) usurer

'wuchern *v/i* (*ge-, h*) grow (*fig* be) rampant; **Wucherung** [ˈvuːxərʊŋ] *f* (-; -en) MED growth

Wuchs [vuːks] *m* (-es; *no pl*) growth; build

wuchs [vuːks] *pret of* **wachsen¹**

Wucht [vʊxt] *f* (-; *no pl*) force; impact

wuchtig [ˈvʊxtɪç] *adj* massive; powerful

wühlen [ˈvyːlən] *v/i* (*ge-, h*) dig; zo root; rummage (**in** *dat* in, through)

Wulst [vʊlst] *m* (-es; **Wülste** [ˈvʏlstə], *f*-; **Wülste**) bulge; roll (*of fat*)

wulstig [ˈvʊlstɪç] *adj* bulging; thick

wund [vʊnt] *adj* MED sore; **~e Stelle** MED sore; **~er Punkt** *fig* sore point

Wunde [ˈvʊndə] *f* (-; -n) MED wound

Wunder [ˈvʊndɐ] *n* (-s; -) miracle, *fig a.* wonder; **~ wirken** work wonders; (**es ist) kein ~, dass du müde bist** no wonder you are tired; **'wunderbar** *adj* wonderful, marvel(l)ous

'Wunderkind *n* infant prodigy

'wunderlich *adj* funny, odd; senile

'wundern *v/refl* (*ge-, h*) be surprised *or* astonished (**über** *acc* at)

'wundervoll *adj* wonderful

'Wundstarrkrampf *m* (-es; *no pl*) MED tetanus

Wunsch [vʊnʃ] *m* (-[e]s; **Wünsche** [ˈvʏnʃə]) wish; request; **auf j-s ~** at s.o.'s request; **auf eigenen ~** at one's own request; (**je) nach ~** as desired

wünschen [ˈvʏnʃən] *v/t* (*ge-, h*) wish; **sich et.** (**zu Weihnachten** *etc*) **~** want s.th. (for Christmas *etc*); **das habe ich mir** (**schon immer) gewünscht** that's what I (always) wanted; **alles, was man sich nur ~ kann** everything one could wish for; **ich wünschte, ich wäre** (**hätte**) **...** I wish I were (had) ...

'wünschenswert *adj* desirable

wurde [ˈvʊrdə] *pret of* **werden**

Würde [ˈvʏrdə] *f* (-; -n) dignity

'würdelos *adj* undignified

'Würdenträger *m* dignitary

'würdevoll *adj* dignified

würdig [ˈvʏrdɪç] *adj* worthy (*gen* of); dignified; **würdigen** [ˈvʏrdɪɡən] *v/t* (*ge-, h*) appreciate; **j-n keines Blickes ~** ignore s.o. completely; **'Würdigung** *f* (-; -en) appreciation

Wurf [vʊrf] *m* (-[e]s; **Würfe** [ˈvʏrfə]) throw; zo litter

Würfel [ˈvʏrfəl] *m* (-s; -) cube (*a.* MATH); dice; **'würfeln** *v/i* (*ge-, h*) throw dice (**um** for); play dice; GASTR dice; **e-e Sechs ~** throw a six

'Würfelzucker *m* lump sugar

'Wurfgeschoss *n* missile

würgen [ˈvʏrɡən] *v/i and v/t* (*ge-, h*) choke; throttle *s.o.*

Wurm [vʊrm] *m* (-[e]s; **Würmer** [ˈvʏrmɐ]) zo worm; **wurmen** [ˈvʊrmən] *F v/t* (*ge-, h*) gall *s.o.*; **'wurmstichig** [ˈvʊrmʃtiçɪç] *adj* worm-eaten

Wurst [vʊrst] *f* (-; **Würste** [ˈvʏrstə]) sausage

Würstchen [ˈvʏrstçən] *n* (-s; -) small

sausage, frankfurter, wiener; hot dog
Würze [ˈvʏrtsə] f (-; -n) spice (a. fig)
Wurzel [ˈvʊrtsəl] f (-; -n) root (a. MATH);
~n schlagen take root (a. fig)
'wurzeln v/i (ge-, h) **~ in** (dat) be rooted
in (a. fig)
'würzen v/t (ge-, h) spice, season, fla-
vo(u)r; **würzig** [ˈvʏrtsɪç] adj spicy,
well-seasoned
wusch [vuːʃ] pret of **waschen**
wusste [ˈvʊstə] pret of **wissen**
Wust [vuːst] F m (-[e]s; no pl) tangled

mass
wüst [vyːst] adj waste; confused; wild,
dissolute
Wüste [ˈvyːstə] f (-; -n) desert
Wut [vuːt] f (-; no pl) rage, fury; **e-e ~
haben** be furious (**auf** acc with)
'Wutanfall m fit of rage
wüten [ˈvyːtən] v/i (ge-, h) rage (a. fig);
~d adj furious (**auf** acc with; **über** acc
at), F mad (at)
'wutschnaubend adj fuming

X, Y

X-Beine [ˈɪksbainə] pl knock-knees; **sie
hat ~** she's knock-kneed
x-beinig [ˈɪksbainɪç] adj knock-kneed
x-be'liebig adj: **jede(r, -s) x-Beliebige
...** any ... you like, F any old ...
'x-mal F adv umpteen times

x-te [ˈɪkstə] adj: **zum ~n Male** for the
umpteenth time
Xylophon [ksyloˈfoːn] n (-s; -e) MUS xy-
lophone
Yacht [jaxt] f (-; -en) MAR yacht
Yoga [ˈjoːga] m, n (-[s]; no pl) yoga

Z

Zacke [ˈtsakə] f (-; -n), **'Zacken** m (-s; -)
(sharp) point; tooth; **zackig** [ˈtsakɪç]
adj serrated; jagged; fig smart
zaghaft [ˈtsaːhaft] adj timid
zäh [tsɛː] adj tough (a. fig); **~flüssig** adj
thick, viscous; fig slow-moving (traffic)
Zähigkeit [ˈtsɛːɪçkait] f (-; no pl) toughness, fig a. stamina
Zahl [tsaːl] f (-; -en) number; figure
'zahlbar adj payable (**an** acc to; **bei** at)
zählbar [ˈtsɛːlbaːɐ] adj countable
zahlen [ˈtsaːlən] v/i and v/t (ge-, h) pay;
~, bitte! the check (Br bill), please!
zählen [ˈtsɛːlən] v/t and v/i (ge-, h) count
(**bis** up to; fig **auf** acc on); **~ zu** rank
with the best etc
'zahlenmäßig 1. adj numerical **2.** adv:
j-m ~ überlegen sein outnumber s.o.
Zähler [ˈtsɛːlɐ] m (-s; -) counter (a.
TECH); MATH numerator; ELECTR etc meter
'Zahlkarte f post deposit (Br paying-in)
slip
'zahllos adj countless

'Zahlmeister m MIL paymaster; MAR
purser
'zahlreich 1. adj numerous **2.** adv in
great number
'Zahltag m payday
'Zahlung f (-; -en) payment
'Zählung f (-; -en) count; POL census
'Zahlungs|aufforderung f request for
payment; **~bedingungen** pl terms of
payment; **~befehl** m order to pay
'zahlungsfähig adj solvent
'Zahlungs|frist f term of payment;
~mittel n currency; **gesetzliches ~** legal tender; **~schwierigkeiten** pl financial difficulties; **~ter,min** m date of
payment
'zahlungsunfähig adj insolvent
'Zählwerk n TECH counter
'Zahlwort n LING numeral
zahm [tsaːm] adj tame (a. fig)
zähmen [ˈtsɛːmən] v/t (ge-, h) tame (a.
fig); **'Zähmung** f (-; no pl) taming
Zahn [tsaːn] m (-[e]s; Zähne [ˈtsɛːnə])
tooth, TECH a. cog; **~arzt** m, **~ärztin** f

dentist, dental surgeon; **~bürste** f toothbrush; **~creme** f toothpaste

zahnen ['tsa:nən] v/i (ge-, h) cut one's teeth, teethe

'**Zahnfleisch** n gums

'**zahnlos** adj toothless

'**Zahn|lücke** f gap between the teeth; **~medi,zin** f dentistry; **~pasta, ~paste** f toothpaste; **~radbahn** f rack railroad; **~schmerzen** pl toothache; **~spange** f MED brace; **~stein** m tartar; **~stocher** m (-s; -) toothpick

Zange ['tsaŋə] f (-; -n) TECH pliers; pincers; tongs; MED forceps; zo pincer

zanken ['tsaŋkən] v/refl (ge-, h) quarrel (**wegen** about; **um** over), fight, argue (about; over)

zänkisch ['tsɛŋkɪʃ] adj quarrelsome

Zäpfchen ['tsɛpfçən] n (-s; -) ANAT uvula; PHARM suppository

zapfen ['tsapfən] v/t (ge-, h) tap

'**Zapfen** m (-s; -) faucet, Br tap; TECH peg, pin; bung; tenon; pivot; BOT cone

'**Zapfenstreich** m MIL tattoo, taps

'**Zapf|hahn** m faucet, Br tap; MOT nozzle; **~säule** f MOT gasoline (Br petrol) pump

zappelig ['tsapəlɪç] adj fidgety

zappeln ['tsapəln] v/i (ge-, h) fidget, wriggle

zappen ['zɛpən] F v/i (ge-, h) TV zap

zart [tsa:ɐt] adj tender; gentle; **~ fühlend** sensitive

'**Zartgefühl** n (-[e]s; no pl) delicacy (of feeling), sensitivity, tact

zärtlich ['tsɛ:ɐtlɪç] adj tender, affectionate (**zu** with); '**Zärtlichkeit** f (-; -en) (no pl) tenderness, affection; caress

Zauber ['tsaubɐ] m (-s; -) magic, spell, charm (all a. fig), fig enchantment; **Zauberei** [tsaubə'rai] f (-; -en) magic, witchcraft; **Zauberer** ['tsaubərɐ] m (-s; -) magician, sorcerer, wizard (a. fig); '**zauberhaft** fig adj enchanting, charming; **Zauberin** ['tsaubərɪn] f (-; -nen) sorceress

'**Zauber|kraft** f magic power; **~künstler** m magician, conjurer; **~kunststück** n conjuring trick

'**zaubern** (ge-, h) **1.** v/i practise magic; do conjuring tricks **2.** v/t conjure (up)

'**Zauberspruch** m spell

zaudern ['tsaudɐn] v/i (ge-, h) hesitate

Zaum [tsaum] m (-[e]s; Zäume ['tsɔymə]) bridle; **im ~ halten** control (**sich** o.s.), keep in check

zäumen ['tsɔymən] v/t (ge-, h) bridle

'**Zaumzeug** n (-[e]s; -e) bridle

Zaun [tsaun] m (-[e]s; Zäune ['tsɔynə]) fence; **~gast** m onlooker; **~pfahl** m pale

z. B. abbr of **zum Beispiel** e.g., for example, for instance

Zebra ['tse:bra] n (-s; -s) zo zebra

'**Zebrastreifen** m MOT zebra crossing

Zeche ['tsɛçə] f (-; -n) check, Br bill; (coal) mine, pit; **die ~ bezahlen müssen** F have to foot the bill

Zeh [tse:] m (-s; -en), **Zehe** ['tse:ə] f (-; -n) ANAT toe; **große (kleine) ~** big (little) toe; '**Zehennagel** m ANAT toenail

'**Zehenspitze** f tip of the toe; **auf ~n gehen** (walk on) tiptoe

zehn [tse:n] adj ten; '**zehnfach** adj tenfold; '**zehnjährig** ['tse:njɛ:rɪç] adj ten-year-old (boy etc); ten-year anniversary etc; absence etc of ten years

Zehnkampf m SPORT decathlon

'**zehnmal** adv ten times; '**zehnte** adj tenth; '**Zehntel** n (-s; -) tenth; '**zehntens** adv tenthly

Zeichen ['tsaiçən] n (-s; -) sign; mark; signal; **zum ~** gen as a token of; **~block** m sketch pad; **~brett** n drawing board; **~dreieck** n MATH set square; **~folge** f IT string; **~lehrer(in)** art teacher; **~setzung** f (-; no pl) LING punctuation; **~sprache** f sign language; **~trickfilm** m (animated) cartoon

zeichnen ['tsaiçnən] v/i and v/t (ge-, h) draw; mark (a. fig); sign; fig leave its mark on s.o.; '**Zeichnen** n (-s; no pl) drawing; PED art; '**Zeichner** ['tsaiçnɐ] m (-s; -) mst graphic artist; draftsman, Br draughtsman; '**Zeichnung** f (-; -en) drawing; diagram; zo marking

Zeigefinger ['tsaigəfɪŋɐ] m ANAT forefinger, index finger; **zeigen** ['tsaigən] (ge-, h) **1.** v/t show (a. sich ...); **2.** v/i: **~ nach** point to; (**mit dem Finger**) **~ auf** (acc) point (one's finger) at; **Zeiger** ['tsaigɐ] m (-s; -) hand; TECH pointer, needle; '**Zeigestock** m pointer

Zeile ['tsailə] f (-; -n) line (a. TV); **j-m ein paar ~n schreiben** drop s.o. a line

Zeit [tsait] f (-; -en) time; age, era; LING tense; **vor einiger ~** some time ago, a while ago; *in letzter* ~ lately, recently; *in der* (*or* zur) ~ *gen* in the days of; ... *aller* ~*en* ... of all time; *die* ~ *ist um* time's up; *e-e* ~ *lang* for some time, for a while; *sich* ~ *lassen* take one's time; *es wird* ~, *dass* ... it's time to *inf*; *das waren noch* ~*en* those were the days; ~ *raubend* → *zeitraubend*; → *zurzeit*

'Zeit|abschnitt *m* period (of time); ~**alter** *n age*; ~**bombe** *f* time bomb (*a. fig*); ~**druck** *m*: *unter* ~ *stehen* be pressed for time; ~**fahren** *n* (*-s; no pl*) cycling: time trials

'zeitgemäß *adj* modern, up-to-date

'Zeitgenosse *m*, 'Zeitgenossin *f*, 'zeitgenössisch ['tsaitgənœsiʃ] *adj* contemporary

'Zeit|geschichte *f* (*-; no pl*) contemporary history; ~**gewinn** *m* (*-[e]s; no pl*) gain of time; ~**karte** *f* season ticket

'Zeitlang *f* → Zeit

zeit'lebens *adv* all one's life

'zeitlich 1. *adj* time ... 2. *adv*: *et.* ~ *pla-nen or abstimmen* time s.th.

'zeitlos *adj* timeless; classic

'Zeit|lupe *f: in* ~ in slow motion; ~**not** *f: in* ~ *sein* be pressed for time; ~**punkt** *m* moment; ~**raffer** *m*: *im* ~ in quick motion

'zeitraubend *adj* time-consuming

'Zeitraum *m* period (of time)

'Zeitschrift *f* magazine

'Zeitung ['tsaitʊŋ] *f* (*-; -en*) (news)paper

'Zeitungs|abonne,ment *n* subscription to a paper; ~**ar,tikel** *m* newspaper article; ~**ausschnitt** *m* (newspaper) clipping (*Br* cutting); ~**junge** *m* paper boy; ~**kiosk** *m* newspaper kiosk; ~**no,tiz** *f* press item; ~**pa,pier** *n* newspaper; ~**stand** *m* newsstand; ~**verkäufer(in)** newsdealer, *Br* news vendor

'Zeitverlust *m* (*-[e]s; no pl*) loss of time

'Zeitverschiebung *f* AVIAT time lag

'Zeitverschwendung *f* waste of time

'Zeitvertreib ['tsaitfɛʁtraip] *m* (*-[e]s; -e*) pastime; *zum* ~ to pass the time

'zeitweilig ['tsaitvailɪç] *adj* temporary

'zeitweise *adv* at times, occasionally

'Zeitwort *n* (*-[e]s; -wörter*) LING verb

'Zeitzeichen *n* radio: time signal

'Zeitzünder *m* MIL time fuse

Zelle ['tsɛlə] *f* (*-; -n*) cell

Zellstoff ['tsɛlʃtɔf] *m*, Zellulose [tsɛlu-

'lo:zə] *f* (*-; -n*) TECH cellulose

Zelt [tsɛlt] *n* (*-[e]s; -e*) tent; zelten ['tsɛl-tən] *v/i* (*ge-, h*) camp; 'Zeltlager *n* camp; 'Zeltplatz *m* campsite

Zement [tse'mɛnt] *m* (*-[e]s; -e*), zemen-tieren [tsemɛn'ti:rən] *v/t* (*no -ge-, h*) cement

Zenit [tse'ni:t] *m* (*-[e]s; no pl*) zenith

zensieren [tsɛn'zi:rən] *v/t* (*no -ge-, h*) censor; PED mark, grade; Zensor ['tsɛnzoːʁ] *m* (*-s; -en* [tsɛn'zo:rən]) censor; Zensur [tsɛn'zu:ʁ] *f* (*-; -en* [tsɛn'zu:rən]) (*no pl*) censorship; PED mark, grade

Zentimeter [tsɛnti'me:tɐ] *n, m* (*-s; -*) centimeter, *Br* centimetre

Zentner ['tsɛntnɐ] *m* (*-s; -*) 50 kilo-grams, metric hundredweight

zentral [tsɛn'tra:l] *adj* central

Zentrale [tsɛn'tra:lə] *f* (*-; -n*) head of-fice; headquarters; TEL switchboard; TECH control room

Zen'tral|heizung *f* central heating; ~**verriegelung** *f* MOT central locking

Zentrum ['tsɛntrʊm] *n* (*-s; Zentren*) center, *Br* centre

Zepter ['tsɛptɐ] *n* (*-s; -*) scepter, *Br* sceptre

zer'brechen *v/i* (*irr, brechen, no -ge-, sein*) *and v/t* (*h*) break; → *Kopf*

zer'brechlich *adj* fragile

zer'bröckeln *v/t* (*no -ge-, h*) *and v/i* (*sein*) crumble

zer'drücken *v/t* (*no -ge-, h*) crush

Zeremonie [tseremo'ni:] *f* (*-; -n*) cere-mony

zeremoniell [tseremo'njɛl] *adj*, Zeremoni'ell *n* (*-s; -e*) ceremonial

Zer'fall *m* (*-[e]s; no pl*) disintegration, decay; zer'fallen *v/i* (*irr, fallen, no -ge-, sein*) disintegrate, decay; ~ *in* (*acc*) break up into

zer|'fetzen *v/t* (*no -ge-, h*) tear to pieces; ~'fressen *v/t* (*irr, fressen, no -ge-, h*) eat (holes in); CHEM corrode; ~'gehen *v/i* (*irr, gehen, no -ge-, sein*) melt, dis-solve; ~'hacken *v/t* (*no -ge-, h*) chop (*a.* ELECTR)

zerknirscht [tsɛɐ'knɪrʃt] *adj* remorse-ful

zer|'knittern *v/t* (*no -ge-, h*) (c)rumple, crease; ~'knüllen *v/t* (*no -ge-, h*) crum-ple up; ~'kratzen *v/t* (*no -ge-, h*) scratch; ~'krümeln *v/t* (*no -ge-, h*) crumble; **~'lassen** v/t (*irr*, *lassen*, *no -ge-*, *h*) melt; **~'legen** v/t (*no -ge-*, *h*) take apart *or* to pieces; TECH dismantle; GASTR carve; CHEM, LING, *fig* analyze, *Br* analyse

zer'lumpt *adj* ragged, tattered

zer'mahlen v/t (*no -ge-*, *h*) grind

zer'mürben v/t (*no -ge-*, *h*) wear down

zer'quetschen v/t (*no -ge-*, *h*) crush

Zerrbild ['tsɛʁbɪlt] *n* caricature

zer'reiben v/t (*irr*, *reiben*, *no -ge-*, *h*) rub to powder, pulverize

zer'reißen (*irr*, *reißen*, *no -ge-*) **1.** v/t (*h*) tear up *or* to pieces; *sich die Hose ~* tear one's trousers **2.** v/i (*sein*) tear; break

zerren ['tsɛrən] (*ge-*, *h*) **1.** v/t tug, drag, pull (*a.* MED); **2.** v/i: *~ an* (*dat*) tug (*or* strain) at

'Zerrung *f* (-; *-en*) MED pulled muscle

zerrütten [tsɛʁ'rʏtən] v/t (*no -ge-*, *h*) ruin; **zer'rüttet** *adj*: *~e Ehe* (*Verhältnisse*) broken marriage (home)

zer'|sägen v/t (*no -ge-*, *h*) saw up; **~schellen** [tsɛʁ'ʃɛlən] v/i (*no -ge-*, *sein*) be smashed, AVIAT *a.* crash; **~'schlagen 1.** v/t (*irr*, *schlagen*, *no -ge-*, *h*) smash (to pieces); *fig* smash; *sich ~* come to nothing **2.** *adj*: *sich ~ fühlen* be (all) worn out, F be dead beat; **~'schmettern** v/t (*no -ge-*, *h*) smash (to pieces), shatter *(a. fig)*; **~'schneiden** v/t (*irr*, *schneiden*, *no -ge-*, *h*) cut (up); **~'setzen** v/t (*no -ge-*, *h*) CHEM decompose (*a. sich ~*); *fig* corrupt, undermine; **~'splittern** v/t (*no -ge-*, *h*) *and* v/i (*sein*) split (up), splinter; shatter; **~'springen** v/i (*irr*, *springen*, *no -ge-*, *sein*) crack; shatter; **~'stampfen** v/t (*no -ge-*, *h*) pound; GASTR mash

zer'stäuben v/t (*no -ge-*, *h*) spray; **Zer·stäuber** [tsɛʁ'ʃtɔybɐ] *m* (*-s*; -) atomizer, sprayer

zer'stören v/t (*no -ge-*, *h*) destroy, ruin (*both a. fig*); **Zer'störer** *m* (*-s*; -) destroyer (*a.* MAR); **zer'störerisch** *adj* destructive; **Zer'störung** *f* (-; *-en*) destruction

zer'streuen v/t *and* v/*refl* (*no -ge-*, *h*) scatter, disperse; break up (*crowd etc*); *fig* take s.o.'s (*refl* one's) mind off things; **zer'streut** *fig adj* absent-minded; **Zer'streutheit** *f* (-; *no pl*) ab-

sent-mindedness; **Zer'streuung** *fig f* (-; *-en*) diversion, distraction

zer'stückeln v/t (*no -ge-*, *h*) cut up *or* (in)to pieces; dismember (*body*)

Zertifikat [tsɛrtifi'kaːt] *n* (-[*e*]*s*; *-e*) certificate

zer'treten v/t (*irr*, *treten*, *no -ge-*, *h*) crush (*a. fig*)

zer'trümmern v/t (*no -ge-*, *h*) smash

zerzaust [tsɛʁ'tsaust] *adj* tousled, dishevel(l)ed

Zettel ['tsɛtəl] *m* (*-s*; -) slip (of paper); note; label, sticker

Zeug [tsɔyk] *n* (-[*e*]*s*; *-e*) stuff (*a.* F); things; *er hat das ~ dazu* he's got what it takes; *dummes ~* nonsense

Zeuge ['tsɔygə] *m* (*-n*; *-n*) witness

'zeugen[1] v/i (*ge-*, *h*) JUR give evidence (*für* for); *fig ~ von* testify to

'zeugen[2] v/t (*ge-*, *h*) BIOL procreate; father

'Zeugen|aussage *f* JUR testimony, evidence; **~bank** *f* (-; *-bänke*) JUR witness stand (*Br* box)

'Zeugin *f* (-; *-nen*) JUR (female) witness

Zeugnis ['tsɔyknɪs] *n* (*-ses*; *-se*) report card, *Br* (school) report; certificate, diploma; reference; *pl* credentials

'Zeugung *f* (-; *-en*) BIOL procreation

z. H(d). *abbr of zu Händen* attn, attention

Zickzack ['tsɪktsak] *m* (-[*e*]*s*; *-e*) (*a. im ~ fahren*) zigzag

Ziege ['tsiːgə] *f* (-; *-n*) ZO (nanny) goat; F *contp* (*blöde*) *~* (silly old) cow

Ziegel ['tsiːgəl] *m* (*-s*; -) brick; tile

'Ziegeldach *n* tiled roof

Ziegelei [tsiːgə'lai] *f* (-; *-en*) brickyard

'Ziegelstein *m* brick

'Ziegen|bock *m* ZO billy goat; **~leder** *n* kid (leather); **~peter** ['tsiːgənpeːtɐ] *m* (*-s*; -) MED mumps

ziehen ['tsiːən] (*irr*, *-ge-*) **1.** v/t (*h*) pull, draw; take off *one's* hat (*vor dat* to) (*a. fig*); AGR grow; pull *or* take out (*aus* of); *j-n ~ an* (*dat*) pull s.o. by; *auf sich ~* attract (*attention etc*); *sich ~* run; stretch; → *Länge, Erwägung* **2.** v/i (*h*) pull (*an dat* at); (*sein*) move; ZO *etc* migrate; go; travel; wander, roam; *es zieht* there's a draft (*Br* draught)

Ziehharmonika ['tsiːharmoːnika] *f* (-; *-s*) MUS accordion

'**Ziehung** f (-; -en) draw
Ziel [tsi:l] n (-[e]s; -e) aim, target, mark (all a. fig), fig a. goal, objective; destination; SPORT finish; **sich ein ~ setzen** set o.s. a goal; **sein ~ erreichen** reach one's goal; **sich zum ~ gesetzt haben, et. zu tun** aim to do or at doing s.th.
'**Zielband** n (-[e]s; -bänder) SPORT tape
zielen ['tsi:lən] v/i (ge-, h) (take) aim (**auf** acc at)
'**Ziellinie** f SPORT finishing line
'**ziellos** adj aimless
'**Zielscheibe** f target, fig a. object
zielstrebig ['tsi:lʃtre:biç] adj purposeful, determined
ziemlich ['tsi:mlıç] **1.** adj quite a **2.** adv rather, fairly, quite, F pretty; **~ viele** quite a few
Zierde ['tsi:ɐdə] f (-; -n) (**zur** as a) decoration; **zieren** ['tsi:rən] v/t (ge-, h) decorate; **sich ~** be coy; make a fuss
zierlich ['tsi:rlıç] adj dainty; petite
Zierpflanze ['tsi:ɐpflantsə] f ornamental plant
Ziffer ['tsıfɐ] f (-; -n) figure
'**Zifferblatt** n dial, face
Zigarette [tsiga'retə] f (-; -n) cigarette
Ziga'retten|auto,mat m cigarette machine; **~stummel** m cigarette end, stub, butt
Zigarre [tsi'garə] f (-; -n) cigar
Zimmer ['tsımɐ] n (-s; -) room; apartment; **~einrichtung** f furniture; **~mädchen** n (chamber)maid; **~mann** m carpenter
'**zimmern** v/t (ge-, h) build, make
'**Zimmer|pflanze** f indoor plant; **~service** m room service; **~suche** f: **auf ~ sein** be looking (or hunting) for a room; **~vermittlung** f accommodation office
zimperlich ['tsımpɐlıç] adj prudish; soft, F sissy
Zimt [tsımt] m (-[e]s; -e) cinnamon
Zink ['tsıŋk] n (-[e]s; no pl) CHEM zinc
Zinke ['tsıŋkə] f (-; -n) tooth; prong
Zinn [tsın] n (-[e]s; no pl) CHEM tin; pewter
Zins [tsıns] m (-es; -en) ECON interest (a. pl); **3% ~ bringen** bear interest at 3%; '**zinslos** adj ECON interest-free;
'**Zinssatz** m ECON interest rate
Zipfel ['tsıpfəl] m (-s; -) corner; point; tail; GASTR end; **~mütze** f pointed cap

zirka ['tsırka] adv about, approximately
Zirkel ['tsırkəl] m (-s; -) circle (a. fig); MATH compasses, dividers
zirkulieren [tsırku'li:rən] v/i (no -ge-, h) circulate
Zirkus ['tsırkʊs] m (-; -se) circus
zirpen ['tsırpən] v/i (ge-, h) chirp
zischen ['tsıʃən] v/i and v/t (ge-, h) hiss; fat etc: sizzle; fig whiz(z)
ziselieren [tsizə'li:rən] v/t (no -ge-, h) TECH chase
Zitat [tsi'ta:t] n (-[e]s; -e) quotation, F quote; **zitieren** [tsi'ti:rən] v/t (no -ge-, h) quote, cite (a. JUR), JUR summon
Zitrone [tsi'tro:nə] f (-; -n) BOT lemon
Zi'tronen|limo,nade f lemon soda or pop, Br (fizzy) lemonade; **~saft** m lemon juice; **~schale** f lemon peel
zitterig ['tsıtərıç] adj shaky; **zittern** ['tsıtɐn] v/i (ge-, h) tremble, shake (both: **vor** dat with)
zivil [tsi'vi:l] adj civil, civilian
Zi'vil n (-s; no pl) civilian clothes; **Polizist in ~** plainclothes policeman
Zi'vildienst m MIL alternative service (in lieu of military service)
Zivilisation [tsiviliza'tsjo:n] f (-; -en) civilization; **zivilisieren** [tsivili'zi:rən] v/t (no -ge-, h) civilize
Zivilist [tsivi'lıst] m (-en; -en) civilian
Zi'vilrecht n (-[e]s; no pl) JUR civil law
Zi'vilschutz m civil defen|se, Br -ce
Znüni ['tsny:ni] Swiss m, n (-s; -) mid-morning snack, tea (or coffee) break
zog [tso:k] pret of **ziehen**
zögern ['tsø:gɐn] v/i (ge-, h) hesitate; '**Zögern** n (-s; no pl) hesitation
Zoll[1] [tsɔl] m (-[e]s; -) inch
Zoll[2] m (-[e]s; Zölle ['tsœlə]) (no pl) customs; duty
'**Zollabfertigung** f customs clearance
'**Zollbeamte** m customs officer
'**Zollerklärung** f customs declaration
'**zollfrei** adj duty-free
'**Zollkon,trolle** f customs examination
'**zollpflichtig** adj liable to duty
'**Zollstock** m (folding) rule
'**Zone** ['tso:nə] f (-; -n) zone
Zoo [tso:] m (-s; -s) zoo
'**Zoohandlung** f pet shop
Zoologe [tsoo'lo:gə] m (-n; -n) zoologist; **Zoologie** [tsoolo'gi:] f (-; no pl) zoology; **Zoo'login** f (-; -nen) zoologist; **zoo'logisch** adj zoological

Zopf [tsɔpf] *m* (-[e]s; *Zöpfe* ['tsœpfə]) plait; pigtail

Zorn [tsɔrn] *m* (-[e]s; *no pl*) anger

zornig ['tsɔrnɪç] *adj* angry

Zote ['tso:tə] *f* (-; -n) filthy joke, obscenity

zottelig ['tsɔtəlɪç] *adj* shaggy

z. T. *abbr of* **zum Teil** partly

zu [tsu:] **1.** *prp* (*dat*) to, toward(s); at; *purpose:* for; **~ Fuß** (*Pferd*) on foot (horseback); **~ Hause** (*Ostern etc*) at home (Easter *etc*); **~ Weihnachten** give *etc* for Christmas; **Tür** (*Schlüssel*) **~ ...** door (key) to ...; **~ m-r Überraschung** to my surprise; **wir sind ~ dritt** there are three of us; **~ zweien** two by two; **~ zwei Euro** at or for two euros; SPORT **1 ~ 1** one all; **2 ~ 1 gewinnen** win two one, win by two goals *etc* to one; → **zum, zur 2.** *adv* too; F closed, shut; **ein ~ großes Risiko** too much of a risk; **~ viel** too much, too many; **~ wenig** too little, too few **3.** *cj* to; **es ist ~ erwarten** it is to be expected

Zubehör ['tsu:bəhø:ɐ] *n* (-[e]s; -e) accessories

'zubereiten *v/t* (*sep, no -ge-, h*) prepare; **'Zubereitung** *f* (-; -en) preparation

'zu|binden *v/t* (*irr, binden, sep, -ge-, h*) tie (up); **~bleiben** *v/i* (*irr, bleiben, sep, -ge-, sein*) stay shut; **~blinzeln** *v/i* (*sep, -ge-, h*) (*dat*) wink at

'Zubringer *m* (-s; -), **~straße** *f* MOT feeder (road), access road

Zucht [tsʊxt] *f* (-; -en) breeding; BOT cultivation; **züchten** ['tsʏçtən] *v/t* (*ge-, h*) zo breed; BOT grow, cultivate; **Züchter(in)** ['tsʏçtɐ, 'tsʏçtərɪn] *m(f)* (-s; -/-; -nen) zo breeder; BOT grower

'Zuchtperle *f* culture(d) pearl

zucken ['tsʊkən] *v/i* (*ge-, h*) jerk; twitch (**mit et.** s.th.); wince; *lightning:* flash

zücken ['tsʏkən] *v/t* (*ge-, h*) draw (*weapon*); F pull out (*one's wallet etc*)

Zucker ['tsʊkɐ] *m* (-s; -) sugar; **~dose** *f* sugar bowl; **~guss** *m* icing, frosting

'zuckerkrank *adj*, **'Zuckerkranke** *m, f* (-n; -n) MED diabetic

'Zuckerkrankheit *f* MED diabetes

'Zuckermais *m* sweet corn

'zuckern *v/t* (*ge-, h*) sugar

'Zuckerrohr *n* BOT sugarcane

'Zuckerrübe *f* BOT sugar beet

'Zuckerwatte *f* candy floss

'Zuckerzange *f* sugar tongs

'Zuckung *f* (-; -en) twitch(ing); tic; convulsion, spasm

'zudecken *v/t* (*sep, -ge-, h*) cover (up)

zudem [tsu'de:m] *adv* besides, moreover

'zudrehen *v/t* (*sep, -ge-, h*) turn off; **j-m den Rücken ~** turn one's back on s.o.

'zudringlich *adj:* **~ werden** F get fresh (**j-m gegenüber** with s.o.)

'zudrücken *v/t* (*sep, -ge-, h*) close, push *s.th.* shut; → **Auge**

zuerst [tsu'ʔeːrst] *adv* first; at first; first (of all), to begin with

'Zufahrt *f* approach; drive(way)

'Zufahrtsstraße *f* access road

'Zufall *m* chance; **durch ~** by chance, by accident; **'zufallen** *v/i* (*irr, fallen, sep, -ge-, sein*) *door etc:* slam (shut); *fig* fall to *s.o.*; **mir fallen die Augen zu** I can't keep my eyes open; **'zufällig 1.** *adj* accidental, chance ... **2.** *adv* by accident, by chance; **~ tun** happen to do

'Zuflucht *f:* **~ suchen** (*finden*) look for (find) refuge *or* shelter (**vor** *dat* from; **bei** with); (**s-e**) **~ nehmen zu** resort to

zufrieden [tsu'fri:dən] *adj* content(ed), satisfied; **~ stellen** satisfy; **~ stellend** satisfactory

zu'frieden|geben *v/refl* (*irr, geben, sep, -ge-, h*): **sich ~ mit** content o.s. with

Zu'friedenheit *f* (-; *no pl*) contentment, satisfaction

zu'frieden|lassen *v/t* (*irr, lassen, sep, -ge-, h*) leave s.o. alone; **~stellen** *v/t* (*sep, -ge-, h*) satisfy; **~stellend** *adj* satisfactory

'zufrieren *v/i* (*irr, frieren, sep, -ge-, sein*) freeze up *or* over

'zufügen *v/t* (*sep, -ge-, h*) do, cause; **j-m Schaden ~** a. harm s.o.

Zufuhr ['tsu:fu:ɐ] *f* (-; -en) supply

Zug [tsu:k] *m* (-[e]s; *Züge* ['tsy:gə]) RAIL train; procession; line; parade; *fig* feature; trait; tendency; *chess etc:* move (*a. fig*); *swimming:* stroke; pull (*a.* TECH), PHYS *a.* tension; *smoking:* puff; draft, *Br* draught; PED stream; **im ~e** *gen* in the course of; **in e-m ~** at one go; **~ um ~** step by step; **in groben Zügen** in broad outlines

'Zugabe *f* addition; THEA encore

'Zugang *m* access (*a. fig*); **'zugänglich**

['tsu:gɛŋlɪç] *adj* accessible (*für* to) (*a. fig*)

'**Zugbrücke** *f* drawbridge

'**zugeben** *v/t* (*irr, geben, sep, -ge-, h*) add; *fig* admit

'**zugehen** *v/i* (*irr, gehen, sep, -ge-, sein*) F *door etc*: close, shut; ~ *auf* (*acc*) walk up to, approach (*a. fig*); *es geht auf 8 Uhr zu* it's getting on for 8; *es ging lustig zu* we had a lot of fun

'**Zugehörigkeit** *f* (-; *no pl*) membership

'**Zügel** ['tsy:gəl] *m* (-*s*; -) rein (*a. fig*)

'**zügeln** 1. *v/t* (*ge-, h*) curb, control, bridle 2. *Swiss v/i* (*ge-, sein*) move

'**Zugeständnis** *n* concession

'**zugestehen** *v/t* (*irr, stehen, sep, no -ge-, h*) concede, grant

'**zugetan** *adj* attached (*dat* to)

'**Zugführer** *m* RAIL conductor, *Br* guard

'**zugig** ['tsu:gɪç] *adj* drafty, *Br* draughty

'**Zugkraft** *f* TECH traction; (*no pl*) attraction, draw, appeal

'**zugkräftig** *adj*: ~ *sein* be a draw

zu'gleich [tsu'glaɪç] *adv* at the same time

'**Zugluft** *f* (-; *no pl*) draft, *Br* draught

'**Zugma,schine** *f* MOT tractor

'**zugreifen** *v/i* (*irr, greifen, sep, -ge-, h*) grab (at) it; *fig* grab the opportunity; *greifen Sie zu!* help yourself!; *mit* ~ lend a hand

'**Zugriffscode** *m* IT access code

'**Zugriffszeit** *f* IT access time

zugrunde [tsu'grʊndə] *adv*: ~ *gehen* (*an dat*) perish (of); *e-r Sache et.* ~ *legen* base s.th. on s.th.; ~ *richten* ruin

zugunsten [tsu'gʊnstən] *prp* (*gen*) in favo(u)r of

zu'gute [tsu'gu:tə] *adv*: ~ *halten* → *zugutehalten*; ~ *kommen* → *zugutekommen*; **~halten** *v/t* (*irr, halten, sep, -ge-, h*): *j-m et.* ~ give s.o. credit for s.th.; make allwances for s.o.'s ...; **~kommen** *v/i* (*irr, kommen, sep, -ge-, sein*): *j-m* ~ be for the benefit of s.o.

'**Zugvogel** *m* ZO bird of passage

'**zuhalten** *v/t* (*irr, halten, sep, -ge-, h*) keep shut; *sich die Ohren* (*Augen*) ~ cover one's ears (eyes) with one's hands; *sich die Nase* ~ hold one's nose

Zuhälter ['tsu:hɛltɐ] *m* (-*s*; -) pimp

Zuhause [tsu'hauzə] *n* (-*s*; *no pl*) home

zu'hause *adv* → *Haus*

'**zuhören** *v/i* (*sep, -ge-, h*) listen (*dat* to)

'**Zuhörer** *m*, '**Zuhörerin** *f* listener, *pl a. the* audience

'**zujubeln** *v/i* (*sep, -ge-, h*) cheer

'**zukleben** *v/t* (*sep, -ge-, h*) seal

'**zuknöpfen** *v/t* (*sep, -ge-, h*) button (up)

'**zukommen** *v/i* (*irr, kommen, sep, -ge-, sein*) ~ *auf* (*acc*) come up to; *fig* be ahead of; *die Dinge auf sich* ~ *lassen* wait and see

Zukunft ['tsu:kʊnft] *f* (-; *no pl*) future (*a.* LING)

'**zukünftig** 1. *adj* future 2. *adv* in future

'**zulächeln** *v/i* (*sep, -ge-, h*) smile at

'**Zulage** *f* bonus

'**zulangen** F *v/i* (*sep, -ge-, h*) tuck in

'**zulassen** *v/t* (*irr, lassen, sep, -ge-, h*) F keep *s.th.* closed; *fig* allow; MOT *etc* license, register; *j-n zu et.* ~ admit s.o. to s.th.; '**zulässig** *adj* admissible (*a.* JUR); ~ *sein* be allowed; '**Zulassung** *f* (-; *-en*) admission; MOT *etc* license, *Br* licence

'**zulegen** *v/t* (*sep, -ge-, h*) add; F *sich ...* ~ get o.s. *s.th.*; adopt (*name*)

zu'letzt [tsu'lɛtst] *adv* in the end; *come etc* last; finally; *wann hast du ihn* ~ *gesehen?* when did you last see him?

zu'liebe [tsu'li:bə] *adv*: *j-m* ~ for s.o.'s sake

zum [tsʊm] *prp zu dem* → *zu*; ~ *ersten Mal* for the first time; *et.* ~ *Kaffee s.th.* with one's coffee; ~ *Schwimmen etc gehen* go swimming *etc*

'**zumachen** F (*sep, -ge-, h*) 1. *v/t* close, shut; button (up) 2. *v/i* close (down)

'**zumauern** *v/t* (*sep, -ge-, h*) brick *or* wall up

zumutbar ['tsu:mu:tbaːɐ] *adj* reasonable; **zu'mute** [tsu'mu:tə] *adv*: *mir ist* ... ~ I feel ...; '**zumuten** *v/t* (*sep, -ge-, h*) *j-m et.* ~ expect s.th. of s.o.; *sich zu viel* ~ overtax o.s.; '**Zumutung** *f*: *das ist e-e* ~ that's asking *or* expecting a bit much

zu'nächst [tsu'nɛːçst] *adv* → *zuerst*

'**zunageln** *v/t* (*sep, -ge-, h*) nail up

'**zunähen** *v/t* (*sep, -ge-, h*) sew up

Zunahme ['tsu:na:mə] *f* (-; *-n*) increase

'**Zuname** *m* surname

'**zünden** ['tsyndən] *v/i* (*ge-, h*) kindle; ELECTR, MOT ignite; fire; **~d** *fig adj* stirring

Zünder ['tsyndɐ] *m* (-*s*; -) MIL fuse; *pl Austrian* matches

Zünd|holz ['tsʏnthɔlts] *n* match; **~ker-ze** *f* MOT spark plug; **~schlüssel** *m* MOT ignition key; **~schnur** *f* fuse

'Zündung *f* (-; *-en*) MOT ignition

'zunehmen *v/i* (*irr*, **nehmen**, *sep*, *-ge-*, *h*) increase (**an** *dat* in); put on weight; *moon*: wax; *days*: grow longer

'Zuneigung *f* (-; *-en*) affection

Zunft [tsʊnft] HIST *f* (-; *Zünfte* ['tsʏnftə]) guild

Zunge [tsʊŋə] *f* (-; *-n*) ANAT tongue; *es liegt mir auf der ~* it's on the tip of my tongue

züngeln ['tsʏŋəln] *v/i* (*ge-*, *h*) *flames*: lick, flicker

'Zungenspitze *f* tip of the tongue

'zunicken *v/i* (*sep*, *-ge-*, *h*) (*dat*) nod at

zunutze [tsu'nʊtsə] *adv*: **sich et. ~ ma-chen** make (good) use of s.th.; take advantage of s.th.

zupfen [tsʊpfən] *v/t and v/i* (*ge-*, *h*) pull (**an** *dat* at), pick, pluck (at) (*a.* MUS)

zur [tsuːɐ] *prp* **zu der → zu**; **~ Schule (Kirche) gehen** go to school (church); **~ Hälfte** half (of it *or* them); **~ Belohnung** etc as a reward *etc*

'zurechnungsfähig *adj* JUR responsible; **'Zurechnungsfähigkeit** *f* (-; *no pl*) JUR responsibility

zu'recht|finden *v/refl* (*irr*, **finden**, *sep*, *-ge-*, *h*) find one's way; *fig* cope, manage; **~kommen** *v/i* (*irr*, **kommen**, *sep*, *-ge-*, *sein*) get along (**mit** with); cope (with); **~legen** *v/t* (*sep*, *-ge-*, *h*) arrange; *fig* **sich et.** ~ think s.th. out; **~machen** *F v/t* (*sep*, *-ge-*, *h*) get ready, prepare, fix; **sich** ~ do o.s. up; **~rücken** *v/t* (*sep*, *-ge-*, *h*) put s.th. straight (*a. fig*)

zu'rechtweisen *v/t* (*irr*, **weisen**, *sep*, *-ge-*, *h*), **Zu'rechtweisung** *f* reprimand

'zu|reden *v/i* (*sep*, *-ge-*, *h*) **j-m** ~ encourage s.o.; **~reiten** *v/t* (*irr*, **reiten**, *sep*, *-ge-*, *h*) break in; **~richten** *F v/t* (*sep*, *-ge-*, *h*) **übel** ~ batter, *a.* beat s.o. up badly, *a.* make a mess of s.th., ruin

zurück [tsu'rʏk] *adv* back; behind (*a. fig*); **~behalten** *v/t* (*irr*, **halten**, *sep*, *no -ge-*, *h*) keep back, retain; **~bekom-men** *v/t* (*irr*, **kommen**, *sep*, *no -ge-*, *h*) get back; **~bleiben** *v/i* (*irr*, **bleiben**, *sep*, *-ge-*, *sein*) stay behind, be left behind; fall behind (*a.* PED *etc*); **~blicken** *v/i* (*sep*, *-ge-*, *h*) look back (**auf** *acc* at, *fig* on); **~bringen** *v/t* (*irr*, **bringen**, *sep*,

-ge-, *h*) bring *or* take back, return; **~da-tieren** *v/t* (*sep*, *no -ge-*, *h*) backdate (**auf** *acc* to); **~fallen** *fig v/i* (*irr*, **fallen**, *sep*, *-ge-*, *sein*) fall behind, SPORT *a.* drop back; **~finden** *v/i* (*irr*, **finden**, *sep*, *-ge-*, *h*) find one's way back (**nach**, **zu** to); *fig* return (to); **~fordern** *v/t* (*sep*, *-ge-*, *h*) reclaim; **~führen** *v/i* (*sep*, *-ge-*, *h*) lead back; ~ **auf** (*acc*) attribute to; **~geben** *v/t* (*irr*, **geben**, *sep*, *-ge-*, *h*) give back, return; **~geblieben** *fig adj* backward; retarded; **~gehen** *v/i* (*irr*, **gehen**, *sep*, *-ge-*, *sein*) go back, return; *fig* decrease; go down, drop; **~gezogen** *fig adj* secluded; **~greifen** *v/i* (*irr*, **greifen**, *sep*, *-ge-*, *h*) ~ **auf** (*acc*) fall back (up)on

zu'rückhalten (*irr*, **halten**, *sep*, *-ge-*, *h*) **1.** *v/t* hold back **2.** *v/refl* control o.s.; be careful; **~d** *adj* reserved

Zu'rückhaltung *f* (-; *no pl*) reserve

zu'rück|kehren *v/i* (*sep*, *-ge-*, *sein*) return; **~kommen** *v/i* (*irr*, **kommen**, *sep*, *-ge-*, *sein*) come back, return (*both fig* **auf** *acc* to); **~lassen** *v/t* (*irr*, **lassen**, *sep*, *-ge-*, *h*) leave (behind); **~legen** *v/t* (*sep*, *-ge-*, *h*) put back; put aside, save (*money*); cover, do (*miles*); **~nehmen** *v/t* (*irr*, **nehmen**, *sep*, *-ge-*, *h*) take back (*a. fig*); **~rufen** (*irr*, **rufen**, *sep*, *-ge-*, *h*) **1.** *v/t* call back (*a.* TEL); ECON recall; *ins Gedächtnis* ~ recall **2.** *v/i* TEL call back; **~schlagen** (*irr*, **schlagen**, *sep*, *-ge-*, *h*) **1.** *v/t* beat off; *tennis*: return; fold back **2.** *v/i* hit back; MIL retaliate (*a. fig*); **~schrecken** *v/i* (*sep*, *-ge-*, *sein*) **~ vor** (*dat*) shrink from; *vor nichts* ~ stop at nothing; **~setzen** *v/t* (*sep*, *-ge-*, *h*) MOT back (up); *fig* neglect s.o.; **~stehen** *v/i* (*irr*, **stehen**, *sep*, *-ge-*, *h*) stand aside; **~stellen** *v/t* (*sep*, *-ge-*, *h*) put back (*a. watch*); put aside; MIL defer; **~strahlen** *v/t* (*sep*, *-ge-*, *h*) reflect; **~treten** *v/i* (*irr*, **treten**, *sep*, *-ge-*, *sein*) step *or* stand back; resign (*von e-m Amt [Posten]* one's office [post]); ECON, JUR withdraw (*von* from); **~weichen** *v/i* (*irr*, **weichen**, *sep*, *-ge-*, *sein*) fall back (*a.* MIL); **~weisen** *v/t* (*irr*, **weisen**, *sep*, *-ge-*, *h*) turn down; JUR dismiss; **~zah-len** *v/t* (*sep*, *-ge-*, *h*) pay back (*a. fig*); **~ziehen** *v/t* (*irr*, **ziehen**, *sep*, *-ge-*, *h*) draw back; *fig* withdraw; *sich* ~ retire, withdraw, MIL *a.* retreat

'Zuruf *m* shout; **'zurufen** *v/t* (*irr*, **rufen**,

sep, -ge-, h) **j-m et. ~** shout s.th. to s.o.

zur'zeit *adv* at the moment, at present

'Zusage *f* promise; assent

'zusagen *v/i and v/t* (*sep, -ge-, h*) accept (an invitation); (*dat*) suit, appeal to; **s-e Hilfe ~** promise to help

zusammen [tsu'zamən] *adv* together; **alles ~** (all) in all; **das macht ~ ...** that makes ... altogether

Zu'sammenarbeit *f* (-; *no pl*) cooperation; **in ~ mit** in collaboration with; **zu'sammenarbeiten** *v/i* (*sep, -ge-, h*) co-operate, collaborate

zu'sammenbeißen *v/t* (*irr, beißen, sep, -ge-, h*) **die Zähne ~** clench one's teeth

zu'sammenbrechen *v/i* (*irr, brechen, sep, -ge-, sein*) break down, collapse (*both a. fig*); **Zu'sammenbruch** *m* breakdown, collapse

zu'sammen|fallen *v/i* (*irr, fallen, sep, -ge-, sein*) coincide; **~falten** *v/t* (*sep, -ge-, h*) fold up

zu'sammenfassen *v/t* (*sep, -ge-, h*) summarize, sum up; **Zu'sammenfassung** *f* (-; *-en*) summary

zu'sammen|fügen *v/t* (*sep, -ge-, h*) join (together); **~gesetzt** *adj* compound; **~halten** *v/i and v/t* (*irr, halten, sep, -ge-, h*) hold together (*a. fig*); F stick together

Zu'sammenhang *m* (-[*e*]s; *-hänge*) connection; context; **im ~ stehen** (*mit*) be connected (with)

zu'sammenhängen *v/i* (*irr, hängen, sep, -ge-, h*) be connected; **~d** *adj* coherent

zu'sammenhang(s)los *adj* incoherent, disconnected

zu'sammen|klappen *v/i* (*sep, -ge-, sein*) *and v/t* (*h*) TECH fold up; F break down; **~kommen** *v/i* (*irr, kommen, sep, -ge-, sein*) meet

Zu'sammenkunft [tsu'zamənkʊnft] *f* (-; *-künfte* [tsu'zamənkʏnftə]) meeting

zu'sammen|legen (*sep, -ge-, h*) **1.** *v/t* combine; fold up **2.** *v/i* club together; **~nehmen** *v/t* (*irr, nehmen, sep, -ge-, h*) muster (up); **sich ~** pull o.s. together; **~packen** *v/t* (*sep, -ge-, h*) pack up; **~passen** *v/i* (*sep, -ge-, h*) harmonize; match; **~rechnen** *v/t* (*sep, -ge-, h*) add up; **~reißen** F *v/refl* (*irr, reißen, sep, -ge-, h*) pull o.s. together; **~rollen** *v/t* (*sep, -ge-, h*) roll up; **sich ~** coil up; **~rot-**

ten [tsu'zamənrɔtən] *v/refl* (*sep, -ge-, h*) band together; **~rücken** (*sep, -ge-*) **1.** *v/t* (*h*) move closer together **2.** *v/i* (*sein*) move up; **~schlagen** *v/t* (*irr, schlagen, sep, -ge-, h*) clap (*hands*); click (*one's heels*); beat *s.o.* up; smash (up)

zu'sammenschließen *v/refl* (*irr, schließen, sep, -ge-, h*) join, unite; **Zu'sammenschluss** *m* union

zu'sammen|schreiben *v/t* (*irr, schreiben, sep, -ge-, h*) write in one word; **~schrumpfen** *v/i* (*sep, -ge-, sein*) shrink

zu'sammensetzen *v/t* (*sep, -ge-, h*) put together; TECH assemble; **sich ~ aus** (*dat*) consist of, be composed of; **Zu'sammensetzung** *f* (-; *-en*) composition; CHEM, LING compound; TECH assembly

zu'sammenstellen *v/t* (*sep, -ge-, h*) put together; arrange

Zu'sammenstoß *m* collision (*a. fig*), crash; impact; *fig* clash; **zu'sammenstoßen** *v/i* (*irr, stoßen, sep, -ge-, sein*) collide (*a. fig*); *fig* clash; **~ mit** run *or* bump into; *fig* have a clash with

zu'sammentreffen *v/i* (*irr, treffen, sep, -ge-, sein*) meet, encounter; coincide (*mit* with); **Zu'sammentreffen** *n* (-*s*; -) meeting; coincidence; encounter

zu'sammen|treten *v/i* (*irr, treten, sep, -ge-, sein*) meet; **~tun** *v/refl* (*irr, tun, sep, -ge-, h*) join (forces), F team up; **~wirken** *v/i* (*sep, -ge-, h*) combine; **~zählen** *v/t* (*sep, -ge-, h*) add up; **~ziehen** (*irr, ziehen, sep, -ge-*) **1.** *v/t and v/refl* (*h*) contract **2.** *v/i* (*sein*) move in (*mit* with); **~zucken** *v/i* (*sep, -ge-, sein*) wince, flinch

'Zusatz *m* addition; *chemical etc* additive; **~... in cpds mst** additional ..., supplementary ...; auxiliary ...; **zusätzlich** ['tsu:zɛtslɪç] *adj* additional, extra

'zuschauen *v/i* (*sep, -ge-, h*) look on (**bei et.** at s.th.); **j-m ~** watch s.o. (**bei et.** doing s.th.)

Zuschauer ['tsu:ʃaʊɐ] *m* (-*s*; -), **'Zuschauerin** *f* (-; *-nen*) spectator; TV viewer, *pl a.* the audience

'Zuschauerraum *m* auditorium

'Zuschlag *m* extra charge; RAIL *etc* excess fare; bonus; *auction*: knocking down; **'zuschlagen** *v/i* (*irr, schlagen,* *sep, -ge-, sein) and v/t (h) door etc:* slam *or* bang shut; *boxing etc:* hit, strike (a blow); *fig* act; *j-m et. ~ auction:* knock s.th. down to s.o.

'**zu**|**schließen** *v/t (irr, schließen, sep, -ge-, h)* lock (up); **~schnallen** *v/t (sep, -ge-, h)* buckle (up); **~schnappen** *v/i (sep, -ge-) (h) dog:* snap; *(sein) door etc:* snap shut; **~schneiden** *v/t (irr, schneiden, sep, -ge-, h)* cut out; cut (to size); **~schnüren** *v/t (sep, -ge-, h)* tie *(or* lace) up; **~schrauben** *v/t (sep, -ge-, h)* screw shut; **~schreiben** *v/t (irr, schreiben, sep, -ge-, h)* ascribe *or* attribute *(dat to)*

'**Zuschrift** *f* letter

zuschulden [tsuˈʃʊldən] *adv: sich et. (nichts) ~ kommen lassen* do s.th. (nothing) wrong

'**Zuschuss** *m* allowance; subsidy

'**zuschütten** *v/t (sep, -ge-, h)* fill up

'**zusehen** → *zuschauen*

zusehends [ˈtsuːzeːənts] *adv* noticeably; rapidly

'**zusetzen** *(sep, -ge-, h)* **1.** *v/t* add; lose *(money)* **2.** *v/i* lose money; *j-m ~* press s.o. (hard)

'**zuspielen** *v/t (sep, -ge-, h)* SPORT pass

'**zuspitzen** *v/t (sep, -ge-, h)* point; *sich ~* become critical

'**Zuspruch** *m (-[e]s; no pl)* encouragement; words of comfort

'**Zustand** *m* condition, state, F shape

zustande [tsuˈʃtandə] *adv: ~ bringen* bring about, manage (to do); *~ kommen* come about; *es kam nicht ~* it didn't come off

'**zuständig** *adj* responsible *(für* for), in charge (of)

'**zustehen** *v/i (irr, stehen, sep, -ge-, h) j-m steht et. (zu tun) zu* s.o. is entitled to (do) s.th.

'**zustellen** *v/t (sep, -ge-, h) post:* deliver; '**Zustellung** *f post:* delivery

'**zustimmen** *v/i (sep, -ge-, h)* agree *(dat* to *s.th.;* with *s.o.);* '**Zustimmung** *f* approval, consent; *(j-s) ~ finden* meet with (s.o.'s) approval

'**zustoßen** *v/i (irr, stoßen, sep, -ge-, sein) j-m ~* happen to s.o.

zutage [tsuˈtaːgə] *adv: ~ bringen (kommen)* bring (come) to light

'**Zutaten** *pl* ingredients

'**zuteilen** *v/t (sep, -ge-, h)* assign, allot;

'**Zuteilung** *f (-; -en)* allotment; ration

'**zutragen** *v/refl (irr, tragen, sep, -ge-, h)* happen

'**zutrauen** *v/t (sep, -ge-, h) j-m et. ~* credit s.o. with s.th.; *sich zu viel ~* overrate o.s.

zutraulich [ˈtsuːtraulɪç] *adj* trusting; zo friendly

'**zutreffen** *v/i (irr, treffen, sep, -ge-, h)* be true; *~ auf (acc)* apply to, go for; *~d adj* true, correct

'**zutrinken** *v/i (irr, trinken, sep, -ge-, h) j-m ~* drink to s.o.

'**Zutritt** *m (-[e]s; no pl)* admission; access; *~ verboten!* no admittance!

zu'**ungunsten** *adv* to s.o.'s disadvantage

zuverlässig [ˈtsuːfɛɐlɛsɪç] *adj* reliable, dependable; safe; '**Zuverlässigkeit** *f (-; no pl)* reliability, dependability

Zuversicht [ˈtsuːfɛɐzɪçt] *f (-; no pl)* confidence; '**zuversichtlich** *adj* confident, optimistic

zuviel → *zu*

zu'**vor** [tsuˈfoːɐ] *adv* before, previously; first

zu'**vorkommen** *v/i (irr, kommen, sep, -ge-, sein)* anticipate; prevent; *j-m ~ a.* F beat s.o. to it; *~d adj* obliging; polite

Zuwachs [ˈtsuːvaks] *m (-es; no pl)* increase, growth; '**zuwachsen** *v/i (irr, wachsen, sep, -ge-, sein)* become overgrown; MED close

zu'**weilen** [tsuˈvailən] *adv* occasionally, now and then

'**zuweisen** *v/t (irr, weisen, sep, -ge-, h)* assign

'**zuwenden** *v/t and v/refl ([irr, wenden,] sep, -ge-, h)* turn to *(a. fig)*

'**Zuwendung** *f (-; -en)* payment; *(no pl)* attention; (loving) care, love, affection

zuwenig → *zu*

'**zuwerfen** *v/t (irr, werfen, sep, -ge-, h)* slam (shut); *j-m et. ~* throw s.o. s.th.; *j-m e-n Blick ~* cast a glance at s.o.

zu'**wider** [tsuˈviːdə] *adj: ... ist mir ~* I hate *or* detest ...; **~handeln** *v/i (sep, -ge-, h) (dat)* act contrary to; violate

'**zu**|**winken** *v/i (sep, -ge-, h)* wave to; signal to; **~zahlen** *v/t (sep, -ge-, h)* pay extra; **~ziehen** *(irr, ziehen, sep, -ge-)* **1.** *v/t (h)* draw *(curtains etc);* pull tight; *fig* consult; **sich ~** MED catch **2.** v/i (sein) move in

zuzüglich ['tsuːtsyːklıç] prp (gen) plus

Zvieri ['tsfiːri] Swiss m, n (-s; -s) afternoon snack, tea or coffee break

zwang [tsvaŋ] pret of **zwingen**

Zwang m (-[e]s; **Zwänge** ['tsvɛŋə]) compulsion, constraint; restraint; coercion; force; **~ sein** be compulsory; **zwängen** ['tsvɛŋən] v/t (ge-, h) press, squeeze, force; '**zwanglos** adj informal; casual; '**Zwanglosigkeit** f (-; no pl) informality

'**Zwangs|arbeit** f JUR hard labo(u)r; **~herrschaft** f (-; no pl) despotism, tyranny; **~lage** f predicament

'**zwangsläufig** adv inevitably

'**Zwangs|maßnahme** f sanction; **~vollstreckung** f JUR compulsory execution; **~vorstellung** f PSYCH obsession

'**zwangsweise** adv by force

zwanzig ['tsvantsıç] adj twenty

'**zwanzigste** adj twentieth

zwar [tsvaːɐ] adv: **ich kenne ihn ~, aber** ... I do know him, but ..., I know him all right, but ...; **und ~** that is (to say), namely

Zweck [tsvɛk] m (-[e]s; -e) purpose, aim; **s-n ~ erfüllen** serve its purpose; **es hat keinen ~** (**zu warten** etc) it's no use (waiting etc); '**zwecklos** adj useless

'**zweckmäßig** adj practical; wise; TECH, ARCH functional; '**Zweckmäßigkeit** f (-; no pl) practicality, functionality

zwecks prp (gen) for the purpose of

zwei [tsvai] adj two

zweibeinig ['tsvaibainıç] adj two-legged

'**Zweibettzimmer** n twin-bedded room

zweideutig ['tsvaidɔytıç] adj ambiguous; off-colo(u)r

Zweier ['tsvaiɐ] m (-s; -) rowing: pair

zweierlei ['tsvaiɐ'lai] adj two kinds of

'**zweifach** adj double, twofold

Zweifa'milienhaus n duplex, Br two-family house

Zweifel ['tsvaifəl] m (-s; -) doubt

'**zweifelhaft** adj doubtful, dubious

'**zweifellos** adv undoubtedly, no or without doubt

'**zweifeln** v/i (ge-, h) **~ an** (dat) doubt s.th., have one's doubts about

Zweig [tsvaik] m (-[e]s; -e) BOT branch

(a. fig); twig; **~geschäft** n, **~niederlassung** f, **~stelle** f branch

'**zweijährig** ['tsvaijɛːrıç] adj two-year-old, of two (years)

'**Zweikampf** m duel

'**zweimal** adv twice

'**zweimalig** adj (twice) repeated

'**zwei|motorig** ['tsvaimotoːrıç] adj twin-engined; **~reihig** ['tsvairaiıç] adj double-breasted (suit); **~schneidig** adj double-edged, two-edged (both a. fig); **~seitig** ['tsvaizaitıç] adj two-sided; reversible; POL bilateral; IT double-sided

'**Zweisitzer** ['tsvaizɪtsɐ] m (-s; -) esp MOT two-seater

'**zwei|sprachig** ['tsvaiʃpraːxıç] adj bilingual; **~stimmig** ['tsvaiʃtımıç] adj MUS ... for two voices; **~stöckig** ['tsvaiʃtœkıç] adj two-storied, Br two-storey ...

zweit [tsvait] adj second; **ein ~er** ... another ...; **jede(r, -s) ~e** ... every other ...; **aus ~er Hand** second-hand; **wir sind zu ~** there are two of us

'**zweitbeste** adj second-best

'**zweiteilig** adj two-piece (suit etc)

zweitens ['tsvaitəns] adv secondly

'**zweitklassig** ['tsvaitklasıç] adj, '**zweitrangig** ['tsvaitraŋıç] adj second-class or -rate

Zwerchfell ['tsvɛrçfɛl] n ANAT diaphragm

Zwerg [tsvɛrk] m (-[e]s; -e ['tsvɛrgə]) dwarf; gnome; fig midget; **~...** in cpds BOT dwarf ...; ZO pygmy ...

Zwetsch(g)e ['tsvɛtʃ(g)ə] f (-; -n) BOT plum

zwicken ['tsvikən] v/t and v/i (ge-, h) pinch, nip

Zwieback ['tsviːbak] m (-[e]s; -e, -bäcke ['tsviːbɛkə]) rusk, zwieback

Zwiebel ['tsviːbəl] f (-; -n) GASTR onion; BOT bulb

Zwiegespräch ['tsviːgəʃprɛːç] n dialog(ue)

'**Zwielicht** n (-[e]s; no pl) twilight

'**Zwiespalt** m (-[e]s; -e) conflict

'**zwiespältig** ['tsviːʃpɛltıç] adj conflicting

'**Zwietracht** f (-; no pl) discord

Zwilling ['tsvilıŋ] m (-s; -e) twin; pl ASTR Gemini; **er ist (ein) ~** he's (a) Gemini

'**Zwillings|bruder** m twin brother;

~schwester *f* twin sister

Zwinge ['tsvɪŋə] *f* (-; -*n*) TECH clamp

zwingen ['tsvɪŋən] *v/t* (*irr, ge-, h*) force, compel; **~d** *adj* compelling; cogent

Zwinger ['tsvɪŋɐ] *m* (-*s*; -) kennels

zwinkern ['tsvɪŋkɐn] *v/i* (*ge-, h*) wink, blink

Zwirn [tsvɪrn] *m* (-[*e*]*s*; -*e*) thread, yarn, twist

zwischen ['tsvɪʃən] *prp* (*dat and acc*) between; among

'zwischen'durch F *adv* in between

'Zwischen|ergebnis *n* intermediate result; **~fall** *m* incident; **~händler** *m* ECON middleman; **~landung** *f* AVIAT stopover; **ohne ~** nonstop

'Zwischen|raum *m* space, interval; **~ruf** *m* (loud) interruption; *pl* heckling; **~rufer** *m* (-*s*; -) heckler; **~spiel** *n* interlude; **~stati,on** *f* stop(over); **~ machen** (*in dat*) stop over (in); **~wand** *f* partition (wall); **~zeit** *f*: **in der~** in the meantime, meanwhile

Zwist [tsvɪst] *m* (-[*e*]*s*; -*e*) discord

zwitschern ['tsvɪtʃɐn] *v/i* (*ge-, h*) twitter, chirp

Zwitter ['tsvɪtɐ] *m* (-*s*; -) BIOL hermaphrodite

zwölf [tsvœlf] *adj* twelve; **um ~ (Uhr)** at twelve (o'clock); at noon; at midnight

'zwölfte *adj* twelfth

Zyankali [tsyaːn'kaːli] *n* (-*s*; *no pl*) CHEM potassium cyanide

Zyklus ['tsyːklʊs] *m* (-; -*klen*) cycle; series, course

Zylinder [tsi'lɪndɐ] *m* (-*s*; -) top hat; MATH, TECH cylinder; **zylindrisch** [tsi-'lɪndrɪʃ] *adj* cylindrical

Zyniker ['tsyːnikɐ] *m* (-*s*; -) cynic

zynisch ['tsyːnɪʃ] *adj* cynical

Zynismus [tsy'nɪsmʊs] *m* (-; -*men*) cynicism

Zypresse [tsy'prɛsə] *f* (-; -*n*) BOT cypress

Zyste ['tsystə] *f* (-; -*n*) MED cyst

z.Z(t). *abbr of* **zur Zeit** at the moment, at present

ENGLISH – GERMAN

A

A, a A, a *n*; *from A to Z* von A bis Z

A *grade* Eins

a, *before vowel*: **an** *indef art* ein(e); per, pro, je; *not a(n)* kein(e); *all of a size* alle gleich groß; *100 dollars a year* 100 Dollar im Jahr; *twice a week* zweimal die *or* in der Woche

a·back: *taken ~* überrascht, verblüfft; bestürzt

a·ban·don aufgeben, preisgeben; verlassen; überlassen

a·base erniedrigen, demütigen

a·base·ment Erniedrigung *f*, Demütigung *f*

a·bashed verlegen

ab·at·toir *Br* Schlachthof *m*

ab·bess REL Äbtissin *f*

ab·bey REL Kloster *n*; Abtei *f*

ab·bot REL Abt *m*

ab·bre·vi·ate (ab)kürzen

ab·bre·vi·a·tion Abkürzung *f*, Kurzform *f*

ABC Abc *n*, Alphabet *n*

ab·di·cate *Amt, Recht etc* aufgeben, verzichten auf (*acc*); *~ (from) the throne* abdanken

ab·di·ca·tion Verzicht *m*; Abdankung *f*

ab·do·men ANAT Unterleib *m*

ab·dom·i·nal ANAT Unterleibs...

ab·duct JUR *j-n* entführen

ab·er·ra·tion Verirrung *f*

a·bet → *aid 1*

ab·hor verabscheuen

ab·hor·rence Abscheu *m* (*of* vor *dat*)

ab·hor·rent zuwider (*to* dat); abstoßend

a·bide *v/i: ~ by the law etc* sich an das Gesetz *etc* halten; *v/t: he can't ~ him* er kann ihn nicht ausstehen

a·bil·i·ty Fähigkeit *f*

ab·jure abschwören; entsagen (*dat*)

a·blaze in Flammen; *fig* glänzend, funkelnd (*with* vor *dat*)

a·ble fähig; geschickt; *be ~ to inf* in der Lage sein zu *inf*, können

a·ble-bod·ied kräftig

ab·nor·mal abnorm, ungewöhnlich; anomal

a·board an Bord; *all ~!* MAR alle Mann *or* Reisenden an Bord!; RAIL alles einsteigen!; *~ a bus* in e-m Bus; *go ~ a train* in

e-n Zug einsteigen

a·bode *a. place of ~* Aufenthaltsort *m*, Wohnsitz *m*; *of or with no fixed ~* ohne festen Wohnsitz

a·bol·ish abschaffen, aufheben

a·bo·li·tion Abschaffung *f*, Aufhebung *f*

A-bomb → *atom(ic) bomb*

a·bom·i·na·ble abscheulich, scheußlich;

a·bom·i·nate verabscheuen; **a·bom·i·na·tion** Abscheu *m*

ab·o·rig·i·nal 1. eingeboren, Ur... **2.** Ureinwohner *m*

ab·o·rig·i·ne Ureinwohner *m*

a·bort *v/t* abbrechen (*a.* MED *Schwangerschaft*); MED *Kind* abtreiben; *v/i* fehlschlagen, scheitern; MED e-e Fehlgeburt haben; **a·bor·tion** MED Fehlgeburt *f*; Schwangerschaftsabbruch *m*, Abtreibung *f*; *have an ~* abtreiben (lassen)

a·bor·tive misslungen, erfolglos

a·bound reichlich vorhanden sein; Überfluss haben, reich sein (*in* an *dat*); voll sein (*with* von)

a·bout 1. *prp* um (... herum); bei (*dat*); (irgendwo) herum in (*dat*); um, gegen, etwa; im Begriff, dabei; über (*acc*) **2.** *adv* herum, umher; in der Nähe; etwa, ungefähr

a·bove 1. *prp* über (*dat or acc*), oberhalb (*gen*); *fig* über, erhaben über (*acc*); *~ all* vor allem **2.** *adv* oben; darüber **3.** *adj* obig, oben erwähnt

a·breast nebeneinander; *keep ~ of, be ~ of fig* Schritt halten mit

a·bridge (ab-, ver)kürzen

a·bridg(e)·ment Kürzung *f*; Kurzfassung *f*

a·broad im *or* ins Ausland; überall(hin)

a·brupt abrupt; jäh; schroff

ab·scess MED Abszess *m*

ab·sence Abwesenheit *f*; Mangel *m*

ab·sent 1. abwesend; fehlend; nicht vorhanden; *be ~* fehlen (*from school* in der Schule; *from work* am Arbeitsplatz); **2.** *~ o.s. from* fernbleiben (*dat*) *or* von; **ab·sent-mind·ed** zerstreut, geistesabwesend

ab·so·lute absolut; unumschränkt; vollkommen; unbedingt; CHEM rein, unver-

mischt
ab·so·lu·tion REL Absolution f
ab·solve freisprechen, lossprechen
ab·sorb absorbieren, aufsaugen, einsaugen; *fig* ganz in Anspruch nehmen
ab·sorb·ing *fig* fesselnd, packend
ab·stain sich enthalten (*from gen*)
ab·ste·mi·ous enthaltsam; mäßig
ab·sten·tion Enthaltung f; POL Stimmenthaltung f
ab·sti·nence Abstinenz f, Enthaltsamkeit f
ab·sti·nent abstinent, enthaltsam
ab·stract 1. abstrakt 2. *das* Abstrakte; Auszug m 3. abstrahieren; entwenden
ab·stract·ed *fig* zerstreut
ab·strac·tion Abstraktion f; abstrakter Begriff
ab·surd absurd; lächerlich
a·bun·dance Überfluss m; Fülle f; Überschwang m
a·bun·dant reich, reichlich
a·buse 1. Missbrauch m; Beschimpfung(en *pl*) f; ~ *of drugs* Drogenmissbrauch m; ~ *of power* Machtmissbrauch m 2. missbrauchen; beschimpfen; **a·bu·sive** beleidigend, Schimpf...
a·but (an)grenzen (*on* an *acc*)
a·byss Abgrund m (*a. fig*)
ac·a·dem·ic 1. Hochschullehrer m 2. akademisch; **a·cad·e·mi·cian** Akademiemitglied n; **a·cad·e·my** Akademie f; ~ *of music* Musikhochschule f
ac·cede: ~ *to* zustimmen (*dat*); *Amt* antreten; *Thron* besteigen
ac·cel·e·rate *v/t* beschleunigen; *v/i* schneller werden, MOT *a.* beschleunigen, Gas geben
ac·cel·e·ra·tion Beschleunigung f
ac·cel·e·ra·tor MOT Gaspedal n
ac·cent 1. Akzent m (*a.* LING); 2. → **ac·cen·tu·ate** akzentuieren, betonen
ac·cept annehmen, akzeptieren; hinnehmen; **ac·cept·a·ble** annehmbar; *person:* tragbar; **ac·cept·ance** Annahme f; Aufnahme f
ac·cess Zugang m (*to* zu); *fig* Zutritt m (*to* bei, zu); IT Zugriff m (*to* auf *acc*)
ac·ces·sa·ry → *accessory*
ac·cess code IT Zugriffskode m
ac·ces·si·ble (leicht) zugänglich
ac·ces·sion (Neu)Anschaffung f (*to* für); Zustimmung f (*to* zu); Antritt m (*e-s Amtes*); ~ *to power* Machtüber-

nahme f; ~ *to the throne* Thronbesteigung f
ac·ces·so·ry JUR Komplize m, Komplizin f, Mitschuldige m, f; *mst pl* Zubehör n, *fashion:* a. Accessoires *pl*, TECH a. Zubehörteile *pl*
ac·cess| road Zufahrts- *or* Zubringerstraße f; ~ **time** IT Zugriffszeit f
ac·ci·dent Unfall m, Unglück n, Unglücksfall m; NUCL Störfall m; *by* ~ zufällig
ac·ci·den·tal zufällig; versehentlich
ac·claim feiern (*as* als)
ac·cla·ma·tion lauter Beifall; Lob n
ac·cli·ma·tize (sich) akklimatisieren *or* eingewöhnen
ac·com·mo·date unterbringen; Platz haben für, fassen; anpassen (*to dat or* an *acc*)
ac·com·mo·da·tion Unterkunft f, Unterbringung f; ~ *of·fice* Zimmervermittlung f
ac·com·pa·ni·ment MUS Begleitung f
ac·com·pa·ny begleiten (*a.* MUS)
ac·com·plice JUR Komplize m, Komplizin f, Helfershelfer(in)
ac·com·plish erreichen; leisten
ac·com·plished fähig, tüchtig
ac·com·plish·ment Fähigkeit f, Talent n
ac·cord 1. Übereinstimmung f; *of one's own* ~ von selbst; *with one* ~ einstimmig 2. übereinstimmen (*with* mit)
ac·cord·ance: *in* ~ *with* entsprechend (*dat*)
ac·cord·ing: ~ *to* laut; nach
ac·cord·ing·ly folglich, also; (dem)entsprechend
ac·cost *j-n* ansprechen
ac·count 1. ECON Rechnung f, Berechnung f; Konto n; Rechenschaft f; Bericht m; *by all* ~*s* nach allem, was man so hört; *of no* ~ ohne Bedeutung; *on no* ~ auf keinen Fall; *on* ~ *of* wegen; *take into* ~, *take* ~ *of* in Betracht *or* Erwägung ziehen, berücksichtigen; *turn s.th. to* (*good*) ~ et. (gut) ausnutzen; *keep* ~*s* die Bücher führen; *call to* ~ zur Rechenschaft ziehen; *give* (*an*) ~ *of* Rechenschaft ablegen über (*acc*); *give an* ~ *of* Bericht erstatten über (*acc*) 2. *v/i:* ~ *for* Rechenschaft über et. ablegen; (sich) erklären
ac·count·a·ble verantwortlich; erklärlich

ac·coun·tant ECON Buchhalter(in)

ac·count·ing ECON Buchführung f

acct abbr of **account** Konto n

ac·cu·mu·late (sich) (an)häufen or ansammeln

ac·cu·mu·la·tion Ansammlung f

ac·cu·mu·la·tor ELECTR Akkumulator m

ac·cu·ra·cy Genauigkeit f

ac·cu·rate genau

ac·cu·sa·tion Anklage f; Anschuldigung f, Beschuldigung f

ac·cu·sa·tive a. ~ **case** LING Akkusativ m

ac·cuse JUR anklagen; beschuldigen (of gen); **the~d** der or die Angeklagte, die Angeklagten pl

ac·cus·er JUR Ankläger(in)

ac·cus·ing anklagend, vorwurfsvoll

ac·cus·tom gewöhnen (**to** an acc)

ac·cus·tomed gewohnt, üblich; gewöhnt (**to** an acc, zu inf)

ace Ass n (a. fig); **have an ~ in the hole** (Br **up one's sleeve**) fig (noch) e-n Trumpf in der Hand haben; **within an ~** um ein Haar

ache 1. schmerzen, wehtun **2.** anhaltender Schmerz

a·chieve zustande bringen; Ziel erreichen; **a·chieve·ment** Zustandebringen n, Leistung f, Ausführung f

ac·id 1. sauer; fig beißend, bissig **2.** CHEM Säure f; **a·cid·i·ty** Säure f

ac·id rain saurer Regen

ac·knowl·edge anerkennen; zugeben; Empfang bestätigen

ac·knowl·edg(e)·ment Anerkennung f; (Empfangs)Bestätigung f; Eingeständnis n

a·corn BOT Eichel f

a·cous·tics Akustik f

ac·quaint bekannt machen; ~ **s.o. with s.th.** j-m et. mitteilen; **be~ed with** kennen; **ac·quaint·ance** Bekanntschaft f; Bekannte m, f

ac·quire erwerben; sich aneignen

ac·qui·si·tion Erwerb m; Anschaffung f, Errungenschaft f

ac·quit JUR freisprechen (of von); ~ **o.s. well** s-e Sache gut machen

ac·quit·tal JUR Freispruch m

a·cre Acre m (4047 qm)

ac·rid scharf, beißend

ac·ro·bat Akrobat(in)

ac·ro·bat·ic akrobatisch

a·cross 1. adv hinüber, herüber; (quer) durch; drüben, auf der anderen Seite; über Kreuz **2.** prp (quer) über (acc); (quer) durch; auf der anderen Seite von (or gen), jenseits (gen); über (dat); **come ~, run ~** fig stoßen auf (acc)

act 1. v/i handeln; sich verhalten or benehmen; (ein)wirken; funktionieren; (Theater) spielen; v/t THEA spielen (a. fig), Stück aufführen; ~ **as** fungieren als **2.** Handlung f, Tat f; JUR Gesetz n; THEA Akt m; **act·ing** THEA Spiel(en) n

ac·tion Handlung f (a. THEA), Tat f; film etc: Action f; Funktionieren n; (Ein-)Wirkung f; JUR Klage f, Prozess m; MIL Gefecht n, Einsatz m; **take ~** handeln

ac·ti·vate v/t aktivieren; **ac·tive** aktiv; tätig, rührig; lebhaft (a. ECON), rege; wirksam

ac·tiv·ist esp POL Aktivist(in)

ac·tiv·i·ty Tätigkeit f; Aktivität f; Betriebsamkeit f; esp ECON Lebhaftigkeit f; ~ **va·ca·tion** Aktivurlaub m

ac·tor Schauspieler m

ac·tress Schauspielerin f

ac·tu·al wirklich, tatsächlich, eigentlich

ac·u·men Scharfsinn m

ac·u·punc·ture MED Akupunktur f

a·cute akut (shortage, pain etc); brennend (problem etc); scharf (hearing etc); scharfsinnig; MATH spitz (angle)

ad F → **advertisement**

ad·a·mant unerbittlich

a·dapt anpassen (**to** dat or an acc); Text bearbeiten (**from** nach); TECH umstellen (**to** auf acc); umbauen (**to** für)

a·dapt·a·ble anpassungsfähig

ad·ap·ta·tion Anpassung f; Bearbeitung f

a·dapt·er, a·dapt·or ELECTR Adapter m

add v/t hinzufügen; ~ **up** zusammenzählen, addieren; v/i: ~ **to** vermehren, beitragen zu, hinzukommen zu; ~ **up** MATH ergeben; F sich summieren; fig e-n Sinn ergeben; ~ **up to** fig hinauslaufen auf (acc)

ad·der ZO Natter f

ad·dict Süchtige m, f; **alcohol** (**drug**) ~ Alkoholsüchtige (Drogen- or Rauschgiftsüchtige); (Fußball- etc) Fanatiker(in), (Film- etc)Narr m

ad·dic·ted süchtig, abhängig (**to** von); **be**

~ **to alcohol (drugs)** alkoholsüchtig (drogenabhängig or -süchtig) sein

ad·dic·tion Sucht f, Süchtigkeit f

ad·di·tion Hinzufügen n; Zusatz m; Zuwachs m; ARCH Anbau m; MATH Addition f; **in** ~ außerdem; **in** ~ **to** außer (dat)

ad·di·tion·al zusätzlich

ad·dress 1. Worte richten (**to** an acc), j-n anreden or ansprechen **2.** Adresse f, Anschrift f; Rede f, Ansprache f

ad·dress·ee Empfänger(in)

ad·ept erfahren, geschickt (**at, in** in dat)

ad·e·qua·cy Angemessenheit f

ad·e·quate angemessen

ad·here (**to**) kleben, haften (an dat); fig festhalten (an dat); **ad·her·ence** Anhaften n; fig Festhalten n; **ad·her·ent** Anhänger(in)

ad·he·sive 1. klebend **2.** Klebstoff m; ~ **plas·ter** MED Heftpflaster n; ~ **tape** Klebeband n, Klebstreifen m; MED Heftpflaster n

ad·ja·cent angrenzend, anstoßend (**to** an acc); benachbart

ad·jec·tive LING Adjektiv n, Eigenschaftswort n

ad·join (an)grenzen an (acc)

ad·journ v/t verschieben, (v/i sich) vertagen; **ad·journ·ment** Vertagung f, Verschiebung f

ad·just anpassen; TECH einstellen, regulieren; **ad·just·a·ble** TECH verstellbar, regulierbar; **ad·just·ment** Anpassung f; TECH Einstellung f

ad·lib aus dem Stegreif (sprechen or spielen)

ad·min·is·ter verwalten; PHARM geben, verabreichen; ~ **justice** Recht sprechen

ad·min·is·tra·tion Verwaltung f; POL Regierung f; Amtsperiode f

ad·min·is·tra·tive Verwaltungs...

ad·min·is·tra·tor Verwaltungsbeamte m

ad·mi·ra·ble bewundernswert; großartig

ad·mi·ral MAR Admiral m

ad·mi·ra·tion Bewunderung f

ad·mire bewundern; verehren

ad·mir·er Verehrer m

ad·mis·si·ble zulässig

ad·mis·sion Eintritt m, Zutritt m; Aufnahme f; Eintrittsgeld n; Eingeständnis n; ~ **free** Eintritt frei

ad·mit v/t zugeben; (her)einlassen (**to,**

into in acc), eintreten lassen; zulassen (**to** zu); **ad·mit·tance** Einlass m, Eintritt m, Zutritt m; **no** ~ Zutritt verboten

ad·mon·ish ermahnen; warnen (**of, against** vor dat)

a·do Getue n, Lärm m; **without more** or **further** ~ ohne weitere Umstände

ad·o·les·cence Jugend f, Adoleszenz f

ad·o·les·cent 1. jugendlich, heranwachsend **2.** Jugendliche m, f

a·dopt adoptieren; übernehmen; ~**ed child** Adoptivkind n

a·dop·tion Adoption f

a·dop·tive par·ents Adoptiveltern pl

a·dor·a·ble F bezaubernd, entzückend

ad·o·ra·tion Anbetung f, Verehrung f

a·dore anbeten, verehren

a·dorn schmücken, zieren

a·dorn·ment Schmuck m, Verzierung f

a·droit geschickt

ad·ult 1. erwachsen **2.** Erwachsene m, f; ~**s only** nur für Erwachsene!; ~ **ed·u·ca·tion** Erwachsenenbildung f

a·dul·ter·ate verfälschen, Wein panschen

a·dul·ter·er Ehebrecher m

a·dul·ter·ess Ehebrecherin f

a·dul·ter·ous ehebrecherisch

a·dul·ter·y Ehebruch m

ad·vance 1. v/i vordringen, vorrücken (a. time); Fortschritte machen; v/t vorrücken; Termin etc vorverlegen; Argument etc vorbringen; Geld vorstrecken, F vorschießen; (be)fördern; Preis erhöhen; Wachstum etc beschleunigen **2.** Vorrücken n, Vorstoß m (a. fig); Fortschritt m; ECON Vorschuss m; Erhöhung f; **in** ~ im Voraus

ad·vanced fortgeschritten; ~ **for one's years** weit or reif für sein Alter

ad·vance·ment Fortschritt m, Verbesserung f

ad·van·tage Vorteil m (a. SPORT); ~ **rule** SPORT Vorteilsregel f; **take** ~ **of** ausnutzen

ad·van·ta·geous vorteilhaft

ad·ven·ture Abenteuer n, Wagnis n

ad·ven·tur·er Abenteurer m

ad·ven·tur·ess Abenteu(r)erin f

ad·ven·tur·ous abenteuerlich; verwegen, kühn

ad·verb LING Adverb n, Umstandswort n

ad·ver·sa·ry Gegner(in)

ad·ver·tise ankündigen, bekannt machen; inserieren; Reklame machen (für)

ad·ver·tise·ment Anzeige f, Inserat n

ad·ver·tis·ing 1. Reklame f, Werbung f **2.** Reklame..., Werbe...; **~ a·gen·cy** Werbeagentur f; **~ cam·paign** Werbefeldzug m

ad·vice Rat(schlag) m; ECON Benachrichtigung f; *take medical ~* e-n Arzt zu Rate ziehen; *take my ~* hör auf mich

ad·vice| cen·ter, Br **~ cen·tre** Beratungsstelle f

ad·vis·a·ble ratsam

ad·vise v/t j-n beraten; j-m raten; esp ECON benachrichtigen, avisieren; v/i sich beraten

ad·vis·er esp Br, **ad·vis·or** Berater m

ad·vi·so·ry beratend

ad·vo·cate 1. befürworten, verfechten **2.** Befürworter(in), Verfechter(in)

aer·i·al 1. luftig; Luft... **2.** Antenne f

aer·i·al| pho·to·graph, **~ view** Luftaufnahme f, Luftbild n

aer·o... Aero..., Luft...

aer·o·bics SPORT Aerobic n

aer·o·drome esp Br Flugplatz m

aer·o·dy·nam·ic aerodynamisch

aer·o·dy·nam·ics Aerodynamik f

aer·o·nau·tics Luftfahrt f

aer·o·plane Br Flugzeug n

aer·o·sol Spraydose f, Sprühdose f

aes·thet·ic etc → *esthetic* etc

a·far: *from ~* von weit her

af·fair Angelegenheit f, Sache f; F Ding n, Sache f; Affäre f

af·fect beeinflussen; MED angreifen, befallen; bewegen, rühren; e-e Vorliebe haben für; vortäuschen

af·fec·tion Liebe f, Zuneigung f

af·fec·tion·ate liebevoll, herzlich

af·fil·i·ate als Mitglied aufnehmen; angliedern

af·fin·i·ty Affinität f; (geistige) Verwandtschaft; Neigung f (*for, to* zu)

af·firm versichern; beteuern; bestätigen; **af·fir·ma·tion** Versicherung f; Beteuerung f; Bestätigung f

af·fir·ma·tive 1. bejahend **2.** *answer in the ~* bejahen

af·fix (*to*) anheften, ankleben (an *acc*); befestigen (an *dat*); beifügen, hinzufügen (*dat*)

af·flict heimsuchen, plagen; *~ed with* geplagt von, leidend an (*dat*)

af·flic·tion Gebrechen n; Elend n, Not f

af·flu·ence Überfluss m; Wohlstand m

af·flu·ent reich, reichlich; **~ so·ci·e·ty** Wohlstandsgesellschaft f

af·ford sich leisten; gewähren, bieten; *I can ~ it* ich kann es mir leisten

af·front 1. beleidigen **2.** Beleidigung f

a·float MAR flott, schwimmend; *set ~* MAR flottmachen; *fig Gerücht etc* in Umlauf setzen

a·fraid: *be ~ of* sich fürchten *or* Angst haben *vor* (*dat*); *I'm ~ she won't come* ich fürchte, sie wird nicht kommen; *I'm ~ I must go now* leider muss ich jetzt gehen

a·fresh von neuem

Af·ri·ca Afrika n; **Af·ri·can 1.** afrikanisch **2.** Afrikaner(in)

af·ter 1. adv hinterher, nachher, danach **2.** prp nach; hinter (*dat*) (... her); **~ all** schließlich (doch) **3.** cj nachdem **4.** adj später; Nach...; **~ ef·fect** MED Nachwirkung f (a. fig)

af·ter·glow Abendrot n

af·ter·math Nachwirkungen pl, Folgen pl

af·ter·noon Nachmittag m; *this ~* heute Nachmittag; *good ~!* guten Tag!

af·ter·taste Nachgeschmack m

af·ter·thought nachträglicher Einfall

af·ter·ward, Br **af·ter·wards** nachher, später

a·gain wieder; wiederum; ferner; **~ and ~, time and ~** immer wieder; *as much ~* noch einmal so viel

a·gainst gegen; an (*dat or acc*); *as ~* verglichen mit; *he was ~ it* er war dagegen

age 1. (Lebens)Alter n; Zeit(alter n) f; Menschenalter n; (*old*) ~ (hohes) Alter; *at the ~ of* im Alter von; *s.o. your ~* in deinem *or* Ihrem Alter; (*come*) *of ~* mündig *or* volljährig (werden); *be over ~* die Altersgrenze überschritten haben; *under ~* minderjährig; unmündig; *wait for ~s* F e-e Ewigkeit warten **2.** alt werden *or* machen

a·ged[1] alt, betagt

aged[2]: *~ twenty* 20 Jahre alt

age·less zeitlos; ewig jung

a·gen·cy Agentur f; Geschäftsstelle f, Büro n

a·gen·da Tagesordnung f

a·gent Agent m (a. POL), Vertreter m; (*Grundstücks- etc*)Makler m; CHEM

Wirkstoff *m*, Mittel *n*

ag·glom·er·ate (sich) zusammenballen; (sich) (an)häufen

ag·gra·vate erschweren, verschlimmern; F ärgern

ag·gre·gate 1. sich belaufen auf (*acc*) **2.** gesamt **3.** Gesamtmenge *f*, Summe *f*; TECH Aggregat *n*

ag·gres·sion Angriff *m*

ag·gres·sive aggressiv, Angriffs...; *fig* energisch

ag·gres·sor Angreifer *m*

ag·grieved verletzt, gekränkt

a·ghast entgeistert, entsetzt

ag·ile flink, behend

a·gil·i·ty Flinkheit *f*, Behendigkeit *f*

ag·i·tate *v/t fig* aufregen, aufwühlen; *Flüssigkeit* schütteln; *v/i* POL agitieren, hetzen (*against* gegen)

ag·i·ta·tion Aufregung *f*; POL Agitation *f*

ag·i·ta·tor POL Agitator *m*

a·go: *a year ~* vor e-m Jahr

ag·o·ny Qual *f*; Todeskampf *m*

a·gree *v/i* übereinstimmen; sich vertragen; einig werden, sich einigen (*on* über *acc*); übereinkommen; *~ to* zustimmen (*dat*), einverstanden sein mit

a·gree·a·ble (*to*) angenehm (für); übereinstimmend (mit)

a·gree·ment Übereinstimmung *f*; Vereinbarung *f*; Abkommen *n*

ag·ri·cul·tur·al landwirtschaftlich

ag·ri·cul·ture Landwirtschaft *f*

a·ground MAR gestrandet; *run ~* stranden, auf Grund laufen

a·head vorwärts, voraus; vorn; *go ~!* nur zu!, mach nur!; *straight ~* geradeaus

aid 1. unterstützen, *j-m* helfen (*in* bei); fördern; *he was accused of ~ing and abetting* JUR er wurde wegen Beihilfe angeklagt **2.** Hilfe *f*, Unterstützung *f*

AIDS, Aids MED Aids *n*

ail kränklich sein; **ail·ment** Leiden *n*

aim 1. *v/i* zielen (*at* auf *acc*, nach); *~ at fig* beabsichtigen; *be ~ing to do s.th.* vorhaben, et. zu tun; *v/t*: *~ at Waffe etc* richten auf *or* gegen (*acc*) **2.** Ziel *n* (*a. fig*); Absicht *f*; *take ~ at* zielen auf (*acc*) *or* nach; **aim·less** ziellos

air¹ 1. Luft *f*; Luftzug *m*; Miene *f*, Aussehen *n*; *by ~* auf dem Luftwege; *in the open ~* im Freien; *on the ~* im Rundfunk *or* Fernsehen; *be on the ~* senden;

in Betrieb sein; *go off the ~* die Sendung beenden (*person*); sein Programm beenden (*station*); *give o.s. ~s, put on ~s* vornehm tun **2.** (aus)lüften; *fig* an die Öffentlichkeit bringen; erörtern

air² MUS Arie *f*, Weise *f*, Melodie *f*

air·bag MOT Airbag *m*

air·base MIL Luftstützpunkt *m*

air·bed Luftmatratze *f*

air·borne AVIAT in der Luft; MIL Luftlande...

air·brake TECH Druckluftbremse *f*

air·bus AVIAT Airbus *m*, Großraumflugzeug *n*

air-con·di·tioned mit Klimaanlage

air-con·di·tion·ing Klimaanlage *f*

air·craft car·ri·er MAR, MIL Flugzeugträger *m*

air·field Flugplatz *m*

air force MIL Luftwaffe *f*

air host·ess AVIAT Stewardess *f*

air jack·et Schwimmweste *f*

air·lift AVIAT Luftbrücke *f*

air·line AVIAT Fluggesellschaft *f*

air·lin·er AVIAT Verkehrsflugzeug *n*

air·mail Luftpost *f*; *by ~* mit Luftpost

air·man MIL Flieger *m*

air·plane Flugzeug *n*

air·pock·et AVIAT Luftloch *n*

air pol·lu·tion Luftverschmutzung *f*

air·port Flughafen *m*

air raid MIL Luftangriff *m*

air-raid| pre·cau·tions MIL Luftschutz *m*; *~* **shel·ter** MIL Luftschutzraum *m*

air route AVIAT Flugroute *f*

air·sick luftkrank

air·space Luftraum *m*

air·strip (behelfsmäßige) Start- und Landebahn

air ter·mi·nal Flughafenabfertigungsgebäude *n*

air·tight luftdicht

air time Sendezeit *f*

air traf·fic AVIAT Flugverkehr *m*

air-traf·fic| con·trol AVIAT Flugsicherung *f*; *~* **con·trol·ler** AVIAT Fluglotse *m*

air·way AVIAT Fluggesellschaft *f*

air·wor·thy AVIAT flugtüchtig

air·y luftig

aisle ARCH Seitenschiff *n*; Gang *m*

a·jar halb offen, angelehnt

a·kin verwandt (*to* mit)

a·lac·ri·ty Bereitwilligkeit *f*

a·larm 1. Alarm(zeichen *n*) *m*; Wecker *m*; Angst *f* **2.** alarmieren; beunruhigen; **~ clock** Wecker *m*

al·bum Album *n* (*a. record*)

al·bu·mi·nous BIOL eiweißhaltig

al·co·hol Alkohol *m*; **al·co·hol·ic 1.** alkoholisch **2.** Alkoholiker(in)

al·co·hol·ism Alkoholismus *m*, Trunksucht *f*

a·lert 1. wachsam; munter **2.** Alarm *m*; Alarmbereitschaft *f*; **on the ~** auf der Hut; in Alarmbereitschaft **3.** warnen (**to** vor *dat*), alarmieren

al·ga BOT Alge *f*

al·ge·bra MATH Algebra *f*

al·i·bi JUR Alibi *n*

a·li·en 1. ausländisch; fremd **2.** Ausländer(in); Außerirdische *m, f*

a·li·en·ate veräußern; entfremden; *esp art:* verfremden; **a·li·en·a·tion** Entfremdung *f*; *esp art:* Verfremdung *f*

a·light 1. in Flammen **2.** aussteigen; absteigen, absitzen; ZO sich niederlassen; AVIAT landen

a·lign (sich) ausrichten (**with** nach)

a·like 1. *adj* gleich **2.** *adv* gleich, ebenso

a·i·mo·ny JUR Unterhalt *m*

a·live lebendig; (noch) am Leben; lebhaft; **~ and kicking** gesund und munter; **be ~ with** wimmeln von

all 1. *adj* all; ganz; jede(r, -s) **2.** *pron* alles; alle *pl* **3.** *adv* ganz, völlig; **~ at once** auf einmal; **~ the better** desto besser; **~ but** beinahe, fast; **~ in** F fertig, ganz erledigt; **~ right** in Ordnung; **for~ that** dessen ungeachtet, trotzdem; **for~ I know** soviel ich weiß; **at~** überhaupt; **not at ~** überhaupt nicht; **the score was two ~** das Spiel stand zwei zu zwei

all-A·mer·i·can typisch amerikanisch; die ganzen USA vertretend

al·lay beruhigen; lindern

al·le·ga·tion *unerwiesene* Behauptung

al·lege behaupten

al·leged angeblich, vermeintlich

al·le·giance Treue *f*

al·ler·gic MED allergisch (**to** gegen)

al·ler·gy MED Allergie *f*

al·le·vi·ate mildern, lindern

al·ley (enge *or* schmale) Gasse; Garten-, Parkweg *m*; *bowling:* Bahn *f*

al·li·ance Bündnis *n*

al·li·ga·tor ZO Alligator *m*

al·lo·cate zuteilen, anweisen

al·lo·ca·tion Zuteilung *f*

al·lot zuteilen, an-, zuweisen

al·lot·ment Zuteilung *f*; Parzelle *f*

al·low erlauben, bewilligen, gewähren; zugeben; ab-, anrechnen, vergüten; **~ for** einplanen, berücksichtigen (*acc*)

al·low·a·ble erlaubt, zulässig

al·low·ance Erlaubnis *f*; Bewilligung *f*; Taschengeld *n*, Zuschuss *m*; Vergütung *f*; *fig* Nachsicht *f*; **make~(s) for s.th.** et. berücksichtigen

al·loy TECH **1.** Legierung *f* **2.** legieren

all-round vielseitig

all-round·er Alleskönner *m*; Allroundsportler *m*, -spieler *m*

al·lude anspielen (**to** auf *acc*)

al·lure locken, an-, verlocken

al·lure·ment Verlockung *f*

al·lu·sion Anspielung *f*

all-wheel drive MOT Allradantrieb *m*

al·ly 1. (sich) vereinigen, verbünden (**to, with** mit); **2.** Verbündete *m, f*, Bundesgenosse *m*, Bundesgenossin *f*; **the Allies** MIL die Alliierten *pl*

al·might·y allmächtig; **the Almighty** REL der Allmächtige

al·mond BOT Mandel *f*

al·most fast, beinah(e)

alms Almosen *n*

a·loft (hoch) (dr)oben

a·lone allein; **let ~, leave ~** in Ruhe lassen, bleiben lassen; **let ~ ...** geschweige denn ...

a·long 1. *adv* weiter, vorwärts; da; dahin; **all ~** die ganze Zeit; **~ with** (zusammen) mit; **come ~** mitkommen, mitgehen; **get ~** vorwärtskommen, weiterkommen; auskommen, sich vertragen (**with s.o.** mit j-m); **take ~** mitnehmen **2.** *prp* entlang (*dat*), längs (*gen*)

a·long·side Seite an Seite; neben

a·loof abseits; reserviert, zurückhaltend, verschlossen; **a·loof·ness** Reserviertheit *f*; Verschlossenheit *f*

a·loud laut

al·pha·bet Alphabet *n*

al·pine (Hoch)Gebirgs..., alpin

al·read·y bereits, schon

al·right → all right

Al·sa·tian *esp Br* ZO Deutscher Schäferhund

al·so auch, ferner

al·tar REL Altar *m*

al·ter ändern, sich (ver)ändern; ab-, umändern; **al·ter·a·tion** Änderung *f* (*to* an *dat*), Veränderung *f*

al·ter·nate 1. abwechseln (lassen) **2.** abwechselnd; **al·ter·nat·ing cur·rent** ELECTR Wechselstrom *m*

al·ter·na·tion Abwechslung *f*; Wechsel *m*

al·ter·na·tive 1. alternativ, wahlweise **2.** Alternative *f*, Wahl *f*, Möglichkeit *f*

al·though obwohl, obgleich

al·ti·tude Höhe *f*; *at an ~ of* in e-r Höhe von

al·to·geth·er im Ganzen, insgesamt; ganz (und gar), völlig

a·lu·min·i·um *Br*, **a·lu·mi·num** Aluminium *n*

al·ways immer, stets

am, AM *abbr of* **before noon** (*Latin* **ante meridiem**) morgens, vorm., vormittags

a·mal·gam·ate (sich) zusammenschließen, ECON *a.* fusionieren

a·mass anhäufen, aufhäufen

am·a·teur Amateur(in); Dilettant(in); Hobby...

a·maze in Erstaunen setzen, verblüffen; **a·maze·ment** Staunen *n*, Verblüffung *f*; **a·maz·ing** erstaunlich

am·bas·sa·dor POL Botschafter *m* (*to* in *e-m Land*); **am·bas·sa·dress** POL Botschafterin *f* (*to* in *e-m Land*)

am·ber Bernstein *m*

am·bi·gu·i·ty Zwei-, Mehrdeutigkeit *f*

am·big·u·ous zwei-, mehr-, vieldeutig

am·bi·tion Ehrgeiz *m*

am·bi·tious ehrgeizig, strebsam

am·ble 1. Passgang *m* **2.** im Passgang gehen *or* reiten; schlendern

am·bu·lance Krankenwagen *m*

a·men *int* REL amen

a·mend verbessern, berichtigen; PARL abändern, ergänzen; **a·mend·ment** Bess(e)rung *f*; Verbesserung *f*; PARL Abänderungsantrag *m*, Ergänzungsantrag *m*; Zusatzartikel *m* zur Verfassung; **a·mends** (Schaden)Ersatz *m*; *make ~* Schadenersatz leisten, es wieder gutmachen; *make ~ to s.o. for s.th.* j-n für et. entschädigen

a·men·i·ty *often pl* Annehmlichkeiten *pl*

A·mer·i·ca Amerika *n*; **A·mer·i·can 1.** amerikanisch **2.** Amerikaner(in)

A·mer·i·can·is·m LING Amerikanismus *m*

A·mer·i·can·ize (sich) amerikanisieren

A·mer·i·can plan Vollpension *f*

a·mi·a·ble liebenswürdig, freundlich

am·i·ca·ble freundschaftlich, *a.* JUR gütlich

a·mid(st) inmitten (*gen*), (mitten) in *or* unter

a·miss verkehrt, falsch, übel; *take s.th. ~ et.* übel nehmen, et. verübeln

am·mo·ni·a CHEM Ammoniak *n*

am·mu·ni·tion Munition *f*

am·nes·ty JUR **1.** Amnestie *f* **2.** begnadigen

a·mok: *run ~* Amok laufen

a·mong(st) (mitten) unter, zwischen

am·o·rous verliebt

a·mount 1. (*to*) sich belaufen (auf *acc*); hinauslaufen (auf *acc*); **2.** Betrag *m*, (Gesamt)Summe *f*; Menge *f*

am·per·age ELECTR Stromstärke *f*

am·ple weit, groß, geräumig; reich, reichlich, beträchtlich

am·pli·fi·ca·tion Erweiterung *f*; PHYS Verstärkung *f*

am·pli·fi·er ELECTR Verstärker *m*

am·pli·fy erweitern; ELECTR verstärken

am·pli·tude Umfang *m*, Weite *f*, Fülle *f*; ELECTR, PHYS Amplitude *f*

am·pu·tate MED amputieren

a·muck → *amok*

a·muse (*o.s.* sich) amüsieren, unterhalten, belustigen

a·muse·ment Unterhaltung *f*, Vergnügen *n*, Zeitvertreib *m*; *~ park* Vergnügungspark *m*, Freizeitpark *m*

a·mus·ing amüsant, unterhaltend

an → *a*

an·a·bol·ic ster·oid PHARM Anabolikum *n*

a·nae·mi·a *Br* → *anemia*

an·aes·thet·ic *Br* → *anesthetic*

a·nal ANAT anal, Anal...

a·nal·o·gous analog, entsprechend

a·nal·o·gy Analogie *f*, Entsprechung *f*

an·a·lyse *esp Br*, **an·a·lyze** analysieren; zerlegen

a·nal·y·sis Analyse *f*

an·arch·y Anarchie *f*, Gesetzlosigkeit *f*; Chaos *n*

a·nat·o·mize MED zerlegen; zergliedern; **a·nat·o·my** MED Anatomie *f*; Zergliederung *f*, Analyse *f*

an·ces·tor Vorfahr *m*, Ahn *m*

an·ces·tress Vorfahrin *f*, Ahnfrau *f*

an·chor MAR **1.** Anker *m*; *at ~* vor Anker

2. verankern

an·chor·man TV Moderator *m*

an·chor·wom·an TV Moderatorin *f*

an·cho·vy ZO Anschovis *f*, Sardelle *f*

an·cient 1. alt, antik; uralt **2.** *the ˷s* HIST die Alten, die antiken Klassiker

and und

an·ec·dote Anekdote *f*

a·ne·mi·a MED Blutarmut *f*, Anämie *f*

an·es·thet·ic MED **1.** betäubend, Narkose… **2.** Betäubungsmittel *n*

an·gel Engel *m*

an·ger 1. Zorn *m*, Ärger *m* (*at* über *acc*); **2.** erzürnen, (ver)ärgern

an·gle¹ Winkel *m* (*a.* MATH)

an·gle² angeln (*for* nach)

an·gler Angler(in)

An·gli·can REL **1.** anglikanisch **2.** Anglikaner(in)

An·glo-Sax·on 1. angelsächsisch **2.** Angelsachse *m*

an·gry zornig, verärgert, böse (*at, with* über *acc*, mit *dat*)

an·guish Qual *f*, Schmerz *m*

an·gu·lar winkelig; knochig

an·i·mal 1. Tier *n* **2.** tierisch; ˷ **lov·er** Tierfreund *m*; ˷ **shel·ter** Tierheim *n*

an·i·mate beleben; aufmuntern, anregen

an·i·mat·ed lebendig; lebhaft, angeregt; ˷ **car·toon** Zeichentrickfilm *m*

an·i·ma·tion Lebhaftigkeit *f*; Animation *f*; Herstellung *f* von Zeichentrickfilmen; IT bewegtes Bild

an·i·mos·i·ty Animosität *f*, Feindseligkeit *f*

an·kle ANAT (Fuß)Knöchel *m*

an·nals Jahrbücher *pl*

an·nex anhängen; annektieren **2.** Anhang *m*; ARCH Anbau *m*

an·ni·ver·sa·ry Jahrestag *m*; Jahresfeier *f*

an·no·tate mit Anmerkungen versehen; kommentieren

an·nounce ankündigen; bekannt geben; *radio*, TV ansagen; durchsagen; **an·nounce·ment** Ankündigung *f*; Bekanntgabe *f*; *radio*, TV Ansage *f*; Durchsage *f*; **an·nounc·er** *radio*, TV Ansager(in), Sprecher(in)

an·noy ärgern; belästigen

an·noy·ance Störung *f*, Belästigung *f*; Ärgernis *n*

an·noy·ing ärgerlich, lästig

an·nu·al 1. jährlich, Jahres… **2.** einjährige Pflanze; Jahrbuch *n*

an·nu·i·ty (Jahres)Rente *f*

an·nul für ungültig erklären, annullieren; **an·nul·ment** Annullierung *f*, Aufhebung *f*

an·o·dyne MED **1.** schmerzstillend **2.** schmerzstillendes Mittel

a·noint REL salben

a·nom·a·lous anomal

a·non·y·mous anonym

an·o·rak Anorak *m*

an·oth·er ein anderer; ein Zweiter; noch eine(r, -s)

an·swer 1. *v/t et.* beantworten; *j-m* antworten; entsprechen (*dat*); *Zweck* erfüllen; TECH *dem Steuer* gehorchen; JUR *e-r Vorladung* Folge leisten; *e-r Beschreibung* entsprechen; ˷ *the bell* or *door* (die Tür) aufmachen; ˷ *the telephone* ans Telefon gehen; *v/i* antworten (*to* auf *acc*); entsprechen (*to* dat); ˷ *for* einstehen für **2.** Antwort *f* (*to* auf *acc*)

an·swer·a·ble verantwortlich

an·swer·ing ma·chine TEL Anrufbeantworter *m*

ant ZO Ameise *f*

an·tag·o·nism Feindschaft *f*

an·tag·o·nist Gegner(in)

an·tag·o·nize bekämpfen; sich *j-n* zum Feind machen

Ant·arc·tic antarktisch

an·te·ced·ent vorhergehend, früher (*to* als)

an·te·lope ZO Antilope *f*

an·ten·na¹ ZO Fühler *m*

an·ten·na² ELECTR Antenne *f*

an·te·ri·or vorhergehend, früher (*to* als); vorder

an·them MUS Hymne *f*

an·ti… Gegen…, gegen … eingestellt, Anti…, anti…

an·ti-air·craft MIL Fliegerabwehr…, Flugabwehr…

an·ti·bi·ot·ic MED Antibiotikum *n*

an·ti·bod·y BIOL Antikörper *m*, Abwehrstoff *m*

an·tic·i·pate voraussehen, ahnen; erwarten; zuvorkommen; vorwegnehmen; **an·tic·i·pa·tion** (Vor)Ahnung *f*; Erwartung *f*; Vorwegnahme *f*; Vorfreude *f*; *in* ˷ im Voraus

an·ti·clock·wise Br entgegen dem Uhrzeigersinn

an·tics Mätzchen *pl*

an·ti·dote Gegengift *n*, Gegenmittel *n*

an·ti·for·eign·er vi·o·lence Gewalt *f* gegen Ausländer

an·ti·freeze Frostschutzmittel *n*

an·ti·lock brak·ing sys·tem MOT Antiblockiersystem *n* (*abbr* **ABS**)

an·ti·mis·sile MIL Raketenabwehr…

an·ti·nu·cle·ar ac·tiv·ist Kernkraftgegner(in)

an·tip·a·thy Abneigung *f*

an·ti·quat·ed veraltet

an·tique 1. antik, alt **2.** Antiquität *f*

an·tique| deal·er Antiquitätenhändler(in); **~ shop** *esp Br*, **~ store** Antiquitätenladen *m*

an·tiq·ui·ty Altertum *n*, Vorzeit *f*

an·ti·sep·tic MED **1.** antiseptisch **2.** antiseptisches Mittel

ant·lers ZO Geweih *n*

a·nus ANAT After *m*

an·vil Amboss *m*

anx·i·e·ty Angst *f*, Sorge *f*

anx·ious besorgt, beunruhigt (*about* wegen); begierig, gespannt (*for* auf *acc*); bestrebt (*to do* zu tun)

an·y 1. *adj and pron* (irgend)eine(r, -s), (irgend)welche(r, -s); (irgend)etwas; jede(r, -s) (beliebige); einige *pl*, welche *pl*; *not* **~** keiner **2.** *adv* irgend(wie), ein wenig, (noch) etwas

an·y·bod·y (irgend)jemand; jeder

an·y·how irgendwie; trotzdem, jedenfalls; wie dem auch sei

an·y·one → *anybody*

an·y·thing (irgend)etwas; alles; **~** *but* alles andere als; **~** *else?* sonst noch etwas?; *not* **~** nichts

an·y·way → *anyhow*

an·y·where irgendwo(hin); überall

a·part einzeln, für sich; beiseite; **~** *from* abgesehen von

a·part·heid POL Apartheid *f*, Politik *f* der Rassentrennung

a·part·ment Wohnung *f*; **~** *build·ing*, **~ house** Mietshaus *n*

ap·a·thet·ic apathisch, teilnahmslos, gleichgültig; **ap·a·thy** Apathie *f*, Teilnahmslosigkeit *f*

ape ZO (Menschen)Affe *m*

ap·er·ture Öffnung *f*

a·pi·a·ry Bienenhaus *n*

a·piece für jedes Stück, pro Stück, je

a·pol·o·gize sich entschuldigen (*for* für; *to* bei); **a·pol·o·gy** Entschuldigung *f*; Rechtfertigung *f*; *make an* **~** (*for s.th.*) sich (für et.) entschuldigen

ap·o·plex·y MED Schlaganfall *m*, F Schlag *m*

a·pos·tle REL Apostel *m*

a·pos·tro·phe LING Apostroph *m*

ap·pal(l) erschrecken, entsetzen

ap·pal·ling erschreckend, entsetzlich

ap·pa·ra·tus Apparat *m*, Vorrichtung *f*, Gerät *n*

ap·par·ent offenbar; anscheinend; scheinbar

ap·pa·ri·tion Erscheinung *f*, Gespenst *n*

ap·peal 1. JUR Berufung *or* Revision einlegen, Einspruch erheben, Beschwerde einlegen; appellieren, sich wenden (*to* an *acc*); **~** *to* gefallen (*dat*), zusagen (*dat*), wirken auf (*acc*); *j-n* dringend bitten (*for* um); **2.** JUR Revision *f*, Berufung *f*; Beschwerde *f*; Einspruch *m*; Appell *m* (*to* an *acc*); Aufruf *m*; Wirkung *f*, Reiz *m*; Bitte *f* (*to* an *acc*; *for* um); **~** *for mercy* JUR Gnadengesuch *n*

ap·peal·ing flehend; ansprechend

ap·pear (er)scheinen; sich zeigen; öffentlich auftreten; sich ergeben *or* herausstellen; **ap·pear·ance** Erscheinen *n*; Auftreten *n*; Äußere *n*, Erscheinung *f*, Aussehen *m*; Anschein *m*, äußerer Schein; *keep up* **~***s* den Schein wahren; *to* or *by all* **~***s* allem Anschein nach

ap·pease besänftigen, beschwichtigen; *Durst etc* stillen; *Neugier* befriedigen

ap·pend an-, hinzu-, beifügen

ap·pend·age Anhang *m*; Anhängsel *n*

ap·pen·di·ci·tis MED Blinddarmentzündung *f*

ap·pen·dix Anhang *m*; *a.* *vermiform* **~** ANAT Wurmfortsatz *m*, Blinddarm *m*

ap·pe·tite (*for*) Appetit *m* (auf *acc*); *fig* Verlangen *n* (nach)

ap·pe·tiz·er Appetithappen *m*, appetitanregendes Gericht *or* Getränk

ap·pe·tiz·ing appetitanregend

ap·plaud applaudieren, Beifall spenden; loben

ap·plause Applaus *m*, Beifall *m*

ap·ple BOT Apfel *m*

ap·ple pie (*warmer*) gedeckter Apfelkuchen

ap·ple sauce Apfelmus *n*; *sl* Schmus *m*,

Quatsch *m*

ap·pli·ance Vorrichtung *f*; Gerät *n*; Mittel *n*

ap·plic·a·ble anwendbar (**to** auf *acc*)

ap·pli·cant Antragsteller(in), Bewerber(in) (**for** um)

ap·pli·ca·tion Anwendung *f* (**to** auf *acc*); Bedeutung *f* (**to** für); Gesuch *n* (**for** um); Bewerbung *f* (**for** um)

ap·ply *v/t* (**to**) (auf)legen, auftragen (auf *acc*); anwenden (auf *acc*); verwenden (für); **~ o.s. to** sich widmen (*dat*); *v/i* (**to**) passen, zutreffen, sich anwenden lassen (auf *acc*); gelten (für); sich wenden (an *acc*); **~ for** sich bewerben um, *et*. beantragen

ap·point bestimmen, festsetzen; verabreden; ernennen (**s.o. governor** j-n zum …); berufen (**to** auf e-n Posten)

ap·point·ment Bestimmung *f*; Verabredung *f*; Termin *m*; Ernennung *f*, Berufung *f*; Stelle *f*; **~ book** Terminkalender *m*

ap·por·tion verteilen, zuteilen

ap·prais·al (Ab)Schätzung *f*

ap·praise (ab)schätzen, taxieren

ap·pre·cia·ble nennenswert, spürbar

ap·pre·ci·ate *v/t* schätzen, würdigen; dankbar sein für; *v/i* im Wert steigen

ap·pre·ci·a·tion Würdigung *f*; Dankbarkeit *f*; (richtige) Beurteilung; ECON Wertsteigerung *f*

ap·pre·hend ergreifen, fassen; begreifen; befürchten; **ap·pre·hen·sion** Ergreifung *f*, Festnahme *f*; Besorgnis *f*; **ap·pre·hen·sive** ängstlich, besorgt (**for** um; **that** dass)

ap·pren·tice 1. Auszubildende *m*, *f*, Lehrling *m*, *Swiss* Lehrtochter *f* **2.** in die Lehre geben; **ap·pren·tice·ship** Lehrzeit *f*, Lehre *f*, Ausbildung *f*

ap·proach 1. *v/i* näher kommen, sich nähern; *v/t* sich nähern (*dat*); herangehen *or* herantreten an (*acc*) **2.** (Heran)Nahen *n*; Einfahrt *f*, Zufahrt *f*, Auffahrt *f*; Annäherung *f*; Methode *f*

ap·pro·ba·tion Billigung *f*, Beifall *m*

ap·pro·pri·ate 1. sich aneignen; verwenden; PARL bewilligen **2.** (**for, to**) angemessen (*dat*), passend (für, zu)

ap·prov·al Billigung *f*; Anerkennung *f*, Beifall *m*; **ap·prove** billigen, anerkennen; **ap·proved** bewährt

ap·prox·i·mate annähernd, ungefähr

a·pri·cot BOT Aprikose *f*

A·pril (*abbr* **Apr**) April *m*

a·pron Schürze *f*

apt geeignet, passend; treffend; begabt; **~ to** geneigt zu

ap·ti·tude (**for**) Begabung *f* (für), Befähigung *f* (für), Talent *n* (zu)

ap·ti·tude test Eignungsprüfung *f*

aq·ua| jog·ging SPORT Aquajogging *n*; **~ plan·ing** *Br* MOT Aquaplaning *n*

a·quar·i·um Aquarium *n*

A·quar·i·us ASTR Wassermann *m*; **he** (**she**) **is** (**an**) **~** er (sie) ist (ein) Wassermann

a·quat·ic Wasser…; **~ plant** Wasserpflanze *f*; **~s**, **~ sports** Wassersport *m*

aq·ue·duct Aquädukt *m*

Ar·ab Araber(in); **A·ra·bi·a** Arabien *n*

Ar·a·bic 1. arabisch **2.** LING Arabisch *n*

ar·a·ble AGR anbaufähig; Acker…

ar·bi·tra·ry willkürlich, eigenmächtig

ar·bi·trate entscheiden, schlichten

ar·bi·tra·tion Schlichtung *f*

ar·bi·tra·tor Schiedsrichter *m*; Schlichter *m*

ar·bo(u)r Laube *f*

arc Bogen *m*; ELECTR Lichtbogen *m*

ar·cade Arkade *f*; Lauben-, Bogengang *m*; Durchgang *m*, Passage *f*

arch¹ 1. Bogen *m*; Gewölbe *n* **2.** (sich) wölben; krümmen

arch² erste(r, -s), oberste(r, -s), Haupt…, Erz…

arch³ schelmisch

ar·cha·ic veraltet

arch·an·gel Erzengel *m*

arch·bish·op REL Erzbischof *m*

ar·cher Bogenschütze *m*

ar·cher·y Bogenschießen *n*

ar·chi·tect Architekt(in)

ar·chi·tec·ture Architektur *f*

ar·chives Archiv *n*

arch·way (Bogen)Gang *m*

arc·tic arktisch, nördlich, Polar…

ar·dent feurig, glühend; *fig* leidenschaftlich, heftig; eifrig

ar·do(u)r Leidenschaft *f*, Glut *f*, Feuer *n*; Eifer *m*

are *du* bist, *wir or sie or Sie* sind, *ihr* seid

ar·e·a (Boden)Fläche *f*; Gegend *f*, Gebiet *n*; Bereich *m*

ar·e·a code TEL Vorwahl(nummer) *f*

a·re·na Arena *f*

Ar·gen·ti·na Argentinien *n*

Argentine

Ar·gen·tine 1. argentinisch **2.** Argentinier(in)

ar·gue argumentieren; streiten; diskutieren; **ar·gu·ment** Argument *n*; Wortwechsel *m*, Auseinandersetzung *f*

ar·id dürr, trocken (*a. fig*)

Ar·ies ASTR Widder *m*; **he (she) is (an) ~** er (sie) ist (ein) Widder

a·rise entstehen; auftauchen, auftreten

ar·is·toc·ra·cy Aristokratie *f*, Adel *m*

ar·is·to·crat Aristokrat(in), Adlige *m*, *f*

ar·is·to·crat·ic aristokratisch, adlig

a·rith·me·tic¹ Rechnen *n*

a·rith·met·ic² arithmetisch, Rechen...

a·rith·met·ic u·nit IT Rechenwerk *n*

ark Arche *f*; **Noah's ~** die Arche Noah

arm¹ ANAT Arm *m*; Armlehne *f*; **keep s.o. at ~'s length** sich j-n vom Leibe halten

arm² MIL (sich) bewaffnen; (auf)rüsten

ar·ma·ment MIL Bewaffnung *f*; Aufrüstung *f*

arm·chair Lehnstuhl *m*, Sessel *m*

ar·mi·stice MIL Waffenstillstand *m*

ar·mo(u)r 1. MIL Rüstung *f*, Panzer *m* (*a. fig*, ZO); **2.** panzern

ar·mo(u)red car gepanzertes Fahrzeug

arm·pit ANAT Achselhöhle *f*

arms Waffen *pl*; Waffengattung *f*; **~ con·trol** Rüstungskontrolle *f*

ar·my MIL Armee *f*, Heer *n*

a·ro·ma Aroma *n*, Duft *m*

a·ro·mat·ic aromatisch, würzig

a·round 1. *adv* (rings)herum, (rund-) herum, ringsumher, überall; umher, herum; in der Nähe; da **2.** *prp* um, um... herum, rund um; in (*dat*) ... herum; ungefähr, etwa

a·rouse (auf)wecken; *fig* aufrütteln, erregen

ar·range (an)ordnen; festlegen, festsetzen; arrangieren (*a.* MUS); vereinbaren; MUS, THEA bearbeiten

ar·range·ment Anordnung *f*; Vereinbarung *f*; Vorkehrung *f*; MUS Arrangement *n*, Bearbeitung *f* (*a.* THEA)

ar·rears Rückstand *m*, Rückstände *pl*

ar·rest JUR **1.** Verhaftung *f*, Festnahme *f* **2.** verhaften, festnehmen

ar·riv·al Ankunft *f*; Erscheinen *n*; Ankömmling *m*; **~s** AVIAT, RAIL *etc* 'Ankunft' (*timetable*); **day of ~** Anreisetag; **ar·rive** (an)kommen, eintreffen, erscheinen; **~ at** *fig* erreichen (*acc*), kom-

men zu

ar·ro·gance Arroganz *f*, Überheblichkeit *f*

ar·ro·gant arrogant, überheblich

ar·row Pfeil *m*

ar·row·head Pfeilspitze *f*

ar·se·nic CHEM Arsen *n*

ar·son JUR Brandstiftung *f*

art 1. Kunst *f* **2.** Kunst...; **~ exhibition** Kunstausstellung *f*; → **arts**

ar·te·ri·al ANAT Schlagader...

ar·te·ri·al road Hauptverkehrsstraße *f*, Verkehrsader *f*

ar·te·ri·o·scle·ro·sis MED Arteriosklerose *f*, Arterienverkalkung *f*

ar·te·ry ANAT Arterie *f*, Schlagader *f*; (Haupt)Verkehrsader *f*

art·ful schlau, verschmitzt

art gal·le·ry Gemäldegalerie *f*

ar·thri·tis MED Arthritis *f*, Gelenkentzündung *f*

ar·ti·choke BOT Artischocke *f*

ar·ti·cle Artikel *m* (*a.* LING)

ar·tic·u·late 1. deutlich (aus)sprechen **2.** deutlich ausgesprochen; gegliedert

ar·tic·u·lat·ed Gelenk...; **~ lorry** *Br* MOT Sattelschlepper *m*

ar·tic·u·la·tion (deutliche) Aussprache; TECH Gelenk *n*

ar·ti·fi·cial künstlich, Kunst...; **~ person** juristische Person

ar·til·le·ry MIL Artillerie *f*

ar·ti·san Handwerker *m*

art·ist Künstler(in)

ar·tis·tic künstlerisch, Kunst...

art·less schlicht; naiv

arts Geisteswissenschaften *pl*; **Arts Department**, *Br* **Faculty of Arts** philosophische Fakultät

as 1. *adv* so, ebenso; wie; als **2.** *cj* (gerade) wie, so wie; ebenso wie; als, während; obwohl, obgleich; da, weil; **~ ...** **~** (eben)so ... wie; **~ for, ~ to** was ... (an-)betrifft; **~ from** von e-m Zeitpunkt an, ab; **~ it were** sozusagen; **~ Hamlet** THEA als Hamlet

as·bes·tos Asbest *m*

as·cend (auf)steigen; ansteigen; besteigen; **as·cen·dan·cy**, **as·cen·den·cy** Überlegenheit *f*; Einfluss *m*

as·cen·sion Aufsteigen *n* (*esp* ASTR); Aufstieg *m*; **As·cen·sion (Day)** REL Himmelfahrt(stag *m*) *f*

as·cent Aufstieg *m*; Besteigung *f*; Steigung *f*

as·cet·ic asketisch

a·sep·tic MED **1.** aseptisch, keimfrei **2.** aseptisches Mittel

ash¹ BOT Esche *f*; Eschenholz *n*

ash² *a.* **ashes** Asche *f*

a·shamed beschämt; *be ~ of* sich schämen für (*acc*)

ash·en Aschen...; aschfahl, aschgrau

a·shore am *or* ans Ufer *or* Land

ash·tray Asch(en)becher *m*

Ash Wednes·day Aschermittwoch *m*

A·sia Asien *n*; **A·sian, A·si·at·ic 1.** asiatisch **2.** Asiat(in)

a·side beiseite (*a.* THEA), seitwärts; *~ from* abgesehen von

ask *v/t* fragen (*s.th.* nach et.); verlangen (*of, from s.o.* von j-m); bitten (*s.o.* [*for*] *s.th.* j-n um et.; *that* darum, dass); erbitten; *~* (*s.o.*) *a question* (j-m) e-e Frage stellen; *v/i ~ for* bitten um; fragen nach; *he ~ed for it or for trouble* er wollte es ja so haben; *to be had for the ~ing* umsonst zu haben sein

a·skew schief

a·sleep schlafend; *be* (*fast, sound*) *~* (fest) schlafen; *fall ~* einschlafen

as·par·a·gus BOT Spargel *m*

as·pect Lage *f*; Aspekt *m*, Seite *f*, Gesichtspunkt *m*

as·phalt 1. Asphalt *m* **2.** asphaltieren

as·pic GASTR Aspik *m*, Gelee *n*

as·pi·rant Bewerber(in)

as·pi·ra·tion Ambition *f*, Bestrebung *f*

as·pire streben (*to, after* nach)

ass ZO Esel *m*

as·sail angreifen; *be ~ed with doubts* von Zweifeln befallen werden

as·sail·ant Angreifer(in)

as·sas·sin (*esp* politischer) Mörder, Attentäter *m*; **as·sas·sin·ate** *esp* POL ermorden; *be ~d* e-m Attentat *or* Mordanschlag zum Opfer fallen; **as·sas·sin·a·tion** (*of*) (*esp* politischer) Mord (an *dat*), Ermordung *f* (*gen*), Attentat *n* (auf *acc*)

as·sault 1. Angriff *m*, Überfall *m* **2.** angreifen, überfallen

as·sem·blage Ansammlung *f*; TECH Montage *f*; **as·sem·ble** (sich) versammeln; TECH montieren

as·sem·bly Versammlung *f*, Gesellschaft *f*; TECH Montage *f*; *~ line* TECH Fließband *n*

as·sent 1. Zustimmung *f* **2.** (*to*) zustimmen (*dat*); billigen (*acc*)

as·sert behaupten; geltend machen; *~ o.s.* sich behaupten, sich durchsetzen

as·ser·tion Behauptung *f*; Erklärung *f*; Geltendmachung *f*

as·sess Kosten *etc* festsetzen; *Einkommen etc* (zur Steuer) veranlagen (*at* mit); *fig* abschätzen, beurteilen

as·sess·ment Festsetzung *f*; (Steuer)Veranlagung *f*; *fig* Einschätzung *f*

as·set ECON Aktivposten *m*; *fig* Plus *n*, Gewinn *m*; *pl* ECON Aktiva *pl*; JUR Vermögen(smasse *f*) *n*; Konkursmasse *f*

as·sid·u·ous emsig, fleißig

as·sign an-, zuweisen; bestimmen; zuschreiben; **as·sign·ment** An-, Zuweisung *f*; Aufgabe *f*; Auftrag *m*; JUR Abtretung *f*; Übertragung *f*

as·sim·i·late (sich) angleichen *or* anpassen (*to, with dat*)

as·sim·i·la·tion Assimilation *f*, Angleichung *f*, Anpassung *f* (*all: to* an *acc*)

as·sist j-m beistehen, helfen; j-n unterstützen; **as·sist·ance** Beistand *m*, Hilfe *f*; **as·sist·ant 1.** stellvertretend, Hilfs... **2.** Assistent(in), Mitarbeiter(in); (*shop*) *~ Br* Verkäufer(in); *~ant referee* SPORT Schiedsrichterassistent(in)

as·so·ci·ate 1. vereinigen, verbinden, zusammenschließen; assoziieren; *~ with* verkehren mit **2.** Teilhaber(in)

as·so·ci·a·tion Vereinigung *f*, Verbindung *f*; Verein *m*

as·sort sortieren, aussuchen, zusammenstellen; **as·sort·ment** ECON (*of*) Sortiment *n* (von), Auswahl *f* (an *dat*)

as·sume annehmen, voraussetzen; übernehmen

as·sump·tion Annahme *f*, Voraussetzung *f*; Übernahme *f*; *the Assumption* REL Mariä Himmelfahrt *f*

as·sur·ance Zusicherung *f*, Versicherung *f*; *esp Br* (Lebens)Versicherung *f*; Sicherheit *f*, Gewissheit *f*; Selbstsicherheit *f*; **as·sure** j-m versichern; *esp Br* j-s *Leben* versichern; **as·sured 1.** sicher **2.** *esp Br* Versicherte *m*, *f*; **as·sur·ed·ly** ganz gewiss

as·te·risk PRINT Sternchen *n*

asth·ma MED Asthma *n*

as·ton·ish in Erstaunen setzen; *be ~ed* erstaunt sein (*at* über *acc*)

astonishing

as·ton·ish·ing erstaunlich
as·ton·ish·ment (Er)Staunen *n*, Verwunderung *f*
as·tound verblüffen
a·stray: go ~ vom Weg abkommen; *fig* auf Abwege geraten; irregehen; **lead ~** *fig* irreführen; verleiten
a·stride rittlings (*of* auf *dat*)
as·trin·gent MED **1.** adstringierend **2.** Adstringens *n*
as·trol·o·gy Astrologie *f*
as·tro·naut Astronaut *m*, (Welt)Raumfahrer *m*
as·tron·o·my Astronomie *f*
as·tute scharfsinnig; schlau
a·sun·der auseinander, entzwei
a·sy·lum Asyl *n*; **right of ~** Asylrecht *n*
a·sy·lum seek·er Asylant(in), Asylbewerber(in)
at *prp place*: in, an, bei, auf; *direction*: auf, nach, gegen, zu; *occupation*: bei, beschäftigt mit, in; *manner, state*: in, bei, zu, unter; *price etc*: für, um; *time, age*: um, bei; **~ the baker's** beim Bäcker; **~ the door** an der Tür; **~ school** in der Schule; **~ 10 dollars** für 10 Dollar; **~ 18** mit 18 (Jahren); **~ the age of** im Alter von; **~ 8 o'clock** um 8 Uhr
a·the·ism Atheismus *m*
ath·lete SPORT (Leicht)Athlet(in)
ath·let·ic SPORT athletisch
ath·let·ics SPORT (Leicht)Athletik *f*
At·lan·tic 1. *a.* **~ Ocean** der Atlantik **2.** atlantisch
at·mo·sphere Atmosphäre *f* (*a. fig*)
at·mo·spher·ic atmosphärisch
at·oll Atoll *n*
at·om Atom *n*; **~ bomb** Atombombe *f*
a·tom·ic atomar, Atom...; **~ age** Atomzeitalter *n*; **~ bomb** Atombombe *f*; **~ en·er·gy** Atomenergie *f*; **~ pile** Atomreaktor *m*; **~ pow·er** Atomkraft *f*; **~-pow·ered** atomgetrieben; **~ waste** Atommüll *m*; **~ weight** CHEM Atomgewicht *n*
at·om·ize atomisieren; *Flüssigkeit* zerstäuben; **at·om·iz·er** Zerstäuber *m*
a·tro·cious grässlich; grausam
a·troc·i·ty Scheußlichkeit *f*; Greueltat *f*
at sign IT at-Zeichen *n*
at·tach *v/t* (**to**) anheften, ankleben (an *acc*), befestigen, anbringen (an *dat*); *Wert, Wichtigkeit etc* beimessen (*dat*); **be ~ed to** *fig* hängen an; **at·tach·ment**

Befestigung *f*; Bindung *f* (**to** an *acc*); Anhänglichkeit *f* (**to** an *acc*)
at·tack 1. angreifen **2.** Angriff *m*; MED Anfall *m*
at·tempt 1. versuchen **2.** Versuch *m*; **an ~ on s.o.'s life** ein Mordanschlag *or* Attentat auf j-n
at·tend *v/t* (ärztlich) behandeln; *Kranke* pflegen; teilnehmen an (*dat*), *Schule, Vorlesung etc* besuchen; *fig* begleiten; *v/i* anwesend sein; erscheinen; **~ to** j-n (*im Laden*) bedienen; **are you being ~ed to?** werden Sie schon bedient?; **~ to s.th.** etwas erledigen; **at·tend·ance** Dienst *m*, Bereitschaft *f*; Pflege *f*; Anwesenheit *f*, Erscheinen *n*; Besucher *pl*, Teilnehmer *pl*; Besuch(erzahl *f*) *m*, Beteiligung *f*; **at·tend·ant** Begleiter(in); Aufseher(in); (Tank-)Wart *m*
at·ten·tion Aufmerksamkeit *f* (*a. fig*); **pay ~** aufpassen
at·ten·tive aufmerksam
at·tic Dachboden *m*; Dachkammer *f*
at·ti·tude (Ein)Stellung *f*; Haltung *f*
at·tor·ney Bevollmächtigte *m*, *f*; JUR (Rechts)Anwalt *m*, (Rechts)Anwältin *f*; **power of ~** Vollmacht *f*
At·tor·ney Gen·e·ral JUR Justizminister; *Br* erster Kronanwalt
at·tract anziehen; *Aufmerksamkeit* erregen; *fig* reizen; **at·trac·tion** Anziehung *f*, Anziehungskraft *f*, Reiz *m*; Attraktion *f*, THEA *etc* Zugnummer *f*, Zugstück *n*; **at·trac·tive** anziehend; attraktiv; reizvoll
at·trib·ute[1] zuschreiben (**to** *dat*); zurückführen (**to** auf *acc*)
at·tri·bute[2] Attribut *n* (*a.* LING), Eigenschaft *f*, Merkmal *n*
at·tune: ~ to *fig* einstellen auf (*acc*)
au·ber·gine BOT Aubergine *f*
au·burn kastanienbraun
auc·tion 1. Auktion *f*, Versteigerung *f* **2.** *mst* **~ off** versteigern
auc·tion·eer Auktionator *m*
au·da·cious unverfroren, dreist
au·dac·i·ty Unverfrorenheit *f*, Dreistigkeit *f*
au·di·ble hörbar
au·di·ence Publikum *n*, Zuhörer *pl*, Zuschauer *pl*, Besucher *pl*, Leser(kreis *m*) *pl*; Audienz *f*
au·di·o·vis·u·al aids audiovisuelle Un-

terrichtsmittel *pl*

au·dit ECON **1.** Buchprüfung *f* **2.** prüfen

au·di·tion MUS Vorsingen *n*; THEA Vorsprechen *n*; *have an ~* vorsingen, THEA vorsprechen

au·di·tor ECON Buchprüfer *m*; UNIV Gasthörer(in)

au·di·to·ri·um Zuhörer-, Zuschauerraum *m*; Vortrags-, Konzertsaal *m*

Aug *abbr of* ***August*** Aug., August *m*

au·ger TECH großer Bohrer

Au·gust (*abbr* ***Aug***) August *m*

aunt Tante *f*

au pair (girl) Au-pair-Mädchen *n*

aus·pic·es: *under the ~ of* unter der Schirmherrschaft (*gen*)

aus·tere streng; enthaltsam; dürftig; einfach, schmucklos

Aus·tra·li·a Australien; **Aus·tra·li·an 1.** australisch **2.** Australier(in)

Aus·tri·a Österreich *n*

Aus·tri·an 1. österreichisch **2.** Österreicher(in)

au·then·tic authentisch; zuverlässig; echt

au·thor Urheber(in); Autor(in), Verfasser(in), Schriftsteller(in)

au·thor·ess Autorin *f*, Verfasserin *f*, Schriftstellerin *f*

au·thor·i·ta·tive gebieterisch, herrisch; maßgebend

au·thor·i·ty Autorität *f*; Nachdruck *m*, Gewicht *n*; Vollmacht *f*; Einfluss *m* (*over* auf *acc*); Ansehen *n*; Quelle *f*; Autorität *f*, Kapazität *f*; *mst pl* Behörde *f*

au·thor·ize *j-n* autorisieren, ermächtigen, bevollmächtigen

au·thor·ship Urheberschaft *f*

au·to Auto *n*

au·to... auto..., selbst..., Auto..., Selbst...

au·to·bi·og·ra·phy Autobiografie *f*

au·to·graph Autogramm *n*

au·to·mat® Automatenrestaurant *n*

au·to·mate automatisieren

au·to·mat·ic 1. automatisch **2.** Selbstladepistole *f*, -gewehr *n*; Auto *n* mit Automatik; *~ tel·ler ma·chine* (*abbr* ***ATM***) Geld-, Bankautomat *m*

au·to·ma·tion TECH Automation *f*

au·tom·a·ton Roboter *m*

au·to·mo·bile Auto *n*, Automobil *n*

au·ton·o·my POL Autonomie *f*

au·top·sy MED Autopsie *f*

au·to·tel·ler Geld-, Bankautomat *m*

au·tumn Herbst *m*

au·tum·nal herbstlich, Herbst...

aux·il·i·a·ry helfend, Hilfs...

a·vail: *to no ~* vergeblich

a·vail·a·ble verfügbar, vorhanden; erreichbar; ECON lieferbar, vorrätig, erhältlich

av·a·lanche Lawine *f*

av·a·rice Habsucht *f*

av·a·ri·cious habgierig

a·venge rächen; **a·veng·er** Rächer(in)

av·e·nue Allee *f*; Boulevard *m*, Prachtstraße *f*

av·e·rage 1. Durchschnitt *m* **2.** durchschnittlich, Durchschnitts...

a·verse abgeneigt (*to dat*)

a·ver·sion Widerwille *m*, Abneigung *f*

a·vert abwenden (*a. fig*)

avian flu Vogelgrippe *f*

a·vi·a·ry Vogelhaus *n*, Voliere *f*

a·vi·a·tion Luftfahrt *f*

a·vi·a·tor Flieger *m*

av·id gierig (*for* nach); begeistert

av·o·ca·do BOT Avocado *f*

a·void (ver)meiden; ausweichen

a·void·ance Vermeidung *f*

a·vow·al Bekenntnis *n*, (Ein)Geständnis *n*

a·wait erwarten, warten auf (*acc*)

a·wake 1. wach, munter **2.** *a.* **a·waken** *v/t* (auf)wecken; *v/i* aufwachen, erwachen;

a·wak·en·ing Erwachen *n*

a·ward 1. Belohnung *f*; Preis *m*, Auszeichnung *f* **2.** zuerkennen, *Preis etc* verleihen

a·ware: *be ~ of s.th.* von etwas wissen, sich e-r Sache bewusst sein; *become ~ of s.th.* etwas merken

a·way weg, fort; (weit) entfernt; immer weiter, d(a)rauflos; SPORT Auswärts...; *~ match* SPORT Auswärtsspiel *n*

awe 1. Furcht *f*, Scheu *f* **2.** *j-m* (Ehr)Furcht *or* großen Respekt einflößen

aw·ful furchtbar, schrecklich

awk·ward ungeschickt, linkisch; unangenehm; unhandlich, sperrig; ungünstig, ungelegen

awl Ahle *f*, Pfriem *m*

aw·ning Plane *f*; Markise *f*

a·wry schief

ax(e) Axt *f*, Beil *n*

ax·is MATH *etc* Achse *f*

ax·le TECH (Rad)Achse *f*, Welle *f*
ay(e) PARL Jastimme *f*

A-Z *Br appr* Stadtplan *m*
az·ure azurblau, himmelblau

B

B, b B, b *n*
b *abbr of* **born** geb., geboren
bab·ble 1. stammeln; plappern, schwatzen; plätschern 2. Geplapper *n*, Geschwätz *n*
babe kleines Kind, Baby *n*; F Puppe *f*
ba·boon ZO Pavian *m*
ba·by 1. Baby *n*, Säugling *m*, kleines Kind; F Puppe *f* 2. Baby..., Kinder...; klein; **~ bug·gy**, **~ car·riage** Kinderwagen *m*; **~changing room** Babywickelraum *m*; **~ food** Babynahrung *f*
ba·by·hood Säuglingsalter *n*
ba·by·ish *contp* kindisch
ba·by·mind·er *Br* Tagesmutter *f*
ba·by·sit babysitten
ba·by·sit·ter Babysitter(in)
bach·e·lor Junggeselle *m*
back 1. Rücken *m*; Rückseite *f*; (Rück)Lehne *f*; hinterer *or* rückwärtiger Teil; SPORT Verteidiger *m* 2. *adj* Hinter..., Rück..., hintere(r, -s), rückwärtig; ECON rückständig; alt, zurückliegend 3. *adv* zurück, rückwärts 4. *v/t* mit e-m Rücken versehen; wetten *or* setzen auf (*acc*); *a*. **~ up** unterstützen; zurückbewegen; MOT zurückstoßen mit; **~ up** IT e-e Sicherungskopie machen von; *v/i often* **~ up** sich rückwärts bewegen, zurückgehen *or* -fahren, MOT *a.* zurückstoßen; **~ in**(**to a parking space**) MOT rückwärts einparken; **~ up** IT e-e Sicherungskopie machen
back·ache Rückenschmerzen *pl*
back·bite verleumden, schlechtmachen
back·bone ANAT Rückgrat *n* (*a. fig*)
back·break·ing erschöpfend, mörderisch
back·chat *Br* freche Antwort(en *pl*)
back·comb *Br* toupieren
back door Hintertür *f*; *fig* Hintertürchen *n*
back·er Unterstützer *m*, Geldgeber *m*
back·fire MOT Früh- *or* Fehlzündung haben; *fig* fehlschlagen
back·ground Hintergrund *m*

back·hand SPORT Rückhand *f*, Rückhandschlag *m*
back·heel·er *soccer:* Hackentrick *m*
back·ing Unterstützung *f*
back num·ber alte Nummer
back·pack *großer* Rucksack
back·pack·er Rucksacktourist(in)
back·pack·ing Rucksacktourismus *m*
back·ped·al brake *Br* Rücktritt *m*, Rücktrittbremse *f*
back seat MOT Rücksitz *m*
back·side Gesäß *n*, F Hintern *m*, Po *m*
back·space (key) IT Rücktaste *f*
back stairs Hintertreppe *f*
back street Seitenstraße *f*
back·stroke Rückenschwimmen *n*
back talk freche Antwort(en *pl*)
back·track *fig* e-n Rückzieher machen
back·up Unterstützung *f*; TECH Ersatzgerät *n*; IT Backup *n*, Sicherungskopie *f*; MOT Rückstau *m*
back·ward 1. *adj* Rück..., Rückwärts...; zurückgeblieben; rückständig; *a* **~ glance** ein Blick zurück 2. *adv a.* **backwards** rückwärts, zurück
back·yard Garten *m* hinter dem Haus; *Br* Hinterhof *m*
ba·con Speck *m*
bac·te·ri·a BIOL Bakterien *pl*
bad schlecht, böse, schlimm; **go ~** schlecht werden, verderben; **he is in a ~ way** es geht ihm schlecht; **he is ~ly off** es geht ihm finanziell schlecht; **~ly wounded** schwer verwundet; **want ~ly** dringend brauchen
badge Abzeichen *n*; Dienstmarke *f*
bad·ger 1. ZO Dachs *m* 2. *j-n* plagen, *j-m* zusetzen
bad·min·ton Federball(spiel *n*) *m*, SPORT Badminton *n*
bad-tempered schlecht gelaunt
bag 1. Beutel *m*, Sack *m*; Tüte *f*; Tasche *f* 2. in e-n Beutel *etc* tun; in Beutel verpacken *or* abfüllen; HUNT zur Strecke bringen; schlottern
bag·gage (Reise)Gepäck *n*; **~ car** RAIL

Gepäckwagen *m*; ~ **check** Gepäckschein *m*; ~ **claim** AVIAT Gepäckausga-
be *f*; ~ **room** RAIL Gepäckaufbewahrung *f*
bag·gy bauschig; ausgebeult
bag·pipes MUS Dudelsack *m*
bail 1. Bürge *m*; JUR Kaution *f*; *be out on*
~ gegen Kaution auf freiem Fuß sein;
go or stand ~ for s.o. für j-n Kaution
stellen 2. ~ *out* JUR j-n gegen Kaution
freibekommen; AVIAT (mit dem Fallschirm) abspringen
bai·liff (Guts)Verwalter *m*; *Br* JUR Ge-
richtsvollzieher *m*
bait 1. Köder *m* (*a. fig*) 2. mit e-m Köder
versehen; *fig* ködern
bake backen, im (Back)Ofen braten;
TECH brennen; dörren
bak·er Bäcker *m*
bak·er·y Bäckerei *f*
bak·ing pow·der Backpulver *n*
bal·ance 1. Waage *f*; Gleichgewicht *n* (*a.
fig*); ECON Bilanz *f*; Saldo *m*, Konto-
stand *m*, Guthaben *n*; Restbetrag *m*;
keep one's ~ das Gleichgewicht halten; *lose one's ~* das Gleichgewicht
verlieren; *fig* die Fassung verlieren; ~
of payments ECON Zahlungsbilanz *f*;
~ *of power* POL Kräftegleichgewicht
n; ~ *of trade* ECON Handelsbilanz *f* 2.
v/t abwägen; im Gleichgewicht halten,
balancieren; ECON ausgleichen; *v/i* balancieren; ECON sich ausgleichen; ~
each other sich die Waage halten
bal·ance sheet ECON Bilanz *f*
bal·co·ny Balkon *m* (*a.* THEA)
bald kahl
bale¹ ECON Ballen *m*
bale²: ~ *out Br* AVIAT (mit dem Fallschirm) abspringen
bale·ful hasserfüllt
balk 1. Balken *m* 2. stutzen; scheuen
ball¹ 1. Ball *m*; Kugel *f*; ANAT (Hand-,
Fuß)Ballen *m*; Knäuel *m, n*; Kloß *m*;
long ~ SPORT langer Pass 2. ballen; sich
zusammenballen
ball² Ball *m*, Tanzveranstaltung *f*
bal·lad Ballade *f*
bal·last 1. Ballast *m* 2. mit Ballast beladen
ball bear·ing TECH Kugellager *n*
bal·let Ballett *n*
bal·lis·tics MIL Ballistik *f*
bal·loon 1. Ballon *m*; Sprech-, Denk-

blase *f* 2. sich (auf)blähen
bal·lot 1. Stimmzettel *m*; (geheime)
Wahl 2. (*for*) stimmen (für), (in gehei-
mer Wahl) wählen (*acc*); ~ **box** Wahlur-
ne *f*; ~ **pa·per** Stimmzettel *m*
ball·point (pen) Kugelschreiber *m*, F
Kuli *m*
ball·room Ballsaal *m*, Tanzsaal *m*
balls V Eier *pl*
balm Balsam *m* (*a. fig*)
balm·y lind, mild
ba·lo·ney F Quatsch *m*
Balt·ics: *the ~* das Baltikum
bal·us·trade Balustrade *f*, Brüstung *f*,
Geländer *n*
bam·boo BOT Bambus(rohr *n*) *m*
bam·boo·zle F betrügen, j-n übers Ohr
hauen
ban 1. (amtliches) Verbot, Sperre *f*; REL
Bann *m* 2. verbieten
ba·nal banal, abgedroschen
ba·na·na BOT Banane *f*
band 1. Band *n*; Streifen *m*; Schar *f*,
Gruppe *f*; *contp* Bande *f*; (Musik)Ka-
pelle *f*, (Tanz-, Unterhaltungs)Orches-
ter *n*, (*Jazz-, Rock*)Band *f* 2. ~ *togeth-*
er sich zusammentun *or* -rotten
ban·dage MED 1. Bandage *f*; Binde *f*;
Verband *m*; (Heft)Pflaster *n* 2. bandagieren; verbinden
'Band-Aid® MED (Heft)Pflaster *n*
B & B *abbr of bed and breakfast* Über-
nachtung *f* mit Frühstück
ban·dit Bandit *m*
band·lead·er MUS Bandleader *m*
band·mas·ter MUS Kapellmeister *m*
ban·dy krumm
ban·dy-legged säbelbeinig, o-beinig
bang 1. heftiger Schlag; Knall *m*; *mst pl*
Pony *m* 2. dröhnend (zu)schlagen
ban·gle Armreif *m*, Fußreif *m*
ban·ish verbannen
ban·ish·ment Verbannung *f*
ban·is·ter *a. pl* Treppengeländer *n*
ban·jo MUS Banjo *m*
bank¹ ECON 1. Bank *f* (*a.* MED); 2. *v/t* bei
e-r Bank einzahlen; *v/i* ein Bankkonto
haben (*with* bei)
bank² (Erd)Wall *m*; Böschung *f*; (*Fluss-*
etc)Ufer *n*; (*Sand-, Wolken*)Bank *f*
bank ac·count Bankkonto *n*
bank bill Banknote *f*, Geldschein *m*
bank·book Sparbuch *n*
bank code ECON Bankleitzahl *f*

bank·er Bankier *m*, Banker *m*; **~'s card** Scheckkarte *f*

bank hol·i·day *Br* gesetzlicher Feiertag *m*

bank·ing ECON **1.** Bankgeschäft *n*, Bankwesen *n* **2.** Bank...

bank note *Br* → **bank bill**

bank rate ECON Diskontsatz *m*

bank·rupt JUR **1.** Konkursschuldner *m* **2.** bankrott; **go~** in Konkurs gehen, Bankrott machen **3.** *j-n*, *Unternehmen* Bankrott machen; **bank·rupt·cy** JUR Bankrott *m*, Konkurs *m*

bank sort·ing code → **bank code**

ban·ner Transparent *n*

banns Aufgebot *n*

ban·quet Bankett *n*

ban·ter necken

bap·tism REL Taufe *f*

bap·tize REL taufen

bar 1. Stange *f*, Stab *m*; SPORT (Tor-, Quer-, Sprung)Latte *f*; Riegel *m*; Schranke *f*, Sperre *f*; *fig* Hindernis *n*; (*Gold- etc*)Barren *m*; MUS Taktstrich *m*; *ein* Takt *m*; dicker Strich; JUR (Gerichts)Schranke *f*; JUR Anwaltschaft *f*; Bar *f*; Lokal *n*, Imbissstube *f*; *pl* Gitter *n*; **a ~ of chocolate** ein Riegel *or* e-e Tafel Schokolade; **a ~ of soap** ein Stück Seife **2.** zuriegeln, verriegeln; versperren; einsperren; (ver)hindern; ausschließen

barb Widerhaken *m*

bar·bar·i·an 1. barbarisch **2.** Barbar(in)

bar·be·cue 1. Bratrost *m*, Grill *m*; Barbecue *n* **2.** auf dem Rost *or* am Spieß braten, grillen

barbed wire Stacheldraht *m*

bar·ber (Herren)Friseur *m*, (-)Frisör *m*

bar code Strichkode *m*

bare 1. nackt, bloß; kahl; leer **2.** entblößen

bare·faced unverschämt, schamlos

bare·foot, bare·foot·ed barfuß

bare·head·ed barhäuptig

bare·ly kaum

bar·gain 1. Geschäft *n*, Handel *m*; vorteilhaftes Geschäft, Gelegenheitskauf *m*; **a (dead)** ~ spottbillig; **it's a ~!** abgemacht! **2.** (ver)handeln; **~ sale** Verkauf *m* zu herabgesetzten Preisen; Ausverkauf *m*

barge 1. Lastkahn *m* **2.** ~ *in* F hereinplatzen (**on** bei)

bark¹ BOT Borke *f*, Rinde *f*

bark² 1. bellen; **~ up the wrong tree** F auf dem Holzweg sein; an der falschen Adresse sein **2.** Bellen *n*

bar·ley BOT Gerste *f*; Graupe *f*

barn Scheune *f*; (Vieh)Stall *m*

ba·rom·e·ter Barometer *n*

bar·on Baron *m*; Freiherr *m*

bar·on·ess Baronin *f*; Freifrau *f*

bar·racks MIL Kaserne *f*; *contp* Mietskaserne *f*

bar·rage Staudamm *m*; MIL Sperrfeuer *n*; *fig* (Wort- *etc*)Schwall *m*

bar·rel Fass *n*, Tonne *f*; (*Gewehr*)Lauf *m*; TECH Trommel *f*, Walze *f*

bar·rel or·gan MUS Drehorgel *f*

bar·ren unfruchtbar; trocken

bar·rette Haarspange *f*

bar·ri·cade 1. Barrikade *f* **2.** verbarrikadieren; sperren

bar·ri·er Schranke *f* (*a. fig*), Barriere *f*, Sperre *f*; Hindernis *n*

bar·ris·ter *Br* JUR Barrister *m*

bar·row Karre *f*

bar·ter 1. Tausch(handel) *m* **2.** tauschen (**for** gegen)

base¹ gemein

base² 1. Basis *f*; Grundlage *f*; Fundament *n*; Fuß *m*; MIL Standort *m*; MIL Stützpunkt *m* **2.** gründen, stützen (**on** auf *acc*)

base³ CHEM Base *f*

base·ball SPORT Baseball(spiel *n*) *m*

base·board Scheuerleiste *f*

base·less grundlos

base·line *tennis etc*: Grundlinie *f*

base·ment ARCH Fundament *n*; Kellergeschoss *n*

bash·ful scheu, schüchtern

ba·sic¹ 1. Grund..., grundlegend **2.** *pl* Grundlagen *pl*

ba·sic² CHEM basisch

ba·sic·al·ly im Grunde

ba·sin Becken *n*, Schale *f*, Schüssel *f*; Tal-, Wasser-, Hafenbecken *n*

ba·sis Basis *f*; Grundlage *f*

bask sich sonnen (*a. fig*)

bas·ket Korb *m*

bas·ket·ball SPORT Basketball(spiel *n*) *m*

bass¹ MUS Bass *m*

bass² ZO (Fluss-, See)Barsch *m*

bas·tard Bastard *m*

baste¹ GASTR mit Fett begießen

baste² (an)heften

bat¹ zo Fledermaus f; *as blind as a ~* stockblind

bat² *baseball, cricket* 1. Schlagholz n, Schläger m; F *right off the ~* sofort 2. am Schlagen sein

batch Stapel m, Stoß m

bate: *with ~d breath* mit angehaltenem Atem

bath 1. (Wannen)Bad n; *pl* Bad n, Badeanstalt f; Badeort m; *have a ~* Br, *take a ~* baden, ein Bad nehmen 2. Br *v/t* j-n baden; *v/i* baden, ein Bad nehmen

bathe *v/t* baden (*a.* MED); *v/i* baden, ein Bad nehmen; schwimmen

bath foam Badeschaum m

bath·ing 1. Baden n 2. Bade…

bath·ing suit → swimsuit

bath·robe Bademantel m; Morgenrock m, Schlafrock m

bath·room Badezimmer n; Toilette f

bath·tub Badewanne f

bat·on Stab m; MUS Taktstock m; Schlagstock m, Gummiknüppel m

bat·tal·i·on MIL Bataillon n

bat·ten Latte f

bat·ter¹ heftig schlagen; misshandeln; verbeulen; *~ down, ~ in* einschlagen

bat·ter² GASTR Rührteig m

bat·ter³ *baseball, cricket:* Schläger m, Schlagmann m

bat·ter·y ELECTR Batterie f; JUR Tätlichkeit f, Körperverletzung f; *assault and ~* JUR tätliche Beleidigung

bat·ter·y charg·er ELECTR Ladegerät n

bat·ter·y-op·er·at·ed ELECTR batteriebetrieben

bat·tle 1. MIL Schlacht f (*of* bei); *fig* Kampf m (*for* um); 2. kämpfen

bat·tle·field,   bat·tle·ground MIL Schlachtfeld n

bat·tle·ments ARCH Zinnen pl

bat·tle·ship MIL Schlachtschiff n

baulk → balk

Ba·va·ri·a Bayern n

Ba·var·i·an 1. bay(e)risch 2. Bayer(in)

bawd·y obszön

bawl brüllen, schreien; *~ s.o. out* mit j-m schimpfen

bay¹ GEOGR Bai f, Bucht f; ARCH Erker m

bay² *a. ~ tree* BOT Lorbeer(baum) m

bay³ 1. zo bellen, Laut geben 2. *hold or keep at ~* j-n in Schach halten; *et.* von sich fernhalten

bay⁴ 1. rotbraun 2. zo Braune m

bay·o·net MIL Bajonett n

bay·ou GEOGR sumpfiger Flussarm

bay win·dow ARCH Erkerfenster n

ba·zaar Basar m

BC *abbr of before Christ* v. Chr., vor Christus

be sein; *to form the passive*: werden; stattfinden; *he wants to ~ a doctor etc* er möchte Arzt *etc* werden; *how much are the shoes?* was kosten die Schuhe?; *that's five dollars* das macht *or* kostet fünf Dollar; *she is reading* sie liest gerade; *there is, there are* es gibt

beach Strand m; *~ ball* Wasserball m; *~ bug·gy* MOT Strandbuggy m

beach·wear Strandkleidung f

bea·con Leucht-, Signalfeuer n

bead (*Glas-, Schweiß- etc*)Perle f; *pl* REL Rosenkranz m

bead·y klein, rund und glänzend

beak zo Schnabel m; TECH Tülle f

beam 1. Balken m; (Licht)Strahl m; AVIAT *etc* Peil-, Leit-, Richtstrahl m 2. ausstrahlen; strahlen (*a. fig with* vor *dat*)

bean BOT Bohne f; *be full of ~s* F aufgekratzt sein; → spill 1

bear¹ zo Bär m

bear² tragen; zur Welt bringen, gebären; ertragen, aushalten; *I can't ~ him (it)* ich kann ihn (es) nicht ausstehen *or* leiden; *~ out* bestätigen

bear·a·ble erträglich

beard Bart m; BOT Grannen pl

beard·ed bärtig

bear·er Träger(in); ECON Überbringer(in), Inhaber(in)

bear·ing Ertragen n; Betragen n; (Körper)Haltung f; *fig* Beziehung f; Lage f, Richtung f, Orientierung f; *take one's ~s* sich orientieren; *lose one's ~s* die Orientierung verlieren

beast (*a. wildes*) Tier; Bestie f

beast·ly scheußlich

beast of prey zo Raubtier n

beat 1. schlagen; (ver)prügeln; besiegen; übertreffen; F *~ s.o. to it* j-m zuvorkommen; *~ it!* F hau ab!; *that ~s all!* das ist doch der Gipfel *or* die Höhe!; *that ~s me* F das ist mir zu hoch; *~ about the bush* wie die Katze um den heißen Brei herumschleichen; *~ down* ECON drücken, herunterhan-

deln; **~ s.o. up** j-n zusammenschlagen
2. Schlag *m*; MUS Takt(schlag) *m*; *jazz*:
Beat *m*; Pulsschlag *m*; Runde *f*, Revier
n **3.** (*dead*) **~** F wie erschlagen, fix und
fertig

beat·en track Trampelpfad *m*; *off the* **~**
ungewohnt, ungewöhnlich

beat·ing (Tracht *f*) Prügel *pl*

beau·ti·cian Kosmetikerin *f*

beau·ti·ful schön

beau·ty Schönheit *f*; *Sleeping Beauty*
Dornröschen *n*; **~ care** Schönheitspflege *f*; **~ par·lo(u)r,** **~ sal·on** Schönheits-
salon *m*

bea·ver ZO Biber *m*; Biberpelz *m*

be·cause weil; **~ of** wegen (*gen*)

beck·on (zu)winken (*dat*)

be·come *v/i* werden (*of* aus); *v/t* sich
schicken für; *j-m* stehen, *j-n* kleiden

be·com·ing passend; schicklich; kleidsam

bed 1. Bett *n*; ZO Lager *n*; AGR Beet *n*;
Unterlage *f*; **~ and breakfast** Zimmer
n mit Frühstück **2. ~ down** sein Nacht-
lager aufschlagen

bed·clothes Bettwäsche *f*

bed·ding Bettzeug *n*; AGR Streu *f*

bed·lam Tollhaus *n*

bed·rid·den bettlägerig

bed·room Schlafzimmer *n*

bed·side: at the ~ am (*a. Kranken*)Bett

bed·side lamp Nachttischlampe *f*

bed·sit F, **bed·sit·ter,** **bed·sit·ting room**
Br möbliertes Zimmer; Einzimmerappartement *n*

bed·spread Tagesdecke *f*

bed·stead Bettgestell *n*

bed·time Schlafenszeit *f*

bee ZO Biene *f*

beech BOT Buche *f*

beech·nut BOT Buchecker *f*

beef GASTR Rindfleisch *n*

beef·bur·ger GASTR *Br* Hamburger *m*

beef tea GASTR (Rind)Fleischbrühe *f*

beef·y F bullig

bee·hive Bienenkorb *m*, Bienenstock *m*

bee·keep·er Imker *m*

bee·line: make a ~ for F schnurstracks
losgehen auf (*acc*)

beep·er TECH Piepser *m*

beer Bier *n*

beet BOT Runkelrübe *f*, Rote Bete, Rote
Rübe

bee·tle ZO Käfer *m*

beet·root BOT *Br* Rote Bete, Rote Rübe

be·fore 1. *adv space*: vorn, voran; *time*:
vorher, früher, schon (früher) **2.** *cj* bevor, ehe, bis **3.** *prp* vor; **be·fore·hand**
zuvor, im Voraus, vorweg

be·friend sich *j-s* annehmen

beg *v/t* et. erbitten (*of s.o.* von j-m); betteln um; *j-n* bitten; *v/i* betteln; (dringend) bitten

be·get (er)zeugen

beg·gar 1. Bettler(in); F Kerl *m* **2.** *it ~s
all description* es spottet jeder Beschreibung

be·gin beginnen, anfangen

be·gin·ner Anfänger(in)

be·gin·ning Beginn *m*, Anfang *m*

be·grudge missgönnen

be·guile täuschen; betrügen (*of, out of*
um); sich *die Zeit* vertreiben

be·half: in (*Br on*) **~ of** im Namen von (*or
gen*)

be·have sich (gut) benehmen

be·hav·io(u)r Benehmen *n*, Betragen *n*,
Verhalten *n*

be·hav·io(u)r·al sci·ence PSYCH Verhal-
tensforschung *f*

be·head enthaupten

be·hind 1. *adv* hinten, dahinter; zurück
2. *prp* hinter (*dat or acc*) **3.** F Hinterteil
n, Hintern *m*

beige beige

be·ing Sein *n*, Dasein *n*, Existenz *f*; (Le-
be)Wesen *n*, Geschöpf *n*; *j-s* Wesen *n*,
Natur *f*

be·lat·ed verspätet

belch 1. aufstoßen, rülpsen; *a.* **~ out**
speien, ausstoßen **2.** Rülpser *m*

bel·fry Glockenturm *m*, -stuhl *m*

Bel·gian 1. belgisch **2.** Belgier(in)

Bel·gium Belgien *n*

be·lief Glaube *m* (*in* an *acc*)

be·liev·a·ble glaubhaft

be·lieve glauben (*in* an *acc*); *I couldn't ~
my ears* (*eyes*) ich traute m-n Ohren
(Augen) nicht

be·liev·er REL Gläubige *m, f*

be·lit·tle *fig* herabsetzen

bell Glocke *f*; Klingel *f*

bell·boy *Br,* **bell·hop** (Hotel)Page *m*

bel·lig·er·ent kriegerisch; streitlustig,
aggressiv; Krieg führend

bel·low 1. brüllen **2.** Gebrüll *n*

bel·lows Blasebalg *m*

bel·ly 1. Bauch *m*; Magen *m* **2. ~ out** (an)-

schwellen lassen; bauschen

bel·ly·ache F Bauchweh *n*

be·long gehören; **~ to** gehören *dat or* zu

be·long·ings Habseligkeiten *pl*, Habe *f*

be·loved 1. (innig) geliebt **2.** Geliebte *m, f*

be·low 1. *adv* unten **2.** *prp* unter (*dat or acc*)

belt 1. Gürtel *m*; Gurt *m*; GEOGR Zone *f*, Gebiet *n*; TECH (Treib)Riemen *m* **2. ~ out** MUS schmettern; *a.* **~ up** den Gürtel (*gen*) zumachen; **~ up** sich anschnallen; **belt·ed** mit e-m Gürtel

belt·way Umgehungsstraße *f*; Ringstraße *f*

be·moan betrauern, beklagen

bench Sitzbank *f*, Bank *f* (*a.* SPORT); TECH Werkbank *f*; JUR Richterbank *f*; Richter *m or pl*

bend Biegung *f*, Kurve *f*; **drive s.o. round the ~** F j-n noch wahnsinnig machen **2.** (sich) biegen *or* krümmen; neigen; beugen; *fig* richten (**to, on** auf *acc*)

be·neath → *below*

ben·e·dic·tion REL Segen *m*

ben·e·fac·tor Wohltäter *m*

be·nef·i·cent wohltätig

ben·e·fi·cial wohltuend, zuträglich, nützlich

ben·e·fit 1. Nutzen *m*, Vorteil *m*; Wohltätigkeitsveranstaltung *f*; (*Sozial-, Versicherungs- etc*)Leistung *f*; (*Arbeitslosen- etc*)Unterstützung *f*; (*Kranken- etc*)Geld *n* **2.** nützen; **~ by, ~ from** Vorteil haben von *or* durch, Nutzen ziehen aus

be·nev·o·lence Wohlwollen *n*

be·nev·o·lent wohltätig; wohlwollend

be·nign MED gutartig

bent 1. ~ on doing entschlossen zu tun **2.** Hang *m*, Neigung *f*; Veranlagung *f*

ben·zene CHEM Benzol *n*

ben·zine CHEM Leichtbenzin *n*

be·queath JUR vermachen

be·quest JUR Vermächtnis *n*

be·reave berauben

be·ret Baskenmütze *f*

ber·ry BOT Beere *f*

berth 1. MAR Liege-, Ankerplatz *m*; Koje *f*; RAIL (Schlafwagen)Bett *n* **2.** MAR festmachen, anlegen

be·seech (inständig) bitten (um); anflehen

be·side *prp* neben (*dat or acc*); **~ o.s.** außer sich (**with** vor); **~ the point, ~ the question** nicht zur Sache gehörig

be·sides 1. *adv* außerdem **2.** *prp* abgesehen von, außer (*dat*)

be·siege belagern

best 1. *adj* beste(r, -s) höchste(r, -s), größte(r, -s), meiste; **~ before** GASTR haltbar bis **2.** *adv* am besten **3.** *der, die, das* Beste; **all the ~!** alles Gute!, viel Glück!; **to the ~ of ...** nach bestem ...; **make the ~ of** das Beste machen aus (*dat*); **at ~** bestenfalls; **be at one's ~** in Hoch- *or* Höchstform sein

best-be·fore date, best-by date Mindesthaltbarkeitsdatum *n*

bes·ti·al *fig* tierisch, bestialisch

be·stow geben, verleihen (**on** *dat*)

best-sell·er Bestseller *m*

bet 1. Wette *f*; **make a ~** e-e Wette abschließen **2.** wetten; **~ s.o. ten dollars** mit j-m um zehn Dollar wetten; **you ~** F und ob!

be·tray verraten (*a. fig*); verleiten

be·tray·al Verrat *m*

be·tray·er Verräter(in)

bet·ter 1. *adj* besser; **he is ~** es geht ihm besser; **~ and ~** immer besser **2.** *das* Bessere; **get the ~ of** die Oberhand gewinnen über (*acc*); *et.* überwinden **3.** *adv* besser; mehr; **do ~ than** es besser machen als; **know ~** es besser wissen; **so much the ~** desto besser; **you had ~ go** Br, F **you ~ go** es wäre besser, wenn du gingest; **~ off** (finanziell) besser gestellt; **he is ~ off than I am** es geht ihm besser als mir **4.** *v/t* verbessern; *v/i* sich bessern

be·tween 1. *adv* dazwischen; **in ~** zwischendurch; F **few and far ~** (ganz) vereinzelt **2.** *prp* zwischen (*dat or acc*); unter (*dat*); **~ you and me** unter uns *or* im Vertrauen (gesagt)

bev·el TECH abkanten, abschrägen

bev·er·age Getränk *n*

bev·y ZO Schwarm *m*, Schar *f*

be·ware (**of**) sich in Acht nehmen (vor *dat*), sich hüten (vor *dat*); **~ of the dog!** Vorsicht, bissiger Hund!

be·wil·der verwirren

be·wil·der·ment Verwirrung *f*

be·witch bezaubern, verhexen

be·yond 1. *adv* darüber hinaus **2.** *prp* jenseits (*gen*); über ... (*acc*) hinaus

bi... zwei, zweifach, zweimal

bi·as Neigung *f*; Vorurteil *n*

bi·as(s)ed voreingenommen; JUR befangen

bi·ath·lete SPORT Biathlet *m*

bi·ath·lon SPORT Biathlon *n*

bib (Sabber)Lätzchen *n*

Bi·ble Bibel *f*

bib·li·cal biblisch, Bibel...

bib·li·og·ra·phy Bibliografie *f*

bi·car·bon·ate *a.* ~ *of soda* CHEM doppeltkohlensaures Natron

bi·cen·te·na·ry *Br*, **bi·cen·ten·ni·al** Zweihundertjahrfeier *f*

bi·ceps ANAT Bizeps *m*

bick·er sich zanken *or* streiten

bi·cy·cle Fahrrad *n*

bid 1. *auction:* bieten **2.** ECON Gebot *n*, Angebot *n*

bi·en·ni·al zweijährlich; BOT zweijährig; **bi·en·ni·al·ly** alle zwei Jahre

bier (Toten)Bahre *f*

big groß; dick, stark; *talk* ~ F den Mund voll nehmen

big·a·my Bigamie *f*

big busi·ness Großunternehmertum *n*

big·head F Angeber *m*

big shot, big·wig F hohes Tier

bike F **1.** (Fahr)Rad *n* **2.** Rad fahren

bik·er Motorradfahrer(in); Radfahrer(in); Radler(in)

bi·lat·er·al bilateral

bile Galle *f* (*a. fig*)

bi·lin·gual zweisprachig

bill¹ ZO Schnabel *m*

bill² ECON Rechnung *f*; POL (Gesetzes)Vorlage *f*; JUR (An)Klageschrift *f*; Plakat *n*; Banknote *f*, (Geld)Schein *m*

bill·board Reklametafel *f*

bill·fold Brieftasche *f*

bil·li·ards Billard(spiel) *n*

bil·li·on Milliarde *f*

bill of de·liv·er·y ECON Lieferschein *m*; ~ of ex·change ECON Wechsel *m*; ~ of sale JUR Verkaufsurkunde *f*

bil·low 1. Woge *f*; (*Rauch- etc*) Schwaden *m* **2.** *a.* ~ *out* sich bauschen *or* blähen

bil·ly goat ZO Ziegenbock *m*

bin (großer) Behälter

bi·na·ry MATH, PHYS *etc* binär, Binär...

bi·na·ry code *n* Binärcode *m*

bi·na·ry num·ber MATH Binärzahl *f*

bind *v/t* (an-, ein-, um-, auf-, fest-, ver-)binden; *a.* vertraglich binden, verpflichten; einfassen; *v/i* binden

bind·er (*esp Buch*)Binder(in); Einband *m*; Aktendeckel *m*

bind·ing 1. bindend, verbindlich **2.** Einband *m*; Einfassung *f*, Borte *f*

bin·go Bingo *n*

bi·noc·u·lars, Fern-, Opernglas *n*

bi·o·chem·is·try Biochemie *f*

bi·o·de·gra·da·ble biologisch abbaubar, umweltfreundlich

bi·og·ra·pher Biograf *m*

bi·og·ra·phy Biografie *f*

bi·o·log·i·cal biologisch

bi·ol·o·gist Biologe *m*, Biologin *f*

bi·ol·o·gy Biologie *f*

bi·o·rhythms Biorhythmus *m*

bi·o·tope Biotop *n*

bi·ped ZO Zweifüßer *m*

birch BOT Birke *f*

bird ZO Vogel *m*

bird·cage Vogelkäfig *m*

bird flu Vogelgrippe *f*

bird of pas·sage ZO Zugvogel *m*

bird of prey ZO Raubvogel *m*

bird sanc·tu·a·ry Vogelschutzgebiet *n*

bird·seed Vogelfutter *n*

bird's-eye view Vogelperspektive *f*

bi·ro® Kugelschreiber *m*

birth Geburt *f*; Herkunft *f*; *give* ~ *to* gebären, zur Welt bringen

birth cer·tif·i·cate Geburtsurkunde *f*

birth con·trol Geburtenregelung *f*

birth·day Geburtstag *m*; *happy* ~*!* alles Gute *or* herzlichen Glückwunsch zum Geburtstag!

birth·mark Muttermal *n*

birth·place Geburtsort *m*

birth·rate Geburtenziffer *f*

bis·cuit *Br* Keks *m*, *n*, Plätzchen *n*

bi·sex·u·al bisexuell

bish·op REL Bischof *m*; *chess:* Läufer *m*

bish·op·ric REL Bistum *n*

bi·son ZO Bison *m*; Wisent *m*

bit Bisschen *n*, Stück(chen) *n*; Gebiss *n* (*am Zaum*); (Schlüssel)Bart *m*; IT Bit *n*; *a* (*little*) ~ ein (kleines) bisschen

bitch ZO Hündin *f*; F *contp* Miststück *n*, Schlampe *f*

bit den·si·ty IT Speicherdichte *f*

bite 1. Beißen *n*; Biss *m*; Bissen *m*, Happen *m*; TECH Fassen *n*, Greifen *n* **2.** (an-)beißen; ZO stechen; GASTR brennen; *fig* schneiden (*cold etc*); beißen (*smoke etc*); TECH fassen, greifen

bit·ter bitter; *fig* verbittert

bit·ters GASTR Magenbitter *m*

biz F → *business*

black 1. schwarz; dunkel; finster; *have s.th. in ~ and white* et. schwarz auf weiß haben *or* besitzen; *be ~ and blue* blaue Flecken haben; *beat s.o. ~ and blue* j-n grün und blau schlagen **2.** schwärzen; *~ out* verdunkeln **3.** Schwarz *n*; Schwärze *f*; Schwarze *m*, *f*

black·ber·ry BOT Brombeere *f*

black·bird ZO Amsel *f*

black·board (Schul-, Wand)Tafel *f*

black box AVIAT Flugschreiber *m*

black cur·rant BOT schwarze Johannisbeere

black·en *v/t* schwärzen; *fig* anschwärzen; *v/i* schwarz werden

black eye blaues Auge, Veilchen *n*

black·head MED Mitesser *m*

black ice Glatteis *n*

black·ing schwarze Schuhwichse

black·leg Br Streikbrecher *m*

black·mail 1. Erpressung *f* **2.** j-n erpressen; **black·mail·er** Erpresser(in)

black mar·ket Schwarzmarkt *m*

black·ness Schwärze *f*

black·out Verdunkelung *f*; Black-out *n*, *m*; ELECTR Stromausfall *m*; Ohnmacht *f*

black pud·ding GASTR Blutwurst *f*

black sheep *fig* schwarzes Schaf

black·smith Schmied *m*

blad·der ANAT Blase *f*

blade TECH Blatt *n*, Schaufel *f*; Klinge *f*; Schneide *f*; BOT Halm *m*

blame 1. Tadel *m*; Schuld *f* **2.** tadeln; *be to ~ for* schuld sein an (*dat*)

blame·less untadelig

blanch *v/t* bleichen; GASTR blanchieren; *v/i* erbleichen, bleich werden

blank 1. leer; unausgefüllt, unbeschrieben; ECON Blanko…; verdutzt **2.** Leere *f*; leerer Raum, Lücke *f*; unbeschriebenes Blatt, Formular *n*; *lottery*: Niete *f*; *~ car·tridge* Platzpatrone *f*; *~ check* (*Br cheque*) ECON Blankoscheck *m*

blan·ket 1. (Woll)Decke *f* **2.** zudecken

blare brüllen, plärren (*radio etc*), schmettern (*trumpet*)

blas·pheme lästern

blas·phe·my Gotteslästerung *f*

blast 1. Windstoß *m*; MUS Ton *m*; TECH Explosion *f*; Druckwelle *f*; Sprengung *f* **2.** sprengen; *fig* zunichtemachen; *~*

off (*into space*) in den Weltraum schießen; *~ off* abheben, starten (*rocket*); *~!* verdammt!; *~ you!* der Teufel soll dich holen!; *~ed* verdammt, verflucht

blast fur·nace TECH Hochofen *m*

blast-off Start *m* (*of a rocket*)

bla·tant offenkundig, eklatant

blaze 1. Flamme(n *pl*) *f*, Feuer *n*; heller Schein; *fig* Ausbruch *m* **2.** brennen, lodern; leuchten

blaz·er Blazer *m*

bla·zon Wappen *n*

bleach bleichen

bleak öde, kahl; rau; *fig* trüb, freudlos, finster

blear·y trübe, verschwommen

bleat ZO **1.** Blöken *n* **2.** blöken

bleed *v/i* bluten; *v/t* MED zur Ader lassen; F schröpfen

bleed·ing MED Blutung *f*; Aderlass *m*

bleep 1. Piepton *m* **2.** j-n anpiepsen

bleep·er Br F Piepser *m*

blem·ish 1. (*a.* Schönheits)Fehler *m*; Makel *m* **2.** entstellen

blend 1. (sich) (ver)mischen; GASTR verschneiden **2.** Mischung *f*; GASTR Verschnitt *m*

blend·er Mixer *m*, Mixgerät *n*

bless segnen; preisen; *be ~ed with* gesegnet sein mit; (*God*) *~ you!* alles Gute!; Gesundheit!; *~ me!*, *~ my heart!*, *~ my soul!* F du meine Güte!

bless·ed selig, gesegnet; F verflixt

bless·ing Segen *m*

blight BOT Mehltau *m*

blind 1. blind (*fig to* gegen[über]); unübersichtlich **2.** Rouleau *n*, Rollo *n*; *the ~* die Blinden *pl* **3.** blenden; *fig* blind machen (*to* für, gegen)

blind al·ley Sackgasse *f*

blind·ers Scheuklappen *pl*

blind·fold 1. blindlings **2.** j-m die Augen verbinden **3.** Augenbinde *f*

blind·ly *fig* blindlings

blind·ness Blindheit *f*; Verblendung *f*

blind·worm ZO Blindschleiche *f*

blink 1. Blinzeln *n* **2.** blinzeln, zwinkern; blinken

blink·ers Br Scheuklappen *pl*

bliss Seligkeit *f*, Wonne *f*

blis·ter MED, TECH **1.** Blase *f* **2.** Blasen hervorrufen auf (*dat*); Blasen ziehen *or* TECH werfen

blitz MIL **1.** heftiger Luftangriff **2.** schwer

bombardieren

bliz·zard Blizzard *m*, Schneesturm *m*

bloat·ed (an)geschwollen, (auf)gedunsen; *fig* aufgeblasen

bloat·er GASTR Bückling *m*

blob Klecks *m*

block 1. Block *m*, Klotz *m*; Baustein *m*, (Bau)Klötzchen *n*; (Schreib-, Notiz-)Block *m*; (Häuser)Block *m*; TECH Verstopfung *f*; *fig geistige etc* Sperre; ~ (of flats) *Br* Wohn-, Mietshaus *n* 2. *a*. ~ up (ab-, ver)sperren, blockieren, verstopfen

block·ade 1. Blockade *f* 2. blockieren

block·bust·er F Kassenmagnet *m*, Kassenschlager *m*

block·head F Dummkopf *m*

block let·ters Blockschrift *f*

blog IT Blog *m*, *n*

blond 1. Blonde *m* 2. blond; hell (skin)

blonde 1. blond 2. Blondine *f*

blood Blut *n*; in cold ~ kaltblütig; ~ bank MED Blutbank *f*; ~ clot MED Blutgerinnsel *n*; ~ cor·pus·cle MED Blutkörperchen *n*

blood·cur·dling grauenhaft

blood do·nor MED Blutspender(in)

blood group MED Blutgruppe *f*

blood·hound ZO Bluthund *m*

blood pres·sure MED Blutdruck *m*

blood·shed Blutvergießen *n*

blood·shot blutunterlaufen

blood test MED Blutprobe *f*

blood·thirst·y blutdürstig

blood ves·sel ANAT Blutgefäß *n*

blood·y blutig; *Br* F verdammt, verflucht

bloom 1. Blume *f*, Blüte *f*; *fig* Blüte(zeit) *f* 2. blühen; *fig* (er)strahlen

blos·som 1. Blüte *f* 2. blühen; *fig* ~ into erblühen zu

blot 1. Klecks *m*; *fig* Makel *m* 2. beklecksen

blotch Klecks *m*; Hautfleck *m*

blotch·y fleckig

blot·ter (Tinten)Löscher *m*

blot·ting pa·per Löschpapier *n*

blouse Bluse *f*

blow[1] Schlag *m* (*a. fig*), Stoß *m*

blow[2] *v/i* blasen, wehen; keuchen, schnaufen; explodieren; platzen (tire); ELECTR durchbrennen; ~ up in die Luft fliegen; explodieren; *v/t*: ~ one's nose sich die Nase putzen; ~ out ausblasen;

~ up sprengen; PHOT vergrößern

blow·dry föhnen

blow·fly ZO Schmeißfliege *f*

blow·pipe Blasrohr *n*

blow·up PHOT Vergrößerung *f*

blud·geon Knüppel *m*

blue 1. blau; F melancholisch, traurig, schwermütig 2. Blau *n*; out of the ~ *fig* aus heiterem Himmel

blue·ber·ry BOT Blau-, Heidelbeere *f*

blue·bot·tle ZO Schmeißfliege *f*

blue-col·lar work·er Arbeiter(in)

blues MUS Blues *m*; F Melancholie *f*; have the ~ F den Moralischen haben

bluff[1] Steilufer *n*

bluff[2] 1. Bluff *m* 2. bluffen

blu·ish bläulich

blun·der 1. Fehler *m*, F Schnitzer *m* 2. e-n (groben) Fehler machen; verpfuschen, F verpatzen

blunt stumpf; *fig* offen

blunt·ly freiheraus

blur [blɜː] 1. *v/t* verwischen; verschmieren; PHOT, TV verwackeln, verzerren; *fig* trüben 2. *v/i* verschwimmen (*a. fig*)

blurt: ~ out herausplatzen mit

blush 1. Erröten *n*, Schamröte *f* 2. erröten, rot werden

blus·ter brausen (wind); *fig* poltern, toben

BO ABBR → body odo(u)r

boar ZO Eber *m*; Keiler *m*

board 1. Brett *n*; (Anschlag)Brett *n*; Konferenztisch *m*; Ausschuss *m*, Kommission *f*; Behörde *f*; Verpflegung *f*; Pappe *f*, Karton *m*; SPORT (Surf)Board *n*; on ~ a train in e-m Zug 2. *v/t* dielen, verschalen; beköstigen; an Bord gehen; MAR entern; RAIL *etc* einsteigen in; *v/i* in Kost sein, wohnen

board·er Kostgänger(in); Pensionsgast *m*; Internatsschüler(in)

board game Brettspiel *n*

board·ing| card AVIAT Bordkarte *f*; ~ house Pension *f*, Fremdenheim *n*; ~ school Internat *n*

board of di·rec·tors ECON Aufsichtsrat *m*

Board of Trade Handelskammer *f*; *Br* Handelsministerium *n*

board·walk Strandpromenade *f*

boast 1. Prahlerei *f* 2. (of, about) sich rühmen (gen), prahlen (mit)

boat Boot *n*; Schiff *n*

bob 1. Knicks *m*; kurzer Haarschnitt; *Br* HIST F Schilling *m* **2.** *v/t* Haar kurz schneiden; *v/i* sich auf und ab bewegen; knicksen

bob·bin Spule *f* (*a.* ELECTR)

bob·sleigh SPORT Bob *m*

bod·ice Mieder *n*; Oberteil *n*

bod·i·ly körperlich

bod·y Körper *m*, Leib *m*; Leiche *f*; JUR Körperschaft *f*; Hauptteil *m*; MOT Karosserie *f*; MIL Truppenkörper *m*

bod·y·guard Leibwache *f*; Leibwächter *m*

bod·y| o·do(u)r (*abbr BO*) Körpergeruch *m*; **~ stock·ing** Body *m*

bod·y·work MOT Karosserie *f*

Boer 1. Bure *m* **2.** Buren...

bog Sumpf *m*, Morast *m*

bo·gus falsch; Schwindel...

boil[1] MED Geschwür *n*, Furunkel *m*, *n*

boil[2] **1.** kochen, sieden **2.** Kochen *n*, Sieden *n*

boil·er (Dampf)Kessel *m*; Boiler *m*

boil·er suit Overall *m*

boil·ing point Siedepunkt *m* (*a. fig*)

bois·ter·ous ungestüm; heftig, laut; lärmend

bold kühn, verwegen; keck, dreist, unverschämt; steil; PRINT fett; *words in* **~ *print*** fett gedruckt; **bold·ness** Kühnheit *f*, Verwegenheit *f*; Dreistigkeit *f*

bol·ster 1. Keilkissen *n* **2. ~ up** fig (unter)stützen, *j-m* Mut machen

bolt 1. Bolzen *m*; Riegel *m*; Blitz(strahl) *m*; plötzlicher Satz, Fluchtversuch *m* **2.** *adv:* **~ upright** kerzengerade **3.** *v/t* verriegeln; F hinunterschlingen; *v/i* davonlaufen, ausreißen; ZO scheuen, durchgehen

bomb 1. Bombe *f*; **the~** die Atombombe **2.** bombardieren; **bom·bard** bombardieren; **bomb·er** AVIAT Bomber *m*; Bombenleger *m*

bomb·proof bombensicher

bomb·shell Bombe *f* (*a. fig*)

bo·nan·za fig Goldgrube *f*

bond Bund *m*, Verbindung *f*; ECON Schuldverschreibung *f*, Obligation *f*; *in* **~** ECON unter Zollverschluss

bond·age Hörigkeit *f*

bonds fig Bande *pl*

bone 1. ANAT Knochen *m*, *pl a.* Gebeine *pl*; ZO Gräte *f* **2.** die Knochen auslösen (aus); entgräten

bon·fire Feuer *n* im Freien; Freudenfeuer *n*

bon·net Haube *f*; *Br* Motorhaube *f*

bo·nus ECON Bonus *m*, Prämie *f*; Gratifikation *f*

bon·y knöchern; knochig

boo *int* buh!; THEA **~ off the stage**, *soccer.* **~ off the park** auspfeifen

boobs *sl* Titten *pl*

boo·by F Trottel *m*

book 1. Buch *n*; Heft *n*; Liste *f*; Block *m* **2.** buchen; eintragen; SPORT verwarnen; *Fahrkarte etc* lösen; *Platz etc* (vor)bestellen, reservieren lassen; *Gepäck* aufgeben; **~ in** *esp Br* sich (*im Hotel*) eintragen; **~ in at** absteigen in (*dat*); **~ed up** ausgebucht, ausverkauft, belegt

book·case Bücherschrank *m*

book·ing Buchen *n*, (Vor)Bestellung *f*; SPORT Verwarnung *f*; **~ clerk** Schalterbeamte *m*, -beamtin *f*; **~ of·fice** Fahrkartenausgabe *f*, -schalter *m*; THEA Kasse *f*

book·keep·er ECON Buchhalter(in)

book·keep·ing ECON Buchhaltung *f*, Buchführung *f*

book·let Büchlein *n*, Broschüre *f*

book·mak·er Buchmacher *m*

book·mark(·er) Lesezeichen *n*

book·sell·er Buchhändler(in)

book·shelf Bücherregal *n*

book·shop *esp Br*, **book·store** Buchhandlung *f*

book·worm fig Bücherwurm *m*

boom[1] ECON **1.** Boom *m*, Aufschwung *m*, Hochkonjunktur *f*, Hausse *f* **2.** e-n Boom erleben

boom[2] MAR Baum *m*, Spiere *f*; TECH (Kran)Ausleger *m*; *film, TV* (Mikrofon)Galgen *m*

boom[3] dröhnen, donnern

boor·ish ungehobelt

boost 1. hochschieben; ECON in die Höhe treiben; ankurbeln; ELECTR verstärken; TECH erhöhen; fig stärken, Auftrieb geben (*dat*) **2.** Erhöhung *f*; Auftrieb *m*; ELECTR Verstärkung *f*

boot[1] Stiefel *m*; *Br* MOT Kofferraum *m*

boot[2]: **~ (up)** IT laden

boot[3]: **to ~** obendrein

boot·ee (*Damen*)Halbstiefel *m*

booth (Markt- *etc*)Bude *f*, (Messe-) Stand *m*; (Wahl- *etc*)Kabine *f*; (Telefon)Zelle *f*

boot·lace Schnürsenkel *m*

boot·y Beute *f*

booze F 1. saufen 2. Zeug *n*; Sauferei *f*

bor·der 1. Rand *m*, Saum *m*, Einfassung *f*; Rabatte *f*; Grenze *f* 2. einfassen; (um)säumen; grenzen (**on** an *acc*)

bore[1] 1. Bohrloch *n*; TECH Kaliber *n* 2. bohren

bore[2] 1. Langweiler *m*; langweilige *or* lästige Sache 2. *j-n* langweilen; **be ~d** sich langweilen

bore·dom Lang(e)weile *f*

bor·ing langweilig

bo·rough Stadtteil *m*; Stadtgemeinde *f*; Stadtbezirk *m*

bor·row (sich) *et.* borgen *or* (aus)leihen

bos·om Busen *m*; *fig* Schoß *m*

boss F 1. Boss *m*, Chef *m* 2. *a.* **~ about, ~ around** herumkommandieren

boss·y F herrisch

bo·tan·i·cal botanisch

bot·a·ny Botanik *f*

botch 1. Pfusch *m* 2. verpfuschen

both beide(s); **~ ... and ...** sowohl ... als (auch) ...

both·er 1. Belästigung *f*, Störung *f*, Plage *f*, Mühe *f* 2. belästigen, stören, plagen; **don't ~!** bemühen Sie sich nicht!

bot·tle 1. Flasche *f* 2. in Flaschen abfüllen; **~ bank** *Br* Altglascontainer *m*

bot·tle·neck *fig* Engpass *m*

bot·tle o·pen·er Flaschenöffner *m*

bot·tom unterster Teil, Boden *m*, Fuß *m*, Unterseite *f*; Grund *m*; F Hintern *m*, Popo *m*; **be at the ~ of s.th.** hinter e-r Sache stecken; **get to the ~ of s.th.** e-r Sache auf den Grund gehen

bough Ast *m*, Zweig *m*

boul·der Geröllblock *m*, Findling *m*

bounce 1. aufprallen *or* aufspringen (lassen); springen, hüpfen, stürmen; ECON F platzen (*check*) 2. Sprung *m*, Satz *m*; F Schwung *m*

bounc·ing kräftig, stramm

bound[1] unterwegs (**for** nach)

bound[2] *mst pl* Grenze *f*, *fig a.* Schranke *f*

bound[3] 1. Sprung *m*, Satz *m* 2. springen, hüpfen; auf-, abprallen

bound·a·ry Grenze *f*

bound·less grenzenlos

boun·te·ous, boun·ti·ful freigebig, reichlich

boun·ty Freigebigkeit *f*; großzügige Spende *f*; Prämie *f*

bou·quet Bukett *n* (*a.* GASTR), Strauß *m*; GASTR Blume *f*

bout SPORT (*Box-, Ring*)Kampf *m*; MED Anfall *m*

bou·tique Boutique *f*

bow[1] 1. Verbeugung *f* 2. *v/i* sich verbeugen *or* verneigen (**to** vor *dat*); *fig* sich beugen *or* unterwerfen (**to** *dat*); *v/t* biegen; beugen, neigen

bow[2] MAR Bug *m*

bow[3] Bogen *m*; Schleife *f*

bow·els ANAT Darm *m*; Eingeweide *pl*

bowl[1] Schale *f*, Schüssel *f*, Napf *m*; (*Zucker*)Dose *f*; Becken *n*; (*Pfeifen-*) Kopf *m*

bowl[2] 1. (*Bowling-, Kegel- etc*)Kugel *f* 2. kegeln; rollen (*bowling ball*); *cricket*: werfen

bow·leg·ged o-beinig

bowl·er[1] Bowlingspieler(in); Kegler(in)

bowl·er[2], *a.* **~ hat** *esp Br* Bowler *m*, F Melone *f*

bowl·ing Bowling *n*; Kegeln *n*; **go ~** kegeln; **~ al·ley** Kegelbahn *f*; **~ ball** Kegelkugel *f*

box[1] Kasten *m*, Kiste *f*; Büchse *f*, Dose *f*, Kästchen *n*; Schachtel *f*; Behälter *m*; TECH Gehäuse *n*; Postfach *n*; *Br* (Telefon)Zelle *f*; JUR Zeugenstand *m*; THEA Loge *f*; MOT, zo Box *f*

box[2] 1. SPORT boxen; F **~ s.o.'s ears** *j-n* ohrfeigen 2. F *a.* **~ on the ear** e-e Ohrfeige

box[3] [boks] BOT Buchsbaum *m*

box·er Boxer *m*

box·ing Boxen *n*, Boxsport *m*

Box·ing Day *Br* der zweite Weihnachtsfeiertag

box num·ber Chiffre(nummer) *f*

box of·fice Theaterkasse *f*

boy Junge *m*, Knabe *m*, Bursche *m*

boy·cott 1. boykottieren 2. Boykott *m*

boy·friend Freund *m*

boy·hood Knabenjahre *pl*, Jugend (-zeit) *f*

boy·ish jungenhaft

boy scout Pfadfinder *m*

bra BH *m* (*Büstenhalter*)

brace 1. TECH Strebe *f*, Stützbalken *m*; (*Zahn*)Klammer *f*, (-)Spange *f* 2. TECH verstreben, versteifen, stützen

brace·let Armband *n*

brac·es *Br* Hosenträger *pl*

brack·et TECH Träger *m*, Halter *m*, Stütze *f*; PRINT Klammer *f*; (*esp Alters-, Steuer*)Klasse *f*; *lower income* ~ niedrige Einkommensgruppe

brack·ish brackig, salzig

brag prahlen (*about* mit)

brag·gart Prahler *m*, F Angeber *m*

braid 1. Zopf *m*; Borte *f*, Tresse *f* **2.** flechten; mit Borte besetzen

brain ANAT Gehirn *n*, *often pl fig a.* Verstand *m*, Intelligenz *f*, Kopf *m*

brain·storm Geistesblitz *m*

brain·wash *j-n* e-r Gehirnwäsche unterziehen

brain·wash·ing Gehirnwäsche *f*

brain·wave *Br* Geistesblitz *m*

brain·y F gescheit

braise GASTR schmoren

brake TECH Bremse *f* **2.** bremsen

brake·light MOT Bremslicht *n*

bram·ble BOT Brombeerstrauch *m*

bran AGR Kleie *f*

branch 1. Ast *m*, Zweig *m*; *fig* Fach *n*; Linie *f* (*des Stammbaumes*); ECON Zweigstelle *f*, Filiale *f* **2.** sich verzweigen; abzweigen

brand 1. ECON (Schutz-, Handels)Marke *f*, Warenzeichen *n*; Markenname *m*; Sorte *f*, Klasse *f*; Brandmal *n* **2.** einbrennen; brandmarken

bran·dish schwingen

brand name ECON Markenname *m*

brand-new nagelneu

bran·dy Kognak *m*, Weinbrand *m*

brass Messing *n*; F Unverschämtheit *f*

brass band MUS Blaskapelle *f*

bras·sière Büstenhalter *m*

brat *contp* Balg *m*, *n*, Gör *n*

brave 1. tapfer, mutig, unerschrocken **2.** trotzen; mutig begegnen (*dat*)

brav·er·y Tapferkeit *f*

brawl 1. Krawall *m*; Rauferei *f* **2.** Krawall machen; raufen

brawn·y muskulös

bray 1. ZO Eselsschrei *m* **2.** ZO schreien; *fig* wiehern

bra·zen unverschämt, unverfroren, frech

Bra·zil Brasilien *n*; **Bra·zil·ian 1.** brasilianisch **2.** Brasilianer(in)

breach 1. Bruch *m*; *fig* Verletzung *f*; MIL Bresche *f* **2.** e-e Bresche schlagen in (*acc*)

bread Brot *n*; *brown* ~ Schwarzbrot *n*; *know which side one's* ~ *is buttered* F s-n Vorteil (er)kennen

breadth Breite *f*

break 1. Bruch *m*; Lücke *f*; Pause *f* (*Br a.* PED), Unterbrechung *f*; (plötzlicher) Wechsel, Umschwung *m*; (*Tages*)Anbruch *m*; *give s.o. a* ~ F j-m e-e Chance geben; *take a* ~ e-e Pause machen; *without a* ~ ununterbrochen **2.** *v/t* (ab-, auf-, durch-, zer)brechen; zerschlagen, kaputt machen; *zo a.* ~ *in* zähmen, abrichten, zureiten; *Gesetz, Vertrag etc* brechen; *Kode etc* knacken; *schlechte Nachricht* (schonend) beibringen; *v/i* brechen (*a. fig*); (zer)brechen, (zer)reißen, kaputtgehen; anbrechen (*Tag*); METEOR umschlagen; *fig* ausbrechen (*into* *in Tränen etc*); ~ *away* ab-, losbrechen; sich losmachen *or* losreißen; ~ *down* ein-, niederreißen, *Haus* abbrechen; zusammenbrechen (*a. fig*); versagen; MOT e-e Panne haben; *fig* scheitern; ~ *in* einbrechen, eindringen; ~ *into* einbrechen in (*ein Haus etc*); ~ *off* abbrechen, *fig a.* Schluss machen mit; ~ *out* ausbrechen; ~ *through* durchbrechen; *fig* den Durchbruch schaffen; ~ *up* abbrechen, beenden, schließen; (sich) auflösen; *fig* zerbrechen, auseinandergehen

break·a·ble zerbrechlich

break·age Bruch *m*

break·a·way 1. Trennung *f* **2.** Splitter...

break·down Zusammenbruch *m* (*a. fig*); TECH Maschinenschaden *m*; MOT Panne *f*; *nervous* ~ MED Nervenzusammenbruch *m*; ~ *lor·ry Br* MOT Abschleppwagen *m*; ~ *ser·vice Br* MOT Pannendienst *m*, Pannenhilfe *f*; ~ *truck Br* MOT Abschleppwagen *m*

break·fast 1. Frühstück *n*; *have* ~ → **2.** frühstücken

break·through *fig* Durchbruch *m*

break·up Aufhebung *f*; Auflösung *f*

breast ANAT Brust *f*; Busen *m*; *fig* Herz *n*

breast·stroke Brustschwimmen *n*

breath Atem(zug) *m*; Hauch *m*; *be out of* ~ außer Atem sein; *waste one's* ~ in den Wind reden

breath·a·lyse *Br*, **breath·a·lyze** F (ins Röhrchen) blasen *or* pusten lassen

breath·a·lys·er® *Br*, **breath·alyz·er®** Alkoholtestgerät *n*, F Röhrchen *n*

breathe atmen
breath·less atemlos
breath·tak·ing atemberaubend
breech·es Kniebund-, Reithosen *pl*
breed 1. ZO Rasse *f*, Zucht *f* **2.** *v/t* BOT, ZO züchten; *v/i* BIOL sich fortpflanzen
breed·er Züchter(in); Zuchttier *n*; PHYS Brüter *m*
breed·ing BIOL Fortpflanzung *f*; (Tier-) Zucht *f*; *fig* Erziehung *f*; (gutes) Benehmen
breeze Brise *f*
breth·ren *esp* REL Brüder *pl*
brew brauen; *Tee* zubereiten, aufbrühen
brew·er (Bier)Brauer *m*
brew·er·y Brauerei *f*
bri·ar → **brier**
bribe 1. Bestechungsgeld *n*, -geschenk *n*; Bestechung *f* **2.** bestechen
brib·er·y Bestechung *f*
brick Ziegel(stein) *m*, Backstein *m*; *Br* Baustein *m*, (Bau)Klötzchen *n*
brick·lay·er Maurer *m*
brick·yard Ziegelei *f*
brid·al Braut…; **bride** Braut *f*
bride·groom Bräutigam *m*
brides·maid Brautjungfer *f*
bridge 1. Brücke *f* **2.** e-e Brücke schlagen über (*acc*); *fig* überbrücken
bri·dle 1. Zaum *m*; Zügel *m* **2.** (auf)zäumen; zügeln; **~ path** Reitweg *m*
brief 1. kurz, bündig **2.** instruieren, genaue Anweisungen geben (*dat*)
brief·case Aktenmappe *f*
briefs Slip *m*
bri·er BOT Dornstrauch *m*; Wilde Rose
bri·gade MIL Brigade *f*
bright hell; glänzend; klar; heiter; lebhaft; gescheit
bright·en *v/t a.* **~ up** heller machen, aufhellen, erhellen; aufheitern; *v/i a.* **~ up** sich aufhellen
bright·ness Helligkeit *f*; Glanz *m*; Heiterkeit *f*; Gescheitheit *f*
brill *Br* F super, toll
bril·liance, **bril·lian·cy** Glanz *m*; *fig* Brillanz *f*
bril·liant 1. glänzend; hervorragend, brillant **2.** Brillant *m*
brim 1. Rand *m*; Krempe *f* **2.** bis zum Rande füllen *or* voll sein
brim·ful(l) randvoll
brine Sole *f*; Lake *f*
bring bringen, mitbringen, herbringen;

j-n dazu bringen (**to do** zu tun); **~ about** zustande bringen; bewirken; **~ forth** hervorbringen; schaffen; **~ on** verursachen; **~ out** herausbringen; **~ round** Ohnmächtigen wieder zu sich bringen; *Kranken* wieder auf die Beine bringen; **~ up** auf-, großziehen; erziehen; zur Sprache bringen
brink Rand *m* (*a. fig*)
brisk flott; lebhaft; frisch
bris·tle 1. Borste *f*; (Bart)Stoppel *f* **2.** *a.* **~ up** sich sträuben; zornig werden; strotzen, wimmeln (**with** von)
bris·tly stoppelig, Stoppel…
Brit F Brite *m*, Britin *f*
Brit·ain Britannien *n*
Brit·ish britisch; **the ~** die Briten *pl*
Brit·on Brite *m*, Britin *f*
brit·tle spröde, zerbrechlich
broach *Thema* anschneiden
broad breit; weit; hell; deutlich (*hint etc*); derb (*humor etc*); stark (*accent*); allgemein; weitherzig; liberal
broad·cast 1. im Rundfunk *or* Fernsehen bringen, ausstrahlen, übertragen; senden **2.** *radio*, TV Sendung *f*
broad·cast·er Rundfunk-, Fernsehsprecher(in)
broad·en verbreitern, erweitern
broad jump SPORT Weitsprung *m*
broad·mind·ed liberal
bro·cade Brokat *m*
bro·chure Broschüre *f*, Prospekt *m*
brogue fester Straßenschuh
broil grillen
broke F pleite, abgebrannt
bro·ken zerbrochen, kaputt; gebrochen (*a. fig*); zerrüttet
brok·en-heart·ed verzweifelt, untröstlich
bro·ker ECON Makler *m*
bron·chi·tis MED Bronchitis *f*
bronze 1. Bronze *f* **2.** bronzefarben; Bronze…
brooch Brosche *f*
brood ZO **1.** Brut *f* **2.** Brut… **3.** brüten (*a. fig*)
brook Bach *m*
broom Besen *m*
broth GASTR Fleischbrühe *f*
broth·el Bordell *n*
broth·er Bruder *m*; **~(s) and sister(s)** Geschwister *pl*

broth·er·hood REL Bruderschaft f
broth·er-in-law Schwager m
broth·er·ly brüderlich
brow ANAT (Augen)Braue f; Stirn f;
GEOGR Rand m
brow·beat einschüchtern
brown 1. braun **2.** Braun n **3.** bräunen;
braun werden
browse grasen, weiden; fig schmökern
bruise 1. MED Quetschung f, blauer
Fleck **2.** quetschen; anstoßen; MED
e-e Quetschung or e-n blauen Fleck
bekommen
brunch Brunch m
brush Bürste f; Pinsel m; ZO (Fuchs-)
Rute f; Scharmützel n; Unterholz n **2.**
bürsten; fegen; streifen; ~ **against** s.o.
j-n streifen; ~ **away**, ~ **off** wegbürsten,
abwischen; ~ **aside**, ~ **away** et. abtun; ~
up (on) fig aufpolieren, auffrischen
brush·wood Gestrüpp n, Unterholz n
brusque brüsk, barsch
Brus·sels sprouts BOT Rosenkohl m
bru·tal brutal, roh
bru·tal·i·ty Brutalität f
brute 1. brutal; **with ~ force** mit roher
Gewalt **2.** Vieh n; F Untier m, Scheusal
n; Rohling m; **brut·ish** fig tierisch
bub·ble 1. Blase f **2.** sprudeln; ~ **bath** Badeschaum m
buck¹ 1. ZO Bock m **2.** bocken
buck² F Dollar m
buck·et Eimer m, Kübel m
buck·le 1. Schnalle f, Spange f **2.** a. ~ **up**
zu-, festschnallen; ~ **on** anschnallen
buck·skin Wildleder n
bud 1. BOT Knospe f; fig Keim m **2.** knospen, keimen
bud·dy F Kamerad m; Kumpel m, Spezi
m
budge v/i sich (von der Stelle) rühren;
v/t (vom Fleck) bewegen
bud·ger·i·gar ZO Wellensittich m
bud·get 1. Budget n, Etat m; PARL Haus-
haltsplan m **2.** preisgünstig; ~ **airline**
Billigflieger m
bud·gie F → **budgerigar**
buf·fa·lo ZO Büffel m
buff·er TECH Puffer m
buf·fet¹ schlagen; ~ **about** durchrütteln,
durchschütteln
buf·fet² Büfett n, Anrichte f
buf·fet³ (Frühstücks- etc)Büfett n; Theke f

bug 1. ZO Wanze f (a. F fig); Insekt n; IT
Programmfehler m **2.** F Wanzen anbringen in (dat); F ärgern
bug·ging| de·vice Abhörgerät n; ~ **op-
e·ra·tion** Lauschangriff m
bug·gy Kinderwagen m; MOT Buggy m
bu·gle MUS Wald-, Signalhorn n
build 1. (er)bauen, errichten **2.** Körper-
bau m, Figur f, Statur f; **build·er** Erbauer m; Bauunternehmer m
build·ing 1. (Er)Bauen n; Bau m, Gebäude n **2.** Bau...; ~ **site** Baustelle f
built-in eingebaut, Einbau...
built-up: ~ **area** bebautes Gelände or
Gebiet; geschlossene Ortschaft
bulb BOT Zwiebel f, Knolle f; ELECTR
(Glüh)Birne f
bulge 1. (Aus)Bauchung f, Ausbuch-
tung f **2.** sich (aus)bauchen; hervor-
quellen
bulk Umfang m, Größe f, Masse f;
Großteil m; **in** ~ ECON lose, unverpackt;
en gros; **bulk·y** sperrig
bull ZO Bulle m, Stier m
bull·dog ZO Bulldogge f
bull·doze planieren; F einschüchtern
bull·doz·er TECH Bulldozer m, Planier-
raupe f
bul·let Kugel f
bul·le·tin Bulletin n, Tagesbericht m
bul·le·tin board Schwarzes Brett
bul·let·proof kugelsicher
bull·fight Stierkampf m
bul·lion Gold-, Silberbarren m
bul·lock ZO Ochse m
bull's-eye: hit the ~ ins Schwarze treffen (a. fig)
bul·ly 1. tyrannische Person, Tyrann m **2.**
einschüchtern, tyrannisieren
bul·wark Bollwerk n (a. fig)
bum F **1.** Gammler m; Tippelbruder m,
Vagabund m; Nichtstuer m **2.** v/t
schnorren; ~ **around** herumgammeln
bum·ble·bee ZO Hummel f
bump 1. heftiger Schlag or Stoß; Beule f;
Unebenheit f **2.** stoßen; rammen, auf
ein Auto auffahren; zusammenstoßen;
holpern; ~ **into** fig j-n zufällig treffen; F
~ **s.o. off** j-n umlegen
bump·er MOT Stoßstange f
bump·y holp(e)rig
bun süßes Brötchen; (Haar)Knoten m
bunch Bund n, Bündel n; F Verein m,
Haufen m; ~ **of flowers** Blumenstrauß

m; **~ of grapes** Weintraube *f*; **~ of keys** Schlüsselbund *m*, -*n*

bun·dle 1. Bündel *n* (*a. fig*), Bund *n* **2.** *v/t a.* **~ up** bündeln

bun·ga·low Bungalow *m*

bun·gee elastisches Seil

bun·gee jump·ing Bungeespringen *n*

bun·gle 1. Pfusch *m* **2.** (ver)pfuschen

bunk Koje *f*; → **~ bed** Etagenbett *n*

bun·ny Häschen *n*

buoy 1. MAR Boje *f* **2.** **~ up** *fig* Auftrieb geben (*dat*)

bur·den 1. Last *f*; Bürde *f* **2.** belasten

bu·reau *Br* Schreibtisch *m*; (Spiegel-)Kommode *f*; Büro *n*

bu·reauc·ra·cy Bürokratie *f*

burg·er GASTR Hamburger *m*

bur·glar Einbrecher *m*

bur·glar·ize einbrechen in (*acc*)

bur·glar·y Einbruch *m*

bur·gle *Br* → **burglarize**

bur·i·al Begräbnis *n*

bur·ly stämmig, kräftig

burn 1. MED Verbrennung *f*, Brandwunde *f*; verbrannte Stelle **2.** (ver-, an-)brennen; **~ down** ab-, niederbrennen; **~ out** ausbrennen; **~ up** auflodern; verbrennen; verglühen (*rocket etc*)

burn·ing brennend (*a. fig*)

burp F rülpsen, aufstoßen; ein Bäuerchen machen (lassen)

bur·row 1. ZO Bau *m* **2.** graben; sich eingraben *or* vergraben

burst 1. Bersten *n*; Riss *m*; *fig* Ausbruch *m* **2.** *v/i* bersten; (zer)platzen; zerspringen; explodieren; **~ from** sich losreißen von; **~ in on** *or* **upon s.o.** bei j-m hereinplatzen; **~ into tears** in Tränen ausbrechen; **~ out** *fig* herausplatzen; *v/t* (auf)sprengen

bur·y begraben, vergraben; beerdigen

bus Omnibus *m*, Bus *m*

bus driv·er Busfahrer *m*

bush Busch *m*; Gebüsch *n*

bush·el Bushel, Scheffel *m* (*Am 35,24 l, Br 36,37 l*)

bush·y buschig

busi·ness Geschäft *n*; Arbeit *f*, Beschäftigung *f*, Beruf *m*, Tätigkeit *f*; Angelegenheit *f*; Sache *f*, Aufgabe *f*; **~ of the day** Tagesordnung *f*; **on ~** geschäftlich, beruflich; **you have no ~ doing** (*or* **to do**) **that** Sie haben kein recht, das zu tun; **that's none of your ~** das

geht Sie nichts an; → **mind** 2

busi·ness hours Geschäftszeit *f*

busi·ness-like geschäftsmäßig, sachlich

busi·ness·man Geschäftsmann *m*

busi·ness trip Geschäftsreise *f*

busi·ness·wom·an Geschäftsfrau *f*

bus stop Bushaltestelle *f*

bust¹ Büste *f*

bust²: **go ~** F pleitegehen

bus·tle 1. geschäftiges Treiben **2.** **~ about** geschäftig hin und her eilen

bus·y 1. beschäftigt; geschäftig; fleißig (**at** bei, an *dat*); belebt (*street*); arbeitsreich (*dat*); TEL besetzt **2.** (*mst* **~ o.s.** sich) beschäftigen (**with** mit)

bus·y·bod·y aufdringlicher Mensch, Gschaftlhuber *m*

bus·y sig·nal TEL Besetztzeichen *n*

but 1. *cj* aber, jedoch; sondern; außer, als; ohne dass; dennoch; **~ then** and(e)rerseits; **he could not ~ laugh** er musste einfach lachen **2.** *prp* außer (*dat*); **all ~ him** alle außer ihm; **the last ~ one** der Vorletzte; **the next ~ one** der Übernächste; **nothing ~** nichts als; **~ for** wenn nicht … gewesen wäre, ohne **3.** *adv* nur; erst, gerade; **all ~** fast, beinahe

butch·er 1. Fleischer *m*, Metzger *m* **2.** (*fig* ab)schlachten

but·ler Butler *m*

butt¹ 1. (*of rifle*) (Gewehr-)Kolben *m*; (*of cigar etc*) (Zigarren-)Stummel *m* (*of cigarette*) (Zigaretten-)Kippe *f*; (*with head etc*) (Kopf-)Stoß *m* **2.** (mit dem Kopf) stoßen; **~ in** F sich einmischen (**on** in *acc*)

butt² (*of wine, beer*) Wein-, Bierfass *n*; (*rainwater tank*) Regentonne *f*

butt³ (*backside*) F Hintern *m*

but·ter 1. Butter *f* **2.** mit Butter bestreichen

but·ter·cup BOT Butterblume *f*

but·ter·fly ZO Schmetterling *m*, Falter *m*

but·tocks ANAT Gesäß *n*, F *or* ZO Hinterteil *n*

but·ton 1. Knopf *m*; Button *m*, (Ansteck)Plakette *f*, Abzeichen *n* **2.** *mst* **~ up** zuknöpfen

but·ton·hole Knopfloch *n*

but·tress Strebepfeiler *m*

buy 1. F Kauf *m* **2.** (an-, ein)kaufen (**of, from** von; **at** bei); Fahrkarte lösen; **~ out** j-n abfinden, auszahlen; *Firma*

aufkaufen; ~ **up** aufkaufen
buy·er Käufer(in); ECON Einkäufer(in)
buzz 1. Summen *n*, Surren *n*; Stimmengewirr *n* **2.** *v/i* summen, surren; ~ **off!** F schwirr ab!, hau ab!
buz·zard ZO Bussard *m*
buzz·er ELECTR Summer *m*
by 1. *prp* (nahe *or* dicht) bei *or* an, neben (**side** ~ **side** Seite an Seite); vorbei *or* vorüber an; *time*: bis um, bis spätestens (**be back** ~ **9.30** sei um 9 Uhr 30 zurück); während, bei (~ **day** bei Tage); per, mit (~ **bus** mit dem Bus; ~ **rail** per Bahn); nach, ...weise (~ **the dozen** dutzendweise); nach, gemäß (~ **my watch** nach *or* auf m-r Uhr); von (~ **nature** von Natur aus); von, durch (**a play** ~ ... ein Stück von ...; ~ **o.s.** allein); um (~ **an inch** um e-n Zoll); MATH mal (**2** ~ **4**); *geteilt durch* (**6** ~ **3**) **2.** *adv* vorbei,

vorüber (**go** ~ vorbeigehen, -fahren; *time*: vergehen); beiseite (**put** ~ beiseitelegen, zurücklegen); ~ **and large** im Großen und Ganzen
by... Neben...; Seiten...
bye, **bye-bye** *int* F Wiedersehen!, tschüs(s)!
by-e·lec·tion PARL Nachwahl *f*
by·gone 1. vergangen **2.** *let* ~*s be* ~*s* lass(t) das Vergangene ruhen
by·pass 1. Umgehungsstraße *f*; MED Bypass *m* **2.** umgehen; vermeiden
by-prod·uct Nebenprodukt *n*
by·road Nebenstraße *f*
by·stand·er Zuschauer(in), *pl die* Umstehenden *pl*
byte IT Byte *n*
by·way Nebenstraße *f*
by·word Inbegriff *m*; **be a** ~ **for** stehen für

C

C, c C, c *n*
C *abbr of* **Celsius** C, Celsius; **centi-grade** hundertgradig
c *abbr of* **cent(s)** Cent *m or pl*; **century** Jh., Jahrhundert *n*; **circa** ca., zirca, ungefähr; **cubic** Kubik...
cab Droschke *f*, Taxi *n*; RAIL Führerstand *m*; MOT Fahrerhaus *n*, *a.* TECH Führerhaus *n*
cab·a·ret Varieteedarbietung(en *pl*) *f*
cab·bage BOT Kohl *m*
cab·in Hütte *f*; MAR Kabine *f*, Kajüte *f*; AVIAT Kanzel *f*
cab·i·net Schrank *m*, Vitrine *f*; POL Kabinett *n*
cab·i·net-mak·er Kunsttischler *m*
cab·i·net meet·ing POL Kabinettssitzung *f*
ca·ble 1. Kabel *n*; (Draht)Seil *n* **2.** telegrafieren; *j-m Geld* telegrafisch anweisen; TV verkabeln
ca·ble car Kabine *f*; Wagen *m*
ca·ble-gram (Übersee)Telegramm *n*
ca·ble| rail·way Drahtseil-, Kabinenbahn *f*; ~ **tel·e·vi·sion**, ~ **TV** Kabelfernsehen *n*
cab rank, **cab·stand** Taxistand *m*
cack·la ZO **1.** Gegacker *n*, Geschnatter *n*

2. gackern, schnattern
cac·tus BOT Kaktus *m*
ca·dence MUS Kadenz *f*; (Sprech-)Rhythmus *m*
ca·det MIL Kadett *m*
cadge Br F schnorren
caf·é, **caf·e** Café *n*
caf·e·te·ri·a Cafeteria *f*, Selbstbedienungsrestaurant *n*, *a.* Kantine *f*, UNIV Mensa *f*
cage 1. Käfig *m*; *mining*: Förderkorb *m* **2.** einsperren
cake 1. Kuchen *m*, Torte *f*; Tafel *f Schokolade*, Stück *n Seife* **2.** ~*d with mud* schmutzverkrustet
ca·lam·i·ty großes Unglück, Katastrophe *f*
cal·cu·late *v/t* kalkulieren; be-, aus-, errechnen; F vermuten; *v/i*: ~ **on** rechnen mit *or* auf (*acc*), zählen auf (*acc*)
cal·cu·la·tion Berechnung *f* (*a. fig*); ECON Kalkulation *f*; *fig* Überlegung *f*
cal·cu·la·tor TECH (Taschen)Rechner *m*
cal·en·dar Kalender *m*
calf¹ ANAT Wade *f*
calf² ZO Kalb *n*
calf·skin Kalb(s)fell *n*
cal·i·ber, *esp Br* **cal·i·bre** Kaliber *n*

call 1. Ruf *m*; TEL Anruf *m*, Gespräch *n*; Ruf *m*, Berufung *f* (**to** in *ein Amt*; auf *e-n Lehrstuhl*); Aufruf *m*, Aufforderung *f*; Signal *n*; (kurzer) Besuch; **on ~** auf Abruf; **be on ~** MED Bereitschaftsdienst haben; **make a ~** telefonieren **2.** *v/t* (herbei)rufen; (ein)berufen; TEL *j-n* anrufen; *j-n* berufen, ernennen (**to** zu); nennen; *Aufmerksamkeit* lenken (**to** auf *acc*); **be ~ed** heißen; **~ s.o. names** j-n beschimpfen, j-n beleidigen; *v/i* rufen; TEL anrufen; e-n (kurzen) Besuch machen (**on s.o., at s.o.'s** [**house**] bei j-m); **~ at a port** MAR e-n Hafen anlaufen; **~ for** rufen nach; *et.* anfordern; *et.* abholen; **to be ~ed for** postlagernd; **~ on** sich an *j-n* wenden (**for** wegen); appellieren an (*acc*) (**to do** zu tun); **~ on s.o.** j-n besuchen

call box Br Telefonzelle *f*
call·er Besucher(in); TEL Anrufer(in)
call-in → **phone-in**
call·ing Berufung *f*; Beruf *m*
cal·lous schwielig; *fig* gefühllos
cal·lus Schwiele *f*
calm 1. still, ruhig **2.** (Wind)Stille *f*, Ruhe *f* **3.** *often* **~ down** besänftigen, (sich) beruhigen
cal·o·rie Kalorie *f*; **high** *or* **rich in ~s** kalorienreich; **low in ~s** kalorienarm, kalorienreduziert
cal·o·rie-con·scious kalorienbewusst
calve ZO kalben
cam·cor·der Camcorder *m*, Kamerarekorder *m*
cam·el ZO Kamel *n*
cam·e·o Kamee *f*; THEA, *film*: kleine Nebenrolle, kurze Szene
cam·e·ra Kamera *f*, Fotoapparat *m*; **~ phone** Fotohandy *n*
cam·o·mile BOT Kamille *f*
cam·ou·flage 1. Tarnung *f* **2.** tarnen
camp 1. (Zelt- *etc*)Lager *n* **2.** lagern; **~ out** zelten, campen
cam·paign 1. MIL Feldzug *m* (*a. fig*); *fig* Kampagne *f*, Aktion *f*; POL Wahlkampf *m* **2.** *fig* kämpfen (**for** für; **against** gegen)
camp bed Br, **camp cot** Feldbett *n*
camp·er (van) Campingbus *m*, Wohnmobil *n*
camp·ground, **camp·site** Lagerplatz *m*; Zeltplatz *m*, Campingplatz *m*

cam·pus Campus *m*, Universitätsgelände *n*
can¹ *v/aux ich* kann, *du* kannst *etc*; dürfen, können
can² 1. Kanne *f*; (Blech-, Konserven-)Dose *f*, (-)Büchse *f* **2.** einmachen, eindosen
Can·a·da Kanada *n*; **Ca·na·di·an 1.** kanadisch **2.** Kanadier(in)
ca·nal Kanal *m* (*a.* ANAT)
ca·nar·y ZO Kanarienvogel *m*
can·cel (durch-, aus)streichen; entwerten; rückgängig machen; absagen; **be ~(l)ed** ausfallen
Can·cer ASTR Krebs *m*; **he** (**she**) **is** (**a**) **~** er (sie) ist (ein) Krebs
can·cer MED Krebs *m*
can·cer·ous MED Krebs..., krebsbefallen
can·cer pa·tient MED Krebskranke *m, f*
can·did aufrichtig, offen
can·di·date Kandidat(in) (**for** für), Bewerber(in) (**for** um)
can·died kandiert
can·dle Kerze *f*; Licht *n*; **burn the ~ at both ends** mit s-r Gesundheit Raubbau treiben
can·dle·stick Kerzenleuchter *m*, Kerzenständer *m*
can·do(u)r Aufrichtigkeit *f*, Offenheit *f*
can·dy 1. Kandis(zucker) *m*; Süßigkeiten *pl* **2.** kandieren; **~ floss** Zuckerwatte *f*; **~ store** Süßwarengeschäft *n*
cane BOT Rohr *n*; (Rohr)Stock *m*
ca·nine Hunde...
canned Dosen..., Büchsen...; **~ fruit** Obstkonserven *pl*
can·ne·ry Konservenfabrik *f*
can·ni·bal Kannibale *m*
can·non MIL Kanone *f*
can·ny schlau
ca·noe 1. Kanu *n*, Paddelboot *n* **2.** Kanu fahren, paddeln
can·on Kanon *m*; Regel *f*
can o·pen·er Dosen-, Büchsenöffner *m*
can·o·py Baldachin *m*
cant Jargon *m*; Phrase(n *pl*) *f*
can·tan·ker·ous F zänkisch, mürrisch
can·teen *esp* Br Kantine *f*; MIL Feldflasche *f*; Besteck(kasten *m*) *n*
can·ter 1. Kanter *m* **2.** kantern
can·vas Segeltuch *n*; Zelt-, Packleinwand *f*; Segel *pl*; PAINT Leinwand *f*; Gemälde *n*

can·vass 1. POL Wahlfeldzug *m*; ECON Werbefeldzug *m* **2.** *v/t* eingehend untersuchen *or* erörtern *or* prüfen; POL werben um (*Stimmen*); *v/i* POL e-n Wahlfeldzug veranstalten

can·yon GEOGR Cañon *m*, Schlucht *f*

cap¹ 1. Kappe *f*; Mütze *f*; Haube *f*; Zündkapsel *f* **2.** (mit e-r Kappe *etc*) bedecken; *fig* krönen; übertreffen

ca·pa·bil·i·ty Fähigkeit *f*

cap·a·ble fähig (*of* zu)

ca·pac·i·ty (Raum)Inhalt *m*; Fassungsvermögen *n*; Kapazität *f*; Aufnahmefähigkeit *f*; (TECH Leistungs)Fähigkeit *f* (*for* ger zu *inf*); *in my ~ as* in meiner Eigenschaft als

cape¹ GEOGR Kap *n*, Vorgebirge *n*

cape² Cape *n*, Umhang *m*

ca·per 1. Kapriole *f*, Luftsprung *m*; *cut ~s → 2.* Freuden- *or* Luftsprünge machen

ca·pil·la·ry ANAT Haar-, Kapillargefäß *n*

cap·i·tal 1. ECON Kapital *n*; Hauptstadt *f*; Großbuchstabe *m* **2.** Kapital...; Tod(es)...; Haupt...; großartig, prima; *~ crime* JUR Kapitalverbrechen *n*

cap·i·tal·ism ECON Kapitalismus *m*

cap·i·tal·ist ECON Kapitalist *m*

cap·i·tal·ize großschreiben; ECON kapitalisieren

cap·i·tal‖ let·ter Großbuchstabe *m*; *~ pun·ish·ment* JUR Todesstrafe *f*

ca·pit·u·late kapitulieren (*to* vor *dat*)

cap·puc·ci·no Cappucino *m*

ca·pri·cious launisch

Cap·ri·corn ASTR Steinbock *m*; *he* (*she*) *is* (*a*) ~ er (sie) ist (ein) Steinbock

cap·size MAR *v/i* kentern; *v/t* zum Kentern bringen

cap·sule Kapsel *f*

cap·tain (An)Führer *m*; MAR, ECON Kapitän *m*; AVIAT Flugkapitän *m*; MIL Hauptmann *m*; SPORT (Mannschafts-) Kapitän *m*, Spielführer *m*

cap·tion Überschrift *f*, Titel *m*; Bildunterschrift *f*; *film:* Untertitel *m*

cap·ti·vate *fig* gefangen nehmen, fesseln; **cap·tive 1.** gefangen; gefesselt; *hold* ~ gefangen halten **2.** Gefangene *m*, *f*; **cap·tiv·i·ty** Gefangenschaft *f*

cap·ture 1. Eroberung *f*; Gefangennahme *f* **2.** fangen, gefangen nehmen; erobern; erbeuten; MAR kapern

car Auto *n*, Wagen *m*; (Eisenbahn-, Straßenbahn)Wagen *m*; Gondel *f* (*of a balloon etc*); Kabine *f*; *by* ~ mit dem Auto, im Auto

car·a·mel Karamell *m*; Karamelle *f*

car·a·van Karawane *f*; *Br* Wohnwagen *m*; *~ site* Campingplatz *m* für Wohnwagen

car·a·way BOT Kümmel *m*

car·bine MIL Karabiner *m*

car·bo·hy·drate CHEM Kohle(n)hydrat *n*

car bomb Autobombe *f*

car·bon CHEM Kohlenstoff *m*; → *carbon copy, carbon paper*

car·bon cop·y Durchschlag *m*

car·bon pa·per Kohlepapier *n*

car·bu·ret·(t)or MOT Vergaser *m*

car·case *Br*, **car·cass** Kadaver *m*, Aas *n*; GASTR Rumpf *m*

car·cin·o·gen·ic MED karzinogen, krebserregend

car·ci·no·ma MED Krebsgeschwulst *f*

card Karte *f*; *play ~s* Karten spielen; *have a ~ up one's sleeve fig* (noch) e-n Trumpf in der Hand haben

card·board Pappe *f*; *~ box* Pappschachtel *f*, Pappkarton *m*

car·di·ac MED Herz...; *~ pace·mak·er* MED Herzschrittmacher *m*

car·di·gan Strickjacke *f*

car·di·nal 1. Grund..., Haupt..., Kardinal...; scharlachrot **2.** REL Kardinal *m*

car·di·nal num·ber MATH Kardinalzahl *f*, Grundzahl *f*

card in·dex Kartei *f*

card phone Kartentelefon *n*

card·sharp·er Falschspieler *m*

car dump Autofriedhof *m*

care 1. Sorge *f*; Sorgfalt *f*; Vorsicht *f*; Obhut *f*, Pflege *f*; *needing* ~ MED pflegebedürftig; *medical* ~ ärztliche Behandlung; *take* ~ *of* aufpassen auf (*acc*); versorgen; *with* ~! Vorsicht! **2.** Lust haben (*to inf* zu *inf*); *~ about* sich kümmern um; ~ *for* sorgen für, sich kümmern um; sich etwas machen aus; *I don't* ~! meinetwegen!; *I couldn't* ~ *less* F es ist mir völlig egal

ca·reer 1. Karriere *f*, Laufbahn *f* **2.** Berufs...; Karriere... **3.** rasen

ca·reers‖ ad·vice Berufsberatung *f*; ~ **ad·vi·sor** Berufsberater *m*; ~ **guid·ance** Berufsberatung *f*; ~ **of·fice** Berufsberatungsstelle *f*; ~ **of·fi·cer** Berufsberater *m*

care·free sorgenfrei, sorglos

care·ful vorsichtig; sorgsam bedacht (*of* auf *acc*); sorgfältig; *be ~!* pass auf!

care·less nachlässig, unachtsam; leichtsinnig, unvorsichtig; sorglos

care·less·ness Nachlässigkeit *f*, Unachtsamkeit *f*; Leichtsinn *m*; Sorglosigkeit *f*

ca·ress 1. Liebkosung *f*; Zärtlichkeit *f* 2. liebkosen, streicheln

care·tak·er Hausmeister *m*; (Haus- *etc*) Verwalter *m*

care·worn abgehärmt, verhärmt

car fer·ry Autofähre *f*

car·go Ladung *f*

car hire *Br* Autovermietung *f*

car·i·ca·ture 1. Karikatur *f*, Zerrbild *n* 2. karikieren

car·i·ca·tur·ist Karikaturist *m*

car·ies, *a.* **dental ~** MED Karies *f*

car me·chan·ic Automechaniker *m*

car·mine Karmin(rot) *n*

car·nap·per F Autoentführer *m*

car·na·tion BOT Nelke *f*

car·ni·val Karneval *m*

car·niv·o·rous ZO fleischfressend

car·ol Weihnachtslied *n*

carp[1] ZO Karpfen *m*

carp[2] nörgeln

car park *esp Br* Parkplatz *m*; Parkhaus *n*

car·pen·ter Zimmermann *m*

car·pet 1. Teppich *m*; **fitted ~** Teppichboden *m*; **sweep s.th. under the ~** *fig* et. unter den Teppich kehren 2. mit Teppich(boden) auslegen

car phone Autotelefon *n*

car pool Fahrgemeinschaft *f*

car pool(·ing) ser·vice Mitfahrzentrale *f*

car·port MOT überdachter Abstellplatz

car rent·al Autovermietung *f*

car re·pair shop Autoreparaturwerkstatt *f*

car·riage Beförderung *f*, Transport *m*; Transportkosten *pl*; Kutsche *f*; *Br* RAIL (Personen)Wagen *m*

car·riage·way Fahrbahn *f*

car·ri·er Spediteur *m*; Gepäckträger *m* (*on a bicycle*); MIL Flugzeugträger *m*

car·ri·er bag *Br* Trag(e)tasche *f*, -tüte *f*

car·ri·on 1. Aas *n* 2. Aas...

car·rot BOT Karotte *f*, Mohrrübe *f*

car·ry *v/t* bringen, führen, tragen (*a. v/i*),

fahren, befördern; (bei sich) haben *or* tragen; *Ansicht* durchsetzen; *Gewinn*, *Preis* davontragen; *Ernte*, *Zinsen* tragen; (weiter)führen, *Mauer* ziehen; *Antrag* durchbringen; *be carried* PARL *etc* angenommen werden; **~ s.th. too far** et. übertreiben, et. zu weit treiben; **get carried away** *fig* die Kontrolle über sich verlieren; sich hinreißen lassen; **~ forward, ~ over** ECON übertragen; **~ on** fortsetzen, weiterführen; ECON betreiben; **~ out, ~ through** aus-, durchführen

car·ry·cot *Br* (Baby)Trag(e)tasche *f*

cart 1. Karren *m*; Wagen *m*; Einkaufswagen *m*; **put the ~ before the horse** *fig* das Pferd beim Schwanz aufzäumen 2. karren

car·ti·lage ANAT Knorpel *m*

cart·load Wagenladung *f*

car·ton Karton *m*; **a ~ of cigarettes** e-e Stange Zigaretten

car·toon Cartoon *m*, *n*; Karikatur *f*; Zeichentrickfilm *m*

car·toon·ist Karikaturist *m*

car·tridge Patrone *f* (*a.* MIL); (Film-) Patrone *f*, (Film)Kassette *f*; Tonabnehmer *m*

cart·wheel: *turn ~s* Rad schlagen

carve GASTR vorschneiden, zerlegen; TECH schnitzen; meißeln

carv·er (Holz)Schnitzer *m*; Bildhauer *m*; GASTR Tranchierer *m*; Tranchiermesser *n*; GASTR *a.* Tranchierbesteck *n*

carv·ing Schnitzerei *f*

car wash Autowäsche *f*; (Auto)Waschanlage *f*, Waschstraße *f*

cas·cade Wasserfall *m*

case[1] 1. Behälter *m*; Kiste *f*, Kasten *m*; Etui *n*; Gehäuse *n*; Schachtel *f*; (Glas-) Schrank *m*; (Kissen)Bezug *m*; TECH Verkleidung *f* 2. in ein Gehäuse *or* Etui stecken; TECH verkleiden

case[2] Fall *m* (*a.* JUR; LING *a.* Kasus *m*; MED (Krankheits)Fall *m*, Patient(in); Sache *f*, Angelegenheit *f*

case·ment Fensterflügel *m*; → **~ window** Flügelfenster *n*

cash 1. Bargeld *n*; Barzahlung *f*; **~ down** gegen bar; **~ on delivery** Lieferung *f* gegen bar; (per) Nachnahme *f* 2. einlösen

cash·book ECON Kassenbuch *n*

cash desk Kasse *f*

cash dis·pens·er *esp Br* Geld-, Bankautomat *m*

cash·ier Kassierer(in)

cash·less bargeldlos

cash ma·chine Geld-, Bankautomat *m*

cash·mere Kaschmir *m*

cash·point *Br* → *cash machine*

cash reg·is·ter Registrierkasse *f*

cas·ing (Schutz)Hülle *f*; Verschalung *f*, Verkleidung *f*, Gehäuse *n*

cask Fass *n*

cas·ket Kästchen *n*; Sarg *m*

cas·sette (*Film-, Band-, Musik*)Kassette *f*; ~ **deck** Kassettendeck *n*; ~ **player** Kassettenrekorder *m*; ~ **ra·di·o** Radiorekorder *m*; ~ **re·cord·er** Kassettenrekorder *m*

cas·sock REL Soutane *f*

cast 1. Wurf *m*; TECH Guss(form *f*) *m*; Abguss *m*, Abdruck *m*; Schattierung *f*, Anflug *m*; Form *f*, Art *f*; Auswerfen *n* (*of a fishing line etc*); THEA Besetzung *f* **2.** (ab-, aus-, hin-, um-, weg)werfen; ZO abwerfen (*skin*); verlieren (*teeth*); verwerfen; gestalten; TECH gießen; *a.* ~ *up* ausrechnen, zusammenzählen; THEA *Stück* besetzen; *Rollen* verteilen (*to* an *acc*); ~ *lots* losen (*for* um); ~ *away* wegwerfen; *be* ~ *down* niedergeschlagen sein; ~ *off Kleidung* ausrangieren; MAR losmachen; *Freund etc* fallen lassen; *knitting*: abketten; *v/i*: ~ *about for*, ~ *around for* suchen (nach), *fig a.* sich umsehen nach

cas·ta·net Kastagnette *f*

cast·a·way Schiffbrüchige *m*, *f*

caste Kaste *f* (*a. fig*)

cast·er Laufrolle *f*; *Br* (*Salz-, Zucker etc*)Streuer *m*

cast i·ron Gusseisen *n*

cast-i·ron gusseisern

cas·tle Burg *f*, Schloss *n*; *chess*: Turm *m*

cast·or → *caster*

cast·or oil PHARM Rizinusöl *n*

cas·trate kastrieren

cas·u·al zufällig; gelegentlich; flüchtig; lässig

cas·u·al·ty Unfall *m*; Verunglückte *m*, *f*, Opfer *n*; MIL Verwundete *m*; Gefallene *m*; *casualties* Opfer *pl*, MIL *mst* Verluste *pl*; ~ **(de·part·ment)** MED Notaufnahme *f*; ~ **ward** MED Unfallstation *f*

cas·u·al wear Freizeitkleidung *f*

cat ZO Katze *f*

cat·a·log, *esp Br* **cat·a·logue 1.** Katalog *m*; Verzeichnis *n*, Liste *f* **2.** katalogisieren

cat·a·lyt·ic con·vert·er MOT Katalysator *m*

cat·a·pult *Br* Schleuder *f*; Katapult *n*, *m*

cat·a·ract Wasserfall *m*; Stromschnelle *f*; MED grauer Star

ca·tarrh MED Katarr(h) *m*

ca·tas·tro·phe Katastrophe *f*

catch 1. Fangen *n*; Fang *m*, Beute *f*; Halt *m*, Griff *m*; TECH Haken *m* (*a. fig*); (Tür)Klinke *f*; Verschluss *m* **2.** *v/t* (auf-, ein)fangen; packen, fassen, ergreifen; überraschen, ertappen; *Blick etc* auffangen; F *Zug etc* (noch) kriegen, erwischen; *et.* erfassen, verstehen; *Atmosphäre etc* einfangen; sich *e-e Krankheit* holen; ~ (*a*) *cold* sich erkälten; ~ *the eye* ins Auge fallen; ~ *s.o.'s eye* j-s Aufmerksamkeit auf sich lenken; ~ *s.o. up* j-n einholen; *be caught up in* verwickelt sein in (*acc*); *v/i* sich verfangen, hängen bleiben; fassen, greifen; TECH ineinandergreifen; klemmen; einschnappen; ~ *up with* einholen

catch·er Fänger *m*

catch·ing packend; MED ansteckend (*a. fig*)

catch·word Schlagwort *n*; Stichwort *n*

catch·y MUS eingängig

cat·e·chis·m REL Katechismus *m*

cat·e·go·ry Kategorie *f*

ca·ter: ~ *for* Speisen und Getränke liefern für; *fig* sorgen für

cat·er·pil·lar ZO Raupe *f*

Cat·er·pil·lar® MOT Raupenfahrzeug *n*; ~ **trac·tor**® MOT Raupenschlepper *m*

cat·gut MUS Darmsaite *f*

ca·the·dral Dom *m*, Kathedrale *f*

Cath·o·lic REL **1.** katholisch **2.** Katholik(in)

cat·kin BOT Kätzchen *n*

cat·tle Vieh *n*; ~ **breed·er** Viehzüchter *m*; ~ **breed·ing** Viehzucht *f*; ~ **dealer** Viehhändler *m*; ~ **mar·ket** Viehmarkt *m*

ca(u)l·dron großer Kessel

cau·li·flow·er BOT Blumenkohl *m*

cause 1. Ursache *f*; Grund *m*; Sache *f* **2.** verursachen; veranlassen

cause·less grundlos

cau·tion 1. Vorsicht *f*; Warnung *f*, Verwarnung *f* **2.** warnen; verwarnen; JUR

belehren
cau·tious behutsam, vorsichtig
cav·al·ry HIST MIL Kavallerie *f*
cave 1. Höhle *f* **2.** *v/i*: **~ in** einstürzen
cav·ern (große) Höhle
cav·i·ty Höhle *f*; MED Loch *n*
caw ZO **1.** krächzen **2.** Krächzen *n*
CD *abbr of* **compact disk** CD *f*; **~ bur·ner** CD-Brenner *m*; **~ play·er** CD--Spieler *m*; **~-ROM** *abbr of* **compact disk read-only memory** CD-ROM; **~-ROM drive** CD-ROM-Laufwerk *n*; **~ vid·e·o** CD-Video *n*; **~ wri·ter** CD--Brenner *m*
cease aufhören; beenden
cease·fire MIL Feuereinstellung *f*; Waffenruhe *f*
cease·less unaufhörlich
cei·ling (Zimmer)Decke *f*; ECON Höchstgrenze *f*, oberste Preisgrenze
cel·e·brate feiern; **cel·e·brat·ed** gefeiert, berühmt (**for** für, wegen)
cel·e·bra·tion Feier *f*
ce·leb·ri·ty Berühmtheit *f*
cel·e·ry BOT Sellerie *m, f*
ce·les·ti·al himmlisch
cel·i·ba·cy Ehelosigkeit *f*
cell BIOL Zelle *f*, ÉLECTR *a.* Element *n*
cel·lar Keller *m*
cel·list MUS Cellist(in)
cel·lo MUS (Violon)Cello *n*
cel·lo·phane® Cellophan® *n*
cel·lu·lar BIOL Zell(en)...
cel·lu·lar phone Handy *n*
Cel·tic keltisch
ce·ment 1. Zement *m*; Kitt *m* **2.** zementieren; (ver)kitten
cem·e·tery Friedhof *m*
cen·sor 1. Zensor *m* **2.** zensieren
cen·sor·ship Zensur *f*
cen·sure 1. Tadel *m*, Verweis *m* **2.** tadeln
cen·sus Volkszählung *f*
cent Hundert *n*; Cent *m* (*1/100 Dollar*); **per ~** Prozent *n*
cen·te·na·ry Hundertjahrfeier *f*, hundertjähriges Jubiläum
cen·ten·ni·al 1. hundertjährig **2.** → **centenary**
cen·ter 1. Zentrum *n*, Mittelpunkt *m*; *soccer*: Flanke *f* **2.** (sich) konzentrieren; zentrieren; **~ back** *soccer*: Vorstopper *m*; **~ for·ward** SPORT Mittelstürmer(in); **~ of grav·i·ty** PHYS Schwerpunkt *m*

cen·ti·grade: **10 degrees ~** 10 Grad Celsius
cen·ti·me·ter, *Br* **cen·ti·me·tre** Zentimeter *m, n*
cen·ti·pede ZO Tausendfüß(l)er *m*
cen·tral zentral; Haupt..., Zentral...; Mittel...; **~ heat·ing** Zentralheizung *f*
cen·tral·ize zentralisieren
cen·tral|lock·ing MOT Zentralverriegelung *f*; **~ res·er·va·tion** *Br* MOT Mittelstreifen *m*
cen·tre *Br* → **center**
cen·tu·ry Jahrhundert *n*
ce·ram·ics Keramik *f*, keramische Erzeugnisse *pl*
ce·re·al 1. Getreide... **2.** BOT Getreide *n*; Getreidepflanze *f*; GASTR Getreideflocken *pl*, Frühstückskost *f*
cer·e·bral ANAT Gehirn...
cer·e·mo·ni·al 1. zeremoniell **2.** Zeremoniell *n*
cer·e·mo·ni·ous zeremoniell; förmlich
cer·e·mo·ny Zeremonie *f*; Feier *f*, Feierlichkeit *f*; Förmlichkeit(en *pl*) *f*
cer·tain sicher, gewiss; zuverlässig; bestimmt; gewisse(r, -s); **cer·tain·ly** sicher, gewiss; *int* sicherlich, bestimmt, natürlich; **cer·tain·ty** Sicherheit *f*, Bestimmtheit *f*, Gewissheit *f*
cer·tif·i·cate Zeugnis *n*; Bescheinigung *f*; **~ of** (**good**) **conduct** Führungszeugnis *n*; **General Certificate of Education advanced level** (**A level**) *Br* PED *appr* Abitur(zeugnis) *n*; **General Certificate of Education ordinary level** (**O level**) *Br* PED *appr* mittlere Reife; **medical ~** ärztliches Attest
cer·ti·fy *et.* bescheinigen; beglaubigen
cer·ti·tude Sicherheit *f*, Bestimmtheit *f*, Gewissheit *f*
CET *abbr of* **Central European Time** MEZ, mitteleuropäische Zeit
cf (*Latin* **confer**) *abbr of* **compare** vgl., vergleiche
CFC *abbr of* **chlorofluorocarbon** FCKW, Fluorchlorkohlenwasserstoff *m*
chafe *v/t* warm reiben; aufreiben, wund reiben; *v/i* (sich durch)reiben, scheuern
chaff AGR Spreu *f*; Häcksel *n*
chaf·finch ZO Buchfink *m*
chag·rin 1. Ärger *m* **2.** ärgern
chain 1. Kette *f*; *fig* Fessel *f* **2.** (an)ket-

ten; fesseln

chain re·ac·tion Kettenreaktion f

chain-smoke F Kette rauchen

chain-smok·er Kettenraucher(in)

chain-smok·ing Kettenrauchen n

chain store Kettenladen m

chair Stuhl m; UNIV Lehrstuhl m; ECON etc Vorsitz m; **be in the ~** den Vorsitz führen; **~ lift** Sessellift m

chair·man Vorsitzende m, Präsident m; Diskussionsleiter m; ECON Br Generaldirektor m

chair·man·ship Vorsitz m

chair·wom·an Vorsitzende f, Präsidentin f; Diskussionsleiterin f

chal·ice REL Kelch m

chalk 1. Kreide f **2.** mit Kreide schreiben or zeichnen

chal·lenge 1. Herausforderung f **2.** herausfordern

chal·len·ger Herausforderer m

cham·ber TECH, PARL etc Kammer f

cham·ber·maid Zimmermädchen n

cham·ber of com·merce ECON Handelskammer f

cham·ois ZO Gämse f

cham·ois (leath·er) Fensterleder n

champ F SPORT → **champion**

cham·pagne Champagner m

cham·pi·on 1. Verfechter(in), Fürsprecher(in); SPORT Meister(in) **2.** verfechten, eintreten für; **cham·pi·on·ship** SPORT Meisterschaft f

chance 1. Zufall m; Chance f, (günstige) Gelegenheit; Aussicht f (**of** auf acc); Möglichkeit f; Risiko n; **by ~** zufällig; **take a ~** es darauf ankommen lassen; **take no ~s** nichts riskieren (wollen) **2.** zufällig **3.** F riskieren

chan·cel·lor Kanzler(in)

chan·de·lier Kronleuchter m

change 1. Veränderung f, Wechsel m; Abwechslung f; Wechselgeld n; Kleingeld n; **for a ~** zur Abwechslung; **~ for the better (worse)** Bess(e)rung f (Verschlechterung f); **2.** v/t (ver)ändern, umändern; (aus)tauschen; (aus-, ver-) tauschen (**for** gegen); umbuchen; MOT, TECH schalten; **~ over** umschalten; umstellen; **~ trains** umsteigen; v/i sich (ver)ändern, wechseln; sich umziehen

change·a·ble veränderlich

change ma·chine Münzwechsler m

change·o·ver Umstellung f (**to** auf acc)

chang·ing room esp SPORT Umkleidekabine f, Umkleideraum m

chan·nel 1. Kanal m (a. fig); (Fernsehetc)Kanal m, (Fernseh- etc)Programm n; fig Weg m **2.** fig lenken

Chan·nel Tun·nel Kanaltunnel m, Eurotunnel m

chant 1. (Kirchen)Gesang m; Singsang m **2.** in Sprechchören rufen

cha·os Chaos n

chap[1] 1. Riss m **2.** rissig machen or werden; aufspringen

chap[2] Br F Bursche m, Kerl m

chap·el ARCH Kapelle f; REL Gottesdienst m

chap·lain REL Kaplan m

chap·ter Kapitel n

char verkohlen

char·ac·ter Charakter m; Ruf m, Leumund m; Schriftzeichen n, Buchstabe m; novel etc: Figur f, Gestalt f; THEA Rolle f; **char·ac·ter·is·tic 1.** charakteristisch (**of** für); **2.** Kennzeichen n; **char·ac·ter·ize** charakterisieren

char·coal Holzkohle f

charge 1. v/t ELECTR (auf)laden; Gewehr etc laden; j-n beauftragen (**with** mit); j-n beschuldigen or anklagen (**with** e-r Sache) (a. JUR); ECON berechnen, verlangen, fordern (**for** für); MIL angreifen; stürmen; **~ s.o. with s.th.** ECON j-m et. in Rechnung stellen; v/i: **~ at s.o.** auf j-n losgehen **2.** Ladung f (a. ELECTR etc); (Spreng)Ladung f; Beschuldigung f, a. JUR Anklage(-punkt m) f; ECON Preis m; Forderung f; Gebühr f; a. pl Unkosten pl, Spesen pl; Verantwortung f; Schützling m, Mündel n, m; **free of ~** kostenlos; **be in ~ of** verantwortlich sein für; **take ~ of** die Leitung etc übernehmen, die Sache in die Hand nehmen

char·ger Aufladegerät n

char·i·ot HIST Streit-, Triumphwagen m

cha·ris·ma Charisma n, Ausstrahlung f, Ausstrahlungskraft f

char·i·ta·ble wohltätig

char·i·ty Nächstenliebe f; Wohltätigkeit f; Güte f, Nachsicht f; milde Gabe

char·la·tan Scharlatan m; Quacksalber m, Kurpfuscher m

charm 1. Zauber m; Charme m, Reiz m; Talisman m, Amulett n **2.** bezaubern, entzücken

charm·ing charmant, bezaubernd

chart (*See-*, *Himmels-*, *Wetter*)Karte *f*; Diagramm *n*, Schaubild *n*; *pl* MUS Charts *pl*, Hitliste(n *pl*) *f*

char·ter 1. Urkunde *f*; Charta *f*; Chartern *n* **2.** chartern, mieten

char·ter flight Charterflug *m*

char·wom·an Putzfrau *f*, Raumpflegerin *f*

chase 1. Jagd *f*; Verfolgung *f* **2.** *v/t* jagen, hetzen; Jagd machen auf (*acc*); TECH ziselieren; *v/i* rasen, rennen

chasm Kluft *f*, Abgrund *m*

chaste keusch; schlicht

chas·tise züchtigen

chas·ti·ty Keuschheit *f*

chat 1. Geplauder *n*, Schwätzchen *n*, Plauderei *f*; IT Chat *m* **2.** plaudern; IT chatten

chat show *Br* TV Talkshow *f*

chat show host *Br* TV Talkmaster *m*

chat·ter 1. plappern; schnattern; klappern **2.** Geplapper *n*; Klappern *n*

chat·ter·box F Plappermaul *n*

chat·ty gesprächig

chauf·feur Chauffeur *m*

chau·vi F Chauvi *m*

chau·vin·ist Chauvinist *m*; F *male* ~ *pig* Chauvi *m*; *contp* Chauvischwein *n*

cheap billig; *fig* schäbig, gemein

cheap·en (sich) verbilligen; *fig* herabsetzen

cheat 1. Betrug *m*, Schwindel *m*; Betrüger(in) **2.** betrügen; F schummeln

check 1. Schach(stellung *f*) *n*; Hemmnis *n*, Hindernis *n* (**on** für); Einhalt *m*; Kontrolle *f* (**on** *gen*); Kontrollabschnitt *m*, -schein *m*; Gepäckschein *m*; Garderobenmarke *f*; ECON Scheck· *m* (**for** über); Häkchen *n* (**on a list** *etc*); ECON Kassenzettel *m*, Rechnung *f*; karierter Stoff **2.** *v/i* (plötzlich) innehalten; ~ **in** sich (*in e-m Hotel*) anmelden; einstempeln; AVIAT einchecken; ~ **out** (*aus e-m Hotel*) abreisen; ausstempeln; ~ **up** (**on**) F (*e-e Sache*) nachprüfen, (*e-e Sache, j-n*) überprüfen; *v/t* hemmen, hindern, aufhalten; zurückhalten; checken, kontrollieren, überprüfen; *auf e-r Liste* abhaken; *Mantel etc* in der Garderobe abgeben; *Gepäck* aufgeben

check card ECON Scheckkarte *f*

checked kariert

check·ers Damespiel *n*

check-in Anmeldung *f*; Einstempeln *n*; AVIAT Einchecken *n*

check-in| coun·ter, ~ desk AVIAT Abfertigungsschalter *m*

check·ing ac·count ECON Girokonto *n*

check·list Check-, Kontrollliste *f*

check·mate 1. (Schach)Matt *n* **2.** (schach)matt setzen

check·out Abreise *f*; Ausstempeln *n*

check-out coun·ter Kasse *f*

check·point Kontrollpunkt *m*

check·room Garderobe *f*; Gepäckaufbewahrung *f*

check-up Überprüfung *f*; MED Check-up *m*, Vorsorgeuntersuchung *f*

cheek ANAT Backe *f*, Wange *f*; *Br* Unverschämtheit *f*; **cheek·y** *Br* frech

cheer 1. Stimmung *f*, Fröhlichkeit *f*; Hoch *n*, Hochruf *m*, Beifall *m*, Beifallsruf *m*; *pl* SPORT Anfeuerungsrufe *pl*; **three ~s!** dreimal hoch!; ~**s!** prost! **2.** *v/t* mit Beifall begrüßen; *a.* ~ **on** anspornen; *a.* ~ **up** aufheitern; *v/i* hoch rufen, jubeln; *a.* ~ **up** Mut fassen; ~ **up!** Kopf hoch!; **cheer·ful** vergnügt

cheer·i·o *int Br* F tschüs(s)!

cheer·lead·er SPORT Einpeitscher *m*, Cheerleader *m*

cheer·less freudlos; unfreundlich

cheer·y vergnügt

cheese Käse *m*

chee·tah ZO Gepard *m*

chef Küchenchef *m*; Koch *m*

chem·i·cal 1. chemisch **2.** Chemikalie *f*

chem·ist Chemiker(in); Apotheker(in); Drogist(in)

chem·is·try Chemie *f*

chem·ist's shop Apotheke *f*; Drogerie *f*

chem·o·ther·a·py MED Chemotherapie *f*

cheque *Br* ECON Scheck *m*; **crossed** ~ Verrechnungsscheck *m*; ~ **ac·count** *Br* Girokonto *n*; ~ **card** *Br* Scheckkarte *f*

cher·ry BOT Kirsche *f*

chess Schach(spiel) *n*; **a game of** ~ e-e Partie Schach

chess·board Schachbrett *n*

chess·man, chess·piece Schachfigur *f*

chest Kiste *f*; Truhe *f*; ANAT Brust *f*, Brustkasten *m*; **get s.th. off one's** ~ F sich et. von der Seele reden

chest·nut 1. BOT Kastanie *f* **2.** kastanienbraun

chest of drawers Kommode *f*

chew (zer)kauen

chew·ing gum Kaugummi *m*

chic schick, *Austrian* fesch

chick zo Küken *n*, junger Vogel; F Biene *f*, Puppe *f* (*girl*)

chick·en zo Huhn *n*; Küken *n*; GASTR (*Brat*)Hähnchen *n*, (*Brat*)Hühnchen *n*

chick·en-heart·ed furchtsam, feige

chick·en pox MED Windpocken *pl*

chic·o·ry BOT Chicorée *m*, *f*

chief 1. oberste(r, -s), Ober..., Haupt..., Chef...; wichtigste(r, -s) **2.** Chef *m*; Häuptling *m*

chief·ly hauptsächlich

chil·blain MED Frostbeule *f*

child Kind *n*; **~ a·buse** JUR Kindesmisshandlung *f*; **~ ben·e·fit** Br Kindergeld *n*; **~birth** Geburt *f*, Niederkunft *f*; **~hood** Kindheit *f*; *from* **~** von Kindheit an; **~ish** kindlich; kindisch; **~like** kindlich; **~mind·er** Tagesmutter *f*; **~seat** Kindersitz *m*, Babysitz *m*

chill 1. kalt, frostig, kühl (*a. fig*) **2.** Frösteln *m*; Kälte *f*, Kühle *f* (*a. fig*); MED Erkältung *f* **3.** abkühlen; *j-n* frösteln lassen; kühlen

chill·y kalt, frostig, kühl (*a. fig*)

chime 1. Glockenspiel *n*; Geläut *n* **2.** läuten; schlagen (*clock*)

chim·ney Schornstein *m*

chim·ney sweep Schornsteinfeger *m*

chimp F, **chim·pan·zee** zo Schimpanse *m*

chin ANAT Kinn *n*; **~ up!** Kopf hoch!, halt die Ohren steif!

chi·na Porzellan *n*

Chi·na China *n*

Chi·nese 1. chinesisch **2.** Chinese *m*, Chinesin *f*; LING Chinesisch *n*; *the* **~** die Chinesen *pl*

chink Ritz *m*, Spalt *m*

chip 1. Splitter *m*, Span *m*, Schnitzel *n*, *m*; dünne Scheibe; Spielmarke *f*; IT Chip *m* **2.** *v/t* schnitzeln; anschlagen, abschlagen; *v/i* abbröckeln

chips (Kartoffel)Chips *pl*; *Br* Pommes frites *pl*, F Fritten *pl*

chi·rop·o·dist Fußpfleger(in), Pediküre *f*

chirp zo zirpen, zwitschern, piepsen

chis·el 1. Meißel *m* **2.** meißeln

chit-chat Plauderei *f*

chiv·al·rous ritterlich

chive(s) BOT Schnittlauch *m*

chlo·ri·nate *Wasser etc* chloren

chlo·rine CHEM Chlor *n*

chlo·ro·fluo·ro·car·bon (*abbr* **CFC**) CHEM Fluorchlorkohlenwasserstoff *m* (*abbr* **FCKW**)

chlor·o·form MED **1.** Chloroform *n* **2.** chloroformieren

choc·o·late Schokolade *f*; Praline *f*; *pl* Pralinen *pl*, Konfekt *n*

choice 1. Wahl *f*; Auswahl *f* **2.** auserlesen, ausgesucht, vorzüglich

choir ARCH, MUS Chor *m*

choke 1. *v/t* (er)würgen, (*a. v/i*) ersticken; **~ back** Ärger *etc* unterdrücken, *Tränen* zurückhalten; **~ down** hinunterwürgen; *a.* **~ up** verstopfen **2.** MOT Choke *m*, Luftklappe *f*

cho·les·te·rol MED Cholesterin *n*

choose (aus)wählen, aussuchen

choos·(e)y *esp Br* wählerisch

chop 1. Hieb *m*, (Handkanten)Schlag *m*; GASTR Kotelett *n* **2.** *v/t* (zer)hacken, hauen; **~ down** fällen; *v/i* hacken

chop·per Hackmesser *n*, Hackbeil *n*; F Hubschrauber *m*

chop·py unruhig (*sea*)

chop·stick Essstäbchen *n*

cho·ral MUS Chor...

cho·rale MUS Choral *m*

chord MUS Saite *f*; Akkord *m*

chore schwierige *or* unangenehme Aufgabe; *pl* Hausarbeit *f*

cho·rus MUS Chor *m*; Kehrreim *m*, Refrain *m*; Tanzgruppe *f*

Christ REL Christus *m*

chris·ten REL taufen

chris·ten·ing REL **1.** Taufe *f* **2.** Tauf...

Chris·tian REL **1.** christlich **2.** Christ(in)

Chris·ti·an·i·ty REL Christentum *n*

Chris·tian name Vorname *m*

Christ·mas Weihnachten *n and pl*; *at* **~** zu Weihnachten; **~ Day** erster Weihnachtsfeiertag; **~ Eve** Heiliger Abend

chrome Chrom *n*

chro·mi·um CHEM Chrom *n*

chron·ic chronisch; ständig, (an)dauernd

chron·i·cle Chronik *f*

chron·o·log·i·cal chronologisch

chro·nol·o·gy Zeitrechnung *f*; Zeitfolge *f*

chub·by F rundlich, pumm(e)lig; pausbäckig

chuck F werfen, schmeißen; **~ out** *j-n*

rausschmeißen; *et.* wegschmeißen; ~ *up Job etc* hinschmeißen

chuck·le 1. ~ *(to o.s.)* (stillvergnügt) in sich hineinlachen **2.** leises Lachen

chum F Kamerad *m*, Kumpel *m*

chum·my F dick befreundet

chump Holzklotz *m*; F Trottel *m*

chunk Klotz *m*, Klumpen *m*

Chun·nel Br → *Channel Tunnel*

church 1. Kirche *f* **2.** Kirch..., Kirchen...

church ser·vice REL Gottesdienst *m*

church·yard Kirchhof *m*

churl·ish grob, flegelhaft

churn 1. Butterfass *n* **2.** buttern; *Wellen* aufwühlen, peitschen

chute Stromschnelle *f*; Rutsche *f*, Rutschbahn *f*; F Fallschirm *m*

ci·der *a.* **hard** ~ Apfelwein *m*; **(sweet)** ~ Apfelmost *m*, Apfelsaft *m*

ci·gar Zigarre *f*

cig·a·rette Zigarette *f*

cinch F todsichere Sache

cin·der Schlacke *f*; *pl* Asche *f*

Cin·de·rel·la Aschenbrödel *n*, Aschenputtel *n*

cin·der track SPORT Aschenbahn *f*

cin·e·cam·e·ra (Schmal)Filmkamera *f*

cin·e·film Schmalfilm *m*

cin·e·ma Br Kino *n*; Film *m*

cin·na·mon Zimt *m*

ci·pher Geheimschrift *f*, Chiffre *f*; Null *f* (*a. fig*)

cir·cle 1. Kreis *m*; THEA Rang *m*; *fig* Kreislauf *m* **2.** (um)kreisen

cir·cuit Kreislauf *m*; ELECTR Stromkreis *m*; Rundreise *f*; SPORT Zirkus *m*; *short* ~ ELECTR Kurzschluss *m*

cir·cu·i·tous gewunden; weitschweifig; ~ *route* Umweg *m*

cir·cu·lar 1. kreisförmig; Kreis... **2.** Rundschreiben *n*; Umlauf *m*; (Post-)Wurfsendung *f*

cir·cu·late *v/i* zirkulieren, im Umlauf sein; *v/t* in Umlauf setzen

cir·cu·lat·ing li·bra·ry Leihbücherei *f*

cir·cu·la·tion (*a.* Blut)Kreislauf *m*, Zirkulation *f*; ECON Umlauf *m*; *newspaper etc:* Auflage *f*

cir·cum·fer·ence (Kreis)Umfang *m*

cir·cum·nav·i·gate umschiffen, umsegeln

cir·cum·scribe MATH umschreiben; *fig* begrenzen

cir·cum·spect umsichtig, vorsichtig

cir·cum·stance Umstand *m*; *pl* (Sach-) Lage *f*, Umstände *pl*; Verhältnisse *pl*; *in or under no* ~*s* unter keinen Umständen, auf keinen Fall; *in or under the* ~*s* unter diesen Umständen

cir·cum·stan·tial ausführlich; umständlich; ~**ev·i·dence** JUR Indizien *pl*, Indizienbeweis *m*

cir·cus Zirkus *m*

CIS *abbr of* **Commonwealth of Independent States** *die* GUS, *die* Gemeinschaft unabhängiger Staaten

cis·tern Wasserbehälter *m*; Spülkasten *m*

ci·ta·tion Zitat *n*; JUR Vorladung *f*

cite zitieren; JUR vorladen

cit·i·zen Bürger(in); Städter(in); Staatsangehörige *m, f*

cit·i·zen·ship Staatsangehörigkeit *f*

cit·y 1. (Groß)Stadt *f*; *the City* die (Londoner) City **2.** städtisch, Stadt...; ~ **cen·tre** Br Innenstadt *f*, City *f*; ~ **coun·cil·(l)or** Stadtrat *m*, Stadträtin *f*; ~ **hall** Rathaus *n*; Stadtverwaltung *f*

civ·ic städtisch, Stadt...

civ·ics PED Staatsbürgerkunde *f*

civ·il staatlich, Staats...; (staats)bürgerlich, Bürger...; zivil, Zivil...; JUR zivilrechtlich; höflich

ci·vil·i·an Zivilist *m*

ci·vil·i·ty Höflichkeit *f*

civ·i·li·za·tion Zivilisation *f*, Kultur *f*

civ·i·lize zivilisieren

civ·il rights (Staats)Bürgerrechte *pl*; ~ **ac·tiv·ist** Bürgerrechtler(in); ~ **move·ment** Bürgerrechtsbewegung *f*

civ·il| ser·vant Staatsbeamte *m*, -beamtin *f*; ~ **ser·vice** Staatsdienst *m*; ~ **war** Bürgerkrieg *m*

clad gekleidet

claim 1. Anspruch *m*; Anrecht *n* (**to** auf *acc*); Forderung *f*; Behauptung *f*; Claim *m* **2.** beanspruchen; fordern; behaupten

clair·voy·ant 1. hellseherisch **2.** Hellseher(in)

clam·ber (mühsam) klettern

clam·my feuchtkalt, klamm

clam·o(u)r 1. Geschrei *n*, Lärm *m* **2.** lautstark verlangen (**for** nach)

clamp TECH Zwinge *f*

clan Clan *m*, Sippe *f*

clan·des·tine heimlich

clang klingen, klirren; erklingen lassen

clank 1. Gerassel n, Geklirr n **2.** rasseln or klirren (mit)

clap 1. Klatschen n; Schlag m, Klaps m **2.** schlagen or klatschen (mit)

clar·et roter Bordeaux(wein); Rotwein m

clar·i·fy v/t (auf)klären, klarstellen; v/i sich (auf)klären, klar werden

clar·i·net MUS Klarinette f

clar·i·ty Klarheit f

clash 1. Zusammenstoß m; Konflikt m **2.** zusammenstoßen; fig nicht zusammenpassen or harmonieren

clasp 1. Haken m, Schnalle f; Schloss n, (Schnapp) Verschluss m; Umklammerung f **2.** einhaken, zuhaken; ergreifen, umklammern

clasp knife Taschenmesser n

class 1. Klasse f; (Bevölkerungs-) Schicht f; (Schul)Klasse f; (Unterrichts)Stunde f; Kurs m; Jahrgang m **2.** (in Klassen) einteilen, einordnen, einstufen

clas·sic 1. Klassiker m **2.** klassisch

clas·si·cal klassisch

clas·sic car Klassiker m

clas·si·fi·ca·tion Klassifizierung f, Einteilung f

clas·si·fied klassifiziert; MIL, POL geheim; **~ ad** Kleinanzeige f

clas·si·fy klassifizieren, einstufen

class·mate Mitschüler(in)

class·room Klassenzimmer n

clat·ter 1. Geklapper n **2.** klappern (mit)

clause JUR Klausel f, Bestimmung f; LING Satz(teil n) m

claw 1. ZO Klaue f, Kralle f; (Krebs-) Schere f **2.** (zer)kratzen; umkrallen, packen

clay Ton m, Lehm m

clean 1. adj rein; sauber, glatt, eben; sl clean **2.** adv völlig, ganz und gar **3.** reinigen, säubern, putzen; **~ out** reinigen; **~ up** gründlich reinigen; aufräumen

clean·er Rein(e)machefrau f, (Fenster- etc)Putzer m; Reinigungsmittel n, Reiniger m; **take to the ~s** et. zur Reinigung bringen; F j-n ausnehmen

clean·ing: do the ~ sauber machen, putzen; **~ la·dy, ~ wom·an** Putzfrau f

clean·li·ness Reinlichkeit f

clean·ly 1. adv sauber **2.** adj reinlich

cleanse reinigen, säubern

cleans·er Putzmittel n, Reinigungsmittel n, Reiniger m

clear 1. klar; hell; rein; deutlich; frei (of von); ECON Netto..., Rein... **2.** v/t reinigen, säubern; Wald lichten, roden; wegräumen (a. **~ away**); Tisch abräumen; räumen, leeren; Hindernis nehmen; SPORT klären; ECON verzollen; JUR freisprechen; IT löschen; v/i klar or hell werden; METEOR aufklaren; sich verziehen (fog); **~ out** aufräumen; ausräumen, entfernen; F abhauen; **~ up** aufräumen; Verbrechen etc aufklären; METEOR aufklaren

clear·ance Räumung f; TECH lichter Abstand; Freigabe f; **~ sale** ECON Räumungsverkauf m, Ausverkauf m

clear·ing Lichtung f

cleave spalten

cleav·er Hackmesser n

clef MUS Schlüssel m

cleft Spalt m, Spalte f

clem·en·cy Milde f, Nachsicht f

clem·ent mild (a. METEOR)

clench Lippen etc (fest) zusammenpressen; Zähne zusammenbeißen; Faust ballen

cler·gy REL Klerus m, die Geistlichen pl

cler·gy·man REL Geistliche m

clerk Verkäufer(in); (Büro- etc)Angestellte m, f, (Bank-, Post)Beamte m, (-)Beamtin f

clev·er klug, gescheit; geschickt

click 1. Klicken n **2.** v/i klicken; zu-, einschnappen; mit der Zunge schnalzen; v/t klicken or einschnappen lassen; mit der Zunge schnalzen; **~ on** IT anklicken

cli·ent JUR Klient(in), Mandant(in); Kunde m, Kundin f, Auftraggeber(in)

cliff Klippe f, Felsen m

cli·mate Klima n

cli·max Höhepunkt m; Orgasmus m

climb klettern; (er-, be)steigen; **~ (up) a tree** auf e-n Baum klettern

climb·er Kletterer m, Bergsteiger(in); BOT Kletterpflanze f

clinch 1. TECH sicher befestigen; (ver)nieten; boxing: umklammern (v/i clinchen); fig entscheiden; **that ~ed it** damit war die Sache entschieden **2.** boxing: Clinch m

cling (to) festhalten (an dat), sich klammern (an acc); sich (an)schmiegen (an *acc)*

cling·film® *esp Br* Frischhaltefolie *f*

clin·ic Klinik *f*

clin·i·cal klinisch

clink 1. Klirren *n*, Klingen *n*; *sl* Knast *m*
2. klingen *or* klirren (lassen); klimpern mit

clip[1] **1.** ausschneiden; *Schafe etc* scheren **2.** Schnitt *m*; Schur *f*; (*Film- etc*) Ausschnitt *m*; (*Video*)Clip *m*

clip[2] **1.** (Heft-, Büro- *etc*)Klammer *f*; (*Ohr*)Klipp *m* **2.** *a. ~ on* anklammern

clip·per: (*a pair of*) *~s* (e-e) (*Nagel- etc*)-
Schere *f*, Haarschneidemaschine *f*

clip·pings Abfälle *pl*, Schnitzel *pl*; (*Zeitungs- etc*)Ausschnitte *pl*

clit·o·ris ANAT Klitoris *f*

cloak 1. Umhang *m* **2.** *fig* verhüllen

cloak·room *Br* Garderobe *f*; Toilette *f*

clock 1. (*Wand-, Stand-, Turm*)Uhr *f*; *9 o'clock* 9 Uhr **2.** SPORT Zeit stoppen; *~ in, ~ on* einstempeln; *~ out, ~ off* ausstempeln; *~ ra·di·o* Radiowecker *m*

clock·wise im Uhrzeigersinn

clock·work Uhrwerk *n*; *like ~* wie am Schnürchen

clod (Erd)Klumpen *m*

clog 1. (Holz)Klotz *m*; Holzschuh *m* **2.** *a. ~ up* verstopfen

clois·ter ARCH Kreuzgang *m*; REL Kloster *n*

close 1. *adj* geschlossen; knapp (*result etc*); genau, gründlich (*inspection etc*); eng (anliegend); stickig, schwül; eng (*friend*), nah (*relative*); *keep a ~ watch on* scharf im Auge behalten (*acc*) **2.** *adv* eng, nahe, dicht; *~ by* ganz in der Nähe, nahe *or* dicht bei **3.** Ende *n*, (Ab)Schluss *m*; *come or draw to a ~* sich dem Ende nähern; Einfriedung *f* **4.** *v/t* (ab-, ver-, zu)schließen, zumachen; ECON schließen; *Straße* (ab)sperren; *v/i* sich schließen; schließen, zumachen; enden, zu Ende gehen; *~ down Geschäft etc* schließen, *Betrieb* stilllegen; *radio*, TV das Programm beenden, Sendeschluss haben; *~ in* bedrohlich nahe kommen; hereinbrechen (*night*); *~ up* (ab-, ver-, zu)schließen; aufschließen, aufrücken

closed geschlossen, F *pred* zu

clos·et (Wand)Schrank *m*

close·up PHOT, *film*: Großaufnahme *f*

clos·ing date Einsendeschluss *m*

clos·ing time Laden-, Geschäftsschluss *m*; Polizeistunde *f* (*of a pub*)

clos·ure Abschluss *m*; *look for ~* mit et. abschließen wollen

clot 1. Klumpen *m*, Klümpchen *n*; *~ of blood* MED Blutgerinnsel *n* **2.** gerinnen; Klumpen bilden

cloth Stoff *m*, Tuch *n*; Lappen *m*

cloth·bound in Leinen gebunden

clothe (an-, be)kleiden; einkleiden

clothes Kleider *pl*, Kleidung *f*; Wäsche *f*

clothes bas·ket Wäschekorb *m*

clothes·horse Wäscheständer *m*

clothes·line Wäscheleine *f*

clothes peg *Br*, **clothes·pin** Wäscheklammer *f*

cloth·ing (Be)Kleidung *f*

cloud 1. Wolke *f*; *fig* Schatten *m* **2.** (sich) bewölken; (sich) trüben

cloud·burst Wolkenbruch *m*

cloud·less wolkenlos

cloud·y bewölkt; trüb; *fig* unklar

clout F Schlag *m*; POL Einfluss *m*

clove[1] GASTR (Gewürz)Nelke *f*; *~ of garlic* Knoblauchzehe *f*

clo·ven hoof ZO Huf *m* der Paarzeher

clo·ver BOT Klee *m*

clown Clown *m*, Hanswurst *m*

club 1. Keule *f*; Knüppel *m*; SPORT Schlagholz *n*; (*Golf*)Schläger *m*; Klub *m*; *pl card game:* Kreuz *n* **2.** einknüppeln auf (*acc*), niederknüppeln

club·foot MED Klumpfuß *m*

cluck ZO **1.** gackern; glucken **2.** Gackern *n*; Glucken *n*

clue Anhaltspunkt *m*, Fingerzeig *m*, Spur *f*

clump 1. Klumpen *m*; (*Baum- etc -*) Gruppe *f* **2.** trampeln

clum·sy unbeholfen, ungeschickt, plump

clus·ter 1. BOT Traube *f*, Büschel *n*; Haufen *m* **2.** sich drängen

clutch 1. Griff *m*; TECH Kupplung *f*; *fig* Klaue *f* **2.** (er)greifen; umklammern

clut·ter *fig* überladen

c/o *abbr of care of* c/o, (wohnhaft) bei

Co *abbr of company* ECON Gesellschaft *f*

coach 1. Reisebus *m*; *Br* RAIL (Personen)Wagen *m*; Kutsche *f*; *~* (*class*) Economyclass *f*; *~ party* (*Bus*) Reisegruppe *f*; SPORT Trainer(in); PED Nach-

hilfelehrer(in) **2.** SPORT trainieren; PED
j-m Nachhilfeunterricht geben
coach·man Kutscher *m*
co·ag·u·late gerinnen (lassen)
coal (Stein)Kohle *f*; *carry ~s to New-castle* F Br Eulen nach Athen tragen
co·a·li·tion POL Koalition *f*; Bündnis *n*,
Zusammenschluss *m*
coal·mine, coal·pit Kohlengrube *f*
coarse grob; rau; derb; ungeschliffen;
gemein
coast 1. Küste *f* **2.** MAR die Küste ent-langfahren; im Leerlauf (*car*) or im
Freilauf (*bicycle*) fahren; rodeln
coast·er brake Rücktritt(bremse *f*) *m*
coast·guard (Angehörige *m* der) Küs-tenwache *f*
coast·line Küstenlinie *f*, -strich *m*
coat 1. Mantel *m*; ZO Pelz *m*, Fell *n*;
(*Farb- etc*)Überzug *m*, Anstrich *m*,
Schicht *f* **2.** (an)streichen, überziehen,
beschichten
coat hang·er Kleiderbügel *m*
coat·ing (*Farb- etc*)Überzug *m*, An-strich *m*; Schicht *f*; Mantelstoff *m*
coat of arms Wappen(schild *m*, *n*) *n*
coax überreden, beschwatzen
cob Maiskolben *m*
cob·bled: *~ street* Straße *f* mit Kopf-steinpflaster
cob·bler (Flick)Schuster *m*
cob·web Spinn(en)gewebe *n*
co·caine Kokain *n*
cock 1. ZO Hahn *m*; V Schwanz *m* **2.** auf-richten
cock·a·too ZO Kakadu *m*
cock·chaf·er ZO Maikäfer *m*
cock·eyed F schielend; (krumm und)
schief
Cock·ney Cockney *m*, waschechter
Londoner
cock·pit AVIAT Cockpit *n*
cock·roach ZO Schabe *f*
cock·sure F übertrieben selbstsicher
cock·tail Cocktail *m*
cock·y großspurig, anmaßend
co·co BOT Kokospalme *f*
co·coa Kakao *m*
co·co·nut BOT Kokosnuss *f*
co·coon (*Seiden*)Kokon *m*
cod ZO Kabeljau *m*, Dorsch *m*
COD *abbr of* **collect** (*Br* **cash**) *on deliv-ery* per Nachnahme
cod·dle verhätscheln, verzärteln

code 1. Kode *m* **2.** verschlüsseln, chiff-rieren; kodieren
cod·fish → *cod*
cod·ing Kodierung *f*
cod·liv·er oil Lebertran *m*
co·ed·u·ca·tion PED Gemeinschaftser-ziehung *f*
co·ex·ist gleichzeitig *or* nebeneinander
bestehen *or* leben
co·ex·ist·ence Koexistenz *f*
cof·fee Kaffee *m*; *black*(*white*) *~* Kaffee
ohne (mit) Milch; *~ bar* Br Café *n*; Im-bissstube *f*; *~ bean* Kaffeebohne *f*; *~
grind·er* Kaffeemühle *f*; *~ machine*
Kaffeeautomat *m*
cof·fee·mak·er Kaffeemaschine *f*
cof·fee| pot Kaffeekanne *f*; *~ shop* Café
n; Imbissstube *f*; *~ ta·ble* Couchtisch *m*
cof·fin Sarg *m*
cog TECH (Rad)Zahn *m*; → **cog·wheel**
TECH Zahnrad *n*
co·her·ence, co·her·en·cy Zusammen-hang *m*
co·her·ent zusammenhängend
co·he·sion Zusammenhalt *m*
co·he·sive (fest) zusammenhaltend
coif·fure Frisur *f*
coil 1. *a.* *~ up* aufrollen, (auf)wickeln;
sich zusammenrollen **2.** Spirale *f* (*a.*
TECH, MED); Rolle *f*, Spule *f*
coin 1. Münze *f* **2.** prägen
co·in·cide zusammentreffen; überein-stimmen; **co·in·ci·dence** (zufälliges)
Zusammentreffen; Zufall *m*
coin-op·e·rat·ed: *~* (*gas*, *Br petrol*)
pump Münztank(automat) *m*
coke Koks *m* (*a.* F *cocaine*)
Coke® F Coke *n*, Cola *n*, *f*, Coca *n*, *f*
cold 1. kalt **2.** MED Erkältung *f*;
catch (*a*) *~* sich erkälten; *have a ~* er-kältet sein
cold-blood·ed kaltblütig
cold cuts GASTR Aufschnitt *m*
cold-heart·ed kaltherzig
cold·ness Kälte *f*
cold sweat Angstschweiß *m*; *he broke
out in a ~* ihm brach der Angstschweiß
aus
cold war POL kalter Krieg
cold wave METEOR Kältewelle *f*
cole-slaw Krautsalat *m*
col·ic MED Kolik *f*
col·lab·o·rate zusammenarbeiten
col·lab·o·ra·tion Zusammenarbeit *f*; *in*

~ with gemeinsam mit

col·lapse 1. zusammenbrechen (*a. fig*), einstürzen; umfallen; *fig* scheitern **2.** Einsturz *m*; *fig* Zusammenbruch *m*

col·lap·si·ble Klapp..., zusammenklappbar

col·lar 1. Kragen *m*; (*Hunde- etc*)Halsband *n* **2.** beim Kragen packen; *j-n* festnehmen, F schnappen

col·lar·bone ANAT Schlüsselbein *n*

col·league Kollege *m*, Kollegin *f*, Mitarbeiter(in)

col·lect *v/t* (ein)sammeln; *Daten* erfassen; *Geld* kassieren; *j-n or et.* abholen; *Gedanken etc* sammeln; *v/i* sich (ver)sammeln; **col·lect·ed** *fig* gefasst

col·lect·ing box Sammelbüchse *f*

col·lec·tion Sammlung *f*; ECON Eintreibung *f*; REL Kollekte *f*; Abholung *f*

col·lec·tive gesammelt; Sammel...; ~ **bargaining** ECON Tarifverhandlungen

col·lec·tive·ly insgesamt; zusammen

col·lec·tor Sammler(in); Steuereinnehmer *m*; ELECTR Stromabnehmer *m*

col·lege College *n*; Hochschule *f*; höhere Lehranstalt

col·lide zusammenstoßen, kollidieren (*a. fig*)

col·lie·ry Kohlengrube *f*

col·li·sion Zusammenstoß *m*, Kollision *f* (*a. fig*)

col·lo·qui·al umgangssprachlich

co·lon LING Doppelpunkt *m*

colo·nel MIL Oberst *m*

co·lo·ni·al·is·m POL Kolonialismus *m*

col·o·nize kolonisieren, besiedeln

col·o·ny Kolonie *f*

col·o(u)r 1. Farbe *f*; *pl* MIL Fahne *f*; MAR Flagge *f*; *what ~ is ...?* welche Farbe hat ...? **2.** *v/t* färben; anmalen, bemalen, anstreichen; *fig* beschönigen; *v/i* sich (ver)färben; erröten

col·o(u)r-blind farbenblind

col·o(u)red bunt; farbig

col·o(u)r·fast farbecht

col·o(u)r film PHOT Farbfilm *m*

col·o(u)r·ful farbenprächtig; *fig* farbig, bunt

col·o(u)r·ing Färbung *f*; Farbstoff *m*; Gesichtsfarbe *f*

col·o(u)r·less farblos

colt ZO (Hengst)Fohlen *n*

col·umn Säule *f*; PRINT Spalte *f*; MIL Kolonne *f*

col·umn·ist Kolumnist(in)

comb 1. Kamm *m* **2.** kämmen; striegeln

com·bat 1. Kampf *m*; *single ~* Zweikampf *m* **2.** kämpfen gegen, bekämpfen; **com·ba·tant** MIL Kämpfer *m*

com·bi·na·tion Verbindung *f*, Kombination *f*; **com·bine 1.** (sich) verbinden **2.** ECON Konzern *m*; AGR *a.* ~ *harvester* Mähdrescher *m*

com·bus·ti·ble 1. brennbar **2.** Brennstoff *m*, Brennmaterial *n*

com·bus·tion Verbrennung *f*

come kommen; *to ~* künftig, kommend; *~ and go* kommen und gehen; *~ to see* besuchen; *~ about* geschehen, passieren; *~ across* auf *j-n or et.* stoßen; *~ along* mitkommen, mitgehen; *~ apart* auseinanderfallen; *~ away* sich lösen, ab-, losgehen (*button etc*); *~ back* zurückkommen; *~ by s.th.* zu et. kommen; *~ down* herunterkommen (*a. fig*); einstürzen; sinken (*prices*); überliefert werden; *~ down with* F erkranken an (*dat*); *~ for* abholen kommen, kommen wegen; *~ forward* sich melden; *~ from* kommen aus; kommen von; *~ home* nach Hause (*Austrian, Swiss a.* nachhause) kommen; *~ in* hereinkommen; eintreffen (*news*); einlaufen (*train*); *~ in!* herein!; *~ loose* sich ablösen, abgehen; *~ off* ab-, losgehen (*button etc*); *~ on!* los!, vorwärts!, komm!; *~ out* herauskommen; *~ over* vorbeikommen (*visitor*); *~ round* vorbeikommen (*visitor*); wieder zu sich kommen; *~ through* durchkommen; *Krankheit etc* überstehen, überleben; *~ to* sich belaufen auf (*acc*); wieder zu sich kommen; *~ up to* entsprechen (*dat*), heranreichen an (*acc*)

come·back Come-back *n*

co·me·di·an Komiker *m*

com·e·dy Komödie *f*, Lustspiel *n*

come·ly attraktiv, gut aussehend

com·fort 1. Komfort *m*, Bequemlichkeit *f*; Trost *m*; *cold ~* schwacher Trost **2.** trösten

com·for·ta·ble komfortabel, behaglich, bequem; tröstlich

com·fort·er Tröster *m*; *esp Br* Schnuller *m*; Steppdecke *f*

com·fort·less unbequem; trostlos

com·fort sta·tion Bedürfnisanstalt *f*

com·ic komisch; Komödien..., Lust-

spiel...; **com·i·cal** komisch, spaßig
com·ics Comics *pl*, Comic-Hefte *pl*
com·ma LING Komma *n*
com·mand 1. Befehl *m*; Beherrschung *f*;
MIL Kommando *n* **2.** befehlen; MIL
kommandieren; verfügen über (*acc*);
beherrschen
com·mand·er MIL Kommandeur *m*, Befehlshaber *m*; ~ **in chief** MIL Oberbefehlshaber *m*
com·mand·ment REL Gebot *n*
com·mand mod·ule Kommandokapsel *f*
com·man·do MIL Kommando *n*
com·mem·o·rate gedenken (*gen*)
com·mem·o·ra·tion: *in* ~ *of* zum Gedenken *or* Gedächtnis an (*acc*)
com·mem·o·ra·tive Gedenk..., Erinnerungs...
com·ment 1. (*on*) Kommentar *m* (zu);
Bemerkung *f* (zu); Anmerkung *f* (zu); *no* ~*!* kein Kommentar! **2.** *v/i* ~ *on* e-n Kommentar abgeben zu, sich äußern über (*acc*); *v/t* bemerken (*that* dass)
com·men·ta·ry Kommentar *m* (*on* zu)
com·men·ta·tor Kommentator *m*, *radio*, TV *a*. Reporter *m*
com·merce ECON Handel *m*
com·mer·cial 1. ECON Handels..., Geschäfts...; kommerziell, finanziell **2.** *radio*, TV Werbespot *m*, Werbesendung *f*; ~ **art** Gebrauchsgrafik *f*; ~ **art·ist** Gebrauchsgrafiker(in)
com·mer·cial·ize kommerzialisieren
com·mer·cial tel·e·vi·sion Werbefernsehen *n*; kommerzielles Fernsehen
com·mis·e·rate: ~ *with* Mitleid empfinden mit
com·mis·e·ra·tion Mitleid *n* (*for* mit)
com·mis·sion 1. Auftrag *m*; Kommission *f*, Ausschuss *m*; ECON Kommission *f*, Provision *f*; Begehung *f* (*of a crime*) **2.** beauftragen; *et*. in Auftrag geben
com·mis·sion·er Beauftragte *m*, *f*; Kommissar(in)
com·mit anvertrauen, übergeben (*to dat*); JUR *j-n* einweisen (*to* in *acc*); *Verbrechen* begehen; *j-n* verpflichten (*to* zu), *j-n* festlegen (*to* auf *acc*)
com·mit·ment Verpflichtung *f*; Engagement *n*
com·mit·tal JUR Einweisung *f*
com·mit·tee Komitee *n*, Ausschuss *m*

com·mod·i·ty ECON Ware *f*, Artikel *m*
com·mon 1. gemeinsam, gemeinschaftlich; allgemein; alltäglich; gewöhnlich, einfach **2.** Gemeindeland *n*; *in* ~ gemeinsam (*with* mit)
com·mon·er Bürgerliche *m*, *f*
com·mon law (ungeschriebenes englisches) Gewohnheitsrecht
com·mon·place 1. Gemeinplatz *m* **2.** alltäglich; abgedroschen
Com·mons: *the* ~, *the House of* ~ Br PARL das Unterhaus
com·mon sense gesunder Menschenverstand
Com·mon·wealth: *the* ~ (*of Nations*) das Commonwealth
com·mo·tion Aufregung *f*; Aufruhr *m*, Tumult *m*
com·mu·nal Gemeinde...; Gemeinschafts...; **com·mune** Kommune *f*
com·mu·ni·cate *v/t* mitteilen; *v/i* sich besprechen; sich in Verbindung setzen (*with s.o.* mit j-m); (durch e-e Tür) verbunden sein
com·mu·ni·ca·tion Mitteilung *f*; Verständigung *f*, Kommunikation *f*; Verbindung *f*; *pl* Kommunikationsmittel *pl*; Verkehrswege *pl*
com·mu·ni·ca·tions sat·el·lite Nachrichtensatellit *m*
com·mu·ni·ca·tive mitteilsam, gesprächig
Com·mu·nion *a*. *Holy* ~ REL (heilige) Kommunion, Abendmahl *n*
com·mu·nis·m POL Kommunismus *m*
com·mu·nist POL **1.** Kommunist(in) **2.** kommunistisch
com·mu·ni·ty Gemeinschaft *f*; Gemeinde *f*
com·mute JUR Strafe *mildernd* umwandeln; RAIL *etc* pendeln
com·mut·er Pendler(in); ~ **train** Pendlerzug *m*, Nahverkehrszug *m*
com·pact 1. Puderdose *f*; MOT Kleinwagen *m* **2.** *adj* kompakt; eng, klein; knapp (*style*); ~ **car** MOT Kleinwagen *m*; ~ **disk** (*abbr CD*) Compact Disc *f*, CD *f*; ~ **disk play·er** CD-Player *m*, CD-Spieler *m*
com·pan·ion Begleiter(in); Gefährte *m*, Gefährtin *f*; Gesellschafter(in); Handbuch *n*, Leitfaden *m*
com·pan·ion·ship Gesellschaft *f*
com·pa·ny Gesellschaft *f*, ECON *a*. Firma

f; MIL Kompanie *f*; THEA Truppè *f*; **keep
s.o. ~** j-m Gesellschaft leisten
com·pa·ra·ble vergleichbar
com·par·a·tive 1. vergleichend; verhältnismäßig **2.** *a.* **~ degree** LING Kompara-
tiv *m*; **com·par·a·tive·ly** vergleichswei-
se; verhältnismäßig
com·pare 1. *v/t* vergleichen; **~d with** im
Vergleich zu; *v/i* sich vergleichen lassen
2. beyond~, without~ unvergleichlich
com·pa·ri·son Vergleich *m*
com·part·ment Fach *n*; RAIL Abteil *n*
com·pass Kompass *m*; **pair of ~es** Zirkel *m*
com·pas·sion Mitleid *n*
com·pas·sion·ate mitleidig
com·pat·i·ble vereinbar; **be~ (with)** passen (zu), zusammenpassen; IT *etc* kompatibel sein (mit)
com·pat·ri·ot Landsmann *m*, Landsmännin *f*
com·pel (er)zwingen
com·pel·ling bezwingend
com·pen·sate *j-n* entschädigen; *et.* ersetzen; ausgleichen
com·pen·sa·tion Ersatz *m*; Ausgleich
m; Schadenersatz *m*, Entschädigung
f; Bezahlung *f*, Gehalt *n*
com·pere *Br* Conférencier *m*
com·pete sich (mit)bewerben (**for** um);
konkurrieren; SPORT (am Wettkampf)
teilnehmen
com·pe·tence Können *n*, Fähigkeit *f*
com·pe·tent fähig, tüchtig; fachkundig,
sachkundig
com·pe·ti·tion Wettbewerb *m*; Konkurrenz *f*
com·pet·i·tive konkurrierend
com·pet·i·tor Mitbewerber(in); Konkur-
rent(in); SPORT (Wettbewerbs-)Teilneh-
mer(in)
com·pile kompilieren, zusammentra-
gen, zusammenstellen
com·pla·cence, com·pla·cen·cy Selbst-
zufriedenheit *f*, Selbstgefälligkeit *f*;
com·pla·cent selbstzufrieden, selbstgefällig
com·plain sich beklagen *or* beschweren
(**about** über *acc*; **to** bei); klagen (**of**
über *acc*)
com·plaint Klage *f*, Beschwerde *f*; MED
Leiden *n*, *pl* MED *a.* Beschwerden *pl*
com·ple·ment 1. Ergänzung *f* **2.** ergänzen

com·ple·men·ta·ry (sich) ergänzend
com·plete 1. vollständig; vollzählig **2.**
vervollständigen; beenden, abschließen
com·ple·tion Vervollständigung *f*; Abschluss *m*; **~ test** PSYCH Lückentext *m*
com·plex 1. zusammengesetzt; komplex, vielschichtig **2.** Komplex *m* (*a.*
PSYCH)
com·plex·ion Gesichtsfarbe *f*, Teint *m*
com·plex·i·ty Komplexität *f*, Viel-
schichtigkeit *f*
com·pli·ance Einwilligung *f*; Befolgung
f; **in ~ with** gemäß (*dat*)
com·pli·ant willfährig
com·pli·cate komplizieren
com·pli·cat·ed kompliziert
com·pli·ca·tion Komplikation *f* (*a.* MED)
com·plic·i·ty JUR Mitschuld *f*, Mittäter-
schaft *f* (**in** an *dat*)
com·pli·ment 1. Kompliment *n*; Empfehlung *f*; Gruß *m* **2.** *v/t* j-m ein Kompliment *or* Komplimente machen (**on**
über *acc*)
com·ply (with) einwilligen (in *acc*); (*e-e
Abmachung etc*) befolgen
com·po·nent Bestandteil *m*; TECH,
ELECTR Bauelement *m*
com·pose zusammensetzen, -stellen;
MUS komponieren; verfassen; **be ~d
of** bestehen *or* sich zusammensetzen
aus; **~ o.s.** sich beruhigen
com·posed ruhig, gelassen
com·pos·er MUS Komponist(in)
com·po·si·tion Zusammensetzung *f*;
MUS Komposition *f*; PED Aufsatz *m*
com·po·sure Fassung *f*, (Gemüts)Ruhe
f
com·pound[1] Lager *n*; Gefängnishof *m*;
(Tier)Gehege *n*
com·pound[2] **1.** Zusammensetzung *f*;
Verbindung *f*; LING zusammengesetz-
tes Wort **2.** zusammengesetzt; **~ interest** ECON Zinseszinsen *pl* **3.** *v/t* zusammensetzen; steigern, *esp* verschlimmern
com·pre·hend begreifen, verstehen
com·pre·hen·si·ble verständlich
com·pre·hen·sion Verständnis *n*; Be-
griffsvermögen *n*, Verstand *m*; **past ~**
unfassbar, unfasslich
com·pre·hen·sive 1. umfassend **2.** *a.* **~
school** *Br* Gesamtschule *f*
com·press zusammendrücken, -pres-

sen; ~*ed air* Druckluft *f*

com·pres·sion PHYS Verdichtung *f*; TECH Druck *m*

com·prise einschließen, umfassen; bestehen aus

com·pro·mise 1. Kompromiss *m* **2.** *v/t* bloßstellen, kompromittieren; *v/i* e-n Kompromiss schließen

com·pro·mis·ing kompromittierend; verfänglich

com·pul·sion Zwang *m*

com·pul·sive zwingend, Zwangs...; PSYCH zwanghaft

com·pul·so·ry obligatorisch; Pflicht..., Zwangs...

com·punc·tion Gewissensbisse *pl*; Reue *f*; Bedenken *pl*

com·pute berechnen; schätzen

com·put·er Computer *m*, Rechner *m*

com·put·er|-aid·ed computergestützt; ~**con·trolled** computergesteuert

com·put·er| game Computerspiel *n*; ~ **graph·ics** Computergrafik *f*

com·put·er·ize (sich) auf Computer umstellen; computerisieren; mit Hilfe e-s Computers errechnen *or* zusammenstellen

com·put·er| pre·dic·tion Hochrechnung *f*; ~ **sci·ence** Informatik *f*; ~ **sci·en·tist** Informatiker *m*; ~ **vi·rus** IT Computervirus *m*

com·rade Kamerad *m*; (Partei)Genosse *m*

con[1] → *contra*

con[2] F reinlegen, betrügen

con·ceal verbergen; verheimlichen

con·cede zugestehen, einräumen

con·ceit Einbildung *f*, Dünkel *m*

con·ceit·ed eingebildet (*of* auf *acc*)

con·cei·va·ble denkbar, begreiflich

con·ceive *v/i* schwanger werden; *v/t* Kind empfangen; sich *et.* vorstellen *or* denken

con·cen·trate (sich) konzentrieren

con·cept Begriff *m*; Gedanke *m*

con·cep·tion Vorstellung *f*, Begriff *m*; BIOL Empfängnis *f*

con·cern 1. Angelegenheit *f*; Sorge *f*; ECON Geschäft *n*, Unternehmen *n* **2.** betreffen, angehen; beunruhigen

con·cerned besorgt; beteiligt (*in* an *dat*)

con·cern·ing *prp* betreffend, hinsichtlich (*gen*), was ... (*acc*) (an)betrifft

con·cert MUS Konzert *n*

con·cert hall Konzerthalle *f*, -saal *m*

con·ces·sion Zugeständnis *n*; Konzession *f*

con·cil·i·a·to·ry versöhnlich, vermittelnd

con·cise kurz, knapp

con·cise·ness Kürze *f*

con·clude schließen, beenden; *Vertrag etc* abschließen; *et.* folgern, schließen (*from* aus); *to be* ~*d* Schluss folgt

con·clu·sion (Ab)Schluss *m*, Ende *n*; Abschluss *m* (*of a contract etc*); (Schluss)Folgerung *f*; → *jump*

con·clu·sive schlüssig

con·coct (zusammen)brauen; *fig* aushecken, ausbrüten

con·coc·tion Gebräu *n*; *fig* Erfindung *f*

con·crete[1] konkret

con·crete[2] **1.** Beton *m* **2.** Beton... **3.** betonieren

con·cur übereinstimmen

con·cur·rence Zusammentreffen *n*; Übereinstimmung *f*

con·cus·sion MED Gehirnerschütterung *f*

con·demn verurteilen (*a.* JUR); verdammen; für unbrauchbar *or* unbewohnbar *etc* erklären; ~ *to death* JUR zum Tode verurteilen; **con·dem·na·tion** Verurteilung *f* (*a.* JUR); Verdammung *f*

con·den·sa·tion Kondensation *f*; Zusammenfassung *f*

con·dense kondensieren; zusammenfassen

con·densed milk Kondensmilch *f*

con·dens·er TECH Kondensator *m*

con·de·scend sich herablassen

con·de·scend·ing herablassend, gönnerhaft

con·di·ment Gewürz *n*, Würze *f*

con·di·tion 1. Zustand *m*; (*körperlicher or* Gesundheits)Zustand *m*; SPORT Kondition *f*, Form *f*; Bedingung *f*; *pl* Verhältnisse *pl*, Umstände *pl*; *on* ~ *that* unter der Bedingung, dass; *out of* ~ in schlechter Verfassung, in schlechtem Zustand **2.** bedingen; in Form bringen

con·di·tion·al 1. (*on*) bedingt (durch), abhängig (von) **2.** *a.* ~ *clause* LING Bedingungs-, Konditionalsatz *m*; *a.* ~ *mood* LING Konditional *m*

con·do → *condominium*

con·dole kondolieren (*with dat*)

con·do·lence Beileid *n*

con·dom Kondom *n*, *m*

con·do·min·i·um Eigentumswohnanlage *f*; Eigentumswohnung *f*

con·done verzeihen, vergeben

con·du·cive dienlich, förderlich (*to dat*)

con·duct 1. Führung *f*; Verhalten *n*, Betragen *n* **2.** führen; PHYS leiten; MUS dirigieren; **~ed tour** Führung *f* (*of* durch); **con·duc·tor** Führer *m*, Leiter *m*; (*Bus-, Straßenbahn*)Schaffner *m*; RAIL Zugbegleiter *m*; MUS Dirigent *m*; PHYS Leiter *m*; ELECTR Blitzableiter *m*

cone Kegel *m*; GASTR Eistüte *f*; BOT Zapfen *m*

con·fec·tion Konfekt *n*

con·fec·tion·er Konditor *m*

con·fec·tion·e·ry Süßigkeiten *pl*, Süß-, Konditoreiwaren *pl*; Konfekt *n*; Konditorei *f*; Süßwarengeschäft *n*

con·fed·e·ra·cy (Staaten)Bund *m*; **the Confederacy** HIST die Konföderation

con·fed·er·ate 1. verbündet **2.** Verbündete *m*, Bundesgenosse *m* **3.** (sich) verbünden

con·fed·er·a·tion Bund *m*, Bündnis *n*; (Staaten)Bund *m*

con·fer *v/t Titel etc* verleihen (*on dat*); *v/i* sich beraten

con·fe·rence Konferenz *f*

con·fess gestehen; beichten

con·fes·sion Geständnis *n*; REL Beichte *f*

con·fes·sion·al REL Beichtstuhl *m*

con·fes·sor REL Beichtvater *m*

con·fi·dant(e) Vertraute *m* (*f*)

con·fide: **~ s.th. to s.o.** j-m et. anvertrauen; **~ in s.o.** sich j-m anvertrauen

con·fi·dence Vertrauen *n*; Selbstvertrauen *n*; **~ man** → **conman**; **~ trickster** Trickbetrüger *m*

con·fi·dent überzeugt, zuversichtlich

con·fi·den·tial vertraulich

con·fine begrenzen, beschränken; einsperren; **be ~d of** entbunden werden von; **con·fine·ment** Haft *f*; Beschränkung *f*; MED Entbindung *f*

con·firm bestätigen; bekräftigen; REL konfirmieren, firmen

con·fir·ma·tion Bestätigung *f*; REL Konfirmation *f*, Firmung *f*

con·fis·cate beschlagnahmen

con·fis·ca·tion Beschlagnahme *f*

con·flict 1. Konflikt *m*, Zwiespalt *m* **2.** im Widerspruch stehen (**with** zu)

con·flict·ing widersprüchlich, zwiespältig

con·form (sich) anpassen (**to** *dat*, an *acc*)

con·found verwirren, durcheinanderbringen

con·front gegenübertreten, -stehen (*dat*); sich stellen (*dat*); konfrontieren

con·fron·ta·tion Konfrontation *f*

con·fuse verwechseln; verwirren; **confused** verwirrt; verlegen; verworren;

con·fu·sion Verwirrung *f*; Verlegenheit *f*; Verwechslung *f*

con·geal erstarren (lassen); gerinnen (lassen)

con·gest·ed überfüllt; verstopft

con·ges·tion MED Blutandrang *m*; *a.* **traffic ~** Verkehrsstockung *f*, Verkehrsstörung *f*, Verkehrsstau *m*

con·grat·u·late beglückwünschen, j-m gratulieren

con·grat·u·la·tion Glückwunsch *m*; **~s!** ich gratuliere!, herzlichen Glückwunsch!

con·gre·gate (sich) versammeln

con·gre·ga·tion REL Gemeinde *f*

con·gress Kongress *m*; **Congress** PARL der Kongress

Con·gress·man PARL Kongressabgeordnete *m*; **Con·gress·wom·an** PARL Kongressabgeordnete *f*

con·ic, con·i·cal *esp* TECH konisch, kegelförmig

co·ni·fer BOT Nadelbaum *m*

con·jec·ture 1. Vermutung *f* **2.** vermuten

con·ju·gal ehelich

con·ju·gate LING konjugieren, beugen

con·ju·ga·tion LING Konjugation *f*, Beugung *f*

con·junc·tion Verbindung *f*; LING Konjunktion *f*, Bindewort *n*

con·junc·ti·vi·tis MED Bindehautentzündung *f*

con·jure zaubern; *Teufel etc* beschwören; **~ up** heraufbeschwören (*a. fig*)

con·jur·er *esp Br* → **conjuror**

con·jur·ing trick Zauberkunststück *n*

con·jur·or Zauberer *m*, Zauberin *f*, Zauberkünstler(in)

con·man Betrüger *m*; Hochstapler *m*

con·nect verbinden; ELECTR anschließen, zuschalten; RAIL, AVIAT *etc* Anschluss haben (**with** an *acc*)

con·nect·ed verbunden; (logisch) zusammenhängend (*speech etc*); *be well ~* gute Beziehungen haben

con·nec·tion, *Br* **con·nex·ion** Verbindung *f*, Anschluss *m* (*a.* ELECTR, RAIL, AVIAT, TEL); Zusammenhang *m*; *mst pl* Beziehungen *pl*, Verbindungen *pl*; Verwandte *pl*

con·quer erobern; (be)siegen

con·quer·or Eroberer *m*

con·quest Eroberung *f* (*a. fig*); erobertes Gebiet

con·science Gewissen *n*

con·sci·en·tious gewissenhaft; Gewissens...; **con·sci·en·tious·ness** Gewissenhaftigkeit *f*

con·sci·en·tious ob·jec·tor MIL Wehrdienstverweigerer *m*

con·scious MED bei Bewusstsein; bewusst; *be ~ of* sich bewusst sein (*gen*)

con·scious·ness Bewusstsein *n* (*a.* MED)

con·script MIL **1.** einberufen **2.** Wehrpflichtige *m*; **con·scrip·tion** MIL Einberufung *f*; Wehrpflicht *f*

con·se·crate REL weihen; widmen

con·se·cra·tion REL Weihe *f*

con·sec·u·tive aufeinanderfolgend; fortlaufend

con·sent 1. Zustimmung *f* **2.** einwilligen, zustimmen

con·se·quence Folge *f*, Konsequenz *f*; Bedeutung *f*

con·se·quent·ly folglich, daher

con·ser·va·tion Erhaltung *f*; Naturschutz *m*; Umweltschutz *m*; *~ area* (Natur)Schutzgebiet *n*

con·ser·va·tion·ist Naturschützer(in); Umweltschützer(in)

con·ser·va·tive 1. erhaltend; konservativ; vorsichtig **2.** *Conservative* POL Konservative *m*, *f*

con·ser·va·to·ry Treibhaus *n*, Gewächshaus *n*; Wintergarten *m*

con·serve erhalten

con·sid·er *v/t* nachdenken über (*acc*); betrachten als, halten für; sich überlegen, erwägen; in Betracht ziehen, berücksichtigen; *v/i* nachdenken, überlegen

con·sid·e·ra·ble ansehnlich, beträchtlich; **con·sid·e·ra·bly** bedeutend, ziemlich, (sehr) viel

con·sid·er·ate rücksichtsvoll

con·sid·e·ra·tion Erwägung *f*, Überle-

gung *f*; Berücksichtigung *f*; Rücksicht (-nahme) *f*; *take into ~* in Erwägung *or* in Betracht ziehen

con·sid·er·ing in Anbetracht (der Tatsache, dass)

con·sign ECON *Waren* zusenden

con·sign·ment ECON (Waren)Sendung *f*; Zusendung *f*

con·sist: *~ in* bestehen in (*dat*); *~ of* bestehen aus

con·sis·tence, **con·sis·ten·cy** Konsistenz *f*, Beschaffenheit *f*; Übereinstimmung *f*; Konsequenz *f*

con·sis·tent übereinstimmend, vereinbar (*with* mit); konsequent; SPORT *etc*: beständig

con·so·la·tion Trost *m*

con·sole trösten

con·sol·i·date festigen; *fig* zusammenschließen, -legen

con·so·nant LING Konsonant *m*, Mitlaut *m*

con·spic·u·ous deutlich sichtbar; auffallend

con·spi·ra·cy Verschwörung *f*

con·spi·ra·tor Verschwörer *m*

con·spire sich verschwören

con·sta·ble *Br* Polizist *m*

con·stant konstant, gleichbleibend; (be)ständig, (an)dauernd

con·stant-care pa·tient MED Pflegefall *m*

con·ster·na·tion Bestürzung *f*

con·sti·pat·ed MED verstopft

con·sti·pa·tion MED Verstopfung *f*

con·sti·tu·en·cy POL *Br* Wählerschaft *f*; Wahlkreis *m*

con·sti·tu·ent (wesentlicher) Bestandteil; POL Wähler(in)

con·sti·tute ernennen, einsetzen; bilden, ausmachen

con·sti·tu·tion POL Verfassung *f*; Konstitution *f*, körperliche Verfassung

con·sti·tu·tion·al konstitutionell; POL verfassungsmäßig

con·strained gezwungen, unnatürlich

con·strict zusammenziehen

con·stric·tion Zusammenziehung *f*

con·struct bauen, errichten, konstruieren

con·struc·tion Konstruktion *f*; Bau *m*, Bauwerk *n*; *under ~* im Bau (befindlich); *~ site* Baustelle *f*

con·struc·tive konstruktiv

con·struc·tor Erbauer *m*, Konstrukteur *m*

con·sul Konsul *m*

con·su·late Konsulat *n*; **~ gen·e·ral** Generalkonsulat *n*

con·sul gen·e·ral Generalkonsul *m*

con·sult *v/t* konsultieren, um Rat fragen; in *e-m Buch* nachschlagen; *v/i* (sich) beraten

con·sul·tant (fachmännischer) Berater; *Br* Facharzt *m*

con·sul·ta·tion Konsultation *f*, Beratung *f*, Rücksprache *f*

con·sult·ing beratend; **~ hours** *Br* MED Sprechstunde *f*; **~ room** *Br* MED Sprechzimmer *n*

con·sume *v/t* Essen *etc* zu sich nehmen, verzehren (*a. fig*); verbrauchen, konsumieren; zerstören, vernichten

con·sum·er ECON Verbraucher(in); **~ so·ci·e·ty** Konsumgesellschaft *f*

con·sum·mate 1. vollendet 2. vollenden; *Ehe* vollziehen

con·sump·tion Verbrauch *m*

cont *abbr of **continued*** Forts., Fortsetzung *f*; fortgesetzt

con·tact 1. Berührung *f*; Kontakt *m*; Ansprechpartner(in), Kontaktperson *f* (*a.* MED); ***make·s** Verbindungen anknüpfen *or* herstellen 2. sich in Verbindung setzen mit, Kontakt aufnehmen mit; **~ lens** Kontaktlinse *f*, -schale *f*, Haftschale *f*

con·ta·gious MED ansteckend (*a. fig*)

con·tain enthalten; *fig* zügeln, zurückhalten; **con·tain·er** Behälter *m*; ECON Container *m*; **con·tain·er·ize** ECON auf Containerbetrieb umstellen; in Containern transportieren

con·tam·i·nate verunreinigen; infizieren, vergiften; (*a.* radioaktiv) verseuchen; ***radioactively ~d** verstrahlt; **~d soil** Altlasten *pl*; **con·tam·i·na·tion** Verunreinigung *f*; Vergiftung *f*; (*a.* radioaktive) Verseuchung

contd *abbr of **continued*** (→ **cont**)

con·tem·plate (nachdenklich) betrachten; nachdenken über (*acc*); erwägen, beabsichtigen

con·tem·pla·tion (nachdenkliche) Betrachtung; Nachdenken *n*

con·tem·pla·tive nachdenklich

con·tem·po·ra·ry 1. zeitgenössisch 2. Zeitgenosse *m*, Zeitgenossin *f*

con·tempt Verachtung *f*

con·temp·ti·ble verachtenswert

con·temp·tu·ous geringschätzig, verächtlich

con·tend kämpfen, ringen (**for** um; **with** mit); **con·tend·er** *esp* SPORT Wettkämpfer(in)

con·tent[1] Gehalt *m*, Aussage *f*, *pl* Inhalt *m*; (**table of**) **~s** Inhaltsverzeichnis *n*

con·tent[2] 1. zufrieden 2. befriedigen; **~ o.s.** sich begnügen

con·tent·ed zufrieden

con·tent·ment Zufriedenheit *f*

con·test 1. (Wett)Kampf *m*; Wettbewerb *m* 2. sich bewerben um; bestreiten, *a.* JUR anfechten

con·tes·tant Wettkämpfer(in), (Wettkampf)Teilnehmer(in)

con·text Zusammenhang *m*

con·ti·nent Kontinent *m*, Erdteil *m*; **the Continent** *Br* das (europäische) Festland; **con·ti·nen·tal** kontinental, Kontinental…

con·tin·gen·cy Möglichkeit *f*, Eventualität *f*; **~ plan** Notplan *m*

con·tin·gent 1. **be ~ on** abhängen von 2. Kontingent *n* (*a.* MIL)

con·tin·u·al fortwährend, unaufhörlich

con·tin·u·a·tion Fortsetzung *f*; Fortbestand *m*, Fortdauer *f*

con·tin·ue *v/t* fortsetzen, fortfahren mit; beibehalten; **to be ~d** Fortsetzung folgt; *v/i* fortdauern; andauern, anhalten; fortfahren, weitermachen

con·ti·nu·i·ty Kontinuität *f*

con·tin·u·ous ununterbrochen; **~ form** LING Verlaufsform *f*

con·tort verdrehen; verzerren

con·tor·tion Verdrehung *f*; Verzerrung *f*

con·tour Umriss *m*

con·tra wider, gegen

con·tra·band ECON Schmuggelware *f*

con·tra·cep·tion MED Empfängnisverhütung *f*

con·tra·cep·tive MED 1. empfängnisverhütend 2. Verhütungsmittel *n*

con·tract 1. Vertrag *m* 2. (sich) zusammenziehen; sich *e-e Krankheit* zuziehen; e-n Vertrag abschließen; sich vertraglich verpflichten

con·trac·tion Zusammenziehung *f*

con·trac·tor *a.* **building ~** Bauunternehmer *m*

con·tra·dict widersprechen (*dat*)

con·tra·dic·tion Widerspruch *m*

con·tra·dic·to·ry (sich) widersprechend

con·tra·ry 1. entgegengesetzt (*to dat*); gegensätzlich; **~ to expectations** wider Erwarten **2.** Gegenteil *n*; **on the ~** im Gegenteil

con·trast 1. Gegensatz *m*; Kontrast *m* **2.** *v/t* gegenüberstellen, vergleichen; *v/i* sich abheben (**with** von, gegen); im Gegensatz stehen (**with** zu)

con·trib·ute beitragen, beisteuern; spenden (**to** für)

con·tri·bu·tion Beitrag *m*; Spende *f*

con·trib·u·tor Beitragende *m*, *f*; Mitarbeiter(in)

con·trib·u·to·ry beitragend

con·trite zerknirscht

con·trive zustande bringen; es fertig bringen

con·trol 1. Kontrolle *f*, Herrschaft *f*, Macht *f*, Gewalt *f*,. Beherrschung *f*; Aufsicht *f*; TECH Steuerung *f*; *mst pl* TECH Steuervorrichtung *f*; **get** (**have, keep**) **under ~** unter Kontrolle bringen (haben, halten); **get out of ~** außer Kontrolle geraten; **lose ~ of** die Herrschaft *or* Gewalt *or* Kontrolle verlieren über **2.** beherrschen, die Kontrolle haben über (*acc*); *e-r Sache* Herr werden, (erfolgreich) bekämpfen; kontrollieren, überwachen; ECON (staatlich) lenken, *Preise* binden; ELECTR, TECH steuern, regeln, regulieren; **~ desk** ELECTR Schalt-, Steuerpult *n*; **~ pan·el** ELECTR Schalttafel *f*; **~ tow·er** AVIAT Kontrollturm *m*, Tower *m*

con·tro·ver·sial umstritten

con·tro·ver·sy Kontroverse *f*, Streit *m*

con·tuse MED sich *et.* prellen *or* quetschen; **con·tu·sion** MED Prellung *f*, Quetschung *f*

con·va·lesce gesund werden, genesen

con·va·les·cence Rekonvaleszenz *f*, Genesung *f*

con·va·les·cent 1. genesend **2.** Rekonvaleszent(in), Genesende *m*, *f*

con·vene (sich) versammeln; zusammenkommen; *Versammlung* einberufen

con·ve·ni·ence Annehmlichkeit *f*, Bequemlichkeit *f*; *Br* Toilette *f*; **all** (**modern**) **~s** aller Komfort; **at your earliest ~** möglichst bald; **con·ve·ni·ent** bequem; günstig, passend

con·vent REL (Nonnen)Kloster *n*

con·ven·tion Zusammenkunft *f*, Tagung *f*, Versammlung *f*; Abkommen *n*; Konvention *f*, Sitte *f*; **con·ven·tion·al** herkömmlich, konventionell

con·verge konvergieren; zusammenlaufen, -strömen

con·ver·sa·tion Gespräch *n*, Unterhaltung *f*

con·ver·sa·tion·al Unterhaltungs...; **~ English** Umgangsenglisch *n*

con·verse sich unterhalten

con·ver·sion Umwandlung *f*, Verwandlung *f*; Umbau *m*; Umstellung *f* (**to** auf *acc*); REL Bekehrung *f*, Übertritt *m*; MATH Umrechnung *f*; **~ ta·ble** Umrechnungstabelle *f*

con·vert (sich) umwandeln *or* verwandeln; umbauen; umstellen (**to** auf *acc*); REL *etc* (sich) bekehren; MATH umrechnen

con·vert·er ELECTR Umformer *m*

con·vert·i·ble 1. umwandelbar, verwandelbar; ECON konvertierbar **2.** MOT Kabrio(lett) *n*

con·vey befördern, transportieren, bringen; überbringen, übermitteln; *Ideen etc* mitteilen, vermitteln

con·vey·ance Beförderung *f*, Transport *m*; Übermittlung *f*; Verkehrsmittel *n*

con·vey·or belt TECH Förderband *n*

con·vict 1. Verurteilte *m*, *f*; Strafgefangene *m*, *f* **2.** JUR (**of**) überführen (*gen*); verurteilen (*wegen*)

con·vic·tion Überzeugung *f*; JUR Verurteilung *f*

con·vince überzeugen

con·voy 1. MAR Geleitzug *m*, Konvoi *m*; MOT (Wagen)Kolonne *f*; (Geleit-)Schutz *m* **2.** Geleitschutz geben (*dat*), eskortieren

con·vul·sion MED Zuckung *f*, Krampf *m*; **con·vul·sive** MED krampfhaft, krampfartig, konvulsiv

coo ZO gurren (*a. fig*)

cook 1. Koch *m*; Köchin *f* **2.** kochen

cook·book Kochbuch *n*

cook·er *Br* Ofen *m*, Herd *m*

cook·e·ry Kochen *n*; Kochkunst *f*

cook·e·ry book *Br* Kochbuch *n*

cook·ie (süßer) Keks, Plätzchen *n*

cook·ing GASTR Küche *f*

cook·y → **cookie**

cool 1. kühl; *fig* kalt(blütig), gelassen;

abweisend; gleichgültig; F klasse, prima, cool **2.** Kühle *f*; F (Selbst)Beherrschung *f* **3.** (sich) abkühlen; **~ down, ~ off** sich beruhigen

coon F zo Waschbär *m*

coop 1. Hühnerstall *m* **2. ~ up, ~ in** einsperren, einpferchen

co-op F Co-op *m*

co·op·e·rate zusammenarbeiten; mitwirken, helfen

co·op·e·ra·tion Zusammenarbeit *f*; Mitwirkung *f*, Hilfe *f*

co·op·e·ra·tive 1. zusammenarbeitend; kooperativ, hilfsbereit; ECON Gemeinschafts…, Genossenschafts… **2.** *a.* **~ society** Genossenschaft *f*; Co-op *m*, Konsumverein *m*; *a.* **~ store** Co-op *m*, Konsumladen *m*

co·or·di·nate 1. koordinieren, aufeinander abstimmen **2.** koordiniert, gleichgeordnet; **co·or·di·na·tion** Koordinierung *f*, Koordination *f*; harmonisches Zusammenspiel

cop F Bulle *m*

cope: ~ with gewachsen sein (*dat*), fertigwerden mit

cop·i·er Kopiergerät *n*, Kopierer *m*

co·pi·ous reich(lich); weitschweifig

cop·per 1. MIN Kupfer *n*; Kupfermünze *f* **2.** kupfern, Kupfer…

cop·pice, copse Gehölz *n*

cop·y 1. Kopie *f*; Abschrift *f*; Nachbildung *f*; Durchschlag *m*; Exemplar *n*; (*Zeitungs*)Nummer *f*; PRINT Satzvorlage *f*; **fair ~** Reinschrift *f* **2.** kopieren; abschreiben, e-e Kopie anfertigen von; IT Daten übertragen; nachbilden; nachahmen

cop·y·book Schreibheft *n*

cop·y·ing Kopier…

cop·y·right Urheberrecht *n*, Copyright *n*

cor·al zo Koralle *f*

cord 1. Schnur *f* (*a.* ELECTR), Strick *m*; Kordsamt *m* **2.** ver-, zuschnüren

cor·di·al¹ Fruchtsaftkonzentrat *n*; MED Stärkungsmittel *n*

cor·di·al² herzlich

cor·di·al·i·ty Herzlichkeit *f*

cord·less schnurlos

cord·less phone schnurloses Telefon

cor·don 1. Kordon *m*, Postenkette *f* **2. ~ off** abriegeln, absperren

cor·du·roy Kord *m*; (*a pair of*) **~s** (e-e)

Kordhose

core 1. Kerngehäuse *n*; Kern *m*, *fig a.* das Innerste **2.** entkernen

core time ECON Kernzeit *f*

cork 1. Kork(en) *m* **2.** *a.* **~ up** zu-, verkorken; **cork·screw** Korkenzieher *m*

corn¹ 1. Korn *n*, Getreide *n*; *a.* **Indian ~** Mais *m* **2.** pökeln

corn² MED Hühnerauge *n*

cor·ner 1. Ecke *f*; Winkel *m*; *esp* MOT Kurve *f*; soccer: Eckball *m*, Ecke *f*; *fig* schwierige Lage, Klemme *f* **2.** Eck… **3.** in die Ecke (*fig* Enge) treiben; **~ kick** *soccer:* Eckball *m*, Eckstoß *m*; **~ shop** *Br* Tante-Emma-Laden *m*

cor·net MUS Kornett *n*; *Br* GASTR Eistüte *f*

corn·flakes Cornflakes *pl*

cor·nice ARCH Gesims *n*, Sims *m*

cor·o·na·ry 1. ANAT Koronar… **2.** F MED Herzinfarkt *m*

cor·o·na·tion Krönung *f*

cor·o·net Adelskrone *f*

cor·po·ral MIL Unteroffizier *m*

cor·po·ral pun·ish·ment körperliche Züchtigung

cor·po·rate gemeinsam; Firmen…

cor·po·ra·tion JUR Körperschaft *f*; Stadtverwaltung *f*; ECON (Aktien)Gesellschaft *f*

corpse Leichnam *m*, Leiche *f*

cor·pu·lent beleibt

cor·ral 1. Korral *m*, Hürde *f*, Pferch *m* **2.** Vieh in e-n Pferch treiben

cor·rect 1. korrekt, richtig, *a.* genau (*time*) **2.** korrigieren, verbessern, berichtigen

cor·rec·tion Korrektur *f*, Verbess(e)rung *f*; Bestrafung *f*

cor·rect·ness Richtigkeit *f*

cor·re·spond (with, to) entsprechen (*dat*), übereinstimmen (mit); korrespondieren (**with** mit)

cor·re·spon·dence Übereinstimmung *f*; Korrespondenz *f*, Briefwechsel *m*; **~ course** Fernkurs *m*

cor·re·spon·dent 1. entsprechend **2.** Briefpartner(in); Korrespondent(in)

cor·re·spon·ding entsprechend

cor·ri·dor Korridor *m*, Gang *m*

cor·rob·o·rate bekräftigen, bestätigen

cor·rode zerfressen; CHEM korrodieren; rosten; **cor·ro·sion** CHEM Korrosion *f*; Rost *m*; **cor·ro·sive** CHEM ätzend; *fig* nagend, zersetzend

cor·ru·gat·ed i·ron Wellblech n

cor·rupt 1. korrupt, bestechlich, käuflich; *moralisch* verdorben **2.** bestechen; *moralisch* verderben

cor·rupt·i·ble korrupt, bestechlich, käuflich

cor·rup·tion Verdorbenheit f; Unredlichkeit f; Korruption f; Bestechlichkeit f; Bestechung f

cor·set Korsett n

cos·met·ic 1. kosmetisch, Schönheits… **2.** kosmetisches Mittel, Schönheitsmittel n

cos·me·ti·cian Kosmetiker(in)

cos·mo·naut Kosmonaut m, (Welt-)Raumfahrer m

cos·mo·pol·i·tan 1. kosmopolitisch **2.** Weltbürger(in)

cost 1. Preis m; Kosten pl; Schaden m **2.** kosten

cost·ly kostspielig; teuer erkauft

cost of liv·ing Lebenshaltungskosten pl

cos·tume Kostüm n, Kleidung f, Tracht f

co·sy Br → **cozy**

cot Feldbett n; Br Kinderbett n

cot·tage Cottage n, (kleines) Landhaus; Ferienhaus n, Ferienhäuschen n

cot·ton 1. Baumwolle f; Baumwollstoff m; (Baumwoll)Garn n, (Baumwoll-)Zwirn m; (Verband)Watte f **2.** baumwollen, Baumwoll…

cot·ton·wood BOT e-e amer. Pappel

cot·ton wool Br (Verband)Watte f

couch Couch f, Sofa n; Liege f

cou·chette RAIL Liegewagenplatz m; a. **~ coach** Liegewagen m

cou·gar ZO Puma m

cough 1. Husten m **2.** husten

coun·cil Rat m, Ratsversammlung f; **~ house** Br gemeindeeigenes Wohnhaus

coun·cil·(l)or Ratsmitglied n, Stadtrat m, Stadträtin f

coun·sel 1. Beratung f; Rat(schlag) m; Br JUR (Rechts)Anwalt m; **~ for the defense** (Br **defence**) Verteidiger m; **~ for the prosecution** Anklagevertreter m **2.** j-m raten; zu et. raten; **~ing center** (Br **~ling centre**) Beratungsstelle f

coun·sel·(l)or (Berufs- etc)Berater(in); JUR (Rechts)Anwalt m

count¹ Graf m

count² 1. Zählung f; JUR Anklagepunkt m **2.** v/t (ab-, auf-, aus-, nach-, zusammen)zählen; aus-, berechnen; *fig* halten für, betrachten als; v/i zählen; gelten; **~ down** Geld hinzählen; den Count-down durchführen für, letzte (Start)Vorbereitungen treffen für; **~ on** zählen auf (acc), sich verlassen auf (acc), sicher rechnen mit

count·down Count-down m, n, letzte (Start)Vorbereitungen pl

coun·te·nance Gesichtsausdruck m; Fassung f, Haltung f

count·er¹ TECH Zähler m; Br Spielmarke f

coun·ter² Ladentisch m; Theke f; (Bank-, Post®)Schalter m

coun·ter³ 1. (ent)gegen, Gegen… **2.** entgegentreten (dat), entgegnen (dat), bekämpfen; abwehren

coun·ter·act entgegenwirken (dat); neutralisieren

coun·ter·bal·ance 1. Gegengewicht n **2.** ein Gegengewicht bilden zu, ausgleichen

coun·ter·clock·wise entgegen dem Uhrzeigersinn

coun·ter·es·pi·o·nage Spionageabwehr f

coun·ter·feit 1. falsch, gefälscht **2.** Fälschung f **3.** Geld, Unterschrift etc fälschen; **~ mon·ey** Falschgeld n

coun·ter·foil Kontrollabschnitt m

coun·ter·mand Befehl etc widerrufen; Ware abbestellen

coun·ter·pane Tagesdecke f

coun·ter·part Gegenstück n; genaue Entsprechung

coun·ter·sign gegenzeichnen

coun·tess Gräfin f

count·less zahllos

coun·try 1. Land n, Staat m; Gegend f, Landschaft f; **in the ~** auf dem Lande **2.** Land…, ländlich

coun·try·man Landbewohner m; Bauer m; a. **fellow ~** Landsmann m

coun·try road Landstraße f

coun·try·side (ländliche) Gegend; Landschaft f

coun·try·wom·an Landbewohnerin f; Bäuerin f; a. **fellow ~** Landsmännin f

coun·ty (Land)Kreis m; Br Grafschaft f; **~ seat** Kreis(haupt)stadt f; **~ town** Br Grafschaftshauptstadt f

coup Coup m; Putsch m

cou·ple 1. Paar *n*; *a ~ of* F ein paar **2.** (zusammen)koppeln; TECH kuppeln; ZO (sich) paaren

cou·pon Gutschein *m*; Kupon *m*, Bestellzettel *m*

cour·age Mut *m*

cou·ra·geous mutig, beherzt

cou·ri·er Kurier *m*; Eilbote *m*; Reiseleiter *m*

course AVIAT, MAR Kurs *m* (*a. fig*); SPORT (*Renn*)Bahn *f*, (*Renn*)Strecke *f*, (*Golf*)Platz *m*; Verlauf *m*; GASTR Gang *m*; Reihe *f*, Zyklus *m*; Kurs *m*, Lehrgang *m*; *of ~* natürlich, selbstverständlich; *the ~ of events* der Gang der Ereignisse, der Lauf der Dinge

court 1. Hof *m*; kleiner Platz; SPORT Platz *m*, (Spiel)Feld *n*; JUR Gericht *n*, Gerichtshof *m*; *go to ~* JUR prozessieren; *take s.o. to ~* JUR gegen j-n prozessieren; j-m den Prozess machen **2.** *j-m* den Hof machen; werben um

cour·te·ous höflich; **cour·te·sy** Höflichkeit *f*; *by ~ of* mit freundlicher Genehmigung von (*or gen*)

court·house Gerichtsgebäude *n*

court·ier Höfling *m*

court·ly höfisch; höflich

court mar·tial MIL Kriegsgericht *n*

court-mar·tial MIL vor ein Kriegsgericht stellen

court·room Gerichtssaal *m*

court·ship Werben *n*

court·yard Hof *m*

cous·in Cousin *m*, Vetter *m*; Cousine *f*, Kusine *f*

cove kleine Bucht

cov·er 1. Decke *f*; Deckel *m*; Buchdeckel *m*, Einband *m*; Umschlag *m*; Titelseite *f*; Hülle *f*; Überzug *m*, Bezug *m*; Schutzhaube *f*, Schutzplatte *f*; Abdeckhaube *f*; Briefumschlag *m*; GASTR Gedeck *n*; Deckung *f*; Schutz *m*; *fig* Tarnung *f*; *take ~* in Deckung gehen; *under plain ~* in neutralem Umschlag; *under separate ~* mit getrennter Post **2.** (be-, zu)decken; einschlagen, einwickeln; verbergen, decken, schützen; ECON (ab)decken; versichern; *Thema* erschöpfend behandeln; *radio*, TV berichten über (*acc*); sich über *e-e Fläche etc* erstrecken; *Strecke* zurücklegen; SPORT *Gegenspieler* decken; *j-n* beschatten; *~ up* ab-, zudecken; *fig* verheimlichen, vertuschen; *~ up for s.o.* j-n decken

cov·er·age Berichterstattung *f* (*of* über *acc*)

cov·er girl Covergirl *n*, Titelblattmädchen *n*

cov·er·ing Decke *f*; Überzug *m*; Hülle *f*; (*Fußboden*)Belag *m*

cov·er sto·ry Titelgeschichte *f*

cow[1] ZO Kuh *f*

cow[2] einschüchtern

cow·ard 1. feig(e) **2.** Feigling *m*

cow·ard·ice Feigheit *f*

cow·ard·ly feig(e)

cow·boy Cowboy *m*

cow·er kauern; sich ducken

cow·herd Kuhhirt *m*

cow·hide Rind(s)leder *n*

cow·house Kuhstall *m*

cowl Mönchskutte *f*; Kapuze *f*; TECH Schornsteinkappe *f*

cow·shed Kuhstall *m*

cow·slip BOT Schlüsselblume *f*; Sumpfdotterblume *f*

cox, cox·swain Bootsführer *m*; *rowing*: Steuermann *m*

coy schüchtern, scheu

coy·ote ZO Kojote *m*, Präriewolf *m*

co·zy 1. behaglich, gemütlich **2.** → *egg cosy, tea cosy*

CPU *abbr of* *central processing unit* IT Zentraleinheit *f*

crab ZO Krabbe *f*, Taschenkrebs *m*

crack 1. Knall *m*; Sprung *m*, Riss *m*; Spalt(e) *f*, Ritze *f*; (heftiger) Schlag *m* **2.** erstklassig **3.** *v/i* krachen, knallen, knacken; (zer)springen; überschnappen (*voice*); *a. ~ up* zusammenbrechen; F *~ up* überschnappen; *get ~ing* F loslegen; *v/t* knallen mit (*Peitsche*), knacken mit (*Fingern*); zerbrechen; *Nuss*, F *Kode, Safe etc* knacken; *~ a joke* e-n Witz reißen; **crack·er** GASTR Cracker *m*, Kräcker *m*; Schwär·mer *m*, Knallfrosch *m*, Knallbonbon *m*, *n*

crack·le knattern, knistern, prasseln

cra·dle 1. Wiege *f* **2.** wiegen; betten

craft[1] Boot(e *pl*) *n*, Schiff(e *pl*) *n*; Flugzeug(e *pl*) *n*; (Welt)Raumfahrzeug(e *pl*) *n*

craft[2] Handwerk *n*, Gewerbe *n*; Schlauheit *f*, List *f*

crafts·man (Kunst)Handwerker *m*

craft·y gerissen, listig, schlau

crag Klippe f, Felsenspitze f

cram v/t (voll)stopfen; nudeln, mästen; mit j-m pauken; v/i pauken, büffeln (**for** für)

cramp 1. MED Krampf m; TECH Klammer f; fig Fessel f **2.** einengen, hemmen

cran·ber·ry BOT Preiselbeere f

crane[1] TECH Kran m

crane[2] **1.** ZO Kranich m **2.** den Hals recken; ~ **one's neck** sich den Hals verrenken (**for** nach)

crank 1. TECH Kurbel f; TECH Schwengel m; F Spinner m, komischer Kauz **2.** (an)kurbeln

crank·shaft TECH Kurbelwelle f

crank·y wack(e)lig; verschroben; schlecht gelaunt

cran·ny Riss m, Ritze f

crape Krepp m, Flor m

crash 1. Krach m, Krachen n; MOT Unfall m, Zusammenstoß m; AVIAT Absturz m; ECON Zusammenbruch m, (Börsen)Krach m **2.** v/t zertrümmern; e-n Unfall haben mit; AVIAT abstürzen mit; v/i krachend einstürzen, zusammenkrachen; esp ECON zusammenbrechen; krachen (**against, into** gegen); MOT zusammenstoßen, verunglücken; AVIAT abstürzen **3.** Schnell..., Sofort...; ~ **bar·ri·er** MOT Leitplanke f; ~ **course** Schnell-, Intensivkurs m; ~ **di·et** radikale Schlankheitskur; ~ **hel·met** Sturzhelm m

crash-land AVIAT e-e Bruchlandung machen (mit); **crash land·ing** AVIAT Bruchlandung f

crate (Latten)Kiste f

cra·ter Krater m; Trichter m

crave sich sehnen (**for, after** nach)

crav·ing heftiges Verlangen

craw·fish → **crayfish**

crawl 1. Kriechen n **2.** kriechen; krabbeln; kribbeln; wimmeln (**with** von); swimming: kraulen; **it makes my skin** ~ F mir läuft e-e Gänsehaut über den Rücken

cray·fish ZO Flusskrebs m

cray·on Zeichen-, Buntstift m

craze Verrücktheit f, F Fimmel m; **be the** ~ Mode sein

cra·zy verrückt (**about** nach)

creak knarren, quietschen

cream 1. GASTR Rahm m, Sahne f; Creme f; fig Auslese f, Elite f **2.** creme

(-farben); **cream·y** sahnig; weich

crease 1. (Bügel)Falte f **2.** (zer)knittern

cre·ate (er)schaffen; hervorrufen; verursachen

cre·a·tion Schöpfung f

cre·a·tive schöpferisch

cre·a·tor Schöpfer m

crea·ture Geschöpf n; Kreatur f

crèche (Kinder)Krippe f; (Weihnachts)Krippe f

cre·den·tials Beglaubigungsschreiben n; Referenzen pl; Zeugnis n; Ausweis m, Ausweispapiere pl

cred·i·ble glaubwürdig

cred·it 1. Glaube(n) m; Ruf m, Ansehen n; Verdienst n; ECON Kredit m; Guthaben n; ~ (**side**) Kredit(seite f) n, Haben n; **on** ~ auf Kredit **2.** j-m glauben; j-m trauen; ECON gutschreiben; ~ **s.o. with s.th.** j-m et. zutrauen; j-m et. zuschreiben

cred·i·ta·ble achtbar, ehrenvoll (**to** für)

cred·it card ECON Kreditkarte f

cred·i·tor ECON Gläubiger m

cred·its film: Vorspann m, Nachspann m

cred·it·wor·thy ECON kreditwürdig

cred·u·lous leichtgläubig

creed REL Glaubensbekenntnis n

creek Bach m; Br kleine Bucht

creep kriechen; schleichen (a. fig); ~ **in** (sich) hinein- or hereinschleichen; sich einschleichen (mistake etc); **it makes my flesh** ~ mir läuft e-e Gänsehaut über den Rücken

creep·er BOT Kriech-, Kletterpflanze f

creep·y unheimlich

cre·mate verbrennen, einäschern

cres·cent Halbmond m

cress BOT Kresse f

crest ZO Haube f, Büschel n; (Hahnen-)Kamm m; Bergrücken m, Kamm m; (Wellen)Kamm m; Federbusch m; **family** ~ Familienwappen n

crest·fal·len niedergeschlagen

cre·vasse GEOL (Gletscher)Spalte f

crev·ice GEOL Riss m, Spalte f

crew AVIAT, MAR Besatzung f, Crew f, MAR Mannschaft f

crib 1. (Futter)Krippe f; Kinderbettchen n; esp Br (Weihnachts)Krippe f; F PED Spickzettel m **2.** F abschreiben, spicken

crick: **a** ~ **in one's back** (**neck**) ein steifer Rücken (Hals)

crick·et¹ zo Grille f

crick·et² SPORT Kricket n

crime JUR Verbrechen n; *coll* Verbrechen pl; ~ **nov·el** Kriminalroman m

crim·i·nal 1. kriminell; Kriminal…, Straf… 2. Verbrecher(in), Kriminelle m, f

crimp kräuseln

crim·son karmesinrot; puterrot

cringe sich ducken

crin·kle 1. Falte f, Fältchen n 2. (sich) kräuseln; knittern

crip·ple 1. Krüppel m 2. zum Krüppel machen; *fig* lähmen

cri·sis Krise f

crisp knusp(e)rig, mürbe; frisch, knackig (*vegetable*); scharf, frisch (*air*); kraus (*hair*)

crisp·bread Knäckebrot n

crisps a. **potato ~** Br (Kartoffel)Chips pl

criss-cross 1. Netz n sich schneidender Linien 2. kreuz und quer ziehen durch; kreuz und quer (ver)laufen

cri·te·ri·on Kriterium n

crit·ic Kritiker(in)

crit·i·cal kritisch; bedenklich

crit·i·cis·m Kritik f (**of** an dat)

crit·i·cize kritisieren; kritisch beurteilen; tadeln

cri·tique Kritik f, Besprechung f, Rezension f

croak zo krächzen; quaken (*both a. fig*)

cro·chet 1. Häkelei f; Häkelarbeit f 2. häkeln

crock·e·ry Geschirr n

croc·o·dile zo Krokodil n

cro·ny F alter Freund

crook 1. Krümmung f; Hirtenstab m; F Gauner m 2. (sich) krümmen *or* biegen; **crook·ed** gekrümmt krumm; F unehrlich, betrügerisch

croon schmachtend singen; summen

croon·er Schnulzensänger(in)

crop 1. AGR (Feld)Frucht f; Ernte f; zo Kropf m; kurzer Haarschnitt; kurz geschnittenes Haar 2. zo abfressen, abweiden; *Haar* kurz schneiden; ~ **up** *fig* plötzlich auftauchen

cross 1. Kreuz n (*a. fig*); BIOL Kreuzung f; *soccer:* Flanke f 2. böse, ärgerlich 3. (sich) kreuzen; *Straße* überqueren; *Plan etc* durchkreuzen; BIOL kreuzen;

~ **off**, ~ **out** ausstreichen, durchstreichen; ~ **o.s.** sich bekreuzigen; ~ **one's arms** die Arme verschränken; ~ **one's legs** die Beine übereinanderschlagen; **keep one's fingers ~ed** den Daumen drücken

cross·bar SPORT Tor-, Querlatte f

cross·breed Mischling m, Kreuzung f

cross-coun·try Querfeldein…, Gelände…; ~ **skiing** Skilanglauf m

cross-ex·am·i·na·tion JUR Kreuzverhör n; **cross-ex·am·ine** JUR ins Kreuzverhör nehmen

cross-eyed: be ~ schielen

cross·ing (*Straßen- etc*)Kreuzung f; Straßenübergang m; Br Fußgängerüberweg m; MAR Überfahrt f

cross·road Querstraße f

cross·roads (*Straßen*)Kreuzung f; *fig* Scheideweg m

cross-sec·tion Querschnitt m

cross·walk Fußgängerüberweg m

cross·wise kreuzweise

cross·word (**puz·zle**) Kreuzworträtsel n

crotch ANAT Schritt m

crotch·et MUS Br Viertelnote f

crouch 1. sich ducken 2. Hockstellung f

crow 1. zo Krähe f; Krähen n 2. krähen

crow·bar TECH Brecheisen n

crowd 1. (Menschen)Menge f; Masse f; Haufen m 2. sich drängen; *Straßen etc* bevölkern; vollstopfen

crowd·ed überfüllt, voll

crown 1. Krone f 2. krönen; *Zahn* überkronen; **to ~ it all** zu allem Überfluss

cru·cial entscheidend, kritisch

cru·ci·fix REL Kruzifix n

cru·ci·fix·ion REL Kreuzigung f

cru·ci·fy REL kreuzigen

crude roh, unbearbeitet; *fig* roh, grob

crude (oil) Rohöl n

cru·el grausam; roh, gefühllos

cru·el·ty Grausamkeit f; ~ **to animals** Tierquälerei f; **society for the prevention of ~ to animals** Tierschutzverein m; ~ **to children** Kindesmisshandlung f

cru·et Essig-, Ölfläschchen n

cruise 1. Kreuzfahrt f, Seereise f 2. kreuzen, e-e Kreuzfahrt *or* Seereise machen; AVIAT, MOT mit Reisegeschwindigkeit fliegen *or* fahren; ~ **mis·sile** MIL Marschflugkörper m

cruis·er Kreuzfahrtschiff n; MIL MAR

Kreuzer *m*; (Funk)Streifenwagen *m*

crumb Krume *f*, Krümel *m*

crum·ble zerkrümeln, zerbröckeln

crum·ple *v/t* zerknittern; *v/i* knittern; zusammengedrückt werden; **~ zone** MOT Knautschzone *f*

crunch geräuschvoll (zer)kauen; knirschen

cru·sade HIST Kreuzzug *m* (*a. fig*)

crush 1. Gedränge *n*; **have a ~ on s.o.** für j-n schwärmen, F in j-n verknallt sein **2.** *v/t* zerquetschen, zermalmen, zerdrücken; TECH zerkleinern, zermahlen; auspressen; *fig* nieder-, zerschmettern, vernichten; *v/i* sich drängen; **~ bar·ri·er** Barriere *f*, Absperrung *f*

crust (Brot)Kruste *f*, (Brot)Rinde *f*

crus·ta·cean ZO Krebs-, Krusten-, Schalentier *n*

crust·y krustig

crutch Krücke *f*

cry 1. Schrei *m*, Ruf *m*; Geschrei *n*; Weinen *n* **2.** schreien, rufen (*for* nach); weinen; heulen, jammern

crypt Gruft *f*, Krypta *f*

crys·tal Kristall *m*; Uhrglas *n*

crys·tal·line kristallen

crys·tal·lize kristallisieren

cub ZO Junge *n*

cube Würfel *m* (*a. MATH*); PHOT Blitzwürfel *m*; MATH Kubikzahl *f*

cube root MATH Kubikwurzel *f*

cu·bic, cu·bi·cal würfelförmig; kubisch; Kubik...

cu·bi·cle Kabine *f*

cuck·oo ZO Kuckuck *m*

cu·cum·ber BOT Gurke *f*; **(as) cool as a ~** F eiskalt, kühl und gelassen

cud AGR wiedergekäutes Futter; **chew the ~** wiederkäuen; *fig* überlegen

cud·dle *v/t* an sich drücken; schmusen mit; *v/i:* **~ up** sich kuscheln *or* schmiegen (*to* an *acc*)

cud·gel 1. Knüppel *m* **2.** prügeln

cue[1] THEA *etc* Stichwort *n* (*a. fig*); *fig* Wink *m*

cue[2] *billiards:* Queue *n*

cuff[1] Manschette *f*; (Hosen-, *Br* Ärmel-) Aufschlag *m*

cuff[2] **1.** Klaps *m* **2.** j-m e-n Klaps geben

cuff link Manschettenknopf *m*

cui·sine GASTR Küche *f*

cul·mi·nate gipfeln (*in* in *dat*)

cu·lottes (*a pair of*) ein) Hosenrock

cul·prit Schuldige *m*, *f*, Täter(in)

cul·ti·vate AGR anbauen, bebauen; kultivieren; *Freundschaft etc* pflegen

cul·ti·vat·ed AGR bebaut; *fig* gebildet, kultiviert

cul·ti·va·tion AGR Kultivierung *f*, Anbau *m*; *fig* Pflege *f*

cul·tu·ral kulturell; Kultur...

cul·ture Kultur *f* (*a. BIOL*); ZO Zucht *f*

cul·tured kultiviert; gezüchtet; Zucht...

cum·ber·some lästig, hinderlich; klobig

cu·mu·la·tive sich (an)häufend, anwachsend; Zusatz...

cun·ning 1. schlau, listig **2.** List *f*, Schlauheit *f*

cup 1. Tasse *f*; Becher *m*; Schale *f*; Kelch *m*; SPORT Cup *m*, Pokal *m* **2.** *die Hand* hohl machen; **she ~ped her chin in her hand** sie stützte das Kinn in die Hand

cup·board (Geschirr-, Speise-, *Br a.* Wäsche-, Kleider)Schrank *m*

cup·board bed Schrankbett *n*

cup fi·nal SPORT Pokalendspiel *n*

cu·po·la ARCH Kuppel *f*

cup tie SPORT Pokalspiel *n*

cup win·ner SPORT Pokalsieger *m*

cur Köter *m*; Schurke *m*

cu·ra·ble MED heilbar

cu·rate REL Hilfsgeistliche *m*

cu·ra·tive heilkräftig; **~ power** Heilkraft *f*

curb 1. Kandare *f* (*a. fig*); Bordstein *m* **2.** an die Kandare legen (*a. fig*); *fig* zügeln

curd *a. pl* Dickmilch *f*, Quark *m*

cur·dle *v/t Milch* gerinnen lassen; *v/i* gerinnen, dick werden; **the sight made my blood ~** bei dem Anblick erstarrte mir das Blut in den Adern

cure 1. MED Kur *f*; (Heil)Mittel *n*; Heilung *f* **2.** MED heilen; GASTR pökeln; räuchern; trocknen

cur·few MIL Ausgangsverbot *n*, -sperre *f*

cu·ri·o Rarität *f*

cu·ri·os·i·ty Neugier *f*; Rarität *f*

cu·ri·ous neugierig; wissbegierig; seltsam, merkwürdig

curl 1. Locke *f* **2.** (sich) kräuseln *or* locken; **curl·er** Lockenwickler *m*; **curl·y** gekräuselt; gelockt, lockig

cur·rant BOT Johannisbeere *f*; GASTR Korinthe *f*

cur·ren·cy ECON Währung *f*; **foreign ~** Devisen *pl*

cur·rent 1. laufend; gegenwärtig, aktuell; üblich, gebräuchlich; **~ events** Tagesereignisse pl **2.** Strömung f, Strom m (both a. fig); ELECTR Strom m; **~ account** Br ECON Girokonto n

cur·ric·u·lum Lehr-, Stundenplan m; **~ vi·tae** Lebenslauf m

cur·ry[1] GASTR Curry m, n

cur·ry[2] Pferd striegeln

curse 1. Fluch m, Verwünschung f **2.** (ver)fluchen, verwünschen

curs·ed verflucht

cur·sor IT Cursor m

cur·so·ry flüchtig, oberflächlich

curt knapp; barsch, schroff

cur·tail Ausgaben etc kürzen; Rechte beschneiden

cur·tain 1. Vorhang m, Gardine f; **draw the~s** die Vorhänge auf- or zuziehen **2.** **~ off** mit Vorhängen abteilen

curt·s(e)y 1. Knicks m **2.** knicksen (**to** vor dat)

cur·va·ture Krümmung f

curve 1. Kurve f; Krümmung f, Biegung f **2.** (sich) krümmen or biegen

cush·ion 1. Kissen n, Polster n **2.** polstern; Stoß etc dämpfen

cuss 1. Fluch m **2.** (ver)fluchen

cus·tard Eiercreme f, Vanillesoße f

cus·to·dy JUR Haft f; Sorgerecht n

cus·tom Brauch m, Gewohnheit f; ECON Kundschaft f

cus·tom·a·ry üblich

cus·tom-built nach Kundenangaben gefertigt

cus·tom·er Kunde m, Kundin f, Auftraggeber(in)

cus·tom house Zollamt n

cus·tom-made maßgefertigt, Maß...

cus·toms Zoll m; **~ clear·ance** Zollabfertigung f; **~ of·fi·cer, ~ of·fi·cial** Zollbeamte m

cut 1. Schnitt m; MED Schnittwunde f; GASTR Schnitte f, Stück n; (Zu)Schnitt m (clothes); TECH Schnitt m, Schliff m; Haarschnitt m; fig Kürzung f, Senkung f; cards: Abheben n **2.** schneiden; ab-, an-, auf-, aus-, be-, durch-, zer-, zuschneiden; Edelstein etc schleifen; Gras mähen, Bäume fällen, Holz hacken; MOT Kurve schneiden; Löhne etc kürzen; Preise herabsetzen, senken; Karten abheben; **~ one's teeth** Zähne bekommen, zahnen; **~ s.o. (dead)** fig F

j-n schneiden; **~ s.o.** or **s.th. short** j-n or et. unterbrechen, j-m ins Wort fallen; **~ across** quer durch ... gehen; **~ back** Pflanze beschneiden, stutzen; einschränken; **~ down** Bäume fällen; verringern, einschränken, reduzieren; **~ in** F sich einmischen, unterbrechen; **~ in on s.o.** MOT j-n schneiden; **~ off** abschneiden; unterbrechen, trennen; Strom etc sperren; **~ out** (her)ausschneiden; Kleid etc zuschneiden; **be ~ out for** wie geschaffen sein für; **~ up** zerschneiden

cut·back Kürzung f

cute F schlau; niedlich, süß

cu·ti·cle Nagelhaut f

cut·le·ry (Ess)Besteck n

cut·let GASTR Kotelett n; (Kalbs-, Schweine)Schnitzel n; Hacksteak n

cut-off date Stichtag m

cut-price, cut-rate ECON herabgesetzt, ermäßigt; Billig...

cut·ter Zuschneider m; (Glas-, Diamant)Schleifer m; Schneidemaschine f, -werkzeug n; film: Cutter(in); MAR Kutter m

cut-throat 1. Mörder m; Killer m **2.** mörderisch

cut·ting 1. schneidend; scharf; TECH Schneid(e)..., Fräs... **2.** Schneiden n; BOT Steckling m; esp Br Ausschnitt m

cut·tings Schnipsel pl; Späne pl

cut·ting torch TECH Schneidbrenner m

Cy·ber·space → virtual reality

cy·cle[1] Zyklus m; Kreis(lauf) m

cy·cle[2] **1.** Fahrrad n **2.** Rad fahren

cy·cle| path, ~ track (Fahr)Radweg m

cy·cling Radfahren n

cy·clist Radfahrer(in); Motorradfahrer(in)

cy·clone Wirbelsturm m

cyl·in·der Zylinder m, TECH a. Walze f, Trommel f

cyn·ic Zyniker(in); **cyn·i·cal** zynisch; **cyn·i·cism** Zynismus m

cy·press BOT Zypresse f

cyst MED Zyste f

czar → tsar

Czech 1. tschechisch; **~ Republic** Tschechien n, Tschechische Republik **2.** Tscheche m, Tschechin f; LING Tschechisch n

D

D, d D, d *n*

d *abbr of* **died** gest., gestorben

dab 1. Klecks *m*, Spritzer *m* **2.** betupfen, abtupfen

dab·ble bespritzen; **~ at, ~ in** sich oberflächlich *or contp* in dilettantischer Weise beschäftigen mit

dachs·hund ZO Dackel *m*

dad F, **dad·dy** F Papa *m*, Vati *m*

dad·dy long·legs ZO Schnake *f*; Weberknecht *m*

daf·fo·dil BOT gelbe Narzisse

dag·ger Dolch *m*; **be at ~s drawn** *fig* auf Kriegsfuß stehen (**with** mit)

dai·ly 1. täglich; **the ~ grind** *or* **rut** das tägliche Einerlei **2.** Tageszeitung *f*; Putzfrau *f*

dain·ty 1. zierlich, reizend; wählerisch **2.** Leckerbissen *m*

dair·y Molkerei *f*; Milchwirtschaft *f*; Milchgeschäft *n*

dai·sy BOT Gänseblümchen *n*

dal·ly: ~ about herumtrödeln

dam 1. (Stau)Damm *m* **2.** *a.* **~ up** stauen, eindämmen

dam·age 1. Schaden *m*, (Be)Schädigung *f*; *pl* JUR Schadenersatz *m* **2.** (be)schädigen

dam·ask Damast *m*

damn 1. verdammen; verurteilen; **~ (it)!** F verflucht!, verdammt! **2.** *adj and adv* F → **damned 3. I don't give a ~** F das ist mir völlig gleich(gültig) *or* egal

dam·na·tion Verdammung *f*; REL Verdammnis *f*

damned F verdammt

damn·ing vernichtend, belastend

damp 1. feucht, klamm **2.** Feuchtigkeit *f* **3.** *a.* **damp·en** an-, befeuchten; dämpfen; **damp·ness** Feuchtigkeit *f*

dance 1. Tanz *m*; Tanzveranstaltung *f* **2.** tanzen

danc·er Tänzer(in)

danc·ing 1. Tanzen *n* **2.** Tanz...

dan·de·li·on BOT Löwenzahn *m*

dan·druff (Kopf)Schuppen *pl*

Dane Däne *m*, Dänin *f*

dan·ger Gefahr *f*; **be out of ~** außer Lebensgefahr sein; **~ ar·e·a** Gefahrenzone *f*, Gefahrenbereich *m*

dan·ger·ous gefährlich

dan·ger zone → **danger area**

dan·gle baumeln (lassen)

Da·nish 1. dänisch **2.** LING Dänisch *n*

dank feucht, nass(kalt)

dare *v/i* es wagen, sich (ge)trauen; **I ~ say** ich glaube wohl; allerdings; **how ~ you!** was fällt dir ein!; untersteh dich!; *v/t et.* wagen

dare·dev·il Draufgänger *m*

dar·ing 1. kühn, verwegen, waghalsig **2.** Mut *m*, Kühnheit *f*, Verwegenheit *f*

dark 1. dunkel; finster; *fig* düster, trüb(e); geheim(nisvoll) **2.** Dunkel *n*, Dunkelheit *f*; **before (at, after) ~** vor (bei, nach) Einbruch der Dunkelheit; **keep s.o. in the ~ about s.th.** j-n über et. im Ungewissen lassen

Dark Ag·es *das* frühe Mittelalter

dark·en (sich) verdunkeln *or* verfinstern

dark·ness Dunkelheit *f*, Finsternis *f*

dark·room PHOT Dunkelkammer *f*

dar·ling 1. Liebling *m* **2.** lieb; F goldig

darn stopfen, ausbessern

dart 1. Wurfpfeil *m*; Sprung *m*, Satz *m*; **~s** Darts **2.** *v/t* werfen, schleudern; *v/i* schießen, stürzen

dart·board Dartsscheibe *f*

dash 1. Schlag *m*; Klatschen *n*; GASTR Prise *f* (*of* salt), Schuss *m* (*of* rum etc), Spritzer *m* (*of* lemon etc); Gedankenstrich *m*; SPORT Sprint *m*; *fig* Anflug *m*; **a ~ of blue** ein Stich ins Blaue; **make a ~ for** losstürzen auf (acc) **2.** *v/t* schleudern, schmettern; *Hoffnung etc* zerstören, zunichtemachen; *v/i* stürmen; **~ off** davonstürzen

dash·board MOT Armaturenbrett *n*

dash·ing schneidig, forsch

da·ta Daten *pl* (*a.* IT), Angaben *pl*; **~ base** IT Datenbank *f*; **~ car·ri·er** Datenträger *m*; **~ in·put** Dateneingabe *f*; **~ me·di·um** Datenträger *m*; **~ mem·o·ry** Datenspeicher *m*; **~ output** Datenausgabe *f*; **~ pro·cess·ing** Datenverarbeitung *f*; **~ pro·tec·tion** JUR Datenschutz *m*; **~ stor·age** Datenspeicher *m*; **~ trans·fer** Datenübertragung *f*

date¹ BOT Dattel *f*

date² 1. Datum *n*; Zeit *f*, Zeitpunkt *m*;

Termin *m*; Verabredung *f*; F (Verabredungs)Partner(in); *out of* ~ veraltet, unmodern; *up to* ~ zeitgemäß, modern, auf dem Laufenden **2.** datieren; F sich verabreden mit, (aus)gehen mit

dat·ed veraltet, überholt

da·tive *a.* ~ *case* LING Dativ *m*, dritter Fall

daub (be)schmieren

daugh·ter Tochter *f*

daugh·ter-in-law Schwiegertochter *f*

daunt entmutigen

dav·en·port Sofa *n*

daw zo Dohle *f*

daw·dle F (herum)trödeln

dawn 1. (Morgen)Dämmerung *f*; *at* ~ bei Tagesanbruch **2.** dämmern; ~ *on fig j-m* dämmern

day Tag *m*; *often pl* (Lebens)Zeit *f*; *any* ~ jederzeit; *these* ~*s* heutzutage; *the other* ~ neulich; *the* ~ *after tomorrow* übermorgen; *the* ~ *before yesterday* vorgestern; *open all* ~ durchgehend geöffnet; *let's call it a* ~*!* machen wir Schluss für heute!, Feierabend!

day·break Tagesanbruch *m*

day care cen·ter (*Br* **cen·tre**) → **day nursery**

day·dream 1. Tag-, Wachtraum *m* **2.** (mit offenen Augen) träumen

day·dream·er Träumer(in)

day·light Tageslicht *n*; *in broad* ~ am helllichten Tag

day nur·se·ry (Kinder)Tagesstätte *f*

day off freier Tag

day re·turn *Br* Tagesrückfahrkarte *f*

day·time: *in the* ~ am Tag, bei Tage

daze 1. blenden; betäuben **2.** *in a* ~ benommen, betäubt

dead 1. tot; unempfindlich (*to* für); matt; blind (*window etc*); erloschen; ECON flau; tot (*capital etc*); völlig, total; *drop* ~ tot umfallen **2.** *adv* völlig, total; plötzlich, abrupt; genau, direkt; ~ *slow* MOT Schritt fahren!; ~ *tired* todmüde **3.** *the* ~ die Toten *pl*

dead·en abstumpfen; (ab)schwächen; dämpfen

dead end Sackgasse *f* (*a. fig*)

dead heat SPORT totes Rennen

dead·line letzter (Ablieferungs)Termin; Stichtag *m*

dead·lock *fig* toter Punkt

dead·locked *fig* festgefahren

dead·ly tödlich

deaf 1. taub **2.** *the* ~ die Tauben *pl*

deaf-and-dumb taubstumm

deaf·en taub machen; betäuben

deaf-mute Taubstumme *m*, *f*

deal 1. F Geschäft *n*, Handel *m*; Menge *f*; *it's a* ~*!* abgemacht!; *a good* ~ ziemlich viel; *a great* ~ sehr viel **2.** *v/t* (aus-, ver-, zu)teilen; *j-m Karten* geben; *j-m e-n Schlag* versetzen; *v/i* handeln (*in* mit *e-r Ware*); *sl* dealen; *cards*: geben; ~ *with* sich befassen mit, behandeln; ECON Handel treiben mit, Geschäfte machen mit; **deal·er** ECON Händler(in); *cards*: Geber(in); *sl* Dealer *m*; **deal·ing** *mst pl* Umgang *m*, Beziehungen *pl*

dean REL, UNIV Dekan *m*

dear 1. teuer; lieb; *Dear Sir* Sehr geehrter Herr ... **2.** Liebste *m*, *f*, Schatz *m*; *my* ~ m-e Liebe, mein Lieber **3.** *int* (oh) ~*!*, ~ *me!* F du liebe Zeit!, ach herrje!; **dear·est** sehnlichst; **dear·ly** innig, von ganzem Herzen; ECON teuer

death Tod *m*; Todesfall *m*

death·bed Sterbebett *n*

death cer·tif·i·cate Totenschein *m*

death·ly tödlich; ~ *still* totenstill

death war·rant JUR Hinrichtungsbefehl *m*; *fig* Todesurteil *n*

de·bar: ~ *s.o. from* j-n ausschließen aus

de·base erniedrigen; mindern

de·ba·ta·ble umstritten

de·bate 1. Debatte *f*, Diskussion *f* **2.** debattieren, diskutieren

deb·it ECON **1.** Soll *n*; (Konto)Belastung *f*; ~ *and credit* Soll und Haben *n* **2.** *j-n*, *ein Konto* belasten

deb·ris Trümmer *pl*, Schutt *m*

debt Schuld *f*; *be in* ~ Schulden haben, verschuldet sein; *be out of* ~ schuldenfrei sein; *get into* ~ sich verschulden, Schulden machen

debt·or Schuldner(in)

de·bug TECH, IT Fehler beseitigen

de·but Debüt *n*

Dec *abbr of* **December** Dez., Dezember *m*

dec·ade Jahrzehnt *n*

dec·a·dent dekadent

de·caf·fein·at·ed koffeinfrei

de·camp F verschwinden

de·cant abgießen; umfüllen

de·cant·er Karaffe *f*

de·cath·lete SPORT Zehnkämpfer *m*

de·cath·lon SPORT Zehnkampf *m*

de·cay 1. zerfallen; verfaulen; kariös *or* schlecht werden (*tooth*) 2. Zerfall *m*; Verfaulen *n*

de·cease *esp* JUR Tod *m*, Ableben *n*

de·ceased *esp* JUR 1. *the* ~ der *or* die Verstorbene; die Verstorbenen *pl* 2. verstorben

de·ceit Betrug *m*; Täuschung *f*

de·ceit·ful betrügerisch

de·ceive betrügen; täuschen

de·ceiv·er Betrüger(in)

De·cem·ber (*abbr* **Dec**) Dezember *m*

de·cen·cy Anstand *m*

de·cent anständig; F annehmbar, (ganz) anständig; F nett

de·cep·tion Täuschung *f*

de·cep·tive trügerisch; *be* ~ täuschen, trügen

de·cide (sich) entscheiden; bestimmen; beschließen, sich entschließen

de·cid·ed entschieden; bestimmt; entschlossen

dec·i·mal MATH 1. *a*. ~ *fraction* Dezimalbruch *m* 2. Dezimal...

de·ci·pher entziffern

de·ci·sion Entscheidung *f*; Entschluss *m*; Entschlossenheit *f*; *make a* ~ e-e Entscheidung treffen; *reach or come to a* ~ zu e-m Entschluss kommen

de·ci·sive entscheidend; ausschlaggebend; entschieden

deck 1. MAR Deck *n*; Spiel *n*, Pack *m* (Spiel)Karten 2. ~ *out* schmücken

deck-chair Liegestuhl *m*

dec·la·ra·tion Erklärung *f*; Zollerklärung *f*; **de·clare** erklären; deklarieren, verzollen

de·clen·sion LING Deklination *f*

de·cline 1. abnehmen, zurückgehen; fallen; verfallen; (höflich) ablehnen; LING deklinieren 2. Abnahme *f*, Rückgang *m*, Verfall *m*

de·cliv·i·ty (Ab)Hang *m*

de·clutch MOT auskuppeln

de·code entschlüsseln

de·com·pose zerlegen; (sich) zersetzen; verwesen

de·con·tam·i·nate entgasen, entgiften, entseuchen, entstrahlen

de·con·tam·i·na·tion Entseuchung *f*

dec·o·rate verzieren, schmücken; tapezieren; (an)streichen; dekorieren

dec·o·ra·tion Verzierung *f*, Schmuck *m*, Dekoration *f*; Orden *m*

dec·o·ra·tive dekorativ; Zier...

dec·o·ra·tor Dekorateur *m*; Maler *m* und Tapezierer *m*

dec·o·rous anständig

de·co·rum Anstand *m*

de·coy 1. Lockvogel *m* (*a, fig*); Köder *m* (*a. fig*) 2. ködern; locken (*into* in *acc*); verleiten (*into* zu)

de·crease 1. Abnahme *f* 2. abnehmen; (sich) vermindern

de·cree 1. Dekret *n*, Erlass *m*, Verfügung *f*; *esp* JUR Entscheid *m*, Urteil *n* 2. verfügen

ded·i·cate widmen

ded·i·cat·ed engagiert

ded·i·ca·tion Widmung *f*; Hingabe *f*

de·duce ableiten; folgern

de·duct *Betrag* abziehen (*from* von); **de·duct·i·ble**: *tax-* steuerlich absetzbar; **de·duc·tion** Abzug *m*; (Schluss)Folgerung *f*, Schluss *m*

deed Tat *f*; Heldentat *f*; JUR (Übertragungs)Urkunde *f*

deep 1. tief (*a. fig*) 2. Tiefe *f*

deep·en (sich) vertiefen, *fig a.* (sich) verstärken

deep freeze 1. tiefkühlen, einfrieren 2. Tiefkühl-, Gefriertruhe *f*

deep-fro·zen tiefgefroren

deep fry frittieren

deep·ness Tiefe *f*

deer ZO Hirsch *m*; Reh *n*

de·face entstellen; unleserlich machen; ausstreichen

def·a·ma·tion Verleumdung *f*

de·fault 1. JUR Nichterscheinen *n* vor Gericht; SPORT Nichtantreten *n*; ECON Verzug *m* 2. s-n Verpflichtungen nicht nachkommen, ECON *a*. im Verzug sein; JUR nicht vor Gericht erscheinen; SPORT nicht antreten

de·feat 1. Niederlage *f* 2. besiegen, schlagen; vereiteln, zunichtemachen

de·fect Defekt *m*, Fehler *m*; Mangel *m*

de·fec·tive mangelhaft; schadhaft, defekt

de·fence *Br* → **defense**

de·fence·less *Br* → **defenseless**

de·fend (*from, against*) verteidigen (gegen), schützen (vor *dat*, gegen)

de·fen·dant Angeklagte *m*, *f*; Beklagte *m*, *f*

de·fend·er Verteidiger(in); SPORT Abwehrspieler(in)

de·fense Verteidigung f (a. MIL, JUR, SPORT), Schutz m; SPORT Abwehr f; **witness for the ~** Entlastungszeuge m

de·fense·less schutzlos, wehrlos

de·fen·sive 1. Defensive f, Verteidigung f, Abwehr f **2.** defensiv; Verteidigungs..., Abwehr...

de·fer aufschieben, verschieben

de·fi·ance Herausforderung f; Trotz m

de·fi·ant herausfordernd; trotzig

de·fi·cien·cy Unzulänglichkeit f; Mangel m

de·fi·cient mangelhaft, unzureichend

def·i·cit ECON Defizit n, Fehlbetrag m

de·file beschmutzen

de·fine definieren; erklären, bestimmen

def·i·nite bestimmt; endgültig, definitiv

def·i·ni·tion Definition f, Bestimmung f, Erklärung f

de·fin·i·tive endgültig, definitiv

de·flect v/t ablenken; *Ball* abfälschen; v/i abweichen

de·form entstellen, verunstalten

de·formed deformiert, verunstaltet; verwachsen

de·for·mi·ty Missbildung f

de·fraud betrügen (*of* um)

de·frost v/t *Windschutzscheibe etc* entfrosten; *Kühlschrank etc* abtauen, *Tiefkühlkost etc* auftauen; v/i ab-, auftauen

deft geschickt, gewandt

de·fy herausfordern; trotzen (*dat*)

de·gen·e·rate 1. entarten **2.** entartet

deg·ra·da·tion Erniedrigung f

de·grade erniedrigen, demütigen

de·gree Grad m; Stufe f; (akademischer) Grad; **by ~s** allmählich; **take one's ~** e-n akademischen Grad erwerben, promovieren

de·hy·drate austrocknen; TECH das Wasser entziehen (*dat*)

de·i·fy vergöttern; vergöttlichen

deign sich herablassen

de·i·ty Gottheit f

de·ject·ed niedergeschlagen, mutlos, deprimiert

de·jec·tion Niedergeschlagenheit f

de·lay 1. Aufschub m; Verzögerung f; RAIL etc Verspätung f **2.** ver-, aufschieben; verzögern; aufhalten; **be ~ed** sich verzögern; RAIL etc Verspätung haben

del·e·gate 1. abordnen, delegieren; *Vollmachten etc* übertragen **2.** Delegierte m, f, bevollmächtigter Vertreter

del·e·ga·tion Übertragung f; Abordnung f, Delegation f

de·lete (aus)streichen; IT löschen

de·lib·e·rate absichtlich, vorsätzlich; bedächtig, besonnen

de·lib·e·ra·tion Überlegung f; Beratung f; Bedächtigkeit f

del·i·ca·cy Delikatesse f, Leckerbissen m; Zartheit f; Feingefühl n, Takt m

del·i·cate delikat (a. fig), schmackhaft; zart; fein; zierlich; zerbrechlich; heikel; empfindlich

del·i·ca·tes·sen Delikatessen pl, Feinkost f; Feinkostgeschäft n

de·li·cious köstlich

de·light 1. Vergnügen n, Entzücken n **2.** entzücken, erfreuen; **~ in** (große) Freude haben an (*dat*)

de·light·ful entzückend

de·lin·quen·cy Kriminalität f

de·lin·quent 1. straffällig **2.** Straffällige m, f; → **juvenile** 1

de·lir·i·ous MED im Delirium, fantasierend; **de·lir·i·um** MED Delirium n

de·liv·er ausliefern, (ab)liefern; *Briefe* zustellen; *Rede etc* halten; befreien, erlösen; **be ~ed of** MED entbunden werden von

de·liv·er·ance Befreiung f

de·liv·er·er Befreier(in)

de·liv·er·y (Ab-, Aus)Lieferung f; post Zustellung f; Halten n (e-r Rede); Vortrag(sweise f) m; MED Entbindung f

de·liv·er·y van Br MOT Lieferwagen m

dell kleines Tal

de·lude täuschen

del·uge Überschwemmung f; fig Flut f

de·lu·sion Täuschung f; Wahn(vorstellung f) m

de·mand 1. Forderung f (**for** nach); Anforderung f (**on** an *acc*); Nachfrage f (**for** nach), Bedarf m (**for** an *dat*); **on ~** auf Verlangen **2.** verlangen, fordern; (*fordernd*) fragen nach; erfordern

de·mand·ing anspruchsvoll

de·ment·ed wahnsinnig

dem·i... Halb..., halb...

de·mil·i·ta·rize entmilitarisieren

dem·o F Demo f

de·mo·bi·lize demobilisieren

de·moc·ra·cy Demokratie f

dem·o·crat Demokrat(in)

dem·o·crat·ic demokratisch

de·mol·ish demolieren; ab-, ein-, niederreißen; zerstören

dem·o·li·tion Demolierung f; Niederreißen n, Abbruch m

de·mon Dämon m; Teufel m

dem·on·strate demonstrieren; beweisen; zeigen; vorführen

dem·on·stra·tion Demonstration f, a. Kundgebung f, a. Vorführung f; **~ car** Br Vorführwagen m

dem·on·stra·tor Demonstrant(in); Vorführer(in); MOT Vorführwagen m

de·mor·al·ize demoralisieren

de·mote degradieren

de·mure ernst, zurückhaltend

den zo Höhle f (a. fig); F Bude f

de·ni·al Ablehnung f; Leugnen n; Verweigerung f; **official ~** Dementi n

den·ims Jeans pl

Den·mark Dänemark n

de·nom·i·na·tion REL Konfession f; ECON Nennwert m

de·note bezeichnen; bedeuten

de·nounce (öffentlich) anprangern

dense dicht; fig beschränkt, begriffsstutzig; **den·si·ty** Dichte f

dent 1. Beule f, Delle f **2.** ver-, einbeulen

den·tal Zahn...;, **plaque** Zahnbelag m; **~ plate** (Zahn)Prothese f; **~ surgeon** Zahnarzt m, Zahnärztin f

den·tist Zahnarzt m, Zahnärztin f

den·tures (Zahn)Prothese f, (künstliches) Gebiss

de·nun·ci·a·tion Denunziation f

de·nun·ci·a·tor Denunziant(in)

de·ny abstreiten, bestreiten, dementieren, (ab)leugnen; j-m et. verweigern, abschlagen

de·o·do·rant De(s)odorant n, Deo n

de·part abreisen; abfahren, abfliegen; abweichen (**from** von)

de·part·ment Abteilung f, UNIV a. Fachbereich m; POL Ministerium n

De·part·ment| of De·fense Verteidigungsministerium n; **~ of State** a. **State Department** Außenministerium n; **~ of the En·vi·ron·ment** Br Umweltministerium n; **~ of the In·te·ri·or** Innenministerium n

de·part·ment store Kaufhaus n, Warenhaus n

de·par·ture Abreise f; RAIL etc Abfahrt f; AVIAT Abflug m; fig Abweichung f; **~s** AVIAT, RAIL etc 'Abfahrt' (timetable); **day of ~** Abreisetag m; **~ gate** AVIAT Flugsteig m; **~ lounge** AVIAT Abflughalle f

de·pend: ~ on sich verlassen auf (acc); abhängen von; ,angewiesen sein auf (acc); **that ~s** das kommt darauf an

de·pend·a·bil·i·ty Zuverlässigkeit f

de·pend·a·ble zuverlässig

de·pen·dant Angehörige m, f

de·pen·dence Abhängigkeit f; Vertrauen n

de·pen·dent 1. (on) abhängig (von); angewiesen (auf acc); **2.** → **dependant**

de·plor·a·ble bedauerlich, beklagenswert; **de·plore** beklagen, bedauern

de·pop·u·late entvölkern

de·port ausweisen, Ausländer a. abschieben; deportieren

de·pose j-n absetzen; JUR unter Eid erklären

de·pos·it 1. absetzen, abstellen; CHEM, GEOL (sich) ablagern or absetzen; deponieren, hinterlegen; ECON Betrag anzahlen **2.** CHEM Ablagerung f, GEOL a. (Erz- etc)Lager n; Deponierung f, Hinterlegung f; ECON Anzahlung f; **make a ~** e-e Anzahlung leisten (**on** für)

dep·ot Depot n; Bahnhof m

de·prave moralisch verderben

de·pre·ci·ate an Wert verlieren

de·press (nieder)drücken; deprimieren, bedrücken

de·pressed deprimiert, niedergeschlagen; ECON flau (market); Not leidend (industry); **~ ar·e·a** ECON Notstandsgebiet n

de·press·ing deprimierend, bedrückend

de·pres·sion Depression f, Niedergeschlagenheit f; ECON Depression f, Flaute f; Senke f, Vertiefung f; METEOR Tief(druckgebiet) n

de·prive: ~ s.o. of s.th. j-m et. entziehen or nehmen; **de·prived** benachteiligt

dept, Dept abbr of **department** Abt., Abteilung f

depth 1. Tiefe f **2.** Tiefen...

dep·u·ta·tion Abordnung f

dep·u·tize: ~ for s.o. j-n vertreten

dep·u·ty (Stell)Vertreter(in); PARL Abgeordnete m, f; a. **~ sheriff** Hilfssheriff m

de·rail: be ~ed entgleisen

de·ranged geistesgestört

der·by F Melone f

der·e·lict heruntergekommen, baufällig

de·ride verhöhnen, verspotten

de·ri·sion Hohn m, Spott m

de·ri·sive höhnisch, spöttisch

de·rive herleiten (*from* von); (sich) ableiten (*from* von); abstammen (*from* von); ~ *pleasure from* Freude finden or haben an (*dat*)

der·ma·tol·o·gist Dermatologe m, Hautarzt m

de·rog·a·to·ry abfällig, geringschätzig

der·rick TECH Derrickkran m; MAR Ladebaum m; TECH Bohrturm m

de·scend herab-, hinabsteigen, herunter-, hinuntersteigen, -gehen, -kommen; AVIAT niedergehen; abstammen, herkommen (*from* von); ~ *on* herfallen über (*acc*); überfallen (*acc*) (*visitor etc*)

de·scen·dant Nachkomme m

de·scent Herab-, Hinuntersteigen n, -gehen n; AVIAT Niedergehen n; Gefälle n; Abstammung f, Herkunft f

de·scribe beschreiben

de·scrip·tion Beschreibung f, Schilderung f; Art f, Sorte f; **de·scrip·tive** beschreibend; anschaulich

des·e·crate entweihen

de·seg·re·gate die Rassentrennung aufheben in (*dat*); **de·seg·re·ga·tion** Aufhebung f der Rassentrennung

des·ert¹ 1. Wüste f 2. Wüsten...

de·sert² v/t verlassen, im Stich lassen; v/i MIL desertieren

de·sert·er MIL Deserteur m

de·ser·tion (JUR a. böswilliges) Verlassen; MIL Fahnenflucht f

de·serve verdienen

de·serv·ed·ly verdientermaßen

de·serv·ing verdienstvoll

de·sign 1. Design n, Entwurf m, (TECH Konstruktions)Zeichnung f; Design n, Muster n; (a. böse)Absicht 2. entwerfen, TECH konstruieren; gestalten; ausdenken; bestimmen, vorsehen (*for* für)

des·ig·nate et. or j-n bestimmen

de·sign·er Designer(in); TECH Konstrukteur m; (*Mode*)Schöpfer(in)

de·sir·a·ble erwünscht, wünschenswert; begehrenswert

de·sire 1. Wunsch m, Verlangen n, Begierde f (*for* nach); 2. wünschen; begehren

de·sist Abstand nehmen (*from* von)

desk Schreibtisch m; Pult n; Empfang m, Rezeption f; Schalter m

desk·top|com·put·er Desktop-Computer m; ~ **pub·lish·ing** (*abbr DTP*) IT Desktop-Publishing n

des·o·late einsam, verlassen; trostlos

de·spair 1. Verzweiflung f; *drive s.o. to* ~ j-n zur Verzweiflung bringen 2. verzweifeln (*of* an *dat*)

de·spair·ing verzweifelt

de·spatch → *dispatch*

des·per·ate verzweifelt; F hoffnungslos, schrecklich

des·per·a·tion Verzweiflung f

des·pic·a·ble verachtenswert, verabscheuungswürdig

de·spise verachten

de·spite trotz (*gen*)

de·spon·dent mutlos, verzagt

des·pot Despot m, Tyrann m

des·sert Nachtisch m, Dessert n

des·ti·na·tion Bestimmung f; Bestimmungsort m

des·tined bestimmt; MAR etc unterwegs (*for* nach)

des·ti·ny Schicksal n

des·ti·tute mittellos

de·stroy zerstören, vernichten; *Tier* töten, einschläfern; **de·stroy·er** Zerstörer(in); MAR MIL Zerstörer m

de·struc·tion Zerstörung f, Vernichtung f; **de·struc·tive** zerstörend, vernichtend; zerstörerisch

de·tach (ab-, los)trennen, (los)lösen

de·tached einzeln, frei or allein stehend; unvoreingenommen; distanziert; ~ *house* Einzelhaus n

de·tach·ment (Los)Lösung f, (Ab-)Trennung f; MIL (Sonder)Kommando n

de·tail 1. Detail n, Einzelheit f; MIL (Sonder)Kommando n; *in* ~ ausführlich 2. genau schildern; MIL abkommandieren

de·tailed detailliert, ausführlich

de·tain aufhalten; JUR in (Untersuchungs)Haft behalten

de·tect entdecken, (heraus)finden

de·tec·tion Entdeckung f

de·tec·tive Kriminalbeamte m, Detektiv m; ~ **nov·el**, ~ **sto·ry** Kriminalroman m

de·ten·tion JUR Haft f; PED Nachsitzen n

de·ter abschrecken (*from* von)

de·ter·gent Reinigungs-, Wasch-, Geschirrspülmittel n

de·te·ri·o·rate (sich) verschlechtern, nachlassen; verderben

de·ter·mi·na·tion Entschlossenheit f, Bestimmtheit f; Entschluss m; Feststellung f, Ermittlung f; **de·ter·mine** et. beschließen, bestimmen; feststellen, ermitteln; (sich) entscheiden; sich entschließen; **de·ter·mined** entschlossen

de·ter·rence Abschreckung f

de·ter·rent 1. abschreckend **2.** Abschreckungsmittel n

de·test verabscheuen

de·throne entthronen

de·to·nate v/t zünden; v/i detonieren, explodieren

de·tour Umweg m; Umleitung f

de·tract: ~ **from** ablenken von; schmälern (acc)

de·tri·ment Nachteil m, Schaden m

deuce cards etc: Zwei f; tennis: Einstand m

de·val·u·a·tion Abwertung f

de·val·ue abwerten

dev·a·state verwüsten

dev·a·stat·ing verheerend, vernichtend; F umwerfend, toll

de·vel·op (sich) entwickeln; Naturschätze, Bauland erschließen; Altstadt etc sanieren; **de·vel·op·er** PHOT Entwickler m; (Stadt)Planer m

de·vel·op·ing Entwicklungs…; ~ **country,** ~ **na·tion** Entwicklungsland n

de·vel·op·ment Entwicklung f; Erschließung f, Sanierung f

de·vi·ate abweichen (**from** von)

de·vi·a·tion Abweichung f

de·vice Vorrichtung f, Gerät n; Plan m, Trick m; **leave s.o. to his own ~s** j-n sich selbst überlassen

dev·il Teufel m (a. fig)

dev·il·ish teuflisch

de·vi·ous abwegig; gewunden; unaufrichtig; ~ **route** Umweg m

de·vise (sich) ausdenken

de·void: ~ **of** ohne (acc)

de·vote widmen (**to** dat); **de·vot·ed** ergeben; hingebungsvoll; eifrig, begeistert; **dev·o·tee** begeisterter Anhänger; **de·vo·tion** Ergebenheit f; Hingabe f; Frömmigkeit f, Andacht f

de·vour verschlingen

de·vout fromm; sehnlichst, innig

dew Tau m; **dew·y** taufeucht, taufrisch

dex·ter·i·ty Gewandtheit f

dex·ter·ous, dex·trous gewandt

di·a·bol·i·cal teuflisch

di·ag·nose diagnostizieren

di·ag·no·sis Diagnose f

di·ag·o·nal 1. diagonal **2.** Diagonale f

di·a·gram Diagramm n, grafische Darstellung

di·al 1. Zifferblatt n; TEL Wählscheibe f; Skala f **2.** TEL wählen; ~ **direct** durchwählen (**to** nach); **direct ~(l)ing** Durchwahl f

di·a·lect Dialekt m, Mundart f

di·al·ling code Br TEL Vorwahl (-nummer) f

di·a·log, Br **di·a·logue** Dialog m, (Zwie)Gespräch n

di·am·e·ter Durchmesser m; **in ~** im Durchmesser

di·a·mond Diamant m; Raute f, Rhombus m; cards: Karo n

di·a·per Windel f

di·a·phragm ANAT Zwerchfell n; OPT Blende f; TEL Membran(e) f

di·ar·rh(o)e·a MED Durchfall m

di·a·ry Tagebuch n

dice 1. Würfel m **2.** GASTR in Würfel schneiden; würfeln

dic·tate diktieren; fig vorschreiben

dic·ta·tion Diktat n

dic·ta·tor Diktator m

dic·ta·tor·ship Diktatur f

dic·tion Ausdrucksweise f, Stil m

dic·tion·a·ry Wörterbuch n

die¹ sterben; zo eingehen, verenden; ~ **of hunger** verhungern; ~ **of thirst** verdursten; ~ **away** sich legen (wind); verklingen (sound); ~ **down** nachlassen; herunterbrennen; schwächer werden; ~ **out** aussterben (a. fig)

die² Würfel m

di·et 1. Diät f; Nahrung f, Kost f; **be on a ~** Diät leben; **put s.o. on a ~** j-m e-e Diät verordnen **2.** Diät leben

di·e·ti·cian Diätassistent(in)

dif·fer sich unterscheiden; anderer Meinung sein (**with, from** als); abweichen

dif·fe·rence Unterschied m; Differenz f; Meinungsverschiedenheit f

dif·fe·rent verschieden; andere(r, -s); anders (**from** als)

dif·fe·ren·ti·ate (sich) unterscheiden

dif·fi·cult schwierig

dif·fi·cul·ty Schwierigkeit *f, pl* Unannehmlichkeiten *pl*

dif·fi·dence Schüchternheit *f*

dif·fi·dent schüchtern

dif·fuse 1. *fig* verbreiten 2. diffus; *esp* PHYS zerstreut; weitschweifig

dif·fu·sion CHEM, PHYS (Zer)Streuung *f*

dig 1. graben; ~ *(up)* umgraben; ~ *(up or out)* ausgraben *(a. fig);* ~ *s.o. in the ribs* j-m e-n Rippenstoß geben 2. F Puff *m,* Stoß *m;* Seitenhieb *m (at* auf *acc)*

di·gest 1. verdauen; ~ *well* leicht verdaulich sein 2. Abriss *m;* Auslese *f,* Auswahl *f;* **di·gest·i·ble** verdaulich; **di·ges·tion** Verdauung *f;* **di·ges·tive** verdauungsfördernd; Verdauungs…

dig·ger *(esp* Gold)Gräber *m*

di·git Ziffer *f; three-~ number* dreistellige Zahl

di·gi·tal digital, Digital…; ~ *camera* Digitalkamera *f;* ~ *clock* Digitaluhr *f;* ~ *television,* ~ *TV* Digitalfernsehen *n* ~ *watch* Digitaluhr *f*

dig·ni·fied würdevoll, würdig

dig·ni·ta·ry Würdenträger(in)

dig·ni·ty Würde *f*

di·gress abschweifen

dike 1. Deich *m,* Damm *m;* Graben *m* 2. eindeichen, eindämmen

di·lap·i·dat·ed verfallen, baufällig, klapp(e)rig

di·late (sich) ausdehnen *or* (aus)weiten; *Augen* weit öffnen

dil·a·to·ry verzögernd, hinhaltend; langsam

dil·i·gence Fleiß *m*

dil·i·gent fleißig, emsig

di·lute 1. verdünnen; *fig* verwässern 2. verdünnt; *fig* verwässert

dim 1. (halb)dunkel, düster; undeutlich, verschwommen; schwach, trüb(e) *(light)* 2. (sich) verdunkeln *or* verdüstern; (sich) trüben; undeutlich werden; ~ *one's headlights* MOT abblenden

dime Zehncentstück *n*

di·men·sion Dimension *f,* Maß *n,* Abmessung *f; pl a.* Ausmaß *n*

di·min·ish (sich) vermindern *or* verringern

di·min·u·tive klein, winzig

dim·ple Grübchen *n*

din Getöse *n,* Lärm *m*

dine essen, speisen; ~ *in* zu Hause essen;

~ *out* auswärts essen, essen gehen

din·er Speisende *m, f;* Gast *m;* Speiselokal *n;* RAIL Speisewagen *m*

din·ghy MAR Jolle *f;* Dingi *n;* Beiboot *n;* Schlauchboot *n*

din·gy schmutzig, schmudd(e)lig

din·ing car RAIL Speisewagen *m*

din·ing room Ess-, Speisezimmer *n*

din·ner (Mittag-, Abend)Essen *n;* Diner *n,* Festessen *n;* ~ *jack·et* Smoking *m;* ~ *par·ty* Dinnerparty *f,* Abendgesellschaft *f;* ~ *ser·vice,* ~ *set* Speiseservice *n,* Tafelgeschirr *n*

din·ner·time Essens-, Tischzeit *f*

di·no F → *dinosaur*

di·no·saur ZO Dinosaurier *m*

dip 1. *v/t* (ein)tauchen; senken; schöpfen; ~ *one's headlights* Br MOT abblenden; *v/i* (unter)tauchen; sinken; sich neigen, sich senken 2. (Ein-, Unter-)Tauchen *n;* F kurzes Bad; Senkung *f,* Neigung *f,* Gefälle *n;* GASTR Dip *m*

diph·ther·i·a MED Diphtherie *f*

di·plo·ma Diplom *n*

di·plo·ma·cy Diplomatie *f*

dip·lo·mat Diplomat *m*

dip·lo·mat·ic diplomatisch

dip·per Schöpfkelle *f*

dire schrecklich; höchste(r, -s), äußerste(r, -s)

di·rect 1. *adj* direkt; gerade; unmittelbar; offen, aufrichtig 2. *adv* direkt, unmittelbar 3. richten; lenken, steuern; leiten; anordnen; *j-n* anweisen; j-m den Weg zeigen; *Brief* adressieren; Regie führen bei; ~ *cur·rent* ELECTR Gleichstrom *m;* ~ *train* durchgehender Zug

di·rec·tion Richtung *f;* Leitung *f,* Führung *f; film etc:* Regie *f; mst pl* Anweisung *f,* Anleitung *f;* ~ *s for use* Gebrauchsanweisung *f; sense of* ~ Ortssinn *m;* ~ *in·di·ca·tor* MOT Fahrtrichtungsanzeiger *m,* Blinker *m*

di·rec·tive Anweisung *f*

di·rect·ly 1. *adv* sofort 2. *cj* F sobald, sowie

di·rec·tor Direktor *m; film etc:* Regisseur(in)

di·rec·to·ry Adressbuch *n*

di·rect speech LING wörtliche Rede

di·rect train durchgehender Zug

dirt Schmutz *m;* (lockere) Erde

dirt cheap F spottbillig

dirt·y 1. schmutzig (*a. fig*) **2.** *v/t* beschmutzen; *v/i* schmutzig werden, schmutzen

dis·a·bil·i·ty Unfähigkeit *f*

dis·a·bled 1. arbeitsunfähig, erwerbsunfähig, invalid(e); MIL kriegsversehrt; *körperlich or geistig* behindert **2. the ~** die Behinderten *pl*

dis·ad·van·tage Nachteil *m*; Schaden *m*; **dis·ad·van·ta·geous** nachteilig, ungünstig

dis·a·gree nicht übereinstimmen; uneinig sein; nicht bekommen (**with s.o.** j-m); **dis·a·gree·a·ble** unangenehm; **dis·a·gree·ment** Verschiedenheit *f*, Unstimmigkeit *f*, Uneinigkeit *f*; Meinungsverschiedenheit *f*

dis·ap·pear verschwinden

dis·ap·pear·ance Verschwinden *n*

dis·ap·point j-n enttäuschen; *Hoffnungen etc* zunichtemachen

dis·ap·point·ing enttäuschend

dis·ap·point·ment Enttäuschung *f*

dis·ap·prov·al Missbilligung *f*

dis·ap·prove missbilligen; dagegen sein

dis·arm *v/t* entwaffnen (*a. fig*); *v/i* MIL, POL abrüsten; **dis·ar·ma·ment** Entwaffnung *f*; MIL, POL Abrüstung *f*

dis·ar·range in Unordnung bringen

dis·ar·ray Unordnung *f*

di·sas·ter Unglück *n*, Unglücksfall *m*, Katastrophe *f*; **~ ar·e·a** Katastrophen-, Notstandsgebiet *n*; **~ con·trol** Katastrophenschutz *m*

di·sas·trous katastrophal, verheerend

dis·be·lief Unglaube *m*; Zweifel *m* (*in* an *dat*); **dis·be·lieve** *et.* bezweifeln, nicht glauben

disc *Br* → **disk**

dis·card *Karten* ablegen, *Kleidung etc a.* ausrangieren; *Freund etc* fallen lassen

di·scern wahrnehmen, erkennen

di·scern·ing kritisch, scharfsichtig

di·scern·ment Scharfblick *m*

dis·charge 1. *v/t* entladen, ausladen; j-n befreien, entbinden; j-n entlassen; *Gewehr etc* abfeuern; von sich geben, ausströmen, -senden, -stoßen; MED absondern; *Pflicht etc* erfüllen; *Zorn etc* auslassen (**on** an *dat*); *v/i* ELECTR sich entladen; sich ergießen, münden (*river*); MED eitern **2.** MAR Entladung *f*; MIL Abfeuern *n*; Ausströmen *n*; MED Absonderung *f*, Ausfluss *m*; Ausstoßen *n*; ELECTR Entladung *f*; Entlassung *f*; Erfüllung *f* (*e-r Pflicht*)

di·sci·ple Schüler *m*; Jünger *m*

dis·ci·pline 1. Disziplin *f* **2.** disziplinieren; **well ~d** diszipliniert; **badly ~d** disziplinlos, undiszipliniert

dis·claim abstreiten, bestreiten; *Verantwortung* ablehnen; JUR verzichten auf (*acc*)

dis·close bekannt geben *or* machen; enthüllen, aufdecken

dis·clo·sure Enthüllung *f*

dis·co Disko *f*

dis·col·o(u)r (sich) verfärben

dis·com·fort 1. Unbehagen *n*; Unannehmlichkeit *f* **2.** j-m Unbehagen verursachen

dis·con·cert aus der Fassung bringen

dis·con·nect trennen (*a. ELECTR*); TECH auskuppeln; ELECTR *Gerät* abschalten; *Gas, Strom, Telefon* abstellen; TEL *Gespräch* unterbrechen

dis·con·nect·ed zusammenhang(s)los

dis·con·so·late untröstlich

dis·con·tent Unzufriedenheit *f*

dis·con·tent·ed unzufrieden

dis·con·tin·ue aufgeben, aufhören mit; unterbrechen

dis·cord Uneinigkeit *f*, Zwietracht *f*, Zwist *m*; MUS Missklang *m*

dis·cord·ant nicht übereinstimmend; MUS unharmonisch, misstönend

dis·co·theque Diskothek *f*

dis·count ECON Diskont *m*; Preisnachlass *m*, Rabatt *m*, Skonto *m, n*

dis·cour·age entmutigen; abschrecken, abhalten, j-m abraten (**from** von)

dis·cour·age·ment Entmutigung *f*; Abschreckung *f*

dis·course 1. Unterhaltung *f*, Gespräch *n*; Vortrag *m* **2.** e-n Vortrag halten (**on** über *acc*)

dis·cour·te·ous unhöflich

dis·cour·te·sy Unhöflichkeit *f*

dis·cov·er entdecken; ausfindig machen, (heraus)finden

dis·cov·er·y Entdeckung *f*

dis·cred·it 1. Zweifel *m*; Misskredit *m*, schlechter Ruf; **bring ~ (up)on** in Verruf bringen **2.** nicht glauben; in Misskredit bringen

di·screet besonnen, vorsichtig; diskret, verschwiegen

di·screp·an·cy Diskrepanz *f*, Widerspruch *m*

di·scre·tion Ermessen *n*, Gutdünken *n*; Diskretion *f*, Verschwiegenheit *f*

di·scrim·i·nate unterscheiden; ~ **against** benachteiligen, diskriminieren; **di·scrim·i·nat·ing** kritisch, urteilsfähig; **di·scrim·i·na·tion** unterschiedliche (*esp* nachteilige) Behandlung; Diskriminierung *f*, Benachteiligung *f*; Urteilsfähigkeit *f*

dis·cus SPORT Diskus *m*

di·scuss diskutieren, erörtern, besprechen; **di·scus·sion** Diskussion *f*, Besprechung *f*

dis·cus| throw SPORT Diskuswerfen *n*; ~ **throw·er** SPORT Diskuswerfer(in)

dis·ease Krankheit *f*

dis·eased krank

dis·em·bark von Bord gehen (lassen); MAR *Waren* ausladen

dis·en·chant·ed: be~ with sich keine Illusionen mehr machen über (*acc*)

dis·en·gage (sich) frei machen; losmachen; TECH auskuppeln, loskuppeln

dis·en·tan·gle entwirren; (sich) befreien

dis·fa·vo(u)r Missfallen *n*; Ungnade *f*

dis·fig·ure entstellen

dis·grace 1. Schande *f*; Ungnade *f* **2.** Schande bringen über (*acc*), *j-m* Schande bereiten

dis·grace·ful schändlich; skandalös

dis·guise 1. verkleiden (**as** als); *Stimme etc* verstellen; *et.* verbergen, verschleiern **2.** Verkleidung *f*; Verstellung *f*; Verschleierung *f*; **in~** maskiert, verkleidet; *fig* verkappt; **in the ~ of** verkleidet als

dis·gust 1. Ekel *m*, Abscheu *m* **2.** (an)ekeln; empören, entrüsten

dis·gust·ing ekelhaft

dish 1. flache Schüssel; (Servier)Platte *f*; GASTR Gericht *n*, Speise *f*; **the ~es** das Geschirr; **wash** or **do the ~es** abspülen, abwaschen **2.** ~ **out** F austeilen; *often* ~ **up** *Speisen* anrichten, auftragen; F *Geschichte etc* auftischen

dish·cloth Geschirrtuch *n*

dis·heart·en entmutigen

di·shev·el(l)ed zerzaust

dis·hon·est unehrlich, unredlich

dis·hon·es·ty Unehrlichkeit *f*; Unredlichkeit *f*

dis·hon·o(u)r 1. Schande *f* **2.** Schande bringen über (*acc*); ECON *Wechsel* nicht honorieren or einlösen

dis·hon·o(u)·ra·ble schändlich, unehrenhaft

dish·wash·er Tellerwäscher *m*, Spüler(in); TECH Geschirrspülmaschine *f*, Geschirrspüler *m*

dish·wa·ter Spülwasser *n*

dis·il·lu·sion 1. Ernüchterung *f*, Desillusion *f* **2.** ernüchtern, desillusionieren; **be~ed with** sich keine Illusionen mehr machen über (*acc*)

dis·in·clined abgeneigt

dis·in·fect MED desinfizieren

dis·in·fec·tant Desinfektionsmittel *n*

dis·in·her·it JUR enterben

dis·in·te·grate (sich) auflösen; verfallen, zerfallen

dis·in·terest·ed uneigennützig, selbstlos; objektiv, unvoreingenommen

disk Scheibe *f*; (Schall)Platte *f*; Parkscheibe *f*; IT Diskette *f*; ANAT Bandscheibe *f*; **slipped ~** MED Bandscheibenvorfall *m*

disk drive IT Diskettenlaufwerk *n*

disk·ette IT Floppy *f*, Diskette *f*

disk jock·ey TECH Diskjockey *m*

disk park·ing MOT Parken *n* mit Parkscheibe

dis·like 1. Abneigung *f*, Widerwille *m* (**of, for** gegen); **take a ~ to s.o.** gegen j-n e-e Abneigung fassen **2.** nicht leiden können, nicht mögen

dis·lo·cate MED sich *den Arm etc* verrenken or ausrenken

dis·loy·al treulos, untreu

dis·mal trüb(e), trostlos, elend

dis·man·tle TECH demontieren

dis·may 1. Schreck(en) *m*, Bestürzung *f*; **in~, with~** bestürzt; **to my~** zu m-r Bestürzung **2.** *v/t* erschrecken, bestürzen

dis·miss *v/t* entlassen; wegschicken; ablehnen; *Thema etc* fallen lassen; JUR abweisen; **dis·miss·al** Entlassung *f*; Aufgabe *f*; JUR Abweisung *f*

dis·mount *v/i* absteigen, absitzen (**from** von); *v/t* demontieren; TECH auseinandernehmen

dis·o·be·di·ence Ungehorsam *m*

dis·o·be·di·ent ungehorsam

dis·o·bey nicht gehorchen, ungehorsam sein (gegen)

dis·or·der Unordnung *f*; Aufruhr *m*; MED Störung *f*

dis·or·der·ly unordentlich; ordnungswidrig; unruhig; aufrührerisch

dis·or·gan·ize durcheinanderbringen; desorganisieren

dis·own nicht anerkennen; *Kind* verstoßen; ablehnen

di·spar·age verächtlich machen, herabsetzen; gering schätzen

di·spar·i·ty Ungleichheit *f*; *~ of or in age* Altersunterschied *m*

dis·pas·sion·ate leidenschaftslos; objektiv

di·spatch 1. schnelle Erledigung; Sendung *f*; Abfertigung *f*; Eile *f*; Botschaft *f*; Bericht *m* **2.** schnell erledigen; absenden, abschicken, *Telegramm etc* aufgeben, abfertigen

di·spel *Menge etc* zerstreuen (*a. fig*), *Nebel* zerteilen

di·spen·sa·ble entbehrlich

di·spen·sa·ry Werks-, Krankenhaus-, Schul-, MIL Lazarettapotheke *f*

dis·pen·sa·tion Austeilung *f*; Befreiung *f*; Dispens *m*; *göttliche* Fügung

di·spense austeilen; *Recht* sprechen; *Arzneien* zubereiten und abgeben; *~ with* auskommen ohne; überflüssig machen; **di·spens·er** Spender *m*, *a.* Abroller *m* (*for adhesive tape etc*), (*Briefmarken- etc*) Automat *m*

di·sperse verstreuen; (sich) zerstreuen

di·spir·it·ed entmutigt

dis·place verschieben; ablösen, entlassen; *j-n* verschleppen; ersetzen; verdrängen

dis·play 1. Entfaltung *f*; (Her)Zeigen *n*; (protzige) Zurschaustellung; IT Display *n*, Bildschirm *m*, Datenanzeige *f*; ECON Display *n*, Auslage *f*; *be on ~* ausgestellt sein **2.** entfalten; zur Schau stellen; zeigen

dis·please *j-m* missfallen

dis·pleased unhgehalten

dis·plea·sure Missfallen *n*

dis·pos·a·ble Einweg...; Wegwerf...

dis·pos·al Beseitigung *f*, Entsorgung *f*; Endlagerung *f*; Verfügung(srecht *n*) *f*; *be* (*put*) *at s.o.'s ~* j-m zur Verfügung stehen (stellen)

dis·pose *v/t* (an)ordnen, einrichten; geneigt machen, bewegen; *v/i*: *~ of* verfügen über (*acc*); erledigen; loswerden; wegschaffen, beseitigen; *Abfall, a. Atommüll etc* entsorgen

dis·posed geneigt; ...gesinnt

dis·po·si·tion Veranlagung *f*

dis·pos·sess enteignen, vertreiben; berauben (*of gen*)

dis·pro·por·tion·ate(·ly) unverhältnismäßig

dis·prove widerlegen

di·spute 1. Disput *m*, Kontroverse *f*; Streit *m*; Auseinandersetzung *f* **2.** streiten (über *acc*); bezweifeln

dis·qual·i·fy unfähig *or* untauglich machen; für untauglich erklären; SPORT disqualifizieren

dis·re·gard 1. Nichtbeachtung *f*; Missachtung *f* **2.** nicht beachten

dis·rep·u·ta·ble übel; verrufen

dis·re·pute schlechter Ruf

dis·re·spect Respektlosigkeit *f*; Unhöflichkeit *f*

dis·re·spect·ful respektlos; unhöflich

dis·rupt unterbrechen

dis·sat·is·fac·tion Unzufriedenheit *f*

dis·sat·is·fied unzufrieden (*with* mit)

dis·sect MED sezieren, zerlegen, zergliedern (*a. fig*)

dis·sen·sion Meinungsverschiedenheit(en *pl*) *f*, Differenz(en *pl*) *f*; Uneinigkeit *f*

dis·sent 1. abweichende Meinung **2.** anderer Meinung sein (*from* als)

dis·sent·er Andersdenkende *m*, *f*

dis·si·dent Andersdenkende *m*, *f*; POL Dissident(in), Regime-, Systemkritiker(in)

dis·sim·i·lar (*to*) unähnlich (*dat*); verschieden (von)

dis·sim·u·la·tion Verstellung *f*

dis·si·pate (sich) zerstreuen; verschwenden

dis·si·pat·ed ausschweifend, zügellos

dis·so·ci·ate trennen; *~ o.s.* sich distanzieren (*from* von)

dis·so·lute → *dissipated*

dis·so·lu·tion Auflösung *f*

dis·solve (sich) auflösen

dis·suade *j-m* abraten (*from* von)

dis·tance 1. Abstand *m*; Entfernung *f*; Ferne *f*; Strecke *f*; *fig* Distanz *f*, Zurückhaltung *f*; *at a ~* von weitem; in einiger Entfernung; *keep s.o. at a ~* j-m gegenüber reserviert sein **2.** hinter sich lassen; *~ race* SPORT Langstreckenlauf *m*; *~ run·ner* SPORT Langstreckenläufer(in), Langstreckler(in)

dis·tant entfernt; fern, Fern...; distanziert

dis·taste Widerwille *m*, Abneigung *f*

dis·taste·ful ekelerregend; unangenehm; *be ~ to s.o.* j-m zuwider sein

dis·tem·per VET Staupe *f*

dis·tend (sich) (aus)dehnen; (auf)blähen; sich weiten

dis·til(l) destillieren

dis·tinct verschieden; deutlich, klar

dis·tinc·tion Unterscheidung *f*; Unterschied *m*; Auszeichnung *f*; Rang *m*

dis·tinc·tive unterscheidend; kennzeichnend, bezeichnend

dis·tin·guish unterscheiden; auszeichnen; *~ o.s.* sich auszeichnen

dis·tin·guished berühmt; ausgezeichnet; vornehm

dis·tort verdrehen; verzerren

dis·tract ablenken; **dis·tract·ed** beunruhigt, besorgt; (*by, with* vor *dat*) außer sich, wahnsinnig; **dis·trac·tion** Ablenkung *f*; Zerstreuung *f*; Wahnsinn *m*; *drive s.o. to ~* j-n wahnsinnig machen

dis·traught → *distracted*

dis·tress 1. Leid *n*, Kummer *m*, Sorge *f*; Not(lage) *f* **2.** beunruhigen, mit Sorge erfüllen

dis·tressed Not leidend; *~ ar·e·a* Notstandsgebiet *n*

dis·tress·ing besorgniserregend

dis·trib·ute ver-, aus-, zuteilen; ECON *Waren* vertreiben, absetzen; *Filme* verleihen; **dis·tri·bu·tion** Ver-, Aus-, Zuteilung *f*; ECON Vertrieb *m*, Absatz *m*; *film:* Verleih *m*

dis·trict Bezirk *m*; Gegend *f*

dis·trust 1. Misstrauen *n* **2.** misstrauen (*dat*); **dis·trust·ful** misstrauisch

dis·turb stören; beunruhigen

dis·turb·ance Störung *f*; Unruhe *f*; *~ of the peace* JUR Störung *f* der öffentlichen Sicherheit und Ordnung; *cause a ~* für Unruhe sorgen; ruhestörenden Lärm machen

dis·turbed geistig gestört; verhaltensgestört

dis·used nicht mehr benutzt (*machinery etc*), stillgelegt (*colliery etc*)

ditch Graben *m*

di·van Diwan *m*; *~ bed* Bettcouch *f*

dive 1. (unter)tauchen; *vom Sprungbrett* springen; e-n Hecht- *or* Kopfsprung machen; hechten (*for* nach); e-n Sturz-

flug machen **2.** *swimming:* Springen *n*; Kopfsprung *m*, Hechtsprung *m*; *soccer:* Schwalbe *f*; AVIAT Sturzflug *m*; F Spelunke *f*; **div·er** Taucher(in); SPORT Wasserspringer(in)

di·verge auseinanderlaufen; abweichen; **di·ver·gence** Abweichung *f*; **di·ver·gent** abweichend

di·verse verschieden; mannigfaltig

di·ver·si·fy verschieden(artig) *or* abwechslungsreich gestalten

di·ver·sion Ablenkung *f*; Zeitvertreib *m*; *Br* MOT Umleitung *f*

di·ver·si·ty Verschiedenheit *f*; Mannigfaltigkeit *f*

di·vert ablenken; *j-n* zerstreuen, unterhalten; *Br Verkehr* umleiten

di·vide 1. *v/t* teilen; ver-, aus-, aufteilen; trennen; MATH dividieren, teilen (*by* durch); *v/i* sich teilen; sich aufteilen; MATH sich dividieren *or* teilen lassen (*by* durch); **2.** GEOGR Wasserscheide *f*

di·vid·ed geteilt; *~ highway* Schnellstraße *f*

div·i·dend ECON Dividende *f*

di·vid·ers (*a pair of ~*) ein Stechzirkel *m*

di·vine göttlich

di·vine ser·vice REL Gottesdienst *m*

div·ing 1. Tauchen *n*; SPORT Wasserspringen *n* **2.** Taucher...

div·ing-board Sprungbrett *n*

div·ing-suit Taucheranzug *m*

di·vin·i·ty Gottheit *f*; Göttlichkeit *f*; Theologie *f*

di·vis·i·ble teilbar

di·vi·sion Teilung *f*; Trennung *f*; Abteilung *f*; MIL, MATH Division *f*

di·vorce 1. (Ehe)Scheidung *f*; *get a ~* sich scheiden lassen (*from* von); **2.** JUR *j-n, Ehe* scheiden; *get ~d* sich scheiden lassen; **di·vor·cee** Geschiedene *m, f*

DIY ABBR → *do-it-yourself*

DIY store Baumarkt *m*

diz·zy schwind(e)lig

do *v/t* tun, machen; (zu)bereiten; *Zimmer* aufräumen; *Geschirr* abwaschen; *Wegstrecke* zurücklegen, schaffen; *~ you know him? no, I don't* kennst du ihn? nein; *what can I ~ for you?* was kann ich für Sie tun?, womit kann ich (Ihnen) dienen?; *~ London* F London besichtigen; *have one's hair done* sich die Haare machen *or* frisieren lassen; *have done reading* fertig sein mit Lesen; *v/i* tun, handeln; sich befinden; genügen; *that will* ~ das genügt; *how* ~ *you* ~*?* guten Tag!; ~ *be quick* beeil dich doch; ~ *you like New York?* I ~ gefällt Ihnen New York? ja; *she works hard, doesn't she?* sie arbeitet viel, nicht wahr?; ~ *well* s-e Sache gut machen; gute Geschäfte machen; ~ *away with* beseitigen, weg-, abschaffen; *do s.o. in* F j-n umlegen; *I'm done in* F ich bin geschafft; ~ *up* Kleid etc zumachen; *Haus* etc instand setzen; *Päckchen* zurechtmachen; ~ *o.s. up* sich zurechtmachen; *I could* ~ *with* ... ich könnte ... brauchen *or* vertragen; ~ *without* auskommen *or* sich behelfen ohne

doc F → *doctor*

do·cile gelehrig; fügsam

dock¹ stutzen, kupieren

dock² 1. MAR Dock *n*; Kai *m*, Pier *m*; JUR Anklagebank *f* 2. *v/t* MAR (ein)docken; *Raumschiff* koppeln; *v/i* MAR anlegen; andocken, ankoppeln (*Raumschiff*)

dock·er Dock-, Hafenarbeiter *m*

dock·ing Docking *n*, Ankopp(e)lung *f*

dock·yard MAR Werft *f*

doc·tor Doktor *m* (*a.* UNIV), Arzt *m*, Ärztin *f*

doc·tor·al: ~ *thesis* UNIV Doktorarbeit *f*

doc·trine Doktrin *f*, Lehre *f*

doc·u·ment 1. Urkunde *f* 2. (urkundlich) belegen; **doc·u·men·ta·ry** 1. urkundlich; *film* etc: Dokumentar... 2. Dokumentarfilm *m*

dodge (rasch) zur Seite springen, ausweichen; F sich drücken (vor *dat*)

dodg·er Drückeberger *m*

doe ZO (Reh)Geiß *f*, Ricke *f*

dog 1. ZO Hund *m* 2. *j-n* beharrlich verfolgen

dog-eared mit Eselsohren (*book*)

dog·ged verbissen, hartnäckig

dog·ma Dogma *n*; Glaubenssatz *m*

dog·mat·ic dogmatisch

do-it-your·self 1. Heimwerken *n* 2. Heimwerker...

do-it-your·self·er Heimwerker *m*

dole 1. milde Gabe; *Br* F Stempelgeld *n*; *go or be on the* ~ *Br* F stempeln gehen 2. ~ *out* sparsam ver- *or* austeilen

dole·ful traurig, trübselig

doll Puppe *f*

dol·lar Dollar *m*

dol·phin ZO Delphin *m*

dome Kuppel *f*

do·mes·tic 1. häuslich; inländisch, einheimisch; zahm 2. Hausangestellte *m*, *f*; ~ *an·i·mal* Haustier *n*

do·mes·ti·cate Tier zähmen

do·mes·tic| flight AVIAT Inlandsflug *m*; ~ **mar·ket** ECON Binnenmarkt *m*; ~ **trade** ECON Binnenhandel *m*; ~ **vi·olence** häusliche Gewalt

dom·i·cile Wohnsitz *m*

dom·i·nant dominierend, (vor)herrschend

dom·i·nate beherrschen; dominieren

dom·i·na·tion (Vor)Herrschaft *f*

dom·i·neer·ing herrisch, tyrannisch

do·nate schenken; stiften; spenden (*a.* MED); **do·na·tion** Schenkung *f*

done getan; erledigt; fertig; GASTR gar

don·key ZO Esel *m*

do·nor Spender(in) (*a.* MED)

do-noth·ing F Nichtstuer *m*

doom 1. Schicksal *n*, Verhängnis *n* 2. verurteilen, verdammen

Dooms·day der Jüngste Tag

door Tür *f*; Tor *n*; *next* ~ nebenan

door·bell Türklingel *f*

door han·dle Türklinke *f*

door·keep·er Pförtner *m*

door·knob Türknauf *m*

door·mat (Fuß)Abtreter *m*

door·step Türstufe *f*

door·way Türöffnung *f*

dope 1. F Stoff *m* (*Rauschgift*); Betäubungsmittel *n*; SPORT Dopingmittel *n*; *sl* Trottel *m* 2. F *j-m* Stoff geben; SPORT dopen; ~ **test** SPORT Dopingkontrolle *f*

dor·mant schlafend, ruhend; untätig

dor·mi·to·ry Schlafsaal *m*; Studentenwohnheim *n*

dor·mo·bile® Campingbus *m*, Wohnmobil *n*

dor·mouse ZO Haselmaus *f*

dose 1. Dosis *f* 2. *j-m* e-e Medizin geben

dot 1. Punkt *m*; Fleck *m*; *on the* ~ F auf die Sekunde pünktlich 2. punktieren; tüpfeln; *fig* sprenkeln; ~*ted line* punktierte Linie

dote: ~ *on* vernarrt sein in (*acc*)

dot·ing vernarrt

doub·le 1. doppelt; Doppel...; zweifach 2. Doppelte *n*; Doppelgänger(in); *film*, TV Double *n* 3. (sich) verdoppeln; *film*,

TV *j-n* doubeln; *a.* ~ *up* falten; *Decke* zusammenlegen; ~ *back* kehrtmachen; ~ *up with* sich krümmen vor (*dat*)

dou·ble-breast·ed zweireihig

dou·ble-check genau nachprüfen

dou·ble chin Doppelkinn *n*

dou·ble-cross ein doppeltes *or* falsches Spiel treiben mit

dou·ble-deal·ing 1. betrügerisch **2.** Betrug *m*

dou·ble-deck·er Doppeldecker *m*

dou·ble-edged zweischneidig (*a. fig*); zweideutig

dou·ble fea·ture *film:* Doppelprogramm *n*

dou·ble-park MOT in zweiter Reihe parken

dou·bles *esp tennis:* Doppel *n*; *men's* ~ Herrendoppel *n*; *women's* ~ Damendoppel *n*

dou·ble-sid·ed IT zweiseitig

doubt 1. *v/i* zweifeln; *v/t* bezweifeln; misstrauen (*dat*) **2.** Zweifel *m*; *be in* ~ *about* Zweifel haben an (*dat*); *no* ~ ohne Zweifel

doubt·ful zweifelhaft

doubt·less ohne Zweifel

douche 1. Spülung *f* (*a.* MED); Spülapparat *m* **2.** spülen (*a.* MED)

dough Teig *m*

dough·nut *appr* Krapfen *m*, Berliner Pfannkuchen, Schmalzkringel *m*

dove ZO Taube *f*

dow·dy unelegant; unmodern

dow·el TECH Dübel *m*

down¹ Daunen *pl*; Flaum *m*

down² 1. *adv* nach unten, herunter, hinunter, herab, hinab, abwärts; unten **2.** *prp* herab, hinab, herunter, hinunter; ~ *the river* flussabwärts **3.** *adj* nach unten gerichtet; deprimiert, niedergeschlagen; ~ *platform* Abfahrtsbahnsteig *m* (*in London*); ~ *train* Zug *m* (von London fort) **4.** *v/t* niederschlagen; *Flugzeug* abschießen; F *Getränk* runterkippen; ~ *tools* die Arbeit niederlegen, in den Streik treten

down·cast niedergeschlagen

down·fall Platzregen *m*; *fig* Sturz *m*

down·heart·ed niedergeschlagen

down·hill 1. *adv* bergab **2.** *adj* abschüssig; *skiing:* Abfahrts... **3.** Abhang *m*; *skiing:* Abfahrt *f*

down pay·ment ECON Anzahlung *f*

down·pour Regenguss *m*, Platzregen *m*

down·right 1. *adv* völlig, ganz und gar, ausgesprochen **2.** *adj* glatt (*lie etc*); ausgesprochen

downs Hügelland *n*

down·stairs die Treppe herunter *or* hinunter; (nach) unten

down·stream stromabwärts

down-to-earth realistisch

down·town 1. *adv* im *or* ins Geschäftsviertel **2.** *adj* im Geschäftsviertel (gelegen *or* tätig); **3.** Geschäftsviertel *n*, Innenstadt *f*, City *f*

down·ward(s) abwärts, nach unten

down·y flaumig

dow·ry Mitgift *f*

doze 1. dösen, ein Nickerchen machen **2.** Nickerchen *n*

doz·en Dutzend *n*

drab trist; düster; eintönig

draft 1. Entwurf *m*; (Luft)Zug *m*; Zugluft *f*; Zug *m*, Schluck *m*; MAR Tiefgang *m*; ECON Tratte *f*, Wechsel *m*; MIL Einberufung *f*; *beer on* ~, ~ *beer* Bier *n* vom Fass, Fassbier *n* **2.** entwerfen; *Brief etc* aufsetzen; MIL einberufen

draft·ee MIL Wehr(dienst)pflichtige *m*

drafts·man TECH Zeichner *m*

drafts·wom·an TECH Zeichnerin *f*

draft·y zugig

drag 1. Schleppen *n*, Zerren *n*; *fig* Hemmschuh *m*; F *et.* Langweiliges **2.** schleppen, zerren, ziehen, schleifen; *a.* ~ *behind* zurückbleiben, nachhinken; ~ *on* weiterschleppen; *fig* sich dahinschleppen; *fig* sich in die Länge ziehen

drag lift Schlepplift *m*

drag·on MYTH Drache *m*

drag·on·fly ZO Libelle *f*

drain 1. Abfluss(kanal) *m*, Abflussrohr *n*; Entwässerungsgraben *m* **2.** *v/t* abfließen lassen; entwässern; austrinken, leeren; *v/i:* ~ *off*, ~ *away* abfließen, ablaufen; **drain·age** Abfließen *n*, Ablaufen *n*, Entwässerung *f*; Entwässerungsanlage *f*, -system *n*

drain·pipe Abflussrohr *n*

drake ZO Enterich *m*, Erpel *m*

dram Schluck *m*

dra·ma Drama *n*; **dra·mat·ic** dramatisch; **dram·a·tist** Dramatiker *m*; **dram·a·tize** dramatisieren

drape 1. drapieren; in Falten legen **2.**

mst **~s** Vorhänge *pl*
drap·er·y *Br* Textilien *pl*
dras·tic drastisch, durchgreifend
draught *Br* → **draft**
draughts *Br* Damespiel *n*
draughts·man *etc* → **draftsman** *etc*
draugh·ty *Br* → **drafty**
draw 1. *v/t* ziehen; *Vorhänge* auf-, zuziehen; *Atem* holen; *Tee* ziehen lassen; *fig Menge* anziehen; *Interesse* auf sich ziehen; zeichnen; *Geld* abheben; *Scheck* ausstellen; *v/i* ziehen; SPORT unentschieden spielen; **~ back** zurückweichen; **~ near** sich nähern; **~ out** *Geld* abheben; *fig* in die Länge ziehen; **~ up** *Schriftstück* aufsetzen; MOT (an)halten; vorfahren **2.** Ziehen *n*; *lottery*: Ziehung *f*; SPORT Unentschieden *n*; Attraktion *f*, Zugnummer *f*
draw·back Nachteil *m*, Hindernis *n*
draw·bridge Zugbrücke *f*
draw·er¹ Schublade *f*, Schubfach *n*
draw·er² Zeichner(in); ECON Aussteller(in)
draw·ing Zeichnen *n*; Zeichnung *f*; **~ board** Reißbrett *n*; **~ pin** *Br* Reißzwecke *f*, Reißnagel *m*, Heftzwecke *f*; **~ room** → **living room**; Salon *m*
drawl gedehnt sprechen
drawn abgespannt; SPORT unentschieden
dread 1. (große) Angst, Furcht *f* **2.** (sich) fürchten
dread·ful schrecklich, furchtbar
dream 1. Traum *m* **2.** träumen
dream·er Träumer(in)
dream·y träumerisch, verträumt
drear·y trübselig; trüb(e); langweilig
dredge 1. (Schwimm)Bagger *m* **2.** (aus)baggern
dredg·er (Schwimm)Bagger *m*
dregs Bodensatz *m*; *fig* Abschaum *m*
drench durchnässen
dress 1. Kleidung *f*; Kleid *n* **2.** (sich) ankleiden *or* anziehen; schmücken, dekorieren; zurechtmachen; GASTR zubereiten, *Salat* anmachen; MED *Wunde* verbinden; *Haare* frisieren; **get ~ed** sich anziehen; **~ s.o. down** F j-m e-e Standpauke halten; **~ up** (sich) fein machen; sich kostümieren *or* verkleiden
dress cir·cle THEA erster Rang
dress de·sign·er Modezeichner(in)
dress·er Anrichte *f*; Toilettentisch *m*

dress·ing An-, Zurichten *n*; Ankleiden *n*; MED Verband *m*; GASTR Dressing *n*, Füllung *f*
dressing-down F Standpauke *f*
dress·ing\| gown *esp Br* Morgenrock *m*, -mantel *m*; SPORT Bademantel *m*; **~ room** THEA *etc* (Künstler)Garderobe *f*; SPORT (Umkleide)Kabine *f*; **~ ta·ble** Toilettentisch *m*
dress·mak·er (Damen)Schneider(in)
dress re·hears·al THEA *etc* Generalprobe *f*
drib·ble tröpfeln (lassen); sabbern, geifern; *soccer*: dribbeln
dried getrocknet, Dörr...
dri·er → **dryer**
drift 1. (Dahin)Treiben *n*; (Schnee)Verwehung *f*; Schnee-, Sandwehe *f*; *fig* Tendenz *f* **2.** (dahin)treiben; wehen; sich häufen
drill 1. TECH Bohrer *m*; MIL Drill *m* (*a. fig*), Exerzieren *n* **2.** bohren; MIL drillen (*a. fig*); **drill·ing site** TECH Bohrgelände *n*, Bohrstelle *f*
drink 1. Getränk *n* **2.** trinken; **~ to s.o.** j-m zuprosten *or* zutrinken
drink-driv·ing *Br* Trunkenheit *f* am Steuer
drink·er Trinker(in)
drinks ma·chine Getränkeautomat *m*
drip 1. Tröpfeln *n*; MED Tropf *m* **2.** tropfen *or* tröpfeln (lassen); triefen
drip-dry bügelfrei
drip·ping Bratenfett *n*
drive 1. Fahrt *f*; Aus-, Spazierfahrt *f*; Zufahrt(sstraße) *f*; (private) Auffahrt; TECH Antrieb *m*; IT Laufwerk *n*; MOT (*Links- etc*)Steuerung *f*; PSYCH Trieb *m*; *fig* Kampagne *f*; *fig* Schwung *m*, Elan *m*, Dynamik *f* **2.** *v/t* treiben; *Auto etc* fahren, lenken, steuern; (im Auto *etc*) fahren; TECH (an)treiben; *a.* **~ off** vertreiben; *v/i* treiben; (Auto) fahren; **~ off** wegfahren; **what are you driving at?** F worauf wollen Sie hinaus?
drive-in 1. Auto...; **~ cinema** *Br*, **~ motion-picture theater** Autokino *n* **2.** Autokino *n*; Drive-in-Restaurant *n*; Autoschalter *m*, Drive-in-Schalter *m*
driv·el 1. faseln **2.** Geschwätz *n*, Gefasel *n*
driv·er MOT Fahrer(in); (*Lokomotiv-*) Führer *m*
driv·er's li·cense Führerschein *m*

driv·ing (an)treibend; TECH Antriebs...,
Treib..., Trieb...; MOT Fahr...

driv·ing force *fig* Triebkraft *f*

driv·ing li·cence *Br* Führerschein *m*

driv·ing test Fahrprüfung *f*

driz·zle 1. Sprühregen *m* **2.** sprühen, nieseln

drone 1. ZO Drohne *f* (*a. fig*) **2.** summen;
dröhnen

droop (schlaff) herabhängen

drop 1. Tropfen *m*; Fallen *n*, Fall *m*; *fig*
Fall *m*, Sturz *m*; Bonbon *m*, *n*; *fruit* ~*s*
Drops *pl* **2.** *v/t* tropfen (lassen); fallen
lassen(*a. fig*); *Brief* einwerfen; *Fahrgast* absetzen; senken; ~ *s.o. a few
lines* j-m ein paar Zeilen schreiben;
v/i tropfen; herab-, herunterfallen;
umsinken, fallen; ~ *in* (kurz) hereinschauen; ~ *off* abfallen; zurückgehen,
nachlassen; F einnicken; ~ *out* herausfallen; aussteigen (*of* aus); *a.* ~ *out of
school* (*university*) die Schule (das
Studium) abbrechen

drop·out Drop-out *m*, Aussteiger *m*;
(Schul-, Studien)Abbrecher *m*

drought Trockenheit *f*, Dürre *f*

drown *v/t* ertränken; überschwemmen;
fig übertönen; *v/i* ertrinken

drow·sy schläfrig; einschläfernd

drudge sich (ab)placken, schuften, sich
schinden; **drudg·e·ry** (stumpfsinnige)
Plackerei *or* Schinderei *or* Schufterei

drug 1. Arzneimittel *n*, Medikament *n*;
Droge *f*, Rauschgift *n*; *be on* ~*s* drogenabhängig *or* drogensüchtig sein;
be off ~*s clean* sein **2.** j-m Medikamente geben; j-n unter Drogen setzen;
ein Betäubungsmittel beimischen
(*dat*); betäuben (*a. fig*); ~ *a·buse* Drogenmissbrauch *m*; Medikamentenmissbrauch *m*; ~ *ad·dict* Drogenabhängige *m*, *f*, Drogensüchtige *m*, *f*;
be a ~ drogenabhängig *or* drogensüchtig sein

drug·gist Apotheker(in); Inhaber(in)
e-s Drugstores

drug·store Apotheke *f*; Drugstore *m*

drug vic·tim Drogentote *m*, *f*

drum 1. MUS Trommel *f*; ANAT Trommelfell *n*; *pl* MUS Schlagzeug *n* **2.** trommeln; **drum·mer** MUS Trommler *m*;
Schlagzeuger *m*

drunk 1. *adj* betrunken; *get* ~ sich betrinken **2.** Betrunkene *m*, *f*; → **drunk-
ard**

drunk·ard Trinker(in), Säufer(in)

drunk driv·ing Trunkenheit *f* am Steuer

drunk·en betrunken; ~ **driv·ing** *Br*
Trunkenheit *f* am Steuer

dry 1. trocken, GASTR *a.* herb; F durstig **2.**
trocknen; dörren; ~ *out* trocknen; e-e
Entziehungskur machen, F trocken
werden; ~ *up* austrocknen; versiegen

dry-clean chemisch reinigen

dry clean·er's chemische Reinigung

dry·er TECH Trockner *m*

dry goods Textilien *pl*

du·al doppelt, Doppel...; ~ **car-
riageway** *Br* Schnellstraße *f*

dub *Film* synchronisieren

du·bi·ous zweifelhaft

duch·ess Herzogin *f*

duck 1. ZO Ente *f*; Ducken *n*; F Schatz *m*
2. (unter)tauchen; (sich) ducken

duck·ling ZO Entchen *n*

due 1. zustehend; gebührend; angemessen; ECON fällig; ~ *to* wegen (*gen*); *be* ~
to zurückzuführen sein auf (*acc*) **2.** *adv*
direkt, genau (*nach Osten etc*)

du·el Duell *n*

dues Gebühren *pl*; Beitrag *m*

du·et MUS Duett *n*

duke Herzog *m*

dull 1. dumm; träge, schwerfällig;
stumpf; matt (*eyes etc*); schwach (*hearing*); langweilig; abgestumpft, teilnahmslos; dumpf; trüb(e); ECON flau
2. stumpf machen *or* werden; (sich)
trüben; mildern, dämpfen; *Schmerz*
betäuben; *fig* abstumpfen

du·ly ordnungsgemäß; gebührend;
rechtzeitig

dumb stumm; sprachlos; F doof, dumm,
blöd

dum(b)·found·ed verblüfft, sprachlos

dum·my Attrappe *f*; Kleider-, Schaufensterpuppe *f*; MOT Dummy *m*, Puppe
f; *Br* Schnuller *m*

dump 1. *v/t* (hin)plumpsen *or* (hin)fallen
lassen; auskippen; *Schutt etc* abladen;
Schadstoffe in e-n Fluss etc einleiten,
im Meer verklappen (*into* in); ECON
Waren zu Dumpingpreisen verkaufen
2. Plumps *m*; Schuttabladeplatz *m*,
Müllkippe *f*, Müllhalde *f*, (Müll)Deponie *f*; **dump·ing** ECON Dumping *n*, Ausfuhr *f* zu Schleuderpreisen

dune Düne *f*

dung AGR 1. Dung *m* 2. düngen
dun·geon (Burg)Verlies *n*
dupe betrügen, täuschen
du·plex 1. doppelt, Doppel... 2. *a.* ~ *apartment* Maisonette *f*, Maisonette-wohnung *f*; *a.* ~ *house* Doppel-, Zwei-familienhaus *n*
du·pli·cate 1. doppelt; ~ *key* Zweit-, Nachschlüssel *m* 2. Duplikat *n*; Zweit-, Nachschlüssel *m* 3. doppelt ausferti-gen; kopieren, vervielfältigen
du·plic·i·ty Doppelzüngigkeit *f*
dur·a·ble haltbar; dauerhaft
du·ra·tion Dauer *f*
du·ress Zwang *m*
dur·ing während
dusk (Abend)Dämmerung *f*
dusk·y dämmerig, düster (*a. fig*); schwärzlich
dust 1. Staub *m* 2. *v/t* abstauben; (be-)streuen; *v/i* Staub wischen, abstauben
dust·bin *Br* Abfall-, Mülleimer *m*; Ab-fall-, Mülltonne *f*; ~ **lin·er** *Br* Müllbeu-tel *m*
dust·cart *Br* Müllwagen *m*
dust cov·er, dust jack·et Schutzum-schlag *m*
dust·er Staubtuch *n*
dust·man *Br* Müllmann *m*
dust·pan Kehrichtschaufel *f*
dust·y staubig
Dutch 1. *adj* holländisch, niederländisch

2. *adv*: *go* ~ getrennte Kasse machen 3. LING Holländisch *n*, Niederländisch *n*; *the* ~ die Holländer *pl*, die Niederlän-der *pl*
Dutch·man Holländer *m*, Niederländer *m*; **Dutch·wom·an** Holländerin *f*, Nie-derländerin *f*
du·ti·a·ble ECON zollpflichtig
du·ty Pflicht *f*; Ehrerbietung *f*; ECON Ab-gabe *f*; Zoll *m*; Dienst *m*; *on* ~ dienst-habend; *be on* ~ Dienst haben; *be off* ~ dienstfrei haben; **du·ty-free** zollfrei
DVD *abbr of* ***Digital Versatile Disk*** DVD; ~ **player** DVD-Player *m*; ~ **re-corder** DVD-Rekorder *m*
dwarf 1. Zwerg(in) 2. verkleinern, klein erscheinen lassen
dwell wohnen; *fig* verweilen (*on* bei)
dwell·ing Wohnung *f*
dwin·dle (dahin)schwinden, abnehmen
dye 1. Farbe *f*; *of the deepest* ~ *fig* von der übelsten Sorte 2. färben
dy·ing 1. sterbend; Sterbe... 2. Sterben *n*; ~ *of forests* Waldsterben *n*
dyke → **dike**[1, 2]
dy·nam·ic dynamisch, kraftgeladen
dy·nam·ics Dynamik *f*
dy·na·mite 1. Dynamit *n* 2. (mit Dyna-mit) sprengen
dys·en·te·ry MED Ruhr *f*
dys·pep·si·a MED Verdauungsstörung *f*

E

E, e E, e *n*
each jede(r, -s); ~ *other* einander, sich; je, pro Person, pro Stück
ea·ger begierig; eifrig
ea·ger·ness Begierde *f*; Eifer *m*
ea·gle ZO Adler *m*; HIST Zehndollar-stück *n*; **ea·gle-eyed** scharfsichtig
ear BOT Ähre *f*; ANAT Ohr *n*; Öhr *n*; Hen-kel *m*
ear·ache Ohrenschmerzen *pl*
ear·drum ANAT Trommelfell *n*
earl *englischer* Graf
ear·lobe ANAT Ohrläppchen *n*
ear·ly früh; Früh...; Anfangs..., erste(r, -s); bald(ig); *as* ~ *as May* schon im Mai; *as* ~ *as possible* so bald wie möglich; ~

on schon früh, frühzeitig
ear·ly bird Frühaufsteher(in)
ear·ly warn·ing sys·tem MIL Frühwarn-system *n*
ear·mark 1. Kennzeichen *n*; Merkmal *n* 2. kennzeichnen; zurücklegen (*for* für)
earn verdienen; einbringen
ear·nest 1. ernst, ernstlich, ernsthaft; ernst gemeint 2. Ernst *m*; *in* ~ im Ernst; ernsthaft
earn·ings Einkommen *n*
ear·phones Ohrhörer *pl*; Kopfhörer *pl*
ear·piece TEL Hörmuschel *f*
ear·ring Ohrring *m*
ear·shot: *within* (*out of*) ~ in (außer) Hörweite

earth 1. Erde f; Land n **2.** v/t ELECTR erden

earth·en irden

earth·en·ware Steingut(geschirr) n

earth·ly irdisch, weltlich; F denkbar

earth·quake Erdbeben n

earth·worm zo Regenwurm m

ease 1. Bequemlichkeit f; (Gemüts)Ruhe f; Sorglosigkeit f; Leichtigkeit f; **at (one's) ~** ruhig, entspannt; unbefangen; **be** or **feel ill at ~** sich (in s-r Haut) nicht wohlfühlen **2.** v/t erleichtern; beruhigen; Schmerzen lindern; v/i mst **~ off, ~ up** nachlassen; sich entspannen (situation etc)

ea·sel Staffelei f

east 1. Ost, Osten m **2.** adj östlich, Ost... **3.** adv nach Osten, ostwärts

East·er Ostern n; Oster...; **~ bun·ny** Osterhase m; **~ egg** Osterei n

eas·ter·ly östlich, Ost...

east·ern östlich, Ost...

east·ward(s) östlich, nach Osten

eas·y leicht; einfach; bequem; gemächlich, gemütlich; ungezwungen; **go ~ on** schonen, sparsam umgehen mit; **go ~, take it ~** sich Zeit lassen; **take it ~!** immer mit der Ruhe!

eas·y chair Sessel m

eas·y·go·ing gelassen; ungezwungen

eat essen; (zer)fressen; **~ out** essen gehen; **~ up** aufessen

eat·a·ble essbar, genießbar

eat·er Esser(in)

eaves Dachrinne f, Traufe f

eaves·drop (heimlich) lauschen or horchen; **~ on** belauschen

ebb 1. Ebbe f **2.** zurückgehen; **~ away** abnehmen; **~ tide** Ebbe f

eb·o·ny Ebenholz n

ec·cen·tric 1. exzentrisch **2.** Exzentriker m, Sonderling m

ec·cle·si·as·tic, ec·cle·si·as·ti·cal geistlich, kirchlich

ech·o 1. Echo n **2.** widerhallen; fig echoen, nachsprechen

e·clipse ASTR (Sonnen-, Mond)Finsternis f; fig Niedergang m

e·co·cide Umweltzerstörung f

e·co·lo·gi·cal ökologisch, Umwelt...

e·col·o·gist Ökologe m

e·col·o·gy Ökologie f

ec·o·nom·ic Wirtschafts..., wirtschaftlich; **~ growth** Wirtschaftswachstum n

e·co·nom·i·cal wirtschaftlich, sparsam

e·co·nom·ics Volkswirtschaft(slehre) f

e·con·o·mist Volkswirt m

e·con·o·mize sparsam wirtschaften (mit)

e·con·o·my 1. Wirtschaft f; Wirtschaftlichkeit f, Sparsamkeit f; Einsparung f **2.** Spar...

e·co·sys·tem Ökosystem n

ec·sta·sy Ekstase f, Verzückung f

ec·stat·ic verzückt

ed·dy 1. Wirbel m **2.** wirbeln

edge 1. Schneide f; Rand m; Kante f; Schärfe f; **be on ~** nervös or gereizt sein **2.** schärfen; (um)säumen; (sich) drängen

edge·ways, edge·wise seitlich, von der Seite

edg·ing Einfassung f; Rand m

edg·y scharf(kantig); F nervös; F gereizt

ed·i·ble essbar, genießbar

e·dict Edikt n

ed·i·fice Gebäude n

ed·it Text herausgeben, redigieren; IT editieren; Zeitung als Herausgeber leiten; **e·di·tion** (Buch)Ausgabe f; Auflage f; **ed·i·tor** Herausgeber(in); Redakteur(in); **ed·i·to·ri·al 1.** Leitartikel m **2.** Redaktions...

EDP abbr of **electronic data processing** EDV, elektronische Datenverarbeitung

ed·u·cate erziehen; unterrichten

ed·u·cat·ed gebildet

ed·u·ca·tion Erziehung f; (Aus)Bildung f; Bildungs-, Schulwesen n; **Ministry of Education** appr Unterrichtsministerium

ed·u·ca·tion·al erzieherisch, pädagogisch, Erziehungs...; Bildungs...

ed·u·ca·tion·(al·)ist Pädagoge m

eel zo Aal m

ef·fect (Aus)Wirkung f; Effekt m, Eindruck m; pl ECON Effekten pl; **be in ~** in Kraft sein; **in ~** in Wirklichkeit; **take ~** in Kraft treten; **ef·fec·tive** wirksam; eindrucksvoll; tatsächlich

ef·fem·i·nate verweichlicht; weibisch

ef·fer·vesce brausen, sprudeln

ef·fer·ves·cent sprudelnd, schäumend

ef·fi·cien·cy Leistung f; Leistungsfähigkeit f; **~ measure** ECON Rationalisierungsmaßnahme f; **ef·fi·cient** wirksam; leistungsfähig, tüchtig

ef·flu·ent Abwasser *n*, Abwässer *pl*

ef·fort Anstrengung *f*, Bemühung *f* (*at* um); Mühe *f*; *without* ~ → **ef·fort·less** mühelos, ohne Anstrengung

ef·fron·te·ry Frechheit *f*

ef·fu·sive überschwänglich

egg¹ Ei *n*; *put all one's* ~*s in one basket* alles vor eine Karte setzen

egg²: ~ *on* anstacheln

egg co·sy *Br* Eierwärmer *m*

egg·cup Eierbecher *m*

egg·head F Eierkopf *m*

egg·plant BOT Aubergine *f*

egg·shell Eierschale *f*

egg tim·er Eieruhr *f*

e·go·is·m Egoismus *m*, Selbstsucht *f*

e·go·ist Egoist(in)

E·gypt Ägypten *n*; **E·gyp·tian 1.** ägyptisch **2.** Ägypter(in)

ei·der·down Eiderdaunen *pl*; Daunendecke *f*

eight 1. acht **2.** Acht *f*

eigh·teen 1. achtzehn **2.** Achtzehn *f*

eigh·teenth achtzehnte(r, -s)

eight·fold achtfach

eighth 1. achte(r, -s) **2.** Achtel *n*

eighth·ly achtens

eigh·ti·eth achtzigste(r, -s)

eigh·ty 1. achtzig; *the eighties* die Achtzigerjahre **2.** Achtzig *f*

ei·ther jede(r, -s) (*von zweien*): eine(r, -s) (*von zweien*); beides; ~ ... *or* entweder ... oder; *not* ~ auch nicht

e·jac·u·late *v/t* Samen ausstoßen; *v/i* ejakulieren; e-n Samenerguss haben

e·jac·u·la·tion Samenerguss *m*

e·ject *j-n* hinauswerfen; TECH ausstoßen, auswerfen

eke: ~ *out Vorräte etc* strecken; *Einkommen* aufbessern; ~ *out a living* sich (mühsam) durchschlagen

e·lab·o·rate 1. sorgfältig (aus)gearbeitet; kompliziert **2.** sorgfältig ausarbeiten

e·lapse verfließen, verstreichen

e·las·tic 1. elastisch, dehnbar; ~ *band Br* → **2.** Gummiring, Gummiband *n*

e·las·ti·ci·ty Elastizität *f*

e·lat·ed begeistert (*at, by* von)

el·bow 1. Ellbogen *m*; (scharfe) Biegung; TECH Knie *n*; *at one's* ~ bei der Hand **2.** mit dem Ellbogen (weg)stoßen; ~ *one's way through* sich (mit den Ellbogen) e-n Weg bahnen durch

el·der¹ **1.** ältere(r, -s) **2.** der, die Ältere;

(Kirchen)Älteste(r) *m*

el·der² BOT Holunder *m*

el·der·ly ältlich, ältere(r, -s)

el·dest älteste(r, -s)

e·lect 1. gewählt **2.** (aus-, er)wählen

e·lec·tion Wahl *f*; ~ *vic·to·ry* POL Wahlsieg *m*; ~ *win·ner* POL Wahlsieger *m*

e·lec·tor Wähler(in); POL Wahlmann *m*; HIST Kurfürst *m*; **e·lec·to·ral** Wähler..., Wahl...; ~ *college* POL Wahlmänner *pl*; ~ *district* POL Wahlkreis *m*; **elec·to·rate** POL Wähler(schaft *f*) *pl*

e·lec·tric elektrisch, Elektro...

e·lec·tri·cal elektrisch; Elektro...; ~ *en·gi·neer* Elektroingenieur *m*, Elektrotechniker *m*; ~ *en·gi·neer·ing* Elektrotechnik *f*

e·lec·tric chair elektrischer Stuhl

e·lec·tri·cian Elektriker *m*

e·lec·tri·ci·ty Elektrizität *f*

e·lec·tric ra·zor Elektrorasierer *m*

e·lec·tri·fy elektrifizieren; elektrisieren (*a. fig*)

e·lec·tro·cute auf dem elektrischen Stuhl hinrichten; durch elektrischen Strom töten

e·lec·tron Elektron *n*

e·lec·tron·ic elektronisch, Elektronen...; ~ *da·ta pro·cess·ing* elektronische Datenverarbeitung

e·lec·tron·ics Elektronik *f*

el·e·gance Eleganz *f*; **el·egant** elegant; geschmackvoll; erstklassig

el·e·ment CHEM Element *n*; Urstoff *m*; (Grund)Bestandteil *m*; *pl* Anfangsgründe *pl*, Grundlage(n *pl*) *f*; Elemente *pl*, Naturkräfte *pl*

el·e·men·tal elementar; wesentlich

el·e·men·ta·ry elementar; Anfangs...; ~ *school* Grundschule *f*

el·e·phant ZO Elefant *m*

el·e·vate erhöhen; *fig* erheben

el·evat·ed erhöht; *fig* gehoben, erhaben

el·e·va·tion Erhebung *f*; Erhöhung *f*; Höhe *f*; Erhabenheit *f*

el·e·va·tor TECH Lift *m*, Fahrstuhl *m*, Aufzug *m*

e·lev·en 1. elf **2.** Elf *f*

e·leventh 1. elfte(r, -s) **2.** Elftel *n*

elf Elf *m*, Elfe *f*; Kobold *m*

e·li·cit *et.* entlocken (*from dat*); ans (Tages)Licht bringen

el·i·gi·ble infrage kommend, geeignet, annehmbar, akzeptabel

e·lim·i·nate entfernen, beseitigen; ausscheiden; **e·lim·i·na·tion** Entfernung *f*, Beseitigung *f*; Ausscheidung *f*

é·lite Elite *f*; Auslese *f*

elk ZO Elch *m*; Wapitihirsch *m*

el·lipse MATH Ellipse *f*

elm BOT Ulme *f*

e·lon·gate verlängern

e·lope (mit s-m *or* s-r Geliebten) ausreißen *or* durchbrennen

el·o·quent redegewandt, beredt

else sonst, weiter; andere(r, -s)

else·where anderswo(hin)

e·lude geschickt entgehen, ausweichen, sich entziehen (*all:* dat); *fig* nicht einfallen (*dat*)

e·lu·sive schwer fassbar

e·ma·ci·ated abgezehrt, ausgemergelt

em·a·nate ausströmen; ausgehen (*from* von); **em·a·na·tion** Ausströmen *n*; *fig* Ausstrahlung *f*

e·man·ci·pate emanzipieren

e·man·ci·pa·tion Emanzipation *f*

em·balm (ein)balsamieren

em·bank·ment (Bahn-, Straßen-) Damm *m*; (Erd)Damm *m*; Uferstraße *f*

em·bar·go ECON Embargo *n*, (Hafen-, Handels)Sperre *f*

em·bark AVIAT, MAR an Bord nehmen *or* gehen, MAR *a.* (sich) einschiffen; *Waren* verladen; **~ on** *et.* anfangen, *et.* beginnen

em·bar·rass in Verlegenheit bringen, verlegen machen, in e-e peinliche Lage bringen; **em·bar·rass·ing** unangenehm, peinlich; verfänglich

em·bar·rass·ment Verlegenheit *f*

em·bas·sy POL Botschaft *f*

em·bed (ein)betten, (ein)lagern

em·bel·lish verschönern; *fig* ausschmücken, beschönigen

em·bers Glut *f*

em·bez·zle unterschlagen

em·bez·zle·ment Unterschlagung *f*

em·bit·ter verbittern

em·blem Sinnbild *n*; Wahrzeichen *n*

em·bod·y verkörpern; enthalten

em·bo·lis·m MED Embolie *f*

em·brace 1. (sich) umarmen; einschließen **2.** Umarmung *f*

em·broi·der (be)sticken; *fig* ausschmücken; **em·broi·der·y** Stickerei *f*; *fig* Ausschmückung *f*

em·broil verwickeln (*in* in *acc*)

e·mend *Texte* verbessern, korrigieren

em·e·rald 1. Smaragd *m* **2.** smaragdgrün

e·merge auftauchen; sich herausstellen *or* ergeben

e·mer·gen·cy 1. Not *f*, Notlage *f*, Notfall *m*, Notstand *m*; **state of ~** POL Ausnahmezustand *m* **2.** Not...; **~ brake** Notbremse *f*; **~ call** Notruf *m*; **~ ex·it** Notausgang *m*; **~ land·ing** AVIAT Notlandung *f*; **~ num·ber** Notruf(nummer *f*) *m*; **~ room** MED Notaufnahme *f*

em·i·grant Auswanderer *m*, *esp* POL Emigrant(in)

em·i·grate auswandern, *esp* POL emigrieren

em·i·gra·tion Auswanderung *f*, *esp* POL Emigration *f*

em·i·nence Berühmtheit *f*, Bedeutung *f*; **Eminence** REL Eminenz *f*

em·i·nent hervorragend, berühmt; bedeutend; **~ly** ganz besonders, äußerst

e·mis·sion Ausstoß *m*, Ausstrahlung *f*, Ausströmen *n*; **~-free** abgasfrei

e·mit aussenden, ausstoßen, ausstrahlen, ausströmen; von sich geben

e·mo·tion (Gemüts)Bewegung *f*, Gefühl *n*, Gefühlsregung *f*; Rührung *f*

e·mo·tion·al emotional; gefühlsmäßig; gefühlsbetont

e·mo·tion·al·ly emotional, gefühlsmäßig; **~ disturbed** seelisch gestört

e·mo·tion·less gefühllos

e·mo·tive word PSYCH Reizwort *n*

em·pe·ror Kaiser *m*

em·pha·sis Gewicht *n*; Nachdruck *m*

em·pha·size nachdrücklich betonen

em·phat·ic nachdrücklich; deutlich; bestimmt

em·pire Reich *n*, Imperium *n*; Kaiserreich *n*

em·pir·i·cal erfahrungsgemäß

em·ploy 1. beschäftigen, anstellen; anverwenden, gebrauchen **2.** Beschäftigung *f*

em·ploy·ee Angestellte *m*, *f*, Arbeitnehmer(in)

em·ploy·er Arbeitgeber(in)

em·ploy·ment Beschäftigung *f*, Arbeit *f*; **~ ad** Stellenanzeige *f*; **~ a·gen·cy** *Br* Arbeitsagentur *f*; **~ of·fice** Arbeitsamt *n*

em·pow·er ermächtigen; befähigen

em·press Kaiserin *f*

emp·tl·ness Leere *f* (*a. fig*)
emp·ty 1. leer (*a. fig*) **2.** leeren, ausleeren, entleeren; sich leeren
em·u·late wetteifern mit; nacheifern (*dat*); es gleichtun (*dat*)
e·mul·sion Emulsion *f*
en·a·ble befähigen, es *j-m* ermöglichen; ermächtigen
en·act *Gesetz* erlassen; verfügen
e·nam·el 1. Email *n*, Emaille *f*; ANAT (Zahn)Schmelz *m*; Glasur *f*, Lack *m*; Nagellack *m* **2.** emaillieren; glasieren; lackieren
en·cased: ~ *in* gehüllt in (*acc*)
en·chant bezaubern; **en·chant·ing** bezaubernd; **en·chant·ment** Bezauberung *f*; Zauber *m*
en·cir·cle einkreisen, umzingeln; umfassen, umschlingen
en·close einschließen, umgeben; beilegen, beifügen
en·clo·sure Einzäunung *f*; Anlage *f*
en·code verschlüsseln, chiffrieren; kodieren
en·com·pass umgeben
en·coun·ter 1. Begegnung *f*; Gefecht *n* **2.** begegnen (*dat*); auf *Schwierigkeiten etc* stoßen; mit *j-m feindlich* zusammenstoßen
en·cour·age ermutigen; fördern
en·cour·age·ment Ermutigung *f*; Anfeuerung *f*; Unterstützung *f*
en·cour·ag·ing ermutigend
en·croach (*on*) eingreifen (in *j-s Recht etc*), eindringen (in *acc*); über Gebühr in Anspruch nehmen (*acc*)
en·croach·ment Ein-, Übergriff *m*
en·cum·ber belasten; (be)hindern
en·cum·brance Belastung *f*
en·cy·clo·p(a)e·di·a Enzyklopädie *f*
end 1. Ende *n*; Ziel *n*, Zweck *m*; *no* ~ *of* unendlich viel(e), unzählige; *at the* ~ *of May* Ende Mai; *in the* ~ am Ende, schließlich; *on* ~ aufrecht; *stand on* ~ zu Berge stehen (*hair*); *to no* ~ vergebens; *go off the deep* ~ F *fig* in die Luft gehen; *make* (*both*) ~*s meet* durchkommen, finanziell über die Runden kommen **2.** enden; beend(-ig)en
en·dan·ger gefährden
en·dear beliebt machen (*to s.o.* bei *j-m*); **en·dear·ing** gewinnend; liebenswert; **en·dear·ment:** *words of* ~, ~*s* zärtliche Worte *pl*

en·deav·o(u)r 1. Bestreben *n*, Bemühung *f* **2.** sich bemühen
end·ing Ende *n*; Schluss *m*; LING Endung *f*
en·dive BOT Endivie *f*
end·less endlos, unendlich; TECH ohne Ende
en·dorse ECON *Scheck etc* indossieren; *et.* vermerken (*on* auf der Rückseite); billigen; **en·dorse·ment** Vermerk *m*; ECON Indossament *n*, Giro *n*
en·dow *fig* ausstatten; ~ *s.o. with s.th.* *j-m* et. stiften; **en·dow·ment** Stiftung *f*; *mst pl* Begabung *f*, Talent *n*
en·dur·ance Ausdauer *f*; *beyond* ~, *past* ~ unerträglich; **en·dure** ertragen
end us·er Endverbraucher *m*
en·e·my 1. Feind *m* **2.** feindlich
en·er·get·ic energisch; tatkräftig
en·er·gy Energie *f*
en·er·gy cri·sis Energiekrise *f*
en·er·gy-sav·ing energiesparend
en·er·gy sup·ply Energieversorgung *f*
en·fold einhüllen; umfassen
en·force (mit Nachdruck, *a.* gerichtlich) geltend machen; *Gesetz etc* durchführen; durchsetzen, erzwingen
en·force·ment ECON, JUR Geltendmachung *f*; Durchsetzung *f*, Erzwingung *f*
en·fran·chise *j-m* das Wahlrecht verleihen
en·gage *v/t j-s Aufmerksamkeit* auf sich ziehen; TECH einrasten lassen; MOT *e-n Gang* einlegen; *j-n* einstellen, anstellen, *Künstler* engagieren; *v/i* TECH einrasten, greifen; ~ *in* sich einlassen auf (*acc*) *or* in (*acc*); sich beschäftigen mit
en·gaged verlobt (*to* mit); beschäftigt (*in, on* mit); besetzt (*a.* Br TEL); ~ *tone or signal* Br TEL Besetztzeichen *n*
en·gage·ment Verlobung *f*; Verabredung *f*; MIL Gefecht *n*
en·gag·ing einnehmend; gewinnend
en·gine Maschine *f*; Motor *m*; RAIL Lokomotive *f*; ~ *driv·er* Br RAIL Lokomotivführer *m*
en·gi·neer 1. Ingenieur *m*, Techniker *m*, Mechaniker *m*; RAIL Lokomotivführer *m*; MIL Pionier *m* **2.** bauen; *fig* (geschickt) in die Wege leiten
en·gi·neer·ing Technik *f*, Ingenieurwesen *n*, Maschinen- und Gerätebau *m*
En·gland England *n*
En·glish 1. englisch **2.** LING Englisch *n*;

the ~ die Engländer *pl*; *in plain* ~ *fig* unverblümt

Eng·lish·man Engländer *m*

Eng·lish·wom·an Engländerin *f*

en·grave (ein)gravieren, (ein)meißeln, (ein)schnitzen; *fig* einprägen

en·grav·er Graveur *m*

en·grav·ing (Kupfer-, Stahl)Stich *m*; Holzschnitt *m*

en·grossed: ~ *in* (voll) in Anspruch genommen von, vertieft *or* versunken in (*acc*)

en·hance erhöhen, verstärken, steigern

e·nig·ma Rätsel *n*

en·ig·mat·ic rätselhaft

en·joy sich erfreuen an (*dat*); genießen; *did you* ~ *it?* hat es Ihnen gefallen?; ~ *o.s.* sich amüsieren, sich gut unterhalten; ~ *yourself!* viel Spaß!; *I* ~ *my dinner* es schmeckt mir; **en·joy·a·ble** angenehm, erfreulich; **en·joy·ment** Vergnügen *n*, Freude *f*; Genuss *m*

en·large (sich) vergrößern *or* erweitern, ausdehnen; PHOT vergrößern; sich verbreiten *or* auslassen (*on* über *acc*)

en·large·ment Erweiterung *f*; Vergrößerung *f* (*a. PHOT*)

en·light·en aufklären, belehren

en·light·en·ment Aufklärung *f*

en·list MIL *v/t* anwerben; *v/i* sich freiwillig melden

en·liv·en beleben

en·mi·ty Feindschaft *f*

en·no·ble adeln; veredeln

e·nor·mi·ty Ungeheuerlichkeit *f*

e·nor·mous ungeheuer

e·nough genug

en·quire, en·qui·ry → *inquire, inquiry*

en·rage wütend machen

en·raged wütend (*at* über *acc*)

en·rap·ture entzücken, hinreißen

en·rap·tured entzückt, hingerissen

en·rich bereichern; anreichern

en·rol(l) (sich) einschreiben *or* eintragen; UNIV (sich) immatrikulieren

en·sign MAR *esp* (National)Flagge *f*; MIL Leutnant *m* zur See

en·sue (darauf-, nach)folgen

en·sure sichern

en·tail mit sich bringen, zur Folge haben

en·tan·gle verwickeln

en·ter *v/t* hinein-, hereingehen, -kommen, -treten in (*acc*), eintreten, einsteigen in (*acc*), betreten; einreisen in (*acc*); MAR, RAIL einlaufen, einfahren in (*acc*); eindringen in (*acc*); *Namen etc* eintragen, einschreiben; SPORT melden, nennen (*for* für); *fig* eintreten in (*acc*), beitreten (*dat*); IT eingeben; *v/i* eintreten, herein-, hineinkommen, herein-, hineingehen; THEA auftreten; sich eintragen *or* einschreiben *or* anmelden (*for* für); SPORT melden, nennen (*for* für)

en·ter key IT Eingabetaste *f*

en·ter·prise Unternehmen *n* (*a. ECON*); ECON Unternehmertum *n*; Unternehmungsgeist *m*; **en·ter·pris·ing** unternehmungslustig; wagemutig; kühn

en·ter·tain unterhalten; bewirten

en·ter·tain·er Entertainer(in), Unterhaltungskünstler(in)

en·ter·tain·ment Unterhaltung *f*; Entertainment *n*; Bewirtung *f*

en·thral(l) fesseln, bezaubern

en·throne inthronisieren

en·thu·si·asm Begeisterung *f*, Enthusiasmus *m*; **en·thu·si·ast** Enthusiast(in); **en·thu·si·as·tic** begeistert, enthusiastisch

en·tice (ver)locken

en·tice·ment Verlockung *f*, Reiz *m*

en·tire ganz, vollständig; ungeteilt

en·tire·ly völlig; ausschließlich

en·ti·tle betiteln; berechtigen (*to* zu)

en·ti·ty Einheit *f*

en·trails ANAT Eingeweide *pl*

en·trance Eintreten *n*, Eintritt *m*; Eingang *m*, Zugang *m*; Zufahrt *f*; Einlass *m*, Eintritt *m*, Zutritt *m*

en·trance¦ ex·am(·i·na·tion) Aufnahmeprüfung *f*; ~ *fee* Eintritt *m*, Eintrittsgeld *n*; Aufnahmegebühr *f*

en·treat inständig bitten, anflehen

en·trea·ty dringende *or* inständige Bitte

en·trench MIL verschanzen (*a. fig*)

en·tre·pre·neur ECON Unternehmer(in); **en·tre·pre·neu·ri·al** ECON unternehmerisch

en·trust anvertrauen (*s.th. to s.o.* j-m et.); *j-n* betrauen (*with* mit)

en·try Eintreten *n*, Eintritt *m*; Einreise *f*; Beitritt *m* (*into* zu); Einlass *m*, Zutritt *m*; Zugang *m*, Eingang *m*, Einfahrt *f*; Eintrag(ung *f*) *m*; Stichwort *n*; SPORT Nennung *f*, Meldung *f*; *no* ~*!* Zutritt verboten!, MOT keine Einfahrt!

en·try per·mit Einreiseerlaubnis *f*, -genehmigung *f*

en·try·phone Türsprechanlage *f*

en·try vi·sa Einreisevisum *n*

en·twine ineinander schlingen

e·nu·me·rate aufzählen

en·vel·op (ein)hüllen, einwickeln

en·ve·lope Briefumschlag *m*

en·vi·a·ble beneidenswert

en·vi·ous neidisch

en·vi·ron·ment Umgebung *f*, *a.* Milieu *n*; Umwelt *f*; **en·vi·ron·men·tal** Milieu...; Umwelt...; **en·vi·ron·mental·ist** Umweltschützer(in)

en·vi·ron·men·tal| law Umweltschutzgesetz *n*; ~ **pol·lu·tion** Umweltverschmutzung *f*

en·vi·ron·ment friend·ly umweltfreundlich

en·vi·rons Umgebung *f*

en·vis·age sich *et.* vorstellen

en·voy Gesandte *m*, Gesandtin *f*

en·vy 1. Neid *m* **2.** beneiden

ep·ic 1. episch **2.** Epos *n*

ep·i·dem·ic MED **1.** seuchenartig; ~ *disease* → **2.** Epidemie *f*, Seuche *f*

ep·i·der·mis ANAT Oberhaut *f*

ep·i·lep·sy MED Epilepsie *f*

ep·i·log, *Br* **ep·i·logue** Epilog *m*, Nachwort *n*

e·pis·co·pal REL bischöflich

ep·i·sode Episode *f*

ep·i·taph Grabinschrift *f*

e·poch Epoche *f*, Zeitalter *n*

eq·ua·ble ausgeglichen (*a.* METEOR)

e·qual 1. gleich; gleichmäßig; ~ *to fig* gewachsen (*dat*); ~ *opportunities* Chancengleichheit *f*; ~ *rights for women* Gleichberechtigung *f* der Frau **2.** Gleiche *m*, *f* **3.** gleichen (*dat*)

e·qual·i·ty Gleichheit *f*

e·qual·i·za·tion Gleichstellung *f*; Ausgleich *m*; **e·qual·ize** gleichmachen, gleichstellen, angleichen; SPORT ausgleichen; **e·qual·iz·er** SPORT Ausgleich *m*, Ausgleichstor *n*, -treffer *m*

eq·ua·nim·i·ty Gleichmut *m*

e·qua·tion MATH Gleichung *f*

e·qua·tor Äquator *m*

e·qui·lib·ri·um Gleichgewicht *n*

e·quip ausrüsten

e·quip·ment Ausrüstung *f*, Ausstattung *f*; TECH Einrichtung *f*; *fig* Rüstzeug *n*

e·quiv·a·lent 1. gleichwertig, äquivalent; gleichbedeutend (*to* mit); **2.** Äquivalent *n*, Gegenwert *m*

e·ra Zeitrechnung *f*; Zeitalter *n*

e·rad·i·cate ausrotten

e·rase ausradieren, ausstreichen, löschen (*a.* IT); *fig* auslöschen

e·ras·er Radiergummi *m*

e·rect 1. aufrecht **2.** aufrichten; *Denkmal etc* errichten; aufstellen

e·rec·tion Errichtung *f*; MED Erektion *f*

er·mine ZO Hermelin *n*

e·rode GEOL erodieren

e·ro·sion GEOL Erosion *f*

e·rot·ic erotisch

err (sich) irren

er·rand Botengang *m*, Besorgung *f*; *go on an ~, run an ~* e-e Besorgung machen

er·rat·ic sprunghaft, unstet, unberechenbar

er·ro·ne·ous irrig

er·ror Irrtum *m*, Fehler *m* (*a.* IT); *in ~* irrtümlicherweise; ~ *of judg(e)ment* Fehleinschätzung *f*; ~*s excepted* ECON Irrtümer vorbehalten; ~ *mes·sage* IT Fehlermeldung *f*

e·rupt ausbrechen (*volcano etc*); durchbrechen (*teeth*); **e·rup·tion** (*Vulkan-*)Ausbruch *m*; MED Ausschlag *m*

ESA *abbr of* **European Space Agency** Europäische Weltraumbehörde

es·ca·late eskalieren; ECON steigen, in die Höhe gehen

es·ca·la·tion Eskalation *f*

es·ca·la·tor Rolltreppe *f*

es·ca·lope GASTR (*esp* Wiener) Schnitzel *n*

es·cape 1. entgehen (*dat*); entkommen, entrinnen (*both dat*); entweichen; *j-m* entfallen **2.** Entrinnen *n*; Entweichen *n*, Flucht *f*; *have a narrow ~* mit knapper Not davonkommen

es·cape chute AVIAT Notrutsche *f*

es·cape key IT Escape-Taste *f*

es·cort 1. MIL Eskorte *f*; Geleit(schutz *m*) *n* **2.** MIL eskortieren; AVIAT, MAR Geleit(schutz) geben; geleiten

es·cutch·eon Wappenschild *m*, *n*

es·pe·cial besondere(r, -s);

es·pe·cial·ly besonders

es·pi·o·nage Spionage *f*

es·pla·nade (*esp* Strand)Promenade *f*

es·say Aufsatz *m*, kurze Abhandlung, Essay *m*, *n*

es·sence Wesen *n*; Essenz *f*; Extrakt *m*

es·sen·tial 1. wesentlich; unentbehrlich **2.** *mst pl* das Wesentliche

es·sen·tial·ly im Wesentlichen, in der Hauptsache

es·tab·lish einrichten, errichten; **~ o.s.** sich etablieren *or* niederlassen; beweisen, nachweisen; **es·tab·lish·ment** Einrichtung *f*, Errichtung *f*; ECON Unternehmen *n*, Firma *f*; **the Establishment** das Establishment, die etablierte Macht, die herrschende Schicht

es·tate (großes) Grundstück, Landsitz *m*, Gut *n*; JUR Besitz *m*, (Erb)Masse *f*, Nachlass *m*; **housing ~** (Wohn)Siedlung *f*; **industrial ~** Industriegebiet *n*; **real ~** Liegenschaften *pl*; **~ a·gent** *Br* Grundstücks-, Immobilienmakler *m*; **~ car** *Br* MOT Kombiwagen *m*

es·teem 1. Achtung *f*, Ansehen *n* (**with** bei); **2.** achten, (hoch) schätzen

es·thet·ic ästhetisch

es·thet·ics Ästhetik *f*

es·ti·mate 1. (ab-, ein)schätzen; veranschlagen **2.** Schätzung *f*; (Kosten)Voranschlag *m*; **es·ti·ma·tion** Meinung *f*; Achtung *f*, Wertschätzung *f*

es·tranged entfremdet

es·trange·ment Entfremdung *f*

es·tu·a·ry weite Flussmündung

etch ätzen; radieren

etch·ing Radierung *f*; Kupferstich *m*

e·ter·nal ewig

e·ter·ni·ty Ewigkeit *f*

e·ther Äther *m*

e·the·re·al ätherisch (*a. fig*)

eth·i·cal sittlich, ethisch

eth·ics Sittenlehre *f*, Ethik *f*

eu·ro Euro *m*

Eu·rope Europa *n*

Eu·ro·pe·an 1. europäisch **2.** Europäer(in); **~ Union** (*abbr EU*) Europäische Union (*abbr* EU)

e·vac·u·ate entleeren; evakuieren; *Haus etc* räumen

e·vade (geschickt) ausweichen (*dat*); umgehen

e·val·u·ate schätzen; abschätzen, bewerten, beurteilen

e·vap·o·rate verdunsten, verdampfen (lassen); **~d milk** Kondensmilch *f*

e·vap·o·ra·tion Verdunstung *f*, Verdampfung *f*

e·va·sion Umgehung *f*, Vermeidung *f*; (*Steuer*)Hinterziehung *f*; Ausflucht *f*

e·va·sive ausweichend; **be ~** ausweichen

eve Vorabend *m*; Vortag *m*; **on the ~ of** unmittelbar vor (*dat*), am Vorabend (*gen*)

e·ven 1. *adj* eben, gleich; gleichmäßig; ausgeglichen; glatt; gerade (*Zahl*); **get ~ with s.o.** es j-m heimzahlen **2.** *adv* selbst, sogar, auch; **not ~** nicht einmal; **~ though, ~ if** wenn auch **3. ~ out** sich einpendeln; sich ausgleichen

eve·ning Abend *m*; **in the ~** am Abend, abends; **~ class·es** Abendkurs *m*, Abendunterricht *m*; **~ dress** Gesellschaftsanzug *m*; Frack *m*, Smoking *m*; Abendkleid *n*

eve·nsong REL Abendgottesdienst *m*

e·vent Ereignis *n*; Fall *m*; SPORT Disziplin *f*; SPORT Wettbewerb *m*; **at all ~s** auf alle Fälle; **in the ~ of** im Falle (*gen*)

e·vent·ful ereignisreich

e·ven·tu·al·(ly) schließlich

ev·er immer (wieder); je(mals); **~ after, ~ since** seitdem; **~ so** F sehr, noch so; **for ~** für immer, auf ewig; **Yours ~, ..., Ever yours, ...** Viele Grüße, dein(e) *or* Ihr(e), ...; **have you ~ been to Boston?** bist du schon einmal in Boston gewesen?

ev·er·green 1. immergrün; unverwüstlich, *esp* immer wieder gern gehört **2.** immergrüne Pflanze; MUS Evergreen *m, n*

ev·er·last·ing ewig

ev·er·more: (**for**) **~** für immer

ev·ery jede(r, -s); alle(r, -s); **~ now and then** von Zeit zu Zeit, dann und wann; **~ one of them** jeder von ihnen; **~ other day** jeden zweiten Tag, alle zwei Tage

ev·ery·bod·y jeder(mann)

ev·ery·day Alltags...

ev·ery·one jeder(mann)

ev·ery·thing alles

ev·ery·where überall(hin)

e·vict JUR zur Räumung zwingen; *j-n* gewaltsam vertreiben

ev·i·dence Beweis(material *n*) *m*, Beweise *pl*; (Zeugen)Aussage *f*; **give ~** (als Zeuge) aussagen; **ev·i·dent** augenscheinlich, offensichtlich

e·vil 1. übel, schlimm, böse **2.** Übel *n*; *das* Böse; **e·vil-mind·ed** bösartig

e·voke (herauf)beschwören; *Erinnerungen* wachrufen

ev·o·lu·tion Entwicklung f; BIOL Evolution f

e·volve (sich) entwickeln

ewe ZO Mutterschaf n

ex prp ECON ab; ~ **works** ab Werk

ex... Ex..., ehemalig

ex·act 1. exakt, genau 2. fordern, verlangen; **ex·act·ing** streng, genau; aufreibend, anstrengend; **ex·act·ly** exakt, genau; ~! ganz recht!, genau!

ex·act·ness Genauigkeit f

ex·ag·ge·rate übertreiben

ex·ag·ge·ra·tion Übertreibung f

ex·am F Examen n

ex·am·i·na·tion Examen n, Prüfung f; Untersuchung f; JUR Vernehmung f, Verhör n; **ex·am·ine** untersuchen; JUR vernehmen, verhören; PED etc prüfen (in in dat; on über acc)

ex·am·ple Beispiel n; Vorbild n, Muster n; for ~ zum Beispiel

ex·as·pe·rate wütend machen

ex·as·pe·rat·ing ärgerlich

ex·ca·vate ausgraben, ausheben, ausschachten

ex·ceed überschreiten; übertreffen

ex·ceed·ing übermäßig

ex·ceed·ing·ly außerordentlich, überaus

ex·cel v/t übertreffen; v/i sich auszeichnen

ex·cel·lence ausgezeichnete Qualität

Ex·cel·len·cy Exzellenz f

ex·cel·lent ausgezeichnet, hervorragend

ex·cept 1. ausnehmen, ausschließen 2. prp ausgenommen, außer; ~ for abgesehen von, bis auf (acc)

ex·cept·ing prp ausgenommen

ex·cep·tion Ausnahme f; Einwand m (to gegen); **make an** ~ e-e Ausnahme machen; **take** ~ **to** Anstoß nehmen an (dat); **without** ~ ohne Ausnahme, ausnahmslos; **ex·cep·tion·al** außergewöhnlich; **ex·cep·tion·al·ly** ungewöhnlich, außergewöhnlich

ex·cerpt Auszug m

ex·cess 1. Übermaß n; Überschuss m; Ausschweifung f 2. Mehr...; ~ **baggage** AVIAT Übergepäck n; ~ **fare** (Fahrpreis)Zuschlag m

ex·ces·sive übermäßig, übertrieben

ex·cess| lug·gage → **excess baggage**; ~ **post·age** Nachgebühr f

ex·change 1. (aus-, ein-, um)tauschen (for gegen); wechseln 2. (Aus-, Um-)Tausch m; (esp Geld)Wechsel m; ECON a. **bill of** ~ Wechsel m; Börse f; Wechselstube f; TEL Fernsprechamt n; ECON **foreign** ~(s) Devisen pl; **rate of** ~ → **exchange rate**; ~ **of·fice** Wechselstube f; ~ **rate** Wechselkurs m; ~ **student** Austauschschüler(in), Austauschstudent(in)

Ex·cheq·uer: Chancellor of the ~ Br Finanzminister m

ex·cise Verbrauchssteuer f

ex·ci·ta·ble reizbar, (leicht) erregbar

ex·cite erregen, anregen; reizen

ex·cit·ed erregt, aufgeregt

ex·cite·ment Aufregung f, Erregung f

ex·cit·ing erregend, aufregend, spannend

ex·claim (aus)rufen

ex·cla·ma·tion Ausruf m, (Auf)Schrei m; ~ **mark** Br, ~ **point** Ausrufe-, Ausrufungszeichen n

ex·clude ausschließen

ex·clu·sion Ausschließung f, Ausschluss m; **ex·clu·sive** ausschließlich; exklusiv; Exklusiv...; ~ **of** abgesehen von, ohne

ex·com·mu·ni·cate REL exkommunizieren; **ex·com·mu·ni·ca·tion** REL Exkommunikation f

ex·cre·ment Kot m

ex·crete MED ausscheiden

ex·cur·sion Ausflug m

ex·cu·sa·ble entschuldbar

ex·cuse 1. entschuldigen; ~ **me** entschuldige(n Sie) 2. Entschuldigung f

ex·di·rec·to·ry num·ber Br TEL Geheimnummer f

ex·e·cute ausführen; vollziehen; MUS vortragen; hinrichten; JUR Testament vollstrecken; **ex·e·cu·tion** Ausführung f; Vollziehung f; JUR (Zwangs-) Vollstreckung f; Hinrichtung f; MUS Vortrag m; **put** or **carry a plan into** ~ e-n Plan ausführen or verwirklichen

ex·e·cu·tion·er JUR Henker m, Scharfrichter m

ex·e·cu·tive 1. vollziehend, ausübend, POL Exekutiv...; ECON leitend 2. POL Exekutive f, vollziehende Gewalt; ECON der, die leitende Angestellte; ~ **board** Geschäftsleitung f;

ex·em·pla·ry vorbildlich

ex·em·pli·fy veranschaulichen

ex·empt 1. befreit, frei **2.** ausnehmen, befreien

ex·er·cise 1. Übung *f;* Ausübung *f;* PED Übung(sarbeit) *f,* Schulaufgabe *f;* MIL Manöver *n;* (körperliche) Bewegung; *do one's ~s* Gymnastik machen; *take ~* sich Bewegung machen **2.** üben; ausüben; (sich) bewegen; sich Bewegung machen; MIL exerzieren

ex·er·cise book Schul-, Schreibheft *n*

ex·ert *Einfluss etc* ausüben; *~ o.s.* sich anstrengen *or* bemühen; **ex·er·tion** Ausübung *f;* Anstrengung *f,* Strapaze *f*

ex·hale ausatmen; *Gas, Geruch etc* verströmen; *Rauch* ausstoßen

ex·haust 1. erschöpfen; *Vorräte* ver-, aufbrauchen **2.** TECH Auspuff *m; a. ~ fumes* TECH Auspuff-, Abgase *pl*

ex·haust·ed erschöpft, aufgebraucht *(supplies),* vergriffen *(book)*

ex·haus·tion Erschöpfung *f*

ex·haus·tive erschöpfend

ex·haust pipe TECH Auspuffrohr *n*

ex·hib·it 1. ausstellen; vorzeigen; *fig* zeigen, zur Schau stellen **2.** Ausstellungsstück *n;* JUR Beweisstück *n*

ex·hi·bi·tion Ausstellung *f;* Zurschaustellung *f*

ex·hil·a·rat·ing erregend, berauschend

ex·hort ermahnen

ex·ile 1. Exil *n;* im Exil Lebende *m, f* **2.** ins Exil schicken

ex·ist existieren; vorhanden sein; leben; bestehen; **ex·ist·ence** Existenz *f;* Vorhandensein *n,* Vorkommen *n;* Leben *n,* Dasein *n;* **ex·ist·ent** vorhanden

ex·it 1. Abgang *m;* Ausgang *m;* (Autobahn)Ausfahrt *f;* Ausreise *f* **2.** *v/i* verlassen; IT (das Programm) beenden; *~ Macbeth* THEA Macbeth (geht) ab

ex·o·dus Auszug *m;* Abwanderung *f; general ~* allgemeiner Aufbruch

ex·on·e·rate entlasten, entbinden, befreien

ex·or·bi·tant übertrieben, maßlos; unverschämt *(price etc)*

ex·or·cize *böse Geister* beschwören, austreiben *(from* aus); befreien *(of* von)

ex·ot·ic exotisch; fremd(artig)

ex·pand ausbreiten; (sich) ausdehnen *or* erweitern; ECON *a.* expandieren

ex·panse weite Fläche, Weite *f*

ex·pan·sion Ausbreitung *f;* Ausdehnung *f,* Erweiterung *f*

ex·pan·sive mitteilsam

ex·pat·ri·ate *j-n* ausbürgern, *j-m* die Staatsangehörigkeit aberkennen

ex·pect erwarten; F annehmen; *be ~ing* in anderen Umständen sein

ex·pec·tant erwartungsvoll; *~ mother* werdende Mutter

ex·pec·ta·tion Erwartung *f;* Hoffnung *f,* Aussicht *f*

ex·pe·di·ent 1. zweckdienlich, zweckmäßig; ratsam **2.** (Hilfs)Mittel *n,* (Not)Behelf *m*

ex·pe·di·tion Expedition *f,* (Forschungs)Reise *f*

ex·pe·di·tious schnell

ex·pel *(from)* vertreiben (aus); ausweisen (aus); ausschließen (von, aus)

ex·pen·di·ture Ausgaben *pl,* (Kosten-) Aufwand *m*

ex·pense Ausgaben *pl; pl* ECON Unkosten *pl,* Spesen *pl,* Auslagen *pl; at the ~ of* auf Kosten *(gen)*

ex·pen·sive kostspielig, teuer

ex·pe·ri·ence 1. Erfahrung *f;* (Lebens-) Praxis *f;* Erlebnis *n* **2.** erfahren, erleben; **ex·pe·ri·enced** erfahren

ex·per·i·ment 1. Versuch *m* **2.** experimentieren; **ex·per·i·men·tal** Versuchs...

ex·pert 1. erfahren, geschickt; fachmännisch **2.** Fachmann *m;* Sachverständige *m, f*

ex·pi·ra·tion Ablauf *m,* Ende *n;* Verfall *m*

ex·pire ablaufen, erlöschen; verfallen

ex·plain erklären

ex·pla·na·tion Erklärung *f*

ex·pli·cit ausdrücklich; ausführlich; offen, deutlich; *(sexually) ~* freizügig *(film etc)*

ex·plode *v/t* zur Explosion bringen; *v/i* explodieren; *fig* ausbrechen *(with* in *acc),* platzen *(with* vor); *fig* sprunghaft ansteigen

ex·ploit 1. (Helden)Tat *f* **2.** ausbeuten; *fig* ausnutzen

ex·ploi·ta·tion Ausbeutung *f,* Auswertung *f,* Verwertung *f,* Abbau *m*

ex·plo·ra·tion Erforschung *f*

ex·plore erforschen

ex·plor·er Forscher(in); Forschungsreisende *m, f*

ex·plo·sion Explosion *f*; *fig* Ausbruch *m*; *fig* sprunghafter Anstieg

ex·plo·sive 1. explosiv; *fig* aufbrausend; *fig* sprunghaft ansteigend **2.** Sprengstoff *m*

ex·po·nent MATH Exponent *m*, Hochzahl *f*; Vertreter(in), Verfechter(in)

ex·port ECON **1.** exportieren, ausführen **2.** Export *m*, Ausfuhr *f*; *mst pl* Export-, Ausfuhrartikel *m*

ex·por·ta·tion ECON Ausfuhr *f*

ex·port·er ECON Exporteur *m*

ex·pose aussetzen; PHOT belichten; *Waren* ausstellen; *j-n* entlarven, bloßstellen, *et.* aufdecken

ex·po·si·tion Ausstellung *f*

ex·po·sure Aussetzen *n*, Ausgesetztsein *n* (**to** *dat*); *fig* Bloßstellung *f*, Aufdeckung *f*, Enthüllung *f*, Entlarvung *f*; PHOT Belichtung *f*; PHOT Aufnahme *f*; **die of ~** an Unterkühlung sterben; **~ me·ter** PHOT Belichtungsmesser *m*

ex·press 1. ausdrücklich, deutlich; Express…, Eil… **2.** Eilbote *m*; Schnellzug *m*; **by ~ → 3.** *adv* durch Eilboten; als Eilgut **4.** äußern, ausdrücken

ex·pres·sion Ausdruck *m*

ex·pres·sion·less ausdruckslos

ex·pres·sive ausdrucksvoll; **be ~ of** *et.* ausdrücken

ex·press let·ter *Br* Eilbrief *m*

ex·press·ly ausdrücklich, eigens

ex·press train Schnellzug *m*

ex·press·way Schnellstraße *f*

ex·pro·pri·ate JUR enteignen

ex·pul·sion (**from**) Vertreibung *f* (aus); Ausweisung *f* (aus)

ex·pur·gate reinigen

ex·qui·site erlesen; fein

ex·tant noch vorhanden

ex·tem·po·re aus dem Stegreif

ex·tem·po·rize aus dem Stegreif sprechen *or* spielen

ex·tend (aus)dehnen, (aus)weiten; *Hand etc* ausstrecken; *Betrieb etc* vergrößern, ausbauen; *Frist, Pass etc* verlängern; sich ausdehnen *or* erstrecken

ex·tend·ed fam·i·ly Großfamilie *f*

ex·ten·sion Ausdehnung *f*; Vergrößerung *f*, Erweiterung *f*; (Frist)Verlängerung *f*; ARCH Erweiterung *f*, Anbau *m*; TEL Nebenanschluss *m*, (-)Apparat *m*; *a.* **~ cord** (*Br* **lead**) ELECTR Verlängerungskabel *n*, -schnur *f*

ex·ten·sive ausgedehnt, umfassend

ex·tent Ausdehnung *f*; Umfang *m*, (Aus)Maß *n*, Grad *m*; **to some ~, to a certain ~** bis zu e-m gewissen Grade; **to such an ~ that** so sehr, dass

ex·ten·u·ate abschwächen, mildern; beschönigen; **extenuating circumstances** JUR mildernde Umstände *pl*

ex·te·ri·or 1. äußerlich, äußere(r, -s), Außen… **2.** *das* Äußere; Außenseite *f*; äußere Erscheinung

ex·ter·mi·nate ausrotten (*a. fig*), vernichten, *Ungeziefer, Unkraut a.* vertilgen

ex·ter·nal äußere(r, -s), äußerlich, Außen…

ex·tinct erloschen; ausgestorben

ex·tinc·tion Erlöschen *n*; Aussterben *n*, Untergang *m*; Vernichtung *f*, Zerstörung *f*

ex·tin·guish (aus)löschen; vernichten

ex·tin·guish·er (*Feuer*)Löscher *m*

ex·tort erpressen (**from** von)

ex·tra 1. *adj* zusätzlich, Extra…, Sonder…; **be ~** gesondert berechnet werden **2.** *adv* extra, besonders; **charge ~ for** *et.* gesondert berechnen **3.** Sonderleistung *f*; *esp* MOT Extra *n*; Zuschlag *m*; Extrablatt *n*; THEA, *film*: Statist(in)

ex·tract 1. Auszug *m* **2.** (heraus)ziehen; herauslocken; ableiten, herleiten

ex·trac·tion (Heraus)Ziehen *n*; Herkunft *f*

ex·tra·dite ausliefern; *j-s* Auslieferung erwirken

ex·tra·di·tion Auslieferung *f*

extra·or·di·na·ry außerordentlich; ungewöhnlich; Sonder…

ex·tra pay Zulage *f*

ex·tra·ter·res·tri·al außerirdisch

ex·tra time SPORT (Spiel)Verlängerung *f*

ex·trav·a·gance Übertriebenheit *f*; Verschwendung *f*; Extravaganz *f*

ex·trav·a·gant übertrieben, überspannt; verschwenderisch; extravagant

ex·treme 1. äußerste(r, -s), größte(r, -s), höchste(r, -s); außergewöhnlich; **~ right** POL rechtsextrem(istisch); **~ right wing** POL rechtsradikal **2.** *das* Äußerste; Extrem *n*; höchster Grad

ex·treme·ly äußerst, höchst

ex·trem·ism POL Extremismus *m*

ex·trem·ist POL Extremist(in)

ex·trem·i·ties Gliedmaßen *pl*, Extremitäten *pl*

ex·trem·i·ty *das* Äußerste; höchste Not; äußerste Maßnahme

ex·tri·cate herauswinden, herausziehen, befreien

ex·tro·vert Extrovertierte *m*, *f*

ex·u·be·rance Fülle *f*; Überschwang *m*; **ex·u·be·rant** reichlich, üppig; überschwänglich; ausgelassen

ex·ult frohlocken, jubeln

eye 1. ANAT Auge *n*; Blick *m*; Öhr *n*; Öse *f*; *see ~ to ~ with s.o.* mit j-m völlig übereinstimmen; *be up to the ~s in work* bis über die Ohren in Arbeit stecken; *with an ~ to s.th.* im Hinblick auf et. 2. ansehen; mustern

eye·ball ANAT Augapfel *m*

eye·brow ANAT Augenbraue *f*

eye·catch·ing ins Auge fallend, auffallend

eye doc·tor F Augenarzt *m*, -ärztin *f*

eye·glass·es *a. pair of ~* Brille *f*

eye·lash ANAT Augenwimper *f*

eye·lid ANAT Augenlid *n*

eye·lin·er Eyeliner *m*

eye·o·pen·er: *that was an ~ to me* das hat mir die Augen geöffnet

eye shad·ow Lidschatten *m*

eye·sight Augen(licht *n*) *pl*, Sehkraft *f*

eye·sore F Schandfleck *m*

eye spe·cial·ist Augenarzt *m*, -ärztin *f*

eye·strain Ermüdung *f or* Überanstrengung *f* der Augen

eye·wit·ness Augenzeuge *m*, -zeugin *f*

F

F, f F, f *n*

fa·ble Fabel *f*; Sage *f*

fab·ric Gewebe *n*, Stoff *m*; Struktur *f*

fab·ri·cate fabrizieren (*mst fig*)

fab·u·lous sagenhaft, der Sage angehörend; fabelhaft

fa·cade, fa·çade ARCH Fassade *f*

face 1. Gesicht *n*; Gesichtsausdruck *m*, Miene *f*; (Ober)Fläche *f*; Vorderseite *f*; Zifferblatt *n*; *~ to ~ with* Auge in Auge mit; *save (lose) one's ~* das Gesicht wahren (verlieren); *on the ~ of it* auf den ersten Blick; *pull a long ~* ein langes Gesicht machen; *have the ~ to do s.th.* die Stirn haben, et. zu tun 2. *v/t* ansehen; gegenüberstehen (*dat*); (hinaus)gehen auf (*acc*); die Stirn bieten (*dat*); einfassen; ARCH bekleiden; *v/i:* *~ about* sich umdrehen

face·cloth, *Br* **face flan·nel** Waschlappen *m*

face-lift Facelifting *n*, Gesichtsstraffung *f*; *fig* Renovierung *f*, Verschönerung *f*

fa·ce·tious witzig

fa·cial 1. Gesichts... 2. Gesichtsbehandlung *f*

fa·cile leicht; oberflächlich

fa·cil·i·tate erleichtern

fa·cil·i·ty Leichtigkeit *f*; Oberflächlichkeit *f*; *mst pl* Erleichterung(en *pl*) *f*; Einrichtung(en *pl*) *f*, Anlage(n *pl*) *f*

fac·ing TECH Verkleidung *f*; *pl* Besatz *m*

fact Tatsache *f*, Wirklichkeit *f*, Wahrheit *f*; Tat *f*; *pl* Daten; *in ~* in der Tat, tatsächlich

fac·tion *esp* POL Splittergruppe *f*; Zwietracht *f*

fac·ti·tious künstlich

fac·tor Faktor *m*

fac·to·ry Fabrik *f*

fac·ul·ty Fähigkeit *f*; Kraft *f*; *fig* Gabe *f*; UNIV Fakultät *f*; Lehrkörper *m*

fad Mode *f*, Modeerscheinung *f*, -torheit *f*; (vorübergehende) Laune

fade (ver)welken (lassen); verschießen, verblassen (*color*); schwinden; immer schwächer werden (*person*); *film, radio,* TV *~ in* auf- *or* eingeblendet werden; auf- *or* einblenden; *~ out* aus- *or* abgeblendet werden; aus- *or* abblenden; *~d jeans* ausgewaschene Jeans *pl*

fail 1. *v/i* versagen; misslingen, fehlschlagen; versiegen; nachlassen; durchfallen (*candidate*); *v/t* im Stich lassen; j-n in e-r Prüfung durchfallen lassen 2. *without ~* mit Sicherheit, ganz bestimmt; **fail·ure** Versagen *n*; Fehlschlag *m*, Misserfolg *m*; Versäumnis *n*; Versager *m*, F Niete *f*

faint 1. schwach, matt 2. ohnmächtig

werden, in Ohnmacht fallen (**with** vor);
3. Ohnmacht *f*

faint-heart·ed verzagt

fair[1] gerecht, ehrlich, anständig, fair;
recht gut, ansehnlich; schön (*weather*);
klar (*sky*); blond (*hair*); hell (*skin*); **play**
~ fair spielen; *fig* sich an die Spielre-
geln halten

fair[2] (Jahr)Markt *m*; Volksfest *n*; Ausstellung *f*, Messe *f*

fair game *fig* Freiwild *n*

fair·ground Rummelplatz *m*

fair·ly gerecht; ziemlich

fair·ness Gerechtigkeit *f*, Fairness *f*

fair play SPORT *and fig* Fair Play *n*, Fairness *f*

fai·ry Fee *f*; Zauberin *f*; Elf *m*, Elfe *f*

fai·ry·land Feen-, Märchenland *n*

fai·ry| sto·ry, ~ tale Märchen *n* (*a. fig*)

faith Glaube *m*; Vertrauen *n*; **faith·ful**
treu (**to** *dat*); *Yours* ~*ly* Hochachtungsvoll (*letter*); **faith·less** treulos

fake 1. Schwindel *m*; Fälschung *f*;
Schwindler *m* **2.** fälschen; imitieren,
nachmachen; vortäuschen, simulieren
3. gefälscht; fingiert

fal·con ZO Falke *m*

fall 1. Fallen *n*, Fall *m*; Sturz *m*; Verfall
m; Einsturz *m*; Herbst *m*; ECON Sinken
n (*of prices etc*); Gefälle *n*; *mst pl* Wasserfall *m* **2.** fallen, stürzen; ab-, einfallen; sinken; sich legen (*wind*); *in e-n
Zustand* verfallen; ~ **ill,** ~ **sick** krank
werden; ~ **in love with** sich verlieben
in (*acc*); ~ **short of** den Erwartungen
etc nicht entsprechen; ~ **back** zurückweichen; ~ **back on** *fig* zurückgreifen
auf (*acc*); ~ **for** hereinfallen auf (*acc*);
F sich *j-n* verknallen; ~ **off** zurückgehen (*business, demand etc*), nachlas-
sen; ~ **on** herfallen über (*acc*); ~ **out** sich
streiten (**with** mit); ~ **through** durchfallen (*a. fig*); ~ **to** reinhauen, tüchtig zugreifen

fal·la·cious trügerisch

fal·la·cy Trugschluss *m*

fall guy F *der* Lackierte, *der* Dumme

fal·li·ble fehlbar

fall·ing star Sternschnuppe *f*

fall-out Fall-out *m*, radioaktiver Niederschlag

fal·low ZO falb; AGR brach(liegend)

false falsch

false·hood, false·ness Falschheit *f*;
Unwahrheit *f*

false start Fehlstart *m*

fal·si·fi·ca·tion (Ver)Fälschung *f*

fal·si·fy (ver)fälschen

fal·si·ty Falschheit *f*, Unwahrheit *f*

fal·ter schwanken; stocken (*voice*);
stammeln; *fig* zaudern

fame Ruf *m*, Ruhm *m*

famed berühmt (**for** wegen)

fa·mil·i·ar 1. vertraut; gewohnt; familiär
2. Vertraute *m*, *f*

fa·mil·i·ar·i·ty Vertrautheit *f*; (plumpe)
Vertraulichkeit

fa·mil·i·ar·ize vertraut machen

fam·i·ly 1. Familie *f* **2.** Familien...,
Haus...; ~ **al·low·ance** → **child benefit**; ~ **doc·tor** Hausarzt *m*; ~ **name** Fa-
milien-, Nachname *m*; ~ **plan·ning** Fa-
milienplanung *f*; ~ **tree** Stammbaum *m*

fam·ine Hungersnot *f*; Knappheit *f* (**of**
an *dat*)

fam·ished verhungert; **be** ~ F am Verhungern sein

fa·mous berühmt

fan[1] **1.** Fächer *m*; Ventilator *m* **2.** (zu)fä-
cheln; anfachen; *fig* entfachen

fan[2] (*Sport- etc*)Fan *m*

fa·nat·ic Fanatiker(in)

fa·nat·i·cal fanatisch

fan belt TECH Keilriemen *m*

fan·ci·er BOT, ZO Liebhaber(in), Züch-
ter(in)

fan·ci·ful fantastisch

fan club Fanklub *m*

fan·cy 1. Fantasie *f*; Einbildung *f*; plötzlicher Einfall, Idee *f*; Laune *f*; Vorliebe
f, Neigung *f* **2.** ausgefallen; Fantasie...
3. sich vorstellen; sich einbilden; ~
that! stell dir vor!, denk nur!; sieh
mal einer an!

fan·cy| ball Kostümfest *n*, Maskenball
m; ~ **dress** (Masken)Kostüm *n*

fan·cy-free → **footloose**

fan·cy goods Modeartikel *pl*, -waren *pl*

fan·cy·work Stickerei *f*

fang ZO Reiß-, Fangzahn *m*; Hauer *m*;
Giftzahn *m*

fan mail Fanpost *f*, Verehrerpost *f*

fan·tas·tic fantastisch

fan·ta·sy Fantasie *f*

far 1. *adj* fern, entfernt, weit **2.** *adv* fern;
weit; (sehr) viel; **as** ~ **as** bis; **in so** ~ **as**
insofern als

far·a·way weit entfernt

fare 1. Fahrgeld *n*; Fahrgast *m*; Verpflegung *f*, Kost *f* **2.** *gut* leben; *he~d well* es (er)ging ihm gut

fare dodg·er Schwarzfahrer(in)

fare·well 1. *int* lebe(n Sie) wohl! **2.** Abschied *m*, Lebewohl *n*

far·fetched *fig* weit hergeholt, gesucht

farm 1. Bauernhof *m*, Gut *n*, Gehöft *n*, Farm *f* **2.** *Land*, *Hof* bewirtschaften

farm·er Bauer *m*, Landwirt *m*, Farmer *m*

farm·hand Landarbeiter(in)

farm·house Bauernhaus *n*

farm·ing 1. Acker..., landwirtschaftlich **2.** Landwirtschaft *f*

farm·stead Bauernhof *m*, Gehöft *n*

farm·yard Wirtschaftshof *m*

far-off entfernt, fern

far right POL rechtsgerichtet

far·sight·ed weitsichtig, *fig a.* weitblickend

fas·ci·nate faszinieren

fas·ci·nat·ing faszinierend

fas·ci·na·tion Zauber *m*, Reiz *m*, Faszination *f*

fas·cism POL Faschismus *m*

fas·cist 1. Faschist *m* **2.** faschistisch

fash·ion Mode *f*; Art *f* und Weise *f*; *be in ~* in Mode sein; *out of ~* unmodern; **fash·ion·a·ble** modisch, elegant; in Mode

fash·ion| pa·rade, ~ show Modenschau *f*

fast¹ 1. Fasten *n* **2.** fasten

fast² 1. schnell; fest; treu; echt, beständig (*color*); flott; *be ~* vorgehen (*watch*)

fast·back MOT (Wagen *m* mit) Fließheck *n*

fast breed·er (re·ac·tor) PHYS Schneller Brüter

fas·ten befestigen, festmachen, anheften, anschnallen, anbinden, zuknöpfen, zu-, verschnüren; *Blick etc* richten (*on* auf *acc*); sich festmachen *or* schließen lassen; **fas·ten·er** Verschluss *m*

fast food Schnellgericht(e *pl*) *n*

fast-food res·tau·rant Schnellimbiss *m*, Schnellgaststätte *f*

fas·tid·i·ous anspruchsvoll, heikel, wählerisch, verwöhnt

fast lane MOT Überholspur *f*

fat 1. fett; dick; fettig, fetthaltig **2.** Fett *n*; *be low in ~* fettarm sein

fa·tal tödlich; verhängnisvoll, fatal (*to* für); **fa·tal·i·ty** Verhängnis *n*; tödlicher Unfall; (Todes)Opfer *n*

fate Schicksal *n*; Verhängnis *n*

fa·ther Vater *m*

Fa·ther Christ·mas *esp Br* der Weihnachtsmann, der Nikolaus

fa·ther·hood Vaterschaft *f*

fa·ther-in-law Schwiegervater *m*

fa·ther·less vaterlos

fa·ther·ly väterlich

fath·om 1. MAR Faden *m* **2.** MAR loten; *fig* ergründen

fath·om·less unergründlich

fa·tigue 1. Ermüdung *f*; Strapaze *f* **2.** ermüden

fat·ten dick *or contp* fett machen *or* werden; mästen; **fat·ty** fett; fettig

fau·cet TECH (Wasser)Hahn *m*

fault Fehler *m*; Defekt *m*; Schuld *f*; *find ~ with* et. auszusetzen haben an (*dat*); *be at ~* Schuld haben

fault·less fehlerfrei, fehlerlos

fault·y fehlerhaft, TECH *a.* defekt

fa·vo(u)r 1. Gunst *f*; Gefallen *m*; Begünstigung *f*; *in ~ of* zu Gunsten von (*or gen*); *do s.o. a ~* j-m e-n Gefallen tun **2.** begünstigen; bevorzugen, vorziehen; wohlwollend gegenüberstehen; SPORT favorisieren; **fa·vo(u)r·a·ble** günstig; **fa·vo(u)r·ite 1.** Liebling *m*; SPORT Favorit *m* **2.** Lieblings...

fawn 1. ZO (Reh)Kitz *n*; Rehbraun *n* **2.** rehbraun

fax 1. Fax *n* **2.** faxen; *~ s.th. (through) to s.o.* j-m et. faxen

fax (ma·chine) Faxgerät *n*

fear 1. Furcht *f* (*of* vor *dat*); Befürchtung *f*; Angst *f* **2.** (be)fürchten; sich fürchten vor (*dat*)

fear·ful furchtsam; furchtbar

fear·less furchtlos

fea·si·ble durchführbar

feast 1. REL Fest *n*, Feiertag *m*; Festessen *n*; *fig* Fest *n*, (Hoch)Genuss *m* **2.** *v/t* festlich bewirten; *v/i* sich gütlich tun (*on* an *dat*), schlemmen

feat große Leistung; (Helden)Tat *f*

fea·ther 1. Feder *f*; *a. pl* Gefieder *n*; *birds of a ~* Leute vom gleichen Schlag; *birds of a ~ flock together* Gleich und Gleich gesellt sich gern; *that is a ~ in his cap* darauf kann er stolz sein **2.** mit Federn polstern *or* schmücken; *Pfeil* fiedern

feath·er·bed verhätscheln

feath·er·brained F hohlköpfig
feath·ered ZO gefiedert
feath·er·weight SPORT Federgewicht *n*, Federgewichtler *m*; Leichtgewicht *n* (*person*)
feath·er·y gefiedert; federleicht
fea·ture 1. (Gesichts)Zug *m*; (charakteristisches) Merkmal; *radio*, TV *etc* Feature *n*; Haupt-, Spielfilm *m* **2.** groß herausbringen; *film:* in der Hauptrolle zeigen; ~ **film** Haupt-, Spielfilm *m*
Feb *abbr of February* Febr., Februar *m*
Feb·ru·a·ry (*abbr* **Feb**) Februar *m*
fed·e·ral POL Bundes...
Fed·e·ral Re·pub·lic of Ger·man·y *die* Bundesrepublik Deutschland (*abbr* **BRD**)
fed·e·ra·tion POL Bundesstaat *m*; Föderation *f*, Staatenbund *m*; ECON, SPORT *etc* (Dach)Verband *m*
fee Gebühr *f*; Honorar *n*; (Mitglieds-)Beitrag *m*; Eintrittsgeld *n*
fee·ble schwach
feed 1. Futter *n*; Nahrung *f*; Fütterung *f*; TECH Zuführung *f*, Speisung *f* **2.** *v/t* füttern; ernähren; TECH *Maschine* speisen; IT eingeben; AGR weiden lassen; *be fed up with s.o.* (*s.th.*) j-n (et.) satthaben; *well fed* wohlgenährt; *v/i* (fr)essen; sich ernähren; weiden
feed·back ELECTR Feed-back *n*, Rückkoppelung *f*; *radio*, TV Reaktion *f*
feed·er Esser *m*
feed·er road Zubringer(straße *f*) *m*
feed·ing bot·tle (Saug)Flasche *f*
feel 1. (sich) fühlen; befühlen; empfinden; sich anfühlen; ~ **sorry for s.o.** j-n bedauern *or* bemitleiden **2.** Gefühl *n*; Empfindung *f*; **feel·er** ZO Fühler *m*; **feel·ing** Gefühl *n*
feign *Interesse etc* vortäuschen, *Krankheit a.* simulieren
feint Finte *f*
fell niederschlagen; fällen
fel·low 1. Gefährte *m*, Gefährtin *f*, Kamerad(in); Gegenstück *n*; F Kerl *m*; *old* ~ F alter Knabe; *the* ~ *of a glove* der andere Handschuh **2.** Mit...; ~ **be·ing** Mitmensch *m*; ~ **cit·i·zen** Mitbürger *m*; ~ **coun·try·man** Landsmann *m*
fel·low·ship Gemeinschaft *f*; Kameradschaft *f*
fel·low trav·el·(l)er Mitreisende *m*, *f*, Reisegefährte *m*, -gefährtin *f*; POL Mitläufer(in)

fel·on JUR Schwerverbrecher *m*
fel·o·ny JUR (schweres) Verbrechen, Kapitalverbrechen *n*
felt Filz *m*; ~ **pen**, ~ **tip**, ~**-tip(ped) pen** Filzstift *m*, Filzschreiber *m*
fe·male 1. weiblich **2.** *contp* Weib *n*, Weibsbild *n*; ZO Weibchen *n*
fem·i·nine weiblich, Frauen...; feminin
fem·i·nism Feminismus *m*
fem·i·nist 1. Feminist(in) **2.** feministisch
fen Fenn *n*, Sumpf-, Marschland *n*
fence 1. Zaun *m*; *sl* Hehler *m* **2.** *v/t:* ~ **in** einzäunen, umzäunen; einsperren; ~ **off** abzäunen; *v/i* SPORT fechten; **fenc·er** SPORT Fechter *m*; **fenc·ing 1.** Einfriedung *f*; SPORT Fechten *n* **2.** Fecht...
fend: ~ **off** abwehren; ~ **for o.s.** für sich selbst sorgen
fend·er Schutzvorrichtung *f*; Schutzblech *n*; MOT Kotflügel *m*; Kamingitter *n*, Kaminvorsetzer *m*
fen·nel BOT Fenchel *m*
fer·ment 1. Ferment *n*; Gärung *f* **2.** gären (lassen)
fer·men·ta·tion Gärung *f*
fern BOT Farn(kraut *n*) *m*
fe·ro·cious wild; grausam
fe·ro·ci·ty Wildheit *f*
fer·ret 1. ZO Frettchen *n*; *fig* Spürhund *m* **2.** herumstöbern; ~ **out** aufspüren, aufstöbern
fer·ry 1. Fähre *f* **2.** übersetzen
fer·ry·boat Fährboot *n*, Fähre *f*
fer·ry·man Fährmann *m*
fer·tile fruchtbar; reich (*of, in* an *dat*)
fer·til·i·ty Fruchtbarkeit *f* (*a. fig*)
fer·ti·lize fruchtbar machen; befruchten; AGR düngen; **fer·ti·liz·er** AGR (*esp* Kunst)Dünger *m*, Düngemittel *n*
fer·vent glühend, leidenschaftlich
fer·vo(u)r Glut *f*; Inbrunst *f*
fes·ter MED eitern
fes·ti·val Fest *n*; Festival *n*, Festspiele *pl*
fes·tive festlich
fes·tiv·i·ty Festlichkeit *f*
fes·toon Girlande *f*
fetch holen; *Preis* erzielen; *Seufzer* ausstoßen; **fetch·ing** F reizend
fete, fête 1. Fest *n*; *village* ~ Dorffest *n* **2.** feiern
fet·id stinkend
fet·ter 1. Fessel *f* **2.** fesseln
feud Fehde *f*

feud·al Feudal..., Lehns...

feu·dal·ism Feudalismus *m*, Feudal-, Lehnssystem *n*

fe·ver MED Fieber *n*; **fe·ver·ish** MED fieb(e)rig, fieberhaft (*a. fig*)

few wenige; *a ~* ein paar, einige; *no fewer than* nicht weniger als; *quite a ~, a good ~* e-e ganze Menge

fi·an·cé Verlobte *m*

fi·an·cée Verlobte *f*

fi·as·co Fiasko *n*

fib F 1. Flunkerei *f*, Schwindelei *f* 2. schwindeln, flunkern

fi·ber, *Br* **fi·bre** Faser *f*

fi·ber·glass TECH Fiberglas *n*, Glasfaser *f*

fi·brous faserig

fick·le wankelmütig; unbeständig

fic·tion Erfindung *f*; Prosaliteratur *f*, Belletristik *f*; Romane *pl*

fic·tion·al erdichtet; Roman...

fic·ti·tious erfunden, fiktiv

fid·dle 1. Fiedel *f*, Geige *f*; *play first (second) ~ esp fig* die erste (zweite) Geige spielen; *(as) fit as a ~* kerngesund 2. MUS fiedeln; *a. ~ about or around (with)* herumfingern (an *dat*), spielen (mit)

fid·dler Geiger(in)

fi·del·i·ty Treue *f*; Genauigkeit *f*

fid·get F nervös machen; (herum)zappeln; **fid·get·y** zapp(e)lig, nervös

field Feld *n*; SPORT Spielfeld *n*; Arbeitsfeld *n*; Gebiet *n*; Bereich *m*; *~ of vision* OPT Gesichtsfeld *n*; *~ e·vents* SPORT Sprung- und Wurfdisziplinen *pl*; *~ glass·es a. pair of ~* Feldstecher *m*, Fernglas *n*; *~ mar·shal* MIL Feldmarschall *m*

field·work praktische (wissenschaftliche) Arbeit, *a.* Arbeit *f* im Gelände; ECON Feldarbeit *f*

fiend Satan *m*, Teufel *m*; F (*Frischluftetc*)Fanatiker(in)

fiend·ish teuflisch, boshaft

fierce wild; scharf; heftig; **fierce·ness** Wildheit *f*, Schärfe *f*, Heftigkeit *f*

fi·er·y feurig; hitzig

fif·teen 1. fünfzehn 2. Fünfzehn *f*

fif·teenth fünfzehnte(r, -s)

fifth 1. fünfte(r, -s) 2. Fünftel *n*

fifth·ly fünftens

fif·ti·eth fünfzigste(r, -s)

fif·ty 1. fünfzig 2. Fünfzig *f*

fif·ty-fif·ty F halbe-halbe

fig BOT Feige *f*

fight 1. Kampf *m*; MIL Gefecht *n*; Schlägerei *f*; *boxing*: Kampf *m*, Fight *m* 2. *v/t* bekämpfen; kämpfen gegen *or* mit, SPORT *a.* boxen gegen; *v/i* kämpfen, sich schlagen; SPORT boxen

fight·er Kämpfer *m*; SPORT Boxer *m*, Fighter *m*; *a. ~ plane* MIL Jagdflugzeug *n*

fight·ing Kampf *m*

fig·u·ra·tive bildlich

fig·ure 1. Figur *f*; Gestalt *f*; Zahl *f*, Ziffer *f*; Preis *m*; *be good at ~s* ein guter Rechner sein 2. *v/t* abbilden, darstellen; F meinen, glauben; sich *et.* vorstellen; *~ out* Problem lösen, F rauskriegen; verstehen; *~ up* zusammenzählen; *v/i* erscheinen, vorkommen; *~ on* rechnen mit; *~ skat·er* Eiskunstläufer(in); *~ skat·ing* Eiskunstlauf *m*

fil·a·ment ELECTR Glühfaden *m*

filch F klauen, stibitzen

file¹ 1. Ordner *m*; Karteikasten *m*; Akte *f*, Akten *pl*; Ablage *f*; IT Datei *f*; Reihe *f*; MIL Rotte *f*; *on ~* bei den Akten 2. *v/t* Briefe etc ablegen, zu den Akten nehmen, einordnen; *Antrag* einreichen, *Berufung* einlegen; *v/i* hintereinander marschieren

file² TECH 1. Feile *f* 2. feilen

file| man·age·ment IT Dateiverwaltung *f*; *~ pro·tec·tion* IT Schreibschutz *m*

fil·et GASTR Filet *n*

fi·li·al kindlich, Kindes...

fil·ing Ablegen *n*

fil·ing cab·i·net Aktenschrank *m*

fill 1. (sich) füllen; an-, aus-, erfüllen, vollfüllen; *Pfeife* stopfen; *Zahn* füllen, plombieren; *~ in* einsetzen; *~ out* (*Br in*) *Formular* ausfüllen; *~ up* vollfüllen; sich füllen 2. Füllung *f*

fil·let → filet

fill·ing Füllung *f*; MED (Zahn)Füllung *f*, Plombe *f*; *~ sta·tion* Tankstelle *f*

fil·ly ZO Stutenfohlen *n*

film 1. Häutchen *n*; Membran(e) *f*; Film *m* (*a.* PHOT); *take or shoot a ~* e-n Film drehen 2. (ver)filmen; sich verfilmen lassen; *~ star esp Br* Filmstar *m*

fil·ter 1. Filter *m* 2. filtern

fil·ter tip Filter *m*; Filterzigarette *f*

fil·ter-tipped: *~ cigarette* Filterzigarette *f*

filth Schmutz *m*

filth·y schmutzig; *fig* unflätig

fin zo Flosse *f*; sport Schwimmflosse *f*

fi·nal 1. letzte(r, -s); End…, Schluss…; endgültig **2.** sport Finale *n*; *mst pl* Schlussexamen *n*, -prüfung *f*

fi·nal dis·pos·al Endlagerung *f*

fi·nal·ist sport Finalist(in)

fi·nal·ly endlich, schließlich; endgültig

fi·nal whis·tle sport Schlusspfiff *m*, Abpfiff *m*

fi·nance 1. Finanzwesen *n*; *pl* Finanzen *pl* **2.** finanzieren

fi·nan·cial finanziell

fi·nan·cier Finanzier *m*

finch zo Fink *m*

find 1. finden; (an)treffen; herausfinden; JUR *j-n* für (*nicht*) *schuldig* erklären; beschaffen, besorgen; **~ out** *v/t et.* herausfinden; *v/i* es herausfinden **2.** Fund *m*, Entdeckung *f*; **find·ings** Befund *m*; JUR Feststellung *f*, Spruch *m*

fine¹ 1. *adj* fein; schön; ausgezeichnet, großartig; *I'm ~* mir geht es gut **2.** *adv* F sehr gut, bestens

fine² 1. Geldstrafe *f*, Bußgeld *n* **2.** zu e-r Geldstrafe verurteilen

fin·ger 1. ANAT Finger *m*; → *cross 3* **2.** betasten, (herum)fingern an (*dat*)

fin·ger·nail ANAT Fingernagel *m*

fin·ger·print Fingerabdruck *m*

fin·ger·tip Fingerspitze *f*

fin·i·cky pedantisch; wählerisch

fin·ish 1. (be)enden, aufhören (mit); *a.* **~ off** vollenden, zu Ende führen, erledigen, *Buch etc* auslesen; *a.* **~ off, ~ up** aufessen, austrinken **2.** Ende *n*, Schluss *m*; sport Endspurt *m*, Finish *n*; Ziel *n*; Vollendung *f*, letzter Schliff

fin·ish·ing line sport Ziellinie *f*

Fin·land Finnland *n*

Finn Finne *m*, Finnin *f*

Finn·ish 1. finnisch **2.** LING Finnisch *n*

fir *a.* **~ tree** BOT Tanne *f*

fir cone BOT Tannenzapfen *m*

fire 1. Feuer *n*; **be on ~** in Flammen stehen, brennen; *catch* **~** Feuer fangen, in Brand geraten; *set on* **~**, *set* **~** *to* anzünden **2.** *v/t* anzünden, entzünden; *fig* anfeuern; abfeuern; *Ziegel etc* brennen; F *j-n* rausschmeißen; heizen; *v/i* Feuer fangen (*a. fig*); feuern

fire a·larm Feueralarm *m*; Feuermelder *m*

fire·arms Schusswaffen *pl*

fire bri·gade *Br* Feuerwehr *f*

fire·bug F Feuerteufel *m*

fire·crack·er Knallfrosch *m*; Knallbonbon *m, n*

fire de·part·ment Feuerwehr *f*

fire en·gine zo Löschfahrzeug *n*

fire es·cape Feuerleiter *f*, -treppe *f*

fire ex·tin·guish·er Feuerlöscher *m*

fire fight·er Feuerwehrmann *m*

fire·guard *Br* Kamingitter *n*

fire hy·drant *Br* Hydrant *m*

fire·man Feuerwehrmann *m*; Heizer *m*

fire·place (offener) Kamin

fire·plug Hydrant *m*

fire·proof feuerfest

fire·rais·ing *Br* Brandstiftung *f*

fire·screen Kamingitter *n*

fire ser·vice *Br* Feuerwehr *f*

fire·side (offener) Kamin

fire sta·tion Feuerwache *f*

fire truck Löschfahrzeug *n*

fire·wood Brennholz *n*

fire·works Feuerwerk *n*

fir·ing squad MIL Exekutionskommando *n*

firm¹ fest; hart; standhaft

firm² Firma *f*

first 1. *adj* erste(r, -s); beste(r, -s) **2.** *adv* erstens; zuerst; **~ of all** an erster Stelle; zu allererst **3.** Erste(r, -s); *at* **~** zuerst, anfangs; *from the* **~** von Anfang an

first aid MED Erste Hilfe; **~ box, ~ kit** Verband(s)kasten *m*

first-born erstgeborene(r, -s), älteste(r, -s)

first class RAIL *etc* 1. Klasse

first-class erstklassig

first floor Erdgeschoss *n*, *Br* erster Stock; → *second floor*

first-hand aus erster Hand

first leg sport Hinspiel *n*

first·ly erstens

first name Vorname *m*

first-rate erstklassig

firth Förde *f*, Meeresarm *m*

fish 1. zo Fisch *m* **2.** fischen, angeln

fish·bone Gräte *f*

fish·er·man Fischer *m*

fish·e·ry Fischerei *f*

fish fin·ger *Br* GASTR Fischstäbchen *n*

fish·hook Angelhaken *m*

fish·ing Fischen *n*, Angeln *n*; **~ line** Angelschnur *f*; **~ rod** Angelrute *f*; **~ tack-**

le Angelgerät *n*
fish·mon·ger *esp Br* Fischhändler *m*
fish stick GASTR Fischstäbchen *n*
fish·y Fisch...; F verdächtig
fis·sion PHYS Spaltung *f*
fis·sure GEOL Spalt *m*, Riss *m*
fist Faust *f*
fit[1] **1.** geeignet, passend; tauglich; SPORT fit, (gut) in Form; *keep* ~ sich fit halten **2.** *v/t* passend machen (*for* für), anpassen; TECH einpassen, einbauen; anbringen; ~ *in* j-m e-n Termin geben, *j-n, et.* einschieben; *a.* ~ *on* anprobieren; *a.* ~ *out* ausrüsten, ausstatten, einrichten (*with* mit); *a.* ~ *up* einrichten (*with* mit); montieren, installieren; *v/i* passen, sitzen (*dress etc*) **3.** Sitz *m*
fit[2] MED Anfall *m*; *give s.o. a* ~ F j-n auf die Palme bringen; j-m e-n Schock versetzen
fit·ful unruhig (*sleep etc*)
fit·ness Tauglichkeit *f*; *esp* SPORT Fitness *f*, (gute) Form; ~ *cen·ter* (*Br* **cen·tre**) Fitnesscenter *n*
fit·ted zugeschnitten; ~ *carpet* Spannteppich *m*, Teppichboden *m*; ~ *kitchen* Einbauküche *f*
fit·ter Monteur *m*; Installateur *m*
fit·ting 1. passend; schicklich **2.** Montage *f*, Installation *f*; *pl* Ausstattung *f*; Armaturen *pl*
five 1. fünf **2.** Fünf *f*
fix 1. befestigen, anbringen (*to* an *dat*); *Preis* festsetzen; fixieren; *Blick etc* richten (*on* auf *acc*); *Aufmerksamkeit etc* fesseln; reparieren, in Ordnung bringen (*a. fig*); *Essen* zubereiten **2.** F Klemme *f*; *sl* Fix *m*
fixed fest; starr
fix·ings GASTR Beilagen *pl*
fix·ture Inventarstück *n*; *lighting* ~ Beleuchtungskörper *m*
fizz zischen, sprudeln
flab·ber·gast F verblüffen; *be* ~*ed* F platt sein
flab·by schlaff
flac·cid schlaff, schlapp
flag[1] **1.** Fahne *f*, Flagge *f* **2.** beflaggen
flag[2] **1.** (Stein)Platte *f*, Fliese *f* **2.** mit (Stein)Platten *or* Fliesen belegen, fliesen
flag[3] nachlassen, erlahmen
flag·pole, flag·staff Fahnenstange *f*
flag·stone (Stein)Platte *f*, Fliese *f*

flake 1. Flocke *f*; Schuppe *f* **2.** *mst* ~ *off* abblättern; F ~ *out* schlappmachen
flak·y flockig; blätt(e)rig
flak·y pas·try GASTR Blätterteig *m*
flame 1. Flamme *f* (*a. fig*); *be in* ~*s* in Flammen stehen **2.** flammen, lodern
flam·ma·ble TECH brennbar, leicht entzündlich, feuergefährlich
flan GASTR Obst-, Käsekuchen *m*
flank 1. Flanke *f* **2.** flankieren
flan·nel Flanell *m*; *Br* Waschlappen *m*; *pl Br* Flanellhose *f*
flap 1. Flattern *n*, (Flügel)Schlag *m*; Klappe *f* **2.** mit *den Flügeln etc* schlagen; flattern
flare 1. flackern; sich weiten; ~ *up* aufflammen; *fig* aufbrausen **2.** Lichtsignal *n*
flash 1. Aufblitzen *n*, Aufleuchten *n*, Blitz *m*; *radio etc*: Kurzmeldung *f*; PHOT F Blitz *m*; F Taschenlampe *f*; *like a* ~ wie der Blitz; *in a* ~ im Nu; *a* ~ *of lightning* ein Blitz **2.** (auf)blitzen *or* aufleuchten (lassen); zucken; rasen, flitzen
flash·back *film*: Rückblende *f*
flash freeze GASTR schnell einfrieren
flash·light PHOT Blitzlicht *n*; Taschenlampe *f*
flash·y protzig; auffallend
flask Taschenflasche *f*
flat[1] **1.** flach, eben, platt; schal; ECON flau; MOT platt (*tire*) **2.** *adv fall* ~ danebengehen; *sing* ~ zu tief singen **3.** Fläche *f*, Ebene *f*; flache Seite; Flachland *n*, Niederung *f*; MOT Reifenpanne *f*
flat[2] *Br* Wohnung *f*
flat-foot·ed plattfüßig
flat·mate *Br* Mitbewohner(in)
flat·ten (ein)ebnen; abflachen; *a.* ~ *out* flach(er) werden
flat·ter schmeicheln (*dat*)
flat·ter·er Schmeichler(in)
flat·ter·y Schmeichelei *f*
fla·vo(u)r 1. Geschmack *m*; Aroma *n*; Blume *f*; *fig* Beigeschmack *m*; Würze *f* **2.** würzen
fla·vo(u)r·ing Würze *f*, Aroma *n*
flaw Fehler *m*, TECH *a.* Defekt *m*
flaw·less einwandfrei, tadellos
flax BOT Flachs *m*
flea ZO Floh *m*
flea mar·ket Flohmarkt *m*
fleck Fleck(en) *m*; Tupfen *m*

fluff

fledged zo flügge

fledg(e)·ling zo Jungvogel m; fig Grünschnabel m

flee fliehen; meiden

fleece 1. Vlies n, esp Schafsfell n **2.** F j-n neppen

fleet MAR Flotte f

flesh Fleisch n; **flesh·y** fleischig; dick

flex¹ esp ANAT biegen

flex² esp Br ELECTR (Anschluss-, Verlängerungs)Kabel n, (-)Schnur f

flex·i·ble flexibel, biegsam; fig anpassungsfähig; ~ **working hours** Gleitzeit f

flex·i·time Br, **flex·time** Gleitzeit f

flick schnippen; schnellen

flick·er 1. flackern; TV flimmern **2.** Flackern n; TV Flimmern n

fli·er AVIAT Flieger m; Reklamezettel m

flight Flucht f; Flug m (a. fig); zo Schwarm m; a. ~ **of stairs** Treppe f; **put to** ~ in die Flucht schlagen; **take (to)** ~ die Flucht ergreifen; ~ **at·tend·ant** AVIAT Flugbegleiter(in); ~ **con·nec·tion** AVIAT Flugverbindung f

flight·less zo flugunfähig

flight| num·ber AVIAT Flugnummer f; ~ **re·cord·er** AVIAT Flugschreiber m

flight·y flatterhaft

flim·sy dünn; zart; fig fadenscheinig

flinch (zurück)zucken, zusammenfahren; zurückschrecken (**from** vor dat)

fling 1. werfen, schleudern; ~ **o.s.** sich stürzen; ~ **open (to)** Tür etc aufreißen (zuschlagen) **2. have a** ~ sich austoben; **have a** ~ **at** es versuchen or probieren mit

flint Feuerstein m

flip schnippen, schnipsen; Münze hochwerfen

flip·pant respektlos, F schnodd(e)rig

flip·per zo Flosse f; Schwimmflosse f

flirt 1. flirten **2. be a** ~ gern flirten

flir·ta·tion Flirt m

flit flitzen, huschen

float 1. v/i (auf dem Wasser) schwimmen, (im Wasser) treiben; schweben; a. ECON in Umlauf sein; v/t schwimmen or treiben lassen; MAR flottmachen; ECON Wertpapiere etc in Umlauf bringen; Währung floaten, den Wechselkurs (gen) freigeben **2.** Festwagen m

float·ing 1. schwimmend, treibend; ECON umlaufend; frei (**exchange rate**);

frei konvertierbar (**currency**) **2.** ECON Floating n

float·ing vot·er POL Wechselwähler(in)

flock 1. zo Herde f (a. REL); Menge f, Schar f **2.** fig strömen

floe (treibende) Eisscholle

flog prügeln, schlagen

flog·ging Tracht f Prügel

flood 1. a. ~ **tide** Flut f; Überschwemmung f **2.** überfluten, überschwemmen

flood·gate Schleusentor n

flood·lights ELECTR Flutlicht n

floor 1. (Fuß)Boden m; Stock m, Stockwerk n, Etage f; Tanzfläche f; → **first floor, second floor**; **take the** ~ das Wort ergreifen **2.** e-n (Fuß)Boden legen in; zu Boden schlagen; fig F j-n umhauen

floor·board (Fußboden)Diele f

floor cloth Putzlappen m

floor·ing (Fuß)Bodenbelag m

floor lamp Stehlampe f

floor lead·er PARL Fraktionsführer m

floor-length bodenlang

floor show Nachtklubvorstellung f

floor·walk·er Aufsicht f

flop 1. sich (hin)plumpsen lassen; F durchfallen, danebengehen, ein Reinfall sein **2.** Plumps m; F Flop m, Reinfall m, Pleite f; Versager m

flop·py (disk) IT Floppy Disk f, Diskette f

flor·id rot, gerötet

flor·ist Blumenhändler(in)

floun·der¹ zo Flunder f

floun·der² zappeln; strampeln; fig sich verhaspeln

flour (feines) Mehl

flour·ish 1. Schnörkel m; MUS Tusch m **2.** v/i blühen, gedeihen; v/t schwenken

flow 1. fließen, strömen; wallen **2.** Fluß m, Strom m (both a. fig)

flow·er 1. Blume f; Blüte f (a. fig) **2.** blühen

flow·er·bed Blumenbeet n

flow·er·pot Blumentopf m

flu F MED Grippe f

fluc·tu·ate schwanken

fluc·tu·a·tion Schwankung f

flue Rauchfang m, Esse f

flu·en·cy Flüssigkeit f; (Rede)Gewandtheit f; **flu·ent** flüssig; gewandt; **speak** ~ **French** fließend Französisch sprechen

fluff 1. Flaum m; Staubflocke f **2.** zo auf-

fluffy 438

plustern; **fluff·y** flaumig

flu·id 1. flüssig **2.** Flüssigkeit *f*

flunk F durchfallen (lassen)

flu·o·res·cent fluoreszierend

flu·o·ride CHEM Fluor *n*

flu·o·rine CHEM Fluor *n*

flur·ry Windstoß *m*; *(Regen-, Schnee-)* Schauer *m*; *fig* Aufregung *f*, Unruhe *f*

flush 1. (Wasser)Spülung *f*; Erröten *n*; Röte *f* **2.** *v/t a.* ~ *out* (aus)spülen; ~ *down* hinunterspülen; ~ *the toilet* spülen; *v/i* erröten, rot werden; spülen **3.** *be* ~ F gut bei Kasse sein

flus·ter 1. nervös machen *or* werden **2.** Nervosität *f*

flute MUS **1.** Flöte *f* **2.** (auf der) Flöte spielen

flut·ter 1. flattern **2.** Flattern *n*; *fig* Erregung *f*

flux *fig* Fluss *m*

fly¹ ZO Fliege *f*

fly² Hosenschlitz *m*; Zeltklappe *f*

fly³ fliegen (lassen); stürmen, stürzen; flattern, wehen; (ver)fliegen *(time)*; *Drachen* steigen lassen; ~ *at s.o.* auf j-n losgehen; ~ *into a passion or rage* in Wut geraten; **fly·er** → *flier*

fly·ing fliegend; Flug...; ~ *sau·cer* fliegende Untertasse; ~ *squad* Überfallkommando *n*; ~ *time* AVIAT Flugzeit *f*; ~ *vis·it* F Stippvisite *f*

fly·o·ver *Br* (Straßen-, Eisenbahn-) Überführung *f*

fly·screen Fliegenfenster *n*

fly·weight *boxing*: Fliegengewicht *n*, Fliegengewichtler *m*

fly·wheel TECH Schwungrad *n*

foal ZO Fohlen *n*

foam 1. Schaum *m* **2.** schäumen; ~ *ex·tin·guish·er* Schaumlöscher *m*, -löschgerät *n*; ~ *rub·ber* Schaumgummi *m*

foam·y schaumig

fo·cus 1. Brennpunkt *m*, *fig a.* Mittelpunkt *m*; OPT, PHOT Scharfeinstellung *f* **2.** OPT, PHOT scharf einstellen; *fig* konzentrieren (*on* auf *acc*)

fod·der AGR (Trocken)Futter *n*

foe POET Feind *m*, Gegner *m*

fog (dichter) Nebel

fog·gy neb(e)lig; *fig* nebelhaft

foi·ble (kleine) Schwäche

foil¹ Folie *f*; *fig* Hintergrund *m*

foil² vereiteln

foil³ *fencing*: Florett *n*

fold¹ 1. Falte *f*; Falz *m* **2.** ...fach, ...fältig **3.** (sich) falten; falzen; *Arme* verschränken; einwickeln; *often* ~ *up* zusammenfalten, -legen, -klappen

fold² AGR Schafhürde *f*, Pferch *m*; REL Herde *f*

fold·er Aktendeckel *m*; Schnellhefter *m*; Faltprospekt *m*, -blatt *n*, Broschüre *f*

fold·ing zusammenlegbar; Klapp...; ~ *bed* Klappbett *n*; ~ *bi·cy·cle* Klapprad *n*; ~ *boat* Faltboot *n*; ~ *chair* Klappstuhl *m*; ~ *door(s)* Falttür *f*

fo·li·age BOT Laub *n*, Laubwerk *n*

folk Leute *pl*; *pl* F *m-e etc* Leute *pl* **2.** Volks...

folk·lore Volkskunde *f*; Volkssagen *pl*; Folklore *f*

folk mu·sic Volksmusik *f*

folk song Volkslied *n*; Folksong *m*

fol·low folgen (*dat*); folgen auf (*acc*); befolgen; verfolgen; *s-m Beruf etc* nachgehen; ~ *up* *e-r Sache* nachgehen; *e-e Sache* weiterverfolgen; *as ~s* wie folgt; **fol·low·er** Nachfolger(in); Verfolger(in); Anhänger(in); **fol·low·ing 1.** Anhängerschaft *f*, Anhänger *pl*; Gefolge *n*; *the* ~ das Folgende; *die Folgenden pl* **2.** folgende(r, -s) **3.** im Anschluss an (*acc*)

fol·ly Torheit *f*

fond zärtlich; vernarrt (*of* in *acc*); *be* ~ *of* gernhaben, lieben

fon·dle liebkosen; streicheln; (ver)hätscheln

fond·ness Zärtlichkeit *f*; Vorliebe *f*

font REL Taufstein *m*, Taufbecken *n*

food Nahrung *f*, Essen *n*; Nahrungs-, Lebensmittel *pl*; AGR Futter *n*

fool 1. Narr *m*, Närrin *f*, Dummkopf *m*; *make a ~ of s.o.* j-n zum Narren halten; *make a ~ of o.s.* sich lächerlich machen **2.** zum Narren halten; betrügen (*out of* um); ~ *about, ~ around* herumtrödeln; Unsinn machen, herumalbern

fool·har·dy tollkühn

fool·ish dumm, töricht; unklug

fool·ish·ness Dummheit *f*

fool·proof kinderleicht; todsicher

foot 1. ANAT Fuß *m* (*a. linear measure* = 30,48 *cm*); Fußende *n*; *on* ~ zu Fuß **2.** F *Rechnung* bezahlen; *have to* ~ *the bill* die Zeche bezahlen müssen; ~ *it* zu Fuß gehen

foot·ball Football(spiel *n*) *m*; *Br* Fußball(spiel *n*) *m*; Football-Ball *m*; *Br* Fußball *m*

foot·bal·ler *Br* Fußballer *m*

foot·ball‖ hoo·li·gan *Br* Fußballrowdy *m*; ~ **play·er** *Br* Fußballspieler *m*

foot·bridge Fußgängerbrücke *f*

foot·fall Tritt *m*, Schritt *m*

foot·hold fester Stand, Halt *m*

foot·ing Halt *m*, Stand *m*; *fig* Grundlage *f*, Basis *f*; *be on a friendly ~ with s.o.* ein gutes Verhältnis zu j-m haben; *lose one's ~* den Halt verlieren

foot·lights THEA Rampenlicht(er *pl*) *n*

foot·note Fußnote *f*

foot·path (Fuß)Pfad *m*, (Fuß)Weg *m*

foot·print Fußabdruck *m*, *pl a.* Fußspur(en *pl*) *f*

foot·sore: *be ~* wunde Füße haben

foot·step Tritt *m*, Schritt *m*; Fußstapfe *f*

foot·wear Schuhwerk *n*, Schuhe *pl*

fop Geck *m*, F Fatzke *m*

for 1. *prp mst* für; *purpose, direction*: zu; nach; *warten, hoffen etc* auf (*acc*); *sich sehnen etc* nach; *cause*: aus, vor (*dat*), wegen; *time*: *~ three days* drei Tage (lang); seit drei Tagen; *distance*: *I walked ~ a mile* ich ging eine Meile (weit); *exchange*: (an)statt; als; *I ~ one* ich zum Beispiel; *~ sure* sicher!, gewiss! **2.** *cj* denn, weil

for·age *a.* ~ *about* (herum)stöbern, (herum)wühlen (*in* in *dat*; *for* nach)

for·ay MIL Einfall *m*, Überfall *m*; *fig* Ausflug *m* (*into politics* in *die Politik*)

for·bid verbieten; hindern

for·bid·ding abstoßend

force 1. Stärke *f*, Kraft *f*, Gewalt *f*, Wucht *f*; *the* (*police*) ~ die Polizei; (*armed*) ~*s* MIL Streitkräfte *pl*; *by ~* mit Gewalt; *come or put into ~* in Kraft treten *or* setzen **2.** *j-n* zwingen; *et.* erzwingen; zwängen; drängen; *Tempo* beschleunigen; ~ *s.th. on s.o.* j-m et. aufzwingen *or* aufdrängen; ~ *o.s. on s.o.* sich j-m aufdrängen; ~ *open* aufbrechen

forced erzwungen; gezwungen, gequält; ~ *land·ing* AVIAT Notlandung *f*

force·ful energisch, kraftvoll; eindrucksvoll, überzeugend

for·ceps MED Zange *f*

for·ci·ble gewaltsam; eindringlich

ford 1. Furt *f* **2.** durchwaten

fore 1. vorder, Vorder…; vorn **2.** Vorderteil *m*, Vorderseite *f*, Front *f*

fore·arm ANAT Unterarm *m*

fore·bear *mst pl* Vorfahren *pl*, Ahnen *pl*

fore·bod·ing (böses) Vorzeichen; (böse) (Vor)Ahnung

fore·cast 1. voraussagen, vorhersehen; *Wetter* vorhersagen **2.** Voraussage *f*; METEOR Vorhersage *f*

fore·fa·ther Vorfahr *m*

fore·fin·ger ANAT Zeigefinger *m*

fore·foot ZO Vorderfuß *m*

fore·gone con·clu·sion ausgemachte Sache; *be a ~ a.* von vornherein feststehen

fore·ground Vordergrund *m*

fore·hand SPORT 1. Vorhand *f*, Vorhandschlag *m* 2. Vorhand…

fore·head ANAT Stirn *f*

for·eign fremd, ausländisch, Außen…, Auslands…; ~ **af·fairs** Außenpolitik *f*; ~ **aid** Auslandshilfe *f*

for·eign·er Ausländer(in)

for·eign‖ lan·guage Fremdsprache *f*; ~ **min·is·ter** POL Außenminister *m*

For·eign Of·fice *Br* POL Außenministerium *n*

for·eign pol·i·cy Außenpolitik *f*

For·eign Sec·re·ta·ry *Br* POL Außenminister *m*

for·eign trade ECON Außenhandel *m*

for·eign work·er Gastarbeiter(in)

fore·knowl·edge vorherige Kenntnis

fore·leg ZO Vorderbein *n*

fore·man TECH Vorarbeiter *m*, Polier *m*; Werkmeister *m*; JUR Sprecher *m*

fore·most vorderste(r, -s), erste(r, -s)

fore·name Vorname *m*

fo·ren·sic JUR Gerichts…; ~ **me·dicine** Gerichtsmedizin *f*

fore·run·ner Vorläufer(in)

fore·see vorhersehen, voraussehen

fore·see·a·ble vorhersehbar

fore·shad·ow ahnen lassen, andeuten

fore·sight Weitblick *m*; (weise) Voraussicht

for·est Wald *m* (*a. fig*); Forst *m*

fore·stall *et.* vereiteln; j-m zuvorkommen

for·est·er Förster *m*

for·est·ry Forstwirtschaft *f*

fore·taste Vorgeschmack *m*

fore·tell vorhersagen

for·ev·er, for ev·er für immer
fore·wom·an TECH Vorarbeiterin *f*
fore·word Vorwort *n*
for·feit verwirken; einbüßen
forge 1. Schmiede *f* 2. fälschen; schmieden
forg·er Fälscher *m*
for·ge·ry Fälschen *n*; Fälschung *f*
for·ge·ry-proof fälschungssicher
for·get vergessen
for·get·ful vergesslich
for·get-me-not BOT Vergissmeinnicht *n*
for·give vergeben, verzeihen
for·give·ness Verzeihung *f*; Vergebung *f*
for·giv·ing versöhnlich; nachsichtig
fork 1. Gabel *f* 2. (sich) gabeln
fork·lift truck MOT Gabelstapler *m*
form 1. Form *f*; Gestalt *f*; Formular *n*, Vordruck *m*; *Br* (Schul)Klasse *f*; Formalität *f*, Kondition *f*, Verfassung *f*; *in great ~* gut in Form 2. (sich) formen, (sich) bilden, gestalten
for·mal förmlich; formell
for·mal dress Gesellschaftskleidung *f*
for·mal·i·ty Förmlichkeit *f*; Formalität *f*
for·mat 1. Aufmachung *f*; Format *n* 2. IT formatieren
for·ma·tion Bildung *f*
form·a·tive bildend; gestaltend; *~ years* Entwicklungsjahre *pl*
for·mat·ting IT Formatierung *f*
for·mer 1. früher; ehemalig 2. *the ~* der *or* die *or* das Erstere
for·mer·ly früher
for·mi·da·ble furchterregend; gewaltig, riesig, gefährlich; schwierig
form teach·er *Br* Klassenlehrer(in), Klassenleiter(in)
for·mu·la Formel *f*; Rezept *n*
for·mu·late formulieren
for·sake aufgeben; verlassen
for·swear abschwören, entsagen (*dat*)
fort MIL Fort *n*, Festung *f*
forth weiter, fort; (her)vor; *and so ~* und so weiter
forth·com·ing bevorstehend, kommend; in Kürze erscheinend (*book*) *or* anlaufend (*film*)
for·ti·eth vierzigste(r, -s)
for·ti·fi·ca·tion Befestigung *f*
for·ti·fy MIL befestigen; *fig* (ver)stärken
for·ti·tude (innere) Kraft *or* Stärke
fort·night *esp Br* vierzehn Tage

for·tress MIL Festung *f*
for·tu·i·tous zufällig
for·tu·nate glücklich; *be~* Glück haben;
for·tu·nate·ly glücklicherweise
for·tune Vermögen *n*; (glücklicher) Zufall, Glück *n*; Schicksal *n*
for·tune-tell·er Wahrsager(in)
for·ty 1. vierzig 2. Vierzig *f*
for·ward 1. *adv* nach vorn, vorwärts 2. *adj* Vorwärts...; fortschrittlich; vorlaut, dreist 3. *soccer*: Stürmer *m* 4. befördern, (ver)senden, schicken; *Brief etc* nachsenden
for·ward·ing a·gent Spediteur *m*
fos·sil GEOL Fossil *n* (*a.* F), Versteinerung *f*
fos·ter-child Pflegekind *n*
fos·ter-par·ents Pflegeeltern *pl*
foul 1. stinkend, widerlich; verpestet, schlecht (*air, water*); GASTR verdorben, faul; schmutzig, verschmutzt; METEOR stürmisch, schlecht; SPORT regelwidrig; *esp Br* F mies 2. SPORT Foul *n*, Regelverstoß *m*; *vicious~* böses *or* übles Foul 3. beschmutzen, verschmutzen; SPORT foulen
found[1] gründen; stiften
found[2] TECH gießen
foun·da·tion ARCH Grundmauer *f*, Fundament *n*; *fig* Gründung *f*, Errichtung *f*; (gemeinnützige) Stiftung; *fig* Grundlage *f*, Basis *f*
found·er[1] Gründer(in); Stifter(in)
foun·der[2] MAR sinken; *fig* scheitern
found·ling JUR Findelkind *n*
foun·dry TECH Gießerei *f*
foun·tain Springbrunnen *m*; (*Wasser-*) Strahl *m*; *~ pen* Füllfederhalter *m*
four 1. vier 2. Vier *f*; *rowing*: Vierer *m*; *on all ~s* auf allen vieren
four star *Br* F Super *n*
four-star pet·rol *Br* Superbenzin *n*
four-stroke en·gine Viertaktmotor *m*
four·teen 1. vierzehn 2. Vierzehn *f*
four·teenth 1. vierzehnte(r, -s)
fourth 1. vierte(r, -s) 2. Viertel *n*
fourth·ly viertens
four-wheel drive MOT Vierradantrieb *m*
fowl ZO Geflügel *n*
fox ZO Fuchs *m*
fox·glove BOT Fingerhut *m*
fox·y schlau, gerissen
frac·tion Bruchteil *m*; MATH Bruch *m*
frac·ture MED 1. (Knochen)Bruch *m* 2.

brechen

fra·gile zerbrechlich

frag·ment Bruchstück *n*

fra·grance Wohlgeruch *m*, Duft *m*

fra·grant wohlriechend, duftend

frail gebrechlich; zerbrechlich; zart, schwach; **frail·ty** Zartheit *f*; Gebrechlichkeit *f*; Schwäche *f*

frame 1. Rahmen *m*; (*Brillen- etc*)Gestell *n*; Körper(bau) *m*; **~ of mind** (Gemüts)Verfassung *f*, (-)Zustand *m* **2.** (ein)rahmen; bilden, formen, bauen; *a*. **~ up** F *j-m* et. anhängen

frame-up F abgekartetes Spiel; Intrige *f*

frame·work TECH Gerüst *n*; *fig* Struktur *f*, System *n*

franc Franc *m*; Franken *m*

France Frankreich *n*

fran·chise POL Wahlrecht *n*; ECON Konzession *f*

frank 1. frei(mütig), offen; **~ly** (**speaking**) offen gesagt **2.** *Brief* freistempeln

frank·fur·ter GASTR Frankfurter (Würstchen *n*) *f*

frank·ness Offenheit *f*

fran·tic hektisch; **be ~** außer sich sein

fra·ter·nal brüderlich

fra·ter·ni·ty Brüderlichkeit *f*; Vereinigung *f*, Zunft *f*; UNIV Verbindung *f*

frat·er·ni·za·tion Verbrüderung *f*

frat·er·nize sich verbrüdern

fraud Betrug *m*; F Schwindel *m*

fraud·u·lent betrügerisch

fray ausfransen, (sich) durchscheuern

freak 1. Missgeburt *f*; Laune *f*; *in cpds* F ...freak *m*, ...fanatiker *m*; Freak *m*, irrer Typ; **~ of nature** Laune *f* der Natur **2.** F *a*. **~ out** durchdrehen, die Nerven verlieren

freck·le Sommersprosse *f*

freck·led sommersprossig

free 1. frei; ungehindert; ungebunden; kostenlos, zum Nulltarif; freigebig; **~ and easy** zwanglos; sorglos; **set ~** freilassen **2.** befreien; freilassen

free climb·ing Freeclimbing *n*

free·dom Freiheit *f*

free fares Nulltarif *m*

free·lance frei, freiberuflich tätig, freischaffend

Free·ma·son Freimaurer *m*

free skat·ing Kür *f*

free·style SPORT Freistil *m*

free time Freizeit *f*

free trade ECON Freihandel *m*; **~ ar·e·a** ECON Freihandelszone *f*

free·way Schnellstraße *f*

free·wheel im Freilauf fahren

freeze 1. *v/i* (ge)frieren; erstarren; *v/t* gefrieren lassen; GASTR einfrieren (*a*. ECON), tiefkühlen **2.** Frost *m*, Kälte *f*; ECON, POL Einfrieren *n*; **wage ~, ~ on wages** ECON Lohnstopp *m*

freeze-dried gefriergetrocknet

freeze-dry gefriertrocknen

freez·er Gefriertruhe *f*, Tiefkühl-, Gefriergerät *n*; Gefrierfach *n*

freez·ing eisig; Gefrier...; **~ com·part·ment** Gefrierfach *n*; **~ point** Gefrierpunkt *m*

freight 1. Fracht *f*; Frachtgebühr *f* **2.** Güter... **3.** beladen; verfrachten

freight car RAIL Güterwagen *m*

freight·er MAR Frachter *m*, Frachtschiff *n*; AVIAT Transportflugzeug *n*

freight train Güterzug *m*

French 1. französisch **2.** LING Französisch *n*; **the ~** die Franzosen *pl*

French doors Terrassen-, Balkontür *f*

French fries GASTR Pommes frites *pl*

French·man Franzose *m*

French win·dows → **French doors**

French·wom·an Französin *f*

fren·zied wahnsinnig, rasend (**with** *vor dat*); hektisch; **fren·zy** Wahnsinn *m*; Ekstase *f*; Raserei *f*

fre·quen·cy Häufigkeit *f*; ELECTR Frequenz *f*

fre·quent 1. häufig **2.** (oft) besuchen

fresh frisch; neu; unerfahren; frech; **fresh·en** auffrischen (*wind*); **~** (**o.s.**) **up** sich frisch machen

fresh·man UNIV Student(in) im ersten Jahr

fresh·ness Frische *f*; Frechheit *f*

fresh wa·ter Süßwasser *n*

fresh-wa·ter Süßwasser...

fret sich Sorgen machen;

fret·ful verärgert, gereizt; quengelig

FRG *abbr of* **Federal Republic of Germany** Bundesrepublik *f* Deutschland

Fri *abbr of* **Friday** Fr., Freitag *m*

fri·ar REL Mönch *m*

fric·tion TECH *etc* Reibung *f* (*a. fig*)

Fri·day (*abbr* **Fri**) Freitag *m*; **on ~** (am) Freitag; **on ~s** freitags

fridge F Kühlschrank *m*

friend Freund(in); Bekannte *m*, *f*; **make**

~s with sich anfreunden mit, Freundschaft schließen mit

friend·ly 1. freund(schaft)lich 2. *esp Br* SPORT Freundschaftsspiel *n*

friend·ship Freundschaft *f*

fries F GASTR Fritten *pl*

frig·ate MAR Fregatte *f*

fright Schreck(en) *m*; *look a* ~ F verboten aussehen; **fright·en** erschrecken; *be* ~*ed* erschrecken (*at, by, of* vor *dat*); Angst haben (*of* vor *dat*)

fright·ful schrecklich, fürchterlich

fri·gid PSYCH frigid(e); kalt, frostig

frill Krause *f*, Rüsche *f*

fringe 1. Franse *f*; Rand *m*; Pony *m* 2. mit Fransen besetzen; ~ **ben·e·fits** ECON Gehalts-, Lohnnebenleistungen *pl*; ~ **e·vent** Randveranstaltung *f*; ~ **group** *soziale* Randgruppe *f*

frisk herumtollen; F *j-n* filzen, durchsuchen; **frisk·y** F lebhaft, munter

friz·zle F GASTR verbrutzeln

frizz·y gekräuselt, kraus

fro: *to and* ~ hin und her

frock REL Kutte *f*

frog ZO Frosch *m*

frog·man Froschmann *m*, MIL *a.* Kampfschwimmer *m*

frol·ic herumtoben, herumtollen

from von; aus; von … aus *or* her; von … (an), seit; aus, vor (*dat*); ~ *9 to 5* (*o'clock*) von 9 bis 5 (Uhr)

front 1. Vorderseite *f*; Front *f* (*a.* MIL); *at the* ~, *in* ~ vorn; *in* ~ *of* vor; *be in* ~ in Führung sein 2. Vorder… 3. *a.* ~ *on*, ~ *to*(*wards*) gegenüberstehen, gegenüberliegen

front·age ARCH (Vorder)Front *f*

front cov·er Titelseite *f*

front door Haustür *f*, Vordertür *f*

front en·trance Vordereingang *m*

fron·tier 1. (Landes)Grenze *f*; HIST Grenzland *n*, Grenze *f* 2. Grenz…

front-page F wichtig, aktuell

front-wheel drive MOT Vorderradantrieb *m*

frost 1. Frost *m*; *a.* **hoar** ~, **white** ~ Reif *m* 2. mit Reif überziehen; *Glas* mattieren; GASTR glasieren mit Zuckerguss überziehen; mit (Puder)Zucker bestreuen

frost·bite MED Erfrierung *f*

frost·bit·ten MED erfroren

frost·ed glass Matt-, Milchglas *n*

frost·y eisig, frostig (*a. fig*)

froth 1. Schaum *m* 2. schäumen; zu Schaum schlagen

froth·y schäumend; schaumig

frown 1. Stirnrunzeln *n*; *with a* ~ stirnrunzelnd 2. *v/i* die Stirn runzeln

fro·zen *adj* (eis)kalt; (ein-, zu)gefroren; Gefrier…

fro·zen foods Tiefkühlkost *f*

fru·gal sparsam; bescheiden; einfach

fruit Frucht *f*; Früchte *pl*; Obst *n*

fruit·er·er Obsthändler *m*

fruit·ful fruchtbar

fruit juice Fruchtsaft *m*

fruit·less unfruchtbar; erfolglos

fruit·y fruchtartig; fruchtig (*wine*)

frus·trate vereiteln; frustrieren

frus·tra·tion Vereitelung *f*; Frustration *f*

fry braten; *fried eggs* Spiegeleier *pl*; *fried potatoes* Bratkartoffeln *pl*

fry·ing pan Bratpfanne *f*

fuch·sia BOT Fuchsie *f*

fuck V ficken, vögeln; ~ *off!* verpiss dich!; *get* ~*ed!* der Teufel soll dich holen!; **fuck·ing** V Scheiß…, verflucht; ~ *hell!* verdammte Scheiße!

fudge GASTR Fondant *m*

fu·el 1. Brennstoff *m*; MOT Treib-, Kraftstoff *m* 2. MOT, AVIAT (auf)tanken

fu·el in·jec·tion en·gine MOT Einspritzmotor *m*

fu·gi·tive 1. flüchtig (*a. fig*) 2. Flüchtling *m*

ful·fil *Br*, **ful·fill** erfüllen; vollziehen; **ful·fil·(l)ing** befriedigend; **ful·fil·(l)·ment** Erfüllung *f*, Ausführung *f*

full 1. voll; ganz; Voll…; ~ *of* voll von, voller; ~ (*up*) (voll) besetzt (*bus etc*); F voll, satt; *house* ~! THEA ausverkauft!; ~ *of o.s.* (ganz) von sich eingenommen 2. *adv* völlig, ganz 3. *in* ~ vollständig, ganz; *write out in* ~ *Wort etc* ausschreiben

full board Vollpension *f*

full dress Gesellschaftskleidung *f*

full-fledged ZO flügge; *fig* richtig

full-grown ausgewachsen

full-length in voller Größe; bodenlang; abendfüllend (*film etc*)

full moon Vollmond *m*

full stop LING Punkt *m*

full time SPORT Spielende *n*

full-time ganztägig, Ganztags…; ~ *job* Ganztagsbeschäftigung *f*

ful·ly voll, völlig, ganz
ful·ly-fledged *Br* → *full-fledged*
ful·ly-'grown *Br* → *full-grown*
fum·ble tasten; fummeln
fume wütend sein
fumes Dämpfe *pl*, Rauch *m*; Abgase *pl*
fum·ing wutschnaubend
fun Scherz *m*, Spaß *m*; *for* ~ aus *or* zum Spaß; *make* ~ *of* sich lustig machen über (*acc*), verspotten
func·tion 1. Funktion *f*; Aufgabe *f*; Veranstaltung *f* **2.** funktionieren
func·tion·a·ry Funktionär *m*
func·tion key IT Funktionstaste *f*
fund ECON Fonds *m*; Geld(mittel *pl*) *n*
fun·da·men·tal 1. Grund..., grundlegend **2.** ~s Grundlage *f*, Grundbegriffe *pl*
fun·da·men·tal·ist Fundamentalist *m*
fu·ne·ral Begräbnis *n*, Beerdigung *f*; ~ **march** MUS Trauermarsch *m*; ~ **o·ration** Trauerrede *f*; ~ **pro·ces·sion** Trauerzug *m*; ~ **ser·vice** Trauerfeier *f*
fun·fair Rummelplatz *m*
fun·gus BOT Pilz *m*, Schwamm *m*
fu·nic·u·lar *a.* ~ *railway* (Draht)Seilbahn *f*
funk·y F irre, schräg, schrill
fun·nel Trichter *m*; MAR, RAIL Schornstein *m*
fun·nies F Comics *pl*
fun·ny komisch, lustig, spaßig; sonderbar
fur Pelz *m*, Fell *n*; MED Belag *m*; TECH Kesselstein *m*
fu·ri·ous wütend
furl *Fahne*, *Segel* aufrollen, einrollen; *Schirm* zusammenrollen
fur·nace TECH Schmelzofen *m*, Hochofen *m*; (Heiz)Kessel *m*
fur·nish einrichten, möblieren; liefern; versorgen, ausrüsten, ausstatten (*with* mit)
fur·ni·ture Möbel *pl*; *sectional* ~ Anbaumöbel *pl*
furred MED belegt, pelzig
fur·ri·er Kürschner *m*
fur·row 1. Furche *f* **2.** furchen
fur·ry pelzig; flauschig
fur·ther 1. weiter **2.** fördern, unterstützen; ~ **ed·u·ca·tion** *Br* Fortbildung *f*, Weiterbildung *f*
fur·ther·more *fig* weiter, überdies
fur·ther·most entfernteste(r, -s), äußerste(r, -s)
fur·tive heimlich, verstohlen
fu·ry Wut *f*, Zorn *m*
fuse 1. Zünder *m*; ELECTR Sicherung *f*; Zündschnur *f* **2.** schmelzen; ELECTR durchbrennen
fuse box ELECTR Sicherungskasten *m*
fu·se·lage (Flugzeug)Rumpf *m*
fu·sion Verschmelzung *f*, Fusion *f*; PHYS *nuclear* ~ Kernfusion *f*
fuss 1. (unnötige) Aufregung; Wirbel *m*, F Theater *n* **2.** sich (unnötig) aufregen; viel Aufhebens machen (*about* um, von); *fuss·y* aufgeregt, hektisch; kleinlich, pedantisch; heikel, wählerisch
fus·ty muffig; *fig* verstaubt
fu·tile nutzlos, zwecklos
fu·ture 1. (zu)künftig **2.** Zukunft *f*; LING Futur *n*, Zukunft *f*; *in* ~ in Zukunft, künftig
fuzz feiner Flaum
fuzz·y kraus, wuschelig; unscharf, verschwommen; flaumig, flauschig

G

G, g G, g *n*
gab F Geschwätz *n*; *have the gift of the* ~ ein gutes Mundwerk haben
gab·ble 1. Geschnatter *n*, Geschwätz *n* **2.** schnattern, schwatzen
ga·ble ARCH Giebel *m*
gad·fly ZO Bremse *f*
gad·get TECH Apparat *m*, Gerät *n*, Vorrichtung *f*; *often contp* technische Spielerei
gag 1. Knebel *m* (*a. fig*); F Gag *m* **2.** knebeln; *fig* mundtot machen
gage 1. Eichmaß *n*; TECH Messgerät *n*, Lehre *f*; TECH Stärke *f*, Dicke *f*; RAIL Spur(weite) *f* **2.** TECH eichen; (ab-, aus)messen
gai·e·ty Fröhlichkeit *f*
gain 1. gewinnen; erreichen, bekom-

men; zunehmen an (dat); vorgehen (um) (watch); ~ **speed** schneller werden; ~ **5 pounds** 5 Pfund zunehmen; ~ **in** zunehmen an (dat) **2.** Gewinn m; Zunahme f; ~ **of time** Zeitgewinn m

gait Gang m, Gangart f; Schritt m

gai·ter Gamasche f

gal F Mädchen n

ga·la 1. Festlichkeit f; Gala (-veranstaltung) f **2.** Gala…

gal·ax·y ASTR Milchstraße f, Galaxis f

gale Sturm m

gall[1] Frechheit f

gall[2] **1.** wund geriebene Stelle **2.** wund reiben or scheuern; fig (ver)ärgern

gal·lant tapfer; galant, höflich

gal·lan·try Tapferkeit f; Galanterie f

gall blad·der ANAT Gallenblase f

gal·le·ry Galerie f; Empore f

gal·ley MAR Galeere f; Kombüse f; a. ~ **proof** PRINT Fahne f, Fahnenabzug m

gal·lon Gallone f (3,79 l, Br 4,55 l)

gal·lop 1. Galopp m **2.** galoppieren (lassen)

gal·lows Galgen m

gal·lows hu·mo(u)r Galgenhumor m

ga·lore in rauen Mengen

gam·ble 1. (um Geld) spielen **2.** Glücksspiel n

gam·bler (Glücks)Spieler(in)

gam·bol 1. Luftsprung m **2.** (herum-)tanzen, (herum)hüpfen

game (Karten-, Ball- etc)Spiel n; (einzelnes) Spiel (a. fig); HUNT Wild n; Wildbret n; pl Spiele pl; PED Sport m

game·keep·er Wildhüter m

game| park, ~ re·serve Wildpark m; Wildreservat n

gan·der ZO Gänserich m

gang 1. (Arbeiter)Trupp m; Gang f, Bande f; Clique f; Horde f **2.** ~ **up** sich zusammentun, contp sich zusammenrotten

gan·gling schlaksig

gang·ster Gangster m

gang| war, ~ war·fare Bandenkrieg m

gang·way Gang m; AVIAT, MAR Gangway f

gaol, gaol·bird, gaol·er Br → **jail** etc

gap Lücke f; Kluft f; Spalte f

gape gähnen; klaffen; gaffen

gar·age 1. Garage f; (Reparatur)Werkstatt f (und Tankstelle f); **2.** Auto in e-r Garage ab- or unterstellen; Auto in die Garage fahren

gar·bage Abfall m, Müll m; ~ **bag** Müllbeutel m; ~ **can** Abfalleimer m, Mülleimer m; Abfalltonne f, Mülltonne f; ~ **truck** Müllwagen m

gar·den Garten m

gar·den·er Gärtner(in)

gar·den·ing Gartenarbeit f

gar·gle gurgeln

gar·ish grell, auffallend

gar·land Girlande f

gar·lic BOT Knoblauch m

gar·ment Kleidungsstück n; Gewand n

gar·nish GASTR garnieren

gar·ret Dachkammer f

gar·ri·son MIL Garnison f

gar·ter Strumpfband n; Sockenhalter m; Strumpfhalter m, Straps m

gas Gas n; F Benzin n, Sprit m

gas·e·ous gasförmig

gash klaffende Wunde

gas·ket TECH Dichtung(sring m) f

gas me·ter Gasuhr f, Gaszähler m

gas·o·lene, gas·o·line Benzin n; ~ **pump** Zapfsäule f

gasp 1. keuchen, röcheln; ~ **(for breath)** nach Atem ringen, F nach Luft schnappen **2.** Keuchen n, Röcheln n

gas sta·tion Tankstelle f

gas stove Gasofen m, Gasherd m

gas·works TECH Gaswerk n

gate Tor n; Pforte f; Schranke f, Sperre f; AVIAT Flugsteig m

gate-crash F uneingeladen kommen (zu); sich ohne zu bezahlen hineinschmuggeln (in acc)

gate·post Tor-, Türpfosten m

gate·way Tor(weg m) n, Einfahrt f

gate·way drug Einstiegsdroge f

gath·er v/t sammeln, Informationen einholen, einziehen; Personen versammeln; ernten, pflücken; zusammenziehen, kräuseln; fig folgern, schließen (from aus); ~ **speed** schneller werden; v/i sich (ver)sammeln; sich (an)sammeln; Versammlung f; Zusammenkunft f

gath·er·ing Versammlung f; Zusammenkunft f

gau·dy auffällig, bunt, grell; protzig

gauge Br → **gage**

gaunt hager; ausgemergelt

gaunt·let Schutzhandschuh m

gauze Gaze f; MED Bandage f, Binde f

gav·el Hammer m

gaw·ky linkisch

gay 1. lustig, fröhlich; bunt, (farben-)prächtig; F schwul **2.** F Schwule *m*

gaze 1. (starrer) Blick **2.** starren; ~ *at* starren auf (*acc*), anstarren

ga·zelle zo Gazelle *f*

ga·zette Amtsblatt *n*

gear TECH Getriebe *n*; MOT Gang *m*; *mst in cpds* Vorrichtung *f*, Gerät *n*; F Kleidung *f*, Aufzug *m*; *shift* (*esp Br change*) ~(*s*) MOT schalten; *shift* (*esp Br change*) *into second* ~ MOT in den zweiten Gang schalten

gear·box MOT Getriebe *n*

gear le·ver *Br*, **gear shift**, **gear stick** *Br* MOT Schalthebel *m*

Gei·ger count·er PHYS Geigerzähler *m*

geld·ing zo Wallach *m*

gem Edelstein *m*

Gem·i·ni ASTR Zwillinge *pl*; *he* (*she*) *is* (*a*) ~ er (sie) ist (ein) Zwilling

gen·der LING Genus *n*, Geschlecht *n*

gene BIOL Gen *n*, Erbfaktor *m*

gen·e·ral 1. allgemein; Haupt..., General... **2.** MIL General *m*; *in* ~ im Allgemeinen; ~ **de·liv·er·y:** (*in care of*) ~ postlagernd; ~ **e·lec·tion** *Br* POL Parlamentswahlen *pl*

gen·e·ral·ize verallgemeinern

gen·er·al·ly im Allgemeinen, allgemein

gen·e·ral prac·ti·tion·er (*abbr GP*) *appr* Arzt *m or* Ärztin *f* für Allgemeinmedizin

gen·e·rate erzeugen; **gen·e·ra·tion** Erzeugung *f*; Generation *f*

gen·e·ra·tor ELECTR Generator *m*; MOT Lichtmaschine *f*

gen·e·ros·i·ty Großzügigkeit *f*

gen·e·rous großzügig; reichlich

gen·et·ic genetisch; ~ *code* BIOL Erbanlage *f*; ~ **en·gin·eer·ing** Gentechnologie *f*; ~ **fin·ger·print** genetischer Fingerabdruck

ge·net·ics BIOL Genetik *f*, Vererbungslehre *f*

ge·ni·al freundlich

gen·i·tive *a.* ~ *case* LING Genitiv *m*, zweiter Fall

ge·ni·us Genie *n*

gen·o·cide Völkermord *m*

gent F *esp Br* Herr *m*; *gents Br* F Herrenklo *n*

gen·tle sanft, zart, sacht; mild

gen·tle·man Gentleman *m*; Herr *m*

gen·tle·man·ly gentlemanlike, vornehm

gen·tle·ness Sanftheit *f*, Zartheit *f*; Milde *f*

gen·try *Br* niederer Adel; Oberschicht *f*

gen·u·ine echt; aufrichtig

ge·og·ra·phy Geografie *f*

ge·ol·o·gy Geologie *f*

ge·om·e·try Geometrie *f*

germ BIOL, BOT Keim *m*; MED Bazillus *m*, Bakterie *f*, (Krankheits)Erreger *m*

Ger·man 1. deutsch **2.** Deutsche *m*, *f*; LING Deutsch *n*; ~ *shep·herd* zo Deutscher Schäferhund

Ger·man·y Deutschland *n*

ger·mi·nate BIOL, BOT keimen (lassen)

ger·und LING Gerundium *n*

ges·tic·u·late gestikulieren

ges·ture Geste *f*, Gebärde *f*

get *v/t* bekommen, erhalten; sich *et.* verschaffen *or* besorgen; erwerben, sich aneignen; holen; bringen; F erwischen; F kapieren, verstehen, checken; *j-n* dazu bringen (*to do* zu tun); *with pp:* lassen; ~ *one's hair cut* sich die Haare schneiden lassen; ~ *going* in Gang bringen; ~ *s.th. ready et.* fertig machen; *have got* haben; *have got to* müssen; *v/i* kommen, gelangen; *with pp or adj:* werden; ~ *tired* müde werden, ermüden; ~ *going* in Gang kommen; *fig* in Schwung kommen; ~ *home* nach Hause kommen; ~ *ready* sich fertig machen; ~ *about* herumkommen; sich herumsprechen *or* verbreiten (*rumor etc*); ~ *ahead of* übertreffen (*acc*); ~ *along* vorwärts-, vorankommen; auskommen (*with* mit *j-m*); zurechtkommen (*with* mit *et.*); ~ *at* herankommen an (*acc*); *what is he getting at?* worauf will er hinaus?; ~ *away* loskommen; entkommen; ~ *away with* davonkommen mit; ~ *back* zurückkommen; *et.* zurückbekommen; ~ *in* hinein-, hereinkommen; einsteigen (in *acc*); ~ *off* aussteigen (aus); davonkommen (*with* mit); ~ *on* einsteigen (in *acc*); → *get along*; ~ *out* herausgehen, hinausgehen; aussteigen (*of* aus); *et.* herausbekommen; ~ *over s.th.* über et. hinwegkommen; ~ *to* kommen nach; ~ *together* zusammenkommen; ~ *up* aufstehen

get·a·way Flucht *f*; ~ *car* Fluchtauto *n*

get-up Aufmachung *f*

gey·ser GEOL Geysir *m*; *Br* TECH Durchlauferhitzer *m*

ghast·ly grässlich; schrecklich; (toten-) bleich

gher·kin Gewürzgurke f

ghet·to Getto n

ghost Geist m, Gespenst n; fig Spur f

ghost·ly geisterhaft

gi·ant 1. Riese m 2. riesig

gib·ber·ish Kauderwelsch n

gib·bet Galgen m

gibe 1. spotten (at über acc); 2. höhnische Bemerkung, Stichelei f

gib·lets GASTR Hühner-, Gänseklein n

gid·di·ness MED Schwindel(gefühl n) m; **gid·dy** schwindelerregend; I feel ~ mir ist schwind(e)lig

gift Geschenk n; Talent n

gift·ed begabt

gift| vouch·er Geschenkgutschein m; ~ **wrap** Geschenkpapier n

gig F MUS Gig m, Auftritt m, Konzert n

gi·gan·tic gigantisch, riesenhaft, riesig, gewaltig

gig·gle 1. kichern 2. Gekicher n

gild vergolden

gill ZO Kieme f; BOT Lamelle f

gim·mick F Trick m; Spielerei f

gin Gin m

gin·ger 1. Ingwer m 2. rötlich or gelblich braun;

gin·ger·bread Lebkuchen m, Pfefferkuchen m

gin·ger·ly behutsam, vorsichtig

gip·sy Br → **gypsy**

gi·raffe ZO Giraffe f

gir·der TECH Tragbalken m

gir·dle Hüfthalter m, Hüftgürtel m

girl Mädchen n

girl·friend Freundin f

girl guide Br Pfadfinderin f

girl·hood Mädchenjahre pl, Jugend f, Jugendzeit f

girl·ish mädchenhaft; Mädchen…

girl scout Pfadfinderin f

girth (Sattel)Gurt m; (a. Körper)Umfang m

gist das Wesentliche, Kern m

give geben; schenken; spenden; Leben hingeben, opfern; Befehl etc geben, erteilen; Hilfe leisten; Schutz bieten; Grund etc angeben; THEA etc geben, aufführen; Vortrag halten; Schmerzen bereiten, verursachen; Grüße etc übermitteln; ~ her my love bestelle ihr herzliche Grüße von mir; ~ birth to zur Welt bringen; ~ s.o. to understand that j-m zu verstehen geben, dass; ~ way nachgeben; Br MOT die Vorfahrt lassen (dat); ~ away hergeben, weggeben, verschenken; j-n, et. verraten; ~ back zurückgeben; ~ in Gesuch etc einreichen; Prüfungsarbeit etc abgeben; nachgeben; aufgeben; ~ off Geruch verbreiten; ausstoßen; ausströmen, verströmen; ~ on(to) führen auf or nach, gehen nach; ~ out aus-, verteilen; esp Br bekannt geben; zu Ende gehen (supplies, strength etc); F versagen (engine etc); ~ up aufgeben; aufhören mit; j-n ausliefern; ~ o.s. up sich (freiwillig) stellen (to the police der Polizei)

give-and-take beiderseitiges Entgegenkommen, Kompromiss(bereitschaft f) m

giv·en: be ~ to neigen zu (dat)

giv·en name Vorname m

gla·cial eisig; Eis…

gla·ci·er Gletscher m

glad froh, erfreut; be ~ of sich freuen über (acc); **glad·ly** gern(e)

glam·o(u)r Zauber m, Glanz m

glam·o(u)r·ous bezaubernd, reizvoll

glance 1. (schneller or flüchtiger) Blick (at auf acc); at a ~ auf e-n Blick 2. (schnell or flüchtig) blicken (at auf acc)

gland ANAT Drüse f

glare 1. grell scheinen or leuchten; wütend starren; ~ at s.o. j-n wütend anstarren 2. greller Schein, grelles Leuchten; wütender Blick

glar·ing fig schreiend

glass 1. Glas n; (Trink)Glas n; Glas (-gefäß) n; (Fern-, Opern)Glas n; Br F Spiegel m; Br Barometer n; (a pair of) ~es (e-e) Brille 2. gläsern; Glas… 3. ~ in, ~ up verglasen

glass case Vitrine f; Schaukasten m

glass·ful ein Glas (voll)

glass·house Gewächs-, Treibhaus n

glass·ware Glaswaren pl

glass·y glasig; glasig

glaze 1. v/t verglasen; glasieren; v/i: a. ~ over glasig werden (eyes) 2. Glasur f

gla·zi·er Glaser m

gleam 1. schwacher Schein, Schimmer m 2. leuchten, schimmern

glean v/t sammeln; v/i Ähren lesen

glee Fröhlichkeit f

glee club Gesangverein m

glee·ful ausgelassen, fröhlich

glen enges Bergtal n

glib gewandt; schlagfertig

glide 1. gleiten; segeln **2.** Gleiten n; AVIAT Gleitflug m; **glid·er** Segelflugzeug n; **glid·ing** Segelfliegen n

glim·mer 1. schimmern **2.** Schimmer m

glimpse 1. (nur) flüchtig zu sehen bekommen **2.** flüchtiger Blick

glint 1. glitzern, glänzen **2.** Glitzern n, Glanz m

glis·ten glitzern, glänzen

glit·ter 1. glitzern, funkeln, glänzen **2.** Glitzern n, Funkeln n, Glanz m

glo·bal Welt..., global, weltumspannend; umfassend; **~ warm·ing** Erwärmung f der Erdatmosphäre

globe (Erd)Kugel f; Globus m

gloom Düsterkeit f; Dunkelheit f; düstere or gedrückte Stimmung

gloom·y düster; hoffnungslos; niedergeschlagen; trübsinnig, trübselig

glo·ri·fi·ca·tion Verherrlichung f

glo·ri·fy verherrlichen

glo·ri·ous ruhmreich, glorreich; herrlich, prächtig

glo·ry Ruhm m; Herrlichkeit f, Pracht f

gloss 1. Glanz m; LING Glosse f **2. ~ over** beschönigen, vertuschen

glos·sa·ry Glossar n

gloss·y glänzend

glove Handschuh m; **~ com·part·ment** MOT Handschuhfach n

glow 1. glühen **2.** Glühen n; Glut f

glow·er finster blicken

glow-worm ZO Glühwürmchen n

glu·cose Traubenzucker m

glue 1. Leim m **2.** kleben

glum bedrückt

glut·ton fig Vielfraß m

glut·ton·ous gefräßig, unersättlich

gnarled knorrig; knotig (hands etc)

gnash knirschen (mit)

gnat ZO (Stech)Mücke f

gnaw (zer)nagen; (zer)fressen

gnome Gnom m; Gartenzwerg m

go 1. gehen, fahren, reisen (to nach); (fort)gehen; gehen, führen (to nach) (road etc); sich erstrecken, gehen (to bis zu); verkehren, fahren (bus etc); TECH gehen, laufen, funktionieren; vergehen (time); harmonieren (with mit), passen (with zu); ausgehen, ablaufen, ausfallen; werden (~ mad; ~

blind); be ~ing to inf im Begriff sein zu inf, tun wollen, tun werden; **~ swim·ming** schwimmen gehen; it is ~ing to rain es gibt Regen; I must be ~ing ich muss gehen; **~ for a walk** e-n Spaziergang machen, spazieren gehen; **~ to bed** ins Bett gehen; **~ to school** zur Schule gehen; **~ to see** besuchen; let ~ loslassen; **~ after** nachlaufen (dat); sich bemühen um; **~ ahead** vorangehen; vorausgehen, vorausfahren; **~ ahead with** beginnen mit; fortfahren mit; **~ at** losgehen auf (acc); **~ away** weggehen; **~ between** vermitteln zwischen (dat); **~ by** vorbeigehen, vorbeifahren; vergehen (time); fig sich halten an (acc), sich richten nach; **~ down** untergehen (sun); **~ for** holen; **~ in** hineingehen; **~ in for an examination** e-e Prüfung machen; **~ off** fortgehen, weggehen; losgehen (gun etc); **~ on** weitergehen, weiterfahren; fig fortfahren (doing zu tun); fig vor sich gehen, vorgehen; **~ out** hinausgehen; ausgehen (with mit); ausgehen (light etc); **~ through** durchgehen, durchnehmen; durchmachen; **~ up** steigen; hinaufgehen, -steigen; **~ without** sich behelfen ohne, auskommen ohne **2.** F Schwung m, Schmiss m; esp Br F Versuch m; it's my ~ esp Br F ich bin dran or an der Reihe; it's a ~! F abgemacht!; have a ~ at s.th. Br F et. probieren

goad fig anstacheln

go-a·head[1]: get the ~ grünes Licht bekommen; give s.o. the ~ j-m grünes Licht geben

go-a·head[2] Br zielstrebig; unternehmungslustig

goal Ziel n (a. fig); SPORT Tor n; keep ~ im Tor stehen; score a ~ ein Tor schießen or erzielen; consolation ~ Ehrentreffer m; own ~ Eigentor n, Eigentreffer m; shot at ~ Torschuss m

goal·ie F, **goal·keep·er** SPORT Torwart m, Torhüter m

goal kick soccer: Abstoß m

goal line SPORT Torlinie f

goal·mouth SPORT Torraum m

goal·post SPORT Torpfosten m

goat ZO Ziege f, Geiß f

gob·ble schlingen; mst ~ up verschlingen (a. fig)

go-be·tween Vermittler(in), Mittelsmann *m*

gob·lin Kobold *m*

god REL *God* Gott *m*; *fig* Abgott *m*

god·child Patenkind *n*

god·dess Göttin *f*

god·fa·ther Pate *m* (*a. fig*), Taufpate *m*

god·for·sak·en *contp* gottverlassen

god·head Gottheit *f*

god·less gottlos

god·like gottähnlich; göttlich

god·moth·er (Tauf)Patin *f*

god·pa·rent (Tauf)Pate, (Tauf)Patin *f*

god·send Geschenk *n* des Himmels

gog·gle glotzen

gog·gle box *Br* F TV Glotze *f*

gog·gles Schutzbrille *f*

go·ings-on F Treiben *n*, Vorgänge *pl*

gold 1. Gold *n* **2.** golden

gold·en *mst* fig golden, goldgelb

gold·finch ZO Stieglitz *m*

gold·fish ZO Goldfisch *m*

gold·smith Goldschmied *m*

golf 1. Golf(spiel) *n* **2.** Golf spielen

golf club Golfschläger *m*; Golfklub *m*

golf course, golf links Golfplatz *m*

gon·do·la Gondel *f*

gone *adj* fort; F futsch; vergangen; tot; F hoffnungslos

good 1. gut; artig; gütig; gründlich; *~ at* geschickt *or* gut in (*dat*); *real ~* F echt gut **2.** Nutzen *m*, Wert *m*; *das* Gute; *do* (*no*) *~* (nichts) nützen; *for ~* für immer; F *what ~ is …?* was nützt …?

good-by(e) 1. *wish s.o. ~*, *say ~ to s.o.* j-m Auf Wiedersehen sagen **2.** *int* (auf) Wiedersehen!

Good Fri·day REL Karfreitag *m*

good-hu·mo(u)red gut gelaunt; gutmütig

good-look·ing gut aussehend

good-na·tured gutmütig

good·ness Güte *f*; *thank ~!* Gott sei Dank!; (*my*) *~!*, *~ gracious!* du meine Güte!, du lieber Himmel!; *for ~' sake* um Himmels willen!; *~ knows* weiß der Himmel

goods ECON Waren *pl*, Güter *pl*

good·will gute Absicht, guter Wille; ECON Firmenwert *m*

good·y F Bonbon *m*, *n*

goose ZO Gans *f*

goose·ber·ry BOT Stachelbeere *f*

goose·flesh, goose pim·ples *fig* Gänsehaut *f*

go·pher ZO Taschenratte *f*; Ziesel *m*

gore durchbohren, aufspießen

gorge 1. ANAT Kehle *f*, Schlund *m*; GEOGR enge (Fels)Schlucht **2.** verschlingen; schlingen, (sich) vollstopfen

gor·geous prächtig

go·ril·la ZO Gorilla *m*

gor·y F blutrünstig

gosh *int* F Mensch!, Mann!

gos·ling ZO junge Gans

go-slow *Br* ECON Bummelstreik *m*

Gos·pel REL Evangelium *n*

gos·sa·mer Altweibersommer *m*

gos·sip 1. Klatsch *m*, Tratsch *m*; Klatschbase *f* **2.** klatschen, tratschen

gos·sip·y geschwätzig; voller Klatsch und Tratsch (*letter etc*)

Goth·ic ARCH **1.** gotisch; *~ novel* Schauerroman *m* **2.** Gotik *f*

gourd BOT Kürbis *m*

gout MED Gicht *f*

gov·ern *v/t* regieren; lenken, leiten; *v/i* herrschen

gov·ern·ess Erzieherin *f*

gov·ern·ment Regierung *f*; Staat *m*

gov·er·nor Gouverneur *m*; Direktor *m*, Leiter *m*; F Alte *m*

gown Kleid *n*; Robe *f*, Talar *m*

grab 1. packen, (hastig *or* gierig) ergreifen, fassen **2.** (hastiger *or* gieriger) Griff; TECH Greifer *m*

grace 1. Anmut *f*, Grazie *f*; Anstand *m*; ECON Frist *f*, Aufschub *m*; Gnade *f*; REL Tischgebet *n* **2.** zieren, schmücken

grace·ful anmutig

grace·less ungraziös

gra·cious gnädig

gra·da·tion Abstufung *f*

grade 1. Grad *m*, Rang *m*; Stufe *f*; ECON Qualität *f*; RAIL *etc* Steigung *f*, Gefälle *n*; PED Klasse *f*; Note *f*, Zensur *f* **2.** sortieren, einteilen; abstufen

grade cross·ing RAIL schienengleicher Bahnübergang

grade school Grundschule *f*

gra·di·ent *Br* RAIL *etc* Steigung *f*, Gefälle *n*

grad·u·al stufenweise, allmählich

grad·u·al·ly nach und nach; allmählich

grad·u·ate 1. UNIV Hochschulabsolvent(in), Akademiker(in); Graduierte *m*, *f*; PED Schulabgänger(in) **2.** abstufen, staffeln; UNIV graduieren; PED die Abschlussprüfung bestehen

grad·u·a·tion Abstufung f, Staffelung f; UNIV Graduierung f; PED Absolvieren n (**from** gen)

graf·fi·ti Graffiti pl, Wandschmierereien pl

graft 1. MED Transplantat n; AGR Pfropfreis n **2.** MED Gewebe verpflanzen, transplantieren; AGR pfropfen

grain (Samen-, esp Getreide)Korn n; Getreide n; (Sand- etc)Körnchen n, (-)Korn n; Maserung f

gram Gramm n

gram·mar Grammatik f

gram·mar school Grundschule f; Br appr (humanistisches) Gymnasium

gram·mat·i·cal grammatisch, Grammatik...

gramme → **gram**

gra·na·ry Kornspeicher m

grand 1. fig großartig; erhaben; groß; Groß..., Haupt... **2.** F Riese m (1000 dollars or pounds)

grand·child Enkel m, Enkelin f

grand·daugh·ter Enkelin f

gran·deur Größe f, Erhabenheit f; Großartigkeit f

grand·fa·ther Großvater m

gran·di·ose großartig

grand·moth·er Großmutter f

grand·par·ents Großeltern pl

grand·son Enkel m

grand·stand SPORT Haupttribüne f

gran·ny F Oma f

grant 1. bewilligen, gewähren; Erlaubnis etc geben; Bitte etc erfüllen; et. zugeben; **take s.th. for ~ed** et. als selbstverständlich betrachten or hinnehmen **2.** Stipendium n; Bewilligung f, Unterstützung f

gran·u·lat·ed körnig, granuliert; ~ **sugar** Kristallzucker m

gran·ule Körnchen n

grape BOT Weinbeere f, Weintraube f

grape·fruit BOT Grapefruit f, Pampelmuse f

grape·vine BOT Weinstock m

graph grafische Darstellung

graph·ic grafisch; anschaulich; ~ **arts** Grafik f; **graph·ics** IT Grafik f

grap·ple ~ **with** kämpfen mit, fig a. sich herumschlagen mit

grasp 1. (er)greifen, packen; fig verstehen, begreifen **2.** Griff m; Reichweite f (a. fig); fig Verständnis n

grass Gras n; Rasen m; Weide(land n) f; sl. Grass n (marijuana)

grass·hop·per ZO Heuschrecke f

grass roots POL Basis f

grass wid·ow Strohwitwe f

grass wid·ow·er Strohwitwer m

gras·sy grasbedeckt, Gras...

grate 1. (Kamin)Gitter n; (Feuer)Rost m **2.** reiben, raspeln; knirschen (mit); ~ **on s.o.'s nerves** an j-s Nerven zerren

grate·ful dankbar

grat·er Reibe f

grat·i·fi·ca·tion Befriedigung f; Freude f; **grat·i·fy** erfreuen; befriedigen

grat·ing[1] kratzend, knirschend, quietschend; schrill; unangenehm

grat·ing[2] Gitter(werk) n

grat·i·tude Dankbarkeit f

gra·tu·i·tous unentgeltlich; freiwillig

gra·tu·i·ty Abfindung f; Gratifikation f; Trinkgeld n

grave[1] ernst; (ge)wichtig; gemessen

grave[2] Grab n

grave·dig·ger Totengräber m

grav·el 1. Kies m **2.** mit Kies bestreuen

grave·stone Grabstein m

grave·yard Friedhof m

grav·i·ta·tion PHYS Gravitation f, Schwerkraft f

grav·i·ty PHYS Schwerkraft f; Ernst m

gra·vy Bratensaft m; Bratensoße f

gray 1. grau **2.** Grau n **3.** grau machen or werden

gray·hound ZO Windhund m

graze[1] Vieh weiden (lassen); (ab)weiden; (ab)grasen

graze[2] **1.** streifen; schrammen; Haut (ab-, auf)schürfen, (auf)schrammen **2.** Abschürfung f, Schramme f; Streifschuss m

grease 1. Fett n; TECH Schmierfett n, Schmiere f **2.** (ein)fetten; TECH schmieren; **greas·y** fett(ig), ölig; speckig; schmierig

great groß; Ur(groß)...; F großartig, super

Great Brit·ain Großbritannien n

great-grand·child Urenkel(in)

great-grand·par·ents Urgroßeltern pl

great·ly sehr

great·ness Größe f

Greece Griechenland n

greed Gier f; **greed·y** gierig (**for** auf acc, nach); habgierig; gefräßig

Greek 1. griechisch **2.** Grieche *m*, Griechin *f*; LING Griechisch *n*

green 1. grün; *fig* grün, unerfahren **2.** Grün *n*; Grünfläche *f*, Rasen *m*; *pl* grünes Gemüse, Blattgemüse *n*

green·back F Dollar *m*

green belt Grüngürtel *m*

green card Arbeitserlaubnis *f*

green·gro·cer *esp Br* Obst- und Gemüsehändler(in)

green·horn F Greenhorn *n*, Grünschnabel *m*

green·house Gewächs-, Treibhaus *n*; ~ ef·fect Treibhauseffekt *m*

green·ish grünlich

greet grüßen; **greet·ing** Begrüßung *f*, Gruß *m*; *pl* Grüße *pl*

gre·nade MIL Granate *f*

grey *Br* → **gray**

grid Gitter *n*; ELECTR *etc* Versorgungsnetz *n*; Gitter(netz) *n* (*map etc*)

grid·i·ron Bratrost *m*

grief Kummer *m*

griev·ance (Grund *m* zur) Beschwerde *f*; Missstand *m*

grieve *v/t* betrüben, bekümmern; *v/i* bekümmert sein; ~ **for** trauern um

griev·ous schwer, schlimm

grill 1. grillen **2.** Grill *m*; Bratrost *m*; GASTR *das* Gegrillte *n*

grim grimmig; schrecklich; erbittert; F schlimm

gri·mace 1. Fratze *f*, Grimasse *f* **2.** Grimassen schneiden

grime Schmutz *m*; Ruß *m*

grim·y schmutzig; rußig

grin 1. Grinsen *n* **2.** grinsen

grind 1. *v/t* (zer)mahlen, zerreiben, zerkleinern; *Messer etc* schleifen; *Fleisch* durchdrehen; ~ **one's teeth** mit den Zähnen knirschen; *v/i* F schuften; pauken, büffeln **2.** Schinderei *f*, F Schufterei *f*; **the daily** ~ das tägliche Einerlei

grind·er (Messer- *etc*)Schleifer *m*; TECH Schleifmaschine *f*; TECH Mühle *f*

grind·stone Schleifstein *m*

grip 1. packen (*a. fig*) **2.** Griff *m*; *fig* Gewalt *f*, Herrschaft *f*; Reisetasche *f*

grip·ping spannend

gris·ly grässlich, schrecklich

gris·tle GASTR Knorpel *m*

grit 1. Kies *m*, (grober) Sand; *fig* Mut *m* **2.** streuen; ~ **one's teeth** die Zähne zusammenbeißen

griz·zly (bear) zo Grislibär *m*, Graubär *m*

groan 1. stöhnen, ächzen **2.** Stöhnen *n*, Ächzen *n*

gro·cer Lebensmittelhändler *m*

gro·cer·ies Lebensmittel *pl*

gro·cer·y Lebensmittelgeschäft *n*

grog·gy F groggy, schwach *or* wackelig (auf den Beinen)

groin ANAT Leiste *f*, Leistengegend *f*

groom 1. Pferdepfleger *m*, Stallbursche *m*; Bräutigam *m* **2.** *Pferde* versorgen, striegeln; pflegen

groove Rinne *f*, Furche *f*; Rille *f*, Nut *f*

grope tasten; F *Mädchen* befummeln

gross 1. dick, feist; grob, derb; ECON Brutto... **2.** Gros *n*

gro·tesque grotesk

ground¹ gemahlen (*coffee etc*); ~ **meat** Hackfleisch *n*

ground² 1. (Erd)Boden *m*, Erde *f*; Boden *m*, Gebiet *n*; SPORT (*Spiel*)Platz *m*; ELECTR Erdung *f*; (Boden)Satz *m*; *fig* Beweggrund *m*; *pl* Grundstück *n*, Park *m*, Gartenanlage *f*; **on the ~(s) of** aufgrund (*gen*); **hold** *or* **stand one's ~** sich behaupten **2.** MAR auflaufen; ELECTR erden; *fig* gründen, stützen; ~ **crew** AVIAT Bodenpersonal *n*; ~ **floor** *esp Br* Erdgeschoss *n*; ~ **forc·es** MIL Bodentruppen *pl*, Landstreitkräfte *pl*

ground·hog zo Amer. Waldmurmeltier *n*

ground·ing ELECTR Erdung *f*; Grundlagen *pl*, Grundkenntnisse *pl*

ground·keep·er SPORT Platzwart *m*

ground·less grundlos

ground·nut *Br* BOT Erdnuss *f*

grounds·man *Br* SPORT Platzwart *m*

ground| staff *Br* AVIAT Bodenpersonal *n*; ~ **sta·tion** Bodenstation *f*

ground·work *fig* Grundlage *f*, Fundament *n*

group 1. Gruppe *f* **2.** (sich) gruppieren

group·ie F Groupie *n*

group·ing Gruppierung *f*

grove Wäldchen *n*, Gehölz *n*

grov·el (am Boden) kriechen

grow *v/i* wachsen; (allmählich) werden; ~ **up** aufwachsen, heranwachsen; *v/t* BOT anpflanzen, anbauen, züchten; ~ **a beard** sich e-n Bart wachsen lassen

grow·er Züchter *m*, Erzeuger *m*

growl knurren, brummen

grown-up 1. erwachsen **2.** Erwachsene *m*, *f*

growth Wachsen *n*, Wachstum *n*; Wuchs *m*, Größe *f*; *fig* Zunahme *f*, Anwachsen *n*; MED Gewächs *n*, Wucherung *f*

grub 1. ZO Larve *f*, Made *f*; F Futter *n* **2.** graben

grub-by schmudd(e)lig

grudge 1. missgönnen (*s.o. s.th.* j-m et.); **2.** Groll *m*

grudg-ing-ly widerwillig

gru-el Haferschleim *m*

gruff grob, schroff, barsch, unwirsch

grum-ble murren, F meckern (*über acc* about, at); ~ *at* schimpfen über (*acc*)

grump-y F schlecht gelaunt, mürrisch, missmutig, verdrießlich, verdrossen

grun-gy F schmudd(e)lig-schlampig; MUS schlecht und laut

grunt 1. grunzen; brummen; stöhnen **2.** Grunzen *n*; Stöhnen *n*

guar-an-tee 1. Garantie *f*; Kaution *f*, Sicherheit *f* **2.** (sich ver)bürgen für; garantieren

guar-an-tor JUR Bürge *m*, Bürgin *f*

guar-an-ty Garantie *f*; Sicherheit *f*

guard 1. Wache *f*, (Wacht)Posten *m*, Wächter *m*; Wärter *m*, Aufseher *m*; Wache *f*, Bewachung *f*; Br Zugbegleiter *m*; Schutz(vorrichtung *f*) *m*; Garde *f*; *be on* ~ Wache stehen; *be on* (*off*) *one's* ~ (nicht) auf der Hut sein **2.** *v/t* bewachen, (be)schützen (*from* vor *dat*); *v/i* sich hüten *or* in Acht nehmen *or* schützen (*against* vor *dat*)

guard-ed vorsichtig, zurückhaltend

guard-i-an 1. JUR Vormund *m* **2.** Schutz...

guard-i-an-ship JUR Vormundschaft *f*

gue(r)-ril-la MIL Guerilla *m*

gue(r)-ril-la war-fare Guerillakrieg *m*

guess 1. (er)raten; vermuten; schätzen; glauben, meinen **2.** Vermutung *f*

guess-work (reine) Vermutung(en *pl*)

guest Gast *m*

guest-house (Hotel)Pension *f*, Fremdenheim *n*

guest-room Gäste-, Fremdenzimmer *n*

guf-faw 1. schallendes Gelächter **2.** schallend lachen

guid-ance Führung *f*; (An)Leitung *f*

guide 1. (Reise-, Fremden)Führer(in); (Reise- *etc*)Führer *m* (*book*); Handbuch (*to* gen); *a* ~ *to London* ein London-Führer **2.** leiten; führen; lenken

guide-book (Reise- *etc*)Führer *m*

guid-ed tour Führung *f*

guide-lines Richtlinien *pl* (*on* gen)

guild HIST Gilde *f*, Zunft *f*

guile-less arglos

guilt Schuld *f*

guilt-less schuldlos, unschuldig (*of* an *dat*)

guilt-y schuldig (*of* gen); schuldbewusst

guin-ea pig ZO Meerschweinchen *n*; *fig* Versuchsperson *f*, F Versuchskaninchen *n*

guise *fig* Gestalt *f*, Maske *f*

gui-tar MUS Gitarre *f*

gulch GEOGR tiefe Schlucht, Klamm *f*

gulf GEOGR Golf *m*; *fig* Kluft *f*

gull ZO Möwe *f*

gul-let ANAT Speiseröhre *f*; Gurgel *f*, Kehle *f*

gulp 1. (großer) Schluck **2.** *often* ~ *down* Getränk hinunterstürzen, *Speise* hinunterschlingen

gum[1] ANAT *mst pl* Zahnfleisch *n*

gum[2] **1.** Gummi *m*, *n*; Klebstoff *m*; Kaugummi *m*; (Frucht)Gummi *m* **2.** kleben

gump-tion F Grips *m*; Schneid *m*

gun 1. Gewehr *n*; Pistole *f*, Revolver *m*; Geschütz *n*, Kanone *f* **2.** ~ *down* niederschießen

gun-fight Feuergefecht *n*, Schießerei *f*

gun-fire Schüsse *pl*; MIL Geschützfeuer *n*

gun li-cence Br, **gun li-cense** Waffenschein *m*

gun-man Bewaffnete *m*

gun-point: *at* ~ mit vorgehaltener Waffe, mit Waffengewalt

gun-pow-der Schießpulver *n*

gun-run-ner Waffenschmuggler *m*

gun-run-ning Waffenschmuggel *m*

gun-shot Schuss *m*; *within* (*out of*) ~ in (außer) Schussweite

gur-gle 1. gurgeln, gluckern, glucksen **2.** Gurgeln *n*, Gluckern *n*, Glucksen *n*

gush 1. strömen, schießen (*from* aus); **2.** Schwall *m*, Strom *m* (*a. fig*)

gust Windstoß *m*, Bö *f*

gust F Eingeweide *pl*; Schneid *m*, Mumm *m*

gut-ter Gosse *f* (*a. fig*), Rinnstein *m*; Dachrinne *f*

guy F Kerl *m*, Typ *m*
guz·zle F saufen; fressen
gym F Fitnesscenter *n*; → *gymnasium*; → *gymnastics*
gym·na·si·um Turn-, Sporthalle *f*
gym·nast Turner(in)
gym·nas·tics Turnen *n*, Gymnastik *f*
gym shirt Turnhemd *n*

gym shorts Turnhose *f*
gy·n(a)e·col·o·gist Gynäkologe *m*, Gynäkologin *f*, Frauenarzt *m*, -ärztin *f*
gy·n(a)e·col·o·gy Gynäkologie *f*, Frauenheilkunde *f*
gyp·sy Zigeuner *m*, Zigeunerin *f*
gy·rate kreisen, sich (im Kreis) drehen, (herum)wirbeln

H

H, h H, h *n*
hab·it (An)Gewohnheit *f*; *esp* (Ordens-) Tracht *f*; *get into* (*out of*) *the ~ of smoking* sich das Rauchen angewöhnen (abgewöhnen); **ha·bit·u·al** gewohnheitsmäßig, Gewohnheits...
hack¹ hacken
hack² *contp* Schreiberling *m*
hack³ *contp* Klepper *m*
hack·er IT Hacker *m*
hack·neyed abgedroschen
had·dock ZO Schellfisch *m*
h(a)e·mor·rhage MED Blutung *f*
hag hässliches altes Weib, Hexe *f*
hag·gard abgespannt; verhärmt, abgehärmt; hager
hag·gle feilschen, handeln
hail 1. Hagel *m* 2. hageln
hail·stone Hagelkorn *n*
hail·storm Hagelschauer *m*
hair *einzelnes* Haar; *coll* Haar *n*, Haare *pl*; *let one's ~ down* F aus sich herausgehen; *without turning a ~* ohne mit der Wimper zu zucken
hair·breadth → *hair's breadth*
hair·brush Haarbürste *f*
hair·cut Haarschnitt *m*
hair·do F Frisur *f*
hair·dress·er Friseur(in)
hair·dri·er, hair·dry·er Trockenhaube *f*; Haartrockner *m*, Föhn *m*
hair·grip *Br* Haarklammer *f*, Haarklemme *f*
hair·less ohne Haare, kahl
hair·pin Haarnadel *f*; *~ bend* MOT Haarnadelkurve *f*
hair·rais·ing haarsträubend
hair's breadth: *by a ~* um Haaresbreite
hair slide *Br* Haarspange *f*
hair·split·ting Haarspalterei *f*

hair·spray Haarspray *m, n*
hair·style Frisur *f*
hair styl·ist Hair-Stylist *m*, Damenfriseur *m*
hair·y behaart, haarig
half 1. Hälfte *f*; *go halves* halbe-halbe machen, teilen 2. halb; *~ an hour* e-e halbe Stunde; *~ a pound* ein halbes Pfund; *~ past ten* halb elf (Uhr); *~ way up* auf halber Höhe
half-breed Halbblut *n*
half-broth·er Halbbruder *m*
half-caste *esp contp* Mischling *m*
half-heart·ed halbherzig
half time SPORT Halbzeit *f*; *~ score* SPORT Halbzeitstand *m*
half·way halb; auf halbem Weg, in der Mitte; *~ line* soccer: Mittellinie *f*
half-wit·ted schwachsinnig
hal·i·but ZO Heilbutt *m*
hall Halle *f*, Saal *m*; Flur, Diele *f*; *esp Br* Herrenhaus *n*; *Br* UNIV Speisesaal *m*; *Br ~ of residence* Studentenheim *n*
hall·mark *fig* Kennzeichen *n*
Hal·low·e'en Abend *m* vor Allerheiligen
hal·lu·ci·na·tion Halluzination *f*
hall·way Halle *f*, Diele *f*; Korridor *m*
ha·lo ASTR Hof *m*; Heiligenschein *m*
halt 1. Halt *m* 2. (an)halten
hal·ter Halfter *m, n*
halt·ing zögernd, stockend
halve halbieren
ham Schinken *m*; *~ and eggs* Schinken mit (Spiegel)Ei
ham·burg·er GASTR Hamburger *m*; Rinderhack *n*
ham·let Weiler *m*
ham·mer 1. Hammer *m* 2. hämmern
ham·mock Hängematte *f*

ham·per¹ (Deckel)Korb *m*; Präsentkorb *m*; Wäschekorb *m*
ham·per² (be)hindern
ham·ster zo Hamster *m*
hand 1. Hand *f* (*a. fig*); Handschrift *f*; (Uhr)Zeiger *m*; *often in cpds* Arbeiter *m*; Fachmann *m*; *card game*: Blatt *n*, Karten *pl*; *change* **~s** den Besitzer wechseln; *give or lend a* **~** mit zugreifen, *j-m* helfen (*with* by); *shake* **~s with** *j-m* die Hand schütteln *or* geben; *at* **~** in Reichweite; nahe; bei der *or* zur Hand; *at first* **~** aus erster Hand; *by* **~** mit der Hand; *on the one* **~** einerseits; *on the other* **~** andererseits; *on the right* **~** rechts; **~s off!** Hände weg!; **~s up!** Hände hoch! **2.** aushändigen, (über)geben, (über)reichen; **~** *around* herumreichen; **~** *down* weitergeben, überliefern; **~** *in* *Prüfungsarbeit etc* abgeben; *Bericht, Gesuch etc* einreichen; **~** *on* weiterreichen, weitergeben; überliefern; **~** *out* austeilen, verteilen; **~** *over* übergeben, aushändigen (*to dat*); **~** *up* hinauf-, heraufreichen; **~bag** Handtasche *f*; **~ bag·gage** Handgepäck *n*; **~ball** SPORT Handball *m*; *soccer*: Handspiel *n*; **~bill** Handzettel *m*, Flugblatt *n*; **~book** Handbuch *n*; **~brake** TECH Handbremse *f*; **~cart** Handwagen *m*; **~cuffs** Handschellen *pl*; **~ful** Handvoll *f*; F Plage *f*
hand·i·cap 1. Handikap *n*, MED *a*. Behinderung *f*, SPORT *a*. Vorgabe *f*; → *mental handicap, physical handicap* **2.** behindern, benachteiligen; **hand·i·capped 1.** gehandikapt, behindert, benachteiligt; → *mental, physical* **2. the ~** MED die Behinderten *pl*
hand·ker·chief Taschentuch *n*
han·dle 1. Griff *m*; Stiel *m*; Henkel *m*; Klinke *f*; *fly off the* **~** F wütend werden **2.** anfassen, berühren; hantieren *or* umgehen mit; behandeln; **~bar(s)** Lenkstange *f*
hand| lug·gage Handgepäck *n*; **~made** handgearbeitet; **~out** Handzettel *m*; Hand-out *n*, Informationsmaterial *n*; **~rail** Geländer *n*; **~s-free-kit** Freisprechanlage *f*; **~shake** Händedruck *m*
hand·some gut aussehend; *fig* ansehnlich, beträchtlich (*sum etc*)
hands-on praktisch

hand| spring Handstandüberschlag *m*; **~stand** Handstand *m*; **~writ·ing** Handschrift *f*; **~writ·ten** handgeschrieben
hand·y zur Hand; geschickt; handlich, praktisch; nützlich; *come in* **~** sich als nützlich erweisen; (sehr) gelegen kommen; **~man** Handwerker *m*; *be a* **~** *a*. handwerklich geschickt sein
hang (auf-, be-, ein)hängen; *Tapete* ankleben; *j-n* (auf)hängen; **~** *o.s.* sich erhängen; **~** *about*, **~** *around* herumlungern; **~** *on* sich klammern (*to* an *acc*) (*a. fig*), festhalten (*to* acc); TEL am Apparat bleiben; **~** *up* TEL einhängen, auflegen; *she hung up on me* sie legte einfach auf
han·gar Hangar *m*, Flugzeughalle *f*
hang·er Kleiderbügel *m*
hang glid·er SPORT (Flug)Drachen *m*; Drachenflieger(in)
hang glid·ing SPORT Drachenfliegen *n*
hang·ing 1. Hänge... **2.** (Er)Hängen *n*
hang·ings Tapete *f*, Wandbehang *m*, Vorhang *m*
hang·man Henker *m*
hang·nail MED Niednagel *m*
hang·o·ver Katzenjammer *m*, Kater *m*
han·ker F sich sehnen (*after, for* nach)
han·kie, han·ky F Taschentuch *n*
hap·haz·ard willkürlich, planlos, wahllos
hap·pen (zufällig) geschehen; sich ereignen, passieren, vorkommen
hap·pen·ing Ereignis *n*, Vorkommnis *n*; Happening *n*
hap·pi·ly glücklich(erweise)
hap·pi·ness Glück *n*
hap·py glücklich; erfreut
hap·py-go-luck·y unbekümmert, sorglos
ha·rangue 1. (Straf)Predigt *f* **2.** *v/t j-m* e-e Strafpredigt halten
har·ass ständig belästigen; schikanieren; aufreiben, zermürben
har·ass·ment ständige Belästigung; Schikane(n *pl*) *f*; → *sexual harassment*
har·bo(u)r 1. Hafen *m*; Zufluchtsort *m* **2.** *j-m* Zuflucht *or* Unterschlupf gewähren; *Groll etc* hegen
hard hart (*a. fig*); fest; schwer, schwierig; heftig, stark; streng (*a. winter*); *fig* nüchtern (*facts etc*); *give s.o. a* **~** *time*

j-m das Leben schwer machen; ~ *of*
hearing schwerhörig; *be ~ on s.th.*
et. strapazieren; ~ *up* F in (Geld)-
Schwierigkeiten, knapp bei Kasse; F
the ~ stuff die harten Sachen (*alcohol,
drugs*)

hard·back gebundene Ausgabe

hard-boiled GASTR hart (gekocht); F *fig*
hart, unsentimental, nüchtern

hard cash Bargeld *n*; klingende Münze

hard core harter Kern; **hard-core** zum
harten Kern gehörend; hart

hard court *tennis*: Hartplatz *m*

hard-cov·er 1. gebunden **2.** Hard Cover
n, gebundene Ausgabe

hard cur·ren·cy ECON harte Währung

hard disk IT Festplatte *f*

hard·en härten; hart machen *or* werden;
(sich) abhärten

hard hat Schutzhelm *m*

hard-head·ed nüchtern, praktisch;
starrköpfig, dickköpfig

hard-heart·ed hartherzig

hard la·bo(u)r JUR Zwangsarbeit *f*

hard line *esp* POL harter Kurs

hard-line *esp* POL hart, kompromisslos

hard·ly kaum

hard·ness Härte *f*; Schwierigkeit *f*

hard·ship Not *f*; Härte *f*; Strapaze *f*

hard shoul·der *Br* MOT Standspur *f*

hard·top MOT Hardtop *n*, *m*

hard·ware Eisenwaren *pl*; Haushalts-
waren *pl*; IT Hardware *f*

hard-wear·ing strapazierfähig

har·dy zäh, robust, abgehärtet; BOT win-
terhart, winterfest

hare ZO Hase *m*

hare·bell BOT Glockenblume *f*

hare·brained verrückt

hare·lip MED Hasenscharte *f*

harm 1. Schaden *m* **2.** verletzen; schaden
(*dat*)

harm·ful schädlich

harm·less harmlos

har·mo·ni·ous harmonisch

har·mo·nize harmonieren; in Einklang
sein *or* bringen

har·mo·ny Harmonie *f*

har·ness 1. (*Pferde- etc*)Geschirr *n* **2.**
anschirren; anspannen (**to** an *acc*)

harp 1. MUS Harfe *f* **2.** MUS Harfe spielen

har·poon 1. Harpune *f* **2.** harpunieren

har·row AGR **1.** Egge *f* **2.** eggen

har·row·ing quälend, qualvoll, erschütternd

harsh rau; grell; streng; schroff, barsch

hart ZO Hirsch *m*

har·vest 1. Ernte(zeit) *f*; (Ernte)Ertrag
m **2.** ernten

har·vest·er MOT Mähdrescher *m*

hash[1] GASTR Haschee *n*

hash[2] F Hasch *n*

hash browns GASTR Brat-, Röstkartof-
feln *pl*

hash·ish Haschisch *n*

hasp TECH Haspe *f*

haste Eile *f*, Hast *f*

has·ten *j-n* antreiben; (sich be)einlen;
et. beschleunigen

hast·y eilig, hastig, überstürzt; voreilig

hat Hut *m*

hatch[1]: *a.* ~ *out* ZO ausbrüten; aus-
schlüpfen

hatch[2] Durchreiche *f*; AVIAT, MAR Luke *f*

hatch·back MOT (Wagen *m* mit) Hecktür
f

hatch·et Beil *n*; *bury the* ~ das Kriegs-
beil begraben

hate 1. Hass *m* **2.** hassen

hate·ful verhasst; abscheulich

ha·tred Hass *m*

haugh·ty hochmütig, überheblich

haul 1. ziehen, zerren; schleppen; befördern, transportieren **2.** Ziehen *n*;
Fischzug *m*, *fig* F *a.* Fang *m*; Beförderung *f*, Transport *m*; Transportweg *m*

haul·age Beförderung *f*, Transport *m*

haul·er, *Br* **haul·i·er** Transportunter-
nehmer *m*

haunch ANAT Hüfte *f*, Hüftpartie *f*, Hin-
terbacke *f*; GASTR Keule *f*

haunt 1. spuken in (*dat*); häufig besuchen; *fig* verfolgen, quälen **2.** häufig
besuchter Ort; Schlupfwinkel *m*

haunt·ing quälend; unvergesslich, eindringlich

have *v/t* haben; erhalten, bekommen;
essen, trinken; ~ *breakfast* frühstücken; ~ *a cup of tea* e-n Tee trinken;
with inf: müssen (*I ~ to go now* ich muss
jetzt gehen); *with object and pp*: lassen
(*I had my hair cut* ich ließ mir die Haare schneiden); ~ *back* zurückbekommen; ~ *on Kleidungsstück* anhaben,
Hut aufhaben; *v/aux* haben; *v/i* often
sein; *I ~ come* ich bin gekommen

ha·ven Hafen *m* (*mst fig*)

hav·oc Verwüstung *f*, Zerstörung *f*; *play*

~ with verwüsten, zerstören; *fig* verheerend wirken auf (*acc*)

hawk[1] ZO Habicht *m*, Falke *m*

hawk[2] hausieren mit; auf der Straße verkaufen; **hawk·er** Hausierer(in); Straßenhändler(in); Drücker(in)

haw·thorn BOT Weißdorn *m*

hay Heu *n*

hay fe·ver MED Heuschnupfen *m*

hay·loft Heuboden *m*

hay·stack Heuhaufen *m*

haz·ard Gefahr *f*, Risiko *n*

haz·ard·ous gewagt, gefährlich, riskant; **~ waste** Sonder-, Giftmüll *m*

haze Dunst(schleier) *m*

ha·zel 1. BOT Hasel(nuss)strauch *m* **2.** (hasel)nussbraun

ha·zel·nut BOT Haselnuss *f*

haz·y dunstig, diesig; *fig* unklar, verschwommen

H-bomb H-Bombe *f*, Wasserstoffbombe *f* .

he 1. er **2.** Er *m*; ZO Männchen *n*; **~-goat** Ziegenbock *m*

head 1. Kopf *m*; (Ober)Haupt *n*; Chef *m*; (An)Führer(in), Leiter(in); Spitze *f*; Kopf(ende *n*) *m*; Kopf *m* (*of a page, nail etc*); Vorderseite *f*; Überschrift *f*; **20 dollars a ~** or **per ~** zwanzig Dollar pro Kopf *or* Person; **40 ~** (*of cattle*) 40 Stück (Vieh); **~s or tails?** Kopf oder Zahl?; **at the ~ of** an der Spitze (*gen*); **~ over heels** kopfüber; bis über beide Ohren (*verliebt sein*); **bury one's ~ in the sand** den Kopf in den Sand stecken; **get it into one's ~ that ...** es sich in den Kopf setzen, dass; **lose one's ~** den Kopf *or* die Nerven verlieren **2.** Ober..., Haupt..., Chef..., oberste(r, -s), erste(r, -s) **3.** *v/t* anführen, an der Spitze stehen von (*or gen*); voran-, vorausgehen (*dat*); (an)führen, leiten; *soccer*: köpfen; *v/i* (**for**) gehen, fahren (nach); lossteuern, losgehen (auf *acc*); MAR Kurs halten (auf *acc*)

head·ache Kopfweh *n*

head·band Stirnband *n*

head·dress Kopfschmuck *m*

head·er Kopfsprung *m*; *soccer*: Kopfball *m*

head·first kopfüber, mit dem Kopf voran; *fig* ungestüm, stürmisch

head·gear Kopfbedeckung *f*

head·ing Überschrift *f*, Titel(zeile *f*) *m*

head·land Landspitze *f*, Landzunge *f*

head·light MOT Scheinwerfer *m*

head·line Schlagzeile *f*; **~s** *radio*, TV *das* Wichtigste in Schlagzeilen

head·long kopfüber; *fig* ungestüm

head·mas·ter *Br* PED Direktor *m*, Rektor *m*

head·mis·tress *Br* PED Direktorin *f*, Rektorin *f*

head-on frontal, Frontal...; **~ collision** MOT Frontalzusammenstoß *m*

head·phones Kopfhörer *pl*

head·quar·ters (*abbr* **HQ**) MIL Hauptquartier *n*; Zentrale *f*

head·rest MOT Kopfstütze *f*

head·set Kopfhörer *pl*

head start SPORT Vorgabe *f*, Vorsprung *m* (*a. fig*)

head·strong halsstarrig

head teach·er → **headmaster, headmistress, principal**

head·wa·ters GEOGR Quellgebiet *n*

head·way Fortschritt(e *pl*) *m*; **make ~** (gut) vorankommen

head·word Stichwort *n*

head·y zu Kopfe steigend, berauschend

heal heilen; **~ over, ~ up** (zu)heilen

heal·ing Heilung *f*; **~ power** Heilkraft *f*

health Gesundheit *f*; **~ cer·tif·i·cate** Gesundheitszeugnis *n*; **~ club** Fitnessklub *m*, Fitnesscenter *n*; **~ food** Reform-, Biokost *f*; **~ food shop** *Br*, **~ food store** Reformhaus *n*, Bioladen *m*

health·ful gesund; heilsam

health| in·su·rance Krankenversicherung *f*; **~ re·sort** Kurort *m*; **~ service** Gesundheitsdienst *m*

health·y gesund

heap 1. Haufe(n) *m* **2.** *a.* **~ up** aufhäufen, *fig a.* anhäufen

hear hören; anhören; *j-m* zuhören; *Zeugen* vernehmen; *Lektion* abhören

hear·er (Zu)Hörer(in)

hear·ing Gehör *n*; Hören *n*; JUR Verhandlung *f*; JUR Vernehmung *f*; *esp* POL Hearing *n*, Anhörung *f*; **within (out of) ~** in (außer) Hörweite

hear·ing aid Hörgerät *n*

hear·say Gerede *n*; **by ~** vom Hörensagen *n*

hearse Leichenwagen *m*

heart ANAT Herz *n* (*a. fig*); Kern *m*; *card games*: Herz(karte *f*) *n*, *pl* Herz *n*; **lose ~** den Mut verlieren; **take ~** sich ein

Herz fassen; **take s.th. to ~** sich et. zu Herzen nehmen; **with a heavy ~** schweren Herzens

heart·ache Kummer *m*

heart at·tack MED Herzanfall *m*; Herzinfarkt *m*

heart·beat Herzschlag *m*

heart·break Leid *n*, großer Kummer

heart·break·ing herzzerreißend

heart·brok·en gebrochen, verzweifelt

heart·burn MED Sodbrennen *n*

heart·en ermutigen

heart fail·ure MED Herzversagen *n*

heart·felt innig, tief empfunden

hearth Kamin *m*

heart·less herzlos

heart·rend·ing herzzerreißend

heart trans·plant MED Herzverpflanzung *f*, Herztransplantation *f*

heart·y herzlich; gesund; herzhaft

heat 1. Hitze *f*; PHYS Wärme *f*; Eifer *m*; ZO Läufigkeit *f*; SPORT (Einzel)Lauf *m*; **preliminary ~** Vorlauf *m* **2.** *v/t* heizen; *a.* **~ up** erhitzen, aufwärmen; *v/i* sich erhitzen (*a. fig*); **heat·ed** geheizt; heizbar; erhitzt, *fig a.* erregt

heat·er Heizgerät *n*, Heizkörper *m*

heath Heide *f*, Heideland *n*

hea·then REL **1.** Heide *m*, Heidin *f* **2.** heidnisch

heath·er BOT Heidekraut *n*; Erika *f*

heat·ing 1. Heizung *f* **2.** Heiz...

heat·proof hitzebeständig

heat shield Hitzeschild *m*

heat·stroke MED Hitzschlag *m*

heat wave Hitzewelle *f*

heave *v/t* (hoch)stemmen, (hoch)hieven; *Anker* lichten; *Seufzer* ausstoßen; *v/i* sich heben und senken, wogen

heav·en Himmel *m*

heav·en·ly himmlisch

heav·y schwer; stark (*rain, smoker, drinker, traffic etc*); hoch (*fine, taxes etc*); schwer (verdaulich); drückend, lastend; Schwer...

heav·y cur·rent ELECTR Starkstrom *m*

heav·y-du·ty TECH Hochleistungs...; strapazierfähig

heav·y-hand·ed ungeschickt

heav·y·weight *boxing:* Schwergewicht *n*, Schwergewichtler *m*

He·brew 1. hebräisch **2.** Hebräer(in); LING Hebräisch *n*

heck·le *Redner* durch Zwischenrufe *or*

Zwischenfragen stören; **heck·ler** Zwischenrufer *m*; **heck·ling** Zwischenrufe

hec·tic hektisch

hedge 1. Hecke *f* **2.** *v/t: a.* **~ in** mit e-r Hecke einfassen; *v/i fig* ausweichen

hedge·hog ZO Stachelschwein *n*; *Br* Igel *m*

hedge·row Hecke *f*

heed 1. beachten, Beachtung schenken (*dat*) **2. give** *or* **pay ~ to, take ~ of** → 1

heed·less: be ~ of nicht beachten, *Warnung etc* in den Wind schlagen

heel 1. ANAT Ferse *f*; Absatz *m*; **down at ~** *fig* abgerissen; heruntergekommen **2.** Absätze machen auf (*acc*)

hef·ty kräftig, stämmig; mächtig (*blow etc*), gewaltig; F saftig (*prices, fine etc*)

heif·er ZO Färse *f*, junge Kuh

height Höhe *f*; (Körper)Größe *f*; Anhöhe *f*; *fig* Höhe(punkt *m*) *f*

height·en erhöhen; vergrößern

heir Erbe *m*; **~ to the throne** Thronerbe *m*, Thronfolger *m*

heir·ess Erbin *f*

heir·loom Erbstück *n*

hel·i·cop·ter AVIAT Hubschrauber *m*, Helikopter *m*

hel·i·port AVIAT Hubschrauberlandeplatz *m*

hell 1. Hölle *f*; **a ~ of a noise** F ein Höllenlärm; **what the ~ ...?** F was zum Teufel ...? **2.** Höllen... **3.** *int* F verdammt!, verflucht!; **hell·ish** F höllisch

hel·lo *int* hallo!

helm MAR Ruder *n*, Steuer *n*

hel·met Helm *m*

helms·man MAR Steuermann *m*

help 1. Hilfe *f*; Hausangestellte *f*; **a call** *or* **cry for ~** ein Hilferuf, ein Hilfeschrei **2.** helfen; **~ o.s.** sich bedienen, zulangen; **I cannot ~** it ich kann es nicht ändern; **I could not ~ laughing** ich musste einfach lachen

help·er Helfer(in)

help·ful hilfreich; nützlich

help·ing Portion *f*

help·less hilflos

help·less·ness Hilflosigkeit *f*

help men·u IT Hilfemenü *n*

hel·ter-skel·ter 1. *adv* holterdiepolter, Hals über Kopf **2.** *adj* überstürzt

helve Stiel *m*, Griff *m*

Hel·ve·tian Schweizer ...

hem 1. Saum *m* **2.** säumen; **~ in** ein-

schließen
hem·i·sphere GEOGR Halbkugel *f*, Hemisphäre *f*
hem·line Saum *m*
hem·lock BOT Schierling *m*
hemp BOT Hanf *m*
hem·stitch Hohlsaum *m*
hen ZO Henne *f*, Huhn *n*; Weibchen *n*
hence daher; *a week* ~ in e-r Woche
hence·forth von nun an
hen house Hühnerstall *m*
hen·pecked hus·band Pantoffelheld *m*
her sie; ihr; ihr(e); sich
her·ald 1. HIST Herold *m* **2.** ankündigen
her·ald·ry Wappenkunde *f*, Heraldik *f*
herb BOT Kraut *n*; Heilkraut *m*
her·ba·ceous BOT krautartig; ~ *plant* Staudengewächs *n*
herb·al BOT Kräuter…, Pflanzen…
her·bi·vore ZO Pflanzenfresser *m*
herd 1. Herde *f* (*a. fig*), Rudel *n* **2.** *v/t* Vieh hüten; *v/i: a.* ~ *together* in e-r Herde leben; sich zusammendrängen
herds·man Hirt *m*
here hier; hierher; ~ *you are* hier (bitte); ~*'s to you!* auf dein Wohl!
here·a·bout(s) hier herum, in dieser Gegend
here·af·ter 1. künftig **2.** *das* Jenseits
here·by hiermit
he·red·i·ta·ry BIOL erblich, Erb…
he·red·i·ty BIOL Erblichkeit *f*; ererbte Anlagen *pl*, Erbmasse *f*
here·in hierin
here·of hiervon
her·e·sy REL Ketzerei *f*
her·e·tic REL Ketzer(in)
here·up·on hierauf, darauf(hin)
here·with hiermit
her·i·tage Erbe *n*
her·maph·ro·dite BIOL Zwitter *m*
her·met·ic TECH hermetisch
her·mit Einsiedler *m*
he·ro Held *m*
he·ro·ic heroisch, heldenhaft, Helden…
her·o·in Heroin *n*
her·o·ine Heldin *f*
her·o·is·m Heldentum *n*
her·on ZO Reiher *m*
her·ring ZO Hering *m*
hers ihrs, ihre(r, -s)
her·self sie selbst, ihr selbst; sich (selbst); *by* ~ von selbst, allein, ohne Hilfe

hes·i·tant zögernd, zaudernd, unschlüssig; **hes·i·tate** zögern, zaudern, unschlüssig sein, Bedenken haben; **hes·i·ta·tion** Zögern *n*, Zaudern *n*, Unschlüssigkeit *f*; *without* ~ ohne zu zögern, bedenkenlos
heterosexual heterosexuell
hew hauen, hacken; ~ *down* fällen, umhauen
hey *int* F he!, heda!
hey·day Höhepunkt *m*, Gipfel *m*; Blüte (-zeit) *f*
hi *inf* F hallo!
hi·ber·nate ZO Winterschlaf halten
hic·cough, hic·cup 1. Schluckauf *m* **2.** den Schluckauf haben
hide¹ (sich) verbergen, verstecken; verheimlichen
hide² Haut *f*, Fell *n*
hide-and-seek Versteckspiel *n*
hide·a·way F Versteck *n*
hid·e·ous abscheulich, scheußlich
hide·out Versteck *n*
hid·ing¹ F Tracht *f* Prügel
hid·ing²: *be in* ~ sich versteckt halten; *go into* ~ untertauchen
hid·ing place Versteck *n*
hi-fi Hi-Fi *n*, Hi-Fi-Gerät *n*, -Anlage *f*
high 1. hoch; groß (*hopes etc*); GASTR angegangen; F blau; F high; *be in* ~ *spirits* in Hochstimmung sein; ausgelassen *or* übermütig sein **2.** METEOR Hoch *n*; Höchststand *m*; High School *f*
high·brow F **1.** Intellektuelle *m*, *f* **2.** (betont) intellektuell
high-cal·o·rie kalorienreich
high-class erstklassig
high·er ed·u·ca·tion Hochschulausbildung *f*
high fi·del·i·ty High Fidelity *f*
high-grade hochwertig; erstklassig
high-hand·ed anmaßend, eigenmächtig
high-heeled hochhackig
high jump SPORT Hochsprung *m*
high jump·er SPORT Hochspringer(in)
high·land Hochland *n*
high·light 1. Höhe-, Glanzpunkt *m* **2.** hervorheben
high·ly *fig* hoch; *think* ~ *of* viel halten von; **high·ly-strung** reizbar, nervös
high·ness *mst fig* Höhe *f*; *Highness* Hoheit *f* (*title*)
high-pitched schrill; steil (*roof*)

high-pow·ered TECH Hochleistungs...;
fig dynamisch

high-pres·sure METEOR, TECH Hochdruck...

high-rank·ing hochrangig

high rise Hochhaus *n*

high road *esp Br* Hauptstraße *f*

high school High School *f*

high sea·son Hochsaison *f*

high so·ci·e·ty High Society *f*

high-spir·it·ed übermütig, ausgelassen

high street *Br* Hauptstraße *f*

high tea *Br* frühes Abendessen

high tech·nol·o·gy Hochtechnologie *f*

high ten·sion ELECTR Hochspannung *f*

high tide Flut *f*

high time: *it is* ~ es ist höchste Zeit

high wa·ter Hochwasser *n*

high·way Highway *m*, Haupt(verkehrs)-
straße *f*; **High·way Code** *Br* Straßenverkehrsordnung *f*

hi·jack 1. *Flugzeug* entführen; *j-n, Geldtransport etc* überfallen **2.** (Flugzeug-)
Entführung *f*; Überfall *m*

hi·jack·er Räuber *m*; (Flugzeug)Entführer(in)

hike 1. wandern **2.** Wanderung *f*

hik·er Wanderer *m*, Wanderin *f*

hik·ing Wandern *n*

hi·lar·i·ous ausgelassen

hi·lar·i·ty Ausgelassenheit *f*

hill Hügel *m*, Anhöhe *f*

hill·bil·ly *contp* Hinterwäldler *m*

hill·ock kleiner Hügel

hill·side (Ab)Hang *m*

hill·top Hügelspitze *f*

hill·y hügelig

hilt Heft *n*, Griff *m*

him ihn; ihm; F er; sich

him·self er *or* ihm *or* ihn selbst; sich;
sich (selbst); *by* ~ von selbst, allein, ohne Hilfe

hind¹ ZO Hirschkuh *f*

hind² Hinter...

hin·der hindern (*from* an *dat*); hemmen

hind·most hinterste(r, -s), letzte(r, -s)

hin·drance Hindernis *n*

Hin·du Hindu *m*

Hin·du·ism Hinduismus *m*

hinge 1. TECH (Tür)Angel *f*, Scharnier *n*
2. ~ *on fig* abhängen von

hint 1. Wink *m*, Andeutung *f*; Tipp *m*;
Anspielung *f*; *take a* ~ e-n Wink verstehen **2.** andeuten; anspielen (*at* auf *acc*)

hip¹ ANAT Hüfte *f*

hip² BOT Hagebutte *f*

hip·po F → **hip·po·pot·a·mus** ZO Flusspferd *n*, Nilpferd *n*

hire 1. *Br Auto etc* mieten, *Flugzeug etc*
chartern; *j-n* anstellen; *j-n* engagieren,
anheuern; ~ *out Br* vermieten **2.** Miete
f; Lohn *m*; *for* ~ zu vermieten; frei

hire car *Br* Leih-, Mietwagen *m*

hire pur·chase: *on* ~ *Br* ECON auf Abzahlung, auf Raten

his sein(e); seins, seine(r, -s)

hiss 1. zischen; fauchen (*cat*); auszischen **2.** Zischen *n*; Fauchen *n*

his·to·ri·an Historiker(in)

his·tor·ic historisch, geschichtlich (bedeutsam); **his·tor·i·cal** historisch, geschichtlich (belegt *or* überliefert); Geschichts...; ~ *novel* historischer Roman

his·to·ry Geschichte *f*; ~ *of civilization*
Kulturgeschichte *f*; *contemporary* ~
Zeitgeschichte *f*

hit 1. schlagen; treffen (*a. fig*); MOT *etc*
j-n, et. anfahren, *et.* rammen; F ~ *it*
off (*with s.o.*) sich (mit j-m) gut vertragen; ~ *on* (zufällig) auf *et.* stoßen, *et.*
finden **2.** Schlag *m*; *fig* (Seiten)Hieb
m; (Glücks)Treffer *m*; Hit *m*

hit-and-run: ~ *driver* (unfall)flüchtiger
Fahrer; ~ *offense* (*Br offence*) Fahrerflucht *f*

hitch 1. befestigen, festmachen, festhaken, anbinden, ankoppeln; ~
up hochziehen; ~ *a ride or lift* im Auto
mitgenommen werden **2.** Ruck *m*, Zug
m; Schwierigkeit *f*, Haken *m*; *without*
a ~ glatt, reibungslos;

hitch·hike per Anhalter fahren, trampen; **hitch·hik·er** Anhalter(in), Tramper(in)

hi-tech → **high tech**

HIV: ~ *carrier* HIV-Positive *m, f*; ~ *negative* HIV-negativ; ~ *positive* HIV-positiv

hive Bienenstock *m*; Bienenschwarm *m*

hoard 1. Vorrat *m*, Schatz *m* **2.** *a.* ~ *up*
horten, hamstern; **hoard·ing** Bauzaun
m; *Br* Reklametafel *f*

hoar·frost (Rau)Reif *m*

hoarse heiser, rau

hoax 1. Falschmeldung *f*; (übler) Scherz
2. *j-n* hereinlegen

hob·ble humpeln, hinken

hob·by Hobby *n*, Steckenpferd *n*
hob·by·horse Steckenpferd *n* (*a. fig*)
hob·gob·lin Kobold *m*
ho·bo F Landstreicher *m*
hock[1] weißer Rheinwein
hock[2] ZO Sprunggelenk *n*
hock·ey SPORT Eishockey *n*; *esp Br* Hockey *n*
hodge·podge Mischmasch *m*
hoe AGR 1. Hacke *f* 2. hacken
hog ZO (Haus-, Schlacht)Schwein *n*
hoist 1. hochziehen; hissen 2. TECH Winde *f*, (Lasten)Aufzug *m*
hold 1. halten; festhalten; *Gewicht etc* tragen, aushalten; zurück-, abhalten (**from** von); *Wahlen, Versammlung etc* abhalten; *Stellung* halten; SPORT *Meisterschaft etc* austragen; *Aktien, Rechte etc* besitzen; *Amt* bekleiden; *Platz* einnehmen; *Rekord* halten; fassen, enthalten; Platz bieten für; der Ansicht sein (**that** dass); halten für; *fig* fesseln, in Spannung halten; (sich) festhalten; anhalten, andauern (*a. fig*); ~ **one's ground**, ~ **one's own** sich behaupten; ~ **the line** TEL am Apparat bleiben; ~ **responsible** verantwortlich machen; ~ **still** still halten; ~ **s.th. against s.o.** j-m et. vorhalten *or* vorwerfen; j-m et. übel nehmen *or* nachtragen; ~ **back** (sich) zurückhalten; *fig* zurückhalten mit; ~ **on** (sich) festhalten (**to** an *dat*); aus-, durchhalten; andauern; TEL am Apparat bleiben; ~ **out** aus-, durchhalten; reichen (*supplies etc*); ~ **up** hochheben; hochhalten; hinstellen (**as** als); aufhalten, verzögern; *j-n, Bank etc* überfallen 2. Griff *m*, Halt *m*; Stütze *f*; Gewalt *f*, Macht *f*, Einfluss *m*; MAR Laderaum *m*, Frachtraum *m*; *catch* (*get*, *take*) ~ *of s.th.* et. ergreifen, et. zu fassen bekommen
hold·er TECH Halter *m*; *esp* ECON Inhaber(in)
hold·ing Besitz *m*; ~ **com·pa·ny** ECON Holding-, Dachgesellschaft *f*
hold·up (Verkehrs)Stockung *f*; (bewaffneter) (Raub)Überfall
hole 1. Loch *n*; Höhle *f*, Bau *m*; *fig* F Klemme *f* 2. durchlöchern
hol·i·day Feiertag *m*; freier Tag; *esp Br mst pl* Ferien *pl*, Urlaub *m*; *be on ~* im Urlaub sein, Urlaub machen; ~ **home** Ferienhaus *n*, Ferienwohnung *f*

hol·i·day·mak·er Urlauber(in)
hol·i·ness Heiligkeit *f*; *His Holiness* Seine Heiligkeit
hol·ler F schreien
hol·low 1. hohl 2. Hohlraum *m*, (Aus)Höhlung *f*; Mulde *f*, Vertiefung *f* 3. ~ **out** aushöhlen
hol·ly BOT Stechpalme *f*
hol·o·caust Massenvernichtung *f*, Massensterben *n*, (*esp* Brand)Katastrophe *f*; *the Holocaust* HIST der Holocaust
hol·ster (Pistolen)Halfter *m*, *n*
ho·ly heilig
ho·ly wa·ter REL Weihwasser *n*
Ho·ly Week REL Karwoche *f*
home 1. Heim *n*; Haus *n*; Wohnung *f*; Zuhause *n*; Heimat *f*; *at ~* zu Hause; *make oneself at ~* es sich bequem machen; *at ~ and abroad* im In- und Ausland 2. *adj* häuslich, Heim... (*a*. SPORT); inländisch, Inlands...; Heimat... 3. *adv* heim, nach Hause; zu Hause; daheim; *fig* ins Ziel, ins Schwarze; *return ~* heimkehren; *strike ~* sitzen, treffen
home ad·dress Privatanschrift *f*
home com·put·er Heimcomputer *m*
home·less heimatlos; obdachlos; ~ *person* Obdachlose *m*, *f*; *shelter for the ~* Obdachlosenasyl *n*
home·ly einfach; unscheinbar, reizlos
home·made selbst gemacht, Hausmacher...
home mar·ket ECON Binnenmarkt *m*
Home| Of·fice *Br* POL Innenministerium *n*; ~ **Sec·re·ta·ry** *Br* POL Innenminister *m*
home·sick: *be ~* Heimweh haben
home·sick·ness Heimweh *n*
home team SPORT Gastgeber *pl*
home·ward *adj* Heim..., Rück...
home·ward(s) *adv* nach Hause
home·work Hausaufgabe(n *pl*) *f*; *do one's ~* s-e Hausaufgaben machen (*a. fig*)
hom·i·cide JUR Mord *m*; Totschlag *m*; Mörder(in)
hom·i·cide squad Mordkommission *f*
ho·mo·ge·ne·ous homogen, gleichartig
ho·mo·sex·u·al 1. homosexuell 2. Homosexuelle *m*, *f*
hone TECH fein schleifen
hon·est ehrlich, rechtschaffen; aufrichtig; **hon·es·ty** Ehrlichkeit *f*, Rechtschaffenheit *f*; Aufrichtigkeit *f*

hon·ey Honig *m*; Liebling *m*, Schatz *m*

hon·ey·comb (Honig)Wabe *f*

hon·eyed *fig* honigsüß

hon·ey·moon 1. Flitterwochen *pl*, Hochzeitsreise *f* **2.** *be ~ing* auf Hochzeitsreise sein

hon·ey·suck·le BOT Geißblatt *n*

honk MOT hupen

hon·or·ar·y Ehren...; ehrenamtlich

hon·o(u)r 1. Ehre *f*; Ehrung *f*, Ehre(n *pl*) *f*; *pl* besondere Auszeichnung(en *pl*); *Your Hono(u)r* JUR Euer Ehren **2.** ehren; auszeichnen; ECON *Scheck etc* honorieren, einlösen

hon·o(u)r·a·ble ehrenvoll, ehrenhaft; ehrenwert

hood Kapuze *f*; MOT Verdeck *n*; (Motor)Haube *f*; TECH (Schutz)Haube *f*

hood·lum F Rowdy *m*; Ganove *m*

hood·wink *j-n* hinters Licht führen

hoof ZO Huf *m*

hook 1. Haken *m*; Angelhaken *m* **2.** an-, ein-, fest-, zuhaken; angeln (*a. fig*)

hooked krumm, Haken...; F süchtig (*on* nach) (*a. fig*); *~ on heroin* (*television*) heroinsüchtig (fernsehsüchtig)

hook·er F Nutte *f*

hoo·li·gan Rowdy *m*

hoo·li·gan·ism Rowdytum *n*

hoop Reif(en) *m*

hoot 1. ZO Schrei *m* (*a. fig*); MOT Hupen *n* **2.** *v/i* heulen; johlen; ZO schreien; MOT hupen; *v/t* auspfeifen, auszischen

Hoo·ver® *Br* **1.** Staubsauger *m* **2.** *mst* **hoover** (staub)saugen

hop¹ 1. hüpfen, hopsen; hüpfen über (*acc*); *be ~ping mad* F e-e Stinkwut haben **2.** Sprung *m*

hop² BOT Hopfen *m*

hope 1. Hoffnung *f* (*of* auf *acc*); **2.** hoffen (*for* auf *acc*); *~ for the best* das Beste hoffen; *I ~ so, let's ~ so* hoffentlich

hope·ful: *be ~ that* hoffen, dass

hope·ful·ly hoffnungsvoll; hoffentlich

hope·less hoffnungslos; verzweifelt

horde Horde *f* (*often contp*)

ho·ri·zon Horizont *m*

hor·i·zon·tal horizontal, waag(e)recht

hor·mone BIOL Hormon *n*

horn ZO Horn *n*, *pl* Geweih *n*; MOT Hupe *f*

hor·net ZO Hornisse *f*

horn·y schwielig; V geil

hor·o·scope Horoskop *n*

hor·ri·ble schrecklich, furchtbar, scheußlich

hor·rid *esp Br* grässlich, abscheulich; schrecklich

hor·rif·ic schrecklich, entsetzlich

hor·ri·fy entsetzen

hor·ror Entsetzen *n*; Abscheu *m*, Horror *m*; F Gräuel *m*

horse ZO Pferd *n*; Bock *m*, Gestell *n*; *wild ~s couldn't drag me there* keine zehn Pferde bringen mich dort hin

horse·back: *on ~* zu Pferde

horse chest·nut BOT Rosskastanie *f*

horse·hair Rosshaar *n*

horse·man (geübter) Reiter

horse·pow·er TECH Pferdestärke *f*

horse race Pferderennen *n*

horse rac·ing Pferderennen *n or pl*

horse·rad·ish BOT Meerrettich *m*

horse·shoe Hufeisen *n*

horse·wom·an (geübte) Reiterin

hor·ti·cul·ture Gartenbau *m*

hose¹ Schlauch *m*

hose² Strümpfe *pl*, Strumpfwaren *pl*

ho·sier·y Strumpfwaren *pl*

hos·pice Sterbeklinik *f*

hos·pi·ta·ble gastfreundlich

hos·pi·tal Krankenhaus *n*, Klinik *f*; *in the ~* im Krankenhaus

hos·pi·tal·i·ty Gastfreundschaft *f*

hos·pi·tal·ize ins Krankenhaus einliefern *or* einweisen

host¹ 1. Gastgeber *m*; BIOL Wirt *m*; *radio*, TV Talkmaster *m*, Showmaster *m*, Moderator(in); *your ~ was ...* durch die Sendung führte Sie ... **2.** *radio*, TV F *Sendung* moderieren

host² Menge *f*, Masse *f*

host³ REL *often* **Host** Hostie *f*

hos·tage Geisel *m*, *f*; *take s.o. ~* j-n als Geisel nehmen

hos·tel *esp Br* UNIV (Wohn)Heim *n*; *mst* **youth ~** Jugendherberge *f*

host·ess Gastgeberin *f*; Hostess *f* (*a. AVIAT*); AVIAT Stewardess *f*

hos·tile feindlich; feindselig (*to* gegen); *~ to foreigners* ausländerfeindlich

hos·til·i·ty Feindseligkeit *f* (*to* gegen); *~ to foreigners* Ausländerfeindlichkeit *f*

hot heiß (*a. fig and sl*); GASTR scharf; warm (*meal*); *fig* hitzig, heftig; ganz neu *or* frisch (*news etc*); *I am or feel ~* mir ist heiß

hot·bed Mistbeet *n*; *fig* Brutstätte *f*

hotch·potch *Br* → *hodgepodge*

hot dog GASTR Hot Dog *n, m*

ho·tel Hotel *n*

hot·head Hitzkopf *m*

hot·house Treib-, Gewächshaus *n*

hot line POL heißer Draht; TEL Hotline *f*

hot·plate Kochplatte *f*

hot spot *esp* POL Unruhe-, Krisenherd *m*

hot spring Thermalquelle *f*

hot-tem·pered jähzornig

hot-wa·ter bot·tle Wärmflasche *f*

hound ZO Jagdhund *m*

hour Stunde *f*; *pl* (*Arbeits*)Zeit *f*, (*Geschäfts*)Stunden *pl*; **hour·ly** stündlich

house 1. Haus *n* **2.** unterbringen

house·bound ans Haus gefesselt

house·break·ing Einbruch *m*

house·hold 1. Haushalt *m* **2.** Haushalts...

house hus·band Hausmann *m*

house·keep·er Haushälterin *f*

house·keep·ing Haushaltung *f*, Haushaltsführung *f*

house·maid Hausangestellte *f*, Hausmädchen *n*

house·man *Br* MED Assistenzarzt *m*, -ärztin *f*

House of Lords *Br* PARL Oberhaus *n*

house plant Zimmerpflanze *f*

house-warm·ing Hauseinweihung *f*, Einzugsparty *f*

house·wife Hausfrau *f*

house·work Hausarbeit *f*

hous·ing Wohnung *f*; ~ **de·vel·op·ment**, *Br* ~ **es·tate** Wohnsiedlung *f*

hov·er schweben; herumlungern; *fig* schwanken

hov·er·craft Hovercraft *n*, Luftkissenfahrzeug *n*

how wie; ~ **are you?** wie geht es dir?; ~ **about...?** wie steht's mit ...?, wie wäre es mit ...?; ~ **do you do?** guten Tag!; ~ **much?** wie viel?; ~ **many** wie viele?

how·ev·er 1. *adv* wie auch (immer) **2.** *cj* jedoch

howl 1. heulen; brüllen, schreien **2.** Heulen *n*; **howl·er** F grober Schnitzer

hub TECH (Rad)Nabe *f*; *fig* Mittelpunkt *m*, Angelpunkt *m*

hub·bub Stimmengewirr *n*; Tumult *m*

hub·by F (Ehe)Mann *m*

huck·le·ber·ry BOT amerikanische Heidelbeere

hud·dle: ~ **together** (sich) zusammendrängen; ~**d up** zusammengekauert

hue[1] Farbe *f*; (Farb)Ton *m*

hue[2]: ~ **and cry** *fig* großes Geschrei, heftiger Protest

huff: **in a** ~ verärgert, verstimmt

hug 1. (sich) umarmen; an sich drücken **2.** Umarmung *f*

huge riesig, riesengroß

hulk F Koloss *m*; sperriges Ding

hull 1. BOT Schale *f*, Hülse *f*; MAR Rumpf *m* **2.** enthülsen, schälen

hul·la·ba·loo Lärm *m*, Getöse *n*

hul·lo *int* hallo!

hum summen; brummen

hu·man 1. menschlich, Menschen... **2.** *a.* ~ **being** Mensch *m*

hu·mane human, menschlich

hu·man·i·tar·i·an humanitär, menschenfreundlich

hu·man·i·ty die Menschheit, die Menschen *pl*; Humanität *f*, Menschlichkeit *f*; *pl* Geisteswissenschaften *pl*; Altphilologie *f*

hu·man·ly: ~ **possible** menschenmöglich

hu·man rights Menschenrechte *pl*

hum·ble 1. demütig; bescheiden **2.** demütigen; **hum·ble·ness** Demut *f*

hum·drum eintönig, langweilig

hu·mid feucht, nass

hu·mid·i·ty Feuchtigkeit *f*

hu·mil·i·ate demütigen, erniedrigen

hu·mil·i·a·tion Demütigung *f*, Erniedrigung *f*

hu·mil·i·ty Demut *f*

hum·ming·bird ZO Kolibri *m*

hu·mor·ous humorvoll, komisch

hu·mo(u)r 1. Humor *m*; Komik *f* **2.** *j-m* s-n Willen lassen; eingehen auf (*acc*)

hump ZO Höcker *m*; MED Buckel *m*

hump·back(ed) → *hunchback(ed)*

hunch 1. → *hump*; dickes Stück; (Vor)Ahnung *f* **2.** *a.* ~ **up** krümmen; ~ **one's shoulders** die Schultern hochziehen

hunch·back Buckel *m*; Bucklige *m, f*

hunch·backed buck(e)lig

hun·dred 1. hundert **2.** Hundert *f*

hun·dredth 1. hundertste(r, -s) **2.** Hundertstel *n*

hun·dred·weight *appr* Zentner *m* (= *50,8 kg*)

Hun·ga·ri·an 1. ungarisch **2.** Ungar(in); LING Ungarisch *n*

Hun·ga·ry Ungarn n
hun·ger 1. Hunger m (a. fig **for** nach); **2.** fig hungern (**for, after** nach)
hun·ger strike Hungerstreik m
hun·gry hungrig
hunk dickes or großes Stück
hunt 1. jagen; Jagd machen auf (acc); verfolgen; suchen (**for, after** nach); ~ **down** zur Strecke bringen; ~ **for** Jagd machen auf (acc); ~ **out,** ~ **up** aufspüren **2.** Jagd f (a. fig), Jagen n; Verfolgung f; Suche f (**for, after** nach)
hunt·er Jäger m; Jagdpferd n
hunt·ing 1. Jagen n **2.** Jagd...
hunt·ing ground Jagdrevier n
hur·dle SPORT Hürde f (a. fig)
hur·dler SPORT Hürdenläufer(in)
hur·dle race SPORT Hürdenrennen n
hurl schleudern; ~ **abuse at s.o.** j-m Beleidigungen ins Gesicht schleudern
hur·rah, hur·ray int hurra!
hur·ri·cane Hurrikan m, Wirbelsturm m; Orkan m
hur·ried eilig, hastig, übereilt
hur·ry 1. v/t schnell or eilig befördern or bringen; often ~ **up** j-n antreiben, hetzen; et. beschleunigen; v/i eilen, hasten; ~ (**up**) sich beeilen; ~ **up!** (mach) schnell! **2.** (große) Eile, Hast f; **be in a ~** es eilig haben
hurt verletzen, verwunden (a. fig); schmerzen, wehtun; schaden (dat)
hurt·ful verletzend
hus·band (Ehe)Mann m
hush 1. int still! **2.** Stille f **3.** zum Schweigen bringen; ~ **up** vertuschen, totschweigen
hush mon·ey Schweigegeld n
husk BOT **1.** Hülse f, Schote f, Schale f **2.** enthülsen, schälen
hus·tle 1. (in aller Eile) wohin bringen or schicken; hasten, hetzen; sich beeilen **2.** ~ **and bustle** Gedränge n; Gehetze n; Betrieb m, Wirbel m

hut Hütte f
hutch Stall m
hy·a·cinth BOT Hyazinthe f
hy·(a)e·na ZO Hyäne f
hy·brid BIOL Mischling m, Kreuzung f
hy·drant Hydrant m
hy·draul·ic hydraulisch
hy·draul·ics hydraulik f
hy·dro... Wasser...
hy·dro·car·bon CHEM Kohlenwasserstoff m
hy·dro·chlor·ic ac·id CHEM Salzsäure f
hy·dro·foil MAR Tragflächenboot n, Tragflügelboot n
hy·dro·gen CHEM Wasserstoff m; ~ **bomb** Wasserstoffbombe f
hy·dro·plane AVIAT Wasserflugzeug n; MAR Gleitboot n
hy·dro·plan·ing MOT Aquaplaning n
hy·e·na ZO Hyäne f
hy·giene Hygiene f
hy·gien·ic hygienisch
hymn Kirchenlied n, Choral m
hype F **1.** a. ~ **up** (übersteigerte) Publicity machen für **2.** (übersteigerte) Publicity; **media ~** Medienrummel m
hy·per... hyper..., übermäßig
hy·per·mar·ket Br Groß-, Verbrauchermarkt m
hy·per·sen·si·tive überempfindlich (**to** gegen)
hy·phen Bindestrich m
hy·phen·ate mit Bindestrich schreiben
hyp·no·tize hypnotisieren
hy·po·chon·dri·ac Hypochonder m
hy·poc·ri·sy Heuchelei f
hyp·o·crite Heuchler(in); **hyp·o·criti·cal** heuchlerisch, scheinheilig
hy·poth·e·sis Hypothese f
hys·te·ri·a MED Hysterie f
hys·ter·i·cal hysterisch
hys·ter·ics hysterischer Anfall; **go into ~** hysterisch werden

I

I, i I, i n
I ich; **it is ~** ich bin es
ice 1. Eis n **2.** Getränke etc mit or in Eis kühlen; GASTR glasieren, mit Zucker-

guss überziehen; ~**d over** zugefroren (lake etc); ~**d up** vereist (road)
ice age Eiszeit f
ice·berg Eisberg m (a. fig)

ice·bound eingefroren

ice cream (Speise)Eis *n*

ice-cream par·lo(u)r Eisdiele *f*

ice cube Eiswürfel *m*

iced eisgekühlt

ice floe Eisscholle *f*

ice hock·ey SPORT Eishockey *n*

ice lol·ly *Br* Eis *n* am Stiel

ice rink (Kunst)Eisbahn *f*

ice show Eisrevue *f*

ice skate Schlittschuh *m*

ice-skate Schlittschuh laufen

i·ci·cle Eiszapfen *m*

ic·ing GASTR Glasur *f*, Zuckerguss *m*; **the ~ on the cake** das Tüpfelchen auf dem i

i·con REL Ikone *f*; IT Icon *n*, (Bild)Symbol *n*

i·cy eisig; vereist

ID *abbr of* **identity** Identität *f*; **ID card** (Personal)Ausweis *m*

i·dea Idee *f*, Vorstellung *f*, Begriff *m*; Gedanke *m*, Idee *f*; **have no ~** keine Ahnung haben

i·deal 1. ideal **2.** Ideal *n*

i·deal·ism Idealismus *m*

i·deal·ize idealisieren

i·den·ti·cal identisch (**to, with** mit); ~ **twins** eineiige Zwillinge *pl*

i·den·ti·fi·ca·tion Identifizierung *f*; ~ (**pa·pers**) Ausweis(papiere *pl*) *m*

i·den·ti·fy identifizieren; ~ **o.s.** sich ausweisen

i·den·ti·kit® **pic·ture** *Br* JUR Phantombild *n*

i·den·ti·ty Identität *f*; ~ **card** (Personal)Ausweis *m*

i·de·o·log·i·cal ideologisch

i·de·ol·o·gy Ideologie *f*

id·i·om Idiom *n*, idiomatischer Ausdruck, Redewendung *f*

id·i·o·mat·ic idiomatisch

id·i·ot Idiot(in), *contp a.* Trottel *m*

id·i·ot·ic idiotisch, F *a.* blödsinnig, schwachsinnig

i·dle 1. untätig; faul, träge; nutzlos; leer, hohl (*talk*); TECH stillstehend, außer Betrieb; MOT leerlaufend, im Leerlauf **2.** faulenzen; MOT leerlaufen; *mst* ~ **away** Zeit vertrödeln

i·dol Idol *n* (*a. fig*) Götzenbild *n*

i·dol·ize abgöttisch verehren, vergöttern

i·dyl·lic idyllisch

if wenn, falls; ob; ~ *I* **were you** wenn ich du wäre

ig·loo Iglu *m, n*

ig·nite anzünden, (sich) entzünden; MOT zünden; **ig·ni·tion** MOT Zündung *f*

ig·ni·tion key MOT Zündschlüssel *m*

ig·no·rance Unkenntnis *f*, Unwissenheit *f*; **ig·no·rant**: **be ~ of s.th.** et. nicht wissen *or* kennen, nichts wissen von et.

ig·nore ignorieren, nicht beachten

ill krank; schlimm, schlecht; **fall ~** krank werden, erkranken

ill-ad·vised schlecht beraten; unklug

ill-bred schlecht erzogen; ungezogen

il·le·gal verboten; JUR illegal, ungesetzlich; ~ **parking** Falschparken *n*

il·le·gi·ble unleserlich

il·le·git·i·mate unehelich; unrechtmäßig

ill feel·ing Verstimmung *f*; **cause ~** böses Blut machen

ill-hu·mo(u)red schlecht gelaunt

il·li·cit unerlaubt, verboten

il·lit·e·rate ungebildet

ill-man·nered ungehobelt, ungezogen

ill-na·tured boshaft, bösartig

ill·ness Krankheit *f*

ill-tem·pered schlecht gelaunt

ill-timed ungelegen, unpassend

ill-treat misshandeln

il·lu·mi·nate beleuchten

il·lu·mi·nat·ing aufschlussreich

il·lu·mi·na·tion Beleuchtung *f*; *pl* Illumination *f*, Festbeleuchtung *f*

il·lu·sion Illusion *f*, Täuschung *f*

il·lu·sive, il·lu·so·ry illusorisch, trügerisch

il·lus·trate illustrieren; bebildern; erläutern, veranschaulichen

il·lus·tra·tion Erläuterung *f*; Illustration *f*; Bild *n*, Abbildung *f*

il·lus·tra·tive erläuternd

il·lus·tri·ous berühmt

ill will Feindschaft *f*

im·age Bild *n*; Ebenbild *n*; Image *n*; bildlicher Ausdruck, Metapher *f*

im·age·ry Bildersprache *f*, Metaphorik *f*

i·ma·gi·na·ble vorstellbar, denkbar

i·ma·gi·na·ry eingebildet, imaginär

i·ma·gi·na·tion Einbildung(skraft) *f*; Vorstellungskraft *f*, -vermögen *n*

i·ma·gi·na·tive ideenreich, einfallsreich; fantasievoll

i·ma·gine sich *j-n or* et. vorstellen; sich et. einbilden

im·bal·ance Unausgewogenheit *f*; POL *etc* Ungleichgewicht *n*

im·be·cile Idiot *m*, Trottel *m*

im·i·tate nachahmen, nachmachen, imitieren; **im·i·ta·tion 1.** Nachahmung *f*, Imitation *f* **2.** nachgemacht, unecht, künstlich, Kunst...

im·mac·u·late unbefleckt, makellos; tadellos, fehlerlos

im·ma·te·ri·al unwesentlich, unerheblich (*to* für)

im·ma·ture unreif

im·mea·su·ra·ble unermesslich

im·me·di·ate unmittelbar; sofortig, umgehend; nächste(r, -s) (*family*)

im·me·di·ate·ly unmittelbar; sofort

im·mense riesig, *fig a.* enorm, immens

im·merse (ein)tauchen; ~ *o.s. in* sich vertiefen in (*acc*)

im·mer·sion Eintauchen *n*

im·mer·sion heat·er Tauchsieder *m*

im·mi·grant Einwanderer *m*, Einwanderin *f*, Immigrant(in); **im·mi·grate** einwandern, immigrieren (*into* in *dat*); **im·mi·gra·tion** Einwanderung *f*, Immigration *f*

im·mi·nent nahe bevorstehend; ~ *danger* drohende Gefahr

im·mo·bile unbeweglich

im·mod·e·rate maßlos

im·mod·est unbescheiden; schamlos, unanständig

im·mor·al unmoralisch

im·mor·tal 1. unsterblich **2.** Unsterbliche *m*, *f*

im·mor·tal·i·ty Unsterblichkeit *f*

im·mo·va·ble unbeweglich; *fig* unerschütterlich; hart, unnachgiebig

im·mune MED immun (*to* gegen); geschützt (*from* vor, gegen); ~ *sys·tem* MED Immunsystem *n*

im·mu·ni·ty MED Immunität *f*

im·mu·nize MED immunisieren, immun machen (*against* gegen)

imp Kobold *m*; F Racker *m*

im·pact Zusammenprall *m*, Anprall *m*; Aufprall *m*; Wucht *f*; *fig* (Ein)Wirkung *f*, (starker) Einfluss (*on* auf *acc*)

im·pair beeinträchtigen

im·part (*to dat*) mitteilen; vermitteln

im·par·tial unparteiisch, unvoreingenommen; **im·par·ti·al·i·ty** Unparteilichkeit *f*, Objektivität *f*

im·pass·a·ble unpassierbar

im·passe *fig* Sackgasse *f*; *reach an* ~ in e-e Sackgasse geraten

im·pas·sioned leidenschaftlich

im·pas·sive teilnahmslos; ungerührt; gelassen

im·pa·tience Ungeduld *f*

im·pa·tient ungeduldig

im·peach JUR anklagen (*for, of, with gen*); JUR anfechten; infrage stellen, in Zweifel ziehen

im·pec·ca·ble untadelig, einwandfrei

im·pede (be)hindern

im·ped·i·ment Hindernis *n* (*to* für); Behinderung *f*

im·pel antreiben; zwingen

im·pend·ing nahe bevorstehend, drohend

im·pen·e·tra·ble undurchdringlich; *fig* unergründlich

im·per·a·tive 1. unumgänglich, unbedingt erforderlich; gebieterisch; LING Imperativ... **2.** *a.* ~ *mood* LING Imperativ *m*, Befehlsform *f*

im·per·cep·ti·ble nicht wahrnehmbar, unmerklich

im·per·fect 1. unvollkommen; mangelhaft **2.** *a.* ~ *tense* LING Imperfekt *n*, 1. Vergangenheit

im·pe·ri·al·ism POL Imperialismus

im·pe·ri·al·ist POL Imperialist *m*

im·per·il gefährden

im·pe·ri·ous herrisch, gebieterisch

im·per·me·a·ble undurchlässig

im·per·son·al unpersönlich

im·per·so·nate *j-n* imitieren, nachahmen; verkörpern, THEA *etc* darstellen

im·per·ti·nence Unverschämtheit *f*, Frechheit *f*

im·per·ti·nent unverschämt, frech

im·per·tur·ba·ble unerschütterlich, gelassen

im·per·vi·ous undurchlässig; *fig* unzugänglich (*to* für)

im·pe·tu·ous ungestüm, heftig; impulsiv; vorschnell

im·pe·tus TECH Antrieb *m*, Impuls *m*

im·pi·e·ty Gottlosigkeit *f*; Pietätlosigkeit *f*, Respektlosigkeit *f* (*to* gegenüber)

im·pinge: ~ *on* sich auswirken auf (*acc*), beeinflussen (*acc*)

im·pi·ous gottlos; pietätlos, respektlos (*to* gegenüber)

im·plac·a·ble unversöhnlich

im·plant MED implantieren, einpflanzen; *fig* einprägen

im·plau·si·ble unglaubwürdig

im·ple·ment 1. Werkzeug *n*, Gerät *n* **2.** ausführen

im·pli·cate *j-n* verwickeln, hineinziehen (*in* in *acc*); **im·pli·ca·tion** Verwicklung *f*; Folge *f*; Andeutung *f*

im·pli·cit vorbehaltlos, bedingungslos; impliziert, (stillschweigend *or* mit) inbegriffen

im·plore *j-n* anflehen; *et.* erflehen

im·ply implizieren, einbeziehen, mit enthalten; andeuten; bedeuten

im·po·lite unhöflich

im·po·li·tic unklug

im·port ECON **1.** importieren, einführen **2.** Import *m*, Einfuhr *f*

im·por·tance Wichtigkeit *f*, Bedeutung *f*; **im·por·tant** wichtig, bedeutend

im·por·ta·tion → *import* 2

im·port du·ty ECON Einfuhrzoll *m*

im·port·er ECON Importeur *m*

im·pose auferlegen, aufbürden (*on dat*); *Strafe* verhängen (*on* gegen); *et.* aufdrängen, aufzwingen (*on dat*); ~ *o.s. on s.o.* sich j-m aufdrängen

im·pos·ing imponierend, eindrucksvoll, imposant

im·pos·si·bil·i·ty Unmöglichkeit *f*

im·pos·si·ble unmöglich

im·pos·ter, *Br* **im·pos·tor** Betrüger(in), *esp* Hochstapler(in)

im·po·tence Unvermögen *n*, Unfähigkeit *f*; Hilflosigkeit *f*; MED Impotenz *f*

im·po·tent unfähig; hilflos; MED impotent

im·pov·e·rish arm machen; *be ~ed* verarmen; verarmt sein

im·prac·ti·ca·ble undurchführbar; unpassierbar

im·prac·ti·cal unpraktisch; undurchführbar

im·preg·na·ble uneinnehmbar

im·preg·nate imprägnieren, tränken; BIOL schwängern

im·press aufdrücken, einprägen (*a. fig*); *j-n* beeindrucken; *be ~ed with* beeindruckt sein von

im·pres·sion Eindruck *m*; Abdruck *m*; *under the ~ that* in der Annahme, dass

im·pres·sive eindrucksvoll

im·print 1. (auf)drücken (*on* auf *acc*); ~ *s.th. on s.o.'s memory* j-m et. ins Gedächtnis einprägen **2.** Abdruck *m*, Eindruck *m*; PRINT Impressum *n*

im·pris·on JUR inhaftieren

im·pris·on·ment Freiheitsstrafe *f*, Gefängnis(strafe *f*) *n*, Haft *f*

im·prob·a·ble unwahrscheinlich

im·prop·er ungeeignet, unpassend; unanständig, unschicklich; unrichtig

im·pro·pri·e·ty Unschicklichkeit *f*

im·prove *v/t* verbessern; *Wert etc* erhöhen, steigern; ~ *on* übertreffen; *v/i* sich (ver)bessern, besser werden, sich erholen; **im·prove·ment** (Ver)Bess(e)rung *f*; Steigerung *f*; Fortschritt *m* (*on* gegenüber *dat*)

im·pro·vise improvisieren

im·pru·dent unklug

im·pu·dence Unverschämtheit *f*

im·pu·dent unverschämt

im·pulse Impuls *m* (*a. fig*); Anstoß *m*, Anreiz *m*; **im·pul·sive** impulsiv

im·pu·ni·ty: *with* ~ straflos, ungestraft

im·pure unrein (*a.* REL), schmutzig; *fig* schlecht, unmoralisch

im·pu·ri·ty Unreinheit *f*

im·pute: ~ *s.th. to s.o.* j-n e-r Sache bezichtigen; j-m et. unterstellen

in 1. *prp place*: in (*dat or acc*), an (*dat*), auf (*dat*): ~ *New York* in New York; ~ *the street* auf der Straße; *put it* ~ *your pocket* steck es in deine Tasche; *time*: in (*dat*), an (*dat*): ~ *1999* 1999; ~ *two hours* in zwei Stunden; ~ *the morning* am Morgen; *state, manner*: in (*dat*), auf (*acc*), mit; ~ *English* auf Englisch; *activity*: in (*dat*), bei (*dat*): ~ *crossing the road* beim Überqueren der Straße; *author*: bei: ~ *Shakespeare* bei Shakespeare; *direction*: in (*acc, dat*), auf (*acc*), zu: *have confidence* ~ Vertrauen haben zu; *purpose*: in (*dat*), zu, als: ~ *defense of* zur Verteidigung *or* zum Schutz von; *material*: in (*dat*), aus, mit: *dressed* ~ *blue* in Blau (gekleidet); *amount etc*: in, von, aus, zu: *three* ~ *all* insgesamt *or* im Ganzen drei; *one* ~ *ten* eine(r, -s) von zehn; nach, gemäß: ~ *my opinion* m-r Meinung nach **2.** *adv* innen, drinnen; hinein, herein; da, (an)gekommen; da, zu Hause **3.** *adj* in (Mode)

in·a·bil·i·ty Unfähigkeit *f*

in·ac·ces·si·ble unzugänglich, unerreichbar (*to* für *or dat*)

in·ac·cu·rate ungenau

in·ac·tive untätig

in·ac·tiv·i·ty Untätigkeit *f*

in·ad·e·quate unangemessen; unzulänglich, ungenügend

in·ad·mis·si·ble unzulässig, unstatthaft

in·ad·ver·tent unbeabsichtigt, versehentlich; *~ly a.* aus Versehen

in·an·i·mate leblos; langweilig

in·ap·pro·pri·ate unpassend, ungeeignet (*for, to* für)

in·apt ungeeignet, unpassend

in·ar·tic·u·late unartikuliert, undeutlich (ausgesprochen), unverständlich; unfähig(, deutlich) zu sprechen

in·at·ten·tive unaufmerksam

in·au·di·ble unhörbar

in·au·gu·ral 1. Eröffnungs..., Antritts...; *~ speech* → 2. Antrittsrede *f*

in·au·gu·rate *j-n* (feierlich) (in sein Amt) einführen; einweihen, eröffnen; einleiten; **in·au·gu·ra·tion** Amtseinführung *f*; Einweihung *f*, Eröffnung *f*; Beginn *m*; ***Inauguration Day*** Tag *m* der Amtseinführung des neu gewählten Präsidenten der USA

in·born angeboren

in·cal·cu·la·ble unberechenbar; unermesslich

in·can·des·cent (weiß) glühend

in·ca·pa·ble unfähig (*of* zu *inf or gen*), nicht imstande (*of doing* zu tun)

in·ca·pac·i·tate unfähig *or* untauglich machen; **in·ca·pac·i·ty** Unfähigkeit *f*, Untauglichkeit *f*

in·car·nate leibhaftig; personifiziert

in·cau·tious unvorsichtig

in·cen·di·a·ry Brand...; *fig* aufwiegelnd, aufhetzend

in·cense¹ REL Weihrauch *m*

in·cense² in Wut bringen, erbosen

in·cen·tive Ansporn *m*, Anreiz *m*

in·ces·sant ständig, unaufhörlich

in·cest Inzest *m*, Blutschande *f*

inch 1. Inch *m (2,54 cm)*, Zoll *m (a. fig)*; *by ~es*, *~ by ~* allmählich; *every ~* durch und durch 2. (sich) zentimeterweise *or* sehr langsam bewegen

in·ci·dence Vorkommen *n*

in·ci·dent Vorfall *m*, Ereignis *n*; POL Zwischenfall *m*

in·ci·den·tal nebensächlich, Neben...; beiläufig; **in·ci·den·tal·ly** nebenbei bemerkt, übrigens

in·cin·e·rate verbrennen

in·cin·e·ra·tor TECH Verbrennungsofen

m; Verbrennungsanlage *f*

in·cise einschneiden; aufschneiden; einritzen, einschnitzen

in·ci·sion (Ein)Schnitt *m*

in·ci·sive schneidend, scharf; *fig* treffend

in·ci·sor ANAT Schneidezahn *m*

in·cite anstiften; aufwiegeln, aufhetzen

in·cite·ment Anstiftung *f*; Aufhetzung *f*, Aufwieg(e)lung *f*

in·clem·ent rau

in·cli·na·tion Neigung *f* (*a. fig*)

in·cline 1. *v/i* sich neigen (*to, towards* nach); *fig* neigen (*to, towards* zu); *v/t* neigen; *fig* veranlassen 2. Gefälle *n*; (Ab)Hang *m*

in·close, in·clos·ure → **enclose, enclosure**

in·clude einschließen, enthalten; aufnehmen (*in in e-e Liste etc*); *the group ~d several ...* zu der Gruppe gehörten einige ...; *tax ~d* inklusive Steuer

in·clud·ing einschließlich

in·clu·sion Einschluss *m*, Einbeziehung *f*; **in·clu·sive** einschließlich, inklusive (*of gen*); *be ~ of* einschließen (*acc*)

in·co·her·ent unzusammenhängend, unklar, unverständlich

in·come ECON Einkommen *n*, Einkünfte *pl*; *~ tax* ECON Einkommensteuer *f*

in·com·ing hereinkommend; ankommend; nachfolgend, neu; *~ mail* Posteingang *m*

in·com·mu·ni·ca·tive verschlossen

in·com·pa·ra·ble unvergleichlich; unvergleichbar

in·com·pat·i·ble unvereinbar; unverträglich; inkompatibel

in·com·pe·tence Unfähigkeit *f*; Inkompetenz *f*; **in·com·pe·tent** unfähig; nicht fachkundig *or* sachkundig; unzuständig, inkompetent

in·com·plete unvollständig; unvollendet

in·com·pre·hen·si·ble unbegreiflich, unfassbar

in·com·pre·hen·sion Unverständnis *n*

in·con·ceiv·a·ble unbegreiflich, unfassbar; undenkbar

in·con·clu·sive nicht überzeugend; ergebnislos, erfolglos

in·con·gru·ous nicht übereinstimmend; unvereinbar

in·con·se·quen·tial unbedeutend

in·con·sid·e·ra·ble unbedeutend

in·con·sid·er·ate unüberlegt; rücksichtslos

in·con·sis·tent unvereinbar; widersprüchlich; inkonsequent

in·con·so·la·ble untröstlich

in·con·spic·u·ous unauffällig

in·con·stant unbeständig, wankelmütig

in·con·test·a·ble unanfechtbar

in·con·ti·nent MED inkontinent

in·con·ve·ni·ence 1. Unbequemlichkeit f; Unannehmlichkeit f, Ungelegenheit f **2.** j-m lästig sein; j-m Umstände machen; **in·con·ve·ni·ent** unbequem; ungelegen, lästig

in·cor·po·rate (sich) vereinigen or zusammenschließen; (mit) einbeziehen; enthalten; eingliedern; Ort eingemeinden; ECON, JUR als Aktiengesellschaft eintragen (lassen)

in·cor·po·rat·ed com·pa·ny ECON Aktiengesellschaft f

in·cor·po·ra·tion Vereinigung f, Zusammenschluss m; Eingliederung f; Eingemeindung f; ECON, JUR Eintragung f als Aktiengesellschaft

in·cor·rect unrichtig, falsch; inkorrekt

in·cor·ri·gi·ble unverbesserlich

in·cor·rup·ti·ble unbestechlich

in·crease 1. zunehmen, (an)wachsen; steigen; vergrößern, vermehren, erhöhen **2.** Vergrößerung f, Erhöhung f, Zunahme f, Zuwachs m, (An)Wachsen n, Steigerung f; **in·creas·ing·ly** immer mehr; ~ **difficult** immer schwieriger

in·cred·i·ble unglaublich

in·cre·du·li·ty Ungläubigkeit f

in·cred·u·lous ungläubig, skeptisch

in·crim·i·nate j-n belasten

in·cu·bate ausbrüten; **in·cu·ba·tor** Brutapparat m; MED Brutkasten m

in·cur sich et. zuziehen, auf sich laden; Schulden machen; Verluste erleiden

in·cu·ra·ble unheilbar

in·cu·ri·ous nicht neugierig, gleichgültig, uninteressiert

in·cur·sion (feindlicher) Einfall; Eindringen n

in·debt·ed (zu Dank) verpflichtet; ECON verschuldet

in·de·cent unanständig, anstößig; JUR unsittlich, unzüchtig; ~ **assault** JUR Sittlichkeitsverbrechen n

in·de·ci·sion Unentschlossenheit f

in·de·ci·sive unentschlossen; unentschieden; unbestimmt, ungewiss

in·deed 1. adv in der Tat, tatsächlich, wirklich; allerdings; **thank you very much** ~! vielen herzlichen Dank! **2.** int ach wirklich?

in·de·fat·i·ga·ble unermüdlich

in·de·fen·si·ble unhaltbar

in·de·fi·na·ble undefinierbar, unbestimmbar

in·def·i·nite unbestimmt; unbegrenzt

in·def·i·nite·ly auf unbestimmte Zeit

in·del·i·cate taktlos; unfein, anstößig

in·dem·ni·fy j-n entschädigen, j-m Schadenersatz leisten (**for** für)

in·dem·ni·ty Entschädigung f

in·dent (ein)kerben, auszacken; PRINT Zeile einrücken

in·de·pen·dence Unabhängigkeit f; Selbstständigkeit f; **Independence Day** Unabhängigkeitstag m

in·de·pen·dent unabhängig; selbstständig

in·de·scri·ba·ble unbeschreiblich

in·de·struc·ti·ble unzerstörbar; unverwüstlich

in·de·ter·mi·nate unbestimmt; unklar, vage

in·dex Index m, (Inhalts-, Namens-, Stichwort)Verzeichnis n, (Sach)Register n; (An)Zeichen n; **cost of living** ~ Lebenshaltungsindex m

in·dex card Karteikarte f

in·dex fin·ger ANAT Zeigefinger m

In·di·a Indien n

In·di·an 1. indisch; neg! indianisch, Indianer… **2.** Inder(in); **American** ~ Indianer(in); ~ **corn** BOT Mais m; ~ **file:** **in** ~ im Gänsemarsch; ~ **sum·mer** Altweibersommer m, Nachsommer m

in·di·a rub·ber Gummi n, m; Radiergummi m

in·di·cate deuten or zeigen auf (acc); TECH anzeigen; MOT blinken; fig hinweisen or hindeuten auf (acc); andeuten; **in·di·ca·tion** (An)Zeichen n, Hinweis m, Andeutung f, Indiz n

in·dic·a·tive a. ~ **mood** LING Indikativ m

in·di·ca·tor TECH Anzeiger m; MOT Richtungsanzeiger m, Blinker m

in·dict JUR anklagen (**for** wegen)

in·dict·ment JUR Anklage f

in·dif·fer·ence Gleichgültigkeit f

in·dif·fer·ent gleichgültig (**to** gegen);

mittelmäßig

in·di·gent arm

in·di·ges·ti·ble unverdaulich

in·di·ges·tion MED Verdauungsstörung f, Magenverstimmung f

in·dig·nant entrüstet, empört, ungehalten (*about, at, over* über *acc*)

in·dig·na·tion Entrüstung f, Empörung f (*about, at, over* über *acc*)

in·dig·ni·ty Demütigung f, unwürdige Behandlung

in·di·rect indirekt; *by ~ means* fig auf Umwegen

in·dis·creet unbesonnen, unbedacht; indiskret; **in·dis·cre·tion** Unbesonnenheit f; Indiskretion f

in·dis·crim·i·nate kritiklos; wahllos

in·dis·pen·sa·ble unentbehrlich, unerlässlich

in·dis·posed indisponiert, unpässlich; abgeneigt; **in·dis·po·si·tion** Unpässlichkeit f; Abneigung f (*to do* zu tun)

in·dis·pu·ta·ble unbestreitbar, unstreitig

in·dis·tinct undeutlich; unklar, verschwommen

in·dis·tin·guish·a·ble nicht zu unterscheiden(d) (*from* von)

in·di·vid·u·al 1. individuell, einzeln, Einzel...; persönlich 2. Individuum n, Einzelne m, f

in·di·vid·u·al·ism Individualismus m

in·di·vid·u·al·ist Individualist(in)

in·di·vid·u·al·i·ty Individualität f, (persönliche) Note

in·di·vid·u·al·ly einzeln, jede(r, -s) für sich; individuell

in·di·vis·i·ble unteilbar

in·dom·i·ta·ble unbezähmbar, nicht unterzukriegen(d)

in·door Haus..., Zimmer..., Innen..., SPORT Hallen...

in·doors im Haus, drinnen; ins Haus (hinein); SPORT in der Halle

in·dorse → *endorse* etc

in·duce j-n veranlassen; verursachen, bewirken; **in·duce·ment** Anreiz m

in·duct einführen, -setzen; **in·duc·tion** Herbeiführung f; Einführung f, Einsetzung f; ELECTR Induktion f

in·dulge nachsichtig sein gegen; e-r Neigung etc nachgeben; *~ in s.th.* sich et. gönnen or leisten; **in·dul·gence** Nachsicht f; Luxus m; REL Ablass m

in·dul·gent nachsichtig, nachgiebig

in·dus·tri·al industriell, Industrie..., Gewerbe..., Betriebs...

in·dus·tri·al ar·e·a Industriegebiet n

in·dus·tri·al·ist Industrielle m, f

in·dus·tri·al·ize industrialisieren

in·dus·tri·ous fleißig

in·dus·try Industrie(zweig m) f; Gewerbe(zweig m) n; Fleiß m

in·ed·i·ble ungenießbar, nicht essbar

in·ef·fec·tive, in·ef·fec·tu·al unwirksam, wirkungslos; unfähig, untauglich

in·ef·fi·cient ineffizient; unfähig, untauglich; unrationell, unwirtschaftlich

in·el·e·gant unelegant

in·el·i·gi·ble nicht berechtigt

in·ept unpassend; ungeschickt; albern, töricht

in·e·qual·i·ty Ungleichheit f

in·ert PHYS träge (*a.* fig); inaktiv

in·er·tia PHYS Trägheit f (*a.* fig)

in·es·cap·a·ble unvermeidlich

in·es·sen·tial unwesentlich, unwichtig (*to* für)

in·es·ti·ma·ble unschätzbar

in·ev·i·ta·ble unvermeidlich

in·ev·i·ta·bly zwangsläufig

in·ex·act ungenau

in·ex·cu·sa·ble unverzeihlich, unentschuldbar

in·ex·haus·ti·ble unerschöpflich; unermüdlich

in·ex·o·ra·ble unerbittlich

in·ex·pe·di·ent unzweckmäßig; nicht ratsam

in·ex·pen·sive billig, preiswert

in·ex·pe·ri·ence Unerfahrenheit f

in·ex·pe·ri·enced unerfahren

in·ex·pert unerfahren; ungeschickt

in·ex·plic·a·ble unerklärlich

in·ex·pres·si·ble unaussprechlich, unbeschreiblich

in·ex·pres·sive ausdruckslos

in·ex·tri·ca·ble unentwirrbar

in·fal·li·ble unfehlbar

in·fa·mous berüchtigt; schändlich, niederträchtig; **in·fa·my** Ehrlosigkeit f; Schande f; Niedertracht f

in·fan·cy frühe Kindheit; *be in its ~* fig in den Kinderschuhen stecken

in·fant Säugling m; kleines Kind, Kleinkind n; **in·fan·tile** kindlich; Kindes..., Kinder...; infantil, kindisch

in·fan·try MIL Infanterie f

in·fat·u·at·ed vernarrt (**with** in acc)

in·fect MED j-n, et. infizieren, j-n anstecken (a. fig); verseuchen, verunreinigen; **in·fec·tion** MED Infektion f, Ansteckung f (a. fig); **in·fec·tious** MED infektiös, ansteckend (a. fig)

in·fer folgern, schließen (**from** aus)

in·fer·ence (Schluss)Folgerung f, (Rück)Schluss m

in·fe·ri·or 1. untergeordnet (**to** dat), niedriger (**to** als); weniger wert (**to** als); minderwertig; **be ~ to s.o.** j-m untergeordnet sein; j-m unterlegen sein **2.** Untergebene m, f

in·fe·ri·or·i·ty Unterlegenheit f; Minderwertigkeit f; **~ com·plex** PSYCH Minderwertigkeitskomplex m

in·fer·nal höllisch, Höllen...

in·fer·no Inferno n, Hölle f

in·fer·tile unfruchtbar

in·fest verseuchen, befallen; fig überschwemmen (**with** mit)

in·fi·del·i·ty (esp eheliche) Untreue

in·fil·trate einsickern in (acc); einschleusen (**into** in acc); POL unterwandern

in·fi·nite unendlich

in·fin·i·tive a. **~ mood** LING Infinitiv m, Nennform f

in·fin·i·ty Unendlichkeit f

in·firm schwach, gebrechlich

in·fir·ma·ry Krankenhaus n; PED etc Krankenzimmer n

in·fir·mi·ty Schwäche f, Gebrechlichkeit f

in·flame entflammen (mst fig); erregen; **become ~d** MED sich entzünden

in·flam·ma·ble brennbar, leicht entzündlich; feuergefährlich

in·flam·ma·tion MED Entzündung f

in·flam·ma·to·ry MED entzündlich; fig aufrührerisch, Hetz...

in·flate aufpumpen, aufblasen, aufblähen (a. fig); ECON Preise etc in die Höhe treiben

in·fla·tion ECON Inflation f

in·flect LING flektieren, beugen

in·flec·tion LING Flexion f, Beugung f

in·flex·i·ble unbiegsam, starr (a. fig); fig inflexibel, unbeweglich, unbeugsam

in·flex·ion Br → **inflection**

in·flict (on) Leid, Schaden etc zufügen (dat); Wunde etc beibringen (dat); Strafe auferlegen (dat), verhängen (über acc); aufbürden, aufdrängen (dat)

in·flic·tion Zufügung f; Verhängung f; Plage f

in·flu·ence 1. Einfluss m **2.** beeinflussen; **in·flu·en·tial** einflussreich

in·flux Zustrom m, Zufluss m, (Waren-) Zufuhr f

in·form benachrichtigen, unterrichten (**of** von), informieren (**of** über acc); **~ against** or **on s.o.** j-n anzeigen; j-n denunzieren

in·for·mal formlos, zwanglos

in·for·mal·i·ty Formlosigkeit f; Ungezwungenheit f

in·for·ma·tion Auskunft f, Information f; Nachricht f

in·for·ma·tive informativ; lehrreich; mitteilsam

in·form·er Denunziant(in); Spitzel m

in·fra·struc·ture Infrastruktur f

in·fre·quent selten

in·fringe: ~ on Rechte, Vertrag etc verletzen, verstoßen gegen

in·fu·ri·ate wütend machen

in·fuse Tee aufgießen

in·fu·sion Aufguss m; MED Infusion f

in·ge·ni·ous genial; einfallsreich; raffiniert; **in·ge·nu·i·ty** Genialität f; Einfallsreichtum m

in·gen·u·ous offen, aufrichtig; naiv

in·got (Gold- etc)Barren m

in·gra·ti·ate: ~ o.s. with s.o. sich bei j-m beliebt machen

in·grat·i·tude Undankbarkeit f

in·gre·di·ent Bestandteil m; GASTR Zutat f

in·hab·it bewohnen, leben in (dat)

in·hab·it·a·ble bewohnbar

in·hab·i·tant Bewohner(in); Einwohner(in)

in·hale einatmen, MED a. inhalieren

in·her·ent innewohnend, eigen (in dat)

in·her·it erben; **in·her·i·tance** Erbe n

in·hib·it hemmen (a. PSYCH), (ver)hindern; **in·hib·it·ed** PSYCH gehemmt; **in·hi·bi·tion** PSYCH Hemmung f

in·hos·pi·ta·ble ungastlich; unwirtlich (region etc)

in·hu·man unmenschlich

in·hu·mane inhuman, menschenunwürdig

in·im·i·cal feindselig (**to** gegen); nachteilig (**to** für)

in·im·i·ta·ble unnachahmlich

in·i·tial 1. anfänglich, Anfangs... **2.** Initiale *f*, (großer) Anfangsbuchstabe

i·ni·tial·ly am *or* zu Anfang, anfänglich

i·ni·ti·ate in die Wege leiten, ins Leben rufen; einführen

i·ni·ti·a·tion Einführung *f*

i·ni·tia·tive Initiative *f*, erster Schritt; **take the ~** die Initiative ergreifen; **on one's own ~** aus eigenem Antrieb

in·ject MED injizieren, einspritzen

in·jec·tion MED Injektion *f*, Spritze *f*

in·ju·di·cious unklug, unüberlegt

in·junc·tion JUR gerichtliche Verfügung

in·jure verletzen, verwunden; schaden (*dat*); kränken; **in·jured 1.** verletzt **2. the ~** die Verletzten *pl*

in·ju·ri·ous schädlich; **be ~ to** schaden (*dat*); **~ to health** gesundheitsschädlich

in·ju·ry MED Verletzung *f*; Kränkung *f*; **~ time** *Br esp soccer:* Nachspielzeit *f*

in·jus·tice Ungerechtigkeit *f*; Unrecht *n*; **do s.o. an ~** j-m unrecht tun

ink Tinte *f*

ink·ling Andeutung *f*; dunkle *or* leise Ahnung

ink pad Stempelkissen *n*

ink·y Tinten…; tinten-, pechschwarz

in·laid eingelegt, Einlege…; **~ work** Einlegearbeit *f*

in·land 1. *adj* inländisch, einheimisch; ECON Binnen… **2.** *adv* landeinwärts

In·land Rev·e·nue *Br* Finanzamt *n*

in·lay Einlegearbeit *f*; MED (Zahn)Füllung *f*, Plombe *f*

in·let GEOGR schmale Bucht; TECH Eingang *m*, Einlass *m*

in·line skate Inliner *m*, Inline Skate *m*

in·mate Insasse *m*, Insassin *f*; Mitbewohner(in)

in·most innerste(r, -s) (*a. fig*)

inn Gasthaus *n*, Wirtshaus *n*

in·nate angeboren

in·ner innere(r, -s); Innen…; verborgen

in·ner·most → *inmost*

in·nings *cricket, baseball:* Spielzeit *f*

inn·keep·er Gastwirt(in)

in·no·cence Unschuld *f*; Harmlosigkeit *f*; Naivität *f*; **in·no·cent** unschuldig; harmlos; arglos, naiv

in·noc·u·ous harmlos

in·no·va·tion Neuerung *f*

in·nu·en·do (versteckte) Andeutung *f*

in·nu·me·ra·ble unzählig, zahllos

i·noc·u·late MED impfen

i·noc·u·la·tion MED Impfung *f*

in·of·fen·sive harmlos

in·op·e·ra·ble MED inoperabel, nicht operierbar; undurchführbar (*plan etc*)

in·op·por·tune inopportun, unangebracht, ungelegen

in·or·di·nate unmäßig

in·pa·tient MED stationärer Patient, stationäre Patientin

in·put Input *m, n,* IT *a.* (Daten)Eingabe *f*, ELECTR *a.* Eingangsleistung *f*

in·quest JUR gerichtliche Untersuchung

in·quire fragen *or* sich erkundigen (nach); **~ into** *et.* untersuchen, prüfen

in·quir·ing forschend; wissbegierig

in·quir·y Erkundigung *f*, Nachfrage *f*; Untersuchung *f*; Ermittlung *f*; **make inquiries** Erkundigungen einziehen

in·qui·si·tion (amtliche) Untersuchung; Verhör *f*; **Inquisition** REL HIST Inquisition *f*

in·quis·i·tive neugierig, wissbegierig

in·roads (*in*[*to*], **on**) Eingriff *m* (in *acc*) Übergriff *m* (auf *acc*)

in·sane geisteskrank, wahnsinnig

in·san·i·ta·ry unhygienisch

in·san·i·ty Geisteskrankheit *f*, Wahnsinn *m*

in·sa·tia·ble unersättlich

in·scrip·tion Inschrift *f*, Aufschrift *f*; Widmung *f*

in·scru·ta·ble unerforschlich, unergründlich

in·sect ZO Insekt *n*; **in·sec·ti·cide** Insektenvertilgungsmittel *n*, Insektizid *n*

in·se·cure unsicher; nicht sicher *or* fest

in·sen·si·ble unempfindlich (**to** gegen); bewusstlos; unempfänglich (**of, to** für), gleichgültig (**of, to** gegen); unmerklich

in·sen·si·tive unempfindlich (**to** gegen); unempfänglich (**of, to** für), gleichgültig (**of, to** gegen)

in·sep·a·ra·ble untrennbar; unzertrennlich

in·sert 1. einfügen, einsetzen, einführen, (hinein)stecken, *Münze* einwerfen; inserieren **2.** (Zeitungs)Beilage *f*, (Buch)Einlage *f*

in·ser·tion Einfügen *n*, Einsetzen *n*, Einführen *n*, Hineinstecken *n*; Einfügung *f*; Einwurf *m*; Anzeige *f*, Inserat *n*

in·sert key IT Einfügetaste *f*

in·shore an *or* nahe der Küste; Küsten…

in·side 1. Innenseite *f; das* Innere; *turn~ out* umkrempeln; auf den Kopf stellen **2.** *adj* innere(r, -s), Innen...; Insider... **3.** *adv* im Inner(e)n, innen, drinnen; *~ of* F innerhalb (*gen*) **4.** *prp* innerhalb, im Inner(e)n

in·sid·er Insider(in), Eingeweihte *m, f*

in·sid·i·ous heimtückisch

in·sight Einsicht *f,* Einblick *m;* Verständnis *n*

in·sig·ni·a Insignien *pl;* Abzeichen *pl*

in·sig·nif·i·cant bedeutungslos; unbedeutend

in·sin·cere unaufrichtig

in·sin·u·ate andeuten, anspielen auf (*acc*); unterstellen; *~ that s.o. ...* j-m unterstellen, dass er ...

in·sin·u·a·tion Anspielung *f,* Andeutung *f,* Unterstellung *f*

in·sip·id geschmacklos, fad

in·sist bestehen, beharren (**on** auf *dat*)

in·sis·tence Bestehen *n,* Beharren *n;* Beharrlichkeit *f*

in·sis·tent beharrlich, hartnäckig

in·sole Einlegesohle *f;* Brandsohle *f*

in·so·lent unverschämt

in·sol·u·ble unlöslich (*substance etc*); unlösbar (*problem etc*)

in·sol·vent ECON zahlungsunfähig, insolvent

in·som·ni·a Schlaflosigkeit *f*

in·spect untersuchen, prüfen, nachsehen; besichtigen, inspizieren

in·spec·tion Prüfung *f,* Untersuchung *f,* Kontrolle *f;* Inspektion *f*

in·spec·tor Aufsichtsbeamte *m,* Inspektor *m;* (Polizei)Inspektor *m,* (Polizei)Kommissar *m*

in·spi·ra·tion Inspiration *f,* (plötzlicher) Einfall; **in·spire** inspirieren, anregen; *Gefühl etc* auslösen

in·stall TECH installieren, einrichten, aufstellen, einbauen, *Leitung* legen; j-n in ein *Amt etc* einsetzen

in·stal·la·tion TECH Installation *f,* Einrichtung *f,* Einbau *m;* TECH *fertige* Anlage *f; fig* Einsetzung *f,* Einführung *f*

in·stall·ment, in·stal·ment Br ECON Rate *f;* (Teil)Lieferung *f;* Fortsetzung *f; radio,* TV Folge *f*

in·stall·ment plan: *buy on the ~* ECON auf Abzahlung *or* Raten kaufen

in·stance Beispiel *n;* (besonderer) Fall; JUR Instanz *f; for ~* zum Beispiel

in·stant 1. Moment *m,* Augenblick *m* **2.** sofortig, augenblicklich

in·stan·ta·ne·ous sofortig, augenblicklich; *death was~* der Tod trat sofort ein

in·stant| cam·e·ra PHOT Sofortbildkamera *f; ~ cof·fee* GASTR Pulver-, Instantkaffee *m*

in·stant·ly sofort, augenblicklich

in·stead stattdessen, dafür; *~ of* anstelle von, (an)statt

in·step ANAT Spann *m,* Rist *m*

in·sti·gate anstiften; aufhetzen; veranlassen; **in·sti·ga·tor** Anstifter(in); (Auf)Hetzer(in)

in·stil Br, **in·still** beibringen, einflößen (*into dat*)

in·stinct Instinkt *m*

in·stinc·tive instinktiv

in·sti·tute Institut *n*

in·sti·tu·tion Institution *f,* Einrichtung *f;* Institut *n;* Anstalt *f*

in·struct unterrichten, -weisen; ausbilden, schulen; informieren; anweisen

in·struc·tion Unterricht *m;* Ausbildung *f,* Schulung *f,* Unterweisung *f;* Anweisung *f,* Instruktion *f;* IT Befehl *m; ~s for use* Gebrauchsanweisung *f; operating ~s* Bedienungsanleitung *f*

in·struc·tive instruktiv, lehrreich

in·struc·tor Lehrer *m;* Ausbilder *m*

in·struc·tress Lehrerin *f;* Ausbilderin *f*

in·stru·ment Instrument *n* (*a.* MUS); Werkzeug *n* (*a. fig*)

in·stru·men·tal MUS Instrumental...; behilflich

in·sub·or·di·nate aufsässig

in·sub·or·di·na·tion Auflehnung *f,* Aufsässigkeit *f*

in·suf·fe·ra·ble unerträglich, unausstehlich

in·suf·fi·cient unzulänglich, ungenügend

in·su·lar Insel...; *fig* engstirnig

in·su·late isolieren; **in·su·la·tion** Isolierung *f;* Isoliermaterial *n*

in·sult 1. Beleidigung *f* **2.** beleidigen

in·sur·ance Versicherung *f;* Versicherungssumme *f;* Absicherung *f* (*against* gegen); *~ com·pa·ny* Versicherungsgesellschaft *f; ~ pol·i·cy* Versicherungspolice *f*

in·sure versichern (*against* gegen)

in·sured: *the ~* der *or* die Versicherte

in·sur·gent 1. aufständisch **2.** Aufständische *m*, *f*

in·sur·moun·ta·ble *fig* unüberwindlich

in·sur·rec·tion Aufstand *m*

in·tact intakt, unversehrt, unbeschädigt, ganz

in·take (*Nahrungs- etc*)Aufnahme *f*; (Neu)Aufnahme(n *pl*) *f*, (Neu)Zugänge *pl*; TECH Einlass(öffnung *f*) *m*

in·te·gral ganz, vollständig; wesentlich

in·te·grate (sich) integrieren; zusammenschließen; eingliedern, einbeziehen; **~d circuit** ELECTR integrierter Schaltkreis

in·te·gra·tion Integration *f*

in·teg·ri·ty Integrität *f*; Vollständigkeit *f*; Einheit *f*

in·tel·lect Intellekt *m*, Verstand *m*

in·tel·lec·tual 1. intellektuell, Verstandes…, geistig 2. Intellektuelle *m*, *f*

in·tel·li·gence Intelligenz *f*; nachrichtendienstliche Informationen *pl*

in·tel·li·gent intelligent, klug

in·tel·li·gi·ble verständlich (**to** für)

in·tem·per·ate unmäßig

in·tend beabsichtigen, vorhaben, planen; **~ed for** bestimmt für *or* zu

in·tense intensiv, stark, heftig

in·ten·si·fy intensivieren; (sich) verstärken

in·ten·si·ty Intensität *f*

in·ten·sive intensiv, gründlich; **~ care u·nit** MED Intensivstation *f*

in·tent 1. gespannt, aufmerksam; **~ on** fest entschlossen zu (*dat*); konzentriert auf (*acc*) 2. Absicht *f*, Vorhaben *n*

in·ten·tion Absicht *f*; JUR Vorsatz *m*

in·ten·tion·al absichtlich, vorsätzlich

in·ter bestatten

in·ter… zwischen, Zwischen…; gegenseitig, einander

in·ter·act aufeinander (ein)wirken, sich gegenseitig beeinflussen

in·ter·ac·tion Wechselwirkung *f*

in·ter·cede vermitteln, sich einsetzen (**with** bei; **for** für)

in·ter·cept abfangen

in·ter·ces·sion Fürsprache *f*

in·ter·change 1. austauschen 2. Austausch *m*; MOT Autobahnkreuz *n*

in·ter·com Sprechanlage *f*

in·ter·course Verkehr *m*; *a.* **sexual ~** (Geschlechts)Verkehr *m*

in·terest 1. Interesse *n* (**in** an *dat*, für); Wichtigkeit *f*, Bedeutung *f*; Vorteil *m*, Nutzen *m*; ECON Anteil *m*, Beteiligung *f*; ECON Zins(en *pl*) *m*; **take an ~ in** sich interessieren für 2. interessieren (**in** für *et*); **in·terest·ed** interessiert (**in** an *dat*); **be ~ in** sich interessieren für

in·terest·ing interessant

in·terest rate ECON Zinssatz *m*

in·ter·face IT Schnittstelle *f*

in·ter·fere sich einmischen (**with** in *acc*); stören; **in·ter·fer·ence** Einmischung *f*; Störung *f*

in·te·ri·or 1. innere(r, -s), Innen…; Binnen…; Inlands… 2. *das* Innere; Interieur *n*; POL innere Angelegenheiten *pl*; **→ Department of the Interior**, **~ dec·o·ra·tor** Innenarchitekt(in)

in·ter·ject *Bemerkung* einwerfen

in·ter·jec·tion Einwurf *m*; Ausruf *m*; LING Interjektion *f*

in·ter·lace (sich) (ineinander) verflechten

in·ter·lop·er Eindringling *m*

in·ter·lude Zwischenspiel *n*; Pause *f*; **~s of bright weather** zeitweilig schön

in·ter·me·di·a·ry Vermittler(in), Mittelsmann *m*

in·ter·me·di·ate in der Mitte liegend, Mittel…, Zwischen…; PED für fortgeschrittene Anfänger

in·ter·ment Beerdigung *f*, Bestattung *f*

in·ter·mi·na·ble endlos

in·ter·mis·sion Unterbrechung *f*; THEA *etc* Pause *f*

in·ter·mit·tent mit Unterbrechungen, periodisch (auftretend); **~ fever** MED Wechselfieber *n*

in·tern[1] internieren

in·tern[2] Assistenzarzt *m*, -ärztin *f*

in·ter·nal innere(r, -s); einheimisch, Inlands…

in·ter·nal-com·bus·tion en·gine Verbrennungsmotor *m*

in·ter·na·tion·al 1. international; Auslands… 2. SPORT Internationale *m*, *f*, Nationalspieler(in); internationaler Wettkampf; Länderspiel *n*; **~ call** TEL Auslandsgespräch *n*; **~ law** JUR Völkerrecht *n*

In·ter·net Internet *n*; **~ ac·cess** Internetzugang *m*; **~ auc·tion** Internetauktion *f*; **~ caf·é** Internetcafé *n*; **~ con·nec·tion** Internetanschluss *m*

in·tern·ist MED Internist *m*

in·ter·per·son·al zwischenmenschlich

in·ter·pret interpretieren, auslegen, erklären; dolmetschen

in·ter·pre·ta·tion Interpretation *f*, Auslegung *f*

in·ter·pret·er Dolmetscher(in)

in·ter·ro·gate verhören, vernehmen; (be)fragen; **in·ter·ro·ga·tion** Verhör *n*, Vernehmung *f*; Frage *f*

in·ter·rog·a·tive LING Interrogativ…, Frage…

in·ter·rupt unterbrechen

in·ter·rup·tion Unterbrechung *f*

in·ter·sect (durch)schneiden; sich schneiden *or* kreuzen; **in·ter·sec·tion** Schnittpunkt *m*; (Straßen)Kreuzung *f*

in·ter·sperse einstreuen, hier und da einfügen

in·ter·state 1. zwischenstaatlich **2.** *a.* **~ highway** Autobahn *f*

in·ter·twine (sich ineinander) verschlingen, sich verflechten

in·ter·val Intervall *n* (*a.* MUS), Abstand *m*; *Br* Pause *f* (*a.* THEA *etc*); *at regular* *~s* in regelmäßigen Abständen

in·ter·vene eingreifen, einschreiten, intervenieren; dazwischenkommen

in·ter·ven·tion Eingreifen *n*, Einschreiten *n*, Intervention *f*

in·ter·view 1. Interview *n*; Einstellungsgespräch *n* **2.** interviewen; ein Einstellungsgespräch führen mit

in·ter·view·ee Interviewte *m*, *f*

in·ter·view·er Interviewer(in)

in·ter·weave (miteinander) verweben

in·tes·tate: *die* **~** JUR ohne Hinterlassung e-s Testaments sterben

in·tes·tine ANAT Darm *m*; *pl* Eingeweide *pl*; *large* **~** Dickdarm *m*; *small* **~** Dünndarm *m*

in·ti·ma·cy Intimität *f*, Vertrautheit *f*; (*a. plumpe*) Vertraulichkeit; intime (*sexuelle*) Beziehungen *pl*

in·ti·mate 1. intim (*a. sexually*); vertraut, eng (*friends etc*); (*a.* plump)vertraulich; innerste(r, -s); gründlich, genau (*knowledge etc*) **2.** Vertraute *m*, *f*

in·tim·i·date einschüchtern

in·tim·i·da·tion Einschüchterung *f*

in·to in (*acc*), in (*acc*) … hinein; gegen (*acc*); MATH in (*acc*); *4* **~** *20 goes five times* 4 geht fünfmal in 20

in·tol·er·a·ble unerträglich

in·tol·er·ance Intoleranz *f*, Unduldsamkeit (*of* gegen)

in·tol·e·rant intolerant, unduldsam (*of* gegen)

in·to·na·tion MUS Intonation *f*, LING *a.* Tonfall *m*

in·tox·i·cat·ed berauscht, betrunken

in·tox·i·ca·tion Rausch *m* (*a. fig*)

in·trac·ta·ble eigensinnig; schwer zu handhaben(d)

in·tran·si·tive LING intransitiv

in·tra·ve·nous MED intravenös

in tray: *in the* **~** im Posteingang *etc*

in·trep·id unerschrocken

in·tri·cate verwickelt, kompliziert

in·trigue 1. Intrige *f* **2.** faszinieren, interessieren; intrigieren

in·tro·duce vorstellen (*to dat*), *j-n* bekannt machen (*to* mit); einführen

in·tro·duc·tion Vorstellung *f*; Einführung *f*; Einleitung *f*, Vorwort *n*; *letter of* **~** Empfehlungsschreiben *n*

in·tro·duc·to·ry Einführungs…; einleitend, Einleitungs…

in·tro·spec·tion Selbstbeobachtung *f*

in·tro·vert PSYCH introvertierter Mensch; **in·tro·vert·ed** PSYCH introvertiert, in sich gekehrt

in·trude (sich) aufdrängen; stören; *am I intruding?* störe ich?; **in·trud·er** Eindringling *m*, Störenfried *m*

in·tru·sion Störung *f*

in·tru·sive aufdringlich

in·tu·i·tion Intuition *f*

in·tu·i·tive intuitiv

In·u·it *a.* **Innuit** Inuit *m*, Eskimo *m*

in·un·date überschwemmen, überfluten (*a. fig*)

in·vade eindringen in (*acc*), einfallen in (*acc*), MIL *a.* einmarschieren in (*acc*); *fig* überlaufen, überschwemmen

in·vad·er Eindringling *m*

in·va·lid[1] **1.** krank; invalid(e) **2.** Kranke *m*; *f*; Invalide *m*, *f*

in·val·id[2] (rechts)ungültig

in·val·i·date JUR für ungültig erkären

in·val·u·a·ble *fig* unschätzbar, unbezahlbar

in·var·i·a·ble unveränderlich

in·var·i·a·bly ausnahmslos

in·va·sion Invasion *f* (*a.* MIL), Einfall *m*, MIL *a.* Einmarsch *m*; *fig* Eingriff *m*, Verletzung *f*

in·vec·tive Schmähung(en *pl*) *f*, Beschimpfung(en *pl*) *f*

in·vent erfinden

in·ven·tion Erfindung f

in·ven·tive erfinderisch; einfallsreich

in·ven·tor Erfinder(in)

in·ven·tory Inventar n, Bestand m; Bestandsliste f; Inventur f

in·verse 1. umgekehrt **2.** Umkehrung f, Gegenteil n; **in·ver·sion** Umkehrung f; LING Inversion f; **in·vert** umkehren

in·ver·te·brate ZO **1.** wirbellos **2.** wirbelloses Tier

in·vert·ed com·mas LING Anführungszeichen pl

in·vest ECON investieren, anlegen

in·ves·ti·gate untersuchen; überprüfen; Untersuchungen or Ermittlungen anstellen (*into* über acc), nachforschen

in·ves·ti·ga·tion Untersuchung f; Ermittlung f, Nachforschung f

in·ves·ti·ga·tor: *private* ~ Privatdetektiv m

in·vest·ment ECON Investition f, (Kapital)Anlage f

in·ves·tor ECON Anleger m

in·vet·e·rate unverbesserlich; hartnäckig

in·vid·i·ous gehässig, boshaft, gemein

in·vig·o·rate stärken, beleben

in·vin·ci·ble unbesiegbar; unüberwindlich

in·vi·o·la·ble unantastbar

in·vis·i·ble unsichtbar

in·vi·ta·tion Einladung f; Aufforderung f

in·vite einladen; auffordern; *Gefahr etc* herausfordern; ~ *s.o. in* j-n hereinbitten; **in·vit·ing** einladend, verlockend

in·voice ECON **1.** (Waren)Rechnung f **2.** in Rechnung stellen, berechnen

in·voke flehen um; *Gott etc* anrufen; beschwören

in·vol·un·ta·ry unfreiwillig; unabsichtlich; unwillkürlich

in·volve verwickeln, hineinziehen (*in* in acc); j-n, et. angehen, betreffen; zur Folge haben, mit sich bringen

in·volved kompliziert, verworren

in·volve·ment Verwicklung f; Beteiligung f

in·vul·ne·ra·ble unverwundbar; fig unanfechtbar

in·ward 1. adj innere(r, -s), innerlich **2.** adv mst ~s einwärts, nach innen

i·o·dine CHEM Jod n

i·on PHYS Ion n

IOU (= *I owe you*) Schuldschein m

IQ abbr of *intelligence quotient* IQ, Intelligenzquotient m

I·ran Iran m; **I·ra·ni·an 1.** iranisch **2.** Iraner(in); LING Iranisch n

I·raq Irak m; **I·ra·qi 1.** irakisch **2.** Iraker(in); LING Irakisch n

i·ras·ci·ble jähzornig

i·rate zornig, wütend

Ire·land Irland n

ir·i·des·cent schillernd

i·ris ANAT Regenbogenhaut f, Iris f; BOT Schwertlilie f, Iris f

I·rish 1. irisch **2.** LING Irisch n; *the* ~ die Iren pl

I·rish·man Ire m

I·rish·wom·an Irin f

i·ron 1. Eisen n; Bügeleisen n; *strike while the* ~ *is hot* fig das Eisen schmieden, solange es heiß ist **2.** eisern (a. fig), Eisen..., aus Eisen **3.** bügeln; ~ *out* ausbügeln

I·ron Cur·tain POL HIST Eiserner Vorhang

i·ron·ic, i·ron·i·cal ironisch, spöttisch

i·ron·ing board Bügelbrett n

i·ron·mon·ger Br Eisenwarenhändler m

i·ron·works TECH Eisenhütte f

i·ron·y Ironie f

ir·ra·tion·al irrational, unvernünftig

ir·rec·on·ci·la·ble unversöhnlich; unvereinbar

ir·re·cov·e·ra·ble unersetzlich; unwiederbringlich

ir·re·fut·a·ble unwiderlegbar

ir·reg·u·lar unregelmäßig; ungleichmäßig; regelwidrig, vorschriftswidrig

ir·rel·e·vant irrelevant, unerheblich, belanglos (*to* für)

ir·rep·a·ra·ble irreparabel, nicht wieder gutzumachen(d)

ir·re·place·a·ble unersetzlich

ir·re·pres·si·ble nicht zu unterdrücken(d); unbezähmbar

ir·re·proach·a·ble einwandfrei, untadelig

ir·re·sist·i·ble unwiderstehlich

ir·res·o·lute unentschlossen

ir·re·spec·tive: ~ *of* ohne Rücksicht auf (acc); unabhängig von

ir·re·spon·si·ble unverantwortlich; verantwortungslos

ir·re·trie·va·ble unwiederbringlich, unersetzlich

ir·rev·e·rent respektlos

ir·rev·o·ca·ble unwiderruflich, endgültig

ir·ri·gate bewässern

ir·ri·ga·tion Bewässerung *f*

ir·ri·ta·ble reizbar

ir·ri·tant Reizmittel *n*

ir·ri·tate reizen; (ver)ärgern

ir·ri·tat·ing ärgerlich

ir·ri·ta·tion Reizung *f*; Verärgerung *f*; Ärger *m* (*at* über *acc*)

is er, sie, es ist

Is·lam der Islam

is·land Insel *f*; *a.* **traffic ~** Verkehrsinsel *f*; **is·land·er** Inselbewohner(in)

isle POET Insel *f*

i·so·late absondern; isolieren

i·so·lat·ed isoliert, abgeschieden; einzeln; **become ~** vereinsamen

i·so·la·tion Isolierung *f*, Absonderung *f*; **~ ward** MED Isolierstation *f*

Is·rael Israel *n*

Is·rae·li 1. israelisch **2.** Israeli *m, f*

is·sue 1. Streitfrage *f*, Streitpunkt *m*; Ausgabe *f*; Erscheinen *n*; JUR Nachkommen(schaft *f*) *pl*; *fig* Ausgang *m*, Ergebnis *n*; **be at ~** zur Debatte stehen; **point at ~** strittiger Punkt **2.** *v/t Zeitung etc* herausgeben; *Banknoten etc* ausgeben; *Dokument etc* ausstellen; *v/i* herauskommen, hervorkommen; herausfließen, herausströmen

it es; *s.th. previously mentioned*: es, er, ihn, sie

I·tal·i·an 1. italienisch **2.** Italiener(in); LING Italienisch *n*

i·tal·ics PRINT Kursivschrift *f*

It·a·ly Italien *n*

itch 1. Jucken *n*, Juckreiz *m* **2.** jucken, kratzen; *I ~ all over* es juckt mich überall; **be ~ing for s.th.** F et. unbedingt (haben) wollen; **be ~ing to** *inf* F darauf brennen zu *inf*

itch·y juckend; kratzend

i·tem Punkt *m* (*on the agenda etc*), Posten *m* (*on a list*); Artikel *m*, Gegenstand *m*; (*Presse-, Zeitungs*)Notiz *f*, (*a. radio*, TV) Nachricht *f*, Meldung *f*

i·tem·ize einzeln angeben *or* aufführen

i·tin·e·ra·ry Reiseweg *m*, Reiseroute *f*; Reiseplan *m*

its sein(e), ihr(e)

it·self sich; sich selbst; selbst; **by ~** (für sich) allein; von selbst; **in ~** an sich

i·vo·ry Elfenbein *n*

i·vy BOT Efeu *m*

J

J, j J, j *n*

jab 1. (hinein)stechen, (hinein)stoßen **2.** Stich *m*, Stoß *m*

jab·ber F (daher)plappern

jack 1. TECH Hebevorrichtung *f*; MOT Wagenheber *m*; *cards*: Bube *m* **2. ~ up** *Auto* aufbocken

jack·al ZO Schakal *m*

jack·ass ZO Esel *m* (*a. fig*)

jack·daw ZO Dohle *f*

jack·et Jacke *f*, Jackett *n*; TECH Mantel *m*; (*Schutz*)Umschlag *m*; (*Platten*)Hülle *f*; **~ potatoes, potatoes** (**boiled**) **in their ~s** Pellkartoffeln *pl*

jack knife 1. Klappmesser *n* **2.** zusammenklappen, zusammenknicken

jack-of-all-trades Hansdampf *m* in allen Gassen

jack·pot Jackpot *m*, Haupttreffer *m*; **hit the ~** F den Jackpot gewinnen; *fig* das große Los ziehen

jade MIN Jade *m, f*; Jadegrün *n*

jag Zacken *m*

jag·ged gezackt, zackig; schartig

jag·u·ar ZO Jaguar *m*

jail 1. Gefängnis *n* **2.** einsperren

jail·bird F Knastbruder *m*

jail·er Gefängnisaufseher *m*

jail·house Gefängnis *n*

jam¹ Konfitüre *f*, Marmelade *f*

jam² **1.** *v/t* (hinein)pressen, (hinein-)quetschen, (hinein)zwängen, *Menschen a.* (hinein)pferchen; (ein)klemmen, (ein)quetschen; *a.* **~ up** blockieren, verstopfen; *Funkempfang* stören; **~ on the brakes** MOT voll auf die Bremse treten; *v/i* sich (hinein)drängen *or* (hinein-) quetschen; TECH sich verklemmen, *brake*: blockieren **2.** Gedränge *n*; TECH Blockierung *f*; Stauung

f, Stockung *f*; **traffic~** Verkehrsstau *m*;
be in a ~ F in der Klemme stecken

jamb (Tür-, Fenster)Pfosten *m*

jam·bo·ree Jamboree *n*, Pfadfindertreffen *n*; Fest *n*

Jan *abbr of* **January** Jan., Januar *m*

jan·gle klimpern *or* klirren (mit)

jan·i·tor Hausmeister *m*

Jan·u·a·ry (ABBR *of* **Jan**) Januar *m*

Ja·pan Japan *n*; **Jap·a·nese 1.** japanisch **2.** Japaner(in); LING Japanisch *n*; **the ~** die Japaner *pl*

jar¹ Gefäß *n*, Krug *m*; (Marmelade- *etc*)- Glas *n*

jar²: ~ on wehtun (*dat*)

jar·gon Jargon *m*, Fachsprache *f*

jaun·dice MED Gelbsucht *f*

jaunt 1. Ausflug *m*, MOT Spritztour *f* **2.** e-n Ausflug *or* e-e Spritztour machen

jaun·ty unbeschwert, unbekümmert; flott

jav·e·lin SPORT Speer *m*; **~ (throw)**, **throwing the ~** SPORT Speerwerfen *n*

jav·e·lin throw·er SPORT Speerwerfer(in)

jaw ANAT Kiefer *m*; *pl* ZO Rachen *m*, Maul *n*; TECH Backen *pl*; **lower ~** ANAT Unterkiefer *m*; **upper ~** ANAT Oberkiefer; **jaw·bone** ANAT Kieferknochen *m*

jay ZO Eichelhäher *m*

jay·walk·er unachtsamer Fußgänger

jazz MUS Jazz *m*

jazz·y F poppig

jeal·ous eifersüchtig (**of** auf *acc*); neidisch; **jeal·ous·y** Eifersucht *f*; Neid *m*

jeans Jeans *pl*

jeer 1. (**at**) höhnische Bemerkung(en) machen (über *acc*); höhnisch lachen (über *acc*); **~ (at)** verhöhnen **2.** höhnische Bemerkung; Hohngelächter *n*

jel·lied GASTR in Aspik, in Sülze

jel·ly Gallert(e *f*) *n*; GASTR Gelee *n*; Aspik *m*, *n*, Sülze *f*; Götterspeise *f*; **~ ba·by** *Br* Gummibärchen *n*; **~ bean** Gummi-, Geleebonbon *m*, *n*

jel·ly·fish ZO Qualle *f*

jeop·ar·dize gefährden

jerk 1. ruckartig ziehen an (*dat*); (zusammen)zucken; sich ruckartig bewegen **2.** (plötzlicher) Ruck; Sprung *m*, Satz *m*; MED Zuckung *f*

jerk·y ruckartig; holprig; rüttelnd

jer·sey Pullover *m*

jest 1. Scherz *m*, Spaß *m* **2.** scherzen, spaßen; **jest·er** HIST (Hof)Narr *m*

jet 1. (Wasser-, Gas- *etc*)Strahl *m*; TECH Düse *f*; AVIAT Jet *m* **2.** (heraus-, hervor)- schießen (**from** aus); AVIAT F jetten; **~ en·gine** AVIAT Düsen-, Strahltriebwerk *n*; **~ plane** AVIAT Düsenflugzeug *n*, Jet *m*

jet-pro·pelled AVIAT mit Düsenantrieb, Düsen...

jet pro·pul·sion AVIAT Düsen-, Strahlantrieb *m*

jet·ty MAR (Hafen)Mole *f*

Jew Jude *m*, Jüdin *f*

jew·el Juwel *n*, *m*, Edelstein *m*

jew·el·er, *Br* **jew·el·ler** Juwelier *m*

jew·el·lery *Br*, **jew·el·ry** Juwelen *pl*; Schmuck *m*

Jew·ess Jüdin *f*

Jew·ish jüdisch

jif·fy: F **in a ~** im Nu, sofort

jig·saw Laubsäge *f*; → **jig·saw puz·zle** Puzzle(spiel) *n*

jin·gle 1. klimpern (mit), bimmeln (lassen) **2.** Klimpern *n*, Bimmeln *n*; Werbesong *m*, Werbespruch *m*

jit·ters: F **the ~** Bammel *m*, e-e Heidenangst; **jit·ter·y** F nervös; ängstlich

job 1. (*einzelne*) Arbeit; Beruf *m*, Beschäftigung *f*, Stellung *f*, Stelle *f*, Arbeit *f*, Job *m* (*a.* IT); Arbeitsplatz *m*; Aufgabe *f*, Sache *f*, Angelegenheit *f*; *a.* **~ work** Akkordarbeit *f*; **by the ~** im Akkord; **out of a ~** arbeitslos **2.** **~ around** jobben; **~ ad**, **~ ad·ver·tisement** Stellenanzeige *f*

job·ber *Br* ECON Börsenspekulant *m*

job cen·tre *Br* Arbeitsamt *n*

job hop·ping häufiger Arbeitsplatzwechsel

job·hunt·ing Arbeitssuche *f*; **be ~** auf Arbeitssuche sein

job·less arbeitslos

jock·ey Jockei *m*

jog 1. stoßen an (*acc*) *or* gegen, *j-n* anstoßen; *mst* **~ along**, **~ on** dahintrotten, dahinzuckeln; SPORT joggen **2.** (leichter) Stoß, Stups *m*; Trott *m*; SPORT Trimmtrab *m*

jog·ger SPORT Jogger(in)

jog·ging SPORT Joggen *n*, Jogging *n*

join 1. *v/t* verbinden, vereinigen, zusammenfügen; sich anschließen (*dat* or *acc*), sich gesellen zu; eintreten in (*acc*), beitreten; teilnehmen *or* sich beteiligen an (*dat*), mitmachen bei; **~ in** einstimmen in; *v/i* sich vereinigen *or* verbinden; **~ in** teilnehmen *or* sich beteiligen (an *dat*), mitmachen (bei) **2.** Verbindungsstelle *f*, Naht *f*

join·er Tischler *m*, Schreiner *m*

joint 1. Verbindungs-, Nahtstelle *f*; ANAT, TECH Gelenk *n*; BOT Knoten *m*; *Br* GASTR Braten *m*; F Laden *m*; Bude *f*, Spelunke *f*; *sl* Joint *m*; *out of ~* MED ausgerenkt; *fig* aus den Fugen **2.** gemeinsam, gemeinschaftlich; Mit...

joint·ed gegliedert; Glieder...

joint-stock com·pa·ny *Br* ECON Kapital- *or* Aktiengesellschaft *f*

joint ven·ture ECON Gemeinschaftsunternehmen *n*

joke 1. Witz *m*; Scherz *m*, Spaß *m*; *practical ~* Streich *m*; *play a ~ on s.o.* j-m e-n Streich spielen **2.** scherzen, Witze machen; **jok·er** Spaßvogel *m*, Witzbold *m*; *cards*: Joker *m*

jol·ly 1. *adj* lustig, fröhlich, vergnügt **2.** *adv Br* F ganz schön; **~ good** prima

jolt 1. e-n Ruck *or* Stoß geben; durchrütteln, durchschütteln; rütteln, holpern (*vehicle*); *fig* aufrütteln **2.** Ruck *m*, Stoß *m*; *fig* Schock *m*

joss stick Räucherstäbchen *n*

jos·tle (an)rempeln; dränge(l)n

jot 1. *not a ~* keine Spur **2.** *~ down* sich schnell *et.* notieren

joule PHYS Joule *n*

jour·nal Journal *n*; (Fach)Zeitschrift *f*; Tagebuch *n*

jour·nal·ism Journalismus *m*

jour·nal·ist Journalist(in)

jour·ney 1. Reise *f* **2.** reisen

jour·ney·man Geselle *m*

joy Freude *f*; *for~* vor Freude

joy·ful freudig; erfreut

joy·less freudlos, traurig

joy·stick AVIAT Steuerknüppel *m*; IT Joystick *m*

jub·i·lant jubelnd, überglücklich

ju·bi·lee Jubiläum *n*

judge 1. JUR Richter(in); SPORT Kampf-, Schieds-, Preisrichter(in); *fig* Kenner(in) **2.** JUR *Fall* verhandeln; urteilen, ein Urteil fällen; beurteilen, einschätzen

judg·ment JUR Urteil *n*; Urteilsvermögen *n*; Meinung *f*, Ansicht *f*; göttliches (Straf)Gericht; *the Last Judgment* REL das Jüngste Gericht

Judgment Day, *a.* *Day of Judgment* REL Tag *m* des Jüngsten Gerichts, Jüngster Tag

ju·di·cial JUR gerichtlich, Justiz...; richterlich

ju·di·cia·ry JUR Richter *pl*

ju·di·cious klug, weise

ju·do SPORT Judo *m*

jug Krug *m*; Kanne *f*, Kännchen *n*

jug·gle jonglieren (mit); ECON *Bücher etc* frisieren; **jug·gler** Jongleur *m*

juice Saft *m*; F Sprit *m*

juic·y saftig; F pikant (*story etc*); F gepfeffert (*price etc*)

juke·box Musikbox *f*, Musikautomat *m*

Jul *abbr of July* Juli *m*

Ju·ly (*abbr Jul*) Juli *m*

jum·ble 1. *a.* *~ together*, *~ up* durcheinanderbringen *or* durcheinanderwerfen **2.** Durcheinander *n*; *~ sale Br* Wohltätigkeitsbasar *m*

jum·bo 1. riesig, Riesen... **2.** AVIAT F Jumbo *m*; *~ jet* AVIAT Jumbo-Jet *m*

jum·bo-sized riesig

jump 1. *v/i* springen; hüpfen; zusammenzucken, -fahren, hochfahren (*at* bei); *~ at the chance* mit beiden Händen zugreifen; *~ to conclusions* voreilige Schlüsse ziehen; *v/t* (hinweg)springen über (*acc*); überspringen; *~ the queue Br* sich vordränge(l)n; *~ the lights* bei Rot über die Kreuzung fahren **2.** Sprung *m*

jump·er[1] SPORT (*Hoch- etc*)Springer(in)

jump·er[2] Trägerrock *m*, Trägerkleid *n*; *Br* Pullover *m*

jump·ing jack Hampelmann *m*

jump·y nervös

Jun *abbr of June* Juni *m*

junc·tion (Straßen)Kreuzung *f*; RAIL Knotenpunkt *m*

junc·ture: *at this~* zu diesem Zeitpunkt

June (*abbr Jun*) Juni *m*

jun·gle Dschungel *m*

ju·ni·or 1. junior; jüngere(r, -s); untergeordnet; SPORT Junioren..., Jugend... **2.** Jüngere *m*, *f*; *~ school Br* Grundschule *f* (*for children aged 7 to 11*)

junk[1] MAR Dschunke *f*

junk[2] F Trödel *m*; Schrott *m*; Abfall *m*; *sl* Stoff *m*

junk food F Junk-Food *n*

junk·ie, junk·y *sl* Junkie *m*, Fixer(in)

junk·yard Schuttabladeplatz *m*;

Schrottplatz *m*
jur·is·dic·tion JUR Gerichtsbarkeit *f*;
Zuständigkeit(sbereich *m*) *f*
ju·ris·pru·dence Rechtswissenschaft *f*
ju·ror JUR Geschworene *m*, *f*
ju·ry JUR *die* Geschworenen *pl*; SPORT *etc*
Jury *f*, Preisrichter *pl*
ju·ry·man JUR Geschworene *m*
ju·ry·wom·an JUR Geschworene *f*
just 1. *adj* gerecht; berechtigt; angemessen **2.** *adv* gerade, (so)eben; genau,
eben; gerade (noch), ganz knapp;
nur, bloß; **~ about** ungefähr, etwa; **~
like that** einfach so; **~ now** gerade

(jetzt), (so)eben
jus·tice Gerechtigkeit *f*; JUR Richter *m*;
Justice of the Peace Friedensrichter
m; **court of ~** Gericht *n*, Gerichtshof *m*
jus·ti·fi·ca·tion Rechtfertigung *f*
jus·ti·fy rechtfertigen
just·ly mit *or* zu Recht
jut: ~ out vorspringen, herausragen
ju·ve·nile 1. jugendlich; Jugend... **2.** Jugendliche *m*, *f*; **~ court** JUR Jugendge-
richt *n*; **~ de·lin·quen·cy** JUR Jugend-
kriminalität *f*; **~ de·lin·quent** JUR straf-
fälliger Jugendlicher, jugendlicher
Straftäter

K

K, k K, k *n*
kan·ga·roo ZO Känguru *n*
ka·ra·te SPORT Karate *n*
keel MAR **1.** Kiel *m* **2. ~ over** umschlagen,
kentern
keen scharf (*a. fig*); schneidend (*cold*);
heftig, stark; lebhaft (*interest*); groß
(*appetite etc*); begeistert, leidenschaftlich; **~ on** versessen *or* scharf auf (*acc*)
keep 1. *v/t* (auf-, fest-, zurück)halten;
(bei)behalten, bewahren; *Gesetze etc*
einhalten, befolgen; *Ware* führen; *Geheimnis* für sich behalten; *Versprechen,
Wort* halten; ECON *Buch* führen; aufheben, aufbewahren; abhalten, hindern
(*from* von); *Tiere* halten; *Bett* hüten; ernähren, erhalten, unterhalten; **~ early
hours** früh zu Bett gehen; **~ one's
head** die Ruhe bewahren; **~ one's temper** sich beherrschen; **~ s.o. company**
j-m Gesellschaft leisten; **~ s.th. from
s.o.** j-m et. vorenthalten *or* verschwei-
gen *or* verheimlichen; **~ time** richtig
gehen (*watch*); MUS Takt halten; *v/i*
bleiben; sich halten; **~ going** weitergehen; **~ smiling** immer nur lächeln!; **~
(on) talking** weitersprechen; **~ (on) try-
ing** es weiterversuchen, es immer wieder versuchen; **~ s.o. waiting** j-n warten lassen; **~ away** (sich) fernhalten
(*from* von); **~ back** zurückhalten (*a.
fig*); **~ from doing s.th.** et. nicht tun;
~ in *Schüler(in)* nachsitzen lassen; **~
off** (sich) fern halten; **~ off!** Betreten

verboten!; **~ on** *Kleidungsstück* anbehalten, anlassen, *Hut* aufbehalten;
Licht brennen lassen; **keep on doing**
fortfahren zu tun; **~ out** nicht hinein-
or hereinlassen; **~ out!** Zutritt verboten!; **~ to** sich halten an (*acc*); **~ up**
fig aufrechterhalten; *Mut* nicht sinken
lassen; fortfahren mit, weitermachen;
~ s.o. up j-n nicht schlafen lassen; **~
it up** so weitermachen; **~ up with**
Schritt halten mit; **~ up with the
Joneses** nicht hinter den Nachbarn
zurückstehen (wollen) **2.** (Lebens)Un-
terhalt *m*; **for ~s** F für immer
keep·er Wärter(in), Wächter(in), Aufse-
her(in); *mst in cpds:* Inhaber(in), Besit-
zer(in); **keep·ing** Verwahrung *f*; Obhut
f; **be in (out of) ~ with ...** (nicht) übereinstimmen mit ...
keep·sake Andenken *n*
keg Fässchen *n*, kleines Fass
ken·nel Hundehütte *f*; **~s** Hundezwin-
ger *m*; Hundepension *f*
kerb *Br* → **curb**
ker·chief (Hals-, Kopf)Tuch *n*
ker·nel BOT Kern *m* (*a. fig*)
ker·o·sene Petroleum *n*
ket·tle Kessel *m*
ket·tle·drum MUS (Kessel)Pauke *f*
key 1. Schlüssel *m* (*a. fig*); (*Schreibma-
schinen-, Klavier- etc*)Taste *f*; MUS Tonart *f* **2.** Schlüssel... **3.** anpassen (**to** an
acc); **~ in** IT *Daten* eingeben; **~ed up**
nervös, aufgeregt, überdreht

key·board Tastatur *f*

key·hole Schlüsselloch *n*

key·note MUS Grundton *m*; *fig* Grundgedanke *m*, Tenor *m*

key ring Schlüsselring *m*

key·stone ARCH Schlussstein *m*; *fig* Grundpfeiler *m*

key·word Schlüssel-, Stichwort *n*

kick 1. (mit dem Fuß) stoßen, treten, e-n Tritt geben *or* versetzen (*dat*); *soccer:* schießen, treten, kicken; strampeln; ausschlagen (*horse*); **~ off** von sich schleudern; *soccer:* anstoßen; **~ out** F rausschmeißen; **~ up** hochschleudern; **~ up a fuss** *or* **row** F Krach schlagen **2.** (Fuß)Tritt *m*; Stoß *m*; *soccer:* Schuss *m*; **free ~** Freistoß *m*; **for ~s** F zum Spaß; **they get a ~ out of it** es macht ihnen e-n Riesenspaß

kick·off *soccer:* Anstoß *m*

kick·out *soccer:* Abschlag *m*

kid[1] ZO Zicklein *n*, Kitz *n*; Ziegenleder *n*; F Kind *n*; **~ brother** F kleiner Bruder

kid[2] *v/t j-n* auf den Arm nehmen; **~ s.o.** j-m et. vormachen; *v/i* Spaß machen; **he is only ~ding** er macht ja nur Spaß; **no ~ding!** im Ernst!

kid gloves Glacéhandschuhe *pl* (*a. fig*)

kid·nap entführen, kidnappen

kid·nap·(p)er Entführer(in), Kidnapper(in)

kid·nap·(p)ing Entführung *f*, Kidnapping *n*

kid·ney ANAT Niere *f*; **~ bean** BOT Kidneybohne *f*, rote Bohne; **~ ma·chine** MED künstliche Niere

kill töten (*a. fig*), umbringen, ermorden; vernichten; ZO schlachten; HUNT erlegen, schießen; **be ~ed in an accident** tödlich verunglücken; **~ time** die Zeit totschlagen; **kill·er** Mörder(in), Killer(in); **kill·ing** mörderisch, tödlich

kill·joy Spielverderber *m*

kiln TECH Brennofen *m*

ki·lo F Kilo *n*

kil·o·gram(me) Kilogramm *n*

kil·o·me·ter, *Br* **kil·o·me·tre** Kilometer *m*

kilt Kilt *m*, Schottenrock *m*

kin Verwandtschaft *f*, Verwandte *pl*; **next of ~** der, die nächste Verwandte, die nächsten Angehörigen *pl*

kind[1] freundlich, liebenswürdig, nett; herzlich

kind[2] Art *f*, Sorte *f*; Wesen *n*; **all ~s of** alle möglichen, allerlei; **nothing of the ~** nichts dergleichen; **~ of** F ein bisschen

kin·der·gar·ten Kindergarten *m*

kind-heart·ed gütig

kin·dle anzünden, (sich) entzünden; *Interesse etc* wecken

kind·ly 1. *adj* freundlich, liebenswürdig, nett **2.** *adv* → 1; freundlicherweise, liebenswürdigerweise, netterweise

kind·ness Freundlichkeit *f*, Liebenswürdigkeit *f*; Gefälligkeit *f*

kin·dred verwandt; **~ spirits** Gleichgesinnte *pl*

king König *m*

king·dom Königreich *n*; REL Reich *n* Gottes; *fig* Reich *n*; **animal ~** Tierreich *n*; **vegetable ~** Pflanzenreich *n*

king·ly königlich

king-size(d) Riesen…

kink Knick *m*; *fig* Tick *m*, Spleen *m*

kink·y spleenig; pervers

ki·osk Kiosk *m*; *Br* Telefonzelle *f*

kip·per GASTR Räucherhering *m*

kiss 1. Kuss *m* **2.** (sich) küssen

kit Ausrüstung *f*; Arbeitsgerät *n*, Werkzeug(e *pl*) *n*; Werkzeugtasche *f*, -kasten *m*; Bastelsatz *m*; **kit bag** Seesack *m*

kitch·en 1. Küche *f* **2.** Küchen…

kitch·en·ette Kleinküche *f*, Kochnische *f*

kitch·en gar·den Küchen-, Gemüsegarten *m*

kite Drachen *m*; ZO Milan *m*; **fly a ~** e-n Drachen steigen lassen

kit·ten ZO Kätzchen *n*

knack Kniff *m*, Trick *m*, F Dreh *m*; Geschick *n*, Talent *n*

knave *card games:* Bube *m*, Unter *m*

knead kneten; massieren

knee ANAT Knie *n*; TECH Knie(stück) *n*

knee·cap ANAT Kniescheibe *f*

knee-deep knietief, bis an die Knie (reichend)

knee joint ANAT Kniegelenk *n* (*a.* TECH)

kneel knien (**to** vor *dat*)

knee-length knielang

knell Totenglocke *f*

knick·er·bock·ers Knickerbocker *pl*, Kniehosen *pl*

knick·ers *Br* F (Damen)Schlüpfer *m*

knick-knack Nippsache *f*

knife 1. Messer *n* **2.** mit e-m Messer ste-

knight

chen *or* verletzen; erstechen

knight 1. Ritter *m*; *chess*: Springer *m* **2.** zum Ritter schlagen

knight·hood Ritterwürde *f*, -stand *m*

knit *v/t* stricken; *a.* **~ together** zusammenfügen, verbinden; **~ one's brows** die Stirn runzeln; *v/i* stricken; MED zusammenwachsen

knit·ting 1. Stricken *n*; Strickzeug *n* **2.** Strick…; **~ nee·dle** Stricknadel *f*

knit·wear Strickwaren *pl*

knob Knopf *m*, Knauf *m*, *runder* Griff; GASTR Stück(chen) *n*

knock 1. schlagen, stoßen; pochen, klopfen; **~ at the door** an die Tür klopfen; **~ about, ~ around** herumstoßen; F sich herumtreiben; F herumliegen; **~ down** *Gebäude etc* abreißen; umstoßen, umwerfen; niederschlagen; anfahren, umfahren; überfahren; mit *dem Preis* heruntergehen; *auction*: et. zuschlagen (**to s.o.** j-m); **be ~ed down** überfahren werden; **~ off** herunter-, abschlagen; F et. hinhauen; F aufhören (mit); F Feierabend *or* Schluss machen; **~ out** herausschlagen, -klopfen, *Pfeife* ausklopfen; *j-n* bewusstlos schlagen; *boxing*: k.o. schlagen; *fig* betäuben (*drug etc*); *fig* F umhauen, schocken; **~ over** umwerfen, umstoßen; überfahren; **be ~ed over** überfahren werden **2.** Schlag *m*, Stoß *m*; Klopfen *n*; **there is a ~** (**on** [*Br* **at**] **the door**) es klopft

knock·er Türklopfer *m*

knock-kneed x-beinig

knock-out *boxing*: K.o. *m*

knoll Hügel *m*

knot 1. Knoten *m*; BOT Astknoten *m*; MAR Knoten *m*, Seemeile *f* **2.** (ver-)knoten, (ver)knüpfen; **knot·ty** knotig; knorrig; *fig* verwickelt, kompliziert

know wissen; können; kennen; erfahren, erleben; (wieder) erkennen; verstehen; **~ French** Französisch können; **~ one's way around** sich auskennen in (*a place etc*); **~ all about it** genau Bescheid wissen; **get to ~** kennenlernen; **~ one's business, ~ the ropes, ~ a thing or two, ~ what's what** F sich auskennen, Erfahrung haben; **you ~** wissen Sie

know-how Know-how *n*, (Sach-, Spezial)Kenntnis(se *pl*) *f*

know·ing klug, gescheit; schlau; verständnisvoll; **know·ing·ly** wissend; wissentlich, absichtlich, bewusst

knowl·edge Kenntnis(se *pl*) *f*; Wissen *n*; **to my ~** meines Wissens; **have a good ~ of** viel verstehen von, sich gut auskennen in (*dat*)

knowl·edge·a·ble: **be very ~ about** viel verstehen von

knuck·le 1. ANAT (Finger)Knöchel *m* **2. ~ down to work** sich an die Arbeit machen

Krem·lin: POL **the ~** der Kreml

L

L, l L, l *n*

L *abbr of* **large** (**size**) groß

lab F Labor *n*

la·bel 1. Etikett *n*, (Klebe- *etc*)Zettel *m*, (-)Schild(chen) *n*; (Schall)Plattenfirma *f* **2.** etikettieren, beschriften; *fig* abstempeln als

la·bor 1. (schwere) Arbeit; Mühe *f*; Arbeiter *pl*, Arbeitskräfte *pl*; MED Wehen *pl* **2.** (schwer) arbeiten; sich bemühen, sich abmühen; sich anstrengen

la·bor·a·to·ry Labor(atorium) *n*; **~ assis·tant** Laborant(in)

la·bored schwerfällig (*style etc*); mühsam (*breathing etc*)

la·bor·er (*esp* Hilfs)Arbeiter *m*

la·bo·ri·ous mühsam; schwerfällig

la·bor u·ni·on Gewerkschaft *f*

la·bour *Br* → **labor**

Labour *Br* POL die Labour Party

la·boured, la·bour·er *Br* → **labored, laborer**

La·bour Par·ty *Br* POL Labour Party *f*

lace 1. Spitze *f*; Borte *f*; Schnürsenkel *m* **2. ~ up** (zu-, zusammen)schnüren; *Schuh* zubinden; **~d with brandy** mit e-m Schuss Weinbrand

la·ce·rate zerschneiden, zerkratzen, aufreißen; *j-s Gefühle* verletzen

lack 1. (**of**) Fehlen *n* (von), Mangel *m* (an

dat); **2.** *v/t* nicht haben; *he~s money* es fehlt ihm an Geld; *v/i* *be ~ing* fehlen; *he is ~ing in courage* ihm fehlt der Mut

lack·lus·ter, *Br* **lack·lus·tre** glanzlos, matt

la·con·ic lakonisch, wortkarg

lac·quer 1. Lack *m*; Haarspray *m*, *n* **2.** lackieren

lad Bursche *m*, Junge *m*

lad·der Leiter *f*; *Br* Laufmasche *f*

lad·der-proof (lauf)maschenfest

la·den (schwer) beladen

la·dle 1. (Schöpf-, Suppen)Kelle *f*, Schöpflöffel *m* **2.** ~ *out Suppe* austeilen

la·dy Dame *f*; *Lady* Lady *f*; ~ *doctor* Ärztin *f*; *Ladies' room*, *Br* *Ladies(')* Damentoilette *f*

la·dy·bird zo Marienkäfer *m*

la·dy·like damenhaft

lag 1. *mst* ~ *behind* zurückbleiben **2.** → *time lag*

la·ger Lagerbier *n*

la·goon Lagune *f*

lair zo Lager *n*, Höhle *f*, Bau *m*

la·i·ty Laien *pl*

lake See *m*

lamb zo **1.** Lamm *n* **2.** lammen

lame 1. lahm (*a. fig*) **2.** lähmen

la·ment 1. jammern, (weh)klagen; trauern **2.** Jammer *m*, (Weh)Klage *f*

lam·en·ta·ble beklagenswert; kläglich

lam·en·ta·tion (Weh)Klage *f*

lam·i·nat·ed laminiert, geschichtet, beschichtet; ~ *glass* Verbundglas *n*

lamp Lampe *f*; Laterne *f*

lamp·post Laternenpfahl *m*

lamp·shade Lampenschirm *m*

lance Lanze *f*

land 1. Land *n*, AGR *a.* Boden *m*, POL *a.* Staat *m*; *by* ~ auf dem Landweg **2.** landen, MAR *a.* anlegen; *Güter* ausladen, MAR *a.* löschen

land a·gent AGR Gutsverwalter *m*

land·ed Land..., Grund...; ~ *gentry* Landadel *m*; ~ *property* Grundbesitz *m*

land·ing AVIAT Landung *f*, Landen *n*, MAR *a.* Anlegen *n*; Treppenabsatz *m*; ~ *field* AVIAT Landeplatz *m*; ~ *gear* AVIAT Fahrgestell *n*; ~ *stage* MAR Landungsbrücke *f*, -steg *m*; ~ *strip* AVIAT Landeplatz *m*

land·la·dy Vermieterin *f*; Wirtin *f*

land·lord Vermieter *m*; Wirt *m*; Grund-

besitzer *m*

land·lub·ber MAR *contp* Landratte *f*

land·mark Wahrzeichen *n*; *fig* Meilenstein *m*

land·own·er Grundbesitzer(in)

land·scape Landschaft *f* (*a. paint*)

land·slide Erdrutsch *m* (*a.* POL); *a ~ victory* POL ein überwältigender Wahlsieg

land·slip (kleiner) Erdrutsch

lane (Feld)Weg *m*; Gasse *f*, Sträßchen *n*; MAR Fahrrinne *f*; AVIAT Flugschneise *f*; SPORT (*einzelne*) Bahn; MOT (Fahr-) Spur *f*; *change ~s* MOT die Spur wechseln; *get in* ~ MOT sich einordnen

lan·guage Sprache *f*

lan·guid matt; träg(e)

lank glatt

lank·y schlaksig

lan·tern Laterne *f*

lap¹ Schoß *m*

lap² SPORT **1.** Runde *f*; ~ *of hono(u)r* Ehrenrunde *f* **2.** *Gegner* überrunden; e-e Runde zurücklegen

lap³ *v/t:* ~ *up* auflecken, aufschlecken; *v/i* plätschern

la·pel Revers *n*, *m*, Aufschlag *m*

lapse 1. Versehen *n*, (kleiner) Fehler *or* Irrtum; Vergehen *n*; Zeitspanne *f*; JUR Verfall *m*; ~ *of memory, memory* ~ Gedächtnislücke *f* **2.** verfallen; JUR verfallen, erlöschen

lar·ce·ny JUR Diebstahl *m*

larch BOT Lärche *f*

lard 1. Schweinefett *n*, Schweineschmalz *n* **2.** *Fleisch* spicken

lar·der Speisekammer *f*, -schrank *m*

large groß; beträchtlich, reichlich; umfassend, weitgehend; *at* ~ in Freiheit, auf freiem Fuß; *fig* (sehr) ausführlich; in der Gesamtheit

large·ly großenteils, größtenteils

large-mind·ed aufgeschlossen, tolerant

large·ness Größe *f*

lar·i·at Lasso *n*, *m*

lark¹ zo Lerche *f*

lark² F Jux *m*, Spaß *m*

lark·spur BOT Rittersporn *m*

lar·va zo Larve *f*

lar·yn·gi·tis MED Kehlkopfentzündung *f*; **lar·ynx** ANAT Kehlkopf *m*

las·civ·i·ous geil, lüstern

la·ser PHYS Laser *m*; ~ *beam* PHYS Laserstrahl *m*; ~ *print·er* IT Laserdrucker *m*; ~ *tech·nol·o·gy* Lasertechnik *f*

lash 1. Peitschenschnur *f*; (Peitschen-)Hieb *m*; Wimper *f* **2.** peitschen (mit); (fest)binden; schlagen; **~ out** (wild) um sich schlagen

las·so Lasso *n, m*

last¹ 1. *adj* letzte(r, -s); vorige(r, -s); **~ but one** vorletzte(r, -s); **~ night** gestern Abend; **letzte Nacht 2.** *adv* zuletzt, an letzter Stelle; **~ but not least** nicht zuletzt, nicht zu vergessen **3.** *der, die, das Letzte*; **at ~** endlich; **to the ~** bis zum Schluss

last² (an-, fort)dauern; (sich) halten; (aus)reichen

last³ (Schuhmacher)Leisten *m*

last·ing dauerhaft; beständig

last·ly zuletzt, zum Schluss

latch 1. Schnappriegel *m*; Schnappschloss *n* **2.** einklinken, zuklinken

latch·key Haus-, Wohnungsschlüssel *m*

late spät; jüngste(r, -s), letzte(r, -s), frühere(r, -s), ehemalig; verstorben; **be ~** zu spät kommen, sich verspäten; **RAIL** etc Verspätung haben; **as ~ as** noch, erst; **of ~** kürzlich; **later on** später

late·ly kürzlich

lath Latte *f*, Leiste *f*

lathe TECH Drehbank *f*

la·ther 1. (Seifen)Schaum *m* **2.** *v/t* einseifen; *v/i* schäumen

Lat·in LING **1.** lateinisch; südländisch **2.** Latein(isch) *n*; **~ A·mer·i·ca** Lateinamerika *n*; **~ A·mer·i·can 1.** lateinamerikanisch **2.** Lateinamerikaner(in)

lat·i·tude GEOGR Breite *f*

lat·ter Letztere(r, -s)

lat·tice Gitter(werk) *n*

lau·da·ble lobenswert

laugh 1. lachen (*at* über *acc*); **~ at s.o.** *a.* j-n auslachen **2.** Lachen *n*, Gelächter *n*

laugh·a·ble lächerlich, lachhaft

laugh·ter Lachen *n*, Gelächter *n*

launch¹ 1. MAR vom Stapel lassen; MIL abschießen, *Rakete a.* starten; *fig Projekt etc* in Gang setzen, starten **2.** MAR Stapellauf *m*; MIL Abschuss *m*, Start *m*

launch² MAR Barkasse *f*

launch·ing → **launch¹** 2; **~ pad** Abschussrampe *f*; **~ site** Abschussbasis *f*

launch pad → **launching pad**

laun·der *Wäsche* waschen (und bügeln); F *esp Geld* waschen

laun·der·ette, **laun·drette** *esp Br*, **laundro·mat**® Waschsalon *m*

laun·dry Wäscherei *f*; Wäsche *f*

laur·el BOT Lorbeer *m* (*a. fig*)

la·va GEOL Lava *f*

lav·a·to·ry Toilette *f*, Klosett *n*; **public ~** Bedürfnisanstalt *f*

lav·en·der BOT Lavendel *m*

lav·ish 1. sehr freigebig, verschwenderisch **2. ~ s.th. on s.o.** j-n mit et. überhäufen *or* überschütten

law Gesetz(e *pl*) *n*; Recht *n*, Rechtssystem *n*; Rechtswissenschaft *f*, Jura; F Bullen *pl* (*police*); F Bulle *m* (*policeman*); Gesetz *n*, Vorschrift *f*; **~ and order** Recht *or* Ruhe und Ordnung

law-a·bid·ing gesetzestreu

law·court Gericht *n*, Gerichtshof *m*

law·ful gesetzlich; rechtmäßig, legitim; rechtsgültig

law·less gesetzlos; gesetzwidrig; zügellos

lawn Rasen *m*

lawn·mow·er Rasenmäher *m*

law·suit JUR Prozess *m*

law·yer JUR (Rechts)Anwalt *m*, (Rechts)Anwältin *f*

lax locker, schlaff; lax, lasch

lax·a·tive MED **1.** abführend **2.** Abführmittel *n*

lay¹ REL weltlich; Laien…

lay² *v/t* legen; *Teppich* verlegen; belegen, auslegen (**with** mit); *Tisch* decken; ZO *Eier* legen; vorlegen (**before** dat); bringen (**before** vor *acc*); *Schuld etc* zuschreiben, zur Last legen (*dat*); *v/i* ZO (Eier) legen; **~ aside** beiseitelegen, zurücklegen; **~ off** *Arbeiter* (*esp* vorübergehend) entlassen; *Arbeit* einstellen; **~ open** darlegen; **~ out** ausbreiten, auslegen; *Garten etc* anlegen; entwerfen, planen; PRINT das Layout (*gen*) machen; **~ up** anhäufen, (an)sammeln; **be laid up** das Bett hüten müssen

lay-by *Br* MOT Parkbucht *f*, Parkstreifen *m*; Parkplatz *m*, Rastplatz *m*

lay·er Lage *f*, Schicht *f*; BOT Ableger *m*

lay·man Laie *m*

lay-off ECON (*esp* vorübergehende) Entlassung

lay·out Grundriss *m*, Lageplan *m*; PRINT Layout *n*, Gestaltung *f*

la·zy faul, träg(e)

LCD *abbr of* **liquid crystal display** Flüssigkristallanzeige *f*

lead¹1. *v/t* führen; (an)führen, leiten; dazu bringen, veranlassen (*to do* zu tun); *v/i* führen; vorangehen; SPORT an der Spitze *or* in Führung liegen; **~ off** anfangen, beginnen; **~ on** j-m et. vormachen *or* weismachen; **~ to** fig führen zu; **~ up to** fig (allmählich) führen zu 2. Führung *f*; Leitung *f*; Spitzenposition *f*; Vorbild *n*, Beispiel *n*; THEA Hauptrolle *f*; Hauptdarsteller(in); (Hunde)Leine *f*; Hinweis *m*, Tipp *m*, Anhaltspunkt *m*; SPORT and fig Führung *f*, Vorsprung *m*; **be in the ~** in Führung sein; **take the ~** in Führung gehen, die Führung übernehmen

lead² CHEM Blei *n*; MAR Lot *n*

lead·ed verbleit, bleihaltig

lead·en bleiern (*a. fig*), Blei...

lead·er (An)Führer(in), Leiter(in); Erste *m*, *f*; Br Leitartikel *m*

lead·er·ship Führung *f*, Leitung *f*

lead-free bleifrei

lead·ing leitend; führend; Haupt...

leaf 1. BOT, PRINT Blatt *n*; (*Tür- etc*)Flügel *m*; (*Tisch*)Klappe *f*, Ausziehplatte *f* 2. **~ through** durchblättern

leaf·let Hand-, Reklamezettel *m*; Prospekt *m*

league POL Bund *m*; SPORT Liga *f*

leak 1. lecken, leck sein; tropfen; **~ out** auslaufen; fig durchsickern 2. Leck *n*, undichte Stelle (*a. fig*)

leak·age Auslaufen *n*

leak·y leck, undicht

lean¹ (sich) lehnen; (sich) neigen; **~ on** sich verlassen auf (*acc*)

lean² 1. mager (*a. fig*) 2. GASTR das Magere; **~ man·age·ment** ECON schlanke Unternehmensstruktur

leap 1. springen; **~ at** fig sich stürzen auf (*acc*) 2. Sprung *m*

leap-frog Bockspringen *n*

leap year Schaltjahr *n*

learn (er)lernen; erfahren, hören

learn·ed gelehrt

learn·er Anfänger(in); Lernende *m*, *f*; **~ driver** Br MOT Fahrschüler(in)

learn·ing Gelehrsamkeit *f*

lease 1. Pacht *f*, Miete *f*; Pacht-, Mietvertrag *m* 2. pachten, mieten; leasen; **~ out** verpachten, vermieten

leash (Hunde)Leine *f*

least 1. *adj* geringste(r, -s), mindeste(r, -s), wenigste(r, -s) 2. *adv* am wenigsten; **~ of all** am allerwenigsten 3. *das* Min-

deste, *das* wenigste; **at ~** wenigstens; **to say the ~** gelinde gesagt

leath·er 1. Leder *n* 2. ledern; Leder...

leave 1. *v/t* (hinter-, über-, ver-, zurück)lassen, übrig lassen; liegen *or* stehen lassen, vergessen; vermachen, vererben; **be left** übrig bleiben, übrig sein; *v/i* (fort-, weg)gehen, abreisen, abfahren, abfliegen; **~ alone** allein lassen; j-n, et. in Ruhe lassen; **~ behind** zurücklassen; **~ on** anlassen; **~ out** draußen lassen; auslassen, weglassen 2. Erlaubnis *f*; Urlaub *m*; Abschied *m*; **on ~** auf Urlaub

leav·en Sauerteig *m*

leaves BOT Laub *n*

leav·ings Überreste *pl*

lech·er·ous geil, lüstern

lec·ture 1. UNIV Vorlesung *f* (**über** acc on); Vortrag *m*; Strafpredigt *f* 2. *v/i* UNIV e-e Vorlesung *or* Vorlesungen halten (**über** acc on; **vor** dat to); e-n Vortrag *or* Vorträge halten; *v/t* j-m e-e Strafpredigt halten

lec·tur·er UNIV Dozent(in); Redner(in)

ledge Leiste *f*, Sims *m*, *n*

leech ZO Blutegel *m*

leek BOT Lauch *m*, Porree *m*

leer 1. anzüglicher *or* lüsterner Seitenblick 2. anzüglich *or* lüstern blicken *or* schielen (**at** nach)

left 1. *adj* linke(r, -s), Links... 2. *adv* links; **turn ~** (sich) nach links wenden; MOT links abbiegen 3. *die* Linke (*a.* POL, *boxing*), Linke *f*; **on the ~** links, auf der linken Seite; **to the ~** (nach) links; **keep to the ~** sich links halten; links fahren

left-hand linke(r, -s)

left-hand drive MOT Linkssteuerung *f*

left-hand·ed linkshändig; für Linkshänder; **be ~** Linkshänder(in) sein

left lug·gage of·fice Br RAIL Gepäckaufbewahrung *f*

left·o·vers (Speise)Reste *pl*

left-wing POL dem linken Flügel angehörend, links..., Links...

leg ANAT Bein *n*; GASTR Keule *f*; MATH Schenkel *m*; **pull s.o.'s ~** F j-n auf den Arm nehmen; **stretch one's ~** sich die Beine vertreten

leg·a·cy fig Vermächtnis *n*, Erbe *n*

le·gal legal, gesetzmäßig; gesetzlich, rechtlich; juristisch, Rechts...

le·gal·i·za·tion Legalisierung f
le·gal·ize legalisieren
le·gal pro·tec·tion Rechtsschutz m
le·ga·tion POL Gesandtschaft f
le·gend Legende f, Sage f
le·gen·da·ry legendär
le·gi·ble leserlich
le·gis·la·tion Gesetzgebung f
le·gis·la·tive POL 1. gesetzgebend, legislativ 2. Legislative f, gesetzgebende Gewalt
le·gis·la·tor POL Gesetzgeber m
le·git·i·mate legitim; gesetzmäßig, rechtmäßig; ehelich
lei·sure freie Zeit; Muße f; *at* ~ ohne Hast; ~ *cen·tre* Br Freizeitzentrum n
lei·sure·ly gemächlich
lei·sure time Freizeit f
lei·sure-time ac·tiv·i·ties Freizeitbeschäftigung f, -gestaltung f
lei·sure·wear Freizeitkleidung f
lem·on BOT 1. Zitrone f 2. Zitronen...
lem·on·ade Zitronenlimonade f
lend j-m et. (ver-, aus)leihen
length Länge f; Strecke f; (Zeit)Dauer f; *at* ~ ausführlich
length·en verlängern, länger machen; länger werden
length·ways, **length·wise** der Länge nach
length·y sehr lang
le·ni·ent mild(e), nachsichtig
lens ANAT, PHOT, PHYS Linse f; PHOT Objektiv n
Lent REL Fastenzeit f
len·til BOT Linse f
Le·o ASTR Löwe m; *he* (*she*) *is* (*a*) ~ er (sie) ist (ein) Löwe
leop·ard ZO Leopard m
le·o·tard (Tänzer)Trikot n
lep·ro·sy MED Lepra f
les·bi·an 1. lesbisch 2. Lesbierin f, F Lesbe f
less 1. *adj and adv* kleiner, geringer, weniger 2. *prp* weniger, minus, abzüglich
less·en (sich) vermindern *or* verringern; abnehmen; herabsetzen
less·er kleiner, geringer
les·son Lektion f; (Unterrichts)Stunde f; *fig* Lehre f; *pl* Unterricht m
let lassen; *esp Br* vermieten, verpachten; ~ *alone* j-n, et. in Ruhe lassen; geschweige denn; ~ *down* hinunterlassen, herunterlassen; *Kleider* verlän-

gern; j-n im Stich lassen, F j-n sitzen lassen; enttäuschen; ~ *go* loslassen; ~ *o.s. go* sich gehenlassen; ~*'s go* gehen wir!; ~ *in* (her)einlassen; ~ *o.s. in for s.th.* sich et. einbrocken, sich auf et. einlassen
le·thal tödlich; Todes...
leth·ar·gy Lethargie f
let·ter Buchstabe m; PRINT Type f; Brief m
let·ter·box *esp Br* Briefkasten m
let·ter car·ri·er Briefträger m
let·tuce BOT (*esp* Kopf)Salat m
leu·k(a)e·mia MED Leukämie f
lev·el 1. *adj* eben; gleich (*a. fig*); ausgeglichen; *be* ~ *with* auf gleicher Höhe sein mit; *my best* F mein Möglichstes 2. Ebene f (*a. fig*), ebene Fläche; Höhe f (*a.* GEOGR), (*Wasser- etc*)Spiegel m, (-)Stand m, (-)Pegel m; Wasserwaage f; *fig* Niveau n, Stufe f; *sea* ~ Meeresspiegel m; *on the* ~ F ehrlich, aufrichtig 3. (ein)ebnen, planieren; dem Erdboden gleichmachen; ~ *at* Waffe richten auf (*acc*); *Beschuldigungen* erheben gegen (*acc*) 4. *adv*: ~ *with* in Höhe (*gen*)
lev·el cross·ing Br schienengleicher Bahnübergang
lev·el-head·ed vernünftig, nüchtern
le·ver Hebel m
lev·y 1. Steuer f, Abgabe f 2. *Steuern* erheben
lewd geil, lüstern; unanständig, obszön
li·a·bil·i·ty ECON, JUR Verpflichtung f, Verbindlichkeit f; ECON, JUR Haftung f, Haftpflicht f; Neigung f (*to* zu), Anfälligkeit f (*to* für); **li·a·ble** ECON, JUR haftbar, haftpflichtig; *be* ~ *for* haften für; *be* ~ *to* neigen zu, anfällig sein für
li·ar Lügner(in)
li·bel JUR 1. (*schriftliche*) Verleumdung *or* Beleidigung 2. (*schriftlich*) verleumden *or* beleidigen
lib·er·al 1. liberal (*a.* POL), aufgeschlossen; großzügig; reichlich 2. Liberale m, f (*a.* POL)
lib·e·rate befreien; **lib·e·ra·tion** Befreiung f; **lib·e·ra·tor** Befreier m
lib·er·ty Freiheit f; *take liberties with* sich Freiheiten gegen j-n herausnehmen; willkürlich mit et. umgehen; *be at* ~ frei sein
Li·bra ASTR Waage f; *he* (*she*) *is* (*a*) ~ er (sie) ist (eine) Waage

likewise

li·brar·i·an Bibliothekar(in)

li·bra·ry Bibliothek *f*; Bücherei *f*

li·cence 1. *Br* → *license* I **2.** e-e Lizenz *or* Konzession erteilen (*dat*); *behördlich* genehmigen

li·cense 1. Lizenz *f*, Konzession *f*; (*Führer*-, *Jagd*-, *Waffen*- etc)Schein *m* **2.** *Br* → *licence* 2

li·cense plate MOT Nummernschild *n*

li·chen BOT Flechte *f*

lick 1. Lecken *n*; Salzlecke *f* **2.** *v/t* ab-, auflecken; F verdreschen, verprügeln; F schlagen, besiegen; *v/i* lecken; züngeln (*flames*)

lic·o·rice Lakritze *f*

lid Deckel *m*; ANAT (Augen)Lid *n*

lie[1] **1.** lügen; **~ *to s.o.*** j-n belügen, j-n anlügen **2.** Lüge *f*; **tell ~s, tell a ~** lügen; **give the ~ to** j-n, et. Lügen strafen

lie[2] **1.** liegen; **let sleeping dogs ~** schlafende Hunde soll man nicht wecken; **~ *behind*** *fig* dahinter stecken; **~ *down*** sich hinlegen **2.** Lage *f* (*a. fig*)

lie-down F Nickerchen *n*

lie-in: **have a ~** *esp Br* F sich gründlich ausschlafen

lieu: **in ~ of** anstelle von (*or gen*)

lieu·ten·ant MIL Leutnant *m*

life Leben *n*; JUR lebenslängliche Freiheitsstrafe; **all her ~** ihr ganzes Leben lang; **for ~** fürs (ganze) Leben; *esp* JUR lebenslänglich

life as·sur·ance *Br* → **life insurance**

life belt Rettungsgürtel *m*

life·boat Rettungsboot *n*

life·guard Bademeister *m*; Rettungsschwimmer *m*

life im·pris·on·ment JUR lebenslängliche Freiheitsstrafe

life in·sur·ance Lebensversicherung *f*

life jack·et Schwimmweste *f*

life·less leblos; matt, schwung-, lustlos

life·like lebensecht

life·long lebenslang

life pre·serv·er Schwimmweste *f*; Rettungsgürtel *m*

life sen·tence JUR lebenslängliche Freiheitsstrafe

life·time Lebenszeit *f*

lift 1. *v/t* (hoch-, auf)heben; erheben; *Verbot etc* aufheben; *Gesicht etc* liften, straffen; F klauen; *v/i* sich heben, steigen (*a. fog*); **~ *off*** starten (*rocket*), AVIAT abheben **2.** (Hoch-, Auf)Heben *n*;

PHYS, AVIAT Auftrieb *m*; *Br* Lift *m*, Aufzug *m*, Fahrstuhl *m*; **give s.o. a ~** j-n (im Auto) mitnehmen; F j-n aufmuntern, j-m Auftrieb geben

lift-off Start *m*, Abheben *n*

lig·a·ment ANAT Band *n*

light[1] **1.** Licht *n* (*a. fig*); Beleuchtung *f*; Schein *m*; Feuer *n*; *fig* Aspekt *m*; *Br mst pl* (Verkehrs)Ampel *f*; **do you have** (*Br* **have you got**) **a ~?** haben Sie Feuer? **2.** *v/t* beleuchten, erleuchten; *a.* **~ *up*** anzünden; *v/i* sich entzünden; **~ *up*** *fig* aufleuchten **3.** hell, licht

light[2] leicht (*a. fig*); **make ~ of s.th.** et. leichtnehmen; et. bagatellisieren

light·en[1] *v/t* erhellen; aufhellen; *v/i* hell(er) werden, sich aufhellen

light·en[2] leichter machen *or* werden; erleichtern

light·er Anzünder *m*; Feuerzeug *n*

light-head·ed (leicht) benommen; leichtfertig, töricht

light-heart·ed fröhlich, unbeschwert

light·house Leuchtturm *m*

light·ing Beleuchtung *f*

light·ness Leichtheit *f*; Leichtigkeit *f*

light·ning Blitz *m*; **like ~** wie der Blitz; **(as) quick as ~** blitzschnell

light·ning| con·duc·tor *Br*, **~ rod** ELECTR Blitzableiter *m*

light·weight SPORT Leichtgewicht *n*, Leichtgewichtler *m*

like[1] **1.** *v/t* gernhaben, mögen; **I ~ it** es gefällt mir; **I ~ her** ich kann sie gut leiden; **how do you ~ it?** wie gefällt es dir?, wie findest du es?; **I ~ that!** *iro* das hab ich gern!; **I should** *or* **would ~ to know** ich möchte gern wissen; *v/i* wollen; (**just**) **as you ~** (ganz) wie du willst; **if you ~** wenn du willst **2. ~s and dislikes** Neigungen und Abneigungen *pl*

like[2] **1.** gleich; wie; ähnlich; **~ that** so; **feel ~** Lust haben auf (*acc*) *or* zu; **what is he ~?** wie ist er?; **that is just ~ him!** das sieht ihm ähnlich! **2.** *der, die, das* Gleiche; **his ~** seinesgleichen; **the ~** dergleichen; **the ~s of you** Leute wie du

like·li·hood Wahrscheinlichkeit *f*

like·ly 1. *adj* wahrscheinlich; geeignet **2.** *adv* wahrscheinlich; **not ~!** F bestimmt nicht!

like·ness Ähnlichkeit *f*; Abbild *n*

like·wise ebenso

lik·ing Vorliebe f

li·lac 1. lila **2.** BOT Flieder m

lil·y BOT Lilie f

lil·y of the val·ley BOT Maiglöckchen n

limb ANAT (Körper)Glied n; BOT Ast m

lime[1] Kalk m

lime[2] BOT Linde f; Limone f

lime·light fig Rampenlicht n

lim·it 1. Limit n, Grenze f; **within ~s** in Grenzen; **off ~s** Zutritt verboten (**to** für); **that is the ~!** F das ist der Gipfel!, das ist (doch) die Höhe!; **go to the ~** bis zum Äußersten gehen **2.** beschränken (**to** auf acc)

lim·i·ta·tion Beschränkung f; fig Grenze f; JUR Verjährung f

lim·it·ed beschränkt, begrenzt; **~ (liability) company** Br ECON Gesellschaft f mit beschränkter Haftung

lim·it·less grenzenlos

limp[1] **1.** hinken, humpeln **2.** Hinken n, Humpeln n

limp[2] schlaff, schlapp, F lappig

line[1] **1.** Linie f, Strich m; Zeile f; Falte f, Runzel f; Reihe f; (Menschen-, a. Auto)Schlange f; (Abstammungs)Linie f; (Verkehrs-, Eisenbahn- etc)Linie f, Strecke f; (Flug- etc)Gesellschaft f; esp TEL Leitung f; MIL Linie f; Fach n, Gebiet n, Branche f; SPORT (Ziel- etc)Linie f; Leine f; Schnur f; Linie f, Richtung f; fig Grenze f; pl THEA Rolle f, Text m; **the ~** der Äquator; **draw the ~** Halt machen, die Grenze ziehen (**at** bei); **the ~ is busy** or **engaged** TEL die Leitung ist besetzt; **hold the ~** TEL bleiben Sie am Apparat; **stand in ~** anstehen, Schlange stehen (**for** um, nach); **2.** lin(i)ieren; Gesicht zeichnen, (zer)furchen; Straße etc säumen; **~ up** (sich) in e-r Reihe or Linie aufstellen, SPORT sich aufstellen; sich anstellen (**for** um, nach)

line[2] Kleid etc füttern; TECH auskleiden, ausschlagen; MOT Bremsen etc belegen

lin·e·ar linear; Längen...

lin·en 1. Leinen n; (Bett-, Tisch- etc -) Wäsche f **2.** leinen, Leinen...

lin·en| clos·et, Br **~ cup·board** Wäscheschrank m

lin·er MAR Linienschiff n; AVIAT Verkehrsflugzeug n

lines·man SPORT Linienrichter m

lines·wom·an SPORT Linienrichterin f

line-up SPORT Aufstellung f; Gegenüberstellung f (zur Identifizierung)

lin·ger verweilen, sich aufhalten; a. **~ on** dahinsiechen; **~ on** noch dableiben; fig fortleben

lin·ge·rie Damenunterwäsche f

lin·ing Futter(stoff m) n; TECH Auskleidung f; MOT (Brems- etc)Belag m

link 1. (Ketten)Glied n; Manschettenknopf m; fig (Binde)Glied n, Verbindung f **2.** a. **~ up** (sich) verbinden

links → golf links

link-up Verbindung f

lin·seed BOT Leinsamen m

lin·seed oil Leinöl n

li·on ZO Löwe m

li·on·ess ZO Löwin f

lip ANAT Lippe f; (Tassen- etc)Rand m; F Unverschämtheit f

lip·stick Lippenstift m

liq·ue·fy (sich) verflüssigen

liq·uid 1. Flüssigkeit f **2.** flüssig; **~ soap** Flüssigseife f

liq·ui·date liquidieren (a. ECON); Schulden tilgen

liq·uid·ize zerkleinern, pürieren

liq·uid·iz·er Mixgerät n, Mixer m

liq·uor Br alkoholische Getränke pl, Alkohol m; Schnaps m, Spirituosen pl

liq·uo·rice Br → licorice

lisp 1. lispeln **2.** Lispeln n

list 1. Liste f, Verzeichnis n; MAR Schlagseite f **2.** (in e-e Liste) eintragen, erfassen; MAR **be ~ing** Schlagseite haben

lis·ten hören; **~ in** Radio hören; **~ in to** et. im Radio (an)hören; **~ in on** Telefongespräch etc abhören or mithören; **~ to** anhören (acc), zuhören (dat); hören auf (acc)

lis·ten·er Zuhörer(in); (Rundfunk)Hörer(in)

list·less teilnahmslos, lustlos

li·ter Liter m, n

lit·e·ral (wort)wörtlich; genau; prosaisch

lit·e·ra·ry literarisch, Literatur...

lit·e·ra·ture Literatur f

lithe geschmeidig, gelenkig

li·tre Br → liter

lit·ter 1. (esp Papier)Abfall m; AGR Streu f; ZO Wurf m; Trage f; Sänfte f **2.** et. herumliegen lassen in (dat) or auf (dat); **be ~ed with** übersät sein mit

lit·ter| bas·ket, **~ bin** Abfallkorb m

lit·tle 1. adj klein; wenig; **the ~ ones** die

loin

Kleinen *pl* **2.** *adv* wenig, kaum **3.** Kleinigkeit *f*; **a~** ein wenig, ein bisschen; **~ by~** (ganz) allmählich, nach und nach; **not a ~** nicht wenig

live¹ leben; wohnen (**with** bei); **~ to see** erleben; **~ on** leben von; weiterleben; **~ up to** s-n *Grundsätzen etc* gemäß leben; *Erwartungen etc* entsprechen; **~ with** mit *j-m* zusammenleben; mit *et.* leben

live² **1.** *adj* lebend, lebendig; richtig, echt; ELECTR Strom führend; *radio*, TV Direkt..., Live-... **2.** *adv* direkt, original, live

live·li·hood (Lebens)Unterhalt *m*

live·li·ness Lebhaftigkeit *f*

live·ly lebhaft, lebendig; aufregend

liv·er ANAT Leber *f* (*a.* GASTR)

liv·e·ry Livree *f*

live·stock Vieh *n*, Viehbestand *m*

liv·id bläulich; F fuchsteufelswild

liv·ing **1.** lebend; **the ~ image of** das genaue Ebenbild (*gen*) **2.** Leben *n*, Lebensweise *f*; Lebensunterhalt *m*; **the ~** die Lebenden *pl*; **standard of ~** Lebensstandard *m*; **earn** *or* **make a ~** (sich) s-n Lebensunterhalt verdienen

liv·ing room Wohnzimmer *n*

liz·ard ZO Eidechse *f*

load **1.** Last *f* (*a. fig*); Ladung *f*; Belastung *f* **2.** *j-n* überhäufen (**with** mit); *Schusswaffe* laden; *a.* **~ up** (auf-, be-, ein)laden

loaf¹ Laib *m* (Brot); Brot *n*

loaf² *a.* **~ about, ~ around** F herumlungern

loaf·er Müßiggänger(in)

loam Lehm *m*; **loam·y** lehmig

loan **1.** (Ver)Leihen *n*; ECON Kredit *m*, Darlehen *n*; Leihgabe *f*; **on ~** leihweise **2.** **~ s.o. s.th., ~ s.th. to s.o.** j-m et. (aus)leihen; et. an j-n verleihen

loath: **be ~ to do s.th.** et. nur (sehr) ungern tun

loathe verabscheuen, hassen

loath·ing Abscheu *m*

lob *esp tennis*: Lob *m*

lob·by **1.** Vorhalle *f*; THEA, *film*: Foyer *n*; Wandelhalle *f*; POL Lobby *f*, Interessengruppe *f* **2.** POL *Abgeordnete etc* beeinflussen

lobe ANAT, BOT Lappen *m*

lob·ster ZO Hummer *m*

lo·cal **1.** örtlich, Orts..., lokal, Lokal...

2. Ortsansässige *m*, *f*, Einheimische *m*, *f*; *Br* F Stammkneipe *f*; **~ call** TEL Ortsgespräch *n*; **~ e·lec·tions** POL Kommunalwahlen *pl*; **~ gov·ern·ment** Gemeindeverwaltung *f*; **~ time** Ortszeit *f*; **~ traf·fic** Orts-, Nahverkehr *m*

lo·cate ausfindig machen; orten; **be ~d** gelegen sein, liegen, sich befinden

lo·ca·tion Lage *f*; Standort *m*; Platz *m* (**for** für); *film*, TV Gelände *n* für Außenaufnahmen; **on ~** auf Außenaufnahme

lock¹ **1.** (*Tür-*, *Gewehr- etc*)Schloss *n*; Schleuse(nkammer) *f*; Verschluss *m*; Sperrvorrichtung *f* **2.** *v/t* zu-, verschließen, zu-, versperren (*a.* **~ up**); umschlingen, umfassen; TECH sperren; *v/i* schließen; abschließbar *or* verschließbar sein; MOT *etc* blockieren; **~ away** wegschließen; **~ in** einschließen, einsperren; **~ out** aussperren; **~ up** abschließen; wegschließen; einsperren

lock² (Haar)Locke *f*

lock·er Spind *m*, Schrank *m*; Schließfach *n*; **~ room** *esp* SPORT Umkleidekabine *f*, Umkleideraum *m*

lock·et Medaillon *n*

lock·out ECON Aussperrung *f*

lock·smith Schlosser *m*

lock·up Arrestzelle *f*

lo·cust ZO Heuschrecke *f*

lodge **1.** Portier-, Pförtnerloge *f*; (*Jagd-*, *Ski- etc*)Hütte *f*; Sommer-, Gartenhaus *n*; (*Freimaurer*)Loge *f* **2.** *v/i* logieren, (*esp* vorübergehend *or* in Untermiete) wohnen, stecken (bleiben) (*bullet etc*); *v/t* aufnehmen, beherbergen, (für die Nacht) unterbringen; *Beschwerde etc* einreichen; *Berufung*, *Protest* einlegen

lodg·er Untermieter(in); **lodg·ing** Unterkunft *f*; *pl esp* möbliertes Zimmer

loft (Dach)Boden *m*; Heuboden *m*; Empore *f*; (*converted*) **~** Loft *m*, Fabriketage *f*

loft·y hoch; erhaben; stolz, hochmütig

log (Holz)Klotz *m*; (*gefällter*) Baumstamm; (Holz)Scheit *n*; → **log·book** MAR Logbuch *n*; AVIAT Bordbuch *n*; MOT Fahrtenbuch *n*

log cab·in Blockhaus *n*, Blockhütte *f*

log·ger·heads: **be at ~** sich streiten, sich in den Haaren liegen (**with** mit)

lo·gic Logik *f*; **lo·gic·al** logisch

loin GASTR Lende(nstück *n*) *f*; *pl* ANAT Lende *f*

loi·ter trödeln; herumlungern

loll hängen (*head*), heraushängen (*tongue*); **~ around** *or* **about** F sich rekeln *or* lümmeln

lol·li·pop GASTR Lutscher *m*; *esp Br* Eis *n* am Stiel; **~ man** *Br* Schülerlotse *m*; **~ woman, ~ lady** *Br* Schülerlotsin *f*

lol·ly GASTR F Lutscher *m*; **ice~** Eis *n* am Stiel

lone·li·ness Einsamkeit *f*

lone·ly einsam; **become ~** vereinsamen

lone·some einsam

long[1] **1.** *adj* lang; weit; langfristig **2.** *adv* lang(e); **as** *or* **so ~ as** solange wie; vorausgesetzt, dass; **~ ago** vor langer Zeit **3.** (e-e) lange Zeit; **for ~** lange; **take ~** lange brauchen *or* dauern

long[2] sich sehnen (**for** nach)

long-dis·tance Fern..., Langstrecken...; **~ call** TEL Ferngespräch *n*; **~ run·ner** SPORT Langstreckenläufer(in)

long·hand Schreibschrift *f*

long·ing 1. sehnsüchtig **2.** Sehnsucht *f*, Verlangen *n*

lon·gi·tude GEOGR Länge *f*

long johns lange Unterhose

long jump SPORT Weitsprung *m*

long-life milk *esp Br* H-Milch *f*

long-range MIL, AVIAT Fern..., Langstrecken...; langfristig

long·shore·man Dock-, Hafenarbeiter *m*

long·sight·ed *esp Br* weitsichtig, *fig a.* weitblickend

long-stand·ing seit langer Zeit bestehend; alt

long-term langfristig, auf lange Sicht

long wave ELECTR Langwelle *f*

long·wear·ing strapazierfähig

long·wind·ed langatmig

look 1. sehen, blicken, schauen (**at, on** auf *acc*, nach); nachschauen, nachsehen; *krank etc* aussehen; nach e-r *Richtung* liegen, gehen (*window etc*); **~ here!** schau mal (her); hör mal (zu)!; **~ like** aussehen wie; **it ~s as if** es sieht (so) aus, als ob; **~ after** aufpassen auf (*acc*); sich kümmern um, sorgen für, *den Haushalt etc* versehen; **~ ahead** nach vorne sehen; *fig* vorausschauen; **~ around** sich umsehen; **~ at** ansehen; **~ back** sich umsehen; *fig* zurückblicken; **~ down** herab-, heruntersehen (*a. fig* **on s.o.** auf j-n); **~ for** suchen; **~**

forward to sich freuen auf (*acc*); **~ in** F hereinschauen (**on** bei); **~ into** untersuchen, prüfen; **~ on** zusehen, zuschauen (*dat*); betrachten, ansehen (**as** als); **~ onto** liegen zu, (hinaus)gehen auf (*acc*) (*window etc*); **~ out** hinaus-, heraussehen; aufpassen, sich vorsehen; ausschauen *or* Ausschau halten (**for** nach); **~ over** *et.* durchsehen; *j-n* mustern; **~ round** sich umsehen; **~ through** *et.* durchsehen; **~ up** aufblicken, aufsehen; *et.* nachschlagen; *j-n* aufsuchen **2.** Blick *m*; Miene *f*, (Gesichts)Ausdruck *m*; (**good**) **~s** gutes Aussehen; **have a ~ at s.th.** sich et. ansehen; **I don't like the ~ of it** es gefällt mir nicht

look·ing glass Spiegel *m*

look·out Ausguck *m*; Ausschau *f*; *fig* F Aussicht(en *pl*) *f*; **be on the ~ for** Ausschau halten nach

loom[1] Webstuhl *m*

loom[2] *a.* **~ up** undeutlich sichtbar werden *or* auftauchen

loop 1. Schlinge *f*, Schleife *f*; Schlaufe *f*; Öse *f*; AVIAT Looping *m*, *n*; IT Schleife *f* **2.** (sich) schlingen

loop·hole MIL Schießscharte *f*; *fig* Hintertürchen *n*; **a ~ in the law** e-e Gesetzeslücke

loose 1. los(e); locker; weit; frei; **let ~** loslassen; freilassen **2. be on the ~** frei herumlaufen

loos·en (sich) lösen *or* lockern; **~ up** SPORT Lockerungsübungen machen

loot 1. Beute *f* **2.** plündern

lop *Baum* beschneiden, stutzen; **~ off** abhauen, abhacken

lop·sid·ed schief; *fig* einseitig

lord Herr *m*, Gebieter *m*; *Br* Lord *m*; **the Lord** REL Gott *m* (der Herr); **the Lord's Prayer** REL das Vaterunser; **the Lord's Supper** REL das (heilige) Abendmahl; **House of Lords** *Br* POL Oberhaus *n*

Lord Mayor *Br* Oberbürgermeister *m*

lor·ry *Br* MOT Last(kraft)wagen *m*, Lastauto *n*, Laster *m*

lose verlieren; verpassen, versäumen; nachgehen (*watch*); **~ o.s.** sich verirren; sich verlieren; **los·er** Verlierer(in); **loss** Verlust *m*; Schaden *m*; **at a ~** ECON mit Verlust; **be at a ~** in Verlegenheit sein (**for** um); **lost** verloren; **be ~** sich verirrt haben, sich nicht mehr zurechtfinden (*a. fig*); *be ~ in thought* in Gedanken versunken sein; *get ~* sich verirren; *get ~! sl* hau ab!

lost-and-found (of·fice), *Br* **lost prop·er·ty of·fice** Fundbüro *n*

lot Los *n*; Parzelle *f*; Grundstück *n*; ECON Partie *f*, Posten *m*; Gruppe *f*, Gesellschaft *f*; Menge *f*, Haufen *m*; Los *n*, Schicksal *n*; *the ~* alles, das Ganze; *a ~ of* F, *~s of* F viel, e-e Menge; *a bad ~* F ein übler Kerl; *cast or draw ~s* losen

loth → *loath*

lo·tion Lotion *f*

lot·te·ry Lotterie *f*

loud laut; *fig* schreiend, grell

loud·mouth *contp* Schwätzer *m*

loud·speak·er Lautsprecher *m*

lounge 1. Wohnzimmer *n*; Aufenthaltsraum *m*, Lounge *f* (*a.* AVIAT); Wartehalle *f* 2. F *contp* sich flegeln; *~ about, ~ around* herumlungern

louse ZO Laus *f*

lou·sy verlaust; F miserabel, saumäßig

lout Flegel *m*, Lümmel *m*, Rüpel *m*

lov·a·ble liebenswert; reizend

love 1. Liebe *f* (*of, for, to, towards* zu); Liebling *m*, Schatz *m*; *tennis*: null; *be in ~ with s.o.* in j-n verliebt sein; *fall in ~ with s.o.* sich in j-n verlieben; *make ~* sich lieben, miteinander schlafen; *give my ~ to her* grüße sie herzlich von mir; *send one's ~ to* j-n grüßen lassen; *~ from ...* herzliche Grüße von ... 2. lieben; gern mögen

love af·fair Liebesaffäre *f*

love·ly (wunder)schön; nett, reizend; F prima

lov·er Liebhaber *m*, Geliebte *m, f*; (*Musik- etc*) Liebhaber(in), (-)Freund(in); *pl* Liebende *pl*, Liebespaar *n*

lov·ing liebevoll, liebend

low 1. *adj* niedrig (*a. fig*); tief (*a. fig*); knapp (*supplies etc*); gedämpft, schwach (*light*); tief (*sound*); leise (*sound, voice*); tief gering(schätzig); ordinär; niedergeschlagen, deprimiert 2. *adv* niedrig; tief (*a. fig*); leise 3. METEOR Tief(druckgebiet) *n*; *fig* Tief(punkt *m*) *n*

low·brow F 1. geistig Anspruchslose *m, f*, Unbedarfte *m, f* 2. geistig anspruchslos, unbedarft

low-cal·o·rie kalorienarm, -reduziert

low-e·mis·sion schadstoffarm

low·er 1. niedriger; tiefer; untere(r, -s), Unter... 2. niedriger machen; herab-, herunterlassen; *Augen, Stimme, Preis etc* senken; *Standard* herabsetzen; *fig* erniedrigen

low-fat fettarm

low-fly·ing plane AVIAT Tieffflieger *m*

low·land Tief-, Flachland *n*

low·ly niedrig

low-necked (tief) ausgeschnitten

low-pitched MUS tief

low-pres·sure METEOR Tiefdruck...; TECH Niederdruck...

low-rise ARCH niedrig (gebaut)

low-spir·it·ed niedergeschlagen

low tide Ebbe *f*

low wa·ter Niedrigwasser *n*

loy·al loyal, treu

loy·al·ty Loyalität *f*, Treue *f*

loz·enge MATH Raute *f*, Rhombus *m*; GASTR Pastille *f*

lu·bri·cant TECH Schmiermittel *n*

lu·bri·cate TECH schmieren, ölen

lu·bri·ca·tion TECH Schmieren *n*, Ölen *n*

lu·cid klar

luck Schicksal *n*; Glück *n*; *bad ~, hard ~, ill ~* Unglück *n*, Pech *n*; *good ~* Glück *n*; *good ~!* viel Glück!; *be in (out of) ~* (kein) Glück haben

luck·i·ly glücklicherweise, zum Glück

luck·y glücklich, Glücks...; *be ~* Glück haben; *~ day* Glückstag *m*; *~ fellow* Glückspilz *m*

lu·cra·tive einträglich, lukrativ

lu·di·crous lächerlich

lug zerren, schleppen

luge SPORT Rennrodeln *n*; Rennrodel *m*, Rennschlitten *m*

lug·gage *esp Br* (Reise)Gepäck *n*; *~ rack esp Br* RAIL *etc* Gepäcknetz *n*, Gepäckablage *f*; *~ van Br* RAIL Gepäckwagen *m*

luke·warm lau(warm); *fig* lau, mäßig, halbherzig

lull 1. beruhigen; sich legen (*storm*); *mst ~ to sleep* einlullen 2. Pause *f*; MAR Flaute *f* (*a. fig*)

lul·la·by Wiegenlied *n*

lum·ba·go MED Hexenschuss *m*

lum·ber[1] schwerfällig gehen; (dahin-) rumpeln (*vehicle*)

lum·ber[2] 1. Bau-, Nutzholz *n*; *esp Br* Gerümpel *n* 2. *v/t ~ s.o. with s.th. Br* F j-m et. aufhalsen

lum·ber·jack Holzfäller *m*, -arbeiter *m*

lum·ber mill Sägewerk *n*

lum·ber room *esp Br* Rumpelkammer *f*

lum·ber·yard Holzplatz *m*, Holzlager *n*

lu·mi·na·ry *fig* Leuchte *f*, Koryphäe *f*

lu·mi·nous leuchtend, Leucht...

lu·mi·nous di·splay Leuchtanzeige *f*

lu·mi·nous paint Leuchtfarbe *f*

lump 1. Klumpen *m*; Schwellung *f*, Beule *f*; MED Geschwulst *f*, Knoten *m*; GASTR Stück *n*; **in the ~** in Bausch und Bogen, pauschal **2.** *v/t:* **~ together** *fig* zusammenwerfen; in e-n Topf werfen; *v/i* Klumpen bilden, klumpen

lump sug·ar Würfelzucker *m*

lump sum Pauschalsumme *f*

lump·y klumpig

lu·na·cy Wahnsinn *m*

lu·nar ASTR Mond...

lu·nar mod·ule Mond(lande)fähre *f*

lu·na·tic *fig* **1.** wahnsinnig, verrückt **2.** Wahnsinnige *m, f*, Verrückte *m, f*

lunch, *formal* **lun·cheon 1.** Lunch *m*, Mittagessen *n* **2.** zu Mittag essen

lunch hour, lunch time Mittagszeit *f*, Mittagspause *f*

lung ANAT Lungenflügel *m*; *pl* die Lunge

lunge sich stürzen (**at** auf *acc*)

lurch 1. taumeln, torkeln **2.** **leave s.o. in the ~** j-n im Stich lassen, F j-n sitzen lassen

lure 1. Köder *m*; *fig* Lockung *f* **2.** ködern, (an)locken

lu·rid grell; grässlich, schauerlich

lurk lauern; **~ about, ~ around** herumschleichen

lus·cious köstlich, lecker; üppig; F knackig

lush saftig, üppig

lust 1. sinnliche Begierde, Lust *f*; Gier *f* **2.** **~ after, ~ for** begehren; gierig sein nach

lus·ter, *Br* **lus·tre** Glanz *m*, Schimmer *m*; **lus·trous** glänzend, schimmernd

lust·y kräftig, robust, vital

lute MUS Laute *f*

Lu·ther·an REL lutherisch

lux·u·ri·ant üppig

lux·u·ri·ate schwelgen (**in** in *dat*)

lux·u·ri·ous luxuriös, Luxus...

lux·u·ry 1. Luxus *m*; Komfort *m*; Luxusartikel *m* **2.** Luxus...

lye Lauge *f*

ly·ing lügnerisch, verlogen

lymph MED Lymphe *f*

lynch lynchen; **~ law** Lynchjustiz *f*

lynx ZO Luchs *m*

lyr·ic 1. lyrisch **2.** lyrisches Gedicht; *pl* Lyrik *f*; (Lied)Text *m*

lyr·i·cal lyrisch, gefühlvoll; schwärmerisch

M

M, m M, m *n*

M *abbr of* **medium (size)** mittelgroß

ma F Mama *f*, Mutti *f*

ma'am → **madam**

ma·cad·am Asphalt *m*

mac·a·ro·ni Makkaroni *pl*

ma·chine 1. Maschine *f* **2.** maschinell herstellen

ma·chine-gun Maschinengewehr *n*

ma·chine-read·a·ble IT maschinenlesbar

ma·chin·e·ry Maschinen *pl*; Maschinerie *f*

ma·chin·ist TECH Maschinist *m*

mach·o *contp* Macho *m*

mack·e·rel ZO Makrele *f*

mac·ro... Makro..., (sehr) groß

mad wahnsinnig, verrückt; VET tollwütig; F wütend; *fig* **be ~ about** wild *or* versessen sein auf (*acc*), verrückt sein nach; **drive s.o. ~** j-n verrückt machen; **go ~** verrückt werden; **like ~** wie verrückt

mad·am gnädige Frau

mad·cap verrückt

mad cow dis·ease VET Rinderwahn (-sinn) *m*

mad·den verrückt *or* rasend machen

mad·den·ing unerträglich; verrückt *or* rasend machend

made: ~ of gold aus Gold

made-to-meas·ure maßgeschneidert

made-up geschminkt; erfunden

mad·house *fig* F Irrenhaus *n*

mad·ly wie verrückt; .F wahnsinnig, schrecklich

mad·man Verrückte *m*

mad·ness Wahnsinn

mad·wom·an Verrückte *f*

mag·a·zine Magazin *n* (*a*. PHOT, MIL), Zeitschrift *f*; Lagerhaus *n*

mag·got zo Made *f*

Ma·gi: *the* (*three*) ~ die (drei) Weisen aus dem Morgenland, die Heiligen Drei Könige

ma·gic 1. Magie *f*, Zauberei *f*; Zauber *m*; *fig* Wunder *n* **2.** *a*. *magical* magisch, Zauber...

ma·gi·cian Magier *m*, Zauberer *m*; Zauberkünstler *m*

ma·gis·trate (Friedens)Richter(in)

mag·na·nim·i·ty Großmut *f*

mag·nan·i·mous großmütig

mag·net Magnet *m*

mag·net·ic magnetisch, Magnet...

mag·nif·i·cent großartig, prächtig

mag·ni·fy vergrößern

mag·ni·fy·ing glass Vergrößerungsglas *n*, Lupe *f*

mag·ni·tude Größe *f*; Wichtigkeit *f*

mag·pie zo Elster *f*

ma·hog·a·ny Mahagoni(holz) *n*

maid (Dienst)Mädchen *n*, Hausangestellte *f*; ~ *of hono(u)r* Hofdame *f*; (erste) Brautjungfer

maid·en Jungfern..., Erstlings...

maid·en name Mädchenname *m*

mail 1. Post(sendung) *f*; *by* ~ mit der Post® **2.** mit der Post® (zu)schicken, aufgeben, *Brief* einwerfen

mail·bag Postsack *m*; Posttasche *f*

mail·box Briefkasten *m*

mail car·ri·er, mail·man Briefträger *m*, Postbote *m*

mail or·der Bestellung *f* bei e-m Versandhaus

mail-or·der| firm, ~ **house** Versandhaus *n*

maim verstümmeln

main 1. Haupt..., wichtigste(r, -s); hauptsächlich; *by* ~ *force* mit äußerster Kraft **2.** *mst pl* Hauptleitung *f*, Hauptgas-, Hauptwasser-, Hauptstromleitung *f*; (Strom)Netz *n*; *in the* ~ in der Hauptsache, im Wesentlichen

main·frame IT Großrechner *m*

main·land Festland *n*

main·ly hauptsächlich

main mem·o·ry IT Hauptspeicher *m*; Arbeitsspeicher *m*

main men·u IT Hauptmenü *n*

main road Haupt(verkehrs)straße *f*

main·spring TECH Hauptfeder *f*; *fig* (Haupt)Triebfeder *f*

main·stay *fig* Hauptstütze *f*

main street Hauptstraße *f*

main·tain (aufrecht)erhalten, beibehalten; instand halten, pflegen, TECH *a*. warten; *Familie etc* unterhalten, versorgen; *et*. behaupten

main·te·nance (Aufrecht)Erhaltung *f*, Instandhaltung *f*, Pflege *f*, TECH *a*. Wartung *f*; Unterhalt *m*

maize *esp Br* BOT Mais *m*

ma·jes·tic majestätisch

ma·jes·ty Majestät *f*; *His* (*Her, Your*) *Majesty* Seine (Ihre, Eure) Majestät

ma·jor 1. größere(r, -s), *fig a*. bedeutend, wichtig; JUR volljährig; *C* ~ MUS C-Dur *n* **2.** MIL Major *m*; JUR Volljährige *m*, *f*; UNIV Hauptfach *n*; MUS Dur *n*; ~ **gen·e·ral** MIL Generalmajor *m*

ma·jor·i·ty Mehrheit *f*, Mehrzahl *f*; JUR Volljährigkeit *f*

ma·jor league *baseball*: oberste Spielklasse

ma·jor road Haupt(verkehrs)straße *f*

make 1. machen; anfertigen, herstellen, erzeugen; (zu)bereiten; (er)schaffen; ergeben; bilden; machen zu; ernennen zu; *Geld* verdienen; sich erweisen als, abgeben (*person*); schätzen auf (*acc*); *Geschwindigkeit* erreichen; *Fehler* machen; *Frieden etc* schließen; *e-e Rede* halten; F *Strecke* zurücklegen; *with inf: j-n* lassen, veranlassen zu, bringen zu, zwingen zu; ~ *it* es schaffen; ~ *do with s.th.* mit et. auskommen, sich mit et. behelfen; *what do you* ~ *of it?* was halten Sie davon?; ~ *believe* vorgeben; ~ *friends with* sich anfreunden mit; ~ *good* wieder gutmachen; *Versprechen etc* halten; ~ *way* Platz machen; ~ *for* zugehen auf (*acc*); sich aufmachen nach; ~ *into* verarbeiten zu; ~ *off* sich davonmachen, sich aus dem Staub machen; ~ *out* *Rechnung, Scheck etc* ausstellen; ausmachen, erkennen; aus *j-m, e-r Sache* klug werden; ~ *over* *Eigentum* übertragen; ~ *up* *et*. zusammenstellen; sich *et*. ausdenken, *et*. erfinden; (sich) zurechtmachen *or* schminken; **~ it up** sich versöhnen *or* wieder vertragen (**with** mit); **~ up one's mind** sich entschließen; **be made up of** bestehen aus, sich zusammensetzen aus; **~ up for** nachholen, aufholen; für *et.* entschädigen **2.** Machart *f*, Bauart *f*; Fabrikat *n*, Marke *f*

make-be·lieve Schein *m*, Fantasie *f*

mak·er Hersteller *m*; *Maker* REL Schöpfer *m*

make·shift 1. Notbehelf *m* **2.** behelfsmäßig, Behelfs...

make-up Make-up *n*, Schminke *f*; Aufmachung *f*; Zusammensetzung *f*

mak·ing Erzeugung *f*, Herstellung *f*, Fabrikation *f*; **be in the ~** noch in Arbeit sein; **have the ~s of** das Zeug haben zu

mal·ad·just·ed nicht angepasst, verhaltensgestört, milieugestört

mal·ad·min·i·stra·tion schlechte Verwaltung; POL Misswirtschaft *f*

mal·con·tent 1. unzufrieden **2.** Unzufriedene *m*, *f*

male 1. männlich **2.** Mann *m*; ZO Männchen *n*

male nurse (Kranken)Pfleger *m*

mal·for·ma·tion Missbildung *f*

mal·ice Bosheit *f*; Groll *m*; JUR böse Absicht, Vorsatz *m*

ma·li·cious boshaft; böswillig

ma·lign verleumden

ma·lig·nant bösartig (*a.* MED); boshaft

mall Einkaufszentrum *n*

mal·le·a·ble TECH verformbar; *fig* formbar

mal·let Holzhammer *m*; (Krocket-, Polo)Schläger *m*

mal·nu·tri·tion Unterernährung *f*; Fehlernährung *f*

mal·o·dor·ous übel riechend

mal·prac·tice Vernachlässigung *f* der beruflichen Sorgfalt; MED falsche Behandlung; (ärztlicher) Kunstfehler

malt Malz *n*

mal·treat schlecht behandeln; misshandeln

mam·mal ZO Säugetier *n*

mam·moth 1. ZO Mammut *n* **2.** Mammut..., Riesen..., riesig

mam·my F Mami *f*

man 1. Mann *m*; Mensch(en *pl*) *m*; Menschheit *f*; F (Ehe)Mann *m*; F Geliebte *m*; (*Schach*)Figur *f*; (*Dame*)Stein *m*; **the ~ on** (*Br* **in**) **the street** der Mann

auf der Straße **2.** (*Raum*)Schiff *etc* bemannen; *Büro etc* besetzen

man·age *v/t Betrieb etc* leiten, führen; *Künstler, Sportler etc* managen; *et.* zustande bringen; es fertigbringen (**to do** zu tun); umgehen (können) mit; mit *j-m, et.* fertigwerden; F *Arbeit, Essen etc* bewältigen, schaffen; *v/i* auskommen (**with** mit; **without** ohne); F es schaffen, zurechtkommen; F es einrichten, es ermöglichen

man·age·a·ble handlich; lenksam

man·age·ment Verwaltung *f*; ECON Management *n*, Unternehmensführung *f*; Geschäftsleitung *f*, Direktion *f*

man·ag·er Verwalter *m*; ECON Manager *m* (*a.* THEA *etc*); Geschäftsführer *m*, Leiter *m*, Direktor *m*; SPORT (Chef-)Trainer *m*; **be a good ~** gut *or* sparsam wirtschaften können

man·a·ge·ri·al ECON geschäftsführend, leitend; **~ position** leitende Stellung; **~ staff** leitende Angestellte *pl*

man·ag·ing ECON geschäftsführend, leitend; **~ di·rec·tor** Generaldirektor *m*, leitender Direktor

man·date Mandat *n*; Auftrag *m*; Vollmacht *f*

man·da·to·ry obligatorisch, zwingend

mane ZO Mähne *f* (*a.* F)

ma·neu·ver *a. fig* **1.** Manöver *n* **2.** manövrieren

mange VET Räude *f*

man·ger AGR Krippe *f*

man·gle 1. (Wäsche)Mangel *f* **2.** mangeln; *j-n* übel zurichten, zerfleischen; *fig Text* verstümmeln

mang·y VET räudig; *fig* schäbig

man·hood Mannesalter *n*; Männlichkeit *f*

ma·ni·a Wahnsinn *m*; *fig* (**for**) Sucht *f* (nach), Leidenschaft *f* (für), Manie *f*, Fimmel *m*; **ma·ni·ac** F Wahnsinnige *m*, *f*, Verrückte *m*, *f*; *fig* Fanatiker(in)

man·i·cure Maniküre *f*, Handpflege *f*

man·i·fest 1. offenkundig **2.** *v/t* offenbaren, manifestieren

man·i·fold mannigfaltig, vielfältig

ma·nip·u·late manipulieren; (geschickt) handhaben

ma·nip·u·la·tion Manipulation *f*

man·kind die Menschheit, die Menschen *pl*

man·ly männlich

man·made vom Menschen geschaffen, künstlich; **~ fiber** Kunstfaser *f*

man·ner Art *f* (und Weise *f*); Betragen *n*, Auftreten *n*; *pl* Benehmen *n*, Umgangsformen *pl*, Manieren *pl*; Sitten *pl*

ma·noeu·vre *Br* → **maneuver**

man·or *Br* (Land)Gut *n*; → **man·or house** Herrenhaus *n*

man·pow·er menschliche Arbeitskraft; Arbeitskräfte *pl*

man·sion (herrschaftliches) Wohnhaus

man·slaugh·ter JUR Totschlag *m*, fahrlässige Tötung

man·tel·piece, **man·tel·shelf** Kaminsims *m*

man·u·al 1. Hand...; mit der Hand (gemacht) 2. Handbuch *n*

man·u·fac·ture 1. erzeugen, herstellen 2. Herstellung *f*, Fertigung *f*; Erzeugnis *n*, Fabrikat *n*

man·u·fac·tur·er Hersteller *m*, Erzeuger *m*

man·u·fac·tur·ing Herstellungs...

ma·nure AGR 1. Dünger *m*, Mist *m*, Dung *m* 2. düngen

man·u·script Manuskript *n*

man·y 1. viel(e); **~ a** manche(r, -s), manch eine(r, -s); **~ times** oft; **as ~** ebenso viel(e) 2. viele; **a good ~** ziemlich viel(e); **a great ~** sehr viele

map 1. (Land- *etc*)Karte *f*; (Stadt- *etc*)Plan *m* 2. e-e Karte machen von; auf e-r Karte eintragen; **~ out** *fig* (bis in die Einzelheiten) (voraus)planen

ma·ple BOT Ahorn *m*

mar beeinträchtigen; verderben

Mar *abbr of* **March** März *m*

mar·a·thon SPORT 1. *a.* **~ race** Marathonlauf *m* 2. Marathon... (*a. fig*)

ma·raud plündern

mar·ble 1. Marmor *m*; Murmel *f* 2. marmorn

march 1. marschieren; *fig* fortschreiten 2. Marsch *m*; *fig* (Fort)Gang *m*; **the ~ of events** der Lauf der Dinge

March (*abbr* **Mar**) März·m

mare ZO Stute *f*

mar·ga·rine, *Br* F **marge** Margarine *f*

mar·gin Rand *m* (*a. fig*); Grenze *f* (*a. fig*); *fig* Spielraum *m*; (Gewinn-, Verdienst)Spanne *f*; **by a wide ~** mit großem Vorsprung; **mar·gin·al** Rand...; **~ note** Randbemerkung *f*

mar·i·hua·na, **mar·i·jua·na** Marihuana

n

ma·ri·na Boots-, Jachthafen *m*

ma·rine Marine *f*; MIL Marineinfanterist *m*

mar·i·ner Seemann *m*

mar·i·tal ehelich, Ehe...

mar·i·tal sta·tus Familienstand *m*

mar·i·time See...; Küsten...; Schifffahrts...

mark¹ 1. Marke *f*, Markierung *f*; (Kenn)Zeichen *n*, Merkmal *n*; (Körper)Mal *n*; Ziel *n* (*a. fig*); Spur *f* (*a. fig*); Fleck *m*; (Fabrik-, Waren)Zeichen *n*, (Schutz-, Handels)Marke *f*; ECON Preisangabe *f*; PED Note *f*, Zensur *f*, Punkt *m*; SPORT Startlinie *f*; *fig* Zeichen *n*; *fig* Norm *f*; **be up to the ~** den Anforderungen gewachsen sein (*person*) *or* genügen (*performance etc*); *gesundheitlich* auf der Höhe sein; **be wide of the ~** weit danebenschießen; *fig* sich gewaltig irren; weit danebenliegen (*estimate etc*); **hit the ~** (das Ziel) treffen; *fig* ins Schwarze treffen; **miss the ~** danebenschießen, das Ziel verfehlen (*a. fig*) 2. markieren, anzeichnen; anzeigen; kennzeichnen; *Waren* auszeichnen; *Preis* festsetzen; Spuren hinterlassen auf (*dat*); Flecken machen auf (*dat*); PED benoten, zensieren; SPORT *Gegenspieler* decken, markieren; **~ my words** denk an m-e Worte; **to the occasion** zur Feier des Tages; **~ time** auf der Stelle treten (*a. fig*); **~ down** notieren, vermerken; *im Preis* herabsetzen; **~ off** abgrenzen; *auf e-r Liste* abhaken; **~ out** *durch Striche etc* markieren; bestimmen (**for** für); **~ up** *im Preis* heraufsetzen

mark² *hist* (*former monetary unit of Germany*) (Deutsche) Mark

marked deutlich, ausgeprägt

mark·er Markierstift *m*; Lesezeichen *n*; SPORT Bewacher(in)

mar·ket 1. Markt *m*; Marktplatz *m*; (Lebensmittel)Geschäft *n*, Laden *m*; ECON Absatz *m*; (**for**) Nachfrage *f* (nach), Bedarf *m* (an *dat*); **on the ~** auf dem Markt *or* im Handel; **put on the ~** auf den Markt *or* in den Handel bringen; (zum Verkauf) anbieten 2. *v/t* auf den Markt *or* in den Handel bringen; verkaufen, vertreiben

mar·ket·a·ble ECON marktgängig

mar·ket gar·den _Br_ Gemüse- und Obstgärtnerei _f_

mar·ket·ing ECON Marketing _n_

mark·ing Markierung _f_; ZO Zeichnung _f_; SPORT Deckung _f_; **man-to-man ~** Manndeckung _f_

marks·man guter Schütze

mar·ma·lade _esp_ Orangenmarmelade _f_

mar·mot ZO Murmeltier _n_

ma·roon 1. kastanienbraun **2.** _auf e-r einsamen Insel_ aussetzen **3.** Leuchtrakete _f_

mar·quee Festzelt _n_

mar·quis Marquis _m_

mar·riage Heirat _f_, Hochzeit _f_ (**to** mit); Ehe _f_; **civil ~** standesamtliche Trauung

mar·ria·ge·a·ble heiratsfähig

mar·riage cer·tif·i·cate Trauschein _m_, Heiratsurkunde _f_

mar·ried verheiratet; ehelich, Ehe...; **~ couple** Ehepaar _n_; **~ life** Ehe(leben _n_) _f_

mar·row ANAT (Knochen)Mark _n_; _fig_ Kern _m_, _das_ Wesentliche

mar·ry _v/t_ heiraten; _Paar_ trauen; **be married** verheiratet sein (**to** mit); **get married** heiraten; sich verheiraten (**to** mit); _v/i_ heiraten

marsh Sumpf(land _n_) _m_, Marsch _f_

mar·shal 1. MIL Marschall _m_; Bezirkspolizeichef _m_ **2.** ordnen; führen

marsh·y sumpfig

mar·ten ZO Marder _m_

mar·tial kriegerisch; Kriegs..., Militär...; **~ arts** asiatische Kampfsportarten _pl_; **~ law** Kriegsrecht _n_

mar·tyr REL Märtyrer(in) (_a. fig_)

mar·vel 1. Wunder _n_ **2.** sich wundern, staunen; **mar·vel·(l)ous** wunderbar; fabelhaft, fantastisch

mar·zi·pan Marzipan _n, m_

mas·ca·ra Wimperntusche _f_

mas·cot Maskottchen _n_

mas·cu·line männlich; Männer...; maskulin (_a._ LING)

mash zerdrücken, zerquetschen

mashed po·ta·toes Kartoffelbrei _m_

mask 1. Maske _f_ (_a._ IT); **2.** maskieren; _fig_ verbergen, verschleiern

masked maskiert; **~ ball** Maskenball _m_

ma·son Steinmetz _m_; _mst_ **Mason** Freimaurer _m_; **ma·son·ry** Mauerwerk _n_

masque THEA HIST Maskenspiel _n_

mas·que·rade 1. Maskerade _f_ (_a. fig_);

Verkleidung _f_ **2.** sich ausgeben (**as** als, für)

mass 1. Masse _f_; Menge _f_; Mehrzahl _f_; **the ~es** die (breite) Masse **2.** (sich) (an)sammeln _or_ (an)häufen **3.** Massen...

Mass REL Messe _f_

mas·sa·cre 1. Massaker _n_ **2.** niedermetzeln

mas·sage 1. Massage _f_ **2.** massieren

mas·seur Masseur _m_

mas·seuse Masseurin _f_, Masseuse _f_

mas·sif (Gebirgs)Massiv _n_

mas·sive massiv; groß, gewaltig

mass me·di·a Massenmedien _pl_

mass-pro·duce serienmäßig herstellen

mass pro·duc·tion Massen-, Serienproduktion _f_

mast MAR Mast _m_; _Br_ ELECTR Sendemast _m_

mas·ter 1. Meister _m_ (_a._ PAINT); Herr _m_; _esp Br_ Lehrer _m_; Original(kopie _f_) _n_; UNIV Magister _m_; **Master of Arts** (_abbr_ **MA**) Magister _m_ Artium; **~ of ceremonies** Conférencier _m_ **2.** Meister...; Haupt...; **~ copy** Originalkopie _f_; **~ tape** TECH Mastertape _n_, Originaltonband _n_ **3.** Herr sein über (_acc_); _Sprache etc_ beherrschen; _Aufgabe etc_ meistern

mas·ter key Hauptschlüssel _m_

mas·ter·ly meisterhaft, virtuos

mas·ter·piece Meisterstück _n_, -werk _n_

mas·ter·y Herrschaft _f_; Oberhand _f_; Beherrschung _f_

mas·tur·bate masturbieren, onanieren

mat[1] 1. Matte _f_; Untersetzer _m_ **2.** sich verfilzen

mat[2] mattiert, matt

match[1] Streichholz _n_, Zündholz _n_

match[2] 1. der, die, das Gleiche; (dazu) passende Sache _or_ Person, Gegenstück _n_; (_Fußball- etc_)Spiel _n_, (_Box- etc -_)Kampf _m_, (_Tennis- etc_)Match _n, m_; Heirat _f_; _gute etc_ Partie (_person_); **be a (no) ~ for s.o.** j-m (nicht) gewachsen sein; **find or meet one's ~** s-n Meister finden **2.** _v/t_ j-m, e-r Sache ebenbürtig _or_ gewachsen sein, gleichkommen; j-m, e-r Sache entsprechen, passen zu; _v/i_ zusammenpassen, übereinstimmen, entsprechen; **gloves to ~** dazu passende Handschuhe

match·box Streichholz-, Zündholzschächtel _f_

match·less unvergleichlich, einzigartig
match·mak·er Ehestifter(in)
match point *tennis etc*: Matchball *m*
mate¹ → *checkmate*
mate² 1. (Arbeits)Kamerad *m*, (-)Kollege *m*; ZO Männchen *n*, Weibchen *n*; MAR Maat *m* 2. ZO (sich) paaren
ma·te·ri·al 1. Material *n*, Stoff *m*; *writing ~s* Schreibmaterial(ien *pl*) *n* 2. materiell; leiblich; wesentlich
ma·ter·nal mütterlich, Mutter...; mütterlicherseits
ma·ter·ni·ty 1. Mutterschaft *f* 2. Schwangerschafts..., Umstands...
ma·ter·ni·ty|leave Mutterschaftsurlaub *m*; *~ ward* Entbindungsstation *f*
math F Mathe *f*
math·e·ma·ti·cian Mathematiker(in)
math·e·mat·ics Mathematik *f*
maths Br F Mathe *f*
mat·i·née THEA *etc* Nachmittagsvorstellung *f*
ma·tric·u·late (sich) immatrikulieren
mat·ri·mo·ni·al ehelich, Ehe...
mat·ri·mo·ny Ehe *f*, Ehestand *m*
ma·trix TECH Matrize *f*
ma·tron Br MED Oberschwester *f*; Hausmutter *f*; Matrone *f*
mat·ter 1. Materie *f*, Material *n*, Substanz *f*, Stoff *m*; MED Eiter *m*; Sache *f*, Angelegenheit *f*; *printed ~* Drucksache *f*; *what's the ~ (with you)?* was ist los (mit dir)?; *no ~ who* gleichgültig, wer; *for that ~* was das betrifft; *a ~ of course* e-e Selbstverständlichkeit; *a ~ of fact* e-e Tatsache; *as a ~ of fact* tatsächlich, eigentlich; *a ~ of form* e-e Formsache; *a ~ of time* e-e Frage der Zeit 2. von Bedeutung sein (*to* für); *it doesn't ~* es macht nichts
mat·ter-of-fact sachlich, nüchtern
mat·tress Matratze *f*
ma·ture 1. reif (*a. fig*) 2. (heran)reifen, reif werden
ma·tu·ri·ty Reife *f* (*a. fig*)
maud·lin rührselig
maul übel zurichten; *fig* verreißen
Maun·dy Thurs·day Gründonnerstag *m*
mauve malvenfarbig, mauve
mawk·ish rührselig
max·i... Maxi..., riesig, Riesen...
max·im Grundsatz *m*
max·i·mum 1. Maximum *n* 2. maximal, Maximal..., Höchst...

May Mai *m*
may *v/aux ich* kann / mag / darf *etc*, *du* kannst / magst / darfst *etc*
may·be vielleicht
may·bug ZO Maikäfer *m*
May Day der 1. Mai
may·on·naise Mayonnaise *f*
mayor Bürgermeister(in)
may·pole Maibaum *m*
maze Irrgarten *m*, Labyrinth *n* (*a. fig*)
me mich; mir; F ich
mead·ow Wiese *f*, Weide *f*
mea·ger, Br **mea·gre** mager (*a. fig*), dürr; dürftig
meal¹ Mahl(zeit *f*) *n*; Essen *n*
meal² Schrotmehl *n*
mean¹ gemein, niederträchtig; geizig, knauserig; schäbig
mean² meinen; sagen wollen; bedeuten; beabsichtigen, vorhaben; *be meant for* bestimmt sein für; *~ well (ill)* es gut (schlecht) meinen
mean³ 1. Mitte *f*, Mittel *n*, Durchschnitt *m* 2. mittlere(r, -s), Mittel..., durchschnittlich, Durchschnitts...
mean·ing 1. Sinn *m*, Bedeutung *f* 2. bedeutungsvoll, bedeutsam
mean·ing·ful bedeutungsvoll; sinnvoll
mean·ing·less sinnlos
means Mittel *n or pl*, Weg *m*; ECON Mittel *pl*, Vermögen *n*; *by all ~* auf alle Fälle, unbedingt; *by no ~* keineswegs, auf keinen Fall; *by ~ of* durch, mit
mean·time 1. inzwischen 2. *in the ~* inzwischen
mean·while inzwischen
mea·sles MED Masern *pl*
mea·sur·a·ble messbar
mea·sure 1. Maß *n* (*a. fig*); TECH Messgerät *n*; MUS Takt *m*; *fig* Maßnahme *f*; *beyond ~* über alle Maßen; *in a great ~* großenteils; *take ~s* Maßnahmen treffen *or* ergreifen 2. (ab-, aus-, ver)messen; *j-m* Maß nehmen; *~ up to* den Ansprüchen (*gen*) genügen; *measured* gemessen; wohlüberlegt; maßvoll
mea·sure·ment (Ver)Messung *f*; Maß *n*; *~ of ca·pac·i·ty* Hohlmaß *n*
mea·sur·ing tape → *tape measure*
meat GASTR Fleisch *n*; *cold ~* kalter Braten
meat·ball GASTR Fleischklößchen *n*
me·chan·ic Mechaniker(in)

mechanical 496

me·chan·i·cal mechanisch; Maschinen...

me·chan·ics PHYS Mechanik f

mech·a·nism Mechanismus m

mech·a·nize mechanisieren

med·al Medaille f; Orden m

med·al·(l)ist SPORT Medaillengewinner(in)

med·dle sich einmischen (**with, in** in acc); **med·dle·some** aufdringlich

me·di·a Medien pl

med·i·ae·val → **medieval**

me·di·an a. ~ **strip** MOT Mittelstreifen m

me·di·ate vermitteln

me·di·a·tion Vermittlung f

me·di·a·tor Vermittler m

med·ic MIL Sanitäter m

med·i·cal 1. medizinisch, ärztlich **2.** ärztliche Untersuchung

med·i·cal cer·tif·i·cate ärztliches Attest

med·i·cated medizinisch

me·di·ci·nal medizinisch, heilkräftig, Heil...

medi·cine Medizin f, a. Arznei f, a. Heilkunde f

med·i·e·val mittelalterlich

me·di·o·cre mittelmäßig

med·i·tate v/i (**on**) nachdenken (über acc); meditieren (über acc); v/t erwägen

med·i·ta·tion Nachdenken n; Meditation f

med·i·ta·tive nachdenklich

Med·i·ter·ra·ne·an Mittelmeer...

me·di·um 1. Mitte f; Mittel n; Medium n **2.** mittlere(r, -s), Mittel..., a. mittelmäßig, GASTR medium, halb gar

med·ley Gemisch n; MUS Medley n, Potpourri n

meek sanft(mütig), bescheiden

meet v/t treffen, sich treffen mit; begegnen (dat); j-n kennenlernen; j-n abholen; zusammentreffen mit, stoßen or treffen auf (acc); Wünschen entgegenkommen, entsprechen; e-r Forderung, Verpflichtung nachkommen; v/i zusammenkommen, -treten; sich begegnen, sich treffen; (feindlich) zusammenstoßen; SPORT aufeinandertreffen; sich kennenlernen; ~ **with** zusammentreffen mit; sich treffen mit; stoßen auf (Schwierigkeiten etc); erleben, erleiden

meet·ing Begegnung f, (Zusammen-) Treffen n; Versammlung f, Konferenz f, Tagung f; ~ **place** Tagungs-, Versammlungsort m; Treffpunkt m

mel·an·chol·y 1. Melancholie f, Schwermut f, Trübsinn m **2.** melancholisch, traurig, trübsinnig, wehmütig

mel·low 1. reif, weich; sanft, mild (light), zart (colors); fig gereift (person) **2.** reifen (lassen) (a. fig); weich or sanft werden

me·lo·di·ous melodisch

mel·o·dra·mat·ic melodramatisch

mel·o·dy MUS Melodie f

mel·on BOT Melone f

melt (zer)schmelzen; ~ **down** einschmelzen

mem·ber Mitglied n, Angehörige m, f; ANAT Glied n, Gliedmaße (männliches) Glied; **Member of Parliament** Br Mitglied n des Unterhauses, Unterhausabgeordnete m, f; **mem·ber·ship** Mitgliedschaft f; Mitgliederzahl f

mem·brane Membran(e) f

mem·o Memo n

mem·oirs Memoiren pl

mem·o·ra·ble denkwürdig

me·mo·ri·al Denkmal n, Ehrenmal n, Gedenkstätte f (**to** für); Gedenkfeier f (**to** für)

mem·o·rize auswendig lernen, sich et. einprägen

mem·o·ry Gedächtnis n; Erinnerung f; Andenken n; IT Speicher m; **in** ~ **of** zum Andenken an (acc)

men·ace 1. (be)drohen **2.** (Be)Drohung f

mend 1. v/t (ver)bessern; ausbessern, reparieren, flicken; ~ **one's ways** sich bessern; v/i sich bessern **2.** ausgebesserte Stelle; **on the** ~ auf dem Wege der Bess(e)rung

men·di·cant REL Bettelmönch m

me·ni·al niedrig, untergeordnet

men·in·gi·tis MED Meningitis f, Hirnhautentzündung f

men·o·pause MED Wechseljahre pl

men·stru·ate menstruieren

men·stru·a·tion Menstruation f

men·tal geistig, Geistes...; seelisch, psychisch; ~ **a·rith·me·tic** Kopfrechnen n; ~ **hand·i·cap** geistige Behinderung; ~ **hos·pi·tal** psychiatrische Klinik

men·tal·i·ty Mentalität f

men·tal·ly: ~ **handicapped** geistig behindert; ~ **ill** geisteskrank

men·tion 1. erwähnen; **don't** ~ **it!** keine

Ursache! **2.** Erwähnung *f*

men·u Speise(n)karte *f*; IT Menü *n*

me·ow ZO miauen

mer·can·tile Handels...

mer·ce·na·ry 1. geldgierig **2.** MIL Söldner *m*

mer·chan·dise 1. Ware(n *pl*) *f* **2.** vermarkten

mer·chan·dis·ing Vermarktung *f*

mer·chant 1. (Groß)Händler *m*, (Groß)Kaufmann *m* **2.** Handels...

mer·ci·ful barmherzig, gnädig

mer·ci·less unbarmherzig, erbarmungslos

mer·cu·ry CHEM Quecksilber *n*

mer·cy Barmherzigkeit *f*, Erbarmen *n*, Gnade *f*

mere, **mere·ly** bloß, nur

merge verschmelzen (*into*, *with* mit); ECON fusionieren

merg·er ECON Fusion *f*

me·rid·i·an GEOGR Meridian *m*; *fig* Gipfel *m*, Höhepunkt *m*

mer·it 1. Verdienst *n*; Wert *m*; Vorzug *m* **2.** verdienen

mer·maid Meerjungfrau *f*, Nixe *f*

mer·ri·ment Fröhlichkeit *f*; Gelächter *n*, Heiterkeit *f*

mer·ry lustig, fröhlich, ausgelassen; *Merry Christmas!* fröhliche *or* frohe Weihnachten

mer·ry-go-round Karussell *n*

mesh 1. Masche *f*; *fig often pl* Netz *n*, Schlingen *pl*; *be in* ~ TECH (ineinander)greifen **2.** TECH (ineinander)greifen; *fig* passen (*with* zu), zusammenpassen

mess 1. Unordnung *f*, Durcheinander *n*; Schmutz *m*, F Schweinerei *f*; F Patsche *f*, Klemme *f*; MIL Messe *f*, Kasino *n*; *make a ~ of* F *fig* verpfuschen, ruinieren, *Pläne etc* über den Haufen werfen **2.** ~ *about*, ~ *around* F herumspielen, herumbasteln (*with* an *dat*); herumgammeln; ~ *up* in Unordnung bringen, durcheinanderbringen; *fig* F verpfuschen, ruinieren, *Pläne etc* über den Haufen werfen

mes·sage Mitteilung *f*, Nachricht *f*; Anliegen *n*, Aussage *f*; *can I take a ~?* kann ich etwas ausrichten?; *get the ~* F kapieren; **mes·sen·ger** Bote *m*

mess·y unordentlich; unsauber, schmutzig

me·tab·o·lis·m MED Stoffwechsel *m*

met·al Metall *n*

me·tal·lic metallisch; Metall...

met·a·mor·pho·sis Metamorphose *f*, Verwandlung *f*

met·a·phor Metapher *f*

me·tas·ta·sis MED Metastase *f*

me·te·or Meteor *m*

me·te·or·o·log·i·cal meteorologisch, Wetter..., Witterungs...; ~ *of·fice* Wetteramt *n*

me·te·o·rol·o·gy Meteorologie *f*, Wetterkunde *f*

me·ter¹ TECH Messgerät *n*, Zähler *m*

me·ter² Meter *m*, *n*; Versmaß *n*

meth·od Methode *f*, Verfahren *n*; System *n*; **me·thod·i·cal** methodisch, systematisch, planmäßig

me·tic·u·lous peinlich genau, übergenau

me·tre *Br* → **meter²**

met·ric metrisch; ~ *sys·tem* metrisches (Maß- und Gewichts)System

me·trop·o·lis Weltstadt *f*

met·ro·pol·i·tan ... der Hauptstadt

met·tle Eifer *m*, Mut *m*, Feuer *n*

mew ZO miauen

Mex·i·can 1. mexikanisch **2.** Mexikaner(in)

Mex·i·co Mexiko *n*

mi·aow ZO miauen

mi·cro... Mikro..., (sehr) klein

mi·cro·chip Mikrochip *m*

mi·cro·e·lec·tron·ics Mikroelektronik *f*

mi·cro·film Mikrofilm *m*

mi·cro·or·gan·ism BIOL Mikroorganismus *m*

mi·cro·phone Mikrofon *n*

mi·cro·pro·ces·sor Mikroprozessor *m*

mi·cro·scope Mikroskop *n*

mi·cro·scop·ic mikroskopisch

mi·cro·wave Mikrowelle *f*; ~ *ov·en* Mikrowellenherd *m*

mid mittlere(r, -s), Mitt(el)...

mid·air: *in* ~ in der Luft

mid·day 1. Mittag *m* **2.** mittägig, Mittag(s)...

mid·dle 1. mittlere(r, -s), Mittel... **2.** Mitte *f*

mid·dle-aged mittleren Alters

Mid·dle Ag·es HIST Mittelalter *n*

mid·dle class(·es) Mittelstand *m*

mid·dle·man ECON Zwischenhändler *m*; Mittelsmann *m*

mid·dle name zweiter Vorname *m*
mid·dle-sized mittelgroß
mid·dle-weight *boxing:* Mittelgewicht *n*, Mittelgewichtler *m*
mid·dling F mittelmäßig, Mittel...; leidlich
mid·field *esp soccer:* Mittelfeld *n*
mid·field·er, mid·field play·er *esp soccer:* Mittelfeldspieler *m*
midge zo Mücke *f*
midg·et Zwerg *m*, Knirps *m*
mid·night Mitternacht *f*; **at ~** um Mitternacht
midst: **in the ~ of** mitten in (*dat*)
mid·sum·mer Hochsommer *m*; ASTR Sommersonnenwende *f*
mid·way auf halbem Wege
mid·wife Hebamme *f*
mid·win·ter Mitte *f* des Winters; ASTR Wintersonnenwende *f*; **in ~** mitten im Winter
might Macht *f*, Gewalt *f*; Kraft *f*
might·y mächtig, gewaltig
mi·grate (aus)wandern, (fort)ziehen (*a.* zo)
mi·gra·tion Wanderung *f* (*a.* zo)
mi·gra·to·ry Wander...; zo Zug...
mike F Mikrofon *n*
mild mild, sanft, leicht
mil·dew BOT Mehltau *m*
mild·ness Milde *f*
mile Meile *f* (*1,6 km*)
mile·age zurückgelegte Meilenzahl or Fahrtstrecke; Meilenstand *m*; *a.* **~ al·lowance** Meilengeld *n*, *appr* Kilometergeld *n*
mile·stone Meilenstein *m* (*a. fig*)
mil·i·tant militant; streitbar, kriegerisch
mil·i·ta·ry 1. militärisch, Militär... **2.** *the* **~** das Militär; **~ gov·ern·ment** Militärregierung *f*; **~ po·lice** (*abbr MP*) Militärpolizei *f*
mi·li·tia Miliz *f*, Bürgerwehr *f*
milk 1. Milch *f*; *it's no use crying over spilt* **~** geschehen ist geschehen **2.** *v/t* melken; *v/i* Milch geben; **~ choc·olate** Vollmilchschokolade *f*
milk·man Milchmann *m*
milk pow·der Milchpulver *n*, Trockenmilch *f*
milk shake Milchmixgetränk *n*
milk tooth ANAT Milchzahn *m*
milk·y milchig; Milch...
Milky Way ASTR Milchstraße *f*

mill 1. Mühle *f*; Fabrik *f* **2.** *Korn etc* mahlen; *Metall* verarbeiten; *Münze* rändeln
mil·le·pede → **millipede**
mill·er Müller *m*
mil·let BOT Hirse *f*
mil·li·ner Hutmacherin *f*, Putzmacherin *f*, Modistin *f*
mil·lion Million *f*
mil·lion·aire Millionär(in)
mil·lionth 1. millionste(r, -s) **2.** Millionstel *n*
mil·li·pede zo Tausendfüß(l)er *m*
mill·stone Mühlstein *m*; *be a ~ round s.o.'s neck fig* j-m ein Klotz am Bein sein
milt zo Milch *f*
mime 1. Pantomime *f*; Pantomime *m* **2.** (panto)mimisch darstellen; **mim·ic 1.** mimisch; Schein... **2.** Imitator *m* **3.** nachahmen; nachäffen; **mim·ic·ry** Nachahmung *f*; zo Mimikry *f*
mince 1. *v/t* zerhacken, (zer)schneiden; *he does not ~ matters or his words* er nimmt kein Blatt vor den Mund; *v/i* tänzeln, trippeln **2.** *a.* **~d meat** Hackfleisch *n*; **minc·er** Fleischwolf *m*
mind 1. Sinn *m*, Gemüt *n*; Herz *n*; Verstand *m*, Geist *m*; Ansicht *f*, Meinung *f*; Absicht *f*, Neigung *f*, Lust *f*; Erinnerung *f*, Gedächtnis *n*; *be out of one's* **~** nicht (recht) bei Sinnen sein; *bear or keep in* **~** (immer) denken an (*acc*), *et.* nicht vergessen; *change one's* **~** es sich anders überlegen, s-e Meinung ändern; *enter s.o.'s* **~** j-m in den Sinn kommen; *give s.o. a piece of one's* **~** j-m gründlich die Meinung sagen; *have (half) a* **~** *to inf* (nicht übel) Lust haben zu *inf*; *lose one's* **~** den Verstand verlieren; *make up one's* **~** sich entschließen, e-n Entschluss fassen; *to my* **~** meiner Ansicht nach **2.** *v/t* achtgeben auf (*acc*); sehen nach, aufpassen auf (*acc*); *et.* haben gegen; **~ the step!** Vorsicht, Stufe!; *mind your own business!* kümmere dich um deine eigenen Angelegenheiten!; *do you* **~** *if I smoke?*, *do you* **~** *my smoking?* haben Sie et. dagegen or stört es Sie, wenn ich rauche?; *would you* **~** *opening the window?* würden Sie bitte das Fenster öffnen?; *would you* **~** *coming* würden Sie bitte kommen?; *v/i* aufpassen; et. dage-

gen haben; ~ (*you*) wohlgemerkt, allerdings; *never* ~! macht nichts!, ist schon gut!; *I don't* ~ meinetwegen, von mir aus

mind·less gedankenlos, blind; unbekümmert (*of* um), ohne Rücksicht (*of* auf *acc*)

mine[1] meins; *that's* ~ das gehört mir

mine[2] **1.** Bergwerk *n*, Mine *f*, Zeche *f*, Grube *f*; MIL Mine *f*; *fig* Fundgrube *f* **2.** *v/i* schürfen, graben (**for** nach); *v/t* Erz, *Kohle* abbauen; MIL verminen

min·er Bergmann *m*, Kumpel *m*

min·e·ral 1. Mineral *n*; *pl Br* Mineralwasser *n* **2.** Mineral…; ~ **oil** Mineralöl *n*; ~ **wa·ter** Mineralwasser *n*

min·gle *v/t* (ver)mischen; *v/i* sich mischen *or* mengen (**with** unter)

min·i… Mini…, Klein(st)…; → *miniskirt*

min·i·a·ture 1. Miniatur(gemälde *n*) *f* **2.** Miniatur…; Klein…; ~ **cam·e·ra** Kleinbildkamera *f*

min·i·mize auf ein Mindestmaß herabsetzen; herunterspielen, bagatellisieren

min·i·mum 1. Minimum *n*, Mindestmaß *n* **2.** minimal, Mindest…

min·ing 1. Bergbau *m* **2.** Berg(bau)…, Bergwerks…; Gruben…

min·i·skirt Minirock *m*

min·is·ter POL Minister(in); Gesandte *m*; REL Geistliche *m*; **min·is·try** POL Ministerium *n*; REL geistliches Amt

mink ZO Nerz *m*

mi·nor 1. kleinere(r, -s), *fig a.* unbedeutend, geringfügig; JUR minderjährig; *A* ~ MUS a-Moll *n*; ~ **key** MUS Moll(tonart *f*) *n* **2.** Minderjährige *m, f*; UNIV Nebenfach *n*; MUS Moll *n*; **mi·nor·i·ty** Minderheit *f*; JUR Minderjährigkeit *f*

min·ster *Br* Münster *n*

mint[1] **1.** Münze *f*, Münzanstalt *f* **2.** prägen

mint[2] BOT Minze *f*

min·u·et MUS Menuett *n*

mi·nus 1. *prp* minus, weniger; F ohne **2.** *adj* Minus… **3.** Minus *n*, *fig a.* Nachteil *m*

min·ute[1] Minute *f*; Augenblick *m*; *in a* ~ sofort; *just a* ~! Moment mal!

mi·nute[2] winzig; sehr genau

min·utes Protokoll *n*; *take* (*or* keep) *the* ~ (das) Protokoll führen

mir·a·cle Wunder *n*

mi·rac·u·lous wunderbar

mi·rac·u·lous·ly wie durch ein Wunder

mi·rage Luftspiegelung *f*, Fata Morgana *f*

mire Schlamm *m*; *drag through the* ~ *fig* in den Schmutz ziehen

mir·ror 1. Spiegel *m* **2.** (wider)spiegeln (*a. fig*)

mis… miss…, falsch, schlecht

mis·ad·ven·ture Missgeschick *n*; Unglück *n*, Unglücksfall *m*

mis·an·thrope, mis·an·thro·pist Menschenfeind(in)

mis·ap·ply falsch an- *or* verwenden

mis·ap·pre·hend missverstehen

mis·ap·pro·pri·ate unterschlagen, veruntreuen

mis·be·have sich schlecht benehmen

mis·cal·cu·late falsch berechnen; sich verrechnen (in *dat*)

mis·car·riage MED Fehlgeburt *f*; Misslingen *n*, Fehlschlag(en *n*) *m*; ~ *of justice* JUR Fehlurteil *n*

mis·car·ry MED e-e Fehlgeburt haben; misslingen, scheitern

mis·cel·la·ne·ous gemischt, vermischt; verschiedenartig

mis·cel·la·ny Gemisch *n*; Sammelband *m*

mis·chief Schaden *m*; Unfug *m*; Übermut *m*

mis·chie·vous boshaft, mutwillig; schelmisch

mis·con·ceive falsch auffassen, missverstehen

mis·con·duct schlechtes Benehmen; schlechte Führung; Verfehlung *f*

mis·con·strue falsch auslegen, missdeuten

mis·de·mea·no(u)r JUR Vergehen *n*

mis·di·rect fehlleiten, irreleiten; *Brief etc* falsch adressieren

mise-en-scène THEA Inszenierung *f*

mi·ser Geizhals *m*

mis·e·ra·ble erbärmlich, kläglich, elend; unglücklich

mi·ser·ly geizig, F knick(e)rig

mis·e·ry Elend *n*, Not *f*

mis·fire versagen (*gun*); MOT fehlzünden, aussetzen; *fig* danebengehen

mis·fit Außenseiter(in)

mis·for·tune Unglück *n*, Unglücksfall *m*; Missgeschick *n*

mis·giv·ing Befürchtung *f*, Zweifel *m*

mis·guid·ed irregeleitet, irrig, unangebracht

mis·hap Unglück *n*; Missgeschick *n*; **without ~** ohne Zwischenfälle

mis·in·form falsch unterrichten

mis·in·ter·pret missdeuten, falsch auffassen *or* auslegen

mis·lay *et.* verlegen

mis·lead irreführen, täuschen; verleiten

mis·man·age schlecht verwalten *or* führen *or* handhaben

mis·place *et.* an e-e falsche Stelle legen *or* setzen; *et.* verlegen; **~d** *fig* unangebracht, deplatziert

mis·print 1. verdrucken **2.** Druckfehler *m*

mis·read falsch lesen; falsch deuten, missdeuten

mis·rep·re·sent falsch darstellen; entstellen, verdrehen

miss 1. *v/t* verpassen, versäumen, verfehlen; übersehen, nicht bemerken; überhören; nicht verstehen *or* begreifen; vermissen; *a.* **~ out** auslassen, übergehen, überspringen; *v/i* nicht treffen; missglücken; **~ out on** *et.* verpassen **2.** Fehlschuss *m*, Fehlstoß *m*, Fehlwurf *m etc*; Verpassen *n*, Verfehlen *n*

Miss Fräulein *n*

mis·shap·en missgebildet

mis·sile 1. Geschoss *n*; Rakete *f* **2.** Raketen...

miss·ing fehlend; **be ~** fehlen, verschwunden *or* weg sein; (MIL *a.* **~ in action**) vermisst; **be~** MIL vermisst sein *or* werden

mis·sion (*Militär- etc*)Mission *f*; *esp* POL Auftrag *m*, Mission *f* (*a.* REL); MIL, AVIAT Einsatz *m*

mis·sion·a·ry REL Missionar *m*

mis·spell falsch buchstabieren *or* schreiben

mis·spend falsch verwenden; vergeuden

mist 1. (feiner *or* leichter) Nebel **2.** **~ over** sich trüben; **~ up** (sich) beschlagen

mis·take 1. verwechseln (**for** mit); verkennen, sich irren in (*dat*); falsch verstehen, missverstehen **2.** Irrtum *m*, Versehen *n*, Fehler *m*; **by ~** aus Versehen, irrtümlich; **mis·tak·en** irrig,

falsch (verstanden); **be ~** sich irren

mis·tle·toe BOT Mistel *f*

mis·tress Herrin *f*; *esp Br* Lehrerin *f*; Geliebte *f*

mis·trust 1. misstrauen (*dat*) **2.** Misstrauen *n* (**of** gegen)

mis·trust·ful misstrauisch

mist·y (leicht) neb(e)lig; *fig* unklar, verschwommen

mis·un·der·stand missverstehen; *j-n* nicht verstehen; **mis·un·der·standing** Missverständnis *n*

mis·use 1. missbrauchen; falsch gebrauchen **2.** Missbrauch *m*

mite ZO Milbe *f*; kleines Ding, Würmchen *n*; **a ~** F ein bisschen

mi·ter, *Br* **mi·tre** REL Mitra *f*, Bischofsmütze *f*

mitt *baseball*: Fanghandschuh *m*; → **mitten** Fausthandschuh *m*

mix 1. (ver)mischen, vermengen; *Getränke* mixen; sich (ver)mischen; sich mischen lassen; verkehren (**with** mit); **~ well** kontaktfreudig sein; **~ up** zusammenmischen, durcheinander mischen; (völlig) durcheinanderbringen; verwechseln (**with** mit); **be ~ed up** verwickelt sein *or* werden (**in** in *acc*); (*geistig*) ganz durcheinander sein **2.** Mischung *f*

mixed gemischt (*a. fig*); vermischt, Misch...

mix·er Mixer *m*; TECH Mischmaschine *f*; *radio*, TV *etc*: Mischpult *n*

mix·ture Mischung *f*; Gemisch *n*

mix-up F Verwechs(e)lung *f*

moan 1. Stöhnen *n* **2.** stöhnen

moat (Burg-, Stadt)Graben *m*

mob 1. Mob *m*, Pöbel *m* **2.** herfallen über (*acc*); *j-n* bedrängen, belagern

mo·bile 1. beweglich; MIL mobil, motorisiert; *fig* lebhaft **2.** → **mobile phone** *or* **telephone**; **~ home** Wohnwagen *m*; **~ phone**, **~ tel·e·phone** Mobiltelefon *n*, Handy *n*

mo·bil·ize mobilisieren, MIL *a.* mobil machen

moc·ca·sin Mokassin *m*

mock 1. *v/t* verspotten; nachäffen; *v/i* sich lustig machen, spotten (**at** über *acc*); **2.** nachgemacht, Schein...

mock·e·ry Spott *m*, Hohn *m*; Gespött *n*

mock·ing·bird ZO Spottdrossel *f*

mode (Art *f* und) Weise *f*; IT Modus *m*,

Betriebsart *f*

mod·el 1. Modell *n*; Muster *n*; Vorbild *n*; Mannequin *n*; Model *n*, (Foto)Modell *n*; TECH Modell *n*, Typ *m*; *male*~ Dressman *m* **2.** Modell..., Muster... **3.** *v/t* modellieren, *a. fig* formen; *Kleider etc* vorführen; *v/i* Modell stehen *or* sitzen; als Mannequin *or* (Foto)Modell *or* Dressman arbeiten

mo·dem IT Modem *m, n*

mod·e·rate 1. (mittel)mäßig; gemäßigt; vernünftig, angemessen **2.** (sich) mäßigen

mod·e·ra·tion Mäßigung *f*

mod·ern modern, neu

mod·ern·ize modernisieren

mod·est bescheiden

mod·es·ty Bescheidenheit *f*

mod·i·fi·ca·tion (Ab-, Ver)Änderung *f*

mod·i·fy (ab-, ver)ändern

mod·u·late modulieren

mod·ule TECH Modul *n*, ELECTR *a.* Baustein *m*; (*Kommando- etc*)Kapsel *f*

moist feucht

moist·en *v/t* anfeuchten, befeuchten; *v/i* feucht werden

mois·ture Feuchtigkeit *f*

mo·lar ANAT Backenzahn *m*

mo·las·ses Sirup *m*

mold¹ Schimmel *m*; Moder *m*; Humus (-boden) *m*

mold² TECH **1.** (Gieß-, Guss-, Press-) Form *f* **2.** gießen; formen

mol·der *a.* ~ *away* vermodern; zerfallen

mold·y verschimmelt, schimm(e)lig; mod(e)rig

mole¹ ZO Maulwurf *m*

mole² Muttermal *n*, Leberfleck *m*

mole³ Mole *f*, Hafendamm *m*

mol·e·cule Molekül *n*

mole·hill Maulwurfshügel *m*; *make a mountain out of a* ~ aus e-r Mücke e-n Elefanten machen

mo·lest belästigen

mol·li·fy besänftigen, beschwichtigen

mol·lusc *Br*, **mol·lusk** ZO Weichtier *n*

mol·ly·cod·dle F verhätscheln, verzärteln

molt (sich) mausern; *Haare* verlieren

mol·ten geschmolzen

mom F Mami *f*, Mutti *f*

mom-and-pop store Tante-Emma-Laden *m*

mo·ment Moment *m*, Augenblick *m*;

Bedeutung *f*; PHYS Moment *n*

mo·men·ta·ry momentan, augenblicklich

mo·men·tous bedeutsam, folgenschwer

mo·men·tum PHYS Moment *n*; Schwung *m*

Mon *abbr of Monday* Mo., Montag *m*

mon·arch Monarch(in), Herrscher(in)

mon·ar·chy Monarchie *f*

mon·as·tery REL (Mönchs)Kloster *n*

Mon·day (*abbr* **Mon**) Montag *m*; *on* ~ (am) Montag; *on* ~*s* montags

mon·e·ta·ry ECON Währungs...; Geld...

mon·ey Geld *n*

mon·ey·box *Br* Sparbüchse *f*

mon·ey·chang·er (Geld)Wechsler *m*; TECH Wechselautomat *m*

mon·ey or·der Post- *or* Zahlungsanweisung *f*

mon·grel ZO Bastard *m, esp* Promenadenmischung *f*

mon·i·tor 1. Monitor *m*; Kontrollgerät *n*, -schirm *m* **2.** abhören; überwachen

monk REL Mönch *m*

mon·key 1. ZO Affe *m*; F (kleiner) Schlingel; *make a* ~ (*out*) *of s.o.* F j-n zum Deppen machen **2.** ~ *about*, ~ *around* F (herum)albern; ~ *about or around with* F herumspielen mit *or* an (*dat*) herummurksen an (*dat*); ~ *wrench* TECH Engländer *m*, Franzose *m*; *throw a* ~ *into s.th.* F et. behindern

mon·o 1. Mono *n*; F Monogerät *n* **2.** Mono...

mon·o... ein..., mono...

mon·o·log, *esp Br* **mon·o·logue** Monolog *m*

mo·nop·o·lize monopolisieren; *fig* an sich reißen

mo·nop·o·ly Monopol *n* (*of* auf *acc*)

mo·not·o·nous monoton, eintönig

mo·not·o·ny Monotonie *f*

mon·soon Monsun *m*

mon·ster 1. Monster *n*, Ungeheuer *n* (*a. fig*); Monstrum *n* **2.** Riesen...

mon·stros·i·ty Ungeheuerlichkeit *f*; Monstrum *n*; **mon·strous** ungeheuer; *mst contp* ungeheuerlich; scheußlich

month Monat *m*; **month·ly 1.** monatlich, Monats... **2.** Monatsschrift *f*

mon·u·ment Monument *n*, Denkmal *n*

mon·u·men·tal monumental; F kolossal, Riesen...; Gedenk...

moo ZO muhen

mooch F schnorren

mood Stimmung f, Laune f; *be in a good* (*bad*) ~ gute (schlechte) Laune haben, gut (schlecht) aufgelegt sein

mood·y launisch; schlecht gelaunt

moon 1. ASTR Mond m **2.** ~ *about*, ~ *around* F herumtrödeln; F ziellos herumstreichen

moon·light Mondlicht n, -schein m

moon·lit mondhell

moor[1] (Hoch)Moor n

moor[2] MAR vertäuen, festmachen

moor·ings MAR Vertäuung f; Liegeplatz m

moose ZO *nordamerikanischer* Elch

mop 1. Mopp m; F (Haar)Wust m **2.** wischen; ~ *up* aufwischen

mope Trübsal blasen

mo·ped *Br* MOT Moped n

mor·al 1. moralisch; Moral..., Sitten... **2.** Moral f, Lehre f; pl Moral f, Sitten pl

mo·rale Moral f, Stimmung f

mor·al·ize moralisieren (*about, on* über acc)

mor·bid morbid, krankhaft

more 1. adj mehr; noch (mehr); *some* ~ *tea* noch etwas Tee **2.** adv mehr; noch; ~ *and* ~ immer mehr; ~ *or less* mehr oder weniger; *once* ~ noch einmal; *the* ~ *so because* umso mehr, da; ~ *important* wichtiger; ~ *often* öfter **3.** Mehr n (*of* an dat); *a little* ~ etwas mehr

mo·rel BOT Morchel f

more·o·ver außerdem, weiter, ferner

morgue Leichenschauhaus n; F (Zeitungs)Archiv n

morn·ing Morgen m; Vormittag m; *good* ~! guten Morgen!; *in the* ~ morgens, am Morgen; vormittags, am Vormittag; *tomorrow* ~ morgen früh or Vormittag

mo·rose mürrisch, verdrießlich

mor·phi·a, mor·phine PHARM Morphium n

mor·sel Bissen m, Happen m; *a* ~ *of* ein bisschen

mor·tal 1. sterblich; tödlich; Tod(es)... **2.** Sterbliche m, f

mor·tal·i·ty Sterblichkeit f

mor·tar[1] Mörtel m

mor·tar[2] Mörser m

mort·gage 1. Hypothek f **2.** mit e-r Hypothek belasten, e-e Hypothek aufnehmen auf (acc)

mor·ti·cian Leichenbestatter m

mor·ti·fi·ca·tion Kränkung f; Ärger m, Verdruss m

mor·ti·fy kränken; ärgern, verdrießen

mor·tu·a·ry Leichenhalle f

mo·sa·ic Mosaik n

Mos·lem → *Muslim*

mosque Moschee f

mos·qui·to ZO Moskito m; Stechmücke f

moss BOT Moos n

moss·y BOT moosig, bemoost

most 1. adj meiste(r, -s), größte(r, -s); die meisten; ~ *people* die meisten Leute **2.** adv am meisten; ~ *of all* am allermeisten; *before adj:* höchst, äußerst; *the* ~ *important point* der wichtigste Punkt **3.** das meiste, *das* Höchste; das meiste, der größte Teil; die meisten pl; *at* (*the*) ~ höchstens; *make the* ~ *of et.* nach Kräften ausnutzen, das Beste herausholen aus

most·ly hauptsächlich, meist(ens)

mo·tel Motel n

moth ZO Motte f

moth-eat·en mottenzerfressen

moth·er 1. Mutter f **2.** bemuttern

moth·er coun·try Vaterland n, Heimatland n; Mutterland n

moth·er·hood Mutterschaft f

moth·er-in-law Schwiegermutter f

moth·er·ly mütterlich

moth·er-of-pearl Perlmutter f, n, Perlmutt n

moth·er tongue Muttersprache f

mo·tif Motiv n

mo·tion 1. Bewegung f; PARL Antrag m; *in quick* ~ *film:* im Zeitraffer; *in slow* ~ *film:* in Zeitlupe; *put or set in* ~ in Gang bringen (*a. fig*), in Bewegung setzen **2.** v/t j-n durch e-n Wink auffordern, j-m ein Zeichen geben; v/i winken

mo·tion·less bewegungslos, unbeweglich

mo·tion pic·ture Film m

mo·ti·vate motivieren, anspornen

mo·ti·va·tion Motivation f, Ansporn m

mo·tive 1. Motiv n, Beweggrund m **2.** treibend (*a. fig*)

mot·ley bunt

mo·to·cross SPORT Motocross n

mo·tor 1. Motor m, fig a. treibende Kraft **2.** Motor...

mo·tor·bike Moped *n*; *Br* F Motorrad *n*
mo·tor·boat Motorboot *n*
mo·tor·cade Auto-, Wagenkolonne *f*
mo·tor·car *Br* Kraftfahrzeug *n*
mo·tor car·a·van *Br* Wohnmobil *n*
mo·tor·cy·cle Motorrad *n*
mo·tor·cy·clist Motorradfahrer(in)
mo·tor home Wohnmobil *n*
mo·tor·ing Autofahren *n*; *school of ~* Fahrschule *f*
mo·tor·ist Autofahrer(in)
mo·tor·ize motorisieren
mo·tor launch Motorbarkasse *f*
mo·tor·way *Br* Autobahn *f*
mot·tled gefleckt, gesprenkelt
mould¹ *Br* → *mold¹*
mould² *Br* → *mold²*
moul·der *Br* → *molder*
mould·y *Br* → *moldy*
moult *Br* → *molt*
mound Erdhügel *m*, Erdwall *m*
mount 1. *v/t* Pferd *etc* besteigen, steigen auf (*acc*); montieren; anbringen, befestigen; *Bild etc* aufziehen, aufkleben; *Edelstein* fassen; *~ed police* berittene Polizei; *v/i* aufsitzen (*rider*); steigen, *fig a.* (an)wachsen; *~ up to* sich belaufen auf (*acc*) **2.** Gestell *n*; Fassung *f*; Reittier *n*, Reitpferd *n*
moun·tain 1. Berg *m*, *pl a.* Gebirge *n* **2.** Berg..., Gebirgs...
moun·tain bike Mountainbike *n*
moun·tain·eer Bergsteiger(in)
moun·tain·eer·ing Bergsteigen *n*
moun·tain·ous bergig, gebirgig
mourn *v/i* trauern (*for, over* um); *v/t* betrauern, trauern um
mourn·er Trauernde *m*, *f*
mourn·ful traurig
mourn·ing Trauer *f*; Trauerkleidung *f*
mouse zo Maus *f* (*a.* IT)
mous·tache → *mustache*
mouth Mund *m*; zo Maul *n*, Schnauze *f*; GEOGR Mündung *f*; Öffnung *f*
mouth·ful *ein* Mundvoll; Bissen *m*
mouth or·gan F Mundharmonika *f*
mouth·piece Mundstück *n*; *fig* Sprachrohr *n*
mouth·wash Mundwasser *n*
mo·va·ble beweglich
move 1. *v/t* (weg)rücken; transportieren; bewegen, rühren (*both a. fig*); *chess etc*: e-n Zug machen mit; PARL beantragen; *~ house* umziehen; *~ heav-*

en and earth Himmel und Hölle in Bewegung setzen; *v/i* sich (fort)bewegen; sich rühren; umziehen (*to* nach); *chess etc*: e-n Zug machen; *~away* weg-, fortziehen; *~ in* einziehen; *~ off* sich in Bewegung setzen; *~ on* weitergehen; *~ out* ausziehen **2.** Bewegung *f*; Umzug *m*; *chess etc*: Zug *m*; *fig* Schritt *m*; *on the ~* in Bewegung; auf den Beinen; *get a ~ on!* F Tempo!, mach(t) schon!, los!
move·a·ble → *movable*
move·ment Bewegung *f* (*a. fig*); MUS Satz *m*; TECH Werk *n*
mov·ie F **1.** Film *m*; Kino *n* **2.** Film..., Kino...; *~ cam·e·ra* Filmkamera *f*; *~ star* Filmstar *m*; *~ thea·ter* Kino *n*
mov·ing sich bewegend, beweglich; *fig* rührend; *~ stair·case* Rolltreppe *f*; *~ van* Möbelwagen *m*
mow mähen
mow·er Mähmaschine *f*, *esp* Rasenmäher *m*
MP3 player MP3–Player *m*
Mr. *abbr of* **Mister** Herr *m*
Mrs. Frau *f*
Ms. Frau *f*
much 1. *adj* viel **2.** *adv* sehr; viel; *~ better* viel besser; *very ~* sehr; *I thought as ~* das habe ich mir gedacht **3.** große Sache; *nothing ~* nichts Besonderes; *make ~ of* viel Wesens machen von; *think ~ of* viel halten von; *I am not ~ of a dancer* F ich bin kein großer Tänzer
muck F *Br* AGR Mist *m*, Dung *m*; *fig* Dreck *m*, Schmutz *m*; F *contp* Fraß *m*
mu·cus (Nasen)Schleim *m*
mud Schlamm *m*, Matsch *m*; Schmutz *m* (*a. fig*)
mud·dle 1. Durcheinander *n*; *be in a ~* durcheinander sein **2.** *a. ~ up* durcheinanderbringen; *~ through* F sich durchwursteln
mud·dy schlammig, trüb; schmutzig; *fig* wirr
mud·guard Kotflügel *m*; Schutzblech *n*
mues·li Müsli *n*
muff Muff *m*
muf·fle Ton *etc* dämpfen; *often ~ up* einhüllen, einwickeln
muf·fler (dicker) Schal; MOT Auspufftopf *m*
mug¹ Krug *m*; Becher *m*; große Tasse; F

Visage *f*; V Fresse *f*

mug² F überfallen und ausrauben

mug·ger F (Straßen)Räuber *m*

mug·ging F Raubüberfall *m*, *esp* Straßenraub *m*

mug·gy schwül

mul·ber·ry BOT Maulbeerbaum *m*; Maulbeere *f*

mule ZO Maultier *n*; Maulesel *m*

mulled: ~ *wine* Glühwein *m*

mul·li·on ARCH Mittelpfosten *m*

mul·ti... viel..., mehr..., Mehrfach..., Multi...

mul·ti·cul·tur·al multikulturell

mul·ti·far·i·ous mannigfaltig, vielfältig

mul·ti·lat·e·ral vielseitig; POL multilateral, mehrseitig

mul·ti·me·di·a multimedial

mul·ti·na·tion·al ECON multinationaler Konzern, F Multi *m*

mul·ti·ple 1. vielfach, mehrfach **2.** MATH Vielfache *n*

mul·ti·pli·ca·tion Vermehrung *f*; MATH Multiplikation *f*; ~ **table** Einmaleins *n*

mul·ti·pli·ci·ty Vielfalt *f*; Vielzahl *f*

mul·ti·ply (sich) vermehren, (sich) vervielfachen; MATH multiplizieren, malnehmen (**by** mit)

mul·ti·pur·pose Mehrzweck...

mul·ti·sto·rey *Br* mehrstöckig; ~ **car park** *Br* Park(hoch)haus *n*

mul·ti·tude Vielzahl *f*

mul·ti·tu·di·nous zahlreich

mum¹ *Br* F Mami *f*, Mutti *f*

mum² 1. *int*: ~'**s the word** Mund halten!, kein Wort darüber! **2.** *adj*: **keep** ~ nichts verraten, den Mund halten

mum·ble murmeln, F nuscheln; mümmeln

mum·mi·fy mumifizieren

mum·my¹ Mumie *f*

mum·my² *Br* F Mami *f*, Mutti *f*

mumps MED Ziegenpeter *m*, Mumps *m*

munch mampfen

mun·dane alltäglich; weltlich

mu·ni·ci·pal städtisch, Stadt..., kommunal, Gemeinde...; ~ **council** Stadt-, Gemeinderat *m*

mu·ni·ci·pal·i·ty Kommunalbehörde *f*; Stadtverwaltung *f*

mu·ral Wandgemälde *n*

mur·der 1. Mord *m*, Ermordung *f* **2.** Mord... **3.** ermorden; F verschandeln

mur·der·er Mörder *m*

mur·der·ess Mörderin *f*

mur·der·ous mörderisch

murk·y dunkel, finster

mur·mur 1. Murmeln *n*; Gemurmel *n*; Murren *n* **2.** murmeln; murren

mus·cle Muskel *m*

mus·cu·lar Muskel...; muskulös

muse¹ (nach)sinnen, (nach)grübeln (**on, over** über *acc*)

muse² *a.* **Muse** Muse *f*

mu·se·um Museum *n*

mush Brei *m*, Mus *n*; Maisbrei *m*

mush·room 1. BOT Pilz *m*, *esp* Champignon *m* **2.** rasch wachsen; ~ **up** *fig* (wie Pilze) aus dem Boden schießen

mu·sic Musik *f*; Noten *pl*; **put** *or* **set to** ~ vertonen

mu·sic·al 1. musikalisch; Musik... **2.** Musical *n*; ~ **box** *esp Br* Spieldose *f*; ~ **in·stru·ment** Musikinstrument *n*

mu·sic| box Spieldose *f*; ~ **cen·ter** (*Br* **cen·ter**) Kompaktanlage *f*; ~ **hall** *Br* Varietee(theater) *n*

mu·si·cian Musiker(in)

mu·sic stand Notenständer *m*

musk Moschus *m*

musk·rat ZO Bisamratte *f*; Bisampelz *m*

Mus·lim 1. Muslim *m*, Moslem *m* **2.** muslimisch, moslemisch

mus·sel ZO (Mies)Muschel *f*

must¹ 1. *v/aux* ich muss, *du* musst *etc*; **you** ~ **not** (F **mustn't**) du darfst nicht **2.** Muss *n*

must² Most *m*

mus·tache Schnurrbart *m*

mus·tard Senf *m*

mus·ter 1. ~ **up** *s-e Kraft etc* aufbieten; *s-n Mut* zusammennehmen **2.** **pass** ~ *fig* Zustimmung finden (**with** bei); den Anforderungen genügen

must·y mod(e)rig, muffig

mu·ta·tion Veränderung *f*; BIOL Mutation *f*

mute 1. stumm **2.** Stumme *m*, *f*; MUS Dämpfer *m*

mu·ti·late verstümmeln

mu·ti·la·tion Verstümmelung *f*

mu·ti·neer Meuterer *m*

mu·ti·nous meuternd; rebellisch

mu·ti·ny 1. Meuterei *f* **2.** meutern

mut·ter 1. murmeln; murren **2.** Murmeln *n*; Murren *n*

mut·ton GASTR Hammel-, Schaffleisch *n*; **leg of** ~ Hammelkeule *f*

native

mut·ton chop GASTR Hammelkotelett *n*
mu·tu·al gegenseitig; gemeinsam
muz·zle 1. ZO Maul *n*, Schnauze *f*; Mündung *f* (*of a gun*); Maulkorb *m* **2.** e-n Maulkorb anlegen (*dat*), *fig a.* j-n mundtot machen
my mein(e)
myrrh BOT Myrrhe *f*
myr·tle BOT Myrte *f*
my·self ich, mich *or* mir selbst; mich; mich (selbst); *by* ~ allein

mys·te·ri·ous rätselhaft, unerklärlich; geheimnisvoll, mysteriös
mys·te·ry Geheimnis *n*, Rätsel *n*; REL Mysterium *n*; ~ *tour* Fahrt *f* ins Blaue
mys·tic 1. Mystiker(in) **2.** → **mystic·al** mystisch
mys·ti·fy verwirren, vor ein Rätsel stellen; *be mystified* vor e-m Rätsel stehen
myth Mythos *m*, Sage *f*
my·thol·o·gy Mythologie *f*

N

N, n N, n *n*
nab F schnappen, erwischen
na·dir ASTR Nadir *m*; *fig* Tiefpunkt *m*
nag¹ 1. nörgeln; ~ (*at*) herumnörgeln an (*dat*) **2.** Nörgler(in)
nag² F Gaul *m*, Klepper *m*
nail 1. ANAT, TECH Nagel *m* **2.** (an-)nageln (*to* an *acc*); ~ **pol·ish** Nagellack *m*; ~ **scis·sors** Nagelschere *f*; ~ **var·nish** *Br* Nagellack *m*
na·ive, na·ïve naiv (*a. art*)
na·ked nackt, bloß; kahl; *fig* ungeschminkt; **nak·ed·ness** Nacktheit *f*
name 1. Name *m*; Ruf *m*; *by* ~ mit Namen, namentlich; *by the* ~ *of* ... namens ...; *what's your* ~? wie heißen Sie?; *call s.o.* ~*s* j-n beschimpfen **2.** (be)nennen; erwähnen; ernennen zu
name·less namenlos; unbekannt
name·ly nämlich
name·plate Namens-, Tür-, Firmenschild *n*
name·sake Namensvetter *m*, Namensschwester *f*
name tag Namensschild *n*
nan·ny Kindermädchen *n*
nan·ny goat ZO Geiß *f*, Ziege *f*
nap 1. Schläfchen *n*; *have or take a* ~ → **2.** ein Nickerchen machen
nape *mst* ~ *of the neck* ANAT Genick *n*, Nacken *m*
nap·kin Serviette *f*
nap·py *Br* Windel *f*
nar·co·sis MED Narkose *f*
nar·cot·ic 1. narkotisch, betäubend, einschläfernd; Rauschgift...; ~ *addiction* Rauschgiftsucht *f* **2.** Narkotikum *n*,

Betäubungsmittel *n*; *often pl* Rauschgift *n*; ~*s squad* Rauschgiftdezernat *n*
nar·rate erzählen; berichten, schildern
nar·ra·tion Erzählung *f*
nar·ra·tive 1. Erzählung *f*; Bericht *m*, Schilderung *f* **2.** erzählend
nar·ra·tor Erzähler(in)
nar·row 1. eng, schmal; beschränkt; knapp **2.** enger *or* schmäler werden *or* machen, (sich) verengen; beschränken, einschränken; **nar·row·ly** mit knapper Not; **nar·row-mind·ed** engstirnig, beschränkt; **nar·row·ness** Enge *f*; Beschränktheit *f*
na·sal nasal; Nasen...
nas·ty ekelhaft, eklig, widerlich (*smell, sight etc*); abscheulich (*weather etc*); böse, schlimm (*accident etc*); hässlich (*character, behavior etc*); gemein, fies; schmutzig, zotig (*language*)
na·tal Geburts...
na·tion Nation *f*, Volk *n*
na·tion·al 1. national, National..., Landes..., Volks... **2.** Staatsangehörige *m, f*; ~ **an·them** Nationalhymne *f*
na·tion·al·i·ty Nationalität *f*, Staatsangehörigkeit *f*
na·tion·al·ize ECON verstaatlichen
na·tion·al‖ park Nationalpark *m*; ~ **so·cial·ism** HIST POL Nationalsozialismus *m*; ~ **so·cial·ist** HIST POL Nationalsozialist *m*; ~ **team** SPORT Nationalmannschaft *f*
na·tion·wide landesweit
na·tive 1. einheimisch, Landes...; heimatlich, Heimat...; eingeboren, Eingeborenen...; angeboren **2.** Eingebo-

rene *m, f;* Einheimische *m, f;* ~ **lan-guage** Muttersprache *f;* ~ **speak·er** Muttersprachler(in)

Na·tiv·i·ty REL *die* Geburt Christi

nat·ty F schick, *Austrian* fesch·

nat·u·ral natürlich; angeboren; Na-tur...; ~ **gas** Erdgas *n*

nat·u·ral·ize naturalisieren, einbürgern

nat·u·ral·ly natürlich; von Natur (aus)

nat·u·ral‖ re·sourc·es Boden- u. Natur-schätze *pl;* ~ **sci·ence** Naturwissen-schaft *f*

na·ture Natur *f;* ~ **con·ser·va·tion** Na-turschutz *m;* ~ **re·serve** Naturschutz-gebiet *n;* ~ **trail** Naturlehrpfad *m*

naugh·ty unartig; unanständig

nau·se·a Übelkeit *f,* Brechreiz *m*

nau·se·ate: ~ *s.o.* j-m Übelkeit verursa-chen; *fig* j-n anwidern

nau·se·at·ing ekelerregend, widerlich

nau·ti·cal nautisch, See...

na·val MIL Flotten..., Marine...; See...; ~ **base** MIL Flottenstützpunkt *m;* ~ **offi-cer** MIL Marineoffizier *m;* ~ **pow·er** MIL Seemacht *f*

nave ARCH Mittel-, Hauptschiff *n*

na·vel ANAT Nabel *m (a. fig)*

nav·i·ga·ble schiffbar

nav·i·gate MAR befahren; AVIAT, MAR steu-ern, lenken

nav·i·ga·tion Schifffahrt *f;* AVIAT, MAR Navigation *f*

nav·i·ga·tor AVIAT, MAR Navigator *m*

na·vy (Kriegs)Marine *f;* Kriegsflotte *f*

na·vy blue Marineblau *n*

nay PARL Gegen-, Neinstimme *f*

Na·zi HIST POL *contp* Nazi *m*

Na·zism HIST POL *contp* Nazismus *m*

near 1. *adj* nahe; kurz; nahe (verwandt); *in the ~ future* in naher Zukunft; *be a ~ miss* knapp scheitern **2.** *adv* nahe, in der Nähe *(a. ~ at hand)*; nahe (bevor-stehend) *(a. ~ at hand)*; beinahe, fast; *~ the station etc* in der Nähe des Bahn-hofs *etc;* ~ *you* in deiner Nähe **3.** *prp* nahe *(dat),* in der Nähe von *(or gen)* **4.** sich nähern, näher kommen *(dat)*

near·by 1. *adj* nahe (gelegen) **2.** *adv* in der Nähe

near·ly beinahe, fast; annähernd

near·sight·ed kurzsichtig

neat ordentlich; sauber; gepflegt; pur *(whisky etc)*

neb·u·lous verschwommen

ne·ces·sar·i·ly notwendigerweise; *not ~* nicht unbedingt

ne·ces·sa·ry notwendig, nötig; unver-meidlich

ne·ces·si·tate *et.* erfordern, verlangen

ne·ces·si·ty Notwendigkeit *f;* (dringen-des) Bedürfnis; Not *f*

neck 1. ANAT Hals *m (a. of bottle etc);* Ge-nick *n,* Nacken *m; be ~ and...* F Kopf an Kopf liegen *(a. fig); be up to one's ~ in debt* F bis zum Hals in Schulden ste-cken **2.** F knutschen, schmusen

neck·er·chief Halstuch *n*

neck·lace Halskette *f*

neck·let Halskettchen *n*

neck·line Ausschnitt *m*

neck·tie Krawatte *f,* Schlips *m*

née: ~ *Smith* geborene Smith

need 1. (*of, for*) (dringendes) Bedürfnis (nach), Bedarf *m* (an *dat*); Notwendig-keit *f;* Mangel *m* (*of, for* an *dat*); Not *f; be in ~ of s.th.* et. dringend brauchen; *in ~* in Not; *in ~ of help* hilfs-, hilfebe-dürftig **2.** *v/t* benötigen, brauchen; *v/aux* brauchen, müssen

nee·dle 1. Nadel *f (a.* BOT, MED); Zeiger *m* **2.** F j-n aufziehen, hänseln

need·less unnötig, überflüssig

nee·dle·wom·an Näherin *f*

nee·dle·work Handarbeit *f*

need·y bedürftig, arm

ne·ga·tion Verneinung *f*

neg·a·tive 1. negativ; verneinend **2.** Ver-neinung *f;* PHOT Negativ *n; answer in the ~* verneinen

ne·glect 1. vernachlässigen; es versäu-men (*doing, to do* zu tun); **2.** Vernach-lässigung *f;* Nachlässigkeit *f*

neg·li·gence Nachlässigkeit *f,* Unacht-samkeit *f;* **neg·li·gent** nachlässig, un-achtsam; lässig, salopp

neg·li·gi·ble unbedeutend

ne·go·ti·ate verhandeln (über *acc*)

ne·go·ti·a·tion Verhandlung *f*

ne·go·ti·a·tor Unterhändler(in)

neigh ZO **1.** wiehern **2.** Wiehern *n*

neigh·bo(u)r Nachbar(in)

neigh·bo(u)r·hood Nachbarschaft *f,* Umgebung *f*

neigh·bo(u)r·ing benachbart, Nach-bar..., angrenzend

neigh·bo(u)r·ly (gut)nachbarlich

nei·ther 1. *adj and pron* keine(r, -s) (von beiden) **2.** *cj* ~ ... *nor* weder ... noch

ne·on CHEM Neon *n*; ~ **lamp** Neonlampe *f*; ~ **sign** Neon-, Leuchtreklame *f*

neph·ew Neffe *m*

nep·o·tism *contp* Vetternwirtschaft *f*

nerd F Trottel *m*; Computerfreak *m*

nerve Nerv *m*; Mut *m*, Stärke *f*, Selbstbeherrschung *f*; F Frechheit *f*; **get on s.o.'s** ~ **s** j-m auf die Nerven gehen *or* fallen; **lose one's** ~ den Mut *or* die Nerven verlieren; **you've got a** ~**!** F Sie haben Nerven!; **nerve·less** kraftlos; mutlos; ohne Nerven, kaltblütig

ner·vous nervös; Nerven...

ner·vous·ness Nervosität *f*

nest 1. Nest *n* **2.** nisten

nes·tle (sich) schmiegen *or* kuscheln (**against, on** an *acc*); *a.* ~ **down** sich behaglich niederlassen, es sich bequem machen (**in** in *dat*)

net[1] **1.** Netz *n*; ~ **curtain** Store *m* **2.** mit e-m Netz fangen *or* abdecken

net[2] **1.** netto, Netto..., Rein... **2.** netto einbringen

Neth·er·lands *die* Niederlande *pl*

net·tle 1. BOT Nessel *f* **2.** F *j-n* ärgern

net·work Netz *n* (*a.* IT), Netzwerk *n*; (*Straßen- etc*)Netz *n*; *radio*, TV Sendernetz *n*; **be in the** ~ IT am Netz sein

neu·ro·sis MED Neurose *f*; **neu·rot·ic** MED **1.** neurotisch **2.** Neurotiker(in)

neu·ter 1. LING sächlich; geschlechtslos **2.** LING Neutrum *n*

neu·tral 1. neutral **2.** Neutrale *m, f*; *a.* ~ **gear** MOT Leerlauf(stellung *f*) *m*

neu·tral·i·ty Neutralität *f*

neu·tral·ize neutralisieren

neu·tron PHYS Neutron *n*

nev·er nie, niemals; **nev·er-end·ing** endlos, nicht enden wollend, unendlich

nev·er·the·less nichtsdestoweniger, dennoch, trotzdem

new neu; frisch; unerfahren; **nothing** ~ nichts Neues

new·born neugeboren

new·com·er Neuankömmling *m*; Neuling *m*

new·ly kürzlich; neu

news Neuigkeit(en *pl*) *f*, Nachricht(en *pl*) *f*

news·a·gent Zeitungshändler(in)

news·boy Zeitungsjunge *m*, Zeitungsausträger *m*

news bul·le·tin Kurznachricht(en *pl*) *f*

news·cast *radio*, TV Nachrichtensendung *f*; **news·cast·er** *radio*, TV Nachrichtensprecher(in)

news deal·er Zeitungshändler(in)

news·flash *radio*, TV Kurzmeldung *f*

news·let·ter Rundschreiben *n*

news·pa·per Zeitung *f*

news·print Zeitungspapier *n*

news·read·er *esp Br* → **newscaster**

news·reel *film*: Wochenschau *f*

news·room Nachrichtenredaktion *f*

news·stand Zeitungskiosk *m*, -stand *m*

news·ven·dor *esp Br* Zeitungsverkäufer(in)

new year Neujahr *n, das* neue Jahr; **New Year's Day** Neujahrstag *m*; **New Year's Eve** Silvester(abend *m*) *m, n*

next 1. *adj* nächste(r, -s); (**the**) ~ **day** am nächsten Tag; ~ **door** nebenan; ~ **but one** übernächste(r, -s); ~ **to** gleich neben *or* nach; beinahe, fast *unmöglich etc* **2.** *adv* als Nächste(r, -s); demnächst, das nächste Mal **3.** *der, die, das* Nächste; → **kin**

next-door (von) nebenan

nib·ble *v/i* knabbern (**at** an *dat*); *v/t* Loch *etc* nagen, knabbern (**in** in *acc*)

nice nett, freundlich; hübsch, schön; *fig* fein (*detail etc*)

nice·ly gut, fein; genau, sorgfältig

ni·ce·ty Feinheit *f*; Genauigkeit *f*

niche Nische *f*

nick 1. Kerbe *f* **2.** (ein)kerben; *j-n* streifen (*bullet*); *Br* F *et.* klauen; *Br* F *j-n* schnappen

nick·el 1. MIN Nickel *n*; Fünfcentstück *n* **2.** TECH vernickeln

nick·el-plate TECH vernickeln

nick-nack → **knick-knack**

nick·name 1. Spitzname *m* **2.** *j-m* den Spitznamen ... geben

niece Nichte *f*

nig·gard Geizhals *m*

nig·gard·ly geizig, knaus(e)rig; schäbig, kümmerlich

night Nacht *f*; Abend *m*; **at** ~**, by** ~**, in the** ~ in der Nacht, nachts

night·cap Schlummertrunk *m*

night·club Nachtklub *m*, Nachtlokal *n*

night·dress (Damen-, Kinder)Nachthemd *n*

night·fall: **at** ~ bei Einbruch der Dunkelheit

night·gown → **nightdress**

night·ie F → *nightdress*

nigh·tin·gale ZO Nachtigall *f*

night·ly (all)nächtlich; (all)abendlich; jede Nacht; jeden Abend

night·mare Albtraum *m* (*a. fig*)

night school Abendschule *f*

night shift Nachtschicht *f*

night·shirt (Herren)Nachthemd *n*

night·time: *in the ~, at ~* nachts

night watch·man Nachtwächter *m*

night·y F → *nightdress*

nil Nichts *n*, Null *f*; *our team won two to ~ or by two goals to ~* (*2-0*) unsere Mannschaft gewann zwei zu null (2:0)

nim·ble flink, gewandt; geistig beweglich

nine 1. neun; *~ to five* normale Dienststunden (von 9-5); *a ~-to-five job* e-e (An)Stellung mit geregelter Arbeitszeit **2.** Neun *f*

nine·pins Kegeln *n*

nine·teen 1. neunzehn **2.** Neunzehn *f*

nine·teenth neunzehnte(r, -s)

nine·ti·eth neunzigste(r, -s)

nine·ty 1. neunzig **2.** Neunzig *f*

ninth 1. neunte(r, -s) **2.** Neuntel *n*

ninth·ly neuntens

nip¹ 1. kneifen, zwicken; F flitzen, sausen; *~ off* F abknipsen; *~ in the bud fig* im Keim ersticken **2.** Kneifen *n*, Zwicken *n*; *it was ~ and tuck* F es war ganz knapp; *there's a ~ in the air today* heute ist es ganz schön kalt

nip² Schlückchen *n* (*of brandy etc*)

nip·per: (*a pair of*) *~s* (e-e) (Kneif)Zange *f*

nip·ple ANAT Brustwarze *f*; (Gummi-)Sauger *m*; TECH Nippel *m*

ni·ter, *Br* **ni·tre** CHEM Salpeter *m*

ni·tro·gen CHEM Stickstoff *m*

no 1. *adv* nein; nicht **2.** *adj* kein(e); *~ one* keiner, niemand; *in ~ time* im Nu, im Handumdrehen **3.** Nein *n*

no·bil·i·ty (Hoch)Adel *m*; *fig* Adel *m*

no·ble adlig; edel, nobel; prächtig

no·ble·man Adlige *m*

no·ble·wom·an Adlige *f*

no·bod·y 1. niemand, keiner **2.** *fig* Niemand *m*, Null *f*

no·cal·o·rie di·et Nulldiät *f*

noc·tur·nal nächtlich, Nacht...

nod 1. nicken (mit); *~ off* einnicken; *have a ~ding acquaintance with s.o.* j-n flüchtig kennen **2.** Nicken *n*

node BOT, MED Knoten *m*

noise 1. Krach *m*, Lärm *m*; Geräusch *n* **2.** *~ about* (*abroad, around*) *Gerücht etc* verbreiten; **noise·less** geräuschlos; **nois·y** laut, geräuschvoll

no·mad Nomade *m*, Nomadin *f*

nom·i·nal nominell; *~ value* ECON Nennwert *m*

nom·i·nate ernennen; nominieren, (zur Wahl) vorschlagen; **nom·i·na·tion** Ernennung *f*; Nominierung *f*

nom·i·na·tive *a. ~ case* LING Nominativ *m*, erster Fall

nom·i·nee Kandidat(in)

non... nicht..., Nicht..., un...

non·al·co·hol·ic alkoholfrei

non·a·ligned POL blockfrei

non·com·mis·sioned of·fi·cer MIL Unteroffizier *m*

non·com·mit·tal unverbindlich

non·con·duc·tor ELECTR Nichtleiter *m*

non·de·script nichtssagend; unauffällig

none 1. *pron* keine(r, -s), niemand **2.** *adv* in keiner Weise, keineswegs

non·en·ti·ty *fig* Null *f*

none·the·less nichtsdestoweniger, dennoch, trotzdem

non·ex·ist·ence Nichtvorhandensein *n*, Fehlen *n*

non·ex·ist·ent nicht existierend

non·fic·tion Sachbücher *pl*

non·flam·ma·ble, **non·in·flam·ma·ble** nicht brennbar

non·in·ter·fer·ence, **non·in·ter·vention** POL Nichteinmischung *f*

non·i·ron bügelfrei

no-non·sense nüchtern, sachlich

non·par·ti·san POL überparteilich; unparteiisch

non·pay·ment ECON Nicht(be)zahlung *f*

non·plus verblüffen

non·pol·lut·ing umweltfreundlich

non·prof·it, *Br* **non·prof·it-mak·ing** gemeinnützig

non·res·i·dent 1. nicht (orts)ansässig; nicht im Hause wohnend **2.** Nichtansässige *m*, *f*; nicht im Hause Wohnende *m*, *f*

non·re·turn·a·ble Einweg...; *~ bot·tle* Einwegflasche *f*

non·sense Unsinn *m*, dummes Zeug

non·skid rutschfest, rutschsicher

non·smok·er Nichtraucher(in)

non·smok·ing Nichtraucher...

non·stick mit Antihaftbeschichtung

non·stop nonstop, ohne Unterbrechung; RAIL durchgehend; AVIAT ohne Zwischenlandung; **~ flight** a. Nonstop-Flug m

non·u·nion nicht (gewerkschaftlich) organisiert

non·vi·o·lence (Politik f der) Gewaltlosigkeit f

non·vi·o·lent gewaltlos

noo·dle Nudel f

nook Ecke f, Winkel m

noon Mittag(szeit f) m; **at ~** um 12 Uhr (mittags)

noose Schlinge f

nope F ne(e), nein

nor → **neither** 2; auch nicht

norm Norm f

nor·mal normal

nor·mal·ize (sich) normalisieren

north 1. Nord, Norden m **2.** adj nördlich, Nord... **3.** adv nach Norden, nordwärts

north·east 1. Nordost, Nordosten m **2.** a. **northeastern** nordöstlich

nor·ther·ly, nor·thern Nord..., nördlich

North Pole Nordpol m

north·ward(s) adv nördlich, nach Norden

north·west 1. Nordwest, Nordwesten m **2.** a. **northwestern** nordwestlich

Nor·way Norwegen n

Nor·we·gian 1. norwegisch **2.** Norweger(in); LING Norwegisch n

nose 1. Nase f; ZO Schnauze f; fig Gespür n **2.** Auto etc vorsichtig fahren; a. **~ about, ~ around** fig F herumschnüffeln (in dat) (**for** nach)

nose·bleed Nasenbluten n; **have a ~** Nasenbluten haben

nose·dive AVIAT Sturzflug m

nos·ey → **nosy**

nos·tal·gia Nostalgie f

nos·tril ANAT Nasenloch n, esp ZO Nüster f

nos·y F neugierig

not nicht; **~ a** kein(e)

no·ta·ble bemerkenswert; beachtlich

no·ta·ry mst **~ public** Notar m

notch 1. Kerbe f; GEOL Engpass m **2.** (ein)kerben

note (mst pl) Notiz f, Aufzeichnung f; Anmerkung f; Vermerk m; Briefchen n, Zettel m; (diplomatische) Note; Banknote f, Geldschein m; MUS Note f; fig Ton m; **take ~s (of)** sich Notizen machen (über acc); **note·book** Notizbuch n; IT Notebook n

not·ed bekannt, berühmt (**for** wegen)

note·pa·per Briefpapier n

note·wor·thy bemerkenswert

noth·ing nichts; **~ but** nichts als, nur; **~ much** F nicht viel; **for ~** umsonst; **to say ~ of** ganz zu schweigen von; **there is ~ like** es geht nichts über (acc)

no·tice 1. Ankündigung f, Bekanntgabe f, Mitteilung f, Anzeige f; Kündigung(sfrist) f; Beachtung f; **give** or **hand in one's ~** kündigen (**to** bei); **give s.o. ~** j-m kündigen; **give s.o. ~ to quit** j-m kündigen; **at six months' ~** mit halbjährlicher Kündigungsfrist; **take (no) ~ of** (keine) Notiz nehmen von, (nicht) beachten; **at short ~** kurzfristig; **until further ~** bis auf Weiteres; **without ~** fristlos **2.** (es) bemerken; (besonders) beachten or achten auf (acc)

no·tice·a·ble erkennbar, wahrnehmbar; bemerkenswert

no·tice·board Br schwarzes Brett

no·ti·fy et. anzeigen, melden, mitteilen; j-n benachrichtigen

no·tion Begriff m, Vorstellung f; Idee f

no·tions Kurzwaren pl

no·to·ri·ous berüchtigt (**for** für)

not·with·stand·ing trotz (gen)

nought Br: **0.4 (~ point four)** 0,4

noun LING Substantiv n, Hauptwort n

nour·ish (er)nähren; fig hegen

nour·ish·ing nahrhaft

nour·ish·ment Ernährung f; Nahrung f

Nov abbr of **November** Nov., November m

nov·el 1. Roman m **2.** (ganz) neu(artig)

nov·el·ist Romanschriftsteller(in)

no·vel·la Novelle f

nov·el·ty Neuheit f

No·vem·ber (abbr **Nov**) November m

nov·ice Anfänger(in), Neuling m; REL Novize m, Novizin f

now 1. adv nun, jetzt; **~ and again**, (**every**) **~ and then** von Zeit zu Zeit, dann und wann; **by ~** inzwischen; **from ~ (on)** von jetzt an; **just ~** gerade eben **2.** cj a. **~ that** nun da; **now·a·days** heutzutage

no·where nirgends

nox·ious schädlich

noz·zle TECH Schnauze f; Stutzen m; Düse f; Zapfpistole f

nu·ance Nuance f
nub springender Punkt
nu·cle·ar Kern..., Atom..., atomar, nuklear, Nuklear...; **~ en·er·gy** PHYS Atomenergie f, Kernenergie f; **~ fis·sion** PHYS Kernspaltung f
nu·cle·ar-free atomwaffenfrei
nu·cle·ar| fu·sion PHYS Kernfusion f; **~ phys·ics** Kernphysik f; **~ pow·er** PHYS Atomkraft f, Kernkraft f
nu·cle·ar-pow·ered atomgetrieben
nu·cle·ar| pow·er plant ELECTR Atomkraftwerk n, Kernkraftwerk n; **~ re·ac·tor** PHYS Atomreaktor m, Kernreaktor m; **~ war** Atomkrieg m; **~ war·head** MIL Atomsprengkopf m; **~ waste** Atommüll m; **~ weap·ons** MIL Atomwaffen pl, Kernwaffen pl
nu·cle·us BIOL, PHYS Kern m (a. fig)
nude 1. nackt **2.** art: Akt m
nudge 1. j-n anstoßen, (an)stupsen **2.** Stups(er) m
nug·get (esp Gold)Klumpen m
nui·sance Plage f, Ärgernis n; Nervensäge f, Quälgeist m; **what a ~!** wie ärgerlich!; **be a ~ to s.o.** j-m lästig fallen, F j-n nerven; **make a ~ of o.s.** den Leuten auf die Nerven gehen or fallen
nukes F Atom-, Kernwaffen pl
null: ~ and void esp JUR null und nichtig
numb 1. starr (**with** vor), taub; fig wie betäubt (**with** vor); **2.** starr or taub machen
num·ber 1. Zahl f, Ziffer f; Nummer f; (An)Zahl f; Ausgabe f; (Bus- etc)Linie f; **sorry, wrong ~** TEL falsch verbunden! **2.** nummerieren; zählen; sich belaufen auf (acc)

num·ber·less zahllos
num·ber·plate esp Br MOT Nummernschild n
nu·me·ral Ziffer f; LING Zahlwort n
nu·me·ra·tor MATH Zähler m
nu·me·rous zahlreich
nun REL Nonne f
nun·ne·ry REL Nonnenkloster n
nurse 1. (Kranken-, Säuglings)Schwester f; Kindermädchen n; (Kranken-)Pflegerin f; **→ male nurse**; a. **wet ~** Amme f **2.** stillen; pflegen; hegen; als Krankenschwester or -pfleger arbeiten; **~ s.o. back to health** j-n gesund pflegen
nur·se·ry Tagesheim n, Tagesstätte f; Baum-, Pflanzschule f; **~ rhyme** Kinderlied n, Kinderreim m; **~ school** Br Vorschule f; **~ slope** skiing: F Idiotenhügel m
nurs·ing Stillen n; (Kranken)Pflege f; **~ bot·tle** (Saug)Flasche f; **~ home** Pflegeheim n
nut BOT Nuss f; TECH (Schrauben)Mutter f; F verrückter Kerl; F Birne f (head)
nut·crack·er(s) Nussknacker m
nut·meg BOT Muskatnuss f
nu·tri·ent 1. Nährstoff m **2.** nahrhaft
nu·tri·tion Ernährung f
nu·tri·tious, nu·tri·tive nahrhaft
nut·shell Nussschale f; (**to put it**) **in a ~** F kurz gesagt, mit e-m Wort
nut·ty voller Nüsse, nussig; Nuss...; F verrückt
ny·lon® Nylon® n; **~ stock·ings** Nylonstrümpfe® pl
nymph Nymphe f

O

O, o O, o n
o Null f
oaf Lümmel m, Flegel m
oak BOT Eiche f
oar Ruder n
oars·man SPORT Ruderer m
oars·wom·an SPORT Ruderin f
o·a·sis Oase f (a. fig)
oath Eid m, Schwur m; Fluch m; **take an ~** e-n Eid leisten or schwören; **be on or**

under ~ JUR unter Eid stehen; **take the ~** JUR schwören
oat·meal Hafermehl n, Hafergrütze f
o·be·di·ence Gehorsam m
o·be·di·ent gehorsam
o·bese fett, fettleibig
o·bes·i·ty Fettleibigkeit f
o·bey gehorchen (dat), folgen (dat); Befehl etc befolgen
o·bit·u·a·ry Nachruf m; a. **~ notice** To-

desanzeige *f*

ob·ject 1. Objekt *n* (*a.* LING); Gegenstand *m*; Ziel *n*, Zweck *m*, Absicht *f*
2. einwenden; *et.* dagegen haben

ob·jec·tion Einwand *m*, Einspruch *m* (*a.* JUR); **ob·jec·tion·a·ble** nicht einwandfrei; unangenehm; anstößig

ob·jec·tive 1. objektiv, sachlich **2.** Ziel *n*; **ob·jec·tive·ness** Objektivität *f*

ob·li·ga·tion Verpflichtung *f*; *be under an ~ to s.o.* j-m (zu Dank) verpflichtet sein; *be under an ~ to do* verpflichtet sein, *et.* zu tun; **ob·lig·a·to·ry** verpflichtend, verbindlich

o·blige nötigen, zwingen; (zu Dank) verpflichten; *~ s.o.* j-m e-n Gefallen tun; *much ~d* besten Dank

o·blig·ing entgegenkommend, gefällig

o·blique schief, schräg; *fig* indirekt

o·blit·er·ate auslöschen; vernichten, völlig zerstören; verdecken

o·bliv·i·on Vergessen(heit *f*) *n*; *fall into ~* in Vergessenheit geraten

o·bliv·i·ous: *be ~ of or to s.th.* sich e-r Sache nicht bewusst sein; *et.* nicht bemerken *or* wahrnehmen

ob·long rechteckig; länglich

ob·nox·ious widerlich

ob·scene obszön, unanständig

ob·scure 1. dunkel, *fig a.* unklar; unbekannt **2.** verdunkeln, verdecken

ob·scu·ri·ty Unbekanntheit *f*; Unklarheit *f*

ob·se·quies Trauerfeier(lichkeiten *pl*) *f*

ob·ser·va·ble wahrnehmbar, merklich; **ob·ser·vance** Beachtung *f*, Befolgung *f*; **ob·ser·vant** aufmerksam; **ob·ser·va·tion** Beobachtung *f*, Überwachung *f*; Bemerkung *f* (*on* über *acc*); **ob·ser·va·to·ry** Observatorium *n*, Sternwarte *f*; **ob·serve** beobachten; überwachen; *Vorschrift etc* beachten, befolgen, einhalten; bemerken, äußern; **ob·serv·er** Beobachter(in)

ob·sess: *be ~ed by or with* besessen sein von; **ob·ses·sion** PSYCH Besessenheit *f*, fixe Idee, Zwangsvorstellung *f*; **ob·ses·sive** PSYCH zwanghaft

ob·so·lete veraltet

ob·sta·cle Hindernis *n*

ob·sti·na·cy Starrsinn *m*

ob·sti·nate hartnäckig; halsstarrig, eigensinnig, starrköpfig

ob·struct verstopfen, versperren; blockieren; behindern

ob·struc·tion Verstopfung *f*; Blockierung *f*; Behinderung *f*

ob·struc·tive blockierend; hinderlich

ob·tain erhalten, bekommen, sich *et.* beschaffen; **ob·tain·a·ble** erhältlich

ob·tru·sive aufdringlich

ob·vi·ous offensichtlich, klar, einleuchtend

oc·ca·sion Gelegenheit *f*; Anlass *m*; Veranlassung *f*; (festliches) Ereignis *n*; *on the ~ of* anlässlich (*gen*)

oc·ca·sion·al gelegentlich; vereinzelt

oc·ca·sion·al·ly gelegentlich, manchmal

Oc·ci·dent *der* Westen, *der* Okzident, *das* Abendland

oc·ci·den·tal abendländisch, westlich

oc·cu·pant Bewohner(in); Insasse *m*, Insassin *f*

oc·cu·pa·tion Beruf *m*; Beschäftigung *f*; MIL, POL Besetzung *f*, Besatzung *f*, Okkupation *f*

oc·cu·py in Besitz nehmen, MIL, POL besetzen; *Raum* einnehmen; in Anspruch nehmen; beschäftigen; *be occupied* bewohnt sein; besetzt sein (*seat*)

oc·cur sich ereignen; vorkommen; *it ~red to me that* es fiel mir ein *or* mir kam der Gedanke, dass

oc·cur·rence Vorkommen *n*; Ereignis *n*; Vorfall *m*

o·cean Ozean *m*, (Welt)Meer *n*

o'clock: (*at*) *five ~* (um) fünf Uhr

Oct *abbr of* **October** Okt., Oktober *m*

Oc·to·ber (*abbr* **Oct**) Oktober *m*

oc·u·lar Augen...

oc·u·list Augenarzt *m*, Augenärztin *f*

OD F *v/i*: *~ on heroin* an e-r Überdosis Heroin sterben

odd sonderbar, seltsam, merkwürdig; einzeln, Einzel...; ungerade (*number*); gelegentlich, Gelegenheits...; *~ jobs* Gelegenheitsarbeiten *pl*; F *30 ~* (et.) über 30, einige 30

odds (Gewinn)Chancen *pl*; *the ~ are 10 to 1* die Chancen stehen 10 zu 1; *the ~ are that* es ist sehr wahrscheinlich, dass; *against all ~* wider Erwarten, entgegen allen Erwartungen; *be at ~* uneins sein (*with* mit); *~ and ends* Krimskrams *m*; **odds-on** hoch, klar (*favorite*), aussichtsreichst (*candidate* *etc*); F *it's ~ that* es sieht ganz so aus, als ob ...

ode Ode *f*

o·do(u)r Geruch *m*

o·do(u)r·less geruchlos

of *prp* von; *origin*: von, aus; *material*: aus; um (**cheat s.o. ~ s.th.** j-n um et. betrügen); *cause*: an (*dat*) (**die ~** sterben an); aus (**~ charity** aus Nächstenliebe); vor (*dat*) (**be afraid ~** Angst haben vor); auf (*acc*) (**be proud ~** stolz sein auf); über (*acc*) (**be glad ~** sich freuen über); nach (**smell ~** riechen nach); von, über (*acc*) (**speak ~ s.th.** von *or* über et. sprechen); an (*acc*) (**think ~ s.th.** an et. denken); **the city ~ London** die Stadt London; **the works ~ Dickens** Dickens' Werke; **your letter ~ ...** Ihr Schreiben vom ...; **five minutes ~ twelve** fünf Minuten vor zwölf

off 1. *adv* fort(...), weg(...); ab(...), ab, abgegangen (*button etc*); weg, entfernt (**3 miles ~**) ab(...), aus–, abgeschaltet; TECH zu; aus(gegangen), alle; aus, vorbei; verdorben (*food*); frei; **I must be ~** ich muss gehen *or* weg; **~ with you!** fort mit dir!; **be ~** ausfallen, nicht stattfinden; **10% ~** ECON 10% Nachlass; **~ and on** ab und zu, hin und wieder; **take a day ~** sich e-n Tag freinehmen; **be well (badly) ~** gut (schlecht) d(a)ran *or* gestellt *or* situiert sein **2.** *prp* fort von, weg von, von (..., ab, weg, herunter); abseits von (*or gen*), von ... weg; MAR *vor der Küste etc*; **be ~ duty** nicht im Dienst sein, dienstfrei haben; **be ~ smoking** nicht mehr rauchen **3.** *adj* frei, arbeits–, dienstfrei; *fig* **have an ~ day** e-n schlechten Tag haben

of·fal GASTR Innereien *pl*

off-col·o(u)r schlüpfrig, zweideutig

of·fence *Br* → **offense**

of·fend beleidigen, kränken; verstoßen (**against** gegen); **of·fend·er** (Übel–, Misse)Täter(in); **first ~** JUR nicht Vorbestrafte *m, f*, Ersttäter(in)

of·fense Vergehen *n*, Verstoß *m*; JUR Straftat *f*; Beleidigung *f*, Kränkung *f*; **take ~** Anstoß nehmen (**at** an *dat*)

of·fen·sive 1. beleidigend, anstößig; widerlich (*smell etc*); MIL Offensiv..., Angriffs... **2.** MIL Offensive *f* (*a. fig*)

of·fer 1. *v/t* anbieten (*a.* ECON); *Preis*,

Möglichkeit *etc* bieten; *Preis, Belohnung* aussetzen; sich bereit erklären (**to do** zu tun); *Widerstand* leisten; *v/i* es *or* sich anbieten **2.** Angebot *n*

off·hand 1. *adj* lässig; Stegreif...; **be ~ with s.o.** F mit j-m kurz angebunden sein **2.** *adv* auf Anhieb, so ohne weiteres

of·fice Büro *n*, Geschäftsstelle *f*, (*Anwalts*)Kanzlei *f*; (*esp* öffentliches) Amt, Posten *m*; *mst* **Office** *esp Br* Ministerium *n*; **~ block** *Br*, **~ build·ing** Bürohaus *n*; **~ hours** Dienstzeit *f*; Geschäfts-, Öffnungszeiten *pl*

of·fi·cer MIL Offizier *m*; (*Polizei- etc*)Beamte *m*, (-)Beamtin *f*

of·fi·cial 1. Beamte *m*, Beamtin *f* **2.** offiziell, amtlich, dienstlich

of·fi·ci·ate amtieren

of·fi·cious übereifrig

off-licence *Br* Wein- und Spirituosenhandlung *f*

off-line IT offline, Offline..., rechnerunabhängig

off-peak: ~ electricity Nachtstrom *m*; **~ hours** verkehrsschwache Stunden *pl*

off sea·son Nebensaison *f*

off·set ECON ausgleichen; verrechnen (**against** mit)

off·shoot BOT Ableger *m*, Sspross *m*

off·shore vor der Küste

off·side SPORT abseits; **~ position** Abseitsposition *f*, Abseitsstellung *f*; **~ trap** Abseitsfalle *f*

off·spring Nachkomme *m*, Nachkommenschaft *f*

off-the-peg *Br*, **off-the-rack** Konfektions..., ... von der Stange

off-the-rec·ord inoffiziell

oh *int* oh!

oil 1. Öl *n*; Erdöl *n* **2.** (ein)ölen, schmieren (*a. fig*)

oil change MOT Ölwechsel *m*

oil·cloth Wachstuch *n*

oil·field Ölfeld *n*

oil paint·ing Ölmalerei *f*; Ölgemälde *n*

oil pan MOT Ölwanne *f*

oil plat·form → **oilrig**

oil pol·lu·tion Ölpest *f*

oil-pro·duc·ing coun·try Ölförderland *n*

oil pro·duc·tion Ölförderung *f*

oil re·fin·e·ry Erdölraffinerie *f*

open

oil·rig (Öl)Bohrinsel f
oil·skins Ölzeug n
oil slick Ölteppich m
oil well Ölquelle f
oil·y ölig; fig schmierig, schleimig
oint·ment Salbe f
OK, o·kay F **1.** adj and int okay(!), o.k.(!), in Ordnung(!) **2.** genehmigen, e-r Sache zustimmen **3.** Okay n, O.K. n, Genehmigung f, Zustimmung f
old 1. alt **2.** the ~ die Alten pl
old age (hohes) Alter; ~ **pen·sion** Rente f, Pension f; ~ **pen·sion·er** Rentner(in), Pensionär(in)
old-fash·ioned altmodisch
old·ish ältlich
old peo·ple's home Altersheim n, Altenheim n
ol·ive BOT Olive f; Olivgrün n
O·lym·pic Games SPORT Olympische Spiele pl
om·i·nous unheilvoll
o·mis·sion Auslassung f; Unterlassung f; Versäumnis n
o·mit auslassen, weglassen; unterlassen
om·nip·o·tent allmächtig
om·nis·ci·ent allwissend
on 1. prp auf (acc or dat) (~ **the table** auf dem or den Tisch); an (dat) (~ **the wall** an der Wand); in (~ **TV** im Fernsehen); direction, target: auf (acc) … (hin), an (acc), nach (dat) … (hin); fig auf (acc) … (hin) (~ **demand** auf Anfrage); time: an (dat) (~ **Sunday** am Sonntag; ~ **the 1st of April** am 1. April); (gleich) nach, bei (~ **his arrival**); gehörig zu, beschäftigt bei (**be** ~ **a committee** e-m Ausschuss angehören); **be** ~ **the „Daily Mail"** bei der "Daily Mail" beschäftigt sein); state: in (dat), auf (dat) (~ **duty** im Dienst; **be** ~ **fire** in Flammen stehen); subject: über (acc) (**talk** ~ **a subject** über ein Thema sprechen); nach (dat) (~ **this model** nach diesem Modell); von (dat) (**live** ~ **s.th.** von et. leben); ~ **the street** auf der Straße; ~ **a train** in e-m Zug; ~ **hearing** it als ich etc es hörte; **have you any money** ~ **you?** hast du Geld bei dir? **2.** adj and adv an (-geschaltet) (light etc), eingeschaltet (radio etc), auf (faucet etc), (dar)auf(legen, -schrauben etc); an(haben, -ziehen) (**have a coat** ~ e-n Mantel anhaben); auf(behalten) (**keep one's hat** ~

den Hut aufbehalten); weiter(gehen, -sprechen etc); **and so** ~ und so weiter; ~ **and** ~ immer weiter; **from this day** ~ von dem Tage an; **be** ~ THEA gegeben werden; film: laufen; radio, TV gesendet werden; **what's** ~? was ist los?
once 1. einmal; einst; ~ **again,** ~ **more** noch einmal; ~ **in a while** ab und zu, hin und wieder; ~ **and for all** ein für alle Mal; **not** ~ kein einziges Mal, keinmal; **at** ~ sofort; auf einmal, gleichzeitig; **all at** ~ plötzlich; **for** ~ diesmal, ausnahmsweise; **this** ~ dieses eine Mal; ~ **upon a time there was …** es war einmal … **2.** sobald
one ein(e); einzig; man; Eins f, eins; ~**'s** sein(e); ~ **day** eines Tages; ~ **another** sich (gegenseitig), einander; ~ **by** ~, ~ **after another,** ~ **after the other** einer nach dem andern; **I for** ~ ich zum Beispiel; **the little** ~**s** die Kleinen pl
one-horse town F contp Nest n
one·self sich (selbst); sich selbst; (all) by ~ ganz allein; **to** ~ ganz für sich (allein)
one-sid·ed einseitig
one-time ehemalig, früher
one-track mind: have a ~ immer nur dasselbe im Kopf haben
one-two soccer: Doppelpass m
one-way Einbahn…; ~ **street** Einbahnstraße f; ~ **tick·et** RAIL etc einfache Fahrkarte, AVIAT einfaches Ticket; ~ **traf·fic** MOT Einbahnverkehr m
on·ion BOT Zwiebel f
on-line IT online, Online…, rechnerabhängig
on·look·er Zuschauer(in)
on·ly 1. adj einzige(r, -s) **2.** adv nur, bloß; erst; ~ **yesterday** erst gestern **3.** cj F nur, bloß
on·rush Ansturm m
on·set Beginn m; MED Ausbruch m
on·slaught (heftiger) Angriff (a. fig)
on·to auf (acc)
on·ward(s) adv vorwärts, weiter; **from now** ~ von nun an
ooze v/i sickern; ~ **away** fig schwinden; v/t absondern; fig ausstrahlen, verströmen
o·paque undurchsichtig; fig unverständlich
o·pen 1. offen, a. geöffnet, a. frei (country etc); öffentlich; fig offen, a. unentschieden, a. freimütig; fig zugänglich,

aufgeschlossen (*to* für *or dat*); **~ all day** durchgehend geöffnet; **in the ~ air** im Freien **2.** *golf, tennis*: offenes Turnier; **in the ~** im Freien; **come out into the ~** *fig* an die Öffentlichkeit treten **3.** *v/t* öffnen, aufmachen, *Buch etc a.* aufschlagen; eröffnen; *v/i* sich öffnen, aufgehen; öffnen, aufmachen (*store*); anfangen, beginnen; **~ into** führen nach *or* in (*acc*); **~ onto** hinausgehen auf (*acc*)

o·pen-air im Freien

o·pen-end·ed zeitlich unbegrenzt

o·pen·er (*Dosen- etc*)Öffner *m*

o·pen-eyed mit großen Augen, staunend

o·pen-hand·ed freigebig, großzügig

o·pen-heart·ed offenherzig

o·pen·ing 1. Öffnung *f*; ECON freie Stelle; Eröffnung *f*, Erschließung *f*, Einstieg *m* **2.** Eröffnungs...; Öffnungs...

o·pen-mind·ed aufgeschlossen

o·pen·ness Offenheit *f*

op·e·ra Oper *f*; **~ glass·es** Opernglas *n*; **~ house** Opernhaus *n*, Oper *f*

op·e·rate *v/i* wirksam sein *or* werden *or* werden; TECH arbeiten, in Betrieb sein, laufen (*machine etc*); MED operieren (**on s.o.** j-n); *v/t Maschine* bedienen, *Schalter etc* betätigen; *Unternehmen, Geschäft* betreiben, führen

op·e·rat·ing| room MED Operationssaal *m*; **~ sys·tem** IT Betriebssystem *n*; **~ thea·tre** *Br* MED Operationssaal *m*

op·e·ra·tion TECH Betrieb *m*, Lauf *m*; Bedienung *f*; ECON Tätigkeit *f*, Unternehmen *n*; MED, MIL Operation *f*; **in ~** TECH in Betrieb; **have an ~** MED operiert werden

op·e·ra·tive wirksam; MED operativ

op·e·ra·tor TECH Bedienungsperson *f*; IT Operator *m*; TEL Vermittlung *f*

o·pin·ion Meinung *f*, Ansicht *f*; Gutachten *n* (**on** über *acc*); **in my ~** meines Erachtens

op·po·nent Gegner(in)

op·por·tune günstig, passend; rechtzeitig

op·por·tu·ni·ty (günstige) Gelegenheit

op·pose sich widersetzen (*dat*)

op·posed entgegengesetzt; **be ~ to** gegen ... sein

op·po·site 1. Gegenteil *n*, Gegensatz *m* **2.** *adj* gegenüberliegend; entgegenge-

setzt **3.** *adv* gegenüber (**to** *dat*); **4.** *prp* gegenüber (*dat*)

op·po·si·tion Widerstand *m*, Opposition *f* (*a.* PARL); Gegensatz *m*

op·press unterdrücken

op·pres·sion Unterdrückung *f*

op·pres·sive (be)drückend; hart, grausam; schwül (*weather*)

op·tic Augen..., Seh...; → **op·ti·cal** optisch; **op·ti·cian** Optiker(in)

op·ti·mism Optimismus *m*

op·ti·mist Optimist(in)

op·ti·mis·tic optimistisch

op·tion Wahl *f*; ECON Option *f*, Vorkaufsrecht *n*; MOT Extra *n*

op·tion·al freiwillig; Wahl...; **be an ~ ex·tra** MOT gegen Aufpreis erhältlich sein; **~ sub·ject** PED *etc* Wahlfach *n*

or oder; **~ else** sonst

o·ral mündlich; Mund...

or·ange 1. BOT Orange *f*, Apfelsine *f* **2.** orange(farben)

or·ange·ade Orangenlimonade *f*

o·ra·tion Rede *f*, Ansprache *f*

or·a·tor Redner(in)

or·bit 1. Kreisbahn *f*, Umlaufbahn *f*; **get** *or* **put into ~** in e-e Umlaufbahn gelangen *or* bringen **2.** *v/t die Erde etc* umkreisen; *v/i* die Erde *etc* umkreisen, sich auf e-r Umlaufbahn bewegen

or·chard Obstgarten *m*

or·ches·tra MUS Orchester *n*; THEA Parkett *n*

or·chid BOT Orchidee *f*

or·dain: **~ s.o.** (**priest**) j-n zum Priester weihen

or·deal Qual *f*, Tortur *f*

or·der 1. Ordnung *f*; Reihenfolge *f*; Befehl *m*, Anordnung *f*; ECON Bestellung *f*, Auftrag *m*; PARL *etc* (Geschäfts)Ordnung *f*; REL *etc* Orden *m*; **~ to pay** ECON Zahlungsanweisung *f*; **in ~ to** *inf* um zu *inf*; **out of ~** TECH nicht in Ordnung, defekt; außer Betrieb; **make to ~** auf Bestellung *or* nach Maß anfertigen **2.** *v/t* j-m befehlen (**to do** zu tun), *et.* befehlen, anordnen; j-n schicken, beordern; MED *j-m et.* verordnen; ECON bestellen; *fig* ordnen, in Ordnung bringen; *v/i* bestellen (*in restaurant*)

or·der·ly 1. ordentlich; *fig* gesittet, friedlich **2.** MED Hilfspfleger *m*

or·di·nal *a.* **~ number** MATH Ordnungszahl *f*

outlet

or·di·nary üblich, gewöhnlich, normal
ore MIN Erz n
or·gan ANAT Organ n (a. fig); MUS Orgel f;
~ do·nor MED Organspender m
or·gan·ic organisch
or·gan·ism Organismus m
or·gan·i·za·tion Organisation f
or·gan·ize organisieren; sich (gewerkschaftlich) organisieren
or·gan·iz·er Organisator(in)
or·gan recip·i·ent MED Organempfän-
ger(in) m(f)
or·gasm Orgasmus m
o·ri·ent 1. *Orient* der Osten, *der* Orient,
das Morgenland **2.** orientieren
o·ri·en·tal 1. orientalisch, östlich **2.** *Ori-*
ental Orientale m, Orientalin f
o·ri·en·tate orientieren
or·i·gin Ursprung m, Abstammung f,
Herkunft f
o·rig·i·nal 1. ursprünglich; Original…;
originell **2.** Original n
o·rig·i·nal·i·ty Originalität f
o·rig·i·nal·ly ursprünglich; originell
o·rig·i·nate v/t schaffen, ins Leben rufen; v/i zurückgehen (*from* auf acc),
(her)stammen (*from* von, aus)
or·na·ment 1. Ornament(e pl) n, Verzie-
rung(en pl) f, Schmuck m; fig Zier(de) f
(*to* für or gen); **2.** verzieren, schmücken
(*with* mit)
or·na·men·tal dekorativ, schmückend,
Zier…
or·nate fig überladen
or·phan 1. Waise f, Waisenkind n **2.** *be*
~ed Waise werden
or·phan·age Waisenhaus n
or·tho·dox orthodox
os·cil·late PHYS schwingen; fig schwanken (*between* zwischen dat)
os·prey ZO Fischadler m
os·ten·si·ble angeblich, vorgeblich
os·ten·ta·tion (protzige) Zurschaustellung; Protzerei f, Prahlerei f
os·ten·ta·tious protzend, prahlerisch
os·tra·cize ächten
os·trich ZO Strauß m
oth·er andere(r, -s); *the ~ day* neulich;
the ~ morning neulich morgens; *every*
~ day jeden zweiten Tag, alle zwei Tage
oth·er·wise anders; sonst
ot·ter ZO Otter m
ought v/aux ich sollte; du solltest etc;
you ~ to have done it Sie hätten es

tun sollen
ounce Unze f (28,35 g)
our unser
ours unsere(r, -s)
our·selves wir or uns selbst; uns (selbst)
oust verdrängen, hinauswerfen (*from*
aus); j-n s-s Amtes entheben
out 1. adv, adj aus; hinaus(gehen, -wer-
fen etc); heraus(kommen etc); aus(brechen etc); draußen, im Freien; nicht zu
Hause; SPORT aus, draußen; aus, vorbei; aus, erloschen; ausverkauft; F
out, aus der Mode; *~ of* aus (… heraus);
zu … hinaus; außerhalb von (or gen);
außer Reichweite etc; außer Atem,
Übung etc; (hergestellt) aus; aus
Furcht etc; *be ~ of bread* kein Brot
mehr haben; *in nine ~ of ten cases*
in neun von zehn Fällen **2.** prp F aus
(… heraus); zu … hinaus **3.** outen
out·bal·ance überwiegen
out·bid überbieten
out·board mo·tor Außenbordmotor m
out·break MED, MIL Ausbruch m
out·build·ing Nebengebäude n
out·burst fig Ausbruch m
out·cast 1. ausgestoßen **2.** Ausgestoße-
ne m, f, Verstoßene m, f
out·come Ergebnis n
out·cry Aufschrei m, Schrei m der Entrüstung
out·dat·ed überholt, veraltet
out·dis·tance hinter sich lassen
out·do übertreffen
out·door adj im Freien, draußen
out·doors adv draußen, im Freien
out·er äußere(r, -s)
out·er·most äußerste(r, -s)
out·er space Weltraum m
out·fit Ausrüstung f, Ausstattung f;
Kleidung f; F (Arbeits)Gruppe f
out·fit·ter Ausstatter m; *men's ~* Her-
renausstatter m
out·go·ing (aus dem Amt) scheidend
out·grow herauswachsen aus (dat); Angewohnheit etc ablegen; größer werden
als
out·house Nebengebäude n
out·ing Ausflug m; Outing n
out·land·ish befremdlich, sonderbar
out·last überdauern, überleben
out·law HIST Geächtete m, f
out·lay (Geld)Auslagen pl, Ausgaben pl
out·let Abfluss m, Abzug m; fig Ventil n

out·line 1. Umriss *m*; Überblick *m* **2.** umreißen, skizzieren

out·live überleben

out·look (Aus)Blick *m*, (Aus)Sicht *f*; Einstellung *f*, Auffassung *f*

out·ly·ing abgelegen, entlegen

out·num·ber in der Überzahl sein; *be ~ed by s.o.* j-m zahlenmäßig unterlegen sein

out-of-date veraltet, überholt

out-of-the-way abgelegen, entlegen; *fig* ungewöhnlich

out·pa·tient MED ambulanter Patient, ambulante Patientin

out·post Vorposten *m*

out·pour·ing (Gefühls)Erguss *m*

out·put ECON Output *m*, Produktion *f*, Ausstoß *m*, Ertrag *m*; IT (Daten)Ausgabe *f*

out·rage 1. Gewalttat *f*, Verbrechen *n*; Empörung *f* **2.** grob verletzen; *j-n* empören; **out·ra·geous** abscheulich; empörend, unerhört

out·right 1. *adj* völlig, gänzlich, glatt (*lie etc*) **2.** *adv* auf der Stelle, sofort; ohne Umschweife

out·run schneller laufen als; *fig* übersteigen, übertreffen

out·set Anfang *m*, Beginn *m*

out·shine überstrahlen, *fig a.* in den Schatten stellen

out·side 1. Außenseite *f*; SPORT Außenstürmer(in); *at the* (*very*) ~ (aller)höchstens; ~ *left* (*right*) SPORT Linksaußen (Rechtsaußen) *m* **2.** *adj* äußere(r, -s), Außen... **3.** *adv* draußen; heraus, hinaus **4.** *prp* außerhalb

out·sid·er Außenseiter(in)

out·size *f* **2.** übergroß

out·skirts Stadtrand *m*, Außenbezirke *pl*

out·spo·ken offen, freimütig

out·spread ausgestreckt, ausgebreitet

out·stand·ing hervorragend; ECON ausstehend; ungeklärt (*problem*); unerledigt (*work*)

out·stay länger bleiben als; → *welcome 4*

out·stretched ausgestreckt

out·strip überholen; *fig* übertreffen

out tray: *in the* ~ im Postausgang *etc*

out·vote überstimmen

out·ward 1. äußere(r, -s); äußerlich **2.** *adv mst* **outwards** auswärts, nach außen; **out·ward·ly** äußerlich

out·weigh *fig* überwiegen

out·wit überlisten, F reinlegen

out·worn veraltet, überholt

o·val 1. oval **2.** Oval *n*

o·va·tion Ovation *f*; *give s.o. a standing* ~ j-m stehende Ovationen bereiten, j-m stehend Beifall klatschen

ov·en Backofen *m*, Bratofen *m*

ov·en-read·y bratfertig

o·ver 1. *prp* über; über (*acc*), über (*acc*) ... (hin)weg; über (*dat*), auf der anderen Seite von (*or gen*); über (*acc*), mehr als **2.** *adv* hinüber, herüber (*to* zu); drüben; darüber, mehr; zu Ende, vorüber, vorbei; über..., um...: *et.* über(*geben etc*); über(*kochen etc*); um(*fallen, -werfen etc*); herum(*drehen etc*); von Anfang bis Ende, durch(*lesen etc*); (gründlich) über(*legen etc*); (*all*) ~ *again* noch einmal; *all* ~ ganz vorbei; ~ *and* ~ (*again*) immer wieder; ~ *and above* obendrein, überdies

o·ver·age zu alt

o·ver·all 1. gesamt, Gesamt...; allgemein; insgesamt **2.** *Br* Arbeitsmantel *m*, Kittel *m*; (*Br* ~s) Overall *m*, Arbeitsanzug *m*; Arbeitshose *f*

o·ver·awe einschüchtern

o·ver·bal·ance umstoßen, umkippen; das Gleichgewicht verlieren

o·ver·bear·ing anmaßend

o·ver·board MAR über Bord

o·ver·bur·den *fig* überlasten

o·ver·cast bewölkt, bedeckt

o·ver·charge überlasten, ELECTR *a.* überladen; ECON *j-m* zu viel berechnen; *Betrag* zu viel verlangen

o·ver·coat Mantel *m*

o·ver·come überwinden, überwältigen; *be* ~ *with emotion* von s-n Gefühlen übermannt werden

o·ver·crowd·ed überfüllt; überlaufen

o·ver·do übertreiben; GASTR zu lange kochen *or* braten; *overdone a.* übergar

o·ver·dose Überdosis *f*

o·ver·draft ECON (Konto)Überziehung *f*; *a.* ~ *facility* Überziehungskredit *m*

o·ver·draw ECON *Konto* überziehen (*by* um)

o·ver·dress (sich) zu fein anziehen; ~*ed* overdressed, zu fein angezogen

o·ver·drive MOT Overdrive *m*, Schongang *m*

o·ver·due überfällig
o·ver·eat zu viel essen
o·ver·es·ti·mate zu hoch schätzen *or* veranschlagen; *fig* überschätzen
o·ver·ex·pose PHOT überbelichten
o·ver·feed überfüttern
o·ver·flow 1. *v/t* überfluten, überschwemmen; *v/i* überlaufen, überfließen; überquellen (**with** von); **2.** TECH Überlauf *m*; Überlaufen *n*, -fließen *n*
o·ver·grown BOT überwachsen, überwuchert
o·ver·hang *v/t* über (*dat*) hängen; *v/i* überhängen
o·ver·haul *Maschine* überholen
o·ver·head 1. *adv* oben, droben **2.** *adj* Hoch..., Ober...; ECON ~ **expenses** *or* **costs** Gemeinkosten *pl*; SPORT Überkopf...; ~ **kick** *soccer*: Fallrückzieher *m* **3.** ECON *esp Br a. pl* Gemeinkosten *pl*
o·ver·hear (zufällig) hören
o·ver·heat·ed überhitzt, überheizt; TECH heiß gelaufen
o·ver·joyed überglücklich
o·ver·lap (sich) überlappen; sich überschneiden
o·ver·leaf umseitig, umstehend
o·ver·load überlasten (*a.* ELECTR), überladen
o·ver·look übersehen; ~**ing the sea** mit Blick aufs Meer
o·ver·night 1. über Nacht; **stay** ~ über Nacht bleiben, übernachten **2.** Nacht..., Übernachtungs...; ~ **bag** Reisetasche *f*
o·ver·pass (Straßen-, Eisenbahn-) Überführung *f*
o·ver·pay zu viel (be)zahlen
o·ver·pop·u·lat·ed übervölkert
o·ver·pow·er überwältigen; ~**ing** *fig* überwältigend
o·ver·rate überbewerten, überschätzen
o·ver·reach: ~ **o.s.** sich übernehmen
o·ver·re·act überreagieren, überzogen reagieren (**to** auf *acc*)
o·ver·re·ac·tion Überreaktion *f*, überzogene Reaktion
o·ver·ride sich hinwegsetzen über (*acc*)
o·ver·rule *Entscheidung etc* aufheben, *Einspruch etc* abweisen
o·ver·run länger dauern als vorgesehen; *Signal* überfahren; **be** ~ **with** wimmeln von

o·ver·seas 1. *adj* überseeisch, Übersee... **2.** *adv* in *or* nach Übersee
o·ver·see beaufsichtigen, überwachen
o·ver·shad·ow *fig* überschatten, in den Schatten stellen
o·ver·sight Versehen *n*
o·ver·size(d) übergroß, überdimensional, in Übergröße(n)
o·ver·sleep verschlafen
o·ver·staffed (personell) überbesetzt
o·ver·state übertreiben
o·ver·state·ment Übertreibung *f*
o·ver·stay länger bleiben als; → **welcome 4**
o·ver·step *fig* überschreiten
o·ver·take überholen; *j-n* überraschen
o·ver·tax zu hoch besteuern; *fig* überbeanspruchen, überfordern
o·ver·throw 1. *Regierung etc* stürzen **2.** (Um)Sturz *m*
o·ver·time ECON Überstunden *pl*; SPORT (Spiel)Verlängerung *f*; **do** ~, **work** ~ Überstunden machen
o·ver·tired übermüdet
o·ver·ture MUS Ouvertüre *f*; Vorspiel *n*
o·ver·turn *v/t* umwerfen, umstoßen; *Regierung etc* stürzen; *v/i* umkippen, MAR kentern
o·ver·view *fig* Überblick *m* (**of** über *acc*)
o·ver·weight 1. Übergewicht *n* **2.** übergewichtig (*person*), zu schwer (**by** um); **be five pounds** ~ fünf Pfund Übergewicht haben
o·ver·whelm überwältigen (*a. fig*)
o·ver·whelm·ing überwältigend
o·ver·work sich überarbeiten; überanstrengen
o·ver·wrought überreizt
o·ver·zeal·ous übereifrig
owe *j-m et.* schulden, schuldig sein; *et.* verdanken
ow·ing: ~ **to** infolge, wegen
owl ZO Eule *f*
own 1. eigen; *my* ~ mein Eigentum; (*all*) **on one's** ~ allein **2.** besitzen; zugeben, (ein)gestehen
own·er Eigentümer(in), Besitzer(in)
own·er-oc·cu·pied *esp Br* eigengenutzt; ~ **flat** Eigentumswohnung *f*
own·er·ship Besitz *m*; Eigentum *n*; Eigentumsrecht *n*
ox ZO Ochse *m*
ox·ide CHEM Oxid *n*, Oxyd *n*
ox·i·dize CHEM oxidieren

ox·y·gen CHEM Sauerstoff *m*; **~ ap·pa·ra·tus** MED Sauerstoffgerät *n*; **~ tent** MED Sauerstoffzelt *n*
oy·ster ZO Auster *f*
o·zone CHEM Ozon *n*

o·zone-friend·ly FCKW-frei, ohne Treibgas
o·zone| hole Ozonloch *n*; **~ lay·er** Ozonschicht *f*; **~ lev·els** Ozonwerte *pl*; **~ shield** Ozonschild *m*

P

P, p P, p *n*
pace 1. Tempo *n*, Geschwindigkeit *f*; Schritt *m*; Gangart *f* (*of a horse*) **2.** *v/t* Zimmer etc durchschreiten; *a.* **~ out** abschreiten; *v/i* (einher)schreiten; **~ up and down** auf und ab gehen
pace·mak·er SPORT Schrittmacher(in); MED Herzschrittmacher *m*
pace·set·ter SPORT Schrittmacher(in)
Pa·cif·ic *a.* **~ Ocean** der Pazifik, der Pazifische *or* Stille Ozean
pac·i·fi·er Schnuller *m*
pac·i·fist Pazifist(in)
pac·i·fy beruhigen, besänftigen
pack 1. Pack(en) *m*, Paket *n*, Bündel *n*; Packung *f*, Schachtel *f*; ZO Meute *f*; Rudel *n*; *contp* Pack *n*, Bande *f*; MED etc Packung *f*; (Karten)Spiel *n*; **a ~ of lies** ein Haufen Lügen **2.** *v/t* ein-, zusammenpacken, abpacken, verpacken (*a.* **~ up**); zusammenpferchen; vollstopfen; *Koffer etc* packen; **~ off** F fort-, wegschicken; *v/i* packen; (sich) drängen (*into* in *acc*); **~ up** zusammenpacken; **send s.o. ~ing** j-n fort- *or* wegjagen
pack·age Paket *n*; Packung *f*; **software ~** IT Software-, Programmpaket *n*
pack·age| deal F Pauschalangebot *n*, -arrangement *n*; **~ hol·i·day** Pauschalurlaub *m*; **~ tour** Pauschalreise *f*
pack·et Päckchen *n*; Packung *f*, Schachtel *f*
pack·ing Packen *n*; Verpackung *f*
pact Pakt *m*, POL *a.* Vertrag *m*
pad 1. Polster *n*; SPORT (*Knie- etc*)Schützer *m*; (*Schreib- etc*)Block *m*; (*Stempel*)Kissen *n*; ZO Ballen *m*; (*Abschuss-*) Rampe *f* **2.** (aus)polstern, wattieren
pad·ding Polsterung *f*, Wattierung *f*
pad·dle 1. Paddel *n*; MAR (Rad)Schaufel *f* **2.** paddeln; plan(t)schen

pad·dock (Pferde)Koppel *f*
pad·lock Vorhängeschloss *n*
pa·gan 1. Heide *m*, Heidin *f* **2.** heidnisch
page[1] **1.** Seite *f* **2.** paginieren
page[2] **1.** (Hotel)Page *m* **2.** j-n ausrufen (lassen)
pag·eant (*a.* historischer) Festzug
pa·gin·ate paginieren
pail Eimer *m*, Kübel *m*
pain 1. Schmerz(en *pl*) *m*; Kummer *m*; *pl* Mühe *f*, Bemühungen *pl*; **be in** (**great**) **~** (große) Schmerzen haben; **be a ~** (**in the neck**) F e-m auf den Wecker gehen; **take ~s** sich Mühe geben **2.** *esp fig* schmerzen; **pain·ful** schmerzhaft, schmerzend; *fig* schmerzlich; peinlich
pain·kill·er Schmerzmittel *n*
pain·less schmerzlos
pains·tak·ing sorgfältig, gewissenhaft
paint 1. Farbe *f*; Anstrich *m* **2.** *v/t* anmalen, bemalen; (an)streichen; *Auto etc* lackieren; *v/i* malen
paint·box Malkasten *m*
paint·brush (Maler)Pinsel *m*
paint·er (*a.* Kunst)Maler(in), Anstreicher(in)
paint·ing Malerei *f*; Gemälde *n*, Bild *n*
pair 1. Paar *n*; **a ~ of ...** ein Paar ..., ein(e) ...; **a ~ of scissors** e-e Schere **2.** *v/i* ZO sich paaren; *a.* **~ off**, **~ up** Paare bilden; *v/t a.* **~ off**, **~ up** paarweise anordnen; **~ off** *zwei Leute* zusammenbringen, verkuppeln
pa·ja·ma(s) (**a pair of**) **~s** (ein) Schlafanzug *m*, (ein) Pyjama *m*
pal Kamerad *m*, F Kumpel *m*, Spezi *m*
pal·ace Palast *m*, Schloss *n*
pal·a·ta·ble schmackhaft (*a. fig*)
pal·ate ANAT Gaumen *m*; *fig* Geschmack *m*
pale[1] **1.** blass, *a.* bleich, *a.* hell (*color*) **2.** blass *or* bleich werden

pale[2] Pfahl *m*; *fig* Grenzen *pl*
pale·ness Blässe *f*
Pal·es·tin·i·an 1. palästinensisch **2.** Palästinenser(in)
pal·ings Lattenzaun *m*
pal·i·sade Palisade *f*; *pl* Steilufer *n*
pal·let TECH Palette *f*
pal·lid blass; **pal·lor** Blässe *f*
palm[1] *a.* ~ **tree** BOT Palme *f*
palm[2] **1.** ANAT Handfläche *f* **2.** *et.* in der Hand verschwinden lassen; ~ **s.th. off on s.o.** F j-m et. andrehen
pal·pa·ble fühlbar, greifbar
pal·pi·tate MED klopfen, pochen
pal·pi·ta·tions MED Herzklopfen *n*
pal·sy MED Lähmung *f*
pal·try armselig
pam·per verwöhnen
pam·phlet Broschüre *f*
pan Pfanne *f*, Topf *m*
pan·a·ce·a Allheilmittel *n*
pan·cake Pfannkuchen *m*
pan·da ZO Panda *m*
pan·da car *Br* (Funk)Streifenwagen *m*
pan·de·mo·ni·um Hölle *f*, Höllenlärm *m*, Tumult *m*, Chaos *n*
pan·der Vorschub leisten (*to* dat)
pane (*Fenster*)Scheibe *f*
pan·el 1. (*Tür*)Füllung *f*, (*Wand*)Täfelung *f*; ELECTR, TECH Instrumentenbrett *n*, (*Schalt-, Kontroll- etc*)Tafel *f*; JUR Liste *f* der Geschworenen; Diskussionsteilnehmer *pl*, Diskussionsrunde *f*; Rateteam *n* **2.** täfeln
pang stechender Schmerz; ~**s of hunger** nagender Hunger; ~**s of conscience** Gewissensbisse *pl*
pan·han·dle 1. Pfannenstiel *m*; GEOGR schmaler Fortsatz **2.** F betteln
pan·ic 1. panisch **2.** Panik *f* **3.** in Panik versetzen *or* geraten
pan·ick·y: F **be** ~ in Panik sein
pan·ic-strick·en von Panik erfasst *or* erfüllt
pan·o·ra·ma Panorama *n*, Ausblick *m*
pan·sy BOT Stiefmütterchen *n*
pant keuchen, schnaufen, nach Luft schnappen
pan·ther ZO Panther *m*; Puma *m*; Jaguar *m*
pan·ties (Damen)Schlüpfer *m*, Slip *m*; Höschen *n*
pan·to·mime THEA Pantomime *f*; *Br* F Weihnachtsspiel *n*

pan·try Speisekammer *f*
pants Hose *f*; *Br* Unterhose *f*; *Br* Schlüpfer *m*
pant·suit Hosenanzug *m*
pan·ty·hose Strumpfhose *f*
pan·ty·lin·er Slipeinlage *f*
pap Brei *m*
pa·pal päpstlich
pa·per 1. Papier *n*; Zeitung *f*; (Prüfungs)Arbeit *f*; UNIV Klausur(arbeit) *f*; Aufsatz *m*; Referat *n*; Tapete *f*; *pl* (Ausweis)Papiere *pl* **2.** tapezieren
pa·per·back Taschenbuch *n*, Paperback *n*
pa·per bag (Papier)Tüte *f*
pa·per·boy Zeitungsjunge *m*
pa·per clip Büro-, Heftklammer *f*
pa·per cup Pappbecher *m*
pa·per·hang·er Tapezierer *m*
pa·per knife *Br* Brieföffner *m*
pa·per mon·ey Papiergeld *n*
pa·per·weight Briefbeschwerer *m*
par: *at* ~ zum Nennwert; *be on a* ~ *with* gleich *or* ebenbürtig sein (*dat*)
par·a·ble Parabel *f*, Gleichnis *n*
par·a·chute Fallschirm *m*
par·a·chut·ist Fallschirmspringer(in)
pa·rade 1. Umzug *m*, *esp* MIL Parade *f*; *fig* Zurschaustellung *f*; *make a* ~ *of fig* zur Schau stellen **2.** ziehen (*through* durch); MIL antreten (lassen), vorbeimarschieren (lassen); zur Schau stellen; ~ (*through*) stolzieren durch
par·a·dise Paradies *n*
par·af·fin *Br* Petroleum *n*
par·a·glid·er SPORT Gleitschirm *m*; Gleitschirmflieger(in); **par·a·glid·ing** SPORT Gleitschirmfliegen *n*
par·a·gon Muster *n* (*of* an *dat*)
par·a·graph Absatz *m*, Abschnitt *m*; (Zeitungs)Notiz *f*
par·al·lel 1. parallel (*to, with* zu); **2.** MATH Parallele *f* (*a. fig*); *without* ~ ohne Parallele, ohnegleichen **3.** entsprechen (*dat*), gleichkommen (*dat*)
par·a·lyse *Br*, **par·a·lyze** MED lähmen, *fig a.* lahmlegen, zum Erliegen bringen; ~**d with** *fig* starr *or* wie gelähmt vor (*dat*)
pa·ral·y·sis MED Lähmung *f*, *fig a.* Lahmlegung *f*
par·a·med·ic MED Sanitäter *m*
par·a·mount größte(r, -s), übergeordnet; *of* ~ *importance* von (aller)größter

Bedeutung *or* Wichtigkeit
par·a·pet Brüstung *f*
par·a·pher·na·li·a (persönliche) Sachen *pl*; Ausrüstung *f*; *esp Br* F Scherereien *pl*
par·a·phrase 1. umschreiben **2.** Umschreibung *f*
par·a·site Parasit *m*, Schmarotzer *m*
par·a·troop·er MIL Fallschirmjäger *m*; *pl* Fallschirmjägertruppe *f*
par·boil halb gar kochen, ankochen
par·cel 1. Paket *n*; Parzelle *f* **2.** ~ *out* aufteilen; ~ *up* (als Paket) verpacken
parch ausdörren, austrocknen; vertrocknen
parch·ment Pergament *n*
par·don 1. JUR Begnadigung *f*; *I beg your* ~ Entschuldigung!, Verzeihung!; erlauben Sie mal!, ich muss doch sehr bitten!; *a.* ~*?* F (wie) bitte? **2.** verzeihen; vergeben; JUR begnadigen; ~ *me* → *I beg your pardon*; F (wie) bitte?
par·don·a·ble verzeihlich
pare sich *die Nägel* schneiden; *Apfel etc* schälen
par·ent Elternteil *m*, Vater *m*, Mutter *f*; *pl* Eltern *pl*; **par·ent·age** Abstammung *f*, Herkunft *f*; **pa·ren·tal** elterlich
pa·ren·the·ses (runde) Klammer
par·ents-in-law Schwiegereltern *pl*
par·ent-teach·er meet·ing PED Elternabend *m*
par·ings Schalen *pl*
par·ish REL Gemeinde *f*
par·ish church REL Pfarrkirche *f*
pa·rish·ion·er REL Gemeindemitglied *n*
park 1. Park *m*, (Grün)Anlage(n *pl*) *f* **2.** MOT parken; *look for somewhere to ~ the car* e-n Parkplatz suchen
par·ka Parka *m*, *f*
park·ing MOT Parken *n*; *no* ~ Parkverbot, Parken verboten; ~ *disk* Parkscheibe *f*; ~ *fee* Parkgebühr *f*; ~ *garage* Park(hoch)haus *n*; ~ *lot* Parkplatz *m*; ~ *lot at·tend·ant* Parkwächter *m*; ~ *me·ter* Parkuhr *f*; ~ *of·fender* Parksünder(in); ~ *space* Parkplatz *m*, Parklücke *f*; ~ *tick·et* Strafzettel *m*
par·ley *esp* MIL Verhandlung *f*
par·lia·ment Parlament *n*
par·lia·men·tar·i·an Parlamentarier(in)
par·lia·men·ta·ry parlamentarisch, Parlaments...
par·lo(u)r *mst in cpds* Salon *m*

pa·ro·chi·al REL Pfarr..., Gemeinde...; *fig* engstirnig, beschränkt
par·o·dy 1. Parodie *f* **2.** parodieren
pa·role JUR **1.** Hafturlaub *m*; bedingte Haftentlassung **2.** ~ *s.o.* j-m Hafturlaub gewähren; j-n bedingt entlassen
par·quet Parkett *n* (*a.* THEA)
par·quet floor Parkett(fuß)boden *m*
par·rot 1. ZO Papagei *m* (*a. fig*) **2.** *et.* (wie ein Papagei) nachplappern
par·ry abwehren, parieren
par·si·mo·ni·ous geizig
pars·ley BOT Petersilie *f*
par·son REL Pfarrer *m*
par·son·age REL Pfarrhaus *n*
part 1. Teil *m*; TECH Teil *n*, Bau-, Ersatzteil *n*; Anteil *m*; Seite *f*, Partei *f*; THEA, *fig* Rolle *f*; MUS Stimme *f*, Partie *f*; GEOGR Gegend *f*, Teil *m*; (Haar)Scheitel *m*; *for my* ~ was mich betrifft; *for the most* ~ größtenteils; meistens; *in* ~ teilweise, zum Teil; *on the* ~ *of* vonseiten, seitens (*gen*); *on my* ~ von m-r Seite; *take* ~ *in s.th.* an e-r Sache teilnehmen; *take s.th. in good* ~ *et.* nicht übel nehmen **2.** *v/t* trennen; (ab-, zer)teilen; einteilen; *Haar* scheiteln; ~ *company* sich trennen (*with* von); *v/i* sich trennen (*with* von); **3.** *adj* Teil... **4.** *adv*: ~ ..., ~ teils ..., teils
par·tial Teil..., teilweise; parteiisch, voreingenommen (*to* für)
par·ti·al·i·ty Parteilichkeit *f*, Voreingenommenheit *f*; Schwäche *f*, besondere Vorliebe (*for* für)
par·tial·ly teilweise, zum Teil
par·tic·i·pant Teilnehmer(in)
par·tic·i·pate teilnehmen, sich beteiligen (*both*: *in* an *dat*)
par·tic·i·pa·tion Teilnahme *f*, Beteiligung *f*
par·ti·ci·ple LING Partizip *n*, Mittelwort *n*
par·ti·cle Teilchen *n*
par·tic·u·lar 1. besondere(r, -s), speziell; genau, eigen, wählerisch **2.** Einzelheit *f*; *pl* nähere Umstände *pl or* Angaben *pl*; Personalien *pl*; *in* ~ insbesondere; **par·tic·u·lar·ly** besonders
part·ing Trennung *f*, Abschied *m*; *esp Br* (Haar)Scheitel *m* **2.** Abschieds...
par·ti·san 1. Parteigänger(in); MIL Partisan(in) **2.** parteiisch
par·ti·tion 1. Teilung *f*; Trennwand *f* **2.** ~

off abteilen, abtrennen

part·ly teilweise, zum Teil

part·ner Partner(in), ECON *a.* Teilhaber(in); **part·ner·ship** Partnerschaft *f*, ECON *a.* Teilhaberschaft *f*

par·tridge ZO Rebhuhn *n*

part-time 1. *adj* Teilzeit…, Halbtags…; *~ worker* → **part-timer 2.** *adv* halbtags

part-tim·er F Teilzeitbeschäftigte *m*, *f*, Halbtagskraft *f*

par·ty Partei *f (a.* POL); *(Arbeits-, Reise-)* Gruppe *f*; *(Rettungs- etc)*Mannschaft *f*; MIL Kommando *n*, Trupp *m*; Party *f*, Gesellschaft *f*; Teilnehmer(in), Beteiligte *m*, *f*; *~* **line** POL Parteilinie *f*; *~* **pol·i·tics** Parteipolitik *f*

pass 1. *v/i* vorbeigehen, -fahren, -kommen, -ziehen *etc* (*by* an *dat*); übergehen (*to* auf *acc*), fallen (*to* an *acc*); vergehen (*pain etc*, *time*); durchkommen, (die Prüfung) bestehen; gelten (*as, for* als), gehalten werden (*as, for*für); PARL Rechtskraft erlangen; unbeanstandet bleiben; SPORT (den Ball) abspielen *or* passen (*to* zu); *card game*: passen (*a. fig*); *let s.o. ~* j-n vorbeilassen; *let s.th. ~* et. durchgehen lassen; *v/t* vorbeigehen, -fahren, -fließen, -kommen, -ziehen *etc* an (*dat*); überholen; *Prüfung* bestehen; *Prüfling* durchkommen lassen; (*mit der Hand*) streichen (*over* über *acc*); *j-m* et. reichen, geben, et. weitergeben; SPORT *Ball* abspielen, passen (*to* zu); *Zeit* verbringen; PARL *Gesetz* verabschieden; *Urteil* abgeben, fällen, JUR *a.* sprechen (*on* über *acc*); *fig* hinausgehen über (*acc*), übersteigen, übertreffen; *~ away* sterben; *~ off* j-n, et. ausgeben (*as* als); *gut etc* verlaufen; *~ out* ohnmächtig werden **2.** Passierschein *m*; Bestehen *n* (*examination*); SPORT Pass *m*, Zuspiel *n*; *(Gebirgs)*Pass *m*; *free ~* Frei(fahr)karte *f*; *things have come to such a ~ that* F die Dinge haben sich derart zugespitzt, dass; *make a ~ at* F Annäherungsversuche machen bei

pass·a·ble passierbar, befahrbar; passabel, leidlich

pas·sage Passage *f*, Korridor *m*, Gang *m*; Durchgang *m*; (See-, Flug)Reise *f*; Durchfahrt *f*, Durchreise *f*; Passage *f (a.* MUS), Stelle *f*; *bird of ~* Zugvogel *m*

pass·book ECON Sparbuch *n*

pas·sen·ger Passagier *m*, Fahrgast *m*, Fluggast *m*, Reisende *m*, *f*, MOT Insasse *m*, Insassin *f*

pass·er·by Passant(in)

pas·sion Leidenschaft *f*; Wut *f*, Zorn *m*; *Passion* REL Passion *f*; *~s ran high* die Erregung schlug hohe Wellen

pas·sion·ate leidenschaftlich

pas·sive passiv; LING passivisch

Pass·o·ver REL Passah(fest) *n*

pass·port (Reise)Pass *m*

pass·word Kennwort *n (a.* IT), MIL *a.* Parole *f*, Losung *f*

past 1. *adj* vergangen; frühere(r, -s); *be~ a.* vorüber sein; *for some time ~* seit einiger Zeit; *~ tense* LING Vergangenheit *f*, Präteritum *n* **2.** *adv* vorüber, vorbei; *go~* vorbeigehen **3.** *prp time*: nach, über (*acc*); über … (*acc*) hinaus; an … (*dat*) vorbei; *half ~ two* halb drei; *~ hope* hoffnungslos **4.** Vergangenheit *f (a.* LING)

pas·ta Teigwaren *pl*

paste 1. Paste *f*; Kleister *m*; Teig *m* **2.** kleben (*to, on* an *acc*); *~ up* ankleben

paste·board Karton *m*, Pappe *f*

pas·tel Pastell(zeichnung *f*) *n*

pas·teur·ize pasteurisieren

pas·time Zeitvertreib *m*, Freizeitbeschäftigung *f*

pas·tor REL Pastor *m*, Pfarrer *m*, Seelsorger *m*; **pas·tor·al** REL seelsorgerisch, pastoral; *~ care* Seelsorge *f*

pas·try GASTR *(Blätter-, Mürbe)*Teig *m*; Feingebäck *n*; *~ cook* Konditor *m*

pas·ture 1. Weide(land *n*) *f* **2.** *v/t* weiden (lassen); *v/i* grasen, weiden

pas·ty¹ *esp Br* GASTR (Fleisch)Pastete *f*

pas·ty² blass, F käsig

pat 1. Klaps *m*; GASTR Portion *f* **2.** tätscheln; klopfen

patch 1. Fleck *m*; Flicken *m*; kleines Stück Land; *in ~es* stellenweise **2.** flicken

pa·tent 1. offenkundig; patentiert; Patent… **2.** Patent *n*; *take out a ~ for s.th.* (sich) et. patentieren lassen **3.** *et.* patentieren lassen

pa·tent·ee Patentinhaber(in)

pa·tent leath·er Lackleder *n*

pa·ter·nal väterlich; väterlicherseits

pa·ter·ni·ty JUR Vaterschaft *f*

path Pfad *m*; Weg *m*

pa·thet·ic mitleiderregend; kläglich, miserabel

pa·tience Geduld *f*; *esp Br* Patience *f*

pa·tient¹ geduldig

pa·tient² MED Patient(in)

pat·i·o Terrasse *f*; Innenhof *m*, Patio *m*

pat·ri·ot Patriot(in)

pat·ri·ot·ic patriotisch

pa·trol 1. Patrouille *f* (*a.* MIL.), Streife *f*, Runde *f*; *on~* auf Patrouille, auf Streife **2.** abpatrouillieren, auf Streife sein in (*dat*), s-e Runde machen in (*dat*)

pa·trol car (Funk)Streifenwagen *m*

pa·trol·man Streifenpolizist *m*; *Br* motorisierter Pannenhelfer

pa·tron Schirmherr *m*; Gönner *m*, Förderer *m*; (Stamm)Kunde *m*; Stammgast *m*; **pat·ron·age** Schirmherrschaft *f*; Förderung *f*; **pat·ron·ess** Schirmherrin *f*; Gönnerin *f*, Förderin *f*; **pat·ron·ize** fördern; (Stamm)Kunde *or* Stammgast sein bei *or* in (*dat*); gönnerhaft *or* herablassend behandeln

pa·tron saint REL Schutzheilige *m, f*

pat·ter prasseln (*rain*); trappeln (*feet*)

pat·tern 1. Muster *n* (*a. fig*); Schema *n* **2.** bilden, formen (*after, on* nach)

paunch (dicker) Bauch

pau·per Arme *m, f*

pause 1. Pause *f* **2.** innehalten, e-e Pause machen

pave pflastern; ~ *the way for* fig den Weg ebnen für

pave·ment Fahrbahn *f*; Belag *m*, Pflaster *n*; *Br* Bürgersteig *m*, Gehsteig *m*

pave·ment ca·fé *Br* Straßencafé *n*

paw 1. ZO Pfote *f*, Tatze *f* **2.** *v/t* Boden scharren; scharren an (*dat*); F betatschen; *v/i* scharren (*at* an *dat*)

pawn¹ *chess:* Bauer *m*; *fig* Schachfigur *f*

pawn² 1. verpfänden, versetzen **2.** *be in* ~ verpfändet *or* versetzt sein

pawn·bro·ker Pfandleiher *m*

pawn·shop Leihhaus *n*, Pfandhaus *n*

pay 1. *v/t et.* (be)zahlen; *j-n* bezahlen; *Aufmerksamkeit* schenken; *Besuch* abstatten; *Kompliment* machen; ~ *attention* achtgeben auf (*acc*); PED aufpassen; ~ *cash* bar bezahlen; *v/i* zahlen; *fig* sich lohnen; ~ *for* (*fig* für) *et.* bezahlen; *fig* büßen; ~ *in* einzahlen; ~ *into* einzahlen auf (*acc*); ~ *off et.* ab(be)zahlen; *j-n* auszahlen **2.** Bezahlung *f*, Gehalt *n*, Lohn *m*

pay·a·ble zahlbar, fällig

pay·day Zahltag *m*

pay·ee Zahlungsempfänger(in)

pay en·ve·lope Lohntüte *f*

pay·ing lohnend

pay·mas·ter MIL Zahlmeister *m*

pay·ment (Be)Zahlung *f*

pay pack·et *Br* Lohntüte *f*

pay phone *Br* Münzfernsprecher *m*

pay·roll Lohnliste *f*

pay·slip Lohn-, Gehaltsstreifen *m*

PC *abbr of personal computer* PC *m*, Personal Computer *m*; *PC user* PC--Benutzer *m*

pea BOT Erbse *f*

peace Friede(n) *m*; Ruhe *f*; JUR öffentliche Ruhe und Ordnung; *at~* in Frieden

peace·a·ble friedlich, friedfertig

peace·ful friedlich

peace·lov·ing friedliebend

peace move·ment Friedensbewegung *f*

peace·time Friedenszeiten *pl*

peach BOT Pfirsich(baum) *m*

pea·cock ZO Pfau *m*, Pfauhahn *m*

pea·hen ZO Pfauhenne *f*

peak Spitze *f*, Gipfel *m*; Schirm *m*; *fig* Höhepunkt *m*, Höchststand *m*

peaked cap Schirmmütze *f*

peak hours Hauptverkehrszeit *f*, Stoßzeit *f*; ELECTR Hauptbelastungszeit *f*

peak| time, ~ *viewing hours* *Br* TV Haupteinschaltzeit *f*, Hauptsendezeit *f*, beste Sendezeit

peal 1. (*Glocken*)Läuten *n*; (*Donner-*)Schlag *m*; ~*s of laughter* schallendes Gelächter **2.** *a.* ~ *out* läuten; krachen

pea·nut BOT Erdnuss *f*; *pl* F lächerliche Summe

pear BOT Birne *f*; Birnbaum *m*

pearl 1. Perle *f*; Perlmutter *f*, Perlmutt *n* **2.** Perlen...

pearl·y perlenartig, Perlen...

peas·ant Kleinbauer *m*

peat Torf *m*

peb·ble Kiesel(stein) *m*

peck picken, hacken; ~ *at one's food* im Essen herumstochern

pe·cu·li·ar eigen, eigentümlich, typisch; eigenartig, seltsam

pe·cu·li·ar·i·ty Eigenheit *f*; Eigentümlichkeit *f*

ped·a·go·gic pädagogisch

ped·al 1. Pedal *n* **2.** das Pedal treten;

(mit dem Rad) fahren, strampeln

pe·dan·tic pedantisch

ped·es·tal Sockel *m*

pe·des·tri·an 1. Fußgänger(in) **2.** Fußgänger…; **~ cross·ing** Fußgängerübergang *m*; **~ mall**, *esp Br* **~ pre·cinct** Fußgängerzone *f*

ped·i·cure Pediküre *f*

ped·i·gree Stammbaum *m* (*a.* ZO)

ped·lar *Br* → *peddler*

pee F **1.** pinkeln **2.** *have* (*or* **go for**) *a* **~** pinkeln (gehen)

peek 1. kurz *or* verstohlen gucken (*at* auf *acc*); **2.** *have or take a* **~** *at* e-n kurzen *or* verstohlenen Blick werfen auf (*acc*)

peel 1. *v/t* schälen; *a.* **~ off** abschälen, *Folie, Tapete etc* abziehen, ablösen; *Kleid* abstreifen; *v/i a.* **~ off** sich lösen (*wallpaper etc*), abblättern (*paint etc*), sich schälen (*skin*) **2.** BOT Schale *f*

peep¹ 1. kurz *or* verstohlen gucken (*at* auf *acc*); *mst* **~ out** (her)vorschauen **2.** *take a* **~** *at* e-n kurzen *or* verstohlenen Blick werfen auf (*acc*)

peep² 1. Piep(s)en *n*; F Piepser *m* **2.** piep(s)en

peep·hole Guckloch *n*; (Tür)Spion *m*

peer angestrengt schauen, spähen; **~** *at s.o.* j-n anstarren

peer·less unvergleichlich, einzigartig

peev·ish verdrießlich, gereizt

peg 1. (Holz)Stift *m*, Zapfen *m*, Pflock *m*; (Kleider)Haken *m*; *Br* (*Wäsche-*) Klammer *f*; (*Zelt*)Hering *m*; *take s.o. down a* **~** (*or two*) F j-m e-n Dämpfer aufsetzen **2.** anpflocken; *Wäsche* anklammern, festklammern

pel·i·can ZO Pelikan *m*; **~ cross·ing** *Br* Ampelübergang *m*

pel·let Kügelchen *n*; Schrotkorn *n*

pelt¹ *v/t* bewerfen, *v/i*: *it's* **~***ing* (*down*), *esp Br it's* **~***ing with rain* es gießt in Strömen

pelt² ZO Fell *n*, Pelz *m*

pel·vis ANAT Becken *n*

pen¹ (*Schreib*)Feder *f*; Füller *m*; Kugelschreiber *m*

pen²1. Pferch *m*, (*Schaf*)Hürde *f* **2.** **~** *in*, **~** *up* Tiere einpferchen, *Personen* zusammenpferchen

pe·nal JUR Straf…; strafbar

pe·nal code JUR Strafgesetzbuch *n*

pe·nal·ize bestrafen

pen·al·ty Strafe *f*, SPORT *a.* Strafpunkt *m*; *soccer*: Elfmeter *m*; **~ ar·e·a**, **~ box** F *soccer*: Strafraum *m*; **~ goal** *soccer*: Elfmetertor *n*; **~ kick** *soccer*: Elfmeter *m*, Strafstoß *m*; **~ shoot-out** *soccer*: Elfmeterschießen *n*; **~ spot** *soccer*: Elfmeterpunkt *m*

pen·ance REL Buße *f*

pen·cil 1. Bleistift *m* **2.** (mit Bleistift) markieren *or* schreiben *or* zeichnen; *Augenbrauen* nachziehen

pen·cil case Federmäppchen *n*

pen·cil sharp·en·er Bleistiftspitzer *m*

pen·dant, pen·dent (Schmuck)Anhänger *m*

pend·ing 1. *prp* bis zu **2.** *adj esp* JUR schwebend

pen·du·lum Pendel *n*

pen·e·trate *v/t* eindringen in (*acc*); dringen durch, durchdringen; *v/i* eindringen (*into* in *acc*); **pen·e·trat·ing** durchdringend; *fig* scharf; scharfsinnig; **pen·e·tra·tion** Durchdringen *n*, Eindringen *n*; *fig* Scharfsinn *m*

pen friend *Br* Brieffreund(in)

pen·guin ZO Pinguin *m*

pe·nin·su·la Halbinsel *f*

pe·nis ANAT Penis *m*

pen·i·tence Buße *f*, Reue *f*

pen·i·tent 1. reuig, bußfertig **2.** REL Büßer(in)

pen·i·ten·tia·ry (Staats)Gefängnis *n*, Strafanstalt *f*

pen·knife Taschenmesser *n*

pen name Schriftstellername *m*, Pseudonym *n*

pen·nant Wimpel *m*

pen·ni·less (völlig) mittellos

pen·ny *Br* Penny *m*

pen pal Brieffreund(in)

pen·sion 1. Rente *f*, Pension *f* **2.** **~** *off* pensionieren, in den Ruhestand versetzen

pen·sion·er Rentner(in), Pensionär(in)

pen·sive nachdenklich

pen·tath·lete SPORT Fünfkämpfer(in)

pen·tath·lon SPORT Fünfkampf *m*

Pen·te·cost REL Pfingsten *n*

pent·house Penthouse *n*, Penthaus *n*

pent-up auf-, angestaut (*emotions*)

pe·o·ny BOT Pfingstrose *f*

peo·ple 1. Volk *n*, Nation *f*; die Menschen *pl*, die Leute *pl*; Leute *pl*, Personen *pl*; man; *the* **~** das (*gemeine*) Volk

2. besiedeln, bevölkern (**with** mit)

peo·ple's re·pub·lic Volksrepublik *f*

pep F **1.** Pep *m*, Schwung *m* **2.** *mst ~ up* j-*n or et.* in Schwung bringen, aufmöbeln

pep·per 1. Pfeffer *m*; BOT Paprikaschote *f* **2.** pfeffern

pep·per cast·er Pfefferstreuer *m*

pep·per·mint BOT Pfefferminze *f*; Pfefferminz *n*

pep·per·y pfeff(e)rig; *fig* hitzig

pep·pill F Aufputschpille *f*

per per, durch; pro, für, je

per·ceive (be)merken, wahrnehmen; erkennen

per cent, per·cent Prozent *n*

per·cen·tage Prozentsatz *m*; F Prozente *pl*, (An)Teil *m*

per·cep·ti·ble wahrnehmbar, merklich; **per·cep·tion** Wahrnehmung *f*; Auffassung *f*, Auffassungsgabe *f*

perch[1] **1.** (Sitz)Stange *f* **2.** (**on**) sich setzen (auf *acc*), sich niederlassen (auf *acc, dat*); F hocken (**on** auf *dat*); ~ *o.s.* F sich hocken (**on** auf *acc*)

perch[2] ZO Barsch *m*

per·co·la·tor Kaffeemaschine *f*

per·cus·sion Schlag *m*; Erschütterung *f*; MUS Schlagzeug *n*; ~ **drill** TECH Schlagbohrer *m*; ~ **in·stru·ment** MUS Schlaginstrument *n*

pe·remp·to·ry herrisch

pe·ren·ni·al ewig, immer während; BOT mehrjährig

per·fect 1. perfekt, vollkommen, vollendet; gänzlich, völlig **2.** vervollkommnen **3.** *a.* ~ *tense* LING Perfekt *n*

per·fec·tion Vollendung *f*; Vollkommenheit *f*, Perfektion *f*

per·fo·rate durchbohren, -löchern

per·form *v/t* verrichten, durchführen, tun; *Pflicht etc* erfüllen; THEA, MUS aufführen, spielen, vortragen; *v/i* THEA *etc* e-e Vorstellung geben, auftreten, spielen; **per·form·ance** Verrichtung *f*, Durchführung *f*; Leistung *f*; THEA, MUS Aufführung *f*, Vorstellung *f*, Vortrag *m*; **per·form·er** THEA, MUS Darsteller(in), Künstler(in)

per·fume 1. Duft *m*; Parfüm *n* **2.** parfümieren; **per·fum·er·y** Parfümerie *f*

per·haps vielleicht

per·il Gefahr *f*; **per·il·ous** gefährlich

pe·ri·od Periode *f*, Zeit *f*, Zeitdauer *f*,

Zeitraum *m*, Zeitspanne *f*; (Unterrichts)Stunde *f*; MED Periode *f*; LING Punkt *m*; ~ **fur·ni·ture** Stilmöbel *pl*

pe·ri·od·ic periodisch

pe·ri·od·i·cal 1. periodisch **2.** Zeitschrift *f*

pe·riph·e·ral IT Peripheriegerät *n*; ~ **e·quip·ment** IT Peripheriegeräte *pl*

pe·riph·e·ry Peripherie *f*, Rand *m*

per·ish umkommen; GASTR schlecht werden, verderben; TECH verschleißen

per·ish·a·ble leicht verderblich

per·ish·a·bles leicht verderbliche Lebensmittel

per·jure: ~ *o.s.* JUR e-n Meineid leisten

per·ju·ry JUR Meineid *m*; **commit** ~ e-n Meineid leisten

perk: ~ **up** *v/i* aufleben, munter werden; *v/t* j-*n* munter machen, F aufmöbeln

perk·y F munter, lebhaft; keck, selbstbewusst

perm 1. Dauerwelle *f*; **get a** ~ → **2. get one's hair ~ed** sich e-e Dauerwelle machen lassen

per·ma·nent 1. (be)ständig, dauerhaft, Dauer... **2.** *a.* ~ **wave** Dauerwelle *f*

per·me·a·ble durchlässig (**to** für)

per·me·ate durchdringen; dringen (**into** in *acc*; **through** durch)

per·mis·si·ble zulässig, erlaubt

per·mis·sion Erlaubnis *f*

per·mis·sive liberal; (sexuell) freizügig; ~ **so·ci·e·ty** tabufreie Gesellschaft

per·mit 1. erlauben, gestatten **2.** Genehmigung *f*

per·pen·dic·u·lar senkrecht; rechtwink(e)lig (**to** zu)

per·pet·u·al fortwährend, ständig, ewig

per·plex verwirren

per·plex·i·ty Verwirrung *f*

per·se·cute verfolgen

per·se·cu·tion Verfolgung *f*

per·se·cu·tor Verfolger(in)

per·se·ver·ance Ausdauer *f*, Beharrlichkeit *f*

per·se·vere beharrlich weitermachen

per·sist beharren (**in** auf *dat*); anhalten

per·sis·tence Beharrlichkeit *f*

per·sis·tent beharrlich; anhaltend

per·son Person *f* (*a.* LING)

per·son·al persönlich (*a.* LING); Personal...; Privat...; ~ **com·pu·ter** (*abbr* **PC**) Personal Computer *m*; ~ **da·ta** Personalien *pl*

per·son·al·i·ty Persönlichkeit *f*; *pl* anzügliche *or* persönliche Bemerkungen *pl*

per·son·al‖ or·ga·ni·zer Notizbuch *n*, Adressbuch *n* und Taschenkalender *m etc* (*in einem*); **~ pro·noun** LING Personalpronomen *n*; **~ ster·e·o** Walkman® *m*

per·son·i·fy personifizieren, verkörpern

per·son·nel Personal *n*, Belegschaft *f*; die Personalabteilung; **~ de·part·ment** Personalabteilung *f*; **~ man·ager** Personalchef *m*

per·spec·tive Perspektive *f*; Fernsicht *f*

per·spi·ra·tion Transpirieren *n*, Schwitzen *n*; Schweiß *m*

per·spire transpirieren, schwitzen

per·suade überreden; überzeugen

per·sua·sion Überredung(skunst) *f*; Überzeugung *f*

per·sua·sive überzeugend

pert keck, kess; schnippisch

per·tain: ~ to s.th. et. betreffen

per·ti·nent sachdienlich, relevant, zur Sache gehörig

per·turb beunruhigen

per·vade durchdringen, erfüllen

per·verse pervers; eigensinnig

per·ver·sion Verdrehung *f*, Perversion *f*

per·ver·si·ty Perversität *f*; Eigensinn *m*

per·vert 1. pervertieren; verdrehen **2.** perverser Mensch

pes·sa·ry MED Pessar *n*

pes·si·mism Pessimismus *m*

pes·si·mist Pessimist(in)

pes·si·mis·tic pessimistisch

pest ZO Schädling *m*; F Nervensäge *f*; F Plage *f*; **~ con·trol** Schädlingsbekämpfung *f*

pes·ter F *j-n* belästigen, *j-m* keine Ruhe lassen

pes·ti·cide Pestizid *n*, Schädlingsbekämpfungsmittel *n*

pet 1. (zahmes) (Haus)Tier; *often contp* Liebling *m* **2.** Lieblings...; Tier... **3.** streicheln; F Petting machen

pet·al BOT Blütenblatt *n*

pet food Tiernahrung *f*

pe·ti·tion 1. Eingabe *f*, Gesuch *n*, (schriftlicher) Antrag **2.** ersuchen; ein Gesuch einreichen (**for** um), e-n Antrag stellen (**for** auf *acc*)

pet name Kosename *m*

pet·ri·fy versteinern

pet·rol *Br* Benzin *n*

pe·tro·le·um Erdöl *n*, Mineralöl *n*

pet·rol‖ pump *Br* Zapfsäule *f*; **~ station** *Br* Tankstelle *f*

pet shop Tierhandlung *f*, Zoogeschäft *n*

pet·ti·coat Unterrock *m*

pet·ting F Petting *n*

pet·tish launisch, gereizt

pet·ty belanglos, unbedeutend, JUR *a.* geringfügig; engstirnig; **~ cash** Portokasse *f*; **~ lar·ce·ny** JUR einfacher Diebstahl

pet·u·lant launisch, gereizt

pew (Kirchen)Bank *f*

pew·ter Zinn *n*; *a.* **~ ware** Zinn (-geschirr) *n*

phan·tom Phantom *n*; Geist *m*

phar·ma·cist Apotheker(in)

phar·ma·cy Apotheke *f*

phase Phase *f*

pheas·ant ZO Fasan *m*

phe·nom·e·non Phänomen *n*, Erscheinung *f*

phi·lan·thro·pist Philanthrop(in), Menschenfreund(in)

phil·is·tine F *contp* **1.** Spießer *m* **2.** spießig

phi·lol·o·gist Philologe *m*, Philologin *f*

phi·lol·o·gy Philologie *f*

phi·los·o·pher Philosoph(in)

phi·los·o·phy Philosophie *f*

phlegm MED Schleim *m*

phone 1. Telefon *n*; **answer the~** ans Telefon gehen; **by~** telefonisch; **on the~** am Telefon; **be on the~** Telefon haben; am Telefon sein **2.** telefonieren, anrufen; **~ book** Telefonbuch *n*; **~ booth**, *Br* **~ box** Telefonzelle *f*; **~ call** Anruf *m*, Gespräch *n*

phone·card Telefonkarte *f*

phone-in *radio*, TV Sendung *f* mit telefonischer Zuhörer- *or* Zuschauerbeteiligung

phone num·ber Telefonnummer *f*

pho·net·ics Phonetik *f*

pho·n(e)y F **1.** Fälschung *f*; Schwindler(in) **2.** falsch, gefälscht, unecht; Schein...

phos·pho·rus CHEM Phosphor *m*

pho·to F Foto *n*, Bild *n*; **in the~** auf dem Foto; **take a~** ein Foto machen (**of** von)

pho·to·cop·i·er Fotokopiergerät *n*

pho·to·cop·y 1. Fotokopie *f* **2.** fotokopieren

pho·to·graph 1. Fotografie *f* **2.** fotografieren

pho·tog·ra·pher Fotograf(in)

pho·tog·ra·phy Fotografie *f*

phras·al verb LING Verb *n* mit Adverb (und Präposition)

phrase 1. (Rede)Wendung *f*, Redensart *f*, idiomatischer Ausdruck **2.** ausdrücken; **phrase·book** Sprachführer *m*

phys·i·cal 1. physisch, körperlich; physikalisch; **~ly handicapped** körperbehindert **2.** ärztliche Untersuchung; **~ ed·u·ca·tion** Leibeserziehung *f*, Sport *m*; **~ ex·am·i·na·tion** ärztliche Untersuchung; **~ hand·i·cap** Körperbehinderung *f*; **~ train·ing** Leibeserziehung *f*, Sport *m*

phy·si·cian Arzt *m*, Ärztin *f*

phys·i·cist Physiker(in)

phys·ics Physik *f*

phy·sique Körper(bau) *m*, Statur *f*

pi·a·nist MUS Pianist(in)

pi·an·o MUS Klavier *n*

pick 1. (auf)hacken; (auf)picken; auflesen, aufnehmen; pflücken; *Knochen* abnagen; bohren *or* stochern in (*dat*); F *Schloss* knacken; aussuchen, auswählen; **~ one's nose** in der Nase bohren; **~ one's teeth** in den Zähnen (herum)stochern; **~ s.o.'s pocket** j-n bestehlen; **have a bone to ~ with s.o.** mit j-m ein Hühnchen zu rupfen haben; **~ out** (sich) *et.* auswählen; ausmachen, erkennen; **~ up** aufheben, auflesen, aufnehmen; aufpicken; *Spur* aufnehmen; *j-n* abholen; *Anhalter* mitnehmen; F *Mädchen* aufreißen; *Kenntnisse, Informationen etc* aufschnappen; sich *e-e Krankheit etc* holen; *a.* **~ up speed** MOT schneller werden **2.** (Spitz)Hacke *f*, Pickel *m*; (Aus)Wahl *f*; **take your** ~ suchen Sie sich etwas aus

pick·a·back huckepack

pick·ax, *Br* **pick·axe** (Spitz)Hacke *f*, Pickel *m*

pick·et 1. Pfahl *m*; Streikposten *m* **2.** Streikposten aufstellen vor (*dat*), mit Streikposten besetzen; Streikposten stehen; **~ fence** Lattenzaun *m*; **~ line** Streikpostenkette *f*

pick·le GASTR **1.** Salzlake *f*; Essigsoße *f*; Essig-, Gewürzgurke *f*; *mst pl esp Br* Pickles *pl*; **be in a** (**pretty**) **~** F (ganz schön) in der Patsche sitzen *or* sein

or stecken **2.** einlegen

pick·lock Einbrecher *m*; TECH Dietrich *m*

pick·pock·et Taschendieb(in)

pick-up Tonabnehmer *m*; Kleintransporter *m*; F (Zufalls)Bekanntschaft *f*

pick·y F wählerisch (**in** *dat* about)

pic·nic 1. Picknick *n* **2.** ein Picknick machen, picknicken

pic·ture 1. Bild *n*; Gemälde *n*; PHOT Aufnahme *f*; Film *m*; *pl esp Br* Kino *n* **2.** darstellen, malen; *fig* sich *j-n*, *et.* vorstellen; **~ book** Bilderbuch *n*; **~ post·card** Ansichtskarte *f*

pic·tur·esque malerisch

pie (*Fleisch- etc*)Pastete *f*; (*mst gedeckter*) (*Apfel- etc*)Kuchen

piece 1. Stück *n*; Teil *n* (*of a machine etc*); Teil *m* (*of a set etc*); *chess*: Figur *f*; *board game*: Stein *m*; (Zeitungs)Artikel *m*, (-)Notiz *f*; **by the** ~ stückweise; **a ~ of advice** ein Rat; **a ~ of news** e-e Neuigkeit; **give s.o. a ~ of one's mind** j-m gründlich die Meinung sagen; **go to ~s** F zusammenbrechen; **take to ~s** auseinandernehmen **2.** **~ together** zusammensetzen, zusammenstückeln; *fig* zusammenfügen

piece·meal schrittweise

piece·work Akkordarbeit *f*; **do ~** im Akkord arbeiten

pier MAR Pier *m*, Landungsbrücke *f*; TECH Pfeiler *m*

pierce durchbohren, durchstechen, durchstoßen; durchdringen

pierc·ing durchdringend, (*Kälte etc a.*) schneidend, (*Schrei a.*) gellend, (*Blick, Schmerz etc a.*) stechend

pi·e·ty Frömmigkeit *f*

pig ZO Schwein *n* (*a.* F); F Ferkel *n*; *sl contp* Bulle *m*

pi·geon ZO Taube *f*

pi·geon·hole 1. Fach *n* **2.** ablegen

pig·gy F Schweinchen *n*

pig·gy·back huckepack

pig·gy bank Sparschwein(chen) *n*

pig·head·ed dickköpfig, stur

pig·let ZO Ferkel *n*

pig·sty Schweinestall *m*, F *contp* Saustall *m*

pig·tail Zopf *m*

pike¹ ZO Hecht *m*

pike² → **turnpike**

pile¹ 1. Stapel *m*, Stoß *m*; F Haufen *m*,

Menge *f*; (*atomic*) ~ Atommeiler *m* **2.** ~
up (an-, auf)häufen, (auf)stapeln, auf-
schichten; sich anhäufen; MOT F aufeinander auffahren

pile² Flor *m*

pile³ Pfahl *m*

piles *Br* F MED Hämorrhoiden *pl*

pile-up MOT Massenkarambolage *f*

pil-fer stehlen, klauen

pil-grim Pilger(in)

pil-grim-age Pilgerfahrt *f*, Wallfahrt *f*

pill PHARM Pille *f*; *the ~* F die (*Antibaby*)-
Pille; *be on the ~* die Pille nehmen

pil-lar Pfeiler *m*; Säule *f*

pil-li-on MOT Soziussitz *m*

pil-lo-ry 1. HIST Pranger *m* **2.** *fig* anprangern

pil-low (Kopf)Kissen *n*

pil-low-case, pil-low slip (Kopf)Kissen-
bezug *m*

pi-lot 1. AVIAT Pilot *m*; MAR Lotse *m* **2.** Versuchs..., Pilot... **3.** lotsen; steuern; ~
film TV Pilotfilm *m*; ~ **scheme** Ver-
suchs-, Pilotprojekt *n*

pimp Zuhälter *m*

pim-ple MED Pickel *m*, Pustel *f*

pin 1. (Steck)Nadel *f*; (*Haar-, Krawat-
ten- etc*)Nadel *f*; Brosche *f*; TECH Bolzen *m*, Stift *m*; *bowling*: Kegel *m*;
Pin *m*; (*Wäsche*)Klammer *f*; *Br*
(*Reiß*)Nagel *m*, (-)Zwecke *f* **2.** (an)hef-
ten, anstecken (*to* an *acc*); befestigen
(*to* an *dat*); pressen, drücken (*against,
to* gegen, an *acc*)

PIN *a.* ~ *number abbr of* **personal identification number** PIN, persönliche
Geheimzahl

pin-a-fore Schürze *f*

pin-ball Flippern *m*; *play* ~ flippern

pin-ball ma-chine Flipper(automat) *m*

pin-cers: (*a pair of* ~ e-e) (Kneif)Zange *f*

pinch 1. *v/t* kneifen, zwicken; F klauen;
v/i drücken **2.** Kneifen *n*, Zwicken *n*;
Prise *f*; *fig* Not(lage) *f*

pin-cush-ion Nadelkissen *n*

pine¹ BOT Kiefer *f*, Föhre *f*

pine² sich sehnen (*for* nach)

pine-ap-ple BOT Ananas *f*

pine cone BOT Kiefernzapfen *m*

pine-tree BOT Kiefer *f*, Föhre *f*

pin-ion ZO Schwungfeder *f*

pink 1. rosa(farben) **2.** Rosa *n*; BOT Nelke
f

pint Pint *n* (*0,47 l, Br 0,57 l*); *Br* F Halbe *f*

pi-o-neer 1. Pionier *m* **2.** den Weg bahnen (für)

pi-ous fromm, religiös

pip¹ *Br* (*Apfel-, Orangen- etc*)Kern *m*

pip² (Piep)Ton *m*

pip³ *on cards etc*: Auge *n*, Punkt *m*

pipe 1. TECH Rohr *n*, Röhre *f*; (*Tabaks*)-
Pfeife *f*; MUS (*Orgel*)Pfeife *f*; *pl Br* F
Dudelsack *m* **2.** (durch Rohre) leiten

pipe-line Rohrleitung *f*; Pipeline *f*

pip-er MUS Dudelsackpfeifer *m*

pip-ing 1. Rohrleitung *f*, Rohrnetz *n* **2.** ~
hot kochend heiß, siedend heiß

pi-quant pikant (*a. fig*)

pique 1. *in a fit of* ~ gekränkt, verletzt,
pikiert **2.** kränken, verletzen; *be* ~*d
a.* pikiert sein

pi-rate 1. Pirat *m*, Seeräuber *m* **2.** unerlaubt kopieren *or* nachdrucken *or*
nachpressen

pi-rate ra-di-o Piratensender *m or pl*

Pis-ces ASTR Fische *pl*; *he* (*she*) *is* (*a*) ~
er (sie) ist (ein) Fisch

piss V **1.** Pisse *f*; *take the* ~ *out of s.o.* j-n
verarschen **2.** pissen; ~ *off!* verpiss
dich!

pis-tol Pistole *f*

pis-ton TECH Kolben *m*

pit¹ 1. Grube *f* (*a.* ANAT), MIN *a.* Zeche *f*;
esp Br THEA Parkett *n*; *a.* **orchestra** ~
THEA Orchestergraben *m*; MED (*esp Pocken*)Narbe *f*; *car racing*: Box *f*; ~ *stop*
Boxenstopp *m* **2.** mit Narben bedecken

pit² 1. BOT Kern *m*, Stein *m* **2.** entkernen,
entsteinen

pitch¹ 1. *v/t* Zelt, *Lager* aufschlagen;
werfen, schleudern; MUS (an)stimmen;
v/i stürzen, fallen; MAR stampfen; sich
neigen (*roof etc*); ~ *in* F sich ins Zeug
legen; kräftig zulangen **2.** *esp Br* SPORT
(Spiel)Feld *n*; MUS Tonhöhe *f*; *fig* Grad
m, Stufe *f*; *esp Br* Stand(platz) *m*; MAR
Stampfen *n*; Neigung *f* (*of a roof etc*)

pitch² Pech *n*

pitch-black, pitch-dark pechschwarz;
stockdunkel

pitch-er¹ Krug *m*

pitch-er² *baseball*: Werfer *m*

pitch-fork Heugabel *f*, Mistgabel *f*

pit-e-ous kläglich

pit-fall Fallgrube *f*; *fig* Falle *f*

pith BOT Mark *n*; weiße innere Haut; *fig*
Kern *m*; **pith-y** markig, prägnant

pit-i-a-ble → **pitiful**

pit·i·ful mitleiderregend, bemitleidenswert; erbärmlich, jämmerlich

pit·i·less unbarmherzig, erbarmungslos

pit·ta bread Fladenbrot n

pit·y 1. Mitleid n (**on** mit); **it is a** (**great**) ~ es ist (sehr) schade; **what a** ~**!** wie schade! **2.** bemitleiden, bedauern

piv·ot 1. TECH Drehzapfen m; fig Dreh- und Angelpunkt m **2.** sich drehen; ~ **on** fig abhängen von

pix·el IT Pixel m

piz·za Pizza f

plac·ard 1. Plakat n; Transparent n **2.** mit Plakaten bekleben

place 1. Platz m, Ort m, Stelle f; Stätte f; Haus n, Wohnung f; Wohnort m; (Arbeits-, Lehr)Stelle f; **in the first** ~ erstens; **in third** ~ SPORT etc auf dem dritten Platz; **in** ~ **of** anstelle von (or gen); **out of** ~ fehl am Platz; **take** ~ stattfinden; **take s.o.'s** ~ j-s Stelle einnehmen **2.** stellen, legen, setzen; Auftrag erteilen (**with** dat), Bestellung aufgeben (**with** bei); **be** ~**d** SPORT sich platzieren (**second** an zweiter Stelle)

place mat Platzdeckchen n, Set n, m

place·ment test Einstufungsprüfung f

place name Ortsname m

plac·id ruhig; gelassen

pla·gia·rize plagiieren

plague 1. Seuche f; Pest f; Plage f **2.** plagen

plaice ZO Scholle f

plaid Plaid n or m

plain 1. adj einfach schlicht; klar (und deutlich); offen (und ehrlich); unscheinbar, wenig anziehend; rein, völlig (nonsense etc) **2.** adv F (ganz) einfach **3.** Ebene f, Flachland n

plain choc·olate Br (zart)bittere Schokolade

plain-clothes … in Zivil

plain·tiff JUR Kläger(in)

plain·tive traurig, klagend

plait esp Br **1.** Zopf m **2.** flechten

plan 1. Plan m **2.** planen; beabsichtigen

plane¹ Flugzeug n; **by** ~ mit dem Flugzeug; **go by** ~ fliegen

plane² 1. flach, eben **2.** MATH Ebene f; fig Stufe f, Niveau n

plane³ 1. Hobel m **2.** hobeln; ~ **down** abhobeln

plan·et ASTR Planet m

plank Planke f, Bohle f; ~ **bed** Pritsche f

plank·ing Planken pl

plant 1. BOT Pflanze f; ECON Werk n, Betrieb m, Fabrik f **2.** (an-, ein)pflanzen; bepflanzen; Garten etc anlegen; aufstellen, postieren; ~ **s.th. on s.o** F j-m et. (Belastendes) unterschieben

plan·ta·tion Plantage f, Pflanzung f; Schonung f

plant·er Plantagenbesitzer(in), Pflanzer(in); Pflanzmaschine f; Übertopf m

plaque Gedenktafel f; MED Zahnbelag m

plas·ter 1. MED Pflaster n; (Ver)Putz m; a. ~ **of Paris** Gips m; **have one's leg in** ~ MED das Bein in Gips haben **2.** verputzen; bekleben; ~ **cast** Gipsabguss m, Gipsmodell n; MED Gipsverband m

plas·tic 1. plastisch; Plastik… **2.** Plastik n, Kunststoff m; → ~ **mon·ey** F Plastikgeld n, Kreditkarten pl; ~ **wrap** Frischhaltefolie f

plate 1. Teller m; Platte f; (Namens-, Nummern- etc)Schild n; (Bild)Tafel f; (Druck)Platte f; Gegenstände pl aus Edelmetall; Doublé n, Dublee n **2.** ~ **d with gold, gold-plated** vergoldet

plat·form Plattform f; RAIL Bahnsteig m; (Redner)Tribüne f, Podium n; POL Plattform f; MOT Pritsche f; **party** ~ POL Parteiprogramm n; **election** ~ POL Wahlprogramm n

plat·i·num CHEM Platin n

pla·toon MIL Zug m

plat·ter (Servier)Platte f

plau·si·ble plausibel, glaubhaft

play 1. Spiel n; Schauspiel n, (Theater)Stück n; TECH Spiel n; fig Spielraum m; **at** ~ beim Spiel(en); **in** ~ im Spiel (ball); **out of** ~ im Aus (ball) **2.** v/i spielen (a. SPORT, THEA etc); v/t Karten, Rolle, Stück etc spielen, SPORT Spiel austragen; ~ **s.o.** SPORT gegen j-n spielen; ~ **the guitar** Gitarre spielen; ~ **a trick on s.o.** j-m e-n Streich spielen; ~ **back** Ball zurückspielen (**to** zu); Tonband abspielen; ~ **s.th. down** verharmlosen, herunterspielen; ~ **off** fig ausspielen (**against** gegen); ~ **on** fig j-s Schwächen ausnutzen

play·back Play-back n, Wiedergabe f, Abspielen n

play·er MUS, SPORT Spieler(in)

play·fel·low *Br* → **playmate**
play·ful verspielt; scherzhaft
play·go·er Theaterbesucher(in)
play·ground Spielplatz *m* (*a. fig*); Schulhof *m*
play·group *Br* Spielgruppe *f*
play·house THEA Schauspielhaus *n*; Spielhaus *n* (*for children*)
play·ing card Spielkarte *f*
play·ing field Sportplatz *m*, Spielfeld *n*
play·mate Spielkamerad(in)
play·pen Laufgitter *n*, Laufstall *m*
play·thing Spielzeug *n*
play·wright Dramatiker(in)
plc, PLC *Br econ abbr of* **public limited company** AG, Aktiengesellschaft *f*
plea: **enter a ~ of** (**not**) **guilty** JUR sich schuldig bekennen (s-e Unschuld erklären)
plead *v/i* (dringend) bitten (**for** um); ~ (**not**) **guilty** JUR sich schuldig bekennen (s-e Unschuld erklären); *v/t a.* JUR ZU s-r Verteidigung *or* Entschuldigung anführen, geltend machen; ~ **s.o.'s case** sich für j-n einsetzen; JUR j-n vertreten
pleas·ant angenehm, erfreulich; freundlich; sympathisch
please 1. *j-m* gefallen; *j-m* zusagen, *j-n* erfreuen; zufriedenstellen; **only to ~ you** nur dir zuliebe; ~ **o.s.** tun, was man will; ~ **yourself!** mach, was du willst! **2.** *int* bitte; (**yes,**) ~ (ja,) bitte; (oh ja,) gerne; ~ **come in!** bitte, treten Sie ein!
pleased erfreut, zufrieden; **be ~ about** sich freuen über (*acc*); **be ~ with** zufrieden sein mit; **I am ~ with it** es gefällt mir; **be ~ to do s.th.** et. gern tun; ~ **to meet you!** angenehm!
pleas·ing angenehm
plea·sure Vergnügen *n*; **at** (**one's**) ~ nach Belieben
pleat (Plissee)Falte *f*
pleat·ed skirt Faltenrock *m*
pledge 1. Pfand *n*; *fig* Unterpfand *n*; Versprechen *n* **2.** versprechen, zusichern
plen·ti·ful reichlich
plen·ty 1. Überfluss *m*; **in** ~ im Überfluss, in Hülle und Fülle; ~ **of** e-e Menge, viel(e), reichlich **2.** F reichlich
pleu·ri·sy MED Brustfell-, Rippenfellentzündung *f*

pli·a·ble, pli·ant biegsam; *fig* flexibel; *fig* leicht beeinflussbar
pli·ers (**a pair of ~** e-e) Beißzange *f*
plight Not *f*, Notlage *f*
plim·soll *Br* Turnschuh *m*
plod *a.* ~ **along** sich dahinschleppen; ~ **away** sich abplagen (**at** mit), schuften
plop F **1.** Plumps *m*, Platsch *m* **2.** plumpsen, (*ins Wasser*) platschen
plot 1. Stück *n* Land, Parzelle *f*, Grundstück *n*; THEA, *film etc*: Handlung *f*; Komplott *n*, Verschwörung *f*; IT grafische Darstellung **2.** *v/i* sich verschwören (**against** gegen); *v/t* planen; einzeichnen
plot·ter IT Plotter *m*
plough *Br*, **plow** AGR **1.** Pflug *m* **2.** (um)pflügen; **plough·share** *Br*, **plow·share** AGR Pflugschar *f*
pluck 1. *v/t Geflügel* rupfen; *mst* ~ **out** ausreißen, ausrupfen, auszupfen; MUS *Saiten* zupfen; ~ **up** (**one's**) **courage** Mut *or* sich ein Herz fassen; *v/i* zupfen (**at** an *dat*); **2.** F Mut *m*, Schneid *m*
pluck·y F mutig
plug 1. Stöpsel *m*; ELECTR Stecker *m*, F Steckdose *f*; F MOT (*Zünd*)Kerze *f* **2.** *v/t* F für *et.* Schleichwerbung machen; *a.* ~ **up** zustöpseln; zustopfen, verstopfen; ~ **in** ELECTR anschließen, einstecken
plug·ging F Schleichwerbung *f*
plum BOT Pflaume *f*; Zwetsch(g)e *f*
plum·age Gefieder *n*
plumb 1. (Blei)Lot *n* **2.** ausloten, *fig a.* ergründen; ~ **in** *esp Br Waschmaschine etc* anschließen **3.** *adj* lotrecht, senkrecht **4.** *adv* F (haar)genau
plumb·er Klempner *m*, Installateur *m*
plumb·ing Klempner-, Installateurarbeit *f*; Rohre *pl*, Rohrleitungen *pl*
plume (Schmuck)Feder *f*; Federbusch *m*; (*Rauch*)Fahne *f*
plump 1. *adj* drall, mollig, rund(lich), F pumm(e)lig **2.** ~ **down** fallen *or* plumpsen (lassen)
plum pud·ding *Br* Plumpudding *m*
plun·der 1. plündern **2.** Plünderung *f*; Beute *f*
plunge 1. (ein-, unter)tauchen; (sich) stürzen (**into** in *acc*); MAR stampfen **2.** (Kopf)Sprung *m*; **take the ~** *fig* den entscheidenden Schritt wagen
plu·per·fect *a.* ~ **tense** LING Plusquam-

perfekt *n*, Vorvergangenheit *f*

plu·ral LING Plural *m*, Mehrzahl *f*

plus 1. *prp* plus, und, *esp* ECON zuzüglich **2.** *adj* Plus…; **~ sign** MATH Plus *n*, Pluszeichen *n* **3.** MATH Plus *n* (*a.* F), Pluszeichen *n*; F Vorteil *m*

plush Plüsch *m*

ply[1] regelmäßig verkehren, fahren (**between** zwischen *dat*)

ply[2] *mst in cpds* TECH Lage *f*, Schicht *f*; **three-~** dreifach (*thread etc*); dreifach gewebt (*carpet*)

ply·wood Sperrholz *n*

pm, PM *abbr of* **after noon** (*Latin* **post meridiem**) nachm., nachmittags, abends

pneu·mat·ic Luft…, pneumatisch; TECH Druck…, Pressluft…

pneu·mat·ic drill Pressluftbohrer *m*

pneu·mo·ni·a MED Lungenentzündung *f*

poach[1] GASTR pochieren; **~ed eggs** verlorene Eier *pl*

poach[2] wildern

poach·er Wilddieb *m*, Wilderer *m*

PO Box Postfach *n*; **write to ~ 225** schreiben Sie an Postfach 225

pock MED Pocke *f*, Blatter *f*

pock·et 1. (Hosen- *etc*)Tasche *f* **2.** *adj* Taschen… **3.** einstecken, in die Tasche stecken; *fig* in die eigene Tasche stecken; **pock·et·book** Notizbuch *n*; Brieftasche *f*

pock·et| cal·cu·la·tor Taschenrechner *m*; **~ knife** Taschenmesser *n*; **~ money** Taschengeld *n*

pod BOT Hülse *f*, Schote *f*

po·di·a·trist Fußpfleger(in)

po·em Gedicht *n*

po·et Dichter(in)

po·et·ic dichterisch

po·et·i·cal dichterisch

po·et·ic jus·tice *fig* ausgleichende Gerechtigkeit

po·et·ry Gedichte *pl*; Poesie *f* (*a. fig*), Dichtkunst *f*, Dichtung *f*

poi·gnant schmerzlich; ergreifend

point 1. Spitze *f*; GEOGR Landspitze *f*; LING, MATH, PHYS, SPORT *etc* Punkt *m*; MATH (Dezimal)Punkt *m*; Grad *m*; MAR (*Kompass*)Strich *m*; *fig* Punkt *m*, Stelle *f*, Ort *m*; Zweck *m*; Ziel *n*, Absicht *f*; springender Punkt; Pointe *f*; **two ~ five (2.5)** 2,5; **~ of view** Stand-, Gesichtspunkt *m*; **be on the ~ of doing**

s.th. im Begriff sein, et. zu tun; **to the ~** zur Sache gehörig; **off** *or* **beside the ~** nicht zur Sache gehörig; **come to the ~** zur Sache kommen; **that's not the ~** darum geht es nicht; **what's the ~?** wozu?; **win on ~s** SPORT nach Punkten gewinnen; **winner on ~s** SPORT Punktsieger *m* **2.** *v/t* (zu)spitzen; *Waffe etc* richten (**at** auf *acc*); **~ one's finger at s.o.** (mit dem Finger) auf j-n zeigen; **~ out** zeigen; *fig* hinweisen *or* aufmerksam machen auf (*acc*); *v/i* (mit dem Finger) zeigen (**at, to** auf *acc*); **~ to** nach e-r Richtung weisen *or* liegen; *fig* hinweisen auf (*acc*)

point·ed spitz; Spitz…; *fig* scharf (*remark etc*); ostentativ

point·er Zeiger *m*; Zeigestock *m*; ZO Pointer *m*, Vorstehhund *m*

point·less sinnlos, zwecklos

points *Br* RAIL Weiche *f*

poise 1. (Körper)Haltung *f*; *fig* Gelassenheit *f* **2.** balancieren; **be ~d** schweben

poi·son 1. Gift *n* **2.** vergiften

poi·son·ous giftig (*a. fig*)

poke 1. *v/t* stoßen; *Feuer* schüren; stecken; *v/i* **~ about**, **~ around** F (herum-) stöbern, (-)wühlen (**in** in *dat*); **2.** Stoß *m*

pok·er Schürhaken *m*

pok·y F eng; schäbig

Po·land Polen *n*

po·lar polar; **~ bear** ZO Eisbär *m*

pole[1] GEOGR Pol *m*

pole[2] Stange *f*; Mast *m*; Deichsel *f*; SPORT (Sprung)Stab *m*

Pole Pole *m*, Polin *f*

pole·cat ZO Iltis *m*; F Skunk *m*, Stinktier *n*

po·lem·ic, po·lem·i·cal polemisch

pole star ASTR Polarstern *m*

pole vault SPORT Stabhochsprung *m*, Stabhochspringen *n*

pole-vault SPORT stabhochspringen

pole vault·er SPORT Stabhochspringer(in)

po·lice 1. Polizei *f* **2.** überwachen

po·lice car Polizeiauto *n*

po·lice·man Polizist *m*

po·lice| of·fi·cer Polizeibeamte *m*, -beamtin *f*, Polizist(in); **~ sta·tion** Polizeiwache *f*, Polizeirevier *n*

po·lice·wom·an Polizistin *f*

pol·i·cy Politik *f*; Taktik *f*; Klugheit *f*; (Versicherungs)Police *f*

po·li·o MED Polio *f*, Kinderlähmung *f*

pol·ish 1. polieren; *Schuhe* putzen; **~ up** aufpolieren (*a. fig*) **2.** Politur *f*; (*Schuh*)Creme *f*; *fig* Schliff *m*

Pol·ish 1. polnisch **2.** LING Polnisch *n*

po·lite höflich

po·lite·ness Höflichkeit *f*

po·lit·i·cal politisch

pol·i·ti·cian Politiker(in)

pol·i·tics Politik *f*

pol·ka MUS Polka *f*

pol·ka·dot gepunktet, getupft

poll 1. (*Meinungs*)Umfrage *f*; Wahlbeteiligung *f*; *a. pl* Stimmabgabe *f*, Wahl *f* **2.** befragen; *Stimmen* erhalten

pol·len BOT Pollen *m*, Blütenstaub *m*

poll·ing Stimmabgabe *f*; Wahlbeteiligung *f*; **~ booth** *esp Br* Wahlkabine *f*; **~ day** Wahltag *m*; **~ place**, *esp Br* **~ station** Wahllokal *n*

polls Wahl *f*; Wahllokal *n*

poll·ster Demoskop(in), Meinungsforscher(in)

pol·lut·ant Schadstoff *m*; **pol·lute** beschmutzen, verschmutzen; verunreinigen; **pol·lut·er** *f.* **environmental ~** Umweltsünder(in); **pol·lu·tion** (*Luft-, Wasser- etc*)Verschmutzung *f*; Verunreinigung *f*

po·lo SPORT Polo *n*

po·lo neck *a.* **~ sweater** *esp Br* Rollkragenpullover *m*

pol·yp ZO, MED Polyp *m*

pol·y·sty·rene® Styropor® *n*

pom·mel (*Sattel- etc*)Knopf *m*

pomp Pomp *m*, Prunk *m*

pom·pous aufgeblasen, wichtigtuerisch; schwülstig (*speech*)

pond Teich *m*, Weiher *m*

pon·der *v/i* nachdenken (**on, over** über *acc*); *v/t* überlegen

pon·der·ous schwerfällig; schwer

pon·toon Ponton *m*

pon·toon bridge Pontonbrücke *f*

po·ny ZO Pony *n*

po·ny·tail Pferdeschwanz *m*

poo·dle ZO Pudel *m*

pool¹ Teich *m*, Tümpel *m*; Pfütze *f*, (*Blut- etc*)Lache *f*; (*Schwimm*)Becken *n*, (*Swimming*)Pool *m*

pool² 1. (*Arbeits-, Fahr*)Gemeinschaft *f*; (*Mitarbeiter- etc*)Stab *m*; (*Fuhr*)Park

m; (*Schreib*)Pool *m*; ECON Pool *m*, Kartell *n*; *card games*: Gesamteinsatz *m*; Poolbillard *n* **2.** *Geld, Unternehmen etc* zusammenlegen; *Kräfte etc* vereinen

pool hall, **pool·room** Billardspielhalle *f*

pools *a.* **football ~** *Br* (Fußball)Toto *n*, *m*

poor 1. arm; dürftig, mangelhaft, schwach **2. the ~** die Armen *pl*

poor·ly 1. *adj esp Br* F kränklich, unpässlich **2.** *adv* ärmlich, dürftig, schlecht, schwach

pop¹ 1. *v/t* zerknallen; F schnell *wohin* tun *or* stecken; *v/i* knallen; (zer)platzen; **~ in** F auf e-n Sprung vorbeikommen; **~ up** (plötzlich) auftauchen **2.** Knall *m*; F Limo *f*

pop² MUS **1.** Pop *m* **2.** Schlager…; Pop…

pop³ F Paps *m*, Papa *m*

pop⁴ *abbr of* **population** Einw., Einwohner *pl*; Einwohnerzahl *f*

pop con·cert MUS Popkonzert *n*

pop·corn Popcorn *n*, Puffmais *m*

Pope REL Papst *m*

pop-eyed F glotzäugig

pop group MUS Popgruppe *f*

pop·lar BOT Pappel *f*

pop mu·sic Popmusik *f*

pop·py BOT Mohn *m*

pop·u·lar populär, beliebt; volkstümlich; allgemein

pop·u·lar·i·ty Popularität *f*, Beliebtheit *f*; Volkstümlichkeit *f*

pop·u·late bevölkern, besiedeln; bewohnen

pop·u·la·tion Bevölkerung *f*

pop·u·lous dicht besiedelt, dicht bevölkert

porce·lain Porzellan *n*

porch überdachter Vorbau; Portal *n*; Veranda *f*

por·cu·pine ZO Stachelschwein *n*

pore¹ Pore *f*

pore²: **~ over** vertieft sein in (*acc*), *et.* eifrig studieren

pork GASTR Schweinefleisch *n*

porn F → **porno**

por·no F **1.** Porno *m* **2.** Porno…

por·nog·ra·phy Pornografie *f*

po·rous porös

por·poise ZO Tümmler *m*

por·ridge Porridge *m*, *n*, Haferbrei *m*

port¹ Hafen *m*; Hafenstadt *f*

port[2] AVIAT, MAR Backbord *n*

port[3] IT Port *m*, Anschluss *m*

port[4] Portwein *m*

por·ta·ble tragbar

por·ter (Gepäck)Träger *m*; *esp Br* Pförtner *m*, Portier *m*; RAIL Schlafwagenschaffner *m*

port·hole MAR Bullauge *n*

por·tion 1. (An)Teil *m*; GASTR Portion *f* **2.** **~ out** aufteilen, verteilen (*among, between* unter *acc*)

port·ly korpulent

por·trait Porträt *n*, Bild *n*, Bildnis *n*

por·tray porträtieren; darstellen; schildern; **por·tray·al** THEA Verkörperung *f*, Darstellung *f*; Schilderung *f*

Por·tu·gal Portugal *n*

Por·tu·guese 1. portugiesisch **2.** Portugiese *m*, Portugiesin *f*; LING Portugiesisch *n*; **the ~** die Portugiesen *pl*

pose 1. *v/t* aufstellen; *Problem, Frage* aufwerfen, *Bedrohung, Gefahr etc* darstellen; *v/i* Modell sitzen *or* stehen; **~ as** sich ausgeben als *or* für **2.** Pose *f*

posh *esp Br* F schick, piekfein

po·si·tion 1. Position *f*, Lage *f*, Stellung *f* (*a. fig*); Stand *m*; *fig* Standpunkt *m* **2.** (auf)stellen

pos·i·tive 1. positiv; bestimmt, sicher, eindeutig; greifbar, konkret; konstruktiv **2.** PHOT Positiv *n*

pos·sess besitzen; *fig* beherrschen

pos·sessed *fig* besessen

pos·ses·sion Besitz *m*; *fig* Besessenheit *f*

pos·ses·sive besitzergreifend; LING possessiv, besitzanzeigend

pos·si·bil·i·ty Möglichkeit *f*

pos·si·ble möglich

pos·si·bly möglicherweise, vielleicht; *if I ~ can* wenn ich irgend kann; *I can't ~ do this* ich kann das unmöglich tun

post[1] **1.** (*Tür-, Tor-, Ziel- etc*)Pfosten *m*; Pfahl *m* **2.** *a.* **~ up** *Plakat etc* anschlagen, ankleben; *be ~ed missing* AVIAT, MAR als vermisst gemeldet werden

post[2] *esp Br* **1.** Post® *f*; Postsendung *f*; *by ~* mit der Post® **2.** mit der Post® (zu-) schicken, aufgeben, *Brief* einwerfen

post[3] **1.** Stelle *f*, Job *m*; Posten *m* **2.** aufstellen, postieren; *esp Br* versetzen, MIL abkommandieren (*to* nach)

post… nach…, Nach…

post·age Porto *n*; **~ stamp** Postwertzeichen *n*, Briefmarke *f*

post·al postalisch, Post®…; **~ or·der** *Br* ECON Postanweisung *f*; **~ vote** POL Briefwahl *f*

post·bag *esp Br* Postsack *m*

post·box *esp Br* Briefkasten *m*

post·card Postkarte *f*; *a.* **picture ~** Ansichtskarte *f*

post·code *Br* Postleitzahl *f*

post·er Plakat *n*; Poster *n, m*

poste res·tante *Br* **1.** Abteilung *f* für postlagernde Sendungen **2.** postlagernd

pos·te·ri·or HUMOR Hinterteil *n*

pos·ter·i·ty die Nachwelt

post-free *esp Br* portofrei

post·hu·mous post(h)um

post·man *esp Br* Briefträger *m*, Postbote *m*

post·mark 1. Poststempel *m* **2.** stempeln, abstempeln

post of·fice Post® *f*; Postamt *n*, -filiale *f*

post of·fice box → **PO Box**

post-paid portofrei

post·pone verschieben, aufschieben

post·pone·ment Verschiebung *f*, Aufschub *m*

post·script Postskript(um) *n*, Nachschrift *f*

pos·ture 1. (Körper)Haltung *f*; Stellung *f* **2.** *fig* sich aufspielen

post·war Nachkriegs…

post·wom·an *esp Br* Briefträgerin *f*, Postbotin *f*

po·sy Sträußchen *n*

pot 1. Topf *m*; Kanne *f*; Kännchen *n* (*Tee etc*); SPORT F Pokal *m* **2.** *Pflanze* eintopfen

po·tas·si·um cy·a·nide CHEM Zyankali *n*

po·ta·to Kartoffel *f*; → **chips, crisps**

pot·bel·ly Schmerbauch *m*

po·ten·cy Stärke *f*; Wirksamkeit *f*, Wirkung *f*; MED Potenz *f*

po·tent PHARM stark; MED potent

po·ten·tial 1. potenziell, möglich **2.** Potenzial *n*, Leistungsfähigkeit *f*

pot·hole MOT Schlagloch *n*

po·tion Trank *m*

pot·ter[1] *Br*: **~ about** herumwerkeln

pot·ter[2] Töpfer(in)

pot·ter·y Töpferei *f*; Töpferware(n *pl*) *f*

pouch Beutel *m* (*a.* ZO); ZO (*Backen*)Tasche *f*

poul·tice MED (warmer) Umschlag *m*

poul·try Geflügel *n*

pounce 1. sich stürzen (**on** auf *acc*); 2. Satz *m*, Sprung *m*

pound[1] Pfund *n* (*453,59 g*); ~ (**sterling**) (*abbr* £) Pfund *n*

pound[2] Tierheim *n*; Abstellplatz *m* für (polizeilich) abgeschleppte Fahrzeuge

pound[3] *v/t* zerstoßen, zerstampfen; trommeln *or* hämmern auf (*acc*) *or* an (*acc*) *or* gegen; *v/i* hämmern (**with** vor *dat*)

pour *v/t* gießen, schütten; ~ **out** ausgießen, ausschütten; Getränk eingießen; *v/i* strömen (*a. fig*)

pout *v/t* Lippen schürzen; *v/i* e-n Schmollmund machen; schmollen

pov·er·ty Armut *f*

pow·der 1. Pulver *n*; Puder *m* 2. pulverisieren; (sich) pudern; ~ **puff** Puderquaste *f*; ~ **room** (Damen)Toilette *f*

pow·er 1. Kraft *f*; Macht *f*; Fähigkeit *f*, Vermögen *n*; Gewalt *f*; JUR Befugnis *f*, Vollmacht *f*; MATH Potenz *f*; ELECTR Strom *m*; **in** ~ POL an der Macht 2. TECH antreiben; ~ **cut** ELECTR Stromsperre *f*; ~ **fail·ure** ELECTR Stromausfall *m*, Netzausfall *m*

pow·er·ful stark, kräftig; mächtig

pow·er·less kraftlos; machtlos

pow·er| plant Elektrizitäts-, Kraftwerk *n*; ~ **pol·i·tics** Machtpolitik *f*; ~ **sta·tion** *Br* Elektrizitäts-, Kraftwerk *n*

prac·ti·ca·ble durchführbar

prac·ti·cal praktisch; ~ **joke** Streich *m*

prac·ti·cal·ly so gut wie

prac·tice 1. Praxis *f*; Übung *f*; Gewohnheit *f*, Brauch *m*; **it is common** ~ es ist allgemein üblich; **put into** ~ in die Praxis umsetzen 2. *v/t* (ein)üben; *als Beruf* ausüben; ~ **law** (**medicine**) als Anwalt (Arzt) praktizieren; *v/i* praktizieren; üben

prac·ticed geübt (**in** in *dat*)

prac·tise *Br* → **practice** 2

prac·tised → **practiced**

prac·ti·tion·er: **general** ~ praktischer Arzt

prai·rie Prärie *f*

prai·rie schoo·ner HIST Planwagen *m*

praise 1. loben, preisen 2. Lob *n*

praise·wor·thy lobenswert

pram *Br* Kinderwagen *m*

prance sich aufbäumen, steigen (*horse*); tänzeln (*horse*); stolzieren

prank Streich *m*

prat·tle: ~ **on** plappern (**about** von)

prawn ZO Garnele *f*

pray beten (**to** zu; **for** für, um)

prayer REL Gebet *n*; *often pl* Andacht *f*; **the Lord's Prayer** das Vaterunser

prayer book REL Gebetbuch *n*

preach predigen (**to** zu, vor *dat*)

preach·er Prediger(in)

pre·am·ble Einleitung *f*

pre·ar·range vorher vereinbaren

pre·car·i·ous prekär, unsicher; gefährlich

pre·cau·tion Vorsichtsmaßnahme *f*; **as a** ~ vorsichtig; **take** ~**s** Vorsichtsmaßnahmen treffen; **pre·cau·tion·a·ry** vorbeugend; vorsorglich

pre·cede voraus-, vorangehen (*dat*)

pre·ce·dence Vorrang *m*

pre·ce·dent Präzedenzfall *m*

pre·cept Regel *f*, Richtlinie *f*

pre·cinct (*Wahl*)Bezirk *m*; (*Polizei*)Revier *n*; *pl* Gelände *n*; *esp Br* (*Einkaufs*)-Viertel *n*; (*Fußgänger*)Zone *f*

pre·cious 1. *adj* kostbar, wertvoll; Edel... (*stone etc*) 2. *adv*: ~ **little** F herzlich wenig

pre·ci·pice Abgrund *m*

pre·cip·i·tate 1. *v/t* (hinunter-, herunter)schleudern; CHEM ausfällen; beschleunigen; stürzen (**into** in *acc*); *v/i* CHEM ausfallen 2. *adj* überstürzt 3. CHEM Niederschlag *m*

pre·cip·i·ta·tion CHEM Ausfällung *f*; METEOR Niederschlag *m*; Überstürzung *f*, Hast *f*

pre·cip·i·tous steil (abfallend); überstürzt

pré·cis Zusammenfassung *f*

pre·cise genau, präzis

pre·ci·sion Genauigkeit *f*; Präzision *f*

pre·clude ausschließen

pre·co·cious frühreif; altklug

pre·con·ceived vorgefasst

pre·con·cep·tion vorgefasste Meinung

pre·cur·sor Vorläufer(in)

pred·a·to·ry ZO Raub...

pre·de·ces·sor Vorgänger(in)

pre·des·ti·na·tion Vorherbestimmung *f*; **pre·des·tined** prädestiniert, vorherbestimmt (**to** für, zu)

pre·de·ter·mine vorherbestimmen; vorher vereinbaren

pre·dic·a·ment missliche Lage, Zwangslage f

pred·i·cate LING Prädikat n, Satzaussage f; **pre·dic·a·tive** LING prädikativ

pre·dict vorhersagen, voraussagen

pre·dic·tion Vorhersage f, Voraussage f; *computer* ~ Hochrechnung f

pre·dis·pose geneigt machen, einnehmen (*in favor of* für); *esp* MED anfällig machen (*to* für)

pre·dis·po·si·tion: ~ *to* Neigung f zu, *esp* MED a. Anfälligkeit f für

pre·dom·i·nant (vor)herrschend, überwiegend

pre·dom·i·nate vorherrschen, überwiegen; die Oberhand haben

pre·em·i·nent hervorragend, überragend

pre·emp·tive ECON Vorkaufs...; MIL Präventiv...

preen ZO *sich or das Gefieder putzen*

pre·fab F Fertighaus n

pre·fab·ri·cate vorfabrizieren, vorfertigen; ~*d house* Fertighaus n

pref·ace 1. Vorwort n (*to* zu); 2. *Buch, Rede etc* einleiten (*with* mit)

pre·fect *Br* PED Aufsichts-, Vertrauensschüler(in)

pre·fer vorziehen (*to dat*), lieber mögen (*to* als), bevorzugen

pref·e·ra·ble: *be* ~ (*to*) vorzuziehen sein (*dat*), besser sein (als)

pref·e·ra·bly vorzugsweise, lieber, am liebsten

pref·e·rence Vorliebe f (*for* für); Vorzug m

pre·fix LING Präfix n, Vorsilbe f

preg·nan·cy MED Schwangerschaft f; ZO Trächtigkeit f

preg·nant MED schwanger; ZO trächtig

pre·heat *Backofen etc* vorheizen

pre·judge *j-n* vorverurteilen; vorschnell beurteilen

prej·u·dice 1. Vorurteil n, Voreingenommenheit f, Befangenheit f; *to the* ~ *of* zum Nachteil *or* Schaden (*gen*) 2. einnehmen (*in favo[u]r of* für; *against* gegen); schaden (*dat*), beeinträchtigen

prej·u·diced (vor)eingenommen, befangen

pre·lim·i·na·ry 1. vorläufig, einleitend, Vor... 2. *pl* Vorbereitungen *pl*

prel·ude Vorspiel n (*a.* MUS)

pre·mar·i·tal vorehelich

pre·ma·ture vorzeitig, verfrüht; *fig* voreilig

pre·med·i·tat·ed JUR vorsätzlich

pre·med·i·ta·tion: *with* ~ JUR vorsätzlich

prem·i·er POL Premier(minister) m

prem·i·ere, prem·i·ère THEA *etc* Premiere f, Ur-, Erstaufführung f

prem·is·es Gelände n, Grundstück n, (*Geschäfts*)Räume *pl*; *on the* ~ an Ort und Stelle, im Haus, im Lokal

pre·mi·um Prämie f, Bonus m

pre·mi·um (gas·o·line) MOT Super n, Superbenzin n

pre·mo·ni·tion (böse) Vorahnung

pre·oc·cu·pa·tion Beschäftigung f (*with* mit)

pre·oc·cu·pied gedankenverloren, geistesabwesend

pre·oc·cu·py (stark) beschäftigen

prep *Br* F PED Hausaufgabe(n *pl*) f

pre·packed, pre·pack·aged abgepackt

pre·paid *post* frankiert, freigemacht; ~ *envelope* Freiumschlag m

prep·a·ra·tion Vorbereitung f (*for* auf *acc*, für); Zubereitung f; CHEM, MED Präparat n

pre·par·a·to·ry vorbereitend

pre·pare *v/t* vorbereiten; GASTR zubereiten; *v/i:* ~ *for* sich vorbereiten auf (*acc*); Vorbereitungen treffen für; sich gefasst machen auf (*acc*)

pre·pared vorbereitet; bereit

prep·o·si·tion LING Präposition f, Verhältniswort n

pre·pos·sess·ing einnehmend, anziehend

pre·pos·ter·ous absurd; lächerlich, grotesk

pre·pro·gram(me) vorprogrammieren

pre·req·ui·site Vorbedingung f, Voraussetzung f

pre·rog·a·tive Vorrecht n

pre·school Vorschule f

pre·scribe *et.* vorschreiben; MED *j-m et.* verschreiben; **pre·scrip·tion** Verordnung f, Vorschrift f; MED Rezept n

pres·ence Gegenwart f, Anwesenheit f; ~ *of mind* Geistesgegenwart f

pres·ent[1] Geschenk n

pre·sent[2] präsentieren; (über)reichen; (über)bringen, (über)geben; schenken; vorbringen, vorlegen; zeigen, vorführen, THEA *etc* aufführen; schildern, darstellen; *j-n, Produkt etc* vorstellen;

Programm etc moderieren

pres·ent³ 1. anwesend; vorhanden; gegenwärtig, jetzig; laufend; vorliegend (*case etc*); **~ tense** LING Präsens *n*, Gegenwart *f* **2.** Gegenwart *f*, LING *a.* Präsens *n*; **at ~** gegenwärtig, zurzeit; **for the ~** vorerst, vorläufig

pre·sen·ta·tion Präsentation *f*; Überreichung *f*; Vorlage *f*; Vorführung *f*, THEA *etc* Aufführung *f*; Schilderung *f*, Darstellung *f*; Vorstellung *f*; *radio*, TV Moderation *f*

pres·ent-day heutig, gegenwärtig, modern

pre·sent·er *esp Br radio*, TV Moderator(in)

pre·sen·ti·ment (böse) Vorahnung

pres·ent·ly zurzeit, jetzt; *Br* bald

pres·er·va·tion Bewahrung *f*; Erhaltung *f*; GASTR Konservierung *f*

pre·ser·va·tive GASTR Konservierungsmittel *n*

pre·serve 1. bewahren, (be)schützen; erhalten; GASTR konservieren, *Obst etc* einmachen, einkochen **2.** (*Jagd*)Revier *n*; *fig* Ressort *n*, Reich *n*; *mst pl* GASTR das Eingemachte

pre·side den Vorsitz haben (**at, over** bei); **pres·i·den·cy** POL Präsidentschaft *f*; Amtszeit *f*; **pres·i·dent** Präsident *m*; ECON Generaldirektor *m*

press 1. *v/t* drücken, pressen; *Frucht* (aus)pressen; drücken auf (*acc*); bügeln; drängen; *j-n* (be)drängen; bestehen auf (*dat*); *v/i* drücken; drängen (*time etc*); (sich) drängen; **~ for** dringen *or* drängen auf (*acc*); **~ on** (zügig) weitermachen **2.** Druck *m* (*a. fig*); (*Wein-etc*)Presse *f*; Bügeln *n*; *die* Presse; *a.* **printing ~** Druckerpresse *f*

press a·gen·cy Presseagentur *f*

press box Pressetribüne *f*

press con·fe·rence Pressekonferenz *f*

press·ing dringend

press of·fice Pressebüro *n*, Pressestelle *f*; **press of·fi·cer** Pressereferent(in)

press re·lease Pressemitteilung *f*

press stud *Br* Druckknopf *m*

press-up *esp Br* SPORT Liegestütz *m*

pres·sure PHYS, TECH *etc* Druck *m* (*a. fig*); **~ cook·er** Dampfkochtopf *m*, Schnellkochtopf *m*

pres·tige Prestige *n*, Ansehen *n*

pre·su·ma·bly vermutlich

pre·sume *v/t* annehmen, vermuten; sich erdreisten *or* anmaßen (**to do** zu tun); *v/i* annehmen, vermuten; anmaßend sein; **~ on** *et.* ausnützen, *et.* missbrauchen

pre·sump·tion Annahme *f*, Vermutung *f*; Anmaßung *f*

pre·sump·tu·ous anmaßend, vermessen

pre·sup·pose voraussetzen

pre·sup·po·si·tion Voraussetzung *f*

pre·tence *Br* → **pretense**; **pre·tend** vortäuschen, vorgeben; sich verstellen; Anspruch erheben (**to** auf *acc*); **she is only ~ing** sie tut nur so; **pre·tend·ed** vorgetäuscht, gespielt; **pre·tense** Verstellung *f*, Vortäuschung *f*; Anspruch *m* (**to** auf *acc*); **pre·ten·sion** Anspruch *m* (**to** auf *acc*); Anmaßung *f*

pre·ter·it(e) LING Präteritum *n*

pre·text Vorwand *m*

pret·ty 1. *adj* hübsch **2.** *adv* ziemlich, ganz schön

pret·zel Brezel *f*

pre·vail vorherrschen, weit verbreitet sein; siegen (**over, against** über *acc*)

pre·vail·ing (vor)herrschend

pre·vent verhindern, verhüten, *e-r Sache* vorbeugen; *j-n* hindern (**from** an *dat*)

pre·ven·tion Verhinderung *f*, Verhütung *f*, Vorbeugung *f*

pre·ven·tive vorbeugend

pre·view *film*, TV Voraufführung *f*; Vorbesichtigung *f*; *film*, TV *etc*: Vorschau *f* (**of** auf *acc*)

pre·vi·ous vorhergehend, vorausgehend, vorherig, vorig; **~ to** bevor, vor (*dat*); **~ knowledge** Vorkenntnisse *pl*

pre·vi·ous·ly vorher, früher

pre-war Vorkriegs...

prey 1. ZO Beute *f*, Opfer *n* (*a. fig*); **be easy ~ for** *or* **to** *fig* e-e leichte Beute sein für **2.** **~ on** ZO Jagd machen auf (*acc*); *fig* nagen an (*dat*); **~ on s.o.'s mind** j-m keine Ruhe lassen

price 1. Preis *m* **2.** den Preis festsetzen für; auszeichnen (**at** mit)

price·less unbezahlbar

price tag Preisschild *n*

prick 1. Stich *m*; V Schwanz *m*; **~s of conscience** Gewissensbisse *pl* **2.** *v/t* (auf-, durch)stechen, stechen in (*acc*); **her conscience ~ed her** sie hatte Gewissensbisse; ~ *up one's ears* die Ohren spitzen; *v/i* stechen

prick·le BOT, ZO Stachel *m*, Dorn *m*

prick·ly stach(e)lig; prickelnd, kribbelnd

pride 1. Stolz *m*; Hochmut *m*; *take* (*a*) ~ *in* stolz sein auf (*acc*) **2.** ~ *o.s. on* stolz sein auf (*acc*)

priest REL Priester *m*

prig Tugendbold *m*

prig·gish tugendhaft

prim steif; prüde

pri·mae·val *esp Br* → **primeval**

pri·ma·ri·ly in erster Linie, vor allem

pri·ma·ry 1. wichtigste(r, -s), Haupt...; grundlegend, elementar, Grund...; Anfangs..., Ur... **2.** POL Vorwahl *f*

pri·ma·ry school *Br* Grundschule *f*

prime 1. MATH Primzahl *f*; *fig* Blüte(zeit) *f*; *in the* ~ *of life* in der Blüte s-r Jahre; *be past one's* ~ s-e besten Jahre hinter sich haben **2.** *adj* erste(r, -s), wichtigste(r, -s), Haupt...; erstklassig **3.** *v/t* TECH grundieren; *j-n* instruieren, vorbereiten; ~ *min·is·ter* (*abbr* POL F *PM*) Premierminister(in), Ministerpräsident(in); ~ *num·ber* MATH Primzahl *f*

prim·er Fibel *f*, Elementarbuch *n*

prime time TV Haupteinschaltzeit *f*, Hauptsendezeit *f*, beste Sendezeit *f*

pri·me·val urzeitlich, Ur...

prim·i·tive erste(r, -s), ursprünglich, Ur...; primitiv

prim·rose BOT Primel *f*, *esp* Schlüsselblume *f*

prince Fürst *m*; Prinz *m*

prin·cess Fürstin *f*; Prinzessin *f*

prin·ci·pal 1. wichtigste(r, -s), hauptsächlich, Haupt... **2.** PED Direktor(in), Rektor(in); THEA Hauptdarsteller(in); MUS Solist(in)

prin·ci·pal·i·ty Fürstentum *n*

prin·ci·ple Prinzip *n*, Grundsatz *m*; *on* ~ grundsätzlich, aus Prinzip

print 1. PRINT Druck *m* (*a. art*); Gedruckte *n*; (*Finger- etc*) Abdruck *m*; PHOT Abzug *m*; bedruckter Stoff; *in* ~ gedruckt; *out of* ~ vergriffen **2.** *v/i* drucken; *v/t* (ab-, auf-, be)drucken; in Druckbuchstaben schreiben; *fig* einprägen (*on dat*); *a.* ~ *off* PHOT abziehen; ~ *out* IT ausdrucken

print·ed mat·ter *post* Drucksache *f*

print·er Drucker *m* (*a.* TECH); ~'s *error* Druckfehler *m*; ~'s *ink* Druckerschwärze *f*; **print·ers** Druckerei *f*

print·ing Drucken *n*; Auflage *f*; ~ *ink* Druckerschwärze *f*; ~ *press* Druckerpresse *f*

print·out IT Ausdruck *m*

pri·or frühere(r, -s); vorrangig

pri·or·i·ty Priorität *f*, Vorrang *m*; MOT Vorfahrt *f*; *give s.th.* ~ et. vordringlich behandeln

prise *esp Br* → **prize²**

prism Prisma *n*

pris·on Gefängnis *n*, Strafanstalt *f*

pris·on·er Gefangene *m*, *f*, Häftling *m*; *hold* ~, *keep* ~ gefangen halten; *take* ~ gefangen nehmen

pri·va·cy Intim-, Privatsphäre *f*; Geheimhaltung *f*

pri·vate 1. privat, Privat...; vertraulich; geheim; ~ *parts* Geschlechtsteile *pl* **2.** MIL gemeiner Soldat; *in* ~ privat; unter vier Augen

pri·va·tion Entbehrung *f*

priv·i·lege Privileg *n*; Vorrecht *n*

priv·i·leged privilegiert

priv·y: *be* ~ *to* eingeweiht sein in (*acc*)

prize¹ 1. (Sieger-, Siegs)Preis *m*, Prämie *f*, Auszeichnung *f*; (*Lotterie*)Gewinn *m* **2.** preisgekrönt; Preis... **3.** (hoch)schätzen

prize²: ~ *open* aufbrechen, aufstemmen

prize·win·ner Preisträger(in)

pro¹ F Profi *m*

pro²: *the* ~ *s and cons* das Pro und Kontra, das Für und Wider

prob·a·bil·i·ty Wahrscheinlichkeit *f*; *in all* ~ höchstwahrscheinlich

prob·a·ble *adj* wahrscheinlich

prob·a·bly *adv* wahrscheinlich

pro·ba·tion Probe *f*, Probezeit *f*; JUR Bewährung *f*, Bewährungsfrist *f*

pro·ba·tion of·fi·cer JUR Bewährungshelfer(in)

probe 1. MED, TECH Sonde *f*; *fig* Untersuchung *f* (*into gen*); **2.** sondieren; (gründlich) untersuchen

prob·lem Problem *n*; MATH *etc* Aufgabe *f*; **prob·lem·at·ic**, **prob·lem·at·i·cal** problematisch

pro·ce·dure Verfahren *n*, Verfahrensweise *f*, Vorgehen *n*

pro·ceed (weiter)gehen, (weiter)fahren; sich begeben (*to* nach, zu); *fig* weitergehen; *fig* fortfahren; *fig* vorgehen;

~ from kommen *or* herrühren von; **~ to do s.th.** sich anschicken *or* daranmachen, et. zu tun

pro·ceed·ing Verfahren *n*, Vorgehen *n*

pro·ceed·ings Vorgänge *pl*, Geschehnisse *pl*; **start** *or* **take** (*legal*) **~ against** JUR (gerichtlich) vorgehen gegen

pro·ceeds ECON Erlös *m*, Ertrag *m*, Einnahmen *pl*

pro·cess 1. Prozess *m*, Verfahren *n*, Vorgang *m*; **in the ~** dabei; **be in ~** im Gange sein; **in ~ of construction** im Bau (befindlich) **2.** TECH *etc* bearbeiten, behandeln; IT *Daten* verarbeiten; PHOT *Film* entwickeln

pro·ces·sion Prozession *f*

pro·ces·sor IT Prozessor *m*; (*Wort-, Text*)Verarbeitungsgerät *n*

pro·claim proklamieren, ausrufen

proc·la·ma·tion Proklamation *f*, Bekanntmachung *f*

pro·cure (sich) *et.* beschaffen *or* besorgen; verkuppeln

prod 1. stoßen; *fig* anstacheln, anspornen (**into** zu); **2.** Stoß *m*

prod·i·gal 1. verschwenderisch **2.** F Verschwender(in)

pro·di·gious erstaunlich, großartig

prod·i·gy Wunder *n*; **child ~** Wunderkind *n*

pro·duce[1] ECON produzieren (*a. film*, TV), herstellen, erzeugen (*a. fig*); hervorholen (**from** aus); *Ausweis etc* (vor)zeigen; *Beweise etc* vorlegen; *Zeugen etc* beibringen; *Gewinn etc* (er)bringen, abwerfen; THEA inszenieren; *fig* hervorrufen, *Wirkung* erzielen

prod·uce[2] *esp* (*Agrar*)Produkt(e *pl*) *n*, (*Agrar*)Erzeugnis(se *pl*) *n*

pro·duc·er Produzent(in) (*a. film*, TV), Hersteller(in); THEA Regisseur(in)

prod·uct Produkt *n*, Erzeugnis *n*

pro·duc·tion ECON Produktion *f* (*a. film*, TV), Erzeugung *f*, Herstellung *f*; Produkt *n*, Erzeugnis *n*; Hervorholen *n*; Vorzeigen *n*, Vorlegen *n*, Beibringung *f*; THEA Inszenierung *f*

pro·duc·tive produktiv (*a. fig*), ergiebig, rentabel; *fig* schöpferisch

pro·duc·tiv·i·ty Produktivität *f*

prof F Prof *m*

pro·fa·na·tion Entweihung *f*

pro·fane 1. (gottes)lästerlich; profan, weltlich **2.** entweihen

pro·fan·i·ty: profanities Flüche *pl*, Lästerungen *pl*

pro·fess vorgeben, vortäuschen; behaupten (**to be** zu sein); erklären

pro·fessed erklärt (*enemy etc*); angeblich

pro·fes·sion (*esp akademischer*) Beruf; Berufsstand *m*

pro·fes·sion·al 1. Berufs..., beruflich; Fach..., fachlich; fachmännisch; professionell **2.** Fachmann *m*, Profi *m*; Berufsspieler(in), -sportler(in), Profi *m*

pro·fes·sor Professor(in); Dozent(in)

pro·fi·cien·cy Können *n*, Tüchtigkeit *f*

pro·fi·cient tüchtig (**at, in** in *dat*)

pro·file Profil *n*; **keep a low ~** Zurückhaltung üben

prof·it 1. Gewinn *m*, Profit *m*; Vorteil *m*, Nutzen *m* **2. ~ by, ~ from** Nutzen ziehen aus, profitieren von

prof·it·a·ble gewinnbringend, einträglich; nützlich, vorteilhaft

prof·it·eer *contp* Profitmacher *m*, Schieber *m*

prof·it shar·ing ECON Gewinnbeteiligung *f*

prof·li·gate verschwenderisch

pro·found *fig* tief; tiefgründig; profund (*knowledge etc*)

pro·fuse (über)reich; verschwenderisch; **pro·fu·sion** Überfülle *f*; **in ~** in Hülle und Fülle

prog·e·ny Nachkommen(schaft *f*) *pl*

prog·no·sis MED Prognose *f*

pro·gram 1. Programm *n* (*a.* IT); *radio*, TV *a.* Sendung *f* **2.** (vor)programmieren; planen; IT programmieren

pro·gram·er IT Programmierer(in)

pro·gramme *Br* → **program**

pro·gram·mer *Br* → **programer**

pro·gress 1. Fortschritt(e *pl*) *m*; **make slow ~** (nur) langsam vorankommen; **be in ~** im Gange sein **2.** fortschreiten; Fortschritte machen

pro·gres·sive progressiv, fortschreitend; fortschrittlich

pro·hib·it verbieten; verhindern

pro·hi·bi·tion Verbot *n*

pro·hib·i·tive Schutz... (*Zoll etc*); unerschwinglich

proj·ect[1] Projekt *n*, Vorhaben *n*

pro·ject[2] *v/i* vorspringen, vorragen, vorstehen; *v/t* werfen, schleudern; planen; projizieren

pro·jec·tile Projektil *n*, Geschoss *n*
pro·jec·tion Vorsprung *m*, vorspringender Teil; Werfen *n*, Schleudern *n*; Planung *f*; *film*: Projektion *f*
pro·jec·tion·ist Filmvorführer *m*
pro·jec·tor *film*: Projektor *m*
pro·le·tar·i·an 1. proletarisch 2. Proletarier(in)
pro·lif·ic fruchtbar
pro·log, *esp Br* **pro·logue** Prolog *m*
pro·long verlängern
prom·e·nade 1. (Strand)Promenade *f* 2. promenieren
prom·i·nent vorspringend, vorstehend; *fig* prominent
pro·mis·cu·ous sexuell freizügig
prom·ise 1. Versprechen *n*; *fig* Aussicht *f* 2. versprechen
prom·is·ing vielversprechend
prom·on·to·ry GEOGR Vorgebirge *n*
pro·mote *j-n* befördern; *Schüler* versetzen; ECON werben für; *Boxkampf, Konzert etc* veranstalten; *et.* fördern; **be ~d** SPORT *esp Br* aufsteigen (**to** in *acc*)
pro·mot·er Promoter(in), Veranstalter(in); ECON Verkaufsförderer *m*
pro·mo·tion Beförderung *f*; PED Versetzung *f*; SPORT Aufstieg *m*; ECON Verkaufsförderung *f*, Werbung *f*
pro·mo·tion(·al) *film* Werbefilm *m*
prompt 1. *j-n* veranlassen (**to do** zu tun); führen zu, *Gefühle etc* wecken; *j-m* vorsagen; THEA *j-m* soufflieren 2. prompt, umgehend, unverzüglich; pünktlich
prompt·er THEA Souffleur *m*, Souffleuse *f*
prone auf dem Bauch *or* mit dem Gesicht nach unten liegend; **be ~ to** *a.* MED neigen zu, anfällig sein für
prong Zinke *f*; (*Geweih*)Sprosse *f*
pro·noun LING Pronomen *n*, Fürwort *n*
pro·nounce aussprechen; erklären für; JUR *Urteil* verkünden
pro·nun·ci·a·tion Aussprache *f*
proof 1. Beweis(e *pl*) *m*, Nachweis *m*; Probe *f*; PRINT Korrekturfahne *f*, *a.* PHOT Probeabzug *m* 2. *adj in cpds* ...fest, ...beständig, ...dicht, ...sicher; → **heatproof, soundproof, waterproof**; **be ~ against** geschützt sein vor (*dat*) 3. imprägnieren
proof·read PRINT Korrektur lesen
proof·read·er PRINT Korrektor(in)
prop 1. Stütze *f* (*a. fig*) 2. *a.* **~ up** stützen;

sich *or et.* lehnen (**against** gegen)
prop·a·gate BIOL sich fortpflanzen *or* vermehren; verbreiten
prop·a·ga·tion Fortpflanzung *f*, Vermehrung *f*; Verbreitung *f*
pro·pel (an)treiben; **pro·pel·lant**, **pro·pel·lent** Treibstoff *m*; Treibgas *n*
pro·pel·ler AVIAT Propeller *m*, MAR *a.* Schraube *f*
pro·pel·ling pen·cil Drehbleistift *m*
pro·pen·si·ty *fig* Neigung *f*
prop·er richtig, passend, geeignet; anständig, schicklich; echt, wirklich, richtig; eigentlich; eigen(tümlich); *esp Br* F ordentlich, tüchtig, gehörig
prop·er| name, **~ noun** Eigenname *m*
prop·er·ty Eigentum *n*, Besitz *m*; Landbesitz *m*, Grundbesitz *m*; Grundstück *n*; *fig* Eigenschaft *f*
proph·e·cy Prophezeiung *f*
proph·e·sy prophezeien
proph·et Prophet *m*
pro·por·tion 1. Verhältnis *n*; (An)Teil *m*; *pl* Größenverhältnisse *pl*, Proportionen *pl*; **in ~ to** im Verhältnis zu 2. (**to**) in das richtige Verhältnis bringen (mit, zu); anpassen (*dat*)
pro·por·tion·al proportional; → **proportionate**
pro·por·tion·ate (**to**) im richtigen Verhältnis (zu), entsprechend (*dat*)
pro·pos·al Vorschlag *m*; (Heirats)Antrag *m*; **pro·pose** *v/t* vorschlagen; beabsichtigen, vorhaben; *Toast* ausbringen (**to** auf *acc*); **~ s.o.'s health** auf j-s Gesundheit trinken; *v/i*: **~ to** *j-m* e-n (Heirats)Antrag machen
prop·o·si·tion Behauptung *f*; Vorschlag *m*, ECON *a.* Angebot *n*
pro·pri·e·ta·ry ECON gesetzlich *or* patentrechtlich geschützt; *fig* besitzergreifend
pro·pri·e·tor Eigentümer *m*, Besitzer *m*, Geschäftsinhaber *m*
pro·pri·e·tress Eigentümerin *f*, Besitzerin *f*, Geschäftsinhaberin *f*
pro·pri·e·ty Anstand *m*; Richtigkeit *f*
pro·pul·sion TECH Antrieb *m*
pro·sa·ic prosaisch, nüchtern, sachlich
prose Prosa *f*
pros·e·cute JUR strafrechtlich verfolgen, (gerichtlich) belangen (**for** wegen)
pros·e·cu·tion JUR strafrechtliche Verfolgung, Strafverfolgung *f*; **the ~** die

Staatsanwaltschaft, die Anklage (-behörde)

pros·e·cu·tor *a.* **public ~** JUR Staatsanwalt *m*, Staatsanwältin *f*

pros·pect 1. Aussicht *f* (*a. fig*); Interessent *m*, ECON möglicher Kunde, potenzieller Käufer **2. ~ for** *mining*: schürfen nach; bohren nach

pro·spec·tive voraussichtlich

pro·spec·tus (Werbe)Prospekt *m*

pros·per gedeihen; ECON blühen, florieren; **pros·per·i·ty** Wohlstand *m*; **pros·per·ous** ECON erfolgreich, blühend, florierend; wohlhabend

pros·ti·tute Prostituierte *f*, Dirne *f*; **male ~** Strichjunge *m*

pros·trate 1. hingestreckt; *fig* am Boden liegend; erschöpft; **~ with grief** gramgebeugt **2.** niederwerfen; *fig* erschöpfen; *fig* niederschmettern

pros·y langweilig; weitschweifig

pro·tag·o·nist Vorkämpfer(in); THEA Hauptfigur *f*, Held(in)

pro·tect (be)schützen (**from** vor *dat*; **against** gegen)

pro·tec·tion Schutz *m*; F Schutzgeld *n*; **~ of animals** Tierschutz; **~ of endangered species** Artenschutz *m*; **~ money** F Schutzgeld *n*; **~ rack·et** F Schutzgelderpressung *f*

pro·tec·tive (be)schützend; Schutz...; **~ cloth·ing** Schutzkleidung *f*; **~ custody** JUR Schutzhaft *f*; **~ du·ty**, **~ tar·iff** ECON Schutzzoll *m*

pro·tec·tor Beschützer *m*; (*Brust- etc -*) Schutz *m*

pro·tec·to·rate POL Protektorat *n*

pro·test 1. Protest *m*; Einspruch *m* **2.** *v/i* protestieren (**against** gegen); *v/t* protestieren gegen; beteuern

Prot·es·tant REL **1.** protestantisch **2.** Protestant(in)

prot·es·ta·tion Beteuerung *f*; Protest *m* (**against** gegen)

pro·to·col Protokoll *n*

pro·to·type Prototyp *m*

pro·tract in die Länge ziehen, hinziehen

pro·trude herausragen, vorstehen (**from** aus); **pro·trud·ing** vorstehend (*a. teeth*); vorspringend (*chin*)

proud stolz (**of** auf *acc*)

prove *v/t* be-, er-, nachweisen; *v/i:* **~** (**to be**) sich herausstellen *or* erweisen als

prov·en bewährt

prov·erb Sprichwort *n*

pro·vide *v/t* versehen, versorgen, beliefern; zur Verfügung stellen, bereitstellen; JUR vorsehen, vorschreiben (**that** dass); *v/i:* **~ against** Vorsorge treffen gegen; JUR verbieten; **~ for** sorgen für; vorsorgen für; JUR *et.* vorsehen

pro·vid·ed: ~ (**that**) vorausgesetzt(, dass)

pro·vid·er Ernährer(in)

prov·ince Provinz *f*; (Aufgaben-, Wissens)Gebiet *n*; **pro·vin·cial 1.** Provinz..., provinziell, *contp* provinzlerisch **2.** *contp* Provinzler(in)

pro·vi·sion Bereitstellung *f*, Beschaffung *f*; Vorkehrung *f*, Vorsorge *f*; Bestimmung *f*, Vorschrift *f*; *pl* Proviant *m*, Verpflegung *f*; **with the ~ that** unter der Bedingung, dass

pro·vi·sion·al provisorisch, vorläufig

pro·vi·so Bedingung *f*, Vorbehalt *m*; **with the ~ that** unter der Bedingung, dass

prov·o·ca·tion Provokation *f*

pro·voc·a·tive provozierend, (*a. sexually*) aufreizend

pro·voke provozieren, reizen

prowl 1. *v/i a.* **~ about**, **~ around** herumschleichen, herumstreifen; *v/t* durchstreifen **2.** Herumstreifen *n*

prowl car (Funk)Streifenwagen *m*

prox·im·i·ty Nähe *f*

prox·y (Handlungs)Vollmacht *f*; (Stell)Vertreter(in), Bevollmächtigte *m, f*; **by ~** durch e-n Bevollmächtigten

prude: **be a ~** prüde sein

pru·dence Klugheit *f*, Vernunft *f*; Besonnenheit *f*

pru·dent klug, vernünftig; besonnen

prud·ish prüde

prune[1] BOT (be)schneiden

prune[2] Backpflaume *f*

prus·sic ac·id CHEM Blausäure *f*

pry[1] neugierig sein; **~ about** herumschnüffeln; **~ into** s-e Nase stecken in (*acc*)

pry[2] → **prize**[2]

psalm REL Psalm *m*

pseu·do·nym Pseudonym *n*, Deckname *m*

psy·chi·a·trist Psychiater(in)

psy·chi·a·try Psychiatrie *f*

psy·cho·a·nal·y·sis Psychoanalyse *f*

psy·cho·log·i·cal psychologisch

psy·chol·o·gist Psychologe *m*, Psycho-

login f
psy·chol·o·gy Psychologie f
psy·cho·so·mat·ic psychosomatisch
pub Br Pub n, m, Kneipe f
pu·ber·ty Pubertät f
pu·bic hair Schamhaare pl
pub·lic 1. öffentlich; allgemein bekannt;
make ~ bekannt machen, an die Öffentlichkeit bringen **2.** die Öffentlichkeit, das Publikum; **in** ~ öffentlich, in
aller Öffentlichkeit
pub·li·ca·tion Bekanntgabe f, Bekanntmachung f; Publikation f, Veröffentlichung f
pub·lic| con·ve·ni·ence Br öffentliche
Bedürfnisanstalt; ~ **en·e·my** Staatsfeind m; ~ **health** öffentliches Gesund-
heitswesen; ~ **hol·i·day** gesetzlicher
Feiertag
pub·lic·i·ty Publicity f, a. Bekanntheit f,
ECON a. Reklame f, Werbung f; ~
depart·ment Werbeabteilung f
pub·lic| li·bra·ry Leihbücherei f; ~ **rela·
tions** (abbr PR) Public Relations pl,
Öffentlichkeitsarbeit f; ~ **school** staat-
liche Schule; Br Public School f; ~
trans·port esp Br, ~ **trans·por·ta·tion**
öffentliche Verkehrsmittel pl
pub·lish bekannt geben or machen; publizieren, veröffentlichen; Buch etc
verlegen, herausgeben
pub·lish·er Verleger(in), Herausge-
ber(in); Verlag m, Verlagshaus n
**pub·lish·er's, pub·lish·ers, publish·
ing house** Verlag m, Verlagshaus n
puck·er a. ~ **up** (sich) verziehen, (sich)
runzeln
pud·ding Br GASTR Nachspeise f, Nachtisch m; (Reis- etc) Auflauf m; (Art)
Fleischpastete f; Pudding m
pud·dle Pfütze f
pu·er·ile infantil, kindisch
puff 1. v/i schnaufen, keuchen; a. ~ **away**
paffen (**at** an dat); ~ **up** (an)schwellen;
v/t Rauch blasen; ~ **out** Kerze etc ausblasen; Rauch etc ausstoßen; Brust her-
ausdrücken **2.** Zug m; (Wind-) Hauch
m, (Wind)Stoß m; (Puder)Quaste f; F
Puste f
puffed sleeve Puffärmel m
puff pas·try GASTR Blätterteig m
puff·y (an)geschwollen; aufgedunsen
pug ZO Mops m
puke F (aus)kotzen

pull 1. Ziehen n; Zug m, Ruck m; Anstieg m, Steigung f; Zuggriff m, Zuglei-
ne f; F Beziehungen pl **2.** ziehen; ziehen an (dat); zerren; reißen; Pflanze
ausreißen; esp Br Bier zapfen; fig anziehen; ~ **ahead of** vorbeiziehen an
(dat), MOT überholen (acc); ~ **away** anfahren (bus etc); ~ **down** Gebäude abreißen; ~ **in** einfahren (train); anhalten;
~ **off** F et. zustande bringen, schaffen; ~
out herausziehen (**of** aus); Tisch ausziehen; RAIL ausfahren, MOT ausscheren; fig sich zurückziehen, aussteigen
(**of** aus); ~ **over** (s-n Wagen) an die or
zur Seite fahren; ~ **round** MED durchbringen; durchkommen; ~ **through**
j-n durchbringen; ~ **o.s. together** sich
zusammennehmen, F sich zusammen-
reißen; ~ **up** MOT anhalten; (an)halten;
~ **up to**, ~ **up with** SPORT j-n einholen
pull date Mindesthaltbarkeitsdatum n
pul·ley TECH Flaschenzug m
pull-in Br F Raststätte f, Rasthaus n
pull-o·ver Pullover m
pull-up SPORT Klimmzug m; **do a** ~ e-n
Klimmzug machen
pulp 1. Fruchtfleisch n; Brei m **2.**
Schund...; ~ **novel** Schundroman m
pul·pit Kanzel f
pulp·y breiig
pul·sate pulsieren, vibrieren
pulse Puls m; Pulsschlag m
pul·ver·ize pulverisieren
pu·ma ZO Puma m
pum·mel mit den Fäusten bearbeiten
pump 1. Pumpe f; (Zapf)Säule f **2.** pumpen; F j-n aushorchen; ~ **up** aufpumpen; ~ **at·tend·ant** Tankwart m
pump·kin BOT Kürbis m
pun 1. Wortspiel n **2.** Wortspiele or ein
Wortspiel machen
punch¹ 1. boxen, (mit der Faust) schlagen **2.** (Faust)Schlag m
punch² 1. lochen; Loch stanzen (**in** in
acc); ~ **in** einstempeln; ~ **out** ausstempeln **2.** Locher m; Lochzange f; Loch-
eisen n
punch³ Punsch m
Punch appr Kasper m, Kasperle n, m;
be as pleased or proud as ~ sich freu-
en wie ein Schneekönig; ~ **and Ju·dy
show** Kasperletheater n
punc·tu·al pünktlich
punc·tu·al·i·ty Pünktlichkeit f

punc·tu·ate interpunktieren

punc·tu·a·tion LING Interpunktion *f*; **~ mark** LING Satzzeichen *n*

punc·ture 1. (Ein)Stich *m*, Loch *n*; MOT Reifenpanne *f* **2.** durchstechen, durchbohren; ein Loch bekommen, platzen; MOT e-n Platten haben

pun·gent scharf, stechend, beißend (*smell, taste*); scharf, bissig (*remark etc*)

pun·ish *j-n* (be)strafen

pun·ish·a·ble strafbar

pun·ish·ment Strafe *f*; Bestrafung *f*

punk Punk *m* (*a.* MUS); Punk(er) *m*

pu·ny schwächlich

pup ZO Welpe *m*, junger Hund

pu·pa ZO Puppe *f*

pu·pil¹ Schüler(in)

pu·pil² ANAT Pupille *f*

pup·pet Handpuppe *f*; Marionette *f* (*a. fig*)

pup·pe·teer Puppenspieler(in)

pup·pet show Marionettentheater *n*, Puppenspiel *n*

pup·py ZO Welpe *m*, junger Hund

pur·chase 1. kaufen; *fig* erkaufen **2.** Kauf *m*; **make ~s** Einkäufe machen

pur·chas·er Käufer(in)

pure rein; pur

pure·bred ZO reinrassig

pur·ga·tive MED **1.** abführend **2.** Abführmittel *n*

pur·ga·to·ry REL Fegefeuer *n*

purge 1. *Partei etc* säubern (**of** von); **2.** Säuberung *f*, Säuberungsaktion *f*

pu·ri·fy reinigen

pu·ri·tan (HIST *Puritan*) **1.** Puritaner(in) **2.** puritanisch

pu·ri·ty Reinheit *f*

purl 1. linke Masche **2.** links stricken

pur·ple purpurn, purpurrot

pur·pose 1. Absicht *f*, Vorsatz *m*; Zweck *m*, Ziel *n*; Entschlossenheit *f*; **on ~** absichtlich; **to no ~** vergeblich **2.** beabsichtigen, vorhaben

pur·pose·ful entschlossen, zielstrebig

pur·pose·less zwecklos; ziellos

pur·pose·ly absichtlich

purr ZO schnurren; MOT summen, surren

purse¹ Geldbeutel *m*, Geldbörse *f*, Portemonnaie *n*; Handtasche *f*; SPORT Siegprämie *f*; *boxing:* Börse *f*

purse²: **~ (up) one's lips** die Lippen schürzen

purs·er MAR Zahlmeister *m*

pur·su·ance: **in (the) ~ of his duty** in Ausübung s-r Pflicht

pur·sue verfolgen; *s-m Studium etc* nachgehen; *Absicht, Politik etc* verfolgen; *Angelegenheit etc* weiterführen

pur·su·er Verfolger(in)

pur·suit Verfolgung *f*; Weiterführung *f*

pur·vey *Lebensmittel etc* liefern

pur·vey·or Lieferant *m*

pus MED Eiter *m*

push 1. stoßen, F schubsen; schieben; *Taste etc* drücken; drängen; (an)treiben; F *Rauschgift* pushen; *fig j-n* drängen (**to do** zu tun); *fig* Reklame machen für; **~ one's way** sich drängen (**through** durch); **~ ahead with** *Plan etc* vorantreiben; **~ along** F sich auf die Socken machen; **~ around** F herumschubsen; **~ for** drängen auf (*acc*); **~ forward with** → **push ahead with**; **~ o.s. forward** *fig* sich in den Vordergrund drängen *or* schieben; **~ in** sich vordrängeln; **~ off!** F hau ab!; **~ on with** → **push ahead with**; **~ out** *fig j-n* hinausdrängen; **~ through** *et.* durchsetzen; **~ up** *Preise etc* hochtreiben **2.** Stoß *m*, F Schubs *m*; (Werbe)Kampagne *f*; F Durchsetzungsvermögen *n*, Energie *f*, Tatkraft *f*

push but·ton TECH Druckknopf *m*, Drucktaste *f*

push·chair *Br* Sportwagen *m*

push·er F *contp* Rauschgifthändler *m*

push·o·ver F Kinderspiel *n*

push-up SPORT Liegestütz *m*

puss F ZO Mieze *f*

pus·sy *a.* **~ cat** F Miezekatze *f*

pus·sy·foot: F **~ about, ~ around** leisetreten, sich nicht festlegen wollen

put legen, setzen, stecken, stellen, tun; *j-n in e-e Lage etc, et. auf den Markt, in Ordnung etc* bringen; *et. in Kraft, in Umlauf etc* setzen; SPORT *Kugel* stoßen; unterwerfen, unterziehen (**to** *dat*); *et.* ausdrücken, *in Worte* fassen; übersetzen (**into** *German* ins Deutsche); *Schuld* geben (**on** *dat*); **~ right** in Ordnung bringen; **~ s.th. before s.o.** *fig* j-m et. vorlegen; **~ to bed** ins Bett bringen; **~ to school** zur Schule schicken; **~ about** *Gerüchte* verbreiten, in Umlauf setzen; **~ across** *et.* verständlich machen; **~ ahead** SPORT in Führung bringen; **~ aside** beiseitelegen; *Ware* zu-

rücklegen; *fig* beiseiteschieben; ~
away weglegen, wegtun; auf-, wegräumen; ~ *back* zurücklegen, -stellen,
-tun; *Uhr* zurückstellen (*by* um); ~
by Geld zurücklegen; ~ *down* v/t hinlegen, niederlegen, hinsetzen, hinstellen; *j-n* absetzen, aussteigen lassen;
(auf-, nieder-) schreiben, eintragen;
zuschreiben (*to dat*); *Aufstand* niederschlagen; (*a. v/i*) AVIAT landen; ~ *forward Plan etc* vorlegen; *Uhr* vorstellen
(*by* um); *fig* vorverlegen (*two days* um
zwei Tage; *to* auf *acc*); ~ *in* v/t hinein-
legen, -stecken, -stellen, *Kassette etc*
einlegen; installieren; *Gesuch etc* einreichen, *Forderung etc a.* geltend machen; *Antrag* stellen; *Arbeit, Zeit* verbringen (*on* mit); *Bemerkung* einwerfen; *v/i* MAR einlaufen (*at* in *acc*); ~
off et. verschieben (*until dat acc*); *j-m*
absagen; *j-n* hinhalten (*with* mit), *j-n*
vertrösten; *j-n* aus dem Konzept bringen; ~ *on Kleider etc* anziehen, *Hut,
Brille* aufsetzen; *Licht, Radio etc* anmachen, einschalten; *Sonderzug* einsetzen; THEA *Stück etc* herausbringen;
et. vortäuschen; F *j-n* auf den Arm nehmen; ~ *on airs* sich aufspielen; ~ *on
weight* zunehmen; ~ *out* v/t hinausle-
gen, -setzen, -stellen; *Hand etc* ausstrecken; *Feuer* löschen; *Licht, Radio etc*
ausmachen (*a. cigarette*), ab-, ausschalten; veröffentlichen, herausgeben; *radio*, TV bringen, senden; *j-n* aus der
Fassung bringen; *j-n* verärgern; *j-m*
Ungelegenheiten bereiten; *j-m* Umstände machen; sich *den Arm etc* verrenken *or.* ausrenken; *v/i* MAR auslaufen; ~ *over* → *put across*; ~ *through*
TEL *j-n* verbinden (*to* mit); durch-, ausführen; ~ *together* zusammenbauen,
-sätzen, -stellen; ~ *up* v/t hinauflegen,
-stellen; *Hand* (hoch)heben; *Zelt etc*
aufstellen; *Gebäude* errichten; *Bild
etc* aufhängen; *Plakat, Bekanntmachung etc* anschlagen; *Schirm* aufspan-
nen; *zum Verkauf* anbieten; *Preis* erhöhen; *Widerstand* leisten; *Kampf* liefern; *j-n* unterbringen, (bei sich) aufnehmen; *v/i* ~ *up at* absteigen in
(*dat*); ~ *up with* sich gefallen lassen;
sich abfinden mit

pu·tre·fy (ver)faulen, verwesen
pu·trid faul, verfault, verwest; F scheußlich, saumäßig
put·ty 1. Kitt *m* **2.** kitten
put-up job F abgekartetes Spiel
puz·zle 1. Rätsel *n*; Geduld(s)spiel *n* **2.**
v/t j-n vor ein Rätsel stellen; verwirren;
be ~*d* vor e-m Rätsel stehen; ~ *out* herausfinden, herausbringen; F austüf-
teln; *v/i* sich den Kopf zerbrechen
(*about, over* über *dat or acc*)
pyg·my 1. Pygmäe *m*, Pygmäin *f*;
Zwerg(in) **2.** *esp* ZO Zwerg...
py·ja·mas *Br* → *pajamas*
py·lon TECH Hochspannungsmast *m*
pyr·a·mid Pyramide *f*
pyre Scheiterhaufen *m*
py·thon ZO Python(schlange) *f*
pyx REL Hostienbehälter *m*

Q

Q, q Q, q *n*
quack[1] ZO **1.** quaken **2.** Quaken *n*
quack[2] *a.* ~ *doctor* Quacksalber *m*, Kurpfuscher *m*; **quack·er·y** Quacksalberei
f, Kurpfuscherei *f*
quad·ran·gle Viereck *n*
quad·ran·gu·lar viereckig
quad·ra·phon·ic quadrophon(isch)
quad·rat·ic MATH quadratisch
quad·ri·lat·er·al MATH **1.** vierseitig **2.**
Viereck *n*
quad·ro·phon·ic → *quadraphonic*

quad·ru·ped ZO Vierfüß(l)er *m*; Vierbeiner *m*
quad·ru·ple 1. vierfach **2.** (sich) vervier-
fachen
quad·ru·plets Vierlinge *pl*
quads Vierlinge *pl*
quag·mire Morast *m*, Sumpf *m*
quail ZO Wachtel *f*
quaint idyllisch, malerisch
quake 1. zittern, beben (*with, for* vor
dat; *at* bei); **2.** F Erdbeben *n*
Quak·er REL Quäker(in)

qual·i·fi·ca·tion Qualifikation *f*, Befähigung *f*, Eignung *f* (*for* für, zu); Voraussetzung *f*; Einschränkung *f*

qual·i·fied qualifiziert, geeignet, befähigt (*for* für); berechtigt; bedingt, eingeschränkt; **qual·i·fy** *v/t* qualifizieren, befähigen (*for* für, zu); berechtigen (*to do* zu tun); einschränken, abschwächen, mildern; *v/i* sich qualifizieren *or* eignen (*for* für; *as* als); SPORT sich qualifizieren (*for* für)

qual·i·ty Qualität *f*; Eigenschaft *f*

qualms Bedenken *pl*, Skrupel *pl*

quan·da·ry: *be in a ~ about what to do* nicht wissen, was man tun soll

quan·ti·ty Quantität *f*, Menge *f*

quan·tum PHYS **1.** Quant *n* **2.** Quanten…

quar·an·tine 1. Quarantäne *f* **2.** unter Quarantäne stellen

quar·rel 1. Streit *m*, Auseinandersetzung *f* **2.** (sich) streiten

quar·rel·some streitsüchtig, zänkisch

quar·ry[1] Steinbruch *m*

quar·ry[2] HUNT Beute *f*, *a. fig* Opfer *n*

quart Quart *n* (*abbr* **qt**) (*0,95 l, Br 1,14 l*)

quar·ter 1. Viertel *n*, vierter Teil; Quartal *n*, Vierteljahr *n*; Viertelpfund *n*; Vierteldollar *m*; SPORT (Spiel)Viertel *n*; (Himmels)Richtung *f*; Gegend *f*, Teil *m*; (Stadt)Viertel *n*; GASTR (*esp* Hinter)Viertel *n*; Gnade *f*, Pardon *m*; *pl* Quartier *n*, Unterkunft *f* (*a.* MIL); *a ~ of an hour* e-e Viertelstunde; *a ~ of* (*Br* **to**) *five* (ein) Viertel vor fünf (4.45); *a ~ after* (*Br* **past**) *five* (ein) Viertel nach fünf (5.15); *at close ~s* in *or* aus nächster Nähe; *from official ~s* von amtlicher Seite **2.** vierteln; *esp* MIL einquartieren (*on* bei)

quar·ter·deck MAR Achterdeck *n*

quar·ter·fi·nals SPORT Viertelfinale *n*

quar·ter·ly 1. vierteljährlich **2.** Vierteljahresschrift *f*

quar·tet(te) MUS Quartett *n*

quartz MIN Quarz *m*; **~ clock** Quarzuhr *f*; **~ watch** Quarz(armband)uhr *f*

qua·ver 1. *v/i* zittern; *v/t et.* mit zitternder Stimme sagen **2.** Zittern *n*

quay MAR Kai *m*

quea·sy: *I feel ~* mir ist übel *or* F mulmig

queen Königin *f*; *card game, chess*: Dame *f*; F Schwule *m*, Homo *m*

queen bee ZO Bienenkönigin *f*

queen·ly wie e-e Königin, königlich

queer komisch, seltsam; F wunderlich; F schwul

quench Durst löschen, stillen

quer·u·lous nörglerisch

que·ry 1. Frage *f*; Zweifel *m* **2.** infrage stellen, in Zweifel ziehen

quest 1. Suche *f* (*for* nach); *in ~ of* auf der Suche nach **2.** suchen (*after, for* nach)

ques·tion 1. Frage *f*, *a.* Problem *n*, *a.* Sache *f*, *a.* Zweifel *m*; *only a ~ of time* nur e-e Frage der Zeit; *this is not the point in ~* darum geht es nicht; *there is no ~ that, it is beyond ~ that* es steht außer Frage, dass; *there is no ~ about this* daran besteht kein Zweifel; *be out of the ~* nicht infrage kommen **2.** befragen (*about* über *acc*); JUR vernehmen, verhören (*about* zu); bezweifeln, in Zweifel ziehen, infrage stellen

ques·tion·a·ble fraglich, zweifelhaft; fragwürdig

ques·tion·er Fragesteller(in)

ques·tion| mark Fragezeichen *n*; **~·mas·ter** *esp Br* Quizmaster *m*

ques·tion·naire Fragebogen *m*

queue *esp Br* **1.** Schlange *f*; → *jump* **2.** *mst ~ up* Schlange stehen, anstehen, sich anstellen

quib·ble sich herumstreiten (*with* mit; *about, over* wegen)

quick 1. *adj* schnell, rasch; aufbrausend, hitzig (*temper*); *be ~!* mach schnell!, beeil dich! **2.** *adv* schnell, rasch **3.** *cut s.o. to the ~ fig* j-n tief verletzen

quick·en (sich) beschleunigen

quick·sand Treibsand *m*

quick-tem·pered aufbrausend, hitzig

quick-wit·ted schlagfertig; geistesgegenwärtig

qui·et 1. ruhig, still; **~**, *please* Ruhe, bitte; *be ~!* sei still! **2.** Ruhe *f*, Stille *f*; *on the ~* F heimlich **3.** *v/t a.* **~** *down* j-n beruhigen; *v/i a.* **~** *down* sich beruhigen

qui·et·en *Br* → *quiet* 3

qui·et·ness Ruhe *f*, Stille *f*

quill ZO (Schwung-, Schwanz)Feder *f*; Stachel *m*

quilt Steppdecke *f*; **quilt·ed** Stepp…

quince BOT Quitte *f*

quin·ine PHARM Chinin *n*

quint F Fünfling *m*

quin·tes·sence Quintessenz *f*; Inbegriff *m*

quin·tet(te) MUS Quintett *n*

quin·tu·ple 1. fünffach **2.** (sich) verfünffachen

quin·tu·plets Fünflinge *pl*

quip 1. geistreiche *or* witzige Bemerkung **2.** witzeln, spötteln

quirk Eigenart *f*, Schrulle *f*; **by some ~ of fate** durch e-e Laune des Schicksals, durch e-n verrückten Zufall

quit F *v/t* aufhören mit; **~ one's job** kündigen; *v/i* aufhören; kündigen

quite ganz, völlig; ziemlich; **~ a few** ziemlich viele; **~ nice** ganz nett, recht nett; **~ (so)!** *esp Br* genau, ganz recht; **be ~ right** völlig recht haben; **she's ~ a beauty** sie ist e-e wirkliche Schönheit

quits F quitt (**with** mit); **call it ~** es gut sein lassen

quit·ter: F **be a ~** schnell aufgeben

quiv·er¹ zittern (**with** vor *dat*; **at** bei)

quiv·er² Köcher *m*

quiz 1. Quiz *n*; Prüfung *f*, Test *m* **2.** ausfragen (**about** über *acc*)

quiz·mas·ter Quizmaster *m*

quiz·zi·cal spöttisch-fragend

quo·ta Quote *f*, Kontingent *n*

quo·ta·tion Zitat *n*; ECON Notierung *f*; Kostenvoranschlag *m*; **~ marks** LING Anführungszeichen *pl*

quote zitieren; *Beispiel etc* anführen; *Preis* nennen; **be ~d at** ECON notieren mit

quo·tient MATH Quotient *m*

R

R, r R, r *n*

rab·bi REL Rabbiner *m*

rab·bit ZO Kaninchen *n*

rab·ble Pöbel *m*, Mob *m*

rab·ble-rous·ing Hetz..., aufwieglerisch

rab·id VET tollwütig; *fig* fanatisch

ra·bies VET Tollwut *f*

rac·coon ZO Waschbär *m*

race¹ Rasse *f*, Rassenzugehörigkeit *f*; (*Menschen*)Geschlecht *n*

race² 1. (Wett)Rennen *n*, (Wett)Lauf *m* **2.** *v/i* an (e-m) Rennen teilnehmen; um die Wette laufen *or* fahren *etc*; rasen, rennen; MOT durchdrehen; *v/t* um die Wette laufen *or* fahren *etc* mit; rasen mit

race car MOT Rennwagen *m*

race·course Rennbahn *f*

race·horse Rennpferd *n*

rac·er Rennpferd *n*; Rennrad *n*, Rennwagen *m*

race ri·ots Rassenunruhen *pl*

race·track Rennbahn *f*

ra·cial rassisch, Rassen...

rac·ing 1. Rennsport *m* **2.** Renn...

rac·ing car *Br* MOT Rennwagen *m*

ra·cism Rassismus *m*

ra·cist 1. Rassist(in) **2.** rassistisch

rack 1. Gestell *n*, (*Geschirr-, Zeitungsetc*)Ständer *m*, RAIL (*Gepäck*)Netz *n*,

MOT (*Dach*)Gepäckständer *m*; HIST Folter(bank) *f* **2. be ~ed by** *or* **with** geplagt *or* gequält werden von; **~ one's brains** sich das Hirn zermartern, sich den Kopf zerbrechen

rack·et¹ *tennis etc*: Schläger *m*

rack·et² F Krach *m*, Lärm *m*; Schwindel *m*, Gaunerei *f*; (*Drogen- etc*)Geschäft *n*; organisierte Erpressung

rack·et·eer Gauner *m*; Erpresser *m*

ra·coon → **raccoon**

rac·y spritzig, lebendig; gewagt (*joke*)

ra·dar TECH Radar *m, n*; **~ screen** Radarschirm *m*; **~ speed check** MOT Radarkontrolle *f*; **~ sta·tion** Radarstation *f*; **~ trap** MOT Radarkontrolle *f*

ra·di·al 1. radial, Radial..., strahlenförmig **2.** MOT Gürtelreifen *m*

ra·di·al| tire, *Br* **~ tyre** → **radial** 2

ra·di·ant strahlend, leuchtend (*a. fig* **with** vor *dat*)

ra·di·ate ausstrahlen; strahlenförmig ausgehen (**from** von)

ra·di·a·tion Ausstrahlung *f*

ra·di·a·tor Heizkörper *m*; MOT Kühler *m*

rad·i·cal 1. radikal (*a.* POL); MATH Wurzel... **2.** POL Radikale *m, f*

ra·di·o 1. Radio(apparat *m*) *n*; Funk *m*; Funkgerät *n*; **by ~** über Funk; **on the ~** im Radio **2.** funken

ra·di·o·ac·tive radioaktiv; **~ waste**

Atommüll *m*, radioaktiver Abfall

ra·di·o·ac·tiv·i·ty Radioaktivität *f*

ra·di·o| ham Funkamateur *m*; **~ play** Hörspiel *n*; **~ set** Radioapparat *m*; **~ sta·tion** Funkstation *f*; Rundfunksender *m*, -station *f*; **~ther·a·py** MED Strahlentherapie *f*, Röntgentherapie *f*; **~ tow·er** Funkturm *m*

rad·ish BOT Rettich *m*; Radieschen *n*

ra·di·us MATH Radius *m*

raf·fle 1. Tombola *f* **2.** *a.* **~ off** verlosen

raft Floß *n*

raf·ter (Dach)Sparren *m*

rag Lumpen *m*, Fetzen *m*; Lappen *m*; *in* **~s** zerlumpt

rage 1. Wut *f*, Zorn *m*; *fly into a* **~** wütend werden; *the latest* **~** F der letzte Schrei; *be all the* **~** F große Mode sein **2.** wettern (*against, at* gegen); wüten, toben

rag·ged zerlumpt; struppig; *fig* stümperhaft

raid 1. (*on*) Überfall *m* (auf *acc*), MIL *a.* Angriff *m* (gegen); Razzia *f* (in *dat*); **2.** überfallen, MIL *a.* angreifen; e-e Razzia machen in (*dat*)

rail 1. Geländer *n*; Stange *f*; (Handtuch)-Halter *m*; (Eisen)Bahn *f*; RAIL Schiene *f*, *pl a.* Gleis *n*; *by* **~** mit der Bahn **2.** **~** *in* einzäunen; **~** *off* abzäunen

rail·ing *often pl* (Gitter)Zaun *m*

rail·road Eisenbahn *f*; **~ line** Bahnlinie *f*; **~ sta·tion** Bahnhof *m*

rail·way *Br* → **railroad**

rain Regen *m*, *pl* Regenfälle *pl*; *the* **~s** die Regenzeit **2.** regnen; *it never* **~s** *but it pours* es kommt immer gleich knüppeldick, ein Unglück kommt selten allein

rain·bow Regenbogen *m*

rain·coat Regenmantel *m*

rain·fall Niederschlag(smenge *f*) *m*

rain for·est GEOGR Regenwald *m*

rain·proof regendicht, wasserdicht

rain·y regnerisch, verregnet, Regen...

raise 1. heben; hochziehen; erheben; *Denkmal etc* errichten; *Staub etc* aufwirbeln; *Gehalt, Miete etc* erhöhen; *Geld* zusammenbringen, beschaffen; *Kinder* aufziehen, großziehen; *Tiere* züchten; *Getreide etc* anbauen; *Frage* aufwerfen, *et.* zur Sprache bringen; *Blockade etc*, *a. Verbot* aufheben **2.** Lohn- *or* Gehaltserhöhung *f*

rai·sin Rosine *f*

rake 1. Rechen *m*, Harke *f* **2.** *v/t*: **~** (*up*) (zusammen)rechen, (zusammen)harken; F *in* scheffeln; *v/i*: **~** *about*, **~** *around* herumstöbern

rak·ish flott, keck, verwegen

ral·ly 1. (sich) (wieder) sammeln; sich erholen (*from* von) (*a.* ECON); **~** *round* sich scharen um **2.** Kundgebung *f*, (Massen)Versammlung *f*; MOT Rallye *f*; *tennis etc*: Ballwechsel *m*

ram 1. ZO Widder *m*, Schafbock *m*; TECH Ramme *f* **2.** rammen

ram·ble 1. wandern, umherstreifen; abschweifen **2.** Wanderung *f*; **ram·bler** Wanderer *m*; BOT Kletterrose *f*

ram·bling weitschweifig; weitläufig; **~ rose** BOT Kletterrose *f*

ramp Rampe *f*; MOT (Autobahn)Auffahrt *f*; (Autobahn)Ausfahrt *f*

ram·page 1. **~** *through* (wild *or* aufgeregt) trampeln durch (*elephant etc*); → **2.** *go on the* **~** *through* randalierend ziehen durch

ram·pant: *be* **~** wuchern (*plant*); grassieren (*in* in *dat*)

ram·shack·le baufällig (*building*); klapp(e)rig (*vehicle*)

ranch Ranch *f*; (Geflügel- *etc*)Farm *f*

ranch·er Rancher *m*; (Geflügel- *etc*) Züchter *m*

ran·cid ranzig

ran·co(u)r Groll *m*, Erbitterung *f*

ran·dom 1. *adj* ziellos, wahllos; zufällig, Zufalls...; **~** *sample* Stichprobe *f* **2.** *at* **~** aufs Geratewohl

range 1. Reich-, Schuss-, Tragweite *f*; Entfernung *f*; *fig* Bereich *m*, *a.* Spielraum *m*, *a.* Gebiet *n*; (*Schieß*)Stand *m*, (-)Platz *m*; (*Berg*)Kette *f*, offenes Weidegebiet; ECON Kollektion *f*, Sortiment *n*; Küchenherd *m*; *at close* **~** aus nächster Nähe; *within* **~** *of vision* in Sichtweite; *a wide* **~** *of ...* eine große Auswahl an ... (*dat*) **2.** *v/i*: **~** *from ...* *to ...*, **~** *between ... and ...* sich zwischen ... und ... bewegen (*prices etc*); *v/t* aufstellen, anordnen

range find·er PHOT Entfernungsmesser *m*

rang·er Förster *m*; Ranger *m*

rank¹ 1. Rang *m* (*a.* MIL), (soziale) Stellung; Reihe *f*; (Taxi)Stand *m*; *of the first* **~** *fig* erstklassig; *the* **~** *and file* *fig* die Basis; *the ~s fig* das Heer, die Masse **2.** *v/t* rechnen, zählen (*among* zu); stellen (*above* über *acc*); *v/i* zählen, gehören (*among* zu); gelten (*as* als)

rank² BOT (üppig) wuchernd; übel riechend, übel schmeckend; *fig* krass (*outsider*), blutig (*beginner*)

ran·kle *fig* nagen, wehtun, F wurmen

ran·sack durchwühlen, durchsuchen; plündern

ran·som 1. Lösegeld *n* **2.** freikaufen, auslösen

rap 1. Klopfen *n*; Klaps *m* **2.** klopfen (an *acc*, auf *acc*)

ra·pa·cious habgierig

rape¹ 1. vergewaltigen **2.** Vergewaltigung *f*

rape² BOT Raps *m*

rap·id schnell, rasch

ra·pid·i·ty Schnelligkeit *f*

rap·ids GEOGR Stromschnellen *pl*

rapt: *with ~ attention* mit gespannter Aufmerksamkeit

rap·ture Entzücken *n*, Verzückung *f*; *go into ~s* in Verzückung geraten

rare¹ selten, rar; dünn (*air*); F Mords...

rare² GASTR blutig (*steak*)

rar·e·fied dünn (*air*)

rar·i·ty Seltenheit *f*; Rarität *f*

ras·cal Schlingel *m*

rash¹ voreilig, vorschnell, unbesonnen

rash² MED (Haut)Ausschlag *m*

rash·er dünne Speckscheibe

rasp 1. raspeln; kratzen **2.** Raspel *f*; Kratzen *n*

rasp·ber·ry BOT Himbeere *f*

rat ZO Ratte *f* (*a. contp*); F *smell a ~* Lunte *or* den Braten riechen

rate 1. Quote *f*, Rate *f*, (Geburten-, Sterbe)Ziffer *f*; (Steuer-, Zins- *etc*)Satz *m*; (Wechsel)Kurs *m*; Geschwindigkeit *f*, Tempo *n*; *at any ~* auf jeden Fall **2.** einschätzen, halten (*as* für); Lob *etc* verdienen; *be ~d as* gelten als

rate of ex·change ECON (Umrechnungs-, Wechsel)Kurs *m*

rate of in·terest ECON Zinssatz *m*

ra·ther ziemlich; eher, vielmehr, besser gesagt; *~! esp Br* F und ob!; *I would or had ~ go* ich möchte lieber gehen

rat·i·fy POL ratifizieren

rat·ing Einschätzung *f*; radio, TV Einschaltquote *f*

ra·ti·o MATH Verhältnis *n*

ra·tion 1. Ration *f* **2.** *et.* rationieren; *~ out* zuteilen (*to dat*)

ra·tion·al rational; vernunftbegabt; vernünftig; verstandesmäßig

ra·tion·al·i·ty Vernunft *f*

ra·tion·al·ize rational erklären; ECON rationalisieren

rat race F endloser Konkurrenzkampf

rat·tle 1. klappern; rasseln *or* klimpern (mit); prasseln (*on* auf *acc*) (*rain etc*); rattern, knattern (*vehicle*); rütteln an (*dat*); F *j-n* verunsichern; *~ at* rütteln an (*dat*); *~ off* F *Gedicht etc* herunterrasseln; F *~ on* quasseln (*about* über *acc*); F *~ through Rede etc* herunterrasseln **2.** Klappern *n* (*etc → 1*); Rassel *f*, Klapper *f*

rat·tle·snake ZO Klapperschlange *f*

rau·cous heiser, rau

rav·age verwüsten

rav·ag·es Verwüstungen *pl*, *a. fig* verheerende Auswirkungen *pl*

rave fantasieren, irrereden; toben; wettern (*against, at* gegen); schwärmen (*about* von)

rav·el (sich) verwickeln *or* verwirren

ra·ven ZO Rabe *m*

rav·e·nous ausgehungert, heißhungrig

ra·vine Schlucht *f*, Klamm *f*

rav·ing mad tobsüchtig

rav·ings irres Gerede, Delirien *pl*

rav·ish·ing *fig* hinreißend

raw GASTR roh, ECON, TECH *a.* Roh...; MED wund; METEOR nasskalt; *fig* unerfahren; *~ vegetables and fruit* Rohkost *f*

raw-boned knochig, hager

raw·hide Rohleder *n*

raw ma·te·ri·al Rohstoff *m*

ray Strahl *m*; *fig* Schimmer *m*

ray·on Kunstseide *f*

ra·zor Rasiermesser *n*; Rasierapparat *m*; *electric ~* Elektrorasierer *m*

ra·zor blade Rasierklinge *f*

ra·zor('s) edge *fig* kritische Lage; *be on a ~* auf des Messers Schneide stehen

re... wieder, noch einmal, neu

reach 1. *v/t* erreichen; reichen *or* gehen bis an (*acc*) *or* zu; *~ down* herunter-, hinunterreichen (*from* von); *~ out Arm etc* ausstrecken; *v/i* reichen, gehen, sich erstrecken; *a. ~ out* greifen, langen (*for* nach); *~ out* die Hand ausstrecken **2.** Reichweite *f*; *within (out of) ~* in (außer) Reichweite; *within easy* ~ leicht erreichbar

re·act reagieren (*to* auf *acc*; CHEM *with* mit); **re·ac·tion** Reaktion *f* (*a.* CHEM)

re·ac·tor PHYS Reaktor *m*

read lesen; TECH (an)zeigen; *Zähler etc* ablesen; UNIV studieren; deuten, verstehen (*as* als); sich *gut etc* lesen (lassen); lauten; ~ (*s.th.*) *to s.o.* j-m (et.) vorlesen

read·a·ble lesbar; leserlich; lesenswert

read·er Leser(in); Lektor(in); Lesebuch *n*

read·i·ly bereitwillig, gern; leicht, ohne weiteres

read·i·ness Bereitschaft *f*

read·ing 1. Lesen *n*; Lesung *f* (*a.* PARL); TECH Anzeige *f*, (*Thermometer- etc -*) Stand *m*; Auslegung *f* **2.** Lese…; ~ *matter* Lesestoff *m*

re·ad·just TECH nachstellen, korrigieren; ~ (*o.s.*) *to* sich wieder anpassen (*dat*) *or* an (*acc*), sich wieder einstellen auf (*acc*)

read·y bereit, fertig; bereitwillig; im Begriff (*to do* zu tun); schnell, schlagfertig; ~ *for use* gebrauchsfertig; *get* ~ (sich) fertig machen

read·y cash → *ready money*

read·y-made Konfektions…

read·y meal Fertiggericht *n*

read·y mon·ey Bargeld *n*

real echt, wirklich, tatsächlich, real; F *for* ~ echt, im Ernst

real es·tate Grundbesitz *m*, Immobilien *pl*; ~ *a·gent* Grundstücks-, Immobilienmakler *m*

re·a·lism Realismus *m*

re·al·ist Realist(in)

re·al·is·tic realistisch

re·al·i·ty Realität *f*, Wirklichkeit *f*

re·a·li·za·tion Erkenntnis *f*; Realisierung *f* (*a.* ECON), Verwirklichung *f*

re·al·ize sich klarmachen, erkennen, begreifen, einsehen; realisieren (*a.* ECON), verwirklichen

real·ly wirklich, tatsächlich; *well*, ~! ich muss schon sagen!; ~? im Ernst?

realm Königreich *n*; *fig* Reich *n*

real·tor Grundstücks-, Immobilienmakler *m*

reap *Getreide etc* schneiden; *Feld* abernten; *fig* ernten

re·ap·pear wieder erscheinen

rear 1. *v/t Kind, Tier* aufziehen, großziehen; *Kopf* heben; *v/i* sich aufbäumen (*horse*) **2.** Rückseite *f*, Hinterseite *f*, MOT Heck *n*; *in* (*Br at*) *the* ~ *of* hinter (*dat*); *bring up the* ~ die Nachhut bilden **3.** hinter, Hinter…, Rück…, MOT *a.* Heck…

rear-end col·li·sion MOT Auffahrunfall *m*

rear·guard MIL Nachhut *f*

rear light MOT Rücklicht *n*

re·arm MIL (wieder) aufrüsten

re·ar·ma·ment MIL (Wieder)Aufrüstung *f*

rear·most hinterste(r, -s)

rear·view mir·ror MOT Rückspiegel *m*

rear·ward 1. *adj* hintere(r, -s), rückwärtig **2.** *adv a.* **rearwards** rückwärts

rear-wheel drive MOT Hinterradantrieb *m*

rear win·dow MOT Heckscheibe *f*

rea·son 1. Grund *m*; Verstand *m*; Vernunft *f*; *by* ~ *of* wegen; *for this* ~ aus diesem Grund; *it stands to* ~ *that* es leuchtet ein, dass **2.** *v/i* vernünftig *or* logisch denken; vernünftig reden (*with* mit); *v/t* folgern, schließen (*that* dass); ~ *s.o. into* (*out of*) *s.th.* j-m et. einreden (ausreden); **rea·son·a·ble** vernünftig; günstig (*price*); ganz gut, nicht schlecht

re·as·sure beruhigen

re·bate ECON Rabatt *m*, (Preis)Nachlass *m*; Rückzahlung *f*

reb·el¹ 1. Rebell(in); Aufständische *m, f* **2.** aufständisch

re·bel² rebellieren, sich auflehnen (*against* gegen)

re·bel·lion Rebellion *f*, Aufstand *m*

re·bel·lous rebellisch, aufständisch

re·birth Wiedergeburt *f*

re·bound 1. abprallen, zurückprallen (*from* von); *fig* zurückfallen (*on* auf *acc.*); **2.** SPORT Abpraller *m*

re·buff 1. schroffe Abweisung, Abfuhr *f* **2.** schroff abweisen

re·build wieder aufbauen (*a. fig*)

re·buke 1. rügen, tadeln **2.** Rüge *f*, Tadel *m*

re·call 1. zurückrufen, abberufen; MOT (in die Werkstatt) zurückrufen; sich erinnern an (*acc*); erinnern an (*acc*) **2.** Zurückrufung *f*, Abberufung *f*; Rückrufaktion *f*; *have total* ~ das absolute Gedächtnis haben; *beyond ~, past ~* unwiederbringlich *or* unwiderruflich vorbei

re·ca·pit·u·late rekapitulieren, (kurz) zusammenfassen

re·cap·ture wieder einfangen (*a. fig*); *Häftling* wieder fassen; MIL zurückerobern

re·cast TECH umgießen; umformen, neu gestalten; THEA *etc* umbesetzen, neu besetzen

re·cede schwinden; *receding chin* fliehendes Kinn

re·ceipt *esp* ECON Empfang *m*, Eingang *m*; Quittung *f*; *pl* Einnahmen *pl*

re·ceive bekommen, erhalten; empfangen; *j-n* aufnehmen (*into* in *acc*); *radio*, TV empfangen; **re·ceiv·er** Empfänger(in); TEL Hörer *m*; JUR Hehler(in); *a. official~Br* JUR Konkursverwalter *m*

re·cent neuere(r, -s); jüngste(r, -s)

re·cent·ly kürzlich, vor kurzem

re·cep·tion Empfang *m*; Aufnahme *f* (*into* in *acc*); *radio*, TV Empfang *m*; *a. ~ desk hotel*: Rezeption *f*, Empfang *m*

re·cep·tion·ist Empfangsdame *f*, -chef *m*; MED Sprechstundenhilfe *f*

re·cep·tive aufnahmefähig; empfänglich (*to* für)

re·cess Unterbrechung *f*, (Schul)Pause *f*; PARL, JUR Ferien *pl*; Nische *f*

re·ces·sion ECON Rezession *f*

re·ci·pe (Koch)Rezept *n*

re·cip·i·ent Empfänger(in)

re·cip·ro·cal wechselseitig, gegenseitig

re·cip·ro·cate *v/i* TECH sich hin- und herbewegen; sich revanchieren; *v/t Einladung etc* erwidern

re·cit·al Vortrag *m*, (*Klavier- etc*)Konzert *n*, (*Lieder*)Abend *m*; Schilderung *f*; **re·ci·ta·tion** Aufsagen *n*, Hersagen *n*; Vortrag *m*; **re·cite** aufsagen, hersagen; vortragen; aufzählen

reck·less rücksichtslos

reck·on *v/t* (aus-, be)rechnen; glauben, schätzen; *~ up* zusammenrechnen; *v/i: ~ on* rechnen mit; *~ with* rechnen mit; *~ without* nicht rechnen mit

reck·on·ing (Be)Rechnung *f*; *be out in one's ~* sich verrechnet haben

re·claim zurückfordern; *Gepäck etc* abholen; *dem Meer etc* Land abgewinnen; TECH wiedergewinnen

re·cline sich zurücklehnen

re·cluse Einsiedler(in)

rec·og·ni·tion (Wieder)Erkennen *n*; Anerkennung *f*

rec·og·nize (wieder) erkennen; anerkennen; zugeben, eingestehen

re·coil 1. zurückschrecken (*from* vor *dat*); 2. Rückstoß *m*

rec·ol·lect sich erinnern an (*acc*)

rec·ol·lec·tion Erinnerung *f* (*of* an *acc*)

rec·om·mend empfehlen (*as* als; *for* für)

rec·om·men·da·tion Empfehlung *f*

rec·om·pense 1. entschädigen (*for* für); 2. Entschädigung *f*

rec·on·cile versöhnen, aussöhnen; in Einklang bringen (*with* mit)

rec·on·cil·i·a·tion Versöhnung *f*, Aussöhnung *f* (*between* zwischen *dat*; *with* mit)

re·con·di·tion TECH (general)überholen

re·con·nais·sance MIL Aufklärung *f*, Erkundung *f*

re·con·noi·ter, *Br* **re·con·noi·tre** MIL erkunden, auskundschaften

re·con·sid·er noch einmal überdenken

re·con·struct wieder aufbauen (*a. fig*); *Verbrechen etc* rekonstruieren

re·con·struc·tion Wiederaufbau *m*; Rekonstruktion *f*

rec·ord[1] Aufzeichnung *f*; JUR Protokoll *n*; Akte *f*; (Schall)Platte *f*; SPORT Rekord *m*; *off the ~* inoffiziell; *have a criminal ~* vorbestraft sein

re·cord[2] aufzeichnen, aufschreiben, schriftlich niederlegen; JUR protokollieren, zu Protokoll nehmen; *auf Schallplatte, Tonband etc* aufnehmen; *Sendung a.* aufzeichnen, mitschneiden

re·cord·er (*Kassetten*)Rekorder *m*; (*Tonband*)Gerät *n*; MUS Blockflöte *f*

re·cord·ing Aufnahme *f*, Aufzeichnung *f*, Mitschnitt *m*

rec·ord play·er Plattenspieler *m*

re·count erzählen

re·cov·er *v/t* wiedererlangen, wiederbekommen, wieder finden; *Kosten etc* wiedereinbringen; *Fahrzeug, Verunglückten etc* bergen; *~ consciousness* MED wieder zu sich kommen, das Bewusstsein wiedererlangen; *v/i* sich erholen (*from* von); **re·cov·er·y** Wiedererlangen *n*; Wiederfinden *n*; Bergung *f*; Genesung *f*; Erholung *f*

rec·re·a·tion Entspannung *f*; Unterhal-

reflect

tung *f*, Freizeitbeschäftigung *f*

re·cruit 1. MIL Rekrut *m*; Neue *m, f*, neues Mitglied **2.** MIL rekrutieren; *Personal* einstellen; *Mitglieder* werben

rec·tan·gle MATH Rechteck *n*

rec·tan·gu·lar rechteckig

rec·ti·fy ELECTR gleichrichten

rec·tor REL Pfarrer *m*

rec·to·ry REL Pfarrhaus *n*

re·cu·pe·rate sich erholen (*from* von) (*a. fig*)

re·cur wiederkehren, wieder auftreten

re·cur·rence Wiederkehr *f*

re·cur·rent wiederkehrend

re·cy·cla·ble TECH recycelbar, wiederverwertbar; **re·cy·cle** TECH *Abfälle* recyceln, wieder verwerten; **~d paper** Recyclingpapier *n*, Umwelt(schutz)-papier *n*; **re·cy·cling** TECH Recycling *n*, Wiederverwertung *f*

red 1. rot **2.** Rot *n*; *be in the* ~ ECON in den roten Zahlen sein

red·breast → *robin*

Red Cres·cent Roter Halbmond

Red Cross Rotes Kreuz

red·cur·rant BOT Rote Johannisbeere

red·den röten, rot färben; rot werden

red·dish rötlich

re·dec·o·rate *Zimmer etc* neu streichen *or* tapezieren

re·deem *Pfand, Versprechen etc* einlösen; REL erlösen

Re·deem·er REL Erlöser *m*, Heiland *m*

re·demp·tion Einlösung *f*; REL Erlösung *f*

re·de·vel·op *Gebäude, Stadtteil* sanieren

red-faced verlegen, mit rotem Kopf

red-hand·ed: *catch s.o.* ~ j-n auf frischer Tat ertappen

red·head F Rotschopf *m*, Rothaarige *f*

red-head·ed rothaarig

red her·ring *fig* falsche Fährte *or* Spur

red-hot rot glühend; *fig* glühend; F brandaktuell (*news etc*)

Red In·di·an *contp* Indianer(in)

red-let·ter day Freuden-, Glückstag *m*

red·ness Röte *f*

re·dou·ble verdoppeln

red tape Bürokratismus *m*, F Amtsschimmel *m*

re·duce verkleinern; *Geschwindigkeit, Risiko etc* verringern, *Steuern etc* senken, *Preis, Waren etc* herabsetzen, reduzieren (*from ... to* von ... auf *acc*),

Gehalt etc kürzen; verwandeln (*to* in *acc*), machen (*to* zu); reduzieren, zurückführen (*to* auf *acc*); **re·duc·tion** Verkleinerung *f*; Verringerung *f*, Senkung *f*, Herabsetzung *f*, Reduzierung *f*, Kürzung *f*

re·dun·dant überflüssig

reed BOT Schilf(rohr) *n*

re·ed·u·cate umerziehen

re·ed·u·ca·tion Umerziehung *f*

reef (Felsen)Riff *n*

reek 1. Gestank *m* **2.** stinken (*of* nach)

reel¹ 1. Rolle *f*, Spule *f* **2.** ~ *off* abrollen, abspulen; *fig* herunterrasseln

reel² sich drehen; (sch)wanken, taumeln, torkeln; *my head ~ed* mir drehte sich alles

re·e·lect wieder wählen

re·en·ter wieder eintreten in (*acc*), wieder betreten; **re·en·try** Wiedereintreten *n*, Wiedereintritt *m*

ref F SPORT Schiri *m*

re·fer: ~ *to* verweisen *or* hinweisen auf (*acc*); j-n verweisen an (*acc*); sich beziehen auf (*acc*); anspielen auf (*acc*); erwähnen (*acc*); nachschlagen in (*dat*)

ref·e·ree SPORT Schiedsrichter *m*, Unparteiische *m*; *boxing:* Ringrichter *m*

ref·er·ence Verweis *m*, Hinweis *m* (*to* auf *acc*); Verweisstelle *f*; Referenz *f*, Empfehlung *f*, Zeugnis *n*; Bezugnahme *f* (*to* auf *acc*); Anspielung *f* (*to* auf *acc*); Erwähnung *f* (*to gen*); Nachschlagen *n* (*to* in *dat*); *list of* ~*s* Quellenangabe *f*; ~ *book* Nachschlagewerk *n*; ~ *li·bra·ry* Handbibliothek *f*; ~ *num·ber* Aktenzeichen *n*

ref·e·ren·dum POL Referendum *n*, Volksentscheid *m*

re·fill 1. wieder füllen, nachfüllen, auffüllen **2.** (*Ersatz*)Mine *f*; (*Ersatz*)Patrone *f*

re·fine TECH raffinieren; *fig* verfeinern, kultivieren; ~ *on* verbessern, verfeinern

re·fined TECH raffiniert; *fig* kultiviert, vornehm

re·fine·ment TECH Raffinierung *f*; *fig* Verbess(e)rung *f*, Verfeinerung *f*; Kultiviertheit *f*, Vornehmheit *f*

re·fin·e·ry TECH Raffinerie *f*

re·flect *v/t* reflektieren, zurückwerfen, -strahlen, (wider)spiegeln; *be* ~*ed in* sich (wider)spiegeln in (*dat*) (*a. fig*);

v/i nachdenken (**on** über *acc*); ~ (**badly**) **on** sich nachteilig auswirken auf (*acc*); ein schlechtes Licht werfen auf (*acc*)

re·flec·tion Reflexion *f*, Zurückwerfung *f*, -strahlung *f*, (Wider)Spiegelung *f* (*a. fig*); Spiegelbild *n*; Überlegung *f*; Betrachtung *f*; **on** ~ nach einigem Nachdenken

re·flec·tive reflektierend; nachdenklich

re·flex Reflex *m*; ~ **ac·tion** Reflexhandlung *f*; ~ **cam·e·ra** PHOT Spiegelreflexkamera *f*

re·flex·ive LING reflexiv, rückbezüglich

re·form 1. reformieren, verbessern; sich bessern 2. Reform *f* (*a.* POL), Besserung *f*; **ref·or·ma·tion** Reformierung *f*, Besserung *f*; **the Reformation** REL die Reformation; **re·form·er** *esp* POL Reformer *m*; REL Reformator *m*

re·fract *Strahlen etc* brechen

re·frac·tion (*Strahlen- etc*)Brechung *f*

re·frain¹: ~ **from** sich enthalten (*gen*), unterlassen (*acc*)

re·frain² Kehrreim *m*, Refrain *m*

re·fresh (**o.s.**) sich) erfrischen, stärken; *Gedächtnis* auffrischen

re·fresh·ing erfrischend (*a. fig*)

re·fresh·ment Erfrischung *f*

re·frig·e·rate TECH kühlen

re·frig·e·ra·tor Kühlschrank *m*

re·fu·el auftanken

ref·uge Zuflucht *f*, Zufluchtsstätte *f*; *Br* Verkehrsinsel *f*

ref·u·gee Flüchtling *m*

ref·u·gee camp Flüchtlingslager *n*

re·fund 1. Rückzahlung *f*, Rückerstattung *f* 2. *Geld* zurückzahlen, zurückerstatten; *Auslagen* ersetzen

re·fur·bish aufpolieren (*a. fig*); renovieren

re·fus·al Ablehnung *f*; Weigerung *f*; Verweigerung *f*

re·fuse¹ *v/t* ablehnen; verweigern; sich weigern, es ablehnen (**to do** zu tun); *v/i* ablehnen; sich weigern

ref·use² Abfall *m*, Abfälle *pl*, Müll *m*

ref·use dump Müllabladeplatz *m*

re·fute widerlegen

re·gain wieder-, zurückgewinnen

re·gale: ~ **s.o. with s.th.** j-n mit et. erfreuen or ergötzen

re·gard 1. Achtung *f*; Rücksicht *f*; *pl* Grüße *pl*; **in this** ~ in dieser Hinsicht; **with** ~ **to** im Hinblick auf (*acc*); hinsichtlich (*gen*); **with kind** ~**s** mit freundlichen Grüßen 2. betrachten (*a. fig*), ansehen; ~ **as** betrachten als, halten für; **as** ~**s** ... was ... betrifft

re·gard·ing bezüglich, hinsichtlich (*gen*)

re·gard·less: ~ **of** ohne Rücksicht auf (*acc*), ungeachtet (*gen*)

regd *abbr of* **registered** ECON eingetragen; *post* eingeschrieben

re·gen·e·rate (sich) erneuern *or* regenerieren

re·gent Regent(in)

re·gi·ment 1. MIL Regiment *n*, *fig a.* Schar *f* 2. reglementieren, bevormunden

re·gion Gegend *f*, Gebiet *n*, Region *f*

re·gion·al regional, örtlich, Orts-

re·gis·ter 1. Register *n*, Verzeichnis *n*, (*Wähler- etc*)Liste *f* 2. *v/t* registrieren, eintragen (lassen); *Messwerte* anzeigen; *Brief etc* einschreiben lassen; *v/i* sich eintragen (lassen)

re·gis·tered let·ter Einschreib(e)brief *m*, Einschreiben *n*

re·gis·tra·tion Registrierung *f*, Eintragung *f*; MOT Zulassung *f*; ~ **fee** Anmeldegebühr *f*; ~ **num·ber** MOT (polizeiliches) Kennzeichen

re·gis·try Registratur *f*

re·gis·try of·fice *esp Br* Standesamt *n*

re·gret 1. bedauern; bereuen 2. Bedauern *n*; Reue *f*; **re·gret·ful** bedauernd; **re·gret·ta·ble** bedauerlich

reg·u·lar 1. regelmäßig; geregelt, geordnet; richtig; normal; MIL Berufs...; ~ **gas** (*Br* **petrol**) MOT Normalbenzin *n* 2. F Stammkunde *m*, Stammkundin *f*; Stammgast *m*; SPORT Stammspieler(in); MIL Berufssoldat *m*; MOT Normal(-benzin) *n*

reg·u·lar·i·ty Regelmäßigkeit *f*

reg·u·late regeln, regulieren; TECH einstellen, regulieren

reg·u·la·tion Reg(e)lung *f*, Regulierung *f*; TECH Einstellung *f*; Vorschrift *f*

reg·u·la·tor TECH Regler *m*

re·hears·al MUS, THEA Probe *f*

re·hearse MUS, THEA proben

reign 1. Regierung *f*, *a. fig* Herrschaft *f* 2. herrschen, regieren

re·im·burse *Auslagen* erstatten, vergüten

rein 1. Zügel *m* 2. ~ **in** *Pferd etc* zügeln; *fig* bremsen

rein·deer zo Ren *n*, Rentier *n*

re·in·force verstärken

re·in·force·ment Verstärkung *f*

re·in·state *j-n* wieder einstellen (*as* als; *in* in *dat*)

re·in·sure rückversichern

re·it·e·rate (ständig) wiederholen

re·ject *j-n*, *et*. ablehnen, *Bitte* abschlagen, *Plan etc* verwerfen; *j-n* ab-, zurückweisen; MED *Organ etc* abstoßen

re·jec·tion Ablehnung *f*; Verwerfung *f*; Zurückweisung *f*; MED Abstoßung *f*

re·joice sich freuen, jubeln (*at*, *over* über *acc*); **re·joic·ing(s)** Jubel *m*

re·join¹ wieder zusammenfügen; wieder zurückkehren zu

re·join² erwidern

re·ju·ve·nate verjüngen

re·kin·dle *Feuer* wieder anzünden; *fig* wieder entfachen

re·lapse 1. zurückfallen, wieder verfallen (*into* in *acc*); rückfällig werden; MED e-n Rückfall bekommen 2. Rückfall *m*

re·late *v/t* erzählen, berichten; in Verbindung *or* Zusammenhang bringen (*to* mit); *v/i* sich beziehen (*to* auf *acc*); zusammenhängen (*to* mit)

re·lat·ed verwandt (*to* mit)

re·la·tion Verwandte *m*, *f*; Beziehung *f* (*between* zwischen *dat*; *to* zu); *pl* diplomatische, *geschäftliche* Beziehungen *pl*; *in or with* ~ *to* in Bezug auf (*acc*)

re·la·tion·ship Verwandtschaft *f*; Beziehung *f*, Verhältnis *n*

rel·a·tive¹ Verwandte *m*, *f*

rel·a·tive² relativ, verhältnismäßig; bezüglich (*to gen*); LING Relativ…, bezüglich

rel·a·tive pro·noun LING Relativpronomen *n*, bezügliches Fürwort

re·lax *v/t Muskeln etc* entspannen; *Griff etc* lockern; *fig* nachlassen in (*dat*); *v/i* sich entspannen, *fig a.* ausspannen; sich lockern

re·lax·a·tion Entspannung *f*; Erholung *f*; Lockerung *f*

re·laxed entspannt, zwanglos

re·lay¹ 1. Ablösung *f*; SPORT Staffel *f*; *radio*, TV Übertragung *f*; ELECTR Relais *n* 2. *radio*, TV übertragen

re·lay² *Kabel*, *Teppich* neu verlegen

re·lay race SPORT Staffel *f*

re·lease 1. entlassen, freilassen, loslassen; freigeben, herausbringen, veröffentlichen; MOT *Handbremse* lösen; *fig* befreien, erlösen 2. Entlassung *f*, Freilassung *f*; Befreiung *f*; Freigabe *f*; Veröffentlichung *f*; TECH, PHOT Auslöser *m*; *film:* often *first* ~ Uraufführung *f*

rel·e·gate verbannen; *be* ~*d* SPORT absteigen (*to* in *acc*)

re·lent nachgeben; nachlassen

re·lent·less unbarmherzig; anhaltend

rel·e·vant relevant, erheblich, wichtig; sachdienlich, zutreffend

re·li·a·bil·i·ty Zuverlässigkeit *f*

re·li·a·ble zuverlässig

re·li·ance Vertrauen *n*; Abhängigkeit *f* (*on* von)

rel·ic Relikt *n*, Überrest *m*; REL Reliquie *f*

re·lief Erleichterung *f*; Unterstützung *f*, Hilfe *f*; Sozialhilfe *f*; Ablösung *f*; Relief *n*; ~ *map* GEOGR Reliefkarte *f*

re·lieve *Schmerz*, *Not* lindern, *j-n*, *Gewissen* erleichtern; *j-n* ablösen

re·li·gion Religion *f*

re·li·gious Religions…; religiös; gewissenhaft

rel·ish 1. *fig* Gefallen *m*, Geschmack *m* (*for* an *dat*); GASTR Würze *f*; Soße *f*; *with* ~ mit Genuss 2. genießen, sich *et*. schmecken lassen; Geschmack *or* Gefallen finden an (*dat*)

re·luc·tance Widerstreben *n*; *with* ~ widerwillig, ungern

re·luc·tant widerstrebend, widerwillig

re·ly: ~ *on* sich verlassen auf (*acc*)

re·main 1. (ver)bleiben; übrig bleiben 2. *pl* (Über)Reste *pl*

re·main·der Rest *m*; Restbetrag *m*

re·make 1. wieder *or* neu machen 2. Remake *n*, Neuverfilmung *f*

re·mand JUR 1. *be* ~*ed in custody* in Untersuchungshaft bleiben 2. *be on* ~ in Untersuchungshaft sein; *prisoner on* ~ Untersuchungsgefangene *m*, *f*

re·mark 1. bemerken, äußern; *v/i* sich äußern (*on* über *acc*, zu) 2. Bemerkung *f*

re·mark·a·ble bemerkenswert; außergewöhnlich

rem·e·dy 1. (Heil-, Hilfs-, Gegen)Mittel *n*; (Ab)Hilfe *f* 2. *Schaden etc* beheben; *Missstand* abstellen; *Situation* bereinigen

re·mem·ber sich erinnern an (*acc*); denken an (*acc*); *please ~ me to her* grüße sie bitte von mir

re·mem·brance Erinnerung *f*; *in ~ of* zur Erinnerung an (*acc*)

re·mind erinnern (*of* an *acc*)

re·mind·er Mahnung *f*

rem·i·nis·cences Erinnerungen *pl* (*of* an *acc*); **rem·i·nis·cent**: *be ~ of* erinnern an (*acc*)

re·mit *Schulden, Strafe* erlassen; *Sünden* vergeben; *Geld* überweisen (*to dat* or an *acc*); **re·mit·tance** ECON Überweisung *f* (*to* an *acc*)

rem·nant (Über)Rest *m*

re·mod·el umformen, umgestalten

re·morse Gewissensbisse *pl*, Reue *f* (*über acc* for)

re·morse·ful zerknirscht, reumütig

re·morse·less unbarmherzig

re·mote fern, entfernt; abgelegen, entlegen; **~ con·trol** TECH Fernlenkung *f*, Fernsteuerung *f*; Fernbedienung *f*

re·mov·al Entfernung *f*; Umzug *m*

re·mov·al van Möbelwagen *m*

re·move *v/t* entfernen (*from* von); *Hut, Deckel etc* abnehmen; *Kleidung* ablegen; beseitigen, aus dem Weg räumen; *v/i* (um)ziehen (*from* von; *to* nach)

re·mov·er (*Flecken- etc*)Entferner *m*

Re·nais·sance *die* Renaissance

ren·der berühmt, schwierig, möglich *etc* machen; *Dienst* erweisen; *Gedicht, Musikstück* vortragen; übersetzen, übertragen (*into* in *acc*); *mst ~ down Fett* auslassen

ren·der·ing *esp Br* → **rendition**

ren·di·tion MUS *etc* Vortrag *m*; Übersetzung *f*, Übertragung *f*

re·new erneuern; *Gespräch etc* wieder aufnehmen; *Kraft etc* wiedererlangen; *Vertrag, Pass* verlängern (lassen)

re·new·al Erneuerung *f*; Verlängerung *f*

re·nounce verzichten auf (*acc*); *s-m Glauben etc* abschwören

ren·o·vate renovieren

re·nown Ruhm *m*; **re·nowned** berühmt (*as* als; *for* wegen, für)

rent¹ 1. Miete *f*; Pacht *f*; Leihgebühr *f*; *for ~* zu vermieten, zu verleihen 2. mieten, pachten (*from* von); *a. ~ out* vermieten, verpachten (*to* an *acc*); *~ed car* Miet-, Leihwagen *m*

rent² Riss *m*

rent·al Miete *f*; Pacht *f*; Leihgebühr *f*; **~ car** Miet-, Leihwagen *m*

re·nun·ci·a·tion Verzicht *m* (*of* auf *acc*); Abschwören *n*

re·pair 1. reparieren, ausbessern; *fig* wieder gutmachen 2. Reparatur *f*; Ausbesserung *f*; *pl* Instandsetzungsarbeiten *pl*; *beyond ~* nicht mehr zu reparieren; *in good* (*bad*) ~ in gutem (schlechtem) Zustand; *be under ~* in Reparatur sein; *the road is under ~* an der Straße wird gerade gearbeitet

rep·a·ra·tion Wiedergutmachung *f*; Entschädigung *f*; *pl* POL Reparationen *pl*

rep·ar·tee Schlagfertigkeit *f*; schlagfertige Antwort(en *pl*) *f*

re·pay *et.* zurückzahlen; *Besuch* erwidern; *et.* vergelten; *j-n* entschädigen

re·pay·ment Rückzahlung *f*

re·peal *Gesetz etc* aufheben

re·peat 1. *v/t* wiederholen; nachsprechen; *~ o.s.* sich wiederholen; *v/i* F aufstoßen (*on s.o.* j-m) (*food*) 2. *radio, TV* Wiederholung *f*; **re·peat·ed** wiederholt; **re·peat·ed·ly** verschiedentlich

re·pel *Angriff, Feind* zurückschlagen; *Wasser etc, fig* j-n abstoßen

re·pel·lent abstoßend

re·pent bereuen

re·pent·ance Reue *f* (*for* über *acc*)

re·pen·tant reuig, reumütig

re·per·cus·sion *mst pl* Auswirkungen *pl* (*on* auf *acc*)

rep·er·toire THEA *etc* Repertoire *n*

rep·er·to·ry the·a·ter (*Br* **the·a·tre**) Repertoiretheater *n*

rep·e·ti·tion Wiederholung *f*

re·place an *j-s* Stelle treten; *j-n, et.* ersetzen; TECH austauschen, ersetzen

re·place·ment TECH Austausch *m*; Ersatz *m*

re·plant umpflanzen

re·play 1. SPORT *Spiel* wiederholen; *Tonband-, Videoaufname etc* abspielen 2. SPORT Wiederholung *f*

re·plen·ish (wieder) auffüllen

re·plete satt; angefüllt, ausgestattet (*with* mit)

rep·li·ca *art*: Originalkopie *f*; Kopie *f*, Nachbildung *f*

re·ply 1. antworten, erwidern (*to* auf *acc*); 2. Antwort *f*, Erwiderung *f* (*to* auf *acc*); *in ~ to* (als Antwort) auf (*acc*)

re·ply cou·pon Rückantwortschein *m*

re·ply-paid en·ve·lope Freiumschlag *m*

re·port 1. Bericht *m*; Meldung *f*, Nachricht *f*; Gerücht *n*; Knall *m*; ~ **card** PED Zeugnis *n* **2.** berichten (über *acc*); (sich) melden; anzeigen; *it is* ~*ed that* es heißt, dass; ~*ed speech* LING indirekte Rede; **re·port·er** Reporter(in), Berichterstatter(in)

re·pose Ruhe *f*; Gelassenheit *f*

re·pos·i·to·ry (Waren)Lager *n*; *fig* Fundgrube *f*, Quelle *f*

rep·re·sent *j-n, Wahlbezirk* vertreten; darstellen; hinstellen (*as, to be* als)

rep·re·sen·ta·tion Vertretung *f*; Darstellung *f*

rep·re·sen·ta·tive 1. repräsentativ (*a.* POL), typisch (*of* für); **2.** (Stell)Vertreter(in); ECON (Handels)Vertreter(in); PARL Abgeordnete *m, f*; *House of Representatives* Repräsentantenhaus *n*

re·press unterdrücken; PSYCH verdrängen; **re·pres·sion** Unterdrückung *f*; PSYCH Verdrängung *f*

re·prieve JUR **1.** *he was ~d* er wurde begnadigt; s-e Urteilsvollstreckung wurde ausgesetzt **2.** Begnadigung *f*; Vollstreckungsaufschub *m*

rep·ri·mand 1. rügen, tadeln (*for* wegen); **2.** Rüge *f*, Tadel *m*, Verweis *m*

re·print 1. neu auflegen *or* drucken, nachdrucken **2.** Neuauflage *f*, Nachdruck *m*

re·pri·sal Repressalie *f*, Vergeltungsmaßnahme *f*

re·proach 1. Vorwurf *m* **2.** vorwerfen (*s.o. with s.th.* j-m et.); Vorwürfe machen; **re·proach·ful** vorwurfsvoll

rep·ro·bate verkommenes Subjekt

re·pro·cess NUCL wieder aufbereiten

re·pro·cess·ing TECH Wiederaufbereitung *f*; ~ **plant** TECH Wiederaufbereitungsanlage *f*

re·pro·duce *v/t* Ton etc wiedergeben; *Bild etc* reproduzieren; ~ *o.s.* → *v/i* BIOL sich fortpflanzen, sich vermehren

re·pro·duc·tion BIOL Fortpflanzung *f*; Reproduktion *f*; Wiedergabe *f*; PED Nacherzählung *f*

re·pro·duc·tive BIOL Fortpflanzungs...

re·proof Rüge *f*, Tadel *m*

re·prove rügen, tadeln (*for* wegen)

rep·tile ZO Reptil *n*

re·pub·lic Republik *f*

re·pub·li·can 1. republikanisch **2.** Republikaner(in)

re·pug·nant widerlich, abstoßend

re·pulse 1. *j-n, Angebot etc* zurückweisen; MIL *Angriff* zurückschlagen **2.** MIL Zurückschlagen *n*; Zurückweisung *f*

re·pul·sion Abscheu *m*, Widerwille *m*; PHYS Abstoßung *f*

re·pul·sive abstoßend, widerlich, widerwärtig; PHYS abstoßend

rep·u·ta·ble angesehen

rep·u·ta·tion (guter) Ruf, Ansehen *n*

re·pute (guter) Ruf

re·put·ed angeblich

re·quest 1. (*for*) Bitte *f* (um), Wunsch *m* (nach); *at the* ~ *of s.o., at s.o.'s* ~ auf j-s Bitte hin; *on* ~ auf Wunsch **2.** um *et.* bitten *or* ersuchen; *j-n* bitten, ersuchen (*to do* zu tun)

re·quest stop *Br* Bedarfshaltestelle *f*

re·quire erfordern; benötigen, brauchen; verlangen; *if* ~*d* wenn nötig

re·quire·ment Erfordernis *n*, Bedürfnis *n*; Anforderung *f*

req·ui·site 1. erforderlich **2.** *mst pl* Artikel *pl*

req·ui·si·tion 1. Anforderung *f*; MIL Requisition *f*, Beschlagnahme *f*; *make a* ~ *for et.* anfordern **2.** anfordern; MIL requirieren, beschlagnahmen

re·sale Wieder-, Weiterverkauf *m*

re·scind JUR *Gesetz, Urteil etc* aufheben

res·cue 1. retten (*from* aus, vor *dat*); **2.** Rettung *f*; Hilfe *f* **3.** Rettungs...

re·search 1. Forschung *f* **2.** forschen; *et.* erforschen

re·search·er Forscher(in)

re·sem·blance Ähnlichkeit *f* (*to* mit; *between* zwischen *dat*)

re·sem·ble ähnlich sein, ähneln (*both*: *dat*)

re·sent übel nehmen, sich ärgern über (*acc*); **re·sent·ful** ärgerlich (*of, at* über *acc*); **re·sent·ment** Ärger *m* (*against, at* über *acc*)

res·er·va·tion Reservierung *f*, Vorbestellung *f*; Vorbehalt *m*; (*Indianer*)Reservat(ion *f*) *n*; (*Wild*)Reservat *n*

re·serve 1. (sich) *et.* aufsparen (*for* für); sich vorbehalten; reservieren (lassen), vorbestellen **2.** Reserve *f* (*a.* MIL); Vorrat *m*; (*Naturschutz-, Wild*)Reservat *n*; SPORT Reservespieler(in); Reserviertheit *f*, Zurückhaltung *f*

re·served zurückhaltend, reserviert

res·er·voir Reservoir *n* (*a. fig of* an *dat*)

re·set *Uhr* umstellen; *Zeiger etc* zurückstellen (**to** auf *acc*)

re·set·tle umsiedeln

re·side wohnen, ansässig sein, s-n Wohnsitz haben

res·i·dence Wohnsitz *m*, Wohnort *m*; Aufenthalt *m*; Residenz *f*; *official ~* Amtssitz *m*; *~* **per·mit** Aufenthaltsgenehmigung *f*, -erlaubnis *f*

res·i·dent 1. wohnhaft, ansässig **2.** Bewohner(in), *in a town etc a.* Einwohner(in); (Hotel)Gast *m*; MOT Anlieger(in)

res·i·den·tial Wohn...; *~* **ar·e·a** Wohngebiet *n*, Wohngegend *f*

re·sid·u·al übrig (geblieben), restlich, Rest...; *~* **pol·lu·tion** Altlasten *pl*

res·i·due Rest *m*, CHEM A. Rückstand *m*

re·sign *v/i* zurücktreten (**from** von); *v/t Amt etc* niederlegen; aufgeben; verzichten auf (*acc*); *~* **o.s. to** sich fügen in (*acc*), sich abfinden mit

res·ig·na·tion Rücktritt *m*; Resignation *f*

re·signed ergeben, resigniert

re·sil·i·ence Elastizität *f*; *fig* Zähigkeit *f*; **re·sil·i·ent** elastisch; *fig* zäh

res·in Harz *n*

re·sist widerstehen (*dat*); Widerstand leisten, sich widersetzen (*both: dat*)

re·sist·ance Widerstand *m* (*a.* ELECTR); MED Widerstandskraft *f*; (*Hitze- etc -*) Beständigkeit *f*, (*Stoß- etc*)Festigkeit *f*

re·sist·ant widerstandsfähig; (*hitze- etc*)beständig, (*stoß- etc*)fest

res·o·lute resolut, entschlossen

res·o·lu·tion Beschluss *m*, PARL *etc a.* Resolution *f*; Vorsatz *m*; Entschlossenheit *f*; Lösung *f*

re·solve 1. beschließen; *Problem etc* lösen; (sich) auflösen; *~* **on** sich entschließen zu **2.** Vorsatz *m*; Entschlossenheit *f*

res·o·nance Resonanz *f*; voller Klang

res·o·nant voll(tönend); widerhallend

re·sort 1. Erholungsort *m*, Urlaubsort *m*; *have ~* **to** → **2.** *~* **to** Zuflucht nehmen zu

re·sound widerhallen (**with** von)

re·source Mittel *n*, Zuflucht *f*; Ausweg *m*; Einfallsreichtum *m*; *pl* Mittel *pl*;

(*natürliche*) Reichtümer *pl*, (*Boden-, Natur*)Schätze *pl*

re·source·ful einfallsreich, findig

re·spect 1. Achtung *f*, Respekt *m* (*both:* **for** vor *dat*); Rücksicht *f* (**for** auf *acc*); Beziehung *f*, Hinsicht *f*; *with ~* **to** ... was ... anbelangt *or* betrifft; *in this ~* in dieser Hinsicht; *give my ~s to* ... e-e Empfehlung an ... (*acc*) **2.** *v/t* respektieren, *a.* achten, *a.* berücksichtigen, beachten

re·spect·a·ble ehrbar, anständig, geachtet; F ansehnlich, beachtlich

re·spect·ful respektvoll, ehrerbietig

re·spec·tive jeweilig; *we went to our ~ places* jeder ging zu seinem Platz

re·spec·tive·ly beziehungsweise

res·pi·ra·tion Atmung *f*

res·pi·ra·tor Atemschutzgerät *n*

re·spite Pause *f*; Aufschub *m*, Frist *f*; *without ~* ohne Unterbrechung

re·splen·dent glänzend, strahlend

re·spond antworten, erwidern (**to** auf *acc*; **that** dass); reagieren, MED *a.* ansprechen (**to** auf *acc*)

re·sponse Antwort *f*, Erwiderung *f* (**to** auf *acc*); *fig* Reaktion *f* (**to** auf *acc*)

re·spon·si·bil·i·ty Verantwortung *f*; *on one's own ~* auf eigene Verantwortung; *sense of ~* Verantwortungsgefühl *n*; *take* (*full*) *~ for* die (volle) Verantwortung übernehmen für

re·spon·si·ble verantwortlich; verantwortungsbewusst; verantwortungsvoll

rest¹ 1. Ruhe(pause) *f*; Erholung *f*; TECH Stütze *f*; (*Telefon*)Gabel *f*; *have or take a ~* sich ausruhen; *set s.o.'s mind at ~* j-n beruhigen **2.** *v/i* ruhen; sich ausruhen; lehnen (**against**, **on** an *dat*); *let s.th. ~* et. auf sich beruhen lassen; *~ on* ruhen auf (*dat*) (*a. fig*); *fig* beruhen auf (*dat*); *v/t* (aus)ruhen (lassen); lehnen (**against** gegen; **on** an *acc*)

**rest² ** Rest *m*; *all the ~ of them* alle Übrigen; *for the ~* im Übrigen

rest ar·e·a MOT Rastplatz *m*

res·tau·rant Restaurant *n*, Gaststätte *f*

rest·ful ruhig, erholsam

rest home Altenpflegeheim *n*; Erholungsheim *n*

res·ti·tu·tion ECON Rückgabe *f*, Rückerstattung *f*

res·tive unruhig, nervös

rest·less ruhelos, rastlos; unruhig

res·to·ra·tion Wiederherstellung *f*; Restaurierung *f*; Rückgabe *f*, Rückerstattung *f*; **re·store** wiederherstellen; restaurieren; zurückgeben, -erstatten; *be ~d (to health)* wieder gesund sein

re·strain (*from*) zurückhalten (von), hindern an (*dat*); *I had to ~ myself* ich musste mich beherrschen (*from doing s.th.* um nicht et. zu tun)

re·strained beherrscht; dezent (*color*)

re·straint Beherrschung *f*, Zurückhaltung *f*; ECON Be-, Einschränkung *f*

re·strict ECON beschränken (*to* auf *acc*), einschränken

re·stric·tion ECON Be-, Einschränkung *f*; *without ~s* uneingeschränkt

rest room Toilette *f*

re·struc·ture umstrukturieren

re·sult 1. Ergebnis *n*, Resultat *n*; Folge *f*; *as a ~ of* als Folge von (*or gen*); *without ~* ergebnislos **2.** folgen, sich ergeben (*from* aus); *~ in* zur Folge haben (*acc*), führen zu

re·sume wieder aufnehmen; fortsetzen; *Platz* wieder einnehmen

re·sump·tion Wiederaufnahme *f*; Fortsetzung *f*

Res·ur·rec·tion REL Auferstehung *f*

re·sus·ci·tate MED wieder beleben

re·sus·ci·ta·tion MED Wiederbelebung *f*

re·tail ECON **1.** Einzelhandel *m*; *by ~* im Einzelhandel **2.** Einzelhandels… **3.** *adv* im Einzelhandel **4.** *v/t* im Einzelhandel verkaufen (*at, for* für); *v/i* im Einzelhandel verkauft werden (*at, for* für); **re·tail·er** ECON Einzelhändler(in)

re·tain (be)halten, bewahren; *Wasser, Wärme* speichern

re·tal·i·ate Vergeltung üben, sich revanchieren; **re·tal·i·a·tion** Vergeltung *f*, Vergeltungsmaßnahmen *pl*

re·tard verzögern, aufhalten, hemmen; (*mentally*) *~ed* (geistig) zurückgeblieben

retch würgen

re·tell nacherzählen

re·think *et.* noch einmal überdenken

re·ti·cent schweigsam, zurückhaltend

ret·i·nue Gefolge *n*

re·tire *v/i* in Rente *or* Pension gehen, sich pensionieren lassen; sich zurückziehen; *~ from business* sich zur Ruhe setzen; *v/t* in den Ruhestand versetzen,

pensionieren; **re·tired** pensioniert, im Ruhestand (lebend); *be ~ a.* in Rente *or* Pension sein; **re·tire·ment** Pensionierung *f*, Ruhestand *m*

re·tir·ing zurückhaltend

re·tort 1. (scharf) entgegnen *or* erwidern **2.** (scharfe) Entgegnung *or* Erwiderung

re·touch PHOT retuschieren

re·trace *Tathergang etc* rekonstruieren; *~ one's steps* denselben Weg zurückgehen

re·tract *v/t Angebot* zurückziehen; *Behauptung* zurücknehmen; *Geständnis* widerrufen; TECH, ZO einziehen; *v/i* TECH, ZO eingezogen werden

re·train umschulen

re·tread MOT **1.** *Reifen* runderneuern **2.** runderneuerter Reifen

re·treat 1. MIL Rückzug *m*; Zufluchtsort *m* **2.** sich zurückziehen; zurückweichen (*from* vor *dat*)

ret·ri·bu·tion Vergeltung *f*

re·trieve zurückholen, wiederbekommen; *Fehler, Verlust etc* wieder gutmachen; HUNT apportieren

ret·ro·ac·tive JUR rückwirkend

ret·ro·grade rückschrittlich

ret·ro·spect: *in ~* im Rückblick

ret·ro·spec·tive rückblickend; JUR rückwirkend

re·try JUR *Fall* erneut verhandeln; neu verhandeln gegen *j-n*

re·turn 1. *v/i* zurückkehren, zurückkommen; zurückgehen; *~ to* auf *ein Thema etc* zurückkommen; in *e-e Gewohnheit etc* zurückfallen; in *e-n Zustand etc* zurückkehren; *v/t* zurückgeben (*to dat*); zurückbringen (*to dat*); zurückschicken, -senden (*to dat or* an *acc*); zurücklegen, -stellen; erwidern; *Gewinn etc* abwerfen; → *verdict* **2.** Rückkehr *f*, *fig* Wiederauftreten *n*; Rückgabe *f*; Zurückbringen *n*; Zurückschicken *n*, -senden *n*; Zurücklegen *n*, -stellen *n*; Erwiderung *f*; (*Steuer*)Erklärung *f*; *tennis etc*: Return *m*, Rückschlag *m*; ECON *a. pl* Gewinn *m*; *Br* → *return ticket*; *Br many happy ~s (of the day)* herzlichen Glückwunsch zum Geburtstag; *by ~ (of post)* umgehend, postwendend; *in ~ for* (als Gegenleistung) für **3.** *adj* Rück…

re·turn·a·ble *in cpds* Mehrweg…; *~ bot-*

tle Pfandflasche *f*

return| game, **~ match** SPORT Rückspiel
n;**re·turn key** IT Eingabetaste *f*; **~ ticket** *Br* RAIL Rückfahrkarte *f*; AVIAT Rückflugticket *n*

re·u·ni·fi·ca·tion POL Wiedervereinigung *f*

re·u·nion Treffen *n*, Wiedersehensfeier
f; Wiedervereinigung *f*

re·us·a·ble wieder verwendbar

rev F MOT **1.** Umdrehung *f*; **~ counter**
Drehzahlmesser *m* **2.** *a*. **~ up** aufheulen
(lassen)

re·val·ue ECON *Währung* aufwerten

re·veal den Blick freigeben auf (*acc*),
zeigen; *Geheimnis etc* enthüllen, aufdecken; **re·veal·ing** aufschlussreich
(*remark etc*); offenherzig (*dress etc*)

rev·el: **~ in** schwelgen in (*dat*); sich weiden an (*dat*)

rev·e·la·tion Enthüllung *f*; REL Offenba-
rung *f*

re·venge 1. Rache *f*; *esp* SPORT Revanche
f; **in ~ for** aus Rache für; **take ~ on s.o.
for s.th.** sich an j-m für et. rächen **2.** rächen; **re·venge·ful** rachsüchtig

rev·e·nue Staatseinkünfte *pl*, Staatsein-
nahmen *pl*

re·ver·be·rate nach-, widerhallen

re·vere (ver)ehren; **rev·e·rence** Verehrung *f*; Ehrfurcht *f* (*for vor dat*)

Rev·e·rend REL Hochwürden *m*

rev·e·rent ehrfürchtig, ehrfurchtsvoll

rev·er·ie (Tag)Träumerei *f*

re·ver·sal Umkehrung *f*; Rückschlag *m*

re·verse 1. *adj* umgekehrt; **in ~ order** in
umgekehrter Reihenfolge **2.** *Wagen* im
Rückwärtsgang fahren *or* rückwärts-
fahren; *Reihenfolge etc* umkehren; *Urteil etc* aufheben; *Entscheidung etc* umstoßen **3.** Gegenteil *n*; MOT Rückwärtsgang *m*; Rückseite *f*, Kehrseite *f* (*of a
coin*); Rückschlag *m*; **~ gear** MOT Rückwärtsgang *m*; **~ side** linke (*Stoff*)Seite
re·vers·i·ble doppelseitig (tragbar)

re·vert: **~ to** in *e-n* Zustand zurückkehren; in *e-e* Gewohnheit *etc* zurückfallen; auf *ein Thema* zurückkommen

re·view 1. Überprüfung *f*; Besprechung
f, Kritik *f*, Rezension *f*; MIL Parade *f*;
PED (Stoff)Wiederholung *f* (**for** für
e-e Prüfung); **2.** überprüfen; besprechen, rezensieren; MIL besichtigen, inspizieren; PED *Stoff* wiederholen (**for**

für *e-e Prüfung*)

re·view·er Kritiker(in), Rezensent(in)

re·vise revidieren, *Ansicht* ändern,
Buch etc überarbeiten; *Br* PED *Stoff*
wiederholen (**for** für *e-e Prüfung*)

re·vi·sion Revision *f*, Überarbeitung *f*;
überarbeitete Ausgabe; *Br* PED
(Stoff-) Wiederholung *f* (**for** für *e-e·
Prüfung*)

re·viv·al Wiederbelebung *f*; Wiederauf-
leben *n*

re·vive wieder beleben; wieder aufleben
(lassen); *Erinnerungen* wachrufen;
MED wieder zu sich kommen; sich erholen

re·voke widerrufen, zurücknehmen,
rückgängig machen

re·volt 1. *v/i* sich auflehnen, revoltieren
(**against** gegen); Abscheu empfinden,
empört sein (**against, at, from** über
acc); *v/t* mit Abscheu erfüllen, abstoßen **2.** Revolte *f*, Aufstand *m*

re·volt·ing abscheulich, abstoßend

rev·o·lu·tion Revolution *f*, Umwälzung
f; ASTR Umlauf *m* (**round** um); TECH
Umdrehung *f*; **number of ~s** Drehzahl
f; **~ counter** Drehzahlmesser *m*; **rev·o·
lu·tion·a·ry 1.** revolutionär; Revolutions... **2.** POL Revolutionär(in)

rev·o·lu·tion·ize revolutionieren

re·volve sich drehen (**on, round** um); **~
around** *fig* sich drehen um

re·volv·er Revolver *m*

re·volv·ing Dreh...; **~ door(s)** Drehtür *f*

re·vue THEA Revue *f*; Kabarett *n*

re·vul·sion Abscheu *m*

re·ward 1. Belohnung *f* **2.** belohnen

re·ward·ing lohnend

re·write neu schreiben, umschreiben

rhap·so·dy MUS Rhapsodie *f*

rhe·to·ric Rhetorik *f*

rheu·ma·tism MED Rheumatismus *m*, F
Rheuma *n*

rhi·no F, **rhi·no·ce·ros** ZO Rhinozeros *n*,
Nashorn *n*

rhu·barb BOT Rhabarber *m*

rhyme 1. Reim *m*; Vers *m*

rhyth·m Rhythmus *m*

rhyth·mic, rhyth·mi·cal rhythmisch

rib ANAT Rippe *f*

rib·bon (*a.* Farb-, Ordens)Band *n*; Streifen *m*; Fetzen *m*

rib cage ANAT Brustkorb *m*

rice BOT Reis *m*

rice pud·ding GASTR Milchreis *m*

rich 1. reich (*in* an *dat*); prächtig, kostbar; GASTR schwer; AGR fruchtbar, fett (*soil*); voll (*sound*); satt (*color*); ~ (*in calories*) kalorienreich **2. the ~** die Reichen *pl*

rick (Stroh-, Heu)Schober *m*

rick·ets MED Rachitis *f*

rick·et·y F *fig* gebrechlich; wack(e)lig

rid befreien (*of* von); **get ~ of** loswerden

rid·den *in cpds* geplagt von

rid·dle[1] Rätsel *n*

rid·dle[2] **1.** grobes Sieb, Schüttelsieb *n* **2.** sieben; durchlöchern, durchsieben

ride 1. *v/i* reiten; fahren (*on* auf *e-m Fahrrad etc*; *on or Br in* in *e-m Bus etc*); *v/t* reiten (auf *dat*); *Fahrrad, Motorrad* fahren, fahren auf (*dat*) **2.** Ritt *m*; Fahrt *f*; **rid·er** Reiter(in); (*Motorrad-, Rad*)Fahrer(in)

ridge GEOGR (*Gebirgs*)Kamm *m*, Grat *m*; ARCH (*Dach*)First *m*

rid·i·cule 1. Spott *m* **2.** lächerlich machen, spotten über (*acc*), verspotten

ri·dic·u·lous lächerlich

rid·ing Reit...

ri·fle[1] Gewehr *n*

ri·fle[2] durchwühlen

rift Spalt *m*, Spalte *f*; *fig* Riss *m*

rig 1. *Schiff* auftakeln; ~ **out** *j-n* ausstaffieren; ~ **up** F (behelfsmäßig) zusammenbauen (*from* aus); **2.** MAR Takelage *f*; TECH Bohrinsel *f*; Γ Aufmachung *f*

rig·ging MAR Takelage *f*

right 1. *adj* recht; richtig; rechte(r, -s), Rechts...; *all ~!* in Ordnung!, gut!; *that's all ~!* das macht nichts!, schon gut!, bitte!; *that's ~!* richtig!, ganz recht!, stimmt!; *be ~* recht haben; *put ~, set ~* in Ordnung bringen; berichtigen, korrigieren **2.** *adv* (nach) rechts; richtig, recht; genau; gerade (-wegs), direkt; ganz, völlig; ~ *away* sofort; ~ *now* im Moment; sofort; ~ *on* geradeaus; *turn ~* (sich) nach rechts wenden; MOT rechts abbiegen **3.** Recht *n*; *die* Rechte (*a.* POL, *boxing*), rechte Seite; *on the ~* rechts, auf der rechten Seite; *to the ~* (nach) rechts; *keep to the ~* sich rechts halten; MOT rechts fahren **4.** aufrichten; *et.* wieder gutmachen; in Ordnung bringen

right an·gle MATH rechter Winkel

right-an·gled MATH rechtwink(e)lig

right·eous gerecht (*anger etc*)

right·ful rechtmäßig

right-hand rechte(r, -s); ~ **drive** MOT Rechtssteuerung *f*

right-hand·ed rechtshändig; für Rechtshänder; *be ~* Rechtshänder(in) sein

right·ly richtig; mit Recht

right of way MOT Vorfahrt *f*, Vorfahrtsrecht *n*; Durchgangsrecht *n*

right-wing POL dem rechten Flügel angehörend, Rechts...

rig·id starr, steif; *fig* streng, strikt

rig·or·ous streng; genau

rig·o(u)r Strenge *f*, Härte *f*

rile F ärgern, reizen

rim Rand *m*; TECH Felge *f*

rim·less randlos

rind (*Zitronen- etc*)Schale *f*; (*Käse*)Rinde *f*; (*Speck*)Schwarte *f*

ring[1] **1.** Ring *m*; Kreis *m*; Manege *f*; (Box)Ring *m*; (Spionage- *etc*)Ring *m* **2.** umringen, umstellen; *Vogel* beringen

ring[2] **1.** läuten; klingeln; klingen (*a. fig*); *Br* TEL anrufen; *the bell is ~ing* es läutet *or* klingelt; ~ *the bell* läuten, klingeln; ~ *back Br* TEL zurückrufen; ~ *for* nach *j-m, et.* läuten; *Arzt etc* rufen; ~ *off Br* TEL (den Hörer) auflegen, Schluss machen; ~ *s.o.* (*up*) *j-n or* bei *j-m* anrufen **2.** Läuten *n*, Klingeln *n*; *fig* Klang *m*; *Br* TEL Anruf *m*; F *give s.o. a* ~ *j-n* anrufen

ring bind·er Ringbuch *n*

ring fin·ger Ringfinger *m*

ring·lead·er Rädelsführer(in)

ring·let (Ringel)Löckchen *n*

ring road *Br* Umgehungsstraße *f*; Ringstraße *f*

ring·side: *at the ~ boxing*: am Ring

rink (Kunst)Eisbahn *f*; Rollschuhbahn *f*

rinse *a.* ~ *out* (aus)spülen

ri·ot 1. Aufruhr *m*; Krawall *m*; *run* ~ randalieren; *run ~ through* randalierend ziehen durch **2.** Krawall machen, randalieren; **ri·ot·er** Aufrührer(in); Randalierer(in); **ri·ot·ous** aufrührerisch; randalierend; ausgelassen, wild

rip 1. *a.* ~ *up* zerreißen; ~ *open* aufreißen; F ~ *s.o. off j-n* neppen **2.** Riss *m*

ripe reif; **rip·en** reifen (lassen)

rip-off F Nepp *m*

rip·ple 1. (sich) kräuseln; plätschern, rie-

rise

seln **2.** kleine Welle; Kräuselung *f*; Plätschern *n*, Rieseln *n*

rise 1. aufstehen, sich erheben; REL auferstehen; aufsteigen (*smoke etc*); sich heben (*curtain, spirits*); ansteigen (*road, river etc*), anschwellen (*river etc*); (an)steigen (*temperature etc*), prices *etc*: *a.* anziehen; stärker werden (*wind etc*); aufgehen (*sun etc, bread etc*); entspringen (*river etc*); *fig* aufsteigen; *fig* entstehen (**from, out of** aus); *a.* **~ up** sich erheben (**against** gegen); **~ to the occasion** sich der Lage gewachsen zeigen **2.** (An)Steigen *n*; Steigung *f*; Anhöhe *f*; ASTR Aufgang *m*; *Br* Lohn- or Gehaltserhöhung *f*; *fig* Anstieg *m*; Aufstieg *m*; **give ~ to** verursachen, führen zu

ris·er: *early* **~** Frühaufsteher(in)

ris·ing 1. Aufstand *m* **2.** aufstrebend

risk 1. Gefahr *f*, Risiko *n*; **at one's own ~** auf eigene Gefahr; **at the ~ of doing s.th.** auf die Gefahr hin, et. zu tun; **be at ~** gefährdet sein; **run the ~ of doing s.th.** Gefahr laufen, et. zu tun; **run a ~, take a ~** ein Risiko eingehen **2.** wagen, riskieren; **risk·y** riskant

rite Ritus *m*; Zeremonie *f*

rit·u·al 1. rituell; Ritual... **2.** Ritual *n*

ri·val 1. Rivale *m*, Rivalin *f*, Konkurrent(in) **2.** Konkurrenz..., rivalisierend **3.** rivalisieren *or* konkurrieren mit; **ri·val·ry** Rivalität *f*; Konkurrenz *f*; Konkurrenzkampf *m*

riv·er Fluss *m*; Strom *m*; **riv·er·side** Flussufer *n*; **by the ~** am Fluss

riv·et 1. TECH Niet *m, n*, Niete *f* **2.** TECH (ver)nieten; *fig* Aufmerksamkeit, *Blick* richten (**on** auf *acc*)

road (Auto-, Land)Straße *f*; *fig* Weg *m*; **on the ~** auf der Straße; unterwegs; THEA auf Tournee

road ac·ci·dent Verkehrsunfall *m*

road·block Straßensperre *f*

road hog F Verkehrsrowdy *m*

road map Straßenkarte *f*

road safe·ty Verkehrssicherheit *f*

road·side Straßenrand *m*; **at the ~, by the ~** am Straßenrand

road toll Straßenbenutzungsgebühr *f*

road·way Fahrbahn *f*

road works Straßenarbeiten *pl*

road·wor·thi·ness Verkehrssicherheit *f*; **road·wor·thy** verkehrssicher

roam *v/i* (umher)streifen, (-)wandern; *v/t* streifen *or* wandern durch

roar 1. Brüllen *n*, Gebrüll *n*; Brausen *n*, Krachen *n*, Donnern *n*; **~s of laughter** brüllendes Gelächter **2.** brüllen; brausen; donnern (*truck, gun etc*)

roast GASTR **1.** *v/t* braten (*a. v/i*); *Kaffee etc* rösten **2.** Braten *m* **3.** *adj* gebraten

roast beef GASTR Rinderbraten *m*

rob *Bank etc* überfallen; *j-n* berauben

rob·ber Räuber *m*

rob·ber·y Raubüberfall *m*, (*Bank-*)Raub *m*, (*Bank*)Überfall *m*

robe *a. pl* Robe *f*, Talar *m*

rob·in ZO Rotkehlchen *n*

ro·bot Roboter *m*

ro·bust robust, kräftig

rock¹ schaukeln, wiegen; erschüttern (*a. fig*)

rock² Fels(en) *m*; Felsen *pl*; GEOL Gestein *n*; Felsbrocken *m*; Stein *m*; *Br* Zuckerstange *f*; *pl* Klippen *pl*; F **on the ~s** in ernsten Schwierigkeiten (*business etc*); kaputt (*marriage etc*); GASTR mit Eis

rock³ *a.* **~ music** Rock(musik *f*) *m*; → **rock 'n' roll**

rock·er Kufe *f*; Schaukelstuhl *m*; *Br* Rocker *m*; **off one's ~** F übergeschnappt

rock·et 1. Rakete *f* **2.** rasen, schießen; *a.* **~ up** hochschnellen, in die Höhe schießen (*prices*)

rock·ing chair Schaukelstuhl *m*

rock·ing horse Schaukelpferd *n*

rock 'n' roll MUS Rock 'n' Roll *m*

rock·y felsig; steinhart

rod Rute *f*; TECH Stab *m*, Stange *f*

ro·dent ZO Nagetier *n*

ro·de·o Rodeo *m, n*

roe ZO *a.* **hard ~** Rogen *m*; *a.* **soft ~** Milch *f*

roe·buck ZO Rehbock *m*

roe deer ZO Reh *n*

rogue Schurke *m*, Gauner *m*; Schlingel *m*, Spitzbube *m*

ro·guish schelmisch, spitzbübisch

role THEA Rolle *f* (*a. fig*)

roll 1. *v/i* rollen; sich wälzen; fahren; MAR schlingern; (g)rollen (*thunder*); *v/t et.* rollen; auf-, zusammenrollen; *Zigarette* drehen; **~ down** Ärmel herunterkrempeln; MOT *Fenster* herunterkurbeln; **~ out** ausrollen; **~ up** aufrollen; (sich) zusammenrollen; *Ärmel* hochkrempeln; MOT *Fenster* hochkurbeln **2.** Rolle *f*; GASTR Brötchen *n*, Semmel *f*; Namens-, Anwesenheitsliste *f*; (G)Rollen *n (of thunder)*; *(Trommel)*-Wirbel *m*; MAR Schlingern *n*

roll call Namensaufruf *m*

roll·er (Locken)Wickler *m*; TECH Rolle *f*, Walze *f*

roll·er coast·er Achterbahn *f*

roll·er skate Rollschuh *m*

roll·er-skate Rollschuh laufen

roll·er-skat·ing Rollschuhlaufen *n*

roll·er tow·el Rollhandtuch *n*

roll·ing pin Nudelholz *n*

roll-on Deoroller *m*

Ro·man 1. römisch **2.** Römer(in)

ro·mance Abenteuer-, Liebesroman *m*; Romanze *f*; Romantik *f*

Ro·mance LING romanisch

Ro·ma·ni·a Rumänien *n*

Ro·ma·ni·an 1. rumänisch **2.** Rumäne *m*, Rumänin *f*; LING Rumänisch *n*

ro·man·tic 1. romantisch **2.** Romantiker(in)

ro·man·ti·cism Romantik *f*

romp *a.* **~ about, ~ around** herumtollen, herumtoben

romp·ers Spielanzug *m*

roof 1. Dach *n*; MOT Verdeck *n* **2.** mit e-m Dach versehen; **~ in, ~ over** überdachen

roof·ing felt Dachpappe *f*

roof-rack MOT Dachgepäckträger *m*

rook[1] ZO Saatkrähe *f*

rook[2] *chess:* Turm *m*

rook[3] F *j-n* betrügen *(of* um)

room 1. Raum *m*, *a.* Zimmer *n*, *a.* Platz *m*; *fig* Spielraum *m* **2.** wohnen

room·er Untermieter(in)

room·ing-house Fremdenheim *n*, Pension *f*

room·mate Zimmergenosse *m*, -genossin *f*

room ser·vice Zimmerservice *m*

room·y geräumig

roost 1. (Hühner)Stange *f*; ZO Schlafplatz *m* **2.** auf der Stange *etc* sitzen *or* schlafen

roost·er ZO (Haus)Hahn *m*

root 1. Wurzel *f*; **take ~** Wurzeln schlagen *(a. fig)* **2.** *v/i* Wurzeln schlagen; wühlen **(for** nach); **~ about** herumwühlen **(among** in *dat*); *v/t* **~ out** *fig* ausrotten; **~ up** mit der Wurzel ausreißen

root·ed: deeply ~ *fig* tief verwurzelt; **stand ~ to the spot** wie angewurzelt dastehen

rope 1. Seil *n*; MAR Tau *n*; Strick *m*; *(Perlen- etc)*Schnur *f*; **give s.o. plenty of ~** j-m viel Freiheit *or* Spielraum lassen; **know the ~s** F sich auskennen; **show s.o. the ~s** F j-n einarbeiten **2.** festbinden **(to** an *dat or acc*); **~ off** (durch ein Seil) absperren *or* abgrenzen; **~ ladder** Strickleiter *f*

ro·sa·ry REL Rosenkranz *m*

rose 1. BOT Rose *f*; Brause *f* **2.** rosarot, rosenrot

ros·trum Redner-, Dirigentenpult *n*

ros·y rosig *(a. fig)*

rot 1. *v/t* (ver)faulen *or* verrotten lassen; *v/i a.* **~ away** (ver)faulen, verrotten, morsch werden **2.** Fäulnis *f*

ro·ta·ry rotierend, sich drehend; Rotations…, Dreh…; **ro·tate** rotieren (lassen), (sich) drehen; turnusmäßig (aus-) wechseln; **ro·ta·tion** Rotation *f*, Drehung *f*; Wechsel *m*

ro·tor TECH Rotor *m*

rot·ten verfault, faul; verrottet, morsch; *fig* miserabel; gemein; **feel ~** F sich mies fühlen

ro·tund rund und dick

rough 1. *adj* rau; uneben *(road etc)*; stürmisch *(sea, crossing, weather)*; grob; barsch; hart; grob, ungefähr *(estimate etc)*; roh, Roh… **2.** *adv* **sleep ~** im Freien übernachten; **play ~** SPORT hart spielen **3.** *golf:* Rough *n*; **write it out in ~ first** zuerst ins Unreine schreiben **4. ~ it** F primitiv *or* anspruchslos leben; **~ out** entwerfen, skizzieren; **~ up** F *j-n* zusammenschlagen

rough·age MED Ballaststoffe *pl*

rough·cast ARCH Rauputz *m*

rough| cop·y Rohentwurf *m*, Konzept *n*; **~ draft** Rohfassung *f*

rough·en rau werden; rau machen, anrauen, aufrauen

rough·ly grob, *fig a.* ungefähr

rough·neck F Schläger *m*

rough·shod: ride ~ over *j-n* rücksichtslos behandeln; sich rücksichtslos über *et.* hinwegsetzen

round 1. *adj* rund; **a ~ dozen** ein rundes Dutzend; **in ~ figures** aufgerundet, abgerundet, rund(e) … **2.** *adv* rund(her)-um, rings(her)um; überall, auf *or* von *or* nach allen Seiten; **turn** ~ sich umdrehen; **invite s.o.** ~ j-n zu sich einladen; ~ **about** F ungefähr; **all (the) year** ~ das ganze Jahr hindurch *or* über; **the other way** ~ umgekehrt **3.** *prp* (rund) um, um (*acc* ... herum); in *or* auf (*dat*) ... herum; **trip** ~ **the world** Weltreise *f* **4.** Runde *f, a.* Rundgang *m*, MED Visite *f, a.* Lage *f* (*beer etc*); Schuss *m*; *esp Br* Scheibe *f* (*bread etc*); MUS Kanon *m* **5.** rund machen, (ab)runden, *Lippen* spitzen; umfahren, fahren um, *Kurve* nehmen; ~ **down** *Zahl etc* abrunden (**to** auf *acc*); ~ **off** *Essen etc* abrunden, beschließen (**with** mit); *Zahl etc* auf- *or* abrunden (**to** auf *acc*); ~ **up** *Vieh* zusammentreiben; *Leute etc* zusammentrommeln; *Zahl etc* aufrunden (**to** auf *acc*)

round·a·bout 1. *Br* MOT Kreisverkehr *m*; *Br* Karussell *n* **2. take a** ~ **route** e-n Umweg machen; **in a** ~ **way** *fig* auf Umwegen

round trip Hin- und Rückfahrt *f*; Hin- und Rückflug *m*

round-trip tick·et Rückfahrkarte *f*; Rückflugticket *n*

round·up Razzia *f*

rouse *j-n* wecken; *fig j-n* aufrütteln, wach rütteln; *j-n* erzürnen, reizen

route Route *f*, Strecke *f*, Weg *m*, (*Bus etc*)Linie *f*

rou·tine 1. Routine *f*; **the same old (daily)** ~ das (tägliche) ewige Einerlei **2.** üblich, routinemäßig, Routine...

rove (umher)streifen, (umher)wandern

row¹ Reihe *f*

row² **1.** rudern **2.** Kahnfahrt *f*

row³ *Br* F **1.** Krach *m*; (lauter) Streit **2.** (sich) streiten

row·boat Ruderboot *n*

row·er Ruderer *m*, Ruderin *f*

row house Reihenhaus *n*

row·ing boat *Br* Ruderboot *n*

roy·al königlich, Königs...

roy·al·ty die königliche Familie; Tantieme *f* (**on** auf *acc*)

rub 1. *v/t* reiben; abreiben; polieren; ~ **dry** trocken reiben; ~ **it in** *fig* F darauf herumreiten; ~ **shoulders with** F verkehren mit; *v/i* reiben, scheuern (**against, on** an *dat*); ~ **down** abreiben, trocken reiben; abschmirgeln, abschleifen; ~ **off** abreiben; abgehen (*paint etc*); ~ **off on(to)** *fig* abfärben

auf (*acc*); ~ **out** *Br* ausradieren **2. give s.th. a** ~ et. abreiben *or* polieren

rub·ber Gummi *n, m*; *esp Br* Radiergummi *m*; Wischtuch *n*; F Gummi *m*

rub·ber band Gummiband *n*

rub·ber din·ghy Schlauchboot *n*

rub·ber·neck F **1.** neugierig gaffen **2.** *a.* **rubbernecker** Gaffer(in), Schaulustige *m, f*

rub·ber·y gummiartig; zäh

rub·bish *Br* Abfall *m*, Abfälle *pl*, Müll *m*; F Schund *m*; Quatsch *m*, Blödsinn *m*; ~ **bin** *Br* Mülleimer *m*; ~ **chute** *Br* Müllschlucker *m*

rub·ble Schutt *m*; Trümmer *pl*

ru·by Rubin *m*; Rubinrot *n*

ruck·sack *esp Br* Rucksack *m*

rud·der AVIAT, MAR Ruder *n*

rud·dy frisch, gesund

rude unhöflich, grob; unanständig (*joke etc*); bös (*shock etc*)

ru·di·men·ta·ry elementar, Anfangs...; primitiv

ru·di·ments Anfangsgründe *pl*

rue·ful reuevoll, reumütig

ruff Halskrause *f* (*a.* ZO)

ruf·fle 1. kräuseln; *Haar* zerzausen; *Federn* sträuben; ~ **s.o.'s composure** j-n aus der Fassung bringen **2.** Rüsche *f*

rug Vorleger *m*, Brücke *f*; *esp Br* dicke Wolldecke

rug·by *a.* ~ **football** SPORT Rugby *n*

rug·ged GEOGR zerklüftet, schroff; TECH robust, stabil; zerfurcht (*face*)

ru·in 1. Ruin *m*; *mst pl* Ruine(n *pl*) *f*, Trümmer *pl* **2.** ruinieren, zerstören

ru·in·ous ruinös

rule 1. Regel *f*; Spielregel *f*; Vorschrift *f*; Herrschaft *f*; Lineal *n*; **against the** ~ **s** regelwidrig; verboten; **as a** ~ in der Regel; **as a** ~ **of thumb** als Faustregel; **work to** ~ Dienst nach Vorschrift tun **2.** *v/t* herrschen über (*acc*); *esp* JUR entscheiden; *Papier* lin(i)ieren; *Linie* ziehen; **be** ~ **d by** *fig* sich leiten lassen von; beherrscht werden von; ~ **out** et. ausschließen; *v/i* herrschen (**over** über *acc*); *esp* JUR entscheiden

rul·er Herrscher(in); Lineal *n*

rum Rum *m*

rum·ble rumpeln (*vehicle*); (g)rollen (*thunder*); knurren (*stomach*)

ru·mi·nant ZO Wiederkäuer *m*

ru·mi·nate zo wiederkäuen

rum·mage F 1. *a.* ~ *about* herumstöbern, herumwühlen (*among, in, through* in *dat*); 2. Ramsch *m*; ~ *sale* Wohltätigkeitsbasar *m*

ru·mo(u)r 1. Gerücht *n*; ~ *has it that* es geht das Gerücht, dass 2. *it is* ~*ed that* es geht das Gerücht, dass; *he is* ~*ed to be* ... man munkelt, er sei ...

rump F Hinterteil *n*

rum·ple zerknittern, zerknüllen, zerwühlen; *Haar* zerzausen

run 1. *v/i* laufen (*a.* SPORT), rennen; fahren, verkehren, gehen (*train, bus etc*); laufen, fließen; zerfließen, zerlaufen (*butter, paint etc*); TECH laufen (*engine*), in Betrieb *or* Gang sein; verlaufen (*road etc*); *esp* JUR gelten, laufen (*for one year* ein Jahr); THEA *etc* laufen (*for three months* drei Monate lang); lauten (*text*); gehen (*melody*); POL kandidieren (*for* für); ~ *dry* austrocknen; ~ *low* knapp werden; ~ *short* knapp werden; ~ *short of gas* (*Br petrol*) kein Benzin mehr haben; *v/t Strecke, Rennen* laufen; *Zug, Bus* fahren *or* verkehren lassen; *Wasser, Maschine etc* laufen lassen; *Geschäft, Hotel etc* führen, leiten; *Zeitungsartikel etc* abdrucken, bringen; ~ *s.o. home* F j-n nach Hause bringen *or* fahren; → *errand*; ~ *across* j-n zufällig treffen; stoßen auf (*acc*); ~ *after* hinterherlaufen, nachlaufen (*dat*); ~ *along!* F ab mit dir!; ~ *away* davonlaufen (*from* vor *dat*); ~ *away with* durchbrennen mit; durchgehen mit (*feelings etc*); ~ *down* MOT anfahren, umfahren; F schlechtmachen; ausfindig machen; ablaufen (*watch*); leer werden (*battery*); ~ *in* Wagen *etc* einfahren; F *Verbrecher* schnappen; ~ *into* laufen *or* fahren gegen; j-n zufällig treffen; *fig* geraten in (*acc*); *fig* sich belaufen auf (*acc*); ~ *off with* → *run away with*; ~ *on* weitergehen, sich hinziehen (*until* bis); F unaufhörlich reden (*about* über *acc*, von); ~ *out* ablaufen (*time etc*); ausgehen, zu Ende gehen (*supplies etc*); ~ *out of gas* (*Br petrol*) kein Benzin mehr haben; ~ *over* MOT überfahren; überlaufen, überfließen; ~ *through* überfliegen, durchgehen, durchlesen; ~ *up Flagge* hissen; *hohe Rechnung, Schulden* machen; ~ *up*

against stoßen auf (*acc*) 2. Lauf *m* (*a.* SPORT); Fahrt *f*; Spazierfahrt *f*; Ansturm *m*, ECON *a.* Run *m* (*on* auf *acc*); THEA *etc* Laufzeit *f*; Laufmasche *f*; Gehege *n*; Auslauf *m*, (*Hühner-*)Hof *m*; SPORT (*Bob-, Rodel-*) Bahn *f*; (*Ski-*)Hang *m*; ~ *of good* (*bad*) *luck* Glückssträhne *f* (Pechsträhne *f*); *in the long* ~ auf die Dauer; *in the short* ~ zunächst; *on the* ~ auf der Flucht

run·a·bout F MOT Stadt-, Kleinwagen *m*

run·a·way Ausreißer(in)

rung Sprosse *f*

run·ner SPORT Läufer(in); Rennpferd *n*; *mst in cpds* Schmuggler(in); (*Schlitten-, Schlittschuh-*)Kufe *f*; Tischläufer *m*; TECH (Gleit)Schiene *f*; BOT Ausläufer *m*; ~ *bean* Br BOT grüne Bohne

run·ning 1. Laufen *n*, Rennen *n*; Führung *f*, Leitung *f* 2. fließend; SPORT Lauf...; *two days* ~ zwei Tage hintereinander; ~ *costs* ECON Betriebskosten *pl*, laufende Kosten *pl*

run·ny F flüssig; laufend (*nose*), tränend (*eyes*)

run-off POL Stichwahl *f*

run-up SPORT Zweite *m, f*, Vizemeister(in)

run·way AVIAT Start- und Landebahn *f*, Rollbahn *f*, Piste *f*

rup·ture 1. Bruch *m* (*a.* MED *and fig*), Riss *m* 2. bersten, platzen; (zer)reißen; ~ *o.s.* MED sich e-n Bruch heben *or* zuziehen

ru·ral ländlich

ruse List *f*, Trick *m*

rush¹ 1. *v/i* hasten, hetzen, stürmen, rasen; ~ *at* losstürzen *or* sich stürzen auf (*acc*); ~ *in* hineinstürzen, hineinstürmen, hereinstürzen, hereinstürmen; ~ *into fig* sich stürzen in (*acc*); *et.* überstürzen; *v/t* antreiben, drängen, hetzen; schnell bringen; *Essen* hinunterschlingen; losstürmen auf (*acc*); *don't* ~ *it* lass dir Zeit dabei 2. Ansturm *m*; Hast *f*, Hetze *f*; Hochbetrieb *m*; ECON stürmische Nachfrage; *what's all the* ~*?* wozu diese Eile *or* Hetze?

rush² BOT Binse *f*

rush hour Rushhour *f*, Hauptverkehrszeit *f*, Stoßzeit *f*

rush-hour traf·fic Stoßverkehr *m*

rusk *esp Br* Zwieback *m*

Rus·sia Russland *n*

Rus·sian 1. russisch **2.** Russe *m*, Russin *f*; LING Russisch *n*

rust 1. Rost *m* **2.** *v/t* (ein-, ver)rosten lassen; *v/i* (ein-, ver)rosten

rus·tic ländlich, bäuerlich; rustikal

rus·tle 1. rascheln (mit), knistern; *Vieh* stehlen **2.** Rascheln *n*

rust·proof rostfrei, nicht rostend

rust·y rostig; *fig* eingerostet

rut¹ 1. (Rad)Spur *f*, Furche *f*; *fig* (alter) Trott; *the daily* ~ das tägliche Einerlei **2.** furchen; *rutted* ausgefahren

rut² ZO Brunft *f*, Brunst *f*

ruth·less unbarmherzig; rücksichtslos, skrupellos

rye BOT Roggen *m*

S

S, s S, s *n*

S *abbr of* **small** (**size**) klein

sa·ber, *Br* **sa·bre** Säbel *m*

sa·ble ZO Zobel *m*; Zobelpelz *m*

sab·o·tage 1. Sabotage *f* **2.** sabotieren

sack 1. Sack *m*; *get the* ~ *Br* F rausgeschmissen werden; *give s.o. the* ~ *Br* F j-n rausschmeißen; *hit the* ~ F sich in die Falle *or* Klappe hauen **2.** in Säcke füllen, einsacken; *Br* F j-n rausschmeißen

sack·cloth, sack·ing Sackleinen *n*

sac·ra·ment REL Sakrament *n*

sa·cred geistlich (*music etc*); heilig

sac·ri·fice 1. Opfer *n* **2.** opfern

sac·ri·lege REL Sakrileg *n*; Frevel *m*

sac·ris·ty REL Sakristei *f*

sad traurig; schmerzlich; schlimm

sad·dle 1. Sattel *m* **2.** satteln

sa·dism Sadismus *m*

sa·dist Sadist(in)

sa·dis·tic sadistisch

sad·ness Traurigkeit *f*

sa·fa·ri Safari *f*; ~ *park* Safaripark *m*

safe 1. sicher **2.** Safe *m, n*, Tresor *m*, Geldschrank *m*

safe con·duct freies Geleit

safe-de·pos·it Tresor *m*

safe-de·pos·it box Schließfach *n*

safe·guard 1. Schutz *m* (*against* gegen, vor *dat*); **2.** schützen (*against, from* gegen, vor *dat*)

safe·keep·ing sichere Verwahrung

safe·ty 1. Sicherheit *f* **2.** Sicherheits-...; ~ *belt* Sicherheitsgurt *m*; ~ *seat belt*; ~ *is·land* Verkehrsinsel *f*; ~ *lock* Sicherheitsschloss *n*; ~ *mea·sure* Sicherheitsmaßnahme *f*; ~ *pin* Sicherheitsnadel *f*

sag sich senken, absacken; durchhängen; (herab)hängen (*shoulders*); *fig*

sinken (*morale*); nachlassen (*interest etc*)

sa·ga·cious scharfsinnig

sa·ga·ci·ty Scharfsinn *m*

sage BOT Salbei *m, f*

Sa·git·tar·i·us ASTR Schütze *m*; *he* (*she*) *is* (*a*) ~ er (sie) ist (ein) Schütze

sail 1. Segel *n*; Segelfahrt *f*; (*Windmühlen*)Flügel *m*; *set* ~ auslaufen (*for* nach); *go for a* ~ segeln gehen **2.** *v/i* MAR segeln, fahren; auslaufen (*for* nach); gleiten, schweben; *go* ~*ing* segeln gehen; *v/t* MAR befahren; *Schiff* steuern, *Boot* segeln

sail·board Surfbrett *n*

sail·boat Segelboot *n*

sail·ing Segeln *n*; Segelsport *m*; *when is the next* ~ *to* ...? wann fährt das nächste Schiff nach ...?; ~ *boat* *Br* Segelboot *n*; ~ *ship* Segelschiff *n*

sail·or Seemann *m*, Matrose *m*; *be a good* (*bad*) ~ (nicht) seefest sein

sail·plane Segelflugzeug *n*

saint Heilige *m, f*

saint·ly heilig, fromm

sake: *for the* ~ *of* ... um ... (*gen*) willen; *for my* ~ meinetwegen; *for God's* ~ F um Gottes willen

sal·a·ble verkäuflich

sal·ad Salat *m*; ~ *dress·ing* Dressing *n*, Salatsoße *f*

sal·a·ried: ~ *employee* Angestellte *m, f*, Gehaltsempfänger(in)

sal·a·ry Gehalt *n*

sale Verkauf *m*; Absatz *m*, Umsatz *m*; (Saison)Schlussverkauf *m*; Auktion *f*, Versteigerung *f*; *for* ~ zu verkaufen; *not for* ~ unverkäuflich; *be on* ~ verkauft werden, erhältlich sein

sale·a·ble → **salable**

sales·clerk (Laden)Verkäufer(in)

sales·girl (Laden)Verkäuferin *f*

sales·man Verkäufer *m*; (Handels-) Vertreter *m*

sales rep·re·sen·ta·tive Handlungsreisende *m*, *f*; (Handels)Vertreter(in)

sales slip ECON Quittung *f*

sales tax ECON Umsatzsteuer *f*

sales·wom·an Verkäuferin *f*; (Handels)Vertreterin *f*

sa·line salzig, Salz…

sa·li·va Speichel *m*

sal·low gelblich

salm·on ZO Lachs *m*

sal·on (*Schönheits- etc*)Salon *m*

sa·loon *Br* MOT Limousine *f*; HIST Saloon *m*; MAR Salon *m*

sa·loon car *Br* MOT Limousine *f*

salt 1. Salz *n* **2.** salzen; (ein)pökeln, einsalzen (*a.* **~ down**); *Straße etc* (mit Salz) streuen **3.** Salz…; gepökelt; salzig, gesalzen

salt·cel·lar *Br* Salzstreuer *m*

salt·pe·ter, *esp Br* **salt·pe·tre** CHEM Salpeter *m*

salt shak·er Salzstreuer *m*

salt wa·ter Salzwasser *n*

salt·y salzig

sal·u·ta·tion Gruß *m*, Begrüßung *f*; Anrede *f*; **sa·lute 1.** MIL salutieren; (be)grüßen **2.** Gruß *m*; MIL Ehrenbezeugung *f*; Salut *m*

sal·vage 1. Bergung *f*; Bergungsgut *n* **2.** bergen (*from* aus); retten (*a. fig*)

sal·va·tion Rettung *f*; REL Erlösung *f*; (Seelen)Heil *n*

Sal·va·tion Ar·my Heilsarmee *f*

salve (Heil)Salbe *f*

same: the ~ derselbe, dieselbe, dasselbe; **all the ~** trotzdem; **it is all the ~ to me** es ist mir ganz egal

sam·ple 1. Muster *n*, Probe *f* **2.** kosten, probieren

san·a·to·ri·um Sanatorium *n*

sanc·ti·fy heiligen

sanc·tion 1. Billigung *f*, Zustimmung *f*; *mst pl* Sanktionen *pl* **2.** billigen, sanktionieren

sanc·ti·ty Heiligkeit *f*

sanc·tu·a·ry Zuflucht *f*, Asyl *n*; ZO Schutzgebiet *n*

sand 1. Sand *m*; *pl* Sandfläche *f* **2.** *Straße etc* mit Sand (be)streuen; TECH schmirgeln

san·dal Sandale *f*

sand·bag Sandsack *m*

sand·bank GEOGR Sandbank *f*

sand·box Sandkasten *m*

sand·cas·tle Sandburg *f*

sand·man Sandmännchen *n*

sand·pa·per Sand-, Schmirgelpapier *n*

sand·pip·er ZO Strandläufer *m*

sand·pit *Br* Sandkasten *m*; Sandgrube *f*

sand·stone GEOL Sandstein *m*

sand·storm Sandsturm *m*

sand·wich 1. Sandwich *n* **2.** **be ~ed between** eingekeilt sein zwischen (*dat*); **~ s.th. in between** *fig* et. einschieben zwischen (*acc or dat*)

sand·y sandig; rotblond

sane geistig gesund; JUR zurechnungsfähig; vernünftig

san·i·tar·i·um → **sanatorium**

san·i·ta·ry hygienisch; Gesundheits…; **~ nap·kin**, *Br* **~ tow·el** (Damen)Binde *f*

san·i·ta·tion sanitäre Einrichtungen *pl*; Kanalisation *f*

san·i·ty geistige Gesundheit; JUR Zurechnungsfähigkeit *f*

San·ta Claus der Weihnachtsmann, der Nikolaus

sap¹ BOT Saft *m*

sap² schwächen

sap·phire Saphir *m*

sar·casm Sarkasmus *m*

sar·cas·tic sarkastisch

sar·dine ZO Sardine *f*

sash¹ Schärpe *f*

sash² Fensterrahmen *m*

sash win·dow Schiebefenster *n*

sas·sy frech

Sat *abbr of* **Saturday** Sa., Samstag *m*, Sonnabend *m*

Sa·tan der Satan

satch·el (Schul)Ranzen *m*; Schultasche *f*

sat·ed *fig* übersättigt

sat·el·lite 1. Satellit *m*; **by or via ~** über Satellit **2.** Satelliten…; **~ dish** F Satellitenschüssel *f*

sat·in Satin *m*

sat·ire Satire *f*

sat·ir·ic, **sat·ir·i·cal** satirisch

sat·i·rist Satiriker(in)

sat·i·rize verspotten

sat·is·fac·tion Befriedigung *f*; Genugtuung *f*, Zufriedenheit *f*

sat·is·fac·to·ry befriedigend, zufrieden-

stellend
sat·is·fy befriedigen, zufrieden stellen;
überzeugen; *be satisfied that* davon
überzeugt sein, dass
sat·u·rate (durch)tränken (*with* mit);
CHEM sättigen (*a. fig*)
Sat·ur·day Sonnabend *m*, Samstag *m*;
on ~ (am) Sonnabend *or* Samstag; *on*
~*s* sonnabends, samstags
sauce Soße *f*
sauce·pan Kochtopf *m*
sau·cer Untertasse *f*
sauc·y *Br* frech
saun·ter bummeln, schlendern
saus·age Wurst *f*; *a.* **small** ~ Würstchen
n
sav·age 1. wild; unzivilisiert **2.** Wilde
m, *f*; **sav·ag·e·ry** Wildheit *f*; Rohheit
f, Grausamkeit *f*
save 1. retten (*from* vor *dat*); Geld, Zeit
etc (ein)sparen; *et.* aufheben, aufsparen (*for* für); *j-m et.* ersparen; IT (ab)-
speichern, sichern; SPORT *Schuss* halten, parieren; *Tor* verhindern **2.** SPORT
Parade *f*
sav·er Retter(in); ECON Sparer(in)
sav·ings ECON Ersparnisse *pl*; ~ **ac·**
count Sparkonto *n*; ~ **bank** Sparkasse
f; ~ **de·pos·it** Spareinlage *f*
sa·vio(u)r Retter(in); *the Savio(u)r* REL
der Erlöser, der Heiland
sa·vo(u)r mit Genuss essen *or* trinken; ~
of fig e-n Beigeschmack haben von
sa·vo(u)r·y schmackhaft
saw 1. Säge *f* **2.** sägen
saw·dust Sägemehl *n*, Sägespäne *pl*
saw·mill Sägewerk *n*
Sax·on 1. (Angel)Sachse *m*, (Angel-)
Sächsin *f* **2.** (angel)sächsisch
say 1. sagen; aufsagen; *Gebet* sprechen;
Vaterunser beten; ~ *grace* das Tischgebet sprechen; *what does your watch*
~*?* wie spät ist es auf deiner Uhr?;
he is said to be ... er soll ... sein; *it*
~*s* es lautet (*letter etc*); *it* ~*s here* hier
heißt es; *it goes without* ~*ing* es versteht sich von selbst; *no sooner said*
than done gesagt, getan; *that is to* ~
das heißt; (*and*) *that's* ~*ing s.th.*
(und) das will was heißen; *you said*
it du sagst es; *you can* ~ *that again!*
das kannst du laut sagen!; *I* ~ sag(en
Sie) mal!; ich muss schon sagen!; *I can't*
~ das kann ich nicht sagen **2.** Mitspra-

cherecht *n* (*in* bei); *have one's* ~ s-e
Meinung äußern, zu Wort kommen;
he always has to have his ~ er muss
immer mitreden
say·ing Sprichwort *n*, Redensart *f*; *as*
the ~ *goes* wie man so (schön) sagt
scab MED, BOT Schorf *m*; *contp* Streik-
brecher(in)
scaf·fold (Bau)Gerüst *n*; Schafott *n*
scaf·fold·ing (Bau)Gerüst *n*
scald 1. sich *die Zunge etc* verbrühen;
Milch abkochen; ~*ing hot* kochend
heiß **2.** MED Verbrühung *f*
scale[1] **1.** Skala *f* (*a. fig*), Grad- *or* Maß-
einteilung *f*; MATH, TECH Maßstab *m* (*a.
fig*); Waage *f*; MUS Skala *f*, Tonleiter *f*;
fig Ausmaß *n*, Umfang *m* **2.** erklettern;
~ *down fig* verringern; ~ *up fig* erhöhen
scale[2] Waagschale *f*; (*a pair of*) ~*s* (e-e)
Waage
scale[3] **1.** ZO Schuppe *f*; TECH Kesselstein
m; *the* ~*s fell from my eyes* es fiel mir
wie Schuppen von den Augen **2.** *Fisch*
(ab)schuppen
scal·lop ZO Kammmuschel *f*
scalp 1. Kopfhaut *f*; Skalp *m* **2.** skalpieren
scal·y ZO schuppig (*a. fig*)
scamp F Schlingel *m*, (kleiner) Strolch
scam·per trippeln; huschen
scan 1. *et.* absuchen (*for* nach); *Zeitung*
etc überfliegen; IT, *radar*, TV abtasten,
scannen **2.** MED *etc* Scanning *n*
scan·dal Skandal *m*; Klatsch *m*
scan·dal·ize: *be* ~*d at s.th.* über et. empört *or* entrüstet sein
scan·dal·ous skandalös; *be* ~ *a.* ein
Skandal sein (*that* dass)
Scan·di·na·vi·a Skandinavien *n*
Scan·di·na·vi·an 1. skandinavisch **2.**
Skandinavier(in)
scan·ner TECH Scanner *m*
scant dürftig, gering
scant·y dürftig, kärglich, knapp
scape·goat Sündenbock *m*
scar MED **1.** Narbe *f* (*a. fig*) **2.** e-e Narbe
or Narben hinterlassen auf (*dat*) *or* fig
bei *j-m*; ~ *over* vernarben
scarce knapp (*food etc*); selten; *be* ~
Mangelware sein (*a. fig*); **scarce·ly**
kaum; **scar·ci·ty** Mangel *m*, Knappheit *f* (*of* an *dat*)
scare 1. erschrecken; *be* ~*d* Angst ha-

ben (*of* vor *dat*); **~ away, ~ off** verjagen,
-scheuchen **2.** Schreck(en) *m*; Panik *f*
scare·crow Vogelscheuche *f* (*a. fig*)
scarf Schal *m*; Hals-, Kopf-, Schulter-
tuch *n*
scar·let scharlachrot; **~ fe·ver** MED
Scharlach *m*
scarred narbig
scath·ing bissig (*remark etc*); vernichtend (*criticism etc*)
scat·ter (sich) zerstreuen (*crowd*); ausstreuen, verstreuen; auseinanderstie-
ben (*birds etc*)
scat·ter·brained F schusselig, schusslig
scat·tered verstreut; vereinzelt
scav·enge: ~ on ZO leben von; **~ for** suchen (nach)
scene Szene *f*; Schauplatz *m*; *pl* THEA
Kulissen *pl*
sce·ne·ry Landschaft *f*, Gegend *f*; THEA
Bühnenbild *n*, Kulissen *pl*
scent 1. Duft *m*, Geruch *m*; *esp Br* Parfüm *n*; HUNT Witterung *f*; Fährte *f*, Spur
f (*a. fig*); *v/t esp Br* parfümieren; **~-
scent·less** geruchlos
scep·ter, *Br* **scep·tre** Zepter *n*
scep·tic, scep·ti·cal *Br* → **skeptic** *etc*
sched·ule 1. Aufstellung *f*, Verzeichnis
n; (*Arbeits-, Stunden-, Zeit- etc*)Plan
m; Fahr-, Flugplan *m*; **ahead of ~**
dem Zeitplan voraus, früher als vorgesehen; **be behind ~** Verspätung haben;
im Verzug *or* Rückstand sein; **on ~**
(fahr-) planmäßig, pünktlich **2. the
meeting is ~d for Monday** die Sitzung
ist für Montag angesetzt; **it is ~d to
take place tomorrow** es soll morgen
stattfinden
sched·uled| de·par·ture (fahr)planmä-
ßige Abfahrt; **~ flight** Linienflug *m*
scheme 1. *esp Br* Programm *n*, Projekt
n; Schema *n*, System *n*; Intrige *f*, Ma-
chenschaft *f* **2.** intrigieren
schmaltz·y F schnulzig
schnit·zel GASTR Wiener Schnitzel *n*
schol·ar Gelehrte *m, f*; UNIV Stipen-
diat(in); **schol·ar·ly** gelehrt
schol·ar·ship Gelehrsamkeit *f*; UNIV
Stipendium *n*
school¹¹ 1. Schule *f* (*a. fig*); UNIV Fakultät
f; Hochschule *f*; **at ~** auf *or* in der Schule; **go to ~** in die *or* zur Schule gehen **2.**
j-n schulen, unterrichten; *Tier* dressieren

school² ZO Schule *f*, Schwarm *m*
school·bag Schultasche *f*
school·boy Schüler *m*
school·child Schulkind *n*
school·fel·low → **schoolmate**
school·girl Schülerin *f*
school·ing (Schul)Ausbildung *f*
school·mate Mitschüler(in), Schulka-
merad(in)
school·teach·er (Schul)Lehrer(in)
school·yard Schulhof *m*
schoo·ner MAR Schoner *m*
sci·ence Wissenschaft *f*; *a*. **natural ~** Na-
turwissenschaft(en *pl*) *f*; **~ fic·tion**
(*abbr* **SF**) Sciencefiction *f*
sci·en·tif·ic (natur)wissenschaftlich; exakt, systematisch
sci·en·tist (Natur)Wissenschaftler(in)
sci-fi F Sciencefiction *f*
scis·sors (*a pair of* **~**) Schere *f*
scoff 1. spotten (*at* über *acc*); **2.** spöttische Bemerkung
scold schimpfen (mit)
scoop 1. Schöpfkelle *f*; (*Mehl- etc* **~**)
Schaufel *f*; (*Eis- etc*)Portionierer *m*;
Kugel *f* (*icecream*); *newspaper, radio,*
TV Exklusivmeldung *f*, F Knüller *m* **2.**
schöpfen, schaufeln; **~ up** aufheben,
hochheben
scoot·er (Kinder)Roller *m*; (*Motor-*)
Roller *m*
scope Bereich *m*; Spielraum *m*
scorch *v/t* ansengen, versengen, verbrennen; ausdörren; *v/i Br* MOT F rasen
score 1. SPORT (Spiel)Stand *m*, (-)Ergeb-
nis *n*; MUS Partitur *f*; Musik *f*; 20
(Stück); *a*. **~ mark** Kerbe *f*, Rille *f*; **what
is the ~?** wie steht es *or* das Spiel?; **the
~ stood at *or* was 3-2** das Spiel stand
3:2; **keep (the) ~** anschreiben; **~s of**
e-e Menge; **four ~ and ten** neunzig;
on that ~ deshalb, in dieser Hinsicht;
have a ~ to settle with s.o. e-e alte
Rechnung mit j-m zu begleichen haben
2. *v/t* SPORT *Punkte, Treffer* erzielen,
Tor a. schießen; *Erfolg, Sieg* erringen;
MUS instrumentieren; *die Musik*
schreiben zu *or* für; einkerben; *v/i*
SPORT e-n Treffer *etc* erzielen, ein Tor
schießen; erfolgreich sein
score·board SPORT Anzeigetafel *f*
scor·er SPORT Torschütze *m*, Torschützin
f; Anschreiber(in)
scorn Verachtung *f*

scorn·ful verächtlich

Scor·pi·o ASTR Skorpion m; **he (she) is (a)** ~ **er** (sie) ist (ein) Skorpion

Scot Schotte m, Schottin f

Scotch 1. schottisch **2.** Scotch m

scot-free: F **get off** ~ ungeschoren davonkommen

Scot·land Schottland n

Scots schottisch; **Scotsman** Schotte m; **Scots·wom·an** Schottin f

Scot·tish schottisch

scoun·drel Schurke m

scour[1] scheuern, schrubben

scour[2] *Gegend* absuchen, durchkämmen (**for** nach)

scourge 1. Geißel f (a. fig) **2.** geißeln, fig a. heimsuchen

scout 1. esp MIL Kundschafter m; Br motorisierter Pannenhelfer; a. **boy** ~ Pfadfinder m; a. **girl** ~ Pfadfinderin f; a. **talent** ~ Talentsucher(in) **2.** ~ **about,** ~ **around** sich umsehen (**for** nach); a. ~ **out** MIL auskundschaften

scowl 1. finsteres Gesicht **2.** finster blicken; ~ **at s.o.** j-n böse or finster anschauen

scram·ble 1. klettern; sich drängeln (**for** zu); **2.** Kletterei f; Drängelei f

scram·bled eggs Rührei(er pl) n

scrap[1] **1.** Stückchen n, Fetzen m; Altmaterial n; Schrott m; pl Abfall m, Speisereste pl **2.** verschrotten; ausrangieren; *Plan etc* aufgeben, fallen lassen

scrap[2] F **1.** Streiterei f; Balgerei f **2.** sich streiten; sich balgen

scrap·book Sammelalbum n

scrape 1. (ab)kratzen, (ab)schaben; sich *die Knie etc* aufschürfen; *Wagen etc* ankratzen; scheuern (**against** an dat); (entlang)streifen; scharren **2.** Kratzen n; Kratzer m, Schramme f; fig Klemme f

scrap heap Schrotthaufen m

scrap met·al Altmetall n, Schrott m

scrap pa·per esp Br Schmierpapier n

scrap val·ue Schrottwert m

scrap·yard Schrottplatz m

scratch 1. (zer)kratzen; abkratzen; *s-n Namen etc* einkratzen; (sich) kratzen; scharren **2.** Kratzer m, Schramme f; Gekratze n; Kratzen n; **from** ~ F ganz von vorn **3.** (bunt) zusammengewürfelt

scratch·pad Notiz-, Schmierblock m

scratch pa·per Schmierpapier n

scrawl 1. kritzeln **2.** Gekritzel n

scraw·ny dürr

scream 1. schreien (**with** vor dat); a. ~ **out** schreien; ~ **with laughter** vor Lachen brüllen **2.** Schrei m; ~**s of laughter** brüllendes Gelächter; **be a** ~ F zum Schreien (komisch) sein

screech 1. kreischen (a. fig), (gellend) schreien **2.** Kreischen n; (gellender) Schrei

screen 1. Wand-, Ofen-, Schutzschirm m; film: Leinwand f; radar, TV, IT Bildschirm m; Fliegenfenster n, -gitter n; fig Tarnung f **2.** abschirmen; film zeigen, *Fernsehprogramm a.* senden; fig j-n decken; fig j-n überprüfen; ~ **off** abtrennen

screen·play Drehbuch n

screen sav·er IT Bildschirmschoner m

screw 1. TECH Schraube f; **he has a** ~ **loose** F bei ihm ist e-e Schraube locker **2.** (an)schrauben (**to** an acc); V bumsen, vögeln; ~ **up** Gesicht verziehen; *Augen* zusammenkneifen; ~ **up one's courage** sich ein Herz fassen

screw·ball F Spinner(in)

screw·driv·er Schraubenzieher m

screw top Schraubverschluss m

scrib·ble 1. (hin)kritzeln **2.** Gekritzel n

scrimp: ~ **and save** jeden Cent zweimal umdrehen

script Manuskript n; film, TV Drehbuch n, Skript n; THEA Text m, Textbuch n; Schrift(zeichen pl) f; Br UNIV (schriftliche) Prüfungsarbeit

Scrip·ture a. **the** ~**s** REL die Heilige Schrift

scroll 1. Schriftrolle f **2.** ~ **down (up)** IT zurückrollen (vorrollen)

scro·tum ANAT Hodensack m

scrub[1] **1.** schrubben, scheuern **2.** Schrubben n, Scheuern n

scrub[2] Gebüsch n, Gestrüpp n

scru·ple 1. Skrupel m, Zweifel m, Bedenken pl **2.** Bedenken haben

scru·pu·lous gewissenhaft

scru·ti·nize genau prüfen; mustern

scru·ti·ny genaue Prüfung; prüfender Blick

scu·ba div·ing (Sport)Tauchen n

scuf·fle 1. Handgemenge n, Rauferei f **2.** sich raufen

scull 1. Skull n; Skullboot n **2.** rudern, skullen

sculp·tor Bildhauer *m*

sculp·ture 1. Bildhauerei *f*; Skulptur *f*, Plastik *f* **2.** hauen, meißeln, formen

scum Schaum *m*; *fig* Abschaum *m*

scurf (Kopf)Schuppen *pl*

scur·ri·lous beleidigend; verleumderisch

scur·ry huschen; trippeln

scur·vy MED Skorbut *m*

scut·tle: ~ *away*, ~ *off* davonhuschen

scythe Sense *f*

sea Meer *n* (*a. fig*), See *f*; *at* ~ auf See; *by* ~ auf dem Seeweg; *by the* ~ am Meer

sea·food GASTR Meeresfrüchte *pl*

sea·gull ZO Seemöwe *f*

seal[1] ZO Robbe *f*, Seehund *m*

seal[2] **1.** Siegel *n*; TECH Plombe *f*; TECH Dichtung *f* **2.** (ver)siegeln; TECH plombieren; abdichten; *fig* besiegeln; ~*ed envelope* verschlossener Briefumschlag; ~ *off Gegend etc* abriegeln

sea lev·el: *above* (*below*) ~ über (unter) dem Meeresspiegel

seal·ing wax Siegellack *m*

seam Naht *f*; Fuge *f*; GEOL Flöz *n*

sea·man Seemann *m*

seam·stress Näherin *f*

sea·plane Wasserflugzeug *n*

sea·port Seehafen *m*; Hafenstadt *f*

sea pow·er Seemacht *f*

search 1. *v/i* suchen (*for* nach); ~ *through* durchsuchen; *v/t j-n, et.* durchsuchen (*for* nach) **2.** Suche *f* (*for* nach); Fahndung *f* (*for* nach); Durchsuchung *f*; *in* ~ *of* auf der Suche nach; **search·ing** prüfend (*look*); eingehend (*examination*)

search·light (Such)Scheinwerfer *m*

search par·ty Suchmannschaft *f*

search war·rant JUR Haussuchungs-, Durchsuchungsbefehl *m*

sea·shore Meeresküste *f*

sea·sick seekrank

sea·side: *at or by the* ~ am Meer; *go to the* ~ ans Meer fahren

sea·side re·sort Seebad *n*

sea·son[1] Jahreszeit *f*; Saison *f*, THEA *etc a.* Spielzeit *f*, (*Jagd-, Urlaubs- etc*)Zeit *f*; *in* (*out of*) ~ in (außerhalb) der (Hoch)Saison; *cherries are now in* ~ jetzt ist Kirschenzeit; *Season's Greetings!* Frohe Weihnachten!; *with the compliments of the* ~ mit den besten Wünschen zum Fest

sea·son[2] *Speise* würzen (*with* mit); *Holz* ablagern

sea·son·al saisonbedingt, Saison...

sea·son·ing GASTR Gewürz *n*

sea·son tick·et RAIL *etc* Dauer-, Zeitkarte *f*; THEA Abonnement *n*

seat 1. Sitz(gelegenheit *f*) *m*; (Sitz)Platz *m*; Sitz(fläche *f*) *m*; Hosenboden *m*; Hinterteil *n*; (*Geschäfts-, Regierungsetc*)Sitz *m*; PARL Sitz *m*; *take a* ~ Platz nehmen; *take one's* ~ s-n Platz einnehmen **2.** *j-n* setzen; Sitzplätze bieten für; *be* ~*ed* sitzen; *please be* ~*ed* bitte nehmen Sie Platz; *remain* ~*ed* sitzen bleiben

seat belt AVIAT, MOT Sicherheitsgurt *m*; *fasten one's* ~ sich anschnallen

sea ur·chin ZO Seeigel *m*

sea·ward(s) seewärts

sea·weed BOT (See)Tang *m*

sea·wor·thy seetüchtig

sec F Augenblick *m*, Sekunde *f*; *just a* ~ Augenblick(, bitte)!

se·cede sich abspalten (*from* von)

se·ces·sion Abspaltung *f*, Sezession *f* (*from* von)

se·clud·ed abgelegen, abgeschieden (*place*); zurückgezogen (*life*)

se·clu·sion Abgeschiedenheit *f*; Zurückgezogenheit *f*

sec·ond[1] **1.** *adj* zweite(r, -s); *every* ~ *day* jeden zweiten Tag, alle zwei Tage; ~ *to none* unerreicht, unübertroffen; *but on* ~ *thought* (*Br thoughts*) aber wenn ich es mir so überlege **2.** *adv* als Zweite(r, -s) **3.** *der, die, das* Zweite; MOT zweiter Gang; Sekundant *m*; *pl* F ECON Waren *pl* zweiter Wahl **4.** *Antrag etc* unterstützen

sec·ond[2] Sekunde *f*; *fig* Augenblick *m*, Sekunde *f*; *just a* ~ Augenblick(, bitte)!

sec·ond·a·ry sekundär, zweitrangig; PED höher

sec·ond-best zweitbeste(r, -s)

sec·ond class RAIL *etc* zweiter Klasse

sec·ond-class zweitklassig

sec·ond floor erster (*Br* zweiter) Stock

sec·ond hand Sekundenzeiger *m*

sec·ond-hand aus zweiter Hand; gebraucht; antiquarisch

sec·ond·ly zweitens

sec·ond-rate zweitklassig

se·cre·cy Verschwiegenheit *f*; Geheimhaltung *f*

se·cret 1. geheim, Geheim…; heimlich; verschwiegen **2.** Geheimnis *n*; *in* ~ heimlich, im Geheimen; *keep s.th. a* ~ et. geheim halten (*from* vor *dat*); *can you keep a* ~**?** kannst du schweigen?

se·cret a·gent Geheimagent(in)

sec·re·ta·ry Sekretär(in); POL Minister(in)

Sec·re·ta·ry of State POL Außenminister(in); *Br* Minister(in)

se·crete MED absondern; **se·cre·tion** MED Sekret *n*; Absonderung *f*

se·cre·tive verschlossen

se·cret·ly heimlich

se·cret ser·vice Geheimdienst *m*

sec·tion Teil *m*; Abschnitt *m*; JUR Paragraf *m*; Abteilung *f*; MATH, TECH Schnitt *m*

sec·tor Sektor *m*, Bereich *m*

sec·u·lar weltlich

se·cure 1. sicher (*against, from* vor *dat*); **2.** *Tür etc* fest verschließen; *et.* sichern (*against, from* vor *dat*)

se·cu·ri·ty Sicherheit *f*; *pl* ECON Wertpapiere *pl*; ~ **check** Sicherheitskontrolle *f*; ~ **mea·sure** Sicherheitsmaßnahme *f*; ~ **risk** Sicherheitsrisiko *n*

se·dan MOT Limousine *f*

se·date ruhig, gelassen

sed·a·tive *mst* MED **1.** beruhigend **2.** Beruhigungsmittel *n*

sed·i·ment (Boden)Satz *m*

se·duce verführen

se·duc·er Verführer(in)

se·duc·tion Verführung *f*

se·duc·tive verführerisch

see¹ *v/i* sehen; nachsehen; *I~!* (ich) verstehe!, ach so!; *you~* weißt du; *let me~* warte mal, lass mich überlegen; *we'll~* mal sehen; *v/t* sehen; besuchen; *j-n* aufsuchen, *j-n* konsultieren; ~ *s.o. home* j-n nach Hause bringen *or* begleiten; ~ *you!* bis dann!, auf bald!; ~ *about* sehen nach, sich kümmern um; ~ *off* j-n verabschieden (*at* am *Bahnhof etc*); ~ *out* j-n hinausbringen, hinausbegleiten; ~ *through* j-n, *et.* durchschauen; *j-m* hinweghelfen über (*acc*); ~ *to it that* dafür sorgen, dass

see² REL Bistum *n*, Diözese *f*; *Holy See* der Heilige Stuhl

seed 1. BOT Same(n) *m*; AGR Saat *f*, Saatgut *n*; (*Apfel- etc*)Kern *m*; SPORT gesetz-ter Spieler, gesetzte Spielerin; *go or run to* ~ BOT schießen; *go to* ~ F herunterkommen, verkommen **2.** *v/t* besäen; entkernen; SPORT *Spieler* setzen; *v/i* BOT in Samen schießen

seed·less BOT kernlos

seed·y F heruntergekommen

seek *Schutz, Wahrheit etc* suchen

seem scheinen; **seem·ing** scheinbar

seep sickern

see·saw Wippe *f*, Wippschaukel *f*

seethe schäumen (*a. fig*); *fig* kochen

see-through durchsichtig

seg·ment Teil *m*, *n*; Stück *n*; Abschnitt *m*; Segment *n*

seg·re·gate trennen

seg·re·ga·tion Rassentrennung *f*

seize *j-n, et.* packen, ergreifen; *Macht etc* an sich reißen; *et.* beschlagnahmen; *et.* pfänden; **sei·zure** Beschlagnahme *f*; Pfändung *f*; MED Anfall *m*

sel·dom *adv* selten

se·lect 1. (aus)wählen **2.** ausgewählt; exklusiv; **se·lec·tion** (Aus)Wahl *f*; ECON Auswahl *f* (*of* an *dat*)

self Ich *n*, Selbst *n*

self-as·sured selbstbewusst, -sicher

self-cen·tered, *Br* **self-cen·tred** egozentrisch

self-col·o(u)red einfarbig

self-con·fi·dence Selbstbewusstsein *n*, Selbstvertrauen *n*

self-con·fi·dent selbstbewusst

self-con·scious befangen, gehemmt, unsicher

self-con·tained (in sich) abgeschlossen; *fig* verschlossen; ~ *flat Br* abgeschlossene Wohnung

self-con·trol Selbstbeherrschung *f*

self-crit·i·cal selbstkritisch

self-de·fence *Br*, **self-de·fense** Selbstverteidigung *f*; *in* ~ in *or* aus Notwehr

self-de·ter·mi·na·tion POL Selbstbestimmung *f*

self-em·ployed selbstständig

self-es·teem Selbstachtung *f*

self-ev·i·dent selbstverständlich; offensichtlich

self-gov·ern·ment POL Selbstverwaltung *f*

self-help Selbsthilfe *f*; ~ **group** Selbsthilfegruppe *f*

self-im·por·tant überheblich

self-in·dul·gent nachgiebig gegen sich

selbst; zügellos
self·in·ter·est Eigennutz *m*
self·ish selbstsüchtig, egoistisch
self·knowl·edge Selbsterkenntnis *f*
self·pit·y Selbstmitleid *n*
self·por·trait Selbstporträt *n*
self·pos·sessed selbstbeherrscht
self·re·li·ant selbstständig
self·re·spect Selbstachtung *f*
self·right·eous selbstgerecht
self·sat·is·fied selbstzufrieden
self·serv·ice 1. mit Selbstbedienung, Selbstbedienungs… **2.** Selbstbedienung *f*
self·stud·y Selbststudium *n*
self·suf·fi·cient ECON autark
self·sup·port·ing finanziell unabhängig
self·willed eigensinnig, eigenwillig
sell *v/t* verkaufen; *v/i* verkauft werden (*at, for* für); sich *gut etc* verkaufen (lassen), gehen; ~ *by* … mindestens haltbar bis …; ~ *off* (*esp* billig) abstoßen; ~ *out* ausverkaufen; *be sold out* ausverkauft sein; ~ *up* *esp Br* sein *Geschäft etc* verkaufen; *sell-by date* Mindesthaltbarkeitsdatum *n*; *sell·er* Verkäufer(in); *good* ~ ECON gut gehender Artikel
sem·blance Anschein *m* (*of* von)
se·men MED Samen(flüssigkeit *f*) *m*, Sperma *n*
se·mes·ter UNIV Semester *n*
sem·i… halb…, Halb…
sem·i·cir·cle Halbkreis *m*
sem·i·co·lon LING Semikolon *n*, Strichpunkt *m*
sem·i·con·duc·tor ELECTR Halbleiter *m*
sem·i·de·tached (house) *Br* Doppelhaushälfte *f*
sem·i·fi·nals SPORT Semi-, Halbfinale *n*
sem·i·nar·y Priesterseminar *n*
sem·i·pre·cious: ~ *stone* Halbedelstein *m*
sem·i·skilled angelernt
sem·o·li·na Grieß *m*
sen·ate POL Senat *m*
sen·a·tor POL Senator *m*
send *et.*, *a.* *Grüße*, *Hilfe etc* senden, schicken (*to dat or an acc*); *Ware etc* versenden, verschicken (*to an acc*); *j-n* schicken (*to* ins *Bett etc*); *with adj or pp*: machen; ~ *word to s.o.* j-m Nachricht geben; ~ *away* fort-, wegschicken; *Brief etc* absenden, abschicken; ~

down *Preise etc* fallen lassen; ~ *for* nach *j-m* schicken, *j-n* kommen lassen; sich *et.* kommen lassen, *et.* anfordern; ~ *in* einsenden, einschicken, einreichen; ~ *off* fort-, wegschicken; *Brief etc* absenden, abschicken; SPORT *j-n* vom Platz stellen; ~ *on* *Brief etc* nachsenden, nachschicken (*to* an *acc*); *Gepäck etc* vorausschicken; ~ *out* hinausschicken; *Einladungen etc* verschicken; ~ *up* *Preise etc* steigen lassen
send·er Absender(in)
se·nile senil; **se·nil·i·ty** Senilität *f*
se·ni·or 1. senior; älter (*to* als); dienstälter; rangälter; Ober… **2.** Ältere *m, f*; UNIV Student(in) im letzten Jahr; *he is my* ~ *by a year* er ist ein Jahr älter als ich; ~ *cit·i·zens* ältere Mitbürger *pl*, Senioren *pl*
se·ni·or·i·ty (höheres) Alter; (höheres) Dienstalter; (höherer) Rang
se·ni·or part·ner ECON Seniorpartner *m*
sen·sa·tion Empfindung *f*; Gefühl *n*; Sensation *f*
sen·sa·tion·al F großartig, fantastisch; sensationell, Sensations…
sense 1. Sinn *m*; Verstand *m*; Vernunft *f*; Gefühl *n*; Bedeutung *f*; *bring s.o. to his* ~*s* j-n zur Besinnung *or* Vernunft bringen; *come to one's* ~*s* zur Besinnung *or* Vernunft kommen; *in a* ~ in gewisser Hinsicht; *make* ~ e-n Sinn ergeben; vernünftig sein; ~ *of duty* Pflichtgefühl *n*; ~ *of security* Gefühl *n* der Sicherheit **2.** fühlen, spüren
sense·less bewusstlos; sinnlos
sen·si·bil·i·ty Empfindlichkeit *f*; *a. pl* Empfindsamkeit *f*, Zartgefühl *n*
sen·si·ble vernünftig; spürbar, merklich; *esp Br* praktisch (*clothes etc*)
sen·si·tive empfindlich; sensibel, empfindsam, feinfühlig
sen·sor TECH Sensor *m*
sen·su·al sinnlich
sen·su·ous sinnlich
sen·tence 1. LING Satz *m*; JUR Strafe *f*, Urteil *n*; *pass or pronounce* ~ das Urteil fällen (*on* über *acc*); **2.** JUR verurteilen (*to* zu)
sen·ti·ment Gefühle *pl*; Sentimentalität *f*; *a. pl* Ansicht *f*, Meinung *f*
sen·ti·ment·al sentimental; gefühlvoll
sen·ti·men·tal·i·ty Sentimentalität *f*
sen·try MIL Wache *f*, (Wach[t])Posten *m*

sep·a·ra·ble trennbar; **sep·a·rate 1.** (sich) trennen; (auf-, ein-, zer)teilen (*into* in *acc*); **2.** getrennt, separat; einzeln; **sep·a·ra·tion** Trennung *f*; (Auf-, Ein-, Zer)Teilung *f*

Sept *abbr of* **September** Sept., September *m*

Sep·tem·ber September *m*

sep·tic MED vereitert, septisch

se·quel Nachfolgeroman *m*, -film *m*, Fortsetzung *f*; *fig* Folge *f*; Nachspiel *n*

se·quence (Aufeinander-, Reihen)Folge *f*; *film*, TV Sequenz *f*, Szene *f*; **~ of tenses** LING Zeitenfolge *f*

ser·e·nade MUS **1.** Serenade *f*, Ständchen *n* **2.** j-m ein Ständchen bringen

se·rene klar; heiter; gelassen

ser·geant MIL Feldwebel *m*; (Polizei-) Wachtmeister *m*

se·ri·al 1. Fortsetzungsroman *m*; (Rundfunk-, Fernseh)Serie *f* **2.** serienmäßig, Serien..., Fortsetzungs...

se·ries Serie *f*, Reihe *f*, Folge *f*; (Buch-) Reihe *f*; (Rundfunk-, Fernseh)Serie *f*, Sendereihe *f*

se·ri·ous ernst, ernsthaft; ernstlich; schwer (*illness*, *damage*, *crime etc*); *be ~* es ernst meinen (*about* mit)

se·ri·ous·ness Ernst *m*, Ernsthaftigkeit *f*; Schwere *f*

ser·mon REL Predigt *f*; F Moral-, Strafpredigt *f*

ser·pen·tine gewunden, kurvenreich

ser·rat·ed zackig, gezackt

se·rum MED Serum *n*

ser·vant Diener(in) (*a. fig*); Dienstmädchen *n*; → *civil servant*

serve 1. *v/t* j-m, s-m Land *etc* dienen; *Dienstzeit* (*a.* MIL) ableisten, *Amtszeit etc* durchlaufen; *j-n, et.* versorgen (*with* mit); *Essen* servieren; *Alkohol* ausschenken; *j-n* (*im Laden*) bedienen; JUR *Strafe* verbüßen; *e-m Zweck* dienen; *e-n Zweck* erfüllen; JUR *Vorladung etc* zustellen (*on s.o.* j-m); *tennis etc*: aufschlagen; *are you being ~d?* werden Sie schon bedient?; (*it*) *~s him right* F (das) geschieht ihm ganz recht; *v/i esp* MIL dienen; servieren; dienen (*as, for* als); *tennis etc*: aufschlagen; *XY to ~ tennis etc*: Aufschlag XY; *~ on a committee* e-m Ausschuss angehören **2.** *tennis etc*: Aufschlag *m*

serv·er *tennis etc*: Aufschläger(in);

GASTR Servierlöffel *m*

ser·vice 1. Dienst *m* (*to* an *dat*); Dienstleistung *f*; (*Post-, Staats-, Telefon- etc*-) Dienst *m*; (*Zug- etc*)Verkehr *m*; ECON Service *m*, Kundendienst *m*; Bedienung *f*; Betrieb *m*; REL Gottesdienst *m*; TECH Wartung *f*, MOT *a.* Inspektion *f*; (*Tee- etc*)Service *n*; JUR Zustellung *f* (*e-r Vorladung*); *tennis etc*: Aufschlag *m*; *pl* MIL Streitkräfte *pl* **2.** TECH warten

ser·vice·a·ble brauchbar; strapazierfähig

ser·vice| ar·e·a MOT (Autobahn)Raststätte *f*; **~ charge** Bedienung *f*, Bedienungszuschlag *m*; **~ sta·tion** Tankstelle *f*; (Reparatur)Werkstatt *f*

ser·vi·ette *esp Br* Serviette *f*

ser·vile sklavisch (*a. fig*); servil, unterwürfig

serv·ing Portion *f*

ser·vi·tude Knechtschaft *f*; Sklaverei *f*

ses·sion Sitzung *f*; Sitzungsperiode *f*; *be in ~* JUR, PARL tagen

set 1. *v/t* setzen, stellen, legen; *in e-n Zustand* versetzen; veranlassen (*doing* zu tun); TECH einstellen, *Uhr* stellen (*by* nach), *Wecker* stellen (*for* auf *acc*); *Tisch* decken; *Preis, Termin etc* festsetzen, festlegen; *Rekord* aufstellen; *Edelstein* fassen (*in* in *dat*); *Ring etc* besetzen (*with* mit); *Flüssigkeit* erstarren lassen; *Haar* legen; *Knochen* einrenken, einrichten; MUS vertonen; PRINT absetzen; *Aufgabe, Frage* stellen; **~ at ease** beruhigen; **~ an example** ein Beispiel geben; **~ s.o. free** j-n freilassen; **~ going** in Gang setzen; **~ s.o. thinking** j-m zu denken geben; **~ one's hopes on** s-e Hoffnung setzen auf (*acc*); **~ s.o.'s mind at rest** j-n beruhigen; **~ great** (*little*) **store by** großen (geringen) Wert legen auf (*acc*); *the novel is ~ in* der Roman spielt in (*dat*); *v/i* ASTR untergehen; fest werden, erstarren; HUNT vorstehen; **~ about doing s.th.** sich daranmachen, et. zu tun; **~ about s.o.** F über j-n herfallen; **~ aside** beiseitelegen; JUR *Urteil etc* aufheben; **~ back** verzögern; *j-n, et.* zurückwerfen (*by two months* um zwei Monate); **~ in** einsetzen; **~ off** aufbrechen, sich aufmachen; hervorheben, betonen; *et.* auslösen; **~ out** arrangieren, herrichten; aufbrechen, sich aufmachen; **~**

out to do s.th. sich daranmachen, et. zu tun; **~** *up* errichten; *Gerät etc* aufbauen; *Firma etc* gründen; *et.* auslösen, verursachen; *j-n* versorgen (**with** mit); sich niederlassen; **~** *o.s. up as* sich ausgeben für **2.** *adj* festgesetzt, festgelegt; F bereit, fertig; starr (*smile etc*); **~** *lunch* or *meal Br* Menü *n*; **~** *phrase* feststehender Ausdruck; *be* **~** *on doing s.th.* (fest) entschlossen sein, et. zu tun; *be all* **~** F startklar sein **3.** Satz *m*; (*Möbel- etc*)Garnitur *f*, (*Tee- etc*)Service *n*; (*Fernseh-*, *Rundfunk-*)Apparat *m*, (-)Gerät *n*; THEA Bühnenbild *n*; *film*, TV Set *n*, *m*; *tennis etc*: Satz *m*; (Personen)Kreis *m*, Clique *f*; (*Kopf- etc*)Haltung *f*; *have a shampoo and* **~** sich die Haare waschen und legen lassen

set·back Rückschlag *m* (**to** für)

set·square *Br* Winkel *m*, Zeichendreieck *n*

set·tee Sofa *n*

set the·o·ry MATH Mengenlehre *f*

set·ting ASTR Untergang *m*; TECH Einstellung *f*; Umgebung *f*; *film etc*: Schauplatz *m*; (*Gold- etc*)Fassung *f*

set·ting lo·tion Haarfestiger *m*

set·tle *v/i* sich niederlassen (**on** auf *acc* or *dat*), sich setzen (**on** auf *acc*) (*a.* **~** *down*); sich niederlassen (**in** in *dat*); sich legen (*dust*); sich setzen (*coffee etc*); sich senken (*building etc*); sich beruhigen (*person, stomach etc*), sich legen (*a.* **~** *down*); sich einigen; *v/t j-n, Nerven etc* beruhigen; vereinbaren; *Frage etc* klären, entscheiden; *Streit etc* beilegen; *Land* besiedeln; *Leute* ansiedeln; *Rechnung* begleichen, bezahlen; *Konto* ausgleichen; *Schaden* regulieren; *s-e Angelegenheiten* in Ordnung bringen; **~** *o.s.* sich niederlassen (**on** auf *acc* or *dat*), sich setzen (**on** auf *acc*); *that* **~** *s it* damit ist der Fall erledigt; *that's* **~** *d then* das ist also klar; **~** *back* sich (gemütlich) zurücklehnen; **~** *down* → *v/i*; sesshaft werden; **~** *down to* sich widmen (*dat*); **~** *for* sich zufriedengeben *or* begnügen mit; **~** *in* sich einleben *or* eingewöhnen; **~** *on* sich einigen auf (*acc*); **~** *up* (be)zahlen; abrechnen (**with** mit)

set·tled fest (*ideas etc*); geregelt (*life*); beständig (*weather*)

set·tle·ment Vereinbarung *f*; Klärung *f*;

Beilegung *f*; Einigung *f*; Siedlung *f*; Besiedlung *f*; Begleichung *f*, Bezahlung *f*; *reach a* **~** sich einigen

set·tler Siedler(in)

sev·en 1. sieben **2.** Sieben *f*

sev·en·teen 1. siebzehn **2.** Siebzehn *f*

sev·en·teenth siebzehnte(r, -s)

sev·enth 1. siebente(r, -s), siebte(r, -s) **2.** Siebentel *n*, Siebtel *n*

sev·enth·ly siebentens, siebtens

sev·en·ti·eth siebzigste(r, -s)

sev·en·ty 1. siebzig **2.** Siebzig *f*

sev·er durchtrennen; abtrennen; *Beziehungen* abbrechen; (zer)reißen

sev·er·al mehrere

sev·er·al·ly einzeln, getrennt

se·vere schwer (*injuries, setback etc*); stark (*pain*); hart, streng (*winter*); streng (*person, discipline etc*); scharf (*criticism etc*); **se·ver·i·ty** Schwere *f*; Stärke *f*; Härte *f*; Strenge *f*; Schärfe *f*

sew nähen

sew·age Abwasser *n*

sew·age works Kläranlage *f*

sew·er Abwasserkanal *m*

sew·er·age Kanalisation *f*

sew·ing 1. Nähen *n*; Näharbeit *f* **2.** Näh...; **~** *ma·chine* Nähmaschine *f*

sex Geschlecht *n*; Sexualität *f*; Sex *m*; Geschlechtsverkehr *m*

sex·ism Sexismus *m*

sex·ist 1. sexistisch **2.** Sexist(in)

sex·ton Küster *m* (und Totengräber *m*)

sex·u·al sexuell, Sexual..., geschlechtlich, Geschlechts...; **~** *har·ass·ment* sexuelle Belästigung; **~** *in·ter·course* Geschlechtsverkehr *m*

sex·u·al·i·ty Sexualität *f*

sex·y F sexy, aufreizend

shab·by schäbig

shack Hütte *f*, Bude *f*; F *contp* Schuppen *m*

shack·les Fesseln *pl*, Ketten *pl* (*both a. fig*)

shade 1. Schatten *m* (*a. fig*); (*Lampen-*)Schirm *m*; Schattierung *f*; Rouleau *n*; *fig* Nuance *f*; *a.* **~** *fig* ein kleines bisschen, e-e Spur **2.** abschirmen (**from** gegen); schattieren; **~** *off* allmählich übergehen (**into** in *acc*)

shad·ow 1. Schatten *m* (*a. fig*); *there's not a* or *the* **~** *of a doubt about it* daran besteht nicht der geringste Zweifel **2.** *j-n* beschatten

shad·ow·y schattig, dunkel; verschwommen, vage, schemenhaft

shad·y schattig; Schatten spendend; F zwielichtig, fragwürdig

shaft (*Pfeil- etc*)Schaft *m*; (*Hammer- etc*)Stiel *m*; TECH Welle *f*; (*Aufzugs-, Bergwerks- etc*)Schacht *m*; (*Sonnen- etc*)Strahl *m*

shag·gy zottig, struppig

shake 1. *v/t* schütteln; rütteln an (*dat*); erschüttern; **~ hands** sich die Hand geben *or* schütteln; *v/i* zittern, beben, wackeln (**with** vor *dat*); **~ down** herunterschütteln; durchsuchen, F filzen; *Br* F kampieren; **~ off** abschütteln; *Erkältung etc* loswerden; **~ up** *Kissen etc* aufschütteln; *Flasche, Flüssigkeit* (durch-)schütteln; *fig* erschüttern **2.** Schütteln *n*; F Milchshake *m*; **~ of the head** Kopfschütteln *n*

shake·down F Erpressung *f*; Durchsuchung *f*, Filzung *f*; *Br* (Not)Lager *n*

shak·en *a.* **~ up** erschüttert

shak·y wack(e)lig; zitt(e)rig

shall *v/aux future*: ich werde, *wir* werden; *in questions*: soll *ich* ...?, sollen *wir* ...?; **~ we go?** gehen wir?

shal·low seicht, flach, *fig a.* oberflächlich; **shal·lows** seichte *or* flache Stelle, Untiefe *f*

sham 1. Farce *f*; Heuchelei *f* **2.** unecht, falsch; vorgetäuscht, geheuchelt **3.** *v/t Mitgefühl etc* vortäuschen, heucheln; *Krankheit etc* simulieren; *v/i* sich verstellen, heucheln; **he's only ~ming** er ist nur so

sham·bles F Schlachtfeld *n*, wüstes Durcheinander, Chaos *n*

shame 1. Scham *f*; Schamgefühl *n*; Schande *f*; **~!** pfui!; **~ on you!** pfui!; schäm dich!; **put to ~** → **2.** beschämen; Schande machen (*dat*)

shame·faced betreten, verlegen

shame·ful beschämend; schändlich

shame·less schamlos

sham·poo 1. Shampoo *n*, Schampon *n*, Schampun *n*; Haarwäsche *f*; → **set 3 2.** *Haare* waschen; *j-m* die Haare waschen; *Teppich etc* schamponieren

shank TECH Schaft *m*; GASTR Hachse *f*

shan·ty¹ Hütte *f*, Bude *f*

shan·ty² Shanty *n*, Seemannslied *n*

shan·ty·town Elendsviertel *n*

shape 1. Form *f*; Gestalt *f*; Verfassung *f*, Zustand *m*; **in good** (**bad**) **~** in gutem (schlechtem) Zustand; **in** (**out of**) **~** SPORT (nicht) gut in Form; **take ~** *fig* Gestalt annehmen **2.** *v/t* formen; gestalten; *v/i a.* **~ up** sich *gut etc* machen

shape·less formlos; ausgebeult

shape·ly wohlgeformt

share 1. Anteil *m* (**in, of** an *dat*); *esp Br* ECON Aktie *f*; **go ~s** teilen; **have a** (**no**) **~ in** (nicht) beteiligt sein an (*dat*) **2.** *v/t* (sich) *et.* teilen (**with** mit); *a.* **~ out** verteilen (**among, between** an *acc*, unter *acc*); *v/i* teilen; **~ in** sich teilen in (*acc*)

share·hold·er *esp Br* ECON Aktionär(in)

shark ZO Hai(fisch) *m*

sharp 1. *adj* scharf (*a. fig*); spitz; abrupt; schneidend (*wind, frost, command, voice, etc*); beißend (*cold, smell etc*); stechend, heftig (*pain*); gescheit; MUS (*um e-n Halbton*) erhöht; **C ~** MUS Cis *n* **2.** *adv* scharf, abrupt; MUS zu hoch; pünktlich, genau; **at eight o'clock ~** Punkt 8 (Uhr)

sharp·en *Messer etc* schärfen, schleifen; *Bleistift etc* spitzen

sharp·en·er (*Messer- etc*)Schärfer *m*; (*Bleistift*)Spitzer *m*

sharp·ness Schärfe *f* (*a. fig*)

sharp·shoot·er Scharfschütze *m*

sharp·sight·ed scharfsichtig

sharp·wit·ted scharfsinnig

shat·ter *v/t* zerschmettern, zerschlagen; *Hoffnungen etc* zerstören; *v/i* zerspringen, zersplittern

shat·ter·ing vernichtend; erschütternd

shat·ter·proof splitterfrei

shave 1. (sich) rasieren; (glatt) hobeln; *j-n, et.* streifen **2.** Rasur *f*; **have a ~** sich rasieren; **that was a close ~** das war knapp, das ist gerade noch einmal gut gegangen!; **shav·en** kahl·geschoren

shav·er (*esp* elektrischer) Rasierapparat *m*

shav·ing 1. Rasieren *n* **2.** Rasier...; **~ bag** Kulturbeutel *m*; **~ brush** Rasierpinsel *m*; **~ cream** Rasiercreme *f*

shav·ings Späne *pl*

shawl Umhängetuch *n*; Kopftuch *n*

she 1. *pron* sie **2.** Sie *f*; ZO Weibchen *n* **3.** *adj in cpds* ZO ...weibchen *n*; **~-bear** Bärin *f*

sheaf Bündel *n*; AGR Garbe *f*

shear 1. scheren **2.** (**a pair of**) **~s** (e-e)

große Schere

sheath (*Schwert- etc*)Scheide *f*; Hülle *f*; *Br* Kondom *n*, *m*; **sheathe** *Schwert etc* in die Scheide stecken; TECH umhüllen, verkleiden, ummanteln

shed[1] Schuppen *m*; Stall *m*

shed[2] *Tränen etc* vergießen; *Blätter etc* verlieren; *fig Hemmungen etc* ablegen; *~ **its skin*** sich häuten; *~ **a few pounds*** ein paar Pfund abnehmen

sheen Glanz *m*

sheep ZO Schaf *n*

sheep·dog ZO Schäferhund *m*

sheep·ish verlegen

sheep·skin Schaffell *n*

sheer rein, bloß; steil, (fast) senkrecht; hauchdünn

sheet Betttuch *n*, (Bett)Laken *n*, Leintuch *n*; (*Glas-, Metall- etc*)Platte *f*; Blatt *n*, Bogen *n*; weite (*Eis- etc*)Fläche; *the rain was coming down in ~s* es regnete in Strömen

sheet light·ning Wetterleuchten *n*

shelf (*Bücher-, Wand- etc*)Brett *n*, (-)Bord *n*; GEOGR Riff *n*; *pl* Regal *n*; *off the ~* gleich zum Mitnehmen

shell 1. (*Austern-, Eier-, Nuss- etc*) Schale *f*; BOT (*Erbsen- etc*)Hülse *f*; (*Muschel f*; (*Schnecken*)Haus *n*; ZO Panzer *m*; MIL Granate *f*; (Geschoss-, Patronen)Hülse *f*; Patrone *f*; TECH Rumpf *m*, Gerippe *n*, ARCH *a.* Rohbau *m* **2.** schälen, enthülsen; mit Granaten beschießen

shell·fish ZO Schal(en)tier *n*

shel·ter 1. Zuflucht *f*, Schutz *m*; Unterkunft *f*, Obdach *n*; MIL Unterstand *m*; *run for~* Schutz suchen; *take~* sich unterstellen (*under* unter *dat*); *bus ~* Wartehäuschen *n* **2.** *v/t* schützen (*from* vor *dat*); *v/i* sich unterstellen

shelve *v/t Bücher* in ein Regal stellen; *Plan etc* aufschieben, zurückstellen; *v/i* sanft abfallen (*garden etc*)

shep·herd 1. Schäfer *m*, Hirt *m* **2.** *j-n* führen

sher·iff Sheriff *m*

shield 1. Schild *m* **2.** *j-n* (be)schützen (*from* vor *dat*); *j-n* decken

shift 1. *v/t et.* bewegen, schieben, *Möbelstück a.* (ver)rücken; *Schuld etc* (ab-) schieben (*onto* auf *acc*); *~ **gear(s)*** MOT schalten; *v/i* sich bewegen; umspringen (*wind*); *fig* sich verlagern *or*

verschieben *or* wandeln; MOT schalten (*into, to* in *acc*); *~ **from one foot to the other*** von e-m Fuß auf den anderen treten; *~ **on one's chair*** auf s-m Stuhl ungeduldig etc hin und her rutschen **2.** *fig* Verlagerung *f*, Verschiebung *f*, Wandel *m*; ECON Schicht *f*; *~ **key*** TECH Umschalttaste *f*; *~ **work·er*** Schichtarbeiter(in)

shift·y F verschlagen

shim·mer schimmern; flimmern

shin 1. *a.* *~bone* ANAT Schienbein *n* **2.** *~ up* hinaufklettern; *~ down* herunterklettern

shine 1. *v/i* scheinen; leuchten; glänzen (*a. fig*); *v/t Schuhe etc* polieren **2.** Glanz *m*

shin·gle[1] grober Strandkies

shin·gle[2] (Dach)Schindel *f*

shin·gles MED Gürtelrose *f*

shin·y blank, glänzend

ship 1. Schiff *n* **2.** verschiffen; ECON verfrachten, versenden

ship·ment ECON Ladung *f*; Verschiffung *f*, Verfrachtung *f*, Versand *m*

ship·own·er Reeder *m*; Schiffseigner *m*

ship·ping Schifffahrt *f*; Schiffsbestand *m*; ECON Verschiffung *f*, Verfrachtung *f*, Versand *m*

ship·wreck Schiffbruch *m*

ship·wrecked *be ~* Schiffbruch erleiden **2.** schiffbrüchig

ship·yard (Schiffs)Werft *f*

shirk sich drücken (vor *dat*)

shirk·er Drückeberger(in)

shirt Hemd *n*

shirt·sleeve 1. Hemdsärmel *m*; *in (one's) ~s* in Hemdsärmeln, hemdsärmelig **2.** hemdsärmelig

shish ke·bab GASTR Schaschlik *m*, *n*

shit V **1.** Scheiße *f* (*a. fig*); *fig* Scheiß *m* **2.** (voll)scheißen

shiv·er 1. zittern (*with* vor *dat*); **2.** Schauer *m*; *pl* MED F Schüttelfrost *m*; *the sight send ~s (up and) down my spine* bei dem Anblick überlief es mich eiskalt

shoal[1] Untiefe *f*; Sandbank *f*

shoal[2] ZO Schwarm *m*

shock[1] **1.** Schock *m* (*a.* MED); Wucht *f*; ELECTR Schlag *m*, (*a.* MED Elektro-) Schock *m*; *be in (a state of) ~* unter Schock stehen **2.** schockieren, empören; *j-m* e-n Schock versetzen

shock² (~ **of hair** Haar)Schopf m

shock ab·sorb·er TECH Stoßdämpfer m.

shock·ing schockierend, empörend, anstößig; F scheußlich

shod·dy minderwertig (goods); gemein, schäbig (trick etc)

shoe 1. Schuh m; Hufeisen n 2. Pferd beschlagen

shoe·horn Schuhanzieher m, -löffel m

shoe·lace Schnürsenkel m

shoe·mak·er Schuhmacher m, Schuster m

shoe·shine boy Schuhputzer m

shoe store (Br **shop**) Schuhgeschäft n

shoe·string Schnürsenkel m

shoot 1. v/t schießen, HUNT a. erlegen; abfeuern, abschießen; erschießen; Riegel vorschieben; j-n fotografieren, aufnehmen, Film drehen; Heroin etc spritzen; ~ **the lights** MOT bei Rot fahren; v/i schießen (**at** auf acc); jagen; fig schießen, rasen; film, TV drehen, filmen; BOT sprießen, treiben 2. BOT Trieb m; Jagd f; Jagdrevier n

shoot·er F Schießeisen n

shoot·ing 1. Schießen n; Schießerei f; Erschießung f; Anschlag m; Jagd f; film, TV Dreharbeiten pl, Aufnahmen pl 2. stechend (pain); ~ **gal·le·ry** Schießbude f; ~ **range** Schießstand m; ~ **star** ASTR Sternschnuppe f

shop 1. Br Laden m, Geschäft n; Werkstatt f; Betrieb m; **talk** ~ fachsimpeln 2. mst **go shopping** einkaufen gehen

shop as·sis·tant Br Verkäufer(in)

shop·keep·er Br Ladenbesitzer(in), Ladeninhaber(in)

shop·lift·er Ladendieb(in)

shop·lift·ing Ladendiebstahl m

shop·per Käufer(in)

shop·ping 1. Einkauf m, Einkaufen n; Einkäufe pl (items bought); **do one's** ~ Br einkaufen, (s-e) Einkäufe machen 2. Einkaufs...; ~ **bag** Einkaufsbeutel m, -tasche f; ~ **cart** Einkaufswagen m; ~ **cen·ter** (Br **cen·tre**) Einkaufszentrum n; ~ **list** Einkaufsliste f, -zettel m; ~ **mall** Einkaufszentrum n; ~ **precinct** Br Fußgängerzone f; ~ **street** Geschäfts-, Ladenstraße f

shop stew·ard ECON gewerkschaftlicher Vertrauensmann

shop·walk·er Br Aufsicht(sperson) f

shop win·dow Schaufenster n

shore¹ Küste f; (See)Ufer n; **on** ~ an Land

shore²: ~ **up** (ab)stützen

short 1. adj kurz; klein (person); kurz angebunden, barsch, schroff (**with** zu); GASTR mürbe; **be** ~ **for** die Kurzform sein von; **be** ~ **of** ... nicht genügend ... haben 2. adv plötzlich, abrupt; ~ **of** außer, außer; **cut** ~ plötzlich unterbrechen; **fall** ~ **of** et. nicht erreichen; **stop** ~ plötzlich innehalten, stutzen; **stop** ~ **of or at** zurückschrecken vor (dat); → **run** 1 3. F Kurzfilm m; ELECTR Kurze m; **called** ... **for** ~ kurz ... genannt; **in** ~ kurz(um)

short·age Knappheit f, Mangel m (**of** an dat)

short·com·ings Unzulänglichkeiten pl, Mängel pl, Fehler pl

short cut Abkürzung f; **take a** ~ (den Weg) abkürzen

short·en v/t (ab-, ver)kürzen; v/i kürzer werden

short·hand Kurzschrift f, Stenografie f

short·ly bald; barsch, schroff; mit wenigen Worten

short·ness Kürze f; Schroffheit f

shorts a. **pair of** ~ Shorts pl; (Herren)Unterhose f

short·sight·ed esp Br kurzsichtig (a. fig)

short sto·ry Kurzgeschichte f

short-tem·pered aufbrausend, hitzig

short-term ECON kurzfristig

short time ECON Kurzarbeit f

short wave ELECTR Kurzwelle f

short-wind·ed kurzatmig

shot Schuss m; Schrot(kugeln pl) m, n; SPORT Kugel f; guter etc Schütze m; soccer etc: Schuss m; basketball etc: Wurf m; tennis, golf: Schlag m; PHOT Schnappschuss m, Aufnahme f; film, TV Aufnahme f, Einstellung f; MED F Spritze f; F Schuss m (of drugs); fig F Versuch m; **a** ~ **of rum** ein Schluck Rum; **I'll have a** ~ **at it** ich probier's mal; **not by a long** ~ F noch lange nicht; → **big shot**

shot·gun Schrotflinte f

shot·gun wed·ding F Mussheirat f

shot put SPORT Kugelstoßen n

shot put·ter SPORT Kugelstoßer(in)

shoul·der 1. ANAT Schulter f; MOT Standspur f 2. schultern; Kosten, Verantwortung etc übernehmen; (mit der Schulter) stoßen; **~ bag** Schulter-, Umhängetasche f; **~ blade** ANAT Schulterblatt n; **~ strap** Träger m; Tragriemen m

shout 1. v/i rufen, schreien (*for* nach; *for help* um Hilfe); **~ at s.o.** j-n anschreien; v/t rufen, schreien **2.** Ruf m, Schrei m

shove 1. stoßen, F schubsen; *et.* schieben, stopfen **2.** Stoß m, F Schubs m

shov·el 1. Schaufel f **2.** schaufeln

show 1. v/t zeigen, vorzeigen, anzeigen; j-n bringen, führen (*to* zu); ausstellen; zeigen, *film etc a.* vorführen **to** a. bringen; v/i zu sehen sein; **be ~ing** gezeigt werden, laufen; **~ around** herumführen; **~ in** herein-, hineinführen, herein-, hineinbringen; **~ off** angeben *or* protzen (mit); vorteilhaft zur Geltung bringen; **~ out** heraus-, hinausführen, heraus-, hinausbringen; **~ round** herumführen; **~ up** v/t herauf-, hinaufführen, herauf-, hinaufbringen; sichtbar machen; j-n entlarven, bloßstellen; *et.* aufdecken; j-n in Verlegenheit bringen; v/i zu sehen sein; F aufkreuzen, auftauchen **2.** THEA *etc* Vorstellung f; Show f; *radio,* TV Sendung f; Ausstellung f; Zurschaustellung f, Demonstration f; *fig leerer* Schein; **be on ~** ausgestellt *or* zu besichtigen sein; **steal the ~ from s.o.** *fig* j-m die Schau stehlen; **make a ~ of** *Anteilnahme, Interesse etc* heucheln; **put up a poor ~** F e-e schwache Leistung zeigen; **be in charge of the whole ~** F den ganzen Laden schmeißen **3.** Muster...

show·biz F, **show busi·ness** Showbusiness n, Showgeschäft n, Unterhaltungsindustrie f

show·case Schaukasten m, Vitrine f

show·down Kraft-, Machtprobe f

show·er 1. (Regen- *etc*)Schauer m; (*Funken*)Regen m; (*Wasser-, Wort- etc*)Schwall m; Dusche f; (Geschenk-) Party f; **have** *or* **take a ~** duschen **2.** v/t j-n mit *et.* überschütten *or* überhäufen; v/i duschen; **~ down** niederprasseln

show jump·er SPORT Springreiter(in)

show jump·ing SPORT Springreiten n

show-off F Angeber(in)

show·room Ausstellungsraum m

show tri·al JUR Schauprozess m

show·y auffallend

shred 1. Fetzen m **2.** zerfetzen; in

(schmale) Streifen schneiden, schnitzeln, schnetzeln; in den Papier- *or* Reißwolf geben; **shred·der** Schnitzelmaschine f; Papier-, Reißwolf m

shrewd scharfsinnig; schlau

shriek 1. (gellend) aufschreien; **~ with laughter** vor Lachen kreischen **2.** (schriller) Schrei

shrill schrill; *fig* heftig, scharf, lautstark

shrimp ZO Garnele f; *fig contp* Knirps m

shrine Schrein m

shrink 1. (ein-, zusammen)schrumpfen (lassen); einlaufen; *fig* abnehmen **2.** F Klapsdoktor m

shrink·age Schrumpfung f; Einlaufen n; *fig* Abnahme f

shrink-wrap einschweißen

shriv·el schrumpfen (lassen); runz(e)lig werden (lassen)

shroud 1. Leichentuch n **2.** *fig* hüllen

Shrove Tues·day Fastnachts-, Faschingsdienstag m

shrub Strauch m, Busch m

shrub·be·ry BOT Strauch-, Buschwerk n, Gebüsch n

shrug 1. *a.* **~ one's shoulders** mit den Achseln *or* Schultern zucken **2.** Achselzucken n, Schulterzucken n

shuck BOT **1.** Hülse f, Schote f; Schale f **2.** enthülsen; schälen

shud·der 1. schaudern **2.** Schauder m

shuf·fle 1. v/t *Karten* mischen; *Papiere etc* umordnen, hierhin oder dorthin legen; **~ one's feet** schlurfen; v/i schlurfen; *Karten* mischen **2.** Schlurfen n, schlurfender Gang; Mischen n

shun j-n, *et.* meiden

shunt *Zug etc* rangieren, verschieben; *a.* **~ off** F j-n abschieben (*to* in *acc*, nach)

shut (sich) schließen; zumachen; **~ down** *Fabrik etc* schließen; **~ off** *Wasser, Gas, Maschine etc* abstellen; **~ up** einschließen; einsperren; *Geschäft* schließen; **~ up!** F halt die Klappe!

shut·ter Fensterladen m; PHOT Verschluss m

shut·tle 1. Pendelverkehr m; (*Raum-*) Fähre f, (-)Transporter m; TECH Schiffchen n **2.** hin- und herbefördern

shut·tle·cock SPORT Federball m

shut·tle ser·vice Pendelverkehr m

shy 1. scheu; schüchtern **2.** scheuen (*at* vor *dat*); **~ away from** *fig* zurückschrecken vor (*dat*)

shy·ness Scheu *f*; Schüchternheit *f*

sick 1. krank; *be ~ esp Br* sich übergeben; *she was or felt ~* ihr war schlecht; *get ~* krank werden; *be off ~* krank (geschrieben) sein; *report ~* sich krank melden; *be ~ of s.th.* F et. satthaben; *it makes me ~* F mir wird schlecht davon, *a. fig* es ekelt *or* widert mich an **2.** *the ~* die Kranken *pl*

sick·bed Krankenbett *n*

sick·en *v/t j-n* anekeln, anwidern; *v/i esp Br* krank werden

sick·le ['sɪkl] Sichel *f*

sick leave: *be on ~* krank (geschrieben) sein, wegen Krankheit fehlen

sick·ly kränklich; ungesund; matt; widerlich (*smell etc*)

sick·ness Krankheit *f*; Übelkeit *f*; *~ ben·e·fit* Krankengeld *n*

side 1. Seite *f*; *esp Br* SPORT Mannschaft *f*; *~ by ~* nebeneinander; *take ~s* Partei ergreifen (*with* für; *against* gegen); **2.** Seiten...; Neben... **3.** Partei ergreifen (*with* für; *against* gegen)

side·board Anrichte *f*, Sideboard *n*

side·car MOT Bei-, Seitenwagen *m*

side dish GASTR Beilage *f*

side·long seitlich; Seiten...; *~ glance* Seitenblick *m*

side street Nebenstraße *f*

side·swipe Seitenhieb *m*

side·track *j-n* ablenken; F *et.* abbiegen; RAIL *etc* rangieren, verschieben

side·walk Bürgersteig *m*, Gehsteig *m*

side·walk ca·fé Straßencafé *n*

side·ways seitlich; seitwärts, nach der *or* zur Seite

sid·ing RAIL Nebengleis *n*

si·dle: *~ up to s.o.* sich an j-n heranschleichen

siege MIL Belagerung *f*; *lay ~ to* belagern (*a. fig*)

sieve 1. Sieb *n* **2.** (durch)sieben

sift (durch)sieben; *a. ~ through fig* sichten, durchsehen, prüfen

sigh 1. seufzen **2.** Seufzer *m*

sight 1. Sehvermögen *n*, Sehkraft *f*, Augenlicht *n*; Anblick *m*; Sicht(weite) *f*; *pl* Visier *n*; Sehenswürdigkeiten *pl*; *at ~*, *on ~* sofort; *at the ~ of* beim Anblick von (*or gen*); *at first ~* auf den ersten Blick; *catch ~ of* erblicken; *know by ~* vom Sehen kennen; *lose ~ of* aus den Augen verlieren; *be (with)in*

~ in Sicht sein (*a. fig*) **2.** sichten

sight-read MUS vom Blatt singen *or* spielen

sight·see·ing Sightseeing *n*, Besichtigung *f* von Sehenswürdigkeiten; *go ~* sich die Sehenswürdigkeiten anschauen; *~ tour* Sightseeingtour *f*, Besichtigungstour *f*, (Stadt)Rundfahrt *f*

sight·se·er Tourist(in)

sight test Sehtest *m*

sign 1. Zeichen *n*; (*Hinweis-, Warn- etc*) Schild *n*; *fig* (An)Zeichen *n* **2.** unterschreiben, unterzeichnen; *Scheck* ausstellen; *~ in* sich eintragen; *~ out* sich austragen

sig·nal 1. Signal *n* (*a. fig*); Zeichen *n* (*a. fig*) **2.** (ein) Zeichen geben; signalisieren

sig·na·to·ry Unterzeichner(in)

sig·na·ture Unterschrift *f*; Signatur *f*; *~ tune* *radio*, TV Kennmelodie *f*

sign·board (Aushänge)Schild *n*

sign·er Unterzeichnete *m*, *f*

sig·net Siegel *n*

sig·nif·i·cance Bedeutung *f*, Wichtigkeit *f*; **sig·nif·i·cant** bedeutend, bedeutsam, wichtig; bezeichnend

sig·ni·fy bedeuten; andeuten

sign·post Wegweiser *m*

si·lence 1. Stille *f*; Schweigen *n*; *~!* Ruhe!; *in ~* schweigend; *reduce to ~* → **2.** zum Schweigen bringen

si·lenc·er TECH Schalldämpfer *m*; *Br* MOT Auspufftopf *m*

si·lent still; schweigend; schweigsam; stumm; *~ part·ner* ECON stiller Teilhaber

sil·i·con CHEM Silizium *n*

sil·i·cone CHEM Silikon *n*

silk 1. Seide *f* **2.** Seiden...

silk·worm ZO Seidenraupe *f*

silk·y seidig; samtig (*voice*)

sill (*Fenster*)Brett *n*

sil·ly 1. albern, töricht, dumm **2.** F Dummerchen *n*

sil·ver 1. Silber *n* **2.** silbern, Silber... **3.** versilbern

sil·ver-plat·ed versilbert

sil·ver·ware Tafelsilber *n*

sil·ver·y silberglänzend; *fig* silberhell

sim·i·lar ähnlich (*to dat*)

sim·i·lar·i·ty Ähnlichkeit *f*

sim·i·le Gleichnis *n*, Vergleich *m*

sim·mer leicht kochen, köcheln; *~ with*

fig kochen vor (*rage etc*), fiebern vor (*excitement etc*); **~ down** F sich beruhigen, F sich abregen

sim·per albern *or* affektiert lächeln

sim·ple einfach, schlicht; leicht; dumm, einfältig; naiv; *the~fact is that ...* es ist einfach e-e Tatsache, dass ...

sim·ple-mind·ed dumm; naiv

sim·plic·i·ty Einfachheit *f*, Schlichtheit *f*; Dummheit *f*; Naivität *f*

sim·pli·fi·ca·tion Vereinfachung *f*

sim·pli·fy vereinfachen

sim·ply einfach; bloß, nur

sim·u·late vortäuschen; MIL, TECH simulieren

sim·ul·ta·ne·ous simultan, gleichzeitig

sin 1. Sünde *f* 2. sündigen

since 1. *adv a.* ***ever ~*** seitdem, seither 2. *prp* seit (*dat*) 3. *cj* seit(dem); da

sin·cere aufrichtig, ehrlich, offen

sin·cer·i·ty Aufrichtigkeit *f*; Offenheit *f*

sin·ew ANAT Sehne *f*

sin·ew·y sehnig; *fig* kraftvoll

sin·ful sündig, sündhaft

sing singen; ***~ s.th. to s.o.*** j-m et. vorsingen

singe (sich et.) ansengen *or* versengen

sing·er Sänger(in)

sing·ing Singen *n*, Gesang *m*

sin·gle 1. einzig; einzeln, Einzel...; einfach; ledig, unverheiratet; ***in ~ file*** im Gänsemarsch 2. *Br* RAIL *etc* einfache Fahrkarte, AVIAT einfaches Ticket (*both a.* ***~ ticket***); Single *f*; Single *m*, Unverheiratete *m*, *f* 3. **~ out** sich herausgreifen

sin·gle-breast·ed einreihig

sin·gle-en·gined AVIAT einmotorig

sin·gle fam·i·ly home Einfamilienhaus *n*

sin·gle fa·ther allein erziehender Vater

sin·gle-hand·ed eigenhändig, allein

sin·gle-lane MOT einspurig

sin·gle-mind·ed zielstrebig, -bewusst

sin·gle moth·er allein erziehende Mutter

sin·gle pa·rent Alleinerziehende *m*, *f*

sin·gle room Einzelzimmer *n*

sin·gles *esp tennis*: Einzel *n*; *a ~* ***match*** ein Einzel; *men's ~* Herreneinzel *n*; *women's ~* Dameneinzel *n*

sin·glet *Br* ärmelloses Unterhemd *or* Trikot

sin·gle-track eingleisig, einspurig

sin·gu·lar 1. einzigartig, einmalig 2. LING Singular *m*, Einzahl *f*

sin·is·ter finster, unheimlich

sink 1. *v/i* sinken, untergehen; sich senken; **~ in** eindringen (*a. fig*); *v/t* versenken; *Brunnen etc* bohren; *Zähne etc* vergraben (*into* in *acc*); 2. Spülbecken *n*, Spüle *f*; Waschbecken *n*

sin·ner Sünder(in)

sip 1. Schlückchen *n* 2. *v/t* nippen an (*dat*) *or* von; schlückchenweise trinken; *v/i* nippen (*at* an *dat or* von)

sir mein Herr; *Dear Sir or Madam* Sehr geehrte Damen und Herren (*address in letters*)

sire ZO Vater *m*, Vatertier *n*

si·ren Sirene *f*

sis·sy F Weichling *m*

sis·ter Schwester *f*; *Br* MED Oberschwester *f*; REL (Ordens)Schwester *f*

sis·ter-hood Schwesternschaft *f*

sis·ter-in-law Schwägerin *f*

sis·ter·ly schwesterlich

sit *v/i* sitzen; sich setzen; tagen; *v/t* j-n setzen; *esp Br Prüfung* ablegen, machen; **~ down** sich setzen; **~ for** *Br Prüfung* ablegen, machen; **~ in** ein Sit-in veranstalten; an e-m Sit-in teilnehmen; **~ in for** j-n vertreten; **~ in on** als Zuhörer teilnehmen an (*dat*); **~ on** sitzen auf (*dat*) (*a. fig*); **~ on a committee** e-m Ausschuss angehören; **~ out** das Ende (*gen*) abwarten; *Krise etc* aussitzen; **~ up** sich *or* j-n aufrichten *or* aufsetzen; aufrecht sitzen; aufbleiben

sit·com → situation comedy

sit-down *a.* **~ strike** Sitzstreik *m*; *a.* **~ demonstration** *or* F **demo** Sitzblockade *f*

site Platz *m*, Ort *m*, Stelle *f*; (*Ausgrabungs*)Stätte *f*; Baustelle *f*

sit-in Sit-in *n*, Sitzstreik *m*

sit·ting Sitzung *f*

sit·ting room *esp Br* Wohnzimmer *n*

sit·u·at·ed: *be* **~** liegen, gelegen sein

sit·u·a·tion Lage *f*, Situation *f*; **~ com·e·dy** TV *etc* Situationskomödie *f*

six 1. sechs 2. Sechs *f*

six·teen 1. sechzehn 2. Sechzehn *f*

six·teenth sechzehnte(r, -s)

sixth 1. sechste(r, -s) 2. Sechstel *n*

sixth·ly sechstens

six·ti·eth sechzigste(r, -s)

six·ty 1. sechzig **2.** Sechzig *f*

size 1. Größe *f*, *fig a*. Ausmaß *n*, Umfang *m* **2.** ~ *up* F abschätzen

siz(e)·a·ble beträchtlich

siz·zle brutzeln

skate 1. Schlittschuh *m*; Rollschuh *m* **2.** Schlittschuh laufen, eislaufen; Rollschuh laufen

skate·board Skateboard *n*

skat·er Eisläufer(in), Schlittschuhläufer(in); Rollschuhläufer(in)

skat·ing Eislaufen *n*, Schlittschuhlaufen *n*; Rollschuhlaufen *n*; *free* ~ Kür *f*, Kürlauf *m*; ~ *rink* (Kunst)Eisbahn *f*; Rollschuhbahn *f*

skel·e·ton Skelett *n*, Gerippe *n*

skep·tic Skeptiker(in)

skep·ti·cal skeptisch

sketch 1. Skizze *f*; THEA *etc* Sketch *m* **2.** skizzieren

skew·er 1. (Brat)Spieß *m* **2.** (auf)spießen

ski 1. Ski *m* **2.** Ski... **3.** Ski fahren *or* laufen

skid 1. MOT rutschen, schleudern **2.** MOT Rutschen *n*, Schleudern *n*; TECH Kufe *f*

skid mark(s) MOT Bremsspur *f*

ski·er Skifahrer(in), Skiläufer(in)

ski goggles Skibrille *f*

ski·ing Skifahren *n*, Skilaufen *n*, Skisport *m*

ski jump (Sprung)Schanze *f*

ski jump·er Skispringer *m*

ski jump·ing Skispringen *n*

skil·ful *Br* → *skillful*

ski lift Skilift *m*

skill Geschicklichkeit *f*, Fertigkeit *f*

skilled geschickt (*at*, *in* in *dat*)

skilled work·er Facharbeiter(in)

skill·ful geschickt

skim Fett *etc* abschöpfen (*a*. ~ *off*); Milch entrahmen; (hin)gleiten über (*acc*); *a*. ~ *over*, ~ *through* Bericht *etc* überfliegen

skim(med) milk Magermilch *f*

skimp *a*. ~ *on* sparen an (*dat*)

skimp·y dürftig; knapp

skin 1. ANAT Haut *f*; ZO Fell *n*; BOT Schale *f* **2.** *Tier* abhäuten; *Zwiebel etc* schälen; *sich das Knie etc* aufschürfen

skin-deep (nur) oberflächlich

skin div·ing Sporttauchen *n*

skin·flint Geizhals *m*

skin·ny F dürr, mager

skin·ny-dip F nackt baden

skip 1. *v/i* hüpfen, springen; seilhüpfen, seilspringen; *v/t et.* überspringen, aus lassen **2.** Hüpfer *m*

skip·per MAR, SPORT Kapitän *m*

skir·mish Geplänkel *n*

skirt 1. Rock *m* **2.** *a*. ~ *(a)round* umgeben; *Problem etc* umgehen

skirt·ing board *Br* Scheuerleiste *f*

ski| run Skipiste *f*; ~ *tow* Schlepplift *m*

skit·tle Kegel *m*

skulk sich herumdrücken, herumschleichen

skull ANAT Schädel *m*

skul(l)·dug·ge·ry F fauler Zauber

skunk ZO Skunk *m*, Stinktier *n*

sky *a*. *skies* Himmel *m*

sky·jack *Flugzeug* entführen

sky·jack·er Flugzeugentführer(in)

sky·lark ZO Feldlerche *f*

sky·light Dachfenster *n*

sky·line Skyline *f*, Silhouette *f*

sky·rock·et F hochschnellen, in die Höhe schießen

sky·scrap·er Wolkenkratzer *m*

slab (*Stein- etc*)Platte *f*; dickes Stück

slack 1. locker; ECON flau; *fig* lax, lasch, nachlässig **2.** bummeln; ~ *off*, ~ *up fig* nachlassen, (*person a*.) abbauen

slack·en *v/t* lockern; verringern; ~ *speed* langsamer werden; *v/i* locker werden; *a*. ~ *off* nachlassen

slacks F Hose *f*

slag TECH Schlacke *f*

sla·lom SPORT Slalom *m*

slam 1. *a*. ~ *shut* zuschlagen, F zuknallen; *a*. ~ *down* F et. knallen (*on* auf *acc*); ~ *on the brakes* F MOT auf die Bremse steigen **2.** Zuschlagen *n*; Knall *m*

slan·der 1. Verleumdung *f* **2.** verleumden; **slan·der·ous** verleumderisch

slang 1. Slang *m*; Jargon *m* **2.** *esp Br* *j-n* wüst beschimpfen

slant 1. schräg legen *or* liegen; sich neigen **2.** schräge Fläche; Abhang *m*; *fig* Einstellung *f*; *at* or *on a* ~ schräg

slant·ing schräg

slap 1. Klaps *m*, Schlag *m* **2.** e-n Klaps geben (*dat*); schlagen; klatschen (*down on* auf *acc*; *against* gegen)

slap·stick THEA Slapstick *m*, Klamauk *m*; ~ *com·e·dy* Slapstickkomödie *f*

slash 1. auf-, zerschlitzen; *Preise* drastisch herabsetzen; *Ausgaben etc* dras-

tisch kürzen; **~ at** schlagen nach **2.**
Hieb *m*; Schlitz *m*

slate 1. Schiefer *m*; Schiefertafel *f*; POL
Kandidatenliste *f* **2.** mit Schiefer decken; *j-n* vorschlagen (**for, to be** als);
et. planen (**for** für)

slaugh·ter 1. Schlachten *n*; *fig* Blutbad
n, Gemetzel *n* **2.** schlachten; *fig* niedermetzeln; **slaugh·ter·house** Schlacht-
haus *n*, Schlachthof *m*

Slav 1. Slawe *m*, Slawin *f* **2.** slawisch

slave 1. Sklave *m*, Sklavin *f* (*a. fig*) **2.** *a.* **~
away** sich abplagen, F schuften

slav·er geifern, sabbern

sla·ve·ry Sklaverei *f*

slav·ish sklavisch

sleaze unsaubere Machenschaften;
Kumpanei *f*; F POL Filz *m*

slea·zy schäbig, heruntergekommen;
anrüchig

sled 1. (*a.* Rodel)Schlitten *m* **2.** Schlitten
fahren, rodeln

sledge *Br* → **sled**

sledge·ham·mer TECH Vorschlagham-
mer *m*

sleek 1. glatt, glänzend; geschmeidig;
MOT schnittig **2.** glätten

sleep 1. Schlaf *m*; *I couldn't get to* **~** ich
konnte nicht einschlafen; *go to* **~** einschlafen (F *a. leg etc*); *put to* **~** Tier einschläfern **2.** *v/i* schlafen; **~ late** lang *or*
länger schlafen; **~ on** *Problem etc* über-
schlafen; **~ with s.o.** mit j-m schlafen;
v/t Schlafgelegenheit bieten für

sleep·er Schlafende *m*, *f*, Schläfer(in);
Br RAIL Schwelle *f*; RAIL Schlafwagen *m*

sleep·ing bag Schlafsack *m*

Sleep·ing Beau·ty Dornröschen *n*

sleep·ing| car Schlafwagen *m*; **~
part·ner** *Br* ECON stiller Teilhaber; **~
pill** PHARM Schlaftablette *f*, -mittel *n*;
~ sick·ness MED Schlafkrankheit *f*

sleep·less schlaflos

sleep·walk·er Schlafwandler(in)

sleep·y schläfrig, müde; verschlafen

sleep·y·head F Schlafmütze *f*

sleet 1. Schneeregen *m*; Graupelschau-
er *m* **2.** *it's~ing* es gibt Schneeregen; es
graupelt

sleeve Ärmel *m*; TECH Manschette *f*,
Muffe *f*; *Br* (*Platten*)Hülle *f*

sleeve·less ärmellos

sleigh (*esp* Pferde)Schlitten *m*

sleight of hand Fingerfertigkeit *f*; *fig*

(Taschenspieler)Trick *m*

slen·der schlank; *fig* mager, dürftig;
schwach (*hope etc*)

slice 1. Scheibe *f*, Stück *n*; *fig* Anteil *m*
(*of* an *dat*); **2.** *a.* **~ up** in Scheiben *or* Stücke schneiden; **~ off** *Stück* abschneiden
(**from** von)

slick 1. gekonnt; geschickt; raffiniert;
glatt (*road etc*) **2.** F (*Öl*)Teppich *m* **3.**
~ down *Haar* glätten, F anklatschen

slick·er Regenmantel *m*

slide 1. gleiten (lassen); rutschen;
schlüpfen; schieben; *let things* **~** *fig·*
die Dinge schleifen lassen **2.** Gleiten
n, Rutschen *n*; Rutsche *f*, Rutschbahn
f; TECH Schieber *m*; PHOT Dia *n*; Ob-
jektträger *m*; (*Erd- etc*)Rutsch *m*; *Br*
(*Haar*)Spange *f*; **~ rule** Rechenschie-
ber *m*; **~ tack·le** *soccer*: Grätsche *f*

slid·ing door Schiebetür *f*

slight 1. leicht, gering(fügig), unbedeutend **2.** beleidigen, kränken **3.** Beleidigung *f*, Kränkung *f*

slim 1. schlank; *fig* gering **2.** *a.* **be slimming, be on a slimming diet** e-e
Schlankheitskur machen, abnehmen

slime Schleim *m*

slim·y schleimig (*a. fig*)

sling 1. aufhängen; F schleudern **2.**
Schlinge *f*; Tragriemen *m*; Tragetuch
n; Schleuder *f*

slip¹ 1. *v/i* rutschen, schlittern; ausgleiten, ausrutschen; schlüpfen; *v/t* sich
losreißen von; **~ s.th. into s.o.'s hand**
j-m et. in die Hand schieben; **~ s.th.**
s.o. j-m et. zuschieben; **~ s.o.'s attention** j-m *or* j-s Aufmerksamkeit entgehen; **~ s.o.'s mind** j-m entfallen; *she
has ~ped a disk* MED sie hat e-n Bandscheibenvorfall; **~ by, ~ past** verstreichen (*time*); **~ off, ~ out of** schlüpfen
aus; **~ on** überstreifen, schlüpfen in
(*acc*) **2.** Ausgleiten *n*, (Aus)Rutschen
n; Versehen *n*; Unterrock *m*; (*Kissen*)
Bezug *m*; **~ of the tongue** Versprecher
m; *give s.o. the* **~** F j-m entwischen

slip² 1. *a.* **~ of paper** Zettel *m*

slip·case Schuber *m*

slip-on 1. *adj* **~ shoe** → **2.** Slipper *m*

slipped disk MED Bandscheibenvorfall
m

slip·per Hausschuh *m*, Pantoffel *m*

slip·per·y glatt, rutschig, glitschig

slip road *Br* MOT → **ramp**

slip·shod schlampig

slit 1. Schlitz *m* **2.** schlitzen; ~ *open* aufschlitzen

slith·er gleiten, rutschen

sliv·er (*Glas- etc*)Splitter *m*

slob·ber sabbern

slo·gan Slogan *m*

sloop MAR Schaluppe *f*

slop 1. *v/t* verschütten; *v/i* überschwappen; schwappen (*over* über *acc*); **2.** *a. pl* schlabb(e)riges Zeug; (*Tee-, Kaffee-*)Rest(e *pl*) *m*; *esp Br* Schmutzwasser *n*

slope 1. (Ab)Hang *m*; Neigung *f*, Gefälle *n* **2.** sich neigen, abfallen

slop·py schlampig; F gammelig; F rührselig

slot Schlitz *m*, (Münz)Einwurf *m*; IT Steckplatz *m*

sloth ZO Faultier *n*

slot ma·chine (Waren-, Spiel)Automat *m*

slouch 1. krumme Haltung; F latschiger Gang **2.** krumm dasitzen *or* dastehen; F latschen

slough[1]: ~ *off* Haut abstreifen, ZO sich häuten

slough[2] Sumpf *m*, Sumpfloch *n*

Slo·vak 1. slowakisch **2.** Slowake *m*, Slowakin *f*; LING Slowakisch *n*

Slo·va·ki·a Slowakei *f*

slov·en·ly schlampig

slow 1. *adj* langsam; begriffsstutzig; ECON schleppend; *be* (*ten minutes*) ~ (zehn Minuten) nachgehen **2.** *adv* langsam **3.** *v/t often* ~ *down*, ~ *up* Geschwindigkeit verringern; *v/i often* ~ *down*, ~ *up* langsamer fahren *or* gehen *or* werden

slow·coach *Br* → **slowpoke**

slow·down ECON Bummelstreik *m*

slow lane MOT Kriechspur *f*

slow mo·tion Zeitlupe *f*

slow-mov·ing kriechend (*traffic*)

slow·poke Langweiler(in)

slow·worm ZO Blindschleiche *f*

sludge Schlamm *m*

slug[1] ZO Nacktschnecke *f*

slug[2] F (*Gewehr- etc*)Kugel *f*; Schluck *m* (*whisky etc*)

slug[3] *j-m* e-n Faustschlag versetzen

slug·gish träge; ECON schleppend

sluice TECH Schleuse *f*

slum *a. pl* Slums *pl*, Elendsviertel *n or pl*

slum·ber POET **1.** schlummern **2.** *a. pl*

Schlummer *m*

slump 1. ECON stürzen (*prices*), stark zurückgehen (*sales etc*); *sit* ~*ed over* zusammengesunken sitzen über (*dat*); ~ *into a chair* sich in e-n Sessel fallen lassen **2.** ECON starker Konjunkturrückgang; ~ *in prices* Preissturz *m*

slur[1] **1.** MUS *Töne* binden; ~ *one's speech* undeutlich sprechen; lallen **2.** undeutliche Aussprache

slur[2] **1.** verleumden **2.** ~ *on s.o.'s reputation* Rufschädigung *f*

slurp F schlürfen

slush Schneematsch *m*; F Kitsch *m*

slush·y F kitschig

slut Schlampe *f*; Nutte *f*

sly gerissen,. schlau, listig; *on the* ~ heimlich

smack[1] **1.** *j-m* e-n Klaps geben; ~ *one's lips* sich (geräuschvoll) die Lippen lecken; ~ *down* F et. hinklatschen **2.** klatschendes Geräusch, Knall *m*; F Schmatz *m* (*kiss*); F Klaps *m*

smack[2]: ~ *of fig* schmecken *or* riechen nach

small 1. *adj and adv* klein; ~ *wonder* (*that*) kein Wunder, dass; *feel* ~ *fig* sich klein (und hässlich) vorkommen **2.** ~ *of the back* ANAT Kreuz *n*; ~ *ad* Kleinanzeige *f*; ~ *arms* Handfeuerwaffen *pl*; ~ *change* Kleingeld *n*; ~ *hours*: *in the* ~ in den frühen Morgenstunden

small-mind·ed engstirnig; kleinlich

small·pox MED Pocken *pl*

small print das Kleingedruckte

small talk Small Talk *m, n*, oberflächliche Konversation; *make* ~ plaudern

small-time F klein, unbedeutend; *in cpds* Schmalspur-

small town Kleinstadt *f*

smart 1. schick, fesch; smart, schlau, clever **2.** wehtun; brennen **3.** (brennender) Schmerz; ~ *al·eck* F Besserwisser(in), Klugscheißer(in)

smart·ness Schick *m*; Schlauheit *f*, Cleverness *f*

smash 1. *v/t* zerschlagen (*a.* ~ *up*); schmettern (*a.* tennis *etc*); *Aufstand etc* niederschlagen, *Drogenring etc* zerschlagen; ~ *up one's car* s-n Wagen zu Schrott fahren; *v/i* zerspringen; ~ *into* prallen an (*acc*) *or* gegen, krachen gegen **2.** Schlag *m*; tennis *etc*: Schmetterball *m*; → *smash hit, smash-up*

smash hit Hit *m*

smash-up MOT, RAIL schwerer Unfall

smear 1. Fleck *m*; MED Abstrich *m*; Verleumdung *f* **2.** (ein-, ver)schmieren; (sich) verwischen; verleumden

smell 1. *v/i* riechen (*at* an *dat*); duften; stinken; *v/t* riechen (an *dat*); **2.** Geruch *m*; Gestank *m*; Duft *m*

smell·y übel riechend, stinkend

smelt *Erz* schmelzen

smile 1. Lächeln *n* **2.** lächeln; ~ *at* j-n anlächeln, *j-m* zulächeln; *j-n, et.* belächeln, lächeln über (*acc*); ~ *to o.s.* schmunzeln

smiley Smiley *n*

smirk (selbstgefällig *or* schadenfroh) grinsen

smith Schmied *m*

smith·e·reens: *smash* (*in*)*to* ~ F in tausend Stücke schlagen *or* zerspringen

smith·y Schmiede *f*

smit·ten verliebt, F verknallt (*with* in *acc*); *be* ~ *by or with fig* gepackt werden von

smock Kittel *m*

smog Smog *m*

smoke 1. Rauch *m*; *have a* ~ eine rauchen **2.** rauchen; räuchern

smok·er Raucher(in), RAIL Raucher *m*, Raucherabteil *n*

smoke-stack Schornstein *m*

smok·ing Rauchen *n*; *no* ~ Rauchen verboten; ~ *com·part·ment* RAIL Raucher *m*, Raucherabteil *n*

smok·y rauchig; verräuchert

smooch F schmusen

smooth 1. glatt (*a. fig*); ruhig (*a. journey etc*); mild (*wine*); *fig* (aal)glatt **2.** *a.* ~ *out* glätten, glatt streichen; ~ *away Falten etc* glätten; *Schwierigkeiten etc* aus dem Weg räumen; ~ *down* glatt streichen

smoth·er ersticken

smo(u)l·der glimmen, schwelen

smudge 1. Schmutzfleck *m* **2.** (be-, ver)-schmieren; (sich) verwischen

smug selbstgefällig

smug·gle schmuggeln (*into* nach; *in* *acc*); **smug·gler** Schmuggler(in)

smut Rußflocke *f*; Schmutz *m* (*a. fig*)

smut·ty *fig* schmutzig

snack Snack *m*, Imbiss *m*; *have a* ~ e-e Kleinigkeit essen

snack bar Snackbar *f*, Imbissstube *f*

snag 1. *fig* Haken *m* **2.** mit *et.* hängen bleiben (*on* an *dat*)

snail ZO Schnecke *f*

snake ZO Schlange *f*

snap 1. *v/i* (zer)brechen, (zer)reißen; *a.* ~ *shut* zuschnappen; ~ *at* schnappen nach; *j-n* anschnauzen; ~ *out of it!* F Kopf hoch!, komm, komm!; ~ *to it!* mach fix!; *v/t* zerbrechen; PHOT F knipsen; ~ *one's fingers* mit den Fingern schnalzen; ~ *one's fingers at fig* keinen Respekt haben vor (*dat*), sich hinwegsetzen über (*acc*); ~ *off* abbrechen; ~ *up et.* schnell entschlossen kaufen; ~ *it up!* mach fix! **2.** Krachen *n*, Knacken *n*, Knall *m*; PHOT F Schnappschuss *m*; Druckknopf *m*; F Schwung *m*; *cold* ~ Kälteeinbruch *m*

snap fas·ten·er Druckknopf *m*

snap·pish *fig* bissig

snap·py modisch, schick; *make it* ~*!* F mach fix!

snap·shot PHOT Schnappschuss *m*

snare 1. Schlinge *f*, Falle *f* (*a. fig*) **2.** in der Schlinge fangen; F *et.* ergattern

snarl 1. knurren; ~ *at s.o.* j-n anknurren **2.** Knurren *n*

snatch 1. *v/t et.* packen; *Gelegenheit* ergreifen; *ein paar Stunden Schlaf etc* ergattern; ~ *s.o.'s handbag* j-m die Handtasche entreißen; *v/i* ~ *at* (schnell) greifen nach; *Gelegenheit* ergreifen **2.** *make a* ~ *at* (schnell) greifen nach; ~ *of conversation* Gesprächsfetzen *m*

sneak 1. *v/i* (sich) schleichen; *Br* F petzen; *v/t* F stibitzen **2.** *Br* F Petze *f*

sneak·er Turnschuh *m*

sneer 1. höhnisch *or* spöttisch grinsen (*at* über *acc*); spotten (*at* über *acc*); **2.** höhnisches *or* spöttisches Grinsen; höhnische *or* spöttische Bemerkung

sneeze 1. niesen **2.** Niesen *n*

snick·er kichern (*at* über *acc*)

sniff 1. *v/i* schniefen; schnüffeln (*at* an *dat*); ~ *at fig* die Nase rümpfen über (*acc*); *v/t Klebstoff etc* schnüffeln, *Kokain etc* schnupfen **2.** Schniefen *n*

snif·fle 1. schniefen **2.** Schniefen *n*; *she's got the* ~*s* F ihr läuft dauernd die Nase

snig·ger *esp Br* → *snicker*

snip 1. Schnitt *m* **2.** durchschnippeln; ~ *off* abschnippeln

snipe[1] zo Schnepfe f
snipe[2] aus dem Hinterhalt schießen (*at* auf *acc*)
snip·er Heckenschütze m
sniv·el greinen, jammern
snob Snob m; **snob·bish** versnobt
snoop: ~ *about*, ~ *around* F herumschnüffeln
snoop·er F Schnüffler(in)
snooze F 1. ein Nickerchen machen 2. Nickerchen n
snore 1. schnarchen 2. Schnarchen n
snor·kel 1. Schnorchel m 2. schnorcheln
snort 1. schnauben 2. Schnauben n
snot·ty nose F Rotznase f
snout zo Schnauze f, Rüssel m
snow 1. Schnee m (*a. sl cocaine*) 2. schneien; *be ~ed in* or *up* eingeschneit sein
snow·ball Schneeball m; ~ *fight* Schneeballschlacht f
snow·board Snowboard n; ~*ing* Snowboardfahren n
snow·bound eingeschneit
snow·capped schneebedeckt
snow·drift Schneewehe f
snow·drop BOT Schneeglöckchen n
snow·fall Schneefall m
snow·flake Schneeflocke f
snow line Schneegrenze f
snow·man Schneemann m
snow·mo·bile Schneemobil n
snow·plough Br, **snow·plow** Schneepflug m
snow·storm Schneesturm m
snow-white schneeweiß
Snow White Schneewittchen n
snow·y schneereich; verschneit
snub *j-n* brüskieren, *j-n* vor den Kopf stoßen
snub nose Stupsnase f
snuff[1] Schnupftabak m
snuff[2] *Kerze* ausdrücken, löschen; ~ *out Leben* auslöschen
snuf·fle schnüffeln, schniefen
snug gemütlich, behaglich; *clothing*: gut sitzend; eng (anliegend)
snug·gle: ~ *up to s.o.* sich an j-n kuscheln; ~ *down in bed* sich ins Bett kuscheln
so so; deshalb; → *hope* 2, *think*; *is that* ~? wirklich?; *an hour or* ~ etwa e-e Stunde; *she is tired -~ am I* sie ist müde - ich auch; ~ *far* bisher

soak *v/t* einweichen (*in* in *dat*); durchnässen; ~ *up* aufsaugen; *v/i* sickern
soak·ing *a.* ~ *wet* völlig durchnässt, F klatschnass
soap 1. Seife f; F → *soap opera* 2. (sich) einseifen
soap op·e·ra radio, TV Seifenoper f
soap·y Seifen...; seifig; *fig* F schmeichlerisch
soar (hoch) aufsteigen; hochragen; zo, AVIAT segeln, gleiten; *fig* in die Höhe schnellen (*prices etc*)
sob 1. schluchzen 2. Schluchzen n
so·ber 1. nüchtern (*a. fig*) 2. ernüchtern; ~ *up* nüchtern machen *or* werden
so-called sogenannt
soc·cer Fußball m
soc·cer hoo·li·gan Fußballrowdy m
so·cia·ble gesellig
so·cial sozial, Sozial...; gesellschaftlich, Gesellschafts...; zo gesellig; ~ *dem·ocrat* POL Sozialdemokrat(in); ~ *insur·ance* Sozialversicherung f
so·cial·ism Sozialismus m
so·cial·ist 1. Sozialist(in) 2. sozialistisch
so·cial·ize *v/i* gesellschaftlich verkehren (*with* mit); *v/t* sozialisieren
so·cial‖ sci·ence Sozialwissenschaft f; ~ *se·cu·ri·ty* Br Sozialhilfe f; *be on* ~ Sozialhilfe beziehen; ~ *ser·vic·es* esp Br Sozialeinrichtungen; ~ *work* Sozialarbeit f; ~ *work·er* Sozialarbeiter(in)
so·ci·e·ty Gesellschaft f; Verein m
so·ci·ol·o·gy Soziologie f
sock Socke f
sock·et ELECTR Steckdose f; Fassung f; (Anschluss)Buchse f; ANAT (Augen-) Höhle f
so·da Soda(wasser) n; (*Orangen- etc*)Limonade f
sod·den aufgeweicht (*ground*); durchweicht (*clothes*)
so·fa Sofa n
soft weich; sanft; leise; gedämpft (*light etc*); F leicht, angenehm, ruhig (*job etc*); alkoholfrei (*drink*); F verweichlicht
soft drink Soft Drink m, alkoholfreies Getränk
soft·en *v/t* weich machen; *Wasser* enthärten; *Ton, Licht, Stimme etc* dämpfen; ~ *up* F *j-n* weich machen; *v/i* weich(er) *or* sanft(er) *or* mild(er) werden
soft-heart·ed weichherzig
soft land·ing weiche Landung

soft·ware IT Software *f*; ~ **pack·age** IT Softwarepaket *n*

soft·y F Softie *m*, Weichling *m*

sog·gy aufgeweicht, matschig

soil[1] Boden *m*, Erde *f*

soil[2] beschmutzen, schmutzig machen

so·lar Sonnen...; ~ **en·er·gy** Solar-, Sonnenenergie *f*; ~ **pan·el** Sonnenkollektor *m*; ~ **sys·tem** Sonnensystem *n*

sol·der TECH (ver)löten

sol·dier Soldat *m*

sole[1] 1. (Fuß-, Schuh)Sohle *f* 2. besohlen

sole[2] ZO Seezunge *f*

sole[3] einzig; alleinig, Allein...

sole·ly (einzig und) allein, ausschließlich

sol·emn feierlich; ernst

so·lic·it bitten um

so·lic·i·tous besorgt (*about, for* um)

sol·id 1. fest; stabil; massiv; MATH körperlich; gewichtig, triftig (*reason etc*), stichhaltig (*argument etc*); solid(e), gründlich (*work etc*); einmütig, geschlossen; *a* ~ *hour* F e-e geschlagene Stunde 2. MATH Körper *m*; *pl* feste Nahrung

sol·i·dar·i·ty Solidarität *f*

so·lid·i·fy fest werden (lassen); *fig* (sich) festigen

so·lil·o·quy Selbstgespräch *n*, *esp* THEA Monolog *m*

sol·i·taire Solitär *m*; Patience *f*

sol·i·ta·ry einsam, (*Leben a.*) zurückgezogen, (*Ort etc a.*) abgelegen; einzig; ~ **con·fine·ment** JUR Einzelhaft *f*

so·lo MUS Solo *n*; AVIAT Alleinflug *m*

so·lo·ist MUS Solist(in)

sol·u·ble CHEM löslich; *fig* lösbar

so·lu·tion CHEM Lösung *f*; *fig* (Auf)Lösung *f*

solve Fall etc lösen

sol·vent 1. ECON zahlungsfähig 2. CHEM Lösungsmittel *n*

som·ber, *Br* **som·bre** düster, trüb(e); *fig* trübsinnig

some (irgend)ein; *pl* einige, ein paar; manche; etwas, ein wenig, ein bisschen; ungefähr; ~ **20 miles** etwa 20 Meilen; ~ **more cake** noch ein Stück Kuchen; **to** ~ **extent** bis zu e-m gewissen Grade

some·bod·y jemand

some·day eines Tages

some·how irgendwie

some·one jemand

some·place irgendwo, irgendwohin

som·er·sault 1. Salto *m*; Purzelbaum *m*; **turn a** ~ → 2. e-n Salto machen; e-n Purzelbaum schlagen

some·thing etwas; ~ **like** ungefähr

some·time irgendwann

some·times manchmal

some·what ein bisschen, ein wenig

some·where irgendwo(hin)

son Sohn *m*; ~ **of a bitch** V Scheißkerl *m*

so·na·ta MUS Sonate *f*

song MUS Lied *n*; Gesang *m*

song·bird ZO Singvogel *m*

son·ic Schall...; ~ **bang** *Br*, ~ **boom** Überschallknall *m*

son-in-law Schwiegersohn *m*

son·net Sonett *n*

so·nor·ous sonor, volltönend

soon bald; **as** ~ **as** sobald; **as** ~ **as possible** so bald wie möglich

soon·er eher, früher; ~ **or later** früher oder später; **the** ~ **the better** je eher, desto besser; **no** ~ **...** **than** kaum ... als; **no** ~ **said than done** gesagt, getan

soot Ruß *m*

soothe beruhigen, beschwichtigen (*a.* ~ **down**); *Schmerzen* lindern, mildern

sooth·ing beruhigend; lindernd

soot·y rußig

sop[1] Beschwichtigungsmittel *n* (**to** für)

sop[2]: ~ **up** aufsaugen

so·phis·ti·cat·ed anspruchsvoll, kultiviert; intellektuell; TECH raffiniert, hoch entwickelt

soph·o·more Student(in) im zweiten Jahr

sop·o·rif·ic einschläfernd

sop·ping *a.* ~ **wet** F klatschnass

sor·cer·er Zauberer *m*, Hexenmeister *m*, Hexer *m*

sor·cer·ess Zauberin *f*, Hexe *f*

sor·cer·y Zauberei *f*, Hexerei *f*

sor·did schmutzig; schäbig

sore 1. weh, wund (*a. fig*); entzündet; F *fig* sauer; **I'm** ~ **all over** mir tut alles weh; ~ **throat** Halsentzündung *f*; **have a** ~ **throat** *a.* Halsschmerzen haben 2. wunde Stelle, Wunde *f*

sor·rel[1] BOT Sauerampfer *m*

sor·rel[2] 1. ZO Fuchs *m* (*horse*) 2. rotbraun

sor·row Kummer *m*, Leid *n*, Schmerz *m*, Trauer *f*

sor·row·ful traurig, betrübt
sor·ry 1. *adj* traurig, jämmerlich; *be or feel ~ for s.o.* j-n bedauern *or* bemitleiden; *I'm ~ for her* sie tut mir leid; *I am ~ to say* ich muss leider sagen; *I'm ~* → **2.** *int* (es) tut mir leid!; Entschuldigung!, Verzeihung!; *~? esp Br* wie bitte?
sort 1. Sorte *f*, Art *f*; *~ of* F irgendwie; *of a ~, of ~s* F so etwas Ähnliches wie; *all ~s of things* alles Mögliche; *nothing of the ~* nichts dergleichen; *what ~ of (a) man is he?* wie ist er?; *be out of ~s* F nicht auf der Höhe *or* auf dem Damm sein; *be completely out of ~s* SPORT F völlig außer Form sein **2.** sortieren; *~ out* aussortieren; *Problem etc* lösen, *Frage etc* klären
SOS SOS *n*; *send an ~* ein SOS funken; *~ call or message* SOS-Ruf *m*
soul Seele *f* (*a. fig*); MUS Soul *m*
sound[1] **1.** Geräusch *n*; Laut *m*; PHYS Schall *m*; *radio*, TV Ton *m*; MUS Klang *m*, Sound *m* **2.** *v/i* (er)klingen, (er)tönen; *sich gut etc* anhören; *v/t* LING (aus)sprechen; MAR (aus)loten; MED abhorchen; *~ one's horn* MOT hupen
sound[2] gesund; intakt, in Ordnung; solid(e), stabil, sicher; klug, vernünftig (*person, advice etc*); gründlich (*training etc*); gehörig (*beating*); vernichtend (*defeat*); fest, tief (*sleep*)
sound| bar·ri·er Schallgrenze *f*, Schallmauer *f*; *~ film* Tonfilm *m*
sound·less lautlos
sound·proof schalldicht
sound·track Filmmusik *f*; Tonspur *f*
sound wave Schallwelle *f*
soup 1. Suppe *f* **2.** *~ up* F *Motor* frisieren
sour 1. sauer; *fig* mürrisch **2.** sauer werden (lassen); *fig* trüben, verbittern
source Quelle *f*, *fig a.* Ursache *f*, Ursprung *m*
south 1. Süd, Süden *m* **2.** *adj* südlich, Süd... **3.** *adv* nach Süden, südwärts
south·east 1. Südost, Südosten *m* **2.** *a.* **south·east·ern** südöstlich
south·er·ly, south·ern südlich, Süd...
south·ern·most südlichste(r, -s)
South Pole Südpol *m*
south·ward(s) südlich, nach Süden
south·west 1. Südwest, Südwesten *m* **2.** *a.* **south·west·ern** südwestlich
sou·ve·nir Souvenir *n*, Andenken *n* (*of an acc*)

sove·reign 1. Monarch(in), Landesherr(in) **2.** POL souverän
sove·reign·ty Souveränität *f*
So·vi·et HIST POL sowjetisch, Sowjet...
sow[1] (aus)säen
sow[2] ZO Sau *f*
soy bean BOT Sojabohne *f*
spa (Heil)Bad *n*
space 1. Raum *m*, Platz *m*; (Welt-)Raum *m*; Zwischenraum *m*; Zeitraum *m* **2.** *a. ~ out* in Abständen anordnen; PRINT sperren
space age Weltraumzeitalter *n*
space bar TECH Leertaste *f*
space cap·sule Raumkapsel *f*
space cen·ter (*Br* **cen·tre**) Raumfahrtzentrum *n*
space·craft (Welt)Raumfahrzeug *n*
space flight (Welt)Raumflug *m*
space·lab Raumlabor *n*
space·man F Raumfahrer *m*; Außerirdische *m*
space probe (Welt)Raumsonde *f*
space re·search (Welt)Raumforschung *f*
space·ship Raumschiff *n*
space shut·tle Raumfähre *f*, Raumtransporter *m*
space sta·tion (Welt)Raumstation *f*
space·suit Raumanzug *m*
space walk Weltraumspaziergang *m*
space·wom·an F (Welt)Raumfahrerin *f*; Außerirdische *f*
spa·cious geräumig
spade Spaten *m*; *card game*: Pik *n*, Grün *n*; *king of ~s* Pikkönig *m*; *call a ~ a ~* das Kind beim (rechten) Namen nennen
Spain Spanien *n*
span 1. Spanne *f*; Spannweite *f* **2.** *Fluss etc* überspannen; *fig* sich erstrecken über (*acc*)
span·gle 1. Flitter *m*, Paillette *f* **2.** mit Flitter *or* Pailletten besetzen; *fig* übersäen (*with* mit)
Span·iard Spanier(in)
span·iel ZO Spaniel *m*
Span·ish 1. spanisch **2.** LING Spanisch *n*; *the ~* die Spanier *pl*
spank *j-m* den Hintern versohlen
spank·ing Tracht *f* Prügel
span·ner *esp Br* Schraubenschlüssel *m*; *put or throw a ~ in the works* F *j-m* in die Quere kommen

spar *boxing*: sparren (**with** mit); *fig* sich ein Wortgefecht liefern (**with** mit)

spare 1. *j-n, et.* entbehren; *Geld, Zeit etc* übrig haben; *keine Kosten, Mühen etc* scheuen; **~ s.o. s.th.** j-m et. ersparen **2.** Ersatz..., Reserve...; überschüssig **3.** MOT Ersatz-, Reservereifen *m*; *esp Br* → **~ part** TECH Ersatzteil *n, m*

spare room Gästezimmer *n*

spare time Freizeit *f*

spar·ing sparsam; *use **~ly** sparsam umgehen mit

spark 1. Funke(n) *m* (*a. fig*) **2.** Funken sprühen

spark·ing plug *Br.* → **spark plug**

spar·kle 1. funkeln, blitzen (**with** vor *dat*); perlen (*drink*) **2.** Funkeln *n*, Blitzen *n*; **spar·kling** funkelnd, blitzend; (geist)sprühend, spritzig; **~ wine** Sekt *m*, Schaumwein *m*

spark plug MOT Zündkerze *f*

spar·row ZO Spatz *m*, Sperling *m*

spar·row·hawk ZO Sperber *m*

sparse spärlich, dünn

spasm MED Krampf *m*; Anfall *m*

spas·mod·ic MED krampfartig; *fig* sporadisch, unregelmäßig

spas·tic MED **1.** spastisch **2.** Spastiker(in)

spa·tial räumlich

spat·ter (be)spritzen

spawn 1. zo laichen; *fig* hervorbringen **2.** zo Laich *m*

speak *v/i* sprechen, reden (**to, with** mit; **about** über *acc*); sprechen (**to** vor *dat*; **about, on** über *acc*); **so to ~** sozusagen; **speaking!** TEL am Apparat!; **~ up** lauter sprechen; *v/t* sprechen, sagen; *Sprache* sprechen

speak·er Sprecher(in), Redner(in)

spear 1. Speer *m* **2.** aufspießen; durchbohren

spear·head Speerspitze *f*; MIL Angriffsspitze *f*; SPORT (Sturm-, Angriffs)Spitze *f*

spear·mint BOT Grüne Minze

spe·cial 1. besondere(r, -s); speziell; Sonder...; Spezial... **2.** Sonderbus *m*, Sonderzug *m*; *radio*, TV Sondersendung *f*; ECON F Sonderangebot *n*; **be on ~** ECON im Angebot sein

spe·cial·ist Spezialist(in), MED *a.* Facharzt *m*, Fachärztin *f* (**in** für)

spe·ci·al·i·ty *Br* → **specialty**

spe·cial·ize sich spezialisieren (*in* auf *acc*)

spe·cial·ty Spezialgebiet *n*; GASTR Spezialität *f*

spe·cies Art *f*, Spezies *f*

spe·cif·ic konkret, präzis; spezifisch, speziell, besondere(r, -s); eigen (**to** *dat*)

spe·ci·fy genau beschreiben *or* angeben *or* festlegen

spe·ci·men Exemplar *n*; Probe *f*, Muster *n*

speck kleiner Fleck, (*Staub*)Korn *n*; Punkt *m* (**on the horizon** am Horizont)

speck·led gefleckt, gesprenkelt

spec·ta·cle Schauspiel *n*; Anblick *m*; (**a pair of**) **~s** (e-e) Brille

spec·tac·u·lar 1. spektakulär **2.** große (*Fernseh- etc*)Show

spec·ta·tor Zuschauer(in)

spec·ter (*fig a. Schreck*)Gespenst *n*

spec·tral geisterhaft, gespenstisch

spec·tre *Br* → **specter**

spec·u·late spekulieren, Vermutungen anstellen (**about, on** über *acc*); ECON spekulieren (**in** mit); **spec·u·la·tion** Spekulation *f* (*a.* ECON), Vermutung *f*; **spec·u·la·tive** spekulativ, ECON *a.* Spekulations...; **spec·u·la·tor** ECON Spekulant(in)

speech Sprache *f*; Rede *f*, Ansprache *f*; **make a ~** e-e Rede halten

speech day *Br* PED (Jahres)Schlussfeier *f*

speech·less sprachlos (**with** vor *dat*)

speed 1. Geschwindigkeit *f*, Tempo *n*, Schnelligkeit *f*; TECH Drehzahl *f*; PHOT Lichtempfindlichkeit *f*; *sl* Speed *n*; MOT *etc* Gang *m*; **five-speed gearbox** Fünfganggetriebe *n*; **at a ~ of** mit e-r Geschwindigkeit von; **at full** *or* **top ~** mit Höchstgeschwindigkeit **2.** *v/i* rasen; **be ~ing** MOT zu schnell fahren; **~ up** beschleunigen, schneller werden; *v/t* rasch bringen *or* befördern; **~ up** *et.* beschleunigen

speed·boat Rennboot *n*

speed·ing MOT zu schnelles Fahren, Geschwindigkeitsüberschreitung *f*

speed lim·it MOT Geschwindigkeitsbegrenzung *f*, Tempolimit *n*

speed·om·e·ter MOT Tachometer *m, n*

speed trap MOT Radarfalle *f*

speed·y schnell, (*reply etc a.*) prompt

spell¹ *a.* **~ out** buchstabieren; (*orthographisch richtig*) schreiben

spell² Weile *f*; (*Husten- etc*)Anfall *m*; **for a ~** e-e Zeit lang; **a ~ of fine weather** e-e Schönwetterperiode; **hot ~** Hitzewelle *f*

spell³ Zauber *m* (*a. fig*)

spell·bound wie gebannt

spell·er IT Speller *m*, Rechtschreibsystem *n*; **be a good** (**bad**) **~** in Rechtschreibung gut (schlecht) sein

spell·ing Buchstabieren *n*; Rechtschreibung *f*; Schreibung *f*, Schreibweise *f*; **~ mis·take** (Recht)Schreibfehler *m*

spend *Geld* ausgeben (**on** für); *Urlaub, Zeit* verbringen

spend·ing Ausgaben *pl*

spend·thrift Verschwender(in)

spent verbraucht

sperm BIOL Sperma *n*, Samen *m*

sphere Kugel *f*; *fig* (*Einfluss- etc*)Sphäre *f*, (*Einfluss- etc*)Bereich *m*, Gebiet *n*

spher·i·cal kugelförmig

spice 1. Gewürz *n*; *fig* Würze *f* **2.** würzen

spick-and-span blitzsauber

spic·y gut gewürzt, würzig; *fig* pikant

spi·der ZO Spinne *f*

spike 1. Spitze *f*; Dorn *m*; Stachel *m*; SPORT Spike *m*, Dorn *m*; *pl* Spikes *pl*, Rennschuhe *pl* **2.** aufspießen

spill 1. *v/t* ausschütten, verschütten; **~ the beans** F alles ausplaudern, singen; → **milk** 1; *v/i fig* strömen (**out of** aus); **~ over** überlaufen; *fig* übergreifen (**into** auf *acc*); **2.** F Sturz *m*

spin 1. *v/t* drehen; *Wäsche* schleudern; *Münze* hochwerfen; *Fäden, Wolle etc* spinnen; **~ out** *Arbeit etc* in die Länge ziehen; *Geld etc* strecken; *v/i* sich drehen; spinnen; **my head was ~ning** mir drehte sich alles; **~ along** MOT dahinrasen; **~ round** herumwirbeln **2.** (schnelle) Drehung; SPORT Effet *m*; TECH Schleudern *n*; AVIAT Trudeln *n*; **be in a** (**flat**) **~** *esp Br* F am Rotieren sein; **go for a ~** MOT F e-e Spritztour machen

spin·ach BOT Spinat *m*

spin·al ANAT Rückgrat...; **~ col·umn** ANAT Wirbelsäule *f*, Rückgrat *n*; **~ cord**, **~ mar·row** ANAT Rückenmark *n*

spin·dle Spindel *f*

spin-dri·er (Wäsche)Schleuder *f*

spin-dry *Wäsche* schleudern

spin-dry·er → **spin-drier**

spine ANAT Wirbelsäule *f*, Rückgrat *n*; ZO Stachel *m*, BOT *a.* Dorn *m*; (*Buch-*

-) Rücken *m*

spin·ning| mill TECH Spinnerei *f*; **~ top** Kreisel *m*; **~ wheel** Spinnrad *n*

spin·ster ältere unverheiratete Frau, *contp* alte Jungfer, spätes Mädchen

spin·y ZO stach(e)lig, BOT *a.* dornig

spi·ral 1. spiralförmig, Spiral... **2.** (*a.* ECON *Preis- etc*)Spirale *f*

spi·ral stair·case Wendeltreppe *f*

spire (*Kirch*)Turmspitze *f*

spir·it Geist *m*; Stimmung *f*, Einstellung *f*; Schwung *m*; Elan *m*; CHEM Spiritus *m*; *mst pl* Spirituosen *pl*

spir·it·ed energisch; erregt (*debate etc*)

spir·it·less temperamentlos; mutlos

spir·its Laune *f*, Stimmung *f*; **be in high ~** in Hochstimmung sein; ausgelassen *or* übermütig sein; **be in low ~** niedergeschlagen sein

spir·i·tu·al 1. geistig; geistlich **2.** MUS Spiritual *n*

spit¹ 1. spucken; knistern (*fire*), brutzeln (*meat etc*); *a.* **~ out** ausspucken; **~ at s.o.** j-n anspucken; **it is ~ting** (**with rain**) es tröpfelt **2.** Spucke *f*

spit² (*Brat*)Spieß *m*; GEOGR Landzunge *f*

spite 1. Bosheit *f*, Gehässigkeit *f*; **out of** *or* **from pure ~** aus reiner Bosheit; **in ~ of** trotz (*gen*) **2.** j-n ärgern

spite·ful boshaft, gehässig

spit·ting im·age Ebenbild *n*; **she is the ~ of her mother** sie ist ihrer Mutter wie aus dem Gesicht geschnitten

spit·tle Speichel *m*, Spucke *f*

splash 1. (be)spritzen; klatschen; plan(t)schen; platschen; **~ down** wassern **2.** Klatschen *n*, Platschen *n*; Spritzer *m*, Spritzfleck *m*; *esp Br* GASTR Spritzer *m*, Schuss *m*

splash·down Wasserung *f*

splay *a.* **~ out** *Finger, Zehen* spreizen

spleen ANAT Milz *f*

splen·did großartig, herrlich, prächtig

splen·do(u)r Pracht *f*

splice miteinander verbinden, *Film etc* (zusammen)kleben

splint MED Schiene *f*; **put in a ~**, **put in ~s** schienen

splin·ter 1. Splitter *m* **2.** (zer)splittern; **~ off** absplittern; *fig* sich abspalten (**from** von)

split 1. *v/t* (zer)spalten; zerreißen; *a.* **~ up** aufteilen (**between** unter *acc*; **into** in *acc*); sich *et.* teilen; **~ hairs** Haarspalterei treiben; **~ one's sides** F sich vor Lachen biegen; *v/i* sich spalten; zerrei-ßen; sich teilen (**into** in *acc*) *a.* **~ up** (**with**) Schluss machen (mit), sich trennen (von) **2.** Riss *m*; Spalt *m*; Aufteilung *f*; *fig* Bruch *m*; *fig* Spaltung *f*

split·ting heftig, rasend (*headache etc*)

splut·ter stottern (*a.* MOT); zischen

spoil 1. *v/t* verderben; ruinieren; *j-n* verwöhnen, *Kind a.* verziehen; *v/i* verderben, schlecht werden **2.** *mst pl* Beute *f*

spoil·er MOT Spoiler *m*

spoil·sport F Spielverderber(in)

spoke TECH Speiche *f*

spokes·man Sprecher *m*

spokes·wom·an Sprecherin *f*

sponge 1. Schwamm *m*; Schnorrer(in); *Br* → **sponge cake 2.** *v/t a.* **~ down** (mit e-m Schwamm) abwaschen; **~ off** weg-, abwischen; **~** (**up**) aufsaugen, aufwischen (**from** von); *et.* schnorren (**from, off, on** von, bei); *v/i* schnorren (**from, off, on** bei)

sponge cake Biskuitkuchen *m*

spong·er Schnorrer(in)

spong·y schwammig; weich

spon·sor 1. Bürge *m*, Bürgin *f*; Sponsor(in), Geldgeber(in); Spender(in) **2.** bürgen für; sponsern

spon·ta·ne·ous spontan

spook F Geist *m*

spook·y F gespenstisch, unheimlich

spool Spule *f*; **~ of thread** Garnrolle *f*

spoon 1. Löffel *m* **2.** löffeln

spoon-feed *Kind etc* füttern

spoon·ful (*ein*) Löffel (voll)

spo·rad·ic sporadisch, gelegentlich

spore BOT Spore *f*

sport 1. Sport *m*; Sportart *f*; F feiner Kerl; *pl* Sport *m* **2.** herumlaufen mit; protzen mit

sports Sport...; **~ car** MOT Sportwagen *m*; **~ cen·ter** (*Br* **cen·tre**) Sportzentrum *n*

sports·man Sportler *m*

sports·wear Sportkleidung *f*

sports·wom·an Sportlerin *f*

spot 1. Punkt *m*, Tupfen *m*; Fleck *m*; MED Pickel *m*; Ort *m*, Platz *m*, Stelle *f*; *radio*, TV (Werbe)Spot *m*; F Spot *m*; **a ~ of** *Br* F ein bisschen; **on the ~** auf der Stelle, sofort; zur Stelle; an Ort und Stelle, vor Ort; auf der Stelle; **soft~** *fig* Schwäche *f* (**for** für); **tender~**

empfindliche Stelle; **weak~** schwacher Punkt; Schwäche *f* **2.** entdecken, sehen

spot check Stichprobe *f*

spot·less tadellos sauber; *fig* untad(e)lig

spot·light Spotlight *n*, Scheinwerfer *m*; Scheinwerferlicht *n*

spot·ted getüpfelt; fleckig

spot·ter Beobachter *m*

spot·ty pick(e)lig

spouse Gatte *m*, Gattin *f*, Gemahl(in)

spout 1. *v/t Wasser etc* (heraus)spritzen; *v/i* spritzen (**from** aus) **2.** Schnauze *f*, Tülle *f*; (*Wasser- etc*)Strahl *m*

sprain MED **1.** sich *et.* verstauchen **2.** Verstauchung *f*

sprat ZO Sprotte *f*

sprawl ausgestreckt liegen *or* sitzen (*a.* **~ out**); sich ausbreiten

spray 1. (be)sprühen; spritzen; sich *die Haare* sprayen; *Parfüm etc* versprühen, zerstäuben **2.** Sprühnebel *m*; Gischt *m*, *f*; Spray *m*, *n*; → **sprayer**

spray can → **spray·er** Sprüh-, Spraydose *f*, Zerstäuber *m*

spread 1. *v/t* ausbreiten, *Arme a.* ausstrecken, *Finger etc* spreizen (*all a.* **~ out**); *Furcht, Krankheit, Nachricht etc* verbreiten, *Gerücht a.* ausstreuen; *Butter etc* streichen (**on** auf *acc*); *Brot etc* (be)streichen (**with** mit); *v/i* sich ausbreiten (*a.* **~ out**); sich erstrecken (**over** über *acc*); sich verbreiten, übergreifen (**to** auf *acc*); sich streichen lassen (*butter etc*) **2.** Ausbreitung *f*, Verbreitung *f*; Ausdehnung *f*; Spannweite *f*; GASTR Aufstrich *m*

spread·sheet IT Tabellenkalkulation *f*, Tabellenkalkulationsprogramm *n*

spree: **go** (**out**) **on a ~** F e-e Sauftour machen; **go on a buying** (*or* **shopping, spending**) **~** wie verrückt einkaufen

sprig BOT kleiner Zweig

spright·ly lebhaft; rüstig

spring 1. *v/i* springen; **~ from** herrühren von; **~ up** aufkommen (*wind*); aus dem Boden schießen (*building etc*); *v/t*: **~ a leak** ein Leck bekommen; **~ a surprise on s.o.** j-n überraschen **2.** Frühling *m*, Frühjahr *n*; Quelle *f*; TECH Feder *f*; Elastizität *f*; Federung *f*; Sprung *m*, Satz *m*; **in** (**the**) **~** im Frühling

spring·board Sprungbrett *n*

spring-clean gründlich putzen, Frühjahrsputz machen (in *dat*)

spring tide Springflut *f*

spring-time Frühling *m*, Frühlingszeit *f*, Frühjahr *n*

spring-y elastisch, federnd

sprin-kle 1. *Wasser etc* sprengen (**on** auf *acc*); *Salz etc* streuen (**on** auf *acc*); *et.* (be)sprengen *or* bestreuen (**with** mit); *it is sprinkling* es tröpfelt **2.** Sprühregen *m*

sprin-kler (*Rasen*)Sprenger *m*; Sprinkler *m*, Berieselungsanlage *f*

sprin-kling: *a* ~ *of* ein bisschen, ein paar

sprint SPORT **1.** sprinten; spurten **2.** Sprint *m*; Spurt *m*

sprint-er SPORT Sprinter(in)

sprite Kobold *m*

sprout BOT **1.** sprießen (*a. fig*), keimen; wachsen lassen **2.** Spross *m*; (*Brussels*) ~*s* Rosenkohl *m*

spruce[1] BOT Fichte *f*; Rottanne *f*

spruce[2] adrett

spry rüstig, lebhaft

spur 1. Sporn *m* (*a.* ZO); *fig* Ansporn *m* (**to** zu); *on the* ~ *of the moment* spontan **2.** *e-m Pferd* die Sporen geben; *often* ~ *on fig* anspornen (**to** zu)

spurt[1] **1.** spurten, sprinten **2.** plötzliche Aktivität, (*Arbeits*)Anfall *m*; Spurt *m*, Sprint *m*

spurt[2] **1.** spritzen (**from** aus); **2.** (*Wasseretc*)Strahl *m*

sput-ter stottern (*a.* MOT); zischen

spy 1. Spion(in) **2.** spionieren, Spionage treiben (**for** für); ~ *into fig* herumspionieren in (*dat*); ~ *on* j-m nachspionieren

spy-hole (Tür)Spion *m*

squab-ble (sich) streiten (**about, over** um, wegen)

squad Mannschaft *f*, Trupp *m*; (*Überfall- etc*)Kommando *n*; Dezernat *n*

squad car (Funk)Streifenwagen *m*

squad-ron MIL, AVIAT Staffel *f*; MAR Geschwader *n*

squal-id schmutzig, verwahrlost, verkommen, armselig

squall Bö *f*

squan-der *Geld, Zeit etc* verschwenden, *Chance* vertun

square 1. Quadrat *n*; Viereck *n*; *öffentlicher Platz*; MATH Quadrat(zahl *f*) *n*; *board game*: Feld *n*; TECH Winkel(maß *n*) *m* **2.** quadratisch, Quadrat...; vier-

eckig; rechtwink(e)lig; eckig (*shoulders etc*); *fig* fair, gerecht; ~ quitt sein **3.** quadratisch *or* rechtwink(e)lig machen (*a.* ~ *off or up*); in Quadrate einteilen (*a.* ~ *off*); MATH *Zahl* ins Quadrat erheben; *Schultern* straffen; *Konto* ausgleichen; *Schulden* begleichen; *fig* in Einklang bringen *or* stehen (**with** mit); ~ *up* F abrechnen; ~ *up to* sich j-m, e-m *Problem etc* stellen

square root MATH Quadratwurzel *f*

squash[1] **1.** zerdrücken, zerquetschen; quetschen, zwängen (**into** in *acc*); ~ *flat* flach drücken, F platt walzen **2.** Gedränge *n*; SPORT Squash *n*

squash[2] BOT Kürbis *m*

squat 1. hocken, kauern; *leer stehendes Haus* besetzen; ~ *down* sich (hin)kauern *or* (hin)hocken **2.** gedrungen, untersetzt; **squat-ter** Hausbesetzer(in)

squaw Squaw *f*

squawk kreischen, schreien; F lautstark protestieren (**about** gegen)

squeak 1. piep(s)en (*mouse etc*); quietschen (*door etc*) **2.** Piep(s)en *n*; Quietschen *n*; **squeak-y** piepsig (*voice*); quietschend (*door etc*)

squeal 1. kreischen (**with** vor *dat*); ~ *on s.o. fig* F j-n verpfeifen **2.** Kreischen *n*; Schrei *m*

squeam-ish empfindlich, zart besaitet

squeeze 1. drücken; auspressen, ausquetschen; (sich) quetschen *or* zwängen (**into** in *acc*); **2.** Druck *m*; GASTR Spritzer *m*; Gedränge *n*

squeez-er (*Frucht*)Presse *f*

squid ZO Tintenfisch *m*

squint schielen; blinzeln

squirm sich winden

squir-rel ZO Eichhörnchen *n*

squirt 1. (be)spritzen **2.** Strahl *m*

stab 1. *v/t* niederstechen; *be* ~ *bed in the arm* e-n Stich in den Arm bekommen; *v/i* stechen (**at** nach) **2.** Stich *m*

sta-bil-i-ty Stabilität *f*; *fig* Dauerhaftigkeit *f*; Ausgeglichenheit *f*

sta-bil-ize (sich) stabilisieren

sta-ble[1] stabil; *fig* dauerhaft; ausgeglichen

sta-ble[2] Stall *m*

stack 1. Stapel *m*, Stoß *m*; ~*s of, a* ~ *of* F jede Menge *Arbeit etc* **2.** stapeln; voll stapeln (**with** mit); ~ *up* aufstapeln

sta-di-um SPORT Stadion *n*

staff 1. Stab *m*; Mitarbeiter(stab *m*) *pl*; Personal *n*, Belegschaft *f*; Lehrkörper *m*; MIL Stab *m* **2.** besetzen (**with** mit)

staff room Lehrerzimmer *n*

stag ZO Hirsch *m*

stage 1. THEA Bühne *f* (*a. fig*); Etappe *f* (*a. fig*), (Reise)Abschnitt *m*; Teilstrecke *f*, Fahrzone *f* (*bus etc*); *fig* Stufe *f*, Stadium *n*, Phase *f* **2.** THEA inszenieren; veranstalten

stage-coach Postkutsche *f*

stage|di·rec·tion THEA Regieanweisung *f*; **~ fright** Lampenfieber *n*; **~ man·ag·er** THEA Inspizient *m*

stag·ger 1. *v/i* (sch)wanken, taumeln, torkeln; *v/t* zo sprachlos machen, F umhauen; *Arbeitszeit etc* staffeln **2.** Wanken *n*, Schwanken *n*, Taumeln *n*

stag·nant stehend (*water*); *esp* ECON stagnierend

stag·nate *esp* ECON stagnieren

stain 1. *v/t* beflecken; (ein)färben; *Holz* beizen; *Glas* bemalen; *v/i* Flecken bekommen, schmutzen **2.** Fleck *m*; TECH Färbemittel *n*; (*Holz*)Beize *f*; Makel *m*

stained glass Bunt-, Farbglas *n*

stain·less nicht rostend, rostfrei

stair (Treppen)Stufe *f*; *pl* Treppe *f*

stair·case, stair·way Treppe *f*; Treppenhaus *n*

stake¹ 1. Pfahl *m*, Pfosten *m*; HIST Marterpfahl *m* **2. ~ off, ~ out** abstecken

stake² 1. Anteil *m*, Beteiligung *f* (**in** an *dat*) (*a.* ECON); (Wett- *etc*)Einsatz *m*; **be at ~** *fig* auf dem Spiel stehen **2.** *Geld etc* setzen (**on** auf *acc*); *Ruf etc* riskieren, aufs Spiel setzen

stale alt(backen); abgestanden, *beer etc*: *a.* schal, *air etc*: *a.* verbraucht

stalk¹ BOT Stängel *m*, Stiel *m*, Halm *m*

stalk² *v/t* sich heranpirschen an (*acc*); verfolgen, hinter *j-m*, *et.* herschleichen; *v/i* stolzieren

stall¹ 1. (*Obst- etc*)Stand *m*, (*Markt- etc*) Bude *f*; AGR Box *f*; *pl* REL Chorgestühl *n*; *Br* THEA Parkett *n* **2.** *v/t Motor* abwürgen; *v/i* absterben

stall² *v/i* Ausflüchte machen; Zeit schinden; *v/t j-n* hinhalten; *et.* hinauszögern

stal·li·on ZO (Zucht)Hengst *m*

stal·wart kräftig, robust; *esp* POL treu

stam·i·na Ausdauer *f*; Durchhaltevermögen *n*, Kondition *f*

stam·mer 1. stottern, stammeln **2.** Stottern *n*, Stammeln *n*

stamp 1. *v/i* sta(m)pfen, trampeln; *v/t Pass etc* (ab)stempeln; *Datum etc* aufstempeln (**on** auf *acc*); *Brief etc* frankieren; *fig j-n* abstempeln (**as** als, zu); **~ one's foot** aufstampfen; **~ out** *Feuer* austreten; TECH ausstanzen **2.** (Brief-) Marke *f*; (*Steuer- etc*)Marke *f*; Stempel *m*; **~ed addressed envelope** Freiumschlag *m*

stam·pede 1. zo wilde Flucht; wilder Ansturm, Massenansturm *m* (**for** auf *acc*); **2.** *v/i* zo durchgehen; *v/t* in Panik versetzen

stanch treu, zuverlässig

stand 1. *v/i* stehen; aufstehen; *fig fest- etc* bleiben; **~ still** still stehen; *v/t* stellen (**on** auf *acc*); aushalten, ertragen; *e-r Prüfung etc* standhalten; *Probe* bestehen; *Chance* haben; *Drink etc* spendieren; **I can't ~ him** (*or* **it**) ich kann ihn (*or* das) nicht ausstehen *or* leiden; **~ around** herumstehen; **~ back** zurücktreten; **~ by** danebenstehen; *fig* zu *j-m* halten; zu *et.* stehen; **~ idly by** tatenlos zusehen; **~ down** verzichten; zurücktreten; JUR den Zeugenstand verlassen; **~ for** stehen für, bedeuten; sich *et.* gefallen lassen, *et.* dulden; *esp Br* kandidieren für; **~ in** einspringen (**for** für); **~ in for s.o.** *a. j-n* vertreten; **~ on** (*fig* be)stehen auf (*dat*); **~ out** hervorstechen; sich abheben (**against** gegen, von); **~ over** überwachen, aufpassen auf (*acc*); **~ together** zusammenhalten, -stehen; **~ up** aufstehen, sich erheben; **~ up for** eintreten *or* sich einsetzen für; **~ up to** *j-m* mutig gegenübertreten, *j-m* die Stirn bieten **2.** (*Obst-, Messe- etc*)Stand *m*; (*Schirm-, Noten-etc*)Ständer *m*; SPORT *etc* Tribüne *f*; (*Taxi*)Stand(platz) *m*; JUR Zeugenstand *m*; **take a ~** *fig* Position beziehen (**on** zu)

stan·dard¹ 1. Norm *f*, Maßstab *m*; Standard *m*, Niveau *n*; **~ of living, living ~** Lebensstandard *m* **2.** normal, Normal...; durchschnittlich, Durchschnitts...; Standard...

stan·dard² Standarte *f*, MOT Stander *m*; HIST Banner *n*

stan·dard·ize vereinheitlichen, *esp* TECH standardisieren, normen

stan·dard lamp *Br* Stehlampe *f*

stand·by 1. Reserve *f*; AVIAT Stand-by *n*; **be on ~** in Bereitschaft stehen **2.** Reserve…, Not…; AVIAT Stand-by…

stand-in *film*, TV Double *n*; Ersatzmann *m*; Vertreter(in)

stand·ing 1. stehend; *fig* ständig; → **ovation 2.** Rang *m*, Stellung *f*; Ansehen *n*, Ruf *m*; Dauer *f*; **of long ~** alt, seit langem bestehend; **~ or·der** ECON Dauerauftrag *m*; **~ room: ~ only** nur noch Stehplätze

stand·off·ish F (sehr) ablehnend, hochnäsig

stand·point *fig* Standpunkt *m*

stand·still Stillstand *m*; **be at a ~** stehen (*car etc*); ruhen (*production etc*); **bring to a ~** Auto *etc* zum Stehen bringen; *Produktion etc* zum Erliegen bringen

stand-up Steh…; **~ fight** Schlägerei *f*

stan·za Strophe *f*

sta·ple¹ 1. Hauptnahrungsmittel *n*; ECON Haupterzeugnis *n* **2.** Haupt…; üblich

sta·ple² 1. Heftklammer *f*; Krampe *f* **2.** heften

sta·pler TECH (Draht)Hefter *m*

star 1. ASTR Stern *m*; PRINT Sternchen *n*; THEA, *sport etc* Star *m* **2.** *v/t* PRINT mit e-m Sternchen kennzeichnen; **~ring …** in der Hauptrolle *or* in den Hauptrollen …; **a film ~ring …** ein Film mit … in der Hauptrolle *or* den Hauptrollen; *v/i* die *or* e-e Hauptrolle spielen (**in** *in dat*)

star·board AVIAT, MAR Steuerbord *n*

starch 1. (*Kartoffel- etc*)Stärke *f*; stärkereiches Nahrungsmittel; (*Wäsche-*)Stärke *f* **2.** *Wäsche* stärken

stare 1. starren; **~ at** *j-n* anstarren **2.** (starrer) Blick, Starren *n*

stark 1. *adj fig* nackt; **be in ~ contrast to** in krassem Gegensatz stehen zu **2.** *adv*: F **~ naked** splitternackt; **~ raving mad**, **~ staring mad** total verrückt

star·light ASTR Sternenlicht *n*

star·ling ZO Star *m*

star·lit stern(en)klar

star·ry Stern…, Sternen…

star·ry-eyed F blauäugig, naiv

start 1. *v/i* anfangen, beginnen (*a.* **~ off**); aufbrechen (**for** nach) (*a.* **~ off, ~ out**); RAIL, MAR ablegen, AVIAT abfliegen, starten; MOT anspringen; TECH anlaufen; SPORT starten; zusammenfahren, -zucken (**at** bei); **to ~ with**

anfangs, zunächst; erstens; **~ from scratch** ganz von vorn anfangen; *v/t* anfangen, beginnen (*a.* **~ off**); in Gang setzen *or* bringen, *Motor etc a.* anlassen, starten **2.** Anfang *m*, Beginn *m*, (*esp* SPORT) Start *m*; Aufbruch *m*; Auffahren *n*, Aufschrecken *n*; **at the ~** am Anfang; SPORT am Start; **for a ~** erstens; **from ~ to finish** von Anfang bis Ende

start·er SPORT Starter(in); MOT Anlasser *m*, Starter *m*; *esp Br* GASTR F Vorspeise *f*; **for ~s** zunächst einmal

start·le erschrecken; überraschen, bestürzen

starv·a·tion Hungern *n*; **die of ~** verhungern; **~ diet** F Fasten-, Hungerkur *f*, Nulldiät *f*

starve hungern (lassen); **~ (to death)** verhungern (lassen); **I'm starving!** *Br* F, **I'm ~d!** F ich komme um vor Hunger!

state 1. Zustand *m*; Stand *m*, Lage *f*; POL (Bundes-, Einzel)Staat *m*; *often* State POL Staat *m* **2.** Staats…, staatlich **3.** angeben, nennen; erklären, JUR aussagen (**that** dass); festlegen, festsetzen

State De·part·ment POL Außenministerium *n*

state·ly gemessen, würdevoll; prächtig

state·ment Statement *n*, Erklärung *f*; Angabe *f*; JUR Aussage *f*; ECON (*Bank-*, *Konto*)Auszug *m*; **make a ~** e-e Erklärung abgeben

state-of-the-art TECH neuest, modernst

states·man POL Staatsmann *m*

stat·ic statisch

sta·tion 1. (*a. Bus-*, *U-*)Bahnhof *m*, Station *f*; (*Forschungs-*, *Rettungs- etc*)Station *f*; Tankstelle *f*; (*Feuer*)Wache *f*; (*Polizei*)Revier *n*; (*Wahl*)Lokal *n*; *radio*, TV Sender *m*, Station *f* **2.** aufstellen, postieren; MIL stationieren

sta·tion·ar·y stehend

sta·tion·er Schreibwarenhändler(in); **sta·tion·er's (shop)** Schreibwarenhandlung *f*; **sta·tion·er·y** Schreibwaren *pl*; Briefpapier *n*

sta·tion·mas·ter RAIL Stations-, Bahnhofsvorsteher *m*

sta·tion wag·on MOT Kombiwagen *m*

sta·tis·ti·cal statistisch

sta·tis·ti·cian Statistiker *m*

sta·tis·tics Statistik(en *pl*) *f*

stat·ue Statue *f*, Standbild *n*

sta·tus Status *m*, Rechtsstellung *f*; (*Fa-*

milien)Stand *m*; Stellung *f*, Rang *m*, Status *m*; ~ **line** IT Statuszeile *f*

stat·ute Gesetz *n*; Statut *n*, Satzung *f*

stat·ute of lim·i·ta·tions JUR Verjährungsfrist *f*; *come under the* ~ verjähren

staunch¹ *Br* → **stanch**

staunch² *Blutung* stillen

stay 1. bleiben (*with s.o.* bei j-m); wohnen (*at* in *dat*; *with s.o.* bei j-m); ~ *put* F sich nicht (vom Fleck) rühren; ~ *away* wegbleiben, sich fernhalten (*from* von); ~ *up* aufbleiben **2.** Aufenthalt *m*; JUR Aussetzung *f*, Aufschub *m*

stead·fast treu, zuverlässig; fest

stead·y 1. *adj* fest; stabil; ruhig (*hand*), gut (*nerves*); gleichmäßig **2.** (sich) beruhigen **3.** *int a.* ~ *on!* *Br* F Vorsicht! **4.** *adv*: *go* ~ *with s.o.* (fest) mit j-m gehen **5.** feste Freundin, fester Freund

steak GASTR Steak *n*; (*Fisch*)Filet *n*

steal stehlen (*a. fig*); sich stehlen, (sich) schleichen (*out of* aus)

stealth: *by* ~ heimlich, verstohlen

stealth·y heimlich, verstohlen

steam 1. Dampf *m*; Dunst *m*; *let off* ~ Dampf ablassen, *fig a.* sich Luft machen **2.** Dampf... **3.** *v/i* dampfen; ~ *up* beschlagen (*mirror etc*); *v/t* GASTR dünsten, dämpfen

steam·boat Dampfboot *n*, Dampfer *m*

steam·er Dampfer *m*, Dampfschiff *n*; Dampf-, Schnellkochtopf *m*

steam·ship Dampfer *m*, Dampfschiff *n*

steel 1. Stahl *m* **2.** ~ *o.s. for* sich wappnen gegen

steel·work·er Stahlarbeiter *m*

steel·works Stahlwerk *n*

steep¹ steil; *fig* stark (*rise etc*); F happig

steep² eintauchen (*in* in *acc*); *Wäsche* (ein)weichen

stee·ple Kirchturm *m*

stee·ple·chase *horse racing*: Hindernisrennen *n*; SPORT Hindernislauf *m*

steer¹ ZO (junger) Ochse

steer² steuern, lenken

steer·ing col·umn MOT Lenksäule *f*

steer·ing wheel MOT Lenkrad *n*, *a.* MAR Steuerrad *n*

stein Maßkrug *m*

stem¹ BOT Stiel *m* (*a. of a wine glass etc*), Stängel *m*; LING Stamm *m* **2.** ~ *from* stammen *or* herrühren von

stench Gestank *m*

sten·cil Schablone *f*; PRINT Matrize *f*

ste·nog·ra·pher Stenotypistin *f*

step 1. Schritt *m* (*a. fig*); Stufe *f*; Sprosse *f*; (*a pair of*) ~*s* (e-e) Tritt- *or* Stufenleiter; *mind the* ~*!* Vorsicht, Stufe!; ~ *by* ~ Schritt für Schritt; *take* ~*s* Schritte *or* et. unternehmen **2.** gehen; treten (*in* in *acc*; *on* auf *acc*); ~ *on it*, ~ *on the gas* MOT F Gas geben, auf die Tube drücken; ~ *aside* zur Seite treten; *fig* Platz machen; ~ *down* *fig* Platz machen; ~ *up* Produktion etc steigern

step-by-step *fig* schrittweise

step·fa·ther Stiefvater *m*

step·lad·der Tritt-, Stufenleiter *f*

step·moth·er Stiefmutter *f*

steppes GEOGR Steppe *f*

step·ping-stone *fig* Sprungbrett *n* (*to* für)

ster·e·o 1. Stereo *n*; Stereogerät *n*, Stereoanlage *f* **2.** Stereo...; ~ **sys·tem** MUS Kompaktanlage *f*

ster·ile steril (*a. fig*), *a.* unfruchtbar, MED *a.* keimfrei

ste·ril·i·ty Sterilität *f* (*a. fig*), Unfruchtbarkeit *f*

ster·il·ize MED sterilisieren

ster·ling das Pfund Sterling

stern¹ streng

stern² MAR Heck *n*

stew 1. *Fleisch, Gemüse* schmoren, *Obst* dünsten; ~*ed apples* Apfelkompott *n* **2.** Eintopf *m*; *be in a* ~ in heller Aufregung sein

stew·ard Ordner *m*; AVIAT, MAR Steward *m*

stew·ard·ess AVIAT, MAR Stewardess *f*

stick¹ trockener Zweig; Stock *m*; ([*Eis*]-*Hockey*)Schläger *m*; (*Besen- etc*-) Stiel *m*; AVIAT (*Steuer*)Knüppel *m*; Stück *n*, Stange *f*, (*Lippen- etc*)Stift *m*, Stäbchen *n*

stick² *v/t* mit e-r *Nadel etc* stechen (*into* in *acc*); *et.* kleben (*on* auf, an *acc*); an-, festkleben (*with* mit); stecken; F tun, stellen, setzen, legen; *I can't* ~ *him* (*or it*) *esp Br* F ich kann ihn (*or* das) nicht ausstehen *or* leiden; *v/i* kleben; kleben bleiben (*to* an *dat*); stecken bleiben; ~ *at nothing* vor nichts zurückschrecken; ~ *by* F bleiben bei; F zu j-m halten; ~ *out* vorstehen; abstehen; *et.* ausstrecken *or* vorstrecken; ~ *to* bleiben bei

stick·er Aufkleber *m*

stick·ing plas·ter *Br* Heftpflaster *n*

stick·y klebrig (**with** von); F heikel, unangenehm

stiff 1. *adj* steif; F stark (*drink etc*); schwer, hart (*task, penalty etc*); hartnäckig (*resistance*); F happig, gepfeffert, gesalzen (*price*); **keep a ~ upper lip** *fig* Haltung bewahren **2.** *adv* äußerst; höchst; **be bored ~** F sich zu Tode langweilen; **be scared ~** e-e wahnsinnige Angst haben; **be worried ~** sich furchtbare Sorgen machen

stiff·en *v/t* Wäsche stärken; versteifen; verstärken; *v/i* steif werden; sich verhärten *or* versteifen

sti·fle ersticken; *fig* unterdrücken

stile Zauntritt *m*

sti·let·to Stilett *n*; **~ heel** Bleistift-, Pfennigabsatz *m*

still¹ 1. *adv* (immer) noch, noch immer; *with comparative:* noch **2.** *cj* dennoch, trotzdem

still² 1. *adj* still; ruhig; GASTR ohne Kohlensäure **2.** *film, TV* Standfoto *n*

still·born MED tot geboren

still life PAINT Stillleben *n*

stilt Stelze *f*; **stilt·ed** *fig* gestelzt

stim·u·lant MED Stimulans *n*, Anregungs-, Aufputschmittel *n*; *fig* Anreiz *m*, Ansporn *m* (**to** für)

stim·u·late MED stimulieren (*a. fig*), anregen, *fig a.* anspornen

stim·u·lus Reiz *m*; *fig* Anreiz *m*, Ansporn *m* (**to** für)

sting 1. stechen (*insect*); brennen (auf *or* in *dat*); **2.** Stachel *m*; Stich *m*; Brennen *n*, brennender Schmerz

stin·gy F knaus(e)rig, knick(e)rig (*person*); mick(e)rig (*meal etc*)

stink 1. stinken (**of** nach); **~ up** (*Br* **out**) verpesten **2.** Gestank *m*

stint: ~ o.s. (**of s.th.**) sich einschränken (mit et.); **~ (on) s.th.** sparen mit et.

stip·u·late zur Bedingung machen; festsetzen, vereinbaren; **stip·u·la·tion** Bedingung *f*; Vereinbarung *f*

stir 1. (um)rühren; (sich) rühren *or* bewegen; *j-n* aufwühlen; **~ up** Unruhe stiften; *Streit* entfachen; *Erinnerungen* wachrufen **2.** **give s.th. a ~** et. umrühren; **cause** (*or* **create**) **a ~** für Aufsehen sorgen

stir·rup Steigbügel *m*

stitch 1. Stich *m*; Masche *f*; MED Seitenstechen *n* **2.** zunähen, *Wunde* nähen (*a. ~ up*); heften

stock 1. Vorrat *m* (**of** an *dat*); GASTR Brühe *f*; *a.* **live~** Viehbestand *m*; (*Gewehr*)Schaft *m*; *fig* Abstammung *f*, Herkunft *f*; ECON Aktie(n *pl*) *f*; *pl* Aktien *pl*, Wertpapiere *pl*; **have s.th. in ~** ECON et. vorrätig *or* auf Lager haben; **take ~** ECON Inventur machen; **take ~ of** *fig* sich klar werden über (*acc*) **2.** ECON *Ware* vorrätig haben, führen; **~ up** sich eindecken *or* versorgen (**on, with** mit); **3.** Serien…; Standard…; stereotyp

stock·breed·er AGR Viehzüchter *m*

stock·breed·ing AGR Viehzucht *f*

stock·brok·er ECON Börsenmakler *m*

stock ex·change ECON Börse *f*

stock·hold·er ECON Aktionär(in)

stock·ing Strumpf *m*

stock mar·ket ECON Börse *f*

stock·pile 1. Vorrat *m* (**of** an *dat*); **2.** e-n Vorrat anlegen an (*dat*)

stock·still regungslos

stock·tak·ing ECON Inventur *f*; *fig* Bestandsaufnahme *f*

stock·y stämmig, untersetzt

stol·id gleichmütig

stom·ach 1. ANAT Magen *m*; Bauch *m*; *fig* Appetit *m* (**for** auf *acc*); **2.** vertragen (*a. fig*)

stom·ach·ache MED Magenschmerzen *pl*, Bauchschmerzen *pl*, Bauchweh *n*

stom·ach up·set MED Magenverstimmung *f*

stone 1. Stein *m*; BOT *a.* Kern *m*; (*Hagel*)Korn *n* **2.** mit Steinen bewerfen; steinigen; entkernen, entsteinen

stone·ma·son Steinmetz *m*

stone·ware Steingut *n*

ston·y steinig; steinern (*face etc*), eisig (*silence*)

stool Hocker *m*, Schemel *m*; MED Stuhl *m*, Stuhlgang *m*

stool·pi·geon F (Polizei)Spitzel *m*

stoop 1. *v/i* sich bücken (*a. ~ down*); gebeugt gehen; **~ to** *fig* sich herablassen *or* hergeben zu **2.** gebeugte Haltung

stop 1. *v/i* (an)halten, stehen bleiben (*a. watch etc*), stoppen; aufhören; *esp Br* bleiben; **~ dead** plötzlich *or* abrupt stehen bleiben; **~ at nothing** vor nichts zurückschrecken; **~ short of** doing, **~**

short **at** *s.th.* zurückschrecken vor (*dat*); *v/t* anhalten, stoppen; aufhören mit; ein Ende machen *or* setzen (*dat*); *Blutung* stillen; *Arbeiten, Verkehr etc* zum Erliegen bringen; *et.* verhindern; *j-n* abhalten (**from** von), hindern (**from** an *dat*); *Rohr etc* verstopfen (*a.* **~ up**); *Zahn* füllen, plombieren; *Scheck* sperren (lassen); **~ by** vorbeischauen; **~ in** vorbeischauen (**at** bei); **~ off** F kurz Halt machen; **~ over** kurz Halt machen; Zwischenstation machen **2.** Halt *m*; (*Bus*)Haltestelle *f*; PHOT Blende *f*; *mst* **full ~** LING Punkt *m*

stop·gap Notbehelf *m*

stop·light MOT Bremslicht *n*; rotes Licht

stop·o·ver Zwischenstation *f*; AVIAT Zwischenlandung *f*

stop·page Unterbrechung *f*, Stopp *m*; Verstopfung *f*; Streik *m*; *Br* (Gehalts-, Lohn)Abzug *m*

stop·per Stöpsel *m*

stop sign MOT Stoppschild *n*

stop·watch Stoppuhr *f*

stor·age ECON Lagerung *f*; Lagergeld *n*; IT Speicher *m*

store 1. (ein)lagern; *Energie* speichern; IT (ab)speichern, sichern; *a.* **~ up** sich e-n Vorrat anlegen an (*dat*) **2.** Vorrat *m*; Lager *n*, Lagerhalle *f*, Lagerhaus *n*; Laden *m*, Geschäft *n*, *esp Br* Kaufhaus *n*, Warenhaus *n*

store·house Lagerhaus *n*; *fig* Fundgrube *f*

store·keep·er Ladenbesitzer(in)

store·room Lagerraum *m*

sto·rey *Br* → **story²**

...sto·reyed *Br*, **...sto·ried** mit ... Stockwerken, ...stöckig

stork ZO Storch *m*

storm 1. Unwetter *n*; Gewitter *n*; Sturm *m* **2.** *v/t* MIL *etc* stürmen; *v/i* stürmen, stürzen; **storm·y** stürmisch

sto·ry¹ Geschichte *f*; Märchen *n* (*a. fig*); Story *f*, *a.* Handlung *f*, *a.* Bericht *m* (**on** über *acc*)

sto·ry² Stock *m*, Stockwerk *n*, Etage *f*

stout korpulent, vollschlank; *fig* unerschrocken; entschieden

stove Ofen *m*, Herd *m*

stow **~ away** verstauen

stow·a·way AVIAT, MAR blinder Passagier

strad·dle rittlings sitzen auf (*dat*)

strag·gle verstreut liegen *or* stehen; BOT

etc wuchern; **~ in** F einzeln eintrudeln

strag·gler Nachzügler(in)

strag·gly verstreut (liegend); BOT *etc* wuchernd; struppig (*mustache etc*)

straight 1. *adj* gerade; glatt (*hair*); pur (*whisky etc*); aufrichtig, offen, ehrlich; *sl* hetero(*sexuell*); *sl* clean, sauber; **put ~** in Ordnung bringen **2.** *adv* gerade; genau, direkt; klar; ehrlich, anständig; **~ ahead** geradeaus; **~ off** F sofort; **~ on** geradeaus; **~ out** F offen, rundheraus **3.** SPORT (*Gegen-, Ziel*)Gerade *f*

straight·en *v/t* gerade machen, (gerade) richten; **~ out** in Ordnung bringen; *v/i* *a.* **~ out** gerade werden; **~ up** sich aufrichten

straight·for·ward aufrichtig; einfach

strain 1. *v/t* *Seil etc* (an)spannen; *sich, Augen etc* überanstrengen; *sich, Muskel etc* zerren; *Gemüse, Tee etc* abgießen; *v/i* sich anstrengen; **~ at** zerren *or* ziehen an (*dat*) **2.** Spannung *f*; Anspannung *f*; Strapaze *f*; *fig* Belastung *f*; MED Zerrung *f*; **strained** MED gezerrt; gezwungen (*smile etc*); gespannt (*relations*); **look ~** abgespannt aussehen

strain·er Sieb *n*

strait GEOGR Meerenge *f*, Straße *f*; *pl fig* Notlage *f*

strait·ened: live in ~ circumstances in beschränkten Verhältnissen leben

strand Strang *m*; Faden *m*; (*Kabel-*)Draht *m*; (*Haar*)Strähne *f*

strand·ed: be ~ MAR gestrandet sein; **be** (*left*) **~** *fig* festsitzen (**in** in *dat*)

strange merkwürdig, seltsam, sonderbar; fremd; **strang·er** Fremde *m*, *f*

stran·gle erwürgen

strap 1. Riemen *m*, Gurt *m*; (*Uhr*)Armband *n*; Träger *m* **2.** festschnallen; anschnallen

stra·te·gic strategisch

strat·e·gy Strategie *f*

stra·tum GEOL Schicht *f* (*a. fig*)

straw Stroh *n*; Strohhalm *m*

straw·ber·ry BOT Erdbeere *f*

stray 1. (herum)streunen; sich verirren; *fig* abschweifen (**from** von); **2.** verirrtes *or* streunendes Tier **3.** verirrt (*bullet, dog etc*); streunend (*dog etc*); vereinzelt

streak 1. Streifen *m*; Strähne *f*; (*Charakter*)Zug *m*; **a ~ of lightning** ein Blitz; **lucky ~** Glückssträhne *f* **2.** flitzen;

streifen
streak·y streifig; GASTR durchwachsen
stream 1. Bach *m*; Strömung *f*; *fig* Strom *m* 2. strömen; flattern, wehen
stream·er Luft-, Papierschlange *f*; Wimpel *m*; IT Streamer *m*
street 1. Straße *f*; **on** (*esp Br* **in**) **the ~** auf der Straße 2. Straßen...
street·car Straßenbahn(wagen *m*) *f*
street sweep·er Straßenkehrer *m*
strength Stärke *f*, Kraft *f*, Kräfte *pl*
strength·en *v/t* (ver)stärken; *v/i* stärker werden
stren·u·ous anstrengend, strapaziös; unermüdlich
stress 1. *fig* Stress *m*; PHYS, TECH Beanspruchung *f*, Belastung *f*, Druck *m*; LING Betonung *f*; *fig* Nachdruck *m* 2. betonen
stress·ful stressig, aufreibend
stretch 1. *v/t* strecken; (aus)weiten, dehnen; spannen; *fig* es nicht allzu genau nehmen mit; **~ out** ausstrecken; **be ful·ly ~ed** *fig* richtig gefordert werden; voll ausgelastet sein; *v/i* sich dehnen, *a.* länger *or* weiter werden; sich dehnen *or* recken *or* strecken; sich erstrecken; **~ out** sich ausstrecken 2. Dehnbarkeit *f*, Elastizität *f*; Strecke *f*; SPORT (Gegen-, Ziel)Gerade *f*; Zeit *f*, Zeitraum *m*, Zeitspanne *f*; **have a ~** sich dehnen *or* recken *or* strecken
stretch·er Trage *f*
strick·en schwer betroffen; **~ with** befallen *or* ergriffen von
strict streng, strikt; genau; **~ly** (**speak·ing**) genau genommen
strict·ness Strenge *f*
stride 1. schreiten, mit großen Schritten gehen 2. großer Schritt
strife Streit *m*
strike 1. *v/t* schlagen; treffen; einschlagen in (*acc*) (*lightning*); Streichholz anzünden; MAR auflaufen auf (*acc*); streichen (**from, off** aus *dat*, von); stoßen auf (*acc*); *j-n* beeindrucken; *j-m* einfallen, in den Sinn kommen; *Münze* prägen; *Saite etc* anschlagen; *Lager, Zelt* abbrechen; *Flagge, Segel* streichen; **~ out** (aus)streichen; **~ up** *Lied etc* anstimmen; *Freundschaft etc* schließen; *v/i* schlagen; einschlagen; ECON streiken; **~** (**out**) **at s.o.** auf *j-n* einschlagen 2. ECON Streik *m*; (*Öl- etc*)Fund *m*; MIL

Angriff *m*; *soccer*: Schuss *m*; **be on ~** streiken; **go on ~** streiken, in den Streik treten; **a lucky ~** ein Glückstreffer
strik·er ECON Streikende *m*, *f*; *soccer*: Stürmer(in)
strik·ing apart; auffallend
string 1. Schnur *f*, Bindfaden *m*; (Schürzen-, Schuh- etc)Band *n*; (Puppenspiel) Faden *m*, Draht *m*; (Perlen- etc)Schnur *f*; MUS, SPORT Saite *f*; (Bogen)Sehne *f*; BOT Faser *f*; IT Zeichenfolge *f*; *fig* Reihe *f*, Serie *f*; **the ~s** MUS die Streichinstrumente *pl*, die Streicher *pl*; **pull a few ~s** *fig* ein paar Beziehungen spielen lassen; **with no ~s attached** *fig* ohne Bedingungen 2. *Perlen etc* aufreihen; *Gitarre etc* besaiten, *Tennisschläger etc* bespannen; *Bohnen* abziehen 3. MUS Streich...; **string bean** BOT grüne Bohne
strin·gent streng
string·y fas(e)rig
strip 1. *v/i: a.* **~ off** sich ausziehen (**to** bis auf *acc*); *v/t* ausziehen; *Farbe etc* abkratzen, *Tapete etc* abreißen (**from, off** von); *a.* **~ down** TECH zerlegen, auseinandernehmen; **~ s.o. of s.th.** *j-m* et. rauben *or* wegnehmen 2. (*Land-, Papier- etc*)Streifen *m*; Strip *m*
stripe Streifen *m*; **striped** gestreift
strive: **~ for** *or* **after** streben nach
stroke 1. streicheln; streichen über (*acc*) 2. Schlag *m* (*a.* SPORT); MED Schlag(-anfall) *m*; (*Pinsel*)Strich *m*; *swimming*: Zug *m*; TECH Hub *m*; **→ four- -stroke engine**; **~ of lightning** Blitzschlag *m*; **a ~ of luck** *fig* ein glücklicher Zufall, ein Glücksfall
stroll 1. bummeln, spazieren 2. Bummel *m*, Spaziergang *m*
stroll·er Bummler(in), Spaziergänger(in); Sportwagen *m*
strong stark (*a.* GASTR, PHARM); kräftig; mächtig; stabil; fest; robust
strong·box (Geld-, Stahl)Kassette *f*
strong·hold Festung *f*; Stützpunkt *m*; *fig* Hochburg *f*
strong-mind·ed willensstark
strong room Tresor(raum) *m*
struc·ture Struktur *f*; (Auf)Bau *m*, Gliederung *f*; Bau *m*, Konstruktion *f*
strug·gle 1. kämpfen, ringen (**with** mit; **for** um); sich abmühen; sich winden, zappeln; **~ against** sich sträuben gegen

2. Kampf *m*

strum klimpern auf (*dat*) (*or* **on** auf *dat*)

strut[1] stolzieren

strut[2] TECH Strebe *f*; Stütze *f*

stub 1. (*Bleistift-, Zigaretten- etc*)Stummel *m*; Kontrollabschnitt *m* **2.** sich *die Zehe* anstoßen; **~ out** *Zigarette* ausdrücken

stub·ble Stoppeln *pl*

stub·bly stoppelig

stub·born eigensinnig, stur; hartnäckig

stub·born·ness Starrsinn *m*

stuck-up F hochnäsig

stud[1] **1.** (*Kragen-, Manschetten*)Knopf *m*; *soccer*: Stollen *m*; Beschlagnagel *m*; Ziernagel *m*; *pl* MOT Spikes *pl* **2. be ~ded with** besetzt sein mit; übersät sein mit; **~ded tires** Spikesreifen *pl*

stud[2] Gestüt *n*

stu·dent Student(in); Schüler(in)

stud farm Gestüt *n*

stud horse zo Zuchthengst *m*

stud·ied wohlüberlegt; gesucht

stu·di·o Studio *n*; Atelier *n*; *a.* **~ apartment**, *Br* **~ flat** Studio *n*, Einzimmerappartement *n*; **~ couch** Schlafcouch *f*

stu·di·ous fleißig

stud·y 1. Studium *n*; Studie *f*, Untersuchung *f*; Arbeitszimmer *n*; *pl* Studium *n* **2.** studieren; lernen (**for** für)

stuff 1. Zeug *n* **2.** (aus)stopfen, stopfen, vollstopfen; füllen (*a.* GASTR); **~ o.s.** F sich vollstopfen; **stuff·ing** Füllung *f* (*a.* GASTR)

stuff·y stickig; spießig; prüde

stum·ble 1. stolpern (**on, over**, *fig* **at, over** über *acc*); **~ across, ~ on** stoßen auf (*acc*) **2.** Stolpern *n*

stump 1. Stumpf *m*; Stummel *m* **2.** stampfen, stapfen

stump·y F kurz und dick

stun betäuben; *fig* sprachlos machen

stun·ning fantastisch; unglaublich

stunt[1] (*das Wachstum gen*) hemmen; **~ed** BIOL verkümmert; **become ~ed** BIOL verkümmern

stunt[2] (*Film*)Stunt *m*; (*gefährliches*) Kunststück; (*Reklame*)Gag *m*

stunt| man *film, TV* Stuntman *m*, Double *n*; **~ wom·an** *film, TV* Stuntwoman *f*, Double *ħ*

stu·pid dumm; F blöd

stu·pid·i·ty Dummheit *f*

stu·por Betäubung *f*; **in a drunken ~** im Vollrausch

stur·dy kräftig, stämmig; *fig* entschlossen, hartnäckig

stut·ter 1. stottern (*a.* MOT); stammeln **2.** Stottern *n*, Stammeln *n*

sty[1] → **pigsty**

sty[2], **stye** MED Gerstenkorn *n*

style 1. Stil *m*; Ausführung *f*; Mode *f* **2.** entwerfen; gestalten

styl·ish stilvoll; modisch, elegant

styl·ist Stilist(in)

Sty·ro·foam® Styropor® *n*

suave verbindlich

sub·con·scious Unterbewusstsein *n*; **~ly** im Unterbewusstsein

sub·di·vi·sion Unterteilung *f*; Unterabteilung *f*

sub·due unterwerfen; *Ärger etc* unterdrücken; **sub·dued** gedämpft (*light, voice etc*); ruhig, still (*person*)

sub·ject 1. Thema *n*; PED, UNIV Fach *n*; LING Subjekt *n*, Satzgegenstand *m*; Untertan(in); Staatsangehörige *m*, *f*, -bürger(in) **2.** *adj*: **~ to** anfällig für; **be ~ to** *a.* neigen zu; **be ~ to** unterliegen (*dat*); abhängen von; **prices ~ to change** Preisänderungen vorbehalten **3.** unterwerfen; **~ to** *e-m Test etc* unterziehen; *der Kritik etc* aussetzen

sub·jec·tion Unterwerfung *f*; Abhängigkeit *f* (**to** von)

sub·ju·gate unterjochen, unterwerfen

sub·junc·tive LING *a.* **~ mood** Konjunktiv *m*

sub·lease, sub·let untervermieten, weitervermieten

sub·lime großartig; *fig* total

sub·ma·chine gun Maschinenpistole *f*

sub·ma·rine 1. unterseeisch **2.** Unterseeboot *n*, U-Boot *n*

sub·merge tauchen; (ein)tauchen (**in** *acc*)

sub·mis·sion Einreichung *f*; *boxing etc*: Aufgabe *f*; Unterwerfung *f* (**to** unter); **sub·mis·sive** unterwürfig

sub·mit *Gesuch etc* einreichen (**to** *dat or* bei); sich fügen (**to** *dat or in acc*); *boxing etc*: aufgeben

sub·or·di·nate 1. untergeordnet (**to** *dat*); **2.** Untergebene *m*, *f* **3. ~ to** unterordnen (*dat*), zurückstellen (hinter *acc*); **~ clause** LING Nebensatz *m*

sub·scribe *v/t Geld* gegen, spenden (**to** für); *v/i*: **~ to** *Zeitung etc* abonnieren;

sub·scrib·er Abonnent(in); TEL Teilnehmer(in); **sub·scrip·tion** Abonnement *n*; (Mitglieds)Beitrag *m*

sub·se·quent später

sub·side sich senken (*building, road etc*); zurückgehen (*flood, demand etc*), sich legen (*storm, anger etc*)

sub·sid·i·a·ry 1. Neben...; ~ *question* Zusatzfrage *f* **2.** ECON Tochtergesellschaft *f*

sub·si·dize subventionieren

sub·si·dy Subvention *f*

sub·sist leben, existieren (**on** von)

sub·sis·tence Existenz *f*

sub·stance Substanz *f* (*a. fig*), Stoff *m*; *das* Wesentliche, Kern *m*

sub·stan·dard minderwertig

sub·stan·tial solid (*furniture etc*); beträchtlich (*salary etc*), (*changes etc a.*) wesentlich; reichlich, kräftig (*meal*)

sub·stan·ti·ate beweisen

sub·stan·tive LING Substantiv *n*, Hauptwort *n*

sub·sti·tute 1. Ersatz *m*; Stellvertreter(in), Vertretung *f*; SPORT Auswechselspieler(in), Ersatzspieler(in) **2.** ~ *s.th. for s.th.* et. durch et. ersetzen, et. gegen et. austauschen *or* auswechseln; ~ *for* einspringen für, *j-n* vertreten **sub·sti·tu·tion** Ersatz *m*; SPORT Austausch *m*, Auswechslung *f*

sub·ter·fuge List *f*

sub·ter·ra·ne·an unterirdisch

sub·ti·tle Untertitel *m*

sub·tle fein (*differences etc*); raffiniert (*plan etc*); scharf (*mind*); scharfsinnig

sub·tract MATH abziehen, subtrahieren (*from* von); **sub·trac·tion** MATH Abziehen *n*, Subtraktion *f*

sub·trop·i·cal subtropisch

sub·urb Vorort *m*, Vorstadt *f*

sub·ur·ban Vorort..., vorstädtisch, Vorstadt...

sub·ver·sive umstürzlerisch, subversiv

sub·way Unterführung *f*; U-Bahn *f*

suc·ceed v/i Erfolg haben, erfolgreich sein, (*plan etc a.*) gelingen; ~ *to* in e-m Amt nachfolgen; ~ *to the throne* auf dem Thron folgen; v/t: ~ *s.o. as* j-s Nachfolger werden als

suc·cess Erfolg *m*

suc·cess·ful erfolgreich

suc·ces·sion Folge *f*; Erb-, Nach-, Thronfolge *f*; *five times in* ~ fünfmal

hintereinander; *in quick* ~ in rascher Folge; **suc·ces·sive** aufeinanderfolgend; **suc·ces·sor** Nachfolger(in); Thronfolger(in)

suc·cu·lent GASTR saftig

such solche(r, -s); derartige(r, -s); so; derart; ~ *a* so ein(e)

suck 1. v/t saugen; lutschen (an *dat*); v/i saugen (*at* an *dat*); **2.** *have or take a* ~ *at* saugen *or* lutschen an (*dat*)

suck·er ZO Saugnapf *m*, Saugorgan *n*; TECH Saugfuß *m*; BOT Wurzelschössling *m*, Wurzelspross *m*; F Trottel *m*, Simpel *m*; Lutscher *m*

suck·le säugen, stillen

suc·tion (An)Saugen *n*; Saugwirkung *f*; ~ *pump* TECH Saugpumpe *f*

sud·den plötzlich, unvermittelt; *all of a* ~ F ganz plötzlich

sud·den·ly plötzlich

suds Seifenschaum *m*

sue JUR *j-n* verklagen (**for** auf *acc*, wegen); klagen (**for** auf *acc*)

suede, **suède** Wildleder *n*, Velours (-leder) *n*

su·et GASTR Nierenfett *n*, Talg *m*

suf·fer v/i leiden (**from** an *dat*, unter *dat*); darunter leiden; v/t erleiden; *Folgen* tragen; **suf·fer·er** Leidende *m, f*; **suf·fer·ing** Leiden *n*; Leid *n*

suf·fi·cient genügend, genug, ausreichend; *be* ~ genügen, (aus)reichen

suf·fix LING Suffix *n*, Nachsilbe *f*

suf·fo·cate ersticken

suf·frage POL Wahl-, Stimmrecht *n*

suf·fuse durchfluten (*light etc*); überziehen (*color etc*)

sug·ar 1. Zucker *m* **2.** zuckern

sug·ar beet BOT Zuckerrübe *f*

sug·ar bowl Zuckerdose *f*

sug·ar·cane BOT Zuckerrohr *n*

sug·ar tongs Zuckerzange *f*

sug·ar·y süß; *fig* süßlich

sug·gest vorschlagen, anregen; hindeuten *or* hinweisen auf (*acc*), schließen lassen auf (*acc*); andeuten

sug·ges·tion Vorschlag *m*, Anregung *f*; Anflug *m*, Spur *f*; Andeutung *f*; PSYCH Suggestion *f*

sug·ges·tive zweideutig (*remark etc*), vielsagend (*look etc*)

su·i·cide Selbstmord *m*; Selbstmörder(in); *commit* ~ Selbstmord begehen

suit 1. Anzug *m*; Kostüm *n*; *card game*:

Farbe f; JUR Prozess m; **follow ~** fig dem Beispiel folgen, dasselbe tun **2.** v/t j-m passen (date etc); j-n kleiden, j-m stehen; et. anpassen (**to** dat); **~ s.th., be ~ed to s.th.** geeignet sein or sich eignen für; **~ yourself!** mach, was du willst!

sui·ta·ble passend, geeignet (**for, to** für)

suit·case Koffer m

suite (Möbel-, Sitz)Garnitur f; Suite f, Zimmerflucht f; MUS Suite f; Gefolge n

sul·fur CHEM Schwefel m

sul·fu·ric ac·id CHEM Schwefelsäure f

sulk schmollen, F eingeschnappt sein

sulk·y schmollend, F eingeschnappt

sul·len mürrisch, verdrossen

sul·phur Br → **sulfur**

sul·phu·ric ac·id Br → **sulfuric acid**

sul·try schwül; aufreizend (look etc)

sum 1. Summe f; Betrag m; (einfache) Rechenaufgabe; **do ~s** rechnen **2. ~ up** zusammenfassen; j-n, et. abschätzen

sum·mar·ize zusammenfassen

sum·ma·ry Zusammenfassung f, (kurze) Inhaltsangabe

sum·mer Sommer m; **in** (**the**) **~** im Sommer; **~ camp** Ferienlager n; **~ hol·i·days** Br Sommerferien pl; **~ school** Ferienkurs m

sum·mer·time Sommer m, Sommerszeit f; **in** (**the**) **~** im Sommer

sum·mer| time esp Br Sommerzeit f; **~ va·ca·tion** Sommerferien pl

sum·mer·y sommerlich, Sommer...

sum·mit Gipfel m (a. ECON, POL, fig); **~ con·fe·rence** POL Gipfelkonferenz f; **~ meet·ing** POL Gipfeltreffen n

sum·mon auffordern; Versammlung etc einberufen; JUR vorladen; **~ up** Kraft, Mut etc zusammenehmen

sum·mons JUR Vorladung f

sump Br MOT Ölwanne f

sump·tu·ous luxuriös, aufwändig

sun 1. Sonne f **2.** Sonnen... **3. ~ o.s.** sich sonnen

Sun abbr of **Sunday** So., Sonntag m

sun·bathe sich sonnen, ein Sonnenbad nehmen

sun·beam Sonnenstrahl m

sun·bed Sonnenbank f

sun·burn Sonnenbrand m

sun cream Sonnencreme f

sun·dae GASTR Eisbecher m

Sun·day (abbr **Sun**) Sonntag m; **on ~** (am) Sonntag; **on ~s** sonntags

sun·dial Sonnenuhr f

sun·dries Diverses, Verschiedenes

sun·dry diverse, verschiedene

sun·glass·es (a pair of **~** e-e) Sonnenbrille f

sunk·en MAR gesunken, versunken; versenkt; tief liegend; eingefallen (cheeks), (a. eyes) eingesunken

sun·light Sonnenlicht n

sun·lit sonnenbeschienen

sun·ny sonnig

sun·rise Sonnenaufgang m; **at ~** bei Sonnenaufgang

sun·roof Dachterrasse f; MOT Schiebedach n

sun·set Sonnenuntergang m; **at ~** bei Sonnenuntergang

sun·shade Sonnenschirm m

sun·shine Sonnenschein m

sun·stroke MED Sonnenstich m

sun·tan (Sonnen)Bräune f; **~ lo·tion** Sonnenschutz m, Sonnencreme f; **~ oil** Sonnenöl n

su·per F super, spitze, klasse

su·per... Über..., über...

su·per·a·bun·dant überreichlich

su·per·an·nu·at·ed pensioniert, im Ruhestand

su·perb ausgezeichnet

su·per·charg·er MOT Kompressor m

su·per·cil·i·ous hochmütig, F hochnäsig

su·per·fi·cial oberflächlich

su·per·flu·ous überflüssig

su·per·hu·man übermenschlich

su·per·im·pose überlagern; Bild etc einblenden (**on** in acc)

su·per·in·tend die (Ober)Aufsicht haben über (acc), überwachen; leiten

su·per·in·tend·ent Aufsicht f, Aufsichtsbeamter m, -beamtin f; Br Kriminalrat m

su·pe·ri·or 1. ranghöher (**to** als); überlegen (**to** dat), besser (**to** als); ausgezeichnet, hervorragend; überheblich, überlegen; **Father Superior** REL Superior m; **Mother Superior** REL Oberin f **2.** Vorgesetzte m, f; **su·peri·or·i·ty** Überlegenheit f (**over** gegenüber)

su·per·la·tive 1. höchste(r, -s), überragend **2.** a. **~ degree** LING Superlativ m

su·per·mar·ket Supermarkt m

su·per·nat·u·ral übernatürlich

su·per·nu·me·ra·ry zusätzlich

su·per·sede ablösen, ersetzen, verdrängen

su·per·son·ic AVIAT, PHYS Überschall...

su·per·sti·tion Aberglaube *m*

su·per·sti·tious abergläubisch

su·per·store Großmarkt *m*

su·per·vene dazwischenkommen

su·per·vise beaufsichtigen, überwachen; **su·per·vi·sion** Beaufsichtigung *f*, Überwachung *f*; *under s.o.'s* ~ unter j-s Aufsicht; **su·per·vi·sor** Aufseher(in), Aufsicht *f*

sup·per Abendessen *n*; *have ~* zu Abend essen; → *lord*

sup·plant verdrängen

sup·ple gelenkig, geschmeidig, biegsam

sup·ple·ment 1. Ergänzung *f*; Nachtrag *m*, Anhang *m*; Ergänzungsband *m*; (*Zeitungs- etc*)Beilage *f* **2.** ergänzen; **sup·ple·men·ta·ry** ergänzend, zusätzlich

sup·pli·er ECON Lieferant(in), *a. pl* Lieferfirma *f*

sup·ply 1. liefern; stellen, sorgen für; *j-n, et.* versorgen, ECON beliefern (*with* mit); **2.** Lieferung *f* (*to* an *acc*); Versorgung *f*; ECON Angebot *n*; *mst pl* Vorrat *m* (*of* an *dat*), *a.* Proviant *m*, MIL Nachschub *m*; *~ and demand* ECON Angebot und Nachfrage

sup·port 1. (ab)stützen, *Gewicht etc* tragen; *Währung* stützen; unterstützen; unterhalten, sorgen für **2.** Stütze *f*; TECH Träger *m*; *fig* Unterstützung *f*

sup·port·er Anhänger(in) (*a.* SPORT), Befürworter(in)

sup·pose 1. annehmen, vermuten; *be ~d to ...* sollen; *what is that ~d to mean?* was soll denn das?; *I ~ so* ich nehme es an, vermutlich **2.** *cj* angenommen; wie wäre es, wenn

sup·posed angeblich, vermeintlich

sup·pos·ing → *suppose* 2

sup·po·si·tion Annahme *f*, Vermutung *f*

sup·pos·i·to·ry PHARM Zäpfchen *n*

sup·press unterdrücken

sup·pres·sion Unterdrückung *f*

sup·pu·rate MED eitern

su·prem·a·cy Vormachtstellung *f*

su·preme höchste(r, -s), oberste(r, -s), Ober...; größte(r, -s)

sur·charge 1. Nachporto *or* e-n Zuschlag erheben (*on* auf *acc*); **2.** Aufschlag *m*, Zuschlag *m* (*on* auf *acc*); Nach-, Strafporto *n* (*on* auf *acc*)

sure 1. *adj* sicher; *~ of o.s.* selbstsicher; *~ of winning* siegessicher; *~ thing!* F (aber) klar!; *be or feel ~* sicher sein; *be ~ to ...* vergiss nicht zu ...; *for ~* ganz sicher *or* bestimmt; *make ~ that* sich (davon) überzeugen, dass; *to be ~* sicher(lich) **2.** *adv* F sicher, klar; *~ enough* tatsächlich

sure·ly sicher(lich)

sure·ty JUR Bürge *m*, Bürgin *f*; Bürgschaft *f*, Sicherheit *f*; *stand ~ for s.o.* für j-n bürgen

surf 1. Brandung *f* **2.** SPORT surfen

sur·face 1. Oberfläche *f*; (*Straßen*)Belag *m* **2.** auftauchen; *Straße* mit e-m Belag versehen **3.** Oberflächen...; *fig* oberflächlich; *~ mail* gewöhnliche Post

surf·board Surfboard *n*, Surfbrett *n*

surf·er Surfer(in), Wellenreiter(in)

surf·ing Surfen *n*, Wellenreiten *n*

surge 1. *fig* Welle *f*, Woge *f*, (*Gefühls*-) Aufwallung *f* **2.** (vorwärts-)drängen; *~* (*up*) aufwallen

sur·geon MED Chirurg(in)

sur·ge·ry MED Chirurgie *f*; operativer Eingriff, Operation *f*; *Br* Sprechzimmer *n*; *Br* Sprechstunde *f*; *a. doctor's ~* Arztpraxis *f*; *~ hours* MED *Br* Sprechstunde(n *pl*) *f*

sur·gi·cal MED chirurgisch

sur·ly mürrisch, unwirsch

sur·name Familienname *m*, Nachname *m*, Zuname *m*

sur·pass *Erwartungen etc* übertreffen

sur·plus 1. Überschuss *m* (*of* an *dat*); **2.** überschüssig

sur·prise 1. Überraschung *f*, Verwunderung *f*; *take s.o. by* ~ j-n überraschen **2.** überraschen; *be ~d at or by* überrascht sein über (*acc*)

sur·ren·der 1. *v/i ~ to* MIL, *a. fig* sich ergeben (*dat*), kapitulieren vor (*dat*); *~ to the police* sich der Polizei stellen; *v/t et.* übergeben, ausliefern (*to dat*); aufgeben, verzichten auf (*acc*); *~ o.s. to the police* sich der Polizei stellen **2.** MIL Kapitulation *f* (*a. fig*); Aufgabe *f*, Verzicht *m*

sur·ro·gate Ersatz *m*

sur·ro·gate moth·er Leihmutter *f*

sur·round umgeben; umstellen

sur·round·ing umliegend

sur·round·ings Umgebung *f*

sur·vey 1. (sich) *et.* betrachten (*a. fig*); *Haus etc* begutachten; *Land* vermessen **2.** Umfrage *f*; Überblick *m* (*of* über *acc*); Begutachtung *f*; Vermessung *f*

sur·vey·or Gutachter *m*; Land(ver)messer *m*

sur·viv·al Überleben *n* (*a. fig*); Überbleibsel *n*; **~ in·stinct** Selbsterhaltungstrieb *m*; **~ kit** Überlebensausrüstung *f*; **~ train·ing** Überlebenstraining *n*

sur·vive überleben; *Feuer etc* überstehen; erhalten bleiben *or* sein

sur·vi·vor Überlebende *m*, *f* (*from, of gen*)

sus·cep·ti·ble empfänglich, anfällig (*both*: **to** für)

sus·pect 1. *j-n* verdächtigen (*of* gen); *et.* vermuten; *et.* anzweifeln, *et.* bezweifeln **2.** Verdächtige *m*, *f* **3.** verdächtig, suspekt

sus·pend *Verkauf, Zahlungen etc* (vorübergehend) einstellen; JUR *Verfahren, Urteil* aussetzen; *Strafe* zur Bewährung aussetzen; *j-n* suspendieren; vorübergehend ausschließen (*from* aus); SPORT *j-n* sperren; (auf)hängen; **be ~ed** schweben; **sus·pend·er** *Br* Strumpfhalter *m*, Straps *m*; Sockenhalter *m*; (*a.* **a pair of**) **~s** Hosenträger *pl*

sus·pense Spannung *f*; **in ~** gespannt, voller Spannung

sus·pen·sion (vorübergehende) Einstellung; Suspendierung *f*; vorübergehender Ausschluss; SPORT Sperre *f*; MOT *etc* Aufhängung *f*; **~ bridge** Hängegebrücke *f*; **~ rail·way** *esp Br* Schwebebahn *f*

sus·pi·cion Verdacht *m*; Verdächtigung *f*; Argwohn *m*, Misstrauen *n*; *fig* Hauch *m*, Spur *f*; **sus·pi·cious** verdächtig; argwöhnisch, misstrauisch; **become ~** Verdacht schöpfen

sus·tain *j-n* stärken; *Interesse etc* aufrechterhalten; *Schaden, Verlust* erleiden; JUR *e-m Einspruch etc* stattgeben

swab MED **1.** Tupfer *m*; Abstrich *m* **2.** *Wunde* abtupfen

swad·dle *Baby* wickeln

swag·ger stolzieren

swal·low¹ 1. schlucken (*a.* F); hinunterschlucken; **~ up** *fig* schlucken, verschlingen **2.** Schluck *m*

swal·low² ZO Schwalbe *f*

swamp 1. Sumpf *m* **2.** überschwemmen; **be ~ed with** *fig* überschwemmt werden mit; **swamp·y** sumpfig

swan ZO Schwan *m*

swank 1. F *esp Br* angeben **2.** F *esp Br* Angeber(in); Angabe *f* **3.** F piekfein

swank·y F piekfein; *esp Br* angeberisch

swap F **1.** (ein)tauschen **2.** Tausch *m*

swarm 1. ZO Schwarm *m* (*a. fig*) **2.** ZO schwärmen; *fig a.* strömen; *a. fig* wimmeln (**with** von)

swar·thy dunkel (*skin*), dunkelhäutig (*person*)

swas·ti·ka Hakenkreuz *n*

swat *Fliege etc* totschlagen

sway 1. *v/i* sich wiegen, schaukeln; **~ between** *fig* schwanken zwischen (*dat*); *v/t* hin- und herbewegen, schwenken, *s-n Körper* wiegen; beeinflussen **2.** Schwanken *n*, Schaukeln *n*

swear fluchen; schwören; **~ at s.o.** j-n wüst beschimpfen; **~ by** *fig* F schwören auf (*acc*); **~ s.o. in** JUR j-n vereidigen

sweat 1. *v/i* schwitzen (**with** vor *dat*); *v/t:* **~ out** *Krankheit* ausschwitzen; **~ blood** F sich abrackern (**over** mit) **2.** Schweiß *m*; F Schufterei *f*; **get in(to) a ~** *fig* F ins Schwitzen geraten *or* kommen

sweat·er Pullover *m*

sweat·shirt Sweatshirt *n*

sweat·y schweißig, verschwitzt; nach Schweiß riechend, Schweiß…; schweißtreibend

Swede Schwede *m*, Schwedin *f*

Swe·den Schweden *n*

Swe·dish 1. schwedisch **2.** LING Schwedisch *n*

sweep 1. *v/t* kehren, fegen; *fig* fegen über (*acc*) (*storm etc*); *Horizont etc* absuchen (**for** nach); *fig Land etc* überschwemmen; **~ along** mitreißen; *v/i* kehren, fegen; rauschen (*person*) **2.** Kehren *n*, Fegen *n*; Hieb *m*, Schlag *m*; F Schornsteinfeger *m*, Kaminkehrer *m*; **give the floor a good ~** den Boden gründlich kehren *or* fegen; **make a clean ~** gründlich aufräumen; SPORT gründlich abräumen

sweep·er (*Straßen*)Kehrer *m*; Kehrmaschine *f*; *soccer*: Libero *m*

sweep·ing durchgreifend (*changes etc*); pauschal, zu allgemein

sweep·ings Kehricht *m*

sweet 1. süß (*a. fig*); lieblich; lieb; **~ nothings** Zärtlichkeiten *pl*; **have a ~ tooth** gern naschen **2.** *Br* Süßigkeit *f*, Bonbon *m, n*; *Br* Nachtisch *m*; **~ corn** *esp Br* BOT Zuckermais *m*

sweet·en süßen

sweet·heart Schatz *m*, Liebste *m, f*

sweet pea BOT Gartenwicke *f*

sweet shop *esp Br* Süßwarengeschäft *n*

swell 1. *v/i a.* **~ up** MED (an)schwellen; *a.* **~ out** sich blähen; *v/t fig Zahl etc* anwachsen lassen; *a.* **~ out** *Segel* blähen **2.** MAR Dünung *f* **3.** F klasse

swell·ing MED Schwellung *f*

swel·ter vor Hitze fast umkommen

swerve 1. schwenken (**to the left** nach links), e-n Schwenk machen; *fig* abweichen (**from** von); **2.** Schwenk *m*, Schwenkung *f*, MOT *etc a.* Schlenker *m*

swift schnell

swim 1. *v/i* schwimmen; *fig* verschwimmen; **my head was ~ming** mir drehte sich alles; *v/t Strecke* schwimmen; *Fluss etc* durchschwimmen **2.** Schwimmen *n*; **go for a ~** schwimmen gehen

swim·mer Schwimmer(in)

swim·ming Schwimmen *n*; **~ bath(s)** *Br* Schwimmbad *n, esp* Hallenbad *n*; **~ cap** Badekappe *f*, Bademütze *f*; **~ costume** Badeanzug *m*; **~ gear** Badezeug *n*; **~ pool** Swimmingpool *m*, Schwimmbecken *n*; **~ things** Badesachen *pl*; **~ trunks** Badehose *f*

swim·suit Badeanzug *m*

swin·dle 1. *j-n* beschwindeln (**out of** um); **2.** Schwindel *m*

swine ZO Schwein *n* (*a.* F *fig*)

swing 1. *v/i* (hin- und her)schwingen; sich schwingen; einbiegen, -schwenken (**into** in *acc*); MUS schwungvoll spielen (**band** *etc*); Schwung haben (*music*); **~ round** sich ruckartig umdrehen; **~ shut** zuschlagen (**door** *etc*); *v/t et., die Arme etc* schwingen **2.** Schwingen *n*; Schaukel *f*; *fig* Schwung *m*; *fig* Umschwung *m*; **in full ~** in vollem Gang

swing door Pendeltür *f*

swin·ish ekelhaft

swipe 1. Schlag *m* **2.** schlagen (**at** nach)

swirl 1. wirbeln **2.** Wirbel *m*

swish¹ 1. *v/i* sausen, zischen; rascheln (*silk etc*); *v/t* mit *dem Schwanz* schlagen **2.** Sausen *n*, Zischen *n*; Rascheln *n*;

Schlagen *n*

swish² *Br* feudal, schick

Swiss 1. schweizerisch, eidgenössisch, Schweizer... **2.** Schweizer(in); **the ~** die Schweizer *pl*

switch 1. ELECTR, TECH Schalter *m*; RAIL Weiche *f*; Gerte *f*, Rute *f*; *fig* Umstellung *f* **2.** ELECTR, TECH (um)schalten (*a.* **~ over**) (**to** auf *acc*); RAIL rangieren; wechseln (**to** zu); **~ off** abschalten, ausschalten; **~ on** anschalten, einschalten

switch·board ELECTR Schalttafel *f*; (Telefon)Zentrale *f*

Swit·zer·land die Schweiz

swiv·el (sich) drehen

swiv·el chair Drehstuhl *m*

swoon in Ohnmacht fallen

swoop 1. *fig* F zuschlagen (*police etc*); *a.* **~ down** ZO herabstoßen (**on** auf *acc*); **~ on** F herfallen über (*acc*) **2.** Razzia *f*

swop F → **swap**

sword Schwert *n*

syc·a·more BOT Bergahorn *m*; Platane *f*

syl·la·ble Silbe *f*

syl·la·bus PED, UNIV Lehrplan *m*

sym·bol Symbol *n*

sym·bol·ic symbolisch

sym·bol·is·m Symbolik *f*

sym·bol·ize symbolisieren

sym·met·ri·cal symmetrisch

sym·me·try Symmetrie *f*

sym·pa·thet·ic mitfühlend; verständnisvoll; wohlwollend

sym·pa·thize mitfühlen; sympathisieren

sym·pa·thiz·er Sympathisant(in)

sym·pa·thy Mitgefühl *n*; Verständnis *n*

sym·pho·ny MUS Sinfonie *f*; **~ orchestra** MUS Sinfonieorchester *n*

symp·tom Symptom *n*

syn·chro·nize *v/t* aufeinander abstimmen; *Uhren, Film* synchronisieren; *v/i* synchron gehen *or* sein

syn·o·nym Synonym *n*

sy·non·y·mous synonym; gleichbedeutend

syn·tax LING Syntax *f*, Satzlehre *f*

syn·the·sis Synthese *f*

syn·thet·ic CHEM synthetisch; **~ fi·ber** (*Br* **fi·bre**) Kunstfaser *f*

Syr·i·a Syrien *n*

sy·ringe MED Spritze *f*

syr·up Sirup *m*

sys·tem System *n*; (*Straßen- etc*)Netz *n*;
Organismus *m*

sys·te·mat·ic systematisch

sys·tem er·ror IT Systemfehler *m*

T

T, t T, t *n*

tab Aufhänger *m*, Schlaufe *f*; Lasche *f*;
Etikett *n*, Schildchen *n*; Reiter *m*; F
Rechnung *f*

ta·ble 1. Tisch *m*; (Tisch)Runde *f*; Tabelle *f*, Verzeichnis *n*; MATH Einmaleins *n*;
at ~ bei Tisch; *at the* ~ am Tisch; *turn
the* ~*s* (*on s.o.*) *fig* den Spieß umdrehen **2.** *fig* auf den Tisch legen; *esp fig*
zurückstellen

ta·ble·cloth Tischdecke *f*, Tischtuch *n*

ta·ble·land GEOGR Tafelland *n*, Plateau
n, Hochebene *f*

ta·ble lin·en Tischwäsche *f*

ta·ble·mat Untersetzer *m*

ta·ble·spoon Esslöffel *m*

tab·let PHARM Tablette *f*; Stück *n*; (*Stein-
etc*)Tafel *f*

ta·ble ten·nis SPORT Tischtennis *n*

ta·ble·top Tischplatte *f*

ta·ble·ware Geschirr *n* und Besteck *n*

tab·loid Boulevardblatt *n*, -zeitung *f*

tab·loid press Boulevardpresse *f*

ta·boo 1. tabu **2.** Tabu *n*

tab·u·lar tabellarisch

tab·u·late tabellarisch (an)ordnen

tab·u·la·tor Tabulator *m*

tach·o·graph MOT Fahrtenschreiber *m*

ta·chom·e·ter MOT Drehzahlmesser *m*

ta·cit stillschweigend

ta·ci·turn schweigsam, wortkarg

tack 1. Stift *m*, (Reiß)Zwecke *f*; Heft-
stich *m* **2.** heften (*to* an *acc*); ~ *on* an-
fügen (*to* dat)

tack·le 1. Problem *etc* angehen; *soccer
etc*: ballführenden *Gegner* angreifen;
j-n zur Rede stellen (*about* wegen);
2. TECH Flaschenzug *m*; (*Angel*)Ge-
rät(e *pl*) *n*; *soccer*: Angriff *m*

tack·y klebrig; F schäbig

tact Takt *m*, Feingefühl *n*

tact·ful taktvoll

tac·tics Taktik *f*

tact·less taktlos

tad·pole ZO Kaulquappe *f*

taf·fe·ta Taft *m*

taf·fy Sahnebonbon *m*, *n*, Toffee *n*

tag 1. Etikett *n*; (*Namens-, Preis*)Schild
n; (Schnürsenkel)Stift *m*; stehende
Redensart *f*; *a.* **question** ~ LING Frage-
anhängsel *n* **2.** etikettieren; *Waren* auszeichnen; anhängen; ~ *along* F mitgehen, mitkommen; ~ *along behind s.o.*
F hinter j-m hertrotten

tail 1. Schwanz *m*; Schweif *m*; hinterer
Teil; F Schatten *m*, Beschatter(in); *pl*
Rück-, Kehrseite *f*; Frack *m*; *put a* ~
on j-n beschatten lassen; *turn* ~ *fig* sich
auf dem Absatz umdrehen; *with one's*
~ *between one's legs fig* mit eingezo-
genem Schwanz **2.** F j-n beschatten; ~
back esp Br MOT sich stauen (*to* bis zu);
~ *off* schwächer werden, abnehmen,
nachlassen

tail·back *esp Br* MOT Rückstau *m*

tail·coat Frack *m*

tail end Ende *n*, Schluss *m*

tail·light MOT Rücklicht *n*

tai·lor 1. Schneider *m* **2.** schneidern

tai·lor-made Maß…; maßgeschneidert
(*a. fig*)

tail pipe TECH Auspuffrohr *n*

tail·wind Rückenwind *m*

taint·ed GASTR verdorben

take 1. *v/t* nehmen; (weg)nehmen; mitnehmen; bringen; MIL, MED einnehmen; *chess etc:* Figur, Stein schlagen;
Gefangene, Prüfung etc machen; UNIV
studieren; *Preis etc* erringen; *Scheck
etc* (an)nehmen; *Rat* annehmen; *et.* hinnehmen; fassen, Platz bieten für; *et.*
aushalten, ertragen; PHOT *et.* aufnehmen, *Aufnahme* machen; *Temperatur*
messen; *Notiz* machen, niederschreiben; *ein Bad, Zug, Bus, Weg etc* nehmen; *Gelegenheit, Maßnahmen* ergreifen; *Mut* fassen; *Zeit, Geduld etc* erfordern, brauchen; *Zeit* dauern; *it took
her four hours* sie brauchte vier Stunden; *I* ~ *it that* ich nehme an, dass; ~ *it or
leave it* F mach, was du willst; ~*n all in
all* im Großen (und) Ganzen; *this seat*

is ~*n* dieser Platz ist besetzt; *be* ~*n by* or *with* angetan sein von; *be* ~*n ill* or *sick* erkranken, krank werden; ~ *to bits* or *pieces et.* auseinandernehmen, zerlegen; ~ *the blame* die Schuld auf sich nehmen; ~ *care* vorsichtig sein, aufpassen; ~ *care!* F mach's gut!; → *care 1*; ~ *hold of* ergreifen; ~ *part* teilnehmen (*in* an *dat*); → *part 1*; ~ *pity on* Mitleid haben mit; ~ *a walk* e-n Spaziergang machen; ~ *my word for it* verlass dich drauf; → *advice, bath 1, break* 1, *lead¹* 2, *message, oath, offense, place* 1, *prisoner, risk* 1, *seat* 1, *step* 1, *trouble* 1, *turn* 2, *etc*; *v/i* MED wirken, anschlagen; ~ *after j-m* nachschlagen, ähneln; ~ *along* mitnehmen; ~ *apart* auseinandernehmen (*a. fig* F), zerlegen; ~ *away* wegnehmen (*from s.o.* j-m); ... *to* ~ *away* Br ... zum Mitnehmen; ~ *back* zurückbringen; zurücknehmen; bei *j-m* Erinnerungen wachrufen; *j-n* zurückversetzen (*to* in *acc*); ~ *down* herunternehmen, abnehmen; *Hose* herunterlassen; auseinandernehmen, zerlegen; (sich) *et.* aufschreiben or notieren; sich *Notizen* machen; *what do you* ~ *me for?* wofür hältst du mich eigentlich?; ~ *from j-m et.* wegnehmen; MATH abziehen von; ~ *in j-n* (bei sich) aufnehmen; *fig et.* einschließen; *Kleidungsstück* enger machen; *et.* begreifen; *j-n* hereinlegen, F *j-n* aufs Kreuz legen; *be* ~*n in by* hereinfallen auf (*acc*); ~ *off Kleidungsstück* ablegen, ausziehen, *Hut etc* abnehmen; *et.* ab-, wegnehmen; abziehen; AVIAT abheben; SPORT abspringen; F sich davonmachen; ~ *a day off* sich e-n Tag freinehmen; ~ *on j-n* einstellen; *Arbeit etc* annehmen; übernehmen; *Farbe, Ausdruck etc* annehmen; sich anlegen mit; ~ *out* herausnehmen, *Zahn* ziehen; *j-n* ausführen, ausgehen mit *j-m*; *Versicherung* abschließen; *s-n Frust etc* auslassen (*on* an *dat*); ~ *over Amt, Macht, Verantwortung etc* übernehmen; die Macht übernehmen; ~ *to* Gefallen finden an (*dat*); ~ *to doing s.th.* anfangen, et. zu tun; ~ *up Vorschlag etc* aufgreifen; *Zeit etc* in Anspruch nehmen, *Platz* einnehmen; *Erzählung etc* aufnehmen; ~ *up doing s.th.* anfangen, sich

mit et. zu beschäftigen; ~ *up with* sich einlassen mit **2.** *film,* TV Einstellung *f;* F Einnahmen *pl*

take·a·way Br **1.** Essen *n* zum Mitmen **2.** Restaurant *n* mit Straßenverkauf

take·off AVIAT Abheben *n,* Start *m;* SPORT Absprung *m*

tak·ings Einnahmen *pl*

tale Erzählung *f;* Geschichte *f;* Lüge *f,* Lügengeschichte *f,* Märchen *n; tell* ~*s* petzen

tal·ent Talent *n,* Begabung *f*

tal·ent·ed talentiert, begabt

tal·is·man Talisman *m*

talk 1. *v/i* reden, sprechen, sich unterhalten (*to, with* mit; *about* über *acc; of* von); ~ *about s.th. a.* et. besprechen; *s.o. to* ~ *to* Ansprechpartner(in); *v/t Unsinn etc* reden; reden *or* sprechen *or* sich unterhalten über (*acc*); ~ *s.o. into s.th.* j-n zu et. überreden; ~ *s.o. out of s.th.* j-m et. ausreden; ~ *s.th. over Problem etc* besprechen (*with* mit); ~ *round j-n* bekehren (*to* zu), umstimmen **2.** Gespräch *n,* Unterhaltung *f* (*with* mit; *about* über *acc*); Vortrag *m;* Sprache *f,* Sprechweise *f;* Gerede *n,* Geschwätz *n; give a* ~ e-n Vortrag halten (*to* vor *dat; about, on* über *acc*); *be the* ~ *of the town* Stadtgespräch sein; *baby* ~ Babysprache *f,* kindliches Gebabbel; → *small talk*

talk·a·tive gesprächig, redselig

talk·er: *be a good* ~ gut reden können

talk·ing-to F Standpauke *f; give s.o. a* ~ j-m e-e Standpauke halten

talk show TV Talkshow *f*

talk-show host TV Talkmaster *m*

tall groß (*person*), hoch (*building etc*)

tal·low Talg *m*

tal·ly¹ SPORT *etc* Stand *m; keep a* ~ *of* Buch führen über (*acc*)

tal·ly² übereinstimmen (*with* mit); *a.* ~ *up* zusammenrechnen, -zählen

tal·on ZO Kralle *f,* Klaue *f*

tame 1. ZO zahm; *fig* fad(e), lahm **2.** ZO zähmen (*a. fig*)

tam·per: ~ *with* sich zu schaffen machen an (*dat*)

tam·pon MED Tampon *m*

tan 1. *Fell* gerben; bräunen; braun werden **2.** Gelbbraun *n;* (Sonnen)Bräune *f* **3.** gelbbraun

tang (scharfer) Geruch *or* Geschmack

tan·gent MATH Tangente *f*; *fly or go off at a ~* plötzlich (vom Thema) abschweifen

tan·ge·rine BOT Mandarine *f*

tan·gi·ble greifbar, *fig a.* handfest, klar

tan·gle 1. (sich) verwirren *or* verheddern, durcheinanderbringen; durcheinanderkommen **2.** Gewirr *n*, *fig a.* Wirrwarr *m*, Durcheinander *n*

tank MOT *etc* Tank *m*; MIL Panzer *m*

tank·ard (Bier)Humpen *m*

tank·er MAR Tanker *m*, Tankschiff *n*; AVIAT Tankflugzeug *n*; MOT Tankwagen *m*

tan·ner Gerber *m*

tan·ne·ry Gerberei *f*

tan·ta·lize *j-n* aufreizen

tan·ta·liz·ing verlockend

tan·ta·mount: *be ~ to* gleichbedeutend sein mit, hinauslaufen auf (*acc*)

tan·trum Wut-, Tobsuchtsanfall *m*

tap¹ 1. TECH Hahn *m*; *beer on ~* Bier *n* vom Fass **2.** *Naturschätze etc* erschließen; *Vorräte etc* angreifen; *Telefon (-leitung)* abhören, F anzapfen; *Fass* anzapfen, anstechen

tap² 1. mit *den Fingern, Füßen* klopfen, mit *den Fingern* trommeln (*on* auf *acc*); antippen; *~ s.o. on the shoulder* j-m auf die Schulter klopfen; *~ on* (leicht) klopfen an (*acc*) *or* auf (*acc*) *or* gegen **2.** (leichtes) Klopfen; Klaps *m*

tap dance Stepptanz *m*

tape 1. (schmales) Band; Kleb(e)streifen *m*; (Magnet-, Video-, Ton)Band *n*; (*Video- etc*)Kassette *f*; (Band)Aufnahme *f*; TV Aufzeichnung *f*; SPORT Zielband *n*; → **red tape 2.** (auf Band) aufnehmen; TV aufzeichnen; *a. ~ up* (mit Klebeband) zukleben

tape deck Tapedeck *n*

tape meas·ure Bandmaß *n*, Maßband *n*, Messband *n*

ta·per *a. ~ off* spitz zulaufen, sich verjüngen; *fig* langsam nachlassen

tape re·cord·er Tonbandgerät *n*

tape re·cord·ing Tonbandaufnahme *f*

ta·pes·try Gobelin *m*, Wandteppich *m*

tape·worm ZO Bandwurm *m*

taps MIL Zapfenstreich *m*

tap wa·ter Leitungswasser *n*

tar 1. Teer *m* **2.** teeren

tare ECON Tara *f*

tar·get (Schieß-, Ziel)Scheibe *f*; MIL Ziel *n* (*a. fig*), ECON *a.* Soll *n*; *fig* Zielscheibe *f*; *~ ar·e·a* MIL Zielbereich *m*; *~ group* Zielgruppe *f*

tar·iff ECON Zoll(tarif) *m*; *esp* Br Preisverzeichnis *n*

tar·mac Asphalt *m*; AVIAT Rollfeld *n*, Rollbahn *f*

tar·nish *v/i* anlaufen; *v/t Ansehen etc* beflecken

tart¹ *esp* Br Obstkuchen *m*; Obsttörtchen *n*; F Flittchen *n*, *sl* Nutte *f*

tart² herb, sauer; scharf (*a. fig*)

tar·tan Tartan *m*; Schottenstoff *m*; Schottenmuster *n*

tar·tar MED Zahnstein *m*; CHEM Weinstein *m*

task Aufgabe *f*; *take s.o. to ~ fig* j-n zurechtweisen (*for* wegen); *~ force* MIL *etc* Sonder-, Spezialeinheit *f*

tas·sel Troddel *f*, Quaste *f*

taste 1. Geschmack *m* (*a. fig*), Geschmackssinn *m*; Kostprobe *f*; Vorliebe *f* (*for* für); **2.** *v/t* kosten, probieren; schmecken; *v/i* schmecken (*of* nach)

taste·ful *fig* geschmackvoll

taste·less geschmacklos (*a. fig*)

tast·y schmackhaft

tat·tered zerlumpt

tat·ters Fetzen *pl*; *in ~* zerfetzt, in Fetzen; *fig* ruiniert

tat·too¹ 1. Tätowierung *f* **2.** (ein)tätowieren

tat·too² MIL Zapfenstreich *m*

taunt 1. verhöhnen, verspotten **2.** höhnische *or* spöttische Bemerkung

Tau·rus ASTR Stier *m*; *he (she) is (a) ~* er (sie) ist (ein) Stier

taut straff; *fig* angespannt

taw·dry (billig und) geschmacklos

taw·ny gelbbraun

tax 1. Steuer *f* (*on* auf *acc*); **2.** besteuern; *j-s Geduld etc* strapazieren

tax·a·ble steuerpflichtig

tax·a·tion Besteuerung *f*

tax e·va·sion Steuerhinterziehung *f*

tax·i 1. Taxi *n*, Taxe *f* **2.** AVIAT rollen

tax·i driv·er Taxifahrer(in)

tax·i rank, tax·i stand Taxistand *m*

tax of·fi·cer Finanzbeamte *m*

tax·pay·er Steuerzahler(in)

tax re·duc·tion Steuersenkung *f*

tax re·turn Steuererklärung *f*

T-bar Bügel *m*; *a. ~ lift* Schlepplift *m*

tea Tee *m*; *have a cup of* ~ e-n Tee trinken; *make some* ~ e-n Tee machen *or* kochen

tea·bag Teebeutel *m*, Aufgussbeutel *m*

teach lehren, unterrichten (in *dat*); *j-m et.* beibringen; unterrichten (*at* an *dat*)

teach·er Lehrer(in)

tea co·sy Teewärmer *m*

tea·cup Teetasse *f*; *a storm in a* ~ *fig* ein Sturm im Wasserglas

team Team *n*, *a.* Arbeitsgruppe *f*, SPORT *a.* Mannschaft *f*, soccer: *a.* Elf *f*

team·ster MOT LKW-Fahrer *m*

team·work Zusammenarbeit *f*, Teamwork *n*; Zusammenspiel *n*

tea·pot Teekanne *f*

tear¹ Träne *f*; *in* ~*s* weinend, in Tränen (aufgelöst)

tear² **1.** *v/t* zerreißen; sich *et.* zerreißen (*on* an *dat*); weg-, losreißen (*from* von); *v/i* (zer)reißen; F rasen, sausen; ~ *down* Plakat etc herunterreißen; Haus etc abreißen; ~ *off* abreißen; sich Kleidung vom Leib reißen; ~ *out* (her)ausreißen; ~ *up* aufreißen; zerreißen **2.** Riss *m*

tear·drop Träne *f*

tear·ful weinend; tränenreich

tear·jerk·er F Schnulze *f*

tea·room Teestube *f*

tease necken, hänseln; ärgern

tea·spoon Teelöffel *m*

teat zo Zitze *f*; *Br* (Gummi)Sauger *m*

tech·ni·cal technisch; fachlich, Fach...

tech·ni·cal·i·ty technische Einzelheit; reine Formsache

tech·ni·cian Techniker(in)

tech·nique Technik *f*, Verfahren *n*

tech·nol·o·gy Technologie *f*; Technik *f*

ted·dy bear Teddybär *m*

te·di·ous langweilig, ermüdend

teem: ~ *with* wimmeln von, strotzen von *or* vor (*dat*)

teen·age(d) im Teenageralter; für Teenager; **teen·ag·er** Teenager *m*

teens: *be in one's* ~ im Teenageralter sein

tee·ny(-wee·ny) F klitzeklein, winzig

tee shirt → *T-shirt*

teethe zahnen

tee·to·tal·(l)er Abstinenzler(in)

tel·e·cast Fernsehsendung *f*

tel·e·com·mu·ni·ca·tions Telekommunikation *f*, Fernmeldewesen *n*

tel·e·gram Telegramm *n*

tel·e·graph **1.** *by* ~ telegrafisch **2.** telegrafieren

tel·e·graph·ic telegrafisch

te·leg·ra·phy Telegrafie *f*

tel·e·phone **1.** Telefon *n* **2.** telefonieren; anrufen; ~ *booth*, ~ *box* *Br* Telefonzelle *f*, Fernsprechzelle *f*; ~ *call* Telefonanruf *n*, Telefongespräch *n*; ~ *di·rec·to·ry* → *phone book*; ~ *number* Telefonnummer *f*

te·leph·o·nist *esp* *Br* Telefonist(in)

tel·e·pho·to lens PHOT Teleobjektiv *n*

tel·e·print·er Fernschreiber *m*

tel·e·scope Teleskop *n*, Fernrohr *n*

tel·e·text Teletext *m*, Videotext *m*

tel·e·type·writ·er Fernschreiber *m*

tel·e·vise im Fernsehen übertragen *or* bringen; **tel·e·vi·sion** **1.** Fernsehen *n*; *a.* ~ *set* Fernsehapparat *m*, -gerät *n*, F Fernseher *m*; *on* ~ im Fernsehen; *watch* ~ fernsehen **2.** Fernseh...

tel·ex **1.** Telex *n*, Fernschreiben *n* **2.** telexen (*to* an *acc*), ein Telex schicken (*dat*)

tell *v/t* sagen; erzählen; erkennen (*by* an *dat*); Namen etc nennen; *et.* anzeigen; *j-m* sagen, befehlen (*to do* zu tun); *I can't* ~ *one from the other, I can't* ~ *them apart* ich kann sie nicht auseinanderhalten; *v/i* sich auswirken (*on* bei, auf *acc*), sich bemerkbar machen; *who can* ~ *?* wer weiß?; *you can never* ~, *you never can* ~ man kann nie wissen; ~ *against* sprechen gegen; von Nachteil sein für; ~ *s.o. off* F mit j-m schimpfen (*for* wegen); ~ *on s.o.* j-n verpetzen *or* verraten

tell·er Kassierer(in)

tell·ing aufschlussreich

tell·tale **1.** verräterisch **2.** F Petze *f*

tel·ly *Br* F Fernseher *m*

te·mer·i·ty Frechheit *f*, Kühnheit *f*

tem·per **1.** Temperament *n*, Wesen *n*, Wesensart *f*; Laune *f*, Stimmung *f*; TECH Härte(grad *m*) *f*; *keep one's* ~ sich beherrschen, ruhig bleiben; *lose one's* ~ die Beherrschung verlieren **2.** TECH Stahl härten

tem·pe·ra·ment Temperament *n*, Naturell *n*, Wesen *n*, Wesensart *f*

tem·pe·ra·men·tal launisch; von Natur aus

tem·pe·rate gemäßigt (*climate*, *region*)

tem·pe·ra·ture Temperatur *f*; **have a ~** MED erhöhte Temperatur *or* Fieber haben

tem·pest POET (heftiger) Sturm

tem·ple¹ Tempel *m*

tem·ple² ANAT Schläfe *f*

tem·po·ral weltlich; LING temporal, der Zeit

tem·po·ra·ry vorübergehend, zeiweilig

tempt *j-n* in Versuchung führen; *j-n* verführen (**to** zu); **temp·ta·tion** Versuchung *f*, Verführung *f*; **tempt·ing** verführerisch

ten 1. zehn **2.** Zehn *f*

ten·a·ble *fig* haltbar

te·na·cious hartnäckig, zäh

ten·ant Pächter(in), Mieter(in)

tend neigen, tendieren (**to** zu); **~ up·wards** e-e steigende Tendenz haben

ten·den·cy Tendenz *f*; Neigung *f*

ten·der¹ empfindlich, *fig a.* heikel; GASTR zart, weich; *sanft, zart, zärtlich*

ten·der² RAIL, MAR Tender *m*

ten·der³ ECON **1.** Angebot *n*; **legal ~** gesetzliches Zahlungsmittel **2.** ein Angebot machen (**for** für)

ten·der·foot F Neuling *m*, Anfänger *m*

ten·der·loin GASTR zartes Lendenstück

ten·der·ness Zartheit *f*; Zärtlichkeit *f*

ten·don ANAT Sehne *f*

ten·dril BOT Ranke *f*

ten·e·ment Mietshaus *n*, *contp* Mietskaserne *f*

ten·nis Tennis *n*; **~ court** Tennisplatz *m*; **~ play·er** Tennisspieler(in)

ten·or MUS, JUR Tenor *m*, JUR *a.* Wortlaut *m*, Sinn *m*; Verlauf *m*

tense¹ LING Zeit(form) *f*, Tempus *n*

tense² gespannt, straff (*rope etc*), (an)gespannt (*a. fig*); (über)nervös, verkrampft (*person*)

ten·sion Spannung *f* (*a.* ELECTR)

tent Zelt *n*

ten·ta·cle ZO Tentakel *m*, *n*, Fangarm *m*

ten·ta·tive vorläufig; vorsichtig, zaghaft

tenth 1. zehnte(r, -s) **2.** Zehntel *n*

tenth·ly zehntens

ten·u·ous *fig* lose (*link, relationship etc*)

ten·ure Besitz *m*, Besitzdauer *f*; **~ of of·fice** Amtsdauer *f*, Dienstzeit *f*

tep·id lau(warm)

term 1. Zeit *f*, Zeitraum *m*, Dauer *f*; JUR Laufzeit *f*; PED, UNIV Semester *n*, *esp Br* Trimester *n*; Ausdruck *m*, Bezeich-

nung *f*; **~ of office** Amtsdauer *f*, Amtsperiode *f*, Amtszeit *f*; *pl* Bedingungen *pl*; **be on good** (**bad**) **~s with** gut (schlecht) auskommen mit; **they are not on speaking ~s** sie sprechen nicht (mehr) miteinander; **come to ~s** sich einigen (**with** mit); **2.** nennen, bezeichnen als

ter·mi·nal 1. End...; letzte(r, -s); MED unheilbar; im Endstadium; **~ly ill** unheilbar krank **2.** RAIL *etc* Endstation *f*; Terminal *m*, *n*; ELECTR Pol *m*; IT Terminal *n*, Datenendstation *f*

ter·mi·nate *v/t* beenden; *Vertrag* kündigen, lösen; MED *Schwangerschaft* unterbrechen; *v/i* enden; ablaufen (*contract*)

ter·mi·na·tion Beendigung *f*; Kündigung *f*, Lösung *f*; Ende *n*; Ablauf *m*

ter·mi·nus RAIL *etc* Endstation *f*

ter·race Terrasse *f*; Häuserreihe *f*; *mst pl esp Br* SPORT Ränge *pl*

ter·raced house *Br* Reihenhaus *n*

ter·res·tri·al irdisch; Erd...; *esp* BOT, ZO Land...

ter·ri·ble schrecklich

ter·rif·ic F toll, fantastisch; irre (*speed, heat etc*)

ter·ri·fy *j-m* schreckliche Angst einjagen

ter·ri·to·ri·al territorial, Gebiets...

ter·ri·to·ry Territorium *n*, (*a.* Hoheits-, Staats)Gebiet *n*

ter·ror Entsetzen *n*; Schrecken *m*; POL Terror *m*; F Landplage *f*; **in ~** in panischer Angst

ter·ror·is·m Terrorismus *m*

ter·ror·ist Terrorist(in)

ter·ror·ize terrorisieren

terse *fig* knapp, kurz (und bündig)

test 1. Test *m*, Prüfung *f*; Probe *f* **2.** testen, prüfen; probieren; *j-s Geduld etc* auf e-e harte Probe stellen

tes·ta·ment: last will and ~ JUR Letzter Wille, Testament *n*

test an·i·mal Versuchstier *n*

test card TV Testbild *n*

test drive MOT Probefahrt *f*

tes·ti·cle ANAT Hoden *m*

tes·ti·fy JUR aussagen

tes·ti·mo·ni·al Referenz *f*

tes·ti·mo·ny JUR Aussage *f*; Beweis *m*

test pi·lot AVIAT Testpilot *m*

test tube CHEM Reagenzglas *n*

tes·ty gereizt

tet·a·nus MED Tetanus *m*, Wundstarr-krampf *m*

teth·er 1. Strick *m*; Kette *f*; *at the end of one's ~* *fig* mit s-n Kräften *or* Nerven am Ende sein **2.** *Tier* anbinden; anketten

text 1. Text *m*; TEL SMS *f*; Kurzmitteilung *f* **2.** eine SMS schicken / schreiben; *I'll ~ you* ich schicke dir eine SMS

text·book Lehrbuch *n*

tex·tile 1. Stoff *m*, *pl* Textilien *pl* **2.** Textil...

text message TEL SMS *f*; Kurzmitteilung *f*; *I'll send you a ~* ich schicke dir eine SMS

tex·ture Textur *f*, Gewebe *n*; Beschaffenheit *f*; Struktur *f*

than als

thank 1. *j-m* danken, sich bei *j-m* bedanken (*for* für); *~ you* danke; *~ you very much* vielen Dank; *no, ~ you* nein, danke; (*yes,*) *~ you* ja, bitte **2.** *~s* Dank *m*; *~s* danke (schön); *no, ~s* nein, danke; *~s to* dank (*gen*), wegen (*gen*)

thank·ful dankbar

thank·less undankbar

that 1. *pron and adj* das; jene(r, -s), der, die, das, derjenige, diejenige, dasjenige **2.** *relative pron* der, die, das, welche(r, -s) **3.** *cj* dass **4.** *adv* F so, dermaßen; *it's ~ simple* so einfach ist das

thatch 1. mit Stroh *or* Reet decken **2.** (Dach)Stroh *n*, Reet *n*; Strohdach *n*, Reetdach *n*

thaw 1. (auf)tauen **2.** Tauwetter *n*; (Auf)Tauen *n*

the 1. der, die, das, *pl* die **2.** *adv*: *~ ... ~ ...* je ... desto ...; *~ sooner ~ better* je eher, desto besser

the·a·ter Theater *n*; UNIV (*Hör*)Saal *m*; MIL (Kriegs)Schauplatz *m*

the·a·ter·go·er Theaterbesucher(in)

the·a·tre *Br* → **theater**; MED Operationssaal *m*

the·at·ri·cal Theater...; *fig* theatralisch

theft Diebstahl *m*

their ihr(e)

theirs der (die, das) ihrige *or* ihre

them sie (*acc pl*); ihnen (*dat*)

theme Thema *n*

them·selves sie (*acc pl*) selbst; sich (selbst)

then 1. *adv* dann; da; damals; *by ~* bis dahin; *from ~ on* von da an; → *every,*

now 1, *there 2*. *adj* damalig

the·o·lo·gian Theologe *m*, Theologin *f*

the·ol·o·gy Theologie *f*

the·o·ret·i·cal theoretisch

the·o·rist Theoretiker *m*

the·o·ry Theorie *f*

ther·a·peu·tic therapeutisch; F wohltuend; gesund

ther·a·pist Therapeut(in)

ther·a·py Therapie *f*

there 1. da, dort; (da-, dort)hin; *~ is, ~ are* es gibt, es ist, *pl* es sind; *~ and then* auf der Stelle; *~ you are* hier bitte; siehst du!, na also! **2.** *int* so; siehst du!, na also!; *~, ~* ist ja gut!

there·a·bout(s) so ungefähr

there·af·ter danach

there·by dadurch

there·fore deshalb, daher; folglich

there·up·on darauf(hin)

ther·mal 1. thermisch, Thermo..., Wärme... **2.** Thermik *f*

ther·mom·e·ter Thermometer *n*

ther·mos® Thermosflasche® *f*

the·sis These *f*; UNIV Dissertation *f*, Doktorarbeit *f*

they sie *pl*; man

thick 1. *adj* dick, (*fog etc a.*) dicht; F dumm; F dick befreundet; *be ~ with* wimmeln von; *~ with smoke* verräuchert; *that's a bit ~!* *esp Br* F das ist ein starkes Stück! **2.** *adv* dick, dicht; *lay it on ~* F dick auftragen **3.** *in the ~ of* mitten in (*dat*); *through ~ and thin* durch dick und dünn; **thick·en** dicker werden, (*fog etc a.*) dichter werden; GASTR eindicken, binden

thick·et Dickicht *n*

thick·head·ed F strohdumm

thick·ness Dicke *f*; Lage *f*, Schicht *f*

thick·set gedrungen, untersetzt

thick-skinned *fig* dickfellig

thief Dieb(in)

thigh ANAT (Ober)Schenkel *m*

thim·ble Fingerhut *m*

thin 1. *adj* dünn; dürr; spärlich, dürftig; schütter (*hair*); schwach, (*excuse etc a.*) fadenscheinig **2.** *adv* dünn **3.** verdünnen; dünner werden, (*fog, hair a.*) sich lichten

thing Ding *n*; Sache *f*; *pl* Sachen *pl*, Zeug *n*; *fig* Dinge *pl*, Lage *f*, Umstände *pl*; *I couldn't see a ~* ich konnte überhaupt nichts sehen; *another ~* et. anderes; *the right* ~ das Richtige

thing·a·ma·jig F Dings(bums) *m, f, n*

think *v/i* denken (*of* an *acc*); nachdenken (*about* über *acc*); *I* ~ *so* ich glaube *or* denke schon; *I'll* ~ *about it* ich überlege es mir; ~ *of* sich erinnern an (*acc*); ~ *of doing s.th.* beabsichtigen *or* daran denken, et. zu tun; *what do you* ~ *of or about ...?* was halten Sie von ...?; *v/t* denken, glauben, meinen; *j-n, et.* halten für; ~ *over* nachdenken über (*acc*), sich *et.* überlegen; ~ *up* sich *et.* ausdenken

think tank Beraterstab *m*, Sachverständigenstab *m*, Denkfabrik *f*

third 1. dritte(r, -s) **2.** Drittel *n*

third·ly drittens

third·rate drittklassig

Third World Dritte Welt

thirst Durst *m*

thirst·y durstig; *be* ~ Durst haben, durstig sein

thir·teen 1. dreizehn **2.** Dreizehn *f*

thir·teenth dreizehnte(r, -s)

thir·ti·eth dreißigste(r, -s)

thir·ty 1. dreißig **2.** Dreißig *f*

this diese(r, -s); ~ *morning* heute Morgen; ~ *is John speaking* TEL hier (spricht) John

this·tle BOT Distel *f*

thong (Leder)Riemen *m*

thorn Dorn *m*

thorn·y dornig; *fig* schwierig, heikel

thor·ough gründlich, genau; fürchterlich (*mess etc*)

thor·ough·bred zo Vollblüter *m*

thor·ough·fare Hauptverkehrsstraße *f*; *no* ~! Durchfahrt verboten!

though 1. *cj* obwohl; (je)doch; *as* ~ als ob **2.** *adv* dennoch, trotzdem

thought Denken *n*; Gedanke *m* (*of* an *acc*); *on second* ~ wenn ich es mir (recht) überlege

thought·ful nachdenklich; rücksichtsvoll, aufmerksam

thought·les gedankenlos; rücksichtslos

thou·sand 1. tausend *2.* Tausend *n*

thou·sandth 1. tausendste(r, -s) **2.** Tausendstel *n*

thrash verdreschen, verprügeln; SPORT F *j-m* e-e Abfuhr erteilen; ~ *about,* ~ *around* sich *im Bett etc* hin und her werfen; um sich schlagen; zappeln (*fish*); ~ *out* Problem *etc* ausdiskutie-

ren

thrash·ing Dresche *f*, Tracht *f* Prügel

thread 1. Faden *m* (*a. fig*); Garn *n*; TECH Gewinde *n* **2.** Nadel einfädeln; *Perlen etc* auffädeln, aufreihen

thread·bare abgewetzt, abgetragen; *fig* abgedroschen

threat Drohung *f*; Bedrohung *f*, Gefahr *f* (*to* gen *or* für)

threat·en (be)drohen

threat·en·ing drohend

three 1. drei **2.** Drei *f*

three·fold dreifach

three·ply → *ply²*

three·score sechzig

three·stage dreistufig

thresh AGR dreschen

thresh·ing ma·chine AGR Dreschmaschine *f*

thresh·old Schwelle *f*

thrift Sparsamkeit *f*

thrift·y sparsam

thrill 1. prickelndes Gefühl; Nervenkitzel *m*; aufregendes Erlebnis **2.** *v/t be* ~*ed* (ganz) hingerissen sein (*at, about* von)

thrill·er Thriller *m*, F Reißer *m*

thrill·ing spannend, fesselnd, packend

thrive gedeihen; *fig* blühen, florieren

throat ANAT Kehle *f*, Gurgel *f*; Rachen *m*; Hals *m*; *clear one's* ~ sich räuspern; → *sore 1*

throb 1. hämmern (*machine*), (*heart etc a.*) pochen, schlagen; pulsieren (*pain*) **2.** Hämmern *n*, Pochen *n*, Schlagen *n*

throm·bo·sis MED Thrombose *f*

throne Thron *m*

throng 1. Schar *f*, Menschenmenge *f* **2.** sich drängen (*in dat*)

throt·tle 1. erdrosseln; ~ *down* MOT, TECH drosseln, Gas wegnehmen **2.** TECH Drosselklappe *f*

through 1. *prp* durch (*acc*); bis (einschließlich); *Monday* ~ *Friday* von Montag bis Freitag **2.** *adv* durch; ~ *and* ~ durch und durch; *put s.o.* ~ *to* TEL *j-n* verbinden mit; *wet* ~ völlig durchnässt **3.** *adj* durchgehend (*train etc*); Durchgangs...

through·out 1. *prp:* ~ *the night* die ganze Nacht hindurch; ~ *the country* im ganzen Land, überall im Land **2.** *adv* ganz, überall; die ganze Zeit (hindurch)

through traf·fic Durchgangsverkehr *m*
through·way *Br* → **thruway**
throw 1. werfen; *Hebel etc* betätigen; *Reiter* abwerfen; *Party* geben, F schmeißen; ~ *a four* e-e Vier würfeln; ~ *off* Jacke *etc* abwerfen; *Verfolger* abschütteln; *Krankheit* loswerden; ~ *on* sich *e-e Jacke etc* (hastig) überwerfen; ~ *out* hinauswerfen; wegwerfen; ~ *up* *v/t* hochwerfen; F *Job etc* hinschmeißen; F (er)brechen; *v/i* F (sich er)brechen **2.** Wurf *m*
throw·a·way Wegwerf..., Einweg...; ~ **pack** Einwegpackung *f*
throw-in *soccer*: Einwurf *m*
thru F → **through**
thrum → **strum**
thrush zo Drossel *f*
thrust 1. *j-n, et.* stoßen (*into* in *acc*); *et.* stecken, schieben (*into* in *acc*); ~ *at* stoßen nach; ~ *s.th. upon s.o.* j-m et. aufdrängen **2.** Stoß *m*; MIL Vorstoß *m*; PHYS Schub *m*, Schubkraft *f*
thru·way Schnellstraße *f*
thud 1. dumpfes Geräusch, Plumps *m* **2.** plumpsen
thug Verbrecher *m*, Schläger *m*
thumb 1. ANAT Daumen *m* **2.** ~ *a lift or ride* per Anhalter fahren, trampen (*to* nach); ~ *through a book* ein Buch durchblättern; *well-thumbed* abgegriffen
thumb·tack Reißzwecke *f*, Reißnagel *m*, Heftzwecke *f*
thump 1. *v/t* j-m e-n Schlag versetzen; ~ *out Melodie* herunterhämmern (*on the piano* auf dem Klavier); *v/i* (heftig) schlagen *or* hämmern *or* pochen (*a. heart*); plumpsen; trampeln **2.** dumpfes Geräusch, Plumps *m*; Schlag *m*
thun·der 1. Donner *m*, Donnern *n* **2.** donnern
thun·der·bolt Blitz *m* und Donner *m*
thun·der·clap Donnerschlag *m*
thun·der·cloud Gewitterwolke *f*
thun·der·ous donnernd (*applause*)
thun·der·storm Gewitter *n*, Unwetter *n*
thun·der·struck wie vom Donner gerührt
Thur(s) *abbr of Thursday* Do., Donnerstag *m*
Thurs·day (*abbr Thur, Thurs*) Donnerstag *m*; *on* ~ (am) Donnerstag; *on* ~*s* donnerstags

thus so, auf diese Weise; folglich, somit; ~ *far* bisher
thwart durchkreuzen, vereiteln
thyme BOT Thymian *m*
thy·roid (gland) ANAT Schilddrüse *f*
tick¹1. Ticken *n*; Haken *m*, Häkchen *n* **2.** *v/i* ticken; *v/t mst* ~ *off* ab-, anhaken
tick² zo Zecke *f*
tick³: *on* ~ *Br* F auf Pump
tick·er·tape pa·rade Konfettiparade *f*
tick·et 1. Fahrkarte *f*, Fahrschein *m*; Flugkarte *f*, Flugschein *m*, Ticket *n*; (*Eintritts-, Theater- etc*)Karte *f*; (*Gepäck*)Schein *m*; Etikett *n*, (*Preis- etc* -) Schild *n*; POL Wahl-, Kandidatenliste *f*; (*a. parking*~) MOT Strafzettel *m* **2.** etikettieren; bestimmen, vorsehen (*for* für)
tick·et·can·cel·(l)ing ma·chine (Fahrschein)Entwerter *m*
tick·et| col·lec·tor (Bahnsteig)Schaffner(in); ~ **machine** Fahrkartenautomat *m*; ~ **of·fice** RAIL Fahrkartenschalter *m*
tick·ing Inlett *n*; Matratzenbezug *m*
tick·le kitzeln
tick·lish kitz(e)lig, *fig a.* heikel
tid·al wave Flutwelle *f*
tid·bit Leckerbissen *m*
tide 1. Gezeiten *pl*; Flut *f*; *fig* Strömung *f*, Trend *m*; *high* ~ Flut *f*; *low* ~ Ebbe *f* **2.** ~ *over fig* j-m hinweghelfen über (*acc*); *j-n* über Wasser halten
ti·dy 1. sauber, ordentlich, aufgeräumt; F hübsch, beträchtlich (*Sum etc*) **2.** *a.* ~ *up* in Ordnung bringen, (*Zimmer a.*) aufräumen; ~ *away* wegräumen, aufräumen
tie 1. Krawatte *f*, Schlips *m*; Band *n*; Schnur *f*; Stimmengleichheit *f*; SPORT Unentschieden *n*; (*Pokal*)Spiel *n*; RAIL Schwelle *f*; *mst pl fig* Bande *pl* **2.** *v/t* an-, festbinden; (sich) *Krawatte etc* binden; *fig* verbinden; *the game was* ~*d* SPORT das Spiel ging unentschieden aus; *v/i: they* ~*d for second place* SPORT *etc* sie belegten gemeinsam den zweiten Platz; ~ *down fig* (an)binden; *j-n* festlegen (*to* auf *acc*); ~ *in with* übereinstimmen mit, passen zu; verbinden *or* koppeln mit; ~ *up Paket etc* verschnüren; *et.* in Verbindung bringen (*with* mit); *Verkehr etc* lahmlegen; *be* ~*d up* ECON fest angelegt sein (*in* in *dat*)

tie·break(·er) *tennis*: Tie-Break *m*, *n*

tie-in (enge) Verbindung, (enger) Zusammenhang; ECON Kopplungsgeschäft *n*; *a book movie~appr* das Buch zum Film

tie-on Anhänge...

tie|pin Krawattennadel *f*

tier (Sitz)Reihe *f*; Lage *f*, Schicht *f*; *fig* Stufe *f*

tie-up (enge) Verbindung, (enger) Zusammenhang; ECON Fusion *f*

ti·ger zo Tiger *m*

tight 1. *adj* fest (sitzend), fest angezogen; straff (*rope etc*); eng (*a. dress etc*); knapp (*a. fig*); F knick(e)rig; F blau; *be in a ~ corner* in der Klemme sein *or* sitzen *or* stecken **2.** *adv* fest; F gut; *hold ~* festhalten; *sleep ~!* F schlaf gut!

tight·en festziehen, anziehen; *Seil etc* straffen; *~ one's belt fig* den Gürtel enger schnallen; *~ up (on) Gesetz etc* verschärfen

tight-fist·ed F knick(e)rig

tights (*Tänzer-, Artisten*)Trikot *n*; *esp Br* Strumpfhose *f*

ti·gress zo Tigerin *f*

tile 1. (Dach)Ziegel *m*; Fliese *f*, Kachel *f* **2.** (mit Ziegeln) decken; fliesen, kacheln

til·er Dachdecker *m*; Fliesenleger *m*

till¹ → *until*

till² (Laden)Kasse *f*

tilt 1. kippen; sich neigen **2.** Kippen *n*; *at a ~* schief, schräg; (*at*) *full ~* F mit Volldampf

tim·ber *Br* Bau-, Nutzholz *n*; Baumbestand *m*, Bäume *pl*; Balken *m*

time 1. Zeit *f*; Uhrzeit *f*; MUS Takt *m*; *Mal n*; *~ after ~, ~ and again* immer wieder; *every ~ I ...* jedes Mal, wenn ich ...; *how many ~s?* wie oft?; *next ~* nächstes Mal; *this ~* diesmal; *three ~s* dreimal; *three ~s four equals or is twelve* drei mal vier ist zwölf; *what's the ~?* wie spät ist es?; *what ~?* um wie viel Uhr?; *all the ~* die ganze Zeit; *at all ~s, at any ~* jederzeit; *at the ~* damals; *at the same ~* gleichzeitig; *at ~s* manchmal; *by the ~* wenn; als; *for a ~* e-e Zeit lang; *for the ~ being* vorläufig, fürs Erste; *from ~ to ~* von Zeit zu Zeit; *have a good ~* sich gut unterhalten *or* amüsieren; *in ~* rechtzeitig; *in no ~ (at all)* im Nu; *on ~* pünktlich; *some~ ago* vor einiger Zeit; *to pass the ~* zum Zeitvertreib; *take one's ~* sich Zeit lassen **2.** *et.* timen (*a.* SPORT); (ab)stoppen; zeitlich abstimmen, den richtigen Zeitpunkt wählen *or* bestimmen für

time| card Stechkarte *f*; *~ clock* Stechuhr *f*; *~ lag* Zeitdifferenz *f*

time-lapse *film*: Zeitraffer...

time·less immer während, ewig; zeitlos

time lim·it Frist *f*

time·ly (recht)zeitig

time sheet Stechkarte *f*

time sig·nal *radio*: Zeitzeichen *n*

time·ta·ble *Br* Fahrplan *m*, Flugplan *m*; Stundenplan *m*; Zeitplan *m*

tim·id ängstlich, furchtsam, zaghaft

tim·ing Timing *n*

tin 1. Zinn *n*; *Br* (Blech-, Konserven)Dose *f*, (-)Büchse *f* **2.** verzinnen; *Br* einmachen, eindosen

tinc·ture Tinktur *f*

tin·foil Stanniol(papier) *n*; Alufolie *f*

tinge 1. tönen; *be ~d with fig* e-n Anflug haben von **2.** Tönung *f*; *fig* Anflug *m*, Spur *f* (*of* von)

tin·gle prickeln, kribbeln

tink·er herumpfuschen, herumbasteln (*at* an *dat*)

tin·kle bimmeln; klirren

tinned *Br* Dosen..., Büchsen...

tinned fruit *Br* Obstkonserven *pl*

tin o·pen·er *Br* Dosenöffner *m*, Büchsenöffner *m*

tin·sel Lametta *n*; Flitter *m*

tint 1. (Farb)Ton *m*, Tönung *f* **2.** tönen

ti·ny winzig

tip¹ 1. Spitze *f*; Filter *m*; *it's on the ~ of my tongue fig* es liegt mir auf der Zunge **2.** mit e-r Spitze versehen

tip² 1. *esp Br* (aus)kippen, schütten; kippen; *~ over* umkippen **2.** *esp Br* (Schutt- *etc*)Abladeplatz *m*, (-)Halde *f*; *Br fig* F Saustall *m*

tip³ 1. Trinkgeld *n* **2.** *j-m* ein Trinkgeld geben

tip⁴ 1. Tipp *m*, Rat(schlag) *m* **2.** tippen auf (*acc*) (*as* als); *~ s.o. off* j-m e-n Tipp *or* Wink geben

tip·sy angeheitert

tip·toe 1. *on ~* auf Zehenspitzen **2.** auf Zehenspitzen gehen

tire¹ MOT Reifen *m*

tire² ermüden, müde machen *or* werden

tired müde; *be ~ of* j-n, et. satt haben

tire·less unermüdlich

tire·some ermüdend; lästig

tis·sue BIOL Gewebe n; Papier(taschen)-
tuch n; → **~ pa·per** Seidenpapier n

tit[1] F *contp* Titte f

tit[2] ZO Meise f

tit·bit *esp Br* → **tidbit**

tit·il·late j-n (*sexuell*) anregen

ti·tle Titel m; JUR (Rechts)Anspruch m
(*to* auf *acc*)

ti·tle·hold·er SPORT Titelhalter(in)

ti·tle page Titelseite f

ti·tle role THEA *etc* Titelrolle f

tit·mouse ZO Meise f

tit·ter 1. kichern 2. Kichern n

to 1. *prp* zu; an (*acc*), auf (*acc*), für, in
(*acc*), in (*dat*), nach; (im Verhältnis *or*
im Vergleich) zu, gegen(über); *extent,
limit, degree*: bis, (bis) zu, (bis) an
(*acc*); *time*: bis, bis zu, bis gegen, vor
(*dat*); *from Monday ~ Friday* von Montag bis Freitag; *a quarter ~ one* (ein)
Viertel vor eins, drei viertel eins; *go
~ Italy* nach Italien fahren; *go ~ school*
in die *or* zur Schule gehen; *have you
ever been ~ Rome?* bist du schon einmal in Rom gewesen?; *~ me etc* mir *etc*;
here's ~ you! auf Ihr Wohl!, prosit! 2.
adv zu; *pull ~ Tür etc* zuziehen; *come ~*
(wieder) zu sich kommen; *~ and fro* hin
und her, auf und ab 3. *with infinitive*:
zu; *intention, aim*: um zu; *~ go* gehen;
easy ~ learn leicht zu lernen; *... ~ earn
money* ... um Geld zu verdienen

toad ZO Kröte f, Unke f

toad·stool BOT ungenießbarer Pilz;
Giftpilz m

toad·y 1. Kriecher(in) 2. *~ to s.o.* *fig* vor
j-m kriechen

toast[1] 1. Toast m 2. toasten; rösten

toast[2] 1. Toast m, Trinkspruch m 2. auf
j-n *or* j-s Wohl trinken

toast·er TECH Toaster m

to·bac·co Tabak m; **to·bac·co·nist** Ta-
bak(waren)händler(in)

to·bog·gan 1. (Rodel)Schlitten m 2. ~
Schlitten fahren, rodeln

to·day 1. *adv* heute; heutzutage; *a week
~, ~ week* heute in e-r Woche, heute in
acht Tagen 2. *~'s paper* die heutige
Zeitung, die Zeitung von heute; *of ~,
~'s* von heute, heutig

tod·dle auf wack(e)ligen *or* unsicheren
Beinen gehen

to-do F *fig* Theater n

toe ANAT Zehe f; Spitze f

toe·nail ANAT Zehennagel m

tof·fee, tof·fy Sahnebonbon m, n, Toffee
n

to·geth·er zusammen; gleichzeitig

toi·let Toilette f; **~ pa·per** Toilettenpa-
pier n; **~ roll** *esp Br* Rolle f Toilettenpa-
pier

to·ken Zeichen n; *as a ~, in ~ of* als *or*
zum Zeichen (*gen*); zum Andenken
an (*acc*); *~ strike* Warnstreik m

tol·e·ra·ble erträglich

tol·e·rance Toleranz f; Nachsicht f

tol·e·rant tolerant (*of, towards* gegenüber)

tol·e·rate tolerieren, dulden; ertragen

toll[1] Benutzungsgebühr f, Maut f;
heavy death ~ große Zahl an Todesop-
fern; *take its ~ (on)* *fig* s-n Tribut fordern (von); s-e Spuren hinterlassen
(bei)

toll[2] läuten

toll-free TEL gebührenfrei

toll road gebührenpflichtige Straße,
Mautstraße f

tom F → **tomcat**

to·ma·to BOT Tomate f

tomb Grab n; Grabmal n; Gruft f

tom·boy Wildfang m

tomb·stone Grabstein m

tom·cat ZO Kater m

tom·fool·e·ry Unsinn m

to·mor·row 1. *adv* morgen; *a week ~, ~
week* morgen in e-r Woche, morgen in
acht Tagen; *~ morning* morgen früh; *~
night* morgen Abend 2. *the day after ~*
übermorgen; *of ~, ~'s* von morgen

ton (*abbr* **t, tn**) Tonne f

tone 1. Ton m; Klang m; (Farb)Ton m;
MUS Note f; MED Tonus m; *fig* Niveau
n 2. *~ down* abschwächen; *~ up* Muskeln *etc* kräftigen

ton·er *for cleansing the face* Gesichts-
wasser n; PRINT Toner m

tongs (*a pair of ~* e-e) Zange f

tongue ANAT, TECH Zunge f; (Mutter)-
Sprache f; Klöppel m (e-r Glocke);
hold one's ~ den Mund halten

ton·ic Tonikum n, Stärkungsmittel n;
Tonic n; MUS Grundton m

to·night heute Abend *or* Nacht

ton·sil ANAT Mandel f

ton·sil·li·tis MED Mandelentzündung *f*; Angina *f*

too zu; zu, sehr; auch (noch)

tool Werkzeug *n*, Gerät *n*; **~ bag** Werkzeugtasche *f*; **~ box** Werkzeugkasten *m*; **~ kit** Werkzeug *n*

tool·mak·er Werkzeugmacher *m*

tool·shed Geräteschuppen *m*

toot *esp* MOT hupen

tooth Zahn *m*

tooth·ache Zahnschmerzen *pl*, Zahnweh *n*

tooth·brush Zahnbürste *f*

tooth·less zahnlos

tooth·paste Zahncreme *f*, Zahnpasta *f*

tooth·pick Zahnstocher *m*

top[1] **1.** oberer Teil; GEOGR Gipfel *m*, Spitze *f*; BOT Krone *f*, Wipfel *m*; Kopfende *n*, oberes Ende; Oberteil *n*; Oberfläche *f*; Deckel *m*; Verschluss *m*; MOT Verdeck *n*; MOT höchster Gang; **at the ~ of the page** oben auf der Seite; **at the ~ of one's voice** aus vollem Hals; **on ~** oben(auf); darauf, F drauf; **on ~ of** (oben) auf (*dat or acc*), über (*dat or acc*) **2.** oberste(r, -s); Höchst…, Spitzen…, Top… **3.** bedecken (**with** mit); *fig* übersteigen; übertreffen; **~ up** Tank *etc* auffüllen; F *j-m* nachschenken

top[2] Kreisel *m* (*toy*)

top hat Zylinder *m*

top-heav·y kopflastig (*a. fig*)

top·ic Thema *n*; **top·ic·al** aktuell

top·ple: *mst* **~ over** umkippen; **~ the government** die Regierung stürzen

top-sy-tur·vy in e-r heillosen Unordnung

torch *Br* Taschenlampe *f*; Fackel *f*

torch·light Fackelschein *m*; **~ procession** Fackelzug *m*

tor·ment 1. Qual *f* **2.** quälen, peinigen, plagen

tor·na·do Tornado *m*, Wirbelsturm *m*

tor·pe·do MIL **1.** Torpedo *m* **2.** torpedieren (*a. fig*)

tor·rent reißender Strom; *fig* Schwall *m*

tor·ren·tial: **~ rain** sintflutartige Regenfälle *pl*

tor·toise ZO Schildkröte *f*

tor·tu·ous gewunden

tor·ture 1. Folter *f*, Folterung *f*; *fig* Qual *f*, Tortur *f* **2.** foltern; *fig* quälen

toss 1. *v/t* werfen; *Münze* hochwerfen; GASTR schwenken; **~ off** F *Bild etc* hin-

hauen; *v/i a.* **~ about, ~ and turn** sich *im Schlaf* hin und her werfen; *a.* **~ up** e-e Münze hochwerfen; **~ for s.th.** um et. losen; **~ one's head** den Kopf zurückwerfen **2.** Wurf *m*; Zurückwerfen *n*; Hochwerfen *n*

tot F Knirps *m*

to·tal 1. völlig, total; ganz, gesamt, Gesamt… **2.** Gesamtbetrag *m*, -menge *f* **3.** sich belaufen auf (*acc*); **~ up** zusammenrechnen, -zählen

tot·ter schwanken, wanken

touch 1. (sich) berühren; anfassen; *Essen etc* anrühren; *fig* herankommen an (*acc*); *fig* rühren; **~ wood!** toi, toi, toi!; **~ down** AVIAT aufsetzen; **~ up** ausbessern; PHOT retuschieren **2.** Tastempfindung *f*; Berührung *f*, MUS *etc* Anschlag *m*; (*Pinsel- etc*)Strich *m*; GASTR Spur *f*; Verbindung *f*, Kontakt *m*; *fig* Note *f*; *fig* Anflug *m*; **a ~ of flu** e-e leichte Grippe; **get in ~ with s.o.** sich mit j-m in Verbindung setzen

touch-and-go F kritisch, riskant, prekär; **it was ~ whether** es stand auf des Messers Schneide, ob

touch·down AVIAT Aufsetzen *n*, Landung *f*

touched gerührt; F leicht verrückt

touch·ing rührend

touch·line *soccer*: Seitenlinie *f*

touch·stone Prüfstein *m* (**of** für)

touch·y empfindlich; heikel (*subject etc*)

tough zäh; widerstandsfähig; *fig* hart; schwierig (*problem, negotiations etc*)

tough·en *a.* **~ up** hart *or* zäh machen *or* werden

tour 1. Tour *f* (**of** durch), (Rund)Reise *f*, (Rund)Fahrt *f*; Ausflug *m*; Rundgang *m* (**of** durch); THEA Tournee *f* (*a.* SPORT); **go on ~** auf Tournee gehen; → **conduct** 2 **2.** bereisen, reisen durch

tour·is·m Tourismus *m*, Fremdenverkehr *m*

tour·ist 1. Tourist(in) **2.** Touristen…; **~ class** AVIAT, MAR Touristenklasse *f*; **~ in·dus·try** Tourismusgeschäft *n*; **~ infor·ma·tion of·fice**, **~ of·fice** Verkehrsverein *m*; **~ sea·son** Reisesaison *f*, Reisezeit *f*

tour·na·ment Turnier *n*

tou·sled zerzaust

tow 1. *Boot etc* schleppen, *Auto etc a.* abschleppen **2.** **give s.o. a ~** j-n abschleppen; **take in** ~ *Auto etc* abschleppen

to·ward, *esp Br* **to·wards** auf (*acc*) …zu, (in) Richtung, zu; *time*: gegen; *fig* gegenüber

tow·el 1. Handtuch *n*, (*Bade- etc*)Tuch *n* **2.** (mit e-m Handtuch) abtrocknen *or* abreiben

tow·er 1. Turm *m* **2.** ~ **above**, ~ **over** überragen; ~ **block** *Br* Hochhaus *n*

tow·er·ing turmhoch; *fig* überragend; **in a ~ rage** rasend vor Zorn

town Stadt *f*; Kleinstadt *f*; **go into** ~ in die Stadt gehen; ~ **cen·tre** *Br* Innenstadt *f*, City *f*; ~ **coun·cil** *Br* Stadtrat *m*; ~ **coun·ci(l)·lor** *Br* Stadtrat *m*, Stadträtin *f*; ~ **hall** Rathaus *n*

town·ie F Städter(in), Stadtmensch *m*

town| plan·ner Stadtplaner(in); ~ **planning** Stadtplanung *f*

towns·peo·ple Städter *pl*, Stadtbevölkerung *f*

tow·rope MOT Abschleppseil *n*

tox·ic toxisch, giftig; Gift…

tox·ic waste Giftmüll *m*

tox·ic waste dump Giftmülldeponie *f*

toy 1. Spielzeug *n*, *pl a.* Spielsachen *pl*, ECON Spielwaren *pl* **2.** Spielzeug…; Miniatur…; Zwerg… **3.** ~ **with** spielen mit (*a. fig*)

trace 1. (durch)pausen; *j-n, et.* ausfindig machen, aufspüren, *et.* finden; *a.* ~ **back** *et.* zurückverfolgen (**to** bis zu); ~ **s.th. to** *et.* zurückführen auf (*acc*) **2.** Spur *f* (*a. fig*)

track 1. Spur *f* (*a. fig*), Fährte *f*; Pfad *m*, Weg *m*; RAIL Gleis *n*, Geleise *n*; TECH Raupe *f*, Raupenkette *f*; SPORT (Renn-, Aschen)Bahn *f*, (*Renn*)Strecke *f*; *tape etc*: Spur *f*; Nummer *f* (*on an LP etc*) **2.** verfolgen; ~ **down** aufspüren; auftreiben

track and field SPORT Leichtathletik *f*

track e·vent SPORT Laufdisziplin *f*

track·ing sta·tion Bodenstation *f*

track·suit Trainingsanzug *m*

tract Fläche *f*, Gebiet *n*; ANAT (*Verdauungs*)Trakt *m*, (*Atem*)Wege *pl*

trac·tion Ziehen *n*, Zug *m*

trac·tion en·gine Zugmaschine *f*

trac·tor Traktor *m*, Trecker *m*

trade 1. Handel *m*; Branche *f*, Gewerbe *n*; (*esp* Handwerks)Beruf *m* **2.** Handel treiben, handeln; ~ **on** ausnutzen; ~ **a·gree·ment** Handelsabkommen *n*

trade·mark Warenzeichen *n*

trade name Markenname *m*, Handelsbezeichnung *f*

trade price Großhandelspreis *m*

trad·er Händler(in)

trades·man (Einzel)Händler *m*; Ladeninhaber *m*; Lieferant *m*

trade(*Br* **trades**)**| u·nion** Gewerkschaft *f*; ~ **u·nion·ist** Gewerkschaftler(in)

tra·di·tion Tradition *f*; Überlieferung *f*

tra·di·tion·al traditionell

traf·fic 1. Verkehr *m*; (*esp* illegaler) Handel (**in** mit); **2.** (*esp* illegal) handeln (**in** mit); ~ **cir·cle** MOT Kreisverkehr *m*; ~ **in·struc·tion** Verkehrsunterricht *m*; ~ **is·land** Verkehrsinsel *f*; ~ **jam** (Verkehrs)Stau *m*, Verkehrsstockung *f*; ~ **light(s)** Verkehrsampel *f*; ~ **offend·er** Verkehrssünder(in); ~ **of·fense** (*Br* **offence**) Verkehrsdelikt *n*; ~ **reg·u·la·tions** Straßenverkehrsordnung *f*; ~ **sign** Verkehrszeichen *n*, -schild *n*; ~ **sig·nal** → **traffic light(s)**; ~ **war·den** *Br* Parküberwacher *m*, Politesse *f*

tra·ge·dy Tragödie *f*

tra·gic tragisch

trail 1. *v/t et.* nachschleifen lassen; verfolgen; SPORT zurückliegen hinter (*dat*) (**by** um); *v/i* sich schleppen; BOT kriechen; SPORT zurückliegen (**by 3-0** 0:3); ~ (**along**) **behind s.o.** hinter j-m herschleifen **2.** Spur *f* (*a. fig*), Fährte *f*; Pfad *m*, Weg *m*; ~ **of blood** Blutspur *f*; ~ **of dust** Staubwolke *f*

trail·er MOT Anhänger *m*; Wohnwagen *m*, Caravan *m*; *film*, TV Trailer *m*, Vorschau *f*; ~ **park** Standplatz *m* für Wohnwagen

train 1. RAIL Zug *m*; Kolonne *f*, Schlange *f*; Schleppe *f*; *fig* Folge *f*, Kette *f*; **by** ~ mit der Bahn, mit dem Zug; ~ **of thought** Gedankengang *m* **2.** *v/t j-n* ausbilden (**as** als, zum), schulen; SPORT trainieren; *Tier* abrichten, dressieren; *Kamera etc* richten (**on** auf *acc*); *v/i* ausgebildet werden (**as** als, zum); SPORT trainieren (**for** für)

train·ee Auszubildende *m*, *f*

train·er Ausbilder(in); ZO Abrichter(in), Dompteur *m*, Dompteuse *f*; SPORT Trainer(in); *Br* Turnschuh *m*

train·ing Ausbildung *f*, Schulung *f*; Abrichten *n*, Dressur *f*; SPORT Training *n*

trait (Charakter)Zug *m*

trai·tor Verräter *m*

tram *Br* Straßenbahn(wagen *m*) *f*

tram·car *Br* Straßenbahnwagen *m*

tramp 1. sta(m)pfen *or* trampeln (durch) **2.** Tramp *m*, Landstreicher *m*, Vagabund *m*; Wanderung *f*; Flittchen *n*; **tram·ple** (zer)trampeln

trance Trance *f*

tran·quil ruhig, friedlich

tran·quil·(l)i·ty Ruhe *f*, Frieden *m*

tran·quil·(l)ize beruhigen

tran·quil·(l)iz·er PHARM Beruhigungsmittel *n*

trans·act *Geschäft* abwickeln, *Handel* abschließen

trans·ac·tion Abwicklung *f*, Abschluss *m*; Geschäft *n*, Transaktion *f*

trans·at·lan·tic transatlantisch, Transatlantik..., Übersee...

tran·scribe abschreiben, kopieren; *Stenogramm etc* übertragen

tran·script Abschrift *f*, Kopie *f*

tran·scrip·tion Umschreibung *f*, Umschrift *f*; Abschrift *f*, Kopie *f*

trans·fer 1. *v/t* (**to**) *Betrieb etc* verlegen (nach); *j-n* versetzen (nach); SPORT *Spieler* transferieren (zu), abgeben (an *acc*); *Geld* überweisen (an *acc*, auf *acc*); JUR *Eigentum, Recht* übertragen (auf *acc*); *v/i* SPORT wechseln (**to** zu); umsteigen (**from ... to ...** von ... auf ... *acc*); **2.** Verlegung *f*; Versetzung *f*; SPORT Transfer *m*, Wechsel *m*; ECON Überweisung *f*; JUR Übertragung *f*; Umsteige(fahr)karte *f*

trans·fer·a·ble übertragbar

trans·fixed *fig* versteinert, starr

trans·form umwandeln, verwandeln

trans·for·ma·tion Umwandlung *f*, Verwandlung *f*

trans·form·er ELECTR Transformator *m*

trans·fu·sion MED Bluttransfusion *f*, Blutübertragung *f*

trans·gress verletzen, verstoßen gegen

tran·sient flüchtig, vergänglich

tran·sis·tor Transistor *m*

tran·sit Transit-, Durchgangsverkehr *m*; ECON Transport *m*; **in ~** unterwegs, auf dem Transport

tran·si·tion Übergang *m*

tran·si·tive LING transitiv

tran·si·to·ry → *transient*

trans·late übersetzen (**from English into German** aus dem Englischen ins

Deutsche)

trans·la·tion Übersetzung *f*

trans·la·tor Übersetzer(in)

trans·lu·cent lichtdurchlässig

trans·mis·sion MED Übertragung *f*; *radio*, TV Sendung *f*; MOT Getriebe *n*

trans·mit *Signale* (aus)senden; *radio*, TV senden; PHYS *Wärme etc* leiten, *Licht etc* durchlassen; MED *Krankheit* übertragen

trans·mit·ter Sender *m*

trans·par·en·cy Durchsichtigkeit *f* (*a. fig*); *fig* Durchschaubarkeit *f*; Dia (-positiv) *n*; Folie *f*; **trans·par·ent** durchsichtig (*a. fig*); *fig* durchschaubar

tran·spire transpirieren, schwitzen; *fig* durchsickern; F passieren

trans·plant 1. umpflanzen, verpflanzen (*a.* MED); MED transplantieren **2.** MED Transplantation *f*, Verpflanzung *f*; Transplantat *n*

trans·port 1. Transport *m*, Beförderung *f*; Beförderungs-, Verkehrsmittel *n or pl*; MIL Transportschiff *n*, -flugzeug *n*, (*Truppen*)Transporter *m* **2.** transportieren, befördern

trans·port·a·ble transportabel, transportfähig

trans·por·ta·tion Transport *m*, Beförderung *f*

trap 1. Falle *f* (*a. fig*); **set a ~ for s.o.** j-m e-e Falle stellen; **shut one's ~, keep one's ~ shut** F die Schnauze halten **2.** (in *or* mit e-r Falle) fangen; *fig* in e-e Falle locken; **be ~ped** eingeschlossen sein

trap·door Falltür *f*; THEA Versenkung *f*

tra·peze Trapez *n*

trap·per Trapper *m*, Fallensteller *m*, Pelztierjäger *m*

trap·pings Rangabzeichen *pl*; *fig* Drum und Dran *n*

trash F Schund *m*; Quatsch *m*, Unsinn *m*; Abfall *m*, Abfälle *pl*, Müll *m*; Gesindel *n*

trash·can Abfall-, Mülleimer *m*; Abfall-, Mülltonne *f*

trash·y Schund...

trav·el 1. *v/i* reisen; fahren; TECH *etc* sich bewegen; *fig* sich verbreiten; *fig* schweifen, wandern; *v/t* bereisen; *Strecke* zurücklegen, fahren **2.** Reisen *n*; *pl* (*esp Auslands*)Reisen *pl*; **~ a·gen·cy** Reisebüro *n*; **~ a·gent** Reisebüroinha-

ber(in); Angestellte *m*, *f* in e-m Reisebüro; **~ a·gent's**, **~ bu·reau** Reisebüro
n
trav·el·(l)er Reisende *m*, *f*
trav·el·(l)er's check (*Br* **cheque**) Rei-
se-, Travellerscheck *m*
trav·el·(l)ing| bag Reisetasche *f*; **~
expens·es** Reisekosten *pl*
trav·el sick·ness Reisekrankheit *f*
trav·es·ty Zerrbild *n*
trawl 1. Schleppnetz *n* **2.** mit dem
Schleppnetz fischen
trawl·er MAR Trawler *m*
tray Tablett *n*; Ablagekorb *m*
treach·er·ous verräterisch; tückisch
treach·er·y Verrat *m*
trea·cle *esp Br* Sirup *m*
tread 1. treten (**on** auf *acc*; **in** *acc*); *Pfad
etc* treten **2.** Gang *m*; Schritt(e *pl*) *m*;
(Reifen)Profil *n*
tread·mill Tretmühle *f* (*a. fig*)
trea·son Landesverrat *m*
trea·sure 1. Schatz *m* **2.** sehr schätzen; in
Ehren halten
trea·sur·er Schatzmeister(in)
trea·sure trove Schatzfund *m*
Trea·su·ry *Br*, **~ De·part·ment** Finanz-
ministerium *n*
treat 1. *j-n, et.* behandeln; umgehen mit;
et. ansehen, betrachten (**as** als); MED
j-n behandeln (**for** gegen); *j-n* einladen
(**to** zu); **~ s.o. to s.th.** *a.* j-m et. spendieren; **~ o.s. to s.th.** sich et. leisten *or*
gönnen; **be ~ed for** MED in ärztlicher
Behandlung sein wegen **2.** (besondere)
Freude *or* Überraschung; **this is my ~**
das geht auf meine Rechnung, ich lade
dich *etc* ein
trea·tise Abhandlung *f*
treat·ment Behandlung *f*
treat·y Vertrag *m*
tre·ble[1] **1.** dreifach **2.** (sich) verdreifachen
tre·ble[2] MUS Knabensopran *m*; *radio*:
(Ton)Höhe *f*
tree BOT Baum *m*
tre·foil BOT Klee *m*
trel·lis BOT Spalier *n*
trem·ble zittern (**with** vor *dat*)
tre·men·dous gewaltig, enorm; F klasse,
toll
trem·or Zittern *n*; Beben *n*
trench Graben *m*; MIL Schützengraben
m

trend Trend *m*, Entwicklung *f*, Tendenz
f; Mode *f*
trend·y F **1.** modern, modisch; **be ~** als
schick gelten, in sein **2.** *esp Br contp*
Schickimicki *m*
tres·pass 1. ~ on *Grundstück etc* unbefugt betreten; *j-s Zeit etc* über Gebühr
in Anspruch nehmen; **no ~ing** Betreten verboten! **2.** unbefugtes Betreten
tres·pass·er: ~s will be prosecuted Betreten bei Strafe verboten!
tres·tle Bock *m*, Gestell *n*
tri·al 1. JUR Prozess *m*, (Gerichts)Ver-
handlung *f*, (-)Verfahren *n*; Erprobung
f, Probe *f*, Prüfung *f*, Test *m*; Plage *f*; **on
~** auf *or* zur Probe; **be on ~** erprobt *or*
getestet werden; **be on ~, stand ~** vor
Gericht stehen (**for** wegen); **by way of ~**
versuchsweise **2.** Versuchs..., Probe...
tri·an·gle Dreieck *n*; Winkel *m*, Zeichendreieck *n*
tri·an·gu·lar dreieckig
tri·ath·lon SPORT Triathlon *n*, *m*, Drei-
kampf *m*
trib·al Stammes...
tribe (Volks)Stamm *m*
tri·bu·nal JUR Gericht(shof *m*) *n*
trib·u·ta·ry GEOGR Nebenfluss *m*
trib·ute: be a ~ to *j-m* Ehre machen; **pay
~ to** *j-m* Anerkennung zollen
trick 1. Trick *m*; (*Karten- etc*)Kunststück
n; Streich *m*; *card game*: Stich *m*;
(merkwürdige) Angewohnheit, Eigenart *f*; **play a ~ on s.o.** j-m e-n Streich
spielen **2.** Trick...; **~ question** Fangfra-
ge *f* **3.** überlisten, F reinlegen
trick·er·y Tricks *pl*
trick·le 1. tröpfeln; rieseln **2.** Tröpfeln *n*;
Rinnsal *n*
trick·ster Betrüger(in), Schwindler(in)
trick·y heikel, schwierig; durchtrieben,
raffiniert
tri·cy·cle Dreirad *n*
tri·dent Dreizack *m*
tri·fle 1. Kleinigkeit *f*; Lappalie *f*; **a ~** ein
bisschen, etwas **2. ~ with** *fig* spielen
mit; **he is not to be ~d with** er lässt
nicht mit sich spaßen
tri·fling geringfügig, unbedeutend
trig·ger Abzug *m*; **pull the ~** abdrücken
trig·ger-hap·py F schießwütig
trill 1. Triller *m* **2.** trillern
trim 1. *Hecke etc* stutzen, beschneiden,
sich *den Bart etc* stutzen; *Kleidungs-*

stück besetzen (*with* mit); **~med with fur** pelzbesetzt, mit Pelzbesatz; **~ off** abschneiden **2. give s.th. a ~** et. stutzen, et. (be)schneiden; **be in good ~** F gut in Form sein **3.** gepflegt

trim·mings Besatz *m*; GASTR Beilagen *pl*

Trin·i·ty REL Dreieinigkeit *f*

trin·ket (*esp* billiges) Schmuckstück

trip 1. *v/i* stolpern (*over* über *acc*); (e-n) Fehler machen; *v/t a*. **~ up** j-m ein Bein stellen (*a. fig*) **2.** (kurze) Reise; Ausflug *m*, Trip *m* (*a. sl*); Stolpern *n*, Fallen *n*

tripe GASTR Kaldaunen *pl*, Kutteln *pl*

trip·le 1. dreifach **2.** verdreifachen

trip·le jump SPORT Dreisprung *m*

trip·lets Drillinge *pl*

trip·li·cate 1. dreifach **2. in ~** in dreifacher Ausfertigung

tri·pod PHOT Stativ *n*

trip·per *esp Br* (*esp Tages*)Ausflügler(in)

trite abgedroschen, banal

tri·umph 1. Triumph *m*, *fig* Sieg *m* (*over* über *acc*); **2.** triumphieren (*over* über *acc*)

tri·um·phal Triumph…

tri·um·phant triumphierend

triv·i·al unbedeutend, bedeutungslos; trivial, alltäglich

trol·ley *esp Br* Einkaufswagen *m*; Gepäckwagen *m*, Kofferkuli *m*; (*Tee- etc*)Wagen *m*; (*supermarket*) **~** Einkaufswagen *m*; **shopping ~** Einkaufsroller *m*

trol·ley·bus Oberleitungsbus *m*, Obus *m*

trom·bone MUS Posaune *f*

troop 1. Schar *f*; *pl* MIL Truppen *pl* **2.** (*herein- etc*)strömen; **~ the colour** *Br* MIL e-e Fahnenparade abhalten

troop·er MIL Kavallerist *m*; Panzerjäger *m*; Polizist *m*

tro·phy Trophäe *f*

trop·ic ASTR, GEOGR Wendekreis *m*; **the ~ of Cancer** der Wendekreis des Krebses; **the ~ of Capricorn** der Wendekreis des Steinbocks

trop·i·cal tropisch, Tropen…

trop·ics Tropen *pl*

trot 1. Trab *m*; Trott *m* **2.** traben (lassen); **~ along** F losziehen

trou·ble 1. Schwierigkeit *f*, Problem *n*, Ärger *m*; Mühe *f*; MED Beschwerden *pl*; *a. pl* POL Unruhen *pl*; *pl* Unannehmlichkeiten *pl*; **be in ~** in Schwierigkei-

ten sein; **get into ~** Schwierigkeiten or Ärger bekommen; j-n in Schwierigkeiten bringen; **get** or **run into ~** in Schwierigkeiten geraten; **have ~ with** Schwierigkeiten or Ärger haben mit; **put s.o. to ~** j-m Mühe or Umstände machen; **take the ~ to do s.th.** sich die Mühe machen, et. zu tun **2.** *v/t* j-n beunruhigen; j-m Mühe or Umstände machen; j-n bemühen (*for* um), bitten (*for* um; *to do* zu tun); **be ~d by** geplagt werden von, leiden an (*dat*); *v/i* sich bemühen (*to do* zu tun), sich Umstände machen (*about* wegen)

trou·ble·mak·er Störenfried *m*, Unruhestifter(in)

trou·ble·some lästig

trou·ble spot *esp* POL Krisenherd *m*

trough Trog *m*; Wellental *n*

trounce SPORT haushoch besiegen

troupe THEA Truppe *f*

trou·ser: (*a pair of*) **~s** (e-e) Hose *f*

trou·ser suit *Br* Hosenanzug *m*

trous·seau Aussteuer *f*

trout ZO Forelle *f*

trow·el (Maurer)Kelle *f*

tru·ant Schulschwänzer(in); **play ~** *Br* (die Schule) schwänzen

truce MIL Waffenstillstand *m* (*a. fig*)

truck 1. MOT Lastwagen *m*; Fernlaster *m*; *Br* RAIL (offener) Güterwagen; Transportkarren *m* **2.** auf or mit Lastwagen transportieren

truck driv·er, **truck·er** MOT Lastwagenfahrer *m*; Fernfahrer *m*

truck farm ECON Gemüse- und Obstgärtnerei *f*

trudge (mühsam) stapfen

true wahr; echt, wirklich; treu (*to dat*); **be ~** wahr sein, stimmen; **come ~** in Erfüllung gehen; wahr werden; **~ to life** lebensecht

tru·ly wahrheitsgemäß; wirklich, wahrhaft; aufrichtig

trump 1. Trumpf(karte *f*) *m*; *pl* Trumpf *m* **2.** mit e-m Trumpf stechen; **~ up** erfinden

trum·pet 1. MUS Trompete *f* **2.** trompeten; *fig* ausposaunen

trun·cheon (Gummi)Knüppel *m*, Schlagstock *m*

trun·dle *Karren etc* ziehen

trunk (Baum)Stamm *m*; Schrankkoffer *m*; ZO Rüssel *m*; ANAT Rumpf *m*; MOT

Kofferraum *m*; ~ **road** *Br* Fernstraße *f*

trunks (*a.* **a pair of** ~ e-e) (*Bade*)Hose *f*; SPORT Shorts *pl*

truss 1. *a.* ~ **up** *j-n* fesseln; GASTR *Geflügel etc* dressieren **2.** MED Bruchband *n*

trust 1. Vertrauen *n* (*in* zu); JUR Treuhand *f*; ECON Trust *m*; Großkonzern *m*; **hold s.th. in** ~ et. treuhänderisch verwalten (*for* für); **place s.th. in s.o.'s** ~ j-m et. anvertrauen **2.** *v/t* (ver)-trauen (*dat*); sich verlassen auf (*acc*); (zuversichtlich) hoffen; ~ **him!** das sieht ihm ähnlich!; *v/i:* ~ **in** vertrauen auf (*acc*); ~ **to** sich verlassen auf (*acc*)

trust-ee JUR Treuhänder(in); Sachverwalter(in)

trust-ful, trust-ing vertrauensvoll

trust-wor-thy vertrauenswürdig, zuverlässig

truth Wahrheit *f*

truth-ful wahr; wahrheitsliebend

try 1. *v/t* versuchen; *et.* (aus)probieren; JUR (über) *e-e Sache* verhandeln; *j-m* den Prozess machen (*for* wegen); *j-n*, *j-s Geduld, Nerven etc* auf *e-e harte Probe* stellen; ~ **s.th. on** *Kleid etc* anprobieren; ~ **s.th. out** *et.* ausprobieren; *v/i* es versuchen; ~ **for** *Br*, ~ **out for** sich bemühen um **2.** Versuch *m*; **give s.o., s.th.** **a** ~ es mit *j-m*, *et.* versuchen; **have a** ~ es versuchen; **try-ing** anstrengend

tsar HIST Zar *m*.

T-shirt T-Shirt *n*

tub Bottich *m*, Zuber *m*, Tonne *f*; Becher *m*; F (*Bade*)Wanne *f*

tub-by F pumm(e)lig

tube Röhre *f* (*a.* ANAT), Rohr *n*; Schlauch *m*; Tube *f*; *Br* F U-Bahn *f* (*in London*); F Röhre *f*, Glotze *f*

tube-less schlauchlos

tu-ber BOT Knolle *f*

tu-ber-cu-lo-sis MED Tuberkulose *f*

tu-bu-lar röhrenförmig

tuck 1. stecken; ~ **away** F wegstecken; ~ **in** *esp Br* F reinhauen, zulangen; ~ **up** (*in bed*) *Kind* ins Bett packen **2.** Biese *f*; Saum *m*; Abnäher *m*

Tue(s) *abbr of* **Tuesday** Di., Dienstag *m*

Tues-day (*abbr* **Tue, Tues**) Dienstag *m*; **on** ~ (am) Dienstag; **on** ~**s** dienstags

tuft (*Gras-, Haar- etc*)Büschel *n*

tug 1. zerren *or* ziehen (an *dat or* **at** an *dat*); **2. give s.th. a** ~ zerren *or* ziehen an (*dat*)

tug-of-war SPORT Tauziehen *n* (*a. fig*)

tu-i-tion Unterricht *m*; Unterrichtsgebühr(en *pl*) *f*

tu-lip BOT Tulpe *f*

tum-ble 1. fallen, stürzen; purzeln (*a. fig*) **2.** Fall *m*, Sturz *m*

tum-ble-down baufällig

tum-bler (Trink)Glas *n*

tu-mid MED geschwollen

tum-my F Bauch *m*, Bäuchlein *n*

tu-mo(u)r MED Tumor *m*

tu-mult Tumult *m*

tu-mul-tu-ous tumultartig, (*applause etc*) stürmisch

tu-na ZO Thunfisch *m*

tune 1. MUS Melodie *f*; **be out of** ~ verstimmt sein **2.** *v/t mst* ~ **in** *Radio etc* einstellen (*to* auf *acc*); *a.* ~ **up** MUS stimmen; *a.* ~ **up** *Motor* tunen; *v/i:* ~ **in** (*das Radio etc*) einschalten; ~ **up** MUS (die Instrumente) stimmen

tune-ful melodisch

tune-less unmelodisch

tun-er *radio*, TV Tuner *m*

tun-nel 1. Tunnel *m* **2.** *Berg* durchtunneln; *Fluss etc* untertunneln

tun-ny ZO Thunfisch *m*

tur-ban Turban *m*

tur-bid trüb (*water*); dick, dicht (*smoke etc*); *fig* verworren, wirr

tur-bine TECH Turbine *f*

tur-bo F, **tur-bo-charg-er** MOT Turbolader *m*

tur-bot ZO Steinbutt *m*

tur-bu-lent turbulent

tu-reen (Suppen)Terrine *f*

turf 1. Rasen *m*; Sode *f*, Rasenstück *n*; **the** ~ die (Pferde)Rennbahn; der Pferderennsport **2.** mit Rasen bedecken

tur-gid MED geschwollen

Turk Türke *m*, Türkin *f*

Tur-key die Türkei

tur-key ZO Truthahn *m*, Truthenne *f*, Pute *f*, Puter *m*; **talk** ~ F offen *or* sachlich reden

Turk-ish 1. türkisch **2.** LING Türkisch *n*

tur-moil Aufruhr *m*

turn 1. *v/t* drehen, herum-, umdrehen; (um)wenden; *Seite* umblättern; *Schlauch etc* richten (**on** auf *acc*); *Antenne* ausrichten (**toward[s]** auf *acc*); *Aufmerksamkeit* zuwenden (**to** *dat*); verwandeln (**into** in *acc*); *Laub etc* färben; *Milch* sauer werden lassen; TECH formen, drechseln; ~ *the corner* um die Ecke biegen; ~ *loose* los-, freilassen; ~ *s.o.'s stomach* j-m den Magen umdrehen; → *inside* 1, *upside down*, *somersault* 1; *v/i* sich (um)drehen; abbiegen; einbiegen (*onto* auf *acc*; *into* in *acc*); MOT wenden; *blass, sauer etc* werden; sich verwandeln, *fig a.* umschlagen (*into, to* in *acc*); → *left* 2, *righ* 2; ~ *against* j-n aufbringen *or* aufhetzen gegen; *fig* sich wenden gegen; ~ *away* (sich) abwenden (*from* von); j-n abweisen, wegschicken; ~ *back* umkehren; j-n zurückschicken; *Uhr* zurückstellen; ~ *down* Radio etc leiser stellen; *Gas etc* klein(er) stellen; *Heizung etc* runterschalten; j-n, *Angebot etc* ablehnen; *Kragen* umschlagen; *Bettdecke* zurückschlagen; ~ *in* v/t zurückgeben; *Gewinn etc* erzielen, machen; *Arbeit* einreichen, abgeben; ~ *o.s. in* sich stellen; *v/i* F sich aufs Ohr legen; ~ *off* v/t *Gas, Wasser etc* abdrehen; *Licht, Radio etc* ausmachen, *Motor* abstellen; F j-n anwidern; F j-m die Lust nehmen; *v/i* abbiegen; ~ *on* *Gas, Wasser etc* aufdrehen; *Gerät* anstellen; *Licht, Radio etc* ausmachen, an-, einschalten; F j-n antörnen, anmachen; ~ *out* v/t *Licht* ausmachen, ausschalten; j-n hinauswerfen; F *Waren* ausstoßen; *Tasche etc* (aus)leeren; *v/i* kommen (*for* zu); sich erweisen *or* herausstellen als; ~ *over* (sich) umdrehen; *Seite* umblättern; wenden; *et.* umkippen; sich *et.* überlegen; j-n, *et.* übergeben (*to* dat); *Waren* umsetzen; ~ *round* sich umdrehen; ~ *one's car round* wenden; ~ *to* sich an j-n wenden; sich zuwenden (dat); ~ *up* *Kragen* hochschlagen; *Ärmel, Saum etc* umschlagen; *Radio etc* lauter stellen; *Gas etc* aufdrehen; *fig* auftauchen **2.** (Um)-Drehung *f*; Biegung *f*, Kurve *f*, Kehre *f*; Abzweigung *f*; *fig* Wende *f*, Wendung *f*; *at every* ~ auf Schritt und Tritt; *by* ~*s* abwechselnd; *in* ~ der Reihe nach; abwechselnd; *it is my* ~ ich bin an der Reihe *or* F dran; *make a left* ~ (nach) links abbiegen; *take* ~*s* sich abwechseln (*at* bei); *take a* ~ *for the better* (*worse*) sich bessern (sich verschlimmern); *do s.o. a good* (*bad*) ~ j-m e-n guten (schlechten) Dienst erweisen

turn·coat Abtrünnige *m*, *f*, Überläufer(in); (*political*) ~ F Wendehals *m*
turn·er Drechsler *m*; Dreher *m*
turn·ing *esp Br* Abzweigung *f*
turn·ing cir·cle MOT Wendekreis *m*
turn·ing point *fig* Wendepunkt *m*
tur·nip BOT Rübe *f*
turn-off Abzweigung *f*
turn·out Besucher(zahl *f*) *pl*, Beteiligung *f*; Wahlbeteiligung *f*; F Aufmachung *f*
turn·o·ver ECON Umsatz *m*; Personalwechsel *m*, Fluktuation *f*
turn·pike (**road**) gebührenpflichtige Schnellstraße
turn·stile Drehkreuz *n*
turn·ta·ble Plattenteller *m*
turn-up *Br* (Hosen)Aufschlag *m*
tur·pen·tine CHEM Terpentin *n*
tur·quoise MIN Türkis *m*
tur·ret ARCH Ecktürmchen *n*; MIL (Panzer)Turm *m*; MAR Gefechtsturm *m*, Geschützturm *m*
tur·tle ZO (See)Schildkröte *f*
tur·tle·dove ZO Turteltaube *f*
tur·tle·neck Rollkragen(pullover) *m*
tusk ZO Stoßzahn *m*; Hauer *m*
tus·sle F Gerangel *n*
tus·sock Grasbüschel *n*
tu·te·lage (An)Leitung *f*; JUR Vormundschaft *f*
tu·tor Privat-, Hauslehrer(in); *Br* UNIV Tutor(in), Studienleiter(in)
tu·to·ri·al *Br* UNIV Tutorenkurs *m*
tux·e·do Smoking *m*
TV 1. TV *n*, Fernsehen *n*; Fernsehgerät *n*, F Fernseher *m*; *on* ~ im Fernsehen; *watch* ~ fernsehen **2.** Fernseh...
twang 1. Schwirren *n*; *mst nasal* ~ näselnde Aussprache **2.** schwirren (lassen)
tweak F zwicken, kneifen
tweet ZO piep(s)en
tweez·ers (*a pair of* ~ e-e) Pinzette *f*
twelfth 1. zwölfte(r, -s) **2.** Zwölftel *n*
twelve 1. zwölf **2.** Zwölf *f*
twen·ti·eth zwanzigste(r, -s)
twen·ty 1. zwanzig **2.** Zwanzig *f*
twice zweimal
twid·dle (herum)spielen mit (*or with* mit); ~ *one's thumbs* Däumchen drehen
twig BOT dünner Zweig, Ästchen *n*

twi·light (*esp* Abend)Dämmerung *f*; Zwielicht *n*, Dämmerlicht *n*

twin 1. Zwilling *m*; *pl* Zwillinge *pl* **2.** Zwillings...; doppelt **3.** *be* **∼ned with** die Partnerstadt sein von

twin-bed·ded room Zweibettzimmer *n*

twin beds zwei Einzelbetten

twin broth·er Zwillingsbruder *m*

twine 1. Bindfaden *m*, Schnur *f* **2.** (sich) schlingen *or* winden (**round** um); *a.* **∼ together** zusammendrehen

twin-en·gined AVIAT zweimotorig

twinge stechender Schmerz, Stechen *n*; *a* **∼ of conscience** Gewissensbisse *pl*

twin·kle 1. glitzern (*stars*), (*a. eyes*) funkeln (**with** vor *dat*); **2.** Glitzern *n*, Funkeln *n*; **with a ∼ in one's eye** augenzwinkernd

twin sis·ter Zwillingsschwester *f*

twin town Partnerstadt *f*

twirl 1. (herum)wirbeln; wirbeln (**round** über *acc*); **2.** Wirbel *m*

twist 1. *v/t* drehen; wickeln (**round** um); *fig* verdrehen; **∼ off** abdrehen; Deckel abschrauben; **∼ one's ankle** (mit dem Fuß) umknicken, sich den Fuß vertreten; *her face was* **∼ed with pain** ihr Gesicht war schmerzverzerrt; *v/i* sich winden, (*river etc a.*) sich schlängeln **2.** Drehung *f*; Biegung *f*; (*überraschende*) Wendung; MUS Twist *m*

twitch 1. *v/t* zucken (mit); *v/i* zucken (**with** vor); zupfen (**at** an *dat*); **2.** Zucken *n*; Zuckung *f*

twit·ter 1. zwitschern **2.** Zwitschern *n*, Gezwitscher *n*; *be all of a* **∼** F ganz aufgeregt sein

two 1. zwei; *the* **∼** *cars* die beiden Autos; *the* **∼** *of us* wir beide; *in* **∼s** zu zweit,

paarweise; *cut in* **∼** in zwei Teile schneiden; *put* **∼** *and* **∼** *together* zwei und zwei zusammenzählen **2.** Zwei *f*

two-edged zweischneidig

two-faced falsch, heuchlerisch

two·fold zweifach

two·pence *Br* zwei Pence *pl*

two·pen·ny *Br* F für zwei Pence

two-piece zweiteilig; **∼ dress** Jackenkleid *n*

two-seat·er AVIAT, MOT Zweisitzer *m*

two-sid·ed zweiseitig

two-sto·ried, *Br* **two-sto·rey** zweistöckig

two-way traf·fic MOT Gegenverkehr *m*

ty·coon (*Industrie- etc*)Magnat *m*

type 1. Art *f*, Sorte *f*; Typ *m*; PRINT Type *f*, Buchstabe *m* **2.** *v/t et.* mit der Maschine schreiben, tippen; *v/i* Maschine schreiben, tippen

type·writ·er Schreibmaschine *f*

type·writ·ten maschine(n)geschrieben

ty·phoid (fe·ver) MED Typhus *m*

ty·phoon Taifun *m*

ty·phus MED Flecktyphus *m*, -fieber *n*

typ·i·cal typisch, bezeichnend (**of** für)

typ·i·fy typisch sein für, kennzeichnen; verkörpern

typ·ing er·ror Tippfehler *m*

typ·ing pool ECON Schreibzentrale *f*

typ·ist Schreibkraft *f*; Maschinenschreiber(in)

ty·ran·ni·cal tyrannisch

tyr·an·nize tyrannisieren

tyr·an·ny Tyrannei *f*

ty·rant Tyrann(in)

tyre *Br* → **tire**[1]

tzar → **tsar**

U

U, u U, u *n*

ud·der ZO Euter *n*

ug·ly hässlich (*a. fig*); bös(e), schlimm (*wound etc*)

ul·cer MED Geschwür *n*

ul·te·ri·or: **∼ motive** Hintergedanke *m*

ul·ti·mate letzte(r, -s), End...; höchste(r, -s)

ul·ti·mate·ly letztlich; schließlich

ul·ti·ma·tum Ultimatum *n*; *deliver an* **∼** *to s.o.* j-m ein Ultimatum stellen

ul·tra-high fre·quen·cy ELECTR Ultrakurzwelle *f*

ul·tra·ma·rine ultramarin

ul·tra·son·ic Ultraschall...

ul·tra·sound PHYS Ultraschall *m*

ul·tra·vi·o·let ultraviolett

um·bil·i·cal cord ANAT Nabelschnur *f*

um·brel·la (Regen)Schirm *m*; *fig* Schutz *m*

um·pire SPORT **1.** Schiedsrichter(in) **2.** als Schiedsrichter(in) fungieren (bei)

un·a·bashed unverfroren

un·a·bat·ed unvermindert

un·a·ble unfähig, außerstande, nicht in der Lage

un·ac·cept·a·ble unzumutbar

un·ac·count·a·ble unerklärlich

un·ac·cus·tomed ungewohnt

un·ac·quaint·ed: *be* ~ *with s.th.* et. nicht kennen, mit e-r Sache nicht vertraut sein

un·ad·vised unbesonnen, unüberlegt

un·af·fect·ed natürlich, ungekünstelt; *be* ~ *by* nicht betroffen sein von

un·aid·ed ohne Unterstützung, (ganz) allein

un·al·ter·a·ble unabänderlich

u·nan·i·mous einmütig; einstimmig

un·an·nounced unangemeldet

un·an·swer·a·ble unwiderlegbar; nicht zu beantworten(d)

un·ap·pe·tiz·ing unappetitlich

un·ap·proach·a·ble unnahbar

un·armed unbewaffnet

un·asked ungestellt (*question*); unaufgefordert, ungebeten (*guest etc*)

un·as·sist·ed ohne (fremde) Hilfe, (ganz) allein

un·as·sum·ing bescheiden

un·at·tached ungebunden, frei

un·at·tend·ed unbeaufsichtigt

un·at·trac·tive unattraktiv, wenig anziehend, reizlos

un·au·thor·ized unberechtigt, unbefugt

un·a·void·a·ble unvermeidlich

un·a·ware: *be* ~ *of s.th.* sich e-r Sache nicht bewusst sein, et. nicht bemerken

un·a·wares: *catch or take s.o.* ~ j-n überraschen

un·bal·ance *j-n* aus dem (seelischen) Gleichgewicht bringen

un·bal·anced unausgeglichen, labil

un·bar aufriegeln, entriegeln

un·bear·a·ble unerträglich; *person*: unausstehlich

un·beat·a·ble unschlagbar

un·beat·en ungeschlagen, unbesiegt

un·be·com·ing unvorteilhaft

un·be·known(st): ~ *to s.o.* ohne j-s Wissen

un·be·liev·a·ble unglaublich

un·bend gerade biegen; sich aufrichten; *fig* aus sich herausgehen, auftauen

un·bend·ing unbeugsam

un·bi·as(s)ed unvoreingenommen; JUR unbefangen

un·bind losbinden

un·blem·ished makellos

un·born ungeboren

un·break·a·ble unzerbrechlich

un·bri·dled *fig* ungezügelt, zügellos; ~ *tongue* lose Zunge

un·bro·ken ununterbrochen; heil, unversehrt; nicht zugeritten (*horse*)

un·buck·le aufschnallen, losschnallen

un·bur·den: ~ *o.s. to s.o.* j-m sein Herz ausschütten

un·but·ton aufknöpfen

un·called-for ungerechtfertigt; unnötig; unpassend

un·can·ny unheimlich

un·cared-for vernachlässigt

un·ceas·ing unaufhörlich

un·cer·e·mo·ni·ous brüsk, unhöflich; überstürzt

un·cer·tain unsicher, ungewiss, unbestimmt; vage; METEOR unbeständig

un·cer·tain·ty Unsicherheit *f*, Ungewissheit *f*

un·chain losketten

un·changed unverändert

un·chang·ing unveränderlich

un·char·i·ta·ble unfair

un·checked ungehindert; ungeprüft

un·chris·tian unchristlich

un·civ·il unhöflich

un·civ·i·lized unzivilisiert

un·cle Onkel *m*

un·com·fort·a·ble unbequem; *feel* ~ sich unbehaglich fühlen

un·com·mon ungewöhnlich

un·com·mu·ni·ca·tive wortkarg, verschlossen

un·com·pre·hend·ing verständnislos

un·com·pro·mis·ing kompromisslos

un·con·cerned: *be* ~ *about* sich keine Gedanken *or* Sorgen machen über (*acc*); *be* ~ *with* uninteressiert sein an (*dat*)

un·con·di·tion·al bedingungslos

un·con·firmed unbestätigt

un·con·scious unbewusst; unbeabsichtigt; MED bewusstlos; *be* ~ *of* sich e-r Sache nicht bewusst sein, nicht bemerken; **un·con·scious·ness** MED Bewusstlosigkeit f

un·con·sti·tu·tion·al verfassungswidrig

un·con·trol·la·ble unkontrollierbar; nicht zu bändigen(d); unbändig (*rage etc*); **un·con·trolled** unkontrolliert

un·con·ven·tion·al unkonventionell

un·con·vinced: *be* ~ nicht überzeugt sein (*about* von)

un·con·vinc·ing nicht überzeugend

un·cooked ungekocht, roh

un·cork entkorken

un·count·a·ble unzählbar

un·coup·le abkoppeln

un·couth *fig* ungehobelt

un·cov·er aufdecken, *fig a.* enthüllen

un·crit·i·cal unkritisch; *be* ~ *of s.th.* e-r Sache unkritisch gegenüberstehen

unc·tion REL Salbung f

unc·tu·ous salbungsvoll

un·cut ungekürzt (*film, novel etc*); ungeschliffen (*diamond etc*)

un·dam·aged unbeschädigt, unversehrt, heil

un·dat·ed undatiert, ohne Datum

un·daunt·ed unerschrocken, furchtlos

un·de·cid·ed unentschieden, offen; unentschlossen

un·de·mon·stra·tive zurückhaltend, reserviert

un·de·ni·a·ble unbestreitbar

un·der 1. *prp* unter (*dat or acc*) **2.** *adv* unten; darunter

un·der·age minderjährig

un·der·bid unterbieten

un·der·brush → *undergrowth*

un·der·car·riage AVIAT Fahrwerk *n*, Fahrgestell *n*

un·der·charge zu wenig berechnen; zu wenig verlangen

un·der·clothes, **un·der·cloth·ing** → *underwear*

un·der·coat Grundierung f

un·der·cov·er: ~ *agent* verdeckter Ermittler

un·der·cut *j-n* (im Preis) unterbieten

un·der·de·vel·oped unterentwickelt; ~ *country* Entwicklungsland *n*

un·der·dog Benachteiligte *m, f*

un·der·done nicht durchgebraten

un·der·es·ti·mate zu niedrig schätzen *or* veranschlagen; *fig* unterschätzen

un·der·ex·pose PHOT unterbelichten

un·der·fed unterernährt

un·der·go erleben, durchmachen; MED

sich *e-r Operation etc* unterziehen

un·der·grad F, **un·der·grad·u·ate** Student(in)

un·der·ground 1. *adv* unterirdisch, unter der Erde **2.** *adj* unterirdisch; *fig* Untergrund… **3.** *esp Br* Untergrundbahn f, U-Bahn f; *by* ~ mit der U-Bahn

un·der·growth Unterholz *n*

un·der·hand, **un·der·hand·ed** heimlich; hinterhältig

un·der·line unterstreichen (*a. fig*)

un·der·ling *contp* Untergebene *m, f*

un·der·ly·ing zugrunde liegend

un·der·mine unterspülen; *fig* untergraben, unterminieren

un·der·neath 1. *prp* unter (*dat or acc*) **2.** *adv* darunter

un·der·nour·ished unterernährt

un·der·pants Unterhose f

un·der·pass Unterführung f

un·der·pay *j-m* zu wenig bezahlen, *j-n* unterbezahlen

un·der·priv·i·leged unterprivilegiert, benachteiligt

un·der·rate unterbewerten, -schätzen

un·der·sec·re·ta·ry POL Staatssekretär *m*

un·der·sell ECON *Ware* verschleudern, unter Wert verkaufen; ~ *o.s. fig* sich schlecht verkaufen

un·der·shirt Unterhemd *n*

un·der·side Unterseite f

un·der·signed: *the* ~ der *or* die Unterzeichnete, die Unterzeichneten *pl*

un·der·size(d) zu klein

un·der·staffed (personell) unterbesetzt

un·der·stand verstehen; erfahren *or* gehört haben (*that* dass); *make o.s. understood* sich verständlich machen; *am I to* ~ *that* soll das heißen, dass; *give s.o. to* ~ *that* *j-m* zu verstehen geben, dass

un·der·stand·a·ble verständlich

un·der·stand·ing 1. Verstand *m*; Verständnis *n*; Abmachung f; Verständigung f; *come to an* ~ e-e Abmachung treffen (*with* mit); *on the* ~ *that* unter der Voraussetzung, dass **2.** verständnisvoll

un·der·state untertreiben, untertrieben darstellen; **un·der·state·ment** Understatement *n*, Untertreibung f

un·der·take *et.* übernehmen; sich verpflichten (*to do* zu tun)

un·der·tak·er Leichenbestatter *m*; Beerdigungs-, Bestattungsinstitut *n*

un·der·tak·ing Unternehmen *n*; Zusicherung *f*

un·der·tone *fig* Unterton *m*; **in an ~** mit gedämpfter Stimme

un·der·val·ue unterbewerten

un·der·wa·ter 1. *adj* Unterwasser... **2.** *adv* unter Wasser

un·der·wear Unterwäsche *f*

un·der·weight 1. Untergewicht *n* **2.** untergewichtig, zu leicht (**by** um); **she is five pounds ~** sie hat fünf Pfund Untergewicht

un·der·world Unterwelt *f*

un·de·served unverdient

un·de·sir·a·ble unerwünscht

un·de·vel·oped unerschlossen (*area*); unentwickelt

un·dies F (Damen)Unterwäsche *f*

un·dig·ni·fied würdelos

un·di·min·ished unvermindert

un·dis·ci·plined undiszipliniert

un·dis·cov·ered unentdeckt

un·dis·guised unverhohlen

un·dis·put·ed unbestritten

un·dis·turbed ungestört

un·di·vid·ed ungeteilt

un·do aufmachen, öffnen; *fig* zunichtemachen; **un·do·ing**: **be s.o.'s ~** j-s Ruin *or* Verderben sein; **un·done** unerledigt; offen; **come ~** aufgehen

un·doubt·ed unbestritten

un·doubt·ed·ly zweifellos, ohne (jeden) Zweifel

un·dreamed-of, **un·dreamt-of** ungeahnt

un·dress sich ausziehen; *j-n* ausziehen

un·due übermäßig

un·du·lat·ing sanft (*hills*)

un·dy·ing ewig

un·earned *fig* unverdient

un·earth ausgraben, *fig a.* ausfindig machen, aufstöbern

un·earth·ly überirdisch; unheimlich; **at an ~ hour** F zu e-r unchristlichen Zeit

un·eas·i·ness Unbehagen *n*

un·eas·y unruhig (*sleep*); unsicher (*peace*); **feel ~** sich unbehaglich fühlen; **I'm ~ about** mir ist nicht wohl bei

un·e·co·nom·ic unwirtschaftlich

un·ed·u·cat·ed ungebildet

un·e·mo·tion·al leidenschaftslos, kühl, beherrscht

un·em·ployed 1. arbeitslos **2.** *the ~* die Arbeitslosen *pl*

un·em·ploy·ment Arbeitslosigkeit *f*; **~ a·gen·cy** *Am* Arbeitsagentur *f*; **~ ben·e·fit** *Br*, **~ com·pen·sa·tion** Arbeitslosengeld *n*

un·end·ing endlos

un·en·dur·a·ble unerträglich

un·en·vi·a·ble wenig beneidenswert

un·e·qual ungleich (*a. fig*), unterschiedlich; *fig* einseitig; **be ~ to** e-r Aufgabe *etc* nicht gewachsen sein

un·e·qual(l)ed unerreicht, unübertroffen

un·er·ring unfehlbar

un·e·ven uneben; ungleich(mäßig); ungerade (*number*)

un·e·vent·ful ereignislos

un·ex·am·pled beispiellos

un·ex·pec·ted unerwartet

un·ex·posed PHOT unbelichtet

un·fail·ing unerschöpflich; nie versagend

un·fair unfair, ungerecht

un·faith·ful untreu (**to** *dat*)

un·fa·mil·i·ar ungewohnt; unbekannt; nicht vertraut (**with** mit)

un·fas·ten aufmachen, öffnen; losbinden

un·fa·vo(u)r·a·ble ungünstig; unvorteilhaft (**for, to** für); negativ, ablehnend

un·feel·ing gefühllos, herzlos

un·fin·ished unvollendet; unfertig; unerledigt

un·fit nicht fit, nicht in Form; ungeeignet, untauglich; unfähig

un·flag·ging unermüdlich, unentwegt

un·flap·pa·ble F nicht aus der Ruhe zu bringen(d)

un·fold auffalten, auseinanderfalten; darlegen, enthüllen; sich entfalten

un·fore·seen unvorhergesehen, unerwartet

un·for·get·ta·ble unvergesslich

un·for·got·ten unvergessen

un·for·tu·nate unglücklich; unglückselig; bedauerlich

un·for·tu·nate·ly leider

un·found·ed unbegründet

un·friend·ly unfreundlich (**to, towards** zu)

un·furl *Fahne* aufrollen, entrollen, *Segel* losmachen

un·fur·nished unmöbliert

un·gain·ly linkisch, unbeholfen

un·god·ly gottlos; *at an ~ hour* F zu e-r unchristlichen Zeit

un·gra·cious ungnädig; unfreundlich

un·grate·ful undankbar

un·guard·ed unbewacht; unbedacht, unüberlegt

un·hap·pi·ly unglücklicherweise, leider; **un·hap·py** unglücklich

un·harmed unversehrt

un·health·y kränklich, nicht gesund; ungesund; *contp* krankhaft, unnatürlich

un·heard: *go ~* keine Beachtung finden, unbeachtet bleiben; **un·heard-of** noch nie da gewesen, beispiellos

un·hinge: *~ s.o.('s mind) fig* j-n völlig aus dem Gleichgewicht bringen

un·ho·ly F furchtbar, schrecklich

un·hoped-for unverhofft, unerwartet

un·hurt unverletzt

u·ni·corn Einhorn *n*

un·i·den·ti·fied unbekannt, nicht identifiziert

u·ni·fi·ca·tion Vereinigung *f*

u·ni·form 1. Uniform *f* **2.** gleichmäßig; einheitlich

u·ni·form·i·ty Einheitlichkeit *f*

u·ni·fy verein(ig)en; vereinheitlichen

u·ni·lat·e·ral *fig* einseitig

un·i·mag·in·a·ble unvorstellbar

un·i·mag·in·a·tive fantasielos, einfallslos

un·im·por·tant unwichtig

un·im·pressed: *remain ~* unbeeindruckt bleiben (*by* von)

un·in·formed nicht unterrichtet *or* eingeweiht

un·in·hab·it·a·ble unbewohnbar

un·in·hab·it·ed unbewohnt

un·in·jured unverletzt

un·in·tel·li·gi·ble unverständlich

un·in·ten·tion·al unabsichtlich, unbeabsichtigt

un·in·terest·ed uninteressiert (*in* an *dat*); *be ~ in a.* sich nicht interessieren für; **un·in·terest·ing** uninteressant

un·in·ter·rupt·ed ununterbrochen

u·nion Vereinigung *f*; Union *f*; Gewerkschaft *f*; **u·nion·ist** Gewerkschaftler(in); **u·nion·ize** (sich) gewerkschaftlich organisieren

u·nique einzigartig; einmalig

u·ni·son: *in ~* gemeinsam

u·nit Einheit *f*; PED Unit *f*, Lehreinheit *f*;

MATH Einer *m*; TECH (Anbau)Element *n*, Teil *n*; *~ furniture* Anbaumöbel *pl*

u·nite verbinden, vereinigen; sich vereinigen *or* zusammentun

u·nit·ed vereinigt, vereint

U·nit·ed King·dom das Vereinigte Königreich (*England, Scotland, Wales and Northern Ireland*)

U·nit·ed States of A·mer·i·ca die Vereinigten Staaten von Amerika

u·ni·ty Einheit *f*; MATH Eins *f*

u·ni·ver·sal allgemein; universal, universell; Welt...

u·ni·verse Universum *n*, Weltall *n*

u·ni·ver·si·ty Universität *f*, Hochschule *f*; *~ grad·u·ate* Akademiker(in)

un·just ungerecht

un·kempt ungekämmt (*hair*); ungepflegt (*clothes etc*)

un·kind unfreundlich

un·known 1. unbekannt (*to dat*); **2.** der, die, das Unbekannte; *~ quan·ti·ty* MATH unbekannte Größe (*a. fig*), Unbekannte *f*

un·law·ful ungesetzlich, gesetzwidrig

un·lead·ed bleifrei

un·learn Ansichten *etc* ablegen, aufgeben

un·less wenn ... nicht, außer wenn ..., es sei denn ...

un·like *prp* im Gegensatz zu; *he is very ~ his father* er ist ganz anders als sein Vater; *that is very ~ him* das sieht ihm gar nicht ähnlich

un·like·ly unwahrscheinlich

un·lim·it·ed unbegrenzt

un·list·ed: *be ~* nicht im Telefonbuch stehen; *~ num·ber* TEL Geheimnummer *f*

un·load entladen, abladen, ausladen; MAR *Ladung* löschen

un·lock aufschließen

un·loos·en losmachen; lockern; lösen

un·loved ungeliebt

un·luck·y unglücklich; *be ~* Pech haben

un·made ungemacht

un·manned unbemannt

un·marked nicht gekennzeichnet; SPORT ungedeckt, frei

un·mar·ried unverheiratet, ledig

un·mask *fig* entlarven

un·matched unübertroffen, unvergleichlich

un·men·tio·na·ble Tabu...; *be ~* tabu

sein

un·mis·tak·a·ble unverkennbar, unver-
wechselbar, untrüglich

un·mo·lest·ed unbehelligt

un·moved ungerührt; **she remained ~
by it** es ließ sie kalt

un·mu·si·cal unmusikalisch

un·named ungenannt

un·nat·u·ral unnatürlich; widernatür-
lich

un·ne·ces·sa·ry unnötig

un·nerve entnerven

un·no·ticed unbemerkt

un·num·bered unnummeriert

un·ob·tru·sive unauffällig, unaufdringlich

un·oc·cu·pied leer (stehend), unbewohnt; unbeschäftigt

un·of·fi·cial inoffiziell

un·pack auspacken

un·paid unbezahlt; *post* unfrei

un·par·al·leled einmalig, beispiellos

un·par·don·a·ble unverzeihlich

un·per·turbed gelassen, ruhig

un·pick *Naht etc* auftrennen

un·placed: **be ~** SPORT sich nicht platzieren können

un·play·a·ble SPORT unbespielbar

un·pleas·ant unangenehm, unerfreulich; unfreundlich

un·plug den Stecker (*gen*) herausziehen

un·pol·ished unpoliert; *fig* ungehobelt

un·pol·lut·ed sauber, unverschmutzt

un·pop·u·lar unpopulär, unbeliebt

un·pop·u·lar·i·ty Unbeliebtheit *f*

un·prac·ti·cal unpraktisch

un·prac·ticed, *Br* **un·prac·tised** unge-
übt

un·prec·e·dent·ed beispiellos, noch nie
da gewesen

un·pre·dict·a·ble unvorhersehbar; unberechenbar (*person*)

un·prej·u·diced unvoreingenommen;
JUR unbefangen

un·pre·med·i·tat·ed nicht vorsätzlich;
unüberlegt

un·pre·pared unvorbereitet

un·pre·ten·tious bescheiden, einfach,
schlicht

un·prin·ci·pled skrupellos, gewissenlos

un·prin·ta·ble nicht druckfähig *or*
druckreif

un·pro·duc·tive unproduktiv, unergie-
big

un·pro·fes·sion·al unprofessionell; un-
fachmännisch

un·prof·it·a·ble unrentabel

un·pro·nounce·a·ble unaussprechbar

un·pro·tect·ed ungeschützt

un·proved, **un·prov·en** unbewiesen

un·pro·voked grundlos

un·pun·ished unbestraft, ungestraft; **go
~** straflos bleiben

un·qual·i·fied unqualifiziert, ungeeignet (**for** für); uneingeschränkt

un·ques·tion·a·ble unbestritten

un·ques·tion·ing bedingungslos

un·quote: **quote … ~** Zitat … Zitat Ende

un·rav·el (sich) auftrennen (*pullover
etc*); entwirren

un·read·a·ble nicht lesenswert, unles-
bar, *a.* unleserlich

un·re·al unwirklich

un·rea·lis·tic unrealistisch

un·rea·son·a·ble unvernünftig; übertrieben, unzumutbar

un·rec·og·niz·a·ble nicht wieder zu er-
kennen(d)

un·re·lat·ed: **be ~** in keinem Zusammenhang stehen (**to** mit)

un·re·lent·ing unvermindert

un·re·li·a·ble unzuverlässig

un·re·lieved ununterbrochen, ständig

un·re·mit·ting unablässig, unaufhörlich

un·re·quit·ed: **~ love** unwiderte Liebe

un·re·served uneingeschränkt; nicht reserviert

un·rest POL *etc* Unruhen *pl*

un·re·strained hemmungslos, ungezügelt

un·re·strict·ed uneingeschränkt

un·ripe unreif

un·ri·val(l)ed unerreicht, unübertroffen, einzigartig

un·roll (sich) aufrollen *or* entrollen; sich
entfalten

un·ruf·fled gelassen, ruhig

un·ru·ly ungebärdig, wild; widerspenstig (*hair*)

un·sad·dle *Pferd* absatteln; *Reiter* abwerfen

un·safe unsicher, nicht sicher

un·said unausgesprochen

un·sal(e)·a·ble unverkäuflich

un·salt·ed ungesalzen

un·san·i·tar·y unhygienisch

un·sat·is·fac·to·ry unbefriedigend

un·sat·u·rat·ed CHEM ungesättigt
un·sa·vo(u)r·y anrüchig, unerfreulich
un·scathed unversehrt, unverletzt
un·screw abschrauben, losschrauben
un·scru·pu·lous skrupellos, gewissenlos
un·seat *Reiter* abwerfen; *j-n s-s Amtes* entheben
un·seem·ly ungebührlich
un·self·ish selbstlos, uneigennützig
un·set·tle durcheinanderbringen; beunruhigen; aufregen
un·set·tled ungeklärt, offen (*question etc*); unsicher (*situation etc*); METEOR unbeständig
un·shak(e)·a·ble unerschütterlich
un·shav·en unrasiert
un·shrink·a·ble nicht eingehend *or* einlaufend
un·sight·ly unansehnlich; hässlich
un·skilled: *~ worker* ungelernter Arbeiter
un·so·cia·ble ungesellig
un·so·cial: *work ~ hours* außerhalb der normalen Arbeitszeit arbeiten
un·so·lic·it·ed unaufgefordert ein- *or* zugesandt, ECON *a.* unbestellt
un·solved ungelöst (*problem etc*)
un·so·phis·ti·cat·ed einfach, schlicht; TECH unkompliziert
un·sound nicht gesund; nicht in Ordnung; morsch; unsicher, schwach; nicht stichhaltig (*argument etc*); *of ~ mind* JUR unzurechnungsfähig
un·spar·ing großzügig, freigebig, verschwenderisch; schonungslos, unbarmherzig
un·speak·a·ble unbeschreiblich, entsetzlich
un·spoiled, **un·spoilt** unverdorben; nicht verwöhnt *or* verzogen
un·sta·ble instabil; unsicher, schwankend; labil (*person*)
un·stead·y wack(e)lig, schwankend, unsicher; unbeständig; ungleichmäßig, unregelmäßig
un·stop *Abfluss etc* frei machen; *Flasche* entstöpseln
un·stressed LING unbetont
un·stuck: *come ~* abgehen, sich lösen; *fig* scheitern
un·stud·ied ungekünstelt, natürlich
un·suc·cess·ful erfolglos, ohne Erfolg; vergeblich

un·suit·a·ble unpassend, ungeeignet; unangemessen
un·sure unsicher; *~ of o.s.* unsicher
un·sur·passed unübertroffen
un·sus·pect·ed unverdächtig; unvermutet; **un·sus·pect·ing** nichts ahnend, ahnungslos
un·sus·pi·cious arglos; unverdächtig, harmlos
un·sweet·ened ungesüßt
un·swerv·ing unbeirrbar, unerschütterlich
un·tan·gle entwirren (*a. fig*)
un·tapped unerschlossen (*resource etc*)
un·teach·a·ble unbelehrbar (*person*); nicht lehrbar
un·ten·a·ble unhaltbar (*theory etc*)
un·think·a·ble undenkbar, unvorstellbar; **un·think·ing** gedankenlos
un·ti·dy unordentlich
un·tie aufknoten, *Knoten etc* lösen; losbinden
un·til *prp, cj* bis; *not ~* erst; erst wenn, nicht bevor
un·time·ly vorzeitig, verfrüht; unpassend, ungelegen
un·tir·ing unermüdlich
un·told *fig* unermesslich
un·touched unberührt, unangetastet
un·true unwahr, falsch
un·trust·wor·thy unzuverlässig, nicht vertrauenswürdig
un·used[1] unbenutzt, ungebraucht
un·used[2]: *be ~ to s.th.* an et. nicht gewöhnt sein, et. nicht gewohnt sein; *be ~ to doing s.th.* es nicht gewohnt sein, et. zu tun
un·u·su·al ungewöhnlich
un·var·nished *fig* ungeschminkt
un·var·y·ing unveränderlich, gleichbleibend
un·veil *Denkmal etc* enthüllen
un·versed unbewandert, unerfahren (*in* in *dat*)
un·voiced unausgesprochen
un·want·ed unerwünscht, ungewollt
un·war·rant·ed ungerechtfertigt
un·washed ungewaschen
un·wel·come unwillkommen
un·well: *be or feel ~* sich unwohl fühlen *or* nicht wohlfühlen
un·whole·some ungesund (*a. fig*)
un·wield·y unhandlich, sperrig
un·will·ing widerwillig; ungern; *be ~ to*

do s.th. et. nicht tun wollen

un·wind (sich) abwickeln; F abschalten, sich entspannen

un·wise unklug

un·wit·ting unwissentlich; unbeabsichtigt

un·wor·thy unwürdig; *he* (*she*) *is ~ of it* er (sie) verdient es nicht, er (sie) ist es nicht wert

un·wrap auswickeln, auspacken

un·writ·ten ungeschrieben

un·yield·ing unnachgiebig

un·zip den Reißverschluss (*gen*) aufmachen

up 1. *adv* herauf, hinauf, aufwärts, nach oben, hoch, in die Höhe; oben; **~ *there*** dort oben; *jump ~ and down* hüpfen; *walk ~ and down* auf und ab gehen, hin und her gehen; **~ *to*** bis zu; *be ~ to s.th.* F et. vorhaben, et. im Schilde führen; *not to be ~ to s.th.* e-r Sache nicht gewachsen sein; *it's ~ to you* das liegt bei dir **2.** *prp* herauf, hinauf; oben auf (*dat*); **~ *the river*** flussaufwärts **3.** *adj* nach oben (gerichtet), Aufwärts...; ASTR aufgegangen; ECON gestiegen; *time:* abgelaufen, um; aufgestanden, F auf; *the ~ train* der Zug nach London; *be ~ and about* F wieder auf den Beinen sein; *what's ~?* F was ist los? **4.** F *v/t* Angebot, *Preis etc* erhöhen **5.** *the ~s and downs* F die Höhen und Tiefen *pl* (*of life* des Lebens)

up-and-com·ing aufstrebend, vielversprechend

up·bring·ing Erziehung *f*

up·com·ing bevorstehend

up·coun·try landeinwärts; im Landesinneren

up·date 1. auf den neuesten Stand bringen; aktualisieren **2.** Lagebericht *m*

up·end hochkant stellen

up·grade *j-n* befördern

up·heav·al *fig* Umwälzung *f*

up·hill aufwärts, bergan; bergauf führend; *fig* mühsam

up·hold *Rechte etc* schützen, wahren; JUR *Urteil* bestätigen

up·hol·ster *Möbel* polstern

up·hol·ster·er Polsterer *m*

up·hol·ster·y Polsterung *f*; Bezug *m*; Polsterei *f*

up·keep Instandhaltung(skosten *pl*) *f*; Unterhalt(ungskosten *pl*) *m*

up·land *mst pl* Hochland *n*

up·lift 1. *j-n* aufrichten, *j-m* Auftrieb geben **2.** Auftrieb *m*

up·on → *on, once 1*

up·per obere(r, -s), Ober...;

up·per·most 1. *adj* oberste(r, -s), größte(r, -s), höchste(r, -s); *be ~* oben sein; *fig* an erster Stelle stehen **2.** *adv* nach oben

up·right aufrecht, *a.* gerade, *fig a.* rechtschaffen

up·ris·ing Aufstand *m*

up·roar Aufruhr *m*; **up·roar·i·ous** lärmend, laut; schallend (*laughter*)

up·root ausreißen, entwurzeln; *fig j-n* herausreißen (*from* aus)

up·set umkippen, umstoßen, umwerfen; *Pläne etc* durcheinanderbringen, stören; *j-n* aus der Fassung bringen; *the fish has ~ me or my stomach* ich habe mir durch den Fisch den Magen verdorben; *be ~* aufgeregt sein; aus der Fassung *or* durcheinander sein; gekränkt *or* verletzt sein

up·shot Ergebnis *n*

up·side down verkehrt herum; *fig* drunter und drüber; *turn ~* umdrehen, *a. fig* auf den Kopf stellen

up·stairs 1. die Treppe herauf *or* hinauf, nach oben; oben **2.** im oberen Stockwerk (gelegen), obere(r, -s)

up·start Emporkömmling *m*

up·state im Norden (e-s Bundesstaats)

up·stream fluss-, stromaufwärts

up·take: F *be quick* (*slow*) *on the ~* schnell begreifen (schwer von Begriff sein)

up-to-date modern; aktuell, auf dem neuesten Stand

up·town in den Wohnvierteln; in die Wohnviertel

up·turn Aufschwung *m*

up·ward(s) aufwärts, nach oben

u·ra·ni·um CHEM Uran *n*

ur·ban städtisch, Stadt...

ur·ban·i·za·tion Verstädterung *f*

ur·chin Bengel *m*

urge 1. *j-n* drängen (*to do* zu tun); drängen auf (*acc*); *a. ~ on j-n* drängen, antreiben **2.** Drang *m*, Verlangen *n*

ur·gen·cy Dringlichkeit *f*

ur·gent dringend; *be ~ a.* eilen

u·ri·nate urinieren; **u·rine** Urin *m*

urn Urne *f*

us uns; *all of* ~ wir alle; *both of* ~ wir beide

us·age Sprachgebrauch *m*; Behandlung *f*; Verwendung *f*, Gebrauch *m*

USB flash drive IT USB-Stick *m*

use 1. *v/t* benutzen, gebrauchen, anwenden, verwenden; (ver)brauchen; ~ *up* auf-, verbrauchen; *v/i*: **I** ~ *d to live here* ich habe früher hier gewohnt **2.** Benutzung *f*, Gebrauch *m*, Verwendung *f*; Nutzen *m*; *be of* ~ nützlich *or* von Nutzen sein (*to* für); *it's no* ~ *doing* es ist nutzlos *or* zwecklos *zu inf*; → *milk 1*

used[1]: *be* ~ *to s.th.* an et. gewöhnt sein, et. gewohnt sein; *be* ~ *to doing s.th.* es gewohnt sein, et. zu tun

used[2] gebraucht; ~ *car* Gebrauchtwagen *m*; ~ *car deal·er* Gebrauchtwagenhändler(in)

use·ful nützlich

use·less nutzlos, zwecklos

us·er Benutzer(in); Verbraucher(in)

us·er-friend·ly benutzer- *or* verbraucherfreundlich

us·er in·ter·face IT Benutzeroberfläche *f*

ush·er 1. Platzanweiser *m*; Gerichtsdiener *m* **2.** *j-n* führen, geleiten (*into* in *acc*; *to* zu)

ush·er·ette Platzanweiserin *f*

u·su·al gewöhnlich, üblich

u·su·al·ly (für) gewöhnlich, normalerweise

u·sur·er Wucherer *m*

u·su·ry Wucher *m*

u·ten·sil Gerät *n*

u·te·rus ANAT Gebärmutter *f*

u·til·i·ty Nutzen *m*; *pl* Leistungen *pl* der öffentlichen Versorgungsbetriebe

u·til·ize nutzen

ut·most äußerste(r, -s), größte(r, -s), höchste(r, -s)

u·to·pi·an utopisch

ut·ter[1] total, völlig

ut·ter[2] äußern, *Seufzer etc* ausstoßen, *Wort* sagen

U-turn MOT Wende *f*; *fig* Kehrtwendung *f*

u·vu·la ANAT (Gaumen)Zäpfchen *n*

V

V, v V, v *n*

va·can·cy freie *or* offene Stelle; *vacancies* Zimmer frei; *no vacancies* belegt

va·cant leer stehend, unbewohnt; frei (*seat etc*); frei, offen (*job*); *fig* leer (*expression, stare etc*)

va·cate *Hotelzimmer* räumen; *Stelle etc* aufgeben

va·ca·tion 1. Ferien *pl*, Urlaub *m*; *esp Br* UNIV Semesterferien *pl*; JUR Gerichtsferien *pl*; *be on* ~ im Urlaub sein, Urlaub machen **2.** Urlaub machen, die Ferien verbringen

va·ca·tion·er, va·ca·tion·ist Urlauber(in)

vac·cin·ate MED impfen

vac·cin·a·tion MED (Schutz)Impfung *f*

vac·cine MED Impfstoff *m*

vac·il·late *fig* schwanken

vac·u·um 1. PHYS Vakuum *n* **2.** F *Teppich, Zimmer etc* saugen; ~ *bot·tle* Thermosflasche® *f*; ~ *clean·er* Staubsauger *m*; ~ *flask Br* Thermosflasche® *f*; ~ *packed* vakuumverpackt

vag·a·bond Vagabund *m*, Landstreicher(in)

va·ga·ry *mst pl* Laune *f*; wunderlicher Einfall

va·gi·na ANAT Vagina *f*, Scheide *f*

va·gi·nal ANAT vaginal, Scheiden…

va·grant Nichtsesshafte *m*, *f*, Landstreicher(in)

vague verschwommen; vage; unklar

vain eingebildet, eitel; vergeblich; *in* ~ vergebens, vergeblich

val·en·tine Valentinskarte *f*

va·le·ri·an BOT, PHARM Baldrian *m*

val·et (Kammer)Diener *m*

val·id stichhaltig, triftig; gültig (*for two weeks* zwei Wochen); JUR rechtsgültig, rechtskräftig; *be* ~ *a.* gelten

va·lid·i·ty (JUR Rechts)Gültigkeit *f*; Stichhaltigkeit *f*, Triftigkeit *f*

val·ley Tal *n*

val·u·a·ble 1. wertvoll **2.** *pl* Wertgegenstände *pl*, Wertsachen *pl*

val·u·a·tion Schätzung *f*; Schätzwert *m* (*on gen*)

val·ue 1. Wert *m*; *be of* ~ wertvoll sein (*to* für); *get* ~ *for money* reell bedient werden **2.** *Haus etc* schätzen (*at* auf *acc*); *j-n*, *j-s Rat etc* schätzen

val·ue-ad·ded tax *Br* ECON (*abbr* **VAT**) Mehrwertsteuer *f*

val·ue·less wertlos

valve TECH, MUS Ventil *n*; ANAT (*Herz- etc*)Klappe *f*

vam·pire Vampir *m*

van MOT Lieferwagen *m*, Transporter *m*; *Br* RAIL (geschlossener) Güterwagen

van·dal Wandale *m*, Vandale *m*

van·dal·ism Wandalismus *m*, Vandalismus *m*

van·dal·ize mutwillig beschädigen *or* zerstören

vane TECH (*Propeller- etc*)Flügel *m*; (*Wetter*)Fahne *f*

van·guard MIL Vorhut *f*

va·nil·la Vanille *f*

van·ish verschwinden

van·i·ty Eitelkeit *f*; ~ **bag** Kosmetiktäschchen *n*; ~ **case** Kosmetikkoffer *m*

va·por·ize verdampfen; verdunsten (lassen)

va·po(u)r Dampf *m*, Dunst *m*; ~ **trail** AVIAT Kondensstreifen *m*

var·i·a·ble 1. variabel, veränderlich; unbeständig, wechselhaft; TECH einstellbar, regulierbar **2.** MATH, PHYS Variable *f*, veränderliche Größe (*both a. fig*)

var·i·ance: *be at* ~ *with* im Gegensatz *or* Widerspruch stehen zu

var·i·ant 1. abweichend, verschieden **2.** Variante *f*; **var·i·a·tion** Abweichung *f*; Schwankung *f*; MUS Variation *f*

var·i·cose veins MED Krampfadern *pl*

var·ied unterschiedlich; abwechslungsreich

va·ri·e·ty Abwechslung *f*; Vielfalt *f*; ECON Auswahl *f*, Sortiment *n* (*of an dat*); BOT, ZO Art *f*; Varietee *n*; *for a* ~ *of reasons* aus den verschiedensten Gründen

var·i·ous verschieden; mehrere, verschiedene

var·nish 1. Lack *m* **2.** lackieren

var·si·ty team SPORT Universitäts-, College-, Schulmannschaft *f*

var·y *v/i* sich (ver)ändern; variieren, auseinandergehen (*opinions etc*) (*on*

über *acc*); ~ *in size* verschieden groß sein; *v/t* (ver)ändern; variieren

vase Vase *f*

vast gewaltig, riesig, (*area a.*) ausgedehnt, weit; **vast·ly** gewaltig, weitaus

vat (großes) Fass, Bottich *m*

VAT *abbr of* **value-added tax** ECON Mehrwertsteuer *f*

vau·de·ville Varietee(theater) *n*

vault¹ ARCH Gewölbe *n*; *a. pl* Stahlkammer *f*, Tresorraum *m*; (*Keller*)Gewölbe *n*; Gruft *f*

vault² 1. ~ (*over*) springen über (*acc*) **2.** *esp* SPORT Sprung *m*

vault·ing| **horse** *gymnastics*: Pferd *n*; ~ **pole** SPORT Sprungstab *m*

VCR *abbr of* **video cassette recorder** Videorekorder *m*, Videogerät *n*

veal GASTR Kalbfleisch *n*; ~ **chop** Kalbskotelett *n*; ~ **cutlet** Kalbsschnitzel *n*; *roast* ~ Kalbsbraten *m*

veer (sich) drehen; MOT ausscheren; ~ *to the right* das Steuer nach rechts reißen

veg·e·ta·ble 1. *mst pl* Gemüse *n* **2.** Gemüse...; Pflanzen...

veg·e·tar·i·an 1. Vegetarier(in) **2.** vegetarisch

veg·e·tate (dahin)vegetieren

veg·e·ta·tion Vegetation *f*

ve·he·mence Vehemenz *f*, Heftigkeit *f*; **ve·he·ment** vehement, heftig

ve·hi·cle Fahrzeug *n*; *fig* Medium *n*

veil 1. Schleier *m* **2.** verschleiern (*a. fig*)

vein ANAT Vene *f*, Ader *f* (*a.* BOT, GEOL, *fig*); *fig* (*Charakter*)Zug *m*; Stimmung *f*

ve·loc·i·ty TECH Geschwindigkeit *f*

ve·lour(s) Velours *m*

vel·vet Samt *m*; **vel·vet·y** samtig

vend·er → **vendor**

vend·ing ma·chine (Verkaufs-, Waren-) Automat *m*

vend·or (*Straßen*)Händler(in), (*Zeitungs- etc*)Verkäufer(in)

ve·neer 1. Furnier *n*; *fig* Fassade *f* **2.** furnieren

ven·er·a·ble ehrwürdig

ven·er·ate verehren

ven·er·a·tion Verehrung *f*

ve·ne·re·al dis·ease MED Geschlechtskrankheit *f*

Ve·ne·tian 1. Venezianer(in) **2.** venezianisch; ~ **blind** (Stab)Jalousie *f*

ven·geance Rache *f*; *take* ~ *on* sich rächen an (*dat*); **with a ~** mächtig, F wie verrückt

ve·ni·al entschuldbar, verzeihlich; REL lässlich

ven·i·son GASTR Wildbret *n*

ven·om ZO Gift *n*, *fig a.* Gehässigkeit *f*

ven·om·ous giftig, *fig a.* gehässig

ve·nous MED venös

vent 1. *v/t s-m* Zorn *etc* Luft machen, *s-e Wut etc* auslassen, abreagieren (**on** an *dat*); **2.** Schlitz *m* (*in a coat etc*); TECH (Abzugs)Öffnung *f*; **give ~ to** *s-m Ärger etc* Luft machen

ven·ti·late (be)lüften; *fig* äußern

ven·ti·la·tion (Be)Lüftung *f*, Ventilation *f*

ven·ti·la·tor Ventilator *m*

ven·tri·cle ANAT Herzkammer *f*

ven·tril·o·quist Bauchredner(in)

ven·ture 1. *esp* ECON Wagnis *n*, Risiko *n*; ECON Unternehmen *n*; → *joint venture* **2.** sich wagen; riskieren

ven·ue SPORT Austragungsort *m*

verb LING Verb *n*, Zeitwort *n*

verb·al mündlich; wörtlich, Wort...

ver·dict JUR (Urteils)Spruch *m*; *fig* Urteil *n*; **bring in** or **return a ~ of** (**not**) **guilty** JUR auf (nicht) schuldig erkennen

ver·di·gris Grünspan *m*

verge 1. Rand *m* (*a. fig*); **be on the ~ of** kurz vor (*dat*) stehen; **be on the ~ of despair** (**tears**) der Verzweiflung (den Tränen) nahe sein **2. ~ on** *fig* grenzen an (*acc*)

ver·i·fy bestätigen; nachweisen; (über-) prüfen

ver·i·ta·ble wahr

ver·mi·cel·li Fadennudeln *pl*

ver·mi·form ap·pen·dix ANAT Wurmfortsatz *m*, Blinddarm *m*

ver·mil·i·on 1. zinnoberrot **2.** Zinnoberrot *n*

ver·min Ungeziefer *n*; Schädlinge *pl*; *fig* Gesindel *n*, Pack *n*

ver·min·ous voller Ungeziefer

ver·nac·u·lar Dialekt *m*, Mundart *f*; **in the ~** im Volksmund

ver·sa·tile vielseitig; vielseitig verwendbar

verse Versdichtung *f*; Vers *m*; Strophe *f*

versed: **be** (**well**) **~ in** beschlagen *or* bewandert sein in (*dat*)

ver·sion Version *f*; TECH Ausführung *f*;

Darstellung *f* (*of an event*); Fassung *f* (*of a film etc*); Übersetzung *f*

ver·sus (*abbr* **v.**, **vs.**) SPORT, JUR gegen

ver·te·bra ANAT Wirbel *m*

ver·te·brate ZO Wirbeltier *n*

ver·ti·cal vertikal, senkrecht

ver·ti·go MED Schwindel *m*; **suffer from ~** an *or* unter Schwindel leiden

verve Elan *m*, Schwung *m*

ver·y 1. *adv* sehr; aller...; **I ~ much hope that** ich hoffe sehr, dass; **the ~ best** das Allerbeste; **for the ~ last time** zum allerletzten Mal **2.** *adj* **the ~** genau der *or* die *or* das; **the ~ opposite** genau das Gegenteil; **the ~ thing** genau das Richtige; **the ~ thought of** schon der *or* der bloße Gedanke an (*acc*)

ves·i·cle MED Bläschen *n*

ves·sel ANAT, BOT Gefäß *n*; Schiff *n*

vest Weste *f*; *Br* Unterhemd *n*; *kugelsichere* Weste

ves·ti·bule (Vor)Halle *f*

ves·tige *fig* Spur *f*

vest·ment Ornat *n*, Gewand *n*, Robe *f*

ves·try REL Sakristei *f*

vet¹ F Tierarzt *m*, Tierärztin *f*

vet² *esp Br* F überprüfen

vet³ MIL F Veteran *m*

vet·e·ran 1. MIL Veteran *m* (*a. fig*) **2.** altgedient; erfahren; **~ car** *Br* Oldtimer *m* (*built before 1905*)

vet·e·ri·nar·i·an Tierarzt *m*, -ärztin *f*

vet·e·ri·na·ry tierärztlich; **~ sur·geon** *Br* Tierarzt *m*, Tierärztin *f*

ve·to 1. Veto *n* **2.** sein Veto einlegen gegen

vexed ques·tion leidige Frage

vi·a über (*acc*), via

vi·a·duct Viadukt *m*, *n*

vi·al (*esp* Arznei)Fläschchen *n*

vibes F Atmosphäre *f*

vi·brant kräftig (*color etc*); pulsierend (*city etc*)

vi·brate *v/i* vibrieren, zittern; flimmern; *fig* pulsieren; *v/t* in Schwingungen versetzen; **vi·bra·tion** Vibrieren *n*, Zittern *n*; *pl* F Atmosphäre *f*

vic·ar REL Pfarrer *m*

vic·ar·age Pfarrhaus *n*

vice¹ Laster *n*

vice² *esp Br* Schraubstock *m*

vice... Vize..., stellvertretend

vice squad Sittendezernat *n*, Sittenpolizei *f*; Rauschgiftdezernat *n*

vi·ce ver·sa: *and* ~ und umgekehrt

vi·cin·i·ty Nähe *f*; Nachbarschaft *f*

vi·cious brutal; bösartig

vi·cis·si·tudes *das* Auf und Ab, *die* Wechselfälle *pl*

vic·tim Opfer *n*

vic·tim·ize (ungerechterweise) bestrafen, ungerecht behandeln; schikanieren

vic·to·ri·ous siegreich

vic·to·ry Sieg *m*

vid·e·o 1. Video *n*; Videokassette *f*; F Videoband *n*; *esp Br* Videorekorder *m*, Videogerät *n*; *on* ~ auf Video **2.** Video... **3.** *esp Br* auf Video aufnehmen, aufzeichnen; ~ **cam·e·ra** Videokamera *f*; ~ **cas·sette** Videokassette *f*; ~ **cassette re·cord·er** → *video recorder*; ~ **clip** Videoclip *m*

vid·e·o·disk Bildplatte *f*

vid·e·o| game Videospiel *n*; ~ **li·brary** Videothek *f*; ~ **re·cord·er** Videorekorder *m*, Videogerät *n*; ~ **re·cord·ing** Videoaufnahme *f*, Videoaufzeichnung *f*; ~ **shop** *Br*, ~ **store** Videothek *f*

vid·e·o·tape 1. Videokassette *f*; Videoband *n* **2.** auf Video aufnehmen, aufzeichnen

vid·e·o·text Bildschirmtext *m*

vie wetteifern (*with* mit; *for* um)

Vi·en·nese 1. Wiener(in) **2.** wienerisch, Wiener...

view 1. Sicht *f* (*of* auf *acc*); Aussicht *f*, (Aus)Blick *m* (*of* auf *acc*); Ansicht *f* (*a.* PHOT), Meinung *f* (*about, on* über *acc*); *fig* Überblick *m* (*of* über *acc*); *a room with a* ~ ein Zimmer mit schöner Aussicht; *be on* ~ ausgestellt *or* zu besichtigen sein; *be hidden from* ~ nicht zu sehen sein; *come into* ~ in Sicht kommen; *in full* ~ *of* direkt vor *j-s* Augen; *in* ~ *of fig* angesichts (*gen*); *in my* ~ m-r Ansicht nach; *keep in* ~ et. im Auge behalten; *with a* ~ *to fig* mit Blick auf (*acc*) **2.** *v/t* Haus *etc* besichtigen; *fig* betrachten (*as* als); *v/i* fernsehen

view·da·ta Bildschirmtext *m*

view·er Fernsehzuschauer(in), F Fernseher(in); TECH (*Dia*)Betrachter *m*

view·find·er PHOT Sucher *m*

view·point Gesichts-, Standpunkt *m*

vig·il (Nacht)Wache *f*

vig·i·lance Wachsamkeit *f*

vig·i·lant wachsam

vig·or·ous energisch; kräftig

vig·o(u)r Energie *f*

Vi·king 1. Wikinger *m* **2.** Wikinger...

vile gemein, niederträchtig; F scheußlich

vil·lage Dorf *n*; ~ **green** Dorfanger *m*

vil·lag·er Dorfbewohner(in)

vil·lain Bösewicht *m*, Schurke *m*; *Br* F Ganove *m*

vin·di·cate *j-n* rehabilitieren; *et.* rechtfertigen; *et.* Bestätigen

vin·dic·tive rachsüchtig, nachtragend

vine BOT (Wein)Rebe *f*; Kletterpflanze *f*

vin·e·gar Essig *m*

vine·grow·er Winzer *m*

vine·yard Weinberg *m*

vin·tage 1. Weinernte *f*, Weinlese *f*; GASTR Jahrgang *m* **2.** GASTR Jahrgangs...; *fig* hervorragend, glänzend; *a 1999* ~ ein 1999er Jahrgang *or* Wein

vin·tage car *esp Br* Oldtimer *m* (*built between 1919 and 1930*)

vi·o·la MUS Bratsche *f*

vi·o·late *Vertrag etc* verletzen, *a. Versprechen* brechen; *Gesetz etc* übertreten; *Ruhe etc* stören; *Grab etc* schänden; **vi·o·la·tion** Verletzung *f*, Bruch *m*, Übertretung *f*

vi·o·lence Gewalt *f*; Gewalttätigkeit *f*; Ausschreitungen *pl*; Heftigkeit *f*

vi·o·lent gewalttätig; gewaltsam; heftig

vi·o·let 1. BOT Veilchen *n* **2.** violett

vi·o·lin MUS Geige *f*, Violine *f*

vi·o·lin·ist Geiger(in), Violinist(in)

VIP *abbr of* ***very important person*** VIP *f*

vi·per ZO Viper *f*, Natter *f*

VIP lounge AVIAT *etc* VIP-Lounge *f*; SPORT Ehrentribüne *f*

vir·gin 1. Jungfrau *f* **2.** jungfräulich, unberührt (*both a. fig*)

Vir·go ASTR Jungfrau *f*; *he* (*she*) *is* (*a*) ~ er (sie) ist Jungfrau

vir·ile männlich; potent

vi·ril·i·ty Männlichkeit *f*; Potenz *f*

vir·tu·al eigentlich, praktisch

vir·tu·al·ly praktisch, so gut wie

vir·tu·al re·al·i·ty IT virtuelle Realität

vir·tue Tugend *f*; Vorzug *m*, Vorteil *m*; *by or in* ~ *of* aufgrund (*gen*), kraft (*gen*); *make a* ~ *of necessity* aus der Not e-e Tugend machen

vir·tu·ous tugendhaft

vir·u·lent MED (akut und) bösartig;

schnell wirkend (*poison*); *fig* bösartig, gehässig

vi·rus MED Virus *n*, *m*

vi·sa Visum *n*, Sichtvermerk *m*

vis·cose Viskose *f*

vis·cous dickflüssig, zähflüssig

vise TECH Schraubstock *m*

vis·i·bil·i·ty Sicht *f*, Sichtverhältnisse *pl*, Sichtweite *f*

vis·i·ble sichtbar; (er)sichtlich

vi·sion Sehkraft *f*; Weitblick *m*; Vision *f*

vi·sion·a·ry 1. weitblickend; eingebildet, unwirklich **2.** Fantast(in), Träumer(in); Seher(in)

vis·it 1. *v/t* j-n besuchen, *Schloss etc a.* besichtigen; *et.* inspizieren; *v/i:* be ~*ing* auf Besuch sein (*with* bei) **2.** Besuch *m*, Besichtigung *f* (*to* gen); Plauderei *f*; *for or on a* ~ auf Besuch; *have a* ~ *from* Besuch haben von; *pay a* ~ *to* j-n besuchen, j-m e-n Besuch abstatten; *Arzt* aufsuchen

vis·it·ing hours MED Besuchszeit *f*

vis·it·or Besucher(in), Gast *m*

vi·sor Visier *n*; Schirm *m*; MOT (*Sonnen-*)Blende *f*

vis·u·al Seh...; visuell; ~ *aids* PED Anschauungsmaterial *n*, Lehrmittel *pl*; ~ *dis·play u·nit* IT Bildschirmgerät *n*, Datensichtgerät *n*; ~ *in·struc·tion* PED Anschauungsunterricht *m*

vis·u·al·ize sich *et.* vorstellen

vi·tal vital, Lebens...; lebenswichtig; unbedingt notwendig; *of* ~ *importance* von größter Wichtigkeit

vi·tal·i·ty Vitalität *f*

vit·a·min Vitamin *n*; ~ *de·fi·cien·cy* Vitaminmangel *m*

vit·re·ous Glas...

vi·va·cious lebhaft, temperamentvoll

viv·id hell (*light*); kräftig, leuchtend (*color*); anschaulich (*description*); lebhaft (*imagination*)

vix·en ZO Füchsin *f*

V-neck V-Ausschnitt *m*

V-necked mit V-Ausschnitt

vo·cab·u·la·ry Vokabular *n*, Wortschatz *m*; Wörterverzeichnis *n*

vo·cal Stimm...; F lautstark; MUS Vokal..., Gesang...; ~ *cords* ANAT Stimmbänder *pl*

vo·cal·ist Sänger(in)

vo·ca·tion Begabung *f* (*for* für); Berufung *f*

vo·ca·tion·al Berufs...; ~ *ed·u·ca·tion* Berufsausbildung *f*; ~ *guid·ance* Berufsberatung *f*; ~ *train·ing* Berufsausbildung *f*

vogue Mode *f*; *be in* ~ Mode sein

voice 1. Stimme *f*; *active* ~ LING Aktiv *n*; *passive* ~ LING Passiv *n* **2.** zum Ausdruck bringen; LING (stimmhaft) aussprechen; *voiced* LING stimmhaft; **voice·less** LING stimmlos

void 1. leer; JUR ungültig; ~ *of* ohne **2.** (Gefühl *n* der) Leere *f*

vol *abbr of* **volume** Bd., Band *m*

vol·a·tile cholerisch (*person*); explosiv (*situation etc*); CHEM flüchtig

vol·ca·no Vulkan *m*

vol·ley 1. Salve *f*; (*Geschoss- etc*)Hagel *m* (*a. fig*); *tennis*: Volley *m*, Flugball *m*; *soccer*: Volleyschuss *m* **2.** *Ball* volley schießen

vol·ley·ball SPORT Volleyball *m*

volt ELECTR Volt *n*

volt·age ELECTR Spannung *f*

vol·u·ble redselig; wortreich

vol·ume Band *m*; Volumen *n*, Rauminhalt *m*; Umfang *m*, große Menge; Lautstärke *f*

vo·lu·mi·nous bauschig (*dress etc*); geräumig; umfangreich (*notes etc*)

vol·un·ta·ry freiwillig; unbezahlt

vol·un·teer 1. *v/i* sich freiwillig melden (*for* zu) (*a.* MIL); *v/t* Hilfe *etc* anbieten; *et.* von sich aus sagen, F herausrücken mit **2.** Freiwillige *m*, *f*; freiwilliger Helfer

vo·lup·tu·ous sinnlich (*lips etc*); aufreizend (*gesture etc*); üppig (*body etc*); kurvenreich (*woman*)

vom·it 1. *v/t* erbrechen; *v/i* (sich *er*)brechen, sich übergeben **2.** Erbrochene *n*

vo·ra·cious unersättlich (*appetite etc*)

vote 1. Abstimmung *f* (*about, on* über *acc*); (Wahl)Stimme *f*; Stimmzettel *m*; *a. pl* Wahlrecht *n*; ~ *of no confidence* Misstrauensvotum *n*; *take a* ~ *on s.th.* über et. abstimmen **2.** *v/i* wählen; ~ *for* (*against*) stimmen für (gegen); ~ *on* abstimmen über (*acc*); *v/t* wählen; *et.* bewilligen; ~ *out of office* abwählen

vot·er Wähler(in)

vot·ing booth Wahlkabine *f*

vouch: ~ *for* (sich *ver*)bürgen für

vouch·er Gutschein *m*, Kupon *m*

vow 1. Gelöbnis *n*; Gelübde *n*; *take a ~,* *make a ~* ein Gelöbnis *or* Gelübde ablegen **2.** geloben, schwören (*to do* zu tun)

vow·el LING Vokal *m*, Selbstlaut *m*

voy·age (See)Reise *f*

vul·gar vulgär, ordinär; geschmacklos

vul·ne·ra·ble *fig* verletzbar, verwundbar; verletzlich; anfällig (*to* für)

vul·ture ZO Geier *m*

W

W, w W, w *n*

wad (*Watte- etc*)Bausch *m*; Bündel *n*; (*Papier- etc*)Knäuel *m, n*

wad·ding Einlage *f*, Füllmaterial *n*

wad·dle watscheln

wade *v/i* waten; *~ through* waten durch; F sich durchkämpfen durch, *et.* durchackern; *v/t* durchwaten

wa·fer (*esp* Eis)Waffel *f*; Oblate *f*; REL Hostie *f*

waf·fle[1] Waffel *f*

waf·fle[2] *Br* F schwafeln

waft *v/i* ziehen (*smell etc*); *v/t* wehen

wag 1. wedeln (mit) **2.** *with a ~ of its tail* schwanzwedelnd

wage[1] *mst pl* (Arbeits)Lohn *m*

wage[2]: *~ (a) war against or on* MIL Krieg führen gegen; *fig* e-n Feldzug führen gegen

wage| earn·er Lohnempfänger(in); Verdiener(in); *~ freeze* Lohnstopp *m*; *~ ne·go·ti·a·tions* Tarifverhandlungen *pl*

wa·ger Wette *f*

wage rise Lohnerhöhung *f*

wag·gle F wackeln (mit)

wag·gon *Br* → **wag·on** Fuhrwerk *n*, Wagen *m*; *Br* RAIL (offener) Güterwagen; (*Tee- etc*)Wagen *m*

wag·tail ZO Bachstelze *f*

wail 1. jammern; heulen (*siren, wind*) **2.** Jammern *n*; Heulen *n*

wain·scot (Wand)Täfelung *f*

waist Taille *f*

waist·coat *esp Br* Weste *f*

waist·line Taille *f*

wait 1. *v/i* warten (*for, on* auf *acc*); *~ for s.o.* a. j-n erwarten; *keep s.o. ~ing* j-n warten lassen; *~ and see!* warte es ab!; *~ on s.o.* j-n bedienen; *~ up* F aufbleiben (*for* wegen); *v/t:* *~ one's chance* auf e-e günstige Gelegenheit warten (*to do* zu tun); *~ one's turn* warten, bis man an der Reihe ist **2.** Wartezeit *f*; *have a long ~* lange warten müssen; *lie in ~ for s.o.* j-m auflauern

wait·er Kellner *m*, Ober *m*; *~, the check* (*Br bill*), *please!* (Herr) Ober, bitte zahlen!

wait·ing Warten *n*; *no ~* MOT Halt(e)verbot *n*; *~ list* Warteliste *f*; *~ room* MED *etc* Wartezimmer *n*; RAIL Wartesaal *m*

wait·ress Kellnerin *f*, Bedienung *f*; *~, the check* (*Br bill*), *please!* Fräulein, bitte zahlen!

wake[1] *v/i a. ~ up* aufwachen, wach werden; *v/t a. ~ up* (auf)wecken; *fig* wachrufen, wecken

wake[2] MAR Kielwasser *n*; *follow in the ~ of fig* folgen auf (*acc*)

wake·ful schlaflos

wak·en *v/i a. ~ up* aufwachen, wach werden; *v/t a. ~ up* (auf)wecken

walk 1. *v/i* (zu Fuß) gehen, laufen; spazieren gehen; wandern; *v/t Strecke* gehen, laufen; j-n bringen (*to* zu; *home* nach Hause); *Hund* ausführen; *Pferd* im Schritt gehen lassen; *~ away →* *walk off; ~ in* hineingehen, hereinkommen; *~ off* fort-, weggehen; *~ off with* F abhauen mit; F *Preis etc* locker gewinnen; *~ out* hinausgehen; (unter Protest) den Saal *etc* verlassen; ECON streiken, in (den) Streik treten; *~ out on s.o.* F j-n verlassen, j-n im Stich lassen; *~ up* hinaufgehen, heraufkommen; *~ up to s.o.* auf j-n zugehen; *~ up!* treten Sie näher! **2.** Spaziergang *m*; Wanderung *f*; Spazier-, Wanderweg *m*; *go for a ~, take a ~* e-n Spaziergang machen, spazieren gehen; *an hour's ~* e-e Stunde Fußweg *or* zu Fuß; *from all ~s of life* Leute aus allen Berufen *or* Schichten

walk·a·way F Spaziergang *m*, leichter Sieg

walk·er Spaziergänger(in); Wanderer *m*, Wand(r)erin *f*; SPORT Geher(in); *be a good* ~ gut zu Fuß sein

walk·ie-talk·ie Walkie-Talkie *n*, tragbares Funksprechgerät

walk·ing Gehen *n*, Laufen *n*; Spazierengehen *n*; Wandern *n*; ~ **pa·pers**: *get one's* ~ F den Laufpass bekommen; ~ **shoes** Wanderschuhe *pl*; ~ **stick** Spazierstock *m*; ~ **tour** Wanderung *f*

Walk·man® Walkman® *m*

walk·out Auszug *m* (*by, of* e-r Delegation *etc*); ECON Ausstand *m*, Streik *m*

walk·over → *walkaway*

walk·up F (Miets)Haus *n* ohne Fahrstuhl; Wohnung *f or* Büro *n etc* in e-m Haus ohne Fahrstuhl

wall 1. Wand *f*; Mauer *f* 2. *a.* ~ *in* mit e-r Mauer umgeben; ~ *up* zumauern

wall cal·en·dar Wandkalender *m*

wall-chart Wandkarte *f*

wal·let Brieftasche *f*

wall-flow·er F Mauerblümchen *n*

wal·lop F *j-m* ein Ding verpassen; SPORT *j-n* erledigen, vernichten (*at* in *dat*)

wal·low sich wälzen; *fig* schwelgen, sich baden (*in* in *dat*)

wall·pa·per 1. Tapete *f* 2. tapezieren

wall-to-wall: ~ *carpet(ing)* Spannteppich *m*, Teppichboden *m*

wal·nut BOT Walnuss(baum *m*) *f*

wal·rus ZO Walross *n*

waltz 1. Walzer *m* 2. Walzer tanzen

wand (*Zauber*)Stab *m*

wan·der (herum)wandern, herumlaufen, umherstreifen; *fig* abschweifen; fantasieren

wane 1. ASTR abnehmen; *fig* schwinden 2. *be on the* ~ *fig* im Schwinden begriffen sein

wan·gle F deichseln, hinkriegen; ~ *s.th. out of s.o.* j-m et. abluchsen; ~ *one's way out of* sich herauswinden aus

want 1. *v/t et.* wollen; *j-n* brauchen; *j-n* sprechen wollen; F *et.* brauchen, nötig haben; *be* ~ *ed* (*polizeilich*) gesucht werden (*for* wegen); *v/i* wollen; *I don't* ~ *to* ich will nicht; *he does not* ~ *for anything* es fehlt ihm an nichts 2. Mangel *m* (*of* an *dat*); Bedürfnis *n*, Wunsch *m*; Not *f*; ~ *ad* Kleinanzeige *f*

want·ed (*polizeilich*) gesucht

wan·ton mutwillig

war Krieg *m* (*a. fig*); *fig* Kampf *m* (*against* gegen)

war·ble ZO trillern

ward 1. MED Station *f*; Br POL Stadtbezirk *m*; JUR Mündel *n* 2. ~ *off Schlag etc* abwehren, *Gefahr etc* abwenden

war·den Aufseher(in); Heimleiter(in); (Gefängnis)Direktor(in)

ward·er Br Aufsichtsbeamte *m*, -beamtin *f*

war·drobe Kleiderschrank *m*; Garderobe *f*

ware·house Lager(haus) *n*

war·fare Krieg *m*; Kriegführung *f*

war·head MIL Spreng-, Gefechtskopf *m*

war·like kriegerisch; Kriegs…

warm 1. *adj* warm, *fig a.* herzlich; *I am* ~, *I feel* ~ mir ist warm 2. *v/t a.* ~ *up* wärmen, sich *die Hände etc* wärmen; *Motor* warm laufen lassen; *v/i a.* ~ *up* warm *or* wärmer werden, sich erwärmen; **warmth** Wärme *f*

warm-up SPORT Aufwärmen *n*

warn warnen (*against, of* vor *dat*); *j-n* verständigen

warn·ing Warnung *f* (*of* vor *dat*); Verwarnung *f*; *without* ~ ohne Vorwarnung; ~ *sig·nal* Warnsignal *n*

warp sich verziehen *or* werfen

war·rant 1. JUR (Durchsuchungs-, Haft*etc*)Befehl *m* 2. *et.* rechtfertigen; ~ *of ar·rest* JUR Haftbefehl *m*

war·ran·ty ECON Garantie(erklärung) *f*; *it's still under* ~ darauf ist noch Garantie

war·ri·or Krieger *m*

war·ship Kriegsschiff *n*

wart MED Warze *f*

war·y vorsichtig

was ich, er, sie, es war; *passive*: ich, er, sie, es wurde

wash 1. *v/t* waschen, sich *die Hände etc* waschen; *v/i* sich waschen; sich *gut etc* waschen (lassen); ~ *up* *v/i* Br abwaschen, (das) Geschirr spülen; *v/t* anschwemmen, anspülen; ~ *one's dirty linen* schmutzige Wäsche waschen 2. Wäsche *f*; MOT Waschanlage *f*, Waschstraße *f*; *be in the* ~ in der Wäsche sein; *give s.th. a* ~ *et.* waschen; *have a* ~ sich waschen

wash·a·ble (ab)waschbar

wash-and-wear bügelfrei; pflegeleicht

wash·ba·sin Br, **wash·bowl** Waschbecken *n*

wash·cloth Waschlappen *m*

wash·er Waschmaschine *f*; TECH Unterlegscheibe *f*

wash·ing 1. Wäsche *f* **2.** Wasch…

wash·ing| ma·chine Waschmaschine *f*; **~ pow·der** Waschpulver *n*, -mittel *n*

washing-up *Br* Abwasch *m*; *do the ~* den Abwasch machen

wash·room Toilette *f*

wasp ZO Wespe *f*

waste 1. Verschwendung *f*; Abfall *m*; Müll *m*; **~ of time** Zeitverschwendung *f*; *hazardous ~, special toxic ~* Sondermüll *m*; *special ~ dump* Sondermülldeponie *f* **2.** *v/t* verschwenden, vergeuden; *j-n* auszehren; *v/i* **~ away** immer schwächer werden (*person*) **3.** überschüssig; Abfall…; brachliegend, öde; *lay ~* verwüsten

waste dis·pos·al Abfall-, Müllbeseitigung *f*; Entsorgung *f*; **~ site** Deponie *f*

waste·ful verschwenderisch

waste| gas Abgas *n*; **~ pa·per** Abfallpapier *n*; Altpapier *n*

waste·pa·per bas·ket Papierkorb *m*

waste pipe Abflussrohr *n*

watch 1. *v/i* zuschauen; **~ for** warten auf (*acc*); **~ out!** pass auf!, Vorsicht!; **~ out for** Ausschau halten nach; sich in Acht nehmen vor (*dat*); *v/t* beobachten; zuschauen bei, sich *et.* ansehen; → *television* **2.** (*Armband-, Taschen*)Uhr *f*; Wache *f*; *keep ~* Wache halten, wachen (*over* über *acc*); *be on the ~ for* Ausschau halten nach; auf der Hut sein vor (*dat*); *keep (a) careful or close ~ on* genau beobachten, scharf im Auge behalten

watch·dog Wachhund *m*

watch·ful wachsam

watch·mak·er Uhrmacher(in)

watch·man Wachmann *m*, Wächter *m*

watch·tow·er Wach(t)turm *m*

wa·ter 1. Wasser *n* **2.** *v/t* Blumen gießen, *Rasen etc* sprengen; *Vieh* tränken; **~ down** verdünnen, verwässern; *fig* abschwächen; *v/i* tränen (*eyes*); *make s.o.'s mouth ~* j-m den Mund wässerig machen

wa·ter bird ZO Wasservogel *m*

wa·ter·col·o(u)r Wasser-, Aquarellfarbe *f*; Aquarellmalerei *f*; Aquarell *n*

wa·ter·course Wasserlauf *m*

wa·ter·cress BOT Brunnenkresse *f*

wa·ter·fall Wasserfall *m*

wa·ter·front Hafenviertel *n*; *along the ~* am Wasser entlang

wa·ter·hole Wasserloch *n*

wa·ter·ing can Gießkanne *f*

wa·ter jump SPORT Wassergraben *m*

wa·ter lev·el Wasserstand *m*

wa·ter lil·y BOT Seerose *f*

wa·ter·mark Wasserzeichen *n*

wa·ter·mel·on BOT Wassermelone *f*

wa·ter| pol·lu·tion Wasserverschmutzung *f*; **~ po·lo** SPORT Wasserball(spiel *n*) *m*

wa·ter·proof 1. wasserdicht **2.** *Br* Regenmantel *m* **3.** imprägnieren

wa·ters Gewässer *pl*; Wasser *pl*

wa·ter·shed GEOGR Wasserscheide *f*; *fig* Wendepunkt *m*

wa·ter·side Ufer *n*

wa·ter ski·ing SPORT Wasserskilaufen *n*

wa·ter·tight wasserdicht, *fig a.* hieb- und stichfest

wa·ter·way Wasserstraße *f*

wa·ter·works Wasserwerk *n*; *turn on the ~* F zu heulen anfangen

wa·ter·y wäss(e)rig

watt ELECTR Watt *n*

wave 1. *v/t* schwenken; winken mit; *Haar* wellen, in Wellen legen; **~ one's hand** winken; **~ s.o. aside** j-n beiseitewinken; *v/i* winken; wehen (*flag etc*); sich wellen (*hair*); **~ at s.o.**, **~ to s.o.** j-m zuwinken **2.** Welle *f* (*a. fig*); Winken *n*

wave·length PHYS Wellenlänge *f* (*a. fig*)

wa·ver flackern; schwanken

wav·y wellig, gewellt

wax¹ 1. Wachs *n*; (*Ohren*)Schmalz *n* **2.** wachsen; bohnern

wax² ASTR zunehmen

wax·en wächsern

wax·works Wachsfigurenkabinett *n*

wax·y wächsern

way 1. Weg *m*; Richtung *f*, Seite *f*; Entfernung *f*, Strecke *f*; Art *f*, Weise *f*; **~s and means** Mittel und Wege *pl*; **~ back** Rückweg *m*, Rückfahrt *f*; **~ home** Heimweg *m*; **~ in** Eingang *m*; **~ out** Ausgang *m*; *be on the ~ to*, *be on one's ~ to* unterwegs sein nach; *by ~ of* über (*acc*), via; *esp Br* statt; *by the ~* übrigens; *give ~* nachgeben; *Br* MOT die Vorfahrt lassen; *in a ~* in gewisser Hinsicht; *in no ~* in keiner Weise;

lead the ~ vorangehen; *let s.o. have his* (*own*) ~ j-m s-n Willen lassen; *lose one's* ~ sich verlaufen *or* verirren; *make* ~ Platz machen (*for* für); *no* ~*!* F kommt überhaupt nicht in Frage!; *out of the* ~ ungewöhnlich; *this* ~ hierhcr; hier entlang **2.** *adv* weit

way·bill ECON Frachtbrief *m*

way·lay *j-m* auflauern; *j-n* abfangen, abpassen

way·ward eigensinnig, launisch

we wir *pl*

weak schwach (*at, in* in *dat*), GASTR *a.* dünn; **weak·en** *v/t* schwächen (*a. fig*); *v/i* schwächer werden; *fig* nachgeben; **weak·ling** Schwächling *m*, F Schlappschwanz *n*; **weak·ness** Schwäche *f*

weal Striemen *m*

wealth Reichtum *m*; *fig* Fülle *f* (*of* von)

wealth·y reich

wean entwöhnen; ~ *s.o. from or off s.th.* j-m et. abgewöhnen

weap·on Waffe *f* (*a. fig*)

wear 1. *v/t* Bart, *Brille, Schmuck etc* tragen, *Mantel etc a.* anhaben, *Hut etc a.* aufhaben; abnutzen, abtragen; ~ *an angry expression* verärgert dreinschauen; *v/i* sich abnutzen, verschleißen; sich gut *etc* halten; *s.th. to* ~ et. zum Anziehen; ~ *away* (sich) abtragen *or* abschleifen; ~ *down* (sich) abtreten (*stairs*), (sich) ablaufen (*heels*), (sich) abfahren (*tires*); abschleifen; j-n zermürben; ~ *off* nachlassen (*pain etc*); ~ *on* sich hinziehen (*all day* über den ganzen Tag); ~ *out* (sich) abnutzen *or* abtragen; *fig* j-n erschöpfen **2.** *often in cpds* Kleidung *f*; *a.* ~ *and tear* Abnutzung *f*, Verschleiß *m*; *the worse for* ~ abgenutzt, verschlissen; F lädiert

wear·i·some ermüdend; langweilig; lästig

wear·y erschöpft, müde; ermüdend, anstrengend; *be* ~ *of s.th.* F et. satthaben

wea·sel ZO Wiesel *n*

weath·er 1. Wetter *n*; Witterung *f* **2.** *v/t* dem Wetter aussetzen; *fig* Krise *etc* überstehen; *v/i* verwittern

weath·er·beat·en verwittert

weath·er| chart METEOR Wetterkarte *f*; ~ **fore·cast** METEOR Wettervorhersage *f*; Wetterbericht *m*

weath·er·man *radio*, TV Wetteransager *m*

weath·er·proof 1. wetterfest **2.** wetterfest machen

weath·er| re·port METEOR Wetterbericht *m*; ~ **sta·tion** METEOR Wetterwarte *f*; ~ **vane** Wetterfahne *f*

weave weben; *Netz* spinnen; *Korb* flechten; ~ *one's way through* sich schlängeln durch; **weav·er** Weber(in)

web Netz *n* (*a. fig*), Gewebe *n*; ZO Schwimmhaut *f*

wed heiraten

Wed(s) *abbr of* **Wednesday** Mi., Mittwoch *m*

wed·ding 1. Hochzeit *f* **2.** Hochzeits..., Braut..., Ehe..., Trau...

wed·ding ring Ehering *m*, Trauring *m*

wedge 1. Keil *m* **2.** verkeilen, mit e-m Keil festklemmen; ~ *in* einkeilen, einzwängen

Wednes·day (*abbr* **Wed, Weds**) Mittwoch *m*; *on* ~ (am) Mittwoch; *on* ~*s* mittwochs

wee[1] F klein, winzig; *a* ~ *bit* ein (kleines) bisschen

wee[2] F **1.** Pipi machen **2.** *do or have a* ~ Pipi machen

weed 1. Unkraut *n* **2.** jäten

weed·kill·er Unkrautvertilgungsmittel *n*

weed·y voll Unkraut; F schmächtig; F rückgratlos

week Woche *f*; ~ *after* ~ Woche um Woche; *a* ~ *today, today* ~ heute in e-r Woche *or* in acht Tagen; *every other* ~ jede zweite Woche; *for* ~*s* wochenlang; *four times a* ~ viermal die Woche; *in a* ~ (*'s time*) in e-r Woche

week·day Wochentag *m*

week·end Wochenende *n*; *on* (*Br at*) *the* ~ am Wochenende; **week·end·er** Wochenendausflügler(in)

week·ly 1. Wochen...; wöchentlich **2.** Wochenblatt *n*, Wochen(zeit)schrift *f*, Wochenzeitung *f*

weep weinen (*for* um *j-n*; *over* über *acc*); MED nässen

weep·ing wil·low BOT Trauerweide *f*

weep·y F weinerlich; rührselig

wee-wee F → **wee**[2]

weigh *v/t* (ab)wiegen; *fig* abwägen (*against* gegen); ~ *anchor* MAR den Anker lichten; *be* ~*ed down with fig* niedergedrückt werden von; *v/i* ... *Kilo etc* wiegen; ~ *on fig* lasten auf (*dat*)

weight 1. Gewicht *n*; Last *f* (*a. fig*); *fig* Bedeutung *f*; *gain ~, put on ~* zunehmen; *lose ~* abnehmen **2.** beschweren

weight·less schwerelos

weight·less·ness Schwerelosigkeit *f*

weight lift·er SPORT Gewichtheber *m*

weight lift·ing SPORT Gewichtheben *n*

weight·y schwer; *fig* schwerwiegend

weir Wehr *n*

weird unheimlich; F sonderbar, verrückt

wel·come 1. *int ~ back!, ~ home!* willkommen zu Hause!; *~ to England!* willkommen in England! **2.** *v/t* begrüßen (*a. fig*), willkommen heißen **3.** *adj* willkommen; *you are ~ to do it* Sie können es gerne tun; *you're ~!* nichts zu danken!, keine Ursache!, bitte sehr! **4.** Empfang *m*, Willkommen *n*; *outstay or overstay one's ~* j-s Gastfreundschaft überstrapazieren *or* zu lange in Anspruch nehmen

weld TECH schweißen

wel·fare Wohl(ergehen) *n*; Sozialhilfe *f*; *be on ~* Sozialhilfe beziehen; *~ state* Wohlfahrtsstaat *m*; *~ work* Sozialarbeit *f*; *~ work·er* Sozialarbeiter(in)

well¹ 1. *adv* gut; gründlich; *as ~* ebenso, auch; *as ~ as ...* sowohl ... als auch ...; nicht nur ..., sondern auch ...; *very ~* also gut, na gut; *~ done!* bravo!; → *off I* **2.** *int* nun, also; *~, ~!* na so was! **3.** *adj* gesund; *feel ~* sich wohlfühlen

well² 1. Brunnen *m*; (*Öl*)Quelle *f*; (*Aufzugs- etc*)Schacht *m* **2.** *a. ~ out* quellen (*from* aus); *tears ~ed* (*up*) *in their eyes* die Tränen stiegen ihnen in die Augen

well-bal·anced ausgeglichen (*person*); ausgewogen (*diet*)

well-be·haved artig, gut erzogen

well-be·ing Wohl(befinden) *n*

well-dis·posed: *be ~ towards s.o.* j-m wohlgesinnt sein

well-done GASTR durchgebraten

well-earned wohlverdient

well-fed gut genährt

well-found·ed (wohl) begründet

well-in·formed gut unterrichtet; gebildet

well-known (wohl) bekannt

well-mean·ing wohlmeinend, gut gemeint; **well-meant** gut gemeint

well-off 1. wohlhabend, vermögend, bessergestellt; *be ~ for* gut versorgt sein mit **2.** *the ~* die Wohlhabenden *pl*

well-read belesen

well-timed (zeitlich) günstig, im richtigen Augenblick

well-to-do wohlhabend, reich

well-worn abgetragen; *fig* abgedroschen

Welsh 1. walisisch **2.** LING Walisisch *n*; *the ~* die Waliser *pl*

welt Striemen *m*

wel·ter Wirrwarr *m*, Durcheinander *n*

wel·ter·weight SPORT Weltergewicht *n*; Weltergewichtler *m*

were *du* warst, *Sie* waren, *wir, sie* waren, *ihr* wart

west 1. West, Westen *m*; *the West* POL der Westen; die Weststaaten *pl* **2.** *adj* westlich, West... **3.** *adv* nach Westen, westwärts; **west·er·ly** West..., westlich; **west·ern 1.** westlich, West... **2.** Western *m*; **west·ward(s)** westlich, nach Westen

wet 1. nass, feucht **2.** Nässe *f* **3.** nass machen, anfeuchten

weth·er ZO Hammel *m*

wet nurse Amme *f*

whack (knallender) Schlag; F Anteil *m*

whacked F fertig, erledigt

whack·ing 1. *Br* F Mords... **2.** (Tracht *f*) Prügel *pl*

whale ZO Wal *m*

wharf Kai *m*

what 1. *pron* was; *~ about ...?* wie wärs mit ...?; *~ for?* wozu?; *so ~?* na und?; *know ~'s ~* F wissen, was Sache ist **2.** *adj* was für ein(e), welche(r, -s); alle, die; alles, was

what·cha·ma·call·it F → *whatsit*

what·ev·er 1. *pron* was (auch immer); alles, was; egal, was **2.** *adj* welche(r, -s) ... auch (immer); *no ... ~* überhaupt kein(e) ...

whats·it F Dings(bums, -da) *m, f, n*

what·so·ev·er → *whatever*

wheat BOT Weizen *m*

whee·dle beschwatzen; *~ s.th. out of s.o.* j-m et. abschwatzen

wheel 1. Rad *n*; MOT, MAR Steuer *n* **2.** schieben, rollen; kreisen; *~ about, ~ (a)round* herumfahren, herumwirbeln

wheel·bar·row Schubkarre(n *m*) *f*

wheel·chair Rollstuhl *m*

wheel clamp MOT Parkkralle *f*

wheeled mit Rädern; fahrbar; *in cpds*

...räd(e)rig

wheeze keuchen, pfeifend atmen

whelp zo Welpe *m*, Junge *n*

when wann; als; wenn; obwohl; *since ~?* seit wann?

when·ev·er wann auch (immer); jedes Mal, wenn

where wo; wohin; *~ ...* (*from*)*?* woher?; *~ ...* (*to*)*?* wohin?; **where·a·bouts 1.** *adv* wo etwa **2.** Verbleib *m*; Aufenthalt *m*, Aufenthaltsort *m*

where·as während, wohingegen

where·by wodurch, womit; wonach

where·u·pon worauf, woraufhin

wher·ev·er wo *or* wohin auch (immer); ganz gleich wo *or* wohin

whet *Messer etc* schärfen; *fig Appetit* anregen

wheth·er ob

whey Molke *f*

which welche(r, -s); der, die, das; was; *~ of you?* wer von euch?

which·ev·er welche(r, -s) auch (immer); ganz gleich, welche(r, -s)

whiff Luftzug *m*; Hauch *m* (*a. fig of* von); Duft *m*, Duftwolke *f*

while 1. Weile *f*; *for a ~* e-e Zeit lang **2.** *cj* während; obwohl **3.** *mst ~ away* sich die Zeit vertreiben (*by doing s.th.* mit et.)

whim Laune *f*

whim·per 1. wimmern; zo winseln **2.** Wimmern *n*; zo Winseln *n*

whim·si·cal wunderlich; launisch

whine 1. zo jaulen; jammern (*about* über *acc*); **2.** zo Jaulen *n*; Gejammer *n*

whin·ny 1. wiehern **2.** Wiehern *n*

whip 1. Peitsche *f*; GASTR Creme *f* **2.** *v/t* (aus)peitschen; GASTR schlagen; *v/i* sausen, flitzen, (*wind*) fegen

whipped| cream Schlagsahne *f*, Schlagrahm *m*; *~ eggs* Eischnee *m*

whip·ping (Tracht *f*) Prügel *pl*

whip·ping boy Prügelknabe *m*

whip·ping cream Schlagsahne *f*, Schlagrahm *m*

whir → *whirr*

whirl 1. wirbeln; *my head is ~ing* mir schwirrt der Kopf **2.** Wirbeln *n*; Wirbel *m* (*a. fig*); *my head's in a ~* mir schwirrt der Kopf

whirl·pool Strudel *m*; Whirlpool *m*

whirl·wind Wirbelsturm *m*

whirr schwirren

whisk 1. schnelle Bewegung; Wedel *m*;

GASTR Schneebesen *m* **2.** GASTR schlagen; *~ its tail* zo mit dem Schwanz schlagen; *~ away Fliegen etc* verscheuchen *or* wegscheuchen; *et.* schnell verschwinden lassen *or* wegnehmen

whis·ker zo Schnurr- *or* Barthaar *n*; *pl* Backenbart *m*

whis·k(e)y Whisky *m*

whis·per 1. flüstern **2.** Flüstern *n*; *say s.th. in a ~* et. im Flüsterton sagen

whis·tle 1. Pfeife *f*; Pfiff *m* **2.** pfeifen

white 1. weiß **2.** Weiß(e) *n*; Weiße *m*, *f*; Eiweiß *n*; *~ bread* Weißbrot *n*; *~ coffee Br* Milchkaffee *m*, Kaffee *m* mit Milch

white-col·lar work·er (Büro)Angestellte *m*, *f*

white lie Notlüge *f*

whit·en weiß machen *or* werden

white·wash 1. Tünche *f* **2.** tünchen, anstreichen; weißen; *fig* beschönigen

whit·ish weißlich

Whit·sun Pfingstsonntag *m*; Pfingsten *n or pl*

Whit Sunday Pfingstsonntag *m*

Whit·sun·tide Pfingsten *n or pl*

whit·tle (zurecht)schnitzen; *~ away Gewinn etc* allmählich aufzehren; *~ down et.* reduzieren (*to auf acc*)

whiz(z) F **1.** *~ by*, *~ past* vorbeizischen, vorbeidüsen **2.** Ass *n*, Kanone *f* (*at* in *dat*); *~ kid* F Senkrechtstarter(in)

who wer; wen; wem; welche(r, -s); der, die, das

who·dun·(n)it F Krimi *m*

who·ev·er wer *or* wen *or* wem auch (immer); egal, wer *or* wen *or* wem

whole 1. *adj* ganz **2.** *das* Ganze; *the ~ of London* ganz London; *on the ~* im Großen (und) Ganzen

whole-heart·ed ungeteilt (*attention*), voll (*support*), ernsthaft (*effort etc*)

whole-heart·ed·ly uneingeschränkt, voll und ganz

whole·meal Vollkorn...; *~ bread* Vollkornbrot *n*

whole·sale ECON **1.** Großhandel *m* **2.** Großhandels...; *~ mar·ket* ECON Großmarkt *m*

whole·sal·er ECON Großhändler *m*

whole·some gesund

whole wheat → *wholemeal*

whol·ly gänzlich, völlig

whoop 1. schreien, *esp* jauchzen; *~ it up* F auf den Putz hauen **2.** (*esp* Freuden)-

Schrei *m*

whoop·ee: F *make* ~ auf den Putz hauen

whoop·ing cough MED Keuchhusten *m*

whore Hure *f*

why warum, weshalb; *that's* ~ deshalb

wick Docht *m*

wick·ed gemein, niederträchtig

wick·er·work Korbwaren *pl*

wick·et *cricket*: Tor *n*

wide 1. *adj* breit; weit offen, aufgerissen (*eyes*); *fig* umfangreich (*knowledge etc*), vielfältig (*interests etc*) **2.** *adv* weit; *go* ~ danebengehen; *go* ~ *of the goal* SPORT am Tor vorbeigehen

wide-an·gle lens PHOT Weitwinkelobjektiv *n*

wide-a·wake hellwach; *fig* aufgeweckt, wach

wide-eyed mit großen *or* aufgerissenen Augen; naiv

wid·en verbreitern; breiter werden

wide-o·pen weit offen, aufgerissen (*eyes*)

wide·spread weit verbreitet

wid·ow Witwe *f*

wid·owed verwitwet; *be* ~ verwitwet sein; Witwe(r) werden

wid·ow·er Witwer *m*

width Breite *f*; Bahn *f*

wield *Einfluss etc* ausüben

wife (Ehe)Frau *f*, Gattin *f*

wig Perücke *f*

wild 1. *adj* wild; stürmisch (*wind, applause etc*); außer sich (*with* vor *dat*); verrückt (*idea etc*); *make a* ~ *guess* einfach drauflosraten; *be* ~ *about* (ganz) verrückt sein nach **2.** *adv*: *go* ~ ausflippen **3.** *in the* ~ in freier Wildbahn; *the* ~*s* die Wildnis

wild·cat ZO Wildkatze *f*

wild·cat strike ECON wilder Streik

wil·der·ness Wildnis *f*

wild·fire: *spread like* ~ sich wie ein Lauffeuer verbreiten

wild·life Tier- und Pflanzenwelt *f*

wil·ful *Br* → **willful**

will[1] *v/aux* ich, *du* will(st) *etc*; *ich* werde ... *etc*

will[2] Wille *m*; Testament *n*; *of one's own free* ~ aus freien Stücken

will[3] durch Willenskraft erzwingen; JUR vermachen

will·ful eigensinnig; absichtlich, *esp* JUR vorsätzlich

will·ing bereit (*to do* zu tun); (bereit)willig

will-o'-the-wisp Irrlicht *n*

wil·low BOT Weide *f*

wil·low·y *fig* gertenschlank

will·pow·er Willenskraft *f*

wil·ly-nil·ly wohl oder übel

wilt verwelken, welk werden

wi·ly gerissen, raffiniert

wimp F Schlappschwanz *m*

win 1. *v/t* gewinnen; ~ *s.o. over* or *round to* j-n gewinnen für; *v/i* gewinnen, siegen; *OK, you* ~ okay, du hast gewonnen **2.** *esp* SPORT Sieg *m*

wince zusammenzucken (*at* bei)

winch TECH Winde *f*

wind[1] **1.** Wind *m*; Atem *m*, Luft *f*; MED Blähungen *pl*; *the* ~ MUS die Bläser *pl* **2.** *j-m* den Atem nehmen *or* verschlagen; HUNT wittern

wind[2] **1.** *v/t* drehen (an *dat*); *Uhr etc* aufziehen; wickeln (*round* um); *v/i* sich winden *or* schlängeln; ~ *down Autofenster etc* herunterdrehen, -kurbeln; *Produktion etc* reduzieren; sich entspannen; ~ *up v/t Autofenster etc* hochdrehen, -kurbeln; *Uhr etc* aufziehen; *Versammlung etc* schließen (*with* mit); *Unternehmen* liquidieren, auflösen; *v/i* F enden, landen; (*esp* s-e Rede) schließen (*by saying* mit den Worten); **2.** Umdrehung *f*

wind·bag F Schwätzer(in)

wind·fall BOT Fallobst *n*; unverhofftes Geschenk; unverhoffter Gewinn

wind·ing gewunden

wind·ing stairs Wendeltreppe *f*

wind in·stru·ment MUS Blasinstrument *n*

wind·lass TECH Winde *f*

wind·mill Windmühle *f*

win·dow Fenster *n*; Schaufenster *n*; Schalter *m*; ~ *clean·er* Fensterputzer *m*; ~ *dress·er* Schaufensterdekorateur(in); ~ *dress·ing* Schaufensterdekoration *f*; *fig* F Mache *f*

win·dow·pane Fensterscheibe *f*

win·dow seat Fensterplatz *m*

win·dow shade Rouleau *n*

win·dow-shop: *go window-shopping* e-n Schaufensterbummel machen

win·dow·sill Fensterbank *f*, -brett *n*

wind·pipe ANAT Luftröhre *f*

wind·screen *Br* MOT Windschutzscheibe *f*; **~ wip·er** *Br* MOT Scheibenwischer *m*

wind·shield MOT Windschutzscheibe *f*; **~ wip·er** MOT Scheibenwischer *m*

wind·surf·ing SPORT Windsurfing *n*, Windsurfen *n*

wind·y windig; MED blähend

wine Wein *m*; **~ cel·lar** Weinkeller *m*; **~ list** Weinkarte *f*; **~ mer·chant** Weinhändler *m*

win·er·y Weinkellerei *f*

wine tast·ing Weinprobe *f*

wing zo Flügel *m*, Schwinge *f*; *Br* MOT Kotflügel *m*; AVIAT Tragfläche *f*; AVIAT MIL Geschwader *n*; *pl* THEA Seitenkulisse *f*

wing·er SPORT Außenstürmer(in), Flügelstürmer(in)

wink 1. zwinkern; **~ at** *j-m* zuzwinkern; *et.* geflissentlich übersehen; **~ one's lights** *Br* MOT blinken **2.** Zwinkern *n*; *I didn't get a ~ of sleep last night, I didn't sleep a ~ last night* ich habe letzte Nacht kein Auge zugetan; → *for·ty 1*

win·ner Gewinner(in), *esp* SPORT Sieger(in)

win·ning 1. einnehmend, gewinnend **2.** *pl* Gewinn *m*

win·ter 1. Winter *m*; *in (the)* **~** im Winter **2.** überwintern; den Winter verbringen; **~ sports** Wintersport *m*

win·ter·time Winter *m*; Winterzeit *f*; *in (the)* **~** im Winter

win·try winterlich; *fig* frostig

wipe (ab-, auf)wischen; **~ off** ab-, wegwischen; **~ out** auswischen; auslöschen, ausrotten; **~ up** aufwischen

wip·er MOT *(Scheiben)*Wischer *m*

wire 1. Draht *m*; ELECTR Leitung *f*; Telegramm *n* **2.** Leitungen verlegen in *(dat)* *(a.* **~ up**)*; *j-m* ein Telegramm schicken; *j-m et.* telegrafieren

wire·less drahtlos, Funk...

wire net·ting Maschendraht *m*

wire-tap *j-n*, *j-s* Telefon abhören

wir·y *fig* drahtig

wis·dom Weisheit *f*, Klugheit *f*

wis·dom tooth Weisheitszahn *m*

wise weise, klug

wise·crack F **1.** Witzelei *f* **2.** witzeln

wise guy F Klugscheißer *m*

wish 1. wünschen; wollen; **~ s.o. well** *j-m* alles Gute wünschen; *if you* **~**

(to) wenn du willst; **~ for s.th.** sich et. wünschen **2.** Wunsch *m* *(for* nach)

wish·ful think·ing Wunschdenken *n*

wish·y-wash·y F labb(e)rig, wäss(e)rig; *fig* lasch *(person)*; verschwommen

wisp *(Gras-, Haar)*Büschel *n*

wist·ful wehmütig

wit Geist *m*, Witz *m*; geistreicher Mensch; *a. pl* Verstand *m*; *be at one's* **~s' end** mit s-r Weisheit am Ende sein

witch Hexe *f*

witch·craft Hexerei *f*

with mit; bei; vor *(dat)*

with·draw *v/t* Geld abheben *(from* von)*; Angebot etc zurückziehen, Anschuldigung etc zurücknehmen; MIL Truppen zurückziehen, abziehen; *v/i* sich zurückziehen; zurücktreten *(from* von)

with·draw·al Rücknahme *f*; *esp* MIL Abzug *m*, Rückzug *m*; Rücktritt *m* *(from* von)*, Ausstieg *m* *(from* aus)*; MED Entziehung *f*, Entzug *m*; *make a* **~** Geld abheben *(from* von)*; **~ cure** MED Entziehungskur *f*; **~ symp·toms** MED Entzugserscheinungen *f*

with·er eingehen *or* verdorren *or* (ver)welken (lassen)

with·hold zurückhalten; **~ s.th. from s.o.** j-m et. vorenthalten

with·in innerhalb *(gen)*

with·out ohne *(acc)*

with·stand *e-m* Angriff etc standhalten; *Beanspruchung etc* aushalten

wit·ness 1. Zeuge *m*, Zeugin *f*; **~ for the defense** *(Br* **defence)** JUR Entlastungszeuge *m*, -zeugin *f*; **~ for the prosecution** JUR Belastungszeuge *m*, -zeugin *f* **2.** Zeuge sein von *et.*; *et.* bezeugen, *Unterschrift* beglaubigen; **~ box** *Br*, **~ stand** JUR Zeugenstand *m*

wit·ti·cis·m geistreiche *or* witzige Bemerkung; **wit·ty** geistreich, witzig

wiz·ard Zauberer *m*; *fig* Genie *n* *(at* in *dat)*

wiz·ened verhutzelt

wob·ble *v/i* wackeln, zittern *(a. voice)*, schwabbeln; MOT flattern; *fig* schwanken; *v/t* wackeln an *(dat)*

woe·ful traurig; bedauerlich

wolf 1. zo Wolf *m*; **lone ~** *fig* Einzelgänger(in) **2.** *a.* **~ down** F *Essen* hinunterschlingen

wom·an Frau *f*; **~ doc·tor** Ärztin *f*; **~ driv·er** Frau *f* am Steuer

wom·an·ish weibisch

wom·an·ly fraulich; weiblich

womb ANAT Gebärmutter f

women's| lib·ber F Emanze f; **~ move·ment** Frauenbewegung f; **~ ref·uge** Br, **~ shel·ter** Frauenhaus n

won·der 1. neugierig or gespannt sein, gern wissen mögen; sich fragen, überlegen; sich wundern, erstaunt sein (*about* über acc); *I ~ if you could help me* vielleicht können Sie mir helfen **2.** Staunen n, Verwunderung f; Wunder n; *do or work ~s* wahre Wunder vollbringen, Wunder wirken (*for* bei)

won·der·ful wunderbar, wundervoll

wont 1. *be ~ to do s.th.* et. zu tun pflegen **2.** *as was his ~* wie es s-e Gewohnheit war

woo umwerben, werben um

wood Holz n; Holzfass n; a. pl Wald m, Gehölz n; *touch ~!* unberufen!, toi, toi, toi!; *he can't see the ~ for the trees* er sieht den Wald vor lauter Bäumen nicht

wood·cut Holzschnitt m

wood·cut·ter Holzfäller m

wood·ed bewaldet

wood·en hölzern (a. fig), aus Holz, Holz…

wood·peck·er ZO Specht m

wood·wind: *the ~* MUS die Holzblasinstrumente pl, die Holzbläser pl; *~ instrument* Holzblasinstrument n

wood·work Holzarbeit f

wood·y waldig; BOT holzig

wool Wolle f

wool·(l)en 1. wollen, Woll… **2.** pl Wollsachen pl, Wollkleidung f

wool·(l)y 1. wollig; fig schwammig **2.** pl F Wollsachen pl

word 1. Wort n; Nachricht f; Losung f, Losungswort n; Versprechen n; Befehl m; pl MUS etc Text m; *have a ~ or a few ~s with s.o.* mit j-m sprechen **2.** et. ausdrücken, *Text* abfassen, formulieren; **word·ing** Wortlaut m

word| or·der LING Wortstellung f; **~ pro·cess·ing** IT Textverarbeitung f; **~ pro·ces·sor** IT Textverarbeitungsgerät n

word·y wortreich, langatmig

work 1. Arbeit f; Werk n; pl TECH Werk n, Getriebe n; ECON Werk n, Fabrik f; *at ~* bei der Arbeit; *be in ~* Arbeit haben; *be out of ~* arbeitslos sein; *go or set*

to ~ an die Arbeit gehen **2.** v/i arbeiten (*at, on* an dat); TECH funktionieren (a. fig); wirken; *~ to rule* Dienst nach Vorschrift tun; v/t j-n arbeiten lassen; *Maschine etc* bedienen, et. betätigen; et. bearbeiten; bewirken; herbeiführen; *~ one's way* sich durcharbeiten or durchkämpfen; *~ off Schulden* abarbeiten; *Wut etc* abreagieren; *~ out* v/t ausrechnen; *Aufgabe* lösen; *Plan etc* ausarbeiten; fig sich et. zusammenreimen; v/i gut gehen, F klappen; aufgehen; F SPORT trainieren; *~ up Zuhörer etc* aufpeitschen, aufwühlen; et. ausarbeiten (*into* zu); *be ~ed up* aufgeregt or nervös sein (*about* wegen)

work·a·ble formbar; fig durchführbar

work·a·day Alltags…

work·a·hol·ic F Arbeitssüchtige m, f

work·bench TECH Werkbank f

work·book PED Arbeitsheft n

work·day Arbeitstag m; Werktag m; *on ~s* werktags

work·er Arbeiter(in); Angestellte m, f

work ex·pe·ri·ence Erfahrung f

work·ing werktätig; Arbeits…; *~ knowledge* Grundkenntnisse pl; *in ~ order* in betriebsfähigem Zustand; *~ class* Arbeiterklasse f; *~ day* → *workday*; *~ hours* Arbeitszeit f

work·ings Arbeits-, Funktionsweise f

work·man Handwerker m

work·man·like fachmännisch

work·man·ship fachmännische Arbeit

work of art Kunstwerk n

work·out F SPORT Training n

work·place Arbeitsplatz m; *at the ~* am Arbeitsplatz

works coun·cil Betriebsrat m

work·sheet PED etc Arbeitsblatt n

work·shop Werkstatt f; Workshop m

work·shy arbeitsscheu

work·sta·tion IT Bildschirmarbeitsplatz m

work-to-rule Br Dienst m nach Vorschrift

world 1. Welt f; *all over the ~* in der ganzen Welt; *bring into the ~* auf die Welt bringen; *do s.o. a or the ~ of good* j-m unwahrscheinlich guttun; *mean all the ~ to s.o.* j-m alles bedeuten; *they are ~s apart* zwischen ihnen liegen Welten; *think the ~ of* große Stücke halten von; *what in the ~ …?* was um alles in

der Welt ...? **2.** Welt...; **~ cham·pi·on**
SPORT Weltmeister *m*; **~ cham·pi·onship** SPORT Weltmeisterschaft *f*
World Cup Fußballweltmeisterschaft *f*;
skiing: Weltcup *m*
world·fa·mous weltberühmt
world lit·er·a·ture Weltlitcratur *f*
world·ly weltlich; irdisch
world·ly·wise weltklug
world| mar·ket ECON Weltmarkt *m*; **~ pow·er** POL Weltmacht *f*; **~ rec·ord**
SPORT Weltrekord *m*; **~ trip** Weltreise
f; **~ war** Weltkrieg *m*
world·wide weltweit; auf der ganzen
Welt
worm 1. ZO Wurm *m* **2.** *Hund etc* entwurmen; **~ one's way through** sich schlängeln *or* zwängen durch; **~ o.s. into
s.o.'s confidence** sich in j-s Vertrauen
einschleichen; **~ s.th. out of s.o.** j-m et.
entlocken
worm-eat·en wurmstichig
worm's-eye view Froschperspektive *f*
worn-out abgenutzt, abgetragen; *fig* erschöpft
wor·ried besorgt, beunruhigt
wor·ry 1. beunruhigen; (sich) Sorgen
machen; **don't ~!** keine Angst!, keine
Sorge! **2.** Sorge *f*
worse schlechter, schlimmer; **~ still** was
noch schlimmer ist; **to make matters ~**
zu allem Übel
wors·en schlechter machen *or* werden,
(sich) verschlechtern
wor·ship 1. Verehrung *f*; Gottesdienst *m*
2. *v/t* anbeten, verehren; *v/i* den Gottesdienst besuchen
wor·ship·(p)er Anbeter(in), Verehrer(in); Kirchgänger(in)
worst 1. *adj* schlechteste(r, -s),
schlimmste(r, -s) **2.** *adv* am schlechtesten, am schlimmsten **3.** der, die, das
Schlechteste *or* Schlimmste; **at (the)
~** schlimmstenfalls
wor·sted Kammgarn *n*
worth 1. wert; **~ reading** lesenswert **2.**
Wert *m*; **worth·less** wertlos
worth·while lohnend; **be ~** sich lohnen
worth·y würdig
would-be Möchtegern...
wound 1. Wunde *f*, Verletzung *f* **2.** verwunden, verletzen
wow *int* F wow!, Mensch!, toll!
wran·gle 1. (sich) streiten **2.** Streit *m*

wrap 1. *v/t a.* **~ up** (ein)packen, (ein)wickeln (**in** *in dat*); *et.* wickeln ([**a**]**round**
um); *v/i:* **~ up** sich warm anziehen **2.**
Umhang *m*
wrap·per (Schutz)Umschlag *m*
wrap·ping Verpackung *f*; **~ pa·per** Einwickel-, Pack-, Geschenkpapier *n*
wrath Zorn *m*
wreath Kranz *m*
wreck 1. MAR Wrack *n* (*a. fig*) **2.** *Pläne etc*
zunichtemachen; **be·ed** MAR zerschellen; Schiffbruch erleiden
wreck·age Trümmer *pl* (*a. fig*), Wrackteile *pl*
wreck·er MOT Abschleppwagen *m*
wreck·ing| com·pa·ny Abbruchfirma *f*;
~ ser·vice MOT Abschleppdienst *m*
wren ZO Zaunkönig *m*
wrench 1. MED sich *das Knie etc* verrenken; **~ s.th. from** *or* **out of s.o.'s hands**
j-m et. aus den Händen winden, j-m et.
entwinden; **~ off** *et.* mit e-m Ruck abreißen *or* wegreißen; **~ open** aufreißen
2. Ruck *m*; MED Verrenkung *f*; *Br* TECH
Schraubenschlüssel *m*
wrest: ~ s.th. from *or* **out of s.o.'s
hands** j-m et. aus den Händen reißen,
j-m et. entreißen *or* entwinden
wres·tle *v/i* SPORT ringen (**with** mit), *fig
a.* kämpfen (**with** mit); *v/t* SPORT ringen
gegen; **wres·tler** SPORT Ringer *m*;
wres·tling SPORT Ringen *n*
wretch *often* HUMOR Schuft *m*, Wicht *m*
wretch·ed elend; (tod)unglücklich;
scheußlich; verdammt, verflixt
wrig·gle *v/i* sich winden; zappeln; **~ out
of** *fig* F sich herauswinden aus; F sich
drücken vor (*dat*); *v/t* mit *den Zehen*
wackeln
wring *j-m die Hand* drücken; *die Hände*
ringen; *den Hals* umdrehen; **~ out** *Wäsche etc* auswringen; **~ s.o.'s heart** j-m
zu Herzen gehen
wrin·kle 1. Falte *f*, Runzel *f* **2.** runzeln;
Nase krausziehen, rümpfen; faltig *or*
runz(e)lig werden
wrist ANAT Handgelenk *n*
wrist·band Bündchen *n*, (Hemd)Manschette *f*; Armband *n*
wrist·watch Armbanduhr *f*
writ JUR Befehl *m*, Verfügung *f*
write schreiben; **~ down** auf-, niederschreiben; **~ off** *j-n*, ECON *et.* abschreiben; **~ out** *Namen etc* ausschreiben;

Bericht etc ausarbeiten; *j-m e-e Quittung etc* ausstellen; **~ pro·tec·tion** IT Schreibschutz *m*

writ·er Schreiber(in), Verfasser(in), Autor(in); Schriftsteller(in)

writhe sich krümmen *or* winden (*in*, *with* vor *dat*)

writ·ing 1. Schreiben *n*; (Hand)Schrift *f*; Schriftstück *n*; *pl* Werke *pl*; *in ~* schriftlich **2.** Schreib…; **~ case** Schreibmappe *f*; **~ desk** Schreibtisch *m*; **~ pad** Schreibblock *m*; **~ pa·per** Briefpapier *n*, Schreibpapier *n*

writ·ten schriftlich

wrong 1. *adj* falsch; unrecht; *be ~* falsch sein, nicht stimmen; unrecht haben; falsch gehen (*watch*); *be on the ~ side of forty* über 40 (Jahre alt) sein; *is anything ~?* ist et. nicht in Ordnung?; *what's ~ with her?* was ist los mit ihr?, was hat sie? **2.** *adv* falsch; *get ~ j-n, et.* falsch verstehen; *go ~* e-n Fehler machen; kaputtgehen; *fig* F schiefgehen **3.** Unrecht *n*; *be in the ~* im Unrecht sein **4.** *j-m* unrecht tun

wrong·ful ungerechtfertigt; gesetzwidrig

wrong-way driv·er MOT F Geisterfahrer(in)

wrought i·ron Schmiedeeisen *n*

wrought-i·ron schmiedeeisern

wry süßsauer (*smile*); ironisch, sarkastisch (*humor etc*)

wt *abbr of* **weight** Gew., Gewicht *n*

WWF *abbr of* **World Wide Fund for Nature** WWF *m*

WYSIWYG *abbr of* **what you see is what you get** IT was du (*auf dem Bildschirm*) siehst, bekommst du (*auch ausgedruckt*)

X

X, x X, x *n*

xen·o·pho·bi·a Fremdenhass *m*; Ausländerfeindlichkeit *f*

XL *abbr of* **extra large** (**size**) extragroß

X·mas F → **Christmas**

X-ray MED **1.** röntgen **2.** Röntgenstrahl *m*; Röntgenaufnahme *f*, -bild *n*; Röntgenuntersuchung *f*

xy·lo·phone MUS Xylophon *n*

Y

Y, y Y, y *n*

yacht MAR **1.** (Segel)Boot *n*; Jacht *f* **2.** segeln; *go ~ing* segeln gehen

yacht club Segelklub *m*, Jachtklub *m*

yacht·ing Segeln *n*, Segelsport *m*

Yan·kee F Yankee *m*, Ami *m*

yap kläffen; F quasseln

yard¹ (*abbr* **yd**) Yard *n* (*91, 44 cm*)

yard² Hof *m*; (*Bau-, Stapel- etc*)Platz *m*; Garten *m*

yard·stick *fig* Maßstab *m*

yarn Garn *n*

yawn 1. gähnen **2.** Gähnen *n*

yeah F ja

year Jahr *n*; *all the ~ round* das ganze Jahr hindurch; *~ after ~* Jahr für Jahr; *~ in ~ out* jahraus, jahrein; *this ~* dieses Jahr; *this ~'s* diesjährige(r, -s)

year·ly jährlich

yearn sich sehnen (*for* nach; *to do* danach, zu tun); **yearn·ing 1.** Sehnsucht *f* **2.** sehnsüchtig

yeast Hefe *f*

yell 1. schreien, brüllen (*with* vor *dat*); **~ at s.o.** j-n anschreien *or* anbrüllen; **~ (out)** *et.* schreien, brüllen **2.** Schrei *m*

yel·low 1. gelb; F feig(e) **2.** Gelb *n*; *at ~* MOT bei Gelb **3.** (sich) gelb färben; gelb werden; vergilben

yel·low fe·ver MED Gelbfieber *n*

yel·low·ish gelblich

Yel·low Pag·es® TEL *die* Gelben Seiten *pl*, Branchenverzeichnis *n*

yel·low press Sensationspresse *f*

yelp 1. (auf)jaulen; aufschreien **2.** (Auf)Jaulen *n*; Aufschrei *m*
yes 1. ja; doch **2.** Ja *n*
yes·ter·day gestern; **~ morning (after-noon)** gestern Morgen (Nachmittag); **the day before ~** vorgestern
yet 1. *adv in questions*: schon; noch; (doch) noch; doch, aber; **as ~** bis jetzt, bisher; **not ~** noch nicht **2.** *cj* aber, doch
yew BOT Eibe *f*
yield 1. *v/t* Früchte tragen; *Gewinn* abwerfen; *Resultat etc* ergeben, liefern; *v/i* nachgeben; **~ to** MOT j-m die Vorfahrt lassen **2.** Ertrag *m*
yip·pee *int* F hurra!
yo·del 1. jodeln **2.** Jodler *m*
yo·ga Joga *m, n,* Yoga *m, n*
yog·h(o)urt, yog·urt Jog(h)urt *m, n*
yoke Joch *n (a. fig)*
yolk (Ei)Dotter *m, n,* Eigelb *n*
you du, ihr, Sie; *(dat)* dir, euch, Ihnen; *(acc)* dich, euch, Sie; man

young 1. jung **2.** ZO Junge *pl*; **with ~** ZO trächtig; **the ~** die jungen Leute *pl,* die Jugend
young·ster Junge *m*
your dein(e); *pl* euer, eure; Ihr(e) *(a. pl)*
yours deine(r, -s); *pl* euer eure(s); Ihre(r, -s) *(a. pl)*; **a friend of ~** ein Freund von dir; **Yours, Bill** Dein Bill
your·self selbst; dir, dich, sich; **by ~** allein
youth Jugend *f*; Jugendliche *m*
youth club Jugendklub *m*
youth·ful jugendlich
youth hos·tel Jugendherberge *f*
yuck·y F *contp* scheußlich
Yu·go·slav HIST **1.** jugoslawisch **2.** Jugoslawe *m,* Jugoslawin *f;* **Yu·go·sla·vi·a** HIST Jugoslawien *n*
yup·pie, yup·py *abbr of* **young upwardly-mobile** *or* **urban professional** junger, aufstrebender *or* städtischer Karrieremensch, Yuppie *m*

Z

Z, z Z, z *n*
zap F *esp computer game etc*: abknallen, fertigmachen; MOT beschleunigen **(from ... to ...** von ... auf *acc* ...); jagen, hetzen; TV *Fernbedienung* bedienen; TV zappen, umschalten; **~ off** abzischen; **~ to** düsen *or* jagen *or* hetzen nach
zap·per TV F Fernbedienung *f*
zap·py *Br* F voller Pep, schmissig, fetzig
zeal Eifer *m*
zeal·ot Fanatiker(in), Eiferer *m,* Eiferin *f;* **zeal·ous** eifrig; **be ~ to do s.th.** eifrig darum bemüht sein, et. zu tun
ze·bra ZO Zebra *n*
ze·bra cross·ing *Br* Zebrastreifen *m*
zen·ith Zenit *m (a. fig)*
ze·ro 1. Null *f;* Nullpunkt *m;* **20 degrees below ~** 20 Grad unter Null **2.** Null...;**~ growth** Nullwachstum *n;* **~ op·tion** POL Nulllösung *f*
zest *fig* Würze *f;* Begeisterung *f;* **~ for life** Lebensfreude *f*
zig·zag 1. Zickzack *m* **2.** Zickzack... **3.** im Zickzack fahren, laufen *etc,* zick-

zackförmig verlaufen
zinc CHEM Zink *n*
zip¹ 1. Reißverschluss *m* **2. ~ the bag open (shut)** den Reißverschluss der Tasche aufmachen (zumachen); **~ s.o. up** j-m den Reißverschluss zumachen
zip² 1. Zischen *n,* Schwirren *n;* F Schwung *m* **2.** zischen, schwirren; **~ by, ~ past** vorbeiflitzen
zip code Postleitzahl *f*
zip fas·ten·er *esp Br* → **zipper**
zip·per Reißverschluss *m*
zo·di·ac ASTR Tierkreis *m;* **signs of the ~** Tierkreiszeichen *pl*
zone Zone *f*
zoo Zoo *m,* Tierpark *m*
zo·o·log·i·cal zoologisch; **~ gar·dens** Tierpark *m,* zoologischer Garten
zo·ol·o·gist Zoologe *m,* Zoologin *f*
zo·ol·o·gy Zoologie *f*
zoom 1. surren; F sausen; F *fig* in die Höhe schnellen; PHOT zoomen; **~ by, ~ past** F vorbeisausen; **~ in on** PHOT *et.* heranholen **2.** Surren *n; a.* **~ lens** PHOT Zoom *n,* Zoomobjektiv *n*

APPENDICES

States of the
Federal Republic of Germany

Baden-Württemberg ['baːdən'vʏrtəmbɛrk] Baden-Württemberg
Bayern ['baɪɐn] Bavaria
Berlin [bɛr'liːn] Berlin
Brandenburg ['brandənbʊrk] Brandenburg
Bremen ['breːmən] Bremen
Hamburg ['hambʊrk] Hamburg
Hessen ['hɛsən] Hesse
Mecklenburg-Vorpommern ['meːklənbʊrk'foːɐpɔmɐn] Mecklenburg-Western Pomerania
Niedersachsen ['niːdɐzaksən] Lower Saxony
Nordrhein-Westfalen ['nɔrtraɪnvɛst'faːlən] North Rhine-Westphalia
Rheinland-Pfalz ['raɪnlant'pfalts] Rhineland-Palatinate
Saarland ['zaːɐlant]: *das ~* the Saarland
Sachsen ['zaksən] Saxony
Sachsen-Anhalt ['zaksən'anhalt] Saxony-Anhalt
Schleswig-Holstein ['ʃleːsvɪç'hɔlʃtaɪn] Schleswig-Holstein
Thüringen ['tyːrɪŋən] Thuringia

States of the Republic of Austria

Burgenland ['bʊrgənlant]: *das ~* the Burgenland
Kärnten ['kɛrntən] Carinthia
Niederösterreich ['niːdɐʔøːstəraɪç] Lower Austria
Oberösterreich ['oːbɐʔøːstəraɪç] Upper Austria
Salzburg ['zaltsbʊrk] Salzburg
Steiermark ['ʃtaɪɐmark]: *die ~* Styria
Tirol [ti'roːl] Tyrol
Vorarlberg ['foːɐʔarlbɛrk] Vorarlberg
Wien [viːn] Vienna

Cantons of the Swiss Confederation

Aargau ['aːrgaʊ]: *der ~* the Aargau
Appenzell [apən'tsɛl] Appenzell
Basel ['baːzəl] Basel, Basle
Bern [bɛrn] Bern(e)
Freiburg ['fraɪbʊrk], *French* **Fribourg** [fri'buːr] Fribourg
Genf [gɛnf], *French* **Genève** [ʒə'nɛːv] Geneva
Glarus ['glaːrʊs] Glarus
Graubünden [graʊ'bʏndən] Graubünden, Grisons
Jura ['juːra]: *der ~* the Jura
Luzern [lu'tsɛrn] Lucerne
Neuenburg ['nɔʏənbʊrk], *French* **Neuchâtel** [nøʃa'tɛl] Neuchâtel
St. Gallen [zaŋkt 'galən] St Gallen, St Gall
Schaffhausen [ʃaf'haʊzən] Schaffhausen
Schwyz [ʃviːts] Schwyz
Solothurn ['zoːlotʊrn] Solothurn
Tessin [tɛ'siːn]: *der ~* the Ticino, *Italian* **Ticino** [ti'tʃiːno]: *das ~* the Ticino
Thurgau ['tuːrgaʊ]: *der ~* the Thurgau
Unterwalden ['ʊntɐvaldən] Unterwalden
Uri ['uːri] Uri
Waadt [vaːt], *French* **Vaud** [vo] Vaud
Wallis ['valɪs], *French* **Valais** [va'lɛ]: *das ~* the Valais, Wallis
Zug [tsuːk] Zug
Zürich ['tsyːrɪç] Zürich

European currency

Germany and Austria

1 euro (€) = 100 cent (ct)

coins

1 ct
2 ct
5 ct
10 ct
20 ct
50 ct
€ 1
€ 2

bills (*Br* bank notes)

€ 5
€ 10
€ 20
€ 50
€ 100
€ 200
€ 500

Switzerland

1 Swiss franc (Sfr) = 100 Rappen (Rp) / centimes (c)

coins

1 Rp
5 Rp
10 Rp
20 Rp
½ Sfr (50 Rp)
1 Sfr
2 Sfr
5 Sfr

bills (*Br* bank notes)

10 Sfr
20 Sfr
50 Sfr
100 Sfr
200 Sfr
1000 Sfr

Numbers

Cardinal numbers

0 null *nought, zero*	**51** einundfünfzig *fifty-one*
1 eins *one*	**60** sechzig *sixty*
2 zwei *two*	**61** einundsechzig *sixty-one*
3 drei *three*	**70** siebzig *seventy*
4 vier *four*	**71** einundsiebzig *seventy-one*
5 fünf *five*	**80** achtzig *eighty*
6 sechs *six*	**81** einundachtzig *eighty-one*
7 sieben *seven*	**90** neunzig *ninety*
8 acht *eight*	**91** einundneunzig *ninety-one*
9 neun *nine*	**100** hundert *a* or *one hundred*
10 zehn *ten*	**101** hunderteins *a hundred and one*
11 elf *eleven*	**200** zweihundert *two hundred*
12 zwölf *twelve*	**300** dreihundert *three hundred*
13 dreizehn *thirteen*	**572** fünfhundertzweiundsiebzig *five hundred and seventy-two*
14 vierzehn *fourteen*	**1000** tausend *a / one thousand*
15 fünfzehn *fifteen*	**1999** neunzehnhundertneunundneunzig *nineteen (hundred and) ninety-nine*
16 sechzehn *sixteen*	
17 siebzehn *seventeen*	
18 achtzehn *eighteen*	**2000** zweitausend *two thousand*
19 neunzehn *nineteen*	**2010** *as year:* zweitausendzehn *two thousand (and) ten*
20 zwanzig *twenty*	
21 einundzwanzig *twenty-one*	**5044** TEL fünfzig vierundvierzig *five O (or zero) double four*
22 zweiundzwanzig *twenty-two*	
30 dreißig *thirty*	**1,000,000** eine Million *one million*
31 einunddreißig *thirty-one*	**2,000,000** zwei Millionen *two million*
40 vierzig *forty*	**1,000,000,000** eine Milliarde *a / one billion*
41 einundvierzig *forty-one*	
50 fünfzig *fifty*	

Ordinal numbers

1. erste *first* (*1st*)
2. zweite *second* (*2nd*)
3. dritte *third* (*3rd*)
4. vierte *fourth* (*4th*)
5. fünfte *fifth* (*5th*) etc .
6. sechste *sixth*
7. siebente *seventh*
8. achte *eighth*
9. neunte *ninth*
10. zehnte *tenth*
11. elfte *eleventh*
12. zwölfte *twelfth*
13. dreizehnte *thirteenth*
14. vierzehnte *fourteenth*
15. fünfzehnte *fifteenth*
16. sechzehnte *sixteenth*
17. siebzehnte *seventeenth*
18. achtzehnte *eighteenth*
19. neunzehnte *nineteenth*
20. zwanzigste *twentieth*
21. einundzwanzigste *twenty-first*
22. zweiundzwanzigste *twenty-second*
23. dreiundzwanzigste *twenty-third*
30. dreißigste *thirtieth*
31. einunddreißigste *thirty-first*

40. vierzigste *fortieth*
41. einundvierzigste *forty-first*
50. fünfzigste *fiftieth*
51. einundfünfzigste *fifty-first*
60. sechzigste *sixtieth*
61. einundsechzigste *sixty-first*
70. siebzigste *seventieth*
71. einundsiebzigste *seventy-first*
80. achtzigste *eightieth*
81. einundachtzigste *eighty-first*
90. neunzigste *ninetieth*
100. hundertste (*one*) *hundredth*
101. hundert(und)erste (*one*) *hundred and first*
200. zweihundertste *two hundredth*
300. dreihundertste *three hundredth*
572. fünfhundert(und)zweiundsiebzigste *five hundred and seventy-second*
1000. tausendste (*one*) *thousandth*
1970. neunzehnhundert(und)siebzigste *nineteen hundred and seventieth*
500 000. fünfhunderttausendste *five hundred thousandth*
1 000 000. millionste (*one*) *millionth*

Fractions, decimals and mathematical calculation methods

$^1/_2$ halb *one / a half*
$^1/_2$ eine halbe Meile *half a mile*
$1^1/_2$ anderthalb / eineinhalb *one and a half*
$2^1/_2$ zweieinhalb *two and a half*
$^1/_3$ ein Drittel *one / a third*
$^2/_3$ zwei Drittel *two thirds*
$^1/_4$ ein Viertel *one fourth, one / a quarter*
$^3/_4$ drei Viertel *three fourths, three quarters*
$1^1/_4$ ein und eine viertel Stunde *one hour and a quarter*
$^1/_5$ ein Fünftel *one / a fifth*
$3^4/_5$ drei vier Fünftel *three and four fifths*
0,4 null Komma vier *point four (.4)*
2,5 zwei Komma fünf *two point five (2.5)*

einfach *single*
  zweifach *double, twofold*
  dreifach *threefold, treble, triple*
  vierfach *fourfold, quadruple*
  fünffach *fivefold, quintuple*

einmal *once*
  zweimal *twice*
  dreimal *three times*
  viermal *four times*
  fünfmal *five times*
  zweimal so viel (so viele) *twice as much (many)*

erstens *first(ly), in the first place*
zweitens *secondly; in the second place*
drittens *thirdly; in the third place*

$2 \times 3 = 6$ zwei mal drei ist sechs, zwei multipliziert mit drei ist sechs *two threes are six, two multiplied by three is six*

$7 + 8 = 15$ sieben plus acht ist fünfzehn *seven plus eight is fifteen*

$10 - 3 = 7$ zehn minus drei ist sieben *ten minus three is seven*

$20 : 5 = 4$ zwanzig (dividiert) durch fünf ist vier *twenty divided by five is four*

German weights and measures

I linear measure

1 mm   *Millimeter* millimeter, *Br* millimetre
- = $1/1000$ meter (*Br* metre)
- = 0.003 feet
- = 0.039 inches

1 cm   *Zentimeter* centimeter, *Br* centimetre
- = $1/100$ meter (*Br* metre)
- = 0.39 inches

1 dm   *Dezimeter* decimeter, *Br* decimetre
- = $1/10$ meter (*Br* metre)
- = 3.94 inches

1 m   *Meter* meter, *Br* metre
- = 1.094 yards
- = 3.28 feet
- = 39.37 inches

1 km   *Kilometer* kilometer, *Br* kilometre
- = 1,000 meters (*Br* metres)
- = 1,093.637 yards
- = 0.621 (statute) miles

1 sm   *Seemeile* nautical mile
- = 1,852 meters (*Br* metres)

II square measure

1 mm²   *Quadratmillimeter* square millimeter (*Br* millimetre)
- = 0.0015 square inches

1 cm²   *Quadratzentimeter* square centimeter (*Br* centimetre)
- = 0.155 square inches

1 m²   *Quadratmeter* square meter (*Br* metre)
- = 1.195 square yards
- = 10.76 square feet

1 a   *Ar* are
- = 100 square meters (*Br* metres)
- = 119.59 square yards
- = 1,076.40 square feet

1 ha   *Hektar* hectare
- = 100 ares
- = 10,000 square meters (*Br* metres)
- = 11,959.90 square yards
- = 2.47 acres

1 km²   *Quadratkilometer* square kilometer (*Br* kilometre)
- = 100 hectares
- = 1,000,000 square meters (*Br* metres)
- = 247.11 acres
- = 0.386 square miles

III cubic measure

1 cm³   *Kubikzentimeter* cubic centimeter (*Br* centimetre)
- = 1,000 cubic millimeters (*Br* millimetres)
- = 0.061 cubic inches

1 dm³   *Kubikdezimeter* cubic decimeter (*Br* decimetre)
- = 1,000 cubic centimeters (*Br* centimetres)
- = 61.025 cubic inches

1 m³   *Kubikmeter*
1 rm   *Raummeter*   } cubic meter (*Br* metre)
1 fm   *Festmeter*
- = 1,000 cubic decimeters (*Br* decimetres)
- = 1.307 cubic yards
- = 35.31 cubic feet

1 RT   *Registertonne* register ton
- = 2.832 m³
- = 100 cubic feet

IV measure of capacity

1 l **Liter** liter, *Br* litre
= 10 deciliters (*Br* decilitres)
= 2.11 pints (*Am*)
= 8.45 gills (*Am*)
= 1.06 quarts (*Am*)
= 0.26 gallons (*Am*)
= 1.76 pints (*Br*)
= 7.04 gills (*Br*)
= 0.88 quarts (*Br*)
= 0.22 gallons (*Br*)

1 hl **Hektoliter** hectoliter, *Br* hectolitre
= 100 liters (*Br* litres)
= 26.42 gallons (*Am*)
= 2.84 bushels (*Am*)
= 22.009 gallons (*Br*)
= 2.75 bushels (*Br*)

V weight

1 mg **Milligramm** milligram(me)
= $^1/_{1000}$ gram(me)
= 0.015 grains

1 g **Gramm** gram(me)
= $^1/_{1000}$ kilogram(me)
= 15.43 grains

1 Pfd **Pfund** pound (German)
= $^1/_2$ kilogram(me)
= 500 gram(me)s
= 1.102 pounds (1b)

1 kg **Kilogramm, Kilo** kilogram(me)
= 1,000 gram(me)s
= 2.204 pounds (1b)

1 Ztr. **Zentner** centner
= 100 pounds (German)
= 50 kilogram(me)s
= 110.23 pounds (1b)
= 1.102 US hundredweights
= 0.98 British hundredweights

1 t **Tonne** ton
= 1,000 kilogram(me)s
= 1.102 US tons
= 0.984 British tons

Conversion tables for temperatures

°C (Celsius)	°F (Fahrenheit)
100	212
95	203
90	194
85	185
80	176
75	167
70	158
65	149
60	140
55	131
50	122
45	113
40	104
35	95
30	86
25	77
20	68
15	59
10	50
5	41
0	32
−5	23
−10	14
−15	5
−17.8	0
−20	−4
−25	−13
−30	−22
−35	−31
−40	−40
−45	−49
−50	−58

Clinical thermometer

°C (Celsius)	°F (Fahrenheit)
42.0	107.6
41.8	107.2
41.6	106.9
41.4	106.5
41.2	106.2
41.0	105.8
40.8	105.4
40.6	105.1
40.4	104.7
40.2	104.4
40.0	104.0
39.8	103.6
39.6	103.3
39.4	102.9
39.2	102.6
39.0	102.2
38.8	101.8
38.6	101.5
38.4	101.1
38.2	100.8
38.0	100.4
37.8	100.0
37.6	99.7
37.4	99.3
37.2	99.0
37.0	98.6
36.8	98.2
36.6	97.9

How to convert Celsius into Fahrenheit and vice versa

To convert Celsius into Fahrenheit multiply by 9, divide by 5 and add 32.

To convert Fahrenheit into Celsius subtract 32, multiply by 5 and divide by 9.

German irregular verbs

infinitive – 3rd person singular – past tense – past participle

backen – backt/bäckt – backte – gebacken

bedingen – bedingt – bedang (bedingte) – bedungen (*conditional*: bedingt)

befehlen – befiehlt – befahl – befohlen

beginnen – beginnt – begann – begonnen

beißen – beißt – biss – gebissen

bergen – birgt – barg – geborgen

bersten – birst – barst – geborsten

bewegen – bewegt – bewog – bewogen

biegen – biegt – bog – gebogen

bieten – bietet – bot – geboten

binden – bindet – band – gebunden

bitten – bittet – bat – gebeten

blasen – bläst – blies – geblasen

bleiben – bleibt – blieb – geblieben

bleichen – bleicht – blich – geblichen

braten – brät – briet – gebraten

brauchen – braucht – brauchte – gebraucht (*v/aux* brauchen)

brechen – bricht – brach – gebrochen

brennen – brennt – brannte – gebrannt

bringen – bringt – brachte – gebracht

denken – denkt – dachte – gedacht

dreschen – drischt – drosch – gedroschen

dringen – dringt – drang – gedrungen

dürfen – darf – durfte – gedurft (*v/aux* dürfen)

empfangen – empfängt – empfing – empfangen

empfehlen – empfiehlt – empfahl – empfohlen

empfinden – empfindet – empfand – empfunden

erlöschen – erlischt – erlosch – erloschen

erschrecken – erschrickt – erschrak – erschrocken

essen – isst – aß – gegessen

fahren – fährt – fuhr – gefahren

fallen – fällt – fiel – gefallen

fangen – fängt – fing – gefangen

fechten – ficht – focht – gefochten

finden – findet – fand – gefunden

flechten – flicht – flocht – geflochten

fliegen – fliegt – flog – geflogen

fliehen – flieht – floh – geflohen

fließen – fließt – floss – geflossen

fressen – frisst – fraß – gefressen

frieren – friert – fror – gefroren

gären – gärt – gor (*esp fig* gärte) – gegoren (*esp fig* gegärt)

gebären – gebärt (gebiert) – gebar – geboren

geben – gibt – gab – gegeben

gedeihen – gedeiht – gedieh – gediehen

gehen – geht – ging – gegangen

gelingen – gelingt – gelang – gelungen

gelten – gilt – galt – gegolten

genesen – genest – genas – genesen

genießen – genießt – genoss – genossen

geschehen – geschieht – geschah – geschehen

gewinnen – gewinnt – gewann – gewonnen

gießen – gießt – goss – gegossen

gleichen – gleicht – glich – geglichen

gleiten – gleitet – glitt – geglitten

glimmen – glimmt – glomm – geglommen

graben – gräbt – grub – gegraben

greifen – greift – griff – gegriffen

haben – hat – hatte – gehabt

halten – hält – hielt – gehalten

hängen – hängt – hing – gehangen

hauen – haut – haute (hieb) – gehauen

heben – hebt – hob – gehoben

heißen – heißt – hieß – geheißen

helfen – hilft – half – geholfen

kennen – kennt – kannte – gekannt

klingen – klingt – klang – geklungen

kneifen – kneift – kniff – gekniffen

kommen – kommt – kam – gekommen

können – kann – konnte – gekonnt (*v/aux* können)

kriechen – kriecht – kroch – gekrochen

laden – lädt – lud – geladen

lassen – lässt – ließ – gelassen (*v/aux* lassen)

laufen – läuft – lief – gelaufen

leiden – leidet – litt – gelitten

leihen – leiht – lieh – geliehen

lesen – liest – las – gelesen
liegen – liegt – lag – gelegen
lügen – lügt – log – gelogen
mahlen – mahlt – mahlte – gemahlen
meiden – meidet – mied – gemieden
melken – melkt – melkte (molk) – ge-molken (gemelkt)
messen – misst – maß – gemessen
misslingen – misslingt – misslang – misslungen
mögen – mag – mochte – gemocht (*v/aux* mögen)
müssen – muss – musste – gemusst (*v/aux* müssen)
nehmen – nimmt – nahm – genommen
nennen – nennt – nannte – genannt
pfeifen – pfeift – pfiff – gepfiffen
preisen – preist – pries – gepriesen
quellen – quillt – quoll – gequollen
raten – rät – riet – geraten
reiben – reibt – rieb – gerieben
reißen – reißt – riss – gerissen
reiten – reitet – ritt – geritten
rennen – rennt – rannte – gerannt
riechen – riecht – roch – gerochen
ringen – ringt – rang – gerungen
rinnen – rinnt – rann – geronnen
rufen – ruft – rief – gerufen
salzen – salzt – salzte – gesalzen (gesalzt)
saufen – säuft – soff – gesoffen
saugen – saugt – sog – gesogen
schaffen – schafft – schuf – geschaffen
schallen – schallt – schallte (scholl) – geschallt (*for* **erschallen** *a.* erschollen)
scheiden – scheidet – schied – geschieden
scheinen – scheint – schien – geschienen
scheißen – scheißt – schiss – geschissen
scheren – schert – schor – geschoren
schieben – schiebt – schob – geschoben
schießen – schießt – schoss – geschossen
schinden – schindet – schund – geschunden
schlafen – schläft – schlief – geschlafen
schlagen – schlägt – schlug – geschlagen
schleichen – schleicht – schlich – geschlichen
schleifen – schleift – schliff – geschliffen
schließen – schließt – schloss – geschlossen

schlingen – schlingt – schlang – geschlungen
schmeißen – schmeißt – schmiss – geschmissen
schmelzen – schmilzt – schmolz – geschmolzen
schneiden – schneidet – schnitt – geschnitten
schreiben – schreibt – schrieb – geschrieben
schreien – schreit – schrie – geschrie(e)n
schreiten – schreitet – schritt – geschritten
schweigen – schweigt – schwieg – geschwiegen
schwellen – schwillt – schwoll – geschwollen
schwimmen – schwimmt – schwamm – geschwommen
schwinden – schwindet – schwand – geschwunden
schwingen – schwingt – schwang – geschwungen
schwören – schwört – schwor – geschworen
sehen – sieht – sah – gesehen
sein – ist – war – gewesen
senden – sendet – sandte – gesandt
sieden – siedet – sott – gesotten
singen – singt – sang – gesungen
sinken – sinkt – sank – gesunken
sinnen – sinnt – sann – gesonnen
sitzen – sitzt – saß – gesessen
sollen – soll – sollte – gesollt (*v/aux* sollen)
spalten – spaltet – spaltete – gespalten (gespaltet)
speien – speit – spie – gespie(e)n
spinnen – spinnt – spann – gesponnen
sprechen – spricht – sprach – gesprochen
sprießen – sprießt – spross – gesprossen
springen – springt – sprang – gesprungen
stechen – sticht – stach – gestochen
stecken – steckt – steckte (stak) – gesteckt
stehen – steht – stand – gestanden
stehlen – stiehlt – stahl – gestohlen
steigen – steigt – stieg – gestiegen
sterben – stirbt – starb – gestorben
stinken – stinkt – stank – gestunken

stoßen – stößt – stieß – gestoßen
streichen – streicht – strich – gestrichen
streiten – streitet – stritt – gestritten
tragen – trägt – trug – getragen
treffen – trifft – traf – getroffen
treiben – treibt – trieb – getrieben
treten – tritt – trat – getreten
trinken – trinkt – trank – getrunken
trügen – trügt – trog – getrogen
tun – tut – tat – getan
überwinden – überwindet – überwand – überwunden
verderben – verdirbt – verdarb – verdorben
verdrießen – verdrießt – verdross – verdrossen
vergessen – vergisst – vergaß – vergessen
verlieren – verliert – verlor – verloren
verschleißen – verschleißt – verschliss – verschlissen
verschwinden – verschwindet – verschwand – verschwunden
verzeihen – verzeiht – verzieh – verziehen
wachsen – wächst – wuchs – gewachsen
wägen – wägt – wog (*rare* wägte) – gewogen (*rare* gewägt)
waschen – wäscht – wusch – gewaschen
weben – webt – wob – gewoben
weichen – weicht – wich – gewichen
weisen – weist – wies – gewiesen
wenden – wendet – wandte – gewandt
werben – wirbt – warb – geworben
werden – wird – wurde – geworden (worden*)
werfen – wirft – warf – geworfen
wiegen – wiegt – wog – gewogen
winden – windet – wand – gewunden
wissen – weiß – wusste – gewusst
wollen – will – wollte – gewollt (*v/aux* wollen)
wringen – wringt – wrang – gewrungen
ziehen – zieht – zog – gezogen
zwingen – zwingt – zwang – gezwungen

* only in connection with the past participles of other verbs, *e.g.* **er ist gesehen worden** he has been seen.

English irregular verbs

infinitive – past tense – past participle

arise – arose – arisen
awake – awoke – awoke*
be – was – been
bear – bore – *getragen*: borne – *geboren*: born
beat – beat – beaten, beat
become – became – become
beget – begot – begotten
begin – began – begun
bend – bent – bent
bereave – bereft* – bereft*
beseech – besought – besought
bet – bet * – bet*
bid – bade, bid – bidden, bid
bide – bode* – bided
bind – bound – bound
bite – bit – bitten
bleed – bled – bled
bless – blest* – blest*
blow – blew – blown
break – broke – broken
breed – bred – bred
bring – brought – brought
build – built – built
burn – burnt* – burnt*
burst – burst – burst
buy – bought – bought
cast – cast – cast
catch – caught – caught
choose – chose – chosen
cleave – cleft, clove* – cleft, cloven*
cling – clung – clung
clothe – clad* – clad*
come – came – come
cost – cost – cost
creep – crept – crept
crow – crew* – crowed
cut – cut – cut
deal – dealt – dealt
dig – dug – dug
dive – dived, *a.* dove – dived
do – did – done
draw – drew – drawn
dream – dreamt* – dreamt*
drink – drank – drunk
drive – drove – driven
dwell – dwelt* – dwelt*
eat – ate – eaten

fall – fell – fallen
feed – fed – fed
feel – felt – felt
fight – fought – fought
find – found – found
fit – fitted, *a.* fit – fitted, *a.* fit
flee – fled – fled
fling – flung – flung
fly – flew – flown
forbid – forbade – forbidden
forget – forgot – forgotten
forsake – forsook – forsaken
freeze – froze – frozen
get – got – got, *a.* gotten
give – gave – given
go – went – gone
grind – ground – ground
grow – grew – grown
hang – hung – hung
have – had – had
hear – heard – heard
heave – hove* – hove*
hew – hewed – hewn*
hide – hid – hidden
hit – hit – hit
hold – held – held
hurt – hurt – hurt
keep – kept – kept
kneel – knelt* – knelt*
knit – knit* – knit*
know – knew – known
lay – laid – laid
lead – led – led
lean – leant* – leant*
leap – leapt* – leapt*
learn – learnt* – learnt*
leave – left – left
lend – lent – lent
let – let – let
lie – lay – lain
light – lit* – lit*
lose – lost – lost
make – made – made
mean – meant – meant
meet – met – met
mow – mowed – mown*
pay – paid – paid
plead – pleaded, *a.* pled – pleaded, *a.* pled

put – put – put
read – read – read
rid – rid – rid
ride – rode – ridden
ring – rang – rung
rise – rose – risen
run – ran – run
saw – sawed – sawn*
say – said – said
see – saw – seen
seek – sought – sought
sell – sold – sold
send – sent – sent
set – set – set
sew – sewed – sewn*
shake – shook – shaken
shave – shaved – shaven*
shear – sheared – shorn
shed – shed – shed
shine – shone – shone
shit – shit – shit
shoe – shod – shod
shoot – shot – shot
show – showed – shown*
shrink – shrank – shrunk
shut – shut – shut
sing – sang – sung
sink – sank – sunk
sit – sat – sat
slay – slew – slain
sleep – slept – slept
slide – slid – slid
sling – slung – slung
slink – slunk – slunk
slit – slit – slit
smell – smelt* – smelt*
sow – sowed – sown*
speak – spoke – spoken
speed – sped* – sped*
spell – spelt* – spelt*
spend – spent – spent
spill – spilt* – spilt*

spin – spun – spun
spit – spat – spat
split – split – split
spoil – spoilt* – spoilt*
spread – spread – spread
spring – sprang, *a.* sprung – sprung
stand – stood – stood
stave – stove* – stove*
steal – stole – stolen
stick – stuck – stuck
sting – stung – stung
stink – stank, stunk – stunk
strew – strewed – strewn*
stride – strode – stridden
strike – struck – struck
string – strung – strung
strive – strove – striven
swear – swore – sworn
sweat – sweat* – sweat*
sweep – swept – swept
swell – swelled – swollen
swim – swam – swum
swing – swung – swung
take – took – taken
teach – taught – taught
tear – tore – torn
tell – told – told
think – thought – thought
thrive – throve* – thriven*
throw – threw – thrown
thrust – thrust – thrust
tread – trod – trodden, trod
wake – woke* – woke(n)*
wear – wore – worn
weave – wove – woven
wed – wedded, wed – wedded, wed
weep – wept – wept
wet – wet* – wet*
win – won – won
wind – wound – wound
wring – wrung – wrung
write – wrote – written

Irregular forms marked with asterisks (*)
can be exchanged for the regular forms.

German declension and conjugation

A. Declension

Order of cases: *nom*, *gen*, *dat*, *acc*, *sg* and *pl.* – Compound nouns and adjectives (e.g. *Eisbär*, *Ausgang*, *abfällig* etc.) inflect like their last elements (*Bär*, *Gang*, *fällig*). *dem* = demonstrative, *imp* = imperative, *ind* = indicative, *perf* = perfect, *pres* = present, *pres p* = present participle, *rel* = relative, *su* = substantive.

I. Nouns

1   Bild   ~(e)s[1]   ~(e)   ~
Bilder[2]   ~   ~n   ~

[1]   *es only*: Geist, Geistes.
[2]   **a, o, u > ä, ö, ü**: Rand, Ränder; Haupt, Häupter; Dorf, Dörfer; Wurm, Würmer.

---

2   Reis*   ~es ['-zəs] ~(e)   ~
Reiser[1] ['-zɐ] ~   ~n   ~

[1]   **a, o > ä, ö**: Glas, Gläser ['glɛːzɐ]; Haus, Häuser ['hɔyzɐ]; Fass, Fässer; Schloss, Schlösser.

*   Fass, Fasse(s).

---

3   Arm   ~(e)s[1,2]   ~(e)[1]   ~
Arme[3]   ~   ~n   ~

[1]   *without* e: Billard, Billard(s).
[2]   *es only*: Maß, Maßes.
[3]   **a, o, u > ä, ö, ü**: Gang, Gänge; Saal, Säle; Gebrauch, Gebräuche [gə'brɔyçə]; Sohn, Söhne; Hut, Hüte.

---

4   Greis[1]*   ~es ['-zəs] ~(e)   ~
Greise[2] ['-zə] ~   ~n   ~

[1]   **s > ss**: Kürbis, Kürbisse(s).
[2]   **a, o, u > ä, ö, ü**: Hals, Hälse; Bass, Bässe; Schoß, Schöße; Fuchs, Füchse; Schuss, Schüsse.

*   Ross, Rosse(s).

---

5   Strahl   ~(e)s[1,2]   ~(e)[2]   ~
Strahlen[3] ~   ~   ~

[1]   *es only*: Schmerz, Schmerzes.
[2]   *without* e: Juwel, Juwel(s).
[3]   Sporn, Sporen.

---

6   Lappen   ~s   ~   ~*
Lappen[1]   ~   ~   ~

[1]   **a, o > ä, ö**: Graben, Gräben; Boden, Böden.

*   *Infinitives used as nouns have no pl*: Geschehen, Befinden etc.

---

7   Maler   ~s   ~   ~
Maler[1]   ~   ~n   ~

[1]   **a, o, u > ä, ö, ü**: Vater, Väter; Kloster, Klöster; Bruder, Brüder.

---

8   Untertan   ~s   ~   ~
Untertanen[1,2] ~   ~   ~

[1]   *with change of accent*: Pro'fessor, Profes'soren [-'soːrən]; 'Dämon ['dɛːmɔn], Dä'monen [dɛ'moːnən].
[2]   *pl* **ien** [-jən]: Kolleg, Kollegien [-'leːgjən]; Mineral, Mineralien.

---

9   Studium   ~s   ~   ~
Studien[1,2] ['-djən] ~   ~   ~

[1]   **a** *and* **o(n) > en**: Drama, Dramen; Stadion, Stadien.
[2]   **on** *and* **um > a**: Lexikon, Lexika; Neutrum, Neutra.

10 Auge   ~s   ~   ~
     Augen   ~   ~   ~

---

11 Genie   ~s[1]*   ~   ~
     Genies[2]*   ~   ~   ~

[1] *without inflection*: Bouillon etc.
[2] *pl* **s** *or* **ta**: Komma, Kommas *or* Kommata; *but*: 'Klima, Klimate [kli'ma:tə] (3).

* **s** *is pronounced*: [ʒe'ni:s].

---

12 Bär*   ~en[1]   ~en[1]   ~en[1]

     Bären   ~   ~   ~

[1] Herr, *sg mst* Herrn; Herz, *gen* Herzens, *acc* Herz.

* ...'**log** *as well as* ... '**loge** (13), e.g. Biolog(e).

---

13 Knabe   ~n[1]   ~n   ~n
     Knaben   ~   ~   ~

[1] **ns**: Name, Namens.

---

14 Trübsal   ~   ~   ~
     Trübsale[1,2,3] ~   ~n   ~

[1] **a, o, u** > **ä, ö, ü**: Hand, Hände; Braut, Bräute; Not, Nöte; Luft, Lüfte; Nuss, Nüsse; *without* **e**: Tochter, Töchter; Mutter, Mütter.
[2] **s** > **ss**: Kenntnis, Kenntnisse; Nimbus, Nimbusse.
[3] **is** *or* **us** > **e**: Kultus, Kulte; *with change of accent*: Di'akonus, Dia'kone [-'ko:nə].

---

15 Blume   ~   ~   ~
     Blumen   ~   ~   ~

...**ee**: e:, *pl* e:ən, *e.g.* I'dee, I'deen.

...**ie** { **stressed syllable**: i:, *pl* i:ən, *e.g.* Batte'rie(n). **unstressed syllable**: jə, *pl* jən, *e.g.* Ar'terie(n).

---

16 Frau   ~   ~   ~
     Frauen[1,2,3]   ~   ~   ~

[1] **in** > **innen**: Freundin, Freun – dinnen.
[2] **a, is, os** *and* **us** > **en**: Firma, Firmen; Krisis, Krisen; Epos, Epen; Genius, Genien; *with change of accent*: 'Heros, He'roen [he'ro:ən]; Di'akonus, Dia'konen [-'ko:nən].
[3] **s** > **ss**: Kirmes, Kirmessen.

II. Proper nouns

17 *In general proper nouns have no* pl.

The following form the gen sg *with* **s**:

1. *Proper nouns without a definite article*: Friedrichs, Paulas, (Friedrich von) Schillers, Deutschlands, Berlins;

2. *Proper nouns, masculine and neuter (except the names of countries) with a definite article and an adjective*: des braven Friedrichs Bruder, des jungen Deutschlands (Söhne).

After **s, sch, ß, tz, x,** *and* **z** *the* gen sg *ends in* **-ens** *or* **'** *(instead of* **'** *it is more advisable to use the definite article or* **von**), e.g. die Werke des [*or* von] Sokrates, Voß *or* Sokrates', Voß' [*not* Sokratessens, *seldom* Vossens] Werke; *but*: die Umgebung von Mainz.
Feminine names ending in a consonant or the vowel **e** *form the* gen sg *with* **(en)s** *or* **(n)s**; *in the* dat *and* acc sg *such names may end in* **(e)n** (pl = **a**).

If a proper noun is followed by a title, only the following forms are inflected:

1. *the title when used* *with* **a definite article**:
der Kaiser Karl   (der Große)
des   ~s ~   (des   ~n)
etc.

2. **the (last) name when used** without **an article:**

Kaiser Karl   (der Große)
~   ~s (des   ~n) etc.
(**but**: Herrn Lehmanns Brief).

III. Adjectives and participles
(also used as nouns*), pronouns, etc.

18

	m	f	n	pl
a) gut	er[1,2]	~e	~es	~e°
	en**	~er	~en**	~er
	em	~er	~em	~en
	en	~e	~es	~e

without article, after prepositions, personal pronouns, and invariables

	m	f	n	pl
b) gut	e[1,2]	~e	~e	~en
	en	~en	~en	~en
	en	~en	~en	~en
	en	~e	~e	~en

with definite article (22) or with pro-noun (21)

	m	f	n	pl
c) gut	er[1,2]	~e	~es	~en
	en	~en	~en	~en
	en	~en	~en	~en
	en	~e	~es	~en

with indefinite article or with pronoun (20)

[1] krass, krasse(r, ~s, ~st etc.).

[2] **a, o, u > ä, ö, ü when forming** the *comp* and *sup*: alt, älter(e, ~es etc.), ältest (der ~e, am ~en); grob, gröber(e, ~es etc.), gröbst (der ~e, am ~en); kurz, kür-zer(e, ~es etc.), kürzest (der ~e, am ~en).

* e.g. Böse(r) *su*: der (die, eine) Böse, ein Böser; Böse(s) *n*: das Böse, **without**

article Böses; **in the same way** Abge-sandte(r) *su*, Angestellte(r) *su* etc.; **in some cases the use varies.**

** **Sometimes the** *gen sg* **ends in ~es** instead of ~en: gutes (**or** guten) Mutes sein.

° **In** böse, böse(r, ~s, ~st etc.) **one** e **is dropped.**

The grades of comparison

The endings of the *comparative* **and** *superlative* **are:**

	reich	schön	*inflected according to* (18²).
comp	reicher	schöner	
sup	reichst	schönst	

After vowels (except e [18°]) **and after** d, s, sch, ß, st, t, tz, x, y, z **the** *sup* **ends in** ~est, **but in unstressed sylla-bles after** d, sch **and** t **generally in** ~st: blau, 'blauest; rund, 'rundest; rasch, 'raschest etc.; **but**: 'dringend, 'drin-gendst; 'närrisch, 'närrischst; ge'eignet, ge'eignetst.

Note. – **The adjectives ending in** ~el, ~en (**except** ~nen) **and** ~er (e.g. dunkel, eben, heiter), **and also the possessive adjectives** unser **and** euer **generally drop** e.

Inflection:

	~e	~em	~en	~er	~es, and
~el >	~le	~lem*	~len*	~ler	~les
~en >	~(e)ne	~(e)nem	~(e)nen	~(e)ner°	~(e)nes
~er >	~(e)re	~rem*	~ren*	~(e)rer°	~(e)res

---

* *or* ~elm, ~eln, ~erm, ~ern; e.g. dunk|el: ~le, ~lem (*or* ~clm), ~len (*or* ~eln), ~ler, ~les; eb|en: ~(e)ne, ~(e)nem etc.; heit|er: ~(e)re, ~rem (*or* ~erm) etc.

° *The inflected comp ends in* ~ner *and* ~rer *only:* eben, ebnere(r, ~s etc.); heiter, heitrere(r, ~s etc.); *but sup* ebenst, heiterst.

19

		1st pers. m, f, n	2nd pers. m, f, n	3rd pers. m	f	n
sg		ich	du	er	sie	es
		meiner*	deiner*	seiner*	ihrer	seiner*
		mir	dir	ihm	ihr	ihm°
		mich	dich	ihn	sie	es°
pl		wir	ihr	sie	(Sie)	
		unser	euer	ihrer	(Ihrer)	
		uns	euch	ihnen	(Ihnen)°	
		uns	euch	sie	(Sie)°	

* *In poetry sometimes without inflection:* gedenke mein!; *also* es *instead of* seiner n (= e-r Sache): ich bin es überdrüssig.

° *Reflexive form:* sich.

20

	m		f	n	pl
mein			~e	~	~e*
dein	es		~er	~es	~er
sein	em		~er	~em	~en
(k)ein	en		~e	~	~e

* *The indefinite article* ein *has no pl*. – *In poetry* mein, dein *and* sein *may stand behind the su without inflection:* die Mutter (Kinder) mein, *or as predicate:* der Hut [*die Tasche, das Buch*] ist mein; *without su:* meiner *m,* meine *f,* mein(e)s *n,* meine *pl etc.: wem gehört der Hut [die Tasche, das Buch]? es ist* meiner (meine, mein[e]s); *or with definite article:* der (die, das) meine, *pl* die meinen (18b). *Regarding* unser *and* euer *see note* (18).

¹ welche(r, s) *as rel pron:* gen sg dessen, deren, *gen pl* deren, *dat pl* denen (23).

* *Used as su,* dies *is preferable to* dieses.

** manch, solch, welch *frequently are uninflected:*

manch	}	guter	(ein guter) Mann	
solch		~en	(~es ~en)	~es
welch		~em	(~em ~en)	~e
			etc. (18)	

Similarly all:

all der (dieser, mein) Schmerz
~ des (~es, ~es) ~es

21

	m		f	n	pl
dies	er		~e	~es*	~e**
jen	es		~er	~es	~er¹
manch	em		~er	~em	~en¹
welch	en		~e	~es*	~e

22

	m	f	n	pl	
	der	die	das	die¹	} definite article
	des	der	des	der	
	dem	der	dem	den	
	den	die	das	die	

¹ derjenige, derselbe – desjenigen, demjenigen, desselben, demselben etc. (18b).

¹ *also* derer, **when used as** *dem pron*

* *also* des.

---

23 *Relative pronoun*

m	f	n	pl
der	die	das	die
dessen*	deren	dessen*	deren¹
dem	der	dem	denen
den	die	das	die

24

wer	was	jemand, niemand
wessen*	wessen	~(e)s
wem	–	~(em°)
wen	was	~(en°)

* *also* wes.

° *preferably without inflection.*

B. Conjugation

In the conjugation tables (25–30) only the simple verbs may be found; in the alphabetical list of the German irregular verbs compound verbs are only included when no simple verb exists (e.g. **beginnen**; **ginnen** does not exist). In order to find the conjugation of any compound verb (with separable or inseparable prefix, regular or irregular) look up the respective simple verb.

Verbs with separable and stressed prefixes such as **'ab-, 'an-, 'auf-, 'aus-, 'bei-, be'vor-, 'dar-, 'ein-, em'por-, ent'gegen-, 'fort-, 'her-, he'rab-** etc. and also **'klar-**[*legen*], **'los-**[*schießen*], **'sitzen** [*bleiben*], **über'hand** [*nehmen*] etc. (but not the verbs derived from compound nouns as *be'antragen* or *be'ratschlagen* from *Antrag* and *Ratschlag* etc.) take the preposition **zu** (in the *inf* and the *pres p*) and the syllable **ge** (in the *pp* and in the passive voice) between the stressed prefix and their root.

Verbs with inseparable and unstressed prefixes such as **be-, emp-, ent-, er-, ge-, ver-, zer-** and generally **miss-** (in spite of its being stressed) take the preposition **zu** before the prefix and drop the syllable **ge** in the *pp* and in the passive voice. The prefixes **durch-, hinter-, über-, um-, unter-, voll-,**

wi(e)der- are separable when stressed and inseparable when unstressed, e.g.

geben: *zu geben, zu gebend; gegeben; ich gebe, du gibst* etc.;

'abgeben: *'abzugeben, 'abzugebend; 'abgegeben; ich gebe (du gibst* etc.*) ab;*

ver'geben: *zu ver'geben, zu ver'gebend; ver'geben; ich ver'gebe, du ver'gibst* etc.;

'umgehen: *'umzugehen, 'umzugehend; 'umgegangen; ich gehe (du gehst* etc.*) um;*

um'gehen: *zu um'gehen, zu um'gehend; um'gangen; ich um'gehe, du um'gehst* etc.

The same rules apply to verbs with two prefixes, e.g.

zu'rückbehalten [see *halten*]: *zu'rückzubehalten, zu'rückzubehaltend; zu-'rückbehalten; ich behalte (du be-hältst* etc.*) zurück;*

wieder 'aufheben [see *heben*]: *wieder 'aufzuheben, wieder 'aufzuhebend; wieder 'aufgehoben; ich hebe (du hebst* etc.*) wieder auf.*

The forms in parentheses ( ) follow the same rules.

a) 'Weak' conjugation

25   loben

pres ind	lobe	lobst	lobt
	loben	lobt	loben
pres subj	lobe	lobest	lobe
	loben	lobet	loben
pret ind	lobte	lobtest	lobte
and *subj*	lobten	lobtet	lobten

imp sg lob(e), *pl* lob(e)t, loben Sie;
inf pres loben; *inf perf* gelobt haben;
pres p lobend; *pp* gelobt (18; 29**).

26   reden

pres ind	rede	redest	redet
	reden	redet	reden
pres subj	rede	redest	rede
	reden	redet	reden
pret ind	redete	redetest	redete
and *subj*	redeten	redetet	redeten

imp sg rede, *pl* redet, reden Sie;
inf pres reden; *inf perf* geredet haben;
pres p redend; *pp* geredet (18; 29**).

27   reisen

preš ind	reise	rei(se)st*	reist
	reisen	reist	reisen
pres subj	reise	reisest	reise
	reisen	reiset	reisen
pret ind	reiste	reistest	reisten
and *subj*	reisten	reistet	reisten

imp sg reise, *pl* reist, reisen Sie;
inf pres reisen; *inf perf* gereist sein *or now
rare* haben; *pres p* reisend; *pp* gereist
(18; 29**).

* **sch:** naschen, nasch(e)st; **ß:** spaßen, spaßt (spaßest); **tz:** ritzen, ritzt (rit-
zest); **x:** hexen, hext (hexest); **z:** reizen,
reizt (reizest); faulenzen, faulenzt (fau-
lenzest).

28   fassen

pres ind	fasse	fasst (fassest)fasst
	fassen	fasst	fassen
pres subj	fasse	fassest	fasse
	fassen	fasset	fassen
pret ind	fasste	fasstest	fasste
and *subj*	fassten	fasstet	fassten

imp sg fasse (fass), *pl* fasst, fassen Sie;
inf pres fassen; *inf perf* gefasst haben;
pres p fassend; *pp* gefasst (18; 29**).

29   handeln

pres ind

| handle* | handelst | handelt |
| handeln | handelt | handeln |

pres subj

| handle* | handelst | handle* |
| handeln | handelt | handeln |

pret ind and *subj*

| handelte | handeltest | handelte |
| handelten | handeltet | handelten |

imp sg handle, *pl* handelt, handeln Sie;
inf pres handeln; *inf perf* gehandelt haben; *pres p* handelnd; *pp* gehandet (18).

  *   **Also** handele; wandern, wand(e)re;
bessern, bessere (bessre); donnern, don-
nere.

  **   *Without* ge, *when the first syllable
is unstressed,* e.g. be'grüßen, be'grüßt;
ent'stehen, ent'standen; stu'dieren,
studiert (*not* gestudiert); trom'peten,
trom'petet (*also when preceded by a
stressed prefix:* 'austrompeten, 'aus-
trompetet, *not* 'ausgetrompetet). *In
some weak verbs the* pp *ends in* en *instead of* t, e.g. mahlen, gemahlen. *With
the verbs* brauchen, dürfen, heißen, helfen, hören, können, lassen, lehren, lernen, machen, mögen, müssen, sehen, sollen, wollen *the* pp *is replaced by* inf
(*without* ge), *when used in connection
with another* inf, e.g. ich habe ihn singen
hören, du hättest es tun können, er hat gehen müssen, ich hätte ihn laufen lassen
sollen.

b) 'Strong' conjugation

30   **fahren**

| *pres ind* | fahre | fährst | fährt |
| | fahren | fahrt | fahren |

| *pres subj* | fahre | fahrest | fahre |
| | fahren | fahret | fahren |

| *pret ind* | fuhr | fuhr(e)st | fuhr |
| | fuhren | fuhrt | fuhren |

| *pres subj* | führe | führest | führe |
| | führen | führet | führen |

imp sg fahr(e), *pl* fahr(e)t, fahren Sie;
inf pres fahren; *inf perf* gefahren haben
or sein;
pres p fahrend; *pp* gefahren (18; 29**).

Proper names

Aachen ['aːxən] Aachen, Aix-la-Cha – pelle
Adler ['aːdlɐ] *Austrian psychologist*
Adria ['aːdria] *die* ~ the Adriatic (Sea)
Afrika ['aːfrika] Africa
Ägäis [ɛ'gɛːɪs] *die* ~ the Aegean (Sea)
Ägypten [ɛ'gʏptən] Egypt
Albanien [al'baːnjən] Albania
Algerien [al'geːrjən] Algeria
Algier ['alʒiːɐ] Algiers
Allgäu ['algɔy] *das* ~ the Al(l)gäu (*region of Bavaria, Germany*)
Alpen ['alpən] *die* ~ *pl* the Alps
Amerika [a'meːrika] America
Anden ['andən] *die* ~ *pl* the Andes
Antillen [an'tɪlən] *die* ~ *pl* the Antilles
Antwerpen [ant'vɛrpən] Antwerp
Apenninen [ape'niːnən] *die* ~ *pl* the Apennines
Argentinien [argɛn'tiːnjən] Argentina, the Argentine
Ärmelkanal ['ɛrməlkanaːl] *der* ~ the English Channel, the Channel
Asien ['aːzjən] Asia
Athen [a'teːn] Athens
Äthiopien [ɛ'tjoːpjən] Ethiopia
Atlantik [at'lantɪk] *der* ~ the Atlantic (Ocean)
Australien [aʊs'traːljən] Australia

Bach [bax] *German composer*
Barlach ['barlax] *German sculptor*
Basel ['baːzəl] Basel, Basle
Bayern ['baɪən] Bavaria
Beethoven ['beːthoːfən] *German composer*
Belgien ['bɛlgjən] Belgium
Berlin [bɛr'liːn] *German city*
Bern [bɛrn] Bern(e)
Bloch [blɔx] *German philosopher*
Böcklin ['bœkliːn] *German painter*
Bodensee ['boːdənzeː] *der* ~ Lake Constance
Böhm [bøːm] *Austrian conductor*
Böhmen ['bøːmən] *hist* Bohemia
Böll [bœl] *German author*
Bonn [bɔn] *German city*
Brahms [braːms] *German composer*
Brasilien [bra'ziːljən] Brazil

Braunschweig ['braʊnʃvaɪk] Braun – schweig, Brunswick
Brecht [brɛçt] *German dramatist*
Bremen ['breːmən] *German city*
Bruckner ['brʊknɐ] *Austrian composer*
Brüssel ['brʏsəl] Brussels
Budapest ['buːdapɛst] *Hungarian city*
Bukarest ['buːkarɛst] Bucharest
Bulgarien [bʊl'gaːrjən] Bulgaria

Calais [ka'lɛː] *die Straße von* ~ the Straits of Dover
Calvin [kal'viːn] *Swiss religious reform – er*
Chile ['tʃiːle] Chile
China ['çiːna] China

Daimler ['daɪmlɐ] *German inventor*
Dänemark ['dɛːnəmark] Denmark
Deutschland ['dɔʏtʃlant] Germany
Diesel ['diːzəl] *German inventor*
Döblin ['døːbliːn] *German author*
Dolomiten [dolo'miːtən] *die* ~ *pl* the Dolomites
Donau ['doːnaʊ] *die* ~ the Danube
Dortmund ['dɔrtmʊnt] *German city*
Dresden ['drɛːsdən] *German city*
Dünkirchen ['dyːnkɪrçən] Dunkirk
Dürer ['dyːrɐ] *German painter*
Dürrenmatt ['dʏrənmat] *Swiss dramatist*
Düsseldorf ['dʏsəldɔrf] *German city*

Egk [ɛk] *German composer*
Eichendorff ['aɪçəndɔrf] *German poet*
Eiger ['aɪgɐ] *Swiss mountain*
Einstein ['aɪnʃtaɪn] *German physicist*
Elbe ['ɛlbə] *die* ~ (*German river*)
Elsass ['ɛlzas] *das* ~ Alsace
England ['ɛŋlant] England
Essen ['esən] *German city*
Europa [ɔy'roːpa] Europe

Finnland ['fɪnlant] Finland
Florenz [flo'rɛnts] Florence
Fontane [fɔn'taːnə] *German author*
Franken ['fraŋkən] Franconia
Frankfurt am Main ['fraŋkfʊrt am 'maɪn] Frankfurt on the Main
Frankfurt an der Oder ['fraŋkfʊrt an

deːʀ 'oːdʊ] Frankfurt on the Oder
Frankreich ['fraŋkraɪç] France
Freud [frɔʏt] *Austrian psychologist*
Frisch [frɪʃ] *Swiss author*

Garmisch ['garmɪʃ] *health resort in Bavaria, Germany*
Genf [gɛnf] Geneva; *er See* Lake Geneva
Genua ['geːnua] Genoa
Goethe ['gøːtə] *German poet*
Grass [gras] *German author*
Griechenland ['griːçənlant] Greece
Grillparzer ['grɪlpartsʊ] *Austrian dramatist*
Grönland ['grøːnlant] Greenland
Gropius ['groːpjʊs] *German architect*
Großbritannien [groːsbri'tanjən] (Great) Britain
Großglockner ['groːsglɔknʊ]: *der* ~ (*Austrian mountain*)
Grünewald ['gryːnəvalt] *German painter*

Haag [haːk]: *Den* ~ The Hague
Hahn [haːn] *German chemist*
Hamburg ['hamburk] *German city*
Händel ['hɛndəl] Handel (*German composer*)
Hannover [ha'noːfʊ] Hanover
Harz [haːʀts]: *der* ~ the Harz (Mountains)
Hauptmann ['hauptman] *German dramatist*
Haydn ['haɪdən] *Austrian composer*
Hegel ['heːgəl] *German philosopher*
Heidegger ['haɪdɛgʊ] *German philosopher*
Heidelberg ['haɪdəlberk] *German city*
Heine ['haɪnə] *German poet*
Heisenberg ['haɪzənberk] *German physicist*
Heißenbüttel ['haɪsənbytəl] *German poet*
Helgoland ['hɛlgolant] Hel(i)goland
Helsinki ['hɛlzɪŋkɪ] *Finnish city*
Hesse ['hɛsə] *German poet*
Hindemith ['hɪndəmɪt] *German composer*
Hölderlin ['hœldɛliːn] *German poet*
Holland ['hɔlant] Holland

Indien ['ɪndjən] India
Inn [ɪn]: *der* ~ (*affluent of the Danube*)

Innsbruck ['ɪnsbrʊk] *Austrian city*
Irak [i'raːk]: *der* ~ Iraq
Iran [i'raːn]: *der* ~ Iran
Irland ['ɪrlant] Ireland
Island ['iːslant] Iceland
Israel ['ɪsrɛl] Israel
Italien [i'taːljən] Italy

Japan ['jaːpan] Japan
Jaspers ['jaspʊs] *German philosopher*
Jordanien [jɔr'daːnjən] Jordan
Jung [jʊŋ] *Swiss psychologist*
Jungfrau ['jʊŋfrau]: *die* ~ (*Swiss mountain*)

Kafka ['kafka] *Czech author*
Kanada ['kanada] Canada
Kant [kant] *German philosopher*
Karlsruhe ['karlsruːə] *German city*
Kärnten ['kɛrntən] Carinthia
Kästner ['kɛstnʊ] *German author*
Kiel [kiːl] *German city*
Klee [kleː] *Swiss-born painter*
Kleist [klaɪst] *German poet*
Koblenz ['koːblɛnts] Koblenz, Coblenz
Kokoschka [ko'kɔʃka] *Austrian painter*
Köln [kœln] Cologne
Kolumbien [ko'lʊmbjən] Colombia
Kolumbus [ko'lʊmbʊs] Columbus
Konstanz ['kɔnstants] Constance
Kopenhagen [koːpən'haːgən] Copenhagen
Kordilleren [kɔrdɪl'jeːrən]: *die* ~ *pl* the Cordilleras
Kreml ['kreːməl]: *der* ~ the Kremlin

Leibniz ['laɪbnɪts] *German philosopher*
Leipzig ['laɪptsɪç] Leipzig, Leipsic
Lessing ['lɛsɪŋ] *German poet*
Libanon ['liːbanɔn]: *der* ~ (the) Lebanon
Liebig ['liːbɪç] *German chemist*
Lissabon ['lɪsabɔn] Lisbon
London ['lɔndɔn] London
Lothringen ['loːtrɪŋən] Lorraine
Lübeck ['lyːbɛk] *German city*
Luther ['lʊtʊ] *German religious reformer*
Luxemburg ['lʊksəmburk] Luxemb(o)urg
Luzern [lu'tsɛrn] Lucerne

Maas [maːs]: *die* ~ the Meuse, the Maas
Madrid [ma'drɪt] Madrid
Mahler ['maːlʊ] *Austrian composer*

Mailand ['maɪlant] Milan
Main [maɪn]: *der ~ (German river)*
Mainz [maɪnts] *German city*
Mann [man] *name of three German authors*
Marokko [ma'rɔko] Morocco
Matterhorn ['matɛhɔrn]: *das ~ (Swiss mountain)*
Meißen· ['maɪsən] Meissen
Menzel ['mɛntsəl] *German painter*
Mexiko ['mɛksiko] Mexico
Mies van der Rohe ['miːs fan deːɐ 'roːə] *German architect*
Mittelmeer ['mɪtəlmeːɐ]: *das ~* the Mediterranean (Sea)
Moldau ['mɔldaʊ]: *die ~* the Vltava; *hist* the Moldau (*Bohemian river*)
Mörike ['møːrɪkə] *German poet*
Mosel ['moːzəl]: *die ~* the Moselle
Mössbauer ['mœsbaʊɐ] *German physicist*
Moskau ['mɔskaʊ] Moscow
Mozart ['moːtsart] *Austrian composer*
München ['mʏnçən] Munich

Neapel [ne'aːpəl] Naples
Neiße ['naɪsə]: *die ~ (German river)*
Neufundland [nɔy'fʊntlant] Newfoundland
Neuseeland [nɔy'zeːlant] New Zealand
Niederlande ['niːdəlandə]: *die ~ pl* the Netherlands
Nietzsche ['niːtʃə] *German philosopher*
Nil [niːl]: *der ~* the Nile
Nordamerika ['nɔrtʔa'meːrika] North America
Nordsee ['nɔrtzeː]: *die ~* the North Sea
Normandie [nɔrman'diː]: *die ~* Normandy
Norwegen ['nɔrveːgən] Norway
Nürnberg ['nʏrnbɛrk] Nuremberg

Oder ['oːdɐ]: *die ~ (German river)*
Orff [ɔrf] *German composer*
Oslo ['ɔslo] Oslo
Ostende [ɔstʔ'ɛndə] Ostend
Österreich ['øːstəraɪç] Austria
Ostsee ['ɔstzeː]: *die ~* the Baltic (Sea)

Palästina [palɛs'tiːna] Palestine
Paris [pa'riːs] Paris
Pfalz [pfalts]: *die ~* the Palatinate
Philippinen [fɪlɪ'piːnən]: *die ~ pl* the Philippines
Planck [plaŋk] *German physicist*
Polen ['poːlən] Poland
Porsche ['pɔrʃə] *German inventor*
Portugal ['pɔrtugal] Portugal
Prag [praːk] Prague
Preußen ['prɔysən] *hist* Prussia
Pyrenäen [pyre'nɛːən]: *die ~ pl* the Pyrenees

Rhein [raɪn]: *der ~* the Rhine
Rilke ['rɪlkə] *Austrian poet*
Rom [roːm] Rome
Röntgen ['rœntgən] *German physicist*
Ruhr [ruːɐ]: *die ~ (German river)*;
Ruhrgebiet ['ruːɐgəbiːt]: *das ~ (industrial center of Germany)*
Rumänien [ru'mɛːnjən] Rumania, Ro(u)mania
Russland ['rʊslant] Russia

Saale ['zaːlə]: *die ~ (German river)*
Saar [zaːɐ]: *die ~ (affluent of the Moselle)*
Salzburg ['zaltsbʊrk] *Austrian city*
Schiller ['ʃɪlɐ] *German poet*
Schönberg ['ʃøːnbɛrk] *Austrian composer*
Schottland ['ʃɔtlant] Scotland
Schubert ['ʃuːbɐt] *Austrian composer*
Schumann ['ʃuːman] *German composer*
Schwaben ['ʃvaːbən] Swabia
Schwarzwald ['ʃvartsvalt]: *der ~* the Black Forest
Schweden ['ʃveːdən] Sweden
Schweiz [ʃvarts]: *die ~* Switzerland
Sibirien [zi'biːrjən] Siberia
Siemens ['ziːməns] *German inventor*
Sizilien [zi'tsiːljən] Sicily
Skandinavien [skandi'naːvjən] Scandinavia
Slowakei [slova'kaɪ]: *die ~* Slovakia
Sofia ['zɔfja] Sofia
Spanien ['ʃpaːnjən] Spain
Spitzweg ['ʃpɪtsveːk] *German painter*
Spranger ['ʃpraŋɐ] *German philosopher*
Stifter ['ʃtɪftɐ] *Austrian author*
Stockholm ['ʃtɔkhɔlm] Stockholm
Storm [ʃtɔrm] *German poet*
Straßburg ['ʃtraːsbʊrk] Strasbourg
Strauß [ʃtraʊs] *Austrian composer*
Strauss [ʃtraʊs] *German composer*
Südamerika ['zyːtʔa'meːrika] South America

Syrien ['zyːrjən] Syria

Themse ['tɛmzə]: **die** ~ the Thames
Tirol [ti'roːl] (the) Tyrol
Tschechien ['tʃɛçjən] Czech Republic
Türkei [tʏr'kaɪ]: **die** ~ Turkey

Ungarn ['ʊŋgarn] Hungary
Ural [u'raːl]: **der** ~ the Urals

Venedig [ve'neːdɪç] Venice
Vereinigte Staaten (von Amerika)
[fɛr'ʔaɪnɪçtə 'ʃtaːtən (fɔn a'meːrika)]:
die Vereinigten Staaten (**von Amerika**) the United States (of America)
Vierwaldstätter See [fiːɐ'valtʃtɛtɐ

'zeː]: **der** ~ Lake Lucerne **Wagner** ['vaː-gnɐ] German composer
Wankel ['vaŋkəl] German inventor
Warschau ['varʃaʊ] Warsaw
Weichsel ['vaɪksəl]: **die** ~ the Vistula
Weiß [vaɪs] German dramatist
Werfel ['vɛrfəl] Austrian author
Weser ['veːzɐ]: **die** ~ (German river)
Wien [viːn] Vienna
Wiesbaden ['viːsbaːdən] German city

Zuckmayer ['tsʊkmaɪɐ] German dramatist
Zweig [tsvaɪk] Austrian author
Zürich ['tsyːrɪç] Zurich
Zypern ['tsyːpɐn] Cyprus

German abbreviations

Abb. *Abbildung* illustration

Abf. *Abfahrt* departure, *abbr* dep.

Abt. *Abteilung* department, *abbr* dept.

a. D. *außer Dienst* retired

ADAC *Allgemeiner Deutscher Automobil-Club* General German Automobile Association

AG *Aktiengesellschaft* (stock) corporation, joint-stock company

allg. *allgemein* general

Ank. *Ankunft* arrival

atü *Atmosphärenüberdruck* atmospheric excess pressure

Bd. *Band* volume, *abbr* vol.; **Bde.** *Bände* volumes, *abbr* vols.

Betr. *Betreff, betrifft letter* : subject, re

BRD *Bundesrepublik Deutschland* Federal Republic of Germany

CDU *Christlich-Demokratische Union* Christian Democratic Union

CSU *Christlich-Soziale Union* Christian Social Union

DB *Deutsche Bahn Germany's main railway operator*

DDR *hist Deutsche Demokratische Republik* German Demoratic Republic

DGB *Deutscher Gewerkschaftsbund* Federation of German Trade Unions

d. h. *das heißt* that is, *abbr* i. e.

DIN *Deutsche Industrie-Norm(en)* German Industrial Standards

DM *hist Deutsche Mark* German Mark(s)

dpa *Deutsche Presse-Agentur* German Press Agency

Dr. *Doktor, abbr* Dr.

DRK *Deutsches Rotes Kreuz* German Red Cross

EDV *Elektronische Datenverarbeitung* electronic data processing, *abbr* EDP

EM *Europameisterschaft* European championship(s)

EU *Europäische Union* European Union, *abbr* EU

e. V. *eingetragener Verein* registered association, incorporated, *abbr* inc.

FDP *Freie Demokratische Partei* Liberal Democratic Party

Forts. *Fortsetzung* continuation

geb. *geboren* born; *geborene ...* née; *gebunden* bound

Ges. *Gesellschaft* association, company; society

gez. *gezeichnet* signed, *abbr* sgd

GmbH *Gesellschaft mit beschränkter Haftung* private limited liability company

h. c. *honoris causa* = ehrenhalber; *academic title* : honorary

Hrsg. *Herausgeber* editor, *abbr* ed.

i. A. *im Auftrage* for, by order, under instruction

Ing. *Ingenieur* engineer

Inh. *Inhaber* proprietor

inkl. *inklusive, einschließlich* inclusive

'Interpol *Internationale Kriminalpolizeiliche Organisation* International Criminal Police Commission

IOK *Internationales Olympisches Komitee* International Olympic Committee, *abbr* IOC

ISBN *Internationale Standardbuchnummer* international standard book number, *abbr* ISBN

i. V. *in Vertretung* by proxy, as a substitute

jr., jun. *junior, der Jüngere* junior *abbr* jr, jun.

Kat *Katalysator* catalytic converter, catalyst, *abbr* cat.

Kfz. *Kraftfahrzeug* motor vehicle

KG *Kommanditgesellschaft* limited

partnership

Kl. *Klasse* class; *school*: form

'Kripo *Kriminalpolizei* Criminal Investigation Department, *abbr* CID

Kto. *Konto* account, *abbr* a/c

lfd. *laufend* current, running

Lfg., Lfrg. *Lieferung* delivery; instal(l)ment, part

Lkw, LKW *Lastkraftwagen* truck, lorry

lt. *laut* according to

MdB *Mitglied des Bundestages* Member of the Bundestag

MEZ *mitteleuropäische Zeit* Central European Time

MS, Ms. *Manuskript* manuscript, *abbr* MS, ms.

mtl. *monatlich* monthly

n. Chr. *nach Christus* after Christ, *abbr* AD

No., Nr. *Numero, Nummer* number, *abbr* No., no

o. B. *ohne Befund* MED without findings

OEZ *osteuropäische Zeit* Eastern European Time, *abbr* EET

PDS *hist Partei des Demokratischen Sozialismus* Party of Democratic Socialism

Pf *hist Pfennig* former German coin : pfennig

Pfd. *Pfund German weight* : pound

PKW, Pkw *Personenkraftwagen* car

PLZ *Postleitzahl* zip code, *Br* post – code

Prof. *Professor* professor

PS *Pferdestärke(n)* horse-power, *abbr* HP, h.p.; *postscriptum, Nachschrift* postscript, *abbr* PS

Rel. *Religion* religion

S. *Seite* page

s. *siehe* see, *abbr* v., vid. (= vide)

Sa. *Summa, Summe* sum, total

sen. *senior, der Ältere* senior

s. o. *siehe oben* see above

sog. *so genannt* so-called

SPD *Sozialdemokratische Partei Deutschlands* Social Democratic Party of Germany

St. *Stück* piece; *Sankt* Saint

Std. *Stunde* hour, *abbr* h

Str. *Straße* street, *abbr* St.

StVO *Straßenverkehrsordnung* (road) traffic regulations, *in GB* : Highway Code

s. u. *siehe unten* see below

tägl. *täglich* daily, per day

Tel. *Telefon* telephone

TH *Technische Hochschule* college *or* institute of technology

TU *Technische Universität* technical university; college *or* institute of technology

TÜV *Technischer Überwachungs – Verein* safety standards authority

u. a. *und andere(s)* and others; *unter anderem or anderen* among other things, inter alia

UKW *Ultrakurzwelle* ultra-short wave, very high frequency, *abbr* VHF

V *Volt* volt; *Volumen* volume

v. Chr. *vor Christus* before Christ, *abbr* BC

vgl. *vergleiche* confer, *abbr* cf.

WAA *Wiederaufbereitungsanlage* reprocessing plant

WEZ *westeuropäische Zeit* Greenwich Mean Time, *abbr* GMT

WG *Wohngemeinschaft* flat share, flat sharing (community)

WM *Weltmeisterschaft* world championship(s); *soccer*: World Cup

z. B. *zum Beispiel* for instance, *abbr* e.g.

z. H(d). *zu Händen* attention of, to be delivered to, care of, *abbr* c/o

z. T. *zum Teil* partly

zus. *zusammen* together

z. Z(t). *zur Zeit* at the time, at present, for the time being